In the *STUDY GUIDE* . . .
resources to ace every test

What better way to study for a test than with a *Study Guide* prepared by the co-author of this textbook. Written by Roger LeRoy Miller and William Eric Hollowell, this comprehensive resource includes:

► Brief introductions and outlines for every chapter

► True-false, fill-in-the-blank, and multiple-choice questions for every chapter, as well as short essay problems to help you test yourself

► Issue Spotters that focus your study

► Sample CPA exam questions

► An appendix at the end of the *Study Guide* containing answers to all questions and Issue Spotters

Bookstore doesn't carry the *Study Guide*?
You can get it online (ISBN: 0-538-47277-7) at **www.cengagebrain.com**.

FREE RESOURCES!

Visit this book's Companion Web Site for many additional study tools
www.cengage.com/blaw/clarkson

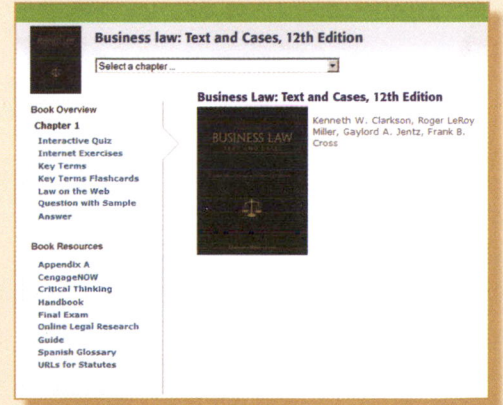

► Answers to selected *Case Problems* from this textbook

► Video clips from the Business Law Digital Video Library (You'll need to view these clips to help you answer *Video Questions* that appear in selected chapters of this book.)

► Interactive self-quizzes for every chapter

► Practical Internet exercises for every chapter

► Court case updates

► Legal reference materials and much more!

BUSINESS LAW
TEXT AND CASES

LEGAL, ETHICAL, GLOBAL, AND CORPORATE ENVIRONMENT

TWELFTH EDITION

Kenneth W. Clarkson
University of Miami

Roger LeRoy Miller
**Institute for University Studies
Arlington, Texas**

Frank B. Cross
**Herbert D. Kelleher
Centennial Professor in Business Law
University of Texas at Austin**

SOUTH-WESTERN
CENGAGE Learning

Australia • Brazil • Japan • Korea • Mexico • Singapore
Spain • United Kingdom • United States

SOUTH-WESTERN
CENGAGE Learning™

BUSINESS LAW
TEXT AND CASES
Legal, Ethical, Global, and
Corporate Environment
TWELFTH EDITION

Kenneth W. Clarkson
Roger LeRoy Miller
Frank B. Cross

Vice President and Editorial Director:
Jack Calhoun

Editor-in-Chief:
Rob Dewey

Senior Acquisitions Editor:
Vicky True-Baker

Senior Developmental Editor:
Jan Lamar

Marketing Director:
Lisa L. Lysne

Marketing Manager:
Laura-Aurora Stopa

Marketing Coordinator:
Nicole Parsons

Senior Marketing Communications Manager:
Sarah Greber

Production Manager:
Bill Stryker

Manager: Senior Media Editor:
Kristen Meere

Manufacturing Buyer:
Kevin Kluck

Editorial Assistant:
Patrick Ian Clark

Compositor:
Parkwood Composition Service

Senior Art Director:
Michelle Kunkler

Internal Designer:
Bill Stryker

Cover Designer:
Stratton Design

For product information and technology assistance, contact us at
Cengage Learning Academic Resource Center
1-800-423-0563

For permission to use material from this text or product, submit all requests online at **www.cengage.com/permissions**.

Further permissions questions can be emailed to
permissionrequest@cengage.com.

ExamView® and ExamView Pro® are registered trademarks of FSCreations, Inc. Windows is a registered trademark of the Microsoft Corporation used herein under license. Macintosh and Power Macintosh are registered trademarks of Apple Computer, Inc., used herein under license.

© 2012, 2009 Cengage Learning. All Rights Reserved.
Cengage Learning WebTutor™ is a trademark of Cengage Learning.

Library of Congress Control Number: 2010936130

Student's Edition:
ISBN-13: 978-0-538-47082-7
ISBN-10: 0-538-47082-8

Instructor's Edition:
ISBN-13: 978-0-538-47081-0
ISBN-10: 0-538-47081-X

South-Western, Cengage Learning
5191 Natorp Blvd.
Mason, OH 45040
USA

Cengage Learning products are represented in Canada by Nelson Education, Ltd.

For your course and learning solutions, visit **www.cengage.com**.

Purchase any of our products at your local college store or at our preferred online store **www.cengagebrain.com**.

Printed in Canada
1 2 3 4 5 6 7 14 13 12 11 10

Contents in Brief

Contents

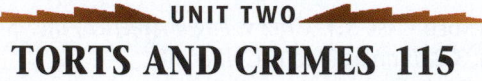

UNIT TWO
TORTS AND CRIMES 115

UNIT THREE
CONTRACTS
AND E-CONTRACTS 205

UNIT FOUR
DOMESTIC AND INTERNATIONAL SALES AND LEASE CONTRACTS 355

UNIT FIVE
NEGOTIABLE
INSTRUMENTS 461

UNIT SIX
CREDITORS' RIGHTS AND BANKRUPTCY 545

UNIT SEVEN
AGENCY AND EMPLOYMENT 623

CONCEPT SUMMARIES

EXHIBITS

EXHIBITS, Continued

SHIFTING LEGAL PRIORITIES FOR BUSINESS

INSIGHT INTO ETHICS

Preface to the Instructor

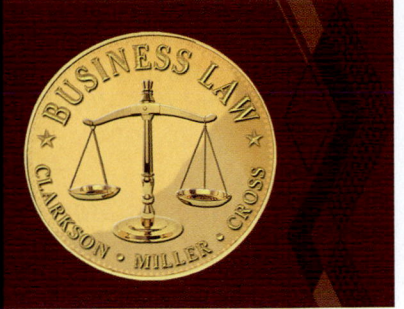

The study of business law and, more generally, the legal environment of business has universal applicability. A student entering any field of business must have at least a passing understanding of business law in order to function in the real world. Additionally, students preparing for a career in accounting, government and political science, economics, and even medicine can use much of the information they learn in a business law and legal environment course. In fact, every individual throughout his or her lifetime can benefit from a knowledge of contracts, real property law, landlord-tenant relationships, and other legal topics. Consequently, we have fashioned this text as a useful "tool for living" for all of your students (including those taking the CPA exam).

For the Twelfth Edition, we have spent a great deal of effort making this book more contemporary, exciting, and visually appealing than ever before. We have also added many new features and special pedagogical devices that focus on the legal, ethical, global, and corporate environments, while addressing core curriculum requirements.

WHAT IS NEW IN THE TWELFTH EDITION

Instructors have come to rely on the coverage, accuracy, and applicability of *Business Law*. To make sure that our text engages your students, solidifies their understanding of legal concepts, and provides the best teaching tools available, we now offer the following items either in the text or in conjunction with the text.

➤ New *Shifting Legal Priorities for Business* Features

For the Twelfth Edition, we have created this new feature that shows students how legal priorities are shifting in the business world. Special emphasis is given to sustainability, ethical trends, and changing managerial responsibilities. Each feature ends with a short section entitled *Managerial*

Implications that points out why the changing priorities discussed in the feature are significant to businesspersons. Topics examined in these features include:

- Prosecuting White-Collar Crime with the Honest-Services Fraud Law (Chapter 9)
- Fair Trade and Environmental Sustainability (Chapter 19)
- The National Export Initiative (Chapter 23)
- SEC Disclosures and Climate Change (Chapter 42)
- The Law of Building "Green"—Sustainable Real Estate Development (Chapter 50)

➤ New *Case in Point* Features

Many instructors use cases to illustrate how the law applies to business. For this edition, we have expanded our in-text discussion of case law by adding at least one new *Case in Point* feature in every chapter. These features present, in paragraph format, the facts and issues of an actual case and then describe the court's decision and rationale. Citations to the cases are included for further reference. The *Case in Point* features are integrated throughout the text to help students better understand how courts apply the principles under discussion in the real world.

➤ New *Debate This* Features

To encourage student participation and motivate your students to think critically about the rationale underlying the law on a particular topic, we have created a special new feature for the Twelfth Edition. Entitled *Debate This,* it consists of a brief statement or question concerning the chapter material that can be used to spur lively classroom or small group discussions, or can be a written assignment. These features follow the *Reviewing* features (discussed shortly) at the end of each chapter. **Suggested pro and con responses to the *Debate This* features can be found in both the *Instructor's Manual* and the *Answers Manual* that accompany this text.**

(The full title of this manual is *Answers to Questions and Case Problems and Alternate Problem Sets with Answers.*)

➤ New Chapter on *Mortgages and Foreclosures after the Recession*

For the Twelfth Edition, we have included an entirely new chapter (Chapter 31) entitled *Mortgages and Foreclosures after the Recession.* This chapter examines some of the mortgage lending practices that contributed to the latest recession and discusses the legal reforms enacted in response to it.

➤ New *Video Questions*

In response to popular demand, we have created eight new *Video Questions* for this edition. As discussed later in this preface, these questions refer students to the text's Web site to view a particular video clip prior to answering a series of questions in the book that relate the video to the chapter material. Some of the new videos are clips from actual movies or television series, such as *Field of Dreams, Midnight Run,* and *Mary Tyler Moore.* Others are from a new Real World Legal series of videos in the Business Law Digital Video Library (discussed later in this preface).

➤ New *Insight into Ethics* Features

For the Twelfth Edition, we have created **many new *Insight into Ethics* features,** which appear in selected chapters and examine the ethical implications of various topics. These features provide valuable insights into how the courts and the law are dealing with specific ethical issues. Each of these features ends with a critical-thinking question that explores some cultural, environmental, political, social, or technological aspect of the issue. The following are some of the topics explored in these features:

- Some Consequences of Caps on Medical Malpractice Awards (Chapter 7)
- How Much Information Must Employers Disclose to Prospective Employees? (Chapter 14)
- Warning Labels for Video Games (Chapter 22)
- Is the Business Judgment Rule Overly Protective? (Chapter 40)
- Should Pharmaceutical Companies Be Allowed to Tweet? (Chapter 44)

➤ Two Critical-Thinking Questions at the End of Nearly Every Case

In every chapter of the Eleventh Edition of *Business Law,* we included one longer case excerpt followed by two questions designed to guide students' analysis of the case and build their legal reasoning skills. For the Twelfth Edition, we continue to offer one longer excerpt—labeled an ***Extended Case***—with two critical-thinking questions in every chapter. These *Extended Cases* may be used for case-briefing assignments and are also tied to the *Special Case Analysis* questions found in every unit of the text.

Because of the popularity of the case-ending questions, we've also included two questions for all cases. These questions may include:

- *What If the Facts Were Different?*
- *Impact of This Case on Today's Law*
- *The Ethical Dimension*
- *The E-Commerce Dimension*
- *The Global Dimension*
- *The Legal Environment Dimension*

Suggested answers to all questions following cases can be found in both the *Instructor's Manual* and the *Answers Manual* that accompany this text.

➤ *Managerial Implications* in Selected Cases

In addition to the critical-thinking questions, we have devised a special new item of case pedagogy for this edition. At the end of selected cases that have particular importance for business managers, we have included a new section entitled *Managerial Implications.* These sections point out the significance of the court's ruling in the case for business owners and managers.

➤ Emphasis on Critical Thinking and Legal Reasoning

Today's business leaders must often think "outside the box" when making business decisions. For this reason, we have included **numerous critical-thinking elements** in the Twelfth Edition that are designed to challenge students' understanding of the materials beyond simple retention. Your students' critical-thinking and legal reasoning skills will be increased as they work through the numerous pedagogical aids in the book. The new *Debate This* features (discussed previously) require critical thinking. In addition, nearly every feature and every case presented in the text conclude with some type of critical-thinking question. These questions include *For Critical Analysis, What If the Facts Were Different?* and the *Ethical, E-Commerce, Global,* and *Legal Environment Dimension* questions discussed previously. They also include the *Special Case Analysis* questions and the questions in the *Reviewing* features, which are described below.

➤ *Special Case Analysis* Questions

Through the years, instructors have frequently requested that we help them teach their business law students how to analyze case law. We discuss the fundamental topic of how to read and understand case law in Chapter 1 and cover **How to Brief Cases and Analyze Case Problems** in Appendix A. For every unit in the text, in the *Questions and Case Problems* at the end of selected chapters, we also provide a *Special Case Analysis* question that is based on the *Extended Case* excerpt in that chapter. These questions are designed to build students' analytical skills.

The *Special Case Analysis* questions test students' ability to perform IRAC (Issue, Rule, Application, and Conclusion) case analysis. Students must identify the legal issue presented in the chapter's *Extended Case,* understand the rule of law, determine how the rule applies to the facts of the case, and describe the court's conclusion. Instructors can assign these questions as homework or use them in class to elicit student participation and teach case analysis.

➤ *Reviewing* Features in Every Chapter

In the Twelfth Edition of *Business Law*, we continue to offer a **Reviewing** feature at the end of every chapter to help solidify students' understanding of the chapter materials. Each *Reviewing* feature presents a hypothetical scenario and then asks a series of questions that require students to identify the issues and apply the legal concepts discussed in the chapter. These features are designed to help students review the chapter topics in a simple and interesting way and see how the legal principles discussed in the chapter affect the world in which they live. An instructor can use these features as the basis for in-class discussion or can encourage students to use them for self-study prior to completing homework assignments. **Suggested answers to the questions posed in the *Reviewing* features can be found in both the *Instructor's Manual* and the *Answers Manual* that accompany this text.**

The *Reviewing* features are also tied to a set of questions for each chapter in the Web-based CengageNOW system, to be discussed next. Students can read through the scenario in the text and then answer the four Applications and Analysis questions online. **By using the CengageNOW system, students can receive instant feedback on their answers to these questions, and instructors will obtain automatically graded assignments that enable them to assess students' understanding of the materials.**

➤ Improved CengageNOW for *Business Law:* Interactive Assignment System

To help students learn how to identify and apply the legal principles they study, we have created an easy-to-use Web-based product for this text. The system provides interactive, automatically graded assignments for every chapter and unit. For each of the fifty-two chapters, we have devised several categories of multiple-choice questions that stress different aspects of the chapter materials. By using the optional CengageNOW system, students can complete the assignments from any location via the Internet and can receive instant feedback on why their answers to questions were incorrect or correct (if the instructor wishes to allow feedback). Instructors can customize the system to meet their own specifications and can track students' progress. CengageNOW offers all of the following:

- **Chapter Review Questions**—The first set of ten to fifteen questions reviews the basic concepts and principles discussed in the chapter. This set often includes questions based on the cases presented in the text.
- **Brief Hypotheticals**—The next group of seven to ten questions gives students practice in spotting the issue and rule of law in the context of a short factual scenario.
- **Legal Reasoning**—The third set contains five questions that require students to analyze the factual situation provided and apply the rules of law discussed in the chapter to arrive at an answer.
- **IRAC Case Analysis**—The next set of four questions for each chapter requires students to perform all the basic elements of legal reasoning (identify the *issue*, determine the *rule* of law, *apply* the rule to the facts presented, and arrive at a *conclusion*).

These questions are based on the *Extended Case* excerpts that appear in each chapter.

- **Application and Analysis**—The final set of four questions is linked to the *Reviewing* features (discussed previously) that appear in every chapter of the text. The student is required to read through the hypothetical scenario, analyze the facts presented, identify the issues in dispute, and apply the rules discussed in the chapter to answer the questions.

- **Essay Questions**—In addition to the multiple-choice questions available on CengageNOW, we now provide essay questions that allow students to compose and submit essays online. Students' essays are automatically recorded to the gradebook so that instructors can quickly and easily evaluate the essays and record grades.

- **Video Questions**—CengageNOW also provides links to the Business Law Digital Video Library so that students can access and view the video clips and answer questions related to the topics in the chapter.

- **Cumulative Questions for Each Unit**—In addition to the questions relating to each chapter, the CengageNOW system provides a set of cumulative questions, entitled "Synthesizing Legal Concepts," for each of the ten units in the text.

- **Additional Advantages of CengageNOW**—Instructors can utilize the system to upload their course syllabi, create and customize homework assignments, keep track of their students' progress, communicate with their students about assignments and due dates, and create reports summarizing the data for an individual student or for the whole class.

➤ Aplia for *Business Law:* Online Homework and Gradebook System

Aplia is an online homework system dedicated to improving learning by increasing student effort and engagement. Aplia encourages business law students to read their text, stay engaged with course material, and master critical-thinking and legal reasoning skills that will serve them well in their future business careers.

Originally created by a professor to enhance his own courses, Aplia has been specially tailored to cover the topics in each chapter of this text. Immediate, detailed feedback for every question helps students learn and improves their performance. Aplia's numerous interactive features help students stay interested in business law, be more prepared for classes, and connect concepts across chapters. Aplia also allows instructors to spend more time teaching and less time reviewing and grading assignments. As your students complete assignments, their scores are imported automatically into your gradebook, where you can easily track class and individual student performance.

Aplia Text, an interactive textbook, contains all the contents of the printed textbook but takes advantage of the digital environment. Features such as flipbook-style navigation allow students to scan through the text easily. They can also highlight the text; listen to audio clips; and view movies, simulations, graphs, and slideshows.

➤ CourseMate

CourseMate brings business law concepts to life with interactive learning, study, and exam preparation tools that support the printed textbook. Built-in engagement tracking tools allow you to assess the study activities of your students. Additionally, CourseMate includes an interactive online textbook, which contains the complete content of the printed textbook enhanced by the many advantages of a digital environment.

➤ Improved Ethics Coverage

For the Twelfth Edition of *Business Law,* we have significantly revised and updated the chapter on ethics and business decision making (Chapter 5). The chapter now presents a more practical, realistic, case-study approach to business ethics and the dilemmas facing businesspersons today.

It also provides step-by-step guidance for making ethical business decisions. The emphasis on ethics is reiterated in materials throughout the text, particularly the *Insight into Ethics* features, the *Focus on Ethics* features that conclude every unit, and the pedagogy that accompanies selected cases and features. We also discuss **corporate governance issues** in the ethics chapter, the corporations chapters, and the *Focus on Ethics* feature at the end of Unit Eight, on business organizations. Finally, each chapter includes a **Question of Ethics** case problem that provides modern-day examples of the kinds of ethical issues faced by businesspersons and explores the ways that courts can resolve them.

➤ More on the Sarbanes-Oxley Act of 2002

In a number of places in this text, we discuss the Sarbanes-Oxley Act of 2002 and the corporate scandals that led to the passage of that legislation. For example, Chapter 5 contains a section examining the requirements of the Sarbanes-Oxley Act relating to confidential reporting systems. In Chapter 42, we discuss this act in the context of securities law and present an exhibit (Exhibit 42–4) containing some of the key provisions of the act relating to corporate accountability with respect to securities transactions. Finally, in Chapter 48, we again look at provisions of the Sarbanes-Oxley Act as they relate to public accounting firms and accounting practices. We also discuss recent attacks on the Sarbanes-Oxley Act in the case *Free Enterprise Fund v. Public Accounting Oversight Board* in the *Shifting Legal Priorities for Business* feature for Chapter 48.

Because the Sarbanes-Oxley Act is a topic of significant concern in today's business climate, we include excerpts and explanatory comments on the act as Appendix H. Students and instructors alike will find it useful to have the provisions of the act immediately available for reference.

BUSINESS LAW ON THE WEB

For the Twelfth Edition of *Business Law,* we offer a text Web site so that users can easily locate the resources they seek.

Resources at the *Business Law* Web Site

When you visit our Web site at **www.cengage.com/blaw/clarkson**, you will find a broad array of teaching/learning resources, including the following:

- *Sample answers* to the *Case Problem with Sample Answer,* which appears in the *Questions and Case Problems* at the end of every chapter. This problem/answer set is designed to help your students learn how to answer case problems by acquainting them with model answers to selected problems. In addition, we offer the answers to the hypothetical *Questions with Sample Answers* on the Web site, as well as in the text (Appendix I).
- *Videos* referenced in the *Video Questions* that appear in selected chapters of this edition of *Business Law.*
- *Internet exercises* for every chapter in the text (at least two per chapter). These exercises have been refocused to provide more practical information to business law students on topics covered in the chapters and to acquaint students with the legal resources that are available online.
- *Interactive quizzes* for every chapter in this text.
- *Legal reference materials* including a "Statutes" page that offers links to the full text of selected statutes referenced in the text, a

Spanish glossary, and links to other important legal resources available for free on the Web.
- *Law on the Web* features that provide links to URLs that discuss topics related to each chapter in the text.
- *Link to our Business Law Digital Video Library* that provides a compendium of more than seventy-five video scenarios and explanations (see below).
- *Online Legal Research Guide* that offers complete yet brief guidance to using the Internet and evaluating information obtained from the Internet as well as hyperlinks to the Web sites discussed.
- *Court case updates* that present summaries of new cases from various legal publications, are continually updated, and are specifically keyed to chapters in this text.

Business Law Digital Video Library

For this edition of *Business Law,* we have included special *Video Questions* at the end of selected chapters. Each of these questions directs students to the text's Web site at **www.cengage.com/blaw/clarkson** to view a video relevant to a topic covered in the chapter. This instruction is followed by a series of questions based on the video.

The videos can be used for homework assignments, discussion starters, or classroom demonstrations and are useful for generating student interest. Some of the videos are clips from actual movies or television series. By watching a video and answering the questions, students will gain an understanding of how the legal concepts they have studied in the chapter apply to the real-life situation portrayed in the video.

The videos are part of our Business Law Digital Video Library. An access code for the videos can be packaged with each new copy of this textbook for no additional charge. If Business Law Digital Video Library access did not come packaged with the textbook, students can purchase it online at **www.cengage.com/blaw/dvl**.

Suggested answers for all of the *Video Questions* are given in both the *Instructor's Manual* and the *Answers Manual* that accompany this text.

ADDITIONAL SPECIAL FEATURES OF THIS TEXT

We have included in *Business Law,* Twelfth Edition, a number of pedagogical devices and special features, including those discussed here.

Concept Summaries

Whenever key areas of the law need additional emphasis, we provide a *Concept Summary*. These summaries have always been a popular pedagogical tool in this text. The text now includes more than fifty of these summaries, many of which have been expanded or revised.

Exhibits

When appropriate, we also illustrate important aspects of the law in graphic form in exhibits. In all, more than one hundred exhibits are featured in *Business Law,* Twelfth Edition. Several of these exhibits are new, and we have modified existing exhibits to achieve better clarity.

Effective Case Formats

For this edition, we have carefully selected recent cases that not only provide on-point illustrations of the legal principles discussed in the chapter but also are of high interest to students. In all, more than 75 percent of the cases in the Twelfth Edition are from 2009 or 2010.

As mentioned, for this edition we have included one *Extended Case* per chapter that is presented entirely in the court's language and does not include any paraphrased section on the case's background and facts or the decision and remedy. The remaining cases in each chapter appear in our usual *Business Law* format, which now includes two case-ending questions (or one question and a *Managerial Implication*) for every case. We also provide bracketed definitions for any terms in the opinion that might be difficult for students to understand. Cases may include one or more of the following sections, a few of which have already been described:

- *Company Profiles*—Certain cases include a profile describing the history of the company involved to give students an awareness of the context of the case before the court. Some profiles include the URL for the company's Web site.
- *What If the Facts Were Different?*—One case in each chapter concludes with this question. The student is asked to decide whether a specified change in the facts of the case would alter its outcome. **Suggested answers to these questions are included in both the *Instructor's Manual* and the *Answers Manual* that accompany this text.**
- *The Ethical [E-Commerce, Global, or Legal Environment] Dimension*—As discussed pre-

viously, these questions ask students to explore different aspects of the issues of the case and help instructors meet core curriculum requirements for business law. **Suggested answers to these questions are included in both the *Instructor's Manual* and the *Answers Manual* that accompany this text.**

- *Impact of This Case on Today's Law*— Because many students are not aware of how some of the older cases presented in this text affect today's court rulings, we include a section at the end of selected landmark cases that clarifies the relevance of the case to modern law.
- *Managerial Implications*—These sections clarify the relevance of a case for business owners or managers.

Case Problems

Nearly every chapter in the Twelfth Edition includes a 2009 or 2010 case problem in the *Questions and Case Problems* that appear at the end of the chapter. These problems are designed to clarify how modern courts deal with the issues discussed in the chapter. In addition, at the request of instructors, we have added a label to every question and case problem that identifies the chapter topic to which the question relates. These labels make it easier for those who wish to assign only certain questions to their students.

Suggested answers to these questions are included in both the *Instructor's Manual* and the *Answers Manual* that accompany this text.

Two *Test Banks* Available

To provide instructors with even greater flexibility in teaching, we offer two separate *Test Banks,* each with a complete set of questions for every chapter of *Business Law,* Twelfth Edition. These two *Test Banks* have been significantly revised, and many new questions have been added. Instructors who would like to alternate the tests they give their students each semester can now do so without having to create additional testing materials. In addition, instructors now have twice as many options for questions in each category (true/false, multiple choice, essay) from which to choose.

Two Questions with Sample Answers in Each Chapter

In response to instructors who would like students to have sample answers available for some of the questions and case problems, we have included two questions with sample answers in each chapter. The *Question with Sample Answer* is a hypothetical question for which students can access a sample answer in Appendix I at the end of the text. Every chapter also has one *Case Problem with Sample Answer* that is based on an actual case and answered on the text's Web site.

THE MOST COMPLETE SUPPLEMENTS PACKAGE AVAILABLE TODAY

This edition of *Business Law* is accompanied by a vast number of teaching and learning supplements. We have already mentioned the CengageNOW for *Business Law*: Interactive Assignment System and the supplemental resources available on the text's Web site at **www.cengage.com/blaw/clarkson**. In addition, the complete teaching/learning package for the Twelfth Edition includes numerous other supplements, including those listed below. For further information on the *Business Law* teaching/learning package, contact your local sales representative or visit the *Business Law* Web site.

Printed Supplements

- *Instructor's Manual*—Includes sections entitled "Additional Cases Addressing This Issue" at the ends of selected case synopses. (Also available on the *Instructor's Resource CD–ROM*, or IRCD.)
- *Study Guide*—Includes essay questions and sample CPA exam questions.
- **Two comprehensive *Test Banks***—*Test Bank 1* and *Test Bank 2* each contain approximately 1,040 multiple-choice questions with answers, more than 1,040 true/false questions with answers, and two short essay questions per chapter (104 in each *Test Bank*). Additionally, there is one question for every *Shifting Legal Priorities* and *Insight into Ethics* feature, and there are two multiple-choice questions for each *Focus on Ethics* section. (Also available on the IRCD.)
- *Answers to Questions and Case Problems and Alternate Problem Sets with Answers*— Provides answers to all questions presented in the text, including the questions in each *Focus on Ethics* section and the *Critical Thinking* questions concluding the *Insight into Ethics* features, as well as alternate problem sets with answers. (Also available on the IRCD.)

Software, Video, and Multimedia Supplements

- *Instructor's Resource CD-ROM* **(IRCD)**— The IRCD includes the following supplements: *Instructor's Manual, Answers Manual, Test Bank 1* and *Test Bank 2*, Case-Problem Cases, Case Printouts, Lecture Outline System, PowerPoint slides, ExamView, *Instructor's Manual* for the *Drama of the Law* video series, *Handbook of Landmark Cases and Statutes in Business Law and the Legal Environment, Handbook on Critical Thinking and Writing in Business Law and the Legal Environment,* and *A Guide to Personal Law.*
- **ExamView Testing Software** (also available on the IRCD).
- **Lecture Outline System** (also available on the IRCD).
- **PowerPoint slides** (also available on the IRCD).
- **WebTutor Advantage and WebTutor Toolbox**—Feature chat, discussion groups, testing, student progress tracking, and business law course materials.
- **Case-Problem Cases** (available only on the IRCD).
- **Transparency acetates** (available only on the IRCD).
- **Westlaw®**—Ten free hours for qualified adopters.
- **Business Law Digital Video Library**— Provides access to more than seventy-five videos, including the *Drama of the Law* videos and video clips from Hollywood movies. Access to our Business Law Digital Video Library is available in an optional package with each new text at no additional cost. If this access did not come with the textbook, students can purchase it at **www.cengage.com/blaw/dvl**.

FOR USERS OF THE ELEVENTH EDITION

First of all, we want to thank you for helping make *Business Law* the best-selling business law text in America today. Second, we want to make you aware of the numerous additions and changes that we have made in this edition—many in response to comments from reviewers. For example, we have added more examples and new *Case in Point* features, and incorporated the latest United States Supreme Court decisions throughout the text as appropriate. We have substantially revised and reorganized the business organizations unit (Unit Eight), particularly the chapters on corporations (Chapter 39 through 41), which have been revised to be more in line with the reality of modern corporate law. We have simplified and streamlined the chapter on securities laws (Chapter 42), and we have revised and reorganized the property chapters (Chapters 49 and 50).

Significantly Revised Chapters

Every chapter of the Twelfth Edition has been revised as necessary to incorporate new developments in the law or to streamline the presentations. A number of new trends in business law are also addressed in the cases and special features of the Twelfth Edition. Other major changes and additions for this edition include the following:

- Chapter 4 (Constitutional Authority to Regulate Business)—This chapter has been thoroughly revised and updated to be more business oriented. New *Case in Point* features have been added throughout, and the privacy materials have been updated to include a new subsection on pretexting.

- Chapter 5 (Ethics and Business Decision Making)—This chapter has been significantly revised, and a new section on the ethical transgressions of financial institutions discusses well-known companies, such as American International Group (AIG). The chapter also provides step-by-step guidance on making ethical business decisions, materials on global business ethics, and a new video question concerning marketing strategies in the pharmaceutical industry. The 2010 United States Supreme Court case involving Jeffrey Skilling, former CEO of Enron Corporation, is presented in the chapter. Other topics include recent bribery scandals, bribery by foreign companies, and Internet attacks on corporate reputations. A new *Shifting Legal Priorities for Business* feature titled *Corporate Social Responsibility May Mean Outbehaving the Competition,* has been added.

- Chapter 6 (Intentional Torts) and Chapter 7 (Negligence and Strict Liability)—Our torts coverage has been revised to be more up to date and business oriented. We have added new materials on tort reform, cyber torts, spam, and the U.S. Safe Web Act in Chapter 6. In Chapter 7, we have reorganized the presentation of causation and damages and included additional coverage on comparative negligence, as well as a new *Insight into Ethics* feature titled *Some*

Consequences of Caps on Medical Malpractice Awards.

- Chapter 8 (Intellectual Property and Internet Law)—The materials on intellectual property rights have been thoroughly revised and updated to reflect the most current laws and trends. We have reworked our discussion of descriptive, generic, and suggestive trademarks for clarity and included an updated discussion of software and business process patents. We have also updated the materials on copyrights in digital information and added a description of cloud computing. The chapter also includes updates on international treaties protecting intellectual property and a *Shifting Legal Priorities for Business* feature on the Anti-Counterfeiting Trade Agreement.

- Chapter 9 (Criminal Law and Cyber Crime)—This chapter has been streamlined and updated. We have added discussions of criminal negligence and strict liability. A *Shifting Legal Priorities for Business* feature titled *Prosecuting White-Collar Crime with Honest-Services Fraud Law* includes a discussion of how the Supreme Court limited the application of this federal law in 2010.

- Chapters 10 through 18 (the Contracts unit)—Throughout this unit, we have added more examples to clarify and enhance our already superb contract law coverage. We have also integrated our discussion of electronic contracts, or e-contracts, into all the chapters in this unit and have revised the text to improve clarity and reduce legalese. We have included up-to-date information and cases that will appeal to your students, such as a case involving the Comedy Club and another involving Amazon.com. Numerous new *Case in Point* features, including one involving Tom Selleck and another involving Mike Tyson, that are intended to garner student interest. Other interesting features include, *Shifting Legal Priorities for Business* features titled *Fair Trade and Environmental Sustainability* and *How Much Information Must Employers Disclose to Prospective Employees?*

- Chapters 19 through 23 (the unit on Domestic and International Sales and Lease Contracts)—We have streamlined and simplified our coverage of the Uniform Commercial Code. We have added numerous new *Cases in Point* and examples throughout the unit to increase student comprehension. We have also expanded our discussion of international sales and lease contracts and now include the International

Law in a Global Economy chapter (Chapter 23) in this unit.

- Chapters 24 through 27 (the unit on Negotiable Instruments)—We have updated this entire unit, particularly Chapters 24 and 27, to accommodate the reality of digital banking and funds transfers. In Chapter 24, we added a *Shifting Legal Priorities for Business* feature titled *Person-to-Person Mobile Payments Aid in Sustainability.* The Check-Clearing in the 21st Century Act (Check 21 Act) has been incorporated into the text. We have also reworked the text, especially in Chapter 26, to clarify and simplify difficult concepts for your students.

- Chapters 28 through 31 (the unit on Creditors' Rights and Bankruptcy)—This unit has been revised to be more up to date and comprehensible and streamlined to focus on materials that students need to know. Chapter 29 (Secured Transactions) was substantially reworked to clarify the general principles and exceptions. The bankruptcy law chapter (Chapter 30), which is based on law after the 2005 Reform Act, has been substantially revised and includes updated dollar amounts of various provisions of the Bankruptcy Code. Chapter 31 (Mortgages and Foreclosures after the Recession) is entirely new to this edition and provides a timely look at the mortgage crisis, predatory lending practices, and the laws enacted to address some of the problems that became evident during the recession.

- Chapter 34 (Employment, Immigration, and Labor Law) and Chapter 35 (Employment Discrimination)—These two chapters covering employment law have been thoroughly updated to include discussions of legal issues facing employers today. Chapter 34 includes new materials on immigration law, which is of increasing importance to employers. It also includes a new section on layoffs and the WARN Act, and covers recent amendments to FMLA leave. We have updated minimum wage figures, as well as Social Security and Medicare percentages, and include current information on privacy rights and genetic testing. A feature titled *The Online Creation and Modification of Employment Contracts* has been added. Chapter 35 includes the latest developments in age and disability discrimination and equal pay legislation. We discuss relevant United States Supreme Court decisions and have reworked the text to simplify and add clarity.

- Chapters 36 through 43 (the Business Organizations unit)—This unit has been substantially revised and updated to improve the flow and clarity and to provide more practical information and recent examples. We have worked to improve the comprehensibility of the materials throughout, including the addition of a new concept summary in Chapter 38. The most significant changes to the unit were made in the corporations chapters (Chapters 39 through 42), which have been revised to reflect modern trends in corporate law. Chapter 39 has been thoroughly revised and includes a new *Shifting Legal Priorities for Business* feature, *The Latest Recession Re-Ignites the Internet Taxation Debate.* We have updated the materials on the Sarbanes-Oxley Act and added discussions of new e-proxy rules and shareholder access. An *Insight into Ethics* feature—*Is the Business Judgment Rule Overly Protective?*—appears in Chapter 40. The chapter on securities law (Chapter 42) was revamped to make this difficult topic more understandable to students. The chapter now includes a practical explanation of the *Howey* test. We have also revised the materials on the registration process to account for well-known seasoned issuers and updated the securities fraud coverage.

- Chapter 44 (Administrative Law)—This chapter has been reworked to underscore the practical significance of administrative law for businesspersons. We present the United States Supreme Court case on fleeting expletives in this chapter, and a feature explores the topic *Should Pharmaceutical Companies Be Allowed to Tweet?*

- Chapter 45 (Consumer Law)—The materials on food labeling and credit cards have been significantly updated. The chapter discusses the Consumer Financial Protection Bureau, the new agency that was established by the 2010 financial reform package. A *Shifting Legal Priorities for Business* feature titled *New Health-Care Law Requires Caloric Information* is included.

- Chapter 46 (Environmental Law)—The materials on air pollution and water pollution have been updated. New subsections discuss how environmental self-audits can help businesses minimize their liability and explain the innocent landowner, or third party, defense to Superfund liability.

- Chapter 47 (Antitrust Law)—We have added new examples and coverage of leading cases throughout the chapter, particularly in the discussions of price fixing, relevant product market, and relevant geographic market. Updated thresholds for interlocking directorates have been incorporated.

- Chapter 48 (Professional Liability and Accountability)—We have added a discussion of the adoption of global accounting rules by the United States and how that may affect an accountant's duty of care in the near future. A *Shifting Legal Priorities for Business* feature titled *Attacking the Essence of the Sarbanes-Oxley Act* appears in the chapter.

- Chapter 50 (Real Property and Landlord-Tenant Relationships)—This chapter has been revised to include more discussion of zoning and includes a new feature titled *The Law of Building "Green"—Sustainable Real Estate Development.*

Acknowledgments for Previous Editions

Since we began this project many years ago, a sizable number of business law professors and others have helped us in various phases of the undertaking. The following reviewers offered numerous constructive criticisms, comments, and suggestions during the preparation of the previous editions.

Jeffrey E. Allen
University of Miami

Judith Anshin
Sacramento City College

Thomas M. Apke
California State University, Fullerton

Raymond August
Washington State University

William Auslen
San Francisco City College

Mary B. Bader
Moorhead State University

Frank Bagan
County College of Morris

John J. Balek
Morton College, Illinois

Michael G. Barth
University of Phoenix

David L. Baumer
North Carolina State University

Barbara E. Behr
Bloomsburg University of Pennsylvania

Robert B. Bennett, Jr.
Butler University

Heidi Boerstler
University of Colorado at Denver

Maria Kathleen Boss
California State University, Los Angeles

Lawrence J. Bradley
University of Notre Dame

Doug Brown
Montana State University

Kristi K. Brown
University of Texas at Austin

William J. Burke
University of Massachusetts, Lowell

Kenneth Burns
University of Miami

Daniel R. Cahoy
Pennsylvania State University

Rita Cain
University of Missouri–Kansas City

Jeanne A. Calderon
New York University

Joseph E. Cantrell
DeAnza College, California

Donald Cantwell
University of Texas at Arlington

Robert Chatov
State University of New York, Buffalo

Nanette C. Clinch
San Jose State University, California

Robert J. Cox
Salt Lake Community College

Thomas Crane
University of Miami

Kenneth S. Culott
University of Texas at Austin

Larry R. Curtis
Iowa State University

Richard Dalebout
Brigham Young University

William H. Daughtrey, Jr.
Virginia Commonwealth University

Michele A. Dunkerley
University of Texas at Austin

O. E. Elmore
Texas A&M University

Robert J. Enders
California State Polytechnic University, Pomona

Michael Engber
Ball State University

David A. Escamilla
University of Texas at Austin

Frank S. Forbes
University of Nebraska at Omaha

Joe W. Fowler
Oklahoma State University

Stanley G. Freeman
University of South Carolina

Christ Gaetanos
State University of New York, Fredonia

Chester S. Galloway
Auburn University

Bob Garrett
American River College, California

Gary L. Giese
University of Colorado at Denver

Thomas Gossman
Western Michigan University

Patrick O. Gudridge
University of Miami School of Law

James M. Haine
University of Wisconsin, Stevens Point

Gerard Halpern
University of Arkansas

Christopher L. Hamilton
Golden West College, California

JoAnn W. Hammer
University of Texas at Austin

Charles Hartman
Wright State University, Ohio

Richard A. Hausler
University of Miami School of Law

Harry E. Hicks
Butler University, Indianapolis

Janine S. Hiller
Virginia Polytechnic Institute and State University

Rebecca L. Hillyer
Chemeketa Community College

E. Clayton Hipp, Jr.
Clemson University

Anthony H. Holliday, Jr.
Howard University

Telford Hollman
University of Northern Iowa

June A. Horrigan
California State University, Sacramento

John P. Huggard
North Carolina State University

Terry Hutchins
Pembroke State University, North Carolina

Robert Jesperson
University of Houston

Bryce J. Jones
Northeast Missouri State University

Margaret Jones
Southwest Missouri State College

Peter A. Karl III
SUNY Institute of Technology at Utica

Jack E. Karns
East Carolina University

Tamra Kempf
University of Miami

Judith Kenney
University of Miami

Barbara Kincaid
Southern Methodist University

Carey Kirk
University of Northern Iowa

Nancy P. Klintworth
University of Central Florida

Kurtis P. Klumb
University of Wisconsin at Milwaukee

Kathleen M. Knutson
College of St. Catherine, St. Paul, Minnesota

M. Alan Lawson
Mt. San Antonio College

Leslie E. Lenn
St. Edwards University

Susan Liebeler
Loyola University

Thomas E. Maher
California State University, Fullerton

Sal Marchionna
Triton College, Illinois

Gene A. Marsh
University of Alabama

Karen Kay Matson
University of Texas at Austin

Woodrow J. Maxwell
Hudson Valley Community College, New York

Bruce E. May
University of South Dakota

Gail McCracken
University of Michigan, Dearborn

John W. McGee
Southwest Texas State University

Cotton Meagher
University of Nevada at Las Vegas

Roger E. Meiners
University of Texas at Arlington

Gerald S. Meisel
Bergen Community College, New Jersey

Richard Mills
Cypress College

David Minars
City University of New York, Brooklyn

Leo Moersen
The George Washington University

Alan Moggio
Illinois Central College

Violet E. Molnar
Riverside City College

James E. Moon
Meyer, Johnson & Moon, Minneapolis

Melinda Ann Mora
University of Texas at Austin

Bob Morgan
Eastern Michigan University

Barry S. Morinaka
Baker College–Michigan

Joan Ann Mrava
Los Angeles Southwest College

Dwight D. Murphey
Wichita State University

Daniel E. Murray
University of Miami School of Law

Paula C. Murray
University of Texas

Gregory J. Naples
Marquette University

George A. Nation III
Lehigh University

Caleb L. Nichols
Western Connecticut State University

John M. Norwood
University of Arkansas

Michael J. O'Hara
University of Nebraska at Omaha

Rick F. Orsinger
College of DuPage, Illinois

Daniel J. O'Shea
Hillsborough Community College

Thomas L. Palmer
Northern Arizona University

Charles M. Patten
University of Wisconsin, Oshkosh

Patricia Pattison
Texas State University, San Marcos

Peyton J. Paxson
University of Texas at Austin

Ralph L. Quinones
University of Wisconsin, Oshkosh

Carol D. Rasnic
Virginia Commonwealth University

Marvin H. Robertson
Harding University

Gary K. Sambol
Rutgers State University

Rudy Sandoval
University of Texas, San Antonio

Sidney S. Sappington
York College of Pennsylvania

Martha Sartoris
North Hennepin Community College

Barbara P. Scheller
Temple University

S. Alan Schlact
Kennesaw State University, Georgia

Lorne H. Seidman
University of Nevada at Las Vegas

Roscoe B. Shain
Austin Peay University

Bennett D. Shulman
Lansing Community College, Michigan

S. Jay Sklar
Temple University

Dana Blair Smith
University of Texas at Austin

Michael Smydra
Oakland Community College–Royal Oak

Arthur Southwick
University of Michigan

Sylvia A. Spade
University of Texas at Austin

John A. Sparks
Grove City College, Pennsylvania

Elisabeth Sperow
California Polytechnic University, San Luis Obispo

Brenda Steuer
North Harris College, Houston

Craig Stilwell
Michigan State University

Irwin Stotsky
University of Miami School of Law

Charles R. B. Stowe
Sam Houston State University

Larry Strate
University of Nevada at Las Vegas

Raymond Mason Taylor
North Carolina State University

H. Allan Tolbert
Central Texas College

Jesse C. Trentadue
University of North Dakota

Edwin Tucker
University of Connecticut

Gary Victor
Eastern Michigan University

William H. Volz
Wayne State University

David Vyncke
Scott Community College, Iowa

William H. Walker
Indiana University–Purdue University, Fort Wayne

Diana Walsh
County College of Morris

Robert J. Walter
University of Texas at El Paso

Gary Watson
California State University, Los Angeles

John L. Weimer
Nicholls State University, Louisiana

Marshall Wilkerson
University of Texas at Austin

Melanie Stallings Williams
California State University–Northridge

Arthur D. Wolfe
Michigan State University

Elizabeth A. Wolfe
University of Texas at Austin

Daniel R. Wrentmore
Santa Barbara City College

Norman Gregory Young
*California State Polytechnic
University, Pomona*

Ronald C. Young
*Kalamazoo Valley Community
College, Michigan*

We would also like to give credit to the following reviewers for their useful input during development of the CengageNOW for *Business Law:* Interactive Assignment System.

Nena Ellison
Florida Atlantic University

Jacqueline Hagerott
Franklin University

Melanie Morris
*Raritan Valley Community
College*

William H. Volz
Wayne State University

Acknowledgments for the Twelfth Edition

In preparing the Twelfth Edition of *Business Law,* we worked closely with the following reviewers, each of whom offered us valuable suggestions for how to improve the text:

Frank Bagan
County College of Morris

Maria Kathleen Boss
*California State University,
Los Angeles*

Nanette C. Clinch
San Jose State University, California

Angela Crossin
Purdue University, Calumet

Larry R. Curtis
Iowa State University

Michael DeAngelis
University of Rhode Island

James Doering
*University of Wisconsin,
Green Bay*

John V. Dowdy
University of Texas at Arlington

Paul Dusseault
*Herkimer County Community
College*

James S. Fargason
Louisiana State University

Debra Johnson
University of Montana at Billings

Barbara Kincaid
Southern Methodist University

Vonda M. Laughlin
Carson-Newman College

Stuart MacDonald
University of Central Oklahoma

Christopher Meakin
University of Texas at Austin

Jamie O'Brien
University of Notre Dame

Michael O'Hara
University of Nebraska at Omaha

Bert K. Robinson
Kennesaw State University

Ira Selkowitz
University of Colorado at Denver

Robert D. Sprague
University of Wyoming

Ray Teske
*University of Texas at
San Antonio*

Melanie Stallings Williams
*California State
University–Northridge*

Norman Gregory Young
*California State Polytechnic
University, Pomona*

We also wish to extend special thanks to the following individuals for their contributions to the Twelfth Edition, specifically for their valuable input for new Chapter 31 and for helping revise Chapter 50:

Robert C. Bird
University of Connecticut

Dean Bredeson
University of Texas at Austin

Corey Ciocchetti
University of Denver

Thomas D. Cavenagh
*North Central College–
Naperville, Illinois*

Joan Gabel
Florida State University

Eric D. Yordy
Northern Arizona University

As in all past editions, we owe a debt of extreme gratitude to the numerous individuals who worked directly with us or at Cengage Learning. In particular, we wish to thank Vicky True and Rob Dewey for their helpful advice and guidance during all of the stages of this new edition. We extend our thanks to Jan Lamar, our longtime developmental editor, for her many useful suggestions and for her efforts in coordinating reviews and ensuring the timely and accurate publication of all supplemental materials. We are also indebted to Laura-Aurora Stopa for her support and excellent marketing advice.

Our production manager and designer, Bill Stryker, made sure that we came out with an error-free, visually attractive Twelfth Edition. We appreciate his efforts more than he can ever imagine. We are also indebted to the staff at Parkwood Composition, our compositor. Their ability to generate the pages for this text quickly and accurately made it possible for us to meet our ambitious printing schedule. We also wish to thank Joy Westberg for her creation of the visual preface.

We especially wish to thank Katherine Marie Silsbee for her management of the entire project, as well as for the application of her superb research and editorial skills. We also thank Lavina Leed Miller for her case research and Roger Meiners for his assistance in finding new case problems. We also wish to thank William Eric Hollowell, who co-authored the *Instructor's Manual,* the *Study Guide,* and the two *Test Banks,* for his excellent research efforts. We were fortunate enough to have the copyediting of Pat Lewis and the proofreading services of Beverly Peavler and Joanne Yost. We are grateful for the efforts of Vickie Reierson and Roxanna Lee for their proofreading and other assistance, which helped to ensure an error-free text. Finally, we thank Suzanne Jasin of K & M Consulting for her many special efforts on this project.

In addition, we would like to give special thanks to all of the individuals who were instrumental in developing and implementing the new CengageNOW for *Business Law:* Interactive Assignment System. These include Rob Dewey, Vicky True, Jan Lamar, Lisa Lysne, and Kristen Meere at Cengage, and Katherine Marie Silsbee, Roger Meiners, Lavina Leed Miller, William Eric Hollowell, Kimberly Wallan, Kristi Wiswell, and Joseph Zavaleta.

Through the years, we have enjoyed an ongoing correspondence with many of you who have found points on which you wish to comment. We continue to welcome all comments and promise to respond promptly. By incorporating your ideas, we can continue to write a business law text that is best for you and best for your students.

K. S. C.
R. L. M.
F. B. C.

Preface to the Student

Welcome to the world of business law and the legal environment. You are about to embark on the study of one of the most important topics you can master in today's changing world. A solid understanding of business law will, of course, help you if you are going into the world of business. If you decide on a career in accounting, economics, finance, political science, or history, understanding how the legal environment works is crucial.

Moreover, in your role as a consumer, you will be faced with some legal issues throughout your lifetime—renting an apartment, buying a house, obtaining a mortgage, and leasing a car, to mention only a few. In your role as an employee (if you don't go into business for yourself), you will need to know what rights you have and what rights you don't have. Even when you contemplate marriage, you will be faced with legal issues.

WHAT YOU WILL FIND IN THIS TEXT

As you thumb through the pages in this text, you will see that we have tried to make your study of business law and the legal environment as efficient and enjoyable as possible. To this end, you will find the following aids:

- **Mastering Terminology**—through *key terms* that are boldfaced, listed at the end of each chapter, and explained fully in the *Glossary* at the end of the book.
- **Understanding Concepts**—through numerous *Concept Summaries* and *exhibits.*
- **Observing the Law in the Context of the Real World**—through new *Case in Point* features within each chapter's text and the *Reviewing* features at the end of every chapter.
- **Seeing How Legal Issues Can Arise**—through *Video Questions* based on Web-available short videos, including some from Hollywood movies.
- **Figuring Out How the Law Is Evolving**—through a feature called *Shifting Legal Priorities for Business.*

- **Determining How the Law Applies to Business Managers**—through the new *Managerial Implications* sections that appear in selected features and cases.
- **Gaining Insight into How the Law Affects or Is Affected by Ethical Issues**—through *Insight into Ethics* features.

The above list, of course, is representative only. You will understand much more of what the law is about as you read through the *court cases* presented in this book, including *Extended Case excerpts,* which will give you a feel for how the courts really decide cases, in the courts' language.

IMPROVING YOUR ABILITY TO PERFORM LEGAL REASONING AND ANALYSIS

Although business law may seem to be a mass of facts, your goal in taking this course should also be an increased ability to use legal reasoning and analysis to figure out how legal situations will be resolved. To this end, you will find the following key learning features to assist you in mastering legal reasoning and analysis:

- *Finding and Analyzing Case Law*—In Chapter 1, you will find a section with this title that explains:
  - Legal citations.
  - The standard elements of a case.
  - The different types of opinions a court can issue.
  - How to read and understand cases.

- *Briefing a Case*—In Appendix A, you will see how to brief and analyze case problems. This explanation will teach you how to break down the elements of a case and will improve your ability to answer the *Case Problems* in each chapter.
- *Questions with Sample Answers*—At the end of each chapter, there is one hypothetical

factual scenario that presents a legal question for which you can access a ***sample answer*** in Appendix I (and also on the text's Web site). This allows you to practice and to see if you are answering the hypothetical questions correctly.

- ***Case Problems with Sample Answers***— Each chapter has a series of chapter-ending ***Case Problems.*** You can find an answer to one problem in each chapter on this book's companion student Web site. You can easily compare your answer to the court's opinion in each real case.

- ***Impact of This Case on Today's Law***— Each case that is considered a landmark concludes with a short section that explains the relevance of older case law to the way courts reason today.

- ***What If the Facts Were Different?***—This section, found at the end of selected cases, encourages you to think about how the outcome of a case might be different if the facts were altered.

- ***The Ethical [E-Commerce, Global, or Legal Environment] Dimension***—Every case in this text concludes with two critical-thinking questions. These *Dimension* questions ask you to explore the law in a variety of contexts to help you meet the specific curriculum requirements for business law students.

- ***Managerial Implications***—When a case has particular importance for business managers, we point out its significance in these special sections.

THE COMPANION STUDENT WEB SITE

The companion student Web site at **www.cengage. com/blaw/clarkson** provides you with short videos on various legal topics and with sample answers to selected case problems. In addition, you will find the following:

- ***Interactive quizzes*** for every chapter.
- A ***Glossary*** of boldfaced terms.
- ***Flashcards*** that provide an optional study tool for reviewing the key terms in every chapter.
- ***Appendix A: How to Brief and Analyze Case Problems*** that will help you analyze

cases. This useful appendix in the book can also be downloaded from the Web site.

- ***Legal reference materials*** including a "Statutes" page that offers links to the full text of selected statutes referenced in the text, a Spanish glossary, and links to other important legal resources available free on the Web.

- ***Internet exercises*** for every chapter in the text (at least two per chapter) that help you learn how to research the law online.

- ***Law on the Web*** features that provide links to Web sites that discuss topics related to each chapter in the text.

- ***Online Legal Research Guide*** that offers complete yet brief guidance to using the Internet and evaluating information obtained from the Internet as well as hyperlinks to the Web sites discussed.

- ***Court case updates*** for follow-up on decisions presented in the text.

INTERACTIVE ASSIGNMENTS ON THE WEB

Some of you may have instructors who provide assignments using either of our interactive Web-based systems, **Aplia or CengageNOW for *Business Law:* Interactive Assignment System.**

Both Aplia and CengageNOW for *Business Law:* Interactive Assignment System allow you to improve your mastery of legal concepts and terminology, legal reasoning and analysis, and much more. Your instructor will give you further information if she or he decides to use a Web-based system.

Of course, whether or not you are using Aplia or CengageNOW, you will wish to consider purchasing the *Study Guide,* which can help you get a better grade in your course (see the inside cover for details).

The law is all around you—and will be for the rest of your life. We hope that you begin your first course in business law and the legal environment with the same high degree of excitement that we, the authors, always have when we work on improving this text, now in its Twelfth Edition. *Business Law* has withstood the test of time— several million students before you have already used and benefited from it.

Dedication

To Sonia and Victor,

You're embarking on
a long journey together.
You each possess all of the
right elements to make it a
joyful and fruitful one.
I am looking forward to
watching your progress.

With great affection,

R. L. M.

To my parents and sisters.

F. B. C.

UNIT ONE

THE LEGAL ENVIRONMENT OF BUSINESS

CONTENTS

BUSINESS LAW

CLARKSON · MILLER · CROSS

CHAPTER 1

Introduction to Law and Legal Reasoning

O ne of the important functions of law in any society is to provide stability, predictability, and continuity so that people can know how to order their affairs. If any society is to survive, its citizens must be able to determine what is legally right and legally wrong. They must know what sanctions will be imposed on them if they commit wrongful acts. If they suffer harm as a result of others' wrongful acts, they must know how they can seek redress. By setting forth the rights, obligations, and privileges of citizens, the law enables individuals to go about their business with confidence and a certain degree of predictability. The stability and predictability created by the law provide an essential framework for all civilized activities, including business activities.

What do we mean when we speak of "the law"? Although the law has various definitions, they are all based on the general observation that **law consists of** *enforceable rules governing relationships among individuals and between individuals and their society.* These "enforceable rules" may consist of unwritten principles of behavior established by a nomadic tribe. They may be set forth in a law code, such as the Code of Hammurabi in ancient Babylon (c. 1780 B.C.E.) or the law code of one of today's European nations. They may consist of written laws and court decisions created by modern legislative and judicial bodies, as in the United States. Regardless of how such rules are created, they all have one thing in common: they establish rights, duties,

and privileges that are consistent with the values and beliefs of their society or its ruling group.

In this introductory chapter, we first look at an important question for any student reading this text: How does the legal environment affect business decision making? We next describe the major sources of American law, the common law tradition, and some basic schools of legal thought. We conclude the chapter with sections offering practical guidance on several topics, including how to find the sources of law discussed in this chapter (and referred to throughout the text) and how to read and understand court opinions.

SECTION 1
BUSINESS ACTIVITIES AND THE LEGAL ENVIRONMENT

As those entering the world of business will learn, laws and government regulations affect virtually all business activities—from hiring and firing decisions to workplace safety, the manufacturing and marketing of products, business financing, and more. To make good business decisions, a basic knowledge of the laws and regulations governing these activities is beneficial—if not essential. Realize also that in today's world, a knowledge of "black-letter" law is not enough. Businesspersons are also pressured to

make ethical decisions. Thus, the study of business law necessarily involves an ethical dimension.

Many Different Laws May Affect a Single Business Transaction

As you will note, each chapter in this text covers a specific area of the law and shows how the legal rules in that area affect business activities. Though compartmentalizing the law in this fashion promotes conceptual clarity, it does not indicate the extent to which a number of different laws may apply to just one transaction.

Consider an example. Suppose that you are the president of NetSys, Inc., a company that creates and maintains computer network systems for business firms, and also markets related software. One day, Hernandez, an operations officer for Southwest Distribution Corporation (SDC), contacts you by e-mail about a possible contract concerning SDC's computer network. In deciding whether to enter into a contract with SDC, you should consider, among other things, the legal requirements for an enforceable contract. Are there different requirements for a contract for services and a contract for products? What are your options if SDC **breaches** (breaks, or fails to perform) the contract? The answers to these questions are part of contract law and sales law.

Other questions might concern payment under the contract. How can you ensure that NetSys will be paid? For example, if payment is made with a check that is returned for insufficient funds, what are your options? Answers to these questions can be found in the laws that relate to negotiable instruments (such as checks) and creditors' rights. Also, a dispute may occur over the rights to NetSys's software, or there may be a question of liability if the software is defective. Questions may even be raised as to whether you and Hernandez had the authority to make the deal in the first place. A disagreement may arise from

other circumstances, such as an accountant's evaluation of the contract. Resolutions of these questions may be found in areas of the law that relate to intellectual property, e-commerce, torts, product liability, agency, business organizations, or professional liability.

Finally, if any dispute cannot be resolved amicably, then the laws and the rules concerning courts and court procedures spell out the steps of a lawsuit. Exhibit 1–1 illustrates the various areas of law that may influence business decision making.

Ethics and Business Decision Making

Merely knowing the areas of law that may affect a business decision is not sufficient in today's business world. Businesspersons must also take ethics into account. As you will learn in Chapter 5, *ethics* generally is defined as the study of what constitutes right or wrong behavior. Today, business decision makers need to consider not just whether a decision is legal, but also whether it is ethical.

Throughout this text, you will learn about the relationship between the law and ethics, as well as about some of the types of ethical questions that

EXHIBIT 1–1 • Areas of the Law That May Affect Business Decision Making

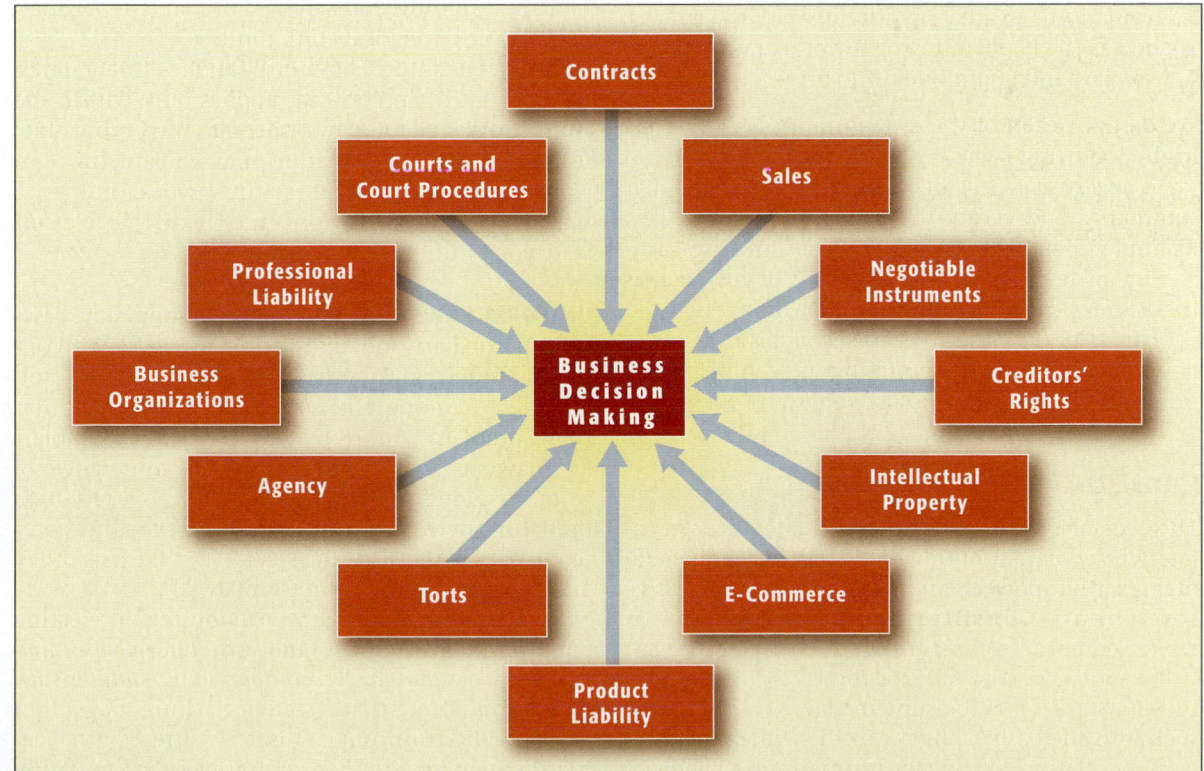

often arise in the business context. For example, the unit-ending *Focus on Ethics* features are devoted solely to the exploration of ethical questions pertaining to topics treated within the unit. We have also included *Ethical Dimension* questions for selected cases that stress the importance of ethical considerations in today's business climate and *Insight into Ethics* features that appear in selected chapters. A *Question of Ethics* case problem is included at the conclusion of every chapter to introduce you to the ethical aspects of specific cases involving real-life situations. Additionally, Chapter 5 offers a detailed look at the importance of ethical considerations in business decision making.

SECTION 2
SOURCES OF AMERICAN LAW

There are numerous sources of American law. *Primary sources of law,* or sources that establish the law, include the following:

1. The U.S. Constitution and the constitutions of the various states.
2. Statutory law—including laws passed by Congress, state legislatures, or local governing bodies.
3. Regulations created by administrative agencies, such as the Food and Drug Administration.
4. Case law and common law doctrines.

We describe each of these important sources of law in the following pages.

Secondary sources of law are books and articles that summarize and clarify the primary sources of law. Examples include legal encyclopedias, treatises, articles in law reviews, and compilations of law, such as the *Restatements of the Law* (which will be discussed shortly). Courts often refer to secondary sources of law for guidance in interpreting and applying the primary sources of law discussed here.

Constitutional Law

The federal government and the states have separate written constitutions that set forth the general organization, powers, and limits of their respective governments. **Constitutional law** is the law as expressed in these constitutions.

According to Article VI of the U.S. Constitution, the Constitution is the supreme law of the land. As such, it is the basis of all law in the United States. A law in violation of the Constitution, if challenged,

will be declared unconstitutional and will not be enforced, no matter what its source. Because of its importance in the American legal system, we present the complete text of the U.S. Constitution in Appendix B.

The Tenth Amendment to the U.S. Constitution reserves to the states all powers not granted to the federal government. Each state in the union has its own constitution. Unless it conflicts with the U.S. Constitution or a federal law, a state constitution is supreme within the state's borders.

Statutory Law

Laws enacted by legislative bodies at any level of government, such as the statutes passed by Congress or by state legislatures, make up the body of law generally referred to as **statutory law.** When a legislature passes a statute, that statute ultimately is included in the federal code of laws or the relevant state code of laws (these codes are discussed later in this chapter).

Statutory law also includes local **ordinances**—statutes (laws, rules, or orders) passed by municipal or county governing units to govern matters not covered by federal or state law. Ordinances commonly have to do with city or county land use (zoning ordinances), building and safety codes, and other matters affecting the local community.

A federal statute, of course, applies to all states. A state statute, in contrast, applies only within the state's borders. State laws thus may vary from state to state. No federal statute may violate the U.S. Constitution, and no state statute or local ordinance may violate the U.S. Constitution or the relevant state constitution.

UNIFORM LAWS The differences among state laws were particularly notable in the 1800s, when conflicting state statutes frequently made trade and commerce among the states difficult. To counter these problems, in 1892 a group of legal scholars and lawyers formed the National Conference of Commissioners on Uniform State Laws (NCCUSL) to draft **uniform laws,** or model laws, for the states to consider adopting. The NCCUSL still exists today and continues to issue uniform laws.

Each state has the option of adopting or rejecting a uniform law. *Only if a state legislature adopts a uniform law does that law become part of the statutory law of that state.* Note that a state legislature may adopt all or part of a uniform law as it is written, or the legislature may rewrite the law however the legislature wishes. Hence, even though many states may have adopted a uniform law, those states' laws may not be entirely "uniform."

The earliest uniform law, the Uniform Negotiable Instruments Law, was completed by 1896 and adopted in every state by the early 1920s (although not all states used exactly the same wording). Over the following decades, other acts were drawn up in a similar manner. In all, more than two hundred uniform acts have been issued by the NCCUSL since its inception. The most ambitious uniform act of all, however, was the Uniform Commercial Code.

THE UNIFORM COMMERCIAL CODE The Uniform Commercial Code (UCC), which was created through the joint efforts of the NCCUSL and the American Law Institute,[1] was first issued in 1952. All fifty states,[2] the District of Columbia, and the Virgin Islands have adopted the UCC. It facilitates commerce among the states by providing a uniform, yet flexible, set of rules governing commercial transactions. The UCC assures businesspersons that their contracts, if validly entered into, normally will be enforced.

As you will read in later chapters, from time to time the NCCUSL revises the articles contained in the UCC and submits the revised versions to the states for adoption. During the 1990s, for example, four articles (Articles 3, 4, 5, and 9) were revised, and two new articles (Articles 2A and 4A) were added. Amendments to Article 1 were approved in 2001 and have now been adopted by a majority of the states. Because of its importance in the area of commercial law, we cite the UCC frequently in this text. We also present the UCC in Appendix C.

Administrative Law

Another important source of American law is **administrative law,** which consists of the rules, orders, and decisions of administrative agencies. An **administrative agency** is a federal, state, or local government agency established to perform a specific function. Administrative law and procedures, which will be examined in detail in Chapter 44, constitute a dominant element in the regulatory environment of business.

Rules issued by various administrative agencies now affect almost every aspect of a business's

operations, including its capital structure and financing, its hiring and firing procedures, its relations with employees and unions, and the way it manufactures and markets its products. Regulations enacted to protect the environment often play a significant role in business operations. See this chapter's *Shifting Legal Priorities for Business* feature on the following page for a discussion of the concept of sustainability and how some environmental regulations encourage it.

FEDERAL AGENCIES At the national level, the cabinet departments of the executive branch include numerous **executive agencies.** The U.S. Food and Drug Administration, for example, is an agency within the U.S. Department of Health and Human Services. Executive agencies are subject to the authority of the president, who has the power to appoint and remove their officers. There are also major **independent regulatory agencies** at the federal level, such as the Federal Trade Commission, the Securities and Exchange Commission, and the Federal Communications Commission. The president's power is less pronounced in regard to independent agencies, whose officers serve for fixed terms and cannot be removed without just cause.

STATE AND LOCAL AGENCIES There are administrative agencies at the state and local levels as well. Commonly, a state agency (such as a state pollution-control agency) is created as a parallel to a federal agency (such as the Environmental Protection Agency). Just as federal statutes take precedence over conflicting state statutes, so federal agency regulations take precedence over conflicting state regulations.

Case Law and Common Law Doctrines

The rules of law announced in court decisions constitute another basic source of American law. These rules include interpretations of constitutional provisions, of statutes enacted by legislatures, and of regulations created by administrative agencies. Today, this body of judge-made law is referred to as **case law.** Case law—the doctrines and principles announced in cases—governs all areas not covered by statutory law or administrative law and is part of our common law tradition. We look at the origins and characteristics of the common law tradition in some detail in the pages that follow.

See *Concept Summary 1.1* on page 7 for a review of the sources of American law.

---

1. This institute was formed in the 1920s and consists of practicing attorneys, legal scholars, and judges.
2. Louisiana has not adopted Articles 2 and 2A (covering contracts for the sale and lease of goods), however.

By now, almost everyone is aware that at the federal, state, and local levels there are numerous statutes that deal with the environment (environmental law will be discussed in Chapter 46). In the last few years, federal, state, and local statutes and administrative regulations have started to embrace the concept of sustainability.

What Does Sustainability Mean?

Although there is no one official definition, *sustainability* generally has been defined as economic development that meets the needs of the present while not compromising the ability of future generations to meet their own needs. By any definition, sustainability is a process rather than a tangible outcome. For business managers, it means that they should engage in long-range planning rather than focusing only on short-run profitability.

Federal Law and Sustainability

Certain provisions of federal environmental laws directly address the topic of sustainability. For example, the Resource Conservation and Recovery Act[a] requires waste minimization as the preferred means of hazardous waste management. Facilities that generate or manage hazardous waste must certify that they have a waste minimization program that reduces the toxicity and quantity of the hazardous waste.

The Pollution Prevention Act (PPA)[b] requires that facilities minimize or eliminate the release of pollutants into the environment whenever feasible. The PPA established a national policy to recycle any pollutants that cannot be prevented.

Finally, the federal Environmental Protection Agency (EPA) has undertaken a major effort to encourage sustainability. The agency's Web site (**www.epa.gov**) devotes numerous pages to sustainability, sustainable development, and sustainable agriculture. The EPA also has a "sector strategies program" that seeks industry-wide environmental gains through innovative actions.

Other nations have enacted legislation that requires sustainability to be taken into account when protecting the environment. An example is the Environmental Protection and Bio-Diversity Conservation Act in Australia.[c]

State Law and Sustainability

At least one state has legislatively committed itself to the concept of sustainable policies. More than a decade ago, the Oregon Sustainability Act was passed. This act officially defines *sustainability* as:

---

a. 42 U.S.C. Sections 6901 *et seq.* (1976).
b. 42 U.S.C. Sections 13101 *et seq.* (1990).
c. This act became effective in 1999 and has been amended many times since.

Using, developing, and protecting resources in a manner that enables people to meet current needs and provides that future generations can also meet future needs, from the joint perspective of environmental, economic, and community objectives.

Oregon's seven-member sustainability board recommends and proposes sustainability legislation and also develops policies and programs related to sustainability.

Where Does the United States Rank in the World Sustainability Index?

Environmental experts from Yale and Columbia universities have created an Environmental Sustainability Index (ESI) that ranks countries according to how well they manage their environments, protect the global commons, and have the capacity to improve their environmental performance. Finland and Norway are at the top of the ESI. The United States ranks forty-fifth. This low ranking is due mainly to excessive waste generation and greenhouse gas emissions in this country.

Some Corporations Take the Lead by Creating the Position of a Chief Sustainability Officer

The giant chemical company DuPont has an official chief sustainability officer (CSO)—a position that did not exist a few years ago. This corporate officer is responsible not only for ensuring that the company complies with all federal, state, local, and international environmental regulations, but also for discovering so-called megatrends that can affect different markets.

DuPont, though best known as a chemical company, also sells agricultural seeds and crop-protection products. One megatrend that its CSO has identified is a growing world population that is going to require more production of corn, soybeans, and other crops from limited acreage. That is where sustainability comes in—producing more with less.

MANAGERIAL IMPLICATIONS

Managers cannot wait until the government tells them what sustainable business practices they must follow. A company that adopts sustainable business practices today not only will promote desirable economic, social, and environmental results, but at the same time will enhance productivity, reduce costs, and thereby increase profitability. A company that has a clear understanding of sustainability will be more competitive as increasing consumer demand for "green" products and global concerns about the environment put pressure on all producers.

CONCEPT SUMMARY 1.1
Sources of American Law

Source	Description
Constitutional Law	The law as expressed in the U.S. Constitution and the state constitutions. The U.S. Constitution is the supreme law of the land. State constitutions are supreme within state borders to the extent that they do not violate a clause of the U.S. Constitution or a federal law.
Statutory Law	Laws (statutes and ordinances) enacted by federal, state, and local legislatures and governing bodies. None of these laws may violate the U.S. Constitution or the relevant state constitution. Uniform laws, when adopted by a state, become statutory law in that state.
Administrative Law	The rules, orders, and decisions of federal, state, or local government administrative agencies.
Case Law and Common Law Doctrines	Judge-made law, including interpretations of constitutional provisions, of statutes enacted by legislatures, and of regulations created by administrative agencies.

SECTION 3
THE COMMON LAW TRADITION

Because of our colonial heritage, much of American law is based on the English legal system, which originated in medieval England and continued to evolve in the following centuries. Knowledge of this system is necessary to understanding the American legal system today.

Early English Courts

The origins of the English legal system—and thus the U.S. legal system as well—date back to 1066, when the Normans conquered England. William the Conqueror and his successors began the process of unifying the country under their rule. One of the means they used to do this was the establishment of the king's courts, or *curiae regis*. Before the Norman Conquest, disputes had been settled according to the local legal customs and traditions in various regions of the country. The king's courts sought to establish a uniform set of customs for the country as a whole. What evolved in these courts was the beginning of the **common law**—a body of general rules that applied throughout the entire English realm. Eventually, the common law tradition became part of the heritage of all nations that were once British colonies, including the United States.

COURTS OF LAW AND REMEDIES AT LAW The early English king's courts could grant only very limited kinds of **remedies** (the legal means to enforce a right or redress a wrong). If one person wronged another in some way, the king's courts could award as compensation one or more of the following: (1) land, (2) items of value, or (3) money. The courts that awarded this compensation became known as **courts of law,** and the three remedies were called **remedies at law.** (Today, the remedy at law normally takes the form of monetary **damages**—an amount given to a party whose legal interests have been injured.) Even though the system introduced uniformity in the settling of disputes, when a complaining party wanted a remedy other than economic compensation, the courts of law could do nothing, so "no remedy, no right."

COURTS OF EQUITY AND REMEDIES IN EQUITY Equity is a branch of law—founded on what might be described as notions of justice and fair dealing—that seeks to supply a remedy when no adequate remedy at law is available. When individuals could not obtain an adequate remedy in a court of law, they petitioned the king for relief. Most of these petitions were decided by an adviser to the king, called a **chancellor,** who had the power to grant new and unique remedies. Eventually, formal chancery courts, or **courts of equity,** were established.

The remedies granted by the equity courts became known as **remedies in equity,** or equitable remedies. These remedies include *specific performance* (ordering a party to perform an agreement as promised), an *injunction* (ordering a party to cease engaging in a specific activity or to undo some wrong or injury), and *rescission* (the cancellation of a contractual obligation). We will discuss these and other equitable remedies in more detail at appropriate points in the chapters that follow, particularly in Chapter 18.

As a general rule, today's courts, like the early English courts, will not grant equitable remedies unless the remedy at law—monetary damages—is inadequate. Suppose that Ted forms a contract (a legally binding agreement—see Chapter 10) to purchase a parcel of land that he thinks will be just perfect for his future home. Further suppose that the seller breaches this agreement. Ted could sue the seller for the return of any deposits or down payment he might have made on the land, but this is not the remedy he really seeks. What Ted wants is to have the court order the seller to perform the contract. In other words, Ted wants the court to grant the equitable remedy of specific performance because monetary damages are inadequate in this situation.

EQUITABLE MAXIMS In fashioning appropriate remedies, judges often were (and continue to be) guided by so-called **equitable maxims**—propositions or general statements of equitable rules. Exhibit 1–2 lists some important equitable maxims. The last maxim listed in that exhibit—"Equity aids the vigilant, not those who rest on their rights"—merits special attention. It has become known as the equitable doctrine of **laches** (a term derived from the Latin *laxus,* meaning "lax" or "negligent"), and it can be used as a defense. A **defense** is an argument raised by the **defendant** (the party being sued) indicating why the **plaintiff** (the suing party) should not obtain the remedy sought. (Note that in equity proceedings, the party bringing a lawsuit is called the **petitioner,** and the party being sued is referred to as the **respondent.**)

The doctrine of laches arose to encourage people to bring lawsuits while the evidence was fresh.

What constitutes a reasonable time, of course, varies according to the circumstances of the case. Time periods for different types of cases are now usually fixed by **statutes of limitations.** After the time allowed under a statute of limitations has expired, no action (lawsuit) can be brought, no matter how strong the case was originally.

Legal and Equitable Remedies Today

The establishment of courts of equity in medieval England resulted in two distinct court systems: courts of law and courts of equity. The courts had different sets of judges and granted different types of remedies. During the nineteenth century, however, most states in the United States adopted rules of procedure that resulted in the combining of courts of law and equity. A party now may request both legal and equitable remedies in the same action, and the trial court judge may grant either or both forms of relief.

The distinction between legal and equitable remedies remains relevant to students of business law, however, because these remedies differ. To seek the proper remedy for a wrong, one must know what remedies are available. Additionally, certain vestiges of the procedures used when there were separate courts of law and equity still exist. For example, a party has the right to demand a jury trial in an action at law, but not in an action in equity. Exhibit 1–3 summarizes the procedural differences (applicable in most states) between an action at law and an action in equity.

The Doctrine of *Stare Decisis*

One of the unique features of the common law is that it is *judge-made* law. The body of principles and doctrines that form the common law emerged over time as judges decided legal controversies.

EXHIBIT 1–2 • Equitable Maxims

1.	*Whoever seeks equity must do equity.* (Anyone who wishes to be treated fairly must treat others fairly.)
2.	*Where there is equal equity, the law must prevail.* (The law will determine the outcome of a controversy in which the merits of both sides are equal.)
3.	*One seeking the aid of an equity court must come to the court with clean hands.* (The plaintiff must have acted fairly and honestly.)
4.	*Equity will not suffer a wrong to be without a remedy.* (Equitable relief will be awarded when there is a right to relief and there is no adequate remedy at law.)
5.	*Equity regards substance rather than form.* (Equity is more concerned with fairness and justice than with legal technicalities.)
6.	*Equity aids the vigilant, not those who rest on their rights.* (Equity will not help those who neglect their rights for an unreasonable period of time.)

EXHIBIT 1–3 • Procedural Differences between an Action at Law and an Action in Equity

PROCEDURE	ACTION AT LAW	ACTION IN EQUITY
Initiation of lawsuit	By filing a complaint	By filing a petition
Parties	Plaintiff and defendant	Petitioner and respondent
Decision	By jury or judge	By judge (no jury)
Result	Judgment	Decree
Remedy	Monetary damages	Injunction, specific performance, or rescission

CASE PRECEDENTS AND CASE REPORTERS When possible, judges attempted to be consistent and to base their decisions on the principles suggested by earlier cases. They sought to decide similar cases in a similar way and considered new cases with care because they knew that their decisions would make new law. Each interpretation became part of the law on the subject and served as a legal **precedent**— that is, a decision that furnished an example or authority for deciding subsequent cases involving identical or similar legal principles or facts.

In the early years of the common law, there was no single place or publication where court opinions, or written decisions, could be found. By the early fourteenth century, portions of the most important decisions from each year were being gathered together and recorded in *Year Books,* which became useful references for lawyers and judges. In the sixteenth century, the *Year Books* were discontinued, and other forms of case publication became available. Today, cases are published, or "reported," in volumes called **reporters,** or *reports*. We describe today's case reporting system in detail later in this chapter.

STARE DECISIS AND THE COMMON LAW TRADITION The practice of deciding new cases with reference to former decisions, or precedents, became a cornerstone of the English and American judicial systems. The practice formed a doctrine known as **stare decisis**[3] (a Latin phrase meaning "to stand on decided cases").

Under this doctrine, judges are obligated to follow the precedents established within their jurisdictions. The term *jurisdiction* refers to a geographic area in which a court or courts have the power to apply the law—see Chapter 2. Once a court has set forth a principle of law as being applicable to a certain set of facts, that court and courts of lower rank (within the same jurisdiction) must adhere to that principle and apply it in future cases involving similar fact patterns. Thus, *stare decisis* has two aspects: first, that decisions made by a higher court are binding on lower courts; and second, that a court should not overturn its own precedents unless there is a compelling reason to do so.

Controlling precedents in a jurisdiction are referred to as binding authorities. A **binding authority** is any source of law that a court must follow when deciding a case. Binding authorities include constitutions, statutes, and regulations that govern the issue being decided, as well as court decisions that are controlling precedents within the jurisdiction. United States Supreme Court case decisions, no matter how old, remain controlling until they are overruled by a subsequent decision of the Supreme Court, by a constitutional amendment, or by congressional legislation (that has not been held unconstitutional).

STARE DECISIS AND LEGAL STABILITY The doctrine of *stare decisis* helps the courts to be more efficient because if other courts have carefully analyzed a similar case, their legal reasoning and opinions can serve as guides. *Stare decisis* also makes the law more stable and predictable. If the law on a given subject is well settled, someone bringing a case to court can usually rely on the court to make a decision based on what the law has been in the past.

DEPARTURES FROM PRECEDENT Although courts are obligated to follow precedents, sometimes a court will depart from the rule of precedent if it decides that the precedent should no longer be followed. If a court decides that a ruling precedent is simply incorrect or that technological or social changes have rendered the precedent inapplicable, the court might rule contrary to the precedent. Cases that overturn precedent often receive a great deal of publicity.

---

3. Pronounced *ster*-ay dih-*si*-ses.

CASE IN POINT The United States Supreme Court expressly overturned precedent when it concluded that separate educational facilities for whites and blacks, which it had previously upheld as constitutional,[4] were inherently unequal.[5] The Court's departure from precedent in this case received a tremendous amount of publicity as people began to realize the ramifications of this change in the law.

Note that judges do have some flexibility in applying precedents. For example, a lower court may avoid applying a precedent set by a higher court in its jurisdiction by distinguishing the two cases based on their facts. When this happens, the lower court's ruling stands unless it is appealed to a higher court and that court overturns the decision.

WHEN THERE IS NO PRECEDENT Occasionally, the courts must decide cases for which no precedents exist, called *cases of first impression*. For example, as you will read throughout this text, the extensive use of the Internet has presented many new and challenging issues for the courts to decide. In deciding cases of first impression, courts often look at *persuasive authorities* (precedents from other jurisdictions) for guidance. A court may also consider a number of factors, including legal principles and policies underlying previous court decisions or existing statutes, fairness, social values and customs, **public policy** (governmental policy based on widely held societal values), and data and concepts drawn from the social sciences. Which of these sources is chosen or receives the greatest emphasis depends on the nature of the case being considered and the particular judge or judges hearing the case.

Stare Decisis and Legal Reasoning

Legal reasoning is the reasoning process used by judges in deciding what law applies to a given dispute and then applying that law to the specific facts or circumstances of the case. Through the use of legal reasoning, judges harmonize their decisions with those that have been made before, as the doctrine of *stare decisis* requires.

Students of business law and the legal environment also engage in legal reasoning. For example, you may be asked to provide answers for some of the case problems that appear at the end of every chapter in this text. Each problem describes the facts of a particular dispute and the legal question at issue. If you are assigned a case problem, you will be asked to determine how a court would answer that question, and why. In other words, you will need to give legal reasons for whatever conclusion you reach.[6] We look here at the basic steps involved in legal reasoning and then describe some forms of reasoning commonly used by the courts in making their decisions.

BASIC STEPS IN LEGAL REASONING At times, the legal arguments set forth in court opinions are relatively simple and brief. At other times, the arguments are complex and lengthy. Regardless of the length of a legal argument, however, the basic steps of the legal reasoning process remain the same. These steps, which you can also follow when analyzing cases and case problems, form what is commonly referred to as the *IRAC method* of legal reasoning. IRAC is an acronym formed from the first letters of the following words: *Issue, Rule, Application,* and *Conclusion.* To apply the IRAC method, you would ask the following questions:

1. *What are the key facts and issues?* Suppose that a plaintiff comes before the court claiming *assault* (the act of wrongfully and intentionally making another person fearful of immediate physical harm—part of a class of actions called *torts*). The plaintiff claims that the defendant threatened her while she was sleeping. Although the plaintiff was unaware that she was being threatened, her roommate heard the defendant make the threat. The legal issue, or question, raised by these facts is whether the defendant's action constitutes the tort of assault, given that the plaintiff was not aware of that action at the time it occurred.

2. *What rules of law apply to the case?* A rule of law may be a rule stated by the courts in previous decisions, a state or federal statute, or a state or federal administrative agency regulation. In our hypothetical case, the plaintiff **alleges** (claims) that the defendant committed a tort. Therefore, the applicable law is the common law of torts— specifically, tort law governing assault (see Chapter 6 for more detail on intentional torts). Case precedents involving similar facts and issues thus would be relevant. Often, more than one rule of law will be applicable to a case.

---

4. See *Plessy v. Ferguson,* 163 U.S. 537, 16 S.Ct. 1138, 41 L.Ed. 256 (1896). A later section in this chapter explains how to read legal citations.
5. *Brown v. Board of Education of Topeka,* 347 U.S. 483, 74 S.Ct. 686, 98 L.Ed. 873 (1954).

6. See Appendix A for further instructions on how to analyze case problems.

3. *How do the rules of law apply to the particular facts and circumstances of this case?* This step is often the most difficult because each case presents a unique set of facts, circumstances, and parties. Although cases may be similar, no two cases are ever identical in all respects. Normally, judges (and lawyers and law students) try to find **cases on point**—previously decided cases that are as similar as possible to the one under consideration. (Because of the difficulty—and importance—of this step in the legal reasoning process, we discuss it in more detail in the next subsection.)

4. *What conclusion should be drawn?* This step normally presents few problems. Usually, the conclusion is evident if the previous three steps have been followed carefully.

FORMS OF LEGAL REASONING Judges use many types of reasoning when following the third step of the legal reasoning process—applying the law to the facts of a particular case. Three common forms of reasoning are deductive reasoning, linear reasoning, and reasoning by analogy.

Deductive Reasoning. Deductive reasoning is sometimes called *syllogistic reasoning* because it employs a **syllogism**—a logical relationship involving a major premise, a minor premise, and a conclusion. For example, consider the hypothetical case presented earlier. In deciding whether the defendant committed assault by threatening the plaintiff while she was sleeping, the judge might point out that "under the common law of torts, an individual must be *aware* of a threat of danger for the threat to constitute assault" (major premise); "the plaintiff in this case was unaware of the threat at the time it occurred" (minor premise); and "therefore, the circumstances do not amount to an assault" (conclusion).

Linear Reasoning. A second form of legal reasoning that is commonly employed might be thought of as "linear" reasoning because it proceeds from one point to another, with the final point being the conclusion. To understand this form of reasoning, imagine a knotted rope, with each knot tying together separate pieces of rope to form a tightly knotted length. As a whole, the rope represents a linear progression of thought logically connecting various points, with the last point, or knot, representing the conclusion. For example, a tenant in an apartment building sues the landlord for damages for an injury resulting from an allegedly inadequately lit stairway.

The court may engage in a reasoning process involving the following "pieces of rope":

1. The landlord, who was on the premises the evening the injury occurred, testifies that none of the other nine tenants who used the stairway that night complained about the lights.

2. The fact that none of the tenants complained is the same as if they had said the lighting was sufficient.

3. That there were no complaints does not prove that the lighting was sufficient but does prove that the landlord had no reason to believe that it was not.

4. The landlord's belief was reasonable because no one complained.

5. Therefore, the landlord acted reasonably and was not negligent with respect to the lighting in the stairway.

From this reasoning, the court concludes that the tenant is not entitled to compensation on the basis of the stairway's allegedly insufficient lighting.

Reasoning by Analogy. Another important type of reasoning that judges use in deciding cases is reasoning by *analogy*. To reason by **analogy** is to compare the facts in the case at hand to the facts in previous cases and, to the extent that the patterns are similar, to apply the same rule of law to the present case. To the extent that the facts are unique, or "distinguishable," different rules may apply. For example, in Case A, the court held that a driver who crossed a highway's center line was negligent. Case B involves a driver who crossed the line to avoid hitting a child. In determining whether Case A's rule applies in Case B, a judge would consider what the reasons were for the decision in A and whether B is sufficiently similar for those reasons to apply. If the judge holds that B's driver is not liable, that judge must indicate why Case A's rule is not relevant to the facts presented in Case B.

There Is No One "Right" Answer

Many people believe that there is one "right" answer to every legal question. In most legal controversies, however, there is no single correct result. Good arguments can often be made to support either side of a legal controversy. Quite often, a case does not involve a "good" person suing a "bad" person. In many cases, both parties have acted in good faith in some measure or in bad faith to some degree.

Additionally, each judge has her or his own personal beliefs and philosophy (see the discussion of schools of jurisprudential thought later in this chapter), which shape the process of legal reasoning, at least to some extent. This means that the outcome of a particular lawsuit before a court cannot be predicted with absolute certainty. In fact, in some cases, even though the weight of the law would seem to favor one party's position, judges, through creative legal reasoning, have found ways to rule in favor of the other party in the interests of preventing injustice.

Legal reasoning and other aspects of the common law tradition are reviewed in *Concept Summary 1.2*.

The Common Law Today

Today, the common law derived from judicial decisions continues to be applied throughout the United States. Common law doctrines and principles, however, govern only areas *not* covered by statutory or administrative law. In a dispute concerning a particular employment practice, for example, if a statute regulates that practice, the statute will apply rather than the common law doctrine that applied prior to the enactment of the statute.

COURTS INTERPRET STATUTES Even in areas governed by statutory law, though, judge-made law continues to be important because there is a significant interplay between statutory law and the

common law. For example, many statutes essentially codify existing common law rules, and regulations issued by various administrative agencies usually are based, at least in part, on common law principles. Additionally, the courts, in interpreting statutory law, often rely on the common law as a guide to what the legislators intended.

Furthermore, how the courts interpret a particular statute determines how that statute will be applied. If you wanted to learn about the coverage and applicability of a particular statute, for example, you would necessarily have to locate the statute and study it. You would also need to see how the courts in your jurisdiction have interpreted and applied the statute. In other words, you would have to learn what precedents have been established in your jurisdiction with respect to that statute. Often, the applicability of a newly enacted statute does not become clear until a body of case law develops to clarify how, when, and to whom the statute applies.

RESTATEMENTS OF THE LAW CLARIFY AND ILLUSTRATE THE COMMON LAW The American Law Institute (ALI) has drafted and published compilations of the common law called *Restatements of the Law,* which generally summarize the common law rules followed by most states. There are *Restatements of the Law* in the areas of contracts, torts, agency,

CONCEPT SUMMARY 1.2
The Common Law Tradition

Aspect	Description
Origins of the Common Law	The American legal system is based on the common law tradition, which originated in medieval England. Following the conquest of England in 1066 by William the Conqueror, king's courts were established throughout England, and the common law was developed in these courts.
Legal and Equitable Remedies	The distinction between remedies at law (money or items of value, such as land) and remedies in equity (including specific performance, injunction, and rescission of a contractual obligation) originated in the early English courts of law and courts of equity, respectively.
Case Precedents and the Doctrine of *Stare Decisis*	In the king's courts, judges attempted to make their decisions consistent with previous decisions, called precedents. This practice gave rise to the doctrine of *stare decisis.* This doctrine, which became a cornerstone of the common law tradition, obligates judges to abide by precedents established in their jurisdictions.
***Stare Decisis* and Legal Reasoning**	Legal reasoning is the reasoning process used by judges in applying the law to the facts and issues of specific cases. Legal reasoning involves becoming familiar with the key facts of a case, identifying the relevant legal rules, applying those rules to the facts, and drawing a conclusion. In applying the legal rules to the facts of a case, judges may use deductive reasoning, linear reasoning, or reasoning by analogy.

trusts, property, restitution, security, judgments, and conflict of laws. The *Restatements,* like other secondary sources of law, do not in themselves have the force of law, but they are an important source of legal analysis and opinion on which judges often rely in making their decisions.

Many of the *Restatements* are now in their second, third, or fourth editions. We refer to the *Restatements* frequently in subsequent chapters of this text, indicating in parentheses the edition to which we are referring. For example, we refer to the third edition of the *Restatement of the Law of Contracts* as simply the *Restatement (Third) of Contracts.*

SECTION 4
SCHOOLS OF JURISPRUDENTIAL THOUGHT

How judges apply the law to specific cases, including disputes relating to the business world, depends in part on their philosophical approaches to law. Part of the study of law, often referred to as **jurisprudence,** involves learning about different schools of jurisprudential thought and discovering how the approaches to law characteristic of each school can affect judicial decision making.

Clearly, a judge's function is not to *make* the laws—that is the function of the legislative branch of government—but to interpret and apply them. From a practical point of view, however, the courts play a significant role in defining the laws enacted by legislative bodies, which tend to be expressed in general terms. Judges thus have some flexibility in interpreting and applying the law. It is because of this flexibility that different courts can, and often do, arrive at different conclusions in cases that involve nearly identical issues, facts, and applicable laws.

The Natural Law School

An age-old question about the nature of law has to do with the finality of a nation's laws, such as the laws of the United States at the present time. For example, what if a particular law is deemed to be a "bad" law by a substantial number of that nation's citizens? Those who adhere to the **natural law** theory believe that a higher or universal law exists that applies to all human beings and that written laws should imitate these inherent principles. If a written law is unjust, then it is not a true (natural) law and need not be obeyed.

The natural law tradition is one of the oldest and most significant schools of jurisprudence. It dates back to the days of the Greek philosopher Aristotle (384–322 B.C.E.), who distinguished between natural law and the laws governing a particular nation. According to Aristotle, natural law applies universally to all humankind.

The notion that people have "natural rights" stems from the natural law tradition. Those who claim that a specific foreign government is depriving certain citizens of their human rights are implicitly appealing to a higher law that has universal applicability. The question of the universality of basic human rights also comes into play in the context of international business operations. For example, U.S. companies that have operations abroad often hire foreign workers as employees. Should the same laws that protect U.S. employees apply to these foreign employees? This question is rooted implicitly in a concept of universal rights that has its origins in the natural law tradition.

The Positivist School

In contrast, *positive,* or national, law (the written law of a given society at a particular point in time) applies only to the citizens of that nation or society. Those who adhere to **legal positivism** believe that there can be no higher law than a nation's positive law. According to the positivist school, there is no such thing as "natural rights." Rather, human rights exist solely because of laws. If the laws are not enforced, anarchy will result. Thus, whether a law is "bad" or "good" is irrelevant. The law is the law and must be obeyed until it is changed—in an orderly manner through a legitimate lawmaking process. A judge with positivist leanings probably would be more inclined to defer to an existing law than would a judge who adheres to the natural law tradition.

The Historical School

The **historical school** of legal thought emphasizes the evolutionary process of law by concentrating on the origin and history of the legal system. This school looks to the past to discover what the principles of contemporary law should be. The legal doctrines that have withstood the passage of time—those that have worked in the past—are deemed best suited for shaping present laws. Hence, law derives its legitimacy and authority from adhering to the standards that historical development has shown to be workable. Adherents of the historical school are more likely than those of other schools to strictly follow decisions made in past cases.

Legal Realism

In the 1920s and 1930s, a number of jurists and scholars, known as *legal realists,* rebelled against the historical approach to law. **Legal realism** is based on the idea that law is just one of many institutions in society and that it is shaped by social forces and needs. The law is a human enterprise, and judges should take social and economic realities into account when deciding cases. Legal realists also believe that the law can never be applied with total uniformity. Given that judges are human beings with unique personalities, value systems, and intellects, different judges will obviously bring different reasoning processes to the same case.

Legal realism strongly influenced the growth of what is sometimes called the **sociological school** of jurisprudence. This school views law as a tool for promoting justice in society. In the 1960s, for example, the justices of the United States Supreme Court played a leading role in the civil rights movement by upholding long-neglected laws calling for equal treatment for all Americans, including African Americans and other minorities. Generally, jurists who adhere to this philosophy of law are more likely to depart from past decisions than are those jurists who adhere to the other schools of legal thought.

Concept Summary 1.3 reviews the schools of jurisprudential thought.

SECTION 5

CLASSIFICATIONS OF LAW

The law may be broken down according to several classification systems. For example, one classification system divides law into substantive law and procedural law. **Substantive law** consists of all laws that define, describe, regulate, and create legal rights and obligations. **Procedural law** consists of all laws that delineate the methods of enforcing the rights established by substantive law. Other classification systems divide law into federal law and state law, private law (dealing with relationships between private entities) and public law (addressing the relationship between persons and their governments), and national law and international law. Here we look at still another classification system, which divides law into civil law and criminal law, as well as at what is meant by the term *cyberlaw.*

Civil Law and Criminal Law

Civil law spells out the rights and duties that exist between persons and between persons and their governments, as well as the relief available when a person's rights are violated. Typically, in a civil case, a private party sues another private party (although

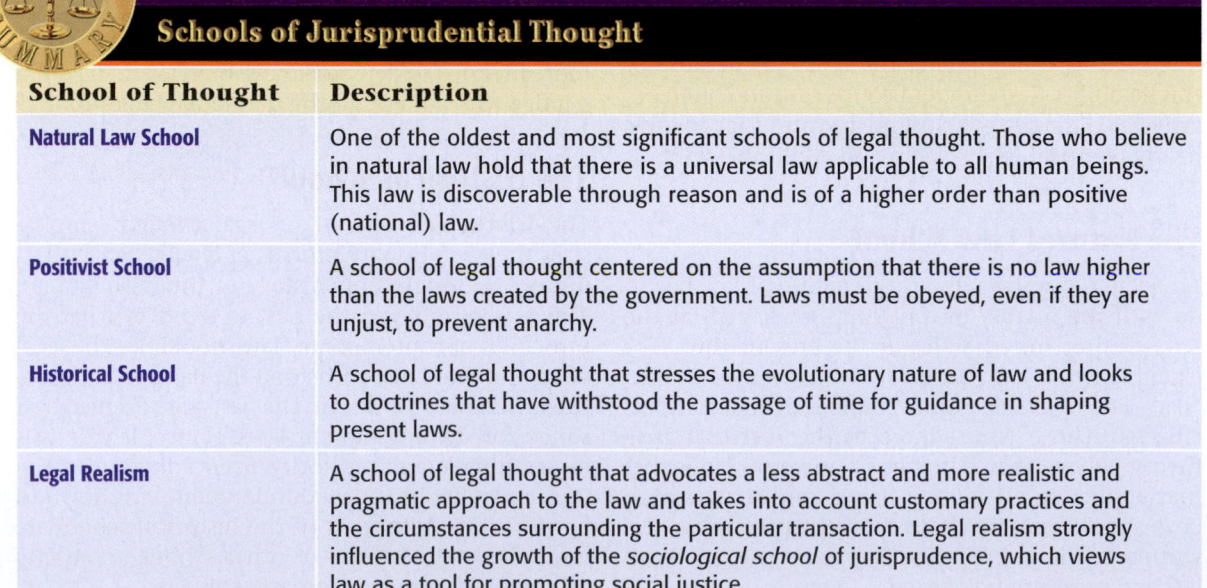

CONCEPT SUMMARY 1.3
Schools of Jurisprudential Thought

School of Thought	Description
Natural Law School	One of the oldest and most significant schools of legal thought. Those who believe in natural law hold that there is a universal law applicable to all human beings. This law is discoverable through reason and is of a higher order than positive (national) law.
Positivist School	A school of legal thought centered on the assumption that there is no law higher than the laws created by the government. Laws must be obeyed, even if they are unjust, to prevent anarchy.
Historical School	A school of legal thought that stresses the evolutionary nature of law and looks to doctrines that have withstood the passage of time for guidance in shaping present laws.
Legal Realism	A school of legal thought that advocates a less abstract and more realistic and pragmatic approach to the law and takes into account customary practices and the circumstances surrounding the particular transaction. Legal realism strongly influenced the growth of the *sociological school* of jurisprudence, which views law as a tool for promoting social justice.

the government can also sue a party for a civil law violation) to make that other party comply with a duty or pay for the damage caused by failure to comply with a duty. Much of the law that we discuss in this text is civil law. Contract law, for example, covered in Chapters 10 through 18, is civil law. The whole body of tort law (see Chapters 6 and 7) is also civil law.

Criminal law, in contrast, is concerned with wrongs committed *against the public as a whole.* Criminal acts are defined and prohibited by local, state, or federal government statutes. Criminal defendants are thus prosecuted by public officials, such as a district attorney (D.A.), on behalf of the state, not by their victims or other private parties. (See Chapter 9 for a further discussion of the distinction between civil law and criminal law.)

Cyberlaw

As mentioned, the use of the Internet to conduct business transactions has led to new types of legal issues. In response, courts have had to adapt traditional laws to situations that are unique to our age. Additionally, legislatures at both the federal and the state levels have created laws to deal specifically with such issues. Frequently, people use the term **cyberlaw** to refer to the emerging body of law that governs transactions conducted via the Internet. Cyberlaw is not really a classification of law, nor is it a new *type* of law. Rather, it is an informal term used to describe both new laws and modifications of traditional laws that relate to the online environment. Throughout this book, you will read how the law in a given area is evolving to govern specific legal issues that arise in the online context.

SECTION 6
HOW TO FIND PRIMARY SOURCES OF LAW

This text includes numerous references, or *citations,* to primary sources of law—federal and state statutes, the U.S. Constitution and state constitutions, regulations issued by administrative agencies, and court cases. A **citation** identifies the publication in which a legal authority—such as a statute or a court decision or other source—can be found. In this section, we explain how you can use citations to find primary sources of law. Note that in addition to being published in sets of books, as described next, most federal and state laws and case decisions are available online.

Finding Statutory and Administrative Law

When Congress passes laws, they are collected in a publication titled *United States Statutes at Large.* When state legislatures pass laws, they are collected in similar state publications. Most frequently, however, laws are referred to in their codified form—that is, the form in which they appear in the federal and state codes. In these codes, laws are compiled by subject.

UNITED STATES CODE The *United States Code* (U.S.C.) arranges all existing federal laws by broad subject. Each of the fifty subjects is given a title and a title number. For example, laws relating to commerce and trade are collected in Title 15, "Commerce and Trade." Titles are subdivided by sections. A citation to the U.S.C. includes both title and section numbers. Thus, a reference to "15 U.S.C. Section 1" means that the statute can be found in Section 1 of Title 15. ("Section" may be designated by the symbol §, and "Sections," by §§.) In addition to the print publication of the U.S.C., the federal government provides a searchable online database of the *United States Code* at **www.gpoaccess.gov/uscode**.

Commercial publications of federal laws and regulations are also available. For example, West Group publishes the *United States Code Annotated* (U.S.C.A.). The U.S.C.A. contains the official text of the U.S.C., plus notes (annotations) on court decisions that interpret and apply specific sections of the statutes. The U.S.C.A. also includes additional research aids, such as cross-references to related statutes, historical notes, and library references. A citation to the U.S.C.A. is similar to a citation to the U.S.C.: "15 U.S.C.A. Section 1."

STATE CODES State codes follow the U.S.C. pattern of arranging law by subject. They may be called codes, revisions, compilations, consolidations, general statutes, or statutes, depending on the preferences of the states. In some codes, subjects are designated by number. In others, they are designated by name. For example, "13 Pennsylvania Consolidated Statutes Section 1101" means that the statute can be found in Title 13, Section 1101, of the Pennsylvania code. "California Commercial Code Section 1101" means that the statute can be found under the subject heading "Commercial Code" of the California code in Section 1101. Abbreviations are often used. For example, "13 Pennsylvania Consolidated Statutes Section 1101" is abbreviated "13 Pa. C.S. § 1101," and "California Commercial Code Section 1101" is abbreviated "Cal. Com. Code § 1101."

ADMINISTRATIVE RULES Rules and regulations adopted by federal administrative agencies are initially published in the *Federal Register,* a daily publication of the U.S. government. Later, they are incorporated into the *Code of Federal Regulations* (C.F.R.). Like the U.S.C., the C.F.R. is divided into fifty titles. Rules within each title are assigned section numbers. A full citation to the C.F.R. includes title and section numbers. For example, a reference to "17 C.F.R. Section 230.504" means that the rule can be found in Section 230.504 of Title 17.

Finding Case Law

Before discussing the case reporting system, we need to look briefly at the court system (which will be discussed in detail in Chapter 2). There are two types of courts in the United States, federal courts and state courts. Both the federal and the state court systems consist of several levels, or tiers, of courts. *Trial courts,* in which evidence is presented and testimony given, are on the bottom tier (which also includes lower courts that handle specialized issues). Decisions from a trial court can be appealed to a higher court, which commonly is an intermediate *court of appeals,* or an *appellate court.* Decisions from these intermediate courts of appeals may be appealed to an even higher court, such as a state supreme court or the United States Supreme Court.

STATE COURT DECISIONS Most state trial court decisions are not published in books (except in New York and a few other states, which publish selected trial court opinions). Decisions from state trial courts are typically filed in the office of the clerk of the court, where the decisions are available for public inspection. Written decisions of the appellate, or reviewing, courts, however, are published and distributed (both in print and via the Internet). As you will note, most of the state court cases presented in this book are from state appellate courts. The reported appellate decisions are published in volumes called *reports* or *reporters,* which are numbered consecutively. State appellate court decisions are found in the state reporters of that particular state. Official reports are published by the state, whereas unofficial reports are privately published.

Regional Reporters. State court opinions appear in regional units of the National Reporter System, published by West Group. Most lawyers and libraries have the West reporters because they report cases more quickly and are distributed more widely than the state-published reporters. In fact, many

states have eliminated their own reporters in favor of West's National Reporter System. The National Reporter System divides the states into the following geographic areas: *Atlantic* (A. or A.2d), *North Eastern* (N.E. or N.E.2d), *North Western* (N.W. or N.W.2d), *Pacific* (P., P.2d, or P.3d), *South Eastern* (S.E. or S.E.2d), *South Western* (S.W., S.W.2d, or S.W.3d), and *Southern* (So., So.2d, or So.3d). (The *2d* and *3d* in the preceding abbreviations refer to *Second Series* and *Third Series,* respectively.) The states included in each of these regional divisions are indicated in Exhibit 1–4, which illustrates West's National Reporter System.

Case Citations. After appellate decisions have been published, they are normally referred to (cited) by the name of the case; the volume, name, and page number of the state's official reporter (if different from West's National Reporter System); the volume, name, and page number of the National Reporter; and the volume, name, and page number of any other selected reporter. (Citing a reporter by volume number, name, and page number, in that order, is common to all citations; often, as in this book, the year the decision was issued will be included in parentheses, just after the citations to reporters.) When more than one reporter is cited for the same case, each reference is called a *parallel citation.*

Note that some states have adopted a "public domain citation system" that uses a somewhat different format for the citation. For example, in Wisconsin, a Wisconsin Supreme Court decision might be designated "2010 WI 40," meaning that the case was decided in the year 2010 by the Wisconsin Supreme Court and was the fortieth decision issued by that court during that year. Parallel citations to the *Wisconsin Reports* and West's *North Western Reporter* are still included after the public domain citation.

Consider the following case citation: *State v. Favoccia,* 119 Conn.App. 1, 986 A.2d 1081 (2010). We see that the opinion in this case can be found in Volume 119 of the official *Connecticut Appellate Reports,* on page 1. The parallel citation is to Volume 986 of the *Atlantic Reporter, Second Series,* page 1,081. In presenting appellate opinions in this text (starting in Chapter 2), in addition to the reporter, we give the name of the court hearing the case and the year of the court's decision. Sample citations to state court decisions are explained in Exhibit 1–5 on pages 18–20.

FEDERAL COURT DECISIONS Federal district (trial) court decisions are published unofficially in West's

EXHIBIT 1–4 • West's National Reporter System—Regional/Federal

Regional Reporters	Coverage Beginning	Coverage
Atlantic Reporter (A. or A.2d)	1885	Connecticut, Delaware, District of Columbia, Maine, Maryland, New Hampshire, New Jersey, Pennsylvania, Rhode Island, and Vermont.
North Eastern Reporter (N.E. or N.E.2d)	1885	Illinois, Indiana, Massachusetts, New York, and Ohio.
North Western Reporter (N.W. or N.W.2d)	1879	Iowa, Michigan, Minnesota, Nebraska, North Dakota, South Dakota, and Wisconsin.
Pacific Reporter (P., P.2d, or P.3d)	1883	Alaska, Arizona, California, Colorado, Hawaii, Idaho, Kansas, Montana, Nevada, New Mexico, Oklahoma, Oregon, Utah, Washington, and Wyoming.
South Eastern Reporter (S.E. or S.E.2d)	1887	Georgia, North Carolina, South Carolina, Virginia, and West Virginia.
South Western Reporter (S.W., S.W.2d, or S.W.3d)	1886	Arkansas, Kentucky, Missouri, Tennessee, and Texas.
Southern Reporter (So., So.2d, or So.3d)	1887	Alabama, Florida, Louisiana, and Mississippi.

Federal Reporters		
Federal Reporter (F., F.2d, or F.3d)	1880	U.S. Circuit Courts from 1880 to 1912; U.S. Commerce Court from 1911 to 1913; U.S. District Courts from 1880 to 1932; U.S. Court of Claims (now called U.S. Court of Federal Claims) from 1929 to 1932 and since 1960; U.S. Courts of Appeals since 1891; U.S. Court of Customs and Patent Appeals since 1929; U.S. Emergency Court of Appeals since 1943.
Federal Supplement (F.Supp. or F.Supp.2d)	1932	U.S. Court of Claims from 1932 to 1960; U.S. District Courts since 1932; U.S. Customs Court since 1956.
Federal Rules Decisions (F.R.D.)	1939	U.S. District Courts involving the Federal Rules of Civil Procedure since 1939 and Federal Rules of Criminal Procedure since 1946.
Supreme Court Reporter (S.Ct.)	1882	United States Supreme Court since the October term of 1882.
Bankruptcy Reporter (Bankr.)	1980	Bankruptcy decisions of U.S. Bankruptcy Courts, U.S. District Courts, U.S. Courts of Appeals, and the United States Supreme Court.
Military Justice Reporter (M.J.)	1978	U.S. Court of Military Appeals and Courts of Military Review for the Army, Navy, Air Force, and Coast Guard.

NATIONAL REPORTER SYSTEM MAP

Federal Supplement (F.Supp. or F.Supp.2d), and opinions from the circuit courts of appeals (reviewing courts) are reported unofficially in West's *Federal Reporter* (F., F.2d, or F.3d). Cases concerning federal bankruptcy law are published unofficially in West's *Bankruptcy Reporter* (Bankr. or B.R.).

EXHIBIT 1-5 • How to Read Citations

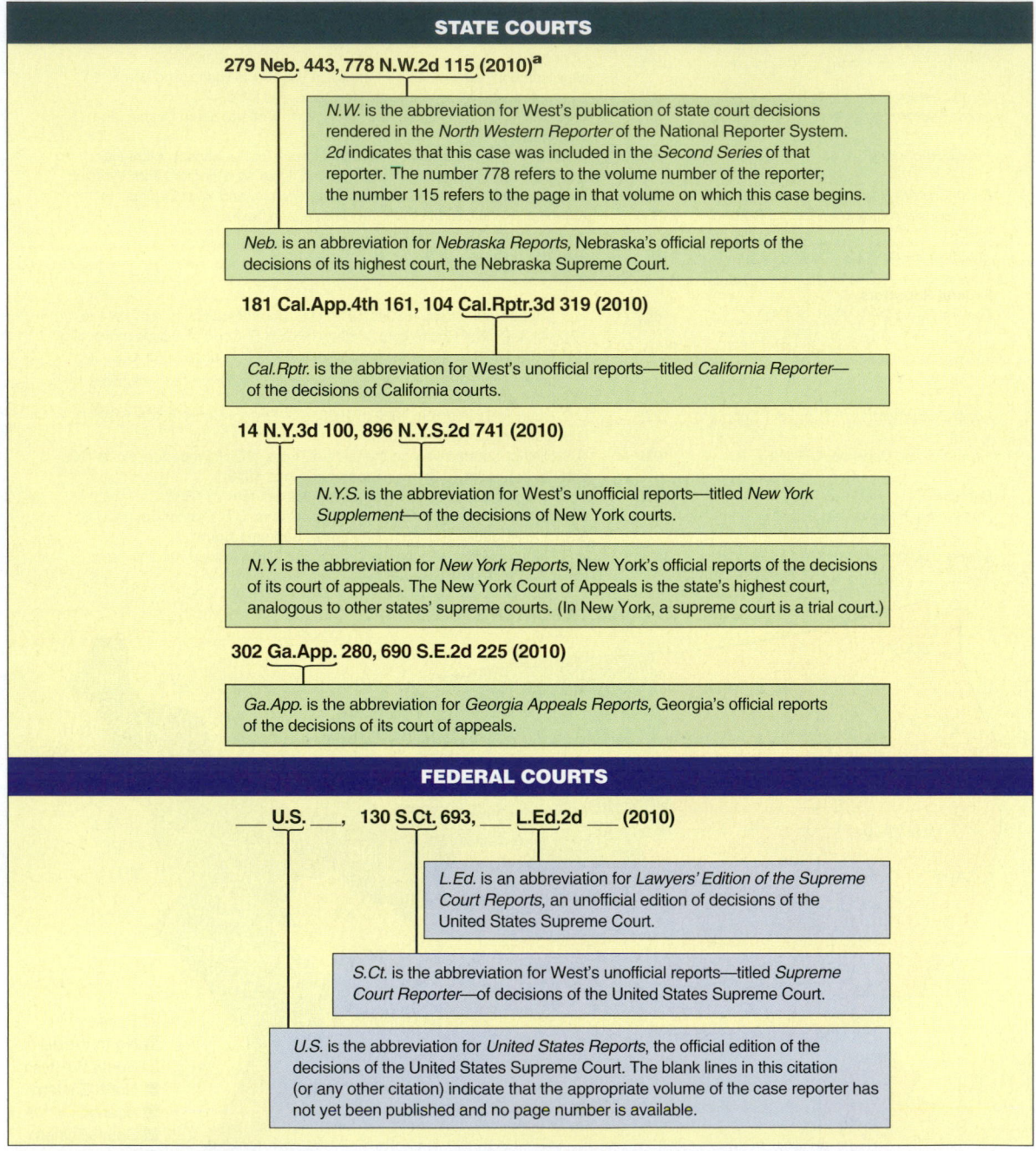

STATE COURTS

279 Neb. 443, 778 N.W.2d 115 (2010)[a]

N.W. is the abbreviation for West's publication of state court decisions rendered in the *North Western Reporter* of the National Reporter System. *2d* indicates that this case was included in the *Second Series* of that reporter. The number 778 refers to the volume number of the reporter; the number 115 refers to the page in that volume on which this case begins.

Neb. is an abbreviation for *Nebraska Reports,* Nebraska's official reports of the decisions of its highest court, the Nebraska Supreme Court.

181 Cal.App.4th 161, 104 Cal.Rptr.3d 319 (2010)

Cal.Rptr. is the abbreviation for West's unofficial reports—titled *California Reporter*—of the decisions of California courts.

14 N.Y.3d 100, 896 N.Y.S.2d 741 (2010)

N.Y.S. is the abbreviation for West's unofficial reports—titled *New York Supplement*—of the decisions of New York courts.

N.Y. is the abbreviation for *New York Reports,* New York's official reports of the decisions of its court of appeals. The New York Court of Appeals is the state's highest court, analogous to other states' supreme courts. (In New York, a supreme court is a trial court.)

302 Ga.App. 280, 690 S.E.2d 225 (2010)

Ga.App. is the abbreviation for *Georgia Appeals Reports,* Georgia's official reports of the decisions of its court of appeals.

FEDERAL COURTS

___ U.S. ___, 130 S.Ct. 693, ___ L.Ed.2d ___ (2010)

L.Ed. is an abbreviation for *Lawyers' Edition of the Supreme Court Reports,* an unofficial edition of decisions of the United States Supreme Court.

S.Ct. is the abbreviation for West's unofficial reports—titled *Supreme Court Reporter*—of decisions of the United States Supreme Court.

U.S. is the abbreviation for *United States Reports,* the official edition of the decisions of the United States Supreme Court. The blank lines in this citation (or any other citation) indicate that the appropriate volume of the case reporter has not yet been published and no page number is available.

a. The case names have been deleted from these citations to emphasize the publications. It should be kept in mind, however, that the name of a case is as important as the specific page numbers in the volumes in which it is found. If a citation is incorrect, the correct citation may be found in a publication's index of case names. In addition to providing a check on errors in citations, the date of a case is important because the value of a recent case as an authority is likely to be greater than that of older cases from the same court.

The official edition of the United States Supreme Court decisions is the *United States Reports* (U.S.), which is published by the federal government. Unofficial editions of Supreme Court cases include West's *Supreme Court Reporter* (S.Ct.) and the *Lawyers' Edition of the Supreme Court Reports* (L.Ed. or L.Ed.2d). Sample citations for federal court decisions are also listed and explained in Exhibit 1–5.

EXHIBIT 1–5 • How to Read Citations, Continued

FEDERAL COURTS (Continued)

590 F.3d 259 (4th Cir. 2010)

> *4th Cir.* is an abbreviation denoting that this case was decided in the U.S. Court of Appeals for the Fourth Circuit.

683 F.Supp.2d 918 (W.D.Wis. 2010)

> *W.D.Wis.* is an abbreviation indicating that the U.S. District Court for the Western District of Wisconsin decided this case.

ENGLISH COURTS

9 Exch. 341, 156 Eng.Rep. 145 (1854)

> *Eng.Rep.* is an abbreviation for *English Reports, Full Reprint,* a series of reports containing selected decisions made in English courts between 1378 and 1865.

> *Exch.* is an abbreviation for *English Exchequer Reports*, which includes the original reports of cases decided in England's Court of Exchequer.

STATUTORY AND OTHER CITATIONS

18 U.S.C. Section 1961(1)(A)

> *U.S.C.* denotes *United States Code*, the codification of *United States Statutes at Large*. The number 18 refers to the statute's U.S.C. title number and 1961 to its section number within that title. The number 1 in parentheses refers to a subsection within the section, and the letter A in parentheses to a subsection within the subsection.

UCC 2–206(1)(b)

> *UCC* is an abbreviation for *Uniform Commercial Code*. The first number 2 is a reference to an article of the UCC, and 206 to a section within that article. The number 1 in parentheses refers to a subsection within the section, and the letter b in parentheses to a subsection within the subsection.

Restatement (Third) of Torts, Section 6

> *Restatement (Third) of Torts* refers to the third edition of the American Law Institute's *Restatement of the Law of Torts*. The number 6 refers to a specific section.

17 C.F.R. Section 230.505

> *C.F.R.* is an abbreviation for *Code of Federal Regulations*, a compilation of federal administrative regulations. The number 17 designates the regulation's title number, and 230.505 designates a specific section within that title.

Continued

UNPUBLISHED OPINIONS Many court opinions that are not yet published or that are not intended for publication can be accessed through Westlaw® (abbreviated in citations as "WL"), an online legal database maintained by West Group. When no citation to a published reporter is available for cases cited in this text, we give the WL citation (see Exhibit 1–5 on the next page for an example).

EXHIBIT 1–5 • How to Read Citations, Continued

WESTLAW® CITATIONS[b]

<u>2010 WL 348005</u>

WL is an abbreviation for Westlaw. The number 2010 is the year of the document that can be found with this citation in the Westlaw database. The number 348005 is a number assigned to a specific document. A higher number indicates that a document was added to the Westlaw database later in the year.

UNIFORM RESOURCE LOCATORS (URLs)

http://www.westlaw.com[c]

The suffix *com* is the top level domain (TLD) for this Web site. The TLD *com* is an abbreviation for "commercial," which usually means that a for-profit entity hosts (maintains or supports) this Web site.

westlaw is the host name—the part of the domain name selected by the organization that registered the name. In this case, West registered the name. This Internet site is the Westlaw database on the Web.

www is an abbreviation for "World Wide Web." The Web is a system of Internet servers that support documents formatted in *HTML* (hypertext markup language) and other formats as well.

http://www.uscourts.gov

This is "The Federal Judiciary Home Page." The host is the Administrative Office of the U.S. Courts. The TLD *gov* is an abbreviation for "government." This Web site includes information and links from, and about, the federal courts.

http://www.law.cornell.edu/index.html

This part of a URL points to a Web page or file at a specific location within the host's domain. This page is a menu with links to documents within the domain and to other Internet resources.

This is the host name for a Web site that contains the Internet publications of the Legal Information Institute (LII), which is a part of Cornell Law School. The LII site includes a variety of legal materials and links to other legal resources on the Internet. The TLD *edu* is an abbreviation for "educational institution" (a school or a university).

http://www.ipl2.org/div/news

This part of the URL points to a static *news* page at this Web site, which provides links to online newspapers from around the world.

div is an abbreviation for "division," which is the way that ipl2 tags the content on its Web site as relating to a specific topic.

The site *ipl2* was formed from the merger of the Internet Public Library and the Librarians' Internet Index. It is an online service that provides reference resources and links to other information services on the Web. The site is supported chiefly by the *iSchool* at Drexel College of Information Science and Technology. The TLD *org* is an abbreviation for "organization" (normally nonprofit).

b. Many court decisions that are not yet published or that are not intended for publication can be accessed through Westlaw, an online legal database.

c. The basic form for a URL is "service://hostname/path." The Internet service for all of the URLs in this text is *http* (hypertext transfer protocol). Because most Web browsers add this prefix automatically when a user enters a host name or a hostname/path, we have generally omitted the *http://* from the URLs listed in this text.

OLD CASE LAW On a few occasions, this text cites opinions from old, classic cases dating to the nineteenth century or earlier; some of these are from the English courts. The citations to these cases may not conform to the descriptions given above because the reporters in which they were originally published were often known by the names of the persons who compiled the reporters.

SECTION 7
HOW TO READ AND UNDERSTAND CASE LAW

The decisions made by the courts establish the boundaries of the law as it applies to almost all business relationships. It thus is essential that businesspersons know how to read and understand case law. The cases that we present in this text have been condensed from the full text of the courts' opinions and are presented in a special format. In approximately two-thirds of the cases, we have summarized the background and facts, as well as the court's decision and remedy, in our own words and have included only selected portions of the court's opinion ("in the language of the court"). In the remaining one-third of the cases, we have provided a longer excerpt from the court's opinion without summarizing the background and facts or decision and remedy. The following sections will provide useful insights into how to read and understand case law.

Case Titles and Terminology

The title of a case, such as *Adams v. Jones,* indicates the names of the parties to the lawsuit. The *v.* in the case title stands for *versus,* which means "against." In the trial court, Adams was the plaintiff—the person who filed the suit. Jones was the defendant. If the case is appealed, however, the appellate court will sometimes place the name of the party appealing the decision first, so the case may be called *Jones v. Adams* if Jones is appealing. Because some appellate courts retain the trial court order of names, it is often impossible to distinguish the plaintiff from the defendant in the title of a reported appellate court decision. You must carefully read the facts of each case to identify the parties. Otherwise, the discussion by the appellate court may be difficult to understand.

The following terms, phrases, and abbreviations are frequently encountered in court opinions and legal publications. Because it is important to understand what is meant by these terms, phrases, and abbreviations, we define and discuss them here.

PARTIES TO LAWSUITS As mentioned previously, the party initiating a lawsuit is referred to as the *plaintiff* or *petitioner,* depending on the nature of the action, and the party against whom a lawsuit is brought is the *defendant* or *respondent.* Lawsuits frequently involve more than one plaintiff and/or defendant.

When a case is appealed from the original court or jurisdiction to another court or jurisdiction, the party appealing the case is called the **appellant.** The **appellee** is the party against whom the appeal is taken. (In some appellate courts, the party appealing a case is referred to as the *petitioner,* and the party against whom the suit is brought or appealed is called the *respondent.*)

JUDGES AND JUSTICES The terms *judge* and *justice* are usually synonymous and represent two designations given to judges in various courts. All members of the United States Supreme Court, for example, are referred to as justices, and justice is the formal title often given to judges of appellate courts, although this is not always the case. In New York, a *justice* is a judge of the trial court (which is called the Supreme Court), and a member of the Court of Appeals (the state's highest court) is called a *judge.* The term *justice* is commonly abbreviated to J., and *justices,* to JJ. A Supreme Court case might refer to Justice Sotomayor as Sotomayor, J., or to Chief Justice Roberts as Roberts, C.J.

DECISIONS AND OPINIONS Most decisions reached by reviewing, or appellate, courts are explained in written **opinions.** The opinion contains the court's reasons for its decision, the rules of law that apply, and the judgment. When all judges or justices unanimously agree on an opinion, the opinion is written for the entire court and can be deemed a *unanimous opinion.* When there is not a unanimous agreement, a *majority opinion* is written; the majority opinion outlines the view supported by the majority of the judges or justices deciding the case.

Often, a judge or justice who wishes to make or emphasize a point that was not made or emphasized in the unanimous or majority opinion will write a *concurring opinion.* This means that the judge or justice agrees, or concurs, with the majority's decision, but for different reasons. When there is not a unanimous opinion, a *dissenting opinion* presents the views of one or more judges who disagree with the majority's decision. The dissenting opinion is important because it may form the basis of the arguments used years later in overruling the precedential majority opinion. Occasionally, a court issues a *per curiam* (Latin for "by the court") opinion, which does not indicate the judge or justice who authored the opinion.

A Sample Court Case

To illustrate the various elements contained in a court opinion, we present an annotated court opinion in Exhibit 1–6 on pages 23–25. The opinion is from an actual case decided by the U.S. Court of Appeals for the Seventh Circuit in 2010.

BACKGROUND OF THE CASE Kevin T. Singer, an inmate at a Wisconsin correctional facility, was a devoted player of Dungeons and Dragons (D&D), a popular fantasy role-playing game. While incarcerated, Singer was able to order and possess D&D materials for two years. In November 2004, however, the prison's gang expert received an anonymous letter stating that Singer and three other inmates were trying to recruit others to join a "gang" dedicated to playing D&D. Prison officials immediately searched Singer's cell, confiscated all of his D&D materials and prohibited him and other inmates from playing D&D. Singer filed a lawsuit in federal district court against the Wisconsin prison alleging that these actions violated his free speech and due process rights. The district court found in favor of the prison when it concluded that the D&D ban was rationally related to a legitimate government interest. Singer appealed to the U.S. Court of Appeals for the Seventh Circuit.

EDITORIAL PRACTICE You will note that triple asterisks (* * *) and quadruple asterisks (* * * *) frequently appear in the opinion. The triple asterisks indicate that we have deleted a few words or sentences from the opinion for the sake of readability or brevity. Quadruple asterisks mean that an entire paragraph (or more) has been omitted. Additionally, when the opinion cites another case or legal source, the citation to the case or other source has been omitted to save space and to improve the flow of the text. These editorial practices are continued in the other court opinions presented in this book. In addition, whenever we present a court opinion that includes a term or phrase that may not be readily understandable, a bracketed definition or paraphrase has been added.

BRIEFING CASES Knowing how to read and understand court opinions and the legal reasoning used by the courts is an essential step in undertaking accurate legal research. A further step is "briefing," or summarizing, the case. Legal researchers routinely brief cases by reducing the texts of the opinions to their essential elements. Generally, when you brief a case, you first summarize the background and facts of the case, as we have done for the cases presented within this text. You then indicate the issue (or issues) before the court. An important element in the case brief is, of course, the court's decision on the issue and the legal reasoning used by the court in reaching that decision. Detailed instructions on how to brief a case are given in Appendix A, which also includes a briefed version of the sample court case presented in Exhibit 1–6.

THE SAMPLE COURT CASE STARTS ON THE FACING PAGE.

EXHIBIT 1–6 • A Sample Court Case

This section contains the citation—the name of the case, the name of the court that heard the case, the year of the decision, and reporters in which the court's opinion can be found.

This line provides the name of the justice (or judge) who authored the court's opinion.

The court divides the opinion into three sections, each headed by a Roman numeral and an explanatory heading. The first section summarizes the factual background of the case.

SINGER v. RAEMISCH

United States Court of Appeals,

Seventh Circuit,

593 F.3d 529 (2010).

TINDER, Circuit Judge.

* * * *

I. Background

Kevin T. Singer is an inmate at Wisconsin's Waupun Correctional Institution. He is also a devoted player of D&D [Dungeons and Dragons], a fantasy role-playing game in which players collectively develop a story around characters whose personae they adopt.

* * * Singer was able to order and possess his D&D materials without incident from June 2002 until November 2004. This all changed on or about November 14, 2004, when Waupun's long-serving Disruptive Group Coordinator, Captain Bruce Muraski, received an anonymous letter from an inmate. The letter expressed concern that Singer and three other inmates were forming a D&D gang and were trying to recruit others to join by passing around their D&D publications and touting the "rush" they got from playing the game. Muraski, Waupun's expert on gang activity, decided to heed the letter's advice and "check into this gang before it gets out of hand."

On November 15, 2004, Muraski ordered Waupun staff to search the cells of the inmates named in the letter. The search of Singer's cell turned up twenty-one books, fourteen magazines, and Singer's handwritten D&D manuscript, all of which were confiscated. * * * In a December 6, 2004, letter to Singer, Muraski informed Singer that "inmates are not allowed to engage in or possess written material that details rules, codes, dogma of games/activities such as 'Dungeons and Dragons' because it promotes fantasy role playing, competitive hostility, violence, addictive escape behaviors, and possible gambling."

Continued

EXHIBIT 1–6 • **A Sample Court Case, Continued**

To *lodge a complaint* is to file the appropriate legal documents with the clerk of a court to initiate a lawsuit.	* * * * * * * Singer **lodged a** * * * **complaint** in federal court * * * . He alleged that his **free speech** and **due process** rights were violated when Waupun officials confiscated his D&D materials and enacted a categorical ban against D&D. * * *
The First Amendment to the U.S. Constitution guarantees the right of *free speech*—to express one's views without governmental restrictions. The Fifth and Fourteenth Amendments guarantee the right to *due process*—to enjoy life, liberty, and property without unfair government interference.	
An *affidavit* is a written or printed voluntary statement of fact, confirmed by the oath or affirmation of the party making it and made before a person having the authority to administer the oath or affirmation.	Singer collected fifteen **affidavits**—from other inmates, his brother, and three role-playing game experts. He contends that the affidavits demonstrate that there is no connection between D&D and gang activity. * * * The prison officials countered Singer's affidavit evidence by submitting an affidavit from Captain Bruce Muraski * * * . Muraski testified * * * that fantasy role-playing games like D&D have "been found to promote competitive hostility, violence, and addictive escape behavior, which can compromise not only the inmate's rehabilitation and effects of positive programming, but endanger the public and jeopardize the safety and security of the institution."
A *summary judgment* is a judgment that a court enters without continuing a trial. This judgment can be entered only if no facts are in dispute and the only question is how the law applies to the facts.	The prison officials moved for **summary judgment** on all of Singer's claims. The district court granted the motion in full, but Singer limits his appeal to the foreclosure of his First Amendment claims.
The second major section of the opinion responds to the plaintiff's appeal.	**II. Discussion**
The court applies the principle established by the *Turner* case—which the United States Supreme Court decided—to the facts of the Singer case. The rulings in cases decided by higher courts are binding on the decisions of lower courts, according to the doctrine of *stare decisis* (see page 9).	* * * * In [*Turner v. Safley*], the [United States] Supreme Court determined that prison regulations that restrict inmates' constitutional rights are nevertheless valid if they are reasonably related to legitimate **penological interests.**
Penological interests relate to the branch of criminology dealing with prison management and the treatment of offenders.	* * * * [Singer] attacks the district court's conclusion that the D&D ban bears a rational relationship to a legitimate governmental interest * * * .
	The sole evidence the prison officials have submitted on this point is the affidavit of Captain Muraski, the gang specialist. Muraski testified that Waupun's prohibition on role-playing and fantasy games * * * was intended to promote prison security because co-operative games can mimic

EXHIBIT 1-6 • **A Sample Court Case, Continued**

Thereof here means "of gangs."

the organization of gangs and lead to the actual development **thereof.** * * * At bottom, his testimony about this policy aim highlighted Waupun's worries about cooperative activity among inmates, particularly that carried out in an organized, **hierarchical** fashion * * * . He [also] testified that D&D can "foster an inmate's obsession with escaping from the real life, correctional environment, fostering hostility, violence and escape behavior," which in turn "can compromise not only the inmate's rehabilitation and effects of positive programming but also endanger the public and jeopardize the safety and security of the institution."

Something that is organized by a rigid, ranked order—here, by a ranked order of inmates depending on who is winning the most.

A *trove* is a collection or treasure.

* * * *

It is true that Singer procured an impressive **trove** of affidavit testimony, including some from role-playing game experts, but none of his **affiants'** testimony addressed the inquiry at issue here. The question is not whether D&D has led to gang behavior in the past; the prison officials concede that it has not. The question is whether the prison officials are rational in their belief that, if left unchecked, D&D could lead to gang behavior among inmates and undermine prison security in the future. Singer's affiants * * * lack the qualifications necessary to determine whether the relationship between the D&D ban and the maintenance of prison security is so remote as to render the policy arbitrary or irrational. In other words, none of them is sufficiently versed in prison security concerns to raise a genuine issue of material fact about their relationship to D&D.

An *affiant* is a person who swears to an affidavit.

* * * *

In the third major section of the opinion, the court states its decision and gives its order.

III. Conclusion

Despite Singer's **large quantum** of affidavit testimony * * * , he has failed to demonstrate a genuine issue of material fact concerning the reasonableness of the relationship between Waupun's D&D ban and the prison's clearly legitimate penological interests. The district court's grant of summary judgment is therefore **AFFIRMED.**

A *large quantum* is a sizeable quantity.

To *affirm* a judgment is to declare that it is valid.

REVIEWING

Introduction to Law and Legal Reasoning

Suppose that the California legislature passes a law that severely restricts carbon dioxide emissions from automobiles in that state. A group of automobile manufacturers files suit against the state of California to prevent the enforcement of the law. The automakers claim that a federal law already sets fuel economy standards nationwide and that fuel economy standards are essentially the same as carbon dioxide emission standards. According to the automobile manufacturers, it is unfair to allow California to impose more stringent regulations than those set by the federal law. Using the information presented in the chapter, answer the following questions.

1. Who are the parties (the plaintiffs and the defendant) in this lawsuit?
2. Are the plaintiffs seeking a legal remedy or an equitable remedy?
3. What is the primary source of the law that is at issue here?
4. Where would you look to find the relevant California and federal laws?

✸ **DEBATE THIS:** *Under the doctrine of* stare decisis, *courts are obligated to follow the precedents established in their jurisdiction unless there is a compelling reason not to. Should U.S. courts continue to adhere to this common law principle, given that our government now regulates so many areas by statute?*

TERMS AND CONCEPTS

	common law 7	jurisprudence 13	public policy 10
	constitutional law 4	laches 8	remedy 7
administrative agency 5	court of equity 7	law 2	remedy at law 7
administrative law 5	court of law 7	legal positivism 13	remedy in equity 7
allege 10	criminal law 15	legal realism 14	reporter 9
analogy 11	cyberlaw 15	legal reasoning 10	respondent 8
appellant 21	damages 7	natural law 13	sociological school 14
appellee 21	defendant 8	opinion 21	*stare decisis* 9
binding authority 9	defense 8	ordinance 4	statute of limitations 8
breach 3	equitable maxims 8	petitioner 8	statutory law 4
case law 5	executive agency 5	plaintiff 8	substantive law 14
case on point 11	historical school 13	precedent 9	syllogism 11
chancellor 7	independent regulatory	procedural law 14	uniform law 4
citation 15	agency 5		
civil law 14			

QUESTIONS AND CASE PROBLEMS

1–1. Sources of Law How does statutory law come into existence? How does it differ from the common law?

1–2. QUESTION WITH SAMPLE ANSWER: Schools of Jurisprudential Thought.

After World War II, an international tribunal of judges convened at Nuremberg, Germany and convicted several Nazis of "crimes against humanity." Assuming that these convicted war criminals had not disobeyed any law of their country and had merely been following their government's orders, what law had they violated? Explain.

• **For a sample answer to Question 1–2, go to Appendix I at the end of this text.**

1–3. Reading Citations Assume that you want to read the entire court opinion in the case of *Pinard v. Dandy Lions,*

LLC, 119 Conn.App. 368, 987 A.2d 406 (2010). Refer to the subsection entitled "Finding Case Law" in this chapter, and then explain specifically where you would find the court's opinion.

1–4. Sources of Law This chapter discussed a number of sources of American law. Which source of law takes priority in the following situations, and why?

(a) A federal statute conflicts with the U.S. Constitution.

(b) A federal statute conflicts with a state constitutional provision.

(c) A state statute conflicts with the common law of that state.

(d) A state constitutional amendment conflicts with the U.S. Constitution.

1–5. *Stare Decisis* In this chapter, we stated that the doctrine of *stare decisis* "became a cornerstone of the English and American judicial systems." What does *stare decisis* mean, and why has this doctrine been so fundamental to the development of our legal tradition?

1–6. Court Opinions What is the difference between a concurring opinion and a majority opinion? Between a concurring opinion and a dissenting opinion? Why do judges and justices write concurring and dissenting opinions, given that these opinions will not affect the outcome of the case at hand, which has already been decided by majority vote?

1–7. The Common Law Tradition Courts can overturn precedents and thus change the common law. Should judges have the same authority to overrule statutory law? Explain.

1–8. Schools of Judicial Thought "The judge's role is not to make the law but to uphold and apply the law." Do you agree or disagree with this statement? Discuss fully the reasons for your answer.

1–9. Remedies Assume that Arthur Rabe is suing Xavier Sanchez for breaching a contract in which Sanchez promised to sell Rabe a painting by Vincent van Gogh for $3 million.

(a) In this lawsuit, who is the plaintiff and who is the defendant?

(b) Suppose that Rabe wants Sanchez to perform the contract as promised. What remedy would Rabe seek from the court?

(c) Now suppose that Rabe wants to cancel the contract because Sanchez fraudulently misrepresented the painting as an original Van Gogh when in fact it is a copy. What remedy would Rabe seek?

(d) Will the remedy Rabe seeks in either situation be a remedy at law or a remedy in equity? What is the difference between legal and equitable remedies?

(e) Suppose that the trial court finds in Rabe's favor and grants one of these remedies. Sanchez then appeals the decision to a higher court. On appeal, which party will be the appellant (or petitioner), and which party will be the appellee (or respondent)?

1–10. A QUESTION OF ETHICS: The Common Law Tradition.

 *On July 5, 1884, Dudley, Stephens, and Brooks— "all able-bodied English seamen"—and a teenage English boy were cast adrift in a lifeboat following a storm at sea. They had no water with them in the boat, and all they had for sustenance were two one-pound tins of turnips. On July 24, Dudley proposed that one of the four in the lifeboat be sacrificed to save the others. Stephens agreed with Dudley, but Brooks refused to consent—and the boy was never asked for his opinion. On July 25, Dudley killed the boy, and the three men then fed on the boy's body and blood. Four days later, a passing vessel rescued the men. They were taken to England and tried for the murder of the boy. If the men had not fed on the boy's body, they would probably have died of starvation within the four-day period. The boy, who was in a much weaker condition, would likely have died before the rest. [Regina v. Dudley and Stephens, 14 Q.B.D. (Queen's Bench Division, England) 273 (1884)]*

(a) The basic question in this case is whether the survivors should be subject to penalties under English criminal law, given the men's unusual circumstances. Were the defendants' actions necessary but unethical? Explain your reasoning. What ethical issues might be involved here?

(b) Should judges ever have the power to look beyond the written "letter of the law" in making their decisions? Why or why not?

LEGAL RESEARCH EXERCISES ON THE WEB

Go to this text's Web site at **www.cengage.com/blaw/clarkson**, select "Chapter 1," and click on "Practical Internet Exercises." There you will find the following Internet research exercises that you can perform to learn more about the topics covered in this chapter.

Practical Internet Exercise 1–1:   Legal Perspective
Internet Sources of Law

Practical Internet Exercise 1–2:   Management Perspective
Online Assistance from Government Agencies

Practical Internet Exercise 1–3:   Social Perspective
The Case of the Speluncean Explorers

CHAPTER 2

Courts and Alternative Dispute Resolution

Today, in the United States there are fifty-two court systems— one for each of the fifty states, one for the District of Columbia, and a federal system. Keep in mind that the federal courts are not superior to the state courts; they are simply an independent system of courts, which derives its authority from Article III, Section 2, of the U.S. Constitution. By the power given to it under Article I of the U.S. Constitution, Congress has extended the federal court system beyond the boundaries of the United States to U.S. territories such as Guam, Puerto Rico,

and the Virgin Islands.[1] As we shall see, the United States Supreme Court is the final controlling voice over all of these fifty-two systems, at least when questions of federal law are involved.

Every businessperson will likely face a lawsuit at some time in his or her career. Thus, anyone involved in business needs to have an understanding of the American court systems,

---
1. In Guam and the Virgin Islands, territorial courts serve as both federal courts and state courts; in Puerto Rico, they serve only as federal courts.

as well as the various methods of dispute resolution that can be pursued outside the courts. In this chapter, after examining the judiciary's role in the American governmental system, we discuss some basic requirements that must be met before a party may bring a lawsuit before a particular court. We then look at the court systems of the United States in some detail. We conclude the chapter with an overview of some alternative methods of settling disputes, including online dispute resolution.

SECTION 1
THE JUDICIARY'S ROLE IN AMERICAN GOVERNMENT

As you learned in Chapter 1, the body of American law includes the federal and state constitutions, statutes passed by legislative bodies, administrative law, and the case decisions and legal principles that form the common law. These laws would be meaningless, however, without the courts to interpret and apply them. This is the essential role of the judiciary—the courts—in the American governmental system: to interpret the laws and apply them to specific situations. (See this chapter's *Insight into Ethics* feature for a discussion of how the availability of "unpublished opinions" over the Internet is changing what some judges consider to be persuasive precedent.)

As the branch of government entrusted with interpreting the laws, the judiciary can decide, among other things, whether the laws or actions

of the other two branches are constitutional. The process for making such a determination is known as **judicial review.** The power of judicial review enables the judicial branch to act as a check on the other two branches of government, in line with the system of checks and balances established by the U.S. Constitution.[2]

The power of judicial review is not mentioned in the U.S. Constitution (although many constitutional scholars conclude that the founders intended the judiciary to have this power). Rather, this power was explicitly established by the United States Supreme Court in 1803 by its decision in *Marbury v. Madison.*[3] In that decision, the Court stated, "It is emphatically

---
2. In a broad sense, judicial review occurs whenever a court "reviews" a case or legal proceeding—as when an appellate court reviews a lower court's decision. When discussing the judiciary's role in American government, however, the term *judicial review* refers to the power of the judiciary to decide whether the actions of the other two branches of government violate the U.S. Constitution.
3. 5 U.S. (1 Cranch) 137, 2 L.Ed. 60 (1803).

INSIGHT INTO ETHICS
How the Internet Is Expanding Precedent

The notion that courts should rely on precedents to decide the outcome of similar cases has long been a cornerstone of U.S. law. Nevertheless, the availability of "unpublished opinions" over the Internet is changing what the law considers to be precedent. An *unpublished opinion* is a decision made by an appellate court that is not intended for publication in a reporter (the bound books that contain court opinions).[a] Courts traditionally have not considered unpublished opinions to be "precedent," binding or persuasive, and attorneys often have not been allowed to refer to these decisions in their arguments.

Increased Online Availability

The number of court decisions not published in printed books has risen dramatically in recent years. Nearly 80 percent of the decisions of the federal appellate courts are unpublished, and the number is equally high in some state court systems. Even though certain decisions are not intended for publication, they are posted ("published") almost immediately on online legal databases, such as Westlaw and Lexis. With the proliferation of free legal databases and court Web sites, the general public also has almost instant access to the unpublished decisions of most courts. This situation has caused many to question why these opinions have no precedential effect.

Should Unpublished Decisions Establish Precedent?

Before the advent of the Internet, not considering unpublished decisions as precedent might have been justified on the ground of fairness. How could lawyers know about unpublished decisions if they were not printed in the case reporters? Now that opinions are so readily available on the Web, however, this justification is no longer valid. Moreover, it now seems unfair *not* to consider these decisions as precedent, given that they are so publicly accessible. Some claim that unpublished decisions could make bad precedents because these decisions frequently are written by staff attorneys and law clerks rather than by judges, so the reasoning may be inferior. If an unpublished decision is considered merely as persuasive precedent, however, then judges who disagree with the reasoning are free to reject the conclusion.

The United States Supreme Court Changed the Federal Rules on Unpublished Opinions

The United States Supreme Court made history in 2006 when it announced that it would allow lawyers to refer to (cite) unpublished decisions in all federal courts. Rule 32.1 of the Federal Rules of Appellate Procedure states that federal courts may not prohibit or restrict the citation of federal judicial opinions that have been designated as "not for publication," "non-precedential," or "not precedent." The rule applies only to federal courts and only to unpublished opinions issued after January 1, 2007. It does not specify the effect that a court must give to one of its unpublished opinions or to an unpublished opinion from another court. Basically, Rule 32.1 simply establishes a uniform rule for all of the federal courts that allows attorneys to cite—and judges to consider as persuasive precedent— unpublished decisions. The rule is a clear example of how technology—the availability of unpublished opinions over the Internet—has affected the law.

---

a. Recently decided cases that are not yet published are also sometimes called *unpublished opinions*, but because these decisions will eventually be printed in reporters, we do not include them here.

CRITICAL THINKING

INSIGHT INTO THE LEGAL ENVIRONMENT
Now that the United States Supreme Court is allowing unpublished decisions to form persuasive precedent in federal courts, should state courts follow? Why or why not?

---

the province and duty of the Judicial Department to say what the law is. . . . If two laws conflict with each other, the Courts must decide on the operation of each. . . . [I]f both [a] law and the Constitution apply to a particular case, . . . the Court must determine which of these conflicting rules governs the case. This is of the very essence of judicial duty." Since the *Marbury v. Madison* decision, the power of judicial review has remained unchallenged. Today, this power is exercised by both federal and state courts.

SECTION 2
BASIC JUDICIAL REQUIREMENTS

Before a lawsuit can be brought before a court, certain requirements must be met. These requirements relate to jurisdiction, venue, and standing to sue. We examine each of these important concepts here.

Jurisdiction

In Latin, *juris* means "law," and *diction* means "to speak." Thus, "the power to speak the law" is the literal meaning of the term **jurisdiction.** Before any court can hear a case, it must have jurisdiction over the person (or company) against whom the suit is brought (the defendant) or over the property involved in the suit. The court must also have jurisdiction over the subject matter of the dispute.

JURISDICTION OVER PERSONS OR PROPERTY

Generally, a particular court can exercise **in personam jurisdiction** (personal jurisdiction) over any person or business that resides in a certain geographic area. A state trial court, for example, normally has jurisdictional authority over residents (including businesses) of a particular area of the state, such as a county or district. A state's highest court (often called the state supreme court[4]) has jurisdictional authority over all residents within the state.

A court can also exercise jurisdiction over property that is located within its boundaries. This kind of jurisdiction is known as **in rem jurisdiction,** or "jurisdiction over the thing." For example, suppose that a dispute arises over the ownership of a boat in dry dock in Fort Lauderdale, Florida. The boat is owned by an Ohio resident, over whom a Florida court normally cannot exercise personal jurisdiction. The other party to the dispute is a resident of Nebraska. In this situation, a lawsuit concerning the boat could be brought in a Florida state court on the basis of the court's *in rem* jurisdiction.

Long Arm Statutes. Under the authority of a state **long arm statute,** a court can exercise personal jurisdiction over certain out-of-state defendants based on activities that took place within the state. Before a court can exercise jurisdiction over an out-of-state defendant under a long arm statute, though, it must be demonstrated that the defendant had sufficient contacts, or *minimum contacts,* with the state to justify the jurisdiction.[5] Generally, this means that the defendant must have enough of a connection to the state for the judge to conclude that it is fair for the state to exercise power over the defendant. For example, if an out-of-state defendant caused an automobile accident or sold defective goods within the state, a court usually will find that

minimum contacts exist to exercise jurisdiction over that defendant. Similarly, a state may exercise personal jurisdiction over a nonresident defendant who is sued for breaching a contract that was formed within the state.

CASE IN POINT An Xbox game system caught fire in Bonnie Broquet's home in Texas and caused substantial personal injuries. Broquet filed a lawsuit in a Texas court against Ji-Haw Industrial Company, a nonresident company that made the Xbox components. Broquet alleged that Ji-Haw's components were defective and had caused the fire. Ji-Haw argued that the Texas court lacked jurisdiction over it, but a state appellate court held that the Texas long arm statute authorized the exercise of jurisdiction over the out-of-state defendant.[6]

Corporate Contacts. Because corporations are considered legal persons, courts use the same principles to determine whether it is fair to exercise jurisdiction over a corporation.[7] A corporation normally is subject to personal jurisdiction in the state in which it is incorporated, has its principal office, and/or is doing business. Courts apply the minimum-contacts test to determine if they can exercise jurisdiction over out-of-state corporations.

The minimum-contacts requirement is usually met if the corporation advertises or sells its products within the state, or places its goods into the "stream of commerce" with the intent that the goods be sold in the state. Suppose that a business is incorporated under the laws of Maine but has a branch office and manufacturing plant in Georgia. The corporation also advertises and sells its products in Georgia. These activities would likely constitute sufficient contacts with the state of Georgia to allow a Georgia court to exercise jurisdiction over the corporation.

Some corporations, however, do not sell or advertise products or place any goods in the stream of commerce. Determining what constitutes minimum contacts in these situations can be more difficult. In the following case, the defendant was a New Jersey corporation that performed machining services on component parts that it received from a North Carolina firm. The North Carolina firm claimed that the services were defective and wanted to sue for breach of contract in a North Carolina court. Did the New Jersey firm have minimum contacts with North Carolina?

---

4. As will be discussed shortly, a state's highest court is often referred to as the state supreme court, but there are exceptions. For example, in New York the supreme court is a trial court.

5. The minimum-contacts standard was first established in *International Shoe Co. v. State of Washington,* 326 U.S. 310, 66 S.Ct. 154, 90 L.Ed. 95 (1945).

6. *Ji-Haw Industrial Co. v. Broquet,* 2008 WL 441822 (Tex.App.—San Antonio 2008).

7. In the eyes of the law, corporations are "legal persons"—entities that can sue and be sued. See Chapter 39.

✳ EXTENDED CASE 2.1 ✳
Southern Prestige Industries, Inc. v. Independence Plating Corp.

Court of Appeals of North Carolina, 690 S.E.2d 768 (2010).
www.nccourts.org[a]

IN THE LANGUAGE OF THE COURT
CALABRIA, Judge.
* * * *

The facts in the instant case [the case before the court] are undisputed. Defendant (Independence Plating Corporation) is a New Jersey corporation that provides anodizing[b] services. Defendant's only office and all of its personnel are located in the state of New Jersey. Defendant does not advertise or otherwise solicit business in North Carolina. Prior to July 2007, defendant had engaged in a longstanding business relationship with Kidde Aerospace ("Kidde"), a North Carolina company.
* * * *

Plaintiff and defendant engaged in frequent transactions between 27 July 2007 and 25 April 2008.

On 18 November 2008, plaintiff initiated an action for breach of contract in [a North Carolina state court]. Plaintiff alleged that defects caused by defendant's anodizing process caused plaintiff's machined parts to be rejected by Kidde. On 6 February 2009, defendant filed, with a supporting affidavit [a written statement, made under oath], a motion to dismiss pursuant to [North Carolina statutory law] for lack of personal jurisdiction. On 18 March 2009, plaintiff filed an affidavit, with supporting exhibits, challenging the assertions in defendant's motion to dismiss. On 4 May 2009, after reviewing the evidence submitted by the parties, the trial court entered an order denying defendant's motion to dismiss. Defendant appeals.

Defendant's only argument on appeal is that the trial court erred in denying its motion to dismiss for lack of personal jurisdiction. Specifically, defendant argues there are insufficient contacts to satisfy the due process of law requirements that are necessary to subject defendant to the personal jurisdiction of North Carolina's courts. We disagree.
* * * *

Neither party contests the findings of fact contained in the trial court's order. * * * Therefore, the only issue to be determined is "whether the trial court's findings of fact support its conclusion of law that the court has personal jurisdiction over defendant. We conduct our review of this issue *de novo* [anew]."

North Carolina courts utilize a two-prong analysis in determining whether personal jurisdiction against a nonresident is properly asserted. Under the first prong of the analysis, we determine if statutory authority for jurisdiction exists under our long-arm statute. If statutory authority exists, we consider under the second prong whether exercise of our jurisdiction comports [is in accordance] with standards of due process.

Defendant has conceded that the facts are sufficient to confer jurisdiction under the North Carolina long arm statute. Therefore, "the inquiry becomes whether plaintiffs' assertion of jurisdiction over defendants complies with due process."

In order to satisfy due process requirements, there must be "certain minimum contacts [between the nonresident defendant and the forum state—that is, the state in which the court is located] such that

the maintenance of the suit does not offend 'traditional notions of fair play and substantial justice.'" In order to establish minimum contacts with North Carolina,

the defendant must have purposefully availed itself of the privilege of conducting activities within the forum state and invoked the benefits and protections of the laws of North Carolina. The relationship between the defendant and the forum state must be such that the defendant should reasonably anticipate being haled into a North Carolina court.

* * * *

* * * Our courts look at the following factors in determining whether minimum contacts exist: (1) the quantity of the contacts, (2) the nature and quality of the contacts, (3) the source and connection of the cause of action to the contacts, (4) the interest of the forum state, and (5) the convenience to the parties.* [Emphasis added.]

In the instant case, the trial court found that the parties "had an ongoing business relationship characterized by frequent transactions between July 27, 2007, and April 25, 2008, as reflected by thirty-two purchase orders." Plaintiff would ship machined parts to defendant, who would then anodize the parts and return them to plaintiff in North Carolina. Defendant sent invoices totaling $21,018.70 to plaintiff in North Carolina, and these invoices were paid from plaintiff's corporate account at a North Carolina bank. Plaintiff filed a breach of contract action against defendant because the machined parts that were shipped to defendant from North Carolina and then anodized

---

a. In the right-hand column of the page, click on "Court Opinions." When that page opens, select the year 2010 under the heading "Court of Appeals Opinions." Scroll down to the case title to access the opinion. The North Carolina court system maintains this Web site.

b. *Anodizing* is a process in which metal is subjected to electrolytic action in order to coat the metal with a protective or decorative film.

EXTENDED CASE CONTINUES ▶

EXTENDED CASE 2.1 CONTINUED ➜

by defendant and shipped back to North Carolina were defective.

"*It is generally conceded that a state has a manifest interest in providing its residents with a convenient forum for redressing injuries inflicted by out-of-state actors.* Thus, North Carolina has a 'manifest interest' in providing the plaintiff 'a convenient forum for redressing injuries inflicted by' defendant, an out-of-state merchant." As for the remaining factor, there is no evidence in the record

that would indicate that it is more convenient for the parties to litigate this matter in a different forum. "Litigation on interstate business transactions inevitably involves inconvenience to one of the parties. When [t]he inconvenience to defendant of litigating in North Carolina is no greater than would be the inconvenience of plaintiff of litigating in [the defendant's state] . . . no convenience factors . . . are determinative[.]" [Emphasis added.]

Therefore, after examining the ongoing relationship between the

parties, the nature of their contacts, the interest of the forum state, the convenience of the parties, and the cause of action, we conclude defendant has "purposely availed" itself of the benefits of doing business in North Carolina and "should reasonably anticipate being haled" into a North Carolina court. We hold that defendant has sufficient minimum contacts with North Carolina to justify the exercise of personal jurisdiction over defendant without violating the due process clause.

Affirmed.

 QUESTIONS

1. What are the factors that the court looked at in determining whether minimum contacts existed between the defendant and the state of North Carolina?
2. Why did the court state that the convenience of the parties was not "determinative" in this case?

JURISDICTION OVER SUBJECT MATTER Subject-matter jurisdiction refers to the limitations on the types of cases a court can hear. Certain courts are empowered to hear certain kinds of disputes.

General and Limited Jurisdiction. In both the federal and the state court systems, there are courts of *general* (unlimited) *jurisdiction* and courts of *limited jurisdiction*. A court of general jurisdiction can decide cases involving a broad array of issues. An example of a court of general jurisdiction is a state trial court or a federal district court. An example of a state court of limited jurisdiction is a probate court. **Probate courts** are state courts that handle only matters relating to the transfer of a person's assets and obligations after that person's death, including issues relating to the custody and guardianship of children. An example of a federal court of limited subject-matter jurisdiction is a bankruptcy court. **Bankruptcy courts** handle only bankruptcy proceedings, which are governed by federal bankruptcy law (see Chapter 30).

A court's jurisdiction over subject matter is usually defined in the statute or constitution creating the court. In both the federal and the state court systems, a court's subject-matter jurisdiction can be limited not only by the subject of the lawsuit but also by the sum in controversy, whether the case is a felony (a more serious type of crime) or a misdemeanor (a less serious type of crime), or whether the proceeding is a trial or an appeal.

Original and Appellate Jurisdiction. A court's subject-matter jurisdiction is also frequently limited to hearing cases at a particular stage of the dispute. Courts in which lawsuits begin, trials take place, and evidence is presented are referred to as *courts of original jurisdiction*. Courts having original jurisdiction are courts of the first instance, or trial courts. In the federal court system, the *district courts* are trial courts. In the various state court systems, the trial courts are known by different names, as will be discussed shortly.

Courts having appellate jurisdiction act as reviewing courts, or appellate courts. In general, cases can be brought before appellate courts only on appeal from an order or a judgment of a trial court or other lower court. In other words, the distinction between courts of original jurisdiction and courts of appellate jurisdiction normally lies in whether the case is being heard for the first time.

JURISDICTION OF THE FEDERAL COURTS Because the federal government is a government of limited powers, the jurisdiction of the federal courts is limited. Federal courts have subject-matter jurisdiction in two situations.

Federal Questions. Article III of the U.S. Constitution establishes the boundaries of federal judicial power. Section 2 of Article III states that "the judicial Power shall extend to all Cases, in Law and Equity, arising under this Constitution, the Laws of the United States, and Treaties made, or which shall be made, under their Authority." In effect, this clause means that whenever a plaintiff's cause of action is based, at least in part, on the U.S. Constitution, a treaty, or a federal law, a **federal question** arises. Any lawsuit involving a federal question comes under the judicial authority of the federal courts and can originate in a federal court. People who claim that their constitutional rights have been violated, for example, can begin their suits in a federal court. Note that in a case based on a federal question, a federal court will apply federal law.

Diversity of Citizenship. Federal district courts can also exercise original jurisdiction over cases involving **diversity of citizenship.** This term applies whenever a federal court has jurisdiction over a case that does not involve a question of federal law. The most common type of diversity jurisdiction has two requirements:[8] (1) the plaintiff and defendant must be residents of different states, and (2) the dollar amount in controversy must exceed $75,000. For purposes of diversity jurisdiction, a corporation is a citizen of both the state in which it is incorporated and the state in which its principal place of business is located. A case involving diversity of citizenship can be filed in the appropriate federal district court. If the case starts in a state court, it can sometimes be transferred, or "removed," to a federal court. A large percentage of the cases filed in federal courts each year are based on diversity of citizenship.

As noted, a federal court will apply federal law in cases involving federal questions. In a case based on diversity of citizenship, in contrast, a federal court will apply the relevant state law (which is often the law of the state in which the court sits).

---

8. Diversity jurisdiction also exists in cases between (1) a foreign country and citizens of a state or of different states and (2) citizens of a state and citizens or subjects of a foreign country. These bases for diversity jurisdiction are less commonly used.

EXCLUSIVE VERSUS CONCURRENT JURISDICTION
When both federal and state courts have the power to hear a case, as is true in suits involving diversity of citizenship, **concurrent jurisdiction** exists. When cases can be tried only in federal courts or only in state courts, **exclusive jurisdiction** exists. Federal courts have exclusive jurisdiction in cases involving federal crimes, bankruptcy, and most patent and copyright claims; in suits against the United States; and in some areas of admiralty law (law governing transportation on ocean waters). State courts also have exclusive jurisdiction over certain subjects—for example, divorce and adoption.

When concurrent jurisdiction exists, a party may choose to bring a suit in either a federal court or a state court. A number of factors can affect a party's decision to litigate in a federal versus a state court—such as the availability of different remedies, the distance to the respective courthouses, or the experience or reputation of a particular judge. For example, if the dispute involves a trade secret, a party might conclude that a federal court—which has exclusive jurisdiction over copyrights, patents, and trademarks—would have more expertise in the matter. A party might also choose a federal court over a state court if he or she is concerned about bias in a state court. In contrast, a plaintiff might choose to litigate in a state court if the court has a reputation for awarding substantial amounts of damages or if the judge is perceived as being pro-plaintiff. The concepts of exclusive and concurrent jurisdiction are illustrated in Exhibit 2–1.

Jurisdiction in Cyberspace

The Internet's capacity to bypass political and geographic boundaries undercuts the traditional basis on which courts assert personal jurisdiction. This basis includes a party's contacts with a court's

EXHIBIT 2–1 • Exclusive and Concurrent Jurisdiction

Exclusive Federal Jurisdiction
(cases involving federal crimes, federal antitrust law, bankruptcy, patents, copyrights, trademarks, suits against the United States, some areas of admiralty law, and certain other matters specified in federal statutes)

Concurrent Jurisdiction
(most cases involving federal questions and diversity-of-citizenship cases)

Exclusive State Jurisdiction
(cases involving all matters not subject to federal jurisdiction—for example, divorce and adoption cases)

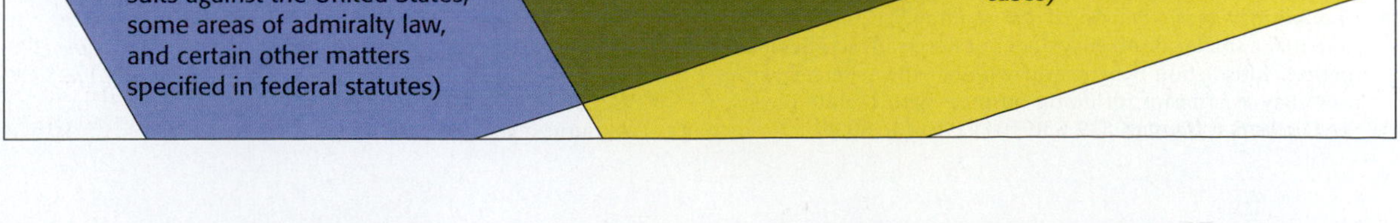

geographic jurisdiction. As already discussed, for a court to compel a defendant to come before it, there must be at least minimum contacts—the presence of a salesperson within the state, for example. Are there sufficient minimum contacts if the only connection to a jurisdiction is an ad on a Web site originating from a remote location?

THE "SLIDING-SCALE" STANDARD Gradually, the courts are developing a standard—called a "sliding-scale" standard—for determining when the exercise of personal jurisdiction over an out-of-state Internet-based defendant is proper. In developing this standard, the courts have identified three types of Internet business contacts: (1) substantial business conducted over the Internet (with contracts and sales, for example); (2) some interactivity through a Web site; and (3) passive advertising. Jurisdiction is proper for the first category, is improper for the third, and may or may not be appropriate for the second.[9] An Internet communication is typically considered passive if people have to voluntarily access it to read the message and active if it is sent to specific individuals. In certain situations, even a single contact can satisfy the minimum-contacts requirement.

CASE IN POINT A Louisiana resident, Daniel Crummey, purchased a used recreational vehicle (RV) from sellers in Texas after viewing photos of it on eBay. The sellers' statements on eBay claimed that "Everything works great on this RV and will provide comfort and dependability for years to come. This RV will go to Alaska and back without problems!" Crummey picked up the RV in Texas, but on the drive back to Louisiana, the RV quit working. He filed a suit in Louisiana against the sellers alleging that the vehicle was defective, but the sellers claimed that the Louisiana court lacked jurisdiction. Because the sellers had used eBay to market and sell the RV to a Louisiana buyer—and had regularly used eBay to sell vehicles to remote parties in the past— the court found that jurisdiction was proper.[10]

INTERNATIONAL JURISDICTIONAL ISSUES Because the Internet is international in scope, international jurisdictional issues have understandably come to the fore. The world's courts seem to be developing a

standard that echoes the requirement of minimum contacts applied by the U.S. courts. Most courts are indicating that minimum contacts—doing business within the jurisdiction, for example—are enough to compel a defendant to appear and that a physical presence is not necessary. The effect of this standard is that a business firm has to comply with the laws in any jurisdiction in which it targets customers for its products. This situation is complicated by the fact that many countries' laws on particular issues—free speech, for example—are very different from U.S. laws.

CASE IN POINT Yahoo operated an online auction site on which Nazi memorabilia, among other things, were offered for sale. In France, the display of any objects depicting symbols of Nazi ideology is illegal and leads to both criminal and civil liability. The International League against Racism and Anti-Semitism filed a suit in Paris against Yahoo for displaying Nazi memorabilia and offering them for sale via its Web site. The French court asserted jurisdiction over Yahoo on the ground that the materials on the company's U.S.–based servers could be viewed on a Web site accessible in France. The French court ordered Yahoo to eliminate all Internet access in France to the Nazi memorabilia offered for sale through its online auctions. Yahoo then took the case to a federal district court in the United States, claiming that the French court's order violated the First Amendment to the U.S. Constitution. Although the federal district court ruled in favor of Yahoo, the U.S. Court of Appeals for the Ninth Circuit reversed. According to the appellate court, U.S. courts lacked personal jurisdiction over the French groups involved. The ruling leaves open the possibility that Yahoo, and anyone else who posts anything on the Internet, could be held answerable to the laws of any country in which the message might be received.[11]

Concept Summary 2.1 reviews the various types of jurisdiction, including jurisdiction in cyberspace.

Venue

Jurisdiction has to do with whether a court has authority to hear a case involving specific persons, property, or subject matter. **Venue**[12] is concerned with the most appropriate location for a trial. For

---

9. For a leading case on this issue, see *Zippo Manufacturing Co. v. Zippo Dot Com, Inc.*, 952 F.Supp. 1119 (W.D.Pa. 1997).

10. *Crummey v. Morgan*, 965 So.2d 497 (La.App. 1 Cir. 2007). But note that a single sale on eBay does not necessarily confer jurisdiction. Jurisdiction depends on whether the seller regularly uses eBay as a means for doing business with remote buyers. See *Boschetto v. Hansing*, 539 F.3d 1011 (9th Cir. 2008).

11. *Yahoo!, Inc. v. La Ligue Contre le Racisme et l'Antisemitisme*, 379 F.3d 1120 (9th Cir. 2004), *cert.* denied, 547 U.S. 1164, 126 S.Ct. 2332, 164 L.Ed.2d 841 (2006).

12. Pronounced *ven*-yoo.

CONCEPT SUMMARY 2.1
Jurisdiction

Type of Jurisdiction	Description
Personal	Exists when a defendant is located within the territorial boundaries within which a court has the right and power to decide cases. Jurisdiction may be exercised over out-of-state defendants under state long arm statutes. Courts have jurisdiction over corporate defendants that do business within the state, as well as corporations that advertise, sell, or place goods into the stream of commerce in the state.
Property	Exists when the property that is subject to a lawsuit is located within the territorial boundaries within which a court has the right and power to decide cases.
Subject Matter	Limits the court's jurisdictional authority to particular types of cases. 1. *Limited jurisdiction*—Exists when a court is limited to a specific subject matter, such as probate or divorce. 2. *General jurisdiction*—Exists when a court can hear cases involving a broad array of issues.
Original	Exists with courts that have the authority to hear a case for the first time (trial courts).
Appellate	Exists with courts of appeal and review. Generally, appellate courts do not have original jurisdiction.
Federal	1. *Federal questions*—A federal court can exercise jurisdiction when the plaintiff's cause of action is based at least in part on the U.S. Constitution, a treaty, or a federal law. 2. *Diversity of citizenship*—A federal court can exercise jurisdiction in cases between citizens of different states when the amount in controversy exceeds $75,000 (or in cases between a foreign country and citizens of a state or of different states and in cases between citizens of a state and citizens or subjects of a foreign country).
Concurrent	Exists when both federal and state courts have authority to hear the same case.
Exclusive	Exists when only state courts or only federal courts have authority to hear a case.
Jurisdiction in Cyberspace	Because the Internet does not have physical boundaries, traditional jurisdictional concepts have been difficult to apply in cases involving activities conducted via the Web. Gradually, the courts are developing standards to use in determining when jurisdiction over a Web site owner or operator in another state is proper. Jurisdictional disputes involving international cyberspace transactions present a significant legal challenge.

example, two state courts (or two federal courts) may have the authority to exercise jurisdiction over a case, but it may be more appropriate or convenient to hear the case in one court than in the other.

Basically, the concept of venue reflects the policy that a court trying a case should be in the geographic neighborhood (usually the county) where the incident leading to the lawsuit occurred or where the parties involved in the lawsuit reside. Venue in a civil case typically is where the defendant resides, whereas venue in a criminal case normally is where the crime occurred. Pretrial publicity or other factors, though, may require a change of venue to another community, especially in criminal cases in which the defendant's right to a fair and impartial jury has been impaired.

Standing to Sue

In order to bring a lawsuit before a court, a party must have **standing to sue,** or a sufficient stake in a matter to justify seeking relief through the court system. In other words, to have standing, a party must have a legally protected and tangible interest at stake in the litigation. The party bringing the lawsuit must have suffered a harm or been threatened with a harm by the action about which she or he has complained. At times, a person can have standing to sue on behalf of another person. Suppose that a child suffers serious injuries as a result of a defectively manufactured toy. Because the child is a minor, another person, such as a parent or a legal guardian, can bring a lawsuit on the child's behalf.

Standing to sue also requires that the controversy at issue be a **justiciable**[13] **controversy**—a controversy that is real and substantial, as opposed to hypothetical or academic.

CASE IN POINT James Bush went to the Federal Bureau of Investigation's (FBI's) office in San Jose, California, and filled out complaint forms indicating that he was seeking records under the Freedom

of Information Act (FOIA—see Chapter 45). When the FBI failed to provide the requested records, Bush filed a lawsuit against the U.S. Department of Justice. The court dismissed the suit, however, finding that no actual controversy existed for the court to decide. Bush had failed to comply with the requirements of the FOIA when he filled out the forms, so the FBI was not obligated to provide any records.[14]

In the following case—involving a suit between a state and an agency of the federal government—the court was asked to determine whether the state's allegations rose to the level of a "concrete, particularized, actual or imminent" injury against the state independent of any harm to private parties.

---

13. Pronounced jus-*tish*-a-bul.

14. *Bush v. U.S. Department of Justice*, 2008 WL 5245046 (N.D.Cal. 2008).

CASE 2.2
Oregon v. Legal Services Corp.

United States Court of Appeals, Ninth Circuit, 552 F.3d 965 (2009).
www.ca9.uscourts.gov[a]

BACKGROUND AND FACTS • The federal government established the Legal Services Corporation (LSC) to provide federal funds to local legal assistance programs for individuals who cannot afford legal services. LSC restricts the use of the funds for some purposes, including participating in class-action lawsuits. The recipients must maintain legal, physical, and financial separation from organizations that engage in these activities. In 2005, in the interest of cutting costs, the state of Oregon directed legal assistance programs in the state to consolidate in situations in which separate organizations provided services in the same geographic area. LSC did not approve of the integration of programs that received its funds with programs that engaged in restricted activities. Oregon filed a suit in a federal district court against LSC, alleging that the state's ability to provide legal services to its citizens was frustrated. The court dismissed the suit "on the merits." Oregon appealed to the U.S. Court of Appeals for the Ninth Circuit.

IN THE LANGUAGE OF THE COURT
Milan D. *SMITH*, Jr., Circuit Judge:
* * * *

* * * In this case there is no burden or injury placed on Oregon. * * * Oregon has not accepted federal funds, nor is it bound by the accompanying restrictions. Oregon is not injured by the federal government's decision to subsidize certain private activities, even if the government attaches impermissible conditions, as is alleged, to the recipients of those funds. *Oregon is only affected by virtue of its interest in the effect of the grant and the conditions on its citizens; it has no independent claim of injury.* [Emphasis added.]

Oregon cannot claim injury simply on the basis that federal subsidies to private parties do not [complement] Oregon's policies. *The state has no standing to sue the federal government to provide voluntary federal subsidies to private parties, and certainly has no standing to sue the federal government to change its conditions for those federal subsidies.* [Emphasis added.]

---

a. In the left-hand column, in the "Decisions" pull-down menu, click on "Opinions." On that page, click on "Advanced Search"; in the "by Case No.:" box, type "06-36012" and click on "Search." In the result, click on the appropriate link to access the opinion. The U.S. Court of Appeals for the Ninth Circuit maintains this Web site.

CASE 2.2 CONTINUED ➡

* * * *

Oregon argues * * * that it has been injured by LSC's regulations, which thwart Oregon's efforts at policy making with regards to Oregon's Legal Service Program. Oregon attempts to analogize [draw comparisons to] its situation to cases recognizing a state's standing to defend its statutes when they are alleged to be unconstitutional or pre-empted by federal regulation. However, those cases are distinguishable, because in this case there is no dispute over Oregon's ability to regulate its legal services program, and no claim that Oregon's laws have been invalidated as a result of the LSC restrictions.

The core of the dispute is whether Oregon should have the ability to control the conditions surrounding a voluntary grant of federal funds to specifically delineated private institutions. Because Oregon has no right, express or reserved, to do so, there is no judicially cognizable [able to be known] injury. Oregon may continue to regulate its legal service programs as it desires, but it cannot depend on voluntary financial support from LSC to * * * any * * * legal services provider within the state if it makes choices that conflict with the LSC * * * regulations.

* * * *

Oregon has failed to allege generalized facts sufficient to show an actual injury for the purposes of establishing its standing in this case. Oregon is not directly affected by the * * * LSC regulations, and is free to avoid any or all indirect effects of those regulations by simply increasing its own taxes to fund its desired policies. * * * Oregon * * * is, therefore, without standing to pursue its claims in this action.

DECISION AND REMEDY • *The U.S. Court of Appeals for the Ninth Circuit agreed that Oregon's complaint should be dismissed, but vacated the judgment and remanded the case for an entry of dismissal based on the plaintiff's lack of standing.*

THE LEGAL ENVIRONMENT DIMENSION • *Under what circumstances might a state suffer an injury that would give it standing to sue to block the enforcement of restrictions on the use of federal funds?*

THE ETHICAL DIMENSION • *Would it be ethical for a state to alter its policies to align with LSC's restrictions in order to continue the funding of local legal services programs? Explain.*

SECTION 3
THE STATE AND FEDERAL COURT SYSTEMS

As mentioned earlier in this chapter, each state has its own court system. Additionally, there is a system of federal courts. Although no two state court systems are exactly the same, the right-hand side of Exhibit 2–2 on the following page illustrates the basic organizational framework characteristic of the court systems in many states. The exhibit also shows how the federal court system is structured. We turn now to an examination of these court systems, beginning with the state courts.

The State Court Systems

Typically, a state court system includes several levels, or tiers, of courts. As indicated in Exhibit 2–2 on the next page, state courts may include (1) local trial courts of limited jurisdiction, (2) state trial courts of general jurisdiction, (3) state courts of appeals (intermediate appellate courts), and (4) the state's highest court (often called the state supreme court). Generally, any person who is a party to a lawsuit has the opportunity to plead the case before a trial court and then, if he or she loses, before at least one level of appellate court. Finally, if the case involves a federal statute or federal constitutional issue, the decision of a state supreme court on that issue may be further appealed to the United States Supreme Court.

The states use various methods to select judges for their courts. Usually, voters elect judges, but in some states judges are appointed. For example, in Iowa, the governor appoints judges, and then the general population decides whether to confirm their appointment in the next general election. The states usually specify the number of years that judges will serve. In contrast, as you will read shortly, judges in the federal court system are appointed by the president of the United States and, if they are confirmed by the Senate, hold office for life—unless they engage in blatantly illegal conduct.

EXHIBIT 2–2 • The State and Federal Court Systems

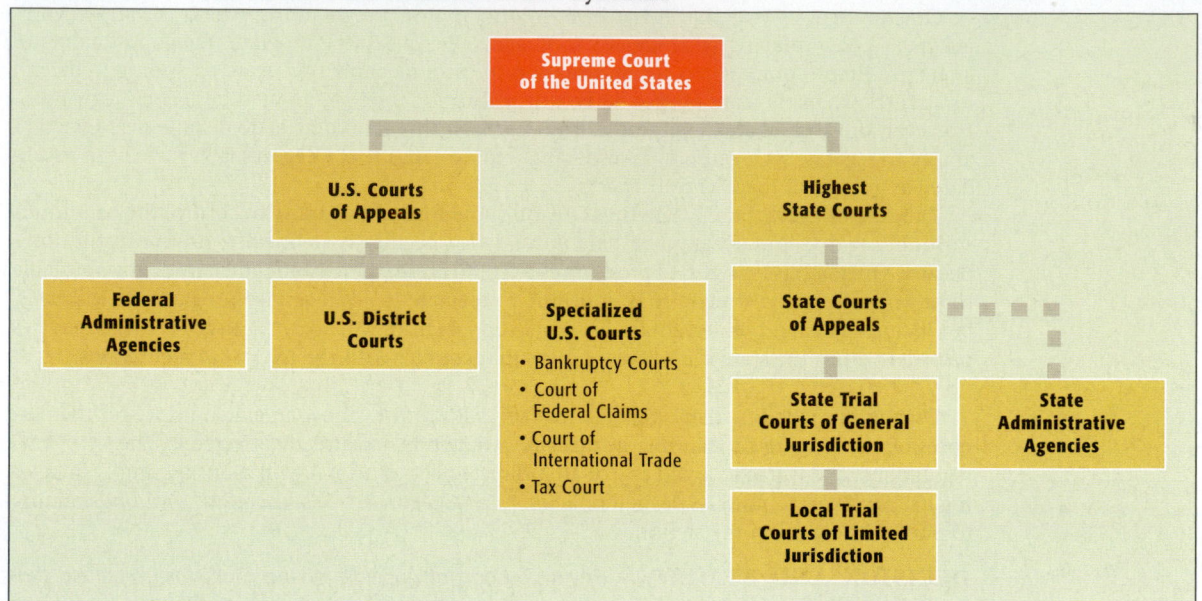

TRIAL COURTS Trial courts are exactly what their name implies—courts in which trials are held and testimony is taken. State trial courts have either general or limited jurisdiction. Trial courts that have general jurisdiction as to subject matter may be called county, district, superior, or circuit courts.[15] State trial courts of general jurisdiction have jurisdiction over a wide variety of subjects, including both civil disputes and criminal prosecutions. In some states, trial courts of general jurisdiction may hear appeals from courts of limited jurisdiction.

Courts of limited jurisdiction as to subject matter are often called special inferior trial courts or minor judiciary courts. **Small claims courts** are inferior trial courts that hear only civil cases involving claims of less than a certain amount, such as $5,000 (the amount varies from state to state). Suits brought in small claims courts are generally conducted informally, and lawyers are not required (in a few states, lawyers are not even allowed). Decisions of small claims courts and municipal courts may sometimes be appealed to a state trial court of general jurisdiction.

Other courts of limited jurisdiction include domestic relations courts, which handle primarily divorce actions and child-custody disputes; local municipal courts, which mainly deal with traffic cases; and probate courts, as mentioned earlier. A

few states have also established Islamic law courts, which are courts of limited jurisdiction that serve the American Muslim community.[16]

APPELLATE, OR REVIEWING, COURTS Every state has at least one court of appeals (appellate court, or reviewing court), which may be an intermediate appellate court or the state's highest court. About three-fourths of the states have intermediate appellate courts. Generally, courts of appeals do not conduct new trials, in which evidence is submitted to the court and witnesses are examined. Rather, an appellate court panel of three or more judges reviews the record of the case on appeal, which includes a transcript of the trial proceedings, and then determines whether the trial court committed an error.

Usually, appellate courts focus on questions of law, not questions of fact. A **question of fact** deals with what really happened in regard to the dispute being tried—such as whether a party actually burned a flag. A **question of law** concerns the application or interpretation of the law—such as whether flag-burning is a form of speech protected by the First Amendment to the U.S. Constitution. Only a judge, not a jury, can rule on questions of law. Appellate courts normally defer (or give weight) to the trial court's findings on questions of fact because the

---

15. The name in Ohio and Pennsylvania is Court of Common Pleas; the name in New York is Supreme Court, Trial Division.

16. See, for example, *Jabri v. Qaddura,* 108 S.W.3d 404 (Tex.App.—Fort Worth 2003); *Abd Alla v. Mourssi,* 680 N.W.2d 569 (Minn. App. 2004).

trial court judge and jury were in a better position to evaluate testimony—by directly observing witnesses' gestures, demeanor, and other nonverbal behavior during the trial. At the appellate level, the judges review the written transcript of the trial, which does not include these nonverbal elements. Thus, an appellate court will not tamper with a trial court's finding of fact unless it is clearly erroneous (contrary to the evidence presented at trial) or when there is no evidence to support the finding.

HIGHEST STATE COURTS The highest appellate court in a state is usually called the supreme court but may be designated by some other name. For example, in both New York and Maryland, the highest state court is called the Court of Appeals. The highest state court in Maine and Massachusetts is the Supreme Judicial Court, and in West Virginia, it is the Supreme Court of Appeals.

The decisions of each state's highest court on all questions of state law are final. Only when issues of federal law are involved can the United States Supreme Court overrule a decision made by a state's highest court. For example, suppose that a city ordinance prohibits citizens from engaging in door-to-door advocacy without first registering with the mayor's office and receiving a permit. Further suppose that a religious group sues the city, arguing that the law violates the freedoms of speech and religion guaranteed by the First Amendment. If the state supreme court upholds the law, the group could appeal the decision to the United States Supreme Court—because a constitutional (federal) issue is involved.

The Federal Court System

The federal court system is basically a three-tiered model consisting of (1) U.S. district courts (trial courts of general jurisdiction) and various courts of limited jurisdiction, (2) U.S. courts of appeals (intermediate courts of appeals), and (3) the United States Supreme Court.

Unlike state court judges, who are usually elected, federal court judges—including the justices of the Supreme Court—are appointed by the president of the United States, subject to confirmation by the U.S. Senate. All federal judges receive lifetime appointments under Article III of the U.S. Constitution, which states that federal judges "hold their offices during good Behaviour." In the entire history of the United States, only seven federal judges have been removed from office through impeachment proceedings.

U.S. DISTRICT COURTS At the federal level, the equivalent of a state trial court of general jurisdiction is the district court. U.S. district courts have original jurisdiction in matters involving a federal question and concurrent jurisdiction with state courts when diversity jurisdiction exists. Federal cases typically originate in district courts. There are other federal courts with original, but special (or limited), jurisdiction, such as the federal bankruptcy courts and others shown in Exhibit 2–2.

There is at least one federal district court in every state. The number of judicial districts can vary over time, primarily owing to population changes and corresponding changes in caseloads. Today, there are ninety-four federal judicial districts. Exhibit 2–3 on the following page shows the boundaries of both the U.S. district courts and the U.S. courts of appeals (discussed next).

U.S. COURTS OF APPEALS In the federal court system, there are thirteen U.S. courts of appeals—referred to as U.S. circuit courts of appeals. Twelve of the federal courts of appeals (including the Court of Appeals for the D.C. Circuit) hear appeals from the federal district courts located within their respective judicial circuits, or geographic boundaries (shown in Exhibit 2–3).[17] The Court of Appeals for the Thirteenth Circuit, called the Federal Circuit, has national appellate jurisdiction over certain types of cases, such as those involving patent law and those in which the U.S. government is a defendant. The decisions of a circuit court of appeals are binding on all courts within the circuit court's jurisdiction and are final in most cases, but appeal to the United States Supreme Court is possible.

UNITED STATES SUPREME COURT At the highest level in the three-tiered federal court system is the United States Supreme Court. According to the language of Article III of the U.S. Constitution, there is only one national Supreme Court. All other courts in the federal system are considered "inferior." Congress is empowered to create other inferior courts as it deems necessary. The inferior courts that Congress has created include the second tier in our model—the U.S. circuit courts of appeals—as well as the district courts and the various federal courts of limited, or specialized, jurisdiction.

---

17. Historically, judges were required to "ride the circuit" and hear appeals in different courts around the country, which is how the name "circuit court" came about.

EXHIBIT 2–3 • Geographic Boundaries of the U.S. Courts of Appeals and U.S. District Courts

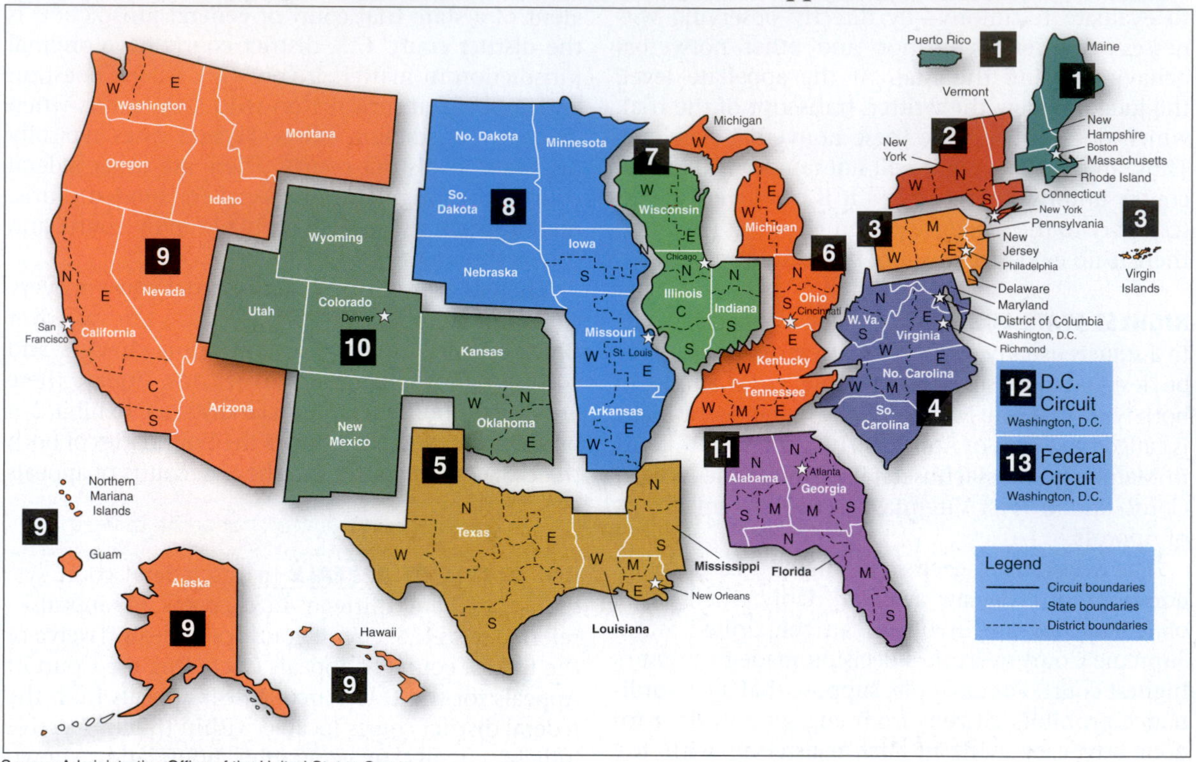

Source: Administrative Office of the United States Courts.

The United States Supreme Court consists of nine justices. Although the Supreme Court has original, or trial, jurisdiction in rare instances (set forth in Article III, Sections 1 and 2), most of its work is as an appeals court. The Supreme Court can review any case decided by any of the federal courts of appeals, and it also has appellate authority over cases involving federal questions that have been decided in the state courts. The Supreme Court is the final arbiter of the Constitution and federal law.

Appeals to the Supreme Court. To bring a case before the Supreme Court, a party requests the Court to issue a writ of *certiorari*.[18] A **writ of *certiorari*** is an order issued by the Supreme Court to a lower court requiring the latter to send it the record of the case for review. The Court will not issue a writ unless at least four of the nine justices approve of it. This is called the **rule of four.** Whether the Court will issue a writ of *certiorari* is entirely within its discretion, and most petitions for writs are denied. (Thousands of cases are filed with the Supreme Court each year, yet it hears, on average, fewer than one

hundred of these cases.)[19] A denial of the request to issue a writ of *certiorari* is not a decision on the merits of a case, nor does it indicate agreement with the lower court's opinion. Also, denial of the writ has no value as a precedent. Denial simply means that the lower court's decision remains the law in that jurisdiction.

Petitions Granted by the Court. Typically, the Court grants petitions in cases that raise important constitutional questions or when the lower courts have issued conflicting decisions on a significant issue. The justices, however, never explain their reasons for hearing certain cases and not others, so it is difficult to predict which type of case the Court might select.

See *Concept Summary 2.2* to review the various types of courts in the federal and state court systems.

---

18. Pronounced sur-shee-uh-*rah*-ree.

19. From the mid-1950s through the early 1990s, the Supreme Court reviewed more cases per year than it has since then. In the Court's 1982–1983 term, for example, the Court issued written opinions in 151 cases. In contrast, during the Court's 2009–2010 term, the Court issued written opinions in only 92 cases.

CONCEPT SUMMARY 2.2
Types of Courts

Type of Court	Description
Trial Courts	Trial courts are courts of original jurisdiction in which actions are initiated. 1. *State courts*—Courts of general jurisdiction can hear any case that has not been specifically designated for another court; courts of limited jurisdiction include, among others, domestic relations courts, probate courts, municipal courts, and small claims courts. 2. *Federal courts*—The federal district court is the equivalent of the state trial court. Federal courts of limited jurisdiction include the bankruptcy courts and others shown in Exhibit 2–2 on page 38.
Intermediate Appellate Courts	Courts of appeals are reviewing courts; generally, appellate courts do not have original jurisdiction. About three-fourths of the states have intermediate appellate courts; in the federal court system, the U.S. circuit courts of appeals are the intermediate appellate courts.
Supreme Courts	The highest state court is that state's supreme court, although it may be called by some other name. Appeal from state supreme courts to the United States Supreme Court is possible only if a federal question is involved. The United States Supreme Court is the highest court in the federal court system and the final arbiter of the Constitution and federal law.

SECTION 4
ALTERNATIVE DISPUTE RESOLUTION

Litigation—the process of resolving a dispute through the court system—is expensive and time consuming. Litigating even the simplest complaint is costly, and because of the backlog of cases pending in many courts, several years may pass before a case is actually tried. For these and other reasons, more and more businesspersons are turning to **alternative dispute resolution (ADR)** as a means of settling their disputes.

The great advantage of ADR is its flexibility. Methods of ADR range from the parties sitting down together and attempting to work out their differences to multinational corporations agreeing to resolve a dispute through a formal hearing before a panel of experts. Normally, the parties themselves can control how they will attempt to settle their dispute, what procedures will be used, whether a neutral third party will be present or make a decision, and whether that decision will be legally binding or nonbinding. ADR also offers more privacy than court proceedings and allows disputes to be resolved relatively quickly.

Today, more than 90 percent of civil lawsuits are settled before trial using some form of ADR. Indeed,

most states either require or encourage parties to undertake ADR prior to trial. Many federal courts have instituted ADR programs as well. In the following pages, we examine the basic forms of ADR. Keep in mind, though, that new methods of ADR—and new combinations of existing methods—are constantly being devised and employed.

Negotiation

The simplest form of ADR is **negotiation,** a process in which the parties attempt to settle their dispute informally, with or without attorneys to represent them. Attorneys frequently advise their clients to negotiate a settlement voluntarily before they proceed to trial. Parties may even try to negotiate a settlement during a trial or after the trial but before an appeal. Negotiation traditionally involves just the parties themselves and (typically) their attorneys. The attorneys, though, are advocates—they are obligated to put their clients' interests first.

Mediation

In **mediation,** a neutral third party acts as a mediator and works with both sides in the dispute to facilitate a resolution. The mediator normally talks with the parties separately as well as jointly, emphasizes points of agreement, and helps the parties to evaluate their options. Although the mediator may propose a solution (called a mediator's proposal), he or she does not make a decision resolving the matter. The mediator, who need not be a lawyer, usually charges a fee for his or her services (which can be split between the parties). States that require parties to undergo ADR before trial often offer mediation as one of the ADR options or (as in Florida) the only option.

One of the biggest advantages of mediation is that it is less adversarial in nature than litigation. In mediation, the mediator takes an active role and attempts to bring the parties together so that they can come to a mutually satisfactory resolution. The mediation process tends to reduce the antagonism between the disputants, allowing them to resume their former relationship while minimizing hostility. For this reason, mediation is often the preferred form of ADR for disputes between business partners, employers and employees, or other parties involved in long-term relationships.

Arbitration

A more formal method of ADR is **arbitration,** in which an arbitrator (a neutral third party or a panel of experts) hears a dispute and imposes a resolution on the parties. Arbitration differs from other forms of ADR in that the third party hearing the dispute makes a decision for the parties. Exhibit 2–4 outlines

the basic differences among the three traditional forms of ADR. Usually, the parties in arbitration agree that the third party's decision will be *legally binding,* although the parties can also agree to *nonbinding* arbitration. (Arbitration that is mandated by the courts often is not binding on the parties.) In nonbinding arbitration, the parties can go forward with a lawsuit if they do not agree with the arbitrator's decision.

THE ARBITRATION PROCESS In some respects, formal arbitration resembles a trial, although usually the procedural rules are much less restrictive than those governing litigation. In a typical arbitration, the parties present opening arguments and ask for specific remedies. Evidence is then presented, and witnesses may be called and examined by both sides. The arbitrator then renders a decision, called an **award.**

An arbitrator's award is usually the final word on the matter. Although the parties may appeal an arbitrator's decision, a court's review of the decision will be much more restricted in scope than an appellate court's review of a trial court's decision. The general view is that because the parties were free to frame the issues and set the powers of the arbitrator at the outset, they cannot complain about the results. The award will be set aside only if the arbitrator's conduct or "bad faith" substantially prejudiced the rights of

EXHIBIT 2–4 • Basic Differences in the Traditional Forms of ADR

TYPE OF ADR	DESCRIPTION	NEUTRAL THIRD PARTY PRESENT	WHO DECIDES THE RESOLUTION
Negotiation	Parties meet informally with or without their attorneys and attempt to agree on a resolution. This is the simplest and least expensive method of ADR.	No	The parties themselves reach a resolution.
Mediation	A neutral third party meets with the parties and emphasizes points of agreement to bring them toward resolution of their dispute. 1. This method of ADR reduces hostility between parties. 2. Mediation is preferred for resolving disputes between business partners, employers and employees, or others involved in long-term relationships.	Yes	The parties, but the mediator may suggest or propose a resolution.
Arbitration	The parties present their arguments and evidence before an arbitrator at a hearing, and the arbitrator renders a decision resolving the parties' dispute. 1. This ADR method is the most formal and resembles a court proceeding because some rules of evidence apply. 2. The parties are free to frame the issues and set the powers of the arbitrator. 3. If the parties agree that the arbitration is binding, then the parties' right to appeal the decision is limited.	Yes	The arbitrator imposes a resolution on the parties that may be either binding or nonbinding.

one of the parties, if the award violates an established public policy, or if the arbitrator exceeded her or his powers (by arbitrating issues that the parties did not agree to submit to arbitration).

ARBITRATION CLAUSES AND STATUTES Almost any commercial matter can be submitted to arbitration. Frequently, parties include an **arbitration clause** in a contract (a written agreement—see Chapter 10) specifying that any dispute arising under the contract will be resolved through arbitration rather than through the court system. Parties can also agree to arbitrate a dispute after it arises.

Most states have statutes (often based, in part, on the Uniform Arbitration Act of 1955) under which arbitration clauses will be enforced, and some state statutes compel arbitration of certain types of disputes, such as those involving public employees. At the federal level, the Federal Arbitration Act (FAA), enacted in 1925, enforces arbitration clauses in contracts involving maritime activity and interstate commerce. Because of the breadth of the commerce clause (see Chapter 4), arbitration agreements involving transactions only slightly connected to the flow of interstate commerce may fall under the FAA. The FAA established a national policy favoring arbitration.

CASE IN POINT Buckeye Check Cashing, Inc., cashes personal checks for consumers in Florida. Buckeye would agree to delay submitting a consumer's check for payment if the consumer paid a "finance charge." For each transaction, the consumer signed an agreement that included an arbitration clause. A group of consumers filed a lawsuit claiming that Buckeye was charging an illegally high rate of interest in violation of state law. Buckeye filed a motion to compel arbitration, which the trial court denied, and the case was appealed. The plaintiffs argued that the entire contract—including the arbitration clause—was illegal and therefore arbitration was not required. The United States Supreme Court found that the arbitration provision was *severable*, or capable of being separated, from the rest of the contract. The Court held that when the challenge is

to the validity of a contract as a whole, and not specifically to an arbitration clause within the contract, an arbitrator must resolve the dispute. This is true even if the contract later proves to be unenforceable, because the FAA established a national policy favoring arbitration and that policy extends to both federal and state courts.[20]

THE ISSUE OF ARBITRABILITY When a dispute arises as to whether the parties to a contract with an arbitration clause have agreed to submit a particular matter to arbitration, one party may file a lawsuit to compel arbitration. The court before which the suit is brought will decide not the basic controversy but rather the issue of *arbitrability*—that is, whether the matter is one that must be resolved through arbitration. If the court finds that the subject matter in controversy is covered by the agreement to arbitrate, then a party may be compelled to arbitrate the dispute. Usually, a court will allow the claim to be arbitrated if the court, in interpreting the relevant statute (the state arbitration statute or the FAA), can find no legislative intent to the contrary.

No party, however, will be ordered to submit a particular dispute to arbitration unless the court is convinced that the party has consented to do so. Additionally, the courts will not compel arbitration if it is clear that the prescribed arbitration rules and procedures are inherently unfair to one of the parties.

The terms of an arbitration agreement can limit the types of disputes that the parties agree to arbitrate. When the parties do not specify limits, however, disputes can arise as to whether the particular matter is covered by the arbitration agreement, and it is up to the court to resolve the issue of arbitrability.

In the following case, the parties had previously agreed to arbitrate disputes involving their contract to develop software, but the dispute involved claims of copyright infringement (see Chapter 8). The question was whether the copyright infringement claims were beyond the scope of the arbitration clause.

---

20. *Buckeye Check Cashing, Inc. v. Cardegna*, 546 U.S. 440, 126 S.Ct. 1204, 163 L.Ed.2d 1038 (2006).

CASE 2.3

NCR Corp. v. Korala Associates, Ltd.

United States Court of Appeals, Sixth Circuit, 512 F.3d 807 (2008).
www.ca6.uscourts.gov[a]

COMPANY PROFILE • In 1884, John H. Patterson founded the National Cash Register Company (NCR), maker of the first mechanical cash registers. In 1906, NCR created a cash register run

---

a. Click on "Opinions Search" and then on "Short Title," and type "NCR." Click on "Submit Query." Next, click on the opinion link in the first column of the row corresponding to the name of this case.

CASE CONTINUES ▶

CASE 2.3 CONTINUED ▶ by an electric motor. By 1914, the company had developed one of the first automated credit systems. By the 1950s, NCR had branched out into transistorized business computers, and later it expanded into liquid crystal displays and data warehousing. Today, NCR is a worldwide provider of automated teller machines (ATMs), integrated hardware and software systems, and related maintenance and support services. More than 300,000 NCR ATMs are installed throughout the world.

BACKGROUND AND FACTS • To upgrade the security of its ATMs, NCR developed a software solution to install in all of its machines. At the same time, Korala Associates, Ltd. (KAL), claimed to have developed a similar security upgrade for NCR's ATMs. Indeed, KAL had entered into a contract with NCR in 1998 (the "1998 Agreement") to develop such software. To facilitate that process, NCR had loaned to KAL a proprietary ATM that contained copyrighted software called APTRA XFS. NCR alleged that KAL had "obtained access to, made unauthorized use of, and engaged in unauthorized copying of the APTRA XFS software." NCR further claimed that KAL had developed its version of the security upgrade only by engaging in this unauthorized activity. When NCR brought a suit claiming copyright infringement, KAL moved to compel arbitration under the terms of the 1998 Agreement. At trial, KAL prevailed. NCR appealed the order compelling arbitration.

IN THE LANGUAGE OF THE COURT
Chief Justice *BATCHELDER* delivered the opinion of the court.
* * * *

The arbitration clause contained within the 1998 Agreement provides that:

> Any controversy or claim arising out of or relating to this contract, or breach thereof, shall be settled by arbitration and judgment upon the award rendered by the arbitrator may be entered in any court having jurisdiction thereof. The arbitrator shall be appointed upon the mutual agreement of both parties failing which both parties will agree to be subject to any arbitrator that shall be chosen by the President of the Law Society.

The parties do not dispute that a valid agreement to arbitrate exists; rather the issue of contention is whether NCR's claims fall within the substantive scope of the agreement.

As a matter of federal law, any doubts concerning the scope of arbitrable issues should be resolved in favor of arbitration. Despite this strong presumption in favor of arbitration, "arbitration is a matter of contract between the parties, and one cannot be required to submit to arbitration a dispute which it has not agreed to submit to arbitration." *When faced with a broad arbitration clause, such as one covering any dispute arising out of an agreement, a court should follow the presumption of arbitration and resolve doubts in favor of arbitration. Indeed, in such a case, only an express provision excluding a specific dispute, or the most forceful evidence of a purpose to exclude the claim from arbitration, will remove the dispute from consideration by the arbitrators.* [Emphasis added.]

* * * It is sufficient that a court would have to reference the 1998 Agreement for part of NCR's direct [copyright] infringement claim. Under these circumstances, we find that the copyright infringement claim as to APTRA XFS falls within the scope of the arbitration agreement.

DECISION AND REMEDY • *The U.S. Court of Appeals for the Sixth Circuit affirmed the part of the district court's decision compelling arbitration of NCR's claims of direct copyright infringement relating to the APTRA XFS software.*

THE LEGAL ENVIRONMENT DIMENSION • *Why did NCR not want its claims decided by arbitration?*

THE ETHICAL DIMENSION • *Could NCR have a claim that KAL engaged in unfair competition because KAL engaged in unethical business practices? (Hint: Unfair competition may occur when one party deceives the public into believing that its goods are the goods of another.) Why or why not?*

MANDATORY ARBITRATION IN THE EMPLOYMENT CONTEXT A significant question in the last several years has concerned mandatory arbitration clauses in employment contracts. Many claim that employees' rights are not sufficiently protected when they are forced, as a condition of being hired, to agree to arbitrate all disputes and thus waive their rights under statutes specifically designed to protect employees.

The United States Supreme Court, however, has held that mandatory arbitration clauses in employment contracts are generally enforceable.[21]

Compulsory arbitration agreements often spell out the rules for a mandatory proceeding. For example, an agreement may address in detail the amount and payment of filing fees and other expenses. Some courts have overturned provisions in employment-related agreements that require the parties to split the costs when an individual worker lacks the ability to pay.[22]

Other Types of ADR

The three forms of ADR just discussed are the oldest and traditionally the most commonly used forms. As mentioned earlier, a variety of new types of ADR have emerged in recent years, including those described here.

1. In **early neutral case evaluation,** the parties select a neutral third party (generally an expert in the subject matter of the dispute) to evaluate their respective positions. The parties explain their positions to the case evaluator, and the case evaluator assesses the strengths and weaknesses of each party's claims.
2. In a **mini-trial,** each party's attorney briefly argues the party's case before the other and a panel of representatives from each side who have the authority to settle the dispute. Typically, a neutral third party (usually an expert in the area being disputed) acts as an adviser. If the parties fail to reach an agreement, the adviser renders an opinion as to how a court would likely decide the issue.
3. Numerous federal courts now hold **summary jury trials,** in which the parties present their arguments and evidence and the jury renders a verdict. The jury's verdict is not binding, but it does act as a guide to both sides in reaching an agreement during the mandatory negotiations that immediately follow the trial.
4. Other alternatives being employed by the courts include summary procedures for commercial litigation and the appointment of special masters to assist judges in deciding complex issues.

---

21. For a landmark decision on this issue, see *Gilmer v. Interstate/Johnson Lane Corp.*, 500 U.S. 20, 111 S.Ct. 1647, 114 L.Ed.2d 26 (1991).
22. See, for example, *Davis v. O'Melveny & Myers, LLC*, 485 F.3d 1066 (9th Cir. 2007); and *Nagrampa v. MailCoups, Inc.*, 469 F.3d 1257 (9th Cir. 2006).

Providers of ADR Services

Both government agencies and private organizations provide ADR services. A major provider of ADR services is the **American Arbitration Association (AAA),** which was founded in 1926 and now handles more than 200,000 claims a year in its numerous offices around the country. Cases brought before the AAA are heard by an expert or a panel of experts in the area relating to the dispute and are usually settled quickly. Generally, about half of the panel members are lawyers. To cover its costs, the AAA charges a fee, paid by the party filing the claim. In addition, each party to the dispute pays a specified amount for each hearing day, as well as a special additional fee in cases involving personal injuries or property loss.

Hundreds of for-profit firms around the country also provide dispute-resolution services. Typically, these firms hire retired judges to conduct arbitration hearings or otherwise assist parties in settling their disputes. The judges follow procedures similar to those of the federal courts and use similar rules. Usually, each party to the dispute pays a filing fee and a designated fee for a hearing session or conference.

Online Dispute Resolution

An increasing number of companies and organizations are offering dispute-resolution services using the Internet. The settlement of disputes in these online forums is known as **online dispute resolution (ODR).** The disputes resolved in these forums have most commonly involved rights to domain names (Web site addresses—see Chapter 8) or the quality of goods sold via the Internet, including goods sold through Internet auction sites.

ODR may be best for resolving small- to medium-sized business liability claims, which may not be worth the expense of litigation or traditional ADR methods. Rules being developed in online forums, however, may ultimately become a code of conduct for everyone who does business in cyberspace. Most online forums do not automatically apply the law of any specific jurisdiction. Instead, results are often based on general, more universal legal principles. As with offline methods of dispute resolution, any party may appeal to a court at any time if the ODR is nonbinding arbitration.

Some cities use ODR as a means of resolving claims against them. For example, New York City hires an ODR provider called Cybersettle to resolve auto accident, sidewalk, and other personal-injury claims made against the city.

INTERNATIONAL DISPUTE RESOLUTION

Businesspersons who engage in international business transactions normally take special precautions to protect themselves in the event that a party with whom they are dealing in another country breaches an agreement. Often, parties to international contracts include special clauses in their contracts providing for how disputes arising under the contracts will be resolved.

Forum-Selection and Choice-of-Law Clauses

As you will read in Chapter 19, parties to international transactions often include forum-selection and choice-of-law clauses in their contracts. These clauses designate the jurisdiction (court or country) where any dispute arising under the contract will be litigated and which nation's law will be applied. When an international contract does not include such clauses, any legal proceedings arising under the contract will be more complex and attended by much more uncertainty. For example, litigation may take place in two or more countries, with each country applying its own national law to the particular transactions.

Furthermore, even if a plaintiff wins a favorable judgment in a lawsuit litigated in the plaintiff's country, the defendant's country could refuse to enforce the court's judgment. As will be discussed in Chapter 23, for reasons of courtesy, the judgment may be enforced in the defendant's country, particularly if the defendant's country is the United States and the foreign court's decision is consistent with U.S. national law and policy. Other nations, however, may not be as accommodating as the United States, and the plaintiff may be left empty handed.

Arbitration Clauses

International contracts also often include arbitration clauses that require a neutral third party to decide any contract disputes. In international arbitration proceedings, the third party may be a neutral entity (such as the International Chamber of Commerce), a panel of individuals representing both parties' interests, or some other group or organization. The United Nations Convention on the Recognition and Enforcement of Foreign Arbitral Awards[23]—which has been implemented in more than 144 countries, including the United States—assists in the enforcement of arbitration clauses, as do provisions in specific treaties among nations. The American Arbitration Association provides arbitration services for international as well as domestic disputes.

---

23. June 10, 1958, 21 U.S.T. 2517, T.I.A.S. No. 6997 (the "New York Convention").

REVIEWING

Courts and Alternative Dispute Resolution

Stan Garner resides in Illinois and promotes boxing matches for SuperSports, Inc., an Illinois corporation. Garner created the concept of "Ages" promotion—a three-fight series of boxing matches pitting an older fighter (George Foreman) against a younger fighter. The concept had titles for each of the three fights, including "Battle of the Ages." Garner contacted Foreman and his manager, who both reside in Texas, to sell the idea, and they arranged a meeting in Las Vegas, Nevada. During the negotiations, Foreman's manager signed a nondisclosure agreement prohibiting him from disclosing Garner's promotional concepts unless the parties signed a contract. Nevertheless, after negotiations fell through, Foreman used Garner's "Battle of the Ages" concept to promote a subsequent fight. Garner filed a suit against Foreman and his manager in a federal district court located in Illinois, alleging breach of contract. Using the information presented in the chapter, answer the following questions.

1. On what basis might the federal district court in Illinois exercise jurisdiction in this case?
2. Does the federal district court have original or appellate jurisdiction?
3. Suppose that Garner had filed his action in an Illinois state court. Could an Illinois state court exercise personal jurisdiction over Foreman or his manager? Why or why not?
4. Assume that Garner had filed his action in a Nevada state court. Would that court have had personal jurisdiction over Foreman or his manager? Explain.

DEBATE THIS: *In this age of the Internet, when people communicate via e-mail, instant text messaging, tweeting, Facebook, and MySpace, is the concept of jurisdiction losing its meaning? Explain your answer.*

TERMS AND CONCEPTS

alternative dispute
    resolution (ADR) 41

American Arbitration
    Association (AAA) 45

arbitration 42

arbitration clause 43

award 42

bankruptcy court 32

concurrent jurisdiction 33

diversity of citizenship 33

early neutral case
    evaluation 45

exclusive jurisdiction 33

federal question 33

in personam jurisdiction 30

in rem jurisdiction 30

judicial review 28

jurisdiction 30

justiciable controversy 36

litigation 41

long arm statute 30

mediation 41

mini-trial 45

negotiation 41

online dispute
    resolution (ODR) 45

probate court 32

question of fact 38

question of law 38

rule of four 40

small claims court 38

standing to sue 35

summary jury trial 45

venue 34

writ of *certiorari* 40

QUESTIONS AND CASE PROBLEMS

2–1. Standing Jack and Maggie Turton bought a house in Jefferson County, Idaho, located directly across the street from a gravel pit. A few years later, the county converted the pit to a landfill. The landfill accepted many kinds of trash that cause harm to the environment, including major appliances, animal carcasses, containers with hazardous content warnings, leaking car batteries, and waste oil. The Turtons complained to the county, but the county did nothing. The Turtons then filed a lawsuit against the county alleging violations of federal environmental laws pertaining to groundwater contamination and other pollution. Do the Turtons have standing to sue? Why or why not?

2–2. QUESTION WITH SAMPLE ANSWER: Appellate Review.

The defendant in a lawsuit is appealing the trial court's decision in favor of the plaintiff. On appeal, the defendant claims that the evidence presented at trial to support the plaintiff's claim was so scanty that no reasonable jury could have found for the plaintiff. Therefore, argues the defendant, the appellate court should reverse the trial court's decision. Will an appellate court ever reverse a trial court's findings with respect to questions of fact? Discuss fully.

• **For a sample answer to Question 2–2, go to Appendix I at the end of this text.**

2–3. Jurisdiction Marya Callais, a citizen of Florida, was walking along a busy street in Tallahassee, Florida, when a large crate flew off a passing truck and hit her, causing numerous injuries. She experienced a great deal of pain and suffering, incurred significant medical expenses, and could not work for six months. She wants to sue the trucking firm for $300,000 in damages. The firm's headquarters are in Georgia, although the company does business in Florida. In what court might Callais bring suit—a Florida state court, a Georgia state court, or a federal court? What factors might influence her decision?

2–4. Jurisdiction Xcentric Ventures, LLC, is an Arizona firm that operates the Web sites RipOffReport.com and BadBusinessBureau.com. Visitors to the sites can buy a copy of a book titled *Do-It-Yourself Guide: How to Get Rip-Off Revenge*. The price ($21.95) includes shipping to anywhere in the United States, including Illinois, to which thirteen copies have been shipped. The sites accept donations and feature postings by individuals who claim to have been "ripped off." Some visitors posted comments about George S. May International Co., a management consulting firm. The postings alleged fraud, larceny, possession of child pornography, and possession of controlled substances (illegal drugs). May filed a suit in a federal district court in Illinois against Xcentric and others, charging, among other things, "false descriptions and representations." The defendants filed a motion to dismiss for lack of jurisdiction. What is the standard for exercising jurisdiction over a party whose only connection to a jurisdiction is over the Web? How would that standard apply in this case? Explain. [*George S. May International Co. v. Xcentric Ventures, LLC*, 409 F.Supp.2d 1052 (N.D.Ill. 2006)]

2–5. Jurisdiction In 2001, Raul Leal, the owner and operator of Texas Labor Contractors in East Texas, contacted Poverty Point Produce, Inc., which operates a sweet potato farm in West Carroll Parish, Louisiana, and offered to provide field workers. Poverty Point accepted the offer. Jeffrey Brown, an owner and field manager for the farm, told Leal the number of workers needed and gave him forms for them to fill out and sign. Leal placed an ad in a newspaper in Brownsville, Texas. Job applicants were directed to Leal's car dealership in Weslaco, Texas, where they were told the details of the work. Leal recruited, among others, Elias Moreno, who lives in the

Rio Grande Valley in Texas, and transported Moreno and the others to Poverty Point's farm. At the farm, Leal's brother Jesse oversaw the work with instructions from Brown, lived with the workers in the on-site housing, and gave them their paychecks. When the job was done, the workers were returned to Texas. Moreno and others filed a suit in a federal district court against Poverty Point and others, alleging, in part, violations of Texas state law related to the work. Poverty Point filed a motion to dismiss the suit on the ground that the court did not have personal jurisdiction. All of the meetings between Poverty Point and the Leals occurred in Louisiana. All of the farmwork was done in Louisiana. Poverty Point has no offices, bank accounts, or phone listings in Texas. It does not advertise or solicit business in Texas. Despite these facts, can the court exercise personal jurisdiction? Explain. [*Moreno v. Poverty Point Produce, Inc.,* 243 F.R.D. 275 (S.D.Tex. 2007)]

2–6. CASE PROBLEM WITH SAMPLE ANSWER: Arbitration Clause.

 *Kathleen Lowden sued cellular phone company T-Mobile USA, Inc., contending that its service agreements were not enforceable under Washington state law. Lowden requested that the court allow a* class-action suit, in which her claims would extend to similarly affected customers. She contended that T-Mobile had improperly charged her fees beyond the advertised price of service and charged her for roaming calls that should not have been classified as roaming. T-Mobile moved to force arbitration in accordance with the provisions that were clearly set forth in the service agreement. The agreement also specified that no class-action suit could be brought, so T-Mobile also asked the court to dismiss the request for a class-action suit. Was T-Mobile correct that Lowden's only course of action was to file arbitration personally? Why or why not? [Lowden v. T-Mobile USA, Inc., 512 F.3d 1213 (9th Cir. 2008)]

- To view a sample answer for Problem 2–6, go to this book's Web site at www.cengage.com/blaw/clarkson, select "Chapter 2," and click on "Case Problem with Sample Answer."

2–7. Arbitration Thomas Baker and others who bought new homes from Osborne Development Corp. sued for multiple defects in the houses they purchased. When Osborne sold the homes, it paid for them to be in a new home warranty program administered by Home Buyers Warranty (HBW). When the company enrolled a home with HBW, it paid a fee and filled out a form that stated the following: "By signing below, you acknowledge that you . . . CONSENT TO THE TERMS OF THESE DOCUMENTS INCLUDING THE BINDING ARBITRATION PROVISION contained therein." HBW then issued warranty booklets to the new homeowners that stated: "Any and all claims, disputes and controversies by or between the Homeowner, the Builder, the Warranty Insurer and/or HBW . . . shall be submitted to arbitration." Were the new homeowners bound by the arbitration agreement, or could they sue the builder, Osborne, in court? Explain. [*Baker v. Osborne Development Corp.,* 159 Cal.App.4th 884, 71 Cal.Rptr.3d 854 (Cal.App. 2008)]

2–8. Arbitration PRM Energy Systems, Inc. (PRM), owned technology patents that it licensed to Primenergy to use and to sublicense in the United States. The agreement stated that all disputes would be settled by arbitration. Kobe Steel of Japan was interested in using the technology at its U.S. subsidiary. PRM directed Kobe to talk to Primenergy about that. Kobe talked to PRM directly about using the technology in Japan, but no agreement was reached. Primenergy then agreed to let Kobe use the technology in Japan without telling PRM. The dispute between PRM and Primenergy about Kobe went to arbitration, as required by the license agreement. In addition, PRM sued Primenergy for fraud and theft of trade secrets. PRM also sued Kobe for using the technology in Japan without its permission. The district court ruled that PRM had to take all complaints about Primenergy to arbitration. PRM also had to take its complaint about Kobe to arbitration because the complaint involved a sublicense Kobe was granted by Primenergy. PRM appealed, contending that the fraud and theft of trade secrets went beyond the license agreement with Primenergy and that Kobe had no right to demand arbitration because it never had a right to use the technology under a license from PRM. Is PRM correct, or must all matters go to arbitration? Why or why not? [*PRM Energy Systems, Inc. v. Primenergy,* 592 F.3d 830 (8th Cir. 2010)]

2–9. A QUESTION OF ETHICS: Agreement to Arbitrate.

 Nellie Lumpkin, who suffered from various illnesses, including dementia, was admitted to the Picayune Convalescent Center, a nursing home. Because of her mental condition, her daughter, Beverly McDaniel, filled out the admissions paperwork and signed the admissions agreement. It included a clause requiring parties to submit to arbitration any disputes that arose. After Lumpkin left the center two years later, she sued, through her husband, for negligent treatment and malpractice during her stay. The center moved to force the matter to arbitration. The trial court held that the arbitration agreement was not enforceable. The center appealed. [Covenant Health & Rehabilitation of Picayune, LP v. Lumpkin, 23 So.3d 1092 (Miss.App. 2009)]

(a) Should a dispute involving medical malpractice be forced into arbitration? This is a claim of negligent care, not a breach of a commercial contract. Is it ethical for medical facilities to impose such a requirement? Is there really any bargaining over such terms?

(b) Should a person with limited mental capacity be held to the arbitration clause agreed to by the next-of-kin who signed on behalf of that person?

2–10. VIDEO QUESTION: Jurisdiction in Cyberspace.

 Go to this text's Web site at www.cengage.com/blaw/clarkson and select "Chapter 2." Click on "Video Questions" and view the video titled *Jurisdiction in Cyberspace.* Then answer the following questions.

(a) What standard would a court apply to determine whether it has jurisdiction over the out-of-state computer firm in the video?

(b) What factors is a court likely to consider in assessing whether sufficient contacts existed when the only connection to the jurisdiction is through a Web site?

(c) How do you think the court would resolve the issue in this case?

LEGAL RESEARCH EXERCISES ON THE WEB

Go to this text's Web site at **www.cengage.com/blaw/clarkson**, select "Chapter 2," and click on "Practical Internet Exercises." There you will find the following Internet research exercises that you can perform to learn more about the topics covered in this chapter.

Practical Internet Exercise 2–1: **Legal Perspective**
Alternative Dispute Resolution

Practical Internet Exercise 2–2: **Management Perspective**
Resolve a Dispute Online

Practical Internet Exercise 2–3: **Historical Perspective**
The Judiciary's Role in American Government

CHAPTER 3

Court Procedures

American and English courts follow the *adversarial system of justice.* Although parties are allowed to represent themselves in court (called *pro se* representation),[1] most parties to lawsuits hire attorneys to represent them. Each lawyer acts as his or her client's advocate, presenting the client's version of the facts in such a way as to convince the judge (or the judge and jury, in a jury trial) that this version is correct.

Most of the judicial procedures that you will read about in the following pages are rooted in the adversarial framework of the American legal system. In this chapter, after a brief overview of judicial procedures, we illustrate the steps involved in a lawsuit with a hypothetical civil case (criminal procedures will be discussed in Chapter 9).

---

1. This right was definitively established in *Faretta v. California,* 422 U.S. 806, 95 S.Ct. 2525, 45 L.Ed.2d 562 (1975).

SECTION 1
PROCEDURAL RULES

The parties to a lawsuit must comply with the procedural rules of the court in which the lawsuit is filed. Although most people, when considering the outcome of a case, think of matters of substantive law, procedural law can have a significant impact on one's ability to assert a legal claim. Procedural rules provide a framework for every dispute and specify what must be done at each stage of the litigation process. Procedural rules are complex, and they vary from court to court and from state to state. There is a set of federal rules of procedure as well as various sets of rules for state courts. Additionally, the applicable procedures will depend on whether the case is a civil or criminal proceeding. All civil trials held in federal district courts are governed by the **Federal Rules of Civil Procedure (FRCP).**[2]

---

2. The United States Supreme Court has authority to establish these rules, as spelled out in 28 U.S.C. Sections 2071–2077. Generally, though, the federal judiciary appoints committees that make recommendations to the Supreme Court. The Court then publishes any proposed changes in the rules and allows for public comment before finalizing the rules.

Stages of Litigation

Broadly speaking, the litigation process has three phases: pretrial, trial, and posttrial. Each phase involves specific procedures, as discussed throughout this chapter. Although civil lawsuits may vary greatly in terms of complexity, cost, and detail, they typically progress through the specific stages charted in Exhibit 3–1.

To illustrate the procedures involved in a civil lawsuit, we will use a simple hypothetical case. The case arose from an automobile accident, which occurred when a car driven by Antonio Carvello, a resident of New Jersey, collided with a car driven by Jill Kirby, a resident of New York. The accident took place at an intersection in New York City. Kirby suffered personal injuries, which caused her to incur medical and hospital expenses as well as lost wages for four months. In all, she calculated that the cost to her of the accident was $100,000.[3] Carvello and Kirby have been unable to agree on a settlement, and Kirby now must decide whether to sue Carvello for the $100,000 compensation she feels she deserves.

---

3. In this example, we are ignoring damages for pain and suffering and for permanent disabilities. Often, plaintiffs in personal-injury cases seek such damages.

EXHIBIT 3-1 • Stages in a Typical Lawsuit

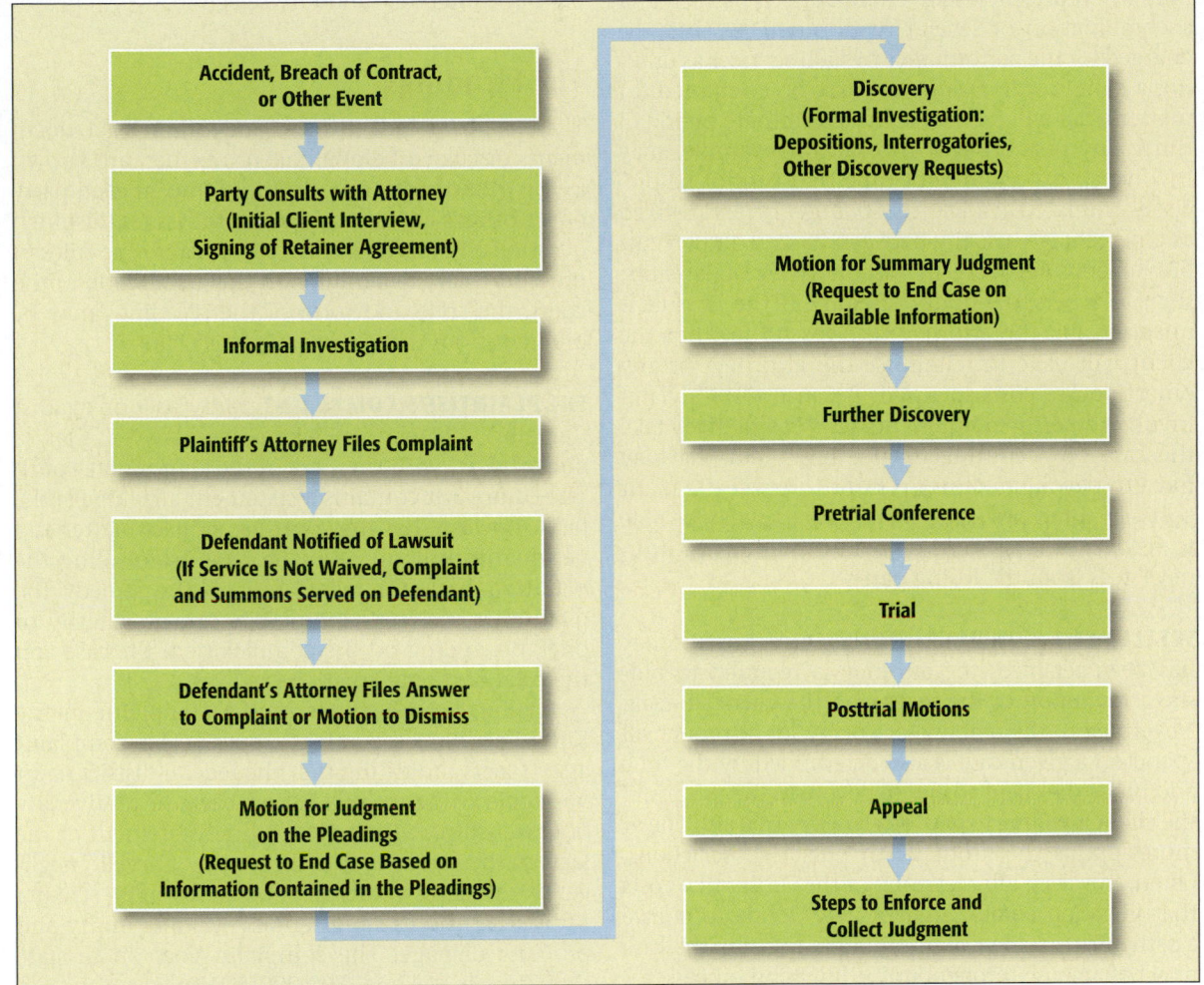

The First Step: Consulting with an Attorney

As mentioned, rules of procedure often affect the outcome of a dispute—a fact that highlights the importance of obtaining the advice of counsel. The first step taken by almost anyone contemplating a lawsuit is to seek the guidance of a qualified attorney.[4] In the hypothetical Kirby-Carvello case, assume that Kirby consults with a lawyer. The attorney will advise her regarding what she can expect in a lawsuit, her probability of success at trial, and the procedures that will be involved. If more than one court would have jurisdiction over the matter, the attorney will also discuss the advantages and disadvantages of filing in a particular court. Depending on the court hearing the case, the attorney will give Kirby an idea of how much time it will take to resolve the dispute through litigation and provide an estimate of the costs involved.

The attorney will also inform Kirby of the legal fees that she will have to pay in an attempt to collect damages from the defendant, Carvello. Attorneys base their fees on such factors as the difficulty of a matter, the amount of time involved, the experience and skill of the attorney in the particular area of the law, and the cost of doing business. In the United States, legal fees range from $175 to $700 per hour or even higher (the average fee per hour is between $200 and $425). In addition, the client is also responsible for paying various expenses related to the case (called "out-of-pocket" costs), including court filing fees, travel expenses, depositions, and the cost of expert witnesses and investigators, for example.

---

4. See Chapter 43 on pages 837 and 838 for a discussion of the importance of obtaining legal counsel and for guidelines on how to locate attorneys and retain their services.

TYPES OF ATTORNEYS' FEES For a particular legal matter, an attorney may charge one type of fee or a combination of several types. *Fixed fees* may be charged for the performance of such services as drafting a simple will. *Hourly fees* may be computed for matters that will involve an indeterminate period of time. Any case brought to trial, for example, may involve an expenditure of time that cannot be precisely estimated in advance. *Contingency fees* are fixed as a percentage (usually between 25 and 40 percent) of a client's recovery in certain types of lawsuits, such as a personal-injury lawsuit.[5] If the lawsuit is unsuccessful, the attorney receives no fee, but the client will have to reimburse the attorney for any out-of-pocket costs incurred. Because Kirby's claim involves a personal injury, her lawyer will likely take the case on a contingency-fee basis, but she may have to pay an amount up front to cover the court costs. In some cases, the winning party may be able to recover at least some portion of her or his attorneys' fees from the losing party.

SETTLEMENT CONSIDERATIONS Once an attorney has been retained, the attorney is required to pursue a resolution of the matter on the client's behalf. Nevertheless, the amount of energy an attorney will spend on a given case is also determined by the time and funds the client wishes to devote to the process. If the client is willing to pay for a lengthy trial and one or more appeals, the attorney may pursue those actions. Often, however, after learning of the substantial costs that litigation entails, a client may decide to pursue a settlement of the claim. Attempts to settle the case may be ongoing throughout the litigation process.

Another important factor in deciding whether to pursue litigation is the defendant's ability to pay the damages sought. Even if Kirby is awarded damages, it may be difficult to enforce the court's judgment if, for example, the amount exceeds the limits of Carvello's automobile insurance policy. (We will discuss the problems involved in enforcing a judgment later in this chapter.)

SECTION 2
PRETRIAL PROCEDURES

The pretrial litigation process involves the filing of the *pleadings,* the gathering of evidence (called

discovery), and possibly other procedures, such as a pretrial conference and jury selection.

The Pleadings

The *complaint* and *answer* (and other legal documents discussed below), taken together, are known as the **pleadings.** The pleadings inform each party of the other's claims and specify the issues (disputed questions) involved in the case. Because the rules of procedure vary depending on the jurisdiction of the court, the style and form of the pleadings may be different from those shown in this chapter.

THE PLAINTIFF'S COMPLAINT Kirby's action against Carvello commences when her lawyer files a **complaint**[6] with the clerk of the appropriate court. The complaint contains a statement alleging (1) the facts showing that the court has subject-matter and personal jurisdiction, (2) the facts establishing the plaintiff's basis for relief, and (3) the remedy the plaintiff is seeking. Complaints can be lengthy or brief, depending on the complexity of the case and the rules of the jurisdiction.

Exhibit 3–2 illustrates how a complaint in the Kirby-Carvello case might appear. The complaint asserts facts indicating that the federal district court has subject-matter jurisdiction because of diversity of citizenship. It then gives a brief statement of the facts of the accident and alleges that Carvello negligently drove his vehicle through a red light, striking Kirby's car and causing serious personal injury and property damage. The complaint goes on to state that Kirby is seeking $100,000 in damages, although in some state civil actions the plaintiff need not specify the amount of damages sought.

Service of Process. Before the court can exercise personal jurisdiction over the defendant (Carvello)—in effect, before the lawsuit can begin—the court must have proof that the defendant was notified of the lawsuit. Formally notifying the defendant of a lawsuit is called **service of process.** The plaintiff must deliver, or serve, a copy of the complaint and a **summons** (a notice requiring the defendant to appear in court and answer the complaint) to the defendant. The summons notifies Carvello that he must file an answer to the complaint within a specified time period (twenty days in the federal courts) or suffer a default judgment against him. A **default judgment** in Kirby's favor

---

5. Note that attorneys may charge a contingency fee in only certain types of cases and are typically prohibited from entering into this type of fee arrangement in criminal cases, divorce cases, and cases involving the distribution of assets after death.

6. Sometimes, the document filed with the court is called a *petition* or a *declaration* instead of a complaint.

EXHIBIT 3-2 • A Typical Complaint

IN THE UNITED STATES DISTRICT COURT
FOR THE SOUTHERN DISTRICT OF NEW YORK

CIVIL NO. 9-1047

JILL KIRBY

Plaintiff,

v.   COMPLAINT

ANTONIO CARVELLO

Defendant.

    The plaintiff brings this cause of action against the defendant, alleging as follows:

1. This action is between the plaintiff, who is a resident of the State of New York, and the defendant, who is a resident of the State of New Jersey. There is diversity of citizenship between the parties.
2. The amount in controversy, exclusive of interest and costs, exceeds the sum of $75,000.
3. On September 10th, 2011, the plaintiff, Jill Kirby, was exercising good driving habits and reasonable care in driving her car through the intersection of Boardwalk and Pennsylvania Avenue, New York City, New York, when the defendant, Antonio Carvello, negligently drove his vehicle through a red light at the intersection and collided with the plaintiff's vehicle.
4. As a result of the collision, the plaintiff suffered severe physical injury, which prevented her from working, and property damage to her car.

    WHEREFORE, the plaintiff demands judgment against the defendant for the sum of $100,000 plus interest at the maximum legal rate and the costs of this action.

By ___*Joseph Roe*___

Joseph Roe
Attorney for Plaintiff
100 Main Street
New York, New York

1/3/12

would mean that she would be awarded the damages alleged in her complaint because Carvello failed to respond to the allegations. A typical summons is shown in Exhibit 3–3 on the following page.

Method of Service. How service of process occurs depends on the rules of the court or jurisdiction in which the lawsuit is brought. Under the Federal Rules of Civil Procedure, anyone who is at least eighteen years of age and is not a party to the lawsuit can serve process in federal court cases. In state courts, the process server is often a county sheriff or an employee of an independent company that provides process service in the local area. Usually, the server hands the summons and complaint to the defendant personally or leaves it at the defendant's residence or place of business. In some states, process can be served by mail if the defendant consents (accepts service). When the defendant cannot be reached, special rules provide for alternative means of service, such as publishing a notice in the local newspaper. In some situations, such as when the defendant is in a foreign country, courts have even allowed service of process via e-mail, as long as it

EXHIBIT 3-3 • A Typical Summons

UNITED STATES DISTRICT COURT
FOR THE SOUTHERN DISTRICT OF NEW YORK

JILL KIRBY

                    Plaintiff,

v.

ANTONIO CARVELLO

                    Defendant.

CIVIL ACTION, FILE NO. 9-1047

SUMMONS

To the above-named Defendant:

You are hereby summoned and required to serve upon Joseph Roe, plaintiff's attorney, whose address is 100 Main Street, New York, NY, an answer to the complaint which is herewith served upon you, within 20 days after service of this summons upon you, exclusive of the day of service. If you fail to do so, judgment by default will be taken against you for the relief demanded in the complaint.

C. H. Hynek
_____
CLERK

January 3, 2012
_____
DATE

John Dolan
_____
BY DEPUTY CLERK

---

is reasonably calculated to provide notice and an opportunity to respond.[7]

In cases involving corporate defendants, the summons and complaint may be served on an officer or on a *registered agent* (representative) of the corporation. The name of a corporation's registered agent

can usually be obtained from the secretary of state's office in the state where the company incorporated its business (and, frequently, from the secretary of state's office in any state where the corporation does business).

Did the plaintiff in the following case effect proper service of the summons and the complaint on an out-of-state corporation?

---

7. See, for example, *Rio Properties, Inc. v. Rio International Interlink,* 284 F.3d 1007 (9th Cir. 2002).

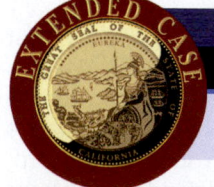

✳ EXTENDED CASE 3.1 ✳
Cruz v. Fagor America, Inc.

California Court of Appeal, Fourth District, 146 Cal.App.4th 488, 52 Cal.Rptr.3d 862 (2007).

IN THE LANGUAGE OF THE COURT

AARON, J. [Judge]
* * * *
    [Alan] Cruz's parents purchased a

pressure cooker from a vendor at the San Diego County Fair [in California] in the summer of 2001. On September 10, 2001, Cruz, who was 16 years old at the time, suffered burns on the left side of his torso and thigh when he attempted

to take the lid off of the pressure cooker. Fagor [America, Inc.] is the American distributor of the pressure cooker.

    On the date of the incident involving the pressure cooker, Cruz's parents sent an e-mail to Fagor to alert the company about what had occurred.

On June 2, 2003, [Fagor] notified Cruz that it was denying liability.

* * * *

Cruz filed a complaint [in a California state court] against Fagor on December 1, 2004, alleging causes of action for negligence and product liability. On December 14, 2004, Cruz, through his attorney, mailed the summons and complaint to Fagor by certified mail, return receipt requested. The envelope was addressed to "Patricio Barriga, Chairman of the Board, FAGOR AMERICA, INC., A Delaware Corporation, 1099 Wall Street, Lyndhurst, NJ 07071-3678."

The return receipt indicates that it was signed by an individual named Tina Hayes on December 22. Fagor did not file an answer.

* * * *

A default judgment [a judgment entered against a defendant who fails to answer or respond to the plaintiff's complaint] in the amount of $259,114.50 was entered against Fagor on May 31, 2005.

Fagor did not make an appearance in the matter until November 29, 2005, when Fagor's attorneys * * * [filed] a motion to set aside the entry of default and default judgment.

* * * *

* * * On February 1, the trial court granted the motion. Cruz [appealed to a state intermediate appellate court] on February 16.

* * * *

* * * The trial court found that service was not effected because there was no proof that the summons and complaint (1) were served on Fagor's designated agent for service; (2) were delivered to the president or other officer, manager, or person authorized to receive service in accordance with [California Civil Procedure Code Section] 416.10; or (3) were served in accordance with [California] Corporations Code Section 2110, which provides for service on a foreign corporation by

hand delivery to an officer or designated agent for service of process.

* * * [But] the proofs of service demonstrate that Cruz served Fagor, an out-of-state corporation, in accordance with [California Civil Procedure Code Section] 415.40. Section 415.40 provides in pertinent part:

> A summons may be served on a person outside this state in any manner provided by this article or by sending a copy of the summons and of the complaint to the person to be served by first-class mail, postage prepaid, requiring a return receipt.

Because Fagor is a corporate entity, Cruz was also required to comply with the mandates of Section 416.10. That section details how a plaintiff is to serve a summons on a corporate defendant and provides in relevant part:

> A summons may be served on a corporation by delivering a copy of the summons and of the complaint: * * * To the president or other head of the corporation, a vice president, a secretary or assistant secretary, a treasurer or assistant treasurer, a general manager, or a person authorized by the corporation to receive service of process.

* * * *

A number of documents in the record establish that Cruz properly served Fagor with process pursuant to California's statutory requirements. The first is a Judicial Counsel of California proof of service form, completed and signed by Cruz's attorney, Harold Thompson. In that form, Thompson states that the summons and complaint were addressed and mailed to Patricio Barriga, the president of Fagor, at 1099 Wall Street, Lyndhurst, New Jersey 07071-3678, which is the address Fagor listed in 2003 with the New York State Department of State—Division of Corporations as its "service of process address."

* * * *Thompson's declaration was properly executed because it shows that Cruz addressed the summons and complaint to a person to be served, as*

listed under Section 416.10. [Emphasis added.]

Cruz also submitted a signed return receipt to establish the fact of actual delivery. A return receipt attached to the proof of service form shows that the envelope was accepted at the Lyndhurst address. The receipt was signed by Hayes.

* * * *

* * * Cruz submitted the declaration of his attorney, Harold Thompson, in which Thompson states that he confirmed with a representative of the United States Postal Service in Lyndhurst, New Jersey, that Hayes regularly receives mail on behalf of Fagor at its Lyndhurst office. This is * * * sufficient to establish that an agent authorized to receive mail on the defendant's behalf received the summons and complaint.

* * * *

* * * *By virtue of her authority to accept mail on Fagor's behalf, Hayes's notice of the action is imputed to Fagor and its officers. Barriga's statement that he did not receive the summons and complaint does not establish that service of process was invalid.* Barriga had constructive knowledge of the existence of the action, and of the summons and complaint, once an individual authorized to receive corporate mail acknowledged service. To hold otherwise would be to ignore the realities of corporate life, in which the duty to sign for mail received often resides with a designated mailroom employee, a receptionist, a secretary, or an assistant. A plaintiff who has provided evidence that a person authorized to receive mail on behalf of a corporation in fact received an item that was mailed to an officer of the corporation should not be held responsible for any failure on the part of the corporate defendant to effectively distribute that mail. [Emphasis added.]

* * * Cruz has * * * satisfied all of the elements necessary to establish effective service.

* * * *

The order of the trial court is reversed.

EXTENDED CASE CONTINUES ➡

EXTENDED CASE 3.1 CONTINUED ➡

 QUESTIONS

1. Suppose that Cruz had misaddressed the envelope but the summons had still reached Hayes, and Cruz could prove it. Would this have been sufficient to establish valid service? Explain.
2. Should a plaintiff be required to serve a defendant with a summons and a copy of a complaint more than once? Why or why not?

Waiver of Formal Service of Process. In many instances, the defendant is already aware that a lawsuit is being filed and is willing to waive (give up) her or his right to be served personally. The Federal Rules of Civil Procedure (FRCP) and many states' rules allow defendants to waive formal service of process, provided that certain procedures are followed. Kirby's attorney, for example, could mail to defendant Carvello a copy of the complaint, along with "Waiver of Service of Summons" forms for Carvello to sign. If Carvello signs and returns the forms within thirty days, formal service of process is waived. Moreover, under the FRCP, defendants who agree to waive formal service of process receive additional time to respond to the complaint (sixty days, instead of twenty days). Some states provide similar incentives to encourage defendants to waive formal service of process and thereby reduce associated costs and foster cooperation between the parties.

THE DEFENDANT'S RESPONSE Typically, the defendant's response to the complaint takes the form of an **answer.** In an answer, the defendant either admits or denies each of the allegations in the plaintiff's complaint and may also set forth defenses to those allegations. Under the federal rules, any allegations that are not denied by the defendant will be deemed by the court to have been admitted. If Carvello admits to all of Kirby's allegations in his answer, a judgment will be entered for Kirby. If Carvello denies Kirby's allegations, the matter will proceed further.

Affirmative Defenses. Carvello can also admit the truth of Kirby's complaint but raise new facts to show that he should not be held liable for Kirby's damages. This is called raising an **affirmative defense.** As will be discussed in subsequent chapters, defendants in both civil and criminal cases can raise affirmative defenses. For example, Carvello could assert Kirby's own negligence as a defense by alleging that Kirby was driving negligently at the time of the accident. In some states, a plaintiff's contributory negligence

operates as a complete defense. In most states, however, the plaintiff's own negligence constitutes only a partial defense (see Chapter 7).

Counterclaims. Carvello could also deny Kirby's allegations and set forth his own claim that the accident occurred as a result of Kirby's negligence and that therefore she owes Carvello for damage to his car. This is appropriately called a **counterclaim.** If Carvello files a counterclaim, Kirby will have to submit an answer to the counterclaim.

Dismissals and Judgments before Trial

Many actions for which pleadings have been filed never come to trial. The parties may, for example, negotiate a settlement of the dispute at any stage of the litigation process. There are also numerous procedural avenues for disposing of a case without a trial. Many of them involve one or the other party's attempts to get the case dismissed through the use of various motions.

A **motion** is a procedural request submitted to the court by an attorney on behalf of her or his client. When one party files a motion with the court, that party must also send to, or serve on, the opposing party a *notice of motion*. The notice of motion informs the opposing party that the motion has been filed. **Pretrial motions** include the motion to dismiss, the motion for judgment on the pleadings, and the motion for summary judgment, as well as the other motions listed in Exhibit 3–4.

MOTION TO DISMISS Either party can file a **motion to dismiss** asking the court to dismiss the case for the reasons stated in the motion, although normally it is the defendant who requests dismissal. A defendant can file a motion to dismiss if the plaintiff's complaint fails to state a claim for which relief (a remedy) can be granted. Such a motion asserts that even if the facts alleged in the complaint are true, they do not give rise to any legal claim against the defendant. For example, if the allegations in Kirby's

EXHIBIT 3-4 • Pretrial Motions

> ### MOTION TO DISMISS
> A motion normally filed by the defendant in which the defendant asks the court to dismiss the case for a specified reason, such as improper service, lack of personal jurisdiction, or the plaintiff's failure to state a claim for which relief can be granted.

> ### MOTION TO STRIKE
> A motion filed by the defendant in which the defendant asks the court to strike (delete) certain paragraphs from the complaint. Motions to strike help to clarify the underlying issues that form the basis for the complaint by removing paragraphs that are redundant or irrelevant to the action.

> ### MOTION TO MAKE MORE DEFINITE AND CERTAIN
> A motion filed by the defendant to compel the plaintiff to clarify the basis of the plaintiff's cause of action. The motion is filed when the defendant believes that the complaint is too vague or ambiguous for the defendant to respond to it in a meaningful way.

> ### MOTION FOR JUDGMENT ON THE PLEADINGS
> A motion that may be filed by either party in which the party asks the court to enter a judgment in his or her favor based on information contained in the pleadings. A judgment on the pleadings will be made only if there are no facts in dispute and the only question is how the law applies to a set of undisputed facts.

> ### MOTION TO COMPEL DISCOVERY
> A motion that may be filed by either party in which the party asks the court to compel the other party to comply with a discovery request. If a party refuses to allow the opponent to inspect and copy certain documents, for example, the party requesting the documents may make a motion to compel production of those documents.

> ### MOTION FOR SUMMARY JUDGMENT
> A motion that may be filed by either party in which the party asks the court to enter judgment in his or her favor without a trial. Unlike a motion for judgment on the pleadings, a motion for summary judgment can be supported by evidence outside the pleadings, such as witnesses' affidavits, answers to interrogatories, and other evidence obtained prior to or during discovery.

complaint do not constitute negligence on Carvello's part, Carvello can move to dismiss the case for failure to state a claim. Defendant Carvello could also file a motion to dismiss on the grounds that he was not properly served, that the court lacked jurisdiction, or that the venue was improper.

If the judge grants the motion to dismiss, the plaintiff generally is given time to file an amended complaint. If the judge denies the motion, the suit will go forward, and the defendant must then file an answer. Note that if Carvello wishes to discontinue the suit because, for example, an out-of-court settlement has been reached, he can likewise move for dismissal. The court can also dismiss a case on its own motion.

MOTION FOR JUDGMENT ON THE PLEADINGS At the close of the pleadings, either party may make a **motion for judgment on the pleadings,** which asks the court to decide the issue solely on the pleadings without proceeding to trial. The judge will grant the motion only when there is no dispute over the facts of the case and the sole issue to be resolved is a

question of law. For example, in the Kirby-Carvello case, if Carvello had admitted to all of Kirby's allegations in his answer and had raised no affirmative defenses, Kirby could file a motion for judgment on the pleadings.

In deciding a motion for judgment on the pleadings, the judge may consider only the evidence contained in the pleadings. In contrast, in a motion for summary judgment, discussed next, the court may consider evidence outside the pleadings, such as sworn statements and other materials that would be admissible as evidence at trial.

MOTION FOR SUMMARY JUDGMENT Either party can file a **motion for summary judgment,** which asks the court to grant a judgment in that party's favor without a trial. As with a motion for judgment on the pleadings, a court will grant a motion for summary judgment only if it determines that no facts are in dispute and the only question is how the law applies to the facts. A motion for summary judgment can be made before or during a trial, but it will be granted only if, when the evidence is viewed in the light most favorable to the other party, there clearly are no facts in contention.

To support a motion for summary judgment, a party can submit evidence obtained at any point before the trial that refutes the other party's factual claim. The evidence may consist of **affidavits** (sworn statements by parties or witnesses) or copies of documents, such as contracts, e-mails, and letters obtained through the course of discovery (discussed next). Of course, the evidence must be *admissible* evidence—that is, evidence that the court would allow to be presented during the trial. As mentioned, the use of additional evidence is one feature that distinguishes the motion for summary judgment from the motion to dismiss and the motion for judgment on the pleadings.

Discovery

Before a trial begins, the parties can use a number of procedural devices to obtain information and gather evidence about the case. Kirby, for example, will want to know how fast Carvello was driving, whether he had been drinking or was under the influence of any medication, and whether he was wearing corrective lenses if he was required by law to do so while driving. The process of obtaining information from the opposing party or from witnesses prior to trial is known as **discovery.** Discovery includes gaining access to witnesses, documents, records, and other types of evidence. In federal courts, the parties are required to make initial disclosures of relevant evidence to the opposing party.

Discovery prevents surprises at trial by giving both parties access to evidence that might otherwise be hidden. This allows the litigants to learn as much as they can about what to expect at a trial before they reach the courtroom. Discovery also serves to narrow the issues so that trial time is spent on the main questions in the case.

The main question in the following case was what a court could do when a plaintiff failed to identify and disclose the names of expert witnesses, even though the court deemed that such witnesses were necessary to establish the plaintiff's claim against the defendants.

CASE 3.2
Blankenship v. Collier
Supreme Court of Kentucky, 302 S.W.3d 665 (2010).
www.courts.ky.gov/supremecourt/minutes.htm[a]

BACKGROUND AND FACTS • In February 2004, Horace Collier was admitted to Caritas Medical Center with abdominal pain. The following day, after undergoing tests and being diagnosed by Dr. Robert Blankenship as having appendicitis, Collier had an appendectomy. One year later, Collier sued Blankenship and Caritas Health Services in a Kentucky state court, contending that they had been negligent because they had failed to evaluate and treat him in a timely manner. Specifically, Collier claimed that he had been ignored for several hours while awaiting treatment and had suffered severe abdominal pain, and that the X-ray of his abdomen had not been stored properly, causing further delay in his diagnosis and treatment. Collier alleged that as a result of the defendants' medical negligence, he had sustained permanent physical and mental injuries, prolonged pain and mental anguish, impairment of his power to earn income, and significant medical expenses. More than nine months later, Collier had not yet disclosed the identities of any expert witnesses who would testify on his behalf, and the court ordered him to do so by January 30, 2006. At Collier's request, this deadline was extended to February 28. Finally, on March 14, 2006, after Collier still had not disclosed any names, the defendants filed motions for summary judgment, arguing that there could be no issue of material fact in this medical malpractice[b] case without expert testimony. The trial court granted the motions. Collier appealed, arguing that summary judgment was inappropriate in this instance because it was being used only as a sanctioning tool to punish him for failing to timely disclose his experts and that there was a "serious question" as to whether he would even need experts to prove his medical malpractice claim. The

---

a. On the page that opens, select "January 21" under the "2010" heading. Scroll down the list to the case title to access the court's opinion. The Supreme Court of Kentucky maintains this Web site.

b. *Medical malpractice* is the term used for the tort of negligence when committed by medical professionals—see Chapter 7.

CASE 3.2 CONTINUED ➤ intermediate appellate court agreed and reversed the trial court's decision. The defendants appealed the decision to the Supreme Court of Kentucky.

IN THE LANGUAGE OF THE COURT
Opinion of the court by Justice *ABRAMSON*.

* * * *

* * * Although a defendant is permitted to move for a summary judgment at any time, this Court has cautioned trial courts not to take up these motions prematurely and to consider summary judgment motions "only after the opposing party has been given ample opportunity to complete discovery." Thus, even though an appellate court always reviews the substance of a trial court's summary judgment ruling *de novo* [anew] * * * to determine whether the record reflects a genuine issue of material fact, *a reviewing court must also consider whether the trial court gave the party opposing the motion an ample opportunity to respond and complete discovery before the court entered its ruling.* In a medical malpractice action, where a sufficient amount of time has expired and the plaintiff has still "failed to introduce evidence sufficient to establish the respective applicable standard of care," then the defendants are entitled to summary judgment as a matter of law. The trial court's determination that a sufficient amount of time has passed and that it can properly take up the summary judgment motion for a ruling is reviewed for an abuse of discretion. [Emphasis added.]

In this case, the issue before this Court is not simply whether Collier had failed to establish a genuine issue of material fact at the time Dr. Blankenship and Caritas filed their summary judgment motions—without a doubt, there is no genuine issue of material fact in the record because Collier has no expert to support his claim of medical negligence. Rather, the more specific issue is whether the trial court was correct to take up the defendants' summary judgment motions and enter a ruling when it did and, secondarily, whether the court was required first either to enter a separate order requiring Collier to obtain expert testimony or to enter an order sanctioning Collier for failing to meet the court's expert disclosure deadline.

Having carefully reviewed the record, we conclude that the defendants' summary judgment motions were properly before the trial court and it did not abuse its discretion in taking them up and deciding to rule on the motions approximately four months after they were filed and seventeen months after the lawsuit was initiated. Collier had completely failed to identify any expert witnesses and could not sustain his burden of proof without expert testimony and, thus, no material issue of fact existed in the record and the defendants were entitled to summary judgment as a matter of law. Because Collier never disputed that a medical expert was necessary to prove his claim of medical negligence and continually represented to the trial court that he would obtain an expert witness, no separate ruling stating the obvious—the need for an expert witness—was required before the court ruled on the defendants' summary judgment motions. Further, * * * the trial court was not required to enter a sanctions order prior to granting the defendants' summary judgment motions.

DECISION AND REMEDY • *The Supreme Court of Kentucky reversed the decision of the lower appellate court and reinstated the trial court's decision. The trial court had not abused its discretion by granting summary judgment for the defendants.*

THE ETHICAL DIMENSION • *Collier contended that there was a "serious question" as to whether he would even need experts to prove his medical malpractice claim. Is it fair to Collier to prevent the trial from proceeding, even though the lack of expert testimony might have made it difficult—if not impossible—for him to win the case? Explain.*

MANAGERIAL IMPLICATIONS • *Business owners and managers should be aware that initiating discovery procedures and responding to discovery requests in a timely fashion are important in any litigation. Although the court in this case claimed that summary judgment was not a sanction imposed on the plaintiff for delays during discovery, one could argue (as a dissenting judge did) that it was indeed a sanction—and a very harsh one. Courts have also dismissed cases when the plaintiffs have caused undue delay by not meeting procedural deadlines.*

DISCOVERY RULES The FRCP and similar state rules set forth the guidelines for discovery activity. Generally, discovery is allowed regarding any matter that is relevant to the claim or defense of any party. Discovery rules also attempt to protect witnesses and parties from undue harassment, and to safeguard privileged or confidential material from being disclosed. Only information that is relevant to the case at hand—or likely to lead to the discovery of relevant information—is discoverable. If a discovery request involves privileged or confidential business information, a court can deny the request and can limit the scope of discovery in a number of ways. For example, a court can require the party to submit the materials to the judge in a sealed envelope so that the judge can decide if they should be disclosed to the opposing party.

DEPOSITIONS Discovery can involve the use of depositions. A **deposition** is sworn testimony by a party to the lawsuit or by any witness, recorded by an authorized court official. The person deposed gives testimony and answers questions asked by the attorneys from both sides. The questions and answers are recorded, sworn to, and signed. These answers, of course, will help the attorneys prepare their cases. Depositions also give attorneys the opportunity to ask immediate follow-up questions and to evaluate how their witnesses will conduct themselves at trial. In addition, depositions can be employed in court to *impeach* (challenge the credibility of) a party or a witness who changes testimony at the trial. A deposition can also be used as testimony if the witness is not available at trial.

INTERROGATORIES Discovery can also involve **interrogatories,** which are written questions for which written answers are prepared and then signed under oath. The main difference between interrogatories and written depositions is that interrogatories are directed to a party to the lawsuit (the plaintiff or the defendant), not to a witness, and the party usually has thirty days to prepare answers. The party's attorney often drafts the answers to interrogatories in a manner calculated to give away as little information as possible. Whereas depositions are useful for eliciting candid responses and answers not prepared in advance, interrogatories are designed to obtain accurate information about specific topics, such as how many contracts were signed and when. The scope of interrogatories is also broader because parties are obligated to answer questions, even if that means disclosing information from their records and files. Note that a court can impose sanctions on

a party who fails to answer interrogatories (or who refuses to respond to other discovery requests).

CASE IN POINT Computer Task Group, Inc. (CTG), hired William Brotby as an information technology consultant. As a condition of his employment, Brotby signed an agreement that restricted his ability to work for CTG's customers if he left CTG. Less than two years later, Brotby left CTG and began working for Alyeska Pipeline Service Company, a CTG client, in breach of the agreement. CTG sued Brotby. During discovery, Brotby refused to respond fully to CTG's interrogatories. He gave contradictory answers, made frivolous objections, filed baseless motions, and never disclosed all the information that CTG sought. The court ordered Brotby to comply with discovery requests five times, but Brotby continued to make excuses and changed his story repeatedly, making it impossible for CTG to establish basic facts with any certainty. Eventually, CTG requested and the court granted a default judgment against Brotby based on his failure to cooperate.[8]

REQUESTS FOR ADMISSIONS One party can serve the other party with a written request for an admission of the truth of matters relating to the trial. Any fact admitted under such a request is conclusively established as true for the trial. For example, Kirby can ask Carvello to admit that his driver's license was suspended at the time of the accident. A request for admission shortens the trial because the parties will not have to spend time proving facts on which they already agree.

REQUESTS FOR DOCUMENTS, OBJECTS, AND ENTRY UPON LAND A party can gain access to documents and other items not in her or his possession in order to inspect and examine them. Carvello, for example, can gain permission to inspect and copy Kirby's car repair bills. Likewise, a party can gain "entry upon land" to inspect the premises.

REQUESTS FOR EXAMINATIONS When the physical or mental condition of one party is in question, the opposing party can ask the court to order a physical or mental examination by an independent examiner. If the court agrees to make the order, the opposing party can obtain the results of the examination. Note that the court will make such an order only when the need for the information outweighs the right to privacy of the person to be examined.

---

8. *Computer Task Group, Inc. v. Brotby,* 364 F.3D 1112 (9th Cir. 2004).

ELECTRONIC DISCOVERY Any relevant material, including information stored electronically, can be the object of a discovery request. The federal rules and most state rules (as well as court decisions) specifically allow individuals to obtain discovery of electronic "data compilations." Electronic evidence, or **e-evidence,** consists of all computer-generated or electronically recorded information, such as e-mail, voice mail, spreadsheets, word-processing documents, and other data. E-evidence can reveal significant facts that are not discoverable by other means. For example, computers automatically record certain information about files—such as who created the file and when, and who accessed, modified, or transmitted it—on their hard drives. This information can only be obtained from the file in its electronic format—not from printed-out versions.

The Federal Rules of Civil Procedures deals specifically with the preservation, retrieval, and production of electronic data. Although traditional means, such as interrogatories and depositions, are still used to find out whether e-evidence exists, a party usually must hire an expert to retrieve the evidence in its electronic format. The expert uses software to reconstruct e-mail exchanges to establish who knew what and when they knew it. The expert can even recover computer files that the user thought had been deleted. Reviewing back-up copies of documents and e-mail can provide useful—and often quite damaging—information about how a particular matter progressed over several weeks or months.

Electronic discovery, or e-discovery, has significant advantages over paper discovery, but it is also time consuming and expensive. These costs are amplified when the parties involved in the lawsuit are large corporations with many offices and employees. Who should pay the costs associated with e-discovery? For a discussion of how the courts are handling this issue, see this chapter's *Shifting Legal Priorities for Business* feature on the next page.

Pretrial Conference

After discovery has taken place and before the trial begins, the attorneys may meet with the trial judge in a **pretrial conference,** or hearing. Usually, the conference consists of an informal discussion between the judge and the opposing attorneys after discovery has taken place. The purpose of the conference is to explore the possibility of a settlement without trial and, if this is not possible, to identify the matters that are in dispute and to plan the course

of the trial. In particular, the parties may attempt to establish ground rules to restrict the number of expert witnesses or discuss the admissibility or costs of certain types of evidence.

The Right to a Jury Trial

The Seventh Amendment to the U.S. Constitution guarantees the right to a jury trial for cases at law in *federal* courts when the amount in controversy exceeds $20. Most states have similar guarantees in their own constitutions (although the threshold dollar amount is higher than $20). The right to a trial by jury need not be exercised, and many cases are tried without a jury. In most states and in federal courts, one of the parties must request a jury, or the judge presumes the parties waive this right. If there is no jury, the judge determines the truth of the facts alleged in the case.

Jury Selection

Before a jury trial commences, a panel of jurors must be selected. Although some types of trials require twelve-person juries, most civil matters can be heard by six-person juries. The jury selection process is known as **voir dire.**[9] During *voir dire* in most jurisdictions, attorneys for the plaintiff and the defendant ask prospective jurors oral questions to determine whether a potential jury member is biased or has any connection with a party to the action or with a prospective witness. In some jurisdictions, the judge may do all or part of the questioning based on written questions submitted by counsel for the parties.

During *voir dire*, a party may challenge a certain number of prospective jurors *peremptorily*—that is, ask that an individual not be sworn in as a juror without providing any reason. Alternatively, a party may challenge a prospective juror *for cause*—that is, provide a reason why an individual should not be sworn in as a juror. If the judge grants the challenge, the individual is asked to step down. A prospective juror, however, may not be excluded by the use of discriminatory challenges, such as those based on racial criteria or gender.

See *Concept Summary 3.1* on page 63 for a review of pretrial procedures.

---

9. Pronounced *vwahr deehr*. These verbs based on Old French mean "to speak the truth." In legal language, the phrase refers to the process of questioning jurors to learn about their backgrounds, attitudes, and similar attributes.

Today, less than 0.5 percent of new information is created on paper. Instead of sending letters and memos, people send e-mails and text messages, creating a massive amount of electronically stored information (ESI). The law requires parties to preserve ESI whenever there is a "reasonable anticipation of litigation."

Why Companies Fail to Preserve Electronic Evidence

Preserving electronic evidence, or e-evidence, can be a challenge, particularly for large corporations that have electronic data scattered across multiple networks, servers, desktops, laptops, handheld devices, and even home computers. Although many companies have policies regarding back-up of office e-mail and computer systems, these may cover only a fraction of the e-discovery requested in a lawsuit.

Technological advances further complicate the situation. Users of BlackBerry devices, for example, can configure them so that messages are transmitted with limited or no archiving rather than going through a company's servers and being recorded. How can a company preserve e-evidence that is never on its servers? In one case, the court held that a company had a duty to preserve transitory "server log data," which exist only temporarily on a computer's memory.[a]

Potential Sanctions and Malpractice Claims

A court may impose sanctions (such as fines) on a party that fails to preserve e-evidence or to comply with e-discovery requests. A firm may be sanctioned if it provides e-mails without the attachments, does not produce all of the e-evidence requested, or fails to suspend its automatic e-mail deletion procedures.[b] Nearly 25 percent of the reported opinions on e-discovery from 2008 involved sanctions for failure to preserve e-evidence.[c] Attorneys who fail to properly advise their clients concerning the duty to preserve e-evidence also often face sanctions and malpractice claims.[d]

Lessons from Intel Corporation

A party that fails to preserve e-evidence may even find itself at such a disadvantage that it will settle a dispute rather than continue litigation. For example, Advanced Micro Devices, Inc. (AMD), sued Intel Corporation, one of the world's largest microprocessor suppliers, for violating antitrust laws. Immediately after the lawsuit was filed, Intel began collecting and preserving the ESI on its servers. Although the company instructed its employees to retain documents and e-mails related to competition with AMD, many employees saved only copies of the e-mails that they had received and not e-mails that they had sent.

In addition, Intel did not stop its automatic e-mail deletion system, causing other information to be lost. In the end, although Intel produced data that, on paper, would have been equivalent to "somewhere in the neighborhood of a pile 137 miles high," its failure to preserve e-evidence led it to settle the dispute in 2008.[e]

MANAGERIAL IMPLICATIONS

Clearly, companies can be accused of intentionally failing to preserve electronic data. As a manager, you have to weigh the cost of retaining data, such as e-mails, against the benefits of having those data available if your company is ever sued.

---

a. See *Columbia Pictures Industries v. Brunnell,* 2007 WL 2080419 (C.D.Cal. 2007).

b. See, for example, *John B. v. Goetz,* 531 F.3d 448 (6th Cir. 2008); and *Wingnut Films, Ltd. v. Katija Motion Pictures,* 2007 WL 2758571 (C.D.Cal. 2007).

c. Sheri Qualters. "25% of Reported E-Discovery Opinions in 2008 Involved Sanction Issues," *National Law Journal.* 12 December 2008: n.p.

d. See, for example, *Qualcomm, Inc. v. Broadcom Corp.,* 539 F.Supp.2d 1214 (S.D.Cal. 2007).

e. See *In re Intel Corp. Microprocessor Antitrust Litigation,* 2008 WL 2310288 (D.Del. 2008). See also *Adams v. Gateway, Inc.,* 2006 WL 2563418 (D. Utah 2006).

SECTION 3
THE TRIAL

Various rules and procedures govern the trial phase of the litigation process. There are rules governing what kind of evidence will or will not be admitted during the trial, as well as specific procedures that the participants in the lawsuit must follow.

Opening Statements

At the beginning of the trial, both attorneys are allowed to make **opening statements** setting forth

CONCEPT SUMMARY 3.1
Pretrial Procedures

Procedure	Description
The Pleadings	1. *The plaintiff's complaint*—The plaintiff's statement of the cause of action and the parties involved, filed with the court by the plaintiff's attorney. After the filing, the defendant is notified of the suit through service of process. 2. *The defendant's response*—The defendant's response to the plaintiff's complaint may take the form of an answer, in which the defendant admits or denies the plaintiff's allegations. The defendant may raise an affirmative defense and/or assert a counterclaim.
Pretrial Motions	1. *Motion to dismiss*—May be made by either party; requests that the judge dismiss the case for reasons that are provided in the motion (such as failure to state a claim for which relief can be granted). 2. *Motion for judgment on the pleadings*—May be made by either party; will be granted only if no facts are in dispute and only questions of law are at issue. 3. *Motion for summary judgment*—May be made by either party; will be granted only if no facts are in dispute and only questions of law are at issue. Unlike the motion for judgment on the pleadings, the motion for summary judgment may be supported by evidence outside the pleadings, such as testimony and other evidence obtained during the discovery phase of litigation.
Discovery	The process of gathering evidence concerning the case; involves (1) *depositions* (sworn testimony by either party or any witness); (2) *interrogatories* (in which parties to the action write answers to questions with the aid of their attorneys); and (3) requests for admissions, documents, examinations, or other information relating to the case. Discovery may also involve electronically recorded information, such as e-mail, voice mail, and other data.
Pretrial Conference	A pretrial hearing, at the request of either party or the court, to identify the matters in dispute after discovery has taken place and to explore the possibility of settling the dispute without a trial. If no settlement is possible, the parties plan the course of the trial.
Jury Selection	In a jury trial, the selection of members of the jury from a pool of prospective jurors. During a process known as *voir dire,* the attorneys for both sides may challenge prospective jurors either for cause or peremptorily (for no cause).

the facts that they expect to prove during the trial. The opening statement provides an opportunity for each lawyer to give a brief version of the facts and the supporting evidence that will be used during the trial. Then the plaintiff's case is presented. In our hypothetical case, Kirby's lawyer would introduce evidence (relevant documents, exhibits, and the testimony of witnesses) to support Kirby's position.

Rules of Evidence

Whether evidence will be admitted in court is determined by the **rules of evidence**—a series of rules that have been created by the courts to ensure that any evidence presented during a trial is fair and reliable. The Federal Rules of Evidence govern the admissibility of evidence in federal courts.

EVIDENCE MUST BE RELEVANT TO THE ISSUES Evidence will not be admitted in court unless it is relevant to the matter in question. **Relevant evidence** is evidence that tends to prove or disprove a fact in question or to establish the degree of probability of a fact or action. For example, evidence that the defendant's gun was in the home of another person when the victim was shot would be relevant—because it would tend to prove that the defendant did not shoot the victim.

HEARSAY EVIDENCE NOT ADMISSIBLE Generally, hearsay is not admissible as evidence. **Hearsay** is testimony someone gives in court about a statement made by someone else who was not under oath at the time of the statement. Literally, it is what someone heard someone else say. For example, if a witness in the Kirby-Carvello case testified in court concerning what he or she heard another observer say about the accident, that testimony would be hearsay, or secondhand knowledge. Admitting hearsay into evidence carries many risks because, even though it may be relevant, there is no way to test its reliability.

In the following case, some of the plaintiff's evidence consisted of printouts of Web pages purporting to indicate how the pages appeared at a prior point in time. The defendant challenged this evidence as hearsay.

CASE 3.3
Novak v. Tucows, Inc.

United States District Court, Eastern District of New York, __ F.Supp.2d __ (2007).

BACKGROUND AND FACTS • In 1997, Robert Novak registered the domain name petswarehouse.com and began selling pet supplies and pets online. Within two years, the site had become one of the most popular sites for pet supplies in the United States. Novak obtained a trademark for the petswarehouse.com name and transferred its registration to Nitin Networks, Inc., which was owned by Tucows, Inc., a Canadian firm that is a domain registrar. In an unrelated matter, John Benn obtained a judgment against Novak in an Alabama state court. On May 1, 2003, on that court's order, Tucows transferred the domain name to the court to satisfy the judgment. After an Alabama intermediate appellate court reversed the judgment, the name was returned to Novak on October 1, 2004. Novak filed a suit in a federal district court against Tucows and Nitin, claiming that the transfer of the name out of his control for seventeen months destroyed his pet-supply business. Novak alleged that the defendants had committed several violations of federal and state law, including trademark infringement. Tucows responded with, among other things, a motion to strike some of Novak's exhibits.

IN THE LANGUAGE OF THE COURT
Joseph F. *BIANCO*, District Judge.
* * * *
    Defendants contend that plaintiff's Exhibits B, J, K, O–R, U and V, which are printouts of Internet pages, constitute inadmissible hearsay and do not fall within any acknowledged exception to the hearsay rule. * * * Defendants [also] objected to Plaintiff's Exhibit 1, as well as to Plaintiff's Exhibits N–R. Plaintiff's Exhibit 1 is a printout from "RegisterSite.com," Nitin's Web site, as it purportedly appeared in 2003. According to plaintiff, he obtained the printout through a Web site called the Internet Archive, which provides access to a digital library of Internet sites. The Internet Archive operates a service called the "Wayback Machine," which purports to allow a user to obtain an archived Web page as it appeared at a particular moment in time. The other contested exhibits include: Exhibit B, an online summary of plaintiff's past and pending lawsuits, obtained via the Wayback Machine; Exhibit J, printouts of comments on a Web message board by [Evgeniy] Pirogov [a Tucows employee]; Exhibit K, a news article from the *Poughkeepsie Journal* Web site featuring [Nitin] Agarwal [the chief executive officer and founder of Nitin]; Exhibit N, Novak's declaration regarding the authenticity of pages printed from the Wayback Machine; Exhibit O, pages printed from the Internet Archive Web site; Exhibit P, pages printed from the Wayback Machine Web site; Exhibits Q, R and U, all of which constitute pages printed from RegisterSite.com via the Wayback Machine; and Exhibit V, a news article from "The Register," a British Web site, regarding Tucows. *Where postings from Internet Web sites are not statements made by declarants testifying at trial and are offered to prove the truth of the matter asserted, such postings generally constitute hearsay under [the Federal Rules of Evidence].* [Emphasis added.]

    Furthermore, in this case, such documents have not been properly authenticated pursuant to [the Federal Rules of Evidence].[a] While plaintiff's declaration purports to cure his inability to authenticate the documents printed from the Internet, he in fact lacks the personal knowledge required to set forth with any certainty that the documents obtained via third-party Web sites

---

a. In this context, *authentication* refers to the requirement that sufficient evidence be introduced to show that these Web pages are what Novak claims.

CASE 3.3 CONTINUED ➡ are, in fact, what he proclaims them to be. This problem is even more acute in the case of documents procured through the Wayback Machine. Plaintiff states that the Web pages archived within the Wayback Machine are based upon "data from third parties who compile the data by using software programs known as crawlers," who then "donate" such data to the Internet Archive, which "preserves and provides access to it." Based upon Novak's assertions, it is clear that the information posted on the Wayback Machine is only as valid as the third-party donating the page decides to make it—the authorized owners and managers of the archived Web sites play no role in ensuring that the material posted in the Wayback Machine accurately represents what was posted on their official Web sites at the relevant time. As Novak proffers neither testimony nor sworn statements attesting to the authenticity of the contested Web page exhibits by any employee of the companies hosting the sites from which plaintiff printed the pages, such exhibits cannot be authenticated as required under the [Federal] Rules of Evidence. Therefore, in the absence of any authentication of plaintiff's Internet printouts, combined with the lack of any assertion that such printouts fall under a viable exception to the hearsay rule, defendants' motion to strike Exhibits B, J, K, N–R, U and V is granted.

DECISION AND REMEDY • *The court granted Tucows's motion to strike Novak's exhibits. Tucows also filed a motion to dismiss Novak's suit altogether based on a clause in the parties' domain name transfer agreement. The clause mandated that all related disputes be litigated in Ontario, Canada, according to Canadian law. The court determined that the clause was valid and reasonable, and granted Tucows's motion to dismiss the suit.*

THE ETHICAL DIMENSION • *Hearsay is literally what a witness says he or she heard another person say. What makes the admissibility of such evidence potentially unethical?*

THE E-COMMERCE DIMENSION • *In this case, the plaintiff offered as evidence printouts of Web pages that he claimed once appeared on others' Web sites. What makes such evidence questionable until proved accurate?*

Examination of Witnesses

Because Kirby is the plaintiff, she has the burden of proving that her allegations are true. Her attorney begins the presentation of Kirby's case by calling the first witness for the plaintiff and examining, or questioning, the witness. (For both attorneys, the types of questions and the manner of asking them are governed by the rules of evidence.) This questioning is called **direct examination.** After Kirby's attorney is finished, the witness is subject to **cross-examination** by Carvello's attorney. Then Kirby's attorney has another opportunity to question the witness in *redirect examination,* and Carvello's attorney may follow the redirect examination with a *recross-examination.* When both attorneys have finished with the first witness, Kirby's attorney calls the succeeding witnesses in the plaintiff's case, each of whom is subject to examination by the attorneys in the manner just described.

EXPERT WITNESSES Both the plaintiff and the defendant may present testimony from one or more expert witnesses—such as forensic scientists, physicians, and psychologists—as part of their cases. An *expert witness* is a person who, by virtue of education, training, skill, or experience, has scientific, technical,

or other specialized knowledge in a particular area beyond that of an average person. In Kirby's case, her attorney might hire an accident reconstruction specialist to establish Carvello's negligence or a physician to confirm the extent of Kirby's injuries.

Normally, witnesses can testify only about the facts of a case—that is, what they personally observed. When witnesses are qualified as experts in a particular field, however, they can offer their opinions and conclusions about the evidence in that field. Expert testimony is an important component of litigation today.

Because numerous experts are available for hire and expert testimony is powerful and effective with juries, there is tremendous potential for abuse. Therefore, in federal courts and most state courts, judges act as gatekeepers to ensure that the experts are qualified and that their opinions are based on scientific knowledge.[10] If a party believes that the opponent's witness

---

10. The requirement that judges act as gatekeepers is known as the *Daubert* standard, named after the case, *Daubert v. Merrell Dow Pharmaceuticals, Inc.,* 43 F.3d 1311 (9th Cir. 1995). A minority of jurisdictions still follow the *Frye* standard, which allows both sides to present all relevant evidence to the jury and then requires the jury to weigh the testimony of experts. See Paul C. Giannelli and Edward J. Imwinkelried. *Scientific Evidence,* 4th ed. (Newark, NJ: LexisNexis, 2007), Sections 1.06 and 1.16.

is not qualified as an expert in the relevant field, that party can make a motion asking the judge to exclude this evidence and prevent the expert witness from testifying in front of the jury.

POTENTIAL MOTION AND JUDGMENT At the conclusion of the plaintiff's case, the defendant's attorney has the opportunity to ask the judge to direct a verdict for the defendant on the ground that the plaintiff has presented no evidence to support her or his claim. This is called a **motion for a judgment as a matter of law** (or a **motion for a directed verdict** in state courts). In considering the motion, the judge looks at the evidence in the light most favorable to the plaintiff and grants the motion only if there is insufficient evidence to raise an issue of fact. (Motions for directed verdicts at this stage of a trial are seldom granted.)

DEFENDANT'S EVIDENCE The defendant's attorney then presents the evidence and witnesses for the defendant's case. Witnesses are called and examined by the defendant's attorney. The plaintiff's attorney has the right to cross-examine them, and there may be a redirect examination and possibly a recross-examination. At the end of the defendant's case, either attorney can move for a directed verdict, and the test again is whether the jury can, through any reasonable interpretation of the evidence, find for the party against whom the motion has been made. After the defendant's attorney has finished introducing evidence, the plaintiff's attorney can present a **rebuttal** by offering additional evidence that refutes the defendant's case. The defendant's attorney can, in turn, refute that evidence in a **rejoinder.**

Closing Arguments, Jury Instructions, and Verdict

After both sides have rested their cases, each attorney presents a closing argument. In the **closing argument,** each attorney summarizes the facts and evidence presented during the trial and indicates why the facts and evidence support his or her client's claim. In addition to generally urging a verdict in favor of the client, the closing argument typically reveals the shortcomings of the points made by the opposing party during the trial.

Attorneys generally present closing arguments whether or not the trial was heard by a jury. If it was a jury trial, the attorneys will have met with the judge prior to closing arguments to determine how the jury will be instructed on the law. The attorneys can refer to these instructions in their closing

arguments. After closing arguments are completed, the judge instructs the jury in the law that applies to the case (these instructions are often called *charges*), and the jury retires to the jury room to deliberate a verdict. In most civil cases, the standard of proof is a *preponderance of the evidence.*[11] In other words, the plaintiff (Kirby in our hypothetical case) need only show that her factual claim is more likely to be true than the defendant's. (As you will read in Chapter 9, in a criminal trial the prosecution has a higher standard of proof to meet—it must prove its case *beyond a reasonable doubt.*)

Once the jury has reached a decision, it issues a **verdict** in favor of one party; the verdict specifies the jury's factual findings. In some cases, the jury also decides on the amount of the *award* (the compensation to be paid to the prevailing party). After the announcement of the verdict, which marks the end of the trial itself, the jurors are dismissed.

See *Concept Summary 3.2* for a review of trial procedures.

SECTION 4
POSTTRIAL MOTIONS

After the jury has rendered its verdict, either party may make a posttrial motion. The prevailing party usually requests that the court enter a judgment in accordance with the verdict. The nonprevailing party frequently files one of the motions discussed next.

Motion for a New Trial

At the end of the trial, the losing party may make a motion to set aside the adverse verdict and any judgment and to hold a new trial. After looking at all the evidence, the judge will grant the **motion for a new trial** only if she or he believes that the jury was in error and that it is not appropriate to grant judgment for the other side. Usually, this occurs when the jury verdict is obviously the result of a misapplication of the law or a misunderstanding of the evidence presented at trial. A new trial can also be granted on the grounds of newly discovered evidence, misconduct by the participants during the trial (such as when a juror has made prejudicial and inflammatory remarks), or an error by the judge.

---

11. Note that some civil claims must be proved by "clear and convincing evidence," meaning that the evidence must show that the truth of the party's claim is *highly* probable. This standard is often applied in situations that present a particular danger of deception, such as allegations of fraud.

CONCEPT SUMMARY 3.2
Trial Procedures

Procedure	Description
Opening Statements	Each party's attorney is allowed to present an opening statement indicating what the attorney will attempt to prove during the course of the trial.
Examination of Witnesses	1. Plaintiff's introduction and direct examination of witnesses, cross-examination by defendant's attorney, possible redirect examination by plaintiff's attorney, and possible recross-examination by defendant's attorney. 2. Both the plaintiff and the defendant may present testimony from one or more expert witnesses. 3. At the close of the plaintiff's case, the defendant may make a motion for a directed verdict (or judgment as a matter of law), which, if granted by the court, will end the trial before the defendant presents witnesses. 4. Defendant's introduction and direct examination of witnesses, cross-examination by plaintiff's attorney, possible redirect examination by defendant's attorney, and possible recross-examination by plaintiff's attorney. 5. Possible rebuttal of defendant's argument by plaintiff's attorney, who presents more evidence. 6. Possible rejoinder by defendant's attorney to meet that evidence.
Closing Arguments, Jury Instructions, and Verdict	Each party's attorney argues in favor of a verdict for his or her client. The judge instructs (or charges) the jury as to how the law applies to the issue, and the jury retires to deliberate. When the jury renders its verdict, this brings the trial to an end.

Motion for Judgment *N.O.V.*

If Kirby wins, and if Carvello's attorney has previously moved for a directed verdict, then Carvello's attorney can now make a **motion for judgment n.o.v.**—from the Latin *non obstante veredicto,* meaning "notwithstanding the verdict." (Federal courts use the term *judgment as a matter of law* instead of *judgment n.o.v.)* Such a motion will be granted only if the jury's verdict was unreasonable and erroneous. If the judge grants the motion, then the jury's verdict will be set aside, and a judgment will be entered in favor of the opposing party (Carvello). If the motion is denied, Carvello may then appeal the case. (Kirby may also appeal the case, even though she won at trial. She might appeal, for example, if she received a smaller monetary award than she had sought.)

SECTION 5
THE APPEAL

Either party may appeal not only the jury's verdict but also the judge's ruling on any pretrial or post-trial motion. Many of the appellate court cases that appear in this text involve appeals of motions for summary judgment or other motions that were denied by trial court judges. Note that a party must have legitimate grounds to file an appeal (some legal error) and that few trial court decisions are reversed on appeal. Moreover, the expenses associated with an appeal can be considerable.[12]

Filing the Appeal

If Carvello decides to appeal the verdict in Kirby's favor, then his attorney must file a *notice of appeal* with the clerk of the trial court within a prescribed period of time. Carvello then becomes the *appellant* or *petitioner.* The clerk of the trial court sends to the reviewing court (usually an intermediate court of appeals) the *record on appeal.* The record contains all the pleadings, motions, and other documents filed with the court and a complete written transcript of the proceedings, including testimony, arguments, jury instructions, and judicial rulings.

Carvello's attorney will file an appellate *brief* with the reviewing court. The **brief** is a formal legal document outlining the facts and issues of the case, the judge's rulings or jury's findings that should be reversed or modified, the applicable law, and arguments on Carvello's behalf (citing applicable statutes

---

12. See, for example, *Phansalkar v. Andersen Weinroth & Co.,* 356 F.3d 188 (2d Cir. 2004).

and relevant cases as precedents). The attorney for the *appellee* (Kirby, in our hypothetical case) usually files an answering brief. Carvello's attorney can file a reply, although it is not required. The reviewing court then considers the case.

Appellate Review

As mentioned in Chapter 2, a court of appeals does not hear any evidence. Rather, it reviews the record for errors of law. Its decision concerning a case is based on the record on appeal and the briefs and arguments. The attorneys present oral arguments, after which the case is taken under advisement. The court then issues a written opinion. In general, appellate courts do not reverse findings of fact unless the findings are unsupported or contradicted by the evidence.

An appellate court has the following options after reviewing a case:

1. The court can *affirm* the trial court's decision. (Most decisions are affirmed.)
2. The court can *reverse* the trial court's judgment if it concludes that the trial court erred or that the jury did not receive proper instructions.

3. The appellate court can *remand* (send back) the case to the trial court for further proceedings consistent with its opinion on the matter.
4. The court might also affirm or reverse a decision *in part*. For example, the court might affirm the jury's finding that Carvello was negligent but remand the case for further proceedings on another issue (such as the extent of Kirby's damages).
5. An appellate court can also *modify* a lower court's decision. If the appellate court decides that the jury awarded an excessive amount in damages, for example, the court might reduce the award to a more appropriate, or fairer, amount.

Appellate courts apply different standards of review depending on the type of issue and the ruling involved. Generally, these standards require the reviewing court to give a certain amount of deference, or weight, to the findings of lower courts on specific issues. The following case illustrates how courts use standards of review.

CASE 3.4
Evans v. Eaton Corp. Long Term Disability Plan

United States Court of Appeals, Fourth Circuit, 514 F.3d 315 (2008).

BACKGROUND AND FACTS • Eaton Corporation is a multinational manufacturing company that funds and administers a long-term disability benefits plan for its employees. Brenda Evans was an employee at Eaton. In 1998, due to severe rheumatoid arthritis, Evans quit her job at Eaton and filed for disability benefits. Eaton paid disability benefits to Evans without controversy prior to 2003, but that year, Evans's disability status became questionable. Her physician had prescribed a new medication that had dramatically improved Evans's arthritis. In addition, Evans had injured her spine in a car accident in 2002 and was claiming to be disabled by continuing back problems as well as arthritis. But diagnostic exams indicated that the injuries to Evans's back were not severe, and she could cook, shop, do laundry, wash dishes, and drive about seven miles a day. By 2004, medical opinion on Evans's condition was mixed. Some physicians who had examined Evans concluded that she was still disabled, but several other physicians had determined that Evans was no longer totally disabled and could work. On that basis, Eaton terminated her disability benefits. Evans filed a complaint in a federal district court alleging violations of the Employee Retirement Income Security Act of 1974 (ERISA, a federal law regulating pension plans that will be discussed in Chapter 34). The district court examined the evidence in great detail and concluded that Eaton had abused its discretion in failing to find Evans's examining physicians' opinions more credible. Eaton appealed.

IN THE LANGUAGE OF THE COURT
WILKINSON, Circuit Judge.
* * * *
    This case turns on a faithful application of the abuse of discretion standard of review, and so we begin with what is most crucial: a clear understanding of what that standard is, and what such standards are for. *The purpose of standards of review*

CASE 3.4 CONTINUED ➡ *is to focus reviewing courts upon their proper role when passing on the conduct of other decision-makers.* Standards of review are thus an elemental expression of judicial restraint, which, in their deferential varieties, safeguard the superior vantage points of those entrusted with primary decisional responsibility. * * * The clear error standard, for example, protects district courts' primacy as triers of fact. * * * Rational basis review protects the political choices of our government's elected branches. And trust law, to which ERISA is so intimately linked, uses the abuse of discretion standard to protect a fiduciary's [one whose relationship is based on trust] decisions concerning the trust funds in his care. [Emphasis added.]

The precise definitions of these various standards, the nuances separating them from one another, "cannot be imprisoned within any forms of words" * * *. But what these and other such standards share is the designation of a primary decision-maker other than the reviewing court, and the instrument, deference, with which that primacy is to be maintained.

* * * In [this] case, the Plan's language giving Eaton "discretionary authority to determine eligibility for benefits" and "the power and discretion to determine all questions of fact * * * arising in connection with the administration, interpretation and application of the Plan" is unambiguous, and Evans does not dispute the standard it requires. Thus the district court functions in this context as a * * * reviewing court with respect to the ERISA fiduciary's decision.
* * * *

*At its immovable core, the abuse of discretion standard requires a reviewing court to show enough deference to a primary decision-maker's judgment that the court does not reverse merely because it would have come to a different result * * *.* The trial judge has discretion in those cases where his ruling will not be reversed simply because an appellate court disagrees. [Emphasis added.]
* * * *

Under no formulation, however, may a court, faced with discretionary language like that in the plan instrument in this case, forget its duty of deference and its secondary rather than primary role in determining a claimant's right to benefits. The abuse of discretion standard in ERISA cases protects important values: the plan administrator's greater experience and familiarity with plan terms and provisions; the enhanced prospects of achieving consistent application of those terms and provisions that results; the desire of those who establish ERISA plans to preserve at least some role in their administration; and the importance of ensuring that funds which are not unlimited go to those who, according to the terms of the plan, are truly deserving.
* * * *

* * * Where an ERISA administrator rejects a claim to benefits on the strength of substantial evidence, careful and coherent reasoning, faithful adherence to the letter of ERISA and the language in the plan, and a fair and searching process, there can be no abuse of discretion—even if another, and arguably a better, decision-maker might have come to a different, and arguably a better, result.
* * * *

So standards of review do matter, for in every context they keep judges within the limits of their role and preserve other decision-makers' functions against judicial intrusion.

DECISION AND REMEDY • *The U.S. Court of Appeals for the Fourth Circuit reversed the district court's award of benefits to Evans and remanded the case with instructions that the district court enter a judgment in favor of Eaton. The district court had incorrectly applied the abuse of discretion standard when reviewing Eaton's termination of Evans's benefits.*

THE ETHICAL DIMENSION • *The appellate court noted in this case that the district court's decision—which granted benefits to Evans—might arguably have been a better decision under the facts. If the court believed that the district court's conclusion was arguably better, then why did it reverse the decision? What does this tell you about the standards for review that appellate judges use?*

WHAT IF THE FACTS WERE DIFFERENT? • *Suppose that it was clear from the evidence on record that the ERISA administrator had not been careful and consistent and had rejected Evans's claim merely because of a personal dislike for Evans. How might this fact have changed the result in this case?*

Higher Appellate Courts

If the reviewing court is an intermediate appellate court, the losing party may decide to appeal the decision to the state's highest court, usually called its supreme court. Although the losing party has a right to ask (petition) a higher court to review the case, the party does not have a right to have the case heard by the higher appellate court. Appellate courts normally have discretionary power and can accept or reject an appeal. Like the United States Supreme Court, state supreme courts generally deny most petitions for appeal.

If the petition is granted, new briefs must be filed before the state supreme court, and the attorneys may be allowed or requested to present oral arguments. Like the intermediate appellate courts, the supreme court can reverse or affirm the lower appellate court's decision or remand the case. At this point, the case typically has reached its end (unless a federal question is at issue and one of the parties has legitimate grounds to seek review by a federal appellate court).

Concept Summary 3.3 reviews the options that the parties may pursue after the trial.

◤◤ SECTION 6 ◤◤
ENFORCING THE JUDGMENT

The uncertainties of the litigation process are compounded by the lack of guarantees that any judgment will be enforceable. Even if the jury awards Kirby the full amount of damages requested ($100,000), for example, Carvello's auto insurance coverage might have lapsed, in which event the company would not pay any of the damages. Alternatively, Carvello's insurance policy might be limited to $50,000, meaning that Carvello personally would have to pay the remaining $50,000.

Requesting Court Assistance in Collecting the Judgment

If the defendant does not have the funds available to pay the judgment, the plaintiff can go back to the court and request that the court issue a *writ of execution*. A **writ of execution** is an order directing the sheriff to seize and sell the defendant's nonexempt assets, or property (certain assets are exempted by law from creditors' actions). The proceeds of the sale are

---

CONCEPT SUMMARY 3.3
Posttrial Options

Procedure	Description
Posttrial Motions	1. *Motion for a new trial*—If the judge believes that the jury was in error but is not convinced that the losing party should have won, the motion normally is granted. It can also be granted on the basis of newly discovered evidence, misconduct by the participants during the trial, or error by the judge. 2. *Motion for judgment n.o.v.* (*"notwithstanding the verdict"*)—The party making the motion must have filed a motion for a directed verdict at the close of the presentation of evidence during the trial; the motion will be granted if the judge is convinced that the jury was in error.
Appeal	Either party can appeal the trial court's judgment to an appropriate court of appeals. 1. *Filing the appeal*—The appealing party must file a notice of appeal with the clerk of the trial court, who forwards the record on appeal to the appellate court. Attorneys file appellate briefs. 2. *Appellate review*—The appellate court does not hear evidence but bases its opinion, which it issues in writing, on the record on appeal and the attorneys' briefs and oral arguments. The court may affirm or reverse all (or part) of the trial court's judgment and/or remand the case for further proceedings consistent with its opinion. Most decisions are affirmed on appeal. 3. *Further review*—In some cases, further review may be sought from a higher appellate court, such as a state supreme court. If a federal question is involved, the case may ultimately be appealed to the United States Supreme Court.

then used to pay the damages owed, and any excess proceeds are returned to the defendant. Alternatively, the nonexempt property itself could be transferred to the plaintiff in lieu of an outright payment. (Creditors' remedies, including those of judgment creditors, as well as exempt and nonexempt property, will be discussed in more detail in Chapter 28.)

Availability of Assets

The problem of collecting a judgment is less pronounced, of course, when a party is seeking to satisfy a judgment against a defendant with substantial assets that can be easily located, such as a major corporation. Usually, one of the factors considered by the plaintiff and his or her attorney before a lawsuit is initiated is whether the defendant has sufficient assets to cover the amount of damages sought. In addition, during the discovery process, attorneys routinely seek information about the location of the defendant's assets that might potentially be used to satisfy a judgment.

REVIEWING

Court Procedures

Ronald Metzgar placed his fifteen-month-old son, Matthew, awake and healthy, in his playpen. Ronald left the room for five minutes and on his return found Matthew lifeless. A toy block had lodged in the boy's throat, causing him to choke to death. Ronald called 911, but efforts to revive Matthew were to no avail. There was no warning of a choking hazard on the box containing the block. Matthew's parents hired an attorney and sued Playskool, Inc., the manufacturer of the block, alleging that the manufacturer had been negligent in failing to warn of the block's hazard. Playskool filed a motion for summary judgment, arguing that the danger of a young child choking on a small block was obvious. Using the information presented in the chapter, answer the following questions.

1. Suppose that the attorney the Metzgars hired agreed to represent them on a contingency-fee basis. What does that mean?
2. How would the Metzgars' attorney likely have served process (the summons and complaint) on Playskool, Inc.?
3. Should Playskool's request for summary judgment be granted? Why or why not?
4. Suppose that the judge denied Playskool's motion and the case proceeded to trial. After hearing all the evidence, the jury found in favor of the defendant. What options do the plaintiffs have at this point if they are not satisfied with the verdict?

DEBATE THIS: *Some consumer advocates argue that attorneys' high contingency fees—sometimes reaching 40 percent—unfairly deprive winning plaintiffs of too much of their awards. Should the government put a cap on contingency fees at, say, 20 percent of the award? Why or why not?*

TERMS AND CONCEPTS

affidavit 58
affirmative defense 56
answer 56
brief 67
closing argument 66
complaint 52
counterclaim 56
cross-examination 65
default judgment 52
deposition 60

direct examination 65
discovery 58
e-evidence 61
Federal Rules of Civil Procedure (FRCP) 50
hearsay 63
interrogatories 60
motion 56
motion for a directed verdict 66
motion for a judgment as a matter of law 66

motion for a new trial 66
motion for judgment *n.o.v.* 67
motion for judgment on the pleadings 57
motion for summary judgment 57
motion to dismiss 56
opening statement 62
pleadings 52
pretrial conference 61

pretrial motion 56
rebuttal 66
rejoinder 66
relevant evidence 63
rules of evidence 63
service of process 52
summons 52
verdict 66
voir dire 61
writ of execution 70

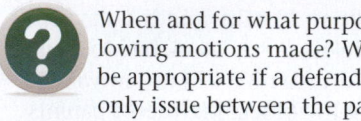

QUESTIONS AND CASE PROBLEMS

3–1. Discovery Rules In the past, the rules of discovery were very restrictive, and trials often turned on elements of surprise. For example, a plaintiff would not necessarily know until the trial what the defendant's defense was going to be. In the last several decades, however, new rules of discovery have substantially changed this situation. Now each attorney can access practically all of the evidence that the other side intends to present at trial, with the exception of certain information—namely, the opposing attorney's work product. Work product is not a precise concept. Basically, it includes all of the attorney's thoughts on the case. Can you see any reason why such information should not be made available to the opposing attorney? Discuss fully.

3–2. QUESTION WITH SAMPLE ANSWER: Motions.

When and for what purpose is each of the following motions made? Which of them would be appropriate if a defendant claimed that the only issue between the parties was a question of law and that the law was favorable to the defendant's position?

  (a) A motion for judgment on the pleadings.
  (b) A motion for a directed verdict.
  (c) A motion for summary judgment.
  (d) A motion for judgment *n.o.v.*

• **For a sample answer to Question 3–2, go to Appendix I at the end of this text.**

3–3. Motion for a New Trial Washoe Medical Center, Inc., admitted Shirley Swisher for the treatment of a fractured pelvis. During her stay, Swisher suffered a fatal fall from her hospital bed. Gerald Parodi, the administrator of her estate, and others filed an action against Washoe seeking damages for the alleged lack of care in treating Swisher. During *voir dire*, when the plaintiffs' attorney returned a few minutes late from a break, the trial judge led the prospective jurors in a standing ovation. The judge joked with one of the prospective jurors, whom he had known in college, about his fitness to serve as a judge and personally endorsed another prospective juror's business. After the trial, the jury returned a verdict in favor of Washoe. The plaintiffs moved for a new trial, but the judge denied the motion. The plaintiffs then appealed, arguing that the tone set by the judge during *voir dire* prejudiced their right to a fair trial. Should the appellate court agree? Why or why not?

3–4. Discovery Advance Technology Consultants, Inc. (ATC), contracted with RoadTrac, LLC, to provide software and client software systems for the products of global positioning satellite (GPS) technology being developed by RoadTrac. RoadTrac agreed to provide ATC with hardware with which ATC's software would interface. Problems soon arose, however. ATC claimed that RoadTrac's hardware was defective, making it difficult to develop the software. RoadTrac contended that its hardware was fully functional and that ATC had simply failed to provide supporting software. ATC told RoadTrac that

it considered their contract terminated. RoadTrac filed a suit in a Georgia state court against ATC alleging breach of contract. During discovery, RoadTrac requested ATC's customer lists and marketing procedures. ATC objected to providing this information because RoadTrac and ATC had become competitors in the GPS industry. Should a party to a lawsuit have to hand over its confidential business secrets as part of a discovery request? Why or why not? What limitations might a court consider imposing before requiring ATC to produce this material?

3–5. Service of Process To establish a Web site, a person must have an Internet service provider or hosting company, register a domain name, and acquire domain name servicing. Pfizer, Inc., Pfizer Ireland Pharmaceuticals, and Warner-Lambert Co. (collectively, Pfizer) filed a suit in a federal district court against Domains By Proxy, Inc., and other persons alleged to be behind two Web sites—www.genericlipitors.com and www.econopetcare.com. Among the defendants were an individual and a company that, according to Pfizer, were located in a foreign country. Without investigating other means of serving these two defendants, Pfizer asked the court for permission to accomplish service of process via e-mail. Under what circumstances is service via e-mail proper? Would it be appropriate in this case? Explain. [*Pfizer, Inc. v. Domains By Proxy, __ F.Supp.2d __ (D.Conn. 2004)*]

3–6. CASE PROBLEM WITH SAMPLE ANSWER: Appellate Review.

BSH Home Appliances Corp. makes appliances under the Bosch, Siemens, Thermador, and Gaggenau brands. To make and market the "Pro 27 Stainless Steel Range," a restaurant-quality range for home use, BSH gave specifications for its burner to Detroit Radiant Products Co. and requested a price for 30,000 units. Detroit quoted $28.25 per unit, offering to absorb all tooling and research and development costs. In 2001 and 2003, BSH sent Detroit two purchase orders, for 15,000 and 16,000 units, respectively. In 2004, after Detroit had shipped 12,886 units, BSH stopped scheduling deliveries. Detroit filed a suit against BSH, alleging breach of contract. BSH argued, in part, that the second purchase order had not added to the first but had replaced it. After a trial, a federal district court issued its "Findings of Fact and Conclusions of Law." The court found that the two purchase orders "required BSH to purchase 31,000 units of the burner at $28.25 per unit." The court ruled that Detroit was entitled to $418,261 for 18,114 unsold burners. BSH appealed to the U.S. Court of Appeals for the Sixth Circuit. Can an appellate court set aside a trial court's findings of fact? Can an appellate court come to its own conclusions of law? What should the court rule in this case? Explain. [Detroit Radiant Products Co. v. BSH Home Appliances Corp., 473 F.3d 623 (6th Cir. 2007)]

• **To view a sample answer for Problem 3–7, go to this book's Web site at www.cengage.com/blaw/clarkson, select "Chapter 3," and click on "Case Problem with Sample Answer."**

3–7. Discovery In October 2004, Rita Peatie filed a suit in a Connecticut state court against Wal-Mart Stores, Inc., to recover for injuries to her head, neck, and shoulder. Peatie claimed that she had been struck two years earlier by a metal cylinder falling from a store ceiling. The parties agreed to nonbinding arbitration. Ten days before the hearing in January 2006, the plaintiff asked for, and was granted, four more months to conduct discovery. On the morning of the rescheduled hearing, she asked for more time, but the court denied this request. The hearing was held, and the arbitrator ruled in Wal-Mart's favor. Peatie filed a motion for a new trial, which was granted. Five months later, she sought through discovery to acquire any photos, records, and reports held by Wal-Mart regarding her alleged injury. The court issued a "protective order" against the request, stating that the time for discovery had long been over. On the day of the trial—four years after the alleged injury—the plaintiff asked the court to lift the order. Should the court do so? Why or why not? [*Peatie v. Wal-Mart Stores, Inc.*, 112 Conn.App. 8, 961 A.2d 1016 (2009)]

3–8. Jury Misconduct Michelle Fleshner worked for Pepose Vision Institute (PVI), a surgical practice. She was fired after she provided information to the Department of Labor about PVI's overtime pay policy. She sued for wrongful termination, and the jury awarded her $125,000. After the trial, a juror told PVI's attorneys that another juror had made anti-Semitic statements during jury deliberations. The comments concerned a witness who testified on PVI's behalf. According to the juror, the other juror said, about the witness: "She is a Jewish witch." "She is a penny-pinching Jew." "She was such a cheap Jew that she did not want to pay Plaintiff unemployment compensation." Another juror confirmed the remarks. PVI filed a motion for a new trial on the basis of juror misconduct. The trial judge held that the comments did not prevent a fair trial from occurring. PVI appealed. Do you think such comments are sufficient to require a new trial, or must a juror's bias be discovered during *voir dire* for it to matter? Explain. [*Fleshner v. Pepose Vision Institute*, 304 S.W.3d 81 (Mo. 2010)]

3–9. A QUESTION OF ETHICS: Service of Process.

Narnia Investments, Ltd., filed a suit in a Texas state court against several defendants, including Harvestons Securities, Inc., a securities dealer. (Securities *are documents evidencing the ownership*

of a corporation, in the form of stock, or debts owed by it, in the form of bonds.) Harvestons is registered with the state of Texas, and thus a party may serve a summons and a copy of a complaint on Harvestons by serving the Texas Securities Commissioner. In this case, the return of service indicated that process was served on the commissioner "by delivering to JoAnn Kocerek defendant, in person, a true copy of this [summons] together with the accompanying copy(ies) of the [complaint]." Harvestons did not file an answer, and Narnia obtained a default judgment against the defendant for $365,000, plus attorneys' fees and interest. Five months after this judgment, Harvestons filed a motion for a new trial, which the court denied. Harvestons appealed to a state intermediate appellate court, claiming that it had not been served in strict compliance with the rules governing service of process. [Harvestons Securities, Inc. v. Narnia Investments, Ltd., 218 S.W.3d 126 (Tex.App.—Houston 2007)]

(a) Harvestons asserted that Narnia's service was invalid, in part, because "the return of service states that process was delivered to 'JoAnn Kocerek'" and did not show that she "had the authority to accept process on behalf of Harvestons or the Texas Securities Commissioner." Should such a detail, if it is required, be strictly construed and applied? Should it apply in this case? Explain.

(b) Whose responsibility is it to see that service of process is accomplished properly? Was it accomplished properly in this case? Why or why not?

3–10. SPECIAL CASE ANALYSIS: Proper Service.
Go to Extended Case 3.1, *Cruz v. Fagor America, Inc.*, 146 Cal.App.4th 488, 52 Cal.Rptr.3d 862 (2007), on pages 54 and 55. Read the excerpt and answer the following questions.

(a) Issue: On what preliminary step to litigation does the issue in this case focus?

(b) Rule of Law: What are the chief requirements for fulfilling the pretrial procedure at the center of the dispute in this case?

(c) Applying the Rule of Law: In applying the rule of law in this case, what did the court infer, and what did that inference imply for the defendant?

(d) Conclusion: Did the court conclude that the plaintiff had met all of the requirements for a favorable judgment in this case? If not, why not?

LEGAL RESEARCH EXERCISES ON THE WEB

Go to this text's Web site at **www.cengage.com/blaw/clarkson**, select "Chapter 3," and click on "Practical Internet Exercises." There you will find the following Internet research exercises that you can perform to learn more about the topics covered in this chapter.

Practical Internet Exercise 3–1:   **Legal Perspective**
Civil Procedure

Practical Internet Exercise 3–2:   **Management Perspective**
Small Claims Courts

Practical Internet Exercise 3–3:   **Technological Perspective**
Virtual Courtrooms

BUSINESS LAW · CLARKSON · MILLER · CROSS

CHAPTER 4

Constitutional Authority to Regulate Business

The U.S. Constitution is the supreme law in this country.[1] As mentioned in Chapter 1, neither Congress nor any state may pass a law that conflicts with the Constitution. Laws that govern business have their origin in the lawmaking authority granted by this document.

In this chapter, we examine some basic constitutional concepts and clauses and their significance for businesspersons. We then look at certain freedoms guaranteed by the first ten amendments to the Constitution—the Bill of Rights—and discuss how these freedoms affect business activities.

1. See Appendix B for the full text of the U.S. Constitution.

SECTION 1
THE CONSTITUTIONAL POWERS OF GOVERNMENT

Following the Revolutionary War, the states—through the Articles of Confederation—created a *confederal form of government* in which the states had the authority to govern themselves and the national government could exercise only limited powers. When problems arose because the nation was facing an economic crisis and state laws interfered with the free flow of commerce, a national convention was called, and the delegates drafted the U.S. Constitution. This document, after its ratification by the states in 1789, became the basis for an entirely new form of government.

A Federal Form of Government

The new government created by the U.S. Constitution reflected a series of compromises made by the convention delegates on various issues. Some delegates wanted sovereign power to remain with the states; others wanted the national government alone to exercise sovereign power. The end result was a compromise—a **federal form of government** in which the national government and the states *share* sovereign power.

The Constitution sets forth specific powers that can be exercised by the national government and provides that the national government has the implied power to undertake actions necessary to carry out its expressly designated powers (or *enumerated powers*). All other powers are expressly "reserved" to the states under the Tenth Amendment to the U.S. Constitution.

As part of their inherent sovereignty, state governments have the authority to regulate affairs within their borders. As mentioned, this authority stems, in part, from the Tenth Amendment, which reserves all powers not delegated to the national government to the states or to the people. State regulatory powers are often referred to as **police powers.** The term does not relate solely to criminal law enforcement but rather refers to the broad right of state governments to regulate private activities to protect or promote the public order, health, safety, morals, and general welfare. Fire and building codes, antidiscrimination laws, parking regulations, zoning restrictions, licensing requirements, and thousands of other state statutes covering almost every aspect of life have been enacted pursuant to states' police powers. Local governments, including cities, also exercise police powers.[2] Generally, state laws enacted pursuant to a state's police powers carry a strong presumption of validity.

---

2. Local governments derive their authority to regulate their communities from the state, because they are creatures of the state. In other words, they cannot come into existence unless authorized by the state to do so.

Relations among the States

The U.S. Constitution also includes provisions concerning relations among the states in our federal system. Particularly important are the *privileges and immunities clause* and the *full faith and credit clause*.

THE PRIVILEGES AND IMMUNITIES CLAUSE Article IV, Section 2, of the U.S. Constitution provides that the "Citizens of each State shall be entitled to all Privileges and Immunities of Citizens in the several States." This clause is often referred to as the interstate **privileges and immunities clause.**[3] It prevents a state from imposing unreasonable burdens on citizens of another state—particularly with regard to means of livelihood or doing business. When a citizen of one state engages in basic and essential activities in another state (the "foreign state"), the foreign state must have a *substantial reason* for treating the nonresident differently from its own residents. Basic activities include transferring property, seeking employment, or accessing the court system. The foreign state must also establish that its reason for the discrimination is *substantially related* to the state's ultimate purpose in adopting the legislation or regulating the activity.[4]

THE FULL FAITH AND CREDIT CLAUSE Article IV, Section 1, of the U.S. Constitution provides that "Full Faith and Credit shall be given in each State to the public Acts, Records, and judicial Proceedings of every other State." This clause, which is referred to as the **full faith and credit clause,** applies only to civil matters. It ensures that rights established under deeds, wills, contracts, and similar instruments in one state will be honored by other states. It also ensures that any judicial decision with respect to such property rights will be honored and enforced in all states.

The full faith and credit clause was originally included in the Articles of Confederation to promote mutual friendship among the people of the various states. In fact, it has contributed to the unity of American citizens because it protects their legal rights as they move about from state to state. It also protects the rights of those to whom they owe obligations, such as a person who is awarded monetary damages by a court. The ability to enforce such rights is extremely important for the conduct of business in a country with a very mobile citizenry.

The Separation of the National Government's Powers

To guard against the possibility that the national government might use its power arbitrarily, the Constitution provided for three branches of government. The legislative branch makes the laws, the executive branch enforces the laws, and the judicial branch interprets the laws. Each branch performs a separate function, and no branch may exercise the authority of another branch.

Additionally, a system of **checks and balances** allows each branch to limit the actions of the other two branches, thus preventing any one branch from exercising too much power. Some examples of these checks and balances include the following:

1. The legislative branch (Congress) can enact a law, but the executive branch (the president) has the constitutional authority to veto that law.
2. The executive branch is responsible for foreign affairs, but treaties with foreign governments require the advice and consent of the Senate.
3. Congress determines the jurisdiction of the federal courts and the president appoints federal judges, with the advice and consent of the Senate, but the judicial branch has the power to hold actions of the other two branches unconstitutional.[5]

The Commerce Clause

To prevent states from establishing laws and regulations that would interfere with trade and commerce among the states, the Constitution expressly delegated to the national government the power to regulate interstate commerce. Article I, Section 8, of the U.S. Constitution explicitly permits Congress "[t]o regulate Commerce with foreign Nations, and among the several States, and with the Indian Tribes." This clause, referred to as the **commerce clause,** has had a greater impact on business than any other provision in the Constitution. The commerce clause provides the basis for the national government's extensive regulation of state and even local affairs.

One of the early questions raised by the commerce clause was whether the word *among* in the

---

3. Interpretations of this clause commonly use the terms *privilege* and *immunity* synonymously. Generally, the terms refer to certain rights, benefits, or advantages enjoyed by individuals.
4. This test was first announced in *Supreme Court of New Hampshire v. Piper,* 470 U.S. 274, 105 S.Ct. 1272, 84 L.Ed.2d 205 (1985). For another example, see *Lee v. Miner,* 369 F.Supp.2d 527 (D.Del. 2005).

---

5. As discussed in Chapter 2, the power of judicial review was established by the United States Supreme Court in *Marbury v. Madison,* 5 U.S. (1 Cranch) 137, 2 L.Ed. 60 (1803).

phrase "among the several States" meant *between* the states or *between and within* the states. For some time, the courts interpreted the commerce clause to apply only to commerce between the states (*interstate* commerce) and not commerce within the states (*intrastate* commerce). In 1824, however, the United States Supreme Court decided the landmark case of *Gibbons v. Ogden.*[6] The Court ruled that commerce within the states could also be regulated by the national government as long as the commerce *substantially affected* commerce involving more than one state.

THE EXPANSION OF NATIONAL POWERS UNDER THE COMMERCE CLAUSE

In *Gibbons v. Ogden,* the Supreme Court expanded the commerce clause to cover activities that "substantially affect interstate commerce." As the nation grew and faced new kinds of problems, the commerce clause became a vehicle for the additional expansion of the national government's regulatory powers. Even activities that seemed purely local in nature came under the regulatory reach of the national government if those activities were deemed to substantially affect interstate commerce.

In 1942, for example, the Supreme Court held that wheat production by an individual farmer intended wholly for consumption on his own farm was subject to federal regulation.[7] In *Heart of Atlanta Motel v. United States,*[8] a landmark case decided in 1964, the Supreme Court upheld the federal government's authority to prohibit racial discrimination nationwide in public facilities, including local motels, based on its powers under the commerce clause. The Court noted that "if it is interstate commerce that feels the pinch, it does not matter how local the operation that applies the squeeze."

THE COMMERCE CLAUSE TODAY

Today, the national government continues to rely on the commerce clause for its constitutional authority to regulate business activities in the United States. The breadth of the commerce clause permits the national government to legislate in areas in which Congress has not explicitly been granted power. In the last twenty years, however, the Supreme Court has begun to curb somewhat the national government's regulatory authority under the commerce clause. In 1995, the Court held—for the first time in sixty years— that Congress had exceeded its regulatory authority

under the commerce clause. The Court struck down an act that banned the possession of guns within one thousand feet of any school because the act attempted to regulate an area that had "nothing to do with commerce."[9] Subsequently, the Court invalidated key portions of two other federal acts on the ground that they exceeded Congress's commerce clause authority.[10]

MEDICAL MARIJUANA LAWS AND THE COMMERCE CLAUSE

In one notable case, however, the Supreme Court did allow the federal government to regulate noncommercial activities taking place wholly within a state's borders.

CASE IN POINT About a dozen states, including California, have adopted "medical marijuana" laws that legalize marijuana for medical purposes. Marijuana possession, however, is illegal under the federal Controlled Substances Act (CSA).[11] After the federal government seized the marijuana that two seriously ill California women were using on the advice of their physicians, the women filed a lawsuit. They argued that it was unconstitutional for the federal statute to prohibit them from using marijuana for medical purposes that were legal within the state. In 2005, however, the United States Supreme Court held that Congress has the authority to prohibit the *intra*state possession and noncommercial cultivation of marijuana as part of a larger regulatory scheme (the CSA).[12] In other words, state laws that allow the use of medical marijuana do not insulate the users from federal prosecution.

THE "DORMANT" COMMERCE CLAUSE

The United States Supreme Court has interpreted the commerce clause to mean that the national government has the *exclusive* authority to regulate commerce that substantially affects trade and commerce among the states. This express grant of authority to the national government, which is often referred to as the "positive" aspect of the commerce clause, implies a negative aspect—that the states do *not* have the authority to regulate interstate commerce.

---

6. 2 U.S. (9 Wheat.) 1, 6 L.Ed. 23 (1824).

7. *Wickard v. Filburn,* 317 U.S. 111, 63 S.Ct. 82, 87 L.Ed. 122 (1942).

8. 379 U.S. 241, 85 S.Ct. 348, 13 L.Ed.2d 258 (1964).

9. The Court held the Gun-Free School Zones Act of 1990 to be unconstitutional in *United States v. Lopez,* 514 U.S. 549, 115 S.Ct. 1624, 131 L.Ed.2d 626 (1995).

10. *Printz v. United States,* 521 U.S. 898, 117 S.Ct. 2365, 138 L.Ed.2d 914 (1997), involving the Brady Handgun Violence Prevention Act of 1993; and *United States v. Morrison,* 529 U.S. 598, 120 S.Ct. 1740, 146 L.Ed.2d 658 (2000), concerning the federal Violence Against Women Act of 1994.

11. 21 U.S.C. Sections 801 *et seq.*

12. *Gonzales v. Raich,* 545 U.S. 1, 125 S.Ct. 2195, 162 L.Ed.2d 1 (2005).

This negative aspect of the commerce clause is often referred to as the "dormant" (implied) commerce clause.

The dormant commerce clause comes into play when state regulations affect interstate commerce. In this situation, the courts weigh the state's interest in regulating a certain matter against the burden that the state's regulation places on interstate commerce. Because courts balance the interests involved, it is difficult to predict the outcome in a particular case.

In the following case, the plaintiffs—a group of California wineries and others—contended that a 2006 Massachusetts statute discriminated against out-of-state wineries in violation of the dormant commerce clause. A federal district court agreed and enjoined (prevented) the enforcement of the statute. The commonwealth of Massachusetts appealed the trial court's decision.

✴ EXTENDED CASE 4.1 ✴
Family Winemakers of California v. Jenkins[a]

United States Court of Appeals, First Circuit, 592 F.3d 1 (2010).
www.ca1.uscourts.gov/opinions/main.php[b]

IN THE LANGUAGE OF THE COURT
LYNCH, Chief Judge.
* * * *

The ratification of the Twenty-first Amendment ended Prohibition[c] and gave states substantial control over the regulation of alcoholic beverages. Most states, including Massachusetts, then imposed a three-tier system to control the sale of alcoholic beverages within their territories. The hallmark of the three-tier system is a rigid, tightly regulated separation between producers, wholesalers, and retailers of alcoholic beverages. Producers can ordinarily sell alcoholic beverages only to licensed in-state wholesalers. Wholesalers then must obtain licenses to sell to retailers. Retailers, which include stores, taverns, restaurants, and bars, must in turn obtain licenses to sell to consumers or to serve alcohol on their premises. Recently, as to wine, Massachusetts has adjusted the separation between these three tiers * * *.
* * * *

Wineries have heralded direct shipping as a supplemental avenue of distribution because of its economic advantages, especially for wineries that do not rank among the fifty to one hundred largest producers. Direct shipping lets consumers directly order wines from the winery, with access to their full range of wines, not just those a wholesaler is willing to distribute. Direct shipping also avoids added steps in the distribution chain, eliminating wholesaler and retailer price markups.

Before 2005, Massachusetts's * * * winery licensing law * * * allowed only in-state wineries to obtain licenses to combine distribution methods through wholesalers, retailers, and direct shipping to consumers. [After the United States Supreme Court] invalidated similar facially discriminatory state laws, [the 2005 Massachusetts law] was held to be invalid under the Commerce Clause.

In 2006, the Massachusetts legislature enacted [a new law regulating wineries, which] does not distinguish on its face between in-state and out-of-state wineries' eligibility for direct shipping licenses, but instead distinguishes between "small" or "large" wineries through [a] 30,000 gallon cap.

* * * *

* * * All wineries producing over 30,000 gallons of wine—all of which are located outside Massachusetts— can apply for a "large winery shipment license[.]" * * * "Large" wineries can either choose to remain completely within the three-tier system and distribute their wines solely through wholesalers, or they can completely opt out of the three-tier system and sell their wines in Massachusetts exclusively through direct shipping [to consumers]. They cannot do both. * * * By contrast, "small" wineries can simultaneously use the traditional wholesaler distribution method, direct distribution to retailers, and direct shipping to reach consumers.

* * * *

* * * *Discrimination under the Commerce Clause "means differential treatment of in-state and out-of-state economic interests that benefits the former and burdens the latter," as opposed to state laws that "regulate * * * evenhandedly with only incidental effects on interstate commerce[.]"* [Emphasis added.]

* * * Plaintiffs argue that Massachusetts's choice of 30,000 gallons as the demarcation [separation]

---

a. The case was brought against Eddie J. Jenkins, the chair of the Massachusetts Alcoholic Beverages Control Commission, in his official capacity.

b. When the page opens, type "Family Winemakers" in the "Short Title *contains*" box and then click on "Submit Search." Select Opinion Number 09-01169P.01A to access the case. The U.S. Court of Appeals for the First Circuit maintains this Web site.

c. The Eighteenth Amendment to the U.S. Constitution, adopted in 1919, prohibited the sale of alcoholic beverages, giving rise to the so-called Prohibition Era. The Twenty-first Amendment, ratified in 1933, repealed the Eighteenth Amendment.

EXTENDED CASE CONTINUES ➧

EXTENDED CASE 4.1 CONTINUED ◆

point between "small" and "large" wineries, along with [a] production exception for fruit wine, has both a discriminatory effect and [a] purpose. The discriminatory effect is because [the law's] definition of "large" wineries encompasses the wineries which produce 98 percent of all wine in the United States, all of which are located out-of-state and all of which are deprived of the benefits of combining distribution methods. All wines produced in Massachusetts, on the other hand, are from "small" wineries that can use multiple distribution methods. Plaintiffs also say that [the law] is discriminatory in purpose because the gallonage cap's particular features, along with legislators' statements and [the law's] process of enactment, show that [the law's] true purpose was to ensure that Massachusetts's wineries obtained advantages over their out-of-state counterparts.

* * * *

* * * State laws that alter conditions of competition to favor in-state interests over out-of-state competitors in a market have long been subject to invalidation.

* * * Here, the totality of the evidence introduced by plaintiffs demonstrates that [the law's] preferential treatment of "small" wineries that produce 30,000 gallons or less of grape wine is discriminatory. Its effect is to significantly alter the terms of competition between in-state and out-of-state wineries to the detriment of the out-of-state wineries that produce 98 percent of the country's wine.

[The 2006 law] confers a clear competitive advantage to "small" wineries, which include all Massachusetts's wineries, and creates a comparative disadvantage for "large" wineries, none of which are in Massachusetts. "Small" wineries that obtain a * * * license can use direct shipping to consumers, retailer distribution, and

wholesaler distribution simultaneously. Combining these distribution methods allows "small" wineries to sell their full range of wines at maximum efficiency because they serve complementary markets. "Small" wineries that produce higher-volume wines can continue distributing those wines through wholesaler relationships. They can obtain new markets for all their wines by distributing their wines directly to retailers, including individual bars, restaurants, and stores. They can also use direct shipping to offer their full range of wines directly to Massachusetts consumers, resulting in greater overall sales.

* * * *

We conclude that [the 2006 law] altered the competitive balance to favor Massachusetts's wineries and disfavor out-of-state competition by design.

* * * *

We *affirm* the judgment of the district court.

 QUESTIONS

1. The court held that the Massachusetts statute discriminated against out-of-state wineries "by design" (intentionally). How can a court determine legislative intent?
2. Suppose that most "small" wineries, as defined by the 2006 Massachusetts law, were located out of state. How could the law be discriminatory in that situation?

The Supremacy Clause and Federal Preemption

Article VI of the U.S. Constitution, commonly referred to as the **supremacy clause,** provides that the Constitution, laws, and treaties of the United States are "the supreme Law of the Land." When there is a direct conflict between a federal law and a state law, the state law is rendered invalid. Because some powers are *concurrent* (shared by the federal government and the states), however, it is necessary to determine which law governs in a particular circumstance.

When Congress chooses to act exclusively in an area in which the federal government and the states have concurrent powers, **preemption** occurs. A valid federal statute or regulation will take precedence over a conflicting state or local law or regulation on

the same general subject. Often, it is not clear whether Congress, in passing a law, intended to preempt an entire subject area against state regulation, and it is left to the courts to determine whether Congress intended to exercise exclusive power over a given area. No single factor is decisive as to whether a court will find preemption. Generally, congressional intent to preempt will be found if a federal law regulating an activity is so pervasive, comprehensive, or detailed that the states have no room to regulate in that area. Also, when a federal statute creates an agency to enforce the law, the agency's rulings on matters that come within its jurisdiction will likely preempt state laws.

CASE IN POINT   The United States Supreme Court heard a case involving a man who alleged that he had been injured by a faulty medical device (a balloon catheter that had been inserted into his artery following a heart attack). The Court found that the Medical Device Amendments of 1976 had included a preemption provision and that the device had passed the U.S. Food and Drug Administration's rigorous premarket approval process. Therefore, the Court ruled that the federal regulation of medical devices preempted the injured party's state common law claims for negligence, strict liability, and implied warranty[13] (see Chapters 7 and 22).

The Taxing and Spending Powers

Article I, Section 8, of the U.S. Constitution provides that Congress has the "Power to lay and collect Taxes, Duties, Imposts, and Excises." Section 8 further requires uniformity in taxation among the states, and thus Congress may not tax some states while exempting others. Traditionally, if Congress attempted to regulate indirectly, by taxation, an area over which it had no authority, the courts would invalidate the tax. Today, however, if a tax measure is reasonable, it generally is held to be within the national taxing power. Moreover, the expansive interpretation of the commerce clause almost always provides a basis for sustaining a federal tax.

Article I, Section 8, also gives Congress its spending power—the power "to pay the Debts and provide for the common Defence and general Welfare of the United States." Congress can spend revenues not only to carry out its expressed powers but also to promote any objective it deems worthwhile, so long as it does not violate the Bill of Rights. The spending power necessarily involves policy choices, with which taxpayers may disagree.

SECTION 2
BUSINESS AND THE BILL OF RIGHTS

The importance of a written declaration of the rights of individuals eventually caused the first Congress of the United States to submit twelve amendments to the U.S. Constitution to the states for approval. Ten of these amendments, commonly known as the **Bill of Rights,** were adopted in 1791 and embody a series of protections for the individual against various types of interference by the federal government.[14] The protections guaranteed by these ten amendments are summarized in Exhibit 4–1 on the following page.[15] Some of these constitutional protections apply to business entities as well. For example, corporations exist as separate legal entities, or *legal persons,* and enjoy many of the same rights and privileges as *natural persons* do.

Limits on Federal and State Governmental Actions

As originally intended, the Bill of Rights limited only the powers of the national government. Over time, however, the United States Supreme Court "incorporated" most of these rights into the protections against state actions afforded by the Fourteenth Amendment to the Constitution. That amendment, passed in 1868 after the Civil War, provides, in part, that "[n]o State shall . . . deprive any person of life, liberty, or property, without due process of law." Starting in 1925, the Supreme Court began to define various rights and liberties guaranteed in the U.S. Constitution as constituting "due process of law," which was required of state governments under the Fourteenth Amendment. Today, most of the rights and liberties set forth in the Bill of Rights apply to state governments as well as the national government. In other words, neither the federal government nor state governments can deprive persons of those rights and liberties.

The rights secured by the Bill of Rights are not absolute. As you can see in Exhibit 4–1 on the next page, many of the rights guaranteed by the first ten amendments are set forth in very general terms. For example, the Second Amendment states that people have a right to keep and bear arms, but it does not explain the extent of this right. As the Supreme Court noted in 2008, this does not mean that people can "keep and carry any weapon whatsoever in any manner whatsoever and for whatever purpose."[16] Legislatures can prohibit the carrying of concealed weapons or certain types of weapons, such as machine guns. Ultimately, it is the United States Supreme Court, as the final interpreter of the Constitution, that gives meaning to these rights and determines their boundaries.

Freedom of Speech

A democratic form of government cannot survive unless people can freely voice their political opinions and criticize government actions or policies.

---

13. *Riegel v. Medtronic, Inc.,* 552 U.S. 312, 128 S.Ct. 999, 169 L.Ed.2d 892 (2008).
14. Another of these proposed amendments was ratified more than two hundred years later (in 1992) and became the Twenty-seventh Amendment to the Constitution. See Appendix B.

15. See the Constitution in Appendix B for the complete text of each amendment.
16. *District of Columbia v. Heller,* ___ U.S. ___, 128 S.Ct. 2783, 171 L.Ed.2d 637 (2008).

EXHIBIT 4–1 • Protections Guaranteed by the Bill of Rights

First Amendment: Guarantees the freedoms of religion, speech, and the press and the rights to assemble peaceably and to petition the government.

Second Amendment: States that the right of the people to keep and bear arms shall not be infringed.

Third Amendment: Prohibits, in peacetime, the lodging of soldiers in any house without the owner's consent.

Fourth Amendment: Prohibits unreasonable searches and seizures of persons or property.

Fifth Amendment: Guarantees the rights to indictment by grand jury, to due process of law, and to fair payment when private property is taken for public use; prohibits compulsory self-incrimination and double jeopardy (being tried again for an alleged crime for which one has already stood trial).

Sixth Amendment: Guarantees the accused in a criminal case the right to a speedy and public trial by an impartial jury and with counsel. The accused has the right to cross-examine witnesses against him or her and to solicit testimony from witnesses in his or her favor.

Seventh Amendment: Guarantees the right to a trial by jury in a civil case involving at least twenty dollars.[a]

Eighth Amendment: Prohibits excessive bail and fines, as well as cruel and unusual punishment.

Ninth Amendment: Establishes that the people have rights in addition to those specified in the Constitution.

Tenth Amendment: Establishes that those powers neither delegated to the federal government nor denied to the states are reserved to the states and to the people.

a. Twenty dollars was forty days' pay for the average person when the Bill of Rights was written.

Freedom of speech, particularly political speech, is thus a prized right, and traditionally the courts have protected this right to the fullest extent possible.

Symbolic speech—gestures, movements, articles of clothing, and other forms of expressive conduct—is also given substantial protection by the courts. For example, the Supreme Court has held that the burning of the American flag as part of a peaceful protest is a constitutionally protected form of expression.[17] Similarly, wearing a T-shirt with a photo of a presidential candidate is a constitutionally protected form of expression.

REASONABLE RESTRICTIONS Expression—oral, written, or symbolized by conduct—is subject to reasonable restrictions. A balance must be struck between a government's obligation to protect its citizens and those citizens' exercise of their rights. Reasonableness is analyzed on a case-by-case basis. If a restriction imposed by the government is content neutral, then a court may allow it. To be content neutral, the restriction must be aimed at combatting some societal problem, such as crime, and not be aimed at suppressing the expressive conduct or its message. Courts have often protected nude dancing as a form of symbolic expression but typically allow content-neutral laws that ban all public nudity.

CASE IN POINT Ria Ora was charged with dancing nude at an annual "anti-Christmas" protest in

Harvard Square in Cambridge, Massachusetts, under a statute banning public displays of open and gross lewdness. Ora argued that the statute was overbroad and unconstitutional, and a trial court agreed. On appeal, a state appellate court upheld the statute as constitutional in situations in which there was an unsuspecting or unwilling audience.[18]

CORPORATE POLITICAL SPEECH Political speech by corporations also falls within the protection of the First Amendment. For example, many years ago the United States Supreme Court struck down as unconstitutional a Massachusetts statute that prohibited corporations from making political contributions or expenditures that individuals were permitted to make.[19] Similarly, the Court has held that a law forbidding a corporation from including inserts with its bills to express its views on controversial issues violates the First Amendment.[20] Corporate political speech continues to be given significant protection under the First Amendment. For example, in 2010 the Court overturned a twenty-year-old precedent when it ruled that corporations can spend freely to support or oppose candidates for president and Congress.[21]

---

17. *Texas v. Johnson,* 491 U.S. 397, 109 S.Ct. 2533, 105 L.Ed.2d 342 (1989).

18. *Commonwealth v. Ora,* 451 Mass. 125, 883 N.E.2d 1217 (2008).

19. *First National Bank of Boston v. Bellotti,* 435 U.S. 765, 98 S.Ct. 1407, 55 L.Ed.2d 707 (1978).

20. *Consolidated Edison Co. v. Public Service Commission,* 447 U.S. 530, 100 S.Ct. 2326, 65 L.Ed.2d 319 (1980).

21. *Citizens United v. Federal Election Commission,* ___ U.S. ___, 130 S.Ct. 876, ___ L.Ed.2d ___ (2010).

COMMERCIAL SPEECH The courts also give substantial protection to *commercial speech,* which consists of communications—primarily advertising and marketing—made by business firms that involve only their commercial interests. The protection given to commercial speech under the First Amendment is less extensive than that afforded to noncommercial speech, however. A state may restrict certain kinds of advertising, for example, in the interest of preventing consumers from being misled. States also have a legitimate interest in roadside beautification and therefore may impose restraints on billboard advertising. For example, in one Florida case, the court found that a law preventing a nude dancing establishment from billboard advertising was constitutionally permissible because it directly advanced a substantial government interest in highway beautification and safety.[22]

Generally, a restriction on commercial speech will be considered valid as long as it meets three criteria: (1) it must seek to implement a substantial government interest, (2) it must directly advance that interest, and (3) it must go no further than necessary to accomplish its objective.

At issue in the following case was whether a government agency had unconstitutionally restricted commercial speech when it prohibited the inclusion of a certain illustration on beer labels.

------

22. *Café Erotica v. Florida Department of Transportation,* 830 So.2d 181 (Fla.App. 1 Dist. 2002); review denied by *Café Erotica/We Dare to Bare v. Florida Department of Transportation,* 845 So.2d 888 (Fla. 2003).

CASE 4.2
Bad Frog Brewery, Inc. v. New York State Liquor Authority

United States Court of Appeals, Second Circuit, 134 F.3d 87 (1998).
www.findlaw.com/casecode/index.html[a]

BACKGROUND AND FACTS • Bad Frog Brewery, Inc., makes and sells alcoholic beverages. Some of the beverages feature labels that display a drawing of a frog making the gesture generally known as "giving the finger." Bad Frog's authorized New York distributor, Renaissance Beer Company, applied to the New York State Liquor Authority (NYSLA) for brand label approval, as required by state law before the beer could be sold in New York. The NYSLA denied the application, in part, because "the label could appear in grocery and convenience stores, with obvious exposure on the shelf to children of tender age." Bad Frog filed a suit in a federal district court against the NYSLA, asking for, among other things, an injunction against the denial of the application. The court granted summary judgment in favor of the NYSLA. Bad Frog appealed to the U.S. Court of Appeals for the Second Circuit.

IN THE LANGUAGE OF THE COURT
Jon O. *NEWMAN,* Circuit Judge:
* * * *

* * * To support its asserted power to ban Bad Frog's labels [NYSLA advances] * * * the State's interest in "protecting children from vulgar and profane advertising" * * * .

[This interest is] substantial * * * . *States have a compelling interest in protecting the physical and psychological well-being of minors* * * * . [Emphasis added.]
* * * *

* * * NYSLA endeavors to advance the state interest in preventing exposure of children to vulgar displays by taking only the limited step of barring such displays from the labels of alcoholic beverages. *In view of the wide currency of vulgar displays throughout contemporary society, including comic books targeted directly at children, barring such displays from labels for alcoholic beverages cannot realistically be expected to reduce children's exposure to such displays to any significant degree.* [Emphasis added.]

* * * If New York decides to make a substantial effort to insulate children from vulgar displays in some significant sphere of activity, at least with respect to materials likely to be seen by

------

a. Under the heading "US Court of Appeals," click on "2nd Circuit Court of Appeals." Enter "Bad Frog Brewery" in the "Party Name Search" box and click on "search." On the resulting page, click on the case name to access the opinion.

CASE CONTINUES ▶

CASE 4.2 CONTINUED ➧ children, NYSLA's label prohibition might well be found to make a justifiable contribution to the material advancement of such an effort, but its currently isolated response to the perceived problem, applicable only to labels on a product that children cannot purchase, does not suffice. * * * A state must demonstrate that its commercial speech limitation is part of a substantial effort to advance a valid state interest, not merely the removal of a few grains of offensive sand from a beach of vulgarity.

* * * *

* * * Even if we were to assume that the state materially advances its asserted interest by shielding children from viewing the Bad Frog labels, it is plainly excessive to prohibit the labels from all use, including placement on bottles displayed in bars and taverns where parental supervision of children is to be expected. Moreover, to whatever extent NYSLA is concerned that children will be harmfully exposed to the Bad Frog labels when wandering without parental supervision around grocery and convenience stores where beer is sold, that concern could be less intrusively dealt with by placing restrictions on the permissible locations where the appellant's products may be displayed within such stores.

DECISION AND REMEDY • *The U.S. Court of Appeals for the Second Circuit reversed the judgment of the district court and remanded the case for the entry of a judgment in favor of Bad Frog. The NYSLA's ban on the use of the labels lacked a "reasonable fit" with the state's interest in shielding minors from vulgarity, and the NYSLA did not adequately consider alternatives to the ban.*

WHAT IF THE FACTS WERE DIFFERENT? • *If Bad Frog had sought to use the offensive label to market toys instead of beer, would the court's ruling likely have been the same? Why or why not?*

THE LEGAL ENVIRONMENT DIMENSION • *Whose interests are advanced by the banning of certain types of advertising?*

UNPROTECTED SPEECH The United States Supreme Court has made it clear that certain types of speech will not be protected under the First Amendment. Speech that violates criminal laws (threatening speech and pornography, for example) is not constitutionally protected. Other unprotected speech includes *fighting words* (speech that is likely to incite others to respond violently).

Speech that harms the good reputation of another, or defamatory speech (see Chapter 6), also is not protected under the First Amendment. To constitute defamation, the speech in question must be an assertion of fact and not merely an opinion. Unlike an opinion, a statement of purported fact can be proved true or false.

Obscene Speech. The First Amendment, as interpreted by the Supreme Court, also does not protect obscene speech. Establishing an objective definition of obscene speech has proved difficult, however, and the Court has grappled from time to time with this problem. In *Miller v. California*,[23] the Supreme Court created a test for legal obscenity, including a set of requirements that must be met for material to be legally obscene. Under this test, material is obscene if (1) the average person finds that it

violates contemporary community standards; (2) the work taken as a whole appeals to a prurient (arousing or obsessive) interest in sex; (3) the work shows patently offensive sexual conduct; and (4) the work lacks serious redeeming literary, artistic, political, or scientific merit.

Because community standards vary widely, the *Miller* test has had inconsistent applications, and obscenity remains a constitutionally unsettled issue. Numerous state and federal statutes make it a crime to disseminate obscene materials, including child pornography.

Online Obscenity. In 2000, Congress enacted the Children's Internet Protection Act (CIPA),[24] which requires public schools and libraries to install **filtering software** on computers to keep children from accessing adult content. Such software is designed to prevent persons from viewing certain Web sites based on a site's Internet address or its **meta tags,** or key words. The CIPA was challenged on constitutional grounds, but in 2003 the Supreme Court held that the act does not violate the First Amendment. The Court concluded that because libraries can disable the filters for any patrons who ask, the system is reasonably flexible

---

23. 413 U.S. 15, 93 S.Ct. 2607, 37 L.Ed.2d 419 (1973).

24. 17 U.S.C. Sections 1701–1741.

and does not burden free speech to an unconstitutional extent.[25]

Due to the difficulties of policing the Internet as well as the constitutional complexities of prohibiting online obscenity through legislation, online obscenity remains a continuing problem in the United States (and worldwide). In 2005, the Federal Bureau of Investigation established an Anti-Porn Squad to target and prosecute companies that distribute child pornography in cyberspace. The Federal Communications Commission has also established new obscenity regulations for television networks. See this chapter's *Insight into Ethics* feature for a discussion of some problems surrounding virtual child pornography.

---

25. *United States v. American Library Association*, 539 U.S. 194, 123 S.Ct. 2297, 156 L.Ed.2d 221 (2003).

INSIGHT INTO ETHICS
Is It Illegal to Distribute Virtual Pornography?

Millions of pornographic images of children are available on the Internet. Some are images of actual children engaged in sexual activity. Others are virtual (computer-generated) pornography—that is, images made to look like children engaged in sexual acts. Whereas child pornography is illegal, the Supreme Court has ruled that virtual pornography is legally protected under the First Amendment because it does not involve the exploitation of real children.[a]

This ruling and the difficulty in distinguishing between real and virtual pornography have created problems for prosecutors. Before they can convict someone of disseminating child pornography on the Internet, they must prove that the images depict real children. To help remedy this problem, Congress enacted the Protect Act of 2003 (here, *Protect* stands for "Prosecutorial Remedies and Other Tools to end the Exploitation of Children Today").[b]

The Protect Act's Pandering Provisions

One of the Protect Act's many provisions prohibits misrepresenting virtual child pornography as actual child pornography. The act's "pandering" provision makes it a crime to knowingly advertise, present, distribute, or solicit "any material or purported material in a manner that reflects the belief, or that is intended to cause another to believe, that the material or purported material" is illegal child pornography.[c] Thus, it may be a crime to intentionally distribute virtual child pornography.

This "pandering" provision was challenged in a 2008 case, *United States v. Williams*.[d] The defendant, Michael Williams, sent a message to an Internet chat room that read "Dad of Toddler has 'good' pics of her an [sic] me for swap of your toddler pics." A law enforcement agent responded by sending Williams a private message that contained photos of a college-aged female, which were computer altered to look like photos of a ten-year-old girl. Williams requested explicit photos of the girl, but the agent did not respond. After that, Williams sent another public message that accused the agent of being a cop and included a hyperlink containing seven pictures of minors engaging in sexually explicit conduct.

Williams was arrested and charged with possession of child pornography and pandering material that appeared to be child pornography. He claimed that the Protect Act's pandering provision was unconstitutionally overbroad and vague. (He later pleaded guilty to the charges but preserved the issue of constitutionality for appeal.)

Is the Protect Act Constitutional?

On appeal, the federal appellate court held that the pandering provision of the Protect Act was unconstitutional because it criminalized speech regarding child pornography. The United States Supreme Court reversed that decision, ruling that the Protect Act was neither unconstitutionally overbroad nor impermissibly vague. The Court held that the statute was valid because it does not prohibit a substantial amount of protected speech. Rather, the act generally prohibits offers to provide, and requests to obtain, child pornography—both of which are unprotected speech. Thus, the act's pandering provision remedied the constitutional defects of its predecessor, which had made it illegal to possess virtual child pornography.

---

a. *Ashcroft v. Free Speech Coalition*, 553 U.S. 234, 122 S.Ct. 1389, 152 L.Ed.2d 403 (2002).
b. 18 U.S.C. Section 2252A(a)(5)(B).
c. 18 U.S.C. Section 2252A(a)(3)(B).
d. 535 U.S. 285, 128 S.Ct. 1830, 170 L.Ed.2d 650 (2008).

CRITICAL THINKING

INSIGHT INTO THE LEGAL ENVIRONMENT
Why should it be illegal to "pander" virtual child pornography when it is not illegal to possess it?

Freedom of Religion

The First Amendment states that the government may neither establish any religion nor prohibit the free exercise of religious practices. The first part of this constitutional provision is referred to as the **establishment clause,** and the second part is known as the **free exercise clause.** Government action, both federal and state, must be consistent with this constitutional mandate.

THE ESTABLISHMENT CLAUSE The establishment clause prohibits the government from establishing a state-sponsored religion, as well as from passing laws that promote (aid or endorse) religion or that show a preference for one religion over another. Although the establishment clause involves the separation of church and state, it does not require a complete separation. Rather, it requires the government to accommodate religions. Federal or state laws that do not promote or place a significant burden on religion are constitutional even if they have some impact on religion. For a government law or policy to be constitutional, it must not have the primary effect of promoting or inhibiting religion.

Can a secular court resolve an internal church dispute over property ownership without becoming impermissibly entangled with questions of religion? The court in the following case faced that question.

CASE 4.3
In re Episcopal Church Cases

California Supreme Court, 45 Cal.4th 467, 87 Cal.Rptr.3d 275 (2009).

BACKGROUND AND FACTS • The Episcopal Church of the United States is divided into regions called dioceses. In 2003, an openly gay man was ordained as bishop of an Episcopal diocese in New Hampshire. Some members of St. James Parish—an Episcopal parish in Los Angeles, California—did not agree with this ordination. The parish's vestry (a board of elected laypersons that, with a rector, governs an Episcopal parish) voted to end its affiliation with the Episcopal Church and to affiliate with the Anglican Church of Uganda. After the disaffiliation, a dispute arose as to who owned the church building that the parish used for worship and the property on which the building stands. To resolve this dispute, the Episcopal Church and others filed a suit in a California state court against St. James and others, with both sides claiming ownership. The court ruled that the parish owned the building and the property, but a state intermediate appellate court reversed this judgment. St. James appealed to the California Supreme Court, arguing, in part, that the parish's name was on the deed to the property.

IN THE LANGUAGE OF THE COURT
CHIN, J. [Justice]
* * * *

* * * State courts must not decide questions of religious doctrine; those are for the church to resolve. Accordingly, if resolution of a property dispute involves a point of doctrine, the court must defer to the position of the highest ecclesiastical authority that has decided the point. *But to the extent the court can resolve a property dispute without reference to church doctrine, it should apply neutral principles of law. The court should consider sources such as the deeds to the property in dispute, * * * the general church's constitution, canons, and rules, and relevant statutes * * * .* [Emphasis added.]
* * * *

St. James Parish holds * * * title to the property in question. That is the fact that defendants rely on most heavily in claiming ownership. On the other hand, from the beginning of its existence, St. James Parish promised to be bound by the constitution and canons of the Episcopal Church. Such commitment is found in the original application to the higher church authorities to organize as a parish * * * .
* * * *

* * * The Episcopal Church's adoption of Canon I.7.4 * * * strongly supports the conclusion that, once defendants left the general church, the property reverted to the general church.
* * * *

[A California state statute] permits the governing instruments of the general church to create an express trust in church property, which Canon I.7.4 does. * * * This statute also compels

CASE 4.3 CONTINUED ➡ the conclusion that the general church owns the property now that defendants have left the general church.

* * * *

Defendants state that, over the years, St. James Parish "purchased additional parcels of property in its own name, with funds donated exclusively by its members." They contend that it would be unjust and contrary to the intent of the members * * * to cause the local parish to "lose its property simply because it has changed its spiritual affiliation." But the matter is not so clear. * * * Did they act over the years intending to contribute to a church that was part of the Episcopal Church or to contribute to St. James Parish even if it later joined a different church? It is impossible to say for sure. Probably different contributors over the years would have had different answers if they had thought about it and were asked. The only intent a secular court can effectively discern is that expressed in legally cognizable documents.

* * * The individual defendants are free to disassociate themselves from the parish and the Episcopal Church and to affiliate themselves with another religious denomination. No court can interfere with or control such an exercise of conscience. The problem lies in defendants' efforts to take the church property with them. This they may not do.

DECISION AND REMEDY • *The California Supreme Court affirmed the appellate court's judgment. The state supreme court applied "neutral principles of law" and concluded that the Episcopal Church, not St. James Parish, owned the property in question.*

THE LEGAL ENVIRONMENT DIMENSION • *Should the court have considered whether the Episcopal Church had abandoned or departed from the tenets of faith and practice that it had held at the time of St. James's affiliation? Why or why not?*

WHAT IF THE FACTS WERE DIFFERENT? • *Suppose that before this property dispute was finally resolved, the church's rules were changed to declare that "all property is held in trust for the local churches." Would the result in this case have been different? Explain.*

THE FREE EXERCISE CLAUSE The free exercise clause guarantees that a person can hold any religious belief that she or he wants, or a person can have no religious belief. This constitutional guarantee generally prevents the government from compelling a person to do something that is contrary to her or his religious beliefs. (Note that the clause applies only to the government—not to individuals and private businesses. See Chapter 35 for a discussion of laws that promote religious freedom in the employment context.)

When religious practices work against public policy and the public welfare, though, the government can act. For example, the government can require that a child receive certain types of vaccinations or medical treatment if his or her life is in danger—regardless of the child's or parent's religious beliefs. When public safety is an issue, an individual's religious beliefs often have to give way to the government's interest in protecting the public. The government's interest must be sufficiently compelling, however.

CASE IN POINT A religious sect in New Mexico follows the practices of a Brazil-based church. Its members ingest hoasca tea as part of a ritual to connect with and better understand God. Hoasca tea, which is brewed from plants native to the Amazon rain forest, contains an illegal hallucinogenic drug. When federal drug agents confiscated the church's shipment of hoasca tea as it entered the country, the church filed a lawsuit claiming that the government had violated its members' right to freely exercise their religion. Ultimately, the Supreme Court ruled that the government had failed to demonstrate a sufficiently compelling interest in barring the sect's sacramental use of hoasca.[26]

Searches and Seizures

The Fourth Amendment protects the "right of the people to be secure in their persons, houses, papers, and effects." Before searching or seizing private property, law enforcement officers must usually obtain a **search warrant**—an order from a judge or other public official authorizing the search or seizure.

SEARCH WARRANTS AND PROBABLE CAUSE To obtain a search warrant, law enforcement officers must

---

26. *Gonzales v. O Centro Espirita Beneficente Uniao Do Vegetal*, 546 U.S. 418, 126 S.Ct. 1211, 163 L.Ed.2d 1017 (2006).

convince a judge that they have reasonable grounds, or probable cause, to believe a search will reveal evidence of a specific illegality. To establish **probable cause,** the officers must have trustworthy evidence that would convince a reasonable person that the proposed search or seizure is more likely justified than not. Furthermore, the Fourth Amendment prohibits *general* warrants. It requires a particular description of whatever is to be searched or seized. General searches through a person's belongings are impermissible. The search cannot extend beyond what is described in the warrant. Although search warrants require specificity, if a search warrant is issued for a person's residence, items that are in that residence may be searched even if they do not belong to that individual.

CASE IN POINT Paycom Billing Services, Inc., an online payment service, stores vast amounts of customer credit-card information. Christopher Adjani, a former Paycom employee, threatened to sell Paycom's confidential client information if the company did not pay him $3 million. Pursuant to an investigation, the Federal Bureau of Investigation (FBI) obtained a search warrant to search Adjani's person, automobile, and residence, including computer equipment. When the FBI agents served the warrant, they discovered evidence of the criminal scheme in the e-mail communications on a computer in Adjani's residence that belonged to Adjani's live-in girlfriend. The court held that the search of the computer was proper given the involvement of computers in the alleged crime.[27]

SEARCHES AND SEIZURES IN THE BUSINESS CONTEXT Because of the strong governmental interest in protecting the public, a warrant normally is not required for seizures of spoiled or contaminated food. Nor are warrants required for searches of businesses in such highly regulated industries as liquor, guns, and strip mining. The standard used for highly regulated industries is sometimes applied in other contexts as well, such as screening for airline travel.

CASE IN POINT Christian Hartwell was attempting to board a flight from Philadelphia to Phoenix, Arizona. When he walked through the security checkpoint, he set off the alarm. Airport security took him aside and eventually discovered that he had two packages of crack cocaine in his pocket. When Hartwell was convicted of possession of drugs, he

appealed, claiming that the airport search was suspicionless and violated his Fourth Amendment rights. A federal appellate court held that airports can be treated as highly regulated industries and that suspicionless checkpoint screening of airline passengers is constitutional.[28]

Generally, government inspectors do not have the right to enter business premises without a warrant, although the standard of probable cause is not the same as that required in nonbusiness contexts. The existence of a general and neutral enforcement plan will normally justify issuance of the warrant. Lawyers and accountants frequently possess the business records of their clients, and inspecting these documents while they are out of the hands of their true owners also requires a warrant.

Self-Incrimination

The Fifth Amendment guarantees that no person "shall be compelled in any criminal case to be a witness against himself." Thus, in any federal or state (because the due process clause extends the protection to state courts) proceeding, an accused person cannot be forced to give testimony that might subject him or her to any criminal prosecution.

The Fifth Amendment's guarantee against self-incrimination extends only to natural persons. Therefore, neither corporations nor partnerships receive Fifth Amendment protection. When a partnership is required to produce business records, it must do so even if the information provided incriminates the individual partners of the firm. In contrast, sole proprietors and sole practitioners (those who fully own their businesses) cannot be compelled to produce their business records. These individuals have full protection against self-incrimination because they function in only one capacity; there is no separate business entity.

━━━◄ **SECTION 3** ►━━━
DUE PROCESS AND EQUAL PROTECTION

Other constitutional guarantees of great significance to Americans are mandated by the *due process clauses* of the Fifth and Fourteenth Amendments and the *equal protection clause* of the Fourteenth Amendment.

---

27. *United States v. Adjani,* 452 F.3d 1140 (9th Cir. 2006); *cert.* denied, 549 U.S. 1025, 127 S.Ct. 568, 166 L.Ed.2d 420 (2006).

28. *United States v. Hartwell,* 436 F.3d 174 (3d Cir. 2006).

Due Process

Both the Fifth and Fourteenth Amendments provide that no person shall be deprived "of life, liberty, or property, without due process of law." The **due process clause** of these constitutional amendments has two aspects—procedural and substantive. Note that the due process clause applies to "legal persons" (that is, corporations), as well as to individuals.

PROCEDURAL DUE PROCESS *Procedural* due process requires that any government decision to take life, liberty, or property must be made equitably; that is, the government must give a person proper notice and an opportunity to be heard. Fair procedures must be used in determining whether a person will be subjected to punishment or have some burden imposed on her or him. Fair procedure has been interpreted as requiring that the person have at least an opportunity to object to a proposed action before an impartial, neutral decision maker (which need not be a judge). Thus, for example, if a driver's license is construed as a property interest, the state must provide some sort of opportunity for the driver to object before suspending or terminating the person's license.

SUBSTANTIVE DUE PROCESS *Substantive* due process protects an individual's life, liberty, or property against certain government actions regardless of the fairness of the procedures used to implement them. Substantive due process limits what the government may do in its legislative and executive capacities. Legislation must be fair and reasonable in content and must further a legitimate governmental objective. Only when state conduct is arbitrary, or shocks the conscience, however, will it rise to the level of violating substantive due process.[29]

If a law or other governmental action limits a fundamental right, the state must have a legitimate and compelling interest to justify its action. Fundamental rights include interstate travel, privacy, voting, marriage and family, and all First Amendment rights. Thus, a state must have a substantial reason for taking any action that infringes on a person's free speech rights.

In situations not involving fundamental rights, a law or action does not violate substantive due process if it rationally relates to any legitimate government purpose. Under this test, almost any business regulation will be upheld as reasonable.

Equal Protection

Under the Fourteenth Amendment, a state may not "deny to any person within its jurisdiction the equal protection of the laws." The United States Supreme Court has interpreted the due process clause of the Fifth Amendment to make the **equal protection clause** applicable to the federal government as well. Equal protection means that the government cannot enact laws that treat similarly situated individuals differently.

Both substantive due process and equal protection require review of the substance of the law or other governmental action rather than review of the procedures used. When a law or action limits the liberty of all persons to do something, it may violate substantive due process; when a law or action limits the liberty of some persons but not others, it may violate the equal protection clause. Thus, for example, if a law prohibits all advertising on the sides of trucks, it raises a substantive due process question; if it makes an exception to allow truck owners to advertise their own businesses, it raises an equal protection issue.

In an equal protection inquiry, when a law or action distinguishes between or among individuals, the basis for the distinction, or classification, is examined. Depending on the classification, the courts apply different levels of scrutiny, or "tests," to determine whether the law or action violates the equal protection clause. The courts use one of three standards: strict scrutiny, intermediate scrutiny, or the "rational basis" test.

STRICT SCRUTINY If a law or action prohibits or inhibits some persons from exercising a fundamental right, the law or action will be subject to "strict scrutiny" by the courts. Under this standard, the classification must be necessary to promote a *compelling state interest.* Also, if the classification is based on a *suspect trait*—such as race, national origin, or citizenship status—it must be necessary to promote a compelling government interest.[30]

Compelling state interests include remedying past unconstitutional or illegal discrimination but do not include correcting the general effects of "society's discrimination." For instance, for a city to give preference to minority applicants in awarding

---

29. See, for example, *Breen v. Texas A&M University,* 485 F.3d 325 (5th Cir. 2007); *Hart v. City of Little Rock,* 432 F.3d 801 (8th Cir. 2005); and *County of Sacramento v. Lewis,* 523 U.S. 833, 118 S.Ct. 1708, 140 L.Ed.2d 1043 (1998).

30. See, for example, *Johnson v. California,* 543 U.S. 499, 125 S.Ct. 1141, 160 L.Ed.2d 949 (2005).

construction contracts, it normally must identify past unconstitutional or illegal discrimination against minority construction firms. Because the policy is based on suspect traits (race and national origin), it will violate the equal protection clause *unless* it is necessary to promote a compelling state interest. Generally, few laws or actions survive strict-scrutiny analysis by the courts.

INTERMEDIATE SCRUTINY Another standard, that of *intermediate scrutiny,* is applied in cases involving discrimination based on gender or legitimacy. Laws using these classifications must be *substantially related to important government objectives.* For example, an important government objective is preventing illegitimate teenage pregnancies. Therefore, because males and females are not similarly situated in this regard—only females can become pregnant—a law that punishes men but not women for statutory rape will be upheld, even though it treats men and women unequally.

The state also has an important objective in establishing time limits (called *statutes of limitation*) for how long after an event a particular type of action can be brought. Such limits prevent persons from bringing fraudulent and stale (outdated) claims.

THE "RATIONAL BASIS" TEST In matters of economic or social welfare, a classification will be considered valid if there is any conceivable *rational basis* on which the classification might relate to a legitimate government interest. It is almost impossible for a law or action to fail the rational basis test. Thus, for example, a city ordinance that in effect prohibits all pushcart vendors, except a specific few, from operating in a particular area of the city will be upheld if the city provides a rational basis—such as reducing the traffic in the particular area—for the ordinance. In contrast, a law that provides unemployment benefits only to people over six feet tall would clearly fail the rational basis test because it could not further any legitimate government objective.

SECTION 4
PRIVACY RIGHTS

The U.S. Constitution does not explicitly mention a general right to privacy. In a 1928 Supreme Court case, *Olmstead v. United States,*[31] Justice Louis

Brandeis stated in his dissent that the right to privacy is "the most comprehensive of rights and the right most valued by civilized men." The majority of the justices at that time, however, did not agree with Brandeis. It was not until the 1960s that the Supreme Court endorsed the view that the Constitution protects individual privacy rights. In a landmark 1965 case, *Griswold v. Connecticut,*[32] the Supreme Court held that a constitutional right to privacy was implied by the First, Third, Fourth, Fifth, and Ninth Amendments.

Federal Statutes Affecting Privacy Rights

In the 1960s, Americans were sufficiently alarmed by the accumulation of personal information in government files that they pressured Congress to pass laws permitting individuals to access their files. Congress responded in 1966 with the Freedom of Information Act, which allows any person to request copies of any information on her or him contained in federal government files. In 1974, Congress passed the Privacy Act, which also gives persons the right to access such information. Since then, Congress has passed numerous other laws protecting individuals' privacy rights with respect to financial transactions, electronic communications, and other activities in which personal information may be gathered and stored by organizations.

Since the 1990s, one of the major concerns of individuals has been how to protect privacy rights in cyberspace and to safeguard private information that may be revealed online (including credit-card numbers and financial information). The increasing value of personal information for online marketers—who are willing to pay a high price for such information to those who collect it—has exacerbated the situation.

PRETEXTING A *pretext* is a false motive put forth to hide the real motive, and *pretexting* is the process of obtaining information by false means. Pretexters may try to obtain personal data by claiming that they are taking a survey for a research firm, a political party, or even a charity. Congress passed the Gramm-Leach-Bliley Act,[33] which made pretexting

---

31. 277 U.S. 438, 48 S.Ct. 564, 72 L.Ed. 944 (1928).

32. 381 U.S. 479, 85 S.Ct. 1678, 14 L.Ed.2d 510 (1965).
33. Also known as the Financial Services Modernization Act, Pub. L. No. 106-102 (1999), 113 Stat. 1338, codified in numerous sections of 12 U.S.C.A. and 15 U.S.C.A.

to obtain financial information illegal. Initially, it was not clear whether that law prohibited lying to obtain *nonfinancial* information for purposes other than identity theft.

This gray area in the law led to a highly publicized scandal involving Patricia C. Dunn, who was then chair of Hewlett-Packard. To find out who had leaked confidential company information to the press, Dunn hired private investigators who used false pretenses to access individuals' personal cell phone records. Dunn claimed that she had not been aware of the investigators' methods and had assumed that they had obtained the information from a public record. Although she was indicted in 2006 for her role in the pretexting, the criminal charges were later dropped. Several civil lawsuits followed. In 2007, the company paid $14.5 million in fines to settle a lawsuit filed by the California attorney general. In 2008, Hewlett-Packard reached a settlement with the New York Times Company and three *BusinessWeek* magazine journalists in connection with the scandal.

To clarify the law on pretexting to gain access to phone records, Congress enacted the Telephone Records and Privacy Protection Act.[34] This act makes it a federal crime to pretend to be someone else or to make false representations for the purpose of obtaining another person's confidential phone records. The Federal Trade Commission investigates and prosecutes violators, who can be fined and sentenced to up to ten years in prison.

MEDICAL INFORMATION Responding to the growing need to protect the privacy of individuals' health records—particularly computerized records— Congress passed the Health Insurance Portability and Accountability Act (HIPAA) of 1996.[35] This act defines and limits the circumstances in which an individual's "protected health information" may be used or disclosed.

HIPAA also requires health-care providers and health-care plans, including certain employers who sponsor health plans, to inform patients of their privacy rights and of how their personal medical information may be used. The act also states that a person's medical records generally may not be used for purposes unrelated to health care—such

as marketing, for example—or disclosed to others without the individual's permission. Covered entities must formulate written privacy policies, designate privacy officials, limit access to computerized health data, physically secure medical records with lock and key, train employees and volunteers on their privacy policies, and sanction those who violate the policies.

THE USA PATRIOT ACT Today, individuals face additional concerns about government intrusions into their privacy. The USA Patriot Act was passed by Congress in the wake of the terrorist attacks of September 11, 2001, and then reauthorized in 2006.[36] The Patriot Act has given government officials increased authority to monitor Internet activities (such as e-mail and Web site visits) and to gain access to personal financial information and student information. Law enforcement officials may now track the telephone and e-mail communications of one party to find out the identity of the other party or parties. To gain access to these communications, the government must certify that the information likely to be obtained by such monitoring is relevant to an ongoing criminal investigation but does not need to provide proof of any wrongdoing.[37] Privacy advocates argue that this law adversely affects the constitutional rights of all Americans, and it has been widely criticized in the media.

Other Laws Affecting Privacy

State constitutions and statutes also protect individuals' privacy rights, often to a significant degree. Privacy rights are also protected under tort law (see Chapter 6). Additionally, the Federal Trade Commission has played an active role in protecting the privacy rights of online consumers (see Chapter 45). The protection of employees' privacy rights, particularly with respect to electronic monitoring practices, is an area of growing concern (see Chapter 34).

---

34. Pub. L. No. 109-476, (2007), 120 Stat. 3568, codified at 18 U.S.C.A. Section 1039.
35. HIPAA was enacted as Pub. L. No. 104-191 (1996) and is codified in 29 U.S.C.A. Sections 1181 *et seq.*

36. The Uniting and Strengthening America by Providing Appropriate Tools Required to Intercept and Obstruct Terrorism Act of 2001, also known as the USA Patriot Act, was enacted as Pub. L. No. 107-56 (2001) and reauthorized by Pub. L. No. 109-173 (2006).
37. See, for example, *American Civil Liberties Union v. National Security Agency,* 493 F.3d 644 (6th Cir. 2007), in which a federal appeals court upheld the government's warrantless monitoring of electronic communications.

REVIEWING

Constitutional Authority to Regulate Business

A state legislature enacted a statute that required any motorcycle operator or passenger on the state's highways to wear a protective helmet. Jim Alderman, a licensed motorcycle operator, sued the state to block enforcement of the law. Alderman asserted that the statute violated the equal protection clause because it placed requirements on motorcyclists that were not imposed on other motorists. Using the information presented in the chapter, answer the following questions.

1. Why does this statute raise equal protection issues instead of substantive due process concerns?

2. What are the three levels of scrutiny that the courts use in determining whether a law violates the equal protection clause?

3. Which standard of scrutiny, or test, would apply to this situation? Why?

4. Applying this standard, or test, is the helmet statute constitutional? Why or why not?

DEBATE THIS: *Legislation aimed at "protecting people from themselves" concerns the individual as well as the public in general. Protective helmet laws are just one example of such legislation. Should individuals be allowed to engage in unsafe activities if they choose to do so?*

TERMS AND CONCEPTS

Bill of Rights 79
checks and balances 75
commerce clause 75
due process clause 87
equal protection clause 87

establishment clause 84
federal form of
    government 74
filtering software 82
free exercise clause 84
full faith and credit
    clause 75

meta tags 82
police powers 74
preemption 78
privileges and immunities
    clause 75

probable cause 86
search warrant 85
supremacy clause 78
symbolic speech 80

QUESTIONS AND CASE PROBLEMS

4–1. Commerce Clause A Georgia state law requires the use of contoured rear-fender mudguards on trucks and trailers operating within Georgia state lines. The statute further makes it illegal for trucks and trailers to use straight mudguards. In approximately thirty-five other states, straight mudguards are legal. Moreover, in Florida, straight mudguards are explicitly required by law. There is some evidence suggesting that contoured mudguards might be a little safer than straight mudguards. Discuss whether this Georgia statute violates any constitutional provisions.

4–2. QUESTION WITH SAMPLE ANSWER: Freedom of Religion.

Thomas worked in the nonmilitary operations of a large firm that produced both military and nonmilitary goods. When the company discontinued the production of nonmilitary

goods, Thomas was transferred to a plant producing military equipment. Thomas left his job, claiming that it violated his religious principles to participate in the manufacture of goods to be used in destroying life. In effect, he argued, the transfer to the military equipment plant forced him to quit his job. He was denied unemployment compensation by the state because he had not been effectively "discharged" by the employer but had voluntarily terminated his employment. Did the state's denial of unemployment benefits to Thomas violate the free exercise clause of the First Amendment? Explain.

• For a sample answer to Question 4–2, go to Appendix I at the end of this text.

4–3. Equal Protection With the objectives of preventing crime, maintaining property values, and preserving the quality of urban life, New York City enacted an ordinance to regulate the locations of commercial establishments that featured adult entertainment. The ordinance expressly applied to female, but not male, topless entertainment. Adele Buzzetti owned the Cozy Cabin, a New York City cabaret that featured female topless dancers. Buzzetti and an anonymous dancer filed a suit in a federal district court against the city, asking the court to block the enforcement of the ordinance. The plaintiffs argued, in part, that the ordinance violated the equal protection clause. Under the equal protection clause, what standard applies to the court's consideration of this ordinance? Under this test, how should the court rule? Why?

4–4. Freedom of Speech Henry Mishkoff is a Web designer whose firm does business as "Webfeats." When Taubman Co. began building a mall called "The Shops at Willow Bend" near Mishkoff's home, Mishkoff registered the domain name "shopsatwillowbend.com" and created a Web site with that address. The site featured information about the mall, a disclaimer indicating that Mishkoff's site was unofficial, and a link to the mall's official site. Taubman discovered Mishkoff's site and filed a suit in a federal district court against him. Mishkoff then registered various other names, including "taubmansucks.com," with links to a site documenting his battle with Taubman. (A Web name with a "sucks.com" moniker attached to it is known as a *complaint name*, and the process of registering and using such names is known as *cybergriping*.) Taubman asked the court to order Mishkoff to stop using all of these names. Should the court grant Taubman's request? On what basis might the court protect Mishkoff's use of the names? [*Taubman Co. v. Webfeats,* 319 F.3d 770 (6th Cir. 2003)]

4–5. CASE PROBLEM WITH SAMPLE ANSWER: Privacy.

*To protect the privacy of individuals identified in information systems maintained by federal agencies, the Privacy Act of 1974 regulates the use of the information. The statute provides for a minimum award of $1,000 for "actual damages sustained" caused by "intentional or willful actions" to the "person entitled to recovery." Buck Doe filed for certain disability benefits with an office of the U.S. Department of Labor (DOL). The application form asked for Doe's Social Security number, which the DOL used to identify his claim on documents sent to groups of claimants, their employers, and the lawyers involved in their cases. This disclosed Doe's Social Security number beyond the limits set by the Privacy Act. Doe filed a suit in a federal district court against the DOL, alleging that he was "torn . . . all to pieces" and "greatly concerned and worried" because of the disclosure of his Social Security number and its potentially "devastating" consequences. He did not offer any proof of actual injury, however. Should damages be awarded in such circumstances solely on the basis of the agency's conduct, or should proof of some actual injury be required? Why? [*Doe v. Chao,* 540 U.S. 614, 124 S.Ct. 1204, 157 L.Ed.2d 1122 (2004)]*

- To view a sample answer for Problem 4–5, go to this book's Web site at **www.cengage.com/blaw/clarkson**, select "Chapter 4," and click on "Case Problem with Sample Answer."

4–6. Supremacy Clause The Federal Communications Act of 1934 grants the right to govern all *interstate* telecommunications to the Federal Communications Commission (FCC) and the right to regulate all *intrastate* telecommunications to the states. The federal Telephone Consumer Protection Act of 1991, the Junk Fax Protection Act of 2005, and FCC rules permit a party to send unsolicited fax ads to recipients with whom the party has an "established business relationship" if those ads include an "opt-out" alternative. Section 17538.43 of California's Business and Professions Code (known as "SB 833") was enacted in 2005 to provide the citizens of California with greater protection than that afforded under federal law. SB 833 omits the "established business relationship" exception and requires a sender to obtain a recipient's express consent (an "opt-in" provision) before faxing an ad to that party into or out of California. The Chamber of Commerce of the United States filed a suit against Bill Lockyer, California's state attorney general, seeking to block the enforcement of SB 833. What principles support the plaintiff's position? How should the court resolve the issue? Explain. [*Chamber of Commerce of the United States v. Lockyer,* 463 F.3d 1076 (E.D.Cal. 2006)]

4–7. Freedom of Speech For decades, New York City has had to deal with the vandalism and defacement of public property caused by unauthorized graffiti. Among other attempts to stop the damage, in December 2005 the city banned the sale of aerosol spray-paint cans and broad-tipped indelible markers to persons under twenty-one years of age and prohibited them from possessing such items on property other than their own. By May 1, 2006, five people—all under age twenty-one—had been cited for violations of these regulations, and 871 individuals had been arrested for actually making graffiti. Artists who wished to create graffiti on legal surfaces, such as canvas, wood, and clothing, included college student Lindsey Vincenty, who was studying visual arts. Unable to buy her supplies in the city or to carry them in the city if she bought them elsewhere, Vincenty and others filed a suit in a federal district court on behalf of themselves and other young artists against Michael Bloomberg, the city's mayor, and others. The plaintiffs claimed that, among other things, the new rules violated their right to freedom of speech. They asked the court to enjoin the enforcement of the rules. Should the court grant this request? Why or why not? [*Vincenty v. Bloomberg,* 476 F.3d 74 (2d Cir. 2007)]

4–8. Due Process In 2006, at the Russ College of Engineering and Technology of Ohio University, a university investigative report found "rampant and flagrant plagiarism" in the theses of mechanical engineering graduate students. Faculty singled out for "ignoring their ethical responsibilities and contributing to an atmosphere of negligence toward issues of academic misconduct" included Jay Gunasekera, professor of mechanical engineering and chair of the department. These findings were publicized in a press conference on May 31. The university prohibited Gunasekera from advising graduate students. He filed a suit in a federal district court against Dennis Irwin, the dean of Russ College, and others, for violating his "due-process rights when they publicized accusations about his role in plagiarism by his graduate student advisees without providing him with a meaningful opportunity to clear his name" in public. Irwin asked the court to dismiss the suit. What does due process require in these circumstances? Why? [*Gunasekera v. Irwin*, 551 F.3d 461 (6th Cir. 2009)]

4–9. Commerce Clause Under the federal Sex Offender Registration and Notification Act (SORNA), sex offenders must register as sex offenders and update their registration when they travel from one state to another. David Hall, a convicted sex offender in New York, moved from New York to Virginia, lived there for part of a year, and then returned to New York. When he returned, he was charged with the federal offense of failing to register as a sex offender while in Virginia, as required by SORNA. In his defense, he claimed that SORNA was unconstitutional because Congress had no authority to criminalize interstate travel where no commerce was involved. The federal district court dismissed the indictment. The government appealed, contending that the statute is valid under the commerce clause. Does that contention seem reasonable? Why or why not? [*United States v. Hall*, 591 F.3d 83 (2d Cir. 2010)]

4–10. A QUESTION OF ETHICS: Defamation.

 Aric Toll owns and manages the Balboa Island Village Inn, a restaurant and bar in Newport Beach, California. Anne Lemen owns the "Island Cottage," a residence across an alley from the Inn. Lemen often complained to the authorities about excessive noise and the behavior of the Inn's customers, whom she called "drunks" and "whores." Lemen referred to Theresa Toll, Aric's wife, as "Madam Whore." Lemen told the Inn's bartender Ewa Cook that Cook "worked for Satan," was "Satan's wife," and was "going to have Satan's children." She told the Inn's neighbors that it was "a whorehouse" with "prostitution going on inside" and that it sold illegal drugs, sold alcohol to minors, made "sex videos," was involved in child pornography, had "Mafia connections," encouraged "lesbian activity," and stayed open until 6:00 A.M. Lemen also voiced her complaints to potential customers, and the Inn's sales dropped more than 20 percent. The Inn filed a suit in a California state court against Lemen, asserting defamation and other claims. [Balboa Island Village Inn, Inc. v. Lemen, 40 Cal.4th 1141, 156 P.3d 339 (2007)]

(a) Are Lemen's statements about the Inn's owners, customers, and activities protected by the U.S. Constitution? Should such statements be protected? In whose favor should the court rule? Why?

(b) Did Lemen behave unethically in the circumstances of this case? Explain.

LEGAL RESEARCH EXERCISES ON THE WEB

Go to this text's Web site at **www.cengage.com/blaw/clarkson**, select "Chapter 4," and click on "Practical Internet Exercises." There you will find the following Internet research exercises that you can perform to learn more about the topics covered in this chapter.

Practical Internet Exercise 4–1:   **Legal Perspective**
                                        Commercial Speech

Practical Internet Exercise 4–2:   **Management Perspective**
                                        Privacy Rights in Cyberspace

CHAPTER 5

Ethics and Business Decision Making

n the early part of the first decade of the 2000s, ethics scandals erupted throughout corporate America. Heads of major corporations (some of which no longer exist) were tried for fraud, conspiracy, conspiracy to commit securities fraud, grand larceny, and obstruction of justice. Former multimillionaires (and even billionaires) who once ran multinational corporations are now serving sentences in federal penitentiaries. The giant energy company Enron in particular dominated headlines. Its investors lost around $60 billion when the company ceased to exist.

Fast-forward to 2009. One man, Bernard Madoff, was convicted of bilking investors out of more than $50 billion through a Ponzi scheme[1] that he had perpetrated for decades. Madoff's victims included not only naïve retirees but also some of the world's biggest and best-known financial institutions, including the Royal Bank of Scotland, France's BNP Paribas, Spain's Banco Santander, and Japan's Nomura. But ethical lapses were not limited to Madoff. Ethical problems in many financial institutions contributed to the onset of the deepest recession since the Great Depression of the 1930s. Not only did some $9 trillion in investment capital evaporate, but millions of workers lost their jobs. The point is clear: the scope and scale of corporate unethical behavior, especially in the financial sector, skyrocketed in the first decade of the twenty-first century—with enormous repercussions for everyone.

The ethics scandals of the last fifteen years have taught businesspersons all over the world that business ethics cannot be taken lightly. Acting ethically in a business context can mean billions of dollars—made or lost—for corporations, shareholders, and employees and can have far-reaching effects on society and the global economy.

---

1. Ponzi schemes are a type of illegal pyramid scheme named after Charles Ponzi, who duped thousands of New England residents into investing in a postage-stamp speculation scheme in the 1920s.

SECTION 1
BUSINESS ETHICS

As you might imagine, business ethics is derived from the concept of ethics. **Ethics** can be defined as the study of what constitutes right or wrong behavior. It is a branch of philosophy focusing on morality and the way moral principles are derived. Ethics has to do with the fairness, justness, rightness, or wrongness of an action.

Business ethics focuses on what is right and wrong behavior in the business world. It has to do with how businesses apply moral and ethical principles to situations that arise in the workplace. Because business decision makers often address more complex ethical issues than they face in their personal lives, business ethics may be more complicated than personal ethics.

Why Is Business Ethics Important?

All of the corporate executives who are sitting behind bars could have avoided these outcomes had they engaged in ethical decision making during their careers. As a result of their crimes, all of their companies suffered losses, and some, such as Enron, were forced to enter bankruptcy, causing thousands of workers to lose their jobs. The corporations, shareholders, and employees who suffered because of those individuals' unethical and criminal behavior certainly paid a high price. Thus, an in-depth understanding of business ethics is important to the long-run viability of any corporation today.

It is also important to the well-being of individual officers and directors and to the firm's employees. Finally, unethical corporate decision making can negatively affect suppliers, consumers, the community, and society as a whole.

At the end of every unit in this book, a series of ethical issues will be presented in features called *Focus on Ethics*. In each of these unit-ending features, we expand on the concepts of business ethics that we present in this chapter.

The Moral Minimum

The minimum acceptable standard for ethical business behavior—known as the **moral minimum**—is normally considered to be compliance with the law In many corporate scandals, had most of the businesspersons involved simply followed the law, they would not have gotten into trouble. Note, though, that in the interest of preserving personal freedom, as well as for practical reasons, the law does not—and cannot—codify all ethical requirements.

As they make business decisions, businesspersons must remember that just because an action is legal does not necessarily make it ethical. For instance, no law specifies the salaries that publicly held corporations can pay their officers. Nevertheless, if a corporation pays its officers an excessive amount relative to other employees, or relative to what officers at other corporations are paid, the executives' compensation might be challenged as unethical. (Executive bonuses can also present ethical problems—see the discussion later in this chapter.)

"Gray Areas" in the Law

In many situations, business firms can predict with a fair amount of certainty whether a given action would be legal. For instance, firing an employee solely because of that person's race or gender would clearly violate federal laws prohibiting employment discrimination. In some situations, though, the legality of a particular action may be less clear. In part, this is because there are so many laws regulating business that it is increasingly possible to violate one of them without realizing it. The law also contains numerous "gray areas," making it difficult to predict with certainty how a court will apply a given law to a particular action.

In addition, many rules of law require a court to determine what is "foreseeable" or "reasonable" in a particular situation. Because a business has no way of predicting how a specific court will decide these issues, decision makers need to proceed with caution and evaluate an action and its consequences from an ethical perspective. The same problem often occurs in cases involving the Internet because it is often unclear how a court will apply existing laws in the context of cyberspace. Generally, if a company can demonstrate that it acted in good faith and responsibly under the circumstances, it has a better chance of successfully defending its action in court or before an administrative law judge in an agency hearing.

Short-Run Profit Maximization

Some people argue that a corporation's only goal should be profit maximization, which will be reflected in a higher market value. When all firms strictly adhere to the goal of profit maximization, resources tend to flow to where they are most highly valued by society. Ultimately, profit maximization, in theory, leads to the most efficient allocation of scarce resources.

Corporate executives and employees have to distinguish, though, between *short-run* and *long-run* profit maximization. In the short run, a company may increase its profits by continuing to sell a product, even though it knows that the product is defective. In the long run, however, because of lawsuits, large settlements, and bad publicity, such unethical conduct will cause profits to suffer. Thus, business ethics is consistent only with long-run profit maximization. An overemphasis on short-term profit maximization is the most common reason that ethical problems occur in business.

CASE IN POINT When the powerful narcotic painkiller OxyContin was first marketed, its manufacturer, Purdue Pharma, claimed that it was unlikely to lead to drug addiction or abuse. Internal company documents later showed that the company's executives knew that OxyContin could be addictive, but kept this risk a secret to boost sales and maximize short-term profits. In 2007, Purdue Pharma and three former executives pleaded guilty to criminal charges that they misled regulators, patients, and physicians about OxyContin's risks of addiction. Purdue Pharma agreed to pay $600 million in fines and other payments. The three former executives agreed to pay $34.5 million in fines and were barred from federal health programs for a period of fifteen years—a ruling that was upheld by an administrative law judge in 2009. Thus, the company's focus on maximizing profits in the short run led to unethical conduct that hurt profits in the long run.

The following case provides an example of unethical—and illegal—conduct that was designed to enhance a company's short-term outlook but in the end destroyed the firm.

CASE 5.1
Skilling v. United States
Supreme Court of the United States ___ U.S. ___, ___ S.Ct. ___, ___ L.Ed.2d ___ (2010).

COMPANY PROFILE • In the 1990s, Enron Corporation was an international, multibillion-dollar enterprise consisting of four businesses that bought and sold energy, owned energy networks, and bought and sold bandwidth capacity. "Wholesale," the division that bought and sold energy, was the most profitable and accounted for 90 percent of Enron's revenues. Jeffrey Skilling—Enron's president, its chief operating officer, and a member of its board of directors—boasted at a conference with financial analysts in January 2001 that Enron's retail energy and bandwidth sales divisions had "sustainable high earnings power." Skilling became Enron's chief executive officer in February 2001.

BACKGROUND AND FACTS • In August 2001, Jeffrey Skilling resigned his position as Enron's CEO. Four months later, Enron filed for bankruptcy. An investigation uncovered a conspiracy to deceive investors about Enron's finances to ensure that its stock price remained high. Among other things, Skilling had shifted more than $2 billion in losses from Enron's struggling divisions to Wholesale. He had overstated Enron's profits in telephone calls to investors and in press releases. To hide more losses, he had arranged deals between Enron's executives and third parties, which he falsely portrayed to Enron's accountants and to the Securities and Exchange Commission as producing income. Skilling was convicted in a federal district court of various crimes, including conspiracy to commit fraud to deprive Enron and its shareholders of the "honest services" of its employees. He was sentenced to 292 months in prison and three years of supervised release, and was ordered to pay $45 million in restitution. Skilling appealed, and the U.S. Court of Appeals for the Fifth Circuit affirmed the trial court's ruling. Skilling appealed to the United States Supreme Court, arguing, among other things, that the honest-services statute is unconstitutionally vague or, in the alternative, that his conduct did not fall within the statute's compass.

IN THE LANGUAGE OF THE COURT
Justice *GINSBURG* delivered the opinion of the Court.
* * * *
[In 1988,] Congress enacted a new statute "specifically to cover * * * the intangible right of honest services" [as a "scheme or artifice to defraud" in laws prohibiting mail and wire fraud].
* * * *
[Before 1988,] the "vast majority" of the honest-services cases involved offenders who, in violation of a fiduciary duty participated in bribery or kickback schemes.
* * * The honest-services doctrine had its genesis [origin] in prosecutions involving bribery allegations.
In view of this history, there is no doubt that Congress intended [the law] to reach *at least* bribes and kickbacks. Reading the statute to proscribe [rule out] a wider range of offensive conduct, we acknowledge, would raise the due process concerns underlying the vagueness doctrine. To preserve the statute without transgressing [breaching] constitutional limitations, we now hold that [the statute] criminalizes *only* the bribe-and-kickback core of the [case law prior to 1988]. [Emphases added by the Court.]
* * * *
The government did not, at any time, allege that Skilling solicited or accepted side payments from a third party in exchange for making * * * misrepresentations [concerning Enron's fiscal health]. It is therefore clear that, as we read [the statute], Skilling did not commit honest-services fraud.
Because the indictment alleged three objects of the conspiracy—honest-services wire fraud, money-or-property wire fraud, and securities fraud—Skilling's conviction is flawed. This determination, however, does not necessarily require reversal of the conspiracy conviction * * *. We leave this dispute for resolution on remand.

CASE CONTINUES ▶

CASE 5.1 CONTINUED ▶ **DECISION AND REMEDY** • *The United States Supreme Court vacated the appellate court's ruling that Skilling's actions had violated the honest-services statute. The Court remanded the case for further proceedings to determine how its decision would affect the other charges against Skilling.*

THE ETHICAL DIMENSION • *During Skilling's tenure at Enron, the mood among the employees must have been upbeat because the company's situation would have appeared "rosy." Is there anything unethical about this situation? Discuss.*

MANAGERIAL IMPLICATIONS • *Just because the Court has reduced the scope of the honest-services fraud doctrine does not mean that federal prosecutors will be unable to indict businesspersons who egregiously violate ethical business practices. There are more than four thousand federal crimes on the books today. Consequently, the federal government will continue to pursue actions that it deems are illegal business practices. The government will simply charge those who are its targets with other federal crimes.*

The Importance of Ethical Leadership

Talking about ethical business decision making is meaningless if management does not set standards. Furthermore, managers must apply the same standards to themselves as they do to the company's employees.

ATTITUDE OF TOP MANAGEMENT One of the most important ways to create and maintain an ethical workplace is for top management to demonstrate its commitment to ethical decision making. A manager who is not totally committed to an ethical workplace rarely succeeds in creating one. Management's behavior, more than anything else, sets the ethical tone of a firm. Employees take their cues from management. For example, an employee who observes a manager cheating on her expense account quickly learns that such behavior is acceptable.

Managers who set unrealistic production or sales goals increase the probability that employees will act unethically. If a sales quota can be met only through high-pressure, unethical sales tactics, employees will try to act "in the best interest of the company" and will continue to behave unethically.

A manager who looks the other way when he knows about an employee's unethical behavior also sets an example—one indicating that ethical transgressions will be accepted. Managers have found that discharging even one employee for ethical reasons has a tremendous impact as a deterrent to unethical behavior in the workplace.

BEHAVIOR OF OWNERS AND MANAGERS Business owners and managers sometimes take more active roles in fostering unethical and illegal conduct. This may indicate to their co-owners, co-managers, employees, and others that unethical business behavior will be tolerated.

Business owners' misbehavior can have negative consequences for themselves and their business. Not only can a court sanction the business owners and managers, but it can also issue an injunction that prevents them from engaging in similar patterns of conduct in the future.

CASE IN POINT Douglas and Brian Baum, along with their father, ran an asset recovery business. The Baums researched various unclaimed funds, tried to locate the rightful owners, and received either a finder's fee or the right to some or all of the funds recovered. The Baums convinced investors—through misrepresentation—to file a meritless lawsuit in a federal district court in Texas. The court later determined that the Baums had maliciously attempted to extort funds and sanctioned them for pretending to be lawyers, lying to the parties and the court, and generally abusing the judicial system. The judge also issued a permanent injunction against all three Baums to prohibit them from filing claims related to the same case without express permission from the judge. When the Baums continued their business in the same manner, the judge expanded the injunction to apply to all claims filed in Texas. The Baums appealed, claiming that the court lacked the power to expand the injunction. The appellate court ruled that federal courts have the power to enjoin (prevent) plaintiffs from future filings when those plaintiffs consistently abuse the court system and harass their opponents.[2]

The following case shows how a manager's sexist attitudes and actions affected the workplace environment. The case also underscores the limitations of the law with respect to this type of unethical business behavior.

---

2. *Baum v. Blue Moon Ventures, LLC,* 513 F.3d 181 (5th Cir. 2008).

✳ EXTENDED CASE 5.2 ✳
Krasner v. HSH Nordbank AG[a]

United States District Court, Southern District of New York, 680 F.Supp.2d 502(2010).

IN THE LANGUAGE OF THE COURT

Gerard E. *LYNCH*, Circuit Judge.

Plaintiff David Krasner brings this action against his former employer, HSH Nordbank AG ("HSH"), and his supervisor while employed there, Roland Kiser, alleging [among other things] sexual discrimination * * * in violation of Title VII of the Civil Rights Act of 1964.[b]

* * * *

Defendant HSH is an international commercial bank, headquartered in Germany, and has offices worldwide, including a branch in New York City.

There, Krasner alleges, he encountered an atmosphere infected with overt sexism, where career "advancement based on sexual favoritism" was accepted, and where male supervisors promoted a sexist and demeaning image of women in the workplace in which women's advancement was governed by a "casting couch." * * * Kiser also pressured male subordinates, such as Krasner, to go to strip clubs with him when on business trips abroad.

* * * *

* * * The primary offender in Krasner's estimation is Kiser, and what takes center stage in the complaint are allegations of a relationship between Kiser and a woman named Melissa Campfield * * * . Kiser, it is alleged, "advance[ed] and promot[ed]" Campfield's career "at the expense of the career advancement and reputations of other far more senior and qualified employees," Krasner included.

* * * *

* * * On September 6, 2007, Krasner lodged a verbal, in-person complaint with * * * the Head of Human Resources, articulating his belief that "Kiser was violating [HSH's] ethics policy by creating a personal conflict of interest" and generally "creating an unprofessional environment."

* * * *

* * * On September 19, Krasner again turned to the Human Resources department, this time with a written complaint, reiterating his belief that Kiser was violating the company's ethics policy and creating an unprofessional environment through his relationship with Campfield.

* * * *

On October 3, HSH concluded its internal investigation of Krasner's complaints and found no violation of law or internal ethics policy. A month later, on November 5, 2007, Krasner was summarily terminated * * * .

Krasner subsequently sought and received a right to sue letter from the Equal Employment Opportunity Commission ("EEOC") and thereafter commenced this lawsuit * * * . Defendants—HSH and Kiser—move to dismiss.

* * * *

The substantive anti-discrimination provision of Title VII prohibits employers from "discriminat[ing] against any individual with respect to his compensation, terms, conditions, or privileges of employment, because of such individual's * * * sex. *One form of gender discrimination prohibited by Title VII is sexual harassment that results in a 'hostile or abusive work environment.' " Under this doctrine,* even if an *"employee does not experience a specific negative action,"* he may have a viable claim under Title VII for sexual discrimination where *"the harassment is so pervasive that it changes the conditions of employment."* [Emphasis added.]

* * * *

Krasner's discrimination claim is founded on allegations that he was subject to a sexually hostile work environment through a combination of "(1) widespread sexual favoritism resulting from Kiser's affair with Campfield; (2) widespread sexual favoritism resulting from other affairs at [HSH]; and (3) sexually harassing and offensive conduct perpetrated by Kiser * * * unrelated to sexual affairs." In addressing these contentions, the parties argue as though a hostile environment is something that exists in some absolute way, like poisonous chemicals in the air, affecting everyone who comes in contact with it. In doing so, the parties all but ignore the prohibited causal factor requirement, which is critical to liability.

Title VII does not prohibit employers from maintaining nasty, unpleasant workplaces, or even ones that are unpleasant for reasons that are sexual in nature. Rather, it prohibits employers from discriminating against an employee (including by subjecting him or her to hostile working conditions) "because of such individual's * * * sex."

* * * *

An examination of Krasner's allegations reveals that he does not contend that he was disparaged or badly treated or subjected to an unpleasant work atmosphere in any way because he is a man. Rather, his complaint is primarily

---

a. *AG* stands for *Actiengesellschaft,* a German term denoting a corporation.

b. Title VII of the federal Civil Rights Act of 1964 prohibits employment discrimination on the basis of race, color, national origin, religion, or gender—see Chapter 35.

EXTENDED CASE CONTINUES ➡

EXTENDED CASE 5.2 CONTINUED ▼

that Kiser and other supervisors advanced a demeaning view of women in the workplace, which Krasner was exposed to and found "objectionable," and which denied "him the opportunity to work in an employment setting free of unlawful harassment."

* * * *

* * * Krasner's claim fails because "none of the alleged acts of harassment committed directly against [Krasner]"—either when viewed in isolation or in conjunction with any potential discrimination against women— "support a claim that [he] is being harassed because he is a *male* employee."

The primary animator of the complaint is what Krasner terms the "egregious effects of Kiser's favoritism" towards Campfield upon plaintiff himself.

Assuming that these actions * * * systematically and pervasively altered the conditions of Krasner's working environment sufficiently to satisfy the objective component of a hostile environment claim, the claim must nevertheless fail because the complaint does not allege that these incidents are in any way related to his gender. Krasner does not allege, and proffers [presents or offers] no facts that remotely suggest, that a female supervisor in his position would not have experienced exactly the same consequences from Kiser's preferential treatment of Campfield.

* * * *

For the foregoing reasons, defendants' motions to dismiss the complaint * * * are granted.

SO ORDERED.

QUESTIONS

1. Why did the court conclude that Krasner did not have a valid claim for "hostile environment" discrimination?
2. Suppose that a female employee had experienced the same type of treatment that Krasner had. Would the female employee succeed in a Title VII claim of gender-based discrimination? Why or why not?

Creating Ethical Codes of Conduct

One of the most effective ways of setting a tone of ethical behavior within an organization is to create an ethical code of conduct. A well-written code of ethics explicitly states a company's ethical priorities and demonstrates the company's commitment to ethical behavior.

The code of conduct indicates the company's commitment to legal compliance, as well as to the welfare of its customers or clients, its employees, and its suppliers. The code also details some specific ways in which the interests and welfare of these different groups will be protected.

ETHICS TRAINING FOR EMPLOYEES For an ethical code to be effective, its provisions must be clearly communicated to employees. Most large companies have implemented ethics training programs, in which managers discuss with employees on a face-to-face basis the firm's policies and the importance of ethical conduct. Some firms hold periodic ethics seminars during which employees can openly discuss any ethical problems that they may be experiencing and learn how the firm's ethical policies apply to those specific problems. Smaller firms should also offer some form of ethics training to employees because if a firm is accused of an ethics violation, the court will consider the presence or absence of such training in evaluating the firm's conduct.

THE SARBANES-OXLEY ACT The Sarbanes-Oxley Act of 2002[3] requires companies to set up confidential systems so that employees and others can "raise red flags" about suspected illegal or unethical auditing and accounting practices. (The Sarbanes-Oxley Act will be discussed in more detail in Chapters 42 and 48, and excerpts from and explanatory comments on this important law appear in Appendix H of this text.)

Some companies have implemented online reporting systems to accomplish this goal. In one such system, employees can click on an icon on their computers that anonymously links them with EthicsPoint, an organization based in Portland, Oregon. Through EthicsPoint, employees can report suspicious accounting practices, sexual harassment, and other possibly unethical behavior. EthicsPoint, in turn, alerts management personnel or the audit committee at the designated company to the possible problem. Those who have used the system say that it is less inhibiting than calling a company's toll-free number.

---

3. 15 U.S.C. Sections 7201 *et seq.*

SECTION 2
ETHICAL TRANSGRESSIONS BY FINANCIAL INSTITUTIONS

One of the best ways to learn the ethical responsibilities inherent in operating a business is to look at the mistakes made by other companies. In the following subsections, we describe some of the worst ethical failures of financial institutions during the latter part of the first decade of the 2000s. Many of these ethical wrongdoings received wide publicity and raised public awareness of the need for ethical leadership in all businesses.

Corporate Stock Buybacks

By now, you are probably aware that many of the greatest financial companies in the United States have either gone bankrupt, been taken over by the federal government, or been bailed out by U.S. taxpayers. What most people do not know is that those same corporations were using their own cash funds to prop up the value of their stock in the years just before the economic crisis that started in 2008.

THE RATIONALE UNDERLYING BUYBACKS The theory behind a **stock buyback** is simple—the management of a corporation believes that the market price of its shares is "below their fair value." Therefore, instead of issuing dividends to shareholders or reinvesting profits, management uses the company's funds to buy its shares in the open market, thereby boosting the price of the stock.

Who benefits from stock buybacks? Although all shareholders benefit somewhat, the main individual beneficiaries are often corporate executives who have been given **stock options,** which enable them to buy shares of the corporation's stock at a set price. When the market price rises above that level, the executives can profit by selling their shares. Although stock buybacks are legal and can serve legitimate purposes, they can easily be abused if managers use them just to increase the stock price in the short term so that they can profit from their options without considering the long-term needs of the company.

THE PREVALENCE OF BUYBACKS From 2005 to 2007, stock buybacks for the top five hundred U.S. corporations added up to $1.4 *trillion.* From 2003 to 2007, the five largest U.S banks bought back close to $100 *billion* in stock. Bank of America Corporation alone bought back $40 billion of its stock (nearly

40 percent of its common stock equity at the end of 2009) during that time period.[4]

In the investment banking business, which almost disappeared entirely in the latter half of 2008, stock buybacks were particularly egregious. In the first half of 2008, Lehman Brothers Holdings was buying back its own stock—in September of that year, it filed for bankruptcy. According to financial writer Liam Denning, Lehman's buybacks were "akin to giving away the fire extinguisher even as your house begins to fill with smoke." Goldman Sachs, another investment bank, bought back $15 billion of its stock in 2007. By the end of 2008, U.S. taxpayers had provided $10 billion in bailout funds to that same company.

Startling Executive Decisions at American International Group

For years, American International Group (AIG) was a respected, conservative, worldwide insurance company based in New York. Then, during the first decade of the 2000s, its managers decided to enter an area in which they had little expertise—the issuance of insurance contracts guaranteeing certain types of complicated financial contracts. When many of those insured contracts failed, AIG experienced multibillion-dollar losses. Ultimately, the company sought a federal bailout that eventually amounted to almost $200 billion of U.S. taxpayers' funds.

While some company executives were testifying before Congress after receiving the funds, other AIG executives spent almost $400,000 on a weeklong retreat at a resort in Monarch Beach, California. In essence, U.S. taxpayers were footing the bill. To most observers, such arrogance was as incomprehensible as it was unethical.

Executive Bonuses

Until the economic crisis began in the latter half of the first decade of the 2000s, the bonuses paid in the financial industry did not make headlines. After all, times were good, and why shouldn't those responsible for record company earnings be rewarded? When investment banks and commercial banks began to fail, however, or had to be bailed out or taken over by the federal government, executive bonuses became an issue of paramount importance.

---

4. This amount was almost as much as the $45 million that Bank of America received from the government bailout under the Troubled Asset Relief Program.

Certainly, the system of rewards in banking became perverse. Executives and others in the industry were paid a percentage of their firm's profits, no matter how risky their investment actions had been. In other words, commissions and bonuses were based on profits from transactions involving risky assets, such as collateralized debt obligations and securities based on subprime and other low-quality mortgages. In some instances, the assets were sold off to investors, but sometimes the firms themselves invested in the risky assets, which in the short run provided high returns. When the subprime mortgage crisis started in 2007, the worldwide house of cards came tumbling down, but those who had created and sold those risky assets suffered no liability—and even received bonuses. Of course, some of those firms that had enjoyed high short-run returns from their risky investments—and paid bonuses based on those profits—found themselves facing bankruptcy.

Consider Lehman Brothers before its bankruptcy. Its chief executive officer, Richard Fuld, Jr., earned almost $500 million between 2000 and the firm's demise in 2008. Even after Lehman Brothers entered into bankruptcy, its new owners, Barclays and Nomura, legally owed $3.5 billion in bonuses to employees still on the payroll. In 2006, Goldman Sachs awarded its employees a total of $16.5 billion in bonuses, or an average of almost $750,000 for each employee.

By 2007, profits on Wall Street had already begun to drop—sometimes dramatically. Citigroup's profits, for example, were down 83 percent from the previous year. Bonuses, in contrast, declined by less than 5 percent. The bonus payout in 2007 for all Wall Street firms combined was $33.2 billion.

SECTION 3
APPROACHES TO ETHICAL REASONING

Each individual, when faced with a particular ethical dilemma, engages in **ethical reasoning**—that is, a reasoning process in which the individual examines the situation at hand in light of his or her moral convictions or ethical standards. Businesspersons do likewise when making decisions with ethical implications.

How do business decision makers decide whether a given action is the "right" one for their firms? What ethical standards should be applied? Broadly speaking, ethical reasoning relating to business traditionally has been characterized by two fundamental approaches. One approach defines ethical behavior in terms of duty, which also implies certain rights. The other approach determines what is ethical in terms of the consequences, or outcome, of any given action. We examine each of these approaches here.

In addition to the two basic ethical approaches, a few theories have been developed that specifically address the social responsibility of corporations. Because these theories also influence today's business decision makers, we conclude this section with a short discussion of the different views of corporate social responsibility.

Duty-Based Ethics

Duty-based ethical standards often are derived from revealed truths, such as religious precepts. They can also be derived through philosophical reasoning.

RELIGIOUS ETHICAL STANDARDS In the Judeo-Christian tradition, which is the dominant religious tradition in the United States, the Ten Commandments of the Old Testament establish fundamental rules for moral action. Other religions have their own sources of revealed truth. Religious rules generally are absolute with respect to the behavior of their adherents. For example, the commandment "Thou shalt not steal" is an absolute mandate for a person who believes that the Ten Commandments reflect revealed truth. Even a benevolent motive for stealing (such as Robin Hood's) cannot justify the act because the act itself is inherently immoral and thus wrong.

KANTIAN ETHICS Duty-based ethical standards may also be derived solely from philosophical reasoning. The German philosopher Immanuel Kant (1724–1804), for example, identified some general guiding principles for moral behavior based on what he believed to be the fundamental nature of human beings. Kant believed that human beings are qualitatively different from other physical objects and are endowed with moral integrity and the capacity to reason and conduct their affairs rationally. Therefore, a person's thoughts and actions should be respected. When human beings are treated merely as a means to an end, they are being treated as the equivalent of objects and are being denied their basic humanity.

A central theme in Kantian ethics is that individuals should evaluate their actions in light of the consequences that would follow if *everyone* in society acted in the same way. This **categorical imperative** can be applied to any action. Suppose that you are deciding whether to cheat on an examination. If you have adopted Kant's categorical imperative, you will decide *not* to cheat because if everyone cheated, the examination (and the entire education system) would be meaningless.

THE PRINCIPLE OF RIGHTS Because a duty cannot exist without a corresponding right, duty-based ethical standards imply that human beings have basic rights. The principle that human beings have certain fundamental rights (to life, freedom, and the pursuit of happiness, for example) is deeply embedded in Western culture. As discussed in Chapter 1, the natural law tradition embraces the concept that certain actions (such as killing another person) are morally wrong because they are contrary to nature (the natural desire to continue living). Those who adhere to this **principle of rights,** or "rights theory," believe that a key factor in determining whether a business decision is ethical is how that decision affects the rights of others. These others include the firm's owners, its employees, the consumers of its products or services, its suppliers, the community in which it does business, and society as a whole.

A potential dilemma for those who support rights theory, however, is that they may disagree on which rights are most important. When considering all those affected by a business decision, for example, how much weight should be given to employees relative to shareholders, customers relative to the community, or employees relative to society as a whole?

In general, rights theorists believe that whichever right is stronger in a particular circumstance takes precedence. Suppose that a firm can either keep a plant open, saving the jobs of twelve workers, or shut the plant down and avoid contaminating a river with pollutants that would endanger the health of thousands of people. In this situation, a rights theorist can easily choose which group to favor. (Not all choices are so clear-cut, however.)

Outcome-Based Ethics: Utilitarianism

"The greatest good for the greatest number" is a paraphrase of the major premise of the utilitarian approach to ethics. **Utilitarianism** is a philosophical theory developed by Jeremy Bentham (1748–1832) and modified by John Stuart Mill (1806–1873)—both British philosophers. In contrast to duty-based ethics, utilitarianism is outcome oriented. It focuses on the consequences of an action, not on the nature of the action itself or on any set of preestablished moral values or religious beliefs.

Under a utilitarian model of ethics, an action is morally correct, or "right," when, among the people it affects, it produces the greatest amount of good for the greatest number. When an action affects the majority adversely, it is morally wrong. Applying the utilitarian theory thus requires (1) a determination of which individuals will be affected by the action in question; (2) a **cost-benefit analysis,** which involves an assessment of the negative and positive effects of alternative actions on these individuals; and (3) a choice among alternative actions that will produce maximum societal utility (the greatest positive net benefits for the greatest number of individuals).

Corporate Social Responsibility

For many years, groups concerned with civil rights, employee safety and welfare, consumer protection, environmental preservation, and other causes have pressured corporate America to behave in a responsible manner with respect to these causes. Thus was born the concept of **corporate social responsibility**—the idea that those who run corporations can and should act ethically and be accountable to society for their actions. Just what constitutes corporate social responsibility has been debated for some time, and there are a number of different theories today.

STAKEHOLDER APPROACH One view of corporate social responsibility stresses that corporations have a duty not just to shareholders, but also to other groups affected by corporate decisions ("stakeholders"). Under this approach, a corporation would consider the impact of its decision on the firm's employees, customers, creditors, suppliers, and the community in which the corporation operates. The reasoning behind this "stakeholder view" is that in some circumstances, one or more of these other groups may have a greater stake in company decisions than the shareholders do. Although this may be true, it is often difficult to decide which group's interests should receive greater weight if the interests conflict.

CORPORATE CITIZENSHIP Another theory of social responsibility argues that corporations should behave as good citizens by promoting goals that society deems worthwhile and taking positive steps toward solving social problems. The idea is that because business controls so much of the wealth and power of this country, business in turn has a responsibility to society to use that wealth and power in socially beneficial ways. Under a corporate citizenship view, companies are judged on how much they donate to social causes, as well as how they conduct their operations with respect to employment discrimination, human rights, environmental concerns, and similar issues.

Some corporations publish annual social responsibility reports, which may also be called corporate sustainability (*sustainability* refers to the capacity to endure) or citizenship reports. For example, the Hitachi Group releases an Annual Corporate Social Responsibility Report that outlines its environmental strategy, including its attempts to reduce carbon dioxide emissions (so-called greenhouse gases). It typically discusses human rights policy and its commitment to human rights awareness. The software company Symantec Corporation issued its first corporate responsibility report in September 2008 to demonstrate its focus on critical environmental, social, and governance issues. Among other things, Symantec pointed out that it had adopted the Calvert Women's Principles, the first global code of corporate conduct designed to empower, advance, and invest in women worldwide.

In the following case, a corporation's board of directors focused solely on the shareholders' profits and failed to check the actions of the firm's chief executive officer. If the board had applied a different set of priorities, the shareholders might have been in a better financial position.

CASE 5.3
Fog Cutter Capital Group, Inc. v. Securities and Exchange Commission
United States Court of Appeals, District of Columbia Circuit, 474 F.3d 822 (2007).

BACKGROUND AND FACTS • The National Association of Securities Dealers (NASD) operates the Nasdaq, an electronic securities exchange, on which Fog Cutter Capital Group was listed.[a] Andrew Wiederhorn had founded Fog Cutter in 1997 to manage a restaurant chain and make other investments. With family members, Wiederhorn controlled more than 50 percent of Fog Cutter's stock. The firm agreed that if Wiederhorn was terminated "for cause," he was entitled only to his salary through the date of termination. If terminated "without cause," he would be owed three times his $350,000 annual salary, three times his largest annual bonus from the previous three years, and any unpaid salary and bonus. "Cause" included the conviction of a felony. In 2001, Wiederhorn became the target of an investigation into the collapse of Capital Consultants, LLC. Fog Cutter then redefined "cause" in his termination agreement to cover only a felony involving Fog Cutter. In June 2004, Wiederhorn agreed to plead guilty to two felonies, serve eighteen months in prison, pay a $25,000 fine, and pay $2 million to Capital Consultants. The day before he entered his plea, Fog Cutter agreed that while he was in prison, he would keep his title, responsibilities, salary, bonuses, and other benefits. It also agreed to a $2 million "leave-of-absence payment." In July, the NASD delisted Fog Cutter from the Nasdaq. Fog Cutter appealed this decision to the Securities and Exchange Commission (SEC), which dismissed the appeal. Fog Cutter petitioned the U.S. Court of Appeals for the District of Columbia Circuit for review.

IN THE LANGUAGE OF THE COURT
RANDOLPH, Circuit Judge.
* * * *

Fog Cutter's main complaint is that the Commission failed to take into account the company's sound business reasons for acting as it did. The decision to enter into the leave-of-absence agreement was, Fog Cutter argues, in the best interest of its shareholders. The company tells us that Wiederhorn's continuing commitment to the company and his return to an active role in the company after his incarceration were essential to preserving Fog Cutter's core business units.
* * * *

* * * Fog Cutter made a deal with Wiederhorn that cost the company $4.75 million in a year in which it reported a $3.93 million net loss. We know as well that Fog Cutter handed

---

a. Securities (stocks and bonds) can be bought and sold through national exchanges. Whether a security is listed on an exchange is subject to the discretion of the organization that operates it. The Securities and Exchange Commission oversees the securities exchanges.

CASE 5.3 CONTINUED ➔ Wiederhorn a $2 million bonus right before he went off to prison, a bonus stemming directly from the consequences of Wiederhorn's criminal activity.

* * * *

Here there was ample evidence supporting the NASD's grounds for taking action against Fog Cutter: Wiederhorn's guilty plea, the leave-of-absence deal and its cost to the company, the Board's determination that Wiederhorn should retain his positions with Fog Cutter, and the concern that Wiederhorn would continue to exert influence on company affairs even while he was in prison. *The decision was in accordance with NASD rules giving the organization broad discretion to determine whether the public interest requires delisting securities in light of events at a company. That rule is obviously consistent with the [law], and NASD's decision did not burden competition.* [Emphasis added.]

Fog Cutter claims that it had to pay Wiederhorn and retain him because if it fired him in light of his guilty plea, it would have owed him $6 million. This scarcely speaks well for the company's case. The potential obligation is a result of an amendment the Board granted Wiederhorn in 2003 while he was under investigation. * * * Before the amendment to Wiederhorn's employment agreement in 2003, termination "for cause" included the conviction of any felony other than a traffic offense. In the 2003 amendment, the relevant provision allowed the Board to terminate Wiederhorn "for cause" upon conviction of a felony involving Fog Cutter. The Board had known about the investigation of Wiederhorn in connection with Capital Consultants for more than two years when it agreed to this amendment.

Fog Cutter thinks NASD's action was "unfair." But it was the company that bowed to Wiederhorn's demand for an amendment to his employment agreement, knowing full well that it was dramatically increasing the cost of firing him. Now it argues that terminating Wiederhorn would have been too expensive. One is reminded of the old saw about the child who murders his parents and then asks for mercy because he is an orphan. The makeup of Fog Cutter's Board was virtually unchanged between the time it amended the employment agreement and entered into the leave-of-absence agreement. It was, to say the least, not arbitrary or capricious for the Commission to find that Wiederhorn exercised thorough control over the Board, and to find this troubling. We agree that the Board provided little or no check on Wiederhorn's conduct, and that the Board's actions only aggravated the concerns Wiederhorn's conviction and imprisonment raised.

That Fog Cutter did not itself violate the [law] and that it disclosed the relevant events does not demonstrate any error in the delisting decision. The NASD's rules state that it may apply criteria more stringent than the minimum [legal] standards for listing. Fog Cutter's disclosure of its arrangements with Wiederhorn did not change the nature of those arrangements, which is what led the NASD to find that the company's actions were contrary to the public interest and a threat to public confidence in the Nasdaq exchange.

DECISION AND REMEDY • *The U.S. Court of Appeals for the District of Columbia Circuit denied Fog Cutter's petition for review of the SEC's decision. The NASD was concerned with "the integrity and the public's perception of the Nasdaq exchange" in light of Wiederhorn's legal troubles and the Fog Cutter board's acquiescence to his demands. The SEC "amply supported these concerns and was well within its authority to dismiss Fog Cutter's" appeal.*

THE ETHICAL DIMENSION • *Should more consideration have been given to the fact that Fog Cutter was not convicted of a violation of the law? Why or why not?*

THE GLOBAL DIMENSION • *What does the decision in this case suggest to foreign investors who may be considering investments in securities listed on U.S. exchanges?*

A WAY OF DOING BUSINESS A survey of U.S. executives undertaken by the Boston College Center for Corporate Citizenship found that more than 70 percent of those polled agreed that corporate citizenship must be treated as a priority. More than 60 percent said that good corporate citizenship added to their companies' profits. Strategist Michelle Bernhart has argued that corporate social responsibility cannot attain its maximum effectiveness unless it is treated as a way of doing business rather than as a special program.

Not all socially responsible activities can benefit a corporation, however. Corporate responsibility is most successful when a company undertakes activities that are relevant and significant to its stakeholders and related to its business operations. For example, the Brazilian firm Companhia Vale do Rio Doce is one of the world's largest diversified metals and mining companies. In 2008, it invested more than $150 million in social projects involving health care, infrastructure, and education. At the same time, it invested more than $300 million in environmental protection. One of its projects involves the rehabilitation of native species in the Amazon Valley. To that end, the company is planting almost 200 million trees in an attempt to restore 1,150 square miles of land where cattle breeding and farming have caused deforestation.

EMPLOYEE RECRUITING AND RETENTION A key corporate stakeholder is a company's workforce, which may include potential employees—job seekers. Surveys of college students about to enter the job market confirm that young people are looking for socially responsible employers. Younger workers are generally altruistic. They want to work for a company that allows them to participate in community projects.

Corporations that engage in meaningful social activities retain workers longer, particularly younger ones. At the accounting firm PKF Texas, for instance, employees support a variety of business, educational, and philanthropic organizations. As a result, this company is able to recruit and retain a younger workforce. Its turnover rate is half the industry average.

SECTION 4
MAKING ETHICAL BUSINESS DECISIONS

As Dean Krehmeyer, executive director of the Business Roundtable's Institute for Corporate Ethics, once said, "Evidence strongly suggests being ethical—doing the right thing—pays." Instilling ethical business decision making into the fabric of a business organization is no small task, even if ethics "pays." The job is to get people to understand that they have to think more broadly about how their decisions will affect employees, shareholders, customers, and even the community. Great companies,

such as Enron and the worldwide accounting firm Arthur Andersen, were brought down by the unethical behavior of a few. A two-hundred-year-old British investment banking firm, Barings Bank, was destroyed by the actions of one employee and a few of his friends. Clearly, ensuring that all employees get on the ethical business decision-making "bandwagon" is crucial in today's fast-paced world.

The George S. May International Company has provided six basic guidelines to help corporate employees judge their actions. Each employee—no matter what her or his level in the organization—should evaluate every action using the following six guidelines:

1. *The law.* Is the action you are considering legal? If you do not know the laws governing the action, then find out. Ignorance of the law is no excuse.
2. *Rules and procedures.* Are you following the internal rules and procedures that have already been laid out by your company? They have been developed to avoid problems. Is what you are planning to do consistent with your company's policies and procedures? If not, stop.
3. *Values.* Laws and internal company policies reinforce society's values. You might wish to ask yourself whether you are attempting to find a loophole in the law or in your company's policies. Next, you have to ask yourself whether you are following the "spirit" of the law as well as the letter of the law or the internal policy.
4. *Conscience.* If you feel any guilt, let your conscience be your guide. Alternatively, ask yourself whether you would be happy to be interviewed by national news media about the action you are going to take.
5. *Promises.* Every business organization is based on trust. Your customers believe that your company will do what it is supposed to do. The same is true for your suppliers and employees. Will your action live up to the commitments you have made to others, both inside the business and outside?
6. *Heroes.* We all have heroes who are role models for us. Is what you are planning on doing an action that your "hero" would take? If not, how would your hero act? That is how you should be acting.

Globalization makes it increasingly difficult for major corporations to differentiate themselves from the competition based solely on their products. See this chapter's *Shifting Legal Priorities for Business* feature for another way that corporations may gain an edge over their competitors.

The worldwide explosion of information technology has made socially responsible behavior more important simply because it has become increasingly difficult to hide bad corporate behavior. In our transparent global economy, corporations that "outbehave" their competition ethically may also outperform them financially.

The Difficulty of Managing a Company's Reputation

Before the advent of the Internet, a corporation that faced an ugly public relations situation—a product that had injured several consumers, for example—simply hired crisis-management consultants and then hid behind lawyers. Today, corporations can no longer manage their reputations the old-fashioned way. Now, when customers are unhappy or employees are disgruntled, they let the entire world know by dashing off a blog posting or putting a video clip on YouTube. In this online environment, corporations cannot control their stories. They can, however, control the way management operates.

Differentiation through "Doing Good"

In today's global economy, companies need to find ways other than through their products or services to differentiate themselves from their competitors. Even if they produce a quality product, chances are that another company somewhere in the world will copy it and sell it for less. Companies must now compete in other areas, including how responsible their behavior is. For instance, how does the company treat its customers and employees?

A key component of responsible behavior is the creation of trust between companies and their customers, employees, and suppliers. Companies that build trust also enjoy higher profits. Numerous studies have shown a strong correlation between the cost of obtaining supplies and the level of trust between the buyer of those raw materials and the seller. The less trust there is between the purchaser and the seller, the higher the procurement costs—and sometimes by a significant margin.

Online Access to the Best Leadership Practices

Fortunately, managers no longer have to create from scratch the best socially responsible leadership practices. The Boston College Center for Corporate Citizenship sponsors an online community where member companies share their best practices for corporate social responsibility. This online community offers user-generated advice and access to numerous business case studies from Boston College's Carroll School of Management. Some of this advice is particularly useful for companies attempting to expand into other countries. Their managers need to understand what social issues matter most in those countries. They can obtain this information from the Center for Corporate Citizenship.

Sustainability Counts, Too

MIT's Sloan School of Management offers custom courses on sustainability. These courses can help managers understand that sustainability is a business opportunity and how to integrate sustainability into their evaluation of risk. One of the first companies to send its executives and directors to this course was Itaú Unibanco S.A., a large Brazilian financial services corporation.

MANAGERIAL IMPLICATIONS

We live in a small world, and it is getting smaller. Managers must recognize that everything they and their co-workers do can be instantaneously communicated around the world. Whenever a manager considers acting in a socially irresponsible way, he or she should envision a YouTube video exposing those actions to millions of viewers.

SECTION 5
PRACTICAL SOLUTIONS TO CORPORATE ETHICS QUESTIONS

Corporate ethics officers and ethics committees require a practical method to investigate and solve specific ethics problems. Ethics consultant Leonard H. Bucklin of Corporate-Ethics.US™ has devised a procedure that he calls Business Process Pragmatism™. It involves five steps:

1. *Inquiry.* Of course, the process must begin with an understanding of the facts. The parties involved might include the mass media, the public, employees, or customers. At this stage, the ethical problem or problems are specified. A list of relevant ethics principles is created.

2. *Discussion.* Here, a list of action options is developed. Each option carries with it certain ethical

principles. In addition, resolution goals should be listed.

3. *Decision.* In this step, those participating in the process craft a consensus decision, or a consensus plan of action, for the corporation.

4. *Justification.* Will the consensus solution withstand moral scrutiny? At this point in the process, reasons should be attached to each proposed action or series of actions. Will the stakeholders involved accept these reasons?

5. *Evaluation.* Do the solutions to the corporate ethics issue satisfy corporate values, community values, and individual values? Ultimately, can the consensus resolution withstand moral scrutiny of the decisions made and the process used to reach those decisions?

SECTION 6
BUSINESS ETHICS ON A GLOBAL LEVEL

Given the various cultures and religions throughout the world, conflicts in ethics frequently arise between foreign and U.S. businesspersons. For example, in certain countries the consumption of alcohol and specific foods is forbidden for religious reasons. Under such circumstances, it would be thoughtless and imprudent for a U.S. businessperson to invite a local business contact out for a drink.

The role played by women in other countries may also present some difficult ethical problems for firms doing business internationally. Equal employment opportunity is a fundamental public policy in the United States, and Title VII of the Civil Rights Act of 1964 prohibits discrimination against women in the employment context (see Chapter 35). Some other countries, however, offer little protection for women against gender discrimination in the workplace, including sexual harassment.

We look here at how the employment practices that affect workers in other countries, particularly developing countries, have created some difficult ethical problems for U.S. sellers of goods manufactured in foreign nations. We also examine some of the ethical ramifications of the U.S. law prohibiting bribery of foreign officials.

The Monitoring of Employment Practices of Foreign Suppliers

Many U.S. businesses contract with companies in developing nations to produce goods, such as shoes and clothing, because the wage rates in those nations are significantly lower than those in the United States. Yet what if a foreign company hires women and children at below-minimum-wage rates, for example, or requires its employees to work long hours in a workplace full of health hazards? What if the company's supervisors routinely engage in workplace conduct that is offensive to women?

Given today's global communications network, few companies can assume that their actions in other nations will go unnoticed by "corporate watch" groups that discover and publicize unethical corporate behavior. As a result, U.S. businesses today usually take steps to avoid such adverse publicity—either by refusing to deal with certain suppliers or by arranging to monitor their suppliers' workplaces to make sure that the employees are not being mistreated.

By providing a forum for complaints, the Internet has increased the potential for damage to the reputation of any major (or minor) corporation at the hands of disgruntled employees or consumers, as well as special interest groups. Wal-Mart and Nike in particular have been frequent targets for advocacy groups that believe that those corporations exploit their workers. Although some of these complaints may be unfounded or exaggerated, the courts generally have refused to consider them defamatory (the tort of defamation will be discussed in Chapter 6). Most courts have regarded online attacks as simply the expression of opinion and therefore a form of speech protected by the First Amendment.

The Foreign Corrupt Practices Act

Another ethical problem in international business dealings has to do with the legitimacy of certain side payments to government officials. In the United States, the majority of contracts are formed within the private sector. In many foreign countries, however, government officials make the decisions on most major construction and manufacturing contracts because of extensive government regulation and control over trade and industry. Side payments to government officials in exchange for favorable business contracts are not unusual in such countries, nor are they considered to be unethical. In the past, U.S. corporations doing business in these nations largely followed the dictum "When in Rome, do as the Romans do."

In the 1970s, however, the U.S. media uncovered a number of business scandals involving large side payments by U.S. corporations to foreign representatives for the purpose of securing advantageous international trade contracts. In response to this unethical behavior, in 1977 Congress passed the Foreign Corrupt Practices Act[5] (FCPA), which prohibits U.S. businesspersons from bribing foreign officials to secure beneficial contracts.

PROHIBITION AGAINST THE BRIBERY OF FOREIGN OFFICIALS The first part of the FCPA applies to all U.S. companies and their directors, officers, shareholders, employees, and agents. This part prohibits the bribery of most officials of foreign governments if the purpose of the payment is to get the official to act in his or her official capacity to provide business opportunities.

The FCPA does not prohibit payment of substantial sums to minor officials whose duties are ministerial. These payments are often referred to as "grease," or facilitating payments. They are meant to accelerate the performance of administrative services that might otherwise be carried out at a slow pace. Thus, for example, if a firm makes a payment to a minor official to speed up an import licensing process, the firm has not violated the FCPA. Generally, the act, as amended, permits payments to foreign officials if such payments are lawful within the foreign country. The act also does not prohibit payments to private foreign companies or other third parties unless the U.S. firm knows that the payments will be passed on to a foreign government in violation of the FCPA.

BRIBERY BY FOREIGN COMPANIES Until a few years ago, the application of the FCPA was confined to

---
5. 15 U.S.C. Sections 78dd-1 *et seq.*

U.S. companies that allegedly bribed foreign officials. More recently, the act has become an instrument for prosecuting foreign companies suspected of bribing officials outside the United States. The U.S. Department of Justice estimates that more than fifty such cases are under investigation or prosecution within this country. Today, the Federal Bureau of Investigation has a five-member team to examine possible violations of U.S. laws by foreign corporations in their attempts to secure business.

ACCOUNTING REQUIREMENTS In the past, bribes were often concealed in corporate financial records. Thus, the second part of the FCPA is directed toward accountants. All companies must keep detailed records that "accurately and fairly" reflect their financial activities. In addition, all companies must have accounting systems that provide "reasonable assurance" that all transactions entered into by the companies are accounted for and legal. These requirements assist in detecting illegal bribes. The FCPA further prohibits any person from making false statements to accountants or false entries in any record or account.

PENALTIES FOR VIOLATIONS The FCPA provides that business firms that violate the act may be fined up to $2 million. Individual officers or directors who violate the FCPA may be fined up to $100,000 (the fine cannot be paid by the company) and may be imprisoned for up to five years.

REVIEWING
Ethics and Business Decision Making

Isabel Arnett was promoted to chief executive officer (CEO) of Tamik, Inc., a pharmaceutical company that manufactures a vaccine called Kafluk, which supposedly provides some defense against bird flu. The company began marketing Kafluk throughout Asia. After numerous media reports that bird flu could soon become a worldwide epidemic, the demand for Kafluk increased, sales soared, and Tamik earned record profits. Tamik's CEO, Arnett, then began receiving disturbing reports from Southeast Asia that in some patients, Kafluk had caused psychiatric disturbances, including severe hallucinations, and heart and lung problems. Arnett was informed that six children in Japan had committed suicide by jumping out of windows after receiving the vaccine. To cover up the story and prevent negative publicity, Arnett instructed Tamik's partners in Asia to offer cash to the Japanese families whose children had died in exchange for their silence. Arnett also refused to authorize additional research within the company to study the potential side effects of Kafluk. Using the information presented in the chapter, answer the following questions.

1. This scenario illustrates one of the main reasons why ethical problems occur in business. What is that reason?

REVIEWING CONTINUES ➡

REVIEWING
Ethics and Business Decision Making, Continued

2. Would a person who adheres to the principle of rights consider it ethical for Arnett not to disclose potential safety concerns and to refuse to perform additional research on Kafluk? Why or why not?

3. If Kafluk prevented fifty Asian people who were infected with bird flu from dying, would Arnett's conduct in this situation be ethical under a utilitarian model of ethics? Why or why not?

4. Did Tamik or Arnett violate the Foreign Corrupt Practices Act in this scenario? Why or why not?

DEBATE THIS: *Executives in large corporations are ultimately rewarded if their companies do well, particularly as evidenced by rising stock prices. Consequently, shouldn't we just let those who run corporations decide what level of negative side effects of their goods or services is "acceptable"?*

TERMS AND CONCEPTS

business ethics 93

categorical imperative 100

corporate social
   responsibility 101

cost-benefit analysis 101

ethical reasoning 100

ethics 93

moral minimum 94

principle of rights 101

stock buyback 99

stock options 99

utilitarianism 101

QUESTIONS AND CASE PROBLEMS

5–1. Business Ethics Jason Trevor owns a commercial bakery in Blakely, Georgia, that produces a variety of goods sold in grocery stores. Trevor is required by law to perform internal tests on food produced at his plant to check for contamination. On three occasions, the tests of food products containing peanut butter were positive for salmonella contamination. Trevor was not required to report the results to U.S. Food and Drug Administration officials, however, so he did not. Instead, Trevor instructed his employees to simply repeat the tests until the results were negative. Meanwhile, the products that had originally tested positive for salmonella were shipped out to retailers. Five people who ate Trevor's baked goods that year became seriously ill, and one person died from a salmonella infection. Even though Trevor's conduct was legal, was it unethical for him to sell goods that had once tested positive for salmonella? If Trevor had followed the six basic guidelines for making ethical business decisions, would he still have sold the contaminated goods? Why or why not?

5–2. QUESTION WITH SAMPLE ANSWER: Approaches to Ethical Reasoning.

Shokun Steel Co. owns many steel plants. One of its plants is much older than the others. Equipment at the old plant is outdated and inefficient, and the costs of production at that plant are now twice as high as at any of Shokun's other plants. Shokun cannot increase the price of its steel because of competition, both domestic and international. The plant employs more than a thousand workers; it is located in Twin Firs, Pennsylvania, which has a population of about forty-five thousand. Shokun is contemplating whether to close the plant. What factors should the firm consider in making its decision? Will the firm violate any ethical duties if it closes the plant? Analyze these questions from the two basic perspectives on ethical reasoning discussed in this chapter.

- **For a sample answer to Question 5–2, go to Appendix I at the end of this text.**

5–3. Ethical Conduct Unable to pay more than $1.2 billion in debt, Big Mountain Metals, Inc., filed a petition to declare bankruptcy in a federal bankruptcy court in July 2009. Among Big Mountain's creditors were several banks, including Bank of New London and Suzuki Bank. The court appointed Morgan Crawford to work as a "disinterested" (neutral) party with Big Mountain and the creditors to resolve their disputes; the court set an hourly fee as Crawford's compensation. Crawford told the banks that he wanted them to pay him an additional percentage fee based on his "success" in finding "new value" to pay Big Mountain's debts. He said that without such a deal, he would not perform his mediation duties. Suzuki Bank agreed; the other banks disputed the deal, but no one told the court. In October 2010, Crawford asked the court for nearly $2.5 million in compensation, including the hourly fees, which totaled about $531,000, and the percentage fees. Big Mountain and others asked the court to deny Crawford any fees on the basis that he had improperly negotiated "secret side agreements." How did Crawford violate his duties as a "disinterested" party? Should he be denied compensation? Why or why not?

5–4. Ethical Conduct Ernest Price suffered from sickle-cell anemia. In 1997, Price asked Dr. Ann Houston, his physician, to prescribe OxyContin, a strong narcotic, for the pain. Over the next several years, Price saw at least ten different physicians at ten different clinics in two cities, and used seven pharmacies in three cities, to obtain and fill simultaneous prescriptions for OxyContin. In March 2001, when Houston learned of these activities, she refused to write more prescriptions for Price. As other physicians became aware of Price's actions, they also stopped writing his prescriptions. Price filed a suit in a Mississippi state court against Purdue Pharma Co. and other producers and distributors of OxyContin, as well as his physicians and the pharmacies that had filled the prescriptions. Price alleged negligence, among other things, claiming that OxyContin's addictive nature caused him injury and that this was the defendants' fault. The defendants argued that Price's claim should be dismissed because it arose from his own wrongdoing. Who should be held *legally* liable? Should any of the parties be considered ethically responsible? Why or why not? [*Price v. Purdue Pharma Co.*, 920 So.2d 479 (Miss. 2006)]

5–5. CASE PROBLEM WITH SAMPLE ANSWER: Ethical Leadership.

In 1999, Andrew Fastow, chief financial officer of Enron Corp., asked Merrill Lynch, an investment firm, to participate in a bogus sale of three barges so that Enron could record earnings of $12.5 million from the sale. Through a third entity, Fastow bought the barges back within six months and paid Merrill for its participation. Five Merrill employees were convicted of conspiracy to commit wire fraud, in part, on an "honest-services" theory. Under this theory, an employee deprives his or her employer of "honest services" when the employee promotes his or her own interests, rather than the interests of the employer. Four of the employees appealed to the U.S. Court of Appeals for the Fifth Circuit, arguing that this charge did not apply to the conduct in which they engaged. The court agreed, reasoning that the barge deal was conducted to benefit Enron, not to enrich the Merrill employees at Enron's expense. Meanwhile, Kevin Howard, chief financial officer of Enron Broadband Services (EBS), engaged in "Project Braveheart," which enabled EBS to show earnings of $111 million in 2000 and 2001. Braveheart involved the sale of an interest in the future revenue of a video-on-demand venture to nCube, a small technology firm, which was paid for its help when EBS bought the interest back. Howard was convicted of wire fraud, in part, on the "honest-services" theory. He filed a motion to vacate his

conviction on the same basis that the Merrill employees had argued. Did Howard act unethically? Explain. Should the court grant his motion? Discuss. [United States v. Howard, 471 F.Supp.2d 772 (S.D.Tex. 2007)]

- To view a sample answer for Problem 5–5, go to this book's Web site at www.cengage.com/blaw/clarkson, select "Chapter 5," and click on "Case Problem with Sample Answer."

5–6. Corporate Social Responsibility Methamphetamine (meth) is an addictive, synthetic drug made chiefly in small toxic labs (STLs) in homes, tents, barns, or hotel rooms. The manufacturing process is dangerous and often results in explosions, burns, and toxic fumes. The government has spent considerable resources to find and eradicate STLs, imprison meth dealers and users, treat addicts, and provide services for families affected by these activities. Meth cannot be made without ephedrine or pseudoephedrine, which are ingredients in cold and allergy medications. Arkansas has one of the highest numbers of STLs in the United States. In an effort to recoup the costs of dealing with the meth epidemic, twenty counties in Arkansas filed a suit in a federal district court against Pfizer, Inc., and other companies that make or distribute cold and allergy medications. What is the defendants' ethical responsibility in this case, and to whom do they owe it? Why? [*Ashley County, Arkansas v. Pfizer, Inc.*, 552 F.3d 659 (8th Cir. 2009)]

5–7. Business Ethics on a Global Scale In the 1990s, Pfizer, Inc., developed a new antibiotic called Trovan (trovafloxacin mesylate). Tests showed that in animals Trovan had life-threatening side effects, including joint disease, abnormal cartilage growth, liver damage, and a degenerative bone condition. In 1996, an epidemic of bacterial meningitis swept across Nigeria. Pfizer sent three U.S. physicians to test Trovan on children who were patients in Nigeria's Infectious Disease Hospital. Pfizer did not obtain the patients' consent, alert them to the risks, or tell them that Médecins Sans Frontières (Doctors Without Borders) was providing an effective conventional treatment at the same site. Eleven children died in the experiment, and others were left blind, deaf, paralyzed, or brain damaged. Rabi Abdullahi and other Nigerian children filed a suit in a U.S. federal district court against Pfizer, alleging a violation of a customary international law norm prohibiting involuntary medical experimentation on humans. Did Pfizer violate any ethical standards? What might Pfizer have done to avert the consequences? Explain. [*Abdullahi v. Pfizer, Inc.*, 562 F.3d 163 (2d Cir. 2009)]

5–8. Violation of Internal Ethical Codes Havensure, LLC, an insurance broker, approached York International to determine whether it could provide insurance for York at a better rate. At the time, York was obtaining its group insurance from Prudential Insurance Co. through Universal Life Resources (ULR), another insurance broker. York allowed Havensure to study its policies. Havensure discovered that the premium Prudential charged included a hidden broker's fee that it used to pay ULR. When Havensure claimed that it could get the insurance at a lower price, York agreed that Havensure could send requests for proposals to various insurance companies. To keep York's business, Prudential offered to match the lowest rate quoted. Prudential also informed York that it must continue to buy the policy through ULR, not through Havensure. York agreed. Havensure then sued Prudential for wrongful interference with a business relationship (a tort that will be discussed in Chapter 6). The trial court held for Prudential. Havensure appealed. The appeals court held that although Prudential had violated its own code of ethics by having a hidden fee for a broker, and might have violated New York insurance law, Havensure still had no case. Why would a court find that a firm that violated its own rules, and might have violated the law, had no obligation for the loss it might have imposed on another firm trying to compete for business? Does this ruling make sense? Why or why not? [*Havensure, LLC v. Prudential Insurance Co. of America*, 595 F.3d 312 (6th Cir. 2010)]

5–9. A QUESTION OF ETHICS: Copyrights.

Steven Soderbergh is the Academy Award–winning director of Erin Brockovich, Traffic, *and many other films. CleanFlicks, LLC, filed a suit in a federal district court against Soderbergh, fifteen other directors, and the Directors Guild of America. The plaintiff asked the court to rule that it had the right to sell DVDs of the defendants' films altered without the defendants' consent to delete scenes of "sex, nudity, profanity and gory violence." CleanFlicks sold or rented the edited DVDs under the slogan "It's About Choice" to consumers, sometimes indirectly through retailers. It would not sell to retailers that made unauthorized copies of the edited films. The defendants, with DreamWorks, LLC, and seven other movie studios that own the copyrights to the films, filed a counterclaim against CleanFlicks and others engaged in the same business, alleging copyright infringement. Those filing the counterclaim asked the court to prevent CleanFlicks and the others from making and marketing altered versions of the films. [CleanFlicks of Colorado, LLC v. Soderbergh, 433 F.Supp.2d 1236 (D.Colo. 2006)]*

(a) Movie studios often edit their films to conform to content and other standards and sell the edited versions to network television and other commercial buyers. In this case, however, the studios objected when CleanFlicks edited the films and sold the altered versions directly to consumers. Similarly,

CleanFlicks made unauthorized copies of the studios' DVDs to edit the films, but objected to others' making unauthorized copies of the altered versions. Is there anything unethical about these apparently contradictory positions? Why or why not?

(b) CleanFlicks and its competitors asserted, among other things, that they were making "fair use" of the studios' copyrighted works. They argued that by their actions "they are criticizing the objectionable content commonly found in current movies and that they are providing more socially acceptable alternatives to enable families to view the films together, without exposing children to the presumed harmful effects emanating from the objectionable content." If you were the judge, how would you view this argument? Is a court the appropriate forum for making determinations of public or social policy? Explain.

5–10. VIDEO QUESTION: Business Ethics.

Go to this text's Web site at **www.cengage.com/blaw/clarkson** and select "Chapter 5." Click on "Video Questions" and view the video titled *Real World Legal: Pharzime, Scene 1 and Scene 2.* Then answer the following questions.

(a) In *Scene 1*, two employees discuss whether to market their company's drug as a treatment for other conditions—even though the U.S. Food and Drug Administration (FDA) approved the drug for treating only epilepsy. One employee argues that marketing the drug for more than the one treatment will increase the company's short-term profits and that obtaining the FDA approval for the other treatments will take too long. What theory describes this employee's perspective?

(b) In *Scene 2*, a new sales rep discusses the company's off-label marketing strategy with a veteran sales rep. Is it unethical or illegal for a sales rep to represent that he is a doctor when he has a doctorate degree in chemistry but is not actually a physician? Explain.

(c) In *Scene 2*, when the new sales rep suggests that they talk with the corporation's legal or human resources department about the drug's safety for off-label uses, how does the woman respond? Does her response encourage ethical conduct? Discuss fully.

LEGAL RESEARCH EXERCISES ON THE WEB

Go to this text's Web site at **www.cengage.com/blaw/clarkson**, select "Chapter 5," and click on "Practical Internet Exercises." There you will find the following Internet research exercises that you can perform to learn more about the topics covered in this chapter.

Practical Internet Exercise 5–1: **Legal Perspective**
Ethics in Business

Practical Internet Exercise 5–2: **Management Perspective**
Environmental Self-Audits

In Chapter 5, we examined the importance of ethical standards in the business context. We also offered suggestions on how business decision makers can create an ethical workplace. Certainly, it is not wrong for a businessperson to try to increase his or her firm's profits. But there are limits, both ethical and legal, to how far businesspersons can go. In preparing for a career in business, you will find that a background in business ethics and a commitment to ethical behavior are just as important as a knowledge of the specific laws that are covered in this text. Of course, no textbook can give an answer to each and every ethical question that arises in the business environment. Nor can it anticipate the types of ethical questions that will arise in the future, as technology and globalization continue to transform the workplace and business relationships.

The most we can do is examine the types of ethical issues that businesspersons have faced in the past and that they are facing today. In the *Focus on Ethics* sections in this book, we provide examples of specific ethical issues that have arisen in various areas of business activity.

In this initial *Focus on Ethics* feature, we look first at the relationship between business ethics and business law. We then examine various obstacles to ethical behavior in the business context. We conclude the feature by exploring the parameters of corporate social responsibility through a discussion of whether corporations have an ethical duty to the community or society at large.

Business Ethics and Business Law

Business ethics and business law are closely intertwined because ultimately the law rests on social beliefs about right and wrong behavior in the business world. Thus, businesspersons, by complying with the law, are acting ethically. Mere legal compliance (the "moral minimum" in terms of business ethics), however, is often not enough. This is because the law does not—and cannot—provide the answers for all ethical questions.

In the business world, numerous actions may be unethical but not necessarily illegal. Consider an example. Suppose that a pharmaceutical company is banned from marketing a particular drug in the United States because of the drug's possible adverse side effects. Yet no law prohibits the company from selling the drug in foreign markets—even though some consumers in those markets may suffer serious health problems as a result of using the drug. At issue here is not whether it would be legal to market the drug in other countries but whether it would be *ethical* to do so. In other words, the law has its limits—it cannot make all ethical decisions for us. Rather, the law assumes that those in business will behave ethically in their day-to-day dealings. If they do not, the courts will not come to their assistance.

Obstacles to Ethical Business Behavior

People sometimes behave unethically in the business context, just as they do in their private lives. Some businesspersons knowingly engage in unethical behavior because they think that they can "get away with it"—that is, no one will ever learn of their unethical actions.

Examples of this kind of unethical behavior include padding expense accounts, casting doubts on the integrity of a rival co-worker to gain a job promotion, stealing company supplies or equipment, and so on. Obviously, these acts are unethical, and many of them are illegal as well. In some situations, however, businesspersons who would choose to act ethically may be deterred from doing so because of situational circumstances or external pressures.

Ethics and the Corporate Environment Individuals in their personal lives normally are free to decide ethical issues as they wish and to follow through on those decisions. In the business world, and particularly in the corporate environment, rarely is such a decision made by *one* person. If you are an officer or a manager of a large company, for example, you will find that the decision as to what is right or wrong for the company is not totally yours to make. Your input may weigh in the decision, but ultimately a corporate decision is a collective undertaking.

Additionally, collective decision making, because it places emphasis on consensus and unity of opinion, tends to hinder individual ethical assertiveness. For example, suppose that a director has ethical misgivings about a planned corporate venture that promises to be highly profitable. If the other directors have no such misgivings, the director who does may be swayed by the others' enthusiasm for the project and downplay her or his own criticisms.

Furthermore, just as no one person makes a collective decision, so no one person (normally) is held accountable for the decision. The corporate enterprise thus tends to shield corporate personnel from both individual exposure to the consequences of their decisions (such as direct contact with someone who suffers harm from a corporate product) and personal accountability for those decisions.

Ethics and Management Much unethical business behavior occurs simply because management does not always make clear what ethical standards and behaviors are expected of the firm's employees. Although most firms now issue ethical policies or codes of

FOCUS ON ETHICS CONTINUES ▶

conduct, these policies and codes are not always effective in creating an ethical workplace. At times, this is because the firm's ethical policies are not communicated clearly to employees or do not bear on the real ethical issues confronting decision makers. Additionally, particularly in a large corporation, unethical behavior in one corporate department may simply escape the attention of those in control of the corporation or the corporate officials responsible for implementing and monitoring the company's ethics program.

Unethical behavior may also occur when corporate management, by its own conduct, indicates that ethical considerations take a second seat. If management makes no attempt to deter unethical behavior—through reprimands or employment terminations, for example—it will be obvious to employees that management is not very serious about ethics. Likewise, if a company gives promotions or salary increases to those who clearly use unethical tactics to increase the firm's profits, then employees who do not resort to such tactics will be at a disadvantage. An employee in this situation may decide that because "everyone else does it," he or she might as well do it too.

Of course, an even stronger encouragement of unethical behavior occurs when employers engage in blatantly unethical or illegal conduct and expect their employees to do so as well. An employee in this situation faces two options, neither of which is satisfactory: participate in the conduct or "blow the whistle" on (inform authorities of) the employer's actions—and, of course, risk being fired. (See Chapter 34 for a more detailed discussion of whistleblowing and its consequences for employees.)

Corporate Social Responsibility

As discussed in Chapter 5, just what constitutes corporate social responsibility has been debated for some time. In particular, questions arise concerning a corporation's ethical obligations to its community and to society as a whole.

A Corporation's Duty to the Community   In some circumstances, the community in which a business enterprise is located is greatly affected by corporate decisions and therefore may be considered a stakeholder. Assume, for example, that a company employs two thousand workers at one of its plants. If the company decides that it would be profitable to close the plant, the employees—and the community—would suffer as a result. To be considered ethical in that situation (and, in some circumstances, to comply with laws governing plant shutdowns), a corporation must take both the employees' needs and the community's needs into consideration when making its decision.

Another ethical question sometimes arises when a firm moves into a community. Does the company have an obligation to evaluate first how its presence will affect that community (even though the community is not a stakeholder yet)? This question has surfaced in regard to the expansion of Wal-Mart Stores, Inc., into smaller communities. Generally, most people in such communities welcome the lower prices and wider array of goods that Wal-Mart offers relative to other, smaller stores in the area. A vocal minority of people in some communities, however, claim that smaller stores often find it impossible to compete with Wal-Mart's prices and thus are forced to go out of business. Many of these smaller stores have existed for years and, according to Wal-Mart's critics, enhance the quality of community life. These critics claim that it is unethical of Wal-Mart to disregard a town's interest in the quality and character of its community life.

In addition to expanding, Wal-Mart has been consolidating some of its smaller stores into large "superstores." As it consolidates, Wal-Mart is closing stores in some of the very towns in which it drove its smaller competitors out of business. This development raises yet another ethical question: Does a store such as Wal-Mart have an obligation to continue operations in a community once it has driven its competitors out of business?

A Corporation's Duty to Society   Perhaps the most disputed area of corporate social responsibility is the nature of a corporation's duty to society at large. Those who contend that corporations should first and foremost attend to the goal of profit maximization would argue that it is by generating profits that a firm can best contribute to society. Society benefits from profit-making activities because profits can only be realized when a firm markets products or services that are desired by society. These products and services enhance the standard of living, and the profits accumulated by successful business firms generate national wealth. Our laws and court decisions promoting trade and commerce reflect the public policy that the fruits of commerce (wealth) are desirable and good. Because our society values wealth as an ethical goal, corporations, by contributing to that wealth, automatically are acting ethically.

Those arguing for profit maximization as a corporate goal also point out that it would be inappropriate to use the power of the corporate business world to further society's goals by promoting social causes. Determinations as to what exactly is in society's best interest involve questions that are essentially political, and therefore the public, through the political process, should have a say in making those determinations. Thus, the legislature—not the corporate boardroom—is the appropriate forum for making such decisions.

Critics of the profit-maximization view believe that corporations should become actively engaged in seeking and furthering solutions to social problems. Because so much of the wealth and power of this country is controlled by business, business in turn has a responsibility to society to use that wealth and power in socially beneficial ways. Corporations should therefore promote human rights, strive for equal treatment of minorities and women in the workplace, take steps to preserve the environment, and generally not profit from activities that society has deemed unethical. The critics also point out that it is ethically irresponsible to leave decisions concerning social welfare up to the government, because many social needs are not being met sufficiently through the political process.

It Pays to Be Ethical

Most corporations today have learned that it pays to be ethically responsible—even if this means less profit in the short run (and it often does). Today's corporations are subject to more intensive scrutiny—by both government agencies and the public—than corporations of the past. "Corporate watch" groups monitor the activities of U.S. corporations, including activities conducted in foreign countries. Through the Internet, complaints about a corporation's practices can easily be disseminated to a worldwide audience. Similarly, dissatisfied customers and employees can voice their complaints about corporate policies, products, or services in Internet chat rooms and other online forums. Thus, if a corporation fails to conduct its operations ethically or to respond quickly to an ethical crisis, its goodwill and reputation (and future profits) will likely suffer as a result.

There are other reasons as well for a corporation to behave ethically. For example, companies that demonstrate a commitment to ethical behavior— by implementing ethical programs, complying with environmental regulations, and promptly investigating product complaints, for example—often receive more lenient treatment from government agencies and the courts. Additionally, investors may shy away from a corporation's stock if the corporation is perceived to be socially irresponsible. Finally, unethical (and/or illegal) corporate behavior may result in government action, such as new laws imposing further requirements on corporate entities.

DISCUSSION QUESTIONS

1. What might be some other deterrents to ethical behavior in the business context, besides those discussed in this *Focus on Ethics* feature?

2. Can you think of a situation in which a business firm may be acting ethically but not in a socially responsible manner? Explain.

3. Why are consumers and the public generally more concerned with ethical and socially responsible business behavior today than they were, say, fifty years ago?

4. Suppose that an automobile manufacturing company has to choose between two alternatives: contributing $1 million annually to the United Way or reinvesting the $1 million in the company. In terms of ethics and social responsibility, which is the better choice?

5. Have Internet chat rooms and online forums affected corporate decision makers' willingness to consider the community and public interest when making choices? Are corporate decision makers more apt to make ethical choices in the cyber age? Explain.

UNIT TWO

✷

TORTS AND CRIMES

CONTENTS

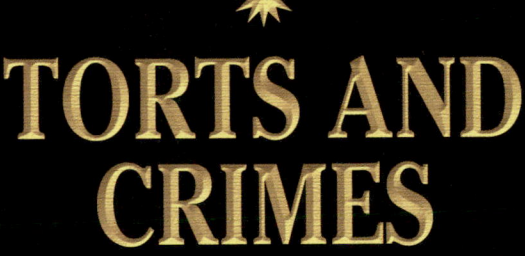

BUSINESS LAW

★ CLARKSON · MILLER · CROSS ★

CHAPTER 6

Intentional Torts and Privacy

Part of doing business today— and, indeed, part of everyday life—is the risk of being involved in a lawsuit. The list of circumstances in which businesspersons can be sued is long and varied. A customer who is injured by a security guard at a business establishment, for example, may attempt to sue the business owner, claiming that the security guard's conduct was wrongful. Any time that one party's allegedly wrongful conduct causes injury to another, an action may arise under the law of *torts* (the word *tort* is French for "wrong"). Through tort law, society compensates those who have suffered injuries as a result of the wrongful conduct of others.

Many of the lawsuits brought by or against business firms are based on the tort theories discussed in this chapter, which covers intentional torts, and the next chapter, which discusses unintentional torts. *Intentional torts* arise from intentional acts, whereas *unintentional torts* often result from carelessness (as when an employee at a store knocks over a display case, injuring a customer). In addition, this chapter discusses how tort law applies to wrongful actions in the online environment. Tort theories also come into play in the context of product liability (liability for defective products), which will be discussed in detail in Chapter 22.

SECTION 1
THE BASIS OF TORT LAW

Two notions serve as the basis of all **torts:** wrongs and compensation. Tort law is designed to compensate those who have suffered a loss or injury due to another person's wrongful act. In a tort action, one person or group brings a lawsuit against another person or group to obtain compensation (monetary damages) or other relief for the harm suffered.

The Purpose of Tort Law

The basic purpose of tort law is to provide remedies for the invasion of various *protected interests*. Society recognizes an interest in personal physical safety, and tort law provides remedies for acts that cause physical injury or that interfere with physical security and freedom of movement. Society recognizes an interest in protecting property, and tort law provides remedies for acts that cause destruction of or damage to property. Society also recognizes an interest in protecting certain intangible interests, such as

personal privacy, family relations, reputation, and dignity, and tort law provides remedies for invasion of these interests.

Damages Available in Tort Actions

Because the purpose of tort law is to compensate the injured party for the damage suffered, you need to have an understanding of the types of damages that plaintiffs seek in tort actions.

COMPENSATORY DAMAGES **Compensatory damages** are intended to compensate or reimburse a plaintiff for actual losses—that is, to make the plaintiff whole and put her or him in the same position that she or he would have been in had the tort not occurred. Compensatory damages awards are often broken down into *special damages* and *general damages*.

Special damages compensate the plaintiff for quantifiable monetary losses, such as medical expenses, lost wages and benefits (now and in the future), extra costs, the loss of irreplaceable items, and the costs of repairing or replacing damaged property.

CASE IN POINT Seaway Marine Transport operates the *Enterprise,* a large cargo ship, which has twenty-two hatches for storing coal. When the *Enterprise* positioned itself to receive a load of coal on the shores of Lake Erie in Ohio, it struck a land-based coal-loading machine operated by Bessemer & Lake Erie Railroad Company. A federal court found Seaway liable for negligence and awarded $522,000 in special damages to compensate Bessemer for the cost of repairing the damage to the loading boom.[1]

General damages compensate individuals (not companies) for the nonmonetary aspects of the harm suffered, such as pain and suffering. A court might award general damages for physical or emotional pain and suffering, loss of companionship, loss of consortium (losing the emotional and physical benefits of a spousal relationship), disfigurement, loss of reputation, or loss or impairment of mental or physical capacity.

PUNITIVE DAMAGES Occasionally, the courts may also award **punitive damages** in tort cases to punish the wrongdoer and deter others from similar wrongdoing. Punitive damages are appropriate only when the defendant's conduct was particularly egregious or reprehensible. Usually, this means that punitive damages are available mainly in intentional tort actions and only rarely in negligence lawsuits (negligence actions will be discussed in Chapter 7). They may be awarded, however, in suits involving *gross negligence,* which can be defined as an intentional failure to perform a manifest duty in reckless disregard of the consequences of such a failure for the life or property of another.

Courts exercise great restraint in granting punitive damages to plaintiffs in tort actions because punitive damages are subject to the limitations imposed by the due process clause of the U.S. Constitution (see Chapter 2). The United States Supreme Court has held that to the extent an award of punitive damages is grossly excessive, it furthers no legitimate purpose and violates due process requirements.[2] Consequently, an appellate court will sometimes reduce the amount of punitive damages awarded to a plaintiff on the ground that it is excessive and thereby violates the due process clause.[3]

Tort Reform

Critics of the current tort law system contend that it encourages trivial and unfounded lawsuits, which clog the courts, and is unnecessarily costly. In particular, they say, damages awards are often excessive and bear little relationship to the actual damage suffered. Such large awards encourage plaintiffs and their lawyers to bring frivolous suits. The result, in the critics' view, is a system that disproportionately rewards a few plaintiffs while imposing a "tort tax" on business and society as a whole. Furthermore, the tax manifests itself in other ways. Because physicians, hospitals, and pharmaceutical companies are worried about medical malpractice suits, they have changed their behavior. Physicians, for example, order more tests than necessary, adding to the nation's health-care costs.

The federal government and a number of states have begun to take some steps toward tort reform. At the federal level, the Class Action Fairness Act (CAFA) of 2005[4] shifted jurisdiction over large interstate tort and product liability class-action lawsuits from the state courts to the federal courts. The intent was to prevent plaintiffs' attorneys from *forum shopping*—looking for a state court known to be sympathetic to their clients' cause and predisposed to award large damages in class-action suits, even though the case might have only a tenuous connection to that jurisdiction.

At the state level, more than half of the states have placed caps ranging from $250,000 to $750,000 on noneconomic (general) damages (for example, pain and suffering), especially in medical malpractice suits. More than thirty states have limited punitive damages, with some imposing outright bans.

SECTION 2
INTENTIONAL TORTS AGAINST PERSONS

An **intentional tort,** as the term implies, requires intent. The **tortfeasor** (the one committing the tort) must intend to commit an act, the consequences of which interfere with the personal or business interests of another in a way not permitted by law. An evil or harmful motive is not required—in fact, the actor may even have a beneficial motive for committing what turns out to be a tortious act. In tort law, *intent* means only that the actor intended the consequences of his or her act or knew with substantial

---

1. *Bessemer & Lake Erie Railroad Co. v. Seaway Marine Transport,* 596 F.3d 357 (6th Cir. 2010).
2. *State Farm Mutual Automobile Insurance Co. v. Campbell,* 538 U.S. 408, 123 S.Ct. 1513, 155 L.Ed.2d 585 (2003).
3. See, for example, *Buell-Wilson v. Ford Motor Co.,* 160 Cal.App.4th 1107, 73 Cal.Rptr.3d 277 (2008).

4. 28 U.S.C. Sections 1711–1715, 1453.

certainty that specific consequences would result from the act. The law generally assumes that individuals intend the *normal* consequences of their actions. Thus, forcefully pushing another—even if done in jest and without any evil motive—is an intentional tort (if injury results), because the object of a strong push can ordinarily be expected to be abruptly displaced.

Intentional torts against persons include assault and battery, false imprisonment, infliction of emotional distress, defamation, invasion of privacy, appropriation, fraudulent misrepresentation, and torts related to misuse of litigation. We discuss these torts in the following subsections.

Assault and Battery

An **assault** is any intentional and unexcused threat of immediate harmful or offensive contact, including words or acts that create in another person a reasonable apprehension of harmful contact. An assault can be completed even if there is no actual contact with the plaintiff, provided that the defendant's conduct creates a reasonable apprehension of imminent harm in the plaintiff. Tort law aims to protect individuals from having to expect harmful or offensive contact.

The *completion* of the act that caused the apprehension, if it results in harm to the plaintiff, is a **battery,** which is defined as an unexcused and harmful or offensive physical contact *intentionally* performed. For example, Ivan threatens Jean with a gun, then shoots her. The pointing of the gun at Jean is an assault; the firing of the gun (if the bullet hits Jean) is a battery. The contact can be harmful, or it can be merely offensive (such as an unwelcome kiss). Physical injury need not occur. The contact can involve any part of the body or anything attached to it—for example, a hat or other item of clothing, a purse, or a chair in which one is sitting. Whether the contact is offensive is determined by the *reasonable person standard.*[5] The contact can be made by the defendant or by some force that the defendant sets in motion—for example, a thrown rock or distributing poisoned food.

If the plaintiff shows that there was contact, and the jury (or judge, if there is no jury) agrees that the contact was offensive, then the plaintiff has a right to compensation. A plaintiff may be compensated for the emotional harm or loss of reputation resulting from a battery, as well as for physical harm. A defendant may raise a number of legally recognized *defenses* (reasons why the plaintiff should not obtain damages) that justify his or her conduct, including self-defense and defense of others.

False Imprisonment

False imprisonment is the intentional confinement or restraint of another person's activities without justification. False imprisonment interferes with the freedom to move without restraint. The confinement can be accomplished through the use of physical barriers, physical restraint, or threats of physical force. Moral pressure does not constitute false imprisonment. It is essential that the person being restrained not agree to the restraint.

Businesspersons often face suits for false imprisonment after they have attempted to confine a suspected shoplifter for questioning. Under the "privilege to detain" granted to merchants in most states, a merchant can use *reasonable force* to detain or delay persons suspected of shoplifting and hold them for the police. Although laws vary from state to state, most states require that any detention be conducted in a *reasonable* manner and for only a *reasonable* length of time. Undue force or unreasonable detention can lead to liability for the business.

Intentional Infliction of Emotional Distress

The tort of *intentional infliction of emotional distress* is an intentional act that amounts to extreme and outrageous conduct resulting in severe emotional distress to another. To be **actionable** (capable of serving as the ground for a lawsuit), the act must be extreme and outrageous to the point that it exceeds the bounds of decency accepted by society.

CASE IN POINT Michael Perkins, an off-duty police officer, went to Wal-Mart to purchase a few items, including a $20 ink cartridge. The cashier, Alicia Jackson, was an acquaintance and apparently scanned the cartridge but then voided it out, so he was not charged for it. Soon after, Wal-Mart's theft prevention staff discovered that Jackson had been involved in an illegal "under-ringing" scheme for some time. In this scheme, a cashier either fails to "ring up" (charge for) merchandise or she scans an item and then voids the transaction. (This allows the cashier's friends to obtain merchandise for free.) Elijah Wilson, the police officer who questioned Jackson, disliked Perkins, and after learning of Perkins's connection to the case, encouraged her to implicate him in the criminal scheme, which she did. Despite claiming no knowledge of the

---

5. The *reasonable person standard* is an "objective" test of how a reasonable person would have acted under the same circumstances. See the subsection entitled "The Duty of Care and Its Breach" in Chapter 7 on pages 137–139.

scheme, Perkins was disciplined at work and charged with a crime; he was later acquitted. The court held that Perkins might be able to prove an intentional infliction of emotional distress claim against Wilson.[6]

Courts in most jurisdictions are wary of emotional distress claims and confine them to situations involving truly outrageous behavior. Acts that cause indignity or annoyance alone usually are not sufficient, but repeated annoyances (such as those experienced by a person who is being stalked), coupled with threats, are enough. When the outrageous conduct consists of speech about a public figure, the First Amendment's guarantee of freedom of speech also limits emotional distress claims.

CASE IN POINT *Hustler* magazine once printed a false advertisement that showed a picture of the late Reverend Jerry Falwell and described him as having lost his virginity to his mother in an outhouse while he was drunk. Falwell sued the magazine for intentional infliction of emotional distress and won, but the United States Supreme Court overturned the decision. The Court held that creators of parodies of public figures are protected under the First Amendment from intentional infliction of emotional distress claims. (The Court used the same standards that apply to public figures in defamation lawsuits, discussed next.)[7]

---

6. *Perkins v. Wal-Mart Stores, Inc.,* ___ So.3d ___, 2010 WL 610627 (Miss.App. 2010).

7. *Hustler Magazine, Inc. v. Falwell,* 485 U.S. 46, 108 S.Ct. 876, 99 L.Ed.2d 41 (1988). For another example of how the courts protect parody, see *Busch v. Viacom International, Inc.,* 477 F.Supp.2d 764 (N.D.Tex. 2007), involving a false endorsement of televangelist Pat Robertson's diet shake.

Defamation

As discussed in Chapter 4, the freedom of speech guaranteed by the First Amendment is not absolute. In interpreting the First Amendment, the courts must balance the vital guarantee of free speech against other pervasive and strong social interests, including society's interest in preventing and redressing attacks on reputation.

Defamation of character involves wrongfully hurting a person's good reputation. The law imposes a general duty on all persons to refrain from making false, defamatory *statements of fact* about others. Breaching this duty in writing or other permanent form (such as a digital recording) involves the tort of **libel.** Breaching this duty orally involves the tort of **slander.** The tort of defamation also arises when a false statement of fact is made about a person's product, business, or legal ownership rights to property.

Often at issue in defamation lawsuits (including online defamation, which will be discussed later in this chapter) is whether the defendant made a statement of fact or a *statement of opinion.* Statements of opinion normally are not actionable because they are protected under the First Amendment. In other words, making a negative statement about another person is not defamation unless the statement is false and represents something as a fact (for example, "Lane cheats on his taxes") rather than a personal opinion (for example, "Lane is a jerk").

Whether an attorney's statement to a reporter about another attorney constituted fact or opinion was at issue in the following case.

✹ EXTENDED CASE 6.1 ✹
Orlando v. Cole

Appeals Court of Massachusetts, 76 Mass.App.Ct. 1112, 921 N.E.2d 566 (2010).

IN THE LANGUAGE OF THE COURT

By the Court
(McHUGH, VUONO & MEADE, JJ. [Justices]).
* * * *

The plaintiff, Joseph M. Orlando, a lawyer, filed a one-count complaint for slander against Garrick F. Cole, who is also a lawyer. The complaint alleges that Orlando suffered harm to his reputation as an attorney as a result of comments made by Cole to newspaper reporters about Orlando's role in a criminal investigation involving Cole's client. Cole filed a motion to dismiss the complaint * * * , which was allowed.

* * * Orlando's complaint and the exhibits attached thereto assert the following facts. In February 2005, Orlando was representing a seventeen-year-old high school student who claimed that her basketball coach, Thomas A. Atwater, sexually assaulted her. Atwater apparently was an acquaintance of Orlando's. After the alleged incident, Atwater, then unrepresented, approached Orlando, admitted that he committed the act, signed an affidavit to that effect, and then went to the police and made a full confession.

* * * A few days later, Orlando spoke to two newspaper reporters,

EXTENDED CASE CONTINUES ➡

EXTENDED CASE 6.1 CONTINUED ⬇

gave them a copy of Atwater's affidavit, and explained the circumstances under which Atwater gave the affidavit. Before publishing their article, the reporters approached Cole, who by this time was representing Atwater in the criminal matter, and asked for Cole's comments. Cole responded that "the affidavit is 'inaccurate' and called Orlando's actions 'deceitful' and 'fraudulent.'" The article further stated, "Cole would not say what he thought was inaccurate in the affidavit." Both Orlando's and Cole's comments were reported together in various publications. Orlando then sued Cole for slander. The complaint alleged that Cole's comments were false, "described conduct by [Orlando] undertaken in his profession and business, and impute an unfitness for or a misconduct in his office or employment."

* * * The standard by which a complaint is measured on a motion to dismiss for failure to state a claim is a lenient one. "The allegations of the complaint, as well as such inferences as may be drawn therefrom in the plaintiff's favor, are to be taken as true." Doubts are resolved in favor of the plaintiff, and the motion must be denied unless it is certain that no set of provable facts could entitle the plaintiff to relief.

We begin with a threshold inquiry into whether the comments are "'reasonably susceptible of a defamatory connotation [implication],' so as to warrant their submission to a jury to determine if in fact the defamatory connotation was conveyed. *A statement is defamatory in the circumstances if it discredits a person in the minds of any considerable and respectable class of the community."* We conclude that the comments at issue are susceptible of a defamatory connotation because each of the terms used— "inaccurate," "fraudulent," and "deceitful"—impl[ies] misconduct. [Emphasis added.]

We now turn to whether Cole's statements were ones of fact, or opinion, or a combination of both. "The determination whether a statement is one of fact or opinion is generally considered a question of law." The distinction is critical because "under the First Amendment, there is no such thing as a false idea. However pernicious [destructive] an opinion may seem, we depend for its correction not on the conscience of judges and juries but on the competition of other ideas. But there is no constitutional value in false statements of fact."

To determine whether a statement is opinion, a court must "examine the statement in its totality in the context in which it was uttered or published." In doing so, "the court must consider all the words used, not merely a particular phrase or sentence. In addition, the court must give weight to cautionary terms used by the person publishing the statement. Finally, the court must consider all of the circumstances surrounding the statement, including the medium by which the statement is disseminated and the audience to which it is published." If the "average reader" could understand the allegedly libelous statements as either fact or opinion, the determination is for the jury.

Cole's allegations that the affidavit signed by Atwater was "inaccurate" and that Orlando's conduct was "fraudulent" and "deceitful" are factual because they are capable of being proved false. These comments were not presented as opinions nor accompanied by any cautionary language. Even if we were to conclude that these statements were an expression of opinion, they appear to be based on undisclosed defamatory facts, namely the unreported private communications between Cole and his new client, Atwater. "Defamation can occur by innuendo as well as by explicit assertion." As previously noted, the terms imply misconduct. *Because, within the context of the article, a reader could view Cole's comments as based on undisclosed defamatory facts, they are not protected under the First Amendment.* [Emphasis added.]

In short, dismissal * * * was premature. * * * We reverse the judgment and remand the case to the [trial court] for further proceedings consistent with this [court's opinion].

 QUESTIONS

1. Orlando sued Cole for slander. Why didn't he sue for libel, given that the comments were reported in various news publications?
2. What did the court mean when it stated that "under the First Amendment there is no such thing as a false idea"?

THE PUBLICATION REQUIREMENT The basis of the tort of defamation is the publication of a statement or statements that hold an individual up to contempt, ridicule, or hatred. *Publication* here means that the defamatory statements are communicated (either intentionally or accidentally) to persons other than the defamed party. If Rodriques writes Andrews a private letter falsely accusing him of embezzling funds, the action does not constitute libel. If Peters falsely states that Gordon is dishonest and incompetent when no one else is around, the action does not constitute slander. In neither case was the message communicated to a third party.

The courts usually have held that even dictating a letter to a secretary constitutes publication, although the publication may be privileged (a concept that will be explained shortly). Moreover, if a third party merely overhears defamatory statements by chance, the courts usually hold that this also constitutes publication. Defamatory statements made via the Internet are actionable as well. Note also that any individual who repeats or republishes defamatory statements normally is liable even if that person reveals the source of the statements.

DAMAGES FOR LIBEL Once a defendant's liability for libel is established, general damages are presumed as a matter of law. General damages are designed to compensate the plaintiff for nonspecific harms such as disgrace or dishonor in the eyes of the community, humiliation, injured reputation, and emotional distress—harms that are difficult to measure. In other words, to recover damages in a libel case, the plaintiff need not prove that he or she was actually injured in any way as a result of the libelous statement.

DAMAGES FOR SLANDER In contrast to cases alleging libel, in a case alleging slander, the plaintiff must prove special damages to establish the defendant's liability. The plaintiff must show that the slanderous statement caused her or him to suffer actual economic or monetary losses. Unless this initial hurdle of proving special damages is overcome, a plaintiff alleging slander normally cannot go forward with the suit and recover any damages. This requirement is imposed in slander cases because oral statements have a temporary quality. In contrast, a libelous (written) statement has the quality of permanence, can be circulated widely, and usually results from some degree of deliberation on the part of the author.

Exceptions to the burden of proving special damages in cases alleging slander are made for certain types of slanderous statements. If a false statement constitutes "slander *per se,*" no proof of special damages is required for it to be actionable. In most states, the following four types of utterances are considered to be slander *per se:*

1. A statement that another has a particular type of disease (historically, leprosy and sexually transmitted diseases, but now also including allegations of mental illness).
2. A statement that another has committed improprieties while engaging in a profession or trade.
3. A statement that another has committed or has been imprisoned for a serious crime.
4. A statement that a person (usually only an unmarried person and sometimes only a woman) is unchaste or has engaged in serious sexual misconduct.

DEFENSES TO DEFAMATION Truth normally is an absolute defense against a defamation charge. In other words, if a defendant in a defamation case can prove that the allegedly defamatory statements of fact were true, normally no tort has been committed. Other defenses to defamation may exist if the speech is *privileged* or concerns a public figure. Note that the majority of defamation actions are filed in state courts, and state laws differ somewhat in the defenses they allow, such as privilege (discussed next).

Privileged Speech. In some circumstances, a person will not be liable for defamatory statements because she or he enjoys a **privilege,** or immunity. With respect to defamation, privileged communications are of two types: absolute and qualified.[8] Only in judicial proceedings and certain government proceedings is an *absolute privilege* granted. For example, statements made by attorneys and judges in the courtroom during a trial are absolutely privileged. So are statements made by government officials during legislative debate, even if the legislators make such statements maliciously—that is, knowing them to be untrue. An absolute privilege is granted in these situations because judicial and government personnel deal with matters that are so much in the public interest that the parties involved should be able to speak out fully and freely and without restriction.

In other situations, a person will not be liable for defamatory statements because he or she has a *qualified,* or *conditional, privilege.* An employer's statements in written evaluations of employees, for example, are protected by qualified privilege. Generally, if the statements are made in good faith and the publication is limited to those who have a legitimate interest in the communication, the statements fall within the area of qualified privilege. The concept of conditional privilege rests on the common law assumption that in some situations, the right to know or speak is equal in importance to the right not to be defamed. If a communication is conditionally privileged, a plaintiff can recover damages only by showing that the privilege was abused.

Public Figures. Public officials who exercise substantial governmental power and any persons in the public limelight are considered **public figures**. In general, public figures are considered "fair game," and false and defamatory statements about them

---

8. Note that the term *privileged communication* in this context is not the same as privileged communication between a professional, such as an attorney, and his or her client. The latter type of privilege will be discussed in Chapter 48, in the context of the liability of professionals.

that are published in the media will not constitute defamation unless the statements are made with **actual malice.** To be made with actual malice, a statement must be made *with either knowledge of its falsity or a reckless disregard of the truth.*[9]

Statements made about public figures, especially when they are communicated via a public medium, usually are related to matters of general public interest. Some public figures, such as politicians, are people who substantially affect all of us. Furthermore, public figures generally have some access to a public medium for answering disparaging falsehoods about themselves; private individuals do not. For these reasons, public figures have a greater burden of proof in defamation cases (they must prove actual malice) than do private individuals.

CASE IN POINT Lynne Spears, the mother of pop star Britney Spears, wrote a book in which she claimed that Sam Lutfi, Britney's former business manager, contributed to a mental breakdown that Britney experienced in 2008. Among other things, the book stated that Lutfi hid psychiatric drugs in Britney's food, disabled her cars and phones, and stole funds from her bank accounts. Lutfi filed a lawsuit for defamation and asserted that Lynne's statements were untrue, disparaging, and made with actual malice. A Los Angeles trial court found that Lutfi was a public figure and had alleged enough evidence in his complaint for the case to go forward to trial. Lynne has appealed that ruling. If the case goes to trial, a central issue will be whether Lynne believed in the truth of her statements or made them with reckless disregard for the truth.[10]

Invasion of Privacy

A person has a right to solitude and freedom from prying public eyes—in other words, to privacy. As mentioned in Chapter 4, the courts have held that certain amendments to the U.S. Constitution imply a right to privacy. Some state constitutions explicitly provide for privacy rights, as do a number of federal and state statutes. Tort law also safeguards these rights through the tort of *invasion of privacy.* Generally, to successfully sue for an invasion of privacy, a person must have a reasonable expectation of privacy, and the invasion must be highly offensive. Four acts can qualify as invasions of privacy:

1. *Appropriation of identity.* Under the common law, using a person's name, picture, or other likeness for commercial purposes without permission is a tortious invasion of privacy. Most states today have also enacted statutes prohibiting *appropriation* (discussed further in the next subsection).

2. *Intrusion into an individual's affairs or seclusion.* For example, invading someone's home or searching someone's personal computer without authorization is an invasion of privacy. This tort has been held to extend to eavesdropping by wiretap, unauthorized scanning of a bank account, compulsory blood testing, and window peeping. One court found that a man who had repeatedly followed a woman (the wife of his girlfriend's former husband), photographed her, and made obscene gestures at her had intruded into her privacy.[11]

3. *False light.* The publication of information that places a person in a false light is another category of invasion of privacy. This could be a story attributing to someone ideas not held or actions not taken by that person. (The publication of such a story could involve the tort of defamation as well.)

4. *Public disclosure of private facts.* This type of invasion of privacy occurs when a person publicly discloses private facts about an individual that an ordinary person would find objectionable or embarrassing. A newspaper account of a private citizen's sex life or financial affairs could be an actionable invasion of privacy, even if the information revealed is true, because it is not of public concern.

Appropriation

The use of another person's name, likeness, or other identifying characteristic, without permission and for the benefit of the user, constitutes the tort of **appropriation** (sometimes referred to as the *right of publicity*). Under the law, normally an individual's right to privacy includes the right to the exclusive use of his or her identity.

CASE IN POINT In one early case, Vanna White, the hostess of the popular *Wheel of Fortune* game show, brought a case against Samsung Electronics America, Inc. Without White's permission, Samsung had included in an advertisement a robotic image dressed in a wig, gown, and jewelry, in a setting that

---

9. *New York Times Co. v. Sullivan,* 376 U.S. 254, 84 S.Ct. 710, 11 L.Ed.2d 686 (1964). As mentioned earlier, the First Amendment protects the creator of a parody from liability for defamation of a public figure.

10. *Lutfi v. Spears,* No. BC 406904 (Sup.Ct.—Los Angeles, Dept. 23, July 7, 2009).

11. *Anderson v. Mergenhagen,* 283 Ga.App. 546, 642 S.E.2d 105 (2007).

resembled the *Wheel of Fortune* set, in a stance for which White is famous. The court ruled in White's favor, holding that the tort of appropriation does not require the use of a celebrity's name or actual likeness. The court stated that Samsung's robot ad left "little doubt" as to the identity of the celebrity that the ad was meant to depict.[12]

DEGREE OF LIKENESS Courts may differ as to the degree of likeness that is required to impose liability for the tort of appropriation. This is particularly true when the plaintiff is claiming appropriation based on a depiction in an animated film or video game.

CASE IN POINT Anthony "Tony" Twist, a former professional hockey player with a reputation for fighting, sued the publishers of the comic book *Spawn*, because it included an evil character named Anthony "Tony Twist" Twistelli. The Missouri Supreme Court held that the use of Tony Twist's name alone was sufficient proof of likeness to support a misappropriation claim.[13] Ultimately, Twist was awarded $15 million in damages.[14]

CASE IN POINT The Naked Cowboy, Robert Burck, has been a street entertainer in New York City's Times Square for more than ten years. He performs for tourists wearing only a white cowboy hat, white cowboy boots, and white underwear and carrying a guitar strategically placed to give the illusion of nudity. Burck has become a well-known persona, appearing in television shows, movies, and video games, and has licensed his name and likeness to certain companies, including Chevrolet. When Mars, Inc., the maker of M&Ms candy, began using a video on billboards in Times Square that depicted a blue M&M dressed exactly like The Naked Cowboy, Burck sued for appropriation. The court held that Mars's creation of a cartoon character dressed in The Naked Cowboy's signature costume did not amount to appropriation by use of Burck's "portrait or picture."[15]

RIGHT OF PUBLICITY AS A PROPERTY RIGHT As mentioned, in many states the common law tort of appropriation has become known as the right of publicity.[16] Rather than being aimed at protecting a person's right to be left alone (privacy), this right aims to protect an individual's pecuniary (financial) interest in the commercial exploitation of his or her identity. In other words, this right allows public figures, celebrities, and entertainers to sue anyone who uses their images for commercial benefit without their permission.

Cases involving the right of publicity generally turn on whether the use was commercial. For instance, if a television news program reports on a celebrity and shows an image of the person, the use likely would not be classified as commercial; in contrast, including the celebrity's image on a poster without his or her permission would be a commercial use.

Because the right of publicity is similar to a property right, most states have concluded that the right is inheritable and survives the death of the person who held the right. Normally, though, the person must provide for the passage of the right to another in her or his will.

Fraudulent Misrepresentation

A misrepresentation leads another to believe in a condition that is different from the condition that actually exists. This is often accomplished through a false or an incorrect statement. Although persons sometimes make misrepresentations accidentally because they are unaware of the existing facts, the tort of **fraudulent misrepresentation,** or *fraud*, involves *intentional* deceit for personal gain. The tort includes several elements:

1. A misrepresentation of material facts or conditions with knowledge that they are false or with reckless disregard for the truth.
2. An intent to induce another party to rely on the misrepresentation.
3. A justifiable reliance on the misrepresentation by the deceived party.
4. Damages suffered as a result of that reliance.
5. A causal connection between the misrepresentation and the injury suffered.

For fraud to occur, more than mere **puffery,** or *seller's talk*, must be involved. Fraud exists only when a person represents as a fact something he or she knows is untrue. For example, it is fraud to claim that the roof of a building does not leak when one

---

12. *White v. Samsung Electronics America, Inc.*, 971 F.2d 1395 (9th Cir. 1992).
13. *Doe v. TCI Cablevision*, 110 S.W.3d 363 (Mo. 2003).
14. The amount of damages was appealed and subsequently affirmed. See *Doe v. McFarlane*, 207 S.W.3d 52 (Mo.App. 2006).
15. Note that Burck was allowed to continue his lawsuit against Mars for violation of trademark law—see Chapter 8. *Burck v. Mars, Inc.*, 571 F.Supp.2d 446 (S.D.N.Y. 2008). See also *Kirby v. Sega of America, Inc.*, 144 Cal.App.4th 47, 50 Cal.Rptr.3d 607 (2006).
16. See, for example, California Civil Code Sections 3344 and 3344.1.

knows that it does. Facts are objectively ascertainable, whereas seller's talk—such as "I am the best accountant in town"—is not, because the speaker is representing a subjective view.

Normally, the tort of fraudulent misrepresentation occurs only when there is reliance on a *statement of fact*. Sometimes, however, reliance on a *statement of opinion* may involve the tort of fraudulent misrepresentation if the individual making the statement of opinion has superior knowledge of the subject matter. For example, when a lawyer makes a statement of opinion about the law in a state in which the lawyer is licensed to practice, a court would construe reliance on the statement to be equivalent to reliance on a statement of fact.

Abusive or Frivolous Litigation

Persons or businesses generally have a right to sue when they have been injured. In recent years, however, an increasing number of meritless lawsuits have been filed simply to harass the defendants. Defending oneself in any legal proceeding can be costly, time consuming, and emotionally draining. Tort law recognizes that people have a right not to be sued without a legally just and proper reason. It therefore protects individuals from the misuse of litigation. Torts related to abusive litigation include malicious prosecution and abuse of process.

If the party that initiated a lawsuit did so out of malice and without probable cause (a legitimate legal reason), and ended up losing that suit, the party can be sued for *malicious prosecution*. In some states, the plaintiff (who was the defendant in the first proceeding) must also prove injury other than the normal costs of litigation, such as lost profits.

Abuse of process can apply to any person using a legal process against another in an improper manner or to accomplish a purpose for which the process was not designed. The key difference between the torts of abuse of process and malicious prosecution is the level of proof. Abuse of process does not require the plaintiff to prove malice or show that the defendant (who was previously the plaintiff) lost in a prior legal proceeding.[17] In addition, abuse of process is not limited to prior litigation. It can be based on the wrongful use of subpoenas, court orders to attach or seize real property, or other types of formal legal process.

Concept Summary 6.1 reviews intentional torts against persons.

---

17. *Palmer v. Diaz,* 214 P.3d 546 (Colo.App. 2009); and *Bernhard-Thomas Building Systems, LLC v. Duncan,* 918 A.2d 889 (Conn. App. 2007).

Most torts can occur in any context, but a few torts, referred to as **business torts,** apply only to wrongful interferences with the business rights of others. Business torts generally fall into two categories—interference with a contractual relationship and interference with a business relationship.

Wrongful Interference with a Contractual Relationship

Three elements are necessary for *wrongful interference with a contractual relationship* to occur:

1. A valid, enforceable contract must exist between two parties.
2. A third party must know that this contract exists.
3. This third party must *intentionally induce* a party to the contract to breach the contract.

CASE IN POINT A landmark case in this area involved an opera singer, Joanna Wagner, who was under contract to sing for a man named Lumley for a specified period of years. A man named Gye, who knew of this contract, nonetheless "enticed" Wagner to refuse to carry out the agreement, and Wagner began to sing for Gye. Gye's action constituted a tort because it interfered with the contractual relationship between Wagner and Lumley. (Of course, Wagner's refusal to carry out the agreement also entitled Lumley to sue Wagner for breach of contract.)[18]

The body of tort law relating to wrongful interference with a contractual relationship has increased greatly in recent years. In principle, any lawful contract can be the basis for an action of this type. The contract could be between a firm and its employees or a firm and its customers. Sometimes, a competitor of a firm draws away one of the firm's key employees. Only if the original employer can show that the competitor knew of the contract's existence, and intentionally induced the breach, can damages be recovered from the competitor.

CASE IN POINT Office Machines, Inc., an office-supply company in Arkansas, filed a lawsuit against Bruce Mitchell and others for wrongful interference with a contractual relationship. Mitchell and the others were former employees of Office Machines

---

18. *Lumley v. Gye,* 118 Eng.Rep. 749 (1853).

CONCEPT SUMMARY 6.1
Intentional Torts against Persons

Name of Tort	Description
Assault and Battery	Any unexcused and intentional act that causes another person to be apprehensive of immediate harm is an assault. An assault resulting in physical contact is a battery.
False Imprisonment	An intentional confinement or restraint of another person's movement without justification.
Intentional Infliction of Emotional Distress	An intentional act that amounts to extreme and outrageous conduct resulting in severe emotional distress to another.
Defamation (Libel or Slander)	A false statement of fact, not made under privilege, that is communicated to a third person and that causes damage to a person's reputation. For public figures, the plaintiff must also prove that the statement was made with actual malice.
Invasion of Privacy	Publishing or otherwise making known or using information relating to a person's private life and affairs, with which the public has no legitimate concern, without that person's permission or approval.
Appropriation	The use of another person's name, likeness, or other identifying characteristic without permission and for the benefit of the user.
Fraudulent Misrepresentation (Fraud)	A false representation made by one party, through misstatement of facts or through conduct, with the intention of deceiving another and on which the other reasonably relies to his or her detriment.
Abusive or Frivolous Litigation	The filing of a lawsuit without legitimate grounds and with malice. Alternatively, the use of a legal process in an improper manner.

who had been negotiating a deal to buy the business. When the deal fell through, the employees quit and started a competing office supply business, hiring several more of Office Machines' employees to work for their competing firm. The court held that hiring workers from a competitor's business did not constitute wrongful interference with a contractual relationship in this situation because the workers had not breached any employment contracts with their former employer.[19]

Wrongful Interference with a Business Relationship

Businesspersons devise countless schemes to attract customers. They are prohibited, however, from unreasonably interfering with another's business in their attempts to gain a greater share of the market.

There is a difference between *competitive practices* and *predatory behavior*—actions undertaken with

the intention of unlawfully driving competitors completely out of the market. Attempting to attract customers in general is a legitimate business practice, whereas specifically targeting the customers of a competitor is more likely to be predatory. For example, the mall contains two athletic shoe stores: Joe's and Sprint. Joe's cannot station an employee at the entrance to Sprint to divert customers to Joe's by telling them that Joe's will beat Sprint's prices. Doing this would constitute the tort of wrongful interference with a business relationship because it would interfere with a prospective economic advantage; such behavior is commonly considered to be an unfair trade practice. If this type of activity were permitted, Joe's would reap the benefits of Sprint's advertising.

Although state laws vary on wrongful interference with a business relationship, generally a plaintiff must prove that the defendant used predatory methods to intentionally harm an established business relationship or prospective economic advantage. The plaintiff must also prove that the defendant's interference caused the plaintiff to suffer economic harm.

---

19. *Office Machines, Inc. v. Mitchell*, 95 Ark.App. 128, 234 S.W.3d 906 (2006).

Defenses to Wrongful Interference

A person will not be liable for the tort of wrongful interference with a contractual or business relationship if it can be shown that the interference was justified, or permissible. Bona fide competitive behavior is a permissible interference even if it results in the breaking of a contract.

For example, if Jerrod's Meats advertises so effectively that it induces Sam's Restaurant to break its contract with Burke's Meat Company, Burke's Meat Company will be unable to recover against Jerrod's Meats on a wrongful interference theory. After all, the public policy that favors free competition through advertising outweighs any possible instability that such competitive activity might cause in contractual relations. Although luring customers away from a competitor through aggressive marketing and advertising strategies obviously interferes with the competitor's relationship with its customers, courts typically allow such activities in the spirit of competition.

SECTION 4

INTENTIONAL TORTS AGAINST PROPERTY

Intentional torts against property include trespass to land, trespass to personal property, conversion, and disparagement of property. These torts are wrongful actions that interfere with individuals' legally recognized rights with regard to their land or personal property. The law distinguishes real property from personal property (see Chapters 49 and 50). *Real property* is land and things permanently attached to the land. *Personal property* consists of all other items, which are basically movable. Thus, a house and lot are real property, whereas the furniture inside a house is personal property. Cash and securities are also personal property.

Trespass to Land

The tort of **trespass to land** occurs any time a person, without permission, enters onto, above, or below the surface of land that is owned by another; causes anything to enter onto the land; or remains on the land or permits anything to remain on it. Actual harm to the land is not an essential element of this tort because the tort is designed to protect the right of an owner to exclusive possession. Common types of trespass to land include walking or driving on another's land; shooting a gun over another's land; throwing rocks at or spraying water on a building that belongs to someone else; building a dam across a river, thereby causing water to back up on someone else's land; and constructing one's building so that it extends onto an adjoining landowner's property.

TRESPASS CRITERIA, RIGHTS, AND DUTIES Before a person can be a trespasser, the real property owner (or other person in actual and exclusive possession of the property, such as a person who is leasing the property) must establish that person as a trespasser. For example, "posted" trespass signs expressly establish as a trespasser a person who ignores these signs and enters onto the property. Any person who enters onto another's property to commit an illegal act (such as a thief entering a lumberyard at night to steal lumber) is established impliedly as a trespasser, without posted signs.

At common law, a trespasser is liable for damages caused to the property and generally cannot hold the owner liable for injuries that the trespasser sustains on the premises. This common law rule is being abandoned in many jurisdictions, however, in favor of a *reasonable duty of care* rule that varies depending on the status of the parties. For example, a landowner may have a duty to post a notice that guard dogs patrol the property. Also, under the "attractive nuisance" doctrine, a landowner may be held liable for injuries sustained by young children on the landowner's property if the children were attracted to the premises by some object, such as a swimming pool or an abandoned building. Finally, an owner can remove a trespasser from the premises—or detain a trespasser on the premises for a reasonable time—through the use of reasonable force without being liable for assault, battery, or false imprisonment.

DEFENSES AGAINST TRESPASS TO LAND Trespass to land involves wrongful interference with another person's real property rights. If it can be shown that the trespass was warranted, however, as when a trespasser enters to assist someone in danger, a defense exists. Another defense exists when the trespasser can show that he or she had a license to come onto the land. A *licensee* is one who is invited (or allowed to enter) onto the property of another for the licensee's benefit. A person who enters another's property to read an electric meter, for example, is a licensee. When you purchase a ticket to attend a movie or sporting event, you are licensed to go onto the property of another to view that movie or event. Note that licenses to enter onto another's property are *revocable* by the property owner. If a property owner asks an electric meter reader to leave and she or he refuses to do so, the meter reader at that point becomes a trespasser.

Trespass to Personal Property

Whenever any individual wrongfully takes or harms the personal property of another or otherwise interferes with the lawful owner's possession and enjoyment of personal property, **trespass to personal property** occurs. This tort may also be called *trespass to chattels* or *trespass to personalty*.[20] In this context, harm means not only destruction of the property, but also anything that diminishes its value, condition, or quality. Trespass to personal property involves intentional meddling with a possessory interest (one arising from possession), including barring an owner's access to personal property. If Kelly takes Ryan's business law book as a practical joke and hides it so that Ryan is unable to find it for several days before the final examination, Kelly has engaged in a trespass to personal property.

If it can be shown that trespass to personal property was warranted, then a complete defense exists. Most states, for example, allow automobile repair shops to hold a customer's car (under what is called an *artisan's lien,* discussed in Chapter 28) when the customer refuses to pay for repairs already completed.

Conversion

Whenever a person wrongfully possesses or uses the personal property of another without permission, the tort of **conversion** occurs. Any act that deprives an owner of personal property or of the use of that property without that owner's permission

and without just cause can be conversion. Even the taking of electronic records and data may form the basis of a common law conversion claim.[21]

Often, when conversion occurs, a trespass to personal property also occurs because the original taking of the personal property from the owner was a trespass, and wrongfully retaining it is conversion. Conversion is the civil side of crimes related to theft, but it is not limited to theft. Even when the rightful owner consented to the initial taking of the property, so no theft or trespass occurred, a failure to return the property may still be conversion. For example, Chen borrows Mark's iPad to use while traveling home from school for the holidays. When Chen returns to school, Mark asks for his iPad back, but Chen says that he gave it to his little brother for Christmas. In this situation, Mark can sue Chen for conversion, and Chen will have to either return the iPad or pay damages equal to its value.

Note that conversion can occur even when a person mistakenly believed that she or he was entitled to the goods. In other words, good intentions are not a defense against conversion. Someone who buys stolen goods, for example, has committed the tort of conversion even if he or she did not know the goods were stolen. If the true owner brings a tort action against the buyer, the buyer must either return the property to the owner or pay the owner the full value of the property (despite having already paid the purchase price to the thief).

The following case involved a university's conversion of the fruits of a professor's work—property created and accumulated over several years. The question before the court was how to make a fair estimate of the property's value.

---

20. Pronounced *per*-sun-ul-tee.

21. See *Thyroff v. Nationwide Mutual Insurance Co.,* 8 N.Y.3d 283, 864 N.E.2d 1272 (2007).

CASE 6.2
Trustees of University of District of Columbia v. Vossoughi
District of Columbia Court of Appeals, 963 A.2d 1162 (2009).

BACKGROUND AND FACTS • Jafar Vossoughi is an expert in applied mechanics and experimental biomechanics, which encompasses the testing of mechanical theories and the creation and use of experimental devices for biomechanical research. In the 1990s, while teaching at the University of the District of Columbia (UDC), Vossoughi set up a laboratory to conduct research. When his employment contract expired, he remained on campus and continued his research. In 2000, without Vossoughi's knowledge, UDC cleaned out the laboratory and threw away most of its contents. Vossoughi filed a suit in a District of Columbia court against UDC, seeking damages for the loss of his course materials, unpublished research data, unique scientific instruments, and other items. He personally testified as

CASE CONTINUES ➡

CASE 6.2 CONTINUED ➡ to the "replacement cost." A jury found UDC liable for conversion (the wrongful taking of someone's personal property) and awarded Vossoughi $1.65 million. UDC appealed.

IN THE LANGUAGE OF THE COURT
GLICKMAN, Associate Judge:
* * * *

The usual and traditional measure of damages for conversion of property is the fair market value of the property at the time of the conversion. * * * But fair market value is not always the test. Sometimes fair market value cannot be determined, or would be inadequate, as when, for example, the article destroyed was unique or possessed qualities the special nature of which could only be appreciated by the owner. Accordingly, *for purposes of awarding adequate compensation for the destruction of property, value means exchange value or the value to the owner if this is greater than the exchange value.* In general, therefore, a person tortiously deprived of property is entitled to damages based upon its special value to him if that is greater than its market value. Where the lost property in such cases is replaceable, it is appropriate to measure damages for its loss by the cost of replacement. [Emphasis added.]

* * * Dr. Vossoughi's course materials, unpublished research and fabricated instruments * * * had great use value to Dr. Vossoughi but no comparable (if any) market value.
* * * *

* * * Dr. Vossoughi based his estimates of the value of the property on the time it would take him to replicate it. This was a conceptually reasonable approach * * * . UDC complains of the vagueness of Dr. Vossoughi's testimony: for example, his estimates were rough approximations, and he did not specify exactly how he valued his or others' time * * * . But our cases have held that an owner is qualified to estimate the value of his property based on his familiarity with its quality and condition * * * . In this case, Dr. Vossoughi certainly had the requisite [necessary] familiarity, and given his experience as a fabricator of instruments, a teacher, a researcher, and a grant recipient, he also had considerable expertise to draw on. His opinions clearly were informed ones. There is nothing to show that his estimates were unrealistic; on the contrary, they were corroborated [substantiated] by [Vossoughi's expert witnesses] Dr. Conway and Dr. Saha.

UDC further argues that Dr. Vossoughi's valuation of his course materials was flawed in [two] respects. First, Dr. Vossoughi admitted his course materials were not salable ("Nobody would buy somebody else's [teaching] notes. It's useless [except] for that particular class."). But * * * the absence of an exchange value does not mean the course materials had no compensable use value to Dr. Vossoughi. Second, Dr. Vossoughi acknowledged having been compensated by * * * UDC from his teaching salary to prepare the course materials and teach the courses. But this fact does not diminish the value of his course materials to Dr. Vossoughi; if anything, it confirms their value.

DECISION AND REMEDY • *The District of Columbia Court of Appeals affirmed the award. Vossoughi's evidence was "not speculative and unreliable." His lost property was difficult to value, but the evidence allowed the jury to make a fair estimate of its worth.*

THE LEGAL ENVIRONMENT DIMENSION • *Should plaintiffs be required to prove the amount of their damages with certainty and exactitude? Why or why not?*

THE ETHICAL DIMENSION • *Did Vossoughi have an ethical duty to reduce the amount of his damages by, for example, retrieving from the trash as much of his property as he could? Discuss.*

Disparagement of Property

Disparagement of property occurs when economically injurious falsehoods are made about another's product or property rather than about another's reputation (as in the tort of defamation). *Disparagement of property* is a general term for torts that can be more specifically referred to as *slander of quality* or *slander of title.*

SLANDER OF QUALITY The publication of false information about another's product, alleging that it is not what its seller claims, constitutes the tort of **slander of quality,** or **trade libel.** To establish trade libel, the plaintiff must prove that the improper publication caused a third person to refrain from dealing with the plaintiff and that the plaintiff sustained economic damages (such as lost profits) as a result.

An improper publication may be both a slander of quality and a defamation of character. For example, a statement that disparages the quality of a product may also, by implication, disparage the character of a person who would sell such a product.

SLANDER OF TITLE When a publication falsely denies or casts doubt on another's legal ownership of property, resulting in financial loss to the property's owner, the tort of **slander of title** occurs. Usually, this is an intentional tort in which someone knowingly publishes an untrue statement about another's ownership of certain property with the intent of discouraging a third person from dealing with the person slandered. For example, it would be difficult for a car dealer to attract customers after competitors published a notice that the dealer's stock consisted of stolen automobiles.

See *Concept Summary 6.2* for a review of intentional torts against property.

SECTION 5
CYBER TORTS

Torts can also be committed in the online environment. Torts committed via the Internet are often called **cyber torts.** Over the years, the courts have had to decide how to apply traditional tort law to torts committed in cyberspace. To date, most cyber torts have involved defamation, so this discussion will focus on how the traditional tort law concerning defamation is being adapted to apply to online defamation.

Identifying the Author of Online Defamation

An initial issue raised by online defamation was simply discovering who was committing it. In the real world, identifying the author of a defamatory remark generally is an easy matter, but suppose that a business firm has discovered that defamatory statements about its policies and products are being posted in an online forum. Such forums allow anyone—customers, employees, or crackpots—to complain about a firm that they dislike while remaining anonymous.

Therefore, a threshold barrier to anyone who seeks to bring an action for online defamation is discovering the identity of the person who posted the defamatory message. An Internet service provider (ISP)—a company that provides connections to the Internet—can disclose personal information about its customers only when ordered to do so by a court. Consequently, businesses and individuals are increasingly bringing lawsuits against "John Does" (John Doe, Jane Doe, and the like are fictitious names used in lawsuits when the identity of a party is not known or when a party wishes to conceal his or her name for privacy reasons). Then, using the authority of the courts, the plaintiffs can obtain from the ISPs the identity of the persons responsible for the defamatory messages.

CONCEPT SUMMARY 6.2
Intentional Torts against Property

Name of Tort	Description
Trespass to Land	The invasion of another's real property without consent or privilege. Once a person is expressly or impliedly established as a trespasser, the property owner has specific rights, which may include the right to detain or remove the trespasser.
Trespass to Personal Property	The intentional interference with an owner's right to use, possess, or enjoy his or her personal property without the owner's consent.
Conversion	The wrongful possession or use of another person's personal property without just cause.
Disparagement of Property	Any economically injurious falsehood that is made about another's product or property; an inclusive term for the torts of *slander of quality* and *slander of title*.

Liability of Internet Service Providers

Recall from the discussion of defamation earlier in this chapter that one who repeats or otherwise republishes a defamatory statement is subject to liability as if he or she had originally published it. Thus, newspapers, magazines, and television and radio stations may be subject to liability for defamatory content that they publish or broadcast, even though the content was prepared or created by others. Applying this rule to cyberspace, however, raises an important issue: Should ISPs be regarded as publishers and therefore be held liable for defamatory messages that are posted by their users in online forums or other arenas?

Before 1996, the courts grappled with this question. Then Congress passed the Communications Decency Act (CDA), which states that "[n]o provider or user of an interactive computer service shall be treated as the publisher or speaker of any information provided by another information content provider."[22] Thus, under the CDA, ISPs generally are treated differently from publishers in print and other media and are not liable for publishing defamatory statements that come from a third party.[23]

Although the courts generally have construed the CDA as providing a broad shield to protect ISPs from liability for third-party content, some courts have started establishing some limits to CDA immunity. In the following case, the court considered the scope of immunity that could be accorded to an online roommate-matching service under the CDA.

---

22. 47 U.S.C. Section 230.
23. For a leading case on this issue, see *Zeran v. America Online, Inc.,* 129 F.3d 327 (4th Cir. 1997); *cert.* denied, 524 U.S. 937, 118 S.Ct. 2341, 141 L.Ed.2d 712 (1998). See also *Hechtman v. Connecticut Department of Public Health,* 2009 WL 5303796 (Conn.Sup. 2009).

CASE 6.3
Fair Housing Council of San Fernando Valley v. Roommate.com, LLC

United States Court of Appeals, Ninth Circuit, 521 F.3d 1157 (2008).

BACKGROUND AND FACTS • Roommate.com, LLC, operates an online roommate-matching Web site at www.roommates.com. (The company uses the singular *Roommate* for its name but the plural *roommates* for its Web site.) The site helps individuals find roommates based on their descriptions of themselves and their roommate preferences. The site has approximately 150,000 active listings and receives about a million user views per day. To become members of Roommate, users respond to a series of online questions, choosing from answers in drop-down and select-a-box menus. Users disclose information about themselves and their roommate preferences based on age, gender, and other characteristics, and on whether children will live in the household. Members can create personal profiles, search lists of compatible roommates, and send "roommail" messages to other members. Roommate also e-mails newsletters to members seeking housing, listing compatible members who have places to rent. The Fair Housing Councils of San Fernando Valley and San Diego, California, filed a suit in a federal district court against Roommate, claiming that the defendant had violated the Fair Housing Act (FHA). The court held that the Communications Decency Act (CDA) barred this claim and dismissed it. The councils appealed to the U.S. Court of Appeals for the Ninth Circuit.

IN THE LANGUAGE OF THE COURT
KOZINSKI, Chief Judge.
* * * *

Section 230 of the CDA immunizes providers of interactive computer services against liability arising from content created by third parties[.] * * * *This grant of immunity applies only if the interactive computer service provider is not also an "information content provider," which is defined as someone who is "responsible, in whole or in part, for the creation or development of" the offending content.* [Emphasis added.]
* * * *

In passing Section 230, Congress sought to [allow] interactive computer services * * * to perform some editing on user-generated content without thereby becoming liable for all defamatory or otherwise unlawful messages that they didn't edit or delete. In other words, Congress sought to immunize the *removal* of user-generated content, not the *creation* of content: "Section

CASE 6.3 CONTINUED ▶ [230] provides 'Good Samaritan' protections from civil liability for providers * * * of an interactive computer service for actions to *restrict* * * * access to objectionable material."

* * * Councils allege that requiring subscribers to disclose their sex, family status and sexual orientation "indicates" an intent to discriminate against them, and thus runs afoul [of the FHA]. Roommate created the questions and choice of answers, and designed its website registration process around them. Therefore, Roommate is undoubtedly the "information content provider" as to the questions and can claim no immunity for posting them on its website, or for forcing subscribers to answer them as a condition of using its services.

* * * *

Councils also claim that requiring subscribers to answer the questions as a condition of using Roommate's services unlawfully "cause[s]" subscribers to make a "statement * * * with respect to the sale or rental of a dwelling that indicates [a] preference, limitation, or discrimination," in violation of [the Fair Housing Act]. The CDA does not grant immunity for inducing third parties to express illegal preferences. Roommate's own acts—posting the questionnaire and requiring answers to it—are entirely its doing and thus Section 230 of the CDA does not apply to them. Roommate is entitled to no immunity.

Councils also charge that Roommate's development and display of subscribers' discriminatory preferences [are] unlawful. Roommate publishes a "profile page" for each subscriber on its website.

* * * *

Here, the part of the profile that is alleged to offend the Fair Housing Act * * * —the information about sex, family status and sexual orientation—is provided by subscribers in response to Roommate's questions, which they cannot refuse to answer if they want to use defendant's services. By requiring subscribers to provide the information as a condition of accessing its service, and by providing a limited set of [available] answers, Roommate becomes much more than a passive transmitter of information provided by others; it becomes the developer, at least in part, of that information. And Section 230 provides immunity only if the interactive computer service does not "creat[e] or develop" the information "in whole or in part."

DECISION AND REMEDY • *The U.S. Court of Appeals for the Ninth Circuit concluded that the CDA does not immunize Roommate for all of the content on its Web site and in its e-mail newsletters. The appellate court reversed the lower court's summary judgment and remanded the case for a determination of whether Roommate's nonimmune publication and distribution of information violate the FHA.*

THE ETHICAL DIMENSION • *Do Internet service providers (ISPs) have an ethical duty to advise their users if the information that the users provide for distribution through the ISPs might violate the law? Explain.*

THE E-COMMERCE DIMENSION • *Should the courts continue to regard the CDA's grant of immunity to ISPs as "quite robust"? Why or why not?*

The Spread of Spam

Businesses and individuals alike are targets of **spam.** Spam refers to the unsolicited "junk e-mails" that flood virtual mailboxes with advertisements, solicitations, and other messages.[24] Considered relatively harmless in the early days of the Internet's popularity, by 2010 spam accounted for roughly 75 percent of all e-mails.

STATE REGULATION OF SPAM In an attempt to combat spam, thirty-six states have enacted laws that prohibit or regulate its use. Many state laws that regulate spam require the senders of e-mail ads to instruct the recipients on how they can "opt out" of further e-mail ads from the same sources. For instance, in some states an unsolicited e-mail ad must include a toll-free phone number or return e-mail address through which the recipient can contact the sender to request that no more ads be e-mailed. Responding to complaints from overwhelmed constituents, a number of jurisdictions have started to pass anti-spamming laws.

---

24. The term *spam* is said to come from a Monty Python song with the lyrics, "Spam spam spam spam, spam spam spam spam, lovely spam, wonderful spam." Like these lyrics, spam online is often considered to be a repetition of worthless text.

THE FEDERAL CAN-SPAM ACT In 2003, Congress enacted the Controlling the Assault of Non-Solicited Pornography and Marketing (CAN-SPAM) Act. The legislation applies to any "commercial electronic mail messages" that are sent to promote a commercial product or service. Significantly, the statute preempts state antispam laws except for those provisions in state laws that prohibit false and deceptive e-mailing practices.

Generally, the act permits the sending of unsolicited commercial e-mail but prohibits certain types of spamming activities, including the use of a false return address and the use of false, misleading, or deceptive information when sending e-mail. The statute also prohibits the use of "dictionary attacks"—sending messages to randomly generated e-mail addresses—and the "harvesting" of e-mail addresses from Web sites through the use of specialized software.

CASE IN POINT In 2007, federal officials arrested Robert Alan Soloway, who was known as the "Spam King" and considered one of the world's most prolific spammers. Soloway had been using *botnets* (networks of software robots, or bots, that run automatically) to send out hundreds of millions of unwanted e-mails. He was charged under anti–identity theft laws for the appropriation of other people's domain names, among other crimes. Soloway pleaded guilty to mail fraud, spam, and failure to pay taxes.[25]

Arresting prolific spammers, however, has done little to curb spam, which continues to flow at a rate of 70 billion messages per day.

THE U.S. SAFE WEB ACT After the CAN-SPAM Act of 2003 prohibited false and deceptive e-mails originating in the United States, spamming from servers located in other nations increased. These cross-border spammers generally were able to escape detection and legal sanctions because the Federal Trade Commission (FTC) lacked the authority to investigate foreign spamming.

Congress sought to rectify the situation by enacting the U.S. Safe Web Act of 2006 (also known as the Undertaking Spam, Spyware, and Fraud Enforcement with Enforcers Beyond Borders Act). The act allows the FTC to cooperate and share information with foreign agencies in investigating and prosecuting those involved in spamming, spyware, and various Internet frauds and deceptions. It also provides ISPs with a "safe harbor" (immunity from liability) for supplying information to the FTC concerning possible unfair or deceptive conduct in foreign jurisdictions.

---

25. "'Spam King of Seattle' Soloway pleads guilty." *SC Magazine.* 17 March 2008: n.p. Web.

REVIEWING
Intentional Torts and Privacy

Two sisters, Darla and Irene, are partners in an import business located in a small town in Rhode Island. Irene is married to a well-known real estate developer and is campaigning to be the mayor of their town. Darla is in her mid-thirties and has never been married. Both sisters travel to other countries to purchase the goods they sell at their retail store. Irene buys Indonesian goods, and Darla buys goods from Africa. After a tsunami destroys many of the cities in Indonesia to which Irene usually travels, she phones one of her contacts there and asks him to procure some items and ship them to her. He informs her that it will be impossible to buy these items now because the townspeople are being evacuated due to a water shortage. Irene is angry and tells the man that if he cannot purchase the goods, he should just take them without paying for them after the town has been evacuated. Darla overhears her sister's instructions and is outraged. They have a falling-out, and Darla decides that she no longer wishes to be in business with her sister. Using the information presented in the chapter, answer the following questions.

1. Suppose that Darla tells several of her friends about Irene's instructing the man to take goods without paying for them after the tsunami disaster. If Irene files a tort action against Darla alleging slander, will her suit be successful? Why or why not?
2. Now suppose that Irene wins the election and becomes the city's mayor. Darla then writes a letter to the editor of the local newspaper disclosing Irene's misconduct. If Irene accuses Darla of committing libel, what defenses could Darla assert?

REVIEWING
Intentional Torts and Privacy, Continued

3. If Irene accepts goods shipped from Indonesia that were wrongfully obtained, has she committed an intentional tort against property? Explain.

4. Suppose now that Irene, who is angry with her sister for disclosing her business improprieties, writes a letter to the editor falsely accusing Darla of having sexual relations with her neighbor's thirteen-year-old son. For what intentional tort or torts could Darla sue Irene in this situation?

⊛ **DEBATE THIS:** *Because of the often anonymous nature of the Internet, defamation has become an outdated legal concept. It's now too difficult to track down the person responsible for the defamatory statement.*

TERMS AND CONCEPTS

actionable 118

actual malice 122

appropriation 122

assault 118

battery 118

business tort 124

compensatory damages 116

conversion 127

cyber tort 129

defamation 119

disparagement of
    property 128

fraudulent
    misrepresentation 123

intentional tort 117

libel 119

privilege 121

public figure 121

puffery 123

punitive damages 117

slander 119

slander of quality 129

slander of title 129

spam 131

tort 116

tortfeasor 117

trade libel 129

trespass to land 126

trespass to personal
    property 127

QUESTIONS AND CASE PROBLEMS

6–1. Defamation Richard is an employee of the Dun Construction Corp. While delivering materials to a construction site, he carelessly backs Dun's truck into a passenger vehicle driven by Green. This is Richard's second accident in six months. When the company owner, Dun, learns of this latest accident, a heated discussion ensues, and Dun fires Richard. Dun is so angry that he immediately writes a letter to the union of which Richard is a member and to all other construction companies in the community, stating that Richard is the "worst driver in the city" and that "anyone who hires him is asking for legal liability." Richard files a suit against Dun, alleging libel on the basis of the statements made in the letters. Discuss the results.

6–2. QUESTION WITH SAMPLE ANSWER: Wrongful Interference.

Lothar owns a bakery. He has been trying to obtain a long-term contract with the owner of Martha's Tea Salons for some time. Lothar starts a local advertising campaign on radio and television and in the newspaper. This advertising campaign is so persuasive that Martha decides to break the contract she has had with Harley's Bakery so that she can patronize Lothar's bakery. Is Lothar liable to Harley's Bakery for the tort of wrongful interference with a contractual relationship? Is Martha liable for this tort?

• **For a sample answer to Question 6–2, go to Appendix I at the end of this text.**

6–3. Intentional Torts against Property Gerrit is a former employee of ABC Auto Repair Co. He enters ABC's repair shop, claiming that the company owes him $800 in back wages. Gerrit argues with ABC's general manager, Steward, and Steward orders him off the property. Gerrit refuses to leave, and Steward tells two mechanics to throw him off the property. Gerrit runs to his truck, but on the way, he grabs some tools valued at $800; then he drives away. Gerrit refuses to return the tools.

(a) Discuss whether Gerrit has committed any torts.

(b) If the mechanics had thrown Gerrit off the property, would ABC be guilty of assault and battery? Explain.

6–4. Trespass to Property America Online, Inc. (AOL), provides services to its customers or members, including the transmission of e-mail to and from other members and across the Internet. To become a member, a person must agree not to use AOL's computers to send bulk, unsolicited, commercial e-mail (spam). AOL uses filters to block spam, but bulk e-mailers sometimes use other software to thwart the filters. National Health Care Discount, Inc. (NHCD), sells discount optical and dental service plans. To generate leads for NHCD's products, sales representatives, who included AOL members, sent more than 300 million pieces of spam through AOL's computer system. Each item cost AOL an estimated $0.00078 in equipment expenses. Some of the spam used false headers and other methods to hide the source. After receiving more than 150,000 complaints from its members, AOL asked NHCD to stop. When the spam continued, AOL filed a suit in a federal district court against NHCD, alleging, in part, trespass to chattels—an unlawful interference with another's rights to possess personal property. AOL asked the court for a summary judgment on this claim. Did the spamming constitute trespass to chattels? Explain. [*America Online, Inc. v. National Health Care Discount, Inc.,* 121 F.Supp.2d 1255 (N.D. Iowa 2000)]

6–5. Intentional Torts against Property Gary Kremen registered the domain name "sex.com" with Network Solutions, Inc., to the name of Kremen's business, Online Classifieds. Later, Stephen Cohen sent Network Solutions a letter that he claimed to have received from Online Classifieds. It stated that "we have no objections to your use of the domain name sex.com and this letter shall serve as our authorization to the Internet registrar to transfer sex.com to your corporation." Without contacting Kremen, Network Solutions transferred the name to Cohen, who subsequently turned sex.com into a lucrative business. Kremen filed a suit in a federal district court against Cohen and others, seeking the name and Cohen's profits. The court ordered Cohen to return the name to Kremen and pay $65 million in damages. Cohen ignored the order and disappeared. Against what other parties might Kremen attempt to obtain relief? Under which theory of intentional torts against property might Kremen be able to file an action? What is the likely result, and why? [*Kremen v. Cohen,* 337 F.3d 1024 (9th Cir. 2003)]

6–6. Invasion of Privacy During the spring and summer of 1999, Edward and Geneva Irvine received numerous "hang-up" phone calls, including three calls in the middle of the night. With the help of their local phone company, the Irvines learned that many of the calls were from the telemarketing department of the *Akron Beacon Journal* in Akron, Ohio. The *Beacon*'s sales force was equipped with an automatic dialing machine. During business hours, the dialer was used to maximize productivity by calling multiple phone numbers at once and connecting a call to a sales representative only after it was answered. After business hours, the *Beacon* programmed its dialer to dial a list of disconnected numbers

to determine whether they had been reconnected. If the dialer detected a ring, it recorded the information and dropped the call. If the automated dialing system crashed, which happened frequently, it redialed the entire list. The Irvines filed a suit in an Ohio state court against the *Beacon* and others, alleging, among other things, an invasion of privacy. In whose favor should the court rule, and why? [*Irvine v. Akron Beacon Journal,* 147 Ohio App.3d 428, 770 N.E.2d 1105 (9 Dist. 2002)]

6–7. Defamation Lydia Hagberg went to her bank, California Federal Bank, FSB, to cash a check made out to her by Smith Barney (SB), an investment services firm. Nolene Showalter, a bank employee, suspected that the check was counterfeit. Showalter called SB and was told that the check was not valid. As she phoned the police, Gary Wood, a bank security officer, contacted SB again and was informed that its earlier statement was "erroneous" and that the check was valid. Meanwhile, a police officer arrived, drew Hagberg away from the teller's window, spread her legs, patted her down, and handcuffed her. The officer searched her purse, asked her whether she had any weapons and whether she was driving a stolen vehicle, and arrested her. Hagberg filed a suit in a California state court against the bank and others, alleging slander. Should the absolute privilege for communications made in judicial or other official proceedings apply to statements made when a citizen contacts the police to report suspected criminal activity? Why or why not? [*Hagberg v. California Federal Bank, FSB,* 32 Cal.4th 350, 7 Cal.Rptr.3d 803 (2004)]

6–8. CASE PROBLEM WITH SAMPLE ANSWER: Emotional Distress.

Between 1996 and 1998, Donna Swanson received several anonymous, handwritten letters that, among other things, accused her husband Alan of infidelity. In 1998, John Grisham, Jr., the author of The Firm *and many other best-selling novels, received an anonymous letter that appeared to have been written by the same person. Grisham and the Swansons suspected Katherine Almy, who soon filed a suit in a Virginia state court against them, alleging, among other things, intentional infliction of emotional distress. According to Almy, Grisham had said that he "really, really wanted to make [her] suffer for writing those letters," and the three devised a scheme to falsely accuse her. They gave David Liebman, a handwriting analyst, samples of Almy's handwriting. These included copies of confidential documents from her children's files at St. Anne's–Belfield School in Charlottesville, Virginia, where Alan Swanson taught and Grisham served on the board of directors. In Almy's view, Grisham influenced Liebman to report that Almy might have written the letters and misrepresented this report as conclusive, which led the police to confront Almy. She claimed that she then suffered severe emotional distress and depression, causing "a complete disintegration of virtually every aspect of her life" and requiring her "to undergo extensive therapy." In response, the defendants asked the court to dismiss the complaint for failure to state a claim. Should the court grant this request? Explain.* [*Almy v. Grisham,* 273 Va. 68, 639 S.E.2d 182 (2007)]

- To view a sample answer for Problem 6–8, go to this book's Web site at www.cengage.com/blaw/clarkson, select "Chapter 6," and click on "Case Problem with Sample Answer."

6–9. Libel and Invasion of Privacy The *Northwest Herald*, a newspaper in Illinois, regularly received e-mail reports from area police departments about criminal arrests. The paper published the information, which is proper because the reports are public records. One day, the *Herald* received an e-mail stating that Carolene Eubanks had been charged with theft and obstruction of justice. The paper put that information into an issue that was to be published four days later. Several hours after the original e-mail had been received, the police issued another e-mail, explaining that Eubanks had not been charged with anything; the correct name was Barbara Bradshaw. Due to a long weekend, no one at the *Herald* noticed the e-mail until after the paper had been published. The following day, five days after the e-mails had been received, the paper published a correction. Eubanks sued the *Herald* for libel and for invasion of privacy. Does Eubanks have a good case for either tort? Why or why not? [*Eubanks v. Northwest Herald Newspapers*, 922 N.E.2d 1196 (App.Ct.Ill. 2010)]

6–10. A QUESTION OF ETHICS: Wrongful Interference with a Contractual Relationship.

White Plains Coat & Apron Co. is a New York–based linen rental business. Cintas Corp. is a nationwide business that rents similar products.

White Plains had five-year exclusive contracts with some of its customers. As a result of Cintas's soliciting of business, dozens of White Plains' customers breached their contracts and entered into rental agreements with Cintas. White Plains demanded that Cintas stop its solicitation of White Plains' customers. Cintas refused. White Plains filed a suit in a federal district court against Cintas, alleging wrongful interference with existing contracts. Cintas argued that it had no knowledge of any contracts with White Plains and had not induced any breach. The court dismissed the suit, ruling that Cintas had a legitimate interest as a competitor to solicit business and make a profit. White Plains appealed to the U.S. Court of Appeals for the Second Circuit. [White Plains Coat & Apron Co. v. Cintas Corp., 8 N.Y.3d 422, 867 N.E.2d 381 (2007)]

(a) What are the two important policy interests at odds in wrongful interference cases? Which of these interests should be accorded priority?

(b) The U.S. Court of Appeals for the Second Circuit asked the New York Court of Appeals to answer a question: Is a general interest in soliciting business for profit a sufficient defense to a claim of wrongful interference with a contractual relationship? What do you think? Why?

LEGAL RESEARCH EXERCISES ON THE WEB

Go to this text's Web site at www.cengage.com/blaw/clarkson, select "Chapter 6," and click on "Practical Internet Exercises." There you will find the following Internet research exercises that you can perform to learn more about the topics covered in this chapter.

Practical Internet Exercise 6–1: **Legal Perspective**
Online Defamation

Practical Internet Exercise 6–2: **Management Perspective**
Legal and Illegal Uses of Spam

CHAPTER 7

Negligence and Strict Liability

The intentional torts discussed in Chapter 6 all involve acts that the tortfeasor (the one committing the tort) intended to commit. In this chapter, we examine the tort of negligence, which involves acts that depart from a reasonable standard of care and therefore create an unreasonable risk of harm to others.

Negligence suits are probably the most prevalent type of lawsuits brought against businesses today. It is therefore essential that businesspersons understand their potential liability for negligent acts. In the concluding pages of this chapter, we also look at another basis for liability

in tort—*strict liability*. Under this tort doctrine, liability depends not on the actor's negligence or intent to harm but on the breach of an absolute duty to make something safe.

SECTION 1
NEGLIGENCE

The tort of **negligence** occurs when someone suffers injury because of another's failure to live up to a required *duty of care*. In contrast to intentional torts, in torts involving negligence, the tortfeasor neither wishes to bring about the consequences of the act nor believes that they will occur. The actor's conduct merely creates a risk of such consequences. If no risk is created, there is no negligence. Moreover, the risk must be foreseeable; that is, it must be such that a reasonable person engaging in the same activity would anticipate the risk and guard against it. In determining what is reasonable conduct, courts consider the nature of the possible harm. Creating a very slight risk of a dangerous explosion might be unreasonable, whereas creating a distinct possibility of someone's burning his or her fingers on a stove might be reasonable.

Many of the actions discussed in the chapter on intentional torts constitute negligence if the element of intent is missing (or cannot be proved). Suppose that Juarez walks up to Maya and intentionally shoves her. Maya falls and breaks her arm as a result. In this situation, Juarez committed an intentional tort (battery). If Juarez carelessly bumps into Maya,

however, and she falls and breaks her arm as a result, Juarez's action constitutes negligence. In either situation, Juarez has committed a tort.

To succeed in a negligence action, the plaintiff must prove each of the following:

1. *Duty.* That the defendant owed a duty of care to the plaintiff.
2. *Breach.* That the defendant breached that duty.
3. *Causation.* That the defendant's breach caused the plaintiff's injury.
4. *Damages.* That the plaintiff suffered a legally recognizable injury.

We discuss each of these four elements of negligence on the following pages.

The Duty of Care and Its Breach

Central to the tort of negligence is the concept of a **duty of care.** This concept arises from the notion that if we are to live in society with other people, some actions can be tolerated and some cannot, and some actions are reasonable and some are not. The basic principle underlying the duty of care is that people are free to act as they please so long as their actions do not infringe on the interests of others.

When someone fails to comply with the duty to exercise reasonable care, a potentially tortious act may have been committed. Failure to live up to a standard of care may be an act (accidentally setting fire to a building) or an omission (neglecting to put out a campfire). It may be a careless act or a carefully performed but nevertheless dangerous act that results in injury. Courts consider the nature of the act (whether it is outrageous or commonplace), the manner in which the act is performed (heedlessly versus cautiously), and the nature of the injury (whether it is serious or slight) in determining whether the duty of care has been breached.

CASE IN POINT Stella Liebeck, an eighty-year-old woman, purchased a cup of coffee at a McDonald's drive-through window. As she removed the lid, Liebeck held the cup between her legs and accidentally spilled the coffee on herself, causing third degree burns. She was hospitalized for eight days and underwent skin grafts but suffered permanent scars. At trial, evidence showed that McDonald's required its restaurants to serve their coffee at 180 to 190 degrees Fahrenheit—10 to 30 degrees hotter than competitors' restaurants. At that temperature, the coffee would cause third-degree burns in two to seven seconds. Based on this evidence, a jury found that McDonald's had breached its duty of care and awarded Liebeck a famously large amount of compensatory and punitive damages.[1] As a result of this case, restaurants have reduced the temperature at which they serve coffee to their customers.

THE REASONABLE PERSON STANDARD Tort law measures duty by the **reasonable person standard.** In determining whether a duty of care has been breached, for example, the courts ask how a reasonable person would have acted in the same circumstances. The reasonable person standard is said to be (though in an

absolute sense it cannot be) objective. It is not necessarily how a particular person *would* act. It is society's judgment of how an ordinarily prudent person *should* act. If the so-called reasonable person existed, he or she would be careful, conscientious, even tempered, and honest. That individuals are required to exercise a reasonable standard of care in their activities is a pervasive concept in business law, and many of the issues dealt with in subsequent chapters of this text have to do with this duty.

In negligence cases, the degree of care to be exercised varies, depending on the defendant's occupation or profession, her or his relationship with the plaintiff, and other factors. Generally, whether an action constitutes a breach of the duty of care is determined on a case-by-case basis. The outcome depends on how the judge (or jury, if it is a jury trial) decides a reasonable person in the position of the defendant would have acted in the particular circumstances of the case. In the following subsections, we examine the degree of care typically expected of landowners and professionals.

THE DUTY OF LANDOWNERS Landowners are expected to exercise reasonable care to protect individuals coming onto their property from harm. In some jurisdictions, landowners may even have a duty to protect trespassers against certain risks. Landowners who rent or lease premises to tenants are expected to exercise reasonable care to ensure that the tenants and their guests are not harmed in common areas, such as stairways, entryways, and laundry rooms (see Chapter 50).

Landowners who rent or lease premises to tenants also have a duty to supply correct information to tenants. If they breach this duty, landowners can be held liable for negligent misrepresentation. Unlike intentional misrepresentation, or fraud, negligent misrepresentation requires only that the person making the statement or omission did not have a reasonable basis for believing its truthfulness.

In the following case, a commercial tenant claimed that the landlord made negligent misrepresentations about the size of a leased space.

---

1. *Liebeck v. McDonald's Restaurants,* No. D-202-CV 9302419, 1995 WL 360309 (N.M. Dist.Ct. 1994). The jury awarded $200,000 in compensatory damages and $2.7 million in punitive damages, which the court reduced to $480,000 ($680,000 total). The parties appealed, but then entered into an out-of-court settlement for an undisclosed amount less than $600,000. See also *Boyle v. Christensen,* 219 P.3d 58 (Utah App. 2009).

CASE 7.1
McClain v. Octagon Plaza, LLC

Court of Appeal of California, Second District, 159 Cal.App.4th 784, 71 Cal.Rptr.3d 885 (2008).

BACKGROUND AND FACTS • Kelly McClain operates a business known as "A+ Teaching Supplies." Ted and Wanda Charanian are the principals of Octagon Plaza, LLC, which owns and manages

CASE CONTINUES ▶

CASE 7.1 CONTINUED ➡ a shopping center in Valencia, California. On February 28, 2003, McClain agreed to lease commercial space in the shopping center. The lease described the size of the unit leased by McClain as "approximately 2,624 square feet," and attached to the lease was a diagram of the shopping center that represented the size of the unit as 2,624 square feet. Because the base rent in the shopping center was $1.45 per square foot per month, McClain's total base rent was $3,804 per month. Moreover, because the unit presumably occupied 23 percent of the shopping center, McClain was responsible for this share of the common expenses. McClain filed a suit, claiming that the Charanians knew that the representations were materially inaccurate. As a result of Octagon's misrepresentations, McClain was induced to enter into a lease that obliged her to pay excess rent. At trial, the Charanians prevailed. McClain appealed.

IN THE LANGUAGE OF THE COURT
MANELLA, J. [Judge]
* * * *

McClain contends that the [first amended claim at trial] adequately alleges a claim for fraud in the inducement, that is, misrepresentation involving a contract in which "the promisor knows what he or she is signing but consent is induced by fraud." We agree. *Generally, "[t]he elements of fraud, which give rise to the tort action for deceit, are (a) misrepresentation (false representation, concealment, or nondisclosure); (b) knowledge of falsity (or 'scienter'); (c) intent to defraud, i.e., to induce reliance; (d) justifiable reliance; and (e) resulting damage."* Claims for negligent misrepresentation deviate from this set of elements. *"The tort of negligent misrepresentation does not require* scienter *or intent to defraud.* It encompasses 'the assertion, as a fact, of that which is not true, by one who has no reasonable ground for believing it to be true', and 'the positive assertion, in a manner not warranted by the information of the person making it, of that which is not true, though he believes it to be true.'"* [Emphasis added.]
* * * *

It is well established that the kind of disclaimer in Paragraph 2.4 [of the commercial lease], which asserts that McClain had an adequate opportunity to examine the leased unit, does not insulate Octagon from liability for fraud or prevent McClain from demonstrating justified reliance on the Charanians' representations.
* * * *

Here, McClain alleges that the Charanians exaggerated the size of her unit by 186 square feet, or 7.6 percent of its actual size, and increased her share of the common expenses by 4 percent through a calculation that understated the size of the shopping center by 965 square feet, or 8.1 percent of its actual size. [These discrepancies] operated to increase the rental payments incurred by McClain's retail business by more than $90,000 over the term of the lease.

DECISION AND REMEDY • *The state intermediate appellate court reversed the trial court's judgment with respect to McClain's claim for misrepresentation.*

THE ETHICAL DIMENSION • *At what point do the misrepresentations about the size of the leased space become unethical—at 1 percent, 2 percent, or more?*

THE LEGAL ENVIRONMENT DIMENSION • *What defense could the shopping center owners raise to counter McClain's claim?*

The Duty to Warn Business Invitees of Risks. Retailers and other firms that explicitly or implicitly invite persons to come onto their premises are usually charged with a duty to exercise reasonable care to protect these **business invitees.** For example, if you entered a supermarket, slipped on a wet floor, and sustained injuries as a result, the owner of the supermarket would be liable for damages if, when you slipped, there was no sign warning that the floor was wet. A court would hold that the business owner was negligent because the owner failed to exercise a reasonable degree of care in protecting the store's customers against foreseeable risks about which the owner knew or *should have known*. That a patron might slip on the wet floor and be injured as a result was a foreseeable risk, and the owner should have taken care to avoid this risk or warn the customer of it (by posting a sign or setting out orange cones, for example).

The landowner also has a duty to discover and remove any hidden dangers that might injure a customer or other invitee. Store owners have a duty to protect customers from slipping and injuring them-selves on merchandise that has fallen off the shelves, for example. Thus, the owners of business premises should evaluate and frequently reassess potential hazards on the property to ensure the safety of busi-ness invitees.

Obvious Risks Provide an Exception. Some risks, of course, are so obvious that an owner need not warn of them. For example, a business owner does not need to warn customers to open a door before attempting to walk through it. Other risks, however, even though they may seem obvious to a business owner, may not be so in the eyes of another, such as a child. In addition, even if a risk is obvious, that does not necessarily excuse a business owner from the duty to protect its customers from foreseeable harm.

CASE IN POINT Giorgio's Grill in Hollywood, Florida, is a restaurant that becomes a nightclub after certain hours. At those times, as the manager of Giorgio's knew, the staff and customers tradition-ally threw paper napkins into the air as the music played. The napkins landed on the floor, but no one picked them up. One night, Jane Izquierdo went to Giorgio's. She had been to the club on prior occasions and knew about the napkin-throwing tradition. Not long after arriving, Izquierdo slipped and fell, break-ing her leg. She required surgery and three months of recovery in a wheelchair. She sued Giorgio's for neg-ligence, but lost at trial because a jury found that the risk of slipping on the napkins was obvious. A state appellate court reversed the lower court's decision, however. The court held that the obviousness of a risk does not discharge a business owner's duty to maintain the premises in a safe condition (although it does discharge the duty to warn).[2]

THE DUTY OF PROFESSIONALS If an individual has knowledge or skill superior to that of an ordinary person, the individual's conduct must be consistent with that status. Professionals—including physi-cians, dentists, architects, engineers, accountants, and lawyers, among others—are required to have a standard minimum level of special knowledge and ability. Therefore, in determining what constitutes reasonable care in the case of professionals, the law takes their training and expertise into account. Thus, an accountant's conduct is judged not by the reasonable person standard, but by the reasonable accountant standard.

If a professional violates his or her duty of care toward a client, the client may bring a suit against the professional, alleging **malpractice,** which is essentially professional negligence. For example, a patient might sue a physician for *medical malpractice*. A client might sue an attorney for *legal malpractice*. The liability of professionals will be examined in fur-ther detail in Chapter 48.

NO DUTY TO RESCUE Although the law requires individuals to act reasonably and responsibly in their relations with one another, a person will not be considered negligent for failing to come to the aid of a stranger in peril. For example, assume that you are walking down a city street and see a pedestrian about to step directly in front of an oncoming bus. You realize that the person has not seen the bus and is unaware of the danger. Do you have a legal duty to warn that individual? No. Although most people would probably concede that, in this situation, the observer has an *ethical* duty to warn, tort law does not impose a general duty to rescue others in peril.

People involved in special relationships, how-ever, have been held to have a duty to rescue other parties within the relationship. A person has a duty to rescue his or her child or spouse if either is in dan-ger, for example. Other special relationships, such as those between teachers and students or hiking and hunting partners, may also give rise to a duty to rescue. In addition, if a person who has no duty to rescue undertakes to rescue another, then the res-cuer is charged with a duty to follow through with due care in the rescue attempt. Most states also have laws that require motorists involved in an automo-bile accident to stop and render aid. Failure to do so is both a tort and a crime.

Causation

Another element necessary to a negligence action is *causation*. If a person breaches a duty of care and someone suffers injury, the person's act must have caused the harm for it to constitute the tort of negligence.

In deciding whether the requirement of causa-tion is met, the court must address two questions:

1. *Is there causation in fact?* Did the injury occur because of the defendant's act, or would it have occurred anyway? If the injury would not have occurred without the defendant's act, then there is causation in fact. **Causation in fact** usually can be determined by use of the *but for* test: "but for" the wrongful act, the injury would not have

---

2. *Izquierdo v. Gyroscope, Inc.,* 946 So.2d 115 (Fla.App. 2007).

occurred. This test determines whether there was an actual cause-and-effect relationship between the act and the injury suffered. In theory, causation in fact is limitless. One could claim, for example, that "but for" the creation of the world, a particular injury would not have occurred. Thus, as a practical matter, the law has to establish limits, and it does so through the concept of proximate cause.

2. *Was the act the proximate, or legal, cause of the injury?* **Proximate cause,** or *legal cause,* exists when the connection between an act and an injury is strong enough to justify imposing liability. Proximate cause asks whether the injuries sustained were foreseeable or too remotely connected to the incident to trigger liability. Judges use proximate cause to limit the scope of the defendant's liability to a subset of the total number of potential plaintiffs that might have been harmed by the defendant's actions. Consider an example. Ackerman carelessly leaves a campfire burning. The fire not only burns down the forest but also sets off an explosion in a nearby chemical plant that spills chemicals into a river, killing all the fish for a hundred miles downstream and ruining the economy of a tourist resort. Should Ackerman be liable to the resort owners? To the tourists whose vacations were ruined? These are questions of proximate cause that a court must decide.

Both of these causation questions must be answered in the affirmative for liability in tort to arise. If a defendant's action constitutes causation in fact but a court decides that the action is not the proximate cause of the plaintiff's injury, the causation requirement has not been met—and the defendant normally will not be liable to the plaintiff.

Questions of proximate cause are linked to the concept of foreseeability because it would be unfair to impose liability on a defendant unless the defendant's actions created a foreseeable risk of injury. Probably the most cited case on the concept of foreseeability and proximate cause is the *Palsgraf* case, which is presented next.

CASE 7.2
Palsgraf v. Long Island Railroad Co.

Court of Appeals of New York, 248 N.Y. 339, 162 N.E. 99 (1928).

BACKGROUND AND FACTS • The plaintiff, Helen Palsgraf, was waiting for a train on a station platform. A man carrying a package was rushing to catch a train that was moving away from a platform across the tracks from Palsgraf. As the man attempted to jump aboard the moving train, he seemed unsteady and about to fall. A railroad guard on the car reached forward to grab him, and another guard on the platform pushed him from behind to help him board the train. In the process, the man's package, which (unknown to the railroad guards) contained fireworks, fell on the railroad tracks and exploded. There was nothing about the package to indicate its contents. The repercussions of the explosion caused scales at the other end of the train platform to fall on Palsgraf, causing injuries for which she sued the railroad company. At the trial, the jury found that the railroad guards had been negligent in their conduct. The railroad company appealed. The appellate court affirmed the trial court's judgment, and the railroad company appealed to New York's highest state court.

IN THE LANGUAGE OF THE COURT
CARDOZO, C.J. [Chief Justice]
* * * *

The conduct of the defendant's guard, if a wrong in its relation to the holder of the package, was not a wrong in its relation to the plaintiff, standing far away. Relatively to her it was not negligence at all.
* * * *

* * * What the plaintiff must show is "a wrong" to herself; i.e., a violation of her own right, and not merely a wrong to someone else[.] * * * *The risk reasonably to be perceived defines the duty to be obeyed[.]* * * * Here, by concession, there was nothing in the situation to suggest to the most cautious mind that the parcel wrapped in newspaper would spread wreckage through the station. If the guard had thrown it down knowingly and willfully, he would not have threatened the plaintiff's safety, so far as appearances could warn him. His conduct would not have

CASE 7.2 CONTINUED ➡ involved, even then, an unreasonable probability of invasion of her bodily security. Liability can be no greater where the act is inadvertent. [Emphasis added.]

    * * * One who seeks redress at law does not make out a cause of action by showing without more that there has been damage to his person. If the harm was not willful, he must show that the act as to him had possibilities of danger so many and apparent as to entitle him to be protected against the doing of it though the harm was unintended. * * * The victim does not sue * * * to vindicate an interest invaded in the person of another. * * * He sues for breach of a duty owing to himself.

    * * * [To rule otherwise] would entail liability for any and all consequences, however novel or extraordinary.

DECISION AND REMEDY • *Palsgraf's complaint was dismissed. The railroad had not been negligent toward her because injury to her was not foreseeable. Had the owner of the fireworks been harmed, and had he filed suit, there could well have been a different result.*

IMPACT OF THIS CASE ON TODAY'S LAW • *The* Palsgraf *case established foreseeability as the test for proximate cause. Today, the courts continue to apply this test in determining proximate cause—and thus tort liability for injuries. Generally, if the victim or the consequences of a harm done were unforeseeable, there is no proximate cause. Note, though, that in the online environment, distinctions based on physical proximity, such as that used by the court in this case, are largely inapplicable.*

INTERNATIONAL DIMENSION Differing Standards of Proximate Cause • *The concept of proximate cause is common among nations around the globe, but its application differs from country to country. French law uses the phrase "adequate cause." An event breaks the chain of adequate cause if the event is both unforeseeable and irresistible. England has a "nearest cause" rule that attributes liability based on which event was nearest in time and space. Mexico bases proximate cause on the foreseeability of the harm but does not require that an event be reasonably foreseeable.*

THE GLOBAL DIMENSION • *What would be the advantages and disadvantages of a universal principle of proximate cause applied everywhere by all courts in all relevant cases? Discuss.*

The Injury Requirement and Damages

For a tort to have been committed, the plaintiff must have suffered a *legally recognizable* injury. To recover damages (receive compensation), the plaintiff must have suffered some loss, harm, wrong, or invasion of a protected interest. Essentially, the purpose of tort law is to compensate for legally recognized harms and injuries resulting from wrongful acts. If no harm or injury results from a given negligent action, there is nothing to compensate—and no tort exists.

    For example, if you carelessly bump into a passerby, who stumbles and falls as a result, you may be liable in tort if the passerby is injured in the fall. If the person is unharmed, however, there normally can be no suit for damages because no injury was suffered.

    Compensatory damages are the norm in negligence cases. Occasionally, though, a court will award punitive damages if the defendant's conduct was *grossly negligent,* meaning that the defendant intentionally failed to perform a duty with reckless disregard of the consequences to others.

SECTION 2
DEFENSES TO NEGLIGENCE

Defendants often defend against negligence claims by asserting that the plaintiffs have failed to prove the existence of one or more of the required elements for negligence. Additionally, there are three basic *affirmative* defenses in negligence cases (defenses that a defendant can use to avoid liability even if the facts are as the plaintiff states): *assumption of risk, superseding cause,* and *contributory and comparative negligence.*

    Note that when a state has enacted a law that places a cap on the amount of noneconomic damages that can be awarded, this law can be similar to a defense because it limits the plaintiff's recovery. This chapter's *Insight into Ethics* feature on the next page discusses some effects of such limitations on damages.

Assumption of Risk

A plaintiff who voluntarily enters into a risky situation, knowing the risk involved, will not be

INSIGHT INTO ETHICS
Some Consequences of Caps on Medical Malpractice Awards

As discussed in Chapter 6, as part of the effort to curb excessive tort litigation, many states have enacted limits on the amount of general noneconomic damages that can be awarded. (Noneconomic damages include damages for pain and suffering, emotional distress, inconvenience, physical impairment, disfigurement, and the like.) Some states also specifically limit damage awards in medical malpractice (professional negligence) cases.

Limitations on Damages

Although placing such caps on damage awards may seem a logical way to reduce the number of negligence cases filed, it raises issues of fairness. Why should a plaintiff who loses a limb, for example, not be able to obtain adequate monetary damages for the mental anguish associated with such an injury? The limits also encourage plaintiffs' attorneys to find ways to avoid these caps, such as by suing other defendants (including nurses and additional health-care professionals) to whom the caps do not apply.

More than half of the states now limit damage awards in medical malpractice cases. For example, California caps noneconomic damages in medical malpractice cases at $250,000—even if the plaintiff dies.[a] States hope that these limitations will reduce the frequency and severity of malpractice claims and thereby reduce health-care expenditures, although there is no definitive scientific evidence showing that damages caps lower health-care costs.[b]

Michigan Nurse Sued for Negligence

As an example of how ethical issues can result from placing caps on medical malpractice claims, consider what happened in one Michigan case. A fifty-two-year-old Michigan farmer developed a blood clot in his leg and underwent emergency surgery at a hospital to remove it. After the surgery, a health-care professional removed the epidural catheter (a tube that enables painkillers to pass into the space surrounding the spinal cord). Eleven minutes later, a nurse came in and gave him a blood thinner called Heparin. According to the standard of care for this procedure, Heparin should not be given until at least one hour after the epidural catheter has been removed to ensure that the catheter site has sufficient time to coagulate and stop bleeding.

In this situation, the Heparin was given too soon and was given continuously for the next twenty-four hours. As a result, the patient experienced bleeding into the epidural space under his skin, and pressure built up in his spinal column. The hospital physicians and nurses failed to recognize the problem, and he was left with a permanent spinal cord injury and paralysis. Because of Michigan's cap on malpractice awards,[c] though, the negligent physician and the hospital responsible for his lifelong injuries were able to settle the claims against them for the legislatively mandated maximum of $717,000 for pain and suffering (and $1.1 million in economic damages).

CRITICAL THINKING
INSIGHT INTO THE SOCIAL ENVIRONMENT
If plaintiffs can still collect significant amounts of economic damages, will the limits on noneconomic damages be effective at reducing the number of negligence lawsuits filed? Why or why not?

---

a. See California Civil Code Section 3333.2.

b. Fred J. Hellinger and William E. Encinosa. "The Impact of State Laws Limiting Malpractice Damage Awards on Health Care Expenditures." *American Journal of Public Health.* August 2006: 1375–1381.

c. Michigan Compiled Laws Section 600.1483.

---

allowed to recover. This is the defense of **assumption of risk.** The requirements of this defense are (1) knowledge of the risk and (2) voluntary assumption of the risk. This defense is frequently asserted when the plaintiff was injured during recreational activities that involve known risk, such as skiing and skydiving. Note that assumption of risk can apply not only to participants in sporting events, but also to spectators and bystanders who are injured while attending those events.

CASE IN POINT Delinda Taylor, who was a Seattle Mariners fan, took her sons to see a Mariners baseball game. They arrived early so that they could watch the players warm up and get their autographs. Taylor was standing by her seat near the foul line watching Mariners' pitcher Freddie Garcia throwing the ball with another player. When she looked away from the field, an errant ball got past Garcia and struck Taylor in the face, causing serious injuries. She filed a negligence lawsuit against the Mariners (Baseball Club of Seattle) to recover for her injuries. The Mariners asserted the defense of assumption of risk. The court ruled that Taylor was familiar with baseball and that she knew about and had voluntarily assumed the risk of getting hit by a thrown baseball.[3]

ASSUMPTION OF RISK CAN BE EXPRESS OR IMPLIED The risk can be assumed by express agreement, or the assumption of risk can be implied by the plaintiff's knowledge of the risk and subsequent

conduct. For example, a driver, Bryan Stewart, knows that there is a risk of being killed or injured in a crash whenever he enters a race. Therefore, a court will deem that Stewart has assumed the risk of racing. Of course, a person does not assume a risk different from or greater than the risk normally carried by the activity. Thus, Stewart does not assume the risk that the banking in the curves of the racetrack will give way during the race because of a construction defect.

In the following case, the plaintiff was driving a beverage cart on a golf course during a golfing event. Does this mean that she was a "participant" in the sport and thus assumed the risk of being hit by a golf ball? That was the issue before the court.

---

3. *Taylor v. Baseball Club of Seattle, LP,* 132 Wash.App. 32, 130 P.3d 835 (2006); see also *Allred v. Capital Area Soccer League, Inc.,* 669 S.E.2d 777 (N.C.App. 2008).

✳ EXTENDED CASE 7.3 ✳
Pfenning v. Lineman

Court of Appeals of Indiana, 922 N.E.2d 45 (2010).
Indianalawblog.com/archives/ind_appct_decisions[a]

IN THE LANGUAGE OF THE COURT
DARDEN, Judge.
* * * *
* * * Whitey's [31 Club], a bar, sponsored a golf scramble at the Elks' golf course in Marion, [Indiana,] on August 19, 2006. * * * Jerry Jones * * * signed up to drive a beverage cart.

The morning of the scramble, Jones invited [his] then-sixteen-year-old [granddaughter, Cassie] Pfenning, to ride in a beverage cart with him during the tournament. With her mother's permission, Pfenning agreed to join Jones.

Upon arriving at the golf course, Jones retrieved a beverage cart for his and Pfenning's use * * * . The cart had a large cooler in the back for drinks but no roof or windshield. Pfenning received no instructions regarding how or where to operate the cart; she was unfamiliar with golf etiquette and had been to a golf course only once before in 1997.

Prior to the start of the scramble, Jones decided to join one of the

teams playing in the scramble as it was short a player. He therefore left Pfenning with his sister, Lottie Kendall. Kendall and Pfenning drove the beverage cart together for a short period of time until Kendall also decided to play in a foursome. Christie Edwards, a Whitey's employee, therefore took Kendall's place in the beverage cart. Pfenning drove the cart, and Edwards dispensed the beverages to the scramble's participants.

Approximately three hours into the tournament, [Joseph] Lineman, a participant in the scramble, hit a drive from the sixteenth hole's tee. * * * Pfenning, who was driving the beverage cart on a cart path near the eighteenth hole, did not hear any warning regarding the ball's approach. After traveling more than two hundred feet, the ball struck Pfenning in the mouth, causing injuries to her mouth, jaw, and teeth.

On February 7, 2007, Pfenning filed a complaint against the Defendants [Lineman, Whitey's, the Elks Club, and others]. She alleged [that the defendants were negligent

in failing to exercise reasonable care for her safety while on the golf course.]
* * * *

As a direct and proximate result of the Defendants' negligent conduct, [Pfenning] suffered painful and permanent injuries and incurred significant medical and dental expenses. Several of [her] teeth were destroyed and her teeth remain missing and/or disfigured.

As a direct and proximate result of the Defendants' negligent conduct, [Pfenning] suffered mental and emotional pain and anguish.

As a direct and proximate result of the Defendants' negligent conduct, [Pfenning]'s ability to function as a whole person has been impaired. The quality of [her] life has been significantly diminished as a result of the Defendants' negligent conduct.
* * *

* * * The trial court [granted] the Defendants' motions for summary judgment.
* * * *

Pfenning asserts that the trial court erred in granting summary

---

a. Scroll down the page to the link given under "February 12, 2010." When the next page opens, click on the case name to access the opinion. The Indiana Law Blog maintains this Web site.

EXTENDED CASE CONTINUES ➡

EXTENDED CASE 7.3 CONTINUED ⬇

judgment in favor of the Defendants. She argues that the Defendants owed her a duty to prevent her from being injured and were negligent in breaching that duty.

* * * *

This court had consistently held that *"there is no duty from one participant in a sports activity to another to prevent injury resulting from an inherent risk of the sport."* [Emphasis added.]

* * * *

Here, Pfenning maintains that she was not a participant in the golf scramble because "she was not playing; she was not watching the event; she was not signed up on a team; nor was she doing anything related to the activity of golf." Thus, she argues that the Defendants owed her a duty to prevent her injury. We disagree.

Pfenning's presence on the golf course was due to the fact there was a golf scramble; she had agreed to function as a driver or rider in a beverage cart provided for the golf scramble; and she performed this function and assisted in providing beverages to players in the golf scramble. If not for the golf scramble, Pfenning would not have been on the golf course the day of the incident. Although not a player herself, she clearly was "part of the sporting event * * * involved[.]"

* * * *

Pfenning, however, also seems to argue that she could not have consented to the inherent risks of golf as "she knew nothing about golf and could not appreciate any risk involved with being near a golf course." We find this argument unavailing [failing to achieve the desired result].

* * * *

Even if we were to assume that Pfenning arrived at the golf course utterly ignorant of the game, the undisputed facts show that Pfenning had been participating in the golf scramble event for approximately three hours prior to being struck by the golf ball. Over this extended time period, she had been delivering beverages to foursomes during play. We find that this supports an inference that Pfenning was aware of the inherent risks of golf; namely, that it involves players hitting golf balls long distances and that some, if not many, of these balls invariably fail to land where intended

Given Pfenning's status as a participant in the golf scramble, with its inherent risks, we find that the Defendants did not owe her a duty.

* * * *

Finding no issues of material fact and that the Defendants are entitled to summary judgment as a matter of law, we conclude that the trial court properly granted summary judgment in favor of the Defendants.

Affirmed.

 QUESTIONS

1. Should the courts distinguish between different levels of participation in a sporting event when determining liability? Explain.
2. Suppose that Pfenning had been riding in the beverage cart with her grandfather when she was struck by the golf ball. In that situation, would the outcome of this case have been any different? Why or why not?

WHEN COURTS DO NOT APPLY ASSUMPTION OF RISK Courts do not apply the assumption of risk doctrine in emergency situations. Nor does it apply when a statute protects a class of people from harm and a member of the class is injured by the harm. For instance, because federal and state statutes protect employees from harmful working conditions, employees do not assume the risks associated with the workplace. An employee who is injured generally will be compensated regardless of fault under state workers' compensation statutes (discussed in Chapter 34).

Superseding Cause

An unforeseeable intervening event may break the causal connection between a wrongful act and an injury to another. If so, the intervening event acts as a **superseding cause**—that is, it relieves a defendant of liability for injuries caused by the intervening event. For example, Derrick, while riding his bicycle, negligently hits Julie, who is walking on the sidewalk. As a result of the impact, Julie falls and fractures her hip. While she is waiting for help to arrive, a small aircraft crashes nearby and explodes, and some of the fiery debris hits her, causing her to sustain severe burns. Derrick will be liable for the damages related to Julie's fractured hip, but normally he will not be liable for the injuries caused by the plane crash—because the risk of a plane crashing nearby and injuring Julie was not foreseeable.

Contributory and Comparative Negligence

All individuals are expected to exercise a reasonable degree of care in looking out for themselves.

In the past, under the common law doctrine of **contributory negligence,** a plaintiff who was also negligent (failed to exercise a reasonable degree of care) could not recover anything from the defendant. Under this rule, no matter how insignificant the plaintiff's negligence was relative to the defendant's negligence, the plaintiff would be precluded from recovering any damages. Today, only a few jurisdictions still hold to this doctrine.

In most states, the doctrine of contributory negligence has been replaced by a **comparative negligence** standard. The comparative negligence standard enables both the plaintiff's and the defendant's negligence to be computed and the liability for damages distributed accordingly. The plaintiff's financial recovery may be reduced, or even prohibited, depending on whether the state has a pure or modified comparative negligence system.

"PURE" COMPARATIVE NEGLIGENCE STATES Some jurisdictions, including California and New York, have adopted a "pure" form of comparative negligence that allows the plaintiff to recover damages even if her or his fault is greater than that of the defendant. Under a pure comparative negligence system, a judge or jury assigns a percentage of fault to each responsible party and then apportions the damages award accordingly.

In states with such systems, even if the plaintiff's percentage of fault is very large, he or she will still be entitled to collect a share of damages from the other responsible party or parties. For example, Jill sustains injuries when her car is struck by Carson's truck. She files a lawsuit. At trial, the jury determines that Jill was also negligent and that Carson was only 20 percent at fault for the accident that caused Jill's injuries. Because they live in a pure comparative negligence state, Jill is entitled to recover 20 percent of the damages she sustained from Carson.

MODIFIED COMPARATIVE FAULT STATES Most jurisdictions in the United States have adopted a modified comparative fault system under which plaintiffs who are largely responsible for their own injuries are not allowed to recover damages. There are two variations of modified comparative fault systems: those that follow a "50 percent rule" and those that follow a "51 percent rule."

Under the 50 percent rule, the plaintiff in a negligence action recovers nothing if she or he was 50 percent or more at fault. Thus, an injured party can recover only if it is determined that his or her responsibility for the injury is 49 percent or less. If

the injured party's level of fault reaches 50 percent, he or she cannot recover *any* damages.

Under the 51 percent rule, the plaintiff in a negligence action recovers nothing if she or he was responsible for *more than half* (51 percent or more) of the accident. Thus, if the plaintiff was 50 percent at fault in causing the injury, then she or he can still recover, but once the plaintiff's level of fault reaches 51 percent, recovery is barred.

SECTION 3
SPECIAL NEGLIGENCE DOCTRINES AND STATUTES

A number of special doctrines and statutes relating to negligence are also important. We examine a few of them here.

Res Ipsa Loquitur

Generally, in lawsuits involving negligence, the plaintiff has the burden of proving that the defendant was negligent. In certain situations, however, the courts may presume that negligence has occurred, in which case the burden of proof rests on the defendant—that is, the defendant must prove that he or she was *not* negligent. The presumption of the defendant's negligence is known as the doctrine of ***res ipsa loquitur,***[4] which translates as "the facts speak for themselves." This doctrine is applied only when the event creating the damage or injury is one that ordinarily does not occur in the absence of negligence.

CASE IN POINT Mary Gubbins underwent abdominal surgery and, following the surgery, suffered nerve damage in her spine near the area of the operation. She was unable to walk or stand for months, and even though she regained some use of her legs through physical therapy, her mobility was impaired and she experienced pain. In her subsequent negligence lawsuit, Gubbins asserted *res ipsa loquitur,* because the injury never would have occurred in the absence of the surgeon's negligence.[5]

For the doctrine of *res ipsa loquitur* to apply, the event must have been within the defendant's power to control, and it must not have been due to any voluntary action or contribution on the part of the plaintiff.

---

4. Pronounced *rayz ihp*-suh *low*-kwuh-tuhr.

5. See, for example, *Gubbins v. Hurson,* 885 A.2d 269 (D.C. 2005).

Negligence *Per Se*

Certain conduct, whether it consists of an action or a failure to act, may be treated as **negligence *per se*** ("in or of itself"). Negligence *per se* may occur if an individual violates a statute or an ordinance providing for a criminal penalty and that violation causes another to be injured. The statute must be designed to prevent the type of injury that the plaintiff suffered, and it must clearly set out what standard of conduct is expected, when and where it is expected, and of whom it is expected. The standard of conduct required by the statute is the duty that the defendant owes to the plaintiff, and a violation of the statute is the breach of that duty.

CASE IN POINT A Delaware statute states that anyone "who operates a motor vehicle and who fails to give full time and attention to the operation of the vehicle" is guilty of inattentive driving. Michael Moore was cited for inattentive driving after he collided with Debra Wright's car when he backed a truck out of a parking space. Moore paid the ticket, which meant that he pleaded guilty to violating the statute. The day after the accident, Wright began having back pain, which eventually required surgery. She sued Moore for damages, alleging negligence *per se*. The Delaware Supreme Court ruled that the inattentive driving statute sets forth a sufficiently specific standard of conduct to warrant application of negligence *per se*.[6]

"Danger Invites Rescue" Doctrine

Sometimes, a person who is trying to avoid harm—such as an individual who swerves to avoid a head-on collision with a drunk driver—ends up causing harm to another (such as a cyclist riding in the bike lane) as a result. In those situations, the original wrongdoer (the drunk driver in this scenario) is liable to anyone who is injured, even if the injury actually resulted from another person's attempt to escape harm. The "danger invites rescue" doctrine extends the same protection to a person who is trying to rescue another from harm—the original wrongdoer is liable for injuries to the individual attempting a rescue.

Under the "danger invites rescue" doctrine, a person who is injured while going to someone else's rescue can sue the person who caused the dangerous situation. The idea is that the rescuer should not be held liable for any damages because he or she did not cause the danger and because danger invites rescue. For example, Ludlam drives down a street and fails to see a stop sign because he is trying to end a squabble between his two young children in the car's backseat. Salter, on the curb near the stop sign, realizes that Ludlam is about to hit a pedestrian walking across the street at the intersection. Salter runs into the street to push the pedestrian out of the way, and Ludlam's vehicle hits Salter instead. Ludlam will be liable for Salter's injury as the rescuer, as well as for any injuries the other pedestrian (or any bystanders) may have sustained.

Special Negligence Statutes

A number of states have enacted statutes prescribing duties and responsibilities in certain circumstances. For example, most states now have what are called **Good Samaritan statutes.**[7] Under these statutes, someone who is aided voluntarily by another cannot turn around and sue the "Good Samaritan" for negligence. These laws were passed largely to protect physicians and medical personnel who volunteer their services in emergency situations to those in need, such as individuals hurt in car accidents.[8] Indeed, the California Supreme Court has interpreted that state's Good Samaritan statute to mean that a person who renders nonmedical aid is not immune from liability.[9] Thus, only medical personnel and persons rendering medical aid in emergencies are protected in California.

Many states have also passed **dram shop acts,**[10] under which a tavern owner or bartender may be held liable for injuries caused by a person who became intoxicated while drinking at the bar or

---

6. *Wright v. Moore*, 931 A.2d 405 (Del.Supr. 2007).

7. These laws derive their name from the Good Samaritan story in the Bible. In the story, a traveler who had been robbed and beaten lay along the roadside, ignored by those passing by. Eventually, a man from the region of Samaria (the "Good Samaritan") stopped to render assistance to the injured person.

8. See, for example, the discussions of various state statutes in *Chamley v. Khokha*, 730 N.W.2d 864 (N.D. 2007), and *Mueller v. McMillian Warner Insurance Co.*, 2006 WI 54, 290 Wis.2d 571, 714 N.W.2d 183 (2006).

9. *Van Horn v. Watson*, 45 Cal.4th 322, 197 P.3d 164, 86 Cal. Rptr.3d 350 (2008).

10. Historically, a dram was a small unit of liquid, and distilled spirits (strong alcoholic liquor) were sold in drams. Thus, a dram shop was a place where liquor was sold in drams.

who was already intoxicated when served by the bartender. Some states' statutes also impose liability on *social hosts* (persons hosting parties) for injuries caused by guests who became intoxicated at the hosts' homes. Under these statutes, it is unnecessary to prove that the tavern owner, bartender, or social host was negligent. Thus, if Jane hosts a Super Bowl party at which Brett, a minor, sneaks alcoholic drinks, Jane is potentially liable for damages resulting from Brett's drunk driving after the party.

SECTION 4
STRICT LIABILITY

Another category of torts is called **strict liability,** or *liability without fault.* Intentional torts and torts of negligence involve acts that depart from a reasonable standard of care and cause injuries. Under the doctrine of strict liability, a person who engages in certain activities can be held responsible for any harm that results to others even if the person used the utmost care. Liability for injury is imposed for reasons other than fault.

Development of Strict Liability

The modern concept of strict liability traces its origins, in part, to the 1868 English case of *Rylands v. Fletcher.*[11] In the coal-mining area of Lancashire, England, the Rylands, who were mill owners, had constructed a reservoir on their land. Water from the reservoir broke through a filled-in shaft of an abandoned coal mine nearby and flooded the connecting passageways in an active coal mine owned by Fletcher. Fletcher sued the Rylands, and the court held that the defendants (the Rylands) were liable, even though the circumstances did not fit within existing tort liability theories. The court held that a "person who for his own purposes brings on his land and collects and keeps there anything likely to do mischief if it escapes . . . is *prima facie*[12] answerable for all the damage which is the natural consequence of its escape."

British courts liberally applied the doctrine that emerged from the *Rylands v. Fletcher* case. Initially, few U.S. courts accepted this doctrine, presumably because the courts were worried about its effect on the expansion of American business. Today, however, the doctrine of strict liability is the norm rather than the exception.

Abnormally Dangerous Activities

Strict liability for damages proximately caused by an abnormally dangerous, or ultrahazardous, activity is one application of strict liability. Courts apply the doctrine of strict liability in these situations because of the extreme risk of the activity. Abnormally dangerous activities are those that involve a high risk of serious harm to persons or property that cannot be completely guarded against by the exercise of reasonable care—activities such as blasting or storing explosives. Even if blasting with dynamite is performed with all reasonable care, there is still a risk of injury. Balancing that risk against the potential for harm, it seems reasonable to ask the person engaged in the activity to pay for injuries caused by that activity. Although there is no fault, there is still responsibility because of the dangerous nature of the undertaking.

Other Applications of Strict Liability

Persons who keep wild animals are strictly liable for any harm inflicted by the animals. The basis for applying strict liability is that wild animals, should they escape from confinement, pose a serious risk of harm to people in the vicinity. An owner of domestic animals (such as dogs, cats, cows, or sheep) may be strictly liable for harm caused by those animals if the owner knew, or should have known, that the animals were dangerous or had a propensity to harm others.

A significant application of strict liability is in the area of product liability—liability of manufacturers and sellers for harmful or defective products. Liability here is a matter of social policy and is based on two factors: (1) the manufacturing company can better bear the cost of injury because it can spread the cost throughout society by increasing prices of goods, and (2) the manufacturing company is making a profit from its activities and therefore should bear the cost of injury as an operating expense. We will discuss product liability in greater detail in Chapter 22. Strict liability is also applied in certain types of *bailments* (a bailment exists when goods are transferred temporarily into the care of another—see Chapter 49).

---

11. 3 L.R.–E & I App. [Law Reports, English & Irish Appeal Cases] (H.L. [House of Lords] 1868).

12. *Prima facie* is Latin for "at first sight." Legally, it refers to a fact that is presumed to be true unless contradicted by evidence.

REVIEWING
Negligence and Strict Liability

Elaine Sweeney went to Ragged Mountain Ski Resort in New Hampshire with a friend. Elaine went snow tubing down a snow-tube run designed exclusively for snow tubers. There were no Ragged Mountain employees present in the snow-tube area to instruct Elaine on the proper use of a snow tube. On her fourth run down the trail, Elaine crossed over the center line between snow-tube lanes, collided with another snow tuber, and was injured. Elaine filed a negligence action against Ragged Mountain seeking compensation for the injuries that she sustained. Two years earlier, the New Hampshire state legislature had enacted a statute that prohibited a person who participates in the sport of skiing from suing a ski-area operator for injuries caused by the risks inherent in skiing. Using the information presented in the chapter, answer the following questions.

1. What defense will Ragged Mountain probably assert?
2. The central question in this case is whether the state statute establishing that skiers assume the risks inherent in the sport bars Elaine's suit. What would your decision be on this issue? Why?
3. Suppose that the court concludes that the statute applies only to skiing and not to snow tubing. Will Elaine's lawsuit be successful? Explain.
4. Now suppose that the jury concludes that Elaine was partly at fault for the accident. Under what theory might her damages be reduced in proportion to the degree to which her actions contributed to the accident and her resulting injuries?

⦿ **DEBATE THIS:** *Each time a state legislature enacts a law that applies the assumption of risk doctrine to a particular sport, participants in that sport suffer.*

TERMS AND CONCEPTS

	comparative negligence 145	Good Samaritan statute 146	reasonable person
	contributory	malpractice 139	standard 137
assumption of risk 142	negligence 145	negligence 136	*res ipsa loquitur* 145
business invitee 138	dram shop act 146	negligence *per se* 146	strict liability 147
causation in fact 139	duty of care 136	proximate cause 140	superseding cause 144

QUESTIONS AND CASE PROBLEMS

7–1. Negligence Shannon's physician gives her some pain medication and tells her not to drive after she takes it, as the medication induces drowsiness. In spite of the doctor's warning, Shannon decides to drive to the store while on the medication. Owing to her lack of alertness, she fails to stop at a traffic light and crashes into another vehicle, causing a passenger in that vehicle to be injured. Is Shannon liable for the tort of negligence? Explain fully.

7–2. QUESTION WITH SAMPLE ANSWER: Duty of Care.

Ruth carelessly parks her car on a steep hill, leaves the car in neutral, and fails to engage the parking brake. The car rolls down the hill and knocks down a power line. The sparks from the broken line ignite a grass fire. The fire spreads until it reaches a barn one mile away. The barn houses dynamite, and the burning barn explodes, causing part of the roof to fall on and injure Jim, a passing motorist. Which element of negligence is of the greatest concern here? What legal doctrine resolves this issue? Will Jim be able to recover damages from Ruth? Explain your answer.

• **For a sample answer to Question 7–2, go to Appendix I at the end of this text.**

7–3. Strict Liability Danny and Marion Klein were injured when part of a fireworks display went astray and exploded near them. They sued Pyrodyne Corp., the pyrotechnic company that was hired to set up and discharge the fireworks, alleging, among other things, that the company should be strictly liable for damages caused by the fireworks display. Will the court agree with the Kleins? What factors will the court consider in making its decision? Discuss fully.

7–4. Negligence *Per Se* A North Carolina Department of Transportation regulation prohibits the placement of telephone booths within a public right-of-way. Despite this regulation, GTE South, Inc., placed a booth in the right-of-way near the intersection of Hillsborough and Sparger Roads in Durham County. A pedestrian, Laura Baldwin, was using the booth when an accident at the intersection caused a dump truck to cross the right-of-way and smash into the booth. Was Baldwin within the class of persons protected by the regulation? If so, did GTE's placement of the booth constitute negligence *per se*? Explain.

7–5. Negligence In July 2004, Emellie Anderson hired Kenneth Whitten, a licensed building contractor, to construct a two-story addition to her home. The bottom floor was to be a garage and the second floor a home office. In August, the parties signed a second contract under which Whitten agreed to rebuild a deck and railing attached to the house and to further improve the office. A later inspection revealed gaps in the siding on the new garage, nails protruding from incomplete framing, improper support for a stairway to the office, and gaps in its plywood flooring. One post supporting the deck was cracked; another was too short. Concrete had not been poured underneath the old posts. A section of railing was missing, and what was installed was warped, with gaps at the joints. Anderson filed a suit in a Connecticut state court against Whitten, alleging that his work was "substandard, not to code, unsafe and not done in a [workmanlike] manner." Anderson claimed that she would have to pay someone else to repair all of the work. Does Whitten's "work" satisfy the requirements for a claim grounded in negligence? Should Anderson's complaint be dismissed, or should she be awarded damages? Explain. [*Anderson v. Whitten*, 100 Conn.App. 730, 918 A.2d 1056 (2007)]

7–6. CASE PROBLEM WITH SAMPLE ANSWER: Defenses to Negligence.

Neal Peterson's entire family skied, and Peterson started skiing at the age of two. In 2000, at the age of eleven, Peterson was in his fourth year as a member of a ski race team. After a race one morning in February, Peterson continued to practice his skills through the afternoon. Coming down a slope very fast, at a point at which his skis were not touching the ground, Peterson collided with David Donahue. Donahue, a forty-three-year-old advanced skier, was skating (skiing slowly) across the slope toward the parking lot. Peterson and Donahue knew that falls, collisions, accidents, and injuries were possible with skiing. Donahue saw Peterson "split seconds" before the impact, which knocked Donahue out of his skis and down the

slope ten or twelve feet. When Donahue saw Peterson lying motionless nearby, he immediately sought help. To recover for his injuries, Peterson filed a suit in a Minnesota state court against Donahue, alleging negligence. Based on these facts, which defense to a claim of negligence is Donahue most likely to assert? How is the court likely to apply that defense and rule on Peterson's claim? Why? [*Peterson ex rel. Peterson v. Donahue*, 733 N.W.2d 790 (Minn.App. 2007)]

• **To view a sample answer for Problem 7–6, go to this book's Web site at www.cengage.com/blaw/clarkson, select "Chapter 7," and click on "Case Problem with Sample Answer."**

7–7. Negligence Mitsubishi Motors North America, Inc., operates an auto plant in Normal, Illinois. In 2003, TNT Logistics Corp. coordinated deliveries of auto parts to the plant, and DeKeyser Express, Inc., transported the parts. On January 21, TNT told DeKeyser to transport three pallets of parts from Trelleborg YSH, Inc., to the plant. DeKeyser dispatched its driver Lola Camp. At Trelleborg's loading dock, Camp noticed that the pallets would fit inside the trailer only if they were stacked. Camp was concerned that the load might shift during transport. DeKeyser dispatcher Ken Kasprzak and TNT supervisor Alan Marten told her that she would not be liable for any damage. Trelleborg loaded the pallets, and Camp drove to TNT's dock in Normal. When she opened the trailer door, the top pallet slipped. As Camp tried to close the door to prevent the pallet from falling, she injured her shoulder and arm. She filed a suit against TNT and Trelleborg, claiming negligence. What is their defense? Discuss. [*Camp v. TNT Logistics Corp.*, 553 F.3d 502 (7th Cir. 2009)]

7–8. Negligence and Multiparty Liability Alice Banks was injured when a chair she was sitting on at an Elks club collapsed. As a result of her injury, Dr. Robert Boyce performed the surgery on her back, fusing certain vertebrae. However, Boyce fused the wrong vertebrae and then had to perform a second surgery to correct the error. Then, during rehabilitation at a nursing home, Banks developed a serious staph infection that required additional surgeries and extensive care and treatment. She sued the Elks club and Boyce for negligence. The Elks club and Boyce filed motions against each other and also sued the nursing home. After complicated holdings by lower courts, the Tennessee Supreme Court reviewed the matter. Did the Elks club have primary liability for all of the injuries suffered by Banks after the initial accident, or did each defendant alone contribute to Banks's injuries? Explain. [*Banks v. Elks Club Pride of Tennessee*, 301 S.W.3d 214 (Sup.Ct.Tenn. 2010)]

7–9. A QUESTION OF ETHICS: Dram Shop Acts.

Donald and Gloria Bowden hosted a late afternoon cookout at their home in South Carolina, inviting mostly business acquaintances. Justin Parks, who was nineteen years old, attended the party. Alcoholic beverages were available to all of the guests, even those who, like Parks, were not minors but were underage. Parks consumed alcohol at the party and left with other

guests. One of these guests detained Parks at the guest's home to give Parks time to "sober up." Parks then drove himself from this guest's home and was killed in a one-car accident. At the time of death, he had a blood alcohol content of 0.291 percent, which exceeded the state's limit for driving a motor vehicle. Linda Marcum, Parks's mother, filed a suit in a South Carolina state court against the Bowdens and others, alleging that they were negligent. [Marcum v. Bowden, 372 S.C. 452, 643 S.E.2d 85 (2007)]

(a) Considering the principles discussed in this chapter, what are arguments in favor of, and against, holding social hosts liable in this situation? Explain.

(b) The states vary widely in assessing liability and imposing sanctions in the circumstances described in this problem. In other words, justice is not equal for parents and other social hosts who serve alcoholic beverages to underage individuals. Why is that?

7–10. VIDEO QUESTION: Negligence.

Go to this text's Web site at **www.cengage.com/ blaw/clarkson** and select "Chapter 7." Click on "Video Questions" and view the video titled *Jaws*. Then answer the following questions.

(a) In the video, the mayor (Murray Hamilton) and a few other men try to persuade Chief Brody (Roy Scheider) not to close the town's beaches. If Brody keeps the beaches open and a swimmer is injured or killed because he failed to warn swimmers about the potential shark danger, has Brody committed the tort of negligence? Explain.

(b) Can Chief Brody be held liable for any injuries or deaths to swimmers under the doctrine of strict liability? Why or why not?

(c) Suppose that Chief Brody goes against the mayor's instructions and warns townspeople to stay off the beach. Nevertheless, several swimmers do not heed his warning and are injured as a result. What defense or defenses could Brody raise under these circumstances if he is sued for negligence?

7–11. SPECIAL CASE ANALYSIS: Assumption of Risk.

Go to Extended Case 7.3, *Pfenning v. Lineman*, 922 N.E.2d 45 (Ind.App. 2010), on pages 143 and 144. Read the excerpt and answer the following questions.

(a) Issue: The focus in this case was the application of the doctrine of assumption of risk to whom and in what circumstances?

(b) Rule of Law: What are the requirements for an injured person to be held liable for his or her injury under the doctrine of assumption of risk?

(c) Applying the Rule of Law: How did the court evaluate the facts in this case to assess liability under the doctrine of assumption of risk?

(d) Conclusion: Among the parties involved in this case, who was held liable for the plaintiff's injury and why?

LEGAL RESEARCH EXERCISES ON THE WEB

Go to this text's Web site at **www.cengage.com/blaw/clarkson**, select "Chapter 7," and click on "Practical Internet Exercises." There you will find the following Internet research exercises that you can perform to learn more about the topics covered in this chapter.

Practical Internet Exercise 7–1:   **Legal Perspective**
Negligence and the *Titanic*

Practical Internet Exercise 7–2:   **Management Perspective**
The Duty to Warn

CHAPTER 8

Intellectual Property and Internet Law

Of significant concern to businesspersons is the need to protect their rights in intellectual property, which in today's world may exceed the value of physical property, such as machines and buildings. **Intellectual property** is any property that results from intellectual, creative processes—that is to say, the products of an individual's mind. Although it is an abstract term for an abstract concept, intellectual property is nonetheless familiar to almost everyone. The information contained in books and computer files is intellec-

tual property. The software you use, the movies you see, and the music you listen to are all forms of intellectual property.

The need to protect creative works was recognized by the framers of the U.S. Constitution more than two hundred years ago: Article I, Section 8, of the U.S. Constitution authorized Congress "[t]o promote the Progress of Science and useful Arts, by securing for limited Times to Authors and Inventors the exclusive Right to their respective Writings and Discoveries." Laws protecting patents, trademarks,

and copyrights are explicitly designed to protect and reward inventive and artistic creativity.

In today's global economy, however, protecting intellectual property in one country is no longer sufficient. Therefore, the United States participates in international agreements to secure ownership rights in intellectual property in other nations. We discuss some of these international agreements at the end of this chapter.

SECTION 1
TRADEMARKS AND RELATED PROPERTY

A **trademark** is a distinctive mark, motto, device, or implement that a manufacturer stamps, prints, or otherwise affixes to the goods it produces so that they can be identified on the market and their origins made known. In other words, a trademark is a source indicator. At common law, the person who

used a symbol or mark to identify a business or product was protected in the use of that trademark. Clearly, by using another's trademark, a business could lead consumers to believe that its goods were made by the other business. The law seeks to avoid this kind of confusion. In this section, we examine various aspects of the law governing trademarks.

In the following classic case concerning Coca-Cola, the defendants argued that the Coca-Cola trademark was entitled to no protection under the law because the term did not accurately represent the product.

CASE 8.1
The Coca-Cola Co. v. The Koke Co. of America

Supreme Court of the United States, 254 U.S. 143, 41 S.Ct. 113, 65 L.Ed. 189 (1920).
www.findlaw.com/casecode/supreme.html[a]

COMPANY PROFILE • John Pemberton, an Atlanta pharmacist, invented a caramel-colored, carbonated soft drink in 1886. His bookkeeper, Frank Robinson, named the beverage Coca-Cola after two of the ingredients, coca leaves and kola nuts. Asa Candler bought the Coca-Cola Company (www.thecoca-colacompany.com) in 1891, and within seven years, he had made the soft drink available throughout the United States, as well as in parts of Canada and Mexico. Candler continued to sell Coke aggressively and to open up new markets, reaching Europe before 1910. In doing so, however, he attracted numerous competitors, some of which tried to capitalize directly on the Coke name.

BACKGROUND AND FACTS • The Coca-Cola Company sought to enjoin (prevent) the Koke Company of America and other beverage companies from, among other things, using the word Koke for their products. The Koke Company of America and other beverage companies contended that the Coca-Cola trademark was a fraudulent representation and that Coca-Cola was therefore not entitled to any help from the courts. The Koke Company and the other defendants alleged that the Coca-Cola Company, by its use of the Coca-Cola name, represented that the beverage contained cocaine (from coca leaves), which it no longer did. The trial court granted the injunction against the Koke Company, but the appellate court reversed the lower court's ruling. Coca-Cola then appealed to the United States Supreme Court.

IN THE LANGUAGE OF THE COURT
Mr. Justice *HOLMES* delivered the opinion of the Court.
 * * * *
 * * * Before 1900 the beginning of [Coca-Cola's] good will was more or less helped by the presence of cocaine, a drug that, like alcohol or caffeine or opium, may be described as a deadly poison or as a valuable [pharmaceutical item, depending on the speaker's purposes]. The amount seems to have been very small,[b] but it may have been enough to begin a bad habit and after the Food and Drug Act of June 30, 1906, if not earlier, long before this suit was brought, it was eliminated from the plaintiff's compound.
 * * * Since 1900 the sales have increased at a very great rate corresponding to a like increase in advertising. The name now characterizes a beverage to be had at almost any soda fountain. It means a single thing coming from a single source, and well known to the community. It hardly would be too much to say that the drink characterizes the name as much as the name the drink. In other words *Coca-Cola probably means to most persons the plaintiff's familiar product to be had everywhere rather than a compound of particular substances.* * * * Before this suit was brought the plaintiff had advertised to the public that it must not expect and would not find cocaine, and had eliminated everything tending to suggest cocaine effects except the name and the picture of [coca] leaves and nuts, which probably conveyed little or nothing to most who saw it. It appears to us that it would be going too far to deny the plaintiff relief against a palpable [readily evident] fraud because possibly here and there an ignorant person might call for the drink with the hope for incipient cocaine intoxication. The plaintiff's position must be judged by the facts as they were when the suit was begun, not by the facts of a different condition and an earlier time. [Emphasis added.]

DECISION AND REMEDY • *The district court's injunction was allowed to stand. The competing beverage companies were enjoined from calling their products Koke.*

---

a. This is the "U.S. Supreme Court Opinions" page within the Web site of the "FindLaw Internet Legal Resources" database. This page provides several options for accessing an opinion. Because you know the citation for this case, you can go to the "Citation Search" box, type in the appropriate volume and page numbers for the *United States Reports* ("254" and "143," respectively, for the *Coca-Cola* case), and click on "Search."

b. In reality, until 1903 the amount of active cocaine in each bottle of Coke was equivalent to one "line" of cocaine.

CASE 8.1 CONTINUED ▶ **IMPACT OF THIS CASE ON TODAY'S LAW** • *In this early case, the United States Supreme Court made it clear that trademarks and trade names (and nicknames for those marks and names, such as the nickname "Coke" for "Coca-Cola") that are in common use receive protection under the common law. This holding is significant historically because it is the predecessor to the federal statute later passed to protect trademark rights—the Lanham Act of 1946, to be discussed next. In many ways, this act represented a codification of common law principles governing trademarks.*

WHAT IF THE FACTS WERE DIFFERENT? • *Suppose that Coca-Cola had been trying to make the public believe that its product contained cocaine. Would the result in this case likely have been different? Why or why not?*

Statutory Protection of Trademarks

Statutory protection of trademarks and related property is provided at the federal level by the Lanham Act of 1946.[1] The Lanham Act was enacted, in part, to protect manufacturers from losing business to rival companies that used confusingly similar trademarks. The Lanham Act incorporates the common law of trademarks and provides remedies for owners of trademarks who wish to enforce their claims in federal court. Many states also have trademark statutes.

TRADEMARK DILUTION Before 1995, federal trademark law prohibited only the unauthorized use of the same mark on competing—or on noncompeting but "related"—goods or services. Protection was given only when the unauthorized use would likely confuse consumers as to the origin of those goods and services. In 1995, Congress amended the Lanham Act by passing the Federal Trademark Dilution Act,[2] which allowed trademark owners to bring suits in federal court for trademark **dilution.** Trademark dilution laws protect "distinctive" or "famous" trademarks (such as Jergens, McDonald's, Dell, and Apple) from certain unauthorized uses even when the use is on noncompeting goods or is unlikely to confuse. More than half of the states have also enacted trademark dilution laws.

SIMILAR MARKS MAY CONSTITUTE TRADEMARK DILUTION A famous mark may be diluted not only by the use of an *identical* mark but also by the use of a *similar* mark.[3] A similar mark is more likely to lessen the value of a famous mark when the companies using the marks provide related goods or compete against each other in the same market.

CASE IN POINT Samantha Lundberg operated "Sambuck's Coffeehouse," a small business in Astoria, Oregon, even though she knew that "Starbucks" is one of the largest coffee chains in the nation. When Starbucks Corporation filed a dilution lawsuit, the federal court ruled that use of the "Sambuck's" mark constituted trademark dilution because it created confusion for consumers. Not only was there a "high degree" of similarity between the marks, but also both companies provided coffee-related services and marketed their services through "stand-alone" retail stores. Therefore, the use of the similar mark (Sambuck's) reduced the value of the famous mark (Starbucks).[4]

Trademark Registration

Trademarks may be registered with the state or with the federal government. To register for protection under federal trademark law, a person must file an application with the U.S. Patent and Trademark Office in Washington, D.C. Under current law, a mark can be registered (1) if it is currently in commerce or (2) if the applicant intends to put it into commerce within six months.

In special circumstances, the six-month period can be extended by thirty months, giving the applicant a total of three years from the date of notice of trademark approval to make use of the mark and file the required use statement. Registration is postponed until the mark is actually used. Nonetheless, during this waiting period, any applicant can legally protect his or her trademark against a third party who previously has neither used the mark nor filed an application for it. Registration is renewable between the fifth and sixth years after the initial registration and every ten years thereafter (every twenty years for those trademarks registered before 1990).

1. 15 U.S.C. Sections 1051–1128.
2. 15 U.S.C. Section 1125.
3. See *Moseley v. V Secret Catalogue, Inc.,* 537 U.S. 418, 123 S.Ct. 1115, 155 L.Ed.2d 1 (2003).
4. *Starbucks Corp. v. Lundberg,* 2005 WL 3183858 (D.Or. 2005).

Trademark Infringement

Registration of a trademark with the U.S. Patent and Trademark Office gives notice on a nationwide basis that the trademark belongs exclusively to the registrant. The registrant is also allowed to use the symbol ® to indicate that the mark has been registered. Whenever that trademark is copied to a substantial degree or used in its entirety by another, intentionally or unintentionally, the trademark has been *infringed* (used without authorization).

When a trademark has been infringed, the owner of the mark has a cause of action against the infringer. To succeed in a trademark infringement action, the owner must show that the defendant's use of the mark created a likelihood of confusion about the origin of the defendant's goods or services. The owner need not prove that the infringer acted intentionally or that the trademark was registered (although registration does provide proof of the date of inception of the trademark's use).

The most commonly granted remedy for trademark infringement is an *injunction* to prevent further infringement. Under the Lanham Act, a trademark owner that successfully proves infringement can recover actual damages, plus the profits that the infringer wrongfully received from the unauthorized use of the mark. A court can also order the destruction of any goods bearing the unauthorized trademark. In some situations, the trademark owner may also be able to recover attorneys' fees.

Distinctiveness of Mark

A trademark must be sufficiently distinct to enable consumers to identify the manufacturer of the goods easily and to distinguish between those goods and competing products.

STRONG MARKS Fanciful, arbitrary, or suggestive trademarks are generally considered to be the most distinctive (strongest) trademarks. Marks that are fanciful, arbitrary, or suggestive are protected as inherently distinctive without demonstrating secondary meaning. These marks receive automatic protection because they serve to identify a particular product's source, as opposed to describing the product itself.

Fanciful and Arbitrary Trademarks. Fanciful trademarks are inherently distinctive and include invented words, such as "Xerox" for one manufacturer's copiers and "Kodak" for another company's photographic products. Arbitrary trademarks are those that use common words in an uncommon way that is nondescriptive, such as "Dutch Boy" as a name for paint. Even a single letter used in a particular style can be an arbitrary trademark.

CASE IN POINT Sports entertainment company ESPN sued Quiksilver, Inc., a maker of surfer clothing, alleging trademark infringement. ESPN claimed that Quiksilver's clothing had used the stylized "X" mark that ESPN uses in connection with the "X Games," a competition focusing on extreme action sports. Quiksilver filed counterclaims for trademark infringement and dilution, arguing that it had a long history of using the stylized X on its products. ESPN created the X Games in the mid-1990s, and Quiksilver has been using the X mark since 1994. ESPN, which has trademark applications pending for the stylized X, asked the court to dismiss Quiksilver's counterclaims. A federal district court ruled that the X on Quiksilver's clothing is clearly an arbitrary mark. Noting that "the two Xs are similar enough that a consumer might well confuse them," the court refused to dismiss Quiksilver's claims and allowed the dispute to go to trial.[5]

Suggestive Trademarks. Suggestive trademarks suggest something about a product's nature, quality, or characteristics, without describing the product directly. These marks require imagination on the part of the consumer to identify the characteristic. For example, "Dairy Queen" suggests an association between its products and milk, but it does not directly describe ice cream. "Blu-ray" is a suggestive mark that is associated with the high-quality, high-definition video contained on a particular optical data storage disc. Although blue-violet lasers are used to read blu-ray discs, the term *blu-ray* does not directly describe the disc.

SECONDARY MEANING Descriptive terms, geographic terms, and personal names are not inherently distinctive and do not receive protection under the law until they acquire a secondary meaning. A secondary meaning may arise when customers begin to associate a specific term or phrase (such as *London Fog*) with specific trademarked items (coats with "London Fog" labels) made by a particular company.

CASE IN POINT Frosty Treats, Inc., sells frozen desserts out of ice cream trucks. The video game series Twisted Metal depicts an ice cream truck with

---

5. *ESPN, Inc. v. Quiksilver, Inc.,* 586 F.Supp.2d 219 (S.D.N.Y. 2008).

a clown character on it that is similar to the clowns on Frosty Treats' trucks. In the last game of the series, the truck bears the label "Frosty Treats." Frosty sued the video game maker for trademark infringement, but the court held that "Frosty Treats" is a descriptive term and is not protected by trademark law unless it has acquired a secondary meaning. To establish secondary meaning, Frosty Treats would have had to show that the public recognized its trademark and associated it with a single source. Because Frosty Treats failed to do so, the court entered a judgment in favor of the video game producer.[6]

Once a secondary meaning is attached to a term or name, a trademark is considered distinctive and is protected. Even a color can qualify for trademark protection, as did the color schemes used by some state university sports teams, including Ohio State University and Louisiana State University.[7]

GENERIC TERMS Generic terms that refer to an entire class of products, such as *bicycle* and *computer,* receive no protection, even if they acquire secondary meanings.[8] A particularly thorny problem arises when a trademark acquires generic use. For example, *aspirin* and *thermos* were originally the names of trademarked products, but today the words are used generically. Other trademarks that have acquired generic use are *escalator, trampoline, raisin bran, dry ice, lanolin, linoleum, nylon,* and *corn flakes.*

Service, Certification, and Collective Marks

A **service mark** is essentially a trademark that is used to distinguish the *services* (rather than the products) of one person or company from those of another. For example, each airline has a particular mark or symbol associated with its name. Titles and character names used in radio and television are frequently registered as service marks.

Other marks protected by law include certification marks and collective marks. A **certification mark** is used by one or more persons, other than the owner, to certify the region, materials, mode of manufacture, quality, or other characteristic of specific goods or services. When used by members of a cooperative, association, or other organization, it is referred to as a **collective mark.** Examples of certification marks are the phrases "Good Housekeeping Seal of Approval" and "UL Tested." Collective marks appear at the ends of motion picture credits to indicate the various associations and organizations that participated in the making of the films. The union marks found on the tags of certain products are also collective marks.

Trade Dress

The term **trade dress** refers to the image and overall appearance of a product. Trade dress is a broad concept and can include either all or part of the total image or overall impression created by a product or its packaging. For example, the distinctive decor, menu, layout, and style of service of a particular restaurant may be regarded as trade dress. Trade dress can also include the layout and appearance of a catalogue, the use of a lighthouse as part of the design of a golf hole, the fish shape of a cracker, or the G-shaped design of a Gucci watch.

Basically, trade dress is subject to the same protection as trademarks. In cases involving trade dress infringement, as in trademark infringement cases, a major consideration is whether consumers are likely to be confused by the allegedly infringing use.

Counterfeit Goods

Counterfeit goods copy or otherwise imitate trademarked goods, but they are not the genuine trademarked goods. The importation of goods that bear counterfeit (fake) trademarks poses a growing problem for U.S. businesses, consumers, and law enforcement. In addition to the negative financial effects on legitimate businesses, certain counterfeit goods, such as pharmaceuticals and nutritional supplements, can present serious public health risks. It is estimated that nearly 7 percent of the goods imported into the United States from abroad are counterfeit.

THE STOP COUNTERFEITING IN MANUFACTURED GOODS ACT The Stop Counterfeiting in Manufactured Goods Act[9] (SCMGA) was enacted to combat counterfeit goods. The act makes it a crime to traffic intentionally in or attempt to traffic in counterfeit goods or services, or to knowingly use a counterfeit mark on or in connection with goods

6. *Frosty Treats, Inc. v. Sony Computer Entertainment America, Inc.,* 426 F.3d 1001 (8th Cir. 2005).

7. *Board of Supervisors of Louisiana State University v. Smack Apparel Co.,* 438 F.Supp.2d 653 (E.D.La. 2006).

8. See, for example, *America Online, Inc. v. AT&T Corp.,* 243 F.3d 812 (4th Cir. 2001).

9. Pub. L. No. 109-181 (2006), which amended 18 U.S.C. Sections 2318–2320.

or services. Before this act, the law did not prohibit the creation or shipment of counterfeit labels that were not attached to any product. Therefore, counterfeiters would make labels and packaging bearing another's trademark, ship the labels to another location, and then affix them to an inferior product to deceive buyers. The SCMGA closed this loophole by making it a crime to knowingly traffic in counterfeit labels, stickers, packaging, and the like, regardless of whether the item is attached to any goods.

COUNTERFEITING PENALTIES Persons found guilty of violating the SCMGA may be fined up to $2 million or imprisoned for up to ten years (or more if they are repeat offenders). If a court finds that the statute was violated, it must order the defendant to forfeit the counterfeit products (which are then destroyed), as well as any property used in the commission of the crime. The defendant must also pay restitution to the trademark holder or victim in an amount equal to the victim's actual loss.

CASE IN POINT Wajdi Beydoun pleaded guilty to conspiring to import cigarette-rolling papers from Mexico that were falsely marked as "Zig-Zags" and selling them in the United States. The court sentenced Beydoun to prison and ordered him to pay $566,267 in restitution. On appeal, the court affirmed the prison sentence but reversed the restitution because the amount exceeded the actual loss suffered by the legitimate sellers of Zig-Zag rolling papers.[10]

Trade Names

Trademarks apply to *products*. The term **trade name** is used to indicate part or all of a business's name, whether the business is a sole proprietorship, a partnership, or a corporation. Generally, a trade name is directly related to a business and its goodwill. A trade name may be protected as a trademark if the trade name is also the name of the company's trademarked product—for example, Coca-Cola. Unless it is also used as a trademark or service mark, a trade name cannot be registered with the federal government. Trade names are protected under the common law, but only if they are unusual or fancifully used. The word *Safeway,* for example, was sufficiently fanciful to obtain protection as a trade name for a grocery chain.

CYBER MARKS

In cyberspace, trademarks are sometimes referred to as **cyber marks.** We turn now to a discussion of how new laws and the courts address trademark-related issues in cyberspace.

Domain Names

As e-commerce expanded worldwide, one issue that emerged involved the rights of a trademark owner to use the mark as part of a domain name. A **domain name** is part of an Internet address—for example, "westlaw.com." Every domain name ends with a generic top level domain (TLD), which is the part of the name to the right of the period that indicates the type of entity that operates the site. For example, *com* is an abbreviation for *commercial*, and *edu* is short for *education*.

The second level domain (SLD)—the part of the name to the left of the period—is chosen by the business entity or individual registering the domain name. Competition for SLDs among firms with similar names and products has led to numerous disputes. By using an identical or similar domain name, parties have attempted to profit from a competitor's goodwill, sell pornography, offer for sale another party's domain name, or otherwise infringe on others' trademarks.

The Internet Corporation for Assigned Names and Numbers (ICANN), a nonprofit corporation, oversees the distribution of domain names and operates an online arbitration system. Due to numerous complaints, ICANN completely overhauled the domain name distribution system and began using a new system in 2009. One of the goals of the new system is to alleviate the problem of *cybersquatting*. **Cybersquatting** occurs when a person registers a domain name that is the same as, or confusingly similar to, the trademark of another and then offers to sell the domain name back to the trademark owner.

Anticybersquatting Legislation

During the 1990s, cybersquatting led to so much litigation that Congress passed the Anticybersquatting Consumer Protection Act (ACPA) of 1999,[11] which amended the Lanham Act—the federal law

---

10. *United States v. Beydoun,* 469 F.3d 102 (5th Cir. 2006).

11. 15 U.S.C. Section 1129.

protecting trademarks discussed earlier. The ACPA makes it illegal for a person to "register, traffic in, or use" a domain name (1) if the name is identical or confusingly similar to the trademark of another and (2) if the one registering, trafficking in, or using the domain name has a "bad faith intent" to profit from that trademark.

THE ONGOING PROBLEM OF CYBERSQUATTING The ACPA was intended to stamp out cybersquatting, but the practice continues to present a problem for businesses today, largely because more TLDs are available and many more companies are registering domain names. Domain name registrars have also proliferated. They charge a fee to businesses and individuals to register new names and to renew annual registrations (often through automated software). Many of these companies also buy and sell expired domain names. All domain name registrars are supposed to relay information about these transactions to ICANN and other companies that keep a master list of domain names. This information is not always transmitted, however. The speed at which domain names change hands and the difficulty in tracking mass automated registrations have created an environment where cybersquatting can flourish.

TYPOSQUATTING Cybersquatters have also developed new tactics, such as **typosquatting,** or registering a name that is a misspelling of a popular brand, such as hotmai.com or myspac.com. Because many Internet users are not perfect typists, Web pages using these misspelled names receive a lot of traffic. More traffic generally means increased profit (advertisers often pay Web sites based on the number of unique visits, or hits), which in turn provides incentive for more cybersquatters. Also, if the misspelling is significant, the trademark owner may have difficulty proving that the name is identical or confusingly similar to the trademark of another as the ACPA requires.

Cybersquatting is costly for businesses, which must attempt to register all variations of a name to protect their domain name rights from would-be cybersquatters and typosquatters. Large corporations may have to register thousands of domain names across the globe just to protect their basic brands and trademarks.

APPLICABILITY AND SANCTIONS OF THE ACPA The ACPA applies to all domain name registrations of trademarks. Successful plaintiffs in suits brought under the act can collect actual damages and profits, or they can elect to receive statutory damages ranging from $1,000 to $100,000.

Although some successful lawsuits have been brought under the ACPA, plaintiffs may encounter roadblocks. Some domain name registrars offer privacy services that hide the true owners of Web sites, making it difficult for trademark owners to identify cybersquatters. Thus, before a trademark owner can bring a suit, he or she has to ask the court for a subpoena to discover the identity of the owner of the infringing Web site. Because of the high costs of court proceedings, discovery, and even arbitration, many disputes over cybersquatting are settled out of court.

Meta Tags

Search engines compile their results by looking through a Web site's key-word field. **Meta tags,** or key words, may be inserted into this field to increase the likelihood that a site will be included in search engine results, even though the site may have nothing to do with the inserted words. Using this same technique, one site may appropriate the key words of other sites with more frequent hits so that the appropriating site will appear in the same search engine results as the more popular sites. Using another's trademark in a meta tag without the owner's permission, however, normally constitutes trademark infringement. Some uses of another's trademark as a meta tag may be permissible if the use is reasonably necessary and does not suggest that the owner authorized or sponsored the use.

CASE IN POINT Terri Welles, a former model who had been "Playmate of the Year" in *Playboy* magazine, established a Web site that used the terms *Playboy* and *Playmate* as meta tags. Playboy Enterprises, Inc. (PEI), which publishes *Playboy*, filed a suit seeking to prevent Welles from using these meta tags. The court determined that Welles's use of PEI's meta tags to direct users to her Web site was permissible because it did not suggest sponsorship and there were no descriptive substitutes for the terms *Playboy* and *Playmate*.[12]

Dilution in the Online World

As discussed earlier, trademark *dilution* occurs when a trademark is used, without authorization, in a way that diminishes the distinctive quality of the mark. Unlike trademark infringement, a claim of dilution

---

12. *Playboy Enterprises, Inc. v. Welles,* 279 F.3d 796 (9th Cir. 2002). See also *Canfield v. Health Communications, Inc.,* 2008 WL 961318 (C.D.Cal. 2008).

does not require proof that consumers are likely to be confused by a connection between the unauthorized use and the mark. For this reason, the products involved need not be similar.

CASE IN POINT In the first case alleging dilution on the Web, a court precluded the use of "candyland.com" as the URL for an adult site. The lawsuit was brought by the company that manufactures the Candyland children's game and owns the "Candyland" mark. Although consumers were not likely to connect candyland.com with the children's game, the court reasoned that the sexually explicit adult site would dilute the value of the "Candyland" mark.[13]

Licensing

One way to avoid litigation and still make use of another's trademark or other form of intellectual property is to obtain a license to do so. A **license** in this context is essentially an agreement, or contract, permitting the use of a trademark, copyright, patent, or trade secret for certain purposes. The party that owns the intellectual property rights and issues the license is the *licensor,* and the party obtaining the license is the *licensee.*

A license grants only the rights expressly described in the license agreement. A licensor might, for example, allow the licensee to use the trademark as part of its company name, or as part of its domain name, but not otherwise use the mark on any products or services. Disputes frequently arise over licensing agreements, particularly when the license involves Internet uses.

CASE IN POINT Perry Ellis International (PEI) owns the "Perry Ellis America" registered trademark (the PEA trademark), which is distinctive and known worldwide as a mark of quality apparel. In 2006, PEI granted URI Corporation an exclusive license to manufacture and distribute footwear using the PEA trademark in Mexico. The agreement required URI to comply with numerous conditions regarding the manufacturing and distribution of the licensed footwear and to sell the shoes only in certain (listed) high-quality stores. URI was not permitted to authorize any other party to use the PEA trademark. Despite this explicit licensing agreement, PEI discovered that footwear bearing its PEA trademark was being sold in discount stores in Mexico. PEI terminated the agreement and filed a lawsuit in a federal district court against URI. PEI was awarded more than $1 million in damages.[14]

Software creators typically license, rather than sell, their software to others. Software licensing agreements frequently include restrictions that prohibit licensees from sharing the software and using it to create similar software. Restrictive licenses enable creators to retain greater control over proprietary software and may offer more protection than intellectual property laws.

SECTION 3
PATENTS

A **patent** is a grant from the government that gives an inventor the right to exclude others from making, using, or selling his or her invention for a period of twenty years from the date of filing the application for a patent. Patents for designs, as opposed to those for inventions, are given for a fourteen-year period. The applicant must demonstrate to the satisfaction of the U.S. Patent and Trademark Office that the invention, discovery, process, or design is novel, useful, and not obvious in light of current technology.

In contrast to patent law in many other countries, in the United States the first person to invent a product or process gets the patent rights rather than the first person to file for a patent on that product or process. Because it can be difficult to prove who invented an item first, however, the first person to file an application is often deemed the first to invent (unless the inventor has detailed prior research notes or other evidence). An inventor can publish the invention or offer it for sale before filing a patent application but must apply for a patent within one year of doing so or forfeit the patent rights.

The period of patent protection begins on the date the patent application is filed, rather than when the patent is issued, which may sometimes be years later. After the patent period ends (either fourteen or twenty years later), the product or process enters the public domain, and anyone can make, sell, or use the invention without paying the patent holder.

Searchable Patent Databases

A significant development relating to patents is the availability online of the world's patent databases. The Web site of the U.S. Patent and Trademark Office

---

13. *Hasbro, Inc. v. Internet Entertainment Group, Ltd.,* 1996 WL 84853 (W.D.Wash. 1996).

14. *Perry Ellis International, Inc. v. URI Corporation,* 2007 WL 3047143 (S.D.Fla. 2007).

(www.uspto.gov) provides searchable databases covering U.S. patents granted since 1976. The Web site of the European Patent Office (www.epo.org) provides online access to 50 million patent documents in more than seventy nations through a searchable network of databases. Businesses use these searchable databases in many ways. Because patents are valuable assets, businesses may need to perform patent searches to list or inventory their assets. Patent searches may also be conducted to study trends and patterns in a specific technology or to gather information about competitors in the industry.

What Is Patentable?

Under federal law, "[w]hoever invents or discovers any new and useful process, machine, manufacture, or composition of matter, or any new and useful improvement thereof, may obtain a patent therefor, subject to the conditions and requirements of

this title."[15] Thus, to be patentable, the item must be novel and not obvious.

In sum, almost anything is patentable, except (1) the laws of nature, (2) natural phenomena, and (3) abstract ideas (including algorithms[16]). Even artistic methods, certain works of art, and the structure of storylines are patentable, provided that they are novel and not obvious. Plants that are reproduced asexually (by means other than from seed), such as hybrid or genetically engineered plants, are patentable in the United States, as are genetically engineered (or cloned) microorganisms and animals.

In the following case, the focus was on the application of the test for proving whether a patent claim was "obvious."

---

15. 35 U.S.C. Section 101.

16. An *algorithm* is a step-by-step procedure, formula, or set of instructions for accomplishing a specific task—such as the set of rules used by a search engine to rank the listings contained within its index in response to a particular query.

✷ EXTENDED CASE 8.2 ✷
KSR International Co. v. Teleflex, Inc.

Supreme Court of the United States, 550 U.S. 398, 127 S.Ct. 1727, 167 L.Ed.2d 705 (2007).

IN THE LANGUAGE OF THE COURT

Justice *KENNEDY* delivered the opinion of the Court.

Teleflex Incorporated * * * sued KSR International Company [in a federal district court] for patent infringement. The patent at issue is entitled "Adjustable Pedal Assembly With Electronic Throttle Control." The patentee is Steven J. Engelgau, and the patent is referred to as "the Engelgau patent." Teleflex holds the exclusive license to the patent.

Claim 4 of the Engelgau patent describes a mechanism for combining an electronic sensor with an adjustable automobile pedal so the pedal's position can be transmitted to a computer that controls the throttle in the vehicle's engine. [KSR designed a pedal assembly for General Motors Corporation (GMC)

to use in its Chevrolet and GMC light trucks.] When Teleflex accused KSR of infringing the Engelgau patent * * *, KSR countered that claim 4 was invalid * * * because its subject matter was obvious.

* * * *

Seeking to resolve the question of obviousness with * * * uniformity and consistency, [the courts have] employed an approach referred to by the parties as the "teaching, suggestion, or motivation" test (TSM test), under which a patent claim is only proved obvious if some motivation or suggestion to combine the prior art teachings can be found in the prior art, the nature of the problem, or the knowledge of a person having ordinary skill in the art. KSR challenges that test, or at least its application in this case.

* * * *

* * * Important for this case are two adjustable pedals disclosed in [other patents]. The Asano patent

reveals a support structure that houses the pedal so that even when the pedal location is adjusted relative to the driver, one of the pedal's pivot points stays fixed. * * * The Redding patent reveals a different, sliding mechanism where both the pedal and the pivot point are adjusted.

[Also important for this case are two] patents involving electronic pedal sensors for computer-controlled throttles. These inventions * * * taught that it was preferable to detect the pedal's position in the pedal assembly, not in the engine. The [Smith] patent disclosed a pedal with an electronic sensor on a pivot point in the pedal assembly.

* * * *

* * * The [Rixon patent] discloses an adjustable pedal assembly with an electronic sensor for detecting the pedal's position.

* * * *

EXTENDED CASE CONTINUES ➡

EXTENDED CASE 8.2 CONTINUED ◆

The District Court granted summary judgment in KSR's favor.

* * * *

* * * The court compared the teachings of the prior art to the claims of Engelgau. It found "little difference." [The] Asano [patent] taught everything contained in claim 4 except the use of a sensor to detect the pedal's position and transmit it to the computer controlling the throttle. That additional aspect was revealed in sources such as * * * sensors [previously] used by Chevrolet.

* * * The District Court [also] held KSR had satisfied the [TSM] test. It reasoned (1) the state of the industry would lead inevitably to combinations of electronic sensors and adjustable pedals, (2) Rixon provided the basis for these developments, and (3) Smith taught a solution to the wire chafing problems in Rixon, namely locating the sensor on the fixed structure of the pedal.

* * * *

* * * [The U.S.] Court of Appeals [for the Federal Circuit] reversed. It ruled the District Court had not been strict enough in applying the [TSM] test, having failed to make "finding[s] as to the specific understanding or principle within the knowledge of a skilled artisan that would have motivated one with no knowledge of [the] invention * * * to attach an electronic control to the support bracket of the Asano assembly."

Here, the Court of Appeals found, the Asano pedal was designed to solve the "constant ratio problem"—that is, to ensure that the force required to depress the pedal is the same no matter how the pedal is adjusted—whereas Engelgau sought to provide a simpler, smaller, cheaper adjustable electronic pedal. As for Rixon, the court explained, that pedal suffered from the problem of wire chafing but was not designed to solve it. In the court's view Rixon did not teach anything helpful to Engelgau's purpose. Smith, in turn, did not relate to adjustable pedals and did not "necessarily go to the issue of motivation to attach the electronic control on the support bracket of the pedal assembly."

* * * *

We begin by rejecting the rigid approach of the Court of Appeals. Throughout this Court's engagement with the question of obviousness, our cases have set forth an expansive and flexible approach inconsistent with the way the Court of Appeals applied its TSM test here.

* * * *For over a half century, the Court has held that a patent for a combination which only unites old elements with no change in their respective functions * * * obviously withdraws what is already known into the field of its monopoly and diminishes the resources available to skillful [persons]. * * * [Emphasis added.]*

* * * *

* * * If a technique has been used to improve one device, and a person of ordinary skill in the art would recognize that it would improve similar devices in the same way, using the technique is obvious unless its actual application is beyond his or her skill.

* * * *

The first error of the Court of Appeals in this case was to * * * [hold] that courts and patent examiners should look only to the problem the patentee was trying to solve.

The second error of the Court of Appeals lay in its assumption that a person of ordinary skill attempting to solve a problem will be led only to those elements of prior art designed to solve the same problem.

* * * *

When we apply the standards we have explained to the instant facts, claim 4 must be found obvious. * * * We see little difference between the teachings of Asano and Smith and the adjustable electronic pedal disclosed in claim 4 of the Engelgau patent. A person having ordinary skill in the art could have combined Asano with a pedal position sensor in a fashion encompassed by claim 4, and would have seen the benefits of doing so.

* * * *

* * * The judgment of the Court of Appeals is reversed, and the case remanded for further proceedings consistent with this opinion.

 QUESTIONS

1. Suppose that a person of ordinary skill creates an item by implementing a predictable variation of another's patented invention. Does the Court's opinion indicate that the item is likely or unlikely to be patentable? Discuss.
2. Based on the Court's reasoning, what other factors should be considered in determining the obviousness of a patent?

PATENTS FOR SOFTWARE At one time, it was difficult for developers and manufacturers of software to obtain patent protection because many software products simply automate procedures that can be performed manually. In other words, it was thought that computer programs did not meet the "novel" and "not obvious" requirements previously mentioned. Also, the basis for software is often a mathematical equation or formula, which is not patentable. In 1981, however, the United States

Supreme Court opened the way for software products to receive patents when it held that it is possible to obtain a patent for a *process* that incorporates a computer program.[17]

PATENTS FOR BUSINESS PROCESSES In a landmark case, *State Street Bank & Trust Co. v. Signature Financial Group, Inc.*,[18] a federal appellate court ruled that business processes were patentable. After the decision in the *State Street* case, numerous technology firms applied for and received patents on business processes or methods. Walker Digital obtained a business process patent for its "Dutch auction" system, which allows Priceline.com users to name their own price for airline tickets and hotels. Amazon.com patented its "one-click" online payment system.

In 2008, however, the court that had decided the *State Street* case made it significantly more difficult to obtain patents for business processes when it reversed its earlier decision and invalidated "pure" business process patents.

CASE IN POINT Two individuals applied to patent a process that used transactions to hedge the risk in commodity trading. The U.S. Patent and Trademark Office denied their application because it was not limited to a machine and did not describe any methods for working out which transactions to perform. The applicants appealed. After soliciting input from numerous interest groups, the U.S. Court of Appeals for the Federal Circuit established a new test for business process patents. Under this test, a business process patent is valid only if it is tied to a particular machine or apparatus or transforms a particular article into a different state or object. Because the process in question failed to meet the machine-or-transformation test, the court upheld the denial of a patent.[19]

Patent Infringement

If a firm makes, uses, or sells another's patented design, product, or process without the patent owner's permission, that firm commits the tort of patent infringement. Patent infringement may occur even though the patent owner has not put the patented product into commerce. Patent infringement may also occur even though not all features or parts of a product are copied. (With respect to a patented process, however, all steps or their equivalent must be copied for infringement to exist.).

Note that, as a general rule, under U.S. law no patent infringement occurs when a patented product is made and sold in another country. The United States Supreme Court has narrowly construed patent infringement as it applies to exported software.

CASE IN POINT AT&T Corporation holds a patent on a device used to digitally encode, compress, and process recorded speech. AT&T brought an infringement case against Microsoft Corporation, which admitted that its Windows operating system incorporated software code that infringed on AT&T's patent. The case reached the United States Supreme Court on the question of whether Microsoft's liability extended to computers made in another country. The Court held that it did not. Microsoft was liable only for infringement in the United States and not for the Windows-based computers produced in foreign locations. The Court reasoned that Microsoft had not "supplied" the software for the computers but had only electronically transmitted a master copy, which the foreign manufacturers then copied and loaded onto the computers.[20]

Remedies for Patent Infringement

If a patent is infringed, the patent holder may sue for relief in federal court. The patent holder can seek an injunction against the infringer and can also request damages for royalties and lost profits. In some cases, the court may grant the winning party reimbursement for attorneys' fees and costs. If the court determines that the infringement was willful, the court can triple the amount of damages awarded (treble damages).

In the past, permanent injunctions were routinely granted to prevent future infringement. In 2006, however, the United States Supreme Court ruled that patent holders are not automatically entitled to a permanent injunction against future infringing activities—the courts have discretion to decide whether equity requires it. According to the Court, a patent holder must prove that it has suffered irreparable injury and that the public interest would not be disserved by a permanent injunction.[21] This decision gives courts discretion to decide what is equitable in the circumstances and allows them to

---

17. *Diamond v. Diehr*, 450 U.S. 175, 101 S.Ct. 1048, 67 L.Ed.2d 155 (1981).
18. 149 F.3d 1368 (Fed.Cir. 1998).
19. *In re Bilski*, 545 F.3d 943 (Fed.Cir. 2008).

20. *Microsoft Corp. v. AT&T Corp.*, 550 U.S. 437, 127 S.Ct. 1746, 167 L.Ed.2d 737 (2007).
21. *eBay, Inc. v. MercExchange, LLC*, 547 U.S. 388, 126 S.Ct. 1837, 164 L.Ed.2d 641 (2006).

consider what is in the public interest rather than just the interests of the parties.

CASE IN POINT In the first case applying this rule, a court found that although Microsoft had infringed on the patent of a small software company, the latter was not entitled to an injunction. According to the court, the small company was not irreparably harmed and could be adequately compensated by damages. Also, the public might suffer negative effects from an injunction because the infringement involved part of Microsoft's widely used Office suite software.[22]

SECTION 4
COPYRIGHTS

A **copyright** is an intangible property right granted by federal statute to the author or originator of a literary or artistic production of a specified type. The Copyright Act of 1976,[23] as amended, governs copyrights. Works created after January 1, 1978, are automatically given statutory copyright protection for the life of the author plus 70 years. For copyrights owned by publishing houses, the copyright expires 95 years from the date of publication or 120 years from the date of creation, whichever comes first. For works by more than one author, the copyright expires 70 years after the death of the last surviving author.[24]

Copyrights can be registered with the U.S. Copyright Office in Washington, D.C. A copyright owner no longer needs to place the symbol © or the term *Copr.* or *Copyright* on the work to have the work protected against infringement. Chances are that if somebody created it, somebody owns it.

What Is Protected Expression?

Works that are copyrightable include books, records, films, artworks, architectural plans, menus, music videos, product packaging, and computer software. To be protected, a work must be "fixed in a durable medium" from which it can be perceived,

reproduced, or communicated. Protection is automatic. Registration is not required.

To obtain protection under the Copyright Act, a work must be original and fall into one of the following categories:

1. Literary works (including newspaper and magazine articles, computer and training manuals, catalogues, brochures, and print advertisements).
2. Musical works and accompanying words (including advertising jingles).
3. Dramatic works and accompanying music.
4. Pantomimes and choreographic works (including ballets and other forms of dance).
5. Pictorial, graphic, and sculptural works (including cartoons, maps, posters, statues, and even stuffed animals).
6. Motion pictures and other audiovisual works (including multimedia works).
7. Sound recordings.
8. Architectural works.

SECTION 102 EXCLUSIONS It is not possible to copyright an *idea*. Section 102 of the Copyright Act specifically excludes copyright protection for any "idea, procedure, process, system, method of operation, concept, principle, or discovery, regardless of the form in which it is described, explained, illustrated, or embodied." Thus, anyone can freely use the underlying ideas or principles embodied in a work. What is copyrightable is the particular way in which an idea is expressed. Whenever an idea and an expression are inseparable, the expression cannot be copyrighted. Generally, anything that is not an original expression will not qualify for copyright protection. Facts widely known to the public are not copyrightable. Page numbers are not copyrightable because they follow a sequence known to everyone. Mathematical calculations are not copyrightable.

COMPILATIONS OF FACTS Unlike ideas, *compilations* of facts are copyrightable. Under Section 103 of the Copyright Act, a compilation is "a work formed by the collection and assembling of preexisting materials or data that are selected, coordinated, or arranged in such a way that the resulting work as a whole constitutes an original work of authorship." The key requirement in the copyrightability of a compilation is originality. If the facts are selected, coordinated, or arranged in an original way, they can qualify for copyright protection. Therefore, the White Pages of a telephone directory do not qualify for copyright protection because the facts (names, addresses, and telephone numbers) are listed in alphabetical order

---

22. *Z4 Technologies, Inc. v. Microsoft Corp.,* 434 F.Supp.2d 437 (E.D.Tex. 2006).
23. 17 U.S.C. Sections 101 *et seq.*
24. These time periods reflect the extensions of the length of copyright protection enacted by Congress in the Copyright Term Extension Act of 1998, 17 U.S.C.A. Section 302. The United States Supreme Court upheld the constitutionality of the act in 2003. See *Eldred v. Ashcroft,* 537 U.S. 186, 123 S.Ct. 769, 154 L.Ed.2d 683 (2003).

rather than being selected, coordinated, or arranged in an original way. The Yellow Pages of a telephone directory, in contrast, may be copyrightable, provided the information is selected, coordinated, or arranged in an original way. Similarly, a compilation of information about yachts listed for sale has qualified for copyright protection.[25]

Copyright Infringement

Whenever the form or expression of an idea is copied, an infringement of copyright has occurred. The reproduction does not have to be exactly the same as the original, nor does it have to reproduce the original in its entirety. If a substantial part of the original is reproduced, the copyright has been infringed.

REMEDIES FOR COPYRIGHT INFRINGEMENT Those who infringe copyrights may be liable for damages or criminal penalties. These range from actual damages or statutory damages, imposed at the court's discretion, to criminal proceedings for willful violations. Actual damages are based on the harm caused to the copyright holder by the infringement, while statutory damages, not to exceed $150,000, are provided for under the Copyright Act. Criminal proceedings may result in fines and/or imprisonment. A court can also issue a permanent injunction against a defendant when the court deems it necessary to prevent future copyright infringement.

CASE IN POINT Rusty Carroll operated an online term paper business, R2C2, Inc., that offered up to 300,000 research papers for sale at nine different Web sites. Individuals whose work was posted on these Web sites without their permission filed a lawsuit against Carroll for copyright infringement. A federal district court in Illinois ruled that an injunction was proper because the plaintiffs had shown that they had suffered irreparable harm and that monetary damages were inadequate to compensate them. Because Carroll had repeatedly failed to comply with court orders regarding discovery, the court found that the copyright infringement was likely to continue unless an injunction was issued. The court therefore issued a permanent injunction prohibiting Carroll and R2C2 from selling any term paper without sworn documentary evidence that the paper's author had given permission.[26]

THE "FAIR USE" EXCEPTION An exception to liability for copyright infringement is made under the "fair use" doctrine. In certain circumstances, a person or organization can reproduce copyrighted material without paying royalties (fees paid to the copyright holder for the privilege of reproducing the copyrighted material). Section 107 of the Copyright Act provides as follows:

> [T]he fair use of a copyrighted work, including such use by reproduction in copies or phonorecords or by any other means specified by [Section 106 of the Copyright Act], for purposes such as criticism, comment, news reporting, teaching (including multiple copies for classroom use), scholarship, or research, is not an infringement of copyright. In determining whether the use made of a work in any particular case is a fair use the factors to be considered shall include–
>
> (1) the purpose and character of the use, including whether such use is of a commercial nature or is for nonprofit educational purposes;
> (2) the nature of the copyrighted work;
> (3) the amount and substantiality of the portion used in relation to the copyrighted work as a whole; and
> (4) the effect of the use upon the potential market for or value of the copyrighted work.

WHAT IS FAIR USE? Because these guidelines are very broad, the courts determine whether a particular use is fair on a case-by-case basis. Thus, even if a person who reproduces copyrighted material believes the fair use exception applies, that person may still be committing a violation. In determining whether a use is fair, courts have often considered the fourth factor to be the most important.

CASE IN POINT The owner of copyrighted music, BMG Music Publishing, granted a license to Leadsinger, Inc., a manufacturer of karaoke devices. The license gave Leadsinger permission to reproduce the sound recordings, but not to reprint the song lyrics, which appeared at the bottom of a TV screen when the karaoke device was used. BMG demanded that Leadsinger pay a "lyric reprint" fee and a "synchronization" fee. Leadsinger refused to pay, claiming that its use of the lyrics was educational and thus did not constitute copyright infringement under the fair use exception. A federal appellate court disagreed. The court held that Leadsinger's display of the lyrics was not a fair use because it would have a negative effect on the value of the copyrighted work.[27]

---

25. *BUC International Corp. v. International Yacht Council, Ltd.,* 489 F.3d 1129 (11th Cir. 2007).

26. *Weidner v. Carroll,* No. 06-782-DRH, U.S. District Court for the Southern District of Illinois, January 21, 2010.

27. *Leadsinger, Inc. v. BMG Music Publishing,* 512 F.3d 522 (9th Cir. 2008).

Copyright Protection for Software

In 1980, Congress passed the Computer Software Copyright Act, which amended the Copyright Act of 1976 to include computer programs in the list of creative works protected by federal copyright law.[28] Generally, the courts have extended copyright protection to those parts of a computer program that can be read by humans, such as the "high-level" language of a source code, and to the binary-language object code, which is readable only by the computer. Additionally, such elements as the overall structure, sequence, and organization of a program have been deemed copyrightable. Not all aspects of software are protected, however. For the most part, courts have not extended copyright protection to the "look and feel"—the general appearance, command structure, video images, menus, windows, and other screen displays—of computer programs.

SECTION 5
COPYRIGHTS IN DIGITAL INFORMATION

Copyright law is probably the most important form of intellectual property protection on the Internet. This is because much of the material on the Internet (including software and database information) is copyrighted, and in order to transfer that material online, it must be "copied." Generally, whenever a party downloads software or music into a computer's random access memory, or RAM, without authorization, a copyright is infringed. Technology has vastly increased the potential for copyright infringement.

CASE IN POINT A musical group used only a few seconds from the guitar solo of another group's copyrighted sound recording, without permission, while recording a rap song that was included in the sound track of a movie. Nevertheless, a federal appellate court held that digitally sampling a copyrighted sound recording of any length constitutes copyright infringement.[29]

Initially, criminal penalties for copyright violations could be imposed only if unauthorized copies were exchanged for financial gain. Yet much piracy of copyrighted materials online was "altruistic" in nature; unauthorized copies were made simply to be shared with others. Then, Congress amended the law and extended criminal liability for the piracy of copyrighted materials to persons who exchange unauthorized copies of copyrighted works without realizing a profit.

Digital Millennium Copyright Act

In 1998, Congress passed further legislation to protect copyright holders—the Digital Millennium Copyright Act (DMCA).[30] The DMCA gave significant protection to owners of copyrights in digital information.[31] Among other things, the act established civil and criminal penalties for anyone who circumvents (bypasses) encryption software or other technological antipiracy protection. Also prohibited are the manufacture, import, sale, and distribution of devices or services for circumvention.

The DMCA provides for exceptions to fit the needs of libraries, scientists, universities, and others. In general, the law does not restrict the "fair use" of circumvention methods for educational and other noncommercial purposes. For example, circumvention is allowed to test computer security, to conduct encryption research, to protect personal privacy, and to enable parents to monitor their children's use of the Internet. The exceptions are to be reconsidered every three years.

The DMCA also limits the liability of Internet service providers (ISPs). Under the act, an ISP is not liable for copyright infringement by its customer *unless* the ISP is aware of the subscriber's violation. An ISP may be held liable only if it fails to take action to shut down the subscriber after learning of the violation. A copyright holder must act promptly, however, by pursuing a claim in court, or the subscriber has the right to be restored to online access.

MP3 and File-Sharing Technology

Soon after the Internet became popular, a few enterprising programmers created software to compress large data files, particularly those associated with music. The best-known compression and decompression system is MP3, which enables music fans to download songs or entire CDs onto their computers or onto portable listening devices, such as iPods or iPhones. The MP3 system also made it possible for music fans to access other music fans' files by engaging in file-sharing via the Internet.

---

28. Pub. L. No. 96-517 (1980), amending 17 U.S.C. Sections 101, 117.
29. *Bridgeport Music, Inc. v. Dimension Films*, 410 F.3d 792 (6th Cir. 2005).
30. 17 U.S.C. Sections 512, 1201–1205, 1301–1332; and 28 U.S.C. Section 4001.
31. This act implemented the World Intellectual Property Organization Copyright Treaty of 1996, which will be discussed later in this chapter on page 169.

File-sharing is accomplished through **peer-to-peer (P2P) networking.** The concept is simple. Rather than going through a central Web server, P2P networking uses numerous personal computers (PCs) that are connected to the Internet. Individuals on the same network can access files stored on one another's PCs through a **distributed network.** Parts of the network may be distributed all over the country or the world, which offers an unlimited number of uses. Persons scattered throughout the country or the world can work together on the same project by using file-sharing programs.

A newer method of sharing files via the Internet is **cloud computing**, which is essentially a subscription-based or pay-per-use service that extends a computer's software or storage capabilities. Cloud computing can deliver a single application through a browser to multiple users, or it might be a utility program to pool resources and provide data storage and virtual servers that can be accessed on demand. Amazon, Facebook, Google, IBM, and Sun Microsystems are using and developing more cloud computing services.

SHARING STORED MUSIC FILES When file-sharing is used to download others' stored music files, copyright issues arise. Recording artists and their labels stand to lose large amounts of royalties and revenues if relatively few CDs are purchased and then made available on distributed networks, from which anyone can get them for free.

CASE IN POINT The issue of file-sharing infringement has been the subject of an ongoing debate since the highly publicized case of *A&M Records, Inc. v. Napster, Inc.*[32] Napster, Inc., operated a Web site with free software that enabled users to copy and transfer MP3 files via the Internet. When firms in the recording industry sued Napster, the court held that Napster was liable for contributory and vicarious[33] (indirect) copyright infringement because it had assisted others in obtaining unauthorized copies of copyrighted music.

In the following case, a group of recording companies sued an Internet user who had downloaded a number of copyrighted songs from the Internet. The user then shared the audio files with others via a P2P network. One of the issues before the court was whether the user was an "innocent infringer"—that is, whether she was innocent of copyright infringement because she was unaware that the works were copyrighted.

---

32. 239 F.3d 1004 (9th Cir. 2001).
33. *Vicarious (indirect) liability* exists when one person is subject to liability for another's actions. A common example occurs in the employment context, when an employer is held vicariously liable by third parties for torts committed by employees in the course of their employment.

CASE 8.3
Maverick Recording Co. v. Harper

United States Court of Appeals, Fifth Circuit, 598 F.3d 193 (2010).
www.ca5.uscourts.gov/Opinions/aspx[a]

COMPANY PROFILE • Recording star Madonna, others in the music business, and Time Warner created Maverick Records in 1992. Initially, the company saw great success with Alanis Morissette, The Prodigy, Candlebox, and the Deftones. It also created the sound track for the movie The Matrix. In a dispute over management of the company, Madonna and another co-owner were bought out. Today, Maverick is a wholly owned subsidiary of Warner Music Group.

BACKGROUND AND FACTS • Maverick Recording Company and several other music-recording firms (the plaintiffs) hired MediaSentry to investigate the infringement of their copyrights over the Internet. During its investigation, MediaSentry discovered that Whitney Harper was using a file-sharing program to share digital audio files with other users of a peer-to-peer network. The shared audio files included a number of the plaintiffs' copyrighted works. The plaintiffs brought an action in a federal court against Harper for copyright infringement. They sought $750 per infringed work, the minimum amount of damages set forth in Section 504(c)(1) of the Copyright Act. Harper asserted that her infringement was "innocent" and that therefore Section 504(c)(2) of the Copyright Act should

---

a. In the box titled "and/or Title contains text," type in "Maverick." On the page that opens, click on the docket number beside the case title to access the opinion. The U.S. Court of Appeals for the Fifth Circuit maintains this Web site.

CASE CONTINUES ▸

CASE 8.3 CONTINUED ▶ apply. That section provides that when an infringer was not aware, and had no reason to believe, that his or her acts constituted copyright infringement, "the court in its discretion may reduce the award of statutory damages to a sum of not less than $200." The trial court granted summary judgment for the plaintiffs on the issue of copyright infringement and enjoined Harper from further downloading and sharing of copyrighted works. The court, however, awarded the plaintiffs only $200 per infringed work. Both parties appealed. Harper claimed that there was insufficient evidence of copyright infringement. The plaintiffs argued that the district court had erred by failing to rule out the innocent infringer defense as a matter of law.

IN THE LANGUAGE OF THE COURT
Edith Brown *CLEMENT*, Circuit Judge:
* * * * *

The uncontroverted [undisputed] evidence is more than sufficient to compel a finding that Harper had downloaded the files: there was no evidence from which a fact-finder could draw a reasonable inference that Harper had *not* downloaded them or that they were something other than audio files. * * * The district court properly rejected Harper's argument that the evidence of infringement was insufficient.

* * * *

* * * The district court held that there was a genuine issue of material fact as to whether Harper was an innocent infringer. * * * Harper averred [asserted] in an affidavit that she did not understand the nature of file-sharing programs and that she believed that listening to music from file-sharing networks was akin to listening to a noninfringing Internet radio station. The district court ruled that this assertion created a triable [capable of being tried before a judge or a jury] issue as to whether Harper's infringement was "innocent" under [Section 504(c)(2) of the Copyright Act].

* * * We hold that the defense was unavailable to her as a matter of law. *The innocent infringer defense is limited by [Section 402(d) of the Copyright Act]: with one exception not relevant here, when a proper copyright notice "appears on the published * * * phonorecords to which a defendant * * * had access, then no weight shall be given to such a defendant's interposition of a defense based on innocent infringement in mitigation of actual or statutory damages."* [Emphasis added.]

The district court acknowledged that Plaintiffs provided proper notice on each of the published phonorecords from which the audio files were taken. * * * Harper contended only that she was too young and naive to understand that the copyrights on published music applied to downloaded music.

These arguments are insufficient to defeat the interposition [interference] of the [Section 402(d)] limitation on the innocent infringer defense. Harper's reliance on her own understanding of copyright law—or lack thereof—is irrelevant in the context of [Section 402(d)]. *The plain language of the statute shows that the infringer's knowledge or intent does not affect its application. Lack of legal sophistication cannot overcome a properly asserted [Section 402(d)] limitation to the innocent infringer defense.* [Emphasis added.]

* * * *

In short, the district court found a genuine issue of fact as to whether Harper intended to infringe Plaintiffs' copyrights, but that issue was not material: [Section 402(d)] forecloses, as a matter of law, Harper's innocent infringer defense. Because the defense does not apply, Plaintiffs are entitled to statutory damages. And because Plaintiffs requested the minimum statutory damages under [Section 504(c)(1)], Harper's culpability is not an issue and there are no issues left for trial. Plaintiffs must be awarded statutory damages of $750 per infringed work.

DECISION AND REMEDY • *The U.S. Court of Appeals for the Fifth Circuit affirmed the trial court's finding of copyright liability, reversed its finding that the innocent infringer defense presented an issue for trial, and remanded the case for further proceedings consistent with the court's opinion. The appellate court concluded that the district court had erred by awarding damages of $200 per infringement because Harper was not an innocent infringer.*

THE ETHICAL DIMENSION • *In this and other cases involving similar rulings, the courts have held that when the published phonorecordings from which audio files were taken contained copyright notices, the innocent infringer defense does not apply. It is irrelevant that the notice is not provided in the online file. Is this fair? Explain.*

MANAGERIAL IMPLICATIONS • *Owners and managers of firms in the business of recording and distributing music face a constant challenge in protecting their copyrights. This is particularly true for audio files in the online environment, where Internet users can easily download a copyrighted song and make it available to P2P file-sharing networks. Among other things, this means that recording companies must be ever vigilant in searching the Web to find infringing uses of works distributed online. Today, it is not uncommon for companies to hire antipiracy firms to investigate the illegal downloading of their copyrighted materials.*

THE EVOLUTION OF FILE-SHARING TECHNOLOGIES

After the *Napster* decision, the recording industry filed and won numerous lawsuits against companies that distribute online file-sharing software. Other companies then developed technologies that allow P2P network users to share stored music files, without paying a fee, more quickly and efficiently than ever. Software such as Morpheus, KaZaA, and LimeWire, for example, provides users with an interface that is similar to a Web browser.[34] When a user performs a search, the software locates a list of peers that have the file available for downloading.

Because of the automated procedures, the companies do not maintain a central index and are unable to determine whether users are exchanging copyrighted files. Nevertheless, the United States Supreme Court has held that companies that distribute file-sharing software intending that it be used to violate copyright laws can be liable for users' copyright infringement.

CASE IN POINT In *Metro-Goldwyn-Mayer Studios, Inc. v. Grokster, Ltd.,*[35] music and film industry organizations sued Grokster, Ltd., and StreamCast Networks, Inc., for contributory and vicarious copyright infringement. The Supreme Court held that anyone who distributes file-sharing software "with the object of promoting its use to infringe copyright, as shown by clear expression or other affirmative steps taken to foster infringement, . . . is liable for the resulting acts of infringement by third parties."

DVDS AND FILE-SHARING

DVDS AND FILE-SHARING File-sharing also creates problems for the motion picture industry, which has lost significant amounts of revenue as a result of pirated DVDs. Nearly one-third of the people in the United States—many of them young men—have illegally copied a movie onto a DVD in violation of copyright laws.[36] Numerous Web sites offer software that facilitates the illegal copying of movies, such as BitTorrent, which enables users to download high-quality files from the Internet.

CASE IN POINT TorrentSpy, a popular BitTorrent indexing Web site, enabled users to locate and exchange files. The Motion Picture Association of America (MPAA) and Columbia Pictures Industries, brought a lawsuit against the operators of TorrentSpy for facilitating copyright infringement. The MPAA also claimed that the operators had destroyed evidence that would reveal the identity of individual infringers. The operators had ignored a court order to keep server logs of the Internet addresses of people who facilitated the trading of files via the site. Because TorrentSpy's operators had willfully destroyed evidence, a federal court found in favor of the MPAA and ordered the defendants to pay a judgment of $111 million.[37]

SECTION 6
TRADE SECRETS

The law of trade secrets protects some business processes and information that are not, or cannot be, patented, copyrighted, or trademarked against appropriation by competitors. A **trade secret** is basically information of commercial value. Trade secrets may include customer lists, plans, research

---

34. In 2005, KaZaA entered into a settlement agreement with four major music companies that had alleged copyright infringement. KaZaA agreed to offer only legitimate, fee-based music downloads. Note also that although the publisher of Morpheus is no longer in business, the software is still available.

35. 545 U.S. 913, 125 S.Ct. 2764, 162 L.Ed.2d 781 (2005). Grokster, Ltd., later settled this dispute out of court and stopped distributing its software.

36. Chris Tribbey. "Report: DVD Piracy Is Growing." *Home Media Magazine*. 7 May 2009.

37. *Columbia Pictures Industries v. Bunnell,* 2007 WL 4877701 (C.D.Cal. 2007). The final judgment awarding damages and issuing a permanent injunction was filed on May 5, 2008 (No. 2:06-CV-01093-FMC-JCx). See David Kravets. "TorrentSpy Dinged $111 Million in MPAA Lawsuit." *Wired.com.* 7 May 2008: n.p. Web.

and development, pricing information, marketing methods, production techniques, and generally anything that makes an individual company unique and that would have value to a competitor.

Unlike copyright and trademark protection, protection of trade secrets extends both to ideas and to their expression. (For this reason, and because a trade secret involves no registration or filing requirements, trade secret protection may be well suited for software.) Of course, the secret formula, method, or other information must be disclosed to some persons, particularly to key employees. Businesses generally attempt to protect their trade secrets by having all employees who use a process or information agree in their contracts, or in confidentiality agreements, never to divulge it.[38]

State and Federal Law on Trade Secrets

Under Section 757 of the *Restatement of Torts,* those who disclose or use another's trade secret, without authorization, are liable to that other party if (1) they discovered the secret by improper means or (2) their disclosure or use constitutes a breach of a duty owed to the other party. The theft of confidential business data by industrial espionage, as when a business taps into a competitor's computer, is a theft of trade secrets without any contractual violation and is actionable in itself.

Trade secrets were protected under the common law, but the protection provided varied from state to state. Today, most states' laws are based on the Uniform Trade Secrets Act,[39] which has been adopted in forty-seven states. Additionally, in 1996 Congress passed the Economic Espionage Act,[40] which made the theft of trade secrets a federal crime. We will examine the provisions and significance of this act in Chapter 9, in the context of crimes related to business.

Trade Secrets in Cyberspace

Computer technology is undercutting many business firms' ability to protect their confidential information, including trade secrets.[41] For example, a dishonest employee could e-mail trade secrets in a company's computer to a competitor or a future employer. If e-mail is not an option, the employee might walk out with the information on a flash pen drive.

For a comprehensive summary of trade secrets and the other forms of intellectual property discussed in this chapter, see Exhibit 8–1.

SECTION 7
INTERNATIONAL PROTECTION FOR INTELLECTUAL PROPERTY

For many years, the United States has been a party to various international agreements relating to intellectual property rights. For example, the Paris Convention of 1883, to which about 172 countries are signatory, allows parties in one country to file for patent and trademark protection in any of the other member countries. Other international agreements in this area include the Berne Convention; the Trade-Related Aspects of Intellectual Property Rights, or, more simply, the TRIPS agreement; and the Madrid Protocol. To learn about a new international treaty being negotiated that will affect international property rights, see this chapter's *Shifting Legal Priorities for Business* feature on page 170.

The Berne Convention

Under the Berne Convention of 1886 (an international copyright agreement), as amended, if a U.S. citizen writes a book, every country that has signed the convention must recognize the U.S. author's copyright in the book. Also, if a citizen of a country that has not signed the convention first publishes a book in one of the 170 countries that have signed, all other countries that have signed the convention must recognize that author's copyright. Copyright notice is not needed to gain protection under the Berne Convention for works published after March 1, 1989.

The laws of many countries, as well as international laws, are being updated to reflect changes

---

38. See, for example, *Verigy US, Inc. v. Mayder,* 2008 WL 564634 (N.D.Cal. 2008); and *Gleeson v. Preferred Sourcing, LLC,* 883 N.E.2d 164 (Ind.App. 2008).

39. The Uniform Trade Secrets Act, as drafted by the National Conference of Commissioners on Uniform State Laws, (NCCUSL), can be found at www.nccusl.org. As with all uniform laws, each state has codified the law within its own state statutory code.

40. 18 U.S.C. Sections 1831–1839.

41. Note that in at least one case, a court has held that customers' e-mail addresses may constitute trade secrets. See *T-N-T Motorsports, Inc. v. Hennessey Motorsports, Inc.,* 965 S.W.2d 18 (Tex.App.—Houston 1998); rehearing overruled (1998); petition dismissed (1998).

EXHIBIT 8-1 • Forms of Intellectual Property

FORM	DEFINITION	HOW ACQUIRED	DURATION	REMEDY FOR INFRINGEMENT
Patent	A grant from the government that gives an inventor exclusive rights to an invention.	By filing a patent application with the U.S. Patent and Trademark Office and receiving its approval.	Twenty years from the date of the application; for design patents, fourteen years.	Monetary damages, including royalties and lost profits, *plus* attorneys' fees. Damages may be tripled for intentional infringements.
Copyright	The right of an author or originator of a literary or artistic work, or other production that falls within a specified category, to have the exclusive use of that work for a given period of time.	Automatic (once the work or creation is put in tangible form). Only the *expression* of an idea (and not the idea itself) can be protected by copyright.	For authors: the life of the author, plus 70 years. For publishers: 95 years after the date of publication or 120 years after creation.	Actual damages plus profits received by the party who infringed *or* statutory damages under the Copyright Act, *plus* costs and attorneys' fees in either situation.
Trademark (Service Mark and Trade Dress)	Any distinctive word, name, symbol, or device (image or appearance), or combination thereof, that an entity uses to distinguish its goods or services from those of others. The owner has the exclusive right to use that mark or trade dress.	1. At common law, ownership created by use of the mark. 2. Registration with the appropriate federal or state office gives notice and is permitted if the mark is currently in use or will be within the next six months.	Unlimited, as long as it is in use. To continue notice by registration, the owner must renew by filing between the fifth and sixth years, and thereafter, every ten years.	1. Injunction prohibiting the future use of the mark. 2. Actual damages *plus* profits received by the party who infringed (can be increased under the Lanham Act). 3. Destruction of articles that infringed. 4. *Plus* costs and attorneys' fees.
Trade Secret	Any information that a business possesses and that gives the business an advantage over competitors (including formulas, lists, patterns, plans, processes, and programs).	Through the originality and development of the information and processes that constitute the business secret and are unknown to others.	Unlimited, so long as not revealed to others. Once revealed to others, it is no longer a trade secret.	Monetary damages for misappropriation (the Uniform Trade Secrets Act also permits punitive damages if willful), *plus* costs and attorneys' fees.

in technology and the expansion of the Internet. Copyright holders and other owners of intellectual property generally agree that changes in the law are needed to stop the increasing international piracy of their property. The World Intellectual Property Organization (WIPO) Copyright Treaty of 1996, a special agreement under the Berne Convention, attempts to update international law governing copyright protection to include more safeguards against copyright infringement via the Internet. The United States signed the WIPO treaty in 1996 and implemented its terms in the Digital Millennium Copyright Act of 1998, which was discussed earlier in this chapter on page 164.

This convention and other international agreements have given some protection to intellectual property on a worldwide level. None of them, however, has been as significant and far reaching in scope as the agreement discussed next.

The TRIPS Agreement

Representatives from more than one hundred nations signed the TRIPS agreement in 1994. The agreement established, for the first time, standards for the international protection of intellectual property rights, including patents, trademarks, and copyrights for movies, computer programs, books, and

In 2008, the United States began negotiating a new international treaty with the European Union, Japan, and Switzerland. By 2010, Australia, Canada, Jordan, Mexico, Morocco, New Zealand, Singapore, South Korea, and the United Arab Emirates had joined in the negotiations. The proposed treaty, called the Anti-Counterfeiting Trade Agreement, would establish its own governing body that is separate and distinct from existing groups, including the World Trade Organization and the World Intellectual Property Organization.

The Goal of the Proposed Treaty

The treaty will apply not only to counterfeit physical goods, such as medications, but also to pirated copyrighted works being distributed via the Internet and other information technology. The goal is to create a new higher standard of enforcement for intellectual property rights that goes beyond the Trade-Related Aspects of Intellectual Property Rights (TRIPS) agreement and encourages international cooperation and information sharing among the signatory countries.

Provisions Being Considered

The specific terms of the treaty have not yet been publicly disclosed, but there is considerable speculation about what it may contain. According to some media reports, one provision may authorize random border searches of electronic devices, such as laptops and iPods, for infringing content. Another provision supposedly would require Internet service providers to provide information about suspected copyright infringers without a warrant. Remember, though, that at this point the actual terms of the treaty are unknown, and the final provisions may differ considerably from the preliminary reports. The impact of the global financial crisis may also have an effect on the negotiations, which finished their seventh round in January 2010.

MANAGERIAL IMPLICATIONS

Managers in companies that create intellectual property for sale must become familiar with the final version of the Anti-Counterfeiting Trade Agreement. Among other things, the agreement may provide additional protection for intellectual property that is downloadable through the Internet.

---

music. The TRIPS agreement provides that each member country of the World Trade Organization must include in its domestic laws broad intellectual property rights and effective remedies (including civil and criminal penalties) for violations of those rights.

NO DISCRIMINATION AGAINST FOREIGN INTELLECTUAL PROPERTY OWNERS Generally, the TRIPS agreement forbids member nations from discriminating against foreign owners of intellectual property rights (in the administration, regulation, or adjudication of such rights). In other words, a member nation cannot give its own nationals (citizens) favorable treatment without offering the same treatment to nationals of all other member countries. For instance, if a U.S. software manufacturer brings a suit for the infringement of intellectual property rights under Germany's national laws, the U.S. manufacturer is entitled to receive the same treatment as a German manufacturer because Germany is a member of the agreement. Each member nation must also ensure that legal procedures are available for parties who wish to bring actions for infringement of intellectual property rights. Additionally, a related document established a mechanism for settling disputes among member nations.

TYPES OF COVERED INTELLECTUAL PROPERTY Particular provisions of the TRIPS agreement relate to patent, trademark, and copyright protection for intellectual property. The agreement specifically provides copyright protection for computer programs by stating that compilations of data, databases, and other materials are "intellectual creations" and are to be protected as copyrightable works. Other provisions relate to trade secrets and the rental of computer programs and cinematographic works.

The Madrid Protocol

In the past, one of the difficulties in protecting U.S. trademarks internationally was the time and expense required to apply for trademark registration in foreign countries. The filing fees and procedures for trademark registration vary significantly among individual countries. The Madrid Protocol, which was signed into law in 2003, may help to resolve these problems. The Madrid Protocol is an international treaty that has been signed by seventy-nine countries. Under its provisions, a U.S. company wishing to register its trademark abroad can submit a single application and designate other member countries in which the company would like to register its mark. The treaty is designed to reduce the costs of international trademark protection by more than 60 percent, according to proponents.

Although the Madrid Protocol may simplify and reduce the cost of trademark registration in foreign countries, it remains to be seen whether it will provide significant benefits to trademark owners. Even with a similar registration process, there is still a question as to whether member countries will enforce the law and protect the mark. Moreover, the cost savings of using the Madrid Protocol may be negated by its requirement that a trademark owner use local agents in the applicable jurisdiction if problems arise.

REVIEWING

Intellectual Property and Internet Law

Two computer science majors, Trent and Xavier, have an idea for a new video game, which they propose to call "Hallowed." They form a business and begin developing their idea. Several months later, Trent and Xavier run into a problem with their design and consult with a friend, Brad, who is an expert in designing computer source codes. After the software is completed but before Hallowed is marketed, a video game called Halo 2 is released for both the Xbox and the Playstation 3 systems. Halo 2 uses source codes similar to those of Hallowed and imitates Hallowed's overall look and feel, although not all the features are alike. Using the information presented in the chapter, answer the following questions.

1. Would the name *Hallowe*d receive protection as a trademark or as trade dress? Explain.
2. If Trent and Xavier had obtained a business process patent on Hallowed, would the release of Halo 2 have infringed on their patent? Why or why not?
3. Based only on the facts described above, could Trent and Xavier sue the makers of Halo 2 for copyright infringement? Why or why not?
4. Suppose that Trent and Xavier discover that Brad took the idea of Hallowed and sold it to the company that produced Halo 2. Which type of intellectual property issue does this raise?

DEBATE THIS: *Congress has amended copyright law several times. Copyright holders now have protection for many decades. Was Congress right in extending these copyright time periods? Why or why not?*

TERMS AND CONCEPTS

certification mark 155
cloud computing 165
collective mark 155
copyright 162

cyber mark 156
cybersquatting 156
dilution 153
distributed network 165
domain name 156
intellectual property 151

license 158
meta tag 157
patent 158
peer-to-peer (P2P)
    networking 165
service mark 155

trade dress 155
trade name 156
trade secret 167
trademark 151
typosquatting 157

QUESTIONS AND CASE PROBLEMS

8–1. Fair Use Professor Wise is teaching a summer seminar in business torts at State University. Several times during the course, he makes copies of relevant sections from business law texts and distributes them to his students. Wise does not realize that the daughter of one of the textbook authors is a member of his seminar. She tells her father about Wise's copying activities, which have taken place without her father's or his publisher's permission. Her father sues Wise for copyright infringement. Wise claims protection under the fair use doctrine. Who will prevail? Explain.

8–2. QUESTION WITH SAMPLE ANSWER: Copyright Infringement.

In which of the following situations would a court likely hold Ursula liable for copyright infringement?

(a) Ursula goes to the library and photocopies ten pages from a scholarly journal relating to a topic on which she is writing a term paper.

(b) Ursula makes blouses, dresses, and other clothes and sells them in her small shop. She advertises some of the outfits as Guest items, hoping that customers might mistakenly assume that they were made by Guess, the well-known clothing manufacturer.

(c) Ursula teaches Latin American history at a small university. She has a digital video recorder and frequently records television programs relating to Latin America and puts them on DVDs. She then takes the DVDs to her classroom so that her students can watch them.

- **For a sample answer to Question 8–2, go to Appendix I at the end of this text.**

8–3. Trademark Infringement Sync Computers, Inc., makes computer-related products under the brand name "Sync," which the company registers as a trademark. Without Sync's permission, E-Product Corp. embeds the Sync mark in E-Product's Web site, in black type on a blue background. This tag causes the E-Product site to be returned at the top of the list of results on a search engine query for "Sync." Does E-Product's use of the Sync mark as a meta tag without Sync's permission constitute trademark infringement? Explain.

8–4. Patent Infringement As a cattle rancher in Nebraska, Gerald Gohl used handheld searchlights to find and help calving animals (animals giving birth) in harsh blizzard conditions. Gohl thought that it would be more helpful to have a portable searchlight mounted on the outside of a vehicle and remotely controlled. He and Al Gebhardt developed and patented practical applications of this idea—the Golight and the wireless, remote-controlled Radio Ray, which could rotate 360 degrees—and formed Golight, Inc., to make and market these products. In 1997, Wal-Mart Stores, Inc., began selling a portable, wireless, remote-controlled searchlight that was identical to the Radio Ray except for a stop piece that prevented the light from rotating more than 351 degrees. Golight sent Wal-Mart a letter claiming that its device infringed Golight's patent. Wal-Mart sold its remaining inventory of the devices and stopped carrying the product. Golight filed a suit in a federal district court against Wal-Mart, alleging patent infringement. How should the court rule? Explain. [*Golight, Inc. v. Wal-Mart Stores, Inc.,* 355 F.3d 1327 (Fed.Cir. 2004)]

8–5. Trade Secrets Briefing.com offers Internet-based analyses of investment opportunities to investors. Richard Green is the company's president. One of Briefing.com's competitors is StreetAccount, LLC (limited liability

company), whose owners include Gregory Jones and Cynthia Dietzmann. Jones worked for Briefing.com for six years until he quit in March 2003 and was a member of its board of directors until April 2003. Dietzmann worked for Briefing.com for seven years until she quit in March 2003. As Briefing.com employees, Jones and Dietzmann had access to confidential business data. For instance, Dietzmann developed a list of contacts through which Briefing.com obtained market information to display online. When Dietzmann quit, she did not return all of the contact information to the company. Briefing.com and Green filed a suit in a federal district court against Jones, Dietzmann, and StreetAccount, alleging that they had appropriated these data and other "trade secrets" to form a competing business. What are trade secrets? Why are they protected? Under what circumstances is a party liable at common law for their appropriation? How should these principles apply in this case? [*Briefing.com v. Jones,* 2006 WY 16, 126 P.3d 928 (2006)]

8–6. CASE PROBLEM WITH SAMPLE ANSWER: Trademarks.

In 1969, Jack Masquelier, a professor of pharmacology, discovered a chemical antioxidant made from the bark of a French pine tree. The substance supposedly assists in nutritional distribution and blood circulation. Horphag Research, Ltd., began to sell the product under the name Pycnogenol, which Horphag registered as a trademark in 1993. Pycnogenol became one of the fifteen best-selling herbal supplements in the United States. In 1999, through the Web site www.healthierlife.com, Larry Garcia began to sell Masquelier's Original OPCs, a supplement derived from grape pits. Claiming that this product was the "true Pycnogenol," Garcia used the mark as a meta tag and a generic term, attributing the results of research on Horphag's product to Masquelier's and altering quotations from scientific literature to substitute the name of Masquelier's product for Horphag's. Customers who purchased Garcia's product contacted Horphag about it, only to learn that they had not bought Horphag's product. Others called Horphag to ask whether Garcia "was selling . . . real Pycnogenol." Horphag filed a suit in a federal district court against Garcia, alleging, among other things, that he was diluting Horphag's mark. What is trademark dilution? Did it occur here? Explain. [Horphag Research, Ltd. v. Garcia, 475 F.3d 1029 (9th Cir. 2007)]

- **To view a sample answer for Problem 8–6, go to this book's Web site at www.cengage.com/blaw/clarkson, select "Chapter 8," and click on "Case Problem with Sample Answer."**

8–7. Copyright Redwin Wilchcombe is a musician and music producer. In 2002, Wilchcombe met Jonathan Smith, known as Lil Jon, a member of Lil Jon & The East Side Boyz (LJESB). Lil Jon and LJESB are under contract to give TeeVee Toons, Inc. (TVT), all rights to LJESB's recordings and Lil Jon's songs. Wilchcombe composed, performed, and recorded a song titled *Tha Weedman* at Lil Jon's request, based on his idea, and with his suggestions for LJESB's album *Kings of Crunk*. They did not discuss payment and Wilchcombe was not paid, but he was given credit on the album as a producer. By 2005, the album had sold 2 million copies. Wilchcombe filed a suit in a federal district court against TVT and the others, alleging copyright infringement. The defendants asserted that they had a license to use the song. Wilchcombe argued that he had never granted a license to anyone. Do these facts indicate that the defendants had a license to use Wilchcombe's song? If so, what does that mean for Wilchcombe's cause? Explain. [*Wilchcombe v. TeeVee Toons, Inc.*, 555 F.3d 949 (11th Cir. 2009)]

8–8. Trade Secrets Peggy Hamilton was a major shareholder in Carbon Processing and Reclamation (CPR), LLC. After a dispute, she sold her interest in the company and signed a confidentiality agreement not to divulge company business to anyone. A year later, when William Jones, the owner of CPR, left on a trip, he let an employee, Jesse Edwards, drive his company car. There were boxes containing some detailed company records in the car. Edwards and his wife, Channon, were in the middle of a divorce, and she suspected him of hiding financial information from her. When Channon saw the boxes in the car her husband was driving, she got a car key from Hamilton, who still had one from when she was an owner. Channon used the key to get into the boxes of company information. Jones then sued Hamilton for breach of the confidentiality agreement, contending that allowing Channon to have access to the files was assisting in the theft of trade secrets. The trial court dismissed the claim, but Jones appealed. Could Hamilton's actions be the basis for a claim of trade secret violation? What factors should be taken into consideration? [*Jones v. Hamilton*, ___ So.3d ___ (Ala.Civ.App. 2010)]

8–9. A QUESTION OF ETHICS: Copyright Infringement.

Custom Copies, Inc., in Gainesville, Florida, is a copy shop that, on request, reproduces and distributes, for profit, material published and owned by others. One of the copy shop's primary activities is the preparation and sale of coursepacks, which contain compilations of readings for college courses. For a particular coursepack, a teacher selects the readings and delivers a syllabus to the copy shop, which obtains the materials from a library, copies them, and then binds and sells the copies. Blackwell Publishing, Inc., in Malden, Massachusetts, publishes books and journals in medicine and other fields and *owns the copyrights to these publications. Blackwell and others filed a suit in a federal district court against Custom Copies, alleging copyright infringement for its "routine and systematic reproduction of materials from plaintiffs' publications, without seeking permission," to compile coursepacks for classes at the University of Florida. The plaintiffs asked the court to issue an injunction and award them damages, as well the profit from the infringement. The defendant filed a motion to dismiss the complaint. [Blackwell Publishing, Inc. v. Custom Copies, Inc.*, ___ F.Supp.2d ___ (N.D.Fla. 2007)]

(a) Custom Copies argued, in part, that creating and selling did not "distribute" the coursepacks. Does a copy shop violate copyright law if it only copies materials for coursepacks? Does the copying fall under the "fair use" exception? Should the court grant the defendant's motion? Why or why not?

(b) What is the potential impact if copies of a book or journal are created and sold without the permission of, and the payment of royalties or a fee to, the copyright owner? Explain.

8–10. VIDEO QUESTION: Protecting Ideas.

Go to this text's Web site at **www.cengage.com/blaw/clarkson** and select "Chapter 8." Click on "Video Questions" and view the video titled *The Jerk*. Then answer the following questions.

(a) In the video, Navin (Steve Martin) creates a special handle for Mr. Fox's (Bill Macy's) glasses. Can Navin obtain a patent or a copyright protecting his invention? Explain your answer.

(b) Suppose that after Navin legally protects his idea, Fox steals it and decides to develop it for himself, without Navin's permission. Has Fox committed infringement? If so, what kind—trademark, patent, or copyright?

(c) Suppose that after Navin legally protects his idea, he realizes he doesn't have the funds to mass-produce the glasses' special handle. Navin therefore agrees to allow Fox to manufacture the product. Has Navin granted Fox a license? Explain.

(d) Assume that Navin is able to manufacture his invention. What might Navin do to ensure that his product is identifiable and can be distinguished from other products on the market?

LEGAL RESEARCH EXERCISES ON THE WEB

Go to this text's Web site at **www.cengage.com/blaw/clarkson**, select "Chapter 8," and click on "Practical Internet Exercises." There you will find the following Internet research exercises that you can perform to learn more about the topics covered in this chapter.

Practical Internet Exercise 8–1: **Legal Perspective**
Unwarranted Legal Threats

Practical Internet Exercise 8–2: **Management Perspective**
Protecting Intellectual Property across Borders

Practical Internet Exercise 8–3: **Technological Perspective**
File-Sharing

CHAPTER 9

Criminal Law and Cyber Crime

The law imposes various sanctions in an effort to ensure that individuals engaged in business in our society can compete and flourish. These sanctions include those imposed by civil law, such as damages for various types of tortious conduct (see Chapters 6 and 7), damages for breach of contract (see Chapter 18), and the equitable remedies (see Chapters 1 and 18). Additional sanctions are imposed under criminal law. Indeed, many statutes regulating business provide for criminal as well as civil penalties. Therefore, criminal law joins civil law as an important element in the legal environment of business.

In this chapter, after explaining some essential differences between criminal law and civil law, we look at how crimes are classified and at the elements that must be present for criminal liability to exist. We then examine the various categories of crimes, the defenses that can be raised to avoid criminal liability, and the rules of criminal procedure. We conclude the chapter with a discussion of crimes that occur in cyberspace, which are often called cyber crimes. Generally, *cyber crime* refers more to the way in which particular crimes are committed rather than to a new category of crimes.

SECTION 1
CIVIL LAW AND CRIMINAL LAW

Recall from Chapter 1 that *civil law* pertains to the duties that exist between persons or between persons and their governments. Criminal law, in contrast, has to do with crime. A **crime** can be defined as a wrong against society proclaimed in a statute and punishable by a fine and/or imprisonment—or, in some cases, death. As mentioned in Chapter 1, because crimes are *offenses against society as a whole,* they are prosecuted by a public official, such as a district attorney (D.A.) or an attorney general (A.G.), not by the victims. Once a crime has been reported, the D.A. typically has the discretion to decide whether to file criminal charges and also determines to what extent to pursue the prosecution or carry out additional investigation.

Major Differences between Civil Law and Criminal Law

Because the state has extensive resources at its disposal when prosecuting criminal cases, there are numerous procedural safeguards to protect the rights of defendants. We look here at one of these safeguards—the higher burden of proof that applies in a criminal case—as well as the harsher sanctions for criminal acts compared with those for civil wrongs. Exhibit 9–1 summarizes these and other key differences between civil law and criminal law.

BURDEN OF PROOF In a civil case, the plaintiff usually must prove his or her case by a *preponderance of the evidence*. Under this standard, the plaintiff must convince the court that based on the evidence presented by both parties, it is more likely than not that the plaintiff's allegation is true.

EXHIBIT 9–1 • Key Differences between Civil Law and Criminal Law

ISSUE	CIVIL LAW	CRIMINAL LAW
Party who brings suit	The person who suffered harm.	The state.
Wrongful act	Causing harm to a person or to a person's property.	Violating a statute that prohibits some type of activity.
Burden of proof	Preponderance of the evidence.	Beyond a reasonable doubt.
Verdict	Three-fourths majority (typically).	Unanimous (almost always).
Remedy	Damages to compensate for the harm or a decree to achieve an equitable result.	Punishment (fine, imprisonment, or death).

In a criminal case, in contrast, the state must prove its case **beyond a reasonable doubt.** If the jury views the evidence in the case as reasonably permitting either a guilty or a not guilty verdict, then the jury's verdict must be not guilty. In other words, the government (prosecutor) must prove beyond a reasonable doubt that the defendant has committed every essential element of the offense with which she or he is charged. If the jurors are not convinced of the defendant's guilt beyond a reasonable doubt, they must find the defendant not guilty. Note also that in a criminal case, the jury's verdict normally must be unanimous—agreed to by all members of the jury—to convict the defendant. (In a civil trial by jury, in contrast, typically only three-fourths of the jurors need to agree.)

CRIMINAL SANCTIONS The sanctions imposed on criminal wrongdoers are also harsher than those that are applied in civil cases. Remember from Chapters 6 and 7 that the purpose of tort law is to enable a person harmed by the wrongful act of another to obtain compensation from the wrongdoer, rather than to punish the wrongdoer. In contrast, criminal sanctions are designed to punish those who commit crimes and to deter others from committing similar acts in the future. Criminal sanctions include fines as well as the much harsher penalty of the loss of one's liberty by incarceration in a jail or prison. Most criminal sanctions also involve probation and sometimes require performance of community service, completion of an educational or treatment program, or payment of restitution. The harshest criminal sanction is, of course, the death penalty.

Civil Liability for Criminal Acts

Some torts, such as assault and battery, provide a basis for a criminal prosecution as well as a civil action in tort. Suppose that Jonas is walking down the street, minding his own business, when a person attacks him. In the ensuing struggle, the attacker stabs Jonas several times, seriously injuring him. A police officer restrains and arrests the assailant. In this situation, the assailant may be subject both to criminal prosecution by the state and to a tort lawsuit brought by Jonas to obtain compensation for his injuries. Exhibit 9–2 on the following page illustrates how the same wrongful act can result in both a civil (tort) action and a criminal action against the wrongdoer.

Classification of Crimes

Depending on their degree of seriousness, crimes are classified as felonies or misdemeanors. **Felonies** are serious crimes punishable by death or by imprisonment for more than one year.[1] Many states also define different degrees of felony offenses and vary the punishment according to the degree.[2] For example, most jurisdictions punish a burglary that involves a forced entry into a home at night more harshly than a burglary that takes place during the day and involves a nonresidential building or structure.

Misdemeanors are less serious crimes, punishable by a fine or by confinement for up to a year. In most jurisdictions, **petty offenses** are considered to be a subset of misdemeanors. Petty offenses are minor violations, such as jaywalking or violations of building codes. Even for petty offenses, however, a

---

1. Some states, such as North Carolina, consider felonies to be punishable by incarceration for at least two years.
2. Although the American Law Institute issued the Model Penal Code in 1962, it is not a uniform code, and each state has developed its own set of laws governing criminal acts. Thus, types of crimes and prescribed punishments may differ from one jurisdiction to another.

EXHIBIT 9–2 • Civil (Tort) Lawsuit and Criminal Prosecution for the Same Act

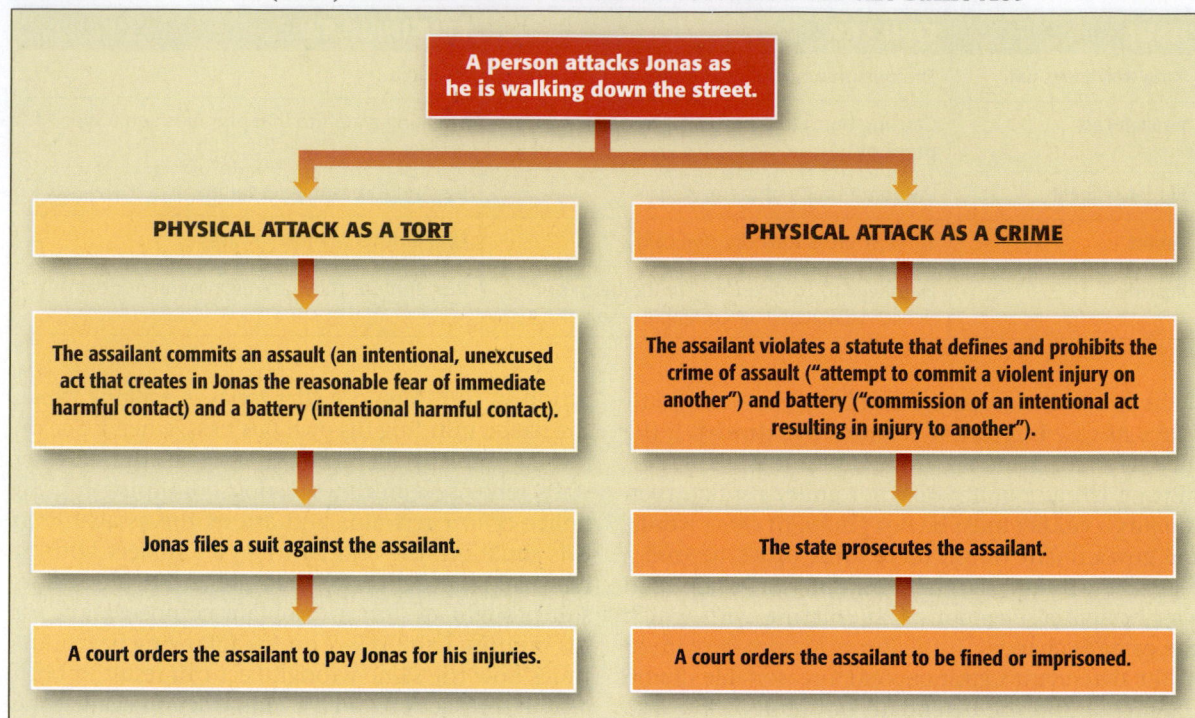

guilty party can be put in jail for a few days, fined, or both, depending on state or local law. Whether a crime is a felony or a misdemeanor can determine in which court the case is tried and, in some states, whether the defendant has a right to a jury trial.

SECTION 2
CRIMINAL LIABILITY

Two elements normally must exist for a person to be convicted of a crime: (1) the performance of a prohibited act and (2) a specified state of mind, or intent, on the part of the actor. Additionally, to establish criminal liability, there usually must be a *concurrence* between the act and the intent. In other words, these two elements must occur together.

For example, a woman intends to kill her husband by poisoning him. On the day she plans to do so, she is driving her husband home from work and swerves to avoid hitting a cat crossing the road. As a result, the car crashes into a tree, killing her husband. Even though she had planned to murder her husband, the woman is not guilty of murder in this situation because the two elements did not occur

together. The woman did not intend to kill her husband by driving the car into a tree.

The Criminal Act

Every criminal statute prohibits certain behavior. Most crimes require an act of *commission*—that is, a person must *do* something in order to be accused of a crime. In criminal law, a prohibited act is referred to as the **actus reus**,[3] or guilty act. In some instances, an act of omission can be a crime, but only when a person has a legal duty to perform the omitted act, such as filing a tax return.

The *guilty act* requirement is based on one of the premises of criminal law—that a person should be punished for harm done to society. For a crime to exist, the guilty act must cause some harm to a person or to property. Thinking about killing someone or about stealing a car may be morally wrong, but the thoughts do no harm until they are translated into action. Of course, a person can be punished for *attempting* murder or robbery, but normally only if he or she has taken substantial steps toward the criminal objective.

---

3. Pronounced *ak*-tuhs *ray*-uhs.

State of Mind

A wrongful mental state (***mens rea***)[4] is also typically required to establish criminal liability. The required mental state, or intent, is indicated in the applicable statute or law. Murder, for example, involves the guilty act of killing another human being, and the guilty mental state is the desire, or intent, to take another's life. For theft, the guilty act is the taking of another person's property, and the mental state involves both the awareness that the property belongs to another and the desire to deprive the owner of it.

CRIMINAL NEGLIGENCE OR RECKLESSNESS A court can also find that the required mental state is present when a defendant's acts are reckless or criminally negligent. A defendant is *criminally reckless* if he or she consciously disregards a substantial and unjustifiable risk. *Criminal negligence* involves the mental state in which the defendant deviates from the standard of care that a reasonable person would use under the same circumstances. The defendant is accused of taking an unjustified, substantial, and foreseeable risk that resulted in harm. Under the Model Penal Code, criminal negligence has occurred if the defendant *should have foreseen* the risk, even if she or he was not actually aware of it.[5]

A homicide is classified as *involuntary manslaughter* when it results from an act of criminal negligence and there is no intent to kill. For example, in 2010, Dr. Conrad Murray, the personal physician of pop star Michael Jackson, was charged with involuntary manslaughter after a coroner determined that Jackson's sudden death in 2009 was the result of drug intoxication. Murray had given Jackson propofol, a powerful anesthetic normally used in surgery, as a sleep aid on the night of his death, even though he knew that Jackson had already taken other sedatives.

STRICT LIABILITY AND OVERCRIMINALIZATION In recent years, an increasing number of laws and regulations have imposed criminal sanctions for strict liability crimes—that is, offenses that do not require a wrongful mental state to establish criminal liability. The federal criminal code now lists more than four thousand criminal offenses, many of which do not require a specific mental state. There are also at least ten thousand federal rules that can be enforced through criminal sanctions, and many of these rules do not require intent. Strict liability crimes are particularly common in environmental laws, laws aimed at combatting illegal drugs, and other laws affecting public health, safety, and welfare. Under federal law, for example, tenants can be evicted from public housing if one of their relatives or guests used illegal drugs—regardless of whether the tenant knew or should have known about the drug activity.[6]

Many states have also enacted laws that punish behavior as criminal without the need to show criminal intent. Under Arizona law, for instance, a hunter who shoots an elk outside the area specified by the permit has committed a crime, regardless of the hunter's intent or knowledge of the law.[7]

Although proponents of such laws argue that they are necessary to protect the public and the environment, critics say laws that criminalize conduct without any required intent have led to *overcriminalization,* or the use of criminal law as the main tool to solve social problems, such as illegal drug use. These critics argue that the removal of the requirement of intent, or malice, from criminal offenses increases the likelihood of people committing crimes unknowingly—and perhaps even innocently. When an honest mistake can lead to a criminal conviction, the idea that crimes are a wrong against society is undermined.

Corporate Criminal Liability

As will be discussed in Chapter 39, a corporation is a legal entity created under the laws of a state. At one time, it was thought that a corporation could not incur criminal liability because, although a corporation is a legal person, it can act only through its agents (corporate directors, officers, and employees). Therefore, the corporate entity itself could not "intend" to commit a crime. Over time, this view has changed. Obviously, corporations cannot be imprisoned, but they can be fined or denied certain legal privileges (such as a license).

LIABILITY OF THE CORPORATE ENTITY Today, corporations normally are liable for the crimes committed by their agents and employees within the course and scope of their employment.[8] For such criminal liability to be imposed, the prosecutor generally must show that the corporation could have

---

4. Pronounced *mehns ray*-uh.
5. Model Penal Code Section 2.02(2)(d).
6. See, for example, *Department of Housing and Urban Development v. Rucker,* 535 U.S. 125, 122 S.Ct. 1230, 152 L.Ed.2d 258 (2002).
7. *State v. Slayton and Remmert,* 1 CA-SA 06-0208 (Ariz.Ct.App. 2007).
8. See Model Penal Code Section 2.07.

prevented the act or that there was authorized consent to, or knowledge of, the act by persons in supervisory positions within the corporation. In addition, corporations can be criminally liable for failing to perform specific duties imposed by law (such as duties under environmental laws or securities laws).

LIABILITY OF THE CORPORATE OFFICERS AND DIRECTORS Corporate directors and officers are personally liable for the crimes they commit, regardless of whether the crimes were committed for their private benefit or on the corporation's behalf. Additionally, corporate directors and officers may be held liable for the actions of employees under their supervision. Under the *responsible corporate officer* doctrine, a court may impose criminal liability on a corporate officer despite whether he or she participated in, directed, or even knew about a given criminal violation.

◄ SECTION 3 ►
TYPES OF CRIMES

Numerous actions are designated as criminal. Federal, state, and local laws provide for the classification and punishment of hundreds of thousands of different criminal acts. Generally, though, criminal acts can be grouped into five broad categories: violent crime (crimes against persons), property crime, public order crime, white-collar crime, and organized crime. Cyber crime—which consists of crimes committed in cyberspace with the use of computers—is, as mentioned earlier in this chapter, less a category of crime than a new way to commit crime. We will examine cyber crime later in this chapter.

Violent Crime

Certain crimes are called *violent crimes,* or crimes against persons, because they cause others to suffer harm or death. Murder is a violent crime. So is sexual assault, or rape. Assault and battery, which were discussed in Chapter 6 in the context of tort law, are also classified as violent crimes. **Robbery**—defined as the taking of money, personal property, or any other article of value from a person by means of force or fear—is also a violent crime. Typically, states have more severe penalties for *aggravated robbery*— robbery with the use of a deadly weapon.

Each of these violent crimes is further classified by degree, depending on the circumstances surrounding the criminal act. These circumstances include the intent of the person committing the crime, whether a weapon was used, and (for crimes other than murder) the level of pain and suffering experienced by the victim.

Property Crime

The most common type of criminal activity is property crime, in which the goal of the offender is some form of economic gain or the damaging of property. Robbery is a form of property crime, as well as a violent crime, because the offender seeks to gain the property of another. We look here at a number of other crimes that fall within the general category of property crime.

BURGLARY Traditionally, **burglary** was defined as breaking and entering the dwelling of another at night with the intent to commit a felony. Originally, the definition was aimed at protecting an individual's home and its occupants. Most state statutes have eliminated some of the requirements found in the common law definition. The time of day at which the breaking and entering occurs, for example, is usually immaterial. State statutes frequently omit the element of breaking, and some states do not require that the building be a dwelling. When a deadly weapon is used in a burglary, the perpetrator can be charged with *aggravated burglary* and punished more severely.

LARCENY Under the common law, the crime of **larceny** involved the unlawful taking and carrying away of someone else's personal property with the intent to permanently deprive the owner of possession. Put simply, larceny is stealing, or theft. Whereas robbery involves force or fear, larceny does not. Therefore, picking pockets is larceny, not robbery. Similarly, taking an employer's products and supplies home for personal use without permission is larceny. (Note that a person who commits larceny generally can also be sued under tort law because the act of taking possession of another's property involves a trespass to personal property.)

Most states have expanded the definition of property that is subject to larceny statutes. Stealing computer programs may constitute larceny even though the "property" consists of magnetic impulses. The theft of natural gas or Internet and television cable service may also be considered larceny. Trade secrets can be subject to larceny statutes.

The common law distinguished between grand and petit larceny depending on the value of the property taken. Many states have abolished this distinction, but in those that have not, grand larceny (or theft of an item having a value greater than a certain amount) is a felony, and petit larceny is a misdemeanor.

ARSON The willful and malicious burning of a building (and, in some states, personal property) owned by another is the crime of **arson.** At common law, arson applied only to burning down another person's house. The law was designed to protect human life. Today, arson statutes have been extended to cover the destruction of any building, regardless of ownership, by fire or explosion. Every state has a special statute that covers the act of burning a building for the purpose of collecting insurance. (Of course, the insurer need not pay the claim when insurance fraud is proved.)

RECEIVING STOLEN GOODS It is a crime to receive stolen goods. The recipient of such goods need not know the true identity of the owner or the thief. All that is necessary is that the recipient knows or should know that the goods are stolen, which implies an intent to deprive the owner of those goods.

FORGERY The fraudulent making or altering of any writing (including electronic records) in a way that changes the legal rights and liabilities of another is **forgery.** If, without authorization, Severson signs Bennett's name to the back of a check made out to Bennett, Severson is committing forgery. Forgery also includes changing trademarks, falsifying public records, counterfeiting, and altering a legal document.

OBTAINING GOODS BY FALSE PRETENSES It is a criminal act to obtain goods by false pretenses, such as buying groceries with a check knowing that one has insufficient funds to cover it. Purchasing goods with someone else's credit-card number without authorization is another example of obtaining goods by false pretenses. Statutes dealing with such illegal activities vary widely from state to state.

Public Order Crime

Historically, societies have always outlawed activities that are considered contrary to public values and morals. Today, the most common public order crimes include public drunkenness, prostitution, gambling, and illegal drug use. These crimes are sometimes referred to as *victimless crimes* because they normally harm only the offender. From a broader perspective,

however, they are deemed detrimental to society as a whole because they may create an environment that gives rise to property and violent crimes.

White-Collar Crime

Crimes occurring in the business context are popularly referred to as white-collar crimes. Although there is no official definition of **white-collar crime,** the term is commonly used to mean an illegal act or series of acts committed by an individual or business entity using some nonviolent means to obtain a personal or business advantage. Usually, this kind of crime takes place in the course of a legitimate business occupation. Corporate crimes fall into this category. Certain property crimes, such as larceny and forgery, may also be white-collar crimes if they occur within the business context. The crimes discussed next normally occur only in the business context.

EMBEZZLEMENT When a person entrusted with another person's property or funds fraudulently appropriates that property or those funds, **embezzlement** occurs. Typically, embezzlement is carried out by an employee who steals funds. Banks are particularly prone to this problem, but embezzlement can occur in any firm. In a number of businesses, corporate officers or accountants have fraudulently converted funds for their own benefit and then "fixed" the books to cover up their crime. Embezzlement is not larceny because the wrongdoer does not *physically* take the property from the possession of another, and it is not robbery because no force or fear is used.

Embezzlement Takes Many Forms. It does not matter whether the embezzler takes the funds from the victim or from a third person. If the financial officer of a large corporation pockets a certain number of checks from third parties that were given to her to deposit into the corporate account, she is embezzling. Even an employer's failure to remit state withholding taxes collected from employees can constitute embezzlement.

CASE IN POINT Dr. Francis H. George owned and operated a medical practice in Virginia. He employed numerous individuals, including nursing assistants, nurse practitioners, and a pediatrician. George withheld funds from his employees' salaries—funds that represented state income taxes owed to Virginia—and deposited them into a bank account that he used to pay his personal and business expenses. He then failed to file withholding tax returns as required by state law and did not send the withheld funds to the state. He was convicted of embezzlement.[9]

Frequently, an embezzler takes a relatively small amount at one time but does so repeatedly over a long period. This might be done by underreporting income or deposits and embezzling the remaining amount, for example, or by creating fictitious

persons or accounts and writing checks to them from the corporate account.

Problems with Prosecution. As a practical matter, an embezzler who returns what has been taken may not be prosecuted because the owner is unwilling to take the time to make a complaint, cooperate with the state's investigative efforts, and appear in court. Also, the owner may not want the crime to become public knowledge. Nevertheless, the intent to return the embezzled property—or its actual return—is not a defense to the crime of embezzlement, as the following case illustrates.

---

9. *George v. Commonwealth of Virginia,* 51 Va.App. 137, 655 S.E.2d 43 (2008).

✳ EXTENDED CASE 9.1 ✳
People v. Sisuphan

Court of Appeal of California, First District, 181 Cal.App.4th 800, 104 Cal.Rptr.3d 654 (2010).
www.courtinfo.ca.gov/opinions[a]

IN THE LANGUAGE OF THE COURT
JENKINS, J. [Judge]
* * * *
As the Director of Finance at Toyota of Marin (the dealership), [Appellant Lou Surivan] Sisuphan managed the financing contracts for vehicle sales and worked with lenders to obtain payment for these transactions. * * * Sisuphan complained repeatedly to management about the performance and attitude of one of the finance managers, Ian McClelland (McClelland). * * * General manager Michael Christian (Christian) opted not to terminate McClelland "because he brought a lot of money into the dealership."

On July 3, 2007, McClelland accepted a large payment from customer Jill Peacock for the vehicle she purchased. Peacock gave him $22,600 in cash and two checks totaling $7,275.51. McClelland prepared a receipt, placed the cash, both checks, and a copy of the receipt in a large manila envelope, and took the envelope to the company safe in Sisuphan's office. McClelland placed the envelope into

the hopper at the top of the safe and turned the handle to rotate the hopper and drop its contents down into the safe. The envelope, which was stuffed with a large amount of cash, did not drop all the way down into the safe and became lodged, with a portion "sticking out." McClelland could not retrieve the envelope or push it completely into the safe, so he decided to cut it and transfer the contents to two envelopes. He * * * asked Sisuphan to keep an eye on the envelope while he went to the showroom. While McClelland was gone, Sisuphan "wiggled" the envelope free, extracted it from the safe, and kept it. When McClelland returned, Sisuphan told him "Hey, no problem, [the envelope] dropped into the safe."

Dealership bookkeepers regularly collected payments from the safe and cross-checked these against carbon copies of the receipts in the receipt book. On the morning of July 5, 2007, one of the bookkeepers discovered in this manner that the payment for the Peacock purchase was missing. She placed a post-it note for Sisuphan on the corresponding page of the receipt

book, inquiring, "Where's money?" She also notified the controller, the general sales manager, and Christian that a payment was missing. When she asked Sisuphan about the missing payment, "he said they were looking into it."

* * * Christian followed up with the customer, made a police report, and filed a claim with the dealership's insurer. He called all the managers together and told them he would not bring criminal charges if the money was returned within twenty-four hours.

On the evening of July 18, 2007, * * * Sisuphan [went] to Christian's office and admitted that he had taken the money. He claimed he had no intention of stealing it and had taken it to get McClelland fired. He said he had not returned the money during the twenty-four-hour amnesty period because he did not believe Christian's assurance that no punitive action would be taken.

The next day, Christian terminated Sisuphan's employment. He prepared a separation report with a narrative that set out the events relating to the missing money and

---

a. From the drop-down menu, select "1st Appellate District," and then click on "View." On the page that opens, scroll down to "P. v. Sisuphan" and click on "PDF" to access the opinion. (Note that "People" is abbreviated "P." in this list.) The California court system maintains this Web site.

EXTENDED CASE 9.1 CONTINUED

included a summary of Sisuphan's confession. Sisuphan reviewed and signed the report without making any changes and repaid the entire sum of cash he had taken. * * * However, "the checks were lost [and] not returned." The customer stopped payment on both checks and reissued them.

A week later, the district attorney filed a criminal complaint against Sisuphan, asserting a felony offense of embezzlement by an employee of property valued in excess of $400 * * * . The matter proceeded to a jury trial on April 15, 2008, and the jury returned a guilty verdict. In June 2008, the trial court sentenced Sisuphan to 120 days in custody and three years probation. Sisuphan filed a timely notice of appeal from the judgment of conviction.

* * * *

The trial court excluded evidence that Sisuphan returned the money to the dealership, concluding it was not relevant, because *return of the property is not a defense to embezzlement.* Sisuphan contends that evidence of repayment was relevant to show he lacked fraudulent intent at the time he took the money and asserts, for this reason, that the trial court's ruling violated his Fifth Amendment right to present a

defense and "all pertinent evidence of significant value to that defense." [Emphasis added.]

Fraudulent intent is an essential element of embezzlement. Although restoration of the property is not a defense, evidence of repayment may be relevant to the extent it shows that a defendant's intent at the time of the taking was not fraudulent. Such evidence is admissible "only when [a] defendant shows a relevant and probative [tending to prove] link in his subsequent actions from which it might be inferred his original intent was innocent." The question before us, therefore, is whether evidence that Sisuphan returned the money reasonably tends to prove he lacked the requisite intent at the time of the taking. [Emphasis added.]

Section 508 [of the California Penal Code], which sets out the offense of which Sisuphan was convicted, provides: "Every clerk, agent, or servant of any person who fraudulently appropriates to his own use, or secretes with a fraudulent intent to appropriate to his own use, any property of another which has come into his control or care by virtue of his employment * * * is guilty of embezzlement." Sisuphan denies he ever intended "to use the [money] to financially better himself, even temporarily" and contends the evidence he sought to

introduce showed "he returned the [money] without having appropriated it to his own use in any way." He argues that this evidence negates fraudulent intent because it supports his claim that he took the money to get McClelland fired and acted "to help his company by drawing attention to the inadequacy and incompetency of an employee." We reject these contentions.

In determining whether Sisuphan's intent was fraudulent at the time of the taking, the issue is not whether he intended to spend the money, but whether he intended to use it for a purpose other than that for which the dealership entrusted it to him. *The offense of embezzlement contemplates a principal's entrustment of property to an agent for certain purposes and the agent's breach of that trust by acting outside his authority in his use of the property.* * * * Sisuphan's undisputed purpose—to get McClelland fired—was beyond the scope of his responsibility and therefore outside the trust afforded him by the dealership. Accordingly, even if the proffered [submitted] evidence shows he took the money for this purpose, it does not tend to prove he lacked fraudulent intent, and the trial court properly excluded this evidence. [Emphasis added.]

* * * *

The judgment is affirmed.

QUESTIONS

1. Given that Sisuphan returned the cash, was it fair of the dealership's general manager to terminate Sisuphan's employment? Why or why not?
2. Why was Sisuphan convicted of embezzlement instead of larceny? What is the difference between these two crimes?

MAIL AND WIRE FRAUD One of the most potent weapons against white-collar criminals is the Mail Fraud Act of 1990.[10] Under this act, it is a federal crime to use the mails to defraud the public. Illegal use of the mails must involve (1) mailing or causing someone else to mail a writing—something written, printed, or photocopied—for the purpose of executing a scheme to defraud and (2) contemplating or organizing a scheme to defraud by false pretenses. If, for example, Johnson advertises by mail the sale of a cure for cancer that he knows to be fraudulent because it has no medical validity, he can be prosecuted for fraudulent use of the mails.

Federal law also makes it a crime (wire fraud) to use wire, radio, or television transmissions to

---

10. 18 U.S.C. Sections 1341–1342.

defraud.[11] Violators may be fined up to $1,000, imprisoned for up to twenty years, or both. If the violation affects a financial institution, the violator may be fined up to $1 million, imprisoned for up to thirty years, or both.

CASE IN POINT Gabriel Sanchez and Timothy Lyons set up six charities and formed a fund-raising company, North American Acquisitions (NAA), to solicit donations on the charities' behalf through telemarketing. NAA raised more than $6 million, of which less than $5,000 was actually spent on charitable causes. The telemarketers kept 80 percent of the donated funds as commissions, the NAA took 10 percent, and most of the rest of the funds went to Sanchez, who spent it on himself. Lyons and Sanchez were both prosecuted for mail fraud and sentenced to serve fifteen years in prison. They appealed. A federal appellate court affirmed their convictions, ruling that the government can use these antifraud laws to prohibit professional fund-raisers from obtaining funds through false pretenses or by making false statements.[12]

Although most fraudulent schemes involve cheating the victim out of tangible property (funds), it can also be a crime to deprive a person of an intangible right to another's honest services. For a discussion of how federal prosecutors are increasingly charging white-collar criminals with "honest-services fraud," and some recent cases on the topic, see this chapter's *Shifting Legal Priorities for Business* feature.

BRIBERY The crime of bribery involves offering to give something of value to a person in an attempt to influence that person, who usually is (but not always) a public official, to act in a way that serves a private interest. Three types of bribery are considered crimes: bribery of public officials, commercial bribery, and bribery of foreign officials. As an element of the crime of bribery, intent must be present and proved. The bribe itself can be anything the recipient considers to be valuable. Realize that the *crime of bribery occurs when the bribe is offered*—it is not required that the bribe be accepted. *Accepting a bribe* is a separate crime.

Commercial bribery involves corrupt dealings between private persons or businesses. Typically, people make commercial bribes to obtain proprietary information, cover up an inferior product, or secure new business. Industrial espionage sometimes involves commercial bribes. For example, a person in one firm may offer an employee in a competing firm some type of payoff in exchange for trade secrets or pricing schedules. So-called kickbacks, or payoffs for special favors or services, are a form of commercial bribery in some situations.

Bribing foreign officials to obtain favorable business contracts is a crime. This crime was discussed in Chapter 5, along with the Foreign Corrupt Practices Act of 1977, which was passed to curb the use of bribery by U.S. businesspersons in securing foreign contracts.

BANKRUPTCY FRAUD Federal bankruptcy law (see Chapter 30) allows individuals and businesses to be relieved of oppressive debt through bankruptcy proceedings. Numerous white-collar crimes may be committed during the many phases of a bankruptcy action. A creditor, for example, may file a false claim against the debtor, which is a crime. Also, a debtor may fraudulently transfer assets to favored parties before or after the petition for bankruptcy is filed. For instance, a company-owned automobile may be "sold" at a bargain price to a trusted friend or relative. Closely related to the crime of fraudulent transfer of property is the crime of fraudulent concealment of property, such as the hiding of gold coins.

INSIDER TRADING An individual who obtains "inside information" about the plans of a publicly listed corporation can often make stock-trading profits by purchasing or selling corporate securities based on this information. *Insider trading* is a violation of securities law and will be considered more fully in Chapter 42. Basically, securities law prohibits a person who possesses inside information and has a duty not to disclose it to outsiders from trading on that information. He or she may not profit from the purchase or sale of securities based on inside information until the information is made available to the public.

THEFT OF OTHER INTELLECTUAL PROPERTY As discussed in Chapter 8, trade secrets constitute a form of intellectual property that for many businesses can be extremely valuable. The Economic Espionage Act of 1996[13] makes the theft of trade secrets a federal crime. The act also makes it a federal crime to buy or possess another person's trade secrets, knowing that the trade secrets were stolen or otherwise acquired without the owner's authorization.

---

11. 18 U.S.C. Section 1343.
12. *United States v. Lyons,* 472 F.3d 1055 (9th Cir. 2007).

13. 18 U.S.C. Sections 1831–1839.

What do former Enron chief executive officer (CEO) Jeffrey Skilling, former Hollinger International CEO Conrad Black, and former Illinois governor Rod Blagojevich have in common? They, along with thousands of other individuals, have been charged under the "honest-services fraud" law. Indeed, 95 percent of the high-profile, white-collar crime cases in recent years have involved individuals who have been charged under this law.

What Is the Honest-Services Fraud Law?

The honest-services fraud law dates back to 1988 and consists of only twenty-eight words. It is known as Section 1346, which refers to the section of Title XVIII of the *United States Code* that defines the offense. The law is broad enough to encompass just about every conceivable white-collar criminal act. Consequently, it has allowed federal prosecutors to attempt to impose criminal penalties on a broad swath of misconduct by public officials and employees, as well as private employees and corporate directors and officers. The key to the law is that it requires individuals to provide the "intangible right of honest services" to their employers. Critics point out that the law is used when the purported crime committed is "fuzzy." When a businessperson is charged with honest-services fraud, there is often a nagging question as to whether the actions involved were truly a crime or just aggressive business behavior.

How Congress Got Involved

Under the U.S. Constitution, the federal government does not have the power to punish fraud directly, but it does have the power to regulate the U.S. mails and interstate commerce. In the 1970s, federal prosecutors started using the federal laws against mail and wire fraud whenever such actions deprived someone of funds or property. Then, a federal prosecutor used the legal theory that a fraudulent action to deprive the public of "honest services" is equivalent to a theft of intangible rights. In 1987, however, the United States Supreme Court rejected this concept of honest services.[a]

Not happy with the Court's ruling, federal prosecutors pleaded with Congress to pass a law. Congress subsequently created a law stating that any scheme to deprive another of honest services will be considered a scheme to defraud. Courts have at times described honest-services fraud as simply the situation in which the public does not get what it wants and deserves—that is, honest, faithful, disinterested services from employees, whether they be public or private.

Interestingly, criminal fraud requires that a victim be cheated out of tangible property, such as money. Honest-services fraud changes that concept. It involves depriving the victim of an intangible right to another's honest services.

The Law Has Been Applied Widely

Federal prosecutors have used the honest-services fraud law since 1988 in a variety of situations. In Texas, federal prosecutors successfully brought a charge against three coaches at Baylor University (a private school) for scheming to obtain scholarships for players. In California, federal prosecutors have used the honest-services legal theory to investigate the hierarchy of the Catholic Archdiocese of Los Angeles. Top church officials are being accused of covering up sexual abuse of minors by priests.

The U.S. Supreme Court Decides

In 2010, the United States Supreme Court issued a ruling that could have a major impact on white-collar crime and political fraud cases in the future. The Court ruled that the honest-services fraud law could not be used against Jeffrey Skilling, who had been convicted for his role in the collapse of Enron.[b] According to the Court, honest-services fraud can only be applied in cases that involve bribes and kickbacks. Because there was no evidence that Skilling had solicited or accepted side payments from a third party in exchange for making misrepresentations about the company, he did not commit honest-services fraud.

The Court did not overturn Skilling's conviction, however. Instead, the Court left it up to the lower court to determine whether Skilling's conviction could be upheld on other grounds. In addition, the Court remanded the honest-services fraud conviction of Conrad Black—the newspaper executive who defrauded his media company—for the same reason.[c] In fact, the Court remanded numerous other honest-services fraud cases for reconsideration in light of its decision.

MANAGERIAL IMPLICATIONS

Although the Court did not strike down the entire honest-services fraud law, the justices significantly narrowed its scope to prevent it from being unconstitutionally vague. Federal prosecutors can still prosecute businesspersons and managers who solicit or accept bribes or kickbacks for honest-services fraud, though. There are also many other federal and state laws that criminalize fraud and certain wrongful business conduct.

a. *McNally v. United States,* 483 U.S. 350, 107 S.Ct. 2875, 97 L.Ed.2d 292 (1987).

b. *Skilling v. United States,* ___ U.S. ___, 130 S.Ct. 2896, ___ L.Ed.2d ___ (2010). See Case 5.1, on pages 95 and 96 of Chapter 5.

c. See *Black v. United States,* ___ U.S. ___, 130 S.Ct. 2963, ___ L.Ed.2d ___ (2010).

Violations of the Economic Espionage Act can result in steep penalties: imprisonment for up to ten years and a fine of up to $500,000. A corporation or other organization can be fined up to $5 million. Additionally, the law provides that any property acquired as a result of the violation, such as airplanes and automobiles, and any property used in the commission of the violation, such as computer servers and other electronic devices, is subject to criminal forfeiture—meaning that the government can take the property. A theft of trade secrets conducted via the Internet, for example, could result in the forfeiture of every computer or other device used to commit or facilitate the violation as well as any assets gained.

The unauthorized copying and use of intellectual property, such as books, films, music, and software—commonly known as pirating—is also a crime under federal law. It has been estimated that 35 percent of all business software is pirated, as is nearly 90 percent of downloaded music. In the United States, digital pirates can be criminally prosecuted under the Digital Millennium Copyright Act.[14] An individual who violates the act for purposes of financial gain can be imprisoned for up to five years and fined up to $500,000 on a first offense. The punishment doubles for any subsequent offense.

Organized Crime

White-collar crime takes place within the confines of the legitimate business world. Organized crime, in contrast, operates *illegitimately* by, among other things, providing illegal goods and services. Traditionally, the preferred markets for organized crime have been gambling, prostitution, illegal narcotics, and loan sharking (lending funds at higher-than-legal interest rates), along with more recent ventures into counterfeiting and credit-card scams.

MONEY LAUNDERING The profits from organized crime and illegal activities amount to billions of dollars a year. These profits come from illegal drug transactions and, to a lesser extent, from racketeering, prostitution, and gambling. Under federal law, banks, savings and loan associations, and other financial institutions are required to report currency transactions involving more than $10,000. Consequently, those who engage in illegal activities face difficulties in depositing their cash profits from illegal transactions.

As an alternative to storing cash from illegal transactions in a safe-deposit box, wrongdoers and racketeers have invented ways to launder "dirty" money to make it "clean." This **money laundering** is done through legitimate businesses. For example, Harris, a successful drug dealer, becomes a partner with a restaurateur. Little by little, the restaurant shows increasing profits. As a partner in the restaurant, Harris is able to report the "profits" of the restaurant as legitimate income on which he pays federal and state taxes. He can then spend those funds without worrying that his lifestyle may exceed the level possible with his reported income.

RICO In 1970, in an effort to curb the entry of organized crime into the legitimate business world, Congress passed the Racketeer Influenced and Corrupt Organizations Act (RICO) as part of the Organized Crime Control Act.[15] The statute makes it a federal crime to (1) use income obtained from racketeering activity to purchase any interest in an enterprise, (2) acquire or maintain an interest in an enterprise through racketeering activity, (3) conduct or participate in the affairs of an enterprise through racketeering activity, or (4) conspire to do any of the preceding activities.

The broad language of RICO has allowed it to be applied in cases that have little or nothing to do with organized crime. In fact, today the statute is used to attack white-collar crimes more often than organized crime. In addition, RICO creates civil as well as criminal liability.

Criminal Provisions. RICO incorporates by reference twenty-six separate types of federal crimes and nine types of state felonies, including many business-related crimes, such as bribery, embezzlement, forgery, mail and wire fraud, and securities fraud.[16] To prove a "pattern of racketeering activity" for purposes of RICO, prosecutors must show that the defendant committed at least two of these offenses. Any individual who is found guilty is subject to a fine of up to $25,000 per violation, imprisonment for up to twenty years, or both. Additionally, the statute provides that those who violate RICO may be required to forfeit (give up) any assets, in the form of property or cash, that were acquired as a result of the illegal activity or that were "involved in" or an "instrumentality of" the activity.

---

14. 17 U.S.C. Sections 2301 *et seq.*

15. 18 U.S.C. Sections 1961–1968.

16. See 18 U.S.C. Section 1961(1)(A). The crimes listed in this section include murder, kidnapping, gambling, arson, robbery, bribery, extortion, money laundering, securities fraud, counterfeiting, dealing in obscene matter, dealing in controlled substances (illegal drugs), and a number of others.

Civil Liability. In the event of a RICO violation, the government can seek civil penalties, including the divestiture of a defendant's interest in a business (called forfeiture) or the dissolution of the business. Moreover, in some cases, the statute allows private individuals to sue violators and potentially recover three times their actual losses (treble damages), plus attorneys' fees, for business injuries caused by a violation of the statute. This is perhaps the most controversial aspect of RICO and one that continues to cause debate in the nation's federal courts. The prospect of receiving treble damages in civil RICO lawsuits has given plaintiffs a financial incentive to pursue businesses and employers for violations.

CASE IN POINT Mohawk Industries, Inc., one of the largest carpeting manufacturers in the United States, was sued by a group of its employees for RICO violations. The employees claimed that Mohawk conspired with recruiting agencies to hire illegal immigrants in an effort to keep labor costs low. The employees argued that this pattern of illegal hiring expanded Mohawk's hourly workforce and resulted in lower wages for the plaintiffs. Mohawk filed a motion to dismiss, arguing that its conduct had not violated RICO. In 2006, however, a federal appellate court ruled that the plaintiffs had presented sufficient evidence of racketeering activity for the case to go to trial.[17]

See *Concept Summary 9.1* for a review of the different types of crimes.

---

17. *Williams v. Mohawk Industries, Inc.,* 465 F.3d 1277 (11th Cir. 2006); *cert.* dismissed, 547 U.S. 516, 126 S.Ct. 2016, 164 L.Ed.2d 776 (2006). For another example, see *Trollinger v. Tyson Foods, Inc.,* 2007 WL 1574275 (E.D.Tenn. 2007).

CONCEPT SUMMARY 9.1
Types of Crimes

Crime Category	Definition and Examples
Violent Crime	1. *Definition*—Crime that causes others to suffer harm or death. 2. *Examples*—Murder, assault and battery, sexual assault (rape), and robbery.
Property Crime	1. *Definition*—Crime in which the goal of the offender is some form of economic gain or the damaging of property; the most common form of crime. 2. *Examples*—Burglary, larceny, arson, receiving stolen goods, forgery, and obtaining goods by false pretenses.
Public Order Crime	1. *Definition*—Crime that is contrary to public values and morals. 2. *Examples*—Public drunkenness, prostitution, gambling, and illegal drug use.
White-Collar Crime	1. *Definition*—An illegal act or series of acts committed by an individual or business entity using some nonviolent means to obtain a personal or business advantage; usually committed in the course of a legitimate occupation. 2. *Examples*—Embezzlement, mail and wire fraud, bribery, bankruptcy fraud, insider trading, and the theft of intellectual property.
Organized Crime	1. *Definition*—A form of crime conducted by groups operating illegitimately to satisfy the public's demand for illegal goods and services (such as gambling and illegal narcotics). 2. *Money laundering*—The establishment of legitimate enterprises through which "dirty" money (obtained through criminal activities, such as illegal drug trafficking) can be "laundered" (made to appear to be legitimate income). 3. *RICO*—The Racketeer Influenced and Corrupt Organizations Act (RICO) of 1970 makes it a federal crime to (a) use income obtained from racketeering activity to purchase any interest in an enterprise, (b) acquire or maintain an interest in an enterprise through racketeering activity, (c) conduct or participate in the affairs of an enterprise through racketeering activity, or (d) conspire to do any of the preceding activities. RICO provides for both civil and criminal liability.

SECTION 4
DEFENSES TO CRIMINAL LIABILITY

Persons charged with crimes may be relieved of criminal liability if they can show that their criminal actions were justified under the circumstances. In certain situations, the law may also allow a person to be excused from criminal liability because she or he lacks the required mental state. We look at several defenses to criminal liability here.

Note that procedural violations (such as obtaining evidence without a valid search warrant) may also operate as defenses. Evidence obtained in violation of a defendant's constitutional rights may not be admitted in court. If the evidence is suppressed, then there may be no basis for prosecuting the defendant.

Justifiable Use of Force

Probably the best-known defense to criminal liability is **self-defense.** Other situations, however, also justify the use of force: the defense of one's dwelling, the defense of other property, and the prevention of a crime. In all of these situations, it is important to distinguish between deadly and nondeadly force. *Deadly force* is likely to result in death or serious bodily harm. *Nondeadly force* is force that reasonably appears necessary to prevent the imminent use of criminal force.

Generally speaking, people can use the amount of nondeadly force that seems necessary to protect themselves, their dwellings, or other property, or to prevent the commission of a crime. Deadly force can be used in self-defense only when the defender *reasonably believes* that imminent death or grievous bodily harm will otherwise result and has no other means of escaping or avoiding the situation. Deadly force normally can be used to defend a dwelling only if the unlawful entry is violent and the person believes deadly force is necessary to prevent imminent death or great bodily harm. In some jurisdictions, however, deadly force can also be used if the person believes it is necessary to prevent the commission of a felony in the dwelling. Note, too, that many states are expanding the situations in which the use of deadly force can be justified.[18]

Necessity

Sometimes, criminal defendants can be relieved of liability by showing that a criminal act was necessary to prevent an even greater harm. Suppose that Jack Trevor is a convicted felon and, as such, is legally prohibited from possessing a firearm. While he and his wife are in a convenience store, a man draws a gun, points it at the cashier, and demands all the cash in the register. Afraid that the man will start shooting, Trevor grabs the gun and holds onto it until police arrive. In this situation, if Trevor is charged with possession of a firearm, he can assert the defense of **necessity.**

Insanity

A person who suffers from a mental illness may be incapable of the state of mind required to commit a crime. Thus, insanity may be a defense to a criminal charge. Note that an insanity defense does not enable a person to avoid imprisonment. It simply means that if the defendant successfully proves insanity, she or he will be placed in a mental institution.

The courts have had difficulty deciding what the test for legal insanity should be, and psychiatrists as well as lawyers are critical of the tests used. Almost all federal courts and some states use the relatively liberal substantial-capacity test set forth in the Model Penal Code:

> A person is not responsible for criminal conduct if at the time of such conduct as a result of mental disease or defect he or she lacks substantial capacity either to appreciate the wrongfulness of his [or her] conduct or to conform his [or her] conduct to the requirements of the law.

Some states use the *M'Naghten* test,[19] under which a criminal defendant is not responsible if, at the time of the offense, he or she did not know the nature and quality of the act or did not know that the act was wrong. Other states use the irresistible-impulse test. A person operating under an irresistible impulse may know an act is wrong but cannot refrain from doing it. Under any of these tests, proving insanity is extremely difficult. For this reason, the insanity defense is rarely used and usually is not successful.

Mistake

Everyone has heard the saying "Ignorance of the law is no excuse." Ordinarily, ignorance of the law or a mistaken idea about what the law requires is not a valid defense. A *mistake of fact,* however, as opposed to a *mistake of law,* can excuse criminal responsibility if it negates the mental state necessary to commit a crime. If, for example, Oliver Wheaton mistakenly

---

18. See, for example, *State v. Sandoval,* 342 Or. 506, 156 P.3d 60 (2007).

19. A rule derived from *M'Naghten's* Case, 8 Eng.Rep. 718 (1843).

walks off with Julie Tyson's briefcase because he thinks it is his, there is no theft. Theft requires knowledge that the property belongs to another. (If Wheaton's act causes Tyson to incur damages, however, she may sue him in a civil action for trespass to personal property or conversion—torts that were discussed in Chapter 6.)

Duress

Duress exists when the *wrongful threat* of one person induces another person to perform an act that he or she would not otherwise have performed. In such a situation, duress is said to negate the mental state necessary to commit a crime because the defendant was forced or compelled to commit the act. Duress can be used as a defense to most crimes except murder. Both the definition of duress and the types of crimes that it can excuse vary among the states, however. Generally, to successfully assert duress as a defense, the defendant must reasonably have believed that he or she was in immediate danger, and the jury (or judge) must conclude that the defendant's belief was reasonable.

Entrapment

Entrapment is a defense designed to prevent police officers or other government agents from enticing persons to commit crimes in order to later prosecute them for those crimes. In the typical entrapment case, an undercover agent *suggests* that a crime be committed and somehow pressures or induces an individual to commit it. The agent then arrests the individual for the crime. For entrapment to be considered a defense, both the suggestion and the inducement must take place. The defense is not intended to prevent law enforcement agents from setting a trap for an unwary criminal; rather, its purpose is to prevent them from pushing the individual into a criminal act. The crucial issue is whether the person who committed a crime was predisposed to commit the illegal act or did so only because the agent induced it.

Statute of Limitations

With some exceptions, such as the crime of murder, statutes of limitations apply to crimes just as they do to civil wrongs. In other words, the state must initiate criminal prosecution within a certain number of years. If a criminal action is brought after the statutory time period has expired, the accused person can raise the statute of limitations as a defense.

The running of the time period in a statute of limitations may be tolled—that is, suspended or stopped temporarily—if the defendant is a minor or is not in the jurisdiction. When the defendant reaches the age of majority or returns to the jurisdiction, the statute revives, meaning that its time period begins to run or to run again.

Immunity

At times, the state may wish to obtain information from a person accused of a crime. Accused persons are understandably reluctant to give information if it will be used to prosecute them, and they cannot be forced to do so. The privilege against **self-incrimination** is guaranteed by the Fifth Amendment to the U.S. Constitution, which reads, in part, "nor shall [any person] be compelled in any criminal case to be a witness against himself." In cases in which the state wishes to obtain information from a person accused of a crime, the state can grant *immunity* from prosecution or agree to prosecute for a less serious offense in exchange for the information. Once immunity is given, the person has an absolute privilege against self-incrimination and therefore can no longer refuse to testify on Fifth Amendment grounds.

Often, a grant of immunity from prosecution for a serious crime is part of the **plea bargaining** between the defending and prosecuting attorneys. The defendant may be convicted of a lesser offense, while the state uses the defendant's testimony to prosecute accomplices for serious crimes carrying heavy penalties.

SECTION 5
CRIMINAL PROCEDURES

Criminal law brings the force of the state, with all of its resources, to bear against the individual. Criminal procedures are designed to protect the constitutional rights of individuals and to prevent the arbitrary use of power on the part of the government.

The U.S. Constitution provides specific safeguards for those accused of crimes. The United States Supreme Court has ruled that most of these safeguards apply not only in federal court but also in state courts by virtue of the due process clause of the Fourteenth Amendment. These protections include the following:

1. The Fourth Amendment protection from unreasonable searches and seizures.

2. The Fourth Amendment requirement that no warrant for a search or an arrest be issued without probable cause.
3. The Fifth Amendment requirement that no one be deprived of "life, liberty, or property without due process of law."
4. The Fifth Amendment prohibition against **double jeopardy** (trying someone twice for the same criminal offense).[20]
5. The Fifth Amendment requirement that no person be required to be a witness against (incriminate) himself or herself.
6. The Sixth Amendment guarantees of a speedy trial, a trial by jury, a public trial, the right to confront witnesses, and the right to a lawyer at various stages in some proceedings.
7. The Eighth Amendment prohibitions against excessive bail and fines and against cruel and unusual punishment.

---

20. The prohibition against double jeopardy means that once a criminal defendant is found not guilty of a particular crime, the government may not indict that person again and retry him or her for the same crime. The prohibition does not preclude the crime victim from bringing a *civil* suit against that same person to recover damages, however. Additionally, a state's prosecution of a crime will not prevent a separate federal prosecution of the same crime, and vice versa.

The Exclusionary Rule

Under what is known as the **exclusionary rule,** any evidence obtained in violation of the constitutional rights spelled out in the Fourth, Fifth, and Sixth Amendments generally is not admissible at trial. All evidence derived from the illegally obtained evidence is known as the "fruit of the poisonous tree," and such evidence normally must also be excluded from the trial proceedings. For example, if a confession is obtained after an illegal arrest, the arrest is the "poisonous tree," and the confession, if "tainted" by the arrest, is the "fruit."

The purpose of the exclusionary rule is to deter police from conducting warrantless searches and engaging in other misconduct. The rule is sometimes criticized because it can lead to injustice. Many a defendant has "gotten off on a technicality" because law enforcement personnel failed to observe procedural requirements. Even though a defendant may be obviously guilty, if the evidence of that guilt was obtained improperly (without a valid search warrant, for example), it normally cannot be used against the defendant in court.

If a suspect is arrested on the basis of a police officer's mistaken belief that there is an outstanding arrest warrant for that individual, should evidence found during a search incident to the arrest be excluded from the trial? This question arose in the following case.

CASE 9.2
Herring v. United States

Supreme Court of the United States, __ U.S. __, 129 S.Ct. 695, 172 L.Ed.2d 496 (2009).
www.findlaw.com/casecode/supreme.html[a]

BACKGROUND AND FACTS • The sheriff's office in Dale County, Alabama, maintains copies of arrest warrants in a computer database. When a warrant is recalled, Sharon Morgan, the warrant clerk, enters this information in the database and discards the physical copy of the warrant. In July 2004, Sandy Pope, the warrant clerk in the sheriff's department in neighboring Coffee County, asked Morgan if there were any outstanding arrest warrants for Bennie Herring. Morgan checked her database and told Pope that there was a warrant. Coffee County officers then arrested Herring. A search revealed methamphetamine in his pocket and an illegal gun in his truck. Meanwhile, Morgan discovered that a mistake had been made: the warrant had been recalled. Herring was charged in a federal district court with illegal possession of a gun and drugs. He filed a motion to exclude the evidence on the ground that his arrest had been illegal. The court denied the motion, the U.S. Court of Appeals for the Eleventh Circuit affirmed the denial, and Herring appealed to the United States Supreme Court.

---

a. In the "Browse Supreme Court Opinions" section, click on "2009." On that page, scroll to the name of the case and click on it to access the opinion. FindLaw maintains this Web site.

CASE 9.2 CONTINUED ➡

IN THE LANGUAGE OF THE COURT
Chief Justice *ROBERTS* delivered the opinion of the Court.
* * * *

* * * We have repeatedly rejected the argument that exclusion [of evidence] is a necessary consequence of a Fourth Amendment violation. Instead we have focused on the efficacy [effectiveness] of the rule in deterring Fourth Amendment violations in the future.

In addition, the benefits of deterrence must outweigh the costs. * * * The principal cost of applying the rule is, of course, letting guilty and possibly dangerous defendants go free.
* * * *

* * * *Evidence should be suppressed only if it can be said that the law enforcement officer had knowledge, or may properly be charged with knowledge, that the search was unconstitutional under the Fourth Amendment.* [Emphasis added.]
* * * *

Indeed, the abuses that gave rise to the exclusionary rule featured *intentional* conduct that was patently unconstitutional. [Emphasis added.]

* * * An error that arises from nonrecurring and attenuated [diluted] negligence is * * * far removed from the core concerns that led us to adopt the rule in the first place.

To trigger the exclusionary rule, police conduct must be sufficiently deliberate that exclusion can meaningfully deter it, and sufficiently culpable [blameworthy] that such deterrence is worth the price paid by the justice system. As laid out in our cases, the exclusionary rule serves to deter deliberate, reckless, or grossly negligent conduct, or in some circumstances recurring or systemic negligence. The error in this case does not rise to that level.
* * * *

* * * [In a previous case, we held that] negligent police miscommunications in the course of acquiring a warrant do not provide a basis to rescind a warrant and render a search or arrest invalid. Here, the miscommunications occurred in a different context—after the warrant had been issued and recalled—but that fact should not require excluding the evidence obtained.
* * * *

We do not suggest that all recordkeeping errors by the police are immune from the exclusionary rule. In this case, however, the conduct at issue was not so objectively culpable as to require exclusion.

DECISION AND REMEDY • *The United States Supreme Court affirmed the lower court's judgment. The exclusionary rule does not apply when a police mistake leading to an unlawful search is the result of an isolated instance of negligence.*

WHAT IF THE FACTS WERE DIFFERENT? • *Suppose that the warrant for Herring's arrest had still been outstanding but had been based on false information. Should the standards applied in this case apply in those circumstances? Explain.*

THE LEGAL ENVIRONMENT DIMENSION • *What does the decision in this case mean for businesses that are subjected to searches by law enforcement personnel?*

The *Miranda* Rule

In regard to criminal procedure, one of the questions many courts faced in the 1950s and 1960s was not whether suspects had constitutional rights—that was not in doubt—but how and when those rights could be exercised. Could the right to be silent (under the Fifth Amendment's protection against self-incrimination) be exercised during pretrial interrogation proceedings or only during the trial?

Were confessions obtained from suspects admissible in court if the suspects had not been advised of their right to remain silent and other constitutional rights?

To clarify these issues, the United States Supreme Court issued a landmark decision in 1966 in *Miranda v. Arizona,* which we present here. Today, the procedural rights required by the Court in this case are familiar to almost every American.

CASE 9.3
Miranda v. Arizona
Supreme Court of the United States, 384 U.S. 436, 86 S.Ct. 1602, 16 L.Ed.2d 694 (1966).

BACKGROUND AND FACTS • On March 13, 1963, Ernesto Miranda was arrested at his home for the kidnapping and rape of an eighteen-year-old woman. Miranda was taken to a Phoenix, Arizona, police station and questioned by two officers. Two hours later, the officers emerged from the interrogation room with a written confession signed by Miranda. A paragraph at the top of the confession stated that the confession had been made voluntarily, without threats or promises of immunity, and "with full knowledge of my legal rights, understanding any statement I make may be used against me." Miranda was at no time advised that he had a right to remain silent and a right to have a lawyer present. The confession was admitted into evidence at the trial, and Miranda was convicted and sentenced to prison for twenty to thirty years. Miranda appealed the decision, claiming that he had not been informed of his constitutional rights. The Supreme Court of Arizona held that Miranda's constitutional rights had not been violated and affirmed his conviction. The *Miranda* case was subsequently reviewed by the United States Supreme Court.

IN THE LANGUAGE OF THE COURT
Mr. Chief Justice *WARREN* delivered the opinion of the Court.

The cases before us raise questions which go to the roots of our concepts of American criminal jurisprudence; the restraints society must observe consistent with the Federal Constitution in prosecuting individuals for crime.
* * * *

At the outset, if a person in custody is to be subjected to interrogation, he must first be informed in clear and unequivocal terms that he has the right to remain silent.
* * * *

The warning of the right to remain silent must be accompanied by the explanation that anything said can and will be used against the individual in court. This warning is needed in order to make him aware not only of the privilege, *but also of the consequences of forgoing it.*
* * * [Emphasis added.]

The circumstances surrounding in-custody interrogation can operate very quickly to overbear the will of one merely made aware of his privilege by his interrogators. Therefore the right to have counsel present at the interrogation is indispensable to the protection of the Fifth Amendment privilege under the system we delineate today.
* * * *

In order fully to apprise a person interrogated of the extent of his rights under this system then, it is necessary to warn him not only that he has the right to consult with an attorney, but also that if he is indigent [without funds] a lawyer will be appointed to represent him. * * * The warning of a right to counsel would be hollow if not couched in terms that would convey to the indigent—the person most often subjected to interrogation—the knowledge that he too has a right to have counsel present.

DECISION AND REMEDY • *The United States Supreme Court held that Miranda could not be convicted of the crime on the basis of his confession because his confession was inadmissible as evidence. For any statement made by a defendant to be admissible, the defendant must be informed of certain constitutional rights prior to police interrogation. If the accused waives his or her rights to remain silent and to have counsel present, the government must demonstrate that the waiver was made knowingly, voluntarily, and intelligently.*

IMPACT OF THIS CASE ON TODAY'S LAW • *Despite considerable criticism and later attempts to overrule the* Miranda *decision through legislation, the requirements stated in this case continue to provide the benchmark by which criminal procedures are judged today. Police officers routinely advise suspects of their "*Miranda *rights" on arrest. When Ernesto Miranda himself was later murdered, the suspected murderer was "read his* Miranda *rights."*

CASE 9.3 CONTINUED ▶ **THE GLOBAL DIMENSION** • *The right to remain silent has long been a legal hallmark in Great Britain as well as in the United States. In 1994, however, the British Parliament passed an act that provides that a criminal defendant's silence may be interpreted as evidence of his or her guilt. British police officers are now required, when making an arrest, to inform the suspect, "You do not have to say anything. But if you do not mention now something which you later use in your defense, the court may decide that your failure to mention it now strengthens the case against you. A record will be made of everything you say, and it may be given in evidence if you are brought to trial." Should U.S. law also change to allow a defendant's silence during questioning to be considered as an indication of guilt? Why or why not?*

Exceptions to the *Miranda* Rule

Although the Supreme Court's decision in the *Miranda* case was controversial, it has survived several attempts by Congress to overrule it.[21] Over time, however, as part of a continuing attempt to balance the rights of accused persons against the rights of society, the Supreme Court has made a number of exceptions to the *Miranda* ruling. For example, the Court has recognized a "public safety" exception, holding that certain statements—such as statements concerning the location of a weapon—are admissible even if the defendant was not given *Miranda* warnings. Additionally, a suspect must unequivocally and assertively ask to exercise her or his right to counsel in order to stop police questioning. Saying, "Maybe I should talk to a lawyer" during an interrogation after being taken into custody is not enough. Police officers are not required to decipher the suspect's intentions in such situations.

Criminal Process

As mentioned earlier in this chapter, a criminal prosecution differs significantly from a civil case in several respects. These differences reflect the desire to safeguard the rights of the individual against the state. Exhibit 9–3 on the next page summarizes the major steps in processing a criminal case. We now discuss three phases of the criminal process—arrest, indictment or information, and trial—in more detail.

ARREST Before a warrant for arrest can be issued, there must be probable cause to believe that the individual in question has committed a crime. As discussed in Chapter 4, *probable cause* can be defined as a substantial likelihood that the person has committed or is about to commit a crime. Note that probable cause involves a likelihood, not just a possibility. Arrests can be made without a warrant if

there is no time to get one, but the action of the arresting officer is still judged by the standard of probable cause.

INDICTMENT OR INFORMATION Individuals must be formally charged with having committed specific crimes before they can be brought to trial. If issued by a grand jury, such a charge is called an **indictment.**[22] A **grand jury** does not determine the guilt or innocence of an accused party; rather, its function is to hear the state's evidence and to determine whether a reasonable basis (probable cause) exists for believing that a crime has been committed and that a trial ought to be held.

Usually, grand juries are called in cases involving serious crimes, such as murder. For lesser crimes, an individual may be formally charged with a crime by an **information,** or criminal complaint. An information will be issued by a government prosecutor if the prosecutor determines that there is sufficient evidence to justify bringing the individual to trial.

TRIAL At a criminal trial, the accused person does not have to prove anything; the entire burden of proof is on the prosecutor (the state). As discussed at the beginning of this chapter, the burden of proof is higher in a criminal case than in a civil case. The prosecution must show that, based on all the evidence, the defendant's guilt is established *beyond a reasonable doubt*. If there is reasonable doubt as to whether a criminal defendant did, in fact, commit the crime with which she or he has been charged, then the verdict must be "not guilty." Note that giving a verdict of "not guilty" is not the same as stating that the defendant is innocent; it merely means that not enough evidence was properly presented to the court to prove guilt beyond a reasonable doubt.

Courts have complex rules about what types of evidence may be presented and how the evidence may be brought out in criminal cases, especially in jury trials. These rules are designed to ensure that

---

21. *Dickerson v. United States,* 530 U.S. 428, 120 S.Ct. 2326, 147 L.Ed.2d 405 (2000).

22. Pronounced in-*dyte*-ment.

EXHIBIT 9–3 • **Major Procedural Steps in a Criminal Case**

ARREST
Police officer takes suspect into custody. Most arrests are made without a warrant. After the arrest, the officer searches the suspect, who is then taken to the police station.

BOOKING
At the police station, the suspect is searched again, photographed, fingerprinted, and allowed at least one telephone call. After the booking, charges are reviewed, and if they are not dropped, a complaint is filed and a magistrate (judge) reviews the case for probable cause.

INITIAL APPEARANCE
The defendant appears before the judge, who informs the defendant of the charges and of his or her rights. If the defendant requests a lawyer and cannot afford one, a lawyer is appointed. The judge sets bail (conditions under which a suspect can obtain release pending disposition of the case).

GRAND JURY
A grand jury determines if there is probable cause to believe that the defendant committed the crime. The federal government and about half of the states require grand jury indictments for at least some felonies.

PRELIMINARY HEARING
In a court proceeding, a prosecutor presents evidence, and the judge determines if there is probable cause to hold the defendant over for trial.

INDICTMENT
An *indictment* is a written document issued by the grand jury to formally charge the defendant with a crime.

INFORMATION
An *information* is a formal criminal charge made by the prosecutor.

ARRAIGNMENT
The defendant is brought before the court, informed of the charges, and asked to enter a plea.

PLEA BARGAIN
A plea bargain is a prosecutor's promise to make concessions (or promise to seek concessions) in return for a defendant's guilty plea. Concessions may include a reduced charge or a lesser sentence.

GUILTY PLEA
In many jurisdictions, most cases that reach the arraignment stage do not go to trial but are resolved by a guilty plea, often as a result of a plea bargain. The judge sets the case for sentencing.

TRIAL
Trials can be either jury trials or bench trials. (In a bench trial, there is no jury, and the judge decides questions of fact as well as questions of law.) If the verdict is "guilty," the judge sets a date for the sentencing. Everyone convicted of a crime has the right to an appeal.

---

evidence presented at trials is relevant, reliable, and not prejudicial toward the defendant.

Federal Sentencing Guidelines

In 1984, Congress passed the Sentencing Reform Act. This act created the U.S. Sentencing Commission, which was charged with the task of standardizing sentences for *federal* crimes. The commission's guidelines, which became effective in 1987, established a range of possible penalties for each federal crime and required the judge to select a sentence from within that range. In other words, the guidelines originally established a mandatory system because judges were not allowed to deviate from the specified sentencing range. Some federal judges felt uneasy about imposing the long prison sentences required by the guidelines on certain criminal defendants, particularly first-time offenders and those convicted in illegal substances cases involving small quantities of drugs.[23]

SHIFT AWAY FROM MANDATORY SENTENCING In 2005, the United States Supreme Court held that certain provisions of the federal sentencing guidelines were unconstitutional.

CASE IN POINT Freddie Booker was arrested with 92.5 grams of crack cocaine in his possession. Booker admitted to police that he had sold an additional 566 grams of crack cocaine, but he was never charged with, or tried for, possession of this additional quantity. Nevertheless, under the federal sentencing guidelines the judge was required to sentence Booker to twenty-two years in prison. The Court ruled that this sentence was unconstitutional because a jury did not find beyond a reasonable doubt that Booker had possessed the additional 566 grams of crack.[24]

Essentially, the Court's ruling changed the federal sentencing guidelines from mandatory to advisory. Depending on the circumstances of the case, a federal trial judge may now depart from the guidelines if she or he believes that it is reasonable to do so.

INCREASED PENALTIES FOR CERTAIN CRIMINAL VIOLATIONS Sentencing guidelines still exist and provide for enhanced punishment for certain types of crimes, including white-collar crimes, violations of the Sarbanes-Oxley Act (discussed in Chapter 5), and violations of securities laws.[25]

In 2009, the Supreme Court considered the sentencing guidelines again and held that a sentencing judge cannot presume that a sentence within the applicable guidelines is reasonable.[26] Before concluding that a particular sentence is reasonable, the court must take into account the various sentencing factors that apply to an individual defendant. When the defendant is a business firm, these factors include the company's history of past violations, management's cooperation with federal investigators, and the extent to which the firm has undertaken specific programs and procedures to prevent criminal activities by its employees.

SECTION 6
CYBER CRIME

The U.S. Department of Justice broadly defines **computer crime** as any violation of criminal law that involves knowledge of computer technology for its perpetration, investigation, or prosecution. A number of the white-collar crimes discussed earlier in this chapter, such as fraud, embezzlement, and the theft of intellectual property, are now committed with the aid of computers and are thus considered computer crimes.

Many computer crimes fall under the broad label of **cyber crime,** which describes any criminal activity occurring via a computer in the virtual community of the Internet. Most cyber crimes are not "new" crimes. Rather, they are existing crimes in which the Internet is the instrument of wrongdoing. Here we look at several types of activity that constitute cyber crimes against persons or property. Other cyber crimes will be discussed in later chapters as they relate to particular topics, such as banking or consumer law.

Cyber Fraud

As pointed out in Chapter 6, fraud is any misrepresentation knowingly made with the intention of deceiving another and on which a reasonable person would and does rely to her or his detriment. **Cyber fraud,** then, is fraud committed over the Internet. Frauds that were once conducted solely by mail or phone can now be found online, and new technology has led to increasingly creative ways to commit fraud.

Sometimes, Internet fraud is just an electronic version of frauds formerly perpetrated by sending letters. For example, the "Nigerian letter fraud scam" is perhaps the longest-running Internet fraud. In this swindle, con artists send e-mails promising the recipients a percentage if they will send funds to help fictitious officials from the African country transfer millions of nonexistent dollars to Western banks. Some versions of the scam reflect current events. In these updated scams, the e-mails may ask for financial help in retrieving the fortune of a

---

23. See, for example, *United States v. Angelos,* 345 F.Supp.2d 1227 (D. Utah 2004).

24. *United States v. Booker,* 543 U.S. 220, 125 S.Ct. 738, 160 L.Ed.2d 621 (2005).

25. The sentencing guidelines were amended in 2003, as required under the Sarbanes-Oxley Act of 2002, to impose stiffer penalties for corporate securities fraud—see Chapter 42.

26. *Nelson v. United States,* ___ U.S. ___, 129 S.Ct. 890, 172 L.Ed.2d 719 (2009).

loved one or an associate who perished in the conflict in Iraq or Afghanistan or during the earthquake in Haiti.

ONLINE AUCTION FRAUD Online auction fraud, in its most basic form, is a simple process. A person puts up an expensive item for auction, on either a legitimate or a fake auction site, and then refuses to send the product after receiving payment. Or, as a variation, the wrongdoer may provide the purchaser with an item that is worth less than the one offered in the auction. The larger online auction sites, such as eBay, try to protect consumers against such schemes by providing warnings about deceptive sellers or offering various forms of insurance. The nature of the Internet, however, makes it nearly impossible to completely block fraudulent auction activity. Because users can assume multiple identities, it is very difficult to pinpoint fraudulent sellers—they will simply change their screen names with each auction.

ONLINE RETAIL FRAUD Somewhat similar to online auction fraud is online retail fraud, in which consumers pay directly (without bidding) for items that are never delivered. Because most consumers will purchase items only from reputable, well-known sites such as Amazon.com, criminals have had to take advantage of some of the complexities of cyberspace to lure unknowing customers. As with other forms of online fraud, it is difficult to determine the actual extent of online sales fraud, but anecdotal evidence suggests that it is a substantial problem.

CASE IN POINT Jeremy Jaynes grossed more than $750,000 per week selling nonexistent or worthless products such as "penny stock pickers" and "Internet history erasers." By the time he was arrested, he had amassed an estimated $24 million from his various fraudulent schemes.[27]

Cyber Theft

In cyberspace, thieves are not subject to the physical limitations of the "real" world. A thief can steal data stored in a networked computer with Internet access from anywhere on the globe. Only the speed of the connection and the thief's computer equipment limit the quantity of data that can be stolen.

IDENTITY THEFT Not surprisingly, there has been a marked increase in identity theft in recent years. **Identity theft** occurs when the wrongdoer steals a form of identification—such as a name, date of birth, or Social Security number—and uses the information to access the victim's financial resources. This crime existed to a certain extent before the widespread use of the Internet. Thieves would rifle through garbage to find credit-card or bank account numbers and then use those numbers to purchase goods or to withdraw funds from the victims' accounts.

The Internet has provided even easier access to private data. Frequent Web surfers surrender a wealth of information about themselves without knowing it. Many Web sites use "cookies" to collect data on those who visit their sites. The data may include the areas of the site the user visits and the links on which the user clicks. Furthermore, Web browsers often store information such as the consumer's name and e-mail address. Finally, every time a purchase is made online, the item is linked to the purchaser's name, allowing Web retailers to amass a database of who is buying what.

PHISHING A distinct form of identity theft known as **phishing** has added a different wrinkle to the practice. In a phishing attack, the perpetrator "fishes" for financial data and passwords from consumers by posing as a legitimate business, such as a bank or credit-card company. The "phisher" sends an e-mail asking the recipient to update or confirm vital information, often with the threat that an account or some other service will be discontinued if the information is not provided. Once the unsuspecting individual enters the information, the phisher can use it to masquerade as that person or to drain his or her bank or credit account.

VISHING When phishing involves some form of voice communication, the scam is known as **vishing.** In one variation, the consumer receives an e-mail saying that there is a problem with an account and that she or he should call a certain telephone number to resolve the problem. Sometimes, the e-mail even says that a telephone call is being requested so that the recipient will know that this is not a phishing attempt. Of course, the goal is to get the consumer to divulge passwords and account information during the call. In one scheme, e-mails seemingly from the Federal Bureau of Investigation asked recipients to call a special telephone number and provide account information. The perpetrators of vishing scams use Voice over Internet Protocol (VoIP) service, which enables telephone calls to be

---

27. *Jaynes v. Commonwealth of Virginia,* 276 Va.App. 443, 666 S.E.2d 303 (2008).

made over the Internet, because it is inexpensive and enables them to easily hide their identity.

EMPLOYMENT FRAUD Cyber criminals also look for victims at online job–posting sites. Claiming to be an employment officer in a well-known company, the criminal sends bogus e-mail messages to job seekers. The messages ask the unsuspecting job seekers to reveal enough information to allow for identity theft. As the recession dragged on into 2010 and the unemployment rate continued to rise, opportunities for employment fraud were also on the increase. For example, the job site Monster.com had to ask its 4.5 million users to change their passwords because cyber thieves had broken into its databases and stolen user identities, passwords, and other data. This theft of personal information was one of Britain's largest cyber theft cases.[28]

CREDIT-CARD CRIME ON THE WEB Credit-card theft was mentioned previously in connection with identity theft. An important point to note, however, is that stolen credit cards are much more likely to hurt merchants and credit-card issuers (such as banks) than consumers. In most situations, the legitimate holders of credit cards are not held responsible for the costs of purchases made with a stolen number (see Chapter 45). That means the financial burden must be borne either by the merchant or by the credit-card company. Most credit-card issuers require merchants to cover the costs—especially if the address to which the goods are sent does not match the billing address of the credit card.

Additionally, companies take risks by storing their online customers' credit-card numbers. In doing so, companies provide quicker service; the consumer can make a purchase by providing a code or clicking on a particular icon without entering a lengthy card number. These electronic warehouses are, however, quite tempting to cyber thieves. Several years ago, for example, an unknown person was able to gain access to computerized records at CardSystems Solutions, a company in Tucson, Arizona, that processes credit-card transactions for small Internet businesses. The breach exposed 40 million credit-card numbers.[29]

Hacking

A **hacker** is someone who uses one computer to break into another. The danger posed by hackers has increased significantly because of **botnets,** or networks of computers that have been appropriated by hackers without the knowledge of their owners. A hacker will secretly install a program on thousands, if not millions, of personal computer "robots," or "bots," that allows him or her to forward transmissions to an even larger number of systems.

MALWARE Botnets are one of the latest forms of **malware**, a term that refers to any program that is harmful to a computer or, by extension, a computer user. A **worm,** for example, is a software program that is capable of reproducing itself as it spreads from one computer to the next. In 2009, in under three weeks, the computer worm called "Conflicker" spread to more than one million personal computers around the world. It was transmitted to some computers through the use of Facebook and Twitter. This worm also infected servers and devices plugged into infected computers via USB ports, such as iPods and pen drives.

A **virus,** another form of malware, is also able to reproduce itself, but must be attached to an "infested" host file to travel from one computer network to another. For example, hackers are now capable of corrupting banner ads that use Adobe's Flash Player. When an Internet user clicks on the banner ad, a virus is installed. Worms and viruses can be programmed to perform a number of functions, such as prompting host computers to continually "crash" and reboot, or otherwise infect the system.

NEW SERVICE-BASED HACKING AVAILABLE AT LOW COST A recent trend in business computer applications is the use of "software as a service." Instead of buying software to install on a computer, the user connects to Web-based software. The user can write e-mails, edit spreadsheets, and the like using his or her Web browser. Cyber criminals have adapted this method and now offer "crimeware as a service."

A would-be thief no longer has to be a computer hacker to create a botnet or steal banking information and credit-card numbers. He or she can rent the online services of cyber criminals to do the work on such sites as NeoSploit. The thief can even target individual groups, such as U.S. physicians or British attorneys. The cost of renting a Web site to do the work is only a few cents per target computer.

---

28. John Bingham. "Monster.com Hacking Follows Tradition of Cyber Theft." *Telegraph.co.uk*. 28 January 2009: n.p. Web.
29. The Federal Trade Commission (FTC) brought charges against the company, which ultimately reached a settlement with the FTC.

CYBERTERRORISM Hackers who break into computers without authorization often commit cyber theft, but sometimes their principal aim is to prove how smart they are by gaining access to others' password-protected computers. **Cyberterrorists** are hackers who, rather than trying to gain attention, strive to remain undetected so that they can exploit computers for a serious impact. Just as "real" terrorists destroyed the World Trade Center towers and a portion of the Pentagon on September 11, 2001, cyberterrorists might explode "logic bombs" to shut down central computers. Such activities obviously can pose a danger to national security.

Cyberterrorists as well as hackers may target businesses. The goals of a hacking operation might include a wholesale theft of data, such as a merchant's customer files, or the monitoring of a computer to discover a business firm's plans and transactions. A cyberterrorist might also want to insert false codes or data. For example, the processing control system of a food manufacturer could be changed to alter the levels of ingredients so that consumers of the food would become ill.

A cyberterrorist attack on a major financial institution, such as the New York Stock Exchange or a large bank, could leave securities or money markets in flux and seriously affect the daily lives of millions of citizens. Similarly, any prolonged disruption of computer, cable, satellite, or telecommunications systems due to the actions of expert hackers would have serious repercussions on business operations—and national security—on a global level.

Prosecution of Cyber Crime

The "location" of cyber crime (cyberspace) has raised new issues in the investigation of crimes and the prosecution of offenders. A threshold issue is, of course, jurisdiction. A person who commits an act against a business in California, where the act is a cyber crime, might never have set foot in California but might instead reside in New York, or even in Canada, where the act may not be a crime. If the crime was committed via e-mail, the question arises as to whether the e-mail would constitute sufficient minimum contacts (see Chapter 2) for the victim's state to exercise jurisdiction over the perpetrator.

Identifying the wrongdoer can also be difficult. Cyber criminals do not leave physical traces, such as fingerprints or DNA samples, as evidence of their crimes. Even electronic "footprints" can be hard to find and follow. For example, e-mail may be sent through a remailer, an online service that guarantees that a message cannot be traced to its source.

For these reasons, laws written to protect physical property are often difficult to apply in cyberspace. Nonetheless, governments at both the state and the federal level have taken significant steps toward controlling cyber crime, both by applying existing criminal statutes and by enacting new laws that specifically address wrongs committed in cyberspace.

The Computer Fraud and Abuse Act

Perhaps the most significant federal statute specifically addressing cyber crime is the Counterfeit Access Device and Computer Fraud and Abuse Act of 1984 (commonly known as the Computer Fraud and Abuse Act, or CFAA).[30] Among other things, this act provides that a person who accesses a computer online, without authority, to obtain classified, restricted, or protected data (or attempts to do so) is subject to criminal prosecution. Such data could include financial and credit records, medical records, legal files, military and national security files, and other confidential information in government or private computers. The crime has two elements: accessing a computer without authority and taking the data.

This theft is a felony if it is committed for a commercial purpose or for private financial gain, or if the value of the stolen data (or computer time) exceeds $5,000. Penalties include fines and imprisonment for up to twenty years. A victim of computer theft can also bring a civil suit against the violator to obtain damages, an injunction, and other relief.

---

30. 18 U.S.C. Section 1030.

REVIEWING
Criminal Law and Cyber Crime

Edward Hanousek worked for Pacific & Arctic Railway and Navigation Company (P&A) as a roadmaster of the White Pass & Yukon Railroad in Alaska. Hanousek was responsible "for every detail of the safe and efficient maintenance and construction of track, structures and marine facilities of the entire railroad," including special projects. One project was a rock quarry, known as "6-mile," above the Skagway River. Next to the quarry, and just beneath the surface, ran a high-pressure oil pipeline owned

REVIEWING

Criminal Law and Cyber Crime, Continued

by Pacific & Arctic Pipeline, Inc., P&A's sister company. When the quarry's backhoe operator punctured the pipeline, an estimated 1,000 to 5,000 gallons of oil were discharged into the river. Hanousek was charged with negligently discharging a harmful quantity of oil into a navigable water of the United States in violation of the criminal provisions of the Clean Water Act (CWA). Using the information presented in the chapter, answer the following questions.

1. Did Hanousek have the required mental state (*mens rea*) to be convicted of a crime? Why or why not?
2. Which theory discussed in the chapter would enable a court to hold Hanousek criminally liable for violating the statute regardless of whether he participated in, directed, or even knew about the specific violation?
3. Could the backhoe operator who punctured the pipeline also be charged with a crime in this situation? Explain.
4. Suppose that at trial, Hanousek argued that he should not be convicted because he was not aware of the requirements of the CWA. Would this defense be successful? Why or why not?

DEBATE THIS: *One legal observer claimed that all Americans may be breaking the law regularly without knowing it because of* overcriminalization, *particularly by the federal government. Should Congress rescind many of the more than four thousand federal crimes now on the books?*

TERMS AND CONCEPTS

actus reus 176
arson 179
beyond a reasonable doubt 175
botnet 195
burglary 178
computer crime 193
crime 174
cyber crime 193

cyber fraud 193
cyberterrorist 196
double jeopardy 188
duress 187
embezzlement 179
entrapment 187
exclusionary rule 188
felony 175
forgery 179
grand jury 191
hacker 195

identity theft 194
indictment 191
information 191
larceny 178
malware 195
mens rea 177
misdemeanor 175
money laundering 184
necessity 186
petty offense 175
phishing 194

plea bargaining 187
robbery 178
self-defense 186
self-incrimination 187
virus 195
vishing 194
white-collar crime 179
worm 195

QUESTIONS AND CASE PROBLEMS

9–1. Types of Cyber Crimes The following situations are similar, but each represents a variation of a particular crime. Identify the crime and point out the differences in the variations.

(a) Chen, posing fraudulently as Diamond Credit Card Co., sends an e-mail to Emily, stating that the company has observed suspicious activity in her account and has frozen the account. The e-mail asks her to reregister her credit-card number and password to reopen the account.

(b) Claiming falsely to be Big Buy Retail Finance Co., Conner sends an e-mail to Dino, asking him to confirm or update his personal security information to prevent his Big Buy account from being discontinued.

(c) Felicia posts her résumé on GotWork.com, an online job–posting site, seeking a position in business and managerial finance and accounting. Hayden, who misrepresents himself as an employment officer with International Bank & Commerce Corp., sends her an e-mail asking for more personal information.

9–2. Property Crimes Which, if any, of the following crimes necessarily involves illegal activity on the part of more than one person?

(a) Bribery
(b) Forgery
(c) Embezzlement
(d) Larceny
(e) Receiving stolen property

9–3. QUESTION WITH SAMPLE ANSWER: Cyber Scam.

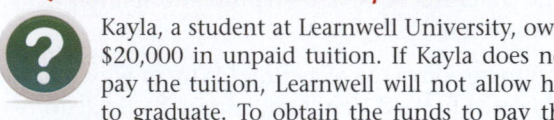

Kayla, a student at Learnwell University, owes $20,000 in unpaid tuition. If Kayla does not pay the tuition, Learnwell will not allow her to graduate. To obtain the funds to pay the debt, she sends e-mail letters to people that she does not personally know asking for financial help to send Milo, her disabled child, to a special school. In reality, Kayla has no children. Is this a crime? If so, which one?

• **For a sample answer to Question 9–3, go to Appendix I at the end of this text.**

9–4. Exclusionary Rule While Charles McFarland was incarcerated in a state prison, two officers questioned him about his connection to a handgun that had been used to shoot two other officers. McFarland was advised of his rights but was not asked whether he was willing to waive those rights. Instead, to induce McFarland to speak, the officers deceived him into believing that "[n]obody is going to give you charges." McFarland made incriminating admissions and was indicted for possessing a handgun as a convicted felon. Should McFarland's statements be suppressed—that is, not be treated as admissible evidence at trial—because he was not asked whether he was willing to waive his rights prior to making his self-incriminating statements? Why or why not? [*United States v. McFarland,* 424 F.Supp.2d 427 (N.D.N.Y. 2006)]

9–5. White-Collar Crime Helm Instruction Co. in Maumee, Ohio, makes custom electrical control systems. In September 1998, Helm hired Patrick Walsh to work as comptroller. Walsh soon developed a close relationship with Richard Wilhelm, Helm's president, who granted Walsh's request to hire Shari Price as an assistant. Wilhelm was not aware that Walsh and Price were engaged in an extramarital affair. Over the next five years, Walsh and Price spent more than $200,000 of Helm's money on themselves. Among other things, Walsh drew unauthorized checks on Helm's accounts to pay his personal credit cards and issued to Price and himself unauthorized salary increases, overtime payments, and tuition reimbursement payments, altering Helm's records to hide the payments. After an investigation, Helm officials confronted Walsh. He denied the affair with Price, claimed that his unauthorized use of Helm's funds was an "interest-free loan," and argued that it was less of a burden on the company to pay his credit cards than to give him the salary increases to which he felt he was entitled. Did Walsh commit a crime? If so, what crime did he commit? Discuss. [*State v. Walsh,* 113 Ohio App.3d 1515, 866 N.E.2d 513 (6 Dist. 2007)]

9–6. CASE PROBLEM WITH SAMPLE ANSWER: Credit Cards.

Oleksiy Sharapka ordered merchandise online using stolen credit cards. He had the items sent to outlets of Mail Boxes, Etc., and then arranged for someone to deliver the items to his house. He subsequently shipped the goods overseas, primarily to Russia. Sharapka was indicted in a federal district court. At the time of his arrest, government agents found in his possession, among other things, more than three hundred stolen credit-card numbers, including numbers issued by American Express. There was evidence that he had used more than ten of the American Express numbers to buy goods worth between $400,000 and $1 million from at least fourteen vendors. Did Sharapka commit any crimes? If so, who were his victims? Explain. [United States v. Sharapka, 526 F.3d 58 (1st Cir. 2008)]

• **To view a sample answer for Problem 9–6, go to this book's Web site at www.cengage.com/blaw/clarkson, select "Chapter 9," and click on "Case Problem with Sample Answer."**

9–7. Intellectual Property Jiri Klimecek was a member of a group that overrode copyright protection in movies, video games, and software, and made them available for download online. Klimecek bought and installed hardware and software to set up a computer server and paid half of the monthly service charges to connect the server to the Internet. He knew that users around the world could access the server to upload and download copyrighted works. He obtained access to Czech movies and music to make them available. Klimecek was indicted in a federal district court for copyright infringement. He claimed that he did not understand the full scope of the operation. Did Klimecek commit a crime? If so, was he a "minor participant" entitled to a reduced sentence? Explain. [*United States v. Klimecek,* __ F.3d __ (7th Cir. 2009)]

9–8. Fourth Amendment Three police officers, including Maria Trevizo, were on patrol in Tucson, Arizona, near a neighborhood associated with the Crips gang, when they pulled over a car with suspended registration. Each officer talked to one of the three occupants. Trevizo spoke with Lemon Johnson, who was wearing clothing consistent with Crips membership. Visible in his jacket pocket was a police scanner, and he said that he had served time in prison for burglary. Trevizo asked him to get out of the car and patted him down "for officer safety." She found a gun. Johnson was charged in an Arizona state court with illegal possession of a weapon. What standard should apply to an officer's patdown of a passenger during a traffic stop? Should a search warrant be required? Could a search proceed solely on the basis of probable cause? Would a reasonable suspicion short of probable cause be sufficient? Discuss. [*Arizona v. Johnson,* __ U.S. __, 129 S.Ct. 781, 172 L.Ed.2d 694 (2009)]

9–9. Sentencing Guidelines Paul Wilkinson worked for a company that sold fuel to various military bases. He paid an employee of a competitor to provide him with information about bids for contracts for which both companies were bidding. The information enabled Wilkinson to rig the bids and win contracts. When the scam was uncovered, he was indicted for conspiracy to defraud the government, to commit wire fraud, and to steal trade secrets. He pleaded guilty to the charges under a plea arrangement. Given the nature of the offenses, the federal sentencing guidelines provide for a prison term of fifty-one to sixty-three months with no possibility of probation. Due to Wilkinson's cooperation, the prosecution recommended fifty-one months. His attorney argued for a term of ten to sixteen months. The judge sentenced Wilkinson to three years' probation and eight hundred hours of community service, but no prison term. The government appealed, arguing that the sentence was too light in violation of the sentencing guidelines. Can a trial judge give such a light sentence under the sentencing guidelines? Explain your answer. [*United States v. Wilkinson*, 590 F.3d 259 (4th Cir. 2010)]

9–10. A QUESTION OF ETHICS: Identity Theft.

Davis Omole had good grades in high school, played on the football and chess teams, and went on to college. Twenty-year-old Omole was also one of the chief architects of a scheme through which more than one hundred individuals were defrauded. Omole worked at a cell phone store where he stole customers' personal information. He and others used the stolen identities to create one hundred different accounts on eBay, through which they held more than three hundred auctions listing for sale items that they did not own and did not intend to sell—cell phones, plasma televisions, stereos, and more. They collected $90,000 through these auctions. To avoid getting caught, they continuously closed and opened the eBay accounts, activated and deactivated cell phone and e-mail accounts, and changed mailing addresses and post office boxes. Omole, who had previously been convicted in a state court for Internet fraud, was convicted in a federal district court of identity theft and wire fraud. [United States v. Omole, 523 F.3d 691 (7th Cir. 2008)]

(a) Before Omole's trial, he sent e-mails to his victims ridiculing them and calling them stupid for having been cheated. During his trial, he displayed contempt for the court. What do these factors show about Omole's ethics?

(b) Under the federal sentencing guidelines, Omole could have been imprisoned for more than eight years, but he received a sentence of only three years, two of which were the mandatory sentence for identity theft. Was this sentence too lenient? Explain.

9–11. VIDEO QUESTION: Criminal Procedures.

Go to this text's Web site at **www.cengage.com/blaw/clarkson** and select "Chapter 9." Click on "Video Questions" and view the video titled *Twelve Angry Men*. Then answer the following questions.

(a) The jurors are deliberating on whether to convict the defendant. One juror says that at the beginning of the trial he felt that the defendant was guilty and that "nobody proved otherwise." Does a criminal defendant have to offer evidence of his or her innocence? What must the prosecution show to establish that a defendant is guilty? How does the burden of proof differ in criminal and civil cases?

(b) It is clear that all of the jurors except one (Henry Fonda) believe that the defendant is guilty. How many jurors does it usually take to render a verdict in a criminal case?

(c) When the holdout juror says that under the U.S. Constitution "the defendant does not even have to open his mouth," to which provision is he referring?

(c) Is it wrong for a group of jurors to bully or persuade another juror of the defendant's guilt or innocence? Explain.

LEGAL RESEARCH EXERCISES ON THE WEB

Go to this text's Web site at **www.cengage.com/blaw/clarkson**, select "Chapter 9," and click on "Practical Internet Exercises." There you will find the following Internet research exercises that you can perform to learn more about the topics covered in this chapter.

Practical Internet Exercise 9–1:   Legal Perspective
Revisiting *Miranda*

Practical Internet Exercise 9–2:   Management Perspective
Hackers

Practical Internet Exercise 9–3:   Global Perspective
Fighting Cyber Crime Worldwide

Ethical and legal concepts are often closely intertwined. This is because the common law, as it evolved in England and then in America, reflected society's values and customs. This connection between law and ethics is clearly evident in the area of tort law, which provides remedies for harms caused by actions that society has deemed wrongful. Criminal law is also rooted in common law concepts of right and wrong behavior, although common law concepts governing criminal acts are now expressed in, or replaced by, federal, state, and local criminal statutes. The number of torts and crimes has continued to expand as new ways to commit wrongs have been discovered.

The laws governing torts, crimes, and intellectual property—the areas of law covered in this unit—constitute an important part of the legal environment of business. In each of these areas, new legal (and ethical) challenges have emerged as a result of developments in technology. Today, we are witnessing some of the challenges posed by the use of new communications networks, particularly the Internet. In this *Focus on Ethics* feature, we look at the ethical dimensions of selected topics discussed in the preceding chapters, including some issues that are unique to the cyber age.

Privacy Rights in an Online World

Privacy rights are protected under constitutional law, tort law, and various federal and state statutes. How to protect privacy rights in the online world, though, has been a recurring problem over the past decade. One difficulty is that individuals today often are not even aware that information about their personal lives and preferences is being collected by Internet companies and other online users. Nor do they know how that information will be used. "Cookies" installed in computers may allow users' Web movements to be tracked. Google now offers a Gmail service that automatically scans and saves information about its users. Persons who purchase goods from online merchants or auctions inevitably must reveal some personal information, often including their credit-card numbers.

The Increased Value of Personal Information   One of the major concerns of consumers in recent years has been the collection and sale of their personal information—sometimes even by third parties with whom the consumers have never had dealings. This information has become increasingly valuable to online marketers, who are willing to pay a high price to those who collect and sell it. Because of consumers' concerns—and the possibility of lawsuits based on privacy laws—businesses marketing goods online need to exercise care. Today, many online businesses create and post on their Web sites a privacy policy disclosing how any information obtained from their customers will be used.

Privacy Rights in the Workplace   Another area of concern is the extent to which employees' privacy rights should be protected in the workplace. Traditionally, employees have been afforded a certain "zone of privacy" in the workplace. For example, the courts have concluded that employees have a reasonable expectation of privacy with respect to personal items contained in their desks or in their lockers. Should this zone of privacy extend to personal e-mail sent via the employer's computer system? This question and others relating to employee privacy rights in today's cyber age will be discussed in greater detail in Chapter 34, in the context of employment law.

Should Civil Liberties Be Sacrificed to Control Crime and Terrorist Activities in the Cyber Age?

In an era when criminal conspirators and terrorists use the Internet to communicate and even to recruit new members, an issue that has come to the forefront is whether it is possible to control many types of crime and terrorist activities without sacrificing some civil liberties. Governments in certain countries, such as Russia, have succeeded in controlling online criminal communications to some extent by monitoring the e-mail and other electronic transmissions of users of specific Internet service providers. In the United States, however, any government attempt to monitor Internet use to detect criminal conspiracies or terrorist activities does not sit well with the American people. The traditional attitude has been that civil liberties must be safeguarded to the greatest extent feasible.

After the terrorist attacks in September 2001, Congress enacted legislation—including the USA Patriot Act, mentioned in Chapter 4—that gave law enforcement personnel more authority to conduct electronic surveillance, such as monitoring Web sites and e-mail exchanges. For a time, it seemed that the terrorist attacks might have made Americans more willing to trade off some of their civil liberties for greater national security. Today, though, many complain that this legislation has gone too far in curbing traditional civil liberties guaranteed by the U.S. Constitution. As terrorists find more ways of using the Internet for their purposes, determining the degree to which individuals should sacrifice personal freedoms in exchange for greater protection will likely become even more difficult.

Global Companies and Censorship Issues—Google China

Doing business on a global level can sometimes involve serious ethical challenges. Consider the ethical firestorm that erupted when Google, Inc., decided to market "Google China" (Google.cn) in 2006. This version of Google's widely used search engine was tailored to the Chinese government's censorship requirements. In China, Web sites that offer pornography, criticism of the government, or information on sensitive topics, such as the Tiananmen Square massacre in 1989, are censored—that is, they cannot be accessed by Web users. Government agencies enforce the censorship and encourage citizens to inform on one another. Thousands of Web sites are shut down each year, and the sites' operators are subject to potential imprisonment.

The Chinese government insists that in restricting access to certain Web sites, it is merely following the lead of other national governments, which also impose controls on information access. As an example, it cites France, which bans access to any Web sites selling or displaying Nazi paraphernalia. The United States itself prohibits the dissemination of certain types of materials, such as child pornography, over the Internet. Furthermore, the U.S. government monitors Web sites and e-mail communications to protect against terrorist threats. How, ask Chinese officials, can other nations point their fingers at China for engaging in a common international practice?

Censorship—The Lesser of Two Evils?

Human rights groups came out strongly against Google's decision, maintaining that the company was seeking profits in a lucrative marketplace at the expense of assisting the Chinese Communist Party in suppressing free speech. Google defended its actions by pointing out that its Chinese search engine at least lets users know which sites are being censored. Google China includes the links to censored sites, but when a user tries to access a link, the program states that it is not accessible.

Google claimed that its approach was essentially the "lesser of two evils": if U.S. companies did not cooperate with the Chinese government, Chinese residents would have less user-friendly Internet access. Moreover, Google asserted that providing Internet access, even if censored, is a step toward more open access in the future because technology is, in itself, a revolutionary force.

China's Cyberattack and Google's Response

Google's attitude changed in late 2009 when it discovered that its software had been the target of a cyberattack that apparently originated in China. David Drummond, senior vice president of corporate development and Google's chief legal officer, informed the public about the attack in an article on the official Google blog on January 12, 2010. Drummond described the attack as "highly sophisticated" and said that it was not limited to Google—some twenty other large companies were similarly targeted. According to Drummond, a primary goal of the attackers apparently was to access the Gmail accounts of Chinese human rights activists. Google also discovered that the accounts of dozens of human rights advocates in the United States, China, and Europe had routinely been accessed by third parties.

Drummond said that the attacks and the surveillance that the investigation has uncovered have led Google to announce a change in its China policy: "We have decided we are no longer willing to continue censoring our results on Google.cn . . . . We recognize that this may well mean having to shut down Google.cn."[1] In March 2010, Google stopped operating Google.cn and automatically redirected users to its Hong Kong servers at Google.com.hk for search services in Chinese.

Although the Chinese government censors results on Google's Hong Kong servers, it nonetheless found Google's auto-redirect policy unacceptable and threatened to revoke Google's license. In June 2010, Google again revised its policy so that it no longer auto-redirects Chinese users to the Hong Kong servers. Instead, Google directs Chinese users to a Web page at which they must elect to use the Hong Kong servers. In addition, Google reopened Google China to host minimal searches for content that does not require censorship—such as for maps, music, and translation services.

Proponents of human rights applauded Google's efforts to avoid censorship of its search content, but others are not so sure. If Google and similar companies refuse to cooperate with governments that engage in censorship, will this transform the World Wide Web? Will the information highway of the future be forced to stop at national borders?

Do Gun Makers Have a Duty to Warn?

One of the issues facing today's courts is how tort law principles apply to harms caused by guns. Across the nation, many plaintiffs have filed negligence actions against gun manufacturers, claiming that gun makers have a duty to warn users of their products of the dangers associated with gun use. Would it be fair to impose such a requirement on gun manufacturers? Some say no, because such dangers are open and obvious. (Recall from Chapter 7 that, generally, there is no duty to warn of open and obvious dangers.) Others contend that warnings could prevent numerous gun accidents.

State courts addressing this issue generally have ruled that manufacturers have no duty to warn users of the obvious risks associated with gun use. For example, New York's highest court has held that a gun manufacturer's duty of care does not extend to those who are

---

1. David Drummond. "A New Approach to China." *The Official Google Blog.* 12 January 2010.

injured by the illegal use of handguns.[2] Some courts, however, have held that gun makers whose marketing or sales practices cause a large influx of guns into the illegal secondary market could be liable under a public nuisance theory.[3]

Pharmacies and the Duty of Care

A significant issue that has surfaced in recent years has to do with whether pharmacies should have a duty of care to third parties. In other words, should pharmacies that dispense mind-altering drugs to known drug abusers be liable to third parties who are injured as a result of the drug users' actions?

The *Sanchez* Case This question came to the fore in a case heard by the Nevada Supreme Court in 2009. The case involved a woman, Patricia Copening, who, while under the influence of the psychotropic drug hydrocodone, caused a car accident that killed Gregory Sanchez, Jr., and seriously injured another person. Copening was arrested and spent nine months in jail.

The families of Sanchez and the injured person sued Copening and, among others, several pharmacies that had filled her prescriptions. These pharmacies had all been notified earlier by the Nevada Prescription Controlled Substance Abuse Prevention Task Force that Copening had obtained approximately 4,500 hydrocodone pills at thirteen different pharmacies between May 2002 and May 2003. The families argued that this notification had created a duty of care on the part of the pharmacies and that they had breached this duty by filling Copening's prescriptions. The trial court disagreed and granted summary judgment for the defendant pharmacies. On appeal, the Nevada Supreme Court affirmed the trial court's decision—the pharmacists owed no duty to third parties.[4]

The Controversy Continues The Nevada Supreme Court's opinion did little to stem the controversy over this issue. For those who argue that such a duty should be imposed, however, Nevada's high court did hold out some hope. In a footnote to the opinion, the court noted that at the time of the accident in 2004, the task force had never advised pharmacies what, if anything, they should do with the information they received about potential drug abusers. In 2006, however, the

Nevada Board of Pharmacy amended its regulations to add detailed instructions on what pharmacists should do in similar situations. The court stated that this change in the regulations "may have created a special relationship that could justify imposing a duty in favor of third parties."

Those who argue against such a duty include, of course, pharmacists and pharmacies. According to Jesse Vivian, a professor in the Department of Pharmacy Practice at Wayne State University in Detroit, had the court held that pharmacies owe a specific duty to protect the general public from the actions of drug-abusing patients, this would have created a zone of risk that would be impossible to define. Such a decision would open the door to unimaginable claims against pharmacies.

Trademark Protection versus Free Speech Rights

Another legal issue involving questions of fairness pits the rights of trademark owners against the right to free speech. The issue is whether a company's ownership rights in a trademark used as a domain name outweigh the free speech rights of others who use a similar domain name to criticize or parody the company. A common tactic of those critical of a company's goods or services is to add the word *sucks* or *stinks* (or some other disparaging term) to the trademark owner's domain name.

A number of companies have sued the owners of such sites for trademark infringement in the hope that a court or an arbitrating panel will order the site owner to cease using the domain name. To date, though, companies have had little success pursuing this alternative. After all, one of the primary reasons trademarks are protected under U.S. law is to prevent customers from becoming confused about the origin of the goods for sale—and a "sucks" site certainly does not create such confusion.

Furthermore, U.S. courts and arbitrators give extensive protection to free speech rights, including the right to express opinions about companies and their products.[5] Even international arbitration panels, when hearing disputes between U.S. parties, give U.S. constitutional law protecting speech significant weight. Consider a case brought before an arbitrating panel of the WIPO (World Intellectual Property Organization) Arbitration and Mediation Center in 2009. In that case, a Web site was created to parody the Sutherland Institute, a Utah public-policy think tank using the

---

2. *Hamilton v. Beretta U.S.A. Corp.,* 96 N.Y.2d 222, 750 N.E.2d 1055, 727 N.Y.S.2d 7 (2001).
3. *City of New York v. Beretta U.S.A. Corp.,* 401 F.Supp.2d 244 (E.D.N.Y. 2005); *City of New York v. Beretta U.S.A. Corp.,* 315 F.Supp.2d 256 (E.D.N.Y. 2004); *Johnson v. Bryco Arms,* 304 F.Supp.2d 383 (E.D.N.Y. 2004); *City of Gary ex rel. King v. Smith & Wesson Corp.,* 801 N.E.2d 1222 (Ind. 2003); and *Ileto v. Glock, Inc.,* 349 F.3d 1191 (9th Cir. 2003).
4. *Sanchez v. Wal-Mart Stores, Inc.,* 221 P.3d 1276 (Nev. 2009).

---

5. Many businesses have concluded that although they cannot control what people say about them, they can make it more difficult for it to be said. Today, businesses commonly register such insulting domain names before the cybergripers themselves can register them.

domain name sutherlandinstitute.org. The parodying site's Web site was at sutherlandinstitute.com, and its home page closely resembled that of the Sutherland Institute. Even though the parodying site's domain name and parts of its Web site were confusingly similar to those of the Sutherland Institute, the WIPO panelists refused to transfer the domain name to the institute. The panelists stated that they "would not rule that the domain name was used in bad faith because the two organizations were from the United States and the U.S. Constitution protects the right to free speech."[6]

Trade Secrets versus Free Speech Rights

Another ongoing issue with ethical dimensions involves the point at which free speech rights come into conflict with the right of copyright holders to protect their property by using encryption technology. This issue came before the California Supreme Court in the case of *DVD Copy Control Association v. Bunner.*[7] Trade associations in the movie industry sued an Internet Web site operator who had posted the code of a computer program that cracked technology used to encrypt DVDs. This posed a significant threat to the movie industry because, by using the code-cracking software, users would be able to duplicate the copyrighted movies stored on the DVDs.

In their suit, the trade associations claimed that the Web site operator had misappropriated trade

secrets. The defendant argued that software programs designed to break encryption programs were a form of constitutionally protected speech. When the case reached the California Supreme Court, the court held that although the First Amendment applies to computer code, computer code is not a form of "pure speech," and the courts can therefore protect it to a lesser extent. The court reinstated a trial court order that enjoined (prevented) the Web site operator from continuing to post the code.

DISCUSSION QUESTIONS

1. Some observers maintain that privacy rights are quickly becoming a thing of the past. In your opinion, is it possible to protect privacy rights in today's online world?

2. Many argue that the federal government should not be allowed to monitor the Internet activities and e-mail exchanges of its citizens without obtaining a warrant. Yet others maintain that in some situations, when time is of the essence, such monitoring may be necessary to keep Americans safe from terrorists. Where should the line be drawn between justifiable and unjustifiable governmental interference with American citizens' civil liberties?

3. Do companies that do business on a global level, such as Google, have an ethical duty to foreign citizens not to suppress free speech, or is it acceptable to censor the information that they provide in other nations at the request of a foreign government?

4. In your opinion, should gun manufacturers have a duty to warn gun users of the dangers of using guns? Would such a warning be effective in preventing gun-related accidents?

5. Generally, do you believe that the law has struck a fair balance between the rights of intellectual property owners and the rights of the public?

---

6. *Sutherland Institute v. Continuative, LLC,* WIPO Arbitration and Mediation Center, Case No. D2009-0893.

7. 31 Cal.4th 864, 4 Cal.Rptr.3d 69 (2003). See also *O'Grady v. Superior Court,* 139 Cal.App.4th 1423, 44 Cal.Rptr.3d 72 (2006), in which a state appellate court distinguished the situation from the *Bunner* case and held that Apple Computer could prevent an online publisher from disclosing confidential information about a product that the company had not yet released.

UNIT THREE

CONTRACTS AND E-CONTRACTS

CONTENTS

BUSINESS LAW

★ CLARKSON · MILLER · CROSS ★

CHAPTER 10

Nature and Terminology

The noted legal scholar Roscoe Pound once said that "[t]he social order rests upon the stability and predictability of conduct, of which keeping promises is a large item."[1] Contract law deals with, among other things, the formation and keeping of promises. A **promise** is a person's manifestation of an intent to act or refrain from acting in a specified way.

Like other types of law, contract law reflects our social values, interests, and expectations at a given point in time. It shows, for example, to what extent our society allows people to make promises or commitments that are legally binding. It distinguishes between promises that create only *moral* obligations (such as a promise to take a friend to lunch) and promises that are legally binding (such as a promise to pay for merchandise purchased).

Contract law also demonstrates which excuses our society accepts for breaking certain types of promises. In addition, it indicates which promises are considered to be contrary to public policy—against the interests of society as a whole—and therefore legally invalid. When the person making a promise is a child or is mentally incompetent, for example, a question will arise as to whether the promise should be enforced. Resolving such questions is the essence of contract law.

1. Roscoe Pound. *Jurisprudence.* Vol. 3 (St. Paul, Minn.: West Publishing Co., 1959), p. 162.

SECTION 1
AN OVERVIEW OF CONTRACT LAW

Before we look at the numerous rules that courts use to determine whether a particular promise will be enforced, it is necessary to understand some fundamental concepts of contract law. In this section, we describe the sources and general function of contract law and introduce the objective theory of contracts.

Sources of Contract Law

The common law governs all contracts except when it has been modified or replaced by statutory law, such as the Uniform Commercial Code (UCC),[2] or by administrative agency regulations. Contracts relating to services, real estate, employment, and

2. See Chapters 1 and 19 for further discussions of the significance and coverage of the UCC. The UCC is presented in Appendix C at the end of this book.

insurance, for example, generally are governed by the common law of contracts.

Contracts for the sale and lease of goods, however, are governed by the UCC—to the extent that the UCC has modified general contract law. The relationship between general contract law and the law governing sales and leases of goods will be explored in detail in Chapter 19. In the discussion of general contract law that follows, we indicate in footnotes the areas in which the UCC has significantly altered common law contract principles.

The Function of Contract Law

No aspect of modern life is entirely free of contractual relationships. You acquire rights and obligations, for example, when you borrow funds, when you buy or lease a house, when you obtain insurance, and when you purchase goods or services. Contract law is designed to provide stability and predictability, as well as certainty, for both buyers and sellers in the marketplace.

Contract law deals with, among other things, the formation and enforcement of agreements between parties (in Latin, *pacta sunt servanda*—"agreements shall be kept"). Clearly, many promises are kept because the parties involved feel a moral obligation to keep them or because keeping a promise is in their mutual self-interest. The **promisor** (the person making the promise) and the **promisee** (the person to whom the promise is made) may also decide to honor their agreement for other reasons. In business agreements, the rules of contract law are often followed to avoid potential disputes.

By supplying procedures for enforcing private contractual agreements, contract law provides an essential condition for the existence of a market economy. Without a legal framework of reasonably assured expectations within which to make long-run plans, businesspersons would be able to rely only on the good faith of others. Duty and good faith are usually sufficient to obtain compliance with a promise, but when price changes or adverse economic factors make compliance costly, these elements may not be enough. Contract law is necessary to ensure compliance with a promise or to entitle the innocent party to some form of relief.

The Definition of a Contract

A **contract** is "a promise or a set of promises for the breach of which the law gives a remedy, or the performance of which the law in some way recognizes as a duty."[3] Put simply, a contract is a legally binding agreement between two or more parties who agree to perform or to refrain from performing some act now or in the future. Generally, contract disputes arise when there is a promise of future performance. If the contractual promise is not fulfilled, the party who made it is subject to the sanctions of a court (see Chapter 18). That party may be required to pay damages for failing to perform the contractual promise; in a few instances, the party may be required to perform the promised act.

The Objective Theory of Contracts

In determining whether a contract has been formed, the element of intent is of prime importance. In contract law, intent is determined by what is called the **objective theory of contracts,** not by the personal or subjective intent, or belief, of a party. The theory is that a party's intention to enter into a legally binding agreement, or contract, is judged by outward, objective facts as interpreted by a *reasonable* person, rather than by the party's own secret, subjective intentions. Objective facts include (1) what the party said when entering into the contract, (2) how the party acted or appeared (intent may be manifested by conduct as well as by oral or written words), and (3) the circumstances surrounding the transaction.

CASE IN POINT Linear Technology Corporation (LTC) makes and sells integrated circuits for use in cell phones and computers. LTC sued its competitor, Micrel, Inc., for patent infringement of a particular chip. In its defense, Micrel claimed that LTC's patent was invalid because LTC had offered to sell the chip commercially before the date on which it could be legally sold. The issue was whether LTC had entered into sales contracts when it solicited input on pricing and accepted distributors' purchase orders using a "will advise" procedure before the critical date. The court ruled that under the objective theory of contracts, no reasonable customer could interpret LTC's requests for information about pricing and potential orders as an offer that could bind LTC to a sale. Therefore, LTC did not violate the ban on sales and could continue its suit against Micrel for patent infringement.[4]

We will also look at the objective theory of contracts in Chapter 11, in the context of contract formation.

SECTION 2
ELEMENTS OF A CONTRACT

The many topics that will be discussed in the following chapters on contract law require an understanding of the basic elements of a valid contract and the way in which a contract is created. It is also necessary to understand the types of circumstances in which even legally valid contracts will not be enforced.

---

3. *Restatement (Second) of Contracts,* Section 1. As mentioned in Chapter 1, *Restatements of the Law* are scholarly books that restate the existing common law principles distilled from court opinions as a set of rules on a particular topic. Courts often refer to the *Restatements* for guidance. The *Restatement of the Law of Contracts* was compiled by the American Law Institute in 1932. The *Restatement,* which is now in its second edition (a third edition is being drafted), will be referred to throughout the following chapters on contract law.

4. *Linear Technology Corp. v. Micrel, Inc.,* 275 F.3d 1040 (Fed.Cir. 2001).

Requirements of a Valid Contract

The following list briefly describes the four requirements that must be met before a valid contract exists. If any of these elements is lacking, no contract will have been formed. (Each requirement will be explained more fully in subsequent chapters.)

1. *Agreement.* An agreement to form a contract includes an *offer* and an *acceptance.* One party must offer to enter into a legal agreement, and another party must accept the terms of the offer.
2. *Consideration.* Any promises made by the parties to the contract must be supported by legally sufficient and bargained-for *consideration* (something of value received or promised, such as money, to convince a person to make a deal).
3. *Contractual capacity.* Both parties entering into the contract must have the contractual *capacity* to do so; the law must recognize them as possessing characteristics that qualify them as competent parties.
4. *Legality.* The contract's purpose must be to accomplish some goal that is legal and not against public policy.

Defenses to the Enforceability of a Contract

Even if all of the requirements listed above are satisfied, a contract may be unenforceable if the following requirements are not met. These requirements typically are raised as *defenses* to the enforceability of an otherwise valid contract.

1. *Voluntary consent.* The consent of both parties must be voluntary. For example, if a contract was formed as a result of fraud, undue influence, mistake, or duress, the contract may not be enforceable (see Chapter 14).

2. *Form.* The contract must be in whatever form the law requires; for example, some contracts must be in writing to be enforceable (see Chapter 15).

SECTION 3
TYPES OF CONTRACTS

There are many types of contracts. In this section, you will learn that contracts can be categorized based on legal distinctions as to formation, performance, and enforceability.

Contract Formation

Contracts can be classified according to how and when they are formed. Exhibit 10–1 shows three such classifications, and the following subsections explain them in greater detail.

BILATERAL VERSUS UNILATERAL CONTRACTS Every contract involves at least two parties. The **offeror** is the party making the offer. The **offeree** is the party to whom the offer is made. Whether the contract is classified as *bilateral* or *unilateral* depends on what the offeree must do to accept the offer and bind the offeror to a contract.

Bilateral Contracts. If the offeree can accept simply by promising to perform, the contract is a **bilateral contract.** Hence, a bilateral contract is a "promise for a promise." No performance, such as payment of funds or delivery of goods, need take place for a bilateral contract to be formed. The contract comes into existence at the moment the promises are exchanged.

For example, Javier offers to buy Ann's digital camcorder for $200. Javier tells Ann that he will give

EXHIBIT 10–1 • Classifications Based on Contract Formation

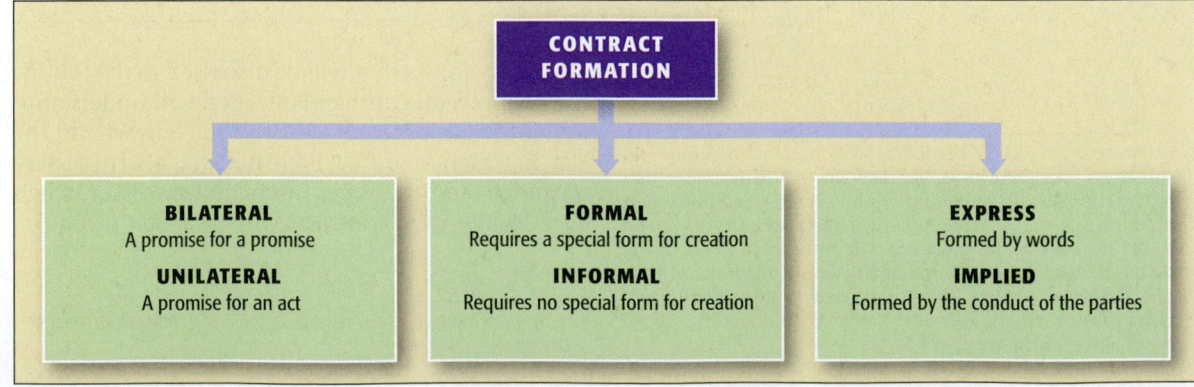

CONTRACT FORMATION		
BILATERAL A promise for a promise	**FORMAL** Requires a special form for creation	**EXPRESS** Formed by words
UNILATERAL A promise for an act	**INFORMAL** Requires no special form for creation	**IMPLIED** Formed by the conduct of the parties

her the $200 for the camcorder next Friday, when he gets paid. Ann accepts Javier's offer and promises to give him the camcorder when he pays her on Friday. Javier and Ann have formed a bilateral contract.

Unilateral Contracts. If the offer is phrased so that the offeree can accept the offer only by completing the contract performance, the contract is a **unilateral contract.** Hence, a unilateral contract is a "promise for an act."[5] In other words, the time of contract formation in a unilateral contract is not the moment when promises are exchanged but the moment when the contract is *performed*. For example, Reese says to Celia, "If you drive my car from New York to Los Angeles, I'll give you $1,000." Only on Celia's completion of the act—bringing the car to Los Angeles—does she fully accept Reese's offer to pay $1,000. If she chooses not to accept the offer to drive the car to Los Angeles, there are no legal consequences.

CASE IN POINT Applicants for vacancies in the police department in Providence, Rhode Island, first

completed a series of tests. The city then sent the most qualified applicants a letter that said it was "a conditional offer of employment" and informed the applicants that they could attend the police training academy if they passed a medical exam. Meanwhile, a new chief of police revised the selection process and rejected some of those who had received this letter. The rejected applicants sued, claiming that the city had breached its contract. The court held that the letter was a unilateral offer that the plaintiffs had accepted by passing the required medical exam. As a remedy for the breach, the court ordered the city to allow the plaintiffs to attend the police academy.[6]

Contests, lotteries, and other competitions involving prizes are examples of offers to form unilateral contracts. If a person complies with the rules of the contest—such as by submitting the right lottery number at the right place and time—a unilateral contract is formed, binding the organization offering the prize to a contract to perform as promised in the offer. If the person fails to comply with the contest rules, however, no binding contract is formed. See this chapter's *Insight into Ethics* feature for a discussion of whether a company can change the advertised prize after the contestants have completed the contest.

---

5. Clearly, a contract cannot be one sided, because by definition an agreement implies the existence of two or more parties. Therefore, the phrase *unilateral contract*, if read literally, is a contradiction in terms. As traditionally used in contract law, however, the phrase refers to the kind of contract that results when only one promise is being made (the promise made by the offeror in return for the offeree's performance).

6. *Ardito v. City of Providence,* 263 F.Supp.2d 358 (D.R.I. 2003).

INSIGHT INTO ETHICS
Is It Right for a Company to Change the Prize Offered in a Contest?

Courts have historically treated contests as unilateral contracts. Unilateral contracts typically cannot be modified by the offeror after the offeree has begun to perform. But this principle may not apply to contest terms if the company sponsoring the contest reserves the right to cancel the contest or change its terms at any time, as Donna Englert learned to her dismay.

Englert entered the "Quarter Million Dollar Challenge" contest sponsored by Nutritional Sciences, LLC. Contestants were to use Nutritional Sciences' products and training plans for thirteen weeks to lose weight and get fit. A panel of judges would then pick winners in certain categories based on their success in transforming their bodies. When Englert was chosen as female runner-up in her age group, she thought that she would receive the advertised prize of $1,500 cash and $500 worth of Nutritional Sciences' products. Instead, the company sent her a "challenge winner agreement" for $250 cash and $250 worth of products. Englert refused to sign the agreement and filed a lawsuit alleging breach of contract. The state trial court dismissed her claim, and she appealed.

The state appellate court observed that the contestant's compliance with the rules of a contest is necessary to form a binding unilateral contract. Here, the contest rules stipulated that "all winners must agree to the regulations outlined specifically for winners before claiming championship or money." Next to this statement was an asterisk corresponding to a note reserving the right of Nutritional Sciences to cancel the contest or alter its terms at any time. Because of this provision, the court ruled that Nutritional Sciences did not breach the contract when it changed the cash prize from $1,500 to $250.[a]

CRITICAL THINKING
INSIGHT INTO THE SOCIAL ENVIRONMENT
Why would a company that changes its advertised prizes have to worry about its reputation?

---

a. *Englert v. Nutritional Sciences, LLC,* 2008 WL 4416597 (Ohio App. 2008).

Revocation of Offers for Unilateral Contracts.
A problem arises in unilateral contracts when the promisor attempts to *revoke* (cancel) the offer after the promisee has begun performance but before the act has been completed. The promisee can accept the offer only on full performance, and under traditional contract principles, an offer may be revoked at any time before the offer is accepted. The present-day view, however, is that an offer to form a unilateral contract becomes irrevocable—cannot be revoked—once performance has begun. Thus, even though the offer has not yet been accepted, the offeror is prohibited from revoking it for a reasonable time period.

For instance, recall the earlier example in which a car is to be driven from New York to Los Angeles. Now suppose that Celia is driving through Nevada and is only a few hundred miles from Los Angeles when Reese calls her on her cell phone and says, "I revoke my offer." Under traditional contract law, Reese's revocation would terminate the offer. Under the modern view of unilateral contracts, however, Reese will not be able to revoke his offer because Celia has undertaken performance and has driven more than 2,500 miles. In these circumstances, Celia can finish driving to Los Angeles and bind Reese to the contract.

FORMAL VERSUS INFORMAL CONTRACTS Another classification system divides contracts into formal contracts and informal contracts. **Formal contracts** are contracts that require a special form or method of creation (formation) to be enforceable.[7] One example is *negotiable instruments*, which include checks, drafts, promissory notes, and certificates of deposit (as will be discussed in Chapter 24). Negotiable instruments are formal contracts because, under the Uniform Commercial Code (UCC), a special form and language are required to create them. *Letters of credit,* which are frequently used in international sales contracts (see Chapter 23), are another type of formal contract. Letters of credit are agreements to pay contingent on the purchaser's receipt of invoices and *bills of lading* (documents evidencing receipt of, and title to, goods shipped).

Informal contracts (also called *simple contracts*) include all other contracts. No special form is required (except for certain types of contracts that must be in writing), as the contracts are usually based on their substance rather than their form.

Typically, businesspersons put their contracts in writing to ensure that there is some proof of a contract's existence should disputes arise.

EXPRESS VERSUS IMPLIED CONTRACTS Contracts may also be categorized as *express* or *implied*. We look here at the differences between these two types of contracts.

Express Contracts. In an **express contract,** the terms of the agreement are fully and explicitly stated in words, oral or written. A signed lease for an apartment or a house is an express written contract. If one classmate calls another on the phone and agrees to buy his textbooks from last semester for $300, an express oral contract has been made.

Implied Contracts. A contract that is implied from the conduct of the parties is called an **implied contract** or an *implied-in-fact contract.* This type of contract differs from an express contract in that the *conduct* of the parties, rather than their words, creates and defines the terms of the contract. (Note that a contract may be a mixture of an express contract and an implied contract. In other words, a contract may contain some express terms, while others are implied.)

CASE IN POINT Lamar Hopkins hired Uhrhahn Construction & Design, Inc., for several projects in building his home. For each project, the parties signed a written contract that was based on a cost estimate and specifications and that required changes to the agreement to be in writing. While the work was in progress, however, Hopkins repeatedly asked Uhrhahn to deviate from the contract specifications, which Uhrhahn did. None of these requests was made in writing. One day, Hopkins asked Uhrhahn to use Durisol blocks instead of the cinder blocks specified in the original contract, indicating that the cost would be the same. Uhrhahn used the Durisol blocks but demanded extra payment when it became clear that the Durisol blocks were more complicated to use. Although Hopkins had paid for the other deviations from the contract that he had orally requested, he refused to pay Uhrhahn for the substitution of the Durisol blocks. Uhrhahn sued for breach of contract. The court found that Hopkins, through his conduct, had waived the provision requiring written contract modification and created an implied contract to pay the extra cost of installing the Durisol blocks.[8]

---

7. See *Restatement (Second) of Contracts,* Section 6, which explains that formal contracts include (1) contracts under seal, (2) recognizances, (3) negotiable instruments, and (4) letters of credit.

8. *Uhrhahn Construction & Design, Inc. v. Hopkins,* 179 P.3d 808 (Utah App. 2008).

Requirements for Implied Contracts. For an implied contract to arise, certain requirements must be met. Normally, if the following conditions exist, a court will hold that an implied contract was formed:

1. The plaintiff furnished some service or property.
2. The plaintiff expected to be paid for that service or property, and the defendant knew or should have known that payment was expected.
3. The defendant had a chance to reject the services or property and did not.

Suppose that you need an accountant to complete your tax return this year. You've noticed that there is an accountant's office in your neighborhood. You drop by the firm's office, explain your problem to an accountant, and learn what fees will be charged. The next day, you return and give the receptionist all of the necessary information and documents, such as W-2 forms. Then you walk out the door without saying anything expressly to the accountant. In this situation, you have entered into an implied contract to pay the accountant the usual and reasonable fees for her services. The contract is implied by your conduct and by hers. She expects to be paid for completing your tax return, and by bringing in the records she will need to do the work, you have implied an intent to pay her.

Contract Performance

Contracts are also classified according to the degree to which they have been performed. A contract that has been fully performed on both sides is called an **executed contract.** A contract that has not been fully performed by the parties is called an **executory contract.** If one party has fully performed but the other has not, the contract is said to be executed on the one side and executory on the other, but the contract is still classified as executory.

For example, Jackson, Inc., agreed to buy ten tons of coal from the Northern Coal Company. Northern delivered the coal to Jackson's steel mill, where it is being burned. At this point, the contract is executed on the part of Northern and executory on Jackson's part. After Jackson pays Northern, the contract will be executed on both sides.

Contract Enforceability

A **valid contract** has the elements necessary to entitle at least one of the parties to enforce it in court. Those elements, as mentioned earlier, consist of (1) an agreement, including an offer and an acceptance of that offer; (2) support by legally sufficient consideration; (3) parties who have the legal capacity to enter into the contract; and (4) a legal purpose. As you can see in Exhibit 10–2, valid contracts may be enforceable, voidable, or unenforceable. Additionally, a contract may be referred to as a *void contract.* We look next at the meaning of the terms *voidable, unenforceable,* and *void* in relation to contract enforceability.

VOIDABLE CONTRACTS A **voidable contract** is a valid contract but one that can be avoided at the option of one or both of the parties. The party having the option can elect either to avoid any duty to

EXHIBIT 10–2 • Enforceable, Voidable, Unenforceable, and Void Contracts

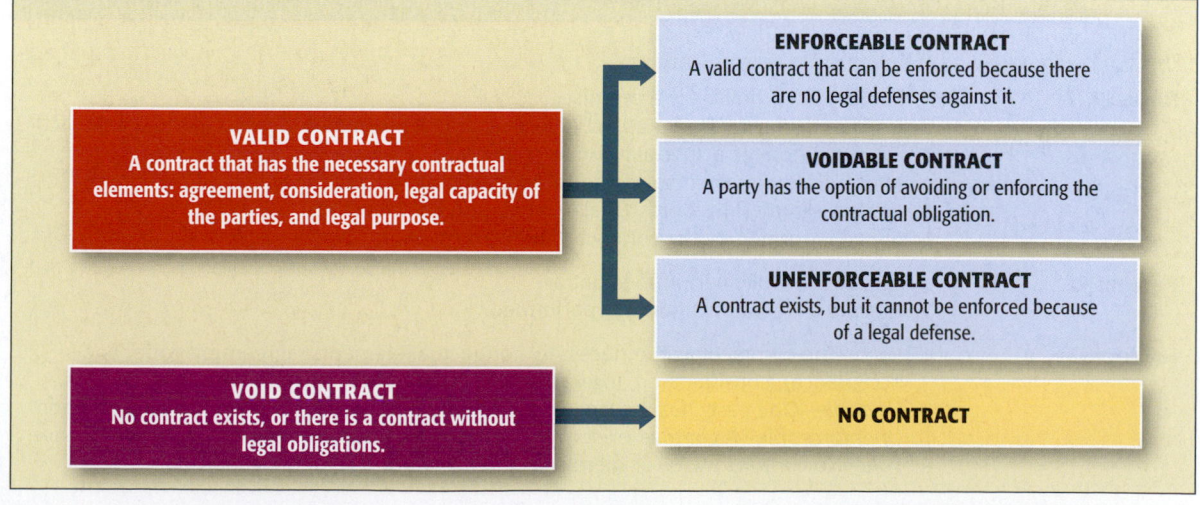

perform or to *ratify* (make valid) the contract. If the contract is avoided, both parties are released from it. If it is ratified, both parties must fully perform their respective legal obligations.

As you will read in Chapter 13, contracts made by minors, mentally incompetent persons, and intoxicated persons may be voidable. For example, contracts made by minors generally are voidable at the option of the minor (with certain exceptions). Additionally, contracts entered into under fraudulent conditions are voidable at the option of the defrauded party. Contracts entered into under legally defined duress or undue influence are also voidable (see Chapter 14).

UNENFORCEABLE CONTRACTS An **unenforceable contract** is one that cannot be enforced because of certain legal defenses against it. It is not unenforceable because a party failed to satisfy a legal requirement of the contract; rather, it is a valid contract rendered unenforceable by some statute or law. For example, certain contracts must be in writing (see Chapter 15), and if they are not, they will not be enforceable except in certain exceptional circumstances.

VOID CONTRACTS A **void contract** is no contract at all. The terms *void* and *contract* are contradictory. A void contract produces no legal obligations on any of the parties. For example, a contract can be void because one of the parties was adjudged by a court to be legally insane (and thus lacked the legal capacity to enter into a contract—see Chapter 13) or because the purpose of the contract was illegal.

To review the various types of contracts, see *Concept Summary 10.1.*

SECTION 4
QUASI CONTRACTS

Express contracts and implied contracts are actual or true contracts formed by the words or actions of the parties. **Quasi contracts,** or contracts *implied in law,* are not actual contracts. The word *quasi* is Latin for "as if" or "analogous to." Quasi contracts are not true contracts because they do not arise from any agreement, express or implied, between the parties themselves. Rather, quasi contracts are fictional contracts that courts can impose on the parties "as if" the parties had entered into an actual contract. They are equitable rather than legal contracts.

Usually, quasi contracts are imposed to avoid the *unjust enrichment* of one party at the expense of another. The doctrine of unjust enrichment is based on the theory that individuals should not be allowed to profit or enrich themselves inequitably at the expense of others. When the court imposes a quasi contract, a plaintiff may recover in **quantum meruit,**[9] a Latin phrase meaning "as much as he or

---

9. Pronounced *kwahn*-tuhm *mehr*-oo-wit.

CONCEPT SUMMARY 10.1
Types of Contracts

Aspect	Definition
Formation	1. *Bilateral*—A promise for a promise. 2. *Unilateral*—A promise for an act (acceptance is the completed performance of the act). 3. *Formal*—Requires a special form for creation. 4. *Informal*—Requires no special form for creation. 5. *Express*—Formed by words (oral, written, or a combination). 6. *Implied*—Formed by the conduct of the parties.
Performance	1. *Executed*—A fully performed contract. 2. *Executory*—A contract not fully performed.
Enforceability	1. *Valid*—The contract has the necessary contractual elements: agreement (offer and acceptance), consideration, legal capacity of the parties, and legal purpose. 2. *Voidable*—One party has the option of avoiding or enforcing the contractual obligation. 3. *Unenforceable*—A contract exists, but it cannot be enforced because of a legal defense. 4. *Void*—No contract exists, or there is a contract without legal obligations.

she deserves." *Quantum meruit* essentially describes the extent of compensation owed under a contract implied in law.

For example, a vacationing physician is driving down the highway and finds Potter lying unconscious on the side of the road. The physician renders medical aid that saves Potter's life. Although the injured, unconscious Potter did not solicit the medical aid and was not aware that the aid had been rendered, Potter received a valuable benefit, and the requirements for a quasi contract were fulfilled. In such a situation, the law will impose a quasi contract, and Potter normally will have to pay the physician for the reasonable value of the medical services rendered.

The following case illustrates an application of the principle of *quantum meruit.*

CASE 10.1
Scheerer v. Fisher

Court of Appeals of North Carolina, 688 S.E.2d 472 (2010).
www.nccourts.org[a]

BACKGROUND AND FACTS • In January 2007, David Scheerer, a licensed real estate agent, told Jack Fisher, the manager of Renaissance Ventures, LLC, that two parcels of property were for sale. Fisher asked Scheerer to investigate the costs of developing the properties, which Scheerer did. After Scheerer had negotiated the terms of sale with the owners of the properties, Fisher executed purchase contracts for the properties for a combined price of $20 million. The contracts stated that the sellers of the properties would pay Scheerer a 2 percent commission. Fisher, who had previously dealt with Scheerer, orally promised to pay Scheerer a 2 percent commission for his role as Fisher's buying agent. In April 2007, through no fault of Scheerer or the sellers, Fisher and Renaissance rescinded (canceled) the offers to buy the properties. Shortly thereafter, Fisher arranged for Anthony Antonio to purchase the properties for substantially less than $20 million and then assign the new purchase contracts to Fisher. (To *assign* is to transfer rights to another—see Chapter 16.) Scheerer and the property sellers had no knowledge of the relationship between Fisher and Antonio. Indeed, during this time, Fisher continued to discuss with Scheerer the amount Fisher would subsequently offer the original sellers for the purchase of the properties and the timing of this subsequent offer. After Antonio bought the properties, he assigned the contracts to Fisher, at which point, Scheerer learned of the relationship. Scheerer, who received no commission from the buyers, only from the sellers, sued Fisher for breach of implied contract and to recover in *quantum meruit* for his services. The trial court dismissed the complaint for failure to state a claim, and Scheerer appealed.

IN THE LANGUAGE OF THE COURT
CALABRIA, Judge.
* * * *

Plaintiffs [Scheerer and his real estate company] argue that the trial court erred in dismissing their claim of *quantum meruit* for failure to state a claim upon which relief can be granted. We agree.
* * * *

"Recovery in *quantum meruit* will not be denied where a contract may be implied from the proven facts but the express contract alleged is not proved." The rationale for allowing a plaintiff to plead both breach of express contract and breach of implied contract is that if the plaintiff "fail[s] to prove the existence of an express contract, [he or] she is not foreclosed from recovery in *quantum meruit* if a contract can be implied and the reasonable value of [his or] her services can be drawn from the evidence."

---

a. In the right-hand column, click on "Court Opinions." When that page opens, click on "2010" under "Court of Appeals Opinions." When the list of 2010 opinions appears, scroll down to "Jan 19, 2010" and click on the case title to access the opinion. The North Carolina courts maintain this Web site.

CASE CONTINUES ➡

CASE 10.1 CONTINUED ➡

To recover in quantum meruit, *plaintiff[s] must show: (1) services were rendered to defendants; (2) the services were knowingly and voluntarily accepted; and (3) the services were not given gratuitously. In short, if plaintiff[s] alleged and proved acceptance of services and the value of those services, [they were] entitled to go to the jury on* quantum meruit. *[Emphasis added.]*

* * * *

The allegations stated by plaintiffs * * *, taken as true, show: (1) plaintiffs provided services to defendants; (2) defendants knowingly and voluntarily accepted the services; (3) plaintiffs did not perform these services gratuitously; (4) defendants were ready, willing and able buyers and in fact closed on the properties after rescinding the first contract and arranging for Antonio to purchase and assign the properties. More importantly, after rescinding the contract but prior to closing, defendant Fisher continued to mislead plaintiffs by continuing discussions for submitting subsequent offers to purchase the properties. The undisputed facts establish conduct demonstrating that defendants took action to deny Scheerer compensation that was earned for the services he rendered. Although the original contract he negotiated failed to close, the law implies a promise to pay some reasonable compensation for services rendered. Plaintiffs' allegations state a valid claim for relief in *quantum meruit*.

DECISION AND REMEDY • *The North Carolina appellate court reversed the trial court's decision and reinstated the case. The plaintiffs had stated a valid claim for recovery in* quantum meruit.

WHAT IF THE FACTS WERE DIFFERENT? • *Suppose that Fisher had not ultimately obtained the properties (through Antonio and the assignment) and had shown no further interest in the properties after he had rescinded the first contract. Would Scheerer still have had a valid claim against Fisher for recovery in* quantum meruit? *Why or why not?*

THE ETHICAL DIMENSION • *Was Fisher's unethical behavior (in misleading Scheerer into believing that he was still interested in making a subsequent offer on the properties) a factor in the court's decision? Explain.*

Limitations on Quasi-contractual Recovery

Although quasi contracts exist to prevent unjust enrichment, the party obtaining the enrichment is not held liable in some situations. Basically, a party who has conferred a benefit on someone else unnecessarily or as a result of misconduct or negligence cannot invoke the principle of quasi contract. The enrichment in those situations will not be considered "unjust."

CASE IN POINT Qwest Wireless, LLC, provides wireless phone services in Arizona and thirteen other states. Qwest marketed and sold handset insurance to its customers, although it did not have a license to sell insurance in Arizona or in any other state. Patrick and Vicki Van Zanen sued Qwest for unjust enrichment based on its receipt of sales commissions for the handset insurance. The court agreed that Qwest had violated the insurance-licensing statute, but found that the commissions did not constitute unjust enrichment because the customers had, in fact, received the insurance. Qwest had not retained a benefit (the commissions) without paying for it

(providing insurance); thus, the Van Zanens and other customers did not suffer unfair detriment.[10]

When an Actual Contract Exists

The doctrine of quasi contract generally cannot be used when there is an *actual contract* that covers the matter in controversy. A remedy already exists if a party is unjustly enriched as a result of a breach of contract: the nonbreaching party can sue the breaching party for breach of contract. For example, Fung contracts with Cameron to deliver a furnace to a building owned by Grant. Fung delivers the furnace, but Cameron never pays Fung. Grant has been unjustly enriched in this situation, to be sure. Fung, however, cannot recover from Grant in quasi contract because Fung had an actual contract with Cameron. Fung already has a remedy—he can sue for breach of contract to recover the price of the furnace from Cameron. The court does not need to impose a quasi contract in this situation to achieve justice.

---

10. *Van Zanen v. Qwest Wireless, LLC*, 522 F.3d 1127 (10th Cir. 2008).

EXHIBIT 10–3 • **Rules of Contract Interpretation**

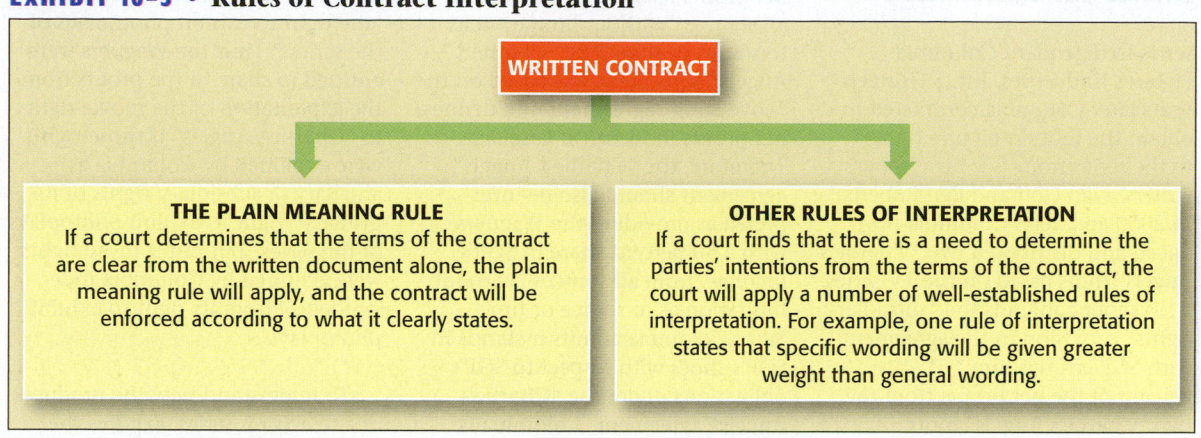

WRITTEN CONTRACT

THE PLAIN MEANING RULE
If a court determines that the terms of the contract are clear from the written document alone, the plain meaning rule will apply, and the contract will be enforced according to what it clearly states.

OTHER RULES OF INTERPRETATION
If a court finds that there is a need to determine the parties' intentions from the terms of the contract, the court will apply a number of well-established rules of interpretation. For example, one rule of interpretation states that specific wording will be given greater weight than general wording.

SECTION 5
INTERPRETATION OF CONTRACTS

Sometimes, parties agree that a contract has been formed but disagree on its meaning or legal effect. One reason this may happen is that one of the parties is not familiar with the legal terminology used in the contract. To an extent, *plain language* laws (enacted by the federal government and a majority of the states) have helped to avoid this difficulty. Sometimes, though, a dispute may arise over the meaning of a contract simply because the rights or obligations under the contract are not expressed clearly—no matter how "plain" the language used.

In this section, we look at some common law rules of contract interpretation. These rules, which have evolved over time, provide the courts with guidelines for deciding disputes over how contract terms or provisions should be interpreted. Exhibit 10–3

provides a brief graphic summary of how these rules are applied.

The Plain Meaning Rule

When a contract's writing is clear and unequivocal, a court will enforce it according to its obvious terms. The meaning of the terms must be determined from *the face of the instrument*—from the written document alone. This is sometimes referred to as *the plain meaning rule*.

Under this rule, if a contract's words appear to be clear and unambiguous, a court cannot consider *extrinsic evidence*—that is, any evidence not contained in the document itself. If a contract's terms are unclear or ambiguous, however, extrinsic evidence may be admissible to clarify the meaning of the contract. The admissibility of such evidence can significantly affect the court's interpretation of ambiguous contractual provisions and thus the outcome of litigation. The following case illustrates these points.

✳ EXTENDED CASE 10.2 ✳
Wagner v. Columbia Pictures Industries, Inc.

California Court of Appeal, Second District, 146 Cal.App.4th 586, 52 Cal.Rptr.3d 898 (2007).

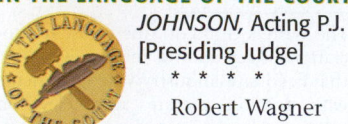

IN THE LANGUAGE OF THE COURT
JOHNSON, Acting P.J. [Presiding Judge]
* * * *
Robert Wagner and Natalie Wood

(the "Wagners") entered into an agreement with Spelling-Goldberg Productions (SGP) "relating to 'Charlie's Angels' (herein called the 'series')." The contract entitled the Wagners to 50 percent of the net profits SGP received as consideration

"for the right to exhibit photoplays of the series and from the exploitation of all ancillary, music and subsidiary rights in connection therewith." SGP subsequently sold its rights and obligations with respect to the "Charlie's Angels"

EXTENDED CASE CONTINUES ➡

EXTENDED CASE 10.2 CONTINUED ⬇

series to defendant Columbia Pictures [Industries, Inc.,] Thirteen years later Columbia contracted to obtain the motion picture rights to the series from * * * the show's writers, Ivan Goff and Ben Roberts. In 2000 and 2003 Columbia produced and distributed two "Charlie's Angels" films based on the TV series.

Wagner contends the "subsidiary rights" provision in the agreement with SGP entitles him * * * to 50 percent of the net profits from the two "Charlie's Angels" films.

Wagner brought this action [in a California state court] against Columbia for breach of contract * * *. Columbia answered and moved for summary [judgment] * * *. The trial court granted that motion * * *. [Wagner appealed this judgment to a state intermediate appellate court.]

* * * *

Wagner introduced evidence of the history of the negotiations underlying the "Charlie's Angels" contract in support of his [contention].

This history begins with a contract the Wagners entered into with SGP to star in a television movie-of-the-week, "Love Song." As compensation for Wagner and Wood acting in "Love Song," SGP agreed to pay them a fixed amount plus one-half the net profits * * *.

* * * *

In the * * * "Love Song" contract net profits were not limited to monies received "for the right to exhibit the Photoplay." Instead they were defined as the net of "all monies received by Producer as consideration for the right to exhibit the Photoplay, and exploitation of all ancillary, music and subsidiary rights in connection therewith."

* * * *

Wagner's argument is simple and straightforward. The net profits provision in the "Love Song" agreement was intended to give the Wagners a one-half share in the

net profits received by SGP "from all sources" without limitation as to source or time. The "Charlie's Angels" agreement was based on the "Love Song" agreement and defines net profits in identical language. Therefore, the "Charlie's Angels" agreement should also be interpreted as providing the Wagners with a 50 percent share in SGP's income "from all sources" without limitation as to source or time. Since Columbia admits it stands in SGP's shoes with respect to SGP's obligations under the "Charlie's Angels" agreement, Columbia is obligated to pay Wagner * * * 50 percent of the net profits derived from the "Charlie's Angels" movies.

* * * *

The problem with Wagner's extrinsic evidence is that it does not explain the ["Charlie's Angels"] contract language, it contradicts it. *Under the parol evidence rule,[a] extrinsic evidence is not admissible to contradict express terms in a written contract or to explain what the agreement was. The agreement is the writing itself. Parol evidence cannot be admitted to show intention independent of an unambiguous written instrument.* [Emphasis added.]

Even if the Wagners and SGP intended the Wagners would share in the net profits "from any and all sources" they did not say so in their contract. What they said in their contract was the Wagners would share in "all monies actually received by Producer, as consideration for the right to exhibit photoplays of the series, and from the exploitation of all ancillary, music and subsidiary rights in connection therewith." For a right to be "subsidiary" or "ancillary," meaning supplementary or subordinate, there must be a primary right to which it relates. The only primary

right mentioned in the contract is "the right to exhibit photoplays of the series." Thus the Wagners were entitled to share in the profits from the exploitation of the movie rights to "Charlie's Angels" if those rights were exploited by Columbia as ancillary or subsidiary rights of its primary "right to exhibit photoplays of the series" but not if those rights were acquired by Columbia independently from its right to exhibit photoplays.

* * * *

To understand how the producer of a television series acquires the motion picture rights in the series it is necessary to understand the Writers Guild of America Minimum Basic Agreement (MBA).[b]

* * * *

The contract between Goff and Roberts and SGP * * * stated: "The parties acknowledge that this agreement is subject to all of the terms and provisions of the applicable [MBA] * * *."

Article 16B of the MBA entitled "Separation of Rights" provided * * * : "[Producer] shall own the exclusive film television rights in the literary material * * *. Writer shall retain all other rights * * * including but not limited to * * * theatrical motion picture * * * rights."

* * * *

Despite the provision in the MBA conferring the motion picture rights in a teleplay on the writers of the teleplay the producer retained a "limited interest in such rights." As relevant here, this "limited interest" consisted of the right of first refusal should the writer decide to offer the movie rights for sale within five years from the date the writer delivered the teleplay to the producer. After the five-year period expired the producer could still purchase the

---

a. As will be discussed in Chapter 15, the *parol evidence rule* prohibits the parties from introducing in court evidence of an oral agreement that contradicts the written terms of a contract.

b. The Writers Guild of America is an association of screen and television writers that negotiates industrywide agreements with motion picture and television producers.

EXTENDED CASE 10.2 CONTINUED ⬇

movie rights but it had to do so on the open market and in competition with any other producer who wanted to purchase those rights.

Consequently, if Columbia had produced "Charlie's Angels" movies based on motion picture rights

* * * SGP had acquired from Goff and Roberts under SGP's right of first refusal Columbia could be said to have "exploited" an ancillary or subsidiary right, i.e., movie-making, in connection with "the right to exhibit photoplays of the series," and the Wagners would be entitled to a share of the movies' profits.

However, * * * there is no evidence SGP ever acquired the motion picture rights to "Charlie's Angels" by exercising its right of first refusal or in any other way connected to its right to exhibit photoplays of the series.

* * * *

The judgment is affirmed.

 QUESTIONS

1. How might the result in this case have been different if the court had admitted the Wagners' evidence of the *Love Song* contract?
2. Under what circumstances would the Wagners have been entitled to a share of the profits from the *Charlie's Angels* movies even though the evidence of the *Love Song* contract was irrelevant?

Other Rules of Interpretation

Generally, a court will interpret the language to give effect to the parties' intent *as expressed in their contract.* This is the primary purpose of the rules of interpretation—to determine the parties' intent from the language used in their agreement and to give effect to that intent. A court normally will not make or remake a contract, nor will it interpret the language according to what the parties *claim* their intent was when they made it. The courts use the following rules in interpreting contractual terms:

1. Insofar as possible, a reasonable, lawful, and effective meaning will be given to all of a contract's terms.
2. A contract will be interpreted as a whole; individual, specific clauses will be considered subordinate to the contract's general intent. All writings that are a part of the same transaction will be interpreted together.
3. Terms that were the subject of separate negotiation will be given greater consideration than standardized terms and terms that were not negotiated separately.
4. A word will be given its ordinary, commonly accepted meaning, and a technical word or term will be given its technical meaning, unless the parties clearly intended something else.[11]

5. Specific and exact wording will be given greater consideration than general language.
6. Written or typewritten terms will prevail over preprinted ones.
7. Because a contract should be drafted in clear and unambiguous language, a party who uses ambiguous expressions is held to be responsible for the ambiguities. Thus, when the language has more than one meaning, it will be interpreted *against* the party who drafted the contract.
8. Evidence of *usage of trade, course of dealing,* and *course of performance* may be admitted to clarify the meaning of an ambiguously worded contract. (These terms will be defined and discussed in more detail in Chapter 19.) When considering custom and usage, a court will look at what is common to the particular business or industry and to the locale where the contract was made or is to be performed. Express terms (terms expressly stated in the contract) are given the greatest weight, followed by course of performance, course of dealing, and custom and usage of trade—in that order.

In the following case, the court was asked to interpret the phrase "increase of hazard" as it appeared in an insurance policy.

---

11. See, for example, *Citizens Communications Co. v. Trustmark Insurance,* 303 F.Supp.2d 197 (D.Conn. 2004).

CASE 10.3
U.S. Bank, N.A.[a] v. Tennessee Farmers Mutual Insurance Company

Tennessee Supreme Court, 277 S.W.3d 381 (2009).
www.tsc.state.tn.us[b]

BACKGROUND AND FACTS • Jessica Robbins bought a house in Humboldt, Tennessee. U.S. Bank, N.A., financed the purchase. Tennessee Farmers Mutual Insurance Company issued the homeowner's insurance policy. The policy included a "standard mortgage clause" that promised payment to the bank unless the house was lost due to an "increase in hazard" that the bank knew of but did not tell the insurer. When Robbins fell behind on her mortgage payments, the bank started foreclosure proceedings. No one told the insurer. Robbins filed for bankruptcy, which postponed the foreclosure (see Chapters 30 and 31 for detailed discussions of bankruptcy, mortgages, and foreclosures). Meanwhile, the house "blew up," in Robbins's words, and was destroyed in a fire caused by chemicals used to make methamphetamine. The bank filed a claim under the policy. The insurer refused to pay. The bank filed a suit in a Tennessee state court against the insurer claiming breach of contract. The insurer argued that it had not been told by the bank of an "increase in hazard"—the foreclosure. The court ruled in favor of the bank, an intermediate appellate court reversed in favor of the insurer, and the bank appealed.

IN THE LANGUAGE OF THE COURT
Sharon G. *LEE,* J. [Justice]
* * * *

Insurance contracts, being subject to the same rules of construction as contracts generally, should be interpreted and enforced as written. *Absent fraud or mistake, the terms of a contract should be given their plain and ordinary meaning, for the primary rule of contract interpretation is to ascertain and give effect to the intent of the parties.* [Emphasis added.]
* * * *

The insurance policy at issue in this case contains a standard mortgage clause. * * * Our task is to interpret the policy language and determine whether this language required the Bank to notify Tennessee Farmers of the commencement of foreclosure proceedings. The precise issue before us is whether the commencement of foreclosure proceedings constitutes an "increase in hazard" which the Bank must report to the insurer or risk invalidation of the policy.
* * * No Tennessee case has squarely addressed the precise issue presented.
* * * *

In similar cases involving standard mortgage clauses requiring notice of an "increase of hazard," courts [in other jurisdictions] have found that the plain meaning of those words do not include an event such as a foreclosure proceeding, but rather, refer to physical conditions on the insured property posing a more hazardous risk to the property.
* * * *

We conclude that the Bank was not required to give notice to Tennessee Farmers of the initiation of foreclosure proceedings, and therefore, the lack of notice does not invalidate the insurance coverage in this case. First, we decline to assume that the mere commencement of foreclosure proceedings, by itself, automatically constitutes an increase in hazard * * *. Notably, the property at issue in this case burned not because of an impending foreclosure sale, but rather due to a mishap during an occupant's production of an illegal substance. Further, the foreclosure that was commenced was stayed pursuant to an order of the bankruptcy court. *Therefore, at the time of the fire, there was no ongoing foreclosure proceeding.* [Emphasis added.]

Second, we decline to read into this policy an obligation to notify the insurer of the commencement of foreclosure. In our view, the insurer is essentially asking us to write a new contract for the parties in accordance with its idea of what the policy should have said. This we decline to do, as our duty is to construe and enforce the policy as written, not make a new contract for the parties on different terms.

---

a. The abbreviation *N.A.* stands for *National Association,* which means the bank was chartered by the federal government under the National Bank Act.

b. In the left-hand column, in the "Court & Ethics Opinions" pull-down menu, select "Supreme Court 1st Quarter 2009." On that page, scroll to the summary of the case and click on "View" to access the opinion. The Tennessee court system maintains this Web site.

CASE 10.3 CONTINUED ▶ **DECISION AND REMEDY** • *The Tennessee Supreme Court reversed the judgment of the appellate court and remanded the case to the trial court. The failure to notify the insurer of the fore-closure did not breach the terms of the policy because the phrase "increase of hazard," by its ordinary meaning, does not include the commencement of foreclosure proceedings.*

THE ETHICAL DIMENSION • *Is it ethical for an insurer to refuse to pay a claim under the terms of a policy that the insurer drafted? Discuss.*

WHAT IF THE FACTS WERE DIFFERENT? • *Suppose that Tennessee Farmers' policy had provided that foreclosure proceedings either voided the coverage or required notification to continue it. Would the result have been different? Explain.*

REVIEWING
Nature and Terminology

Mitsui Bank hired Ross Duncan as a branch manager in one of its Southern California locations. At that time, Duncan received an employee handbook informing him that Mitsui would review his performance and salary level annually. In 2008, Mitsui decided to create a new lending program to help financially troubled businesses stay afloat. Duncan was appointed to be the credit development officer (CDO) for the new program and was given a written compensation plan. According to the plan, his compensation would be based on the program's success and would include bonuses and commissions based on the volume of loans and sales. The written plan also stated, "This compensation plan will be reviewed and potentially amended after one year and will be subject to such review and amendment annually thereafter." Duncan's efforts as CDO were successful, and the business-lending program he developed grew to represent 25 percent of Mitsui's business in 2009 and 40 percent in 2010. Nevertheless, Mitsui refused to give Duncan a raise in 2009. In fact, Mitsui amended his compensation plan to reduce his compensation significantly and to change his performance evaluation schedule to every six months. When he had still not received a raise by 2011, Duncan resigned as CDO and filed a lawsuit alleging breach of contract. Using the information presented in the chapter, answer the following questions.

1. What are the four requirements of a valid contract?
2. Did Duncan have a valid contract with Mitsui for employment as CDO? If so, was it a bilateral or a unilateral contract?
3. What are the requirements of an implied contract?
4. Can Duncan establish an implied contract based on the employment manual or the written compensation plan? Why or why not?

✹ DEBATE THIS: *Companies should be able to make or break employment contracts whenever and however they wish.*

TERMS AND CONCEPTS

bilateral contract 208

contract 207

executed contract 211

executory contract 211

express contract 210

formal contract 210

implied contract 210

informal contract 210

objective theory of
  contracts 207

offeree 208

offeror 208

promise 206

promisee 207

promisor 207

quantum meruit 212

quasi contract 212

unenforceable contract 212

unilateral contract 209

valid contract 211

void contract 212

voidable contract 211

QUESTIONS AND CASE PROBLEMS

10–1. Express versus Implied Contracts
Everett McCleskey, a local businessperson, is a good friend of Al Miller, the owner of a local candy store. Every day on his lunch hour, McCleskey goes into Miller's candy store and stays about five minutes. After looking at the candy and talking with Miller, McCleskey usually buys one or two candy bars. One afternoon, McCleskey goes into Miller's candy shop, looks at the candy, and picks up a $1 candy bar. Seeing that Miller is very busy, he waves the candy bar at Miller without saying a word and walks out. Is there a contract? If so, classify it within the categories presented in this chapter.

10–2. QUESTION WITH SAMPLE ANSWER: Implied Contract.

Janine was hospitalized with severe abdominal pain and placed in an intensive care unit. Her doctor told the hospital personnel to order around-the-clock nursing care for Janine. At the hospital's request, a nursing services firm, Nursing Services Unlimited, provided two weeks of in-hospital care and, after Janine was sent home, an additional two weeks of at-home care. During the at-home period of care, Janine was fully aware that she was receiving the benefit of the nursing services. Nursing Services later billed Janine $4,000 for the nursing care, but Janine refused to pay on the ground that she had never contracted for the services, either orally or in writing. In view of the fact that no express contract was ever formed, can Nursing Services recover the $4,000 from Janine? If so, under what legal theory? Discuss.

• **For a sample answer to Question 10–2, go to Appendix I at the end of this text.**

10–3. Types of Contracts Burger Baby restaurants engaged Air Advertising to fly an advertisement above the Connecticut beaches. The advertisement offered $1,000 to any person who could swim from the Connecticut beaches to Long Island in less than a day. At 10:00 A.M. on October 10, Air Advertising's pilot flew a sign above the Connecticut beaches that read: "Swim across the Sound and Burger Baby pays $1,000." On seeing the sign, Davison dived in. About four hours later, when he was about halfway across the Sound, Air Advertising flew another sign over the Sound that read: "Burger Baby revokes." Davison completed the swim in another six hours. Is there a contract between Davison and Burger Baby? Can Davison recover anything?

10–4. Interpretation of Contracts East Mill Associates (EMA) was developing residential "units" in East Brunswick, New Jersey, within the service area of the East Brunswick Sewerage Authority (EBSA). The sewer system required an upgrade to the Ryder's Lane Pumping Station to accommodate the new units. EMA agreed to pay "fifty-five percent (55%) of the total cost" of the upgrade. At the time, the estimated cost to EMA was $150,000 to $200,000. Impediments to the project arose, however, substantially increasing the cost. Among other things, the pumping station had to be moved to accommodate a widened road nearby. The upgrade was delayed for almost three years. When it was completed, EBSA asked EMA for $340,022.12, which represented 55 percent of the total cost. EMA did not pay. EBSA filed a suit in a New Jersey state court against EMA for breach of contract. What rule should the court apply to interpret the parties' contract? How should that rule be applied? Why? [*East Brunswick Sewerage Authority v. East Mill Associates, Inc.*, 365 N.J.Super. 120, 838 A.2d 494 (A.D. 2004)]

10–5. CASE PROBLEM WITH SAMPLE ANSWER: Contract Enforceability.

California's Subdivision Map Act (SMA) prohibits the sale of real property until a map of its subdivision is filed with, and approved by, the appropriate state agency. In November 2004, Black Hills Investments, Inc., entered into two contracts with Albertson's, Inc., to buy two parcels of property in a shopping center development. Each contract required that "all governmental approvals relating to any lot split [or] subdivision" be obtained before the sale but permitted Albertson's to waive this condition. Black Hills made a $133,000 deposit on the purchase. A few weeks later, before the sales were complete, Albertson's filed with a local state agency a map that subdivided the shopping center into four parcels, including the two that Black Hills had agreed to buy. In January 2005, Black Hills objected to concessions that Albertson's had made to a buyer of one of the other parcels, told Albertson's that it was terminating its deal, and asked for a return of its deposit. Albertson's refused. Black Hills filed a suit in a California state court against Albertson's, arguing that the contracts were void. Are these contracts valid, voidable, unenforceable, or void? Explain. [Black Hills Investments, Inc. v. Albertson's, Inc., 146 Cal.App.4th 883, 53 Cal.Rptr.3d 263 (4 Dist. 2007)]

• **To view a sample answer for Problem 10–5, go to this book's Web site at www.cengage.com/blaw/clarkson, select "Chapter 10," and click on "Case Problem with Sample Answer."**

10–6. Interpretation of Contracts Lisa and Darrell Miller married in 1983 and had two children, Landon and Spencer. The Millers divorced in 2003 and entered into a joint custody implementation plan (JCIP). Under the JCIP, Darrell agreed to "begin setting funds aside for the minor children to attend post-secondary education necessary to pay tuition, books, supplies, and room and board not to exceed four (4) years." After Landon's eighteenth birthday, Darrell filed a petition to reduce the amount of the child support that he was paying to Lisa. In response, she asked the court to order Darrell to pay the boys' college expenses but offered no evidence to support the request. Darrell contended that the JCIP was not clear on this point. Do the rules of contract interpretation, applied to the phrasing of the Millers' JCIP, support Lisa's request or Darrell's contention? Explain. [*Miller v. Miller, 1 So.3d 815 (La.App. 2009)*]

10–7. *Quantum Meruit* Robert Gutkowski, a sports marketing expert, met numerous times with George Steinbrenner, the owner of the New York Yankees, and other Yankees executives over a ten-year period to help launch the Yankees Entertainment and Sports Network (YES Network). He was a paid consultant during that time. When the parties quit working together, Gutkowski sued, contending that he had been promised an ownership share in YES as part of the compensation for his work. While he was a paid consultant, he was not given a share of YES or hired as a regular executive. He contended that, by industry standards, a reasonable value for his services would be a 2 to 3 percent ownership share. There was no written contract for such a share, but Gutkowski claimed he was due that to prevent unjust enrichment of the Yankees for exploiting his expertise. Does Gutkowski have a good claim for payment based on *quantum meruit?* Explain. [*Gutkowski v. Steinbrenner, 680 F.Supp.2d 602 (S.D.N.Y. 2010)*]

10–8. A QUESTION OF ETHICS: Unilateral Contracts.

International Business Machines Corp. (IBM) hired Niels Jensen in 2000 as a software sales representative. In 2001, IBM presented a new "Software Sales Incentive Plan" (SIP) at a conference for its sales employees. A brochure given to the attendees stated, "There are no caps to your earnings; the more you sell, . . . the more earnings for you." The brochure outlined how the plan worked and referred the employees to the "Sales Incentives" section of IBM's corporate intranet for more details. Jensen was given a "quota letter" that said he would be paid $75,000 as a base salary and, if he attained his quota, an additional $75,000 as incentive pay. In September, Jensen closed a deal with the Internal Revenue Service that was worth more than $24 million to IBM. Relying on the SIP brochure, Jensen estimated his commission to be $2.6 million. IBM paid him less than $500,000, however. Jensen filed a suit in a federal district court, contending that the SIP brochure and quota letter constituted a unilateral offer that became a binding contract when Jensen closed the sale. In view of these facts, consider the following questions. [Jensen v. International Business Machines Corp., 454 F.3d 382 (4th Cir. 2006)]

(a) Would it be fair to the employer in this case to hold that the SIP brochure and the quota letter created a unilateral contract if IBM did not *intend* to create such a contract? Would it be fair to the employee to hold that *no* contract was created? Explain.

(b) The "Sales Incentives" section of IBM's intranet included a clause providing that "management will decide if an adjustment to the payment is appropriate" when an employee closes a large transaction. Jensen's quota letter stated, "[The SIP] program does not constitute a promise by IBM to make any distributions under it. IBM reserves the right to adjust the program terms or to cancel or otherwise modify the program at any time." How do these statements affect your answers to the above questions? From an ethical perspective, would it be fair to hold that a contract exists despite these statements?

10–9. SPECIAL CASE ANALYSIS: Rules of Interpretation.
Go to Extended Case 10.2, *Wagner v. Columbia Pictures Industries, Inc., 146 Cal.App.4th 586, 52 Cal.Rptr.3d 898 (2 Dist. 2007)*, on pages 215–217. Read the excerpt and answer the following questions.

(a) **Issue:** The dispute between the parties centered on which contract and asked what question?

(b) **Rule of Law:** What rule concerning the interpretation of a contract and the admission of evidence did the court apply in this case?

(c) **Applying the Rule of Law:** How did the intent of the contracting parties and the language in their contract affect the application of the rule of law?

(d) **Conclusion:** Did the court resolve the dispute in the plaintiff's favor? Why or why not?

LEGAL RESEARCH EXERCISES ON THE WEB

Go to this text's Web site at **www.cengage.com/blaw/clarkson**, select "Chapter 10," and click on "Practical Internet Exercises." There you will find the following Internet research exercises that you can perform to learn more about the topics covered in this chapter.

Practical Internet Exercise 10–1: Legal Perspective
Contracts and Contract Provisions

Practical Internet Exercise 10–2: Management Perspective
Implied Employment Contracts

Practical Internet Exercise 10–3: Historical Perspective
Contracts in Ancient Mesopotamia

CHAPTER 11

Agreement in Traditional and E-Contracts

Contract law developed over time, through the common law tradition, to meet society's need to know with certainty what kinds of promises, or contracts, will be enforced and the point at which a valid and binding contract is formed. For a contract to be considered valid and enforceable, the requirements listed in Chapter 10 must be met. In this chapter, we look closely at the first of these requirements, *agreement*.

Agreement is required to form a contract, regardless of whether it is formed in the traditional way, through the exchange of paper documents, or online, through the exchange of electronic messages or documents. In today's world, many contracts are formed via the Internet. We discuss online offers and acceptances and examine some laws that have been created to apply to electronic contracts, or *e-contracts*, in the latter part of this chapter.

SECTION 1
AGREEMENT

An essential element for contract formation is **agreement**—the parties must agree on the terms of the contract and manifest to each other their *mutual assent* (agreement) to the same bargain. Ordinarily, agreement is evidenced by two events: an *offer* and an *acceptance*. One party offers a certain bargain to another party, who then accepts that bargain. The agreement does not necessarily have to be in writing. Both parties, however, must manifest their assent, or voluntary consent, to the same bargain. Once an agreement is reached, if the other elements of a contract are present (consideration, capacity, and legality—discussed in subsequent chapters), a valid contract is formed, generally creating enforceable rights and duties between the parties.

Because words often fail to convey the precise meaning intended, the law of contracts generally adheres to the *objective theory of contracts,* as discussed in Chapter 10. Under this theory, a party's words and conduct are held to mean whatever a reasonable person in the offeree's position would think they meant.

Requirements of the Offer

An **offer** is a promise or commitment to do or refrain from doing some specified action in the future. As mentioned in Chapter 10, the parties to a contract are the *offeror,* the one who makes an offer or proposal to another party, and the *offeree,* the one to whom the offer or proposal is made. Under the common law, three elements are necessary for an offer to be effective:

1. The offeror must have a serious intention to become bound by the offer.
2. The terms of the offer must be reasonably certain, or definite, so that the parties and the court can ascertain the terms of the contract.
3. The offer must be communicated to the offeree.

Once an effective offer has been made, the offeree's acceptance of that offer creates a legally binding contract (providing the other essential elements for a valid and enforceable contract are present).

INTENTION The first requirement for an effective offer is a serious intent on the part of the offeror. Serious intent is not determined by the subjective intentions, beliefs, and assumptions of the offeror.

Rather, it is determined by what a reasonable person in the offeree's position would conclude that the offeror's words and actions meant. Offers made in obvious anger, jest, or undue excitement do not meet the serious-and-objective-intent test because a reasonable person would realize that a serious offer was not being made. Because these offers are not effective, an offeree's acceptance does not create an agreement.

Suppose that Linda and Dena ride to school each day in Dena's new automobile, which has a market value of $20,000. One cold morning, they get into the car, but Dena cannot get the car started. She yells in anger, "I'll sell this car to anyone for $500!" Linda drops $500 on Dena's lap. A reasonable person—taking into consideration Dena's frustration and the obvious difference in value between the market price of the car and the proposed purchase price—would realize that Dena's offer was not made with serious and objective intent. No agreement was formed.

In the classic case presented next, the court considered whether an offer made "after a few drinks" met the serious-and-objective-intent requirement.

CASE 11.1
Lucy v. Zehmer
Supreme Court of Appeals of Virginia, 196 Va. 493, 84 S.E.2d 516 (1954).

BACKGROUND AND FACTS • W.O. Lucy, the plaintiff, filed a suit against A. H. and Ida Zehmer, the defendants, to compel the Zehmers to transfer title of their property, known as the Ferguson Farm, to the Lucys (W.O. and his wife) for $50,000, as the Zehmers had allegedly agreed to do. Lucy had known A.H. Zehmer for fifteen or twenty years and for the last eight years or so had been anxious to buy the Ferguson Farm from him. One night, Lucy stopped in to visit the Zehmers in the combination restaurant, filling station, and motor court they operated. While there, Lucy tried to buy the Ferguson Farm once again. This time he tried a new approach. According to the trial court transcript, Lucy said to Zehmer, "I bet you wouldn't take $50,000 for that place." Zehmer replied, "Yes, I would too; you wouldn't give fifty." Throughout the evening, the conversation returned to the sale of the Ferguson Farm for $50,000. At the same time, the men continued to drink whiskey and engage in light conversation. Eventually, Lucy enticed Zehmer to write up an agreement to the effect that the Zehmers would sell the Ferguson Farm to Lucy for $50,000 complete. Later, Lucy sued Zehmer to compel him to go through with the sale. Zehmer argued that he had been drunk and that the offer had been made in jest and hence was unenforceable. The trial court agreed with Zehmer, and Lucy appealed.

IN THE LANGUAGE OF THE COURT
BUCHANAN, J. [Justice] delivered the opinion of the court.
* * * *

In his testimony, Zehmer claimed that he "was high as a Georgia pine," and that the transaction "was just a bunch of two doggoned drunks bluffing to see who could talk the biggest and say the most." That claim is inconsistent with his attempt to testify in great detail as to what was said and what was done.
* * * *

The appearance of the contract, the fact that it was under discussion for forty minutes or more before it was signed; Lucy's objection to the first draft because it was written in the singular, and he wanted Mrs. Zehmer to sign it also; the rewriting to meet that objection and the signing by Mrs. Zehmer; the discussion of what was to be included in the sale, the provision for the examination of the title, the completeness of the instrument that was executed, the taking possession of it by Lucy with no request or suggestion by either of the defendants that he give it back, are facts which furnish persuasive evidence that the execution of the contract was a serious business transaction rather than a casual, jesting matter as defendants now contend.
* * * *

In the field of contracts, as generally elsewhere, *we must look to the outward expression of a person as manifesting his intention rather than to his secret and unexpressed intention.* The law

CASE CONTINUES ➡

CASE 11.1 CONTINUED ➡ imputes to a person an intention corresponding to the reasonable meaning of his words and acts. [Emphasis added.]

* * * *

Whether the writing signed by the defendants and now sought to be enforced by the complainants was the result of a serious offer by Lucy and a serious acceptance by the defendants, or was a serious offer by Lucy and an acceptance in secret jest by the defendants, in either event it constituted a binding contract of sale between the parties.

DECISION AND REMEDY • *The Supreme Court of Appeals of Virginia determined that the writing was an enforceable contract and reversed the ruling of the lower court. The Zehmers were required by court order to follow through with the sale of the Ferguson Farm to the Lucys.*

IMPACT OF THIS CASE ON TODAY'S LAW • *This is a classic case in contract law because it illustrates so clearly the objective theory of contracts with respect to determining whether a serious offer was intended. Today, the courts continue to apply the objective theory of contracts and routinely cite* Lucy v. Zehmer *as a significant precedent in this area.*

WHAT IF THE FACTS WERE DIFFERENT? • *Suppose that the day after Lucy signed the purchase agreement for the farm, he decided that he did not want it after all, and Zehmer sued Lucy to perform the contract. Would this change in the facts alter the court's decision that Lucy and Zehmer had created an enforceable contract? Why or why not?*

The concept of intention can be further clarified through an examination of the types of expressions and statements that are *not* offers. We look at these expressions and statements in the subsections that follow.

Expressions of Opinion. An expression of opinion is not an offer. It does not indicate an intention to enter into a binding agreement.

CASE IN POINT George Hawkins took his son to Edward McGee, a physician, and asked McGee to operate on the son's hand. McGee said that the boy would be in the hospital three or four days and that the hand would *probably* heal a few days later. The son's hand did not heal for a month, but the father did not win a suit for breach of contract. The court held that McGee had not made an offer to heal the son's hand in a few days. He had merely expressed an opinion as to when the hand would heal.[1]

Statements of Future Intent. A statement of an *intention* to do something in the future is not an offer. If Samir says, "I *plan* to sell my stock in Novation, Inc., for $150 per share," no contract is created if John "accepts" and tenders the $150 per share for the stock. Samir has merely expressed his intention to enter into a future contract for the sale of the stock. If John accepts and tenders the $150 per share, no contract is formed because a reasonable

person would conclude that Samir was only *thinking about* selling his stock, not *promising* to sell it.

Preliminary Negotiations. A request or invitation to negotiate is not an offer. It only expresses a willingness to discuss the possibility of entering into a contract. Statements such as "Will you sell Blythe Estate?" or "I wouldn't sell my car for less than $5,000" are examples. A reasonable person in the offeree's position would not conclude that these statements indicated an intention to enter into a binding obligation. Likewise, when the government or private firms require construction work, they invite contractors to submit bids. The *invitation* to submit bids is not an offer, and a contractor does not bind the government or private firm by submitting a bid. (The bids that the contractors submit are offers, however, and the government or private firm can bind the contractor by accepting the bid.)

Advertisements. In general, advertisements (including representations made in mail-order catalogues, price lists, and circulars) are treated not as offers to contract but as invitations to negotiate.[2]

CASE IN POINT An advertisement on the *Science NOW* Web site asked readers to submit "news tips," which the organization would then investigate for possible inclusion in its magazine or on the Web site. Erik Trell, a professor and physician, submitted

---

1. *Hawkins v. McGee,* 84 N.H. 114, 146 A. 641 (1929).

2. *Restatement (Second) of Contracts,* Section 26, Comment b.

a manuscript in which he claimed to have solved a famous mathematical problem. When *Science NOW* did not publish the information, Trell filed a lawsuit for breach of contract. He claimed that the *Science NOW* ad was an offer, which he had accepted by submitting his manuscript. The court dismissed Trell's suit, holding that the ad was not an offer, but merely an invitation.[3]

Price lists are another form of invitation to negotiate or trade. A seller's price list is not an offer to sell at that price; it merely invites the buyer to offer to buy at that price. In fact, the seller usually puts "prices subject to change" on the price list. Only in rare circumstances will a price quotation be construed as an offer.

Although most advertisements and the like are treated as invitations to negotiate, this does not mean that an advertisement can never be an offer. On some occasions, courts have construed advertisements to be offers because the ads contained definite terms that invited acceptance (such as an ad offering a reward for the return of a lost dog).

Auctions. In an auction, a seller "offers" goods for sale through an auctioneer, but this is not an offer to form a contract. Rather, it is an invitation asking bidders to submit offers. In the context of an auction, a bidder is the offeror, and the auctioneer is the offeree. The offer is accepted when the auctioneer strikes the hammer. Before the fall of the hammer, a bidder may revoke (take back) her or his bid, or the auctioneer may reject that bid or all bids. Typically, an auctioneer will reject a bid that is below the price the seller is willing to accept.

When the auctioneer accepts a higher bid, he or she rejects all previous bids. Because rejection terminates an offer (as will be discussed later), those bids represent offers that have been terminated. Thus, if the highest bidder withdraws her or his bid before the hammer falls, none of the previous bids is reinstated. If the bid is not withdrawn or rejected, the contract is formed when the auctioneer announces, "Going once, going twice, sold!" (or something similar) and lets the hammer fall.

Auctions with and without Reserve. Auctions traditionally have been referred to as either "with reserve" or "without reserve." In an auction with reserve, the seller (through the auctioneer) may withdraw the goods at any time before the auctioneer

closes the sale by announcement or by the fall of the hammer. All auctions are assumed to be auctions with reserve unless the terms of the auction are explicitly stated to be *without reserve*. In an auction without reserve, the goods cannot be withdrawn by the seller and must be sold to the highest bidder. In auctions with reserve, the seller may reserve the right to confirm or reject the sale even after "the hammer has fallen." In this situation, the seller is obligated to notify those attending the auction that sales of goods made during the auction are not final until confirmed by the seller.[4]

Agreements to Agree. Traditionally, agreements to agree—that is, agreements to agree to the material terms of a contract at some future date—were not considered to be binding contracts. The modern view, however, is that agreements to agree may be enforceable agreements (contracts) if it is clear that the parties intended to be bound by the agreements. In other words, under the modern view the emphasis is on the parties' intent rather than on form.

CASE IN POINT After a person was injured and nearly drowned on a water ride at one of its amusement parks, Six Flags, Inc., filed a lawsuit against the manufacturer that had designed that ride. The defendant-manufacturer claimed that there was no binding contract between the parties, only preliminary negotiations that were never formalized into a construction contract. The court, however, held that a faxed document specifying the details of the water ride, along with the parties' subsequent actions—such as beginning construction and handwriting notes on the fax—was sufficient to show an intent to be bound. Because of the court's finding, the manufacturer was required to provide insurance for the water ride at Six Flags, and its insurer was required to defend Six Flags in the personal-injury lawsuit that arose out of the incident.[5]

Increasingly, the courts are holding that a preliminary agreement constitutes a binding contract if the parties have agreed on all essential terms and no disputed issues remain to be resolved.[6] In contrast, if the parties agree on certain major terms but leave other terms open for further negotiation, a

---

3. *Trell v. American Association for the Advancement of Science,* ___ F.Supp.2d ___ (W.D.N.Y. 2007).

4. These rules apply under both the common law of contracts and the Uniform Commercial Code (UCC)—see UCC 2–328.

5. *Six Flags, Inc. v. Steadfast Insurance Co.,* 474 F.Supp.2d 201 (D.Mass. 2007).

6. See, for example, *Tractebel Energy Marketing, Inc. v. AEP Power Marketing, Inc.,* 487 F.3d 89 (2d Cir. 2007); and *Florine On Call, Ltd. v. Fluorogas Limited,* No. 01-CV-186 (W.D.Tex. 2002), contract issue affirmed on appeal at 380 F.3d 849 (5th Cir. 2004).

preliminary agreement is binding only in the sense that the parties have committed themselves to negotiate the undecided terms in good faith in an effort to reach a final agreement.[7]

---

7. See, for example, *MBH, Inc. v. John Otte Oil & Propane, Inc.,* 727 N.W.2d 238 (Neb.App. 2007); and *Barrand v. Whataburger, Inc.,* 214 S.W.3d 122 (Tex.App.—Corpus Christi 2006).

The following case concerned a dispute over an agreement to settle a case during a trial. One party claimed that the agreement, which was formed via e-mail, was binding, and the other party claimed that it was merely an agreement to agree or to work out the terms of a settlement in the future. Can an exchange of e-mails create a complete and unambiguous agreement?

CASE 11.2
Basis Technology Corp. v. Amazon.com, Inc.

Appeals Court of Massachusetts, 71 Mass.App.Ct. 29, 878 N.E.2d 952 (2008).

BACKGROUND AND FACTS • Basis Technology Corporation created software and provided technical services for Amazon.com, Inc.'s, Japanese-language Web site. The agreement between the two companies allowed for separately negotiated contracts for additional services that Basis might provide to Amazon. At the end of 1999, Basis and Amazon entered into stock-purchase agreements. Later, Amazon objected to certain actions related to the securities that Basis sold. Basis sued Amazon for various claims involving these securities and for failing to pay for services performed by Basis that were not included in the original agreement. During the trial, the two parties appeared to reach an agreement to settle out of court via a series of e-mail exchanges outlining the settlement. When Amazon reneged, Basis served a motion to enforce the proposed settlement. The trial judge entered a judgment against Amazon, which appealed.

IN THE LANGUAGE OF THE COURT
SIKORA, J. [Judge]

* * * *

* * * On the evening of March 23, after the third day of evidence and after settlement discussions, Basis counsel sent an e-mail with the following text to Amazon counsel:

> [Amazon counsel]—This e-mail confirms the essential business terms of the settlement between our respective clients * * *. Basis and Amazon agree that they promptly will take all reasonable steps to memorialize in a written agreement, to be signed by individuals authorized by each party, the terms set forth below, as well as such other terms that are reasonably necessary to make these terms effective.
>
> * * * *
>
> [Amazon counsel], please contact me first thing tomorrow morning if this e-mail does not accurately summarize the settlement terms reached earlier this evening. See you tomorrow morning when we report this matter settled to the Court.

At 7:26 A.M. on March 24, Amazon counsel sent an e-mail with a one-word reply: "correct." Later in the morning, in open court and on the record, both counsel reported the result of a settlement without specification of the terms.

On March 25, Amazon's counsel sent a facsimile of the first draft of a settlement agreement to Basis's counsel. The draft comported with all the terms of the e-mail exchange, and added some implementing and boilerplate [standard contract provisions] terms.

* * * *

[Within a few days, though,] the parties were deadlocked. On April 21, Basis served its motion to enforce the settlement agreement. Amazon opposed. * * * The motion and opposition presented the issues whether the e-mail terms were sufficiently complete and definite to form an agreement and whether Amazon had intended to be bound by them.

* * * *

We examine the text of the terms for the incompleteness and indefiniteness charged by Amazon. *Provisions are not ambiguous simply because the parties have developed different interpretations of them.* [Emphasis added.]

* * * *

CASE 11.2 CONTINUED ➡ We must interpret the document as a whole. In the preface to the enumerated terms, Basis counsel stated that the "e-mail confirms the essential business terms of the settlement between our respective clients," and that the parties "agree that they promptly will take all reasonable steps to memorialize" those terms. Amazon counsel concisely responded, "correct." Thus the "essential business terms" were resolved. The parties were proceeding to "memorialize" or record the settlement terms, not to create them.

    * * * *

To ascertain intent, a court considers the words used by the parties, the agreement taken as a whole, and surrounding facts and circumstances. The essential circumstance of this disputed agreement is that it concluded a trial.

    * * * As the trial judge explained in her memorandum of decision, she "terminated" the trial; she did not suspend it for exploratory negotiations. She did so in reliance upon the parties' report of an accomplished agreement for the settlement of their dispute.

    * * * *

In sum, the deliberateness and the gravity attributable to a report of a settlement, especially during the progress of a trial, weigh heavily as circumstantial evidence of the intention of a party such as Amazon to be bound by its communication to the opposing party and to the court.

DECISION AND REMEDY • *The Appeals Court of Massachusetts affirmed the trial court's finding that Amazon intended to be bound by the terms of the March 23 e-mail. That e-mail constituted a complete and unambiguous statement of the parties' desire to be bound by the settlement terms.*

WHAT IF THE FACTS WERE DIFFERENT? • *Suppose that the attorneys for both sides had simply had a phone conversation that included all of the terms to which they actually agreed in their e-mail exchanges. Would the court have ruled differently? Why or why not?*

THE LEGAL ENVIRONMENT DIMENSION • *What does the result in this case suggest that a businessperson should do before she or he agrees to a settlement of a legal dispute?*

DEFINITENESS OF TERMS The second requirement for an effective offer involves the definiteness of its terms. An offer must have reasonably definite terms so that a court can determine if a breach has occurred and give an appropriate remedy. The specific terms required depend, of course, on the type of contract. Generally, a contract must include the following terms, either expressed in the contract or capable of being reasonably inferred from it:

1. The identification of the parties.
2. The identification of the object or subject matter of the contract (also the quantity, when appropriate), including the work to be performed, with specific identification of such items as goods, services, and land.
3. The consideration to be paid.
4. The time of payment, delivery, or performance.

An offer may invite an acceptance to be worded in such specific terms that the contract is made definite. For example, Marcus Business Machines contacts Best Corporation and offers to sell "from one to ten MacCool copying machines for $1,600 each; state the number desired in acceptance." Best Corporation agrees to buy two copiers. Because the quantity is specified in the acceptance, the terms are definite and the contract is enforceable.

When the parties have clearly manifested an intent to form a contract, courts sometimes are willing to supply a missing term in a contract, especially a sales contract.[8] But a court will not rewrite a contract if the parties' expression of intent is too vague or uncertain to be given any precise meaning.

COMMUNICATION The third requirement for an effective offer is communication—the offer must be communicated to the offeree. Ordinarily, one cannot agree to a bargain without knowing that it exists. For example, Tolson advertises a reward for the return of her lost cat. Dirk, not knowing of the reward, finds the cat and returns it to Tolson. Usually, Dirk cannot

---

8. See Chapter 19 and UCC 2–204. Note that Article 2 of the UCC specifies different rules relating to the definiteness of terms used in a contract for the sale of goods. In essence, Article 2 modifies general contract law by requiring *less* specificity.

recover the reward because an essential element of a reward contract is that the one who claims the reward must have known it was offered. A few states would allow recovery of the reward, but not on contract principles—Dirk would be allowed to recover on the basis that it would be unfair to deny him the reward just because he did not know about it.

The following case illustrates the importance of the communication requirement in contract formation.

✳ EXTENDED CASE 11.3 ✳
Alexander v. Lafayette Crime Stoppers, Inc.

Court of Appeal of Louisiana, Third District, 28 So.3d 1253 (2010).
www.la3circuit.org/opinions.htm[a]

IN THE LANGUAGE OF THE COURT
AMY, Judge.
* * * *

In the summer of 2002, after several South Louisiana women had been murdered, the Multi Agency Homicide Task Force (Task Force) was established to investigate these murders, believed to be committed by the same individual referred to as the South Louisiana Serial Killer. In April 2003, the Baton Rouge Crime Stoppers (BRCS) began publicizing a reward offer in newspapers, television stations, and billboards around the Baton Rouge area regarding the South Louisiana Serial Killer. A short time later, Lafayette Crime Stoppers (LCS) also publicized a reward offer. Both reward offers provided an expiration date of August 1, 2003.

According to the plaintiffs' petition, on July 9, 2002, Dianne Alexander was attacked in her home in St. Martin Parish. Ms. Alexander's son, Herman Alexander, arrived home during the attack and chased the attacker from the property. Ms. Alexander reported the attack to local police and, later, both Ms. Alexander and her son described the attacker to the St. Martin Sheriff's Department.

According to his investigative report, Lieutenant Boyd, the lead investigator on Ms. Alexander's

attack, began to suspect that Ms. Alexander's attacker could be the same man identified as the South Louisiana Serial Killer, after investigators linked the death of a Lafayette woman to the suspected serial killer. In May 2003, Lieutenant Boyd shared information regarding Ms. Alexander's attack with the Lafayette Sheriff's Department, who in turn shared the information with the Task Force.

On May 22, 2003, Ms. Alexander was interviewed by an FBI agent assisting the Task Force. Based upon that interview, a composite sketch was drawn and released to the public on May 23, 2003. Investigators believed the composite sketch matched the description of a possible suspect in an investigation being handled by the Louisiana Attorney General's Office and the Zachary Police Department. On May 25, 2003, a photo lineup was prepared and presented to Ms. Alexander, who identified her attacker as the same man suspected in the Zachary investigation, Derrick Todd Lee.

On or about August 14, 2003, Ms. Alexander contacted LCS and sought to collect the advertised award; however, LCS informed her she was ineligible to receive the award. On February 22, 2006, Ms. Alexander and her son filed a lawsuit against BRCS and LCS, alleging that the defendants owed them $100,000 and $50,000, respectively,

for the information they provided to the defendants. The defendants filed motions for summary judgment asserting that a valid contract never existed between the parties. Specifically, the defendants argued that the plaintiffs never provided information to Crime Stoppers via the tipster hotline and thus did not comply with the "form, terms, or conditions required by the Crime Stoppers' offers[.]" The trial court granted the defendants' motions for summary judgment, finding that the offer from Crime Stoppers was conditioned on the information being provided to the defendant entities rather than law enforcement.

The plaintiffs appeal, asserting that there is a genuine issue of material fact that the LCS and BRCS offers contained a requirement that acceptance of the reward must be done through the Crime Stoppers' tipline.

* * * *

The offer made by LCS in a May 14, 2003 press release, reads [in part] as follows:

* * * *

In order to qualify for the reward, the tipster must provide information which leads to the arrest, DNA match, and the formal filing of charges against a suspect through grand jury indictment or Bill of Information. In addition, the qualifying tip must be received prior to midnight, August 1, 2003.

---

a. Under "2010," click on "February." When that page opens, select "February 3, 2010." When you reach the page for February 3, 2010, scroll down the list to the case title and click on the docket number (CA 09-00927) to access this opinion. The judicial branch of the Louisiana state government maintains this Web site.

EXTENDED CASE 11.3 CONTINUED ➡

The offer from BRCS, as published in the *Morning Advocate,* reads [in part] as follows:

> Crime Stoppers, Inc. $100,000 reward for information on the South Louisiana Serial Killer. A $100,000 reward will be given for information leading to the arrest and indictment of the South Louisiana Serial Killer.

Both LCS and BRCS offers were irrevocable offers because they specified a period of time for acceptance. Louisiana Civil Code Article 1934 provides that "acceptance of an irrevocable offer is effective when received by the offeror." *Acceptance is received when it comes into the possession of a person authorized by the offeror to receive it, or when it is deposited in a place the offeror has indicated as the place where communications of that kind are to be deposited for him.* [Emphasis added.]

The plaintiffs argue that there is a genuine issue of material fact as

to whether they accepted the Crime Stoppers' reward offers; however, the plaintiffs admit that they did not contact either Crime Stopper organization before August 1, 2003. The plaintiffs argue that they accepted the offers by performance when they provided information about the serial killer to law enforcement. Further, the plaintiffs contend that this performance is a customary manner of accepting reward offers from Crime Stopper organization[s].

In the present matter, the plaintiffs' acceptance of the reward offers must have been received by the defendants (offerors) by the time prescribed in the offer (August 1, 2003) in the place where communications of that kind were to be deposited (the phone number cited in the offers). The record contains no evidence indicating the defendants were notified by the plaintiffs in the time and manner indicated in the offer. While the plaintiffs may have provided information related to the arrest or indictment

of Derrick Todd Lee to local law enforcement and the Task Force, there is no indication in the offer that either of those parties were the offerors of the reward or persons authorized to receive acceptance on their behalf.

* * * [As to the plaintiffs' argument that providing information to law enforcement is a customary manner of accepting reward offers from Crime Stoppers,] [w]hile acceptance may be valid if customary in similar transactions, according to [Louisiana law], it must be "customary in similar transactions at the time and place the offer is *received.*" (Emphasis added [by the court].) As indicated above, there is no evidence in the record that the defendants received any acceptance of the offer. Accordingly, no contract was formed between the parties.

* * * *

For the foregoing reasons, the judgment granting the defendants' motions for summary judgment is affirmed.

 QUESTIONS

1. Suppose that the plaintiffs had learned about the reward offer after the killer had already been arrested and indicted due to their assistance but *before* the August 1, 2003, deadline. If they had then called in their information on the tip line, would they have been legally entitled to claim the reward in this circumstance? Explain.
2. The plaintiffs argued that "providing information to law enforcement is a customary manner of accepting reward offers from Crime Stoppers." How did the court respond to this argument?

Termination of the Offer

The communication of an effective offer to an offeree gives the offeree the power to transform the offer into a binding, legal obligation (a contract) by an acceptance. This power of acceptance does not continue forever, though. It can be terminated either by the action of the parties or by operation of law.

TERMINATION BY ACTION OF THE PARTIES An offer can be terminated by the action of the parties in any of three ways: by revocation, by rejection, or by counteroffer.

Revocation of the Offer by the Offeror. The offeror's act of withdrawing (revoking) an offer is

known as **revocation.** Unless an offer is irrevocable (discussed shortly), the offeror usually can revoke the offer (even if he or she has promised to keep it open) as long as the revocation is communicated to the offeree before the offeree accepts. Revocation may be accomplished by express repudiation of the offer (for example, with a statement such as "I withdraw my previous offer of October 17") or by performance of acts that are inconsistent with the existence of the offer and are made known to the offeree (for example, selling the offered property to another person in the presence of the offeree).

The general rule followed by most states is that a revocation becomes effective when the offeree or the offeree's *agent* (a person acting on behalf of the offeree) actually receives it. Therefore, a letter of revocation mailed on April 1 and delivered at the offeree's residence or place of business on April 3 becomes effective on April 3.

An offer made to the general public can be revoked in the same manner that the offer was originally communicated. Suppose that an electronics retailer offers a $10,000 reward to anyone providing information leading to the apprehension of the persons who burglarized the store's downtown branch. The offer is published in three local papers and four papers in neighboring communities. To revoke the offer, the retailer must publish the revocation in all seven of the papers in which it published the offer. The revocation is then accessible to the general public, even if some particular offeree does not know about it.

Irrevocable Offers. Although most offers are revocable, some can be made irrevocable—that is, they cannot be revoked. Increasingly, courts refuse to allow an offeror to revoke an offer when the offeree has changed position because of justifiable reliance on the offer (under the doctrine of *detrimental reliance,* or *promissory estoppel,* which will be discussed in Chapter 12). In some circumstances, "firm offers" made by merchants may also be considered irrevocable—see the discussion of the "merchant's firm offer" in Chapter 19.

Another form of irrevocable offer is an option contract. An **option contract** is created when an offeror promises to hold an offer open for a specified period of time in return for a payment (consideration) given by the offeree. An option contract takes away the offeror's power to revoke the offer for the period of time specified in the option.

Option contracts are also frequently used in conjunction with the sale or lease of real estate. For example, Tyrell agrees to lease a house from Jackson, the property owner. Included in the lease contract is a clause stating that Tyrell is paying an additional $15,000 for an option to purchase the property within a specified period of time. If Tyrell decides not to purchase the house after the specified period has lapsed, he loses the $15,000, and Jackson is free to sell the property to another buyer.

Rejection of the Offer by the Offeree. If the offeree rejects the offer—by words or by conduct—the offer is terminated. Any subsequent attempt by the offeree to accept will be construed as a new offer, giving the original offeror (now the offeree) the power of acceptance. As with a revocation, a rejection of an offer is effective only when it is actually received by the offeror or the offeror's agent.

Merely inquiring about an offer does not constitute rejection. Suppose that Raymond offers to buy Francie's PlayStation 3 with the stereoscopic 3D update for $300, and Francie responds, "Is that your best offer?" or "Will you pay me $375 for it?" A reasonable person would conclude that Francie did not reject the offer but simply made an inquiry for further consideration of the offer. She can still accept and bind Raymond to the $300 purchase price. When the offeree merely inquires as to the firmness of the offer, there is no reason to presume that he or she intends to reject it.

Counteroffer by the Offeree. A **counteroffer** is a rejection of the original offer and the simultaneous making of a new offer. Suppose that Burke offers to sell his home to Lang for $270,000. Lang responds, "Your price is too high. I'll offer to purchase your house for $250,000." Lang's response is called a counteroffer because it rejects Burke's offer to sell at $270,000 and creates a new offer by Lang to purchase the home at a price of $250,000.

At common law, the **mirror image rule** requires the offeree's acceptance to match the offeror's offer exactly—to mirror the offer. Any change in, or addition to, the terms of the original offer automatically terminates that offer and substitutes the counteroffer. The counteroffer, of course, need not be accepted; but if the original offeror does accept the terms of the counteroffer, a valid contract is created.[9]

TERMINATION BY OPERATION OF LAW The power of the offeree to transform the offer into a binding, legal obligation can be terminated by operation of law through the occurrence of any of the following events:

1. Lapse of time.
2. Destruction of the specific subject matter of the offer.
3. Death or incompetence of the offeror or the offeree.
4. Supervening illegality of the proposed contract.

Lapse of Time. If the offer states that it will be left open until a particular date, then the offer will terminate at midnight on that day. If the offer states

---

9. The mirror image rule has been greatly modified in regard to sales contracts. Section 2–207 of the UCC provides that a contract is formed if the offeree makes a definite expression of acceptance (such as signing the form in the appropriate location), even though the terms of the acceptance modify or add to the terms of the original offer (see Chapter 19).

that it will be left open for a number of days, such as ten days, this time period normally begins to run when the offer is actually received by the offeree, not when it is formed or sent. When the offer is delayed (through the misdelivery of mail, for example), the period begins to run from the date the offeree would have received the offer, but only if the offeree knows or should know that the offer is delayed.[10]

If the offer does not specify a time for acceptance, the offer terminates at the end of a *reasonable* period of time. What constitutes a reasonable period of time depends on the subject matter of the contract, business and market conditions, and other relevant circumstances. An offer to sell farm produce, for example, will terminate sooner than an offer to sell farm equipment because farm produce is perishable and subject to greater fluctuations in market value.

Destruction of the Subject Matter. An offer is automatically terminated if the specific subject matter of the offer is destroyed before the offer is accepted.[11] If Johnson offers to sell his prize greyhound to Rizzo, for example, but the dog dies before Rizzo can accept, the offer is automatically terminated. Johnson does not have to tell Rizzo that the animal has died for the offer to terminate.

Death or Incompetence of the Offeror or Offeree. An offeree's power of acceptance is terminated when the offeror or offeree dies or is deprived of legal capacity to enter into the proposed contract, *unless the offer is irrevocable*. A revocable offer is personal to both parties and cannot pass to the heirs, guardian, or estate of either. This rule applies whether or not the other party had notice of the death or incompetence.

Supervening Illegality of the Proposed Contract. A statute or court decision that makes an offer illegal automatically terminates the offer.[12] For example, Lee offers to lend Kim $10,000 at an annual interest rate of 15 percent. Before Kim can accept the offer, a law is enacted that prohibits interest rates higher than 12 percent. Lee's offer is automatically terminated. (If the statute is enacted after Kim accepts the offer, a valid contract is formed, but the contract may still be unenforceable—see Chapter 13.)

Concept Summary 11.1 provides a review of the ways in which an offer can be terminated.

---

10. *Restatement (Second) of Contracts,* Section 49.
11. *Restatement (Second) of Contracts,* Section 36.

12. *Restatement (Second) of Contracts,* Section 36.

CONCEPT SUMMARY 11.1
Methods by Which an Offer Can Be Terminated

By Action of the Parties—

1. *Revocation*—Unless the offer is irrevocable, it can be revoked at any time before acceptance without liability. Revocation is not effective until received by the offeree or the offeree's agent. Some offers, such as a merchant's firm offer and option contracts, are irrevocable. Also, in some situations, an offeree's detrimental reliance or partial performance will cause a court to rule that the offeror cannot revoke the offer.
2. *Rejection*—Accomplished by words or actions that demonstrate a clear intent not to accept the offer; not effective until received by the offeror or the offeror's agent.
3. *Counteroffer*—A rejection of the original offer and the making of a new offer.

By Operation of Law—

1. *Lapse of time*—The offer terminates at the end of the time period specified in the offer or, if no time period is stated in the offer, at the end of a reasonable time period.
2. *Destruction of the subject matter*—When the specific subject matter of the offer is destroyed before the offer is accepted, the offer automatically terminates.
3. *Death or incompetence of the offeror or offeree*—If the offeror or offeree dies or becomes incompetent, this offer terminates (unless the offer is irrevocable).
4. *Supervening illegality*—When a statute or court decision makes the proposed contract illegal, the offer automatically terminates.

Acceptance

Acceptance is a voluntary act by the offeree that shows assent (agreement) to the terms of an offer. The offeree's act may consist of words or conduct. The acceptance must be unequivocal and must be communicated to the offeror.

UNEQUIVOCAL ACCEPTANCE To exercise the power of acceptance effectively, the offeree must accept unequivocally. This is the *mirror image rule* previously discussed. If the acceptance is subject to new conditions or if the terms of the acceptance change the original offer, the acceptance may be deemed a counteroffer that implicitly rejects the original offer.

An acceptance may be unequivocal even though the offeree expresses dissatisfaction with the contract. For example, "I accept the offer, but I wish I could have gotten a better price" is an effective acceptance. So, too, is "I accept, but can you shave the price?" In contrast, the statement "I accept the offer but only if I can pay on ninety days' credit" is not an unequivocal acceptance and operates as a counteroffer, rejecting the original offer.

Certain terms, when included in an acceptance, will not change the offer sufficiently to constitute rejection. Suppose that in response to an art dealer's offer to sell a painting, the offeree, Ashton Gibbs, replies, "I accept; please send a written contract." Gibbs is requesting a written contract but is not making it a condition for acceptance. Therefore, the acceptance is effective without the written contract. In contrast, if Gibbs replies, "I accept *if* you send a written contract," the acceptance is expressly conditioned on the request for a writing, and the statement is not an acceptance but a counteroffer. (Notice how important each word is!)[13]

SILENCE AS ACCEPTANCE Ordinarily, silence cannot constitute acceptance, even if the offeror states, "By your silence and inaction, you will be deemed to have accepted this offer." This general rule applies because an offeree should not be obligated to act affirmatively to reject an offer when no consideration has passed to the offeree to impose such a duty.

In some instances, however, the offeree does have a duty to speak. In these situations, her or his silence or inaction will operate as an acceptance.

Silence may be an acceptance when an offeree takes the benefit of offered services even though he or she had an opportunity to reject them and knew that they were offered with the expectation of compensation. For example, John is a student who earns extra income by washing store windows. John taps on the window of a store, catches the attention of the store's manager, and points to the window and raises his cleaner, signaling that he will be washing the window. The manager does nothing to stop him. Here, the store manager's silence constitutes an acceptance, and an implied contract is created. The store is bound to pay a reasonable value for John's work.

Silence can also operate as acceptance when the offeree has had prior dealings with the offeror. Suppose that a business routinely receives shipments from a certain supplier and always notifies that supplier when defective goods are rejected. In this situation, silence regarding a shipment will constitute acceptance.

COMMUNICATION OF ACCEPTANCE In a bilateral contract, communication of acceptance is necessary because acceptance is in the form of a promise (not performance), and the contract is formed when the promise is made (rather than when the act is performed). Communication of acceptance is not necessary if the offer dispenses with the requirement, however, or if the offer can be accepted by silence.

Because a unilateral contract calls for the full performance of some act, acceptance is usually evident, and notification is therefore unnecessary. Nevertheless, exceptions do exist, such as when the offeror requests notice of acceptance or has no way of determining whether the requested act has been performed.

MODE AND TIMELINESS OF ACCEPTANCE In bilateral contracts, acceptance must be timely. The general rule is that acceptance in a bilateral contract is timely if it is made before the offer is terminated. Problems may arise, though, when the parties involved are not dealing face to face. In such situations, the offeree should use an authorized mode of communication.

The Mailbox Rule. Acceptance takes effect, thus completing formation of the contract, at the time the offeree sends or delivers the communication via the mode expressly or impliedly authorized by the offeror. This is the so-called **mailbox rule,** which the majority of courts follow. Under this rule, if the

---

13. As noted in Footnote 9, in regard to sales contracts, the UCC provides that an acceptance may still be valid even if some terms are added. The new terms are simply treated as proposed additions to the contract.

authorized mode of communication is the mail, then an acceptance becomes valid when it is dispatched (placed in the control of the U.S. Postal Service)—*not* when it is received by the offeror. (Note, however, that if the offer stipulates when acceptance will be effective, then the offer will not be effective until the time specified.)

The mailbox rule does not apply to instantaneous forms of communication, such as when the parties are dealing face to face, by telephone, or by fax. There is still some uncertainty in the courts as to whether e-mail should be considered an instantaneous form of communication to which the mailbox rule does not apply. If the parties have agreed to conduct transactions electronically and if the Uniform Electronic Transactions Act (UETA—discussed later in this chapter) applies, then e-mail is considered sent when it either leaves the control of the sender or is received by the recipient. This rule takes the place of the mailbox rule when the UETA applies but essentially allows an e-mail acceptance to become effective when sent (as it would if sent by U.S. mail).

Authorized Means of Acceptance. A means of communicating acceptance can be expressly authorized by the offeror or impliedly authorized by the facts and circumstances surrounding the situation or by law.[14] An acceptance sent by means not expressly or impliedly authorized normally is not effective until it is received by the offeror.

When an offeror specifies how acceptance should be made (for example, by overnight delivery), *express authorization* is said to exist, and the contract is not formed unless the offeree uses that specified mode of acceptance. Moreover, both offeror and offeree are bound in contract the moment this means of acceptance is employed. For example, Shaylee & Perkins, a Massachusetts firm, offers to sell a container of antique furniture to Leaham's Antiques in Colorado. The offer states that Leaham's must accept the offer via FedEx overnight delivery. The acceptance is effective (and a binding contract is formed) the moment that Leaham's gives the overnight envelope containing the acceptance to the FedEx driver.

If the offeror does not expressly authorize a certain mode of acceptance, then acceptance can be made by *any reasonable means*.[15] Courts look at the

---

14. *Restatement (Second) of Contracts,* Section 30, provides that an offer invites acceptance "by any medium reasonable in the circumstances," unless the offer is specific about the means of acceptance.
15. *Restatement (Second) of Contracts,* Section 30. This is also the rule under UCC 2–206(1)(a).

prevailing business usages and the surrounding circumstances to determine whether the mode of acceptance used was reasonable. Usually, the offeror's choice of a particular means in making the offer implies that the offeree can use the *same* or a *faster* means for acceptance. Thus, if the offer is made via priority mail, it would be reasonable to accept the offer via priority mail or by a faster method, such as by fax or FedEx.

Substitute Method of Acceptance. If the offeror authorizes a particular method of acceptance, but the offeree accepts by a different means, the acceptance may still be effective if the substituted method serves the same purpose as the authorized means. The acceptance is not effective on dispatch, though, and no contract will be formed until the acceptance is received by the offeror. For example, an offer specifies acceptance by FedEx overnight delivery, but the offeree instead accepts by UPS overnight delivery. The substitute method of acceptance will still be effective, but the contract will not be formed until the offeror receives the UPS delivery (rather than the day before, when the letter was given to the carrier).

SECTION 2
AGREEMENT IN E-CONTRACTS

As previously noted, numerous contracts are formed online. Electronic contracts, or **e-contracts,** must meet the same basic requirements (agreement, consideration, contractual capacity, and legality) as paper contracts. Disputes concerning e-contracts, however, tend to center on contract terms and whether the parties voluntarily agreed to those terms.

Online contracts may be formed not only for the sale of goods and services but also for *licensing.* The "sale" of software generally involves a license, or a right to use the software, rather than the passage of title (ownership rights) from the seller to the buyer. For example, Galynn wants to obtain software that will allow her to work on spreadsheets on her BlackBerry. She goes online and purchases GridMagic. During the transaction, she has to click on several on-screen "I agree" boxes to indicate that she understands that she is purchasing only the right to use the software and will not obtain any ownership rights. After she agrees to these terms (the licensing agreement), she can download the software.

As you read through the following subsections, keep in mind that although we typically refer to the offeror and the offeree as a *seller* and a *buyer,* in many online transactions these parties would be more accurately described as a *licensor* and a *licensee.*

Online Offers

Sellers doing business via the Internet can protect themselves against contract disputes and legal liability by creating offers that clearly spell out the terms that will govern their transactions if the offers are accepted. All important terms should be conspicuous and easy to view.

DISPLAYING THE OFFER The seller's Web site should include a hypertext link to a page containing the full contract so that potential buyers are made aware of the terms to which they are assenting. The contract generally must be displayed online in a readable format, such as a twelve-point typeface. All provisions should be reasonably clear. Suppose that Netquip sells a variety of heavy equipment, such as trucks and trailers, on its Web site. Because Netquip's pricing schedule is very complex, the schedule must be fully provided and explained on the Web site. In addition, the terms of the sale (such as any warranties and the refund policy) must be fully disclosed.

PROVISIONS TO INCLUDE An important rule to keep in mind is that the offeror (the seller) controls the offer and thus the resulting contract. The seller should therefore anticipate the terms he or she wants to include in a contract and provide for them in the offer. In some instances, a standardized contract form may suffice. At a minimum, an online offer should include the following provisions:

1. *Acceptance of terms.* A clause that clearly indicates what constitutes the buyer's agreement to the terms of the offer, such as a box containing the words "I accept" that the buyer can click. (Mechanisms for accepting online offers will be discussed in detail later in the chapter.)
2. *Payment.* A provision specifying how payment for the goods (including any applicable taxes) must be made.
3. *Return policy.* A statement of the seller's refund and return policies.
4. *Disclaimer.* Disclaimers of liability for certain uses of the goods. For example, an online seller of business forms may add a disclaimer that the seller does not accept responsibility for the buyer's reliance on the forms rather than on an attorney's advice.

5. *Limitation on remedies.* A provision specifying the remedies available to the buyer if the goods are found to be defective or if the contract is otherwise breached. Any limitation of remedies should be clearly spelled out.
6. *Privacy policy.* A statement indicating how the seller will use the information gathered about the buyer.
7. *Dispute resolution.* Provisions relating to dispute settlement, such as an arbitration clause or a forum-selection clause (discussed next).

DISPUTE-SETTLEMENT PROVISIONS Online offers frequently include provisions relating to dispute settlement. For example, the offer might include an arbitration clause specifying that any dispute arising under the contract will be arbitrated in a designated forum.

Many online contracts contain a **forum-selection clause** indicating the forum, or location (such as a court or jurisdiction), in which contract disputes will be resolved. As discussed in Chapter 2, significant jurisdictional issues may arise when parties are at a great distance, as they often are when they form contracts via the Internet. A forum-selection clause will help to avert future jurisdictional problems and also help to ensure that the seller will not be required to appear in court in a distant state.

CASE IN POINT Before advertisers can place ads through Google, Inc., they must agree to certain terms that are displayed in an online window. These terms include a forum-selection clause, which provides that any dispute is to be "adjudicated in Santa Clara County, California." Lawrence Feldman, who advertised through Google, complained that he was overcharged and filed a lawsuit against Google in a federal district court in Pennsylvania. The court held that Feldman had agreed to the forum-selection clause in Google's online contract and transferred the case to a court in Santa Clara County.[16]

Some online contracts might also include a *choice-of-law clause* in which the parties specify that any dispute arising out of the contract will be settled in accordance with the law of a particular jurisdiction, such as a state or country. As will be discussed in Chapter 23, choice-of-law clauses are particularly common in international contracts, but they may also appear in e-contracts to specify which state's laws will govern in the United States.

---

16. *Feldman v. Google, Inc.,* 513 F.Supp.2d 229 (E.D.Pa. 2007).

Online Acceptances

The *Restatement (Second) of Contracts*, which, as noted earlier, is a compilation of common law contract principles, states that parties may agree to a contract "by written or spoken words or by other action or by failure to act."[17] The Uniform Commercial Code (UCC), which governs sales contracts, has a similar provision. Section 2–204 of the UCC states that any contract for the sale of goods "may be made in any manner sufficient to show agreement, including conduct by both parties which recognizes the existence of such a contract."

CLICK-ON AGREEMENTS The courts have used the *Restatement* and UCC provisions to conclude that a binding contract can be created by conduct, including the act of clicking on a box indicating "I accept" or "I agree" to accept an online offer. The agreement resulting from such an acceptance is often called a **click-on agreement** (sometimes referred to as a *click-on license* or *click-wrap agreement*). Exhibit 11–1 shows a portion of a typical click-on agreement that accompanies a software package.

Generally, the law does not require that the parties have read all of the terms in a contract for it to be effective. Therefore, clicking on a box that states "I agree" to certain terms can be enough. The terms may be contained on a Web site through which the buyer is obtaining goods or services, or they may appear on a computer screen when software is loaded from a CD-ROM or DVD or downloaded from the Internet.

SHRINK-WRAP AGREEMENTS With a **shrink-wrap agreement** (or *shrink-wrap license*), the terms are expressed inside the box in which the goods are packaged. (The term *shrink-wrap* refers to the plastic that covers the box.) Usually, the party who opens the box is told that she or he agrees to the terms by keeping whatever is in the box. Similarly, when a purchaser opens a software package, he or she agrees to abide by the terms of the limited license agreement. In most instances, a shrink-wrap agreement is not between a retailer and a buyer, but between the manufacturer of the hardware or software and the ultimate buyer-user of the product. The terms generally concern warranties, remedies, and other issues associated with the use of the product.

---

17. *Restatement (Second) of Contracts*, Section 19.

EXHIBIT 11–1 • A Click-On Agreement Sample

This exhibit illustrates an online offer to form a contract. To accept the offer, the user simply clicks on the "I Accept" button.

Shrink-Wrap Agreements and Enforceable Contract Terms. In some cases, the courts have enforced the terms of shrink-wrap agreements in the same way as the terms of other contracts. These courts have reasoned that by including the terms with the product, the seller proposed a contract. The buyer could accept this contract by using the product after having an opportunity to read the terms. Thus, a buyer's failure to object to terms contained within a shrink-wrapped software package may constitute an acceptance of the terms by conduct. Also, it seems practical from a business's point of view to enclose a full statement of the legal terms of a sale with the product rather than to read the statement over the phone, for example, when a buyer calls to order the product.

Shrink-Wrap Terms That May Not Be Enforced. Nevertheless, the courts have sometimes refused to enforce certain terms included in shrink-wrap agreements because the buyers did not expressly consent to them. One factor that courts consider important is whether the parties form their contract before or after the seller communicates the terms of the shrink-wrap agreement to the buyer. If a buyer orders a product over the telephone, for instance, and is not informed of an arbitration clause or forum-selection clause at that time, the buyer clearly has not expressly agreed to these terms. If the buyer discovers the clauses *after* the parties entered into their contract, a court may conclude that those terms were proposals for additional terms and were not part of the contract.

BROWSE-WRAP TERMS Like the terms of click-on agreements, **browse-wrap terms** can occur in transactions conducted over the Internet. Unlike click-on agreements, however, browse-wrap terms do not require Internet users to assent to the terms before, say, downloading or using certain software. In other words, a person can install the software without clicking "I agree" to the terms of a license. Browse-wrap terms are often unenforceable because they do not satisfy the agreement requirement of contract formation.[18]

CASE IN POINT Netscape Communications Corporation provided free downloadable software called "SmartDownload" on its Web site to those who indicated, by clicking on a designated box, that they wished to obtain it. On the Web site's download page was a reference to a license agreement that the user could view only by scrolling to the next screen. In other words, the user did not have to agree to the terms of the license before downloading the software. One of the terms required all disputes to be submitted to arbitration in California. When a group of users filed a lawsuit against Netscape in New York, the court held that the arbitration clause in the browse-wrap license agreement was unenforceable because users were not required to indicate their assent to the agreement.[19]

E-Signature Technologies

Today, numerous technologies allow electronic documents to be signed. An **e-signature** has been defined as "an electronic sound, symbol, or process attached to or logically associated with a record and executed or adopted by a person with the intent to sign the record."[20] Thus, e-signatures include encrypted digital signatures, names (intended as signatures) at the ends of e-mail messages, and clicks on a Web page (if the clicks include some means of identification). The technologies for creating e-signatures generally fall into one of two categories, *digitized handwritten signatures* and *public-key-infrastructure–based digital signatures*.

A digitized signature is a graphical image of a handwritten signature. Often, a person creates such a signature using a digital pen and pad, such as an ePad, and special software. For security reasons, the strokes of a person's signature can be measured by software to authenticate the identity of the person signing (this is referred to as *signature dynamics*).

In a public-key infrastructure (such as an asymmetric cryptosystem), two mathematically linked but different keys are generated—a private signing key and a public validation key. A digital signature is created when the signer uses the private key to create a unique mark on an electronic document. The appropriate software enables the recipient of the document to use the public key to verify the identity of the signer. A **cybernotary**, or legally recognized certification authority, issues the key pair, identifies the owner of the keys, and certifies the validity of the public key. The cybernotary also serves as a repository for public keys.

State Laws Governing E-Signatures

Most states have laws governing e-signatures. The problem is that state e-signature laws are not uniform. Some states—California is a notable example—prohibit many types of documents from being signed with e-signatures, whereas other states are more permissive. Some states recognize only digital signatures as valid, while others permit additional types of e-signatures.

In an attempt to create more uniformity among the states, in 1999 the National Conference of Commissioners on Uniform State Laws and the American Law Institute promulgated the Uniform Electronic Transactions Act (UETA). To date, the UETA has been adopted, at least in part, by forty-eight states. Among other things, the UETA declares that a signature may not be denied legal effect or enforceability solely because it is in electronic form. (The provisions of the UETA will be discussed in more detail shortly.)

Federal Law on E-Signatures and E-Documents

In 2000, Congress enacted the Electronic Signatures in Global and National Commerce Act (E-SIGN Act),[21] which provides that no contract, record, or signature may be "denied legal effect" solely because it is in electronic form. In other words, under this law, an electronic signature is as valid as a signature on paper, and an e-document can be as enforceable as a paper one.

For an e-signature to be enforceable, the contracting parties must have agreed to use electronic signatures. For an electronic document to be valid, it must be in a form that can be retained and accurately reproduced.

---

18. See, for example, *Jesmer v. Retail Magic, Inc.*, 863 N.Y.S.2d 737 (2008).

19. *Specht v. Netscape Communications Corp.*, 306 F.3d 17 (2d Cir. 2002).

20. This definition is from the Uniform Electronic Transactions Act, which will be discussed later in this chapter.

21. 15 U.S.C. Sections 7001 *et seq.*

The E-SIGN Act does not apply to all types of documents. Contracts and documents that are exempt include court papers, divorce decrees, evictions, foreclosures, health-insurance terminations, prenuptial agreements, and wills. Also, the only agreements governed by the UCC that fall under this law are those covered by Articles 2 and 2A (sales and lease contracts) and UCC 1–107 and 1–206. Despite these limitations, the E-SIGN Act significantly expanded the possibilities for contracting online.

Partnering Agreements

One way that online sellers and buyers can prevent disputes over signatures in their e-contracts, as well as disputes over the terms and conditions of those contracts, is to form partnering agreements. In a **partnering agreement,** a seller and a buyer who frequently do business with each other agree in advance on the terms and conditions that will apply to all transactions subsequently conducted electronically. The partnering agreement can also establish special access and identification codes to be used by the parties when transacting business electronically.

A partnering agreement reduces the likelihood that disputes will arise under the contract, because the buyer and the seller have agreed in advance to the terms and conditions that will accompany each sale. Furthermore, if a dispute does arise, a court or arbitration forum will be able to refer to the partnering agreement when determining the parties' intent.

SECTION 3
THE UNIFORM ELECTRONIC TRANSACTIONS ACT

As noted earlier, the Uniform Electronic Transactions Act (UETA) was set forth in 1999. It represents one of the first comprehensive efforts to create uniform laws pertaining to e-commerce.

The primary purpose of the UETA is to remove barriers to e-commerce by giving the same legal effect to electronic records and signatures as is currently given to paper documents and signatures. As mentioned earlier, the UETA broadly defines an *e-signature* as "an electronic sound, symbol, or process attached to or logically associated with a record and executed or adopted by a person with the intent to sign the record."[22] A **record** is "information that is inscribed on a tangible medium or that is stored

in an electronic or other medium and is retrievable in perceivable [visual] form."[23]

The Scope and Applicability of the UETA

The UETA does not create new rules for electronic contracts but rather establishes that records, signatures, and contracts may not be denied enforceability solely due to their electronic form. The UETA does not apply to all writings and signatures. It covers only electronic records and electronic signatures *relating to a transaction*. A *transaction* is defined as an interaction between two or more people relating to business, commercial, or governmental activities.[24]

The act specifically does not apply to wills or testamentary trusts (see Chapter 52) or to transactions governed by the UCC (other than those covered by Articles 2 and 2A).[25] In addition, the provisions of the UETA allow the states to exclude its application to other areas of law.

The UETA does not apply to a transaction unless each of the parties has previously agreed to conduct transactions by electronic means. The agreement need not be explicit, however; it can be implied by the conduct of the parties and the surrounding circumstances.[26] For example, a party's agreement can be inferred from a letter or other writing or from some verbal communication. Furthermore, a person who has previously agreed to an electronic transaction can also withdraw his or her consent and refuse to conduct further business electronically. The parties can also agree to opt-out of all or some of the terms of the UETA, but if they do not, then the UETA terms will govern their electronic transactions.

The Federal E-SIGN Act and the UETA

As described earlier, Congress passed the E-SIGN Act in 2000, a year after the UETA was presented to the states for adoption. Thus, a significant issue was to what extent the federal E-SIGN Act preempted the UETA as adopted by the states.

The E-SIGN Act[27] refers explicitly to the UETA and provides that if a state has enacted the uniform version of the UETA, it is not preempted by the E-SIGN Act. In other words, if the state has enacted the UETA without modification, state law will govern.

---

22. UETA 102(8).

23. UETA 102(15).
24. UETA 2(12) and 3.
25. UETA 3(b).
26. UETA 5(b), and Comment 4B.
27. 15 U.S.C. Section 7002(2)(A)(i).

The problem is that many states have enacted non-uniform (modified) versions of the UETA, largely for the purpose of excluding other areas of state law from the UETA's terms. The E-SIGN Act specifies that those exclusions will be preempted to the extent that they are inconsistent with the E-SIGN Act's provisions.

The E-SIGN Act explicitly allows the states to enact alternative requirements for the use of electronic records or electronic signatures. Generally, however, the requirements must be consistent with the provisions of the E-SIGN Act, and the state must not give greater legal status or effect to one specific type of technology. Additionally, if a state enacts alternative requirements *after* the E-SIGN Act was adopted, the state law must specifically refer to the E-SIGN Act. The relationship between the UETA and the E-SIGN Act is illustrated in Exhibit 11–2.

Attributing Electronic Signatures

Under the UETA, if an electronic record or signature is the act of a particular person, the record or signature may be attributed to that person. If a person typed her or his name at the bottom of an e-mail purchase order, that name would qualify as a "signature" and be attributed to the person whose name appeared. Just as in paper contracts, one may use any relevant evidence to prove that the record or signature is or is not the act of the person.[28]

---

28. UETA 9.

If any issues arise relating to agency, authority, forgery, or contract formation, the UETA provides that other state laws control. Also, if state laws require a document to be notarized, the UETA allows the electronic signature of a notary public to fulfill this requirement.

The Effect of Errors

The UETA encourages, but does not require, the use of security procedures (such as encryption) to verify changes to electronic documents and to correct errors. If the parties have agreed to a security procedure and one party does not detect an error because he or she did not follow the procedure, the conforming party can legally avoid the effect of the change or error. If the parties have not agreed to use a security procedure, then other state laws (including contract law governing mistakes—see Chapter 14) will determine the effect of the error on the parties' agreement.

To avoid the effect of errors, a party must promptly notify the other party of the error and of her or his intent not to be bound by the error. In addition, the party must take reasonable steps to return any benefit received: parties cannot avoid a transaction if they have benefited.

Timing

Section 15 of the UETA sets forth provisions relating to the sending and receiving of electronic records. These provisions apply unless the parties agree to different terms. Under Section 15, an electronic record

EXHIBIT 11–2 • The E-SIGN Act and the UETA

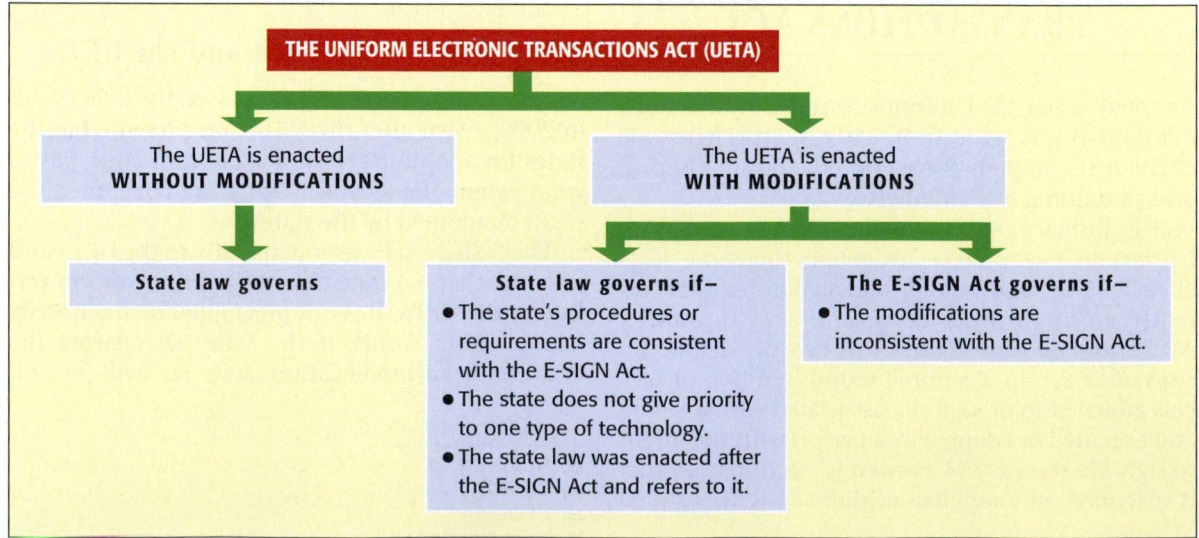

is considered *sent* when it is properly directed to the intended recipient in a form readable by the recipient's computer system. Once the electronic record leaves the control of the sender or comes under the control of the recipient, the UETA deems it to have been sent. An electronic record is considered *received* when it enters the recipient's processing system in a readable form—*even if no individual is aware of its receipt.*

Additionally, the UETA provides that, unless otherwise agreed, an electronic record is to be sent from or received at the party's principal place of business. If a party has no place of business, the provision authorizes the place of sending or receipt to be the party's residence. If a party has multiple places of business, the record should be sent from or received at the location that has the closest relationship to the underlying transaction.

SECTION 4
INTERNATIONAL TREATIES AFFECTING E-CONTRACTS

Today, much of the e-commerce conducted on a worldwide basis involves buyers and sellers from the United States. The preeminence of U.S. law in this area is likely to be challenged in the future, however, as Internet use continues to expand worldwide. Already, several international organizations have created their own regulations for global Internet transactions.

For example, the United Nations Convention on the Use of Electronic Communications in International Contracts was completed in 2005. A major goal of this convention is to improve commercial certainty by determining an Internet user's location for legal purposes. The convention also establishes standards for creating functional equivalence between electronic communications and paper documents. The convention also provides that e-signatures will be treated as the equivalent of signatures on paper documents.

Another treaty relevant to e-contracts is the Hague Convention on the Choice of Court Agreements. Although this convention does not specifically address e-commerce and applies only to business-to-business transactions, not business-to-consumer transactions, it will provide more certainty regarding jurisdiction and recognition of judgments by other nations' courts. Such matters are important to both offline and online transactions, so the convention should enhance e-commerce as well as other forms of international trade.

REVIEWING
Agreement in Traditional and E-Contracts

Shane Durbin wanted to have a recording studio custom-built in his home. He sent invitations to a number of local contractors to submit bids on the project. Rory Amstel submitted the lowest bid, which was $20,000 less than any of the other bids Durbin received. Durbin called Amstel to ascertain the type and quality of the materials that were included in the bid and to find out if he could substitute a superior brand of acoustic tiles for the same bid price. Amstel said he would have to check into the price difference. The parties also discussed a possible start date for construction. Two weeks later, Durbin changed his mind and decided not to go forward with his plan to build a recording studio. Amstel filed a suit against Durbin for breach of contract. Using the information presented in the chapter, answer the following questions.

1. Did Amstel's bid meet the requirements of an offer? Explain.
2. Was there an acceptance of the offer? Why or why not?
3. Suppose that the court determines that the parties did not reach an agreement. Further suppose that Amstel, in anticipation of building Durbin's studio, had purchased materials and refused other jobs so that he would have time in his schedule for Durbin's project. Under what theory discussed in the chapter might Amstel attempt to recover these costs?
4. How is an offer terminated? Assuming that Durbin did not inform Amstel that he was rejecting the offer, was the offer terminated at any time described here? Explain.

DEBATE THIS: *The terms and conditions in click-on agreements are so long and detailed that no one ever reads the agreement. Therefore, the act of clicking on "Yes, I agree" is not really an acceptance.*

TERMS AND CONCEPTS

acceptance 232

agreement 222

browse-wrap terms 235

click-on agreement 235

counteroffer 230

cybernotary 236

e-contract 233

e-signature 236

forum-selection clause 234

mailbox rule 232

mirror image rule 230

offer 222

option contract 230

partnering agreement 237

record 237

revocation 229

shrink-wrap agreement 235

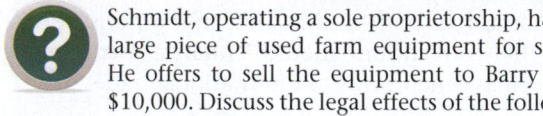

QUESTIONS AND CASE PROBLEMS

11–1. Agreement Ball writes to Sullivan and inquires how much Sullivan is asking for a specific forty-acre tract of land Sullivan owns. In a letter received by Ball, Sullivan states, "I will not take less than $60,000 for the forty-acre tract as specified." Ball immediately sends Sullivan a fax stating, "I accept your offer for $60,000 for the forty-acre tract as specified." Discuss whether Ball can hold Sullivan to a contract for the sale of the land.

11–2. QUESTION WITH SAMPLE ANSWER: Offer and Acceptance.

Schmidt, operating a sole proprietorship, has a large piece of used farm equipment for sale. He offers to sell the equipment to Barry for $10,000. Discuss the legal effects of the following events on the offer:

(a) Schmidt dies prior to Barry's acceptance, and at the time he accepts, Barry is unaware of Schmidt's death.

(b) The night before Barry accepts, fire destroys the equipment.

(c) Barry pays $100 for a thirty-day option to purchase the equipment. During this period, Schmidt dies, and later Barry accepts the offer, knowing of Schmidt's death.

(d) Barry pays $100 for a thirty-day option to purchase the equipment. During this period, Barry dies, and Barry's estate accepts Schmidt's offer within the stipulated time period.

- **For a sample answer to Question 11–2, go to Appendix I at the end of this text.**

11–3. Online Acceptance Anne is a reporter for *Daily Business Journal*, a print publication consulted by investors and other businesspersons. She often uses the Internet to perform research for the articles that she writes for the publication. While visiting the Web site of Cyberspace Investments Corp., Anne reads a pop-up window that states, "Our business newsletter, *E-Commerce Weekly*, is available at a one-year subscription rate of $5 per issue. To subscribe, enter your e-mail address below and click 'SUBSCRIBE.' By subscribing, you agree to the terms of the subscriber's agreement. To read this agreement, click 'AGREEMENT.'" Anne enters her e-mail address, but does not click on "AGREEMENT" to read the terms. Has Anne entered into an enforceable contract to pay for *E-Commerce Weekly*? Explain.

11–4. Revocation On Thursday, Dennis mailed a letter to Tanya's office offering to sell his car to her for $3,000. On Saturday, having changed his mind, Dennis sent a fax to Tanya's office revoking his offer. Tanya did not go to her office over the weekend and thus did not learn about the revocation until Monday morning, just a few minutes after she had mailed a letter of acceptance to Dennis. When Tanya demanded that Dennis sell his car to her as promised, Dennis claimed that no contract existed because he had revoked his offer prior to Tanya's acceptance. Is Dennis correct? Explain.

11–5. CASE PROBLEM WITH SAMPLE ANSWER: Offer.

In August 2000, in California, Terry Reigelsperger sought treatment for pain in his lower back from chiropractor James Siller. Reigelsperger felt better after the treatment and did not intend to return for more, although he did not mention this to Siller. Before leaving the office, Reigelsperger signed an "informed consent" form that read, in part, "I intend this consent form to cover the entire course of treatment for my present condition and for any future condition(s) for which I seek treatment." He also signed an agreement that required the parties to submit to arbitration "any dispute as to medical malpractice. . . . This agreement is intended to bind the patient and the health care provider . . . who now or in the future treat[s] the patient." Two years later, Reigelsperger sought treatment from Siller for a different condition relating to his cervical spine and shoulder. Claiming malpractice with respect to the second treatment, Reigelsperger filed a suit in a California state court against Siller. Siller asked the court to order the dispute to be submitted to arbitration. Did Reigelsperger's lack of intent to return to Siller after his first treatment affect the enforceability of the arbitration agreement and consent form? Why or why not? [Reigelsperger v. Siller, 40 Cal.4th 574, 150 P.3d 764, 53 Cal.Rptr.3d 887 (2007)]

- **To view a sample answer for Problem 11–5, go to this book's Web site at www.cengage.com/blaw/clarkson, select "Chapter 11," and click on "Case Problem with Sample Answer."**

11–6. Online Acceptances Internet Archive (IA) is devoted to preserving a record of resources on the Internet for future generations. IA uses the "Wayback Machine" to automatically browse Web sites and reproduce their contents in an archive. IA does not ask the owners' permission before copying their material but will remove it on request. Suzanne Shell, a resident of Colorado, owns www.profane-justice.org, which is dedicated to providing information to individuals accused of child abuse or neglect. The site warns, "IF YOU COPY OR DISTRIBUTE ANYTHING ON THIS SITE YOU ARE ENTERING INTO A CONTRACT." The terms, which can be accessed only by clicking on a link, include, among other charges, a fee of $5,000 for each page copied "in advance of printing." Neither the warning nor the terms require a user to indicate assent. When Shell discovered that the Wayback Machine had copied the contents of her site—approximately eighty-seven times between May 1999 and October 2004—she asked IA to remove the copies from its archive and pay her $100,000. IA removed the copies and filed a suit in a federal district court against Shell, who responded, in part, with a counterclaim for breach of contract. IA filed a motion to dismiss this claim. Did IA contract with Shell? Explain. [*Internet Archive v. Shell*, 505 F.Supp.2d 755 (D.Colo. 2007)]

11–7. Acceptance Evelyn Kowalchuk, an eighty-eight-year-old widow, and her son, Peter, put their savings into accounts managed by Matthew Stroup. Later, they initiated an arbitration proceeding before the National Association of Securities Dealers (NASD), asserting that Stroup fraudulently or negligently handled their accounts. They asked for an award of $832,000. After the hearing, but before a decision was rendered, Stroup offered to pay the Kowalchuks $285,000, and they e-mailed their acceptance. Stroup signed a settlement agreement and faxed it to the Kowalchuks for their signatures. Meanwhile, the NASD issued an award in the Kowalchuks' favor for $88,788. Stroup immediately told them that he was withdrawing his settlement "offer." When Stroup did not pay according to its terms, the Kowalchuks filed a suit in a New York state court against him for breach of contract. Did these parties have a contract? Why or why not? [*Kowalchuk v. Stroup*, 873 N.Y.S.2d 43 (N.Y.A.D. 1 Dept. 2009)]

11–8. Offer and Acceptance In 1996, Troy Blackford was gambling at Prairie Meadows Casino when he destroyed a slot machine. After pleading guilty to criminal mischief, Blackford was banned from the casino. In 1998, Blackford was found in the casino, escorted out, and charged with trespass. In 2006, he gambled at the casino again and won $9,387. When Blackford went to collect his winnings, casino employees learned who he was and refused to pay. He sued for breach of contract, contending that he and the casino had an enforceable contract because he had accepted its offer to gamble. The casino argued that it had not made an offer and in fact had banned Blackford from the premises. The trial court held

in favor of the casino. The appellate court reversed and ordered a new trial. The casino appealed to the Iowa high court for review. Did the casino make a valid offer to Blackford to gamble and thus create an enforceable contract between them? Explain your answer. [*Blackford v. Prairie Meadows Racetrack and Casino*, 778 N.W.2d 184 (Sup.Ct. Iowa 2010)]

11–9. A QUESTION OF ETHICS: E-Contract Disputes.

In 2000 and 2001, Dewayne Hubbert, Elden Craft, Chris Grout, and Rhonda Byington bought computers from Dell Corp. through its Web site. Before buying, Hubbert and the others configured their own computers. To make a purchase, each buyer completed forms on five Web pages. On each page, Dell's "Terms and Conditions of Sale" were accessible by clicking on a blue hyperlink. A statement on three of the pages read, "All sales are subject to Dell's Term[s] and Conditions of Sale," but a buyer was not required to click an assent to the terms to complete a purchase. The terms were also printed on the backs of the invoices and on separate documents contained in the shipping boxes with the computers. Among those terms was a "Binding Arbitration" clause. The computers contained Pentium 4 microprocessors, which Dell advertised as the fastest, most powerful Intel Pentium processors available. In 2002, Hubbert and the others filed a suit in an Illinois state court against Dell, alleging that this marketing was false, misleading, and deceptive. The plaintiffs claimed that the Pentium 4 microprocessor was slower and less powerful, and provided less performance, than either a Pentium III or an AMD Athlon, and at a greater cost. Dell asked the court to compel arbitration. [*Hubbert v. Dell Corp.*, 359 Ill.App.3d 976, 835 N.E.2d 113, 296 Ill.Dec. 258 (5 Dist. 2005)]

(a) Should the court enforce the arbitration clause in this case? If you were the judge, how would you rule on this issue?

(b) In your opinion, do shrink-wrap, click-on, and browse-wrap terms impose too great a burden on purchasers? Why or why not?

(c) An ongoing complaint about shrink-wrap, click-on, and browse-wrap terms is that sellers (often large corporations) draft them and buyers (typically individual consumers) do not read them. Should purchasers be bound in contract by terms that they have not even read? Why or why not?

11–10. VIDEO QUESTION: Agreements.

Go to this text's Web site at **www.cengage.com/ blaw/clarkson** and select "Chapter 11." Click on "Video Questions" and view the video titled *Real World Legal: Jack's Restaurant, Scene 2.* Then answer the following questions.

(a) In regards to the sale of Jack's Restaurant, Jack (the seller) says that he is going to retain the rights to the restaurant's frozen food line. The buyers, however, thought that their sales agreement included the rights to all of the restaurant's signature dishes— whether fresh or frozen. Did the parties have an "agreement to agree" on the terms of the sale of the restaurant? Why or why not?

(b) Suppose that Jack previously offered to sell the restaurant to these particular buyers and they had all agreed on the price and date for delivery. Would such an offer meet the definiteness requirement, even if no terms pertained to the frozen food line? Explain.

(c) Does Jack's statement that he intended to retain his rights to the frozen food line revoke any earlier offer he may have made to sell the restaurant to these individuals? Why or why not?

(d) Did the buyers unequivocally accept the terms of the offer that Jack expressed in this scene? Explain.

LEGAL RESEARCH EXERCISES ON THE WEB

Go to this text's Web site at **www.cengage.com/blaw/clarkson**, select "Chapter 11," and click on "Practical Internet Exercises." There you will find the following Internet research exercises that you can perform to learn more about the topics covered in this chapter.

Practical Internet Exercise 11–1:   **Legal Perspective**
                                           Contract Terms

Practical Internet Exercise 11–2:   **Management Perspective**
                                           Sample Contracts

Practical Internet Exercise 11–3:   **Management Perspective**
                                           Offers and Advertisements

CHAPTER 12
✳
Consideration

The fact that a promise has been made does not mean the promise can or will be enforced. Under Roman law, a promise was not enforceable without some sort of *causa*—that is, a reason for making the promise that was also deemed to be a sufficient reason for enforcing it. Under the common law, a primary basis for the enforcement of promises is consideration. **Consideration usually is defined as the value (such as cash) given in return for a promise (in a bilateral contract) or in return for a performance (in a unilateral contract).**

SECTION 1
ELEMENTS OF CONSIDERATION

Often, consideration is broken down into two parts: (1) something of *legally sufficient value* must be given in exchange for the promise; and (2) usually, there must be a *bargained-for* exchange.

Legal Value

The "something of legally sufficient value" may consist of (1) a promise to do something that one has no prior legal duty to do, (2) the performance of an action that one is otherwise not obligated to undertake, or (3) the refraining from an action that one has a legal right to undertake (called a **forbearance**). Consideration in bilateral contracts normally consists of a promise in return for a promise, as explained in Chapter 10. For example, in a contract for the sale of goods, the seller promises to ship specific goods to the buyer, and the buyer promises to pay for those goods when they are received. Each of these promises constitutes consideration for the contract.

In contrast, unilateral contracts involve a promise in return for a performance. Suppose that Anita said to her neighbor, "When you finish painting the garage, I will pay you $100." Anita's neighbor paints the garage. The act of painting the garage is the consideration that creates Anita's contractual obligation to pay her neighbor $100.

What if, in return for a promise to pay, a person refrains from pursuing harmful habits (a forbearance), such as the use of tobacco and alcohol? Does such forbearance constitute legally sufficient consideration? This was the issue before the court in the following case, which is one of the classics in contract law with respect to consideration.

CASE 12.1
Hamer v. Sidway

Court of Appeals of New York, Second Division, 124 N.Y. 538, 27 N.E. 256 (1891).

BACKGROUND AND FACTS • William E. Story, Sr., was the uncle of William E. Story II. In the presence of family members and guests invited to a family gathering, the elder Story promised to pay his nephew $5,000 ($72,000 in today's dollars) if he would refrain from drinking, using tobacco, swearing, and playing cards or billiards for money until he reached the age of twenty-one. (Note that in 1869, when this contract was formed, it was legal in New York to drink and play cards for money before the

CASE CONTINUES ▶

CASE 12.1 CONTINUED ▶ age of twenty-one.) The nephew agreed and fully performed his part of the bargain. When he reached the age of twenty-one, he wrote and told his uncle that he had kept his part of the agreement and was therefore entitled to $5,000. The uncle replied that he was pleased with his nephew's performance, writing, "I have no doubt but you have, for which you shall have five thousand dollars, as I promised you. I had the money in the bank the day you was twenty-one years old that I intend for you, and you shall have the money certain. . . . P.S. You can consider this money on interest." The nephew received his uncle's letter and thereafter consented that the money should remain with his uncle according to the terms and conditions of the letter. The uncle died about twelve years later without having paid his nephew any part of the $5,000 and interest. The executor of the uncle's estate (Sidway, the defendant in this action) claimed that there had been no valid consideration for the promise and therefore refused to pay the $5,000 (plus interest) to Hamer, a third party to whom the nephew had transferred his rights in the note. The court reviewed the case to determine whether the nephew had given valid consideration under the law.

IN THE LANGUAGE OF THE COURT
PARKER, J. [Justice]
* * * *

* * * Courts will not ask whether the thing which forms the consideration does in fact benefit the promisee or a third party, or is of any substantial value to any one. It is enough that something is promised, done, forborne, or suffered by the party to whom the promise is made as consideration for the promise made to him. *In general a waiver of any legal right at the request of another party is a sufficient consideration for a promise.* Any damage, or suspension, or forbearance of a right will be sufficient to sustain a promise. * * * Now, applying this rule to the facts before us, the promisee used tobacco, occasionally drank liquor, and he had a legal right to do so. That right he abandoned for a period of years upon the strength of the promise of the testator [his uncle] that for such forbearance he would give him $5,000. We need not speculate on the effort which may have been required to give up the use of those stimulants. It is sufficient that he restricted his lawful freedom of action within certain prescribed limits upon the faith of his uncle's agreement * * *. [Emphasis added.]

DECISION AND REMEDY • *The court ruled that the nephew had provided legally sufficient consideration by giving up smoking, drinking, swearing, and playing cards or billiards for money until he reached the age of twenty-one and was therefore entitled to the funds.*

IMPACT OF THIS CASE ON TODAY'S LAW • *Although this case was decided more than a century ago, the principles enunciated in the case remain applicable to contracts formed today, including online contracts. For a contract to be valid and binding, consideration must be given, and that consideration must be something of legally sufficient value.*

WHAT IF THE FACTS WERE DIFFERENT? • *If the nephew had not had a legal right to engage in the behavior that he agreed to forgo, would the result in this case have been different? Explain.*

Bargained-for Exchange

The second element of consideration is that it must provide the basis for the bargain struck between the contracting parties. The item of value must be given or promised by the promisor (offeror) in return for the promisee's promise, performance, or promise of performance.

This element of bargained-for exchange distinguishes contracts from gifts. For example, Roberto says to his son, "In consideration of the fact that you are not as wealthy as your brothers, I will pay you $5,000." The fact that the word *consideration* is used does not, by itself, mean that consideration has been given. Indeed, this is not an enforceable promise because the son does not have to do anything in order to receive the promised $5,000. Because the son does not need to give Roberto something of legal value in return for his promise, there is no bargained-for exchange. Rather, Roberto has simply stated his motive for giving his son a gift.

ADEQUACY OF CONSIDERATION

Legal sufficiency of consideration involves the requirement that consideration be something of legally sufficient value in the eyes of the law. Adequacy of consideration involves how much consideration is given. Essentially, adequacy of consideration concerns the fairness of the bargain.

Courts Typically Will Not Consider Adequacy

On the surface, when the items exchanged are of unequal value, fairness would appear to be an issue. In general, however, a court will not question the adequacy of consideration based solely on the comparative value of the things exchanged. In other words, the determination of whether consideration exists does not depend on a comparison of the values of the things exchanged. Something need not be of direct economic or financial value to be considered legally sufficient consideration. In many situations, the exchange of promises and potential benefits is deemed sufficient as consideration.

Under the doctrine of freedom of contract, courts leave it up to the parties to decide what something is worth, and parties are usually free to bargain as they wish. If people could sue merely because they had entered into an unwise contract, the courts would be overloaded with frivolous suits.

Inadequate Consideration May Cause a Court to Examine Whether Voluntary Consent Was Lacking

When there is a large disparity in the amount or value of the consideration exchanged, the inadequate consideration may raise a red flag for a court to look more closely at the bargain. This is because shockingly inadequate consideration can indicate that fraud, duress, or undue influence was involved or that the element of bargained-for exchange was lacking. It may also cause a judge to question whether the contract is so one sided that it is *unconscionable*,[1] a concept that will be discussed further in Chapter 13.

Judges are troubled about enforcing unequal bargains, and it is the courts' task to police contracts

and make sure that there was not some defect in a contract's formation that negates mutual assent. If an elderly person sells her Mercedes-Benz convertible to her neighbor for $5,000 even though it is worth well over $50,000, the disparity in value may indicate that the sale involved undue influence or fraud. A judge would thus want to make sure that the person voluntarily entered into this agreement.

AGREEMENTS THAT LACK CONSIDERATION

Sometimes, one of the parties (or both parties) to an agreement may think that consideration has been exchanged when in fact it has not. Here, we look at some situations in which the parties' promises or actions do not qualify as contractual consideration.

Preexisting Duty

Under most circumstances, a promise to do what one already has a legal duty to do does not constitute legally sufficient consideration.[2] The preexisting legal duty may be imposed by law or may arise out of a previous contract. A sheriff, for example, cannot collect a reward for providing information leading to the capture of a criminal if the sheriff already has a legal duty to capture the criminal.

Likewise, if a party is already bound by contract to perform a certain duty, that duty cannot serve as consideration for a second contract.[3] For example, Bauman-Bache, Inc., begins construction on a seven-story office building and after three months demands an extra $75,000 on its contract. If the extra $75,000 is not paid, the contractor will stop working. The owner of the land, finding no one else to complete the construction, agrees to pay the extra $75,000. The agreement is unenforceable because it is not supported by legally sufficient consideration; Bauman-Bache had a preexisting contractual duty to complete the building.

UNFORESEEN DIFFICULTIES The rule regarding preexisting duty is meant to prevent extortion and the so-called holdup game. What happens, though, when an honest contractor who has contracted

---

1. Pronounced un-*kon*-shun-uh-bul.

2. See *Foakes v. Beer*, 9 App.Cas. 605 (1884); and *Corben v. What Music Holdings, Ltd.*, 2003 WL 22073940 (Chan. Div.).
3. See, for example, *Braude & Margulies, P.C. v. Fireman's Fund Insurance Co.*, 468 F.Supp.2d 190 (D.D.C. 2007).

with a landowner to construct a building runs into extraordinary difficulties that were totally unforeseen at the time the contract was formed? In the interests of fairness and equity, the courts sometimes allow exceptions to the preexisting duty rule. Therefore, if a landowner agrees to pay extra compensation to the contractor for overcoming unforeseen difficulties (such as having to use special digging equipment to remove an unforeseen obstacle), the court may refrain from applying the preexisting duty rule and enforce the agreement. When the unforeseen difficulties that give rise to a contract modification are the types of risks ordinarily assumed in business, however, the courts will usually assert the preexisting duty rule.

RESCISSION AND NEW CONTRACT The law recognizes that two parties can mutually agree to rescind, or cancel, their contract, at least to the extent that it is executory (still to be carried out). **Rescission**[4] is the unmaking of a contract so as to return the parties to the positions they occupied before the contract was made. Sometimes, parties rescind a contract and make a new contract at the same time. When this occurs, it is often difficult to determine whether there was consideration for the new contract, or whether the parties had a preexisting duty under the previous contract. If a court finds there was a preexisting duty, then the new contract will be invalid because there was no consideration.

Past Consideration

Promises made in return for actions or events that have already taken place are unenforceable. These promises lack consideration in that the element of bargained-for exchange is missing. In short, you can bargain for something to take place now or in the future but not for something that has already taken place. Therefore, **past consideration** is no consideration.

Suppose that Elsie, a real estate agent, does her friend Judy a favor by selling Judy's house and not charging a commission. Later, Judy says to Elsie, "In return for your generous act, I will pay you $3,000." This promise involves past consideration. Consequently, a court would not enforce it. Judy is simply creating a situation in which she presents a gift to Elsie.

CASE IN POINT Jamil Blackmon became friends with Allen Iverson when Iverson was a high school student who showed tremendous promise as an athlete. One evening, Blackmon suggested that Iverson use "The Answer" as a nickname in the summer league basketball tournaments. Blackmon said that Iverson would be "The Answer" to all of the National Basketball Association's woes. Later that night, Iverson said that he would give Blackmon 25 percent of any proceeds from the merchandising of products that used "The Answer" as a logo or a slogan. Because Iverson's promise was made in return for past consideration, it was unenforceable; in effect, Iverson stated his intention to give Blackmon a gift.[5]

As you will read in Chapter 13, an employer will often ask an employee to sign a *noncompete agreement*, also called a *covenant not to compete*. Under such an agreement, the employee agrees not to work for competitors of the employer for a certain period of time after the employment relationship ends. In the following case, the court had to decide if continued employment constituted valid consideration for a noncompete agreement or if it was past consideration.

---

4. Pronounced reh-*sih*-zhen.

5. *Blackmon v. Iverson,* 324 F.Supp.2d 602 (E.D.Pa. 2003).

CASE 12.2
Access Organics, Inc. v. Hernandez
Supreme Court of Montana, 341 Mont. 73, 175 P.3d 899 (2008).

BACKGROUND AND FACTS • Bonnie Poux hired Andy Hernandez to sell organic produce for her sole proprietorship, Access Organics, Inc. Four months later, he was promoted to sales manager. Soon after, he signed a noncompete agreement in which he agreed "not to directly or indirectly compete with the business . . . for a period of two years following termination of employment." Later, the business encountered financial difficulties. Hernandez left and went into business with another former employee to compete with Access Organics in the sale of produce in the same part of Montana. Poux then sued to enforce the noncompete agreement. The trial court found that Hernandez had violated the noncompete agreement and ordered him not to compete directly with Access Organics for the

CASE 12.2 CONTINUED ➧ two-year period called for in the agreement. The court held that the agreement was valid because it was supported by consideration, which was continued employment at Access Organics at the time the agreement was signed. Hernandez appealed.

IN THE LANGUAGE OF THE COURT
W. William *LEAPHART,* Justice.

* * * *

Hernandez argues that the non-compete agreement is invalid and unenforceable, because it is not supported by good consideration. Access Organics contends that Hernandez's salary and continued employment supplied sufficient consideration.

Consideration exists if the employee enters into the non-compete agreement at the time of hiring. During pre-employment negotiations, the employee and the employer engage in a bargained-for exchange: the employer obtains the desired non-compete agreement, and in return, the employee receives employment. The non-compete agreement is simply a condition of employment which the employee takes into account when accepting or rejecting the employment offer. Here, the agreement purports to offer employment in exchange for Hernandez's promise not to compete: "as an inducement for Access Organics * * * to employ Andy Hernandez, he * * * hereby agrees not to * * * compete * * *."

However, Hernandez signed the agreement more than four months after accepting his initial employment offer from Access Organics. The record clearly shows that the agreement was not signed as part of Access Organics's pre-employment negotiations with Hernandez. The basic precepts of black letter contract law teach us that "past consideration is not sufficient to support a promise." *Thus, prior work may not serve as consideration. Access Organics's initial offer of employment to Hernandez is past consideration and may not serve as consideration for the non-compete agreement signed four months later.* [Emphasis added.]

However, "afterthought agreements"—non-compete agreements signed by employees after the date of hire—are not automatically invalid. *Non-compete agreements entered into by existing employees may be supported by independent consideration.* For example, an employer may provide an employee with a raise or promotion in exchange for signing a non-compete agreement. In such instances, the salary increase or promotion serves as good consideration. Access to trade secrets or other confidential information may also suffice as a form of good consideration. In each of these examples, the employee receives a benefit which constitutes good consideration in exchange for his or her promise not to compete. [Emphasis added.]

* * * *

When a current employee is required to sign a non-compete agreement, the employer and employee are not on equal bargaining ground: the employee is vulnerable to heavy economic pressure to sign the agreement in order to keep his job. Thus, in the context of non-compete agreements, we require clear evidence that the employee received good consideration in exchange for bargaining away some of his post-employment freedom to practice the profession or trade of his choice.

* * * *

We conclude that the covenant not to compete between Andy Hernandez and Access Organics is unenforceable for lack of consideration. Thus, the District Court erred in determining that the agreement was enforceable as a matter of law. Since the agreement is unenforceable as a matter of law, the District Court also erred in granting the preliminary injunction against Hernandez. Thus, we reverse and remand for further proceedings consistent with this opinion.

DECISION AND REMEDY • *Montana's highest court held that the noncompete agreement between the employer and the employee was invalid because it was not supported by consideration. Because no contract had been formed, the trial court's injunction enforcing the agreement against Hernandez was removed.*

THE LEGAL ENVIRONMENT DIMENSION • *How could Access Organics have obtained a noncompete agreement from Hernandez that would have been enforced?*

THE ETHICAL DIMENSION • *Would an economic recession and global financial crisis excuse a former employee from having to comply with a noncompete clause that he or she had signed? Why or why not?*

Illusory Promises

If the terms of the contract express such uncertainty of performance that the promisor has not definitely promised to do anything, the promise is said to be *illusory*—without consideration and unenforceable. A promise is illusory when it fails to bind the promisor. For example, the president of Tuscan Corporation says to her employees, "All of you have worked hard, and if profits continue to remain high, a 10 percent bonus at the end of the year will be given—if management thinks it is warranted." The employees continue to work hard, and profits remain high, but no bonus is given. This is an *illusory promise,* or no promise at all, because performance depends solely on the discretion of the president (the management). There is no bargained-for consideration. The statement indicates only that management may or may not do something in the future. The president is not obligated now or later.

OPTION-TO-CANCEL CLAUSES Sometimes, option-to-cancel clauses in term contracts present problems in regard to consideration. When the promisor has the option to cancel the contract before performance has begun, then the promise is illusory. For example, Abe contracts to hire Chris for one year at $5,000 per month, reserving the right to cancel the contract at any time. On close examination of these words, you can see that Abe has not actually agreed to hire Chris, as Abe could cancel without liability before Chris started performance. This contract is therefore illusory.

But if Abe instead reserves the right to cancel the contract at any time *after* Chris has begun performance by giving Chris *thirty days' notice,* the promise is not illusory. Abe, by saying that he will give Chris thirty days' notice, is relinquishing the opportunity (legal right) to hire someone else instead of Chris for a thirty-day period. If Chris works for one month, at the end of which Abe gives him thirty days' notice, Chris has an enforceable claim for $10,000 in salary.[6]

REQUIREMENTS AND OUTPUT CONTRACTS Problems with consideration may also arise in other types of contracts because of uncertainty of performance.[7] Uncertain performance is characteristic of requirements and output contracts, for example. In a *requirements contract,* a buyer and a seller agree that the buyer will purchase from the seller all of the goods of a designated type that the buyer needs, or requires. In an *output contract,* the buyer and seller agree that the buyer will purchase from the seller all of what the seller produces, or the seller's output. These types of contracts will be discussed further in Chapter 19.

Concept Summary 12.1 provides a convenient summary of the main aspects of consideration.

6. For another example, see *Vanegas v. American Energy Services,* 302 S.W.3d 299 (Tex. 2009).
7. See, for example, *Johnson Controls, Inc. v. TRW Vehicle Safety Systems,* 491 F.Supp.2d 707 (E.D.Mich. 2007).

CONCEPT SUMMARY 12.1
Consideration

Elements of Consideration	Consideration is the value given in exchange for a promise. A contract cannot be formed without sufficient consideration. Consideration is often broken down into two elements: 1. *Legal value*—Something of legally sufficient value must be given in exchange for a promise. This may consist of a promise, a performance, or a forbearance. 2. *Bargained-for exchange*—There must be a bargained-for exchange.
Adequacy of Consideration	Adequacy of consideration relates to how much consideration is given and whether a fair bargain was reached. Courts will inquire into the adequacy of consideration (if the consideration is legally sufficient) only when fraud, undue influence, duress, or the lack of a bargained-for exchange may be involved.
Agreements That Lack Consideration	Consideration is lacking in the following situations: 1. *Preexisting duty*—Consideration is not legally sufficient if one is either by law or by contract under a *preexisting duty* to perform the action being offered as consideration for a new contract. 2. *Past consideration*—Actions or events that have already taken place do not constitute legally sufficient consideration. 3. *Illusory promises*—When the nature or extent of performance is too uncertain, the promise is rendered illusory and unenforceable.

SECTION 4

SETTLEMENT OF CLAIMS

Businesspersons and others often enter into contracts to settle legal claims. It is important to understand the nature of consideration given in these kinds of settlement agreements, or contracts. Claims are commonly settled through an *accord and satisfaction,* in which a debtor offers to pay a lesser amount than the creditor purports to be owed. Claims may also be settled by the signing of a *release* or a *covenant not to sue.*

Accord and Satisfaction

In an **accord and satisfaction,** a debtor offers to pay, and a creditor accepts, a lesser amount than the creditor originally claimed was owed. The *accord* is the agreement under which one of the parties undertakes to give or perform, and the other to accept, in satisfaction of a claim, something other than that on which the parties originally agreed. *Satisfaction* is the performance (usually payment) that takes place after the accord is executed. A basic rule is that there can be no satisfaction unless there is first an accord. For accord and satisfaction to occur, the amount of the debt *must be in dispute.*

LIQUIDATED DEBTS If a debt is *liquidated,* accord and satisfaction cannot take place. A **liquidated debt** is one whose amount has been ascertained, fixed, agreed on, settled, or exactly determined. For example, Barbara Kwan signs an installment loan contract with her banker in which she agrees to pay a specified rate of interest on a specified amount of borrowed funds at monthly intervals for two years. Because the total obligation is precisely known to both parties, it is a liquidated debt.

Suppose that Kwan has missed her last two payments on the loan and the creditor demands that she pay the overdue debt. Kwan makes a partial payment and states that she believes this payment is all she should have to pay and that the debt will be satisfied if the creditor accepts the payment. In the majority of states, acceptance of a lesser sum than the entire amount of a liquidated debt is *not* satisfaction, and the balance of the debt is still legally owed. The reason for this rule is that the debtor has given no consideration to satisfy the obligation of paying the balance to the creditor—because the debtor has a preexisting legal obligation to pay the entire debt.

UNLIQUIDATED DEBTS An *unliquidated debt* is the opposite of a liquidated debt. The amount of the debt is *not* settled, fixed, agreed on, ascertained, or determined, and reasonable persons may differ over the amount owed. In these circumstances, acceptance of payment of a lesser sum operates as satisfaction, or discharge, of the debt because there is valid consideration—the parties give up a legal right to contest the amount in dispute.

Release

A **release** is a contract in which one party forfeits the right to pursue a legal claim against the other party. It bars any further recovery beyond the terms stated in the release. Releases will generally be binding if they are (1) given in good faith, (2) stated in a signed writing (which is required in many states), and (3) accompanied by consideration.[8]

Clearly, an individual is better off knowing the extent of his or her injuries or damages before signing a release. For example, Lucy's car is damaged in an automobile accident caused by Donovan's negligence. Donovan offers to give her $3,000 if she will release him from further liability resulting from the accident. Lucy believes that this amount will cover her damage, so she agrees and signs the release. Later, Lucy discovers that it will cost $4,200 to repair her car. Can Lucy collect the balance from Donovan?

The answer normally is no; Lucy is limited to the $3,000 specified in the release. Why? The reason is that a valid contract existed. Lucy and Donovan both voluntarily agreed to the terms in the release, and sufficient consideration was present. The consideration was the legal right Lucy forfeited to sue to recover damages, should they be more than $3,000, in exchange for Donovan's promise to give her $3,000.

Covenant Not to Sue

Unlike a release, a **covenant not to sue** does not always bar further recovery. The parties simply substitute a contractual obligation for some other type of legal action based on a valid claim. Suppose (continuing the earlier example) that Lucy agrees with Donovan not to sue for damages in a tort action if he will pay for the damage to her car. If Donovan fails to pay, Lucy can bring an action against him for breach of contract.

---

8. Under the Uniform Commercial Code (UCC), a written, signed waiver or renunciation by an aggrieved party discharges any further liability for a breach, even without consideration.

SECTION 5

EXCEPTIONS TO THE CONSIDERATION REQUIREMENT

There are some exceptions to the rule that only promises supported by consideration are enforceable. The following types of promises may be enforced despite the lack of consideration:

1. Promises that induce detrimental reliance, under the doctrine of *promissory estoppel*.
2. Promises to pay debts that are barred by a statute of limitations.
3. Promises to make charitable contributions.

Promissory Estoppel

Under the doctrine of **promissory estoppel** (also called *detrimental reliance*), a person who has reasonably and substantially relied on the promise of another may be able to obtain some measure of recovery. This doctrine is applied in a wide variety of contexts in which a promise is otherwise unenforceable, such as when a promise is not supported by consideration. Under this doctrine, a court may enforce an otherwise unenforceable promise to avoid the injustice that would otherwise result.

REQUIREMENTS TO STATE A CLAIM For the promissory estoppel doctrine to be applied, the following elements are required:

1. There must be a clear and definite promise.
2. The promisor should have expected that the promisee would rely on the promise.
3. The promisee reasonably relied on the promise by acting or refraining from some act.
4. The promisee's reliance was definite and resulted in substantial detriment.
5. Enforcement of the promise is necessary to avoid injustice.

If these requirements are met, a promise may be enforced even though it is not supported by consideration.[9] In essence, the promisor will be e*stopped* (prevented) from asserting the lack of consideration as a defense.

Promissory estoppel is similar in some ways to the doctrine of quasi contract that was discussed in Chapter 10. In both situations, a court is acting in the interests of equity and imposes contract obligations on the parties to prevent unfairness even though no actual contract exists. The difference is that with quasi contracts, no promise was made at all; whereas with promissory estoppel, a promise was made and relied on, but it was unenforceable.

APPLICATION OF THE DOCTRINE Promissory estoppel was originally applied to situations involving gifts (I promise to pay you $1,000 a week so that you will not have to work) and donations to charities (I promise to contribute $50,000 a year to the Raising Giants orphanage). Later, courts began to apply the doctrine to avoid inequity or hardship in other situations, including business transactions.

CASE IN POINT The U.S. Air Force solicited bids for construction of a new building in Anchorage, Alaska. A general contractor, Vern Hickel, contacted eight different subcontractors to find the lowest price on electrical work. Alaska Bussell Electric Company, an electrical subcontractor, told Hickel that it would do the work for $477,498. Hickel reasonably relied on this amount when he submitted his primary bid for the entire project to the Air Force and won the contract. Subsequently, Alaska Bussell realized that it had made a mistake and refused to perform the work for Hickel for $477,498. Hickel had to hire another subcontractor at a substantially higher cost. Under the doctrine of promissory estoppel, Hickel can sue Alaska Bussell for the cost difference because he had detrimentally relied on Alaska Bussell's bid, even though there was no consideration for Alaska Bussell's promise to do the work for $477,498.[10]

In the following case, a tenant of a shopping plaza informed the plaza's owner that it wished to expand its business and to lease more space. After the plaza owner had spent a considerable amount of time and funds to accommodate the tenant, the tenant refused to lease the additional space. Whether the plaza owner could recover its costs under a theory of promissory estoppel was the issue before the court.

---

9. *Restatement (Second) of Contracts*, Section 90.

10. See *Alaska Bussell Electric Co. v. Vern Hickel Construction Co.*, 688 P.2d 576 (1984); also see *Commerce Bancorp, Inc. v. BK International Insurance Brokers, Ltd.*, 490 F.Supp.2d 556 (D.N.J. 2007).

✳ EXTENDED CASE 12.3 ✳
1861 Group, LLC v. Wild Oats Markets, Inc.

United States District Court, Eastern District of Missouri, ___ F.Supp.2d ___ (2010).

IN THE LANGUAGE OF THE COURT

Donald J. *STOHR,*
District Judge.

* * * *

Plaintiff is a company that owns a shopping plaza called Lammert Center located at 8801–8845 Ladue Road, St. Louis, Missouri. Defendant leased a portion of Lammert Center and operated a grocery business out of that space.

In March 2000, defendant advised plaintiff that it wanted to expand its operations and lease additional space in Lammert Center. At that time, defendant occupied its portion of Lammert Center pursuant to a sublease with Schnuck Markets, Inc. In response to defendant's interest in leasing additional space, plaintiff advised defendant that it would need to relocate other existing Lammert Center tenants to accommodate defendant's plan, which would in turn require plaintiff to terminate or modify existing leases. Plaintiff also advised defendant that it would need to negotiate modifications to lease agreements with several new tenants that were on the verge of agreeing to lease space at Lammert Center. Plaintiff advised defendant that it would incur substantial costs and lost rent to accommodate defendant's plan. Plaintiff advised defendant that expansion into new space would require defendant to terminate its sublease and sign a new lease. Plaintiff advised defendant that by terminating the sublease and signing a new lease plaintiff would incur substantial costs and the loss of valuable corporate guarantees backing defendant's sublease.

As a result of its communications with plaintiff, defendant knew that plaintiff would incur significant costs, lost rents, and other losses in order to accommodate defendant's plan to expand. Defendant promised plaintiff on several occasions that it would continue to negotiate in good faith to enter, ultimately, into a new lease. Plaintiff relied on defendant's promises that it would negotiate in good faith and sign a lease in relocating two existing Lammert Center tenants, incurring costs associated with reconfiguring the rental spaces, terminating leases, and forgiving amounts owed to plaintiff in the process. In addition to relocating other tenants, plaintiff incurred costs in connection with efforts to rework defendant's sublease.

In January 2001, plaintiff, defendant, and Schnuck Markets entered into a termination agreement, in which defendant's sublease with Schnuck Markets and Schnuck Markets's lease with plaintiff would terminate if plaintiff and defendant were able to agree to a new lease by April 30, 2001. The parties agreed to extend that deadline to June 30, 2001, on April 17, 2001, but then on April 20, 2001, defendant cancelled its agreement to extend the deadline. On April 24, 2001, defendant advised plaintiff that it was not going forward with its plan to expand and that it did not intend to enter into a new lease. Defendant also orally advised plaintiff that its plan to expand was only temporarily postponed and that it would like plaintiff to reintroduce the issue of a new lease in one year. Approximately one year later, plaintiff approached defendant about the plan to expand and defendant's promise to negotiate a new lease. Defendant indicated orally that it was not yet ready to expand but would revisit the issue at some point in the future. Ultimately, plaintiff and defendant never agreed to a new lease, and plaintiff alleges that it is entitled to an award of damages of not less than $1,350,000 plus interest, attorney fees, expenses, and costs incurred as a result of its reliance on defendant's promises.

* * * *

In its instant motion [the motion before the court], defendant moves the Court to dismiss Count VII, which is labeled as a claim for promissory estoppel by plaintiff.

Under Missouri law, *to state a claim for promissory estoppel, a plaintiff must allege (1) a promise, (2) on which the plaintiff relied to its detriment, (3) in a way the promisor expected or should have expected, and (4) the reliance resulted in an injustice which can be cured only by enforcement of the promise.* The promise giving rise to the cause of action must be definite, and the promise must be made in a contractual sense. [Emphasis added.]

* * * *

* * * [The plaintiff] has alleged that: (1) defendant promised that if plaintiff made additional space in Lammert Center available to accommodate an expansion, defendant would enter into a new lease with plaintiff after a good faith negotiation of the terms; (2) plaintiff relied on this promise to its detriment when it incurred various costs to make the expanded space available to defendant; (3) defendant was aware of plaintiff's actions to make the expanded space available and was aware that plaintiff's actions were in response to defendant's promise; and (4) plaintiff would suffer the injustice of uncompensated expenditures made in reliance on defendant's promise if defendant's promise is not enforced. The Court finds that such allegations support each of the elements of a claim of promissory estoppel * * *.

* * * *

EXTENDED CASE CONTINUES ➡

EXTENDED CASE 12.3 CONTINUED ↴

[Defendant argues] that a promise to negotiate is not definite or certain enough to permit recovery. * * * Under Missouri law, *for a promise to be actionable under a theory of promissory estoppel, it must be definite and made in a contractual sense.* That is, it must be "as definite and delineated as an offer under contract law." [Emphasis added.]

In this case, * * * the Court reads the allegations such that

defendant promised that it would enter into a new lease if plaintiff made the necessary changes to Lammert Center. That promise was only limited by the requirement that both parties negotiate the terms of the lease in good faith, which is to say that defendant was not promising to sign any lease that plaintiff put in front of it. Rather, once defendant promised it would enter a new lease if plaintiff made the new space available, it was bound to make a good faith effort to reach

an agreement on the terms of the lease. Under these allegations, the Court finds that the alleged promise was sufficiently definite to support a claim for promissory estoppel.

* * * *

For the above stated reasons, IT IS HEREBY ORDERED that defendant's motion to dismiss Count VII of plaintiff's complaint is denied.

QUESTIONS

1. The defendant argued that the promise to renew the lease was not sufficiently definite to support a claim for promissory estoppel. How did the court respond to this argument?
2. Suppose that the plaintiff's costs in accommodating the defendant's request had been $5,000 instead of $1,350,000. Would the outcome of this case have been any different? Why or why not?

Promises to Pay Debts Barred by a Statute of Limitations

Statutes of limitations in all states require a creditor to sue within a specified period to recover a debt. If the creditor fails to sue in time, recovery of the debt is barred by the statute of limitations. A debtor who promises to pay a previous debt even though recovery is barred by the statute of limitations makes an enforceable promise. *The promise needs no consideration.* (Some states, however, require that it be in writing.) In effect, the promise extends the limitations period, and the creditor can sue to recover the entire debt or at least the amount promised. The promise can be implied if the debtor acknowledges the barred debt by making a partial payment.

Charitable Subscriptions

Subscriptions to religious, educational, and charitable institutions are promises to make gifts. Traditionally,

these promises were unenforceable because they are not supported by legally sufficient consideration. A gift, after all, is the opposite of bargained-for consideration. The modern view, however, is to make exceptions to the general rule by applying the doctrine of promissory estoppel.

For example, a church solicits and receives pledges (commitments to contribute funds) from church members to erect a new church building. On the basis of these pledges, the church purchases land, hires architects, and makes other contracts that change its position. Because of the church's detrimental reliance, a court may enforce the pledges under the theory of promissory estoppel. Alternatively, a court may find consideration in the fact that each promise was made in reliance on the other promises of support or that the trustees, by accepting the subscriptions, impliedly promised to complete the proposed undertaking.

REVIEWING

Consideration

John operates a motorcycle repair shop from his home but finds that his business is limited by the small size of his garage. Driving by a neighbor's property, he notices a for-sale sign on a large, metal-sided garage. John contacts the neighbor and offers to buy the building, hoping that it can be dismantled and moved to his own property. The neighbor accepts John's payment and makes a

REVIEWING
Consideration, Continued

generous offer in return: if John will help him dismantle the garage, which will take a substantial amount of time, he will help John reassemble it after it has been transported to John's property. They agree to have the entire job completed within two weeks. John spends every day for a week working with his neighbor to disassemble the building. In his rush to acquire a larger workspace, he turns down several lucrative repair jobs. Once the disassembled building has been moved to John's property, however, the neighbor refuses to help John reassemble it as he originally promised. Using the information presented in the chapter, answer the following questions.

1. Are the basic elements of consideration present in the neighbor's promise to help John reassemble the garage? Why or why not?
2. Suppose that the neighbor starts to help John but then realizes that, because of the layout of John's property, putting the building back together will take much more work than dismantling it took. Under which principle discussed in the chapter might the neighbor be allowed to ask for additional compensation?
3. What if John's neighbor made his promise to help reassemble the garage at the time he and John were moving it to John's property, saying, "Since you helped me take it down, I will help you put it back up." Would John be able to enforce this promise? Why or why not?
4. Under what doctrine discussed in the chapter might John seek to recover the profits he lost when he declined to do repair work for one week?

⊛ **DEBATE THIS:** *Courts should not be able to decide on the adequacy of consideration. A deal is a deal.*

TERMS AND CONCEPTS

	consideration 243	liquidated debt 249	release 249
	covenant not to sue 249	past consideration 246	rescission 246
accord and satisfaction 249	forbearance 243	promissory estoppel 250	

QUESTIONS AND CASE PROBLEMS

12–1. Preexisting Duty Tabor is a buyer of file cabinets manufactured by Martin. Martin's contract with Tabor calls for delivery of fifty file cabinets at $40 per cabinet in five equal installments. After delivery of two installments (twenty cabinets), Martin informs Tabor that because of inflation, Martin is losing money and will promise to deliver the remaining thirty cabinets only if Tabor will pay $50 per cabinet. Tabor agrees in writing to do so. Discuss whether Martin can legally collect the additional $100 on delivery to Tabor of the next installment of ten cabinets.

12–2. QUESTION WITH SAMPLE ANSWER: Preexisting Duty.

Bernstein owns a lot and wants to build a house according to a particular set of plans and specifications. She solicits bids from building contractors and receives three bids: one

from Carlton for $160,000, one from Friend for $158,000, and one from Shade for $153,000. She accepts Shade's bid. One month after beginning construction of the house, Shade contacts Bernstein and informs her that because of inflation and a recent price hike for materials, he will not finish the house unless Bernstein agrees to pay an extra $13,000. Bernstein reluctantly agrees to pay the additional sum. After the house is finished, however, Bernstein refuses to pay the extra $13,000. Discuss whether Bernstein is legally required to pay this additional amount.

• For a sample answer to Question 12–2, go to Appendix I at the end of this text.

12–3. Consideration Daniel, a recent college graduate, is on his way home for the Christmas holidays from his new job. He gets caught in a snowstorm and is taken in by an elderly couple, who provide him with food and shelter. After the snowplows have cleared the road, Daniel proceeds home. Daniel's father, Fred, is most appreciative of the elderly couple's action and in a letter promises to pay them $500. The elderly couple, in need of funds, accept Fred's offer. Then, because of a dispute between Daniel and Fred, Fred refuses to pay the elderly couple the $500. Discuss whether the couple can hold Fred liable in contract for the services rendered to Daniel.

12–4. Illusory Promises Costello hired Sagan to drive his racing car in a race. Sagan's friend Gideon promised to pay Sagan $3,000 if she won the race. Sagan won the race, but Gideon refused to pay the $3,000. Gideon contended that no legally binding contract had been formed because he had received no consideration from Sagan in exchange for his promise to pay. Sagan sued Gideon for breach of contract, arguing that winning the race was the consideration given in exchange for Gideon's promise to pay. What rule of law discussed in this chapter supports Gideon's claim?

12–5. Accord and Satisfaction Merrick grows and sells blueberries. Maine Wild Blueberry Co. agreed to buy all of Merrick's crop under a contract that left the price unliquidated. Merrick delivered the berries, but a dispute arose over the price. Maine Wild sent Merrick a check with a letter stating that the check was the "final settlement." Merrick cashed the check but filed a suit for breach of contract, claiming that he was owed more. What will the court likely decide in this case? Why?

12–6. Consideration In 1995, Helikon Furniture Co. appointed Tom Gaede as an independent sales agent for the sale of its products in parts of Texas. The parties signed a one-year contract that specified, among other things, the commissions that Gaede would receive. More than a year later, although the parties had not signed a new contract, Gaede was still representing Helikon when it was acquired by a third party. Helikon's new management allowed Gaede to continue to perform for the same commissions and sent him a letter stating that it would make no changes in its sales representatives "for at least the next year." Three months later, in December 1997, the new managers sent Gaede a letter proposing new terms for a contract. Gaede continued to sell Helikon products until May 1997, when he received a letter effectively reducing the amount of his commissions. Gaede filed a suit in a Texas state court against Helikon, alleging breach of contract. Helikon argued, in part, that there was no contract because there was no consideration. In whose favor should the court rule, and why? [*Gaede v. SK Investments, Inc.*, 38 S.W.3d 753 (Tex.App.—Houston [14 Dist.] 2001)]

12–7. Settlement of Claims Shoreline Towers Condominium Owners Association in Gulf Shores, Alabama, authorized Resort Development, Inc. (RDI), to manage Shoreline's property. On Shoreline's behalf, RDI obtained a property insurance policy from Zurich American Insurance Co. In October 1995, Hurricane Opal struck Gulf Shores. RDI

filed claims with Zurich regarding damage to Shoreline's property. Zurich determined that the cost of the damage was $334,901. Zurich then subtracted an applicable $40,000 deductible and sent checks to RDI totaling $294,901. RDI disputed the amount. Zurich eventually agreed to issue a check for an additional $86,000 in return for RDI's signing a "Release of All Claims." Later, contending that the deductible had been incorrectly applied and that this was a breach of contract, among other things, Shoreline filed a suit against Zurich in a federal district court. How, if at all, should the agreement reached by RDI and Zurich affect Shoreline's claim? Explain. [*Shoreline Towers Condominium Owners Association, Inc. v. Zurich American Insurance Co.*, 196 F.Supp.2d 1210 (S.D.Ala. 2002)]

12–8. CASE PROBLEM WITH SAMPLE ANSWER: Adequacy of Consideration.

 As a child, Martha Carr once visited her mother's 108-acre tract of unimproved land in Richland County, South Carolina. In 1968, Betty and Raymond Campbell leased the land. Carr, a resident of New York, was diagnosed as having schizophrenia and depression in 1986, was hospitalized five or six times, and subsequently took prescription drugs for the illnesses. In 1996, Carr inherited the Richland property and, two years later, contacted the Campbells about selling the land. Carr asked Betty about the value of the land, and Betty said that the county tax assessor had determined that the land's agricultural value was $54,000. The Campbells knew at the time that the county had assessed the total property value at $103,700 for tax purposes. A real estate appraiser found that the real market value of the property was $162,000. On August 6, Carr signed a contract to sell the land to the Campbells for $54,000. Believing the price to be unfair, however, Carr did not deliver the deed. The Campbells filed a suit in a South Carolina state court against Carr, seeking specific performance of the contract. At trial, an expert real estate appraiser testified that the real market value of the property was $162,000 at the time of the contract. Under what circumstances will a court examine the adequacy of consideration? Are those circumstances present in this case? Should the court enforce the contract between Carr and the Campbells? Explain. [*Campbell v. Carr*, 361 S.C. 258, 603 S.E.2d 625 (S.C.App. 2004)]

• To view a sample answer for Problem 12–8, go to this book's Web site at www.cengage.com/blaw/clarkson, select "Chapter 12," and click on "Case Problem with Sample Answer."

12–9. Rescission In 2002, Farrokh and Scheherezade Sharabianlou were looking for a location for a printing business. They signed a purchase agreement to buy a building owned by Berenstein Associates for $2 million and deposited $115,000 in escrow until the time of the final purchase. The agreement contained a clause requiring an environmental assessment of the property. This study indicated the presence of tricholoroethene and other chemicals used in dry cleaning, and it recommended further study of the contamination. Because of this issue, the bank would not provide financing for the purchase. When the deal fell apart, the Berensteins sued for breach of contract. The Sharabianlous sought the return of their $115,000 deposit and rescission of the contract. The trial court awarded the Berensteins $428,660 in damages due to the reduced value of their property when it was later sold to another party at a lower price. The Sharabianlous appealed. Do they have a good argument for rescission? Explain your answer. [*Sharabianlou v. Karp*, 181 Cal.App.4th 1133, 105 Cal. Rptr.3d 300 (1st Dist. 2010)]

12–10. A QUESTION OF ETHICS: Promissory Estoppel.

John Sasson and Emily Springer met in January 2002. John worked for the U.S. Army as an engineer. Emily was an attorney with a law firm. Six months later, John bought a townhouse in Randolph, New Jersey, and asked Emily to live with him. She agreed but retained the ownership of her home in Monmouth Beach. John paid the mortgage and the other expenses on the townhouse. He urged Emily to quit her job and work from "our house." In May 2003, Emily took John's advice and started her own law practice. In December, John made her the beneficiary of his $150,000 individual retirement account (IRA) and said that he would give her his 2002 BMW M3 car

before the end of the next year. He proposed to her in September 2004, giving her a diamond engagement ring and promising to "take care of her" for the rest of her life. Less than a month later, John was critically injured by an accidental blow to his head during a basketball game and died. On behalf of John's estate, which was valued at $1.1 million, his brother Steven filed a complaint in a New Jersey state court to have Emily evicted from the townhouse. Given these facts, consider the following questions. [In re Estate of Sasson, 387 N.J.Super. 459, 904 A.2d 769 (App.Div. 2006)]

(a) Based on John's promise to "take care of her" for the rest of her life, Emily claimed that she was entitled to the townhouse, the BMW, and an additional portion of John's estate. Under what circumstances would such a promise constitute a valid, enforceable contract? Does John's promise meet these requirements? Why or why not?

(b) Whether or not John's promise is legally binding, is there an ethical basis on which it should be enforced? Is there an ethical basis for *not* enforcing it? Are there any circumstances under which a promise of support should be—or should *not* be—enforced? Discuss.

LEGAL RESEARCH EXERCISES ON THE WEB

Go to this text's Web site at **www.cengage.com/blaw/clarkson**, select "Chapter 12," and click on "Practical Internet Exercises." There you will find the following Internet research exercises that you can perform to learn more about the topics covered in this chapter.

Practical Internet Exercise 12–1: **Legal Perspective**
Legal Value of Consideration

Practical Internet Exercise 12–2: **Management Perspective**
Promissory Estoppel

Practical Internet Exercise 12–3: **Global Perspective**
Contract Consideration in Canada

CHAPTER 13

✴ Capacity and Legality

In addition to agreement and consideration, for a contract to be deemed valid the parties to the contract must have **contractual capacity**—the legal ability to enter into a contractual relationship. Courts generally presume the existence of contractual capacity, but in some situations, when a person is young or mentally incompetent, capacity is lacking or may be questionable. Similarly, contracts calling for the performance of an illegal act are illegal and thus void—they are not contracts at all. In this chapter, we examine contractual capacity and some aspects of illegal bargains.

Realize that capacity and legality are not inherently related other than that they are both contract requirements. We treat these topics in one chapter merely for convenience and reasons of space.

SECTION 1
CONTRACTUAL CAPACITY

Historically, the law has given special protection to those who bargain with the inexperience of youth and those who lack the degree of mental competence required by law. A person who has been determined by a court to be mentally incompetent, for example, cannot form a legally binding contract with another party. In other situations, a party may have the capacity to enter into a valid contract but also have the right to avoid liability under it. For example, minors—or *infants,* as they are commonly referred to in legal terminology—usually are not legally bound by contracts. In this section, we look at the effect of youth, intoxication, and mental incompetence on contractual capacity.

Minors

Today, in almost all states, the **age of majority** (when a person is no longer a minor) for contractual purposes is eighteen years.[1] In addition, some states provide for the termination of minority on marriage. Minority status may also be terminated by a minor's

emancipation, which occurs when a child's parent or legal guardian relinquishes the legal right to exercise control over the child. Normally, minors who leave home to support themselves are considered emancipated. Several jurisdictions permit minors to petition a court for emancipation themselves. For business purposes, a minor may petition a court to be treated as an adult.

The general rule is that a minor can enter into any contract that an adult can, provided that the contract is not one prohibited by law for minors (for example, the sale of tobacco or alcoholic beverages). A contract entered into by a minor, however, is voidable at the option of that minor, subject to certain exceptions. To exercise the option to avoid a contract, a minor need only manifest an intention not to be bound by it. The minor avoids the contract by disaffirming it.

A MINOR'S RIGHT TO DISAFFIRM The legal avoidance, or setting aside, of a contractual obligation is referred to as **disaffirmance.** To disaffirm, a minor must express his or her intent, through words or conduct, not to be bound to the contract. The minor must disaffirm the entire contract, not merely a portion of it. For example, the minor cannot decide to keep part of the goods purchased under a contract and return the remaining goods.

---

1. The age of majority may still be twenty-one for other purposes, such as the purchase and consumption of alcohol.

A contract can ordinarily be disaffirmed at any time during minority[2] or for a reasonable period after reaching majority. What constitutes a "reasonable" time may vary. Two months would probably be considered reasonable, but except in unusual circumstances, a court may not find it reasonable for a minor to wait a year or more after coming of age to disaffirm. If an individual fails to disaffirm an executed contract within a reasonable time after reaching the age of majority, a court will likely hold that the contract has been ratified (*ratification* will be discussed shortly).

Note that an adult who enters into a contract with a minor cannot avoid his or her contractual duties on the ground that the minor can do so. Unless the minor exercises the option to disaffirm the contract, the adult party normally is bound by it.

A MINOR'S OBLIGATIONS ON DISAFFIRMANCE

Although all states' laws permit minors to disaffirm contracts (with certain exceptions), states differ on the extent of a minor's obligations on disaffirmance. Courts in most states hold that the minor need only return the goods (or other consideration) subject to the contract, provided the goods are in the minor's possession or control. Even if the minor returns damaged goods, the minor often is entitled to disaffirm the contract and obtain a full refund of the purchase price.

A growing number of states place an additional duty on the minor to restore the adult party to the position she or he held before the contract was made. These courts may hold a minor responsible for damage, ordinary wear and tear, and depreciation of goods that the minor used prior to disaffirmance.

CASE IN POINT Sixteen-year-old Joseph Dodson bought a pickup truck from a used-car dealer. Although the truck developed mechanical problems nine months later, Dodson continued to drive it until it stopped running altogether. Then Dodson disaffirmed the contract and attempted to return the truck to the dealer for a full refund. The dealer refused to accept the pickup or refund the purchase price. Dodson filed a suit. Ultimately, the Tennessee Supreme Court allowed Dodson to disaffirm the contract but required him to compensate the seller for the depreciated value—not the purchase price—of the pickup.[3]

---

2. In some states, however, a minor who enters into a contract for the sale of land cannot disaffirm the contract until she or he reaches the age of majority.
3. *Dodson v. Shrader,* 824 S.W.2d 545 (Tenn.Sup.Ct. 1992) is a seminal case on this subject. See also *Restatement (Third) of Restitution,* Sections 16 and 33.

EXCEPTIONS TO A MINOR'S RIGHT TO DISAFFIRM

State courts and legislatures have carved out several exceptions to the minor's right to disaffirm. Some contracts, such as marriage contracts and contracts to enlist in the armed services, cannot be avoided as a matter of law, on the ground of public policy. Other contracts may not be disaffirmed for other reasons, including those discussed here.

Misrepresentation of Age. Suppose that a minor tells a seller that she is twenty-one years old when she is really seventeen. Ordinarily, minors can disaffirm contracts even when they have misrepresented their age. Nevertheless, a growing number of states have enacted laws to prohibit disaffirmance in such situations. In some states, misrepresentation of age is enough to prohibit disaffirmance. Other states prohibit disaffirmance by minors who misrepresented their age while engaged in business as an adult. Still other states prevent minors who misrepresented their age from disaffirming a contract unless they can return the consideration received.

Contracts for Necessaries. A minor who enters into a contract for necessaries may disaffirm the contract but remains liable for the reasonable value of the goods. **Necessaries** include whatever is reasonably needed to maintain the minor's standard of living. In general, food, clothing, shelter, and medical services are necessaries. What is a necessary for one minor, however, may be a luxury for another, depending on the minors' customary living standard. In addition, what a court considers to be a necessary may depend on what the minor's parents provide. For example, if Shannon is a minor whose parents provide her with a residence, then a contract that Shannon enters to lease an apartment normally will not be classified as a contract for necessaries.

Generally, then, for a contract to qualify as a contract for necessaries, (1) the item contracted for must be necessary for the minor's subsistence, (2) the value of the necessary item must be appropriate to maintain the minor's standard of living, and (3) the minor must not be under the care of a parent or guardian who is required to supply this item. Unless these three criteria are met, the minor can disaffirm the contract *without* being liable for the reasonable value of the goods used.

CASE IN POINT Harun Fountain, a minor, was accidentally shot in the back of the head by a playmate and suffered serious injuries, for which he was awarded damages. Fountain received extensive life-saving medical services from Yale Diagnostic Radiology, but his mother refused to pay the $17,694 bill for those services. Yale Diagnostic therefore filed a lawsuit against Fountain directly. The court held that when necessary medical services are rendered to a minor whose parents do not pay for them, equity and justice demand that the minor be responsible for payment of these necessary services.[4]

RATIFICATION In contract law, **ratification** is the act of accepting and giving legal force to an obligation that previously was not enforceable. A minor who has reached the age of majority can ratify a contract expressly or impliedly. *Express* ratification takes place when the individual, on reaching the age of majority, states orally or in writing that he or she intends to be bound by the contract. *Implied* ratification takes place when the minor, on reaching the age of majority, indicates an intent to abide by the contract.

For example, Lin enters into a contract to sell her laptop to Andrew, a minor. If, on reaching the age of majority, Andrew writes a letter to Lin stating that he still agrees to buy the laptop, he has *expressly* ratified the contract. If, instead, Andrew takes possession of the laptop as a minor and continues to use it well after reaching the age of majority, he has *impliedly* ratified the contract.

If a minor fails to disaffirm a contract within a reasonable time after reaching the age of majority,

then the court must determine whether the conduct constitutes ratification or disaffirmance. Generally, a contract that is *executed* (fully performed by both parties) is presumed to be ratified. A contract that is still *executory* (not yet fully performed by both parties) normally is considered to be disaffirmed.

PARENTS' LIABILITY As a general rule, parents are not liable for contracts made by minor children acting on their own. This is why businesses ordinarily require parents to cosign any contract made with a minor. The parents then become personally obligated under the contract to perform the conditions of the contract, even if their child avoids liability. (Although minors normally are personally liable for their own torts, in some states parents can also be held liable for a minor's torts, especially if they failed to exercise proper parental control.)

Concept Summary 13.1 reviews the rules relating to contracts by minors.

Intoxication

Intoxication is a condition in which a person's normal capacity to act or think is inhibited by alcohol or some other drug. A contract entered into by an intoxicated person can be either voidable or valid (and thus enforceable).[5] If the person was sufficiently intoxicated to lack mental capacity, then

---

4. *Yale Diagnostic Radiology v. Estate of Harun Fountain,* 267 Conn. 351, 838 A.2d 179 (2004).

5. Note that if an alcoholic makes a contract while sober, there is no lack of capacity. See *Wright v. Fisher,* 32 N.W. 605 (Mich. 1887).

CONCEPT SUMMARY 13.1
Contracts by Minors

Concept	Description
General Rule	Contracts entered into by minors are *voidable* at the option of the minor.
Rules of Disaffirmance	A minor may disaffirm the contract at any time while still a minor and within a reasonable time after reaching the age of majority. Most states do not require restitution.
Exceptions to Basic Rules of Disaffirmance	1. *Misrepresentation of age (or fraud)*—In many jurisdictions, misrepresentation of age prohibits the right of disaffirmance. 2. *Necessaries*—Minors remain liable for the reasonable value of necessaries (goods and services). 3. *Ratification*—After reaching the age of majority, a person can ratify a contract that he or she formed as a minor, becoming fully liable thereon.

the agreement may be voidable even if the intoxication was purely voluntary. If, despite intoxication, the person understood the legal consequences of the agreement, the contract will be enforceable. Courts look at objective indications of the situation to determine if the intoxicated person possessed or lacked the required capacity.

For the contract to be voidable, the person must prove that the intoxication impaired her or his reason and judgment so severely that she or he did not comprehend the legal consequences of entering into the contract. In addition, the person claiming intoxication must be able to return all consideration received. As a practical matter, courts rarely permit contracts to be avoided on the ground of intoxication because it is difficult to determine whether a party was sufficiently intoxicated to avoid legal duties.

DISAFFIRMANCE If a contract is voidable because one party was intoxicated, that person has the option of disaffirming it while intoxicated and for a reasonable time after becoming sober (just as a minor may disaffirm during minority and for a reasonable period thereafter). To avoid the contract in most states, the person claiming intoxication must be able to return all consideration received unless the contract involves necessaries. Contracts for necessaries are voidable, but the intoxicated person is liable in quasi contract for the reasonable value of the consideration received (see Chapter 12).

RATIFICATION An intoxicated person, after becoming sober, may ratify a contract expressly or impliedly, just as a minor may do on reaching majority. Implied ratification occurs when a person enters into a contract while intoxicated and fails to disaffirm the contract within a *reasonable* time after becoming sober. Acts or conduct inconsistent with an intent to disaffirm—such as the continued use of property purchased under a voidable contract—will also ratify the contract.

See *Concept Summary 13.2* for a review of the rules relating to contracts by intoxicated persons.

Mental Incompetence

Contracts made by mentally incompetent persons can be void, voidable, or valid. We look here at the circumstances that determine which of these classifications apply.

WHEN THE CONTRACT WILL BE VOID If a court has previously determined that a person is mentally incompetent and has appointed a guardian to represent the individual, any contract made by the mentally incompetent person is *void*—no contract exists. Only the guardian can enter into binding legal obligations on behalf of the mentally incompetent person.

WHEN THE CONTRACT WILL BE VOIDABLE If a court has not previously judged a person to be mentally incompetent but in fact the person was incompetent at the time the contract was formed, the contract may be voidable. A contract is *voidable* if the person did not know he or she was entering into

---

CONCEPT SUMMARY 13.2
Contracts by Intoxicated Persons

Concept	Description
General Rules	If a person was sufficiently intoxicated to lack the mental capacity to comprehend the legal consequences of entering into the contract, the contract may be *voidable* at the option of the intoxicated person. If, despite intoxication, the person understood these legal consequences, the contract will be enforceable.
Disaffirmance	An intoxicated person may disaffirm the contract at any time while intoxicated and for a reasonable time after becoming sober but must make full restitution. Contracts for necessaries are voidable, but the intoxicated person is liable for the reasonable value of the goods or services.
Ratification	After becoming sober, a person can ratify a contract that she or he formed while intoxicated, becoming fully liable thereon.

the contract or lacked the mental capacity to comprehend its nature, purpose, and consequences. The contract can be avoided only by the mentally incompetent person, not by the other party. The contract may then be disaffirmed or ratified (if the person regains mental competence). Like intoxicated persons, mentally incompetent persons must return any consideration and pay for the reasonable value of any necessaries they receive.

For example, Milo, who had not been previously declared incompetent by a judge, agrees to sell twenty lots in a prime residential neighborhood to Anastof. At the time of entering into the contract, Milo is mentally incompetent and is confused over which lots he is selling and how much they are worth. As a result, he contracts to sell the properties for substantially less than their market value. If the court finds that Milo was unable to understand the nature and consequences of the contract, Milo can avoid the sale, provided that he returns any consideration he received.

WHEN THE CONTRACT WILL BE VALID A contract entered into by a mentally incompetent person (whom a court has not previously declared incompetent) may also be *valid* if the person had capacity *at the time the contract was formed*. An otherwise incompetent person who understands the nature, purpose, and consequences of a contract at the time of entering into it is bound by it. Some people who are incompetent due to age or illness have *lucid intervals*—temporary periods of sufficient intelligence, judgment, and will—during which they will be considered to have legal capacity to enter into contracts.

See *Concept Summary 13.3* for a review of the rules relating to contracts entered into by mentally incompetent persons.

SECTION 2
LEGALITY

Legality is the fourth requirement for a valid contract to exist. For a contract to be valid and enforceable, it must be formed for a legal purpose. A contract to do something that is prohibited by federal or state statutory law is illegal and, as such, void from the outset and thus unenforceable. A contract or a clause in a contract can also be illegal even in the absence of a specific statute prohibiting the action promised by the contract. Additionally, a contract to commit a tortious act—such as an agreement to engage in fraudulent misrepresentation (see Chapter 6)—is contrary to public policy and therefore illegal and unenforceable.

Contracts Contrary to Statute

Statutes often set forth rules specifying which terms and clauses may be included in contracts and which are prohibited. We now examine several ways in which contracts may be contrary to statute and thus illegal.

CONTRACTS TO COMMIT A CRIME Any contract to commit a crime is a contract in violation of a statute. Thus, a contract to sell illegal drugs in violation of criminal laws is unenforceable, as is a contract to cover up a corporation's violation of the Sarbanes-Oxley Act (see Chapter 5). Similarly, a contract to smuggle undocumented workers from another country into the United States for an employer is illegal (see Chapter 34), as is a contract to dump hazardous waste in violation of environmental laws (see Chapter 46). If the object or performance of the contract is rendered illegal by statute *after* the contract has been

CONCEPT SUMMARY 13.3	
Contracts by Mentally Incompetent Persons	
Concept	**Description**
Void	If a court has declared a person to be mentally incompetent and has appointed a legal guardian, any contract made by that person is void from the outset.
Voidable	If a court has *not* declared a person mentally incompetent, but that person lacked the capacity to comprehend the subject matter, nature, and consequences of the agreement, then the contract is voidable at that person's option.
Valid	If a court has *not* declared a person mentally incompetent and that person was able to understand the nature and effect of the contract at the time it was formed, then the contract is valid and enforceable.

entered into, the contract is considered to be discharged by law. (See the discussion of impossibility or impracticability of performance in Chapter 17.)

USURY Almost every state has a statute that sets the maximum rate of interest that can be charged for different types of transactions, including ordinary loans. A lender who makes a loan at an interest rate above the lawful maximum commits **usury.** Although usurious contracts are illegal, most states simply limit the interest that the lender may collect on the contract to the lawful maximum interest rate in that state. In a few states, the lender can recover the principal amount of the loan but no interest.

Usury statutes place a ceiling on allowable rates of interest, but states can make exceptions to facilitate business transactions. For example, many states exempt corporate loans from the usury laws, and nearly all states allow higher interest rate loans for borrowers who could not otherwise obtain funds.

In reaction to the latest economic recession, the Federal Reserve System (see Chapter 27) instituted wide-ranging restrictions on the way banks and other credit-card issuers can price their products and adjust those prices to changing credit conditions. These federal regulations established a system of price controls that are analogous to a federal usury law because they establish upper limits on prices—that is, on interest rates and fees on credit cards.[6]

GAMBLING Gambling is the creation of risk for the purpose of assuming it. Any scheme that involves the distribution of property by chance among persons who have paid valuable consideration for the opportunity (chance) to receive the property is gambling. Traditionally, the states have deemed gambling contracts illegal and thus void. It is sometimes difficult, however, to distinguish a gambling contract from the risk sharing inherent in almost all contracts.

All states have statutes that regulate gambling, and many states allow certain forms of gambling, such as horse racing, poker machines, and charity-sponsored bingo. In addition, nearly all states allow state-operated lotteries and gambling on Native American reservations. Even in states that permit certain types of gambling, though, courts often find that gambling contracts are illegal.

CASE IN POINT Casino gambling is legal in Louisiana, as are video poker machines. Nevertheless, Louisiana courts refused to enforce certain contracts relating to the installation of video poker machines. Gaming Venture, Inc. (GVI), had entered into two contracts with Tastee Restaurant Corporation: a licensing agreement and an agreement that authorized GVI to install poker machines in various Tastee locations. When several Tastee restaurants refused to install the machines, GVI sued for breach of contract. The state appellate court held that the two agreements were illegal gambling contracts and therefore void because GVI had failed to get the prior approval of the state video gaming commission.[7]

ONLINE GAMBLING In the past, this "mixed bag" of gambling laws presented a legal quandary: Can citizens in a state that does not allow gambling place bets through a Web site located in a state that does? After all, states have no constitutional authority over activities that take place in other states. Complicating the problem was the fact that many Internet gambling sites are located outside the United States in countries where Internet gambling is legal, and no state government has authority over activities that take place in other countries.

In 2006, Congress, concerned about money laundering stemming from online gambling, the problem of addiction, and underage gambling, passed legislation that greatly strengthened efforts to reduce online gaming. The Unlawful Internet Gambling Enforcement Act of 2006 cuts off the cash flow to Internet gambling sites by barring electronic payments, such as credit-card transactions, at those sites.[8] The reaction by the online gambling industry was swift and dramatic. After the passage of this bill, many foreign-based companies suspended the use of real money on the Web sites serving the United States. Without the incentive of playing for cash, the sites have lost their appeal for most clients.

Property, including funds, involved in illegal gambling can be seized under federal law through a civil forfeiture action. A defendant may assert a defense to reclaim the property, but should a criminal fugitive—a person who is evading custody in a criminal proceeding—be entitled to file such a claim? That was the question in the following case.

---

6. The Credit Card Accountability, Responsibility, and Disclosure Act of 2009, Pub. L. No. 111-24, 123 Stat. 1734. This law, which codifies many of the Federal Reserve's regulations, will be discussed in Chapter 45 in the context of consumer law.

7. *Gaming Venture, Inc. v. Tastee Restaurant Corp.*, 996 So.2d 515 (La. App. 5 Cir. 2008).

8. 31 U.S.C. Sections 5361 *et seq.*

CASE 13.1
United States v. $6,976,934.65, Plus Interest Deposited into Royal Bank of Scotland International

United States Court of Appeals, District of Columbia Circuit, 554 F.3d 123 (2009).
www.cadc.uscourts.gov/internet/home.nsf[a]

BACKGROUND AND FACTS • William Scott operated World Wide Tele-Sports, an Internet sports–betting service based on a Caribbean island. In 1998, the United States charged Scott with soliciting and accepting wagers from U.S. residents through illegal offshore Web sites. Unable to arrest Scott, who lived abroad, the government followed some of the proceeds from the enterprise to an account at the Royal Bank of Scotland International (RBSI) held by Soulbury Limited, a British corporation of which Scott was the majority shareholder. The United States filed a civil action in a federal district court, seeking the forfeiture of $6,976,934.65, plus interest, from RBSI's account with a U.S. bank. Soulbury denied that the funds were linked to Scott and filed a claim for the funds. Meanwhile, in 2005, Scott was indicted on money laundering charges related to the gambling violations. Under the Civil Asset Forfeiture Reform Act, also known as the *fugitive disentitlement statute,* a court can dismiss a claim in a civil forfeiture case based on a defendant's evasion of a separate criminal proceeding. The government filed a motion to dismiss Soulbury's claim under the fugitive disentitlement statute. The court issued a summary judgment in the government's favor. Soulbury appealed.

IN THE LANGUAGE OF THE COURT
GRIFFITH, Circuit Judge:
* * * *

[One issue in the application of the fugitive disentitlement statute is] whether the civil forfeiture action is "related" to the criminal prosecution being evaded.
* * * *

We think [the] standard to govern the "related" element * * * is found in the statute that provides for civil forfeiture of property related to a criminal prosecution. That statute specifies the circumstances in which the government may bring a civil forfeiture action to recover property related to a crime. The natural reading of "related" in the fugitive disentitlement statute is that the civil forfeiture action must be one in which the government is proceeding * * * to recover property "involved in," "derived from," "traceable to," "obtained by," or "used to facilitate" a crime for which the defendant is evading prosecution. In other words, *the question is whether the facts that underlie the prosecution being evaded also form the basis for the forfeiture action.* [Emphasis added.]

Applying that test, both the 1998 and 2005 prosecutions of Scott are unquestionably "related" to this forfeiture action. The 1998 criminal complaint charged Scott with * * * [illegally] "using a wire communication facility for the transmission in interstate and foreign commerce of bets and wagers on sporting events and contests, and for the transmission of a wire communication which entitled the recipient to receive money and credit as a result of bets and wagers." The charge was based on Scott's operation of an Internet sports betting service called World Wide Tele-Sports from 1997 to 1998. The 2005 indictment included the same charge against Scott * * * and also charged [him] with international money laundering. The civil forfeiture complaint * * * is based on, *inter alia* [among other things], charges of international money laundering with intent to promote a specified unlawful activity. The "specified unlawful activity" being promoted is the * * * violation alleged in the 1998 criminal complaint.

Soulbury has not raised a genuine issue of material fact as to the relation between the two criminal prosecutions and this civil forfeiture case. Thus, * * * the district court * * * correctly granted summary judgment as to this element.

DECISION AND REMEDY • *The federal appellate court found that the indictments against Scott were sufficiently "related" to the civil forfeiture action for the fugitive disentitlement statute to*

---

a. In the middle of the page, click on the "Opinions" box. On the page that opens, select "January" from the "Month:" menu and "2009" from the "Year:" menu, and click on "Go!" Scroll to the name of the case and click on its number to access the opinion. The U.S. Court of Appeals for the District of Columbia Circuit maintains this Web site.

CASE 13.1 CONTINUED ➡ *apply, but the court also determined that other issues of fact still had to be decided. Consequently, the court reversed the grant of summary judgment and remanded the case.*

THE GLOBAL DIMENSION • *Does the global reach of the Internet justify a court's assertion of authority over activities that occur in another jurisdiction? Why or why not?*

THE ETHICAL DIMENSION • *Do you believe that civil forfeiture statutes, like the one involved in this case, are effective deterrents of future criminal violations? Explain.*

LICENSING STATUTES All states require members of certain professions—including physicians, lawyers, real estate brokers, accountants, architects, electricians, and stockbrokers—to have licenses. Some licenses are obtained only after extensive schooling and examinations, which indicate to the public that a special skill has been acquired. Others require only that the applicant be of good moral character and pay a fee.

Whether a contract with an unlicensed person is legal and enforceable depends on the purpose of the licensing statute. If the statute's purpose is to protect the public from unauthorized practitioners (such as unlicensed attorneys and electricians, for example), then a contract involving an unlicensed practitioner is generally illegal and unenforceable. If the statute's purpose is merely to raise government revenues, however, a contract with an unlicensed person (such as a landscape architect or a massage therapist) may be enforced and the unlicensed practitioner fined.

Contracts Contrary to Public Policy

Although contracts involve private parties, some are not enforceable because of the negative impact they would have on society. Examples include a contract to commit a tortious act, such as invading another person's privacy; a contract to commit an immoral act, such as selling a child; and a contract that prohibits marriage. We look here at certain types of business contracts that are often said to be *contrary to public policy.*

CONTRACTS IN RESTRAINT OF TRADE Contracts in restraint of trade (anticompetitive agreements) usually adversely affect the public policy that favors competition in the economy. Typically, such contracts also violate one or more federal or state antitrust statutes.[9] An exception is recognized when the restraint is reasonable and is contained in an ancillary (secondary, or subordinate) clause in a contract. Such restraints often are included in contracts for the sale of an ongoing business and employment contracts.

Covenants Not to Compete and the Sale of an Ongoing Business. Many contracts involve a type of restraint called a **covenant not to compete,** or a restrictive covenant (promise). A covenant not to compete may be created when a seller agrees not to open a new store in a certain geographic area surrounding the old store. Such an agreement enables the seller to sell, and the purchaser to buy, the goodwill and reputation of an ongoing business without having to worry that the seller will open a competing business a block away. Provided the restrictive covenant is reasonable and is an ancillary part of the sale of an ongoing business, it is enforceable.

Covenants Not to Compete in Employment Contracts. Sometimes, agreements not to compete (also referred to as *noncompete agreements*) are included in employment contracts. People in middle- or upper-level management positions commonly agree not to work for competitors or not to start competing businesses for a specified period of time after termination of employment. Such agreements are legal in most states so long as the specified period of time (of restraint) is not excessive in duration and the geographic restriction is reasonable. What constitutes a reasonable time period may be shorter in the online environment than in conventional employment contracts because the restrictions apply worldwide. To be reasonable, a restriction on competition must protect a legitimate business interest and must not be any greater than necessary to protect that interest.

CASE IN POINT Safety and Compliance Management, Inc. (S&C), provides drug- and alcohol-testing services. S&C hired Angela Burgess primarily to retrieve specimens from clients and transport them to the lab. She signed a covenant not to compete "in any area of business" conducted by S&C for a period of two years from the date of termination. When Burgess quit her job at S&C and went to work at a nearby hospital as a medical assistant, S&C filed a lawsuit claiming that she had breached the noncompete agreement. The hospital also offered drug-testing services, and Burgess sometimes collected specimens from patients. The court, however, found

---

9. Federal statutes include the Sherman Antitrust Act, the Clayton Act, and the Federal Trade Commission Act (see Chapter 47).

that because S&C's noncompete agreement failed to specify the activities that Burgess was prohibited from performing, it was too broad and indefinite to be enforceable. The agreement was unreasonable because it imposed a greater limitation on Burgess than was necessary for S&C's protection.[10]

---

10. *Stultz v. Safety and Compliance Management, Inc.,* 285 Ga.App. 799, 648 S.E.2d 129 (2007).

The contract in the following case provided an exclusive license to open and operate comedy clubs under a certain famous trademark. It included a covenant not to compete. The question was whether the restraint was reasonable.

CASE 13.2
Comedy Club, Inc. v. Improv West Associates

United States Court of Appeals, Ninth Circuit, 553 F.3d 1277 (2009).
www.ca9.uscourts.gov[a]

BACKGROUND AND FACTS • Improv West Associates is the founder of the Improv Comedy Club and owner of the "Improv" trademark. Comedy Club, Inc. (CCI), owns and operates restaurants and comedy clubs. Improv West granted CCI an exclusive license to open four Improv clubs per year in 2001, 2002, and 2003. Their agreement prohibited CCI from opening any non-Improv comedy clubs "in the contiguous United States" until 2019. When CCI failed to open eight clubs by the end of 2002, Improv West commenced arbitration. The arbitrator's award in 2005 stated that CCI had forfeited its right to open Improv clubs but that the parties' agreement had not terminated and the covenant not to compete was enforceable—CCI could not open any new comedy clubs for its duration. A federal district court confirmed the award, and CCI appealed.

IN THE LANGUAGE OF THE COURT
GOULD, Circuit Judge:
* * * *

The basic outline of what the arbitrator did, terminating an exclusive right to open Improv clubs nationwide, because of contractually inadequate performance contrary to the agreed schedule, while keeping in force the restrictive covenant makes sense in so far as CCI should not have an exclusive license on Improv clubs absent complying with designated performance. And so long as CCI was running some Improv clubs, a restrictive covenant to some degree could protect Improv West from damage caused by improper competition. Because we cannot say that there is no basis in the record for the arbitrator's decision, we hold that the arbitrator's award is not completely irrational.
* * * *

CCI's "business" is operating full-service comedy clubs. CCI currently operates at least seven Improv clubs. As interpreted by the arbitrator, the * * * covenant not to compete applies geographically to the contiguous United States, and does not end until 2019. Thus, the covenant not to compete has dramatic geographic and temporal [time-related] scope. Combined with the arbitrator's ruling that CCI forfeited its rights to use the Improv marks license in any new location, the practical effect of the arbitrator's award * * * is that for more than fourteen years the entire contiguous United States comedy club market, except for CCI's current Improv clubs, is off limits to CCI. This forecloses competition in a substantial share of the comedy club business.
* * * *

* * * *The economic restraint of [this covenant] on competition is too broad to be countenanced [tolerated]* * * *. The covenant not to compete must be more narrowly tailored to relate to the areas in which CCI is operating Improv clubs under the license agreement.* [Emphasis added.]

---

a. In the left-hand column, in the "Decisions" pull-down menu, click on "Opinions." On that page, click on "Advanced Search." Type "05-55739" in the "by Case No.:" box, and click on "Search." In the result, click on the "01/29/2009" link to access the opinion. The U.S. Court of Appeals for the Ninth Circuit maintains this Web site.

CASE 13.2 CONTINUED ➡   However, we do not void the entire * * * covenant not to compete. * * * We weigh CCI's right to operate its business against Improv West's interest to protect and maintain its trademark, trade name and goodwill. This balance tilts in favor of Improv West with regard to counties where CCI is operating an Improv club.

Therefore, we hold that the district court should vacate [set aside] the arbitrator's [award] as to any county where CCI does not currently operate an Improv club, but uphold [the covenant] in those counties where CCI currently operates Improv clubs. Nationwide CCI may open and operate non-Improv comedy clubs in all those counties where it does not currently operate an Improv club. However, CCI may not open or operate any non-Improv clubs in those counties where it currently owns or operates Improv clubs.

DECISION AND REMEDY • *The federal appellate court reversed part of the lower court's confirmation of the award and remanded the case. A covenant not to compete in the comedy club business for fourteen years in forty-eight states is too broad to be enforced.*

THE ETHICAL DIMENSION • *Should companies or any subsidiaries affiliated with CCI be subject to the covenant not to compete? Would it be unethical to impose such a requirement? Discuss.*

THE LEGAL ENVIRONMENT DIMENSION • *Why would a business such as Improv West include a covenant not to compete in such an agreement as the contract at issue in this case? Explain.*

Enforcement Problems. The laws governing the enforceability of covenants not to compete vary significantly from state to state. In some states, such as Texas, such a covenant will not be enforced unless the employee has received some benefit in return for signing the noncompete agreement. This is true even if the covenant is reasonable as to time and area. If the employee receives no benefit, the covenant will be deemed void. California prohibits altogether the enforcement of covenants not to compete.

Occasionally, depending on the jurisdiction, courts will *reform* covenants not to compete. If a covenant is found to be unreasonable in time or geographic area, the court may convert the terms into reasonable ones and then enforce the reformed covenant. This presents a problem, however, in that the judge has implicitly become a party to the contract. Consequently, courts usually resort to contract *reformation* only when necessary to prevent undue burdens or hardships.

UNCONSCIONABLE CONTRACTS OR CLAUSES A court does not ordinarily look at the fairness or equity of a contract. For example, the courts generally do not inquire into the adequacy of consideration (as discussed in Chapter 12). Persons are assumed to be reasonably intelligent, and the courts will not come to their aid just because they have made an unwise or foolish bargain. In certain circumstances, however, bargains are so oppressive that the courts relieve innocent parties of part or all of their duties. Such bargains are deemed **unconscionable** because they are so unscrupulous or grossly unfair as to be "void of conscience."[11] A contract can be unconscionable on either procedural or substantive grounds, as discussed in the following subsections and illustrated graphically in Exhibit 13–1 on the following page.

Procedural Unconscionability. *Procedural* unconscionability often involves inconspicuous print, unintelligible language ("legalese"), or the lack of an opportunity to read the contract or ask questions about its meaning. This type of unconscionability typically arises when a party's lack of knowledge or understanding of the contract terms deprived him or her of any meaningful choice.

Procedural unconscionability can also occur when there is such disparity in bargaining power between the two parties that the weaker party's consent is not voluntary. This type of situation often involves an *adhesion contract* (see Chapter 14), which is a contract written exclusively by one party (the dominant party, usually the seller or creditor) and presented to the other (the adhering party, usually the buyer

---

11. The Uniform Commercial Code incorporated the concept of unconscionability in Sections 2–302 and 2A–108. These provisions, which apply to contracts for the sale or lease of goods, will be discussed in Chapter 19.

EXHIBIT 13–1 • Unconscionability

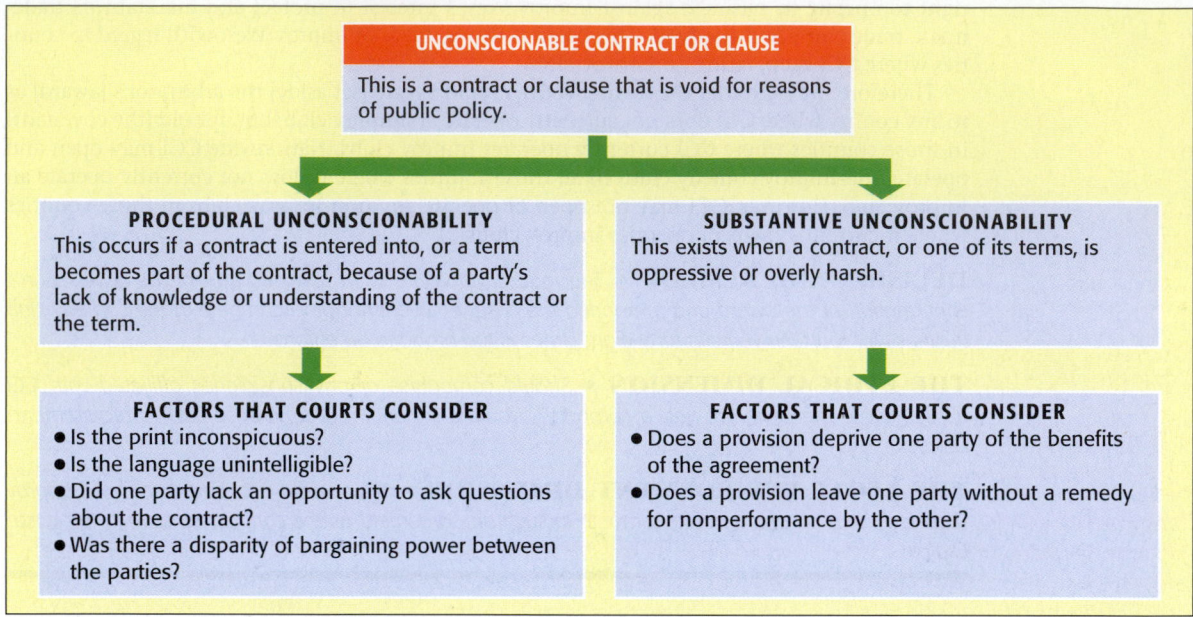

or borrower) on a take-it-or-leave-it basis.[12] In other words, the adhering party has no opportunity to negotiate the terms of the contract. Not all adhesion contracts are unconscionable, only those that unreasonably favor the drafter.[13]

Substantive Unconscionability. *Substantive* unconscionability characterizes those contracts, or portions of contracts, that are oppressive or overly harsh. Courts generally focus on provisions that deprive one party of the benefits of the agreement or leave that party without a remedy for nonperformance by the other. For example, a person with little income and only a fourth-grade education agrees to purchase a refrigerator for $4,500 and signs a two-year installment contract. The same type of refrigerator usually sells for $900 on the market. Despite the general rule that the courts will not inquire into the adequacy of consideration, some courts have held that this type of contract is unconscionable because

the contract terms are so oppressive as to "shock the conscience" of the court.[14]

Substantive unconscionability can arise in a wide variety of business contexts. For example, a contract clause that gives the business entity free access to the courts but requires the other party to arbitrate any dispute with the firm may be unconscionable.[15] Similarly, an arbitration clause in a credit-card agreement that prevents credit cardholders from obtaining relief for abusive debt-collection practices under consumer law may be unconscionable.[16] Contracts drafted by insurance companies and cell phone providers have been struck down as substantively unconscionable when they included provisions that were overly harsh or one sided.[17]

In the following case, the question was whether an arbitration clause was both procedurally and substantively unconscionable.

---

12. For a classic case involving an adhesion contract, see *Henningsen v. Bloomfield Motors, Inc.*, 32 N.J. 358, 161 A.2d 69 (1960).

13. See, for example, *Thibodeau v. Comcast Corp.*, 2006 PA Super. 346, 912 A.2d 874 (2006).

14. See, for example, *Jones v. Star Credit Corp.*, 59 Misc.2d 189, 298 N.Y.S.2d 264 (1969). This case will be presented in Chapter 19 as Case 19.3 on pages 272 and 273.

15. See, for example, *Wisconsin Auto Title Loans, Inc. v. Jones,* 290 Wis.2d 514, 714 N.W.2d 155 (2006).

16. See, for example, *Coady v. Cross County Bank,* 2007 WI App 26, 299 Wis.2d 420, 729 N.W.2d 732 (2007).

17. See, for example, *Gatton v. T-Mobile USA, Inc.,* 152 Cal.App.4th 571, 61 Cal.Rptr.3d 344 (2007); *Kinkel v. Cingular Wireless, LLC,* 223 Ill.2d 1, 857 N.E.2d 250, 306 Ill.Dec. 157 (2006); and *Aul v. Golden Rule Insurance Co.,* 737 N.W.2d 24 (Wis.App. 2007).

✳ EXTENDED CASE 13.3 ✳
Lhotka v. Geographic Expeditions, Inc.

California Court of Appeal, First District, 181 Cal.App.4th 816, 104 Cal.Rptr.3d 844 (2010).
www.courtinfo.ca.gov/opinions[a]

IN THE LANGUAGE OF THE COURT

SIGGINS, J. [Judge]

* * * *

Jason Lhotka was thirty-seven years old when he died of an altitude-related illness while on a GeoEx [Geographic Expeditions, Inc.] expedition up Mount Kilimanjaro with his mother, plaintiff Sandra Menefee. GeoEx's limitation of liability and release form, which both Lhotka and Menefee signed as a requirement of participating in the expedition, provided that each of them released GeoEx from all liability in connection with the trek and waived any claims for liability "to the maximum extent permitted by law." The release * * * reads: "I understand that all Trip Applications are subject to acceptance by GeoEx in San Francisco, California, USA. I agree that in the unlikely event a dispute of any kind arises between me and GeoEx, the following conditions will apply: (a) the dispute will be submitted to a neutral third-party mediator in San Francisco, California, with both parties splitting equally the cost of such mediator. If the dispute cannot be resolved through mediation, then (b) the dispute will be submitted for binding arbitration to the American Arbitration Association in San Francisco, California; (c) the dispute will be governed by California law; and (d) the maximum amount of recovery to which I will be entitled under any and all circumstances will be the sum of the land and air cost of my trip with GeoEx. I agree that this is a fair and reasonable limitation on the

damages, of any sort whatsoever, that I may suffer. I agree to fully indemnify [compensate] GeoEx for all of its costs (including attorneys' fees) if I commence an action or claim against GeoEx based upon claims I have previously released or waived by signing this release." Menefee paid $16,831 for herself and Lhotka to go on the trip.

A letter from GeoEx president James Sano that accompanied the limitation of liability and release explained that the form was mandatory and that, on this point, "our lawyers, insurance carriers and medical consultants give us no discretion. A signed, unmodified release form is required before any traveler may join one of our trips. * * * My review of other travel companies' release forms suggests that our forms are not a whole lot different from theirs."

After her son's death, Menefee sued GeoEx for wrongful death and alleged various theories of liability including fraud, gross negligence and recklessness, and intentional infliction of emotional distress. GeoEx moved to compel arbitration.

The trial court found the arbitration provision was unconscionable * * * and on that basis denied the motion. It ruled: "The agreement at issue is both procedurally and substantively unconscionable * * *.

This appeal timely followed.

* * * *

We turn * * * to GeoEx's contention that the court erred when it found the arbitration agreement unconscionable. Although the issue arises here in a relatively novel setting, the basic legal framework is well established.

"Unconscionability has generally been recognized to include an absence of meaningful choice on the part of one of the parties together with contract terms which are unreasonably favorable to the other party. Phrased another way, *unconscionability has both a procedural and a substantive element. The procedural element requires oppression or surprise.* * * * *The substantive element concerns whether a contractual provision reallocates risks in an objectively unreasonable or unexpected manner.*" * * * [Emphasis added.]

GeoEx argues the arbitration agreement involved neither the oppression nor surprise aspects of procedural unconscionability. GeoEx argues the agreement was not oppressive because plaintiffs made no showing of an "industry-wide requirement that travel clients must accept an agreement's terms without modification" and "they fail[ed] even to attempt to negotiate" with GeoEx. We disagree. GeoEx's argument cannot reasonably be squared with its own statements advising participants that they must sign an *unmodified* release form to participate in the expedition; that GeoEx's "lawyers, insurance carriers and medical consultants give [it] no discretion" on that point; and *that other travel companies were no different.* In other words, GeoEx led the plaintiffs to understand not only that its terms and conditions were nonnegotiable, but that plaintiffs would encounter the same requirements with any other travel company. This is a sufficient basis for us to conclude the plaintiffs lacked bargaining power.

GeoEx also contends its terms were not oppressive, apparently as a

---

a. From the drop-down menu, select "1st Appellate District," and then click on "View." On the page that opens, scroll down the list to the case title (decided January 29, 2010) to access the opinion. The California court system maintains this Web site.

EXTENDED CASE CONTINUES ➡

EXTENDED CASE 13.3 CONTINUED ⬇

matter of law, because Menefee and Lhotka could have simply decided not to trek up Mount Kilimanjaro. It argues that contracts for recreational activities can *never* be unconscionably oppressive because, unlike agreements for necessities such as medical care or employment, a consumer of recreational activities *always* has the option of [forgoing] the activity. The argument has some initial resonance [significance], but on closer inspection we reject it as unsound.

* * * *

Here, certainly, plaintiffs could have chosen not to sign on with the expedition. That option, like any availability of market alternatives, is relevant to the existence, and degree, of oppression. But we must also consider the other circumstances surrounding the execution of the agreement. GeoEx presented its limitation of liability and release form as mandatory and unmodifiable, and essentially told plaintiffs that any other travel provider would

impose the same terms. "Oppression arises from an inequality of bargaining power which results in no real negotiation and an absence of meaningful choice * * * ." GeoEx presented its terms as both nonnegotiable and *no different than what plaintiffs would find with any other provider.* Under these circumstances, plaintiffs made a sufficient showing to establish at least a minimal level of oppression to justify a finding of procedural unconscionability. [Emphasis in original.]

* * * [We now] address whether the substantive unconscionability of the GeoEx contract warrants the trial court's ruling.

* * * *

The arbitration provision in GeoEx's release * * * guaranteed that plaintiffs could not possibly obtain anything approaching full recompense for their harm by limiting any recovery they could obtain to the amount they paid GeoEx for their trip. In addition to a limit on their recovery, plaintiffs, residents of Colorado, were required to mediate and arbitrate in San Francisco—all

but guaranteeing both that GeoEx would never be out more than the amount plaintiffs had paid for their trip, and that any recovery plaintiffs might obtain would be devoured by the expense they incur in pursuing their remedy. The release also required plaintiffs to indemnify GeoEx for its costs and attorney fees for defending any claims covered by the release of liability form. Notably, there is no reciprocal limitation on damages or indemnification obligations imposed on GeoEx. Rather than providing a neutral forum for dispute resolution, GeoEx's arbitration scheme provides a potent disincentive for an aggrieved client to pursue any claim, in any forum—and may well guarantee that GeoEx wins even if it loses. Absent reasonable justification for this arrangement—and none is apparent—we agree with the trial court that the arbitration clause is so one-sided as to be substantively unconscionable.

* * * *

The order denying GeoEx's motion to compel arbitration is affirmed.

QUESTIONS

1. What did the judge mean when he said that GeoEx's one-sided arbitration scheme "may well guarantee that GeoEx wins even if it loses"?
2. Did the fact that the terms of the release were nonnegotiable contribute to its procedural unconscionability or its substantive unconscionability? Explain.

EXCULPATORY CLAUSES Often closely related to the concept of unconscionability are **exculpatory clauses,** which release a party from liability in the event of monetary or physical injury *no matter who is at fault.* Indeed, courts sometimes refuse to enforce such clauses on the ground that they are unconscionable. Exculpatory clauses found in rental agreements for commercial property are frequently held to be contrary to public policy, and such clauses are almost always unenforceable in residential property leases. Courts also usually hold that exculpatory clauses are against public policy in the employment context. Thus, employers frequently cannot enforce exculpatory clauses in contracts with employees or

independent contractors (see Chapter 32) to avoid liability for work-related injuries.[18]

Although courts view exculpatory clauses with disfavor, they do enforce such clauses when they do not contravene public policy, are not ambiguous, and do not claim to protect parties from liability for intentional misconduct. Businesses such as health clubs, racetracks, amusement parks, skiing facilities, horse-rental operations, golf-cart concessions, and skydiving organizations frequently use exculpatory clauses to limit their liability for patrons' injuries.

---

18. See, for example, *Speedway SuperAmerica, LLC v. Erwin,* 250 S.W.3d 339 (2008).

Because these services are not essential, the firms offering them are sometimes considered to have no relative advantage in bargaining strength, and anyone contracting for their services is considered to do so voluntarily.

DISCRIMINATORY CONTRACTS Contracts in which a party promises to discriminate on the basis of race, color, national origin, religion, gender, age, or disability are contrary to both statute and public policy. They are also unenforceable.[19] For example, if a property owner promises in a contract not to sell the property to a member of a particular race, the contract is unenforceable. The public policy underlying these prohibitions is very strong, and the courts are quick to invalidate discriminatory contracts.

Exhibit 13–2 illustrates the types of contracts that may be illegal because they are contrary to statute or public policy.

Effect of Illegality

In general, an illegal contract is void—that is, the contract is deemed never to have existed, and the

---

19. The major federal statute prohibiting discrimination is the Civil Rights Act of 1964, 42 U.S.C. Sections 2000e–2000e-17. For a discussion of this act and other acts prohibiting discrimination in the employment context, see Chapter 35.

courts will not aid either party. In most illegal contracts, both parties are considered to be equally at fault—*in pari delicto*.[20] If the contract is executory (not yet fulfilled), neither party can enforce it. If it has been executed, neither party can recover damages.

Generally, the courts are not concerned if one wrongdoer in an illegal contract is unjustly enriched at the expense of the other—except under certain circumstances. The main reason for this hands-off attitude is the belief that a plaintiff who has broken the law by entering into an illegal bargain should not be allowed to obtain help from the courts. Another justification is the hoped-for deterrent effect: a plaintiff who suffers a loss because of an illegal bargain will presumably be deterred from entering into similar illegal bargains in the future.

There are exceptions to the general rule that neither party to an illegal bargain can sue for breach and neither party can recover for performance rendered. We look at these exceptions next.

JUSTIFIABLE IGNORANCE OF THE FACTS When one of the parties is relatively innocent (has no reason to know that the contract is illegal), that party can often recover any benefits conferred in a partially

---

20. Pronounced in *pah*-ree deh-*lick*-tow.

EXHIBIT 13–2 • Contract Legality

CONTRACTS CONTRARY TO STATUTE		CONTRACTS CONTRARY TO PUBLIC POLICY	
USURIOUS LOANS Illegal if the interest rate exceeds legal limit	**CONTRACTS BY UNLICENSED PERSONS** May not be enforceable depending on the purpose of the statute	**CONTRACTS IN RESTRAINT OF TRADE** Normally unenforceable, unless the restraint is reasonable under the circumstances, such as in some covenants not to compete	**ADHESION CONTRACTS** May be unenforceable if entered into because of one party's superior bargaining power
GAMBLING CONTRACTS Illegal depending on state statute			**EXCULPATORY CLAUSES** May be deemed unconscionable
CONTRACTS TO COMMIT A CRIME Always illegal		**CONTRACTS TO COMMIT A TORT** Always unenforceable	**DISCRIMINATORY CONTRACTS** Illegal when discrimination is based on race, religion, national origin, or gender
		UNCONSCIONABLE CONTRACTS Must not be so unfair as to be oppressive	

executed contract. In this situation, the courts will not enforce the contract but will allow the parties to return to their original positions.

A court may sometimes permit an innocent party who has fully performed under the contract to enforce the contract against the guilty party. For example, a trucking company contracts with Gillespie to carry crates filled with goods to a specific destination for the normal fee of $5,000. The trucker delivers the crates and later finds out that they contained illegal goods. Although the law specifies that the shipment, use, and sale of the goods were illegal, the trucker, being an innocent party, can still legally collect the $5,000 from Gillespie.

MEMBERS OF PROTECTED CLASSES When a statute is clearly designed to protect a certain class of people, a member of that class can enforce a contract in violation of the statute even though the other party cannot. For example, flight attendants and pilots are subject to a federal statute that prohibits them from flying more than a certain number of hours every month. If an attendant or a pilot exceeds the maximum, the airline must nonetheless pay for those extra hours of service.

Other examples of statutes designed to protect a particular class of people are state statutes that regulate the sale of insurance. If an insurance company violates a statute when selling insurance, the purchaser can still enforce the policy and recover from the insurer.

WITHDRAWAL FROM AN ILLEGAL AGREEMENT If the illegal part of a bargain has not yet been performed, the party rendering performance can withdraw from the contract and recover the performance or its value. For example, Sam and Jim decide to wager (illegally) on the outcome of a boxing match. Each deposits cash with a stakeholder, who agrees to pay the winner of the bet. At this point, each party has performed part of the agreement, but the illegal element of the agreement will not occur until the funds are paid to the winner. Before that payment occurs, either party is entitled to withdraw from the bargain by giving notice of repudiation to the stakeholder.

CONTRACT ILLEGAL THROUGH FRAUD, DURESS, OR UNDUE INFLUENCE Often, one party to an illegal contract is more at fault than the other. When a party has been induced to enter into an illegal bargain by fraud, duress, or undue influence on the part of the other party to the agreement, that party will be allowed to recover for the performance or its value.

SEVERABLE, OR DIVISIBLE, CONTRACTS A contract that is *severable,* or divisible, consists of distinct parts that can be performed separately, with separate consideration provided for each part. With an *indivisible* contract, in contrast, complete performance by each party is essential, even if the contract contains a number of seemingly separate provisions.

If a contract is divisible into legal and illegal portions, a court may enforce the legal portion but not the illegal one, so long as the illegal portion does not affect the essence of the bargain. This approach is consistent with the courts' basic policy of enforcing the legal intentions of the contracting parties whenever possible. For example, Cole signs an employment contract that includes an overly broad and thus illegal covenant not to compete. In that situation, a court might allow the employment contract to be enforceable but reform the unreasonably broad covenant by converting its terms into reasonable ones. Alternatively, the court could declare the covenant illegal (and thus void) and enforce the remaining employment terms.

REVIEWING
Capacity and Legality

Renee Beaver started racing go-karts competitively in 2007, when she was fourteen. Many of the races required her to sign an exculpatory clause to participate, which she or her parents regularly signed. In 2010, she participated in the annual Elkhart Grand Prix, a series of races in Elkhart, Indiana. During the event in which she drove, a piece of foam padding used as a course barrier was torn from its base and ended up on the track. A portion of the padding struck Beaver in the head, and another portion was thrown into oncoming traffic, causing a multikart collision during which she sustained severe injuries.

REVIEWING
Capacity and Legality, Continued

Beaver filed an action against the race organizers for negligence. The organizers could not locate the exculpatory clause that Beaver had supposedly signed. Race organizers argued that she must have signed one to enter the race, but even if she had not signed one, her actions showed her intent to be bound by its terms. Using the information presented in the chapter, answer the following questions.

1. Did Beaver have the contractual capacity to enter a contract with an exculpatory clause? Why or why not?
2. Assuming that Beaver did, in fact, sign the exculpatory clause, did she later disaffirm or ratify the contract? Explain.
3. Now assume that Beaver stated that she was eighteen years old at the time that she signed the exculpatory clause. How might this affect Beaver's ability to disaffirm or ratify the contract?
4. If Beaver did not actually sign the exculpatory clause, could a court conclude that she impliedly accepted its terms by participating in the race? Why or why not?

DEBATE THIS: *After agreeing to an exculpatory clause or purchasing some item, such as a computer, minors often seek to avoid the contracts. Today's minors are far from naïve and should not be allowed to avoid their contractual obligations.*

TERMS AND CONCEPTS

age of majority 256
contractual capacity 256
covenant not
   to compete 263
disaffirmance 256
emancipation 256
exculpatory clause 268
necessaries 257
ratification 258
unconscionable 265
usury 261

QUESTIONS AND CASE PROBLEMS

13–1. Intoxication After Kira had had several drinks one night, she sold Charlotte a diamond necklace worth thousands of dollars for just $100. The next day, Kira offered the $100 to Charlotte and requested the return of her necklace. Charlotte refused to accept the $100 or return the necklace, claiming that there was a valid contract of sale. Kira explained that she had been intoxicated at the time the bargain was made and thus the contract was voidable at her option. Was Kira correct? Explain.

13–2. QUESTION WITH SAMPLE ANSWER: Covenants Not to Compete.

A famous New York City hotel, Hotel Lux, is noted for its food as well as its luxury accommodations. Hotel Lux contracts with a famous chef, Chef Perlee, to become its head chef at $10,000 per month. The contract states that should Perlee leave the employment of Hotel Lux for any reason, he will not work as a chef for any hotel or restaurant in New York, New Jersey, or Pennsylvania for a period of one year. During the first six months of the contract, Hotel Lux heavily advertises Perlee as its head chef, and business at the hotel is excellent. Then a dispute arises between the hotel management and Perlee, and Perlee terminates his employment. One month later, he is hired by a famous New Jersey restaurant just across the New York state line. Hotel Lux learns of Perlee's employment through a large advertisement in a New York City newspaper. It seeks to enjoin (prevent) Perlee from working in that restaurant as a chef for one year. Discuss how successful Hotel Lux will be in its action.

- **For a sample answer to Question 13–2, go to Appendix I at the end of this text.**

13–3. Capacity Joanne is a seventy-five-year-old widow who survives on her husband's small pension. Joanne has become increasingly forgetful, and her family worries that she may have Alzheimer's disease (a brain disorder that seriously affects a person's ability to carry out daily activities). No physician has diagnosed her, however, and no court has ruled on Joanne's legal competence. One day while she is out shopping, Joanne stops by a store that is having a sale on pianos and enters into a fifteen-year installment contract to buy a grand piano. When the piano arrives the next day, Joanne seems confused and repeatedly asks the deliveryperson why a piano is being delivered. Joanne claims that she does not recall buying a piano. Explain whether this contract is void, voidable, or valid. Can Joanne avoid her contractual obligation to buy the piano? If so, how?

13–4. Unconscionability Frank Rodziewicz was driving a Volvo tractor-trailer on Interstate 90 in Lake County, Indiana, when he struck a concrete barrier. His tractor-trailer became stuck on the barrier, and the Indiana State Police contacted Waffco Heavy Duty Towing, Inc., to assist in the recovery of the truck. Before beginning work, Waffco told Rodziewicz that it would cost $275 to tow the truck. There was no discussion of labor or any other costs. Rodziewicz told Waffco to take the truck to a local Volvo dealership. Within a few minutes, Waffco pulled the truck off the barrier and towed it to Waffco's nearby towing yard. Rodziewicz was soon notified that, in addition to the $275 towing fee, he would have to pay $4,070 in labor costs and that Waffco would not release the truck until payment was made. Rodziewicz paid the total amount. Disputing the labor charge, however, he filed a suit in an Indiana state court against Waffco, alleging, in part, breach of contract. Was the towing contract unconscionable? Would it make a difference if the parties had discussed the labor charge before the tow? Explain. [*Rodziewicz v. Waffco Heavy Duty Towing, Inc.*, 763 N.E.2d 491 (Ind.App. 2002)]

13–5. Covenant Not to Compete Gary Forsee was an executive officer with responsibility for the U.S. operations of BellSouth Corp., a company providing global telecommunications services. Under a covenant not to compete, Forsee agreed that for a period of eighteen months after termination from employment, he would not "provide services . . . in competition with [BellSouth] . . . to any person or entity which provides products or services identical or similar to products and services provided by [BellSouth] . . . within the territory." *Territory* was defined to include the geographic area in which Forsee provided services to BellSouth. The *services* included "management, strategic planning, business planning, administration, or other participation in or providing advice with respect to the communications services business." Forsee announced his intent to resign and accept a position as chief executive officer of Sprint Corp., a competitor of BellSouth. BellSouth filed a suit in a Georgia state court against Forsee, claiming, in part, that his acceptance of employment with Sprint would violate the covenant not to compete. Is the covenant legal?

Should it be enforced? Why or why not? [*BellSouth Corp. v. Forsee*, 265 Ga.App. 589, 595 S.E.2d 99 (2004)]

13–6. CASE PROBLEM WITH SAMPLE ANSWER: Misrepresentation of Age.

*Millennium Club, Inc., operates a tavern in South Bend, Indiana. In January 2003, Pamela Avila and other minors gained admission by misrepresenting themselves to be at least twenty-one years old. According to the club's representatives, the minors used false driver's licenses, "fraudulent transfer of a stamp used to gain admission by another patron or other means of false identification." To gain access, the minors also signed affidavits falsely attesting to the fact that they were aged twenty-one or older. When the state filed criminal charges against the club, the club filed a suit in an Indiana state court against Avila and more than two hundred others, charging that they had misrepresented their ages and seeking damages of $3,000 each. The minors filed a motion to dismiss the complaint. Should the court grant the motion? What are the competing policy interests in this case? If the club was not careful in checking minors' identification, should it be allowed to recover? If the club reasonably relied on the minors' representations, should the minors be allowed to avoid liability? Discuss. [*Millennium Club, Inc. v. Avila*, 809 N.E.2d 906 (Ind.App. 2004)]*

• To view a sample answer for Problem 13–6, go to this book's Web site at www.cengage.com/blaw/clarkson, select "Chapter 13," and click on "Case Problem with Sample Answer."

13–7. Licensing Statutes Under California law, a contract to manage a professional boxer must be in writing, and the manager must be licensed by the State Athletic Commission. Marco Antonio Barrera is a professional boxer and two-time world champion. In May 2003, José Castillo, who was not licensed by the state, orally agreed to assume Barrera's management. He "understood" that he would be paid in accord with the "practice in the professional boxing industry, but in no case less than ten percent (10%) of the gross revenue" that Barrera generated as a boxer and through endorsements. Among other accomplishments, Castillo negotiated an exclusive promotion contract for Barrera with Golden Boy Promotions, Inc., which is owned and operated by Oscar De La Hoya. Castillo also helped Barrera settle three lawsuits and resolve unrelated tax problems so that Barrera could continue boxing. Castillo did not train Barrera, pick his opponents, or arrange his fights, however. When Barrera abruptly stopped communicating with Castillo, Castillo filed a suit in a California state court against Barrera and others, alleging breach of contract. Under what circumstances is a contract with an unlicensed practitioner enforceable? Is the alleged contract in this case enforceable? Why or why not? [*Castillo v. Barrera*, 146 Cal.App.4th 1317, 53 Cal.Rptr.3d 494 (2 Dist. 2007)]

13–8. Unconscionable Contracts or Clauses Roberto Basulto and Raquel Gonzalez, who did not speak English, responded to an ad on Spanish-language television sponsored by Hialeah Automotive, LLC, which does business as Potamkin Dodge. Potamkin's staff understood that Basulto and Gonzalez did not speak or read English and conducted the entire transaction in Spanish. They explained the English-language contract, but did not explain an accompanying arbitration agreement. This agreement limited the amount of damages that the buyers could seek in court to less than $5,000, but did not limit Potamkin's right to pursue greater damages. Basulto and Gonzalez bought a Dodge Caravan and signed the contract in blank (meaning that some parts were left blank). Potamkin later filled in a lower trade-in allowance than agreed and refused to change it. The buyers returned the van—having driven it a total of seven miles—and asked for a return of their trade-in vehicle, but it had been sold. The buyers filed a suit in a Florida state court against Potamkin. The dealer sought arbitration. Was the arbitration agreement unconscionable? Why or why not? [*Hialeah Automotive, LLC v. Basulto*, 156 Fla. 92, 22 So.3d 586 (3 Dist. 2009)]

13–9. Substantive Unconscionability Erica Bishop lived in public housing with her children. Her lease stated that only she and her children, who were listed on the lease, could live in the apartment, and that she was responsible for the actions of all household members. Any violations of the lease by any household member, including criminal activity, would be grounds for eviction. Bishop's son Derek committed an armed robbery at a store next to the apartment building. Bishop was given thirty days to vacate the apartment due to breach of the lease. She sued, arguing that Derek had moved out of the apartment months before the robbery, but she admitted he had been in the apartment right before the robbery. The trial court held that since Derek had visited the apartment right before the robbery, he was a household member and Bishop had to vacate. She appealed, contending that the lease was invalid because it was substantively unconscionable. Does Erica have grounds for a reversal in her favor? Discuss. [*Bishop v. Housing Authority of South Bend*, 920 N.E.2d 772 (Ind.App. 2010)]

13–10. A QUESTION OF ETHICS: Covenants Not to Compete.

Retina Consultants, P.C., is a medical practice that specializes in retina eye surgery. This company hired Brendan Coleman as a software engineer in 2000. Prior to his hiring at Retina Consultants, Coleman had created and marketed a software billing program called Clinex. During his stay with Retina Consultants, physicians worked with Coleman to modify his Clinex program to better suit the company's needs. The new program was called Clinex-RE. While employed, Coleman signed an agreement which stated ownership of Clinex remained with Coleman while that of Clinex-RE remained with Retina Consultants. Within the document was the following sentence: "Coleman will not distribute, vend or license to any ophthalmologist or optometrist the Clinex software or any computer application competitive with the Clinex-RE software without the written consent of Retina Consultants." In essence, Coleman agreed to a covenant not to compete (noncompete clause). After quitting his job with Retina Consultants, Coleman attempted to license Clinex and Clinex-RE to other ophthalmologists. He also refused to provide the necessary passwords for Retina Consultants to use Clinex and Clinex-RE. Furthermore, he used the company's trade secrets and withdrew funds from a company banking account, among other actions. At trial, the court entered a judgment enjoining Coleman from marketing the software that was in competition with the software he had developed for Retina Consultants. The court also obligated Coleman to return the funds taken from the company's bank account. Coleman appealed. [*Coleman v. Retina Consultants, P.C., 286 Ga. 317, 687 S.E.2d 457 (2009)*]

(a) Should the court uphold the noncompete clause? If so, why? If not, why not?

(b) Should the court require Coleman to return the funds he withdrew from the company's accounts? Discuss fully.

(c) Did Coleman's behavior after he left the company influence the court's decision? Explain your answer.

LEGAL RESEARCH EXERCISES ON THE WEB

Go to this text's Web site at **www.cengage.com/blaw/clarkson**, select "Chapter 13," and click on "Practical Internet Exercises." There you will find the following Internet research exercises that you can perform to learn more about the topics covered in this chapter.

Practical Internet Exercise 13–1: **Legal Perspective**
Covenants Not to Compete

Practical Internet Exercise 13–2: **Management Perspective**
Minors and the Law

Practical Internet Exercise 13–3: **Social Perspective**
Online Gambling

CHAPTER 14

Mistakes, Fraud, and Voluntary Consent

An otherwise valid contract may still be unenforceable if the parties have not genuinely agreed to its terms. As mentioned in Chapter 10, a lack of *voluntary consent* (assent) can be used as a defense to the contract's enforceability.

Voluntary consent may be lacking because of a mistake, misrepresentation, undue influence, or duress—in other words, because there is no true "meeting of the minds." Generally, a party who demonstrates that he or she did not truly agree to the terms of a

contract can choose either to carry out the contract or to rescind (cancel) it and thus avoid the entire transaction. In this chapter, we examine the kinds of factors that may indicate a lack of voluntary consent.

SECTION 1
MISTAKES

We all make mistakes, so it is not surprising that mistakes are made when contracts are formed. In certain circumstances, contract law allows a contract to be avoided on the basis of mistake. It is important to distinguish between *mistakes of fact* and *mistakes of value or quality.* Only a mistake of fact makes a contract voidable.

Mistakes of Fact

Mistakes of fact occur in two forms—*bilateral* and *unilateral*. A bilateral, or mutual, mistake is made by *both* of the contracting parties. A unilateral mistake is made by only *one* of the parties. We look next at these two types of mistakes and illustrate them graphically in Exhibit 14–1.

BILATERAL (MUTUAL) MISTAKES OF FACT A bilateral mistake of fact is a "mutual misunderstanding concerning a basic assumption on which the contract was made."[1] When both parties are mistaken about the same material fact, the contract can be rescinded

by either party. Normally, the contract is voidable by the adversely affected party. For example, Gilbert contracts to sell Magellan three tracts of undeveloped land for $6 million on the basis of a surveyor's report showing the layout and acreage. After agreeing to the price, the parties discover that the surveyor made an error and that the tracts actually contain 10 percent more acreage than reported. In this situation, Gilbert can seek rescission (cancellation) of the contract based on mutual mistake. The same result—rescission—would occur if both parties had mistakenly believed that the tracts of land were adjoining but they were not.[2]

A word or term in a contract may be subject to more than one reasonable interpretation. If the parties to the contract attach materially different meanings to the term, a court may allow the contract to be rescinded because there has been no true "meeting of the minds."[3]

---

2. See, for example, *Rawson v. UMLIC VP, LLC,* 933 So.2d 1206 (Fla.App. 2006).

3. The only way for a court to find out the meaning that each party attached to the contract term is to allow the parties to introduce *parol evidence,* which is basically oral testimony about the terms of their agreement. Parol evidence will be discussed in Chapter 15.

---

1. *Restatement (Second) of Contracts,* Section 152.

EXHIBIT 14–1 • Mistakes of Fact

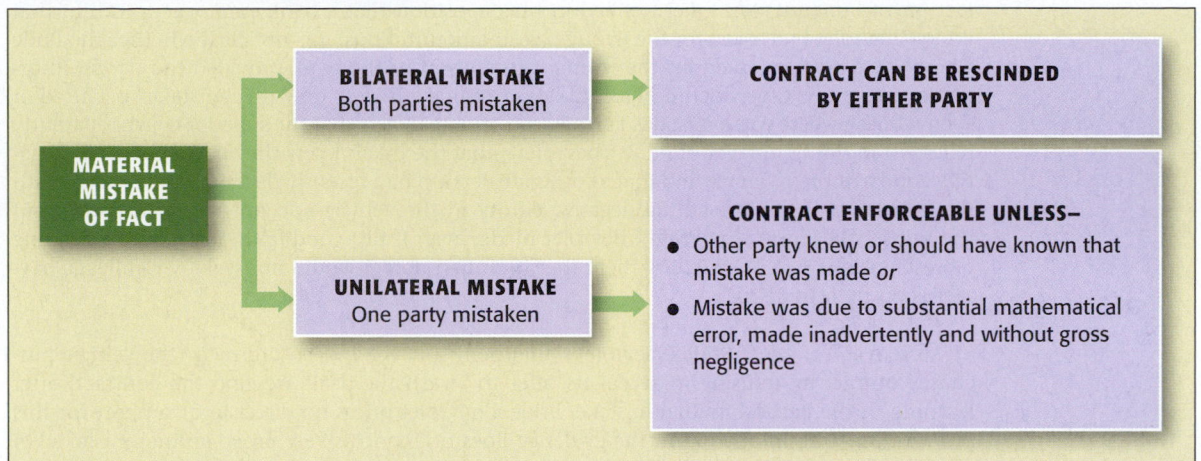

CASE IN POINT In 1864, Wichelhaus agreed to buy a shipment of Surat cotton from Raffles, "to arrive 'Peerless' from Bombay." There were two ships named *Peerless* sailing from Bombay, India, however. Wichelhaus was referring to the *Peerless* that sailed in October; Raffles meant a different *Peerless* that sailed in December. When Raffles tried to deliver the goods in December, Wichelhaus refused to accept them, and a lawsuit followed. The court held in favor of Wichelhaus, concluding that a mutual mistake had

been made because the parties had attached materially different meanings to an essential term of the contract.[4]

In the following case, the court had to grapple with the question of whether a mutual mistake of fact had occurred.

_____

4. *Raffles v. Wichelhaus,* 159 Eng.Rep. 375 (1864).

CASE 14.1
Inkel v. Pride Chevrolet-Pontiac, Inc.

Supreme Court of Vermont, 945 A.2d 855 (2008).

BACKGROUND AND FACTS • Normand and Brandy Inkel, who live in Vermont, called Pride Chevrolet-Pontiac, Inc., in Boston about buying a new Chevy Tahoe. They said that they would trade in a high-mileage vehicle they had leased. The sales representative told them that the high-mileage penalty would probably not apply as the lease was from a bank, not a dealership. When the Inkels took delivery of the new Tahoe and left their old vehicle at Pride, the price on the contract was $41,200. In small print on the back of the agreement was a provision that the buyer was responsible for any problems with the trade-in vehicle. A month after the sale, Pride told the Inkels they owed another $16,435 because of a misunderstanding with the leasing company about the high-mileage charge. The Inkels refused to pay. Pride demanded that they return the Tahoe and wanted to cancel the deal; the Inkels refused. The Inkels then sued Pride for breach of contract and other claims. A Vermont trial court held that a mutual mistake had been made in the contract and that the Inkels should have agreed to undo the deal. The court granted summary judgment for Pride and ordered the Inkels to pay damages. They appealed.

IN THE LANGUAGE OF THE COURT
BURGESS, Justice.
* * * *

The evidence submitted in connection with the parties' cross motions for summary judgment does not establish what happened in the instant case [the case under discussion]. Although the superior court [the trial court] stated in a footnote that it

CASE CONTINUES ➡

CASE 14.1 CONTINUED ➡ was undisputed that the Chittenden Bank was negligent in giving Pride Chevrolet an incorrect payoff amount, Mr. Inkel testified in his deposition that a bank employee told him that Pride Chevrolet had asked for the wrong payoff amount. Thus, it is not clear whether the Pride Chevrolet employee asked for the wrong information or the bank provided the wrong information. In short, the evidentiary record does not make it clear how the "mistake" occurred or even whether there was a mistake. Further, the principal facts that the superior court apparently relied on in ruling in favor of Pride Chevrolet—that the Inkels knew they had substantial negative equity in their vehicle and that another dealership had recently declined to negotiate with them because of the substantial negative equity in the vehicle—do not necessarily undercut the Inkels' allegation that Pride Chevrolet made, even if [in] good-faith, false and misleading representations * * * by telling them that their lien holder would not seek over-mileage payments on their trade-in.

* * * *

Moreover, we reject Pride Chevrolet's argument that the Inkels "affirmed" the vehicle purchase contract by refusing to accept its offer to "wash the deal" [rescind the contract] after learning of the parties' mutual mistake. Pride Chevrolet offers no direct legal support for this proposition, and, in any event, the evidence does not conclusively prove mutual mistake. *"A mutual mistake must be a mistake reciprocally involving both parties, a mistake independently made by both parties." "A mistake by one party coupled with ignorance thereof does not constitute mutual mistake."* [Emphasis added.]

Given the current state of the record, whether the Inkels merely accepted Pride Chevrolet's statements as true or took advantage of the dealer's mistaken beliefs, the existence of mutual mistake is questionable at best. Further, even assuming that the parties' mistake was mutual, Pride Chevrolet failed to demonstrate that the offer to "wash the deal" was a legitimate offer to rescind the contract. Pride Chevrolet presented no evidence indicating precisely when the offer was made, who made the offer, or what terms, if any, were offered.

DECISION AND REMEDY • *The Vermont high court reversed in favor of the Inkels, holding that it was not clear that a mutual mistake was made. For a court to find that a mutual mistake occurred, evidence would have to be produced at trial to show that both parties were mistaken about the same facts.*

THE ETHICAL DIMENSION • *If a Pride sales representative led the Inkels to believe that the dealership did not care about the excessive miles on the trade-in vehicle, should Pride be willing to incur the loss? Why or why not?*

WHAT IF THE FACTS WERE DIFFERENT? • *Suppose that the provision making the buyers responsible for any problems with the trade-in vehicle was clearly visible on the face of the contract that the Inkels signed (rather than being in small print on the back). How might this have changed the outcome of this case?*

UNILATERAL MISTAKES OF FACT A unilateral mistake occurs when only one of the contracting parties is mistaken about a material fact. Generally, a unilateral mistake does not afford the mistaken party any right to relief from the contract. Normally, the contract is enforceable. For example, DeVinck intends to sell his motor home for $32,500. When he learns that Benson is interested in buying a used motor home, DeVinck faxes Benson an offer to sell the vehicle to him. When typing the fax, however, DeVinck mistakenly keys in the price of $23,500. Benson immediately sends DeVinck a fax accepting DeVinck's offer. Even though DeVinck intended to

sell his motor home for $32,500, his unilateral mistake falls on him. He is bound in contract to sell the motor home to Benson for $23,500.

There are at least two exceptions to this general rule.[5] First, if the *other* party to the contract knows or should have known that a mistake of fact was made, the contract may not be enforceable. In the above example, if Benson knew that DeVinck intended to sell his motor home for $32,500, then DeVinck's

---

5. *The Restatement (Second) of Contracts,* Section 153, liberalizes the general rule to take into account the modern trend of allowing avoidance even though only one party has been mistaken.

unilateral mistake (stating $23,500 in his offer) can render the resulting contract unenforceable.

The second exception arises when a unilateral mistake of fact was due to a mathematical mistake in addition, subtraction, division, or multiplication and was made inadvertently and without gross (extreme) negligence. The clerical error must be readily provable, though. If a contractor's bid was significantly low because he or she made a mistake in addition when totaling the estimated costs, any contract resulting from the bid normally may be rescinded. Of course, in both situations, the mistake must still involve some *material fact.*

Mistakes of Value

If a mistake concerns the future market value or quality of the object of the contract, the mistake is one of *value,* and the contract normally is enforceable. Mistakes of value can be bilateral or unilateral, but either way, they do not serve as a basis for avoiding a contract. For example, Renée buys a violin from Ian for $250. Although the violin is very old, neither party believes that it is particularly valuable. Later, however, an antiques dealer informs the parties that the violin is rare and worth thousands of dollars. Here, both parties were mistaken, but the mistake is a mistake of *value* rather than a mistake of *fact* that would justify contract rescission. This would be true even if, at the time of contracting, only Ian believed that the violin was not particularly valuable (a unilateral mistake) and Renée thought it was rare and worth more than $250.

The reason that mistakes of value or quality have no legal significance is that value is variable. Depending on the time, place, and other circumstances, the same item may be worth considerably different amounts. When parties form a contract, their agreement establishes the value of the object of their transaction—for the moment. Each party is considered to have assumed the risk that the value will change in the future or prove to be different from what he or she thought. Without this rule, almost any party who did not receive what she or he considered a fair bargain could argue mistake.

<hr>

SECTION 2
FRAUDULENT MISREPRESENTATION

<hr>

Although fraud is a tort (see Chapter 6), it also affects the authenticity of the innocent party's consent to the contract. When an innocent party is fraudulently induced to enter into a contract, the contract normally can be avoided because that party has not *voluntarily* consented to its terms.[6] Ordinarily, the innocent party can either rescind the contract and be restored to her or his original position or enforce the contract and seek damages for any harms resulting from the fraud.

Generally, fraudulent misrepresentation refers only to misrepresentation that is consciously false and is intended to mislead another. The person making the fraudulent misrepresentation knows or believes that the assertion is false or knows that she or he does not have a basis (stated or implied) for the assertion.[7] Typically, fraudulent misrepresentation consists of the following elements:

1. A misrepresentation of a material fact must occur.
2. There must be an intent to deceive.
3. The innocent party must justifiably rely on the misrepresentation.

Additionally, to collect damages, a party must have been harmed as a result of the misrepresentation.

Misrepresentation Has Occurred

The first element of proving fraud is to show that misrepresentation of a material fact has occurred. This misrepresentation can occur by words or actions. For example, the statement "This sculpture was created by Michelangelo" is a misrepresentation of fact if another artist sculpted the statue. Similarly, if a customer asks to see only paintings by the decorative artist Paul Wright and the owner immediately leads the customer over to paintings that were not done by Wright, the owner's actions can be a misrepresentation.

STATEMENT OF FACT VERSUS OPINION To constitute fraud, the misrepresentation must involve a material fact. What if a party to the contract is merely stating her or his opinion?

Statements of Opinion Do Not Qualify. Statements of opinion and representations of future facts (predictions) generally are not subject to claims of fraud. Every person is expected to exercise care and judgment when entering into contracts, and the law will not come to the aid of one who simply makes an unwise bargain. Statements such as "This land will be worth twice as much next year" or "This car

<hr>

6. *Restatement (Second) of Contracts,* Sections 163 and 164.
7. *Restatement (Second) of Contracts,* Section 162.

will last for years and years" are statements of opinion, not fact. Contracting parties should recognize them as opinions and not rely on them. A fact is objective and verifiable; an opinion is usually subject to debate. Therefore, a seller of goods is allowed to use *puffery* to sell his or her wares without liability for fraud.

Opinions from Experts Can Qualify.

In certain situations, such as when a naïve purchaser relies on an opinion from an expert, the innocent party may be entitled to rescission or reformation. (*Reformation* is an equitable remedy granted by a court in which the terms of a contract are altered to reflect the true intentions of the parties—see Chapter 18.)

CASE IN POINT Audrey E. Vokes, a widow without family, attended a dance party at an Arthur Murray dance school in 1961. The dance instructor praised Vokes's grace and poise, and convinced her that she had the potential to become an accomplished dancer. Over a period of sixteen months, the instructor sold her 2,302 hours of dancing lessons for a total amount of $31,090.45 (equivalent to $140,000 in 2011). When it became clear to Vokes that she did not, in fact, have the potential to be an excellent dancer, she filed a suit against the school, alleging fraudulent misrepresentation. The court held that because the dance school had superior knowledge about a person's dance potential, the instructor's statements could be considered statements of fact rather than opinion.[8]

MISREPRESENTATION BY CONDUCT

Misrepresentation also arises when a party takes specific action to conceal a fact that is material to the contract.[9] Therefore, if a seller, by her or his actions, prevents a buyer from learning of some fact that is material to the contract, such behavior constitutes misrepresentation by conduct.

CASE IN POINT Actor Tom Selleck contracted to purchase a horse named Zorro for his daughter from Dolores Cuenca. Cuenca acted as though Zorro was fit to ride in competitions, when in reality the horse suffered from a medical condition. Selleck filed a lawsuit against Cuenca for wrongfully concealing the horse's condition and won. In 2009, a jury awarded Selleck more than $187,000 for Cuenca's misrepresentation by conduct.[10]

---

8. *Vokes v. Arthur Murray, Inc.*, 212 So.2d 906 (Fla.App. 1968).
9. *Restatement (Second) of Contracts*, Section 160.
10. *Selleck v. Cuenca*, Case No. GIN056909, North County of San Diego, California, decided September 9, 2009.

MISREPRESENTATION OF LAW

Misrepresentation of law *ordinarily* does not entitle a party to relief from a contract. For example, Camara has a parcel of property that she is trying to sell to Pike. Camara knows that a local ordinance prohibits the construction of anything higher than ten stories on the property. Nonetheless, she tells Pike, "You can build a condominium one hundred stories high if you want to." Pike buys the land and later discovers that Camara's statement was false. Normally, Pike cannot avoid the contract, because under the common law, people are assumed to know state and local laws. Additionally, a layperson should not rely on a statement made by a nonlawyer about a point of law.

Exceptions to this rule occur when the misrepresenting party is in a profession that is known to require greater knowledge of the law than the average citizen possesses. For example, if Camara, in the preceding example, had been a lawyer or a real estate broker, her misrepresentation of the area's zoning laws probably would have constituted fraud.

MISREPRESENTATION BY SILENCE

Ordinarily, neither party to a contract has a duty to come forward and disclose facts. Therefore, courts typically do not set aside contracts because a party did not volunteer pertinent information. Suppose that Jim is selling a car that has been in an accident and has been repaired. He does not need to volunteer this information to a potential buyer. If, however, the purchaser asks Jim if the car has had extensive bodywork and he lies, he has committed a fraudulent misrepresentation.

Nevertheless, if a seller knows of a serious potential problem that the buyer cannot reasonably be expected to discover, the seller may have a duty to speak. Generally, the seller must disclose only *latent defects*—that is, defects that could not readily be ascertained. Thus, termites in a house may not be a latent defect, because a buyer could discover their presence through a termite inspection. Also, when the parties are in a *fiduciary relationship* (a relationship founded on trust and confidentiality, such as between a physician and patient or attorney and client), there is a duty to disclose material facts. Failure to do so may constitute fraud.

In the following case, a student sought to rescind a pair of mortgages on a New York condominium on the ground that the apartment had been a gift and that she had been defrauded into signing the loan documents.

CASE 14.2
Rosenzweig v. Givens

New York Supreme Court, Appellate Division, 62 A.D.3d 1, 879 N.Y.S.2d 387 (2009).
www.courts.state.ny.us/decisions/index.shtml[a]

BACKGROUND AND FACTS • Radiah Givens, a student, was involved in a romantic relationship with Joseph Rosenzweig, an attorney nineteen years her senior. In 2002, she moved into an apartment on which he made the down payment and acted as the lender for two mortgages totaling $285,300. His attorney had her sign the mortgage documents, but Rosenzweig made the payments and paid the household expenses. In 2004, Givens and Rosenzweig married in Jamaica. A year later, he forged her signature to obtain a bank loan for $150,000. She soon learned of the forgery and discovered that from the beginning of their relationship he had been married to someone else, with whom he had children. The Givens-Rosenzweig marriage was annulled. Rosenzweig then filed a suit in a New York state court against Givens to collect on the mortgages. The court issued a summary judgment in Rosenzweig's favor. Givens appealed, claiming that the apartment had been a gift.

IN THE LANGUAGE OF THE COURT
MOSKOWITZ, J. [Justice]
* * * *

Defendant contends that the apartment was a gift to her from plaintiff. She contends that she was a student at the time of the transaction and that plaintiff knew she could not make the monthly payments. * * * Defendant explains that plaintiff induced her to sign the mortgage documents by claiming her signature was necessary to effectuate the gift. She says she never questioned this because he was a lawyer and she loved and trusted him.
* * * *

* * * Agreements between spouses * * * involve a fiduciary relationship requiring the utmost of good faith. * * * Although the parties were not married on the day defendant signed the mortgage agreements, their relationship, as their eventual marriage demonstrates, was sufficiently analogous [equivalent] to at least raise a question as to whether or not a fiduciary relationship existed to raise the level of scrutiny of this transaction * * *. *Thus, defendant has detailed circumstances that raise an issue of fact about whether a fiduciary relationship existed between the parties, including their romantic involvement that resulted in a marriage (albeit a sham one because plaintiff was a bigamist), their age difference and that plaintiff was a lawyer.* [Emphasis added.]

Reasoning that these were mortgage documents, the [lower] court, without discovery, dismissed defendant's claims that she was fraudulently induced to sign them on the ground that her allegations did not rise to the level of fraud. However, this analysis fails to take into account the highly unusual circumstances of this case * * *. Given the surrounding circumstances, especially the nature of the parties' relationship, defendant has sufficiently raised an issue of fact about whether plaintiff tricked her into signing the mortgage documents by claiming they were merely a formality to effectuate his gift to her. That defendant did not have her own lawyer, but relied on a friend of plaintiff, further raises questions about this transaction.
* * * *

The record also contains indications that plaintiff did intend the apartment as a gift. For example, plaintiff did not demand payment from defendant for three years and then not until their relationship was disintegrating because defendant had discovered that plaintiff had forged her signature on a loan application and had another wife. * * * *Moreover, it would be unusual for someone who intended to make a loan to also provide the down payment, pay the maintenance and pay most other household expenses.* * * * Given that the marriage was a sham and that plaintiff forged defendant's signature on a loan application for $150,000, it is plausible that plaintiff did trick defendant into thinking he was gifting her the apartment. [Emphasis added.]

---

a. In the left-hand column, in the "Appellate Divisions" list, click on "1st Dept." On that page, in the "Archives" section, in the "2009" pull-down menu, select "January." In the result, scroll to "Cases Decided January 8, 2009" and click on the name of the case to access the opinion.

CASE CONTINUES ➡

CASE 14.2 CONTINUED ▶   **DECISION AND REMEDY** • *The state intermediate appellate court reversed the lower court's judgment and remanded the case for discovery and trial. Rosenzweig could have committed fraud against Givens.*

WHAT IF THE FACTS WERE DIFFERENT? • *Suppose that the difference in the parties' ages was reversed so that Rosenzweig was nineteen years Givens's junior. Should this affect the outcome in the case? Explain.*

THE ETHICAL DIMENSION • *Could Rosenzweig be characterized as a scoundrel? If so, should this influence the decision in this case? Discuss.*

Intent to Deceive

The second element of fraud is knowledge on the part of the misrepresenting party that facts have been falsely represented. This element, normally called **scienter,**[11] or "guilty knowledge," signifies that there was an *intent to deceive*. *Scienter* clearly exists if a party knows a fact is not as stated. *Scienter* also exists if a party makes a statement that he or she believes is not true or makes a statement recklessly, without regard to whether it is true or false. Finally, this element is met if a party says or implies that a statement is made on some basis, such as personal knowledge or personal investigation, when it is not.

CASE IN POINT   Robert Sarvis, a convicted felon, applied for a position as an adjunct professor two weeks after his release from prison. On his résumé, he lied about his work history by representing that he had been the president of a corporation for fourteen years and had taught business law at another college. After he was hired and began working, Sarvis's probation officer alerted the school to his criminal history. The school immediately fired Sarvis, and he brought a lawsuit against the school for breaching his employment contract. The court held in the school's favor because Sarvis had not fully disclosed his personal history, he clearly had an intent to deceive, and the school had justifiably relied on his misrepresentations.[12]

INNOCENT MISREPRESENTATION   If a person makes a statement that she or he believes to be true but that actually misrepresents material facts, the person is guilty only of an **innocent misrepresentation,** not of fraud. When an innocent misrepresentation occurs, the aggrieved party can rescind the contract but usually cannot seek damages. For example, Parris tells Roberta that a tract of land contains 250 acres. Parris is mistaken—the tract contains only 215 acres—but Parris had no knowledge of the mistake. Roberta relies on the statement and contracts to buy the land. Even though the misrepresentation is innocent, Roberta can avoid the contract if the misrepresentation is material.

In the following case, a party sought to rescind a deed based on misrepresentation. The issue before the court was whether an intent to deceive is necessary for fraudulent misrepresentation to occur.

---

11. Pronounced sy-*en*-ter.

12. *Sarvis v. Vermont State Colleges*, 172 Vt. 76, 772 A.2d 494 (2001).

✳ EXTENDED CASE 14.3 ✳
Eaton v. Waldrop

Court of Civil Appeals of Alabama, ____ So.3d ____ (2010).

IN THE LANGUAGE OF THE COURT

MOORE, Judge.
* * * *
On December 16, 2005, James M.

Eaton, Jr., and Marguerite Eaton [his mother] * * * filed a complaint against [Bobby Joe] Waldrop alleging, among other things, that Waldrop had fraudulently induced James to deed certain property

situated in Jefferson County ("the property") to Waldrop and Marguerite, jointly with a right of survivorship, and that Waldrop had subsequently fraudulently induced Marguerite to transfer her interest

EXTENDED CASE 14.3 CONTINUED ➡

in the property to Waldrop. James and Marguerite requested that the court set aside the deed executed by James transferring the property to Marguerite and Waldrop * * *. Marguerite subsequently died, and James, as the executor of her estate [the person designated in her will to handle her affairs on her death], was substituted as a plaintiff.

* * * The trial court conducted a bench [without a jury] trial on June 11, 2009. At the conclusion of James's case-in-chief, Waldrop moved for a judgment as a matter of law, arguing that James had failed to prove that Waldrop had made a representation "with intent to deceive." The trial court granted that motion, and * * * James filed his notice of appeal * * *.

On appeal, James * * * argues that the trial court erred in granting Waldrop's motion * * * because, he says, the law does not require him to prove an intent to deceive in order to obtain a rescission of a deed based on fraud.

James cites [Alabama Code 1975, Section 6-5-101 and a previous case] in support of his argument that intent to deceive is not a necessary element of fraud. Section 6-5-101 provides: "Misrepresentations of a material fact made willfully to deceive, or recklessly without knowledge, and acted on by the opposite party, *or if made by mistake and innocently and acted on by the opposite party,* constitute legal fraud." (Emphasis added [by the court].)

* * * The Alabama Supreme Court, citing [Section] 6-5-101 stated that "a false representation, even if made innocently or by mistake, operates as a legal fraud if it is a material fact that is acted upon with belief in its truth." We also note that our [state] supreme court has applied [Section] 6-5-101 in an action to set aside a deed. * * * Accordingly, we conclude that Alabama law does not require a plaintiff seeking rescission of a deed based on an allegation of fraud to prove intent to deceive.

In this case, James presented evidence indicating that Marguerite, his mother, had deeded him certain

real property. Marguerite and Waldrop then moved into a mobile home on that property with the permission of James. Waldrop soon began requesting that James deed to Waldrop and Marguerite the parcel of property on which the mobile home rested. James consented to Waldrop's request only after Waldrop had represented that he and Marguerite had married, which was not true. James testified that he never would have executed the deed transferring the property jointly to Marguerite and Waldrop * * * if he had known the truth. In the present context, that evidence presented a *prima facie* case [a case in which the evidence compels the plaintiff's conclusion if the defendant produces no evidence to disprove it] of misrepresentation without further proof of Waldrop's intent to deceive. Thus, the trial court erred in granting Waldrop's motion * * *.

* * * *

Based on the foregoing, we reverse the trial court's judgment * * * and remand this cause for a new trial consistent with this opinion.

QUESTIONS

1. Why was James arguing on appeal that intent to deceive was not a requirement for fraud? Given that Waldrop had told James that he and Marguerite were married, when in fact they weren't, couldn't intent to deceive be inferred? Discuss.
2. Recall from Chapter 1 that there are two types of remedies: equitable remedies and remedies at law. Is rescission an equitable remedy or a remedy at law? Why is rescission an appropriate remedy in this case?

NEGLIGENT MISREPRESENTATION Sometimes, a party makes a misrepresentation through carelessness, believing the statement is true. If the party fails to exercise reasonable care in uncovering or disclosing the facts or does not use the skill and competence that her or his business or profession requires, such a mispresentation may constitute **negligent misrepresentation.** For example, an operator of a weight scale certifies the weight of Sneed's commodity, even though the scale's accuracy has not been checked in more than a year.

In almost all states, such negligent misrepresentation is equal to *scienter,* or knowingly making a misrepresentation. In effect, negligent misrepresentation is treated as fraudulent misrepresentation,

even though the misrepresentation was not purposeful. In negligent misrepresentation, culpable ignorance of the truth supplies the intention to mislead, even if the defendant can claim, "I didn't know."

Reliance on the Misrepresentation

The third element of fraud is reasonably *justifiable reliance* on the misrepresentation of fact. The deceived party must have a justifiable reason for relying on the misrepresentation, and the misrepresentation must be an important factor (but not necessarily the sole factor) in inducing that party to enter into the contract. Suppose that to rent a car, an eighteen-year-old misrepresents his age and presents a false driver's license listing his age as twenty-two. In this situation, the car rental agency would be justified in relying on the misrepresentation (provided that the proof of identity was not visibly false).[13]

Reliance is not justified if the innocent party knows the true facts or relies on obviously extravagant statements. If a used-car dealer says, "This old Cadillac will get fifty miles to the gallon," the potential buyer normally will not be justified in relying on the statement. Suppose, however, that Merkel, a bank director, induces O'Connell, a co-director, to sign a statement that the bank has sufficient assets to meet its liabilities by telling O'Connell, "We have plenty of assets to satisfy our creditors." This statement is false. If O'Connell knows the true facts or, as a bank director, should know the true facts, he is not justified in relying on Merkel's statement. If O'Connell does not know the true facts, however, *and has no way of finding them out,* he may be justified in relying on the statement.

The same rule applies to defects in property sold. If the defects are of the kind that would be obvious on inspection, the buyer cannot justifiably rely on the seller's representations. If the defects are hidden or latent, as previously discussed, the buyer is justified in relying on the seller's statements.

Should employers also be held liable for misrepresentations they make to prospective employees? See this chapter's *Insight into Ethics* feature for a discussion of this issue.

Injury to the Innocent Party

Most courts do not require a showing of injury when the action is to rescind the contract. These courts hold that because rescission returns the parties to the positions they held before the contract was made, a showing of injury to the innocent party is unnecessary.

To recover damages caused by fraud, however, proof of harm is universally required. The measure of damages is ordinarily equal to the property's value had it been delivered as represented, less the actual price paid for the property. Additionally, because fraud actions necessarily involve wrongful conduct, courts may also award *punitive damages,* or *exemplary damages.*[14] As discussed in Chapter 6,

---

13. See, for example, *Fogel v. Enterprise Leasing Co. of Chicago,* 353 Ill.App.3d 165, 817 N.E.2d 1135, 288 Ill.Dec. 485 (2004).

14. See, for example, *McIver v. Bondy's Ford, Inc.,* 963 So.2d 136 (Ala. App. 2007); and *Alexander v. Meduna,* 47 P.3d 206 (Wyo. 2002).

INSIGHT INTO ETHICS
How Much Information Must Employers Disclose to Prospective Employees?

One of the problems employers face is that it is not always clear what information they should disclose to prospective employees. To lure qualified workers, employers are often tempted to "promise the moon" and paint their companies' prospects as bright. Employers must be careful, though, to avoid any conduct that could be interpreted by a court as intentionally deceptive. In particular, they must avoid making any statements about their companies' future prospects or financial health that they know to be false. If they do make a false statement on which a prospective employee relies to her or his detriment, they may be sued for fraudulent misrepresentation.

In one case, for example, an employee accepted a job with a brokerage firm because he relied on assurances that the firm was not about to be sold. In fact, negotiations to sell the firm were under way at the time he was hired. The employee filed a fraud claim against the firm and won, and the trial court awarded him more than $6 million in damages.[a]

In another case, Kevin Helmer filed a fraud lawsuit against Bingham Toyota Isuzu and Bob Clark, his supervisor at the firm. Helmer claimed that he was fraudulently induced to leave a prior job with another Toyota dealership due to false promises made to him by Clark concerning the amount of compensation that he would receive at Bingham Toyota. A jury found in Helmer's favor, awarding him $450,913 in compensatory damages and $1.5 million in punitive damages. (Later, the court reduced the punitive damages award to $675,000.)[b]

CRITICAL THINKING
INSIGHT INTO THE LEGAL ENVIRONMENT
Why would an employer risk the possibility of a lawsuit by providing a prospective employee with false information?

---

a. *McConkey v. AON Corp.,* 354 N.J.Super. 25, 804 A.2d 572 (A.D. 2002).

b. *Helmer v. Bingham Toyota Isuzu,* 129 Cal.App.4th 1121, 29 Cal. Rptr.3d 136 (2005).

punitive damages are intended to punish the defendant and are granted to a plaintiff over and above compensation for the proved, actual loss. Because of the potential for punitive damages, which normally are not available in contract actions, plaintiffs often include a claim for fraudulent misrepresentation in their contract disputes.

SECTION 3
UNDUE INFLUENCE

Undue influence arises from special kinds of relationships in which one party can greatly influence another party, thus overcoming that party's free will. A contract entered into under excessive or undue influence lacks voluntary consent and is therefore voidable.[15]

How Undue Influence May Occur

There are various types of relationships in which one party may dominate another party, thus unfairly influencing him or her. Minors and elderly people, for example, are often under the influence of guardians (persons who are legally responsible for another). If a guardian induces a young or elderly ward (a person whom the guardian looks after) to enter into a contract that benefits the guardian, the guardian may have exerted undue influence. Undue influence can arise from a number of fiduciary relationships, such as physician-patient, parent-child, husband-wife, or guardian-ward.

The essential feature of undue influence is that the party being taken advantage of does not, in reality, exercise free will in entering into a contract. It is not enough that a person is elderly or suffers from some physical or mental impairment. There must be clear and convincing evidence that the person did not act out of her or his free will.[16] Similarly, the existence of a fiduciary relationship alone is insufficient to prove undue influence.[17]

The Presumption of Undue Influence

When the dominant party in a fiduciary relationship benefits from that relationship, a presumption of undue influence arises. In a relationship of trust and confidence, such as that between an attorney and a client, the dominant party (the attorney) must exercise the utmost good faith in dealing with the other party. When a contract enriches the dominant party, the court will often *presume* that the contract was made under undue influence.

For example, if a guardian enters into a contract on behalf of the ward that financially benefits the guardian and the ward challenges the contract, a presumption arises that the guardian has taken advantage of the ward. To rebut (refute) this presumption successfully, the guardian has to show that full disclosure was made to the ward, that consideration was adequate, and that the ward received, if available, independent and competent advice before completing the transaction. Unless the presumption can be rebutted, the contract will be rescinded.

SECTION 4
DURESS

Agreement to the terms of a contract is not voluntary if one of the parties is *forced* into the agreement. The use of threats to force a party to enter into a contract is referred to as *duress*. In addition, blackmail or extortion to induce consent to a contract constitutes duress. Duress is both a defense to the enforcement of a contract and a ground for the rescission of a contract.

The Threatened Act Must Be Wrongful or Illegal

To establish duress, there must be proof of a threat to do something that the threatening party has no right to do. Generally, for duress to occur, the threatened act must be wrongful or illegal and it must render the person incapable of exercising free will. A threat to exercise a legal right, such as the right to sue someone, ordinarily does not constitute duress.

For example, Joan accidentally drives into Olin's car at a stoplight. Joan has no automobile insurance, but she has substantial assets. At the scene, Olin claims to have suffered whiplash and tells Joan that he will agree not to file a lawsuit against her if she pays him $5,000. Joan initially refuses, but Olin says, "If you don't pay me $5,000 right now, I'm going to sue you for $25,000." Joan then gives Olin a check for $5,000 to avoid the lawsuit. The next day, Joan stops payment on the check. When Olin later sues to enforce their oral settlement agreement for $5,000, Joan claims duress as a defense to

---

15. *Restatement (Second) of Contracts,* Section 177.
16. See, for example, *Bailey v. Turnbow,* 273 Va. 262, 639 S.E.2d 291 (2007); and *Hooten v. Jensen,* 94 Ark.App. 130, 227 S.W.3d 431 (2006).
17. See, for example, *Landers v. Sgouros,* 224 S.W.3d 651 (Mo.App. 2007); and *Ware v. Ware,* 161 P.3d 1188 (Alaska 2007).

its enforcement. In this situation, because Olin had a right to sue Joan, his threat to sue her does not constitute duress. A court would not consider the threat of a civil suit to be duress.

Economic Duress

Economic need generally is not sufficient to constitute duress, even when one party exacts a very high price for an item that the other party needs. If the party exacting the price also creates the need, however, *economic duress* may be found.

For example, the Internal Revenue Service (IRS) assesses a large tax and penalty against Weller. Weller retains Eyman, the accountant who prepared the tax returns on which the assessment was based, to challenge the assessment. Two days before the deadline for filing a reply with the IRS, Eyman declines to represent Weller unless he signs a very high contingency-fee agreement for the services. In this situation, a court might find that the agreement was unenforceable because of economic duress. Although Eyman has threatened only to withdraw his services, something that he is legally entitled to do, he is responsible for delaying the withdrawal until the last days before the deadline. Because it would be impossible at that late date to obtain adequate representation elsewhere, Weller would be forced either to sign the contract or to lose his right to challenge the IRS assessment.

SECTION 5
ADHESION CONTRACTS AND UNCONSCIONABILITY

Questions concerning voluntary consent may arise when the terms of a contract are dictated by a party with overwhelming bargaining power and the signer must agree to those terms or go without the commodity or service in question. As explained in Chapter 13, such contracts, which are written *exclusively* by one party and presented to the other party on a take-it-or-leave-it basis, are often referred to as **adhesion contracts**. These contracts often use standard forms, which give the adhering party no opportunity to negotiate the contract terms.

Standard-Form Contracts

Standard-form contracts often contain fine-print provisions that shift a risk ordinarily borne by one party to the other. A variety of businesses use such contracts. Life insurance policies, residential leases, loan agreements, and employment agency contracts are often standard-form contracts. To avoid enforcement of the contract or of a particular clause, the aggrieved party must show that the parties had substantially unequal bargaining positions and that enforcement would be manifestly unfair or oppressive. If the required showing is made, the contract or particular term is deemed *unconscionable* and is not enforced.

CASE IN POINT Sherry Simpson signed a standard-form contract with Addy's Harbor Dodge, a car dealership, when she traded in her automobile for a new vehicle. Above the signature line was a statement indicating that there were additional terms and conditions on the opposite page. Simpson did not read these terms, which contained an arbitration clause that also limited the damages she could recover in the event of a dispute. Simpson later filed a lawsuit, claiming that Addy's had misrepresented the trade-in value of her vehicle, artificially increased the purchase price, and failed to provide all promised rebates. Addy's filed a motion to compel arbitration, which the court denied. The court refused to enforce the arbitration provision on the ground that it was unconscionable. Not only was it oppressive, one sided, and inconspicuous, but it also required Simpson to give up statutory remedies.[18]

Unconscionability and the Courts

Technically, unconscionability under Section 2–302 of the Uniform Commercial Code (UCC) applies only to contracts for the sale of goods. Many courts, however, have broadened the concept and applied it in other situations.

Although unconscionability was discussed in Chapter 13, it is important to note here that the UCC gives courts a great degree of discretion to invalidate or strike down a contract or clause as being unconscionable. As a result, some states have *not* adopted Section 2–302 of the UCC. In those states, the legislature and the courts prefer to rely on traditional notions of fraud, undue influence, and duress.

See *Concept Summary 14.1* for a review of all of the factors that may indicate a lack of voluntary consent.

---

18. *Simpson v. MSA of Myrtle Beach, Inc.*, 373 S.C. 14, 644 S.E.2d 663 (2007).

CONCEPT SUMMARY 14.1
Voluntary Consent

Problems of Assent	Rule
Mistakes	1. *Bilateral (mutual) mistake*—If both parties are mistaken about a material fact, such as the identity of the subject matter, either party can avoid the contract. If the mistake relates to the value or quality of the subject matter, either party can enforce the contract. 2. *Unilateral mistake*—Generally, the mistaken party is bound by the contract, unless the other party knows or should have known of the mistake, or the mistake is an inadvertent mathematical error in addition, subtraction, or the like that is committed without gross negligence.
Fraudulent Misrepresentation	Three elements are necessary to establish fraudulent misrepresentation: 1. A misrepresentation of a material fact has occurred. 2. There has been an intent to deceive. 3. The innocent party has justifiably relied on the misrepresentation.
Undue Influence and Duress	1. *Undue influence*—Arises from special relationships, such as fiduciary relationships, in which one party's free will has been overcome by the undue influence of another. Usually, the contract is voidable. 2. *Duress*—Defined as the use of threats to force a party to enter into a contract out of fear; for example, the threat of violence or economic pressure. The party forced to enter into the contract can rescind the contract.
Adhesion Contracts and Unconscionability	Concerns one-sided bargains in which one party has substantially superior bargaining power and can dictate the terms of a contract. Unconscionability typically occurs as a result of the following: 1. *Standard-form contracts*—In which a fine-print provision purports to shift a risk normally borne by one party to the other (for example, a liability disclaimer). 2. *Take-it-or-leave-it adhesion contracts*—In which the buyer has no choice but to agree to the seller's dictated terms if the buyer is to procure certain goods or services.

REVIEWING
Mistakes, Fraud, and Voluntary Consent

Chelene had been a caregiver for Marta's eighty-year-old mother, Janis, for nine years. Shortly before Janis passed away, Chelene convinced her to buy Chelene's house for Marta. The elderly woman died before the papers were signed, however. Four months later, Marta used her inheritance to buy Chelene's house without having it inspected. The house was built in the 1950s, and Chelene said it was in "perfect condition." Nevertheless, one year after the purchase, the basement started leaking. Marta had the paneling removed from the basement walls and discovered that the walls were bowed inward and cracked. Marta then had a civil engineer inspect the basement walls, and he found that the cracks had been caulked and painted over before the paneling was installed. He concluded that the "wall failure" had existed "for at least thirty years" and that the basement walls were "structurally unsound." Using the information presented in the chapter, answer the following questions.

1. Can Marta obtain rescission of the contract based on undue influence? If the sale to Janis had been completed before her death, could Janis have obtained rescission based on undue influence? Explain.

REVIEWING CONTINUES ➡

REVIEWING

Mistakes, Fraud, and Voluntary Consent, *Continued*

2. Can Marta sue Chelene for fraudulent misrepresentation? Why or why not? What element(s) might be lacking?

3. Now assume that Chelene knew that the basement walls were cracked and bowed and that she had hired someone to install paneling before she offered to sell the house. Did she have a duty to disclose this defect to Marta? Could a court find that Chelene's silence in this situation constituted misrepresentation? Explain.

4. If Chelene knew about the problem with the walls but did not know that the house was structurally unsound, could she be liable for negligent misrepresentation? Why or why not?

5. Can Marta avoid the contract on the ground that both parties made a mistake about the condition of the house? Explain.

✹ **DEBATE THIS:** *The concept of* caveat emptor *("let the buyer beware") should be applied to all sales, including those for real property.*

TERMS AND CONCEPTS

innocent misrepresentation 280

scienter 280

voluntary consent 274

adhesion contract 284

negligent misrepresentation 281

QUESTIONS AND CASE PROBLEMS

14–1. Undue Influence Juan is an elderly man who lives with his nephew, Samuel. Juan is totally dependent on Samuel's support. Samuel tells Juan that unless he transfers a tract of land he owns to Samuel for a price 35 percent below its market value, Samuel will no longer support and take care of him. Juan enters into the contract. Discuss fully whether Juan can set aside this contract.

14–2. QUESTION WITH SAMPLE ANSWER: Fraudulent Misrepresentation.

? Grano owns a forty-room motel on Highway 100. Tanner is interested in purchasing the motel. During the course of negotiations, Grano tells Tanner that the motel netted $30,000 during the previous year and that it will net at least $45,000 the next year. The motel books, which Grano turns over to Tanner before the purchase, clearly show that Grano's motel netted only $15,000 the previous year. Also, Grano fails to tell Tanner that a bypass to Highway 100 is being planned that will redirect most traffic away from the front of the motel. Tanner purchases the motel. During the first year under Tanner's operation,

the motel nets only $18,000. At this time, Tanner learns of the previous low profitability of the motel and the planned bypass. Tanner wants Grano to return the purchase price. Discuss fully Tanner's probable success in getting his funds back.

- **For a sample answer to Question 14–2, go to Appendix I at the end of this text.**

14–3. Voluntary Consent Discuss whether either of the following contracts will be unenforceable on the ground that voluntary consent is lacking:

(a) Simmons finds a stone in his pasture that he believes to be quartz. Jenson, who also believes that the stone is quartz, contracts to purchase it for $10. Just before delivery, the stone is discovered to be a diamond worth $1,000.

(b) Jacoby's barn is burned to the ground. He accuses Goldman's son of arson and threatens to have the prosecutor bring a criminal action unless Goldman agrees to pay him $5,000. Goldman agrees to pay.

14–4. Negligent Misrepresentation Cleveland Chiropractic College (CCC) promised prospective students that CCC would provide clinical training and experience—a critical part of a chiropractic education and a requirement for graduation and obtaining a license to practice. Specifically, CCC expressly promised that it would provide an ample variety of patients. CCC knew, however, that it did not have the ability to provide sufficient patients, as evidenced by its report to the Council on Chiropractic Education, an accreditation body through which chiropractic colleges monitor and certify themselves. In that report, CCC said that patient recruitment was the "joint responsibility" of the college and the student. During the 1990s, most of the "patients" that students saw were healthy persons whom the students recruited to be stand-in patients. After graduating and obtaining licenses to practice, Michael Troknya and nineteen others filed a suit in a federal district court against CCC, alleging, among other things, negligent misrepresentation. What are the elements of this cause of action? Are they satisfied in this case? Why or why not? [*Troknya v. Cleveland Chiropractic Clinic,* 280 F.3d 1200 (8th Cir. 2002)]

14–5. Duress The law firm of Traystman, Coric and Keramidas represented Andrew Daigle in a divorce in Norwich, Connecticut. Scott McGowan, an attorney with the firm, handled the two-day trial. After the first day of the trial, McGowan told Daigle to sign a promissory note in the amount of $26,973, which represented the amount that Daigle then owed to the firm, or McGowan would withdraw from the case and Daigle would be forced to get another attorney or to continue the trial by himself. Daigle said that he wanted another attorney, Martin Rutchik, to see the note. McGowan urged Daigle to sign it and assured him that a copy would be sent to Rutchik. Feeling that he had no other choice, Daigle signed the note. When he did not pay, the law firm filed a suit in a Connecticut state court against him. Daigle asserted that the note was unenforceable because he had signed it under duress. What are the requirements for the use of duress as a defense to a contract? Are the requirements met here? What might the law firm argue in response to Daigle's assertion? Explain. [*Traystman, Coric and Keramidas v. Daigle,* 84 Conn.App. 843, 855 A.2d 996 (2004)]

14–6. CASE PROBLEM WITH SAMPLE ANSWER: Fraudulent Misrepresentation.

According to the student handbook at Cleveland Chiropractic College (CCC) in Missouri, academic misconduct *includes "selling . . . any copy of any material intended to be used as an instrument of academic evaluation in advance of its initial administration." Leonard Verni was enrolled at CCC in Dr. Aleksandr Makarov's dermatology class. Before the first examination, Verni was reported to be selling copies of the test. CCC investigated and concluded that Verni had committed academic misconduct. He was dismissed from CCC, which informed him of his right to an appeal. According to the handbook, at the hearing on appeal a student could have an attorney or other adviser, present witnesses' testimony and other evidence, and "question any testimony . . . against him/her." At his hearing, however, Verni did not bring his attorney,*

present evidence on his behalf, or question any adverse witnesses. When the dismissal was upheld, Verni filed a suit in a Missouri state court against CCC and others, claiming, in part, fraudulent misrepresentation. Verni argued that because he "relied" on the handbook's "representation" that CCC would follow its appeal procedure, he was unable to properly refute the charges against him. Can Verni succeed with this argument? Explain. [Verni v. Cleveland Chiropractic College, *212 S.W.3d 150 (Mo. 2007)*]

- To view a sample answer for Problem 14–6, go to this book's Web site at www.cengage.com/blaw/clarkson, select "Chapter 14," and click on "Case Problem with Sample Answer."

14–7. Fraudulent Misrepresentation Peggy Williams helped eighty-seven-year-old Melvin Kaufman care for Elsie Kaufman, his wife and Williams's great aunt, for several years before her death. Melvin then asked Williams to "take care of him the rest of his life." He conveyed his house to her for "Ten and No/100 Dollars ($10.00), and other good and valuable consideration," according to the deed, and executed a power of attorney in her favor. When Melvin returned from a trip to visit his brother, however, Williams had locked him out of the house. He filed a suit in a Texas state court, alleging fraud. He claimed that he had deeded the house to her in exchange for her promise of care, but that she had not taken care of him and had not paid him the ten dollars. Williams admitted that she had not paid the ten dollars, but argued that she had made no such promise, that Melvin had given her the house when he had been unable to sell it, and that his trip had been intended as a move. Do these facts show fraud? If so, what would be the appropriate remedy? Explain. [*Williams v. Kaufman,* 275 S.W.3d 637 (Tex.App.—Beaumont 2009)]

14–8. Fraudulent Misrepresentation Ricky and Sherry Wilcox hired Esprit Log and Timber Frame Homes to build a log house, which the Wilcoxes intended to sell. They paid Esprit $125,260 for materials and services. They eventually sold the home for $1,620,000 but sued Esprit due to construction delays. The logs were supposed to arrive at the construction site precut and predrilled, but that did not happen. So it took five extra months to build the house while the logs were cut and drilled one by one. The Wilcoxes claimed that the interest they paid on a loan for the extra construction time cost them about $200,000. The jury agreed and awarded them that much in damages, plus $250,000 in punitive damages and $20,000 in attorneys' fees. Esprit appealed, claiming that the evidence did not support the verdict because the Wilcoxes had sold the house for a good price. Is Esprit's argument credible? Why or why not? How should the court rule? [*Esprit Log and Timber Frame Homes, Inc. v. Wilcox,* 302 Ga.App. 550, 691 S.E.2d 344 (2010)]

14–9. A QUESTION OF ETHICS: Mistake.

On behalf of BRJM, LLC, Nicolas Kepple offered Howard Engelsen $210,000 for a parcel of land known as lot five on the north side of Barnes Road in Stonington, Connecticut. Engelsen's company, Output Systems, Inc., owned the land. Engelsen had the lot

surveyed and obtained an appraisal. The appraiser valued the property at $277,000, after determining that it was 3.0 acres in size and thus could not be subdivided because it did not meet the town's minimum legal requirement of 3.7 acres for subdivision. Engelsen responded to Kepple's offer with a counteroffer of $230,000, which Kepple accepted. On May 3, 2002, the parties signed a contract. When Engelsen refused to go through with the deal, BRJM filed a suit in a Connecticut state court against Output, seeking specific performance and other relief. The defendant asserted the defense of mutual mistake on at least two grounds. [BRJM, LLC v. Output Systems, Inc., 100 Conn.App. 143, 917 A.2d 605 (2007)]

(a) In the counteroffer, Engelsen asked Kepple to remove from their contract a clause requiring written confirmation of the availability of a "free split," which meant that the property could be subdivided without the town's prior approval. Kepple agreed. After signing the contract, Kepple learned that the property was *not* entitled to a free split. Would this circumstance qualify as a mistake on which the *defendant* could avoid the contract? Discuss.

(b) After signing the contract, Engelsen obtained a second appraisal that established the size of lot five as 3.71 acres, which meant that it could be subdivided, and valued the property at $490,000. Can the defendant avoid the contract on the basis of a mistake in the first appraisal? Explain.

14–10. VIDEO QUESTION: Mistake.

Go to this text's Web site at **www.cengage.com/blaw/clarkson** and select "Chapter 14." Click on "Video Questions" and view the video titled *Mistake*. Then answer the following questions.

(a) What kind of mistake is involved in the dispute shown in the video (bilateral or unilateral, mistake of fact or mistake of value)?

(b) According to the chapter, in what two situations would the supermarket be able to rescind a contract to sell peppers to Melnick at the incorrectly advertised price?

(c) Does it matter if the price that was advertised was a reasonable price for the peppers? Why or why not?

LEGAL RESEARCH EXERCISES ON THE WEB

Go to this text's Web site at **www.cengage.com/blaw/clarkson**, select "Chapter 14," and click on "Practical Internet Exercises." There you will find the following Internet research exercises that you can perform to learn more about the topics covered in this chapter.

Practical Internet Exercise 14–1: Legal Perspective
Negligent Misrepresentation and *Scienter*

Practical Internet Exercise 14–2: Management Perspective
Fraudulent Misrepresentation

Practical Internet Exercise 14–3: Economic Perspective
Economic Duress

CHAPTER 15

The Statute of Frauds— Writing Requirement and Electronic Records

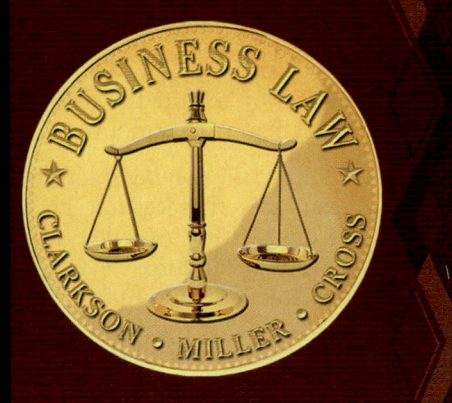

As discussed in Chapter 14, a contract that is otherwise valid may still be unenforceable if the parties have not voluntarily consented to its terms. An otherwise valid contract may also be unenforceable for another reason—because it is not in the proper form. For example, certain types of contracts are required to be in writing or evidenced by a memorandum, note, or electronic record (*record* was defined in Chapter 11 on page 237). The writing requirement does not mean that an agreement must be a formal written contract. All that is necessary is some written proof that a contract exists, such as an e-mail exchange evidencing the agreement. Under what is called the **Statute of Frauds**, certain agreements are required by law to be in writing or evidenced by a record. If there is no written evidence of the contract, it may not be enforceable.

In this chapter, we examine the kinds of contracts that require a writing under the Statute of Frauds and some exceptions to the writing requirement. We also discuss the *parol evidence rule,* which courts follow when determining whether evidence that is extraneous, or external, to written contracts may be admissible at trial. Though not inherently related to the Statute of Frauds, the parol evidence rule has general application in contract law. We cover these topics within this one chapter primarily for reasons of convenience and space.

SECTION 1
THE ORIGINS OF THE STATUTE OF FRAUDS

At early common law, parties to a contract were not allowed to testify. This led to the practice of hiring third party witnesses. As early as the seventeenth century, the English recognized the many problems presented by this practice and enacted a statute to help deal with them. The statute, passed by the English Parliament in 1677, was known as "An Act for the Prevention of Frauds and Perjuries." The act established that certain types of contracts, to be enforceable, had to be evidenced by a writing and signed by the party against whom enforcement was sought. The primary purpose of the statute was to ensure that, for certain types of contracts, there was reliable evidence of the contracts and their terms.

Today, every state has a statute, modeled after the English act, that stipulates what types of contracts must be in writing or evidenced by a writing.

Although the statutes vary slightly from state to state, all states require certain types of contracts to be in writing or evidenced by a written (or electronic) memorandum signed (or acknowledged) by the party against whom enforcement is sought, unless certain exceptions apply. (These exceptions will be discussed later in this chapter.) In this text, we refer to these statutes collectively as the Statute of Frauds. The actual name of the Statute of Frauds is misleading because it neither applies to fraud nor invalidates any type of contract. Rather, it denies enforceability to certain contracts that do not comply with its requirements.

SECTION 2
CONTRACTS THAT FALL WITHIN THE STATUTE OF FRAUDS

The following types of contracts are said to fall "within" or "under" the Statute of Frauds and therefore are required to be in writing or evidenced by a written memorandum or record:

1. Contracts involving interests in land.
2. Contracts that cannot by their terms be performed within one year from the day after the date of formation.
3. Collateral, or secondary, contracts, such as promises to answer for the debt or duty of another and promises by the administrator or executor of an estate to pay a debt of the estate personally—that is, out of her or his own pocket.
4. Promises made in consideration of marriage.
5. Under the Uniform Commercial Code (UCC—see Chapter 19), contracts for the sale of goods priced at $500 or more.

Contracts Involving Interests in Land

A contract calling for the sale of land is not enforceable unless it is in writing or evidenced by a written memorandum. Land is *real property* and includes all physical objects that are permanently attached to the soil, such as buildings, fences, trees, and the soil itself (see Chapter 50). The Statute of Frauds operates as a *defense* to the enforcement of an oral contract for the sale of land. For example, if Sam contracts orally to sell Fair Oaks to Beth but later decides not to sell, under most circumstances Beth cannot enforce the contract.

The Statute of Frauds also requires written evidence of contracts for the transfer of other interests in land. For example, mortgage agreements and leases (see Chapter 31) normally must be written. Similarly, an agreement that includes an option to purchase real property must be in writing for the option to be enforced.[1]

Generally, for a land sale contract to be enforceable under the Statute of Frauds, the contract must describe the property being transferred with sufficient certainty. Whether a contract for the sale of land met this requirement was at issue in the following case.

---

1. See, for example, *Stickney v. Tullis-Vermillion,* 165 Ohio App.3d 480, 847 N.E.2d 29 (2006).

✷ EXTENDED CASE 15.1 ✷
Salim v. Solaiman

Court of Appeals of Georgia, 302 Ga. App. 607, 691 S.E.2d 389 (2010).

IN THE LANGUAGE OF THE COURT

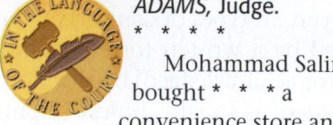

ADAMS, Judge.
* * * *
Mohammad Salim bought * * * a convenience store and gas station * * * . He made some improvements to the property and then offered it for sale. Talat Solaiman and Sabina Chowdhury approached Salim about buying the property in December 2006. After negotiating a purchase price of $975,000, the parties signed a handwritten document memorializing the terms of the agreement and on December 26, signed a more formal, typewritten "Purchase and Sale Agreement" prepared by Solaiman and Chowdhury.

The typed agreement * * * described [the property] simply as "the property and business (known as BP Food Mart) located at 199 Upper Riverdale Road, Jonesboro, GA 30236." The agreement set a closing date of January 5, 2007 and required Solaiman and Chowdhury to pay a $25,000 "security deposit" to be applied toward the down payment. But the agreement did not specify what would happen to the security deposit in the event the sale failed to close.

* * * Solaiman and Chowdhury conducted due diligence [investigation], including visiting the store and speaking to store clerks, vendors and customers. They also ordered a title search on the property and paid $2,000 for an application to renew the store's alcoholic beverage license in their name.

* * * The closing did not occur on January 5. And after receiving the title report in mid-January, Solaiman and Chowdhury decided that they no longer wanted to buy the property. They notified Salim of their decision and asked for reimbursement of the security deposit and the alcohol license renewal fee. * * * Salim refused to repay the funds, and Solaiman and Chowdhury filed this action [for breach of contract] in December 2007.

The trial court issued judgment in favor of Solaiman and Chowdhury after finding the parties' purchase agreement to be unenforceable because "it does not sufficiently describe the real property to be purchased."
* * * *
The requirement that a contract to purchase real property include an adequate property description arises under the Statute of Frauds. To comply with the Statute, an agreement for the sale of land "must be in writing and must provide a sufficiently definite description of the property to be sold. Specifically, such a contract must describe the

EXTENDED CASE 15.1 CONTINUED ◆

*property * * * with the same degree of certainty as that required in a deed conveying realty."* The property description must demonstrate "with sufficient certainty" the grantor's intention with regard to the quantity and location of the land to be conveyed, "so that its identification is practicable * * * ." To be enforceable, therefore, the purchase agreement in this case was required to

either "describe the particular tract or provide a key by which it may be located with the aid of extrinsic [outside] evidence." To suffice as a key, the description "must open the door to extrinsic [outside] evidence which leads unerringly to the land in question." But if the words in the agreement, "when aided by extrinsic evidence, fail to locate and identify a certain tract of land, the description fails and the instrument is void." [Emphasis added.]

The property description contained in the four corners of the purchase agreement clearly fails to identify the land at issue with the requisite certainty as it merely provides a street address.

* * * *

Accordingly, we affirm the trial court's holding that the parties' purchase agreement was void for lack of an adequate property description.

QUESTIONS

1. Why was Salim arguing that the contract should be deemed enforceable when he was being sued for breach of contract?
2. What might Salim have done to ensure that the sales contract would be enforceable?

The One-Year Rule

Contracts that cannot, *by their own terms,* be performed within one year *from the day after* the contract is formed must be in writing to be enforceable.[2] Suppose that Superior University forms a contract with Kimi San stating that San will teach three courses in history during the coming academic year (September 15 through June 15). If the contract is formed in March, it must be in writing to be enforceable—because it cannot be performed within one year. If the contract is not formed until July, however, it does not have to be in writing to be enforceable—because it can be performed within one year.

The key for determining whether an oral contract is enforceable under the one-year rule is whether performance is *possible* within one year from the day after the date of contract formation—not whether the agreement is *likely* to be performed within one year. When performance of a contract is objectively impossible during the one-year period, the oral contract will be unenforceable. When performance is objectively possible within a year, the contract does not fall within the Statute of Frauds. For example, an oral contract for lifetime employment does not fall within the Statute of Frauds because an employee who is hired "for life" can die within a year, so the contract can be performed within one year.[3] Exhibit 15–1 on the following page graphically illustrates the one-year rule.

CASE IN POINT Babyback's International, Inc., makes ready-to-eat barbeque foods that are sold in grocery stores. Babyback's and the Coca-Cola Company were involved in a co-marketing arrangement in which their products were placed together in stores in the Indianapolis area. Because of the success of the Indianapolis program, the parties began to negotiate another co-marketing contract for the Louisville area. Babyback's faxed a proposed contract to Coca-Cola that summarized their oral agreement, but Coca-Cola did not sign the agreement, which was to continue for multiple years. Because the agreement could not be performed within a year and because Coca-Cola had not signed the fax, the court ruled that the oral agreement was unenforceable.[4]

Collateral Promises

A **collateral promise,** or secondary promise, is one that is ancillary (subsidiary) to a principal transaction or primary contractual relationship. In other words, a collateral promise is one made by a third party to assume the debts or obligations of a primary party to a contract if that party does not perform. Any collateral promise of this nature falls under the Statute of Frauds and therefore must be in writing to be enforceable. To understand this concept, it is important to distinguish between primary and secondary promises and obligations.

---

2. *Restatement (Second) of Contracts,* Section 130.
3. See, for example, *Gavegnano v. TLT Construction Corp.,* 67 Mass. App.Ct. 1102, 851 N.E.2d 1133 (2006).

4. *Coca-Cola Co. v. Babyback's International, Inc.,* 841 N.E.2d 557 (Ind. 2006).

EXHIBIT 15–1 • The One-Year Rule

Under the Statute of Frauds, contracts that by their terms are impossible to perform within one year from the day after the date of contract formation must be in writing to be enforceable. Put another way, if it is at all possible to perform an oral contract within one year from the day after the contract is made, the contract will fall outside the Statute of Frauds and be enforceable.

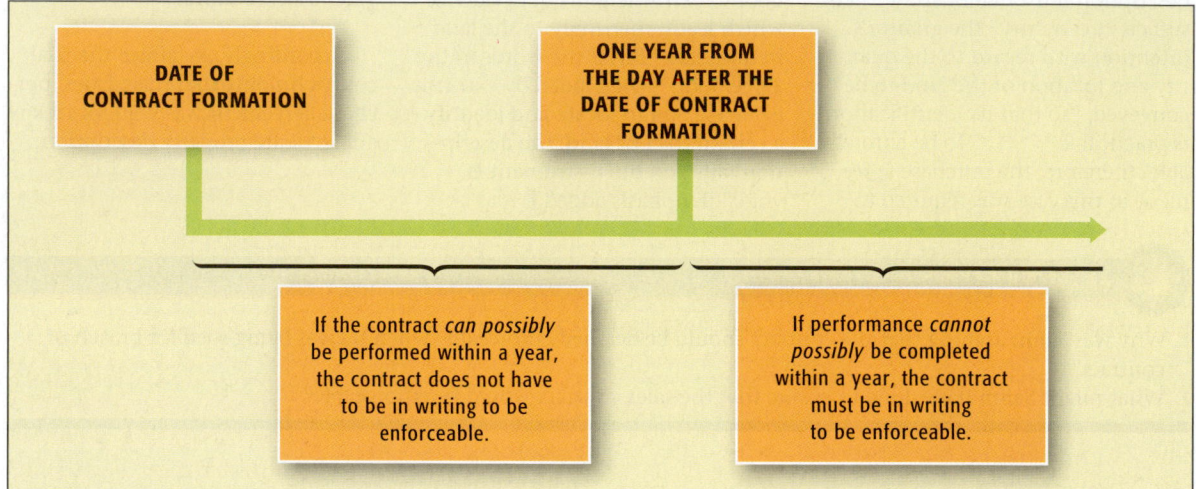

PRIMARY VERSUS SECONDARY OBLIGATIONS As a general rule, a contract in which a party assumes a primary obligation does not need to be in writing to be enforceable. For example, Bancroft forms an oral contract with Corrine's Flowers to send his mother a dozen roses for Mother's Day. Bancroft's oral contract with Corrine's provides that he will pay for the roses when he receives the bill for the flowers. Bancroft is a direct party to this contract and has incurred a *primary* obligation under the contract. Because he is a party to the contract and has a primary obligation to Corrine's, this contract does *not* fall under the Statute of Frauds and does not have to be in writing to be enforceable. If Bancroft fails to pay the florist and the florist sues him for payment, Bancroft cannot raise the Statute of Frauds as a defense.

In contrast, a contract in which a party assumes a secondary obligation does have to be in writing to be enforceable. For example, Bancroft's mother borrows $10,000 from the International Bank on a promissory note payable six months later. Bancroft promises the bank officer handling the loan that he will pay the $10,000 *only if his mother does not pay the loan on time.* Bancroft, in this situation, becomes what is known as a *guarantor* on the loan—that is, he is guaranteeing to the bank that he will pay back the loan if his mother fails to do so—and has incurred a *secondary* obligation. This kind of collateral promise, in which the guarantor states that he or she will become responsible only if the primary party does not perform, must be in writing to be enforceable.

Exhibit 15–2 illustrates the concept of a collateral promise. (We will return to the concept of guaranty and the distinction between primary and secondary obligations in Chapter 28, in the context of creditors' rights.)

AN EXCEPTION–THE "MAIN PURPOSE" RULE An oral promise to answer for the debt of another is covered by the Statute of Frauds *unless* the guarantor's main purpose in incurring a secondary obligation is to secure a personal benefit. This type of contract need not be in writing.[5] The assumption is that a court can infer from the circumstances of a particular case whether the "leading objective" of the promisor was to secure a personal benefit and thus, in effect, to answer for her or his own debt.

Consider an example. Braswell contracts with Custom Manufacturing Company to have some machines custom-made for Braswell's factory. She promises Newform Supply, Custom's supplier, that if Newform continues to deliver the materials to Custom for the production of the custom-made machines, she will guarantee payment. This promise need not be in writing, even though the effect may be to pay the debt of another. This is because Braswell's main purpose in forming the contract is to secure a benefit for herself (her factory).

Another typical application of the main purpose rule occurs when one creditor guarantees a debtor's

---

5. *Restatement (Second) of Contracts,* Section 116.

EXHIBIT 15–2 • Collateral Promises

A collateral (secondary) promise is one made by a third party (C, in this exhibit) to a creditor (B, in this exhibit) to pay the debt of another (A, in this exhibit), who is primarily obligated to pay the debt. Under the Statute of Frauds, collateral promises must be in writing to be enforceable.

debt to another creditor to forestall litigation. A creditor might do this because it allows the debtor to remain in business long enough to generate profits sufficient to pay *both* creditors. In this situation, the guaranty does not need to be in writing to be enforceable.

Promises Made in Consideration of Marriage

A unilateral promise to make a monetary payment or to give property in consideration of a promise to marry must be in writing. Baumann promises to pay Villard $10,000 if Villard marries Baumann's daughter. Because the promise is in consideration of marriage, it must be in writing to be enforceable.

The same rule applies to **prenuptial agreements**—agreements made before marriage that define each partner's ownership rights in the other partner's property. A couple might make such an agreement if, for example, a prospective wife wishes to limit the amount her prospective husband can obtain if the marriage ends in divorce. Prenuptial agreements must be in writing to be enforceable. In addition, most states will not enforce a premarital agreement against a person unless she or he voluntarily entered into the agreement after the other party reasonably disclosed his or her assets.[6]

---

6. In 1983, the National Conference of Commissioners on Uniform State Laws issued the Uniform Prenuptial Agreements Act (UPAA) and the act has now been adopted by a majority of states. The act provides that when a prenuptial agreement was voluntarily entered into in writing after a fair and reasonable disclosure of assets, it is enforceable in every state, not just the state in which the parties married.

Contracts for the Sale of Goods

The Uniform Commercial Code (UCC) includes Statute of Frauds provisions that require written evidence or an electronic record of a contract for the sale of goods priced at $500 or more. A writing that will satisfy the UCC requirement need only state the quantity term; other terms agreed on can be omitted or even stated imprecisely in the writing, as long as they adequately reflect both parties' intentions. A written memorandum or series of communications evidencing a contract will suffice.

The sales contract will not be enforceable for any quantity greater than that set forth in the writing. In addition, the writing must have been signed by the person against whom enforcement is sought—that is, by the person who refuses to perform or the one being sued. Beyond these two requirements, the writing normally need not designate the buyer or the seller, the terms of payment, or the price. Requirements of the Statute of Frauds under the UCC will be discussed in more detail in Chapter 19.

Exceptions to the Statute of Frauds

Exceptions to the applicability of the Statute of Frauds are made in certain circumstances. We describe those situations here.

PARTIAL PERFORMANCE A court may grant *specific performance* (performance of the contract according to its precise terms) of an oral contract to transfer an interest in land when the contract has been partially performed. For instance, when the purchaser has paid part of the price, taken possession of the property, and made permanent improvements to it, the parties clearly cannot be returned to the positions they occupied before the contract was formed. Whether a court will enforce an oral contract for an interest in land when partial performance has taken place usually is determined by the degree of harm that would be suffered if the court chose *not* to enforce the oral contract. In some states, mere reliance on certain types of oral contracts is enough to remove them from the Statute of Frauds.[7]

Under the UCC, an oral contract for the sale of goods is enforceable to the extent that a seller accepts payment or a buyer accepts delivery of the goods.[8] The existence and extent of a contract to supply computer kiosks for use in school cafeterias were in dispute in the following case.

---

7. *Restatement (Second) of Contracts,* Section 129.

8. UCC 2–201(3)(c). See Chapter 19.

CASE 15.2
School-Link Technologies, Inc. v. Applied Resources, Inc.
United States District Court, District of Kansas, 471 F.Supp.2d 1101 (2007).

BACKGROUND AND FACTS • Applied Resources, Inc. (ARI), makes computer hardware for point-of-sale systems—kiosks consisting of computers encased in chassis on which card readers or other payment devices are mounted. School-Link Technologies, Inc. (SLT), sells food-service technology to schools. In August 2003, the New York City Department of Education (NYCDOE) asked SLT to propose a cafeteria payment system that included kiosks. SLT asked ARI to participate in a pilot project, orally promising ARI that it would be the exclusive supplier of as many as 1,500 kiosks if the NYCDOE awarded the contract to SLT. ARI agreed. SLT intended to cut ARI out of the deal, however, and told the NYCDOE that SLT would be making its own kiosks. Meanwhile, SLT paid ARI in advance for a certain number of goods but insisted on onerous terms for a written contract, to which ARI would not agree. ARI suspended production of the prepaid items and refused to refund more than $55,000 that SLT had paid. SLT filed a suit in a federal district court against ARI. ARI responded with, among other things, a counterclaim for breach of contract, asserting that SLT had failed to use ARI as an exclusive supplier as promised. ARI sought to recover the expenses it had incurred for the pilot project and the amount of profit that it would have realized on the entire deal. SLT filed a motion for summary judgment on this claim.

IN THE LANGUAGE OF THE COURT
John W. *LUNGSTRUM,* United States District Judge.
 * * * *

SLT raises several arguments as to why it is entitled to summary judgment on ARI's breach of * * * contract claim. SLT relies, first, on the statute of frauds. Contracts for the sale of goods over $500 generally must be in writing and must be signed by the party against whom enforcement is sought. Because the NYCDOE contract undisputedly involved the sale of goods in excess of $500, the parties' oral contract that ARI would be the exclusive supplier of kiosks for the project is not enforceable in the absence of an applicable exception to this general rule.

ARI contends that the statute of frauds does not apply with respect to goods which have been received and accepted * * * . *[Under] one of the exceptions to the statute of frauds * * * a contract which would otherwise be unenforceable for lack of a writing but which is valid in other respects is enforceable * * * with respect to goods for which payment has been made and accepted or which have been received and accepted.* This exception allows partial performance to serve as a substitute for the required writing, but only for goods which have been received and accepted or for which payment has been made and accepted. Here, the goods which arguably fall within that definition are those supplied by ARI for the pilot project with the NYCDOE because those goods were received and accepted by SLT. Consequently, SLT's motion for summary judgment based on the statute of frauds is denied with respect to those goods. [Emphasis added.]

SLT's motion based on the statute of frauds is granted, however, with respect to ARI's claim that it was to be the exclusive supplier for 1,500 kiosks for the NYCDOE project. * * * The non-

CASE 15.2 CONTINUED ➡ pilot program kiosks do not fall within the ambit [realm] of [the partial performance exception to the Statute of Frauds] because those goods were not received and accepted, nor was payment made and accepted for them. ARI has not directed the court's attention to any other evidence which demonstrates a genuine issue of material fact with respect to any other statute of frauds exception. Accordingly, the court's analysis of ARI's breach of oral contract claim is narrowed to the goods ARI supplied for SLT's pilot project with the NYCDOE, as the remaining aspect of that claim is barred by the statute of frauds.

DECISION AND REMEDY • *The court denied SLT's motion for summary judgment on ARI's counterclaim for breach of contract "with respect to goods which SLT already received and accepted, the goods for the pilot program with the NYCDOE." Under the partial performance exception to the Statute of Frauds, an oral contract for a sale of goods that would otherwise be unenforceable for the lack of a writing is enforceable to the extent that the seller delivers the goods and the buyer accepts them.*

THE ETHICAL DIMENSION • *On what additional theories could ARI's request for relief be based in this case? What common thread underlies these theories?*

THE LEGAL ENVIRONMENT DIMENSION • *Could ARI have successfully asserted a claim against SLT based on fraudulent misrepresentation? Explain.*

ADMISSIONS In some states, if a party against whom enforcement of an oral contract is sought "admits" in pleadings, testimony, or otherwise in court that a contract for sale was made, the contract will be enforceable.[9] A contract subject to the UCC will be enforceable, but only to the extent of the quantity admitted.[10] For example, the president of Ashley Corporation admits under oath that an oral agreement was made with Com Best to buy certain business equipment for $10,000. In this situation, a court will enforce the agreement only to the extent admitted (the $10,000), even if Com Best claims that the agreement involved $20,000 of equipment.

PROMISSORY ESTOPPEL In some states, an oral contract that would otherwise be unenforceable under the Statute of Frauds may be enforced under the doctrine of promissory estoppel. Recall from Chapter 12 that if a promisor makes a promise on which the promisee justifiably relies to his or her detriment, a court may *estop* (prevent) the promisor from denying that a contract exists. Section 139 of the *Restatement (Second) of Contracts* provides that in these circumstances, an oral promise can be enforceable notwithstanding the Statute of Frauds. For the promise to be enforceable, the promisee must have justifiably relied on it to her or his detriment, the reliance must have been foreseeable to the person making the promise, and enforcing the promise must be the only way to avoid injustice.

(Note the similarities between this exception and the doctrine of partial performance discussed previously: both require reasonable reliance and operate to estop a party from claiming that no contract exists.)

SPECIAL EXCEPTIONS UNDER THE UCC Special exceptions to the applicability of the Statute of Frauds apply to sales contracts. Oral contracts for customized goods may be enforced in certain circumstances. Another exception has to do with oral contracts *between merchants* that have been confirmed in a written memorandum. We will examine these exceptions in more detail in Chapter 19, when we discuss the UCC provisions regarding the Statute of Frauds.

Exhibit 15–3 on the next page graphically summarizes the types of contracts that fall under the Statute of Frauds and the various exceptions that apply.

SECTION 3
SUFFICIENCY OF THE WRITING

A written contract will satisfy the writing requirement of the Statute of Frauds. A *written memorandum* (written or electronic evidence of the oral contract) signed by the party against whom enforcement is sought will also satisfy the writing requirement. The signature need not be placed at the end of the document but can be anywhere in the writing; it can even be initials rather than the full name. As discussed in Chapter 11, there are many ways to create signatures

---

9. *Restatement (Second) of Contracts*, Section 133.
10. UCC 2–201(3)(b).

EXHIBIT 15–3 • Contracts Subject to the Statute of Frauds

BUSINESS CONTRACTS THAT MUST BE IN WRITING TO BE ENFORCEABLE			
Contracts for the sale of goods priced at $500 or more	**Contracts involving interests in land**	**Contracts that cannot be performed within one year**	**Contracts containing collateral promises**
EXCEPTIONS • Customized goods • Admissions (quantity) • Partial performance • Merchants' contracts confirmed in writing	**EXCEPTIONS** • Partial performance • Admissions[a] • Promissory estoppel[a]	**EXCEPTIONS** • Admissions[a] • Promissory estoppel[a]	**EXCEPTIONS** • Main purpose rule • Admissions[a] • Promissory estoppel[a]

a. Some states follow Section 133 (on admissions) and Section 139 (on promissory estoppel) of the *Restatement (Second) of Contracts.*

electronically, and electronic signatures, such as a person's name typed at the bottom of an e-mail message, generally satisfy the Statute of Frauds.

What Constitutes a Writing?

A writing can consist of any order confirmation, invoice, sales slip, check, fax, or e-mail—or such items in combination. The written contract need not consist of a single document to constitute an enforceable contract. One document may incorporate another document by expressly referring to it. Several documents may form a single contract if they are physically attached, such as by staple, paper clip, or glue. Several documents may form a single contract even if they are only placed in the same envelope.

For example, Simpson orally agrees to sell some land next to a shopping mall to Terro Properties. Simpson gives Terro an unsigned memo that contains a legal description of the property, and Terro gives Simpson an unsigned first draft of their contract. Simpson sends Terro a signed letter that refers to the memo and to the first and final drafts of the contract. Terro sends Simpson an unsigned copy of the final draft of the contract with a signed check stapled to it. Together, the documents can constitute a writing sufficient to satisfy the Statute of Frauds and bind both parties to the terms of the contract as evidenced by the writings.

What Must Be Contained in the Writing?

A memorandum or note evidencing the oral contract need only contain the essential terms of the contract, not every term. There must, of course, also be some indication that the parties voluntarily agreed to the terms. A faxed memo of the terms of an agreement could be sufficient if it showed that there was a meeting of the minds and that the faxed terms were not just part of the preliminary negotiations.[11]

As mentioned earlier, under the UCC, a writing evidencing a contract for the sale of goods need only state the quantity and be signed by the party to be charged. Under most state Statute of Frauds provisions, the writing must also name the parties and identify the subject matter, the consideration, and the essential terms with reasonable certainty. In addition, contracts for the sale of land often are required to state the price and describe the property with sufficient clarity to allow them to be determined without reference to outside sources.

Note that because only the party against whom enforcement is sought must have signed the writing, a contract may be enforceable by one of its parties but not by the other. For example, Rock orally agrees to buy Betty Devlin's lake house and lot for

---

11. See, for example, *Coca-Cola Co. v. Babyback's International, Inc.,* cited in Footnote 4.

$150,000. Devlin writes Rock a letter confirming the sale by identifying the parties and the essential terms of the sales contract—price, method of payment, and legal address—and signs the letter. Devlin has made a written memorandum of the oral land contract. Because she has signed the letter, she normally can be held to the oral contract by Rock. Devlin cannot enforce the contract against Rock, however, because he has not signed or entered into a written contract or memorandum and can assert the Statute of Frauds as a defense.

▰▰▰ SECTION 4 ▰▰▰

THE PAROL EVIDENCE RULE

Sometimes, a written contract does not include—or contradicts—an oral understanding reached by the parties before or at the time of contracting. For instance, a landlord might tell a person who agrees to rent an apartment that she or he can have a cat, whereas the lease contract clearly states that no pets are allowed. If a dispute later arises over whether or not the tenant can have a cat, can the landlord's oral statements be introduced into evidence? In determining the outcome of such disputes, the courts look to a common law rule governing the admissibility in court of oral evidence, or *parol evidence.*

Under the **parol evidence rule,** if a court finds that the parties intended their written contract to be a complete and final statement of their agreement, then it will not allow either party to present parol evidence (testimony or other evidence of communications between the parties that are not contained in the contract itself).[12]

CASE IN POINT Pittsburgh Steelers Sports, Inc., sent Ronald Yocca a brochure that offered to sell stadium builder licenses (SBLs), which granted the right to buy season tickets to the Pittsburgh Steelers football games. Prices varied, depending on the seats' locations, which were indicated by small diagrams. Yocca applied for an SBL, listing his seating preferences. The Steelers sent him a letter notifying him where his seat was located, but the diagram showed different seating sections than were shown in the SBL brochure. The Steelers also sent Yocca documents setting forth the terms of the SBL agreement, which included a clause that read, "This Agreement contains the entire agreement of the parties." Yocca signed the documents as required. When Yocca went to the stadium and discovered that his seat was not where he expected it to be, based on the brochure, he filed a lawsuit for breach of contract. The court, however, concluded that the brochure was not part of the parties' contract and dismissed the suit. The SBL documents that Yocca had signed constituted the parties' entire contract and, under the parol evidence rule, could not be supplemented by previous negotiations or agreements.[13]

Exceptions to the Parol Evidence Rule

Because of the rigidity of the parol evidence rule, the courts have created the following exceptions:

1. *Contracts subsequently modified.* Evidence of any *subsequent modification* (oral or written) of a written contract can be introduced into court. Keep in mind that the oral modifications may not be enforceable if they come under the Statute of Frauds—for example, if they increase the price of the goods for sale to $500 or more or increase the term for performance to more than one year. Also, oral modifications will not be enforceable if the original contract provides that any modification must be in writing.[14]
2. *Voidable or void contracts.* Oral evidence can be introduced in all cases to show that the contract was voidable or void (for example, induced by mistake, fraud, or misrepresentation). The reason is simple: if deception led one of the parties to agree to the terms of a written contract, oral evidence attesting to the fraud should not be excluded. Courts frown on bad faith and are quick to allow such evidence when it establishes fraud.
3. *Contracts containing ambiguous terms.* When the terms of a written contract are ambiguous and require interpretation, evidence is admissible to show the meaning of the terms.
4. *Incomplete contracts.* When the written contract is incomplete in that it lacks one or more of the essential terms, the courts allow evidence to "fill in the gaps."
5. *Prior dealing, course of performance, or usage of trade.* Under the UCC, evidence can be introduced to explain or supplement a written contract by showing a prior dealing, course of performance, or usage of trade.[15] This is because when buyers

---

12. *Restatement (Second) of Contracts,* Section 213.

13. *Yocca v. Pittsburgh Steelers Sports, Inc.,* 578 Pa. 479, 854 A.2d 425 (2004).
14. UCC 2–209(2), (3).
15. UCC 1–205, 2–202.

and sellers deal with each other over extended periods of time, certain customary practices develop. These practices are often overlooked in the writing of the contract, so courts allow the introduction of evidence to show how the parties have acted in the past. Usage of trade—practices and customs generally followed in a particular industry—can also shed light on the meaning of certain contract provisions, and thus evidence of trade usage may be admissible. We will discuss these terms in further detail in Chapter 19, in the context of sales contracts.

6. *Contracts subject to an orally agreed-on condition precedent.* As you will read in Chapter 17, sometimes the parties agree that a condition must be fulfilled before a party is required to perform the contract. This is called a *condition precedent*. If the parties have orally agreed on a condition precedent and the condition does not conflict with the terms of a written agreement, then a court may allow parol evidence to prove the oral condition. The parol evidence rule does not apply here because the existence of the entire written contract is subject to an orally agreed-on condition. Proof of the condition does not alter or modify the written terms but affects the *enforceability* of the written contract.

CASE IN POINT A city has a renewable contract to lease property for an airport from a business. After a dispute arises, the parties agree to settle it by amending the lease agreement subject to the approval of the city council. The city amends the lease, but the business refuses to sign it, contending that the council has not approved it. Because the council's approval is a condition precedent to the formation of the settlement contract, the parol evidence rule does not apply. Thus, oral evidence is admissible to show that no agreement exists as to the terms of the settlement.[16]

7. *Contracts with an obvious or gross clerical (or typographic) error that clearly would not represent the agreement of the parties.* Parol evidence is admissible to correct an obvious typographic error. Suppose that Davis agrees to lease 1,000 square feet of office space from Stone Enterprises at the current monthly rate of $3 per square foot. The signed written lease provides for a monthly lease payment of $300 rather than the $3,000 agreed to by the parties. Because the error is obvious, Stone Enterprises would be allowed to admit parol evidence to correct the mistake.

In the following case, the court addressed the issue of whether parol evidence could be admitted to clarify the parties' intent in a sale of property.

---

16. *Castroville Airport, Inc. v. City of Castroville,* 974 S.W.2d 207 (Tex. App.—San Antonio 1998).

CASE 15.3
Watkins v. Schexnider

Court of Appeal of Louisiana, Third Circuit, 31 So.3d 609 (2010).
www.la3circuit.org/opinions.htm[a]

BACKGROUND AND FACTS • In 2000, Pamela Watkins purchased a home from Sandra Schexnider. The home purchase agreement stated, among other things, that Watkins would pay off the balance of the mortgage in monthly payments until the note was paid in full. "Then the house will be hers." The agreement also stipulated that Watkins would pay for insurance on the property. Watkins regularly paid the note and insurance. The home was destroyed following Hurricane Rita in 2005, and the mortgage was satisfied by the insurance proceeds. Watkins claimed that she owned the land, but Schexnider refused to transfer title to her. Schexnider asserted that she had sold only the house to Watkins, not the land. Watkins filed a petition in a Louisiana state court for specific performance of the agreement.[b] The trial court denied her claim for specific performance, concluding that the "clear wording of the contract" indicated that Watkins was purchasing only the house, not the land. Because the contract was clear on its face, the court refused to admit parol evidence to the contrary. Watkins appealed.

---

a. Click on "February" in the 2010 list, and then select "February 10, 2010." When you reach the page for February 10, 2010, scroll down the list to the case title and docket number (CA 09-00744) to access the opinion. The judicial branch of the Louisiana state government maintains this Web site.

b. *Specific performance* is an equitable remedy that requires a party who has breached (broken) a contract to perform the specific terms promised in the contract—see Chapters 1 and 18.

CASE 15.3 CONTINUED ➡️

IN THE LANGUAGE OF THE COURT
GREMILLION, Judge.
* * * *

Although the general rule is that parol evidence will not be allowed in interpreting a contract, it has been allowed in many instances in order to discern the intention of the parties in contracts to sell immovable property. * * * A panel of this court recently summarized the pertinent law regarding contract interpretation:

* * * *

* * * *When the words of a contract are clear, explicit, and lead to no absurd consequences, the contract must be interpreted within its four corners and cannot be explained or contradicted by parol evidence. However, when a word in a contract is not clear, testimony or other evidence may be considered to determine the parties' intent and interpret the contract * * *.* [Emphasis added.]

* * * *

Admittedly, the contract itself refers to the "home" and "house" multiple times. However, it references "the property" in terms of maintaining an insurance policy. The agreement was drafted by a lay person. * * * The fact that Schexnider, the person who wrote the contract, is claiming that the agreement only conveyed the house, yet failed to put any such provision in the contract, can only be interpreted as ambiguous. It seems clear that if a party intends to sell only a house and not the land on which it sits, she would so note and provide for the details of the manner in which the underlying land is to be used. Otherwise, the home buyer is left in a quandary of having no idea what the terms of the land rental agreement is, such as when it begins, the cost, the limitations on the land, and various other matters pertaining to use of another person's land. This situation surely leads to absurd consequences as it leaves a buyer susceptible [vulnerable] to the landowner's whim and further leads to instability of transactions involving immovables [real property].

Accordingly, we find that parol evidence should have been allowed to determine the true intent of the parties regarding the underlying land. We now consider the evidence adduced [used as a means of proof in an argument] at trial.

Watkins testified that, as of the time of trial, she had resided in the home for eight years. Watkins testified that Schexnider always indicated that the sale included the house, its contents, and the land. * * * She stated that Schexnider walked her around the property indicating the boundary lines. Watkins stated that Schexnider always indicated that the sale included the land and that she would have never purchased a home that sat on someone else's land.

* * * Watkins testified that * * * the house was completely destroyed following Hurricane Rita's landfall in September 2005, but that she and her husband returned to the property the following February and lived in a FEMA [Federal Emergency Management Agency] trailer. She testified that she and her husband began repairing the property. She estimates that they spent approximately $15,000 repairing the property, but could only provide $9,000 worth of receipts. Pictures of the remodeled barn that Watkins converted into a living area were admitted into evidence.

* * * *

Marla Raffield, Watkins' daughter-in-law, testified that she was present the day that Schexnider pointed out the whole property line. Raffield said that Schexnider indicated a survey would be done once the land was paid for so that Watkins could "verify her land with the court." Raffield said that Schexnider never indicated that she was only selling the house.

Having reviewed all of the evidence, we are certain that, at the time Watkins and Schexnider confected [prepared] the "Home Purchase Agreement" the land was included as part of the sale.

DECISION AND REMEDY • *The Court of Appeal of Louisiana held that parol evidence should have been admitted to clarify the meaning of the contract. In light of the parol evidence, the court concluded that the parties intended to transfer ownership of both the house and the land, and ordered that title to the property be transferred to Watkins.*

THE ETHICAL DIMENSION • *The parol evidence rule is centuries old and is an important rule of contract law. Why should the courts allow exceptions to this rule?*

CASE CONTINUES ➡️

CASE 15.3 CONTINUED ➧ **MANAGERIAL IMPLICATIONS** • *Although the contract at issue in this case was written in simple terms by a party with only a high school education, the case contains an important message for businesspersons. No matter how sophisticated and complex the agreement, it is important to make sure that your intentions are made clear by the written words. Otherwise, a judge may determine the issue, and you may not agree with the judge's conclusion. Additionally, if the party you are contracting with states a term or condition orally, and you agree to it, always make sure that the term or condition is included in the written contract. Finally, as you will read shortly, parties can add a clause to their contract stating that the contract is fully integrated, meaning that the contract represents a complete and final record of the parties' agreement. When a contract is fully integrated, parol evidence normally is not admissible.*

Integrated Contracts

The key in determining whether parol evidence will be allowed is whether the written contract is intended to be a complete and final statement of the terms of the agreement. If it is so intended, it is referred to as an **integrated contract,** and extraneous evidence (evidence derived from sources outside the contract itself) is excluded.

An integrated contract can be either completely or partially integrated. If it contains all of the terms of the parties' agreement, then it is completely integrated. If it contains only some of the terms that the parties agreed on and not others, it is partially integrated. If the contract is only partially integrated, evidence of consistent additional terms is admissible to supplement the written agreement.[17] Note that for both complete and partially integrated contracts, courts exclude any evidence that *contradicts*

the writing and allow parol evidence only to add to the terms of a partially integrated contract. Exhibit 15–4 illustrates the relationship between integrated contracts and the parol evidence rule.

━━━━━ **SECTION 5** ━━━━━
THE STATUTE OF FRAUDS IN THE INTERNATIONAL CONTEXT

As you will read in Chapter 19, the Convention on Contracts for the International Sale of Goods (CISG) governs international sales contracts between citizens of countries that have ratified the convention (agreement). Article 11 of the CISG does not incorporate any Statute of Frauds provisions. Rather, it states that a "contract for sale need not be concluded in or evidenced by writing and is not subject to any other requirements as to form."

---

17. *Restatement (Second) of Contracts,* Section 216; and UCC 2–202.

EXHIBIT 15–4 • **The Parol Evidence Rule**

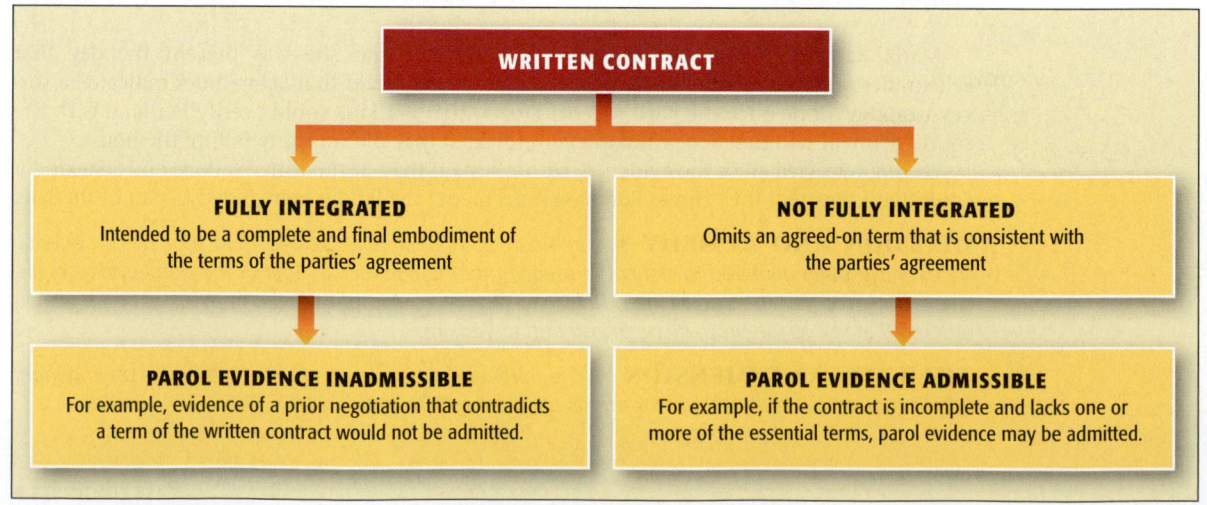

Article 11 accords with the legal customs of most nations, which no longer require contracts to meet certain formal or writing requirements to be enforceable. Ironically, even England, the nation that created the original Statute of Frauds in 1677, has repealed all of it except the provisions relating to collateral promises and to transfers of interests in land. Many other countries that once had such statutes have also repealed all or parts of them. Some countries, such as France, have never required certain types of contracts to be in writing.

REVIEWING
The Statute of Frauds—Writing Requirement and Electronic Records

Charter Golf, Inc., manufactures and sells golf apparel and supplies. Ken Odin had worked as a Charter sales representative for six months when he was offered a position with a competing firm. Charter's president, Jerry Montieth, offered Odin a 10 percent commission "for the rest of his life" if Ken would turn down the offer and stay on with Charter. He also promised that Odin would not be fired unless he was dishonest. Odin turned down the competitor's offer and stayed with Charter. Three years later, Charter fired Odin for no reason. Odin sued, alleging breach of contract. Using the information presented in the chapter, answer the following questions.

1. Would a court likely decide that Odin's employment contract falls within the Statute of Frauds? Why or why not?
2. Assume that the court does find that the contract falls within the Statute of Frauds and that the state in which the court sits recognizes every exception to the Statute of Frauds discussed in the chapter. What exception provides Odin with the best chance of enforcing the oral contract in this situation?
3. Now suppose that Montieth had taken out a pencil, written "10 percent for life" on the back of a register receipt, and handed it to Odin. Would this satisfy the Statute of Frauds? Why or why not?
4. Assume that Odin had signed a written employment contract at the time he was hired to work for Charter, but it was not completely integrated. Would a court allow Odin to present parol evidence of Montieth's subsequent promises?

DEBATE THIS: *Many countries have eliminated the Statute of Frauds except for sales of real estate. The United States should do the same.*

TERMS AND CONCEPTS

integrated contract   300
parol evidence rule   297
prenuptial agreement   293
Statute of Frauds   289
collateral promise   291

QUESTIONS AND CASE PROBLEMS

15–1. The One-Year Rule On May 1, by telephone, Yu offers to hire Benson to perform personal services. On May 5, Benson returns Yu's call and accepts the offer. Discuss fully whether this contract falls under the Statute of Frauds in the following circumstances:

(a) The contract calls for Benson to be employed for one year, with the right to begin performance immediately.

(b) The contract calls for Benson to be employed for nine months, with performance of services to begin on September 1.

(c) The contract calls for Benson to submit a written research report, with a deadline of two years for submission.

15–2. QUESTION WITH SAMPLE ANSWER: Collateral Promises.

Mallory promises a local hardware store that she will pay for a lawn mower that her brother is purchasing on credit if the brother fails to pay the debt. Must this promise be in writing to be enforceable? Why or why not?

• **For a sample answer to Question 15–2, go to Appendix I at the end of this text.**

15–3. The One-Year Rule

On January 1, Damon, for consideration, orally promised to pay Gary $300 a month for as long as Gary lived, with the payments to be made on the first day of every month. Damon made the payments regularly for nine months and then made no further payments. Gary claimed that Damon had breached the oral contract and sued Damon for damages. Damon contended that the contract was unenforceable because, under the Statute of Frauds, contracts that cannot be performed within one year must be in writing. Discuss whether Damon will succeed in this defense.

15–4. Collateral Promises

Jeremy took his mother on a special holiday to Mountain Air Resort. Jeremy was a frequent patron of the resort and was well known by its manager. The resort required each of its patrons to make a large deposit to ensure payment of the room rental. Jeremy asked the manager to waive the requirement for his mother and told the manager that if his mother for any reason failed to pay the resort for her stay there, he would cover the bill. Relying on Jeremy's promise, the manager waived the deposit requirement for Jeremy's mother. After she returned home from her holiday, Jeremy's mother refused to pay the resort bill. The resort manager tried to collect the sum from Jeremy, but Jeremy also refused to pay, stating that his promise was not enforceable under the Statute of Frauds. Is Jeremy correct? Explain.

15–5. Oral Contracts

Jason Knapp, doing business as Knapp Associates, hired Barbara Meade as an independent contractor in March 2009. The parties orally agreed on the terms of employment, including payment to Meade of a share of the company's income, but they did not put anything in writing. In March 2011, Meade quit. Knapp then told Meade that she was entitled to $9,602.17—25 percent of the difference between the accounts receivable and the accounts payable as of Meade's last day. Meade disagreed and demanded more than $63,500—25 percent of the revenue from all invoices, less the cost of materials and outside processing, for all the years that she worked for Knapp. Knapp refused. Meade filed a lawsuit in a state court against Knapp, alleging breach of contract. In Knapp's response and at the trial, he testified that the parties had an oral contract under which Meade was entitled to 25 percent of the difference between accounts receivable and payable as of the date

of Meade's termination. Did the parties have an enforceable contract? How should the court rule, and why?

15–6. Interests in Land

Sierra Bravo, Inc., and Shelby's, Inc., entered into a written "Waste Disposal Agreement" under which Shelby's allowed Sierra to deposit on Shelby's land waste products, harmful materials, and debris removed by Sierra in the construction of a highway. Later, Shelby's asked Sierra why it had not constructed a waterway and a building pad suitable for a commercial building on the property, as they had orally agreed. Sierra denied any such agreement. Shelby's filed a suit in a Missouri state court against Sierra, alleging breach of contract. Sierra contended that any oral agreement was unenforceable under the Statute of Frauds. Sierra argued that because the right to *remove* minerals from land is considered a contract for the sale of an interest in land to which the Statute of Frauds applies, the Statute of Frauds should apply to the right to *deposit* soil on another person's property. How should the court rule, and why? [*Shelby's, Inc. v. Sierra Bravo, Inc.*, 68 S.W.3d 604 (Mo.App.S.D. 2002)]

15–7. CASE PROBLEM WITH SAMPLE ANSWER: The Parol Evidence Rule.

Novell, Inc., owned the source code for DR DOS, a computer operating system that Microsoft Corp. targeted with allegedly anticompetitive practices in the early 1990s. Novell worried that if it filed a suit, Microsoft would retaliate with further alleged unfair practices. Consequently, Novell sold DR DOS to Canopy Group, Inc., a Utah corporation. The purposes of the sale were to obligate Canopy to bring an action against Microsoft and to allow Novell to share in the recovery without revealing its role. Novell and Canopy signed two documents—a contract of sale, obligating Canopy to pay $400,000 for rights to the source code, and a temporary license, obligating Canopy to pay at least $600,000 in royalties, which included a percentage of any recovery from the suit. Canopy settled the dispute with Microsoft, deducted its expenses, and paid Novell the remainder of what was due. Novell filed a suit in a Utah state court against Canopy, alleging breach of contract for Canopy's deduction of expenses. Canopy responded that it could show that the parties had an oral agreement on this point. On what basis might the court refuse to consider this evidence? Is that the appropriate course in this case? Explain. [*Novell, Inc. v. Canopy Group, Inc.*, 2004 UT App. 162, 92 P.3d 768 (2004)]

• **To view a sample answer for Problem 15–7, go to this book's Web site at www.cengage.com/blaw/clarkson, select "Chapter 15," and click on "Case Problem with Sample Answer."**

15–8. Contract for a Sale of Goods

Milton Blankenship agreed in writing to buy 15 acres of Ella Mae Henry's junkyard property for $15,000 per acre with a ten-year option to buy ~~an adjoining 55 acres~~. Blankenship orally agreed to (1) begin operating a car skeleton–processing plant within six to fifteen months; (2) buy as many car skeletons generated by the yard as Henry wanted to sell him, at a certain premium over the market price; and (3) allow all junk vehicles on the property to remain until they were processed at the new plant. Blankenship never operated such a plant, never bought any vehicles from the yard, and demanded that all vehicles be removed from the property. To obtain the remaining 28.32 acres, Blankenship filed a suit in a Georgia state court against Henry, who responded with a counterclaim for breach of contract. Under oath during discovery, Henry testified that their oral agreement allowed him to sell "as many of the car skeletons generated by the Henry junkyard" as he wished, and Blankenship testified that he had agreed to buy as many skeletons as Henry was willing to sell. Does the Statute of Frauds undercut or support Henry's counterclaim? Explain. [*Henry v. Blankenship,* 284 Ga.App. 578, 644 S.E.2d 419 (2007)]

15–9. The Parol Evidence Rule When Hurricane Katrina hit the Gulf Coast in 2005, Evangel Temple Assembly of God in Wichita Falls, Texas, contacted Wood Care Centers, Inc., about leasing a facility it owned to house evacuees from the hurricane. Evangel and Wood Care reached an agreement and signed a twenty-year lease at $10,997 per month. One clause said that Evangel could terminate the lease at any time by giving Wood Care notice and paying 10 percent of the balance remaining on the lease. Another clause stated that if the facility was not given a property tax exemption, Evangel had the option to terminate the lease. Nine months later, the last of the evacuees left the facility, and Evangel notified Wood Care that it would end the lease. Wood Care demanded the 10 percent payment. Evangel claimed that it did not need to make the payment because if the facility converted back to a "non-church" use, it would lose its tax-exempt status and Evangel could simply terminate the lease. Evangel's pastor testified that the parties understood that this would be the scenario at the time the lease was signed. The trial court held that Evangel owed nothing. Wood Care appealed, contending that the trial court improperly allowed parol evidence to interpret the contract. Was the trial court's acceptance of parol evidence correct? Why or why not? [*Wood Care Centers, Inc. v. Evangel Temple Assembly of God of Wichita Falls,* 307 S.W.3d 816303 (Tex.App.—Fort Worth 2010)]

15–10. A QUESTION OF ETHICS: The Parol Evidence Rule.

William Williams is an attorney in Birmingham, Alabama. In 1997, Robert Shelborne asked Williams to represent him in a deal in London, England, from which Shelborne expected to receive

$31 million. Shelborne agreed to pay Williams a fee of $1 million. Their overseas contact was Robert Tundy, who said that he was with the "Presidency" in London. Tundy said that a tax of $100,010 would have to be paid for Shelborne to receive the $31 million. Shelborne asked James Parker, a former co-worker, to lend him $50,000. Shelborne signed a note agreeing to pay Parker $100,000 within seventy-two hours. Parker, Shelborne, and Williams wired the $50,000 to an account at Chase Manhattan Bank. They never heard from Tundy again. No $31 million was transferred to Shelborne, who soon disappeared. Williams then learned that no "Presidency" existed in London. Whenever Parker asked Williams about the note, Williams assured him that he would be paid. On Parker's behalf, Williams filed a suit in an Alabama state court against Shelborne, seeking the amount due on the note and damages. The court entered a judgment against the defendant for $200,000, but there were no assets from which to collect it. [*Parker v. Williams,* 977 So.2d 476 (Ala. 2007)]

(a) Parker filed a suit in an Alabama state court against Williams, alleging, among other things, breach of contract. Parker offered as evidence a tape recording of a phone conversation in which Williams guaranteed Shelborne's loan. Is the court likely to rule in Parker's favor on the contract claim? Why or why not?

(b) In response to Parker's suit, Williams filed a counterclaim, seeking unpaid attorneys' fees relating to the suit that Williams filed against Shelborne on Parker's behalf. The court ruled against Williams on this claim. He appealed to the Alabama Supreme Court but failed to supply a transcript of the trial on his counterclaim, as it was his duty to do. Is the appellate court likely to rule in his favor? Why or why not?

(c) The sham deal at the center of this case is known to law enforcement authorities as advance fee fraud, commonly referred to as a "419 scam." The victim is promised a transfer of funds from an overpaid contract, or some other suspect source, but is asked to pay a tax or other fee first. Among the parties attracted by the 419 scam in this case, who, if anyone, behaved ethically? Discuss.

LEGAL RESEARCH EXERCISES ON THE WEB

Go to this text's Web site at **www.cengage.com/blaw/clarkson**, select "Chapter 15," and click on "Practical Internet Exercises." There you will find the following Internet research exercises that you can perform to learn more about the topics covered in this chapter.

Practical Internet Exercise 15-1: Legal Perspective
Promissory Estoppel and the Statute of Frauds

Practical Internet Exercise 15-2: Management Perspective
"Get It in Writing"

CHAPTER 16

Third Party Rights

Once it has been determined that a valid and legally enforceable contract exists, attention can turn to the rights and duties of the parties to the contract. A contract is a private agreement between the parties who have entered into it, and traditionally these parties alone have rights and liabilities under the contract. This principle is referred to as privity of contract. A *third party*—one who is not a direct party to a particular contract—normally does not have rights under that contract.

There are exceptions to the rule of privity of contract. For example, privity of contract between a seller and a buyer is no longer a requirement to recover damages under product liability laws (see Chapter 22). In this chapter, we look at two other exceptions. One exception allows a party to a contract to transfer the rights or duties arising from the contract to another person through an *assignment* (of rights) or a *delegation* (of duties). The other exception involves a *third party beneficiary contract*—a contract in which the parties to the contract intend that the contract benefit a third party.

SECTION 1
ASSIGNMENTS AND DELEGATIONS

In a bilateral contract, the two parties have corresponding rights and duties. One party has a *right* to require the other to perform some task, and the other has a *duty* to perform it. The transfer of contractual *rights* to a third party is known as an **assignment.** The transfer of contractual *duties* to a third party is known as a **delegation.** An assignment or a delegation occurs *after* the original contract was made.

Assignments

Assignments are important because they are involved in many types of business financing. Banks, for example, frequently assign their rights to receive payments under their loan contracts to other firms, which pay for those rights. If Tia obtains a loan from a bank to purchase a car, she may later receive a notice from the bank stating that it has transferred (assigned) its rights to receive payments on the loan to another firm. When it is time to repay the loan, Tia must make the payments to that other firm.

Financial institutions that make *mortgage loans* (loans to enable prospective home buyers to purchase land or a home) often assign their rights to collect the mortgage payments to a third party, such as GMAC Mortgage. Following the assignment, the home buyers are notified that they must make future payments not to the bank that loaned them the funds but to the third party. Millions of dollars change hands daily in the business world in the form of assignments of rights in contracts. If it were not possible to transfer contractual rights, many businesses could not continue to operate.

TERMINOLOGY In an assignment, the party assigning the rights to a third party is known as the **assignor,**[1] and the party receiving the rights is the **assignee.**[2] Other traditional terms used to describe the parties in assignment relationships are **obligee** (the person to whom a duty, or obligation, is owed) and **obligor** (the person who is obligated to perform the duty).

---

1. Pronounced uh-*sye*-nore.
2. Pronounced uh-*sye*-nee.

THE EFFECT OF AN ASSIGNMENT When rights under a contract are assigned unconditionally, the rights of the assignor are extinguished.[3] The third party (the assignee) has a right to demand performance from the other original party to the contract. The assignee takes only those rights that the assignor originally had, however.

Suppose that Brower is obligated by contract to pay Horton $1,000. In this situation, Brower is the obligor because she owes an obligation, or duty, to Horton. Horton is the obligee, the one to whom the obligation, or duty, is owed. Now suppose that Horton assigns his right to receive the $1,000 to Kuhn. Horton is the assignor, and Kuhn is the assignee. Kuhn now becomes the obligee because Brower owes Kuhn the $1,000. Here, a valid assignment of a debt exists. Kuhn (the assignee-obligee) is entitled to enforce payment in court if Brower (the obligor) does not pay him the $1,000. These concepts are illustrated in Exhibit 16–1.

RIGHTS ASSIGNED ARE SUBJECT TO THE SAME DEFENSES The assignee's rights are subject to the defenses that the obligor has against the assignor. Assume that in the preceding scenario, Brower owes Horton the $1,000 under a contract in which Brower agreed to buy Horton's MacBook Pro laptop. When Brower decided to purchase the laptop, she relied on Horton's fraudulent misrepresentation that the computer had eight megabytes of memory. When Brower discovers that the computer has only four megabytes of memory, she tells Horton that she is going to return the laptop to him and cancel the contract. Even though Horton has assigned his "right" to receive the $1,000 to Kuhn, Brower need not pay Kuhn the $1,000—Brower can raise the defense of Horton's fraudulent misrepresentation to avoid payment.

FORM OF THE ASSIGNMENT In general, an assignment can take any form, oral or written. Naturally, it is more difficult to prove that an oral assignment occurred, so it is practical to put all assignments in writing. Of course, assignments covered by the Statute of Frauds must be in writing to be enforceable. For example, an assignment of an interest in land must be in writing to be enforceable. In addition, most states require contracts for the assignment of wages to be in writing.[4]

The circumstances in the following case illustrate some of the problems that can arise with oral assignments. The case also stands for the principle that an assignment, like any contract, must have consideration—in this case, a dance center's assumption of a choreographer's legal and financial duties associated with her choreography.

---

3. *Restatement (Second) of Contracts,* Section 317.

4. See, for example, California Labor Code Section 300. There are other assignments that must be in writing as well.

EXHIBIT 16–1 • Assignment Relationships

In the assignment relationship illustrated here, Horton assigns his *rights* under a contract that he made with Brower to a third party, Kuhn. Horton thus becomes the *assignor* and Kuhn the *assignee* of the contractual rights. Brower, the *obligor*, now owes performance to Kuhn instead of Horton. Horton's original contract rights are extinguished after assignment.

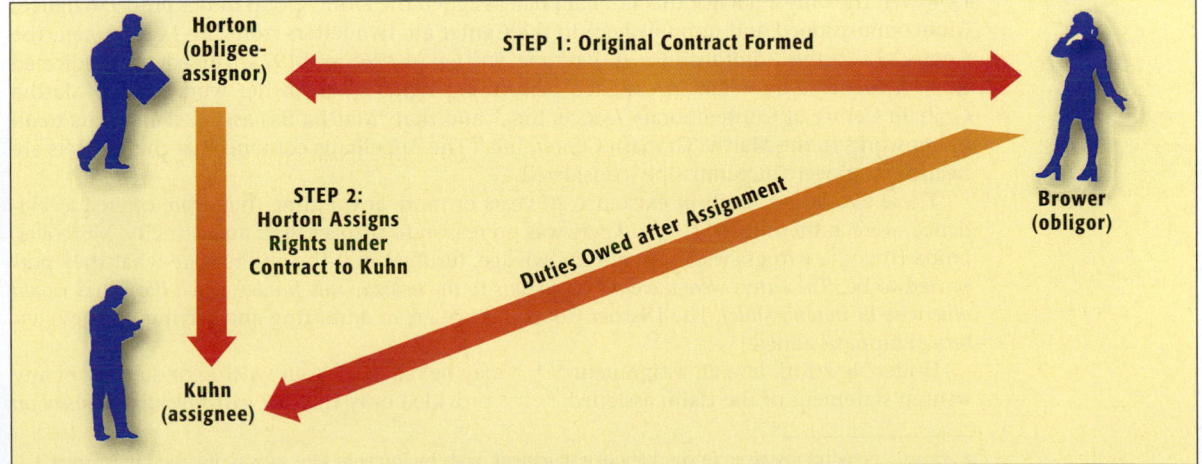

Horton
(obligee-
assignor)

STEP 1: Original Contract Formed

STEP 2:
Horton Assigns
Rights under
Contract to Kuhn

Duties Owed after Assignment

Brower
(obligor)

Kuhn
(assignee)

CASE 16.1
Martha Graham School and Dance Foundation, Inc. v. Martha Graham Center of Contemporary Dance, Inc.
United States Court of Appeals, Second Circuit, 380 F.3d 624 (2004).

BACKGROUND AND FACTS • Martha Graham's career as a dancer, dance instructor, and choreographer began in the first third of the twentieth century. In the 1920s, she started a dance company and a dance school and choreographed works on commission. In the 1940s, she funded the Martha Graham Center of Contemporary Dance, Inc. (the Center). She sold her school to the Martha Graham School of Contemporary Dance, Inc. (the School), in 1956. By 1980, the Center encompassed the School. In 1989, two years before her death, Graham executed a will in which she gave Ronald Protas, the Center's general director, "any rights or interests" in "dance works, musical scores [and] scenery sets." After her death, Protas asserted ownership of all of Graham's dances and related property. In 1999, the Center's board removed Protas and, due to financial problems, suspended operations. Meanwhile, Protas founded the Martha Graham School and Dance Foundation, Inc., and began licensing Graham's dances. When the School reopened in 2001, Protas and his foundation filed a suit in a federal district court against the Center and others to enjoin their use of, among other things, seventy of the dances. The Center responded, in part, that Graham had assigned the dances to it. The court ruled that twenty-one of the dances had been assigned to the Center. The plaintiffs appealed to the U.S. Court of Appeals for the Second Circuit.

IN THE LANGUAGE OF THE COURT
Jon O. *NEWMAN,* Circuit Judge.
* * * *

The Appellants contend that the District Court erred in finding that Graham assigned to the Center 21 dances, * * * which were created before 1956, unpublished at the time of assignment, and not commissioned. We disagree.
* * * *

Although there is no document memorializing Graham's assignment of copyright in her pre-1956 dances to the Center, the District Court was entitled to find that Graham assigned to the Center, orally or in writing, her copyrights in her noncommissioned pre-1956 dances that were not published at the time she assigned them.

The District Court relied on several items of evidence to reach its conclusion. For example, Jeannette Roosevelt, former President of the Center's board of directors, testified that Graham had given the dances to the Center prior to 1965 or 1966, when she joined the board. There was additional evidence that the Center acted as the owner of the dances by entering into contracts with third parties, and that Graham was aware of this and did not object. Other evidence showed that the Center received royalties for the dances and treated them as its assets. However, the only evidence that Graham had assigned the entire group of her pre-1956 dances (noncommissioned and unpublished) to the Center are two letters from Lee Leatherman, the Center's Executive Administrator at that time, written in 1968 and 1971. These letters indicated that "[r]ecently Miss Graham assigned performing rights to all of her works to the Martha Graham Center of Contemporary Dance, Inc.," and that "Martha has assigned all rights to all of her works to the Martha Graham Center, Inc." The Appellants contend that these letters are hearsay[a] and were impermissibly considered

These two letters, both in existence 20 years or more at the time they were offered as evidence, were authenticated * * * . There was no reason to suspect their authenticity. Moreover, Linda Hodes, a witness with relevant knowledge, testified that the letters were what they purported to be. *The letters were therefore exceptions to the hearsay rule [under which the letters would otherwise be inadmissible].* The District Court did not err in admitting and relying on these letters. [Emphasis added.]

Under New York law, an assignment * * * may be made without writing or delivery of any written statement of the claim assigned, * * * provided only that *the assignment is founded on*

---
a. *Hearsay* is testimony given in court about a statement made by someone else, as was discussed in Chapter 3.

CASE 16.1 CONTINUED ▶ *a valid consideration between the parties.* The District Court was entitled to find that Graham received consideration for the assignment of her pre-1956 dances. Graham benefited from the Center's assumption of the legal and financial duties associated with her choreography; assigning to the Center the copyrights in her dances gave her what she wished—freedom from the responsibilities of copyright registration and renewal, licensing, collection of royalties, and archival tasks. [Emphasis added.]

The District Court was entitled to find that Graham assigned her pre-1956 dances * * * to the Center sometime between 1957 and the mid-1960s.

DECISION AND REMEDY • *The U.S. Court of Appeals for the Second Circuit affirmed the lower court's judgment on this issue, "commend[ing] the District Court for its careful rulings on the many issues in this complicated case." The appellate court held that Graham had received consideration for her assignment of certain dances and that, although the assignment had been oral, it had been reliably proved by written testimony.*

WHAT IF THE FACTS WERE DIFFERENT? • *Suppose that Graham had not benefited from the Center's assumption of the duties associated with her choreography. Would the alleged assignment have been valid? Why or why not?*

THE E-COMMERCE DIMENSION • *If Graham's dances had existed as part of a database available only over the Internet, would the principles applied in this case, and the way in which they were applied, have been different? Why or why not?*

RIGHTS THAT CANNOT BE ASSIGNED As a general rule, all rights can be assigned. Exceptions are made, however, under certain circumstances. Some of these exceptions are described next.

When a Statute Prohibits Assignment. When a statute expressly prohibits assignment of a particular right, that right cannot be assigned. Suppose that Quincy is an employee of Specialty Computer, Inc. Specialty Computer is an employer under workers' compensation statutes in this state, and thus Quincy is a covered employee. Quincy is injured on the job and begins to collect monthly workers' compensation checks (see Chapter 34 for a discussion of workers' compensation laws). In need of a loan, Quincy borrows from Draper, assigning to Draper all of her future workers' compensation benefits. A state statute prohibits the assignment of *future* workers' compensation benefits, and thus such rights cannot be assigned.

When a Contract Is Personal in Nature. If a contract is for personal services, the rights under the contract normally cannot be assigned unless all that remains is a monetary payment.[5] For example, Brower signs a contract to be a tutor for Horton's children. Horton then attempts to assign to Kuhn his right to Brower's services. Kuhn cannot enforce the contract against Brower. Kuhn's children may be more difficult to tutor than Horton's; thus, if Horton could assign his rights to Brower's services to Kuhn, it would change the nature of Brower's obligation. Because personal services are unique to the person rendering them, rights to receive personal services are likewise unique and cannot be assigned.

Note that when legal actions involve personal rights, they are considered personal in nature and cannot be assigned. For instance, personal-injury tort claims generally are nonassignable as a matter of public policy. If Elizabeth is injured by Randy's defamation, she cannot assign her right to sue Randy for damages to someone else.

CASE IN POINT Accrued Financial Services, Inc. (AFS), conducts audits on behalf of tenants in commercial buildings to determine if the landlords have overcharged the tenants. As part of AFS's standard contract, the tenants assign their rights to file lawsuits against the landlord to AFS. AFS performed an audit for tenants of Prime Retail, Inc., and subsequently brought a lawsuit against Prime Retail. The court, however, held that it was against public policy to allow tenants to assign their right to file legal claims against their landlord to AFS. Therefore, the purported assignment was illegal, and the contract was unenforceable.[6]

---

5. *Restatement (Second) of Contracts,* Sections 317 and 318.

6. *Accrued Financial Services, Inc. v. Prime Retail, Inc.,* 298 F.3d 291 (4th Cir. 2002).

When an Assignment Will Significantly Change the Risk or Duties of the Obligor. A right cannot be assigned if the assignment will significantly increase or alter the risks to or the duties of the obligor (the party owing performance under the contract).[7] For example, Horton has a hotel, and to insure it, he takes out a policy with Southeast Insurance. The policy insures against fire, theft, floods, and vandalism. Horton attempts to assign the insurance policy to Kuhn, who also owns a hotel. The assignment is ineffective because it substantially alters Southeast Insurance's *duty of performance*. An insurance company evaluates the particular risk of a certain party and tailors its policy to fit that risk. If the policy is assigned to a third party, the insurance risk is materially altered because the insurance company may have no information on the third party. Therefore, the assignment will not operate to give Kuhn any rights against Southeast Insurance.

When the Contract Prohibits Assignment. When a contract specifically stipulates that a right cannot be assigned, then *ordinarily* it cannot be assigned. Whether an *antiassignment clause* is effective depends, in part, on how it is phrased. A contract that states that any assignment is void effectively prohibits any assignment. Note that restraints on the power to assign operate only against the parties themselves. They do not prohibit an assignment by operation of law, such as an assignment pursuant to bankruptcy or death.

The general rule that a contract can prohibit assignment has several exceptions.

1. A contract cannot prevent an assignment of the right to receive funds. This exception exists to encourage the free flow of funds and credit in modern business settings.
2. The assignment of rights in real estate often cannot be prohibited because such a prohibition is contrary to public policy in most states. Prohibitions of this kind are called restraints against **alienation** (transfer of land ownership).
3. The assignment of *negotiable instruments* (see Chapter 24) cannot be prohibited.
4. In a contract for the sale of goods, the right to receive damages for breach of contract or payment of an account owed may be assigned even though the sales contract prohibits such an assignment.[8]

NOTICE OF ASSIGNMENT Once a valid assignment of rights has been made, the assignee (the third party to whom the rights have been assigned) should notify the obligor (the one owing performance) of the assignment. For instance, in the previously discussed example, when Horton assigns to Kuhn his right to receive the $1,000 from Brower, Kuhn should notify Brower, the obligor, of the assignment. Giving notice is not legally necessary to establish the validity of the assignment: an assignment is effective immediately, whether or not notice is given. Two major problems arise, however, when notice of the assignment is not given to the obligor.

1. If the assignor assigns the same right to two different persons, the question arises as to which one has priority—that is, which one has the right to the performance by the obligor. Although the rule most often observed in the United States is that the first assignment in time is the first in right, some states follow the English rule, which basically gives priority to the first assignee who gives notice.
2. Until the obligor has notice of an assignment, the obligor can discharge his or her obligation by performance to the assignor (the obligee), and performance by the obligor to the assignor (obligee) constitutes a discharge to the assignee. Once the obligor receives proper notice, however, only performance to the assignee can discharge the obligor's obligations. In the Horton-Brower-Kuhn example, assume that Brower, the obligor, is not notified of Horton's assignment of his rights to Kuhn. Brower subsequently pays Horton the $1,000. Although the assignment was valid, Brower's payment to Horton discharges the debt. Kuhn's failure to give notice to Brower of the assignment has caused Kuhn to lose the right to collect the cash from Brower. If, however, Kuhn had given Brower notice of the assignment, Brower's payment to Horton would not have discharged the debt, and Kuhn would have had a legal right to require payment from Brower.

Delegations

Just as a party can transfer rights through an assignment, a party can also transfer duties. Duties are not assigned, however; they are *delegated*. Normally, a delegation of duties does not relieve the party making the delegation (the **delegator**) of the obligation to perform in the event that the party to whom the duty has been delegated (the **delegatee**) fails to perform. No special form is required to create a valid delegation

---

7. Section 2–210(2) of the Uniform Commercial Code (UCC).
8. UCC 2–210(2).

of duties. As long as the delegator expresses an intention to make the delegation, it is effective; the delegator need not even use the word *delegate*. Exhibit 16–2 illustrates delegation relationships.

DUTIES THAT CANNOT BE DELEGATED As a general rule, any duty can be delegated. There are, however, some exceptions to this rule. Delegation is prohibited in the circumstances discussed next.

When the Duties Are Personal in Nature.

When special trust has been placed in the obligor or when performance depends on the personal skill or talents of the obligor, contractual duties cannot be delegated. For example, Horton, who is impressed with Brower's ability to perform veterinary surgery, contracts with Brower to have her perform surgery on Horton's prize-winning stallion in July. Brower later decides that she would rather spend the summer at the beach, so she delegates her duties under the contract to Kuhn, who is also a competent veterinary surgeon. The delegation is not effective without Horton's consent, no matter how competent Kuhn is, because the contract is for *personal* performance.

In contrast, nonpersonal duties may be delegated. Assume that Brower contracts with Horton to pick up and deliver heavy construction machinery to Horton's property. Brower delegates this duty to Kuhn, who is in the business of delivering heavy

machinery. This delegation is effective because the performance required is of a *routine* and *nonpersonal* nature.

When Performance by a Third Party Will Vary Materially from That Expected by the Obligee.

When performance by a third party will vary materially from that expected by the obligee under the contract, contractual duties cannot be delegated. Suppose that Alex Payton is a wealthy philanthropist who recently established a charitable foundation. Payton has known Brent Murdoch for twenty years and knows that Murdoch shares his beliefs on many humanitarian issues. He contracts with Murdoch to be in charge of allocating funds among various charitable causes. Six months later, Murdoch is experiencing health problems and delegates his duties to Drew Cole. Payton does not approve of Cole as a replacement. In this situation, Payton can claim the delegation was not effective because it *materially altered his expectations* under the contract. Payton had reasonable expectations about the types of charities to which Murdoch would give the foundation's funds, and the substitution of Cole's performance materially changed those expectations.

When the Contract Prohibits Delegation.

When the contract expressly prohibits delegation by including an *antidelegation clause*, the duties cannot

EXHIBIT 16–2 • Delegation Relationships

In the delegation relationship illustrated here, Brower delegates her *duties* under a contract that she made with Horton to a third party, Kuhn. Brower thus becomes the *delegator* and Kuhn the *delegatee* of the contractual duties. Kuhn now owes performance of the contractual duties to Horton. Note that a delegation of duties normally does not relieve the delegator (Brower) of liability if the delegatee (Kuhn) fails to perform the contractual duties.

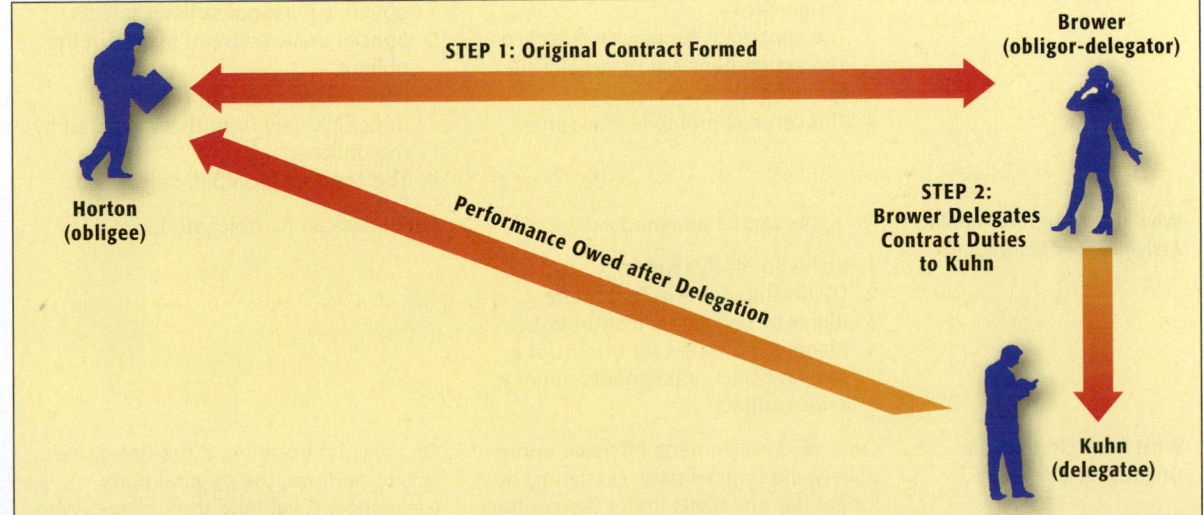

be delegated. R.W. Stern Company contracts with Jan Pearson, a certified public accountant, to perform its annual audits for the next five years. If the contract prohibits delegation, then Pearson cannot delegate her duty to perform the audit to another accountant at the same firm. In some situations, however, when the duties are completely impersonal in nature, courts have held that the duties can be delegated notwithstanding an antidelegation clause.

EFFECT OF A DELEGATION   If a delegation of duties is enforceable, the obligee must accept performance from the delegatee. Consider again the example in which Brower delegates to Kuhn the duty to pick up and deliver heavy construction machinery to Horton's property. In that situation, Horton (the obligee) must accept performance from Kuhn (the delegatee) because the delegation was effective. The obligee can legally refuse performance from the delegatee only if the duty is one that cannot be delegated.

As noted, a valid delegation of duties does not relieve the delegator of obligations under the contract. Thus, in the above example, if Kuhn (the delegatee) fails to perform, Brower (the delegator) is still liable to Horton (the obligee). The obligee can also hold the delegatee liable if the delegatee made a promise of performance that will directly benefit the obligee. In this situation, there is an "assumption of duty" on the part of the delegatee, and breach of this duty makes the delegatee liable to the obligee. For example, if Kuhn (the delegatee) promises Brower (the delegator), in a contract, to pick up and deliver the construction equipment to Horton's property but fails to do so, Horton (the obligee) can sue Brower, Kuhn, or both. Although there are many exceptions, the general rule today is that the obligee can sue both the delegatee and the delegator.

Concept Summary 16.1 outlines the basic principles of the laws governing assignments and delegations.

Assignment of "All Rights"

When a contract provides for an "assignment of all rights," this wording may create both an assignment of rights and a delegation of duties.[9] Therefore, when general words are used (for example, "I assign the contract" or "I assign all my rights under the contract"), the contract normally is construed as

---

9. *Restatement (Second) of Contracts,* Section 328; UCC 2–210(3), (4).

CONCEPT SUMMARY 16.1
Assignments and Delegations

Which Rights Can Be Assigned, and Which Duties Can Be Delegated?	All rights can be assigned *unless*: 1. A statute expressly prohibits assignment. 2. The contract is for personal services. 3. The assignment will materially alter the obligor's risk or duties. 4. The contract prohibits assignment.	All duties can be delegated *unless*: 1. Performance depends on the obligor's personal skills or talents. 2. Special trust has been placed in the obligor. 3. Performance by a third party will materially vary from that expected by the obligee. 4. The contract prohibits delegation.
What If the Contract Prohibits Assignment or Delegation?	No rights can be assigned *except*: 1. Rights to receive funds. 2. Ownership rights in real estate. 3. Rights to negotiable instruments. 4. Rights to damages for breach of a sales contract or payments under a sales contract.	No duties can be delegated.
What Is the Effect on the Original Party's Rights?	On a valid assignment, effective immediately, the original party (assignor) no longer has any rights under the contract.	On a valid delegation, if the delegatee fails to perform, the original party (delegator) is liable to the obligee (who may also hold the delegatee liable).

implying both an assignment of the assignor's rights and a delegation of any duties of performance owed by the assignor under the contract being assigned. Thus, the assignor remains liable if the assignee fails to perform the contractual obligations.

SECTION 2
THIRD PARTY BENEFICIARIES

Another exception to the doctrine of privity of contract arises when the contract is intended to benefit a third party. When the original parties to the contract agree that the contract performance should be rendered to or directly benefit a third person, the third person becomes an *intended* **third party beneficiary** of the contract. As the **intended beneficiary** of the contract, the third party has legal rights and can sue the promisor directly for breach of the contract.

Who, though, is the promisor? In a bilateral contract, both parties to the contract make promises that can be enforced, so the court has to determine which party made the promise that benefits the third party—that person is the promisor. Allowing a third party to sue the promisor directly in effect circumvents the "middle person" (the promisee) and thus reduces the burden on the courts. Otherwise, the third party would sue the promisee, who would then sue the promisor.

CASE IN POINT The classic case that gave third party beneficiaries the right to bring a suit directly against a promisor was decided in 1859. The case involved three parties—Holly, Lawrence, and Fox. Holly had borrowed $300 from Lawrence. Shortly thereafter, Holly loaned $300 to Fox, who in return promised Holly that he would pay Holly's debt to Lawrence on the following day. When Lawrence failed to obtain the $300 from Fox, he sued Fox to recover the funds. The court had to decide whether Lawrence could sue Fox directly (rather than suing Holly). The court held that when "a promise [is] made for the benefit of another, he for whose benefit it is made may bring an action for its breach."[10]

Types of Intended Beneficiaries

The law distinguishes between *intended* beneficiaries and *incidental* beneficiaries. Only intended beneficiaries acquire legal rights in a contract.

CREDITOR BENEFICIARY One type of intended beneficiary is a *creditor beneficiary*. Like the plaintiff in the *Case in Point* just discussed, a creditor beneficiary benefits from a contract in which one party (the promisor) promises another party (the promisee) to pay a debt that the promisee owes to a third party (the creditor beneficiary).

For example, Jay Carrera owns a business firm that is making monthly payments on equipment bought from Speedwell. Carerra sells the firm to Miller, who agrees in their contract to take over the payments to Speedwell for the equipment. Speedwell is a creditor beneficiary and can sue Miller directly to enforce the contract and obtain payment on the debt.

In the following case, the court had to decide whether an aggrieved owner of a condominium unit was an intended third party beneficiary of another owner's contract with the condominium association.

---

10. *Lawrence v. Fox*, 20 N.Y. 268 (1859).

IN THE LANGUAGE OF THE COURT
Opinion by Justice
SMITH.
* * * *
[Autumn] Allan
and [Aslan] Koraev

✳ **EXTENDED CASE 16.2** ✳
Allan v. Nersesova

Court of Appeals of Texas, Dallas, 307 S.W.3d 564 (2010).
www.5thcoa.courts.state.tx.us[a]

both owned units in the Boardwalk on the Parkway Condominiums. Allan's unit was directly beneath Koraev's.* * * Between March 2005 and July 2007, Allan's unit suffered eight incidents of water and sewage incursion as a result of plumbing

problems and misuse of appliances in Koraev's unit. Allan sued Koraev [and Ekaterina Nersesova, who was the property manager for Koraev's unit] on a variety of causes of action, including * * * breach of contract.

a. In the left-hand column, select "Search Opinions." When that page opens, key in the title of this case and click on the "Search" box. From the search results, click on the file number that precedes the case title to access the opinion. The Fifth District Court of Appeals in Dallas, Texas, maintains this Web site.

EXTENDED CASE CONTINUES ➡

EXTENDED CASE 16.2 CONTINUED ◆

The jury found for Allan on her claims for breach of contract against Koraev * * *. Koraev moved for judgment notwithstanding the verdict, asserting Allan failed to prove as a matter of law the existence of a contract between her and Koraev. The trial court granted the motion[.]

* * * *

* * * Allan contends the trial court erred by rendering judgment notwithstanding the verdict on her breach of contract claim.

* * * *

Allan asserted that the [governing documents of the condominium] formed a contract between each unit owner and the Owners' Association. [The governing documents] * * * required Koraev to comply with the terms of the governing documents, and the Bylaws and Rules and Regulations made Koraev liable for any damage he caused to another unit.

* * * *

* * * Because Allan was not in privity of contract with Koraev, she has standing to bring a breach of contract claim only if she demonstrated she was a third-party beneficiary.

A third party, such as Allan, may sue to enforce a contract as a third-party beneficiary only if the contracting parties entered into the contract directly and primarily for the third party's benefit. * * * There are three types of third-party beneficiaries—donee, creditor, and incidental. * * * A party is a creditor beneficiary if no intent to make a gift appears from the contract, but performance will satisfy an actual or asserted duty of the promisee to the beneficiary, such as an indebtedness, contractual obligation, or other legally enforceable commitment to the third party, and *the promisee must intend that the beneficiary will have the right to enforce the contract.* [Emphasis added.]

* * * *

* * * Paragraph 19 of the Declaration [one of the governing documents] stated, "Each Owner shall comply strictly with the provisions of the [governing documents.] * * * Failure to comply with any of the same shall be grounds for an action to recover sums due, for damages or injunctive relief or both, and for reimbursement of all attorneys' fees incurred in connection therewith, which action shall be maintainable by the Managing Agent or Board of Directors in the name of the Association, in behalf of the Owners or, in a proper case, *by an aggrieved owner.*" [Emphasis added.]

* * * Allan's testimony about the damages she suffered as a result of Koraev and his tenants' breach of the governing documents established that she was an aggrieved owner.

* * * *

* * * Koraev's failure to perform the contract between himself and the Association was a breach of his duty not to cause damage to Allan's unit. As an intended creditor beneficiary, Allan had standing to bring suit against Koraev for his breach of the governing documents.

We conclude the governing documents made Allan an intended creditor beneficiary of the contract between Koraev and the Association and granted her authority to bring suit for Koraev's breach of those documents. Accordingly, we conclude the trial court erred by granting Koraev's motion for judgment notwithstanding the verdict on Allan's claim for breach of contract.

QUESTIONS

1. Why did the court use the term *creditor beneficiary* to describe Allan?
2. Suppose that Allan had sued Koraev for negligence. Would she have been successful? Discuss your answer.

DONEE BENEFICIARY Another type of intended beneficiary is a *donee beneficiary*. When a contract is made for the express purpose of giving a *gift* to a third party, the third party (the donee beneficiary) can sue the promisor directly to enforce the promise.[11] The most common donee beneficiary contract is a life insurance contract. Suppose that Akins (the promisee) pays premiums to Standard Life, a life insurance company, and Standard Life (the promisor) promises to pay a certain amount on Akins's death to anyone Akins designates as a beneficiary.

The designated beneficiary is a donee beneficiary under the life insurance policy and can enforce the promise made by the insurance company to pay her or him on Akins's death.

Most third party beneficiaries do not fit neatly into either the creditor beneficiary or the donee beneficiary category. Thus, the modern view adopted by the *Restatement (Second) of Contracts* does not draw clear lines between the types of intended beneficiaries. Today, courts frequently distinguish only between *intended beneficiaries* (who can sue to enforce contracts made for their benefit) and *incidental beneficiaries* (who cannot sue, as will be discussed shortly).

---

11. This principle was first enunciated in *Seaver v. Ransom,* 224 N.Y. 233, 120 N.E. 639 (1918).

When the Rights of an Intended Beneficiary Vest

An intended third party beneficiary cannot enforce a contract against the original parties until the rights of the third party have *vested,* which means the rights have taken effect and cannot be taken away. Until these rights have vested, the original parties to the contract—the promisor and the promisee—can modify or rescind the contract without the consent of the third party.

When do the rights of third parties vest? The majority of courts hold that the rights vest when any of the following occurs:

1. The third party materially changes his or her position in justifiable reliance on the promise.
2. The third party brings a lawsuit on the promise.
3. The third party demonstrates her or his consent to the promise at the request of the promisor or promisee.[12]

If the contract expressly reserves to the contracting parties the right to cancel, rescind, or modify the contract, the rights of the third party beneficiary are subject to any changes that result. If the original contract reserves the right to revoke the promise or change the beneficiary, the vesting of the third party's rights does not terminate that power.[13] For example, in most life insurance contracts, the policyholder reserves the right to change the designated beneficiary.

Intended versus Incidental Beneficiaries

The benefit that an **incidental beneficiary** receives from a contract between two parties is

unintentional. Because the benefit is *unintentional,* an incidental beneficiary cannot sue to enforce the contract. Exhibit 16–3 illustrates the distinction between intended beneficiaries and incidental beneficiaries.

In determining whether a third party beneficiary is an intended or an incidental beneficiary, the courts focus on intent, as expressed in the contract language and implied by the surrounding circumstances. Any beneficiary who is not deemed an intended beneficiary is considered incidental. Although no single test can embrace all possible situations, courts often apply the *reasonable person* test: Would a reasonable person in the position of the beneficiary believe that the promisee intended to confer on the beneficiary the right to enforce the contract? In addition, the presence of one or more of the following factors strongly indicates that the third party is an intended beneficiary to the contract:

1. Performance is rendered directly to the third party.
2. The third party has the right to control the details of performance.
3. The third party is expressly designated as a beneficiary in the contract.

In the following case, a national beauty pageant organization and one of its state affiliates agreed that the national organization would accept the winner of the state contest as a competitor in the national pageant. When the state winner was asked to resign her title, she filed a suit to enforce the agreement to have herself declared a contestant in the national pageant. The national organization argued that she was an incidental, not an intended, beneficiary of the agreement.

---

12. *Restatement (Second) of Contracts,* Section 311.
13. Defenses against third party beneficiaries are given in the *Restatement (Second) of Contracts,* Section 309.

EXHIBIT 16–3 • Third Party Beneficiaries

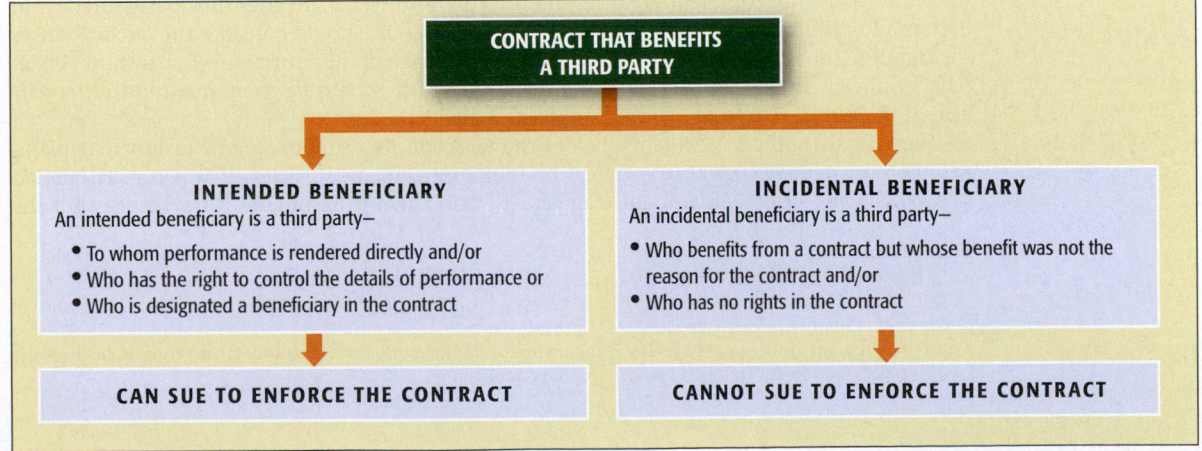

CASE 16.3
Revels v. Miss America Organization

Court of Appeals of North Carolina, 182 N.C.App. 334, 641 S.E.2d 721 (2007).
www.aoc.state.nc.us/www/public/html/opinions.htm[a]

COMPANY PROFILE • In 1921, businesses in Atlantic City, New Jersey, sponsored a "Miss America" contest as a publicity stunt to extend the summer tourist season. The stunt soon evolved into an event with contestants from all the states vying for the title of Miss America. More than twelve thousand women participate each year in the local and state events that culminate in the selection of the fifty-two national finalists. To succeed requires commitment, hard work, and talent. In 1945, the nonprofit Miss America Organization (MAO) offered its first scholarship. Today, MAO is the largest provider of scholarships to young women in the world, awarding more than $45 million in cash and tuition assistance annually.

BACKGROUND AND FACTS • Miss North Carolina Pageant Organization, Inc. (MNCPO), is a franchisee of Miss America Organization (MAO). Under the Miss America Organization Official Franchise Agreement, MNCPO conducts a public contest (the State Finals) to select Miss North Carolina and to prepare Miss North Carolina for participation in the Miss America pageant (the National Finals).[b] In return, MAO "accepts the winner of the State Finals . . . as a contestant in the National Finals." On June 22, 2002, MNCPO designated Rebekah Revels "Miss North Carolina 2002." On July 19, MAO received an anonymous e-mail (which was later determined to have been sent by Revels's ex-boyfriend) implying that she had formerly cohabited with a "male non-relative" and that nude photos of her existed. Revels confirmed the existence of the photos. On July 22, MAO and MNCPO asked Revels to resign as Miss North Carolina and told her that if she refused, she would be excluded from competing in the National Finals. On July 23, she resigned. She then filed a suit in a North Carolina state court against MAO, MNCPO, and others, asserting, among other things, breach of contract. The court issued a summary judgment in MAO's favor. Revels appealed this judgment to a state intermediate appellate court.

IN THE LANGUAGE OF THE COURT
McCULLOUGH, Judge.
* * * *

Plaintiff contends on appeal that there was sufficient evidence that she is a third-party beneficiary under the franchise agreement between MAO and MNCPO to establish that there is a genuine issue of material fact [and thus for her claim to proceed to trial].

In order to assert rights as a third-party beneficiary under the franchise agreement, plaintiff must show she was an intended beneficiary of the contract. This Court has held that *in order to establish a claim as a third-party beneficiary, plaintiff must show: (1) that a contract exists between two persons or entities; (2) that the contract is valid and enforceable; and (3) that the contract was executed for the direct, and not incidental, benefit of the third party.* A person is a direct beneficiary of the contract if the contracting parties intended to confer a legally enforceable benefit on that person. It is not enough that the contract, in fact, benefits the third party, if, when the contract was made, the contracting parties did not intend it to benefit the third party directly. In determining the intent of the contracting parties, the court should consider the circumstances surrounding the transaction as well as the actual language of the contract. When a third person seeks enforcement of a contract made between other parties, *the contract must be construed strictly against the party seeking enforcement.* [Emphasis added.]

There was insufficient evidence before the trial court to support a conclusion that plaintiff was an intended beneficiary under the franchise agreement. Plaintiff was not designated as a beneficiary under the franchise agreement and there is absolutely no evidence that the

---

a. In the "Court of Appeals Opinions" section, click on "2007." In the result, scroll to the "20 March 2007" section and click on the name of the case to access the opinion. The North Carolina Administrative Office of the Courts maintains this Web site.

b. A *franchise* is an arrangement by which the owner of a trademark or other intellectual property licenses the use of the mark to another party under specific conditions.

CASE 16.3 CONTINUED ➡ franchise agreement was executed for her direct benefit. The franchise agreement does provide that MAO will accept the winner of the North Carolina pageant as a contestant in the national finals. However, this evidence is insufficient to establish a showing of intent on the parties to make plaintiff an intended beneficiary. Further, the evidence adduced tended to show that the primary intent of the franchise agreement was to ensure uniformity among all franchisees and it provided the incidental benefit of allowing the winner of MNCPO's contest to compete in the national finals.

DECISION AND REMEDY • *The court affirmed the lower court's judgment in favor of MAO. Revels was an incidental beneficiary of the agreement between MAO and MNCPO. That the agreement provided that MAO would accept the winner of the State Finals as a contestant in the National Finals did not establish that the two organizations intended to make the winner a direct beneficiary of the agreement. Because Revels was not an intended beneficiary, she could not maintain an action against MAO based on the agreement.*

THE GLOBAL DIMENSION • *If the agreement between MAO and MNCPO had involved a third party—an international pageant organization—would this have been a basis for concluding that Revels was an intended third party beneficiary? Why or why not?*

THE E-COMMERCE DIMENSION • *How might Revels's third party status with respect to the agreement between MAO and MNCPO have been affected if the contracting parties had conducted their business online? Explain.*

REVIEWING
Third Party Rights

Myrtle Jackson owns several commercial buildings that she leases to businesses, one of which is a restaurant. The lease states that tenants are responsible for securing all necessary insurance policies but the landlord is obligated to keep the buildings in good repair. The owner of the restaurant, Joe McCall, tells his restaurant manager to purchase insurance, but the manager never does so. Jackson tells her son-in-law, Rob Dunn, to perform any necessary maintenance for the buildings. Dunn knows that the ceiling in the restaurant needs repair but fails to do anything about it. One day a customer, Ian Faught, is dining in the restaurant when a chunk of the ceiling falls on his head and fractures his skull. Faught files suit against the restaurant and discovers that there is no insurance policy in effect. Faught then files a suit against Jackson, arguing that he is an intended third party beneficiary of the lease provision requiring insurance and thus can sue Jackson for failing to enforce the lease (which requires the restaurant to carry insurance). Using the information presented in the chapter, answer the following questions.

1. Can Jackson delegate her duty to maintain the buildings to Dunn? Why or why not?
2. Who can be held liable for Dunn's failure to fix the ceiling, Jackson or Dunn?
3. Was Faught an intended third party beneficiary of the lease between Jackson and McCall? Why or why not?
4. Suppose that Jackson tells Dan Stryker, a local builder to whom she owes $50,000, that he can collect the rents from the buildings' tenants until the debt is satisfied. Is this a valid assignment? Why or why not?

✹ **DEBATE THIS:** *As a matter of public policy, personal-injury tort claims cannot be assigned. This public policy is wrong and should be changed.*

TERMS AND CONCEPTS

alienation 308

assignee 304

assignment 304

assignor 304

delegatee 308

delegation 304

delegator 308

incidental beneficiary 313

intended beneficiary 311

obligee 304

obligor 304

privity of contract 304

third party beneficiary 311

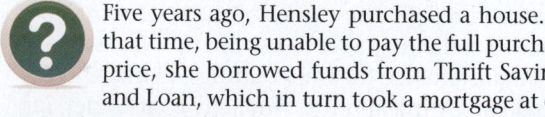

QUESTIONS AND CASE PROBLEMS

16–1. Third Party Beneficiary Alexander has been accepted as a freshman at a college two hundred miles from his home for the fall semester. Alexander's wealthy uncle, Michael, decides to give Alexander a car for Christmas. In November, Michael makes a contract with Jackson Auto Sales to purchase a new car for $18,000 to be delivered to Alexander just before the Christmas holidays, in mid-December. The title to the car is to be in Alexander's name. Michael pays the full purchase price, calls Alexander and tells him about the gift, and takes off for a six-month vacation in Europe. Is Alexander an intended third party beneficiary of the contract between Michael and Jackson Auto Sales? Suppose that Jackson Auto Sales never delivers the car to Alexander. Does Alexander have the right to sue Jackson Auto Sales for breaching its contract with Michael? Explain.

16–2. QUESTION WITH SAMPLE ANSWER: Assignment.

Five years ago, Hensley purchased a house. At that time, being unable to pay the full purchase price, she borrowed funds from Thrift Savings and Loan, which in turn took a mortgage at 6.5 percent interest on the house. The mortgage contract did not prohibit the assignment of the mortgage. Then Hensley secured a new job in another city and sold the house to Sylvia. The purchase price included payment to Hensley of the value of her equity and the assumption of the mortgage debt still owed to Thrift. At the time the contract between Hensley and Sylvia was made, Thrift did not know about or consent to the sale. On the basis of these facts, if Sylvia defaults in making the house payments to Thrift, what are Thrift's rights? Discuss.

• **For a sample answer to Question 16–2, go to Appendix I at the end of this text.**

16–3. Assignment Marsala, a college student, signs a one-year lease agreement that runs from September 1 to August 31. The lease agreement specifies that the lease cannot be assigned without the landlord's consent. In late May, Marsala decides not to go to summer school and assigns the balance of the lease (three months) to a close friend, Fred. The landlord objects to the assignment and denies Fred access to the apartment. Marsala claims that Fred is financially sound and should be allowed the full rights and privileges of an assignee. Discuss fully who is correct, the landlord or Marsala.

16–4. Delegation Inez has a specific set of plans to build a sailboat. The plans are detailed, and any boatbuilder can construct the boat. Inez secures bids, and the low bid is made by the Whale of a Boat Corp. Inez contracts with Whale to build the boat for $4,000. Whale then receives unexpected business from elsewhere. To meet the delivery date in the contract with Inez, Whale delegates its obligation to build the boat, without Inez's consent, to Quick Brothers, a reputable boatbuilder. When the boat is ready for delivery, Inez learns of the delegation and refuses to accept delivery, even though the boat is built to her specifications. Discuss fully whether Inez is obligated to accept and pay for the boat. Would your answer be any different if Inez had not had a specific set of plans but had instead contracted with Whale to design and build a sailboat for $4,000? Explain.

16–5. Third Party Beneficiary Acciai Speciali Terni USA, Inc. (AST), hired a carrier to ship steel sheets and coils from Italy to the United States on the *M/V Berane*. The ship's receipt for the goods included a forum-selection clause, which stated that any dispute would be "decided in the country where the carrier has his principal place of business." The receipt also contained a "Himalaya" clause, which extended "every right, exemption from liability, defense and immunity" that the carrier enjoyed to those acting on the carrier's behalf. Transcom Terminals, Ltd., was the U.S. stevedore—that is, Transcom off-loaded the vessel and stored the cargo for eventual delivery to AST. Finding the cargo damaged, AST filed a suit in a federal district court against Transcom and others, charging, among other things, negligence in the off-loading. Transcom filed a motion to dismiss on the basis of the forum-selection clause. Transcom argued that it was an intended third party beneficiary of this provision through the Himalaya clause. Is Transcom correct? What should the court rule? Explain. [*Acciai Speciali Terni USA, Inc. v. M/V Berane,* 181 F.Supp.2d 458 (D.Md. 2002)]

16–6. CASE PROBLEM WITH SAMPLE ANSWER: Intended versus Incidental Beneficiaries.

The National Collegiate Athletic Association (NCAA) regulates intercollegiate amateur athletics among the more than 1,200 colleges and universities with whom it contracts. Among other things, the NCAA maintains rules of eligibility for student participation in intercollegiate athletic events. Jeremy Bloom, a high school football and track star, was recruited to play football at the University of Colorado (CU). Before enrolling, he competed in Olympic and professional World Cup skiing events, becoming the World Cup champion in freestyle moguls. During the Olympics, Bloom appeared on MTV and was offered other paid entertainment opportunities, including a chance to host a show on Nickelodeon. Bloom was also paid to endorse certain ski equipment and contracted to model clothing for Tommy Hilfiger. On Bloom's behalf, CU asked the NCAA to waive its rules restricting student-athlete endorsement and media activities. The NCAA refused, and Bloom quit the activities to play football for CU. He filed a suit in a Colorado state court against the NCAA, however, asserting breach of contract on the ground that its rules permitted these activities if they were needed to support a professional athletic career. The NCAA responded that Bloom did not have standing to pursue this claim. What contract has allegedly been breached in this case? Is Bloom a party to this contract? If not, is he a third party beneficiary of it, and if so, is his status intended or incidental? Explain. [Bloom v. National Collegiate Athletic Association, *93 P.3d 621 (Colo.App. 2004)*]

- **To view a sample answer for Problem 16–6, go to this book's Web site at www.cengage.com/blaw/clarkson, select "Chapter 16," and click on "Case Problem with Sample Answer."**

16–7. Third Party Beneficiary The National Association for Stock Car Auto Racing, Inc. (NASCAR), sanctions stock car races. NASCAR and Sprint Nextel Corp. agreed that Sprint would become the official series sponsor of the NASCAR NEXTEL Cup Series in 2004. The agreement granted sponsorship exclusivity to Sprint and contained a list of competitors that were barred from sponsoring series events. Excepted were existing sponsorships: in "Driver and Car Owner Agreements" between NASCAR and the cars' owners, NASCAR promised to "preserve and protect" those sponsorships, which could continue and be renewed at the owners' option, despite Sprint's exclusivity. RCR Team #31, LLC, owns the #31 Car in the series. Cingular Wireless LLC (a Sprint competitor), had been #31 Car's primary sponsor since 2001. In 2007, Cingular changed its name to AT&T Mobility, LLC, and proposed a new paint scheme for the #31 Car that called for the Cingular logo to remain on the hood while the AT&T logo would be added on the rear quarter panel. NASCAR rejected the proposal. AT&T filed a suit in a federal district court against NASCAR, claiming, in part, that NASCAR was in breach of its Driver and Car Owner Agreement with RCR. Can AT&T maintain an action against NASCAR based on this agreement? Explain.

[*AT&T Mobility, LLC v. National Association for Stock Car Auto Racing, Inc.*, 494 F.3d 1356 (11th Cir. 2007)]

16–8. Assignment and Delegation Bruce Albea Contracting, Inc., was the general contractor on a state highway project. Albea and the companies that agreed to guarantee the financial liabilities involved here (called sureties) agreed to be liable for all work on the project. Albea subcontracted with APAC-Southeast, Inc., an asphalt company. The contract stated that it could not be assigned without Albea's consent. Later, Albea and APAC got into a dispute because APAC wanted to be paid more for its asphalt. APAC then sold and assigned its assets, including the contract, to Matthews Contracting Company. Albea was informed of the assignment and did not approve it but allowed Matthews to work. Matthews demanded higher payments for asphalt, and Albea agreed because no other contractor would step in at the original price. Albea suffered a loss on the job and could not pay its bills, so Albea's sureties paid Matthews $2.7 million for work performed. APAC sued Albea and its sureties for $1.2 million for work it had performed before the contract was delegated to Matthews. The trial court granted APAC $1.2 million. On appeal, the defendants argued that APAC had breached the contract by assignment without consent. Did APAC breach the contract with Albea? Did Albea owe APAC anything? Explain your answers. [*Western Surety Co. v. APAC-Southeast, Inc.*, 302 Ga.App. 654, 691 S.E.2d 234 (2010)]

16–9. A QUESTION OF ETHICS: Assignment.

In 1984, James Grigg's mother was killed in a car accident. Royal Insurance Co. of America agreed to pay Grigg a number of monthly payments, as well as two lump-sum payments of $50,000 due May 1, 1995, and May 1, 2005. Royal contracted with Safeco Life Insurance Co. to make the payments. In 1997, Grigg assigned the 2005 payment of $50,000 to Howard Foley for $10,000. Neither Grigg nor Foley notified Safeco or Royal. Four years later, Grigg offered to sell Settlement Capital Corp. (SCC) his interest in the 2005 payment. On SCC's request, an Idaho state court approved the transfer. Foley later notified Safeco of his interest in the payment, and in 2005, the court approved an arrangement by which Foley and SCC would share the $50,000. Shortly before the 2005 payment was made, however, it was revealed that Grigg had also tried to sell his interest to Canco Credit Union, whose manager, Timothy Johnson, had paid Grigg for it. Later, Johnson assigned the interest to Robert Chris, who used it as collateral for a loan from Canco. Foley filed a suit in an Idaho state court against Grigg, asking the court to determine who, among these parties, was entitled to the 2005 payment. [Foley v. Grigg, *144 Idaho 530, 164 P.3d 180 (2007)*]

(a) If the court applies the rule most often observed in the United States, who is likely to be awarded the $50,000? If the court applies the English rule, who will have priority to the payment?

(b) Regardless of the legal principles to be applied, was there a violation of ethics in these circumstances? Explain.

16–10. VIDEO QUESTION: Third Party Beneficiaries.

Go to this text's Web site at **www.cengage.com/blaw/clarkson** and select "Chapter 16." Click on "Video Questions" and view the video titled *Third Party Beneficiaries*. Then answer the following questions.

(a) Discuss whether a valid contract was formed when Oscar and Vinny bet on the outcome of a football game. Would Vinny be able to enforce the contract in court?

(b) Is the Fresh Air Fund an incidental or intended beneficiary? Why?

(c) Can Maria sue to enforce Vinny's promise to donate Oscar's winnings to the Fresh Air Fund?

LEGAL RESEARCH EXERCISES ON THE WEB

Go to this text's Web site at **www.cengage.com/blaw/clarkson**, select "Chapter 16," and click on "Practical Internet Exercises." There you will find the following Internet research exercises that you can perform to learn more about the topics covered in this chapter.

Practical Internet Exercise 16–1: **Legal Perspective**
New York's Leading Decisions

Practical Internet Exercise 16–2: **Management Perspective**
Professional Liability to Third Parties

Just as rules are necessary to determine when a legally enforceable contract exists, so also are they required to determine when one of the parties can justifiably say, "I have fully performed, so I am now discharged from my obligations under this contract." The legal environment of business requires the identification of some point at which the parties can reasonably know that their duties have ended.

The most common way to **discharge,** or terminate, one's contractual duties is by the **performance** of those duties. For example, a buyer and seller enter into an agreement via e-mail for the sale of a 2011 Lexus for $39,000. This contract will be discharged by performance when the buyer pays $39,000 to the seller and the seller transfers possession of the Lexus to the buyer.

The duty to perform under any contract (including e-contracts) may be *conditioned* on the occurrence or nonoccurrence of a certain event, or the duty may be *absolute.* In the first part of this chapter, we look at conditions of performance and the degree of performance required. We then examine some other ways in which a contract can be discharged, including discharge by agreement of the parties and discharge by operation of law.

SECTION 1
CONDITIONS

In most contracts, promises of performance are not expressly conditioned or qualified. Instead, they are *absolute promises*. They must be performed, or the parties promising the acts will be in breach of contract. In some situations, however, performance is contingent on the occurrence or nonoccurrence of a certain event. A **condition** is a possible future event, the occurrence or nonoccurrence of which will trigger the performance of a legal obligation or terminate an existing obligation under a contract.[1] If this condition is not satisfied, the obligations of the parties are discharged. Suppose that Alfonso offers to purchase a painting from Jerome only if an independent appraisal indicates that it is worth at least $10,000. Jerome accepts Alfonso's offer. Their obligations (promises) are conditioned on the outcome

of the appraisal. Should the condition not be satisfied (for example, if the appraiser deems the market value of the painting to be only $5,000), the parties' obligations to each other are discharged and cannot be enforced.

Three types of conditions can be present in contracts: conditions *precedent*, conditions *subsequent*, and *concurrent* conditions. Conditions are also classified as *express* or *implied*.

Conditions Precedent

A condition that must be fulfilled before a party's performance can be required is called a **condition precedent.** The condition precedes the absolute duty to perform, as in the Jerome-Alfonso example just discussed. Real estate contracts frequently are conditioned on the buyer's ability to obtain financing. For example, Fisher promises to buy Calvin's house if Salvation Bank approves Fisher's mortgage application. The Fisher-Calvin contract is therefore subject to a condition precedent—the bank's approval of Fisher's mortgage application. If the bank does not approve the application, the contract will

---

1. *The Restatement (Second) of Contracts,* Section 224, defines a condition as "an event, not certain to occur, which must occur, unless its nonoccurrence is excused, before performance under a contract becomes due."

fail because the condition precedent was not met. Insurance contracts frequently specify that certain conditions, such as passing a physical examination, must be met before the insurance company will be obligated to perform under the contract.

Conditions Subsequent

When a condition operates to terminate a party's absolute promise to perform, it is called a **condition subsequent.** The condition follows, or is subsequent to, the time that the absolute duty to perform arose. If the condition occurs, the party's duty to perform is discharged. For example, a law firm hires Julie Koker, a recent law school graduate and newly licensed attorney. Their contract provides that the firm's obligation to continue employing Koker is discharged if Koker fails to maintain her license to practice law. This is a condition subsequent because a failure to maintain the license would discharge a duty that has already arisen.

Generally, conditions precedent are common; conditions subsequent are rare. The *Restatement (Second) of Contracts* does not use the terms *condition subsequent* and *condition precedent* but refers to both simply as conditions.[2]

Concurrent Conditions

When each party's performance is conditioned on the other party's performance or tender of performance (offer to perform), there are **concurrent conditions.** Concurrent conditions occur only when the contract calls for the parties to perform their respective duties *simultaneously*. For example, if a buyer promises to pay for goods when the seller delivers them, the parties' promises to perform are mutually dependent. The buyer's duty to pay for the goods does not become absolute until the seller either delivers or tenders the goods. Likewise, the seller's duty to deliver the goods does not become absolute until the buyer tenders or actually makes payment. Therefore, neither can recover from the other for breach without first tendering performance.

Express and Implied Conditions

Conditions can also be classified as express or implied in fact. *Express conditions* are provided for by the parties' agreement. Although no particular words are necessary, express conditions are normally prefaced by the words *if, provided, after,* or *when.*

CASE IN POINT Alejandro Alvarado's automobile insurance policy stated that, if involved in an accident, the insured must cooperate with the insurance company in the defense of any claim or lawsuit. When Alvarado was involved in an accident, he notified the insurance company that a negligence lawsuit had been filed against him, but then failed to cooperate in his defense and did not appear in court for the trial. The court entered a judgment against him, which prejudiced the rights of the insurance company. In this situation, a Texas appellate court found that the cooperation clause was a condition precedent to coverage under the policy. Because Alvarado did not cooperate with the insurer, the accident was not covered under the policy, and the company was not liable for the damages awarded.[3]

Implied conditions are understood to be part of the agreement, but they are not found in the express language of the agreement. Courts may imply conditions from the purpose of the contract or from the intent of the parties. Conditions are often implied when they are necessarily inherent in the actual performance of the contract.

SECTION 2
DISCHARGE BY PERFORMANCE

The great majority of contracts are discharged by performance. The contract comes to an end when both parties fulfill their respective duties by performing the acts they have promised. Performance can also be accomplished by *tender*. **Tender** is an unconditional offer to perform by a person who is ready, willing, and able to do so. Therefore, a seller who places goods at the disposal of a buyer has tendered delivery and can demand payment. A buyer who offers to pay for goods has tendered payment and can demand delivery of the goods. Once performance has been tendered, the party making the tender has done everything possible to carry out the terms of the contract. If the other party then refuses to perform, the party making the tender can sue for breach of contract.

Types of Performance

There are two basic types of performance—*complete performance* and *substantial performance*. A contract

---

2. *Restatement (Second) of Contracts,* Section 224.

3. *Progressive County Mutual Insurance Co. v. Trevino,* 202 S.W.3d 811 (Tex.App.—San Antonio 2006).

may stipulate that performance must meet the personal satisfaction of either the contracting party or a third party. Such a provision must be considered in determining whether the performance rendered satisfies the contract.

COMPLETE PERFORMANCE

When a party performs exactly as agreed, there is no question as to whether the contract has been performed. When a party's performance is perfect, it is said to be complete.

Normally, conditions expressly stated in a contract must be fully satisfied for complete performance to take place. For example, most construction contracts require the builder to meet certain specifications. If the specifications are conditions, complete performance is required to avoid material breach (*material breach* will be discussed shortly). If the conditions are met, the other party to the contract must then fulfill her or his obligation to pay the builder. If the specifications are not conditions and if the builder, without the other party's permission, fails to comply with the specifications, performance is not complete. What effect does such a failure have on the other party's obligation to pay? The answer is part of the doctrine of substantial performance.

SUBSTANTIAL PERFORMANCE

A party who in good faith performs substantially all of the terms of a contract can enforce the contract against the other party under the doctrine of substantial performance. Note that good faith is required. Intentional failure to comply with the terms is a breach of the contract.

Confers Most of the Benefits Promised.

Generally, to qualify as substantial, the performance must not vary greatly from the performance promised in the contract, and it must create substantially the same benefits as those promised in the contract. If the omission, variance, or defect in performance is unimportant and can easily be compensated for by awarding damages, a court is likely to hold that the contract has been substantially performed.

Courts decide whether the performance was substantial on a case-by-case basis, examining all of the facts of the particular situation. For example, in a construction contract, a court would look at the intended purpose of the structure and the expense required to bring the structure into complete compliance with the contract. Thus, the exact point at which performance is considered substantial varies.

Entitles the Other Party to Damages.

Because substantial performance is not perfect, the other party is entitled to damages to compensate for the failure to comply with the contract. The measure of the damages is the cost to bring the object of the contract into compliance with its terms, if that cost is reasonable under the circumstances. If the cost is unreasonable, the measure of damages is the difference in value between the performance that was rendered and the performance that would have been rendered if the contract had been performed completely.

The following classic case emphasizes that there is no exact formula for deciding when a contract has been substantially performed.

✳ EXTENDED CASE 17.1 ✳
Jacob & Youngs v. Kent

Court of Appeals of New York, 230 N.Y. 239, 129 N.E. 889 (1921).

IN THE LANGUAGE OF THE COURT

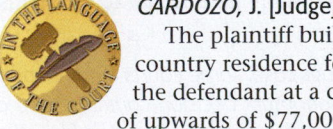

CARDOZO, J. [Judge]
The plaintiff built a country residence for the defendant at a cost of upwards of $77,000, and now sues to recover a balance of $3,483.46, remaining unpaid. The work of construction ceased in June, 1914, and the defendant then began to occupy the dwelling. There was no complaint of defective performance until March, 1915. One of

the specifications for the plumbing work provides that—

> All wrought-iron pipe must be well galvanized, lap welded pipe of the grade known as "standard pipe" of Reading manufacture.

The defendant learned in March, 1915, that some of the pipe, instead of being made in Reading, was the product of other factories. The plaintiff was accordingly directed by the architect to do the work anew. The plumbing was then encased

within the walls except in a few places where it had to be exposed. Obedience to the order meant more than the substitution of other pipe. It meant the demolition at great expense of substantial parts of the completed structure. The plaintiff left the work untouched, and asked for a certificate that the final payment was due. Refusal of the certificate was followed by this suit [in a New York state court].

EXTENDED CASE CONTINUES ➤

EXTENDED CASE 17.1 CONTINUED ◆

The evidence sustains a finding that the omission of the prescribed brand of pipe was neither fraudulent nor willful. It was the result of the oversight and inattention of the plaintiff's subcontractor. Reading pipe is distinguished from Cohoes pipe and other brands only by the name of the manufacturer stamped upon it at intervals of between six and seven feet. Even the defendant's architect, though he inspected the pipe upon arrival, failed to notice the discrepancy. The plaintiff tried to show that the brands installed, though made by other manufacturers, were the same in quality, in appearance, in market value, and in cost as the brand stated in the contract—that they were, indeed, the same thing, though manufactured in another place. The evidence was excluded, and a verdict directed for the defendant. The [state intermediate appellate court] reversed, and granted a new trial.

We think the evidence, if admitted, would have supplied some basis for the inference that the defect was insignificant in its relation to the project. The courts never say that one who makes a contract fills the measure of his duty by less than full performance. They do say, however, that *an omission, both trivial and innocent, will sometimes be atoned for by allowance of the resulting damage,*

and will not always be the breach of a condition * * * . [Emphasis added.]

* * * Where the line is to be drawn between the important and the trivial cannot be settled by a formula. In the nature of the case precise boundaries are impossible. The same omission may take on one aspect or another according to its setting. Substitution of equivalents may not have the same significance in fields of art on the one side and in those of mere utility on the other. Nowhere will change be tolerated, however, if it is so dominant or pervasive as in any real or substantial measure to frustrate the purpose of the contract. There is no general license to install whatever, in the builder's judgment, may be regarded as "just as good." The question is one of degree, to be answered, if there is doubt, by the triers of the facts, and, if the inferences are certain, by the judges of the law. *We must weigh the purpose to be served, the desire to be gratified, the excuse for deviation from the letter, the cruelty of enforced adherence. Then only can we tell whether literal fulfillment is to be implied by law as a condition.* [Emphasis added.]

In the circumstances of this case, we think the measure of the allowance is not the cost of replacement, which would be great, but the difference in value, which would be either nominal or nothing. Some of the exposed

sections might perhaps have been replaced at moderate expense. The defendant did not limit his demand to them, but treated the plumbing as a unit to be corrected from cellar to roof. In point of fact, the plaintiff never reached the stage at which evidence of the extent of the allowance became necessary. The trial court had excluded evidence that the defect was unsubstantial, and in view of that ruling there was no occasion for the plaintiff to go further with an offer of proof. We think, however, that the offer, if it had been made, would not of necessity have been defective because directed to difference in value. It is true that in most cases the cost of replacement is the measure. The owner is entitled to the money which will permit him to complete, unless the cost of completion is grossly and unfairly out of proportion to the good to be attained. When that is true, the measure is the difference in value. * * * The rule that gives a remedy in cases of substantial performance with compensation for defects of trivial or inappreciable importance has been developed by the courts as an instrument of justice. The measure of the allowance must be shaped to the same end.

The order should be affirmed, and judgment absolute directed in favor of the plaintiff upon the stipulation, with costs in all courts.

QUESTIONS

1. The New York Court of Appeals found that Jacob & Youngs had substantially performed the contract. To what, if any, remedy was Kent entitled?
2. A requirement of substantial performance is good faith. Did Jacob & Youngs substantially perform all of the terms of the contract in good faith? Why or why not?

IMPACT OF THIS CASE ON TODAY'S LAW • *At the time of the* Jacob & Youngs *case, some courts did not apply the doctrine of substantial performance to disputes involving breaches of contract. This landmark decision contributed to a developing trend toward equity and fairness in those circumstances. Today, an unintentional and trivial deviation from the terms of a contract will not prevent its enforcement but will permit an adjustment in the value of its performance.*

PERFORMANCE TO THE SATISFACTION OF ANOTHER

Contracts often state that completed work must personally satisfy one of the parties or a third person. The question then is whether this satisfaction

becomes a condition precedent, requiring actual personal satisfaction or approval for discharge, or whether the performance need only satisfy a *reasonable person* (substantial performance).

When the Contract Is Personal. When the subject matter of the contract is *personal,* a contract to be performed to the satisfaction of one of the parties is conditioned, and performance must actually satisfy that party. For example, contracts for portraits, works of art, and tailoring are considered personal. Therefore, only the personal satisfaction of the party fulfills the condition—unless a court finds that the party is expressing dissatisfaction simply to avoid payment or otherwise is not acting in good faith.

Reasonable Person Standard. Most other contracts need to be performed only to the satisfaction of a reasonable person unless they *expressly state otherwise.* When such contracts require performance to the satisfaction of a third party (for example, "to the satisfaction of Robert Ames, the supervising engineer"), the courts are divided. A majority of courts require the work to be satisfactory to a reasonable person, but some courts hold that the personal satisfaction of the third party designated in the contract (Robert Ames, in this example) must be met. Again, the personal judgment must be made honestly, or the condition will be excused.

When a contract requires one party to meet the other party's demand, what percentage of compliance constitutes substantial performance? Does the duty of good faith require that this demand be put ahead of other customers' needs? Those were the questions in the following case.

CASE 17.2
Wisconsin Electric Power Co. v. Union Pacific Railroad Co.

United States Court of Appeals, Seventh Circuit, 557 F.3d 504 (2009).
www.ca7.uscourts.gov[a]

BACKGROUND AND FACTS • In 1999, Wisconsin Electric Power Company (WEPCO) contracted with Union Pacific Railroad to transport coal to WEPCO's plants from mines in Colorado. Each month, WEPCO was to inform Union Pacific how many tons of coal (within a certain maximum) it wanted shipped the next month. Union Pacific was to make "good faith reasonable efforts" to meet the schedule. The contract also required WEPCO to supply the railcars. When WEPCO did not supply the railcars, however, Union Pacific used its own railcars and delivered 84 percent of the requested coal. Claiming that the minimum percentage should have exceeded 90 percent and that Union Pacific was shipping less than that because other customers paid higher rates, WEPCO filed a suit in a federal district court against Union Pacific for breach of contract. The court issued a summary judgment in the defendant's favor. WEPCO appealed.

IN THE LANGUAGE OF THE COURT
POSNER, Circuit Judge.
* * * *

* * * The contract required WEPCO to notify the railroad monthly of how many tons of coal (within the maximum tonnage specified by the contract) it wanted shipped the next month, and "the parties agree to make good faith reasonable efforts to meet the Monthly Shipping Schedule." Nowhere did the contract require the railroad to comply with the schedule; it merely had to make, in good faith, a reasonable effort to do so. [The contract] did require the railroad to transport tonnages specified by WEPCO, but only if WEPCO supplied the railcars for the shipment, and it did not; the railroad did; during the period in which WEPCO charges that the railroad was acting in bad faith, the railroad transported in its own cars 84 percent of the total shipments of coal requested by WEPCO.

Not enough, argues WEPCO. Without specifying the minimum percentage that would have demonstrated good faith, it argues that it would have exceeded 90 percent. It says that the railroad shipped less because it had other customers who paid higher rates. WEPCO invokes the legal duty of good faith in the performance of a contract. *The duty entails the avoidance of conduct such as evasion of the spirit of the bargain, lack of diligence and slacking off, willful rendering*

---

a. In the left-hand column, click on "Opinions." On that page, in the "Case Number:" boxes, type "08 2693" and click on "List Case(s)." In the result, click on the appropriate link to access the opinion. The U.S. Court of Appeals for the Seventh Circuit maintains this Web site.

CASE CONTINUES ➡

CASE 17.2 CONTINUED ➡ *of imperfect performance, abuse of a power to specify terms, and interference with or failure to cooperate in the other party's performance.* [Emphasis added.]

But the duty of good faith does not require your putting one of your customers ahead of the others, even if the others are paying you more. Parties are not prevented from protecting their respective economic interests.

* * * *A duty of good faith does not mean that a party vested with a clear right is obligated to exercise that right to its own detriment for the purpose of benefiting another party to the contract.* And it certainly doesn't mean exercising that right to the detriment of another party with which it has a contract. * * * WEPCO invites the court to undertake an unmanageable judicial task—that of working out an equitable allocation of Union Pacific's railcars among its various customers. [Emphasis added.]

DECISION AND REMEDY • *The U.S. Court of Appeals for the Seventh Circuit affirmed the lower court's judgment. Union Pacific did not breach its duty of good faith. In this instance, "84 percent" constituted substantial performance of the contract.*

THE ECONOMIC DIMENSION • *Why would a different customer have paid a higher rate than WEPCO to Union Pacific for the transport of resources or other products?*

THE ETHICAL DIMENSION • *Should a contracting party relax the terms of the contract if the other party has trouble performing them? Discuss.*

Material Breach of Contract

A **breach of contract** is the nonperformance of a contractual duty. The breach is *material* when performance is not at least substantial.[4] If there is a material breach, then the nonbreaching party is excused from the performance of contractual duties and can sue for damages resulting from the breach. If the breach is *minor* (not material), the nonbreaching party's duty to perform can sometimes be suspended until the breach has been remedied, but the duty to perform is not entirely excused. Once the minor breach has been cured, the nonbreaching party must resume performance of the contractual obligations.

Any breach entitles the nonbreaching party to sue for damages, but only a material breach discharges the nonbreaching party from the contract. The policy underlying these rules allows contracts to go forward when only minor problems occur but allows them to be terminated if major difficulties arise.

CASE IN POINT Su Yong Kim sold an apartment building in Portland, Oregon. At the time of the sale, the building's plumbing violated the city's housing code. Therefore, a clause in the contract stated that the seller (Kim) would correct the violations within eight months. A year later, Kim still had not made the necessary repairs. The buyers stopped making the payments due under the contract, and the dispute ended up in court. The court found that the seller's failure to make the required repairs was a material breach because it defeated the purpose of the contract. The buyers had purchased the building to lease it to tenants, but instead they were losing tenants and being fined by the city due to the substandard plumbing. Because Kim's breach was material, the buyers did not have to continue to perform their obligation to make payments under the contract.[5]

Anticipatory Repudiation

Before either party to a contract has a duty to perform, one of the parties may refuse to carry out his or her contractual obligations. This is called **anticipatory repudiation**[6] of the contract. When an anticipatory repudiation occurs, it is treated as a material breach of the contract, and the nonbreaching party is permitted to bring an action for damages immediately, even though the scheduled time for performance under the contract may still be in the future. Until the nonbreaching party treats an early repudiation as a breach, however, the repudiating party can retract her or his anticipatory repudiation by proper notice and restore the parties to their original obligations.[7]

---

4. *Restatement (Second) of Contracts,* Section 241.

5. *Kim v. Park,* 192 Or.App. 365, 86 P.3d 63 (2004).
6. *Restatement (Second) of Contracts,* Section 253; Section 2–610 of the Uniform Commercial Code (UCC).
7. See UCC 2–611.

RATIONALE FOR TREATING REPUDIATION AS BREACH An anticipatory repudiation is treated as a present, material breach for two reasons. First, the nonbreaching party should not be required to remain ready and willing to perform when the other party has already repudiated the contract. Second, the nonbreaching party should have the opportunity to seek a similar contract elsewhere and may have a duty to do so to minimize his or her loss.[8]

ANTICIPATORY REPUDIATION AND MARKET PRICES Quite often, anticipatory repudiation occurs when performance of the contract would be extremely unfavorable to one of the parties because of a sharp fluctuation in market prices.

For example, Martin Corporation enters into an e-contract to manufacture and sell 100,000 personal computers to ComAge, a retailer of computer equipment. Delivery is to be made two months from the date of the contract. One month later, three inventory suppliers raise their prices to Martin. Because of these higher prices, Martin stands to lose $500,000 if it sells the computers to ComAge at the contract price. Martin immediately e-mails ComAge, stating that it cannot deliver the 100,000 computers at the contract price. Even though you may sympathize with Martin, its e-mail is an anticipatory repudiation of the contract. ComAge can treat the repudiation as a material breach and immediately pursue remedies, even though the contract delivery date is still a month away.

Time for Performance

If no time for performance is stated in the contract, a *reasonable time* is implied.[9] If a specific time is stated, the parties must usually perform by that time. Unless time is expressly stated to be vital, however, a delay in performance will not destroy the performing party's right to payment.[10] When time is expressly stated to be "of the essence" or vital, the parties normally must perform within the stated time period because the time element becomes a condition. Even when the contract states that time is of the essence, a court may find that a party who fails to complain about

the other party's delay has waived the breach of the time provision.

SECTION 3
DISCHARGE BY AGREEMENT

Any contract can be discharged by agreement of the parties. The agreement can be contained in the original contract, or the parties can form a new contract for the express purpose of discharging the original contract.

Discharge by Rescission

As mentioned in previous chapters, *rescission* is the process by which a contract is canceled or terminated and the parties are returned to the positions they occupied prior to forming it. For **mutual rescission** to take place, the parties must make another agreement that also satisfies the legal requirements for a contract. There must be an *offer,* an *acceptance,* and *consideration.* Ordinarily, if the parties agree to rescind the original contract, their promises not to perform the acts stipulated in the original contract will be legal consideration for the second contract (the rescission).

Agreements to rescind most executory contracts (in which neither party has performed) are enforceable, even if the agreement is made orally and even if the original agreement was in writing. Under the Uniform Commercial Code (UCC), however, agreements to rescind a contract for the sale of goods, regardless of price, must be in writing (or contained in an electronic record) when the contract requires a written rescission.[11] Agreements to rescind contracts involving transfers of realty also must be evidenced by a writing or other record.

When one party has fully performed, an agreement to cancel the original contract normally will *not* be enforceable unless there is additional consideration. Because the performing party has received no consideration for the promise to call off the original bargain, additional consideration is necessary to support a rescission contract.

Discharge by Novation

A contractual obligation may also be discharged through novation. A **novation** occurs when both of the parties to a contract agree to substitute a third

---

8. The doctrine of anticipatory repudiation first arose in the landmark case of *Hochster v. De La Tour,* 2 Ellis and Blackburn Reports 678 (1853), when an English court recognized the delay and expense inherent in a rule requiring a nonbreaching party to wait until the time of performance before suing on an anticipatory repudiation.

9. See UCC 2–204.

10. See, for example, *Manganaro Corp. v. Hitt Contracting, Inc.,* 193 F.Supp.2d 88 (D.D.C. 2002).

11. UCC 2–209(2), (4).

party for one of the original parties. The requirements of a novation are as follows:

1. A previous valid obligation.
2. An agreement by all parties to a new contract.
3. The extinguishing of the old obligation (discharge of the prior party).
4. A new contract that is valid.

For example, Union Corporation contracts to sell its pharmaceutical division to British Pharmaceuticals, Ltd. Before the transfer is completed, Union, British Pharmaceuticals, and a third company, Otis Chemicals, execute a new agreement to transfer all of British Pharmaceuticals' rights and duties in the transaction to Otis Chemicals. As long as the new contract is supported by consideration, the novation will discharge the original contract (between Union and British Pharmaceuticals) and replace it with the new contract (between Union and Otis Chemicals).

A novation expressly or impliedly revokes and discharges a prior contract. The parties involved may expressly state in the new contract that the old contract is now discharged. If the parties do not expressly discharge the old contract, it will be impliedly discharged if the new contract's terms are inconsistent with the old contract's terms. It is this immediate discharge of the prior contract that distinguishes a novation from both an accord and satisfaction, which will be discussed shortly, and an assignment of all rights, discussed in Chapter 16 on pages 310 and 311.

Discharge by Settlement Agreement

A compromise, or settlement agreement, that arises out of a genuine dispute over the obligations under an existing contract will be recognized at law. Such an agreement will be substituted as a new contract, and it will either expressly or impliedly revoke and discharge the obligations under any prior contract. In contrast to a novation, a substituted agreement does not involve a third party. Rather, the two original parties to the contract form a different agreement to substitute for the original one.

Discharge by Accord and Satisfaction

For a contract to be discharged by accord and satisfaction, the parties must agree to accept performance that is different from the performance originally promised. As discussed in Chapter 12, an *accord* is a contract to perform some act to satisfy an existing contractual duty that is not yet discharged.[12] A

---

12. *Restatement (Second) of Contracts,* Section 281.

---

satisfaction is the performance of the accord agreement. An accord and its satisfaction discharge the original contractual obligation.

Once the accord has been made, the original obligation is merely suspended. The obligor (the one owing the obligation) can discharge the obligation by performing either the obligation agreed to in the accord or the original obligation. If the obligor refuses to perform the accord, the obligee (the one to whom performance is owed) can bring an action on the original obligation or seek a decree compelling specific performance on the accord.

For example, Frazer has a judgment against Ling for $8,000. Later, both parties agree that the judgment can be satisfied by Ling's transfer of his automobile to Frazer. This agreement to accept the auto in lieu of $8,000 in cash is the accord. If Ling transfers the car to Frazer, the accord is fully performed, and the debt is discharged. If Ling refuses to transfer the car, the accord is breached. Because the original obligation is merely suspended, Frazer can sue Ling to enforce the original judgment for $8,000 in cash or bring an action for breach of the accord.

SECTION 4
DISCHARGE BY OPERATION OF LAW

Under certain circumstances, contractual duties may be discharged by operation of law. These circumstances include material alteration of the contract, the running of the statute of limitations, bankruptcy, and the impossibility or impracticability of performance.

Alteration of the Contract

To discourage parties from altering written contracts, the law operates to allow an innocent party to be discharged when the other party has materially altered a written contract without consent. For example, a party alters a material term of a contract, such as the stated quantity or price, without the knowledge or consent of the other party. In this situation, the party who was unaware of the alteration can treat the contract as discharged or terminated.

Statutes of Limitations

As mentioned earlier in this text, statutes of limitations restrict the period during which a party can sue on a particular cause of action. After the applicable limitations period has passed, a suit can no longer be brought. For example, the limitations period for bringing suits for breach of oral contracts usually is two to three years; for written or otherwise recorded contracts, four to five years; and for recovery of amounts awarded in judgments, ten to twenty years, depending on state law. Lawsuits for breach of a contract for the sale of goods generally must be brought within four years after the cause of action has accrued.[13] By their original agreement, the parties can reduce this four-year period to not less than one year, but they cannot agree to extend it.

Bankruptcy

A proceeding in bankruptcy attempts to allocate the debtors' assets to the creditors in a fair and equitable fashion. Once the assets have been allocated, the debtor receives a **discharge in bankruptcy.** A discharge in bankruptcy will ordinarily bar enforcement of most of the debtor's contracts by the creditors. Partial payment of a debt *after* discharge in bankruptcy will not revive the debt. (Bankruptcy will be discussed in detail in Chapter 30.)

Impossibility or Impracticability of Performance

After a contract has been made, supervening events (such as a fire) may make performance impossible in an objective sense. This is known as **impossibility of performance** and can discharge a contract.[14] Performance may also become so difficult or costly due to some unforeseen event that a court will consider it commercially unfeasible, or impracticable.

OBJECTIVE IMPOSSIBILITY OF PERFORMANCE *Objective impossibility* ("It can't be done") must be distinguished from *subjective impossibility* ("I'm sorry, I simply can't do it"). For example, subjective impossibility occurs when a party cannot deliver goods on time because of freight car shortages or cannot make payment on time because the bank is closed. In effect, in each of these situations the party is saying, "It is impossible for *me* to perform," not "It is impossible for *anyone* to perform." Accordingly, such excuses do not discharge a contract, and the

nonperforming party is normally held in breach of contract.

Note that to justify nonperformance of the contract, the supervening event must have been unforeseeable at the time of the contract's formation. Parties are supposed to consider foreseeable events, such as floods in a flood zone, at the time of contracting and allocate those risks accordingly through insurance and other means. Three basic types of situations, however, may qualify as grounds for the discharge of contractual obligations based on impossibility of performance:[15]

1. *When one of the parties to a personal contract dies or becomes incapacitated prior to performance.* For example, Fred, a famous dancer, contracts with Ethereal Dancing Guild to play a leading role in its new ballet. Before the ballet can be performed, Fred becomes ill and dies. His personal performance was essential to the completion of the contract. Thus, his death discharges the contract and his estate's liability for his nonperformance.

2. *When the specific subject matter of the contract is destroyed.* For example, A-1 Farm Equipment agrees to sell Gudgel the green tractor on its lot and promises to have it ready for Gudgel to pick up on Saturday. On Friday night, however, a truck veers off the nearby highway and smashes into the tractor, destroying it beyond repair. Because the contract was for this specific tractor, A-1's performance is rendered impossible owing to the accident.

3. *When a change in law renders performance illegal.* For example, a contract to build an apartment building becomes impossible to perform when the zoning laws are changed to prohibit the construction of residential rental property at the planned location. A contract to paint a bridge using lead paint becomes impossible when the government passes new regulations forbidding the use of lead paint on bridges.[16]

TEMPORARY IMPOSSIBILITY An occurrence or event that makes performance temporarily impossible operates to suspend performance until the impossibility ceases. Then, ordinarily, the parties must perform the contract as originally planned. If, however, the lapse of time and the change in circumstances surrounding the contract make it substantially more burdensome for the parties to perform the promised

---

13. Section 2–725 of the UCC contains this four-year limitation period. A cause of action in sales contracts generally accrues when the breach occurs, regardless of the aggrieved party's lack of knowledge of the breach. A breach of warranty normally occurs when the seller delivers the goods to the buyer.

14. *Restatement (Second) of Contracts,* Section 261.

15. *Restatement (Second) of Contracts,* Sections 262–266; UCC 2–615.

16. *M.J. Paquet, Inc. v. New Jersey Department of Transportation,* 171 N.J. 378, 794 A.2d 141 (2002).

INSIGHT INTO ETHICS
When Is Impossibility of Performance a Valid Defense?

The doctrine of impossibility of performance is applied only when the parties could not have reasonably foreseen, at the time the contract was formed, the event or events that rendered performance impossible. In some cases, the courts may seem to go too far in holding that the parties should have foreseen certain events or conditions, thus precluding the parties from avoiding contractual obligations under the doctrine of impossibility of performance.

Actually, courts today are more likely to allow parties to raise this defense than courts in the past, which rarely excused parties from performance under this doctrine. Indeed, until the latter part of the nineteenth century, courts were reluctant to discharge a contract

even when performance appeared to be impossible. Generally, the courts must balance the freedom of parties to contract (and thereby assume the risks involved) against the injustice that may result when certain contractual obligations are enforced. If the courts allowed parties to raise impossibility of performance as a defense to contractual obligations more often, freedom of contract would suffer.

CRITICAL THINKING
INSIGHT INTO THE SOCIAL ENVIRONMENT
Why might those entering into contracts be worse off in the long run if the courts increasingly accept impossibility of performance as a defense?

acts, the contract is discharged.[17] Sometimes, it can be difficult to predict how a court will—or should—rule in a particular situation, as discussed in this chapter's *Insight into Ethics* feature.

CASE IN POINT Keefe Hurwitz contracted to sell his home in Madisonville, Louisiana, to Wesley and Gwendolyn Payne for a price of $241,500 on August 22, 2005. Four days later, Hurricane Katrina made landfall and caused extensive damage to the house. When Hurwitz refused to pay the cost of the necessary repairs, estimated at $60,000, the Paynes filed a lawsuit to enforce the contract. Hurwitz claimed that Hurricane Katrina had made it impossible for him to perform and had discharged his duties under the contract. The court, however, ruled that Hurricane Katrina had caused only a temporary impossibility. Hurwitz was required to pay for the necessary repairs and to perform the contract as written. In other words, he could not obtain a higher purchase price to offset the cost of the repairs.[18]

COMMERCIAL IMPRACTICABILITY When a supervening event does not render performance objectively impossible, but does make it much more

difficult or expensive to perform than the parties originally contemplated, the courts may excuse the parties' obligations under the contract. For someone to invoke the doctrine of **commercial impracticability** successfully, however, the anticipated performance must become *extremely* difficult or costly.[19]

The added burden of performance not only must be extreme but also *must not have been known by the parties when the contract was made*. In one classic case, for example, a court held that a contract could be discharged because a party would otherwise have to pay ten times more than the original estimate to excavate a certain amount of gravel.[20] In another case, the court allowed a party to rescind a contract for the sale of land because of a potential problem with contaminated groundwater under the land. The court found that "the potential for substantial and unbargained-for" liability made contract performance economically impracticable.[21]

In the following case, a contract called for an illegal act, although the parties did not know this at the time the contract was formed. Given that the contract could not be performed legally, could performance be excused on the basis of impossibility of performance or commercial impracticability, or was the contract void from the outset? These were the questions before the court.

---

17. For a leading case involving temporary impossibility, see *Autry v. Republic Productions,* 30 Cal.2d 144, 180 P.2d 888 (1947). An actor's contract became temporarily impossible to perform when he was drafted to serve in World War II. After he returned, his duty to perform was discharged because the value of the dollar had declined, making performance substantially burdensome to him.

18. *Payne v. Hurwitz,* 978 So.2d 1000 (La.App. 1st Cir. 2008).

19. *Restatement (Second) of Contracts,* Section 264.

20. *Mineral Park Land Co. v. Howard,* 172 Cal. 289, 156 P. 458 (1916).

21. *Cape-France Enterprises v. Estate of Peed,* 305 Mont. 513, 29 P.3d 1011 (2001).

CASE 17.3
Merry Homes, Inc. v. Chi Hung Luu

Court of Appeals of Texas, Houston, ___ S.W.3d ___ (2010).
www.morelaw.com/verdicts[a]

BACKGROUND AND FACTS • Chi Hung Luu leased premises in Houston, Texas, from Merry Homes, Inc., with the intention of opening a bar and nightclub on the property. The lease provided that Luu could only use the premises for operating a nightclub or bar and for no other purpose. The lease also prohibited Luu from using the premises for, among other things, "any activity that violated any applicable federal, state, or local law." After he signed the lease, Luu submitted an application for a liquor license to the city of Houston. The city denied the application because a city ordinance prohibited the sale of alcoholic beverages where the premises were located, which was fewer than three hundred feet from a public school. The city suggested that Luu take advantage of the "restaurant exception" to the law, which allowed restaurants in such areas to serve alcoholic beverages. Luu considered the restaurant possibility but decided that it would not be financially feasible. When Merry Homes refused to cancel the lease and refund Luu's $6,000 security deposit, Luu brought an action against Merry Homes in a Texas state court. Luu sought a declaratory judgment that the lease was void because it could not be performed legally. Merry Homes counterclaimed for breach of contract and sought to recover eight months of unpaid rent. The trial court declared the lease void, and Merry Homes appealed.

IN THE LANGUAGE OF THE COURT
Jane *BLAND,* Justice.
   * * * *

   * * * * The Texas Alcoholic Beverages Code authorizes counties and cities to adopt regulations prohibiting the sale of alcohol within 300 feet of a public school. The City of Houston has adopted such a regulation.

Although the lease, on its face, does not require violation of the law, the only permissible use of the premises under the lease's terms is impossible and illegal, given the location of the premises relative to a school. As Luu cannot obtain a liquor license and therefore cannot perform under the lease without violating the statute and ordinance, the trial court properly determined that this lease is void for illegality.

Merry Homes [argues] * * * that Luu unconditionally bound himself to perform under the lease, and thus the City of Houston's refusal to grant a liquor license should not excuse his performance, especially because the City's denial is a contingency that Luu should have anticipated.
   * * * *

   * * * Merry Homes contends that the trial court's decision to declare the lease void cannot be affirmed on the basis of impossibility of performance. Merry Homes relies on Section 10(c) of the lease, which provides that Luu will satisfy himself that the premises can be used for the intended purposes, and thus is bound to perform. *We first note that Section 261 of the [Restatement (Second) of Contracts] only applies to supervening events [events occurring after the contract's formation] that render performance impracticable, not preexisting conditions and events.* The trial court found that the ordinance prohibiting the sale of alcohol on Luu's premises[,] which renders Luu's performance illegal and impracticable[,] existed before the parties executed the lease, and therefore Section 266 of the *Restatement* applies. [Emphasis added.]

Section 266(1) provides:

Where, at the time a contract is made, a party's performance under it is impracticable without his fault because of [a] fact of which he has no reason to know and the nonexistence of which is a basic assumption on which the contract is made, no duty to render that performance arises, unless the language or circumstances indicate the contrary.

---

a. From the "Select a State" menu, select Texas. From the "Select Field to Search" menu, select "Case Caption." Enter "Merry Homes" in the search box and then click "Go." On the page that opens, click on the link to access the court's opinion. Attorney Kent Morlan of Morlan & Associates, P.C., maintains this Web site.

CASE CONTINUES ▶

CASE 17.3 CONTINUED ▶   * * * Although Section 266 excuses performance as impracticable based upon a preexisting condition "of which [the party] has no reason to know," we previously held that "a contract to do a thing which cannot be performed without a violation of the law is void, *whether the parties knew the law or not.*" (Emphasis added [by the court].) The Texas Supreme Court "has long recognized Texas'[s] strong public policy in favor of preserving the freedom of contract." Freedom of contract, however, is not unlimited: "As a rule, parties have the right to contract as they see fit as long as their agreement does not violate the law or public policy." Merry Homes cannot indirectly receive benefits—monthly rental payments—from what the law says it cannot do directly.

DECISION AND REMEDY • *The Court of Appeals of Texas affirmed the trial court's judgment. The lease was void and unenforceable because it could not be performed without violating the law.*

WHAT IF THE FACTS WERE DIFFERENT? • *Suppose that Luu had decided to use the premises for a restaurant, but the wording of the lease had not changed. In this situation, if Luu sought to cancel the lease, would Merry Homes succeed in a suit for breach of contract? Discuss your answer.*

THE ETHICAL DIMENSION • *"Ignorance of the law is no excuse." How does this case affirm that adage?*

FRUSTRATION OF PURPOSE A theory closely allied with the doctrine of commercial impracticability is the doctrine of **frustration of purpose.** In principle, a contract will be discharged if supervening circumstances make it impossible to attain the purpose both parties had in mind when they made the contract. As with commercial impracticability and impossibility, the supervening event must not have been reasonably foreseeable at the time the contract was formed. In contrast to impracticability, which usually involves an event that increases the cost or difficulty of performance, frustration of purpose typically involves an event that decreases the value of what a party receives under the contract.[22]

See Exhibit 17–1 for a summary of the ways in which a contract can be discharged.

---

22. See, for example, *East Capitol View Community Development Corp., Inc. v. Robinson,* 941 A.2d 1036 (D.C.App. 2008).

EXHIBIT 17–1 • **Contract Discharge**

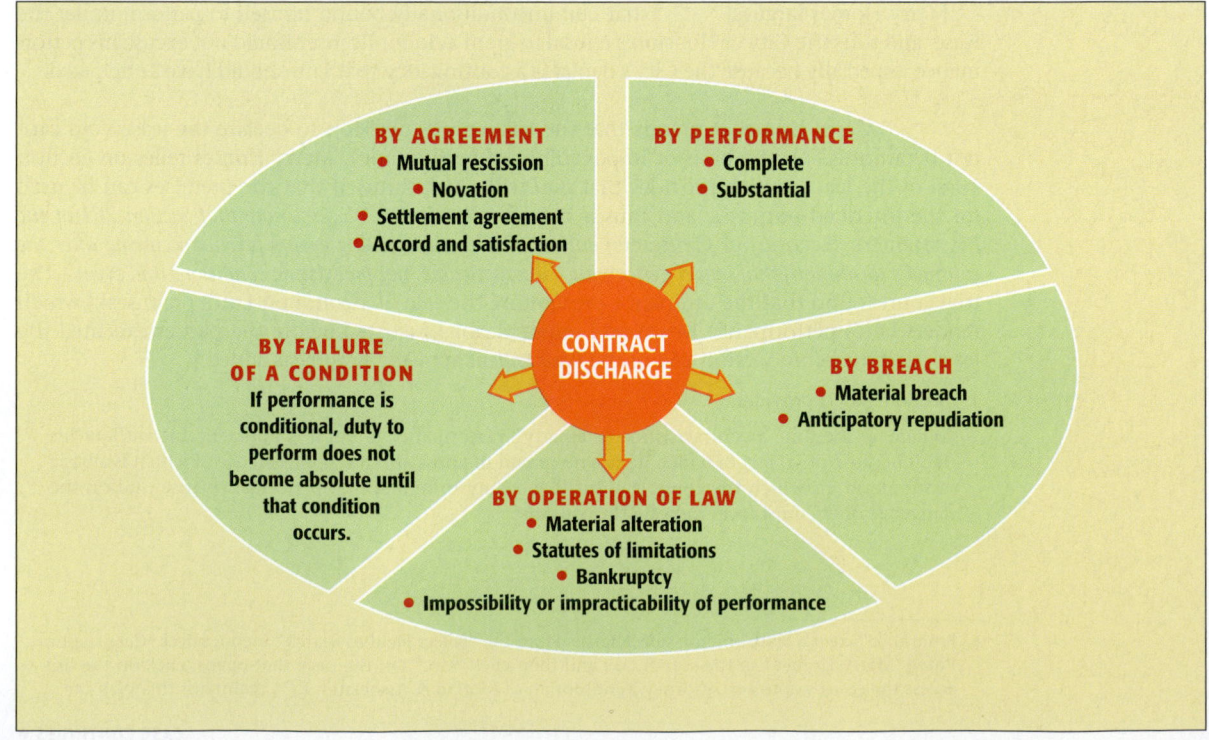

REVIEWING

Performance and Discharge in Traditional and E-Contracts

Val's Foods signs a contract to buy 1,500 pounds of basil from Sun Farms, a small organic herb grower, as long as an independent organization inspects the crop and certifies that it contains no pesticide or herbicide residue. Val's has a contract with several restaurant chains to supply pesto and intends to use Sun Farms' basil in the pesto to fulfill these contracts. While Sun Farms is preparing to harvest the basil, an unexpected hailstorm destroys half the crop. Sun Farms attempts to purchase additional basil from other farms, but it is late in the season and the price is twice the normal market price. Sun Farms is too small to absorb this cost and immediately notifies Val's that it will not fulfill the contract. Using the information presented in the chapter, answer the following questions.

1. Suppose that the basil does not pass the chemical-residue inspection. Which concept discussed in the chapter might allow Val's to refuse to perform the contract in this situation?

2. Under which legal theory or theories might Sun Farms claim that its obligation under the contract has been discharged by operation of law? Discuss fully.

3. Suppose that Sun Farms contacts every basil grower in the country and buys the last remaining chemical-free basil anywhere. Nevertheless, Sun Farms is able to ship only 1,475 pounds to Val's. Would this fulfill Sun Farms' obligations to Val's? Why or why not?

4. Now suppose that Sun Farms sells its operations to Happy Valley Farms. As a part of the sale, all three parties agree that Happy Valley will provide the basil as stated under the original contract. What is this type of agreement called?

⚙ DEBATE THIS: *The doctrine of commercial impracticability should be abolished.*

TERMS AND CONCEPTS

anticipatory repudiation 324
breach of contract 324
commercial
   impracticability 328

concurrent conditions 320
condition 319
condition precedent 319
condition subsequent 320
discharge 319

discharge in bankruptcy 327
frustration of purpose 330
impossibility of
   performance 327
mutual rescission 325

novation 325
performance 319
tender 320

QUESTIONS AND CASE PROBLEMS

17–1. Conditions of Performance The Caplans own a real estate lot, and they contract with Faithful Construction, Inc., to build a house on it for $360,000. The specifications list "all plumbing bowls and fixtures . . . to be Crane brand." The Caplans leave on vacation, and during their absence Faithful is unable to buy and install Crane plumbing fixtures. Instead, Faithful installs Kohler brand fixtures, an equivalent in the industry. On completion of the building contract, the Caplans inspect the work, discover the substitution, and refuse to accept the house, claiming Faithful has breached the conditions set forth in the specifications. Discuss fully the Caplans' claim.

17–2. QUESTION WITH SAMPLE ANSWER: Discharge by Agreement.

Junior owes creditor Iba $1,000, which is due and payable on June 1. Junior has been in a car accident, has missed a great deal of work, and consequently will not have the funds on June 1. Junior's father, Fred, offers to pay Iba $1,100 in four equal installments if Iba will discharge Junior from any further liability on the debt. Iba accepts. Is this transaction a novation or an accord and satisfaction? Explain.

• **For a sample answer to Question 17–2, go to Appendix I at the end of this text.**

17–3. Anticipatory Repudiation ABC Clothiers, Inc., has a contract with Taylor & Sons, a retailer, to deliver one thousand summer suits to Taylor's place of business on or before May 1. On April 1, Taylor senior receives a letter from ABC informing him that ABC will not be able to make the delivery as scheduled. Taylor is very upset, as he had planned a big ad campaign. He wants to file a suit against ABC immediately (on April 2). Taylor's son Tom tells his father that filing a lawsuit is not proper until ABC actually fails to deliver the suits on May 1. Discuss fully who is correct, Taylor or Tom.

17–4. Impossibility of Performance In the following situations, certain events take place after the contracts are formed. Discuss whether each of these contracts is discharged because the events render the contracts impossible to perform.

(a) Jimenez, a famous singer, contracts to perform in your nightclub. He dies prior to performance.

(b) Raglione contracts to sell you her land. Just before title is to be transferred, she dies.

(c) Oppenheim contracts to sell you one thousand bushels of apples from her orchard in the state of Washington. Because of a severe frost, she is unable to deliver the apples.

(d) Maxwell contracts to lease a service station for ten years. His principal income is from the sale of gasoline. Because of an oil embargo by foreign oil-producing nations, gasoline is rationed, cutting sharply into Maxwell's gasoline sales. He cannot make his lease payments.

17–5. Implied Conditions Heublein, Inc., makes wines and distilled spirits. Tarrant Distributors, Inc., agreed to distribute Heublein brands. When problems arose, the parties entered mediation. Under a settlement agreement, Heublein agreed to pay Tarrant the amount of its "net loss" as determined by Coopers & Lybrand, an accounting firm, according to a specified formula. The parties agreed that Coopers & Lybrand's calculation would be "final and binding." Heublein disagreed with Coopers & Lybrand's calculation, however, and refused to pay. The parties asked a court to rule on the dispute. Heublein argued that the settlement agreement included an implied condition precedent that Coopers & Lybrand would correctly apply the specified formula before Heublein would be obligated to pay. Tarrant pointed to the clause stating that the calculation would be "final and binding." With whom will the court agree, and why?

17–6. Frustration of Purpose Train operators and other railroad personnel use signaling systems to ensure safe train travel. Reading Blue Mountain & Northern Railroad Co. (RBMN) and Norfolk Southern Railway Co. entered into a contract for the maintenance of a signaling system that serviced a stretch of track near Jim Thorpe, Pennsylvania. The system included a series of poles, similar to telephone poles, suspending wires above the tracks. The contract provided that "the intent of the parties is to maintain the existing . . . facilities" and split the cost equally. In December 2002, a severe storm severed the wires and destroyed most of the poles. RBMN and Norfolk discussed replacing the old system, which they agreed was antiquated, inefficient, dangerous to rebuild, and expensive, but they could not agree on an alternative. Norfolk installed an entirely new system and filed a suit in a federal district court against RBMN to recover half of the cost. RBMN filed a motion for summary judgment, asserting, in part, the doctrine of frustration of purpose. What is this doctrine? Does it apply in this case? How should the court rule on RBMN's motion? Explain. [*Norfolk Southern Railway Co. v. Reading Blue Mountain & Northern Railroad Co.*, 346 F.Supp.2d 720 (M.D.Pa. 2004)]

17–7. CASE PROBLEM WITH SAMPLE ANSWER: Material Breach.

 *Kermit Johnson formed FB&I Building Products, Inc., in Watertown, South Dakota, to sell building materials. In December 1998, FB&I contracted with Superior Truss & Components in Minneota, Minnesota, "to exclusively sell Superior's open-faced wall panels, floor panels, roof trusses and other miscellaneous products." In March 2000, FB&I agreed to exclusively sell Component Manufacturing Co.'s building products in Colorado. Two months later, Superior learned of FB&I's deal with Component and terminated its contract with FB&I. That contract provided that on cancellation, "FB&I will be entitled to retain the customers that they continue to sell and service with Superior products." Superior refused to honor this provision. Between the cancellation of FB&I's contract and 2004, Superior made $2,327,528 in sales to FB&I customers without paying a commission. FB&I filed a suit in a South Dakota state court against Superior, alleging, in part, breach of contract and seeking the unpaid commissions. Superior insisted that FB&I had materially breached their contract, excusing Superior from performing. In whose favor should the court rule and why?* [FB&I Building Products, Inc. v. Superior Truss & Components, a Division of Banks Lumber, Inc., 2007 SD 13, 727 N.W.2d 474 (S.D. 2007)]

- To view a sample answer for Problem 17–7, go to this book's Web site at www.cengage.com/blaw/clarkson, select "Chapter 17," and click on "Case Problem with Sample Answer."

17–8. Material Breach Roger Bannister was the director of technical and product development for Bemis Co. He signed a covenant not to compete that prohibited him from working for a "conflicting organization" for eighteen months following his termination, but required Bemis to pay his salary if he was unable to find a job "consistent with his abilities and education." Bemis terminated Bannister. Mondi Packaging, a Bemis competitor, told him that it would like to offer him a job but could not do so because of the the noncompete agreement. Bemis released Bannister from the agreement with respect to "all other companies than Mondi" and refused to pay his salary. Nine months later, Bannister accepted a position with Bancroft Bag, Inc., another Bemis competitor. He filed a suit in a federal district court against his former employer. Do these facts show a material breach of contract? If so, what is the appropriate remedy? Explain. [*Bannister v. Bemis Co., Inc.*, 556 F.3d 882 (8th Cir. 2009)]

17–9. Condition Precedent Just Homes, LLC (JH), hired Mike Building & Contracting, Inc., to do $1.35 million worth of renovation work on three homes. Community Preservation Corporation (CPC) supervised Mike's work on behalf of JH. The contract stated that in the event of a dispute, JH would have to obtain the project architect's certification to justify terminating Mike. As construction progressed, relations between Mike and CPC worsened. At a certain point in the project, Mike requested partial payment, and CPC recommended that JH not make it. Mike refused to continue work without further payment. JH evicted Mike from the project. Mike sued for breach of contract. JH contended that it had the right to terminate the contract due to CPC's negative reports and Mike's failure to agree with the project's engineer. Mike moved for summary judgment for the amounts owed for work performed, claiming that JH had not fulfilled the condition precedent—that is, JH never obtained the project architect's certification for Mike's termination. Which of the two parties involved breached the contract? Explain your answer. [*Mike Building & Contracting, Inc. v. Just Homes, LLC,* 27 Misc.3d 833, 901 N.Y.S.2d 458 (2010)]

17–10. A QUESTION OF ETHICS: Conditions.

King County, Washington, hired Frank Coluccio Construction Co. (FCCC) to act as general contractor for a public works project involving the construction of a small utility tunnel under the Duwamish Waterway. FCCC hired Donald B. Murphy Contractors, Inc. (DBM), as a subcontractor. DBM was responsible for constructing an access shaft at the eastern end of the tunnel. Problems arose during construction, including a "blow-in" of the access shaft that caused it to fill with water, soil, and debris. FCCC and DBM incurred substantial

*expenses from the repairs and delays. Under the project contract, King County was supposed to buy an insurance policy to "insure against physical loss or damage by perils included under an 'All-Risk' Builder's Risk policy." Any claim under this policy was to be filed through the insured. King County, which had general property damage insurance, did not obtain an all-risk builder's risk policy. For the losses attributable to the blow-in, FCCC and DBM submitted builder's risk claims, which the county denied. FCCC filed a suit in a Washington state court against King County, alleging, among other claims, breach of contract. [*Frank Coluccio Construction Co., Inc. v. King County, 136 Wash.App. 751, 150 P.3d 1147 (Div. 1 2007)]*

(a) King County's property damage policy specifically excluded, at the county's request, coverage of tunnels. The county drafted its contract with FCCC to require the all-risk builder's risk policy and authorize itself to "sponsor" claims. When FCCC and DBM filed their claims, the county secretly colluded with its property damage insurer to deny payment. What do these facts indicate about the county's ethics and legal liability in this situation?

(b) Could DBM, as a third party to the contract between King County and FCCC, maintain an action on the contract against King County? Discuss.

(c) All-risk insurance is a promise to pay on the "fortuitous" happening of a loss or damage from any cause except those that are specifically excluded. Payment usually is not made on a loss that, at the time the insurance was obtained, the claimant subjectively knew would occur. If a loss results from faulty workmanship on the part of a contractor, should the obligation to pay under an all-risk policy be discharged? Explain.

LEGAL RESEARCH EXERCISES ON THE WEB

Go to this text's Web site at **www.cengage.com/blaw/clarkson**, select "Chapter 17," and click on "Practical Internet Exercises." There you will find the following Internet research exercises that you can perform to learn more about the topics covered in this chapter.

Practical Internet Exercise 17–1: **Legal Perspective**
Anticipatory Repudiation

Practical Internet Exercise 17–2: **Management Perspective**
Commercial Impracticability

CHAPTER 18

Breach of Contract and Remedies

When one party breaches a contract, the other party—the nonbreaching party—can choose one or more of several remedies. A *remedy* is the relief provided for an innocent party when the other party has breached the contract. It is the means employed to enforce a right or to redress an injury.

The most common remedies available to a nonbreaching party include damages, rescission and restitution, specific performance, and reformation. As discussed in Chapter 1, a distinction is made between *remedies at law* and *remedies in equity.* Today, the remedy at law normally is monetary damages, which are discussed in the first part of this chapter.

Equitable remedies include rescission and restitution, specific performance, and reformation, all of which will be examined later in the chapter. Usually, a court will not award an equitable remedy unless the remedy at law is inadequate. Special legal doctrines and concepts relating to remedies will be discussed in the final pages of this chapter.

SECTION 1
DAMAGES

A breach of contract entitles the nonbreaching party to sue for monetary damages. As discussed in Chapter 6, tort law damages are designed to compensate a party for harm suffered as a result of another's wrongful act. In the context of contract law, damages compensate the nonbreaching party for the loss of the bargain. Often, courts say that innocent parties are to be placed in the position they would have occupied had the contract been fully performed.[1]

Realize at the outset, though, that collecting damages through a court judgment requires litigation, which can be expensive and time consuming. Also keep in mind that court judgments are often difficult to enforce, particularly if the breaching party does not have sufficient assets to pay the damages awarded (as discussed in Chapter 3). For these reasons, most parties settle their lawsuits for damages (or other remedies) prior to trial.

Types of Damages

There are four broad categories of damages:

1. Compensatory (to cover direct losses and costs).
2. Consequential (to cover indirect and foreseeable losses).
3. Punitive (to punish and deter wrongdoing).
4. Nominal (to recognize wrongdoing when no monetary loss is shown).

Compensatory and punitive damages were discussed in Chapter 6 in the context of tort law. Here, we look at these types of damages, as well as consequential and nominal damages, in the context of contract law.

COMPENSATORY DAMAGES Damages that compensate the nonbreaching party for the *loss of the bargain* are known as *compensatory damages.* These damages compensate the injured party only for damages actually sustained and proved to have arisen directly from the loss of the bargain caused by the breach of contract. They simply replace what was lost because of the wrong or damage and, for this reason, are often said to "make the person whole."

---

1. *Restatement (Second) of Contracts,* Section 347.

The standard measure of compensatory damages is the difference between the value of the breaching party's promised performance under the contract and the value of her or his actual performance. This amount is reduced by any loss that the injured party has avoided, however.

To illustrate: Wilcox contracts to perform certain services exclusively for Hernandez during the month of March for $4,000. Hernandez cancels the contract and is in breach. Wilcox is able to find another job during the month of March but can earn only $3,000. He can sue Hernandez for breach and recover $1,000 as compensatory damages. Wilcox can also recover from Hernandez the amount that he spent to find the other job. Expenses that are caused directly by a breach of contract—such as those incurred to obtain performance from another source—are known as **incidental damages.**

The measurement of compensatory damages varies by type of contract. Certain types of contracts deserve special mention. They are contracts for the sale of goods, land contracts, and construction contracts.

Sale of Goods. In a contract for the sale of goods, the usual measure of compensatory damages is an amount equal to the difference between the contract price and the market price.[2] For example, Medik Laboratories contracts to buy ten model UTS network servers from Cal Industries for $4,000 each. Cal Industries, however, fails to deliver the ten servers to Medik. The market price of the servers at the time Medik learns of the breach is $4,500. Therefore, Medik's measure of damages is $5,000 (10 × $500), plus any incidental damages (expenses) caused by the breach. When the buyer breaches and the seller has not yet produced the goods, compensatory damages normally equal lost profits on the sale, not the difference between the contract price and the market price.

Sale of Land. Ordinarily, because each parcel of land is unique, the remedy for a seller's breach of a contract for a sale of real estate is specific performance—that is, the buyer is awarded the parcel of property for which she or he bargained (*specific performance* will be discussed more fully later in this chapter). When this remedy is unavailable (because the seller has sold the property to someone else, for example) or when the buyer is the party in breach, the measure of damages is typically the difference between the contract price and the market price of the land. The majority of states follow this rule.

A minority of states follow a different rule when the seller breaches the contract and the breach is not deliberate.[3] When the breach was not willful, these states limit the prospective buyer's damages to a refund of any down payment made plus any expenses incurred (such as fees for title searches, attorneys, and escrows). This rule effectively returns purchasers to the positions they occupied prior to the sale, rather than giving them the benefit of the bargain.

Construction Contracts. The measure of damages in a building or construction contract varies depending on which party breaches and when the breach occurs. The owner can breach at three different stages—before performance has begun, during performance, or after performance has been completed.

If the owner breaches *before performance has begun,* the contractor can recover only the profits that would have been made on the contract (that is, the total contract price less the cost of materials and labor). If the owner breaches *during performance,* the contractor can recover the profits plus the costs incurred in partially constructing the building. If the owner breaches *after the construction has been completed,* the contractor can recover the entire contract price, plus interest.

When the construction contractor breaches the contract—either by failing to undertake construction or by stopping work partway through the project—the measure of damages is the cost of completion, which includes reasonable compensation for any delay in performance. If the contractor finishes late, the measure of damages is the loss of use. The rules concerning the measurement of damages in breached construction contracts are summarized in Exhibit 18–1 on the following page.

Construction Contracts and Economic Waste. If the contractor substantially performs, a court may use the cost-of-completion formula, but only

---

2. More specifically, the amount is the difference between the contract price and the market price at the time and place at which the goods were to be delivered or tendered. See UCC [Uniform Commercial Code] 2–708 and 2–713.

3. "Deliberate" breaches include the seller's failure to convey (transfer title) the land because the market price has gone up. "Nondeliberate" breaches include the seller's failure to convey the land because of a problem with the title, such as the discovery of an unknown *easement* that gives another a right of use over the property (see Chapter 50).

EXHIBIT 18–1 • Measurement of Damages—Breach of Construction Contracts

PARTY IN BREACH	TIME OF BREACH	MEASUREMENT OF DAMAGES
Owner	Before construction has begun.	Profits (contract price less cost of materials and labor).
Owner	During construction.	Profits, plus costs incurred up to time of breach.
Owner	After construction is completed.	Full contract price, plus interest.
Contractor	Before construction has begun.	Cost in excess of contract price to complete work.
Contractor	Before construction is completed.	Generally, all costs incurred by owner to complete.

if requiring completion will not entail unreasonable economic waste. *Economic waste* occurs when the cost of repairing or completing the performance as required by the contract greatly outweighs the benefit to the owner. Suppose that a contractor discovers that it will cost $20,000 to move a large coral rock eleven inches as specified in the contract. Because changing the rock's position will alter the appearance of the project only a trifle, a court would likely conclude that full completion would involve economic waste. Thus, the contractor will not be required to pay the entire $20,000 to complete performance.

CONSEQUENTIAL DAMAGES Foreseeable damages that result from a party's breach of contract are called **consequential damages,** or *special damages*. They differ from compensatory damages in that they are caused by special circumstances beyond the contract itself. They flow from the consequences, or results, of a breach.

When a seller fails to deliver goods, knowing that the buyer is planning to use or resell those goods immediately, a court may award consequential damages for the loss of profits from the planned resale. (The buyer will also recover compensatory damages for the difference between the contract price and the market price of the goods.)

To recover consequential damages, the breaching party must know (or have reason to know) that special circumstances will cause the non-breaching party to suffer an additional loss. This rule was enunciated in the following classic case. In reading this decision, it is helpful to understand that in the mid-nineteenth century, large flour mills customarily kept more than one main crankshaft on hand in the event that one broke and had to be repaired.

CASE 18.1
Hadley v. Baxendale
Court of Exchequer, 156 Eng.Rep. 145 (1854).

BACKGROUND AND FACTS • The Hadleys (the plaintiffs) ran a flour mill in Gloucester, England. The main crankshaft attached to the steam engine in the mill broke, causing the mill to shut down. The crankshaft had to be sent to a foundry located in Greenwich so that a new shaft could be made to fit the other parts of the engine. Baxendale, the defendant, was a common carrier that transported the shaft from Gloucester to Greenwich. The freight charges were collected in advance, and Baxendale promised to deliver the shaft the following day. It was not delivered for a number of days, however. As a consequence, the mill was closed for several days. The Hadleys sued to recover the profits lost during that time. Baxendale contended that the loss of profits was "too remote" to be recoverable. The court held for the plaintiffs, and the jury was allowed to take into consideration the lost profits. The defendant appealed.

IN THE LANGUAGE OF THE COURT
ALDERSON, J. [Judge]
* * * *

* * * Where two parties have made a contract which one of them has broken, the damages which the other party ought to receive in respect of such breach of contract should be such as may fairly and reasonably be considered either arising naturally, [that

CASE 18.1 CONTINUED ▶ is,] according to the usual course of things, from such breach of contract itself, or such as may reasonably be supposed to have been in the contemplation of both parties, at the time they made the contract, as the probable result of the breach of it. Now, if the special circumstances under which the contract was actually made were communicated by the plaintiffs to the defendants, and thus known to both parties, the damages resulting from the breach of such a contract, *which they would reasonably contemplate,* would be the amount of injury which would ordinarily follow from a breach of contract under these special circumstances so known and communicated. * * * Now, in the present case, if we are to apply the principles above laid down, we find that the only circumstances here communicated by the plaintiffs to the defendants at the time the contract was made, were, that the article to be carried was the broken shaft of a mill, and that the plaintiffs were the millers of that mill. * * * Special circumstances were here never communicated by the plaintiffs to the defendants. It follows, therefore, that the loss of profits here cannot reasonably be considered such a consequence of the breach of contract as could have been fairly and reasonably contemplated by both the parties when they made this contract. [Emphasis added.]

DECISION AND REMEDY • *The Court of Exchequer ordered a new trial. According to the court, to collect consequential damages, the plaintiffs would have to have given express notice of the special circumstances that caused the loss of profits.*

IMPACT OF THIS CASE ON TODAY'S LAW • *This case established the rule that when damages are awarded, compensation is given only for those injuries that the defendant could reasonably have foreseen as a probable result of the usual course of events following a breach. Today, the rule enunciated by the court in this case still applies. To recover consequential damages, the plaintiff must show that the defendant had reason to know or foresee that a particular loss or injury would occur.*

THE E-COMMERCE DIMENSION • *If a Web merchant loses business due to a computer system's failure that can be attributed to malfunctioning software, can the merchant recover the lost profits from the software maker? Explain.*

PUNITIVE DAMAGES Punitive, or exemplary, damages generally are not recoverable in contract law, even for an intentional breach of contract. Because punitive damages are designed to punish a wrongdoer and set an example to deter similar conduct in the future, they have no legitimate place in contract law. A contract is simply a civil relationship between the parties, so breaching a contract is not a crime; nor does it necessarily harm society (as torts do). Thus, a court will not award punitive damages but will compensate one party for the loss of the bargain—no more and no less.

In a few situations, however, when a person's actions constitute both a breach of contract and a tort, punitive damages may be available. For example, some parties, such as an engineer and her client, may establish by contract a certain reasonable standard or duty of care. Failure to live up to that standard is a breach of contract, and the act itself may constitute negligence. Similarly, some intentional torts, such as fraud, may be tied to a breach of the terms of a contract and enable the injured party to seek punitive damages. Additionally, when an insurance company exhibits bad faith in failing to settle a claim on behalf of the insured party, courts may award punitive damages. Overall, though, punitive damages are almost never available in contract disputes.

NOMINAL DAMAGES When no actual damage or financial loss results from a breach of contract and only a technical injury is involved, the court may award **nominal damages** to the innocent party. Awards of nominal damages are often small, such as one dollar, but they do establish that the defendant acted wrongfully. Most lawsuits for nominal damages are brought as a matter of principle under the theory that a breach has occurred and some damages must be imposed regardless of actual loss.

Assume that Jackson contracts to buy potatoes from Stanley at fifty cents a pound. Stanley breaches the contract and does not deliver the potatoes. In the meantime, the price of potatoes has fallen. Jackson is able to buy them in the open market at half the price he contracted for with Stanley. He is clearly better off because of Stanley's breach. Thus, because Jackson sustained only a technical injury and suffered no monetary loss, he is likely to be awarded only nominal damages if he brings a suit for breach of contract.

Mitigation of Damages

In most situations, when a breach of contract occurs, the innocent injured party is held to a duty to mitigate, or reduce, the damages that he or she suffers. Under this doctrine of **mitigation of damages,** the duty owed depends on the nature of the contract.

For example, some states require a landlord to use reasonable means to find a new tenant if a tenant abandons the premises and fails to pay rent. If an acceptable tenant is found, the landlord is required to lease the premises to this tenant to mitigate the damages recoverable from the former tenant. The former tenant is still liable for the difference between the amount of the rent under the original lease and the rent received from the new tenant. If the landlord has not taken the reasonable steps necessary to find a new tenant, a court will likely reduce any award made by the amount of rent the landlord could have received had such reasonable means been used.

In the majority of states, a person whose employment has been wrongfully terminated owes a duty to mitigate the damages suffered because of the employer's breach of the employment contract. In other words, a wrongfully terminated employee has a duty to take a similar job if one is available. If the employee fails to do this, the damages awarded will be equivalent to the person's salary less the income he or she would have received in a similar job obtained by reasonable means. The employer has the burden of proving that such a job existed and that the employee could have been hired. Normally, the employee is under no duty to take a job of a different type and rank.

Liquidated Damages Provisions

A **liquidated damages** provision in a contract specifies that a certain dollar amount is to be paid in the event of a *future* default or breach of contract. (*Liquidated* means determined, settled, or fixed.) For example, a provision requiring a construction contractor to pay $300 for every day he or she is late in completing the project is a liquidated damages provision.

Liquidated damages provisions are frequently used in construction contracts. They are also common in contracts for the sale of goods.[4] In addition, contracts with entertainers and professional athletes often include liquidated damages provisions. For example, in 2010 a television network settled its contract dispute with *The Tonight Show* host Conan O'Brien for $33 million—somewhat less than the $40 million he would have potentially received in liquidated damages if the dispute had gone to court and he had prevailed.

LIQUIDATED DAMAGES VERSUS PENALTIES Liquidated damages differ from penalties. A **penalty** specifies a certain amount to be paid in the event of a default or breach of contract and is designed to penalize the breaching party. Liquidated damages provisions usually are enforceable. In contrast, if a court finds that a provision calls for a penalty, the agreement as to the amount will not be enforced, and recovery will be limited to actual damages.

In the following case, the issue before the court was whether a clause in a contract was an enforceable liquidated damages provision or an unenforceable penalty.

---

4. Section 2–718(1) of the UCC specifically authorizes the use of liquidated damages provisions.

✹ EXTENDED CASE 18.2 ✹
B-Sharp Musical Productions, Inc. v. Haber

New York Supreme Court, 27 Misc.3d 41, 899 N.Y.S.2d 792 (2010).

IN THE LANGUAGE OF THE COURT
PER CURIAM [By the whole court].
* * * * *
Plaintiff [B-Sharp Musical Productions, Inc.,] and defendant James Haber entered into a contract pursuant to which plaintiff agreed to provide a designated 16-piece band on a specified date to perform at Mr.

Haber's son's bar mitzvah. Mr. Haber was to pay approximately $30,000 for the band's services. The contract contained a liquidated damages clause stating, in pertinent part, "If [the contract] is terminated in writing by [Mr. Haber] for any reason within ninety (90) days prior to the engagement, the remaining balance of the contract will be immediately due and payable. If [the contract] is terminated in writing by [Mr. Haber]

for any reason before the ninety (90) days period, 50 percent of the balance will be immediately due and payable."

Less than 90 days prior to the date of the bar mitzvah, Mr. Haber sent a letter to plaintiff notifying it that he was canceling the contract. After Mr. Haber refused plaintiff's demand that he pay the remaining amount due under the contract—approximately $25,000—plaintiff

EXTENDED CASE 18.2 CONTINUED ▼

commenced this action against Mr. Haber and his wife, defendant Jill Haber. Civil Court granted plaintiff's motion for summary judgment on its cause of action to enforce the liquidated damages clause and denied defendants' cross motion for partial summary judgment dismissing that cause of action and the complaint as against Mrs. Haber.

Given the nature of the contract and the particular circumstances underlying this case, Civil Court correctly determined that the subject provision of the contract is an enforceable liquidated damages clause, not an unenforceable penalty. "The clause, which in effect uses an estimate of [plaintiff's] chances of rebooking the [band] as the measure of [its] probable loss in the event of a cancellation, reflects an understanding that although the

expense and possibility of rebooking a canceled [performance] could not be ascertained [determined] with certainty, *as a practical matter the expense would become greater, and the possibility would become less, the closer to the [performance] the cancellation was made, until a point was reached, [90] days before [the performance], that any effort to rebook could not be reasonably expected.*" [Emphasis added.]

Defendants' argument that the cause of action to enforce the liquidated damages clause must be dismissed because the clause does not comply with the type size requirement of CPLR [New York's Civil Practice Law Rules] 4544 is without merit. In an effort to demonstrate that the clause did not comply with the statutory type size requirement, defendants submitted a copy of the contract with the image of a ruler imprinted in the margin. However, defendants failed to establish that

the type size of the copy they submitted is identical to that of the original contract, a critical failure given the precision with which type size must be measured and calculated. Therefore, defendants failed to raise a triable [one that could go before a judge or jury] issue as to whether the clause violated the statutory type size requirement.

We agree with defendants that the complaint should be dismissed against Mrs. Haber. The contract was signed only by Mr. Haber, and no triable issue exists as to whether Mr. Haber executed the contract as Mrs. Haber's agent. We note in this connection that an agency relationship may not be implied or inferred solely by reason of the marital relationship of the couple.

This constitutes the decision and order of the court.

QUESTIONS

1. In deciding whether a clause provides for liquidated damages or a penalty, should the courts ever consider the circumstances that caused the nonperforming party to breach the contract? Explain.
2. Why did the court determine that the contract clause at issue was an enforceable liquidated damages clause and not an unenforceable penalty clause?

ENFORCEABILITY To determine if a particular provision is for liquidated damages or for a penalty, a court asks two questions:

1. When the contract was entered into, was it apparent that damages would be difficult to estimate in the event of a breach?
2. Was the amount set as damages a reasonable estimate and not excessive?[5]

If the answers to both questions are yes, the provision normally will be enforced. If either answer is no, the provision usually will not be enforced.

CASE IN POINT Winthrop Resources Corporation leased nearly $9 million worth of computer equipment to Eaton Hydraulics. When Eaton failed to meet its payment obligations and did not take proper care of the leased equipment, Winthrop filed a lawsuit for breach of the contract. The contract included a liquidated damages provision that valued the computer equipment at more than four times

its market value. Eaton challenged the provision, claiming that it called for an unenforceable penalty. According to the court, the amount of actual damages was difficult to ascertain at the time the contract was formed because of the "speculative nature of the value of computers at termination of lease schedules." Therefore, the court ruled that the liquidated damages clause was enforceable and required Eaton to pay nearly $4 million to Winthrop.[6]

SECTION 2
EQUITABLE REMEDIES

Sometimes, damages are an inadequate remedy for a breach of contract. In these situations, the nonbreaching party may ask the court for an equitable remedy. Equitable remedies include rescission and restitution, specific performance, and reformation.

---

5. *Restatement (Second) of Contracts*, Section 356(1).

6. *Winthrop Resources Corp. v. Eaton Hydraulics, Inc.*, 361 F.3d 465 (8th Cir. 2004).

Rescission and Restitution

As discussed in Chapter 17 on page 325, *rescission* is essentially an action to undo, or terminate, a contract—to return the contracting parties to the positions they occupied prior to the transaction.[7] When fraud, a mistake, duress, undue influence, misrepresentation, or lack of capacity to contract is present, unilateral rescission is available. Rescission may also be available by statute.[8] The failure of one party to perform entitles the other party to rescind the contract. The rescinding party must give prompt notice to the breaching party.

RESTITUTION Generally, to rescind a contract, both parties must make **restitution** to each other by returning goods, property, or funds previously conveyed.[9] If the property or goods can be returned, they must be. If the goods or property have been consumed, restitution must be made in an equivalent dollar amount.

Essentially, restitution involves the plaintiff's recapture of a benefit conferred on the defendant that has unjustly enriched her or him. For example, Katie pays $10,000 to Bob in return for Bob's promise to design a house for her. The next day, Bob calls Katie and tells her that he has taken a position with a large architectural firm in another state and cannot design the house. Katie decides to hire another architect that afternoon. Katie can obtain restitution of the $10,000.

RESTITUTION IS NOT LIMITED TO RESCISSION CASES Restitution may be appropriate when a contract is rescinded, but the right to restitution is not limited to rescission cases. Because an award of restitution basically returns something to its rightful owner, a party can seek restitution in actions for breach of contract, tort actions, and other types of actions. For example, restitution can be obtained when funds or property have been transferred by mistake or because of fraud or incapacity. Similarly, restitution might be available when there has been misconduct by a party in a confidential or other special relationship. Even in criminal cases a court can order restitution of funds or property obtained through embezzlement, conversion, theft, or copyright infringement.

Specific Performance

The equitable remedy of **specific performance** calls for the performance of the act promised in the contract. This remedy is attractive to a nonbreaching party because it provides the exact bargain promised in the contract. It also avoids some of the problems inherent in a suit for damages, such as collecting a judgment and arranging another contract. In addition, the actual performance may be more valuable than the monetary damages.

Normally, however, specific performance will not be granted unless the party's legal remedy (monetary damages) is inadequate.[10] For this reason, contracts for the sale of goods rarely qualify for specific performance. The legal remedy—monetary damages—is ordinarily adequate in such situations because substantially identical goods can be bought or sold in the market. Only if the goods are unique will a court grant specific performance. For example, paintings, sculptures, or rare books or coins are so unique that monetary damages will not enable a buyer to obtain substantially identical substitutes in the market.

SALE OF LAND A court may grant specific performance to a buyer in an action for a breach of contract involving the sale of land. In this situation, the legal remedy of monetary damages may not compensate the buyer adequately because every parcel of land is unique: the same land in the same location obviously cannot be obtained elsewhere. Only when specific performance is unavailable (such as when the seller has sold the property to someone else) will monetary damages be awarded instead.

CASE IN POINT Howard Stainbrook entered into a contract to sell Trent Low forty acres of mostly timbered land for $45,000. Low agreed to pay for a survey of the property and other costs in addition to the price. He gave Stainbrook a check for $1,000 to show his intent to fulfill the contract. One month later, Stainbrook died. His son David became the executor of the estate. After he discovered that the timber on the property was worth more than $100,000, David asked Low to withdraw his offer to buy the forty acres. Low refused and filed a suit against David seeking specific performance of the

---

7. The rescission discussed here is *unilateral* rescission, in which only one party wants to undo the contract. In mutual rescission, both parties agree to undo the contract. Mutual rescission discharges the contract; unilateral rescission generally is available as a remedy for breach of contract.

8. The Federal Trade Commission and many states have rules or statutes allowing consumers to unilaterally rescind contracts made at home with door-to-door salespersons. Rescission is allowed within three business days for any reason or for no reason at all. See, for example, California Civil Code Section 1689.5.

9. *Restatement (Second) of Contracts*, Section 370.

10. *Restatement (Second) of Contracts*, Section 359.

contract. The court found that because Low had substantially performed his obligations under the contract and offered to perform the rest, he was entitled to specific performance.[11]

CONTRACTS FOR PERSONAL SERVICES Personal-service contracts require one party to work personally for another party. Courts generally refuse to grant specific performance of personal-service contracts because to order a party to perform personal services against his or her will amounts to a type of involuntary servitude.[12]

Moreover, the courts do not want to monitor contracts for personal services, which usually require the exercise of personal judgment or talent. For example, if Nicole contracted with a surgeon to perform surgery to remove a tumor on her brain, and he refused, the court would not compel (and she certainly would not want) the surgeon to perform under those circumstances. A court cannot assure meaningful performance in such a situation.[13]

---

11. *Stainbrook v. Low,* 842 N.E.2d 386 (Ind.App. 2006).
12. Involuntary servitude, or slavery, is contrary to the public policy expressed in the Thirteenth Amendment to the U.S. Constitution. A court can, however, enter an order (injunction) prohibiting a person who breached a personal-service contract from engaging in similar contracts for a period of time in the future.
13. Similarly, courts often refuse to order specific performance of construction contracts because courts are not set up to operate as construction supervisors or engineers.

If a contract is not deemed personal, the remedy at law of monetary damages may be adequate if substantially identical service (such as lawn mowing) is available from other persons.

Reformation

Reformation is an equitable remedy used when the parties have *imperfectly* expressed their agreement in writing. Reformation allows a court to rewrite the contract to reflect the parties' true intentions.

WHEN FRAUD OR MUTUAL MISTAKE IS PRESENT Courts order reformation most often when fraud or mutual mistake (for example, a clerical error) is present. Typically, a party seeks reformation so that some other remedy may then be pursued. To illustrate: If Carson contracts to buy a certain parcel of land from Malboa but their contract mistakenly refers to a different parcel of land and not the one being sold, the contract does not reflect the parties' intentions. Accordingly, a court can reform the contract so that it conforms to the parties' intentions and accurately refers to the parcel of land being sold. Carson can then, if necessary, show that Malboa has breached the contract as reformed. She can at that time request an order for specific performance.

In the following case, a court was asked to reform a deed eight months after the transaction in which the deed played a principal part.

CASE 18.3
Drake v. Hance

Court of Appeals of North Carolina, 673 S.E.2d 411 (2009).
www.nccourts.org[a]

BACKGROUND AND FACTS • In June 2005, Eric and Debra Hance agreed to buy Garry and Wanda Drake's home in Monroe, North Carolina. The contract described the property as "#15 Legacy Lake." The deed, however, listed "lot 15, Legacy Lake" and "lot 11, Legacy Lake." Lot 15 is the property on which the home sits. Lot 11 is a vacant lot across the street. After the sale, the deed was filed with the appropriate state office. Eight months later, when the Drakes tried to sell lot 11 to a third party, they learned that it had been listed on the Hances' deed. The Drakes told the Hances, who denied that any mistake had been made. Claiming that they had intended to sell only lot 15, the Drakes filed a suit in a North Carolina state court against the Hances. The attorney who closed the sale testified that the deed was drafted improperly. The court reformed it. The Hances appealed.

---

a. In the "Favorites" column, click on "Court Opinions." On that page, in the "Court of Appeals Opinions" section, click on "2009." In the result, scroll to "3 March 2009" and click on the name of the case to access the opinion. The North Carolina Administrative Office of the Courts maintains this Web site.

CASE CONTINUES ➡

CASE 18.3 CONTINUED ➡

IN THE LANGUAGE OF THE COURT
CALABRIA, Judge.
* * * *

A deed is a written document that on its face conveys title or an interest in real property. A deed is an integrated document and the parties may not introduce oral or written evidence to contradict its terms.

However, if a party can show a mutual mistake was made in the execution of a deed, in this case due to the error of the draftsman, parol evidence is competent evidence to show the true intentions of the parties. *If the evidence is strong, cogent, and convincing that the deed, as recorded, did not reflect the agreement between the parties due to a mutual mistake caused by a drafting error, a deed can be reformed.* [Emphasis added.]

In the present case, the closing attorney improperly prepared the deed due to an error in his office. The court found that repeated attempts were made to contact the defendants to correct the error but were unsuccessful. More importantly, the defendants, at that time, did not dispute that an error had been made. The trial court found the closing attorney's testimony "exceptionally persuasive," and we agree.

* * * The evidence of an error by the draftsman was strong, cogent, and convincing. The trial court did not err in reforming the deed based on this evidence.

Competent evidence supports the trial court's findings that the parties contracted for the sale of lot 15 only, and that the attorney erred when drafting the deed that included both lots. The trial court did not err in admitting parol evidence to determine the intent of the parties, and did not err in reforming the deed when presented evidence of the attorney's mistake.

DECISION AND REMEDY • *The state intermediate appellate court affirmed the lower court's action. The parties had contracted for the sale of only one lot. The deed could be reformed based on the testimony of the party who drafted it.*

THE E-COMMERCE DIMENSION • *Is a mistake such as the one in this case likely to occur when software is used to draft a document? Why or why not?*

THE ETHICAL DIMENSION • *What may have motivated the defendants in this case to assert that there was no mistake in the deed? Discuss.*

Exhibit 18–2 graphically summarizes the remedies, including reformation, that are available to the nonbreaching party.

ORAL CONTRACTS AND COVENANTS NOT TO COMPETE Courts also frequently reform contracts in two other situations. The first involves two parties who have made a binding oral contract. They further agree to put the oral contract in writing, but in doing so, they make an error in stating the terms. Normally, a court will allow into evidence the correct terms of the oral contract, thereby reforming the written contract.

The second situation occurs when the parties have executed a written covenant not to compete (discussed in Chapter 13 on page 263). If the covenant is for a valid and legitimate purpose (such as the sale of a business) but the area or time restraints of the covenant are unreasonable, some courts will reform the restraints by making them reasonable and will enforce the entire contract as reformed. Other courts, however, will throw out the entire restrictive covenant as illegal.

SECTION 3

RECOVERY BASED ON QUASI CONTRACT

In some situations, when no actual contract exists, a court may step in to prevent one party from being unjustly enriched at the expense of another party. As discussed in Chapter 10 on pages 212 and 213, quasi contract is a legal theory under which an obligation is imposed in the absence of an agreement. The legal obligation arises because the law considers that the party accepting the benefits has made an implied promise to pay for them. Generally, when one party has conferred a benefit on another party, justice requires that the party receiving the benefit pay the reasonable value for it. The party conferring

EXHIBIT 18-2 • Remedies for Breach of Contract

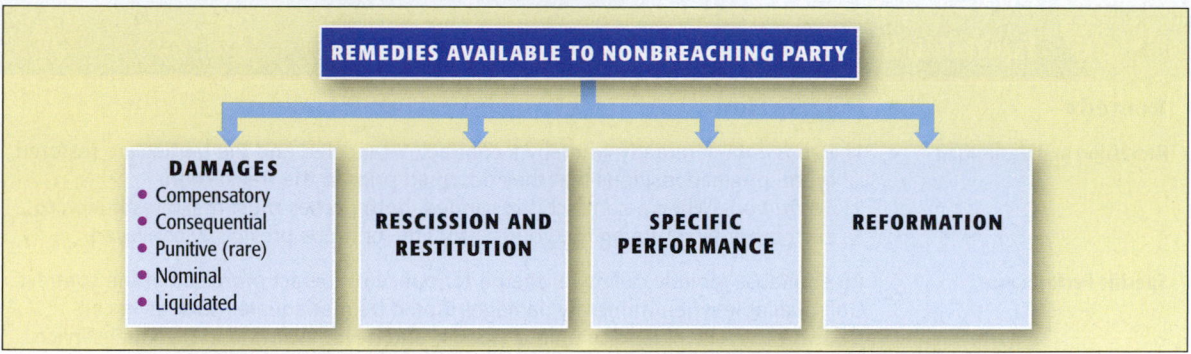

the benefit can recover in *quantum meruit,* which means "as much as he or she deserves."

When Quasi Contract Is Used

Quasi contract allows a court to act as if a contract exists when there is no actual contract or agreement between the parties. A court can also use this theory when the parties entered into a contract, but it is unenforceable for some reason. Quasi-contractual recovery is often granted when one party has partially performed under a contract that is unenforceable. It provides an alternative to suing for damages and allows the party to recover the reasonable value of the partial performance, measured in some cases according to the benefit received and in others according to the detriment suffered.

For example, Ericson contracts to build two oil derricks for Petro Industries. The derricks are to be built over a period of three years, but the parties do not make a written contract. Thus, the Statute of Frauds will bar enforcement of the contract.[14] After Ericson completes one derrick, Petro Industries informs him that it will not pay for the derrick. Ericson can sue Petro Industries under the theory of quasi contract.

The Requirements of Quasi Contract

To recover under the theory of quasi contract, the party seeking recovery must show the following:

1. The party has conferred a benefit on the other party.
2. The party conferred the benefit with the reasonable expectation of being paid.

3. The party did not act as a volunteer in conferring the benefit.
4. The party receiving the benefit would be unjustly enriched if allowed to retain the benefit without paying for it.

Applying these requirements to the example just given, Ericson can sue in quasi contract because all of the conditions for quasi-contractual recovery have been fulfilled. Ericson conferred a benefit on Petro Industries by building the oil derrick. Ericson built the derrick with the reasonable expectation of being paid and was not intending to act as a volunteer. The derrick conferred an obvious benefit on Petro Industries. Petro Industries would be unjustly enriched if it was allowed to keep the derrick without paying Ericson for the work. Therefore, Ericson should be able to recover in *quantum meruit* the reasonable value of the oil derrick that was built, which is ordinarily equal to its fair market value.

Concept Summary 18.1 on the following page reviews all of the equitable remedies, including quasi contract, that may be available in the event that a contract is breached.

◢◣ SECTION 4 ◢◣

ELECTION OF REMEDIES

In many cases, a nonbreaching party has several remedies available. When the remedies are inconsistent with one another, the common law of contracts requires the party to choose which remedy to pursue. This is called *election of remedies*.

The Purpose of the Doctrine

The purpose of the doctrine of election of remedies is to prevent double recovery. Suppose that

---

14. Contracts that by their terms cannot be performed within one year must be in writing to be enforceable (see Chapter 15).

CONCEPT SUMMARY 18.1
Equitable Remedies

Remedy	Description
Rescission and Restitution	1. *Rescission*—A remedy whereby a contract is canceled and the parties are restored to the original positions that they occupied prior to the transaction. 2. *Restitution*—When a contract is rescinded, both parties must make restitution to each other by returning the goods, property, or funds previously conveyed.
Specific Performance	An equitable remedy calling for the performance of the act promised in the contract. Only available when monetary damages would be inadequate—such as in contracts for the sale of land or unique goods—and never available in personal-service contracts.
Reformation	An equitable remedy allowing a contract to be reformed, or rewritten, to reflect the parties' true intentions. Available when an agreement is imperfectly expressed in writing, such as when a mutual mistake has occurred.
Recovery Based on Quasi Contract	An equitable theory under which a party who confers a benefit on another with the reasonable expectation of being paid can seek a court order for the fair market value of the benefit conferred.

McCarthy agrees in writing to sell his land to Tally. Then McCarthy changes his mind and repudiates the contract. Tally can sue for compensatory damages *or* for specific performance. If Tally could seek compensatory damages in addition to specific performance, she would recover twice for the same breach of contract. The doctrine of election of remedies requires Tally to choose the remedy she wants, and it eliminates any possibility of double recovery. In other words, the election doctrine represents the legal embodiment of the adage "You can't have your cake and eat it, too."

The doctrine has often been applied in a rigid and technical manner, leading to some harsh results. For example, Beacham is fraudulently induced to buy a parcel of land for $150,000. He spends an additional $10,000 moving onto the land and then discovers the fraud. Instead of suing for damages, Beacham sues to rescind the contract. The court allows Beacham to recover the purchase price of $150,000 in restitution, but not the additional $10,000 in moving expenses (because the seller did not receive this payment, he or she will not be required to return it). So Beacham suffers a net loss of $10,000 on the transaction. If Beacham had elected to sue for damages instead of seeking the remedy of rescission and restitution, he could have recovered the $10,000 as well as the $150,000.

The UCC's Rejection of the Doctrine

Because of the many problems associated with the doctrine of election of remedies, the UCC expressly rejects it.[15] As will be discussed in Chapter 21, remedies under the UCC are not exclusive but are cumulative in nature and include all the available remedies for breach of contract.

Pleading in the Alternative

Although the nonbreaching party must ultimately elect which remedy to pursue, modern court procedures do allow plaintiffs to plead their cases "in the alternative" (pleadings were discussed in Chapter 3 on page 52). In other words, when the plaintiff originally files a lawsuit, he or she can ask the court to order either rescission (and restitution) or damages. At trial, the party can elect the remedy that is most beneficial or appropriate, or the judge can order one remedy and not another. This process still prevents double recovery because the party can be awarded only one of the remedies requested.

SECTION 5
WAIVER OF BREACH

Under certain circumstances, a nonbreaching party may be willing to accept a defective performance of the contract. This knowing relinquishment of a legal right (that is, the right to require satisfactory and full performance) is called a **waiver.**

---

15. See UCC 2–703 and 2–711.

Consequences of a Waiver of Breach

When a waiver of a breach of contract occurs, the party waiving the breach cannot take any later action on it. In effect, the waiver erases the past breach; the contract continues as if the breach had never occurred. Of course, the waiver of breach of contract extends only to the matter waived and not to the whole contract.

Reasons for Waiving a Breach

Businesspersons often waive breaches of contract to get whatever benefit is still possible out of the contract. For instance, a seller contracts with a buyer to deliver to the buyer ten thousand tons of coal on or before November 1. The contract calls for the buyer to pay by November 10 for coal delivered. Because of a coal miners' strike, coal is hard to find. The seller breaches the contract by not tendering delivery until November 5. The buyer will likely choose to waive the seller's breach, accept delivery of the coal, and pay as contracted.

Waiver of Breach and Subsequent Breaches

Ordinarily, a waiver by a contracting party will not operate to waive subsequent, additional, or future breaches of contract. This is always true when the subsequent breaches are unrelated to the first breach. For example, an owner who waives the right to sue for late completion of a stage of construction does not waive the right to sue for failure to comply with engineering specifications on the same job.

A waiver will be extended to subsequent defective performance, however, if a reasonable person would conclude that similar defective performance in the future will be acceptable. Therefore, a *pattern of conduct* that waives a number of successive breaches will operate as a continued waiver. To change this result, the nonbreaching party should give notice to the breaching party that full performance will be required in the future.

The party who has rendered defective or less-than-full performance remains liable for the damages caused by the breach of contract. In effect, the waiver operates to keep the contract going. The waiver prevents the nonbreaching party from declaring the contract at an end or rescinding the contract. The contract continues, but the nonbreaching party can recover damages caused by the defective or less-than-full performance.

SECTION 6
CONTRACT PROVISIONS LIMITING REMEDIES

A contract may include provisions stating that no damages can be recovered for certain types of breaches or that damages will be limited to a maximum amount. The contract may also provide that the only remedy for breach is replacement, repair, or refund of the purchase price. Provisions stating that no damages can be recovered are called *exculpatory clauses* (see Chapter 13 on page 268). Provisions that affect the availability of certain remedies are called *limitation-of-liability clauses*.

The UCC Allows Sales Contracts to Limit Remedies

The UCC provides that in a contract for the sale of goods, remedies can be limited. We will examine the UCC provisions on limited remedies in Chapter 21, in the context of the remedies available on the breach of a contract for the sale or lease of goods.[16]

Enforceability of Limitation-of-Liability Clauses

Whether a limitation-of-liability clause in a contract will be enforced depends on the type of breach that is excused by the provision. For example, a provision excluding liability for fraudulent or intentional injury will not be enforced. Likewise, a clause excluding liability for illegal acts, acts that are contrary to public policy, or violations of law will not be enforced.

CASE IN POINT Engineering Consulting Services, Ltd. (ECS), contracted with RSN Properties, Inc, a real estate developer, to perform soil studies for $2,200 and render an opinion on the use of septic systems in a particular subdivision being developed. A clause in the contract limited ECS's liability to RSN to the value of the engineering services or the sum of $50,000, whichever was greater. ECS concluded that most of the lots were suitable for septic systems. RSN proceeded with the development in reliance on ECS's conclusions, which turned out to be incorrect. RSN filed a breach of contract lawsuit against ECS and argued that the limitation of liability was against public policy and unenforceable. The court, however, held that the "contract represented a

---

16. See UCC 2–719(1).

reasonable allocation of risks in an arm's-length business transaction, and did not violate public policy for professional engineering practice." The court therefore enforced the limitation-of-liability clause.[17]

A clause that excludes liability for negligence may be enforced in some situations when the parties have roughly equal bargaining positions.[18] If the limitation-of-liability clause is contained in a contract between persons with unequal bargaining power or is part of an adhesion contract, then it may not be enforced.

---

17. *RSN Properties, Inc. v. Engineering Consulting Services, Ltd.,* 301 Ga.App. 52, 686 S.E.2d 853 (2009).

18. See, for example, *Asch Webhosting, Inc. v. Adelphia Business Solutions Investment, LLC,* 2007 WL 2122044 (D.N.J. 2007); and *Lucier v. Williams,* 366 N.J.Super. 485, 841 A.2d 907 (2004).

REVIEWING
Breach of Contract and Remedies

Kyle Bruno enters a contract with X Entertainment to be a stuntman in a movie. Bruno is widely known as the best motorcycle stuntman in the business, and the movie to be produced, *Xtreme Riders*, has numerous scenes involving high-speed freestyle street-bike stunts. Filming is set to begin August 1 and end by December 1 so that the film can be released the following summer. Both parties to the contract have stipulated that the filming must end on time to capture the profits from the summer movie market. The contract states that Bruno will be paid 10 percent of the net proceeds from the movie for his stunts. The contract also includes a liquidated damages provision, which specifies that if Bruno breaches the contract, he will owe X Entertainment $1 million. In addition, the contract includes a limitation-of-liability clause stating that if Bruno is injured during filming, X Entertainment's liability is limited to nominal damages. Using the information presented in the chapter, answer the following questions.

1. One day, while Bruno is preparing for a difficult stunt, he gets into an argument with the director and refuses to perform any stunts at all. Can X Entertainment seek specific performance of the contract? Why or why not?
2. Suppose that while performing a high-speed wheelie on a motorcycle, Bruno is injured by the intentionally reckless act of an X Entertainment employee. Will a court be likely to enforce the limitation-of-liability clause? Why or why not?
3. What factors would a court consider to determine whether the $1 million liquidated damages provision constitutes valid damages or is a penalty?
4. Suppose that the contract had no liquidated damages provision (or the court refused to enforce it) and X Entertainment breached the contract. The breach caused the release of the film to be delayed until the fall. Could Bruno seek consequential (special) damages for lost profits from the summer movie market in that situation? Explain.

✹ DEBATE THIS: *Courts should always uphold limitation-of-liability clauses, whether or not the two parties to the contract had equal bargaining power.*

TERMS AND CONCEPTS

	incidental damages 335	nominal damages 337	restitution 340
	liquidated damages 338	penalty 338	specific performance 340
consequential damages 336	mitigation of damages 338	reformation 341	waiver 344

QUESTIONS AND CASE PROBLEMS

18–1. Liquidated Damages Cohen contracts to sell his house and lot to Windsor for $100,000. The terms of the contract call for Windsor to pay 10 percent of the purchase price as a deposit toward the purchase price, or a down payment. The terms further stipulate that if the buyer breaches the contract, Cohen will retain the deposit as liquidated damages. Windsor pays the deposit, but because her expected financing of the $90,000 balance falls through, she breaches the contract. Two weeks later Cohen sells the house and lot to Ballard for $105,000. Windsor demands her $10,000 back, but Cohen refuses, claiming that Windsor's breach and the contract terms entitle him to keep the deposit. Discuss who is correct.

18–2. QUESTION WITH SAMPLE ANSWER: Specific Performance.

In which of the following situations would specific performance be an appropriate remedy? Discuss fully.

(a) Thompson contracts to sell her house and lot to Cousteau. Then, on finding another buyer willing to pay a higher purchase price, she refuses to deed the property to Cousteau.

(b) Amy contracts to sing and dance in Fred's nightclub for one month, beginning May 1. She then refuses to perform.

(c) Hoffman contracts to purchase a rare coin owned by Erikson, who is breaking up his coin collection. At the last minute, Erikson decides to keep his coin collection intact and refuses to deliver the coin to Hoffman.

(d) ABC Corp. has three shareholders: Panozzo, who owns 48 percent of the stock; Chang, who owns another 48 percent; and Ryan, who owns 4 percent. Ryan contracts to sell her 4 percent to Chang. Later, Ryan refuses to transfer the shares to Chang.

• For a sample answer to Question 18–2, go to Appendix I at the end of this text.

18–3. Mitigation of Damages Lauren Barton, a single mother with three children, lived in Portland, Oregon. Cynthia VanHorn also lived in Oregon until she moved to New York City to open and operate an art gallery. VanHorn asked Barton to manage the gallery under a one-year contract for an annual salary of $72,000. To begin work, Barton relocated to New York. As part of the move, Barton transferred custody of her children to her husband, who lived in London, England. In accepting the job, Barton also forfeited her husband's alimony and child-support payments, including unpaid amounts of nearly $30,000. Before Barton started work, VanHorn repudiated the contract. Unable to find employment for more than an annual salary of $25,000, Barton moved to London to be near her children. Barton filed a suit in an Oregon state court against VanHorn, seeking damages for breach

of contract. Should the court hold, as VanHorn argued, that Barton did not take reasonable steps to mitigate her damages? Why or why not?

18–4. CASE PROBLEM WITH SAMPLE ANSWER: Damages.

Tyna Ek met Russell Peterson in Seattle, Washington. Peterson persuaded Ek to buy a boat that he had once owned, the O'Hana Kai, which was in Juneau, Alaska. Ek paid $43,000 for the boat, and in January 2000, the parties entered into a contract. In the contract, Peterson agreed to make the vessel seaworthy so that within one month it could be transported to Seattle, where he would pay its moorage costs. He would also renovate the boat at his own expense in return for a portion of the profit on its resale in 2001. At the time of the resale, Ek would recover her costs, after which she would reimburse Peterson for his expenses. Ek loaned Peterson her cell phone so that they could communicate while he prepared the vessel for the trip to Seattle. In March, Peterson, who was still in Alaska, borrowed $4,000 from Ek. Two months later, Ek began to receive unanticipated, unauthorized bills for vessel parts and moorage, the use of her phone, and charges on her credit card. She went to Juneau to take possession of the boat. Peterson moved it to Petersburg, Alaska, where he registered it under a false name, and then to Taku Harbor, where the police seized it. Ek filed a suit in an Alaska state court against Peterson, alleging breach of contract and seeking damages. If the court finds in Ek's favor, what should her damages include? Discuss. [Peterson v. Ek, 93 P.3d 458 (Alaska 2004)]

• To view a sample answer for **Problem 18–4**, go to this book's Web site at **www.cengage.com/blaw/clarkson**, select "Chapter 18," and click on "Case Problem with Sample Answer."

18–5. Waiver of Breach In May 1998, RDP Royal Palm Hotel, L.P., contracted with Clark Construction Group, Inc., to build the Royal Palms Crowne Plaza Resort in Miami Beach, Florida. The deadline for "substantial completion" was February 28, 2000, but RDP could ask for changes, and the date would be adjusted accordingly. During construction, Clark faced many setbacks, including a buried seawall, contaminated soil, the unforeseen deterioration of the existing hotel, and RDP's issue of hundreds of change orders. Clark requested extensions of the deadline, and RDP agreed, but the parties never specified a date. After the original deadline passed, RDP continued to issue change orders, Clark continued to perform, and RDP accepted the work. In March 2002, when the resort was substantially complete, RDP stopped paying Clark. Clark stopped working. RDP hired another contractor to finish the resort, which opened in May. RDP filed a suit in a federal district court against Clark, alleging, among other things, breach of contract for the two-year delay in the resort's completion. In whose favor should the court rule, and why? Discuss. [*RDP Royal Palm Hotel, L.P. v. Clark Construction Group, Inc., __ F.3d __ (11th Cir. 2006)*]

18–6. Remedies On July 7, 2000, Frances Morelli agreed to sell to Judith Bucklin a house at 126 Lakedell Drive in Warwick, Rhode Island, for $77,000. Bucklin made a deposit on the house. The closing at which the parties would exchange the deed for the price was scheduled for September 1. The agreement did not state that "time is of the essence," but it did provide, in "Paragraph 10," that "[i]f Seller is unable to [convey good, clear, insurable, and marketable title], Buyer shall have the option to: (a) accept such title as Seller is able to convey without abatement or reduction of the Purchase Price, or (b) cancel this Agreement and receive a return of all Deposits." An examination of the public records revealed that the house did not have marketable title. Wishing to be flexible, Bucklin offered Morelli time to resolve the problem, and the closing did not occur as scheduled. Morelli decided "the deal is over" and offered to return the deposit. Bucklin refused and, in mid-October, decided to exercise her option under Paragraph 10(a). She notified Morelli, who did not respond. Bucklin filed a suit in a Rhode Island state court against Morelli. In whose favor should the court rule? Should damages be awarded? If not, what is the appropriate remedy? Why? [*Bucklin v. Morelli*, 912 A.2d 931 (R.I. 2007)]

18–7. Quasi Contract Middleton Motors, Inc., a struggling Ford dealership in Madison, Wisconsin, sought managerial and financial assistance from Lindquist Ford, Inc., a successful Ford dealership in Bettendorf, Iowa. While the two dealerships negotiated the terms for the services and a cash infusion, Lindquist sent Craig Miller, its general manager, to assume control of Middleton. After about a year, the parties had not agreed on the terms, Lindquist had not invested any money, Middleton had not made a profit, and Miller was fired without being paid. Lindquist and Miller filed a suit in a federal district court against Middleton based on quasi contract, seeking to recover Miller's pay for his time. What are the requirements to recover on a theory of quasi-contract? Which of these requirements is most likely to be disputed in this case? Why? [*Lindquist Ford, Inc. v. Middleton Motors, Inc.*, 557 F.3d 469 (7th Cir. 2009)]

18–8. Liquidated Damages and Penalties Planned Pethood Plus, Inc., is a veterinarian-owned clinic. It borrowed $389,000 from KeyBank at an interest rate of 9.3 percent per year for ten years. The loan had a "prepayment penalty" clause that clearly stated that if the loan was repaid early, a specific formula would be used to assess a lump-sum payment to extinguish the obligation. The sooner the loan was paid off, the higher the prepayment penalty. After a year, the veterinarians decided to pay off the loan. KeyBank invoked a prepayment penalty of $40,525.92, which was equal to 10.7 percent of the balance due. The veterinarians sued, contending that the prepayment requirement was unenforceable because it was a penalty. The bank countered that the amount was not a penalty but liquidated damages and that the sum was reasonable. The trial court agreed with the bank, and the veterinarians appealed. Was the loan's prepayment charge reasonable, and should it have been enforced? Why or why not? [*Planned Pethood Plus, Inc. v. KeyCorp, Inc.*, 228 P.3d 262 (Colo.App. 2010)]

18–9. A QUESTION OF ETHICS: Remedies.

In 2004, Tamara Cohen, a real estate broker, began showing property in Manhattan to Steven Galistinos, who represented comedian Jerry Seinfeld and his wife, Jessica. According to Cohen, she told Galistinos that her commission would be 5 or 6 percent, and he agreed. According to Galistinos, there was no such agreement. Cohen spoke with Maximillan Sanchez, another broker, about a townhouse owned by Ray and Harriet Mayeri. According to Cohen, Sanchez said that the commission would be 6 percent, which they agreed to split equally. Sanchez later acknowledged that they had agreed to split the fee, but claimed that they had not discussed a specific amount. On a Friday in February 2005, Cohen showed the townhouse to Jessica. According to Cohen, she told Jessica that the commission would be 6 percent, with the Seinfelds paying half, and Jessica agreed. According to Jessica, there was no such conversation. Later that day, Galistinos asked Cohen to arrange for the Seinfelds to see the premises again. Cohen told Galistinos that her religious beliefs prevented her from showing property on Friday evenings or Saturdays before sundown. She suggested the following Monday or Tuesday, but Galistinos said that Jerry would not be available and asked her to contact Carolyn Liebling, Jerry's business manager. Cohen left Liebling a message. Over the weekend, the Seinfelds toured the building on their own and agreed to buy the property for $3.95 million. Despite repeated attempts, they were unable to contact Cohen. [*Cohen v. Seinfeld*, 15 Misc.3d 1118(A), 839 N.Y.S.2d 432 (Sup. 2007)]

(a) The contract between the Seinfelds and the Mayeris stated that the sellers would pay Sanchez's fee and the "buyers will pay buyer's real estate broker's fees." The Mayeris paid Sanchez $118,500, which is 3 percent of $3.95 million. The Seinfelds refused to pay Cohen. She filed a suit in a New York state court against them, asserting, among other things, breach of contract. Should the court order the Seinfelds to pay Cohen? If so, is she entitled to a full commission even though she was not available to show the townhouse when the Seinfelds wanted to see it? Explain.

(b) What obligation do parties involved in business deals owe to each other with respect to their religious beliefs? How might the situation in this case have been avoided?

18–10. VIDEO QUESTION: Remedies.

Go to this text's Web site at **www.cengage.com/ blaw/clarkson** and select "Chapter 18." Click on "Video Questions" and view the video titled *Midnight Run*. Then answer the following questions.

(a) In the video, Eddie (Joe Pantoliano) and Jack (Robert De Niro) negotiate a contract for Jack to find The Duke, a mob accountant who embezzled funds, and bring him back for trial. Assume that the contract is valid. If Jack breaches the contract by failing to bring in The Duke, what kinds of remedies, if any, can Eddie seek? Explain your answer.

(b) Would the equitable remedy of specific performance be available to either Jack or Eddie in the event of a breach? Why or why not?

(c) Now assume that the contract between Eddie and Jack is unenforceable. Nevertheless, Jack performs his side of the bargain (brings in The Duke). Can Jack recover from Eddie in this situation under the theory of quasi contract ? Why or why not?

LEGAL RESEARCH EXERCISES ON THE WEB

Go to this text's Web site at **www.cengage.com/blaw/clarkson**, select "Chapter 18," and click on "Practical Internet Exercises." There you will find the following Internet research exercises that you can perform to learn more about the topics covered in this chapter.

Practical Internet Exercise 18–1: **Legal Perspective**
Contract Damages and Contract Theory

Practical Internet Exercise 18–2: **Management Perspective**
The Duty to Mitigate

Generally, as you read in Chapter 5, a responsible business manager will evaluate a business transaction on the basis of three criteria—legality, profitability, and ethics. But what does acting ethically mean in the area of contracts? If you enter into a contract with an individual who fails to look after her or his own interests, is that your fault? Should you be doing something about it? If the contract happens to be to your advantage and to the other party's detriment, do you have a responsibility to correct the situation?

Suppose that your neighbor puts a "For sale" sign on her car and offers to sell it for $6,000. You learn that she is moving to another state and needs the extra cash to help finance the move. You know that she could easily get $10,000 for the car, and you consider purchasing it and then reselling it at a profit. But you also discover that your neighbor is completely unaware that she has priced the car significantly below its *Blue Book* value. Are you ethically obligated to tell her that she is essentially giving away $4,000 if she sells you the car for only $6,000?

This kind of situation, transplanted into the world of commercial transactions, raises an obvious question: At what point should the sophisticated businessperson cease looking after his own economic welfare and become "his brother's keeper," so to speak?

Freedom of Contract and Freedom from Contract

The answer to the question just raised is not simple. On the one hand, a common ethical assumption in our society is that individuals should be held responsible for the consequences of their own actions, including their contractual promises. This principle is expressed in the legal concept of freedom of contract. On the other hand, another common assumption in our society is that individuals should not harm one another by their actions. This is the basis of both tort law and criminal law.

In the area of contract law, ethical behavior often involves balancing these principles. In the above example, if you purchased the car and your neighbor later learned its true value and sued you for the difference, very likely no court of law would find that the contract should be rescinded. At times, however, courts will hold that the principle of freedom *of* contract should give way to the principle of freedom *from* contract, a doctrine based on the assumption that people should not be harmed by the actions of others. We look next at some examples of situations in which parties to contracts may be excused from performance under their contracts to prevent injustice.

Impossibility of Performance
The doctrine of impossibility of performance is based to some extent on the ethical question of whether one party should suffer

economic loss when it is impossible to perform a contract. The rule that one is "bound by his or her contracts" is not followed when performance becomes impossible. This doctrine, however, is applied only when the parties themselves did not consciously assume the risk of the events that rendered performance impossible. Furthermore, this doctrine rests on the assumption that the party claiming the defense of impossibility has acted ethically.

A contract is discharged, for example, if it calls for the delivery of a particular car and, through no fault of either party, this car is stolen and completely demolished in an accident. Yet the doctrine would not excuse performance if the party who agreed to sell the car caused its destruction by her or his negligence.

Before the late nineteenth century, courts were reluctant to discharge a contract even when performance was literally impossible. Just as society's ethics changes with the passage of time, however, the law also changes to reflect society's new perceptions of ethical behavior.[1] Today, courts are much more willing to discharge a contract when its performance has become literally impossible. Holding a party in breach of contract, when performance has become impossible through no fault of that party, no longer coincides with society's notions of fairness.

Unconscionability
The doctrine of unconscionability is a good example of how the law attempts to enforce ethical behavior. Under this doctrine, a contract may be deemed to be so unfair to one party as to be unenforceable—even though that party voluntarily agreed to the contract's terms. Unconscionable action, like unethical action, defies precise definition. Information about the particular facts and specific circumstances surrounding the contract is essential. For example, a court might find that a contract made with a marginally literate consumer was unfair and unenforceable but might uphold the same contract made with a major business firm.

Section 2–302 of the Uniform Commercial Code, which incorporates the common law concept of unconscionability, similarly does not define the concept with any precision. Rather, it leaves it to the courts to determine when a contract is so one sided and unfair to one party as to be unconscionable and thus unenforceable.

Usually, courts will do all that they can to save contracts rather than render them unenforceable. Only in extreme situations, as when a contract or clause is so one sided as to "shock the conscience" of the court,

---

1. A leading English case in which the court held that a defendant was discharged from the duty to perform due to impossibility of performance is *Taylor v. Caldwell,* 122 Eng.Rep. 309 (K.B. [King's Bench] 1863).

will a court hold a contract or contractual clause unconscionable.

Exculpatory Clauses   In some situations, courts have also refused to enforce exculpatory clauses on the ground that they are unconscionable or contrary to public policy. An *exculpatory clause* attempts to excuse a party from liability in the event of monetary or physical injury, no matter who is at fault. In some situations, such clauses are upheld. Generally, the law permits parties to assume, by express agreement, the risks inherent in certain activities. For example, a health club can require its members to sign a clause releasing the club from any liability for injuries the members might incur while using the club's equipment and facilities. Likewise, an exculpatory clause releasing a ski resort from liability for skiing accidents would likely be enforced.[2] In such situations, exculpatory clauses make it possible for a firm's owner to stay in business—by shifting some of the liability risks from the business to the customer.

Nonetheless, some jurisdictions take a dubious view of exculpatory clauses, particularly when the agreement is between parties with unequal bargaining power, such as a landlord and a tenant or an employer and an employee. Frequently, courts will hold that an exculpatory clause that attempts to exempt an employer from *all* liability for negligence toward its employees is against public policy and thus void.[3] The courts reason that disparity in bargaining power and economic necessity force the employee to accept the employer's terms. Also, if a plaintiff can prove that an exculpatory clause is ambiguous, the courts generally will not enforce the clause.[4]

Covenants Not to Compete

In today's complicated, technological business world, knowledge learned on the job, including trade secrets, has become a valuable commodity. To prevent this knowledge from falling into the hands of competitors, more and more employers are requiring their employees to sign covenants not to compete. The increasing number of lawsuits over noncompete clauses in employment contracts has caused many courts to reconsider the reasonableness of these covenants.

Generally, the courts have few problems with enforcing a covenant not to compete that is ancillary to the sale of a business as long as the covenant's terms are reasonable. After all, part of what is being sold is the business's reputation and goodwill. If, after the sale, the seller opens a competing business nearby, the value of the original business to the purchaser could be greatly diminished.

More difficult for the courts is determining whether covenants not to compete in the employment context should be enforced. Often, this determination involves balancing the interests of the employer against the interests of the employee. Employers have a legitimate interest in protecting their trade secrets, customer lists, and other knowledge key to their businesses' success from falling into the hands of competitors. At the same time, employees should not be unreasonably restricted in their ability to work in their chosen profession or trade. Inevitably, issues of fairness arise in deciding such issues.

Jurisdictional Differences in Enforcement   Jurisdictions vary in their approach to covenants not to compete. Many jurisdictions will enforce noncompete covenants in the employment context if (1) the limitations placed on an employee are reasonable as to time and geographic area, and (2) the limitations do not impose a greater restraint than necessary to protect the goodwill or other business interests of the employer.[5] In a number of jurisdictions, if a court finds that a restraint in a noncompete covenant is not reasonable in light of the circumstances, it will reform the unreasonable provision and then enforce it. For example, a court might rewrite an unreasonable restriction by reducing the time period during which a former employee cannot compete from three years to one year and then enforce the reformed agreement.[6]

Other jurisdictions are not so "employer friendly" and refuse to enforce unreasonable covenants. Under California law, covenants not to compete are illegal, as are a number of other types of agreements that have a similar effect.[7] Other western states also tend to regard noncompete covenants with suspicion. For example, the Washington Supreme Court has refused to reform

---

2. *Myers v. Lutsen Mountains Corp.,* 587 F.3d 891 (8th Cir. 2009).
3. See, for example, *City of Santa Barbara v. Superior Court,* 62 Cal. Rptr.3d 527, 161 P.3d 1095 (2007); and *Health Net of California, Inc. v. Department of Health Services,* 113 Cal.App.4th 224, 6 Cal. Rptr.3d 235 (2003).
4. See, for example, *Tatman v. Space Coast Kennel Club, Inc.,* 27 So.3d 108 (Fla.App. 5 Dist. 2010).
5. See *Drummond American, LLC v. Share Corp.,* ___ F.Supp.2d ___ (E.D.Tex., 2010); and TEKsystems, Inc. v. Bolton, ___ F.Supp.2d ___ (D.Md. 2010).
6. See, for example, *Estee Lauder Companies v. Batra,* 430 F.Supp.2d 158 (S.D.N.Y. 2006); *National Café Services, Ltd. v. Podaras,* 148 S.W.3d 194 (Tex.App.—Waco 2004); *Pathfinder Communications Corp. v. Macy,* 795 N.E.2d 1103 (Ind.App. 2003); and *Health Care Enterprises, Inc. v. Levy,* 715 So.2d 341 (Fla.App.4th 1998).
7. For a discussion of these agreements, including "no hire" agreements (which prevent employees who have left a firm from hiring other employees from the firm to work in a competing business), see *Thomas Weisel Partners, LLC v. BNP Paribas,* ___ F.Supp.2d ___ (N.D.Cal. 2010).

FOCUS ON ETHICS CONTINUES ➤

noncompete covenants that are unreasonable and lacking in consideration.[8]

Courts in Arizona and Texas have reached similar conclusions.[9]

Do Noncompete Covenants Stifle Innovation? One of the reasons that the courts usually look closely at covenants not to compete and evaluate them on a case-by-case basis is the strong public policy favoring competition in this country. Some scholars claim that covenants not to compete, regardless of how reasonable they are, may stifle competition and innovation.

Consider, for example, the argument put forth some years ago by Ronald Gilson, a Stanford University professor of law and business. He contended that California's prohibition on covenants not to compete helped to explain why technological innovation and economic growth skyrocketed in California's Silicon Valley in the late 1990s, while technological development along Massachusetts's Route 128 languished during the same time period. According to Gilson, the different legal rules regarding covenants not to compete in California and Massachusetts were a "critical" factor in explaining why one area saw so much innovation and transfer of technology knowledge and the other area did not.[10]

Oral Contracts and Promissory Estoppel

Oral contracts are made every day. Many—if not most—of them are carried out, and no problems arise. Occasionally, however, oral contracts are not performed, and one party decides to sue the other. Sometimes, to prevent injustice, the courts will enforce oral contracts under the theory of promissory estoppel. Ethical standards certainly underlie this doctrine, under which a person who has reasonably relied on the promise of another to his or her detriment can often obtain some measure of recovery. Essentially, promissory estoppel allows a variety of oral promises to be enforced even though they lack what is formally regarded as consideration.

An oral promise made by an insurance agent to a business owner, for example, may be binding if the owner relies on that promise to her or his detriment. Employees who rely to their detriment on an employer's promise may be able to recover under the doctrine of promissory estoppel. A contractor who, when bidding for a job, relies on a subcontractor's promise to perform certain construction work at a certain price may be able to recover, on the basis of promissory estoppel, any damages sustained because of the subcontractor's failure to perform. These are but a few of the many examples in which the courts, in the interests of fairness and justice, have estopped a promisor from denying that a contract existed.

Oral Contracts and the Statute of Frauds

The courts sometimes use the theory of promissory estoppel to remove a contract from the Statute of Frauds. As you learned in Chapter 15, the Statute of Frauds was originally enacted in England in 1677. The act was intended to prevent harm to innocent parties by requiring written evidence of agreements concerning important transactions.

Until the Statute of Frauds was passed, the English courts had enforced oral contracts on the strength of oral testimony by witnesses. Under these conditions, it was not too difficult to evade justice by procuring "convincing" witnesses to support the claim that a contract had been created and then breached. The possibility of fraud in such actions was enhanced by the fact that seventeenth-century English courts did not allow oral testimony to be given by the parties to a lawsuit—or by any parties with an interest in the litigation, such as husbands or wives. Defense against actions for breach of contract was thus limited to written evidence or the testimony of third parties.

Detrimental Reliance Under the Statute of Frauds, if a contract is oral when it is required to be in writing, it will not, as a rule, be enforced by the courts. An exception to this rule is made if a party has reasonably relied, to his or her detriment, on the oral contract. Enforcing an oral contract on the basis of a party's reliance arguably undercuts the essence of the Statute of Frauds. The reason that such an exception is made is to prevent the statute—which was created to prevent injustice—from being used to promote injustice. Nevertheless, this use of the doctrine is controversial—as is the Statute of Frauds itself.

Criticisms of the Statute of Frauds Since its inception more than three hundred years ago, the statute has been criticized by some because, although it was created to protect the innocent, it can also be used as a technical defense by a party breaching a genuine, mutually agreed-on oral contract—if the contract falls within the Statute of Frauds. For this reason, some legal scholars believe the act has caused more injustice than it has prevented. Thus, exceptions are sometimes

---

8. See, for example, *Labriola v. Pollard Group, Inc.*, 152 Wash.2d 828, 100 P.3d 791 (2004).

9. *Bandera Drilling Co., Inc. v. Sledge Drilling Corp.*, 293 S.W.3d 867 (Tex.App.—Eastland 2009); and *Varsity Gold, Inc. v. Porzio*, 202 Ariz. 355, 45 P.3d 352 (2002).

10. Ronald J. Gilson. "The Legal Infrastructure of High Technology Industrial Districts: Silicon Valley, Route 128, and Covenants Not to Compete." *New York University Law Review.* June 1999: 575–579.

made—such as under the doctrine of promissory estoppel—to prevent unfairness and inequity. Generally, the courts are slow to apply the statute if doing so will result in obvious injustice. In some instances, this has required a good deal of inventiveness on the part of the courts.

DISCUSSION QUESTIONS

1. Suppose that you contract to purchase steel at a fixed price per ton. Before the contract is performed, a lengthy steelworkers' strike causes the price of steel to triple from the price specified in the contract. If you demand that the supplier fulfill the contract, the supplier will go out of business. What are your ethical obligations in this situation? What are your legal rights?

2. Many countries have no Statute of Frauds, and even England, the country that created the original act, has repealed it. Should the United States do likewise? What are some of the costs and benefits to society of the Statute of Frauds?

3. In determining whether an exculpatory clause should be enforced, why does it matter whether the contract containing the clause involves essential services (such as transportation) or nonessential services (such as skiing or other leisure-time activities)?

4. Employers often include covenants not to compete in employment contracts to protect their trade secrets. What effect, if any, will the growth in e-commerce have on the reasonability of covenants not to compete?

UNIT FOUR

DOMESTIC AND INTERNATIONAL SALES AND LEASE CONTRACTS

CONTENTS

BUSINESS LAW

CLARKSON · MILLER · CROSS

CHAPTER 19

The Formation of Sales and Lease Contracts

When we turn to contracts for the sale and lease of goods, we move away from common law principles and into the area of statutory law. State statutory law governing sales and lease transactions is based on the Uniform Commercial Code (UCC), which, as mentioned in Chapter 1, has been adopted as law by all of the states.[1]

---

1. Louisiana has not adopted Articles 2 and 2A, however.

We open this chapter with a discussion of the UCC's Article 2 (on sales) and Article 2A (on leases) as a background to the topic of this chapter, which is the formation of contracts for the sale and lease of goods. The goal of the UCC is to simplify and to streamline commercial transactions, allowing parties to form sales and lease contracts without observing the same degree of formality used in forming other types of contracts.

Today, businesses often engage in sales and lease transactions on a global scale. Because international sales transactions are increasingly commonplace, we conclude the chapter with an examination of the United Nations Convention on Contracts for the International Sale of Goods (CISG), which governs international sales contracts. The CISG is a model uniform law that applies only when a nation has adopted it, just as the UCC applies only to the extent that it has been adopted by a state.

SECTION 1
THE UNIFORM COMMERCIAL CODE

In the early years of this nation, sales law varied from state to state, and this lack of uniformity complicated the formation of multistate sales contracts. The problems became especially troublesome in the late nineteenth century as multistate contracts became the norm. For this reason, numerous attempts were made to produce a uniform body of laws relating to commercial transactions. The National Conference of Commissioners on Uniform State Laws (NCCUSL) drafted two uniform ("model") acts that were widely adopted by the states: the Uniform Negotiable Instruments Law (1896) and the Uniform Sales Act (1906). Several other proposed uniform acts followed, although most were not as widely adopted.

In the 1940s, the NCCUSL recognized the need to integrate the half dozen or so uniform acts covering commercial transactions into a single, comprehensive body of statutory law. The NCCUSL developed the Uniform Commercial Code (UCC) to serve that purpose. First issued in 1949, the UCC facilitates commercial transactions by making the laws governing sales and lease contracts clearer, simpler, and more readily applicable to the numerous difficulties that can arise during such transactions.

Comprehensive Coverage of the UCC

The UCC is the single most comprehensive codification of the broad spectrum of laws involved in a total commercial transaction. The UCC views the entire "commercial transaction for the sale of and payment for goods" as a single legal occurrence having numerous facets.

You can gain an idea of the UCC's comprehensiveness by looking at the titles of the articles of the UCC in Appendix C. As you will note, Article 1, titled General Provisions, sets forth definitions and general principles applicable to commercial transactions, including an obligation to perform in "good faith" all contracts falling under the UCC [UCC 1–304]. Article 1 thus provides the basic groundwork for the remaining articles, each of which focuses on a particular aspect of commercial transactions.

A Single, Integrated Framework for Commercial Transactions

The UCC attempts to provide a consistent and integrated framework of rules to deal with all the phases *ordinarily arising* in a commercial sales transaction from start to finish. A simple example will illustrate how several articles of the UCC can apply to a single commercial transaction. Suppose that a consumer—a person who purchases goods primarily for personal or household use—buys a stainless steel bottom-freezer refrigerator from an appliance store. The consumer agrees to pay for the refrigerator on an installment plan.

Because the transaction involves a contract for the sale of goods, Article 2 will apply. If the consumer gives a check as the down payment on the purchase price, it will be negotiated and ultimately passed through one or more banks for collection. This process is the subject matter of Article 3, Negotiable Instruments, and Article 4, Bank Deposits and Collections. If the appliance store extends credit to the consumer through an installment plan, it may retain a *lien* (a legal right or interest) on the refrigerator (the collateral, which is the property pledged as security against a debt). If so, then Article 9, Secured Transactions, will be applicable (*secured transactions* will be discussed in detail in Chapter 29).

Suppose, in addition, that the appliance company must obtain the refrigerator from the manufacturer's warehouse before shipping it by common carrier to the consumer. The storage and shipment of goods are the subject matter of Article 7, Documents of Title. To pay the manufacturer, which is located in another state, for the refrigerator supplied, the appliance company may use a letter of credit—the subject matter of Article 5.

Periodic Revisions of the UCC

Various articles and sections of the UCC are periodically revised or supplemented to clarify certain rules or to establish new rules when changes in business customs have rendered the existing UCC provisions inapplicable. For example, because of the increasing importance of leases of goods in the commercial context, Article 2A, governing leases, was added to the UCC. To clarify the rights of parties to commercial fund transfers, particularly electronic fund transfers, Article 4A was issued.

Articles 3 and 4, covering negotiable instruments and banking, underwent a significant revision in the 1990s, as did Articles 5, 8, and 9. Because of other changes in business practices and in the law, the NCCUSL has recommended the repeal of Article 6 (on bulk transfers) and has offered a revised Article 6 to those states that prefer not to repeal it. Article 1 was revised in 2001, and the NCCUSL approved amendments to Articles 3 and 4 in 2002.

SECTION 2
THE SCOPE OF ARTICLE 2— THE SALE OF GOODS

Article 2 of the UCC (as adopted by state statutes) governs **sales contracts,** or contracts for the sale of goods. To facilitate commercial transactions, Article 2 modifies some of the common law contract requirements that were discussed in the previous chapters. To the extent that it has not been modified by the UCC, however, the common law of contracts also applies to sales contracts. For example, the common law requirements for a valid contract—agreement (offer and acceptance), consideration, capacity, and legality—that were summarized in Chapter 10 and discussed at length in Chapters 11 through 13 are also applicable to sales contracts. Thus, you should reexamine these common law principles when studying the law of sales.

In general, the rule is that whenever a conflict arises between a common law contract rule and the state statutory law based on the UCC, the UCC controls. In other words, when a UCC provision addresses a certain issue, the UCC rule governs; when the UCC is silent, the common law governs. The relationship between general contract law and the law governing sales of goods is illustrated in Exhibit 19–1 on the following page.

In regard to Article 2, keep two points in mind. First, Article 2 deals with the sale of *goods;* it does not deal with real property (real estate), services, or intangible property such as stocks and bonds. Thus, if the subject matter of a dispute is goods, the UCC governs. If it is real estate or services, the common law applies. Second, in some situations, the rules may vary quite a bit, depending on whether the buyer or the seller is a *merchant.* We look now at how the UCC defines a *sale, goods,* and *merchant status.*

EXHIBIT 19–1 • The Law Governing Contracts
This exhibit graphically illustrates the relationship between general contract law and statutory law (UCC Articles 2 and 2A) governing contracts for the sale and lease of goods. Sales contracts are not governed exclusively by Article 2 of the UCC but are also governed by general contract law whenever it is relevant and has not been modified by the UCC.

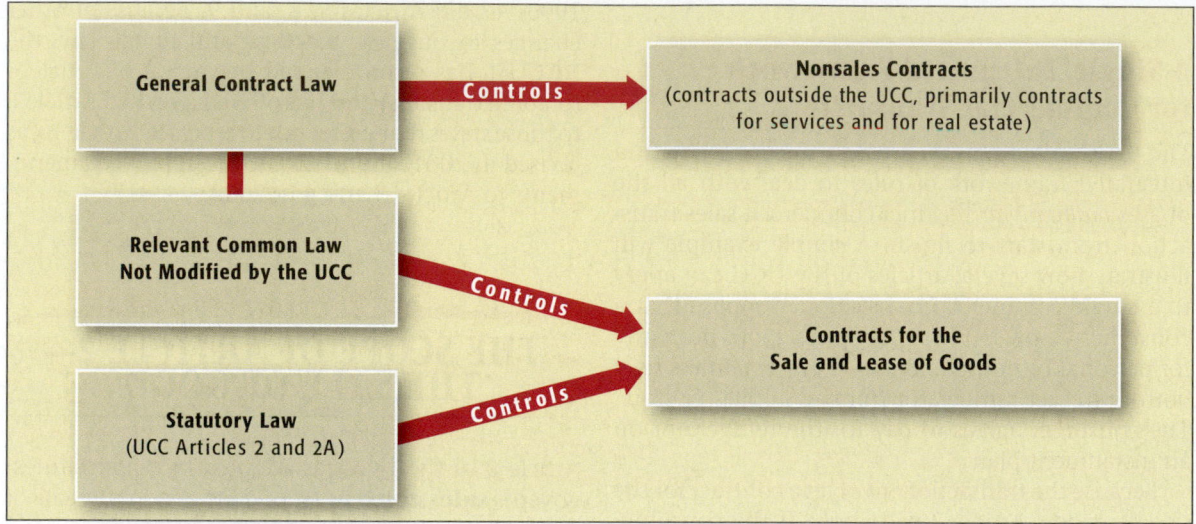

What Is a Sale?

The UCC defines a **sale** as "the passing of title [evidence of ownership rights] from the seller to the buyer for a price" [UCC 2–106(1)]. The price may be payable in cash or in other goods or services.

What Are Goods?

To be characterized as a *good,* an item of property must be *tangible,* and it must be *movable.* **Tangible property** has physical existence—it can be touched or seen. Intangible property—such as corporate stocks and bonds, patents and copyrights, and ordinary contract rights—has only conceptual existence and thus does not come under Article 2. A *movable* item can be carried from place to place. Hence, real estate is excluded from Article 2.

Two areas in particular give rise to disputes over whether the object of a contract is goods and thus whether Article 2 is applicable. One problem concerns *goods associated with real estate,* such as crops or timber, and the other concerns contracts involving a combination of *goods and services.*

GOODS ASSOCIATED WITH REAL ESTATE Goods associated with real estate often fall within the scope of Article 2. Section 2–107 provides the following rules:

1. A contract for the sale of minerals or the like (including oil and gas) or a structure (such as

a building) is a contract for the sale of goods if *severance, or separation, is to be made by the seller.* If the *buyer* is to sever (separate) the minerals or structures from the land, the contract is considered to be a sale of real estate governed by the principles of real property law, not the UCC.

2. A sale of growing crops (such as potatoes, carrots, and wheat) or timber to be cut is a contract for the sale of goods *regardless of who severs them.*

3. Other "things attached" to real property but capable of severance (separation) without material harm to the land are considered to be goods *regardless of who severs them.*[2] Examples of "things attached" that are severable without harm to realty include a window air conditioner in a house and tables and stools in a restaurant. Thus, the removal and sale of these items would be considered a sale of goods. The test is whether removal will cause substantial harm to the real property to which the item is attached.

CASE IN POINT Homeowners in Colorado installed underground radiant heating systems to warm indoor flooring or melt snow and ice under driveways and sidewalks. When the systems began

---

2. The UCC avoids the term *fixtures* here because of the numerous definitions of the word. In general, a fixture is anything so firmly or permanently attached to land or to a building as to become a part of it. Once personal property becomes a fixture, real estate law governs. See Chapter 50.

to leak as a result of the hardening of a hose called Entran II, the homeowners filed a lawsuit against the maker of the systems and against Goodyear Tire and Rubber Company, the maker of the hose. The homeowners asserted various contract claims under Colorado's version of the UCC. Goodyear argued that the UCC did not apply because Entran II was used in the construction of underground systems that were covered by flooring or cement, and thus the hose was not a "good." The court, however, ruled that because the hose was an existing and movable good at the time the contract was made, it was a "good" under the UCC. The UCC applied to the contract even though Entran II was later incorporated into real property (under flooring).[3]

GOODS AND SERVICES COMBINED In cases involving contracts in which goods and services are combined, courts have reached different results. For example, is providing blood to a patient during an operation a "sale of goods" or the "performance of a medical service"? Some courts say it is a good; others say it is a service. Because the UCC does not provide the answers to such questions, the courts generally use the **predominant-factor test** to determine whether a contract is primarily for the sale of goods

or for the sale of services.[4] This determination is important because if a court decides that a mixed contract is primarily a goods contract, *any* dispute, even a dispute over the services portion, will be decided under the UCC. Likewise, any disagreement over a predominantly services contract will not be decided using the UCC, even if the dispute involves the goods portion of the contract.

For example, an accounting firm contracts to purchase customized software from Micro Systems. The contract states that half of the purchase price is for Micro's professional services and the other half is for the goods (the software). If a court determines that the contract is predominantly for the software, rather than the services to customize the software, the court will hold that the transaction falls under Article 2. Conversely, if the court finds that the services are predominant, it will hold that the transaction is not governed by the UCC.

If an entire business—including a truck and its equipment—is sold, but the contract does not specify what portion of the sale price relates to the goods, does Article 2 of the UCC still apply to the transaction? That was the main issue in the following case.

---

3. *Loughridge v. Goodyear Tire and Rubber Co.*, 192 F.Supp.2d 1175 (D.Colo. 2002).

4. UCC 2–314(1) does stipulate that serving food or drinks is a "sale of goods" for purposes of the implied warranty of merchantability, as will be discussed in Chapter 22. The UCC also specifies that selling unborn animals or rare coins qualifies as a "sale of goods."

CASE 19.1
Jannusch v. Naffziger

Appellate Court of Illinois, Fourth District, 379 Ill.App.3d 381, 883 N.E.2d 711 (2008).

BACKGROUND AND FACTS • Gene and Martha Jannusch ran Festival Foods, which provided concessions at events around Illinois and Indiana. They owned a truck, a trailer, freezers, roasters, chairs, tables, a fountain service, signs, and lighting. Lindsey and Louann Naffziger were interested in buying the concessions business. They met with the Jannusches and orally agreed to a price of $150,000. The Naffzigers paid $10,000 down with the balance to come from a bank loan. They took possession of the equipment and began to use it immediately in Festival Foods operations at various events, even though Gene Jannusch kept the titles to the truck and trailer in his name. Gene Jannusch was paid to attend two events with the Naffzigers to provide advice about running the operation. After six events, and at the end of the outdoor season, the Naffzigers returned the truck and all the equipment to its storage location and wanted out of the deal. They said the business did not generate as much income as they expected. The Jannusches sued the Naffzigers for the balance due on the purchase price. The trial court held that the Uniform Commercial Code (UCC) governed the case but that there was not enough evidence to show that the parties had a sufficient meeting of the minds to form a contract. The Jannusches appealed.

CASE CONTINUES ➡

CASE 19.1 CONTINUED ➡

IN THE LANGUAGE OF THE COURT
Charles J. *REYNARD,* Judge Presiding.
* * * *

Defendants [the Naffzigers] argue the UCC should not apply because this case involves the sale of a business rather than just the sale of goods. The "predominant purpose" test is used to determine whether a contract for both the sale of goods and the rendition of services falls within the scope of Article 2 of the UCC.

* * * *

Defendants argue that nothing was said in the contract about allocating a price for good will, a covenant not to compete, allocating a price for the equipment, how to release liens, what would happen if there was no loan approval, and other issues. Defendants argue these are essential terms for the sale of a business and the Internal Revenue Service requires that parties allocate the sales price. "None of these items were even discussed much less agreed to. There is not an enforceable agreement when there are so many essential terms missing. A contract may be enforced even though some contract terms may be missing or left to be agreed upon, but if the essential terms are so uncertain that there is no basis for deciding whether the agreement has been kept or broken, there is no contract."

The essential terms were agreed upon in this case. The purchase price was $150,000, and the items to be transferred were specified. No essential terms remained to be agreed upon; the only action remaining was the performance of the contract. Defendants took possession of the items to be transferred and used them as their own. *"Rejection of goods must be within a reasonable time after their delivery or tender. It is ineffective unless the buyer seasonably [within a reasonable amount of time] notifies the seller"* [UCC 2–602(1)]. Defendants paid $10,000 of the purchase price. The fact that defendants were disappointed in the income from the events they operated is not inconsistent with the existence of a contract. [Emphasis added.]

The trial court noted that "the parties have very different views about what transpired in the course of the contract-formation discussions." It is not necessary that the parties share a subjective understanding as to the terms of the contract; the parties' conduct may indicate an agreement to the terms. The conduct in this case is clear. Parties discussing the sale of goods do not transfer those goods and allow them to be retained for a substantial period before reaching agreement. Defendants replaced equipment, reported income, paid taxes, and paid Gene for his time and expenses, all of which is inconsistent with the idea that defendants were only "pursuing buying the business." An agreement to make an agreement is not an agreement, but there was clearly more than that here.

* * * The parties' agreement could have been fleshed out with additional terms, but the essential terms were agreed upon. [Naffziger] admitted there was an agreement to purchase Festival Foods for $150,000 but could not recall specifically making an oral agreement on any particular date. "An agreement sufficient to constitute a contract for sale may be found even though the moment of its making is undetermined" [UCC 2–204(2)]. *Returning the goods at the end of the season was not a rejection of plaintiffs' offer to sell; it was a breach of contract.* [Emphasis added.]

We conclude there was an agreement to sell Festival Foods for the price of $150,000 and that defendants breached that agreement. We reverse the circuit court's judgment and remand for the entry of an order consistent with this opinion.

DECISION AND REMEDY • *The appeals court reversed the decision of the trial court, finding that a contract had been formed under the UCC and that the Naffzigers had breached it. The primary value of the contract was in the goods, not the value of the business; the parties agreed on a price; and the Naffzigers took possession of the business. They had no right to return it.*

WHAT IF THE FACTS WERE DIFFERENT? • *Suppose that the contract had stated that the truck and other equipment were worth $50,000 and the goodwill value of the business was worth $100,000. Would that have changed the outcome of this case? Why or why not?*

MANAGERIAL IMPLICATIONS • *This case illustrates how important it is to anticipate the factors that courts consider in determining whether Article 2 of the UCC applies. The facts of each situation are carefully considered. For example, even though the purchase of software may appear to be a purchase of goods, if the contract also provides for installing and modifying the software, a court might construe the contract as predominantly for services. For the managers involved in purchasing or selling the software, this would mean that the UCC does not apply, which may be a very important consideration in some transactions.*

Who Is a Merchant?

Article 2 governs the sale of goods in general. It applies to sales transactions between all buyers and sellers. In a limited number of instances, though, the UCC presumes that special business standards ought to be imposed because of merchants' relatively high degree of commercial expertise.[5] Such standards do not apply to the casual or inexperienced seller or buyer (consumer). Section 2–104 sets forth three ways in which merchant status can arise:

1. A merchant is a person who *deals in goods of the kind* involved in the sales contract. Thus, a retailer, a wholesaler, or a manufacturer is a merchant of the goods sold in his or her business. A merchant for one type of goods is not necessarily a merchant for another type. For example, a sporting goods retailer is a merchant when selling tennis rackets but not when selling a used computer.

2. A merchant is a person who, by occupation, holds himself or herself out as having knowledge and skill unique to the practices or goods involved in the transaction. This broad definition may include banks or universities as merchants.

3. A person who *employs a merchant as a broker, agent, or other intermediary* has the status of merchant in that transaction. Hence, if an art collector hires a broker to purchase or sell art for her, the collector is considered a merchant in the transaction.

In summary, a person is a **merchant** when she or he, acting in a mercantile capacity, possesses or uses an expertise specifically related to the goods being sold. This basic distinction is not always clearcut. For example, state courts appear to be split on whether farmers should be considered merchants.[6] In some states, courts have held that the drafters of the UCC did not intend to include farmers as merchants. In other states, farmers are considered merchants because they sell products or livestock on a regular basis.

CASE IN POINT Steve Hammer and Ron Howe placed 150 breeding heifers with Kevin Thompson for grazing. Thompson resold the cattle to Roger Morris, who then resold them to other parties. Hammer and Howe filed a lawsuit against Morris and others alleging conversion (see Chapter 6 on page 127). In his defense, Morris argued that he bought the cattle from Thompson, whom he believed was a cattle "order buyer," meaning a middleman who purchases cattle specifically to resell them to others. A Kansas state court decided that because Thompson had previously acted as a cattle order buyer, he was a merchant, even though there had been a lapse of time between his order-buying transactions. Therefore, Thompson was held to the higher standard of conduct that is required of merchants under the UCC.[7]

SECTION 3

THE SCOPE OF ARTICLE 2A—LEASES

In the past few decades, leases of personal property (goods) have become increasingly common. Consumers and business firms lease automobiles, industrial equipment, items for use in the home (such as floor polishers), and many other types of goods. Article 2A of the UCC was created to fill the need for uniform guidelines in this area. Article 2A covers any transaction that creates a lease of goods or a sublease of goods [UCC 2A–102, 2A–103(1)(k)]. Article 2A is essentially a repetition of Article 2, except that it applies to leases of goods rather than sales of goods and thus varies to reflect differences between sales and lease transactions. (Note that Article 2A is not concerned with leases of real property, such as land or buildings. The laws governing these types of transactions will be examined in Chapter 50.)

Definition of a Lease Agreement

Article 2A defines a **lease agreement** as a lessor and lessee's bargain with respect to the lease of goods, as found in their language and as implied by other circumstances [UCC 2A–103(1)(k)]. A **lessor** is one who transfers the right to the possession and use of goods under a lease [UCC 2A–103(1)(p)]. A **lessee** is one who acquires the right to the possession and use of goods under a lease [UCC 2A–103(1)(o)]. In other words, the lessee is the party who is leasing the goods from the lessor. Article 2A applies to all types of leases of goods. Special rules apply to certain types of leases, however, including consumer leases and finance leases.

---

5. The provisions that apply only to merchants deal principally with the Statute of Frauds, firm offers, confirmatory memoranda, warranties, and contract modification. These special rules reflect expedient business practices commonly known to merchants in the commercial setting. They will be discussed later in this chapter.

6. See one court's discussion of this issue in *R. F. Cunningham & Co. v. Driscoll,* 7 Misc.3d 234, 790 N.Y.S.2d 368 (2005).

7. *Hammer v. Thompson,* 35 Kan.App.2d 165, 129 P.3d 609 (2006).

Consumer Leases

A *consumer lease* involves three elements: (1) a lessor who regularly engages in the business of leasing or selling; (2) a lessee (except an organization) who leases the goods "primarily for a personal, family, or household purpose"; and (3) total lease payments that are less than $25,000 [UCC 2A–103(1)(e)]. In the interest of providing special protection for consumers, certain provisions of Article 2A apply only to consumer leases. For example, one provision states that a consumer may recover attorneys' fees if a court determines that a term in a consumer lease contract is unconscionable [UCC 2A–108(4)(a)].

Finance Leases

A *finance lease* involves a lessor, a lessee, and a supplier. The lessor buys or leases goods from the supplier and leases or subleases them to the lessee [UCC 2A–103(1)(g)]. Typically, in a finance lease, the lessor is simply financing the transaction. For example, Marlin Corporation wants to lease a crane for use in its construction business. Marlin's bank agrees to purchase the equipment from Jennco, Inc., and lease the equipment to Marlin. In this situation, the bank is the lessor-financer, Marlin is the lessee, and Jennco is the supplier.

Article 2A, unlike ordinary contract law, makes the lessee's obligations under a finance lease irrevocable and independent from the financer's obligations [UCC 2A–407]. In other words, the lessee must perform and continue to make lease payments even if the leased equipment turns out to be defective. The lessee must look almost entirely to the supplier for any recovery.

CASE IN POINT American Transit Insurance Company (ATIC) arranged to lease telephone equipment through a finance lease. Siemens Credit Corporation obtained the equipment from the manufacturer and then leased the equipment to ATIC. When the equipment turned out to be defective, ATIC stopped making the lease payments. Siemens then sued ATIC, which argued that requiring it to make payments on defective equipment was unconscionable. According to the court, though, the lease clearly qualified as a finance lease under Article 2A, and thus ATIC was obligated to make all payments due under the lease regardless of the performance of the leased equipment. The court said that ATIC's claims could be brought only against the manufacturer, not against the lessor (Siemens).[8]

---

8. *Siemens Credit Corp. v. American Transit Insurance Co.*, 2001 WL 40775 (S.D.N.Y. 2001).

SECTION 4

THE FORMATION OF SALES AND LEASE CONTRACTS

In regard to the formation of sales and lease contracts, the UCC modifies the common law in several ways. We look here at how Articles 2 and 2A of the UCC modify common law contract rules. Remember, though, that parties to sales contracts are basically free to establish whatever terms they wish. The UCC comes into play when the parties either fail to provide certain terms in their contract or wish to change the effect of the UCC's terms in the contract's application. The UCC makes this very clear time and again by its use of such phrases as "unless the parties otherwise agree" and "absent a contrary agreement by the parties."

Offer

In general contract law, the moment a definite offer is met by an unqualified acceptance, a binding contract is formed. In commercial sales transactions, the verbal exchanges, correspondence, and actions of the parties may not reveal exactly when a binding contractual obligation arises. The UCC states that an agreement sufficient to constitute a contract can exist even if the moment of its making is undetermined [UCC 2–204(2), 2A–204(2)].

OPEN TERMS According to general contract law, an offer must be definite enough for the parties (and the courts) to ascertain its essential terms when it is accepted. In contrast, the UCC states that a sales or lease contract will not fail for indefiniteness even if one or more terms are left open as long as (1) the parties intended to make a contract and (2) there is a reasonably certain basis for the court to grant an appropriate remedy [UCC 2–204(3), 2A–204(3)].

Suppose that Mike agrees to lease a highly specialized computer work station from CompuQuik. Mike and one of CompuQuik's sales representatives sign a lease agreement that leaves some of the details blank, to be "worked out" the following week, when the leasing manager will be back from vacation. In the meantime, CompuQuik obtains the necessary equipment from one of its suppliers and spends several days modifying the equipment to suit Mike's needs. When the leasing manager returns, she calls Mike and tells him that his work station is ready. Mike says he is no longer interested in the work station, as he has arranged to lease the same equipment for a lower price from another firm. CompuQuik sues Mike to recover its costs in obtaining and modifying the equipment, and one of the issues before the court is whether the parties had an enforceable contract. The court will likely hold that they did, based on their intent and conduct, despite the blanks in their written agreement.

Relative to the common law of contracts, the UCC has radically lessened the requirement of definiteness of terms. Keep in mind, though, that if too many terms are left open, a court may find that the parties did not intend to form a contract.

Open Price Term. If the parties have not agreed on a price, the court will determine a "reasonable price at the time for delivery" [UCC 2–305(1)]. If either the buyer or the seller is to determine the price, the price is to be fixed in good faith [UCC 2–305(2)]. Under the UCC, *good faith* means honesty in fact and the observance of reasonable commercial standards of fair dealing in the trade [UCC 2–103(1)(b)]. The concepts of *good faith* and *commercial reasonableness* permeate the UCC. (The obligations of good faith and commercial reasonableness in sales and lease contracts will be examined in Chapter 22.) For a discussion of how sellers might charge slightly higher prices for goods in the interest of promoting "fair trade," see this chapter's *Shifting Legal Priorities for Business* feature on the next page.

Sometimes, the price fails to be fixed through the fault of one of the parties. In that situation, the other party can treat the contract as canceled or fix a reasonable price. For example, Perez and Merrick enter into a contract for the sale of goods and agree that Perez will fix the price. Perez refuses to specify the price. Merrick can either treat the contract as canceled or set a reasonable price [UCC 2–305(3)].

Open Payment Term. When the parties do not specify payment terms, payment is due at the time and place at which the buyer is to receive the goods [UCC 2–310(a)]. The buyer can tender payment using any commercially normal or acceptable means, such as a check or credit card. If the seller demands payment in cash, however, the buyer must be given a reasonable time to obtain it [UCC 2–511(2)]. This is especially important when the contract states a definite and final time for performance.

Open Delivery Term. When no delivery terms are specified, the buyer normally takes delivery at the seller's place of business [UCC 2–308(a)]. If the seller has no place of business, the seller's residence

is used. When goods are located in some other place and both parties know it, delivery is made there. If the time for shipment or delivery is not clearly specified in the sales contract, then the court will infer a "reasonable" time for performance [UCC 2–309(1)].

Duration of an Ongoing Contract. A single contract might specify successive performances but not indicate how long the parties are required to deal with each other. In this situation, either party may terminate the ongoing contractual relationship. Nevertheless, principles of good faith and sound commercial practice call for reasonable notification before termination so as to give the other party sufficient time to seek a substitute arrangement [UCC 2–309(2), (3)].

Options and Cooperation with Regard to Performance. When specific shipping arrangements have not been made but the contract contemplates shipment of the goods, the *seller* has the right to make these arrangements in good faith, using commercial reasonableness in the situation [UCC 2–311].

When terms relating to an assortment of goods are omitted from a sales contract, the buyer can specify the assortment. For example, Harley and Babcock contract for the sale of one thousand pens. The pens come in a variety of colors, but the contract is silent as to which colors are ordered. Babcock, the buyer, has the right to take whatever colors he wishes. Babcock, however, must exercise good faith and commercial reasonableness in making the selection [UCC 2–311].

Open Quantity Term. Normally, if the parties do not specify a quantity, a court will have no basis for determining a remedy. This is because there is almost no way to determine objectively what is a reasonable quantity of goods for someone to purchase (whereas a court can objectively determine a reasonable price for particular goods by looking at the market). The UCC recognizes two exceptions in requirements and output contracts [UCC 2–306(1)].

In a **requirements contract,** the buyer agrees to purchase and the seller agrees to sell all or up to a stated amount of what the buyer *needs* or *requires*. There is implicit consideration in a requirements contract because the buyer gives up the right to buy from any other seller, and this forfeited right creates a legal detriment. Requirements contracts are common in the business world and normally are enforceable. If, however, the buyer promises to purchase only if he or she *wishes* to do so, or if the buyer

Sales contracts, whether domestic or international, involve the transfer of a quantity of goods at a price. But sales contracts can do more than that. Thanks to the Fair Trade movement, they can also benefit poor farmers in developing countries and promote environmentally sustainable farming practices.

What Is the Fair Trade Movement?

The origins of the Fair Trade movement can be traced to an effort in Europe almost fifty years ago to provide relief to refugees and other poor communities by selling their handicrafts. But the movement only began to expand in the 1980s when the "Fair Trade" label was developed in the Netherlands to identify coffee produced under certain conditions. Today, the Fairtrade Labeling Organizations International determines minimum "fair" prices that ensure that small producers can earn a living wage. Products obtained at these prices can bear the Fair Trade label. Retailers can still charge any price they wish, but because they pay more for products with the Fair Trade label, they usually pass these costs on to consumers in the form of slightly higher prices.

TransFair U.S.A. founder Paul Rice describes the Fair Trade movement this way: "Fair Trade creates the opportunity for businesses to increase their profits through socially responsible business practices, for consumers to vote with every purchase for a more equitable world, and for farmers to view themselves not as an anonymous cog in the world market, but as a valuable contributor to a global society."

The Principles of Fair Trade

Under the Fair Trade system, low-income farmers and artisans in developing countries form alliances with importers and marketers in Western Europe and North America. Participants must agree to certain basic principles:

- Producers must receive a stable minimum price for their products.

- Forced or child labor will not be used.
- Production methods must be environmentally friendly.

When these standards are met, international certification bodies allow the products to carry a Fair Trade logo, such as the well-known label borne by some coffee imported into the United States.

Emphasis on Environmental Sustainability

As mentioned, only producers who agree to use environmentally sustainable farming methods can sell their products through the Fair Trade system. The farmers must agree to preserve valuable ecosystems for future generations. The use of harmful chemicals and genetically modified organisms is strictly prohibited.

According to Paulette Stenzel, professor of international business law at the Eli Broad College of Business at Michigan State University, "Fair Trade is simply one way of carrying out business, which takes into account all aspects of sustainability, especially of the producers." Stenzel argues that businesses must take responsibility for environmental and socioeconomic outcomes that are directly related to their activities: "Today, many companies realize that sustainability efforts must be based on the triple bottom line of economy, social equity, and environment."

MANAGERIAL IMPLICATIONS

Today, Fair Trade certification is available in the United States for coffee, cocoa and chocolate, tea and herbs, fresh fruit, sugar, rice, and vanilla. As more consumers become aware of the movement, sales of Fair Trade products are likely to grow. Collaboration between Fair Trade producers and retail outlets in the United States is a key aspect of the movement. Marketing managers at large retail companies may find that their bottom lines will improve if they seek products bearing the Fair Trade label for their customers.

---

reserves the right to buy the goods from someone other than the seller, the promise is illusory (without consideration) and unenforceable by either party.[9]

In an **output contract,** the seller agrees to sell and the buyer agrees to buy all or up to a stated amount of what the seller *produces*. Again, because

the seller essentially forfeits the right to sell goods to another buyer, there is implicit consideration in an output contract.

The UCC imposes a *good faith limitation* on requirements and output contracts. The quantity under such contracts is the amount of requirements or the amount of output that occurs during a *normal* production period. The actual quantity purchased or sold cannot be unreasonably disproportionate to

---

9. See, for example, *In re Anchor Glass Container Corp.,* 345 Bankr. 765 (M.D.Fla. 2006).

normal or comparable prior requirements or output [UCC 2–306].

MERCHANT'S FIRM OFFER Under regular contract principles, an offer can be revoked at any time before acceptance. The major common law exception is an *option contract* (discussed in Chapter 11 on page 230), in which the offeree pays consideration for the offeror's irrevocable promise to keep the offer open for a stated period. The UCC creates a second exception, which applies only to firm offers for the sale or lease of goods made by a merchant (regardless of whether or not the offeree is a merchant).

When a Merchant's Firm Offer Arises. A **firm offer** arises when a merchant-offeror gives *assurances in a signed writing* that the offer will remain open. The merchant's firm offer is irrevocable without the necessity of consideration[10] for the stated period or, if no definite period is stated, a reasonable period (neither to exceed three months) [UCC 2–205, 2A–205].

To illustrate: Osaka, a used-car dealer, writes a letter to Bennett on January 1, stating, "I have a used 2010 Suzuki on the lot that I'll sell you for $20,500 any time between now and January 31." By January 18, Osaka has heard nothing from Bennett, so he sells the Suzuki to another person. On January 23, Bennett tenders $20,500 to Osaka and asks for the car. When Osaka tells him the car has already been sold, Bennett claims that Osaka has breached a valid contract. Bennett is right. Osaka is a merchant of used cars and assured Bennett in a signed writing that he would keep his offer open until the end of January. Thus, Bennett's acceptance on January 23 created a contract, which Osaka breached.

The Offer Must Be in Writing and Signed by the Offeror. It is necessary that the offer be both *written* and *signed* by the offeror.[11] When a firm offer is contained in a form contract prepared by the offeree, the offeror must also sign a separate assurance of the firm offer. This requirement ensures that the offeror will be made aware of the offer. For instance, an offeree might respond to an initial offer by sending its own form contract containing a clause stating that the offer will remain open for three months. If the firm offer is buried amid copious language in one of the pages of the offeree's form contract, the offeror may inadvertently sign the contract without realizing that it contains a firm offer. This would defeat the purpose of the rule—which is to give effect to a merchant's deliberate intent to be bound to a firm offer.

Acceptance

Under the UCC, acceptance of an offer to buy, sell, or lease goods generally may be made in any reasonable manner and by any reasonable means. We examine the UCC's provisions governing acceptance in detail in the subsections that follow.

METHODS OF ACCEPTANCE The general common law rule is that an offeror can specify, or authorize, a particular means of acceptance, making that means the only one effective for contract formation. Under the common law, if the offer is accepted by an improper means of communication, normally it is considered a counteroffer rather than an acceptance. (For a review of the requirements relating to the mode and timeliness of acceptance, see Chapter 11 on pages 232 and 233.) Only when the offeror does not specify an authorized means of acceptance will courts applying general contract law consider whether the acceptance was by reasonable means. The UCC, in contrast, gives effect to all acceptances communicated by reasonable means.

Any Reasonable Means. When the offeror does not specify a means of acceptance, the UCC provides that acceptance can be made by any means of communication that is reasonable under the circumstances [UCC 2–206(1), 2A–206(1)]. This is also the basic rule under the common law of contracts (see Chapter 11).

For example, Anodyne Corporation writes a letter to Bethlehem Industries offering to lease $5,000 worth of goods. The offer states that Anodyne will keep the offer open for only ten days from the date of the letter. Before the ten days have lapsed, Bethlehem sends Anodyne an acceptance by fax. The fax is misdirected by someone at Anodyne's offices and does not reach the right person at Anodyne until after the ten-day deadline has passed. Has a valid contract been formed? The answer is probably yes, because acceptance by fax appears to be a commercially reasonable mode of acceptance under the circumstances. Acceptance would be effective on Bethlehem's transmission of the fax, which occurred before the offer lapsed.

---

10. If the offeree pays consideration, then an option contract (not a merchant's firm offer) is formed.
11. *Signed* includes any symbol executed or adopted by a party with a present intention to authenticate a writing [UCC 1–201(37)]. A complete signature is not required.

Promise to Ship or Prompt Shipment. The UCC permits an offeree to accept an offer to buy goods "either by a prompt *promise* to ship or by the prompt or current shipment of conforming or non-conforming goods" [UCC 2–206(1)(b)]. *Conforming* goods are goods that accord with the contract's terms; *nonconforming* goods do not.

The seller's prompt shipment of *nonconforming goods* constitutes both an *acceptance* (a contract) and a *breach* of that contract. This rule does not apply if the seller **seasonably** (within a reasonable amount of time) notifies the buyer that the nonconforming shipment is offered only as an *accommodation,* or as a favor. The notice of accommodation must clearly indicate to the buyer that the shipment does not constitute an acceptance and that therefore no contract has been formed.

Assume that Barrymore orders one thousand *black* fans from Stroh. Stroh ships one thousand *blue* fans to Barrymore, notifying Barrymore that these are sent as an accommodation because Stroh has only blue fans in stock. The shipment of blue fans is not an acceptance but a counteroffer, and a contract will be formed only if Barrymore accepts the blue fans. If, however, Stroh ships one thousand blue fans instead of black *without* notifying Barrymore that the goods are being shipped as an accommodation, Stroh's shipment acts as both an acceptance of Barrymore's offer and a breach of the resulting contract. Barrymore may sue Stroh for any appropriate damages.

COMMUNICATION OF ACCEPTANCE Under the common law, because a unilateral offer invites acceptance by performance, the offeree need not notify the offeror of performance unless the offeror would not otherwise know about it. In other words, a unilateral offer can be accepted by beginning performance. The UCC is more stringent than the common law in this regard because it requires notification. Under the UCC, if the offeror is not notified within a reasonable time that the offeree has accepted the contract by beginning performance, then the offeror can treat the offer as having lapsed before acceptance [UCC 2–206(2), 2A–206(2)].

ADDITIONAL TERMS Recall from Chapter 11 on page 230 that under the common law, the mirror image rule requires that the terms of the acceptance exactly match those of the offer. Thus, if Alderman makes an offer to Beale, and Beale in turn accepts but adds some slight modification, there is no contract. The UCC dispenses with the mirror image rule. Generally, the UCC takes the position that if the offeree's response indicates a *definite* acceptance of the offer, a contract is formed, *even if the acceptance includes terms additional to or different from those contained in the offer* [UCC 2–207(1)]. Whether the additional terms become part of the contract depends, in part, on whether the parties are nonmerchants or merchants.

Rules When One Party or Both Parties Are Nonmerchants. If one (or both) of the parties is a *nonmerchant,* the contract is formed according to the terms of the original offer and not according to the additional terms of the acceptance [UCC 2–207(2)]. For instance, Tolsen offers in writing to sell his iPad and thirteen additional apps to Valdez for $1,500. Valdez e-mails a reply to Tolsen, stating, "I accept your offer to purchase your iPad and the thirteen additional apps for $1,500. I *would like* a box of laser printer paper and two extra toner cartridges to be included in the purchase price." Valdez has given Tolsen a definite expression of acceptance (creating a contract), even though the acceptance also *suggests* an added term for the offer. Because Tolsen is not a merchant, the additional term is merely a proposal (suggestion), and Tolsen is not legally obligated to comply with that term.

Rules When Both Parties Are Merchants. The drafters of the UCC created a special rule for merchants to avoid the "battle of the forms," which occurs when two merchants exchange separate standard forms containing different contract terms. Under UCC 2–207(2), in contracts *between merchants*, the additional terms *automatically* become part of the contract *unless* one of the following conditions arises:

1. The original offer expressly limited acceptance to its terms.
2. The new or changed terms materially alter the contract.
3. The offeror objects to the new or changed terms within a reasonable period of time.

When determining whether an alteration is material, courts consider several factors. Generally, if the modification does not involve any unreasonable element of surprise or hardship for the offeror, a court will hold that the modification did not materially alter the contract. Courts also consider the parties' prior dealings.

For example, Woolf has ordered meat from Tupman sixty-four times over a two-year period. Each time, Woolf placed the order over the phone, and Tupman mailed first a confirmation form, and then an invoice, to Woolf. Tupman's confirmation form and invoice have always included an arbitration clause. If Woolf places another order and fails to pay for the meat, the court will likely hold that the additional term—the arbitration provision—did not materially alter the contract, because Woolf should not have been surprised by the term. The result might be different, however, if the parties had dealt with each other on only two prior occasions and the arbitration clause had been included on the back of a faxed invoice but not in the confirmation form.

Conditioned on Offeror's Assent. Regardless of merchant status, the UCC provides that the offeree's expression cannot be construed as an acceptance if it contains additional or different terms and is expressly *conditioned* on the offeror's assent to those terms [UCC 2–207(1)]. For example, Philips offers to sell Hundert 650 pounds of turkey thighs at a specified price and with specified delivery terms. Hundert responds, "I accept your offer for 650 pounds of turkey thighs *on the condition that you agree to give me ninety days to pay for them.*" Hundert's response will be construed not as an acceptance but as a counteroffer, which Philips may or may not accept.

Additional Terms May Be Stricken. The UCC provides yet another option for dealing with conflicting terms in the parties' writings. Section 2–207(3) states that conduct by both parties that recognizes the existence of a contract is sufficient to establish a contract for sale even though the writings of the parties do not otherwise establish a contract. In this situation, "the terms of the particular contract will consist of those terms on which the writings of the parties agree, together with any supplementary terms incorporated under any other provisions of this Act." In a dispute over contract terms, this provision allows a court simply to strike from the contract those terms on which the parties do not agree.

Suppose that SMT Marketing orders goods over the phone from Brigg Sales, Inc., which ships the goods to SMT with an acknowledgment form (confirming the order). SMT accepts and pays for the goods. The parties' writings do not establish a contract, but there is no question that a contract exists. If a dispute arises over the terms, such as the extent of any warranties, UCC 2–207(3) provides the governing rule.

As noted previously, the fact that a merchant's acceptance frequently contains terms that add to or even conflict with those of the offer is often referred to as the "battle of the forms." Although the UCC tries to eliminate this battle, the problem of differing contract terms still arises in commercial settings, particularly when contracts are based on the merchants' standard forms, such as order forms and confirmation forms.

Consideration

The common law rule that a contract requires consideration also applies to sales and lease contracts. Unlike the common law, however, the UCC does not require a contract modification to be supported by new consideration. The UCC states that an agreement modifying a contract for the sale or lease of goods "needs no consideration to be binding" [UCC 2–209(1), 2A–208(1)].

MODIFICATIONS MUST BE MADE IN GOOD FAITH Of course, any contract modification must be made in good faith [UCC 1–304]. For example, Allied, Inc., agrees to lease a new recreational vehicle (RV) to Diane Lee for a stated monthly payment. Subsequently, a sudden shift in the market makes it difficult for Allied to lease the new RV to Lee at the contract price without suffering a loss. Allied tells Lee of the situation, and she agrees to pay an additional sum for the lease of the RV. Later, Lee reconsiders and refuses to pay more than the original price. Under the UCC, Lee's promise to modify the contract needs no consideration to be binding. Hence, she is bound by the modified contract.

In this example, a shift in the market is a *good faith* reason for contract modification. What if there really was no shift in the market, however, and Allied knew that Lee needed the RV immediately but refused to deliver it unless Lee agreed to pay an additional amount? This attempt at extortion through modification without a legitimate commercial reason would be ineffective because it would violate the duty of good faith. Allied would not be permitted to enforce the higher price.

WHEN MODIFICATION WITHOUT CONSIDERATION DOES REQUIRE A WRITING In some situations, an agreement to modify a sales or lease contract without consideration must be in writing to be enforceable. For example, if the contract itself specifies that any changes to the contract must be in a signed writing, only those changes agreed to in a signed writing are enforceable. If a consumer (nonmerchant buyer) is dealing with a merchant and the merchant supplies the form that contains the prohibition against oral modification, the consumer must sign a separate acknowledgment of the clause [UCC 2–209(2), 2A–208(2)].

Also, under Article 2, any modification that brings a sales contract under the Statute of Frauds must usually be in writing to be enforceable. Thus, if an oral contract for the sale of goods priced at $400 is modified so that the goods are priced at $600, the modification must be in writing to be enforceable [UCC 2–209(3)]. (This is because the UCC's Statute of Frauds provision, as you will read shortly, requires a written record of sales contracts for goods priced at $500 or more.) Nevertheless, if the buyer accepts delivery of the goods after the oral modification, he or she is bound to the $600 price [UCC 2–201(3)(c)]. (Unlike Article 2, Article 2A does not say whether a lease as modified needs to satisfy the Statute of Frauds.)

The Statute of Frauds

As discussed in Chapter 15, the Statute of Frauds requires that certain types of contracts, to be enforceable, must be in writing or be evidenced by a written memorandum or record. The UCC contains Statute of Frauds provisions covering sales and lease contracts. Under these provisions, sales contracts for goods priced at $500 or more and lease contracts requiring total payments of $1,000 or more must be in writing to be enforceable [UCC 2–201(1), 2A–201(1)]. (These low threshold amounts may eventually be raised.)

SUFFICIENCY OF THE WRITING The UCC has greatly relaxed the requirements for the sufficiency of a writing to satisfy the Statute of Frauds. A writing or a memorandum will be sufficient as long as it indicates that the parties intended to form a contract and as long as it is signed by the party (or agent of the party) against whom enforcement is sought. The contract normally will not be enforceable beyond the quantity of goods shown in the writing, however. All other terms can be proved in court by oral testimony. For leases, the writing must reasonably identify and describe the goods leased and the lease term.

SPECIAL RULES FOR CONTRACTS BETWEEN MERCHANTS Once again, the UCC provides a special rule for merchants in sales transactions (there is no corresponding rule that applies to leases under Article 2A). Merchants can satisfy the Statute of Frauds if, after the parties have agreed orally, one of the merchants sends a signed written confirmation to the other merchant within a reasonable time.

The communication must indicate the terms of the agreement, and the merchant receiving the confirmation must have reason to know of its contents. Generally, courts hold that it is sufficient if a merchant sends an e-mail confirmation of the agreement.[12] Unless the merchant who receives the confirmation gives written notice of objection to its contents within ten days after receipt, the writing is sufficient against the receiving merchant, even though she or he has not signed it [UCC 2–201(2)].

For example, Alfonso is a merchant-buyer in Cleveland. He contracts over the telephone to purchase $6,000 worth of spare aircraft parts from Goldstein, a merchant-seller in New York City. Two days later, Goldstein sends a written and signed confirmation detailing the terms of the oral contract, and Alfonso subsequently receives it. If Alfonso does not notify Goldstein in writing of his objection to the contents of the confirmation within ten days of receipt, Alfonso cannot raise the Statute of Frauds as a defense against the enforcement of the oral contract.

EXCEPTIONS The UCC defines three exceptions to the writing requirements of the Statute of Frauds. An oral contract for the sale of goods priced at $500 or more or the lease of goods involving total payments of $1,000 or more will be enforceable despite the absence of a writing in the circumstances described next [UCC 2–201(3), 2A–201(4)].

Specially Manufactured Goods. An oral contract is enforceable if (1) it is for goods that are *specially manufactured* for a particular buyer or specially manufactured or obtained for a particular lessee, (2) these goods are *not suitable for resale or lease* to others in the ordinary course of the seller's or lessor's business, and (3) the seller or lessor has *substantially started to manufacture* the goods or has made commitments for the manufacture or procurement of the goods. In these situations, once the seller or lessor has taken action, the buyer or lessee cannot repudiate the agreement claiming the Statute of Frauds as a defense.

Suppose that Womach orders custom-made draperies for her new boutique. The price is $9,000, and the contract is oral. When the merchant-seller manufactures the draperies and tenders delivery to Womach, she refuses to pay for them, even though the job has been completed on time. Womach claims that she is not liable because the contract was oral. Clearly, if the unique style and color of the draperies make it improbable that the seller can find another buyer, Womach is liable to the seller.

---

12. See, for example, *Bazak International Corp. v. Tarrant Apparel Group*, 378 F.Supp.2d 377 (S.D.N.Y. 2005); and *Great White Bear, LLC v. Mervyns, LLC*, 2007 WL 1295747 (S.D.N.Y. 2007).

Note that the seller must have made a substantial beginning in manufacturing the specialized item prior to the buyer's repudiation. In addition, the court must be convinced by evidence of the terms of the oral contract.

Admissions. An oral contract for the sale or lease of goods is enforceable if the party against whom enforcement is sought admits in pleadings, testimony, or other court proceedings that a sales or lease contract was made. In this situation, the contract will be enforceable even though it was oral, but enforceability will be limited to the quantity of goods admitted.

For example, Lane and Salazar negotiate an agreement over the telephone. During the negotiations, Lane requests a delivery price for five hundred gallons of gasoline and a separate price for seven hundred gallons of gasoline. Salazar replies that the price would be the same, $3.10 per gallon. Lane orally orders five hundred gallons. Salazar honestly believes that Lane ordered seven hundred gallons and tenders that amount. Lane refuses the shipment of seven hundred gallons, and Salazar sues for breach. In his pleadings and testimony, Lane admits that an oral contract was made, but only for five hundred gallons. Because Lane admits the existence of the oral contract, Lane cannot plead the Statute of Frauds as a defense. The contract is enforceable, however, only to the extent of the quantity admitted (five hundred gallons).

Is it possible to admit to a contract in court and also assert the Statute of Frauds as a defense? That was the position of the one of the parties in the following case.

CASE 19.2
Glacial Plains Cooperative v. Lindgren

Court of Appeals of Minnesota, 759 N.W.2d 661 (2009).
www.lawlibrary.state.mn.us/archive[a]

COMPANY PROFILE • Glacial Plains Cooperative is a locally owned agricultural cooperative based in west central Minnesota. Glacial Plains employs fifty to one hundred workers, who supply grain marketing, seed, energy, feed, and agronomy products and services. Recent annual sales have averaged between $50 million and $100 million. The cooperative also offers short-term, low-interest loans and other financial products to its members. Glacial Plains' motto is "Solid Performance and Returning Cash to Member Owners."

BACKGROUND AND FACTS • Gerald Lindgren, a farmer, agreed by phone to sell grain to Glacial Plains Cooperative. They reached four agreements: two for the delivery of 9,000 and 10,000 bushels of soybeans in the fall of 2006, one for the delivery of 65,000 bushels of corn in the same season, and one for the sale of 30,000 bushels of corn in the fall of 2007. Glacial Plains sent Lindgren four written—but unsigned—contracts. Lindgren made the soybean deliveries and part of the first corn delivery, but sold the rest of his corn to another dealer. Glacial Plains bought corn elsewhere, paying a higher price, and filed a suit in a Minnesota state court against Lindgren for breach of contract. During a deposition and in papers filed with the court, Lindgren acknowledged his oral agreements with Glacial Plains and admitted that he did not fully perform. He argued, nonetheless, that the agreements were unenforceable because they were not signed. The court denied Lindgren's defense. He appealed.

IN THE LANGUAGE OF THE COURT
KLAPHAKE, Judge.
* * * *

Appellant argues that the oral corn agreements are not enforceable because they violate the Statute of Frauds. Minnesota's version of the UCC provides that a contract for the sale of goods for the price of $500 or more is not enforceable "unless there is

---

a. In the "Court of Appeals Opinions" box, click on "Index by Release Date." On that page, in the "Published" column in the "2009" section, select "January–March." In the result, scroll to "January 27, 2009" and click on the docket number of the case to access the opinion. The Minnesota State Law Library maintains this Web site.

CASE CONTINUES ➧

CASE 19.2 CONTINUED ➡ some writing sufficient to indicate that a contract for sale has been made between the parties and signed by the party against whom enforcement is sought."

Respondent argues that the oral agreements fall within * * * the admission exception.

The admission exception to the code's statute of frauds is found in [Minnesota Statutes Section 36.2-201(3)(b), Minnesota's version of UCC 2–201(3)(b)], which provides that even when there is no signed writing sufficient to satisfy the writing requirement, *the Statute of Frauds will not act to abolish the contract "if the party against whom enforcement is sought admits in pleading, testimony or otherwise in court that a contract for sale was made."* The exception was created to reduce the risk of fraud: Where the making of a contract is admitted in court, no additional writing is necessary for protection against fraud, and the contract becomes enforceable notwithstanding the provisions of the statute of frauds. [Emphasis added.]

Appellant has made such an admission here. During his deposition and in his summary judgment papers, appellant acknowledged that he made two oral agreements in April 2006 for the sale of corn to be delivered in 2006 and 2007, and that he operated under the assumption that he was obligated under these agreements throughout the summer of 2006. He further admitted that he * * * decided [the unsigned contracts] were unenforceable, and stopped performing on the 2006 corn contract and never performed on the 2007 corn agreement. * * * Based on these admissions by appellant, we conclude that the admission exception applies here, removing the agreement from the UCC statute of frauds.

* * * Meeting the Minnesota Statute of Frauds does not prove the terms of the contract; meeting the Statute of Frauds simply removes the defense and allows a jury to determine the issue of whether the parties entered into an agreement and its terms.

DECISION AND REMEDY • *The state intermediate appellate court affirmed the lower court's decision. The appellate court remanded the case for a determination of the terms of the contracts.*

WHAT IF THE FACTS WERE DIFFERENT? • *Suppose that Lindgren had admitted to a lesser quantity than he had orally promised to Glacial Plains but that other proof of the true terms was available. What might have been the result? Explain your answer.*

THE LEGAL ENVIRONMENT DIMENSION • *Lindgren entered into an agreement in the spring of 2006 to deliver corn to Great Plains in the fall of 2007. Should the court have denied the enforcement of this agreement under the one-year rule? Explain.*

Partial Performance. An oral contract for the sale or lease of goods is enforceable if payment has been made and accepted or goods have been received and accepted. This is the "partial performance" exception. The oral contract will be enforced at least to the extent that performance *actually* took place.

CASE IN POINT Quality Pork International formed an oral contract with Rupari Food Services, Inc., which buys and sells food products to retail operations. Quality was to ship three orders of pork to Star Food Processing, Inc., and Rupari was to pay for the products. Quality shipped the pork to Star and sent invoices to Rupari. Rupari billed Star for all three orders but paid Quality only for the first two. Quality filed a suit against Rupari to recover $44,051.98, the cost of the third order. Rupari argued that because the parties did not have a written agreement, there was no enforceable contract. The court held that even though Rupari had not signed a written contract or purchase order, it had accepted the goods and partially performed the contract by paying for the first two shipments. Rupari's conduct was sufficient to prove the existence of a contract, and the court required Rupari to pay for the last shipment.[13]

The exceptions just discussed and other ways in which sales law differs from general contract law are summarized in Exhibit 19–2.

Parol Evidence

When the parties to a contract set forth its terms in a confirmatory memorandum or in other writing that is intended as a complete and final statement of their agreement, it is considered *fully integrated* (see Chapter 15 on page 230). The terms of a fully integrated contract cannot be contradicted by evidence of any prior agreements or contemporaneous oral agreements. If, however, the writing contains some

---

13. *Quality Pork International v. Rupari Food Services, Inc.,* 267 Neb. 474, 675 N.W.2d 642 (2004).

EXHIBIT 19–2 • Major Differences between Contract Law and Sales Law

	CONTRACT LAW	**SALES LAW**
Contract Terms	Contract must contain all material terms.	Open terms are acceptable if parties intended to form a contract, but the contract is not enforceable beyond quantity term.
Acceptance	Mirror image rule applies. If additional terms are added in acceptance, a counteroffer is created.	Additional terms will not negate acceptance unless acceptance is expressly conditioned on assent to the additional terms.
Contract Modification	Modification requires consideration.	Modification does not require consideration.
Irrevocable Offers	Option contracts (with consideration).	Merchants' firm offers (without consideration).
Statute of Frauds Requirements	All material terms must be included in the writing.	Writing is required only for sale of goods priced at $500 or more, but the contract is not enforceable beyond the quantity specified. Merchants can satisfy the writing by a confirmation evidencing their agreement. *Exceptions:* 1. Specially manufactured goods. 2. Admissions by party against whom enforcement is sought. 3. Partial performance.

of the terms the parties agreed on but not others, then the contract is not fully integrated.

When a court finds that the terms of a contract are *not fully integrated,* then the court may allow evidence of *consistent additional terms* to explain or supplement the terms stated in the contract. The court may also allow the parties to submit evidence of *course of dealing, usage of trade,* or *course of performance* [UCC 2–202, 2A–202].

COURSE OF DEALING AND USAGE OF TRADE Under the UCC, the meaning of any agreement, evidenced by the language of the parties and by their actions, must be interpreted in light of commercial practices and other surrounding circumstances. In interpreting a commercial agreement, the court will assume that the course of dealing between the parties and the general usage of trade were taken into account when the agreement was phrased.

A **course of dealing** is a sequence of actions and communications between the parties to a particular transaction that establishes a common basis for their understanding [UCC 1–303(b)]. A course of dealing is restricted to the sequence of conduct between the parties in their transactions previous to the agreement. The UCC states, "A course of performance or course of dealing between the parties

or usage of trade in the vocation or trade in which they are engaged or of which they are or should be aware is relevant in ascertaining the meaning of the parties' agreement, may give particular meaning to specific terms of the agreement, and may supplement or qualify the terms of the agreement" [UCC 1–303(d)].

Usage of trade is defined as any practice or method of dealing having such regularity of observance in a place, vocation, or trade as to justify an expectation that it will be observed with respect to the transaction in question [UCC 1–303(c)]. The express terms of an agreement and an applicable course of dealing or usage of trade will be construed to be consistent with each other whenever reasonable. When such a construction is *unreasonable,* however, the express terms in the agreement will prevail [UCC 1–303(e)].

COURSE OF PERFORMANCE The conduct that occurs under the terms of a particular agreement is called a **course of performance** [UCC 1–303(a)]. Presumably, the parties themselves know best what they meant by their words, and the course of performance actually carried out under their agreement is the best indication of what they meant [UCC 2–208(1), 2A–207(1)].

For example, Janson's Lumber Company contracts with Lopez to sell Lopez a specified number of two-by-fours. The lumber in fact does not measure 2 inches by 4 inches but rather $1^7/8$ inches by $3^3/4$ inches. Janson's agrees to deliver the lumber in five deliveries, and Lopez, without objection, accepts the lumber in the first three deliveries. On the fourth delivery, however, Lopez objects that the two-by-fours do not measure precisely 2 inches by 4 inches.

The course of performance in this transaction—that is, the fact that Lopez accepted three deliveries without objection under the agreement—is relevant in determining that here a "two-by-four" actually means a "$1^7/8$-by-$3^3/4$." Janson's can also prove that two-by-fours need not be exactly 2 inches by 4 inches by applying usage of trade, course of dealing, or both. Janson's can, for example, show that in previous transactions, Lopez took $1^7/8$-inch-by-$3^3/4$-inch lumber without objection. In addition, Janson's can show that in the trade, two-by-fours are commonly $1^7/8$ inches by $3^3/4$ inches.

RULES OF CONSTRUCTION The UCC provides *rules of construction* for interpreting contracts. Express terms, course of performance, course of dealing, and usage of trade are to be construed together when they do not contradict one another. When such a construction is unreasonable, however, the following order of priority controls: (1) express terms, (2) course of performance, (3) course of dealing, and (4) usage of trade [UCC 1–303(e), 2–208(2), 2A–207(2)].

Unconscionability

As discussed in Chapters 13 and 14, an unconscionable contract is one that is so unfair and one sided that it would be unreasonable to enforce it. The UCC allows a court to evaluate a contract or any clause in a contract, and if the court deems it to have been unconscionable *at the time it was made,* the court can do any of the following [UCC 2–302, 2A–108]:

1. Refuse to enforce the contract.
2. Enforce the remainder of the contract without the unconscionable part.
3. Limit the application of the unconscionable term to avoid an unconscionable result.

The following landmark case illustrates an early application of the UCC's unconscionability provisions.

✳ EXTENDED CASE 19.3 ✳
Jones v. Star Credit Corp.

Supreme Court of New York, Nassau County, 59 Misc.2d 189, 298 N.Y.S.2d 264 (1969).

IN THE LANGUAGE OF THE COURT
Sol M. *WACHTLER,* Justice.

On August 31, 1965 the plaintiffs, who are welfare recipients, agreed to purchase a home freezer unit for $900 as the result of a visit from a salesman representing Your Shop At Home Service, Inc. With the addition of the time credit charges, credit life insurance, credit property insurance, and sales tax, the purchase price totaled $1,234.80. Thus far the plaintiffs have paid $619.88 toward their purchase. The defendant claims that with various added credit charges paid for an extension of time there is a balance of $819.81 still due from the plaintiffs. The uncontroverted proof at the trial established that the freezer unit, when purchased, had a maximum retail value of approximately $300. The question is whether this transaction and the resulting contract could be considered unconscionable within the meaning of section 2–302 of the Uniform Commercial Code * * *.

* * * *

There was a time when the shield of *caveat emptor* ["let the buyer beware"] would protect the most unscrupulous in the marketplace—a time when the law, in granting parties unbridled latitude to make their own contracts, allowed exploitive and callous practices which shocked the conscience of both legislative bodies and the courts.

* * * *

The law is beginning to fight back against those who once took advantage of the poor and illiterate without risk of either exposure or interference.

* * * *

Section 2–302 of the Uniform Commercial Code enacts the moral sense of the community into the law of commercial transactions. It authorizes the court to find, as a matter of law, that a contract or a clause of a contract was "unconscionable at the time it was made," and upon so finding the court may refuse to enforce the contract, excise the objectionable clause or limit the application of the clause to avoid an unconscionable result. The principle * * * is one of the prevention of oppression and unfair surprise. It permits a court to accomplish directly what heretofore was often accomplished by construction of

EXTENDED CASE 19.3 CONTINUED ➡

language, manipulations of fluid rules of contract law and determinations based upon a presumed public policy.

* * * *

Fraud, in the instant case, is not present; nor is it necessary under the statute. The question which presents itself is whether or not, under the circumstances of this case, the sale of a freezer unit having a retail value of $300 for $900 ($1,439.69 including credit charges and $18 sales tax) is unconscionable as a matter of law. The court believes it is.

* * * *

Concededly, deciding [this case] is substantially easier than explaining it. No doubt, the mathematical disparity between $300, which presumably includes a reasonable profit margin, and $900, which is exorbitant on its face, carries the greatest weight. Credit charges alone exceed

by more than $100 the retail value of the freezer. These alone may be sufficient to sustain the decision. Yet, a caveat [warning] is warranted lest we reduce the import of Section 2–302 solely to a mathematical ratio formula. It may, at times, be that; yet it may also be much more. The very limited financial resources of the purchaser, known to the sellers at the time of the sale, is entitled to weight in the balance. Indeed, the value disparity itself leads inevitably to the felt conclusion that knowing advantage was taken of the plaintiffs. In addition, *the meaningfulness of choice essential to the making of a contract can be negated by a gross inequality of bargaining power.* [Emphasis added.]

There is no question about the necessity and even the desirability of installment sales and the extension of credit. Indeed, there are many, including welfare recipients, who would be deprived of even the

most basic conveniences without the use of these devices. Similarly, the retail merchant selling on installment or extending credit is expected to establish a pricing factor which will afford a degree of protection commensurate with the risk of selling to those who might be default prone. However, neither of these accepted premises can clothe the sale of this freezer with respectability.

* * * *

Having already [been] paid more than $600 toward the purchase of this $300 freezer unit, it is apparent that the defendant has already been amply compensated. In accordance with the statute, the application of the payment provision should be limited to amounts already paid by the plaintiffs and the contract be reformed and amended by changing the payments called for therein to equal the amount of payment actually so paid by the plaintiffs.

QUESTIONS

1. Why would the seller's knowledge of the buyers' limited resources support a finding of unconscionability?
2. Why didn't the court rule that the buyers, as adults, had made a decision of their own free will and therefore were bound by the terms of the contract, regardless of the difference between the freezer's contract price and its retail value?

IMPACT OF THIS CASE ON TODAY'S LAW • *This early classic case illustrates the approach that many courts take today when deciding whether a sales contract is unconscionable—an approach that focuses on "excessive" price and unequal bargaining power. Most of the litigants who have used UCC 2–302 successfully could demonstrate both an absence of meaningful choice and contract terms that were unreasonably favorable to the other party.*

Concept Summary 19.1 on the next page reviews the concepts and rules related to the formation of sales and lease contracts.

SECTION 5
CONTRACTS FOR THE INTERNATIONAL SALE OF GOODS

International sales contracts between firms or individuals located in different countries may be

governed by the 1980 United Nations Convention on Contracts for the International Sale of Goods (CISG). The CISG governs international contracts only if the countries of the parties to the contract have ratified the CISG and if the parties have not agreed that some other law will govern their contract. As of 2010, the CISG had been adopted by seventy countries, including the United States, Canada, Mexico, some Central and South American countries, China, Japan, and most European nations. That means that the CISG is the uniform international sales law of countries that account for more than two-thirds of all global trade.

CONCEPT SUMMARY 19.1
The Formation of Sales and Lease Contracts

Concept	Description
Offer and Acceptance	1. *Offer—* a. Not all terms have to be included for a contract to be formed. b. The price does not have to be included for a contract to be formed. c. Particulars of performance can be left open. d. An offer by a merchant in a signed writing with assurances that the offer will not be withdrawn is irrevocable without consideration (for up to three months). 2. *Acceptance—* a. Acceptance may be made by any reasonable means of communication; it is effective when dispatched. b. The acceptance of a unilateral offer can be made by a promise to ship or by the shipment of conforming or nonconforming goods. c. Acceptance by performance requires notice within a reasonable time; otherwise, the offer can be treated as lapsed. d. A definite expression of acceptance creates a contract even if the terms of the acceptance modify the terms of the offer.
Consideration	A modification of a contract for the sale of goods does not require consideration.
Requirements under the Statute of Frauds	1. All contracts for the sale of goods priced at $500 or more must be in writing. A writing is sufficient as long as it indicates a contract between the parties and is signed by the party against whom enforcement is sought. A contract is not enforceable beyond the quantity shown in the writing. 2. When written confirmation of an oral contract between merchants is not objected to in writing by the receiver within ten days, the oral contract is enforceable. 3. Exceptions to the requirement of a writing exist in the following situations: a. When the oral contract is for specially manufactured or obtained goods not suitable for resale or lease to others and the seller or lessor has made commitments for the manufacture or procurement of the goods. b. If the defendant admits in pleadings, testimony, or other court proceedings that an oral contract for the sale or lease of goods was made, then the contract will be enforceable to the extent of the quantity of goods admitted. c. The oral agreement will be enforceable to the extent that payment has been received and accepted or to the extent that goods have been received and accepted.
Parol Evidence Rule	1. The terms of a clearly and completely worded written contract cannot be contradicted by evidence of prior agreements or contemporaneous oral agreements. 2. Evidence is admissible to clarify the terms of a writing in the following situations: a. If the contract terms are ambiguous. b. If evidence of course of dealing, usage of trade, or course of performance is necessary to learn or to clarify the intentions of the parties to the contract.

Applicability of the CISG

Essentially, the CISG is to international sales contracts what Article 2 of the UCC is to domestic sales contracts. As discussed in this chapter, in domestic transactions the UCC applies when the parties to a contract for a sale of goods have failed to specify in writing some important term concerning price, delivery, or the like. Similarly, whenever the parties to international transactions have failed to specify in writing the precise terms of a contract, the CISG will be applied. Unlike the UCC, the CISG does not apply to consumer sales, and neither the UCC nor the CISG applies to contracts for services.

Businesspersons must take special care when drafting international sales contracts to avoid problems caused by distance, including language differences and differences in national laws. The appendix following this chapter (pages 380–383) shows an actual international sales contract used by Starbucks Coffee Company. The contract illustrates many of the special terms and clauses that are typically contained in international contracts for the sale of goods. Annotations in this appendix explain the meaning and significance of specific clauses in the contract. (See Chapter 23 for a discussion of other laws that frame global business transactions.)

A Comparison of CISG and UCC Provisions

The provisions of the CISG, although similar for the most part to those of the UCC, differ from them in some respects. In the event that the CISG and the UCC are in conflict, the CISG applies (because it is a treaty of the national government and therefore is supreme—see the discussion of the supremacy clause of the U.S. Constitution in Chapter 4).

The major differences between the CISG and the UCC in regard to contract formation concern the mirror image rule, irrevocable offers, the Statute of Frauds, and the time of contract formation. We discuss these differences in the subsections that follow. CISG provisions relating to risk of loss, performance, remedies, and warranties will be discussed in the following chapters as those topics are examined.

THE MIRROR IMAGE RULE Under the UCC, a definite expression of acceptance that contains additional terms can still result in the formation of a contract, unless the additional terms are conditioned on the assent of the offeror. In other words, the UCC does away with the mirror image rule in domestic sales contracts.

Article 19 of the CISG provides that a contract can be formed even though the acceptance contains additional terms, unless the additional terms materially alter the contract. Under the CISG, however, the definition of a "material alteration" includes almost any change in the terms. If an additional term relates to payment, quality, quantity, price, time and place of delivery, extent of one party's liability to the other, or the settlement of disputes, the CISG considers the added term a material alteration. In effect, then, the CISG requires that the terms of the acceptance mirror those of the offer.

Therefore, as a practical matter, businesspersons undertaking international sales transactions should not use the sale or purchase forms that they customarily use for transactions within the United States. Instead, they should draft specific forms to suit the needs of the particular transactions.

IRREVOCABLE OFFERS UCC 2–205 provides that a merchant's firm offer is irrevocable, even without consideration, if the merchant gives assurances in a signed writing. In contrast, under the CISG, an offer can become irrevocable without a signed writing. Article 16(2) of the CISG provides that an offer will be irrevocable if the offeror simply states orally that the offer is irrevocable or if the offeree reasonably relies on the offer as being irrevocable. In both of these situations, the offer will be irrevocable even without a writing and without consideration.

THE STATUTE OF FRAUDS As mentioned previously, the UCC's Statute of Frauds provision [UCC 2–201] requires that contracts for the sale of goods priced at $500 or more be evidenced by a written record signed by the party against whom enforcement is sought. Article 11 of the CISG, however, states that a contract of sale "need not be concluded in or evidenced by writing and is not subject to any other requirements as to form. It may be proved by any means, including witnesses." Article 11 of the CISG accords with the legal customs of most nations, which no longer require contracts to meet certain formal or writing requirements to be enforceable.

TIME OF CONTRACT FORMATION Under the common law of contracts, an acceptance is effective on dispatch, so a contract is created when the acceptance is transmitted. The UCC does not alter this so-called mailbox rule. Under the CISG, in contrast, a contract is created not at the time the acceptance is transmitted but only on its *receipt* by the offeror. (The offer becomes *irrevocable,* however, when the acceptance is sent.) Article 18(2) states that an acceptance by return promise "becomes effective at the moment the indication of assent reaches the offeror." Under Article 18(3), the offeree may also bind the offeror by performance even without giving any notice to the offeror. The acceptance becomes effective "at the moment the act is performed." Thus, it is the offeree's reliance, rather than the communication of acceptance to the offeror, that creates the contract.

Special Provisions in International Contracts

Language and legal differences among nations can create various problems for parties to international contracts when disputes arise. It is possible to avoid these problems by including in a contract special provisions relating to choice of language, choice of forum, choice of law, and the types of events that may excuse the parties from performance.

CHOICE OF LANGUAGE A deal struck between a U.S. company and a company in another country frequently involves two languages. One party may not understand complex contractual terms that are written in the other party's language. Translating the terms poses its own problems, as typically many phrases are not readily translatable into another language. To make sure that no disputes arise out of this language problem, an international sales contract should include a **choice-of-language clause,** designating the official language by which the contract will be interpreted in the event of disagreement. The clause might also specify that the agreement is to be translated into, say, Spanish; that the translation is to be ratified by both parties; and that the foreign company can rely on the translation. If arbitration is anticipated, an additional clause must be added to indicate the official language that will be used at the arbitration proceeding.

CHOICE OF FORUM A forum-selection clause designates the forum (place, or court) in which any disputes that arise under the contract will be litigated. Including a forum-selection clause in an international contract is especially important because when several countries are involved, litigation may be sought in courts in different nations. There are no universally accepted rules regarding the jurisdiction of a particular court over subject matter or parties to a dispute, although the adoption of the 2005 Choice of Court Convention should help resolve certain issues. A forum-selection clause should indicate the specific court that will have jurisdiction. The forum does not necessarily have to be within the geographic boundaries of either party's nation.

Under certain circumstances, a forum-selection clause will not be valid. Specifically, if the clause denies one party an effective remedy, is the product of fraud or unconscionable conduct, causes substantial inconvenience to one of the parties, or violates public policy, the clause will not be enforced.

CHOICE OF LAW A contractual provision designating the applicable law, called a **choice-of-law clause,** is typically included in every international contract. At common law (and in European civil law systems—see Chapter 23), parties are allowed to choose the law that will govern their contractual relationship, provided that the law chosen is the law of a jurisdiction that has a substantial relationship to the parties and to the business transaction.

Under the UCC, parties may choose the law that will govern the contract as long as the choice is "reasonable." Article 6 of the CISG, however, imposes no limitation on the parties in their choice of what law will govern the contract, and the 1986 Hague Convention on the Law Applicable to Contracts for the International Sale of Goods—often referred to as the Choice-of-Law Convention—allows unlimited autonomy in the choice of law. Whenever a choice of law is not specified in a contract, the Hague Convention indicates that the law of the country where the seller's place of business is located will govern.

FORCE MAJEURE CLAUSE Every contract, and particularly those involving international transactions, should include a *force majeure* **clause.** The meaning of the French term *force majeure* is "impossible or irresistible force"—sometimes loosely defined as "an act of God." *Force majeure* clauses commonly stipulate that in addition to acts of God, a number of other eventualities (such as governmental orders or regulations, embargoes, or extreme shortages of materials) may excuse a party from liability for nonperformance.

REVIEWING

The Formation of Sales and Lease Contracts

Guy Holcomb owns and operates Oasis Goodtime Emporium, an adult entertainment establishment. Holcomb wanted to create an adult Internet system for Oasis that would offer customers adult theme videos and "live" chat room programs using performers at the club. On May 10, Holcomb signed a work order authorizing Thomas Consulting Group (TCG) "to deliver a working prototype of a customer chat system, demonstrating the integration of live video and chatting in a Web browser." In exchange for creating the prototype, Holcomb agreed to pay TCG $64,697. On May 20, Holcomb

REVIEWING

The Formation of Sales and Lease Contracts, Continued

signed an additional work order in the amount of $12,943 for TCG to install a customized firewall system. The work orders stated that Holcomb would make monthly installment payments to TCG, and both parties expected the work would be finished by September. Due to unforeseen problems largely attributable to system configuration and software incompatibility, the project required more time than anticipated. By the end of the summer, the Web site was still not ready, and Holcomb had fallen behind in his payments to TCG. TCG threatened to cease work and file a suit for breach of contract unless the bill was paid. Rather than make further payments, Holcomb wanted to abandon the Web site project. Using the information presented in the chapter, answer the following questions.

1. Would a court be likely to decide that the transaction between Holcomb and TCG was covered by the Uniform Commercial Code (UCC)? Why or why not?
2. Would a court be likely to consider Holcomb a merchant under the UCC? Why or why not?
3. Did the parties have a valid contract under the UCC? Were any terms left open in the contract? If so, which terms? How would a court deal with open terms?
4. Suppose that Holcomb and TCG meet in October in an attempt to resolve their problems. At that time, the parties reach an oral agreement that TCG will continue to work without demanding full payment of the past due amounts and Holcomb will pay TCG $5,000 per week. Assuming the contract falls under the UCC, is the oral agreement enforceable? Why or why not?

DEBATE THIS: *The UCC should require the same degree of definiteness of terms, especially with respect to price and quantity, as contract law does.*

TERMS AND CONCEPTS

choice-of-language
  clause 376
choice-of-law clause 376
course of dealing 371

course of performance 371
firm offer 365
force majeure clause 376
lease agreement 361
lessee 361
lessor 361

merchant 361
output contract 364
predominant-factor
  test 359
requirements contract 363
sale 358

sales contract 357
seasonably 366
tangible property 358
usage of trade 371

QUESTIONS AND CASE PROBLEMS

19–1. Statute of Frauds Fresher Foods, Inc., orally agreed to purchase one thousand bushels of corn for $1.25 per bushel from Dale Vernon, a farmer. Fresher Foods paid $125 down and agreed to pay the remainder of the purchase price on delivery, which was scheduled for one week later. When Fresher Foods tendered the balance of $1,125 on the scheduled day of delivery and requested the corn, Vernon refused to deliver it. Fresher Foods sued Vernon for damages, claiming that Vernon had breached their oral contract. Can Fresher Foods recover? If so, to what extent?

19–2. QUESTION WITH SAMPLE ANSWER: Acceptance.

Flint, a retail seller of television sets, orders one hundred Color-X sets from manufacturer Martin. The order specifies the price and that the television sets are to be shipped by Hummingbird Express on or before October 30. Martin receives the order on October 5. On October 8, Martin writes Flint a letter indicating that the order was received and that the sets will be shipped as directed, at the specified price. Flint receives this letter on October 10. On October 28, Martin, in preparing the shipment, discovers it has only ninety Color-X sets in stock. Martin ships the ninety Color-X sets and ten television sets of a different model, stating clearly on the invoice that the ten are being shipped only as an accommodation. Flint claims Martin is in breach of contract. Martin claims that the shipment was not an acceptance and therefore no contract was formed. Explain who is correct, and why.

- **For a sample answer to Question 19–2, go to Appendix I at the end of this text.**

19–3. Additional Terms Strike offers to sell Bailey one thousand shirts for a stated price. The offer declares that shipment will be made by the Dependable Truck Line. Bailey replies, "I accept your offer for one thousand shirts at the price quoted. Delivery to be by Yellow Express Truck Line." Both Strike and Bailey are merchants. Three weeks later, Strike ships the shirts by the Dependable Truck Line, and Bailey refuses shipment. Strike sues for breach of contract. Bailey claims (a) that there never was a contract because the reply, which included a modification of carriers, did not constitute an acceptance and (b) that even if there had been a contract, Strike would have been in breach owing to having shipped the shirts by Dependable, contrary to the contract terms. Discuss fully Bailey's claims.

19–4. Goods and Services Combined Propulsion Technologies, Inc., a Louisiana firm doing business as PowerTech Marine Propellers, markets small steel boat propellers that are made by a unique tooling method. Attwood Corp., a Michigan firm, operated a foundry (a place where metal is cast) in Mexico. In 1996, Attwood offered to produce castings of the propellers. Attwood promised to maintain quality, warrant the castings against defects, and obtain insurance to cover liability. In January 1997, the parties signed a letter that expressed these and other terms— Attwood was to be paid per casting, and twelve months' notice was required to terminate the deal—but the letter did not state a quantity. PowerTech provided the tooling. Attwood produced rough castings, which PowerTech refined by checking each propeller's pitch; machining its interior; grinding, balancing, and polishing the propeller; and adding serial numbers and a rubber clutch. In October, Attwood told PowerTech that the foundry was closing. PowerTech filed a suit in a federal district court against Attwood, alleging, among other things, breach of contract. One of the issues was whether their deal was subject to Article 2 of the Uniform Commercial Code. What type of transactions does Article 2 cover? Does the arrangement between PowerTech and Attwood qualify? Explain. [*Propulsion Technologies, Inc. v. Attwood Corp.,* 369 F.3d 896 (5th Cir. 2004)]

19–5. Offer In 1998, Johnson Controls, Inc. (JCI), began buying auto parts from Q.C. Onics Ventures, LP. For each part, JCI would inform Onics of its need and ask the price. Onics would analyze the specifications, contact its suppliers, and respond with a formal quotation. A quote listed a part's number and description, the price per unit, and an estimate of units available for a given year. A

quote did not state payment terms, an acceptance date, timing of performance, warranties, or quantities. JCI would select a supplier and issue a purchase order for a part. The purchase order required the seller to supply all of JCI's requirements for the part but gave the buyer the right to end the deal at any time. Using this procedure, JCI issued hundreds of purchase orders. In July 2001, JCI terminated its relationship with Onics and began buying parts through another supplier. Onics filed a suit in a federal district court against JCI, alleging breach of contract. Which documents—the price quotations or the purchase orders—constituted offers? Which were acceptances? What effect would the answers to these questions have on the result in this case? Explain. [*Q.C. Onics Ventures, LP v. Johnson Controls, Inc.,* __ F.Supp.2d __ (N.D.Ind. 2006)]

19–6. CASE PROBLEM WITH SAMPLE ANSWER: Parol Evidence.

 Clear Lakes Trout Co. operates a fish hatchery in Idaho. Rodney and Carla Griffith are trout growers. Clear Lakes agreed to sell "small trout" to the Griffiths, who agreed to sell the trout back when they had grown to "market size." At the time, in the trade "market size" referred to fish approximating one-pound live weight. The parties did business without a written agreement until September 1998, when they executed a contract with a six-year duration. The contract did not define "market size." All went well until September 11, 2001, after which there was a demand for larger fish. Clear Lakes began taking deliveries later and in smaller loads, leaving the Griffiths with overcrowded ponds and other problems. In 2003, the Griffiths refused to accept more fish and filed a suit in an Idaho state court against Clear Lakes, alleging breach of contract. Clear Lakes argued that there was no contract because the parties had different interpretations of "market size." Clear Lakes claimed that "market size" varied according to whatever its customers demanded. The Griffiths asserted that the term referred to fish of about one-pound live weight. Is outside evidence admissible to explain the terms of a contract? Are there any exceptions that could apply in this case? If so, what is the likely result? Explain. [*Griffith v. Clear Lakes Trout Co.,* 143 Idaho 733, 152 P.3d 604 (Idaho 2007)]

- **To view a sample answer for Problem 19–6, go to this book's Web site at www.cengage.com/blaw/clarkson, select "Chapter 19," and click on "Case Problem with Sample Answer."**

19–7. Additional Terms Continental Insurance Co. issued a policy to cover shipments by Oakley Fertilizer, Inc. Oakley agreed to ship three thousand tons of fertilizer by barge from New Orleans, Louisiana, to Ameropa North America in Caruthersville, Missouri. Oakley sent Ameropa a contract form that set out these terms and stated that title and risk (discussed in Chapter 20) would pass to the buyer after the seller was paid for the goods. Ameropa e-mailed a different form that set out the same essential terms but stated that title and risk of loss would pass to the buyer when the goods were loaded onto the barges in New Orleans. The cargo was loaded onto barges but had not yet been delivered when it was damaged in

Hurricane Katrina. Oakley filed a claim for the loss with Continental but was denied coverage. Oakley filed a suit in a Missouri state court against the insurer. Continental argued that title and risk passed to Ameropa before the damage as specified in the buyer's form under Section 2–207(3) of the Uniform Commercial Code because the parties did not have a valid contract under UCC 2–207(1). Apply UCC 2–207 on additional terms in an acceptance to these facts. Is Continental correct? Explain. [*Oakley Fertilizer, Inc. v. Continental Insurance Co.*, 276 S.W.3d 342 (Mo.App.E.D. 2009)]

19–8. A QUESTION OF ETHICS: Contract Terms.

Daniel Fox owned Fox and Lamberth Enterprises, Inc., a kitchen and bath remodeling business, in Dayton, Ohio. Fox leased a building from Carl and Bellulah Hussong. Craftsmen Home Improvement, Inc., also remodeled baths and kitchens. When Fox planned to close his business, Craftsmen expressed an interest in buying his showroom assets. Fox set a price of $50,000. Craftsmen's owners agreed and gave Fox a list of the desired items and "A Bill of Sale" that set the terms for payment. The parties did not discuss Fox's arrangement with the Hussongs, but Craftsmen expected to negotiate a new lease and extensively modified the premises, including removing some of the displays to its own showroom. When the Hussongs and Craftsmen could not agree on new terms, Craftsmen told Fox that the deal was off. [Fox & Lamberth Enterprises, Inc. v. Craftsmen Home Improvement, Inc., __ Ohio App.3d __, __ N.E.2d __ (2 Dist. 2006)]

(a) In Fox's suit in an Ohio state court for breach of contract, Craftsmen raised the Statute of Frauds as a defense. What are the requirements of the Statute of Frauds? Did the deal between Fox and Craftsmen meet these requirements? Did it fall under one of the exceptions? Explain.

(b) Craftsmen also claimed that the predominant factor of its agreement with Fox was a lease for the Hussongs' building. What is the "predominant-factor" test? Does it apply here? In any event, is it fair to hold a party to a contract to buy a business's assets when the buyer cannot negotiate a favorable lease of the premises on which the assets are located? Discuss.

19–9. VIDEO QUESTION: Sales and Lease Contracts.

Go to this text's Web site at **www.cengage.com/blaw/clarkson** and select "Chapter 19." Click on "Video Questions" and view the video titled *Sales and Lease Contracts: Price as a Term.* Then answer the following questions.

(a) Is Anna correct in assuming that a contract can exist even though the sales price for the computer equipment was not specified? Explain.

(b) According to the Uniform Commercial Code, what conditions must be satisfied in order for a contract to be formed when certain terms are left open? What terms (in addition to price) can be left open?

(c) Are the e-mail messages that Anna refers to sufficient proof of the contract?

(d) Would parol evidence be admissible?

LEGAL RESEARCH EXERCISES ON THE WEB

Go to this text's Web site at **www.cengage.com/blaw/clarkson**, select "Chapter 19," and click on "Practical Internet Exercises." There you will find the following Internet research exercises that you can perform to learn more about the topics covered in this chapter.

Practical Internet Exercise 19–1: **Legal Perspective**
Is It a Contract?

Practical Internet Exercise 19–2: **Management Perspective**
A Checklist for Sales Contracts

An Example of a Contract for the International Sale of Coffee

OVERLAND COFFEE IMPORT CONTRACT
OF THE
GREEN COFFEE ASSOCIATION
OF
NEW YORK CITY, INC.*

Contract Seller's No.: __504617__
Buyer's No.: __P9264__
Date: __10/11/12__

SOLD BY: __XYZ Co.__

TO: __Starbucks__

QUANTITY: __Five Hundred__ (__500__) Tons of __Mexican__ coffee (Bags)
weighing about __152.117 lbs.__ per bag.

PACKAGING: Coffee must be packed in clean sound bags of uniform size made of sisal, henequen, jute, burlap, or similar woven material, without inner lining or outer covering of any material properly sewn by hand and/or machine. Bulk shipments are allowed if agreed by mutual consent of Buyer and Seller.

DESCRIPTION: __High grown Mexican Altura__

PRICE: At __Ten/$10.00 dollars__ U.S. Currency, per __lb.__ net, (U.S. Funds)
Upon delivery in Bonded Public Warehouse at __Laredo, TX__
(City and State)

PAYMENT: __Cash against warehouse receipts__

Bill and tender to DATE when all import requirements and governmental regulations have been satisfied, and coffee delivered or discharged (as per contract terms). Seller is obliged to give the Buyer two (2) calendar days free time in Bonded Public Warehouse following but not including date of tender.

ARRIVAL: During __December__ via __truck__
(Period)   (Method of Transportation)
from __Mexico__ for arrival at __Laredo, TX, USA__
(Country of Exportation)   (Country of Importation)
Partial shipments permitted.

ADVICE OF ARRIVAL: Advice of arrival with warehouse name and location, together with the quantity, description, marks and place of entry, must be transmitted directly, or through Seller's Agent/Broker, to the Buyer or his Agent/ Broker. Advice will be given as soon as known but not later than the fifth business day following arrival at the named warehouse. Such advice may be given verbally with written confirmation to be sent the same day.

WEIGHTS: (1) DELIVERED WEIGHTS: Coffee covered by this contract is to be weighed at location named in tender. Actual tare to be allowed.
(2) SHIPPING WEIGHTS: Coffee covered by this contract is sold on shipping weights. Any loss in weight exceeding __1/2__ percent at location named in tender is for account of Seller at contract price.
(3) Coffee is to be weighed within fifteen (15) calendar days after tender. Weighing expenses, if any, for account of __Seller__ (Seller or Buyer)

MARKINGS: Bags to be branded in English with the name of Country of Origin and otherwise to comply with laws and regulations of the Country of Importation, in effect at the time of entry, governing marking of import merchandise. Any expense incurred by failure to comply with these regulations to be borne by Exporter/Seller.

RULINGS: The "Rulings on Coffee Contracts" of the Green Coffee Association of New York City, Inc., in effect on the date this contract is made, is incorporated for all purposes as a part of this agreement, and together herewith, constitute the entire contract. No variation or addition hereto shall be valid unless signed by the parties to the contract.
Seller guarantees that the terms printed on the reverse hereof, which by reference are made a part hereof, are identical with the terms as printed in By-Laws and Rules of the Green Coffee Association of New York City, Inc., heretofore adopted.
Exceptions to this guarantee are:

ACCEPTED: COMMISSION TO BE PAID BY:
__XYZ Co.__   __Seller__
                          Seller
BY_____*DM*_____
                          Agent
__Starbucks__
                          Buyer
BY_____   __ABC Brokerage__
                          Agent   Broker(s)
When this contract is executed by a person acting for another, such person hereby represents that he is fully authorized to commit his principal.

* Reprinted with permission of The Green Coffee Association of New York City, Inc.

An Example of a Contract for the International Sale of Coffee

1 This is a contract for a sale of coffee to be *imported* internationally. If the parties have their principal places of business located in different countries, the contract may be subject to the United Nations Convention on Contracts for the International Sale of Goods (CISG). If the parties' principal places of business are located in the United States, the contract may be subject to the Uniform Commercial Code (UCC).

2 Quantity is one of the most important terms to include in a contract. Without it, a court may not be able to enforce the contract. See Chapter 19.

3 Weight per unit (bag) can be exactly stated or approximately stated. If it is not so stated, usage of trade in international contracts determines standards of weight.

4 Packaging requirements can be conditions for acceptance and payment. Bulk shipments are not permitted without the consent of the buyer.

5 A description of the coffee and the "Markings" constitute express warranties. Warranties in contracts for domestic sales of goods are discussed generally in Chapter 22. International contracts rely more heavily on descriptions and models or samples.

6 Under the UCC, parties may enter into a valid contract even though the price is not set. Under the CISG, a contract must provide for an exact determination of the price.

7 The terms of payment may take one of two forms: credit or cash. Credit terms can be complicated. A cash term can be simple, and payment can be made by any means acceptable in the ordinary course of business (for example, a personal check or a letter of credit). If the seller insists on actual cash, the buyer must be given a reasonable time to get it. See Chapter 21.

8 *Tender* means the seller has placed goods that conform to the contract at the buyer's disposition. What constitutes a valid tender is explained in Chapter 21. This contract requires that the coffee meet all import regulations and that it be ready for pickup by the buyer at a "Bonded Public Warehouse." (A *bonded warehouse* is a place in which goods can be stored without payment of taxes until the goods are removed.)

9 The delivery date is significant because, if it is not met, the buyer may hold the seller in breach of the contract. Under this contract, the seller is given a "period" within which to deliver the goods, instead of a specific day. The seller is also given some time to rectify goods that do not pass inspection (see the "Guarantee" clause on page two of the contract). For a discussion of the remedies of the buyer and seller, see Chapter 21.

10 As part of a proper tender, the seller (or its agent) must inform the buyer (or its agent) when the goods have arrived at their destination. The responsibilities of agents are set out in Chapters 32 and 33.

11 In some contracts, delivered and shipped weights can be important. During shipping, some loss can be attributed to the type of goods (spoilage of fresh produce, for example) or to the transportation itself. A seller and buyer can agree on the extent to which either of them will bear such losses. See Chapter 49 for a discussion of the liability of common carriers for loss during shipment.

12 Documents are often incorporated in a contract by reference, because including them word for word can make a contract difficult to read. If the document is later revised, the entire contract might have to be reworked. Documents that are typically incorporated by reference include detailed payment and delivery terms, special provisions, and sets of rules, codes, and standards.

13 In international sales transactions, and for domestic deals involving certain products, brokers are used to form the contracts. When so used, the brokers are entitled to a commission. See Chapter 32.

(Continued)

An Example of a Contract for the International Sale of Coffee

TERMS AND CONDITIONS

14 — ARBITRATION: All controversies relating to, in connection with, or arising out of this contract, its modification, making or the authority or obligations of the signatories hereto, and whether involving the principals, agents, brokers, or others who actually subscribe hereto, shall be settled by arbitration in accordance with the "Rules of Arbitration" of the Green Coffee Association of New York City, Inc., as they exist at the time of the arbitration (including provisions as to payment of fees and expenses). Arbitration is the sole remedy hereunder, and it shall be held in accordance with the law of New York State, and judgment of any award may be entered in the courts of that State, or in any other court of competent jurisdiction. All notices or judicial service in reference to arbitration or enforcement shall be deemed given if transmitted as required by the aforesaid rules.

15 — GUARANTEE: (a) If all or any of the coffee is refused admission into the country of importation by reason of any violation of governmental laws or acts, which violation existed at the time the coffee arrived at Bonded Public Warehouse, seller is required, as to the amount not admitted and as soon as possible, to deliver replacement coffee in conformity to all terms and conditions of this contract, excepting only the Arrival terms, but not later than thirty (30) days after the date of the violation notice. Any payment made and expenses incurred for any coffee denied entry shall be refunded within ten (10) calendar days of denial of entry, and payment shall be made for the replacement delivery in accordance with the terms of this contract. Consequently, if Buyer removes the coffee from the Bonded Public Warehouse, Seller's responsibility as to such portion hereunder ceases.
(b) Contracts containing the overstamp "No Pass-No Sale" on the face of the contract shall be interpreted to mean: If any or all of the coffee is not admitted into the country of Importation in its original condition by reason of failure to meet requirements of the government's laws or Acts, the contract shall be deemed null and void as to that portion of the coffee which is not admitted in its original condition. Any payment made and expenses incurred for any coffee denied entry shall be refunded within ten (10) calendar days of denial of entry.

16 — CONTINGENCY: This contract is not contingent upon any other contract.

CLAIMS: Coffee shall be considered accepted as to quality unless within *fifteen* (15) calendar days after delivery at Bonded Public Warehouse or within *fifteen* (15) calendar days after all Government clearances have been received, whichever is later, either:
(a) Claims are settled by the parties hereto, or,
(b) Arbitration proceedings have been filed by one of the parties in accordance with the provisions hereof.
(c) If neither (a) nor (b) has been done in the stated period or if any portion of the coffee has been removed from the Bonded Public Warehouse before representative sealed samples have been drawn by the Green Coffee Association of New York City, Inc., in accordance with its rules, Seller's responsibility for quality claims ceases for that portion so removed.
17 — (d) Any question of quality submitted to arbitration shall be a matter of allowance only, unless otherwise provided in the contract.

18 — DELIVERY: (a) No more than three (3) chops may be tendered for each lot of 250 bags.
(b) Each chop of coffee tendered is to be uniform in grade and appearance. All expense necessary to make coffee uniform shall be for account of seller.
(c) Notice of arrival and/or sampling order constitutes a tender, and must be given not later than the fifth business day following arrival at Bonded Public Warehouse stated on the contract.

INSURANCE: Seller is responsible for any loss or damage, or both, until Delivery and Discharge of coffee at the Bonded Public Warehouse in the Country of Importation.

All Insurance Risks, costs and responsibility are for Seller's Account until Delivery and Discharge of coffee at the Bonded Public Warehouse in the Country of Importation.

Buyer's insurance responsibility begins from the day of importation or from the day of tender, whichever is later.

19 — FREIGHT: Seller to provide and pay for all transportation and related expenses to the Bonded Public Warehouse in the Country of Importation.

20 — EXPORT DUTIES/TAXES: Exporter is to pay all Export taxes, duties or other fees or charges, if any, levied because of exportation.

IMPORT DUTIES/TAXES: Any Duty or Tax whatsoever, imposed by the government or any authority of the Country of Importation, shall be borne by the Importer/Buyer.

21 — INSOLVENCY OR FINANCIAL FAILURE OF BUYER OR SELLER: If, at any time before the contract is fully executed, either party hereto shall meet with creditors because of inability generally to make payment of obligations when due, or shall suspend such payments, fail to meet his general trade obligations in the regular course of business, shall file a petition in bankruptcy or, for an arrangement, shall become insolvent, or commit an act of bankruptcy, then the other party may at his option, expressed in writing, declare the aforesaid to constitute a breach and default of this contract, and may, in addition to other remedies, decline to deliver further or make payment or may sell or purchase for the defaulter's account, and may collect damage for any injury or loss, or shall account for the profit, if any, occasioned by such sale or purchase.

This clause is subject to the provisions of (11 USC 365 (e) 1) if invoked.

22 — BREACH OR DEFAULT OF CONTRACT: In the event either party hereto fails to perform, or breaches or repudiates this agreement, the other party shall subject to the specific provisions of this contract be entitled to the remedies and relief provided for by the Uniform Commercial Code of the State of New York. The computation and ascertainment of damages, or the determination of any other dispute as to relief, shall be made by the arbitrators in accordance with the Arbitration Clause herein.

23 — Consequential damages shall not, however, be allowed.

An Example of a Contract for the International Sale of Coffee

14 Arbitration is the settling of a dispute by submitting it to a disinterested party (other than a court), which renders a decision. The procedures and costs can be provided for in an arbitration clause or incorporated through other documents. To enforce an award rendered in an arbitration, the winning party can "enter" (submit) the award in a court "of competent jurisdiction." For a general discussion of arbitration and other forms of dispute resolution (other than courts), see Chapter 2.

15 When goods are imported internationally, they must meet certain import requirements before being released to the buyer. Because of this, buyers frequently want a guaranty clause that covers the goods not admitted into the country and that either requires the seller to replace the goods within a stated time or allows the contract for those goods not admitted to be void. See Chapter 17.

16 In the "Claims" clause, the parties agree that the buyer has a certain time within which to reject the goods. The right to reject is a right by law and does not need to be stated in a contract. If the buyer does not exercise the right within the time specified in the contract, the goods will be considered accepted. See Chapter 21.

17 Many international contracts include definitions of terms so that the parties understand what they mean. Some terms are used in a particular industry in a specific way. Here, the word *chop* refers to a unit of like-grade coffee beans. The buyer has a right to inspect ("sample") the coffee. If the coffee does not conform to the contract, the seller must correct the nonconformity. See Chapter 21.

18 The "Delivery," "Insurance," and "Freight" clauses, with the "Arrival" clause on page one of the contract, indicate that this is a destination contract. The seller has the obligation to deliver the goods to the destination, not simply deliver them into the hands of a carrier. Under this contract, the destination is a "Bonded Public Warehouse" in a specific location. The seller bears the risk of loss until the goods are delivered at their destination. Typically, the seller will have bought insurance to cover the risk. See Chapter 20 for a discussion of delivery terms and the risk of loss and Chapter 51 for a general discussion of insurance.

19 Delivery terms are commonly placed in all sales contracts. Such terms determine who pays freight and other costs and, in the absence of an agreement specifying otherwise, who bears the risk of loss. International contracts may use these delivery terms, or they may use INCOTERMS, which are published by the International Chamber of Commerce. For example, the INCOTERM DDP (delivered duty paid) requires the seller to arrange shipment, obtain and pay for import or export permits, and get the goods through customs to a named destination.

20 Exported and imported goods are subject to duties, taxes, and other charges imposed by the governments of the countries involved. International contracts spell out who is responsible for these charges.

21 This clause protects a party if the other party should become financially unable to fulfill the obligations under the contract. Thus, if the seller cannot afford to deliver, or the buyer cannot afford to pay, for the stated reasons, the other party can consider the contract breached. This right is subject to "11 USC 365(e)(1)," which refers to a specific provision of the U.S. Bankruptcy Code dealing with executory contracts. Bankruptcy provisions are covered in Chapter 30.

22 In the "Breach or Default of Contract" clause, the parties agreed that the remedies under this contract are the remedies (except for consequential damages) provided by the UCC, as in effect in the state of New York. The amount and "ascertainment" of damages, as well as other disputes about relief, are to be determined by arbitration. Breach of contract and contractual remedies in general are explained in Chapter 21. Arbitration is discussed in Chapter 2.

23 Three clauses frequently included in international contracts (see Chapter 19) are omitted here. There is no choice-of-language clause designating the official language to be used in interpreting the contract terms. There is no choice-of-forum clause designating the place in which disputes will be litigated, except for arbitration (law of New York State). Finally, there is no *force majeure* clause relieving the sellers or buyers from nonperformance due to events beyond their control.

CHAPTER 20

Title, Risk, and Insurable Interest

Before the creation of the Uniform Commercial Code (UCC), *title*—the right of ownership—was the central concept in sales law, controlling all issues of rights and remedies of the parties to a sales contract. There were numerous problems with this concept, however. For example, it was frequently difficult to determine when title actually passed from the seller to the buyer, and therefore it was also difficult to predict which party a court would decide had title at the time of a loss. Because of such problems, the UCC divorced the question of title as completely as possible from the question of the rights and obligations of buyers, sellers, and third parties (such as subsequent purchasers, creditors, or the tax collector).

In some situations, title is still relevant under the UCC, and the UCC has special rules for assigning title. These rules will be discussed in the sections that follow. In most situations, however, the UCC has replaced the concept of title with three other concepts: identification, risk of loss, and insurable interest.

In lease contracts, of course, the lessor-owner of the goods retains title. Hence, the UCC's provisions relating to passage of title do not apply to leased goods. Other concepts discussed in this chapter, though, including identification, risk of loss, and insurable interest, relate to lease contracts as well as to sales contracts.

SECTION 1
IDENTIFICATION

Before any interest in specific goods can pass from the seller or lessor to the buyer or lessee, the goods must be (1) in existence and (2) identified as the specific goods designated in the contract [UCC 2–105(2)]. **Identification** takes place when specific goods are designated as the subject matter of a sales or lease contract. Title and risk of loss cannot pass to the buyer from the seller unless the goods are identified to the contract. (As mentioned, title to leased goods remains with the lessor—or, if the owner is a third party, with that party.) Identification is significant because it gives the buyer or lessee the right to insure (or to have an insurable interest in) the goods and the right to recover from third parties who damage the goods. Once the goods are in existence, the parties can agree in their contract on when identification will take place. If they do not so specify, the UCC will determine when identification takes place [UCC 2–501(1), 2A–217].

Existing Goods

If the contract calls for the sale or lease of specific and ascertained goods that are already in existence, identification takes place at the time the contract is made. For example, Litco, LLC, contracts to purchase or lease a fleet of five cars by their vehicle identification numbers (VINs). Because the cars are identified by their VINs, identification has taken place, and Litco acquires an insurable interest in them at the time of contracting.

Future Goods

Any goods that are not in existence at the time of contracting are known as future goods. If a sale or lease involves unborn animals to be born within twelve months after contracting, identification takes place when the animals are conceived. If a sale involves crops that are to be harvested within twelve months (or the next harvest season occurring after contracting, whichever is longer), identification takes place when the crops are planted. Otherwise, identification takes place when the crops begin to grow. In a sale or lease of any other future goods, identification occurs when the goods are shipped, marked, or otherwise designated by the seller or lessor as the goods to which the contract refers.

CASE IN POINT Gordon Bonner signed a contract with Ronnie Carman to build a forty-six-foot motorboat for $278,950. The contract required progress payments but did not contain any specific provisions regarding delivery (which, as you will read shortly, can determine when title to the goods passes to the buyer). After nearly three years, with the boat still not completed, Carman filed for bankruptcy. The bankruptcy trustee wanted to sell the unfinished boat to pay Carman's creditors, but Bonner claimed that the boat—which was still on Carman's business premises—was his. The court held that under the UCC, the boat constituted future goods because it did not exist at the time the contract was signed. In addition, title had not passed to Bonner, because the boat had not been identified to the contract—for example, by listing its hull number in the contract or by later marking or designating it as Bonner's. Therefore, the bankruptcy trustee could sell it and distribute the funds to Carman's creditors.[1]

Goods That Are Part of a Larger Mass

Goods that are part of a larger mass are identified when the goods are marked, shipped, or somehow designated by the seller or lessor as the particular goods to pass under the contract. Suppose that a buyer orders 10,000 pairs of men's jeans from a lot that contains 90,000 articles of clothing for men, women, and children. Until the seller separates the 10,000 pairs of jeans from the other items, title and risk of loss remain with the seller.

A common exception to this rule involves fungible goods. **Fungible goods** are goods that are alike naturally, by agreement, or by trade usage. Typical examples include specific grades or types of wheat, oil, and wine, which usually are stored in large containers. If the owners of these goods hold title as tenants in common (owners having shares undivided from the entire mass jointly owned—see Chapter 49), a seller-owner can pass title and risk of loss to the buyer without actually separating the goods. The buyer replaces the seller as an owner in common [UCC 2–105(4)].

For example, Alvarez, Braudel, and Carpenter are farmers. They deposit, respectively, 5,000 bushels, 3,000 bushels, and 2,000 bushels of grain of the same grade and quality in a grain elevator. The three become owners in common, with Alvarez owning 50 percent of the 10,000 bushels, Braudel 30 percent, and Carpenter 20 percent. Alvarez contracts to sell her 5,000 bushels of grain to Treyton. Because the goods are fungible, she can pass title and risk of loss to Treyton without physically separating the 5,000 bushels. Treyton now becomes an owner in common with Braudel and Carpenter.

SECTION 2
WHEN TITLE PASSES

Once goods exist and are identified, the provisions of UCC 2–401 apply to the passage of title. In nearly all subsections of UCC 2–401, the words "unless otherwise explicitly agreed" appear, meaning that any explicit understanding between the buyer and the seller determines when title passes. Without an explicit agreement to the contrary, *title passes to the buyer at the time and the place the seller performs by delivering the goods* [UCC 2–401(2)]. For example, if a person buys cattle at a livestock auction, title will pass when the cattle are physically delivered to him or her (unless, of course, the parties agree otherwise).[2]

Shipment and Destination Contracts

Unless otherwise agreed, delivery arrangements can determine when title passes from the seller to the buyer. In a **shipment contract,** the seller is required or authorized to ship goods by carrier, such as a trucking company. Under a shipment contract, the seller is required only to deliver the goods into the hands of a carrier, and title passes to the buyer at the time and place of shipment [UCC 2–401(2)(a)]. Generally, *a contract is assumed to be a shipment contract if nothing to the contrary is stated in the contract.*

---

1. *In re Carman,* 399 Bankr. 158 (D.Md. 2009). For another case in which a boat was held to be future goods, see *Gonsalves v. Montgomery,* 2006 WL 2711540 (N.D.Cal. 2006).

2. See, for example, *In re Stewart,* 274 Bankr. 503 (2002).

In a **destination contract,** the seller is required to deliver the goods to a particular destination, usually directly to the buyer, but sometimes to another party designated by the buyer. Title passes to the buyer when the goods are *tendered* at that destination [UCC 2–401(2)(b)]. As you will read in Chapter 21, *tender of delivery* occurs when the seller places or holds conforming goods at the buyer's disposal (with any necessary notice), enabling the buyer to take possession [UCC 2–503(1)].

Delivery without Movement of the Goods

Sometimes, a sales contract does not call for the seller to ship or deliver the goods (such as when the buyer is to pick up the goods). In that situation, the passage of title depends on whether the seller must deliver a **document of title,** such as a bill of lading or a warehouse receipt, to the buyer. A *bill of lading*[3] is a receipt for goods that is signed by a carrier and serves as a contract for the transportation of the goods. A *warehouse receipt* is a receipt issued by a warehouser for goods stored in a warehouse.

When a document of title is required, title passes to the buyer *when and where the document is delivered.* Thus, if the goods are stored in a warehouse, title passes to the buyer when the appropriate documents are delivered to the buyer. The goods never move. In fact, the buyer can choose to leave the goods at the same warehouse for a period of time, and the buyer's title to those goods will be unaffected.

When no document of title is required, and delivery is made without moving the goods, title passes at the time and place the sales contract is made, if the goods have already been identified. If the goods have not been identified, title does not pass until identification occurs. Suppose that Juarez sells lumber to Bodan. They agree that Bodan will pick up the lumber at the yard. If the lumber has been identified (segregated, marked, or in any other way distinguished from all other lumber), title passes to Bodan when the contract is signed. If the lumber is still in large storage bins at the mill, title does not pass to Bodan until the particular pieces of lumber to be sold under this contract are identified [UCC 2–401(3)].

---

3. The term *bill of lading* has been used by international carriers for many years and is derived from *bill,* which historically referred to a schedule of costs for services, and the verb *to lade,* which means to load cargo onto a ship or other form of transportation.

Sales or Leases by Nonowners

Problems occur when persons who acquire goods with imperfect titles attempt to sell or lease them. Sections 2–402 and 2–403 of the UCC deal with the rights of two parties who lay claim to the same goods sold with imperfect titles. Generally, a buyer acquires at least whatever title the seller has to the goods sold.

These same UCC sections also protect lessees. Obviously, a lessee does not acquire whatever title the lessor has to the goods; rather, the lessee acquires a right to possess and use the goods—that is, a *leasehold interest.* A lessee acquires whatever leasehold interest the lessor has or has the power to transfer, subject to the lease contract [UCC 2A–303, 2A–304, 2A–305].

VOID TITLE A buyer may unknowingly purchase goods from a seller who is not the owner of the goods. If the seller is a thief, the seller's title is void—legally, no title exists. Thus, the buyer acquires no title, and the real owner can reclaim the goods from the buyer. The same result would occur if the goods were leased instead, because the lessor would have no leasehold interest to transfer.

If Saki steals a valuable necklace owned by Macy, Saki has a *void title* to that necklace. If Saki sells the necklace to Valdez, Macy can reclaim it from Valdez even though Valdez acted in good faith and honestly was not aware that the necklace was stolen. (Note that Valdez may file a tort claim against Saki under these circumstances, but here we are only discussing title to the goods.) Article 2A contains similar provisions for leases.

VOIDABLE TITLE A seller has a *voidable title* if the goods that he or she is selling were obtained by fraud, paid for with a check that was later dishonored, purchased from a minor, or purchased on credit when the seller was *insolvent.* (Under the UCC, a person is **insolvent** when that person ceases to pay his or her debts in the ordinary course of business, cannot pay his or her debts as they become due, or is insolvent within the meaning of federal bankruptcy law [UCC 1–201(23)].)

Good Faith Purchasers. In contrast to a seller with void title, a seller with voidable title has the power to transfer good title to a good faith purchaser for value. A **good faith purchaser** is one who buys without knowledge of circumstances that would make a person of ordinary prudence inquire about the validity of the seller's title to the goods.

One who purchases *for value* gives legally sufficient consideration (value) for the goods purchased. The original owner normally cannot recover goods from a good faith purchaser for value [UCC 2–403(1)].[4] If the buyer of the goods is not a good faith purchaser for value, then the actual owner of the goods can reclaim them from the buyer (or from the seller, if the goods are still in the seller's possession). Exhibit 20–1 illustrates these concepts.

Voidable Title and Leases. The same rules apply in situations involving leases. A lessor with voidable title has the power to transfer a valid leasehold interest to a good faith lessee for value. The real owner cannot recover the goods, except as permitted by the terms of the lease. The real owner can, however, receive all proceeds arising from the lease and can obtain a transfer of the rights that the lessor had under the lease, including the right to the return of the goods when the lease expires [UCC 2A–305(1)].

THE ENTRUSTMENT RULE Entrusting goods to a merchant *who deals in goods of that kind* gives the merchant the power to transfer all rights to *a buyer in the ordinary course of business* [UCC 2–403(2)]. This is known as the **entrustment rule.** Entrusting

includes both turning over the goods to the merchant and leaving purchased goods with the merchant for later delivery or pickup [UCC 2–403(3)]. Article 2A provides a similar rule for leased goods [UCC 2A–305(2)]. A buyer in the ordinary course of business is a person who—in good faith and without knowledge that the sale violates the rights of another party—buys goods in the ordinary course from a merchant (other than a pawnbroker) in the business of selling goods of that kind [UCC 1–201(9)].

The entrustment rule basically allows innocent buyers to obtain legitimate title to goods purchased from merchants even if the merchants do not have good title. Assume that Jan leaves her watch with a jeweler to be repaired. The jeweler sells both new and used watches. The jeweler sells Jan's watch to Kim, a customer who is unaware that the jeweler has no right to sell it. Kim, as a good faith buyer, gets good title against Jan's claim of ownership.[5] Kim, however, obtains only those rights held by the person entrusting the goods (Jan).

Now suppose instead that Jan had stolen the watch from Greg and then left it with the jeweler to be repaired. The jeweler then sold it to Kim. Kim would obtain good title against Jan, who entrusted

---

4. The real owner could sue the person who initially obtained voidable title to the goods.

5. Jan can sue the jeweler for the tort of conversion (or trespass to personal property) to obtain damages equivalent to the cash value of the watch (see Chapter 6 on page 127).

EXHIBIT 20–1 • **Void and Voidable Titles**
If goods are transferred from their owner to another by theft, the thief acquires no ownership rights. Because the thief's title is *void,* a later buyer can acquire no title, and the owner can recover the goods. If the transfer occurs by fraud, the transferee acquires a *voidable* title. A later good faith purchaser for value can acquire good title, and the original owner cannot recover the goods.

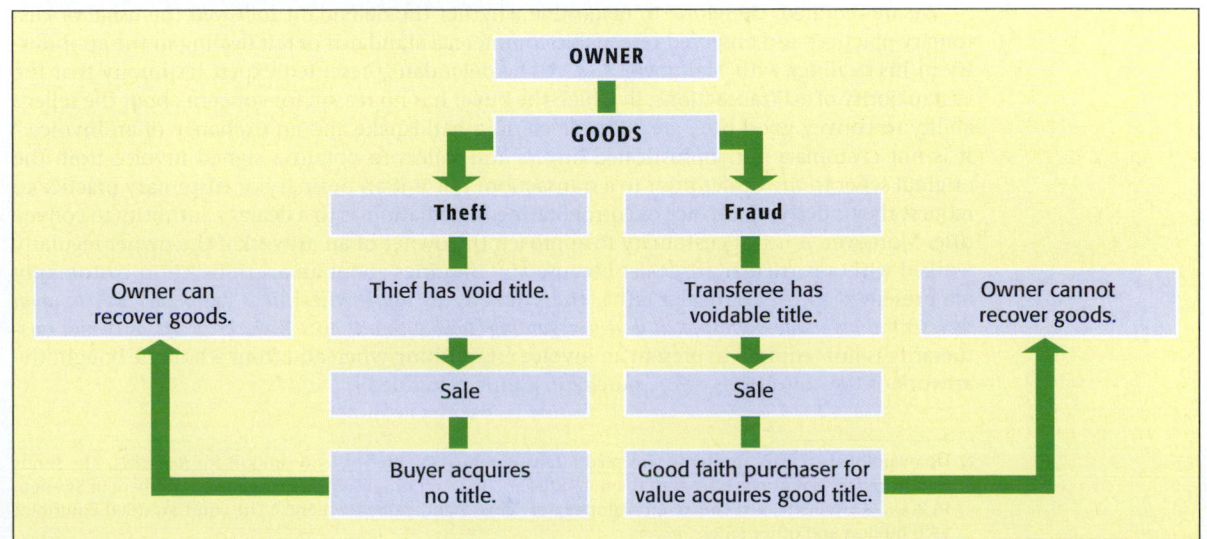

the watch to the jeweler, but not against Greg (the real owner), who neither entrusted the watch to Jan nor authorized Jan to entrust it.

A nonowner's sale of *Red Elvis,* an artwork by Andy Warhol, was at the center of the dispute in the following case.

CASE 20.1
Lindholm v. Brant
Supreme Court of Connecticut, 283 Conn. 65, 925 A.2d 1048 (2007).

BACKGROUND AND FACTS • In 1987, Kerstin Lindholm of Greenwich, Connecticut, bought a silkscreen by Andy Warhol titled *Red Elvis* from Anders Malmberg, a Swedish art dealer, for $300,000. In 1998, Lindholm loaned *Red Elvis* to the Guggenheim Museum in New York City for an exhibition to tour Europe. Peter Brant, who was on the museum's board of trustees and also a Greenwich resident, believed that Lindholm was the owner. Stellan Holm, a Swedish art dealer who had bought and sold other Warhol works with Brant, told him, however, that Malmberg had bought it and would sell it for $2.9 million. Malmberg refused Brant's request to provide a copy of an invoice between Lindholm and himself on the ground that such documents normally and customarily are not disclosed in art deals. To determine whether Malmberg had good title, Brant hired an attorney to search the Art Loss Register (an international database of stolen and missing artworks) and other sources. No problems were found, but Brant was cautioned that this provided only "minimal assurances." Brant's attorney drafted a formal contract, which conditioned payment on the delivery of *Red Elvis* to a warehouse in Denmark. The exchange took place in April 2000.[a] Lindholm filed a suit in a Connecticut state court against Brant, alleging conversion, among other things. The court issued a judgment in Brant's favor. Lindholm appealed to the Connecticut Supreme Court.

IN THE LANGUAGE OF THE COURT
SULLIVAN, J. [Justice]
* * * *
* * * "A person buys goods in the ordinary course if the sale to the person comports with the usual or customary practices in the kind of business in which the seller is engaged or with the seller's own usual or customary practices * * *" [according to Connecticut General Statutes Annotated Section 42a-1-201(9), (Connecticut's version of UCC 1–201(9)]. *A person buys goods in good faith if there is "honesty in fact and the observance of reasonable commercial standards of fair dealing" in the conduct or transaction concerned* [under Section 42a-1-201(20)]. [Emphasis added.]

We are required, therefore, to determine whether the defendant followed the usual or customary practices and observed reasonable commercial standards of fair dealing in the art industry in his dealings with Malmberg. * * * The defendant presented expert testimony that the vast majority of art transactions, in which the buyer has no reason for concern about the seller's ability to convey good title, are "completed on a handshake and an exchange of an invoice." It is not customary for sophisticated buyers and sellers to obtain a signed invoice from the original seller to the dealer prior to a transaction, nor is it an ordinary or customary practice to request the underlying invoice or corroborating information as to a dealer's authority to convey title. Moreover, it is not customary to approach the owner of an artwork if the owner regularly worked with a particular art dealer because any inquiries about an art transaction customarily are presented to the art dealer rather than directly to the [owner]. *It is customary to rely upon representations made by respected dealers regarding their authority to sell works of art.* A dealer customarily is not required to present an invoice establishing when and from whom he bought the artwork or the conditions of the purchase. [Emphasis added.]

---

a. Unaware of this deal, Lindholm accepted a Japanese buyer's offer of $4.6 million for *Red Elvis.* The funds were wired to Malmberg, who kept them. Lindholm filed a criminal complaint against Malmberg in Sweden. In 2003, a Swedish court convicted Malmberg of "gross fraud embezzlement." The court awarded Lindholm $4.6 million and other relief.

CASE 20.1 CONTINUED ▶   We are compelled to conclude, however, that the sale from Malmberg to the defendant was unlike the vast majority of art transactions. * * * Under such circumstances, a handshake and an exchange of invoice is not sufficient to confer status as a buyer in the ordinary course.

* * * *

* * * A merchant buyer has a heightened duty of inquiry when a reasonable merchant would have doubts or questions regarding the seller's authority to sell. * * * In the present case, the defendant had concerns about Malmberg's ability to convey good title to *Red Elvis* because he believed that Lindholm might have had a claim to the painting. The defendant also was concerned that Malmberg had not yet acquired title to the painting * * * .

Because of his concern that Lindholm might make a claim to *Red Elvis,* the defendant took the extraordinary step of hiring counsel to conduct an investigation and to negotiate a formal contract of sale on his behalf. * * * Such searches typically are not conducted during the course of a normal art transaction and, therefore, provided the defendant with at least some assurance that Lindholm had no claims to the painting.

Moreover, * * * both Malmberg and Holm had reputations as honest, reliable, and trustworthy art dealers. * * * The defendant had little reason to doubt Malmberg's claim that he was the owner of *Red Elvis,* and any doubts that he did have reasonably were allayed [reduced] by relying on Holm's assurances that Malmberg had bought the painting from the plaintiff * * * .

The defendant's concerns were further allayed when Malmberg delivered *Red Elvis* to a * * * warehouse in Denmark, the delivery location the parties had agreed to in the contract of sale. At the time of the sale, the painting was on loan to the Guggenheim, whose policy it was to release a painting on loan only to the true owner, or to someone the true owner had authorized to take possession. * * * We conclude that these steps were sufficient to conform to reasonable commercial standards for the sale of artwork under the circumstances and, therefore, that the defendant had status as a buyer in the ordinary course of business.

DECISION AND REMEDY • *The Connecticut Supreme Court affirmed the judgment of the lower court. The state supreme court concluded that "on the basis of all the circumstances surrounding this sale," Brant was a buyer in the ordinary course of business and, therefore, took all rights to* Red Elvis *under UCC 2–403(2).*

THE ETHICAL DIMENSION • *How did the "usual and customary" methods of dealing in the art business help Malmberg deceive the other parties in this case? What additional steps might those parties have taken to protect themselves from such deceit?*

THE GLOBAL DIMENSION • *Considering the international locales in this case, why was Lindholm able to bring an action against Brant in Connecticut?*

SECTION 3
RISK OF LOSS

Under the UCC, risk of loss does not necessarily pass with title. When risk of loss passes from a seller or lessor to a buyer or lessee is generally determined by the contract between the parties. Sometimes, the contract states expressly when the risk of loss passes. At other times, it does not, and a court must interpret the existing terms to ascertain whether the risk has passed. When no provision in the contract indicates when risk passes, the UCC provides special rules, based on delivery terms, to guide the courts.

Delivery with Movement of the Goods—Carrier Cases

When the contract involves movement of the goods through a common carrier but does not specify when risk of loss passes, the courts first look for specific delivery terms in the contract. The terms that have traditionally been used in contracts are listed and defined in Exhibit 20–2 on the next page. *Unless the parties agree otherwise,* these terms will determine which party will pay the costs of delivering the goods and who will bear the risk of loss. If the contract does not include these terms, then the courts must decide whether the contract is a shipment or a destination contract.

EXHIBIT 20–2 • Contract Terms—Definitions

The contract terms listed and defined in this exhibit help to determine which party will bear the costs of delivery and when risk of loss will pass from the seller to the buyer.

F.O.B. (free on board)—Indicates that the selling price of goods includes transportation costs to the specific F.O.B. place named in the contract. The seller pays the expenses and carries the risk of loss to the F.O.B. place named [UCC 2–319(1)]. If the named place is the place from which the goods are shipped (for example, the seller's city or place of business), the contract is a shipment contract. If the named place is the place to which the goods are to be shipped (for example, the buyer's city or place of business), the contract is a destination contract.

F.A.S. (free alongside ship)—Requires that the seller, at his or her own expense and risk, deliver the goods alongside the vessel in the manner usual in that port or on a dock designated and provided by the buyer [UCC 2–319(2)]. An F.A.S. contract is essentially an F.O.B. contract for ships.

C.I.F. or **C.&F.** (cost, insurance, and freight or just cost and freight)—Requires, among other things, that the seller "put the goods in possession of a carrier" before risk passes to the buyer [UCC 2–320(2)]. (These are basically pricing terms, and the contracts remain shipment contracts, not destination contracts.)

Delivery ex-ship (delivery from the carrying vessel)—Means that risk of loss does not pass to the buyer until the goods are properly unloaded from the ship or other carrier [UCC 2–322].

SHIPMENT CONTRACTS In a shipment contract, the seller or lessor is required or authorized to ship goods by carrier, but is not required to deliver them to a particular destination. The risk of loss in a shipment contract passes to the buyer or lessee when the goods are delivered to the carrier [UCC 2–509(1)(a), 2A–219(2)(a)].

For example, a seller in Texas sells five hundred cases of grapefruit to a buyer in New York, F.O.B. Houston (free on board in Houston, which means that the buyer pays the transportation charges from Houston—see Exhibit 20–2). The contract authorizes shipment by carrier; it does not require that the seller tender the grapefruit in New York. Risk passes to the buyer when conforming goods are properly placed in the possession of the carrier. If the goods are damaged in transit, the loss is the buyer's. (Actually, buyers have recourse against carriers, subject to certain limitations, and they may insure the goods from the time the goods leave the seller.)

The following case illustrates how the application of a contract's delivery term can affect a buyer's recovery for goods damaged in transit.

✳ EXTENDED CASE 20.2 ✳
Spray-Tek, Inc. v. Robbins Motor Transportation, Inc.

United States District Court, Western District of Wisconsin, 426 F.Supp.2d 875 (2006).

IN THE LANGUAGE OF THE COURT
SHABAZ, District Judge.
* * * *
    Plaintiff Spray-Tek, Inc., is engaged in the business of commercial dehydration of food flavor, pharmaceutical and soft chemical products. In 2003 plaintiff entered into a contract with Niro, Inc. (hereinafter Niro) in which Niro was to design and manufacture a fourteen-foot diameter cone-bottom drying chamber (hereinafter drying chamber) for plaintiff. Pursuant to the terms of the contract Niro was

also responsible for shipping the drying chamber from its facility in Hudson, Wisconsin, to plaintiff's facility in Bethlehem, Pennsylvania. The contract stated in relevant part:

* * * *

For one (1) Niro-Bowen * * * drying chamber, * * * F.O.B. points of manufacture in the U.S.A. * * *

Price * * * $1,161,500.00

* * * *

IX. RISKS OF LOSS. The Purchaser shall bear the risk of loss of or damage to the equipment and parts after delivery of the equipment and parts to the job site or

to the shipping point if delivery F.O.B. shipping point is specified.

    On October 14, 2004 Niro's representative Mr. David Thoen contacted defendant Robbins Motor Transportation, Inc., to obtain an estimate for transporting the drying chamber to plaintiff. Mr. Thoen spoke with Mr. Robert Kauffman, Jr., who serves as defendant's Southwest Regional Terminal Manager. * * * Mr. Kauffman prepared and sent an estimate to Niro.

    Mr. Thoen signed the estimate and faxed it back to defendant * * *.

    On October 18, 2004 defendant arrived at Niro's facility in Hudson,

EXTENDED CASE 20.2 CONTINUED ➡

Wisconsin, and the drying chamber was loaded onto its trailer. Niro prepared a Bill of Lading * * *.

* * * *

On or about October 28, 2004, the drying chamber was damaged while it was in transit * * * in Baltimore, Maryland. Accordingly, the drying chamber never arrived at plaintiff's facility in Bethlehem, Pennsylvania. The drying chamber was damaged when it struck an overpass and became dislodged from defendant's vehicle. It was inspected and declared a total loss. Accordingly, Niro manufactured a replacement drying chamber for plaintiff and invoiced it $233,100.00 in replacement costs.

* * * *

[Spray-Tek filed a suit in a federal district court against Robbins under a federal statute known as the Carmack Amendment to recover the replacement cost and other expenses.] The Carmack Amendment * * * states in relevant part:

A carrier providing transportation or service * * * shall issue a receipt or bill of lading for property it receives for transportation under this part. That carrier * * * [is] liable to the person entitled to recover under the receipt or bill of lading.

The purpose of the Carmack Amendment is to establish uniform federal guidelines designed in part to remove the uncertainty surrounding a carrier's liability when damage occurs to a shipper's interstate shipment.

Under the Carmack Amendment plaintiff bears the burden of establishing a *prima facie* case [legally sufficient case] which requires it to demonstrate: (1) delivery to

the carrier in good condition; (2) arrival in damaged condition; and (3) the amount of damages. * * * The excepted causes [relieving a carrier of liability] are: (1) acts of God; (2) the public enemy; (3) acts of the shipper himself; (4) public authority; or (5) the inherent vice or nature of the goods.

Defendant concedes that it received the drying chamber in good condition. Accordingly, plaintiff's first element of its *prima facie* case is established.

* * * *

It is undisputed that the drying chamber was damaged when it struck an overpass and became dislodged from defendant's vehicle. Additionally, it is undisputed that after the accident the drying chamber was inspected and declared a total loss.

An * * * argument defendant asserts concerning plaintiff's second element of its *prima facie* case is that plaintiff cannot demonstrate it owned the drying chamber during transport. However, the contract plaintiff entered into with Niro establishes that it was the owner of the drying chamber when it was damaged. The contract provided that the terms of sale were "F.O.B. points of manufacture in the U.S.A." According to * * * David Brand who serves as plaintiff's vice-president and general manager "F.O.B. points of manufacture" means that the drying chamber became plaintiff's property once it was "placed on board the delivery truck at its point of manufacture in Hudson, Wisconsin."

Mr. Brand's assertion * * * is reinforced by the provision in the contract concerning risks of loss. * * * The "F.O.B. points of manufacture" language * * *

demonstrates that plaintiff bore the risk of loss once the drying chamber departed from Niro's Hudson, Wisconsin, facility. * * * Accordingly, plaintiff established the second element of its *prima facie* case.

Finally, defendant asserts plaintiff cannot meet its burden of establishing the third element of its *prima facie* case because it failed to demonstrate what "it is obligated to pay for the dryer." However, * * * Niro invoiced plaintiff $233,100.00 for the replacement dryer. Accordingly, plaintiff established the third element of its *prima facie* case because its amount of damages is $233,100.00.

Plaintiff met its burden of establishing a *prima facie* case under the Carmack Amendment. * * * Defendant concedes it failed to produce any evidence establishing that damage to the shipment was due to one of the excepted causes. Accordingly, plaintiff is entitled to summary judgment on the issue of defendant's liability under the Carmack Amendment.

* * * *

* * * There remains a genuine issue of material fact concerning the issue of whether defendant provided Niro with a reasonable opportunity to choose between two different levels of liability.

* * * *

* * * The October 14, 2004, estimate does not contain a term or condition limiting defendant's liability. However, the Bill of Lading limits defendant's liability * * *. Accordingly, when the two documents are viewed together as a whole the Court concludes the contract is ambiguous and its interpretation must be reserved for the fact finder [at trial].

 QUESTIONS

1. Would the result have been different if the contract between Spray-Tek and Niro had specified "F.O.B. Bethlehem, Pennsylvania"? Explain.
2. One of the elements required to establish a carrier's liability is a showing that the goods arrived in damaged condition. Should Robbins Motor Transportation have been absolved of liability in this case on the ground that the drying chamber never arrived at its final destination? Why or why not?

DESTINATION CONTRACTS In a destination contract, the risk of loss passes to the buyer or lessee when the goods are tendered to the buyer or lessee at the specified destination [UCC 2–509(1)(b), 2A–219(2)(b)]. In the preceding example involving the cases of grapefruit, if the contract had been a destination contract, F.O.B. New York, risk of loss during transit to New York would have been the seller's. Risk of loss would not have passed to the buyer until the carrier tendered the goods to the buyer in New York.

Whether a contract is a shipment contract or a destination contract can have significant consequences for the parties. When an agreement is ambiguous as to whether it is a shipment or a destination contract, courts normally will presume that it is a shipment contract. The parties must use clear and explicit language to overcome this presumption and create a destination contract.

Delivery without Movement of the Goods

The UCC also addresses situations in which the contract does not require the goods to be shipped or moved. Frequently, the buyer or lessee is to pick up the goods from the seller or lessor, or the goods are to be held by a bailee. A *bailment* is a temporary delivery of personal property, without passage of title, into the care of another, called a *bailee*. Under the UCC, a bailee is a party who—by a bill of lading, warehouse receipt, or other document of title—acknowledges possession of goods and/or contracts to deliver them. For example, a warehousing company or a trucking company may be a bailee.[6]

GOODS HELD BY THE SELLER When the seller keeps the goods for pickup, a document of title usually is not used. If the seller is not a merchant, the risk of loss to goods held by the seller passes to the buyer on *tender of delivery* [UCC 2–509(3)]. This means that the seller bears the risk of loss until he or she makes the goods available to the buyer and notifies the buyer that the goods are ready to be picked up. If the seller is a merchant, risk of loss to goods held by the seller passes to the buyer when the buyer *actually takes physical possession of the goods* [UCC 2–509(3)]. In other words, the merchant bears the risk of loss between the time the contract is formed and the time the buyer picks up the goods.

CASE IN POINT Henry Ganno purchased a twelve-foot beam at a lumberyard, and an employee at the lumberyard loaded it onto Ganno's truck. A sign at the lumberyard stated that the store did not secure loads for customers, but Ganno did not tie down or otherwise secure the beam to his truck. After he drove onto the highway, the beam fell out of his truck. While he was trying to retrieve the beam, he was struck by another vehicle and injured. Ganno sued the lumberyard for negligence, but the court held that Ganno—not the lumberyard—bore the risk of loss and injury after he left the lumberyard's premises. Once the truck was loaded, the risk of loss passed to Ganno under the UCC because he had taken physical possession of the goods.[7]

With respect to leases, the risk of loss passes to the lessee on the lessee's receipt of the goods if the lessor—or supplier, in a finance lease (see Chapter 19 on page 362)—is a merchant. Otherwise, the risk passes to the lessee on tender of delivery [UCC 2A–219(2)(c)]. For example, Erikson Crane leases a helicopter from Jevis, Ltd., which is in the business of renting aircraft. While Erikson's pilot is on the way to Idaho to pick up the helicopter, the helicopter is damaged during an unexpected storm. In this situation, Jevis is a merchant-lessor, so it bears the risk of loss to the leased helicopter until Erikson takes possession of the helicopter.

GOODS HELD BY A BAILEE When a bailee is holding goods that are to be delivered under a contract without being moved, the goods are usually represented by a document of title, such as a bill of lading or a warehouse receipt.[8] Risk of loss passes to the buyer when (1) the buyer receives a negotiable document of title for the goods, (2) the bailee acknowledges the buyer's right to possess the goods, or (3) the buyer receives a nonnegotiable document of title or a writing (record) directing the bailee to hand over the goods *and* the buyer has had a *reasonable time* to present the document to the bailee and demand the goods. Obviously, if the bailee refuses to honor the document, the risk of loss remains with the seller [UCC 2–503(4)(b), 2–509(2)].

With respect to leases, if goods held by a bailee are to be delivered without being moved, the risk of loss

---

6. See Chapter 49 for a detailed discussion of the law of bailments.

7. *Ganno v. Lanoga Corp.*, 119 Wash.App. 310, 80 P.3d 180 (2003).

8. A negotiable document of title actually stands for the goods it covers, so any transfer of the goods requires the surrender of the document. In contrast, a nonnegotiable document of title merely serves as evidence of the goods' existence.

passes to the lessee on acknowledgment by the bailee of the lessee's right to possession of the goods [UCC 2A–219(2)(b)].

Concept Summary 20.1 reviews the rules for when title and risk of loss pass to the buyer or lessee when the seller or lessor is not required to ship or deliver the goods.

Conditional Sales

Buyers and sellers can form sales contracts that are conditioned either on the buyer's approval of the goods or on the buyer's resale of the goods. Under such contracts, the buyer is in possession of the goods, and disputes can arise over which party should bear the loss if the goods are damaged or stolen. Disputes may also arise over whether the goods being held by the buyer are subject to claims of the buyer's creditors.

SALE ON APPROVAL In a **sale on approval,** a seller offers to sell goods to a buyer (who is usually not a merchant) and sends the goods to the buyer on a trial basis. The goods are delivered primarily so that the prospective buyer can use the goods and be convinced of their appearance or performance. The term *sale* here is misleading, because only an *offer* to sell has been made, along with a bailment created by the buyer's possession.

In a sale on approval, title and risk of loss remain with the seller until the buyer accepts (approves) the offer by any act inconsistent with the *trial* purpose or the seller's ownership (such as retaining the goods beyond the trial period). If the buyer does not wish to accept, the buyer may notify the seller of that fact within the trial period, and the return is made at the seller's expense and risk [UCC 2–327(1)]. Goods held on approval are not subject to the claims of the buyer's creditors until acceptance.

For example, Brad orders a Bowflex TreadClimber over the Internet, and the manufacturer allows him to try it risk-free for thirty days. If Brad decides to keep the TreadClimber, then the sale is complete, but if he returns it within thirty days, there will be no sale and he will not be charged. If Brad files for bankruptcy within the thirty-day period and still has the TreadClimber in his possession, his creditors may not attach (seize) the TreadClimber, because he has not accepted it yet.

CONCEPT SUMMARY 20.1
Delivery without Movement of the Goods

Concept	Description

Goods Not Represented by a Document of Title	Unless otherwise agreed, if the goods are not represented by a document of title, title and risk pass as follows:
	1. Title passes on the formation of the contract [UCC 2–401(3)(b)].
	2. Risk of loss passes to the buyer or lessee:
	  a. If the seller or lessor is a merchant, risk passes on the buyer's or lessee's *receipt* of the goods.
	  b. If the seller or lessor is a nonmerchant, risk passes to the buyer or lessee on the seller's or lessor's *tender* of delivery of the goods [UCC 2–509(3), 2A–219(2)(c)].

Goods Represented by a Document of Title	Unless otherwise agreed, if the goods are represented by a document of title, title and risk pass to the buyer when any of the following occurs: 1. The buyer receives a negotiable document of title for the goods. 2. The bailee acknowledges the buyer's right to possess the goods. 3. The buyer receives a nonnegotiable document of title or a writing (record) directing the bailee to hand over the goods and the buyer has had a reasonable time to present the document to the bailee and demand the goods [UCC 2–503(4)(b), 2–509(2)].
Leased Goods Held by a Bailee	If leased goods held by a bailee are to be delivered without being moved, the risk of loss passes to the lessee on acknowledgment by the bailee of the lessee's right to possession of the goods [UCC 2A–219(2)(b)].

SALE OR RETURN In a **sale or return,** in contrast, the sale is completed but the buyer has an option to return the goods and undo the sale. Sale-or-return contracts often arise when a merchant purchases goods primarily for resale, but has the right to return part or all of the goods in lieu of payment if the goods fail to be resold. Basically, a sale or return is a sale of goods in the present that may be undone at the buyer's option within a specified time period.

Because the buyer receives possession at the time of the sale, title and risk of loss pass to the buyer and remain with the buyer unless the goods are returned within the time period specified. If the buyer decides to return the goods within this time period, the return is made at the buyer's risk and expense. Goods held under a sale-or-return contract are subject to the claims of the buyer's creditors while they are in the buyer's possession.

Consignments

Under a **consignment,** the owner of goods (the *consignor*) delivers them to another (the *consignee*) to be sold or kept. The consignee essentially acts as an agent (agency will be discussed in Chapter 32)

of the consignor-owner and holds the goods as a bailee. Consignments are common in business. For example, a wholesale diamond company might give diamonds to a retailer on consignment, or a pharmaceutical company might provide drugs to a sales representative on consignment.[9] A consignment is similar to a sale or return in that a merchant takes possession of goods for resale, but a consignment normally results in a bailment rather than a sale.

Before the adoption of the 2001 amendments to the UCC, consignments were treated as a sale or return and governed by Article 2. Since these amendments, however, Article 9 on secured transactions (see Chapter 29) generally has governed consignment transactions, with some exceptions. For example, Article 9 does not cover consignments of goods that are considered "consumer goods" immediately before delivery. If neither Article 2 nor Article 9 govern such consignments, what law applies to them? This was the issue before the court in the following case.

---

9. See, for example, *Forest Diamonds, Inc. v. Aminov Diamonds, LLC,* ___ F.Supp.2d ___, 2010 WL 148615 (S.D.N.Y. 2010); and *Christopher v. SmithKlein Beecham Corp.,* 2010 WL 396300 (D.Ariz. 2010).

CASE 20.3
In re Music City RV, LLC

Supreme Court of Tennessee, 304 S.W.3d 806 (2010).
www.tsc.state.tn.us/OPINIONS/TSC/sc1qtr2010.shtml[a]

BACKGROUND AND FACTS • Dudley King and eight other unrelated individuals consigned their recreational vehicles (RVs) for sale on the lot of Music City RV, LLC (MCRV). Subsequently, an involuntary Chapter 7 bankruptcy petition was filed against MCRV by some of its creditors (this type of bankruptcy proceeding will be discussed in Chapter 30). At the time of the bankruptcy, all of the consigned RVs were still on MCRV's premises. Given that Article 9 of the UCC does not cover consignments that consist of consumer goods, the question before the bankruptcy court was whether the transaction was covered by Article 2 of the UCC. Because there were no precedents to guide the bankruptcy court on this issue, the court submitted the question to the Supreme Court of Tennessee for its decision.

IN THE LANGUAGE OF THE COURT
Sharon G. *LEE,* J. [Justice]
* * * *
In the case at bar [the case before the court], the parties agree that Article 9 does not apply because the consigned RVs were "consumer goods," defined by the UCC as "goods that are used or bought for use primarily for personal, family, or household purposes," and apparently the bankruptcy court agreed.

---

a. On the page that opens, scroll down to "Cases posted the week of 1/18/2010" to find the case title, and click on "View" to access the opinion. The Tennessee Supreme Court maintains this Web site.

CASE 20.3 CONTINUED ➡   Regarding the consignment transactions in the instant case, consignor Mr. King argues that the effect of the 2001 Amendment[s] to [Tennessee's law corresponding to UCC Section 2–326] was to remove *all* consignment transactions from the province of Article 2 of the UCC. Accordingly, *because the transactions at issue do not fall within Article 9's definition of "consignment," the UCC does not apply and the consignments here are governed by the common law of bailment.* The Bankruptcy Trustee argues that the 2001 Amendment[s] did not remove all consignments from [Section 2–326]. Consequently, those consignment transactions that do not fall within Article 9's definition of "consignment" continue to be governed by Article 2, and each consignment transaction should be deemed a "sale or return" by operation of [Section 2–326]. Our review of the statutory language at issue and the Official Comments to the UCC persuades us that Mr. King's position is correct. [Emphasis added.]

* * * *

As an initial matter, we note that [UCC Section 2–326] no longer makes reference to consignments, nor does it describe a transaction that could be characterized as a "consignment." A "classic consignment" has been described as a transaction where "the owner of goods delivers possession to a bailee [one to whom person property is entrusted for a particular purpose] who is also given the power to sell the goods to its customers. Title remains with the consignor until the goods are sold to the ultimate buyer and the consignee is free to return any unsold goods to the consignor."

Further, [UCC 2–326] expressly applies to situations where "delivered goods may be returned *by the buyer* even though they conform to the contract." (Emphasis added [by the court]). Subsection (2) of the statute similarly refers to "the buyer" in describing applicable transactions: "(g)oods held on approval are not subject to the claims of *the buyer's* creditors until acceptance; goods held on sale or return are subject to such claims while in *the buyer's* possession." (Emphasis added [by the court]). Article 2 of the UCC as adopted in Tennessee defines "buyer" as "a person who buys or contracts to buy goods." In this case, there is no indication that MCRV contracted to buy the RVs at issue, but rather, as a consignee, MCRV agreed to take possession and to try to sell them to a third party for a commission. Similarly, there was no "sale" as defined at [UCC 2–106] as "the passing of title from the seller to the buyer for a price." MCRV was not a buyer of the RVs, and it consequently follows that [UCC Section 2–326] does not apply under the circumstances of this case.

DECISION AND REMEDY • *The Supreme Court of Tennessee concluded that the consignment of an RV by a consumer (not another business) to a Tennessee RV dealer, for the purpose of selling that RV to a third person, is not a transaction covered under Section 2–326 of the UCC, as adopted in Tennessee. Rather, the transaction is covered by the law of bailments.*

WHAT IF THE FACTS WERE DIFFERENT? • *Suppose that the goods on consignment were not consumer goods but goods owned by a business enterprise. How would that change in the facts affect the court's decision?*

THE ECONOMIC DIMENSION • *How does the answer to the question before the court affect the consignors?*

WHO HOLDS TITLE TO CONSIGNED GOODS? If the consignee sells consigned goods, title passes to the buyer, and the consignee must pay the consignor for the goods sold. The consignee typically receives a commission for selling the goods. If the consignee does not sell or keep the goods, they may simply be returned to the consignor. Although the goods are in the possession of the consignee, the consignee does not hold title to them. The consignor-owner can retake the goods from the consignee at any time.

CREDITORS' CLAIMS TO CONSIGNED GOODS As previously mentioned, the question of whether the goods being held on consignment are subject to the claims of creditors is now governed by Article 9 of the UCC. Generally, if the owner of the consigned goods has filed a *financing statement* (see Chapter 29) covering the goods, then that party's creditors can assert claims against the goods. If the owner-consignor has not filed a financing statement, then the creditors of the dealer who is in possession of the consigned goods can assert claims against the goods. The goods are not subject to claims by the consignee-dealer's creditors, however, if the creditors know that the consignee is in the business of regularly selling the goods of others on consignment [UCC 9–102(20)].[10]

Risk of Loss When a Sales or Lease Contract Is Breached

When a sales or lease contract is breached, the transfer of risk operates differently depending on which party breaches. Generally, the party in breach bears the risk of loss.

WHEN THE SELLER OR LESSOR BREACHES If the goods are so nonconforming that the buyer has the right to reject them, the risk of loss does not pass to the buyer until the defects are *cured* (that is, until the goods are repaired, replaced, or discounted in price by the seller—see Chapter 21) or until the buyer accepts the goods in spite of their defects (thus waiving the right to reject). For example, suppose that a buyer orders black refrigerators from a seller, F.O.B. seller's plant. The seller ships white refrigerators instead. The white refrigerators (nonconforming goods) are damaged in transit. The risk of loss falls on the seller. Had the seller shipped black refrigerators (conforming goods) instead, the risk would have fallen on the buyer [UCC 2–510(1)].

---

10. See *Fariba v. Dealer Services Corp.*, 178 Cal.App.4th 156, 100 Cal. Rptr.3d 219 (2009); and *Italian Designer Import Outlet, Inc. v. New York Central Mutual Fire Insurance Co.*, 26 Misc.3d 631, 891 N.Y.S.2d 260 (2009).

If a buyer accepts a shipment of goods and later discovers a defect, acceptance can be revoked. The revocation allows the buyer to pass the risk of loss back to the seller, at least to the extent that the buyer's insurance does not cover the loss [UCC 2–510(2)].

Article 2A provides a similar rule for leases. If the tender or delivery of goods is so nonconforming that the lessee has the right to reject them, the risk of loss remains with the lessor (or the supplier) until cure or acceptance [UCC 2A–220(1)(a)]. If the lessee, after acceptance, rightfully revokes her or his acceptance of the goods, the risk of loss passes back to the lessor or supplier to the extent that the lessee's insurance does not cover the loss [UCC 2A–220(1)(b)].

WHEN THE BUYER OR LESSEE BREACHES The general rule is that when a buyer or lessee breaches a contract, the risk of loss *immediately shifts* to the buyer or lessee. This rule has three important limitations [UCC 2–510(3), 2A–220(2)]:

1. The seller or lessor must already have identified the contract goods.
2. The buyer or lessee bears the risk for only a *commercially reasonable time* after the seller or lessor has learned of the breach.
3. The buyer or lessee is liable only to the extent of any deficiency in the seller's or lessor's insurance coverage.

See *Concept Summary 20.2* for a review of the rules on who bears the risk of loss when a contract is breached.

CONCEPT SUMMARY 20.2
Risk of Loss When a Sales or Lease Contract Is Breached

Concept	Description
When the Seller or Lessor Breaches the Contract	If the seller or lessor breaches by tendering nonconforming goods that the buyer or lessee has a right to reject, the risk of loss does not pass to the buyer or lessee until the defects are cured or the buyer accepts the goods (thus waiving the right to reject) [UCC 2–510(1), 2A–220(1)].
When the Buyer or Lessee Breaches the Contract	If the buyer or lessee breaches the contract, the risk of loss to identified goods immediately shifts to the buyer or lessee. Limitations to this rule are as follows [UCC 2–510(3), 2A–220(2)]: 1. The seller or lessor must have already identified the contract goods. 2. The buyer or lessee bears the risk for only a commercially reasonable time after the seller or lessor has learned of the breach. 3. The buyer or lessee is liable only to the extent of any deficiency in the seller's or lessor's insurance coverage.

SECTION 4
INSURABLE INTEREST

Parties to sales and lease contracts often obtain insurance coverage to protect against damage, loss, or destruction of goods. Any party purchasing insurance, however, must have a sufficient interest in the insured item to obtain a valid policy. Insurance laws—not the UCC—determine sufficiency. The UCC is helpful, though, because it contains certain rules regarding insurable interests in goods.

Insurable Interest of the Buyer or Lessee

A buyer or lessee has an **insurable interest** in *identified goods*. The moment the contract goods are identified by the seller or lessor, the buyer or lessee has a special property interest that allows the buyer or lessee to obtain the necessary insurance coverage for those goods even before the risk of loss has passed [UCC 2–501(1), 2A–218(1)]. Identification can be made at any time and in any manner agreed to by the parties. If the parties do not explicitly agree on identification in their contract, then the UCC provisions on identification that were previously discussed in this chapter apply. For example, in March a farmer sells a cotton crop that she hopes to harvest in October. If the contract does not specify otherwise, the buyer acquires an insurable interest in the crop when it is planted because the goods (the cotton crop) are identified to the sales contract at that time [UCC 2–501(1)(c)].

Insurable Interest of the Seller or Lessor

A seller has an insurable interest in goods as long as he or she retains title to the goods. Even after title passes to a buyer, a seller who has a security interest in the goods (a right to secure payment—see Chapter 29) still has an insurable interest and can insure the goods [UCC 2–501(2)]. Thus, both the buyer and the seller can have an insurable interest in identical goods at the same time. Of course, the buyer or seller must sustain an actual loss to have the right to recover from an insurance company. In regard to leases, the lessor retains an insurable interest in leased goods unless the lessee exercises an option to buy, in which event the risk of loss passes to the lessee [UCC 2A–218(3)].

REVIEWING
Title, Risk, and Insurable Interest

In December, Mendoza agreed to buy the broccoli grown on one hundred acres of Willow Glen's one-thousand-acre broccoli farm. The sales contract specified F.O.B. Willow Glen's field by Falcon Trucking. The broccoli was to be planted in February and harvested in March of the following year. Using the information presented in the chapter, answer the following questions.

1. At what point is a crop of broccoli identified to the contract under the Uniform Commercial Code? Why is identification significant?
2. When does title to the broccoli pass from Willow Glen to Mendoza under the contract terms? Why?
3. Suppose that while in transit, Falcon's truck overturns and spills the entire load. Who bears the loss, Mendoza or Willow Glen?
4. Suppose that instead of buying fresh broccoli, Mendoza had contracted with Willow Glen to purchase one thousand cases of frozen broccoli from Willow Glen's processing plant. The highest grade of broccoli is packaged under the "FreshBest" label, and everything else is packaged under the "FamilyPac" label. Further suppose that although the contract specified that Mendoza was to receive FreshBest broccoli, Falcon Trucking delivered FamilyPac broccoli to Mendoza. If Mendoza refuses to accept the broccoli, who bears the loss?

DEBATE THIS: *The distinction between shipment and destination contracts for the purpose of deciding who will bear the risk of loss should be eliminated in favor of a rule that always requires the buyer to obtain insurance for the goods being shipped.*

TERMS AND CONCEPTS

	document of title 386	identification 384	sale or return 394
	entrustment rule 387	insolvent 386	shipment contract 385
consignment 394	fungible goods 385	insurable interest 397	
destination contract 386	good faith purchaser 386	sale on approval 393	

QUESTIONS AND CASE PROBLEMS

20–1. Risk of Loss Mackey orders from Pride one thousand cases of Greenie brand peas from lot A at list price to be shipped F.O.B. Pride's city via Fast Freight Lines. Pride receives the order and immediately sends Mackey an acceptance of the order with a promise to ship promptly. Pride later separates the one thousand cases of Greenie peas and prints Mackey's name and address on each case. The peas are placed on Pride's dock, and Fast Freight is notified to pick up the shipment. The night before the pickup by Fast Freight, through no fault of Pride's, a fire destroys the one thousand cases of peas. Pride claims that title passed to Mackey at the time the contract was made and that risk of loss passed to Mackey when the goods were marked with Mackey's name and address. Discuss Pride's contentions.

20–2. QUESTION WITH SAMPLE ANSWER: Risk of Loss.

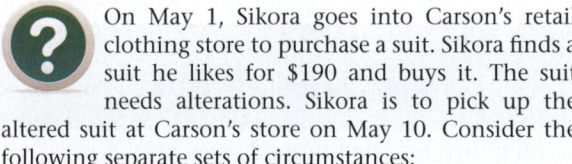

On May 1, Sikora goes into Carson's retail clothing store to purchase a suit. Sikora finds a suit he likes for $190 and buys it. The suit needs alterations. Sikora is to pick up the altered suit at Carson's store on May 10. Consider the following separate sets of circumstances:

(a) One of Carson's major creditors obtains a judgment on the debt Carson owes and has the court issue a writ of execution (a court order to seize a debtor's property to satisfy a debt) to collect on that judgment all clothing in Carson's possession. Discuss Sikora's rights in the suit under these circumstances.

(b) On May 9, through no fault of Carson's, the store burns down, and all contents are a total loss. Between Carson and Sikora, who suffers the loss of the suit destroyed by the fire? Explain.

• **For a sample answer to Question 20–2, go to Appendix I at the end of this text.**

20–3. Sale or Return Zeke, who sells lawn mowers, tells Stasio, a regular customer, about a special promotional campaign. On receipt of a $50 down payment, Zeke will sell Stasio a new Universal lawn mower for $200, even though it normally sells for $350. Zeke also says that if Stasio does not like the performance of the lawn mower, he can return it within thirty days, and Zeke will refund the $50 down payment. Stasio pays the $50 and takes the mower. On the tenth day, the lawn mower is stolen through no fault of Stasio's. Stasio calls Zeke and demands the return of his $50. Zeke claims that Stasio should suffer the risk of loss and that he still owes Zeke $150 for the rest of the purchase price. Discuss who is correct, Stasio or Zeke.

20–4. Risk of Loss H.S.A. II, Inc., made parts for motor vehicles. Under an agreement with Ford Motor Co., Ford provided steel to H.S.A. to make Ford parts. Ford's purchase orders for the parts contained the term "FOB Carrier Supplier's [Plant]." GMAC Business Credit, L.L.C., loaned money to H.S.A. under terms that guaranteed payment would be made—if the funds were not otherwise available—from H.S.A.'s inventory, raw materials, and finished goods. H.S.A. filed for bankruptcy on February 2, 2000, and ceased operations on June 20, when it had in its plant more than $1 million in finished goods for Ford. Ford sent six trucks to H.S.A. to pick up the goods. GMAC halted the removal. The parties asked the bankruptcy court to determine whose interest had priority. GMAC contended, among other things, that Ford did not have an interest in the goods because there had not yet been a sale. Ford responded that under its purchase orders, title and risk of loss transferred on completion of the parts. In whose favor should the court rule, and why? [*In re H.S.A. II, Inc.*, 271 Bankr. 534 (E.D.Mich. 2002)]

20–5. CASE PROBLEM WITH SAMPLE ANSWER: Entrustment Rule.

William Bisby gave an all-terrain vehicle (ATV) to Del City Cycle in Enid, Oklahoma, to sell on his behalf. Joseph Maddox bought the ATV but paid for it with a check written on a closed checking account. The bank refused to honor the check. Before Del City or Bisby could reclaim the ATV, however, Maddox sold it to Aaron Jordan, who sold it to Shannon Skaggs. In November 2003, the Enid Police Department seized the ATV from Skaggs. Bisby filed a suit in an Oklahoma state court against the state and Skaggs, claiming that he was the owner of the ATV and asking the court to return it to him. Skaggs objected. Is there a distinction between the ownership interests of a party who steals an item and those of a party who acquires the item with a check that is not honored? What was the status of Skaggs's title, if any, to the ATV? Among the many parties involved in this case, which one should the court rule is the owner of "good" title to the ATV? Why? [State v. Skaggs, 140 P.3d 576 (Okla.Civ.App. Div. 3 2006)]

- To view a sample answer for Problem 20–5, go to this book's Web site at www.cengage.com/blaw/clarkson, select "Chapter 20," and click on "Case Problem with Sample Answer."

20–6. Shipment and Destination Contracts In 2003, Karen Pearson and Steve and Tara Carlson agreed to buy a 2004 Dynasty recreational vehicle (RV) from DeMartini's RV Sales in Grass Valley, California. On September 29, Pearson, the Carlsons, and DeMartini's signed a contract providing that "seller agrees to deliver the vehicle to you on the date this contract is signed." The buyers made a payment of $145,000 on the total price of $356,416 the next day, when they also signed a form acknowledging that the RV had been inspected and accepted. They agreed to return later to have the RV transported out of state for delivery (to avoid paying state sales tax on the purchase). On October 7, Steve Carlson returned to DeMartini's to ride with the seller's driver to Nevada to consummate the out-of-state delivery. When the RV developed problems, Pearson and the Carlsons filed a suit in a federal district court against the RV's manufacturer, Monaco Coach Corp., alleging, in part, breach of warranty under state law. The applicable statute is expressly limited to goods sold in California. Monaco argued that this RV had been sold in Nevada. How does the Uniform Commercial Code (UCC) define a sale? What does the UCC provide with respect to the passage of title? How do these provisions apply here? Discuss. [*Carlson v. Monaco Coach Corp.*, 486 F.Supp.2d 1127 (E.D.Cal. 2007)]

20–7. A QUESTION OF ETHICS: Void and Voidable Titles.

Kenneth West agreed to sell his car, a 1975 Corvette, to a man representing himself as Robert Wilson. In exchange for a cashier's check, West signed over the Corvette's title to Wilson and gave him the car. Ten days later, when West learned that the cashier's check was a forgery, he filed a stolen vehicle report with the police. The police could not immediately locate Wilson or the Corvette, however, and the case grew cold. Nearly two and a half years later, the police found the Corvette in the possession of Tammy Roberts, who also had the certificate of title. She said that she had bought the car from her brother, who had obtained it through an ad in a newspaper. West filed a suit in a Colorado state court against Roberts to reclaim the car. The court applied Colorado Revised Statutes Section 4-2-403 (Colorado's version of Section 2–403 of the Uniform Commercial Code) to determine the vehicle's rightful owner. [West v. Roberts, 143 P.3d 1037 (Colo. 2006)]

(a) Under UCC 2–403, what title, if any, to the Corvette did "Wilson" acquire? What was the status of Roberts's title, if any, assuming that she bought the car without knowledge of circumstances that would make a person of ordinary prudence inquire about the validity of the seller's title? In whose favor should the court rule? Explain.

(b) If the original owner of a vehicle relinquishes it due to fraud, should he or she be allowed to recover the vehicle from a good faith purchaser? If not, which party or parties might the original owner sue for recovery? What is the ethical principle underlying your answer to these questions? Discuss.

20–8. VIDEO QUESTION: Risk of Loss.

Go to this text's Web site at www.cengage.com/blaw/clarkson and select "Chapter 20." Click on "Video Questions" and view the video titled *Risk of Loss*. Then answer the following questions.

(a) Does Oscar have a right to refuse the shipment because the lettuce is wilted? Why or why not? What type of contract is involved in this video?

(b) Does Oscar have a right to refuse the shipment because the lettuce is not organic butter crunch lettuce? Why or why not?

(c) Assume that you are in Oscar's position—that is, you are buying produce for a supermarket. What different approaches might you take to avoid having to pay for a delivery of wilted produce?

20–9. SPECIAL CASE ANALYSIS: Delivery Terms.
Go to Extended Case 20.2, *Spray-Tek, Inc. v. Robbins Motor Transportation, Inc.*, 426 F.Supp.2d 875 (W.D.Wis. 2006), on pages 390 and 391. Read the excerpt and answer the following questions.

(a) **Issue:** What contract provision was at the heart of the dispute between the parties to this case, and why?

(b) **Rule of Law:** What rule of law did the court apply to interpret this provision?

(c) **Applying the Rule of Law:** How did the court apply this rule to interpret the provision at the center of this case?

(d) **Conclusion:** Did the court resolve the dispute between these parties with respect to determining who suffered the loss and how much that loss was? Explain.

LEGAL RESEARCH EXERCISES ON THE WEB

Go to this text's Web site at **www.cengage.com/blaw/clarkson**, select "Chapter 20," and click on "Practical Internet Exercises." There you will find the following Internet research exercises that you can perform to learn more about the topics covered in this chapter.

Practical Internet Exercise 20–1: **Legal Perspective**
The Entrustment Rule

Practical Internet Exercise 20–2: **Management Perspective**
Passage of Title

CHAPTER 21

Performance and Breach of Sales and Lease Contracts

The performance that is required of the parties under a sales or lease contract consists of the duties and obligations each party has under the terms of the contract. The basic obligation of the seller or lessor is to transfer and deliver the goods as stated in the contract, and the basic duty of the buyer or lessee is to accept and pay for the goods.

Keep in mind that "duties and obligations" under the terms of the contract include those specified by the agreement, by custom, and by the Uniform Commercial Code (UCC). Thus, parties to a sales or lease contract may be bound not only by terms they expressly agreed on, but also by terms implied by custom, such as a customary method of weighing or measuring particular goods. In addition, the UCC sometimes imposes terms on parties to a sales contract, such as the requirement that a seller find a substitute carrier to deliver goods to the buyer if the agreed-on carrier becomes unavailable. In this chapter, we examine the basic performance obligations of the parties under a sales or lease contract.

Sometimes, circumstances make it difficult for a person to carry out the promised performance, leading to a breach of the contract. When a breach occurs, the aggrieved party looks for remedies—which we examine in the second half of the chapter. The UCC provides a range of possible remedies, from retaining the goods to requiring the breaching party's performance under the contract. Generally, these remedies are designed to put the aggrieved party "in as good a position as if the other party had fully performed." Note that in contrast to the common law of contracts, remedies under the UCC are *cumulative* in nature. In other words, an innocent party to a breached sales or lease contract is not limited to one exclusive remedy.

SECTION 1
PERFORMANCE OBLIGATIONS

As discussed in previous chapters, the obligations of good faith and commercial reasonableness underlie every sales and lease contract.

The UCC's Good Faith Provision

The UCC's good faith provision, which can never be disclaimed, reads as follows: "Every contract or duty within this Act imposes an obligation of good faith in its performance or enforcement" [UCC 1–304]. *Good faith* means honesty in fact. For a merchant, it means honesty in fact and the observance of reasonable commercial standards of fair dealing in the trade [UCC 2–103(1)(b)]. In other words, merchants are held to a higher standard of performance or duty than are nonmerchants.

Good Faith and Contract Performance

The principle of good faith applies to both parties and provides a framework for the entire agreement. If a sales contract leaves open some particulars of performance, for instance, the parties must exercise good faith and commercial reasonableness when later specifying the details. The *Focus on Ethics* feature on pages 457–460 at the end of this unit explores the ethical implications of the UCC's good faith standard.

In performing a sales or lease contract, the basic obligation of the seller or lessor is to *transfer and deliver conforming goods*. The basic obligation of the buyer or lessee is to *accept and pay for conforming goods* in accordance with the contract [UCC 2–301, 2A–516(1)]. Overall performance of a sales or lease contract is controlled by the agreement between the parties. When the contract is unclear and disputes arise, the courts look to the UCC and impose standards of good faith and commercial reasonableness.

SECTION 2
OBLIGATIONS OF THE SELLER OR LESSOR

As stated, the basic duty of the seller or lessor is to deliver the goods called for under the contract to the buyer or lessee.

Tender of Delivery

Goods that conform to the contract description in every way are called **conforming goods.** To fulfill the contract, the seller or lessor must either deliver or tender delivery of conforming goods to the buyer or lessee. **Tender of delivery** occurs when the seller or lessor makes conforming goods available to the buyer or lessee and gives the buyer or lessee whatever notification is reasonably necessary to enable the buyer or lessee to take delivery [UCC 2–503(1), 2A–508(1)].

Tender must occur at a *reasonable hour* and in a *reasonable manner*. For example, a seller cannot call the buyer at 2:00 A.M. and say, "The goods are ready. I'll give you twenty minutes to get them." Unless the parties have agreed otherwise, the goods must be tendered for delivery at a reasonable hour and kept available for a reasonable period of time to enable the buyer to take possession of them [UCC 2–503(1)(a)].

Normally, all goods called for by a contract must be tendered in a single delivery—unless the parties have agreed that the goods may be delivered in several lots or *installments* (to be discussed shortly) [UCC 2–307, 2–612, 2A–510]. Hence, an order for 1,000 shirts cannot be delivered two shirts at a time. If, however, the parties agree that the shirts will be delivered in four orders of 250 each as they are produced (for summer, fall, winter, and spring stock), then tender of delivery may occur in this manner.

Place of Delivery

The buyer and seller (or lessor and lessee) may agree that the goods will be delivered to a particular destination where the buyer or lessee will take possession. If the contract does not designate the place of delivery, then the goods must be made available to the buyer at the *seller's place of business* or, if the seller has none, the *seller's residence* [UCC 2–308(a)]. If, at the time of contracting, the parties know that the goods identified to the contract are located somewhere other than the seller's business, then the *location of the goods* is the place for their delivery [UCC 2–308(b)].

For example, Li Wan and Boyd both live in San Francisco. In San Francisco, Li Wan contracts to sell Boyd five used trucks, which both parties know are located in a Chicago warehouse. If nothing more is specified in the contract, the place of delivery for the trucks is Chicago. Li Wan may tender delivery either by giving Boyd a negotiable or nonnegotiable document of title or by obtaining the bailee's (warehouser's) acknowledgment that the buyer is entitled to possession.[1]

Delivery via Carrier

In many instances, attendant circumstances or delivery terms in the contract (such as F.O.B. or F.A.S. terms; see Exhibit 20–2 on page 390) make it apparent that the parties intend that a carrier be used to move the goods. In contracts involving a carrier, a seller can complete performance of the obligation to deliver the goods in two ways—through a shipment contract or through a destination contract.

SHIPMENT CONTRACTS Recall from Chapter 20 that a *shipment contract* requires or authorizes the seller to ship goods by a carrier. The contract does not require that the seller deliver the goods at a particular destination [UCC 2–319, 2–509(1)(a)]. Unless otherwise agreed, the seller must do the following:

1. Place the goods into the hands of the carrier.
2. Make a contract for their transportation that is reasonable according to the nature of the goods and their value. (For example, certain types of goods need refrigeration in transit.)
3. Obtain and promptly deliver or tender to the buyer any documents necessary to enable the buyer to obtain possession of the goods from the carrier.

---

1. If the seller delivers a nonnegotiable document of title or merely instructs the bailee in a writing (record) to release the goods to the buyer without the bailee's acknowledgment of the buyer's rights, this is also a sufficient tender, unless the buyer objects [UCC 2–503(4)]. Risk of loss, however, does not pass until the buyer has had a reasonable amount of time in which to present the document or the instructions. See Chapter 20.

4. Promptly notify the buyer that shipment has been made [UCC 2–504].

If the seller does not make a reasonable contract for transportation or fails to notify the buyer of the shipment, the buyer can reject the goods, but only if a *material loss* of the goods or a significant *delay* results. Suppose that a contract involves the shipment of fresh fruit, such as strawberries, but the seller does not arrange for refrigerated transportation. In this situation, if the fruit spoils during transport, a material loss will likely result. (Of course, the parties are free to make agreements that alter the UCC's rules and allow the buyer to reject goods for other reasons.)

DESTINATION CONTRACTS In a *destination contract,* the seller agrees to deliver conforming goods to the buyer at a particular destination. The goods must be tendered at a reasonable hour and held at the buyer's disposal for a reasonable length of time. The seller must also give the buyer appropriate notice. In addition, the seller must provide the buyer with any documents of title necessary to enable the buyer to obtain delivery from the carrier. Sellers often do this by tendering the documents through ordinary banking channels [UCC 2–503].

The Perfect Tender Rule

As previously noted, the seller or lessor has an obligation to ship or tender *conforming goods,* which the buyer or lessee is then obligated to accept and pay for according to the terms of the contract [UCC 2–507]. Under the common law, the seller was obligated to deliver goods that conformed with the terms of the contract in every detail. This was called the **perfect tender rule.** The UCC preserves the perfect tender doctrine by stating that if goods or tender of delivery fails *in any respect* to conform to the contract, the buyer or lessee has the right to accept the goods, reject the entire shipment, or accept part and reject part [UCC 2–601, 2A–509].

For example, a lessor contracts to lease fifty Comclear monitors to be delivered at the lessee's place of business on or before October 1. On September 28, the lessor discovers that it has only thirty Comclear monitors in inventory but will have another twenty Comclear monitors within the next two weeks. The lessor tenders delivery of the thirty Comclear monitors on October 1, with the promise that the other monitors will be delivered within two weeks. Because the lessor has failed to make a perfect tender of fifty Comclear monitors, the lessee has the right to reject the entire shipment and hold the lessor in breach.

Exceptions to the Perfect Tender Rule

Because of the rigidity of the perfect tender rule, several exceptions to the rule have been created, some of which we discuss here.

AGREEMENT OF THE PARTIES Exceptions to the perfect tender rule may be established by agreement. If the parties have agreed, for example, that defective goods or parts will not be rejected if the seller or lessor is able to repair or replace them within a reasonable period of time, the perfect tender rule does not apply.

CURE The UCC does not specifically define the term **cure,** but it refers to the right of the seller or lessor to repair, adjust, or replace defective or nonconforming goods [UCC 2–508, 2A–513]. When any delivery is rejected because of nonconforming goods and the time for performance has not yet expired, the seller or lessor can attempt to "cure" the defect *within the contract time for performance* [UCC 2–508(1), 2A–513(1)]. To do so, the seller or lessor must seasonably (timely) notify the buyer or lessee of the intention to cure.

Reasonable Grounds Required When Time for Performance Has Expired. Once the time for performance under the contract has expired, the seller or lessor can still exercise the right to cure if he or she has *reasonable grounds to believe that the nonconforming tender will be acceptable to the buyer or lessee* [UCC 2–508(2), 2A–513(2)]. For example, if in the past a buyer frequently accepted a particular substitute for a good when the good ordered was not available, the seller has reasonable grounds to believe the buyer will again accept the substitute. Even if the buyer had rejected the substitute good on a particular occasion, the seller nonetheless has reasonable grounds to believe that the substitute will be acceptable. A seller or lessor will sometimes tender nonconforming goods with some type of price allowance, which can serve as the "reasonable grounds" to believe that the buyer or lessee will accept the nonconforming tender.

A Restriction on the Buyer's or Lessee's Right of Rejection. The right to cure substantially restricts the right of the buyer or lessee to reject goods. For example, if a lessee refuses a tender of goods as nonconforming but does not disclose the nature of the defect to the lessor, the lessee cannot later assert the defect as a defense if the defect is one that the lessor could have cured. Generally, buyers and lessees must act in good faith and state specific reasons for refusing to accept goods [UCC 2–605, 2A–514].

SUBSTITUTION OF CARRIERS When an agreed-on manner of delivery (such as the use of a particular carrier to transport the goods) becomes impracticable or unavailable through no fault of either party, but a commercially reasonable substitute is available, this substitute performance is sufficient tender to the buyer and must be used [UCC 2–614(1)]. For example, a sales contract calls for the delivery of a large piece of machinery to be shipped by ABC Truck Lines on or before June 1. The contract terms clearly state the importance of the delivery date. The employees of ABC Truck Lines go on strike. The seller must make a reasonable substitute tender, perhaps by another trucking firm or by air freight, if it is available. Note that the seller normally is responsible for any additional shipping costs, unless contrary arrangements have been made in the sales contract.

INSTALLMENT CONTRACTS An **installment contract** is a single contract that requires or authorizes delivery in two or more separate lots to be accepted and paid for separately. With an installment contract, a buyer or lessee can reject an installment *only if the nonconformity substantially impairs the value* of the installment and cannot be cured [UCC 2–307, 2–612(2), 2A–510(1)]. If the buyer or lessee fails to notify the seller or lessor of the rejection, however, and subsequently accepts a nonconforming installment, the contract is reinstated [UCC 2–612(3), 2A–510(2)].

The entire installment contract is breached only when one or more nonconforming installments *substantially* impair the value of the *whole contract*. The UCC strictly limits rejection to instances of *substantial* nonconformity. Suppose that an installment contract involves parts of a machine. The first part is necessary for the operation of the machine, but when it is delivered, it is irreparably defective. The failure of this first installment will be a breach of the whole contract because the machine will not operate without the first part. The situation would likely be different, however, if the contract

had called for twenty carloads of plywood and only 9 percent of one of the carloads of plywood had deviated from the thickness specifications in the contract.

The point to remember is that the UCC significantly alters the right of the buyer or lessee to reject the entire contract if the contract requires delivery to be made in several installments. Only a *substantial* nonconformity will allow the buyer or lessee to reject the contract (unless, of course, the parties agree that breach of an installment constitutes a breach of the entire contract).

COMMERCIAL IMPRACTICABILITY As discussed in Chapter 17 on page 328, occurrences unforeseen by either party when a contract was made may make performance commercially impracticable. When this occurs, the perfect tender rule no longer applies. According to UCC 2–615(a) and 2A–405(a), a delay in delivery or nondelivery in whole or in part is not a breach if performance has been made impracticable "by the occurrence of a contingency the nonoccurrence of which was a basic assumption on which the contract was made." The seller or lessor must, however, notify the buyer or lessee as soon as practicable that there will be a delay or nondelivery.

Foreseeable versus Unforeseeable Contingencies. The doctrine of commercial impracticability does not extend to problems that could have been foreseen. An increase in cost resulting from inflation, for instance, does not in and of itself excuse performance, as this kind of foreseeable risk is ordinarily assumed by a seller or lessor conducting business. The nonoccurrence of the contingency must have been a basic assumption on which the contract was made [UCC 2–615, 2A–405].

For example, a major oil company that receives its oil from the Middle East has a contract to supply a buyer with one hundred thousand barrels of oil. Because of an oil embargo by the Organization of Petroleum Exporting Countries, the seller is unable to secure oil from the Middle East or any other source to meet the terms of the contract. This situation comes fully under the commercial impracticability exception to the perfect tender doctrine.

Can unanticipated increases in a seller's costs that make performance "impracticable" constitute a valid defense to performance on the basis of commercial impracticability? The court dealt with this question in the following case.

CASE 21.1
Maple Farms, Inc. v. City School District of Elmira

Supreme Court of New York, 76 Misc.2d 1080, 352 N.Y.S.2d 784 (1974).

BACKGROUND AND FACTS • On June 15, 1973, Maple Farms, Inc., formed an agreement with the city school district of Elmira, New York, to supply the school district with milk for the 1973–1974 school year. The agreement was in the form of a requirements contract, under which Maple Farms would sell to the school district all the milk the district required at a fixed price—which was the June market price of milk. By December 1973, the price of raw milk had increased by 23 percent over the price specified in the contract. This meant that if the terms of the contract were fulfilled, Maple Farms would lose $7,350. Because it had similar contracts with other school districts, Maple Farms stood to lose a great deal if it was held to the price stated in the contracts. When the school district would not agree to release Maple Farms from its contract, Maple Farms brought an action in a New York state court for a declaratory judgment (a determination of the parties' rights under a contract). Maple Farms contended that the substantial increase in the price of raw milk was an event not contemplated by the parties when the contract was formed and that, given the increased price, performance of the contract was commercially impracticable.

IN THE LANGUAGE OF THE COURT
Charles B. *SWARTWOOD,* Justice.
* * * *

* * * [The doctrine of commercial impracticability requires first that] a contingency—something unexpected—must have occurred. Second, the risk of the unexpected occurrence must not have been allocated either by agreement or by custom.

* * * Here we find that the contingency causing the increase of the price of raw milk was not totally unexpected. The price from the low point in the year 1972 to the price on the date of the award of the contract in June 1973 had risen nearly 10%. And *any businessman should have been aware of the general inflation in this country during the previous years* * * * . [Emphasis added.]

* * * Here the very purpose of the contract was to guard against fluctuation of price of half pints of milk as a basis for the school budget. Surely had the price of raw milk fallen substantially, the defendant could not be excused from performance. We can reasonably assume that the plaintiff had to be aware of escalating inflation. It is chargeable with knowledge of the substantial increase of the price of raw milk from the previous year's low. * * * It nevertheless entered into this agreement with that knowledge. It did not provide in the contract any exculpatory clause to excuse it from performance in the event of a substantial rise in the price of raw milk. On these facts the risk of a substantial or abnormal increase in the price of raw milk can be allocated to the plaintiff.

DECISION AND REMEDY • *The New York trial court ruled that inflation and fluctuating prices did not render performance impracticable in this case and granted summary judgment in favor of the school district.*

IMPACT OF THIS CASE ON TODAY'S LAW • *This classic case illustrates the UCC's commercial impracticability doctrine as courts still apply it today. Under this doctrine, increased cost alone does not excuse performance unless the rise in cost is due to some unforeseen contingency that alters the essential nature of the performance.*

WHAT IF THE FACTS WERE DIFFERENT? • *Suppose that the court had ruled in the plaintiff's favor. How might that ruling have affected the plaintiff's contracts with other parties?*

Partial Performance. Sometimes, the unforeseen event only *partially* affects the capacity of the seller or lessor to perform, and thus the seller or lessor can *partially* fulfill the contract but cannot tender total performance. In this event, the seller or lessor is required to allocate in a fair and reasonable manner any remaining production and deliveries among its regular customers and those to whom it is contractually obligated to deliver the goods [UCC 2–615(b), 2A–405(b)]. The buyer or lessee must receive notice of the allocation and has the right to accept or reject it [UCC 2–615(c), 2A–405(c)].

For example, a Florida orange grower, Best Citrus, Inc., contracts to sell this season's production to a number of customers, including Martin's grocery chain. Martin's contracts to purchase two thousand crates of oranges. Best Citrus has sprayed *some* of its orange groves with a chemical called Karmoxin. The U.S. Department of Agriculture discovers that persons who eat products sprayed with Karmoxin may develop cancer and issues an order prohibiting the sale of these products. Best Citrus picks all the oranges not sprayed with Karmoxin, but the quantity is insufficient to meet all the contracted-for deliveries. In this situation, Best Citrus is required to allocate its production. It notifies Martin's that it cannot deliver the full quantity specified in the contract and indicates the amount it will be able to deliver. Martin's can either accept or reject the allocation, but Best Citrus has no further contractual liability.

CASE IN POINT By contract, Hoosier Energy Rural Electric Cooperative was required to make lease payments to John Hancock Life Insurance Company for sixty-three years. The lease payments were guaranteed by Ambac Assurance Corporation, but when the latest global financial crisis struck, Ambac's credit rating was downgraded. Under the terms of the contract, this meant that Hoosier would have to pay $120 million to John Hancock or find another guarantor within a very short time. Hoosier went to court, claiming commercial impracticability, among other things. Hoosier argued that the obstacles it faced in finding another guarantor were the product of the credit crisis, were not anticipated, and could not have been guarded against. The court agreed and issued an injunction that prevented John Hancock from obtaining the $120 million, even though Hoosier had agreed to the payment when it entered into the contract.[2]

DESTRUCTION OF IDENTIFIED GOODS

Sometimes, an unexpected event, such as a fire, totally destroys goods through no fault of either party and before risk passes to the buyer or lessee. In such a situation, *if the goods were identified at the time the contract was formed*, the parties are excused from performance [UCC 2–613, 2A–221]. If the goods are only partially destroyed, however, the buyer or lessee can inspect them and either treat the contract as void or accept the damaged goods with a reduction in the contract price.

Consider an example. Atlas Sporting Equipment agrees to lease to River Bicycles sixty bicycles of a particular model that has been discontinued. No other bicycles of that model are available. River specifies that it needs the bicycles to rent to tourists. Before Atlas can deliver the bicycles, they are destroyed by a fire. In this situation, Atlas is not liable to River for failing to deliver the bicycles. Through no fault of either party, the goods were destroyed before the risk of loss passed to the lessee. The loss was total, so the contract is avoided. Clearly, Atlas has no obligation to tender the bicycles, and River has no obligation to pay for them.

ASSURANCE AND COOPERATION

Two other exceptions to the perfect tender doctrine apply equally to both parties to sales and lease contracts: the right of assurance and the duty of cooperation.

The Right of Assurance. The UCC provides that if one of the parties to a contract has "reasonable grounds" to believe that the other party will not perform as contracted, she or he may *in writing* "demand adequate assurance of due performance" from the other party. Until such assurance is received, she or he may "suspend" further performance without liability. What constitutes "reasonable grounds" is determined by commercial standards. If such assurances are not forthcoming within a reasonable time (not to exceed thirty days), the failure to respond may be treated as a *repudiation* of the contract [UCC 2–609, 2A–401].

CASE IN POINT Two companies that made road-surfacing materials, Koch Materials and Shore Slurry Seal, Inc., entered into a contract. Koch obtained a license to use Novachip, a special material made by Shore, and Shore agreed to buy all of its asphalt from Koch for the next seven years. A few years into the contract term, Shore notified Koch that it was planning to sell its assets to Asphalt Paving Systems, Inc. Koch demanded assurances that Asphalt Paving would continue the deal, but Shore refused to provide assurances. The court held that Koch could treat Shore's failure to give assurances as a repudiation and sue Shore for breach of contract.[3]

---

2. *Hoosier Energy Rural Electric Cooperative, Inc. v. John Hancock Life Insurance Co.*, 588 F.Supp.2d 919 (S.D.Ind. 2008).

3. *Koch Materials Co. v. Shore Slurry Seal, Inc.*, 205 F.Supp.2d 324 (D.N.J. 2002).

The Duty of Cooperation. Sometimes, the performance of one party depends on the cooperation of the other. The UCC provides that when such cooperation is not forthcoming, the other party can suspend his or her own performance without liability and hold the uncooperative party in breach or proceed to perform the contract in any reasonable manner [UCC 2–311(3)].

Suppose that Amati is required by contract to deliver twelve hundred Model K washing machines to locations in the state of California to be specified later by Farrell. Deliveries are to be made on or before October 1. Amati has repeatedly requested the delivery locations, but Farrell has not responded. The twelve hundred Model K machines are ready for shipment on October 1, but Farrell still refuses to give Amati the delivery locations. Amati does not ship on October 1. Can Amati be held liable? The answer is no. Amati is excused for any resulting delay of performance because of Farrell's failure to cooperate.

◣ SECTION 3 ◢
OBLIGATIONS OF THE BUYER OR LESSEE

The main obligation of the buyer or lessee under a sales or lease contract is to pay for the goods tendered in accordance with the contract. Once the seller or lessor has adequately tendered delivery, the buyer or lessee is obligated to accept the goods and pay for them according to the terms of the contract.

Payment

In the absence of any specific agreements, the buyer or lessee must make payment at the time and place the goods are *received* [UCC 2–310(a), 2A–516(1)]. When a sale is made on credit, the buyer is obliged to pay according to the specified credit terms (for example, 60, 90, or 120 days), not when the goods are received. The credit period usually begins on the *date of shipment* [UCC 2–310(d)]. Under a lease contract, a lessee must make the lease payment that was specified in the contract [UCC 2A–516(1)].

Payment can be made by any means agreed on between the parties—cash or any other method generally acceptable in the commercial world. If the seller demands cash when the buyer offers a check, credit card, or the like, the seller must permit the buyer reasonable time to obtain legal tender [UCC 2–511].

Right of Inspection

Unless the parties otherwise agree, or for C.O.D. (collect on delivery) transactions, the buyer or lessee has an absolute right to inspect the goods before making payment. This right allows the buyer or lessee to verify that the goods tendered or delivered conform to the contract. If the goods are not as ordered, the buyer or lessee has no duty to pay. *An opportunity for inspection is therefore a condition precedent to the right of the seller or lessor to enforce payment* [UCC 2–513(1), 2A–515(1)].

Inspection can take place at any reasonable place and time and in any reasonable manner. Generally, what is reasonable is determined by custom of the trade, past practices of the parties, and the like. The buyer bears the costs of inspecting the goods but can recover the costs from the seller if the goods do not conform and are rejected [UCC 2–513(2)].

The following case focuses on the buyer's right to inspect the goods before acceptance, as well as the buyer's right to reject nonconforming goods.

✴ EXTENDED CASE 21.2 ✴
Romero v. Scoggin-Dickey Chevrolet-Buick, Inc.

Court of Appeals of Texas, Amarillo, ____ S.W.3d ____ (2010).
www.7thcoa.courts.state.tx.us[a]

IN THE LANGUAGE OF THE COURT

Patrick A. *PIRTLE,* Justice.
* * * *
* * * Jessie Romero went to the

Scoggin-Dickey Chevrolet-Buick, Inc., dealership in Lubbock, Texas, and sought to purchase a 2006 Silverado pickup from Fred Morales. Romero proposed to purchase the pickup by assigning the dealership the factory rebates, supplying two

trade-in vehicles (a 2003 Mitsubishi Montero SP and a 2002 Chevrolet Silverado pickup), and paying the cash difference. At the time of the negotiations, Romero did not have the proposed trade-in vehicles on the lot for inspection by Scoggin-Dickey.

---

a. In the right-hand column, under "Case Information," select "Opinion Search." When that page opens, fill out the "Case Number" boxes with "09," "0086," and "CV." In the "Date Written" box, enter "2/9/2010." Next, in the "Opinion Text" box, type "Romero." Then click on "Search." On the next page, select "View Opinion" to read the case. The Texas Seventh Court of Appeals in Amarillo, Texas, maintains this Web site.

EXTENDED CASE 21.2 CONTINUED ⬇

After negotiating a value for the trade-in vehicles, Romero and Morales signed a contract order wherein Scoggin-Dickey agreed to sell Romero the 2006 Silverado pickup for $21,888. In return, Romero agreed to trade in two vehicles having a combined net value of $15,000, assign factory rebates totaling $3,000, and pay $4,333.52 in cash.

Romero paid the cash, assigned the rebates, and took possession of the 2006 Silverado pickup. At that time, Romero did not deliver the trade-in vehicles to Scoggin-Dickey, nor did Scoggin-Dickey transfer title to the 2006 Silverado pickup to Romero. Subsequently, Romero showed Morales the location of the [Mitsubishi] Montero. After several weeks passed, Romero informed Morales that the 2002 Silverado pickup was located at a body shop. The pickup was not in running condition and was eventually towed by wrecker to Scoggin-Dickey.

After inspecting the trade-in vehicles, Scoggin-Dickey determined the Montero and 2002 Silverado pickup had little, or no, commercial value.

Thereafter, Scoggin-Dickey took back the 2006 Silverado pickup and made two settlement offers to Romero pertaining to a partial refund of his down payment. Romero rejected the offers and filed suit.

* * * The trial court concluded, as a matter of law, that Scoggin-Dickey had a right to inspect the trade-in vehicles under [the Texas Code's equivalent to UCC Section 2–513] and, upon inspection, had validly exercised their right to reject the vehicles tendered by Romero.

* * * *

* * * Romero [argued on appeal, among other things, that] Scoggin-Dickey had no legal right to inspect and/or reject the trade-in vehicles after the contract order was executed[.]

* * * *

* * * *Unless the parties agree otherwise, a buyer has a right to inspect goods identified to a contract for sale at any reasonable place and time and in any reasonable manner prior to payment or acceptance of the goods. This is an implied condition in all contracts for sale.* Moreover, if the goods are nonconforming, the buyer also has "an absolute right to reject." Thus, the trial court correctly held, as a matter

of law, that Scoggin-Dickey had a right to inspect Romero's trade-in vehicles to verify ownership, make, model, and value, even after the contract order was executed. If the trade-in vehicles did not conform to their description in the contract order, Scoggin-Dickey had a right to reject any nonconforming vehicle. [Emphasis added.]

* * * Execution of the contract order did not constitute a "sale" because there was no present transfer of ownership of the 2006 Silverado pickup to Romero or a transfer of ownership of the two trade-in vehicles in full payment of the purchase price to Scoggin-Dickey. Rather, the contract order was a *contract for sale,* [that is,] "a contract to sell goods at a future time"; or conditional sale. * * * Under these facts, the trial court could conclude that the parties intended that vehicle ownership pass in the future when the balance of the purchase price was paid to Scoggin-Dickey, [that is, when] Romero tendered two trade-in vehicles conforming to their description in the contract order.

* * * *

The trial court's judgment is affirmed.

 QUESTIONS

1. Why didn't the "contract order" signed by the parties constitute a binding contract for the sale of goods?
2. According to the court, "Romero and Scoggin-Dickey were both buyers and sellers." What did the court mean by this statement?

Acceptance

Once the buyer or lessee has had a reasonable opportunity to inspect the goods, the buyer or lessee can demonstrate acceptance of the delivered goods by words or conduct. A buyer or lessee who indicates to the seller or lessor that either the goods are conforming or he or she will retain them in spite of their nonconformity has accepted the goods [UCC 2–606(1)(a), 2A–515(1)(a)]. Acceptance of the goods is presumed when the buyer or lessee *fails to reject* the goods within a reasonable period of time [UCC 2–602(1), 2–606(1)(b), 2A–515(1)(b)].

In sales contracts, if the buyer *performs any act inconsistent with the seller's ownership,* then the buyer will be deemed to have accepted the goods. For example, any use or resale of the goods—except for the limited purpose of testing or inspecting the goods—generally constitutes an acceptance [UCC 2–606(1)(c)].

Partial Acceptance

If some of the goods delivered do not conform to the contract and the seller or lessor has failed to cure, the buyer or lessee can make a *partial* acceptance [UCC 2–601(c), 2A–509(1)]. The same is true if the nonconformity was not reasonably discoverable before acceptance. (In the latter situation, the buyer or lessee may be able to revoke the acceptance, as will be discussed later in this chapter.)

A buyer or lessee cannot accept less than a single commercial unit, however. The UCC defines a *commercial unit* as a unit of goods that, by commercial usage, is viewed as a "single whole" for purposes of sale and that cannot be divided without materially impairing the character of the unit, its market value, or its use [UCC 2–105(6), 2A–103(1)(c)]. A commercial unit can be a single article (such as a machine), a

set of articles (such as a suite of furniture), a quantity (such as a bale, a gross, or a carload), or any other unit treated in the trade as a single whole.

See *Concept Summary 21.1* for a review of the obligations of both parties to a sales or lease contract.

SECTION 4
ANTICIPATORY REPUDIATION

What if, before the time for contract performance, one party clearly communicates to the other the intention *not* to perform? As discussed in Chapter 17

CONCEPT SUMMARY 21.1
Performance of Sales and Lease Contracts

Concept	Description
Obligations of the Seller or Lessor	1. The seller or lessor must tender *conforming* goods to the buyer or lessee at a *reasonable hour* and in a *reasonable manner.* Under the perfect tender doctrine, the seller or lessor must tender goods that conform exactly to the terms of the contract [UCC 2–503(1), 2A–508(1)]. 2. If the seller or lessor tenders nonconforming goods and the buyer or lessee rejects them, the seller or lessor may *cure* (repair or replace the goods) within the contract time for performance [UCC 2–508(1), 2A–513(1)]. Even if the time for performance under the contract has expired, the seller or lessor has a reasonable time to substitute conforming goods without liability if the seller or lessor has reasonable grounds to believe the nonconforming tender will be acceptable to the buyer or lessee [UCC 2–508(2), 2A–513(2)]. 3. If the agreed-on means of delivery becomes impracticable or unavailable, the seller must substitute an alternative means (such as a different carrier) if a reasonable one is available [UCC 2–614(1)]. 4. If a seller or lessor tenders nonconforming goods in any one installment under an installment contract, the buyer or lessee may reject the installment only if the nonconformity substantially impairs its value and cannot be cured. The entire installment contract is breached only when one or more installments *substantially* impair the value of the *whole* contract [UCC 2–612, 2A–510]. 5. When performance becomes commercially impracticable owing to circumstances unforeseen when the contract was formed, the perfect tender rule no longer applies [UCC 2–615, 2A–405].
Obligations of the Buyer or Lessee	1. On tender of delivery by the seller or lessor, the buyer or lessee must pay for the goods at the time and place the goods are *received*, unless the sale is made on credit. Payment can be made by any method generally acceptable in the commercial world, but the seller can demand cash [UCC 2–310, 2–511]. 2. Unless otherwise agreed or in C.O.D. shipments, the buyer or lessee has an absolute right to inspect the goods before acceptance [UCC 2–513(1), 2A–515(1)]. 3. The buyer or lessee can manifest acceptance of delivered goods in words or by conduct, such as by failing to reject the goods after having had a reasonable opportunity to inspect them. A buyer will be deemed to have accepted goods if he or she performs any act inconsistent with the seller's ownership [UCC 2–606(1), 2A–515(1)].

on pages 324 and 325, such an action is a breach of the contract by *anticipatory repudiation*.

Suspension of Performance Obligations

When anticipatory repudiation occurs, the nonbreaching party has a choice of two responses: (1) treat the repudiation as a final breach by pursuing a remedy or (2) wait to see if the repudiating party will decide to honor the contract despite the avowed intention to renege [UCC 2–610, 2A–402]. In either situation, the nonbreaching party may suspend performance.

A Repudiation May Be Retracted

The UCC permits the breaching party to "retract" his or her repudiation (subject to some limitations). This can be done by any method that clearly indicates the party's intent to perform. Once retraction is made, the rights of the repudiating party under the contract are reinstated. There can be no retraction, however, if since the time of the repudiation the other party has canceled or materially changed position or otherwise indicated that the repudiation is final [UCC 2–611, 2A–403].

On April 1, Cora, who owns a small inn, purchases a suite of furniture from Tom Horton, proprietor of Horton's Furniture Warehouse. The contract states that "delivery must be made on or before May 1." On April 10, Tom informs Cora that he cannot make delivery until May 10 and asks her to consent to the modified delivery date. In this situation, Cora has the option of either treating Tom's notice of late delivery as a final breach of contract and pursuing a remedy or agreeing to the later delivery date. Suppose that Cora does neither for two weeks. On April 24, Tom informs Cora that he will be able to deliver the furniture by May 1 after all. In effect, he has retracted his repudiation, reinstating the rights and obligations of the parties under the original contract. Note that if Cora had indicated after Tom's repudiation that she was canceling the contract, he would not have been able to retract his repudiation.

SECTION 5
REMEDIES OF THE SELLER OR LESSOR

When the buyer or lessee is in breach, the seller or lessor has numerous remedies under the UCC. Generally, the remedies available to the seller or lessor depend on the circumstances existing at the time of the breach. The most pertinent considerations are which party has possession of the goods, whether the goods are in transit, and whether the buyer or lessee has rejected or accepted the goods.

When the Goods Are in the Possession of the Seller or Lessor

Under the UCC, if the buyer or lessee breaches the contract before the goods have been delivered, the seller or lessor has the right to pursue the following remedies:

1. Cancel (rescind) the contract.
2. Resell the goods and sue to recover damages.
3. Sue to recover the purchase price or lease payments due.
4. Sue to recover damages for the buyer's nonacceptance of goods.

THE RIGHT TO CANCEL THE CONTRACT If the buyer or lessee breaches the contract, the seller or lessor can choose to simply cancel the contract [UCC 2–703(f), 2A–523(1)(a)]. The seller or lessor must notify the buyer or lessee of the cancellation, and at that point all remaining obligations of the seller or lessor are discharged. The buyer or lessee is not discharged from all remaining obligations, however; he or she is in breach, and the seller or lessor can pursue remedies available under the UCC for breach.

THE RIGHT TO WITHHOLD DELIVERY In general, sellers and lessors can withhold delivery or discontinue performance of their obligations under sales or lease contracts when the buyers or lessees are in breach. This is true whether a buyer or lessee has wrongfully rejected or revoked acceptance of contract goods (which will be discussed later in this chapter), failed to make a payment, or repudiated the contract [UCC 2–703(a), 2A–523(1)(c)]. The seller or lessor can also refuse to deliver the goods to a buyer or lessee who is insolvent (unable to pay debts as they become due) unless the buyer or lessee pays in cash [UCC 2–702(1), 2A–525(1)].

THE RIGHT TO RESELL OR DISPOSE OF THE GOODS When a buyer or lessee breaches or repudiates the contract while the seller or lessor is in possession of the goods, the seller or lessor can resell or dispose of the goods. The seller can retain any profits made as a result of the sale and can hold the buyer or lessee liable for any loss [UCC 2–703(d), 2–706(1), 2A–523(1)(e), 2A–527(1)].

The seller must give the original buyer reasonable notice of the resale, unless the goods are perishable or will rapidly decline in value [UCC 2–706(2), (3)]. A good faith purchaser in a resale takes the goods free of any of the rights of the original buyer, even if the seller fails to comply with this requirement [UCC 2–706(5)]. The UCC encourages the resale of the goods because although the buyer is liable for any deficiency, the seller is not accountable to the buyer for any profits made on the resale [UCC 2–706(6)].

Unfinished Goods. When the goods contracted for are unfinished at the time of the breach, the seller or lessor can either (1) cease manufacturing the goods and resell them for scrap or salvage value or (2) complete the manufacture and resell or dispose of the goods, holding the buyer or lessee liable for any deficiency. In choosing between these two alternatives, the seller or lessor must exercise reasonable commercial judgment in order to mitigate the loss and obtain maximum value from the unfinished goods [UCC 2–704(2), 2A–524(2)]. Any resale of the goods must be made in good faith and in a commercially reasonable manner.

Measure of Damages. In sales transactions, the seller can recover any deficiency between the resale price and the contract price, along with *incidental damages* (see Chapter 18), defined as those costs to the seller resulting from the breach [UCC 2–706(1), 2–710]. The resale can be private or public, and the goods can be sold as a unit or in parcels.

In lease transactions, the lessor may lease the goods to another party and recover from the original lessee, as damages, any unpaid lease payments up to the beginning date of the lease term under the new lease. The lessor can also recover any deficiency between the lease payments due under the original lease contract and those under the new lease contract, along with incidental damages [UCC 2A–527(2)].

THE RIGHT TO RECOVER THE PURCHASE PRICE OR LEASE PAYMENTS DUE Under the UCC, an unpaid seller or lessor can bring an action to recover the purchase price or the payments due under the lease contract, plus incidental damages [UCC 2–709(1), 2A–529(1)]. If a seller or lessor is unable to resell or dispose of the goods and sues for the contract price or lease payments due, the goods must be held for the buyer or lessee. The seller or lessor can resell the goods at any time prior to collecting the judgment from the buyer or lessee. If the goods are resold, the net proceeds from the sale must be credited to the buyer or lessee because of the duty to mitigate damages.

Suppose that Southern Realty contracts with Gem Point, Inc., to purchase one thousand pens with Southern Realty's name inscribed on them. Gem Point tenders delivery of the pens, but Southern Realty wrongfully refuses to accept them. In this situation, Gem Point can bring an action for the purchase price because it delivered conforming goods, and Southern Realty refused to accept or pay for the goods. Gem Point obviously cannot resell the pens inscribed with the buyer's business name, so this situation falls under UCC 2–709. Gem Point is required to make the pens available for Southern Realty, but can resell them (in the event that it can find a buyer) at any time prior to collecting the judgment from Southern Realty.

THE RIGHT TO RECOVER DAMAGES FOR THE BUYER'S NONACCEPTANCE If a buyer or lessee repudiates a contract or wrongfully refuses to accept the goods, a seller or lessor can bring an action to recover the damages sustained. Ordinarily, the amount of damages equals the difference between the contract price or lease payments and the market price or lease payments at the time and place of tender of the goods, plus incidental damages [UCC 2–708(1), 2A–528(1)]. When the ordinary measure of damages is inadequate to put the seller or lessor in as good a position as the buyer's or lessee's performance would have, the UCC provides an alternative. In that situation, the proper measure of damages is the lost profits of the seller or lessor, including a reasonable allowance for overhead and other expenses [UCC 2–708(2), 2A–528(2)].

When the Goods Are in Transit

When the seller or lessor has delivered the goods to a carrier or a bailee but the buyer or lessee has not yet received them, the goods are said to be *in transit*. If, while the goods are in transit, the seller or lessor learns that the buyer or lessee is insolvent, the seller or lessor can stop the carrier or bailee from delivering the goods, regardless of the quantity of goods shipped. If the buyer or lessee is in breach but is not insolvent, the seller or lessor can stop the goods in transit only if the quantity shipped is at least a carload, a truckload, a planeload, or a larger shipment [UCC 2–705(1), 2A–526(1)].

To stop delivery, the seller or lessor must *timely notify* the carrier or other bailee that the goods are to be returned or held for the seller or lessor. If the carrier has sufficient time to stop delivery, the goods must be held and delivered according to the instructions of the seller or lessor, who is liable to the carrier for any additional costs incurred [UCC 2–705(3), 2A–526(3)].

The seller or lessor has the right to stop delivery of the goods under UCC 2–705(2) and 2A–526(2) until the time when:

1. The buyer or lessee receives the goods.
2. The carrier or the bailee acknowledges the rights of the buyer or lessee in the goods (by reshipping or holding the goods for the buyer or lessee, for example).
3. A negotiable document of title covering the goods has been properly transferred to the buyer in a sales transaction, giving the buyer ownership rights in the goods [UCC 2–705(2)].

Once the seller or lessor reclaims the goods in transit, she or he can pursue the remedies allowed to sellers and lessors when the goods are in their possession.

When the Goods Are in the Possession of the Buyer or Lessee

When the buyer or lessee has breached a sales or lease contract and the goods are in his or her possession, the seller or lessor can sue to recover the purchase price of the goods or the lease payments due, plus incidental damages [UCC 2–709(1), 2A–529(1)].

In some situations, a seller may also have a right to reclaim the goods from the buyer. For example, in a sales contract, if the buyer has received the goods on credit and the seller discovers that the buyer is insolvent, the seller can demand the return of the goods [UCC 2–702(2)]. Ordinarily, the demand must be made within ten days of the buyer's receipt of the goods.[4] The seller's right to reclaim the goods is subject to the rights of a good faith purchaser or other subsequent buyer in the ordinary course of business who purchases the goods from the buyer before the seller reclaims them.

In regard to lease contracts, if the lessee is in default (fails to make payments that are due, for example), the lessor may reclaim the leased goods that are in the lessee's possession [UCC 2A–525(2)].

[4.] The seller can demand and reclaim the goods at any time, though, if the buyer misrepresented his or her solvency in writing within three months prior to the delivery of the goods.

REMEDIES OF THE BUYER OR LESSEE

When the seller or lessor breaches the contract, the buyer or lessee has numerous remedies available under the UCC. Like the remedies available to sellers and lessors, the remedies available to buyers and lessees depend on the circumstances existing at the time of the breach.

When the Seller or Lessor Refuses to Deliver the Goods

If the seller or lessor refuses to deliver the goods to the buyer or lessee, the basic remedies available to the buyer or lessee include the right to:

1. Cancel (rescind) the contract.
2. Recover goods that have been paid for if the seller or lessor is insolvent.
3. Sue to obtain specific performance if the goods are unique or if damages are an inadequate remedy.
4. Buy other goods (obtain *cover*—defined on page 413) and recover damages from the seller.
5. Sue to obtain identified goods held by a third party (*replevy* goods—defined on page 413).
6. Sue to recover damages.

THE RIGHT TO CANCEL THE CONTRACT When a seller or lessor fails to make proper delivery or repudiates the contract, the buyer or lessee can cancel, or rescind, the contract. The buyer or lessee is relieved of any further obligations under the contract but retains all rights to other remedies against the seller or lessor [UCC 2–711(1), 2A–508(1)(a)]. (The right to cancel the contract is also available to a buyer or lessee who has rightfully rejected goods or revoked acceptance, as will be discussed shortly.)

THE RIGHT TO RECOVER THE GOODS If a buyer or lessee has made a partial or full payment for goods that remain in the possession of the seller or lessor, the buyer or lessee can recover the goods if the seller or lessor becomes insolvent within ten days after receiving the first payment and if the goods are identified to the contract. To exercise this right, the buyer or lessee must tender to the seller or lessor any unpaid balance of the purchase price or lease payments [UCC 2–502, 2A–522].

THE RIGHT TO OBTAIN SPECIFIC PERFORMANCE A buyer or lessee can obtain specific performance if the goods are unique or the remedy at law (monetary damages) is inadequate [UCC 2–716(1), 2A–521(1)]. Ordinarily, an award of damages is sufficient to place a buyer or lessee in the position she or he would have occupied if the seller or lessor had fully performed. When the contract is for the purchase of a particular work of art or a similarly unique item, however, damages may not be sufficient. Under these circumstances, equity requires that the seller

or lessor perform exactly by delivering the particular goods identified to the contract (the remedy of specific performance).

Animals are items of property and can be classified as "goods." An animal such as a pet likely seems unique to its owner. But does a pet possess the quality of uniqueness necessary for an award of specific performance? That was the question in the following case.

CASE 21.3
Houseman v. Dare

Superior Court of New Jersey, Appellate Division, 405 N.J.Super. 538, 966 A.2d 24 (2009).
www.lawlibrary.rutgers.edu/search.shtml[a]

BACKGROUND AND FACTS • Doreen Houseman and Eric Dare were together for thirteen years. They bought a house and were engaged to marry. They also bought a pedigreed dog for $1,500, which they registered with the American Kennel Club as joint owners. When Dare decided to end the relationship, they agreed that he could pay Houseman for her interest in the house and she would move out. They also agreed that she could take the dog. She asked him to put the agreement about the dog in writing, but he told her that she could trust him. She allowed him to take the dog for visits. After one such visit, Dare kept the dog. Houseman filed a suit in a New Jersey state court against Dare. In a summary judgment, the court concluded that specific performance is not available as a remedy for the breach of an oral agreement about the possession of a dog and awarded Houseman $1,500. She appealed.

IN THE LANGUAGE OF THE COURT
GRALL, J.A.D. [Judge, Appellate Division]
* * * *

The court's conclusion that specific performance is not, as a matter of law, available to remedy a breach of an oral agreement about possession of a dog reached by its joint owners is not sustainable. The remedy of specific performance can be invoked to address a breach of an enforceable agreement when money damages are not adequate to protect the * * * interest of the injured party.

Specific performance is generally recognized as the appropriate remedy when an agreement concerns possession of property such as heirlooms, family treasures and works of art that induce a strong sentimental attachment. That is so because money damages cannot compensate the injured party for the special subjective benefits he or she derives from possession.
* * * *

The special subjective value of personal property worthy of recognition by a court of equity is sentiment explained by facts and circumstances—such as the party's relationship with the donor or prior associations with the property—that give rise to the special affection. * * * *Pets have special subjective value to their owners.* [Emphasis added.]

There is no reason for a court of equity to be more wary in resolving competing claims for possession of a pet based on one party's sincere affection for and attachment to it than in resolving competing claims based on one party's sincere sentiment for an inanimate object based upon a relationship with the donor. In both types of cases, a court of equity must consider the

---

a. Under "Resources," select "Search by party name." On the page that opens, in the left column, check "Appellate Division." In the right column, in the "First Name:" box, type "Houseman," and click on "Submit Form." In the result, click on "Click here to get this document" to access the opinion. The Rutgers University School of Law in Camden, New Jersey, maintains this Web site.

CASE 21.3 CONTINUED ➡ interests of the parties pressing competing claims for possession and public policies that may be implicated by an award of possession.

* * * *

We conclude that the trial court erred by declining to consider the relevance of the oral agreement alleged on the ground that a pet is property. Agreements about property jointly held by cohabitants are material in actions concerning its division. They may be specifically enforced when that remedy is appropriate.

DECISION AND REMEDY • *The state intermediate appellate court reversed the lower court's decision and remanded the case for trial. A dog can have the unique value essential to an award of specific performance for the breach of an oral agreement concerning its ownership.*

WHAT IF THE FACTS WERE DIFFERENT? • *In Dare's response to Houseman's complaint, he admitted that he had orally promised her that she could have the dog. Suppose that he had not admitted to this promise. On what principle should a trial court base a finding that one of the parties is more credible on this point?*

THE ETHICAL DIMENSION • *What might the award to Houseman of the value of the dog instead of its possession mean to Dare, and what might it indicate to others who could be tempted to breach their agreements?*

THE RIGHT OF COVER In certain situations, buyers and lessees can protect themselves by obtaining **cover**—that is, by buying or leasing substitute goods for those that were due under the contract. This option is available when the seller or lessor repudiates the contract or fails to deliver the goods. (Cover is also available when a buyer or lessee has rightfully rejected goods or revoked acceptance, to be discussed shortly.)

In obtaining cover, the buyer or lessee must act in good faith and without unreasonable delay [UCC 2–712, 2A–518]. After purchasing or leasing substitute goods, the buyer or lessee can recover from the seller or lessor the difference between the cost of cover and the contract price (or lease payments), plus incidental and consequential damages, less the expenses (such as delivery costs) that were saved as a result of the breach [UCC 2–712, 2–715, 2A–518]. *Consequential damages* are any losses suffered by the buyer or lessee that the seller or lessor had reason to know about at the time of contract formation. Consequential damages can also include any injury to the buyer's or lessee's person or property proximately resulting from the contract's breach [UCC 2–715(2), 2A–520(2)].

Buyers and lessees are not required to cover, and failure to do so will not bar them from using any other remedies available under the UCC. A buyer or lessee who fails to cover, however, risks collecting a lower amount of consequential damages. A court may reduce the consequential damages by the amount of the loss that could have been avoided had the buyer or lessee purchased or leased substitute goods.

THE RIGHT TO REPLEVY GOODS Buyers and lessees also have the right to replevy goods. **Replevin**[5] is an action to recover identified goods in the hands of a party who is unlawfully withholding them. At common law, *replevin* refers to a legal proceeding to recover specific personal property that has been unlawfully taken. Under the UCC, a buyer or lessee can replevy goods identified to the contract if the seller or lessor has repudiated or breached the contract. To maintain an action to replevy goods, buyers and lessees must usually show that they were unable to cover for the goods after making a reasonable effort [UCC 2–716(3), 2A–521(3)].

THE RIGHT TO RECOVER DAMAGES If a seller or lessor repudiates the contract or fails to deliver the goods, the buyer or lessee can sue for damages. The measure of recovery is the difference between the contract price (or lease payments) and the market price of the goods (or lease payments that could be obtained for the goods) at the time the buyer (or lessee) *learned* of the breach. The market price or market lease payments are determined at the place where the seller or lessor was supposed to deliver the goods. The buyer or lessee can also recover incidental and consequential damages less the expenses that were saved as a result of the breach [UCC 2–713, 2A–519].

Consider an example. Schilling orders ten thousand bushels of wheat from Valdone for $7.00 per

---

5. Pronounced ruh-*pleh*-vun, derived from the Old French word *plevir,* meaning "to pledge."

bushel, with delivery due on June 14 and payment due on June 20. Valdone does not deliver on June 14. On June 14, the market price of wheat is $7.50 per bushel. Schilling chooses to do without the wheat. He sues Valdone for damages for nondelivery. Schilling can recover $0.50 × 10,000, or $5,000, plus any expenses the breach has caused him. The measure of damages is the market price on the day Schilling was to have received delivery less the contract price. (Any expenses Schilling saved by the breach would be deducted from the damages.)

When the Seller or Lessor Delivers Nonconforming Goods

When the seller or lessor delivers nonconforming goods, the buyer or lessee has several remedies available under the UCC.

THE RIGHT TO REJECT THE GOODS If either the goods or the tender of the goods by the seller or lessor fails to conform to the contract in any respect, the buyer or lessee can reject all of the goods or any commercial unit of the goods [UCC 2–601, 2A–509]. If the buyer or lessee rejects the goods, she or he may then obtain cover or cancel the contract, and may seek damages just as if the seller or lessor had refused to deliver the goods (see the earlier discussion of these remedies).

CASE IN POINT Jorge Jauregui contracted to buy a new Kawai RX5 piano for $24,282 from Bobb's Piano Sales & Service, Inc. When the piano was delivered with "unacceptable damage," Jauregui rejected it and filed a lawsuit for breach of contract. The court ruled that Bobb's had breached the contract by delivering nonconforming goods. Jauregui was entitled to damages equal to the contract price with interest, plus the sales tax, delivery charge, and attorneys' fees.[6]

Timeliness and Reason for Rejection Are Required. The buyer or lessee must reject the goods within a reasonable amount of time after delivery or tender of delivery and must seasonably (timely) notify the seller or lessor [UCC 2–602(1), 2A–509(2)]. If the buyer or lessee fails to reject the goods within a reasonable amount of time, acceptance will be presumed. The buyer or lessee must also designate defects that are ascertainable by

reasonable inspection. Failure to do so precludes the buyer or lessee from using such defects to justify rejection or to establish breach when the seller or lessor could have cured the defects if they had been disclosed seasonably [UCC 2–605, 2A–514].

Duties of Merchant Buyers and Lessees When Goods Are Rejected. What happens if a *merchant buyer or lessee* rightfully rejects goods and the seller or lessor has no agent or business at the place of rejection? In that situation, the merchant buyer or lessee has a good faith obligation to follow any reasonable instructions received from the seller or lessor with respect to the goods [UCC 2–603, 2A–511]. The buyer or lessee is entitled to be reimbursed for the care and cost entailed in following the instructions. The same requirements hold if the buyer or lessee rightfully revokes her or his acceptance of the goods at some later time [UCC 2–608(3), 2A–517(5)]. (Revocation of acceptance will be discussed shortly.)

If no instructions are forthcoming and the goods are perishable or threaten to decline in value quickly, the buyer or lessee can resell the goods. The buyer or lessee must exercise good faith and can take appropriate reimbursement and a selling commission (not to exceed 10 percent of the gross proceeds) from the proceeds [UCC 2–603(1), (2); 2A–511(1)]. If the goods are not perishable, the buyer or lessee may store them for the seller or lessor or reship them to the seller or lessor [UCC 2–604, 2A–512].

REVOCATION OF ACCEPTANCE Acceptance of the goods precludes the buyer or lessee from exercising the right of rejection, but it does not necessarily prevent the buyer or lessee from pursuing other remedies. In certain circumstances, a buyer or lessee is permitted to *revoke* his or her acceptance of the goods.

Acceptance of a lot or a commercial unit can be revoked if the nonconformity *substantially* impairs the value of the lot or unit *and* if one of the following factors is present:

1. Acceptance was predicated on the reasonable assumption that the nonconformity would be cured, and it has not been cured within a reasonable period of time [UCC 2–608(1)(a), 2A–517(1)(a)].
2. The buyer or lessee did not discover the nonconformity before acceptance, either because it was difficult to discover before acceptance or because assurances made by the seller or lessor that the goods were conforming kept the buyer or lessee from inspecting the goods [UCC 2–608(1)(b), 2A–517(1)(b)].

---

6. *Jauregui v. Bobb's Piano Sales & Service, Inc.*, 922 So.2d 303 (Fla. App. 2006).

Revocation of acceptance is not effective until notice is given to the seller or lessor. Notice must occur within a reasonable time after the buyer or lessee either discovers or *should have discovered* the grounds for revocation. Additionally, revocation must occur before the goods have undergone any substantial change (such as spoilage) not caused by their own defects [UCC 2–608(2), 2A–517(4)]. Once acceptance is revoked, the buyer or lessee can pursue remedies, just as if the goods had been rejected.

THE RIGHT TO RECOVER DAMAGES FOR ACCEPTED GOODS   A buyer or lessee who has accepted nonconforming goods may also keep the goods and recover for any loss "resulting in the ordinary course of events . . . as determined in any manner which is reasonable" [UCC 2–714(1), 2A–519(3)]. To do so, the buyer or lessee must notify the seller or lessor of the breach within a reasonable time after the defect was or should have been discovered. Failure to give notice of the defects (breach) to the seller or lessor bars the buyer or lessee from pursuing any remedy [UCC 2–607(3), 2A–516(3)]. In addition, the parties to a sales or lease contract can insert a provision requiring the buyer or lessee to give notice of any defects in the goods within a prescribed period.

When the goods delivered are not as promised, the measure of damages equals the difference between the value of the goods as accepted and their value if they had been delivered as warranted, unless special circumstances show proximately caused damages of a different amount [UCC 2–714(2), 2A–519(4)]. The buyer or lessee is also entitled to incidental and consequential damages when appropriate [UCC 2–714(3), 2A–519(3)]. The UCC further permits the buyer or lessee, with proper notice to the seller or lessor, to deduct all or any part of the damages from the price or lease payments still due under the contract [UCC 2–717, 2A–516(1)].

CASE IN POINT   James Fitl attended a sports-card show in San Francisco, California, where he met Mark Strek, an exhibitor at the show. Fitl bought a 1952 Mickey Mantle Topps baseball card for $17,750 from Strek, who had represented that the card was in near-mint condition. Strek delivered it to Fitl in Nebraska, and Fitl placed it in a safe-deposit box. Two years later, Fitl sent the card to Professional Sports Authenticators (PSA), a sports-card grading service. PSA told Fitl that the card was ungradable because it had been discolored and doctored. Fitl complained to Strek, who refused to refund the purchase price because of the amount of time that had gone by. Fitl then filed a lawsuit, and the court awarded him

$17,750, plus his court costs. Strek appealed. The Nebraska Supreme Court affirmed Fitl's right to recover damages. The court held that Fitl had reasonably relied on Strek's representation that the card was "authentic," which it was not, and that Fitl had given Strek timely notice of the card's defects when they were discovered.[7]

SECTION 7
ADDITIONAL PROVISIONS AFFECTING REMEDIES

The parties to a sales or lease contract can vary their respective rights and obligations by contractual agreement. For example, a seller and buyer can expressly provide for remedies in addition to those provided in the UCC. The parties can also specify remedies in lieu of those provided in the UCC, or they can change the measure of damages. As under the common law of contracts, they may also include clauses in their contracts providing for liquidated damages in the event of a breach or a delay in performance (see Chapter 18 on page 338).

Additionally, a seller can stipulate that the buyer's only remedy on the seller's breach will be repair or replacement of the item, or the seller can limit the buyer's remedy to return of the goods and refund of the purchase price. In sales and lease contracts, an agreed-on remedy is in addition to those provided in the UCC unless the parties expressly agree that the remedy is exclusive of all others [UCC 2–719(1), 2A–503(1), (2)].

Exclusive Remedies

If the parties state that a remedy is *exclusive,* then it is the sole remedy. For example, Standard Tool Company agrees to sell a pipe-cutting machine to United Pipe & Tubing Corporation. The contract limits United's remedy exclusively to repair or replacement of any defective parts. Thus, repair or replacement of defective parts is the buyer's only remedy under this contract.

When circumstances cause an exclusive remedy to fail in its essential purpose, however, it is no longer exclusive, and the buyer or lessee may pursue other remedies available under the UCC

---

7. *Fitl v. Strek,* 269 Neb. 51, 690 N.W.2d 605 (2005).

[UCC 2–719(2), 2A–503(2)]. In the example just given, suppose that Standard Tool Company was unable to repair a defective part, and no replacement parts were available. In this situation, because the exclusive remedy failed in its essential purpose, the buyer could pursue other remedies available under the UCC.

Consequential Damages

As discussed earlier in this chapter on page 413, consequential damages are special damages that compensate for indirect losses (such as lost profits) resulting from a breach of contract that were reasonably forseeable. Under the UCC, parties to a contract can limit or exclude consequential damages, provided the limitation is not unconscionable. When the buyer or lessee is a consumer, any limitation of consequential damages for personal injuries resulting from consumer goods is *prima facie* (presumptively) unconscionable. The limitation of consequential damages is not necessarily unconscionable when the loss is commercial in nature—for example, lost profits and property damage [UCC 2–719(3), 2A–503(3)].

Lemon Laws

Purchasers of defective automobiles—often referred to as "lemons"—may have remedies in addition to those offered by the UCC. All of the states and the District of Columbia have enacted *lemon laws*. Basically, lemon laws provide that if an automobile under warranty has a defect that significantly affects the vehicle's value or use, and the defect is not remedied by the seller within a specified number of opportunities (usually three or four), the buyer is entitled to a new car, replacement of defective parts, or return of all consideration paid.

In most states, lemon laws require an aggrieved new-car owner to notify the dealer or manufacturer of the problem and to provide the dealer or manufacturer with an opportunity to solve it. If the problem remains, the owner must then submit complaints to the arbitration program specified in the manufacturer's warranty before taking the case to court. Decisions by arbitration panels are binding on the manufacturer—that is, cannot be appealed by the manufacturer to the courts—but usually are not binding on the purchaser. All arbitration boards must meet state and/or federal standards of impartiality, and some states have established mandatory government-sponsored arbitration programs for lemon-law disputes.

SECTION 8

DEALING WITH INTERNATIONAL CONTRACTS

Because buyers and sellers (or lessees and lessors) engaged in international business transactions may be separated by thousands of miles, special precautions are often taken to ensure performance under international contracts. Sellers and lessors want to avoid delivering goods for which they might not be paid. Buyers and lessees desire the assurance that sellers and lessors will not be paid until there is evidence that the goods have been shipped. Thus, **letters of credit** frequently are used to facilitate international business transactions.

Letter-of-Credit Transactions

In a simple letter-of-credit transaction, the *issuer* (a bank) agrees to issue a letter of credit and to ascertain whether the *beneficiary* (seller or lessor) performs certain acts. In return, the *account party* (buyer or lessee) promises to reimburse the issuer for the amount paid to the beneficiary. The transaction may also involve an *advising bank* that transmits information and a *paying bank* that expedites payment under the letter of credit. See Exhibit 21–1 for an illustration of a letter-of-credit transaction.

Under a letter of credit, the issuer is bound to pay the beneficiary (seller or lessor) when the beneficiary has complied with the terms and conditions of the letter of credit. The beneficiary looks to the issuer, not to the account party (buyer or lessee), when it presents the documents required by the letter of credit. Typically, the letter of credit will require that the beneficiary deliver a *bill of lading* (the carrier's contract) to prove that shipment has been made. Letters of credit assure beneficiaries (sellers or lessors) of payment while at the same time assuring account parties (buyers or lessees) that payment will not be made until the beneficiaries have complied with the terms and conditions of the letter of credit.

The basic principle behind letters of credit is that payment is made against the documents presented by the beneficiary and not against the facts that the documents purport to reflect. Thus, in a letter-of-credit transaction, the issuer (bank) does not police the underlying contract; the letter of credit is independent of the underlying contract between the buyer and the seller. Eliminating the need for the bank (issuer) to inquire into whether actual conditions have been satisfied greatly reduces the costs of letters of credit.

EXHIBIT 21-1 • A Letter-of-Credit Transaction

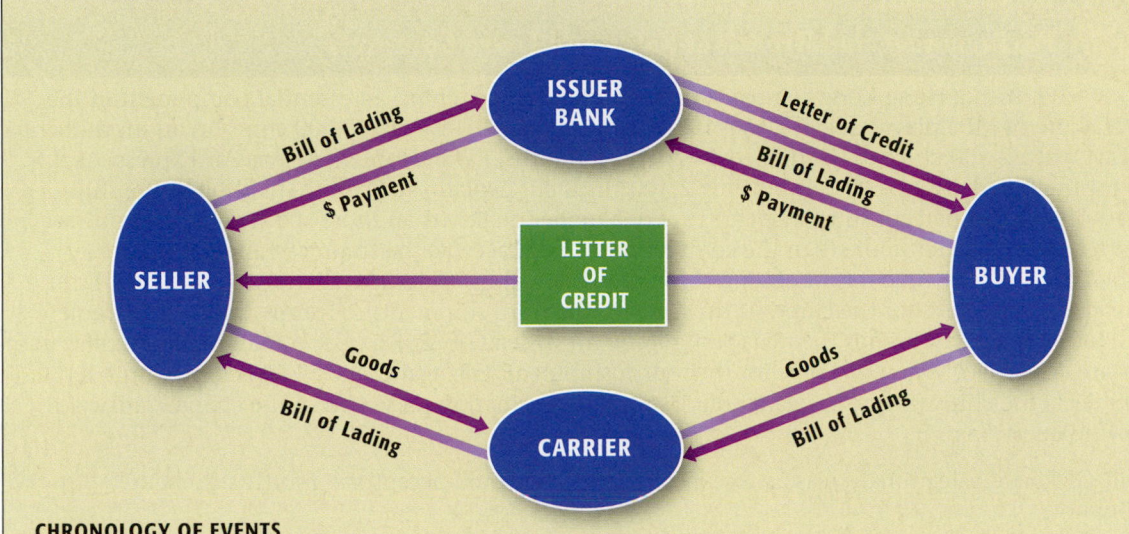

CHRONOLOGY OF EVENTS

1. Buyer contracts with issuer bank to issue a letter of credit; this sets forth the bank's obligation to pay on the letter of credit and buyer's obligation to pay the bank.

2. Letter of credit is sent to seller informing seller that on compliance with the terms of the letter of credit (such as presentment of necessary documents—in this example, a bill of lading), the bank will issue payment for the goods.

3. Seller delivers goods to carrier and receives a bill of lading.

4. Seller delivers the bill of lading to issuer bank and, if the document is proper, receives payment.

5. Issuer bank delivers the bill of lading to buyer.

6. Buyer delivers the bill of lading to carrier.

7. Carrier delivers the goods to buyer.

8. Buyer settles with issuer bank.

Remedies for Breach of International Sales Contracts

The United Nations Convention on Contracts for the International Sale of Goods (CISG) provides international sellers and buyers with remedies very similar to those available under the UCC. Article 74 of the CISG provides for money damages, including foreseeable consequential damages, on a contract's breach. As under the UCC, the measure of damages normally is the difference between the contract price and the market price of the goods.

Under Article 49, the buyer is permitted to avoid obligations under the contract if the seller breaches the contract or fails to deliver the goods during the time specified in the contract or later agreed on by the parties. Similarly, under Article 64, the seller can avoid obligations under the contract if the buyer breaches the contract, fails to accept delivery of the goods, or fails to pay for the goods.

The CISG also allows for specific performance as a remedy under Article 28, which provides that "one party is entitled to require performance of any obligation by the other party." This statement is then qualified, however. Article 28 goes on to state that a court may grant specific performance as a remedy only if it would do so "under its own law in respect of similar contracts of sale not governed by this Convention." As already discussed, in the United States the equitable remedy of specific performance will normally be granted only if no adequate remedy at law (monetary damages) is available and the goods are unique in nature. In other countries, such as Germany, however, specific performance is a commonly granted remedy for breach of contract.

REVIEWING

Performance and Breach of Sales and Lease Contracts

GFI, Inc., a Hong Kong company, makes audio decoder chips, an essential component in the manufacture of MP3 players. Egan Electronics contracts with GFI to buy 10,000 chips on an installment contract, with 2,500 chips to be shipped every three months, F.O.B. Hong Kong, via Air Express. At the time for the first delivery, GFI delivers only 2,400 chips but explains to Egan that although the shipment is less than 5 percent short, the chips are of a higher quality than those specified in the contract and are worth 5 percent more than the contract price. Egan accepts the shipment and pays GFI the contract price. At the time for the second shipment, GFI makes a shipment identical to the first. Egan again accepts and pays for the chips. At the time for the third shipment, GFI ships 2,400 of the same chips, but this time GFI sends them via Hong Kong Air instead of Air Express. While in transit, the chips are destroyed. When it is time for the fourth shipment, GFI again sends 2,400 chips, but this time Egan rejects the chips without explanation. Using the information presented in the chapter, answer the following questions.

1. Did GFI have a legitimate reason to expect that Egan would accept the fourth shipment? Why or why not?
2. Did the substitution of carriers in the third shipment constitute a breach of the contract by GFI? Explain.
3. Suppose that the silicon used for the chips becomes unavailable for a period of time. Consequently, GFI cannot manufacture enough chips to fulfill the contract, but does ship as many as it can to Egan. Under what doctrine might a court release GFI from further performance of the contract?
4. Under the UCC, does Egan have a right to reject the fourth shipment? Why or why not?

⚙ **DEBATE THIS:** *If a contract specifies a particular carrier, then the shipper must use that carrier or be in breach of the contract—no exceptions should ever be allowed.*

TERMS AND CONCEPTS

	cover 413	letter of credit 416	tender of delivery 401
conforming goods 401	cure 402	perfect tender rule 402	
	installment contract 403	replevin 413	

QUESTIONS AND CASE PROBLEMS

21–1. Remedies of the Seller or Lessor Ames contracts to ship to Curley one hundred Model Z television sets. The terms of delivery are F.O.B. Ames's city, by Green Truck Lines, with delivery on or before April 30. On April 15, Ames discovers that because of an error in inventory control, all Model Z sets have been sold, and the stock has not been replenished. Ames has Model X, a similar but slightly more expensive unit, in stock. On April 16, Ames ships one hundred Model X sets, with notice that Curley will be charged the Model Z price. Curley (in a proper manner) rejects the Model X sets when they are tendered on April 18. Ames does not wish to be held in breach of contract, even though he has tendered nonconforming goods. Discuss Ames's options.

21–2. QUESTION WITH SAMPLE ANSWER: Anticipatory Repudiation.

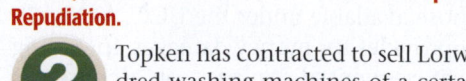

Topken has contracted to sell Lorwin five hundred washing machines of a certain model at list price. Topken is to ship the goods on or before December 1. Topken produces one thousand washing machines of this model but has not yet prepared Lorwin's shipment. On November 1, Lorwin repudiates the contract. Discuss the remedies available to Topken.

• **For a sample answer to Question 21–2, go to Appendix I at the end of this text.**

21–3. Remedies of the Buyer or Lessee Lehor collects antique cars. He contracts to purchase spare parts for a 1938 engine from Beem. These parts are not made anymore and are scarce. To obtain the contract with Beem, Lehor agrees to pay 50 percent of the purchase price in advance. Lehor sends the payment on May 1, and Beem receives it on May 2. On May 3, Beem, having found another buyer willing to pay substantially more for the parts, informs Lehor that he will not deliver as contracted. That same day, Lehor learns that Beem is insolvent. Discuss fully any possible remedies available to Lehor to enable him to take possession of these parts.

21–4. CASE PROBLEM WITH SAMPLE ANSWER: Limitation of Remedies.

 Eaton Corp. bought four air-conditioning units from Trane Co., an operating division of American Standard, Inc., in 1998. The contract stated in part, "NEITHER PARTY SHALL BE LIABLE FOR . . . CONSEQUENTIAL DAMAGES." Trane was responsible for servicing the units. During the last ten days of March 2003, Trane's employees serviced and inspected the units, changed the filters and belts, and made a materials list for repairs. On April 3, a fire occurred at Eaton's facility, extensively damaging the units and the facility, although no one was hurt. Alleging that the fire started in the electric motor of one of the units, and that Trane's faulty servicing of the units caused the fire, Eaton filed a suit in a federal district court against Trane. Eaton asserted breach of contract, among other claims, and sought consequential damages. Trane filed a motion for summary judgment, based on the limitation-of-remedies clause. What are consequential damages? Can these be limited in some circumstances? Is the clause valid in this case? Explain. [Eaton Corp. v. Trane Carolina Plains, 350 F.Supp.2d 699 (D.S.C. 2004)]

- **To view a sample answer for Problem 21–4, go to this book's Web site at www.cengage.com/blaw/clarkson, select "Chapter 21," and click on "Case Problem with Sample Answer."**

21–5. Remedies of the Buyer

L.V.R.V., Inc., sells recreational vehicles (RVs) in Las Vegas, Nevada, as Wheeler's Las Vegas RV. In September 1997, Wheeler's sold a Santara RV made by Coachmen Recreational Vehicle Co. to Arthur and Roswitha Waddell. The Waddells hoped to spend two or three years driving around the country, but almost immediately—and repeatedly—they experienced problems with the RV. Its entry door popped open. Its cooling and heating systems did not work properly. Its batteries did not maintain a charge. Most significantly, its engine overheated when ascending a moderate grade. The Waddells took the RV to Wheeler's service department for repairs. Over the next year and a half, the RV spent more than seven months at Wheeler's. In March 1999, the Waddells filed a complaint in a Nevada state court against the dealer to revoke their acceptance of the RV. What are the requirements for a buyer's revocation of acceptance? Were the requirements met in this case? In whose favor should the court rule? Why? [Waddell v. L.V.R.V., Inc., 122 Nev. 15, 125 P.3d 1160 (2006)]

21–6. Additional Provisions Affecting Remedies

Nomo Agroindustrial Sa De CV is a farm company based in Mexico that grows tomatoes, cucumbers, and other vegetables to sell in the United States. In the early part of the first decade of the 2000s, Nomo's tomato plants contracted a disease: tomato spotted wilt virus (TSWV). To obtain a crop that was resistant to TSWV, Nomo contacted Enza Zaden North America, Inc., an international corporation that manufactures seeds. Enza's brochures advertised—and Enza told Nomo—that its Caiman variety was resistant to TSWV. Based on these assurances, Nomo bought Caiman seeds. The invoice, which Nomo's representative signed, limited any damages to the purchase price of the seeds. The plants germinated from the Caiman seeds contracted TSWV, which destroyed Nomo's entire tomato crop. Nomo filed a suit in a federal district court against Enza, seeking to recover for the loss. Enza argued, in part, that any damages were limited to the price of the seeds. Can parties agree to limit their remedies under the Uniform Commercial Code? If so, what are Nomo's best arguments against the enforcement of the limitations clause in Enza's invoice? What should the court rule on this issue? Why? [Nomo Agroindustrial Sa De CV v. Enza Zaden North America, Inc., 492 F.Supp.2d 1175 (D.Ariz. 2007)]

21–7. Obligations of the Seller

Flint Hills Resources, LP, a refiner of crude oil, agreed to buy "approximately 1,000 barrels per day" of Mexican natural gas condensate from JAG Energy, Inc., an oil broker. Four months into the contract, Pemex, the only authorized seller of freshly extracted Mexican condensate, warned Flint Hills that some companies might be selling stolen Mexican condensate. Fearing potential criminal liability, Flint Hills refused to accept more deliveries from JAG without proof of the title to its product. JAG promised to forward documents showing its chain of title. After several weeks, when JAG did not produce the documents, Flint Hills canceled their agreement. JAG filed a suit in a federal district court against Flint Hills, alleging breach of contract. Did Flint Hills have a right to demand assurance of JAG's title to its product? If so, did Flint Hills act reasonably in exercising that right? Explain. [Flint Hills Resources LP v. JAG Energy, Inc., 559 F.3d 373 (5th Cir. 2009)]

21–8. Breach and Damages

Before Chad DeRosier could build a house on his undeveloped property, he needed to have some fill dirt deposited on the land. Utility Systems of America, Inc., was doing roadwork nearby, and DeRosier asked Utility if it would like to deposit extra fill dirt on his property. Utility said it would, and DeRosier obtained the necessary permit. The permit was for 1,500 cubic yards of fill dirt, the amount that DeRosier needed. DeRosier gave Utility a copy of the permit. Later, DeRosier found 6,500 cubic yards of fill dirt on his land and had to have 5,000 cubic yards of it removed. Utility denied responsibility but said that it would remove the fill dirt for $9,500. DeRosier filed a suit against Utility and hired another company to remove the fill dirt and to do certain foundation work. He paid $46,629 to that contractor. The district court held that Utility had breached its contract and ordered it to pay DeRosier $22,829 in general damages and $8,000 in consequential damages. Utility appealed. In view of the fact that Utility charged nothing for the fill dirt, did a breach of contract occur? If a breach occurred, should the damages be greater than $9,500? Can consequential damages be justified? Discuss. [*DeRosier v. Utility Systems of America, Inc.,* 780 N.W.2d 1 (Minn.App. 2010)]

21–9. A QUESTION OF ETHICS: Revocation.

Scotwood Industries, Inc., sells calcium chloride flake for use in ice melt products. Between July and September 2004, Scotwood delivered thirty-seven shipments of flake to Frank Miller & Sons, Inc. After each delivery, Scotwood billed Miller, which paid thirty-five of the invoices and processed 30 to 50 percent of the flake. In August, Miller began complaining about the product's quality. Scotwood assured Miller that it would remedy the situation. Finally, in October, Miller told Scotwood, "This is totally unacceptable. We are willing to discuss Scotwood picking up the material." Miller claimed that the flake was substantially defective because it was chunked. Calcium chloride maintains its purity for up to five years, but if it is exposed to and absorbs moisture, it chunks and becomes unusable. In response to Scotwood's suit to collect payment on the unpaid invoices, Miller filed a counterclaim in a federal district court for breach of contract, seeking to recover based on revocation of acceptance, among other
things. [*Scotwood Industries, Inc. v. Frank Miller & Sons, Inc.,* 435 F.Supp.2d 1160 (D.Kan. 2006)]

(a) What is revocation of acceptance? How does a buyer effectively exercise this option? Do the facts in this case support this theory as a ground for Miller to recover damages? Why or why not?

(b) Is there an ethical basis for allowing a buyer to revoke acceptance of goods and recover damages? If so, is there an ethical limit to this right? Discuss.

21–10. VIDEO QUESTION: Letter of Credit.

Go to this text's Web site at **www.cengage.com/ blaw/clarkson** and select "Chapter 21." Click on "Video Questions" and view the video titled *International: Letter of Credit.* Then answer the following questions.

(a) Do banks always require the same documents to be presented in letter-of-credit transactions? If not, who dictates what documents will be required in the letter of credit?

(b) At what point does the seller receive payment in a letter-of-credit transaction?

(c) What assurances does a letter of credit provide to the buyer and the seller involved in the transaction?

LEGAL RESEARCH EXERCISES ON THE WEB

Go to this text's Web site at **www.cengage.com/blaw/clarkson**, select "Chapter 21," and click on "Practical Internet Exercises." There you will find the following Internet research exercises that you can perform to learn more about the topics covered in this chapter.

Practical Internet Exercise 21–1: **Legal Perspective**
International Performance Requirements

Practical Internet Exercise 21–2: **Social Perspective**
Lemon Laws

Practical Internet Exercise 21–3: **Management Perspective**
The Right to Reject Goods

CHAPTER 22

✳

Warranties and Product Liability

Warranty is an age-old concept. In sales and lease law, a warranty is an assurance or guarantee by the seller or lessor of certain facts concerning the goods being sold or leased. The Uniform Commercial Code (UCC) has numerous rules governing product warranties as they occur in sales and lease contracts and specifies several types of warranties, each of which we examine in this chapter.

Because a warranty imposes a duty on the seller or lessor, a breach of warranty is a breach of the seller's or lessor's promise. Assuming that the parties have not agreed to limit or modify the remedies available, if the seller or lessor breaches a warranty, the buyer or lessee can sue to recover damages from the seller or lessor. Under some circumstances, a breach of warranty can allow the buyer or lessee to rescind (cancel) the agreement.

Breach of warranty actions are a subset of product liability claims. Product liability encompasses the contract theory of warranty, as well as the tort theories of negligence, misrepresentation, and strict liability (discussed in Chapters 6 and 7). Manufacturers and sellers of goods can be held liable for products that are defective or unreasonably dangerous. Goods can be defective in a number of ways, including manufacturing defects, design defects, and inadequate warnings. We examine product liability in the second part of the chapter. Because warranty law protects buyers, some of whom are consumers, warranty law is also part of the broad body of consumer protection law that will be discussed in Chapter 45.

SECTION 1
TYPES OF WARRANTIES

Most goods are covered by some type of warranty designed to protect buyers. Articles 2 (on sales) and 2A (on leases) of the UCC designate several types of warranties that can arise in a sales or lease contract, including warranties of title, express warranties, and implied warranties. In the following subsections, we discuss these types of warranties as well as a federal statute that is designed to prevent deception and make warranties more understandable.

Warranties of Title

Under the UCC, three types of title warranties—*good title, no liens,* and *no infringements*—can automatically arise in sales and lease contracts [UCC 2–312, 2A–211]. Normally, a seller or lessor can disclaim or modify these title warranties only by including *specific language* in the contract. For example, sellers may assert that they are transferring only such rights, title, and interest as they have in the goods.

GOOD TITLE In most sales, sellers warrant that they have good and valid title to the goods sold and that the transfer of the title is rightful [UCC 2–312(1)(a)]. Suppose that Alexis steals goods from Camden and sells them to Emma, who does not know that they are stolen. If Camden discovers that Emma has the goods, then he has the right to reclaim them from Emma. When Alexis sold Emma the goods, Alexis *automatically* warranted to Emma that the title conveyed was valid and that its transfer was rightful. Because a thief has no title to stolen goods, Alexis breached the warranty of title imposed by UCC 2–312(1)(a) and became liable to the buyer for appropriate damages. (See pages 386–389 in Chapter 20 for a detailed discussion of sales by nonowners.)

NO LIENS A second warranty of title protects buyers and lessees who are *unaware* of any encumbrances (claims, charges, or liabilities—usually called *liens*[1]) against goods at the time the contract is made [UCC 2–312(1)(b), 2A–211(1)]. This warranty protects buyers who, for example, unknowingly purchase goods that are subject to a creditor's security interest (a *security interest* in this context is an interest in the goods that secures payment or performance of an obligation—see Chapter 29). If a creditor legally repossesses the goods from a buyer *who had no actual knowledge of the security interest,* the buyer can recover from the seller for breach of warranty. (A buyer who has *actual knowledge of a security interest* has no recourse against a seller.)

Consider an example. Henderson buys a used boat from Loring for cash. A month later, Barish proves that she has a valid security interest in the boat and that Loring, who has missed five payments, is in default. Barish then repossesses the boat from Henderson. Henderson demands his cash back from Loring. Under Section 2–312(1)(b), Henderson has legal grounds to recover from Loring because the seller of goods warrants that the goods are delivered free from any security interest or other lien of which the buyer has no knowledge.

Article 2A affords similar protection for lessees. Section 2A–211(1) provides that during the term of the lease, no claim of any third party will interfere with the lessee's enjoyment of the leasehold interest.

NO INFRINGEMENTS Finally, when the seller or lessor is a merchant, he or she automatically warrants that the buyer or lessee takes the good *free of infringements*. In other words, a merchant promises that the goods delivered are free from any copyright, trademark, or patent claims of a third person[2] [UCC 2–312(3), 2A–211(2)].

If this warranty is breached and the buyer is sued by the party holding copyright, trademark, or patent rights in the goods, the buyer *must notify the seller* of the litigation within a reasonable time to enable the seller to decide whether to defend the lawsuit. If the seller states in a writing (or record) that she or he has decided to defend and agrees to bear all expenses, then the buyer must turn over control of

the litigation to the seller; otherwise, the buyer is barred from any remedy against the seller for liability established by the litigation [UCC 2–607(3)(b), 2–607(5)(b)].

In situations that involve leases rather than sales, Article 2A provides for the same notice of infringement litigation [UCC 2A–516(3)(b), 2A–516(4)(b)]. There is an exception for leases to individual consumers for personal, family, or household purposes. A consumer who fails to notify the lessor within a reasonable time does not lose his or her remedy against the lessor for whatever liability is established in the litigation [UCC 2A–516(3)(b)].

Express Warranties

A seller or lessor can create an **express warranty** by making representations concerning the quality, condition, description, or performance potential of the goods. Under UCC 2–313 and 2A–210, express warranties arise when a seller or lessor indicates any of the following:

1. That the goods conform to any *affirmation* (a declaration that something is true) *of fact* or *promise* that the seller or lessor makes to the buyer or lessee about the goods. Such affirmations or promises are usually made during the bargaining process. Statements such as "these drill bits will *easily* penetrate stainless steel—and without dulling" are express warranties.

2. That the goods conform to any *description* of them. For example, a label that reads "Crate contains one 150-horsepower diesel engine" or a contract that calls for the delivery of a "wool coat" creates an express warranty that the content of the goods sold conforms to the description.

3. That the goods conform to any *sample or model* of the goods shown to the buyer or lessee.

Express warranties can be found in a seller's or lessor's advertisement, brochure, or promotional materials, in addition to being made orally or in an express warranty provision in a sales or lease contract.

BASIS OF THE BARGAIN To create an express warranty, a seller or lessor does not have to use formal words such as *warrant* or *guarantee*. It is only necessary that a reasonable buyer or lessee would regard the representation as being part of the basis of the bargain [UCC 2–313(2), 2A–210(2)]. Just what constitutes the basis of the bargain is hard to say. The UCC does not define the concept, and it is a question of fact in each case whether a representation was made

---

1. Pronounced *leens*. Liens will be discussed in detail in Chapter 28.
2. Recall from Chapter 19 that a *merchant* is defined in UCC 2–104(1) as a person who deals in goods of the kind involved in the sales contract or who, by occupation, presents himself or herself as having knowledge or skill peculiar to the goods involved in the transaction.

at such a time and in such a way that it induced the buyer or lessee to enter into the contract. Therefore, if an express warranty is not intended, the marketing agent or salesperson should not promise too much.

STATEMENTS OF OPINION AND VALUE Only statements of fact create express warranties. A seller or lessor who makes a statement that merely relates to the value or worth of the goods, or states an opinion about or recommends the goods, does not create an express warranty [UCC 2–313(2), 2A–210(2)].

Suppose that a seller claims that "this is the best used car to come along in years; it has four new tires and a 250-horsepower engine just rebuilt this year." The seller has made several *affirmations of fact* that can create a warranty: The automobile has an engine; it has a 250-horsepower engine; the engine was rebuilt this year; there are four tires on the automobile; and the tires are new.

The seller's *opinion* that the vehicle is "the best used car to come along in years," however, is known as "puffery" and creates no warranty. (*Puffery* is an expression of opinion by a seller or lessor that is not made as a representation of fact.) A statement relating to the value of the goods, such as "it's worth a fortune" or "anywhere else you'd pay $10,000 for it," usually does not create a warranty.

An Exception for Statements of Opinion by Experts. Although normally giving an opinion is not a warranty, if the seller or lessor is an expert and gives an opinion as an expert to a layperson, then a warranty may be created. For example, Stephen is an art dealer and an expert in seventeenth-century paintings. If Stephen states to Lauren, a purchaser, that in his opinion a particular painting is a Rembrandt, Stephen has warranted the accuracy of his opinion.

Puffery versus Express Warranties. It is not always easy to determine whether a statement constitutes an express warranty or puffery. The reasonableness of the buyer's or lessee's reliance appears to be the controlling criterion in many cases. For example, a salesperson's statements that a ladder will "never break" and will "last a lifetime" are so clearly improbable that no reasonable buyer should rely on them. Additionally, the context in which a statement is made may be relevant in determining the reasonableness of a buyer's or lessee's reliance. A reasonable person is more likely to rely on a written statement made in an advertisement than on a statement made orally by a salesperson.

CASE IN POINT A tobacco farmer read an advertisement for Chlor-O-Pic, a chemical fumigant, which stated that, if applied as directed, Chlor-O-Pic would give "season-long control with application in fall, winter, or spring" against black shank disease, a fungal disease that destroys tobacco crops. The farmer bought Chlor-O-Pic and applied it as directed to his tobacco crop. Nonetheless, the crop developed black shank disease. The farmer sued the manufacturer of Chlor-O-Pic, arguing that he had purchased the product in reliance on a "strong promise" of "season-long control." The court found that the manufacturer's strong promise had created an express warranty and that the farmer was entitled to the value of the damaged crop.[3]

Implied Warranties

An **implied warranty** is one that *the law derives* by inference from the nature of the transaction or the relative situations or circumstances of the parties. Under the UCC, merchants impliedly warrant that the goods they sell or lease are merchantable and, in certain circumstances, fit for a particular purpose. In addition, an implied warranty may arise from a course of dealing or usage of trade. We examine these three types of implied warranties in the following subsections.

IMPLIED WARRANTY OF MERCHANTABILITY Every sale or lease of goods made by a merchant who deals in goods of the kind sold or leased automatically gives rise to an **implied warranty of merchantability** [UCC 2–314, 2A–212]. Thus, a merchant who is in the business of selling ski equipment makes an implied warranty of merchantability every time he sells a pair of skis. A neighbor selling her skis at a garage sale does not (because she is not in the business of selling goods of this type).

Merchantable Goods. To be *merchantable,* goods must be "reasonably fit for the ordinary purposes for which such goods are used." They must be of at least average, fair, or medium-grade quality. The quality must be comparable to quality that will pass without objection in the trade or market for goods of the same description. To be merchantable, the goods must also be adequately packaged and labeled, and they must conform to the promises or affirmations of fact made on the container or label, if any. Of course, merchants

---

3. *Triple E, Inc. v. Hendrix & Dail, Inc.,* 344 S.C. 186, 543 S.E.2d 245 (2001). See also *Nomo Agroindustrial Sa De CV v. Enza Zaden North America, Inc.,* 492 F.Supp.2d 1175 (D.Ariz. 2007).

are not absolute insurers against *all* accidents arising in connection with the goods. For example, a bar of soap is not unmerchantable merely because a user could slip and fall by stepping on it.

Knowledge of Defect Not Required. The warranty of merchantability may be breached even though the merchant did not know or could not have discovered that a product was defective (not merchantable). For example, Christine contracts to purchase a log home package from Milde, a log home dealer. The dealer provides the logs and other materials and constructs the home. Immediately after Christine moves into the house, she finds that due to a defective waterproofing product used on the logs, the exterior walls leak when it rains, staining and discoloring the interior walls. Even though Milde did not know that the waterproofing product was defective, he can be held liable because the waterproofing product was not reasonably fit for its ordinary purpose—that is, making the house waterproof.

CASE IN POINT Darrell Shoop bought a Dodge Dakota truck that had been manufactured by DaimlerChrysler Corporation. Almost immediately, he had problems with the truck. During the first eighteen months, the engine, suspension, steering, transmission, and other components required repairs twelve times, including at least five times for the same defect, which remained uncorrected.

Shoop eventually traded in the truck and filed a lawsuit against DaimlerChrysler for breach of the implied warranty of merchantability. The court held that Shoop could maintain an action against DaimlerChrysler and use the fact that the truck had required a significant number of repairs as evidence that it was unmerchantable.[4]

Merchantable Food. The UCC treats the serving of food or drink to be consumed on or off the premises as a sale of goods subject to the implied warranty of merchantability [UCC 2–314(1)]. "Merchantable" food is food that is fit to eat on the basis of consumer expectations. For example, the courts assume that consumers should reasonably expect to find on occasion bones in fish fillets, cherry pits in cherry pie, a nutshell in a package of shelled nuts, and the like—because such substances are natural to the ingredients or the finished food product. In contrast, consumers would not reasonably expect to find an inchworm in a can of peas or a piece of glass in a soft drink—because these substances are *not* natural to the food product.

In the following classic case, the court had to determine whether one should reasonably expect to find a fish bone in fish chowder.

---

4. *Shoop v. DaimlerChrysler Corp.*, 371 Ill.App.3d 1058, 864 N.E.2d 785, 309 Ill.Dec. 544 (2007).

CASE 22.1
Webster v. Blue Ship Tea Room, Inc.
Supreme Judicial Court of Massachusetts, 347 Mass. 421, 198 N.E.2d 309 (1964).

BACKGROUND AND FACTS • Blue Ship Tea Room, Inc., was located in Boston in an old building overlooking the ocean. Webster, who had been born and raised in New England, went to the restaurant and ordered fish chowder. The chowder was milky in color. After three or four spoonfuls, she felt something lodged in her throat. As a result, she underwent two esophagoscopies; in the second esophagoscopy, a fish bone was found and removed. Webster filed a suit against the restaurant in a Massachusetts state court for breach of the implied warranty of merchantability. The jury rendered a verdict for Webster, and the restaurant appealed to the state's highest court.

IN THE LANGUAGE OF THE COURT
REARDON, Justice.

[The plaintiff] ordered a cup of fish chowder. Presently, there was set before her "a small bowl of fish chowder." * * * After 3 or 4 [spoonfuls] she was aware that something had lodged in her throat because she "couldn't swallow and couldn't clear her throat by gulping and she could feel it." This misadventure led to two esophagoscopies [procedures in which a telescope-like instrument is used to look into the throat] at the Massachusetts General Hospital, in the second of which, on April 27, 1959, a fish bone was found and removed. The sequence of events produced injury to the plaintiff which was not insubstantial.

CASE 22.1 CONTINUED ➡   We must decide whether a fish bone lurking in a fish chowder, about the ingredients of which there is no other complaint, constitutes a breach of implied warranty under applicable provisions of the Uniform Commercial Code * * *. As the judge put it in his charge [jury instruction], "Was the fish chowder fit to be eaten and wholesome? * * * Nobody is claiming that the fish itself wasn't wholesome. * * * But the bone of contention here—I don't mean that for a pun—but was this fish bone a foreign substance that made the fish chowder unwholesome or not fit to be eaten?"

* * * *

[We think that it] is not too much to say that a person sitting down in New England to consume a good New England fish chowder embarks on a gustatory [taste-related] adventure which may entail the removal of some fish bones from his bowl as he proceeds. We are not inclined to tamper with age-old recipes by any amendment reflecting the plaintiff's view of the effect of the Uniform Commercial Code upon them. We are aware of the heavy body of case law involving foreign substances in food, but we sense a strong distinction between them and those relative to unwholesomeness of the food itself, [such as] tainted mackerel, and a fish bone in a fish chowder. * * * We consider that the joys of life in New England include the ready availability of fresh fish chowder. We should be prepared to cope with the hazards of fish bones, the occasional presence of which in chowders is, it seems to us, to be anticipated, and which, in the light of a hallowed tradition, do not impair their fitness or merchantability.

DECISION AND REMEDY • *The Supreme Judicial Court of Massachusetts "sympathized with a plaintiff who has suffered a peculiarly New England injury" but entered a judgment for the defendant, Blue Ship Tea Room. A fish bone in fish chowder is not a breach of the implied warranty of merchantability.*

IMPACT OF THIS CASE ON TODAY'S LAW • *This classic case, phrased in memorable language, was an early application of the UCC's implied warranty of merchantability to food products. The case established the rule that consumers should expect to find, on occasion, elements of food products that are natural to the product (such as fish bones in fish chowder). Courts today still apply this rule.*

THE E-COMMERCE DIMENSION • *If Webster had made the chowder herself from a recipe that she had found on the Internet, could she have successfully brought an action against its author for a breach of the implied warranty of merchantability? Explain.*

IMPLIED WARRANTY OF FITNESS FOR A PARTICULAR PURPOSE The **implied warranty of fitness for a particular purpose** arises when *any* seller or lessor (merchant or nonmerchant) knows the particular purpose for which a buyer or lessee will use the goods *and* knows that the buyer or lessee is relying on the skill and judgment of the seller or lessor to select suitable goods [UCC 2–315, 2A–213].

Particular versus Ordinary Purpose. A "particular purpose" of the buyer or lessee differs from the "ordinary purpose for which goods are used" (merchantability). Goods can be merchantable but unfit for a particular purpose. For example, you need a gallon of paint to match the color of your living room walls—a light shade somewhere between coral and peach. You take a sample to your local hardware store and request a gallon of paint of that color. Instead, you are given a gallon of bright blue paint. Here, the salesperson has not breached any warranty of implied merchantability—the bright blue paint is of high quality and suitable for interior walls—but she or he has breached an implied warranty of fitness for a particular purpose.

Knowledge and Reliance Requirements. A seller or lessor need not have actual knowledge of the buyer's or lessee's particular purpose. It is sufficient if a seller or lessor "has reason to know" the purpose. For an implied warranty to be created, however, the buyer or lessee must have *relied* on the skill or judgment of the seller or lessor in selecting or furnishing suitable goods. Moreover, the seller or lessor must have reason to know that the buyer or lessee is relying on her or his judgment or skill.

For example, Bloomberg leases a computer from Future Tech, a lessor of technical business equipment. Bloomberg tells the clerk that she wants a computer that will run a complicated new engineering graphics program at a realistic speed. Future Tech leases

Bloomberg an Architex One computer with a CPU speed of only 2.4 gigahertz, even though a speed of at least 3.8 gigahertz would be required to run Bloomberg's graphics program at a "realistic speed." After discovering that it takes forever to run her program, Bloomberg wants a full refund. Here, because Future Tech has breached the implied warranty of fitness for a particular purpose, Bloomberg normally will be able to recover. The clerk knew specifically that Bloomberg wanted a computer with enough speed to run certain software and was relying on the clerk's judgment. Furthermore, Bloomberg relied on the clerk to furnish a computer that would fulfill this purpose. Because Future Tech did not do so, the warranty was breached.

WARRANTIES IMPLIED FROM PRIOR DEALINGS OR TRADE CUSTOM   Implied warranties can also arise (or be excluded or modified) as a result of course of dealing or usage of trade [UCC 2–314(3), 2A–212(3)]. In the absence of evidence to the contrary, when both parties to a sales or lease contract have knowledge of a well-recognized trade custom, the courts will infer that both parties intended for that custom to apply to their contract. For instance, if the industrywide custom is to lubricate a new car before it is delivered and a dealer fails to do so, the dealer can be held liable to a buyer for damages resulting from the breach of an implied warranty. (This, of course, would also be negligence on the part of the dealer.)

Magnuson-Moss Warranty Act

The Magnuson-Moss Warranty Act of 1975[5] was designed to prevent deception in warranties by making them easier to understand. The act modifies UCC warranty rules to some extent when *consumer* transactions are involved. The UCC, however, remains the primary codification of warranty rules for commercial transactions. Under the Magnuson-Moss Warranty Act, no seller is *required* to give a written warranty for consumer goods sold. If a seller chooses to make an express written warranty, however, and the cost of the consumer goods is more than $25, the warranty must be labeled as either "full" or "limited."

A *full warranty* requires free repair or replacement of any defective part. If the product cannot be repaired within a reasonable time, the consumer has the choice of a refund or a replacement without charge. A full warranty can be for an unlimited or

limited time period, such as a "full twelve-month warranty." A *limited warranty* is one in which the buyer's recourse is limited in some fashion, such as to replacement of an item. The fact that only a limited warranty is being given must be conspicuously stated.

The Magnuson-Moss Act further requires the warrantor to make certain disclosures fully and conspicuously in a single document in "readily understood language." The seller must disclose the name and address of the warrantor, specifically what is warranted, and the procedures for enforcing the warranty. The seller must also clarify that the buyer has legal rights and explain limitations on warranty relief.

See *Concept Summary 22.1* on the facing page for a review of the various types of warranties.

◣◤ SECTION 2 ◣◤
OVERLAPPING WARRANTIES

Sometimes, two or more warranties are made in a single transaction. An implied warranty of merchantability, an implied warranty of fitness for a particular purpose, or both can exist in addition to an express warranty. For example, when a sales contract for a new car states that "this car engine is warranted to be free from defects for 36,000 miles or thirty-six months, whichever occurs first," there is an express warranty against all defects, as well as an implied warranty that the car will be fit for normal use.

When the Warranties Are Consistent

The rule under the UCC is that express and implied warranties are construed as *cumulative* if they are consistent with one another [UCC 2–317, 2A–215]. Courts will interpret two or more overlapping warranties as being consistent, and thus cumulative, if this interpretation is reasonable. If the warranties are not consistent with one another, then the court looks at the intention of the parties to determine which warranty is dominant.

Conflicting Warranties

If the warranties are inconsistent, the courts usually apply the following rules to interpret which warranty is most important:

1. Express warranties displace inconsistent implied warranties, except implied warranties of fitness for a particular purpose.

---

5. 15 U.S.C. Sections 2301–2312.

CONCEPT SUMMARY 22.1
Types of Warranties

Concept	Description
Warranties of Title	The UCC provides for the following warranties of title [UCC 2–312, 2A–211]: 1. *Good title*—A seller warrants that he or she has the right to pass good and rightful title to the goods. 2. *No liens*—A seller warrants that the goods sold are free of any encumbrances (claims, charges, or liabilities—usually called *liens*). A lessor warrants that the lessee will not be disturbed in her or his possession of the goods by the claims of a third party. 3. *No infringements*—A merchant-seller warrants that the goods are free of infringement claims (claims that a patent, trademark, or copyright has been infringed) by third parties. Lessors make similar warranties.
Express Warranties	An express warranty arises under the UCC when a seller or lessor indicates any of the following as part of the sale or bargain [UCC 2–313, 2A–210]: 1. An affirmation of fact or promise. 2. A description of the goods. 3. A sample or model shown as conforming to the contract goods.
Implied Warranty of Merchantability	When a seller or lessor is a merchant who deals in goods of the kind sold or leased, the seller or lessor warrants that the goods sold or leased are properly packaged and labeled, are of proper quality, and are reasonably fit for the ordinary purposes for which such goods are used [UCC 2–314, 2A–212].
Implied Warranty of Fitness for a Particular Purpose	An implied warranty of fitness for a particular purpose arises when the buyer's or lessee's purpose or use is known by the seller or lessor, and the buyer or lessee purchases or leases the goods in reliance on the seller's or lessor's selection [UCC 2–315, 2A–213].
Other Implied Warranties	Other implied warranties can arise as a result of course of dealing or usage of trade [UCC 2–314(3), 2A–212(3)].
Magnuson-Moss Warranty Act	An express written warranty covering consumer goods priced at more than $25, *if made,* must be labeled as either a full warranty or a limited warranty. A full warranty requires free repair or replacement of defective parts and refund or replacement for goods that cannot be repaired in a reasonable time. A limited warranty is one in which the buyer's recourse is limited in some fashion, such as to replacement of an item. Sellers must make certain disclosures to buyers and must state any limitations on a warranty clearly, conspicuously, and in readily understood language.

2. Samples take precedence over inconsistent general descriptions.
3. Exact or technical specifications displace inconsistent samples or general descriptions.

For example, Innova, Ltd., leases a computer from Vernon Computer Source. The contract contains an express warranty concerning the speed of the CPU and the application programs that the computer is capable of running. Innova does not realize that the speed expressly warranted in the contract is insufficient for its needs until it tries to run the software and the computer slows to a crawl. Innova files an action claiming that Vernon has breached the implied warranty of fitness for a particular purpose because Innova made it clear that it was leasing the computer to perform certain tasks. In this situation, Innova normally will prevail. Although the express warranty on CPU speed takes precedence over the implied warranty of merchantability, it normally does not take precedence over an implied warranty of fitness for a particular purpose.

WARRANTY DISCLAIMERS AND LIMITATIONS ON LIABILITY

The UCC generally permits warranties to be disclaimed or limited by specific and unambiguous language, provided that this is done in a manner that protects the buyer or lessee from surprise. Because each type of warranty is created in a different way, the manner in which a seller or lessor can disclaim warranties varies with the type of warranty.

Express Warranties

A seller or lessor can disclaim all oral express warranties by including in the contract a written (or an electronically recorded) disclaimer in language that is clear and conspicuous, and called to a buyer's or lessee's attention [UCC 2–316(1), 2A–214(1)]. This allows the seller or lessor to avoid false allegations that oral warranties were made, and it ensures that only representations made by properly authorized individuals are included in the bargain.

Note, however, that a buyer or lessee must be made aware of any warranty disclaimers or modifications *at the time the contract is formed*. In other words, any oral or written warranties—or disclaimers—made during the bargaining process cannot be modified at a later time by the seller or lessor without the consent of the buyer or lessee.

Implied Warranties

Generally, unless circumstances indicate otherwise, the implied warranties of merchantability and fitness are disclaimed by an expression such as "as is" or "with all faults." The phrase must be one that in common understanding for *both* parties calls the buyer's or lessee's attention to the fact that there are no implied warranties [UCC 2–316(3)(a), 2A–214(3)(a)]. (Note, however, that some states have passed consumer protection statutes that forbid "as is" sales or make it illegal to disclaim warranties of merchantability on consumer goods.)

CASE IN POINT Mandy Morningstar advertised a "lovely, eleven-year-old mare" with extensive jumping ability for sale. After examining the horse twice, Sue Hallett contracted to buy the horse. She signed a contract that described the horse as an eleven-year-old mare and as being sold "as is." Shortly after the purchase, a veterinarian determined that the horse was actually sixteen years old and in no condition for jumping. Hallett stopped payment, and Morningstar filed a lawsuit for breach of contract. The court held that the statement in the contract describing the horse as eleven years old constituted an express warranty, which Morningstar had breached. Although the "as is" clause effectively disclaimed any implied warranties (of merchantability and fitness for a particular purpose, such as jumping), the court ruled that it did not disclaim the express warranty concerning the horse's age.[6]

DISCLAIMER OF THE IMPLIED WARRANTY OF MERCHANTABILITY To specifically disclaim an implied warranty either of merchantability or of fitness, a seller or lessor must mention the word *merchantability*. The disclaimer need not be written, but if it is, the writing (or record) must be conspicuous [UCC 2–316(2), 2A–214(4)]. Under the UCC, a term or clause is conspicuous when it is written or displayed in such a way that a reasonable person would notice it. Conspicuous terms include words set in capital letters, in a larger font size, or in a different color so as to be set off from the surrounding text.

DISCLAIMER OF THE IMPLIED WARRANTY OF FITNESS To disclaim an implied warranty of fitness for a particular purpose, the disclaimer must be in a writing (or record) and must be conspicuous. The writing does not have to mention the word *fitness*; it is sufficient if, for example, the disclaimer states, "There are no warranties that extend beyond the description on the face hereof."

Buyer's or Lessee's Examination or Refusal to Inspect

If a buyer or lessee actually examines the goods (or a sample or model) as fully as desired before entering into a contract, or refuses to examine the goods on the seller's or lessor's request that he or she do so, *there is no implied warranty with respect to defects that a reasonable examination would reveal or defects that are found on examination* [UCC 2–316(3)(b), 2A–214(2)(b)].

Assume that Joplin buys a lamp at Gershwin's Home Store. No express warranties are made. Gershwin asks Joplin to inspect the lamp before buying it, but she refuses. Had Joplin inspected the lamp, she would have noticed that the base was obviously cracked and the electrical cord was pulled loose. If the lamp later cracks or starts a fire in Joplin's home and causes damage, she normally will not be able to hold Gershwin's liable for breach of the warranty of

---

6. *Morningstar v. Hallett,* 858 A.2d 125 (Pa.Super.Ct. 2004).

merchantability. Because she refused to examine the lamp as Gershwin requested, Joplin will be deemed to have assumed the risk that it was defective.

Warranty Disclaimers and Unconscionability

The UCC sections dealing with warranty disclaimers do not refer specifically to unconscionability as a factor. Ultimately, however, the courts will test warranty disclaimers with reference to the UCC's unconscionability standards [UCC 2–302, 2A–108]. Such things as lack of bargaining position, "take-it-or-leave-it" choices, and a buyer's or lessee's failure to understand or know of a warranty disclaimer will be relevant to the issue of unconscionability.

Statutes of Limitations

A cause of action for breach of contract under the UCC must be commenced *within four years after the cause of action accrues*—that is, within four years after the breach occurs. The parties can reduce this period to not less than one year in their original agreement, but they *cannot* extend it beyond four years [UCC 2–725(1), 2A–506(1)]. An action for breach of warranty accrues when the seller or lessor *tenders* delivery, even if the buyer or lessee is unaware of the breach at that time [UCC 2–725(2), 2A–506(2)]. In addition, the nonbreaching party usually must notify the breaching party within a reasonable time after discovering the breach or be barred from pursuing any remedy [UCC 2–607(3)(a), 2A–516(3)].

SECTION 4
PRODUCT LIABILITY

Those who make, sell, or lease goods can be held liable for physical harm or property damage caused by those goods to a consumer, user, or bystander. This is called **product liability.** Product liability may be based on the warranty theories just discussed, as well as on the theories of negligence, misrepresentation, and strict liability. Note that multiple theories of liability can be, and often are, asserted in the same case. We look here at product liability based on negligence and on misrepresentation.

Product Liability Based on Negligence

In Chapter 7, *negligence* was defined as the failure to exercise the degree of care that a reasonable, prudent person would have exercised under the circumstances. If a manufacturer fails to exercise "due care" to make a product safe, a person who is injured by the product may sue the manufacturer for negligence.

DUE CARE MUST BE EXERCISED Due care must be exercised in designing the product, selecting the materials, using the appropriate production process, assembling and testing the product, and placing adequate warnings on the label informing the user of dangers of which an ordinary person might not be aware. The duty of care also extends to the inspection and testing of any purchased components that are used in the product sold by the manufacturer.

PRIVITY OF CONTRACT NOT REQUIRED A product liability action based on negligence does not require the injured plaintiff and the negligent defendant-manufacturer to be in *privity of contract* (see Chapter 16 on page 304). In other words, the plaintiff and the defendant need not be directly involved in a contractual relationship with one another. Thus, any person who is injured by a product may bring a negligence suit even though he or she was not the one who actually purchased the product. A manufacturer, seller, or lessor is liable for failure to exercise due care to *any person* who sustains an injury proximately caused by a negligently made (defective) product. Relative to the long history of the common law, this exception to the privity requirement is a fairly recent development—it dates to the early part of the twentieth century.[7]

Product Liability Based on Misrepresentation

When a user or consumer is injured as a result of a manufacturer's or seller's fraudulent misrepresentation, the basis of liability may be the tort of fraud. In this situation, the misrepresentation must have been made knowingly or with reckless disregard for the facts. The intentional mislabeling of packaged cosmetics, for instance, or the intentional concealment of a product's defects would constitute fraudulent misrepresentation. The misrepresentation must be of a material fact, and the seller must have intended to induce the buyer's reliance on the misrepresentation. Misrepresentation on a label or advertisement is enough to show an intent to induce the reliance of anyone who may use the product. In addition, the buyer must have relied on the misrepresentation.

---

7. A landmark case in this respect is *MacPherson v. Buick Motor Co.,* 217 N.Y. 382, 111 N.E. 1050 (1916).

SECTION 5
STRICT PRODUCT LIABILITY

Under the doctrine of *strict liability* (discussed in Chapter 7), people may be liable for the results of their acts regardless of their intentions or their exercise of reasonable care. In addition, liability does not depend on privity of contract. The injured party does not have to be the buyer or a third party beneficiary (see Chapter 16), as required under contract warranty theory. In the 1960s, courts applied the doctrine of strict liability in several landmark cases involving manufactured goods, and it has since become a common method of holding manufacturers liable.

Strict Product Liability and Public Policy

The law imposes strict product liability as a matter of public policy. This public policy rests on the threefold assumption that (1) consumers should be protected against unsafe products; (2) manufacturers and distributors should not escape liability for faulty products simply because they are not in privity of contract with the ultimate user of those products; and (3) manufacturers, sellers, and lessors of products are in a better position to bear the costs associated with injuries caused by their products—costs that they can ultimately pass on to all consumers in the form of higher prices.

California was the first state to impose strict product liability in tort on manufacturers. In a landmark decision, *Greenman v. Yuba Power Products, Inc.,*[8] the California Supreme Court set out the reason for applying tort law rather than contract law (including laws governing warranties) in cases involving consumers who were injured by defective products. According to the *Greenman* court, the "purpose of such liability is to [e]nsure that the costs of injuries resulting from defective products are borne by the manufacturers . . . rather than by the injured persons who are powerless to protect themselves." Today, the majority of states recognize strict product liability, although some state courts limit its application to situations involving personal injuries (rather than property damage).

The Requirements for Strict Product Liability

The courts often look to the *Restatements of the Law* for guidance, even though the *Restatements* are not

---

8. 59 Cal.2d 57, 377 P.2d 897, 27 Cal.Rptr. 697 (1962).

binding authorities. Section 402A of the *Restatement (Second) of Torts,* which was originally issued in 1964, has become a widely accepted statement of how the doctrine of strict liability should be applied to sellers of goods (including manufacturers, processors, assemblers, packagers, bottlers, wholesalers, distributors, retailers, and lessors).

The bases for an action in strict liability that are set forth in Section 402A of the *Restatement (Second) of Torts* can be summarized as a series of six requirements, which is listed here. Depending on the jurisdiction, if these requirements are met, a manufacturer's liability to an injured party can be almost unlimited.

1. The product must be in a *defective condition* when the defendant sells it.
2. The defendant must normally be engaged in the *business of selling* (or otherwise distributing) that product.
3. The product must be *unreasonably dangerous* to the user or consumer because of its defective condition (in most states).
4. The plaintiff must incur *physical harm* to self or property by use or consumption of the product.
5. The defective condition must be the *proximate cause* of the injury or damage.
6. The *goods must not have been substantially changed* from the time the product was sold to the time the injury was sustained.

PROVING A DEFECTIVE CONDITION Under these requirements, in any action against a manufacturer, seller, or lessor, the plaintiff need not show why or in what manner the product became defective. The plaintiff does, however, have to prove that the product was defective at the time it left the hands of the seller or lessor and that this defective condition made it "unreasonably dangerous" to the user or consumer. Unless evidence can be presented to support the conclusion that the product was defective when it was sold or leased, the plaintiff will not succeed. If the product was delivered in a safe condition and subsequent mishandling made it harmful to the user, the seller or lessor normally is not strictly liable.

UNREASONABLY DANGEROUS PRODUCTS The *Restatement* recognizes that many products cannot be made entirely safe for all uses; thus, sellers or lessors are liable only for products that are *unreasonably* dangerous. A court could consider a product so defective as to be an **unreasonably dangerous product** in either of the following situations:

1. The product was dangerous beyond the expectation of the ordinary consumer.
2. A less dangerous alternative was *economically* feasible for the manufacturer, but the manufacturer failed to produce it.

As will be discussed next, a product may be unreasonably dangerous due to a flaw in the manufacturing process, a design defect, or an inadequate warning.

Product Defects

Because Section 402A of the *Restatement (Second) of Torts* did not clearly define such terms as *defective* and *unreasonably dangerous,* these terms have been subject to different interpretations by different courts. In 1997, to address these concerns, the American Law Institute issued the *Restatement (Third) of Torts: Products Liability.* This *Restatement* defines the three types of product defects that have traditionally been recognized in product liability law—manufacturing defects, design defects, and inadequate warnings.

MANUFACTURING DEFECTS According to Section 2(a) of the *Restatement (Third) of Torts,* a product "contains a manufacturing defect when the product departs from its intended design even though all possible care was exercised in the preparation and marketing of the product." Basically, a manufacturing defect is a departure from a product's design specifications that results in products that are physically flawed, damaged, or incorrectly assembled. A glass bottle that is made too thin and explodes in a consumer's face is an example of a product with a manufacturing defect.

Usually, such defects occur when a manufacturer fails to assemble, test, or adequately check the quality of a product. Liability is imposed on the manufacturer (and on the wholesaler and retailer) regardless of whether the manufacturer's quality control efforts were "reasonable." The idea behind holding defendants strictly liable for manufacturing defects is to encourage greater investment in product safety and stringent quality control standards. Cases involving allegations of a manufacturing defect are often decided based on the opinions and testimony of experts.

CASE IN POINT While Kevin Schmude was standing on an eight-foot ladder that he had purchased, it collapsed and he was seriously injured. He filed a lawsuit against the ladder's maker, Tricam Industries, Inc., based on a manufacturing defect. Experts testified that the preexisting holes in the ladder's top cap did not properly line up with the holes in the rear right rail and backing plate. As a result of the misalignment, the rivet at the rear legs of the ladder was more likely to fail. A jury concluded that this manufacturing defect made the ladder unreasonably dangerous and awarded Schmude more than $677,000 in damages.[9]

DESIGN DEFECTS Unlike a product with a manufacturing defect, a product with a design defect is made in conformity with the manufacturer's design specifications but nevertheless results in injury to the user because the design itself was faulty. A product "is defective in design when the foreseeable risks of harm posed by the product could have been reduced or avoided by the adoption of a reasonable alternative design by the seller or other distributor, or a predecessor in the commercial chain of distribution, and the omission of the alternative design renders the product not reasonably safe."[10]

For example, after a massive recall of Toyota vehicles in 2009 due to problems with purportedly unintended acceleration, owners of recalled cars filed numerous product liability lawsuits against Toyota. Some of these lawsuits claimed that the Japanese automaker negligently manufactured the cars or made fraudulent misrepresentations concerning the electronic throttle control system used in the cars. In 2010, Toyota admitted that there was in fact a design defect that caused some Prius models to have brake problems.

Test for Design Defects. To successfully assert a design defect, a plaintiff has to show that a reasonable alternative design was available and that the defendant's failure to adopt the alternative design rendered the product not reasonably safe. In other words, a manufacturer or other defendant is liable only when the harm was reasonably preventable.

Factors to Be Considered. According to the *Restatement,* a court can consider a broad range of factors, including the magnitude and probability of the foreseeable risks as well as the relative advantages and disadvantages of the product as it was designed and as it could have been designed. Basically, most courts engage in a risk-utility analysis, determining whether the risk of harm from the product as designed outweighs its utility to the user and to the public.

---

9. *Schmude v. Tricam Industries, Inc.,* 550 F.Supp.2d 846 (E.D.Wis. 2008).
10. *Restatement (Third) of Torts: Products Liability,* Section 2(b).

CASE IN POINT Jodie Bullock smoked cigarettes manufactured by Philip Morris for forty-five years. When she was diagnosed with lung cancer, Bullock brought a product liability suit against Philip Morris. She presented evidence that by the late 1950s, scientists had proved that smoking caused lung cancer. Nonetheless, Philip Morris had issued full-page announcements stating that there was no proof that smoking caused cancer and that "numerous scientists" questioned "the validity of the statistics." At trial, the judge instructed the jury to consider the gravity of the danger posed by the design, as well as the likelihood that the danger would cause injury. The jury found that there was a defect in the design of the cigarettes and that they had been negligently designed. It awarded Bullock $850,000 in compensatory damages and $28 million in punitive damages. Philip Morris appealed, claiming that no evidence had been offered to show that there was a safer design for cigarettes, but the reviewing court found that the jury had been properly instructed. The court affirmed the award but remanded the case for a reconsideration of the proper amount of punitive damages.[11]

INADEQUATE WARNINGS A product may also be deemed defective because of inadequate instructions or warnings. A product will be considered defective "when the foreseeable risks of harm posed by the product could have been reduced or avoided by the provision of reasonable instructions or warnings by the seller or other distributor, or a predecessor in the commercial chain of distribution, and the omission of the instructions or warnings renders the product not reasonably safe."[12]

Important factors for a court to consider include the risks of a product, the "content and comprehensibility" and "intensity of expression" of warnings and instructions, and the "characteristics of expected user groups."[13] Courts apply a "reasonableness" test to determine if the warnings adequately alert consumers to the product's risks. For example, children will likely respond readily to bright, bold, simple warning labels, whereas educated adults might need more detailed information.

An action alleging that a product is defective due to an inadequate label can be based on state law. (For a discussion of a case involving a state law that required warning labels on violent video games, see this chapter's *Insight into Ethics* feature on page 434.) Can a state-law claim still be asserted if a federal agency approved the label? That was the question in the following case.

---

11. *Bullock v. Philip Morris USA, Inc.*, 159 Cal.App.4th 655, 71 Cal. Rptr.3d 775 (2008).

12. *Restatement (Third) of Torts: Products Liability*, Section 2(c).

13. *Restatement (Third) of Torts: Products Liability*, Section 2, Comment h.

CASE 22.2
Wyeth v. Levine

Supreme Court of the United States, __ U.S. __, 129 S.Ct. 1187, 173 L.Ed.2d 51 (2009).
www.findlaw.com/casecode/supreme.html[a]

BACKGROUND AND FACTS • Diane Levine, a professional guitar player and pianist, visited Plainfield Health Center in Vermont for treatment of a migraine headache. A physician's assistant gave her Phenergan (an antihistamine used to treat nausea) with a syringe—the intravenous-push (IV-push) method. The drug's label, which the U.S. Food and Drug Administration (FDA) had approved, did not warn that this method was more risky than the IV-drip method. Phenergan entered Levine's artery and, because the drug is corrosive, led to gangrene and the amputation of her forearm. She filed a suit in a Vermont state court against Wyeth, the drug's manufacturer, alleging that the label's warning was inadequate. Levine was awarded damages of $7.4 million. The Vermont Supreme Court affirmed the result. Wyeth appealed.

IN THE LANGUAGE OF THE COURT
Justice *STEVENS* delivered the opinion of the Court.
* * * *

Wyeth first argues that Levine's state-law claims are pre-empted because it is impossible for it to comply with both the state-law duties underlying those claims

---

a. In the "Browse Supreme Court Opinions" section, click on "2009." On that page, scroll to the name of the case and click on it to access the opinion. FindLaw maintains this Web site.

CASE 22.2 CONTINUED ➡ and its federal labeling duties. * * * Generally speaking, a manufacturer may only change a drug label after the FDA approves a supplemental application. There is, however, an FDA regulation that permits a manufacturer to make certain changes to its label before receiving the agency's approval. Among other things, this * * * regulation provides that if a manufacturer is changing a label to "add or strengthen a contraindication, warning, precaution, or adverse reaction" * * * , it may make the labeling change upon filing its supplemental application with the FDA; it need not wait for FDA approval.

* * * *

* * * *The* * * *regulation permitted Wyeth to unilaterally strengthen its warning, and the mere fact that the FDA approved Phenergan's label does not establish that it would have prohibited such a change.* [Emphasis added.]

* * * *

Wyeth also argues that requiring it to comply with a state-law duty to provide a stronger warning about IV-push administration would obstruct the purposes and objectives of federal drug labeling regulation.

* * * The most glaring problem with this argument is that all evidence of Congress' purposes is to the contrary. Building on its 1906 Act, Congress enacted the [Food, Drug and Cosmetic Act (FDCA) in 1938] to bolster consumer protection against harmful products. Congress did not provide a federal remedy for consumers harmed by unsafe or ineffective drugs in the 1938 statute or in any subsequent amendment. Evidently, it determined that widely available state rights of action provided appropriate relief for injured consumers. It may also have recognized that state-law remedies further consumer protection by motivating manufacturers to produce safe and effective drugs and to give adequate warnings.

If Congress thought state-law suits posed an obstacle to its objectives, it surely would have enacted an express pre-emption provision at some point during the FDCA's 70-year history. * * * Its silence on the issue, coupled with its certain awareness of the prevalence of state tort litigation, is powerful evidence that Congress did not intend FDA oversight to be the exclusive means of ensuring drug safety and effectiveness.

DECISION AND REMEDY • *The United States Supreme Court affirmed the lower court's decision. The FDA's approval of Phenergan's label did not preempt Levine's claim against the drug's manufacturer.*

WHAT IF THE FACTS WERE DIFFERENT? • *Suppose that the Phenergan label had contained a stronger warning against the IV-push method without explicitly stating that the method should not be used. Would the result in Levine's case have been the same? Discuss.*

THE LEGAL ENVIRONMENT DIMENSION • *In a 2006 preamble to a regulation, for the first time the FDA expressed the opinion that state-law actions "threaten [the] FDA's statutorily prescribed role as the expert Federal agency responsible for evaluating and regulating drugs." What might have motivated this dramatic change in the agency's traditional position?*

Obvious Risks. There is no duty to warn about risks that are obvious or commonly known. Warnings about such risks do not add to the safety of a product and could even detract from it by making other warnings seem less significant. As will be discussed later in the chapter, the obviousness of a risk and a user's decision to proceed in the face of that risk may be a defense in a product liability suit based on an inadequate warning.

CASE IN POINT Sixteen-year-old Gary Crosswhite attempted to do a back flip on a trampoline in his backyard and accidentally landed on his head and neck. The fall fractured his spine and resulted in paraplegia. Crosswhite filed a strict product liability lawsuit against the manufacturer, in which he claimed that the trampoline was defective because of inadequate warnings and instructions. The court found that there were nine warning labels affixed to the trampoline, an instruction manual with safety warnings, and a placard attached to the entrance that advised users not to do flips. These warnings were sufficient to make the risks obvious and insulate the manufacturer from liability for Crosswhite's injuries.[14]

---

14. *Crosswhite v. Jumpking, Inc.,* 411 F.Supp.2d 1228 (D.Or. 2006).

INSIGHT INTO ETHICS
Warning Labels for Video Games

The video game industry uses a voluntary rating system that includes six age-specific labels. Should video game makers also be required to attach labels to their games that warn parents of excessive violence? When California legislated this requirement, video software dealers sued.

The act defined a violent video game as one in which "the range of options available to a player includes killing, maiming, dismembering, or sexually assaulting an image of a human being." While agreeing that some video games are unquestionably violent by everyday standards, the trial court pointed out, as did the federal court that heard the appeal, that many video games are based on popular novels or motion pictures and have complex plot lines. Accordingly, the court found that the definition of a violent video game was unconstitutionally vague and thus violated the First Amendment's guarantee of freedom of speech. The court also noted the existence of the voluntary rating system.

The state appealed, but the U.S. Court of Appeals for the Ninth Circuit also found that the statute's definition of a violent video game was unconstitutionally broad.[a] The appeals court noted that other federal circuit courts had already ruled against extending restrictions on sex-based content to restrictions on violence in video games.[b]

CRITICAL THINKING
INSIGHT INTO THE SOCIAL ENVIRONMENT
Why would some legislators believe that the six-part voluntary labeling system for video games is not sufficient to protect minors?

---

a. *Video Software Dealers Association v. Schwarzenegger,* 556 F.3d 950 (9th Cir. 2009).
b. See, for example, *Interactive Digital Software Association v. St. Louis County,* 329 F.3d 954 (8th Cir. 2003).

Nevertheless, risks that may seem obvious to some users will not be obvious to all users, especially when the users are likely to be children. A young child may not be able to read or understand warning labels or comprehend the risk of certain activities. Therefore, if a child is permanently injured by diving into a shallow, aboveground pool, the manufacturer cannot escape liability simply by having a warning label on the box in which the pool was shipped. To avoid liability, the manufacturer would have to prove that the warnings it provided were adequate to make the risk of injury obvious to a young child using the pool.[15]

Foreseeable Misuses. Generally, a seller must warn those who purchase its product of the harm that can result from the foreseeable misuse of the product as well. The key is the foreseeability of the misuse. Sellers are not required to take precautions against every conceivable misuse of a product, just those that are foreseeable.

Market-Share Liability

Ordinarily, in all product liability claims, a plaintiff must prove that the defective product that caused his or her injury was the product of a specific defendant. In a few situations, however, courts have dropped this requirement when plaintiffs could not prove which of many distributors of a harmful product supplied the particular product that caused the injuries.

CASE IN POINT John Smith, a resident of Hawaii, was a hemophiliac. Because of his condition, Smith received injections of a blood protein known as anti-hemophiliac factor (AHF) concentrate. Smith later tested positive for the acquired immune deficiency syndrome (AIDS) virus. Because it was not known which manufacturer was responsible for the particular AHF received by Smith, the court held that all of the manufacturers of AHF could be held liable under the theory of **market-share liability.**[16]

Courts in many jurisdictions do not recognize this theory of liability because they believe that it deviates too significantly from traditional legal principles.[17] In jurisdictions that do recognize market-share liability,

---

16. *Smith v. Cutter Biological, Inc.,* 72 Haw. 416, 823 P.2d 717 (1991). See also *Sutowski v. Eli Lilly & Co.,* 82 Ohio St.3d 347, 696 N.E.2d 187 (1998); and *In re Methyl Tertiary Butyl Ether ("MTBE") Products Liability Litigation,* 447 F.Supp.2d 289 (S.D.N.Y. 2006).
17. For the Illinois Supreme Court's position on market-share liability, see *Smith v. Eli Lilly & Co.,* 137 Ill.2d 222, 560 N.E.2d 324 (1990). Pennsylvania law also does not recognize market-share liability. See *Bortell v. Eli Lilly & Co.,* 406 F.Supp.2d 1 (D.D.C. 2005).

---

15. See, for example, *Bunch v. Hoffinger Industries, Inc.,* 123 Cal. App.4th 1278, 20 Cal.Rptr.3d 780 (2004).

it is usually applied in cases involving drugs or chemicals, when it is difficult or impossible to determine which company made a particular product.

Other Applications of Strict Product Liability

Almost all courts extend the strict liability of manufacturers and other sellers to injured bystanders. Thus, if a defective forklift that will not go into reverse injures a passerby, that individual can sue the manufacturer for product liability (and possibly bring a negligence action against the forklift operator as well).

Strict product liability also applies to suppliers of component parts. For example, suppose that General Motors buys brake pads from a subcontractor and puts them in Chevrolets without changing their composition. If those pads are defective, both the supplier of the brake pads and General Motors will be held strictly liable for the injuries caused by the defects.

SECTION 6
DEFENSES TO PRODUCT LIABILITY

Defendants in product liability suits can raise a number of defenses. One defense, of course, is to show that there is no basis for the plaintiff's claim. For example, in a product liability case based on negligence, if a defendant can show that the plaintiff has *not* met the requirements (such as causation)

for an action in negligence, generally the defendant will not be liable. Similarly, in a case involving strict product liability, a defendant can claim that the plaintiff failed to meet one of the requirements. For example, if the defendant establishes that the goods were altered after they were sold, normally the defendant will not be held liable.[18] Defendants may also assert the defenses discussed next.

Assumption of Risk

Assumption of risk can sometimes be used as a defense in a product liability action. To establish such a defense, the defendant must show that (1) the plaintiff knew and appreciated the risk created by the product defect and (2) the plaintiff voluntarily assumed the risk, even though it was unreasonable to do so. For example, if a buyer failed to heed a seller's product recall, the buyer may be deemed to have assumed the risk of the product defect that the seller offered to cure. (See Chapter 7 for a more detailed discussion of assumption of risk.)

In the following case, an injured user of a tanning booth had signed an exculpatory clause stating that she was using the booth at her own risk and that she released the manufacturer, among others, from any liability for any injuries. The issue before the court was whether an exculpatory clause can relieve a manufacturer from strict product liability.

---

18. See, for example, *Edmondson v. Macclesfield L-P Gas Co.,* 642 S.E.2d 265 (N.C.App. 2007); and *Pichardo v. C. S. Brown Co.,* 35 A.D.3d 303, 827 N.Y.S.2d 131 (N.Y.App. 2006).

✴ EXTENDED CASE 22.3 ✴
Boles v. Sun Ergoline, Inc.

Supreme Court of Colorado, 223 P.3d 724 (2010).
www.cobar.org/ors.cfm[a]

IN THE LANGUAGE OF THE COURT

Justice *COATS* delivered the opinion of the court.

* * * *

Savannah Boles brought suit against Sun Ergoline, Inc., asserting a strict products liability claim for personal injury. Sun Ergoline moved for

summary judgment, countering that Boles's claim was barred by a release she signed prior to using its product. The trial court agreed and granted Sun Ergoline's motion on the basis of the following undisputed facts.

Executive Tans operated an upright tanning booth manufactured by Sun Ergoline. Prior to using the booth, Boles signed a

release form provided by Executive Tans that contained the following exculpatory agreement: "I have read the instructions for proper use of the tanning facilities and do so at my own risk and hereby release the owners, operators, franchiser, or manufacturers, from any damage or harm that I might incur due to use of the facilities." After entering

---

a. Under the heading "Opinions," select "Colorado Supreme Court Opinions." When that page opens, select "February 8, 2010" from the list of dates under the heading "Cases published announced on." When that page appears, scroll down the page to the case title and click on the link to view the opinion. The Colorado Bar Association maintains this Web site.

EXTENDED CASE CONTINUES ➡

EXTENDED CASE 22.3 CONTINUED ◆

the booth, several of Boles's fingers came in contact with an exhaust fan located at the top of the booth, partially amputating them.

On direct appeal, the court of appeals affirmed. * * * [It found] that the language of the release was broad enough to include any damage or harm that might occur due to Boles's use of the facilities [and] * * * found no violation of public policy.

We granted Boles's petition for a writ of *certiorari* [a request by the losing party asking the higher court to hear the case] challenging the court of appeals' determination that the exculpatory agreement barred her strict products liability claim.

* * * *

"Strict products liability" has been described as a "term of art that reflects the judgment that products liability is a discrete area of tort law which borrows from both negligence and warranty" but "is not fully congruent with classical tort or contract law." Rather than resting on negligence principles, it "is premised on the concept of enterprise liability for casting a

defective product into the stream of commerce." *In strict products liability, the focus is on the nature of the product rather than the conduct of either the manufacturer or the person injured.* [Emphasis added.]

As such, strict products liability evolved to accommodate, and is driven by, public policy considerations surrounding the relationship between manufacturers and consumers in general, rather than any particular transaction or contract for sale. In addition to the typical inaccessibility of information and inequality of bargaining power inherent in any disclaimer or ordinary consumer's agreement to release a manufacturer, a claim for strict products liability is also premised on a number of public policy considerations that would be flatly thwarted [prevented] by legitimizing such disclaimers or exculpatory agreements. Not least among these is the deliberate provision of economic incentives for manufacturers to improve product safety and take advantage of their unique "position to spread the risk of loss among all who use the product."

* * * The *Second Restatement of Torts* clearly indicates that exculpatory agreements between a manufacturer and an end-user can have no effect. * * * The *Third Restatement* would even more emphatically prohibit "contractual exculpations" from barring or reducing otherwise valid products liability claims for personal injuries by ordinary consumers against sellers or distributors of new products.

There appears to be virtually universal agreement on this point among the other jurisdictions considering the question.

* * * An agreement releasing a manufacturer from strict products liability for personal injury, in exchange for nothing more than an individual consumer's right to have or use the product, necessarily violates the public policy of this jurisdiction and is void.

* * * *

Because the lower courts erred * * * in finding the exculpatory agreement in this case enforceable, the judgment of the court of appeals is reversed with directions to remand for further proceedings consistent with this opinion.

 QUESTIONS

1. What did the court mean when it stated that strict product liability laws are "not fully congruent" with classical tort law?
2. Why would the enforcement of the exculpatory clause in this case conflict with the rationale underlying strict product liability?

Product Misuse

Similar to the defense of voluntary assumption of risk is that of **product misuse,** which occurs when a product is used for a purpose for which it was not intended. Here, in contrast to assumption of risk, the injured party *does not know that the product is dangerous for a particular use.* The courts have severely limited this defense, however. Even if the injured party does not know about the inherent danger of using the product in a wrong way, if the misuse is reasonably foreseeable, the seller must take measures to guard against it. For example, it is reasonably foreseeable that a child might misuse a product without

understanding the danger of doing so. Thus, if a child is playing with a BIC lighter and starts a fire that causes injury to another person, the manufacturer cannot escape liability by claiming that the child misused the lighter.[19]

Comparative Negligence (Fault)

Developments in the area of comparative negligence, or fault (see Chapter 7), have also affected the doctrine of strict liability. In the past, the plaintiff's

---

19. See, for example, *Price v. BIC Corp.*, 702 A.2d 330 (Sup.Ct.N.H. 1997).

conduct was never a defense to liability for a defective product. Today, courts in many jurisdictions will consider the negligent or intentional actions of both the plaintiff and the defendant when apportioning liability and damages.[20] This means that a defendant may be able to limit at least some of its liability if it can show that the plaintiff's misuse of the product contributed to his or her injuries. When proved, comparative negligence differs from other defenses in that it does not completely absolve the defendant of liability, but it can reduce the total amount of damages that will be awarded to the plaintiff. Note that some jurisdictions allow only intentional conduct to affect a plaintiff's recovery, whereas other states allow ordinary negligence to be used as a defense to product liability.

CASE IN POINT Dan Smith, a mechanic, was not wearing a hard hat at work when he was asked to start the diesel engine of an air compressor. Because the compressor was an older model, he had to prop open a door to start it. When the engine started, the door fell from its position and hit Smith's head. The injury caused him to suffer from seizures. Smith sued the manufacturer, claiming that the engine was defectively designed. The manufacturer contended that Smith had been negligent by failing to wear a hard hat and propping open the door in an unsafe manner. Although Smith argued that ordinary negligence could not be used as a defense in product liability cases, the court ruled that defendants can use the plaintiff's ordinary negligence to reduce their liability proportionately.[21]

Commonly Known Dangers

The dangers associated with certain products (such as matches and sharp knives) are so commonly known that, as already mentioned, manufacturers need not warn users of those dangers. If a defendant succeeds in convincing the court that a plaintiff's injury resulted from a *commonly known danger,* the defendant will not be liable.

CASE IN POINT In 1957, Marguerite Jamieson was injured when an elastic exercise rope slipped off her foot and struck her in the eye, causing a detachment of the retina. Jamieson claimed that the manufacturer should be liable because it had failed to warn users

that the exerciser might slip off a foot in such a manner. The court stated that to hold the manufacturer liable in these circumstances "would go beyond the reasonable dictates of justice in fixing the liabilities of manufacturers." After all, stated the court, "almost every physical object can be inherently dangerous or potentially dangerous in a sense. . . . A manufacturer cannot manufacture a knife that will not cut or a hammer that will not mash a thumb or a stove that will not burn a finger. The law does not require [manufacturers] to warn of such common dangers."[22]

Knowledgeable User

A related defense is the *knowledgeable user* defense. If a particular danger (such as electrical shock) is or should be commonly known by particular users of a product (such as electricians), the manufacturer need not warn these users of the danger.

CASE IN POINT The parents of teenagers who had become overweight and developed health problems filed a product liability suit against McDonald's. The teenagers claimed that the fast-food chain had failed to warn customers of the adverse health effects of eating its food. The court rejected this claim, however, based on the knowledgeable user defense. The court found that it is well known that the food at McDonald's contains high levels of cholesterol, fat, salt, and sugar and is therefore unhealthful. The court's opinion, which thwarted future lawsuits against fast-food restaurants, stated: "If consumers know (or reasonably should know) the potential ill health effects of eating at McDonald's, they cannot blame McDonald's if they, nonetheless, choose to satiate their appetite with a surfeit [excess] of supersized McDonald's products."[23]

Statutes of Limitations and Repose

As previously discussed, statutes of limitations restrict the time within which an action may be brought. The statute of limitations for product liability cases varies according to state law, and unlike warranty claims, product liability claims are not subject to the UCC's limitation period. Usually, the injured party must bring a product liability claim within two to four years. Often, the running of the prescribed period is *tolled* (that is, suspended) until the party suffering an injury has discovered it or should have discovered it. To ensure that sellers and manufacturers will not be left vulnerable to lawsuits

20. See, for example, *State Farm Insurance Companies v. Premier Manufactured Systems, Inc.,* 213 Ariz. 419, 142 P.3d 1232 (2006); and *Industrial Risk Insurers v. American Engineering Testing, Inc.,* 318 Wis.2d 148, 769 N.W.2d 82 (Wis.App. 2009).

21. *Smith v. Ingersoll-Rand Co.,* 14 P.3d 990 (Alaska 2000).

22. *Jamieson v. Woodward & Lothrop,* 247 F.2d 23 (D.C.Cir. 1957).

23. *Pelman v. McDonald's Corp.,* 237 F.Supp.2d 512 (S.D.N.Y. 2003).

indefinitely, many states have passed laws, called **statutes of repose,** that place *outer* time limits on product liability actions. For example, a statute of repose may require that claims be brought within twelve years from the date of sale or manufacture of the defective product. If the plaintiff does not bring an action before the prescribed period expires, the seller cannot be held liable.

REVIEWING

Warranties and Product Liability

Shalene Kolchek bought a Great Lakes Spa from Val Porter, a dealer who was selling spas at the state fair. Porter told Kolchek that Great Lakes spas were "top of the line" and "the Cadillac of spas" and indicated that the spa she was buying was "fully warranted for three years." Kolchek signed an installment contract; then Porter handed her the manufacturer's paperwork and arranged for the spa to be delivered and installed for her. Three months later, Kolchek noticed that one corner of the spa was leaking onto her new deck and causing damage. She complained to Porter, but he did nothing about the problem. Kolchek's family continued to use the spa. Using the information presented in the chapter, answer the following questions.

1. Did Porter's statement that the spa was "top of the line" and "the Cadillac of spas" create any type of warranty? Why or why not?
2. If the paperwork provided to Kolchek after her purchase indicated that the spa had no warranty, would this be an effective disclaimer under the Uniform Commercial Code? Explain.
3. One night, Kolchek's six-year-old daughter, Litisha, was in the spa with her mother. Litisha's hair became entangled in the spa's drain, and she was sucked down and held underwater for a prolonged period, causing her to suffer brain damage. Under which theory or theories of product liability can Kolchek sue Porter to recover for Litisha's injuries?
4. If Kolchek had negligently left Litisha alone in the spa prior to the incident described in the previous question, what defense to liability might Porter assert?

DEBATE THIS: *No express warranties should be created by the oral statements made by salespersons about a product.*

TERMS AND CONCEPTS

express warranty 422

implied warranty 423

implied warranty of fitness
  for a particular
  purpose 425

implied warranty of
  merchantability 423

market-share liability 434

product liability 429

product misuse 436

statute of repose 438

unreasonably dangerous
  product 430

QUESTIONS AND CASE PROBLEMS

22–1. Implied Warranties Moon, a farmer, needs to install a two-thousand-pound piece of equipment in his barn. This will require lifting the equipment thirty feet up into a hayloft. Moon goes to Davidson Hardware and tells Davidson that he needs some heavy-duty rope to be used on his farm. Davidson recommends a one-inch-thick nylon rope, and Moon purchases two hundred feet of it. Moon ties the rope around the piece of equipment; puts the rope through a pulley; and, with a tractor, lifts the equipment off the ground. Suddenly, the rope breaks. The equipment crashes to the ground and is severely damaged. Moon files a suit against Davidson for breach of the implied warranty of fitness for a particular purpose. Discuss how successful Moon will be in his suit.

22–2. QUESTION WITH SAMPLE ANSWER: Product Liability.

Jason Clark, an experienced hunter, bought a paintball gun. Clark practiced with the gun and knew how to screw in the carbon dioxide cartridge, pump the gun, and use its safety and trigger. Although Clark was aware that he could purchase protective eyewear, he chose not to buy it. Clark had taken gun safety courses and understood that it was "common sense" not to shoot anyone in the face. Clark's friend, Chris Wright, also owned a paintball gun and was similarly familiar with the gun's use and its risks. Clark, Wright, and their friends played a game that involved shooting paintballs at cars whose occupants also had the guns. One night, while Clark and Wright were cruising with their guns, Wright shot at Clark's car, but hit Clark in the eye. Clark filed a product liability lawsuit against the manufacturer of Wright's paintball gun to recover for the injury. Clark claimed that the gun was defectively designed. During the trial, Wright testified that his gun "never malfunctioned." In whose favor should the court rule? Why?

• **For a sample answer to Question 22–2, go to Appendix I at the end of this text.**

22–3. Defenses to Product Liability Baxter manufactures electric hair dryers. Julie purchases a Baxter dryer from her local Ace Drugstore. Cox, a friend and guest in Julie's home, has taken a shower and wants to dry her hair. Julie tells Cox to use the new Baxter hair dryer that she has just purchased. As Cox plugs in the dryer, sparks fly out from the motor, and sparks continue to fly as she operates it. Despite this, Cox begins drying her hair. Suddenly, the entire dryer ignites into flames, severely burning Cox's scalp. Cox sues Baxter on the basis of negligence and strict liability in tort. Baxter admits that the dryer was defective but denies liability, particularly because Cox was not the person who purchased the dryer. In other words, Cox had no contractual relationship with Baxter. Discuss the validity of Baxter's defense. Are there any other defenses that Baxter might assert to avoid liability? Discuss fully.

22–4. Express Warranties Videotape is recorded magnetically. The magnetic particles that constitute the recorded image are bound to the tape's polyester base. The binder that holds the particles to the base breaks down over time. This breakdown, which is called sticky shed syndrome, causes the image to deteriorate. The Walt Disney Co. made many of its movies available on tape. Buena Vista Home Entertainment, Inc., sold the tapes, which it described as part of a "Gold Collection" or "Masterpiece Collection." The advertising included such statements as "Give Your Children the Memories of a Lifetime—Collect Each Timeless Masterpiece!" and "Available for a Limited Time Only!" Charmaine Schreib and others who bought the tapes filed a suit in an Illinois state court against Disney and Buena Vista, alleging, among other things, breach of warranty. The plaintiffs claimed that

the defendants' marketing promised the tapes would last for generations. In reality, the tapes were as subject to sticky shed syndrome as other tapes. Did the ads create an express warranty? In whose favor should the court rule on this issue? Explain. [*Schreib v. The Walt Disney Co.,* __ N.E.2d __ (Ill.App. 1 Dist. 2006)]

22–5. CASE PROBLEM WITH SAMPLE ANSWER: Product Liability.

Bret D'Auguste was an experienced skier when he rented equipment to ski at Hunter Mountain Ski Bowl, Inc., owned by Shanty Hollow Corp., in New York. The adjustable retention/release value for the bindings on the rented equipment was set at a level that, according to skiing industry standards, was too low—meaning that the skis would be released too easily—given D'Auguste's height, weight, and ability. When D'Auguste entered a "double black diamond," or extremely difficult, trail, he noticed immediately that the surface consisted of ice and almost no snow. He tried to exit the steeply declining trail by making a sharp right turn, but in the attempt, his left ski snapped off. D'Auguste lost his balance, fell, and slid down the mountain, striking his face and head against a fence along the trail. According to a report by a rental shop employee, one of the bindings on D'Auguste's skis had a "cracked heel housing." D'Auguste filed a suit in a New York state court against Shanty Hollow and others, including the bindings' manufacturer, on a theory of strict product liability. The manufacturer filed a motion for summary judgment. On what basis might the court grant the motion? On what basis might the court deny the motion? How should the court rule? Explain. [D'Auguste v. Shanty Hollow Corp., 26 A.D.3d 403, 809 N.Y.S.2d 555 (2 Dept. 2006)]

• **To view a sample answer for Problem 22–5, go to this book's Web site at www.cengage.com/blaw/clarkson, select "Chapter 22," and click on "Case Problem with Sample Answer."**

22–6. Implied Warranties Peter and Tanya Rothing operated Diamond R Stables near Belgrade, Montana, where they bred, trained, and sold horses. Arnold Kallestad owned a ranch in Gallatin County, Montana, where he grew hay and grain, and raised Red Angus cattle. For more than twenty years, Kallestad had sold between three hundred and one thousand tons of hay annually, sometimes advertising it for sale in the *Bozeman Daily Chronicle*. In 2001, the Rothings bought hay from Kallestad for $90 a ton. They received delivery on April 23. In less than two weeks, at least nine of the Rothings' horses exhibited symptoms of poisoning that was diagnosed as botulism. Before the outbreak was over, nineteen animals had died. Robert Whitlock, associate professor of medicine and the director of the Botulism Laboratory at the University of Pennsylvania, concluded that Kallestad's hay was the source. The Rothings filed a suit in a Montana state court against Kallestad, claiming, in part, breach of the implied warranty of merchantability. Kallestad asked the court to dismiss this claim on the ground that, if botulism had been present, it had been in no way foreseeable. Should the court grant this request? Why or why not? [*Rothing v. Kallestad,* 337 Mont. 193, 159 P.3d 222 (2007)]

22–7. Defenses to Product Liability Terry Kunkle and VanBuren High hosted a Christmas party in Berkeley County, South Carolina. Guests had drinks and hors d'oeuvres at a residence and adjourned to dinner in a barn across a public road. Brandon Stroud ferried the guests to the barn in a golf car made by Textron, Inc. The golf car was not equipped with lights, and Textron did not warn against its use on public roads at night. South Carolina does not require golf cars to be equipped with lights, but does ban their operation on public roads at night. As Stroud attempted to cross the road at 8:30 P.M., his golf car was struck by a vehicle driven by Joseph Thornley. Stroud was killed. His estate filed a suit in a South Carolina state court against Textron, alleging strict product liability and product liability based on negligence. The estate claimed that the golf car was defective and unreasonably dangerous. What might Textron assert in its defense? Explain. [*Moore v. Barony House Restaurant, LLC*, 382 S.C. 35, 674 S.E.2d 500 (S.C.App. 2009)]

22–8. Product Liability Yun Tung Chow tried to unclog a floor drain in the kitchen of the restaurant where he worked. He used a drain cleaner called Lewis Red Devil Lye that contained crystalline sodium hydroxide. The product label said to wear eye protection, to put one tablespoon of lye directly into the drain, and to keep one's face away from the drain because there could be dangerous backsplash. Without eye protection, Chow mixed three tablespoons of lye in a can and poured that mixture down the drain while bending over it. Liquid splashed back into his face, causing injury. He brought a product liability suit based on inadequate warnings and design defect. The trial court granted summary judgment to the manufacturer, and Chow appealed. An expert for Chow stated that the product was defective because it had a tendency to backsplash. Is that a convincing argument? Why or why not? [*Yun Tung Chow v. Reckitt & Coleman, Inc.*, 69 A.D.3d 413, 891 N.Y.S.2d 402 (N.Y.A.D. 1 Dept. 2010)]

22–9. A QUESTION OF ETHICS: Dangerous Products.

Susan Calles lived with her four daughters, Amanda, age eleven, Victoria, age five, and Jenna and Jillian, age three. In March 1998, Calles bought an Aim N Flame utility lighter, which she stored on the top shelf of her kitchen cabinet. A trigger can ignite the Aim N Flame after an "ON/OFF" switch is slid to the "on" position.

On the night of March 31, Calles and Victoria left to get videos. Jenna and Jillian were in bed, and Amanda was watching television. Calles returned to find fire trucks and emergency vehicles around her home. Robert Finn, a fire investigator, determined that Jenna had started a fire using the lighter. Jillian suffered smoke inhalation, was hospitalized, and died on April 21. Calles filed a suit in an Illinois state court against Scripto-Tokai Corp., which distributed the Aim N Flame, and others. In her suit, which was grounded, in part, in strict liability claims, Calles alleged that the lighter was an "unreasonably dangerous product." Scripto filed a motion for summary judgment. [*Calles v. Scripto-Tokai Corp.*, 224 Ill.2d 247, 864 N.E.2d 249, 309 Ill.Dec. 383 (2007)]

(a) A product is unreasonably dangerous when it is dangerous beyond the expectation of the ordinary consumer. Whose expectation—Calles's or Jenna's—applies? Does the lighter pass this test? Explain.

(b) Calles presented evidence as to the likelihood and seriousness of injury from lighters that do not have child-safety devices. Scripto argued that the Aim N Flame is an alternative source of fire and is safer than a match. Calles admitted that she knew the dangers presented by lighters in the hands of children. Scripto admitted that it had been a defendant in several suits for injuries under similar circumstances. How should the court rule? Why?

22–10. VIDEO QUESTION: Warranties.

Go to this text's Web site at **www.cengage.com/blaw/clarkson** and select "Chapter 22." Click on "Video Questions" and view the video titled *Matilda*. Then answer the following questions.

(a) What warranties of title arise in the sales of used cars by dealers?

(b) In the video, a father (Danny DeVito) uses a tool to turn back the numbers on a vehicle's odometer. When he sells this car, if he tells the buyer the mileage is only 60,000 knowing that it is really 120,000, has he breached an express warranty? What if the seller did not make any oral statements about the car's mileage, could the buyer claim an express warranty existed? Explain.

(c) What would a person who buys the car in the video have to show to prove that the seller breached the implied warranty of merchantability?

LEGAL RESEARCH EXERCISES ON THE WEB

Go to this text's Web site at **www.cengage.com/blaw/clarkson**, select "Chapter 22," and click on "Practical Internet Exercises." There you will find the following Internet research exercises that you can perform to learn more about the topics covered in this chapter.

Practical Internet Exercise 22–1: **Legal Perspective**
Product Liability Litigation

Practical Internet Exercise 22–2: **Management Perspective**
The Duty to Warn

International business transactions are not unique to the modern world. Commerce has always crossed national borders. What is new in our day is the dramatic growth in world trade and the emergence of a global business community. Because exchanges of goods, services, and ideas (intellectual property) on a global level are now routine, students of business law and the legal environment should be familiar with the laws pertaining to international business transactions.

Laws affecting the international legal environment of business include both international law and national law. **International law** can be defined as a body of law—formed as a result of international customs, treaties, and organizations—that governs relations among or between nations. International law may be public, creating standards for the nations themselves; or it may be private, establishing international standards for private transactions that cross national borders. **National law** is the law of a particular nation, such as Brazil, Germany, Japan, or the United States.

In this chapter, we examine how both international law and national law frame business operations in the global context. We also look at some selected areas relating to business activities in a global context, including common types of international business transactions, export and import controls, and the role of trade agreements. We conclude the chapter with a discussion of the application of certain U.S. laws in a transnational setting.

SECTION 1
INTERNATIONAL LAW

The major difference between international law and national law is that government authorities can enforce national law. What government, however, can enforce international law? By definition, a *nation* is a sovereign entity—which means that there is no higher authority to which that nation must submit. If a nation violates an international law and persuasive tactics fail, other countries or international organizations have no recourse except to take coercive actions—from severance of diplomatic relations and boycotts to, as a last resort, war—against the violating nation.

In essence, international law attempts to reconcile the need of each country to be the final authority over its own affairs with the desire of nations to benefit economically from trade and harmonious relations with one another. Sovereign nations can,

and do, voluntarily agree to be governed in certain respects by international law for the purpose of facilitating international trade and commerce, as well as civilized discourse. As a result, a body of international law has evolved. In this section, we examine the primary sources and characteristics of that body of law, as well as some important legal principles and doctrines that have been developed over time to facilitate dealings among nations.

Sources of International Law

Basically, there are three sources of international law: international customs, treaties and international agreements, and international organizations and conferences. We look at each of these sources here.

INTERNATIONAL CUSTOMS One important source of international law consists of the international customs that have evolved among nations in their relations with one another. Article 38(1) of the

Statute of the International Court of Justice refers to an international custom as "evidence of a general practice accepted as law." The legal principles and doctrines that you will read about shortly are rooted in international customs and traditions that have evolved over time in the international arena.

TREATIES AND INTERNATIONAL AGREEMENTS

Treaties and other explicit agreements between or among foreign nations provide another important source of international law. A **treaty** is an agreement or contract between two or more nations that must be authorized and ratified by the supreme power of each nation. Under Article II, Section 2, of the U.S. Constitution, the president has the power "by and with the Advice and Consent of the Senate, to make Treaties, provided two-thirds of the Senators present concur."

A *bilateral* agreement, as the term implies, is an agreement formed by two nations to govern their commercial exchanges or other relations with one another. A *multilateral* agreement is formed by several nations. For example, regional trade associations such as the Andean Common Market, the Association of Southeast Asian Nations, and the European Union are the result of multilateral trade agreements.

INTERNATIONAL ORGANIZATIONS

In international law, the term **international organization** generally refers to an organization composed mainly of officials of member nations and usually established by treaty. The United States is a member of more than one hundred multilateral and bilateral organizations, including at least twenty through the United Nations. These organizations adopt resolutions, declarations, and other types of standards that often require nations to behave in a particular manner. The General Assembly of the United Nations, for example, has adopted numerous nonbinding resolutions and declarations that embody principles of international law. Disputes with respect to these resolutions and declarations may be brought before the International Court of Justice. That court, however, normally has authority to settle legal disputes only when nations voluntarily submit to its jurisdiction.

The United Nations Commission on International Trade Law has made considerable progress in establishing uniformity in international law as it relates to trade and commerce. One of the commission's most significant creations to date is the 1980 Convention on Contracts for the International Sale of Goods (CISG). Recall from Chapters 19 through 22 that the CISG is similar to Article 2 of the Uniform Commercial Code in that it is designed to settle disputes between parties to sales contracts. It spells out the duties of international buyers and sellers that will apply if the parties have not agreed otherwise in their contracts. The CISG governs only sales contracts between trading partners in nations that have ratified the CISG.

Common Law and Civil Law Systems

Companies operating in foreign nations are subject to the laws of those nations. In addition, international disputes often are resolved through the court systems of foreign nations. Therefore, businesspersons should understand that legal systems around the globe generally are divided into *common law* and *civil law* systems. Exhibit 23–1 on the facing page lists some of the nations that use civil law systems and some that use common law systems.

COMMON LAW SYSTEMS

As discussed in Chapter 1, in a *common law* system, the courts independently develop the rules governing certain areas of law, such as torts and contracts. These common law rules apply to all areas not covered by statutory law. Although the common law doctrine of *stare decisis* obligates judges to follow precedential decisions in their jurisdictions, courts may modify or even overturn precedents when deemed necessary.

CIVIL LAW SYSTEMS

In contrast to common law countries, most of the European nations, as well as nations in Latin America, Africa, and Asia, base their legal systems on Roman civil law, or "code law." The term *civil law,* as used here, refers not to civil as opposed to criminal law but to *codified* law—an ordered grouping of legal principles enacted into law by a legislature or other governing body.

In a **civil law system**, the primary source of law is a statutory code. Courts interpret the code and apply the rules to individual cases, but courts may not depart from the code and develop their own laws. Judicial precedents are not binding, as they are in a common law system. In theory, the law code sets forth all of the principles needed for the legal system. Trial procedures also differ in civil law systems. Unlike judges in common law systems, judges in civil systems often actively question witnesses.

ISLAMIC LEGAL SYSTEMS

A third, less prevalent, legal system is common in Islamic countries, where the law is often influenced by *sharia,* the religious law of Islam. *Sharia* is a comprehensive code of

EXHIBIT 23–1 • The Legal Systems of Selected Nations

CIVIL LAW		COMMON LAW	
Argentina	Indonesia	Australia	Nigeria
Austria	Iran	Bangladesh	Singapore
Brazil	Italy	Canada	United Kingdom
Chile	Japan	Ghana	United States
China	Mexico	India	Zambia
Egypt	Poland	Israel	
Finland	South Korea	Jamaica	
France	Sweden	Kenya	
Germany	Tunisia	Malaysia	
Greece	Venezuela	New Zealand	

principles that governs both the public and the private lives of persons of the Islamic faith, directing many aspects of day-to-day life, including politics, economics, banking, business law, contract law, and social issues. Although *sharia* affects the legal codes of many Muslim countries, the extent of its impact and its interpretation vary widely. In some Middle Eastern nations, aspects of *sharia* have been codified and are enforced by national judicial systems.

International Principles and Doctrines

Over time, a number of legal principles and doctrines have evolved and are employed—to a greater or lesser extent—by the courts of various nations to resolve or reduce conflicts that involve a foreign element. The three important legal principles discussed below are based primarily on courtesy and respect, and are applied in the interests of maintaining harmonious relations among nations.

THE PRINCIPLE OF COMITY Under the principle of **comity,** one nation will defer and give effect to the laws and judicial decrees of another country, as long as they are consistent with the law and public policy of the accommodating nation. For example, a Swedish seller and a U.S. buyer have formed a contract, which the buyer breaches. The seller sues the buyer in a Swedish court, which awards damages. The buyer's assets, however, are in the United States and cannot be reached unless the judgment is enforced by a U.S. court. In this situation, if a U.S. court determines that the procedures and laws applied in the Swedish court are consistent with U.S. national law and policy, the U.S. court will likely defer to, and enforce, the foreign court's judgment.

CASE IN POINT After Karen Goldberg's husband was killed in a terrorist bombing of a bus in Israel, she filed a lawsuit in a federal court in New York

against UBS AG, a Switzerland-based global financial services company with many offices in the United States. Goldberg claimed that UBS was liable under the U.S. Anti-Terrorism Act for aiding and abetting the murder of her husband because it provided financial services to the international terrorist organizations responsible for his murder. UBS argued that the case should be transferred to a court in Israel, which would offer a remedy "substantially the same" as the one available in the United States. The court refused to transfer the case, however, because that would require an Israeli court to take evidence and judge the emotional damage suffered by Goldberg, "raising distinct concerns of comity and enforceability." U.S. courts hesitate to impose U.S. law on foreign courts when such law is "an unwarranted intrusion" on the policies governing a foreign nation's judicial system.[1]

One way to understand the principle of comity (and the *act of state doctrine,* which will be discussed shortly) is to consider the relationships among the states in our federal form of government. Each state honors (gives "full faith and credit" to) the contracts, property deeds, wills, and other legal obligations formed in other states, as well as judicial decisions with respect to such obligations. On a global basis, nations similarly attempt to honor judgments rendered in other countries when it is feasible to do so. Of course, in the United States the states are constitutionally required to honor other states' actions, whereas, internationally, nations are not *required* to honor the actions of other nations.

THE ACT OF STATE DOCTRINE The **act of state doctrine** provides that the judicial branch of one country will not examine the validity of public acts

---

1. *Goldberg v. UBS AG,* 690 F.Supp.2d 92 (E.D.N.Y. 2010).

committed by a recognized foreign government within the latter's own territory.

When a Foreign Government Takes Private Property.

The act of state doctrine can have important consequences for individuals and firms doing business with, and investing in, other countries. This doctrine is frequently employed in cases involving **expropriation,** which occurs when a government seizes a privately owned business or privately owned goods for a proper public purpose and awards just compensation. When a government seizes private property for an illegal purpose and without just compensation, the taking is referred to as a **confiscation.** The line between these two forms of taking is sometimes blurred because of differing interpretations of what is illegal and what constitutes just compensation.

For example, Flaherty, Inc., a U.S. company, owns a mine in Brazil. The government of Brazil seizes the mine for public use and claims that the profits Flaherty has already realized from the mine constitute just compensation. Flaherty disagrees, but the act of state doctrine may prevent that company's recovery in a U.S. court. Note that in a case alleging that a foreign government has wrongfully taken the plaintiff's property, the defendant government has the burden of proving that the taking was an expropriation, not a confiscation.

Doctrine May Immunize a Foreign Government's Actions.

When applicable, both the act of state doctrine and the doctrine of *sovereign immunity,* which we discuss next, tend to shield foreign nations from the jurisdiction of U.S. courts. As a result, firms or individuals who own property overseas generally have little legal protection against government actions in the countries where they operate.

THE DOCTRINE OF SOVEREIGN IMMUNITY

When certain conditions are satisfied, the doctrine of **sovereign immunity** exempts foreign nations from the jurisdiction of the U.S. courts. In 1976, Congress codified this rule in the Foreign Sovereign Immunities Act (FSIA).[2] The FSIA exclusively governs the circumstances in which an action may be brought in the United States against a foreign nation, including attempts to attach a foreign nation's property. Because the law is jurisdictional in nature, a plaintiff generally has the burden of showing that a defendant is not entitled to sovereign immunity.

Section 1605 of the FSIA sets forth the major exceptions to the jurisdictional immunity of a foreign state. A foreign state is not immune from the jurisdiction of U.S. courts in the following situations:

1. When the foreign state has waived its immunity either explicitly or by implication.
2. When the foreign state has engaged in commercial activity within the United States or in commercial activity outside the United States that has "a direct effect in the United States."
3. When the foreign state has committed a tort in the United States or has violated certain international laws.

When courts apply the FSIA, questions frequently arise as to whether an entity is a "foreign state" and what constitutes a "commercial activity." Under Section 1603 of the FSIA, a *foreign state* includes both a political subdivision of a foreign state and an instrumentality (department or agency of any branch of a government) of a foreign state. Section 1603 broadly defines a *commercial activity* as a regular course of commercial conduct, transaction, or act that is carried out by a foreign state within the United States. Section 1603, however, does not describe the particulars of what constitutes a commercial activity. Thus, the courts are left to decide whether a particular activity is governmental or commercial in nature.

SECTION 2
DOING BUSINESS INTERNATIONALLY

A U.S. domestic firm can engage in international business transactions in a number of ways. The simplest way is for U.S. firms to **export** their goods and services to foreign markets. Alternatively, a U.S. firm can establish foreign production facilities to be closer to the foreign market or markets in which its products are sold. The advantages may include lower labor costs, fewer government regulations, and lower taxes and trade barriers. A domestic firm can also obtain revenues by licensing its technology to an existing foreign company or by selling franchises to overseas entities.

Exporting

Exporting can take two forms: direct exporting and indirect exporting. In *direct exporting,* a U.S.

---

2. 28 U.S.C. Sections 1602–1611.

company signs a sales contract with a foreign purchaser that provides for the conditions of shipment and payment for the goods. (International contracts for the purchase and sale of goods, as well as the use of letters of credit to make payments in international transactions, were discussed in Chapters 19 through 22.) If sufficient business develops in a foreign country, a U.S. company may establish a specialized marketing organization there by appointing a foreign agent or a foreign distributor. This is called *indirect exporting*.

When a U.S. firm wishes to limit its involvement in an international market, it will typically establish an *agency relationship* with a foreign firm (*agency* will be discussed in Chapter 32). The foreign firm then acts as the U.S. firm's agent and can enter contracts in the foreign location on behalf of the principal (the U.S. company).

When a foreign country represents a substantial market, a U.S. firm may wish to appoint a distributor located in that country. The U.S. firm and the distributor enter into a **distribution agreement**—a contract setting out the terms and conditions of the distributorship, such as price, currency of payment, guarantee of supply availability, and method of payment. Disputes concerning distribution agreements may involve jurisdictional or other issues, as well as contract law.

In response to the latest economic recession, the U.S. government has taken a greater interest in the export of goods and services to foreign markets by U.S. companies. For a discussion of a recent federal initiative to encourage exports, see this chapter's *Shifting Legal Priorities for Business* feature on the following page.

Manufacturing Abroad

An alternative to direct or indirect exporting is the establishment of foreign manufacturing facilities. Typically, U.S. firms establish manufacturing plants abroad when they believe that by doing so they will reduce costs—particularly for labor, shipping, and raw materials—and thereby be able to compete more effectively in foreign markets. Foreign firms have done the same in the United States. Sony, Nissan, and other Japanese manufacturers have established U.S. plants to avoid import duties that the U.S. Congress may impose on Japanese products entering this country.

A U.S. firm can conduct manufacturing operations in other countries in several ways. They include licensing, franchising, and investing in a wholly owned subsidiary or a joint venture.

LICENSING A U.S. firm may license a foreign manufacturing company to use its copyrighted, patented, or trademarked intellectual property or trade secrets. Like any other licensing agreement (see Chapters 8 and 11), a licensing agreement with a foreign-based firm calls for a payment of royalties on some basis—such as so many cents per unit produced or a certain percentage of profits from units sold in a particular geographic territory. For example, the Coca-Cola Bottling Company licenses firms worldwide to employ (and keep confidential) its secret formula for the syrup used in its soft drink; in return, the company receives a percentage of the income gained from the sale of Coca-Cola by those firms.

The licensing of intellectual property rights benefits all parties to the transaction. The firm that receives the license can take advantage of an established reputation for quality. The firm that grants the license receives income from the foreign sales of its products and also establishes a global reputation. Once a firm's trademark is known worldwide, the demand for other products manufactured or sold by that firm may increase—obviously, an important consideration.

FRANCHISING Franchising is a well-known form of licensing. As you will read in Chapter 36, in a franchise arrangement, the owner of a trademark, trade name, or copyright (the franchisor) licenses another (the franchisee) to use the trademark, trade name, or copyright, under certain conditions or limitations, in the selling of goods or services. In return, the franchisee pays a fee, which is usually based on a percentage of gross or net sales. Examples of international franchises include Holiday Inn and Hertz.

INVESTING IN A WHOLLY OWNED SUBSIDIARY OR A JOINT VENTURE Another way to expand into a foreign market is to establish a wholly owned subsidiary firm in a foreign country. In many European countries, a subsidiary would likely take the form of a *société anonyme* (S.A.), which is similar to a U.S. corporation. In German-speaking nations, it would be called an *Aktiengesellschaft* (A.G.). When a wholly owned subsidiary is established, the parent company, which remains in the United States, retains complete ownership of all of the facilities in the foreign country, as well as total authority and control over all phases of the operation.

A U.S. firm can also expand into international markets through a joint venture. In a joint venture, the U.S. company owns only part of the operation; the rest is owned either by local owners in the foreign country or by another foreign entity. All of the firms involved in a joint venture share responsibilities, as

Although the United States is one of the world's major exporters, exports make up a much smaller share of annual output in the United States than they do in our most important trading partners. In an effort to increase this nation's exports, in 2010 the Obama administration created the National Export Initiative (NEI) with a goal of doubling U.S. exports by 2015. Some commentators believe that another goal of the NEI is to reduce outsourcing—the practice of having manufacturing or other activities performed in lower-wage countries such as China and India. Especially in view of the higher unemployment rate, there is increasing concern that U.S. jobs are being shipped overseas.

The Export Promotion Cabinet

An important component of the NEI is the Export Promotion Cabinet, which reports directly to the president. The cabinet's members include officials from the Departments of Agriculture, Commerce, and State, as well as from the Small Business Administration, the U.S. Export-Import Bank, and the Office of the U.S. Trade Representative. All members must submit detailed plans to the president that outline the steps that they will take to increase U.S. exports.

Increased Efforts to Promote Exports

The U.S. Commerce Department will play a leading role in the NEI and is receiving increased funding to do so. More than three hundred trade experts from the department will serve as advocates for U.S. companies and will help some twenty thousand "client companies" increase their export sales. In addition, the Commerce Department's International Trade Administration will play a more active role in promoting U.S. exports in the emerging high-growth markets of Brazil, China, and India. Finally, the department will identify market opportunities in fast-growing sectors, such as environmental goods and services, biotechnology, and renewable energy.

Increased Export Financing

Under the NEI, the U.S. Export-Import Bank is increasing the financing that it makes available to small and medium-sized businesses by 50 percent. In the initial phase of the NEI, the bank added hundreds of new small-business clients that sell a wide variety of products, from sophisticated polymers to date palm trees and nanotechology-based cosmetics. In addition, the administration has proposed that $30 billion be used to boost lending to small businesses, especially for export purposes.

Removing the Economic Blind Spot

Officials at the Commerce Department believe that in the past the United States has had an economic "blind spot" toward exports. The U.S. government has not placed as much emphasis on exports as the governments of many trading partners, which actively promote their nations' exports. As a result, other countries have been able to slowly chip away at the United States' international competitiveness. One way to improve the situation is to remove barriers that deny U.S. companies fair access to foreign markets. To this end, the government will pursue trade agreements that improve market access for U.S. workers, firms, farmers, and ranchers. In addition, while remaining committed to a rule-based international trading system, the government will continue to combat unfair tariffs and nontariff barriers.

MANAGERIAL IMPLICATIONS

Managers in companies that are now outsourcing or are thinking of doing so may wish to reconsider. Increasingly, the federal government is taking a stance against outsourcing. As long as unemployment remains high in the United States, the emphasis will be on the creation of jobs at home. These efforts will often be backed by subsidies and access to federally supported borrowing initiatives.

---

well as profits and liabilities. (See Chapter 38 for a more detailed discussion of joint ventures.)

SECTION 3
REGULATION OF SPECIFIC BUSINESS ACTIVITIES

Doing business abroad can affect the economies, foreign policies, domestic politics, and other national interests of the countries involved. For this reason, nations impose laws to restrict or facilitate international business. Controls may also be imposed by international agreements.

Investment Protections

Firms that invest in foreign nations face the risk that the foreign government may expropriate the investment property. Expropriation, as mentioned earlier in this chapter, occurs when property is taken and the owner is paid just compensation for what is taken. This generally does not violate observed principles of international law. Confiscating property without compensation (or without adequate compensation), however, normally violates these principles. Few remedies are available for confiscation of property by a foreign government. Claims are often resolved by lump-sum settlements after negotiations between the United States and the taking nation.

To counter the deterrent effect that the possibility of confiscation may have on potential investors, many countries guarantee compensation to foreign investors if property is taken. A guaranty can be in the form of national constitutional or statutory laws or provisions in international treaties. As further protection for foreign investments, some countries provide insurance for their citizens' investments abroad.

Export Controls

The U.S. Constitution provides in Article I, Section 9, that "No Tax or Duty shall be laid on Articles exported from any State." Thus, Congress cannot impose any export taxes. Congress can, however, use a variety of other devices to restrict or encourage exports. Congress may set export quotas on various items, such as grain being sold abroad. Under the Export Administration Act of 1979,[3] the flow of technologically advanced products and technical data can be restricted.

While restricting certain exports, the United States (and other nations) also use incentives and subsidies to stimulate other exports and thereby aid domestic businesses. Under the Export Trading Company Act of 1982,[4] for example, U.S. banks are encouraged to invest in export trading companies, which are formed when exporting firms join together to export a line of goods. The Export-Import Bank of the United States provides financial assistance, primarily in the form of credit guaranties given to commercial banks that in turn lend funds to U.S. exporting companies.

Import Controls

All nations have restrictions on imports, and the United States is no exception. Restrictions include strict prohibitions, quotas, and tariffs. Under the Trading with the Enemy Act of 1917,[5] for example, no goods may be imported from nations that have been designated enemies of the United States. Other laws prohibit the importation of illegal drugs, books that urge insurrection against the United States, and agricultural products that pose dangers to domestic crops or animals.

The importation of goods that infringe U.S. patents is also prohibited. The International Trade Commission is the government agency that investigates allegations that imported goods infringe U.S. patents and imposes penalties if necessary. In the following case, the court considered an appeal from a company that had been fined more than $13.5 million for importing certain disposable cameras.

---

3. 50 U.S.C. Sections 2401–2420.

4. 15 U.S.C. Sections 4001, 4003.
5. 12 U.S.C. Section 95a.

CASE 23.1
Fuji Photo Film Co. v. International Trade Commission

United States Court of Appeals, Federal Circuit, 474 F.3d 1281 (2007).

BACKGROUND AND FACTS • Fuji Photo Film Company owns fifteen patents for "lens-fitted film packages" (LFFPs), popularly known as disposable cameras. An LFFP consists of a plastic shell preloaded with film. To develop the film, a consumer gives the LFFP to a film processor and receives back the negatives and prints, but not the shell. Fuji makes and sells LFFPs. Jazz Photo Corporation collected used LFFP shells in the United States, shipped them abroad to insert new film, and imported refurbished shells back into the United States for sale. The International Trade Commission (ITC) determined that Jazz's resale of shells originally sold outside the United States infringed Fuji's patents. In 1999, the ITC issued a cease-and-desist order to stop the imports. While the order was being disputed at the ITC and in the courts, between August 2001 and December 2003 Jazz imported and sold 27 million refurbished LFFPs. Fuji complained to the ITC, which fined Jazz more than $13.5 million. Jack Benun, Jazz's chief operating officer, appealed to the U.S. Court of Appeals for the Federal Circuit.

CASE CONTINUES ▶

CASE 23.1 CONTINUED ▶

IN THE LANGUAGE OF THE COURT
DYK, Circuit Judge.
* * * *

* * * The Commission concluded that 40% of the LFFPs in issue were first sold abroad * * * . This conclusion was supported by substantial evidence. It was based on * * * the identifying numbers printed on the LFFPs and Fuji's production and shipping databases to determine where samples of Fuji-type LFFPs with Jazz packaging (i.e., ones that were refurbished by Jazz) were first sold.

Benun urges that the Commission's decision in this respect was not supported by substantial evidence, primarily arguing that Jazz's so-called informed compliance program required a finding in Jazz's favor. Benun asserts that this program tracked shells from collection through the refurbishment process to sale and insured that only shells collected from the United States were refurbished for sale here. The Commission rejected this argument for two reasons. First, it concluded that the program was too disorganized and incomplete to provide credible evidence that Jazz only refurbished shells collected from the United States. Second, the Commission concluded that at most the program could insure that Jazz only refurbished LFFPs collected from the United States, not LFFPs that were first sold here.

Responding to the second ground, Benun urges that proof that Jazz limited its activities to shells collected in the United States was sufficient * * * because Fuji "infected the pool" of camera shells collected in the United States by taking actions that made it difficult for Jazz and Benun to insure that these shells were from LFFPs first sold here. These actions allegedly included allowing [one company] to import cameras with Japanese writing on them for sale in the United States; allowing [that company] to import spent shells into the United States for recycling; and allowing tourists to bring cameras first sold abroad into the United States for personal use. Under these circumstances, Benun argues that a presumption should arise that shells collected in the United States were first sold here. However, the Commission found that the number of shells falling into these categories was insignificant, and that finding was supported by substantial evidence. Moreover, *there was evidence that Jazz treated substantial numbers of its own shells collected in the United States * * * as having been sold in the United States even though it knew that 90% of these shells were first sold abroad * * * .* [Emphasis added.]

In any event, the Commission's first ground—that the program was too incomplete and disorganized to be credible—was supported by substantial evidence. Since there was no suggestion that the incomplete and disorganized nature of the program was due to Fuji's actions, this ground alone was sufficient to justify a conclusion that Benun had not carried his burden to prove [the refurbished LFFPs had been sold first in the United States].

DECISION AND REMEDY • *The U.S. Court of Appeals for the Federal Circuit held that Jazz had violated the cease-and-desist order, affirming this part of the ITC's decision. The court concluded, among other things, that "substantial evidence supports the finding that the majority of the cameras were first sold abroad."*

WHAT IF THE FACTS WERE DIFFERENT? • *Suppose that, after this decision, Jazz fully compensated Fuji for the infringing sales of LFFPs. Would Jazz have acquired the right to refurbish those LFFPs in the future? Explain.*

THE GLOBAL DIMENSION • *How does the prohibition against importing goods that infringe U.S. patents protect those patents outside the United States?*

QUOTAS AND TARIFFS Limits on the amounts of goods that can be imported are known as **quotas.** At one time, the United States had legal quotas on the number of automobiles that could be imported from Japan. Today, Japan "voluntarily" restricts the number of automobiles exported to the United States. **Tariffs** are taxes on imports. A tariff is usually a percentage of the value of the import, but

it can be a flat rate per unit (such as per barrel of oil). Tariffs raise the prices of imported goods, causing some consumers to purchase more domestically manufactured goods instead of imports.

Sometimes, countries impose tariffs on goods from a particular nation in retaliation for political acts. For example, in 2009 Mexico imposed tariffs of 10 to 20 percent on ninety products exported from the

United States in retaliation for the Obama administration's cancellation of a cross-border trucking program. The program had been instituted to comply with a provision in the North American Free Trade Agreement (to be discussed shortly) that called for Mexican trucks to eventually be granted full access to U.S. highways. U.S. truck drivers opposed the program, however, and consumer protection groups claimed that the Mexican trucks posed safety issues.

President Barack Obama signed legislation that cut off funding for the program, but asked his trade representative to look into creating a new program for cross-border transportation.

In the following case, an importer provided invoices that understated the value of its imports and resulted in lower tariffs than would have been paid on the full value of the goods. Was this fraud or negligence?

CASE 23.2
United States v. Inn Foods, Inc.

United States Court of Appeals, Federal Circuit, 560 F.3d 1338 (2009).
www.cafc.uscourts.gov[a]

COMPANY PROFILE • Inn Foods, Inc. (www.innfoods.com), was established in 1976 as a subsidiary of the VPS Companies, Inc. Inn Foods imports frozen fruits and vegetables into the United States from sources worldwide. At its plants in California and Texas, the company blends, custom packages, flavors, and seasons vegetables, pasta, potatoes, rice, fruits, and other food products. Each year, Inn Foods sells more than 157 million pounds of food. Its customers include buyers in the food service industry, industrial food markets, and retail food markets at locations around the globe.

BACKGROUND AND FACTS • Between 1987 and 1990, Inn Foods imported frozen produce from six Mexican growers who agreed to issue invoices that understated the value of the produce. For each understated invoice, Inn Foods sent an order confirmation that estimated the produce's actual market value. Inn Foods later remitted the difference to the growers. Through this double-invoicing system, Inn Foods undervalued its purchases by approximately $3.5 million and paid lower tariff taxes as a result. During an investigation by U.S. Customs and Border Protection, Inn Foods' accounting supervisor denied the existence of the double invoices. The federal government filed an action in the U.S. Court of International Trade against Inn Foods. The court held the defendant liable for fraud and assessed the amount of the unpaid taxes—$624,602.55—plus an additional penalty of $7.5 million. Inn Foods appealed, claiming that it had acted negligently, not fraudulently.

IN THE LANGUAGE OF THE COURT
DYK, Circuit Judge.
* * * * *

Initially we note that the record fully supports the trade court's determination that Inn Foods knew that the invoice for each shipment of produce was grossly undervalued, and hence false. The Mexican grower sent Inn Foods a copy of the undervalued "factura" invoice; that "factura" invoice was used to value the entries for Customs purposes. There was evidence that the growers specifically informed Inn Foods of the undervaluation. As the trade court noted, for example, a letter * * * from one of the Mexican growers stated that "we ship * * * Broccoli Spears at 0.50/lb" but that "my invoice * * * will read * * * 0.28/lb." Moreover, upon receipt of the undervalued factura, a * * * manager * * * adjusted the prices to reflect the true and higher estimate. This higher amount was entered into Inn Foods's accounting system. Inn Foods then sent an order confirmation to the Mexican grower with the higher price, retaining a copy of both the undervalued and true invoices for its files. *Thus, one invoice served to bring the produce into the United States at a reduced cost and * * * the second to keep accurate accounting records.* [Emphasis added.]

---

a. In the link at the top of the page, click on "Opinions & orders." On that page, click on "2009." In the result, scroll to "2009/3/27" and click on the name of the case to access the opinion. The U.S. Court of Appeals for the Federal Circuit maintains this Web site.

CASE CONTINUES ➡

CASE 23.2 CONTINUED ➡   The existence of the double invoices was also concealed. * * * [For example,] during the initial Customs investigation, Inn Foods's accounting supervisor—with what must have been full knowledge of the falsity of the statement—denied outright the existence of a second invoice reflecting a price higher than the amount reported to Customs. This concealment, too, points strongly to fraudulent intent.

The record also makes clear, and Inn Foods does not contest, that Inn Foods knew the false invoices would be used to enter goods into the United States.

DECISION AND REMEDY • *The U.S. Court of Appeals for the Federal Circuit affirmed the lower court's judgment. The evidence showed that Inn Foods "knowingly entered goods by means of a material false statement."*

WHAT IF THE FACTS WERE DIFFERENT? • *Suppose that after Inn Foods learned of the investigation, the company told U.S. Customs and Border Protection that it was working to correct the "errors" and would "advise" as soon as that happened. Would this have undercut the government's case? Why or why not?*

THE LEGAL ENVIRONMENT DIMENSION • *Inn Foods passed on the cost savings from the lower duties to the growers when it paid them the difference between the understated value of the products and their actual value. Should this in any way absolve Inn Foods of liability for fraud? Explain your answer.*

ANTIDUMPING DUTIES The United States has laws specifically directed at what it sees as unfair international trade practices. **Dumping,** for example, is the sale of imported goods at "less than fair value." *Fair value* is usually determined by the price of those goods in the exporting country. Foreign firms that engage in dumping in the United States hope to undersell U.S. businesses to obtain a larger share of the U.S. market. To prevent this, an extra tariff—known as an *antidumping duty*—may be assessed on the imports.

Two U.S. government agencies are instrumental in imposing antidumping duties: the International Trade Commission (ITC) and the International Trade Administration (ITA). The ITC assesses the effects of dumping on domestic businesses and then makes recommendations to the president concerning temporary import restrictions. The ITA, which is part of the Department of Commerce, decides whether imports were sold at less than fair value. The ITA's determination establishes the amount of antidumping duties, which are set to equal the difference between the price charged in the United States and the price charged in the exporting country. A duty may be retroactive to cover past dumping.

Trade Agreements That Minimize Trade Barriers

Restrictions on imports are also known as *trade barriers*. The elimination of trade barriers is sometimes seen as essential to the world's economic well-being. Most of the world's leading trading nations are members of the World Trade Organization (WTO), which was established in 1995. To minimize trade barriers among nations, each member country of the WTO is required to grant **normal trade relations (NTR) status** (formerly known as *most-favored-nation status*) to other member countries. This means that each member is obligated to treat other members at least as well as it treats the country that receives its most favorable treatment with regard to imports or exports. Various regional trade agreements and associations also help to minimize trade barriers between nations.

THE EUROPEAN UNION (EU) The European Union (EU) arose out of the 1957 Treaty of Rome, which created the Common Market, a free trade zone comprising the nations of Belgium, France, Italy, Luxembourg, the Netherlands, and West Germany. Today, the EU is a single integrated European trading unit made up of twenty-seven European nations.

The EU has its own governing authorities. These include the Council of Ministers, which coordinates economic policies and includes one representative from each nation; a commission, which proposes regulations to the council; and an elected assembly, which oversees the commission. The EU also has its own court, the European Court of Justice, which can review each nation's judicial decisions and is the ultimate authority on EU law.

The EU has gone a long way toward creating a new body of law to govern all of the member nations—although some of its efforts to create uniform laws have been confounded by nationalism. The council and the commission issue regulations, or directives, that define EU law in various areas, such as environmental law, product liability, anticompetitive practices, and corporations. The directives normally are binding on all member countries.

THE NORTH AMERICAN FREE TRADE AGREEMENT (NAFTA)

The North American Free Trade Agreement (NAFTA) created a regional trading unit consisting of Canada, Mexico, and the United States. The goal of NAFTA is to eliminate tariffs among these three nations on substantially all goods by reducing the tariffs incrementally over a period of time. NAFTA gives the three countries a competitive advantage by retaining tariffs on goods imported from countries outside the NAFTA trading unit. Additionally, NAFTA provided for the elimination of barriers that traditionally have prevented the cross-border movement of services, such as financial and transportation services. NAFTA also attempts to eliminate citizenship requirements for the licensing of accountants, attorneys, physicians, and other professionals.

THE CENTRAL AMERICA–DOMINICAN REPUBLIC–UNITED STATES FREE TRADE AGREEMENT (CAFTA-DR)

The Central America–Dominican Republic–United States Free Trade Agreement (CAFTA-DR) was formed by Costa Rica, the Dominican Republic, El Salvador, Guatemala, Honduras, Nicaragua, and the United States. Its purpose is to reduce trade tariffs and improve market access among all of the signatory nations, including the United States. Legislatures from all seven countries have approved the CAFTA-DR, despite significant opposition in certain nations.

SECTION 4
U.S. LAWS IN A GLOBAL CONTEXT

The internationalization of business raises questions about the extraterritorial application of a nation's laws—that is, the effect of the country's laws outside its boundaries. To what extent do U.S. domestic laws apply to other nations' businesses? To what extent do U.S. domestic laws apply to U.S. firms doing business abroad? Here, we discuss the extraterritorial application of certain U.S. laws, including antitrust laws, tort laws, and laws prohibiting employment discrimination.

U.S. Antitrust Laws

U.S. antitrust laws (to be discussed in Chapter 47) have a wide application. They may *subject* firms in foreign nations to their provisions, as well as *protect* foreign consumers and competitors from violations committed by U.S. citizens. Section 1 of the Sherman Act—the most important U.S. antitrust law—provides for the extraterritorial effect of the U.S. antitrust laws. The United States is a major proponent of free competition in the global economy. Thus, any conspiracy that has a *substantial effect* on U.S. commerce is within the reach of the Sherman Act. The law applies even if the violation occurs outside the United States, and foreign governments as well as businesses can be sued for violations. Before U.S. courts will exercise jurisdiction and apply antitrust laws, however, it must be shown that the alleged violation had a substantial effect on U.S. commerce.

CASE IN POINT An investigation by the U.S. government revealed that a number of companies that manufactured and sold thermal fax paper on the global market had met in Japan and reached a price-fixing agreement (an agreement to set prices—see Chapter 47). A Florida company that uses thermal fax paper filed a lawsuit against New Oji Paper Company, a Japanese-based manufacturer that had participated in the conspiracy. Although New Oji is based in a foreign nation, it sold fax paper in the United States. Thus, its agreement to sell paper at above-normal prices throughout North America had a *substantial restraining effect* on U.S. commerce. Therefore, the Supreme Court of Florida ruled that it had jurisdiction over New Oji, even though all of the price-fixing activities took place outside the United States.[6]

International Tort Claims

The international application of tort liability is growing in significance and controversy. An increasing number of U.S. plaintiffs are suing foreign (or U.S.) entities for torts that these entities have allegedly committed overseas. Often, these cases involve human rights violations by foreign governments. The Alien Tort Claims Act (ATCA),[7] adopted in 1789, allows even foreign citizens to bring civil suits in U.S. courts for injuries caused by violations of the law of nations or a treaty of the United States.

---

6. *Execu-Tech Business Systems, Inc. v. New Oji Paper Co.,* 752 So.2d 582 (Fla. 2000).
7. 28 U.S.C. Section 1350.

Since 1980, foreign plaintiffs have increasingly used the ATCA to bring actions against companies operating in nations such as Colombia, Ecuador, Egypt, Guatemala, India, Indonesia, Nigeria, and Saudi Arabia. Some of these cases have involved alleged environmental destruction. In addition, mineral companies in Southeast Asia have been sued for collaborating with oppressive government regimes.

The following case involved claims against hundreds of corporations that allegedly "aided and abetted" the government of South Africa in maintaining its apartheid (racially discriminatory) regime.

✳ EXTENDED CASE 23.3 ✳
Khulumani v. Barclay National Bank, Ltd.

United States Court of Appeals, Second Circuit, 504 F.3d 254 (2007).

IN THE LANGUAGE OF THE COURT

PER CURIAM [By the whole court].

* * * *

The plaintiffs in this action bring claims under the Alien Tort Claims Act ("ATCA") against approximately fifty corporate defendants and hundreds of "corporate Does" [including Bank of America, N.A.; Barclay National Bank, Ltd.; Citigroup, Inc.; Credit Suisse Group; Deutsche Bank A.G.; General Electric Company; IBM Corporation; and Shell Oil Company]. The plaintiffs argue that these defendants actively and willingly collaborated with the government of South Africa in maintaining a repressive, racially based system known as "apartheid," which restricted the majority black African population in all areas of life while providing benefits for the minority white population.

Three groups of plaintiffs filed ten separate actions in multiple federal district courts asserting these apartheid-related claims. One group, the Khulumani Plaintiffs, filed a complaint against twenty-three domestic and foreign corporations, charging them with various violations of international law. The other two groups, the Ntsebeza and Digwamaje Plaintiffs, brought

class action claims on behalf of the "victims of the apartheid related atrocities, human rights' violations, crimes against humanity and unfair [and] discriminatory forced labor practices."

* * * All of the actions [were transferred to a federal district court in] the Southern District of New York * * *. Thirty-one of the fifty-five defendants in the Ntsebeza and Digwamaje actions * * * [and] eighteen of the twenty-three defendants in [the Khulumani] action * * * filed * * * motion[s] to dismiss.

* * * *

Ruling on the defendants' motions to dismiss, the district court held that the plaintiffs failed to establish subject matter jurisdiction under the ATCA. * * * The district court therefore dismissed the plaintiffs' complaints in their entirety. * * * The plaintiffs filed timely notices of appeal [with the U.S. Court of Appeals for the Second Circuit].

* * * *

* * * [This court] vacate[s] the district court's dismissal of the plaintiffs' ATCA claims because the district court erred in holding that aiding and abetting violations of customary international law cannot provide a basis for ATCA jurisdiction. *We hold that * * * a plaintiff*

may plead a theory of aiding and abetting liability under the ATCA. * * *
[The majority of the judges on the panel that heard this case agreed on the result but differed on the reasons, which were presented in two concurring opinions. One judge believed that liability on these facts is "well established in international law," citing such examples as the Rome Statute of the International Criminal Court. Another judge stated that grounds existed in such resources of U.S. law as Section 876(b) of the *Restatement (Second) of Torts,* under which liability could be assessed in part for "facilitating the commission of human rights violations by providing the principal tortfeasor with the tools, instrumentalities, or services to commit those violations."] [Emphasis added.]

* * * *

* * * We decline to affirm the dismissal of plaintiffs' ATCA claims on the basis of the prudential concerns[a] raised by the defendants. * * * The Supreme Court [has] identified two different respects in which courts should consider prudential concerns in deciding whether to hear claims brought under the ATCA.[b] First, * * * courts should consider prudential concerns in the context of determining whether to recognize a cause of action under the ATCA. Specifically,

---

a. The term *prudential concerns* refers to the defendants' arguments that the plaintiffs do not have standing to pursue their case in a U.S. court. Here, *prudential* means that the arguments are based on judicially (or legislatively) created principles rather than on the constitutionally based requirements set forth in Article III of the U.S. Constitution.

b. The court is referring to the United States Supreme Court decision in *Sosa v. Alvarez-Machain,* 542 U.S. 692, 124 S.Ct. 2739, 159 L.Ed.2d 718 (2004). In the *Sosa* case, the Court outlined the need for caution in deciding actions under the ATCA and said that the "potential implications for the foreign relations of the United States of recognizing such causes should make courts particularly wary of impinging [encroaching] on the discretion of the Legislative and Executive Branches in managing foreign affairs."

EXTENDED CASE 23.3 CONTINUED ◆

* * * the determination whether a norm is sufficiently definite to support a cause of action should (and, indeed, inevitably must) involve an element of judgment about the practical consequences of making that cause available to litigants in the federal courts. Second, * * * in certain cases, other prudential principles might operate to limit the availability of relief in the federal courts for violations of customary international law.

* * * *

One such principle * * * [is] a policy of case-specific deference to the political branches [of the U.S. government]. *This policy of judicial deference to the Executive Branch on questions of foreign policy has long been established under the prudential justiciability doctrine known as the political question doctrine. Another prudential doctrine that the defendants raise in this case is international comity.* This doctrine * * * asks whether adjudication of the case by a United States court would offend amicable working relationships with a foreign country. [Emphasis added.]

* * * *

We decline to address these case-specific prudential doctrines now and instead remand to the district court to allow it to engage in the first instance in the careful "case-by-case" analysis that questions of this type require.

* * * *

* * * We VACATE the district court's dismissal of the plaintiffs' ATCA claims * * * and REMAND for further proceedings consistent with this opinion.

QUESTIONS

1. What are the ramifications for the defendants of the ruling in this case?
2. How might such "prudential concerns" as the principle of comity affect the eventual outcome?

Antidiscrimination Laws

As will be explained in Chapter 35, federal laws in the United States prohibit discrimination on the basis of race, color, national origin, religion, gender, age, and disability. These laws, as they affect employment relationships, generally apply extraterritorially. Since 1984, for example, the Age Discrimination in Employment Act of 1967 has covered U.S. employees working abroad for U.S. employers. The Americans with Disabilities Act of 1990, which requires employers to accommodate the needs of workers with disabilities, also applies to U.S. nationals working abroad for U.S. firms.

For some time, it was uncertain whether the major U.S. law regulating discriminatory practices in the workplace, Title VII of the Civil Rights Act of 1964, applied extraterritorially. The Civil Rights Act of 1991 addressed this issue. The act provides that Title VII applies extraterritorially to all U.S. employees working for U.S. employers abroad. Generally, U.S. employers must abide by U.S. discrimination laws unless to do so would violate the laws of the country where their workplaces are located. This "foreign laws exception" allows employers to avoid being subjected to conflicting laws.

REVIEWING

International Law in a Global Economy

Robco, Inc., was a Florida arms dealer. The armed forces of Honduras contracted to purchase weapons from Robco over a six-year period. After the government was replaced and a democracy installed, the Honduran government sought to reduce the size of its military, and its relationship with Robco deteriorated. Honduras refused to honor the contract and purchase the inventory of arms, which Robco could sell only at a much lower price. Robco filed a suit in a federal district court in the United States to recover damages for this breach of contract by the government of Honduras. Using the information presented in the chapter, answer the following questions.

REVIEWING CONTINUES ➤

REVIEWING

International Law in a Global Economy, Continued

1. Should the Foreign Sovereign Immunities Act (FSIA) preclude this lawsuit? Why or why not?

2. Does the act of state doctrine bar Robco from seeking to enforce the contract? Explain.

3. Suppose that prior to this lawsuit, the new government of Honduras had enacted a law making it illegal to purchase weapons from foreign arms dealers. What doctrine of deference might lead a U.S. court to dismiss Robco's case in that situation?

4. Now suppose that the U.S. court hears the case and awards damages to Robco, but the government of Honduras has no assets in the United States that can be used to satisfy the judgment. Under which doctrine might Robco be able to collect the damages by asking another nation's court to enforce the U.S. judgment?

☀ DEBATE THIS: *The U.S. federal courts are accepting too many lawsuits initiated by foreigners that concern matters not relevant to this country.*

TERMS AND CONCEPTS

act of state doctrine 443

civil law system 442

comity 443

confiscation 444

distribution agreement 445

dumping 450

export 444

expropriation 444

international law 441

international organization 442

national law 441

normal trade relations (NTR) status 450

quota 448

sovereign immunity 444

tariff 448

treaty 442

QUESTIONS AND CASE PROBLEMS

23–1. Comity In 1995, France implemented a law that makes the use of the French language mandatory in certain legal documents. Documents relating to securities offerings, such as prospectuses, for example, must be written in French. So must instruction manuals and warranties for goods and services offered for sale in France. Additionally, all agreements entered into with French state or local authorities, with entities controlled by state or local authorities, and with private entities carrying out a public service (such as providing utilities) must be written in French. What kinds of problems might this law pose for U.S. businesspersons who wish to form contracts with French individuals or business firms?

23–2. QUESTION WITH SAMPLE ANSWER: Dumping.

The U.S. pineapple industry alleged that producers of canned pineapple from the Philippines were selling their canned pineapple in the United States for less than its fair market value

(dumping). The Philippine producers also exported other products, such as pineapple juice and juice concentrate, which used separate parts of the same fresh pineapple, so they shared raw material costs, according to the producers' own financial records. To determine fair value and antidumping duties, the pineapple industry argued that a court should calculate the Philippine producers' cost of production and allocate a portion of the shared fruit costs to the canned fruit. The result of this allocation showed that more than 90 percent of the canned fruit sales were below the cost of production. Is this a reasonable approach to determining the production costs and fair market value of canned pineapple in the United States? Why or why not?

• **For a sample answer to Question 23–2, go to Appendix I at the end of this text.**

23–3. Comity E&L Consulting, Ltd., is a U.S. corporation that sells lumber products in New Jersey, New York, and Pennsylvania. Doman Industries, Ltd., is a Canadian corporation that also sells lumber products, including green hem-fir, a durable product used for home building. Doman supplies more than 95 percent of the green hem-fir for sale in the northeastern United States. In 1990, Doman contracted to sell green hem-fir through E&L, which received monthly payments plus commissions. In 1998, Sherwood Lumber Corp., a New York firm and an E&L competitor, approached E&L about a merger. The negotiations were unsuccessful. According to E&L, Sherwood and Doman then conspired to monopolize the green hem-fir market in the United States. When Doman terminated its contract with E&L, the latter filed a suit in a federal district court against Doman, alleging violations of U.S. antitrust law. Doman filed for bankruptcy in a Canadian court and asked the U.S. court to dismiss E&L's suit, in part, under the principle of comity. What is the principle of comity? On what basis would it apply in this case? What would be the likely result? Discuss. [*E&L Consulting, Ltd. v. Doman Industries, Ltd.,* 360 F.Supp.2d 465 (E.D.N.Y. 2005)]

23–4. Dumping A newspaper printing press system is more than a hundred feet long, stands four or five stories tall, and weighs 2 million pounds. Only about ten of the systems are sold each year in the United States. Because of the size and cost, a newspaper may update its system, rather than replace it, by buying "additions." By the 1990s, Goss International Corp. was the only domestic maker of the equipment in the United States and represented the entire U.S. market. Tokyo Kikai Seisakusho (TKSC), a Japanese corporation, makes the systems in Japan. In the 1990s, TKSC began to compete in the U.S. market, forcing Goss to cut its prices below cost. TKSC's tactics included offering its customers "secret" rebates on prices that were ultimately substantially less than the products' actual market value in Japan. According to TKSC office memos, the goal was to "win completely this survival game" against Goss, the "enemy." Goss filed a suit in a federal district court against TKSC and others, alleging illegal dumping. At what point does a foreign firm's attempt to compete with a domestic manufacturer in the United States become illegal dumping? Was that point reached in this case? Discuss. [*Goss International Corp. v. Man Roland Druckmaschinen Aktiengesellschaft,* 434 F.3d 1081 (8th Cir. 2006)]

23–5. Comity Jan Voda, M.D., a resident of Oklahoma City, Oklahoma, owns three U.S. patents related to guiding catheters for use in interventional cardiology, as well as corresponding foreign patents issued by the European Patent Office, Canada, France, Germany, and Great Britain. Voda filed a suit in a federal district court against Cordis Corp., a U.S. firm, alleging infringement of the U.S. patents under U.S. patent law and of the corresponding foreign patents under the patent law of the various foreign countries. Cordis admitted, "The XB catheters have been sold domestically and internationally since 1994. The XB catheters were manufactured in Miami Lakes, from 1993 to 2001 and have been manufactured in Juarez, Mexico, since 2001." Cordis argued, however, that Voda could not assert infringement claims

under foreign patent law because the court did not have jurisdiction over such claims. Which of the important international legal principles discussed in this chapter would be most likely to apply in this case? How should the court apply it? Explain. [*Voda v. Cordis Corp.,* 476 F.3d 887 (Fed.Cir. 2007)]

23–6. CASE PROBLEM WITH SAMPLE ANSWER: Sovereign Immunity.

When Ferdinand Marcos was president of the Republic of the Philippines, he put assets into a company called Arelma. Its holdings are in New York. A group of plaintiffs, referred to as the Pimentel class, brought a class-action suit in a U.S. district court for human rights violations by Marcos. They won a judgment of $2 billion and sought to attach Arelma's assets to help pay the judgment. At the same time, the Republic of the Philippines established a commission to recover property wrongfully taken by Marcos. A court in the Philippines was convened to determine whether Marcos's property, including Arelma, should be forfeited to the Republic or to other parties. The Philippine government, in opposition to the Pimentel judgment, moved to dismiss the U.S. court proceedings. The district court refused, and the U.S. Court of Appeals for the Ninth Circuit agreed that the Pimentel class should take the assets. The Republic of the Philippines appealed. What are the key international legal issues? [Republic of the Philippines v. Pimentel, 553 U.S. 851, 128 S.Ct. 2180, 171 L.Ed.2d 131 (2008)]

- **To view a sample answer for Problem 23–6, go to this book's Web site at www.cengage.com/blaw/clarkson, select "Chapter 23," and click on "Case Problem with Sample Answer."**

23–7. Dumping Nuclear power plants use low enriched uranium (LEU) as fuel. LEU consists of feed uranium enriched by energy to a certain assay—the percentage of the isotope necessary for a nuclear reaction. The amount of energy is described by an industry standard as a "separative work unit" (SWU). A nuclear utility may buy LEU from an enricher, or the utility may provide an enricher with feed uranium and pay for the SWUs necessary to produce LEU. Under an SWU contract, the LEU returned to the utility may not be exactly the uranium the utility provided. This is because feed uranium is fungible and trades like a commodity (such as wheat or corn), and profitable enrichment requires the constant processing of undifferentiated stock. Foreign enrichers, including Eurodif, S.A., allegedly exported LEU to the United States and sold it for "less than fair value." Did this constitute dumping? Explain. If so, what could be done to prevent it? [*United States v. Eurodif, S.A.,* __ U.S. __, 129 S.Ct. 878, 172 L.Ed.2d 679 (2009)]

23–8. International Agreements and Jurisdiction The plaintiffs in this case were descendants of Holocaust victims who had lived in various countries in Europe. Before the Holocaust, the plaintiffs' ancestors had purchased insurance policies from Assicurazioni Generali, S.P.A., an Italian insurance company. When Generali refused to pay benefits under the policies, the plaintiffs, who were U.S. citizens and the beneficiaries of these policies, sued for breach of the insurance contracts. Due to certain agreements among nations after World War II, such lawsuits could not be filed for many years. In 2000, however, the United States agreed that Germany could establish a foundation—the International Commission on Holocaust-Era Insurance Claims, or ICHEIC—that would compensate victims who had suffered losses at the hands of the Germans during the war. Whenever a German company was sued in a U.S. court based on a Holocaust-era claim, the U.S. government would inform the court that the matter should be referred to the ICHEIC as the exclusive forum and remedy for the resolution. There was no such agreement with Italy, however. The plaintiffs sued the Italy-based Generali in a U.S. district court. The court dismissed the suit, and the plaintiffs appealed. Did the plaintiffs have to take their claim to the ICHEIC rather than sue in a U.S. court? Why or why not? [*In re Assicurazioni Generali, S.P.A.,* 592 F.3d 113 (2d Cir. 2010)]

23–9. A QUESTION OF ETHICS: Sovereign Immunity.

On December 21, 1988, Pan Am Flight 103 exploded 31,000 feet in the air over Lockerbie, Scotland, killing all 259 passengers and crew on board and 11 people on the ground. Among those killed was Roger Hurst, a U.S. citizen. An investigation determined that a portable radio-cassette player packed in a brown Samsonite suitcase smuggled onto the plane was the source of the explosion. The explosive device was constructed with a digital timer specially made for, and bought by, Libya. Abdel Basset Ali Al-Megrahi, a Libyan government official and an employee of the Libyan Arab Airline (LAA), was convicted by the Scottish High Court of Justiciary on criminal charges that he planned and executed the bombing in association with members of the Jamahiriya Security Organization (JSO) (an

agency of the Libyan government that performs security and intelligence functions) or the Libyan military. Members of the victims' families filed a suit in a U.S. district court against the JSO, the LAA, Al-Megrahi, and others. The plaintiffs claimed violations of U.S. federal law, including the Anti-Terrorism Act, and state law, including the intentional infliction of emotional distress. [Hurst v. Socialist People's Libyan Arab Jamahiriya, 474 F.Supp.2d 19 (D.D.C. 2007)]

(a) Under what doctrine, codified in which federal statute, might the defendants claim to be immune from the jurisdiction of a U.S. court? Should this law include an exception for "state-sponsored terrorism"? Why or why not?

(b) The defendants agreed to pay $2.7 billion, or $10 million per victim, to settle all claims for "compensatory death damages." The families of eleven victims, including Hurst, were excluded from the settlement because they were "not wrongful death beneficiaries under applicable state law." These plaintiffs continued the suit. The defendants filed a motion to dismiss. Should the motion be granted on the ground that the settlement bars the plaintiffs' claims? Explain.

23–10. SPECIAL CASE ANALYSIS: Alien Torts Claims Act.

Go to Extended Case 23.3, *Khulumani v. Barclay National Bank, Ltd.,* 504 F.3d 254 (2d Cir. 2007), on pages 452–453. Read the excerpt and answer the following questions.

(a) **Issue:** What was the plaintiffs' claim in this case?

(b) **Rule of Law:** On what U.S. law did the plaintiffs base this claim, and what was the defendants' response?

(c) **Applying the Rule of Law:** How did the trial court respond to the parties' contentions, what was the appellate court's position, and why?

(d) **Conclusion:** Did the court issue an ultimate ruling with respect to the plaintiffs' claim in this case? Explain.

LEGAL RESEARCH EXERCISES ON THE WEB

Go to this text's Web site at **www.cengage.com/blaw/clarkson**, select "Chapter 23," and click on "Practical Internet Exercises." There you will find the following Internet research exercises that you can perform to learn more about the topics covered in this chapter.

Practical Internet Exercise 23–1: **Legal Perspective**
      The World Trade Organization

Practical Internet Exercise 23–2: **Management Perspective**
      Overseas Business Opportunities

Transactions involving the sale or lease of goods make up a great deal of the business activity in the commercial and manufacturing sectors of our economy. Articles 2 and 2A of the Uniform Commercial Code (UCC) govern the sale or lease of goods in every state except Louisiana. Many of the UCC's provisions express our ethical standards.

Good Faith and Commercial Reasonableness

The concepts of good faith and commercial reasonableness permeate the UCC and help to prevent unethical behavior by businesspersons. These two key concepts are read into every contract and impose certain duties on all parties. Additionally, reasonability in the formation, performance, and termination of contracts underlies almost all of the UCC's provisions.

As an example, consider the UCC's approach to open terms. Section 2–311(1) states that when a term is to be specified by one of the parties, "any such specification must be made in good faith and within limits set by commercial reasonableness." The requirement of commercial reasonableness means that the term subsequently supplied by one party should not come as a surprise to the other. The party filling in the missing term may not take advantage of the opportunity to add a term that will be beneficial to himself or herself (and detrimental to the other party) and then demand a contractual performance that the other party totally failed to anticipate. Under the UCC, the party filling in the missing term is not allowed to deviate from what is commercially reasonable in the context of the transaction. Courts frequently look to course of dealing, usage of trade, and the surrounding circumstances in determining what is commercially reasonable in a given situation.

Good Faith in Output and Requirements Contracts

The obligation of good faith is particularly important in so-called output and requirements contracts. UCC 2–306 states that "quantity" in these contracts "means such actual output or requirements as may occur in good faith." For example, Mandrow's Machines, which assembles personal computers, has a requirements contract with Advanced Tech Circuit Boards, under which Advanced Tech is to supply Mandrow's with all of the circuit boards it needs. If Mandrow's suddenly quadruples the size of its business, it cannot insist that Advanced Tech supply all of its requirements, as specified in the original contract.

As another example, assume that the market price of the goods subject to a requirements contract rises rapidly and dramatically because of an extreme shortage of materials necessary to their production. The buyer could claim that her needs are equivalent to the seller's entire output. Then, after buying all of the seller's output at the contract price (which is substantially below the market price), the buyer could turn around and sell the goods that she does not need at the higher market price. Under the UCC, this type of unethical behavior is prohibited, even though the buyer in this instance has not technically breached the contract.

Bad Faith Not Required for Breach

A party can breach the obligation of good faith under the UCC even if the party did not show "bad faith"—that is, even when there is no proof that the party was dishonest. For example, in one case a large manufacturer of recreational boats, Genmar Holdings, Inc., purchased Horizon, a small company that produced a particular type of fishing boat. At the time of the purchase, Genmar executives promised that Horizon boats would be the company's "champion" and vowed to keep Horizon's key employees on as managers. The contract required Genmar to pay Horizon a lump sum in cash and also to pay "earn-out consideration" under a specified formula for five years. The "earn-out" amount would depend on the number of Horizon brand boats sold and on annual gross revenues.

One year after the sale, Genmar renamed the Horizon brand boats "Nova" and told employees to give priority to producing Genmar brand boats over the Nova boats. Because the Genmar boats were more difficult and time consuming to make than the Nova boats, gross revenues and production decreased, and Genmar was not required to pay the "earn-out" amounts. Eventually, Genmar fired the former Horizon employees and stopped manufacturing the Nova boats entirely. The former employees filed a suit alleging that Genmar had breached the implied covenant of good faith and fair dealing. Genmar argued that it could not have violated good faith because there was no proof that it had engaged in fraud, deceit, or misrepresentation. The court held for the plaintiffs, however, and the decision was affirmed on appeal.[1] It is possible for a party to breach its good faith obligations under the UCC even if the party did not engage in fraud, deceit, or misrepresentation.

Commercial Reasonableness

Under the UCC, the concept of good faith is closely linked to commercial reasonableness. All commercial actions—including the performance and enforcement of contract obligations—must display commercial reasonableness. A merchant is expected to act in a reasonable manner according to reasonable commercial customs. The reliance of the UCC's drafters on commercial customs, or usage

---

1. *O'Tool v. Genmar Holdings, Inc.*, 387 F.3d 1188 (10th Cir. 2004).

FOCUS ON ETHICS CONTINUES ▶

of trade, as a guideline to reasonable behavior in a given trade or industry indicates the importance of commercial reasonableness in sales law.

The concept of commercial reasonableness is clearly expressed in the doctrine of commercial impracticability. Under this doctrine, which is related to the common law doctrine of impossibility of performance, a party's nonperformance of a contractual obligation may be excused when, because of unforeseen circumstances, performance of the contract becomes impracticable. The courts make clear, however, that performance will not be excused under this doctrine unless the nonperforming party has made every reasonable effort to fulfill his or her obligations.

The Concept of the Good Faith Purchaser

The concept of the good faith purchaser reflects the UCC's emphasis on protecting innocent parties. Suppose, for example, that you innocently and in good faith purchase a boat for a fair market price from someone who appears to have good title. Under the UCC, you are protected from the possibility that the real owner—from whom the seller may have fraudulently obtained the boat—will later appear and demand his boat back. (Note that nothing prevents the true owner from bringing suit against the party who defrauded him.)

Ethical questions arise, though, when both parties to a dispute over title to goods are good faith purchasers. For example, suppose that a car dealer purchases a used car in good faith for value and sells it to a customer, also a good faith purchaser. If it turns out that there was actually a lien on the vehicle and the true owner claims title to the car, which of these two good faith purchasers should lose out? Here, a court would likely look to trade usage for guidance. In one case involving this situation, the court noted that in the used-car industry, it is customary for the seller to reimburse the buyer when the seller cannot deliver good title to a vehicle. According to the court, this custom is consistent with public policy. Car dealers are better able than buyers to investigate irregularities in title, so the risk of forged title documents "can and should be borne by dealers rather than purchasers."[2]

Another ethical issue is raised when the purchaser of goods is not quite so innocent. Suppose that the purchaser has reason to suspect that the seller may not have good title to the goods being sold but nonetheless goes ahead with the transaction because it is a "good deal." Has this buyer crossed the boundary that separates the good faith purchaser from one who

purchases in bad faith? This boundary is important in the law of sales because the UCC will not be a refuge for those who purchase in bad faith. The term *good faith purchaser* means just that—one who enters into a contract for the purchase of goods without knowing, or having any reason to know, that there is anything shady or illegal about the deal.

Unconscionability

The doctrine of unconscionability is a good example of how the law attempts to enforce ethical behavior. This doctrine suggests that some contracts may be so unfair to one party as to be unenforceable, even though that party originally agreed to the contract's terms. Section 2–302 of the UCC provides that a court will consider the fairness of contracts and may hold that a contract or any clause of a contract was unconscionable at the time it was made. If a court makes such a determination, it may refuse to enforce the contract, enforce the contract without the unconscionable clause, or limit the application of the clause so as to avoid an unconscionable result.

The Test for Unconscionability The UCC does not define the term *unconscionability*. The drafters of the UCC, however, have added explanatory comments to the relevant sections, and these comments serve as guidelines for applying the UCC. Comment 1 to Section 2–302 suggests that the basic test for unconscionability is whether, under the circumstances existing at the time of the contract's formation, the clause in question was so one sided as to be unconscionable. This test is to be applied against the general commercial background of the contract.

Unconscionability—A Case Example In one case applying Section 2–302, a New York appellate court held that an arbitration clause was unconscionable and refused to enforce it. Gateway 2000, Inc., which sold computers and software directly to consumers, included in its retail agreements a clause specifying that any dispute arising out of the contract had to be arbitrated in Chicago, Illinois, in accordance with the arbitration rules of the International Chamber of Commerce (ICC).

A number of consumers who had purchased Gateway products became incensed when they learned that the ICC rules required advance fees of $4,000 (more than the cost of most Gateway products) and that the $2,000 registration fee was nonrefundable—even if the consumer prevailed at the arbitration. Additionally, the consumers would have to pay travel expenses to Chicago. In the class-action litigation against Gateway that followed, the New York court agreed with the consumers that the "egregiously

---

2. *Superior, Inc. v. Arrington,* 2009 Ark.App. 875 (2009).

[flagrantly] oppressive" arbitration clause was unconscionable: "Barred from resorting to the courts by the arbitration clause in the first instance, the designation of a financially prohibitive forum effectively bars consumers from this forum as well; consumers are thus left with no forum at all in which to resolve a dispute."[3]

Warranties

A seller or lessor has not only a legal obligation to provide safe products but also an ethical one. When faced with the possibility of increasing safety at no extra cost, every ethical businessperson will certainly opt for a safer product. An ethical issue arises, however, when producing a safer product means higher costs. To some extent, our warranty laws serve to protect consumers from sellers who may be tempted to neglect ethical concerns if what they are doing is both legal and profitable.

Express and Implied Warranties The UCC recognizes both express and implied warranties. Under UCC 2–314 and 2A–212, goods sold by a merchant or leased by a lessor must be fit for the ordinary purposes for which such goods are used, be of proper quality, and be properly labeled and packaged. The UCC injects greater fairness into contractual situations by recognizing descriptions as express warranties. Hence, a seller or lessor of goods may be held to have breached a contract if the goods fail to conform to the description. In this way, the UCC acknowledges that a buyer or lessee may often reasonably believe that a seller or lessor is warranting his or her product, even though the seller or lessor does not use a formal word such as *warrant* or *guarantee*. Thus, the law imposes an ethical obligation on sellers and lessors in a statutory form.

Warranty Disclaimers The UCC requirement that warranty disclaimers be sufficiently conspicuous to catch the eye of a reasonable purchaser is based on the ethical premise that sellers of goods should not take advantage of unwary consumers, who may not always read the "fine print" on standard purchase order forms. As discussed in Chapter 22, if a seller or lessor, when attempting to disclaim warranties, fails to meet the specific requirements imposed by the UCC, the warranties will not be effectively disclaimed. Before the UCC was adopted by the states, purchasers of automobiles frequently signed standard-form purchase agreements drafted by the auto manufacturer without learning the meaning of all the fine print until later.

---

3. *Brower v. Gateway 2000, Inc.*, 246 A.D.2d 246, 676 N.Y.S.2d 569 (1998). See also *DeFontes v. Dell, Inc.*, 984 A.2d 1061 (R.I. 2009).

Freedom of Contract versus Freedom from Contract—Revisited Although freedom of contract reflects a basic ethical principle in our society, courts have made it clear that when such freedom leads to gross unfairness, it should be curbed. (Several examples of the exceptions to freedom of contract that courts will make were offered in the *Focus on Ethics* feature at the end of Unit Three.) Nonetheless, before the UCC was in effect, courts generally would not intervene in cases involving warranty disclaimers in fine print or otherwise "hidden" in a standard purchase order form. Exceptions were made only when the resulting unfairness "shocked the conscience" of the court. By obligating sellers and lessors to meet specific requirements when disclaiming warranties, the UCC has made dealing fairly with buyers and lessees—already an ethical obligation of all sellers and lessors of goods—a legal obligation as well.

Today, if a warranty disclaimer unfairly "surprises" a purchaser or a lessee, chances are that the disclaimer was not sufficiently conspicuous. In this situation, the unfairness of the bargain need not be so great as to "shock the court's conscience" before a remedy will be granted.

International Transactions

Conducting business internationally presents unique challenges including, at times, ethical challenges. This is understandable, given that laws and cultures vary from one country to another. Consider the role of women. In the United States, equal employment opportunity is a fundamental public policy. This policy is clearly expressed in Title VII of the Civil Rights Act of 1964 (to be discussed in Chapter 35), which prohibits discrimination against women in the employment context. Some other countries, however, largely reject any professional role for women. Consequently, U.S. women conducting business transactions in those countries may encounter difficulties. For example, when the World Bank sent a delegation that included women to negotiate with the Central Bank of Korea, the Koreans were surprised and offended. They thought that the presence of women meant that the negotiations were not being taken seriously.

There are also some important ethical differences among nations. In Islamic countries, for example, the consumption of alcohol and certain foods is forbidden by the Islamic religion. Thus, it would be thoughtless and imprudent to invite a Saudi Arabian business contact out for a drink. Additionally, in many foreign nations, gift giving is a common practice between contracting companies or between companies and government officials. To Americans, such gift giving may look suspiciously like an unethical (and possibly illegal) bribe. This cultural difference has been an

FOCUS ON ETHICS CONTINUES ▶

important source of friction in international business, particularly since the U.S. Congress passed the Foreign Corrupt Practices Act in 1977 (discussed in Chapters 5 and 9). This act prohibits U.S. business firms from offering certain side payments to foreign officials to secure favorable contracts.

DISCUSSION QUESTIONS

1. Review the UCC provisions that apply to the topics discussed in Chapters 19 through 22. Discuss fully how various UCC provisions, excluding the provisions discussed above, reflect social values and ethical standards.
2. How can a court objectively measure good faith and commercial reasonableness?
3. Generally, the courts determine what constitutes "reasonable" behavior in disputes between contract parties over this issue. Should the UCC be more specific in defining what will be deemed reasonable in particular circumstances so that the courts do not have to decide the issue? Why or why not?
4. Why does the UCC protect innocent persons (good faith purchasers) who buy goods from sellers with voidable title but not innocent persons who buy goods from sellers with void title?
5. Should U.S. firms doing business internationally send female employees to foreign nations that reject any role for women in business? Why or why not? How can a U.S. company accommodate the culture of foreign nations and still treat its own employees equally?

UNIT FIVE

NEGOTIABLE INSTRUMENTS

CONTENTS

CHAPTER 24

The Function and Creation of Negotiable Instruments

Most commercial transactions that take place in the modern business world would be inconceivable without negotiable instruments. A negotiable instrument can function as a substitute for cash or as an extension of credit. For example, when a buyer writes a check to pay for goods, the check serves as a substitute for cash. When a buyer gives a seller a promissory note in which the buyer promises to pay the seller the purchase price within sixty days, the seller has essentially extended credit to the buyer for a sixty-day period.

For a negotiable instrument to operate *practically* as either a substitute for cash or a credit device, or both, it is essential that the instrument be *easily transferable without danger of being uncollectible.* This is a fundamental function of negotiable instruments. Each rule described in the following pages can be examined in light of this function.

The law governing negotiable instruments grew out of commercial necessity. In the medieval world, merchants engaging in foreign trade used *bills of exchange* to finance and conduct their affairs, rather than risk transporting gold or coins. The merchants developed their own set of rules, which eventually became a distinct set of laws known as the *Lex Mercatoria* (Law Merchant).

The Law Merchant was later codified in England and is the forerunner of Article 3 of the Uniform Commercial Code (UCC).

Article 3 imposes special requirements for the form and content of *negotiable instruments.* These requirements are discussed throughout this chapter and in Chapters 25 and 26. Article 3 also governs the process of *negotiation* (the transfer of an instrument from one party to another) and the parties' responsibilities in negotiation, as will be discussed. Article 4 of the UCC, which governs bank deposits and collections, will be covered in Chapter 27. The revised Articles 3 and 4 are included in their entirety in Appendix C.

SECTION 1
TYPES OF NEGOTIABLE INSTRUMENTS

A **negotiable instrument** is a signed writing (or record) that contains an unconditional promise or order to pay an exact amount, either on demand or at a specific future time. Most negotiable instruments are paper documents, which is why they are sometimes referred to as *commercial paper.* UCC 3–104(b) defines an *instrument* as a "negotiable instrument."[1] For that reason, whenever the term *instrument* is used in this book, it refers to a negotiable instrument.

The UCC specifies four types of negotiable instruments: *drafts, checks, notes,* and *certificates of deposit*

(CDs). These instruments, which are summarized briefly in Exhibit 24–1 on the facing page, frequently are divided into the two classifications that we will discuss in the following subsections: *orders to pay* (drafts and checks) and *promises to pay* (promissory notes and CDs).

Negotiable instruments may also be classified as either demand instruments or time instruments. A *demand instrument* is payable on demand—that is, it is payable immediately after it is issued and thereafter for a reasonable period of time.[2] **Issue** is "the first delivery of an instrument by the maker or drawer

---

1. Note that all of the references to Article 3 of the UCC in this chapter are to the 1990 version of Article 3, which has been adopted by almost all of the states.

2. "A promise or order is 'payable on demand' if it (i) states that it is payable on demand or at sight, or otherwise indicates that it is payable at the will of the holder, or (ii) does not state any time of payment" [UCC 3–108(a)]. The UCC defines a *holder* as "the person in possession of a negotiable instrument that is payable either to bearer or to an identified person [who] is the person in possession" [UCC 1–201(21)(A)]. The term *bearer* will be defined later in this chapter.

EXHIBIT 24–1 • Basic Types of Negotiable Instruments

INSTRUMENTS	CHARACTERISTICS	PARTIES
ORDERS TO PAY **Draft**	An order by one person to another person or to bearer [UCC 3–104(e)].	*Drawer*—The person who signs or makes the order to pay [UCC 3–103(a)(3)].
Check	A draft drawn on a bank and payable on demand [UCC 3–104(f)].[a] (With certain types of checks, such as cashier's checks, the bank is both the drawer and the drawee—see Chapter 27 for details.)	*Drawee*—The person to whom the order to pay is made [UCC 3–103(a)(2)]. *Payee*—The person to whom payment is ordered.
PROMISES TO PAY **Promissory note**	A promise by one party to pay money to another party or to bearer [UCC 3–104(e)].	*Maker*—The person who promises to pay [UCC 3–103(a)(5)].
Certificate of deposit	A note made by a bank acknowledging a deposit of funds made payable to the holder of the note [UCC 3–104(j)].	*Payee*—The person to whom the promise is made.

a. Under UCC 4–105(1), banks include savings banks, savings and loan associations, credit unions, and trust companies (organizations that perform the fiduciary functions of trusts and agencies).

. . . for the purpose of giving rights on the instrument to any person" [UCC 3–105]. All checks are demand instruments because, by definition, they must be payable on demand. A *time instrument* is payable at a future date.

Drafts and Checks (Orders to Pay)

A **draft** is an unconditional written order that involves *three parties*. The party creating the draft (the **drawer**) orders another party (the **drawee**) to pay money, usually to a third party (the **payee**). The most common type of draft is a check, but drafts other than checks may be used in commercial transactions.

TIME DRAFTS AND SIGHT DRAFTS A *time draft* is payable at a definite future time. A *sight draft* (or demand draft) is payable on sight—that is, when it is presented to the drawee (usually a bank or financial institution) for payment. A sight draft may be payable on acceptance. **Acceptance** is the drawee's written promise to pay the draft when it comes due. Usually, an instrument is accepted by writing the word *accepted* across its face, followed by the date of acceptance and the signature of the drawee. A draft can be both a time and a sight draft; such a draft is payable at a stated time after sight. An example would be a draft that states that it is payable ninety days after sight.

Exhibit 24–2 on the following page shows a typical time draft. For the drawee to be obligated to honor the order, the drawee must be obligated to the drawer either by agreement or through a debtor-creditor relationship. For example, on January 16, OurTown Real Estate orders $1,000 worth of office supplies from Eastman Supply Company, with payment due April 16. Also on January 16, OurTown sends Eastman a draft drawn on its account with the First National Bank of Whiteacre as payment. In this scenario, the drawer is OurTown, the drawee is OurTown's bank (First National Bank of Whiteacre), and the payee is Eastman Supply Company. First National Bank is obligated to honor the draft because of its account agreement with OurTown Real Estate.

TRADE ACCEPTANCES A trade acceptance is a type of draft that is frequently used in the sale of goods. In a **trade acceptance,** the seller of the goods is both the drawer and the payee. The buyer to whom credit is extended is the drawee. Essentially, the draft orders the buyer to pay a specified amount to the seller, usually at a stated time in the future.

For example, Jackson Street Bistro buys its restaurant supplies from Osaka Industries. When Jackson requests supplies, Osaka creates a draft ordering Jackson to pay Osaka for the supplies within ninety days and sends it along with the supplies. When the supplies arrive, Jackson accepts the draft by signing its face and is then obligated to make the payment. This signed draft is a trade acceptance and can be

EXHIBIT 24-2 • A Typical Time Draft

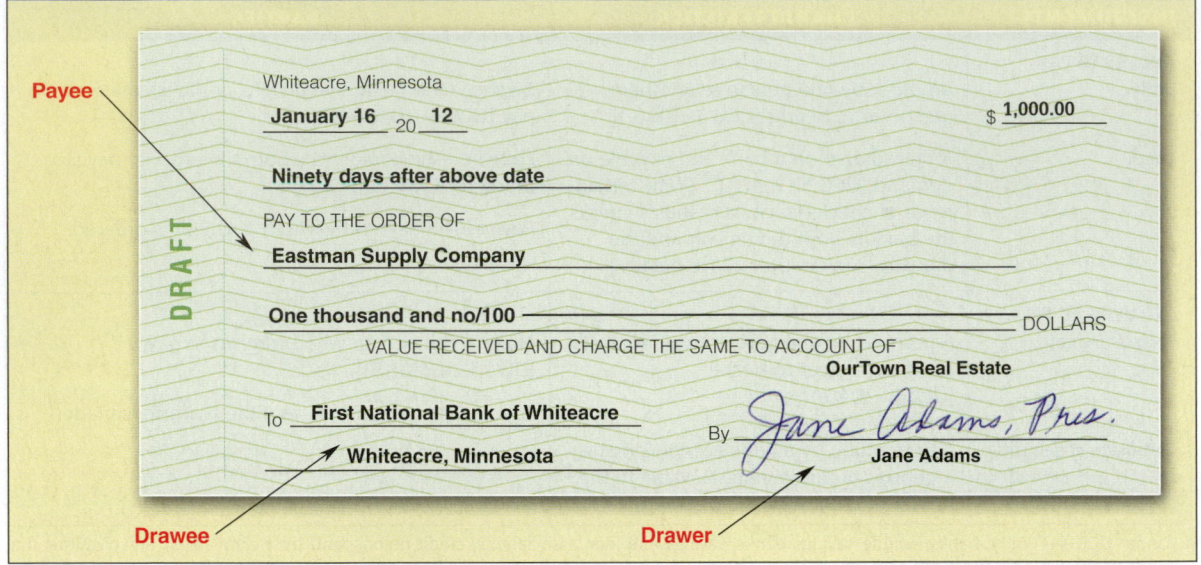

sold to a third party (on the *commercial money market*—the market that businesses use for short-term borrowing) if Osaka needs cash before the payment is due.

When a draft orders the buyer's bank to pay, it is called a **banker's acceptance.** Banker's acceptances are commonly used in international trade.

CHECKS As mentioned, the most commonly used type of draft is a **check.** The writer of the check is the drawer, the bank on which the check is drawn is the drawee, and the person to whom the check is made payable is the payee. Checks are demand instruments because they are payable on demand. For a discussion of how payments made via mobile phones can replace checks and also promote sustainability, see this chapter's *Shifting Legal Priorities for Business* feature on the facing page.

Checks will be discussed more fully in Chapter 27, but it should be noted here that with certain types of checks, such as *cashier's checks,* the bank is both the drawer and the drawee. The bank customer purchases a cashier's check from the bank—that is, pays the bank the amount of the check—and indicates to whom the check should be made payable. The bank, not the customer, is the drawer of the check, as well as the drawee. A cashier's check functions the same as cash because the bank has committed itself to paying the stated amount on demand.

Note also that while checks are still commonly used in the United States, their negotiability is questionable in other nations. In many European nations, including Austria, France, Germany, and the Netherlands, people write fewer checks today. Instead, they rely on direct bank transfers and electronic payments (both of which will be discussed in Chapter 27). The shift away from checks in Europe has been spurred by the European Union's low-cost electronic payment system, which is much faster and more efficient than the systems available in the United States.

Promissory Notes (Promises to Pay)

A **promissory note** is a written promise made by one person (the **maker** of the promise) to pay another (usually a payee) a specified sum. A promissory note, which is often referred to simply as a *note,* can be made payable at a definite time or on demand. It can name a specific payee or merely be payable to bearer (bearer instruments will be discussed later in this chapter). For example, on April 30, Laurence and Margaret Roberts, who are called co-makers, sign a writing unconditionally promising to pay "to the order of" the First National Bank of Whiteacre $3,000 (with 8 percent interest) on or before June 29. This writing is a promissory note. A typical promissory note is shown in Exhibit 24–3 on the facing page.

CASE IN POINT Joseph Cotton borrowed funds from a bank for his education and signed a promissory note for their repayment. The bank assigned the note to the U.S. Department of Education, and Cotton failed to pay the debt. The government then

Approximately 70 billion checks are written and processed each year in the United States. All of these checks are written on paper, and some of them are transported in physical form for long distances within the U.S. banking system—a process that requires airplane and truck fuel. Thus, whenever we make payments by some electronic means instead of by checks, trees do not have to be cut down to make paper, and fossil fuels do not have to be used to transport the checks. Many people, especially younger ones, have already embraced online shopping and electronic banking. Now they seem poised to take another step toward sustainability.

Person-to-Person Mobile Phone Payments

Mobile phones have long been commonplace in the United States, but today many U.S. residents are using their mobile phones to buy goods or pay for services. Banks are facilitating the process by adding person-to-person payments to their existing mobile and online banking offerings. For example, if you loan your classmate $50, he can now repay you by sending the payment to your e-mail address or cell phone number. The 80 million people who have PayPal accounts have been conducting similar transactions worldwide for several years. PayPal allows its members to transfer funds over their cell phones.

Mobile Phone Payments Are Part of a Growing Trend

Banking is just one part of our interrelated business world that, whether consciously or not, is moving toward sustainability. Whenever an industry or company creates a new service that avoids the need for paper, we can enjoy that service at a lower resource cost, thereby improving our future resource wealth. The move to use electronic substitutes for checks is part of this trend. Indeed, the day may come when paper checks will no longer be accepted.

MANAGERIAL IMPLICATIONS

Although there is no current legislation that requires banks and other businesses to reduce their use of paper, some may be enacted in the near future. Given that sustainability appears to be a priority for the Obama administration and Congress, such legislation is likely to be proposed. Managers can start now to reduce the amount of paper that their employees use by encouraging more paperless communication as well as more electronic presentations concerning finance, human resources, and other topics.

---

received a court order allowing it to garnish (take a percentage of) Cotton's wages and his federal income tax refund. Cotton filed a lawsuit seeking to avoid payment and claiming that the debt was invalid because he had not signed any document promising to pay the government. He also argued that the note lacked consideration because the school had closed down before he had completed his education. The court found that failure of consideration is not a defense in student loan cases, because the student

EXHIBIT 24-3 • A Typical Promissory Note

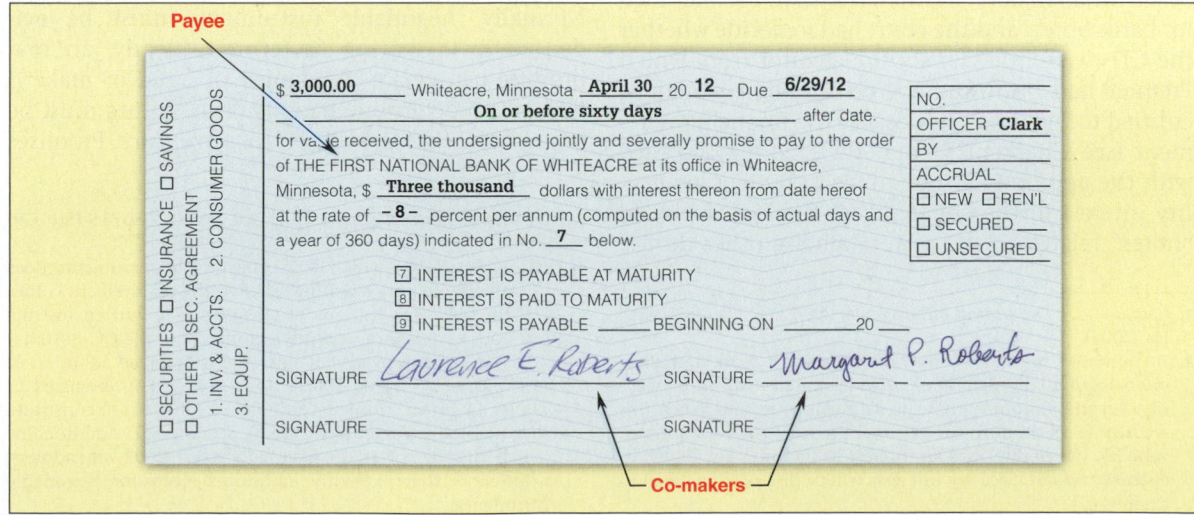

receives the funds in exchange for the promise to repay them. The court also found that the signature on Cotton's employment records matched the one on the bank's note, which had been validly assigned to the government. Thus, the government was entitled to enforce the note.[3]

Promissory notes are used in a variety of credit transactions. Often, a promissory note will carry the name of the transaction involved. For example, a note may be secured by personal property, such as an automobile. This type of note is referred to as a *collateral note* because property pledged as security for the satisfaction of a debt is called *collateral*.[4] A note payable in installments, such as installment payments for a large-screen 3D LCD television over a twelve-month period, is called an *installment note*.

Certificates of Deposit (Promises to Pay)

A **certificate of deposit (CD)** is a type of note issued when a party deposits funds with a bank, and the bank promises to repay the funds, with interest, on a certain date [UCC 3–104(j)]. The bank is the maker of the note, and the depositor is the payee. For example, on February 15, Sara Levin deposits $5,000 with the First National Bank of Whiteacre. The bank promises to repay the $5,000, plus 3.25 percent annual interest, on August 15.

CASE IN POINT Premier Interval Resorts, Inc., borrowed $42 million secured by a deed of trust on a Nevada casino that was to be purchased with the $42 million. In addition, to provide collateral to comply with Nevada's workers' compensation laws (to be discussed in Chapter 34), Premier deposited two CDs at Bank West, one for $2.5 million and the other for $350,000. Shortly after that, Premier filed for bankruptcy, and the court had to decide whether the CDs were notes. If so, the creditor from which Premier had borrowed the $42 million would be entitled to the proceeds because the financing statement (see Chapter 29) that the creditor had filed with the appropriate state office to protect its security interest in the collateral for the loan included "notes" related to the casino, among other things.

The court found that because Nevada's version of the UCC defined a CD as a promise of payment, or a note, and because the CDs related to the casino, they were incorporated by reference in the financing statement. Therefore, the creditor was entitled to the proceeds from the CDs.[5]

Because CDs are time deposits, the purchaser-payee typically is not allowed to withdraw the funds before the date of maturity (except in limited circumstances, such as disability or death). If a payee wants to access the funds before the maturity date, he or she can sell (negotiate) the CD to a third party. Certificates of deposit in small denominations (for amounts up to $100,000) are often sold by savings and loan associations, savings banks, commercial banks, and credit unions. Exhibit 24–4 on the facing page shows a typical small CD.

SECTION 2
REQUIREMENTS FOR NEGOTIABILITY

For an instrument to be negotiable, it must meet the following requirements:

1. Be in writing.
2. Be signed by the maker or the drawer.
3. Be an unconditional promise or order to pay.
4. State a fixed amount of money.
5. Be payable on demand or at a definite time.
6. Be payable to order or to bearer, unless it is a check.

Written Form

Normally, negotiable instruments must be evidenced by a writing or record.[6] Clearly, an oral promise can create the danger of fraud or make it difficult to determine liability. The writing must be on material that lends itself to *permanence*. Promises

---

3. *Cotton v. U.S. Department of Education,* 2006 WL 3313753 (M.D. Fla. 2006).

4. To minimize the risk of loss when making a loan, a creditor often requires the debtor to provide some *collateral,* or security, beyond a promise that the debt will be repaid. When this security takes the form of personal property (such as a motor vehicle), the creditor has an interest in the property known as a *security interest.* Security interests will be discussed in detail in Chapter 29.

5. *In re Premier Interval Resorts, Inc.,* 2003 WL 22880715 (5th Cir. 2003).

6. UCC Section 3–104, which defines negotiable instruments, does not explicitly require a writing. The writing requirement comes from the UCC's definitions of an *order* (as a written instruction) and a *promise* (as a written undertaking) [UCC 3–103(a)(6), (9)]. Note, however, that since the widespread adoption of the Uniform Electronic Transactions Act (UETA), discussed in Chapter 11, an electronic record may be sufficient to constitute a negotiable instrument (see UETA Section 16). Additionally, a small number of states have adopted a 2002 amendment to Article 3 that explicitly authorizes electronic negotiable instruments.

EXHIBIT 24-4 • A Typical Small Certificate of Deposit

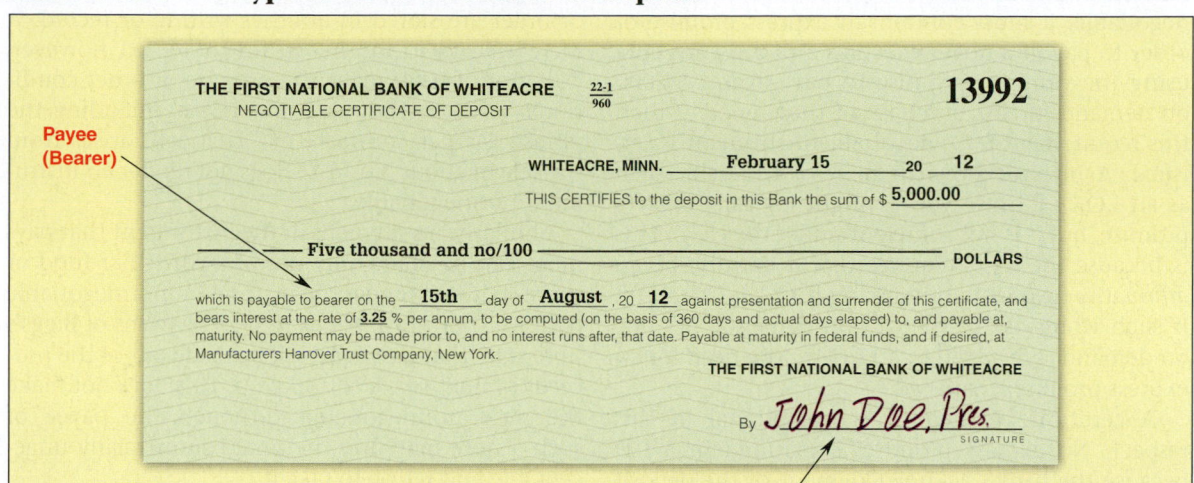

carved in blocks of ice or inscribed in the sand or on other impermanent surfaces would not qualify as negotiable instruments. The UCC nevertheless gives considerable leeway as to what can be a negotiable instrument. Checks and notes have been written on napkins, menus, tablecloths, shirts, and a variety of other materials.

The writing must also have *portability*. Although the UCC does not explicitly state this requirement, if an instrument is not movable, it obviously cannot meet the requirement that it be freely transferable. For example, suppose that Cullen writes on the side of a cow, "I, Cullen, promise to pay to Merrill or her order $500 on demand." Technically, this would meet the requirements of a negotiable instrument—except for portability. Because a cow cannot easily be transferred in the ordinary course of business, the "instrument" is nonnegotiable.

Signatures

For an instrument to be negotiable, it must be signed by (1) the maker if it is a note or a certificate of deposit or (2) the drawer if it is a draft or a check [UCC 3–103(a)(3), (5)]. If a person signs an instrument as an authorized *agent* for the maker or drawer, the maker or drawer has effectively signed the instrument [UCC 3–402]. (Agents' signatures will be discussed in Chapter 26.)

SIGNATURE REQUIREMENTS The UCC is quite lenient with regard to what constitutes a signature. Almost any symbol executed or adopted by a person with the intent to authenticate a written

or electronic document can be a **signature** [UCC 1–201(39)]. A signature can be made manually or by means of some device, such as a rubber stamp or thumbprint, and can consist of any name, including a trade or assumed name, or a word, mark, or symbol [UCC 3–401(b)]. If necessary, parol evidence (discussed in Chapter 15) is admissible to identify the signer. When the signer is identified, the signature becomes effective.

Although there are almost no limitations on the manner in which a signature can be made, one should be careful about receiving an instrument that has been signed in an unusual way. Oddities on a negotiable instrument can open the door to disputes and lead to litigation. Furthermore, an unusual signature clearly will decrease the *marketability* of an instrument because it creates uncertainty.

PLACEMENT OF THE SIGNATURE The location of the signature on the document is unimportant, although the usual place is the lower right-hand corner. A *handwritten* statement on the body of the instrument, such as "I, Kammie Orlik, promise to pay Janis Tan," is sufficient to act as a signature.

Unconditional Promise or Order to Pay

The terms of the promise or order must be included in the writing on the face of a negotiable instrument. The terms must also be *unconditional*—that is, they cannot be conditioned on the occurrence or nonoccurrence of some other event or agreement [UCC 3–104(a)].

PROMISE OR ORDER For an instrument to be negotiable, it must contain an express promise or order to pay. If a buyer executes a promissory note using the words "I promise to pay Alvarez $1,000 on demand for the purchase of these goods," then this requirement for a negotiable instrument is satisfied. A mere acknowledgment of the debt, such as an I.O.U. ("I owe you"), might logically *imply* a promise, but it is not sufficient under the UCC. This is because the UCC requires that a promise be an *affirmative* (express) undertaking [UCC 3–103(a)(9)]. If such words as "to be paid on demand" or "due on demand" are added to an I.O.U., the need for an express promise is satisfied.

A certificate of deposit is exceptional in this respect. No express promise is required in a CD because the bank's acknowledgment of the deposit and the other terms of the instrument clearly indicate a promise by the bank to repay the sum of money [UCC 3–104(j)].

An *order* is associated with three-party instruments, such as checks, drafts, and trade acceptances. An order directs a third party to pay the instrument as drawn. In the typical check, for example, the word *pay* (to the order of a payee) is a command to the drawee bank to pay the check when presented, and thus it is an order. A command, such as "pay," is mandatory even if it is accompanied by courteous words, as in "Please pay" or "Kindly pay." Generally, the language used must indicate that a command, or order, is being given. Stating "I wish you would pay" does not fulfill this requirement. An order may be addressed to one person or to more than one person, either jointly ("to A *and* B") or alternatively ("to A *or* B") [UCC 3–103(a)(6)]. (The effect of naming alternative or joint payees will be discussed in Chapter 25.)

UNCONDITIONALITY OF THE PROMISE OR ORDER A negotiable instrument's utility as a substitute for cash or as a credit device would be dramatically reduced if it had conditional promises attached to it. No one could safely purchase the instrument without first investigating whether the condition was satisfied, and doing so would be time consuming and expensive. Also, this would restrict the instrument's transferability. Therefore, only instruments with *unconditional* promises or orders can be negotiable [UCC 3–104(a)].

A promise or order is conditional (and *not* negotiable) if it states (1) an express condition to payment, (2) that the promise or order is subject to or governed by another writing (or record), or (3) that

the rights or obligations with respect to the promise or order are stated in another writing or record. A mere *reference* to another writing or record, however, does not of itself make the promise or order conditional [UCC 3–106(a)]. For example, including the phrase "as per contract" or "This debt arises from the sale of goods X and Y" does not render an instrument nonnegotiable.

Similarly, a statement in the instrument that payment can be made only out of a particular fund or source will not render the instrument nonnegotiable [UCC 3–106(b)(ii)]. For example, the terms of Biggs's note state that payment will be made out of the proceeds of next year's cotton crop. This does not make the note nonnegotiable—although the payee of such a note may find the note commercially unacceptable and refuse to take it.

If the payment is to be made from a fund that does not yet exist, however, or is conditioned on the occurrence of some future event, then the instrument will be nonnegotiable. For example, Duffy's note promises to pay Sherman from the trust account that Duffy will establish when he receives the proceeds from his father's estate. This promise is conditional, and the note is nonnegotiable.

A Fixed Amount of Money

Negotiable instruments must state with certainty a fixed amount of money, with or without interest or other charges described in the promise or order, to be paid at the time the instrument is payable [UCC 3–104(a)]. This requirement ensures that the value of the instrument can be determined with clarity and certainty.

FIXED AMOUNT The term *fixed amount* (sometimes called *sum certain*) means that the amount must be ascertainable from the face of the instrument. Interest may be stated as a fixed or variable rate. A demand note payable with 10 percent interest meets the requirement of a fixed amount because its amount can be determined at the time it is payable [UCC 3–104(a)].

The rate of interest may also be determined with reference to information that is not contained in the instrument if that information is readily ascertainable by reference to a formula or a source described in the instrument [UCC 3–112(b)]. For example, an instrument that is payable at the *legal rate of interest* (a rate of interest fixed by statute) is negotiable. Mortgage notes tied to a variable rate of interest (a rate that fluctuates as a result of market conditions) can also be negotiable.

PAYABLE IN MONEY UCC 3–104(a) provides that a fixed amount is to be *payable in money*. The UCC defines money as "a medium of exchange authorized or adopted by a domestic or foreign government as a part of its currency" [UCC 1–201(24)]. An instrument payable in the United States with a face amount stated in a foreign currency can be paid in the foreign money or in the equivalent in U.S. dollars [UCC 3–107].

Suppose that the maker of a note promises "to pay on demand $1,000 in U.S. gold." Gold is not a medium of exchange adopted by the U.S. government, so the note is nonnegotiable because it is not payable in money. The same result occurs if the maker promises "to pay $1,000 and fifty magnums of 1994 Chateau Lafitte-Rothschild wine" because the instrument is not payable *entirely* in money. An instrument payable in government bonds or in shares of IBM stock is nonnegotiable because neither is a medium of exchange recognized by the U.S. government. The statement "Payable in $1,000 U.S. currency or an equivalent value in gold" would render the instrument nonnegotiable if the maker reserved the option of paying in money *or* gold. If the instrument left the option to the payee, some legal scholars argue that it would be negotiable.

Payable on Demand or at a Definite Time

A negotiable instrument must "be payable on demand or at a definite time" [UCC 3–104(a)(2)]. To determine the value of a negotiable instrument, it is necessary to know when the maker, drawee, or *acceptor* is required to pay (an **acceptor** is a drawee who has accepted, or agreed to pay, an instrument when it is presented later for payment). It is also necessary to know when the obligations of secondary parties, such as *indorsers,*[7] will arise. Furthermore, it is necessary to know when an instrument is due in order to calculate when the statute of limitations may apply [UCC 3–118(a)]. Finally, with an interest-bearing instrument, it is necessary to know the exact interval during which

the interest will accrue to determine the instrument's value at the present time.

PAYABLE ON DEMAND Instruments that are payable on demand include those that contain the words "Payable at sight" or "Payable upon presentment." **Presentment** means a demand made by or on behalf of a person entitled to enforce an instrument to either pay or accept the instrument [UCC 3–501]. Thus, presentment occurs when a person brings the instrument to the appropriate party for payment or acceptance.

The very nature of the instrument may indicate that it is payable on demand. For example, a check, by definition, is payable on demand [UCC 3–104(f)]. If no time for payment is specified and the person responsible for payment must pay on the instrument's presentment, the instrument is payable on demand [UCC 3–108(a)].

CASE IN POINT Patrick Gowin was an employee of a granite countertop business owned by John Stathis. In November 2000, Gowin signed a promissory note agreeing to pay $12,500 in order to become a co-owner of the business. The note was dated January 15, 2000 (ten months before it was signed) and required him to make installment payments starting in February 2000. Stathis told Gowin not to worry about the note and never requested any payments. Gowin continued working at the business until 2002 and then quit. Stathis claimed that Gowin did not own any interest in the business because he had never paid the $12,500. When Gowin brought a lawsuit, the court reasoned that because compliance with the stated dates was impossible, the note effectively did not state a date for its payment and therefore was a demand note under UCC 3–108(a). The court also concluded that because no demand for payment had been made, Gowin's obligation to make it had not arisen and the termination of his ownership interest in the granite business was improper.[8]

In the following case, the issue before the court was whether a promissory note was a demand note.

---

7. We should note that because the UCC uses the spelling *indorse* (*indorsement,* and the like), rather than the more common spelling *endorse* (*endorsement,* and the like), we adopt the UCC's spelling here and in other chapters in this text. Indorsers will be discussed in Chapter 25.

---

8. *Gowin v. Granite Depot, LLC,* 272 Va. 246, 634 S.E.2d 714 (2006).

☀ EXTENDED CASE 24.1 ☀
Reger Development, LLC v. National City Bank

United States Court of Appeals, Seventh Circuit, 592 F.3d 759 (2010).
www.ca7.uscourts.gov[a]

IN THE LANGUAGE OF THE COURT

FLAUM, Circuit Judge.

* * * *

* * * Plaintiff-appellant Reger Development, LLC * * * is an Illinois limited liability company involved in real estate development. Kevin Reger is Reger Development's principal and sole member. Defendant-appellee National City Bank * * * had lent money to Reger Development for several previous projects. In June 2007, National City offered the company a line of credit to fund potential development opportunities. * * * Reger Development then executed the form contract, which was structured as a promissory note ("Note") * * *.

The main question in this case is whether the Note entitles National City to demand payment from Reger Development at will. * * * [One of the contract clauses reads, in part:]

PAYMENT: Borrower will pay this loan in full immediately upon Lender's demand.

* * * *

The Note [continues on] to reference payment on lender's demand several times in other provisions. * * * [About a year later, National City asked Reger Development to pay down some of the loan and] notified appellant that it would be reducing the amount of cash available through the line of credit * * *.

Kevin Reger "expressed surprise" about these developments and asked if National City would call the line of credit if Reger Development did not agree to the requests. The bank acknowledged that Reger Development was not in default but stated that "there is a possibility that we may demand payment of the line."

Reger Development then filed a complaint in Illinois state court accusing National City of breaching the terms of the Note. * * *Appellee removed the case to the Northern District of Illinois under diversity jurisdiction and then successfully moved to dismiss the complaint for failure to state a cause of action under which relief could be granted. * * * Reger Development [appealed].

* * * *

While Illinois law generally holds that "a covenant of fair dealing and good faith is implied into every contract absent express disavowal," *the duty to act in good faith does not apply to lenders seeking payment on demand notes.* In light of this controlling law, appellant's complaint appears vacuous [lacking in content]. Reger Development's allegations are "that National City breached the Contract Documents by arbitrarily and capriciously (1) demanding payment under the Line of Credit even though Reger Development was in good standing and (2) unilaterally changing and attempting to change the fundamental terms of the Contract Documents without Reger Development's consent." Reger

Development [points] to several provisions in the Note that it believes to be fundamentally inconsistent with the nature of a demand instrument. These include * * * the prepayment clause, which allows the borrower to pay down "all or a portion of the amount owed earlier than it is due;" and the clause that grants National City the right to access the borrower's financial information. Reger Development describes the latter as a "financial insecurity" provision that conditions the right to demand payment on some economic cause. [Emphasis added.]

We are not persuaded by the suggestion that these references * * * somehow overpower the repeated, explicit contract language setting forth the lender's right to demand payment at any time. A bank that wishes to call the Note can specify some future date on which it needs payment as a "due date." Failure to pay at that point in time, as well as failure to make monthly interest payments required by the Note, would constitute default, but *the mere use of the terms "due date" or "default" would not alter the nature of the agreement.* * * * The language merely reinforces National City's right to collect scheduled monthly interest payments and does not deviate from the structure of a demand note. [Emphasis added.]

* * * *

For the foregoing reasons, we AFFIRM the district court's grant of National City's motion to dismiss the Reger Development complaint.

a. Select "Opinions" under the "Case Information" heading. When the page opens, enter "09" and "2821" in the "Case Number" boxes, and click on "List Case(s)." On the page that appears next, click on the link to the case number to access the opinion. The U.S. Court of Appeals for the Seventh Circuit maintains this Web site.

QUESTIONS

1. In its opinion, the court pointed out that "the duty to act in good faith does not apply to lenders seeking payment on demand notes." Why not?
2. If National City had demanded "payment of the line" instead of just indicating that there was a possibility it might do so in the future, would the outcome of this case have been any different? Explain.

PAYABLE AT A DEFINITE TIME If an instrument is not payable on demand, to be negotiable it must be payable at a definite time. An instrument is payable at a definite time if it states that it is payable (1) on a specified date, (2) within a definite period of time (such as thirty days) after being presented for payment, or (3) on a date or time readily ascertainable at the time the promise or order is issued [UCC 3–108(b)]. The maker or drawee is under no obligation to pay until the specified time.

When an instrument is payable by the maker or drawer *on or before* a stated date, it is clearly payable at a definite time. The maker or drawer has the *option* of paying before the stated maturity date, but the payee can still rely on payment being made by the maturity date. The option to pay early does not violate the definite-time requirement. For example, John gives Ernesto an instrument dated May 1, 2011, that indicates on its face that it is payable *on or before* May 1, 2012. This instrument satisfies the definite-time requirement.

In contrast, an instrument that is undated and made payable "one month after date" is clearly nonnegotiable. There is no way to determine the maturity date from the face of the instrument. Whether the time period is a month or a year, if the date is uncertain, the instrument is not payable at a definite time. Thus, an instrument that states, "One year after the death of my grandfather, Jeremy Adams, I promise to pay to the order of Lucy Harmon $5,000. [Signed] Jacqueline Wells," is nonnegotiable.

ACCELERATION CLAUSE An **acceleration clause** allows a payee or other holder of a time instrument to demand payment of the entire amount due, with interest, if a certain event occurs, such as a default in payment of an installment when due. (A **holder** is any person in possession of a negotiable instrument that is payable either to the bearer or to an identified person that is the person in possession [UCC 1–201(20)].)

Assume that Martin lends $1,000 to Ruth, who makes a negotiable note promising to pay $100 per month for eleven months. The note contains an acceleration provision that permits Martin or any holder to immediately demand all the payments plus the interest owed to date if Ruth fails to pay an installment in any given month. If, for example, Ruth fails to make the third payment and Martin accelerates the unpaid balance, the note will be due and payable in full. Ruth will owe Martin the remaining principal plus any unpaid interest to that date.

Under the UCC, instruments that include acceleration clauses are negotiable because (1) the exact value of the instrument can be ascertained and (2) the instrument will be payable on a specified date if the event allowing acceleration does not occur [UCC 3–108(b)(ii)]. Thus, the specified date is the outside limit used to determine the value of the instrument.

In the following case, the question was whether a party entitled to installment payments on a promissory note that contained an acceleration clause waived the right to exercise this provision when the party accepted late payments from the maker.

CASE 24.2
Foundation Property Investments, LLC v. CTP, LLC

Court of Appeals of Kansas, 37 Kan.App.2d 890, 159 P.3d 1042 (2007).
www.kscourts.org/Cases-and-Opinions/opinions[a]

BACKGROUND AND FACTS • In April 2004, CTP, LLC, bought a truck stop in South Hutchinson, Kansas. As part of the deal, CTP borrowed $96,000 from Foundation Property Investments, LLC. The loan was evidenced by a promissory note, which provided that CTP was to make monthly payments of $673.54 between June 1, 2004, and June 1, 2009. The note stated that on default in any payment "the whole amount then unpaid shall become immediately due and payable at the option of the holder without notice." CTP paid the first four installments on or before the due dates, but beginning in October 2004, CTP paid the next nine installments late. In July 2005, citing the late payments, Foundation demanded full payment of the note by the end of the month. CTP responded that the parties' course of dealing permitted payments to be made beyond their due dates. Foundation filed a suit in a Kansas state court against CTP to collect the note's full amount. CTP asserted that Foundation had waived its right to accelerate the note by its acceptance of late payments. The court determined

---

a. In the menu at the left, click on "Search by Docket Number." In the result, in the right column, click on "96000 – 96999." On the next page, scroll to "96697" and click on the number to access the opinion. The Kansas courts, Washburn University School of Law Library, and University of Kansas School of Law Library maintain this Web site.

CASE CONTINUES ▶

CASE 24.2 CONTINUED ▶ that Foundation was entitled to payment of the note in full, plus interest and attorneys' fees and costs, for a total of $110,975.58, and issued a summary judgment in Foundation's favor. CTP appealed to a state intermediate appellate court.

IN THE LANGUAGE OF THE COURT
GREEN, J. [Judge]

* * * *

The general rule is that where a [note] contains an acceleration clause relating to default of a required payment, the [holder] is entitled because of such default to enforce the acceleration clause at once according to its terms. * * * However, *an acceleration clause may be waived. A waiver is the intentional relinquishment of a known right, and intention may be inferred from conduct.* [Emphasis added.]

* * * *

* * * Foundation argues that the provisions of the note should be strictly construed against CTP, because it was the drafter of the note. Foundation also points to one of the note's provisions: "Upon default in payment of any interest, or any installment of principal, the whole amount then unpaid shall become immediately due and payable at the option of the holder without notice." Foundation argues that under this provision, CTP expressly waived demand of payment and notice of nonpayment.

Foundation's arguments afford no basis for saying that it did not waive the condition of prompt payment by routinely accepting late payments. There is no dispute that CTP drafted the note or that the language of the note allowed Foundation to accelerate payment at its option, without notice to CTP. The fact that the note affords Foundation the option to accelerate, however, does not mean that Foundation could not waive the acceleration clause, especially when the note does not contain an anti-waiver provision. Consequently, the question that we must determine is whether Foundation waived the option to accelerate based on its pattern of accepting late payments from CTP.

CTP argues that Foundation's acceptance of late payments over 9 months' time (October 2004–June 2005) established a course of dealing by which late payments would be accepted. *Course of dealing is defined [in Kansas Statutes Annotated Section 84-1-205(1), Kansas's version of UCC 1–205(1)] as a "sequence of previous conduct between the parties to a particular transaction which is fairly to be regarded as establishing a common basis of understanding for interpreting their expressions and other conduct."* [Emphasis added.]

Foundation alleges that course of dealing cannot be found in the present case because this concept * * * only relates to conduct between the parties that occurs before the agreement in question.

Contrary to Foundation's argument, * * * the course of dealing concept is applicable * * *. Absent an anti-waiver provision in the note or actual notice that future late payments will not be accepted, a previous practice of accepting late payments precludes acceleration of the note.

In the present case, there is nothing in the record to indicate that Foundation ever objected to CTP's late payments before the July 2005 letter stating that Foundation was exercising its option to accelerate payment on the note. Foundation's action of accepting late payments from CTP was inconsistent with its claim or right to receive prompt payments. Accordingly, the trial court incorrectly determined that Foundation's conduct did not constitute a waiver of its right of acceleration.

Foundation, however, suggests that CTP suffered no detrimental reliance because Foundation's delay in accelerating the payment actually benefited CTP: the principal balance was less than it would have been had Foundation exercised the acceleration clause upon any of CTP's previous late payments. Nevertheless, CTP had reasonably relied on Foundation accepting late payments without exercising the acceleration clause. Moreover, CTP will clearly suffer prejudice if forced to now pay the note in full. It would be inequitable to permit Foundation to accelerate the entire note without Foundation first giving notice to CTP that Foundation would no longer accept late payments.

DECISION AND REMEDY • *The state intermediate appellate court held that Foundation's acceptance of late payments constituted a waiver of its right to exercise the note's acceleration clause. The appellate court reversed the lower court's ruling and remanded the case with instructions to enter a judgment in CTP's favor.*

CASE 24.2 CONTINUED ➡ **THE E-COMMERCE DIMENSION** • *If Foundation had sent CTP an e-mail threatening to accelerate the note each time CTP's payment was late, would this have been sufficient to support the holder's eventual demand for full payment? Why or why not?*

THE GLOBAL DIMENSION • *Suppose that Foundation was an entity based outside the United States. Could it have successfully claimed, in attempting to enforce the acceleration clause, that it had not given CTP notice because it was not aware of Kansas law? Discuss.*

EXTENSION CLAUSE The reverse of an acceleration clause is an **extension clause,** which allows the date of maturity to be extended into the future [UCC 3–108(b)(iii), (iv)]. To keep the instrument negotiable, the interval of the extension must be specified if the right to extend the time of payment is given to the maker or the drawer of the instrument. If, however, the holder of the instrument can extend the time of payment, the extended maturity date need not be specified.

Suppose that Alek executes a note that reads, "The maker has the right to postpone the time of payment of this note beyond its definite maturity date of January 1, 2012. This extension, however, shall be for no more than a reasonable time." A note with this language is not negotiable because it does not satisfy the definite-time requirement. The right to extend is the maker's, and the maker has not indicated when the note will become due after the extension.

In contrast, suppose that Alek's note reads, "The holder of this note at the date of maturity, January 1, 2012, can extend the time of payment until the following June 1 or later, if the holder so wishes." This note is a negotiable instrument. The length of the extension does not have to be specified because the option to extend is solely that of the holder. After January 1, 2012, the note is, in effect, a demand instrument.

Payable to Order or to Bearer

Because one of the functions of a negotiable instrument is to serve as a substitute for cash, freedom to transfer is essential. To ensure a proper transfer, the instrument must be "payable to order or to bearer" at the time it is issued or first comes into the possession of the holder [UCC 3–104(a)(1)]. An instrument is not negotiable unless it meets this requirement.

ORDER INSTRUMENTS An **order instrument** is an instrument that is payable (1) "to the order of an identified person" or (2) "to an identified person or order" [UCC 3–109(b)]. An identified person is the person "to whom the instrument is initially payable" as determined by the intent of the maker or drawer [UCC 3–110(a)]. The identified person, in turn, may transfer the instrument to whomever he or she wishes. Thus, the maker or drawer is agreeing to pay either the person specified on the instrument or whomever that person might designate. In this way, the instrument retains its transferability. Suppose that an instrument states, "Payable to the order of James Yung" or "Pay to James Yung or order." Clearly, the maker or drawer has indicated that payment will be made to Yung or to whomever Yung designates. The instrument is negotiable.

Note that in order instruments, the person specified must be identified with *certainty* because the transfer of an order instrument requires the indorsement, or signature, of the payee. An *indorsement* is a signature placed on an instrument, such as on the back of a check, generally for the purpose of transferring one's ownership rights in the instrument. Indorsements will be discussed at length in Chapter 25. An order instrument made "Payable to the order of my nicest cousin," for instance, is not negotiable because it does not clearly specify the payee.

BEARER INSTRUMENTS A **bearer instrument** is an instrument that does not designate a specific payee [UCC 3–109(a)]. The term **bearer** refers to a person in possession of an instrument that is payable to bearer or indorsed in blank (with a signature only, as will be discussed in Chapter 25) [UCC 1–201(5), 3–109(a), 3–109(c)]. This means that the maker or drawer agrees to pay anyone who presents the instrument for payment. Any instrument containing terms such as the following is a bearer instrument:

1. "Payable to the order of bearer."
2. "Payable to Simon Reed or bearer."
3. "Payable to bearer."
4. "Pay cash."
5. "Pay to the order of cash."

In addition, an instrument that "indicates that it is not payable to an identified person" is a bearer instrument [UCC 3–109(a)(3)]. Thus, an instrument that is "payable to X" can be negotiated as a bearer instrument, as though it were payable to cash. Similarly, an instrument that is "payable to Batman" is negotiable as a bearer instrument because it is obvious that it is payable to a *nonexistent person*. The UCC does not accept an instrument issued to a *nonexistent organization* as payable to bearer, however [UCC 3–109, Comment 2]. Therefore, an instrument "payable to the order of the Camrod Company," if no such company exists, would not be a bearer instrument or an order instrument and, in fact, would not qualify as a negotiable instrument.

See *Concept Summary 24.1* below for a convenient review of the basic rules governing negotiability.

CONCEPT SUMMARY 24.1
Requirements for Negotiability

Requirements	Basic Rules
Must Be in Writing UCC 3–103(6), (9)	A writing can be on anything that is readily transferable and that has a degree of permanence.
Must Be Signed by the Maker or Drawer UCC 1–201(39) UCC 3–103(a)(3), (5) UCC 3–401(b) UCC 3–402	1. The signature can be anywhere on the face of the instrument. 2. It can be in any form (such as a word, mark, or rubber stamp) that purports to be a signature and authenticates the writing. 3. A signature may be made in a representative capacity.
Must Be a Definite Promise or Order UCC 3–103(a)(6), (9) UCC 3–104(a)	1. A promise must be more than a mere acknowledgment of a debt. 2. The words "I/We promise" or "Pay" meet this criterion.
Must Be Unconditional UCC 3–106	1. Payment cannot be expressly conditional on the occurrence of an event. 2. Payment cannot be made subject to or governed by another agreement.
Must Be an Order or Promise to Pay a Fixed Amount UCC 3–104(a) UCC 3–107 UCC 3–112(b)	An amount may be considered a fixed sum even if payable in installments, with a fixed or variable rate of interest, or at a foreign exchange rate.
Must Be Payable in Money UCC 3–104(a)	1. Any medium of exchange recognized as the currency of a government is money. 2. The maker or drawer cannot retain the option to pay the instrument in money *or* something else.
Must Be Payable on Demand or at a Definite Time UCC 3–104(a)(2) UCC 3–108(a), (b), (c)	1. Any instrument that is payable on sight, presentment, or issue or that does not state any time for payment is a demand instrument. 2. An instrument is still payable at a definite time, even if it is payable on or before a stated date or within a fixed period after sight or if the drawer or maker has the option to extend the time for a definite period. 3. Acceleration clauses do not affect the negotiability of the instrument.
Must Be Payable to Order or to Bearer UCC 3–104(a)(1) UCC 3–109 UCC 3–110(a)	1. An order instrument must identify the payee with reasonable certainty. 2. An instrument whose terms indicate payment to no particular person is payable to bearer.

SECTION 3
FACTORS THAT DO NOT AFFECT NEGOTIABILITY

Certain ambiguities or omissions will not affect the negotiability of an instrument. Article 3's rules for interpreting ambiguous terms include the following:

1. Unless the date of an instrument is necessary to determine a definite time for payment, the fact that an instrument is undated does not affect its negotiability. A typical example is an undated check, which is still negotiable. If a check is not dated, under the UCC its date is the date of its issue, meaning the date on which the drawer first delivers the check to another person to give that person rights on the check [UCC 3–113(b)].

2. Antedating or postdating an instrument does not affect its negotiability [UCC 3–113(a)]. *Antedating* occurs when a party puts a date on an instrument that precedes the actual calendar date. *Postdating* occurs when a party puts a date on an instrument that is after the actual date. For example, Crenshaw draws a check on his account at First Bank, payable to Sung Imports. He postdates the check by fifteen days. Sung Imports can immediately negotiate the check, and, unless Crenshaw tells First Bank otherwise, the bank can charge the amount of the check to Crenshaw's account [UCC 4–401(c)].

3. Handwritten terms outweigh typewritten and printed terms (preprinted terms on forms, for example), and typewritten terms outweigh printed terms [UCC 3–114]. For example, your check (like most checks) has printed on it "Pay to the order of" with a blank next to it. In handwriting, you insert in the blank "Anita Delgado or bearer." The handwritten terms will outweigh the printed form (an order instrument), and the check will be a bearer instrument.

4. Words outweigh figures unless the words are ambiguous [UCC 3–114]. This rule becomes important when the numerical amount and the written amount on a check differ. Suppose that Paruzzo issues a check payable to Cheaper Appliance Company. For the amount, she fills in the number "$100" but writes out the words "One thousand and 00/100" dollars. The check is payable in the amount of $1,000.

5. When an instrument simply states "with interest" and does not specify a particular interest rate, the interest rate is the *judgment rate of interest* (a rate of interest fixed by statute that is applied to a monetary judgment awarded by a court until the judgment is paid or terminated) [UCC 3–112(b)].

6. A check is negotiable even if there is a notation on it stating that it is "nonnegotiable" or "not governed by Article 3." Any other instrument, however, can be made nonnegotiable by the maker's or drawer's conspicuously noting on it that it is "nonnegotiable" or "not governed by Article 3" [UCC 3–104(d)].

REVIEWING
The Function and Creation of Negotiable Instruments

Robert Durbin, a student, borrowed funds from a bank for his education and signed a promissory note for their repayment. The bank lent the funds under a federal program designed to assist students at postsecondary institutions. Under this program, repayment ordinarily begins nine to twelve months after the student borrower fails to carry at least one-half of the normal full-time course load at his or her school. The federal government guarantees that the note will be fully repaid. If the student defaults on the repayment, the lender presents the current balance—principal, interest, and costs—to the government. When the government pays the balance, it becomes the lender, and the borrower owes the government directly. After Durbin defaulted on his note, the government paid the lender the balance due and took possession of the note. Durbin then refused to pay the government, claiming that the government was not the holder of the note. The government filed a suit in a federal district court against Durbin to collect the amount due. Using the information presented in the chapter, answer the following questions.

1. Using the categories discussed in the chapter, what type of negotiable instrument was the note that Durbin signed (an order to pay or a promise to pay)? Explain.

REVIEWING CONTINUES ▶

REVIEWING

The Function and Creation of Negotiable Instruments, Continued

2. Suppose that the note did not state a specific interest rate but instead referred to a statute that established the maximum interest rate for government-guaranteed school loans. Would the note fail to meet the requirements for negotiability in that situation? Why or why not?

3. For the government to be a holder, which method must have been used to transfer the instrument from the bank to the government?

4. Suppose that in court, Durbin argues that because the school closed down before he could finish his education, there was a failure of consideration: he did not get something of value in exchange for his promise to pay. Assuming that the government is a holder of the promissory note, would this argument likely be successful against it? Why or why not?

⚫ DEBATE THIS: *An amendment to the 2010 health-care reform bill eliminated privately provided student loans guaranteed by the federal government. Now all student loans come directly from the government. Students will benefit.*

TERMS AND CONCEPTS

acceleration clause 471

acceptance 463

acceptor 469

banker's acceptance 464

bearer 473

bearer instrument 473

certificate of
    deposit (CD) 466

check 464

draft 463

drawee 463

drawer 463

extension clause 473

holder 471

issue 462

maker 464

negotiable instrument 462

order instrument 473

payee 463

presentment 469

promissory note 464

signature 467

trade acceptance 463

QUESTIONS AND CASE PROBLEMS

24–1. Negotiable Instruments Sabrina Runyan writes the following note on a sheet of paper: "I, the undersigned, do hereby acknowledge that I owe Leo Woo one thousand dollars, with interest, payable out of the proceeds of the sale of my horse, Lightning, next month. Payment is to be made on or before six months from date." Discuss specifically why this is not a negotiable instrument.

24–2. QUESTION WITH SAMPLE ANSWER: Negotiability.

Juan Sanchez writes the following note on the back of an envelope: "I, Juan Sanchez, promise to pay Kathy Martin or bearer $500 on demand." Is this a negotiable instrument? Discuss fully.

- **For a sample answer to Question 24–2, go to Appendix I at the end of this text.**

24–3. Promissory Notes A college student, Austin Keynes, wished to purchase a new entertainment system from Friedman Electronics, Inc. Because Keynes did not have the cash to pay for the entertainment system, he offered to sign a note promising to pay $150 per month for the next six months. Friedman Electronics, eager to sell the system to Keynes, agreed to accept the promissory note, which read, "I, Austin Keynes, promise to pay to Friedman Electronics or its order the sum of $150 per month for the next six months." The note was signed by Austin Keynes. About a week later, Friedman Electronics, which was badly in need of cash, signed the back of the note and sold it to the First National Bank of Halston. Give the specific designation of each of the three parties on this note.

24–4. Bearer Instruments Adam's checks are imprinted with the words "Pay to the order of" followed by a blank. Adam fills in an amount on one of the checks and signs it, but he does not write anything in the blank following the "Pay to the order of" language. Adam gives this check to Beth. On another check, Adam writes in the blank "Carl or bearer." Which, if either, of these checks is a bearer instrument, and why?

24–5. Negotiability In October 1998, Somerset Valley Bank notified Alfred Hauser, president of Hauser Co., that the bank had begun to receive what appeared to be Hauser Co. payroll checks. None of the payees were Hauser Co. employees, however, and Hauser had not written the checks or authorized anyone to sign them on his behalf. Automatic Data Processing, Inc., provided payroll services for Hauser Co. and used a facsimile signature on all its payroll checks. Hauser told the bank not to cash the checks. In early 1999, Robert Triffin, who deals in negotiable instruments, bought eighteen of the checks, totaling more than $8,800, from various check-cashing agencies. The agencies stated that they had cashed the checks expecting the bank to pay them. Each check was payable to a bearer for a fixed amount, on demand, and did not state any undertaking by the person promising payment other than the payment of money. Each check bore a facsimile drawer's signature stamp identical to Hauser Co.'s authorized stamp. Each check had been returned to an agency marked "stolen check" and stamped "do not present again." When the bank refused to cash the checks, Triffin filed a suit in a New Jersey state court against Hauser Co. Were the checks negotiable instruments? Why or why not? [*Triffin v. Somerset Valley Bank,* 343 N.J.Super. 73, 777 A.2d 993 (2001)]

24–6. Negotiability In October 1996, Robert Hildebrandt contracted with Harvey and Nancy Anderson to find a tenant for the Andersons' used-car lot. The Andersons agreed to pay Hildebrandt "a commission equal in amount to five percent up to first three years of lease." On December 12, Paramount Automotive, Inc., agreed to lease the premises for three years at $7,500 per month, and the Andersons signed a promissory note, which stated that they would pay Hildebrandt $13,500, plus interest, in consecutive monthly installments of $485 until the total sum was paid. The note contained an acceleration clause. In a separate agreement, Paramount promised to pay $485 of its monthly rent directly to Hildebrandt. Less than a year later, Paramount stopped making payments to all parties. To enforce the note, Hildebrandt filed a suit in an Oregon state court against the Andersons. One issue in the case was whether the note was a negotiable instrument. The Andersons claimed that it was not, because it was not "unconditional," arguing that their obligation to make payments on the note was conditioned on their receipt of rent from Paramount. Are the Andersons correct? Explain. [*Hildebrandt v. Anderson,* 180 Or.App. 192, 42 P.3d 355 (2002)]

24–7. Cashier's Checks In July 1981, Southeast Bank in Miami, Florida, issued five cashier's checks, totaling $450,000, to five payees, including Roberto Sanchez. Two months later, in Colombia, South America, Sanchez gave the checks to Juan Diaz. In 1991, Southeast failed. Under federal law, notice must be mailed to a failed bank's depositors, who then have eighteen months to file a claim for their funds. Under an "Assistance Agreement,"

First Union National Bank agreed to assume Southeast's liability for outstanding cashier's checks and other items. First Union received funds to pay these items but was required to return the funds if, within eighteen months after Southeast's closing, payment for any item had not been claimed. In 1996, in Colombia, Diaz gave the five cashier's checks that he had received from Sanchez to John Acevedo in payment of a debt. In 2001, Acevedo tendered these checks to First Union for payment. Does First Union have to pay? Would it make any difference if the required notice had not been mailed? Why or why not? [*Acevedo v. First Union National Bank,* 357 F.3d 1244 (11th Cir. 2004)]

24–8. CASE PROBLEM WITH SAMPLE ANSWER: Negotiability.

 In September 2001, Cory Babcock and Honest Air Conditioning & Heating, Inc., bought a new 2001 Chevrolet Corvette from Cox Chevrolet in Sarasota, Florida. Their retail installment sales contract (RISC) required monthly payments until $52,516.20 was paid. The RISC imposed many other conditions on the buyers and seller with respect to the payment for, and handling of, the Corvette. Cox assigned the RISC to General Motors Acceptance Corp. (GMAC). In August 2002, the buyers sold the car to Florida Auto Brokers, which agreed to pay the balance due on the RISC. The check to GMAC for this amount was dishonored for insufficient funds, however, after the vehicle's title had been forwarded. GMAC filed a suit in a Florida state court against Honest Air and Babcock, seeking $35,815.26 as damages for breach of contract. The defendants argued that the RISC was a negotiable instrument. A ruling in their favor on this point would reduce any damages due GMAC to less than the Corvette's current value. What are the requirements for an instrument to be negotiable? Does the RISC qualify? Explain. [General Motors Acceptance Corp. v. Honest Air Conditioning & Heating, Inc., *933 So.2d 34 (Fla.App. 2 Dist. 2006)]*

- **To view a sample answer for Problem 24–8, go to this book's Web site at www.cengage.com/blaw/clarkson, select "Chapter 24," and click on "Case Problem with Sample Answer."**

24–9. A QUESTION OF ETHICS: Promissory Notes.

 In November 2000, Monay Jones signed a promissory note in favor of a mortgage company in the amount of $261,250, using the deed to her home in Denver, Colorado, as collateral. Fifth Third Bank soon became the holder of the note. After Jones defaulted on the payment, in September 2001 she and the bank agreed to raise the note's balance to $280,231.23. She again defaulted. In November, the bank received a check from a third party as payment on Jones's note. It was the bank's policy to refuse personal checks in payoff of large debts. The bank representative who worked on Jones's account noted receipt of the check in the bank's records and forwarded it to the "payoff department." A week later, the bank discovered that the check had been lost without having been posted to Jones's account or submitted for payment. The bank notified Jones, and both parties searched, without success, for a copy of the check or evidence of the identity of its maker, the drawee bank, or the amount. In late 2002, the bank filed a suit in a

Colorado state court to foreclose on Jones's home. She insisted that the note had been paid in full by a cashier's check issued by an Arkansas bank at the request of her deceased aunt. [Fifth Third Bank v. Jones, 168 P.3d 1 (Colo.App. 2007)]

(a) What evidence supports a finding that Jones gave the bank a check? Does it seem more likely that the check was a cashier's check or a personal check? Would it be fair for a court to find that the check had paid the note in full?

(b) Under UCC 3–310, if a cashier's check or other certified check "is taken for an obligation, the obligation is discharged." The bank argued that it had not "taken [Jones's check] for an obligation" because the bank's internal administrative actions were still pending when the check was lost. Would it be fair for the court to rule in the bank's favor based on this argument? Why or why not?

24–10. VIDEO QUESTION: Negotiable Instruments.

 Go to this text's Web site at **www.cengage.com/blaw/clarkson** and select "Chapter 24." Click on "Video Questions" and view the video titled *Negotiable Instruments*. Then answer the following questions.

(a) Who is the maker of the promissory note discussed in the video?

(b) Is the note in the video payable on demand or at a definite time?

(c) Does the note contain an unconditional promise or order to pay?

(d) If the note does not meet the requirements of negotiability, can Onyx assign the note (assignment was discussed in Chapter 16) to the bank in exchange for cash?

LEGAL RESEARCH EXERCISES ON THE WEB

Go to this text's Web site at **www.cengage.com/blaw/clarkson**, select "Chapter 24," and click on "Practical Internet Exercises." There you will find the following Internet research exercises that you can perform to learn more about the topics covered in this chapter.

Practical Internet Exercise 24–1: **Legal Perspective**
Overview of Negotiable Instruments

Practical Internet Exercise 24–2: **Management Perspective**
Banks and Bank Accounts

CHAPTER 25

Transferability and Holder in Due Course

O nce issued, a negotiable instrument can be transferred to others by *assignment* or by *negotiation*. Recall from Chapter 16 that an assignment is a transfer of rights under a contract. Under contract law principles, a transfer by assignment to an assignee gives the assignee only those rights that the assignor possessed. Any defenses that can be raised against an assignor can normally be raised against the assignee. This same rule applies when a negotiable instrument, such as

a promissory note, is transferred by assignment to an assignee: the assignee receives only those rights in the instrument that the assignor had prior to the assignment.

In contrast, when an instrument is transferred by **negotiation**, the Uniform Commercial Code (UCC) provides that the transferee (the person to whom the instrument is transferred) becomes a *holder* [UCC 3–201(a)]. A holder receives, at the very least, the rights of the previous possessor [UCC 3–203(b),

3–305]. But unlike an assignment, a transfer by negotiation can make it possible for a holder to receive *more* rights in the instrument than the prior possessor had [UCC 3–305]. A holder who receives greater rights is known as a *holder in due course,* a concept we discuss in this chapter. First, though, we look at the requirements for negotiation and examine the various types of *indorsements* that are used when order instruments are negotiated.

SECTION 1

NEGOTIATION

As just described, negotiation is the transfer of an instrument in such form that the transferee becomes a holder. There are two methods of negotiating an instrument so that the receiver becomes a holder. The method used depends on whether the instrument is an *order instrument* or a *bearer instrument.*

Negotiating Order Instruments

An order instrument contains the name of a payee capable of indorsing, as in "Pay to the order of Elliot Goodseal." If an instrument is an order instrument, it is negotiated by delivery with any necessary indorsements (*indorsements* will be discussed shortly). For example, the Welpac Corporation issues a payroll check "to the order of Elliot Goodseal." Goodseal takes the check to the bank, signs his name on the back (an indorsement), gives it to the teller (a

delivery), and receives cash. Goodseal has negotiated the check to the bank [UCC 3–201(b)].

Negotiating order instruments requires both delivery and indorsement. If Goodseal had taken the check to the bank and delivered it to the teller without signing it, the transfer would not qualify as a negotiation. In that situation, the transfer would be treated as an assignment, and the bank would become an assignee rather than a holder. In fact, whenever a transfer fails to qualify as a negotiation because it fails to meet one or more of the requirements of a negotiable instrument, it is treated as an assignment.

Negotiating Bearer Instruments

If an instrument is payable to bearer, it is negotiated by delivery—that is, by transfer into another person's possession. Indorsement is not necessary [UCC 3–201(b)]. The use of bearer instruments thus involves a greater risk of loss or theft than the use of order instruments.

Assume that Alonzo Cruz writes a check payable to "cash," thus creating a bearer instrument. Cruz then hands the check to Blaine Parrington (a delivery). Parrington puts the check in his wallet, which is subsequently stolen. The thief now has possession of the check. At this point, the thief has no rights in the check. If the thief "delivers" the check to an innocent third person, however, negotiation will be complete. All rights to the check will pass *absolutely* to that third person, and Parrington will lose all right to recover the proceeds of the check from that person [UCC 3–306]. Of course, Parrington can recover his funds from the thief, if the thief can be found.

SECTION 2

INDORSEMENTS

An indorsement is required whenever an order instrument is negotiated. An **indorsement** is a signature with or without additional words or statements. It is most often written on the back of the instrument itself. If there is no room on the instrument, the indorsement can be written on a separate piece of paper (called an *allonge*) that is firmly affixed to the instrument, such as with staples. A paper firmly attached to a negotiable instrument is part of the instrument [UCC 3–204(a)].

A person who transfers a note or a draft by signing (indorsing) it and delivering it to another person is an **indorser.** The person to whom the check is indorsed and delivered is the **indorsee.** For example, Luisa Parks receives a graduation check for $100. She can transfer the check to her mother (or to anyone) by signing it on the back. Luisa is an indorser. If Luisa indorses the check by writing "Pay to Avery Parks," Avery Parks is the indorsee.

Here, we examine four categories of indorsements: blank, special, qualified, and restrictive. Note that a single indorsement may have characteristics of more than one category. In other words, these categories are not mutually exclusive.

Blank Indorsements

A **blank indorsement** does not specify a particular indorsee and can consist of a mere signature [UCC 3–205(b)]. Hence, a check payable "to the order of Mark Deitsch" can be indorsed in blank simply by writing Deitsch's signature on the back

of the check. Exhibit 25–1 below shows a blank indorsement.

EXHIBIT 25–1 • A Blank Indorsement

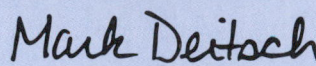

An order instrument indorsed in blank becomes a bearer instrument and can be negotiated by delivery alone [UCC 3–205(b)]. In other words, as will be discussed later, a blank indorsement converts an order instrument to a bearer instrument, which anybody can cash. Suppose that Rita Chou indorses in blank a check payable to her order and then loses it on the street. If Schaefer finds the check, he can sell it to Duncan for value without indorsing it. This constitutes a negotiation because Schaefer has made delivery of a bearer instrument (which was an order instrument until it was indorsed in blank).

Special Indorsements

A **special indorsement** contains the signature of the indorser and identifies the person to whom the indorser intends to make the instrument payable; that is, it names the indorsee [UCC 3–205(a)]. For example, words such as "Pay to the order of Russell Clay" or "Pay to Russell Clay," followed by the signature of the indorser, are sufficient. When an instrument is indorsed in this way, it is an order instrument.

To avoid the risk of loss from theft, a holder may convert a blank indorsement to a special indorsement by writing, above the signature of the indorser, words identifying the indorsee [UCC 3–205(c)]. This changes the bearer instrument back to an order instrument. For example, a check is made payable to Hal Cohen. He signs his name on the back of the check—a blank indorsement—and negotiates the check by delivering it to William Hunter. Hunter is not able to cash the check immediately but wants to avoid any risk should he lose the check. He therefore writes "Pay to William Hunter" above Cohen's blank indorsement. In this manner, Hunter has converted Cohen's blank indorsement into a special indorsement. Further negotiation now requires William Hunter's indorsement, plus delivery. Exhibit 25–2 on the facing page shows a special indorsement.

EXHIBIT 25–2 • A Special Indorsement

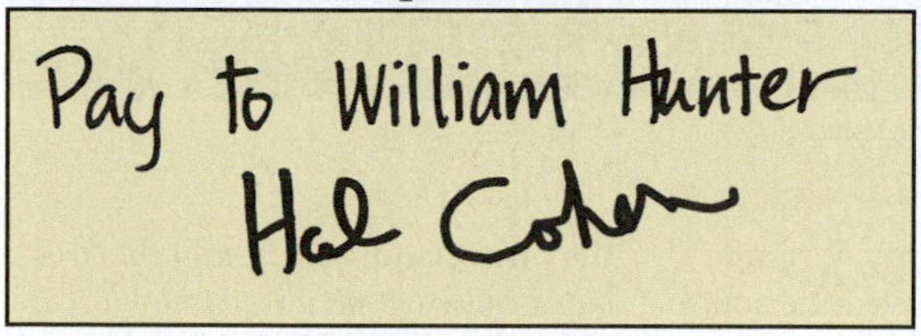

Pay to William Hunter
Hal Cohen

Qualified Indorsements

Generally, an indorser, *merely by indorsing,* impliedly promises to pay the holder, or any subsequent indorser, the amount of the instrument in the event that the drawer or maker defaults on the payment [UCC 3–415(a)]. Usually, then, indorsements are *unqualified indorsements.* In other words, the indorser is guaranteeing payment of the instrument in addition to transferring title to it. An indorser who does not wish to be liable on an instrument can use a **qualified indorsement** to disclaim this liability [UCC 3–415(b)]. The notation "without recourse" is commonly used to create a qualified indorsement.

Suppose that a check is made payable to the order of Sarah Jacobs. Sarah wants to negotiate the check to Allison Jong but does not want to assume liability for the check's payment. Sarah could create a qualified indorsement by indorsing the check as follows: "Pay to Allison Jong, without recourse, [signed] Sarah Jacobs" (see Exhibit 25–3 below).

EXHIBIT 25–3 • A Qualified Indorsement

Pay to Allison Jong,
without recourse
Sarah Jacobs

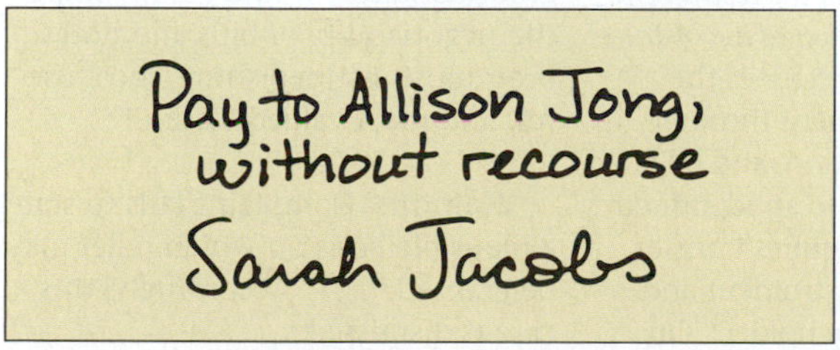

THE EFFECT OF QUALIFIED INDORSEMENTS Qualified indorsements are often used by persons (agents) acting in a representative capacity. For example, insurance agents sometimes receive checks payable to them that are really intended as payment to the insurance company. The agent is merely indorsing the payment through to the insurance company and should not be required to make good on a check if it is later dishonored. The "without recourse" indorsement relieves the agent from any liability on the check. If the instrument is dishonored, the holder cannot recover from the agent who indorsed "without recourse" unless the indorser breached one

of the transfer warranties that will be discussed in Chapter 26. These warranties relate to good title, authorized signature, no material alteration, and other requirements.

SPECIAL VERSUS BLANK QUALIFIED INDORSEMENTS
A qualified indorsement ("without recourse") can be accompanied by either a special indorsement or a blank indorsement. A special qualified indorsement includes the name of the indorsee as well as the words "without recourse," as shown in Exhibit 25–3 in the left column below. The special indorsement makes the instrument an order instrument, and it requires an indorsement, plus delivery, for negotiation. A blank qualified indorsement ("without recourse, [signed] Jennie Cole") makes the instrument a bearer instrument, and only delivery is required for negotiation. In either situation, the instrument still transfers title and can be further negotiated.

CASE IN POINT Chester Crow executed a promissory note payable "to the order of The First National Bank of Shreveport or bearer" in the amount of $21,578.42. More than ten years later, Credit Recoveries, Inc., filed a suit alleging that Crow still owed $7,222.57 on the note. Crow responded that Premier Bank, the successor to First National Bank of Shreveport, had canceled the note. Crow also argued that although Credit Recoveries was in possession of the note, it was not listed as the payee and had not proved it owned the note. On the back of the note was the following qualified indorsement: "Pay to the Order of Credit Recoveries, Inc., without recourse [signed, the vice president of] Premier Bank." The trial court dismissed the case, but the state appellate court held that because the note was made payable to bearer (or to the bank), it was bearer paper and could have been transferred by mere delivery to Credit Recoveries. Any later indorsement did not change the fact that Credit Recoveries had title to, and was a holder of, the note. Credit Recoveries was entitled to present the note as evidence at trial, and the trial court should have admitted it and then allowed Crow to present any defenses he had to payment of the note.[1]

The following case illustrates the effect of a blank qualified indorsement.

---

1. *Credit Recoveries, Inc. v. Crow,* 862 So.2d 1146 (La.App. 2 Cir. 2003).

✹ EXTENDED CASE 25.1 ✹
Hammett v. Deutsche Bank National Co.

United States District Court, Eastern District of Virginia, ___ F.Supp.2d ___ (2010).

IN THE LANGUAGE OF THE COURT
Liam *O'GRADY*, District Judge.
* * * *

On October 6, 2005 Plaintiffs [Vernon Hammett and others] purchased a residential property in Alexandria. As part of that transaction, Plaintiffs executed a promissory note (the "Note") in the amount of $475,000 and a deed of trust[a] (the "Deed") securing the note in favor of Encore Credit Corporation ("Encore").

The Note was presented to the Court with an attached "allonge"[b] which contains a blank endorsement which reads: "Pay To The Order Of ___ Without Recourse Encore Credit Corp. A California Corporation." Defendants [Deutsche Bank National Company and others] are now in possession of the Note.

At some point after executing the Note and the Deed, Plaintiffs "refused" to continue paying on their obligation under the Note. Defendants then initiated foreclosure proceedings[c] on the Property. Defendant Deutsche Bank * * * subsequently purchased the property at the foreclosure sale * * * .

* * * *

Plaintiffs filed their Complaint on September 8, 2009 in the Circuit Court for Fairfax County, Virginia. Defendants then removed the action to this Court and filed motions to dismiss on January 13, 2010 and February 25, 2010, respectively.

* * * *

Plaintiffs allege that the entities which foreclosed on their home are not entitled as a matter of law to do so. Specifically, Plaintiffs allege that "Defendants have no legal or equitable right or interest in the Promissory Note and/or the Deed of Trust * * * . However, nothing in Plaintiffs' conclusory [convincing, but not definitive] allegations provides a plausible basis for relief after considering the settled law of negotiable instruments or the enforcement of a deed of trust securing notes after their negotiation.

Under Virginia law, *the holder of an instrument or a nonholder in possession of the instrument with the same rights as the holder may enforce the instrument. Further, an individual may be "entitled to enforce the instrument even though the person is not the owner of the instrument or is in wrongful possession of the instrument."* An individual becomes the "holder" of an instrument through the process of negotiation, and if "an instrument is payable to an identified person, negotiation requires transfer of possession of the instrument and its endorsement by the holder." On the other hand, *if an instrument has a blank endorsement, it is considered "payable to bearer," and it may be negotiated by transfer of possession alone.* In this case, the face of the Note shows that the Note has a blank endorsement. Accordingly, it may be negotiated by a simple change in possession and enforced by its current possessor, Deutsche Bank. [Emphasis added.]

Further, absent a contrary provision, notes are generally freely transferable, and the transferee retains the right to enforce the instrument. The explicit terms of the Note at issue here indicate that it is freely transferable. ("I understand that the Lender may transfer this Note. The Lender or anyone who takes this Note by transfer and who is entitled to receive payments under this Note is called the Note Holder").

By their own allegations, Plaintiffs admit they "refused to pay" on the Note. * * * To permit the parties to the [instrument] to object to its payment, on any of the grounds stated, would greatly impair the negotiability of bills and notes[,] their most distinguishing, most useful, and most valued feature."

* * * *

Plaintiffs' Complaint fails to state a plausible basis on which relief may be granted. * * * Accordingly, this case is dismissed.

---

a. As you will read in Chapter 50, a *deed* is a document by which real property, or realty, is transferred from one party to another. With a *deed of trust,* a type of instrument in use in some states, legal title to real property is held by one or more trustees. A deed of trust is used to secure the repayment of funds or to meet some other condition.

b. An *allonge* (pronounced uh-*lonj*) is a piece of paper firmly attached to a negotiable instrument, on which indorsements can be made if there is no room on the instrument.

c. Mortgages and foreclosure proceedings will be discussed in Chapter 31.

✹ QUESTIONS

1. How do the requirements for negotiation of an instrument with a blank qualified indorsement, as was used in this case, differ from those for negotiation of an instrument with a special qualified indorsement?
2. Suppose that the indorsement at issue in this case had been written on a separate document that was not firmly affixed to the note. Would this document have constituted an allonge? Would Deutsche Bank be entitled to enforce the note? Explain.

Restrictive Indorsements

A **restrictive indorsement** requires the indorsee to comply with certain instructions regarding the funds involved but does not prohibit further negotiation of the instrument [UCC 3–206(a)]. Although most indorsements are nonrestrictive, many forms of restrictive indorsements exist, including those discussed here.

INDORSEMENTS PROHIBITING FURTHER INDORSEMENT

An indorsement such as "Pay to Julie Diaz only, [signed] Thomas Fasulo" does not destroy negotiability. Diaz can negotiate the paper to a holder just as if it had read "Pay to Julie Diaz, [signed] Thomas Fasulo" [UCC 3–206(a)]. If the holder gives value, this type of restrictive indorsement has the same legal effect as a special indorsement.

CONDITIONAL INDORSEMENTS When payment depends on the occurrence of some event specified in the indorsement, the instrument has a conditional indorsement [UCC 3–204(a)]. For example, Ken Barton indorses a check as follows: "Pay to Lars Johansen if he completes the renovation of my kitchen by June 1, 2012, [signed] Ken Barton." Barton has created a conditional indorsement.

Article 3 states that an indorsement conditioning the right to receive payment "does not affect the right of the indorsee to enforce the instrument" [UCC 3–206(b)]. A person paying or taking an instrument for value (*taking for value* will be discussed later in the chapter) can disregard the condition without liability.

The effect of a conditional indorsement, which appears on the back of an instrument, differs from the effect of conditional language that appears on the *face* (front) of an instrument. As noted, conditional instruments do not prevent further negotiation. In contrast, an instrument with conditional language on its face is not negotiable, because it does not meet the requirement that a negotiable instrument must contain an unconditional promise to pay.

INDORSEMENTS FOR DEPOSIT OR COLLECTION A common type of restrictive indorsement makes the indorsee (almost always a bank) a collecting agent of the indorser [UCC 3–206(c)]. Exhibit 25–4 (above right) illustrates this type of indorsement on a check payable and issued to Marcel Dumont. In particular, the indorsements "For deposit only" and "For collection only" have the effect of locking the instrument into the bank collection process. Only a bank can acquire the rights of a holder following one of these indorsements until the item has been specially indorsed by a bank to a person who is not a bank [UCC 3–206(c), 4–201(b)]. A bank's liability for

EXHIBIT 25–4 • "For Deposit Only" and "For Collection Only" Indorsements

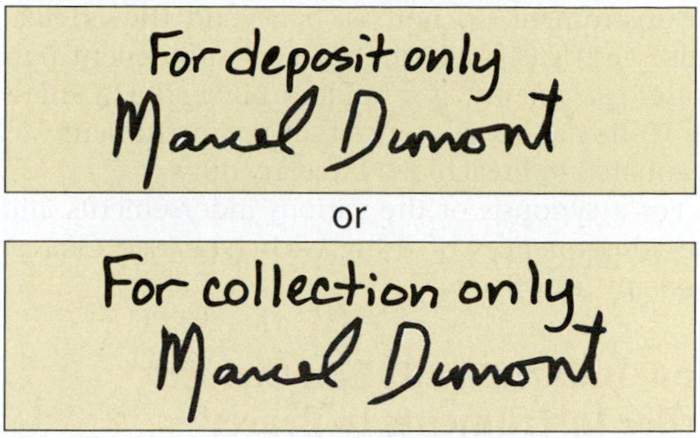

payment of an instrument with a restrictive indorsement of this kind will be discussed in Chapter 27.

TRUST (AGENCY) INDORSEMENTS Indorsements to persons who are to hold or use the funds for the benefit of the indorser or a third party are called **trust indorsements** (also known as *agency indorsements*) [UCC 3–206(d), (e)]. For example, Ralph Zimmer asks his accountant, Stephanie Contento, to pay some bills for him while he is out of the country. He indorses a check, drawn by a friend, to Stephanie Contento "as agent for Ralph Zimmer." This trust (agency) indorsement obligates Contento to use the funds from his friend's check only for the benefit of Zimmer.

The result of a trust indorsement is that legal rights in the instrument are transferred to the original indorsee. To the extent that the original indorsee pays or applies the proceeds consistently with the indorsement (for example, in an indorsement stating "Pay to Ellen Cook in trust for Roger Callahan"), the indorsee is a holder and can become a holder in due course (a status that will be described shortly). Sample trust (agency) indorsements are shown in Exhibit 25–5.

EXHIBIT 25–5 • Trust (Agency) Indorsements

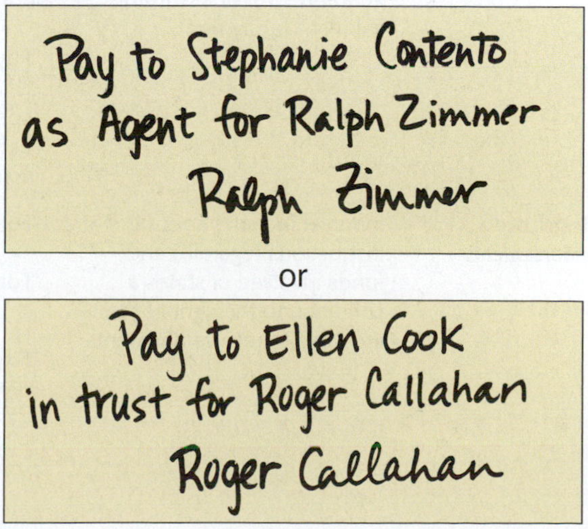

The fiduciary restrictions—restrictions mandated by a relationship involving trust and loyalty—on the instrument do not reach beyond the original indorsee [UCC 3–206(d), (e)]. Any subsequent purchaser can qualify as a holder in due course unless he or she has actual notice that the instrument was negotiated in breach of a fiduciary duty.

For a synopsis of the various indorsements and the consequences of using each type, see *Concept Summary 25.1* below.

How Indorsements Can Convert Order Instruments to Bearer Instruments and Vice Versa

Earlier we saw that order instruments and bearer instruments are negotiated differently. The method used for negotiation depends on the character of the instrument *at the time the negotiation takes place.* Indorsement can convert an order instrument into a bearer instrument. For example, a check originally payable to "cash" but subsequently indorsed with the words "Pay to Arnold" must be negotiated as an order instrument (by indorsement and delivery), even though it was previously a bearer instrument [UCC 3–205(a)].

As mentioned earlier, an instrument payable to the order of a named payee and indorsed in blank becomes a bearer instrument [UCC 3–205(b)]. For example, a check made payable to the order of Jessie Arnold is issued to Arnold, and Arnold indorses it by signing her name on the back. The instrument, which is now a bearer instrument, can be negotiated by delivery without indorsement. Arnold can negotiate the check to whomever she wishes merely by delivery, and that person can negotiate by delivery

---

CONCEPT SUMMARY 25.1
Types of Indorsements and Their Effect

Type of Indorsement	Description	Examples	Legal Effect
Blank Indorsements	Indorser does not identify the person to whom the instrument is payable; can consist of a mere signature.	"Elana Guiterrez" "Mark Deitsch"	Creates a bearer instrument, which can be negotiated by delivery alone.
Special Indorsements	Indorser identifies the person to whom the instrument is payable.	"Pay to the order of Russell Clay" "Pay to William Hunter"	Creates an order instrument; negotiation requires indorsement and delivery.
Qualified Indorsements	Indorser includes words indicating that he or she is not guaranteeing or assuming liability for payment.	"Without recourse, Elana Guitterez" (blank qualified indorsement) "Pay to Allison Jong without recourse, Sarah Jacobs" (special qualified indorsement, which creates an order instrument)	Relieves indorser of any liability for payment of the instrument; frequently used by agents or others acting on behalf of another.
Restrictive Indorsements	Indorser includes specific instructions regarding the funds involved or states a condition to the right of the indorsee to receive payment.	"For deposit only" "For collection only"	Only a bank can become a holder of instruments that are indorsed for deposit or collection.
		"Pay to Stephanie Contento as agent for Ralph Zimmer" "Pay to Ellen Cook in trust for Roger Callahan"	In a trust indorsement, the third party agent or trustee has the rights of a holder but has fiduciary duties to use the funds consistently with the indorsement.

without indorsement. If Arnold loses the check after she indorses it, anyone who finds the check can negotiate it further.

Similarly, a bearer instrument can be converted into an order instrument through indorsement. Suppose that Arnold takes the check that she indorsed in blank (now a bearer instrument) and negotiates it, by delivery, to Jonas Tolling. Tolling indorses the check "Pay to Mark Hyatt, [signed] Jonas Tolling." By adding this special indorsement, Tolling has converted the check into an order instrument. The check can be further negotiated only by indorsement (by Mark Hyatt) and delivery [UCC 3–205(b)]. Exhibit 25–6 below illustrates how an indorsement can convert an order instrument into a bearer instrument and vice versa.

SECTION 3
MISCELLANEOUS INDORSEMENT PROBLEMS

Of course, a significant problem occurs when an indorsement is forged or unauthorized. The UCC rules concerning unauthorized or forged signatures and indorsements will be discussed in Chapter 26 in the context of signature liability. These rules will be examined again in Chapter 27 in the context of the bank's liability for payment of an instrument containing an unauthorized signature. Here we look at some other difficulties that may arise with indorsements.

Misspelled Names

An indorsement should be identical to the name that appears on the instrument. A payee or indorsee whose name is misspelled can indorse with the misspelled name, the correct name, or both [UCC 3–204(d)]. For example, if Marie Ellison receives a check payable to the order of Mary Ellison, she can indorse the check either "Marie Ellison" or "Mary Ellison." The usual practice is to indorse with the name as it appears on the instrument followed by the correct name.

Instruments Payable to Entities

A negotiable instrument can be drawn payable to an entity such as an estate, a partnership, or an organization. In this situation, an authorized representative of the entity can negotiate the instrument. For example, a check may read "Pay to the order of the Red Cross." An authorized representative of the Red Cross can negotiate this check. Similarly, negotiable paper can be payable to a public officer. For example, checks reading "Pay to the order of the County Tax Collector" or "Pay to the order of Larry White, Receiver of Taxes" can be negotiated by whoever holds the office [UCC 3–110(c)].

Alternative or Joint Payees

An instrument payable to two or more persons *in the alternative* (for example, "Pay to the order of Ying or Mifflin") requires the indorsement of only one of

EXHIBIT 25–6 • Converting an Order Instrument to a Bearer Instrument and Vice Versa

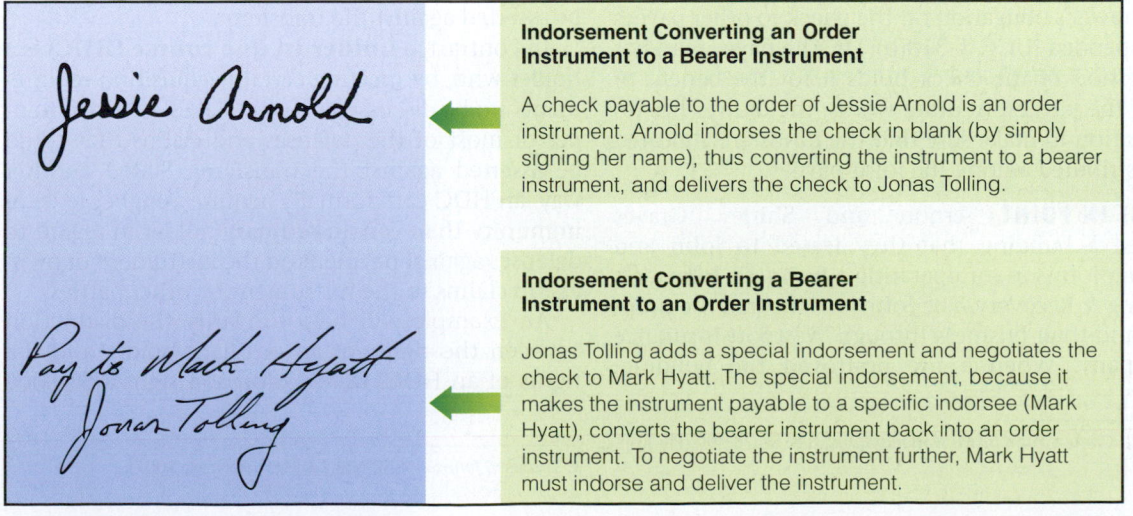

Indorsement Converting an Order Instrument to a Bearer Instrument

A check payable to the order of Jessie Arnold is an order instrument. Arnold indorses the check in blank (by simply signing her name), thus converting the instrument to a bearer instrument, and delivers the check to Jonas Tolling.

Indorsement Converting a Bearer Instrument to an Order Instrument

Jonas Tolling adds a special indorsement and negotiates the check to Mark Hyatt. The special indorsement, because it makes the instrument payable to a specific indorsee (Mark Hyatt), converts the bearer instrument back into an order instrument. To negotiate the instrument further, Mark Hyatt must indorse and deliver the instrument.

the payees [UCC 3–110(d)]. If, however, an instrument is made payable to two or more persons *jointly* (for example, "Pay to the order of Bridgette and Tony Van Horn"), all of the payees' indorsements are necessary for negotiation.

ALTERNATIVE PAYEES PRESUMED IF THE INSTRUMENT IS AMBIGUOUS

If an instrument payable to two or more persons does not clearly indicate whether it is payable in the alternative or payable jointly, then "the instrument is payable to the persons alternatively" [UCC 3–110(d)]. The same principles apply to special indorsements that identify more than one person to whom the indorser intends to make the instrument payable [UCC 3–205(a)].

CASE IN POINT Hyatt Corporation hired Skyscraper Building Maintenance, LLC, to perform maintenance services. Skyscraper asked Hyatt to make checks for the services payable to Skyscraper and J&D Financial Corporation, but two of the checks issued by Hyatt were made payable to "J&D Financial Corp. Skyscraper Building Maint." Parties listed in this manner—without an "and" or "or" between them—are referred to as *stacked payees*. The checks were indorsed only by Skyscraper and negotiated by a bank. J&D and Hyatt filed a lawsuit claiming that the checks were payable *jointly* and thus required indorsement by both payees. The bank argued that the checks were payable to J&D and Skyscraper *alternatively*. The court found that the bank was not liable. A check payable to stacked payees is ambiguous and thus payable alternatively, with indorsement by only one of the payees, under UCC 3–110(d).[2]

SUSPENSION OF THE DRAWER'S OBLIGATION

When a drawer gives one alternative or joint payee a check, the drawer's obligation on the check to other payees is suspended [UCC 3–310(b)(1)]. The payee who has possession of the check holds it for the benefit of all of the payees. In other words, the drawer has no obligation to make sure that the funds are allocated or distributed among the joint payees.

CASE IN POINT Vernon and Shirley Graves owned a building that they leased to John and Tamara Johnson for operating a business, Johnson's Towing & Recovery. The Johnsons insured the property and their business through Westport Insurance Company. When a fire destroyed the building, Westport Insurance agreed to pay $98,000 in three payments with the checks co-payable to Johnson's Towing and Vernon Graves. Westport issued two checks, for $30,000 and $29,000, and delivered them to Vernon, who deposited them in his account. A third check was tendered to the Johnsons, but they did not remit the funds to the Graveses, who subsequently filed a lawsuit against the Johnsons and Westport. The court dismissed the lawsuit, holding that the parties had agreed that the insurance company would issue the checks to joint payees and that Westport had complied with this agreement. Once Westport sent the checks to one of the joint payees, its obligation to the other joint payees was suspended until the check was either paid or dishonored.[3]

SECTION 4
HOLDER IN DUE COURSE (HDC)

One of the important distinctions in the law governing negotiable instruments is that between a holder and a *holder in due course* (HDC). Often, whether a holder is entitled to obtain payment will depend on whether she or he is an HDC. Here, we first look briefly at the difference between an ordinary holder and an HDC. Then we examine the requirements for HDC status.

Holder versus Holder in Due Course

When an instrument is transferred, an ordinary holder obtains only those rights that the transferor had in the instrument, as mentioned previously. In this respect, a holder has the same status as an assignee (see Chapter 16). Like an assignee, a holder normally is subject to the same defenses that could be asserted against the transferor.

In contrast, a **holder in due course (HDC)** is a holder who, by meeting certain acquisition requirements (to be discussed shortly), takes an instrument *free* of most of the defenses and claims that could be asserted against the transferor. Stated another way, an HDC can normally acquire a higher level of immunity than can an ordinary holder in regard to defenses against payment on the instrument or ownership claims to the instrument by other parties.

An example will help to clarify the distinction between the rights of an ordinary holder and the rights of an HDC. Debby Morrison signs a $10,000

---

2. *Hyatt Corp. v. Palm Beach National Bank*, 840 So.2d 300 (Fla.App. 2003).

3. *Graves v. Johnson*, 862 N.E.2d 716 (Ind.App. 2007).

note payable to Alex Jerrod in payment for some ancient Roman coins. Jerrod negotiates the note to Beverly Larson, who promises to pay Jerrod for it in thirty days. During the next month, Larson learns that Jerrod has breached his contract with Morrison by delivering coins that were not from the Roman era, as promised, and for this reason, Morrison will not honor the $10,000 note. Whether Larson can hold Morrison liable on the note depends on whether Larson has met the requirements for HDC status. If Larson has met these requirements and thus has HDC status, she is entitled to payment on the note. If Larson has not met these requirements, she has the status of an ordinary holder, and Morrison's defense against payment to Jerrod will also be effective against Larson.

Requirements for HDC Status

The basic requirements for attaining HDC status are set forth in UCC 3–302. An HDC must first be a holder of a negotiable instrument and must have taken the instrument (1) for value, (2) in good faith, and (3) without notice that it is defective (such as when the instrument is overdue, dishonored, irregular, or incomplete). We now examine each of these requirements.

TAKING FOR VALUE An HDC must have given value for the instrument [UCC 3–302(a)(2)(i), 3–303]. A person who receives an instrument as a gift or inherits it has not met the requirement of value. In these situations, the person normally becomes an ordinary holder and does not possess the rights of an HDC.

Under UCC 3–303(a), a holder takes an instrument for value if the holder has done any of the following:

1. Performed the promise for which the instrument was issued or transferred.
2. Acquired a security interest or other lien in the instrument, excluding a lien obtained by a judicial proceeding (see Chapters 28 and 29).
3. Taken the instrument in payment of, or as security for, an **antecedent claim** (preexisting obligation). For example, Zon owes Dwyer $2,000 on a past-due account. If Zon negotiates a $2,000 note signed by Gordon to Dwyer and Dwyer accepts it to discharge the overdue account balance, Dwyer has given value for the instrument.
4. Given a negotiable instrument as payment. For example, Martin has issued a $5,000 negotiable promissory note to Paulene. The note is due six months from the date issued. Paulene needs cash

and does not want to wait until the maturity date to collect. She negotiates the note to her friend Kristen, who pays $2,000 in cash and writes Paulene a check—a negotiable instrument—for the balance of $3,000. Kristen has given full value for the note by paying $2,000 in cash and issuing Paulene the check for $3,000.
5. Given an irrevocable commitment (such as a letter of credit, described in Chapter 21 on page 416) as payment.

Value Is Distinguishable from Consideration. The concept of value in the law of negotiable instruments is not the same as the concept of consideration in the law of contracts. Although an executory promise (a promise to give value in the future) is clearly valid consideration to support a contract, it does not constitute sufficient value to make the promisor an HDC.

If a person promises to perform or give value in the future, that person is not an HDC. A holder takes an instrument for value *only to the extent that the promise has been performed* [UCC 3–303(a)(1)]. Therefore, in the Morrison-Jerrod-Larson example presented earlier Larson is not an HDC because she did not take the instrument (Morrison's note) for value—she has not yet paid Jerrod for the note. Thus, Morrison's defense of breach of contract is valid against Larson as well as against Jerrod. If Larson had paid Jerrod for the note at the time of transfer (given value), she would be an HDC and could have held Morrison liable on the note even though Morrison has a valid defense against Jerrod. Exhibit 25–7 on the following page illustrates these concepts.

Exceptions. In a few situations, the holder may pay for the instrument but does not acquire HDC status. For example, when the instrument is purchased at a judicial sale, such as a bankruptcy or creditor's sale, the holder will not be an HDC. Similarly, if the instrument is acquired as a result of taking over a trust or estate (as administrator), or as part of a corporate purchase of assets, the holder will have only the rights of an ordinary holder [UCC 3–302(c)].

TAKING IN GOOD FAITH The second requirement for HDC status is that the holder must take the instrument in *good faith* [UCC 3–302(a)(2)(ii)]. This means that the holder must have acted honestly in the process of acquiring the instrument. UCC 3–103(a)(4) defines *good faith* as "honesty in fact and the observance of reasonable commercial standards of fair dealing" [UCC 3–103(a)(4)].

EXHIBIT 25–7 • Taking for Value

By exchanging defective goods (coins that were not Roman) for the note, Jerrod breached his contract with Morrison. Morrison could assert this defense if Jerrod presented the note to her for payment. Jerrod exchanged the note for Larson's promise to pay in thirty days, however. Because Larson did not take the note for value, she is not a holder in due course. Thus, Morrison can assert against Larson the defense of Jerrod's breach when Larson submits the note to Morrison for payment. In contrast, if Larson had taken the note for value, Morrison could not assert that defense and would be liable to pay the note.

The good faith requirement applies only to the *holder*. It is immaterial whether the transferor acted in good faith. Thus, even a person who takes a negotiable instrument from a thief may become an HDC if the person acquired the instrument in good faith and had no reason to be suspicious of the transaction. The purchaser must have honestly believed that the instrument was not defective, however. If a person purchases a $10,000 note for $300 from a stranger on a street corner, the issue of good faith can be raised on the grounds of both the suspicious circumstances and the grossly inadequate consideration (value).

In the following case, the court had to determine whether a check had been accepted in good faith.

CASE 25.2
Georg v. Metro Fixtures Contractors, Inc.
Supreme Court of Colorado, 178 P.3d 1209 (2008).

BACKGROUND AND FACTS • Clinton Georg employed Cassandra Demery as a bookkeeper at his business, Freestyle, until he discovered that she had embezzled more than $200,000 and had failed to pay $240,000 in state and federal taxes owed by Freestyle. Georg fired Demery and said that if she did not repay the embezzled funds, he would notify the authorities. Demery went to work as a bookkeeper for Metro Fixtures, a company owned by her parents. Without authorization, she wrote a check to Freestyle for $189,000 out of Metro's account and deposited it to Freestyle's checking account. She told Georg that the check was a loan to her from her family to enable her to repay him. Georg used the funds to pay his back taxes. Two years later, Metro discovered Demery's theft and sued Georg and Freestyle for *conversion* (see Chapter 6), as Demery had no authority to take the funds. The trial court held that Freestyle was a holder in due course (HDC) and granted summary judgment. Metro appealed. The appeals court reversed, holding that because Demery had deposited the check directly into Freestyle's account, Freestyle could not have been an HDC, as it never had actual possession of the check. Georg and Freestyle appealed.

IN THE LANGUAGE OF THE COURT
HOBBS, Justice.
* * * *

A check is a negotiable instrument. The holder in due course doctrine is designed to encourage the transfer and usage of checks and facilitate the flow of capital. *An entity may qualify as a holder in due course even if the instrument at issue may have passed through the hands of a thief.* [Emphasis added.] A holder in due course must meet five conditions: (1) be a holder; (2) of a negotiable instrument who took it; (3) for value; (4) in good faith; (5) without notice of certain problems with the instrument.

To be a holder one must meet two conditions * * *: (1) he or she must have possession (2) of an instrument drawn, issued, or indorsed to him or her. Possession is an element designed to

CASE 25.2 CONTINUED ➡ prevent two or more claimants from qualifying as holders who could take free of the other party's claim of ownership. With rare exceptions, those claiming to be holders have physical ownership of the instrument in question.

An otherwise authorized signature on a negotiable instrument is not converted into an unauthorized forgery when an agent, authorized to sign negotiable instruments in his principal's name, abuses that authority by negotiating the instrument to a holder in due course for the agent's own personal benefit.

Section 4–201(a) [of Colorado's UCC statute] states that a collecting bank "is an agent or subagent of the owner of the item." Further, the statute states, "This provision applies regardless of the form of indorsement or lack of indorsement * * *." A check payable to a party and deposited in that party's account makes the party the "owner" of the check under the UCC. Further, the [well-known] treatise on the UCC speaks to a collecting bank as an agent for the owner's possession:

> Sometimes the one claiming to be a holder in due course will not have possession of the instrument at the time of the suit. When a collecting bank holds the check, the solution is simple for section 4-201 makes that bank the agent of the owner of the check. *Under traditional analysis, the agent's possession would be the owner's possession and thus the owner would have "possession."*

Thus, there are circumstances wherein requiring actual physical possession of the instrument would be problematic and constructive possession applies. *Nevertheless, a determination of constructive possession should occur only when delivery is clearly for an identifiable person under circumstances excluding any other party as a holder in due course.* [Emphasis added.]

* * * *

Colorado's UCC intends to promote reliability on issued instruments, not to undermine their efficacy by placing the burden on the person to whom it is issued to determine a check's validity. Metro's recourse is not against Freestyle, but rather against its agent employee for breaching her fiduciary duty to the company.

Having reviewed the holder in due course elements in light of the undisputed facts of the case, we determine that Freestyle was a holder with constructive possession of a negotiable instrument, which was given for value and taken in good faith without notice of a forgery or an unauthorized signature. Accordingly, we reverse the judgment of the court of appeals and remand with directions that the court of appeals return this case to the district court for entry of judgment in favor of Freestyle.

DECISION AND REMEDY • *The Colorado Supreme Court reinstated the verdict of the trial court and held that Freestyle had received the check in good faith, not knowing it involved theft. Demery was the wrongdoer in this case, and either Metro or Freestyle would have to absorb the loss. Because Freestyle had no reason to know of the theft and Metro did not take steps to prevent it, the loss should fall on Metro.*

WHAT IF THE FACTS WERE DIFFERENT? • *Suppose that Demery had gone to work for a company with which she had no relationship and had stolen funds from it to pay Georg. Would Georg then be the more innocent party? Why or why not?*

THE ETHICAL DIMENSION • *Since Georg knew that Demery had previously embezzled funds from Freesytle when she was an employee, shouldn't he have been suspicious about the source of the funds that Demery was using to repay Freestyle? Why did the court conclude that Freestyle acted in good faith in accepting the check?*

TAKING WITHOUT NOTICE The final requirement for HDC status concerns notice of defects. A person cannot be an HDC if she or he knows or has reason to know that the instrument is defective in any one of the following ways [UCC 3–302(a)]:

1. It is overdue.

2. It has been dishonored.
3. It is part of a series in which at least one instrument has an uncured (uncorrected) default.
4. The instrument contains an unauthorized signature or has been altered.
5. There is a defense against the instrument or a claim to the instrument.

6. The instrument is so incomplete or irregular as to call into question its authenticity.[4]

A holder will be deemed to have notice if she or he (1) has actual knowledge of the defect; (2) has received a notice of the defect (such as a letter from a bank identifying the serial numbers of stolen bearer instruments); or (3) has reason to know that a defect exists, given all the facts and circumstances known at the time in question [UCC 1–201(25)]. The holder must also have received the notice "at a time and in a manner that gives a reasonable opportunity to act on it" [UCC 3–302(f)]. A purchaser's knowledge of certain facts, such as insolvency proceedings against the maker or drawer of the instrument, does not constitute notice that the instrument is defective [UCC 3–302(b)].

Overdue Demand Instruments.

What constitutes notice that an instrument is overdue depends on whether it is a demand instrument (payable on demand) or a time instrument (payable at a definite time). A purchaser has notice that a *demand instrument* is overdue if he or she either takes the instrument knowing that demand has been made or takes the instrument an unreasonable length of time after its date. For a check, a "reasonable time" is ninety days after the date of the check. For all other demand instruments, what will be considered a reasonable time depends on the circumstances [UCC 3–304(a)].

Overdue Time Instruments.

Normally, a *time instrument* is overdue on the day after its due date; hence, anyone who takes a time instrument after the due date is on notice that it is overdue [UCC 3–304(b)].[5] Thus, if a promissory note due on May 15 is purchased on May 16, the purchaser will be an ordinary holder, not an HDC. If an instrument states that it is "Payable in thirty days," counting begins the day after the instrument is dated. For example, a note dated December 1 that is payable in thirty days is due by midnight on December 31. If the payment date falls on a Sunday or holiday, the instrument is payable on the next business day.

A series of notes issued at the same time with successive maturity dates is overdue when any note in the series is overdue. This serves to notify prospective purchasers that they cannot qualify as HDCs [UCC 3–302(a)(2)(iii)].

If the principal is to be paid in installments, the default or nonpayment of any one installment will make the instrument overdue and provide notice to prospective purchasers of the default. The instrument will remain overdue until the default is cured [UCC 3–304(b)(1)]. An instrument does not become overdue if there is a default on a payment of interest only, however [UCC 3–304(c)]. For this reason, most installment notes provide that any payment shall be applied first to interest and then the balance to the principal. This serves as notice that any installment payment for less than the full amount results in a default on an installment payment toward the principal.

Dishonored Instruments.

An instrument is *dishonored* when the party to whom the instrument is presented refuses to pay it. If a holder knows or has reason to know that an instrument has been dishonored, the holder is on notice and cannot claim HDC status [UCC 3–302(a)(2)]. Thus, a person who takes a check clearly stamped "insufficient funds" is put on notice. Conversely, if a person purchasing an instrument does not know and has no reason to know that it has been dishonored, the person is *not* put on notice and therefore can become an HDC.

For example, suppose that Gonzalez holds a demand note dated September 1 on Apex, Inc., a local business firm. On September 17, she demands payment, and Apex refuses (that is, dishonors the instrument). On September 22, Gonzalez negotiates the note to Brenner, a purchaser who lives in another state. Brenner does not know, and has no reason to know, that the note has been dishonored. Because Brenner is *not* put on notice, Brenner can become an HDC.

Notice of Claims or Defenses.

A holder cannot become an HDC if he or she has notice of any claim to the instrument or defense against it [UCC 3–302(a)(2)(v), (vi)]. Knowledge of claims or defenses can be imputed (attributed) to the purchaser if these claims or defenses are apparent on the face of the instrument or if the purchaser otherwise had reason to know of them from facts surrounding the transaction.[6] For example, a potential purchaser who knows

---

4. Section 302(1)(c) of the unrevised Article 3 provided that HDC protection is lost if a holder has notice that an instrument is overdue or has been dishonored or if there is a claim to or a defense against it.

5. A time instrument also becomes overdue the day after an accelerated due date, unless the purchaser has no reason to know that the due date has been accelerated [UCC 3–302(a)(2)(iii), 3–304(b)(3)].

6. If an instrument contains a statement required by a statute or an administrative rule to the effect that the rights of a holder or transferee are subject to the claims or defenses that the issuer could assert against the original payee, the instrument is negotiable, but there cannot be an HDC of the instrument. See UCC 3–106(d) and the discussion of federal limitations on HDC rights in Chapter 26.

that the maker of a note has breached the underlying contract with the payee cannot thereafter purchase the note as an HDC.

Knowledge of one defense precludes a holder from asserting HDC status in regard to all other defenses. For example, Litton, knowing that the note he has taken has a forged indorsement, presents it to the maker for payment. The maker refuses to pay on the ground of breach of the underlying contract. The maker can assert this defense against Litton even though Litton had no knowledge of the breach, because Litton's knowledge of the forgery alone prevents him from being an HDC in *any* circumstances.

What steps should a bank take to determine that there are no defenses against the payment of a check? In the following case, a bank phoned the issuer of a cashier's check (a check on which the bank is both the drawer and the drawee—see Chapter 27) to confirm that it was "good," and the court had to determine whether this was sufficient.

CASE 25.3
South Central Bank of Daviess County v. Lynnville National Bank

Indiana Court of Appeals, 901 N.E.2d 576 (2009).

COMPANY PROFILE • South Central Bank of Kentucky can trace its beginnings to 1889, when Deposit Bank of Monroe County was chartered. In 1972, James Bale bought Deposit Bank with the goal of providing more banking services to rural Kentucky. Over the next thirty-five years, South Central grew from a single branch with $10 million in assets to a bank holding company composed of five individually chartered banks with more than twenty-six offices across the state and assets of more than $800 million. The organization's motto—"Hometown banking . . . there is a difference"—epitomizes the banks' focus on the needs of the people in the communities they serve.

BACKGROUND AND FACTS • Lynnville National Bank in Lynnville, Indiana, issued a cashier's check for $31,917.55 payable to Landmark Housing Center, Inc. The check represented a loan to Bryan and Lisa Fisher to buy a manufactured home. The same day, Landmark deposited the check into its account with South Central Bank of Daviess County in Owensboro, Kentucky. South Central phoned Lynnville and, on confirmation of the date, amount, and payee of the check, paid its entire amount. Two days later, Lynnville learned that Landmark was unable to fulfill its contract with the Fishers. Lynnville then told South Central that payment on the cashier's check would be refused. South Central filed a suit in an Indiana state court against Lynnville, seeking to recover the amount of the check, plus interest and fees. The court entered a summary judgment in the defendant's favor. South Central appealed.

IN THE LANGUAGE OF THE COURT
BAKER, Chief Judge.
* * * *
Indiana Code Section 26-1-3.1-411 [Indiana's version of UCC 3–411] governs situations in which an obligated bank wrongfully refuses to pay a cashier's check. * * * Only under certain, very specific circumstances is a bank entitled to stop payment on a cashier's check * * *. None of those circumstances occurred in this case. Lynnville's obligation to pay was clear and it was able to pay, but it refused payment on the check as an accommodation to the Fishers, who had no right to make that request.

Lynnville relies on the defense of fraud as its basis for stopping payment on the cashier's check. But * * * Lynnville cannot maintain an action of its own against Landmark for fraud. Lynnville was never a victim of fraud.
* * * *
Moreover, South Central argues that it was a holder in due course (HDC) of the cashier's check, which would further limit the defenses available to Lynnville.

On June 1, when a Landmark representative presented the cashier's check to South Central, South Central took the instrument for value and in good faith. * * * Acting with an abundance of caution, South Central telephoned Lynnville to confirm the date, amount, and payee of the

CASE CONTINUES ➡

CASE 25.3 CONTINUED ➡ check. Although South Central was not required to do so—and, to be clear, we do not intend to imply that the holder of a cashier's check is required to make such a phone call—that act certainly means that South Central was without notice of any problems with the instrument. Indeed, at that time, *Lynnville* was without notice of any problems with the instrument. Therefore, when South Central accepted the cashier's check on June 1, it became an HDC.

Because South Central is an HDC, the only defenses that could be raised by Lynnville are the "real" defenses enumerated by Indiana Code Section 26-1-3.1-305 [UCC 3–305]. * * * *None of these defenses apply to Lynnville.* [Emphasis added.]

* * * Landmark's fraud on the Fishers does not automatically spill over to South Central[,] who had absolutely no knowledge of what Landmark did or did not promise the Fishers * * *. There is absolutely nothing in the cashier's check that in any way indicated what type of transaction was involved or what, if anything, had been promised to the Fishers. * * * It could not be clearer that Lynnville was not entitled to stop payment on the cashier's check. It has no valid defense for that action.

DECISION AND REMEDY • *The state intermediate appellate court reversed the lower court's judgment and remanded the case for the entry of a judgment in South Central's favor for the amount of the check, plus expenses and interest, and for a determination of consequential damages. South Central took the check without notice of any defense against its payment.*

WHAT IF THE FACTS WERE DIFFERENT? • *Suppose that Landmark had a history of unreliability as a South Central customer. Would South Central's acceptance of the check have then constituted a failure to act reasonably? Explain your answer.*

THE LEGAL ENVIRONMENT DIMENSION • *How would a decision in favor of Lynnville have affected the status of a cashier's check as a substitute for cash?*

Incomplete Instruments. A purchaser cannot become an HDC of an instrument so incomplete on its face that an element of negotiability is lacking (for example, the amount is not filled in) [UCC 3–302(a)(1)]. Minor omissions (such as the omission of the date—see Chapter 24) are permissible because these do not call into question the validity of the instrument [UCC 3–113(b)].

Similarly, when a person accepts an instrument that has been completed without knowing that it was incomplete when issued, the person can take it as an HDC [UCC 3–115(b), 3–302(a)(1)]. Even if an instrument that is originally incomplete is later completed in an unauthorized manner, an HDC can still enforce the instrument as completed [UCC 3–407(c)].

To illustrate: Peyton asks Brittany to buy a textbook for him when she goes to the campus bookstore. Peyton writes a check payable to the campus store, leaves the amount blank, and tells Brittany to fill in the price of the textbook. The cost of the textbook is $85. If Brittany fills in the check for $150 before she gets to the bookstore, the bookstore cashier sees only a properly completed instrument.

Therefore, because the bookstore had no notice that the check was incomplete when it was issued, the bookstore can take the check for $150 and become an HDC. (Material alterations will be discussed in Chapter 26.)

Irregular Instruments. Any irregularity on the face of an instrument (such as an obvious forgery or alteration) that calls into question its validity or ownership, or that creates an ambiguity as to the party to pay, will bar HDC status. A difference between the handwriting used in the body of a check and that used in the signature will not in and of itself make an instrument irregular. Antedating or postdating a check or stating the amount in digits but failing to write out the numbers normally will not make a check irregular [UCC 3–113(a)].[7] Visible evidence that a maker's or drawer's signature is forged,

---

7. Note that some courts have held that the postdating of a check may raise substantial suspicions about its authenticity, particularly if it is a commercial check. See, for example, *Bay Shore Check Cashing Corp. v. Landscapes by North East Construction Corp.*, 776 N.Y.S.2d 742 (N.Y.Dist. 2004).

however, will disqualify a purchaser from HDC status. Nevertheless, a good forgery of a signature or a careful alteration can go undetected by reasonable examination. In that situation, the purchaser can qualify as an HDC [UCC 3–302(a)(1)].

Losses that result from well-crafted forgeries usually fall on the party to whom the forger transferred the instrument (assuming, of course, that the forger cannot be found). This means that a bank that accepts a check for deposit despite apparent evidence on the check's face that it is irregular will bear the loss if the check later turns out to be forged.

CASE IN POINT First Service Title Agency (FSTA) issued three checks drawn on its account with Key Bank in conjunction with a real estate transaction. The next day, FSTA discovered that the real estate transaction had been fraudulent and put stop-payment orders (see Chapter 27 on page 523) on all three checks. Meanwhile, Randall Davis, who had accounts at Firstar Bank, N.A., but was not a party to any of the checks, presented the checks to Firstar for payment. The checks had multiple indorsements that appeared to be in the same handwriting and were marked "for deposit only." Without further inquiry, Firstar paid the checks and sent them to Key Bank, which returned the three checks to Firstar with the notation "payment stopped." Claiming that it was an HDC, Firstar filed a suit against FSTA for failure to pay the checks. The court found that Firstar was not an HDC because the checks were irregular and Firstar had failed to exercise ordinary care to determine if the checks were forged or otherwise deficient before it had paid them. FTSA could, therefore, successfully assert its defenses to Firstar's demand for payment.[8]

SECTION 5
HOLDER THROUGH AN HDC

A person who does not qualify as an HDC but who derives his or her title through an HDC can acquire the rights and privileges of an HDC. This rule, which is sometimes called the **shelter principle,** is set out in UCC 3–203(b):

---

8. *Firstar Bank, N.A. v. First Service Title Agency, Inc.,* 2004 WL 1906851 (Ohio App. 2004).

Transfer of an instrument, whether or not the transfer is a negotiation, vests in the transferee any right of the transferor to enforce the instrument, including any right as a holder in due course, but the transferee cannot acquire rights of a holder in due course by a transfer, directly or indirectly, from a holder in due course if the transferee engaged in fraud or illegality affecting the instrument.

The Purpose of the Shelter Principle

The shelter principle extends the benefits of HDC status and is designed to aid the HDC in readily disposing of the instrument. Anyone, no matter how far removed from an HDC, who can ultimately trace her or his title back to an HDC comes within the shelter principle. Normally, a person who acquires an instrument from an HDC or from someone with HDC rights receives HDC rights on the legal theory that the transferee of an instrument receives at least the rights that the transferor had. By extending the benefits of HDC status, the shelter principle promotes the marketability and free transferability of negotiable instruments.

Limitations on the Shelter Principle

There are some limitations on the shelter principle. Certain persons who formerly held instruments cannot improve their positions by later reacquiring the instruments from HDCs [UCC 3–203(b)]. If a holder participated in fraud or illegality affecting the instrument, or had notice of a claim or defense against an instrument, that holder is not allowed to improve her or his status by repurchasing the instrument from a later HDC.

To illustrate: Matthew and Carla collaborate to defraud Dina. Dina is induced to give Carla a negotiable note payable to Carla's order. Carla then specially indorses the note for value to Larry, an HDC. Matthew and Carla split the proceeds. Larry negotiates the note to Stuart, another HDC. Stuart then negotiates the note for value to Matthew. Matthew, even though he obtained the note through an HDC, is not a holder through an HDC because he participated in the original fraud and can never acquire HDC rights in this note.

See *Concept Summary 25.2* on the following page for a review of the requirements for HDC status.

CONCEPT SUMMARY 25.2
Rules and Requirements for HDC Status

Basic Requirements	Rules
Must Be a *Holder*	A *holder* is defined as a person in possession of an instrument "if the instrument is payable to bearer or, in the cases of an instrument payable to an identified person, if the identified person is in possession" [UCC 1–201(20)].
Must Take *for Value*	A holder gives *value* by doing any of the following [UCC 3–303]: 1. Performing the promise for which the instrument was issued or transferred. 2. Acquiring a security interest or other lien in the instrument (other than a lien obtained by a judicial proceeding). 3. Taking the instrument in payment of, or as security for, an antecedent debt. 4. Giving a negotiable instrument as payment. 5. Giving an irrevocable commitment as payment.
Must Take *in Good Faith*	*Good faith* is defined for purposes of revised Article 3 as "honesty in fact and the observance of reasonable commercial standards of fair dealing" [UCC 3–103(a)(4)].
Must Take *without Notice*	A holder must not be *on notice* that the instrument is defective in any of the following ways [UCC 3–302, 3–304]: 1. The instrument is overdue. 2. The instrument has been dishonored. 3. There is an uncured (uncorrected) default with respect to another instrument issued as part of the same series. 4. The instrument contains an unauthorized signature or has been altered. 5. There is a defense against the instrument or a claim to the instrument. 6. The instrument is so irregular or incomplete as to call into question its authenticity.
Shelter Principle– Holder through a Holder in Due Course	A holder who cannot qualify as an HDC has the rights of an HDC if he or she derives title through an HDC [UCC 3–203(b)].

REVIEWING

Transferability and Holder in Due Course

The Brown family owns several companies, including the J. H. Stevedoring Company and Penn Warehousing and Distribution, Inc. Many aspects of the companies' operations and management are intertwined. Dennis Bishop worked for J. H. and Penn for more than ten years until by 2011, he had become the financial controller at J. H., where he was responsible for approving invoices for payment and reconciling the corporate checkbook. In December 2012, Bishop began stealing from Penn and J. H. by writing checks on the corporate accounts and using the funds for his own benefit (committing the crime of embezzlement). Several members of the Brown family signed the checks for Bishop without hesitation because he was a longtime, trusted employee. Over the next two years, Bishop embezzled $1,209,436, of which $670,632 was used to buy horses from the Fasig-Tipton Company and Fasig-Tipton Midlantic, Inc., with Penn and J. H. checks made payable to those firms. When Bishop's fraud was revealed, J. H. and Penn filed a suit in a federal district court against the Fasig-Tipton firms (the defendants) to recover the amounts of the checks made payable to them. Using the information presented in the chapter, answer the following questions.

1. What method was most likely used to negotiate the instruments described here?

REVIEWING

Transferability and Holder in Due Course, Continued

2. Suppose that all of the checks issued to the defendants were made payable to "Fasig-Tipton Co., Fasig-Tipton Midlantic, Inc." Under the Uniform Commercial Code, were the instruments payable jointly or in the alternative? Why is this significant?

3. Do the defendants in this situation (the two Fasig-Tipton firms) meet the requirements of an HDC? Why or why not?

4. In whose favor should the court rule, and why?

DEBATE THIS: *We should eliminate the status of holder in due course for those who possess negotiable instruments.*

TERMS AND CONCEPTS

antecedent claim 487

blank indorsement 480

holder in due
  course (HDC) 486

indorsee 480

indorser 480

indorsement 480

negotiation 479

qualified indorsement 481

restrictive indorsement 483

shelter principle 493

special indorsement 480

trust indorsement 483

QUESTIONS AND CASE PROBLEMS

25–1. Indorsements A check drawn by Cullen for $500 is made payable to the order of Jordan and issued to Jordan. Jordan owes his landlord $500 in rent and transfers the check to his landlord with the following indorsement: "For rent paid, [signed] Jordan." Jordan's landlord has contracted to have Deborah do some landscaping on the property. When Deborah insists on immediate payment, the landlord transfers the check to Deborah without indorsement. Later, to pay for some palm trees purchased from Better-Garden Nursery, Deborah transfers the check with the following indorsement: "Pay to Better-Garden Nursery, without recourse, [signed] Deborah." Better-Garden Nursery sends the check to its bank indorsed "For deposit only, [signed] Better-Garden Nursery."

(a) Classify each of these indorsements.

(b) Was the transfer from Jordan's landlord to Deborah, without indorsement, an assignment or a negotiation? Explain.

25–2. QUESTION WITH SAMPLE ANSWER: Holder in Due Course.

Celine issues a ninety-day negotiable promissory note payable to the order of Hayden. The amount of the note is left blank, pending a determination of the amount that Hayden will need to purchase a used car for Celine. Celine authorizes any amount not to exceed $2,000. Hayden, without authority, fills in the note in the amount of $5,000 and thirty days later sells the note to First National Bank of Oklahoma for $4,850. Hayden does not buy the car and leaves the state. First National Bank has no knowledge that the instrument was incomplete when issued or that Hayden had no authority to complete the instrument in the amount of $5,000.

(a) Does the bank qualify as a holder in due course? If so, for what amount? Explain.

(b) If Hayden had sold the note to a stranger in a bar for $500, would the stranger qualify as a holder in due course? Explain.

• **For a sample answer to Question 25–2, go to Appendix I at the end of this text.**

25–3. Holder in Due Course Through negotiation, Emilio has received from dishonest payees two checks with the following histories:

(a) The drawer issued a check to the payee for $9. The payee cleverly altered the numeral amount on the check from $9 to $90 and the written word from "nine" to "ninety."

(b) The drawer issued a check to the payee without filling in the amount. The drawer authorized the payee to fill in the amount for no more than $90. The payee filled in the amount of $900. Discuss whether Emilio, by giving value to the payees, can qualify as a holder in due course of these checks.

25–4. Negotiation Bertram writes a check for $200 payable to "cash." He puts the check in his pocket and drives to the bank to cash the check. As he gets out of his car in the bank's parking lot, the check slips out of his pocket and falls to the pavement. Jerrod walks by moments later, picks up the check, and later that day delivers it to Amber, to whom he owes $200. Amber indorses the check "For deposit only, [signed] Amber Dowel" and deposits it into her checking account. In light of these circumstances, answer the following questions:

(a) Is the check a bearer instrument or an order instrument?

(b) Did Jerrod's delivery of the check to Amber constitute a valid negotiation? Why or why not?

(c) What type of indorsement did Amber make?

(d) Does Bertram have a right to recover the $200 from Amber? Explain.

25–5. Alternative or Joint Payees Hartford Mutual Insurance Co. issued a check for $60,150 payable to "Andrew Michael Bogdan, Jr., Crystal Bogdan, Oceanmark Bank FSB, Goodman-Gable-Gould Company." The check was to pay a claim related to the Bogdans' commercial property. Besides the Bogdans, the payees were the mortgage holder (Oceanmark) and the insurance agent who adjusted the claim. The Bogdans and the agent indorsed the check and cashed it at Provident Bank of Maryland. Meanwhile, Oceanmark sold the mortgage to Pelican National Bank, which asked Provident to pay it the amount of the check. Provident refused. Pelican filed a suit in a Maryland state court against Provident, arguing that the check had been improperly negotiated. Was this check payable jointly or in the alternative? Whose indorsements were required to cash it? In whose favor should the court rule? Explain. [*Pelican National Bank v. Provident Bank of Maryland*, 381 Md. 327, 849 A.2d 475 (2004)]

25–6. Holder in Due Course Robert Triffin bought a number of dishonored checks from McCall's Liquor Corp., Community Check Cashing II, LLC (CCC), and other licensed check-cashing businesses in New Jersey. Seventeen of the checks had been dishonored as counterfeit. In an attempt to recover on the items, Triffin met with the drawer, Automatic Data Processing, Inc. (ADP). At the meeting, Triffin said that he knew the checks were counterfeit. When ADP refused to pay, Triffin filed suits in New Jersey state courts to collect, asserting claims totaling $11,021.33. With each complaint were copies of assignment agreements corresponding to each check. Each agreement stated, among other things, that the seller was a holder in due course (HDC) and had assigned its rights in the check to Triffin. ADP had not previously seen these agreements. A private investigator determined that the forms attached to the McCall's and CCC checks had not been signed by their

sellers but that Triffin had scanned the signatures into his computer and pasted them onto the agreements. ADP claimed fraud. Does Triffin qualify as an HDC? If not, did he acquire the rights of an HDC under the shelter principle? As for the fraud claim, which element of fraud would ADP be least likely to prove? [*Triffin v. Automatic Data Processing, Inc.*, 394 N.J.Super. 237, 926 A.2d 362 (App.Div. 2007)]

25–7. CASE PROBLEM WITH SAMPLE ANSWER: Holder in Due Course.

American International Group, Inc. (AIG), an insurance company, issued a check to Jermielem Merriwether in connection with a personal-injury matter. Merriwether presented the check to A-1 Check Cashing Emporium for payment. A-1's clerk forgot to have Merriwether sign the check. When he could not reach Merriwether and ask him to come back to A-1 to sign the check, the clerk printed Merriwether's name on the back and deposited the check for collection. When the check was not paid, A-1 sold it to Robert Triffin, who is in the business of buying dishonored checks. When Triffin could not get the check honored, he sued AIG, contending that he, through A-1, had the right to collect on the check as a holder in due course (HDC). The trial court rejected that claim. Triffin appealed. On what basis could he claim HDC status? [Triffin v. American International Group, Inc., ___ A.2d ___ (N.J.Super. 2008)]

• **To view a sample answer for Problem 25–7, go to this book's Web site at www.cengage.com/blaw/clarkson, select "Chapter 25," and click on "Case Problem with Sample Answer."**

25–8. Transfer and Holder in Due Course Germanie Fequiere executed and delivered a promissory note in the principal amount of $240,000 to BNC Mortgage. As security for the note, Fequiere executed and delivered a mortgage on real property. BNC indorsed the promissory note in blank. Several years later, when Fequiere failed to make payments on the note, Chase Home Finance, LLC—the holder in due course of the note and holder of the mortgage—moved to foreclose on the property. In defense, Fequiere asserted that Chase could not foreclose on the property because the mortgage on the property had not been properly transferred from BNC to Chase. Assuming that is true, does it mean that Chase, as holder of the negotiable note, cannot foreclose on the collateral (the property secured by the mortgage)? Explain your answer. [*Chase Home Finance, LLC v. Fequiere*, 119 Conn.App. 570, 989 A.2d 606 (2010)]

25–9. A QUESTION OF ETHICS: Indorsements.

As an assistant comptroller for Interior Crafts, Inc., in Chicago, Illinois, Todd Leparski was authorized to receive checks from Interior's customers and deposit the checks into Interior's account. Between October 2000 and February 2001, Leparski stole more than $500,000 from Interior by indorsing the checks "Interior Crafts—For Deposit Only" but depositing some of them into his own account at Marquette Bank through an automated teller machine owned by Pan American Bank.

Marquette alerted Interior, which was able to recover about $250,000 from Leparski. Interior also recovered $250,000 under its policy with American Insurance Co. To collect the rest of the missing funds, Interior filed a suit in an Illinois state court against Leparski and the banks. The court ruled in favor of Interior, and Pan American appealed to a state intermediate appellate court. [Interior Crafts, Inc. v. Leparski, 366 Ill.App.3d 1148, 853 N.E.2d 1244, 304 Ill.Dec. 878 (3 Dist. 2006)]

(a) What type of indorsement is "Interior Crafts—For Deposit Only"? What is the obligation of a party that receives a check with this indorsement? Does the fact that Interior authorized Leparski to indorse its checks but not to deposit those checks into his own account absolve Pan American of liability? Explain.

(b) From an ethical perspective, how might a business firm such as Interior discourage an employee's thievery such as Leparski's acts in this case? Discuss.

25–10. VIDEO QUESTION: Indorsements.

Go to this text's Web site at **www.cengage.com/blaw/clarkson** and select "Chapter 25." Click on "Video Questions" and view the video titled *Negotiability & Transferability: Indorsing Checks.* Then answer the following questions.

(a) According to the instructor in the video, what are the two reasons why banks generally require a person to indorse a check that is made out to cash (a bearer instrument), even when the check is signed in the presence of the teller?

(b) Suppose that your friend makes out a check payable to cash, signs it, and hands it to you. You take the check to your bank and indorse the check with your name and the words "without recourse." What type of indorsement is this? How does this indorsement affect the bank's rights?

(c) Now suppose that you go to your bank and write a check on your account payable to cash for $500. The teller gives you the cash without asking you to indorse the check. After you leave, the teller slips the check into his pocket. Later, the teller delivers it (without an indorsement) to his friend Carol in payment for a gambling debt. Carol takes your check to her bank, indorses it, and deposits the money. Discuss whether Carol is a holder in due course.

LEGAL RESEARCH EXERCISES ON THE WEB

Go to this text's Web site at **www.cengage.com/blaw/clarkson**, select "Chapter 25," and click on "Practical Internet Exercises." There you will find the following Internet research exercises that you can perform to learn more about the topics covered in this chapter.

Practical Internet Exercise 25–1: Legal Perspective
Electronic Negotiable Instruments

Practical Internet Exercise 25–2: Management Perspective
Holder in Due Course

CHAPTER 26

Liability, Defenses, and Discharge

iability on a negotiable instrument can arise either from a person's signature on the instrument *(signature liability)* or from the warranties that are implied when the person presents the instrument for negotiation *(warranty liability)*. A person who signs a negotiable instrument is potentially liable for payment of the amount stated on the instrument. Unlike signature liability, warranty liability does not require a signature and extends to both signers and nonsigners. A breach of warranty can occur when the instrument is transferred or presented for payment.

This chapter focuses on the liability *of the instrument itself or the warranties* *connected with the transfer or present-* *ment of the instrument*, as opposed to the liability on any underlying contract. Suppose that Donna agrees to buy one thousand Blu-ray discs from Luis and issues a check to Luis in payment. The liability discussed in this chapter does not relate directly to the contract (for instance, whether the Blu-ray discs are of proper quality or fit for the purpose for which they are intended). The liability discussed here is the one in connection with the *check* (such as what recourse Luis will have if Donna's bank refuses to pay the check due to insufficient funds in her account or her order to stop payment on the check).

The first part of this chapter covers the liability of the parties who sign instruments—for example, drawers of drafts and checks, makers of notes and certificates of deposit, and indorsers. It also covers the liability of accommodation parties and the warranty liability of those who transfer instruments and present instruments for payment.

The chapter then examines the defenses that can be raised to avoid liability on an instrument and the effect that holder in due course (HDC) status has on those defenses. The final section in the chapter looks at some of the ways in which parties can be *discharged* from liability on negotiable instruments.

SECTION 1
SIGNATURE LIABILITY

The key to liability on a negotiable instrument is a signature. As discussed in Chapter 24 on page 467, the Uniform Commercial Code (UCC) broadly defines a signature as any name, word, mark, or symbol executed or adopted by a person with the present intention to authenticate a writing [UCC 1–209(39), 3–401(b)]. A signature can be made manually or by use of any device or machine.

The general rule is that every party, except a qualified indorser,[1] who signs a negotiable instrument is

either primarily or secondarily liable for payment of that instrument when it comes due. Signature liability is contractual liability—no person will be held contractually liable for an instrument that he or she has not signed personally or through an authorized representative (agent) [UCC 3–401(a)]. The following subsections discuss primary and secondary liability, as well as the conditions that must be met before liability can arise.

Primary Liability

A person who is primarily liable on a negotiable instrument is absolutely required to pay the instrument—unless, of course, he or she has a valid defense to payment. Liability is immediate when the instrument is signed or issued. No action by the holder of the instrument is required. Only *makers*

---

1. A qualified indorser—one who indorses "without recourse"— undertakes no obligation to pay [UCC 3–415(b)]. A qualified indorser merely assumes warranty liability, which will be discussed later in this chapter.

and *acceptors* of instruments are primarily liable [UCC 3–412, 3–413].

MAKERS The maker of a promissory note unconditionally promises to pay the note according to its terms. It is the maker's promise to pay that renders the instrument negotiable. If the instrument was incomplete when the maker signed it, the maker is obligated to pay it according to either its stated terms or terms that were agreed on and later filled in to complete the instrument [UCC 3–115, 3–407, 3–412].

For example, Tristan executes a preprinted promissory note to Sharon, without filling in the due-date blank. If Sharon does not complete the form by adding the date, the note will be payable on demand. If Sharon subsequently writes in a due date that Tristan authorized, the note is payable on the stated due date. In either situation, Tristan (the maker) is obligated to pay the note. (Note that if Sharon fills in a date that Tristan did not authorize, Tristan can claim a defense to payment—material alteration, which will be discussed later in this chapter.)

ACCEPTORS An *acceptor* is a drawee who promises to pay an instrument when it is presented later for payment, as mentioned in Chapter 24. Once a drawee *accepts* a draft (usually by writing "accepted" across its face and signing it), the drawee becomes an acceptor and is obligated to pay the draft when it is presented for payment [UCC 3–409(a)]. The drawee's acceptance is a promise to pay that places the drawee in almost the same position as the maker of a promissory note [UCC 3–413]. Failure to pay an accepted draft when presented leads to primary signature liability for the drawee-acceptor.

Acceptance of a check is called *certification,* as will be discussed in Chapter 27. Certification is not necessary on checks, and a bank is under no obligation to certify checks. If it does certify a check, however, the drawee bank occupies the position of an acceptor and is primarily liable on the check to any holder [UCC 3–409(d)].

Secondary Liability

Drawers and *indorsers* are secondarily liable. On a negotiable instrument, secondary liability is similar to the liability of a guarantor in a simple contract (described in Chapter 28) in the sense that it is *contingent liability*. In other words, a drawer or an indorser will be liable *only if* the party that is primarily responsible for paying the instrument refuses to do so—that is, **dishonors** the instrument. On drafts and checks,

a drawer's secondary liability does not arise until the drawee fails to pay or to accept the instrument, whichever is required. With regard to promissory notes, an indorser's secondary liability does not arise until the maker, who is primarily liable, has defaulted on the instrument [UCC 3–412, 3–415].

Thus, dishonor of an instrument triggers the liability of parties who are secondarily liable on the instrument—that is, the drawer and *unqualified* indorsers. For example, Lee writes a check for $1,000 on her account at Western Bank payable to the order of Carerra. Carerra indorses and delivers the check, for value, to Deere. Deere deposits the check into his account at Universal Bank, but the bank returns the check to Deere marked "insufficient funds," thus dishonoring the check. The question for Deere is whether the drawer (Lee) or the drawee-indorser (Carerra) can be held liable on the check after the bank has dishonored it. The answer to the question depends on whether certain conditions for secondary liability have been satisfied.

Parties are secondarily liable on a negotiable instrument *only if* the following events occur:[2]

1. The instrument is properly and timely presented.
2. The instrument is dishonored.
3. Timely notice of dishonor is given to the secondarily liable party.[3]

PROPER PRESENTMENT As discussed in Chapter 24, *presentment* occurs when a person presents an instrument either to the party liable on the instrument for payment or to a drawee for acceptance. The UCC requires that a holder present the instrument to the appropriate party, in a timely fashion, and give reasonable identification if requested [UCC 3–414(f), 3–415(e), 3–501]. The party to whom the instrument must be presented depends on the type of instrument involved. A note or certificate of deposit (CD) must be presented to the maker for payment. A draft is presented to the drawee for acceptance, payment, or both. A check is presented to the drawee (bank) for payment [UCC 3–501(a), 3–502(b)].

Presentment can be made by any commercially reasonable means, including oral, written, or electronic communication [UCC 3–501(b)]. It is ordinarily effective when the demand for payment or

---

2. An instrument can be drafted to include a waiver of the presentment and notice of dishonor requirements [UCC 3–504]. Presume, for simplicity's sake, that such waivers have *not* been incorporated into the instruments described in this chapter.
3. Note that these requirements are necessary for a secondarily liable party to have *signature* liability on a negotiable instrument, but they are not necessary for a secondarily liable party to have *warranty* liability (to be discussed later in this chapter).

acceptance is received (unless presentment takes place after an established cutoff hour, in which case it may be treated as occurring on the next business day).

TIMELY PRESENTMENT Timeliness is important for proper presentment [UCC 3–414(f), 3–415(e), 3–501(b)(4)]. Failure to present an instrument on time is a common reason for improper presentment and can lead to unqualified indorsers being discharged from secondary liability. A reasonable time for presentment is determined by the nature of the instrument, any usage of banking or trade, and the facts of the particular case.

If the instrument is payable on demand, the holder should present it for payment or acceptance within a reasonable time. For domestic, uncertified checks, the UCC establishes a presumptively reasonable time period [UCC 3–414(f), 3–415(e)]. An ordinary check should be presented for payment within thirty days of its date or the date that it was indorsed. A drawer is *not* automatically discharged from liability for checks presented after thirty days, but the holder must be able to prove that the presentment after that time was reasonable.[4]

The time for proper presentment for different types of instruments is shown in Exhibit 26–1 below.

DISHONOR As mentioned previously, an instrument is dishonored when payment or acceptance of the instrument is refused or cannot be obtained within the prescribed time. An instrument is also dishonored when the required presentment is excused (as it would be, for example, if the maker had died) and the instrument is not properly accepted or paid [UCC 3–502(e), 3–504].

In certain situations, a delay in payment or a refusal to pay an instrument will *not* dishonor the instrument. When presentment is made after an established cutoff hour (not earlier than 2:00 P.M.), for instance, a bank can postpone payment until the following business day without dishonoring the instrument [UCC 3–501(b)(4)]. In addition, when the holder refuses to exhibit the instrument, to give reasonable identification, or to sign a receipt for the payment on the instrument, a bank's refusal to pay does not dishonor the instrument [UCC 3–501(b)(2)]. Returning an instrument because it lacks a proper indorsement also is not a dishonor [UCC 3–501(b)(3)(i)].

PROPER NOTICE Once an instrument has been dishonored, proper notice must be given to secondary parties (drawers and indorsers) for them to be held liable. Notice may be given in any reasonable manner, including an oral, written, or electronic communication, as well as notice written or stamped on the instrument itself [UCC 3–503(b)].[5] If the party giving notice is a bank, it must give any necessary notice before its midnight deadline (midnight of the next banking day after receipt) [UCC 3–503(c)]. Notice by any party other than a bank must be given within thirty days following the day of dishonor or the day on which the person who is secondarily liable received notice of dishonor [UCC 3–503(c)].

Accommodation Parties

An **accommodation party** is one who signs an instrument for the purpose of lending his or her name as credit to another party on the instrument [UCC 3–419(a)]. Requiring an accommodation party

---

4. For a seminal case in which a state's highest court held that presentment more than thirty days after the date of an uncertified check did not discharge the liability of the drawer, see *Grist v. Osgood*, 90 Nev. 165, 521 P.2d 368 (1974).

5. Written notice is preferable because a secondary party may claim that an oral notice was never received. Also, to give proper notice of the dishonor of a foreign draft (a draft drawn in one country and payable in another country), a formal notice called a *protest* is required [UCC 3–505(b)].

EXHIBIT 26–1 • Time for Proper Presentment

TYPE OF INSTRUMENT	FOR ACCEPTANCE	FOR PAYMENT
Time	On or before due date.	On due date.
Demand	Within a reasonable time (after date of issue or after secondary party becomes liable on the instrument).	Within a reasonable time.
Check	Not applicable.	Within thirty days of its date, to hold drawer secondarily liable. Within thirty days of indorsement, to hold indorser secondarily liable.

is one way to secure against nonpayment of a negotiable instrument. When a person (such as a parent) cosigns a promissory note with the maker (such as the parent's son or daughter), the cosigner is an *accommodation party,* and the maker is the *accommodated party.*

If the accommodation party signs on behalf of the *maker,* he or she is an *accommodation maker* and is primarily liable on the instrument. For example, if Alex takes out a loan to purchase a car and his uncle cosigns the note, the uncle becomes primarily liable on the instrument. In other words, Alex's uncle is guaranteeing payment, and the bank can seek payment directly from the uncle.

If, however, the accommodation party signs on behalf of a *payee or other holder* (usually to make the instrument more marketable), she or he is an *accommodation indorser* and, as an indorser, is secondarily liable. For example, suppose that Frank Huston applies to Northeast Bank for a $20,000 loan to start a small business. Huston's lender (who has possession of the note) has Finch Smith, who has invested in Huston's business, sign the note. In this situation, Smith is an indorser, and his liability is secondary—that is, the lender must pursue Huston first before seeking payment from Smith. If Smith ends up paying the amount due on the note, he has a right to reimbursement from Huston (the accommodated party) [UCC 3–419(e)].

Authorized Agents' Signatures

The general law of agency, covered in Chapters 32 and 33, applies to negotiable instruments. Questions often arise as to the liability on an instrument signed by an agent. An **agent** is a person who agrees to represent or act for another, called the **principal.** Agents can sign negotiable instruments, just as they can sign contracts, and thereby bind their principals [UCC 3–401(a)(ii), 3–402(a)]. Without such a rule, all corporate commercial business would stop, as every corporation can and must act through its agents. Certain requirements must be met, however, before the principal becomes liable on the instrument. A basic requirement to hold the principal liable on the instrument is that the agent must be *authorized* to sign the instrument on the principal's behalf.

LIABILITY OF THE PRINCIPAL Generally, an authorized agent binds a principal on an instrument if the agent *clearly names* the principal in the signature (by writing, mark, or some symbol). In this situation, the UCC presumes that the signature is authorized and genuine [UCC 3–308(a)]. The agent may or may not add his or her own name, but if the signature shows clearly that it is made on behalf of a specific principal, the agent is not liable on the instrument [UCC 3–402(b)(1)].

For example, either of the following signatures by Sandra Binney as agent for Bob Aronson will bind Aronson on the instrument:

1. Aronson, by Binney, agent.
2. Aronson.

If Binney (the agent) signs just her own name, however, she will be personally liable to a holder in due course (HDC) who has no notice of her agency status. An agent can escape liability to ordinary holders if the agent proves that the original parties did not intend the agent to be liable on the instrument [UCC 3–402(a), (b)(2)].[6] In either situation, the principal is bound if the party entitled to enforce the instrument can prove the agency relationship.

LIABILITY OF THE AGENT An authorized agent may be held personally liable on a negotiable instrument in three situations. First, as noted above, if the agent signed the agent's own name on the instrument with no indication that she or he was signing as an agent, an HDC can hold the agent personally liable. Second, an agent may be liable if the agent signed in both the agent's name and the principal's name but nothing on the instrument indicated the agency relationship. For example, if Binney signs the instrument "Sandra Binney, Bob Aronson" or "Aronson, Binney," she may be held personally liable because it is not clear that there is an agency relationship.

CASE IN POINT Hugh Caraway was the president of Internacional Realty, Inc. When Internacional hired Land Design Studio to landscape an apartment complex, Caraway signed a promissory note as "Hugh Caraway, Internacional Realty, Inc." When Internacional did not make any payments on the note, Land Design filed a suit against both Caraway and Internacional. Caraway claimed that he had signed the note as an agent and should not be personally liable for the debt. The court ruled that Caraway was personally liable on the note because there was no indication that he was signing as an agent for Internacional.[7]

The third situation in which an agent may be liable is when the agent indicates agency status in signing a negotiable instrument but fails to name the principal (for example, "Sandra Binney, agent")

---

6. See UCC 3–402, Comment 1.
7. *Caraway v. Land Design Studio,* 47 S.W.3d 696 (Tex.App.—Austin 2001).

[UCC 3–402(b)(2)]. Obviously, to protect against potential liability, an authorized agent should disclose on the instrument the identity of the principal and also indicate that the agent is signing in a representative capacity.

CHECKS SIGNED BY AGENTS An important exception to the rules on agent liability is made for checks that are signed by agents. If an agent signs his or her own name on a *check that is payable from the account of the principal,* and the principal is identified on the check, the agent will not be personally liable on the check [UCC 3–402(c)]. Suppose that Binney, who is *authorized* to draw checks on Aronson Company's account, signs a check that is preprinted with Aronson Company's name. The signature reads simply "Sandra Binney." In this situation, Binney will not be personally liable on the check.

The following case illustrates the rule for determining liability when an agent signs his own name to a check that is preprinted with the name of the principal.

CASE 26.1
Jeanmarie v. Peoples

Court of Appeal of Louisiana, Fourth Circuit, 34 So.3d 945 (2010).
www.la4th.org/caseSearch.aspx[a]

BACKGROUND AND FACTS • On August 26, 2005, Anthony and Alcibia Jeanmarie sold property located in New Orleans to Melanie Murray. As part of the transaction, Encore Credit Corporation provided two loans to Murray, for $104,000 and $26,000. Murray secured each loan with a mortgage (mortgages will be discussed in Chapter 31) in favor of Encore. Mark Peoples, through his company, Pyramid Title, LLC, handled the closing of the sale. At the closing, a check was drawn on the Pyramid escrow account[b] in the sum of $110,303.86, payable to the Jeanmaries. The Jeanmaries deposited the check in their account, but two days later the check was returned because there were insufficient funds in Pyramid's escrow account to cover the check. Peoples stated that one of the reasons for the shortage of funds in the escrow account was that Encore Credit had not "timely funded" the $26,000 loan, which would normally be in the account. The Jeanmaries filed an action in a Louisiana state court, seeking payment from both Pyramid Title, LLC, and Peoples personally. Peoples contended that he should not be held liable because he had signed the Pyramid check to the Jeanmaries in his representative capacity. The trial court held for the Jeanmaries, and Peoples and Pyramid submitted a motion for a new trial. When the trial court denied that motion, Peoples and Pyramid appealed.

IN THE LANGUAGE OF THE COURT
Joan Bernard *ARMSTRONG,* Chief Judge.
* * * *

The record contains an undisputed copy of the check in question. It bears the title, "Pyramid Title LLC Escrow Account." Mr. Peoples does not contest the fact that the check bears his signature upon the line entitled "Authorized Signature." [Louisiana's equivalent to UCC 3–402] concerning signatures affixed in a representative capacity provides as follows:

§ 3–402. Signature by representative
* * * *

(c) *If a representative signs the name of the representative as drawer of a check without indication of the representative status and the check is payable from an account of the represented person who is identified on the check, the signer is not liable on the check if the signature is an authorized signature of the represented person.* [Emphasis added.]

---

a. On the drop-down menu for "Appellate Court Case Year," enter 2009, which was the year in which the case was accepted for review by the court. In the box for the "Appellate Court Case Number," enter "1059" and click on "Go." When the case title and other case information appear at the bottom of the page, click on "Download Opinion." The Louisiana court system maintains this Web site.

b. Until a sale of real property, or real estate, is finalized (closed), funds paid by the buyer to the seller, such as a down payment, as well as funds to be paid to the seller by a financing institution, are typically held in an *escrow account.* The concept of escrow and the utilization of escrow accounts in the sale of real property will be discussed in Chapter 50.

CASE 26.1 CONTINUED ➡ Comment No. 3 of the Uniform Commercial Code found under [Louisiana's equivalent to UCC 3–402] shows that [the section] quoted above is the paragraph applicable to the fact situation found in the instant case:

> 3. Subsection (c) * * * states that if the check identifies the represented person, the agent who signs on the signature line does not have to indicate agency status. Virtually all checks used today are in personalized form that identify the person on whose account the check is drawn. In this case, nobody is deceived into thinking that the person signing the check is meant to be liable.

In the instant case, the check clearly identifies the represented person at the top in boldface and a large font as Pyramid Title LLC * * *.

The signature line is entitled, "AUTHORIZED SIGNATURE," a designation not typically found on personal checks. It is patent [obvious] on the face of the check that Mark Peoples signed as the authorized signatory for Pyramid Title and not in his personal capacity * * *. There is nothing subtle, obscure or ambiguous about this.

DECISION AND REMEDY • *The Louisiana appellate court held that it was clear from the face of the instrument that Peoples had signed the check in his representative capacity and thus was not personally liable on the instrument. The court vacated the trial court's ruling on this issue and remanded the case for further proceedings consistent with its opinion.*

WHAT IF THE FACTS WERE DIFFERENT? • *Suppose that the name Pyramid Title, LLC, had not been included on the face of the check. Would Peoples have been personally liable for payment of the check in that situation? Why or why not?*

THE ECONOMIC DIMENSION • *Should Encore Credit Corporation's failure to "timely fund" the $26,000 loan be taken into consideration by the court when determining whether Peoples could be held personally liable on the check to the Jeanmaries? Discuss fully.*

Unauthorized Signatures

Unauthorized signatures arise in two situations—when a person forges another person's name on a negotiable instrument and when an agent who lacks the authority signs an instrument on behalf of a principal. The general rule is that an unauthorized signature is wholly inoperative and will not bind the person whose name is signed or forged. Suppose that Pablo finds Veronica's checkbook lying on the street, writes out a check to himself, and forges Veronica's signature. If a bank negligently fails to ascertain that Veronica's signature is not genuine and cashes the check for Pablo, the bank generally will be liable to Veronica for the amount. (The liability of banks for paying instruments with forged signatures will be discussed further in Chapter 27.)

Similarly, if an agent lacks the authority to sign the principal's name or has exceeded the authority given by the principal, the signature does not bind the principal but will bind the "unauthorized signer" [UCC 3–403(a)]. For example, Maya Campbell is the principal, and Lena Shem is her agent. Shem, without authority, signs a promissory note as follows: "Maya Campbell, by Lena Shem, agent." Because Maya Campbell's "signature" is unauthorized, Campbell cannot be held liable, but Shem is liable to a holder of the note. This would be true even if

Shem had signed the note "Maya Campbell," without indicating any agency relationship. In either situation, the unauthorized signer, Shem, is liable on the instrument.

EXCEPTIONS TO THE GENERAL RULE There are two exceptions to the general rule that an unauthorized signature will not bind the person whose name is signed:

1. When the person whose name is signed *ratifies* (affirms) the signature, he or she will be bound [UCC 3–403(a)]. The parties involved need not be principal and agent. For example, a mother may ratify her daughter's forgery of the mother's signature so that the daughter will not be prosecuted for forgery. A person can ratify an unauthorized signature either expressly (by affirming the validity of the signature) or impliedly (by other conduct, such as keeping any benefits received in the transaction or failing to repudiate the signature).
2. When the negligence of the person whose name was forged substantially contributed to the forgery, a court may not allow the person to deny the effectiveness of an unauthorized signature [UCC 3–115, 3–406, 4–401(d)(2)]. For example, Rob, the owner of a business, leaves his signature stamp and a blank check on an office counter. An

employee uses the stamp to fill in the check and cashes it. Rob can be estopped (prevented), on the basis of his negligence, from denying liability for payment of the check. Whatever loss occurs, however, may be allocated between certain parties on the basis of *comparative negligence* [UCC 3–406(b)]. If Rob, in this example, can demonstrate that the bank was negligent in paying the check, a court may require the bank to bear a portion of the loss. (The liability of the parties in this type of situation will be discussed further in Chapter 27.)

WHEN THE HOLDER IS A HOLDER IN DUE COURSE A person who forges a check or signs an instrument without authorization can be held personally liable for payment by a holder in due course, or HDC [UCC 3–403(a)]. This is true even if the name of the person signing the instrument without authorization does not appear on the instrument. For example, if Michel Vuillard signs "Paul Richman" without Richman's authorization, Vuillard is personally liable just as if he had signed his own name. Vuillard's liability is limited, however, to persons who in good faith pay the instrument or take it for value. A holder who knew the signature was unauthorized would not qualify as an HDC (because of the good faith requirement) and thus could not recover from Vuillard on the instrument. (The defenses that are effective against ordinary holders versus HDCs will be discussed in detail later in this chapter.)

Special Rules for Unauthorized Indorsements

Generally, when an indorsement is forged or unauthorized, the burden of loss falls on the first party to take the instrument with the forged or unauthorized indorsement. The reason for this general rule is that the first party to take an instrument is in the best position to prevent the loss.

For example, Jenny Nilson steals a check drawn on Universal Bank and payable to the order of Inga Leed. Nilson indorses the check "Inga Leed" and presents the check to Universal Bank for payment. The bank, without asking Nilson for identification, pays the check, and Nilson disappears. In this situation, Leed will not be liable on the check, because her indorsement was forged. The bank will bear the loss, which it might have avoided if it had requested identification from Nilson.

This general rule has two important exceptions. These exceptions arise when an indorsement is made by an *imposter* or by a *fictitious payee*.

IMPOSTERS An **imposter** is one who, by her or his personal appearance or use of the mails, Internet, telephone, or other communication, induces a maker or drawer to issue an instrument in the name of an impersonated payee. If the maker or drawer believes the imposter to be the named payee at the time of issue, the indorsement by the imposter is not treated as unauthorized when the instrument is transferred to an innocent party. This is because the maker or drawer *intended* the imposter to receive the instrument. In this situation, under the UCC's *imposter rule,* the imposter's indorsement will be effective—that is, not considered a forgery—insofar as the drawer or maker is concerned [UCC 3–404(a)].

The comparative negligence standard mentioned previously also applies to situations involving imposters [UCC 3–404(d)]. Thus, if a bank fails to exercise ordinary care in cashing a check made out to an imposter, the drawer may be able to recover a portion of the loss from the bank.

CASE IN POINT Jennifer Pennington was an employee at Cablecast. Part of her job was to indorse checks that her employer received in the mail with the Cablecast deposit stamp, prepare the deposit slip, and take the checks to be deposited at City National Bank. On discovering that Pennington had deposited checks payable to Cablecast into her personal account at Premier Bank, Cablecast filed a suit against Premier, claiming that the bank had failed to act in good faith and to exercise ordinary care in handling the checks. The court ruled that there was no evidence that the bank had not acted in good faith. Pennington had represented that she was doing business as Cablecast, and the bank had no reason to doubt her statements or suspect her of wrongdoing. The bank had also observed commercially reasonable standards in its handling of the checks, so it was not negligent. Therefore, the court held that the employer, not the bank, would bear the loss because it was in the best position to prevent the unauthorized indorsement.[8]

FICTITIOUS PAYEES When a person causes an instrument to be issued to a payee who will have *no interest* in the instrument, the payee is referred to as a **fictitious payee.** A fictitious payee can be a person or firm that does not truly exist, or it may be an identifiable party that will not acquire any interest in the instrument. Under the UCC's

---

8. *Cablecast Magazine v. Premier Bank, N.A.,* 729 So.2d 1165 (La. App. 1 Cir. 1999).

fictitious payee rule, the payee's indorsement is not treated as a forgery, and an innocent holder can hold the maker or drawer liable on the instrument [UCC 3–404(b), 3–405].

Situations involving fictitious payees most often arise when (1) a dishonest employee deceives the employer into signing an instrument payable to a party with no right to receive payment on the instrument or (2) a dishonest employee or agent has the authority to issue an instrument on behalf of the employer and issues a check to a party who has no interest in the instrument.

How a Fictitious Payee Can Be Created—An Example.

Assume that Goldstar Aviation, Inc., gives its bookkeeper, Leslie Rose, general authority to issue company checks drawn on First State Bank so that Rose can pay employees' wages and other corporate bills. Rose decides to cheat Goldstar out of $10,000 by issuing a check payable to the Del Rey Company, a supplier of aircraft parts. Rose does not intend Del Rey to receive any of the funds, nor is Del Rey entitled to the payment. Rose indorses the check in Del Rey's name and deposits the check in an account that she opened in West National Bank in the name "Del Rey Co." West National Bank accepts the check and collects payment from the drawee bank, First State Bank. First State Bank charges Goldstar's account $10,000. Rose transfers $10,000 out of the Del Rey account and closes the account. Goldstar discovers the fraud and demands that the account be recredited.

Who Bears the Loss?

According to the UCC's fictitious payee rule, Rose's indorsement in the name of a payee with no interest in the instrument is "effective," so there is no "forgery" [UCC 3–404(b)(2)]. Under this provision, West National Bank is protected in paying on the check, and the drawee bank is protected in charging Goldstar's account. Thus, the employer-drawer, Goldstar, will bear the loss. Of course, Goldstar has recourse against Rose, if she has not absconded with the funds. Additionally, if Goldstar can prove that West National Bank's failure to exercise reasonable care contributed substantially to the loss, the bank may be required to bear a proportionate share of the loss under the UCC's comparative negligence standard [UCC 3–404(d)]. Thus, West National Bank could be liable for a portion of the loss if it failed to exercise ordinary care in its dealings with Rose.

Regardless of whether a dishonest employee actually signs the check or merely supplies his or her employer with names of fictitious creditors (or with true names of creditors having fictitious debts), the result is the same under the UCC. Suppose that Dan Symes draws up the payroll list from which employees' salary checks are written. He fraudulently adds the name Penny Trip (a real person but a fictitious employee) to the payroll, thereby causing checks to be issued to her. Trip cashes the checks and shares the proceeds with Symes. Again, it is the employer-drawer who bears the loss.

For a synopsis of the rules relating to signature liability, see *Concept Summary 26.1* on the following page.

SECTION 2
WARRANTY LIABILITY

In addition to the signature liability, transferors make certain implied warranties regarding the instruments that they are negotiating. Warranty liability arises even when a transferor does not indorse (sign) the instrument [UCC 3–416, 3–417]. Warranty liability is particularly important when a holder cannot hold a party liable on her or his signature, such as when a person delivers a bearer instrument. *Unlike secondary signature liability, warranty liability is not subject to the conditions of proper presentment, dishonor, or notice of dishonor.*

Warranties fall into two categories: those that arise from the *transfer* of a negotiable instrument and those that arise on *presentment*. Both transfer and presentment warranties attempt to shift liability back to the wrongdoer or to the person who dealt face to face with the wrongdoer and thus was in the best position to prevent the wrongdoing.

Transfer Warranties

Under UCC 3–416, one who transfers an instrument for consideration makes the following five **transfer warranties** to all subsequent transferees and holders who take the instrument in good faith (with some exceptions, as will be noted shortly):

1. The transferor is entitled to enforce the instrument.
2. All signatures are authentic and authorized.
3. The instrument has not been altered.
4. The instrument is not subject to a defense or claim of any party that can be asserted against the transferor.

CONCEPT SUMMARY 26.1
Signature Liability

Concept	Description
Primary and Secondary Liability	Every party (except a qualified indorser) who signs a negotiable instrument is either primarily or secondarily liable for payment of the instrument when it comes due. 1. *Primary liability*—Makers and acceptors are primarily liable [UCC 3–409, 3–412, 3–413]. 2. *Secondary liability*—Drawers and indorsers are secondarily liable [UCC 3–414, 3–415, 3–501, 3–502, 3–503]. Parties who are secondarily liable on an instrument promise to pay on that instrument only if the following events occur: a. The instrument is properly and timely presented. b. The instrument is dishonored. c. Timely notice of dishonor is given.
Accommodation Parties	An *accommodation party* is one who signs an instrument for the purpose of lending his or her name as credit to another party on the instrument [UCC 3–419]. Accommodation *makers* are primarily liable; accommodation *indorsers* are secondarily liable.
Agents' Signatures	An *agent* is a person who agrees to represent or act for another, called the *principal*. Agents can sign negotiable instruments and thereby bind their principals. Liability on the instrument depends on whether the agent is authorized and on whether the agent's representative capacity and the principal's identity are both indicated on the instrument [UCC 3–401, 3–402, 3–403]. Agents need not indicate their representative capacity on *checks*—provided the checks clearly identify the principal and are drawn on the principal's account.
Unauthorized Signatures	An unauthorized signature is wholly inoperative as the signature of the person whose name is signed *unless:* 1. The person whose name is signed ratifies (affirms) it or is precluded from denying it [UCC 3–115, 3–403, 3–406, 4–401]. 2. The instrument has been negotiated to a holder in due course [UCC 3–403].
Special Rules for Unauthorized Indorsements	An unauthorized indorsement will not bind the maker or drawer of the instrument except in the following circumstances: 1. When an imposter induces the maker or drawer of an instrument to issue it to the imposter *(imposter rule)* [UCC 3–404(a)]. 2. When a person causes an instrument to be issued to a payee who will have *no interest* in the instrument *(fictitious payee rule)* [UCC 3–404(b), 3–405].

5. The transferor has no knowledge of any bankruptcy proceedings against the maker, the acceptor, or the drawer of the instrument.[9]

---

9. A 2002 amendment to UCC 3–416(a) adds a sixth warranty: "with respect to a remotely created consumer item, that the person on whose account the item is drawn authorized the issuance of the item in the amount for which the item is drawn." UCC 3–103(16) defines a "remotely created consumer item" as an item, such as a check, drawn on a consumer account, that is not created by the payor bank and does not contain the drawer's handwritten signature. Suppose that a telemarketer submits an instrument to a bank for payment, claiming that the consumer on whose account the instrument purports to be drawn authorized it over the phone. Under this amendment, which has been adopted in only a few states, a bank that accepts and pays the instrument warrants to the next bank in the collection chain that the consumer authorized the item in that amount.

Note that for transfer warranties to arise, an instrument *must be transferred for consideration.* For example, Quality Products Corporation sells goods to Royal Retail Stores, Inc., and receives in payment Royal Retail's note. Quality then sells the note, for value, to Superior Finance Company. In this situation, the instrument has been transferred for consideration.

PARTIES TO WHOM WARRANTY LIABILITY EXTENDS
The manner of transfer and the type of negotiation that are used determine how far a transfer warranty will run and whom it will cover. Transfer of an order instrument by indorsement and delivery extends warranty liability to any subsequent holder who

takes the instrument in good faith. The warranties of a person who, for consideration, transfers *without indorsement* (by delivery of a bearer instrument), however, will extend only to the immediate transferee [UCC 3–416(a)].

Suppose that Wylie forges Kim's name as a maker of a promissory note. The note is made payable to Wylie. Wylie indorses the note in blank, negotiates it for consideration to Bret, and then leaves the country. Bret, without indorsement, delivers the note for consideration to Fern. Fern, also without indorsement, delivers the note for consideration to Rick. On Rick's presentment of the note to Kim, the forgery is discovered. Rick can hold Fern (the immediate transferor) liable for breach of the warranty that all signatures are genuine. Rick cannot hold Bret liable because Bret is not Rick's immediate transferor; rather, Bret is a prior nonindorsing transferor.

Note that if Wylie had added a special indorsement ("Payable to Bret") instead of a blank indorsement, the instrument would have remained an order instrument. In that situation, Bret would have had to indorse the instrument to negotiate it to Fern, and his transfer warranties would extend to all subsequent holders, including Rick. This example shows the importance of the distinction between transfer by indorsement and delivery (of an order instrument) and transfer by delivery only, without indorsement (of a bearer instrument).

For a synopsis of the rules on transfer warranty liability, see *Concept Summary 26.2* below.

RECOVERY FOR BREACH OF WARRANTY A transferee or holder who takes an instrument in good faith can sue on the basis of breach of a warranty as soon as he or she has reason to know of the breach [UCC 3–416(d)]. Notice of a claim for breach of warranty must be given to the warrantor within thirty days after the transferee or holder has reason to know of the breach and the identity of the warrantor, or the warrantor is not liable for any loss caused by a delay [UCC 3–416(c)]. The transferee or holder can recover damages for the breach in an amount equal to the loss suffered (but not more than the amount of the instrument), plus expenses and any loss of interest caused by the breach [UCC 3–416(b)].

These warranties can be disclaimed with respect to any instrument except a check [UCC 3–416(c)]. In the check-collection process, discussed in Chapter 27, banks rely on these warranties. For all other instruments, the immediate parties can agree to a disclaimer, and an indorser can disclaim by including in the indorsement such words as "without warranties."

Presentment Warranties

Any person who presents an instrument for payment or acceptance makes the following **presentment warranties** to any other person who in good faith pays or accepts the instrument [UCC 3–417(a), (d)]:

1. The person obtaining payment or acceptance is entitled to enforce the instrument or is authorized

CONCEPT SUMMARY 26.2

Transfer Warranty Liability for Transferors Who Receive Consideration

Transferors	Transferees to Whom Warranties Extend If Consideration Is Received
Indorsers Who Receive Consideration	Five transfer warranties extend to *all* subsequent holders: 1. The transferor is entitled to enforce the instrument. 2. All signatures are authentic and authorized. 3. The instrument has not been altered. 4. The instrument is not subject to a defense or claim of any party that can be asserted against the transferor. 5. The transferor has no knowledge of insolvency proceedings against the maker, acceptor, or drawer of the instrument.
Nonindorsers Who Receive Consideration	Same as for indorsers, but warranties extend *only* to the *immediate transferee*.

to obtain payment or acceptance on behalf of a person who is entitled to enforce the instrument. (This is, in effect, a warranty that there are no missing or unauthorized indorsements.)

2. The instrument has not been altered.

3. The person obtaining payment or acceptance has no knowledge that the signature of the drawer of the instrument is unauthorized.[10]

These warranties are referred to as *presentment warranties* because they protect the person to whom the instrument is presented. They often have the effect of shifting liability back to the party that was in the best position to prevent the wrongdoing. The second and third warranties do not apply to makers, acceptors, and drawers. It is assumed that a drawer or a maker will recognize his or her own signature and that a maker or an acceptor will recognize whether an instrument has been materially altered. Presentment warranties cannot be disclaimed with respect to checks, and a claim for breach must be given to the warrantor within thirty days after the claimant knows or has reason to know of the breach and the identity of the warrantor, or the warrantor is not liable for any loss caused by a delay [UCC 3–417(e)].

---

10. As discussed in Footnote 9, the 2002 amendments to Article 3 of the UCC provide additional protection for "remotely created consumer items," such as a check drawn on a personal account that the account holder authorized over the phone but did not physically sign.

SECTION 3
DEFENSES AND LIMITATIONS

Depending on whether a holder or a holder in due course (HDC)—or a holder through an HDC—makes the demand for payment, certain defenses can bar collection from persons who would otherwise be liable on an instrument. There are two general categories of defenses—*universal defenses* and *personal defenses*, which are discussed below and summarized in Exhibit 26–2 below.

Universal Defenses

Universal defenses (also called *real defenses*) are valid against *all* holders, including HDCs and holders through HDCs. Universal defenses include those described in the following subsections.

FORGERY Forgery of a maker's or drawer's signature cannot bind the person whose name is used unless that person ratifies (approves or validates) the signature or is precluded from denying it (because the forgery was made possible by the maker's or drawer's negligence, for example) [UCC 3–401(a), 3–403(a)]. Thus, when a person forges an instrument, the person whose name is forged has no liability to pay any holder or any HDC the value of the forged instrument.

EXHIBIT 26–2 • Defenses against Liability on Negotiable Instruments

UNIVERSAL (REAL) DEFENSES	PERSONAL (LIMITED) DEFENSES
Valid against all holders, including holders in due course	Valid against ordinary holders but not against holders in due course
1. Forgery. 2. Fraud in the execution. 3. Material alteration. 4. Discharge in bankruptcy. 5. Minority, if the contract is voidable. 6. Illegality, mental incapacity, or duress, if the contract is void under state law.	1. Breach of contract (including breach of contract warranties). 2. Lack or failure of consideration. 3. Fraud in the inducement (ordinary fraud). 4. Illegality, mental incapacity, or duress, if the contract is voidable. 5. Previous payment or cancellation of the instrument. 6. Unauthorized completion of an incomplete instrument and nondelivery of the instrument.

FRAUD IN THE EXECUTION If a person is deceived into signing a negotiable instrument, believing that she or he is signing something other than a negotiable instrument (such as a receipt), *fraud in the execution* (or inception) is committed against the signer [UCC 3–305(a)(1)(iii)]. For example, Connor, a salesperson, asks Javier, a customer, to sign a paper, which Connor says is a receipt for the delivery of goods that Javier is picking up from the store. In fact, the paper is a promissory note, but Javier is unfamiliar with the English language and does not realize this. In this situation, even if the note is negotiated to an HDC, Javier has a valid defense against payment.

This defense cannot be raised, however, if a reasonable inquiry would have revealed the nature and terms of the instrument. Thus, the signer's age, experience, and intelligence are relevant because they frequently determine whether the signer should have understood the nature of the transaction before signing.

MATERIAL ALTERATION An alteration is *material* if it changes the contract terms between two parties *in any way.* Examples include any unauthorized addition of words or numbers or other changes to complete an incomplete instrument that affect the obligation of a party to the instrument [UCC 3–407(a)]. Making any change in the amount, the date, or the rate of interest—even if the change is only one penny, one day, or 1 percent—is material.

It is not a material alteration, however, to correct the maker's address or to draw a red line across the instrument to indicate that an auditor has checked it. It is also not a material alteration to change the figures on a check so that they agree with the written amount. If the alteration is not material, any holder is entitled to enforce the instrument according to its original terms.

A Complete or Partial Defense. Material alteration is a *complete defense* against an ordinary holder but only a *partial defense* against an HDC. An ordinary holder can recover nothing on an instrument that has been materially altered [UCC 3–407(b)]. In contrast, when the holder is an HDC and an original term, such as the monetary amount payable, has been *altered,* the HDC can enforce the instrument against the maker or drawer according to the original terms but not for the altered amount [UCC 3–407(c)(i)].

In the following case, a note that allowed for an extension for payment expired. Its maker and payee then executed a second note, which the payee insisted was only an extension of the time for payment but which in reality increased the balance due. The question before the court was whether the second note materially altered the first.

✳ EXTENDED CASE 26.2 ✳
Keesling v. T.E.K. Partners, LLC

Indiana Court of Appeals, 861 N.E.2d 1246 (2007).

IN THE LANGUAGE OF THE COURT
NAJAM, Judge.
* * * *

In January 1998, Heritage Land [Company] and M.G. Financial [Services of Indiana, Inc.,] formed Heritage/M.G.[, LLC,] for the purpose of developing a residential neighborhood known as Ironwood Estates in Delaware County[, Indiana]. On May 25, 1999, Heritage/M.G. executed * * * [a] note to Peoples Bank and Trust Company, custodian for the James Henke, I.R.A. ("Henke I.R.A."), in the amount of $300,000 to partially finance the development. The final installment under the note was due June 1, 2001. [The note authorized an extension of the time for payment.] The signatories [included Thomas McMullen, on behalf of Heritage/M.G., and Larry and Vivian Keesling.]

Heritage/M.G. did not complete the payments under the original note by the June 2001 deadline. On January 3, 2002, the balance due on the note was $48,228.69.

Then, on May 24, 2002, * * * without the knowledge or consent of the Keeslings * * *, Heritage/M.G. executed [a] second note to the Henke I.R.A. in the amount of $102,000. * * * No payments were ever made on the second note.

Accordingly, on September 2, 2004, 1st National Bank and Trust Company, [which had succeeded Peoples Bank] as custodian for the Henke I.R.A., filed * * * [a complaint in an Indiana state court] against the Keeslings [and others]. On October 25, 2004, the Henke I.R.A. assigned * * * both the original note and the second note to T.E.K. [Partners, LLC] * * *. On November 19, 2004, the trial court entered an order substituting T.E.K. for 1st National Bank as plaintiff. Following a * * * trial, the trial court * * * concluded in relevant part that * * * T.E.K. is

EXTENDED CASE CONTINUES ➡

EXTENDED CASE 26.2 CONTINUED ➡

entitled to judgment * * * in the sum of $365,905.07 plus $10,000 in attorney fees, for a total judgment of $375,905.07. * * * The Keeslings * * * bring this appeal [to a state intermediate appellate court].

* * * *

In sum, the Keeslings * * * contend that because they were accommodation parties on the original note, and the second note constitutes a material alteration of the original note, they are discharged from further personal liability under the original note, and they have no liability under the second note.

* * * *A guaranty is * * * a promise to answer for the debt, default, or miscarriage of another person. It is an agreement collateral to the debt itself and represents a conditional promise whereby the guarantor promises to pay only if the principal debtor fails to pay.* [Emphasis added.]

* * * *

Under Indiana common-law principles, when parties cause a material alteration of an underlying obligation without the consent of the guarantor, the guarantor is discharged from further liability * * * . *A material alteration which will effect a discharge of the guarantor must be a change which alters the legal identity of the principal's contract, substantially increases the risk of loss to the guarantor, or places the guarantor in a different position. The change must be binding.* [Emphasis added.]

Here, Heritage/M.G. is the principal obligor. The Keeslings are guarantors on the original note payable to the Henke I.R.A., which was the original obligee. As guarantors,

the Keeslings are accommodation parties.

* * * *

The original note was past due. * * * T.E.K. maintains that the second note merely extended the time for payment of the original note, as authorized by that note, and did not constitute a material alteration of the original obligation. The trial court agreed, finding that the second note for $102,000 was merely given "to evidence the current amount of monies then due and owing" under the original note "and extend the due date for payment" of the original note. Those findings are clearly erroneous.

* * * The evidence shows that * * * on May 24, 2002, * * * McMullen, on behalf of Heritage/ M.G., executed the second note for $102,000 payable to the Henke I.R.A. * * * . McMullen, who signed both notes, testified that the "difference [between $48,228.69 and $102,000] was used to pay vendors," as well as to pay "interest and stuff."

The evidence clearly shows that the second note did not merely extend the time of payment on the "current amount of monies then due and owing" on the original note. Instead, the facts demonstrate that the second note included additional money to "pay the bills."

The second note also capitalized interest due on the original note, that is, it converted interest due on the original note to principal in the second note. The capitalization of interest meant that the contract interest rate of 12% and the default interest rate of 24% would be charged against the interest added to the second note, thereby

compounding the payment of interest and the effective interest rate. In itself, this capitalization of interest was a material alteration.

Thus, the second note not only added new debt but increased the total principal draws beyond the $300,000 face amount of the original note. [James] Henke testified that under the original note, his I.R.A. was committed to advance "up to $300,000" for the project. The Henke I.R.A. advanced two $130,000 draws to Heritage/M.G. under the original note, for a total of $260,000. But the second note of $102,000 brought total draws to $362,000 * * * which was $62,000 more in draws than the original note authorized.

* * * *

* * * The original note was an unambiguous "promise to pay * * * the sum of $300,000." The note contains a promise to pay a sum certain and does not provide for total draws greater than that sum. The original note was not a revolving line of credit. The accommodation parties assumed the risk of a $300,000 loan, not some multiple of $300,000.

* * * *

In sum, the second note constitutes a material alteration of the original obligation. As such, the Keeslings * * * are discharged from their personal liability on the original note, and they have no liability for the additional sums advanced under the second note, which they did not sign. We reverse the trial court's judgment [against the Keeslings] * * * .

QUESTIONS

1. If the court had affirmed the judgment in favor of T.E.K., against whom might the Keeslings have had a right of recourse?

2. What might the parties who executed the second note have done at the time to avoid the outcome in this case?

An HDC Can Enforce an Incomplete Instrument That Was Subsequently Altered. Note that if the instrument was originally incomplete and was later completed in an unauthorized manner, alteration can no longer be claimed as a defense against an HDC, and the HDC can enforce the instrument as completed [UCC 3–407(b), (c)]. This is because a drawer or maker who has issued an incomplete instrument normally will be held responsible for such an alteration, which could have been avoided by the exercise of greater care. If the alteration is readily apparent (such as a number changed on the face of a check), then obviously the holder has notice of some defect or defense and therefore cannot be an HDC (and therefore cannot enforce the instrument) [UCC 3–302(a)(1), (2)(iv)].

DISCHARGE IN BANKRUPTCY Discharge in bankruptcy (see Chapter 30) is an absolute defense on any instrument regardless of the status of the holder [UCC 3–305(a)(1)(iv)]. This defense exists because the purpose of bankruptcy is to finally settle all of the insolvent party's debts.

MINORITY Minority, or infancy, is a universal defense only to the extent that state law recognizes it as a defense to a simple contract. Because state laws on minority vary, so do determinations of whether minority is a universal defense against an HDC [UCC 3–305(a)(1)(i)]. (See Chapter 13 for further discussion of the contractual liability of minors.)

ILLEGALITY Certain types of illegality constitute universal defenses, whereas others are personal defenses. If a statute provides that an illegal transaction is void, then the defense is universal—that is, absolute against both an ordinary holder and an HDC. If the law merely makes the instrument voidable, then the illegality is a personal defense against an ordinary holder, but not against an HDC [UCC 3–305(a)(1)(ii)].

MENTAL INCAPACITY If a court has declared a person to be mentally incompetent, then any instrument issued by that person is void. The instrument is void *ab initio* (from the beginning) and unenforceable by any holder or HDC [UCC 3–305(a)(1)(ii)]. Mental incapacity in these circumstances is a universal defense. If a court has not declared a person to be mentally incompetent, then mental incapacity operates as a personal defense against ordinary holders but not against HDCs.

EXTREME DURESS When a person signs and issues a negotiable instrument under such extreme duress as an immediate threat of force or violence (for example, at gunpoint), the instrument is void and unenforceable by any holder or HDC [UCC 3–305(a)(1)(ii)]. (Ordinary duress is a defense against ordinary holders but not against HDCs.)

Personal Defenses

Personal defenses (sometimes called *limited defenses*), such as those described next, are used to avoid payment to an ordinary holder of a negotiable instrument, but not to an HDC or a holder through an HDC.

BREACH OF CONTRACT OR BREACH OF WARRANTY
When there is a breach of the underlying contract for which the negotiable instrument was issued, the maker of a note can refuse to pay it, or the drawer of a check can order his or her bank to stop payment on the check. Breach of warranty can also be claimed as a defense to liability on the instrument.

For example, Elias purchases two dozen pairs of athletic shoes from De Soto. The shoes are to be delivered in six weeks. Elias gives De Soto a promissory note for $1,000, which is the price of the shoes. The shoes arrive, but many of them are stained, and the soles of several pairs are coming apart. Elias has a defense to liability on the note on the basis of breach of contract and breach of warranty. (Recall from Chapter 22 that a seller impliedly promises that the goods being sold are at least merchantable.) If, however, the note is no longer in the hands of the payee-seller (De Soto) but is presented for payment by an HDC, the maker-buyer (Elias) will not be able to plead breach of contract or warranty as a defense against liability on the note.

LACK OR FAILURE OF CONSIDERATION The absence of consideration (value) may be a successful defense in some instances [UCC 3–303(b), 3–305(a)(2)]. For example, Tony gives Cleo, as a gift, a note that states, "I promise to pay you $100,000," and Cleo accepts the note. No consideration is given in return for Tony's promise, and a court will not enforce the promise.

Similarly, if delivery of goods becomes impossible, a party who has issued a draft or note under the contract has a defense for not paying it. Thus, in the hypothetical athletic-shoe transaction described previously, if the shoes were lost in an accident and delivery became impossible, De Soto could not subsequently enforce Elias's promise to pay the $1,000 promissory note. If the note was in the hands of an HDC, however, Elias's defense would not be available against the HDC.

FRAUD IN THE INDUCEMENT (ORDINARY FRAUD) A person who issues a negotiable instrument based on false statements by the other party will be able to avoid payment on that instrument, unless the holder is an HDC. To illustrate: Weston agrees to purchase

Carla's used tractor for $26,500. Carla, knowing her statements to be false, tells Weston that the tractor is in good working order and that it has been used for only one harvest. In addition, she tells Weston that she owns the tractor free and clear of all claims. Weston pays Carla $4,500 in cash and issues a negotiable promissory note for the balance. As it turns out, Carla still owes the original seller $10,000 on the purchase of the tractor, and the tractor is subject to a valid security interest (discussed in Chapter 29). In addition, the tractor is three years old and has been used in three harvests.

In this situation, Weston can refuse to pay the note if it is held by an ordinary holder. If, however, Carla has negotiated the note to an HDC, Weston must pay the HDC. Of course, Weston can then sue Carla to recover the funds.

ILLEGALITY As mentioned, if a statute provides that an illegal transaction is voidable, the defense is personal. For example, some states make contracts in restraint of trade voidable. Thus, an instrument given in payment of a contract to restrain trade in those states is voidable and operates as a personal defense (only against ordinary holders).

MENTAL INCAPACITY If a maker or drawer issues a negotiable instrument while mentally incompetent but before a court has declared him or her to be so, the instrument is voidable. In this situation, mental incapacity serves as a personal defense (only against ordinary holders).

OTHER PERSONAL DEFENSES A number of other personal defenses can be used to avoid payment to an ordinary holder, but not an HDC, of a negotiable instrument, including the following:

1. Discharge by previous payment or cancellation [UCC 3–601(b), 3–602(a), 3–603, 3–604].
2. Unauthorized completion of an incomplete instrument [UCC 3–115, 3–302, 3–407, 4–401(d)(2)].
3. Nondelivery of the instrument [UCC 1–201(14), 3–105(b), 3–305(a)(2)].
4. Ordinary duress or undue influence rendering the contract voidable [UCC 3–305(a)(1)(ii)].

Federal Limitations on HDC Rights

The federal government limits HDC rights in certain circumstances because of the harsh effects that the HDC rules can sometimes have on consumers. Under the HDC doctrine, a consumer who purchased a defective product (such as a defective automobile) would continue to be liable to HDCs even

if the consumer returned the defective product to the retailer. For example, to buy a used truck with a one-year warranty, Brian pays $5,000 down and signs a promissory note to the dealer, for the remaining $15,000. The truck turns out to be defective, but the dealer has already sold the note to an HDC. Thus, even if Brian returns the truck to the dealer, under the HDC doctrine, he would remain liable to the HDC for $15,000 because his claim of breach of warranty is a personal defense. To protect consumers who purchased defective products, the Federal Trade Commission (FTC) adopted Rule 433.[11]

FTC RULE 433 FTC Rule 433 severely limits the rights of HDCs that purchase instruments arising out of *consumer credit* transactions. The rule applies to consumers who purchase goods or services for personal, family, or household use using a consumer credit contract. The FTC regulation attempts to prevent a consumer from being required to make payment for a defective product to a third party HDC of a promissory note that formed part of the contract with the dealer who sold the defective good.

Rule 433 requires the following provision to be included in boldface type in a consumer credit contract:

NOTICE

ANY HOLDER OF THIS CONSUMER CREDIT CONTRACT IS SUBJECT TO ALL CLAIMS AND DEFENSES WHICH THE DEBTOR COULD ASSERT AGAINST THE SELLER OF GOODS OR SERVICES OBTAINED PURSUANT HERETO OR WITH THE PROCEEDS HEREOF. RECOVERY HEREUNDER BY THE DEBTOR SHALL NOT EXCEED AMOUNTS PAID BY THE DEBTOR HEREUNDER.

EFFECT OF THE RULE When a negotiable instrument contains the required notice, a consumer is allowed to bring any defense that she or he has against the seller of a product against a subsequent holder as well. In essence, FTC Rule 433 places an HDC of the instrument in the position of a contract assignee. The rule makes the buyer's duty to pay conditional on the seller's full performance of the contract. It also clearly reduces the degree of transferability of negotiable instruments resulting from consumer credit contracts. An instrument that contains this notice or a similar statement required by law may remain negotiable, but there cannot be an HDC of such an instrument [UCC 3–106(d)].

There is a loophole, however, in that FTC Rule 433 does not prohibit third parties from purchasing

---

11. 16 C.F.R. Section 433.2. The rule was enacted in 1976 pursuant to the FTC's authority under the Federal Trade Commission Act, 15 U.S.C. Sections 41–58.

notes or credit contracts that do *not* contain the required notice. So, if a third party purchases an instrument arising from a consumer credit transaction that lacks the required notice, that third party normally is not subject to the buyer's defenses against the seller. Thus, some consumers remain unprotected by the FTC rule.[12]

SECTION 4

DISCHARGE

Discharge from liability on an instrument can occur in several ways, including by payment, by cancellation, and, as previously discussed, by material alteration. Discharge can also occur if a party reacquires an instrument, if a holder impairs another party's right of recourse, or if a holder surrenders collateral without consent.

Discharge by Payment or Tender of Payment

All parties to a negotiable instrument will be discharged when the party primarily liable on it pays to a holder the full amount due [UCC 3–602, 3–603].[13] The liability of all parties is also discharged when the drawee of an unaccepted draft or check makes payment in good faith to the holder. Payment by any other party (for example, an indorser) discharges only the liability of that party and subsequent parties. The party making such a payment still has the right to recover on the instrument from any prior parties.[14]

---

12. A 2002 amendment to UCC 3–305(e) closes this loophole, but only a minority of the states have adopted the amendment. The amendment makes a third party holder in possession of a note or other instrument that was supposed to include this notice subject to a buyer's defenses against a seller even if the instrument did not include the notice.

13. This is true even if the payment is made with knowledge of a claim to the instrument by another person unless the payor knows that "payment is prohibited by injunction or similar process of a court of competent jurisdiction" or, in most situations, "the party making payment accepted, from a person having a claim to the instrument, indemnity against loss resulting from refusal to pay the person entitled to enforce the instrument" [UCC 3–602(a), (b)(1)].

14. Under the 2002 amendment to UCC 3–602(b), when a party entitled to enforce an instrument transfers it without giving notice to the parties obligated to pay it, and one of those parties pays the transferor, that payment is effective. For example, Roberto borrows $5,000 from Consumer Finance Company on a note payable to the lender. Consumer Finance transfers the note to Delta Investment Corporation but continues to collect payments from Roberto. Under this amendment, those payments effectively discharge Roberto to the extent of their amount.

A party will not be discharged when paying in bad faith to a holder who acquired the instrument by theft or who obtained the instrument from someone else who acquired it by theft (unless, of course, the person has the rights of an HDC) [UCC 3–602(b)(2)].

If a tender of payment is made to a person entitled to enforce the instrument and the tender is refused, indorsers and accommodation parties whose rights to seek reimbursement are impaired (impairment of the right of recourse is discussed shortly) are discharged to the extent of the amount of the tender [UCC 3–603(b)]. If a tender of payment of an amount due on an instrument is made to a person entitled to enforce the instrument, the obligor's obligation to pay interest after the due date on the amount tendered is discharged [UCC 3–603(c)].

Discharge by Cancellation or Surrender

Intentional cancellation of an instrument discharges the liability of all parties [UCC 3–604]. Intentionally writing "Paid" across the face of an instrument cancels it. Intentionally tearing up an instrument cancels it. If a holder intentionally crosses out a party's signature, that party's liability and the liability of subsequent indorsers who have already indorsed the instrument are discharged. Materially altering an instrument may discharge the liability of all parties, as previously discussed [UCC 3–407(b)]. (An HDC may be able to enforce a materially altered instrument against its maker or drawer according to the instrument's *original* terms, however.)

Destruction or mutilation of a negotiable instrument is considered cancellation only if it is done with the intention of eliminating obligation on the instrument [UCC 3–604(a)(i)]. Thus, if destruction or mutilation occurs by accident, the instrument is not discharged, and the original terms can be established by parol evidence [UCC 3–309]. A note's holder may also discharge the obligation by surrendering the note to the person to be discharged—provided that the holder intended to eliminate the obligation [UCC 3–604(a)(i)].

CASE IN POINT Edith Mark bought a Ford pickup and signed a loan contract and promissory note with Huntington National Bank to finance the purchase. She had made twenty of the sixty-six payments required on the loan when she received the original agreement, stamped "PAID," in the mail, along with the title certificate. Mark stopped making payments on the loan, and the bank filed a lawsuit. Mark argued that the note had been discharged by surrender, but the bank claimed that the documents were returned to her due to an inadvertent clerical error. The court held that because the bank did not intend to discharge the note when it returned the documents to Mark, the surrender did not constitute a valid cancellation of the note.[15]

Discharge by Reacquisition

A person who reacquires an instrument that he or she held previously discharges all intervening indorsers against subsequent holders who do not qualify as HDCs [UCC 3–207]. Of course, the person reacquiring the instrument may be liable to subsequent holders if the instrument is dishonored.

Discharge by Impairment of Recourse

Discharge can also occur when a party's right of recourse is impaired [UCC 3–605]. A *right of recourse* is a right to seek reimbursement. Ordinarily, when a holder collects the amount of an instrument from an indorser, the indorser has a right of recourse against prior indorsers, the maker or drawer, and accommodation parties. If the holder has adversely affected the indorser's right to seek reimbursement from these other parties, however, the indorser is not liable on the instrument (to the extent that the indorser's right of recourse is impaired). This occurs when, for example, the holder releases or agrees not to sue a party against whom the indorser has a right of recourse. It also occurs when a holder agrees to an extension of the instrument's due date or to some other material modification that results in a loss to the

indorser with respect to the right of recourse [UCC 3–605(c), (d)].[16]

Discharge by Impairment of Collateral

Sometimes, a party to an instrument gives collateral as security that her or his performance will occur. When a holder "impairs the value" of that collateral without the consent of the parties who would benefit from the collateral in the event of nonpayment, those parties to the instrument are discharged to the extent of the impairment [UCC 3–605(e), (f)].

For example, Jerome and Myra sign a note as co-makers, putting up Jerome's property as collateral. The note is payable to Montessa. Montessa is required by law to file a financing statement (discussed in Chapter 29) with the state to put others on notice of her interest in Jerome's property as collateral for the note. If Montessa fails to file the statement and Jerome goes through bankruptcy—which results in his property's being sold to pay other debts and leaves him unable to pay anything on the note—Montessa has impaired the value of the collateral to Myra, who is discharged to the extent of that impairment.

In other words, when Jerome goes through bankruptcy, Montessa's earlier failure to file the statement prevents her from taking possession of the collateral, selling it, and crediting the amount owed on the note. Myra, as co-maker, is then responsible only for any remaining indebtedness, instead of the entire unpaid balance. Thus, Myra is discharged to the extent that the proceeds from the sale of the collateral would have discharged her liability on the note.

---

15. *Huntington National Bank v. Mark,* 2004 WL 1627029 (Ohio App. 2004).

16. The 2002 amendments to UCC 3–605 essentially apply the principles of suretyship and guaranty (to be discussed in Chapter 28) to circumstances that involve the impairment of the right of recourse of "secondary obligors," which include indorsers and accommodation parties. One important difference from the principles of suretyship and guaranty, however, is that under amended UCC 3–605(a), the release of a principal obligor by a person entitled to enforce a check grants a complete discharge to an indorser of the check without requiring proof of harm.

CHAPTER 26 REVIEWING

REVIEWING
Liability, Defenses, and Discharge

Nancy Mahar was the office manager at Golden Years Nursing Home, Inc. She was given a signature stamp to issue checks to the nursing home's employees for up to $100 as advances on their pay. The checks were drawn on Golden Years' account at First National Bank. Over a seven-year period,

REVIEWING

Liability, Defenses, and Discharge, Continued

Mahar wrote a number of checks to employees exclusively for the purpose of embezzling funds for herself. She forged the employees' indorsements on the checks, signed her name as a second indorser, and deposited the checks in her personal account at Star Bank. The employees whose names were on the checks never actually requested them. When the scheme was uncovered, Golden Years filed a suit against Mahar, Star Bank, and others to recover the funds. Using the information presented in the chapter, answer the following questions.

1. With regard to signature liability, which provision of the Uniform Commercial Code (UCC) discussed in this chapter applies to this scenario?
2. What is the rule set forth by that provision?
3. Under the UCC, which party, Golden Years or Star Bank, must bear the loss in this situation? Why?
4. Based on these facts, describe any transfer or presentment warranties that Mahar may have violated.

⊛ **DEBATE THIS:** *Because signature stamps create so many opportunities for embezzlement, they should be banned.*

TERMS AND CONCEPTS

accommodation party 500

agent 501
dishonor 499
fictitious payee 504

imposter 504
personal defense 511
presentment warranty 507

principal 501
transfer warranty 505
universal defense 508

QUESTIONS AND CASE PROBLEMS

26–1. Material Alteration Williams purchased a used car from Stein for $1,000. Williams paid for the car with a check (written in pencil) payable to Stein for $1,000. Stein, through careful erasures and alterations, changed the amount on the check to read $10,000 and negotiated the check to Boz. Boz took the check for value, in good faith, and without notice of the alteration and thus met the Uniform Commercial Code's requirements for the status of a holder in due course. Can Williams successfully raise the universal (real) defense of material alteration to avoid payment on the check? Explain.

26–2. Signature Liability Waldo makes out a negotiable promissory note payable to the order of Grace. Grace indorses the note by writing on it "Without recourse, Grace" and transfers the note for value to Adam. Adam, in need of cash, negotiates the note to Keith by indorsing it with the words "Pay to Keith, Adam." On the due date, Keith presents the note to Waldo for payment, only to learn that Waldo has filed for bankruptcy and will have

all debts (including the note) discharged. Discuss fully whether Keith can hold Waldo, Grace, or Adam liable on the note.

26–3. QUESTION WITH SAMPLE ANSWER: Defenses.

Niles sold Kennedy a small motorboat for $1,500, maintaining to Kennedy that the boat was in excellent condition. Kennedy gave Niles a check for $1,500, which Niles indorsed and gave to Frazier for value. When Kennedy took the boat for a trial run, she discovered that the boat leaked, needed to be painted, and required a new motor. Kennedy stopped payment on her check, which had not yet been cashed. Niles has disappeared. Can Frazier recover from Kennedy as a holder in due course? Discuss.

• **For a sample answer to Question 26–3, go to Appendix I at the end of this text.**

26–4. Signature Liability Gil makes out a $900 negotiable promissory note payable to Ben. By special indorsement,

Ben transfers the note for value to Jess. By blank indorsement, Jess transfers the note for value to Pam. By special indorsement, Pam transfers the note for value to Adrien. In need of cash, Adrien transfers the instrument for value by blank indorsement back to Jess. When told that Ben has left the country, Jess strikes out Ben's indorsement. Later she learns that Ben is a wealthy restaurant owner in Baltimore and that Gil is financially unable to pay the note. Jess contends that, as a holder in due course, she can hold Ben, Pam, or Adrien liable on the note. Discuss fully Jess's contentions.

26–5. Agents' Signatures Robert Helmer and Percy Helmer, Jr., were authorized signatories on the corporate checking account of Event Marketing, Inc. The Helmers signed a check drawn on Event Marketing's account and issued to Rumarson Technologies, Inc. (RTI), in the amount of $24,965. The check was signed on July 13, 1998, but dated August 14. When RTI presented the check for payment, it was dishonored due to insufficient funds. RTI filed a suit in a Georgia state court against the Helmers to collect the amount of the check. Claiming that the Helmers were personally liable on Event Marketing's check, RTI filed a motion for summary judgment. Can an authorized signatory on a corporate account be held personally liable for corporate checks returned for insufficient funds? Are the Helmers liable in this case? Discuss. [*Helmer v. Rumarson Technologies, Inc.*, 245 Ga.App. 598, 538 S.E.2d 504 (2000)]

26–6. Defenses On September 13, 1979, Barbara Shearer and Barbara Couvion signed a note for $22,500, with interest at 11 percent, payable in monthly installments of $232.25 to Edgar House and Paul Cook. House and Cook assigned the note to Southside Bank in Kansas City, Missouri. In 1997, the note was assigned to Midstates Resources Corp., which assigned the note to the Cadle Co. in 2000. According to the payment history that Midstates gave to Cadle, the interest rate on the note was 12 percent. A Cadle employee noticed the discrepancy and recalculated the payments at 11 percent. When Shearer and Couvion refused to make further payments on the note, Cadle filed a suit in a Missouri state court against them to collect. Couvion and Shearer responded that they had made timely payments on the note, that Cadle and the previous holders had failed to accurately apply the payments to the reduction of principal and interest, and that the note "is either paid in full and satisfied or very close to being paid in full and satisfied." Is the makers' answer sufficient to support a verdict in their favor? If so, on what ground? If not, why not? [*The Cadle Co. v. Shearer*, 69 S.W.3d 122 (Mo.App.W.D. 2002)]

26–7. CASE PROBLEM WITH SAMPLE ANSWER: Agents' Signatures.

Ameripay, LLC, is a payroll services company that, among other things, issues payroll checks to the employees of its clients. In July 2002, Nu Tribe Radio Networks, Inc. (NTRN), based in New York City, hired Ameripay. Under their agreement, Ameripay set up an account on NTRN's behalf at Commerce Bank. NTRN agreed to deposit funds in the account to cover its payroll obligations. Arthur Piacentini, an owner of Ameripay, was an authorized signatory on the account. On the checks, NTRN was the only identified company, and Piacentini's signature appeared without indicating his status. At the end of the month, four NTRN employees cashed their payroll checks, which Piacentini had signed, at A-1 Check Cashing Emporium, Inc. The checks were returned dishonored. Ameripay had stopped their payment because it had not received the funds from NTRN. A-1 assigned its interest in the checks to Robert Triffin, who filed a suit in a New Jersey state court against Ameripay. Between a principal and an agent, what principles determine which party is liable for the amount of an unpaid instrument? How do those principles apply in this case? Is Ameripay liable? Why or why not? [Triffin v. Ameripay, LLC, 368 N.J.Super. 587, 847 A.2d 628 (App. Div. 2004)]

- **To view a sample answer for Problem 26–7, go to this book's Web site at www.cengage.com/blaw/clarkson, select "Chapter 26," and click on "Case Problem with Sample Answer."**

26–8. Accommodation Parties Donald Goosic, a building contractor in Nebraska, did business as "Homestead" builders. To construct a house "on spec" (without a pre-construction buyer), Donald obtained materials from Sack Lumber Co. on an open account. When Donald "got behind in his payments," his wife, Frances, cosigned a note payable to Sack for $43,000, the outstanding balance on the account. Donald made payments on the note until he obtained a discharge of his debts in a bankruptcy proceeding to which Frances was not a party. Less than a year later, Sack filed a suit in a Nebraska state court against Frances to collect on the note. She contended that she was an accommodation party, not a maker, and thus was not liable because the applicable statute of limitations had run. She testified that Donald "made more debt than . . . money" and that she was "paying the bills out of [her] income." The Goosics' most recent tax returns showed only losses relating to Homestead. Under the Uniform Commercial Code, a person receiving only an indirect benefit from a transaction can qualify as an accommodation party. How would you rule on this question of fact? Why? [*Sack Lumber Co. v. Goosic*, 15 Neb.App. 529, 732 N.W.2d 690 (2007)]

26–9. Unauthorized Indorsements Stephen Schor, an accountant in New York City, advised his client, Andre Romanelli, Inc., to open an account at J. P. Morgan Chase Bank, N.A., to obtain a favorable interest rate on a line of credit. Romanelli's representative signed a signature card, which he gave to Schor. When the accountant later told Romanelli that the rate was not favorable, the firm told him not to open the account. Schor signed a blank line on the signature card, changed the mailing address to his office, and opened the account in Romanelli's name. In a purported attempt to obtain credit for the firm elsewhere, Schor had its principals write checks payable to themselves for more than $4.5 million, ostensibly to pay taxes. He indorsed and deposited the checks in the

Chase account and eventually withdrew and spent the funds. Romanelli filed a suit in a New York state court against Chase and other banks, alleging that a drawer is not liable on an unauthorized indorsement. Is this the rule? What are its exceptions? Which principle applies to these facts, and why? [*Andre Romanelli, Inc. v. Citibank, N.A.*, 60 A.D.3d 428, 875 N.Y.S.2d 14 (1 Dept. 2009)]

26–10. A QUESTION OF ETHICS: Primary and Secondary Liability.

Clarence Morgan, Jr., owned Easy Way Automotive, a car dealership in D'Lo, Mississippi. Easy Way sold a truck to Loyd Barnard, who signed a note for the amount of the price payable to Trustmark National Bank in six months. Before the note came due, Barnard returned the truck to Easy Way, which sold it to another buyer. Using some of the proceeds from the second sale, Easy Way sent a check to Trustmark to pay Barnard's note. Meanwhile, Barnard obtained another truck from Easy Way, financed through another six-month note payable to Trustmark. After eight of these deals, some of which involved more than one truck, an Easy Way check to Trustmark was

dishonored. In a suit in a Mississippi state court, Trustmark sought to recover the amounts of two of the notes from Barnard. Trustmark had not secured titles to two of the trucks covered by the notes, however, and this complicated Barnard's efforts to reclaim the vehicles from the later buyers. [Trustmark National Bank v. Barnard, *930 So.2d 1281 (Miss.App. 2006)*]

(a) On what basis might Barnard be liable on the Trustmark notes? Would he be primarily or secondarily liable? Could this liability be discharged on the theory that Barnard's right of recourse had been impaired when Trustmark did not secure titles to the trucks covered by the notes? Explain.

(b) Easy Way's account had been subject to other recent overdrafts, and a week after the check to Trustmark was returned for insufficient funds, Morgan committed suicide. At the same time, Barnard was unable to obtain a mortgage because the unpaid notes affected his credit rating. How do the circumstances of this case underscore the importance of practicing business ethics?

LEGAL RESEARCH EXERCISES ON THE WEB

Go to this text's Web site at **www.cengage.com/blaw/clarkson**, select "Chapter 26," and click on "Practical Internet Exercises." There you will find the following Internet research exercises that you can perform to learn more about the topics covered in this chapter.

Practical Internet Exercise 26–1: **Legal Perspective**
Fictitious Payees

Practical Internet Exercise 26–2: **Management Perspective**
FTC Rule 433

Checks are the most common type of negotiable instruments regulated by the Uniform Commercial Code (UCC). Checks are convenient to use because they serve as a substitute for cash. Although debit cards now account for more retail payments than do checks, commercial checks remain an integral part of the U.S. economic system.

Articles 3 and 4 of the UCC govern issues relating to checks. As noted in the preceding chapters, Article 3 establishes the requirements for all negotiable instruments, including checks. Article 3 also sets forth the rights and responsibilities of parties to negotiable instruments. Article 4 establishes a framework for deposit and checking agreements between a bank and its customers. Article 4 also governs the relationships of banks with one another as they process checks for payment. A check therefore may fall within the scope of Article 3 and yet be subject to the provisions of Article 4 while in the course of collection. If a conflict arises between Articles 3 and 4, Article 4 controls [UCC 4–102(a)].

In this chapter, we first identify the legal characteristics of checks and the legal duties and liabilities that arise when a check is issued. Then we examine the check-collection process. Increasingly, credit cards, debit cards, and other devices and methods for transferring funds electronically are being used to pay for goods and services. In the latter part of this chapter, we look at the law governing electronic fund transfers.

SECTION 1
CHECKS

A **check** is a special type of draft that is drawn on a bank, ordering the bank to pay a fixed amount of money on demand [UCC 3–104(f)]. Article 4 defines a *bank* as "a person engaged in the business of banking, including a savings bank, savings and loan association, credit union or trust company" [UCC 4–105(1)]. If a nonbank institution (such as a brokerage firm) handles a check for payment or for collection, the check is not covered by Article 4.

Recall from the preceding chapters that a person who writes a check is called the *drawer*. The drawer is usually a depositor in the bank on which the check is drawn. The person to whom the check is payable is the *payee*. The bank or financial institution on which the check is drawn is the *drawee*. Thus, if Anne Tomas writes a check on her checking account to pay her college tuition, she is the drawer, her bank is the drawee, and her college is the payee.

Between the time a check is drawn and the time it reaches the drawee, the effectiveness of the check may be altered by some event—for example, the drawer may die or order payment not to be made, or the account on which the check is drawn may be depleted. To avoid this problem, a payee may insist on payment by an instrument that has already been accepted by the drawee, such as a cashier's check, a traveler's check, or a certified check.

Cashier's Checks

Checks are usually three-party instruments, but on some checks, the bank serves as both the drawer *and* the drawee. For example, when a bank draws a check on itself, the check is called a **cashier's check** and is a negotiable instrument on issue (see Exhibit 27–1 on the facing page) [UCC 3–104(g)]. Normally, a cashier's check indicates a specific payee. In effect, with a cashier's check, the bank assumes responsibility for paying the check, thus making the check more readily acceptable as a substitute for cash.

EXHIBIT 27-1 • A Cashier's Check

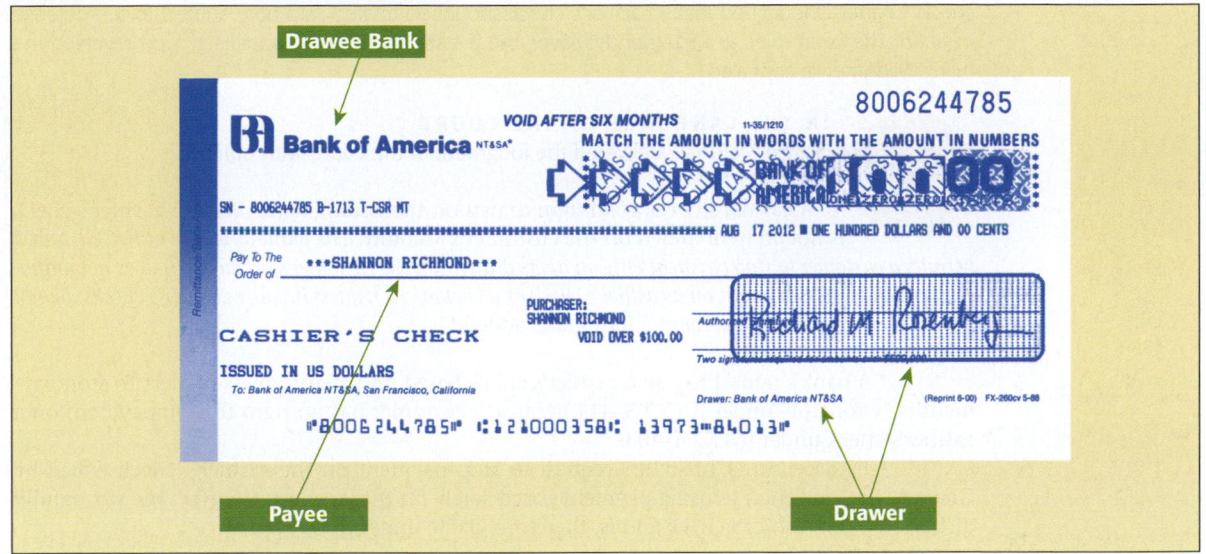

*The abbreviation *NT&SA* stands for National Trust and Savings Association. The Bank of America NT&SA is a subsidiary of Bank of America Corporation, which is engaged in financial services, insurance, investment management, and other businesses.

For example, Blake needs to pay a moving company $8,000 for moving his household goods to his new home in another state. The moving company requests payment in the form of a cashier's check. Blake goes to a bank (he need not have an account at the bank) and purchases a cashier's check, payable to the moving company, in the amount of $8,000. Blake has to pay the bank the $8,000 for the check, plus a small service fee. He then gives the check to the moving company.

Cashier's checks are commonly used in business to pay for real estate transactions or to make tax payments because payment is immediately credited (the payee need not wait to see if the check "clears"). Except in very limited circumstances, the issuing bank *must*

honor its cashier's checks when they are presented for payment. If a bank wrongfully dishonors a cashier's check, a holder can recover from the bank all expenses incurred, interest, and consequential damages [UCC 3–411]. This same rule applies if a bank wrongfully dishonors a certified check (to be discussed shortly) or a *teller's check*. (A *teller's check* is similar to a cashier's check except that usually it is drawn by a bank on another bank [UCC 3–104(h)]. A teller's check may be used when a person withdraws funds from one bank to transfer to an account at another bank.)

Rather than being treated as the equivalent of cash, should a cashier's check be treated as a note with all of the applicable defenses? That was the contention in the following case.

CASE 27.1
MidAmerica Bank, FSB v. Charter One Bank, FSB

Illinois Supreme Court, 232 Ill.2d 560, 905 N.E.2d 839 (2009).

BACKGROUND AND FACTS • Mary Christelle was the mother of David Hernandez, president of Essential Technologies of Illinois (ETI). Christelle bought a $50,000 cashier's check from Charter One Bank payable to ETI. ETI deposited the check into its account with MidAmerica Bank. Four days later, Christelle asked Charter One to stop payment (see pages 523 and 524) on the cashier's check. Charter One agreed and refused to honor the check. MidAmerica returned the check to ETI. Within two weeks, ETI's account had a negative balance of $52,000. MidAmerica closed the account and filed a

CASE CONTINUES ▶

CASE 27.1 CONTINUED ▶ suit in an Illinois state court against Charter One, alleging that it had wrongfully dishonored the cashier's check. Charter One argued that a cashier's check should be treated as a note subject to the defense of fraud. The court ruled in MidAmerica's favor, but a state intermediate appellate court reversed the ruling. MidAmerica appealed.

IN THE LANGUAGE OF THE COURT
Justice *KILBRIDE* delivered the judgment of the court, with opinion.
* * * *
A cashier's check is an item drawn on the issuing bank. Thus, a cashier's check is not an item drawn on the customer's account. *The plain language of [UCC] 4–403 permits a customer to stop payment only on items drawn "on the customer's account." It does not authorize a bank to stop payment on a cashier's check at a customer's request because cashier's checks are not drawn "on the customer's account."* [Emphasis added.]
* * * *
* * * A bank's refusal to pay a cashier's check based on its customer's request to stop payment is "wrongful" under [UCC] 3–411 because a customer has no right to stop payment on a cashier's check under [UCC] 4–403.
* * * By accepting Christelle's request to stop payment on the cashier's check issued by Charter One, and then refusing payment based solely on that request, Charter One wrongfully dishonored the cashier's check and is, therefore, liable under [UCC] 3–411.
* * * *
* * * Charter One submits that * * * revisions [to UCC Article 3] changed the law from treating cashier's checks as "cash equivalents" to treating them as "demand notes." Charter One argues that all defenses to the enforcement of a note now apply to cashier's checks.
* * * *
* * * [Under the UCC,] cashier's checks are treated as drafts to reflect common commercial usage, but [the] liability of the "drawer" is the same as the "maker" of a note. This is because a bank issuing a cashier's check is both the drawer and [the] drawee of the check. The UCC provides that cashier's checks are drafts, not notes. * * * *The liability of a bank is that of the maker of a note because issuance of a cashier's check establishes the bank as both drawer and drawee, representing that it will honor the draft when presented.* Thus the * * * revisions * * * do not represent a change in the former law. [Emphasis added.]
* * * *
The UCC comment preceding Article 3 explains that cashier's checks are to be treated as "cash equivalents." We therefore reject Charter One's argument that * * * revisions to the UCC changed the law to treat cashier's checks as "demand notes."
* * * *
Charter One, nonetheless, attempts to assert defenses to support its dishonor of the cashier's check, arguing that the cashier's check was procured by fraud. To the contrary, the record does not show that Charter One had knowledge of any fraud when it dishonored the cashier's check.

DECISION AND REMEDY • *The Illinois Supreme Court reversed the lower court's decision, awarded MidAmerica the amount of the check, and remanded the case for a determination of interest and fees. Except in limited circumstances, none of which applied here, a bank can obtain payment on a cashier's check over the drawee bank's stop-payment order.*

WHAT IF THE FACTS WERE DIFFERENT? • *Suppose that the court had accepted Charter One's argument that a cashier's check should be treated as a note and the bank had presented proof of fraud in the procurement of the check. What might have been the result in this case? Explain.*

MANAGERIAL IMPLICATIONS • *It is worth noting that no one—managers and consumers alike—can treat stop-payment orders casually. These orders have to be for a valid cause, such as fraud or nondelivery of merchandise or services purchased. Moreover, when a cashier's check is involved, as the court determined in this case, there virtually is never a valid reason to place a stop-payment order on a cashier's check, and banks normally should ignore such orders.*

Traveler's Checks

A **traveler's check** is an instrument that is payable on demand, drawn on or payable at a financial institution (such as a bank), and designated as a traveler's check. The issuing institution is directly obligated to accept and pay its traveler's check according to the check's terms. Traveler's checks are designed as a safe substitute for cash when a person is on vacation or traveling and are issued for a fixed amount, such as $20, $50, or $100. The purchaser is required to sign the check at the time it is purchased and again at the time it is used [UCC 3–104(i)]. Today, instead of issuing traveler's checks, most major banks purchase and issue American Express traveler's checks for their customers (see Exhibit 27–2 below).

Certified Checks

A **certified check** is a check that has been *accepted* by the bank on which it is drawn [UCC 3–409(d)]. When a drawee bank agrees to certify a check, it immediately charges the drawer's account with the amount of the check and transfers those funds to its own certified-check account. In effect, the bank is agreeing in advance to accept that check when it is presented for payment and to make payment from those funds reserved in the certified-check account. Essentially, certification prevents the bank from denying liability. It is a promise that sufficient funds are on deposit and *have been set aside* to cover the check.

To certify a check, the bank writes or stamps the word *certified* on the face of the check and typically writes the amount that it will pay.[1] Either the drawer or the holder (payee) of a check can request certification, but the drawee bank is not required to certify a check. A bank's refusal to certify a check is not a dishonor of the check [UCC 3–409(d)]. Once a check is certified, the drawer and any prior indorsers are completely discharged from liability on the check [UCC 3–414(c), 3–415(d)]. Only the certifying bank is required to pay the instrument.

SECTION 2
THE BANK-CUSTOMER RELATIONSHIP

The bank-customer relationship begins when the customer opens a checking account and deposits funds that the bank will use to pay for checks written by the customer. Essentially, three types of relationships come into being, as discussed next.

Creditor-Debtor Relationship

A creditor-debtor relationship is created between a customer and a bank when, for example, the customer makes cash deposits into a checking account. When a customer makes a deposit, the customer becomes a creditor, and the bank a debtor, for the amount deposited.

---

1. If the certification does not state an amount, and the amount is later increased and the instrument negotiated to a holder in due course (HDC), the obligation of the certifying bank is the amount of the instrument when it was taken by the HDC.

EXHIBIT 27–2 • An American Express Traveler's Check

Agency Relationship

An agency relationship also arises between the customer and the bank when the customer writes a check on his or her account. In effect, the customer is ordering the bank to pay the amount specified on the check to the holder when the holder presents the check to the bank for payment. In this situation, the bank becomes the customer's agent and is obligated to honor the customer's request. Similarly, if the customer deposits a check into his or her account, the bank, as the customer's agent, is obligated to collect payment on the check from the bank on which the check was drawn.

Contractual Relationship

Whenever a bank-customer relationship is established, certain contractual rights and duties arise. The contractual rights and duties of the bank and the customer depend on the nature of the transaction. These rights and duties are discussed in detail in the following pages.

SECTION 3
THE BANK'S DUTY TO HONOR CHECKS

When a banking institution provides checking services, it agrees to honor the checks written by its customers, with the usual stipulation that sufficient funds must be available in the account to pay each check. When a drawee bank *wrongfully* fails to honor a check, it is liable to its customer for damages resulting from its refusal to pay [UCC 4–402(b)]. To sue for wrongful dishonor, the customer does not have to prove that the bank breached its contractual commitment or was negligent.

The customer's agreement with the bank includes a general obligation to keep sufficient funds on deposit to cover all checks written. The customer is liable to the payee or to the holder of a check in a civil suit if a check is dishonored for insufficient funds. If intent to defraud can be proved, the customer can also be subject to criminal prosecution for writing a bad check.

When the bank properly dishonors a check for insufficient funds, it has no liability to the customer. The bank may rightfully refuse payment on a customer's check in other circumstances as well. We look here at the rights and duties of both the bank and its customers in specific situations.

Overdrafts

When the bank receives an item properly payable from its customer's checking account but the account contains insufficient funds to cover the amount of the check, the bank has two options. It can either (1) dishonor the item or (2) pay the item and charge the customer's account, thus creating an **overdraft,** providing that the customer has authorized the payment and the payment does not violate any bank-customer agreement [UCC 4–401(a)].[2] The bank can subtract the difference (plus a service charge) from the customer's next deposit because the check carries with it an enforceable implied promise to reimburse the bank.

When a check "bounces," a holder can resubmit the check, hoping that at a later date sufficient funds will be available to pay it. The holder must notify any indorsers on the check of the first dishonor, however; otherwise, they will be discharged from their signature liability, as discussed in Chapter 26.

A bank can expressly agree with a customer to accept overdrafts through what is sometimes called an "overdraft protection agreement." If such an agreement is formed, any failure of the bank to honor a check because it would create an overdraft breaches this agreement and is treated as a wrongful dishonor [UCC 4–402(a), (b)].

Postdated Checks

A bank may also charge a postdated check against a customer's account, unless the customer notifies the bank, in a timely manner, not to pay the check until the stated date. (Indeed, banks today typically ignore the dates on checks and treat them as demand instruments unless they have received notice from a customer that a check was postdated.) The notice of postdating must be given in time to allow the bank to act on the notice before committing itself to pay on the check.

The UCC states that the bank should treat the notice like a stop-payment order (to be discussed shortly). If the bank fails to act on the customer's notice and charges the customer's account before the date on the postdated check, the bank may be liable for any damages incurred by the customer. Damages include those that result from the dishonor of checks that are subsequently presented for

---

2. When customers have a joint account, the bank cannot hold any customer on the account liable for payment of an overdraft unless that customer has signed the check or has benefited from the proceeds of the check [UCC 4–401(b)].

payment and are dishonored for insufficient funds [UCC 4–401(c)].

Stale Checks

Commercial banking practice regards a check that is presented for payment more than six months from its date as a **stale check.** A bank is not obligated to pay an uncertified check presented more than six months from its date [UCC 4–404]. When receiving a stale check for payment, the bank has the option of paying or not paying the check. If a bank pays a stale check in good faith without consulting the customer, the bank has the right to charge the customer's account for the amount of the check.

Death or Incompetence of a Customer

Neither the death nor the incompetence of a customer revokes a bank's authority to pay an item until the bank knows of the situation and has had reasonable time to act on the notice [UCC 4–405]. Thus, if, at the time a check is issued or its collection is undertaken, a bank does not know that the customer who wrote the check has been declared incompetent, the bank can pay without incurring liability.

Even when a bank knows of the death of its customer, for ten days after the *date of death* it can pay or certify checks drawn on or before the date of death. Without this provision, banks would constantly be required to verify the continued life and competence of their drawers. An exception to the rule is made if a person claiming an interest in the account of the deceased customer, such as an heir or an executor of the estate (see Chapter 52), orders the bank to stop payment.

Stop-Payment Orders

A **stop-payment order** is an order by a customer to her or his bank not to pay a certain check.[3] Only a customer or a "person authorized to draw on the account" can order the bank not to pay the check when it is presented for payment [UCC 4–403(a)]. A customer has no right to stop payment on a check that has already been certified (or accepted) by a bank, however. Also, a stop-payment order must be received within a reasonable time and in a reasonable manner to permit the bank to act on it [UCC 4–403(a)]. Although a stop-payment order can be given orally,

usually by phone, the order is binding on the bank for only fourteen calendar days unless confirmed in writing.[4] A written stop-payment order (see Exhibit 27–3 on the following page) or an oral order confirmed in writing is effective for six months, at which time it must be renewed in writing [UCC 4–403(b)].

BANK'S LIABILITY FOR WRONGFUL PAYMENT If the bank pays the check over the customer's properly instituted stop-payment order, the bank will be obligated to recredit the customer's account. In addition, if the bank's payment over a stop-payment order causes subsequent checks written on the drawer's account to "bounce," the bank will be liable for the resultant costs the drawer incurs. The bank is liable only for the amount of the actual loss suffered by the drawer because of the wrongful payment, however [UCC 4–403(c)].

Assume that Mike Murano orders one hundred cell phones from Advanced Communications, Inc., at $50 each. Murano pays in advance for the phones with a check for $5,000. Later that day, Advanced Communications tells Murano that it will not deliver the phones as arranged. Murano immediately calls the bank and stops payment on the check. Two days later, in spite of this stop-payment order, the bank inadvertently honors Murano's check to Advanced Communications for the undelivered phones. The bank will be liable to Murano for the full $5,000.

The result would be different, however, if Advanced Communications had delivered and Murano had accepted ninety-nine phones. Because Murano would have owed Advanced Communications $4,950 for the goods delivered, Murano's actual loss would be only $50. Consequently, the bank would be liable to Murano for only $50.

CUSTOMER'S LIABILITY FOR WRONGFUL STOP-PAYMENT ORDER A stop-payment order has its risks for a customer. The drawer must have a *valid legal ground* for issuing such an order; otherwise, the holder can sue the drawer for payment. Moreover, defenses sufficient to refuse payment to a payee may not be valid grounds to prevent payment to a subsequent holder in due course [UCC 3–305, 3–306]. A person who wrongfully stops payment on a check not only will be liable to the payee for the amount of the check but also may be liable for consequential damages incurred by the payee as a result of the wrongful stop-payment order.

---

3. Note that although this discussion focuses on checks, the right to stop payment is not limited to checks; it extends to any item payable by any bank. See Official Comment 3 to UCC 4–403.

---

4. Some states do not recognize oral stop-payment orders; the orders must be in writing.

EXHIBIT 27–3 • A Stop-Payment Order

BI **Bank of America**

Checking Account
Stop-Payment Order

To: Bank of America NT&SA
I want to stop payment on the following check(s).

ACCOUNT NUMBER: ⬜⬜⬜⬜⬜⬜ — ⬜⬜⬜⬜⬜

SPECIFIC STOP

*ENTER DOLLAR AMOUNT: _____ *CHECK NUMBER: _____

THE CHECK WAS SIGNED BY: _____

THE CHECK IS PAYABLE TO: _____

THE REASON FOR THIS STOP PAYMENT IS: _____

STOP RANGE (Use for lost or stolen check(s) only.)

DOLLAR AMOUNT: 000

*ENTER STARTING CHECK NUMBER: _____ *END CHECK NUMBER: _____

THE REASON FOR THIS STOP PAYMENT IS: _____

I agree that this order (1) is effective only if the above check(s) has (have) not yet been cashed or paid against my account, (2) will end six months from the date it is delivered to you unless I renew it in writing, and (3) is not valid if the check(s) was (were) accepted on the strength of my Bank of America courtesy-check guarantee card by a merchant participating in that program. I also agree (1) to notify you immediately to cancel this order if the reason for the stop payment no longer exists or (2) that closing the account on which the check(s) is (are) drawn automatically cancels this order.

IF ANOTHER BRANCH OF THIS BANK OR ANOTHER PERSON OR ENTITY BECOMES A "HOLDER IN DUE COURSE" OF THE ABOVE CHECK, I UNDERSTAND THAT PAYMENT MAY BE ENFORCED AGAINST THE CHECK'S MAKER (SIGNER).

*I CERTIFY THE AMOUNT AND CHECK NUMBER(S) ABOVE ARE CORRECT.

☐ I have written a replacement check (number and date of check).

_____

(Optional—please circle one: Mr., Ms., Mrs., Miss) CUSTOMER'S SIGNATURE **X** _____ DATE _____

BANK USE ONLY

TRANCODE:

☐ 21—ENTER STOP PAYMENT (SEE OTHER SIDE TO REMOVE)

NON READS: _____
UNPROC. STMT HIST: _____
PRIOR STMT CYCLE: _____
HOLDS ON COOLS: _____
REJECTED CHKS: _____
LARGE ITEMS: _____
FEE COLLECTED: _____
DATE ACCEPTED: _____
TIME ACCEPTED: _____

Forged Drawers' Signatures

When a bank pays a check on which the drawer's signature is forged, generally the bank suffers the loss.[5] A bank may be able to recover at least some of the loss from the customer, however, if the customer's negligence substantially contributed to the forgery. A bank may also obtain partial recovery from the forger of the check (if he or she can be found) or from the holder who presented the check for payment (if the holder knew that the signature was forged).

THE GENERAL RULE A forged signature on a check has no legal effect as the signature of a drawer [UCC 3–403(a)]. For this reason, banks require a signature card from each customer who opens a checking account. Signature cards allow a bank to verify whether the signatures on its customers' checks are genuine. The general rule is that the bank must recredit the customers' account when it pays on a forged signature. (Banks today normally verify signatures only on checks that exceed a certain threshold, such as $2,500 or some higher amount. Even

though a bank sometimes incurs liability costs when it has paid forged checks, the costs of verifying the signature on every check would be much higher.)

Note that a bank may contractually shift to the customer the risk of forged checks created by the use of facsimile or other nonmanual signatures. For example, the contract might stipulate that the customer is solely responsible for maintaining security over any device affixing a signature. The contract might also provide that any nonmanual signature is effective as the customer's signature regardless of whether the person who affixed the signature was authorized to do so.

CUSTOMER NEGLIGENCE When a customer's negligence substantially contributes to a forgery, the bank normally will not be obligated to recredit the customer's account for the amount of the check [UCC 3–406(a)]. If negligence on the part of the bank (or other "person") paying the instrument or taking it for value or for collection substantially contributed to the customer's loss, however, the customer's liability may be reduced by the amount of the loss caused by the bank's negligence [UCC 3–406(b)].

Suppose that CompuNet, Inc., uses a check-writing machine to write its payroll and business

---

5. Each year, check fraud costs banks many billions of dollars—more than the combined losses from credit-card fraud, theft from automated teller machines, and armed robberies.

checks. A CompuNet employee uses the machine to create a check for $10,000 payable to himself, and CompuNet's bank subsequently honors it. CompuNet asks the bank to recredit $10,000 to its account for incorrectly paying on a forged check. If the bank can show that CompuNet failed to take reasonable care in controlling access to the check-writing equipment, the bank will not be required to recredit the account for the amount of the forged check. If CompuNet can show that negligence on the part of the bank contributed substantially to the loss, however, then CompuNet's liability may be reduced proportionately.

In the following case, an employee opened a bogus bank account and fraudulently deposited his employer's checks in it for years. The court had to determine if the bank should have requested written authorization from the company before opening the account.

CASE 27.2
Auto-Owners Insurance Co. v. Bank One

Supreme Court of Indiana, 879 N.E.2d 1086 (2008).

BACKGROUND AND FACTS • Kenneth Wulf worked in the claims department of Auto-Owners Insurance Company for ten years. When the department received checks, a staff member would note them in the file and send them on to headquarters. Wulf opened a checking account at Bank One in the name of "Auto-Owners, Kenneth B. Wulf." Over a period of eight years, he deposited $546,000 worth of checks that he had stolen from Auto-Owners and indorsed with a stamp that read "Auto-Owners Insurance Deposit Only." When the scam was finally discovered, Auto-Owners sued Bank One, contending that it had failed to exercise ordinary care in opening the account because it had not asked for documentation to show that Wulf was authorized to open an account in the name of Auto-Owners. The lower courts rejected that argument and granted summary judgment for Bank One. Auto-Owners appealed.

IN THE LANGUAGE OF THE COURT
SULLIVAN, Justice.
* * * *
   We begin with the question of whether Bank One exercised ordinary care. * * * Auto-Owners claims that Bank One should have invested more energy in confirming Wulf's legitimacy when Wulf opened a bank account in Auto-Owners's name in 1991. However, [UCC 3–]405(b) makes no mention of a bank's responsibilities when opening an account for a new customer. Rather, subsection (b) requires ordinary care from a bank in the "paying" or "taking" of an instrument.
* * * *
   Even if Bank One did not demonstrate ordinary care in its acceptance of the checks proffered [submitted] by Wulf, Auto-Owners must still show that such a lack of ordinary care "substantially contributed" to its losses.
   * * * Thus, *to determine whether conduct has substantially contributed to a loss, we follow the second comment to [UCC 3–406] and ask whether the opening of the bank account was (1) a contributing factor to Auto-Owners's loss and (2) whether the opening of the bank account was a substantial factor in bringing the loss about.* * * * We will view the conduct of Bank One "in its entirety." [Emphasis added.]
   * * * Other than the lack of procedure used in opening the bank account in 1991, Bank One appears to have followed required protocol in depositing checks from Wulf. Even if we assume that Bank One's conduct in opening the account was a contributing factor to Auto-Owners's loss, and meets the first part of the "substantially contributed" test, * * * Bank One's conduct was not a substantial factor in bringing that loss about under the second part of the test. In other words, when viewed in its entirety Bank One's conduct does not meet the "substantially contributed" test. * * * Auto Owners was the substantial contributor to its own losses * * * with its less than rigorous monitoring of its files and incoming checks.

CASE CONTINUES ➡

CASE 27.2 CONTINUED ▶   * * * We agree with the trial court's determination that Bank One was entitled to summary judgment and that Auto-Owners is not entitled to a trial * * *.

DECISION AND REMEDY • *Indiana's highest court affirmed the lower court's decision granting summary judgment to Bank One. Bank One's conduct did not "substantially contribute" to bringing about the losses suffered by Auto-Owners. The bank breached no duty to the insurance company by opening Wulf's checking account.*

THE LEGAL ENVIRONMENT DIMENSION • *What reasonable steps could Auto-Owners have taken to prevent such internal fraud?*

WHAT IF THE FACTS WERE DIFFERENT? • *Would the outcome in this case have been changed if Auto-Owners had never given Wulf (and other staff members) the authority to deposit checks to its bank account? Why or why not?*

Timely Examination of Bank Statements Required. Banks typically send or make available (such as with online statements) to their customers monthly statements detailing the activity in their checking accounts. In the past, banks routinely included the canceled checks themselves (or photocopies of the canceled checks) with the statement sent to the customer. Today, most banks simply provide the customer with information (check number, amount, and date of payment) on the statement that will allow the customer to reasonably identify each check that the bank has paid [UCC 4–406(a), (b)]. If the bank retains the canceled checks, it must keep the checks—or legible images of them—for seven years [UCC 4–406(b)]. The customer may obtain a copy of a canceled check from the bank during this period of time.

The customer has a duty to examine promptly bank statements (and canceled checks or photocopies, if they are included) with reasonable care on receipt and to report any alterations or forged signatures [UCC 4–406(c)]. The customer is also obligated to report any alteration or forgery in the signatures of indorsers (to be discussed shortly). If the customer fails to fulfill her or his duty and the bank suffers a loss as a result, the customer will be liable for the loss [UCC 4–406(d)].

Consequences of Failure to Detect Forgeries. Sometimes, the same wrongdoer forges the customer's signature on a series of checks. In that situation, to recover for all of the forged items, the customer must discover and report the first forged check to the bank within thirty calendar days of the receipt or availability of the bank statement [UCC 4–406(d)(2)]. Failure to notify the bank within this time period discharges the bank's liability for all forged checks that it pays prior to notification.

CASE IN POINT Joseph Montanez, an employee at Espresso Roma Corporation, used stolen software and blank checks to generate company checks on his home computer. The series of forged checks spanned a period of more than two years and totaled more than $330,000. When the bank statements containing the forged checks arrived in the mail, Montanez removed the checks so that the forgeries would go undetected. Eventually, Espresso Roma discovered the forgeries and asked the bank to recredit its account. When the bank refused, litigation ensued. The court held that the bank was not liable for the forged checks because Espresso Roma had failed to report the first forgeries within thirty days, as required by the UCC.[6]

Negligence and the Bank's Duty of Care. In one situation, a bank customer can escape liability, at least in part, for failing to notify the bank of forged or altered checks within the required thirty-day period. That situation occurs when the customer can prove that the bank was also negligent—that is, that the bank failed to exercise ordinary care. Then the bank, too, will be liable, and the loss will be allocated between the bank and the customer on the basis of comparative negligence [UCC 4–406(e)]. In other words, even though a customer may have been negligent, the bank may still have to recredit the customer's account for a portion of the loss if the bank failed to exercise ordinary care.

The UCC defines *ordinary care* as the "observance of reasonable commercial standards, prevailing in the area in which [a] person is located, with respect to the business in which that person is engaged" [UCC 3–103(a)(7)]. As mentioned earlier, it is customary in

---

6. *Espresso Roma Corp. v. Bank of America, N.A.*, 100 Cal.App.4th 525, 124 Cal.Rptr.2d 549 (2002).

the banking industry to examine signatures only on checks that exceed a certain amount. Thus, a bank's failure to verify the authenticity of a signature on a particular check does not necessarily mean that it has breached its duty to exercise ordinary care.

The plaintiff in the following case alleged that his father's bank had breached the duty of care when it added a signatory to his father's bank account. The central question before the court had to do with how the required standard of care was to be determined.

✳ EXTENDED CASE 27.3 ✳
Schultz v. Bank of America, N.A.

Court of Appeals of Maryland, 413 Md. 15, 990 A.2d 1078 (2010).
www.courts.state.md.us/opinions.html[a]

IN THE LANGUAGE OF THE COURT
GREENE, J. [Judge]
* * * *

[Melvin] Schultz died on July 5, 2005, at the age of 81. * * * Before he died * * * he developed some sort of relationship with [Robin] Holbrook, who had moved into Schultz's home. Holbrook was apparently acting as Schultz's caregiver, but Petitioner [Stephen Schultz, Melvin Schultz's son and personal representative[b]] alleges that Holbrook also took advantage of Schultz by having her name added to Schultz's account with the Bank [of America, N.A.]. Petitioner has advanced two theories as to how this occurred, one in which Holbrook coerced Schultz into adding her name to his account and another in which Holbrook had her name added through forgery. There is no dispute that Holbrook's name was in fact added to Schultz's account and that she made withdrawals from the account.

Petitioner filed suit against the Bank, alleging that the Bank negligently handled Schultz's account * * *. At trial, * * * a handwriting expert examined several of Schultz's known signatures and the signature card that was used to add Holbrook's name to Schultz's bank account. He opined that the

signature purporting to be Schultz's on the signature card was not the signature that Schultz used in the normal course of business. He also testified that several checks drawn on Schultz's account appeared to have been forged with Schultz's signature.

Petitioner * * * testified to the deterioration in Schultz's health, and * * * that the signatures on some checks drawn from Schultz's bank account were not authentic. He also explained that there had been activity on Schultz's ATM account after Schultz met Holbrook, even though Schultz never used an ATM.

* * * *

* * * The trial court denied the Bank's motion [for summary judgment], concluding that expert testimony was unnecessary to establish the standard of care on the facts of this case, [and] that there was sufficient evidence to submit the negligence claim to the jury * * *.

[At trial, the jury found in Schultz's favor. The bank appealed, and the Court of Special Appeals (an intermediate appellate court) reversed the trial court's judgment. Schultz then appealed to Maryland's highest state court, the Court of Appeals.]

* * * *

In a negligence case, there are four elements that the plaintiff must prove to prevail: "a duty owed to

him [or her] (or to a class of which he [or she] is a part), a breach of that duty, a legally cognizable causal relationship between the breach of duty and the harm suffered, and damages." *In regard to the duty a bank owes to its customers when disbursing the customers' funds, banks are not to be held strictly liable for every wrongful disbursement.* Instead, our case law and the comments to the Maryland Uniform Commercial Code ("Commercial Code") establish that a duty of "ordinary care" applies. The Commercial Code defines "ordinary care" as the "1) observance of reasonable commercial standards, 2) which prevail in the area in which the person is located, 3) with respect to the business in which the person is engaged." A bank customer may bring a negligence suit against a bank for a violation of this duty of ordinary care. [Emphasis added.]

* * * *

In this case, Petitioner's negligence claim is based on his allegation that the Bank failed to satisfy its duty of ordinary care in regard to its handling of Schultz's checking account. Specifically at issue in this appeal is Petitioner's claim that the Bank did not satisfy that duty when it "fail[ed] to properly add Holbrook to the account and verify her and [Schultz's] identities."

The Bank argues that expert testimony was necessary to establish

EXTENDED CASE CONTINUES ➡

EXTENDED CASE 27.3 CONTINUED ➡

the Bank's standard of care, while Petitioner contends that * * * no expert testimony was necessary to explain the Bank's standard of care to the jury. We disagree with Petitioner's contention * * * . To explain [the process of adding names to bank accounts], a plaintiff must produce expert testimony from someone familiar with the process from a bank's perspective. Petitioner also failed to provide evidence of the reasonable commercial banking standards that prevail specifically in the relevant geographical area of the Bank, as required by the ordinary care standard. Finally, banking practices are changing in the era of the Internet and other electronic banking practices. Bank procedures may not be the same today as they were just

a few years ago, which also means that an expert may be necessary to explain to the trier of fact [a judge or jury] what duty a bank owes to a customer.

* * * *

When negligence is alleged against a bank, * * * expert testimony is ordinarily necessary to establish the applicable standard of care. Such testimony is not necessary when the bank's alleged negligence, if proven, so obviously deviated from the applicable standard of care that the trier of fact could appreciate the deviation without an expert's assistance. The alleged negligence in this case, however, involved internal banking procedures that the trier of fact could not be expected to appreciate. Petitioner should have provided expert testimony to explain to the jury what banks ordinarily do

to protect their customers from imposters when adding a name to the customer's account, so that the jury could then decide whether the Bank had acted in accordance with the duty of ordinary care. Instead, Petitioner provided no testimony on this issue at all. Without expert testimony to explain the duty of ordinary care, the jury could not know whether to hold the Bank accountable for failing to protect its customer's account. Petitioner therefore failed to provide any competent evidence of the duty owed to him, a necessary element of a negligence claim, and the trial court should not have submitted this claim to the jury. We agree with the Court of Special Appeals that the trial court should have granted the Bank's motion for judgment.

Judgment of the court of special appeals affirmed.

 QUESTIONS

1. "Expert testimony should not be required to inform jurors of what a reasonable standard of care should be in commonplace banking transactions." Do you agree with this statement? Why or why not?
2. Suppose that both Schultz *and* the bank had been found negligent in the addition of Holbrook's name to Schultz's account. In this situation, which party would be liable for any damages resulting from the negligence? Explain.

One-Year Time Limit. Regardless of the degree of care exercised by the customer or the bank, the UCC places an absolute time limit on the liability of a bank for paying a check with a customer's forged signature. A customer who fails to report her or his forged signature within one year from the date that the statement was made available for inspection loses the legal right to have the bank recredit her or his account [UCC 4–406(f)]. The parties can also agree in their contract to a lower time limit, but the UCC stipulates that the bank has no liability on forged instruments after one year.

CASE IN POINT Wanda Williamson, a clerk at Visiting Nurses Association of Telfair County, Inc. (VNA), was responsible for making VNA bank deposits, but she was not a signatory on the association's account. Over a four-year period, Williamson embezzled more than $250,000 from VNA by forging its indorsement on checks, cashing them at the bank, and keeping a portion of the proceeds.

Williamson was eventually arrested and convicted. VNA then filed a lawsuit against the bank, claiming that it had been negligent in allowing Williamson to cash the checks. The court dismissed the case because VNA had failed to report the forged indorsements within the prescribed time period. Not only did UCC 4–406(f) preclude the action, but the bank's contract with VNA had also included a clause stating that customers had to report a forgery within sixty days. Thus, the bank was not liable.[7]

OTHER PARTIES FROM WHOM THE BANK MAY RECOVER As noted earlier, a forged signature on a check has no legal effect as the signature of a drawer; a forged signature, however, is effective as the signature of the unauthorized signer [UCC 3–403(a)]. Therefore, when a bank pays a check on which the

---

7. *Security State Bank v. Visiting Nurses Association of Telfair County, Inc.*, 568 S.E.2d 491 (Ga.App. 2002).

drawer's signature is forged, the bank has a right to recover from the party who forged the signature. The bank may also have a right to recover from a party (its customer or a collecting bank—to be discussed later in this chapter) who transferred a check bearing a forged drawer's signature and received payment (see the discussion of transfer warranties in Chapter 26). This right is limited, however, in that the bank cannot recover from a person who took the check in good faith and for value or who in good faith changed position in reliance on the payment or acceptance [UCC 3–418(c)].

Checks Bearing Forged Indorsements

A bank that pays a customer's check bearing a forged indorsement must recredit the customer's account or be liable to the customer (drawer) for breach of contract. Suppose that Cameron issues a $500 check "to the order of Sophia." Margo steals the check, forges Sophia's indorsement, and cashes the check. When the check reaches Cameron's bank, the bank pays it and debits Cameron's account. The bank must recredit Cameron's account for the $500 because it failed to carry out Cameron's order to pay "to the order of Sophia" [UCC 4–401(a)]. Of course, Cameron's bank can in turn recover—for breach of warranty (see Chapter 26 on page 507)—from the bank that cashed the check when Margo presented it [UCC 4–207(a)(2)].

Eventually, *the loss usually falls on the first party to take the instrument bearing the forged indorsement* because a forged indorsement does not transfer title. Thus, anyone who takes an instrument with a forged indorsement cannot become a holder.

The customer, in any event, has a duty to report forged indorsements promptly. The bank is relieved of liability if the customer fails to report the forged indorsements within three years of receiving the bank statement that contained the forged items [UCC 4–111].[8]

Altered Checks

The customer's instruction to the bank is to pay the exact amount on the face of the check to the holder. The bank has an implicit duty to examine checks before making final payments. If it fails to detect an alteration, it is liable to its customer for the loss

because it did not pay as the customer ordered. The loss is the difference between the original amount of the check and the amount actually paid. Suppose that a check written for $11 is raised to $111. The customer's account will be charged $11 (the amount the customer ordered the bank to pay). The bank will normally be responsible for the remaining $100 [UCC 4–401(d)(1)].

CUSTOMER NEGLIGENCE   As in a situation involving a forged drawer's signature, a customer's negligence can shift the loss when payment is made on an altered check (unless the bank was also negligent). For example, a person may carelessly write a check and leave large gaps around the numbers and words where additional numbers and words can be inserted (see Exhibit 27–4 on the following page).

Similarly, a person who signs a check and leaves the dollar amount for someone else to fill in is barred from protesting when the bank unknowingly and in good faith pays whatever amount is shown [UCC 4–401(d)(2)]. Finally, if the bank can trace its loss on successive altered checks to the customer's failure to discover the initial alteration, then the bank can reduce its liability for reimbursing the customer's account [UCC 4–406].[9]

In every situation involving a forged drawer's signature or an alteration, a bank must observe reasonable commercial standards of care in paying on a customer's checks [UCC 4–406(e)]. The customer's contributory negligence can be asserted only if the bank has exercised ordinary care.

OTHER PARTIES FROM WHOM THE BANK MAY RECOVER   The bank is entitled to recover the amount of loss (including expenses and any loss of interest) from a transferor who, by presenting a check for payment, warrants that the check has not been altered.[10] This rule has two exceptions. If the bank is the drawer (as it is on a cashier's check), it cannot recover on this ground from the presenting party if the party is a holder in due course (HDC) acting in

---

8. This is a general statute of limitations for all actions under Article 4; it provides that any lawsuit must be brought within three years of the time that the cause of action arises.

9. The bank's defense is the same whether the successive payments were made on a forged drawer's signature or on altered checks. The bank must prove that prompt notice would have prevented its loss. For example, notification might have alerted the bank not to pay further items or might have enabled it to catch the forger.

10. Usually, the party presenting an instrument for payment is the payee, a holder, a bank customer, or a collecting bank. A bank's customers include its account holders, which may include other banks [UCC 4–104(a)(5)]. As will be discussed later in this chapter, a *collecting bank* is any bank handling an item for collection except the bank on which the check is drawn [UCC 4–105(5)].

EXHIBIT 27–4 • A Poorly Filled-Out Check

good faith [UCC 3–417(a)(2), 4–208(a)(2)]. The reason is that an instrument's drawer is in a better position than an HDC to know whether the instrument has been altered.

Similarly, an HDC who presents a certified check for payment in good faith does not warrant to the check's certifier that the check was not altered before the HDC acquired it [UCC 3–417(a)(2), 4–208(a)(2)]. Consider an example. Alan, the drawer, draws a check for $500 payable to Pam, the payee. Pam alters the amount to $5,000. National City Bank, the drawee, certifies the check for $5,000. Pam negotiates the check to Jordan, an HDC. The drawee bank pays Jordan $5,000. On discovering the mistake, the bank cannot recover from Jordan the $4,500 paid by mistake, even though the bank was not in a superior position to detect the alteration. This is in accord with the purpose of certification, which is to obtain the definite obligation of a bank to honor a definite instrument.

For a synopsis of the rules governing the honoring of checks, see *Concept Summary 27.1* on the facing page.

SECTION 4
THE BANK'S DUTY TO ACCEPT DEPOSITS

A bank has a duty to its customer to accept the customer's deposits of cash and checks. When checks are deposited, the bank must make the funds represented by those checks available within certain time frames. A bank also has a duty to collect payment on any checks payable or indorsed to its customer and deposited by the customer into his or her account. Cash deposits made in U.S. currency are received into the customer's account without being subject to further collection procedures.

Availability Schedule for Deposited Checks

The Expedited Funds Availability Act (EFAA) of 1987[11] and Regulation CC,[12] which was issued by the Federal Reserve Board of Governors (the *Federal Reserve System* will be discussed shortly) to implement the act, require that any local check deposited must be available for withdrawal by check or as cash within one business day from the date of deposit. A check is classified as a local check if the first bank to receive the check for payment and the bank on which the check is drawn are located in the same check-processing region (regions are designated by the Federal Reserve Board of Governors). For nonlocal checks, the funds must be available for withdrawal within not more than five business days. Note that under the Check Clearing in the 21st Century Act (the Check 21 Act will be discussed later in this chapter), a bank will have to credit a customer's account as soon as the bank receives the funds.

---

11. 12 U.S.C. Sections 4001–4010.
12. 12 C.F.R. Sections 229.1–229.42.

CONCEPT SUMMARY 27.1
Honoring Checks

Situation	Basic Rules
Wrongful Dishonor [UCC 4–402]	The bank is liable to its customer for actual damages proved if it wrongfully dishonors a check due to its own mistake.
Overdraft [UCC 4–401]	The bank has a right to charge a customer's account for any item properly payable, even if the charge results in an overdraft.
Postdated Check [UCC 4–401]	The bank may charge a postdated check against a customer's account, unless the customer notifies the bank of the postdating in time to allow the bank to act on the notice before the bank commits itself to pay on the check.
Stale Check [UCC 4–404]	The bank is not obligated to pay an uncertified check presented more than six months after its date, but the bank may do so in good faith without liability.
Death or Incompetence of a Customer [UCC 4–405]	So long as the bank does not know of the death or incompetence of a customer, the bank can pay an item without liability. Even with knowledge of a customer's death, a bank can honor or certify checks (in the absence of a stop-payment order) for ten days after the date of the customer's death.
Stop-Payment Order [UCC 4–403]	The customer (or a "person authorized to draw on the account") must institute a stop-payment order in time for the bank to have a reasonable opportunity to act. A customer has no right to stop payment on a check that has been certified or accepted by the bank, however, and can be held liable for stopping payment on any check without a valid legal ground.
Forged Signature or Alteration [UCC 4–406]	The customer has a duty to examine account statements with reasonable care on receipt and to notify the bank promptly of any unauthorized signatures or alterations. The customer's failure to report promptly an unauthorized signature or alteration will discharge the bank's liability—unless the bank failed to exercise reasonable care (and then the bank may be responsible for some portion of the loss). The customer is prevented from holding the bank liable after one year for unauthorized customer signatures or alterations and after three years for unauthorized indorsements.

In addition, the EFAA requires the following:

1. That funds be available on the next business day for cash deposits and wire transfers, government checks, the first $100 of a day's check deposits, cashier's checks, certified checks, and checks for which the banks receiving and paying the checks are branches of the same institution.

2. That the first $100 of any deposit be available for cash withdrawal on the opening of the *next business day* after deposit. If a local check is deposited, the next $400 is to be available for withdrawal by no later than 5:00 P.M. on the next business day. If, for example, Heidi deposits a local check for $500 on Monday, she can withdraw $100 in cash at the opening of the business day on Tuesday, and an additional $400 must be available for withdrawal by no later than 5:00 P.M. on Wednesday.

A different availability schedule applies to deposits made at *nonproprietary* automated teller machines (ATMs). These are ATMs that are not owned or operated by the bank receiving the deposits. Basically, a five-day hold is permitted on all deposits, including cash deposits, made at nonproprietary ATMs. Other exceptions also exist. For example, a banking institution has eight days to make funds available in new accounts (those open less than thirty days) and has an extra four days on deposits that exceed $5,000 (except deposits of government and cashier's checks).

Some commentators argue that making funds available more quickly has encouraged fraud. See this chapter's *Insight into Ethics* feature below for a discussion of this issue.

Interest-Bearing Accounts

Under the Truth-in-Savings Act (TISA) of 1991[13] and Regulation DD,[14] the act's implementing regulation, banks must pay interest based on the full balance of a customer's interest-bearing account each day. For example, Nigel has an interest-bearing checking account with First National Bank. Nigel keeps a $500 balance in the account for most of the month but withdraws all but $50 the day before the bank posts the interest. The bank cannot pay interest on just the $50. The interest must be adjusted to account for the entire month, including those days when Nigel's balance was higher.

Before opening a deposit account, new customers must be provided certain information. The information, which must also appear in all advertisements, includes the following:

1. The minimum balance required to open an account and to be paid interest.
2. The interest, stated in terms of the annual percentage yield on the account.
3. How interest is calculated.

---

13. 12 U.S.C. Sections 4301–4313.
14. 12 C.F.R. Sections 230.1–230.9.

4. Any fees, charges, and penalties and how they are calculated.

Also, under the TISA and Regulation DD, a customer's monthly statement must disclose the interest earned on the account, any fees that were charged, how the fees were calculated, and the number of days that the statement covers.

The Traditional Collection Process

Usually, deposited checks involve parties who do business at different banks, but sometimes checks are written between customers of the same bank. Either situation brings into play the bank collection process as it operates under Article 4 of the UCC. The check-collection process described in the following subsections will be modified as the banking industry implements Check 21, which will be discussed shortly.

DESIGNATIONS OF BANKS INVOLVED IN THE COLLECTION PROCESS The first bank to receive a check for payment is the **depositary bank.**[15] For example, when a person deposits a tax-refund check

---

15. All definitions in this section are found in UCC 4–105. The terms *depositary* and *depository* have different meanings in the banking context. A depository bank is a *physical place* (a bank or other institution) in which deposits or funds are held or stored.

INSIGHT INTO ETHICS
Expedited Funds and an Increase in Check Fraud

Since the Expedited Funds Availability Act (EFAA) was enacted, millions of people have fallen prey to various types of check fraud. In a common scam, the fraudsters contact an individual—via e-mail, telephone, or letter—and say that they will send that person a check for a certain amount if he or she agrees to wire some of the funds back to them, typically to cover "fees and taxes." The victim receives a check and deposits it in his or her account. A day or so later, when the law says the funds must be made available, the victim confirms that the funds are in his or her bank account and wires the requested amount back to the fraudsters.

Unfortunately, by the time the bank discovers the check is a fake and notifies the customer, he or she has already sent thousands of dollars to the fraudsters. Because the check was counterfeit, the bank has no

liability on it, and the loss falls to the customer. The incidence of these scams is increasing, largely because the fraudsters know that the law requires U.S. banks to make the funds available soon after checks are deposited, even if those checks later prove to be counterfeit.

Moreover, technology has improved fraudsters' ability to create checks that look real. Although the EFAA was intended to protect bank customers, it now appears to be having the opposite effect—making them a target for increased fraud.

CRITICAL THINKING

INSIGHT INTO THE BUSINESS ENVIRONMENT
Why would banks say that they, too, are worse off because of the EFAA?

from the Internal Revenue Service into a personal checking account at the local bank, that bank is the depositary bank. The bank on which a check is drawn (the drawee bank) is called the **payor bank.** Any bank except the payor bank that handles a check during some phase of the collection process is a **collecting bank.** Any bank except the payor bank or the depositary bank to which an item is transferred in the course of this collection process is called an **intermediary bank.**

During the collection process, any bank can take on one or more of the various roles of depositary, payor, collecting, or intermediary bank. To illustrate: Brooke, a buyer in New York, writes a check on her New York bank and sends it to David, a seller in San Francisco. David deposits the check in his San Francisco bank account. David's bank is both a *depositary bank* and a *collecting bank.* Brooke's bank in New York is the *payor bank.* As the check travels from San Francisco to New York, any *collecting bank* handling the item in the collection process (other than the ones acting as depositary bank and payor bank) is also called an *intermediary bank.* Exhibit

27–5 below illustrates how various banks function in the check-collection process.

CHECK COLLECTION BETWEEN CUSTOMERS OF THE SAME BANK
An item that is payable by the depositary bank that receives it (which in this situation is also the payor bank) is called an "on-us item." Usually, a bank issues a "provisional credit" for on-us items within the same day. If the bank does not dishonor the check by the opening of the second banking day following its receipt, the check is considered paid [UCC 4–215(e)(2)].

CHECK COLLECTION BETWEEN CUSTOMERS OF DIFFERENT BANKS
Once a depositary bank receives a check, it must arrange to present the check, either directly or through intermediary banks, to the appropriate payor bank. Each bank in the collection chain must pass the check on before midnight of the next banking day following its receipt [UCC 4–202(b)].[16]

---

16. A bank may take a "reasonably longer time" in certain circumstances, such as a power failure that disrupts the bank's computer system [UCC 4–202(b)].

EXHIBIT 27–5 • The Check-Collection Process

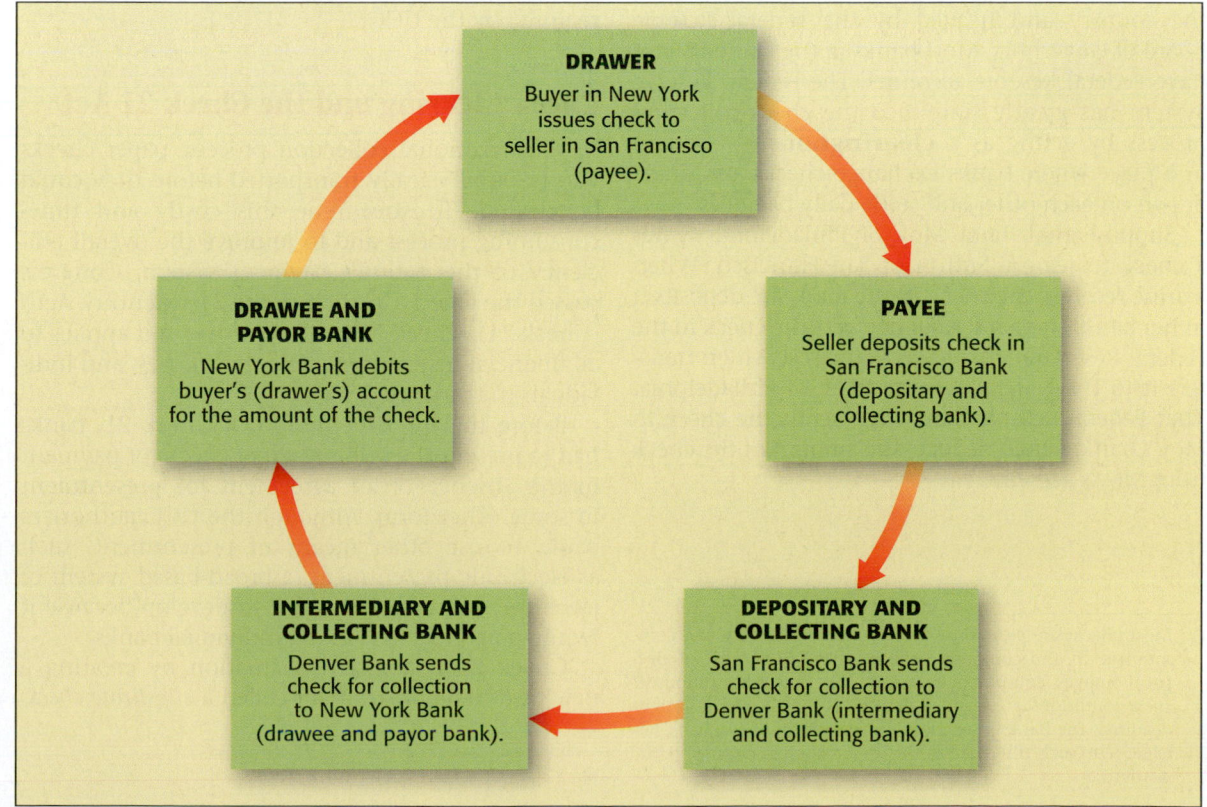

A "banking day" is any part of a day on which the bank is open to carry on substantially all of its banking functions. Thus, if only a bank's drive-through facilities are open, a check deposited on Saturday will not trigger a bank's midnight deadline until the following Monday. When the check reaches the payor bank, that bank is liable for the face amount of the check, unless the payor bank dishonors the check or returns it by midnight of the next banking day following receipt [UCC 4–302].[17]

Because of this deadline and because banks need to maintain an even work flow in the many items they handle daily, the UCC permits what is called *deferred posting*. According to UCC 4–108, "a bank may fix an afternoon hour of 2:00 P.M. or later as a cutoff hour for the handling of money and items and the making of entries on its books." Any checks received after that hour "may be treated as being received at the opening of the next banking day." Thus, if a bank's "cutoff hour" is 3:00 P.M., a check received by a payor bank at 4:00 P.M. on Monday will be deferred for posting until Tuesday. In this situation, the payor bank's deadline will be midnight Wednesday.

HOW THE FEDERAL RESERVE SYSTEM CLEARS CHECKS
The **Federal Reserve System** is a network of twelve district banks, which are located around the country and headed by the Federal Reserve Board of Governors. Most banks in the United States have Federal Reserve accounts. The Federal Reserve System has greatly simplified the check-collection process by acting as a **clearinghouse**—a system or a place where banks exchange checks and drafts drawn on each other and settle daily balances.

Suppose that Tami Moy of Philadelphia writes a check to Jeanne Sutton of San Francisco. When Jeanne receives the check in the mail, she deposits it in her bank. Her bank then deposits the check in the Federal Reserve Bank of San Francisco, which transfers it to the Federal Reserve Bank of Philadelphia. That Federal Reserve bank then sends the check to Moy's bank, which deducts the amount of the check from Moy's account.

ELECTRONIC CHECK PRESENTMENT In the past, most checks were processed manually—the employees of each bank in the collection chain would physically handle each check that passed through the bank for collection or payment. Today, most checks are processed electronically—a practice that has been facilitated by Check 21 (to be discussed next). Whereas manual check processing can take days, *electronic check presentment* can be done on the day of the deposit. With electronic check presentment, items are encoded with information (such as the amount of the check) that is read and processed by other banks' computers. In some situations, a check may be retained at its place of deposit, and only its image or description is presented for payment [UCC 4–110].

A bank that encodes information on an item after the item has been issued warrants to any subsequent bank or payor that the encoded information is correct [UCC 4–209]. This is also true for a bank that retains an item and presents an image or description of the item for payment.

Regulation CC provides that a returned check must be encoded with the routing number of the depositary bank, the amount of the check, and other information. The regulation further states that a check must still be returned within the deadlines required by the UCC.

Check Clearing and the Check 21 Act

In the traditional collection process, paper checks had to be physically transported before they could be cleared. To streamline this costly and time-consuming process and to improve the overall efficiency of the nation's payment system, Congress passed the Check Clearing in the 21st Century Act[18] (Check 21). Check 21 is a federal law and applies to all financial institutions, other businesses, and individuals in the United States.

Before the implementation of Check 21, banks had to present the original paper check for payment in the absence of an agreement for presentment in some other form. Although the UCC authorizes banks to use other means of presentment, such as electronic presentment, a broad-based system of electronic presentment failed to develop because it required agreements among individual banks.

Check 21 changed the situation by creating a new negotiable instrument called a *substitute check*.

---

17. Most checks are cleared by a computerized process, and communication and computer facilities may fail because of electrical outages, equipment malfunction, or other conditions. If such conditions arise and a bank fails to meet its midnight deadline, the bank is "excused" from liability if the bank has exercised "such diligence as the circumstances require" [UCC 4–109(d)].

18. 12 U.S.C. Sections 5001–5018.

Although the act did not require banks to change their current check-collection practices, its creation of substitute checks has certainly facilitated the use of electronic check processing. In addition, since Check 21, bank customers cannot demand that their original canceled checks be returned with their monthly statements, nor can anyone refuse to accept a substitute check as proof of payment.

WHAT IS A SUBSTITUTE CHECK? A substitute check is a paper reproduction of the front and back of an original check that contains all of the same information required on checks for automated processing. Banks create a substitute check from a digital image of an original check. Every substitute check must include the following statement somewhere on it: "This a legal copy of your check. You can use it in the same way you would use the original check." See Exhibit 27–6 below for an example of a substitute check.

In essence, those financial institutions that exchange digital images of checks do not have to send the original paper checks. They can simply transmit the information electronically and replace the original checks with the substitute checks. Banks that do not exchange checks electronically are required to accept substitute checks in the same way that they accept original checks.

Because the original check can be destroyed after a substitute check is created, the financial system can prevent the check from being paid twice and reduce the expense of paper storage and retrieval. Nevertheless, at least for quite a while, not all checks will be converted to substitute checks. Thus, if a bank returns canceled checks to deposit holders at the end of each month, some of those returned checks may be substitute checks, and some may be original canceled paper checks.

REDUCED "FLOAT" TIME Sometimes, individuals and businesses write checks even though they have insufficient funds in their accounts to cover those checks. Such check writers are relying on the "float," or the time between when a check is written and when the amount is actually deducted from their account. When all checks had to be physically transported, the float time could be several days, but as Check 21 has been implemented, the time required to process checks (the float time) has been substantially reduced. Consequently, account holders who plan to cover their checks after writing them may experience unexpected overdrafts.

FASTER ACCESS TO FUNDS The Expedited Funds Availability Act (mentioned earlier in this chapter) requires that the Federal Reserve Board revise the availability schedule for funds from deposited checks to correspond to reductions in check-processing time. Therefore, as the speed of check processing increases under Check 21, the Federal Reserve Board will reduce the maximum time that a bank can hold funds from deposited checks before making them available to the depositor. Thus, account holders will have faster access to their deposited funds.

EXHIBIT 27–6 • An Example of Substitute Check

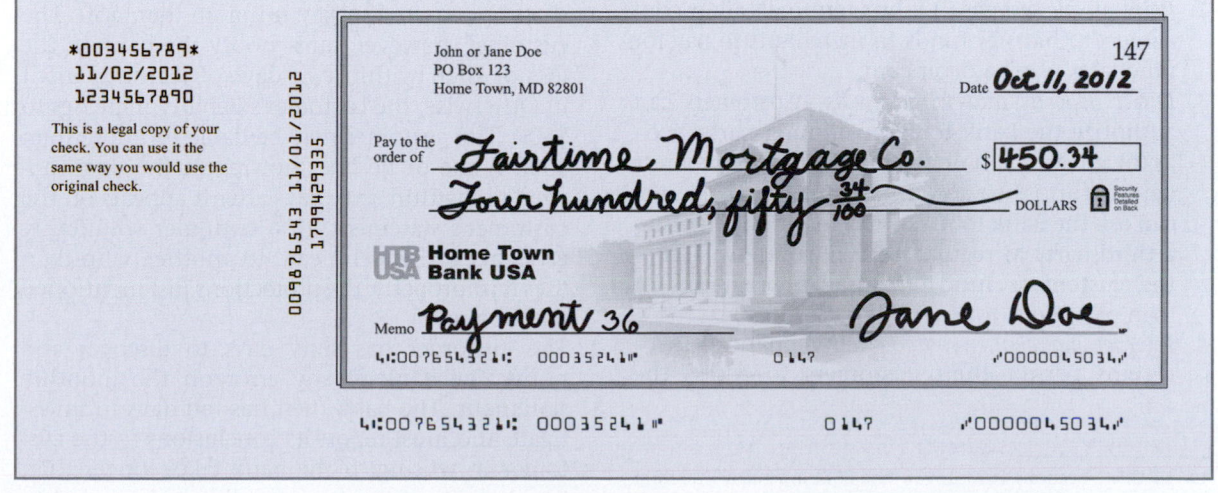

▲◣▲▲ SECTION 5 ◣▲▲▲
ELECTRONIC FUND TRANSFERS

The application of computer technology to banking, in the form of electronic fund transfer systems, has helped to reduce the mountains of paperwork previously required to process fund transfers. An **electronic fund transfer (EFT)** is a transfer of funds made by the use of an electronic terminal, a telephone, a computer, or magnetic tape. The law governing EFTs depends on the type of transfer involved. Consumer fund transfers are governed by the Electronic Fund Transfer Act (EFTA) of 1978.[19] Commercial fund transfers are governed by Article 4A of the UCC.

Although electronic banking offers numerous benefits, it also poses difficulties on occasion. It is difficult to issue stop-payment orders with electronic banking. Also, fewer records are available to prove or disprove that a transaction took place, and the possibilities for tampering with a person's private banking information have increased.

Types of EFT Systems

Most banks offer EFT services to their customers. The following are the most common types of EFT systems used by bank customers:

1. *Automated teller machines* (ATMs)—The machines are connected online to the bank's computers. A customer inserts a **debit card** (a plastic card, also called an *ATM card*) issued by the bank and keys in a *personal identification number* (PIN) to access her or his accounts and conduct banking transactions.
2. *Point-of-sale systems*—Online terminals allow consumers to transfer funds to merchants to pay for purchases using a debit card.
3. *Direct deposits and withdrawals*—Customers can authorize the bank to allow another party, such as the government or an employer, to make direct deposits into their accounts. Similarly, a customer can ask the bank to make automatic payments to a third party at regular, recurrent intervals from the customer's funds (insurance premiums or loan payments, for example).
4. *Internet payment systems*—Many financial institutions permit their customers to access the

institution's computer system via the Internet and direct a transfer of funds between accounts or pay a particular bill, such as a utility bill. Payments can be made on a onetime or a recurring basis. The *Shifting Legal Priorities for Business* feature in Chapter 24 on page 465 discussed how many customers now use their mobile phones to access the Internet and direct their banks to make online payments.

Consumer Fund Transfers

The Electronic Fund Transfer Act (EFTA) provides a basic framework for the rights, liabilities, and responsibilities of users of EFT systems. Additionally, the act gave the Federal Reserve Board authority to issue rules and regulations to help implement the act's provisions. The Federal Reserve Board's implemental regulation is called **Regulation E.**

The EFTA governs financial institutions that offer electronic transfers of funds involving customer accounts. The types of accounts covered include checking accounts, savings accounts, and any other asset accounts established for personal, family, or household purposes. Telephone transfers are covered by the EFTA only if they are made in accordance with a prearranged plan under which periodic or recurring transfers are contemplated.

DISCLOSURE REQUIREMENTS The EFTA is essentially a disclosure law benefiting consumers. The act requires financial institutions to inform consumers of their rights and responsibilities, including those listed here, with respect to EFT systems.

1. If a customer's debit card is lost or stolen and used without her or his permission, the customer shall be required to pay no more than $50. The customer, however, must notify the bank of the loss or theft within two days of learning about it. Otherwise, the customer's liability increases to $500. The customer may be liable for more than $500 if she or he does not report the unauthorized use within sixty days after it appears on the customer's statement. (If a customer voluntarily gives her or his debit card to another, who then uses it improperly, the protections just mentioned do not apply.)
2. The customer has sixty days to discover and notify the bank of any error on the monthly statement. The bank then has ten days to investigate and must report its conclusions to the customer in writing. If the bank takes longer than ten days, it must return the disputed amount to

---

19. 15 U.S.C. Sections 1693–1693r. The EFTA amended Title IX of the Consumer Credit Protection Act.

the customer's account until it finds the error. If there is no error, the customer is required to return the funds to the bank.

3. The bank must furnish receipts for transactions made through computer terminals, but it is not obligated to do so for telephone transfers.

4. The bank must provide a monthly statement for every month in which there is an electronic transfer of funds. Otherwise, the bank must provide a statement every quarter. The statement must show the amount and date of the transfer, the names of the retailers or other third parties involved, the location or identification of the terminal, and the fees. Additionally, the statement must give an address and a phone number for inquiries and error notices.

5. Any preauthorized payment for utility bills and insurance premiums can be stopped three days before the scheduled transfer if the customer notifies the financial institution orally or in writing. (The institution may require the customer to provide written confirmation within fourteen days of an oral notification.) For other EFT transactions, however, the EFTA does not provide for the reversal of an electronic transfer of funds once the transfer has occurred.

UNAUTHORIZED TRANSFERS Because of the vulnerability of EFT systems to fraudulent activities, the EFTA clearly defined what constitutes an unauthorized transfer. Under the act, a transfer is unauthorized if (1) it is initiated by a person who has no actual authority to initiate the transfer, (2) the consumer receives no benefit from it, and (3) the consumer did not furnish the person "with the card, code, or other means of access" to his or her account. Gaining unauthorized access to an EFT system constitutes a federal felony, and those convicted may be fined up to $10,000 and sentenced to as long as ten years in prison.

VIOLATIONS AND DAMAGES Banks must strictly comply with the terms of the EFTA and are liable for any failure to adhere to its provisions. For a bank's violation of the EFTA, a consumer may recover both actual damages (including attorneys' fees and costs) and punitive damages of not less than $100 and not more than $1,000. In a class-action suit, up to $500,000 or 1 percent of the institution's net worth can be awarded as punitive damages. Failure to investigate an error in good faith makes the bank liable for treble damages (three times the amount of damages). Even when a customer has sustained no actual damage, the bank may be liable for legal

costs and punitive damages if it fails to follow the proper procedures outlined by the EFTA for error resolution.

Commercial Fund Transfers

Funds are also transferred electronically "by wire" between commercial parties. In fact, payments made via wire transfers amount to more than $1 trillion a day—an amount that far exceeds the dollar volume of payments made by other means. The two major wire payment systems are the Federal Reserve wire transfer network (Fedwire) and the New York Clearing House Interbank Payments Systems (CHIPS).

Commercial wire transfers are governed by Article 4A of the UCC, which has been adopted by most of the states. Article 4A uses the term *funds transfer* rather than *wire transfer* to describe the overall payment transaction. The full text of Article 4A is presented in Appendix C.

As an example of the type of funds transfer covered by Article 4A, assume that American Industries, Inc., owes $5 million to Chandler Corporation. Instead of sending Chandler a check or some other instrument that would enable Chandler to obtain payment, American Industries tells its bank, North Bank, to credit $5 million to Chandler's account in South Bank. North Bank debits American Industries' North Bank account and wires $5 million to South Bank with instructions to credit $5 million to Chandler's South Bank account. In more complex transactions, additional banks would be involved.

SECTION 6
E-MONEY AND ONLINE BANKING

New forms of electronic payments (e-payments) have the potential to replace *physical* cash—coins and paper currency—with *virtual* cash in the form of electronic impulses. This is the unique promise of **digital cash,** which consists of funds stored on microchips and other computer devices. Online banking has also become commonplace in today's world. In a few minutes, anybody with the proper software can access his or her account, transfer funds, write "checks," pay bills, monitor investments, and even buy and sell stocks. Various forms of electronic money, or **e-money,** are emerging, as discussed in the following subsections.

Stored-Value Cards

The simplest kind of e-money system uses *stored-value cards*. These are plastic cards embossed with magnetic strips containing magnetically encoded data. You may have purchased a stored-value card (called a fare card) to pay your fare to ride on mass transit, such as a subway or train, in a major metropolitan area like New York or San Diego. In some applications, for instance, gift cards for retailers such as Home Depot or Starbucks, a stored-value card can be used only to purchase goods and services offered by the specific card issuer.

Prepaid credit cards and prepaid ATM cards are further examples of stored-value cards. A prepaid credit or ATM card has no link to a bank account. The purchaser simply pays a specific amount to the card provider, and that amount is loaded onto the card. The user can then access those funds anywhere in the world without having to provide identification or have a bank account. Students, travelers and persons without bank accounts can use prepaid cards as a convenient and safe substitute for cash. There is a growing concern, however, that criminals (especially drug traffickers) are using these stored-value cards to launder money and move illicit funds across international borders.

Smart Cards

Another form of e-money is the smart card. **Smart cards** are plastic cards containing computer microchips that can hold much more information than magnetic strips. A smart card carries and processes security programming. This capability gives smart cards a technical advantage over stored-value cards. The microprocessors on smart cards can also authenticate the validity of transactions. Retailers can program electronic cash registers to confirm the authenticity of a smart card by examining a unique digital signature stored on its microchip. (Digital signatures were discussed in Chapter 11.)

Online Banking Services

Most customers use three kinds of online banking services: bill consolidation and payment, transferal of funds among accounts, and applications for loans. Customers typically must appear in person to finalize the terms of a loan, however. Generally, customers are not yet able to deposit and withdraw funds online, although smart cards may eventually allow people to do so (withdrawing funds and depositing them onto the card as needed).

Since the late 1990s, several banks have operated exclusively on the Internet. These "virtual banks" have no physical branch offices. Because few individuals are equipped to send funds to virtual banks via smart-card technology, the virtual banks have accepted deposits through physical delivery systems, such as the U.S. Postal Service, FedEx, or UPS.

Privacy Protection

At the present time, it is not clear which, if any, laws apply to the security of e-money payment information and e-money issuers' financial records. The Federal Reserve has decided not to impose Regulation E, which governs certain electronic fund transfers, on e-money transactions. Federal laws prohibiting unauthorized access to electronic communications might apply, however. For example, the Electronic Communications Privacy Act of 1986[20] prohibits any person from knowingly divulging to any other person the contents of an electronic communication while that communication is in transmission or in electronic storage.

E-MONEY ISSUERS' FINANCIAL RECORDS Under the Right to Financial Privacy Act of 1978,[21] before a financial institution may give financial information about an individual to a federal agency, he must explicitly consent. If he does not, a federal agency wishing to access his financial records normally must obtain a warrant. A digital cash issuer may be subject to this act if that issuer is deemed to be (1) a bank by virtue of its holding customer funds or (2) any entity that issues a physical card similar to a credit or debit card.

CONSUMER FINANCIAL DATA In 1999, Congress passed the Financial Services Modernization Act,[22] also known as the Gramm-Leach-Bliley Act, in an attempt to delineate how financial institutions can treat customer data. In general, the act and its rules[23] place restrictions and obligations on financial institutions to protect consumer data and privacy. Every financial institution must provide its customers with information on its privacy policies and practices. No financial institution can disclose nonpublic personal information about a consumer to an unaffiliated third party unless the act's disclosure and opt-out requirements are met.

---

20. 18 U.S.C. Sections 2510–2521.
21. 12 U.S.C. Sections 3401 *et seq.*
22. 12 U.S.C. Sections 24a, 248b, 1820a, 1828b, and others.
23. 12 C.F.R. Part 40.

REVIEWING

Checks and Banking in the Digital Age

RPM Pizza, Inc., issued a check for $96,000 to Systems Marketing for an advertising campaign. A few days later, RPM decided not to go through with the deal and placed a written stop-payment order on the check. RPM and Systems had no further contact for many months. Three weeks after the stop-payment order expired, however, Toby Rierson, an employee at Systems, cashed the check. Bank One Cambridge, RPM's bank, paid the check with funds from RPM's account. Because of the amount of the check, and because the check was more than six months old (stale), the signature on the check should have been specially verified according to standard banking procedures and Bank One's own policies, but it was not. RPM filed a suit in a federal district court against Bank One to recover the amount of the check. Using the information presented in the chapter, answer the following questions.

1. How long is a written stop-payment order effective? What else could RPM have done to prevent this check from being cashed?
2. What would happen if it turned out that RPM did not have a legitimate reason for stopping payment on the check?
3. What are a bank's obligations with respect to stale checks? Should Bank One have contacted RPM before paying the check? Why or why not?
4. Assume that Rierson's indorsement on the check was a forgery. Would a court be likely to hold the bank liable for the amount of the check because it failed to verify the signature on the check? Why or why not?

⚙ **DEBATE THIS:** *To reduce fraud, checks that utilize mechanical or electronic signature systems should not be honored.*

TERMS AND CONCEPTS

cashier's check 518
certified check 521
check 518
clearinghouse 534

collecting bank 533
debit card 536
depositary bank 532
digital cash 537
electronic fund
   transfer (EFT) 536

e-money 537
Federal Reserve System 534
intermediary bank 533
overdraft 522
payor bank 533

Regulation E 536
smart card 538
stale check 523
stop-payment order 523
traveler's check 521

QUESTIONS AND CASE PROBLEMS

27–1. Forged Signatures Roy Supply, Inc., and R. M. R. Drywall, Inc., had checking accounts at Wells Fargo Bank. Both accounts required all checks to carry two signatures—that of Edward Roy and that of Twila June Moore, both of whom were executive officers of both companies. Between January 2009 and March 2010, the bank honored hundreds of checks on which Roy's signature was forged by Moore. On January 31, 2011, Roy and the two corporations notified the bank of the forgeries and then filed a suit in a California state court against the bank, alleging negligence. Who is liable for the amounts of the forged checks? Why?

27–2. QUESTION WITH SAMPLE ANSWER: Customer Negligence.

Gary goes grocery shopping and carelessly leaves his checkbook in his shopping cart. His checkbook, with two blank checks remaining, is stolen by Dolores. On May 5, Dolores forges Gary's name on a check for $10 and cashes the check at Gary's bank, Citizens Bank of Middletown. Gary has not reported the loss of his blank checks to his bank. On June 1, Gary receives his monthly bank statement and copies of canceled checks from Citizens Bank, including the forged check, but he does not examine the canceled checks. On June 20, Dolores forges Gary's last check. This check is for $1,000 and is cashed at Eastern City Bank, a bank with which Dolores has previously done business. Eastern City Bank puts the check through the collection process, and Citizens Bank honors it. On July 1, on receipt of his bank statement and canceled checks covering June transactions, Gary discovers both forgeries and immediately notifies Citizens Bank. Dolores cannot be found. Gary claims that Citizens Bank must recredit his account for both checks, as his signature was forged. Discuss fully Gary's claim.

- **For a sample answer to Question 27–2, go to Appendix I at the end of this text.**

27–3. Bank's Duty to Honor Checks On January 5, Brian drafts a check for $3,000 drawn on Southern Marine Bank and payable to his assistant, Shanta. Brian puts last year's date on the check by mistake. On January 7, before Shanta has had a chance to go to the bank, Brian is killed in an automobile accident. Southern Marine Bank is aware of Brian's death. On January 10, Shanta presents the check to the bank, and the bank honors the check by payment to Shanta. Later, Brian's widow, Joyce, claims that because the bank knew of Brian's death and also because the check was by date more than one year old the bank acted wrongfully when it paid Shanta. Joyce, as executor of Brian's estate and sole heir by his will, demands that Southern Marine Bank recredit Brian's estate for the check paid to Shanta. Discuss fully Southern Marine's liability in light of Joyce's demand.

27–4. Electronic Fund Transfers Yannuzzi has a checking account at Texas Bank. She frequently uses her debit card to obtain cash from the bank's automated teller machines. She always withdraws $50 when she makes a withdrawal, but she never withdraws more than $50 in any one day. When she received the April statement on her account, she noticed that on April 13 two withdrawals for $50 each had been made from the account. Believing this to be a mistake, she went to her bank on May 10 to inform it of the error. A bank officer told her that the bank would investigate and advise her as to the result. On May 26, the bank officer called her and said that bank personnel were having trouble locating the error but would continue to try to find it. On June 20, the bank sent her a full written report telling her that no error had been made. Yannuzzi, unhappy with the bank's explanation, filed a suit against the bank, alleging that it had violated the Electronic Fund Transfer Act. What was the outcome of the suit? Would it matter if the bank could show that on the day in question it deducted $50 from Yannuzzi's account to cover a check that cleared the bank on that day—a check that Yannuzzi had written to a local department store?

27–5. CASE PROBLEM WITH SAMPLE ANSWER: Forgery.

In December 1999, Jenny Triplett applied for a bookkeeping position with Spacemakers of America, Inc., in Atlanta, Georgia. Spacemakers hired Triplett and delegated to her all responsibility for maintaining the company checkbook and reconciling it with the monthly statements from SunTrust Bank. Triplett also handled invoices from vendors. Spacemakers' president, Dennis Rose, reviewed the invoices and signed the checks to pay them, but no other employee checked Triplett's work. By the end of her first full month of employment, Triplett had forged six checks totaling more than $22,000, all payable to Triple M Entertainment, which was not a Spacemakers vendor. By October 2000, Triplett had forged fifty-nine more checks, totaling more than $475,000. A SunTrust employee became suspicious of an item that required sight inspection under the bank's fraud detection standards, which exceeded those of other banks in the area. Triplett was arrested. Spacemakers filed a suit in a Georgia state court against SunTrust. The bank filed a motion for summary judgment. On what basis could the bank avoid liability? In whose favor should the court rule, and why? [Spacemakers of America, Inc. v. SunTrust Bank, 271 Ga.App. 335, 609 S.E.2d 683 (2005)]

- **To view a sample answer for Problem 27–5, go to this book's Web site at www.cengage.com/blaw/clarkson, select "Chapter 27," and click on "Case Problem with Sample Answer."**

27–6. Forged Indorsements In 1994, Brian and Penny Grieme bought a house in Mandan, North Dakota. They borrowed for the purchase through a loan program financed by the North Dakota Housing Finance Agency (NDHFA). The Griemes obtained insurance for the house from Center Mutual Insurance Co. When a hailstorm damaged the house in 2001, Center Mutual determined that the loss was $4,378 and issued a check for that amount, drawn on Bremer Bank, N.A. The check's payees included Brian Grieme and the NDHFA. Grieme presented the check for payment to Wells Fargo Bank of Tempe, Arizona. The back of the check bore his signature and in handprinted block letters the words "ND Housing Finance." The check was processed for collection and paid, and the canceled check was returned to Center Mutual. By the time the insurer learned that NDHFA's indorsement had been forged, the Griemes had canceled their policy, defaulted on their loan, and filed for bankruptcy. The NDHFA filed a suit in a North Dakota state court against Center Mutual for the amount of the check. Who is most likely to suffer the loss in this case? Why? [State ex rel. North Dakota Housing Finance Agency v. Center Mutual Insurance Co., 720 N.W.2d 425 (N.Dak. 2006)]

27–7. Bank's Duty to Honor Checks Sheila Bartell was arrested on various charges related to burglary, the possession for sale of methamphetamine, and other crimes. She pleaded guilty in a California state court to some charges in exchange for the dismissal of others and an agreement to reimburse the victims. The victims included "Rita E.," who reported that her checkbook had been stolen and her signature forged on three checks totaling $590. Wells Fargo Bank had "covered" the checks and credited her account, however, so the court ordered Bartell to pay the bank. Bartell appealed, arguing that the bank was not entitled to restitution. What principles apply when a person forges a drawer's signature on a check? Is the bank entitled to recover from the defendant? Explain. [*People v. Bartell,* 170 Cal.App.4th 1258, 88 Cal.Rptr.3d 844 (3 Dist. 2009)]

27–8. Bank's Duty of Care Arnett Gertrude, a widow with no children, lived with her sister and her nephew Jack Scriber. When Gertrude was diagnosed with cancer, she added Scriber as an authorized signatory to her checking account at Salyersville National Bank and gave him power of attorney. Shortly before Gertrude died, Scriber wrote checks on the account to withdraw nearly all of the $600,000 in the account and transferred the funds into his own account. After Gertrude's death, Bobbie Caudill, the administrator of the estate, discovered the withdrawals. Caudill sued the bank for aiding Scriber in the conversion of Gertrude's funds. The bank's defense was that Scriber had power of attorney over Gertrude's finances and had the power to write checks on the account, so the bank had to honor the checks that Scriber had written. The estate argued that the bank had breached its duty to Gertrude to guard against such obvious misappropriation. The trial court held for the bank. Did the bank breach its duty to Gertrude? Why or why not? [*Caudill v. Salyersville National Bank,* ____ S.W.3d ____ (Ky.App. 2010)]

27–9. A QUESTION OF ETHICS: Forged Drawer's Signature.

From the 1960s, James Johnson served as Bradley Union's personal caretaker and assistant, and was authorized by Union to handle his banking transactions. Louise Johnson, James's wife, wrote checks on Union's checking account to pay his bills, normally signing the checks "Brad Union." Branch Banking & Trust Co. (BB&T) managed Union's account. In December 2000, on the basis of Union's deteriorating mental and physical condition,

*a North Carolina state court declared him incompetent. Douglas Maxwell was appointed as Union's guardian. Maxwell "froze" Union's checking account and asked BB&T for copies of the canceled checks, which were provided by July 2001. Maxwell believed that Union's signature on the checks had been forged. In August 2002, Maxwell contacted BB&T, which refused to recredit Union's account. Maxwell filed a suit on Union's behalf in a North Carolina state court against BB&T. [*Union v. Branch Banking & Trust Co., 176 N.C.App. 711, 627 S.E.2d 276 (2006)]*

(a) Before Maxwell's appointment, BB&T sent monthly statements and canceled checks to Union, and Johnson reviewed them, but no unauthorized signatures were ever reported. On whom can liability be imposed in the case of a forged drawer's signature on a check? What are the limits set by Section 4–406(f) of the Uniform Commercial Code? Should Johnson's position, Union's incompetence, or Maxwell's appointment affect the application of these principles? Explain.

(b) Why was this suit brought against BB&T? Is BB&T liable? If not, who is? Why? Regardless of any violations of the law, did anyone act unethically in this case? If so, who and why?

27–10. SPECIAL CASE ANALYSIS: Bank's Duty of Care.
Go to Extended Case 27.3, *Schultz v. Bank of America, N.A.,* 413 Md. 15, 990 A.2d 1078 (2010) on pages 527–528. Read the excerpt and answer the following questions.

(a) **Issue:** This case was about determining whether a bank was negligent in handling a certain transaction for its customer. What was this transaction, and what was the specific issue before the court?

(b) **Rule of Law:** What rule of law was applicable to this case's circumstances?

(c) **Applying the Rule of Law:** How did the rule of law apply to the specific circumstances in this case?

(d) **Conclusion:** After applying the rule of law to the facts, what did the court conclude?

LEGAL RESEARCH EXERCISES ON THE WEB

Go to this text's Web site at **www.cengage.com/blaw/clarkson**, select "Chapter 27," and click on "Practical Internet Exercises." There you will find the following Internet research exercises that you can perform to learn more about the topics covered in this chapter.

Practical Internet Exercise 27–1: Legal Perspective
Smart Cards

Practical Internet Exercise 27–2: Management Perspective
Check Fraud

Articles 3 and 4 of the Uniform Commercial Code (UCC), which deal with negotiable instruments, constitute an important part of the law governing commercial transactions. These articles reflect several fundamental ethical principles. One principle is that individuals should be protected against harm caused by the misuse of negotiable instruments. Another basic principle—and one that underlies the entire concept of negotiable instruments—is that the laws governing the use of negotiable instruments should be practical and reasonable to encourage the free flow of commerce.

Here, we look first at some of the ethical implications of the concept of a holder in due course (HDC). We then examine some other ethical issues that frequently arise in relation to these instruments.

Ethics, the HDC Concept, and *Ort v. Fowler*

The drafters of Article 3 did not create the HDC concept out of thin air. Indeed, under the common law, courts had often restricted the extent to which defenses could successfully be raised against a good faith holder of a negotiable instrument. As an example, consider a classic 1884 case, *Ort v. Fowler.*[1]

Case Background Ort, a farmer, was working alone in his field one day, when he was approached by a stranger who claimed to be the statewide agent for a manufacturer of iron posts and wire fencing. The two men conversed for some time, and eventually the stranger persuaded the farmer to act as an area representative for the manufacturer. The stranger then completed two documents for Ort to sign, telling him that they were identical copies of an agreement in which Ort agreed to represent the manufacturer.

Because the farmer did not have his glasses with him and could read only with great difficulty, he asked the stranger to read the document to him. The stranger then purported to do so, not mentioning that the document was a promissory note. Both men signed each document. The stranger later negotiated the promissory note he had fraudulently obtained from Ort to a party that today we would refer to as an HDC. When this party brought suit against him, Ort attempted to defend on the basis of fraud in the execution.

The Court's Decision The Kansas court that decided the issue entertained three possible views. One was that because Ort never *intended* to execute a note, he should not be held liable for doing so. A second view was that the jury should decide, as a question of fact, whether Ort was guilty of negligence under the circumstances. The third view was that because Ort possessed

---

1. 31 Kan. 478, 2 P. 580 (1884).

all of his faculties and was able to read the English language, signing a promissory note solely in reliance on a stranger's assurances that it was a different instrument constituted negligence.

This third view was the one adopted by the court in 1884. The court held that Ort's negligence had contributed to the fraud and that such negligence precluded Ort from raising fraud as a defense against payment on the note. Today, the UCC expresses essentially the same reasoning: fraud is a defense against an HDC only if the injured party signed the instrument "with neither knowledge nor a reasonable opportunity to learn of its character or its essential terms" [UCC 3–305(a)(1)(iii)].

The Reasoning of the HDC Concept Although it may not seem fair that an innocent victim should have to suffer the consequences of another's fraudulent act, the UCC assumes that it would be even less fair if an HDC could not collect payment. The reasoning behind this assumption is that an HDC, as a third party, is less likely to have been responsible for—or to have had an opportunity to protect against—the fraud in the underlying transaction.

In general, the HDC doctrine, like other sections of the UCC, reflects the philosophy that when two or more innocent parties are at risk, the burden should fall on the party that was in the best position to prevent the loss. For businesspersons, the HDC doctrine means that they should exercise caution when they issue and accept commercial paper in order to protect against the risk of loss through fraud.

Good Faith in Negotiable Instruments Law

Clearly, the principle of good faith reflects ethical principles. The most notable application of the good faith requirement in negotiable instruments law is, of course, the HDC doctrine. Traditionally, to acquire the protected status of an HDC, a holder must have acquired an instrument in good faith. Other transactions subject to Articles 3 and 4 also require good faith—as, indeed, do all transactions governed by the UCC.

The Importance of Good Faith A party that acts in bad faith may be precluded from seeking shelter under UCC provisions that would otherwise apply, such as the fictitious payee rule or the imposter rule. Cases often turn on whether a party exercised good faith, as a case decided by Maryland's courts illustrates.

The bank in this case, American General Financial Services, Inc., was contacted by telephone by a man who represented himself to be Ronald E. Wilder—although later it was discovered that he was an imposter. The man wanted to obtain a loan for $20,000 to renovate his property and supplied Wilder's personal information and copies of his tax returns to complete the loan application. The bank ran a credit check on Wilder and, finding that he had excellent credit, approved an $18,000 loan. The imposter then came to the bank, presented a driver's license with his photo and Ronald Wilder's personal information to a bank employee, and obtained the check.

Later that day, the imposter took the $18,000 check to a check-cashing business, State Security Check Cashing, Inc., to cash it. He presented the same false identification that he had used at the bank, and a State Security employee examined the check and reviewed the loan documents before giving the man the face value of the check (less State Security's fee). The day after the loan check was negotiated, the real Ronald E. Wilder informed American General that someone had fraudulently applied for a loan in his name. When he learned about the check written to the imposter, Wilder placed a stop-payment order on the check. American General then refused to pay State Security, who sued to recover for payment of the check's proceeds to the imposter.

The court had to decide which party—the bank or the check-cashing company—was liable for the amount of the check. Good faith was the controlling issue. American General claimed that State Security had not taken the check in good faith, because "suspicious circumstances" surrounded the transaction. After all, reasonable persons do not cash $18,000 loan checks at check-cashing establishments, which charge very high fees ($900 in this case). The bank argued that State Security should have taken additional steps to verify the check or at least have waited until the check cleared before disbursing the funds. The trial court agreed: State Security was in the best position to prevent the loss and should not have immediately paid out the funds. Because State Security had not exercised good faith or due care, it was not an HDC and was precluded from asserting the imposter rule.

State Security appealed, and the reviewing court reversed. The appellate court found that the bank had not shown that State Security had failed to exercise good faith when it cashed the check in reliance on the same documents that the bank had seen. This meant that State Security was an HDC and that the imposter rule applied. Therefore, the appellate court ruled that American General was liable for the $18,000.[2]

How Should Good Faith Be Tested?
There has long been a division of opinion as to how good faith should be measured or tested. At one end of the spectrum of

views is the position that the test of good faith should be subjective in nature. In other words, as long as a person acts honestly, no matter how negligent or foolish the conduct may be, that person is acting in good faith. At the other end of the spectrum is the "objective" test of good faith. Under this test, honesty in itself is not enough. A party must also act reasonably under the circumstances.

Over time, the pendulum seems to have swung from one end of the spectrum to the other. When the UCC was initially drafted, the definition of *good faith* set forth in UCC 1–201(19) established a subjective test for good faith. It defined good faith as "honesty in fact in the conduct or transaction concerned." The only UCC article that incorporated a more objective test for good faith was Article 2. Section 2–103(1)(b) defined good faith as both honesty in fact *and* the observance of reasonable commercial standards of fair dealing in the trade. Under this test, a person who acts honestly in fact but does not observe reasonable commercial standards of fair dealing will not meet the good faith requirement. This more objective measure of good faith has since been incorporated into other articles of the UCC, including Articles 3, 4, and 4A.

Criticisms of the Objective Standard
Some critics claim that while the subjective test of "honesty in fact" is manageable, the objective test that requires the "observance of reasonable commercial standards" opens the door to potentially endless litigation. After all, it is difficult to determine what is commercially reasonable in a given context until you hear what others in that commercial situation have to say. Thus, parties to a dispute can nearly always make some kind of good faith argument, and any time the issue is raised, litigation can result.

How Good Faith Standards Can Affect HDC Status
Whether the objective or the subjective standard of good faith is used has considerable impact on HDC status, as an example will illustrate. Mitchell was a farmer who operated a multistate farming operation on leased property. Runnells, a grain broker, had sold Mitchell's 2001 grain crop. Mitchell instructed Runnells to use the crop proceeds to draw checks payable to Mitchell's various landlords in fulfillment of his rent obligations. The checks totaled more than $153,000. The landlords accepted the checks in payment of the farmer's rent—completely unaware that Mitchell had already pledged the proceeds from the sale of his crops as collateral for a loan from Agriliance (security interests will be discussed in Chapter 29). Agriliance filed a lawsuit in a federal court against Runnells and the various landlords for conversion (wrongful taking of personal property—see Chapter 6 on page 127).

---

2. *State Security Check Cashing, Inc. v. American General Financial Services, Inc.,* 409 Md. 81, 972 A.2d 882 (2009).

FOCUS ON ETHICS CONTINUES ▶

According to the UCC, an HDC takes a negotiable instrument free of any claim to the instrument, including claims of prior secured parties. Thus, the outcome of the case depended on whether Runnells and the landlords were HDCs. Under the subjective standard, the landlords were HDCs because they took the checks without actual knowledge of Agriliance's claim to the crop proceeds. The objective standard, however, dictated a different result. Because it is common for farmers to put their crops up as collateral for loans, the court held that reasonable commercial standards of fair dealing required Mitchell's creditors (Runnells and the landlords) to conduct a search of the public records. Such a search would have revealed the existence of Agriliance's prior secured claim. Runnells and the landlords could not be HDCs in this case because they failed to meet the objective element of good faith. The court, therefore, ruled that Agriliance was entitled to the crop proceeds.[3]

Efficiency versus Due Care

A major problem faced by today's banking institutions is how to verify customer signatures on the billions of checks that are processed by the banking system each month. If a bank fails to verify a signature on a check it receives for payment and the check turns out to be forged, the bank will normally be held liable to its customer for the amount paid. But how can banks possibly examine, item by item, each signature on every check that they pay?

The banks' solution to this problem is simply to not examine all signatures. Instead, computers are programmed to verify signatures only on checks exceeding a certain threshold amount, such as $2,500 or perhaps some higher figure. Checks for less than the threshold amount are selected for signature verification only on

a random basis. In other words, serious attention is restricted to serious matters. As a result, many, if not most, checks are paid without signature verification. This practice, which has become an acceptable standard in today's banking industry, is economically efficient for banks. Even though liability costs are sometimes incurred—when forged checks are paid—the total costs involved in verifying the authenticity of each and every signature would be far higher.

Some people have argued that banks using such procedures are not exercising due care in handling their customers' accounts. Under the UCC, banks are held to a standard of "ordinary care." At one time in the banking industry, ordinary care was generally interpreted to mean that a bank had a duty to inspect *all* signatures on checks. But what constitutes ordinary care in today's world? Does a bank exercise ordinary care if it follows the prevailing industry practice of examining signatures on only a few, randomly selected checks payable for under a certain amount? Or does ordinary care still mean that a bank should examine each signature?

DISCUSSION QUESTIONS

1. Because the UCC offers special protection to HDCs, innocent makers of notes or drawers of checks in fraudulent transactions often have no legal recourse. From an ethical standpoint, how could you justify to the "losers" in such situations the provisions of the UCC that fail to protect them? Can you think of a way in which such problems could be handled more fairly or ethically than they are under the UCC?

2. What do you think would result if the law was changed to allow personal defenses to be successfully raised against HDCs? Who would lose, and who would gain? How would such a change in the law affect the flow of commerce in this country?

3. Do you think that the UCC's provisions have struck an appropriate balance between the interests of banks and those of bank customers? Why or why not?

---

3. *Agriliance, L.L.C. v. Runnells Grain Elevator, Inc.,* 272 F.Supp.2d 800 (S.D. Iowa 2003).

UNIT SIX

CREDITORS' RIGHTS AND BANKRUPTCY

CONTENTS

BUSINESS LAW

CLARKSON · MILLER · CROSS

CHAPTER 28

Creditors' Rights and Remedies

Normally, creditors have no problem collecting the debts owed to them. When disputes arise over the amount owed, however, or when the debtor simply cannot or will not pay, what happens? What remedies are available to creditors when a debtor defaults (fails to pay as promised)? In this chapter, we focus on some basic laws that assist the debtor and creditor in resolving their dispute without resorting to bankruptcy (see Chapter 30) or mortgage foreclosure (see Chapter 31). In Chapter 29, we will discuss the remedies that are available only to secured creditors (those whose loans are supported or backed by collateral) under Article 9 of the Uniform Commercial Code (UCC).

SECTION 1
LAWS ASSISTING CREDITORS

Both the common law and statutory laws other than Article 9 of the UCC create various rights and remedies for creditors. We discuss here some of these rights and remedies, including liens, garnishment, and creditors' composition agreements.

Liens

A **lien** is an encumbrance on (claim against) property to satisfy a debt or protect a claim for the payment of a debt. As mentioned, liens may arise under the common law (usually by possession of the property) or under statutory law. Statutory liens include *mechanic's liens,* whereas *artisan's liens* were recognized at common law. *Judicial liens* are those that represent a creditor's efforts to collect on a debt before or after a judgment is entered by a court.

Liens are a very important tool for creditors because they generally take priority over other claims against the same property (priority of claims will be discussed in depth in Chapter 29). In fact, mechanic's and artisan's liens normally take priority over creditors who have a *perfected* security interest in the property. (As you will read in Chapter 29, a creditor who has perfected a security interest in property—by filing a financing statement, for example—usually prevails against other parties with an interest in the same property, except for certain lienholders.)

MECHANIC'S LIENS When a person contracts for labor, services, or materials to be furnished for the purpose of making improvements on real property but does not immediately pay for the improvements, the creditor can place a **mechanic's lien** on the property. This creates a special type of debtor-creditor relationship in which the real estate itself becomes security for the debt.

For example, a painter agrees to paint a house for a homeowner for an agreed-on price to cover labor and materials. If the homeowner refuses to pay or pays only a portion of the charges, a mechanic's lien against the property can be created. The painter is then a lienholder, and the real property is encumbered (burdened) with the mechanic's lien for the amount owed. If the homeowner does not pay the lien, the property can be sold to satisfy the debt. Notice of the *foreclosure* (the process by which the creditor deprives the debtor of his or her property—see Chapter 31) and sale must be given to the debtor in advance, however.

Note that state law governs the procedures that must be followed to create a mechanic's (or other statutory) lien. Generally, the lienholder must file a written notice of lien against the particular property involved. The notice of lien must be filed within a specific time period, measured from the last date on which materials or labor was provided (usually within 60 to 120 days). If the property owner fails to pay the debt, the lienholder is entitled to foreclose on the real estate on which the work or materials were provided and to sell it to satisfy the debt. The sale proceeds are used to pay the debt and the costs of the legal proceedings; the surplus, if any, is paid to the former owner.

ARTISAN'S LIENS An **artisan's lien** is a device created at common law through which a creditor can recover payment from a debtor for labor and materials furnished in the repair of personal property. In contrast to a mechanic's lien, an artisan's lien is *possessory*. This means that the lienholder ordinarily must have retained possession of the property and have expressly or impliedly agreed to provide the services on a cash, not a credit, basis. The lien remains in existence as long as the lienholder maintains possession, and the lien is terminated once possession is *voluntarily* surrendered—unless the surrender is only temporary.[1] As mentioned, artisan's liens usually take priority over other creditors' claims to the same property.

<mark>CASE IN POINT</mark> Erie Power Technologies, Inc., hired Shaw Group to design and fabricate steam generators for Erie's power plant. Erie delivered the necessary materials for the development of the generators and made several payments to Shaw as the work progressed. Shaw completed the fabrication of the materials in its possession, but Erie made no further payments and filed for bankruptcy. Under the bankruptcy reorganization plan (see Chapter 30), Erie was required to pay Shaw $320,000 for completing the generators. Erie then filed a lawsuit to recover that payment, claiming that those funds should have gone to other secured creditors who had priority over Shaw. The court held that Shaw had a common law artisan's lien in the goods that it possessed and had added value to them. Because the artisan's lien took priority over the claims of other secured creditors, the court granted a summary judgment in favor of Shaw.[2]

Modern statutes permit the holder of an artisan's lien to foreclose and sell the property subject to the lien to satisfy the debt. As with a mechanic's lien, the lienholder is required to give notice to the owner of the property prior to foreclosure and sale. The sale proceeds are used to pay the debt and the costs of the legal proceedings, and the surplus, if any, is paid to the former owner.[3]

JUDICIAL LIENS When a debt is past due, a creditor can bring a legal action against the debtor to collect the debt. If the creditor is successful in the action, the court awards the creditor a judgment against the debtor (usually for the amount of the debt plus any interest and legal costs incurred in obtaining the judgment). Frequently, however, the creditor is unable to collect the awarded amount.

To ensure that a judgment in the creditor's favor will be collectible, the creditor is permitted to request that certain nonexempt property of the debtor be seized to satisfy the debt. (As will be discussed later in this chapter, under state or federal statutes some kinds of property are exempt from attachment by creditors.) A court's order to seize the debtor's property is known as a *writ of attachment* if it is issued prior to a judgment in the creditor's favor. If the order is issued after a judgment, it is referred to as a *writ of execution*.

Writ of Attachment. In the context of judicial liens, **attachment** refers to a court-ordered seizure and taking into custody of property prior to the securing of a judgment for a past-due debt. (As you will read in Chapter 29, attachment means something different in the context of secured transactions.[4]) Normally, attachment is a *prejudgment* remedy, occurring either at the time a lawsuit is filed or immediately afterwards. To attach before a judgment, a creditor must comply with the specific state's statutory restrictions and requirements. The due process clause of the Fourteenth Amendment to the U.S. Constitution also applies and requires that the debtor be given notice and an opportunity to be heard (see Chapter 4).

The creditor must have an enforceable right to payment of the debt under law and must follow certain procedures. Otherwise, the creditor can be liable for damages for wrongful attachment. Typically, the creditor must file with the court an *affidavit* (a

---

1. Involuntary surrender of possession by a lienholder, such as when a police officer seizes goods from a lienholder, does not terminate the lien.

2. *In re Erie Power Technologies, Inc.,* 364 Bankr. 896 (W.D.Pa. 2007).

3. An artisan's lien has priority over a filed statutory lien (such as a title lien on an automobile or a lien filed under Article 9 of the UCC) and a bailee's lien (such as a storage lien).

4. In secured transactions, *attachment* refers to the process through which a security interest becomes effective and enforceable against a debtor with respect to the debtor's collateral [UCC 9–203].

written statement, made under oath) stating that the debtor has failed to pay and indicating the statutory grounds under which attachment is sought. The creditor must also post a bond to cover at least the court costs, the value of the property attached, and the value of the loss of use of that property suffered by the debtor. When the court is satisfied that all the requirements have been met, it issues a **writ of attachment,** which directs the sheriff or other officer to seize nonexempt property. If the creditor prevails at trial, the seized property can be sold to satisfy the judgment.

Writ of Execution.

If a creditor obtains a judgment against the debtor and the debtor will not or cannot pay the judgment, the creditor is entitled to go back to the court and request a **writ of execution.** A writ of execution is an order that directs the sheriff to seize (levy) and sell any of the debtor's nonexempt real or personal property that is within the court's geographic jurisdiction (usually the county in which the courthouse is located). The proceeds of the sale are used to pay the judgment, accrued interest, and costs of the sale. Any excess is paid to the debtor. The debtor can pay the judgment and redeem the nonexempt property at any time before the sale takes place. (Because of exemption laws and bankruptcy laws, however, many judgments are practically uncollectible.)

Garnishment

An order for **garnishment** permits a creditor to collect a debt by seizing property of the debtor that is held by a third party. In a garnishment proceeding, the third party—the person or entity on whom the garnishment judgment is served—is called the *garnishee.* Typically, the garnishee is the debtor's employer, and the creditor is seeking a judgment so that part of the debtor's usual paycheck will be paid to the creditor. In some situations, however, the garnishee is a third party that holds funds belonging to the debtor (such as a bank) or has possession of, or exercises control over, funds or other types of property owned by the debtor. A creditor can garnish almost all types of property, including tax refunds, pensions, and trust funds—so long as the property is not exempt from garnishment and is in the possession of a third party.

GARNISHMENT PROCEEDINGS State law governs garnishment actions, so the specific procedures vary from state to state. According to the laws in many states, the judgment creditor needs to obtain only one order of garnishment, which will then apply continuously to the judgment debtor's weekly wages until the entire debt is paid. Garnishment can be a prejudgment remedy, requiring a hearing before a court, but it is most often a postjudgment remedy.

LAWS LIMITING THE AMOUNT OF WAGES SUBJECT TO GARNISHMENT Both federal and state laws limit the amount that can be taken from a debtor's weekly take-home pay through garnishment proceedings.[5] Federal law provides a minimal framework to protect debtors from losing all their income to pay judgment debts.[6] State laws also provide dollar exemptions, and these amounts are often larger than those provided by federal law. Under federal law, an employer cannot dismiss an employee because his or her wages are being garnished.

The question in the following case was whether payments to an independent contractor (see Chapter 32) for services performed could be garnished.

---

5. A few states (for example, Texas) do not permit garnishment of wages by private parties except under a child-support order.
6. For example, the federal Consumer Credit Protection Act, 15 U.S.C. Sections 1601–1693r, provides that a debtor can retain either 75 percent of his or her disposable earnings per week or an amount equivalent to thirty hours of work paid at federal minimum wage rates, whichever is greater.

CASE 28.1
Indiana Surgical Specialists v. Griffin
Court of Appeals of Indiana, 867 N.E.2d 260 (2007).

BACKGROUND AND FACTS • Helen Griffin owed Indiana Surgical Services a certain amount. When the debt was not paid, Indiana Surgical filed a suit in an Indiana small claims court against Griffin. Griffin did not answer the complaint. In 2001, the court issued a default judgment against her. Four years later, Indiana Surgical learned that Griffin worked for MDS Courier Services. On Indiana Surgical's request, the court issued a garnishment order against MDS to "withhold from the earnings of" Griffin the appropriate amount until her debt was paid. MDS responded:

CASE 28.1 CONTINUED ➡ MDS Courier Services, Inc. employs drivers on a "contract" basis, therefore, drivers are not actual employees, but rather "contracted" to do a particular job. Because of this, we are not responsible for any payroll deductions including garnishments.

Indiana Surgical asked the court to hold MDS in contempt. Dawn Klingenberger, an MDS manager, testified that Griffin was a subcontractor of MDS, called as needed, compensated per job at "thirty-five percent of whatever she does," and paid on a biweekly basis. The court ruled that "the judgment debtor is a subcontractor, and not an employee," and that her earnings could not be garnished. Indiana Surgical appealed to a state intermediate appellate court.

IN THE LANGUAGE OF THE COURT
MAY, Judge.
* * * *

Indiana Surgical argues the trial court erred by declining to enforce the garnishment order issued to MDS on the ground Griffin was a "subcontractor" and not an employee of MDS. Indiana Surgical asserts the trial court's "distinction between wages subject to withholding and other earnings" is not supported in law. Under the facts of this case, we agree.

Garnishment refers to "any legal or equitable proceedings through which the earnings of an individual are required to be withheld by a garnishee, by the individual debtor, or by any other person for the payment of a judgment" [under Indiana Code Section 24-4.5-5-105(1)(b)].

Earnings are [defined in Indiana Code Section 24-4.5-1-301(9) as] "compensation paid or payable for personal services, whether denominated as wages, salary, commission, bonus, or otherwise, and includes periodic payments under a pension or retirement program."[a] In discussing the [provision in the Consumer Credit Protection Act that is the] federal counterpart to the Indiana statute, the [United States] Supreme Court stated: *"There is every indication that Congress, in an effort to avoid the necessity of bankruptcy, sought to regulate garnishment in its usual sense as a levy on periodic payments of compensation needed to support the wage earner and his family on a week-to-week, month-to-month basis."* [Emphasis added.]

Griffin received "periodic payments of compensation" for her personal services as a courier. These payments were earnings that could be garnished through a garnishment order. The trial court erred to the extent it held otherwise. We reverse and remand for further proceedings including, but not limited to, a determination of MDS's liability for payments made to Griffin after Indiana Surgical acquired an equitable lien upon service of process in [garnishment proceedings]. In light of our holding, the trial court should also determine whether MDS should be held in contempt of the garnishment order.

DECISION AND REMEDY • *The state intermediate appellate court held that payments for the services of an independent contractor fell within the applicable definition of* earnings *and thus Griffin's earnings as an independent contractor could be garnished. The court reversed the decision of the lower court and remanded the case.*

THE ETHICAL DIMENSION • *Should some people be exempt from garnishment orders? Explain why or why not.*

THE LEGAL ENVIRONMENT DIMENSION • *Building contractors and subcontractors are typically classified as independent contractors. Could payments to these parties also fall within the definition of* earnings *applied in this case? Discuss.*

---

a. Indiana's definition of *earnings* is included in the part of the Indiana Code known as the Uniform Consumer Credit Code, which was derived from the federal Consumer Credit Protection Act. The federal provision defining earnings is identical.

Creditors' Composition Agreements

Creditors may contract with the debtor for discharge of the debtor's liquidated debts (debts that are definite, or fixed, in amount) on payment of a sum less than that owed. These agreements are referred to as **creditors' composition agreements** (or *composition agreements*) and usually are held to be enforceable unless they are formed under duress.

Concept Summary 28.1 on the following page provides a synopsis of the remedies available to creditors.

CONCEPT SUMMARY 28.1
Remedies Available to Creditors

Remedy	Description
Liens	1. *Mechanic's lien*—A lien placed on an owner's real estate for labor, services, or materials furnished for improvements made to the realty. 2. *Artisan's lien*—A lien placed on an owner's personal property for labor performed or value added to that property. 3. *Judicial liens*— a. Writ of attachment—A court-ordered seizure of property prior to a court's final determination of the creditor's rights to the property. Creditors must strictly comply with applicable state statutes to obtain a writ of attachment. b. Writ of execution—A court order directing the sheriff to seize (levy) and sell a debtor's nonexempt real or personal property to satisfy a court's judgment in the creditor's favor.
Garnishment	A collection remedy that allows the creditor to attach a debtor's funds (such as wages owed or bank accounts) and property that are held by a third person.
Creditors' Composition Agreement	A contract between a debtor and her or his creditors by which the debtor's debts are discharged by payment of a sum less than the amount that is actually owed.

◄── SECTION 2 ──►
SURETYSHIP AND GUARANTY

When a third person promises to pay a debt owed by another in the event that the debtor does not pay, either a *suretyship* or a *guaranty* relationship is created. Exhibit 28–1 on the facing page illustrates these relationships. The third person's creditworthiness becomes the security for the debt owed. At common law, there were significant differences in the liability of a surety and a guarantor, as discussed in the following subsections. Today, however, the distinctions outlined here have been abolished in some states.

Suretyship

A contract of strict **suretyship** is a promise made by a third person to be responsible for the debtor's obligation. It is an express contract between the **surety** (the third party) and the creditor. In the strictest sense, the surety is primarily liable for the debt of the principal. This means that the creditor can demand payment from the surety from the moment the debt is due and that the creditor need not exhaust all legal remedies against the principal debtor before holding the surety responsible for payment.

For example, Roberto Delmar wants to borrow from the bank to buy a used car. Because Roberto is still in college, the bank will not lend him the funds unless his father, José Delmar, who has dealt with the bank before, will cosign the note (add his signature to the note, thereby becoming a surety and thus jointly liable for payment of the debt). When José Delmar cosigns the note, he becomes primarily liable to the bank. On the note's due date, the bank can seek payment from either Roberto or José Delmar, or both jointly.

Guaranty

With a suretyship arrangement, the surety is *primarily* liable for the debtor's obligation. With a guaranty arrangement, the **guarantor**—the third person making the guaranty—is *secondarily* liable. The guarantor can be required to pay the obligation *only after the principal debtor defaults,* and usually only after the creditor has made an attempt to collect from the debtor. The guaranty contract terms determine the extent and time of the guarantor's liability.

For example, a corporation, BX Enterprises, needs to borrow to meet its payroll. The bank is skeptical about the creditworthiness of BX and requires Dawson, its president, who is a wealthy businessperson and owner of 70 percent of BX Enterprises, to sign an agreement making herself personally liable for payment if BX does not pay off the loan. As a guarantor of the loan, Dawson cannot be held liable until BX Enterprises is in default.

EXHIBIT 28–1 • Suretyship and Guaranty Parties

In a suretyship or guaranty arrangement, a third party promises to be responsible for a debtor's obligations. A third party who agrees to be responsible for the debt even if the primary debtor does not default is known as a surety; a third party who agrees to be *secondarily* responsible for the debt—that is, responsible only if the primary debtor defaults—is known as a guarantor. As noted in Chapter 15, normally a promise of guaranty (a collateral, or secondary, promise) must be in writing to be enforceable.

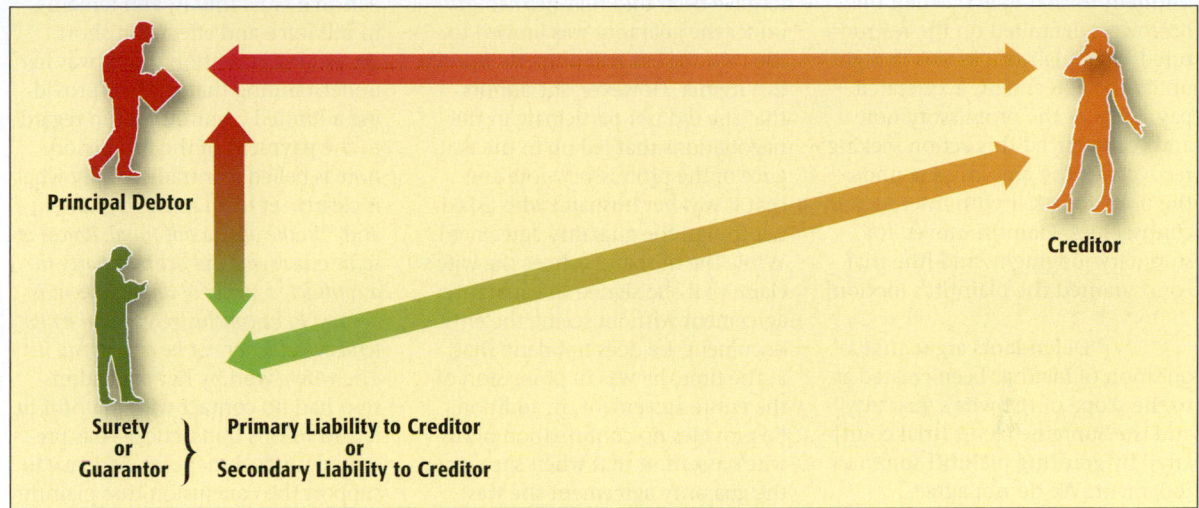

Principal Debtor

Creditor

Surety or Guarantor } Primary Liability to Creditor or Secondary Liability to Creditor

Under the Statute of Frauds, a guaranty contract between the guarantor and the creditor must be in writing (recorded) to be enforceable unless the *main purpose* exception (discussed in Chapter 15) applies.[7] At common law, a suretyship agreement did not need to be in writing to be enforceable, and oral surety agreements were sufficient. Today, however, some states require a writing (or electronic record) to enforce a suretyship.

In the following case, a guarantor claimed that she did not understand the full extent of her liability under a guaranty agreement at the time she signed it. Did her alleged ignorance of the terms of the agreement excuse her from liability for the debt after the primary debtor's default? That was the issue before the court.

---

7. Briefly, the main purpose exception provides that if the main purpose of the guaranty agreement is to benefit the guarantor, then the contract need not be in writing to be enforceable.

☀ EXTENDED CASE 28.2 ☀
Overseas Private Investment Corp. v. Kim

New York Supreme Court, Appellate Division, 69 A.D.3d 1185, 895 N.Y.S.2d 217 (2010).
www.courts.state.ny.us/decisions/index.shtml[a]

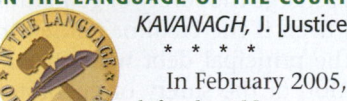

IN THE LANGUAGE OF THE COURT
KAVANAGH, J. [Justice]
* * * *

In February 2005, defendant Nam Koo Kim (hereinafter the husband), as sole owner of

Majestic Group Korea, Ltd., entered into a loan agreement on behalf of the company with plaintiff [the Overseas Private Investment Corporation] to borrow $1,500,000 for the purposes of financing a "Ruby Tuesday's" restaurant in South Korea. The husband and his

wife, defendant Hee Sun Kim (hereinafter the wife), issued personal guaranties for the loan. In October 2005, Majestic defaulted on the loan and a restructured loan and assumption agreement was executed by the parties and included a promissory note by the husband to pay plaintiff

---

a. In the left-hand column of the page, select "3rd Dept." under the heading "Appellate Decisions." When the next page opens, select "January 2010" from the drop-down menu in the upper-left corner, and then click on "Decisions" in the January 21 calendar box. Scroll down the list to the case title to access its opinion. The New York Supreme Court maintains this Web site.

EXTENDED CASE CONTINUES ➡

EXTENDED CASE 28.2 CONTINUED ➡

$1,517,000 in the event of a default. Once again, the wife agreed to personally guaranty the terms of the note and signed a written commitment to that effect. When the borrowers defaulted on the restructured loan, plaintiff, as was its right under the agreement, accelerated payments of the promissory note and commenced this action seeking recovery of the amount due under the note, together with interest and counsel fees. Plaintiff moved for summary judgment, and [the trial court granted the plaintiff's motion].

* * * *

* * * Defendants argue that a question of fact has been created as to the scope of the wife's guaranty and the Supreme Court [trial court] erred by granting plaintiff summary judgment. We do not agree.

A party is entitled to a judgment on a guaranty of a note if it proves that there has been a default on the payment of a promissory note and the party against whom judgment has been sought has executed a valid guaranty warranting the payment of the amount due under that note.

In her defense, the wife argues that when she signed the guaranty she was only provided with the last page of the agreement and claims to have been told that her liability under the guaranty was limited to the value of her real property interest in Virginia. However, she admits that she did not participate in the negotiations that led up to the issuance of the promissory note and that it was her husband who asked her to sign the guaranty agreement. While the husband echoes the wife's claim that she signed the guaranty agreement without seeing the entire document, he does not deny that, at the time, he was in possession of the entire agreement. In addition, he provides no confirmation of his wife's assertion that when she signed the guaranty agreement she was told that her legal obligation was limited to the value of her real estate interest in Virginia. In addition, the terms of the guaranty are clear on its face and specifically provide that the wife has guaranteed full payment of the promissory note. In fact,

immediately above the wife's signature is an acknowledgment to the effect that she "has received a copy of this Restructured Loan Deferral Letter, agrees to all terms and conditions hereof, and confirms that the Personal Guaranty is, and remains, in full force and effect." In short, the wife's contention that it was her understanding that she was providing a limited commitment in regard to the payment of the promissory note is belied [contradicted] by what is clearly set forth in the document and, *"in the absence of fraud, duress or some other wrongful act by a party to a contract, a signer of an agreement is deemed to be conclusively bound by its terms whether or not he or she read it."* The wife—who by her own admission had no contact with plaintiff in regard to this transaction—has presented no documentary evidence to support the conclusion that plaintiff used duress or fraud to procure her signature on this document. As such, she is bound by the terms of her guaranty. [Emphasis added.]

* * * *

ORDERED that the order is affirmed, with costs.

 QUESTIONS

1. If the guaranty agreement had not been in writing, would the agreement have been enforceable? Explain.
2. A guarantor can be required to pay a debt only after the principal debtor defaults. Which party was the principal debtor in this case?

Actions Releasing the Surety and the Guarantor

The actions that will release the surety from an obligation are basically the same as those that will discharge the guarantor. Making any material modification to the terms of the original contract—without the consent of the surety or guarantor—will discharge the surety or guarantor's obligation. (The extent to which the surety or guarantor is discharged depends on whether he or she was compensated, and to what extent he or she suffered a loss from the modification. For example, a father who receives no consideration in return for acting as a surety on his daughter's loan will be completely discharged if the loan contract is modified without his consent.) Similarly, if a creditor surrenders the collateral to the debtor or impairs the collateral without

the consent of the surety or guarantor, these acts can reduce the obligation of the surety or guarantor.

Naturally, any payment of the principal obligation by the debtor or by another person on the debtor's behalf will discharge the surety or guarantor from the obligation. Even if the creditor refused to accept payment of the principal debt when it was tendered, the obligation of the surety or guarantor can be discharged (if the creditor knew about the suretyship or guaranty).

Defenses of the Surety and the Guarantor

Generally, the surety or guarantor can also assert any of the defenses available to the principal debtor to avoid liability on the obligation to the creditor. A few exceptions do exist, however. The surety or guarantor cannot assert the principal debtor's incapacity or bankruptcy as a defense, nor can the surety assert the statute of limitations as a defense.

Obviously, a surety or guarantor may also have his or her own defenses—for example, incapacity or bankruptcy. If the creditor fraudulently induced the person to act as a surety or guarantor on the debt, the surety or guarantor can assert fraud as a defense. In most states, the creditor has a legal duty to inform the surety, before the formation of the suretyship contract, of material facts known by the creditor that would substantially increase the surety's risk. Failure to so inform may constitute fraud and renders the suretyship obligation voidable.

Rights of the Surety and the Guarantor

When the surety or guarantor pays the debt owed to the creditor, he or she acquires certain rights, as discussed next.

THE RIGHT OF SUBROGATION The surety or guarantor has the legal **right of subrogation.** Simply stated, this means that any right that the creditor had against the debtor now becomes the right of the surety or guarantor. Included are creditor rights in bankruptcy, rights to collateral possessed by the creditor, and rights to judgments obtained by the creditor. In short, the surety or guarantor now stands in the shoes of the creditor and may pursue any remedies that were available to the creditor against the debtor.

CASE IN POINT Guerrero Brothers, Inc. (GBI), contracted with the Public School System (PSS) to build a high school. Century Insurance Company (CIC) agreed to provide GBI with the required payment and performance bonds on the project. Thus, CIC acted as a surety of GBI's performance and promised to finish the project if GBI defaulted. Four years after construction began, PSS terminated GBI's contract for default, and CIC fulfilled GBI's obligations by finishing construction of the school. Numerous disputes arose, and litigation ensued. Ultimately, PSS agreed to pay GBI $500,000 in contract funds. CIC then filed an action against GBI and PSS to recover the $867,867.16 it claimed PSS owed it for finishing the school. The court found that CIC, as a performing surety, was entitled to the remaining contract funds through the right of subrogation. It had performed GBI's obligations and therefore stepped into GBI's shoes and had the right to obtain payment from PSS.[8]

8. *Century Insurance Co. v. Guerrero Brothers, Inc.,* 2010 WL 997112 (N.Mariana Islands 2010).

THE RIGHT OF REIMBURSEMENT The surety or guarantor has a **right of reimbursement** from the debtor. Basically, the surety is entitled to receive from the debtor all outlays made on behalf of the suretyship arrangement. Such outlays can include expenses incurred as well as the actual amount of the debt paid to the creditor.

THE RIGHT OF CONTRIBUTION Two or more sureties are called **co-sureties.** When a co-surety pays more than her or his proportionate share on a debtor's default, she or he is entitled to recover from the other co-sureties the amount paid above that surety's obligation. This is the **right of contribution.** Generally, a co-surety's liability either is determined by agreement or, in the absence of agreement, is set at the maximum liability under the suretyship contract.

For example, assume that two co-sureties are obligated under a suretyship contract to guarantee the debt of a debtor. Together, the sureties' maximum liability is $25,000. Surety A's maximum liability is $15,000, and surety B's is $10,000. The debtor owes $10,000 and is in default. Surety A pays the creditor the entire $10,000. In the absence of agreement, Surety A can recover $4,000 from Surety B ($10,000/$25,000 × $10,000 = $4,000, Surety B's obligation).

SECTION 3
PROTECTION FOR DEBTORS

The law protects debtors as well as creditors. Certain property of the debtor, for example, is exempt under state law from creditors' actions. Consumer protection statutes (see Chapter 45) also protect debtors' rights. Of course, bankruptcy laws, which will be discussed in Chapter 30, are designed specifically to assist debtors in need of help.

In most states, certain types of real and personal property are exempt from execution or attachment. State exemption statutes usually include both real and personal property.

Exempted Real Property

Probably the most familiar exemption is the **homestead exemption.** Each state permits the debtor to retain the family home, either in its entirety or up to a specified dollar amount, free from the claims of unsecured creditors or trustees in bankruptcy. (Note that federal bankruptcy law now places a cap on the amount that debtors filing bankruptcy can claim is exempt under their states' homestead exemption—see Chapter 30 for details.)

For example, Beere owes Veltman $40,000. The debt is the subject of a lawsuit, and the court awards Veltman a judgment of $40,000 against Beere. Beere's homestead is valued at $50,000, and the homestead exemption is $25,000. There are no outstanding mortgages or other liens on his homestead. To satisfy the judgment debt, Beere's family home is sold at public auction for $45,000. The proceeds of the sale are distributed as follows:

1. Beere is given $25,000 as his homestead exemption.
2. Veltman is paid $20,000 toward the judgment debt, leaving a $20,000 deficiency judgment (that is, "leftover debt") that can be satisfied from any other nonexempt property (personal or real) that Beere may own, if permitted by state law.

In a few states, statutes allow the homestead exemption only if the judgment debtor has a family. If a judgment debtor does not have a family, a creditor may be entitled to collect the full amount realized from the sale of the debtor's home. In addition, note that the homestead exemption interacts with other areas of law and can sometimes operate to cancel out a portion of a lien on a debtor's real property.

CASE IN POINT Antonio Stanley purchased a modular home from Yates Mobile Services Corporation. When Stanley failed to pay the purchase price of the home, Yates obtained a judicial lien against Stanley's property in the amount of $165,138.05. Stanley then filed for bankruptcy and asserted the homestead exemption. The court found that Stanley was entitled to avoid the lien to the extent that it impaired his exemption. Using a bankruptcy law formula, the court determined that the total impairment was $143,639.05 and that Stanley could avoid paying this amount to Yates. Thus, Yates was left with a judicial lien on Stanley's home in the amount of $21,499.[9]

Exempted Personal Property

Personal property that is most often exempt from satisfaction of judgment debts includes the following:

1. Household furniture up to a specified dollar amount.
2. Clothing and certain personal possessions, such as family pictures or a Bible.
3. A vehicle (or vehicles) for transportation (at least up to a specified dollar amount).
4. Certain classified animals, usually livestock but including pets.
5. Equipment that the debtor uses in a business or trade, such as tools or professional instruments, up to a specified dollar amount.

---

9. *In re Stanley,* __ Bankr. __, 2010 WL 2103441 (M.D.N.C. 2010).

REVIEWING
Creditors' Rights and Remedies

Air Ruidoso, Ltd., operated a commuter airline and air charter service between Ruidoso, New Mexico, and airports in Albuquerque and El Paso. Executive Aviation Center, Inc., provided services for airlines at the Albuquerque International Airport. When Air Ruidoso failed to pay more than $10,000 that it owed on its account for fuel, oil, and oxygen, Executive Aviation took possession of Air Ruidoso's plane, claiming that it had a lien on the plane. Using the information presented in the chapter, answer the following questions.

1. Can Executive Aviation establish an artisan's lien on the plane? Why or why not?
2. Suppose that Executive Aviation files a lawsuit in court against Air Ruidoso for the $10,000 past-due debt. What two methods discussed in this chapter would allow the court to seize Air Ruidoso's plane to satisfy the debt?
3. Suppose that Executive Aviation discovers that Air Ruidoso has sufficient assets in one of its bank accounts to pay the past-due amount. How might Executive Aviation attempt to obtain access to these funds?
4. Suppose that a clause in the contract between Air Ruidoso and Executive Aviation provides that "if the airline becomes insolvent, Braden Fasco, the chief executive officer of Air Ruidoso, agrees to cover its outstanding debts." Is this a suretyship or a guaranty agreement?

DEBATE THIS: *Because writs of attachment are a prejudgment remedy for nonpayment of a debt, they are unfair and should be abolished.*

TERMS AND CONCEPTS

artisan's lien 547	creditors' composition agreement 549	homestead exemption 553	right of subrogation 553

artisan's lien 547

attachment 547

co-surety 553

creditors' composition
    agreement 549

default 546

garnishment 548

guarantor 550

homestead exemption 553

lien 546

mechanic's lien 546

right of contribution 553

right of reimbursement 553

right of subrogation 553

surety 550

suretyship 550

writ of attachment 548

writ of execution 548

QUESTIONS AND CASE PROBLEMS

28–1. Liens Sylvia takes her car to Caleb's Auto Repair Shop. A sign in the window states that all repairs must be paid for in cash unless credit is approved in advance. Sylvia and Caleb agree that Caleb will repair Sylvia's car engine and put in a new transmission. No mention is made of credit. Because Caleb is not sure how much engine repair will be necessary, he refuses to give Sylvia an estimate. He repairs the engine and puts in a new transmission. When Sylvia comes to pick up her car, she learns that the bill is $2,500. Sylvia is furious, refuses to pay Caleb that amount, and demands possession of her car. Caleb insists on payment. Discuss the rights of both parties in this matter.

28–2. QUESTION WITH SAMPLE ANSWER: Judicial Liens.

Kanahara is employed part-time by the Cross-Bar Packing Corp. and earns take-home pay of $400 per week. He is $2,000 in debt to the Holiday Department Store for goods purchased on credit over the past eight months. Most of this property is nonexempt and is now in Kanahara's apartment. Kanahara is in default on his payments to Holiday. Holiday learns that Kanahara has a girlfriend in another state and that he plans to give her most of this property for Christmas. Discuss what actions are available to and should be taken by Holiday to collect the debt owed by Kanahara.

• **For a sample answer to Question 28–2, go to Appendix I at the end of this text.**

28–3. Mechanic's Lien Grant is the owner of a relatively old home valued at $45,000. He notices that the bathtubs and fixtures are leaking and need to be replaced. He contracts with Jane's Plumbing to replace the bathtubs and fixtures. Jane replaces them, and on June 1 she submits her bill of $4,000 to Grant. Because of financial difficulties, Grant does not pay the bill. Grant's only asset is his home, but his state's homestead exemption is $40,000. Discuss fully Jane's remedies in this situation.

28–4. Garnishment Susan Guinta is a real estate salesperson. Smythe Cramer Co. went to an Ohio state court and obtained a garnishment order to attach Guinta's personal earnings. The order was served on Russell Realtors to attach sales commissions that Russell owed

to Guinta. Russell objected, arguing that commissions are not personal earnings and are therefore exempt from attachment under a garnishment of personal earnings. An Ohio statute defines *personal earnings* as "money, or any other consideration or thing of value, that is paid or due to a person in exchange for work, labor, or personal services provided by the person to an employer." An *employer* is "a person who is required to withhold taxes out of payments of personal earnings made to a judgment debtor." Russell does not withhold taxes from its salespersons' commissions. Under a federal statute, *earnings* means "compensation paid or payable for personal services, whether denominated as wages, salary, commission, bonus, or otherwise." When the federal definition is more restrictive and results in a smaller garnishment, that definition is controlling. Property other than personal earnings may be subject to garnishment without limits. How should the court rule regarding Russell's objection? Why? [*Smythe Cramer Co. v. Guinta*, 116 Ohio Misc.2d 20, 762 N.E.2d 1083 (2001)]

28–5. CASE PROBLEM WITH SAMPLE ANSWER: Liens.

Karen and Gerald Baldwin owned property in Rapid City, South Dakota, which they leased to Wyoming Alaska Corp. (WACO) for use as a gas station and convenience store. The lease obligated the Baldwins to make repairs, but WACO was authorized to make necessary repairs. After seventeen years, the property was run-down. The store's customers were tripping over chunks of concrete in the parking lot. An underground gasoline storage tank was leaking. The store's manager hired Duffield Construction, Inc., to install a new tank and make other repairs. The Baldwins saw the new tank sitting on the property before the work began. When WACO paid only a small portion of the cost, Duffield filed a mechanic's lien and asked a South Dakota state court to foreclose on the property. The Baldwins disputed the lien, arguing that they had not requested the work. What is the purpose of a mechanic's lien? Should property owners who do not contract for improvements be liable for the cost under such a lien? How might property owners protect themselves against a lien for work that they do not request? Explain. [Duffield Construction, Inc. v. Baldwin, 679 N.W.2d 477 (S.D. 2004)]

• **To view a sample answer for Problem 28–5, go to this book's Web site at <u>www.cengage.com/blaw/clarkson</u>, select "Chapter 28," and click on "Case Problem with Sample Answer."**

28–6. Attachment In 2004 and 2005, Kent Avery, on behalf of his law firm—the Law Office of Kent Avery, LLC—contracted with Marlin Broadcasting, LLC, to air commercials on WCCC-FM, 106.9 "The Rock." Avery, who was the sole member of his firm, helped to create the ads, which solicited direct contact with "defense attorney Kent Avery," featured his voice, and repeated his name and experience to make potential clients familiar with him. When WCCC was not paid for the broadcasts, Marlin filed a suit in a Connecticut state court against Avery and his firm, alleging an outstanding balance of $35,250. Pending the court's hearing of the suit, Marlin filed a request for a writ of attachment. Marlin offered in evidence the parties' contracts, the ads' transcripts, and WCCC's invoices. Avery contended that he could not be held personally liable for the cost of the ads. Marlin countered that the ads unjustly enriched Avery by conferring a personal benefit on him to Marlin's detriment. What is the purpose of attachment? What must a creditor prove to obtain a writ of attachment? Did Marlin meet this test? Explain. [*Marlin Broadcasting, LLC v. Law Office of Kent Avery, LLC,* 101 Conn.App. 638, 922 A.2d 1131 (2007)]

28–7. Liens Autolign Manufacturing Group, Inc., was a plastic injection molder that made parts for the auto industry. Because of a fire at its plant, Autolign subcontracted its work to several other companies to produce parts for its customers. Autolign provided the subcontractors with molds it owned so that they could produce the exact parts needed. The subcontractors produced the parts for Autolign, which it then sold to automakers. Shortly afterward, Autolign ceased operations. The subcontractors sued Autolign for breach of contract, claiming that they were never paid for the parts that they had produced for Autolign. The subcontractors asserted a statutory "molder's lien" on the molds in their possession. A molder's lien is similar to an artisan's lien in that it is possessory, but was established by a Michigan statute rather than common law. One of Autolign's creditors, Wamco 34, Ltd., argued that the molds were its property because the molds were used to secure repayment of a debt that Autolign owed to Wamco. The trial court held that Wamco was a secured creditor and that its interest had priority over the plaintiffs' lien in the molds. The subcontractors appealed. Which party had the superior claim? Explain your answer. [*Delta Engineered Plastics, LLC v. Autolign Manufacturing Group, Inc.,* 286 Mich.App. 115, 777 N.W.2d 502 (2010)]

28–8. A QUESTION OF ETHICS: Guaranty.

 73-75 Main Avenue, LLC, agreed to lease a portion of the commercial property at 73 Main Avenue, Norwalk, Connecticut, to PP Door Enterprise, Inc. Nan Zhang, as manager of PP Door, signed the lease agreement. The lessor required the principal officers of PP Door to execute personal guaranties. In addition, the principal officers agreed to provide the lessor with credit information. Apparently, both the lessor and the principals of PP Door signed the lease and guaranty agreements that were sent to PP Door's office. When PP Door failed to make monthly payments, 73-75 Main Avenue filed a suit against PP Door and its owner, Ping Ying Li. At trial, Li testified that she was the sole owner of PP Door but denied that Zhang was its manager. She also denied signing the guaranty agreement. She claimed that she had signed the credit authorization form because Zhang had told her he was too young to have good credit. Li claimed to have no knowledge of the lease agreement. She did admit, however, that she had paid the rent. She claimed that Zhang had been in a car accident and had asked her to help pay his bills, including the rent at 73 Main Avenue. Li further testified that she did not see the name PP Door on the storefront of the leased location. [73-75 Main Avenue, LLC v. PP Door Enterprise, Inc., *120 Conn.App. 150, 991 A.2d 650 (2010)*]

(a) Li argued that she was not liable on the lease agreement because Zhang was not authorized to bind her to the lease. Do the facts support Li? Why or why not?

(b) Li claimed that the guaranty for rent was not enforceable against her. Why might the court agree?

28–9. SPECIAL CASE ANALYSIS: Guaranty.

Go to Extended Case 28.2, *Overseas Private Investment Corp. v. Kim,* 69 A.D.3d 1185, 895 N.Y.S.2d 217 (2010) on pages 551–552. Read the excerpt and answer the following questions.

(a) Issue: The main issue concerned the enforceability of a guaranty agreement. Who was arguing that the agreement should not be enforced, and on what grounds?

(b) Rule of Law: What are the requirements for a guaranty agreement to be enforceable?

(c) Applying the Rule of Law: How did the court apply the rule of law to the guaranty agreement in this case?

(d) Conclusion: After applying the rule of law, what did the court conclude? Who benefited from the court's decision, the plaintiff or the defendants?

LEGAL RESEARCH EXERCISES ON THE WEB

Go to this text's Web site at **www.cengage.com/blaw/clarkson**, select "Chapter 28," and click on "Practical Internet Exercises." There you will find the following Internet research exercises that you can perform to learn more about the topics covered in this chapter.

Practical Internet Exercise 28–1: Legal Perspective
Debtor-Creditor Relations

Practical Internet Exercise 28–2: Management Perspective
Mechanic's Liens

CHAPTER 29

✳

Secured Transactions

Whenever the payment of a debt is guaranteed, or *secured,* by personal property owned by the debtor or in which the debtor has a legal interest, the transaction becomes known as a secured transaction. The concept of the secured transaction is as basic to modern business practice as the concept of credit. Logically, sellers and lenders do not want to risk nonpayment, so they usually will not sell goods or lend funds unless the promise of payment is somehow guaranteed. Indeed, business as we know it could not exist without laws permitting and governing secured transactions.

Article 9 of the Uniform Commercial Code (UCC) governs secured transactions in personal property. Personal property includes accounts, agricultural liens, *chattel paper* (any writing evidencing a debt secured by personal property), commercial assignments of $1,000 or more, *fixtures* (certain property that is attached to land), instruments, and other types of intangible property, such as patents.

Article 9 does not cover creditor devices such as liens (see Chapter 28) and real property mortgages (see Chapter 31).

In this chapter, we first look at the terminology of secured transactions. We then discuss how the rights and duties of creditors and debtors are created and enforced under Article 9. As will become evident, the law of secured transactions tends to favor the rights of creditors, but it also offers debtors some protections, though to a lesser extent.

SECTION 1
THE TERMINOLOGY OF SECURED TRANSACTIONS

The UCC's terminology has been uniformly adopted in all documents used in situations involving secured transactions. The following is a brief summary of the UCC's definitions of terms relating to secured transactions:

1. A **secured party** is any creditor who has a *security interest* in the debtor's collateral. This creditor can be a seller, a lender, a cosigner, or even a buyer of accounts or chattel paper [UCC 9–102(a)(72)].
2. A **debtor** is the party who owes payment or other performance of a secured obligation [UCC 9–102(a)(28)].
3. A **security interest** is the interest in the collateral (such as personal property, fixtures, or accounts) that secures payment or performance of an obligation [UCC 1–201(37)].

4. A **security agreement** is an agreement that creates or provides for a security interest [UCC 9–102(a)(73)].
5. **Collateral** is the subject of the security interest [UCC 9–102(a)(12)].
6. A **financing statement**—referred to as the UCC-1 form—is the document that is normally filed to give public notice to third parties of the secured party's security interest [UCC 9–102(a)(39)].

Together, these basic definitions form the concept under which a debtor-creditor relationship becomes a secured transaction relationship (see Exhibit 29–1 on the following page).

SECTION 2
CREATION OF A SECURITY INTEREST

A creditor has two main concerns if the debtor defaults: (1) Can the debt be satisfied through the

EXHIBIT 29–1 • Secured Transactions—Concept and Terminology
In a security agreement, a debtor and a creditor agree that the creditor will have a security interest in collateral in which the debtor has rights. In essence, the collateral secures the loan and ensures the creditor of payment should the debtor default.

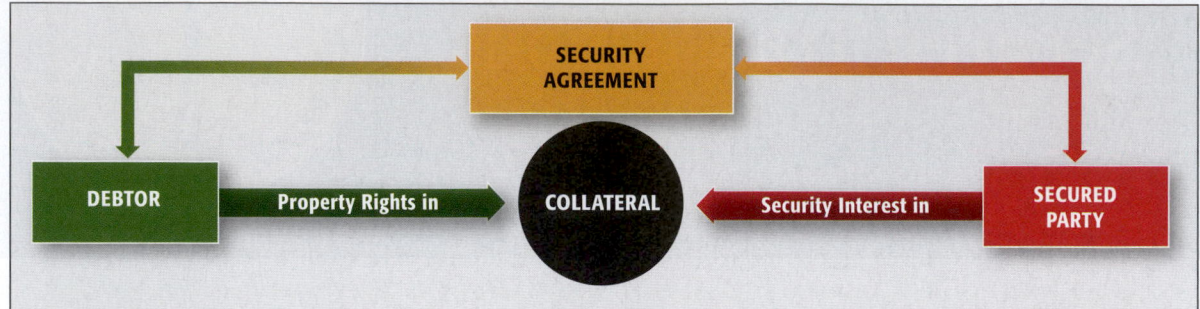

possession and (usually) sale of the collateral? (2) Will the creditor have priority over any other creditors or buyers who may have rights in the same collateral? These two concerns are met through the creation and perfection of a security interest. We begin by examining how a security interest is created.

To become a secured party, the creditor must obtain a security interest in the collateral of the debtor. Three requirements must be met for a creditor to have an enforceable security interest:

1. Unless the creditor has possession of the collateral, there must be a written or authenticated security agreement that clearly describes the collateral subject to the security interest and is signed or authenticated by the debtor.
2. The secured party must give the debtor something of value.
3. The debtor must have rights in the collateral.

Once these requirements have been met, the creditor's rights are said to *attach* to the collateral. **Attachment** gives the creditor an enforceable security interest in the collateral [UCC 9–203].[1]

For example, if Sam applies for a credit card at a local department store, the application will likely contain a clause stating that the store will retain a security interest in the goods that he buys with the card until he has paid for the goods in full. This application would be considered a written security agreement, which is the first requirement for an enforceable security interest. The goods that Sam buys with the card are the collateral (the second requirement), and his ownership interest in those goods is the right that he has in them (the third requirement). Thus, the

requirements for an enforceable security interest are met. When Sam buys something with the card, the store's rights attach to it.

Written or Authenticated Security Agreement

When the collateral is *not* in the possession of the secured party, the security agreement must be either written or *authenticated,* and it must describe the collateral. **Authentication** is the act of signing, executing, or adopting any symbol on an electronic record that verifies that the person signing has the intent to adopt or accept the record [UCC 9–102(a)(7)]. If the security agreement is in writing or authenticated, *only the debtor's signature or authentication* is required to create the security interest. The reason authentication is acceptable is to provide for electronic filing (the filing process will be discussed later).

A security agreement must contain a description of the collateral that reasonably identifies it. Generally, such phrases as "all the debtor's personal property" or "all the debtor's assets" would *not* constitute a sufficient description [UCC 9–108(c)].

Secured Party Must Give Value

The secured party must give something of value to the debtor. Under the UCC, value can include a binding commitment to extend credit and, in general, any consideration sufficient to support a simple contract [UCC 1–204]. Normally, the value given by a secured party involves a direct loan or a commitment to sell goods on credit.

Debtor Must Have Rights in the Collateral

The debtor must have rights in the collateral; that is, the debtor must have some ownership interest

---

1. As was mentioned on page 547 in Chapter 28, the term *attachment* has a different meaning in secured transactions than it does in the context of judicial liens. In judicial liens, attachment refers to a court-ordered seizure and taking into custody of property prior to the securing of a court judgment for a past-due debt.

or right to obtain possession of that collateral. The debtor's rights can represent either a current or a future legal interest in the collateral. For example, a retail seller–debtor can give a secured party a security interest not only in existing inventory owned by the retailer but also in *future* inventory to be acquired by the retailer.

SECTION 3
PERFECTION OF A SECURITY INTEREST

Perfection is the legal process by which secured parties protect themselves against the claims of third parties who may wish to have their debts satisfied out of the same collateral. Whether a secured party's security interest is perfected or unperfected can have serious consequences for the secured party if, for example, the debtor defaults on the debt or files for bankruptcy. What if the debtor has borrowed from two different creditors and used the same property as collateral for both loans? If the debtor defaults on both loans, which of the two creditors has first rights to the collateral? In this situation, the creditor with a perfected security interest will prevail.

Perfection usually is accomplished by filing a financing statement with the office of the appropriate government official. In some circumstances, however, a security interest becomes perfected even though no financing statement is filed.

Perfection by Filing

The most common means of perfection is by filing a *financing statement*—a document that gives public notice to third parties of the secured party's security interest—with the office of the appropriate government official. The security agreement itself can also be filed to perfect the security interest. The financing statement must provide the names of the debtor and the secured party, and must indicate the collateral covered by the financing statement. A uniform financing statement form (see Exhibit 29–2 on the next page) is used in all states [UCC 9–521].

Communication of the financing statement to the appropriate filing office, together with payment of the correct filing fee, or acceptance of the financing statement by the filing officer constitutes a filing [UCC 9–516(a)]. The word *communication* means that the filing can be accomplished electronically [UCC 9–102(a)(18)]. Once completed, filings are indexed by the name of the debtor so that they can be located by subsequent searchers. A financing statement may be filed even before a security agreement is made or a security interest attaches [UCC 9–502(d)].

THE DEBTOR'S NAME The UCC requires that a financing statement be filed under the name of the debtor [UCC 9–502(a)(1)]. Slight variations in names normally will not be considered misleading if a search of the filing office's records, using a standard computer search engine routinely used by that office, would disclose the filings [UCC 9–506(c)].[2] If the debtor is identified by the correct name at the time when the financing statement is filed, the secured party's interest retains its priority even if the debtor's name later changes. Because most states use electronic filing systems, UCC 9–503 sets out detailed rules for determining when the debtor's name as it appears on a financing statement is sufficient.

Specific Types of Debtors. For corporations, which are organizations that have registered with the state, the debtor's name on the financing statement must be "the name of the debtor indicated on the public record of the debtor's jurisdiction of organization" [UCC 9–503(a)(1)]. If the debtor is a trust or a trustee with respect to property held in trust, the filed financing statement must disclose this information and must provide the trust's name as specified in its official documents [UCC 9–503(a)(3)]. For all others, the filed financing statement must disclose "the individual or organizational name of the debtor" [UCC 9–503(a)(4)(A)]. As used here, the word *organization* includes unincorporated associations, such as clubs and some churches, as well as joint ventures and general partnerships. If an organizational debtor does not have a group name, the names of the individuals in the group must be listed.

Trade Names. In general, providing only the debtor's trade name (or fictitious name) in a financing statement is *not* sufficient for perfection [UCC 9–503(c)]. Assume that a loan is being made to a sole proprietorship owned by Peter Jones. The trade, or fictitious, name is Pete's Plumbing. A financing statement filed in the trade name Pete's Plumbing

---

2. If the name listed in the financing statement is so inaccurate that a search using the standard search engine will not disclose the debtor's name, the financing statement is deemed seriously misleading under UCC 9–506. See also UCC 9–507, which governs the effectiveness of financing statements found to be seriously misleading.

EXHIBIT 29-2 • **The Uniform Commercial Code Financing Statement**

UCC FINANCING STATEMENT
FOLLOW INSTRUCTIONS (front and back) CAREFULLY

A. NAME & PHONE OF CONTACT AT FILER [optional]

B. SEND ACKNOWLEDGMENT TO: (Name and Address)

THE ABOVE SPACE IS FOR FILING OFFICE USE ONLY

1. DEBTOR'S EXACT FULL LEGAL NAME   insert only one debtor name (1a or 1b) - do not abbreviate or combine names

1a. ORGANIZATION'S NAME				

OR

1b. INDIVIDUAL'S LAST NAME	FIRST NAME	MIDDLE NAME	SUFFIX

1c. MAILING ADDRESS	CITY	STATE	POSTAL CODE	COUNTRY

1d. SEE INSTRUCTIONS	ADD'L INFO RE ORGANIZATION DEBTOR	1e. TYPE OF ORGANIZATION	1f. JURISDICTION OF ORGANIZATION	1g. ORGANIZATIONAL ID #, if any
				□ NONE

2. ADDITIONAL DEBTOR'S EXACT FULL LEGAL NAME - insert only one debtor name (2a or 2b)   do not abbreviate or combine names

2a. ORGANIZATION'S NAME				

OR

2b. INDIVIDUAL'S LAST NAME	FIRST NAME	MIDDLE NAME	SUFFIX

2c. MAILING ADDRESS	CITY	STATE	POSTAL CODE	COUNTRY

2d. SEE INSTRUCTIONS	ADD'L INFO RE ORGANIZATION DEBTOR	2e. TYPE OF ORGANIZATION	2f. JURISDICTION OF ORGANIZATION	2g. ORGANIZATIONAL ID #, if any
				□ NONE

3. SECURED PARTY'S NAME (or NAME of TOTAL ASSIGNEE of ASSIGNOR S/P)   insert only one secured party name (3a or 3b)

3a. ORGANIZATION'S NAME				

OR

3b. INDIVIDUAL'S LAST NAME	FIRST NAME	MIDDLE NAME	SUFFIX

3c. MAILING ADDRESS	CITY	STATE	POSTAL CODE	COUNTRY

4. This FINANCING STATEMENT covers the following collateral:

5. ALTERNATIVE DESIGNATION [if applicable]: □ LESSEE/LESSOR   □ CONSIGNEE/CONSIGNOR   □ BAILEE/BAILOR   □ SELLER/BUYER   □ AG. LIEN   □ NON-UCC FILING

6. □ This FINANCING STATEMENT is to be filed [for record] (or recorded) in the REAL ESTATE RECORDS.   Attach Addendum [if applicable]   7. Check to REQUEST SEARCH REPORT(S) on Debtor(s) [ADDITIONAL FEE] [optional]   □ All Debtors   □ Debtor 1   □ Debtor 2

8. OPTIONAL FILER REFERENCE DATA

FILING OFFICE COPY — UCC FINANCING STATEMENT (FORM UCC1) (REV. 05/22/02)   International Association of Commercial Administrators (IACA)

NATIONAL UCC FINANCING STATEMENT (FORM UCC1) (REV. 01/01/08) would *not* be sufficient because it does not identify Peter Jones as the actual debtor. As will be discussed in Chapter 36, a sole proprietorship (such as Pete's Plumbing) is not a legal entity distinct from the person who owns it. The reason for this rule is to ensure that the debtor's name on a financing statement is one that prospective lenders can locate and recognize in future searches.

CHANGES IN THE DEBTOR'S NAME If the debtor's name changes, the financing statement remains effective for collateral the debtor acquired before or within four months after the name change. Unless an amendment to the financing statement is filed within this four-month period, collateral acquired by the debtor after the four-month period is unperfected [UCC 9–507(b) and (c)]. A one-page uniform financing statement amendment form is available for filing name changes and for other purposes (see the discussion of amendments later in this chapter) [UCC 9–521].

DESCRIPTION OF THE COLLATERAL The UCC requires that both the security agreement and the financing statement contain a description of the collateral in which the secured party has a security interest. The security agreement must describe the collateral because no security interest in goods can exist unless the parties agree on which goods are subject to the security interest. The financing statement must also describe the collateral to provide public notice of the fact that certain goods of the debtor are subject to a security interest. Other parties who might later wish to lend funds to the debtor or buy the collateral can thus learn of the security interest by checking with the state or local office in which a financing statement for that type of collateral would be filed. For land-related security interests, a legal description of the realty is also required [UCC 9–502(b)].

Sometimes, the descriptions in the two documents differ, with the description in the security agreement being more precise than the description in the financing statement, which is allowed to be more general. For example, a security agreement for a commercial loan to a manufacturer may list all of the manufacturer's equipment subject to the loan by serial number, whereas the financing statement may simply state "all equipment owned or hereafter acquired."

The UCC permits broad, general descriptions in the financing statement, such as "all assets" or "all personal property." Usually, if a financing statement accurately describes the agreement between the secured party and the debtor, the description is sufficient [UCC 9–504].

WHERE TO FILE In most states, a financing statement must be filed centrally in the appropriate state office, such as the office of the secretary of state, in the state where the debtor is located. Filing in the county where the collateral is located is required only when the collateral consists of timber to be cut; fixtures; or items to be extracted, such as oil, coal, gas, and minerals [UCC 9–301(3) and (4), 9–502(b)].

The state in which a financing statement should be filed depends on the *debtor's location,* not the location of the collateral (as was required under the unrevised Article 9) [UCC 9–301]. The debtor's location is determined as follows [UCC 9–307]:

1. For an *individual debtor,* it is the state of the debtor's principal residence.
2. For an organization registered with the state, such as a corporation or limited liability company, it is the state in which the organization is registered. For example, if a debtor is incorporated in Delaware and has its chief executive office in New York, a secured party would file the financing statement in Delaware because that is where the debtor's business is registered.
3. For all other entities, it is the state in which the business is located or, if the debtor has more than one office, the place from which the debtor manages its business operations and affairs (the office of its chief executive).

CONSEQUENCES OF AN IMPROPER FILING Any improper filing renders the secured party's interest unperfected and reduces the secured party's claim in bankruptcy to that of an unsecured creditor. For example, if the debtor's name on the financing statement is inaccurate or if the collateral is not sufficiently described on the filing statement, the filing may not be effective.

CASE IN POINT Corona Fruits & Veggies, Inc., sublet farmland to Armando Munoz Juarez, a strawberry farmer, and loaned funds to Juarez for payroll and production expenses. The sublease and other documents set out Juarez's full name, but Juarez generally went by the name "Munoz" and signed the sublease "Armando Munoz." Corona filed financing statements that identified the debtor as "Armando Munoz." In December, Juarez contracted to sell strawberries to Frozsun Foods, Inc., which advanced funds secured by a financing statement that identified the debtor as "Armando Juarez." By the next July, Juarez owed Corona $230,482.52 and Frozsun $19,648.52. When Juarez did not repay his debt, Corona took possession of the farmland, harvested and sold the strawberries, and kept the proceeds. Corona and Frozsun then filed a suit against Juarez to collect the rest. At trial, Frozsun presented evidence that it had conducted a debtor name search for "Juarez" and had not discovered Corona's financing statement. The court concluded that the "Armando Munoz" debtor name in Corona's financing statement was seriously misleading. Frozsun's interest thus took priority because its financing statement was recorded properly.[3]

Perfection without Filing

In two types of situations, security interests can be perfected without filing a financing statement. The first occurs when the collateral is transferred into the possession of the secured party. The second occurs when the security interest is one of a limited number under the UCC that can be perfected on attachment (without a filing and without possession of the goods) [UCC 9–309]. The phrase *perfected on attachment* means that these security interests are automatically perfected at the time of their creation. Two

of the most common security interests that are perfected on attachment are a *purchase-money security interest* in consumer goods (defined and explained shortly) and an assignment of a beneficial interest in a decedent's estate [UCC 9–309(1), (13)].

Where or how to perfect a security interest sometimes depends on the classification or definition of the collateral. Collateral is generally divided into two classifications: *tangible collateral* (collateral that can be seen, felt, and touched) and *intangible collateral* (collateral that consists of or generates rights). Exhibit 29–3 below and on the facing page summarizes the various classifications of collateral and the methods of perfecting a security interest in collateral falling within each of those classifications.[4]

PERFECTION BY POSSESSION In the past, one of the most frequently used means of obtaining financing under the common law was to **pledge** certain

---

3. *Corona Fruits and Veggies, Inc. v. Frozsun Foods, Inc.,* 143 Cal. App.4th 319, 48 Cal.Rptr.3d 868 (2006).

4. There are additional classifications, such as agricultural liens, commercial tort claims, and investment property. For definitions of these types of collateral, see UCC 9–102(a)(5), (a)(13), and (a)(49).

EXHIBIT 29–3 • Types of Collateral and Methods of Perfection

TANGIBLE COLLATERAL		METHOD OF PERFECTION
All things that are movable at the time the security interest attaches (such as livestock) or that are attached to the land, including timber to be cut and growing crops.		
1. Consumer Goods [UCC 9–301, 9–303, 9–309(1), 9–310(a), 9–313(a)]	Goods used or bought primarily for personal, family, or household purposes—for example, household furniture [UCC 9–102(a)(23)].	For purchase-money security interest, attachment (that is, the creation of a security interest) is sufficient; for boats, motor vehicles, and trailers, filing or compliance with a certificate-of-title statute is required; for other consumer goods, general rules of filing or possession apply.
2. Equipment [UCC 9–301, 9–310(a), 9–313(a)]	Goods bought for or used primarily in business (and not part of inventory or farm products)—for example, a delivery truck [UCC 9–102(a)(33)].	Filing or (rarely) possession by secured party.
3. Farm Products [UCC 9–301, 9–310(a), 9–313(a)]	Crops (including aquatic goods), livestock, or supplies produced in a farming operation—for example, ginned cotton, milk, eggs, and maple syrup [UCC 9–102(a)(34)].	Filing or (rarely) possession by secured party.
4. Inventory [UCC 9–301, 9–310(a), 9–313(a)]	Goods held by a person for sale or under a contract of service or lease; raw materials held for production and work in progress [UCC 9–102(a)(48)].	Filing or (rarely) possession by secured party.
5. Accessions [UCC 9–301, 9–310(a), 9–313(a)]	Personal property that is so attached, installed, or fixed to other personal property (goods) that it becomes a part of these goods—for example, a DVD player installed in an automobile [UCC 9–102(a)(1)].	Filing or (rarely) possession by secured party (same as personal property being attached).

EXHIBIT 29-3 • Types of Collateral and Methods of Perfection, Continued

INTANGIBLE COLLATERAL		METHOD OF PERFECTION
Nonphysical property that exists only in connection with something else.		
1. Chattel Paper [UCC 9–301, 9–310(a), 9–312(a), 9–313(a), 9–314(a)]	A writing or writings (record or records) that evidence both a monetary obligation and a security interest in goods and software used in goods—for example, a security agreement or a security agreement and promissory note. *Note:* If the record or records consist of information stored in an electronic medium, the collateral is called *electronic chattel paper.* If the information is inscribed on a tangible medium, it is called *tangible chattel paper* [UCC 9–102(a)(11), (a)(31), and (a)(78)].	Filing or possession or control by secured party.
2. Instruments [UCC 9–301, 9–309(4), 9–310(a), 9–312(a) and (e), 9–313(a)]	A negotiable instrument, such as a check, note, certificate of deposit, draft, or other writing that evidences a right to the payment of money and is not a security agreement or lease but rather a type that can ordinarily be transferred (after indorsement, if necessary) by delivery [UCC 9–102(a)(47)].	Except for temporary perfected status, filing or possession. For the sale of promissory notes, perfection can be by attachment (automatically on the creation of the security interest).
3. Accounts [UCC 9–301, 9–309(2) and (5), 9–310(a)]	Any right to receive payment for the following: (a) any property, real or personal, sold, leased, licensed, assigned, or otherwise disposed of, including intellectual licensed property; (b) services rendered or to be rendered, such as contract rights; (c) policies of insurance; (d) secondary obligations incurred; (e) use of a credit card; (f) winnings of a government-sponsored or government-authorized lottery or other game of chance; and (g) health-care insurance receivables, defined as an interest or claim under a policy of insurance to payment for health-care goods or services provided [UCC 9–102(a)(2) and (a)(46)].	Filing required except for certain assignments that can be perfected by attachment (automatically on the creation of the security interest).
4. Deposit Accounts [UCC 9–104, 9–304, 9–312(b), 9–314(a)]	Any demand, time, savings, passbook, or similar account maintained with a bank [UCC 9–102(a)(29)].	Perfection by control, such as when the secured party is the bank in which the account is maintained or when the parties have agreed that the secured party can direct the disposition of funds in a particular account.
5. General Intangibles [UCC 9–301, 9–309(3), 9–310(a) and (b)(8)]	Any personal property (or debtor's obligation to make payments on such) other than that defined above [UCC 9–102(a)(42)], including software that is independent from a computer or other good [UCC 9–102(a)(44), (a)(61), and (a)(75)].	Filing only (for copyrights, with the U.S. Copyright Office), except a sale of a payment intangible by attachment (automatically on the creation of the security interest).

collateral as security for the debt and transfer the collateral into the creditor's possession. When the debt was paid, the collateral was returned to the debtor. Although the debtor usually entered into a written security agreement, oral security agreements were also enforceable as long as the secured party possessed the collateral.

Article 9 of the UCC retained the common law pledge and the principle that the security agreement need not be in writing to be enforceable if the collateral is transferred to the secured party [UCC 9–310, 9–312(b), 9–313]. For example, Sheila borrows $4,000 from Trent to pay for a needed medical procedure. As security on the loan, she gives him a promissory note on which she is the payee. Even though the agreement to hold the note as collateral was oral, Trent has a perfected security interest. He does not need to file a financing statement, because he has possession of the note. No other creditor of Sheila's can attempt to recover the promissory note from Trent in payment for other debts.

For most collateral, possession by the secured party is impractical because then the debtor cannot use or derive income from the property to pay off the debt. For example, Jason, a farmer, takes out a loan to finance the purchase of a corn harvester and uses the equipment as collateral. Clearly, the purpose of the purchase would be defeated if Jason transferred the collateral into the creditor's possession because he would not be able to use the equipment to harvest his corn. Certain items, however, such as stocks, bonds, negotiable instruments, and jewelry, are commonly transferred into the creditor's possession when they are used as collateral for loans.

PERFECTION BY ATTACHMENT—THE PURCHASE-MONEY SECURITY INTEREST IN CONSUMER GOODS

Under the UCC, fourteen types of security interests are perfected automatically at the time they are created [UCC 9–309]. The most common of these is the **purchase-money security interest (PMSI).** A PMSI in consumer goods is created when a person buys goods primarily for personal, family, or household purposes, and the seller or lender agrees to extend credit for part or all of the purchase price of the goods. The entity that extends the credit and obtains the PMSI can be either the seller (a store, for example) or a financial institution that lends the buyer the funds with which to purchase the goods [UCC 9–102(a)(2)].

Automatic Perfection. A PMSI in consumer goods is perfected automatically at the time of a credit sale— that is, at the time the PMSI is created. The seller in this situation does not need to do anything more to perfect her or his interest. For example, Jamie purchases a Whirlpool Duet steam washer and dryer from West Coast Appliance for $2,500. Unable to pay the entire amount in cash, Jamie signs a purchase agreement to pay $1,000 down and $100 per month until the balance, plus interest, is fully paid. West Coast Appliance is to retain a security interest in the appliances until full payment has been made. Because the security interest was created as part of the purchase agreement with a consumer, it is a PMSI, and West Coast Appliance's security interest is automatically perfected.

Exceptions to Automatic Perfection. There are two exceptions to the rule of automatic perfection for PMSIs. First, certain types of security interests that are subject to other federal or state laws may require additional steps to be perfected [UCC 9–311]. For example, many jurisdictions have certificate-of-title statutes that establish perfection requirements for security interests in certain goods, including automobiles, trailers, boats, mobile homes, and farm tractors. If a consumer in these jurisdictions purchases a boat, for example, the secured party will need to file a certificate of title with the appropriate state official to perfect the PMSI.

A second exception involves PMSIs in nonconsumer goods, such as a business's inventory or livestock, which are not automatically perfected [UCC 9–324]. These types of PMSIs will be discussed later in this chapter in the context of priorities.

Effective Time Duration of Perfection

A financing statement is effective for five years from the date of filing [UCC 9–515]. If a **continuation statement** is filed *within six months prior to* the expiration date, the effectiveness of the original statement is continued for another five years, starting with the expiration date of the first five-year period [UCC 9–515(d), (e)]. The effectiveness of the statement can be continued in the same manner indefinitely. Any attempt to file a continuation statement outside the six-month window will render the continuation ineffective, and the perfection will lapse at the end of the five-year period.

If a financing statement lapses, the security interest that had been perfected by the filing now becomes unperfected. A purchaser for value can take the property that was used as collateral as if the security interest had never been perfected [UCC 9–515(c)].

For a synopsis of the rules for creating and perfecting a security interest, see *Concept Summary 29.1* on the facing page.

SECTION 4
THE SCOPE OF A SECURITY INTEREST

As previously mentioned, a security interest can cover property in which the debtor has ownership or possessory rights in the present or in the future. Therefore, security agreements can cover the proceeds of the sale of collateral, after-acquired property, and future advances, as discussed next.

Proceeds

Proceeds are the cash or property received when collateral is sold or disposed of in some other way

CONCEPT SUMMARY 29.1
Creating and Perfecting a Security Interest

Concept	Description
Creating a Security Interest	1. Unless the creditor has possession of the collateral, there must be a written or authenticated security agreement signed or authenticated by the debtor and describing the collateral subject to the security interest. 2. The secured party must give value to the debtor. 3. The debtor must have rights in the collateral—some ownership interest or right to obtain possession of the specified collateral.

Perfecting a Security Interest	1. *Perfection by filing*—The most common method of perfection is by filing a financing statement containing the names of the secured party and the debtor and indicating the collateral covered by the financing statement.
	  a. Communication of the financing statement to the appropriate filing office, together with the correct filing fee, constitutes a filing.
	  b. The financing statement must be filed under the name of the debtor; fictitious (trade) names normally are not sufficient.
	2. *Perfection without filing*—
	  a. By transfer of collateral—The debtor can transfer possession of the collateral to the secured party. For example, a *pledge* is this type of transfer.
	  b. By attachment—A limited number of security interests are perfected by attachment, such as a purchase-money security interest (PMSI) in consumer goods. If the secured party has a PMSI in consumer goods (bought for personal, family, or household purposes), the secured party's security interest is perfected automatically.

[UCC 9–102(a)(64)]. A security interest in the collateral gives the secured party a security interest in the proceeds acquired from the sale of that collateral. For example, People's Bank has a perfected security interest in the inventory of a retail seller of heavy farm machinery. The retailer sells a tractor out of this inventory to Jacob Dunn, who is by definition *a buyer in the ordinary course of business* (this term will be discussed later in the chapter). Dunn agrees, in a security agreement, to make monthly payments to the retailer for a period of twenty-four months. If the retailer goes into default on the loan from the bank, the bank is entitled to the remaining payments Dunn owes to the retailer as proceeds.

A security interest in proceeds perfects automatically on the *perfection* of the secured party's security interest in the original collateral and remains perfected for twenty days after the debtor receives the proceeds. One way to extend the twenty-day automatic perfection period is to provide for such extended coverage in the original security agreement [UCC 9–315(c), (d)]. This is typically done when the collateral is the type that is likely to be sold, such as a retailer's inventory—for example, of computers or cell phones. The UCC also permits a security interest in identifiable cash proceeds to remain perfected after twenty days [UCC 9–315(d)(2)].

After-Acquired Property

After-acquired property is property that the debtor acquired after the execution of the security agreement. The security agreement may provide for a security interest in after-acquired property, such as a debtor's inventory [UCC 9–204(1)]. A secured party whose security interest is in existing inventory knows that the debtor will sell that inventory, thereby reducing the collateral subject to the security interest.

Generally, the debtor will purchase new inventory to replace the inventory sold. The secured party wants this newly acquired inventory to be subject to the original security interest. Thus, the after-acquired property clause continues the secured party's claim to any inventory acquired thereafter. (This is not to say that the original security interest will take priority over the rights of all other creditors with regard to this after-acquired inventory, as will be discussed later.)

To illustrate: Amato buys factory equipment from Bronson on credit, giving as security an interest in all of her equipment—both what she is buying and what she already owns. The security agreement with Bronson contains an after-acquired property clause. Six months later, Amato pays cash to another seller of factory equipment for additional equipment. Six months after that, Amato goes out of business before she has paid off her debt to Bronson. Bronson has a security interest in all of Amato's equipment, even the equipment bought from the other seller.

Future Advances

Often, a debtor will arrange with a bank to have a *continuing line of credit* under which the debtor can borrow funds intermittently. Advances against lines of credit can be subject to a properly perfected security interest in certain collateral. The security agreement may provide that any future advances made against that line of credit are also subject to the security interest in the same collateral [UCC 9–204(c)]. Future advances need not be of the same type or otherwise related to the original advance to benefit from this type of **cross-collateralization.**[5] Cross-collateralization occurs when an asset that is not the subject of a loan is used to collateralize that loan.

For example, Stroh is the owner of a small manufacturing plant with equipment valued at $1 million. He has an immediate need for $40,000 of working capital, so he obtains a loan from Midwestern Bank and signs a security agreement, putting up all of his equipment as security. The bank properly perfects its security interest. The security agreement provides that Stroh can borrow up to $500,000 in the future, using the same equipment as collateral for any future advances. In this situation, Midwestern Bank does not have to execute a new security agreement and perfect a security interest in the collateral each time an advance is made, up to a cumulative total of $500,000. For priority purposes, each advance is perfected as of the date of the *original* perfection.

The Floating-Lien Concept

A security agreement that provides for a security interest in proceeds, in after-acquired property, or in collateral subject to future advances by the secured party (or in all three) is often characterized as a **floating lien.** This type of security interest continues in the collateral or proceeds even if the collateral is sold, exchanged, or disposed of in some other way.

A FLOATING LIEN IN INVENTORY Floating liens commonly arise in the financing of inventories. A creditor is not interested in specific pieces of inventory, which are constantly changing, so the lien "floats" from one item to another, as the inventory changes.

Consider an example. Cascade Sports, Inc., a corporation formed in Oregon, operates as a cross-country ski dealer and has a line of credit with Portland First

Bank to finance an inventory of cross-country skis. Cascade and Portland First enter into a security agreement that provides for coverage of proceeds, after-acquired inventory, present inventory, and future advances. Portland First perfects its security interest in the inventory by filing centrally with the office of the secretary of state in Oregon. One day, Cascade sells a new pair of the latest cross-country skis and receives a used pair in trade. That same day, Cascade purchases two new pairs of cross-country skis from a local manufacturer for cash. Later that day, to meet its payroll, Cascade borrows $8,000 from Portland First Bank under the security agreement.

Portland First has a perfected security interest in the used pair of skis under the proceeds clause, has a perfected security interest in the two new pairs of skis purchased from the local manufacturer under the after-acquired property clause, and has the new amount of funds advanced to Cascade secured on all of the above collateral by the future-advances clause. All of this is accomplished under the original perfected security interest. The various items in the inventory have changed, but Portland First still has a perfected security interest in Cascade's inventory. Hence, it has a floating lien in the inventory.

A FLOATING LIEN IN A SHIFTING STOCK OF GOODS The concept of the floating lien can also apply to a shifting stock of goods. The lien can start with raw materials, follow them as they become finished goods and inventories, and continue as the goods are sold and are turned into accounts receivable, chattel paper, or cash.

SECTION 5
PRIORITIES

When more than one party claims an interest in the same collateral, which has priority? The UCC sets out detailed rules to answer this question. Although in many situations the party who has a perfected security interest will have priority, there are exceptions that give priority rights to another party, such as a buyer in the ordinary course of business.

General Rules of Priority

The basic rule is that when more than one security interest has been perfected in the same collateral, the first security interest to be perfected (or filed) has priority over any security interests that are perfected later. If only one of the conflicting security interests has been perfected, then that security interest has priority. If none of the security interests have been perfected, then

---

5. See Official Comment 5 to UCC 9–204.

the first security interest that attaches has priority. The UCC's rules of priority can be summarized as follows:

1. *A perfected security interest has priority over unsecured creditors and unperfected security interests.* When two or more parties have claims to the same collateral, a perfected secured party's interest has priority over the interests of most other parties [UCC 9–322(a)(2)]. This includes priority to the proceeds from a sale of collateral resulting from a bankruptcy (giving the perfected secured party rights superior to those of the bankruptcy trustee, as will be discussed in Chapter 30).

2. *Conflicting perfected security interests.* When two or more secured parties have perfected security interests in the same collateral, generally the first to perfect (by filing or taking possession of the collateral) has priority [UCC 9–322(a)(1)].

   CASE IN POINT Rebel Rents, Inc., bought snorkel equipment to use as inventory in its rental business and gave Textron Financial Corporation, which financed the purchase, a security interest in the equipment and its proceeds. Later that year, General Electric Capital Corporation (GECC) loaned Rebel up to $25 million and obtained a security interest in substantially all of Rebel's assets, including its inventory and proceeds. On January 5, 2001, GECC filed a financing statement to perfect its interest. Textron filed its financing statement on January 16. Rebel filed a petition for bankruptcy in 2002 but obtained $430,661 from operating its business after the filing. Textron claimed that because its security interest was created first, it was entitled to the $430,661. The court, however, ruled that GECC's security interest had priority because of the date of perfection. Although Textron's security interest was created first, it was not perfected until January 16. GECC's financing statement was filed on January 5—eleven days before Textron's financing statement was filed.[6]

3. *Conflicting unperfected security interests.* When two conflicting security interests are unperfected, the first to attach (be created) has priority [UCC 9–322(a)(3)]. This is sometimes called the "first-in-time" rule.

   CASE IN POINT Ag Venture Financial Services, Inc., made multiple loans to a family-owned dairy farm, Montagne Heifers, Inc. (MHI). Michael Montagne owned the business, and his wife and son were shareholders and employees. In 2005, MHI executed a promissory note and security agreement in favor of Ag Venture, which listed all of MHI's accounts, equipment, farm products, inventory, livestock, and proceeds as collateral. In 2006, Montagne and his wife separated, and he signed a separation agreement that gave her some funds and certain parcels of land. In 2007, Montagne gave his son a promissory note for $100,000 in exchange for his shares in MHI; the note listed all of MHI's equipment, inventory, livestock, and proceeds as collateral. Also in 2007, Montagne sold a herd of dairy cows for $500,000 and gave his former wife a check for $240,000. In 2008, Montagne filed a petition for bankruptcy, and a dispute arose over which party (Ag Venture or Montagne's son or former wife) was entitled to the proceeds from the 2007 sale of the cows. The court held that because Ag Venture's security interest in the proceeds was the first in time to *attach* (it was created in 2005), Ag Venture had first priority to the proceeds.[7]

In the following case, the court had to determine which of two conflicting security interests in a manufactured (mobile) home took priority.

---

6. *In re Rebel Rents, Inc.*, 307 Bankr. 171 (C.D.Cal. 2004).
7. *In re Montagne*, 417 Bankr. 214 (D.Vt. 2009).

✳ EXTENDED CASE 29.1 ✳
Citizens National Bank of Jessamine County v. Washington Mutual Bank

Court of Appeals of Kentucky, 309 S.W.3d 792 (2010).
apps.courts.ky.gov/supreme/sc_opinions.shtm[a]

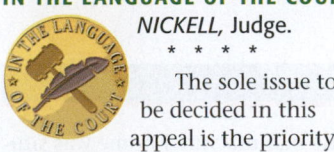

IN THE LANGUAGE OF THE COURT
NICKELL, Judge.
* * * *

The sole issue to be decided in this appeal is the priority of competing liens in and to a manufactured [mobile] home located on, but not attached to, a parcel of real estate which is the subject of a foreclosure action.

The land and mobile home were both previously owned by Rose Day.

On February 18, 1999, Ms. Day conveyed [transferred] the real estate to Anthony Reynolds and Kim Reynolds by deed, which was thereafter duly recorded in the Garrard County Clerk's Office. The deed description does not mention the mobile home;

---

a. In the left-hand column, in the "Enter Search Request" box, key in "April 9, 2010." Then click on "Search." Select the highlighted link to docket number "2008-CA-000155" in the left-hand column to access the case. The Kentucky appellate court system maintains this Web site.

EXTENDED CASE CONTINUES ➡

EXTENDED CASE 29.1 CONTINUED ➡

but it is clear from the record that the Reynolds were purchasing both from Ms. Day. The Reynolds further executed a mortgage to Washington Mutual Bank's predecessor in interest that was recorded shortly after the deed conveying a security interest in the * * * property. There is no question the Washington Mutual Bank has a valid and first lien on the real property.[b] There is no specific mention of the mobile home on the mortgage. Additionally, the Reynolds did not obtain a title certificate to the mobile home in their name. The evidence reveals that at the time of filing of the Complaint in this action by Washington Mutual, the mobile home was still titled in Ms. Day's name. There was no title lien statement issued in favor of Washington Mutual, or its predecessors in interest. The parties acknowledge that the mobile home was never legally affixed to the real property so as to remove it from the motor vehicle title records and change its character from personal property to real property.

On or about May 30, 2002, the Reynolds executed a second mortgage encumbering [burdening] the real property in favor of Citizens. Once again there was no description of the mobile home in the mortgage and no title lien statement issued in favor of Citizens. The Reynolds subsequently defaulted on both loans prompting the filing of the present litigation.

The Complaint was filed by Washington Mutual on April 16, 2007, claiming lien priority on both

the real estate and the manufactured home. On April 19, 2007, the Plaintiff [Washington Mutual] recorded a *lis pendens*[c] notice with the Garrard County Clerk's Office claiming an interest in both the real estate and the mobile home. The *lis pendens* and its amendment both identified Citizens National Bank of Jessamine County as an interested party. Further, Citizens was listed as a party defendant and properly served with the Complaint. On May 16, 2007, after being served with the Complaint, Citizens and the Reynolds executed a Title Lien Statement regarding the mobile home, which was recorded in the Garrard County Clerk's Office on August 14, 2007.

The master commissioner * * * determined that [the relevant Kentucky statute concerning the *lis pendens*] applied equally to real and personal property. Without further citation to authority, the master commissioner found "the filing of the Complaint and *lis pendens* by Washington Mutual created a priority claim in the mobile home." * * * The master commissioner concluded Washington Mutual's claims to the real estate and the manufactured home should be given priority over all other claims.

* * * *

[The trial court confirmed the master commissioner's report, and this appeal followed.]

Citizens contends the trial court erred in confirming the master commissioner's report as it was based on the erroneous conclusion that the

filing of a complaint and *lis pendens* created a priority lien on the manufactured home. Citizens contends the purpose of a *lis pendens* is to provide notice of a claim and applies only to interests in real estate.

* * * *

We agree with Citizens. Kentucky's *lis pendens* statute clearly applies only to real estate.

* * * As adopted in this Commonwealth, the UCC does not allow for the filing of a *lis pendens* on personal property such as the manufactured home in issue here.

* * * *KRS [Kentucky Revised Statutes] 186A.190 provides that the sole means of perfecting a security interest in personal property for which a certificate of title is issued is by placing a notation of the lien on the certificate of title.* There is no dispute Citizens has so perfected its lien but Washington Mutual has not. *It is fundamental that unperfected security interests are subordinate to perfected security interests.* This is true regardless of Citizens' knowledge of Washington Mutual's filing of a notice of *lis pendens* and any claim set up by such filing because, as we stated earlier, the notice of *lis pendens* applied only to the real estate which was the subject of the underlying foreclosure action, and not the manufactured home situated thereon. *Because Washington Mutual has failed to perfect its lien under the mandates of KRS 186A.190, its interest in the Reynolds' manufactured home must necessarily give way to Citizens' perfected claim.* The master commissioner's findings were incorrect and the trial court erred in not so finding. [Emphasis added.]

* * * *

For the foregoing reasons, the judgment of the Garrard Circuit Court is reversed and the cause remanded for entry of a judgment consistent with this opinion.

---

b. *Real property* (realty) consists of land and everything attached to it. All other property is regarded as *personal property*. In this case, the manufactured home, because it was not affixed to the land, is classified as personal property.

c. The term *lis pendens* (pronounced lease *pen*-dense) is Latin for "suit pending." It is a written notice, filed with the court and recorded with the county recorder, stating that a lawsuit has been initiated concerning the title to certain real property.

QUESTIONS

1. According to the court, which of the two security interests in the *land* on which the manufactured home was situated had priority? Why?

2. Suppose that the manufactured home had been affixed to the land and regarded as real property. In that situation, which of the two security interests would have taken priority? Why?

Exceptions to the General Rule

Under some circumstances, on the debtor's default, the perfection of a security interest will *not* protect a secured party against certain other third parties having claims to the collateral. For example, the UCC provides that in some instances a PMSI, properly perfected,[8] will prevail over another security interest in after-acquired collateral, even though the other was perfected first. We discuss several significant exceptions to the general rules of priority in the following subsections.

BUYERS IN THE ORDINARY COURSE OF BUSINESS

Under the UCC, a person who buys "in the ordinary course of business" takes the goods free from any security interest created by the seller *even if the security interest is perfected and the buyer knows of its existence* [UCC 9–320(a)]. In other words, a buyer in the ordinary course will have priority even if a previously perfected security interest exists as to the goods. The rationale for this rule is obvious: if buyers could not obtain the goods free and clear of any security interest the merchant had created, for example, in inventory, the free flow of goods in the marketplace would be hindered.

A **buyer in the ordinary course of business** is a person who in good faith, and without knowledge that the sale violates the rights of another in the goods, buys in ordinary course from a person in the business of selling goods of that kind [UCC 1–201(9)]. Note that the buyer can know about the existence of a perfected security interest, so long as he or she does not know that buying the goods violates the rights of any third party.

CASE IN POINT Dublin Auto Sales granted a security interest in its inventory to Heartland Bank for a $300,000 line of credit. Heartland perfected its security interest by filing financing statements with the appropriate state offices. Dublin Auto used $9,000 of its credit to buy a 1997 Ford F-150 and $13,000 to buy a 1999 Jeep Cherokee and delivered the certificates of title, which designated Dublin Auto as the owner, to Heartland. In March 2002, Dublin Auto sold the F-150 for $15,386.63 to Joe and Michael Murphy, and the Jeep for $14,045 to Michael Laxton. National City Bank financed both purchases. New certificates of title designated the buyers as the owners and Heartland as the "first lienholder." Heartland received none of the funds from the sales and consequently filed a suit in an Ohio state court against National City and others, seeking a declaration that its security interest in the vehicles took priority. The court, however, ruled in National City's favor. Because the Murphys and Laxton were buyers in the ordinary course of business, Heartland's security interest in the motor vehicles at issue was extinguished when the vehicles were sold to them.[9]

PMSI IN GOODS OTHER THAN INVENTORY AND LIVESTOCK

An important exception to the first-in-time rule involves certain types of collateral, such as equipment, that is not inventory (or livestock) and in which one of the secured parties has a perfected PMSI [UCC 9–324(a)]. Suppose that Sandoval borrows funds from West Bank, signing a security agreement in which she puts up all of her present and after-acquired equipment as security. On May 1, West Bank perfects this security interest (which is not a PMSI). On July 1, Sandoval purchases a new piece of equipment from Zylex Company on credit, signing a security agreement. The delivery date for the new equipment is August 1.

Zylex thus has a PMSI in the new equipment (which is not part of its inventory), but the PMSI is not in consumer goods and thus is not automatically perfected. If Sandoval defaults on her payments to both West Bank and Zylex, which of them has priority with regard to the new piece of equipment? Generally, West Bank would have priority because its interest perfected first in time. In this situation, however, as long as Zylex perfected its PMSI in the new equipment within twenty days after Sandoval took possession on August 1, Zylex has priority.

PMSI IN INVENTORY

Another important exception to the first-in-time rule has to do with security interests in inventory. A perfected PMSI in inventory has priority over a conflicting security interest in the same inventory, provided that the holder of the PMSI notifies the holder of the conflicting security interest on or before the time the debtor takes possession of the inventory [UCC 9–324(b)].

Suppose that on May 1, SNS Electronics borrows funds from West Bank. SNS signs a security agreement that puts up all of its present inventory and any inventory thereafter acquired as collateral. West Bank perfects its interest (not a PMSI) on that date. On June 10, SNS buys new inventory from Martin,

---

8. Recall that, with some exceptions (such as motor vehicles), a PMSI in *consumer goods* is automatically perfected—no filing is necessary. A PMSI that is *not* in consumer goods must still be perfected, however.

9. *Heartland Bank v. National City Bank,* 171 Ohio App.3d 132, 869 N.E.2d 746 (2007).

Inc., a manufacturer, to use for its Fourth of July sale. SNS makes a down payment for the new inventory and signs a security agreement giving Martin a PMSI in the new inventory as collateral for the remaining debt. Martin delivers the inventory to SNS on June 28, but SNS's Fourth of July sale is a disaster, and most of its inventory remains unsold. In August, SNS defaults on its payments to both West Bank and Martin.

Does West Bank or Martin have priority with respect to the new inventory delivered to SNS on June 28? If Martin has not perfected its security interest by June 28, West Bank's after-acquired collateral clause has priority because it was the first to be perfected (on May 1). If, however, Martin has perfected *and* gives proper notice of its security interest to West Bank before SNS takes possession of the goods on June 28, Martin has priority.

BUYERS OF THE COLLATERAL The UCC recognizes that there are certain types of buyers whose interest in purchased goods could conflict with those of a perfected secured party on the debtor's default. These include buyers in the ordinary course of business (as discussed), as well as buyers of farm products, instruments, documents, or securities. The UCC sets down special rules of priority for these types of buyers.

Exhibit 29–4 on the facing page describes the various rules regarding the priority of claims to a debtor's collateral.

SECTION 6

RIGHTS AND DUTIES OF DEBTORS AND CREDITORS

The security agreement itself spells out most of the rights and duties of the debtor and the secured party. The UCC, however, imposes some rights and duties that are applicable in the absence of a valid security agreement that states the contrary.

Information Requests

At the time of filing, a secured party has the option of furnishing a *copy* of the financing statement being filed to the filing officer and requesting that the filing officer make a note of the file number, the date, and the hour of the original filing on the copy [UCC 9–523(a)]. The filing officer must send this copy to the person designated by the secured party or to the debtor, if the debtor makes the request. The filing officer must also give information to a person who is contemplating obtaining a security interest from a prospective debtor [UCC 9–523(c), (d)]. If requested, the filing officer must issue a certificate that provides information on possible perfected financing statements with respect to the named debtor.[10]

Release, Assignment, and Amendment

A secured party can release all or part of any collateral described in the financing statement, thereby terminating its security interest in that collateral. The release is recorded by filing a uniform amendment form [UCC 9–512, 9–521(b)]. A secured party can also assign all or part of the security interest to a third party (the assignee). The assignee becomes the secured party of record if the assignment is filed by use of a uniform amendment form [UCC 9–514, 9–521(a)].

If the debtor and the secured party agree, they can amend the filing—to add or substitute new collateral, for example—by filing a uniform amendment form that indicates the file number of the initial financing statement [UCC 9–512(a)]. The amendment does not extend the time period of perfection, but if new collateral is added, the perfection date (for priority purposes) for the new collateral begins on the date the amendment is filed [UCC 9–512(b), (c)].

Confirmation or Accounting Request by Debtor

The debtor may believe that the amount of the unpaid debt or the list of the collateral subject to the security interest is inaccurate. The debtor has the right to request a confirmation of the unpaid debt or list of collateral [UCC 9–210]. The debtor is entitled to one request without charge every six months.

The secured party must comply with the debtor's confirmation request by authenticating and sending to the debtor an accounting within fourteen days after the request is received. Otherwise, the secured party can be held liable for any loss suffered by the debtor, plus $500 [UCC 9–210, 9–625(f)].

10. The filing officer will charge a fee for the certification and for any information copies provided [UCC 9–525(d)].

EXHIBIT 29-4 • Priority of Claims to a Debtor's Collateral

PARTIES	PRIORITY
Perfected Secured Party versus **Unsecured Parties and Creditors**	A perfected secured party's interest has priority over the interests of most other parties, including unsecured creditors, unperfected secured parties, subsequent lien creditors, trustees in bankruptcy, and buyers who do not purchase the collateral in the ordinary course of business.
Perfected Secured Party versus **Perfected Secured Party**	Between two perfected secured parties in the same collateral, the general rule is that the first in time of perfection is the first in right to the collateral [UCC 9–322(a)(1)].
Perfected Secured Party versus **Perfected PMSI**	A PMSI, even if second in time of perfection, has priority providing that the following conditions are met: 1. *Other collateral*—A PMSI has priority, providing it is perfected within twenty days after the debtor takes possession [UCC 9–324(a)]. 2. *Inventory*—A PMSI has priority if it is perfected and proper written or authenticated notice is given to the other security-interest holder on or before the time the debtor takes possession [UCC 9–324(b)]. 3. *Software*—Applies to a PMSI in software only if used in goods subject to a PMSI. If the goods are inventory, priority is determined the same as for inventory; if they are not, priority is determined as for goods other than inventory [UCC 9–103(c), 9–324(f)].
Perfected Secured Party versus **Purchaser of Debtor's Collateral**	1. *Buyer of goods in the ordinary course of the seller's business*—Buyer prevails over a secured party's security interest, even if perfected and even if the buyer knows of the security interest [UCC 9–320(a)]. 2. *Buyer of consumer goods purchased outside the ordinary course of business*—Buyer prevails over a secured party's interest, even if perfected by attachment, providing the buyer purchased as follows: a. For value. b. Without actual knowledge of the security interest. c. For use as a consumer good. d. Prior to the secured party's perfection by *filing* [UCC 9–320(b)]. 3. *Buyer of chattel paper*—Buyer prevails if the buyer: a. Gave new value in making the purchase. b. Took possession in the ordinary course of the buyer's business. c. Took without knowledge of the security interest [UCC 9–330]. 4. *Buyer of instruments, documents, or securities*—Buyer who is a holder in due course, a holder to whom negotiable documents have been duly negotiated, or a bona fide purchaser of securities has priority over a previously perfected security interest [UCC 9–330(d), 9–331(a)]. 5. *Buyer of farm products*—Buyer from a farmer takes free and clear of perfected security interests unless, where permitted, a secured party files centrally an effective financing statement (EFS) or the buyer receives proper notice of the security interest before the sale.
Unperfected Secured Party versus **Unsecured Creditor**	An unperfected secured party prevails over unsecured creditors and creditors who have obtained judgments against the debtor but who have not begun the legal process to collect on those judgments [UCC 9–201(a)].

Termination Statement

When the debtor has fully paid the debt, if the secured party perfected the security interest by filing, the debtor is entitled to have a termination statement filed. Such a statement demonstrates to the public that the filed perfected security interest has been terminated [UCC 9–513].

Whenever consumer goods are involved, the secured party *must* file a termination statement (or, alternatively, a release) within one month of the final payment or within twenty days of receiving the debtor's authenticated demand, whichever is earlier [UCC 9–513(b)].

When the collateral is other than consumer goods, on an authenticated demand by the debtor, the secured party must either send a termination statement to the debtor or file such a statement within twenty days [UCC 9–513(c)]. Otherwise, when the collateral is not consumer goods, the secured party is not required to file or to send a termination statement. Whenever a secured party fails to file or send the termination statement as requested, the debtor can recover $500 plus any additional loss suffered [UCC 9–625(e)(4), (f)].

<hr>

SECTION 7
DEFAULT

<hr>

Article 9 defines the rights, duties, and remedies of the secured party and of the debtor on the debtor's default. If the secured party fails to comply with his or her duties, the debtor is afforded particular rights and remedies under the UCC.

The topic of default is of great concern to secured lenders and to the lawyers who draft security agreements. What constitutes *default* is not always clear. In fact, Article 9 does not define the term. Consequently, parties are encouraged in practice—and by the UCC—to include in their security agreements the standards under which their rights and duties will be measured [UCC 9–601, 9–603]. In so doing, parties can stipulate the conditions that will constitute a default. Often, these critical terms are shaped by creditors themselves with an attempt to provide the maximum protection possible. The parties cannot agree to waive or alter certain UCC provisions, however, such as those involving the debtor's right to an accounting or disposition of collateral [UCC 9–602]. The terms may also not run counter to the UCC's provisions regarding good faith and unconscionability.

Any breach of the terms of the security agreement can constitute default. Nevertheless, default occurs most commonly when the debtor fails to meet the scheduled payments that the parties have agreed on or when the debtor becomes bankrupt.

Basic Remedies

The rights and remedies of secured parties under Article 9 are *cumulative* [UCC 9–601(c)]. Therefore, if a creditor is unsuccessful in enforcing rights by one method, she or he can pursue another method. Generally, a secured party's remedies can be divided into the two basic categories discussed next.

REPOSSESSION OF THE COLLATERAL—THE SELF-HELP REMEDY On the debtor's default, a secured party can take possession (peacefully or by court order) of the collateral covered by the security agreement [UCC 9–609(b)]. This provision, because it allows the secured party to take peaceful possession of the collateral without the use of the judicial process, is often referred to as the "self-help" provision of Article 9. This provision has been controversial, largely because the UCC does not define what constitutes *peaceful possession*. The general rule, however, is that the collateral has been taken peacefully if the secured party has taken it without committing (1) trespass onto land, (2) assault and/or battery, or (3) breaking and entering. On taking possession, the secured party may either retain the collateral for satisfaction of the debt [UCC 9–620] or resell the goods and apply the proceeds toward the debt [UCC 9–610].

JUDICIAL REMEDIES Alternatively, a secured party can relinquish the security interest and use any judicial remedy available, such as obtaining a judgment on the underlying debt, followed by execution and levy. (**Execution** is the implementation of a court's decree or judgment. **Levy** is the obtaining of funds by legal process through the seizure and sale of nonexempt property, usually done after a writ of execution has been issued. This writ was discussed in Chapter 28 on page 548.) Execution and levy are rarely undertaken unless the collateral is no longer in existence or has declined so much in value that it is worth substantially less than the amount of the debt and the debtor has other assets available that may be legally seized to satisfy the debt [UCC 9–601(a)].[11]

If a customer finances a purchase through a bank loan, returns the item, and refuses to make the loan payments, what are the rights of the bank (the secured party)? That was one of the issues in the following case.

<hr>

11. Some assets are exempt from creditors' claims under state statutes (see Chapter 28) or bankruptcy laws (see Chapter 30).

CASE 29.2
First National Bank of Litchfield v. Miller

Supreme Court of Connecticut, 285 Conn. 294, 939 A.2d 572 (2008).

BACKGROUND AND FACTS • The Millers wanted to buy a boat from Norwest Marine, so they made a deposit and signed a form contract. Title and ownership were to pass when the Millers made full payment, although delivery would occur earlier. The agreement stated that the Millers had inspected and accepted the boat and that the document constituted the entire agreement between the parties. The Millers needed financing and contacted First National Bank of Litchfield to begin the loan process. The Millers signed a loan agreement with the bank, which sent Norwest full payment for the boat. When the Millers took delivery of the boat, it did not run properly, so they returned it to Norwest for repairs. After the repairs were completed, the Millers refused to accept the boat, claiming that it was not satisfactory. They told the bank that they did not want the boat, and they stopped making loan payments. The bank sued, contending that the Millers had breached the retail contract by refusing to make monthly payments. The Millers filed claims against the bank and Norwest asserting that they had committed fraud. The trial court held for the bank, awarding it the full amount owed under the loan contract, plus attorneys' fees. The Millers appealed, and the appellate court reversed and remanded. The case was certified to the state's highest court for review.

IN THE LANGUAGE OF THE COURT
SCHALLER, Justice.
* * * *

[UCC 2–606] defines what constitutes acceptance of goods: "Acceptance of goods occurs when the buyer (a) after a reasonable opportunity to inspect the goods signifies to the seller that the goods are conforming or that he will take or retain them in spite of their nonconformity; or (b) fails to make an effective rejection as provided by subsection (1) of section 42a–2–602, but such acceptance does not occur until the buyer has had a reasonable opportunity to inspect them; or (c) does any act inconsistent with the seller's ownership; but if such act is wrongful as against the seller it is an acceptance only if ratified by him."

The record reveals that the trial court had ample support for its finding that the Millers had accepted the boat. The court based its finding both on the fact that the Millers had signed both the purchase agreement and the retail installment contract and on the numerous actions by the Millers, subsequent to the purchase of the boat, that were inconsistent with Norwest's ownership of the boat. The purchase agreement provided that the Millers had inspected the boat at the time that they signed the agreement and that they were satisfied with it. This representation by the Millers to Norwest supports the trial court's finding of acceptance because it indicates that the Millers, "after a reasonable opportunity to inspect the goods," had signified to Norwest "that the goods [were] conforming * * *." The retail installment contract also contained a representation by Norwest that the boat had been accepted by the Millers. Although the Millers did not make this representation, they signed the retail installment contract, which was a pre-printed form that contained the representation under a section of the contract entitled, "Seller's Agreement with Lender."

The court also grounded its decision on an independent basis for finding acceptance, namely, that the Millers had engaged in acts inconsistent with Norwest's ownership of the boat. The court expressly grounded this finding on evidence that the Millers had obtained a temporary certificate of registration of the boat in their names. The record reveals additional facts that provide support for this aspect of the trial court's finding, including the Millers' request that Norwest install a depth finder and radio on the boat and paint the bottom of the boat. Based on the record before the trial court, its conclusion that the Millers had accepted the boat was not clearly erroneous.

CASE CONTINUES ▶

CASE 29.2 CONTINUED ➧ **DECISION AND REMEDY** • *The court reinstated the verdict of the trial court, holding that the Millers had accepted delivery of the boat under the UCC. They had signed a purchase agreement providing that they had inspected the boat and were satisfied with it. The Millers could not claim they had never taken delivery of the boat, and they were therefore responsible for the loan they had accepted.*

THE LEGAL ENVIRONMENT DIMENSION • *How could Norwest and the bank have avoided the problem that arose in this case?*

THE ETHICAL DIMENSION • *Why should the Millers be held responsible for a statement that Norwest made in the retail installment contract, which said the boat had been accepted by the Millers?*

Disposition of Collateral

Once default has occurred and the secured party has obtained possession of the collateral, the secured party has several options. The secured party can (1) retain the collateral in full or partial satisfaction of the debt (subject to limitations, discussed next) or (2) sell, lease, license, or otherwise dispose of the collateral in any commercially reasonable manner and apply the proceeds toward satisfaction of the debt [UCC 9–602(7), 9–603, 9–610(a), 9–613, 9–620]. Any sale is always subject to procedures established by state law.

RETENTION OF COLLATERAL BY THE SECURED PARTY

The UCC acknowledges that parties are sometimes better off if they do not sell the collateral. Therefore, a secured party may retain the collateral unless it consists of consumer goods and the debtor has paid 60 percent or more of the purchase price in a PMSI or debt in a non-PMSI (as will be discussed shortly) [UCC 9–620(e)].

This general right is subject to several conditions, however. The secured party must notify the debtor of its proposal to retain the collateral. Notice is required unless the debtor has signed a statement renouncing or modifying her or his rights *after default* [UCC 9–620(a), 9–621]. If the collateral is consumer goods, the secured party does not need to give any other notice. In all other situations, the secured party must also send notice to any other secured party from whom the secured party has received written or authenticated notice of a claim of interest in the collateral in question. The secured party must also send notice to any **junior lienholder** (one holding a lien that is subordinate to one or more other liens on the same property) who has filed a statutory lien (such as a mechanic's lien—see Chapter 28) or a security interest in the collateral ten days before the debtor consented to the retention [UCC 9–621].

If, within twenty days after the notice is sent, the secured party receives an objection sent by a person entitled to receive notification, the secured party must sell or otherwise dispose of the collateral (disposition procedures will be discussed shortly). If no such written objection is received, the secured party may retain the collateral in full or partial satisfaction of the debtor's obligation [UCC 9–620(a), 9–621].

CONSUMER GOODS

When the collateral is consumer goods and the debtor has paid 60 percent of the purchase price on a PMSI or loan amount, the secured party must sell or otherwise dispose of the repossessed collateral within ninety days [UCC 9–620(e), (f)]. Failure to comply opens the secured party to an action for conversion or other liability under UCC 9–625(b) and (c) unless the consumer-debtor signed a written statement *after default* renouncing or modifying the right to demand the sale of the goods [UCC 9–624].

DISPOSITION PROCEDURES

A secured party who does not choose to retain the collateral or who is required to sell it must resort to the disposition procedures prescribed under UCC 9–602(7), 9–603, 9–610(a), and 9–613. The UCC allows substantial flexibility with regard to disposition. A secured party may sell, lease, license, or otherwise dispose of any or all of the collateral in its present condition or following any commercially reasonable preparation or processing [UCC 9–610(a)].

The collateral can be disposed of at public or private proceedings, but every aspect of the disposition's method, manner, time, and place must be commercially reasonable [UCC 9–610(b)]. The secured party must notify the debtor and other specified parties in writing ahead of time about the sale or disposition of the collateral. Notification is not required if the collateral is perishable, will decline rapidly in value, or is of a type customarily sold on a recognized market [UCC 9–611(b), (c)]. The debtor may waive the right to receive this notice, but only after default [UCC 9–624(a)].

The secured party may purchase the collateral at a public sale, but not at a private sale—unless the collateral is of a kind customarily sold on a recognized market or is the subject of widely distributed standard price quotations [UCC 9–610(c)]. If the secured party does not dispose of the collateral in a commercially reasonable manner and the price paid for the collateral is affected, a court can reduce the amount of any deficiency that the debtor owes to the secured party [UCC 9–626(a)(3)].

Under the UCC, the secured party must meet a high standard when disposing of collateral. Although obtaining a satisfactory price is the purpose of requiring the secured party to resell collateral in a commercially reasonable way, price is only one aspect, as the following case makes clear.

CASE 29.3
Hicklin v. Onyx Acceptance Corp

Delaware Supreme Court, 970 A.2d 244 (2009).
www.courts.state.de.us/Courts[a]

COMPANY PROFILE • Onyx Acceptance Corporation (www.onyxacceptance.com) was founded in 1993 and is headquartered in Foothill Ranch, California. Onyx and its wholly owned subsidiaries operate as an automobile finance company in the United States. Together, they provide an independent source to automobile dealers to finance their customers' purchases of new and used vehicles. The company's markets include automotive manufacturers, banks, savings associations, independent finance companies, credit unions, and leasing companies. In addition, Onyx purchases, securities, and services motor vehicle retail installment contracts originated by franchised and select independent automobile dealerships. It also acquires contracts that are collateralized by late model used and new automobiles. Today, Onyx Acceptance Corporation operates as a subsidiary of Capital One Financial Corp. This group has approximately 12,000 dealerships and eighteen auto finance centers throughout the country.

BACKGROUND AND FACTS • Shannon Hicklin bought a 1993 Ford Explorer under an installment sales contract. When she fell three payments behind—still owing $5,741.65—Onyx Acceptance Corporation repossessed the car. The car was sold for $1,500 at a private auction held by ABC Washington-Dulles, LLC. After the costs of repossession and sale were deducted from these proceeds, a deficiency of $5,018.88 remained. Onyx filed a suit in a Delaware state court to collect this amount from Hicklin. To establish that the sale was commercially reasonable, Onyx offered proof only of the price. The court found that the fair market value of the car at the time of the sale was $2,335 and held that the sale was commercially reasonable solely because the auction price was more than 50 percent of this estimated market value. The court granted Onyx a deficiency judgment, which a state intermediate appellate court affirmed. Hicklin appealed.

IN THE LANGUAGE OF THE COURT
JACOBS, Justice.
* * * *

The UCC does not specifically define the term "commercially reasonable." Whether or not a secured party's disposition of collateral action was commercially reasonable must be considered on a case-by-case basis.

* * * *To be commercially reasonable the actions must be in keeping with prevailing trade practice among reputable and responsible business and commercial enterprises engaged in the same or similar businesses.* [Emphasis added.]
* * * *

Onyx could prove that its sale of Hicklin's car was commercially reasonable * * * in one of two ways. First, it could show that every aspect of the sale was conducted in a commercially reasonable manner, as Section 9–610(b) prescribes. Second, it could [show under UCC 9–627(b)(3)] that it sold the car in accordance with the accepted practices of reputable dealers in that type of property.

---

a. In the left-hand column, click on "Supreme Court." On that page, in the "Opinions" pull-down menu, select "Supreme." In the result, in the "Year" pull-down menu, select "2009." In the "Search For:" box, type "Hicklin" and click on "Search." When that page opens, click on the name of the case to access the opinion. The Delaware Judicial Information Center maintains this Web site.

CASE CONTINUES ▶

CASE 29.3 CONTINUED ▶   * * * *

* * * Because *every aspect* of a sale must be "commercially reasonable," showing that the sale grossed over 50% of the collateral's value, without more, will not establish the secured party's compliance with [UCC] 9–610(b). Therefore, the [lower courts] reversibly erred by holding that the sale of Hicklin's car for over 50% of its * * * fair market value, without more, was "commercially reasonable."

* * * *

* * * The sale of a car to the highest bidder at a poorly publicized, sparsely attended, and inconveniently located auction would not be meaningful; but a sale to the highest bidder at a highly publicized, well-attended auction run by a highly regarded auctioneer in a convenient location would be. Onyx has failed to adduce [cite as proof] any evidence that would permit a fact-finder to determine whether the ABC auction represented the former or the latter kind of auction. *Without proof of the specific auction procedures that were followed, a secured party cannot satisfy its burden of establishing commercial reasonableness.* [Emphasis added.]

* * * *

Nor has Onyx proved commercial reasonableness by establishing conformity with accepted practices in the trade.

DECISION AND REMEDY • *The Delaware Supreme Court reversed the lower court's judgment and remanded the case. The price obtained on a sale of repossessed collateral does not prove, without more, that the sale was commercially reasonable.*

THE ETHICAL DIMENSION • *Why does UCC 9–627(b)(3) require that a sale be conducted in conformity with reasonable commercial practices among dealers in the type of property that was the subject of the disposition?*

WHAT IF THE FACTS WERE DIFFERENT? • *Suppose that Onyx had argued that private auctions generally yield higher prices, and because Hicklin's car was sold at a private auction, the sale must have been commercially reasonable. Should the court have ruled in favor of the creditor on this ground? Explain your answer.*

PROCEEDS FROM DISPOSITION Proceeds from the disposition of collateral after default on the underlying debt are distributed in the following order:

1. Reasonable expenses incurred by the secured party in repossessing, storing, and reselling the collateral.
2. Balance of the debt owed to the secured party.
3. Junior lienholders who have made written or authenticated demands.
4. Unless the collateral consists of accounts, payment intangibles, promissory notes, or chattel paper, any surplus goes to the debtor [UCC 9–608(a); 9–615(a), (e)].

NONCASH PROCEEDS Whenever the secured party receives noncash proceeds from the disposition of collateral after default, the secured party must make a value determination and apply this value in a commercially reasonable manner [UCC 9–608(a)(3), 9–615(c)].

DEFICIENCY JUDGMENT Often, after proper disposition of the collateral, the secured party still has not collected all that the debtor owes. Unless otherwise agreed, the debtor normally is liable for any deficiency, and the creditor can obtain a **deficiency judgment** from a court to collect the deficiency. Note, however, that if the underlying transaction is a sale of accounts, chattel paper, or promissory notes, the debtor is *not* entitled to any surplus or liable for any deficiency unless that right is granted by the security agreement [UCC 9–615(e)].

REDEMPTION RIGHTS At any time before the secured party disposes of the collateral or enters into a contract for its disposition, or before the debtor's obligation has been discharged through the secured party's retention of the collateral, the debtor or any other secured party can exercise the right of *redemption* of the collateral. To redeem the collateral, the debtor or other secured party must tender the entire obligation that is owed plus any reasonable expenses and attorneys' fees incurred by the secured party in retaking and maintaining the collateral [UCC 9–623].

Concept Summary 29.2 on the facing page provides a review of the secured party's remedies on the debtor's default.

CONCEPT SUMMARY 29.2
Remedies of the Secured Party on the Debtor's Default

Concept	Description

Repossession of the Collateral	The secured party may take possession (peacefully or by court order) of the collateral covered by the security agreement and then pursue one of two alternatives:
	1. Retain the collateral (unless the collateral is consumer goods and the debtor has paid 60 percent of the selling price on a PMSI or 60 percent of the debt on a non-PMSI). To retain the collateral, the secured party must—
	  a. Give notice to the debtor if the debtor has not signed a statement renouncing or modifying his or her rights after default. With consumer goods, no other notice is necessary.
	  b. Send notice to any other secured party who has given written or authenticated notice of a claim to the same collateral or who has filed a security interest or a statutory lien ten days before the debtor consented to the retention. If an objection is received within twenty days from the debtor or any other secured party given notice, the creditor must dispose of the collateral according to the requirements of UCC 9–602, 9–603, 9–610, and 9–613. Otherwise, the creditor may retain the collateral in full or partial satisfaction of the debt.
	2. Dispose of the collateral in accordance with the requirements of UCC 9–602(7), 9–603, 9–610(a), and 9–613. To do so, the secured party must—
	  a. Dispose of (sell, lease, or license) the goods in a commercially reasonable manner.
	  b. Notify the debtor and (except in sales of consumer goods) other identified persons, including those who have given notice of claims to the collateral to be sold (unless the collateral is perishable or will decline rapidly in value).
	  c. Apply the proceeds in the following order:
	    (1) Expenses incurred by the secured party in repossessing, storing, and reselling the collateral.
	    (2) The balance of the debt owed to the secured party.
	    (3) Junior lienholders who have made written or authenticated demands.
	    (4) Surplus to the debtor (unless the collateral consists of accounts, payment intangibles, promissory notes, or chattel paper).

Judicial Remedies	The secured party may relinquish the security interest and proceed with any judicial remedy available, such as obtaining a judgment on the underlying debt, followed by execution and levy on the nonexempt assets of the debtor.

REVIEWING
Secured Transactions

Paul Barton owned a small property-management company, doing business as Brighton Homes. In October, Barton went on a spending spree. First, he bought a Bose surround-sound system for his home from KDM Electronics. The next day, he purchased a Wilderness Systems kayak and roof rack from Outdoor Outfitters, and the day after that he bought a new Toyota 4-Runner financed through Bridgeport Auto. Two weeks later, Barton purchased six new iMac computers for his office, also from KDM Electronics. Barton bought each of these items under an installment sales contract. Six months later, Barton's property-management business was failing, and he could not make the payments due on any of these purchases and thus defaulted on the loans. Using the information presented in the chapter, answer the following questions.

REVIEWING CONTINUES ➡

REVIEWING
Secured Transactions, Continued

1. For which of Barton's purchases (the surround-sound system, the kayak, the 4-Runner, and the six iMacs) would the creditor need to file a financing statement to perfect its security interest?
2. Suppose that Barton's contract for the office computers mentioned only the name *Brighton Homes*. What would be the consequences if KDM Electronics filed a financing statement that listed only Brighton Homes as the debtor's name?
3. Which of these purchases would qualify as a PMSI in consumer goods?
4. Suppose that after KDM Electronics repossesses the surround-sound system, it decides to keep the system rather than sell it. Can KDM do this under Article 9? Why or why not?

DEBATE THIS: *A financing statement that does not have the debtor's exact name should still be effective because creditors should always be protected when debtors default.*

TERMS AND CONCEPTS

after-acquired property 565

attachment 558

authentication 558

buyer in the ordinary course
    of business 569

collateral 557

continuation statement 564

cross-collateralization 566

debtor 557

deficiency judgment 576

execution 572

financing statement 557

floating lien 566

junior lienholder 574

levy 572

perfection 559

pledge 562

proceeds 564

purchase-money security
    interest (PMSI) 564

secured party 557

secured transaction 557

security agreement 557

security interest 557

QUESTIONS AND CASE PROBLEMS

29–1. Priorities Redford is a seller of electric generators. He purchases a large quantity of generators from a manufacturer, Mallon Corp., by making a down payment and signing an agreement to make the balance of payments over a period of time. The agreement gives Mallon Corp. a security interest in the generators and the proceeds. Mallon Corp. properly files a financing statement on its security interest. Redford receives the generators and immediately sells one of them to Garfield on an installment contract, with payment to be made in twelve equal installments. At the time of the sale, Garfield knows of Mallon's security interest. Two months later, Redford goes into default on his payments to Mallon. Discuss Mallon's rights against Garfield in this situation.

29–2. Perfection of a Security Interest Marsh has a prize horse named Arabian Knight. Marsh is in need of working capital. She borrows $50,000 from Mendez, who takes possession of Arabian Knight as security for the loan.

No written agreement is signed. Discuss whether, in the absence of a written agreement, Mendez has a security interest in Arabian Knight. If Mendez does have a security interest, is it a perfected security interest?

29–3. QUESTION WITH SAMPLE ANSWER: The Scope of a Security Interest.

Edward owned a retail sporting goods shop. A new ski resort was being constructed in his area, and to take advantage of the potential business, Edward decided to expand his operations. He borrowed a large sum from his bank, which took a security interest in his present inventory and any after-acquired inventory as collateral for the loan. The bank properly perfected the security interest by filing a financing statement. Edward's business was profitable, so he doubled his inventory. A year later, just a few months after the ski resort had opened, an avalanche destroyed the ski slope and lodge. Edward's business consequently took a turn for the worse, and he defaulted on his debt to the bank. The bank then sought possession of his entire inventory, even though the inventory was now twice as large as it had been when the loan was made. Edward claimed that the bank had rights to only half of his inventory. Is Edward correct? Explain.

- **For a sample answer to Question 29–3, go to Appendix I at the end of this text.**

29–4. Security Interest In St. Louis, Missouri, in August 2000, Richard Miller orally agreed to loan Jeff Miller $35,000 in exchange for a security interest in a 1999 Kodiak dump truck. The Millers did not put anything in writing concerning the loan, its repayment terms, or Richard's security interest or rights in the truck. Jeff used the amount of the loan to buy the truck, which he kept in his possession. In June 2004, Jeff filed a petition to obtain a discharge of his debts in bankruptcy. Richard claimed that he had a security interest in the truck and thus was entitled to any proceeds from its sale. What are a creditor's main concerns on a debtor's default? How does a creditor satisfy these concerns? What are the requirements for a creditor to have an enforceable security interest? Have these requirements been met in this case? Considering these points, what is the court likely to rule with respect to Richard's claim? [*In re Miller*, 320 Bankr. 911 (E.D.Mo. 2005)]

29–5. Creating a Security Interest In 2002, Michael Sabol, doing business in the recording industry as Sound Farm Productions, applied to Morton Community Bank in Bloomington, Illinois, for a $58,000 loan to expand his business. Besides the loan application, Sabol signed a promissory note that referred to the bank's rights in "any collateral." Sabol also signed a letter that stated, "the undersigned does hereby authorize Morton Community Bank to execute, file and record all financing statements, amendments, termination statements and all other statements authorized by Article 9 of the Illinois Uniform Commercial Code, as to any security interest." Sabol did not sign any other documents, including the financing statement, which contained a description of the collateral. Less than three years later, without having repaid the loan, Sabol filed a petition in a federal bankruptcy court to declare bankruptcy. The bank claimed a security interest in Sabol's sound equipment. What are the elements of an enforceable security interest? What are the requirements of each of those elements? Does the bank have a valid security interest in this case? Explain. [*In re Sabol*, 337 Bankr. 195 (C.D.Ill. 2006)]

29–6. Default Primesouth Bank issued a loan to Okefenokee Aircraft, Inc. (OAI), to buy a plane. OAI executed a note in favor of Primesouth in the amount of $161,306.25 plus interest. The plane secured the note. When OAI defaulted, Primesouth repossessed the plane. Instead of disposing of the collateral and seeking a deficiency judgment, however, the bank retained possession of the plane and filed a suit in a Georgia state court against OAI to enforce the note. OAI did not deny that it had defaulted on the note or dispute the amount due. Instead, OAI argued that Primesouth Bank was not acting in a commercially reasonable manner. According to OAI, the creditor must sell the collateral and apply the proceeds against the debt. What is a secured creditor's obligation in these circumstances? Can the creditor retain the collateral and seek a judgment for the amount of the underlying debt, or is a sale required? Discuss. [*Okefenokee Aircraft, Inc. v. Primesouth Bank*, 296 Ga.App. 782, 676 S.E.2d 394 (2009)]

29–7. CASE PROBLEM WITH SAMPLE ANSWER: Purchase-Money Security Interest.

In 2007, James Cavazos purchased a new Mercedes vehicle from a dealer and gave JPMorgan Chase Bank (Chase) a purchase-money security interest (PMSI) in the car. The state recorded Chase's lien on the original certificate of title. Cavazos then forged a release of the lien against the title and received a certified copy of the original title. In reliance on that title, NXCESS Motor Cars, Inc., bought the car. It sold the car to Xavier Valeri, who granted a PMSI to U.S. Bank. NXCESS warranted that the title was free of all liens. When a new title was issued, Chase learned of Cavazos's forgery. It sued Cavazos, Valeri, and U.S. Bank for conversion (see page 127 in Chapter 6). Chase demanded possession of the vehicle and that Cavazos repay the loan. Valeri and U.S. Bank contended that they were buyers in the ordinary course of business and had good title to the Mercedes because the state had provided a title free of liens and claims. Cavazos is liable on the loan, but who has the right to possess the car? Which PMSI dominates? Explain your answers. [NXCESS Motor Cars, Inc. v. JPMorgan Chase Bank, N.A., ___ S.W.3d ___ (Tex.App.— Houston 2010)]

- **To view a sample answer for Problem 29–7, go to this book's Web site at www.cengage.com/blaw/clarkson, select "Chapter 29," and click on "Case Problem with Sample Answer."**

29–8. A QUESTION OF ETHICS: Priorities.

In 1995, Mark Denton cosigned a $101,250 loan issued by the First Interstate Bank (FIB) in Missoula, Montana, to Denton's friend Eric Anderson. Denton's business assets—a mini-warehouse operation—secured the loan. On his own, Anderson obtained a $260,000 U.S. Small Business Administration (SBA) loan from FIB at the same time. The purpose of both loans was to buy logging equipment so that Anderson could start a business. In 1997, the business failed. As a consequence, FIB repossessed and sold the equipment and applied the proceeds to the SBA loan. FIB then asked Denton to pay the other loan's outstanding balance ($98,460), plus interest. When Denton refused, FIB initiated proceedings to obtain his business assets. Denton filed a suit in a Montana state court against FIB, claiming, in part, that Anderson's equipment was the collateral for the loan that FIB was attempting to collect from Denton. [Denton v. First Interstate Bank of Commerce, 2006 MT 193, 333 Mont. 169, 142 P.3d 797 (2006)]

(a) Denton's assets served as the security for Anderson's loan because Anderson had nothing to offer. When the loan was obtained, Dean Gillmore, FIB's loan officer, explained to them that if Anderson defaulted, the proceeds from the sale of the logging equipment would be applied to the SBA loan first. Under these circumstances, is it fair to hold Denton liable for the unpaid balance of Anderson's loan? Why or why not?

(b) Denton argued that the loan contract was unconscionable and constituted a "contract of adhesion." What makes a contract unconscionable? Did the transaction between the parties in this case qualify? What is a "contract of adhesion"? Was this deal unenforceable on that basis? Explain.

29–9. VIDEO QUESTION: Secured Transactions.

Go to this text's Web site at **www.cengage.com/blaw/clarkson** and select "Chapter 29." Click on "Video Questions" and view the video titled *Secured Transactions*. Then answer the following questions.

(a) This chapter lists three requirements for creating a security interest. In the video, which requirement does Laura assert has not been met?

(b) What, if anything, must the bank have done to perfect its interest in the editing equipment?

(c) If the bank exercises its self-help remedy to repossess Onyx's editing equipment, does Laura have any chance of getting it back? Explain.

(d) Assume that the bank had a perfected security interest and repossessed the editing equipment. Also assume that the purchase price (and the loan amount) for the equipment was $100,000, of which Onyx had paid $65,000. Discuss the rights and duties of the bank with regard to the collateral in this situation.

29–10. SPECIAL CASE ANALYSIS: Security Interests.

Go to Extended Case 29.1, *Citizens National Bank of Jessamine County v. Washington Mutual Bank,* 309 S.W.3d 792 (2010), on pages 567–568. Read the excerpt and answer the following questions.

(a) **Issue:** This case involved conflicting security interests in the same collateral. What was the collateral, and why was it difficult to decide which creditor's security interest took priority?

(b) **Rule of Law:** What did the court have to decide before determining which rule governing priorities applied to the conflicting security interests in this case?

(c) **Applying the Rule of Law:** The court decided that one party had perfected its security interest in the collateral and the other had not. How did this decision affect the application of the rule of law?

(d) **Conclusion:** In which party's favor did the court rule? Explain your answer.

LEGAL RESEARCH EXERCISES ON THE WEB

Go to this text's Web site at **www.cengage.com/blaw/clarkson**, select "Chapter 29," and click on "Practical Internet Exercises." There you will find the following Internet research exercises that you can perform to learn more about the topics covered in this chapter.

Practical Internet Exercise 29–1: **Legal Perspective**
Repossession

Practical Internet Exercise 29–2: **Management Perspective**
Filing Financial Statements

CHAPTER 30

Bankruptcy Law

Historically, debtors had few rights. At one time, debtors who could not pay their debts as they came due faced harsh consequences, including imprisonment and involuntary servitude. Today, in contrast, debtors have numerous rights, some of which were discussed in Chapters 28 and 29. In this chapter, we look at another significant right of debtors: the right to petition for bankruptcy relief under federal law.

The number of petitions for bankruptcy filed each year in the United States rose dramatically from 1980 until 2005, when bankruptcy reform legislation significantly reduced individual bankruptcy filings. In recent years, bankruptcy filings have jumped again as a result of the economic recession that swept the country in 2008 and 2009. In this chapter, you will read about the different types of relief offered under federal bankruptcy law and about the basic bankruptcy procedures required for specific types of relief.

SECTION 1
THE BANKRUPTCY CODE

Bankruptcy relief is provided under federal law. Although state laws may play a role in bankruptcy proceedings, particularly state laws governing property, the governing law is based on federal legislation.

Congressional authority to provide bankruptcy relief for debtors is based on Article I, Section 8, of the U.S. Constitution, which gives Congress the power to establish "uniform laws on the subject of bankruptcies throughout the United States." Federal bankruptcy legislation was first enacted in 1898 and since then has undergone several modifications.

Bankruptcy law before 2005 was based on the Bankruptcy Reform Act of 1978, as amended—hereinafter called the Bankruptcy Code or, more simply, the Code. In 2005, Congress enacted the Bankruptcy Reform Act,[1] which significantly overhauled certain provisions of the Bankruptcy Code.

Goals of Bankruptcy Law

Modern bankruptcy law is designed to accomplish two main goals. The first is to provide relief and protection to debtors who have "gotten in over their heads." The second is to provide a fair means of distributing a debtor's assets among all creditors. Thus, the law attempts to balance the rights of the debtor and the creditors.

Although the twin goals of bankruptcy remain the same, the balance between them has shifted somewhat under the 2005 reform legislation. That law was enacted, in part, because of the growing concern that the 1978 act allowed too many debtors to avoid paying their debts. Thus, one of the major goals of the 2005 legislation was to require more consumers to pay as many of their debts as they possibly could instead of having those debts fully extinguished in bankruptcy.

Bankruptcy Courts

Bankruptcy proceedings are held in federal bankruptcy courts, which are under the authority of U.S. district courts, and rulings from bankruptcy courts can be appealed to the district courts. Essentially, a bankruptcy court fulfills the role of an administrative

---

1. The full title of the act was the Bankruptcy Abuse Prevention and Consumer Protection Act of 2005, Pub. L. No. 109-8, 119 Stat. 23 (April 20, 2005).

court for the federal district court concerning matters in bankruptcy. The bankruptcy court holds the proceedings required to administer the estate of the debtor in bankruptcy (the *estate* consists of the debtor's assets, as will be discussed shortly).

Bankruptcy court judges are appointed for terms of fourteen years. A bankruptcy court can conduct a jury trial if the appropriate district court has authorized it and the parties to the bankruptcy consent. Bankruptcy courts follow the Federal Rules of Bankruptcy Procedure rather than the Federal Rules of Civil Procedure (discussed in Chapter 3).

Types of Bankruptcy Relief

The Bankruptcy Code is contained in Title 11 of the *United States Code* and has eight chapters. Chapters 1, 3, and 5 of the Code contain general definitional provisions, as well as provisions governing case administration, creditors, the debtor, and the estate. These three chapters normally apply to all kinds of bankruptcies.

Four chapters of the Code set forth the most important types of relief that debtors can seek:

1. Chapter 7 provides for **liquidation** proceedings (the selling of all nonexempt assets and the distribution of the proceeds to the debtor's creditors).
2. Chapter 11 governs reorganizations.
3. Chapter 12 (for family farmers and family fishermen) and 13 (for individuals) provide for the adjustment of debts by persons with regular incomes.[2]

In the following pages, we look at the specific type of bankruptcy relief provided under Chapters 7, 11, 12, and 13 of the Code. Note that a debtor (except for a municipality) need not be insolvent[3] to file for bankruptcy relief under the Bankruptcy Code. Anyone obligated to a creditor can declare bankruptcy.

Special Requirements for Consumer-Debtors

Recall from Chapter 29 that a consumer-debtor is a debtor whose debts result primarily from the purchase of goods for personal, family, or household use. To ensure that a consumer-debtor is aware of the types of relief available, the Code requires that the clerk of the court give all consumer-debtors written notice of the general purpose, benefits, and costs of each chapter under which they might proceed. In addition, the clerk must provide consumer-debtors with information on the types of services available from credit counseling agencies. In practice, most of these steps are handled by an attorney, not by court clerks.

SECTION 2
LIQUIDATION PROCEEDINGS

Liquidation under Chapter 7 of the Bankruptcy Code is probably the most familiar type of bankruptcy proceeding and is often referred to as an *ordinary,* or *straight, bankruptcy*. Put simply, a debtor in a liquidation bankruptcy turns all assets over to a **bankruptcy trustee,** a person appointed by the court to manage the debtor's funds. The trustee sells the nonexempt assets and distributes the proceeds to creditors. With certain exceptions, the remaining debts are then **discharged** (extinguished), and the debtor is relieved of the obligation to pay the debts.

Any "person"—defined as including individuals, partnerships, and corporations[4]—may be a debtor in a liquidation proceeding. A husband and wife may file jointly for bankruptcy under a single petition. Insurance companies, banks, savings and loan associations, investment companies licensed by the Small Business Administration, and credit unions *cannot* be debtors in a liquidation bankruptcy, however. Other chapters of the Bankruptcy Code or other federal or state statutes apply to them.

A straight bankruptcy can be commenced by the filing of either a voluntary or an involuntary **petition in bankruptcy**—the document that is filed with a bankruptcy court to initiate bankruptcy proceedings. If a debtor files the petition, the bankruptcy is voluntary. If one or more creditors file a petition to force the debtor into bankruptcy, the bankruptcy is involuntary. We discuss both voluntary and involuntary bankruptcy proceedings under Chapter 7 in the following subsections.

Voluntary Bankruptcy

To bring a voluntary petition in bankruptcy, the debtor files official forms designated for that purpose

---

2. There are no Chapters 2, 4, 6, 8, or 10 in Title 11. Such "gaps" are not uncommon in the *United States Code*. They occur because chapter numbers (or other subdivisional unit numbers) are sometimes reserved for future use when a statute is enacted. (A gap may also appear if a law has been repealed.)

3. The inability to pay debts as they become due is known as *equitable* insolvency. *Balance sheet* insolvency, which exists when a debtor's liabilities exceed assets, is not the test. Thus, debtors whose cash-flow problems become severe may petition for bankruptcy voluntarily or be forced into involuntary bankruptcy even though their assets far exceed their liabilities.

4. The definition of *corporation* includes unincorporated companies and associations. It also covers labor unions.

in the bankruptcy court. Current bankruptcy law specifies that before debtors can file a petition, they must receive credit counseling from an approved nonprofit agency within the 180-day period preceding the date of filing. Debtors filing a Chapter 7 petition must include a certificate proving that they have received individual or group counseling from an approved agency within the last 180 days (roughly six months).

A consumer-debtor who is filing for liquidation bankruptcy must confirm the accuracy of the petition's contents. The debtor must also state in the petition, at the time of filing, that he or she understands the relief available under other chapters of the Code and has chosen to proceed under Chapter 7. Attorneys representing the consumer-debtors must file an affidavit stating that they have informed the debtors of the relief available under each chapter of the Bankruptcy Code. In addition, the attorneys must reasonably attempt to verify the accuracy of the consumer-debtors' petitions and schedules (described below). Failure to do so is considered perjury.

CHAPTER 7 SCHEDULES The voluntary petition must contain the following schedules:

1. A list of both secured and unsecured creditors, their addresses, and the amount of debt owed to each.
2. A statement of the financial affairs of the debtor.
3. A list of all property owned by the debtor, including property that the debtor claims is exempt.
4. A list of current income and expenses.
5. A certificate of credit counseling (as discussed previously).
6. Proof of payments received from employers within sixty days prior to the filing of the petition.
7. A statement of the amount of monthly income, itemized to show how the amount is calculated.
8. A copy of the debtor's federal income tax return for the most recent year ending immediately before the filing of the petition.

The official forms must be completed accurately, sworn to under oath, and signed by the debtor. To conceal assets or knowingly supply false information on these schedules is a crime under the bankruptcy laws.

With the exception of tax returns, failure to file the required schedules within forty-five days after the filing of the petition (unless an extension of up to forty-five days is granted) will result in an automatic dismissal of the petition. The debtor has up to seven days before the date of the first creditors' meeting to provide a copy of the most recent tax returns to the trustee.

TAX RETURNS DURING BANKRUPTCY In addition, a debtor may be required to file a tax return at the end of each tax year while the case is pending and to provide a copy to the court. This may be done at the request of the court or of the **U.S. trustee**—a government official who performs administrative tasks that a bankruptcy judge would otherwise have to perform, including supervising the work of the bankruptcy trustee. Any *party in interest* (a party, such as a creditor, who has a valid interest in the outcome of the proceedings) may make this request as well. Debtors may also be required to file tax returns during Chapter 11 and 13 bankruptcies.

SUBSTANTIAL ABUSE–MEANS TEST In the past, a bankruptcy court could dismiss a Chapter 7 petition for relief (discharge of debts) if the use of Chapter 7 would constitute a "substantial abuse" of bankruptcy law. Today, the law provides a *means test* to determine a debtor's eligibility for Chapter 7. The purpose of the test is to keep upper-income people from abusing the bankruptcy process by filing for Chapter 7, as was thought to have happened in the past. The test forces more people to file for Chapter 13 bankruptcy rather than have their debts discharged under Chapter 7. Exhibit 30–1 on the following page outlines the essentials of the means test, but there are exceptions that apply in a small number of cases.

The Basic Formula. A debtor wishing to file for bankruptcy must complete the means test to determine whether she or he qualifies for Chapter 7. The debtor's average monthly income in recent months is compared with the median income in the geographic area in which the person lives. (The U.S. Trustee Program provides these data at its Web site.) If the debtor's income is below the median income, the debtor usually is allowed to file for Chapter 7 bankruptcy, as there is no presumption of bankruptcy abuse.

Applying the Means Test to Future Disposable Income. If the debtor's income is above the median income, then further calculations must be made to determine whether the person will have sufficient disposable income in the future to repay at least some of his or her unsecured debts. *Disposable income* is calculated by subtracting living expenses and secured debt payments, such as mortgage payments, from monthly income. In making this calculation, the debtor's recent monthly income is presumed to continue for the next sixty months. Living expenses

EXHIBIT 30–1 • The Means Test to Determine Chapter 7 Eligibility

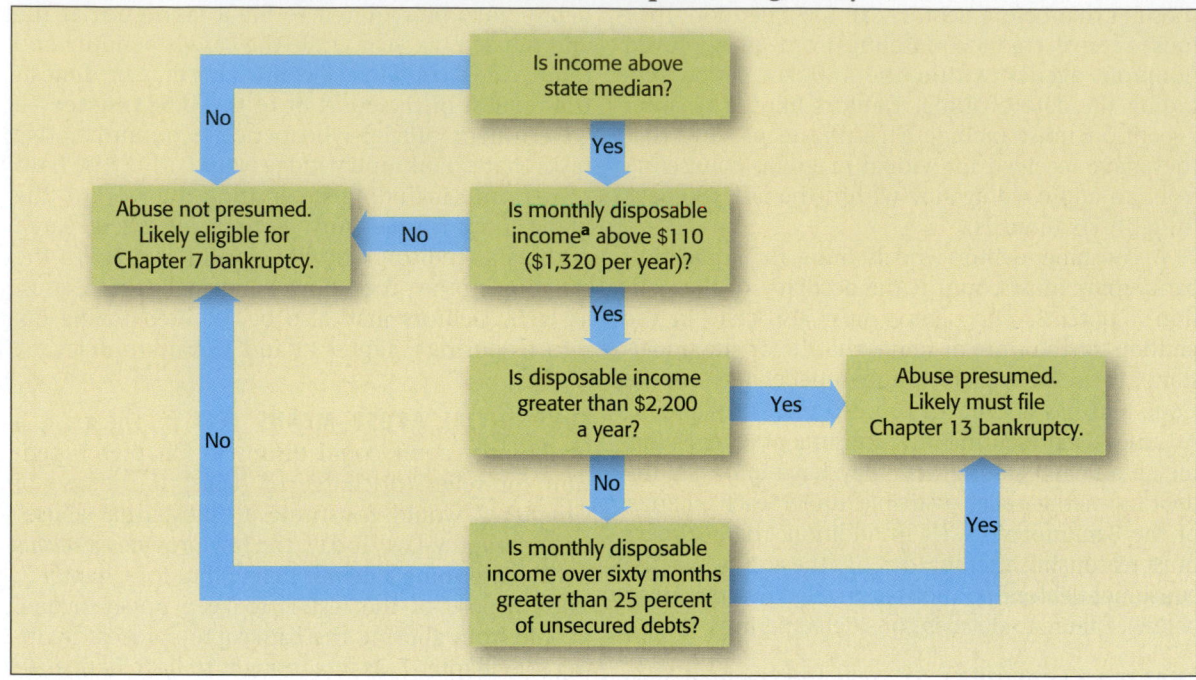

a. Income minus living expenses and secured debt payments equals *disposable income.*

are the amounts allowed under formulas used by the Internal Revenue Service (IRS). The IRS allowances include modest allocations for food, clothing, housing, utilities, transportation (including a car payment), health care, and other necessities. (The U.S. Trustee Program's Web site also provides these amounts.) The allowances do not include expenditures for items such as cell phones and cable television service.

Once future disposable income has been estimated, that amount is used to determine whether the debtor will have income that could be applied to unsecured debts. As shown in Exhibit 30–1 above, the debtor will fall into one of the following categories, based on his or her disposable income (these amounts are adjusted annually):

- If disposable income is less than $110 per month ($1,320 per year), no abuse is presumed, and the debtor will likely be allowed to file for Chapter 7 bankruptcy.
- If disposable income is more than $110 per month ($1,320 per year), then the debtor will have income that could be applied to unsecured debts, and Chapter 13 bankruptcy may be required.
- If disposable income is more than $183 per month ($2,200 per year), then abuse is presumed, and

Chapter 13 bankruptcy will be required, except in unusual cases.[5]
- If disposable income is between $1,320 and $2,200 per year and the total over sixty months (five years) is greater than 25 percent of the debtor's unsecured debts, then abuse is presumed, and Chapter 13 is required. If the total over sixty months is less than 25 percent of the unsecured debts, then Chapter 7 bankruptcy is allowed.

To a large extent, this system follows the prior law on substantial abuse. The court may also consider the debtor's bad faith or other circumstances indicating abuse.

ADDITIONAL GROUNDS FOR DISMISSAL As noted, a debtor's voluntary petition for Chapter 7 relief may be dismissed for substantial abuse or for failing to provide the necessary documents (such as schedules and tax returns) within the specified time. In addition, a motion to dismiss a Chapter 7 filing might be granted in two other situations. First, if the debtor has been convicted of a violent crime or a drug-trafficking offense, the victim can file a motion to dismiss the

---

5. A debtor can rebut (refute) the presumption of abuse by demonstrating special circumstances that justify additional expenses, such as anticipated medical costs not covered by health insurance.

voluntary petition.[6] Second, if the debtor fails to pay post-petition domestic-support obligations (which include child and spousal support), the court may dismiss the debtor's petition.

ORDER FOR RELIEF   If the voluntary petition for bankruptcy is found to be proper, the filing of the petition will itself constitute an **order for relief.** (An order for relief is a court's grant of assistance to a petitioner.) Once a consumer-debtor's voluntary petition has been filed, the trustee and creditors must be given notice of the order for relief by mail not more than twenty days after entry of the order.

Involuntary Bankruptcy

An involuntary bankruptcy occurs when the debtor's creditors force the debtor into bankruptcy proceedings.[7] For an involuntary action to be filed, the following requirements must be met: If the debtor has twelve or more creditors, three or more of these creditors having unsecured claims totaling at least $14,425 must join in the petition. If a debtor has fewer than twelve creditors, one or more creditors having a claim totaling $14,425 or more may file.[8]

If the debtor challenges the involuntary petition, a hearing will be held, and the bankruptcy court will enter an order for relief if it finds either of the following:

1. The debtor is not paying debts as they come due.
2. A general receiver, assignee, or custodian took possession of, or was appointed to take charge of,

substantially all of the debtor's property within 120 days before the filing of the petition.

If the court grants an order for relief, the debtor will be required to supply the same information in the bankruptcy schedules as in a voluntary bankruptcy.

An involuntary petition should not be used as an everyday debt-collection device, and the Code provides penalties for the filing of frivolous petitions against debtors. If the court dismisses an involuntary petition, the petitioning creditors may be required to pay the costs and attorneys' fees incurred by the debtor in defending against the petition. If the petition was filed in bad faith, damages can be awarded for injury to the debtor's reputation. Punitive damages may also be awarded.

Automatic Stay

The moment a petition, either voluntary or involuntary, is filed, an **automatic stay,** or suspension, of almost all actions by creditors against the debtor or the debtor's property normally goes into effect. In other words, once a petition has been filed, creditors cannot contact the debtor by phone or mail or start any legal proceedings to recover debts or to repossess property. (In some circumstances, a secured creditor or other party in interest may petition the bankruptcy court for relief from the automatic stay, as will be discussed shortly.)

The Code provides that if a creditor *knowingly* violates the automatic stay (a willful violation), any injured party, including the debtor, is entitled to recover actual damages, costs, and attorneys' fees, and may be awarded punitive damages as well. Until the bankruptcy proceeding is closed or dismissed, the automatic stay prohibits a creditor from taking any act to collect, assess, or recover a claim against the debtor that arose before the filing of the petition.

Did a university's refusal to provide a transcript unless a debt was paid constitute an act in violation of the automatic stay? That was the issue in the following case.

---

6. Note that the court may not dismiss a case on this ground if the debtor's bankruptcy is necessary to satisfy a claim for a domestic-support obligation.
7. An involuntary case cannot be filed against a charitable institution or a farmer (an individual or business that receives more than 50 percent of gross income from farming operations).
8. 11 U.S.C. Section 303. The amounts stated in this chapter are in accordance with those computed on April 1, 2010.

CASE 30.1
In re Kuehn

United States Court of Appeals, Seventh Circuit, 563 F.3d 289 (2009).
www.ca7.uscourts.gov[a]

BACKGROUND AND FACTS • Stefanie Kuehn, an art teacher, obtained a master's degree at Cardinal Stritch University in Wisconsin. But when Kuehn asked for a transcript—which was required to

---

a. In the left-hand column, click on "Opinions." On that page, in the "Case Number:" boxes, type "07" and "3954" and click on "List Case(s)." In the result, click on the appropriate link to access the opinion.

CASE CONTINUES ➡

CASE 30.1 CONTINUED ▶ receive an increase in salary from her school district—the university refused because she owed more than $6,000 in tuition. Kuehn offered to pay the nominal transcript fee but not the tuition. She then filed a petition in a federal bankruptcy court, listing the university as her only creditor. While the case was pending, she again asked for a transcript. The university once more refused unless she paid the tuition. Kuehn complained to the court, which ordered the university to provide a transcript. A federal district court affirmed the order. The university appealed.

IN THE LANGUAGE OF THE COURT
EASTERBROOK, Chief Judge.
* * * *

* * * *[If] providing a transcript is an implicit part of the educational contract, covered by the fee for the course hours, [then] Kuehn * * * has a contract or property right for which she has already paid.* (Well, she hasn't paid, but her obligation to do so has been [stayed by the bankruptcy petition] so it comes to the same thing.) The University cannot charge Kuehn extra if the fee for instruction covers transcripts, too. Then the University's refusal to certify a transcript of Kuehn's grades would be an act to collect the discharged debt and would violate * * * the automatic stay. [Emphasis added.]

Well, then, does Kuehn have a property interest because a certified transcript is part of the package of goods and services that a college offers in exchange for tuition? Property interests are created and defined by state law unless a federal law requires a different result. Nothing in the Bankruptcy Code creates or alters property rights in grades or the right to receive a transcript. Other federal law addresses privacy concerns but not property interests. What remain are state statutes and common law.

* * * *

Wisconsin courts have not considered whether a student has a contract or property right to receive a transcript. No Wisconsin statute is on point. *Under Wisconsin common law, property rights may arise from custom and usage. Universities have consistently provided transcripts at or around cost.* A transcript currently sets students back $4 at Cardinal Stritch University, $3 at Harvard University, and nothing at the University of Chicago if delivered electronically (otherwise $12). Fees at other universities are similar. We could not find any case in any court where a university had asserted that it could charge a student more than cost for a transcript, and, as far as we can tell, no university has ever tried to profit by charging a fee based on the transcript's effect on a student's future income. [Emphasis added.]

* * * *

Kuehn's property right might be limited to her grades, * * * and not include a right to receive a transcript from the University certifying those grades. But the custom of universities has been to provide certified transcripts, and for good reason. Intangible grades are worthless without proof. Kuehn's school district increases compensation only after it receives a certified transcript. Other employers have similar policies. * * * A right to receive a certified copy of a transcript is essential to a meaningful property right in grades.

* * * *

* * * We conclude that Kuehn has a state-law right to receive a certified copy of her transcript. The University's refusal to honor that right until Kuehn paid her back tuition was an act to collect a debt and thereby violated the automatic stay.

DECISION AND REMEDY • *The U.S. Court of Appeals for the Seventh Circuit affirmed the lower court's order. Kuehn had a right to a copy of her transcript, and the university's refusal to honor that right until she paid her tuition was an act to collect a debt in violation of the automatic stay.*

WHAT IF THE FACTS WERE DIFFERENT? • *Suppose that instead of offering to pay for a transcript, Kuehn had tried to obtain one on credit. Would the university's refusal to provide one on that basis have led to the same result? Why or why not?*

THE ETHICAL DIMENSION • *Some might say that higher education institutions should be able to use all methods possible to collect unpaid tuition, including withholding certified grade transcripts. What ethical issues would this approach raise?*

THE ADEQUATE PROTECTION DOCTRINE Underlying the Code's automatic-stay provision for a secured creditor is a concept known as *adequate protection*. The **adequate protection doctrine,** among other things, protects secured creditors from losing their security as a result of the automatic stay. The bankruptcy court can provide adequate protection by requiring the debtor or trustee to make periodic cash payments or a one-time cash payment (or to provide additional collateral or replacement liens) to the extent that the stay may actually cause the value of the property to decrease.

EXCEPTIONS TO THE AUTOMATIC STAY The Code provides several exceptions to the automatic stay. Collection efforts can continue for domestic-support obligations, which include any debt owed to or recoverable by a spouse, a former spouse, a child of the debtor, that child's parent or guardian, or a governmental unit. In addition, proceedings against the debtor related to divorce, child custody or visitation, domestic violence, and support enforcement are not stayed. Also excepted are investigations by a securities regulatory agency (see Chapter 42) and certain statutory liens for property taxes.

LIMITATIONS ON THE AUTOMATIC STAY A secured creditor or other party in interest can petition the bankruptcy court for relief from the automatic stay. If a creditor or other party requests relief from the stay, the stay will automatically terminate sixty days after the request, unless the court grants an extension[9] or the parties agree otherwise. Also, the automatic stay on secured debts (see Chapter 29) will terminate thirty days after the petition is filed if the debtor filed a bankruptcy petition that was dismissed within the prior year. Any party in interest can request that the court extend the stay by showing that the filing is in good faith.

If the debtor had two or more bankruptcy petitions dismissed during the prior year, the Code presumes bad faith, and the automatic stay does *not* go into effect until the court determines that the petition was filed in good faith. In addition, the automatic stay on secured property terminates forty-five days after the creditors' meeting (to be discussed shortly) unless the debtor redeems or reaffirms certain debts (*reaffirmation* will be discussed later in this chapter). In other words, the debtor cannot keep the

secured property (such as a financed automobile), even if she or he continues to make payments on it, without reinstating the rights of the secured party to collect on the debt.

Bankruptcy Estate

On the commencement of a liquidation proceeding under Chapter 7, a *bankruptcy estate* (sometimes called an *estate in property*) is created. This task is performed by the bankruptcy trustee, as described next. The estate consists of all the debtor's interests in property currently held, wherever located. It also includes community property (property jointly owned by a husband and wife in certain states—see Chapter 50), property transferred in a transaction voidable by the trustee, proceeds and profits from the property of the estate, and certain after-acquired property. Interests in certain property—such as gifts, inheritances, property settlements (from divorce), and life insurance death proceeds—to which the debtor becomes entitled *within 180 days after filing* may also become part of the estate. Withholdings for employee benefit plan contributions are excluded from the estate. Generally, though, the filing of a bankruptcy petition fixes a dividing line: property acquired prior to the filing of the petition becomes property of the estate, and property acquired after the filing of the petition, except as just noted, remains the debtor's.

The Bankruptcy Trustee

Promptly after the order for relief in the liquidation proceeding has been entered, a trustee is appointed. The basic duty of the trustee is to collect and reduce to cash the property in the bankruptcy estate that is not exempt. (Exemptions will be discussed later in the chapter.) The trustee is held accountable for administering the debtor's estate to preserve the interests of both the debtor and unsecured creditors. To enable the trustee to accomplish this duty, the Code gives the trustee certain powers, stated in both general and specific terms. These powers must be exercised within two years of the order for relief.

DUTIES FOR MEANS TESTING The trustee is required to promptly review all materials filed by the debtor to determine if there is substantial abuse. Within ten days after the first meeting of the creditors (held soon after the order for relief is granted, as discussed later), the trustee must file a statement indicating whether the case is presumed to be an abuse under

---

9. The court might grant an extension, for example, on a motion by the trustee that the property is of value to the estate.

the means test. The trustee must provide a copy of this statement to all creditors within five days. When there is a presumption of abuse, the trustee must either file a motion to dismiss the petition (or convert it to a Chapter 13 case) or file a statement setting forth the reasons why a motion would not be appropriate. If the debtor owes a domestic-support obligation (such as child support), the trustee is required to provide written notice of the bankruptcy to the claim holder (a former spouse, for example).

THE TRUSTEE'S POWERS The trustee has the power to require persons holding the debtor's property at the time the petition is filed to deliver the property to the trustee.[10] To enable the trustee to implement this power, the Code provides that the trustee has rights *equivalent* to those of certain other parties, such as a creditor who has a judicial lien. This power of a trustee, which is equivalent to that of a lien creditor, is known as *strong-arm power*.

In addition, the trustee has specific *powers of avoidance*—that is, the trustee can set aside (avoid) a sale or other transfer of the debtor's property, taking it back as a part of the debtor's estate. These powers include voidable rights available to the debtor, preferences, and fraudulent transfers by the debtor. Each is discussed in more detail below. In addition, a trustee can avoid certain statutory liens (creditors' claims against the debtor's property).

The debtor shares most of the trustee's avoidance powers. Thus, if the trustee does not take action to enforce one of the rights just mentioned, the debtor in a liquidation bankruptcy can enforce that right.[11]

VOIDABLE RIGHTS A trustee steps into the shoes of the debtor. Thus, any reason that a debtor can use to obtain the return of her or his property can be used by the trustee as well. These grounds include fraud, duress, incapacity, and mutual mistake.

For example, Ben sells his boat to Tara. Tara gives Ben a check, knowing that she has insufficient funds in her bank account to cover the check. Tara has committed fraud. Ben has the right to avoid that transfer

and recover the boat from Tara. If Ben files for bankruptcy relief under Chapter 7, the trustee can exercise the same right to recover the boat from Tara, and the boat becomes a part of the debtor's estate.

PREFERENCES A debtor is not permitted to transfer property or to make a payment that favors—or gives a **preference** to—one creditor over others. The trustee is allowed to recover payments made both voluntarily and involuntarily to one creditor in preference over another.

To have made a preferential payment that can be recovered, an *insolvent* debtor must have transferred property, for a *preexisting* debt, within *ninety days* prior to the filing of the bankruptcy petition. The transfer must have given the creditor more than the creditor would have received as a result of the bankruptcy proceedings. The Code presumes that a debtor is insolvent during the ninety-day period before filing a petition.

If a **preferred creditor** (one who has received a preferential transfer from the debtor) has sold the property to an innocent third party, the trustee cannot recover the property from the innocent party. The preferred creditor, however, generally *can* be held accountable for the value of the property.

Preferences to Insiders. Sometimes, the creditor receiving the preference is an **insider**—an individual, a partner, a partnership, a corporation, or an officer or a director of a corporation (or a relative of one of these) who has a close relationship with the debtor. In this situation, the avoidance power of the trustee is extended to transfers made within *one year* before filing. (If the transfer was fraudulent, as will be discussed shortly, the trustee can avoid transfers made within *two years* before filing.) Note, however, that if the transfer occurred before the ninety-day period, the trustee is required to prove that the debtor was insolvent at the time it occurred or that the transfer was made to or for the benefit of an insider.

What Constitutes a Preference? Not all transfers are preferences. To be a preference, the transfer must be made for something other than current consideration. Most courts generally assume that payment for services rendered *within fifteen days* before the payment is not a preference. If a creditor receives payment in the ordinary course of business from an individual or business debtor, such as payment of last month's cell phone bill, the bankruptcy trustee cannot recover the payment.

To be recoverable, a preference must be a transfer for an antecedent (preexisting) debt, such as a year-old landscaping bill. In addition, the Code permits a

---

10. Usually, though, the trustee takes constructive, rather than actual, possession of the debtor's property. For example, to obtain control of a debtor's business inventory, a trustee might change the locks on the doors to the business and hire a security guard.

11. Under a Chapter 11 bankruptcy (to be discussed later), for which no trustee other than the debtor generally exists, the debtor has the same avoidance powers as a trustee under Chapter 7. Under Chapters 12 and 13 (also to be discussed later), a trustee must be appointed.

consumer-debtor to transfer any property to a creditor up to a total value of $5,850 without the transfer's constituting a preference. Payment of domestic-support debts does not constitute a preference.

FRAUDULENT TRANSFERS The trustee may avoid fraudulent transfers or obligations if they (1) were made within two years of the filing of the petition, or (2) were made with actual intent to hinder, delay, or defraud a creditor. For example, a debtor who is thinking about petitioning for bankruptcy sells her gold jewelry, worth $10,000, to a friend for $500. The friend agrees that in the future he will "sell" the collection back to the debtor for the same amount. This is a fraudulent transfer that the trustee can undo.

Transfers made for less than reasonably equivalent consideration are also vulnerable if the debtor thereby became insolvent or was left engaged in business with an unreasonably small amount of capital. When a fraudulent transfer is made outside the Code's two-year limit, creditors may seek alternative relief under state laws. Some state laws may allow creditors to recover for transfers made up to three years before the filing of a petition.

In the following case, a trustee alleged that severance payments—that is, compensation paid to an employee who is fired—made to the chief executive officer of a company reorganizing under Chapter 11 constituted both an unlawful preference to an insider and a fraudulent transfer under the Code.

✳ EXTENDED CASE 30.2 ✳
In the Matter of TransTexas Gas Corp.
United States Court of Appeals, Fifth Circuit, 597 F.3d 298 (2010).
www.ca5.uscourts.gov/Opinions.aspx[a]

IN THE LANGUAGE OF THE COURT

Leslie H. *SOUTHWICK*, Circuit Judge.
* * * *
TransTexas Gas Corporation was engaged in [the] exploration, production, and transmission of oil and natural gas. In April 1999, TransTexas filed for Chapter 11 bankruptcy protection. The reorganization plan provided that the company would enter a three-year Employment Agreement with John Stanley, Sr., the company's founder. Stanley would serve as Chief Executive Officer and be one of the five directors * * *.

The Employment Agreement provided that Stanley could be terminated beginning two years after its execution * * * [and] would be entitled to severance pay. If he were dismissed for reasons other than cause, he would receive three million dollars. If he were terminated

for cause, his payment would be one and a half million dollars. If he voluntarily resigned, he would be paid no severance.
* * * In February 2001, a law firm retained by the Board to investigate allegations of Stanley's wrongdoing found that he could validly be dismissed for cause.
* * * *
Between January and March 2002, Stanley remained CEO and a member of the Board as he negotiated the terms of his departure. In March, Stanley and TransTexas agreed that he would resign. On March 14, 2002, the Board executed a "Separation Agreement." It explicitly superseded [replaced] his Employment Agreement. He was to be paid three million dollars in installments. Stanley received $2,270,794.90 before the payments ceased.
* * * *
As a result of its financial deterioration, TransTexas in November 2002 filed a second Chapter 11

proceeding in the bankruptcy court for the Southern District of Texas.
* * * Under the plan, a liquidating trust was established with U.S. Bank as the liquidating trustee.

U.S. Bank filed an adversary proceeding against Stanley, seeking to avoid the severance payments.
* * * The bankruptcy court held that the severance payments constituted both unlawful preferences under Section 547(b) and fraudulent transfers pursuant to Section 548
* * *.

On appeal, the district court agreed in most respects. * * * [The court held] that Stanley's severance payments were avoidable as fraudulent transfers pursuant to Section 548 * * *, but not as preferential transfers under Section 547(b).

On appeal now, * * * U.S. Bank seeks reversal of the district court's holding that the transfers were not preferential under Section 547(b). Stanley argues for reversal of the holding that the severance

---
a. In the box for the docket number, enter "08-41128" and then click on "Search." When the search result appears, select the highlighted docket number to access the opinion. The U.S. Court of Appeals for the Fifth Circuit maintains this Web site.

EXTENDED CASE CONTINUES ➡

EXTENDED CASE 30.2 CONTINUED ⬦

payments were fraudulent transfers under Section 548 * * *.

* * * *

An avoidable fraudulent transfer requires (a) an obligation (b) incurred by the debtor for the benefit of an insider (c) made or incurred within two years before the date of petition where the debtor either (d) incurred such obligation with actual intent to hinder, delay or defraud a creditor, or (e) received less than reasonably equivalent value in exchange for such obligation while the debtor was insolvent or made for the benefit of an insider under an employment contract and not in the ordinary course of business. [Emphasis added.]

Two elements are clearly satisfied. The severance payments made to Stanley after his dismissal were obligations incurred by TransTexas within two years of its petition date.

Superficially, it would appear that the third element of Stanley's being an insider is beyond question. That element is challenged, though, on the basis that at the time of the actual payments, Stanley had left the company and was no longer an insider.

* * * *

Under Section 548, it is enough that Stanley was an insider either at the time of the transfer of the funds or at the time the company incurred such obligation. The language of the statute makes that evident. A "trustee may avoid any transfer (including any transfer to or for the benefit of an insider under an employment contract)," if the debtor "(A) made such transfer or *incurred such obligation*" with the requisite intent, "or (B)(i) received less than a reasonably equivalent value in exchange for such transfer or *obligation*" (emphases added [by the court]).

* * * *

Stanley was indisputably an insider at the time he entered into the relevant obligation. That is enough for Section 548.

* * * *

The bankruptcy court found there was no value to the 2002 agreement to pay three million dollars. The district court assigned some value to the exchange, such as Stanley's release and covenant not to sue. Stanley suggests that by agreeing to "go quietly," he provided benefit to the company.

* * * *

TransTexas did not receive reasonably equivalent value for providing Stanley greater compensation than required by the terms of the Employment Agreement. The district court agreed that even under the most favorable circumstances, Stanley could only have been entitled to $1.5 million under the Employment Agreement, basing that on the conclusion that there was good cause for terminating him. There is simply too much disparity [difference] between TransTexas's payments and any concessions Stanley may have made for his expedient [convenient] exit from the company.

* * * *

[As to the insolvency of TransTexas,] the language in Section 548 regarding fraudulent transfers [makes it] clear that there are different ways in which such transfers can occur. One alternative is that a transfer has been made when the debtor was insolvent. Another alternative is [that] the transfer be made "to or for the benefit of an insider, or incurred such obligation to or for the benefit of an insider, under an employment contract and not in the ordinary course of business." That latter provision applies. As we have discussed, Stanley was an insider at the time the obligation was incurred.

* * * *

* * * [We] AFFIRM the district court on the basis that TransTexas's payments to Stanley were avoidable fraudulent transfers under Section 548.

QUESTIONS

1. What might Stanley have meant when he said that by agreeing to "go quietly," he provided a benefit to the company?
2. Stanley argued that he was not an insider because he was no longer employed by the company when the severance payments were made. How did the court respond to this argument?

Exemptions

As just described, the trustee takes control over the debtor's property in a Chapter 7 bankruptcy, but an individual debtor is entitled to exempt (exclude) certain property from the bankruptcy. The Bankruptcy Code exempts the following property:[12]

1. Up to $21,625 in equity in the debtor's residence and burial plot (the homestead exemption).
2. Interest in a motor vehicle up to $3,450.
3. Interest, up to $550 for a particular item, in household goods and furnishings, wearing apparel, appliances, books, animals, crops, and musical instruments (the aggregate total of all items is limited to $11,525).
4. Interest in jewelry up to $1,450.
5. Interest in any other property up to $1,150, plus any unused part of the $21,625 homestead exemption up to $10,825.

---

12. The dollar amounts stated in the Bankruptcy Code are adjusted automatically every three years on April 1 based on changes in the Consumer Price Index. The adjusted amounts are rounded to the nearest $25. The amounts stated in this chapter are in accordance with those computed on April 1, 2010.

6. Interest in any tools of the debtor's trade up to $2,175.
7. A life insurance contract owned by the debtor (other than a credit life insurance contract).
8. Certain interests in accrued dividends and interest under, or loan value of, life insurance contracts owned by the debtor, not to exceed $11,525.
9. Professionally prescribed health aids.
10. The right to receive Social Security and certain welfare benefits, alimony and support, certain retirement funds and pensions, and education savings accounts held for specific periods of time.
11. The right to receive certain personal-injury and other awards up to $21,625.

Individual states have the power to pass legislation precluding debtors from using the federal exemptions within the state; a majority of the states have done this (see Chapter 28). In those states, debtors may use only state, not federal, exemptions. In the rest of the states, an individual debtor (or a husband and wife filing jointly) may choose either the exemptions provided under state law or the federal exemptions.

The Homestead Exemption

As mentioned in Chapter 28, the 2005 reforms significantly changed the law for those debtors seeking to use state homestead exemption statutes. In six states, including Florida and Texas, homestead exemptions allowed debtors petitioning for bankruptcy to shield *unlimited* amounts of equity in their homes from creditors. The Code now places limits on the amount that can be claimed as exempt in bankruptcy. In addition, a debtor must have lived in a state for two years before filing the bankruptcy petition to be able to use the state homestead exemption (prior law required only six months).

In general, if the debtor acquired the homestead within three and a half years preceding the date of filing, the maximum equity exempted is $146,450, even if state law would permit a higher amount. Note, however, that a debtor who has violated securities laws (see Chapter 42) or been convicted of a felony may not be able to claim the exemption. Similarly, the court can prevent a debtor who has committed any criminal act, intentional tort, or other misconduct that caused serious physical injury or death to another individual in the previous five years from using the homestead exemption.

Creditors' Meeting

In addition to creating and preserving the bankruptcy estate, the bankruptcy trustee has several duties in regard to the creditors. One is to hold the creditors' meeting. Within a reasonable time after the order for relief has been granted (not less than twenty days or more than forty days), the trustee must call a meeting of the creditors listed in the schedules filed by the debtor. The bankruptcy judge does not attend this meeting. The debtor is required to attend (unless excused by the court) and to submit to examination under oath by the creditors and the trustee. At the meeting, the trustee ensures that the debtor is aware of the potential consequences of bankruptcy and of his or her ability to file for bankruptcy under a different chapter of the Bankruptcy Code.

Creditors' Claims

To be entitled to receive a portion of the debtor's estate, each creditor normally files a *proof of claim* with the bankruptcy court clerk within ninety days of the creditors' meeting.[13] The proof of claim lists the creditor's name and address, as well as the amount that the creditor asserts is owed to the creditor by the debtor. A creditor need not file a proof of claim if the debtor's schedules list the creditor's claim as liquidated (exactly determined) and the creditor does not dispute the amount of the claim. A proof of claim is necessary if there is any dispute concerning the claim.

Distribution of Property

In the next step in a Chapter 7 bankruptcy, the trustee distributes the bankruptcy estate to the creditors. In the distribution of the debtor's estate, secured creditors take priority over unsecured creditors. The Code provides that a consumer-debtor, within thirty days of filing a liquidation petition or before the date of the first meeting of the creditors (whichever is first), must file with the clerk a statement of intention with respect to the secured collateral. The statement must indicate whether the debtor will retain the collateral or surrender the collateral to the secured party. Also, if applicable, the debtor must specify whether the collateral will be claimed as exempt property and whether the debtor intends to redeem the property or reaffirm the debt

---

13. This ninety-day rule applies in Chapter 12 and Chapter 13 bankruptcies as well.

secured by the collateral. The trustee is obligated to enforce the debtor's statement within forty-five days after it is filed.

In a bankruptcy case in which the debtor has no assets (called a "no-asset case"), creditors are notified of the debtor's petition for bankruptcy but are instructed not to file a claim. In no-asset cases, the unsecured creditors will receive no payment, and most, if not all, of these debts will be discharged.

DISTRIBUTION TO SECURED CREDITORS The rights of perfected secured creditors were discussed on pages 572–577 in Chapter 29. If the collateral is surrendered to the secured party, the secured creditor can enforce the security interest either by accepting the property in full satisfaction of the debt or by selling the collateral and using the proceeds to pay off the debt. Thus, the secured party has priority over unsecured parties as to the proceeds from the disposition of the collateral. Should the collateral be insufficient to cover the secured debt owed, the secured creditor becomes an unsecured creditor for the difference.

DISTRIBUTION TO UNSECURED CREDITORS Bankruptcy law establishes an order of priority for classes of debts owed to *unsecured* creditors, and they are paid in the order of their priority. Each class must be fully paid before the next class is entitled to any of the remaining proceeds. If there are insufficient proceeds to pay fully all the creditors in a class, the proceeds are distributed *proportionately* to the creditors in that class, and classes lower in priority receive nothing. In almost all cases, the funds will be insufficient to pay all creditors. The order of priority among classes of unsecured creditors is as follows (some of these classes involve cases against bankrupt businesses):

1. Claims for domestic-support obligations, such as child support and alimony.
2. Administrative expenses, including court costs, trustee fees, and attorneys' fees.
3. In an involuntary bankruptcy, expenses incurred by the debtor in the ordinary course of business.
4. Unpaid wages, salaries, and commissions earned within ninety days of the filing of the petition; the amount is capped for each claimant.
5. Unsecured claims for contributions to be made to employee benefit plans; the amount is capped for each claimant.
6. Consumer deposits given to the debtor before the petition was filed; the amount is capped for each claimant.

7. Certain taxes and penalties owed to government units, such as income and property taxes.
8. Claims for death or personal injury resulting from the unlawful operation of a motor vehicle.
9. Claims of general creditors.

If any amount remains after the priority classes of creditors have been satisfied, it is turned over to the debtor.

Discharge

From the debtor's point of view, the primary purpose of liquidation is to obtain a fresh start through a discharge of debts. Certain debts, however, are not dischargeable in bankruptcy. Also, certain debtors may not qualify to have all debts discharged in bankruptcy. These situations are discussed next.

EXCEPTIONS TO DISCHARGE Discharge of a debt may be denied because of the nature of the claim or the conduct of the debtor. Claims that are not dischargeable in bankruptcy include the following:

1. Claims for back taxes accruing within two years prior to bankruptcy.
2. Claims for amounts borrowed by the debtor to pay federal taxes or any nondischargeable taxes.[14]
3. Claims against property or funds obtained by the debtor under false pretenses or by false representations.
4. Claims by creditors who were not notified of the bankruptcy; these claims did not appear on the schedules the debtor was required to file.
5. Claims based on fraud[15] or misuse of funds by the debtor while acting in a fiduciary capacity or claims involving the debtor's embezzlement or larceny.
6. Domestic-support obligations and property settlements as provided for in a separation agreement or divorce decree.

---

14. Taxes accruing within three years prior to bankruptcy are nondischargeable, including federal and state income taxes, employment taxes, taxes on gross receipts, property taxes, excise taxes, customs duties, and any other taxes for which the government claims the debtor is liable in some capacity. See 11 U.S.C. Sections 507(a)(8) and 523(a)(1).
15. Even if a debtor who is sued for fraud settles the lawsuit, the United States Supreme Court has held that the amount due under the settlement agreement may not be discharged in bankruptcy because of the underlying fraud. See *Archer v. Warner*, 538 U.S. 314, 123 S.Ct. 1462, 155 L.Ed.2d 454 (2003).

7. Claims for amounts due on a retirement account loan.
8. Claims based on willful or malicious conduct by the debtor toward another or the property of another.
9. Certain government fines and penalties.
10. Certain student loans or obligations to repay funds received as an educational benefit, scholarship, or stipend—unless payment of the loans imposes an undue hardship on the debtor and the debtor's dependents. (For an example of what constitutes undue hardship, see the *Case in Point* feature that follows this list.)
11. Consumer debts of more than $600 for luxury goods or services owed to a single creditor incurred within ninety days of the order for relief.
12. Cash advances totaling more than $875 that are extensions of open-end consumer credit obtained by the debtor within seventy days of the order for relief.
13. Judgments against a debtor as a result of the debtor's operation of a motor vehicle while intoxicated.
14. Fees or assessments arising from property in a homeowners' association, as long as the debtor retained an interest in the property.
15. Taxes with respect to which the debtor failed to provide required or requested tax documents.

CASE IN POINT Keldric Mosley incurred student loans while attending Alcorn State University and then joined the U.S. Army Reserve Officers' Training Corps. He was injured during training and resigned from the Corps because of medical problems related to his injuries. Mosley worked briefly for several employers, but depressed and physically limited by his injuries, he was unable to keep any of the jobs. A federal bankruptcy court granted him a discharge under Chapter 7, but it did not include the student loans. By 2004, Mosley was homeless and had a monthly income of $210 in disability benefits, but he still owed $45,000 in student loans. He asked the bankruptcy court to reopen his case and discharge his student loans based on undue hardship. The court held that Mosley's medical problems, lack of skills, and "dire living conditions" made it unlikely that he would be able to hold a job and repay the loans. The court therefore discharged the debt, reasoning that Mosley could not maintain a minimal standard of living if forced to repay the loans.[16]

---

16. *In re Mosley,* 494 F.3d 1320 (11th Cir. 2007).

OBJECTIONS TO DISCHARGE In addition to the exceptions to discharge previously discussed, a bankruptcy court may also deny the discharge based on the debtor's conduct. In such a situation, the assets of the debtor are still distributed to the creditors, but the debtor remains liable for the unpaid portion of all claims. Grounds for a denial of discharge of the debtor include the following:

1. The debtor's concealment or destruction of property with the intent to hinder, delay, or defraud a creditor.
2. The debtor's fraudulent concealment or destruction of financial records.
3. The grant of a discharge to the debtor within eight years before the petition was filed.
4. The debtor's failure to complete the required consumer education course.
5. Proceedings in which the debtor could be found guilty of a felony (basically, a court may not discharge any debt until the completion of felony proceedings against the debtor).

EFFECT OF A DISCHARGE The primary effect of a discharge is to void, or set aside, any judgment on a discharged debt and prohibit any action to collect a discharged debt. A discharge does not affect the liability of a co-debtor. (For a discussion of how some debts that were discharged in bankruptcy have still appeared on debtors' credit reports, see this chapter's *Insight into Ethics* feature on the next page.)

REVOCATION OF DISCHARGE On petition by the trustee or a creditor, the bankruptcy court can, within one year, revoke the discharge decree if it is discovered that the debtor acted fraudulently or dishonestly during the bankruptcy proceedings. The revocation renders the discharge void, allowing creditors not satisfied by the distribution of the debtor's estate to proceed with their claims against the debtor.

Reaffirmation of Debt

An agreement to pay a debt dischargeable in bankruptcy is called a **reaffirmation agreement.** A debtor may wish to pay a debt—for example, a debt owed to a family member, physician, bank, or some other creditor—even though the debt could be discharged in bankruptcy. Also, as noted previously, a debtor cannot retain secured property while continuing to pay without entering into a reaffirmation agreement.

When a bankruptcy judge discharges certain debts, they are no longer supposed to appear on debtors' credit reports. Nonetheless, many credit-card companies and other creditors have been keeping debts active even after they have been discharged in bankruptcy. Not surprisingly, some aggressive entrepreneurs have found a way to profit from this practice. Companies with names such as eCast Settlement and Max Recovery purchase discharged debt obligations at pennies on the dollar. Then they pursue the debtors and pressure them to pay the debts even though they have been discharged. Some of these companies have been successful enough to become publicly traded on the New York Stock Exchange.

The fact that discharged debt does not have a zero dollar value indicates that some consumers have been repaying these debts. As the number of bankruptcies rose during the latest recession, the market price of fully discharged Chapter 7 debt actually increased—to about seven cents on the dollar.

One federal district court judge, though, has had enough. In a class-action lawsuit, plaintiffs claimed that credit reporting agencies had violated the federal Fair Credit Reporting Act (see Chapter 45) by failing to follow reasonable procedures that ensured accurate reporting of debts discharged in Chapter 7 bankruptcies. The court agreed and ordered the agencies to revise their procedures.[a] Today, credit agencies must automatically report all prebankruptcy debt as "discharged," unless the debt is nondischargable. Although the purchasers of discharged debt may still attempt to pressure consumers into paying debts that they do not owe, the change in the credit bureaus' procedures may give consumers additional help in their efforts to rebuild their lives after bankruptcy.

CRITICAL THINKING
INSIGHT INTO THE ECONOMIC ENVIRONMENT
About six years ago, one could buy debt that had been discharged in bankruptcy for less than five cents on the dollar. Why has the price increased to seven cents on the dollar?

a. *White v. Experian Information Solutions,* No. 05-CV-1-70 DOC (C.D.Cal. 2008).

THE REAFFIRMATION PROCESS To be enforceable, reaffirmation agreements must be made before the debtor is granted a discharge. The agreement must be signed and filed with the court. Court approval is required unless the debtor is represented by an attorney during the negotiation of the reaffirmation and submits the proper documents and certifications. Even when the debtor is represented by an attorney, court approval may be required if it appears that the reaffirmation will result in undue hardship on the debtor. When court approval is required, a separate hearing will take place. The court will approve the reaffirmation only if it finds that the agreement will not result in undue hardship to the debtor and that the reaffirmation is consistent with the debtor's best interests.

REAFFIRMATION DISCLOSURES To discourage creditors from engaging in abusive reaffirmation practices, the law provides specific language for disclosures that must be given to debtors entering into reaffirmation agreements. Among other things, these disclosures explain that the debtor is not required to reaffirm any debt, but that liens on secured property, such as mortgages and cars, will remain in effect even if the debt is not reaffirmed.

The reaffirmation agreement must disclose the amount of the debt reaffirmed, the rate of interest, the date payments begin, and the right to rescind. The disclosures also caution the debtor: "Only agree to reaffirm a debt if it is in your best interest. Be sure you can afford the payments you agree to make." The original disclosure documents must be signed by the debtor, certified by the debtor's attorney, and filed with the court at the same time as the reaffirmation agreement. A reaffirmation agreement that is not accompanied by the original signed disclosures will not be effective.

SECTION 3
REORGANIZATIONS

The type of bankruptcy proceeding most commonly used by corporate debtors is the Chapter 11 *reorganization*. In a reorganization, the creditors and the debtor formulate a plan under which the debtor pays a portion of the debts and is discharged of the remainder. The debtor is allowed to continue in business. Although this type of bankruptcy is generally a corporate reorganization, any debtor (except a stockbroker or a commodities broker) who is eligible for Chapter 7 relief is eligible for relief under Chapter 11. Railroads are also eligible.

In 1994, Congress established a "fast-track" Chapter 11 procedure for small-business debtors whose liabilities do not exceed $2.19 million and who do not own or manage real estate. The fast track enables a debtor to avoid the appointment of a creditors' committee and also shortens the filing periods and relaxes certain other requirements. Because the process is shorter and simpler, it is less costly.

The same principles that govern the filing of a liquidation (Chapter 7) petition apply to reorganization (Chapter 11) proceedings. The case may be brought either voluntarily or involuntarily. The automatic-stay provisions and adequate protection doctrine apply in reorganizations as well. An exception from the automatic stay is triggered if the debtor files for bankruptcy again within two years and new grounds for dismissal (such as substantial abuse) or conversion of the case are established.

Workouts

In some instances, to avoid bankruptcy proceedings, creditors may prefer private, negotiated adjustments of creditor-debtor relations, also known as **workouts.** Often, these out-of-court workouts are much more flexible and thus more conducive to a speedy settlement. Speed is critical because delay is one of the most costly elements in any bankruptcy proceeding. Another advantage of workouts is that they avoid the various administrative costs of bankruptcy proceedings.

Focus Is on the Best Interests of the Creditors

After a petition for Chapter 11 bankruptcy has been filed, a bankruptcy court, after notice and a hearing, can dismiss or suspend all proceedings at any time if dismissal or suspension would better serve the interests of the creditors. The Code also allows a court, after notice and a hearing, to dismiss a case under reorganization "for cause." Cause includes the absence of a reasonable likelihood of rehabilitation, the inability to effect a plan, and an unreasonable

delay by the debtor that is prejudicial to (may harm the interests of) creditors.[17]

Debtor in Possession

On entry of the order for relief, the debtor generally continues to operate the business as a **debtor in possession (DIP).** The court, however, may appoint a trustee (often referred to as a *receiver*) to operate the debtor's business if gross mismanagement of the business is shown or if appointing a trustee is in the best interests of the estate.

The DIP's role is similar to that of a trustee in a liquidation.[18] The DIP is entitled to avoid preferential payments made to creditors and fraudulent transfers of assets. The DIP has the power to decide whether to cancel or assume obligations under prepetition executory contracts (those that are not yet performed) or unexpired leases. The DIP can also exercise a trustee's strong-arm powers.

Creditors' Committees

As soon as practicable after the entry of the order for relief, a creditors' committee of unsecured creditors is appointed.[19] This committee often is composed of the biggest suppliers to the business. The committee may consult with the trustee or the DIP concerning the administration of the case or the formulation of the plan. Additional creditors' committees may be appointed to represent special interest creditors.

Generally, no orders affecting the estate will be entered without the consent of the committee or after a hearing in which the judge is informed of the committee's position. As mentioned earlier, businesses with debts of less than $2.19 million that do not own or manage real estate can avoid creditors' committees. In these cases, orders can be entered without a committee's consent.

The Reorganization Plan

A reorganization plan to rehabilitate the debtor is a plan to conserve and administer the debtor's assets in the hope of an eventual return to successful

---

17. See 11 U.S.C. Section 1112(b). Debtors are not prohibited from filing successive petitions, however. A debtor whose petition is dismissed, for example, can file a new Chapter 11 petition (which may be granted unless it is filed in bad faith).
18. 11 U.S.C. Section 544(a).
19. If the debtor has filed a reorganization plan accepted by the creditors, the trustee may decide not to call a meeting of the creditors.

operation and solvency. The plan must be fair and equitable and must do the following:

1. Designate classes of claims and interests.
2. Specify the treatment to be afforded the classes. (The plan must provide the same treatment for all claims in a particular class.)
3. Provide an adequate means for execution. (Individual debtors are required to utilize post-petition assets as necessary to execute the plan.)
4. Provide for payment of tax claims over a five-year period.

FILING THE PLAN Only the debtor may file a plan within the first 120 days after the date of the order for relief. This period may be extended, but not beyond eighteen months from the date of the order for relief. If the debtor does not meet the 120-day deadline or obtain an extension, and if the debtor fails to procure the required creditor consent (discussed below) within 180 days, any party may propose a plan. The plan need not provide for full repayment to unsecured creditors. Instead, creditors receive a percentage of each dollar owed to them by the debtor. If a small-business debtor chooses to avoid a creditors' committee, the time for the debtor's filing is 180 days.

ACCEPTANCE AND CONFIRMATION OF THE PLAN
Once the plan has been developed, it is submitted to each class of creditors for acceptance. For the plan to be adopted, each class that is adversely affected by the plan must accept it. A class has accepted the plan when a majority of the creditors, representing two-thirds of the amount of the total claim, vote to approve it. Confirmation is conditioned on the debtor's certification that all postpetition domestic-support obligations have been paid in full.

Even when all classes of creditors accept the plan, the court may refuse to confirm it if it is not "in the best interests of the creditors." The plan can also be modified on the request of the debtor, the trustee, the U.S. trustee, or a holder of an unsecured claim. If an unsecured creditor objects to the plan, specific rules apply to the value of property to be distributed under the plan. Tax claims must be paid over a five-year period.

Even if only one class of creditors has accepted the plan, the court may still confirm the plan under the Code's so-called **cram-down provision.** In other words, the court may confirm the plan over the objections of a class of creditors. Before the court can exercise this right of cram-down confirmation, it must be demonstrated that the plan does not discriminate unfairly against any creditors and is fair and equitable.

DISCHARGE The plan is binding on confirmation; however, the law provides that confirmation of a plan does not discharge an individual debtor. *For individual debtors, the plan must be completed before discharge will be granted,* unless the court orders otherwise. For all other debtors, the court may order discharge at any time after the plan is confirmed. At this time, the debtor is given a reorganization discharge from all claims not protected under the plan. This discharge does not apply to any claims that would be denied discharge under liquidation.

SECTION 4
BANKRUPTCY RELIEF UNDER CHAPTER 13 AND CHAPTER 12

In addition to bankruptcy relief through liquidation and reorganization, the Code also provides for individuals' repayment plans (Chapter 13) and family-farmer and family-fisherman debt adjustments (Chapter 12).

Individuals' Repayment Plans

Chapter 13 of the Bankruptcy Code provides for "Adjustment of Debts of an Individual with Regular Income." Individuals (not partnerships or corporations) with regular income who owe fixed (liquidated) unsecured debts of less than $360,475 or fixed secured debts of less than $1,081,400 may take advantage of bankruptcy repayment plans. Among those eligible are salaried employees; sole proprietors; and individuals who live on welfare, Social Security, fixed pensions, or investment income. Many small-business debtors have a choice of filing under either Chapter 11 or Chapter 13. Repayment plans offer some advantages because they are less expensive and less complicated than reorganization or liquidation proceedings.

FILING THE PETITION A Chapter 13 repayment plan case can be initiated only by the debtor's filing of a voluntary petition or by court conversion of a Chapter 7 petition (because of a finding of substantial abuse under the means test, for example). Certain liquidation and reorganization cases may be converted to repayment plan cases with the consent of the debtor.[20] A trustee, who will make payments under the plan, must be appointed. On the filing of a repayment plan petition, the automatic stay previously discussed takes effect. Although the stay applies to all or part of the debtor's consumer debt, it does not apply to any business debt incurred by the debtor or to any domestic-support obligations.

GOOD FAITH REQUIREMENT The Bankruptcy Code imposes the requirement of good faith on a debtor at both the time of the filing of the petition and the time of the filing of the plan. The Code does not define good faith, but if the circumstances on the whole indicate bad faith, a court can dismiss a debtor's Chapter 13 petition.

CASE IN POINT Roger and Pauline Buis bought an air show business, including a helicopter. They decorated the helicopter as "Otto the Clown" and operated the business as Otto Airshows. Several years later, a competitor won a defamation lawsuit against the Buises and Otto Airshows. The Buises then stopped doing business as Otto Airshows and formed a new firm, Prop and Rotor Aviation, Inc., to which they leased the Otto equipment. Within a month, they filed a bankruptcy petition under Chapter 13. The plan and the schedules failed to mention the lawsuit, the equipment lease, and several other items. The court therefore dismissed the Buises' petition due to bad faith. The debtors had not included all of their assets and liabilities on their initial petition, and they had timed its filing to avoid payment on the defamation judgment.[21]

THE REPAYMENT PLAN A plan of rehabilitation by repayment must provide for the following:

1. The turning over to the trustee of such future earnings or income of the debtor as is necessary for execution of the plan.
2. Full payment through deferred cash payments of all claims entitled to priority, such as taxes.[22]
3. Identical treatment of all claims within a particular class. (The Code permits the debtor to list co-debtors, such as guarantors or sureties, as a separate class.)

The repayment plan may provide either for payment of all obligations in full or for payment of a lesser amount. The length of the payment plan can be three or five years, depending on the debtor's family income. If the debtor's family income is greater than the median family income in the relevant geographic area under the means test, the term of the proposed plan must be for five years.[23] The term may not exceed five years.

The debtor must begin making payments under the proposed plan within thirty days after the plan has been *filed* and must continue to make "timely" payments from her or his disposable income. Failure of the debtor to make timely payments or to commence payments within the thirty-day period will allow the court to convert the case to a liquidation bankruptcy or to dismiss the petition.

CONFIRMATION OF THE PLAN After the plan is filed, the court holds a confirmation hearing, at which interested parties (such as creditors) may object to the plan. The hearing must be held at least twenty days, but no more than forty-five days, after the meeting of the creditors. The debtor must have filed all prepetition tax returns and paid all postpetition domestic-support obligations before a court will confirm any plan. The court will confirm a plan with respect to each claim of a secured creditor under any of the following circumstances:

1. If the secured creditors have accepted the plan.
2. If the plan provides that secured creditors retain their liens until there is payment in full or until the debtor receives a discharge.
3. If the debtor surrenders the property securing the claims to the creditors.

In addition, for a motor vehicle purchased within 910 days before the petition is filed, the plan must provide that a creditor with a purchase-money security interest (PMSI—see page 564 in Chapter 29) retains its lien until the entire debt is paid. For PMSIs on other personal property, the payment plan must cover debts incurred within a one-year period preceding the filing.

DISCHARGE After the debtor has completed all payments, the court grants a discharge of all debts provided for by the repayment plan. Except for allowed claims not provided for by the plan, certain long-term debts provided for by the plan, certain tax claims, payments on retirement accounts, and

---

20. A Chapter 13 repayment plan may be converted to a Chapter 7 liquidation at the request of the debtor or, under certain circumstances, by a creditor "for cause." A Chapter 13 case may be converted to a Chapter 11 case after a hearing.
21. *In re Buis,* 337 Bankr. 243 (N.D.Fla. 2006).
22. As with a Chapter 11 reorganization plan, full repayment of all claims is not always required.

---

23. See 11 U.S.C. Section 1322(d) for details on when the court will find that the Chapter 13 plan should extend to a five-year period.

claims for domestic-support obligations, all other debts are dischargeable. Under prior law, a discharge of debts under a Chapter 13 repayment plan was sometimes referred to as a "superdischarge" because it allowed the discharge of fraudulently incurred debt and claims resulting from malicious or willful injury. The 2005 reforms, however, deleted most of the "superdischarge" provisions, especially for debts based on fraud or taxes. Today, debts related to injury or property damage caused while driving under the influence of alcohol or drugs are also nondischargeable.

CASE IN POINT James Ellett owed $18,000 in personal income taxes to the state of California at the time he petitioned for Chapter 13 bankruptcy. Ellett listed the debt in his petition but misstated the last digit of his Social Security number (SSN). Because of this error, the California Franchise Tax Board (FTB) did not receive any notice of Ellett's bankruptcy and never filed a proof of claim or received any distribution through his repayment plan. After Ellett completed the repayment plan and received a discharge, the FTB attempted to collect the tax debt. Ellett filed a lawsuit seeking a court declaration that the debt to the FTB had been discharged. The court ruled against him, and he appealed. A federal appellate court concluded that because of Ellett's negligence in listing an erroneous SSN on his bankruptcy petition, the FTB had been never notified of his bankruptcy; thus, the tax debt was not discharged.[24]

In the following case, the issue before the United States Supreme Court was whether the discharge of certain student loan debt had been rendered void by a legal error on the part of the bankruptcy court.

---

24. *Ellett v. Stanislaus,* 506 F.3d 774 (9th Cir. 2007). (Stanislaus was the name of the director of the Franchise Tax Board.)

CASE 30.3
United Student Aid Funds, Inc. v. Espinosa

Supreme Court of the United States, ___U.S.___, 130 S.Ct. 1367, 176 L.Ed.2d 158 (2010).
www.supremecourtus.gov[a]

BACKGROUND AND FACTS • Francisco Espinosa filed a petition for an individual repayment plan under Chapter 13 of the Bankruptcy Code. The plan proposed that Espinosa would repay only the principal of his student loan debt and that the interest on the loan would be discharged once the principal was repaid. Under Chapter 13, a student loan cannot be discharged unless the bankruptcy court finds that payment of the debt would constitute an undue hardship for the debtor. Despite this requirement, no undue hardship hearing was requested by Espinosa, by the court, or by United Student Aid Funds, Inc. (United), the creditor. United received notice of the plan but did not object to it. In addition, United failed to file an appeal after the bankruptcy court subsequently confirmed the plan. Years later, however, United filed a motion under Federal Rule of Civil Procedure 60(b)(4) asking the bankruptcy court to rule that its order confirming the plan was void because the order was issued in violation of the laws and rules governing bankruptcy. The court denied the petition and ordered United to cease its collection efforts. United appealed to the U.S. District Court for the District of Arizona, which reversed the bankruptcy court's ruling. On further appeal, the U.S. Court of Appeals for the Ninth Circuit reversed the district court's judgment. United appealed to the United States Supreme Court.

IN THE LANGUAGE OF THE COURT
Justice *THOMAS* delivered the opinion of the Court.
* * * *

A discharge under Chapter 13 "is broader than the discharge received in any other chapter." Chapter 13 nevertheless restricts or prohibits entirely the discharge of certain types of debts. As relevant here, [Section] 1328(a) [of the Bankruptcy Code] provides that when a debtor has completed the repayments required by a confirmed plan,

---

a. In the left-hand column, select "Opinions" and click on "Latest Slip Opinions." When that page opens, scroll down the list to the date 3/23/10 and click on the case title to access the case. The Supreme Court of the United States maintains this Web site.

CASE 30.3 CONTINUED ▶ a bankruptcy court "shall grant the debtor a discharge of all debts provided for by the plan or disallowed under Section 502 of this title, except," *inter alia* [among others], "any debt * * * of the kind specified in [Section] 523(a)(8). [That section], in turn, specifies certain student loan debts "unless excepting such debt from discharge * * * would impose an undue hardship on the debtor and the debtor's dependents." * * * *[The] Bankruptcy Rules require a party seeking to determine the dischargeability of a student loan debt to commence an adversary proceeding by serving a summons and complaint on affected creditors.* We must decide whether the Bankruptcy Court's order confirming Espinosa's plan is "void" under Federal Rule of Civil Procedure 60(b)(4) because the Bankruptcy Court confirmed the plan without complying with these requirements. [Emphasis added.]

The Bankruptcy Court's order confirming Espinosa's proposed plan was a final judgment, from which United did not appeal. * * * Rule 60(b)(4)—the provision under which United brought this motion—authorizes the court to relieve a party from a final judgment if "the judgment is void."

* * * *

"A judgment is not void * * * simply because it is or may have been erroneous." Similarly, a motion under Rule 60(b)(4) is not a substitute for a timely appeal. Instead, Rule 60(b)(4) applies only in the rare instance where a judgment is premised either on a certain type of jurisdictional error or on a violation of due process that deprives a party of notice or the opportunity to be heard.

* * * *

Unable to demonstrate a jurisdictional error or a due process violation, United and the Government, as *amicus* [friend of the court], urge us to expand the universe of judgment defects that support Rule 60(b)(4) relief. Specifically, they contend that the Bankruptcy Court's confirmation order is void because the court lacked statutory authority to confirm Espinosa's plan absent a finding of undue hardship.

* * * *

*Given the Code's clear * * * requirement for an undue hardship determination, the Bankruptcy Court's failure to find undue hardship before confirming Espinosa's plan was a legal error. But the order remains enforceable and binding on United because United had notice of the error and failed to object or timely appeal.* [Emphasis added.]

United's response—that it had no obligation to object to Espinosa's plan until Espinosa served it with the summons and complaint the Bankruptcy Rules require—is unavailing [fails to achieve the desired result]. Rule 60(b)(4) does not provide a license for litigants to sleep on their rights. United had actual notice of the filing of Espinosa's plan, its contents, and the Bankruptcy Court's subsequent confirmation of the plan. In addition, United filed a proof of claim regarding Espinosa's student loan debt, thereby submitting itself to the Bankruptcy Court's jurisdiction with respect to that claim. United therefore forfeited its arguments regarding the validity of service or the adequacy of the Bankruptcy Court's procedures by failing to raise a timely objection in that court.

DECISION AND REMEDY • *The United States Supreme Court affirmed the judgment of the U.S. Court of Appeals for the Ninth Circuit. The bankruptcy court's order confirming Espinosa's Chapter 13 repayment plan was not void, and the student loan debt was thus discharged.*

THE ETHICAL DIMENSION • *At one point, United argued that if the Court failed to declare the bankruptcy court's order void, it would encourage dishonest debtors to abuse the Chapter 13 process. How might such abuse occur? Discuss whether the possibility of such abuse should affect the Court's decision.*

MANAGERIAL IMPLICATIONS • *Business owners and managers should be aware that courts generally have little sympathy for those who "sleep on their rights." In this case, the creditor could have objected to the plan, but it did not. The creditor also could have appealed the confirmation order, but it did not. Only years later did the creditor seek to have the confirmation order declared void. To protect their rights, businesspersons should take care, if a client or other debtor petitions for bankruptcy relief, to respond to any notices received from the debtor or the bankruptcy court in a timely fashion.*

Family Farmers and Fishermen

In 1986, to help relieve economic pressure on small farmers, Congress created Chapter 12 of the Bankruptcy Code. In 2005, Congress extended this protection to family fishermen, modified its provisions somewhat, and made it a permanent chapter in the Bankruptcy Code (previously, the statutes authorizing Chapter 12 had to be periodically renewed by Congress).

DEFINITIONS For purposes of Chapter 12, a *family farmer* is one whose gross income is at least 50 percent farm dependent and whose debts are at least 50 percent farm related. The total debt for a family farmer must not exceed $3,792,650. A partnership or closely held corporation (see Chapter 39) at least 50 percent owned by the farm family can also qualify as a family farmer.[25]

A *family fisherman* is defined as one whose gross income is at least 50 percent dependent on commercial fishing operations[26] and whose debts are at least 80 percent related to commercial fishing. The total debt for a family fisherman must not exceed $1,757,475. As with family farmers, a partnership or closely held corporation can also qualify.

FILING THE PETITION The procedure for filing a family-farmer or family-fisherman bankruptcy plan is very similar to the procedure for filing a repayment plan under Chapter 13. The debtor must file a plan not later than ninety days after the order for relief. The filing of the petition acts as an automatic stay against creditors' and co-obligors' actions against the estate.

A farmer or fisherman who has already filed a reorganization or repayment plan may convert it to a Chapter 12 plan. The debtor may also convert a Chapter 12 plan to a liquidation plan.

CONTENT AND CONFIRMATION OF THE PLAN The content of a plan under Chapter 12 is basically the same as that of a Chapter 13 repayment plan. Generally, the plan must be confirmed or denied within forty-five days of filing.

Court confirmation of the plan is the same as for a repayment plan. The plan must provide for payment of secured debts at the value of the collateral. If the secured debt exceeds the value of the collateral, the remaining debt is unsecured. For unsecured debtors, the plan must be confirmed if either (1) the value of the property to be distributed under the plan equals the amount of the claim or (2) the plan provides that all of the debtor's disposable income to be received in a three-year period (or longer, by court approval) will be applied to making payments. Disposable income is all income received less amounts needed to support the farmer or fisherman and his or her family and to continue the farming or commercial fishing operation. Completion of payments under the plan discharges all debts provided for by the plan.

See *Concept Summary 30.1* below and on the facing page for a comparison of bankruptcy procedures under Chapters 7, 11, 12, and 13.

---

25. Note that for a corporation or partnership to qualify under Chapter 12, at least 80 percent of the value of the firm's assets must consist of assets related to the farming operation.
26. Commercial fishing operations include catching, harvesting, or raising fish, shrimp, lobsters, urchins, seaweed, shellfish, or other aquatic species or products.

CONCEPT SUMMARY 30.1
Forms of Bankruptcy Relief Compared

Issue	Chapter 7	Chapter 11	Chapters 12 and 13
Purpose	Liquidation	Reorganization	Adjustment
Who Can Petition	Debtor (voluntary) or creditors (involuntary).	Debtor (voluntary) or creditors (involuntary).	Debtor (voluntary) only.
Who Can Be a Debtor	Any "person" (including partnerships, corporations, and municipalities) except railroads, insurance companies, banks, savings and loan	Any debtor eligible for Chapter 7 relief; railroads are also eligible. Individuals have specific rules and limitations.	*Chapter 12*—Any family farmer (one whose gross income is at least 50 percent farm dependent and whose debts are at least 50 percent farm related) or family fisherman (one whose gross income is at

CONCEPT SUMMARY 30.1
Forms of Bankruptcy Relief Compared, Continued

Issue	Chapter 7	Chapter 11	Chapters 12 and 13
Purpose	Liquidation	Reorganization	Adjustment
Who Can Be a Debtor—Continued	institutions, investment companies licensed by the Small Business Administration, and credit unions. Farmers and charitable institutions cannot be involuntarily petitioned. If the court finds the petition to be a substantial abuse of the use of Chapter 7, the debtor may be required to convert to a Chapter 13 repayment plan.		least 50 percent dependent on commercial fishing operations and whose debts are at least 80 percent related to commercial fishing) or any partnership or closely held corporation at least 50 percent owned by a family farmer or fisherman, when total debt does not exceed a specified amount ($3,792,650 for farmers and $1,757,475 for fishermen). *Chapter 13*—Any individual (not partnerships or corporations) with regular income who owes fixed (liquidated) unsecured debts of less than $360,475 or fixed secured debts of less than $1,081,400.
Procedure Leading to Discharge	Nonexempt property is sold, and the proceeds are distributed (in order) to priority groups. Dischargeable debts are terminated.	Plan is submitted; if it is approved and followed, debts are discharged.	Plan is submitted and must be approved if the value of the property to be distributed equals the amount of the claims or if the debtor turns over disposable income for a three-year or five-year period; if the plan is followed, debts are discharged.
Advantages	On liquidation and distribution, most debts are discharged, and the debtor has an opportunity for a fresh start.	Debtor continues in business. Creditors can accept the plan, or it can be "crammed down" on them. The plan allows for the reorganization and liquidation of debts over the plan period.	Debtor continues in business or possession of assets. If the plan is approved, most debts are discharged after the plan period.

REVIEWING
Bankruptcy Law

Three months ago, Janet Hart's husband of twenty years died of cancer. Although he had medical insurance, he left Janet with outstanding medical bills of more than $50,000. Janet has worked at the local library for the past ten years, earning $1,500 per month. Since her husband's death, Janet also receives $1,500 in Social Security benefits and $1,100 in life insurance proceeds every month, for a total monthly income of $4,300. After she pays the mortgage payment of $1,500 and the amounts due

REVIEWING CONTINUES ▶

REVIEWING
Bankruptcy Law, Continued

on other debts, Janet has barely enough left to buy groceries for her family (she has two teenage daughters at home). She decides to file for Chapter 7 bankruptcy, hoping for a fresh start. Using the information presented in the chapter, answer the following questions.

1. What must Janet do *before* filing a petition for relief under Chapter 7?
2. How much time does Janet have after filing the bankruptcy petition to submit the required schedules? What happens if Janet does not meet the deadline?
3. Assume that Janet files a petition under Chapter 7. Further assume that the median family income in the geographic area in which Janet lives is $49,300. What steps would a court take to determine whether Janet's petition is presumed to be "substantial abuse" using the means test?
4. Suppose that the court determines that no *presumption* of substantial abuse applies in Janet's case. Nevertheless, the court finds that Janet does have the ability to pay at least a portion of the medical bills out of her disposable income. What would the court likely order in that situation?

DEBATE THIS: *Rather than being allowed to file Chapter 7 bankruptcy petitions, individuals and couples should always be forced to make an effort to pay off their debts through Chapter 13.*

TERMS AND CONCEPTS

adequate protection doctrine 587
automatic stay 585
bankruptcy trustee 582
cram-down provision 596
debtor in possession (DIP) 595
discharge 582
insider 588
liquidation 582
order for relief 585
petition in bankruptcy 582
preference 588
preferred creditor 588
reaffirmation agreement 593
U.S. trustee 583
workout 595

QUESTIONS AND CASE PROBLEMS

30–1. Voluntary versus Involuntary Bankruptcy
Burke has been a rancher all her life, raising cattle and crops. Her ranch is valued at $500,000, almost all of which is exempt under state law. Burke has eight creditors and a total indebtedness of $70,000. Two of her largest creditors are Oman ($30,000 owed) and Sneed ($25,000 owed). The other six creditors have claims of less than $5,000 each. A drought has ruined all of Burke's crops and forced her to sell many of her cattle at a loss. She cannot pay off her creditors.
(a) Under the Bankruptcy Code, can Burke, with a $500,000 ranch, voluntarily petition herself into bankruptcy? Explain.
(b) Could either Oman or Sneed force Burke into involuntary bankruptcy? Explain.

30–2. QUESTION WITH SAMPLE ANSWER: Preferences.

 Peaslee is not known for his business sense. He started a greenhouse and nursery business two years ago, and because of his lack of

experience, he soon was in debt to a number of creditors. On February 1, Peaslee borrowed $5,000 from his father to pay some of these creditors. On May 1, Peaslee paid back the $5,000, depleting his working capital. One creditor, the Cool Springs Nursery Supply Corp., had extended credit to Peaslee on numerous purchases. Cool Springs pressured Peaslee for payment, and on July 1, Peaslee paid Cool Springs half the amount owed. On September 1, Peaslee voluntarily petitioned himself into bankruptcy. The trustee in bankruptcy claims that both Peaslee's father and Cool Springs must turn over to the debtor's estate the amounts Peaslee paid to them. Discuss fully the trustee's claims.

• **For a sample answer to Question 30–2, go to Appendix I at the end of this text.**

30–3. Distribution of Property Montoro petitioned himself into voluntary bankruptcy. There were three major claims against his estate. One was made by Carlton, a friend who held Montoro's negotiable promissory note for $2,500; one was made by Elmer, an employee who was owed three months' back wages of $4,500; and one was made by the United Bank of the Rockies on an unsecured loan of $5,000. In addition, Dietrich, an accountant retained by the trustee, was owed $500, and property taxes of $1,000 were owed to Rock County. Montoro's nonexempt property was liquidated, with proceeds of $5,000. Discuss fully what amount each party will receive, and why.

30–4. Exceptions to Discharge Between 1988 and 1992, Lorna Nys took out thirteen student loans, totaling about $30,000, to finance an associate of arts degree in drafting from the College of the Redwoods and a bachelor of arts degree from Humboldt State University (HSU) in California. In 1996, Nys began working at HSU as a drafting technician. As a "Drafter II," the highest-paying drafting position at HSU, Nys's gross income in 2002 was $40,244. She was fifty-one years old. Her net monthly income was $2,299.33, and she had $2,295.05 in monthly expenses, including saving $140 for her retirement, which she planned for age sixty-five. When Educational Credit Management Corp. (ECMC) began to collect payments on Nys's student loans, she filed a Chapter 7 petition in a federal bankruptcy court, seeking a discharge of the loans. ECMC argued that Nys did not show any "additional circumstances" that would impede her ability to repay. What is the standard for the discharge of student loans under Chapter 7? Does Nys meet that standard? Why or why not? [*In re Nys*, 446 F.3d 938 (9th Cir. 2006)]

30–5. Substantial Abuse James Stout, a professor of economics and business at Cornell College in Iowa City, Iowa, filed a petition in bankruptcy under Chapter 7, seeking to discharge about $95,000 in credit-card debts. At the time, Stout had been divorced for ten years and had custody of his children: Z. S., who attended college, and G. S., who was twelve years old. Stout's ex-wife did not contribute child support. According to Stout, G. S. was an "elite" ice-skater who practiced twenty hours a week and had placed between first and third at more than forty competitive events. He had decided to home school G. S., whose academic achievements were average for her grade level despite her frequent absences from public school. His petition showed monthly income of $4,227 and expenses of $4,806. The expenses included annual home school costs of $8,400 and annual skating expenses of $6,000. They did not include Z. S.'s college costs, such as airfare for his upcoming studies in Europe, and other items. The trustee allowed monthly expenses of $3,227—with nothing for skating—and asked the court to dismiss the petition. Can the court grant this request? Should it? If so, what might it encourage Stout to do? Explain. [*In re Stout*, 336 Bankr. 138 (N.D. Iowa 2006)]

30–6. CASE PROBLEM WITH SAMPLE ANSWER: Discharge in Bankruptcy.

Rhonda Schroeder married Gennady Shvartsshteyn (Gene) in 1997. Gene worked at Royal Courier and Air Domestic Connect in Illinois, where Melissa Winyard also worked in 1999 and 2000.

During this time, Gene and Winyard had an affair. A year after leaving Royal, Winyard filed a petition in a federal bankruptcy court under Chapter 7 and was granted a discharge of her debts. Sometime later, in a letter to Schroeder who had learned of the affair, Winyard wrote, "I never intentionally wanted any of this to happen. I never wanted to disrupt your marriage." Schroeder obtained a divorce and, in 2005, filed a suit in an Illinois state court against Winyard, alleging "alienation of affection." Schroeder claimed that there had been "mutual love and affection" in her marriage until Winyard engaged in conduct intended to alienate her husband's affection. Schroeder charged that Winyard "caused him to have sexual intercourse with her," resulting in "the destruction of the marital relationship." Winyard filed a motion for summary judgment on the ground that any liability on her part had been discharged in her bankruptcy. Is there an exception to discharge for "willful and malicious conduct"? If so, does Schroeder's claim qualify? Discuss. [Schroeder v. Winyard, 375 Ill.App.3d 358, 873 N.E.2d 35, 313 Ill.Dec. 740 (2 Dist. 2007)]

- To view a sample answer for Problem 30–6, go to this book's Web site at **www.cengage.com/blaw/clarkson**, select "Chapter 30," and click on "Case Problem with Sample Answer."

30–7. Discharge in Bankruptcy Cathy Coleman took out loans to complete her college education. After graduation, Coleman was irregularly employed as a teacher before filing a petition in a federal bankruptcy court under Chapter 13. The court confirmed a five-year plan under which Coleman was required to commit all of her disposable income to paying the student loans. Less than a year later, she was laid off. Still owing more than $100,000 to Educational Credit Management Corp., Coleman asked the court to discharge the debt on the ground that it would be undue hardship for her to pay it. Under Chapter 13, when is a debtor normally entitled to a discharge? Are student loans dischargeable? If not, is "undue hardship" a legitimate ground for an exception? With respect to a debtor, what is the goal of bankruptcy? With these facts and principles in mind, what argument could be made in support of Coleman's request? [*In re Coleman*, 560 F.3d 1000 (9th Cir. 2009)]

30–8. Discharge in Bankruptcy Caroline McAfee loaned $400,000 to Carter Oaks Crossing. Joseph Harman, president of Carter Oaks Crossing, signed a promissory note providing that the company would repay the amount with interest in installments beginning in 1999 and ending by 2006. Harman signed a personal guaranty for the note. Carter Oaks Crossing defaulted on the note, so McAfee sued Harman for payment under the guaranty. Harman moved for summary judgment on the ground that McAfee's claim against him had been discharged in his Chapter 7 bankruptcy case, filed after 1999 but before the default on the note. The guaranty was not listed among Harman's debts in the bankruptcy filing. Would the obligation under the guaranty have been discharged in bankruptcy, as Harman claimed? Why or why not? [*Harman v. McAfee*, 302 Ga.App. 698, 691 S.E.2d 586 (2010)]

30–9. A QUESTION OF ETHICS: Discharge in Bankruptcy.

In October 1994, Charles Edwards formed ETS Payphones, Inc., to sell and lease pay phones as investment opportunities—an investor would buy a phone from ETS, which would lease it back. ETS promised returns of 14 to 15 percent but consistently lost money. To meet its obligations to existing investors, ETS had to continually attract new investors. Eventually, ETS defrauded thousands of investors of more than $300 million. Edwards transferred the funds from ETS to himself. In 2000, ETS filed a petition in a federal bankruptcy court to declare bankruptcy. Darryl Laddin was appointed trustee. On the debtor's behalf, Laddin filed a suit against Reliance Trust Co. and others, alleging, among other things, that the defendants helped defraud investors by "ignoring the facts" and "funneling" the investors' funds to ETS, causing it to "incur millions of dollars in additional debt." Laddin sought treble (triple) damages. [Official Committee of Unsecured Creditors of PSA, Inc. v. Edwards, *437 F.3d 1145 (11th Cir. 2006)]*

(a) The defendants argued, in part, that the doctrine of *in pari delicto,* which provides that a wrongdoer may not profit from his or her wrongful acts, barred Laddin's claim. Who should be considered ethically responsible for the investors' losses? Explain.

(b) Laddin contended that his actions, as trustee on behalf of the debtor, should not be subject to the doctrine of *in pari delicto* because that doctrine depends on the "personal malfeasance of the individual seeking to recover." The defendants filed a motion to dismiss Laddin's complaint. Do you think that the court should rule in favor of Laddin or the defendants? Why?

30–10. VIDEO QUESTION: Bankruptcy.

Go to this text's Web site at **www.cengage.com/ blaw/clarkson** and select "Chapter 30." Click on "Video Questions" and view the video titled *Field of Dreams.* Then answer the following questions.

(a) Before this scene, the movie makes clear that Ray (Kevin Costner) is unable to pay his bills, but he has not filed a voluntary petition for bankruptcy. What would be required for Ray's creditors to force him into an involuntary bankruptcy?

(b) If Ray did file a voluntary petition for a Chapter 7 bankruptcy, what exemptions might protect him from "losing everything" and being evicted as the man indicated in this scene? How much equity in the farm home could Ray claim as exempt if he filed the petition?

(c) What are the requirements for Ray to qualify as a family farmer under Chapter 12 of the Bankruptcy Code?

(d) How would the results of a Chapter 12 bankruptcy differ from those of a Chapter 7 bankruptcy for Ray?

LEGAL RESEARCH EXERCISES ON THE WEB

Go to this text's Web site at **www.cengage.com/blaw/clarkson**, select "Chapter 30," and click on "Practical Internet Exercises." There you will find the following Internet research exercises that you can perform to learn more about the topics covered in this chapter.

Practical Internet Exercise 30–1:   Legal Perspective
Bankruptcy

Practical Internet Exercise 30–2:   Management Perspective
Bankruptcy Alternatives

CHAPTER 31

Mortgages and Foreclosures after the Recession

During the early years of the twenty-first century, the United States experienced one of the biggest real estate bubbles in its history as prices of homes in many areas increased at unprecedented rates. The bubble started to shrink in 2006 and was still deflating in 2011. As a result of the collapse of the housing market and the financial crisis that accompanied it, the United States and much of the rest of the world suffered through what is now called the Great Recession. Although the recession may be over by the time you read this, the real estate market is still in turmoil in countless areas. Many people have lost their homes to foreclosure because they could not make the payments; others can afford the payments but choose not to because they owe more on the properties than those properties are worth.

This chapter examines the rights and obligations that apply to homeowners and their lenders. The chapter begins with a discussion of *mortgages*—the loans that lenders provide to enable borrowers to purchase real property (*real property* will be discussed in Chapter 50). Next, we examine the laws that protect borrowers when they obtain mortgages. The chapter concludes with a discussion of the options that lenders and homeowners have when the homeowners cannot continue to make their mortgage payments.

SECTION 1
MORTGAGES

When individuals purchase real property, they typically borrow funds from a financial institution for part or all of the purchase price. A **mortgage** is a written instrument that gives the creditor (the *mortgagee*) an interest in, or lien on, the property being acquired by the debtor (the *mortgagor*) as security for the debt's payment. Here, we look first at the different types of mortgages, including some new varieties that helped to inflate the housing bubble. Then we consider some of the ways that creditors protect their interest in the property and examine some of the most important provisions in a typical mortgage document.

Types of Mortgages

Mortgage loans are contracts, and as such, they come in a variety of forms. Lenders offer various types of mortgages to meet the needs of different borrowers. In recent decades, the expansion of home ownership became a political goal, and lenders were encouraged to become more creative in devising new types of mortgages. In many instances, these new mortgages were aimed at borrowers who could not qualify for traditional mortgages and lacked the funds to make a **down payment** (the part of the purchase price that is paid up front in cash).

In general, these mortgages, which include some adjustable-rate mortgages, interest-only mortgages, and balloon mortgages, feature a low initial interest rate. Often, the borrower hopes to refinance—pay off the original mortgage and obtain a new one at more favorable terms—within a few years. When the housing bubble burst and house prices began to decline, however, refinancing became more difficult than many borrowers had anticipated.

FIXED-RATE MORTGAGES *Fixed-rate mortgages* are the simplest mortgage loans. A **fixed-rate mortgage** is a standard mortgage with a fixed, or unchanging, rate of interest. Payments on the loan remain the same for the duration of the mortgage, which ranges from fifteen to forty years. Lenders determine the interest rate based on a variety of factors, including the borrower's credit history, credit score, income, and debts. Today, for a borrower to qualify for a standard fixed-rate mortgage loan, lenders typically require that the monthly mortgage payment (including principal, interest, taxes, and insurance) not exceed 28 percent of the person's gross income.

ADJUSTABLE-RATE MORTGAGES The rate of interest paid by the borrower changes periodically with an **adjustable-rate mortgage (ARM).** Typically, the initial interest rate for an ARM is set at a relatively low fixed rate for a specified period, such as a year or three years. After that time, the interest rate adjusts annually or by some other period, such as biannually or monthly. ARMs generally are described in terms of the initial fixed period and the adjustment period. For example, if the interest rate is fixed for three years and then adjusts annually, the mortgage is called a 3/1 ARM; if the rate adjusts annually after five years, the mortgage is a 5/1 ARM.

The interest rate adjustment is calculated by adding a certain number of percentage points (called the margin) to an index rate (one of various government interest rates). The margin and index rate are specified in the mortgage loan documents. For example, Greta and Marcus obtain a 3/1 ARM to purchase a home. After three years, when the first adjustment is to be made, the index rate is 6 percent. If the margin specified in the loan documents is 3 percentage points, the fully indexed interest rate for the ARM would be 9 percent. Most ARMs, however, have lifetime interest rate caps that limit the amount that the rate can rise over the duration of the loan.

Some ARMs also have caps that stipulate the maximum increase that can occur at any particular adjustment period. In the Greta and Marcus example above, if the initial interest rate was 5 percent and the loan stipulated that the rate could rise no more than 3 percentage points in one adjustment period, the interest rate after three years would increase to 8 percent, not 9 percent, because of the cap. Note that the interest rate could be adjusted downward as well as upward; if the index rate was 1 percent, the adjusted rate would potentially fall to 4 percent, although some ARMs also limit the amount that the rate can fall.

INTEREST-ONLY (IO) MORTGAGES With an **interest-only (IO) mortgage,** the borrower can choose to pay only the interest portion of the monthly payments and forgo paying any of the principal for a specified period of time. (IO loans can be for fixed-rate or adjustable-rate mortgages.) This IO payment usually is available for three to ten years. After the IO payment option is exhausted, the borrower's payment increases to include payments on the principal.

SUBPRIME MORTGAGES During the late 1990s and the first decade of the 2000s, *subprime lending* increased significantly. A **subprime mortgage** is a loan made to a borrower who does not qualify for a standard mortgage. Often, such borrowers have poor credit scores or high current *debt-to-income ratios*—that is, the total amount owed as a percentage of current after-tax income. Subprime mortgages are riskier than traditional mortgages and have a higher default rate. Consequently, lenders charge a higher interest rate for subprime loans. Subprime mortgages can be fixed-rate, adjustable-rate, or IO loans. Subprime lending allows many people who could not otherwise purchase real property to do so, but at a higher risk to the lender.

CONSTRUCTION LOANS A **construction loan** is similar to a mortgage in many ways—for example, this type of loan comes in all varieties, including fixed-rate and adjustable-rate loans. Rather than purchasing an existing home, the borrower uses the funds from a construction loan to build a new home. Construction loans are often set up with a schedule of "draws." For example, Joel and Jennie borrow funds to purchase real estate and build a home. The first draw of funds pays for the land. Subsequent draws occur when the foundation is laid, when the framing for the structure is finished, when the exterior is completed, and finally when the interior is completed and the contractor turns the house over to the couple for occupancy.

PARTICIPATION LOANS In some instances, a lender may be interested in receiving more than standard principal and interest payments for a loan. In exchange for more desirable loan terms (for example, lower interest rates or lower down payment requirements), a borrower may agree to give the lender some equity (ownership) rights in a purchase. Such a loan agreement, called a **participation loan** (also referred to as an *equity participation loan*), typically gives the lender a right to receive a percentage of revenue, rental income, or resale income from the property.

BALLOON MORTGAGES Similar to an ARM, a **balloon mortgage** starts with low payments for a specified period, usually seven to ten years. At the end of that period, a large balloon payment for the entire balance of the mortgage loan is due. Because the balloon payment is often very large, many borrowers refinance when this payment is due. A potential disadvantage is that the lender will set the interest rate of the refinanced loan at whatever the market dictates at that time. As a result, the payments may be higher than they would have been if the buyer had initially obtained a fixed-rate mortgage instead of a balloon mortgage.

HYBRID AND REVERSE MORTGAGES A variety of other less common mortgages are also available. One example is a **hybrid mortgage** (also called a *two-step mortgage*), which starts as a fixed-rate mortgage and then converts into an ARM.

With a **reverse mortgage,** instead of borrowing funds from a bank to buy a home, existing homeowners take cash for the equity in their home. The mortgage does not need to be repaid until the home is sold or the owner dies. Reverse mortgages are geared toward older borrowers (over the age of sixty-two) who have substantial equity in their homes. By converting a portion of that equity into cash, the homeowners can supplement their retirement income.

Home Equity Loans

Home equity refers to the portion of a home's value that is "paid off." For example, if Susanna has a home valued at $200,000 and owes the bank $120,000 on her mortgage, she has 40 percent equity in her house ($80,000/$200,000 = 40 percent). With a **home equity loan,** a bank accepts the borrower's equity as *collateral,* which can be seized if the loan is not repaid on time. If Susanna takes out a $30,000 home equity loan, the amount is added to the amount of her mortgage ($30,000 + $120,000 = $150,000), so she now has only $50,000 (25 percent) equity in her $200,000 home.

Borrowers often take out home equity loans to obtain funds to renovate the property itself. Others obtain home equity loans to pay off debt, such as credit-card debt, that carries a higher interest rate than they will pay on the home equity loan. This strategy can lead to problems, however, if the borrower cannot keep up the payments. Many Americans who lost their homes during the Great Recession were able to pay their original mortgage loans, but not their home equity loans. From the lender's perspective, a home equity loan is riskier than a mortgage loan because home equity loans are *subordinated,* which means that they take a lower priority in any proceeding that occurs if the homeowner fails to make the payments on the primary mortgage.

Creditor Protection

When creditors grant mortgages, they are advancing a significant amount of funds for a number of years. Consequently, creditors take a number of steps to protect their interest. One precaution is to require debtors to obtain private mortgage insurance if they do not make a down payment of at least 20 percent of the purchase price. For example, if a borrower makes a down payment of only 5 percent of the purchase price, the creditor might require insurance covering 15 percent of the cost. Then, if the debtor defaults, the creditor repossesses the house and receives reimbursement from the insurer for the covered portion of the loan.

In addition, the creditor will record the mortgage with the appropriate office in the county where the property is located. Recording ensures that the creditor is officially on record as holding an interest in the property. In essence, recording a mortgage perfects the lender's security interest in the property (see page 559 in Chapter 29). A lender that fails to record a mortgage could find itself in the position of an unsecured creditor.

Mortgages normally are lengthy documents that include a number of provisions. Many of these provisions are aimed at protecting the creditor's investment.

STATUTE OF FRAUDS Because a mortgage involves a transfer of real property, it must be in writing to comply with the Statute of Frauds (see page 290 in Chapter 15). Most mortgages today are highly formal documents that follow similar formats, but a mortgage is not required to follow any particular form. Indeed, as long as the mortgage satisfies the Statute of Frauds, it generally will be effective.

IMPORTANT MORTGAGE PROVISIONS Mortgage documents ordinarily contain all or most of the following terms:

1. *The terms of the underlying loan.* These include the loan amount, the interest rate, the period of repayment, and other important financial terms, such as the margin and index rate for an ARM. Many lenders include a **prepayment penalty clause,** which requires the borrower to pay a penalty if the mortgage is repaid in full within a certain period. A prepayment penalty helps to protect the lender should the borrower refinance within a short time after obtaining a mortgage.

2. *Provisions relating to the maintenance of the property.* Because the mortgage conveys an interest in the property to the lender, the lender will require the

borrower to maintain the property in such a way that the lender's investment is protected.

3. *A statement obligating the borrower to maintain* **homeowners' insurance** (*also known as* hazard insurance) *on the property.* This type of insurance protects the lender's interest in the event of a loss due to certain hazards, such as fire or storm damages.

4. *A list of the nonloan financial obligations to be borne by the borrower.* For example, the borrower typically is required to pay all property taxes, assessments, and other claims against the property.

5. *A provision requiring that the borrower pay certain obligations.* For example, a borrower may be required to pay some or all of the taxes, insurance, assessments, or other expenses associated with the property in advance or through the lender. In this way, the lender is assured that the funds for these expenses will be available when the bills come due.

Although a record number of homeowners have failed to keep up with their mortgage payments in recent years, courts have continued to enforce the terms of plainly written financing documents. Even in today's more protective environment, borrowers cannot avoid the clear meaning of terms in financing documents, even when the effect may be harsh.

SECTION 2
REAL ESTATE FINANCING LAW

During the real estate boom in the first decade of the 2000s, some lenders were less than honest with borrowers about the loan terms they were signing. As a result, many individuals failed to understand how much the monthly payments on ARMs, interest-only mortgages, and other exotic types of loans might increase. In addition, fees and penalties often were not properly disclosed. In an effort to provide more protection for borrowers, Congress and the Federal Reserve Board have instituted a number of new requirements, mostly in the form of required disclosures. Here, we examine some of the most important statutes that provide protection for borrowers. First, though, we look at some of the practices that led to the enactment of these statutes.

Predatory Lending and Other Improper Practices

The general term *predatory lending* is often used to describe situations in which borrowers are the victims of loan terms or lending procedures that are excessive, deceptive, or not properly disclosed. Predatory lending typically occurs during the loan origination process. It includes a number of practices ranging from failure to disclose terms to providing misleading information to outright dishonesty.

Two specific types of improper practices are often at the core of a violation. *Steering and targeting* occurs when the lender manipulates a borrower into accepting a loan product that benefits the lender but is not the best loan for the borrower. For example, a lender may steer a borrower toward an ARM, even though the buyer qualifies for a fixed-rate mortgage. *Loan flipping* occurs when a lender convinces a homeowner to refinance soon after obtaining a mortgage. Such early refinancing rarely benefits the homeowner and may, in fact, result in prepayment penalties.

The Truth-in-Lending Act (TILA)

The Truth-in-Lending Act (TILA) of 1968[1] requires lenders to disclose the terms of a loan in clear, readily understandable language so that borrowers can make rational choices. (We will discuss the TILA in more detail in Chapter 45 in the context of consumer law.) With respect to real estate transactions, the TILA applies only to residential loans.

REQUIRED DISCLOSURES The major terms that must be disclosed under the TILA include the loan principal; the interest rate at which the loan is made; the **annual percentage rate,** or **APR** (the actual cost of the loan on a yearly basis); and all fees and costs associated with the loan. The TILA requires that these disclosures be made on standardized forms and based on uniform formulas of calculation. Certain types of loans—including ARMs, reverse mortgages, open-ended home equity loans, and high-interest loans—have specially tailored disclosure requirements. The Mortgage Disclosure Improvement Act (MDIA) of 2008[2] amended the TILA to strengthen the disclosures required for ARMs, which, as mentioned earlier, played a leading role in the recent real estate meltdown.

---

1. 15 U.S.C. Sections 1601–1693r.
2. The Mortgage Disclosure Improvement Act is contained in Sections 2501 through 2503 of the Housing and Economic Recovery Act of 2008, Pub. L. No. 110-289, enacted on July 30, 2008. Congress then amended its provisions as part of the Emergency Economic Stabilization Act of 2008 (also known as the Bailout Bill), Pub. L. No. 110-343, enacted on October 3, 2008.

PROHIBITIONS AND REQUIREMENTS The TILA prohibits certain lender abuses and creates certain borrower rights. Among the prohibited practices is the charging of prepayment penalties on most subprime mortgages and home equity loans.

The TILA also addresses other unfair, abusive, or deceptive home mortgage–lending practices. For example, lenders may not coerce an **appraiser** (an individual who specializes in determining the value of specified real or personal property) into misstating the value of a property on which a loan is to be issued. Also, a loan cannot be advertised as a fixed-rate loan if, in fact, its rate or payment amounts will change.

Right to Rescind. A mortgage cannot be finalized until at least seven days after a borrower has received the TILA paperwork. Even if all required disclosures are provided, the TILA gives the borrower the right to rescind (cancel) a mortgage within three business days. According to the 2008 amendments, Sunday is the only day of the week that is not a business day. If the lender fails to provide material TILA disclosures, including the three-day right to rescind, the rescission period lasts up to three years.

Written Representations. The TILA requirements apply to the written materials the lender provides, not to any oral representations. If a lender provides the required TILA disclosures, a borrower who fails to read the relevant documents cannot claim fraud, even if the lender orally misrepresented the terms of the loan.

CASE IN POINT Patricia Ostolaza and José Diaz owned a home on which they had two mortgage loans and a home equity line of credit provided by Bank of America. Anthony Falcone called them and said that he could refinance their mortgages in a manner that would reduce their monthly payments. Falcone said that he represented Bank of America when in fact he represented Countrywide Home Loans, Inc. At the closing of the new loan, the homeowners were given all of the relevant documents, including the TILA disclosure statement. The documents accurately stated the monthly payment under the new loan, which was higher than the couple's original payments. The homeowners later filed a lawsuit against Falcone and Countrywide Bank, alleging fraud. The trial court dismissed the suit, and the appellate court upheld the dismissal because the homeowners had been given the opportunity to read all of the relevant documents, but had not done so.[3]

---

3. *Ostolaza-Diaz v. Countrywide Bank, N.A.,* 2010 WL 95145 (4th Cir. 2010).

Protection for High-Cost Mortgage Loan Recipients

In the last twenty years, lenders have provided many high-cost and high-fee mortgage products to people who could not easily obtain credit under other loan programs. These loans are commonly known as HOEPA loans, named after the Home Ownership and Equity Protection Act (HOEPA) of 1994,[4] which amended the TILA to create this special category of loans. The rules pertaining to HOEPA loans are contained in Section 32 of *Regulation Z,* enacted by the Federal Reserve Board to implement the TILA (see Chapter 45).

A loan can qualify for protection under HOEPA either because it carries a high rate of interest or because it entails high fees for the borrower. HOEPA applies if the APR disclosed for the loan exceeds the interest rates of **Treasury securities** (or bonds) of comparable maturity by more than 8 percentage points for a first mortgage and 10 percentage points for a second mortgage. HOEPA can also apply when the total fees paid by the consumer exceed 8 percent of the loan amount or a set dollar amount (based on changes in the consumer price index), whichever is larger.

SPECIAL CONSUMER PROTECTIONS If a loan qualifies for HOEPA protection, the consumer must receive several disclosures in addition to those required by the TILA. The lender must disclose the APR, the regular payment amount, and any required balloon payments. For loans with a variable rate of interest, the lender must disclose that the rate and monthly payments may increase and state the potential maximum monthly payment. These disclosures must be provided at least three business days before the loan is finalized.

In addition, the lender must provide a written notice stating that the consumer need not complete the loan simply because he or she received the disclosures or signed the loan application. Borrowers must also be informed that they could lose their home (and all funds invested in it) if they default on the loan.

HOEPA also prohibits lenders from engaging in certain practices, such as requiring balloon payments for loans with terms of five years or less. Loans that result in negative amortization are also prohibited. **Negative amortization** occurs when the monthly payments are insufficient to cover the interest due on the loan. The difference is then

---

4. 15 U.S.C. Sections 1637 and 1647.

added to the principal, so the balance owed on the loan increases over time.

HOEPA also provides the borrower with protection when the original lender assigns the mortgage to a third party. For most purposes, HOEPA eliminates the status of holder in due course and its accompanying defenses (see Chapter 25) for a **mortgage assignee.** To encourage an assignee to scrutinize an assigned loan carefully, the assignee is subject to all claims and defenses that the borrower could have asserted against the original lender.

REMEDIES AND LIABILITIES For HOEPA violations, consumers can obtain damages in an amount equal to all finance charges and fees paid if the lender's failure to disclose is deemed material. Any failure to comply with HOEPA provisions also extends the borrower's right to rescind the loan for up to three years.

Whether a particular loan is covered by HOEPA and thus is entitled to the statute's significant protections can have important ramifications because it can determine whether a lender can foreclose on a loan. In the following case, a consumer challenged the foreclosure of her home by claiming that the bank had not met all of the requirements under HOEPA.

CASE 31.1
Bank of New York v. Parnell

Court of Appeal of Louisiana, Fifth Circuit, 32 So.3d 877 (2010).
www.fifthcircuit.org/Opinions.aspx[a]

BACKGROUND AND FACTS • Kathleen Parnell executed a promissory note and mortgage in favor of EquiCredit Corporation of America on May 9, 2001. Later that year, EquiCredit assigned its rights to the Bank of New York. On June 19, 2003, Parnell's attorney wrote a letter to the Bank of New York on behalf of Parnell providing a notice of rescission. The letter stated that rescission was proper because the loan was governed by the Home Ownership and Equity Protection Act (HOEPA) and that EquiCredit had failed to deliver required material disclosures. These disclosures included documents stating that Parnell did not need to enter into the loan and that she could lose her home as a result of entering into the loan. The bank responded that the loan was not large enough to trigger HOEPA disclosures but that, in any event, Parnell had received full and accurate disclosures. Later, the bank filed a petition alleging that Parnell was in default and that it was accelerating the payments due under the mortgage. Subsequently, the trial judge directed the sheriff to seize and sell the property secured by the mortgage. Parnell filed a petition to stop the seizure and sale. The bank filed a motion for summary judgment in its favor, which the court granted. Parnell appealed.

IN THE LANGUAGE OF THE COURT
Fredericka Homberg *WICKER,* Judge.
* * * *

Congress enacted the Truth in Lending Act to assure a meaningful disclosure of credit terms so that the consumer will be able to compare more readily the various credit terms available to him and avoid the uninformed use of credit, and to protect the consumer against inaccurate and unfair credit billing and credit card practices. Accordingly, *the Act requires creditors to provide borrowers with clear and accurate disclosures of terms dealing with things like finance charges, annual percentage rates of interest, and the borrower's rights. A creditor's failure to comply with these disclosure requirements may result in actual and statutory damages.* Additionally, if a creditor fails to provide a consumer with material disclosures when the loan is secured by the consumer's "principal dwelling," the consumer has "the right to rescind the transaction until midnight of the third business day following the consummation of the transaction or the delivery of the information and rescission forms required * * * whichever is later." If the required material disclosures are not delivered, the rescission period expires "three years after the date

---

a. Select "Search by Case Number" in the list of options. When that page opens, enter "09" and "439" in the two boxes for the case number. When the case title appears in the box below, click on the Adobe Reader icon to view the case. The Louisiana court system maintains this Web site.

CASE 31.1 CONTINUED ➡ of consummation [completion] of the transaction or upon the sale of the property, whichever occurs first." [Emphasis added.]

The Truth in Lending Act as amended by HOEPA and Regulation Z of the Federal Reserve Board provides that when a consumer loan violates the Act, the consumer is entitled to rescind the loan, to recover monies and other property given to the creditor, and to [cancel] any mortgages made in connection with the loan.

* * * *

TILA was enacted in 1968 to aid the unsophisticated consumer so that he would not be easily misled as to the total costs of financing. Consequently, it is not surprising that courts have held that TILA, as a remedial statute which is designed to balance the scales, [and] "thought to be weighed in favor of lenders," is to be liberally construed in favor of borrowers. Nonetheless, finding that TILA's protections were still inadequate, Congress added the protections and requirements of the Home Ownership and Equity Protection Act ("HOEPA") in 1994. HOEPA was designed to address the problem of "reverse redlining," that is, the targeting of persons for "credit on unfair terms" based on their income, race, or ethnicity. In an attempt to even the playing field, Congress enacted HOEPA to ensure that consumers understand the terms of such loans and are protected from high pressure sales tactics[.] * * * The legislation requires creditors making High Cost Mortgages to provide a special, streamlined High Cost Mortgage disclosure three days before consummation of the transaction. The bill also prohibits High Cost Mortgages from including certain terms such as prepayment penalties and balloon payments that have proven particularly problematic.

Accordingly, we find that the trial judge erred in granting summary judgment insofar as the HOEPA claim.

DECISION AND REMEDY • *The appellate court overturned the lower court's grant of summary judgment and sent the case back to the lower court for a full trial on the issue.*

THE LEGAL ENVIRONMENT DIMENSION • *The Truth-in-Lending Act, HOEPA, and other consumer protection laws exist to protect purchasers from unscrupulous lenders or sellers. As consumers become better informed about these issues, will these laws still be needed? Discuss.*

WHAT IF THE FACTS WERE DIFFERENT? • *If the lender had been dealing with a borrower who was a professor of finance at Harvard, would the appellate judge have ruled the same way? Why or why not?*

Protection for Higher-Priced Mortgage Loans

In 2008, the Federal Reserve Board enacted an amendment to Regulation Z that created a second category of expensive loans, called Higher-Priced Mortgage Loans (HPMLs). Only mortgages secured by a consumer's principal home qualify to receive the HPML designation.

REQUIREMENTS TO QUALIFY To be an HPML, a mortgage must have an APR that exceeds the *average prime offer rate* for a comparable transaction by 1.5 percentage points or more if the loan is a first lien on a dwelling. (The **average prime offer rate** is the rate offered to the best-qualified borrowers as established by a survey of lenders.) If the loan is secured by a subordinate lien on a home, then the APR must exceed the average prime offer rate by 3.5 percentage points or more in order to be considered an HPML.

Mortgages excluded from coverage include those for the initial construction of a home, temporary or *bridge loans* that are one year or shorter in duration, home equity lines of credit, and reverse mortgages. (**Bridge loans** are short-term loans that allow a buyer to make a down payment on a new home before selling her or his current home.)

SPECIAL PROTECTIONS FOR CONSUMERS As with a HOEPA loan, consumers receiving an HPML receive additional protections. First, lenders cannot make an HPML based on the value of the consumer's home without verifying the consumer's ability to repay the loan. This verification is typically accomplished through review of the consumer's financial records such as tax returns, bank account statements, and payroll records. The creditor must also verify the consumer's other credit obligations.

Second, prepayment penalties are severely restricted for HPMLs. Prepayment penalties are allowed only if they are limited to two years, and they will not even apply if the source of the pre-payment funds is a refinancing by the creditor or the creditor's affiliate. Additionally, lenders must establish *escrow accounts* for borrowers' payments for homeowners' insurance and property taxes for all first mortgages. (An escrow account holds funds to be paid to a third party—see Chapter 50). Finally, lenders cannot structure a loan specifically to evade the HPML protections.

SECTION 3
FORECLOSURES

If a homeowner **defaults,** or fails to make mortgage payments, the lender has the right to foreclose on the mortgaged property. **Foreclosure** is a process that allows a lender to legally repossess and auction off the property that is securing a loan.[5] Foreclosure is expensive and time consuming, however, and generally benefits neither the borrowers, who lose their homes, nor the lenders, which face the prospect of losses on their loans. Therefore, various methods to avoid foreclosure have been developed. We look first at some of these methods and then turn to the fore-closure process itself.

How to Avoid Foreclosure

In the past, especially during the Great Depression of the 1930s, a number of alternatives to foreclosure have been developed. More recently, as foreclosures have become more common than at any time since the Great Depression, Congress has intervened to aid in the modification of mortgage loans.

FORBEARANCE AND WORKOUT AGREEMENTS The first preforeclosure option a borrower has is called forbearance. **Forbearance** is the postponement, for a limited time, of part or all of the payments on a loan in jeopardy of foreclosure. Such payment waivers had their origins in the Great Depression. A lender grants forbearance when it expects that, during the forbearance period, the borrower can solve the problem by securing a new job, selling the property, or finding another acceptable solution.

When a borrower fails to make payments as required, the lender may attempt to negotiate a workout. As noted in Chapter 30, a *workout* is a voluntary process to cure the default in some fashion. The parties may even create a formal **workout agreement**—a written document that describes the rights and responsibilities of the parties as they try to resolve the default without proceeding to fore-closure. In such an agreement, the lender will likely agree to delay seeking foreclosure or other legal rights. In exchange, the borrower may agree to provide financial information to the lender on which a workout might be constructed. Whether a workout is possible or preferable to foreclosure depends on many factors, including the value of the property, the amount of the unpaid principal, the market in which the property will be sold, the relationship of the lender and the borrower, and the financial condition of the borrower.

HOUSING AND URBAN DEVELOPMENT ASSISTANCE A lender may be able to work with the borrower to obtain an interest-free loan from the U.S. Department of Housing and Urban Development (HUD) to bring the mortgage current. HUD assistance may be available if the loan is at least four months (but not more than twelve months) delinquent, if the property is not in foreclosure, and if the borrower is able to make full mortgage payments. When the lender files a claim, HUD pays the lender the amount necessary to make the mortgage current. The borrower executes a note to HUD, and a lien for the second loan is placed on the property. The promissory note is interest free and comes due if the property is sold.

SHORT SALES When an owner is unable to make mortgage payments, a lender may agree to a **short sale**—that is, a sale of the property for less than the balance of the mortgage loan. Typically, the borrower has to show some hardship, such as the loss of job, a decline in the value of the home, a divorce, or a death in the household. In a short sale, the borrower sells the real property with the permission of the lender, often for an amount less than the balance due on the mortgage loan. The lender receives the proceeds of the sale, and the borrower still owes the balance of the debt to the lender, unless the lender specifically agrees to forgive the remaining debt. In 2007, Congress passed the Mortgage Forgiveness Debt Relief Act,[6] which eliminated income taxes on the forgiven debt. (Ordinarily, forgiven debt must be reported as income that is subject to federal income tax.)

A short sale can offer several advantages. Although the borrower's credit rating is affected, the

---

5. Lenders other than those holding a first mortgage on a property may also foreclose. For example, a roofing company holding a mechanic's lien for the unpaid cost of a new roof can foreclose on the property.

6. Pub. L. No. 110-142, December 7, 2007.

negative impact is less than it would be with a fore-closure, which generally remains on the borrower's credit report for seven years.[7] The short sale process also avoids the expense of foreclosure for the lender and the trauma of being evicted from the home for the homeowner. But because the lender often has approval rights in a short sale, the sale process can take much longer than a standard real estate trans-action. In addition, although the parties' losses are mitigated, the borrower still loses her or his home.

SALE AND LEASEBACK In some situations, the home-owner may be able to sell the property to an investor who is looking for an income property. The owner sells the property to the investor and then leases it back at an amount that is less than the monthly mortgage payment. The owner-seller uses the pro-ceeds of the sale to pay off the mortgage and still has the use and possession of the property. In some circumstances, this strategy can also be used to raise capital when there is no risk of loss of the property.

HOME AFFORDABLE MODIFICATION PROGRAM In 2009, the U.S. Treasury Department launched the Home Affordable Modification Program (HAMP) to encourage private lenders to modify mortgages so as to lower the monthly payments of borrowers who are in default. The program may share in the costs of modifying the loan and provides incentives to lend-ers based on successful loan modification. A series of steps must be taken to determine debtor eligibility, the appropriate method for reducing the mortgage burden, and the possibility of forbearance of part of the mortgage loan.

Determination If a Homeowner Qualifies.
HAMP modifications are not available for every mort-gage. To qualify, the loan must have originated on or before January 1, 2009, the home must be occu-pied by the owner, and the unpaid balance may not exceed $729,750 for a single-unit property.[8] The homeowner must be facing financial hardship and be either more than sixty days late on mortgage pay-ments or at risk of imminent default. Homeowners are required to verify their hardship through appro-priate documentation.

In addition, the home must be the homeowner's primary residence. Investor-owned homes, vacant homes, and condemned properties are not eligible under the program. Borrowers in active litigation

related to their mortgage may take advantage of the program without waiving their legal rights.

Steps Taken to Alleviate the Mortgage Burden.
The purpose of HAMP is not to force lenders to for-give all high-risk mortgages, but rather to reduce monthly mortgage payments to a level that the homeowner can reasonably pay. The goal is to reduce the debtor's mortgage payment to 31 percent of his or her gross monthly income.

The loan is then restructured by adding any delinquencies (such as accrued interest, past-due taxes, or unpaid insurance premiums) to the princi-pal amount. This increases the number of payments but eliminates the delinquencies by spreading them over the life of the loan. Once the loan is restruc-tured, lenders try to incrementally lower the mort-gage interest rate to a level at which the payments are less than 31 percent of the debtor's income. If the lender cannot reach the 31 percent target by lower-ing the interest rate to 2 percent, then the lender can **reamortize** the loan (change the way the pay-ments are configured), extending the schedule of payments for up to forty years.

Borrowers who qualify under HAMP then begin a ninety-day trial period to determine their ability to make three modified monthly mortgage payments. If they succeed, the lender offers them permanent modifications.

VOLUNTARY CONVEYANCE Under some circum-stances, the parties might benefit from a **deed in lieu of foreclosure,** by which the property is con-veyed (transferred) to the lender in satisfaction of the mortgage. A property that is worth close to the outstanding loan principal and on which no other loans have been taken might be the subject of such a conveyance.

Although the lender faces the risk that it may ultimately sell the property for less than the loan amount, the lender avoids the time, risk, and expense of foreclosure litigation. The borrower who gives the property to the lender without a fight also avoids the foreclosure process and may preserve a better credit rating than if he or she had been forced to give up the property involuntarily.

FRIENDLY FORECLOSURE Another way for the par-ties to avoid a contested foreclosure is to engage in a friendly foreclosure. In such a transaction, the bor-rower in default agrees to submit to the court's juris-diction, to waive any defenses as well as the right to appeal, and to cooperate with the lender. This process takes longer than a voluntary conveyance,

---

7. Credit reporting agencies also claim that a foreclosure looks much worse on a credit report than a bankruptcy.
8. Higher limits are allowed for properties with two to four units.

but all of the parties have greater certainty as to the finality of the transaction with respect to others who might have a financial interest in the property.

PREPACKAGED BANKRUPTCY Bankruptcy allows a borrower to escape payment of some debts (see Chapter 30). A prepackaged bankruptcy allows a debtor to negotiate terms with all of her or his creditors in advance. The package of agreements is then submitted to the bankruptcy court for approval. This approach to bankruptcy will likely save considerable time and expense for all parties involved, although the creditors are also likely to receive less than full payment on their particular debts.

The Foreclosure Procedure

If all efforts to find another solution fail, the lender will proceed to foreclosure—a process that dates back to English law. A formal foreclosure is necessary to extinguish the borrower's *equitable right of redemption* (discussed later). Generally, two types of foreclosure are used in the United States: **judicial foreclosure** and **power of sale foreclosure.** In a judicial foreclosure, which is available in all states, a court supervises the process. In a power of sale foreclosure, the lender is allowed to foreclose on and sell the property without judicial supervision. Only a few states permit power of sale foreclosures because borrowers have less protection when a court does not supervise the process.

ACCELERATION CLAUSES In a strict foreclosure, the lender may seek only the amount of the missed payments, not the entire loan amount. Therefore, lenders almost always include an *acceleration clause* in their loan documents. An **acceleration clause** allows the lender to call the entire loan due—even if only one payment is late or missed. Thus, with an acceleration clause, the lender can foreclose only once on the entire amount of the loan rather than having to foreclosure on smaller amounts over a period of time as each payment is missed.

NOTICE OF DEFAULT AND OF SALE To initiate a foreclosure, a lender must record a **notice of default** with the appropriate county office. The borrower is then on notice of a possible foreclosure and can take steps to pay the loan and cure the default. If the loan is not paid within a reasonable time (usually three months), the borrower will receive a **notice of sale.** In addition, the notice of sale usually is posted on the property, recorded with the county, and announced in the newspaper.

The property is then sold in an auction on the courthouse steps at the time and location indicated in the notice of sale. The buyer generally has to pay cash within twenty-four hours for the property. If the procedures are not followed precisely, the parties may have to resort to litigation to establish clear ownership of the property. The following case illustrates how the notice requirements work.

☀ EXTENDED CASE 31.2 ☀
Mitchell v. Valteau

Court of Appeal of Louisiana, Fourth Circuit, 30 So.3d 1108 (2010).
www.la4th.org/Opinions.aspx[a]

IN THE LANGUAGE OF THE COURT
Patricia Rivet *MURRAY,* Judge.
* * * *
 On April 30, 2001, Dr. Mitchell borrowed $143,724 to purchase a house and the lot on which it was located * * * (the "Property"). [The loan] * * * was secured by a mortgage on

the Property. * * * The mortgage contained [a clause] providing for the acceleration of the amount secured and the sale of the property in the event of a default on the loan.
 In 2006, Dr. Mitchell defaulted on her mortgage payments. On December 15, 2006, [the lending bank] commenced an executory proceeding * * * . The trial court ordered the issuance of a writ of

seizure and sale.
 On January 23, 2007, Dr. Mitchell was served personally with the notice of seizure, which stated that a sheriff's sale was tentatively scheduled for November 2, 2007.
 Subsequently, * * * Dr. Mitchell and [the bank] entered into a [repayment agreement that postponed the seizure and sale of the property while the agreement was in place].

---

a. From the search mode choices, select "Search Cases by Published Date" and in the "Sort By" drop-down menu, select "Date Published." Then select "Click for Calendar." Using the arrow at the top of the calendar, go to January 2010, then click on "27." Scroll through the list at the bottom of the page to the case title and click on "Download" to access the opinion. The Louisiana court system maintains this Web site.

EXTENDED CASE 31.2 CONTINUED ➡

* * * Although Dr. Mitchell made a few (about two) payments, she was unable to comply with the payment terms of the repayment agreement.

On July 19, 2007, the trial court ordered that the original petition be amended and that an amended writ of seizure be issued. On September 7, 2007, the sheriff issued an amended notice of seizure. * * * The sheriff attempted to serve Dr. Mitchell at her residence on seven occasions. Because the sheriff was unable to serve Dr. Mitchell, [the court appointed a receiver who] accepted service on Dr. Mitchell's behalf.

On January 3, 2008, the Property was sold at a sheriff's sale * * *.

* * * *

On April 11, 2008, Dr. Mitchell filed a Petition to Annul Executory Proceedings and Judicial Sale, and for Damages for Wrongful Seizure [against Sheriff Paul Valteau, Jr., the lending bank, and others].

On November 18, 2008, [the bank] filed a motion for summary judgment. Following a hearing, the trial court granted the motion and rendered judgment dismissing all the parties. [Dr. Mitchell appealed.]

* * * *

A creditor seeking to enforce a mortgage or privilege on property by executory process must file a petition praying for the seizure and sale of the property affected by the mortgage or privilege. * * * In this case, [the bank] filed a petition for executor process and attached thereto authentic evidence

satisfying all three requirements for obtaining an order of seizure and sale: a copy of the note, mortgage agreement, and a certified copy of the assignment of the mortgage note to it. * * * It is undisputed that Dr. Mitchell was served with the initial notice of seizure. Dr. Mitchell, however, contends that the sheriff also was required to serve her with the amended notice of seizure from which her property was seized and sold. [Emphasis added.]

Resolution of the issue of whether service of the amended notice of seizure was required turns on construction of several * * * statutory provisions. La. C.C.P. Art. [Louisiana Code of Civil Procedure Article] 2721 provides that the sheriff must serve upon the defendant "a written notice of the seizure of the property. ["] La. C.C.P. Art. 2293(B) also provides that the sheriff shall serve "a notice of seizure."

* * * *

Construing La. R.S. [Louisiana Revised Statutes] 13:3852 and La. C.C.P. Art. 2293(B) * * * [a prior court] rejected a debtor's argument that she was entitled to a second notice of seizure when the first sale was delayed.

* * * [There,] the court * * * reasoned that the debtor had defaulted under the terms of the mortgage and that the creditor had validly exercised its right to have the property seized and sold in accord with the executor process provisions. * * * The court further reasoned that read together

La. C.C.P. Art 2293(B)—which requires service of "a written notice of seizure of the property"—and La. R.S. 13:3852—which requires [that] the notice include "the date of the first scheduled sale of the property"—mandate that "upon seizure of their property, a defendant receive a written notice that informs them of the first scheduled sale date." * * * The court still further reasoned that there was no Louisiana authority for requiring a creditor to provide a debtor with notice of a rescheduled judicial sale.

The situation in this case is analogous to the situation presented in the [referenced] case. Dr. Mitchell defaulted on her loan agreement and [the bank] established its right to proceed by executory process to seize and sell the Property. Dr. Mitchell was served with a notice of seizure. Thereafter, she entered into the repayment agreement, [which] expressly provided that the executor proceeding would be placed on hold for the time the repayment agreement was in place. The agreement also provided for the resumption of the foreclosure in the event of a default in its terms, which Dr. Mitchell acknowledged occurred. When the executory proceeding was resumed, there was no obligation to serve Dr. Mitchell with another notice of seizure.

* * * We thus find the trial court correctly concluded that there was no requirement that Dr. Mitchell be served with the amended notice of seizure.

QUESTIONS

1. What are the purposes of the notice provisions in the Louisiana code? Did this court stay true to those purposes? Explain your answer.
2. How might the lender have avoided the dispute in this case?

DEFICIENCY JUDGMENTS If any equity remains after the foreclosed property is sold, the borrower is often able to keep the difference between the sale price and the mortgage amount. If the sale amount is not enough to cover the loan amount, the lender can ask a court for a *deficiency judgment* (a judgment against the borrower for the amount of debt remaining unpaid after the collateral is sold, as discussed in Chapter 29). A deficiency judgment requires the borrower to make up the difference to the lender over time. (Note that some states do not allow deficiency judgments for mortgaged residential real estate.)

Redemption Rights

Borrowers in every state have the right to purchase the property after default by paying the full amount of the debt, plus any interest and costs that have accrued, before the foreclosure sale. This is referred to as the buyer's **equitable right of redemption.** Equitable redemption allows a defaulting borrower to gain title and regain possession of a property.[9] The idea behind equitable redemption is that it is only fair, or equitable, for the borrower to have a chance to regain possession after default. Although many critics question the utility of this right, all states still allow for an equitable right of redemption.

Some states have passed laws that entitle a borrower to repurchase property even *after* a judicial foreclosure.[10] This is called a **statutory right of redemption,** and it may be exercised even if the property was purchased at auction by a third party.

Generally, the borrower may exercise this right for up to one year from the time the house is sold at a foreclosure sale.[11] The borrower[12] must pay the price at which the house was sold at the foreclosure sale (the redemption price), plus taxes, interest, and assessments, as opposed to the balance owed on the foreclosed loan.

Some states allow the borrower to retain possession of the property after the foreclosure sale until the statutory redemption period ends. If the borrower does not exercise the right of redemption, the new buyer receives title to and possession of the property. The statutes creating this right were enacted to drive up sale prices at foreclosure auctions on the theory that third parties would offer prices too high for defaulting borrowers to afford. Instead, in many states, the statutory right of redemption has created a strong disincentive for potential buyers to tie up their funds in an uncertain transaction.

---

9. Note that a foreclosure proceeding is the legal means by which a lender terminates the borrower's equitable right of redemption.
10. This right of redemption is not available after a power of sale foreclosure.

11. Some states do not allow a borrower to waive the statutory right of redemption. This means that a buyer at auction must wait one year to obtain title to, and possession of, a foreclosed property.
12. Some states also allow the spouse of a defaulting borrower or creditors holding liens on the property to purchase the property under the statutory right of redemption.

REVIEWING
Mortgages and Foreclosures after the Recession

Al and Betty Smith's home is valued at $200,000. They have paid off their mortgage and own the house outright—that is, they have 100 percent home equity. They lost most of their savings when the stock market declined during the Great Recession. Now they want to start a new business and need funds, so they decide to obtain a home equity loan. They borrow $150,000 for ten years at an interest rate of 12 percent. On the date they take out the loan, a ten-year Treasury bond is yielding 3 percent. The Smiths pay a total of $10,000 in fees to Alpha Bank. The Smiths are not given any notice that they can lose their home if they do not meet their obligations under the loan. Two weeks after completing the loan, the Smiths change their minds and want to rescind the loan.

1. Is the Smiths' loan covered by the Truth-in-Lending Act as amended by the Home Ownership and Equity Protection Act? Why or why not?
2. Do the Smiths have a right to rescind the loan two weeks after the fact, or are they too late? Explain.
3. Assume now that Alpha Bank gave the Smiths all of the required notices before the loan was completed. If all other facts remain the same, do the Smiths have a right to rescind? Discuss your answer.
4. Suppose now that the Smiths never rescind the loan and that they default four years later while still owing Alpha Bank $120,000. The bank forecloses and raises only $110,000 when the house is sold at auction. If the state where the Smiths live follows the majority rule, can Alpha Bank seek the remaining $10,000 from the Smiths?

DEBATE THIS: *Federal legislation enacted in the past few years has unfairly benefited homeowners who should not have bought such expensive houses and taken on so much debt.*

TERMS AND CONCEPTS

acceleration clause 614

adjustable-rate
  mortgage (ARM) 606

annual percentage
  rate (APR) 608

appraiser 609

average prime offer rate 611

balloon mortgage 606

bridge loan 611

construction loan 606

deed in lieu of
  foreclosure 613

default 612

down payment 605

equitable right of
  redemption 616

fixed-rate mortgage 605

forbearance 612

foreclosure 612

home equity loan 607

homeowners' insurance 608

hybrid mortgage 607

interest only
  (IO) mortgage 606

judicial foreclosure 614

mortgage 605

mortgage assignee 610

negative amortization 609

notice of default 614

notice of sale 614

participation loan 606

power of sale
  foreclosure 614

prepayment penalty
  clause 607

reamortize 613

reverse mortgage 607

short sale 612

statutory right of
  redemption 616

subprime mortgage 606

Treasury securities 609

workout agreement 612

QUESTIONS AND CASE PROBLEMS

31–1. Disclosure Requirements Rancho Mortgage, Inc., is planning a new advertising campaign designed to attract homebuyers in a difficult economic environment. Rancho wants to promote its new loan product, which offers a fixed interest rate for the first five years and then switches to a variable rate of interest. Rancho believes that Spanish-speaking homebuyers have been underserved in recent years, and it wants to direct its ads to that market. What must Rancho say (and not say) in its advertising campaigns about the structure of the loan product, and in what language? What language should Rancho use in its Truth-in-Lending disclosures? Why?

31–2. QUESTION WITH SAMPLE ANSWER: Real Estate Financing.

Jane Lane refinanced her mortgage with Central Equity, Inc. Central Equity split the transaction into two separate loan documents with separate Truth-in-Lending disclosure statements and settlement statements. Two years later, Lane sought to exercise her right to rescission under the Home Ownership and Equity Protection Act (HOEPA), but Central Equity refused. Central Equity responded that the original transactions comprised two separate loan transactions and because neither loan imposed sufficient fees and costs to trigger HOEPA, its protections did not apply. Lane claims that if the costs and fees were combined into a single transaction (which Lane expected the loan to be), they would surpass the HOEPA threshold and trigger its protections. In turn, because Central Equity did not provide the necessary disclosures under HOEPA, Lane argues that she can properly rescind under its provisions. Is Lane correct? Does loan splitting allow the lender to count each loan transaction with a borrower separately for HOEPA purposes? Why or why not?

• **For a sample answer to Question 31–2, go to Appendix I at the end of this text.**

31–3. Lender's Options In 2008, Frank relocated and purchased a home in a beautiful mountain town. The home was five years old, and Frank purchased it for $450,000. He paid $90,000 as a down payment and financed the remaining $360,000 of the purchase price with a loan from Bank of Town. Frank signed mortgage documents that gave Bank of Town a mortgage interest in the home. Frank made payments on the loan for three years. But the housing market declined significantly, and Frank's home is now valued at only $265,000. The balance due on his loan is $354,000. In addition to the decline in housing prices, the economy has slowed, and the booming business that Frank started when he bought the home has experienced a decrease in revenues. It seems inevitable that Frank will not be able to make his mortgage payments. Discuss Bank of Town's options in this situation.

31–4. Home Ownership and Equity Protection Act Michael and Edith Jones owned a home that went into foreclosure. During this time, they were contacted by a representative of Rees-Max, whose notice read: "There are only a few months to go in your redemption period! Your options to save the equity in your home are fading. Call me immediately for a no-bull, no-obligation assessment of your situation. Even if you have been 'promised' by a mortgage broker or investor that they will help, CALL ME . . . ." The Joneses contacted Rees-Max, and they entered into a sale and leaseback transaction. Rees-Max would purchase the property from the Joneses, the Joneses would lease the property for a few months, and then the Joneses would purchase the property back from Rees-Max on a contract. The property was appraised at

$278,000 and purchased by Rees-Max for $214,000, with more than $30,000 in fees. The Joneses disputed these fees, and Rees-Max moved to evict them. The agreement did not use the terms *debt, security,* or *mortgage,* and the documents stated that no security interest was granted. Does this transaction constitute a mortgage that would receive protection under the Truth-in-Lending Act and the Home Ownership and Equity Protection Act? Why or why not? [*Jones v. Rees-Max, LLC,* 514 F.Supp.2d 1139 (D.Minn. 2007)]

31–5. Right of Rescission George and Mona Antanuos obtained a mortgage loan secured with rental property from the First National Bank of Arizona. At the closing, they received from the bank a "Notice of Right to Cancel," informing them of their three-day rescission period under the Truth-in-Lending Act (TILA). The following day, according to the Antanuoses, they informed the lender via fax that they wished to exercise their right to rescind. The lender refused to rescind the agreement. George and Mona sued the bank. In federal court, the Antanuoses did not dispute that a consumer's right to rescind under the TILA applies only to the consumer's original dwelling and that they had used their commercial property as a security interest. Instead, the Antanuoses argued that the bank was prohibited from denying them the rescission right because they relied to their detriment on the bank's disclosure, which would have been required under the TILA. Would the court be convinced? Explain. [*Antanuos v. First National Bank of Arizona,* 508 F.Supp.2d 466 (E.D.Va. 2007)]

31–6. Mortgage Foreclosure In January 2003, Gary Ryder and Washington Mutual Bank, F.A., executed a note in which Ryder promised to pay $2,450,000, plus interest at a rate that could vary from month to month. The amount of the first payment was $10,933. The note was to be paid in full by February 1, 2033. A mortgage on Ryder's real property at 345 Round Hill Road in Greenwich, Connecticut, in favor of the bank secured his obligations under the note. The note and mortgage required that he pay the taxes on the property, which he did not do in 2004 and 2005. The bank notified him that he was in default and, when he failed to act, paid $50,095.92 in taxes, penalties, interest, and fees. Other disputes arose between the parties, and Ryder filed a suit in a federal district court against the bank, alleging, in part, breach of contract. He charged, among other things, that some of his timely payments were not processed and were subjected to incorrect late fees, forcing him to make excessive payments and ultimately resulting in "non-payment by Ryder." The bank filed a counterclaim, seeking to foreclose on the mortgage. What should a creditor be required to prove to foreclose on mortgaged property? What would be a debtor's most effective defense? Which party in this case is likely to prevail on the bank's counterclaim? Why? [*Ryder v. Washington Mutual Bank, F.A.,* 501 F.Supp.2d 311 (D.Conn. 2007)]

31–7. CASE PROBLEM WITH SAMPLE ANSWER: Wrongful Foreclosure.

After a series of bankruptcies and foreclosures, Wells Fargo Home Mortgage, the mortgagee, foreclosed on the debtors' home and purchased it for $33,500. The debtors then filed a complaint against Wells Fargo and certain related entities, claiming wrongful foreclosure and breach of contract. The debtors sought damages, specific performance, and other remedies. The dispute grew out of a loan note for $51,300 that the plaintiffs had executed with Southern Atlantic Financial Services, Inc. In exchange for that loan, the plaintiffs gave Southern Atlantic a security interest in their home. Southern Atlantic transferred its interest in the property and the note to GE Capital Mortgage Services, Inc. On September 30, 2000, Wells Fargo Home Mortgage started servicing this loan for GE. Wells Fargo acquired the loan from GE on December 1, 2004. When the plaintiffs did not make all of the required payments, Wells Fargo sought relief from a stay to file a foreclosure because the debtors were in arrears on the mortgage. The parties agreed that Wells Fargo could have relief from the stay if the debtors failed to make all future payments. Claiming default, Wells Fargo then filed a foreclosure and bought the property at the sale. The debtors filed a complaint alleging that the price paid was shockingly insufficient and constituted wrongful foreclosure and a breach of fiduciary duty. Under what circumstances is a foreclosure sale unfair? Does a property foreclosure sale have to realize the market price? The amount owed on the note? Discuss. [*In re Sharpe,* 425 Bankr. 620 (N.D.Ala. 2010)]

• **To view a sample answer for Problem 31–7, go to this book's Web site at www.cengage.com/blaw/clarkson, select "Chapter 31," and click on "Case Problem with Sample Answer."**

31–8. Foreclosure on Mortgage and Liens LaSalle Bank loaned $8 million to Cypress Creek to build an apartment complex. The loan was secured by a mortgage. Cypress Creek hired contractors to provide concrete work, plumbing, carpentry, and other construction services. Cypress Creek went bankrupt, owing LaSalle $3 million. The contractors recorded mechanic's liens (see page 546 in Chapter 28) when they did not get paid for their work. The property was sold to LaSalle at a sheriff's sale for $1.3 million. The contractors claimed that they should be paid the amounts they were owed out of the $1.3 million and that the mechanic's liens should be satisfied before any funds were distributed to LaSalle for its mortgage. The trial court distributed the $1.3 million primarily to LaSalle, with only a small fraction going to the contractors. Do the liens come before the mortgage in priority of payment? Discuss. [*LaSalle Bank v. Cypress Creek,* 925 N.E.2d 233 (Ill.App.3d 2010)]

31–9. A QUESTION OF ETHICS: Predatory Lending.

Peter Sutton owned a home that was subject to two mortgages, but his only source of income was a $1,080 monthly Social Security benefit. In an effort to reduce his mortgage payments, which exceeded

$1,400 per month, he sought a refinancing loan through an Apex Mortgage Services mortgage broker. According to Sutton, the broker led him to believe that he could receive, from Countrywide Home Loans, Inc., a refinancing loan with payments of $428 per month. The broker, however, ultimately arranged for Sutton to receive an adjustable-rate loan from Countrywide; the loan required monthly payments that started at more than $1,000 per month and were subject to further increases. Sutton also alleged that the broker reported his monthly income as four times the actual amount and failed to inform Sutton about the existence of a prepayment penalty. Sutton signed forms stating that he agreed to the terms of the loan arranged by the broker. He claimed, however, that he did not understand the terms of the loan until after the closing. As compensation for brokering Sutton's loan, Countrywide paid Apex $7,270, which included a yield-spread premium of $4,710. (A yield-spread premium *is a form of compensation*

paid to a broker by a lender for providing a borrower with a loan that carries an interest rate above the lender's par rate.) Sutton sued the broker and lender claiming violations of federal law. [Sutton v. Countrywide Home Loans, Inc., ___ F.3d ___ (11th Cir. 2009)]

(a) Who is ethically responsible for Sutton's predicament? To what extent does Sutton have a duty to read and understand what he signs? Discuss.

(b) Sutton argued that because the broker provided services that were of no value to Sutton, the broker should not receive the yield-spread premium. Do you agree? Why or why not?

(c) Did Countrywide, the lender, have any ethical obligation to monitor the activities of the broker? Would the result have been different if Countrywide had intervened before the documents were signed? Explain.

LEGAL RESEARCH EXERCISES ON THE WEB

Go to this text's Web site at **www.cengage.com/blaw/clarkson**, select "Chapter 31," and click on "Practical Internet Exercises." There you will find the following Internet research exercises that you can perform to learn more about the topics covered in this chapter.

Practical Internet Exercise 31–1: **Legal Perspective**
Federal Loan Modification Program

Practical Internet Exercise 31–2: **Management Perspective**
Understanding the Truth-in-Lending Act

We have certainly come a long way from the period in our history when debtors' prisons existed. Today, debtors are in a much more favorable position—they can file for protection under bankruptcy law. Indeed, after the Bankruptcy Reform Act of 1978 was passed, some claimed that we had gone too far toward protecting debtors and had made it too easy for them to avoid paying what they legally owed. Critics of the 2005 Bankruptcy Reform Act were concerned that the pendulum had swung too far in the opposite direction—favoring creditors' interests and making it too difficult for debtors to obtain a fresh start. Clearly, it is hard to protect the rights of both debtors and creditors at the same time, and laws governing debtor-creditor relationships have traditionally been perceived, by one group or another, as being unfair.

It is obviously impossible for the law to protect both debtors and creditors at all times under all circumstances. Attempts to balance the rights of both groups necessarily raise questions of fairness and justice. In this *Focus on Ethics* feature, we look at several aspects of debtor-creditor relationships that frequently involve issues of fairness, and we examine the ethical ramifications of the bankruptcy reform legislation for debtors and creditors.

"Self-Help" Repossession

Section 9–503 of the Uniform Commercial Code (UCC) states that "[u]nless otherwise agreed, a secured party has on default the right to take possession of the collateral. In taking possession, a secured party may proceed without judicial process if this can be done without breach of the peace." The underlying rationale for this "self-help" provision of Article 9 is that it simplifies the process of repossession for creditors and reduces the burden on the courts. Because the UCC does not define "breach of the peace," however, it is not always easy to predict what behavior will constitute such a breach.

One problem is that the debtor may not realize what is happening when agents of the creditor show up to repossess the collateral. Often, to avoid confrontation with the debtor and any potential violence or breach of the peace, a secured creditor will arrange to have the collateral repossessed during the night or in the early-morning hours, when the repossession effort is least likely to be observed. But a debtor who awakens in the night and sees his or her car being towed away may not realize that it is being repossessed.

At the same time, repossession can be risky for the creditor; if the repossession results in a breach of the peace, the creditor may be liable for substantial damages. Inevitably, repossession attempts will occasionally result in confrontations with the debtor. Indeed, some contend that the self-help provision encourages violence by providing an incentive for debtors to incite creditors to breach the peace, which may entitle the debtors to damages.

Ethics and Bankruptcy

As we have discussed, the first goal of bankruptcy law is to provide relief and protection to debtors. Society generally has concluded that everyone should be given the chance to start over. But how far should society go in allowing debtors to avoid obligations that they voluntarily incurred?

Consider the concept of bankruptcy from the point of view of the creditor. The creditor has extended a transfer of purchasing power from herself or himself to the debtor. That transfer of purchasing power represents a transfer of an asset for an asset. The debtor obtains the asset of funds, goods, or services, and the creditor obtains the asset of a *secured* or *unsecured* legal obligation to repay. Once the debtor is in bankruptcy, voluntarily or involuntarily, the asset that the creditor owns most often has a diminished value. Indeed, in many circumstances, that asset has no value. Yet the easier it becomes for debtors to discharge their debts under bankruptcy laws, the greater will be the incentive for debtors to use such laws to avoid paying amounts that are legally owed.

Clearly, bankruptcy law is a balancing act between providing a second chance for debtors and ensuring that creditors are given reasonable protection. Understandably, ethical issues arise in the process.

Bankruptcy and Economics

Among other things, when the number of bankruptcies increases, creditors incur higher risks in making loans—because bankruptcy shifts the cost of the debt from the debtor to the creditor. To compensate for these higher risks, creditors take one or more of the following actions: increase the interest rates charged to everyone, require additional security (collateral), or become more selective in granting credit. Thus, with more lenient bankruptcy laws, debtors who find themselves in bankruptcy will be better off, but debtors who will never be in bankruptcy will be worse off. Ethical concerns regarding this trade-off must be matched with the economic concerns of other groups of individuals affected by the law, especially in the economic environment after the Great Recession.

Consequences of Bankruptcy Under bankruptcy law, filing for personal bankruptcy (particularly under Chapter 7) is difficult. Although the stigma attached to bankruptcy today is less than it once was, bankruptcy is never easy for debtors. Many debtors feel a sense of shame and failure when they petition for bankruptcy. After all, bankruptcy is a matter of public record, and there is no way to avoid a certain amount of publicity. In one case, for example, a couple who filed for Chapter 7 bankruptcy wanted to use their attorney's mailing address in another town on their bankruptcy schedules in an effort to prevent an elderly parent and one of their employers from learning about the bankruptcy. The court, however, held that debtors are not entitled to be protected from publicity surrounding the filing of their cases.[1]

A court in another case held that the public interest in information involving a particular bankruptcy debtor (Gitto Global Corporation) was important enough to justify disclosing a previously sealed report from a bankruptcy examiner. In essence, the court gave the media access to the bankruptcy examiner's report on the misconduct of more than 120 individuals at the debtor company.[2]

Bankruptcy also has other consequences for debtors, including blemished credit ratings for up to ten years and higher interest charges for new debts, such as those incurred through the purchase of cars or homes. Some private employers may even refuse to hire a job applicant who has filed for bankruptcy. The courts provide little relief for applicants who are denied a job for this reason.[3]

Thus, bankruptcy can have adverse effects for both debtors and creditors. Because of the consequences of bankruptcy, debtors do not always get the fresh start promised by bankruptcy law. At the same time, creditors rarely are able to recover all that is owed them once a debtor petitions for bankruptcy.

Investment Risk Management and Bankruptcy In the years leading up to the Great Recession, many investors opted to invest most or all of their funds in risky propositions that promised to yield ultra-high returns. Rather than simply seeking a healthy profit, these investors were looking for extraordinary gains. Too often, they were so certain of success that they failed to manage the risk of investment by diversifying their portfolios or holding some funds in reserve. Many were so overconfident that they borrowed additional funds to invest. When the recession hit, however, those risky investments came crashing down, and many investors were left unable to pay their debts and had to file for bankruptcy.

The combination of overdependence on credit and overconfidence in investments helped bring on the global economic crisis from which the United States has not yet fully recovered. What these investors lacked was a sense of self-sufficiency and a clear understanding of the importance of minimizing debt. A person or firm that minimizes debt and is financially self-reliant will be less affected by fluctuations in the market or difficulties in obtaining credit, and therefore will be less likely to be bankrupted in a recession.

DISCUSSION QUESTIONS

1. Do you think that the law favors debtors at the expense of creditors or vice versa? Is there any way to achieve a better balance between the interests of creditors and those of debtors?

2. So long as a breach of the peace does not result, a lender may repossess goods on the debtor's default under the self-help provision of Article 9. Do you think that debtors have a right to be told in advance about a planned repossession? Some observers argue that the self-help remedy under Article 9 should be abolished. Do you agree? Why or why not?

3. Is it unethical to avoid paying one's debts by going into bankruptcy? Does a person have a moral responsibility to pay his or her debts? Discuss.

4. Are borrowers better off as a result of the bankruptcy reform legislation? Why or why not?

5. How does minimizing business or personal debt help prevent bankruptcies in a recession?

---

1. *In the Matter of Laws,* 223 Bankr. 714 (D.Neb. 1998).
2. *In re Gitto Global Corp.,* 422 F.3d 1 (D.Mass. 2005).
3. See, for example, *In re Potter,* 354 Bankr. 301 (D.Ala. 2006); and *In re Stinson,* 285 Bankr. 239 (W.D.Va. 2002).

UNIT SEVEN

AGENCY AND EMPLOYMENT

CONTENTS

BUSINESS LAW

CLARKSON · MILLER · CROSS

One of the most common, important, and pervasive legal relationships is that of **agency**. In an agency relationship involving two parties, one of the parties, called the *agent*, agrees to represent or act for the other, called the *principal*. The principal has the right to control the agent's conduct in matters entrusted to the agent. By using agents, a principal can conduct multiple business operations simultaneously in various locations. Thus, for example, contracts that bind the principal can be made at different places with different persons at the same time.

A familiar example of an agent is a corporate officer who serves in a representative capacity for the owners of the corporation. In this capacity, the officer has the authority to bind the principal (the corporation) to a contract. In fact, agency law is essential to the existence and operation of a corporate entity because only through its agents can a corporation function and enter into contracts.

Most employees are also considered to be agents of their employers. Thus, some of the concepts of employment law that you will learn about in Chapters 34 and 35 are based on agency law. Indeed, agency relationships permeate the business world. For that reason, an understanding of the law of agency is crucial to understanding business law.

SECTION 1
AGENCY RELATIONSHIPS

Section 1(1) of the *Restatement (Third) of Agency*[1] defines *agency* as "the fiduciary relation [that] results from the manifestation of consent by one person to another that the other shall act in his [or her] behalf and subject to his [or her] control, and consent by the other so to act." In other words, in a principal-agent relationship, the parties have agreed that the agent will act *on behalf and instead of* the principal in negotiating and transacting business with third parties.

The term **fiduciary** is at the heart of agency law. This term can be used both as a noun and as an adjective. When used as a noun, it refers to a person having a duty created by his or her undertaking to act primarily for another's benefit in matters connected with the undertaking. When used as an adjective, as in the phrase *fiduciary relationship*, it means that the relationship involves trust and confidence.

Agency relationships commonly exist between employers and employees. Agency relationships may sometimes also exist between employers and independent contractors who are hired to perform special tasks or services.

Employer-Employee Relationships

Normally, all employees who deal with third parties are deemed to be agents. A salesperson in a department store, for instance, is an agent of the store's owner (the principal) and acts on the owner's behalf. Any sale of goods made by the salesperson to a customer is binding on the principal. Similarly, most representations of fact made by the salesperson with respect to the goods sold are binding on the principal.

Because employees who deal with third parties generally are deemed to be agents of their employers, agency law and employment law overlap considerably. Agency relationships, though, as will become apparent, can exist outside an employer-employee

---

1. The *Restatement (Third) of Agency* is an authoritative summary of the law of agency and is often referred to by judges in their decisions and opinions.

relationship, and thus agency law has a broader reach than employment law does.

Employment laws (state and federal) apply only to the employer-employee relationship. Statutes governing Social Security, withholding taxes, workers' compensation, unemployment compensation, workplace safety, employment discrimination, and other aspects of employment (see Chapters 34 and 35) are applicable only when an employer-employee relationship exists. *These laws do not apply to an independent contractor.*

Employer–Independent Contractor Relationships

Independent contractors are not employees because, by definition, those who hire them have no control over the details of their work performance. Section 2 of the *Restatement (Third) of Agency* defines an **independent contractor** as follows:

> [An independent contractor is] a person who contracts with another to do something for him [or her] but who is not controlled by the other nor subject to the other's right to control with respect to his [or her] physical conduct in the performance of the undertaking. He [or she] may or may not be an agent.

Building contractors and subcontractors are independent contractors; a property owner who hires a contractor and subcontractors to complete a project does not control the details of the way they perform their work. Truck drivers who own their vehicles and hire out on a per-job basis are independent contractors, but truck drivers who drive company trucks on a regular basis usually are employees.

The relationship between a principal and an independent contractor may or may not involve an agency relationship. To illustrate: An owner of real estate who hires a real estate broker to negotiate the sale of her property not only has contracted with an independent contractor (the real estate broker) but also has established an agency relationship for the specific purpose of selling the property. Another example is an insurance agent, who is both an independent contractor and an agent of the insurance company for which he or she sells policies. (Note that an insurance *broker,* in contrast, normally is an agent of the person obtaining insurance and not of the insurance company.)

Determination of Employee Status

The courts are frequently asked to determine whether a particular worker is an employee or an independent contractor. How a court decides this issue can have a significant effect on the rights and liabilities of the parties. For example, employers are required to pay certain taxes, such as Social Security and unemployment taxes, for employees but not for independent contractors.

CRITERIA USED BY THE COURTS In deciding whether a worker is categorized as an employee or an independent contractor, courts often consider the following questions:

1. How much control does the employer exercise over the details of the work? (If the employer exercises considerable control over the details of the work and the day-to-day activities of the worker, this indicates employee status. This is perhaps the most important factor weighed by the courts in determining employee status.)
2. Is the worker engaged in an occupation or business distinct from that of the employer? (If so, this points to independent-contractor, not employee, status.)
3. Is the work usually done under the employer's direction or by a specialist without supervision? (If the work is usually done under the employer's direction, this indicates employee status.)
4. Does the employer supply the tools at the place of work? (If so, this indicates employee status.)
5. For how long is the person employed? (If the person is employed for a long period of time, this indicates employee status.)
6. What is the method of payment—by time period or at the completion of the job? (Payment by time period, such as once every two weeks or once a month, indicates employee status.)
7. What degree of skill is required of the worker? (If a great degree of skill is required, this may indicate that the person is an independent contractor hired for a specialized job and not an employee.)

Sometimes, workers may benefit from having employee status—for tax purposes and to be protected under certain employment laws, for example. As mentioned earlier, federal statutes governing employment discrimination apply only when an employer-employee relationship exists. Protection under employment-discrimination statutes provides a significant incentive for workers to claim that they are employees rather than independent contractors.

CASE IN POINT A Puerto Rican television station, WIPR, contracted with Victoria Lis Alberty-Vélez to co-host a television show. Alberty-Vélez signed a new contract for every new episode, each of which required her to work a certain number of days. She was under no other commitment to work for WIPR and was free to pursue other opportunities during the weeks between filming. WIPR did not withhold any taxes from the lump-sum amount it paid her for each contract. When Alberty-Vélez became pregnant, WIPR stopped contracting with her. She filed a lawsuit claiming that WIPR was discriminating against her in violation of federal employment-discrimination laws, but the court found in favor of WIPR. Because the parties had structured their relationship through the use of repeated fixed-length contracts and had described the woman as an independent contractor on tax documents, she could not maintain an employment-discrimination suit.[2]

Whether a worker is an employee or an independent contractor can also affect the employer's liability for the worker's actions. In the following case, the court had to determine the status of a taxi driver whose passengers were injured in a collision.

---

2. *Alberty-Vélez v. Corporación de Puerto Rico para la Difusión Pública,* 361 F.3d 1 (1st Cir. 2004).

CASE 32.1
Lopez v. El Palmar Taxi, Inc.

Court of Appeals of Georgia, 297 Ga.App. 121, 676 S.E.2d 460 (2009).

BACKGROUND AND FACTS • El Palmar Taxi, Inc., requires its drivers to supply their own cabs, which must display El Palmar's logo. The drivers pay gas, maintenance, and insurance costs, as well as a fee to El Palmar. They are expected to follow certain rules—dress neatly, for example—and to comply with the law, including licensing regulations, but they can work when they want for as long as they want. El Palmar may dispatch a driver to pick up a fare, or the driver can look for a fare. Mario Julaju drove a taxi under a contract with El Palmar that described him as an independent contractor. El Palmar sent Julaju to pick up Maria Lopez and her children. During the ride, Julaju's cab collided with a truck. To recover for their injuries, the Lopezes filed a suit in a Georgia state court against El Palmar. The employer argued that it was not liable because Julaju was an independent contractor. The court ruled in El Palmar's favor. The plaintiffs appealed.

IN THE LANGUAGE OF THE COURT
PHIPPS, Judge.
* * * *
In the complaint, Lopez alleged that she, accompanied by her children, hired El Palmar to transport them safely to their destination. * * * In its * * * answer, El Palmar denied this allegation and stated that Lopez had hired an independent contractor for transportation, not El Palmar.
* * * *

As a general rule, an employer is not responsible for [the actions of] its employee when the employee exercises an independent business and is not subject to the immediate direction and control of the employer. *To determine whether the relationship of the parties is that of employer and servant or that of employer and independent contractor, the primary test is whether the employer retains the right to control the time, manner and method of executing the work.* [Emphasis added.]

Here, Julaju executed an agreement with * * * El Palmar Taxi that he would work for El Palmar as an independent contractor. The only restrictions the contract imposed on him were to comply with all federal, state and local laws requiring business permits, certificates and licenses and to refrain from operating under the company's name in any jurisdiction where the vehicle could not legally be operated.

The evidence does not show that El Palmar assumed control over the time, manner or method of Julaju's work. He was free to work when and for as long as he wanted, he was not required to accept fares from El Palmar, he could obtain his own fares and he could work anywhere the taxi could legally be operated. The fact that the cars he drove displayed the El Palmar logo and the fact that he received calls from El Palmar are not sufficient to create an employer-employee relationship.

* * * The car [Julaju] drove the day of the collision was not owned by El Palmar. Thus, El Palmar cannot be held liable for Julaju's [actions] under the theory that Julaju was El Palmar's employee.

CASE 32.1 CONTINUED ◆ **DECISION AND REMEDY** • *The state intermediate appellate court affirmed this part of the lower court's decision. A taxi driver who is not subject to the control of the taxi company is an independent contractor. But the appellate court reversed the judgment in El Palmar's favor on other grounds and remanded the case for trial.*

WHAT IF THE FACTS WERE DIFFERENT? • *Suppose that El Palmar had limited its driver to a set schedule in a specific area of the city and allowed him to pick up only certain passengers. Would these facts have established Julaju as an employee? Why or why not?*

MANAGERIAL IMPLICATIONS • *When an employment contract clearly designates one party as an independent contractor, the relationship between the parties is presumed to be that of employer and independent contractor. But this is only a presumption. Evidence can be introduced to show that the employer exercised sufficient control to establish the other party as an employee. The Internal Revenue Service is becoming increasingly aggressive in pursuing cases involving independent contractor versus employee status. Thus, from a tax perspective, business managers need to ensure that all independent contractors fully control their own work.*

CRITERIA USED BY THE IRS The Internal Revenue Service (IRS) has established its own criteria for determining whether a worker is an independent contractor or an employee. Although the IRS once considered twenty factors in determining a worker's status, guidelines today encourage IRS examiners to look closely at just one of those factors—the degree of control the business exercises over the worker.

The IRS tends to scrutinize closely a firm's classification of its workers, because, as mentioned, employers can avoid certain tax liabilities by hiring independent contractors instead of employees. Even when a firm has classified a worker as an independent contractor, the IRS may decide that the worker is actually an employee. In that situation, the employer will be responsible for paying any applicable Social Security, withholding, and unemployment taxes. Microsoft Corporation, for example, was once ordered to pay back payroll taxes for hundreds of temporary workers who had contractually agreed to work for Microsoft as independent contractors.[3]

EMPLOYEE STATUS AND "WORKS FOR HIRE" Under the Copyright Act of 1976, any copyrighted work created by an employee within the scope of her or his employment at the request of the employer is a "work for hire," and the employer owns the copyright to the work. In contrast, when an employer hires an independent contractor—a freelance artist, writer, or computer programmer, for example—the independent contractor normally owns the copyright. In this situation, the employer can own the copyright only if the parties agree in writing that the work is a "work for hire" and the work falls into one of nine specific categories, including audiovisual and other works.

CASE IN POINT Artisan House, Inc., hired a professional photographer, Steven H. Lindner, owner of SHL Imaging, Inc., to take pictures of its products for the creation of color slides to be used by Artisan's sales force. Lindner controlled his own work and carefully chose the lighting and angles used in the photographs. When Lindner later discovered that Artisan had published the photographs in a catalogue and brochures without his permission, he had SHL register the photographs with the copyright office and file a lawsuit for copyright infringement. Artisan claimed that its publication of the photographs was authorized because they were works for hire. The court, however, decided that SHL was an independent contractor and owned the copyright to the photographs. SHL had only given Artisan permission (a license) to provide the photographs to its sales reps, not to reproduce them in other publications. Because Artisan had used the photographs in an unauthorized manner, the court ruled that Artisan was liable for copyright infringement.[4]

◄◄◄ **SECTION 2** ►►►
FORMATION OF THE AGENCY RELATIONSHIP

Agency relationships normally are *consensual*—that is, they come about by voluntary consent and agreement between the parties. Generally, the agreement

---

3. *Vizcaino v. U.S. District Court for the Western District of Washington,* 173 F.3d 713 (9th Cir. 1999).

4. *SHL Imaging, Inc. v. Artisan House, Inc.,* 117 F.Supp.2d 301 (S.D.N.Y. 2000).

need not be in writing,[5] and consideration is not required.

A person must have contractual capacity to be a principal.[6] Those who cannot legally enter into contracts directly should not be allowed to do so indirectly through an agent. Any person can be an agent, however, regardless of whether he or she has the capacity to contract (including minors).

An agency relationship can be created for any legal purpose. An agency relationship created for a purpose that is illegal or contrary to public policy is unenforceable. If Archer (as principal) contracts with Burke (as agent) to sell illegal narcotics, the agency relationship is unenforceable because selling illegal narcotics is a felony and is contrary to public policy. It is also illegal for physicians and other licensed professionals to employ unlicensed agents to perform professional actions.

An agency relationship can arise in four ways: by agreement of the parties, by ratification, by estoppel, and by operation of law. We look here at each of these possibilities.

Agency by Agreement

Most agency relationships are based on an express or implied agreement that the agent will act for the principal and that the principal agrees to have the agent so act. An agency agreement can take the form of an express written contract or be created by an oral agreement. For example, Henry asks Grace, a gardener, to contract with others for the care of his lawn on a regular basis. If Grace agrees, an agency relationship exists between Henry and Grace for the lawn care.

An agency agreement can also be implied by conduct. For example, a hotel expressly allows only Hans Cooper to park cars, but Hans has no employment contract there. The hotel's manager tells Hans when to work, as well as where and how to park the cars. The hotel's conduct manifests a willingness to have Hans park its customers' cars, and Hans can infer from the hotel's conduct that he has authority to act as a parking valet. Thus, there is an implied agreement that Hans is an agent of the hotel and provides valet parking services for hotel guests.

At issue in the following case was whether an agency relationship arose when a man, who was being hospitalized, asked his wife to sign the admissions papers for him.

---

5. There are two main exceptions to the statement that agency agreements need not be in writing. An agency agreement must be in writing (1) whenever agency authority empowers the agent to enter into a contract that the Statute of Frauds requires to be in writing (this is called the *equal dignity rule*, to be discussed in the next chapter) and (2) whenever an agent is given power of attorney.

6. Note that some states allow a minor to be a principal. When a minor is permitted to be a principal, any resulting contracts will be voidable by the minor principal but *not* by the adult third party.

CASE 32.2
Laurel Creek Health Care Center v. Bishop

Court of Appeals of Kentucky, ___ S.W.3d ___ (2010).
courts.ky.gov/courtofappeals[a]

BACKGROUND AND FACTS • Gilbert Bishop was admitted to Laurel Creek Health Care Center suffering from various physical ailments. During an examination, Bishop told Laurel Creek staff that he could not use his hands well enough to write or hold a pencil, but he was otherwise found to be mentally competent. Bishop's sister, Rachel Combs, testified that when she arrived at the facility, she offered to sign the admissions forms, but Laurel Creek employees told her that it was their policy to have the patient's spouse sign the admissions papers if the patient was unable to do so. Combs also testified that Bishop asked her to get his wife, Anna, so that she could sign his admissions papers. Combs then brought Anna to the hospital, and Anna signed the admissions paperwork, which contained a provision for mandatory arbitration. Subsequently, Bishop went into cardiopulmonary arrest and died. Following his death, Bishop's family brought an action in a Kentucky state court against Laurel Creek for negligence. Laurel Creek asked the trial court to order the parties to proceed to arbitration in accordance with the mandatory arbitration provision

---

a. Select "Searchable Opinions" from the "Related Content" list on the right side of the screen. On the page that opens, under "Select Search Category," choose "Court of Appeals Opinions (1996+)"; then enter "2009-CA-001055" in the "Enter Search Request" box and click on "Search." In the "Search Results" list, select the highlighted link to access the case. The Kentucky Court of Appeals maintains this Web site.

CASE 32.2 CONTINUED ◆ contained in the admissions paperwork signed by Anna. The trial court denied the request on the ground that Anna was not Bishop's agent and had no legal authority to make decisions for him. Laurel Creek appealed.

IN THE LANGUAGE OF THE COURT
LAMBERT, Judge.
* * * *
　　Laurel Creek first argues that this is a case of actual agency and that Anna Bishop had actual authority as Gilbert's agent to sign the admissions paperwork and is therefore bound by the arbitration agreement therein.
* * * *
We agree with Laurel Creek that Gilbert created an actual agency relationship between him and his wife. According to his sister, Rachel, Gilbert specifically asked that his wife be brought to the nursing home so that she could sign the admissions documents for him, and Anna acted upon that delegation of authority and signed the admissions papers. This is consistent with the creation of actual authority as described in the *Restatement (Third) of Agency*, [Section] 2.01, Comment c (2006). The Restatement explains the rationale for the creation of actual agency in three steps. *First,* "the principal manifests assent to be affected by the agent's action." In the instant case, Gilbert asked that Anna come to the hospital to sign the papers for him. *Second,* "*the agent's actions establish the agent's consent to act on the principal's behalf.*" Here, Anna signed all the admissions papers per her husband's request and therefore consented to act on Gilbert's behalf. *Third, by acting within such authority, the agent affects the principal's legal relations with third parties.* Clearly here, Anna's actions affected Gilbert's relations with Laurel Creek, a third party. [Emphasis added.]
* * * *
* * * * The evidence indicates that Gilbert indicated to Laurel Creek that he was physically incapable of signing the documents but was of sound mental capacity and wanted his wife to sign the documents on his behalf. When Gilbert communicated this to his sister, and the sister brought Anna in to sign the documents, Gilbert created an agency relationship upon which Laurel Creek relied.

DECISION AND REMEDY • *The Kentucky Court of Appeals reversed the trial court's judgment and remanded the case for further proceedings consistent with its opinion. An actual agency relationship between Bishop and his wife, Anna, had been formed, and the trial court had erred when it found otherwise.*

THE ECONOMIC DIMENSION • *Which party benefited from the court's ruling? Why?*

THE LEGAL ENVIRONMENT DIMENSION • *Laurel Creek argued that even if there was no actual agency relationship, an implied agency relationship existed. Is this argument valid? Why or why not?*

Agency by Ratification

On occasion, a person who is in fact not an agent (or who is an agent acting outside the scope of her or his authority) may make a contract on behalf of another (a principal). If the principal approves or affirms that contract by word or by action, an agency relationship is created by *ratification*. Ratification involves a question of intent, and intent can be expressed by either words or conduct. The basic requirements for ratification will be discussed in Chapter 33.

Agency by Estoppel

When a principal causes a third person to believe that another person is the principal's agent, and the third person acts to his or her detriment in reasonable reliance on that belief, the principal is "estopped to deny" (prevented from denying) the agency relationship. In such a situation, the principal's actions have created the *appearance* of an agency that does not in fact exist. The third person must prove that he or she *reasonably* believed that an agency relationship existed, however.[7] Facts and circumstances must show that an ordinary, prudent person familiar with business practice and custom would have been justified in concluding that the agent had authority.

CASE IN POINT Marsha and Jerry Wiedmaier owned Wiedmaier, Inc., a corporation that operated a truck stop. Their son, Michael, did not own any interest in the corporation but had worked at the truck stop as a fuel operator. Michael decided to form his own business called Extreme Diecast, LLC. To obtain a line of credit with Motorsport Marketing, Inc., which sells racing memorabilia, Michael asked his mother to sign the credit application form. After Marsha had signed as "Secretary-Owner" of Wiedmaier, Inc., Michael added his name to the list of corporate owners and faxed the form to Motorsport. Later, when Michael stopped making payments on the merchandise he had ordered, Motorsport sued Wiedmaier, Inc., for the unpaid balance. The court ruled that Michael was an apparent agent of Wiedmaier, Inc., because the credit application had caused Motorsport to reasonably believe that Michael was acting as Wiedmaier's agent in ordering merchandise.[8]

---

7. These concepts also apply when a person who is in fact an agent undertakes an action that is beyond the scope of her or his authority, as will be discussed in Chapter 33.
8. *Motorsport Marketing, Inc. v. Wiedmaier, Inc.,* 195 S.W.3d 492 (Mo. App. 2006).

Note that the acts or declarations of a purported *agent* in and of themselves do not create an agency by estoppel. Rather, it is the deeds or statements of the *principal* that create an agency by estoppel. Thus, in the *Case in Point* feature just discussed, if Marsha Wiedmaier had not signed the credit application on behalf of the principal-corporation, then Motorsport would not have been justified in believing that Michael was Wiedmaier's agent.

Agency by Operation of Law

The courts may find an agency relationship in the absence of a formal agreement in other situations as well. This may occur in family relationships, such as when one spouse purchases certain basic necessaries and charges them to the other spouse's account. The courts often rule that a spouse is liable for payment for the necessaries because of either a social policy or a legal duty to supply necessaries to family members.

Agency by operation of law may also occur in emergency situations, when the agent is unable to contact the principal and the agent's failure to act outside the scope of her or his authority would cause the principal substantial loss. For example, a railroad engineer may contract on behalf of his or her employer for medical care for an injured motorist hit by the train.

Concept Summary 32.1 below reviews the various ways that agencies are formed.

CONCEPT SUMMARY 32.1
Formation of the Agency Relationship

Method of Formation	Description
By Agreement	The agency relationship is formed through express consent (oral or written) or implied by conduct.
By Ratification	The principal either by act or by agreement ratifies the conduct of a person who is not in fact an agent.
By Estoppel	The principal causes a third person to believe that another person is the principal's agent, and the third person acts to his or her detriment in reasonable reliance on that belief.
By Operation of Law	The agency relationship is based on a social or legal duty (such as the need to support family members) or formed in emergency situations when the agent is unable to contact the principal and failure to act outside the scope of the agent's authority would cause the principal substantial loss.

SECTION 3

DUTIES OF AGENTS AND PRINCIPALS

Once the principal-agent relationship has been created, both parties have duties that govern their conduct. As discussed previously, the principal-agent relationship is *fiduciary*—based on trust. In a fiduciary relationship, each party owes the other the duty to act with the utmost good faith. In this section, we examine the various duties of agents and principals.

Agent's Duties to the Principal

Generally, the agent owes the principal five duties—performance, notification, loyalty, obedience, and accounting.

PERFORMANCE An implied condition in every agency contract is the agent's agreement to use reasonable diligence and skill in performing the work. When an agent fails to perform his or her duties, liability for breach of contract may result. The degree of skill or care required of an agent is usually that expected of a reasonable person under similar circumstances. Generally, this is interpreted to mean ordinary care. If an agent has represented herself or himself as possessing special skills, however, the agent is expected to exercise the degree of skill claimed. Failure to do so constitutes a breach of the agent's duty.

Not all agency relationships are based on contract. In some situations, an agent acts gratuitously—that is, without payment. A gratuitous agent cannot be liable for breach of contract, as there is no contract; he or she is subject only to tort liability. Once a gratuitous agent has begun to act in an agency capacity, he or she has the duty to continue to perform in that capacity in an acceptable manner and is subject to the same standards of care and duty to perform as other agents.

For example, Bower's friend Alcott is a real estate broker. Alcott offers to sell Bower's farm at no charge. If Alcott never attempts to sell the farm, Bower has no legal cause of action to force her to do so. If Alcott does find a buyer, however, but negligently fails to follow through with the sales contract, causing the buyer to seek other property, then Bower can sue Alcott for negligence.

NOTIFICATION An agent is required to notify the principal of all matters that come to her or his attention concerning the subject matter of the agency. This is the *duty of notification,* or the duty to inform. Suppose that Perez, an artist, is about to negotiate a contract to sell a series of paintings to Barber's Art Gallery for $25,000. Perez's agent learns that Barber is insolvent and will be unable to pay for the paintings. The agent has a duty to inform Perez of Barber's insolvency because it is relevant to the subject matter of the agency, which is the sale of Perez's paintings. Generally, the law assumes that the principal is aware of any information acquired by the agent that is relevant to the agency—regardless of whether the agent actually passes on this information to the principal. It is a basic tenet of agency law that notice to the agent is notice to the principal.

LOYALTY Loyalty is one of the most fundamental duties in a fiduciary relationship. Basically, the agent has the duty to act *solely for the benefit of his or her principal* and not in the interest of the agent or a third party. For example, an agent cannot represent two principals in the same transaction unless both know of the dual capacity and consent to it. The duty of loyalty also means that any information or knowledge acquired through the agency relationship is confidential. It is a breach of loyalty to disclose such information either during the agency relationship or after its termination. Typical examples of confidential information are trade secrets and customer lists compiled by the principal.

In short, the agent's loyalty must be undivided. The agent's actions must be strictly for the benefit of the principal and must not result in any secret profit for the agent.

CASE IN POINT Don Cousins contracted with Leo Hodgins, a real estate agent, to negotiate the purchase of an office building. While working for Cousins, Hodgins discovered that the property owner would sell the building only as a package deal with another parcel. Hodgins then formed a company to buy the two properties and resell the building to Cousins. When Cousins discovered these actions, he filed a lawsuit alleging that Hodgins had breached his fiduciary duties. The court ruled in Cousins's favor. As a real estate agent, Hodgins had a duty to communicate all offers to his principal and not to secretly purchase the property and then resell it to his principal. Hodgins was required to act in Cousins's best interests and could only become the purchaser in this situation with Cousins's knowledge and approval.[9]

In the following case, an employer alleged that a former employee had breached his duty of loyalty by planning a competing business while still working for the employer.

---

9. *Cousins v. Realty Ventures, Inc.,* 844 So.2d 860 (La.App. 5 Cir. 2003).

✴ EXTENDED CASE 32.3 ✴
Taser International, Inc. v. Ward

Court of Appeals of Arizona, Division 1, 224 Ariz. 389, 231 P.3d 921 (2010).
www.cofad1.state.az.us[a]

IN THE LANGUAGE OF THE COURT
PORTLEY, Judge.
* * * *

Taser International develops and manufactures electronic control devices, commonly called stun guns, and accessories for electronic control devices, including a personal video and audio recording device called TASER CAM. Taser sells its products to the military, law enforcement, corrections, private security, and the general public.

[Steve] Ward was employed full-time with Taser from January 1, 2004, to July 24, 2007, and served as Taser's vice president of marketing during the time relevant to this appeal. He was an at-will employee,[b] and he did not sign any employment contract, non-compete agreement, or non-disclosure agreement.
* * * *

In December 2006, Ward began exploring whether he could personally develop the concept of an eyeglass-mounted camera. He sought legal advice about whether he could permissibly develop such a camera independent of Taser, and hired patent counsel to conduct a patent search on the idea.

Between April 2007 and his resignation approximately four months later, Ward shifted his exploration to the concept of a clip-on camera device, after learning that the eyeglass-mounted concept was already patent protected. He directed patent counsel to conduct a patent search on the modified idea. He communicated with JAM-Proactive, a product development company,

about the design and development of a clip-on camera device, and he received a detailed product development proposal from JAM-Proactive on June 12, 2007. Prior to his resignation, Ward planned to leave Taser to form a new business, and completed substantial work on a business plan to develop, market, and sell a clip-on camera device.

Ward resigned on July 24, 2007.
* * * He formed Vievu LLC on August 23, 2007, and Vievu now markets a clip-on camera device to general consumers and law enforcement. Ten months after Ward resigned, Taser announced the AXON, a product that provides an audio-video record of an incident from the visual perspective of the person involved.

[Taser filed a suit against Ward in an Arizona state court alleging, among other things, that Ward had breached his duty of loyalty to Taser. Taser moved for summary judgment in its favor, which the court granted. Ward appealed.]
* * * *

"In Arizona, an employee/agent owes his or her employer/principal a fiduciary duty." *"It is too plain to need discussion that an agent is under the duty to act with entire good faith and loyalty for the furtherance of the interests of his principal in all matters concerning or affecting the subject of his agency, and if he fails to do so, he is responsible to his principal for any loss resulting therefrom."* [Emphasis added.]

One aspect of this broad principle is that an employee is precluded from actively competing with his or her employer during the period of employment.

Although an employee may not compete prior to termination, "[the employee] may take action [during employment], not otherwise wrongful, to prepare for competition following termination of the agency relationship." Preparation cannot take the form of "acts in direct competition with the employer's business."

The line separating mere preparation from active competition may be difficult to discern in some cases, and we must "focus on the nature of the defendant's preparations to compete." [Emphasis added.]
* * * *

It is undisputed that, prior to his resignation, Ward did not solicit or recruit any Taser employees, distributors, customers, or vendors; he did not buy, sell, or incorporate any business; he did not acquire office space or other general business services; he did not contact or enter into any agreements with suppliers or manufacturers for his proposed clip-on camera; and he did not sell any products. However, Ward did begin developing a business plan, counseled with several attorneys, explored and abandoned the concept of an eyeglass-mounted camera device, and engaged, to some extent, in the exploration and development of a clip-on camera device.

Ward argues that his pre-termination activities did not constitute active competition but were merely lawful preparation for a future business venture. Taser contends, however, that "this case is not about just investigating computer software, acquiring a line

---

a. On the page that opens, select "Opinions Div 1" from the list of topics in the left-hand column. Select "Civil" from the list of categories. Scroll down the resulting list to the case title, and click on the link to access the opinion. The Arizona Court of Appeals maintains this Web site.

b. *Employment at will* is a common law doctrine under which either party may terminate an employment relationship at any time for any reason, unless a contract specifies otherwise.

EXTENDED CASE 32.3 CONTINUED ◆

of credit, securing office space, or getting prices on telephones * * * [but] about developing a rival design during employment, knowing full well TASER has sold such a device and continues to develop a second-generation product."

Upon review, we agree with Ward that certain of his pre-termination activities are qualitatively different than "direct competition" and cannot form the basis for liability.

* * * *

However, assuming Taser was engaged in the research and development of a recording device during Ward's employment, assuming Ward knew or should have known of those efforts, and assuming Taser's device would compete with Ward's concept, substantial design and development efforts by Ward during his employment would constitute direct competition with the business activities of Taser and would violate his duty of loyalty. In the context of a business which engages in research, design, development, manufacture,

and marketing of products, we cannot limit "competition" to just actual sales of competing products.

Summary judgment on this theory is nevertheless improper because a genuine issue of material fact exists as to the extent of Ward's pre-termination design and development efforts.

* * * *

For the foregoing reasons, we reverse the grant of summary judgment entered in favor of Taser * * * and remand for further proceedings.

 QUESTIONS

1. Why was it unclear whether Ward's pretermination actions constituted direct competition with his employer or were mere planning activities?
2. Suppose that Ward's planning and development efforts were focused on a product that in no way would compete with Taser's products. Would such efforts have breached his duty of loyalty to Taser in any way? Explain fully.

OBEDIENCE When acting on behalf of the principal, an agent has a duty to follow all lawful and clearly stated instructions of the principal. Any deviation from such instructions is a violation of this duty. During emergency situations, however, when the principal cannot be consulted, the agent may deviate from the instructions without violating this duty. Whenever instructions are not clearly stated, the agent can fulfill the duty of obedience by acting in good faith and in a manner reasonable under the circumstances.

ACCOUNTING Unless an agent and a principal agree otherwise, the agent has a duty to keep and make available to the principal an account of all property and funds received and paid out on behalf of the principal. This includes gifts from third parties in connection with the agency. For example, a gift from a customer to a salesperson for prompt deliveries made by the salesperson's firm, in the absence of a company policy to the contrary, belongs to the firm. The agent has a duty to maintain separate accounts for the principal's funds and the agent's personal funds, and the agent must not intermingle the funds in these accounts. Whenever a licensed professional (such as an attorney) violates this duty to account, he or she may be subject to disciplinary proceedings carried out by the appropriate regulatory institution

(such as the state bar association) in addition to being liable to the principal (the professional's client) for failure to account.

Principal's Duties to the Agent

The principal also has certain duties to the agent. These duties relate to compensation, reimbursement and indemnification, cooperation, and safe working conditions.

COMPENSATION In general, when a principal requests certain services from an agent, the agent reasonably expects payment. The principal therefore has a duty to pay the agent for services rendered. For example, when an accountant or an attorney is asked to act as an agent, an agreement to compensate the agent for this service is implied. The principal also has a duty to pay that compensation in a timely manner. Unless the agency relationship is gratuitous and the agent does not act in exchange for payment, the principal must pay the agreed-on value for the agent's services. If no amount has been expressly agreed on, then the principal owes the agent the customary compensation for such services.

REIMBURSEMENT AND INDEMNIFICATION Whenever an agent disburses funds to fulfill the request of the principal or to pay for necessary expenses in the course of reasonable performance of her or his agency duties, the principal has the duty to reimburse the agent for these payments.[10] Agents cannot recover for expenses incurred by their own misconduct or negligence, though.

Subject to the terms of the agency agreement, the principal has the duty to *indemnify* (compensate) an agent for liabilities incurred because of authorized and lawful acts and transactions. For example, if the agent, on the principal's behalf, forms a contract with a third party, and the principal fails to perform the contract, the third party may sue the agent for damages. In this situation, the principal is obligated to compensate the agent for any costs incurred by the agent as a result of the principal's failure to perform the contract.

Additionally, the principal must indemnify the agent for the value of benefits that the agent confers on the principal. The amount of indemnification usually is specified in the agency contract. If it is not, the courts will look to the nature of the business and the type of loss to determine the amount. Note that this rule applies to acts by gratuitous agents as well.

COOPERATION A principal has a duty to cooperate with the agent and to assist the agent in performing his or her duties. The principal must do nothing to prevent that performance. For example, when a principal grants an agent an exclusive territory, it creates an *exclusive agency,* in which the principal cannot compete with the agent or appoint or allow another agent to compete. If the principal does so, it violates the exclusive agency, and the principal is exposed to liability for the agent's lost profits. Suppose that Akers (the principal) creates an exclusive agency by granting Johnson (the agent) a territory within which only Johnson may sell Akers's products. If Akers begins to sell the products himself within Johnson's territory or permits another agent to do so, Akers has violated the exclusive agency and can be held liable for Johnson's lost profits.

SAFE WORKING CONDITIONS The common law requires the principal to provide safe working premises, equipment, and conditions for all agents and employees. The principal has a duty to inspect working areas and to warn agents and employees about any unsafe situations. When the agent is an employee, the employer's liability is frequently covered by state workers' compensation insurance, and federal and state statutes often require the employer to meet certain safety standards (see Chapter 34).

SECTION 4
RIGHTS AND REMEDIES OF AGENTS AND PRINCIPALS

In general, for every duty of the principal, the agent has a corresponding right, and vice versa. When one party to the agency relationship violates his or her duty to the other party, the remedies available to the nonbreaching party arise out of contract and tort law. These remedies include monetary damages, termination of the agency relationship, an injunction, and required accountings.

Agent's Rights and Remedies against the Principal

The agent has the right to be compensated, to be reimbursed and indemnified, and to have a safe working environment. An agent also has the right to perform agency duties without interference by the principal.

TORT AND CONTRACT REMEDIES Remedies of the agent for breach of duty by the principal follow normal contract and tort remedies. For example, Aaron Hart, a builder who has just constructed a new house, contracts with a real estate agent, Fran Boller, to sell the house. The contract calls for the agent to have an exclusive ninety-day listing and to receive 6 percent of the selling price when the home is sold. Boller holds several open houses and shows the home to a number of potential buyers. One month before the ninety-day listing terminates, Hart agrees to sell the house to another buyer—not one to whom Boller has shown the house—after the ninety-day listing expires. Hart and the buyer agree that Hart will reduce the price of the house by 3 percent because he will sell it directly and thus will not have to pay Boller's commission. In this situation, if Boller learns of Hart's actions, she can terminate the agency relationship and sue Hart for damages, including the 6 percent commission she should have earned on the sale of the house.

---

10. This principle applies to acts by gratuitous agents as well. If a finder of a dog that becomes sick takes the dog to a veterinarian and pays the required fees for the veterinarian's services, the gratuitous agent is entitled to be reimbursed for those fees by the owner of the dog.

DEMAND FOR AN ACCOUNTING An agent can also withhold further performance and demand that the principal give an accounting. For example, a sales agent may demand an accounting if the agent and principal disagree on the amount of commissions the agent should have received for sales made during a specific period of time.

NO RIGHT TO SPECIFIC PERFORMANCE When the principal-agent relationship is not contractual, the agent has no right to specific performance. An agent can recover for past services and future damages but cannot force the principal to allow him or her to continue acting as an agent.

Principal's Rights and Remedies against the Agent

In general, a principal has contract remedies for an agent's breach of fiduciary duties. The principal also has tort remedies if the agent engages in misrepresentation, negligence, deceit, libel, slander, or trespass. In addition, any breach of a fiduciary duty by an agent may justify the principal's termination of the agency. The main actions available to the principal are constructive trust, avoidance, and indemnification.

CONSTRUCTIVE TRUST Anything that an agent obtains by virtue of the employment or agency relationship belongs to the principal. An agent commits a breach of fiduciary duty if he or she secretly retains benefits or profits that, by right, belong to the principal. For example, Lee, a purchasing agent for Metcalf, receives cash rebates from a customer. If Lee keeps the rebates for himself, he violates his fiduciary duty to his principal, Metcalf. On finding out about the cash rebates, Metcalf can sue Lee and recover them.

AVOIDANCE When an agent breaches the agency agreement or agency duties under a contract, the principal has a right to avoid any contract entered into with the agent. This right of avoidance is at the election of the principal.

INDEMNIFICATION In certain situations, when a principal is sued by a third party for an agent's negligent conduct, the principal can sue the agent for indemnification—that is, for an equal amount of damages. The same holds true if the agent violates the principal's instructions. For example, Parker (the principal) owns a used-car lot where Moore (the agent) works as a salesperson. Parker tells Moore to make no warranties for the used cars. Moore is eager to make a sale to Walters, a customer, and adds a 50,000-mile warranty for the car's engine. Parker may still be liable to Walters for engine failure, but if Walters sues Parker, Parker normally can then sue Moore for indemnification for violating his instructions.

Sometimes, it is difficult to distinguish between instructions of the principal that limit an agent's authority and those that are merely advice. For example, Gutierrez (the principal) owns an office supply company, and Logan (the agent) is the manager. Gutierrez tells Logan, "Don't purchase any more inventory this month." Gutierrez goes on vacation. A large order comes in from a local business, and the inventory on hand is insufficient to meet it. What is Logan to do? In this situation, Logan probably has the inherent authority to purchase more inventory despite Gutierrez's command. It is unlikely that Logan would be required to indemnify Gutierrez in the event that the local business subsequently canceled the order.

REVIEWING
Agency Formation and Duties

James Blatt hired Marilyn Scott to sell insurance for the Massachusetts Mutual Life Insurance Co. Their contract stated, "Nothing in this contract shall be construed as creating the relationship of employer and employee." The contract was terminable at will by either party. Scott financed her own office and staff, was paid according to performance, had no taxes withheld from her checks, and could legally sell products of Massachusetts Mutual's competitors. But when Blatt learned that Scott was simultaneously selling insurance for Perpetual Life Insurance Corp., one of Massachusetts Mutual's fiercest competitors, Blatt withheld client contact information from Scott that would have assisted her

REVIEWING CONTINUES ➡

REVIEWING

Agency Formation and Duties, Continued

insurance sales for Massachusetts Mutual. Scott complained to Blatt that he was inhibiting her ability to sell insurance for Massachusetts Mutual. Blatt subsequently terminated their contract. Scott filed a suit in a New York state court against Blatt and Massachusetts Mutual. Scott claimed that she had lost sales for Massachusetts Mutual—and her commissions—as a result of Blatt's withholding contact information from her. Using the information presented in the chapter, answer the following questions.

1. Who is the principal and who is the agent in this scenario? By which method was an agency relationship formed between Scott and Blatt?
2. What facts would the court consider most important in determining whether Scott was an employee or an independent contractor?
3. How would the court most likely rule on Scott's employee status? Why?
4. Which of the four duties that Blatt owed Scott in their agency relationship has probably been breached?

⚙ DEBATE THIS: *All works created by independent contractors should be considered works for hire under copyright law.*

TERMS AND CONCEPTS

fiduciary 624

independent contractor 625

agency 624

QUESTIONS AND CASE PROBLEMS

32–1. Agency Formation Paul Gett is a well-known, wealthy financial expert living in the city of Torris. Adam Wade, Gett's friend, tells Timothy Brown that he is Gett's agent for the purchase of rare coins. Wade even shows Brown a local newspaper clipping mentioning Gett's interest in coin collecting. Brown, knowing of Wade's friendship with Gett, contracts with Wade to sell a rare coin valued at $25,000 to Gett. Wade takes the coin and disappears with it. On the payment due date, Brown seeks to collect from Gett, claiming that Wade's agency made Gett liable. Gett does not deny that Wade was a friend, but he claims that Wade was never his agent. Discuss fully whether an agency was in existence at the time the contract for the rare coin was made.

32–2. QUESTION WITH SAMPLE ANSWER: Duty of Loyalty.

Peter hires Alice as an agent to sell a piece of property he owns. The price is to be at least $30,000. Alice discovers that the fair market value of Peter's property is actually at least $45,000 and could be higher because a shopping mall is going to be built nearby. Alice forms a real estate partnership with her cousin Carl, and she prepares for Peter's signature a contract for the sale of the property to Carl for $32,000. Peter signs the contract. Just before closing and passage of title, Peter learns about the shopping mall and the increased fair market value of his property. Peter refuses to deed the property to Carl. Carl claims that Alice, as agent, solicited a price above that agreed on when the agency was created and that the contract is therefore binding and enforceable. Discuss fully whether Peter is bound to this contract.

- **For a sample answer to Question 32–2, go to Appendix I at the end of this text.**

32–3. Principal's Remedies against Agent Ankir is hired by Jamison as a traveling salesperson. Ankir not only solicits orders but also delivers the goods and collects payments from his customers. Ankir deposits all payments in his private checking account and at the end of each month draws sufficient cash from his bank to cover the payments made. Jamison is totally unaware of this procedure. Because of a slowdown in the economy, Jamison tells all his salespeople to offer 20 percent discounts on orders. Ankir solicits orders, but he offers only 15 percent discounts, pocketing the extra 5 percent paid by customers. Ankir has not lost any orders by this practice, and he is rated as one of Jamison's top salespersons. Jamison learns of Ankir's actions. Discuss fully Jamison's rights in this matter.

32–4. Agency Formation Ford Motor Credit Co. is a subsidiary of Ford Motor Co. with its own offices, officers, and directors. Ford Credit buys contracts and leases of automobiles entered into by dealers and consumers. Ford Credit also provides inventory financing for dealers' purchases of Ford and non-Ford vehicles and makes loans to Ford and non-Ford dealers. Dealers and consumers are not required to finance their purchases or leases of Ford vehicles through Ford Credit. Ford Motor is not a party to the agreements between Ford Credit and its customers and does not directly receive any payments under those agreements. Also, Ford Credit is not subject to any agreement with Ford Motor "restricting or conditioning" its ability to finance the dealers' inventories or the consumers' purchases or leases of vehicles. A number of plaintiffs filed a product liability suit in a Missouri state court against Ford Motor. Ford Motor claimed that the court did not have venue. The plaintiffs asserted that Ford Credit, which had an office in the jurisdiction, acted as Ford's "agent for the transaction of its usual and customary business" there. Is Ford Credit an agent of Ford Motor? Discuss. [*State ex rel. Ford Motor Co. v. Bacon,* 63 S.W.3d 641 (Mo. 2002)]

32–5. Agent's Duties to Principal Sam and Theresa Daigle decided to build a home in Cameron Parish, Louisiana. To obtain financing, they contacted Trinity United Mortgage Co. At a meeting with Joe Diez on Trinity's behalf, on July 18, 2001, the Daigles signed a temporary loan agreement with Union Planters Bank. Diez assured them that they did not need to make payments on this loan until their house was built and permanent financing had been secured. Because the Daigles did not make payments on the Union loan, Trinity declined to make the permanent loan. Meanwhile, Diez left Trinity's employ. On November 1, the Daigles moved into their new house. They tried to contact Diez at Trinity but were told that he was unavailable and would get back to them. Three weeks later, Diez came to the Daigles' home and had them sign documents that they believed were to secure a permanent loan but that were actually an application with Diez's new employer. Union filed a suit in a Louisiana state court against the Daigles for failing to pay on its loan. The Daigles paid Union, obtained permanent financing through another source, and filed a suit against Trinity to recover the cost. Who should have told the Daigles that Diez was no longer Trinity's agent? Could Trinity be liable to the Daigles on this basis? Explain. [*Daigle v. Trinity United Mortgage, L.L.C.,* 890 So.2d 583 (La.App. 3 Cir. 2004)]

32–6. Principal's Duties to Agent Josef Boehm was an officer and the majority shareholder of Alaska Industrial Hardware, Inc. (AIH), in Anchorage, Alaska. In August 2001, Lincolnshire Management, Inc., in New York, created AIH Acquisition Corp. to buy AIH. The three firms signed a "commitment letter" to negotiate "a definitive stock purchase agreement" (SPA). In September, Harold Snow and Ronald Braley began to work, on Boehm's behalf, with Vincent Coyle, an agent for AIH Acquisition, to produce an SPA. They exchanged many drafts and dozens of e-mails. Finally, in February 2002, Braley told Coyle that Boehm would sign the SPA "early next week." That did not occur, however, and at the end of March, after more negotiations and drafts, Boehm demanded a larger payment. AIH Acquisition agreed, and, following more work by the agents, another SPA was drafted. In April, the parties met in Anchorage. Boehm still refused to sign. AIH Acquisition and others filed a suit in a federal district court against AIH. Did Boehm violate any of the duties that principals owe to their agents? If so, which duty, and how was it violated? Explain. [*AIH Acquisition Corp., LLC v. Alaska Industrial Hardware, Inc.,* __ F.Supp.2d __ (S.D.N.Y. 2004)]

32–7. CASE PROBLEM WITH SAMPLE ANSWER: Agent's Duties to Principal.

In July 2001, John Warren viewed a condominium in Woodland Hills, California, as a potential buyer. Hildegard Merrill was the agent for the seller. Because Warren's credit rating was poor, Merrill told him he needed a co-borrower to obtain a mortgage at a reasonable rate. Merrill said that her daughter Charmaine would "go on title" until the loan and sale were complete if Warren would pay her $10,000. Merrill also offered to defer her commission on the sale as a loan to Warren so that he could make a 20 percent down payment on the property. He agreed to both plans. Merrill applied for and secured the mortgage in Charmaine's name alone by misrepresenting her daughter's address, business, and income. To close the sale, Merrill had Warren remove his name from the title to the property. In October, Warren moved into the condominium, repaid Merrill the amount of her deferred commission, and began paying the mortgage. Within a few months, Merrill had Warren evicted. Warren filed a suit in a California state court against Merrill and Charmaine. Who among these parties was in an agency relationship? What is the basic duty that an agent owes a principal? Was the duty breached here? Explain. [Warren v. Merrill, *143 Cal.App.4th 96, 49 Cal. Rptr.3d 122 (2 Dist. 2006)*]

- **To view a sample answer for Problem 32–7, go to this book's Web site at www.cengage.com/blaw/clarkson, select "Chapter 32," and click on "Case Problem with Sample Answer."**

32–8. Agent's Duties to Principal Su Ru Chen owned the Lucky Duck Fortune Cookie Factory in Everett, Massachusetts, which made Chinese-style fortune cookies for restaurants. In November 2001, Chen listed the business for sale with Bob Sun, a real estate broker, for $35,000. Sun's daughter Frances and her fiancé, Chiu Chung Chan, decided that Chan would buy the business. Acting as a broker on Chen's (the seller's) behalf, Frances asked about the Lucky Duck's finances. Chen said that each month the business sold at least 1,000 boxes of cookies at a $2,000 profit. Frances negotiated a price of $23,000, which Chan (her fiancé) paid. When Chan began to operate the Lucky Duck, it became clear that the demand for the cookies was actually about 500 boxes per month—a rate at which the business would suffer losses. Less than two months later, the factory closed. Chan filed a suit in a Massachusetts state court against Chen, alleging fraud, among other things. Chan's proof included Frances's testimony as to what Chen had said to her. Chen objected to the admission of this testimony. What is the basis for this objection? Should the court admit the testimony? Why or why not? [*Chan v. Chen*, 70 Mass.App.Ct. 79, 872 N.E.2d 1153 (2007)]

32–9. Agency by Ratification Wesley Hall, an independent contractor managing property for Acree Investments, Ltd., lost control of a fire he had set to clear ten acres of Acree land. The runaway fire burned seventy-eight acres of Earl Barrs's property. Russell Acree, one of the owners of Acree Investments, had previously owned the ten acres, but he had put it into the company and was no longer the principal owner. Hall had worked for Russell Acree in the past and had told the state forestry department that he was burning the land for Acree. Barrs sued Russell Acree for the acts of his agent, Hall. In his suit, Barrs noted that Hall had been an employee of Russell Acree, Hall had talked about burning the land "for Acree," Russell Acree had apologized to Barrs for the fire, and Acree Investments had not been identified as the principal property owner until Barrs had filed his lawsuit. Barrs argued that those facts were sufficient to create an agency by ratification to impose liability on Russell Acree. Was Barrs's agency by ratification claim valid? Why or why not? [*Barrs v. Acree*, 691 S.E.2d 575 (Ga.App. 2010)]

32–10. A QUESTION OF ETHICS: Agency Formation and Duties.

 Emergency One, Inc. (EO), makes fire and rescue vehicles. Western Fire Truck, Inc., contracted with EO to be its exclusive dealer in Colorado and Wyoming through December 2003. James Costello, a Western salesperson, was authorized to order EO vehicles for his customers. Without informing Western, Costello e-mailed EO about Western's difficulties in obtaining cash to fund its operations. He asked about the viability of Western's contract and his possible employment with EO. On EO's request, and in disregard of Western's instructions, Costello sent some payments for EO vehicles directly to EO. In addition, Costello, with EO's help, sent a competing bid to a potential Western customer. EO's representative e-mailed Costello, "You have my permission to kick [Western's] ass." In April 2002, EO terminated its contract with Western, which, after reviewing Costello's e-mail, fired Costello. Western filed a suit in a Colorado state court against Costello and EO, alleging, among other things, that Costello breached his duty as an agent and that EO aided and abetted the breach. [Western Fire Truck, Inc. v. Emergency One, Inc., *134 P.3d 570 (Colo.App. 2006)]*

(a) Was there an agency relationship between Western and Costello? Western required monthly reports from its sales staff, but Costello did not report regularly. Does this indicate that Costello was *not* Western's agent? In determining whether an agency relationship exists, is the *right* to control or the *fact* of control more important? Explain.

(b) Did Costello owe Western a duty? If so, what was the duty? Did Costello breach it? If so, how?

(c) A Colorado state statute allows a court to award punitive damages in "circumstances of fraud, malice, or willful and wanton conduct." Did any of these circumstances exist in this case? Should punitive damages be assessed against either defendant? Why or why not?

LEGAL RESEARCH EXERCISES ON THE WEB

Go to this text's Web site at **www.cengage.com/blaw/clarkson**, select "Chapter 32," and click on "Practical Internet Exercises." There you will find the following Internet research exercises that you can perform to learn more about the topics covered in this chapter.

Practical Internet Exercise 32–1: **Legal Perspective**
Employees or Independent Contractors?

Practical Internet Exercise 32–2: **Management Perspective**
Problems with Using Independent Contractors

CHAPTER 33

✷

Agency Liability and Termination

As discussed in the previous chapter, the law of agency focuses on the special relationship that exists between a principal and an agent—how the relationship is formed and the duties the principal and agent assume once the relationship is established. This chapter deals with another important aspect of agency law—the liability of principals and agents to third parties.

We look first at the liability of principals for contracts formed by agents with third parties. Generally, the liability of the principal will depend on whether the agent was authorized to form the contract. The second part of the chapter deals with an agent's liability to third parties in contract and tort, and the principal's liability to third parties because of an agent's torts. The chapter concludes with a discussion of how agency relationships are terminated.

SECTION 1
SCOPE OF AGENT'S AUTHORITY

The liability of a principal to third parties with whom an agent contracts depends on whether the agent had the authority to enter into legally binding contracts on the principal's behalf. An agent's authority can be either *actual* (express or implied) or *apparent*. If an agent contracts outside the scope of his or her authority, the principal may still become liable by ratifying the contract.

Express Authority

Express authority is authority declared in clear, direct, and definite terms. Express authority can be given orally or in writing.

THE EQUAL DIGNITY RULE In most states, the **equal dignity rule** requires that if the contract being executed is or must be in writing, then the agent's authority must also be in writing. Failure to comply with the equal dignity rule can make a contract voidable *at the option of the principal*. The law regards the contract at that point as a mere offer. If the principal decides to accept the offer, the acceptance must be ratified, or affirmed, in writing.

Assume that Paloma (the principal) orally asks Austin (the agent) to sell a ranch that Paloma owns. Austin finds a buyer and signs a sales contract (a contract for an interest in realty must be in writing) on behalf of Paloma to sell the ranch. The buyer cannot enforce the contract unless Paloma subsequently ratifies Austin's agency status in writing. Once the contract is ratified, either party can enforce rights under the contract.

Modern business practice allows an exception to the equal dignity rule. An executive officer of a corporation normally is not required to obtain written authority from the corporation to conduct *ordinary* business transactions. The equal dignity rule does not apply when the agent acts in the presence of the principal or when the agent's act of signing is merely perfunctory (token or customary). Thus, if Healy (the principal) negotiates a contract but is called out of town the day it is to be signed and orally authorizes Santini to sign, the oral authorization is sufficient.

POWER OF ATTORNEY Giving an agent a **power of attorney** confers express authority.[1] The power of attorney is a written document and is usually notarized. (A document is notarized when a **notary public**—a public official authorized to attest to the authenticity of signatures—signs

and dates the document and imprints it with her or his seal of authority.) Most states have statutory provisions for creating a power of attorney. A power of attorney can be special (permitting the agent to perform specified acts only), or it can be general (permitting the agent to transact all business for the principal). Because of the extensive authority granted to an agent by a general power of attorney (see Exhibit 33–1 below), it should be used with great caution and usually only in exceptional circumstances. Ordinarily, a power of

---

1. An agent who holds a power of attorney is called an *attorney-in-fact* for the principal. The holder does not have to be an attorney-at-law (and often is not).

EXHIBIT 33–1 • A Sample General Power of Attorney

GENERAL POWER OF ATTORNEY

Know All Men by These Presents:

That I, _____ , hereinafter referred to as PRINCIPAL, in the County of _____
State of _____ , do(es) appoint _____ as my true and lawful attorney.

In principal's name, and for principal's use and benefit, said attorney is authorized hereby;

(1) To demand, sue for, collect, and receive all money, debts, accounts, legacies, bequests, interest, dividends, annuities, and demands as are now or shall hereafter become due, payable, or belonging to principal, and take all lawful means, for the recovery thereof and to compromise the same and give discharges for the same;

(2) To buy and sell land, make contracts of every kind relative to land, any interest therein or the possession thereof, and to take possession and exercise control over the use thereof;

(3) To buy, sell, mortgage, hypothecate, assign, transfer, and in any manner deal with goods, wares and merchandise, choses in action, certificates or shares of capital stock, and other property in possession or in action, and to make, do, and transact all and every kind of business of whatever nature;

(4) To execute, acknowledge, and deliver contracts of sale, escrow instructions, deeds, leases including leases for minerals and hydrocarbon substances and assignments of leases, covenants, agreements and assignments of agreements, mortgages and assignments of mortgages, conveyances in trust, to secure indebtedness or other obligations, and assign the beneficial interest thereunder, subordinations of liens or encumbrances, bills of lading, receipts, evidences of debt, releases, bonds, notes, bills, requests to reconvey deeds of trust, partial or full judgments, satisfactions of mortgages, and other debts, and other written instruments of whatever kind and nature, all upon such terms and conditions as said attorney shall approve.

GIVING AND GRANTING to said attorney full power and authority to do all and every act and thing whatsoever requisite and necessary to be done relative to any of the foregoing as fully to all intents and purposes as principal might or could do if personally present.

All that said attorney shall lawfully do or cause to be done under the authority of this power of attorney is expressly approved.

Dated: _____   /s/_____

State of _____   } SS.
    County of _____
On _____ , before me, the undersigned, a Notary Public in and for said
State, personally appeared _____
_____
known to me to be the person _____ whose name _____ subscribed
to the within instrument and acknowledged that _____ executed the same.
                                                    (Seal) _____
Witness my hand and official seal.   Notary Public in and for said State.

attorney terminates on the incapacity or death of the person giving the power.[2]

Implied Authority

An agent has the **implied authority** to do what is reasonably necessary to carry out express authority and accomplish the objectives of the agency. Authority can also be implied by custom or inferred from the position the agent occupies. For example, Archer is employed by Packard Grocery to manage one of its stores. Packard has not expressly stated that Archer has authority to contract with third persons. Nevertheless, authority to manage a business implies authority to do what is reasonably required (as is customary or can be inferred from a manager's position) to operate the business. This includes forming contracts to hire employees, to buy merchandise and equipment, and to advertise the products sold in the store.

In general, implied authority is authority customarily associated with the position occupied by the agent or authority that can be inferred from the express authority given to the agent to perform fully his or her duties. For example, an agent has authority to solicit orders for goods sold by the principal. The agent, however, does not carry any goods with him when soliciting orders, and thus generally would not have the authority to collect payments for the goods. The test is whether it was reasonable for the agent to believe that she or he had the authority to enter into the contract in question.

Also note that an agent's implied authority cannot contradict his or her express authority. Thus, if

_____
2. A *durable* power of attorney, however, continues to be effective despite the principal's incapacity. An elderly person, for example, might grant a durable power of attorney to provide for the handling of property and investments or specific health-care needs should he or she become incompetent (see Chapter 52).

a principal has limited an agent's authority—by forbidding a manager to enter into contracts to hire additional workers, for example—then the fact that managers customarily would have such authority is irrelevant.

Apparent Authority

Actual authority (express or implied) arises from what the principal makes clear *to the agent*. Apparent authority, in contrast, arises from what the principal causes a third party to believe. An agent has **apparent authority** when the principal, by either word or action, causes a *third party* reasonably to believe that the agent has authority to act, even though the agent has no express or implied authority.

A PATTERN OF CONDUCT   Apparent authority usually comes into existence through a principal's pattern of conduct over time. For example, Ashley is a traveling salesperson with the authority to solicit orders for a principal's goods. Because she does not carry any goods with her, she normally would not have the implied authority to collect payments from customers on behalf of the principal. Suppose that she does accept payments from Cabo Enterprises, however, and submits them to the principal's accounting department for processing. If the principal does nothing to stop Ashley from continuing this practice, a pattern develops over time, and the principal confers apparent authority on Ashley to accept payments from Cabo.

In the following case, an employee misappropriated more than $1 million from her employer by using his credit card without authorization over a number of years. The issue before the court was whether the employee had apparent authority to use the card.

CASE 33.1
Azur v. Chase Bank, USA

United States Court of Appeals, Third Circuit, 601 F.3d 212 (2010).
www.ca3.uscourts.gov[a]

BACKGROUND AND FACTS • ATM Corporation of America, Inc. (ATM), manages settlement services for large national lenders. Francis Azur, the founder of ATM, served as its president and chief executive officer until September 2007, when ATM was sold. In July 1997, ATM hired Michelle Vanek to be Azur's personal assistant. Vanek's responsibilities included opening Azur's personal bills, preparing and

_____
a. Under "Opinions and Oral Arguments," select "Search for Opinions." When the search page appears, type "Azur" in the search box and click on "Go." When the case information appears at the bottom of the search page, click on the highlighted link to the PDF to access the case. The U.S. Court of Appeals for the Third Circuit maintains this Web site.

CASE CONTINUES ▶

CASE 33.1 CONTINUED ▶ presenting checks for Azur to sign, balancing Azur's checking and savings accounts, and reviewing his credit-card and bank statements. Vanek also had access to Azur's credit-card number so that she could make purchases for him. Over a period of seven years, Vanek withdrew unauthorized cash advances of between $200 and $700, typically twice a day, from Azur's credit-card account with Chase Bank, USA. The fraudulent charges were reflected on at least sixty-five monthly billing statements sent by Chase to Azur, and Vanek paid the bills by either writing checks and forging Azur's signature or making online payments from Azur's checking account. In all, Vanek misappropriated more than $1 million from Azur. When Azur discovered Vanek's fraudulent scheme in 2006, he terminated her employment and closed the Chase account. Azur sued Chase, seeking reimbursement of the fraudulent charges under Section 1643 of the Truth-in-Lending Act, or TILA.[b] A magistrate judge concluded that Azur's claim failed because Vanek had apparent authority to use Azur's credit card. The trial court—a U.S. district court—agreed and granted Chase's motion for summary judgment on this issue. Azur appealed.

IN THE LANGUAGE OF THE COURT
FISHER, Circuit Judge.
* * * *

* * * [Section 1643 of the TILA] provides that "[a] cardholder shall be liable for the unauthorized use of a credit card" in certain circumstances. The term *"unauthorized use" is defined as the "use of a credit card by a person other than the cardholder who does not have actual, implied, or apparent authority for such use and from which the cardholder receives no benefit."* [Emphasis added.]

To determine whether apparent authority exists, we turn to applicable state agency law. * * * Citing the *Restatement (Second) of Agency*, the Pennsylvania Supreme Court has explained as follows:

> Apparent authority is power to bind a principal which the principal has not actually granted but which he leads persons with whom his agent deals to believe that he has granted. Persons with whom the agent deals can reasonably believe that the agent has power to bind his principal if, for instance, the principal knowingly permits the agent to exercise such power or if the principal holds the agent out as possessing such power.

* * * *

* * * A cardholder may, in certain circumstances, vest a fraudulent user with the apparent authority to use a credit card by enabling the continuous payment of the credit card charges over a period of time.

Here, Azur's negligent omissions led Chase to reasonably believe that the fraudulent charges were authorized. Although Azur may not have been aware that Vanek was using the Chase credit card, or even that the Chase credit card account existed, Azur knew that he had a Dollar Bank checking account, and he did not review his Dollar Bank statements or exercise any other oversight over Vanek, his employee. * * * Had Azur occasionally reviewed his statements, Azur would have likely noticed that checks had been written to Chase. Because Chase reasonably believed that a prudent business person would oversee his employees in such a manner, Chase reasonably relied on the continuous payment of the fraudulent charges.

DECISION AND REMEDY • *The U.S. Court of Appeals for the Third Circuit affirmed the trial court's judgment, holding that Azur had vested Vanek with apparent authority to use the Chase credit card.*

THE ETHICAL DIMENSION • *The TILA essentially is a consumer-protection law. How does allowing a credit-card company to avoid liability—if a card user has apparent authority to use the card—protect consumers?*

MANAGERIAL IMPLICATIONS • *Business owners and managers should take precautions to avoid being held liable, under a theory of apparent authority, for unauthorized credit-card charges made by their employees. Any employee who has access to the employer's credit-card number, credit-card statements, bank accounts, and other financial data should be carefully supervised. The employer should periodically review bank statements and credit-card payments to ensure that no checks have been forged and that all payments to credit-card companies are for authorized charges.*

---

b. Among other things, the Truth-in-Lending Act (TILA) protects holders of credit cards from liability for the fraudulent use of their credit cards. (See Chapter 45 for a detailed discussion of this consumer-protection statute.)

APPARENT AUTHORITY AND ESTOPPEL The doctrine of agency by estoppel (introduced in Chapter 32) may be applied in situations in which a principal has given a third party reason to believe that an agent has authority to act. If the third party changes position to his or her detriment in good faith reliance on the principal's representations, the principal may be *estopped* (prevented) from denying that the agent had authority.

In the following case, the court applied the doctrine of estoppel to a situation involving a question of apparent authority or, as the court referred to it, "ostensible authority."

CASE 33.2
Ermoian v. Desert Hospital

Court of Appeal of California, Fourth District, 152 Cal.App.4th 475, 61 Cal.Rptr.3d 754 (2007).

BACKGROUND AND FACTS • In 1990, Desert Hospital in California established a comprehensive perinatal services program (CPSP) to provide obstetrical care to women who were uninsured (*perinatal* is often defined as relating to the period from about the twenty-eighth week of pregnancy to around one month after birth). The CPSP was set up in an office suite across from the hospital and named "Desert Hospital Outpatient Maternity Services Clinic." The hospital contracted with a corporation controlled by Dr. Morton Gubin, which employed Dr. Masami Ogata, to provide obstetrical services. In January 1994, Jackie Shahan went to the hospital's emergency room because of cramping and other symptoms. The emergency room physician told Shahan that she was pregnant and referred her to the clinic. Shahan visited the clinic throughout her pregnancy. On May 15, Shahan's baby, Amanda Ermoian, was born with brain abnormalities that left her severely mentally retarded and unable to care for herself. Her conditions could not have been prevented, treated, or cured *in utero*. Through a guardian, Amanda filed a suit in a California state court against the hospital and others, alleging "wrongful life." She claimed that the defendants negligently failed to inform her mother of her abnormalities before her birth, depriving her mother of the opportunity to make an informed choice to terminate the pregnancy. The court ruled in the defendants' favor, holding, among other things, that the hospital was not liable because Drs. Gubin and Ogata were not its employees. Amanda appealed to a state intermediate appellate court, contending that the physicians were the hospital's "ostensible agents."

IN THE LANGUAGE OF THE COURT
KING, J. [Judge]
* * * *

Agency may be either actual or ostensible [apparent]. Actual agency exists when the agent is really employed by the principal. Here, there was evidence that the physicians were not employees of the Hospital, but were physicians with a private practice who contracted with the Hospital to perform obstetric services at the clinic. The written contract between the Hospital and Dr. Gubin's corporation (which employed Dr. Ogata) describes Dr. Gubin and his corporation as "independent contractors with, and not as employees of, [the] Hospital." [Maria Sterling, a registered nurse at the clinic and Shahan's CPSP case coordinator] testified that Drs. Gubin and Ogata, not the Hospital, provided the obstetric services to the clinic's patients. Donna McCloudy, a director of nursing [who set up the CPSP] at the Hospital, testified that while the Hospital provided some aspects of the CPSP services, "independent physicians * * * provided the obstetrical care * * * ." Based upon such evidence, the [trial] court reasonably concluded that the physicians were not the employees or actual agents of the Hospital for purposes of vicarious [indirect] liability.

Ostensible [apparent] agency on the other hand, may be implied from the facts of a particular case, and if a principal by his acts has led others to believe that he has conferred authority upon an agent, he cannot be heard to assert, as against third parties who have relied thereon in good faith, that he did not intend to confer such power * * * . The doctrine establishing the principles of liability for the acts of an ostensible agent rests on the doctrine of estoppel. *The essential elements are representations by the principal, justifiable reliance thereon by a third party,*

CASE CONTINUES ▶

CASE 33.2 CONTINUED ▶ *and change of position or injury resulting from such reliance.* Before recovery can be had against the principal for the acts of an ostensible agent, the person dealing with an agent must do so with belief in the agent's authority and this belief must be a reasonable one. Such belief must be generated by some act or neglect by the principal sought to be charged and the person relying on the agent's apparent authority must not be guilty of neglect. [Emphasis added.]

* * * *

Here, the Hospital held out the clinic and the personnel in the clinic as part of the Hospital. Furthermore, it was objectively reasonable for Shahan to believe that Drs. Gubin and Ogata were employees of the Hospital. The clinic was located across the street from the Hospital. It used the same name as the Hospital and labeled itself as an outpatient clinic. Numerous professionals at the clinic were employees of the Hospital. [Carol Cribbs, a comprehensive perinatal health worker at the clinic] and Sterling indicated to Shahan that they were employees of the Hospital and that the program was run by the Hospital. Sterling personally set up all of Shahan's appointments at the main Hospital rather than giving Shahan a referral for the various tests. Shahan was referred by individuals in the emergency room specifically to Dr. Gubin. When she called for an appointment she was told by the receptionist that she was calling the Hospital outpatient clinic which was the clinic of Dr. Gubin. On days when Shahan would see either Dr. Gubin or Dr. Ogata at the clinic, she would also see either Cribbs or Sterling, whom she knew were employed by the Hospital.

* * * At her first appointment she signed a document titled "patient rights and responsibilities," which would unambiguously lead a patient to the conclusion that the clinic "was a one-stop shop for the patient," and that all individuals at the clinic were connected with the Hospital. All of Shahan's contacts with the physicians were at the Hospital-run clinic. Most, if not all, of the physician contacts occurred in conjunction with the provision of other services by either Sterling or Cribbs. The entire appearance created by the Hospital, and those associated with it, was that the Hospital was the provider of the obstetrical care to Shahan.

DECISION AND REMEDY • *The state intermediate appellate court decided that, contrary to the lower court's finding, Drs. Gubin and Ogata were "ostensible agents of the Hospital." The appellate court affirmed the lower court's ruling, however, on Amanda's "wrongful life" claim, concluding that the physicians were not negligent in failing to advise Shahan to have an elective abortion.*

THE ETHICAL DIMENSION • *Does a principal have an ethical responsibility to inform an unaware third party that an apparent (ostensible) agent does not in fact have authority to act on the principal's behalf?*

THE E-COMMERCE DIMENSION • *Could Amanda have established Drs. Gubin and Ogata's apparent authority if Desert Hospital had maintained a Web site that advertised the services of the CPSP clinic and stated clearly that the physicians were not its employees? Explain.*

Emergency Powers

When an unforeseen emergency demands action by the agent to protect or preserve the property and rights of the principal, but the agent is unable to communicate with the principal, the agent has emergency power. For example, Fulsom is an engineer for Pacific Drilling Company. While Fulsom is acting within the scope of his employment, he is severely injured in an accident at an oil rig many miles from home. Acosta, the rig supervisor, directs Thompson, a physician, to give medical aid to Fulsom and to charge Pacific for the medical services. Acosta, an agent, has no express or implied authority to bind the principal, Pacific Drilling, for Thompson's medical services. Because of the emergency situation, however, the law recognizes Acosta as having authority to act appropriately under the circumstances.

Ratification

Ratification occurs when the principal affirms, or accepts responsibility for, an agent's *unauthorized* act. When ratification occurs, the principal is bound to the agent's act, and the act is treated as if it had been authorized by the principal *from the outset.* Ratification can be either express or implied.

If the principal does not ratify the contract, the principal is not bound, and the third party's agreement with the agent is viewed as merely an unaccepted offer. Because the third party's agreement is an unaccepted offer, the third party can revoke it at any time, without liability, before the principal ratifies the contract. The agent, however, may be liable to the third party for misrepresenting her or his authority.

The requirements for ratification can be summarized as follows:

1. The agent must have acted on behalf of an identified principal who subsequently ratifies the action.
2. The principal must know all of the material facts involved in the transaction. If a principal ratifies a contract without knowing all of the facts, the principal can rescind (cancel) the contract.[3]
3. The principal must affirm the agent's act in its entirety.
4. The principal must have the legal capacity to authorize the transaction at the time the agent engages in the act and at the time the principal ratifies. The third party must also have the legal capacity to engage in the transaction.
5. The principal's affirmation (ratification) must occur before the third party withdraws from the transaction.

6. The principal must observe the same formalities when ratifying the act as would have been required to authorize it initially.

Concept Summary 33.1 below summarizes the rules concerning an agent's authority to bind the principal and a third party.

SECTION 2

LIABILITY FOR CONTRACTS

Liability for contracts formed by an agent depends on how the principal is classified and on whether the actions of the agent were authorized or unauthorized. Principals are classified as disclosed, partially disclosed, or undisclosed.[4]

A **disclosed principal** is a principal whose identity is known by the third party at the time the contract is made by the agent. A **partially disclosed principal** is a principal whose identity is not known by the third party, but the third party knows that the agent is or may be acting for a principal at the time the contract is made. An **undisclosed principal** is a principal whose identity is totally unknown by the third party, and the third party has no knowledge that the agent is acting in an agency capacity at the time the contract is made.

---

3. If the third party has changed position in reliance on the apparent contract, however, the principal can rescind but must reimburse the third party for any costs.

4. *Restatement (Third) of Agency*, Section 1.04 (2).

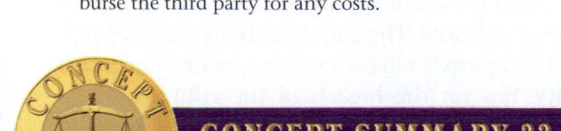

CONCEPT SUMMARY 33.1
Authority of an Agent to Bind the Principal and a Third Party

Authority of Agent	Definition	Effect on Principal and Third Party
Express Authority	Authority expressly given by the principal to the agent.	Principal and third party are bound in contract.
Implied Authority	Authority implied (1) by custom, (2) from the position in which the principal has placed the agent, or (3) because such authority is necessary if the agent is to carry out expressly authorized duties and responsibilities.	Principal and third party are bound in contract.
Apparent Authority	Authority created when the conduct of the principal leads a third party to believe that the principal's agent has authority.	Principal and third party are bound in contract.
Unauthorized Acts	Acts committed by an agent that are outside the scope of his or her express, implied, or apparent authority.	Principal and third party are not bound in contract—*unless* the principal ratifies prior to the third party's withdrawal.

Authorized Acts

If an agent acts within the scope of her or his authority, normally the principal is obligated to perform the contract regardless of whether the principal was disclosed, partially disclosed, or undisclosed. Whether the agent may also be held liable under the contract, however, depends on the disclosed, partially disclosed, or undisclosed status of the principal.

DISCLOSED OR PARTIALLY DISCLOSED PRINCIPAL A disclosed or partially disclosed principal is liable to a third party for a contract made by the agent. If the principal is disclosed, the agent has no contractual liability for the nonperformance of the principal or the third party. If the principal is partially disclosed, in most states the agent is also treated as a party to the contract, and the third party can hold the agent liable for contractual nonperformance.[5]

CASE IN POINT Walgreens leased commercial property at a mall owned by Kedzie Plaza Associates to operate a drugstore. A property management company, Taxman Corporation, signed the lease on behalf of the principal, Kedzie. The lease required the landlord to keep the sidewalks free of snow and ice, so Taxman, on behalf of Kedzie, contracted with another company to remove ice and snow from the sidewalks surrounding the Walgreens store. When a Walgreens employee slipped on ice outside the store and was injured, she sued Taxman, among others, for negligence. Because the principal's identity (Kedzie) was fully disclosed in the snow-removal contract, however, the court ruled that the agent, Taxman, could not be held liable. Taxman did not assume a contractual obligation to remove the snow but merely retained a contractor to do so on behalf of the owner.[6]

UNDISCLOSED PRINCIPAL When neither the fact of an agency relationship nor the identity of the principal is disclosed, the undisclosed principal is bound to perform just as if the principal had been fully disclosed at the time the contract was made.

When a principal's identity is undisclosed and the agent is forced to pay the third party, the agent is entitled to be *indemnified* (compensated) by the principal. The principal had a duty to perform, even though his or her identity was undisclosed,[7] and failure to do so will make the principal ultimately liable.

Once the undisclosed principal's identity is revealed, the third party generally can elect to hold either the principal or the agent liable on the contract.

Conversely, the undisclosed principal can require the third party to fulfill the contract, *unless* (1) the undisclosed principal was expressly excluded as a party in the written contract; (2) the contract is a negotiable instrument signed by the agent with no indication of signing in a representative capacity;[8] or (3) the performance of the agent is personal to the contract, allowing the third party to refuse the principal's performance.

Unauthorized Acts

If an agent has no authority but nevertheless contracts with a third party, the principal cannot be held liable on the contract. It does not matter whether the principal was disclosed, partially disclosed, or undisclosed. The person who acted as an agent is liable, however. For example, Updike signs a contract for the purchase of a truck, purportedly acting as an agent under authority granted by Parker. In fact, Parker has not given Updike any such authority. Parker refuses to pay for the truck, claiming that Updike had no authority to purchase it. The seller of the truck is entitled to hold Updike liable for payment.

If an agent for a disclosed or partially disclosed principal contracts with a third party without authorization, the third party who relied on the agency status can also hold the agent liable for breaching the *implied warranty of authority*. The agent's liability here is based on the third party's reliance on the agent's purported authority, not on the breach of the contract itself.[9] For example, Pinnell, a reclusive artist, hires Auber to solicit offers for particular paintings from various galleries, but does not authorize her to enter into sales agreements. Olaf, a gallery owner, offers to buy two of Pinnell's paintings for an upcoming show. If Auber draws up a sales contract with Olaf, she impliedly warrants that she has the authority to enter into sales contracts on behalf of Pinnell. If Pinnell does not agree to ratify Auber's sales contract, Olaf cannot hold Pinnell liable, but he can hold Auber liable for breaching the implied warranty of authority.

Note that if the third party knows at the time the contract is made that the agent does not have authority, then the agent is not liable. Similarly, if the agent expressed to the third party *uncertainty* as to the extent of her or his authority, the agent is not personally liable.

---

5. *Restatement (Third) of Agency,* Section 6.02.
6. *McBride v. Taxman Corp.,* 327 Ill.App.3d 992, 765 N.E.2d 51 (2002).
7. If the agent is a gratuitous agent, and the principal accepts the benefits of the agent's contract with a third party, then the principal will be liable to the agent on the theory of quasi contract (see Chapter 10).

8. Under the Uniform Commercial Code (UCC), only the agent is liable if the instrument neither names the principal nor shows that the agent signed in a representative capacity [UCC 3–402(b)(2)].
9. The agent is not liable on the contract, because the agent was never intended personally to be a party to the contract.

Actions by E-Agents

Although in the past standard agency principles applied only to *human* agents, today these same agency principles also apply to e-agents. An electronic agent, or **e-agent,** is a semiautonomous computer program that is capable of executing specific tasks. E-agents used in e-commerce include software that can search through many databases and retrieve only relevant information for the user.

The Uniform Electronic Transactions Act (UETA), which was discussed on pages 233 to 239 in Chapter 11, sets forth provisions relating to the principal's liability for the actions of e-agents. According to Section 15 of the UETA, e-agents can enter into binding agreements on behalf of their principals—at least, in those states that have adopted the act. Thus, if consumers place an order over the Internet, and the company (principal) takes the order via an e-agent, the company cannot later claim that it did not receive the order.

The UETA also stipulates that if an e-agent does not provide an opportunity to prevent errors at the time of the transaction, the other party to the transaction can avoid the transaction. Therefore, if an e-agent fails to provide an on-screen confirmation of a purchase or sale, the other party can avoid the effect of any errors. For example, Bigelow wants to purchase three copies of three different books (a total of nine items). The e-agent mistakenly records an order for thirty-three of a single book and does not provide an on-screen verification of the order. If thirty-three books are then sent to Bigelow, he can avoid the contract to purchase them.

SECTION 3

LIABILITY FOR TORTS AND CRIMES

Obviously, any person, including an agent, is liable for his or her own torts and crimes. Whether a principal can also be held liable for an agent's torts and crimes depends on several factors, which we examine here. In some situations, a principal may be held liable not only for the torts of an agent, but also for torts committed by an independent contractor.

Principal's Tortious Conduct

A principal who acts through an agent may be liable for harm resulting from the principal's own negligence or recklessness. Therefore, a principal may be liable if he or she gives improper instructions, authorizes the use of improper materials or tools, or establishes improper rules that result in the agent's committing a tort. For instance, Peter knows that Audrey's driver's license has been suspended but nevertheless tells her to use the company truck to deliver some equipment to a customer. If someone is injured as a result, Peter will be liable for his own negligence in instructing Audrey to drive without a valid license.

Principal's Authorization of Agent's Tortious Conduct

Similarly, a principal who authorizes an agent to commit a tort may be liable to persons or property injured thereby, because the act is considered to be the principal's. For example, Pagani directs his agent, Atkin, to cut the corn on specific acreage, which neither of them has the right to do. The harvest is therefore a trespass (a tort), and Pagani is liable to the owner of the corn.

Note that an agent acting at the principal's direction can be liable as a *tortfeasor* (one who commits a wrong, or tort), along with the principal, for committing the tortious act even if the agent was unaware that the act was wrong. Assume in the above example that Atkin, the agent, did not know that Pagani lacked the right to harvest the corn. Atkin can still be held liable to the owner of the field for damages, along with Pagani, the principal.

Liability for Agent's Misrepresentation

A principal is exposed to tort liability whenever a third person sustains a loss due to the agent's misrepresentation. The principal's liability depends on whether the agent was actually or apparently authorized to make representations and whether the representations were made within the scope of the agency. The principal is always directly responsible for an agent's misrepresentation made within the scope of the agent's authority.

Suppose that Ainsley is a demonstrator for Pavlovich's products. Pavlovich sends Ainsley to a home show to demonstrate the products and to answer questions from consumers. Pavlovich has given Ainsley authority to make statements about the products. If Ainsley makes only true representations, all is fine. But if he makes false claims, Pavlovich will be liable for any injuries or damages sustained by third parties in reliance on Ainsley's false representations.

APPARENT IMPLIED AUTHORITY When a principal has placed an agent in a position of apparent authority—making it possible for the agent to defraud a third party—the principal may also be liable for the agent's fraudulent acts. For example, Joan Ableman is a loan officer at First Security Bank. In the ordinary course of her job, Ableman approves and services loans and has access to the credit records of all customers. Ableman falsely represents to a borrower, McMillan, that the bank feels insecure about McMillan's loan and intends to call it in unless McMillan provides additional collateral, such as stocks and bonds. McMillan gives Ableman numerous stock certificates, which Ableman keeps in her own possession and later uses as collateral to take out a personal loan. The bank is liable to McMillan for any losses sustained on the stocks even though the bank was unaware of the fraudulent scheme.

If, in contrast, Ableman had been a recently hired junior bank teller rather than a loan officer when she told McMillan that the bank required additional security for the loan, McMillan would not have been justified in relying on her representation. In that situation, the bank normally would not be liable to McMillan for any the losses sustained.

As will be discussed in Chapter 37, partners in a partnership generally have the apparent implied authority to act as agents on behalf of the firm. Thus, if one of the partners commits a tort or a crime, the partnership itself—and often the other partners personally—can be held liable for the loss.

CASE IN POINT Selheimer & Company, a securities broker-dealer that operated as a partnership, provided various financial services. The managing partner, Perry Selheimer, embezzled funds that clients had turned over to the firm for investment. After Selheimer was convicted, other partners in the firm claimed that they were not liable for losses resulting from his illegal activities. The court, however, held that Selheimer had apparent implied authority to act in the ordinary course of the partnership's business. Thus, the firm, as principal, was liable, and under the law of partnerships, the personal assets of

the individual partners could be used to cover the firm's liability.[10]

INNOCENT MISREPRESENTATION Tort liability based on fraud requires proof that a material misstatement was made knowingly and with the intent to deceive. An agent's *innocent* mistakes occurring in a contract transaction or involving a warranty contained in the contract can provide grounds for the third party's rescission of the contract and the award of damages. Moreover, justice dictates that when a principal knows that an agent is not accurately advised of facts but does not correct either the agent's or the third party's impressions, the principal is directly responsible to the third party for resulting damages. The point is that the principal is always directly responsible for an agent's misrepresentation made within the scope of authority.

Liability for Agent's Negligence

Under the doctrine of **respondeat superior,**[11] the principal-employer is liable for any harm caused to a third party by an agent-employee within the scope of employment. This doctrine imposes **vicarious liability,** or indirect liability, on the employer—that is, liability without regard to the personal fault of the employer for torts committed by an employee in the course or scope of employment.[12] Third parties injured through the negligence of an employee can sue either that employee or the employer, if the employee's negligent conduct occurred while the employee was acting within the scope of employment.

When an agent commits a negligent act, can the agent, as well as the principal, be held liable? That was the issue in the following case.

---

10. *In re Selheimer & Co.,* 319 Bankr. 395 (E.D.Pa. 2005).
11. Pronounced ree-*spahn*-dee-uht soo-*peer*-ee-your. The doctrine of *respondeat superior* applies not only to employer-employee relationships but also to other principal-agent relationships in which the principal has the right of control over the agent.
12. The theory of *respondeat superior* is similar to the theory of strict liability covered in Chapter 7.

✳ EXTENDED CASE 33.3 ✳
Warner v. Southwest Desert Images, LLC

Court of Appeals of Arizona, 218 Ariz. 121, 180 P.3d 986 (2008).

IN THE LANGUAGE OF THE COURT

J. William *BRAMMER,* Jr., Judge.
  * * * Southwest Desert Images, LLC (SDI) was hired

by Warner's employer, Aegis Communications (Aegis), to perform landscaping and weed control. On September 29, 2003, SDI employee [David] Hoggatt began spraying an herbicide on weeds on the property around Aegis's building. * * * After

approximately an hour and a half of spraying, Hoggatt was informed that people inside Aegis's building were complaining. The herbicide spray had entered the building through its air conditioning system and had circulated throughout

EXTENDED CASE 33.3 CONTINUED ◆

the building. After being informed of the situation, Hoggatt stopped spraying. Emergency services arrived as the building was being evacuated. Employees in the building complained of respiratory problems and itching and burning eyes.

Prior to and during the evacuation, [an Aegis employee, Catherine] Warner began having difficulty breathing, was coughing violently, and felt burning in her eyes, nose, and throat. As she exited the building, Warner began to feel faint and felt "extreme chest pain" and heart palpitations. Warner had had [two heart attacks in the past], and had undergone heart surgery in May 2003. * * * She was then transported by ambulance to the hospital, where she was treated and released after about four hours. * * * [It was later determined that Warner had suffered a heart attack on the day of the evacuation. She continued to experience health complications that she blamed on exposure to the spray.]

Warner sued SDI for negligence in September 2004, later amending her complaint to include * * *

Hoggatt [and several others as defendants].

* * * *

The jury found SDI to be completely responsible for the injuries Warner suffered by inhaling the herbicide. * * * It awarded Warner $3,825 in compensatory damages and costs against SDI. [Warner appealed.]

On the last day of trial, the court entered a directed verdict in favor of Hoggatt because "the evidence [wa]s undisputed that Mr. Hoggatt [had] acted within the scope of his employment for [SDI]," and, thus, that SDI was "clearly liable in situation for whatever damages the jury does find in this matter." There was no dispute at trial that Hoggatt had been negligent * * *.

We agree with Warner that "there was no legal basis for the court's decision to dismiss Hoggatt from the action." *It is well-established law that an agent will not be excused from responsibility for tortious conduct merely because he is acting for his principal.* [Also, as stated in the *Restatement (Third) of Agency*], "An agent is subject to liability to a third party harmed by the agent's tortious conduct. Unless an applicable statute provides otherwise, an actor remains

subject to liability although the actor acts * * * within the scope of employment." [Emphasis added.]

Hoggatt cites no authority suggesting this rule should not apply in this case. He does, however, argue the error was harmless. * * * Hoggatt asserts Warner was not prejudiced [injured] because "the jury apportioned one hundred percent of the fault to SDI. Adding other possible parties to the jury verdict form would not have changed the outcome of this case." We agree that including Hoggatt as a defendant throughout the trial could not have changed Warner's damage award, and Warner does not argue otherwise. Nor is there a need for the jury to apportion fault between Hoggatt and SDI—the liability of those parties is joint and several.

That the error does not warrant a new trial, however, does not mean it was not prejudicial to Warner. She has a right to recover her damages from Hoggatt, and his improper dismissal has deprived her of that right. Accordingly, we reverse the trial court's grant of a directed verdict in Hoggatt's favor and amend the judgment in Warner's favor to show it is against Hoggatt as well.

QUESTIONS

1. Why should Hoggatt be personally liable if he merely followed the instructions of his employer, SDI, given that the employer is better able financially to pay the judgment and may have insurance that covers the matter?
2. How could SDI reduce the likelihood of similar lawsuits occurring in the future?

RATIONALE UNDERLYING THE DOCTRINE OF *RESPONDEAT SUPERIOR* At early common law, a servant (employee) was viewed as the master's (employer's) property. The master was deemed to have absolute control over the servant's acts and was held strictly liable for them, no matter how carefully the master supervised the servant. The rationale for the doctrine of *respondeat superior* is based on the social duty that requires every person to manage his or her affairs, whether accomplished by the person or through agents, so as not to injure another. Liability is imposed on employers because they are deemed to be in a better financial position to bear the loss. The superior financial position carries with it the duty to be responsible for damages.

Generally, public policy requires that an injured person be afforded effective relief, and a business enterprise is usually better able to provide that relief than is an individual employee. Employers normally carry liability insurance to cover any damages awarded as a result of such lawsuits. They are also able to spread the cost of risk over the entire business enterprise.

The doctrine of *respondeat superior*, which the courts have applied for nearly two centuries, continues to have practical implications in all situations involving principal-agent (employer-employee) relationships. Today, the small-town grocer with one clerk and the multinational corporation with thousands of employees are equally subject to the doctrinal demand of "let the master respond." (Keep this principle in mind when you read through Chapters 34 and 35.)

THE SCOPE OF EMPLOYMENT The key to determining whether a principal may be liable for the torts of an agent under the doctrine of *respondeat superior* is whether the torts are committed within the scope of the agency or employment. Courts may consider the following factors in determining whether a particular act occurred within the course and scope of employment:

1. Whether the employee's act was authorized by the employer.
2. The time, place, and purpose of the act.
3. Whether the act was one commonly performed by employees on behalf of their employers.
4. The extent to which the employer's interest was advanced by the act.
5. The extent to which the private interests of the employee were involved.
6. Whether the employer furnished the means or instrumentality (for example, a truck or a machine) by which an injury was inflicted.
7. Whether the employer had reason to know that the employee would perform the act in question and whether the employee had done it before.
8. Whether the act involved the commission of a serious crime.

THE DISTINCTION BETWEEN A "DETOUR" AND A "FROLIC" A useful insight into the concept of "scope of employment" may be gained from Judge Baron Parke's classic distinction between a "detour" and a "frolic" in the case of *Joel v. Morison* (1834).[13] In this case, the English court held that if a servant merely took a detour from his master's business, the master will be responsible. If, however, the servant was on a "frolic of his own" and not in any way "on his master's business," the master will not be liable.

Consider an example. Mandel, a traveling salesperson, while driving his employer's vehicle to call on a customer, decides to stop at the post office—which is one block off his route—to mail a personal letter. As Mandel approaches the post office, he negligently runs into a parked vehicle owned by

Chan. In this situation, because Mandel's detour from the employer's business is not substantial, he is still acting within the scope of employment, and the employer is liable. The result would be different, though, if Mandel had decided to pick up a few friends for cocktails in another city and in the process had negligently run his vehicle into Chan's. In that circumstance, the departure from the employer's business would be substantial, and the employer normally would not be liable to Chan for damages. Mandel would be considered to have been on a "frolic" of his own.

EMPLOYEE TRAVEL TIME An employee going to and from work or to and from meals usually is considered to be outside the scope of employment. In contrast, all travel time of traveling salespersons or others whose jobs require them to travel normally is considered to be within the scope of employment for the duration of the business trip, including the return trip home, unless there is a significant departure from the employer's business.

NOTICE OF DANGEROUS CONDITIONS The employer is charged with knowledge of any dangerous conditions discovered by an employee and pertinent to the employment situation. Suppose that Brad, a maintenance employee in an apartment building, notices a lead pipe protruding from the ground in the building's courtyard. Brad neglects either to fix the pipe or to inform his employer of the danger. John trips on the pipe and is injured. The employer is charged with knowledge of the dangerous condition regardless of whether Brad actually informed the employer. That knowledge is imputed to the employer by virtue of the employment relationship.

BORROWED SERVANTS Employers sometimes lend the services of their employees to other employers. Suppose that an employer leases ground-moving equipment to another employer and sends along an employee to operate the machinery. Who is liable for injuries caused by the employee's negligent actions on the job site?

Liability turns on *which employer had the primary right to control* the employee at the time the injuries occurred. Generally, the employer who rents out the equipment is presumed to retain control over her or his employee. If the rental is for a relatively long period of time, however, control may be deemed to pass to the employer who is renting the equipment and presumably controlling and directing the employee.

---

13. 6 Car. & P. 501, 172 Eng.Rep. 1338 (1834).

Liability for Agent's Intentional Torts

Most intentional torts that employees commit have no relation to their employment; thus, their employers will not be held liable. Nevertheless, under the doctrine of *respondeat superior,* the employer can be liable for intentional torts of the employee that are committed within the course and scope of employment, just as the employer is liable for negligence. For example, an employer is liable when an employee (such as a "bouncer" at a nightclub or a security guard at a department store) commits the tort of assault and battery or false imprisonment while acting within the scope of employment.

In addition, an employer who knows or should know that an employee has a propensity for committing tortious acts is liable for the employee's acts even if they would not ordinarily be considered within the scope of employment. For example, if an employer hires a bouncer knowing that he has a history of arrests for criminal assault and battery, the employer may be liable if the employee viciously attacks a patron in the parking lot after hours.

An employer is also liable for permitting an employee to engage in reckless actions that can injure others. For example, an employer observes an employee smoking while filling containerized trucks with highly flammable liquids. Failure to stop the employee will cause the employer to be liable for any injuries that result if a truck explodes. Needless to say, most employers purchase liability insurance to cover their potential liability for employee conduct in many situations (see Chapter 51).

Liability for Independent Contractor's Torts

Generally, an employer is not liable for physical harm caused to a third person by the negligent act of an independent contractor in the performance of the contract. This is because the employer does not have *the right to control* the details of an independent contractor's performance. Courts make an exception to this rule when the contract involves unusually hazardous activities, such as blasting operations, the transportation of highly volatile chemicals, or the use of poisonous gases. In these situations, an employer cannot be shielded from liability merely by using an independent contractor. Strict liability is imposed on the employer-principal as a matter of law. Also, in some states, strict liability may be imposed by statute.

Liability for Agent's Crimes

An agent is liable for his or her own crimes. A principal or employer is not liable for an agent's or employee's crime simply because the agent or employee committed the crime while otherwise acting within the scope of authority or employment. An exception to this rule is made when the principal or employer participated in the crime by conspiracy or other action. In some jurisdictions, under specific statutes, a principal may be liable if an agent, in the course and scope of employment, violates regulations such as those governing sanitation, prices, weights, and the sale of liquor.

SECTION 4
TERMINATION OF AN AGENCY

Agency law is similar to contract law in that both an agency and a contract may be terminated by an act of the parties or by operation of law. Once the relationship between the principal and the agent has ended, the agent no longer has the right (*actual* authority) to bind the principal. For an agent's *apparent* authority to be terminated, though, third persons may also need to be notified that the agency has been terminated.

Termination by Act of the Parties

An agency relationship may be terminated by act of the parties in any of the following ways:

1. *Lapse of time.* When an agency agreement specifies the time period during which the agency relationship will exist, the agency ends when that time period expires. For example, Akers signs an agreement of agency with Janz "beginning January 1, 2012, and ending December 31, 2014." The agency is automatically terminated on December 31, 2014. If no definite time is stated, then the agency continues for a reasonable time and can be terminated at will by either party. What constitutes a reasonable time depends on the circumstances and the nature of the agency relationship.

2. *Purpose achieved.* If an agent is employed to accomplish a particular objective, such as the purchase of breeding stock for a cattle rancher, the agency automatically ends after the cattle have been purchased. If more than one agent is employed to accomplish the same purpose, such as the sale of real estate, the first agent to complete the sale

automatically terminates the agency relationship for all the others.

3. *Occurrence of a specific event.* When an agency relationship is to terminate on the happening of a certain event, the agency automatically ends when the event occurs. For example, if Posner appoints Rubik to handle her business affairs while she is away, the agency automatically terminates when Posner returns.

4. *Mutual agreement.* The parties to an agency can cancel (rescind) their contract by mutually agreeing to terminate the agency relationship, whether the agency contract is in writing or whether it is for a specific duration.

5. *Termination by one party.* As a *general* rule, either party can terminate the agency relationship—because agency is a consensual relationship, and thus neither party can be compelled to continue in the relationship. The agent's act is said to be a *renunciation* of authority. The principal's act is a *revocation* of authority. Although both parties may have the *power* to terminate the agency, they may not possess the *right* to terminate and therefore may be liable for breach of contract, or *wrongful termination.*

WRONGFUL TERMINATION Wrongful termination can subject the canceling party to a lawsuit for breach of contract. For example, Rawlins has a one-year employment contract with Munro to act as agent in return for $65,000. Although Munro has the *power* to discharge Rawlins before the contract period expires, if he does so, he can be sued for breaching the contract because he had no *right* to terminate the agency.

Even in an agency at will—that is, an agency that either party may terminate at any time—the principal who wishes to terminate must give the agent *reasonable* notice. The notice must be at least sufficient to allow the agent to recoup his or her expenses and, in some situations, to make a normal profit.

AGENCY COUPLED WITH AN INTEREST A special rule applies in an *agency coupled with an interest.* This type of agency is not an agency in the usual sense because it is created for the agent's benefit instead of for the principal's benefit. For example, Julie borrows $5,000 from Rob, giving Rob some of her jewelry and signing a letter authorizing him to sell the jewelry as her agent if she fails to repay the loan. After Julie receives the $5,000 from Rob, she attempts to revoke his authority to sell the jewelry as her agent. Julie will not succeed in this attempt because a principal cannot revoke an agency created for the agent's benefit.

An agency coupled with an interest should not be confused with a situation in which the agent merely derives proceeds or profits from the sale of the subject matter. For example, an agent who merely receives a commission from the sale of real property does not have a beneficial interest in the property itself.

NOTICE OF TERMINATION When an agency has been terminated by act of the parties, it is the principal's duty to inform any third parties who know of the existence of the agency that it has been terminated (notice of the termination may be given by others, however).

Although an agent's actual authority ends when the agency is terminated, an agent's *apparent authority* continues until the third party receives notice (from any source) that such authority has been terminated. If the principal knows that a third party has dealt with the agent, the principal is expected to notify that person *directly.* For third parties who have heard about the agency but have not yet dealt with the agent, *constructive notice* is sufficient.[14]

No particular form is required for notice of termination of the principal-agent relationship to be effective. The principal can personally notify the agent, or the agent can learn of the termination through some other means. For example, Manning bids on a shipment of steel, and Stone is hired as an agent to arrange transportation for the shipment. When Stone learns that Manning has lost the bid, Stone's authority to make the transportation arrangement terminates. If the agent's authority is written, however, normally it must be revoked in writing (unless the written document contained an expiration date).

Termination by Operation of Law

Certain events terminate agency authority automatically because their occurrence makes it impossible for the agent to perform or improbable that the principal would continue to want performance. We look at these events here. Note that when an agency terminates by operation of law, there is no duty to notify third persons—unless the agent's authority is coupled with an interest.

1. *Death or insanity.* The general rule is that the death or insanity of either the principal or the agent automatically and immediately terminates an ordinary agency relationship.[15] Knowledge of

---

14. With *constructive notice* of a fact, knowledge of the fact is imputed by law to a person if he or she could have discovered the fact by proper diligence. Constructive notice is often accomplished by publication in a newspaper.

15. An exception to this rule exists in the bank-customer relationship. A bank, as agent, can continue to exercise specific types of authority even after the customer's death or insanity, and can continue to pay checks drawn by the customer for ten days after death (see page 523 in Chapter 27).

the death or insanity is not required. For example, Grey sends Bosley to Japan to purchase a rare book. Before Bosley makes the purchase, Grey dies. Bosley's agent status is terminated at the moment of Grey's death, even though Bosley does not know that Grey has died. (Some states, however, have enacted statutes that change the common law rule to require an agent's knowledge of the principal's death before termination.)

An agent's transactions that occur after the death of the principal normally are not binding on the principal's estate. Assume that McCoy had an individual checking account and that he later authorized his live-in girlfriend, Kaye, to write checks on that account. The girlfriend is merely McCoy's agent and is not a joint account holder. If McCoy dies, Kaye's authority to write checks on the account is terminated. Thus, if Kaye writes checks on this account after McCoy's death, McCoy's estate is not bound by her acts. If the bank was aware of McCoy's death and paid the checks, it will be liable to the estate for the amount of the checks.[16]

2. *Impossibility.* When the specific subject matter of an agency is destroyed or lost, the agency terminates. For example, Gonzalez employs Arnez to sell Gonzalez's house. Prior to any sale, the house is destroyed by fire. Arnez's agency and authority to sell the house terminate. Similarly, when it is impossible for the agent to perform the agency lawfully because of a change in the law, the agency terminates.

3. *Changed circumstances.* When an event occurs that has such an unusual effect on the subject matter of the agency that the agent can reasonably infer that the principal will not want the agency to continue, the agency terminates. Suppose that Baird hires Joslen to sell a tract of land for $40,000. Subsequently, Joslen learns that there is oil under the land and that the land is therefore worth $1 million. The agency and Joslen's authority to sell the land for $40,000 are terminated.

4. *Bankruptcy.* If either the principal or the agent petitions for bankruptcy, the agency is *usually* terminated. In certain circumstances, such as when the agent's financial status is irrelevant to the purpose of the agency, the agency relationship may continue. *Insolvency* (the inability to pay debts when they come due or when liabilities exceed assets), as distinguished from bankruptcy, does not necessarily terminate the relationship.

5. *War.* When the principal's country and the agent's country are at war with each other, the agency is terminated. In this situation, the agency is automatically suspended or terminated because there is no way to enforce the legal rights and obligations of the parties.

See *Concept Summary 33.2* below and on the following page for a synopsis of the rules governing the termination of an agency.

---

16. See, for example, *Sturgill v. Virginia Citizens Bank*, 223 Va. 394, 291 S.E.2d 207 (1982).

CONCEPT SUMMARY 33.2
Termination of an Agency

Method of Termination	Rules	Termination of Agent's Authority
Act of the Parties		
1. Lapse of time.	Automatic at end of the stated time.	
2. Purpose achieved.	Automatic on the completion of the purpose.	**Notice to Third Parties Required—**
3. Occurrence of a specific event.	Normally automatic on the happening of the event.	1. Direct to those who have dealt with agency.
4. Mutual agreement.	Mutual consent required.	2. Constructive to all others.
5. At the option of one party (revocation, if by principal; renunciation, if by agent).	Either party normally has a right to terminate the agency but may lack the power to do so; wrongful termination can lead to liability for breach of contract.	

CONCEPT SUMMARY CONTINUES ➡

CONCEPT SUMMARY 33.2
Termination of an Agency, Continued

Method of Termination	Rules	Termination of Agent's Authority
Operation of Law		
1. Death or insanity.	Automatic on the death or insanity of either the principal or the agent (except when the agency is coupled with an interest).	
2. Impossibility—destruction of the specific subject matter.	Applies any time the agency cannot be performed because of an event beyond the parties' control.	
3. Changed circumstances.	Events so unusual that it would be inequitable to allow the agency to continue to exist.	**No Notice Required–** Automatic on the happening of the event.
4. Bankruptcy.	Bankruptcy petition (not mere insolvency) usually terminates the agency.	
5. War between principal's country and agent's country.	Automatically suspends or terminates agency—no way to enforce legal rights.	

REVIEWING
Agency Liability and Termination

Lynne Meyer, on her way to a business meeting and in a hurry, stopped at a Buy-Mart store for a new pair of nylons to wear to the meeting. There was a long line at one of the checkout counters, but a cashier, Valerie Watts, opened another counter and began loading the cash drawer. Meyer told Watts that she was in a hurry and asked Watts to work faster. Instead, Watts, only slowed her pace. At this point, Meyer hit Watts. It is not clear whether Meyer hit Watts intentionally or, in an attempt to retrieve the nylons, hit her inadvertently. In response, Watts grabbed Meyer by the hair and hit her repeatedly in the back of the head, while Meyer screamed for help. Management personnel separated the two women and questioned them about the incident. Watts was immediately fired for violating the store's no-fighting policy. Meyer subsequently sued Buy-Mart, alleging that the store was liable for the tort (assault and battery) committed by its employee. Using the information presented in the chapter, answer the following questions.

1. Under what doctrine discussed in this chapter might Buy-Mart be held liable for the tort committed by Watts?
2. What is the key factor in determining whether Buy-Mart is liable under this doctrine?
3. How is Buy-Mart's potential liability affected by whether Watts's behavior constituted an intentional tort or a tort of negligence?
4. Suppose that when Watts applied for the job at Buy-Mart, she disclosed in her application that she had previously been convicted of felony assault and battery. Nevertheless, Buy-Mart hired Watts as a cashier. How might this fact affect Buy-Mart's liability for Watts's actions?

⊛ **DEBATE THIS:** *The doctrine of* respondeat superior *should be modified to make agents solely liable for some of their tortious acts.*

TERMS AND CONCEPTS

apparent authority 641

disclosed principal 645

e-agent 647

equal dignity rule 639

express authority 639

implied authority 641

notary public 640

partially disclosed
   principal 645

power of attorney 640

ratification 644

respondeat superior 648

undisclosed principal 645

vicarious liability 648

QUESTIONS AND CASE PROBLEMS

33–1. Agent's Authority Adam is a traveling salesperson for Peter Petri Plumbing Supply Corp. Adam has express authority to solicit orders from customers and to offer a 5 percent discount if payment is made within thirty days of delivery. Petri has said nothing to Adam about extending credit. Adam calls on a new prospective customer, John's Plumbing Firm. John tells Adam that he will place a large order for Petri products if Adam will give him a 10 percent discount with payment due in equal installments thirty, sixty, and ninety days from delivery. Adam says he has authority to make such a contract. John calls Petri and asks if Adam is authorized to make contracts giving a discount. No mention is made of payment terms. Petri replies that Adam has authority to give discounts on purchase orders. On the basis of this information, John orders $10,000 worth of plumbing supplies and fixtures. The goods are delivered and are being sold. One week later, John receives a bill for $9,500, due in thirty days. John insists he owes only $9,000 and can pay it in three equal installments, at thirty, sixty, and ninety days from delivery. Discuss the liability of Petri and John only.

33–2. QUESTION WITH SAMPLE ANSWER: Unauthorized Acts.

Janell Arden is a purchasing agent–employee for the A&B Coal Supply partnership. Arden has authority to purchase the coal needed by A&B to satisfy the needs of its customers. While Arden is leaving a coal mine from which she has just purchased a large quantity of coal, her car breaks down. She walks into a small roadside grocery store for help. While there, she encounters Will Wilson, who owns 360 acres back in the mountains with all mineral rights. Wilson, in need of cash, offers to sell Arden the property for $1,500 per acre. On inspection of the property, Arden forms the opinion that the subsurface contains valuable coal deposits. Arden contracts to purchase the property for A&B Coal Supply, signing the contract "A&B Coal Supply, Janell Arden, agent." The closing date is August 1. Arden takes the contract to the partnership. The managing partner is furious, as A&B is not in the property business. Later, just before closing, both Wilson and the partnership learn that the value of the land is at

least $15,000 per acre. Discuss the rights of A&B and Wilson concerning the land contract.

• **For a sample answer to Question 33–2, go to Appendix I at the end of this text.**

33–3. Ratification by Principal Springer was a political candidate running for Congress. He was operating on a tight budget and instructed his campaign staff not to purchase any campaign materials without his explicit authorization. In spite of these instructions, one of his campaign workers ordered Dubychek Printing Co. to print some promotional materials for Springer's campaign. When the printed materials arrived, Springer did not return them but instead used them during his campaign. When Springer failed to pay for the materials, Dubychek sued for recovery of the price. Springer contended that he was not liable on the sales contract because he had not authorized his agent to purchase the printing services. Dubychek argued that the campaign worker was Springer's agent and that the worker had authority to make the printing contract. Additionally, Dubychek claimed that even if the purchase was unauthorized, Springer's use of the materials constituted ratification of his agent's unauthorized purchase. Is Dubychek correct? Explain.

33–4. *Respondeat Superior* ABC Tire Corp. hires Arnez as a traveling salesperson and assigns him a geographic area and time schedule in which to solicit orders and service customers. Arnez is given a company car to use in covering the territory. One day, Arnez decides to take his personal car to cover part of his territory. It is 11:00 A.M., and Arnez has just finished calling on all customers in the city of Tarrytown. His next appointment is at 2:00 P.M. in the city of Austex, twenty miles down the road. Arnez starts out for Austex, but halfway there he decides to visit a former college roommate who runs a farm ten miles off the main highway. Arnez is enjoying his visit with his former roommate when he realizes that it is 1:45 P.M. and that he will be late for the appointment in Austex. Driving at a high speed down the country road to reach the main highway, Arnez crashes his car into a tractor, severely injuring Thomas, the driver of the tractor. Thomas claims that he can hold ABC Tire

Corp. liable for his injuries. Discuss fully ABC's liability in this situation.

33–5. Liability for Independent Contractor's Torts Dean Brothers Corp. owns and operates a steel drum manufacturing plant. Lowell Wyden, the plant superintendent, hired Best Security Patrol, Inc. (BSP), a security company, to guard Dean property and "deter thieves and vandals." Some BSP security guards, as Wyden knew, carried firearms. Pete Sidell, a BSP security guard, was not certified as an armed guard but nevertheless brought his gun, in a briefcase, to work. While working at the Dean plant on October 31, 2010, Sidell fired his gun at Tyrone Gaines, in the belief that Gaines was an intruder. The bullet struck and killed Gaines. Gaines's mother filed a lawsuit claiming that her son's death was the result of BSP's negligence, for which Dean was responsible. What is the plaintiff's best argument that Dean is responsible for BSP's actions? What is Dean's best defense? Explain.

33–6. Principal's Liability for Contracts In 1998, William Larry Smith signed a lease for certain land in Chilton County, Alabama, owned by Sweet Smitherman. The lease stated that it was between "Smitherman, and WLS, Inc., d/b/a [doing business as] S&H Mobile Homes," and the signature line identified the lessee as "WLS, Inc. d/b/a S&H Mobile Homes . . . By: William Larry Smith, President." The amount of the rent was $5,000, payable by the tenth of each month. All of the checks that Smitherman received for the rent identified the owner of the account as "WLS Corporation d/b/a S&H Mobile Homes." Nearly four years later, Smitherman filed a suit in an Alabama state court against William Larry Smith, alleging that he owed $26,000 in unpaid rent. Smith responded, in part, that WLS was the lessee and that he was not personally responsible for the obligation to pay the rent. Is Smith a principal, an agent, both a principal and an agent, or neither? In any event, in the lease, is the principal disclosed, partially disclosed, or undisclosed? With the answers to these questions in mind, who is liable for the unpaid rent, and why? Discuss. [*Smith v. Smitherman,* 887 So.2d 285 (Ala.Civ.App. 2004)]

33–7. CASE PROBLEM WITH SAMPLE ANSWER: Apparent Authority.

Lee Dennegar and Mark Knutson lived in Dennegar's house in Raritan, New Jersey. Dennegar paid the mortgage and other household expenses. With Dennegar's consent, Knutson managed their household's financial affairs and the "general office functions concerned with maintaining the house." Dennegar allowed Knutson to handle the mail and "to do with it as he chose." Knutson wrote checks for Dennegar to sign, although Knutson signed Dennegar's name to many of the checks with Dennegar's consent. AT&T Universal issued a credit card in Dennegar's name in February 2001. Monthly statements were mailed to Dennegar's house, and payments were sometimes made on those statements. Knutson died in June 2003. The unpaid charges on the card of $14,752.93 were assigned to New Century Financial Services. New Century filed a suit in a New Jersey state court against Dennegar to collect the unpaid amount. Dennegar claimed that he never applied for or used the card and knew nothing about it. Under what theory could Dennegar be liable for the charges? Explain. [*New Century Financial Services, Inc. v. Dennegar, 394 N.J.Super. 595, 928 A.2d 48 (A.D. 2007)*]

- To view a sample answer for Problem 33–7, go to this book's Web site at www.cengage.com/blaw/clarkson, select "Chapter 33," and click on "Case Problem with Sample Answer."

33–8. Undisclosed Principal Homeowners Jim and Lisa Criss hired Kevin and Cathie Pappas, doing business as Outside Creations, to undertake a landscaping project. Kevin signed the parties' contract as "Outside Creations Rep." The Crisses made payments on the contract with checks payable to Kevin, who deposited them in his personal account—there was no Outside Creations account. Later, alleging breach of contract, the Crisses filed a suit in a Georgia state court against the Pappases. The defendants contended that they could not be liable because the contract was not with them personally. They claimed that they were the agents of Forever Green Landscaping and Irrigation, Inc., which had been operating under the name "Outside Creations" at the time of the contract and had since filed for bankruptcy. The Crisses pointed out that the name "Forever Green" was not in the contract. Can the Pappases be liable on this contract? Why or why not? [*Pappas v. Criss, 296 Ga.App. 803, 676 S.E.2d 21 (2009)*]

33–9. Liability Based on Actual or Apparent Authority Summerall Electric Co. and other subcontractors were hired by National Church Services, Inc. (NCS), which was the general contractor on a construction project for the Church of God at Southaven. As work progressed, payments from NCS to the subcontractors were late and eventually stopped altogether. The church had paid NCS in full for the entire project beforehand, but apparently NCS had mismanaged the project. When payments from NCS stopped, the subcontractors filed *mechanic's liens* (see page 546 in Chapter 28) for the value of the work they had performed but for which they had not been paid. The subcontractors sued the church, contending that it was liable for the payments because NCS was its agent on the basis of either actual or apparent authority. Was NCS an agent for the church, thereby making the church liable to the subcontractors? Explain your reasoning. [*Summerall Electric Co. v. Church of God at Southaven,* 25 So.3d 1090 (App.Miss. 2010)]

33–10. A QUESTION OF ETHICS: Power of Attorney.

Warren Davis lived with Renee Brandt in a house that Davis owned in Virginia Beach, Virginia. At Davis's request, attorney Leigh Ansell prepared, and Davis acknowledged, a durable power of attorney appointing Ansell to act as Davis's attorney-in-fact. Ansell was authorized to sign "any . . . instrument of . . . deposit" and "any contract . . . relating to . . . personal property." Ansell could act "in any circumstances as fully and effectively as I could do as part of my normal, every-day business affairs if acting personally." A few days later, at Davis's direction, Ansell prepared, and Davis signed, a will that gave Brandt the right to occupy, rent-free, the house in which she and Davis lived *"so long as she lives in the premises."* The will's other chief beneficiaries were Davis's daughters, Sharon Jones and Jody Clark. According to Ansell, Davis intended to *"take care of [Brandt] outside of this will"* and asked Ansell to designate Brandt the beneficiary *"payable on death" (POD) of Davis's $250,000 certificate of deposit (CD).* The CD had no other named beneficiary. Less than two months later, Davis died. A suit between Brandt and Davis's daughters ensued in a Virginia state court. *[Jones v. Brandt, 274 Va. 131, 645 S.E.2d 312 (2007)]*

(a) Should the language in a power of attorney be interpreted broadly or strictly? Why?

(b) In this case, did Ansell have the authority under the power of attorney to change the beneficiary of Davis's CD? Explain.

(c) Ansell advised Davis by letter that he had complied with the instruction to designate Brandt the beneficiary of the CD. Davis made no objection. Based on these facts, what theory might apply to validate the designation?

LEGAL RESEARCH EXERCISES ON THE WEB

Go to this text's Web site at **www.cengage.com/blaw/clarkson**, select "Chapter 33," and click on "Practical Internet Exercises." There you will find the following Internet research exercises that you can perform to learn more about the topics covered in this chapter.

Practical Internet Exercise 33–1: **Legal Perspective**
Power of Attorney

Practical Internet Exercise 33–2: **Management Perspective**
Liability in Agency Relationships

Until the early 1900s, most employer-employee relationships were governed by the common law. Even today, under the common law *employment-at-will doctrine,* private employers are generally free to hire and fire workers at will, unless doing so violates an employee's contractual or statutory rights. Now, however, there are numerous statutes and administrative agency regulations that regulate the workplace. Thus, to a large extent, statutory law has displaced common law doctrines.

In this chapter, we look at the most significant laws regulating employment relationships. We deal with other important laws regulating the workplace—those that prohibit employment discrimination—in the next chapter.

SECTION 1
EMPLOYMENT AT WILL

Traditionally, employment relationships have generally been governed by the common law doctrine of **employment at will.** Under this doctrine, either party may terminate the employment relationship at any time and for any reason, unless doing so would violate the provisions of an employment contract or a statute. The majority of U.S. workers continue to have the legal status of "employees at will." In other words, this common law doctrine is still in widespread use, and only one state (Montana) does not apply the doctrine.

Nonetheless, as mentioned in the chapter introduction, federal and state statutes governing employment relationships prevent the doctrine from being applied in a number of circumstances. Today, an employer is not permitted to fire an employee if doing so would violate a federal or state employment statute, such as one prohibiting employment termination for discriminatory reasons (see Chapter 35). Note that the distinction made under agency law (discussed in Chapter 32) between employee status and independent-contractor status is important here. The employment laws that will be discussed in this chapter and in Chapter 35 apply only to the employer-employee relationship. They do not apply to independent contractors.

Exceptions to the Employment-at-Will Doctrine

Under the employment-at-will doctrine, as mentioned, an employer may hire and fire employees at will (regardless of the employees' performance) without liability, unless the decision violates the terms of an employment contract or statutory law. Because of the harsh effects of the employment-at-will doctrine for employees, courts have carved out various exceptions to this doctrine. These exceptions are based on contract theory, tort theory, and public policy.

EXCEPTIONS BASED ON CONTRACT THEORY Some courts have held that an *implied* employment contract exists between the employer and the employee. If the employee is fired outside the terms of the implied contract, he or she may succeed in an action for breach of contract even though no written employment contract exists.

For example, an employer's manual or personnel bulletin may state that, as a matter of policy, workers will be dismissed only for good cause. If the employee is aware of this policy and continues to work for the employer, a court may find that there is an implied contract based on the terms stated in the manual or bulletin. Generally, the key consideration in determining whether an employment manual creates an implied contractual obligation is the employee's reasonable expectations.

Courts in a few states have gone further and held that all employment contracts contain an implied covenant of good faith. This means that both sides promise to abide by the contract in good faith. If an employer fires an employee for an arbitrary or unjustified reason, the employee can claim that the covenant of good faith was breached and the contract violated.

Increasingly, employers and their employees are negotiating the terms of employment contracts via e-mail and other forms of electronic communication. See this chapter's *Shifting Legal Priorities for Business* feature on the next page for a discussion of whether the promises that employers make to employees in e-mail exchanges are enforceable in court.

EXCEPTIONS BASED ON TORT THEORY In some situations, the discharge of an employee may give rise to an action for wrongful discharge under tort theories. Abusive discharge procedures may result in a lawsuit for intentional infliction of emotional distress or defamation. In addition, some courts have permitted workers to sue their employers under the tort theory of fraud. Under this theory, an employer may be held liable for making false promises to a prospective employee if the person detrimentally relies on the employer's representations by taking the job.

Suppose that an employer induces a prospective employee to leave a lucrative position and move to another state by offering "a long-term job with a thriving business." In fact, the employer is having significant financial problems. Furthermore, the employer is planning a merger that will result in the elimination of the position offered to the prospective employee. If the person takes the job in reliance on the employer's representations and is laid off shortly thereafter, he or she may be able to bring an action against the employer for fraud.[1]

EXCEPTIONS BASED ON PUBLIC POLICY Most often, a common law exception to the employment-at-will doctrine is made on the basis of public policy. Courts may apply this exception when an employer fires a worker for reasons that violate a fundamental public policy of the jurisdiction. Generally, the courts require

that the public policy involved be expressed clearly in the statutory law governing the jurisdiction.

For example, employers with fifty or more employees are required by the federal Family and Medical Leave Act (FMLA—see page 664) to give employees up to twelve weeks of unpaid family or medical leave per year. Mila's employer has only forty employees and thus is not covered by the law. Nonetheless, if Mila is fired from her job because she takes three weeks of unpaid family leave to help her son through a difficult surgery, a court may deem that the employer's actions violated the public policy expressed in the FMLA.

An exception may also be made when an employee "blows the whistle" on an employer's wrongdoing. **Whistleblowing** occurs when an employee tells government authorities, upper-level managers, or the media that her or his employer is engaged in some unsafe or illegal activity. Whistleblowers on occasion have been protected from wrongful discharge for reasons of public policy.[2] Normally, however, whistleblowers seek protection from retaliatory discharge under federal and state statutory laws, such as the Whistleblower Protection Act of 1989.[3]

Wrongful Discharge

Whenever an employer discharges an employee in violation of an employment contract or a statutory law protecting employees, the employee may bring an action for **wrongful discharge.** Even if an employer's actions do not violate any express employment contract or statute, the employer may still be subject to liability under a common law doctrine, such as a tort theory or agency. For example, if an employer discharges a female employee and publicly discloses private facts about her sex life to her co-workers, the employee could bring a wrongful discharge suit based on an invasion of privacy (see Chapter 6).

────────── **SECTION 2** ──────────
WAGE AND HOUR LAWS

In the 1930s, Congress enacted several laws regulating the wages and working hours of employees. In 1931, Congress passed the Davis-Bacon Act,[4] which requires contractors and subcontractors working on

---

1. See, for example, *Helmer v. Bingham Toyota Isuzu,* 129 Cal. App.4th 1121, 29 Cal.Rptr.3d 136 (2005).

2. See, for example, *Wendeln v. The Beatrice Manor, Inc.,* 271 Neb. 373, 712 N.W.2d 226 (2006).

3. 5 U.S.C. Section 1201.

4. 40 U.S.C. Sections 276a–276a-5.

Today, e-mail is used in nearly every aspect of the employment environment—from workplace communications to negotiations of contracts with employees. As you learned in Chapter 15, under the one-year rule of the Statute of Frauds, most employment contracts must be in writing. But electronic communications, including e-mail, instant messages, text messages, and even Twitter, can be used as evidence to show that a contract existed or that the parties modified their contract.

Moreover, although many employment contracts include traditional integration clauses stating that the contract can be modified only by a signed writing, such a clause may not necessarily prevent e-mail modifications. Under the federal E-Sign Act and the Uniform Electronic Transactions Act (both discussed in Chapter 11), what constitutes a signed writing has changed. A court cannot refuse to enforce a contract solely because it is contained in an electronic record, and a name typed at the end of an e-mail can be a signature.

E-Mail Evidence That an Employment Contract Existed

The court applied this rule in a recent case. Robert Moroni negotiated a deal to provide consulting services for Medco Health Solutions, Inc., a third party administrator of prescription-drug plans. Medco sent Moroni an e-mail setting forth the details of the parties' agreement. Moroni e-mailed a counteroffer, proposing that he would work on Medco's projects two days a week for thirteen months, in exchange for $17,000 per month ($204,000 annually), plus travel expenses. Medco accepted via e-mail, and Moroni began performing the contract, but Medco refused to pay him. Moroni sued for breach of contract. Medco argued that no enforceable contract existed and that the e-mail exchange showed only an agreement to agree. The court, however, ruled that the e-mail amounted to an agreement to the essential terms of an employment contract.[a]

E-Mail Modifications of an Employment Contract

In another case, Arthur Stevens sold his public relations firm in New York to Publicis, S.A., a French global communications company. (*S.A.* stands for *Société Anonyme,* the French equivalent of a U.S. corporation.) The sale involved two contracts: a stock purchase agreement (SPA) and an employment contract. Stevens received an initial payment of more than $3 million under the SPA and stood to receive additional payments of up to $4 million over the next three years, depending on the new company's earnings. The employment contract allowed Stevens to stay on as chief executive officer (CEO) of the new company for three years and contained an integration clause that required any modification to be in a signed writing.

Within six months of the sale, however, the new company had lost $900,000 and was not meeting revenue and profit targets. Stevens was removed as CEO and given the option of leaving the firm or staying to develop new business. An agent of Publicis then e-mailed Stevens another option, giving him specific information on the responsibilities he could assume. Within a day, Stevens sent an e-mail stating, "I accept your proposal with total enthusiasm and excitement." The message also said that he was "psyched" about his new position. Nevertheless, Stevens later sued Publicis, claiming that it had breached the terms of his original employment contract by not keeping him on as CEO. The court, however, held that in the e-mail exchanges, Stevens had accepted the proposed modification of his employment contract in a signed writing. Because the e-mail modification was binding, Stevens could not sue Publicis.[b]

MANAGERIAL IMPLICATIONS

Communication with potential and actual employees via Twitter, instant messaging, Facebook, MySpace, and e-mail has become common. Managers must understand that a court may review the entire thread of such communications and determine that the exchange is sufficient to create an agreement about the essential terms of a contract. Thus, any form of online communication about a job or a modification of an employment agreement must be treated as if it were part of actual contract negotiations.

a. *Moroni v. Medco Health Solutions, Inc.,* 2008 WL 3539476 (E.D.Mich. 2008).

b. *Stevens v. Publicis, S.A.,* 50 A.D.3d 253, 854 N.Y.S.2d 690 (1 Dept. 2008).

federal government construction projects to pay "prevailing wages" to their employees. In 1936, the Walsh-Healey Act[5] was passed. This act requires that a minimum wage, as well as overtime pay at 1.5 times regular pay rates, be paid to employees of manufacturers or suppliers entering into contracts with agencies of the federal government.

In 1938, Congress passed the Fair Labor Standards Act (FLSA).[6] This act extended wage-hour requirements to cover all employers engaged in interstate

5. 41 U.S.C. Sections 35–45.

6. 29 U.S.C. Sections 201–260.

commerce or in the production of goods for interstate commerce, plus selected other types of businesses. Here, we examine the FLSA's provisions in regard to child labor, minimum wages, and overtime.

Child Labor

The FLSA prohibits oppressive child labor. Children under fourteen years of age are allowed to do certain types of work, such as deliver newspapers, work for their parents, and be employed in the entertainment and (with some exceptions) agricultural areas. Children who are fourteen or fifteen years of age are allowed to work, but not in hazardous occupations. There are also numerous restrictions on how many hours per day and per week children can work.

Working times and hours are not restricted for persons between the ages of sixteen and eighteen, but they cannot be employed in hazardous jobs or in jobs detrimental to their health and well-being. None of these restrictions apply to those over the age of eighteen.

Minimum Wages

The FLSA provides that a **minimum wage** of $7.25 per hour must be paid to employees in covered industries. Congress periodically revises this minimum wage.[7] Under the FLSA, employers who customarily furnish food or lodging to employees can deduct the reasonable cost of those services from the employees' wages.

Overtime Provisions and Exemptions

Under the FLSA, any employee who works more than forty hours per week must be paid no less than 1.5 times her or his regular pay for all hours over forty. Note that the FLSA overtime provisions apply only after an employee has worked more than forty hours per *week*. Thus, employees who work for ten hours a day, four days per week, are not entitled to overtime pay, because they do not work more than forty hours per week.

Certain employees—usually administrative, executive, and professional employees, as well as outside salespersons and computer programmers—are exempt from the FLSA's overtime provisions. Employers are not required to pay overtime wages to exempt employees. An employer can voluntarily pay overtime to ineligible employees but cannot waive or reduce the overtime requirements of the FLSA.

An executive employee is one whose primary duty is management. An employee's primary duty is determined by what he or she does that is of principal value to the employer, not by how much time the employee spends doing particular tasks. An employer cannot deny overtime wages to an employee based only on the employee's job title, however, and must be able to show that the employee's primary duty qualifies her or him for an exemption.[8]

CASE IN POINT Starbucks hired Kevin Keevican as a barista to wait on customers, operate the cash register, make drinks, and clean the equipment. Eventually, he was promoted to manager. As manager, Keevican worked seventy hours a week for $650 to $800, a 10 to 20 percent bonus, and fringe benefits, such as paid sick leave, which were not available to baristas. Keevican quit and, along with other former managers, filed a claim against Starbucks for unpaid overtime. The managers admitted that they had performed many managerial tasks, but argued that they had spent 70 to 80 percent of their time on barista chores and thus were not executive employees. The court, however, found that each manager was "the single highest-ranking employee in his [or her] particular store and was responsible on site for that store's day-to-day overall operations." Therefore, each manager's primary duty was managerial, and Starbucks was not required to pay overtime.[9]

The exemptions from the overtime-pay requirement do not apply to manual laborers or to licensed nurses, police, firefighters, and other public-safety workers. White-collar workers who earn more than $100,000 per year, computer programmers, dental hygienists, and insurance adjusters are typically exempt, though they must also meet certain other criteria.

In the following case, the issue before the court was whether an employee of a pharmaceutical company was an administrative employee and therefore exempt from the overtime requirements of the FLSA.

---

7. Note that many state and local governments also have minimum-wage laws. These laws may provide for minimum-wage rates higher than the federal rate.

8. See, for example, *Slusser v. Vantage Builders, Inc.*, 576 F.Supp.2d 1207 (D.N.M. 2008).

9. *Mims v. Starbucks Corp.*, 2007 WL 10369 (S.D.Tex. 2007).

☀ EXTENDED CASE 34.1 ☀
Smith v. Johnson and Johnson

United States Court of Appeals, Third Circuit, 593 F.3d 280 (2010).
www.ca3.uscourts.gov[a]

IN THE LANGUAGE OF THE COURT

GREENBERG, Circuit Judge.

* * * *

* * * McNeill Pediatrics, a J&J [Johnson and Johnson] wholly owned subsidiary, employed [Patty Lee] Smith in the position of Senior Professional Sales Representative. In essence, Smith's position required her to travel to various doctors' offices and hospitals where she extolled the benefit of J&J's pharmaceutical drug Concerta to the prescribing doctors. * * * Smith, however, did not sell Concerta (a controlled substance) directly to the doctors, as such sales are prohibited by law.

J&J gave Smith a list of target doctors that it created and told her to complete an average of ten visits per day, visiting every doctor on her target list at least once each quarter. To schedule visits with reluctant doctors, Smith had to be inventive and cultivate relationships with the doctor's staff, an endeavor in which she found that coffee and donuts were useful tools. J&J left the itinerary and order of Smith's visits to the target doctors to her discretion. * * * J&J gave her a budget for these visits and she could use the money in the budget to take the doctors to lunch or to sponsor seminars.

* * * *

In Smith's deposition she made it clear that she appreciated the freedom and responsibility that her position provided. Though a supervisor accompanied Smith during the doctor visits on a few days each quarter, by her own calculation Smith was unsupervised 95% of the time. As Smith explained during her deposition, "it was really up to me to run the territory the way I wanted to. And it was not a micromanaged type of job. I had pretty much the ability to work it the way I wanted to work it." According to Smith's job description, she was required to plan and prioritize her responsibilities in a manner that maximized business results. J&J witnesses testified (and J&J documents confirmed) that Smith was the "expert" on her own territory and was supposed to develop a strategic plan to achieve higher sales.

* * * *

Smith earned a base salary of $66,000 but was not paid overtime, though J&J, at its discretion, could award her a bonus.

Smith filed suit seeking overtime pay under the Fair Labor Standards Act ("FLSA"). * * * J&J moved for summary judgment, arguing that she was not entitled to overtime pay under the FLSA because she was exempt from that statute under * * * the "administrative employee" exemption. [The court granted J&J's motion, and Smith appealed.]

* * * *

Under the FLSA, employees who work more than 40 hours per week are entitled to overtime pay unless they fall within one of the FLSA's exemptions. * * * The District Court held that the administrative employee exemption applied to Smith, so we focus on the regulations describing that exemption.

Under the administrative employee exemption, anyone employed in a bona fide administrative capacity is exempt from the FLSA's overtime requirements. The Secretary [of Labor] has defined an administrative employee as someone:

(1) Compensated on a salary or fee basis at a rate of not less than $455 per week * * * exclusive of board, lodging or other facilities;

(2) Whose primary duty is the performance of office or non-manual work directly related to the management or general business operations of the employer or the employer's customers; and

(3) Whose primary duty includes the exercise of discretion and independent judgment with respect to matters of significance. [Emphasis added.]

The parties agree that Smith's salary qualifies her for the administrative employee exemption, but dispute her qualification for that exemption under the remaining two sections.

We find that the administrative employee exemption applies to Smith. While testifying at her deposition Smith elaborated on the independent and managerial qualities that her position required. Her non-manual position required her to form a strategic plan designed to maximize sales in her territory. We think that this requirement satisfied the "directly related to the management or general business operations of the employer" provision of the administrative employee exemption because it involved a high level of planning and foresight, and the strategic plan that Smith developed guided the execution of her remaining duties.

When we turn to the "exercise of discretion and independent judgment with respect to matters of significance" requirement, we note that Smith executed nearly all of her duties without direct oversight. In fact, she described herself as the manager of her own business who could

---

a. In the "Opinions and Oral Arguments" box, select "Opinion Archives." When that page opens, select "February" in the list under "2010 Decision." Scroll down the list of "Precedential" cases in the left-hand column and click on the highlighted case title to access the opinion. The U.S. Court of Appeals for the Third Circuit maintains this Web site.

EXTENDED CASE 34.1 CONTINUED ➡

run her own territory as she saw fit. Given these descriptions, we conclude

that Smith was subject to the administrative employee exemption.

* * * *

The District Court's order * * * will be affirmed * * *.

QUESTIONS

1. Is it unfair to exempt employees to deprive them of overtime wages? Why or why not?
2. J&J argued that Smith was exempt under either the administrative employee exemption or the outside salesperson exemption. The district court found, though, that Smith did not qualify for the outside salesperson exemption. What single fact might have made Smith ineligible for the outside salesperson exemption?

SECTION 3
LAYOFFS

During the latest economic recession in the United States, mass layoffs of workers resulted in high unemployment rates. Later in this chapter, we will discuss unemployment insurance, which helps some workers manage financially until they can find another job. In this section, we discuss the laws pertaining to employee layoffs, an area that is increasingly the subject of litigation.

The Worker Adjustment and Retraining Notification Act

Since 1988, the Worker Adjustment and Retraining Notification Act,[10] or the WARN Act, has required large businesses to provide sixty days' notice before implementing a mass layoff or closing a plant that employs more than fifty full-time workers. This federal law applies to employers with at least one hundred full-time employees. It is intended to give workers advance notice so that they can start looking for a new job while they are still employed.

The WARN Act defines the term *mass layoff* as a reduction in force that, during any thirty-day period, results in an employment loss of either:

1. At least 33 percent of the full-time employees at a single job site and at least fifty employees; or
2. At least five hundred full-time employees.

An *employment loss* is defined as a layoff that exceeds six months or a reduction in hours of work of more than 50 percent during each month of any six-month period.

---
10. 29 U.S.C. Sections 2101 *et seq.*

NOTIFICATION REQUIREMENTS The WARN Act requires that advance notice of the layoff be sent to the affected workers *or* their representative (if the workers are members of a labor union), as well as to state and local government authorities. The state and local authorities are notified so that they can provide resources, such as job training, to displaced workers. Employers must also provide notice to part-time and seasonal employees who are being laid off, even though these workers do not count in determining whether the act's provisions are triggered. Note also that even companies that are planning to file for bankruptcy normally must provide notice under the WARN Act before implementing a mass layoff. Nevertheless, employers can sometimes avoid the WARN notice requirements by staggering layoffs over many months or various locations.

REMEDIES FOR VIOLATIONS An employer that orders a mass layoff or plant closing in violation of the WARN Act can be fined up to $500 for each day of the violation. Employees can recover back pay for each day of the violation (up to sixty days), plus reasonable attorneys' fees. An employee can also recover benefits under an employee benefit plan, including the cost of medical expenses that would have been covered by the plan. (Employees who are laid off may also claim that the layoff was discriminatory in violation of the laws described in Chapter 35 if it disproportionately affects members of a protected class, such as minorities or women.)

State Laws May Also Require Layoff Notices

Many states also have statutes requiring employers to provide notice before initiating mass layoffs, and these laws may have different and even stricter requirements than the WARN Act. In New York, for instance, companies with fifty or more employees must provide ninety days' notice before any layoff that affects twenty-five or more full-time employees. The law in Illinois applies to companies with seventy-five or more employees and requires sixty days' advance notice of any layoff that affects twenty-five or more full-time employees at one plant or two hundred and fifty employees.

SECTION 4
FAMILY AND MEDICAL LEAVE

In 1993, Congress passed the Family and Medical Leave Act (FMLA)[11] to allow employees to take time off work for family or medical reasons. A majority of the states also have legislation allowing for a leave from employment for family or medical reasons, and many employers maintain private family-leave plans for their workers. The FMLA does not supersede any state or local law that provides more generous family- or medical-leave protection. In 2009, significant changes to the FMLA created new categories of leave for military caregivers and for qualifying exigencies that arise due to military service.

Coverage and Application

The FMLA requires employers who have fifty or more employees to provide an employee with up to twelve weeks of unpaid family or medical leave during any twelve-month period. The FMLA expressly covers private and public (government) employees who have worked for their employers for at least a

---

11. 29 U.S.C. Sections 2601, 2611–2619, 2651–2654.

year.[12] An employee may take *family leave* to care for a newborn baby or a child recently placed for adoption or foster care.[13] An employee can take *medical leave* when the employee or the employee's spouse, child, or parent has a serious health condition requiring care.

In addition, an employee caring for a family member with a serious injury or illness incurred as a result of military duty can now take up to twenty-six weeks of *military caregiver leave* within a twelve-month period.[14] An employee can also take up to twelve weeks of *qualifying exigency leave* to handle specified nonmedical emergencies when a spouse, parent, or child is on, or called to, active military duty.[15]

Benefits and Protections

When an employee takes FMLA leave, the employer must continue the worker's health-care coverage on the same terms as if the employee had continued to work. On returning from FMLA leave, most employees must be restored to their original position or to a comparable position (with nearly equivalent pay and benefits, for example). An important exception allows the employer to avoid reinstating a *key employee*—defined as an employee whose pay falls within the top 10 percent of the firm's workforce.

Employees suffering from addiction to drugs or alcohol pose a special problem under the FMLA. Under what circumstances do days off resulting from the addiction, as opposed to days off for medical treatment in a medical facility, count as part of protected leave? That issue was addressed in the following case.

---

12. Note that changes to the FMLA rules allow employees who have taken a break from their employment to qualify for FMLA leave if they worked a total of twelve months during the previous seven years. See 29 C.F.R. Section 825.110(b)(1-2).
13. The foster care must be state sanctioned for such an arrangement to fall within the coverage of the FMLA.
14. 29 C.F.R. Section 825.200.
15. 29 C.F.R. Section 825.126.

CASE 34.2
Darst v. Interstate Brands Corp.
United States Court of Appeals, Seventh Circuit, 512 F.3d 903 (2008).

BACKGROUND AND FACTS • Krzysztof Chalimoniuk worked for Interstate Brands Corporation (IBC) for fifteen years before he was fired for excessive absenteeism. Chalimoniuk, an alcoholic, sought treatment for his condition. He requested leave under the Family and Medical Leave Act (FMLA) from July 29 to August 14, 2000, to deal with the problem. From August 4 to 11, he was hospitalized for treatment of alcohol dependence and withdrawal. When he failed to return to work on August 15, he was fired for being absent. IBC noted that he was also absent from July 29 to August 3, when he

CASE 34.2 CONTINUED ➧ was not hospitalized, and those days were counted as improper absences because he had already exceeded the number of days he could miss under the company's leave policy. Chalimoniuk sued, contending that IBC had violated his FMLA rights. During the course of litigation, Chalimoniuk filed for bankruptcy, and his claim against IBC became part of the bankruptcy estate. Richard Darst, as trustee for the estate, continued to prosecute the claim. The district court granted summary judgment in favor of IBC. Darst appealed.

IN THE LANGUAGE OF THE COURT
ROEVNER, Circuit Judge.
* * * *

The substantive law at issue is the FMLA. Under the FMLA, eligible employees are entitled to up to twelve weeks of unpaid leave per year for absence due to, among other things, a "Serious Health Condition" that renders the employee unable to perform the functions of his or her job. To ensure the entitlement, the FMLA makes it "unlawful for any employer to interfere with, restrain, or deny the exercise of or the attempt to exercise, any right provided." When an employee alleges a deprivation of the substantive guarantees of the FMLA, the employee must establish, by a preponderance of the evidence, an entitlement to the disputed leave. Because the district court resolved the case on a motion for summary judgment, Chalimoniuk need only raise a genuine issue of material fact regarding his entitlement to FMLA leave on the relevant dates.

A Serious Health Condition is defined as an illness, injury, impairment, or physical or mental condition that involves either (1) inpatient care in a hospital, hospice, or residential medical facility; or (2) continuing treatment by a health care provider. Although the statute itself does not specifically address whether alcoholism [and] substance abuse constitute serious health conditions, Department of Labor regulations that implement the statute provide the answer. *As we noted above, substance abuse may be a Serious Health Condition under certain conditions but FMLA leave may be taken only for treatment for substance abuse. On the other hand, absence because of the employee's use of the substance, rather than for treatment, does not qualify for FMLA leave. Under this regulation, Chalimoniuk was entitled to FMLA leave only for treatment for substance abuse.* Because of the final sentence in the regulation, the parties argue over whether Chalimoniuk was intoxicated on July 31, August 2 or August 3, but we will assume for the purposes of summary judgment that he was not intoxicated on those days. Even if he was sober on those days, however, he has provided no explanation for his absence that would excuse the absence under IBC's point system except that he was in treatment for alcoholism. [Emphasis added.]
* * * *

Dr. Pfeifer [Chalimoniuk's physician] confirmed that Chalimoniuk received inpatient treatment at [the hospital] from August 4 until August 11. He produced no records and had no recollection of treating Chalimoniuk prior to that time. Chalimoniuk provided an affidavit from Dr. Pfeifer stating the doctor's belief that "treatment" for alcoholism begins when the patient takes the first step towards seeking professional help. According to Dr. Pfeifer, this includes the first phone call to the health care provider seeking evaluation, treatment or referral. Based on his training and experience as a medical doctor, Dr. Pfeifer averred [asserted] that Chalimoniuk's treatment therefore began on July 29, when he first contacted his physician's office. *Under the FMLA, however, "treatment" is a defined term that does not include actions such as calling to make an appointment. Treatment would include examinations to determine if a serious health condition exists and evaluation of the condition.* But Chalimoniuk has produced no evidence that he was being examined or evaluated on July 29, August 2 or August 3. Treatment does not include "any activities that can be initiated without a visit to a health care provider." Chalimoniuk complains that memories have faded since the time of his termination, that his doctors could have testified regarding his treatment on those days if he had known closer to the time that the company was challenging the fact of treatment on the days in question. But Chalimoniuk knew as of August 15, days after his treatment ended, that the company was denying him FMLA leave for all of the days he was absent except the period of his hospitalization. He had ample opportunities to preserve any relevant evidence. Thus, because Chalimoniuk has produced no evidence that he received any treatment as that term is defined by the FMLA on the days in question, he was not entitled to FMLA leave on those dates. Because he had exceeded the number of points allowable

CASE CONTINUES ➧

CASE 34.2 CONTINUED ▶ under IBC's absenteeism policy, the defendants were free to terminate his employment without running afoul of the FMLA. [Emphasis added.]

DECISION AND REMEDY • *The appeals court affirmed that Chalimoniuk's employer did not violate his FMLA leave by dismissing him for excessive absences. FMLA leave covered the days he was receiving medical treatment, not the days he missed work prior to or after the treatment.*

THE ETHICAL DIMENSION • *Did IBC take unfair advantage of the "letter of the law" by not granting Chalimoniuk a little more leave time? After all, he was, in fact, dealing with his problem. Explain your answer.*

THE LEGAL ENVIRONMENT DIMENSION • *Although IBC won this case, defending against the lawsuit was costly. How can employers avoid such litigation?*

Violations

An employer that violates the FMLA can be required to provide various remedies, including (1) damages for lost wages and benefits, denied compensation, and actual monetary losses (such as the cost of providing for care of a family member) up to an amount equivalent to the employee's wages for twelve weeks; (2) job reinstatement; and (3) promotion, if a promotion was denied.

In addition, a successful plaintiff is entitled to court costs and attorneys' fees; if bad faith on the part of the employer is shown, the plaintiff may also receive two times the amount of damages awarded by the judge or jury. Supervisors can also be held personally liable, as employers, for violations of the act.

Employers generally are required to notify employees when an absence will be counted against leave authorized under the act. If an employer fails to provide such notice, and the employee consequently is damaged because he or she did not receive notice, the employer may be sanctioned.[16]

SECTION 5
WORKER HEALTH AND SAFETY

Under the common law, employees who were injured on the job had to file lawsuits against their employers to obtain recovery. Today, numerous state and federal statutes protect employees from the risk of accidental injury, death, or disease resulting from their employment. This section discusses the primary federal statute governing health and safety in the workplace, along with state workers' compensation acts.

The Occupational Safety and Health Act

At the federal level, the primary legislation protecting employees' health and safety is the Occupational Safety and Health Act of 1970,[17] which is administered by the Occupational Safety and Health Administration (OSHA). Congress passed this act in an attempt to ensure safe and healthful working conditions for practically every employee in the country.

REQUIREMENTS The act imposes a general duty on employers to keep workplaces safe. To this end, OSHA has established specific safety standards that employers must follow depending on the industry. For instance, OSHA regulations require the use of safety guards on certain mechanical equipment and set maximum levels of exposure to substances in the workplace that may be harmful to a worker's health. The act also requires that employers post certain notices in the workplace, perform prescribed recordkeeping, and submit specific reports.

For instance, employers with eleven or more employees are required to keep occupational injury and illness records for each employee. Each record must be made available for inspection when requested by an OSHA compliance officer. Whenever a work-related injury or disease occurs, employers must make reports directly to OSHA. If an employee dies or five or more employees are hospitalized because of a work-related incident, the employer must notify the U.S. Department of Labor within forty-eight hours. A company that fails to do so will be fined. Following the incident, a complete inspection of the premises is mandatory.

ENFORCEMENT PROCEDURES AND VIOLATIONS OSHA compliance officers may enter and inspect the facilities of any establishment covered by the

---

16. *Ragsdale v. Wolverine World Wide, Inc.*, 535 U.S. 81, 122 S.Ct. 1155, 152 L.Ed.2d 167 (2002).

17. 29 U.S.C. Sections 553, 651–678.

Occupational Safety and Health Act.[18] Employees may also file complaints of violations. Under the act, an employer cannot discharge an employee who files a complaint or who, in good faith, refuses to work in a high-risk area if bodily harm or death might result.

Criminal penalties for willful violation of the Occupational Safety and Health Act are limited. Employers may also be prosecuted under state laws, however. In other words, the act does not preempt state and local criminal laws.[19]

State Workers' Compensation Laws

State **workers' compensation laws** establish an administrative procedure for compensating workers injured on the job. Instead of suing, an injured worker files a claim with the administrative agency or board that administers local workers' compensation claims.

Most workers' compensation statutes are similar. No state covers all employees. Typically, domestic workers, agricultural workers, temporary employees, and employees of common carriers (companies that provide transportation services to the public) are excluded, but minors are covered. Usually, the statutes allow employers to purchase insurance from a private insurer or a state fund to pay workers' compensation benefits in the event of a claim. Most states also allow employers to be *self-insured*—that is, employers that show an ability to pay claims do not need to buy insurance.

WORKERS' COMPENSATION REQUIREMENTS In general, the only requirements to recover benefits under state workers' compensation laws are:

1. The existence of an employment relationship.
2. An *accidental* injury that *occurred on the job or in the course of employment,* regardless of fault. (If an employee is injured while commuting to or from work, the injury usually will not be considered

to have occurred on the job or in the course of employment and hence will not be covered.)

An injured employee must notify her or his employer promptly (usually within thirty days of the accident). Generally, an employee must also file a workers' compensation claim with the appropriate state agency or board within a certain period (sixty days to two years) from the time the injury is first noticed, rather than from the time of the accident.

WORKERS' COMPENSATION VERSUS LITIGATION An employee who accepts workers' compensation benefits is prohibited from suing for injuries caused by the employer's negligence. By barring lawsuits for negligence, workers' compensation laws also prevent employers from raising common law defenses to negligence, such as contributory negligence or assumption of risk, to avoid liability. A worker may sue an employer who *intentionally* injures the worker, however.

SECTION 6
INCOME SECURITY

Federal and state governments participate in insurance programs designed to protect employees and their families from the financial impact of retirement, disability, death, hospitalization, and unemployment. The key federal law on this subject is the Social Security Act of 1935.[20]

Social Security

The Social Security Act of 1935 provides for old-age (retirement), survivors', and disability insurance. The act is therefore often referred to as OASDI. Both employers and employees must "contribute" under the Federal Insurance Contributions Act (FICA)[21] to help pay for benefits that will partially make up for the employees' loss of income on retirement.

The basis for the employee's and the employer's contribution is the employee's annual wage base—the maximum amount of the employee's wages that is subject to the tax. The employer withholds the employee's FICA contribution from the employee's wages and then matches this contribution. The

---

18. In 1978, the United States Supreme Court held that warrantless inspections violate the warrant clause of the Fourth Amendment to the U.S. Constitution. See *Marshall v. Barlow's, Inc.*, 436 U.S. 307, 98 S.Ct. 1816, 56 L.Ed.2d 305 (1978). Although this case has not been overruled, the Supreme Court subsequently indicated that statutory inspection programs can provide a constitutionally adequate substitute for a warrant. See *Donovan v. Dewey*, 452 U.S. 594, 101 S.Ct. 2534, 69 L.Ed.2d 262 (1981).

19. *Pedraza v. Shell Oil Co.*, 942 F.2d 48 (1st Cir. 1991); cert. denied, 502 U.S. 1082, 112 S.Ct. 993, 117 L.Ed.2d 154 (1992). See also *In re Welding Fume Products Liability Litigation*, 364 F.Supp.2d 669 (N.D. Ohio 2005).

20. 42 U.S.C. Sections 301–1397e.
21. 26 U.S.C. Sections 3101–3125.

annual wage base is adjusted each year as needed to take into account the rising cost of living. In 2010, employers were required to withhold 6.2 percent of each employee's wages, up to a maximum wage base of $106,800, and to match this contribution.

Retired workers are eligible to receive monthly payments from the Social Security Administration, which administers the Social Security Act. Social Security benefits are fixed by statute but increase automatically with increases in the cost of living.

Medicare

Medicare, a federal government health-insurance program, is administered by the Social Security Administration for people sixty-five years of age and older and for some under age sixty-five who are disabled. It originally had two parts, one pertaining to hospital costs and the other to nonhospital medical costs, such as visits to physicians' offices. Medicare now offers additional coverage options and a prescription-drug plan. People who have Medicare hospital insurance can obtain additional federal medical insurance if they pay small monthly premiums, which increase as the cost of medical care rises.

As with Social Security, both the employer and the employee contribute to Medicare, but the programs differ in that there is no cap on the amount of wages subject to the Medicare tax. In 2010, both the employer and the employee were required to pay 1.45 percent of *all* wages and salaries to finance Medicare. Thus, for Social Security and Medicare together, in 2010 the employer and employee each paid 7.65 percent of the first $106,800 of income (6.2 percent for Social Security + 1.45 percent for Medicare), for a combined total of 15.3 percent. In addition, all wages and salaries above $106,800 were taxed at a combined (employer and employee) rate of 2.9 percent for Medicare.[22] Self-employed persons pay both the employer and the employee portions of the Social Security and Medicare taxes (15.3 percent of income up to $106,800 and 2.9 percent of income above that amount in 2010).

Private Pension Plans

The major federal statute regulating employee retirement plans set up by employers is the Employee Retirement Income Security Act (ERISA) of 1974.[23] This act empowers a branch of the U.S. Department of Labor to enforce its provisions governing employers who have private pension funds for their employees. ERISA created the Pension Benefit Guaranty Corporation (PBGC), an independent federal agency, to provide timely and uninterrupted payment of voluntary private pension benefits. The pension plans pay annual insurance premiums (at set rates adjusted for inflation) to the PBGC, which then pays benefits to participants in the event that a plan is unable to do so. Under the Pension Protection Act of 2006,[24] the director of the PBGC is appointed by the president and confirmed by the Senate.

ERISA does not require an employer to establish a pension plan. When a plan exists, however, ERISA provides standards for its management. A key provision of ERISA concerns vesting. **Vesting** gives an employee a legal right to receive pension benefits at some future date when she or he stops working. Before ERISA was enacted, some employees who had worked for companies for as long as thirty years received no pension benefits when their employment terminated because those benefits had not vested. ERISA establishes complex vesting rules. Generally, however, all of an employee's contributions to a pension plan vest immediately, and the employee's rights to the employer's contributions vest after five years of employment.

In an attempt to prevent mismanagement of pension funds, ERISA has established rules on how they must be invested. Managers must choose investments cautiously and must diversify the plan's investments to minimize the risk of large losses. ERISA also includes detailed record-keeping and reporting requirements.

Unemployment Compensation

To ease the financial impact of unemployment, the United States has a system of unemployment insurance. The Federal Unemployment Tax Act (FUTA) of 1935[25] created a state-administered system that provides unemployment compensation to eligible

---

22. Note that as a result of the 2010 health-care reform legislation (the Health Care and Education Reconciliation Act of 2010, H.R. 4872), not only are Medicare tax rates expected to rise, but also the applicable compensation base will expand to include more than just salary incomes. For instance, starting in 2012, there will be a 3.8 percent Medicare payroll tax on investment income for families making more than $250,000 per year.

---

23. 29 U.S.C. Sections 1001 *et seq.*
24. The Pension Protection Act amended 26 U.S.C. Sections 430–432, 436, 4966, 4967, 6039I, 6050U, 6050V, 6695A, 6720B, 7443B; and 29 U.S.C. Sections 1082–1085, 1202a.
25. 26 U.S.C. Sections 3301–3310.

individuals. Under this system, employers pay into a fund, and the proceeds are paid out to qualified unemployed workers. The FUTA and state laws require employers that fall under the provisions of the act to pay unemployment taxes at regular intervals.

To be eligible for unemployment compensation, a worker must be willing and able to work. Workers who have been fired for misconduct or who have voluntarily left their jobs are not eligible for benefits. In the past, workers had to be actively seeking employment to continue receiving benefits. Due to the high unemployment rates after the Great Recession, however, President Barack Obama announced measures that allow jobless persons to retain their unemployment benefits while pursuing additional education and training (rather than seeking employment).

COBRA

For workers whose jobs have been terminated—and who are thus no longer eligible for group health-insurance plans—federal law also provides a right to continued health-care coverage. The Consolidated Omnibus Budget Reconciliation Act (COBRA) of 1985[26] prohibits an employer from eliminating a worker's medical, optical, or dental insurance on the voluntary or involuntary termination of the worker's employment.

Employers, with some exceptions, must inform employees of COBRA's provisions when they face termination or a reduction of hours that would affect their eligibility for coverage under the plan. Only workers fired for gross misconduct are excluded from protection.

PROCEDURES A worker has sixty days (beginning with the date that the group coverage would stop) to decide whether to continue with the employer's group insurance plan. If the worker chooses to discontinue the coverage, then the employer has no further obligation. If the worker chooses to continue coverage, though, the employer is obligated to keep the policy active for up to eighteen months (twenty-nine months if the worker is disabled). The coverage provided must be the same as that enjoyed by the worker prior to the termination or reduction of work. If family members were originally included, for instance, COBRA prohibits their exclusion.

PAYMENT The worker does not receive the insurance coverage for free. Generally, an employer can require the employee to pay all of the premiums, plus a 2 percent administrative charge. In 2009, however, the law was changed to provide for certain workers who involuntarily lost their jobs.[27] These employees can be charged no more than 35 percent of the premiums. The employer receives a tax credit as reimbursement for the remaining 65 percent of the premiums.

If the worker fails to pay the required premiums (or if the employer completely eliminates its group benefit plan), the employer is relieved of further responsibility. (The employer is also relieved of the obligation if the worker becomes eligible for Medicare or obtains coverage under another health plan, such as a spouse's or new employer's plan.) An employer that does not comply with COBRA risks substantial penalties, such as a tax of up to 10 percent of the annual cost of the group plan or $500,000, whichever is less.

Employer-Sponsored Group Health Plans

The Health Insurance Portability and Accountability Act (HIPAA),[28] which was discussed in Chapter 4 in the context of its privacy protections, contains provisions that affect employer-sponsored group health plans. HIPAA does not require employers to provide health insurance, but it does establish requirements for those that do provide such coverage. For instance, HIPAA strictly limits an employer's ability to exclude coverage for *preexisting conditions*. It also requires employers to give credit to employees for previous health coverage (including COBRA coverage) to decrease any waiting period before their coverage becomes effective.

In addition, HIPAA restricts the manner in which covered employers collect, use, and disclose the health information of employees and their families. Employers must train employees, designate privacy officials, and distribute privacy notices to ensure that employees' health information is not disclosed to unauthorized parties. Failure to comply with HIPAA regulations can result in civil penalties of up to $100 per person per violation (with a cap of $25,000 per year). The employer is also subject to

---

26. 29 U.S.C. Sections 1161–1169.

27. These changes were made by the American Recovery and Reinvestment Act (Stimulus Bill) of 2009, Pub. L. No. 111-5, 123 Stat. 115 (February 17, 2009). The provisions for workers who involuntarily lost their jobs were originally set to end in 2009 but were later extended through November 2010.

28. 29 U.S.C. Sections 1181 *et seq.*

criminal prosecution for certain types of HIPAA violations and can face up to $250,000 in criminal fines and imprisonment for up to ten years if convicted.

SECTION 7
EMPLOYEE PRIVACY RIGHTS

In the last thirty years, concerns about the privacy rights of employees have arisen in response to the sometimes invasive tactics used by employers to monitor and screen workers. Perhaps the greatest privacy concern in today's employment arena has to do with electronic monitoring of employees' activities.

Electronic Monitoring

According to the American Management Association, more than two-thirds of employers engage in some form of electronic monitoring of their employees. This surveillance may include monitoring employees' e-mails, blogs, instant messages, tweets, Internet use, and computer files; video-recording employee job performance; and recording and reviewing telephone conversations, voice mail, and text messages.

Various specially designed software products have made it easier for an employer to track employees' Internet use, including the specific Web sites visited and the time spent surfing the Web. Indeed, inappropriate Web surfing seems to be a primary concern for employers. More than 75 percent of them are monitoring workers' Web connections. Filtering software, which was discussed in Chapter 4, can be used to prevent access to certain Web sites, such as sites containing sexually explicit images. Private employers are generally free to use filtering software to block access to certain Web sites because the First Amendment's protection of free speech prevents only *government employers* from restraining speech by blocking Web sites.

EMPLOYEE PRIVACY PROTECTION Recall from Chapter 4 that the United States Supreme Court has inferred a personal right to privacy from the constitutional guarantees provided by the First, Third, Fourth, Fifth, and Ninth Amendments to the Constitution. Tort law (see Chapters 6 and 7), state constitutions, and a number of state and federal statutes also provide for privacy rights.

When determining whether an employer should be held liable for violating an employee's privacy rights, the courts generally weigh the employer's interests against the employee's reasonable expectation of privacy. Normally, if employees are informed that their communications are being monitored, they cannot reasonably expect those communications to be private. If employees are not informed that certain communications are being monitored, however, the employer may be held liable for invading their privacy. For this reason, most employers that engage in electronic monitoring notify their employees about the monitoring.

Nevertheless, establishing a general privacy policy may not sufficiently protect an employer who monitors other forms of communications that the policy fails to mention. Similarly, notifying employees that their e-mails may be monitored may not protect an employer who monitors text messages. Courts also look at other factors when deciding if the employee had a reasonable expectation of privacy. For instance, if the employer provided the e-mail system or blog that the employee used for communications, a court will typically hold that the employee did not have a reasonable expectation of privacy.

ELECTRONIC COMMUNICATIONS PRIVACY ACT The major statute governing electronic monitoring by employers is the Electronic Communications Privacy Act (ECPA) of 1986.[29] This act amended existing federal wiretapping law to cover electronic forms of communications, such as communications via cell phones and e-mail. The ECPA prohibits the intentional interception of any wire or electronic communication or the intentional disclosure or use of the information obtained by the interception. Excluded from coverage are any electronic communications through devices that are "furnished to the subscriber or user by a provider of wire or electronic communication service" and that are being used by the subscriber or user, or by the provider of the service, "in the ordinary course of its business."

This "business-extension exception" to the ECPA allows an employer to monitor employees' electronic communications in the ordinary course of business. It does not, however, permit an employer to monitor employees' personal communications. Nevertheless, under another exception to the ECPA, an employer may avoid liability if the employees consent to having their electronic communications intercepted by the employer. Thus, by simply requiring employees to sign forms indicating that they consent to such monitoring, an employer can avoid liability for monitoring employees' personal communications.

---

29. 18 U.S.C. Sections 2510–2521.

STORED COMMUNICATIONS Part of the ECPA is known as the Stored Communications Act (SCA).[30] The SCA prohibits intentional and unauthorized access to *stored* electronic communications and sets forth criminal and civil sanctions for violators. A person can violate the SCA by intentionally accessing a stored electronic communication or by intentionally exceeding the authorization given to access the communication. To prove a violation, however, an individual must show that the other party (for example, an employer) lacked the authority to access the stored communication. Proving this lack of authority may be difficult at times, especially when an employer provided the electronic communication device.

CASE IN POINT Jeff Quon, a police sergeant for Ontario, California, was issued a pager with wireless text-messaging services provided by Arch Wireless Operating Company. Although the city had a general policy that employees should not use work computers, Internet, and e-mail for personal matters, it did not expressly mention the pagers or text messaging. On several occasions, Quon paid the city overage charges for exceeding the limit on text messages. Without Quon's knowledge, his supervisors obtained transcripts of his stored text messages from Arch Wireless to determine whether any of the texts were personal. When Quon learned that the city had read his personal texts, he filed a lawsuit against the city and Arch Wireless for violating his privacy rights. A federal appellate court ruled that Quon had a reasonable expectation of privacy in his text messages that were temporarily stored by Arch Wireless, a third party provider. Therefore, Arch Wireless should not have provided transcripts to the city without his authorization. On appeal, the United States Supreme Court reversed that ruling, finding that the search of Quon's text messages was reasonable. Because the police department had a written policy, which Quon admitted that he understood applied to the pagers, he should have had no reasonable expectation of privacy.[31]

Other Types of Monitoring

In addition to monitoring their employees' online activities, employers also engage in other types of employee screening and monitoring practices. The practices discussed next often have been challenged as violations of employee privacy rights.

LIE-DETECTOR TESTS At one time, many employers required employees or job applicants to take polygraph examinations (lie-detector tests). In 1988, Congress passed the Employee Polygraph Protection Act,[32] which generally prohibits employers from requiring or causing employees or job applicants to take lie-detector tests or suggesting or requesting that they do so. The act also restricts employers' ability to use or ask about the results of any lie-detector test or to take any negative employment action based on the results.

Employers excepted from these prohibitions include federal, state, and local government employers; certain security service firms; and companies manufacturing and distributing controlled substances. Other employers may use polygraph tests when investigating losses attributable to theft, including embezzlement and the theft of trade secrets.

DRUG TESTING In the interests of public safety and to reduce unnecessary costs, many employers, including the government, require their employees to submit to drug testing. Government (public) employers, of course, are constrained in drug testing by the Fourth Amendment to the U.S. Constitution, which prohibits unreasonable searches and seizures (see Chapter 4). Drug testing of public employees is allowed by statute for transportation workers and is normally upheld by the courts when drug use in a particular job may threaten public safety. Also, when there is a reasonable basis for suspecting public employees of drug use, courts often find that drug testing does not violate the Fourth Amendment.

The Fourth Amendment does not apply to drug testing conducted by private employers.[33] Hence, the privacy rights and drug testing of private-sector employees are governed by state law, which varies from state to state. Many states have statutes that allow drug testing by private employers but put restrictions on when and how the testing may be performed. A collective bargaining agreement (discussed later in this chapter) may also provide protection against drug testing (or authorize drug testing under certain conditions). The permissibility of a private employee's drug test often hinges on whether the employer's testing was reasonable. Random drug tests and even "zero-tolerance" policies (which deny a "second chance" to employees who test positive for drugs) have been held to be reasonable.[34]

30. 18 U.S.C. Sections 2701–2711.
31. *City of Ontario, California v. Quon,* __ U.S. __, 130 S.Ct. 2619, __ L.Ed.2d __ (2010).
32. 29 U.S.C. Sections 2001 *et seq.*
33. See *Chandler v. Miller,* 520 U.S. 305, 117 S.Ct. 1295, 137 L.Ed.2d 513 (1997).
34. See *CITGO Asphalt Refining Co. v. Paper, Allied-Industrial, Chemical, and Energy Workers International Union Local No. 2–991,* 385 F.3d 809 (3d Cir. 2004).

GENETIC TESTING A serious privacy issue arose when some employers began conducting genetic testing of employees or prospective employees in an effort to identify individuals who might develop significant health problems in the future. To date, however, only a few cases involving this issue have come before the courts.

CASE IN POINT Lawrence Berkeley Laboratory screened prospective employees for the gene that causes sickle-cell anemia, although the applicants were not informed of this. When the prospective employees subsequently sued the laboratory, a federal appellate court held that they had a cause of action for violation of their privacy rights. The case was later settled for $2.2 million.[35]

In 2008, to prevent the improper use of genetic information by employers and health insurance providers, Congress passed the Genetic Information Nondiscrimination Act (GINA).[36] Under GINA, employers cannot make decisions about hiring, firing, job placement, or promotion based on the results of genetic testing. GINA also prohibits group health plans and insurers from denying coverage or charging higher premiums based solely on a genetic predisposition to develop a disease in the future.

SECTION 8
IMMIGRATION LAW

The United States did not have any laws restricting immigration until the late nineteenth century. In recent years, immigration law has become an area of increasing concern for businesses as the number of immigrants—especially illegal immigrants—to the United States has grown. An estimated 11 to 12 million illegal immigrants now live in the United States. The great majority of these illegal immigrants came to find jobs, but U.S. employers face serious penalties if they hire illegal immigrants. Thus, an understanding of the immigration laws has become increasingly important for businesses. Today, the most important laws affecting the employment relationship are the Immigration Reform and Control Act (IRCA) of 1986[37] and the Immigration Act of 1990.[38]

The Immigration Reform and Control Act

When the IRCA was enacted in 1986, it provided amnesty to certain groups of illegal aliens living in the United States at the time. It also established a system that sanctions employers that hire illegal immigrants who lack work authorization. The IRCA makes it illegal to hire, recruit, or refer for a fee someone not authorized to work in this country. Through Immigration and Customs Enforcement officers, the federal government conducts random compliance audits and engages in enforcement actions against employers who hire illegal immigrants.

I-9 EMPLOYMENT VERIFICATION To comply with IRCA requirements, an employer must perform **I-9 verifications** for new hires, including those hired as "contractors" or "day workers" if they work under the employer's direct supervision. The employer must complete Form I-9, Employment Eligibility Verification, which is available from U.S. Citizenship and Immigration Services,[39] for each worker within three days of his or her commencement of employment. The three-day period allows the employer to check the form's accuracy and to review and verify documents establishing the prospective worker's identity and eligibility for employment in the United States.

The employer must attest, under penalty of perjury, that an employee produced documents establishing his or her identity and legal employability. Acceptable documents include a U.S. passport establishing the person's citizenship or a document authorizing a foreign citizen to work in the United States, such as a permanent resident card or an *Alien Registration Receipt* (discussed on the facing page).

Note that most legal actions alleging violations of I-9 rules are brought against employees. An employee must state on the I-9 form that she or he is a U.S. citizen or otherwise authorized to work in the United States. If the employee enters false information on the form or presents false documentation, the employer can fire the worker, who then may be subject to deportation.

The IRCA prohibits "knowing" violations, including situations in which an employer "should have known" that the worker was unauthorized. Good faith is a defense under the statute, and employers

---

35. *Norman-Bloodsaw v. Lawrence Berkeley Laboratory,* 135 F.3d 1260 (9th Cir. 1998).

36. 26 U.S.C. Section 9834; 42 U.S.C. Sections 300gg-53, 1320d-9, 2000ff-1 to 2000ff-11.

37. 29 U.S.C. Section 1802.

38. This act amended various provisions of the Immigration and Nationality Act of 1952, 8 U.S.C. Sections 1101 *et seq.*

39. U.S. Citizenship and Immigration Services is a federal agency that is part of the U.S. Department of Homeland Security.

are legally entitled to rely on a document authorizing a person to work that reasonably appears on its face to be genuine, even if it is later established to be counterfeit.

ENFORCEMENT The IRCA rules are enforced by U.S. Immigration and Customs Enforcement (ICE), a federal agency that was established in 2003 as the largest investigative arm of the U.S. Department of Homeland Security. ICE has a general inspection program that conducts random compliance audits. Other audits may occur if the agency receives a written complaint alleging that an employer has committed violations. Government inspections include a review of an employer's file of I-9 forms. The government does not need a subpoena or a warrant to conduct such an inspection.

If an investigation reveals a possible violation, ICE will bring an administrative action and issue a Notice of Intent to Fine, which sets out the charges against the employer. The employer has a right to a hearing on the enforcement action if it files a request within thirty days. This hearing is conducted before an *administrative law judge* (see Chapters 1 and 44), and the employer has a right to counsel and to *discovery* (see Chapter 3). A typical defense in such actions is good faith or substantial compliance with the documentation provisions. Although the federal government increased its enforcement actions significantly during the Bush administration, the Obama administration shifted the focus away from enforcement actions and toward reforming immigration laws.

PENALTIES An employer who violates the law by hiring an unauthorized alien is subject to substantial penalties. The employer can be fined up to $2,200 for each unauthorized employee for a first offense, $5,000 per employee for a second offense, and up to $11,000 for subsequent offenses. Employers who have engaged in a "pattern or practice of violations" are subject to criminal penalties, which include additional fines and imprisonment for up to ten years. A company may also be barred from future government contracts for violations. In determining the penalty, ICE considers the seriousness of the violation (such as intentional falsification of documents) and the employer's past compliance. ICE regulations also identify factors that will mitigate or aggravate the penalty under certain circumstances, such as whether the employer cooperated in the investigation or is a small business.

The Immigration Act

U.S. immigration laws have long included provisions that permit businesses to hire foreign workers with special qualifications when there are not enough qualified workers available in the United States. The Immigration Act of 1990 placed caps on the number of visas (entry permits) that can be issued to immigrants each year.

Most temporary visas are set aside for workers who can be characterized as "persons of extraordinary ability," members of the professions holding advanced degrees, or other skilled workers and professionals. To hire such an individual, an employer must submit a petition to U.S. Citizenship and Immigration Services, which determines whether the job candidate meets the legal standards. Each visa is for a specific job, and there are legal limits on the employee's ability to switch jobs once he or she is in the United States.

I-551 ALIEN REGISTRATION RECEIPTS A company seeking to hire a noncitizen worker may do so if the worker is self-authorized. This means that the worker either is a lawful permanent resident or has a valid temporary Employment Authorization Document. A lawful permanent resident can prove his or her status to an employer by presenting an **I-551 Alien Registration Receipt,** known as a green card, or a properly stamped foreign passport. Many immigrant workers are not already self-authorized, and an employer that wishes to hire them may obtain labor certification, or green cards, for them. To gain authorization for hiring a foreign worker, the employer must show that no U.S. worker is qualified, willing, and able to take the job. Approximately fifty thousand new green cards are issued each year. A green card can be obtained only for a person who is being hired for a permanent, full-time position. (A separate authorization system provides for the temporary entry and hiring of nonimmigrant visa workers.)

THE H-1B VISA PROGRAM The most common and controversial visa program today is the H-1B visa system. To obtain an H1-B visa, the potential employee must be qualified in a "specialty occupation," which is defined as involving highly specialized knowledge and the attainment of a bachelor's or higher degree or its equivalent. The recipients of these visas include many high-tech workers, such as computer programmers and electronics specialists. Individuals with H-1B visas can stay in the United States for three to six years and work only for the sponsoring employer.

LABOR CERTIFICATION Before an employer can submit an H-1B application, it must file a Labor Certification application on a form known as ETA 9035. The employer must agree to provide a wage level at least equal to the wages offered to other individuals with similar experience and qualifications, and must attest that the hiring will not adversely affect other workers similarly employed. The employer is required to inform U.S. workers of the intent to hire a foreign worker by posting the form. The U.S. Department of Labor reviews the applications and may reject them for omissions or inaccuracies.

H-2, O, L, AND E VISAS Other specialty temporary visas are available for other categories of employees. H-2 visas provide for workers performing agricultural labor of a seasonal nature. O visas provide entry for persons who have "extraordinary ability in the sciences, arts, education, business or athletics which has been demonstrated by sustained national or international acclaim." L visas allow a company's foreign managers or executives to work inside the United States. E visas permit the entry of certain foreign investors or entrepreneurs.

SECTION 9
LABOR UNIONS

In the 1930s, in addition to the wage and hour laws discussed earlier, Congress enacted several other laws regulating employment relationships. These laws protect employees' rights to join labor unions, to bargain with management over the terms and conditions of employment, and to conduct strikes.

Federal Labor Laws

Federal labor laws governing union-employer relations have developed considerably since the first law was enacted in 1932. Initially, the laws were concerned with protecting the rights and interests of workers. Subsequent legislation placed some restraints on unions and granted rights to employers. We look here at four major federal statutes regulating union-employer relations.

NORRIS-LAGUARDIA ACT Congress protected peaceful strikes, picketing, and boycotts in 1932 in the Norris-LaGuardia Act.[40] The statute restricted the power of federal courts to issue injunctions against unions engaged in peaceful strikes. In effect, this act declared a national policy permitting employees to organize.

NATIONAL LABOR RELATIONS ACT One of the foremost statutes regulating labor is the National Labor Relations Act (NLRA) of 1935.[41] This act established the rights of employees to engage in collective bargaining and to strike. The act also specifically defined a number of employer practices as unfair to labor:

1. Interference with the efforts of employees to form, join, or assist labor organizations or to engage in concerted activities for their mutual aid or protection.
2. An employer's domination of a labor organization or contribution of financial or other support to it.
3. Discrimination in the hiring of or the awarding of tenure to employees for reason of union affiliation.
4. Discrimination against employees for filing charges under the act or giving testimony under the act.
5. Refusal to bargain collectively with the duly designated representative of the employees.

The National Labor Relations Board. To ensure that employees' rights would be protected, the NLRA established the National Labor Relations Board (NLRB). The NLRB has the authority to investigate employees' charges of unfair labor practices and to file complaints against employers in response to these charges. When violations are found, the NLRB may also issue a **cease-and-desist order**—an order compelling the employer to stop engaging in unfair practices. Cease-and-desist orders can be enforced by a federal appellate court if necessary. Disputes over alleged unfair labor practices are first decided by the NLRB and may then be appealed to a federal court.

Under the NLRA, employers and unions have a duty to bargain in good faith. Bargaining over certain subjects is mandatory, and a party's refusal to bargain over these subjects is an unfair labor practice that can be reported to the NLRB. In one case, for example, an employer was required to bargain with the union over the use of hidden video surveillance cameras.[42]

Workers Protected by the NLRA. To be protected under the NLRA, an individual must be an

---

40. 29 U.S.C. Sections 101–110, 113–115.

41. 20 U.S.C. Sections 151–169.
42. *National Steel Corp. v. NLRB,* 324 F.3d 928 (7th Cir. 2003).

employee or a job applicant (otherwise, the NLRA's ban on discrimination in regard to hiring would mean little). Additionally, the United States Supreme Court has held that individuals who are hired by a union to organize a company (union organizers) are to be considered employees of the company for NLRA purposes.[43]

LABOR-MANAGEMENT RELATIONS ACT The Labor-Management Relations Act (LMRA) of 1947[44] was passed to proscribe certain unfair union practices, such as the *closed shop*. A **closed shop** is a firm that requires union membership as a condition of employment. Although the act made the closed shop illegal, it preserved the legality of the union shop. A **union shop** is a firm that does not require union membership as a prerequisite for employment but can, and usually does, require that workers join the union after a specified amount of time on the job.

The LMRA also prohibited unions from refusing to bargain with employers, engaging in certain types of picketing, and *featherbedding* (causing employers to hire more employees than necessary). In addition, the act allowed individual states to pass their own **right-to-work laws**—laws making it illegal for union membership to be required for *continued* employment in any establishment. Thus, union shops are technically illegal in the twenty-two states that have right-to-work laws.

LABOR-MANAGEMENT REPORTING AND DISCLOSURE ACT The Labor-Management Reporting and Disclosure Act (LMRDA) of 1959[45] established an employee bill of rights and reporting requirements for union activities. The act strictly regulates unions' internal business procedures, including elections. For example, the LMRDA requires unions to hold regularly scheduled elections of officers using secret ballots. Former convicts are prohibited from holding union office. Moreover, union officials are accountable for union property and funds. Members have the right to attend and to participate in union meetings, to nominate officers, and to vote in most union proceedings.

The act also outlawed **hot-cargo agreements,** in which employers voluntarily agree with unions not to handle, use, or deal in goods of other employers produced by nonunion employees. The act made all such boycotts (called **secondary boycotts**) illegal.

Union Organization

Forming a union requires support from a majority of the employees in a defined bargaining unit, such as all of the workers at a specific automotive plant or all of the nurses employed by a particular hospital. Typically, the first step union organizers (unionizers) take is to have the workers that the union is seeking to represent sign authorization cards. An **authorization card** usually states that the worker desires to have a certain union, such as the United Auto Workers, represent the workforce. If a majority of the workers sign authorization cards, the organizers can present the cards to the employer and ask for formal recognition of the union. The employer is not required to recognize the union at this point, but it may do so voluntarily on a showing of majority support. (Under pro-union legislation that has been proposed in the U.S. Congress, the employer would be required to recognize the union as soon as a majority of the workers had signed authorization cards—without holding an election, as described next.[46])

UNION ELECTIONS If the employer refuses to voluntarily recognize the union after a majority of the workers sign authorization cards—or if fewer than 50 percent of the workers sign authorization cards—the union organizers present the cards to the NLRB with a petition for an election. For an election to be held, the unionizers must demonstrate that at least 30 percent of the workers to be represented support a union or an election on unionization.

The proposed union must also represent an *appropriate bargaining unit*. Not every group of workers can form a single union. One key requirement to being an appropriate bargaining unit is a *mutuality of interest* among all the workers to be represented by the union. Factors considered in determining whether there is a mutuality of interest include the *similarity of the jobs* of all the workers to be unionized and their physical location.

If all of these requirements are met, an election is held. The NLRB supervises the election and ensures secret voting and voter eligibility. If the proposed union receives majority support in a fair election, the NLRB certifies the union as the bargaining representative for the employees.

UNION ELECTION CAMPAIGNS Many disputes between labor and management arise during union election campaigns. Generally, the employer has control

---

43. *NLRB v. Town & Country Electric, Inc.,* 516 U.S. 85, 116 S.Ct. 450, 133 L.Ed.2d 371 (1995).
44. 29 U.S.C. Sections 141 *et seq.*
45. 29 U.S.C. Sections 401 *et seq.*

---

46. If the proposed Employee Free Choice Act (or Card Check Bill) becomes law, some of the information here may change.

over unionizing activities that take place on company property and during working hours. Thus, the employer may limit the campaign activities of union supporters as long as the employer has a legitimate business reason for doing so. The employer may also reasonably limit the times and places that union solicitation occurs, provided that the employer is not discriminating against the union.

Suppose that a union is seeking to organize clerks at a department store owned by Amanti Enterprises. Amanti can prohibit all union solicitation in areas of the store open to the public because the unionizing activities could interfere with the store's business. It can also restrict union-related activities to coffee breaks and lunch hours. Amanti cannot, however, allow solicitation for charitable causes during work hours or in the public part of the store if it prohibits union-related solicitation.

An employer may campaign among its workers against the union, but the NLRB carefully monitors and regulates the tactics used by management. If the employer issued threats ("If the union wins, you'll all be fired") or engaged in other unfair labor practices, the NLRB may certify the union even though it lost the election. Alternatively, the NLRB may ask a court to order a new election.

During a campaign, employers cannot undertake certain types of surveillance of workers or even create the impression of observing workers to identify union sympathizers. Not all management tactics will be deemed illegal, however. In the following case, the question was whether managers' brief interruptions of unionizing activities constituted illegal surveillance in violation of the National Labor Relations Act.

CASE 34.3
Local Joint Executive Board of Las Vegas v. National Labor Relations Board
United States Court of Appeals, Ninth Circuit, 515 F.3d 942 (2008).

BACKGROUND AND FACTS • Aladdin Gaming, LLC, operates a hotel and casino in Las Vegas, Nevada. On May 30, 2003, Local Joint Executive Board of Las Vegas and two other unions began an open campaign to organize Aladdin's housekeeping, food, and beverage departments. On two occasions during this campaign, human resources managers at Aladdin (Tracy Sapien and Stacey Briand) approached union organizers who were discussing unionization with employees in an employee dining room during a lunch break. Sapien and Briand interrupted the organizers while they were obtaining signatures on authorization cards and asked whether the employees had been fully informed of the facts before signing. The unions filed a complaint with the National Labor Relations Board (NLRB) claiming that the managers' actions were illegal surveillance in violation of the National Labor Relations Act (NLRA). The NLRB ruled in favor of Aladdin, and the unions appealed.

IN THE LANGUAGE OF THE COURT
CALLAHAN, Circuit Judge:
* * * *

Section 8(a)(1) of the NLRA states that "it shall be an unfair labor practice for an employer (1) to interfere with, restrain, or coerce employees in the exercise of the rights guaranteed in section 157 of this title." The [NLRB] has interpreted Section 8(a)(1) to make observation of union activity unlawful, "if the observation goes beyond casual and becomes unduly intrusive." * * * *"The test for determining whether an employer engages in unlawful surveillance or whether it creates the impression of surveillance is an objective one and involves the determination of whether the employer's conduct, under the circumstances, was such as would tend to interfere with, restrain or coerce employees* in the exercise of the rights guaranteed under Section 7 of the [National Labor Relations] Act." [Emphasis added.]
* * * *

There is no evidence that either Ms. Sapien or Ms. Briand used threats, force, or promises of benefits that would strip their speech of the protections of Section 8(c). Ms. Sapien attempted to give the buffet servers additional facts to consider before signing the union cards. Ms. Briand told Ms. Felix [an employee] that Ms. Bueno [another employee] should not sign a union card without fully understanding the consequences and provided her opinion that the union may not be able to deliver on its promises. Ms. Felix voluntarily translated Ms. Briand's comments for Ms. Bueno. After Ms. Felix explained the translation, Ms. Briand left.

CASE 34.3 CONTINUED ▶ **DECISION AND REMEDY** • *The federal appellate court denied the unions' petition for review, concluding that the managers' brief interruptions of organizing activity did not constitute illegal surveillance.*

WHAT IF THE FACTS WERE DIFFERENT? • *If management employees had interrupted union-organizing activities twenty-five times rather than just two, would the outcome of this case have been different? Why or why not?*

THE LEGAL ENVIRONMENT DIMENSION • *An administrative law judge (ALJ) originally ruled that the two brief verbal interruptions by the company's human resources managers were in violation of the National Labor Relations Act. Why might the ALJ have made this ruling?*

Collective Bargaining

If the NLRB certifies the union, the union becomes the *exclusive bargaining representative* of the workers. The central legal right of a union is to engage in collective bargaining on the members' behalf. **Collective bargaining** is the process by which labor and management negotiate the terms and conditions of employment, including wages, benefits, working conditions, and other matters. Collective bargaining allows union representatives elected by the union members to speak on their behalf at the bargaining table.

When a union is officially recognized, it may demand to bargain with the employer and negotiate new terms or conditions of employment. In collective bargaining, as in most other business negotiations, each side uses its economic power to pressure or persuade the other side to grant concessions.

Bargaining does not mean that one side must give in to the other or that compromises must be made. It does mean that a demand to bargain with the employer must be taken seriously and that both sides must bargain in good faith. Good faith bargaining requires that management must be willing to meet with union representatives and consider the union's wishes when negotiating a contract. Examples of bad faith bargaining on the part of management include engaging in a campaign among workers to undermine the union, constantly shifting positions on disputed contract terms, and sending bargainers who lack authority to commit the company to a contract. If an employer (or a union) refuses to bargain in good faith without justification, it has committed an unfair labor practice, and the other party may petition the NLRB for an order requiring good faith bargaining.

Strikes

Even when labor and management have bargained in good faith, they may be unable to reach a final agreement. When extensive collective bargaining has been conducted and an impasse results, the union may call a strike against the employer to pressure it into making concessions. In a **strike,** the unionized employees leave their jobs and refuse to work. The workers also typically picket the workplace, walking or standing outside the facility with signs stating their complaints.

A union may strike when the employer has engaged in unfair labor practices, but most strikes are economic strikes, which are initiated because the union wants a better contract. For example, in 2010 the union representing workers at the Disneyland Hotel organized a hunger strike to draw attention to a prolonged contract dispute over workers' health-care benefits and workloads. After two years of negotiations with the hotel, the workers still had no signed contract for health-care benefits.

THE RIGHT TO STRIKE The right to strike is guaranteed by the NLRA, within limits, and strike activities, such as picketing, are protected by the free speech guarantee of the First Amendment to the U.S. Constitution. Persons who are not employees have a right to participate in picketing an employer. The NLRA also gives workers the right to refuse to cross a picket line of fellow workers who are engaged in a lawful strike. Employers are permitted to hire replacement workers to substitute for the striking workers.

STRIKER RIGHTS AFTER A STRIKE ENDS An important issue concerns the rights of strikers after a strike ends. In a typical economic strike, the employer has a right to hire permanent replacements during the strike and need not terminate the replacement workers when the economic strikers seek to return to work. In other words, striking workers are not guaranteed the right to return to their jobs after the strike if satisfactory replacement workers have been found.

If the employer has not hired replacement workers to fill the strikers' positions, however, then the employer must rehire the economic strikers to fill any vacancies. Employers may not discriminate against former economic strikers, and those who are rehired retain their seniority rights. Different rules apply when a union strikes because the employer has engaged in unfair labor practices. In this situation, the employer may still hire replacements but must give the strikers back their jobs once the strike is over.

REVIEWING

Employment, Immigration, and Labor Law

Rick Saldona began working as a traveling salesperson for Aimer Winery in 1988. Sales constituted 90 percent of Saldona's work time. Saldona worked an average of fifty hours per week but received no overtime pay. In June 2011, Saldona's new supervisor, Caesar Braxton, claimed that Saldona had been inflating his reported sales calls and required Saldona to submit to a polygraph test. Saldona reported Braxton to the U.S. Department of Labor, which prohibited Aimer from requiring Saldona to take a polygraph test for this purpose. In August 2011, Saldona's wife, Venita, fell from a ladder and sustained a head injury while employed as a full-time agricultural harvester. Saldona delivered to Aimer's Human Resources Department a letter from his wife's physician indicating that she would need daily care for several months, and Saldona took leave until December 2011. Aimer had sixty-three employees at that time. When Saldona returned to Aimer, he was informed that his position had been eliminated because his sales territory had been combined with an adjacent territory. Using the information presented in the chapter, answer the following questions.

1. Would Saldona have been legally entitled to receive overtime pay at a higher rate? Why or why not?
2. What is the maximum length of time Saldona would have been allowed to take leave to care for his injured spouse?
3. Under what circumstances would Aimer have been allowed to require an employee to take a polygraph test?
4. Would Aimer likely be able to avoid reinstating Saldona under the *key employee* exception? Why or why not?

🌀 **DEBATE THIS:** *The U.S. labor market is highly competitive, so state and federal laws that require overtime pay are unnecessary and should be abolished.*

TERMS AND CONCEPTS

authorization card 675
cease-and-desist order 674
closed shop 675
collective bargaining 677

employment at will 658
hot-cargo agreement 675
I-9 verification 672
I-551 Alien Registration
    Receipt 673
minimum wage 661

right-to-work law 675
secondary boycott 675
strike 677
union shop 675
vesting 668
whistleblowing 659

workers' compensation
    law 667
wrongful discharge 659

QUESTIONS AND CASE PROBLEMS

34–1. Unfair Labor Practices Consolidated Stores is undergoing a unionization campaign. Prior to the union election, management states that the union is unnecessary to protect workers. Management also provides bonuses and wage increases to the workers during this period. The employees reject the union. Union organizers protest that the wage increases during the election campaign unfairly prejudiced the

vote. Should these wage increases be regarded as an unfair labor practice? Discuss.

34–2. QUESTION WITH SAMPLE ANSWER: Wrongful Discharge.

Denton and Carlo were employed at an appliance plant. Their job required them to perform occasional maintenance work while standing on a wire mesh twenty feet above the plant floor. Other employees had fallen through the mesh, and one of them had been killed by the fall. When their supervisor told them to perform tasks that would likely involve walking on the mesh, Denton and Carlo refused because they feared they might suffer bodily injury or death. Because they refused to do the requested work, the two employees were fired from their jobs. Was their discharge wrongful? If so, under what federal employment law? To what federal agency or department should they turn for assistance?

• **For a sample answer to Question 34–2, go to Appendix I at the end of this text.**

34–3. Federal Medical Leave Act Jennifer Willis worked for Coca Cola Enterprises, Inc. (CCE), in Louisiana as a senior account manager. On a Monday in May 2003, Willis called her supervisor to tell him that she was sick and would not be able to work that day. She also said that she was pregnant, but she did not say she was sick because of the pregnancy. On Tuesday, she called to ask where to report to work and was told that she could not return without a doctor's release. She said that she had a doctor's appointment on "Wednesday," which her supervisor understood to be the next day. Willis meant the *following* Wednesday. For more than a week, Willis did not contact CCE. When she returned to work, she was told that she had violated CCE's "No Call/No Show" policy. Under this policy "an employee absent from work for three consecutive days without notifying the supervisor during that period will be considered to have voluntarily resigned." She was fired. Willis filed a suit in a federal district court against CCE under the Family and Medical Leave Act (FMLA). To be eligible for FMLA leave, an employee must inform an employer of the reason for the leave. Did Willis meet this requirement? Did CCE's response to Willis's absence violate the FMLA? Explain. [*Willis v. Coca Cola Enterprises, Inc.*, 445 F.3d 413 (5th Cir. 2006)]

34–4. Unemployment Insurance Mary Garas, a chemist, sought work in Missouri through Kelly Services, Inc. Kelly is a staffing agency that places individuals in jobs of varying duration with other companies. Through Kelly, Garas worked at Merial Co. from April 2005 to February 2006. After the assignment ended, Garas asked Kelly for more work. Meanwhile, she filed a claim for unemployment benefits with the Missouri Division of Employment Security (DES). In March, Kelly recruiter Rebecca Cockrum told Garas about a temporary assignment with Celsis Laboratory. Garas said that she would prefer a "more stable position," but later asked Cockrum to submit her résumé to Celsis. Before the employer responded, Kelly told the DES that Garas had refused suitable work. Under a Missouri state statute, a claim for unemployment benefits must be denied if "the claimant failed without good cause . . . to accept suitable work when offered the claimant . . . by an employer by whom the individual was formerly employed." The DES denied Garas's claim for benefits. She filed an appeal with a state court. Was the DES's denial right or wrong?

Why? [*Garas v. Kelly Services, Inc.*, 211 S.W.3d 149 (Mo. App.E.D. 2007)]

34–5. CASE PROBLEM WITH SAMPLE ANSWER: Immigration.

*Nicole Tipton and Sadik Seferi owned and operated a restaurant in Iowa. Acting on a tip from the local police, agents of Immigration and Customs Enforcement executed search warrants at the restaurant and at an apartment where some restaurant workers lived. The agents discovered six undocumented aliens working at the restaurant and living together. When the I-9 forms for the restaurant's employees were reviewed, none were found for the six aliens. They were paid in cash while other employees were paid by check. The jury found Tipton and Seferi guilty of hiring and harboring illegal aliens. Both were given prison terms. The defendants challenged the conviction, contending that they did not violate the law because they did not know that the workers were unauthorized aliens. Was that argument credible? Why or why not? [*United States v. Tipton*, 518 F.3d 591 (8th Cir. 2008)]*

• **To view a sample answer for Problem 34–5, go to this book's Web site at** <u>www.cengage.com/blaw/clarkson</u>**, select "Chapter 34," and click on "Case Problem with Sample Answer."**

34–6. Immigration Work Status Mohammad Hashmi, a citizen of Pakistan, entered the United States in 2002 on a student visa. Two years later, when he applied for a job at CompuCredit, he completed an I-9 form and checked the box to indicate that he was "a citizen or national of the United States." Soon after submitting that form, he married a U.S. citizen. Several months later, the federal immigration services claimed that Hashmi had misrepresented himself as a U.S. citizen. Hashmi contended that he had not misrepresented himself. At an administrative hearing, he testified that when he filled out the I-9 form he believed that he was a "national of the United States" because he was legally in the country under a student visa and was going to marry a U.S. citizen. He requested that his immigration status be adjusted to account for the fact that he was employed and married to an American. The immigration judge rejected that request and found that Hashmi had made a false claim on the I-9 form. He ruled that Hashmi was "inadmissible" to the United States and that his legal status in the country could not be amended because of his marriage or employment. Hashmi appealed. Was it reasonable for Hashmi to think he was a U.S. national? Should his visa status be changed because of his marriage and employment? Why or why not? [*Hashmi v. Mukasey*, 533 F.3d 700 (8th Cir. 2008)]

34–7. Vesting The United Auto Workers (UAW) represents workers at Caterpillar, Inc., and negotiates labor contracts on their behalf. A 1988 labor agreement provided lifetime no-cost medical benefits for retirees but did not state when the employees' rights to those benefits vested. This agreement expired in 1991. Caterpillar and the UAW did not reach a new agreement until 1998. Under the new agreement, retiree medical benefits were subject to certain limits, and retirees were to be responsible for paying some of the costs. Workers who retired during the period when no agreement was in force filed a suit in a federal district court to obtain benefits under the 1988 agreement. Review the Employee Retirement Income Security Act vesting rules for private pension plans on page 668. What is the most plausible application of those rules to these facts? Why? [*Winnett v. Caterpillar, Inc.,* 553 F.3d 1000 (6th Cir. 2009)]

34–8. Unfair Labor Practices The Laborers' International Union of North America, Local 578, and Shaw Stone & Webster Construction, Inc., were parties to a collective bargaining agreement that covered workers at the company. The agreement contained a union-security provision that required all company employees who were represented by the union to join the union. If an employee failed to join or pay union dues, the union would request that the employee be fired. After Sebedeo Lopez went to work for Shaw Stone, he failed to pay his union initiation fee and monthly dues. Lopez's shop steward told him to pay these fees, although the amount owed was unclear. He was also told that the union was pressing the company to fire him. Lopez agreed to pay the fees and left a money order for $200 at the union's office, but the union claimed that it did not find the money order. Lopez promised to pay another $215 in a few days, but the union demanded his immediate dismissal. Shaw Stone fired him on the spot. Lopez complained to the National Labor Relations Board (NLRB), which brought unfair labor practice charges against the union. An administrative law judge ruled against the union, and the NLRB agreed. The union appealed. Was the union guilty of unfair labor practices under the National Labor Relations Act by having Lopez fired? Why or why not? [*Laborers' International Union of North America, Local 578 v. National Labor Relations Board,* 594 F.3d 732 (10th Cir. 2010)]

34–9. A QUESTION OF ETHICS: Workers' Compensation Law.

 In 1999, after working for Atchison Leather Products, Inc., in Kansas for ten years, Beverly Tull began to complain of hand, wrist, and shoulder pain. Atchison recommended that she contact a certain physician, who in April 2000 diagnosed the condition as carpal tunnel syndrome "severe enough" for surgery. In August, Tull filed a claim with the state workers' compensation board. Because Atchison changed workers' compensation insurance companies every year, a dispute arose as to which company should pay Tull's claim. Fearing liability, no insurer would authorize treatment, and Tull was forced to delay surgery until December. The board granted her

temporary total disability benefits for the subsequent six weeks that she missed work. On April 23, 2002, Berger Co. bought Atchison. The new employer adjusted Tull's work so that it was less demanding and stressful, but she continued to suffer pain. In July, a physician diagnosed her condition as permanent. The board granted her permanent partial disability benefits. By May 2005, the bickering over the financial responsibility for Tull's claim involved five insurers—four of which had each covered Atchison for a single year and one of which covered Berger. [Tull v. Atchison Leather Products, Inc., 37 Kan.App.2d 87, 150 P.3d 316 (2007)]

(a) When an injured employee files a claim for workers' compensation, a proceeding is held to assess the injury and determine the amount of compensation. Should a dispute between insurers over the payment of the claim be resolved in the same proceeding? Why or why not?

(b) The board designated April 23, 2002, as the date of Tull's injury. What is the reason for determining the date of a worker's injury? Should the board in this case have selected this date or a different date? Why?

(c) How should the board assess liability for the payment of Tull's medical expenses and disability benefits? Would it be appropriate to impose joint and several liability on the insurers (holding each of them responsible for the full amount of damages), or should the individual liability of each of them be determined? Explain.

34–10. VIDEO QUESTION: Employment at Will.

 Go to this text's Web site at **www.cengage.com/ blaw/clarkson** and select "Chapter 34." Click on "Video Questions" and view the video titled *Employment at Will.* Then answer the following questions.

(a) In the video, Laura asserts that she can fire Ray "for any reason; for no reason." Is this true? Explain your answer.

(b) What exceptions to the employment-at-will doctrine are discussed in the chapter? Does Ray's situation fit any of these exceptions?

(c) Would Ray be protected from wrongful discharge under whistleblowing statutes? Why or why not?

(d) Assume that you are the employer in this scenario. What arguments can you make that Ray should not be able to sue for wrongful discharge in this situation?

LEGAL RESEARCH EXERCISES ON THE WEB

Go to this text's Web site at **www.cengage.com/blaw/clarkson**, select "Chapter 34," and click on "Practical Internet Exercises." There you will find the following Internet research exercises that you can perform to learn more about the topics covered in this chapter.

Practical Internet Exercise 34–1: Management Perspective
Workplace Monitoring and Surveillance

Practical Internet Exercise 34–2: Historical Perspective
Labor Unions and Labor Law

CHAPTER 35

Employment Discrimination

O ut of the 1960s civil rights movement to end racial and other forms of discrimination grew a body of law protecting employees against discrimination in the workplace. This protective legislation further eroded the employment-at-will doctrine, which was discussed in Chapter 34. In the past several decades, judicial decisions, administrative agency actions, and legislation have restricted the ability of both employers and unions to discriminate against workers on the basis of race, color, religion, national origin, gender, age, or disability. A class of persons defined by one or more of these criteria is known as a **protected class.**

Several federal statutes prohibit **employment discrimination** against members of protected classes. The most important statute is Title VII of the Civil Rights Act of 1964.[1] Title VII prohibits employment discrimination on the basis of race, color, religion, national origin, and gender. The Age Discrimination in Employment Act of 1967[2] and the Americans with Disabilities Act of 1990[3] prohibit discrimination on the basis of age and disability, respectively. As was discussed in Chapter 23, the protections afforded under these laws also extend to U.S. citizens who are working abroad for U.S. firms or for companies that are controlled by U.S. firms.

This chapter focuses on the kinds of discrimination prohibited by these federal statutes. Note, however, that discrimination against employees on the basis of any of the above-mentioned criteria may also violate state human rights statutes or other state laws prohibiting discrimination.

1. 42 U.S.C. Sections 2000e–2000e-17.
2. 29 U.S.C. Sections 621–634.
3. 42 U.S.C. Sections 12102–12118.

SECTION 1
TITLE VII OF THE CIVIL RIGHTS ACT OF 1964

Title VII of the Civil Rights Act of 1964 and its amendments prohibit job discrimination against employees, applicants, and union members on the basis of race, color, national origin, religion, and gender at any stage of employment. It prohibits discrimination in the hiring process, as well as in discipline procedures, discharge, promotion, and benefits. Title VII applies to employers with fifteen or more employees, labor unions with fifteen or more members, labor unions that operate hiring halls (to which members go regularly to be assigned jobs as they become available), employment agencies, and state and local governing units or agencies.

The United States Supreme Court has also ruled that an employer with fewer than fifteen employees is not automatically shielded from a lawsuit filed under Title VII.[4] A special section of the act prohibits discrimination in most federal government employment. When Title VII applies to the employer, any employee—including an undocumented (alien) worker—can bring an action for employment discrimination.

The Equal Employment Opportunity Commission

The Equal Employment Opportunity Commission (EEOC) monitors compliance with Title VII. A victim of alleged discrimination must first file a claim with the EEOC before a lawsuit can be brought against the employer. The EEOC may investigate the dispute and attempt to obtain the parties' voluntary consent

4. *Arbaugh v. Y&H Corp.*, 546 U.S. 500, 126 S.Ct. 1235, 163 L.Ed.2d 1097 (2006).

to an out-of-court settlement. If a voluntary agreement cannot be reached, the EEOC may file a suit against the employer on the employee's behalf.

The EEOC does not investigate every claim of employment discrimination. Generally, it takes only "priority cases," such as cases that affect many workers and cases involving retaliatory discharge (firing an employee in retaliation for submitting a claim with the EEOC). If the EEOC decides not to investigate a claim, the victim may bring his or her own lawsuit against the employer.

Intentional and Unintentional Discrimination

Title VII of the Civil Rights Act of 1964 prohibits both intentional and unintentional discrimination.

INTENTIONAL DISCRIMINATION Intentional discrimination by an employer against an employee is known as **disparate-treatment discrimination.** Because intent may sometimes be difficult to prove, courts have established certain procedures for resolving disparate-treatment cases. Suppose that a woman applies for employment with a construction firm and is rejected. If she sues on the basis of disparate-treatment discrimination in hiring, she must show that (1) she is a member of a protected class, (2) she applied and was qualified for the job in question, (3) she was rejected by the employer, and (4) the employer continued to seek applicants for the position or filled the position with a person not in a protected class.

If the woman can meet these relatively easy requirements, she has made out a ***prima facie* case** of illegal discrimination. Making out a *prima facie* case of discrimination means that the plaintiff has met her initial burden of proof and will win unless the employer can present a legally acceptable defense. (Defenses to claims of employment discrimination will be discussed later in this chapter.) The burden then shifts to the employer-defendant, who must articulate a legal reason for not hiring the plaintiff. For example, the employer might say that the plaintiff was not hired because she lacked sufficient experience or training. To prevail, the plaintiff must then show that the employer's reason is a *pretext* (not the true reason) and that discriminatory intent actually motivated the employer's decision.

UNINTENTIONAL DISCRIMINATION Employers often use interviews and tests to choose from among a large number of applicants for job openings.

Minimum educational requirements are also common. Some employer practices, such as those involving educational requirements, may have an unintended discriminatory impact on a protected class. **Disparate-impact discrimination** occurs when a protected group of people is adversely affected by an employer's practices, procedures, or tests, even though they do not appear to be discriminatory.

In a disparate-impact discrimination case, the complaining party must first use one of two statistical methods to show that the employer's practices, procedures, or tests are discriminatory in effect. Under the *pool of applicants* test, a plaintiff can prove a disparate impact by showing that the percentage of the protected class in the employer's workforce does not reflect the percentage of that group in the pool of qualified individuals available in the local labor market. Alternatively, a plaintiff can prove disparate impact by comparing the *selection rates* of members of a protected class with the selection rates of nonmembers, regardless of the relative percentages of the two groups in the employer's workforce. Under EEOC guidelines, a selection rate for a protected class that is less than four-fifths, or 80 percent, of the rate for the group with the highest rate of hiring generally will be regarded as evidence of disparate impact.

Once a disparate impact has been proved using one of these methods, the plaintiff must show a causal link between the employer's practice and the discriminatory effect. This establishes a *prima facie* case, and the burden of proof then shifts to the employer to show that the practices or procedures in question were justified.

Discrimination Based on Race, Color, and National Origin

Title VII prohibits employers from discriminating against employees or job applicants on the basis of race, color, or national origin. Although there has been some uncertainty in the federal courts about what constitutes race versus national origin discrimination, race is interpreted broadly to apply to the ancestry or ethnic characteristics of a group of persons, such as Native Americans. The national origin provisions make it unlawful to discriminate against persons based on their birth in another country, such as Iraq or the Philippines, or their ancestry or culture, such as Hispanic.

If an employer's standards or policies for selecting or promoting employees have a discriminatory effect on employees or job applicants in these protected classes, then a presumption of illegal discrimination arises. To avoid liability, the employer must then show that its standards or policies have a substantial, demonstrable relationship to realistic qualifications for the job in question.

CASE IN POINT Jiann Min Chang was an instructor at Alabama Agricultural and Mechanical University (AAMU). When AAMU terminated his employment, Chang filed a lawsuit claiming discrimination based on national origin. Chang established a *prima facie* case because he (1) was a member of a protected class, (2) was qualified for the job, (3) suffered an adverse employment action, and (4) was replaced by someone outside his protected class (a non-Asian instructor). When the burden of proof shifted to the employer, however, AAMU showed that Chang had argued with a university vice president and refused to comply with her instructions. The court ruled that the university had not renewed Chang's contract for a legitimate reason—insubordination—and therefore was not liable for unlawful discrimination.[5]

REVERSE DISCRIMINATION Note that Title VII also protects against *reverse discrimination*—that is, discrimination against majority group individuals, such as white males. For example, if an African American woman fired several white men from their management positions at a school district, the district could be held liable for reverse discrimination unless it had articulated a legitimate, nondiscriminatory reason for its actions.[6]

In 2009, the United States Supreme Court issued a decision that will have a significant impact on disparate-impact and reverse discrimination litigation. Employers may find the application of the ruling somewhat confusing, however, because the Court found that an employer had engaged in reverse discrimination when it discarded test results in an attempt to avoid unlawful discrimination.

CASE IN POINT The fire department in New Haven, Connecticut, administered a test to determine which firefighters were eligible for promotions. No African Americans and only two Hispanic firefighters passed the test. Fearing that it would be sued for racial discrimination if it used the test results for promotions, the city refused to certify (and basically discarded) the results. The white firefighters (and one Hispanic) who had passed the test then sued the city, claiming reverse discrimination. The lower courts found in favor of the city, but the United States Supreme Court reversed. The Court held that the city's race-conscious, discriminatory actions were not justified. An employer can engage in intentional discrimination to remedy unintentional discrimination only if the employer has "a strong basis in evidence" to believe that it will be successfully sued for disparate-impact discrimination. Mere fear of litigation was not a sufficient reason for the city to discard its test results. The city subsequently promoted all the firefighters involved in the lawsuit.[7]

POTENTIAL SECTION 1981 CLAIMS Victims of racial or ethnic discrimination may also have a cause of action under 42 U.S.C. Section 1981. This section, which was enacted as part of the Civil Rights Act of 1866 to protect the rights of freed slaves, prohibits discrimination on the basis of race or ethnicity in the formation or enforcement of contracts. Because employment is often a contractual relationship, Section 1981 can provide an alternative basis for a plaintiff's action and is potentially advantageous because it does not place a cap on damages (see page 688).

Discrimination Based on Religion

Title VII of the Civil Rights Act of 1964 also prohibits government employers, private employers, and unions from discriminating against persons because of their religion. Employers cannot treat their employees more or less favorably based on their religious beliefs or practices and cannot require employees to participate in any religious activity (or forbid them from participating in one).

If an employee's religion prohibits her or him from working on a certain day of the week or at a certain type of job, the employer must make a reasonable attempt to accommodate these religious requirements. Employers must reasonably accommodate an employee's sincerely held religious belief even if the belief is not based on the doctrines of a traditionally recognized religion, such as Christianity or Judaism, or denomination, such as Baptist.

Discrimination Based on Gender

Under Title VII, as well as under other federal acts (including the Equal Pay Act of 1963, which is

---

5. *Jiann Min Chang v. Alabama Agricultural and Mechanical University,* 2009 WL 3403180 (11th Cir. 2009).

6. See, for example, *Johnston v. School District of Philadelphia,* 2006 WL 999966 (E.D.Pa. 2006).

7. *Ricci v. DeStefano,* ___ U.S. ___, 129 S.Ct. 2658, 174 L.Ed.2d 490 (2009).

discussed next), employers are forbidden from discriminating against employees on the basis of gender. Employers are prohibited from classifying jobs as male or female and from advertising in help-wanted columns that are designated male or female unless the employer can prove that the gender of the applicant is essential to the job. Employers also cannot have separate male and female seniority lists or refuse to promote employees based on their gender.

Generally, to succeed in a suit for gender discrimination, a plaintiff must demonstrate that gender was a determining factor in the employer's decision to hire, fire, or promote him or her. Typically, this involves looking at all of the surrounding circumstances.

CASE IN POINT The EEOC filed a lawsuit against a plastics manufacturer, Polycon Industries, Inc. The EEOC alleged that the company had reserved higher-paying production jobs for male employees and refused to promote female workers to these jobs because of their gender. The EEOC decided to pursue the case when it received complaints from women who had applied for production jobs but had never even been interviewed.[8]

The Pregnancy Discrimination Act of 1978,[9] which amended Title VII, expanded the definition of gender discrimination to include discrimination based on pregnancy. Women affected by pregnancy, childbirth, or related medical conditions must be treated—for all employment-related purposes, including the receipt of benefits under employee benefit programs—the same as other persons not so affected but similar in ability to work.

EQUAL PAY ACT The Equal Pay Act of 1963[10] prohibits employers from engaging in gender-based wage discrimination. For the act's equal pay requirements to apply, the male and female employees must work at the same establishment doing similar work. The work need not be identical, provided that it involves substantial equality in skill, effort, responsibility, and working conditions. To determine whether the Equal Pay Act has been violated, a court will look at the primary duties of the two jobs, focusing on the job content rather than the job description.[11] If the

court finds that the wage differential is based on a permissible practice, such as a seniority or merit system, it does not violate the Equal Pay Act.

2009 EQUAL PAY LEGISLATION More than four decades after the Equal Pay Act was enacted, there is still a significant gap between the wages earned by male and female employees in the United States. Women typically earn about three-quarters of what men earn. This continuing disparity prompted Congress to pass the Paycheck Fairness Act of 2009, which closed some loopholes in the Equal Pay Act that allowed employers to justify wage discrimination if it was based on any factor other than gender. The Paycheck Fairness Act clarifies the defenses that employers may offer and prohibits the use of gender-based differentials in assessing an employee's education, training, or experience. The act also provides additional remedies for wage discrimination, including compensatory and punitive damages, which are available as remedies for discrimination based on race and national origin.

In another 2009 action, Congress responded to a 2007 decision by the United States Supreme Court that required a plaintiff alleging wage discrimination to file a complaint within 180 days of the decision that set the discriminatory pay.[12] Congress rejected this limit when it enacted the Lilly Ledbetter Fair Pay Act of 2009.[13] The act makes discriminatory wages actionable under federal law regardless of when the discrimination began. Each time a person is paid discriminatory wages, benefits, or other compensation, a cause of action arises (and the plaintiff has 180 days from that date to file a complaint). In other words, if a plaintiff continues to work for the employer while receiving discriminatory wages, the time period for filing a complaint is basically unlimited.

Constructive Discharge

The majority of Title VII complaints involve unlawful discrimination in decisions to hire or fire employees. In some situations, however, employees who leave their jobs voluntarily can claim that they were "constructively discharged" by the employer. **Constructive discharge** occurs when the employer causes the employee's working conditions to be so intolerable that a reasonable person in the employee's position would feel compelled to quit.

---

8. Case No. 2:09-cv-00141-RL-PRC, filed in the U.S. District Court for the Northern District of Indiana, Hammond Division.
9. 42 U.S.C. Section 2000e(k).
10. 29 U.S.C. Section 206(d).
11. For an illustration of the factors courts consider in wage-discrimination claims under the Equal Pay Act, see *Beck-Wilson v. Principi,* 441 F.3d 353 (6th Cir. 2006).

12. *Ledbetter v. Goodyear Tire Co.,* 550 U.S. 618, 127 S.Ct. 2162, 167 L.Ed.2d 982 (2007).
13. Pub. L. No. 111-2, 123 Stat. 5 (January 5, 2009), amending 42 U.S.C. Section 2000e-5[e].

PROVING CONSTRUCTIVE DISCHARGE The plaintiff must present objective proof of intolerable working conditions, which the employer knew or had reason to know about yet failed to correct within a reasonable time period. Courts generally also require the employee to show causation—that the employer's unlawful discrimination caused the working conditions to be intolerable. Put a different way, the employee's resignation must be a foreseeable result of the employer's discriminatory action. Although courts weigh the facts on a case-by-case basis, employee demotion is one of the most frequently cited reasons for a finding of constructive discharge, particularly when the employee was subjected to humiliation.

For example, Khalil's employer humiliates him by informing him in front of his co-workers that he is being demoted to an inferior position. Khalil's co-workers then continually insult, harass, and make derogatory remarks to him about his national origin (he is from Iraq). The employer is aware of this discriminatory treatment but does nothing to remedy the situation, despite repeated complaints from Khalil. After several months, Khalil quits his job and files a Title VII claim. In this situation, Khalil would likely have sufficient evidence to maintain an action for constructive discharge in violation of Title VII.

APPLIES TO ALL TITLE VII DISCRIMINATION Note that constructive discharge is a theory that plaintiffs can use to establish any type of discrimination claims under Title VII, including race, color, national origin, religion, gender, pregnancy, and sexual harassment. Constructive discharge has also been successfully used in situations that involve discrimination based on age or disability (both of which will be discussed later in this chapter). Constructive discharge is most commonly asserted in cases involving sexual harassment, however.

When constructive discharge is claimed, the employee can pursue damages for loss of income, including back pay. These damages ordinarily are not available to an employee who left a job voluntarily.

Sexual Harassment

Title VII also protects employees against **sexual harassment** in the workplace. Sexual harassment can take two forms: *quid pro quo* harassment and hostile-environment harassment. *Quid pro quo* is a Latin phrase that is often translated as "something in exchange for something else." *Quid pro quo* harassment occurs when sexual favors are demanded in return for job opportunities, promotions, salary increases, or other benefits. According to the United States Supreme Court, hostile-environment harassment occurs when "the workplace is permeated with discriminatory intimidation, ridicule, and insult, that is sufficiently severe or pervasive to alter the conditions of the victim's employment and create an abusive working environment."[14]

The courts determine whether the sexually offensive conduct was sufficiently severe or pervasive to create a hostile environment on a case-by-case basis. Typically, a single incident of sexually offensive conduct is not enough to permeate the work environment (although there have been exceptions when the conduct was particularly objectionable).[15] Note also that if the employee who is alleging sexual harassment has signed an employment contract containing an arbitration clause (see Chapter 3), she or he will most likely be required to arbitrate the claim.[16]

HARASSMENT BY SUPERVISORS For an employer to be held liable for a supervisor's sexual harassment, the supervisor normally must have taken a *tangible employment action* against the employee. A **tangible employment action** is a significant change in employment status or benefits, such as when an employee is fired, refused a promotion, demoted, or reassigned to a position with significantly different responsibilities. Only a supervisor, or another person acting with the authority of the employer, can cause this sort of harm. A co-worker cannot dock another employee's pay, demote her or him, or set conditions for continued employment, for example. A constructive discharge also qualifies as a tangible employment action.[17]

THE *ELLERTH/FARAGHER* AFFIRMATIVE DEFENSE In 1998, the United States Supreme Court issued several important rulings that have had a lasting impact on cases involving alleged sexual harassment by supervisors.[18] The Court held that an employer (a city) was liable for a supervisor's harassment of employees even though the employer was unaware of the

---

14. *Harris v. Forklift Systems,* 510 U.S. 17, 114 S.Ct. 367, 126 L.Ed.2d 295 (1993). See also *Baker v. Via Christi Regional Medical Center,* 491 F.Supp.2d 1040 (D.Kan. 2007).
15. See, for example, *Pomales v. Celulares Telefonica, Inc.,* 447 F.3d 79 (1st Cir. 2006); and *Fontanez-Nunez v. Janssen Ortho, LLC,* 447 F.3d 50 (1st Cir. 2006).
16. See, for example, *EEOC v. Cheesecake Factory, Inc.,* 2009 WL 1259359 (D.Ariz. 2009).
17. See, for example, *Pennsylvania State Police v. Suders,* 542 U.S. 129, 124 S.Ct. 2342, 159 L.Ed.2d 204 (2004).
18. *Burlington Industries, Inc. v. Ellerth,* 524 U.S. 742, 118 S.Ct. 2257, 141 L.Ed.2d 633 (1998); and *Faragher v. City of Boca Raton,* 524 U.S. 775, 118 S.Ct. 2275, 141 L.Ed.2d 662 (1998).

behavior. Although the city had a written policy against sexual harassment, it had not distributed the policy to its employees and had not established any complaint procedures for employees who felt that they had been sexually harassed. In another case, the Court held that an employer can be liable for a supervisor's sexual harassment even though the employee does not suffer adverse job consequences.

The Court's decisions in these cases established what has become known as the *Ellerth/Faragher* affirmative defense to charges of sexual harassment. The defense has two elements:

1. The employer must have taken reasonable care to prevent and promptly correct any sexually harassing behavior (by establishing effective harassment policies and complaint procedures, for example).
2. The plaintiff-employee must have unreasonably failed to take advantage of preventive or corrective opportunities provided by the employer to avoid harm.

An employer that can prove both elements will not be liable for a supervisor's harassment.

RETALIATION BY EMPLOYERS Employers sometimes retaliate against employees who complain about sexual harassment or other Title VII violations. Retaliation can take many forms. An employer might demote or fire the person, or otherwise change the terms, conditions, and benefits of employment. Title VII prohibits retaliation, and employees can sue their employers when it occurs. In a *retaliation claim*, an individual asserts that she or he has suffered a harm as a result of making a charge, testifying, or participating in a Title VII investigation or proceeding. In a 2009 decision, the United States Supreme Court held that Title VII's retaliation protection extends to an employee who speaks out about discrimination not on her or his own initiative, but in answering questions during an employer's internal investigation of another employee's complaint.[19]

At one time, the courts disagreed as to whether the plaintiff had to show that the challenged action adversely affected the terms or conditions of *employment* to prove retaliation. In the following case, the United States Supreme Court resolved the question of whether Title VII's ban on retaliation covers acts that are not job related.

---

19. *Crawford v. Metropolitan Government of Nashville and Davidson County, Tennessee,* __ U.S. __, 129 S.Ct. 846, 172 L.Ed.2d 650 (2009).

✳ EXTENDED CASE 35.1 ✳
Burlington Northern and Santa Fe Railroad Co. v. White

Supreme Court of the United States, 548 U.S. 53, 126 S.Ct. 2405, 165 L.Ed.2d 345 (2006).

IN THE LANGUAGE OF THE COURT

Justice *BREYER* delivered the opinion of the Court.

* * * *

* * * Sheila White [was] the only woman working in the Maintenance of Way department at [Burlington Northern & Santa Fe Railway Company's] Tennessee Yard.

In September 1997, White complained to Burlington officials that her * * * supervisor, Bill Joiner, had repeatedly told her that women should not be working in the Maintenance of Way department. [Joiner was disciplined. White

was reassigned from forklift duty to "track laborer" tasks.]

* * * *

On October 10, White filed a complaint with the Equal Employment Opportunity Commission (EEOC * * *).

[In December, White's supervisor, Percy Sharkey, complained to Burlington officials that White had been insubordinate. She was suspended without pay but reinstated after an investigation and awarded back pay for the period of the suspension. White filed a second charge with the EEOC.]

* * * *

* * * [Later,] White filed this Title VII action against Burlington

in federal [district] court. * * * She claimed that Burlington's actions—(1) changing her job responsibilities, and (2) suspending her * * * without pay—amounted to unlawful retaliation in violation of Title VII. A jury found in White's favor * * * [and] awarded her $43,500 in * * * damages * * * .

* * * [On appeal, the U.S. Court of Appeals for the Sixth Circuit held that Title VII's antiretaliation ban is limited to acts that adversely affect the terms, conditions, or benefits of employment, and] affirmed the District Court's judgment in White's favor on both retaliation claims. [Burlington appealed to the United States Supreme Court.]

EXTENDED CASE 35.1 CONTINUED ◆

* * * *

* * * The language of the [antidiscrimination] provision differs from that of the anti-retaliation provision in important ways.

The * * * words in the [antidiscrimination] provision—"hire," "discharge," "compensation, terms, conditions, or privileges of employment," "employment opportunities," and "status as an employee"—explicitly limit the scope of that provision to actions that affect employment or alter the conditions of the workplace. No such limiting words appear in the anti-retaliation provision.

* * * The two provisions differ not only in language but in purpose as well. The anti-discrimination provision seeks a workplace where individuals are not discriminated against because of their racial, ethnic, religious, or gender-based status. *The anti-retaliation provision seeks to secure that primary objective by preventing* an employer from interfering (through retaliation) with an employee's efforts to secure or advance enforcement of the Act's basic guarantees. The [antidiscrimination] provision seeks to prevent injury to individuals based on who they are, i.e., their status. *The anti-retaliation provision seeks to prevent harm to individuals based on what they do, i.e., their conduct.* [Emphasis added.]

To secure the first objective, Congress did not need to prohibit anything other than employment-related discrimination.

But one cannot secure the second objective by focusing only upon employer actions and harm that concern employment and the workplace. * * * *An employer can effectively retaliate against an employee by taking actions not directly related to his employment or by causing him harm outside the workplace.* * * * [Emphasis added.]

* * * *

* * * We conclude that * * * the anti-retaliation provision extends beyond workplace-related or employment-related retaliatory acts * * * .

* * * *

* * * A plaintiff must show that a reasonable employee would have found the challenged action materially adverse, which in this context means it well might have dissuaded a reasonable worker from making or supporting a charge of discrimination.

* * * *

* * * [In this case,] the track labor duties were by all accounts more arduous and dirtier; * * * the forklift operator position required more qualifications, which is an indication of prestige; and * * * the forklift operator position was objectively considered a better job and the male employees resented White for occupying it. Based on this record, a jury could reasonably conclude that the reassignment of responsibilities would have been materially adverse to a reasonable employee.

* * * *

For these reasons, the judgment of the Court of Appeals is affirmed.

QUESTIONS

1. Why did the Court evaluate the language of Title VII's antidiscrimination and antiretaliation provisions?
2. What was the Court's interpretation of those provisions?

HARASSMENT BY CO-WORKERS AND OTHERS When the harassment of co-workers, rather than supervisors, creates a hostile working environment, an employee may still have a cause of action against the employer. Normally, though, the employer will be held liable only if it knew or should have known about the harassment and failed to take immediate remedial action.

Occasionally, a court may also hold an employer liable for harassment by *nonemployees* if the employer knew about the harassment and failed to take corrective action. Suppose that Gordon, who owns and manages a Great Bites restaurant, knows that one of his regular customers, Dean, repeatedly harasses Sharon, a waitress. If Gordon does nothing and permits the harassment to continue, he may be liable under Title VII even though Dean is not an employee of the restaurant.

CASE IN POINT Kathleen Torres-Negrón, a sales representative at Merck & Company, Inc., was temporarily assigned to work in Mexico at Merck-Mexico (a subsidiary of Merck). She claimed that she was being sexually harassed and informed the supervisor in Mexico. When she filed a lawsuit, Merck argued that it should not be liable because the alleged harassers were employed by Merck-Mexico and not by the U.S.-based Merck. Although the trial court granted a summary judgment in Merck's favor, an appellate court held that there was a sufficient issue of fact as to whether Merck and Merck-Mexico could be considered a single employer for purposes of a Title VII claim. Thus, the court ruled that there was enough evidence of Merck's control over the alleged harassers for the employee to take her case to a jury.[20]

SAME-GENDER HARASSMENT In 1998, in the landmark case *Oncale v. Sundowner Offshore Services, Inc.,*[21] the Supreme Court held that Title VII protection extends to situations in which individuals are sexually harassed by members of the same gender. It can be difficult, though, to prove that the harassment in same-gender cases is "based on sex." When the victim is homosexual, some courts have found that the harasser's conduct does not qualify as sexual harassment under Title VII because it was based on the employee's sexual orientation, not on his or her "sex."[22] It is easier to establish a case of same-gender harassment when the harasser is homosexual.[23]

Although federal law (Title VII) does not prohibit discrimination or harassment based on a person's sexual orientation, a growing number of states have enacted laws that prohibit sexual orientation discrimination in private employment.[24] Many companies have also voluntarily established nondiscrimination policies that include sexual orientation.

Online Harassment

Employees' online activities can create a hostile working environment in many ways. Racial jokes, ethnic slurs, or other comments contained in e-mail, text or instant messages, and blog posts can become the basis for a claim of hostile-environment harassment or other forms of discrimination. A worker who regularly sees sexually explicit images on a co-worker's computer screen may find the images offensive and claim that they create a hostile working environment.[25] Nevertheless, employers may be able to avoid liability for online harassment by taking prompt remedial action.

CASE IN POINT While working at WorldCom Corporation, Angela Daniels received racially harassing e-mailed jokes from another employee. Shortly afterward, the company issued a warning to the offending employee about the proper use of the e-mail system and held two meetings to discuss company policy on the use of the system. In Daniels's suit against WorldCom for racial discrimination, a federal district court concluded that the employer was not liable for its employee's racially harassing e-mails because the employer took prompt remedial action.[26]

Remedies under Title VII

Employer liability under Title VII may be extensive. If the plaintiff successfully proves that unlawful discrimination occurred, he or she may be awarded reinstatement, back pay, retroactive promotions, and damages. Compensatory damages are available only in cases of intentional discrimination. Punitive damages may be recovered against a private employer only if the employer acted with malice or reckless indifference to an individual's rights. The statute limits the total amount of compensatory and punitive damages that plaintiffs can recover from specific employers (ranging from $50,000 from employers with one hundred or fewer employees to $300,000 from employers with more than five hundred employees).

SECTION 2
DISCRIMINATION BASED ON AGE

Age discrimination is potentially the most widespread form of discrimination, because anyone—regardless of race, color, national origin, or gender—could be a victim at some point in life. The Age Discrimination in Employment Act (ADEA) of 1967, as amended, prohibits employment discrimination on the basis of age against individuals forty years of age or older. The act also prohibits mandatory retirement for nonmanagerial workers. The United States Supreme Court has made it clear that the text and the legislative history of the ADEA show that it was meant to protect relatively older workers from discrimination that gives an unfair advantage to the relatively young. For the act to apply, an employer must have twenty or more employees, and the employer's business activities must affect interstate commerce. The EEOC administers the ADEA, but the act also permits private causes of action against employers for age discrimination.

20. *Torres-Negrón v. Merck & Company, Inc.,* 488 F.3d 34 (1st Cir. 2007).

21. 523 U.S. 75, 118 S.Ct. 998, 140 L.Ed.2d 207 (1998).

22. See, for example, *McCown v. St. John's Health System,* 349 F.3d 540 (8th Cir. 2003); and *Rene v. MGM Grand Hotel, Inc.,* 305 F.3d 1061 (9th Cir. 2002).

23. See, for example, *Tepperwien v. Entergy Nuclear Operations, Inc.,* 606 F.Supp.2d 427 (S.D.N.Y. 2009).

24. See, for example, 775 Illinois Compiled Statutes 5/1–103.

25. See, for example, *Doe v. XYC Corp.,* 382 N.J.Super. 122 (App. Div. 2005).

26. *Daniels v. WorldCom Corp.,* 1998 WL 91261 (N.D.Tex. 1998). See also *Musgrove v. Mobil Oil Corp.,* 2003 WL 21653125 (N.D.Tex. 2003).

Procedures under the ADEA

The burden-shifting procedure under the ADEA differs from the procedure under Title VII as a result of a United States Supreme Court decision, which dramatically changed the burden of proof in age discrimination cases.[27] As explained earlier, if the plaintiff in a Title VII case can show that the employer was motivated, at least in part, by unlawful discrimination, the burden of proof shifts to the employer to articulate a legitimate nondiscriminatory reason for the challenged action. Thus, in cases in which the employer has a "mixed motive" for discharging an employee, the employer has the burden of proving its reason was legitimate.

Under the ADEA, in contrast, a plaintiff must show that the unlawful discrimination was not just *a* reason but *the* reason for the adverse employment action. In other words, the employee has the burden of persuasion to establish *but for* causation—that is, that age discrimination was, in fact, the reason for the adverse decision. Thus, to establish a *prima facie* case, the plaintiff must show that she or he (1) was a member of the protected age group, (2) was qualified for the position from which she or he was discharged, and (3) was discharged because of age discrimination. Then the burden shifts to the employer. If the employer offers a legitimate reason for its action, then the plaintiff must show that the stated reason is only a pretext for the employer's decision. The following case illustrates this process.

---

27. *Gross v. FBL Financial Services, Inc.,* ___ U.S. ___, 129 S.Ct. 2343, 174 L.Ed.2d 119 (2009).

CASE 35.2
Mora v. Jackson Memorial Foundation, Inc.

United States Court of Appeals, Eleventh Circuit, 597 F.3d 1201 (2010).
www.ca11.uscourts.gov/opinions/search.php[a]

BACKGROUND AND FACTS • Josephine Mora was sixty-two years old when she was fired from her job as a fund-raiser for Jackson Memorial Foundation, Inc. Mora's supervisor had become dissatisfied with Mora's work and recommended that she be fired. The foundation's chief executive officer, Mr. Rodriguez, agreed. Later, though, Rodriguez decided to give Mora a different position in his office "where he could observe her more closely." Mora worked with Rodriguez for a month, and more errors and issues with professionalism supposedly arose. Mora contended that when Rodriguez fired her, he told her, "I need someone younger I can pay less." A former employee stated that she had heard this conversation, adding that she heard Rodriguez say to Mora, "You are very old, you are very inept. What you should be doing is taking care of old people. They really need you. I need somebody younger that I can pay less and I can control." Another former employee stated that Rodriguez explained to her and another employee that Mora was "too old to be working here anyway." Rodriguez denied that he had made these statements, and one of the employees substantiated Rodriguez's version of events. Mora sued the foundation in a federal district court for wrongful termination under the Age Discrimination in Employment Act (ADEA). The foundation moved for summary judgment, arguing that regardless of the discrimination issue, Mora still would have been terminated for poor job performance. The district court granted the motion, and Mora appealed.

IN THE LANGUAGE OF THE COURT
PER CURIAM [By the Whole Court].
* * * *

   After Plaintiff [Mora] appealed, the Supreme Court, in *Gross v. FBL Financial Services, Inc.,*[b] clarified the nature of ADEA claims. The Supreme Court concluded that ADEA claims are not subject to the burden-shifting protocol set forth for Title VII suits in

---

a. In the box titled "Search by Case Number or Docket Number," enter "08-16113"—the case docket number. In the search results, click on the link to the docket number to access the opinion. The U.S. Court of Appeals for the Eleventh Circuit maintains this Web site.

b. ___U.S.___, 129 S.Ct. 2343, 174 L.Ed.2d 119 (2009).

CASE CONTINUES ➧

CASE 35.2 CONTINUED ▶ *Price Waterhouse v. Hopkins.*^c The ADEA requires that "age [be] the reason that the employer decided to act." *Because an ADEA plaintiff must establish "but for" causality, no "same decision" affirmative defense [the argument that the same decision—to fire someone, for example—would have been made regardless of the alleged discrimination] can exist: the employer either acted "because of" the plaintiff's age or it did not.* [Emphasis added.]

Because the Supreme Court has excluded the whole idea of a "mixed motive" ADEA claim—and the corresponding "same decision" defense—we need not consider the district court's analysis of Defendant's [the foundation's] affirmative defense. Instead, * * * we look to determine whether a material factual question exists on this record about whether Defendant discriminated against her. We say "Yes."

* * * *

A plaintiff in an ADEA claim may "establish a claim of illegal age discrimination through either direct evidence or circumstantial evidence." Plaintiff's testimony that Rodriguez fired her because she was "too old" was substantiated by the affidavits of two other employees of Defendant. Rodriguez and Quevedo [another employee] testified that no such comments were made * * *.

The resolution of this case depends on whose account of the pertinent conversations a jury would credit. We conclude that a reasonable juror could accept that Rodriguez made the discriminatory-sounding remarks and that the remarks are sufficient evidence of a discriminatory motive which was the "but for" cause of Plaintiff's dismissal. Summary judgment for Defendant was therefore incorrect.

We have considered cases factually similar to Plaintiff's. In [one case], we concluded that statements from a county official who "didn't want to hire any old pilots" were direct evidence of discrimination * * *. In [another case], we likewise concluded that an employer's statement that he wanted "aggressive, young men like himself to be promoted" was circumstantial evidence of discrimination.

While these cases were litigated under the now-defunct ADEA mixed motive theory, they remain instructive. Plaintiff's situation is similar. A reasonable juror could find that Rodriguez's statements should be taken at face value and that he fired Plaintiff because of her age.

DECISION AND REMEDY • *The U.S. Court of Appeals for the Eleventh Circuit vacated (set aside) the decision of the trial court and remanded the case for further proceedings. Because there was a "disputed question of material fact" as to whether the plaintiff had been fired because of her age, the defendant was not entitled to summary judgment.*

THE ETHICAL DIMENSION • *Is the court's decision in this case fair to employers? Why or why not?*

MANAGERIAL IMPLICATIONS • *Business owners and supervisory personnel should be careful to avoid statements regarding an employee's age that may sound discriminatory. If the employee later has to be dismissed due to poor performance, comments about his or her age may become the basis for an age discrimination lawsuit.*

---

c. 490 U.S. 228, 109 S.Ct. 1775, 104 L.Ed.2d 268 (1989).

Replacing Older Workers with Younger Workers

Numerous age discrimination cases have been brought against employers who, to cut costs, replaced older, higher-salaried employees with younger, lower-salaried workers. Whether a firing is discriminatory or simply part of a rational business decision to prune the company's ranks is not always clear. Companies typically defend a decision to discharge a worker by asserting that the worker could no longer perform her or his duties or that the worker's skills were no longer needed.

A plaintiff must prove only that the discharge was motivated by age bias. The plaintiff does not need to prove that she or he was replaced by a person "outside the protected class" (under the age of forty years), as long as the replacement worker is younger than the plaintiff.[28] The issue in all ADEA cases is whether age discrimination has, in fact, occurred, regardless of the age of the replacement worker. Nevertheless, the bigger the age gap, the more likely the plaintiff is to succeed in showing age discrimination.

When an older worker who is laid off as part of a restructuring subsequently files a suit against the company for age discrimination, he or she must present evidence that the layoff was motivated by age bias. Relevant evidence that will be allowed at trial might include testimony from other employees or former employees concerning the company's attitudes toward the workers' ages.[29]

State Employees Not Covered by the ADEA

Generally, the states are immune under the Eleventh Amendment from lawsuits brought by private individuals in federal court—unless a state consents to the suit. This immunity stems from the United States Supreme Court's interpretation of the Eleventh Amendment (the text of this amendment is included in Appendix B).

CASE IN POINT In two cases, professors and librarians contended that their employers—two Florida state universities—denied them salary increases and other benefits because they were getting old and their successors could be hired at a lower cost. The universities claimed that as agencies of a sovereign state, they could not be sued without the state's consent. The cases ultimately reached the United States Supreme Court, which held that the Eleventh Amendment bars private parties from suing state employers for violations of the ADEA.[30]

State immunity under the Eleventh Amendment is not absolute, as the Court explained in 2004. In some situations, such as when fundamental rights are at stake, Congress has the power to abrogate (abolish) state immunity to private suits through legislation that unequivocally shows Congress's intent to subject states to private suits.[31] Generally, though, the Court has found that state employers are immune from private suits brought by employees under the ADEA (for age discrimination), the Americans with Disabilities Act (for disability-based discrimination),[32] and the Fair Labor Standards Act.[33] As explained in Chapter 34, state employers are not immune from the requirements of the Family and Medical Leave Act.[34]

SECTION 3
DISCRIMINATION BASED ON DISABILITY

The Americans with Disabilities Act (ADA) of 1990 is designed to eliminate discriminatory employment practices that prevent otherwise qualified workers with disabilities from fully participating in the national labor force. The ADA prohibits disability-based discrimination in all workplaces with fifteen or more workers (with the exception of state government employers, who are generally immune under the Eleventh Amendment, as was just discussed). Basically, the ADA requires that employers "reasonably accommodate" the needs of persons with disabilities unless to do so would cause the employer to suffer an "undue hardship." In 2008, Congress enacted the ADA Amendments Act,[35] which broadened the coverage of the ADA's protections, as discussed shortly.

Procedures under the ADA

To prevail on a claim under the ADA, a plaintiff must show that he or she (1) has a disability, (2) is otherwise qualified for the employment in question, and (3) was excluded from the employment solely because of the disability. As in Title VII cases, the plaintiff must pursue his or her claim through the EEOC before filing an action in court for a violation of the ADA. The EEOC may decide to investigate and perhaps even sue the employer on behalf of the employee. The EEOC can bring a suit on behalf of the employee under the ADA even if the employee signed an arbitration agreement with the employer.[36]

---

28. *O'Connor v. Consolidated Coin Caterers Corp.*, 517 U.S. 308, 116 S.Ct. 1307, 134 L.Ed.2d 433 (1996).

29. See, for example, *Sprint/United Management Co. v. Mendelsohn*, 552 U.S. 379, 128 S.Ct. 1140, 170 L.Ed.2d 1 (2008).

30. *Kimel v. Florida Board of Regents*, 528 U.S. 62, 120 S.Ct. 631, 145 L.Ed.2d 522 (2000).

31. *Tennessee v. Lane*, 541 U.S. 509, 124 S.Ct. 1978, 158 L.Ed.2d 820 (2004).

32. *Board of Trustees of the University of Alabama v. Garrett*, 531 U.S. 356, 121 S.Ct. 955, 148 L.Ed.2d 866 (2001).

33. *Alden v. Maine*, 527 U.S. 706, 119 S.Ct. 2240, 144 L.Ed.2d 636 (1999).

34. *Nevada Department of Human Resources v. Hibbs*, 538 U.S. 721, 123 S.Ct. 1972, 155 L.Ed.2d 953 (2003).

35. 42 U.S.C. Sections 12103 and 12205a.

36. This was the Supreme Court's ruling in *EEOC v. Waffle House, Inc.*, 534 U.S. 279, 122 S.Ct. 754, 151 L.Ed.2d 755 (2002).

If the EEOC decides not to sue, then the employee may do so. Plaintiffs in lawsuits brought under the ADA may seek many of the same remedies that are available under Title VII. These include reinstatement, back pay, a limited amount of compensatory and punitive damages (for intentional discrimination), and certain other forms of relief. Repeat violators may be ordered to pay fines of up to $100,000.

What Is a Disability?

The ADA broadly defines *persons with disabilities* as persons with physical or mental impairments that "substantially limit" their everyday activities. More specifically, the ADA defines a *disability* as "(1) a physical or mental impairment that substantially limits one or more of the major life activities of such individuals; (2) a record of such impairment; or (3) being regarded as having such an impairment."

Health conditions that have been considered disabilities under federal law include blindness, alcoholism, heart disease, cancer, muscular dystrophy, cerebral palsy, paraplegia, diabetes, acquired immune deficiency syndrome (AIDS), testing positive for the human immunodeficiency virus (HIV, the virus that causes AIDS), and morbid obesity (which exists when an individual's weight is two times the normal weight for his or her height). The ADA excludes from coverage certain conditions, such as kleptomania (the obsessive desire to steal).

AN INITIAL NARROW INTERPRETATION Although the ADA's definition of disability is broad, United States Supreme Court rulings from 1999 to 2007 interpreted that definition narrowly and made it harder for employees to establish a disability under the act. In 1999, the Supreme Court held that severe myopia, or nearsightedness, which can be corrected with lenses, does not qualify as a disability under the ADA.[37] In 2002, the Supreme Court held that repetitive-stress injuries (such as carpal tunnel syndrome) ordinarily do not constitute a disability under the ADA.[38] After that ruling, the courts began focusing on how the person functioned when using corrective devices or taking medication, not on how the person functioned without these measures.[39]

2008 AMENDMENTS BROADEN DEFINITION In response to the Supreme Court's limiting decisions, Congress decided to amend the ADA in 2008. Basically, the amendments reverse the Court's restrictive interpretation of disability under the ADA and prohibit employers from considering mitigating measures or medications when determining if an individual has a disability. As a result, disability is now determined on a case-by-case basis.

A condition may fit the definition of disability in one set of circumstances, but not in another. What makes the difference in an individual situation? The court in the following case answered that question.

---

37. *Sutton v. United Airlines, Inc.,* 527 U.S. 471, 119 S.Ct. 2139, 144 L.Ed.2d 450 (1999).
38. *Toyota Motor Manufacturing, Kentucky, Inc. v. Williams,* 534 U.S. 184, 122 S.Ct. 681, 151 L.Ed.2d 615 (2002). This case was invalidated by the 2008 amendments to the ADA.
39. See, for example, *Orr v. Wal-mart Stores, Inc.,* 297 F.3d 720 (8th Cir. 2002).

CASE 35.3
Rohr v. Salt River Project Agricultural Improvement and Power District

United States Court of Appeals, Ninth Circuit, 555 F.3d 850 (2009).
www.ca9.uscourts.gov[a]

BACKGROUND AND FACTS • Diabetes is a chronic disease associated with an increased risk of heart disease, stroke, high blood pressure, blindness, kidney disease, nervous system disease, and amputations, among other things. Larry Rohr has type 2 diabetes, which results from the body's failure to use insulin properly. He tires quickly and suffers from high blood pressure, deteriorating vision, and loss of feeling in his hands and feet. Insulin injections, other medicine, blood tests, and a strict diet are fixtures of his daily life. If he fails to follow this regimen, his blood sugar rises to a level that aggravates his disease. At the time of his diagnosis, he was a welding metallurgy specialist for the Salt River Project Agricultural Improvement and Power District, which provides utility services to homes in Arizona. Due to the effort required to manage his diabetes, particularly his strict diet schedule, Rohr's physician forbade

---

a. In the left-hand column, click on "Decisions" and then on "Opinions." When that page opens, click on "Advanced Search." In the "by Case No.:" box, type "06-16527" and click on "Search." In the result, click on the case title to access the opinion.

CASE 35.3 CONTINUED ▶ his assignment to tasks involving overnight, out-of-town travel. Salt River told Rohr that this would prevent him from performing the essential functions of his job, such as responding to power outages. Rohr was asked to transfer, apply for disability benefits, or take early retirement. He filed a suit in a federal district court against Salt River, alleging discrimination. The court issued a summary judgment in the employer's favor. Rohr appealed.

IN THE LANGUAGE OF THE COURT
BAER, Senior District Judge:

* * * *

The ADA defines "disability," in pertinent part, as "a physical or mental impairment that substantially limits one or more of the major life activities of such individual." Diabetes is a "physical impairment" because it affects the digestive, hemic [blood] and endocrine systems, and eating is a "major life activity." Whether Rohr's diabetes substantially limits his eating is an individualized inquiry. *Once an impairment is found, the issue is whether Rohr's diabetes substantially limits his activity of eating.* [Emphasis added.]

* * * * *

To determine whether an insulin-dependent type 2 diabetic like Rohr is substantially limited in his eating, we must compare the condition, manner or duration under which he can eat as compared to the condition, manner or duration under which the average person in the general population can eat.

* * * *

Finally, we must consider not only whether the symptoms of Rohr's diabetes substantially limit one of his major life activities, but also whether his efforts to mitigate [diminish] the disease constitute a substantial limitation.

* * * *

* * * For people like Rohr, who must treat their diabetes with insulin, the failure to take insulin will result in severe problems and eventually death. Insulin injections themselves can be dangerous. * * * It is difficult to determine how much insulin to take, as the necessary amount varies depending on the food and activity level. * * * To obtain the appropriate balance, Rohr must test his blood glucose levels * * * numerous times a day.

If daily insulin injections alone more or less stabilized Rohr's blood sugar levels, such that any limitation imposed on his diet would be minor, then Rohr's major life activity of eating might not be substantially limited. However, [there are] substantial limitations on his eating in spite of his medicine and insulin. He must snack regularly, plan his daily schedule around his diet, avoid skipping meals and eat immediately when he feels dizzy or light-headed. * * * Straying from a diet for more than one or two meals is not a cause for medical concern for most people, and skipping a meal, or eating a large one, does not expose them to the risk of fainting. * * * For Rohr, the effort required to control his diet is itself substantially limiting.

DECISION AND REMEDY • *The U.S. Court of Appeals for the Ninth Circuit vacated the lower court's judgment and remanded the case for trial. Diabetes satisfies the ADA's definition of "disability" if it significantly restricts an individual's eating.*

THE E-COMMERCE DIMENSION • *If Rohr could have monitored his condition and regimen through a cell phone or other portable Internet connection, would the result in this case likely have been affected? Explain.*

THE LEGAL ENVIRONMENT DIMENSION • *Salt River argued that type 1 diabetes is harder to control than Rohr's type 2 diabetes. Assuming this is true, would it support a conclusion that Rohr does not suffer from a disability? Why or why not?*

Reasonable Accommodation

The ADA does not require that employers accommodate the needs of job applicants or employees with disabilities who are not otherwise qualified for the work. If a job applicant or an employee with a disability, with reasonable accommodation, can perform essential job functions, however, the employer must make the accommodation. Required modifications may include installing ramps for a wheelchair, establishing flexible working hours, creating or modifying job assignments, and designing or improving training materials and procedures.

Generally, employers should give primary consideration to employees' preferences in deciding what accommodations should be made.

UNDUE HARDSHIP Employers who do not accommodate the needs of persons with disabilities must demonstrate that the accommodations would cause *undue hardship* in terms of being significantly difficult or expensive for the employer. Usually, the courts decide whether an accommodation constitutes an undue hardship on a case-by-case basis.

For example, Bryan Lockhart, who uses a wheelchair, works for a cell phone company that provides parking for its employees. Lockhart informs the company supervisors that the parking spaces are so narrow that he is unable to extend the ramp on his van that allows him to get in and out of the vehicle. Lockhart therefore requests that the company reasonably accommodate his needs by paying a monthly fee for him to use a larger parking space in an adjacent lot. In this situation, a court would likely find that it would not be an undue hardship for the employer to pay for additional parking for Lockhart.

JOB APPLICATIONS AND PHYSICAL EXAMS Employers must modify their job-application and selection process so that those with disabilities can compete for jobs with those who do not have disabilities. For instance, a job announcement might be modified to allow job applicants to respond by e-mail or letter, as well as by telephone, so that it does not discriminate against potential applicants with hearing impairments.

Employers are restricted in the kinds of questions they may ask on job-application forms and during preemployment interviews. In addition, employers cannot require persons with disabilities to submit to preemployment physicals unless such exams are required of all other applicants. An employer can condition an offer of employment on the applicant's successfully passing a medical examination, but can only disqualify the applicant if the medical problems discovered would make it impossible for the applicant to perform the job. For example, when filling the position of delivery truck driver, a company cannot screen out all applicants who are unable to meet the U.S. Department of Transportation's hearing standard. The company would first have to prove that drivers who are deaf are not qualified to perform the essential job function of driving safely and pose a higher risk of accidents than drivers who are not deaf.[40]

SUBSTANCE ABUSERS Drug addiction is considered a disability under the ADA because it is a substantially limiting impairment. Those who are actually using illegal drugs are not protected by the act, however. The ADA protects only persons with *former* drug addictions—those who have completed or are now in a supervised drug-rehabilitation program. Individuals who have used drugs casually in the past are not protected under the act. They are not considered addicts and therefore do not have a disability (addiction).

People suffering from alcoholism are protected by the ADA. Employers cannot legally discriminate against employees simply because they suffer from alcoholism. Of course, employers have the right to prohibit the use of alcohol in the workplace and can require that employees not be under the influence of alcohol while working. Employers can also fire or refuse to hire a person who is an alcoholic if he or she poses a substantial risk of harm either to himself or herself or to others and the risk cannot be reduced by reasonable accommodation.

HEALTH-INSURANCE PLANS Workers with disabilities must be given equal access to any health insurance provided to other employees. Nevertheless, an employer can put a limit, or cap, on health-care payments under its group health policy as long as the cap is applied equally to all insured employees and does not discriminate on the basis of disability. Whenever a group health-care plan makes a disability-based distinction in its benefits, the plan violates the ADA (unless the employer can justify its actions under the business necessity defense, as will be discussed later in this chapter).

Association Discrimination

The ADA contains an "association provision" that protects qualified individuals from employment discrimination based on an identified disability of a person with whom the qualified individual is known to have a relationship or an association.[41] The purpose of this provision is to prevent employers from taking adverse employment actions based on stereotypes or assumptions about individuals who associate with people who have disabilities. An employer cannot, for instance, refuse to hire the parent of a child with a disability based on the assumption that the person will miss work too often or be unreliable.

To establish a *prima facie* case of association discrimination under the ADA, the plaintiff must show that she or he (1) was qualified for the job, (2) was subjected to an adverse employment action, and

---

40. See, for example, *Bates v. United Parcel Service, Inc.*, 465 F.3d 1069 (9th Cir. 2006).

41. 42 U.S.C. Section 12112(b)(4).

(3) was known by her or his employer to have a relative or an associate with a disability.

CASE IN POINT Randall Francin had worked at Mosby, Inc., for twelve years before his wife was diagnosed with amyotrophic lateral sclerosis (Lou Gehrig's disease). He discussed his rights for leave under the Family and Medical Leave Act (see Chapter 34) with a company representative. Early in 2004, Francin received a "merit award increase" in salary and subsequently discussed his wife's illness with his supervisor. In September 2004, Francin was fired. Francin filed a lawsuit claiming that Mosby had discriminated against him because of his association with a person with a disability. Although the trial court granted a summary judgment for Mosby, the appellate court found that there was sufficient evidence that Francin's wife's illness was a contributing factor to his termination for the case to go to trial. Thus, summary judgment was inappropriate.[42]

SECTION 4
DEFENSES TO EMPLOYMENT DISCRIMINATION

The first line of defense for an employer charged with employment discrimination is to assert that the plaintiff has failed to meet his or her initial burden of proving that discrimination occurred. As noted, plaintiffs bringing cases under the ADEA may find it difficult to meet this initial burden because they must prove that age discrimination was, in fact, the reason for their employer's decision to discharge them.

Once a plaintiff succeeds in proving that discrimination occurred, then the burden shifts to the employer to justify the discriminatory practice. Often, employers attempt to justify the discrimination by claiming that it was the result of a business necessity, a bona fide occupational qualification, or a seniority system. Alternatively, they may assert that employee misconduct should limit their liability. In some situations, as noted earlier, an effective antiharassment policy and prompt remedial action when harassment occurs may shield employers from liability for sexual harassment under Title VII.

Business Necessity

An employer may defend against a claim of disparate-impact (unintentional) discrimination by asserting that a practice that has a discriminatory effect is a **business necessity.** If requiring a high school diploma, for example, is shown to have a discriminatory effect, an employer might argue that a high school education is necessary for workers to perform the job at a required level of competence. If the employer can demonstrate to the court's satisfaction that a definite connection exists between a high school education and job performance, then the employer normally will succeed in this business necessity defense.

Bona Fide Occupational Qualification

Another defense applies when discrimination against a protected class is essential to a job—that is, when a particular trait is a **bona fide occupational qualification (BFOQ).** Race, color, and national origin, however, can never be BFOQs.

Generally, courts have restricted the BFOQ defense to instances in which the employee's gender or religion is essential to the job. For example, a women's clothing store might legitimately hire only female salespersons if part of a salesperson's job involves assisting clients in the store's dressing rooms. Similarly, the Federal Aviation Administration can legitimately impose age limits for airline pilots—but an airline cannot impose weight limits only on female flight attendants.

Seniority Systems

An employer with a history of discrimination may have no members of protected classes in upper-level positions. Even if the employer now seeks to be unbiased, it may face a lawsuit from members of protected classes claiming that they should be promoted ahead of schedule to compensate for past discrimination. If no present intent to discriminate is shown, however, and if promotions or other job benefits are distributed according to a fair **seniority system** (in which workers with more years of service are promoted first or laid off last), the employer normally has a good defense against the suit.

According to the United States Supreme Court, this defense may also apply to claims of discrimination under the ADA. A baggage handler who had injured his back requested an assignment to a mailroom position at U.S. Airways, Inc. The airline refused to give the employee the position because another employee had seniority. The Court sided with U.S. Airways. If an employee with a disability requests an accommodation that conflicts with an employer's seniority system, the accommodation generally will not be considered "reasonable" under the ADA.[43]

---

42. *Francin v. Mosby, Inc.,* 248 S.W.3d 619 (Mo. 2008).

43. *U.S. Airways, Inc. v. Barnett,* 535 U.S. 391, 122 S.Ct. 1516, 152 L.Ed.2d 589 (2002).

After-Acquired Evidence of Employee Misconduct

In some situations, employers have attempted to avoid liability for employment discrimination on the basis of "after-acquired evidence"—that is, evidence that the employer discovers after a lawsuit is filed—of an employee's misconduct. Suppose that an employer fires a worker, who then sues the employer for employment discrimination. During pretrial investigation, the employer learns that the employee made material misrepresentations on his employment application—misrepresentations that, had the employer known about them, would have served as a ground to fire the individual. Can this after-acquired evidence be used as a defense?

According to the United States Supreme Court, after-acquired evidence of wrongdoing cannot be used to shield an employer entirely from liability for employment discrimination. It may, however, be used to limit the amount of damages for which the employer is liable.[44]

SECTION 5
AFFIRMATIVE ACTION

Federal statutes and regulations providing for equal opportunity in the workplace were designed to reduce or eliminate discriminatory practices with respect to hiring, retaining, and promoting employees. **Affirmative action** programs go a step further and attempt to "make up" for past patterns of discrimination by giving members of protected classes preferential treatment in hiring or promotion. During the 1960s, all federal and state government agencies, private companies that contracted to do business with the federal government, and institutions that received federal funding were required to implement affirmative action policies.

Title VII of the Civil Rights Act of 1964 neither requires nor prohibits affirmative action. Thus, most private companies and organizations have not been required to implement affirmative action policies, though many have done so voluntarily. Affirmative action programs have been controversial, however, particularly when they result in reverse discrimination against members of a majority group, such as white males.

Constitutionality of Affirmative Action Programs

Because of their inherently discriminatory nature, affirmative action programs may violate the equal protection clause of the Fourteenth Amendment to the U.S. Constitution. The United States Supreme Court has held that any federal, state, or local government affirmative action program that uses racial or ethnic classifications as the basis for making decisions is subject to strict scrutiny by the courts.[45] Recall from Chapter 4 that strict scrutiny is the highest standard, which means that most programs do not survive a court's analysis under this test.

Today, an affirmative action program normally is constitutional only if it attempts to remedy past discrimination and does not make use of quotas or preferences. Furthermore, once such a program has succeeded in the goal of remedying past discrimination, it must be changed or dropped.

Affirmative Action in Schools

Most of the affirmative action cases that have reached the United States Supreme Court in the last twenty years have involved university admissions programs and schools, rather than business employers. Generally, the Court has found that a school admissions policy that *automatically* awards minority group applicants a specified number of points violates the equal protection clause.[46] A school can, however, "consider race or ethnicity more flexibly as a 'plus' factor in the context of individualized consideration of each and every applicant."[47] In other words, it is unconstitutional for schools to apply a mechanical formula that gives "diversity bonuses" based on race or ethnicity.

CASE IN POINT In 2007, the Supreme Court ruled on two cases involving the use of racial classifications to assign students to schools. Two school districts (in Seattle, Washington, and Jefferson County, Kentucky) had adopted student assignment plans that relied on race to determine which schools certain children would attend. The Seattle plan classified children as "white" or "nonwhite" and used the racial classifications as a "tiebreaker" to determine which school students would attend. The Jefferson

---

44. *McKennon v. Nashville Banner Publishing Co.,* 513 U.S. 352, 115 S.Ct. 879, 130 L.Ed.2d 852 (1995). See also *EEOC v. Dial Corp.,* 469 F.3d 735 (8th Cir. 2006).

45. See the landmark decision in *Adarand Constructors, Inc. v. Peña,* 515 U.S. 200, 115 S.Ct. 2097, 132 L.Ed.2d 158 (1995).

46. *Gratz v. Bollinger,* 539 U.S. 244, 123 S.Ct. 2411, 156 L.Ed.2d 257 (2003).

47. *Grutter v. Bollinger,* 539 U.S. 306, 123 S.Ct. 2325, 156 L.Ed.2d 304 (2003).

County plan classified students as "black" or "other" to assign them to schools. When parents claimed that the racial preferences violated the equal protection clause, the Court held that the school districts had failed to show that the use of racial classifications was necessary to achieve their stated goal of racial diversity. Hence, the Court found that both districts' affirmative action programs were unconstitutional.[48]

---

48. The Court consolidated the two cases and issued one opinion for both. See, *Parents Involved in Community Schools v. Seattle School District No. 1,* 551 U.S. 701, 127 S.Ct. 2738, 168 L.Ed.2d 508 (2007).

REVIEWING
Employment Discrimination

Amaani Lyle, an African American woman, was hired by Warner Brothers Television Productions to be a scriptwriters' assistant for the writers of *Friends,* a popular, adult-oriented television series. One of her essential job duties was to type detailed notes for the scriptwriters during brainstorming sessions in which they discussed jokes, dialogue, and story lines. The writers then combed through Lyle's notes after the meetings for script material. During these meetings, the three male scriptwriters told lewd and vulgar jokes and made sexually explicit comments and gestures. They often talked about their personal sexual experiences and fantasies, and some of these conversations were then used in episodes of *Friends.*

During the meetings, Lyle never complained that she found the writers' conduct offensive. After four months, Lyle was fired because she could not type fast enough to keep up with the writers' conversations during the meetings. She filed a suit against Warner Brothers, alleging sexual harassment and claiming that her termination was based on racial discrimination. Using the information presented in the chapter, answer the following questions.

1. Would Lyle's claim of racial discrimination be for intentional (disparate-treatment) or unintentional (disparate-impact) discrimination? Explain.
2. Can Lyle establish a *prima facie* case of racial discrimination? Why or why not?
3. When Lyle was hired, she was told that typing speed was extremely important to the position. At the time, she maintained that she could type eighty words per minute, so she was not given a typing test. It later turned out that Lyle could type only fifty words per minute. What impact might typing speed have on Lyle's lawsuit?
4. Lyle's sexual-harassment claim is based on the hostile working environment created by the writers' sexually offensive conduct at meetings that she was required to attend. The writers, however, argue that their behavior was essential to the "creative process" of writing for *Friends,* a show that routinely contained sexual innuendos and adult humor. Which defense discussed in the chapter might Warner Brothers assert using this argument?

DEBATE THIS: *Members of minority groups and women have made enough economic progress in the last several decades that they no longer need special legislation to protect them.*

TERMS AND CONCEPTS

affirmative action 696
bona fide occupational qualification (BFOQ) 695
business necessity 695

constructive discharge 684
disparate-impact discrimination 682
disparate-treatment discrimination 682

employment discrimination 681
prima facie case 682
protected class 681
seniority system 695

sexual harassment 685
tangible employment action 685

QUESTIONS AND CASE PROBLEMS

35–1. Title VII Violations Discuss fully whether either of the following actions would constitute a violation of Title VII of the 1964 Civil Rights Act, as amended:

(a) Tennington, Inc., is a consulting firm and has ten employees. These employees travel on consulting jobs in seven states. Tennington has an employment record of hiring only white males.

(b) Novo Films is making a movie about Africa and needs to employ approximately one hundred extras for this picture. To hire these extras, Novo advertises in all major newspapers in Southern California. The ad states that only African Americans need apply.

35–2. QUESTION WITH SAMPLE ANSWER: Religious Discrimination.

When Kayla Caldwell got a job as a cashier at a Costco store, she wore multiple pierced earrings and had four tattoos, but she had no facial piercings. Over the next two years, Caldwell engaged in various forms of body modification, including facial piercing and cutting. Then Costco revised its dress code to prohibit all facial jewelry, except earrings. Caldwell was told that she would have to remove her facial jewelry. She asked for a complete exemption from the code, asserting that she was a member of the Church of Body Modification and that eyebrow piercing was part of her religion. She was told to remove the jewelry, cover it, or go home. She went home and was later discharged for her absence. Based on these facts, will Caldwell be successful in a lawsuit against Costco for religious discrimination in violation of Title VII? Does an employer have an obligation to accommodate its employees' religious practices? If so, to what extent?

• **For a sample answer to Question 35–2, go to Appendix I at the end of this text.**

35–3. Discrimination Based on Gender For twenty years, Darlene Jespersen worked as a bartender at Harrah's Casino in Reno, Nevada. In 2000, Harrah's implemented a "Personal Best" program that included new grooming standards. Among other requirements, women were told to wear makeup "applied neatly in complimentary colors." Jespersen, who never wore makeup off the job, felt so uncomfortable wearing it on the job that it interfered with her ability to perform. Unwilling to wear makeup and not qualifying for another position at Harrah's with similar compensation, Jespersen quit her job. She filed a suit in a federal district court against Harrah's Operating Co., the casino's owner, alleging that the makeup policy discriminated against women in violation of Title VII of the Civil Rights Act of 1964. Harrah's argued that any burdens under the new program fell equally on both genders, citing the "Personal Best" short-hair standard that applied only to men. Jespersen responded by describing her personal reaction to the makeup policy

and emphasizing her exemplary record during her tenure at Harrah's. In whose favor should the court rule? Why? [*Jespersen v. Harrah's Operating Co.*, 444 F.3d 1104 (9th Cir. 2006)]

35–4. Discrimination Based on Disability Cerebral palsy limits Steven Bradley's use of his legs. He uses forearm crutches for short-distance walks and a wheelchair for longer distances. Standing for more than ten or fifteen minutes is difficult. With support, however, Bradley can climb stairs and get on and off a stool. His condition also restricts the use of his fourth finger to, for example, type, but it does not limit his ability to write—he completed two years of college. His grip strength is normal, and he can lift heavy objects. In 2001, Bradley applied for a "greeter" or "cashier" position at a Wal-Mart Stores, Inc., Supercenter in Richmond, Missouri. The job description stated, "No experience or qualification is required." Bradley indicated that he was available for full- or part-time work from 4:00 P.M. to 10:00 P.M. any evening. His employment history showed that he currently worked as a proofreader and that he had previously worked as an administrator. His application was rejected, according to Janet Daugherty, the personnel manager, based on his "work history" and the "direct threat" that he posed to the safety of himself and others. Bradley claimed, however, that the store refused to hire him due to his disability. What steps must Bradley follow to pursue his claim? What does he need to show to prevail? Is he likely to meet these requirements? Discuss. [*EEOC v. Wal-Mart Stores, Inc.*, 477 F.3d 561 (8th Cir. 2007)]

35–5. Defenses to Employment Discrimination The Milwaukee County Juvenile Detention Center established a new policy that required each unit of the facility to be staffed at all times by at least one officer of the same gender as the detainees housed at a unit. The purpose of the policy, administrators said, was to reduce the likelihood of sexual abuse of juveniles by officers of the other gender. Because there were many more male units in the center than female units, the policy had the effect of reducing the number of shifts available for women officers and increasing the number of shifts for men. Two female officers sued for gender discrimination. The district court held for the county, finding that the policy of assignment was based on a bona fide occupational qualification (BFOQ) and so was not illegal gender discrimination. The officers appealed. What would be evidence that the county had a valid BFOQ? [*Henry v. Milwaukee County*, 539 F.3d 573 (7th Cir. 2008)]

35–6. CASE PROBLEM WITH SAMPLE ANSWER: Sexual Harassment.

The Metropolitan Government of Nashville and Davidson County, Tennessee (Metro), began looking into rumors of sexual harassment by the Metro School District's employee relations director, Gene Hughes. Veronica Frazier, a Metro human resources officer,

asked Vicky Crawford, a Metro employee, whether she had witnessed "inappropriate behavior" by Hughes. Crawford described several instances of sexually harassing behavior. Two other employees also reported being sexually harassed by Hughes. Metro took no action against Hughes, but soon after completing the investigation, Metro accused Crawford of embezzlement and fired her. The two other employees were also fired. Crawford filed a suit in a federal district court against Metro, claiming retaliation under Title VII. What arguments can be made that Crawford's situation does or does not qualify as a retaliation claim under Title VII? Discuss. [Crawford v. Metropolitan Government of Nashville and Davidson County, Tennessee, __ U.S. __, 129 S.Ct. 846, 172 L.Ed.2d 650 (2009)]

- **To view a sample answer for Problem 35–6, go to this book's Web site at www.cengage.com/blaw/clarkson, select "Chapter 35," and click on "Case Problem with Sample Answer."**

35–7. Discrimination Based on Gender Brenda Lewis had been employed for two years at Heartland Inns of America, LLC, and gradually worked her way up the management ladder. Lewis, who described herself as a tomboy, was commended for her good work. When she moved to a different Heartland hotel, the director of operations, Barbara Cullinan, told one of the owners that Lewis was not a "good fit" for the front desk because she was not feminine enough. Cullinan told various people that the hotel wanted "pretty" girls at the front desk. Cullinan then informed Lewis that her hiring had not been done properly and that she would need to undergo another interview. Soon after the interview, Cullinan fired Lewis. The reason given in a letter was that Lewis was hostile during the interview. Lewis sued Heartland for gender discrimination based on unlawful gender stereotyping. The district court dismissed the suit. Lewis appealed. Does her claim fall under Title VII's prohibition against discrimination based on gender? Why or why not? [*Lewis v. Heartland Inns of America, LLC*, 591 F.3d 1033 (8th Cir. 2010)]

35–8. A QUESTION OF ETHICS: Discrimination Based on Disability.

Titan Distribution, Inc., employed Quintak, Inc., to run its tire mounting and distribution operation in Des Moines, Iowa. Robert Chalfant worked for Quintak as a second shift supervisor at Titan. He suffered a heart attack in 1992 and underwent heart bypass surgery in 1997. He also had arthritis. In July 2002, Titan decided to fire Quintak. Chalfant applied to work at Titan. On his application, he described himself as disabled. After a physical exam, Titan's physician concluded that Chalfant could work in his current capacity, and he was notified that he would be hired. Despite the notice, Nadis Barucic, a Titan employee, wrote "not pass px" at the top of Chalfant's application, and he was not hired. He took a job with AMPCO Systems, a parking ramp management company. This work involved walking up to five miles a day and lifting more weight than he had at Titan. In September, Titan eliminated its second shift. Chalfant filed a suit in a federal district court

against Titan, in part, under the Americans with Disabilities Act (ADA). Titan argued that it had not hired Chalfant because he did not pass the physical, but no one—including Barucic—could explain why she had written "not pass px" on his application. Later, Titan claimed that Chalfant was not hired because the entire second shift was going to be eliminated. [Chalfant v. Titan Distribution, Inc., 475 F.3d 982 (8th Cir. 2007)]

(a) What must Chalfant establish to make his case under the ADA? Can he meet these requirements? Explain.

(b) In employment-discrimination cases, punitive damages can be appropriate when an employer acts with malice or reckless indifference toward an employee's protected rights. Would an award of punitive damages to Chalfant be appropriate in this case? Discuss.

35–9. VIDEO QUESTION: Employment Discrimination.

Go to this text's Web site at **www.cengage.com/blaw/clarkson** and select "Chapter 35." Click on "Video Questions" and view the video titled *Mary Tyler Moore*. Then answer the following questions.

(a) In the video, Mr. Grant (Ed Asner) asks Mary (Mary Tyler Moore) some personal questions during a job interview, including why she is not married and what religion she practices. He also tells her that he "figured he'd hire a man." Can Mary make out a *prima facie* case of gender or religious discrimination based on these questions? Why or why not?

(b) Can Mary prove a *prima facie* case of age discrimination because Mr. Grant asked her age during the interview and then implied that she was "hedging" about her age? What would she need to prove under the Age Discrimination in Employment Act?

(c) How does the fact that Mr. Grant hired Mary as an associate producer affect her ability to establish a case of employment discrimination?

(d) Mr. Grant says that he will hire Mary to see if it works out but fire her if he does not like her or if she does not like him at the end of this trial period. Can he do that? Explain. If he fired Mary a few weeks later, would this affect Mary's ability to sue for employment discrimination? Why or why not?

35–10. SPECIAL CASE ANALYSIS: Sexual Harassment.

Go to Extended Case 35.1, *Burlington Northern and Santa Fe Railway Co. v. White*, 548 U.S. 53, 126 S.Ct. 2405, 165 L.Ed.2d 345 (2006), on pages 686 and 687. Read the excerpt and answer the following questions.

(a) Issue: What was the plaintiff's complaint, the defendant's response, and the chief legal dispute between them?

(b) Rule of Law: Which provisions of Title VII did the Court consider, and which rule of statutory interpretation governed the Court's consideration?

(c) **Applying the Rule of Law:** How did the Court interpret these provisions, and how did that interpretation apply to the circumstances in this case?

(d) **Conclusion:** Based on its application of the principles in this case, what did the Court conclude?

LEGAL RESEARCH EXERCISES ON THE WEB

Go to this text's Web site at **www.cengage.com/blaw/clarkson**, select "Chapter 35," and click on "Practical Internet Exercises." There you will find the following Internet research exercises that you can perform to learn more about the topics covered in this chapter.

Practical Internet Exercise 35–1: **Legal Perspective**
Americans with Disabilities

Practical Internet Exercise 35–2: **Management Perspective**
Equal Employment Opportunity

Practical Internet Exercise 35–3: **Social Perspective**
Religious and National Origin Discrimination

Ethical principles—and challenging ethical issues—pervade the areas of agency and employment. As you read in Chapter 32, when one person agrees to act on behalf of another, as an agent does in an agency relationship, that person assumes certain ethical responsibilities. Similarly, the principal also assumes certain ethical duties. In essence, agency law gives legal force to the ethical duties arising in an agency relationship. Although agency law also focuses on the rights of agents and principals, those rights are framed by the concept of duty—that is, an agent's duty becomes a right for the principal, and vice versa. Significantly, many of the duties of the principal and agent are negotiable when they form their contract. In forming a contract, the principal and the agent can extend or abridge many of the ordinary duties owed in such a relationship.

Employees who deal with third parties are also deemed to be agents and thus share the ethical (and legal) duties imposed under agency law. In the employment context, however, it is not always possible for an employee to negotiate favorable employment terms. Often, an employee who is offered a job must either accept the job on the employer's terms or look elsewhere for a position. Although numerous federal and state statutes protect employees, in some situations employees still have little recourse against their employers. At the same time, employers complain that statutes regulating employment relationships impose so many requirements that they find it hard to exercise a reasonable amount of control over their workplaces.

The Agent's Duty to the Principal

The very nature of the principal-agent relationship is one of trust. Because of the nature of this relationship, which we call a fiduciary relationship, an agent is considered to owe certain duties to the principal. These duties include being loyal and obedient, informing the principal of important facts concerning the agency, accounting to the principal for property or funds received, and performing with reasonable diligence and skill.

Thus, ethical conduct would prevent an agent from representing two principals in the same transaction, making a secret profit from the agency relationship, or failing to disclose the agent's interest in property being purchased by the principal. The expected ethical conduct of the agent has evolved into rules that, if breached, cause the agent to be held legally liable.

Does an Agent Also Have a Duty to Society? A question that sometimes arises is whether an agent's obligation extends beyond the duty to the principal and includes a duty to society as well. Consider, for example, the situation faced by an employee who knows that her employer is engaging in an unethical—or even illegal—practice, such as marketing an unsafe product. Does the employee's duty to the principal include keeping silent about this practice, which may harm users of the product? Does the employee have a duty to protect consumers by disclosing this information to the public, even if she loses her job as a result? Some scholars have argued that many of the greatest evils in the past thirty years have been accomplished in the name of duty to the principal.

Does an Agent's Breach of Loyalty Terminate the Agent's Authority? Suppose that an employee-agent who is authorized to access company trade secrets contained in computer files takes those secrets to a competitor for whom the employee is about to begin working. Clearly, in this situation the agent has violated the ethical—and legal—duty of loyalty to the principal. Does this breach of loyalty mean that the employee's act of accessing the trade secrets was unauthorized? The question has significant implications because if the act was unauthorized, the employee will be subject to state and federal laws prohibiting unauthorized access to computer information and data. If the act was authorized, the employee will not be subject to such laws.

To date, most courts have ruled that an agent's authority continues, even though there was a breach of loyalty. In one case, for example, three employees of Lockheed Martin Corporation copied confidential information and trade secrets from Lockheed's computer network onto compact discs and BlackBerries (personal digital assistants). Lockheed had authorized the employee-agents to access these files but was understandably upset when the three resigned and went to work for a competitor, taking the trade secrets with them. Lockheed sued the former agents under the Computer Fraud and Abuse Act (discussed in Chapter 6), arguing that they had accessed the data without authorization. The federal district court, however, held that the individuals did have authorization to access the computer network and did not lose this authorization when they breached the duty of loyalty. Therefore, the court dismissed the case.[1]

The Principal's Duty to the Agent

Just as agents owe certain duties to their principals, so do principals owe duties to their agents, such as compensation and reimbursement for job-related expenses. Principals also owe their agents a duty of cooperation. One might expect principals to cooperate

---

1. *Lockheed Martin Corp. v. Speed,* 2006 WL 2683058 (M.D.Fla. 2006). See also *Cenveo Corp. v. CelumSolutions Software GMBH & Co. KG,* 504 F.Supp.2d 574 (D.Minn. 2007).

FOCUS ON ETHICS CONTINUES ▶

with their agents out of self-interest, but this does not always happen.

Suppose that a principal hires an agent on commission to sell a building, and the agent puts considerable time and expense into finding a buyer. If the principal changes his mind and decides to retain the building, he may try to prevent the agent from completing the sale. Is such action ethical? Does it violate the principal's duty of cooperation? What alternatives would the principal have?

Although a principal is legally obligated to fulfill certain duties to the agent, these duties do not include any specific duty of loyalty. Some argue that employers' failure to be loyal to their employees has resulted in a reduction in employee loyalty to employers. After all, they maintain, why should an employee be loyal to an employer's interests over the years when the employee knows that the employer has no corresponding legal duty to be loyal to the employee's interests? Employers who do show a sense of loyalty toward their employees—for example, by not laying off longtime, faithful employees when business is slow or when those employees could be replaced by younger workers at lower cost—base that loyalty primarily on ethical, not legal, considerations.

Respondeat Superior

Agency relationships have ethical ramifications for third parties as well as for agents and principals. A legal concept that addresses the effect of agency relationships on third parties is the doctrine of *respondeat superior*. This doctrine raises a significant ethical question: Why should innocent employers be required to assume responsibility for the tortious, or wrongful, actions of their agent-employees? The answer has to do with the courts' perception that when one of two innocent parties must suffer a loss, the party in the better position to prevent that loss should bear the burden. In an employment relationship, for example, the employer has more control over the employee's behavior than a third party to the relationship does.

Another reason for retaining the doctrine of *respondeat superior* in our laws is that the employer is assumed to be better able to pay any damages incurred by a third party. One of our society's shared beliefs is that an injured party should be afforded the most effective relief possible. Thus, even though an employer may be absolutely innocent, the employer has "deeper pockets" than the employee and will be more likely to have the funds necessary to make the injured party whole.

Immigration Reform

Unauthorized (illegal) workers make up 5 percent of the total U.S. workforce and 12 percent of the workers in the construction industry. The federal government during the Bush administration significantly stepped up enforcement actions (raids) to combat the growing number of illegal immigrants. The raids targeted workers in many industries, including food processing and packaging firms, contractors (landscape, cleaning, and janitorial services), construction firms, temporary employment services, and fast-food restaurants. Often, the unauthorized workers were performing jobs that no one else wanted because the jobs paid low wages or involved substandard conditions.

As a result of these raids, many immigrant workers were detained and deported, their families were torn apart, the businesses for which they worked were disrupted, and some managers faced prison terms. The impact of these raids on immigrants—in a nation founded by immigrants—has led many U.S. citizens to believe that reforming the immigration laws is a moral imperative. Many believe that it is unethical to imprison and deport these impoverished and unrepresented workers—who often were already being exploited by their U.S. employers.

When President Barack Obama took office, he promised to reform immigration law. His goals were to decrease bureaucracy, increase efficiency, and boost the number of immigrant workers with legal status in the United States in an effort to keep families together and meet employers' needs for workers. Although the number of workplace raids has decreased, the Obama administration's policies have not resulted in more favorable treatment of immigrant workers. For example, in September 2009, American Apparel, a U.S.-based clothing company, laid off more than 1,600 workers in Los Angeles rather than face fines for employing undocumented workers.[2]

Problems with I-9 Verification

Verifying a person's eligibility to work in the United States can be a complicated and costly process for employers. The most recent I-9 form (see Chapter 34) specifies the documents that an employer may accept to verify employment eligibility and identification. At the same time, it is illegal for an employer to discriminate against foreign-born workers by requiring them to provide a driver's license or Social Security card to prove their identity. If an employer relies on the documents a worker provides to prove identity and eligibility (such a school photo identification card) and these documents later prove to be fraudulent or invalid, the employer can be sanctioned for hiring a person that

---

2. "Immigration Reforms: How a Broken System Breaks Communities," *Making Contact,* a production of the National Radio Project, January 26, 2010.

the employer "should have known" was unauthorized. Thus, employers are forced to choose between violating antidiscrimination laws and risking sanctions for violating immigration laws. It is an ethical dilemma with no easy answer.

Discrimination against Transgender Persons

Although some states have laws that specifically ban discrimination based on gender identity, most courts have held that federal law (Title VII, discussed in Chapter 35) does *not* protect transgender persons from discrimination. This situation may be changing, however, now that one federal court has extended Title VII protection against gender discrimination to transsexuals. Diane Schroer (previously David Schroer) was born male but always identified with the female gender. Schroer, who has master's degrees in history and international relations, served twenty-five years in the military and was a commander of special forces. After retiring with top-secret clearance, Schroer applied for a terrorism specialist position at the Library of Congress. At the job interview, Schroer dressed as a man and received the highest interview score of all eighteen candidates. The selection committee unanimously voted to offer the job to Schroer.

Schroer then met with her future supervisor and explained that she had been diagnosed with gender identity disorder and was planning to have sex reassignment surgery. The next day, the Library of Congress withdrew its offer to hire Schroer. When Schroer sued alleging gender discrimination, the Library claimed that it had withdrawn its offer because Schroer was untrustworthy and would be unable to receive the needed security clearance. The court, however, found that these reasons were pretexts (excuses) and ruled in favor of Schroer. The court held that the Library had refused to hire Schroer because her appearance and background did not comport with the selection committee's stereotypes about how women and men should act and appear. The court concluded that the revocation of the job offer violated Title VII; it was discrimination "because of sex" even though Title VII does not include transsexuals as a protected class. In 2009, Schroer was awarded nearly $500,000 in back pay and damages.[3]

DISCUSSION QUESTIONS

1. How much obedience and loyalty does an agent-employee owe to an employer? What if the employer engages in an activity—or requests that the employee engage in an activity—that violates the employee's ethical standards but does not violate any public policy or law? In such a situation, does an employee's duty to abide by her or his own ethical standards override the employee's duty of loyalty to the employer?

2. When an agent acts in violation of his or her ethical or legal duty to the principal, should that action terminate the agent's authority to act on behalf of the principal? Why or why not?

3. If an agent-employee injures a third party during the course of employment, under the doctrine of *respondeat superior,* the employer may be held liable for the employee's action even though the employer did not authorize the action and was not even aware of it. Is it fair to hold the employer liable in this situation? Would it be more equitable if the employee alone was held liable for his or her tortious (legally wrongful) actions to third parties, even when the actions were committed within the scope of employment?

4. How should immigration law be reformed? Does the United States have any ethical duties to undocumented (illegal) aliens who come here to work? How can the law be fair and balance the rights of immigrants, their families, the companies that employ them, and U.S. citizens?

5. Should the law prohibit discrimination against transgender persons? Why or why not?

---

3. *Schroer v. Billington,* 577 F.Supp.2d 293 (D.D.C. 2008).

UNIT EIGHT

BUSINESS ORGANIZATIONS

CONTENTS

CHAPTER 36

Sole Proprietorships and Franchises

Anyone who starts a business must first decide which form of business organization will be most appropriate for the new endeavor. In making this decision, the **entrepreneur** (one who initiates and assumes the financial risk of a new enterprise) needs to consider a number of factors, especially (1) ease of creation, (2) the liability of the owners, (3) tax considerations, and (4) the need for capital. In studying this unit, keep these factors in mind as you read about the various business organizational forms available to entrepreneurs. You may also find it helpful to refer to Exhibit 41–4 on pages 807 and 808, which compares the major

business forms in use today with respect to these and other factors.

Traditionally, entrepreneurs have relied on three major business forms—the sole proprietorship, the partnership, and the corporation. In this chapter, we examine the sole proprietorship form of business. We also look at franchises, which are widely used today. The franchise is not actually a separate organizational form. Rather, it is a contractual arrangement, and the parties to a franchise contract may use any one of several organizational forms—for example, the parties may be a sole proprietor and a corporation or two corporations.

In Chapter 37, we will examine the second major traditional business form, the partnership, as well as some newer variations on partnerships. In Chapter 38, we will look at the limited liability company (LLC), a relatively new and increasingly popular form of business enterprise, and other special forms of business.

The third major traditional form—the corporation—will be discussed in Chapters 39 through 42. We conclude this unit with a chapter (Chapter 43) discussing practical legal information that all businesspersons should know, particularly those operating small businesses.

SECTION 1
SOLE PROPRIETORSHIPS

The simplest form of business is a **sole proprietorship.** In this form, the owner is the business; thus, anyone who does business without creating a separate business organization has a sole proprietorship. More than two-thirds of all U.S. businesses are sole proprietorships. They are usually small enterprises—about 99 percent of the sole proprietorships in the United States have revenues of less than $1 million per year. Sole proprietors can own and manage any type of business from an informal, home-office undertaking to a large restaurant or construction firm.

Advantages of the Sole Proprietorship

A major advantage of the sole proprietorship is that the proprietor owns the entire business and receives

all of the profits (because she or he assumes all of the risk). In addition, starting a sole proprietorship is often easier and less costly than starting any other kind of business, as few legal formalities are required.[1] No documents need to be filed with the government to start a sole proprietorship (though a state business license may be required to operate certain types of businesses).

This form of business organization also offers more flexibility than does a partnership or a corporation. The sole proprietor is free to make any decision he or she wishes concerning the business—such as whom to hire, when to take a vacation, and what kind of business to pursue. In addition, the proprietor can sell or transfer all or part of the business to another party at any time and does not need

---

1. Although starting a sole proprietorship involves fewer legal formalities than other business organizational forms, even small sole proprietorships may need to comply with zoning requirements, obtain licenses, and the like.

approval from anyone else (as would be required from partners in a partnership or normally from shareholders in a corporation).

A sole proprietor pays only personal income taxes (including Social Security and Medicare taxes) on the business's profits, which are reported as personal income on the proprietor's personal income tax return. Sole proprietors are also allowed to establish certain retirement accounts that are tax-exempt until the funds are withdrawn, usually after age fifty-nine and a half.

Disadvantages of the Sole Proprietorship

The major disadvantage of the sole proprietorship is that the proprietor alone bears the burden of any losses or liabilities incurred by the business enterprise. In other words, the sole proprietor has unlimited liability, or legal responsibility, for all obligations that arise in doing business. Any lawsuit against the business or its employees can lead to unlimited personal liability for the owner of a sole proprietorship. Creditors can go after the owner's personal assets to satisfy any business debts. This unlimited liability is a major factor to be considered in choosing a business form.

The sole proprietorship also has the disadvantage of lacking continuity on the death of the proprietor. When the owner dies, so does the business—it is automatically dissolved. Another disadvantage is that in raising capital, the proprietor is limited to his or her personal funds and any personal loans that he or she can obtain.

The personal liability of the owner of a sole proprietorship was at issue in the following case. The case involved the federal Cable Communications Act, which prohibits a commercial establishment from broadcasting television programs to its patrons without authorization. The court had to decide whether the owner of a sole proprietorship that installed a satellite television system was personally liable for violating this act by identifying a restaurant as a "residence" for billing purposes.

CASE 36.1
Garden City Boxing Club, Inc. v. Dominguez

United States District Court, Northern District of Illinois, Eastern Division, __ F.Supp.2d __ (2006).

BACKGROUND AND FACTS • Garden City Boxing Club, Inc. (GCB), which is based in San Jose, California, owned the exclusive right to broadcast several prizefights, via closed-circuit television, including a match between Oscar De La Hoya and Fernando Vargas on September 14, 2002. GCB sold the right to receive the broadcasts to bars and other commercial venues. The fee was $20 multiplied by an establishment's maximum fire code occupancy. Antenas Enterprises in Chicago, Illinois, sells and installs satellite television systems under a contract with DISH Network. After installing a system, Antenas sends the buyer's address and other identifying information to DISH. In January 2002, Luis Garcia, an Antenas employee, identified a new customer as Jose Melendez at 220 Hawthorn Commons in Vernon Hills. The address was a restaurant—Mundelein Burrito—but Garcia designated the account as residential. Mundelein's patrons watched the De La Hoya–Vargas match on September 14, as well as three other fights on other dates, for which the restaurant paid only the residential rate to DISH and nothing to GCB. GCB filed a suit in a federal district court against Luis Dominguez, the sole proprietor of Antenas, to collect the fee.

IN THE LANGUAGE OF THE COURT
LEINENWEBER, J. [Judge]
* * * *

　　Section 605(a) [of the Cable Communications Act] states "[a]n authorized intermediary of a communication violates the Act when it divulges communication through an electronic channel to one other than the addressee." Mundelein Burrito was clearly a commercial establishment. The structure of the building, an exterior identification sign, and its location in a strip mall made this obvious. Mundelein Burrito paid only the residential fee for the four fights it broadcast to its patrons. It was not an authorized addressee of any of the four fights. By improperly listing Mundelein Burrito as a residence, Antenas Enterprises allowed

CASE CONTINUES ➡

CASE 36.1 CONTINUED ◆ the unauthorized broadcast of the [De La Hoya–Vargas fight], and three additional fights, to Mundelein Burrito. Antenas Enterprises is liable under [Section] 605 of the Act.

* * * *

The unauthorized broadcast of the four separate events deprived GCB of the full value of its business investment. * * * [Under the Cable Communications Act] an aggrieved party * * * may recover an award of damages "for each violation of [Section 605(a)] involved in the action in a sum of not less than $1,000 or more than $10,000, as the court considers just." If the violation was willful and for purposes of commercial advantage or private financial gain, the court in its discretion may increase the award of damages—by an amount not more than $100,000. The court must award attorneys' fees to the prevailing party.

GCB argues that the Antenas Enterprises failure to properly list Mundelein Burrito resulted in four separate violations. According to the license fee charged for each of the four fights that were illegally broadcast by Mundelein Burrito, the proper amount would have been $20.00 times the maximum fire code occupancy (46) or $3,680.00. Instead, due to the improper identification of the account as residential, Mundelein Burrito paid only $184.40 to broadcast the four events. GCB did not receive any of the $184.40.

* * * [Considering] the willfulness of the defendant's conduct and the deterrent value of the sanction imposed * * * twice the amount of actual damages is reasonable for this case. Therefore, Antenas Enterprises is liable to GCB for the sum of $7,360.00. Pursuant to the Act, GCB is also entitled to reasonable attorneys' fees.

* * * *

GCB argues Luis Dominguez is personally liable for Antenas Enterprises' violation of [Section] 605 of the Act. The term "person" in the Act means an "individual, partnership, association, joint stock company, trust, corporation or governmental entity."

Antenas Enterprises is a sole proprietorship, owned by Dominguez. *A sole proprietor is personally responsible for actions committed by his employees within the scope of their employment.* Accordingly, Dominguez is personally liable for the damages caused by the violation of [Section] 605 of the Act. [Emphasis added.]

DECISION AND REMEDY • *The court issued a summary judgment in GCB's favor, holding that the plaintiff was entitled to the amount of Mundelein's fee, for which Dominguez was personally liable, plus damages and attorneys' fees.*

WHAT IF THE FACTS WERE DIFFERENT? • *If Mundelein had identified itself as a residence when ordering the satellite system, how might the result in this case have been different?*

THE GLOBAL DIMENSION • *Because the Internet has made it possible for sole proprietorships to do business worldwide without greatly increasing their costs, should they be considered, for some purposes, the equivalent of other business forms? Why or why not?*

SECTION 2
FRANCHISES

Instead of setting up a sole proprietorship to market their own products or services, many entrepreneurs opt to purchase a franchise. A **franchise** is an arrangement in which the owner of a trademark, a trade name, or a copyright licenses others to use the trademark, trade name, or copyright in the selling of goods or services. A **franchisee** (a purchaser of a franchise) is generally legally independent of the **franchisor** (the seller of the franchise). At the same time, the franchise is economically dependent on the franchisor's integrated business system.

In other words, a franchisee can operate as an independent businessperson but still obtain the advantages of a regional or national organization. Today, franchising companies and their franchisees account for a significant portion of all retail sales in this country. Well-known franchises include McDonald's, 7-Eleven, and Holiday Inn. Franchising has also become a popular way for businesses to expand their operations internationally because franchisees can operate abroad without violating the legal restrictions that many nations impose on foreign ownership of businesses.

Types of Franchises

Many different kinds of businesses now sell franchises, and numerous types of franchises are available. Generally, though, franchises fall into one of three classifications: distributorships, chain-style business operations, and manufacturing or processing-plant arrangements.

DISTRIBUTORSHIP In a *distributorship,* a manufacturer (the franchisor) licenses a dealer (the franchisee) to sell its product. Often, a distributorship covers an exclusive territory. An example is an automobile dealership or a beer distributorship, such as a distributorship for Anheuser-Busch products.

CHAIN-STYLE BUSINESS OPERATION In a *chain-style business operation,* a franchise operates under a franchisor's trade name and is identified as a member of a select group of dealers that engage in the franchisor's business. The franchisee is generally required to follow standardized or prescribed methods of operation. Often, the franchisor insists that the franchisee maintain certain standards of performance. In addition, the franchisee may be required to obtain materials and supplies exclusively from the franchisor. McDonald's and most other fast-food chains are examples of this type of franchise. Chain-style franchises are also common in service-related businesses, including real estate brokerage firms, such as Century 21, and tax-preparation services, such as H&R Block, Inc.

MANUFACTURING ARRANGEMENT In a *manufacturing,* or *processing-plant, arrangement,* the franchisor transmits to the franchisee the essential ingredients or formula to make a particular product. The franchisee then markets the product either at wholesale or at retail in accordance with the franchisor's standards. Examples of this type of franchise include Coca-Cola and other soft-drink bottling companies.

Laws Governing Franchising

Because a franchise relationship is primarily a contractual relationship, it is governed by contract law. If the franchise exists primarily for the sale of products manufactured by the franchisor, the law governing sales contracts as expressed in Article 2 of the Uniform Commercial Code applies (see Chapters 19 through 22). Additionally, the federal government and most states have enacted laws governing certain aspects of franchising. Generally, these laws are designed to protect prospective franchisees from dishonest franchisors and to prevent franchisors from terminating franchises without good cause.

FEDERAL REGULATION OF FRANCHISES The federal government regulates franchising through laws that apply to specific industries and through the Franchise Rule, created by the Federal Trade Commission (FTC).

Industry-Specific Standards. Congress has enacted laws that protect franchisees in certain industries, such as automobile dealerships and service stations. These laws protect the franchisee from unreasonable demands and bad faith terminations of the franchise by the franchisor. If an automobile manufacturer–franchisor terminates a franchise because of a dealer-franchisee's failure to comply with unreasonable demands (for example, failure to attain an unrealistically high sales quota), the manufacturer may be liable for damages.[2] Similarly, federal law prescribes the conditions under which a franchisor of service stations can terminate the franchise.[3] Federal antitrust laws (to be discussed in Chapter 47) also apply in certain circumstances to prohibit certain types of anticompetitive agreements.

The Franchise Rule. The FTC's Franchise Rule requires franchisors to disclose certain material facts that a prospective franchisee needs in order to make an informed decision concerning the purchase of a franchise.[4] The rule was designed to enable potential franchisees to weigh the risks and benefits of an investment. The rule requires the franchisor to make numerous written disclosures to prospective franchisees, but franchisors can provide online disclosure documents as long as they met certain requirements. Prospective franchisees must be able to download or save all electronic disclosure documents.

Under the Franchise Rule, all representations made to a prospective franchisee must have a reasonable basis. If a franchisor provides projected earnings figures, the franchisor must indicate whether the figures are based on actual data or hypothetical examples. (The rule does not require franchisors to provide potential earnings figures, however, as discussed in the *Insight into Ethics* feature on the following page.) If a franchisor makes sales or earnings projections based on actual data for a specific franchise location, the franchisor must disclose the number and percentage of its existing franchises that have achieved this result.

Franchisors are required to explain termination, cancellation, and renewal provisions of the franchise contract to potential franchisees before the agreement is signed. In addition, a franchisor must

---

2. Automobile Dealers' Franchise Act of 1965, also known as the Automobile Dealers' Day in Court Act, 15 U.S.C. Sections 1221 *et seq.*
3. Petroleum Marketing Practices Act (PMPA) of 1979, 15 U.S.C. Sections 2801 *et seq.* See Extended Case 36.3 on pages 714 and 715.
4. 16 C.F.R. Section 436.1.

INSIGHT INTO ETHICS
Information on Potential Earnings Provided by Franchisors

Entrepreneurs who are thinking about investing in a franchise almost invariably ask, "How much will I make?" Surprisingly, the law does not require franchisors to provide any estimate of, or actual data on, the earnings potential of a franchise. Franchisors can voluntarily choose to provide earnings data on their uniform disclosure documents but are not required to do so. If franchisors do make earnings claims, as mentioned in the text, they must indicate whether these figures are actual or hypothetical, follow specific rules, and have a reasonable basis for these claims. About 75 percent of franchisors choose not to provide information about earnings potential.

The failure of the FTC's Franchise Rule to require disclosure of earnings potential has led to many complaints from franchisees. After all, some franchisees invest their life savings in franchises that ultimately fail because of unrealistic earnings expectations. Moreover, the franchisee may be legally responsible to continue operating and paying the franchisor even when the business is not turning a profit.

For instance, Thomas Anderson asked the franchisor, Rocky Mountain Chocolate Factory, Inc. (RMCF), and five of its franchisees for earnings information before he entered into a franchise agreement, but he did not receive any data. When his chocolate franchise failed to become profitable, Anderson and his partner were ordered by a court to pay $33,109 in past due royalties and interest to RMCF (plus court costs and expenses).[a]

CRITICAL THINKING

INSIGHT INTO THE BUSINESS ENVIRONMENT
If the law required franchisors to provide estimates of potential earnings, would there be more or less growth in the number of franchises? Explain your answer.

---

a. *Rocky Mountain Chocolate Factory, Inc. v. SDMS, Inc.,* 2009 WL 579516 (D.Colo. 2009).

---

provide disclosures concerning any lawsuits that it has filed against franchisees and settlement agreements that it has entered into with them. Those who violate the Franchise Rule are subject to substantial civil penalties, and the FTC can sue on behalf of injured parties to recover damages.

STATE PROTECTION FOR FRANCHISEES State legislation varies but often is aimed at protecting franchisees from unfair practices and bad faith terminations by franchisors. Approximately fifteen states have laws similar to the federal rules that require franchisors to provide presale disclosures to prospective franchisees.[5]

Some state laws also require that a disclosure document (known as the Franchise Disclosure Document, or FDD) be registered or filed with a state official. State laws may also require that a franchisor submit advertising aimed at prospective franchisees to the state for approval. To protect franchisees, a state law might require the disclosure of information such as

the actual costs of operation, recurring expenses, and profits earned, along with facts substantiating these figures. State deceptive trade practices acts (see Chapter 45) may also apply and prohibit certain types of actions on the part of franchisors. To protect franchisees against arbitrary or bad faith terminations, state law may prohibit termination without "good cause" or require that certain procedures be followed in terminating a franchising relationship.

CASE IN POINT FMS, Inc., entered into a franchise agreement with Samsung Construction Equipment North America to become an authorized dealership for the sale of Samsung-brand equipment. Volvo Construction Equipment North America, Inc., purchased Samsung's business and eventually modified and rebranded the construction equipment so that it could be sold under its own name. When Volvo canceled FMS's franchise agreement, FMS filed a lawsuit alleging that Volvo, among other things, had violated Maine's franchise law, which prohibits termination of a franchise without "good cause." A federal appellate court, however, found that because Volvo was no longer manufacturing the Samsung-brand equipment, it did have good cause to terminate FMS's franchise. Although the statute would have prevented Volvo from terminating the FMS

---

5. These states include California, Hawaii, Illinois, Indiana, Maryland, Michigan, Minnesota, New York, North Dakota, Oregon, Rhode Island, South Dakota, Virginia, Washington, and Wisconsin.

franchise as to the Samsung-brand equipment, the statute did not apply to the rebranded equipment.[6]

The Franchise Contract

The franchise relationship is defined by a contract between the franchisor and the franchisee. The franchise contract specifies the terms and conditions of the franchise and spells out the rights and duties of the franchisor and the franchisee. If either party fails to perform its contractual duties, that party may be subject to a lawsuit for breach of contract. Furthermore, if a franchisee is induced to enter into a franchise contract by the franchisor's fraudulent misrepresentation, the franchisor may be liable for damages. Generally, statutes and the case law governing franchising tend to emphasize the importance of good faith and fair dealing in franchise relationships.

Because each type of franchise relationship has its own characteristics, it is difficult to describe the broad range of details a franchising contract may include. We look next at some of the major issues that typically are addressed in a franchise contract.

PAYMENT FOR THE FRANCHISE The franchisee ordinarily pays an initial fee or lump-sum price for the franchise license (the privilege of being granted a franchise). This fee is separate from the various products that the franchisee purchases from or through the franchisor. In some industries, the franchisor relies heavily on the initial sale of the franchise for realizing a profit. In other industries, the continued dealing between the parties brings profit to both. In most situations, the franchisor receives a stated percentage of the annual (or monthly) sales or annual volume of business done by the franchisee. The franchise agreement may also require the franchisee to pay a percentage of the franchisor's advertising costs and certain administrative expenses.

BUSINESS PREMISES The franchise agreement may specify whether the premises for the business must be leased or purchased outright. Sometimes, a building must be constructed to meet the terms of the agreement. Certainly, the agreement will specify whether the franchisor or the franchisee is responsible for supplying equipment and furnishings for the premises.

LOCATION OF THE FRANCHISE Typically, the franchisor determines the territory to be served. Some franchise contracts give the franchisee exclusive rights, or "territorial rights," to a certain geographic area. Other franchise contracts, while defining the territory allotted to a particular franchise, either specifically state that the franchise is nonexclusive or are silent on the issue of territorial rights.

Many franchise cases involve disputes over territorial rights, and the implied covenant of good faith and fair dealing often comes into play in this area of franchising. If the franchise contract does not grant the franchisee exclusive territorial rights and the franchisor allows a competing franchise to be established nearby, the franchisee may suffer a significant loss in profits. In this situation, a court may hold that the franchisor's actions breached an implied covenant of good faith and fair dealing.

BUSINESS ORGANIZATION As part of the franchise agreement, the franchisor may require that the business use a particular organizational form and capital structure. The franchise agreement may also set out standards of operation in such aspects of the business as sales quotas, quality, and record keeping. Additionally, a franchisor may retain stringent control over the training of personnel involved in the operation and over administrative aspects of the business.

QUALITY CONTROL The day-to-day operation of the franchise business normally is left up to the franchisee. Nonetheless, the franchise agreement may provide for some degree of supervision and control by the franchisor so that it can protect the franchise's name and reputation. When the franchise prepares a product, such as food, or provides a service, such as motel accommodations, the contract often states that the franchisor will establish certain standards for the facility. Typically, the contract will state that the franchisor is permitted to make periodic inspections to ensure that the standards are being maintained.

As a general rule, the validity of a provision permitting the franchisor to establish and enforce certain quality standards is unquestioned. Because the franchisor has a legitimate interest in maintaining the quality of the product or service to protect its name and reputation, it can exercise greater control in this area than would otherwise be tolerated. If a franchisor exercises too much control over the operations of its franchisees, however, the franchisor risks potential liability under agency law for the tortious acts of the franchisees' employees (see Chapter 33).

---

6. *FMS, Inc. v. Volvo Construction Equipment North America, Inc.*, 557 F.3d 758 (7th Cir. 2009).

PRICING ARRANGEMENTS Franchises provide the franchisor with an outlet for the firm's goods and services. Depending on the nature of the business, the franchisor may require the franchisee to purchase certain supplies from the franchisor at an established price.[7] A franchisor cannot, however, set the prices at which the franchisee will resell the goods because such price setting may be a violation of state or federal antitrust laws, or both. A franchisor can suggest retail prices but cannot mandate them.

◤▬▬▬ SECTION 3 ▬▬▬◢
FRANCHISE TERMINATION

The duration of the franchise is a matter to be determined between the parties. Generally, a franchise relationship starts with a short trial period, such as a year, so that the franchisee and the franchisor can determine whether they want to stay in business with one another. Usually, the franchise agreement specifies that termination must be "for cause," such as the death or disability of the franchisee, insolvency of the franchisee, breach of the franchise agreement, or failure to meet specified sales quotas. Most franchise contracts provide that notice of termination must be given. If no set time for termination is specified, then a reasonable time, with notice, is implied. A franchisee must be given reasonable time to wind up the business—that is, to do the accounting and return the copyright or trademark or any other property of the franchisor.

A franchise agreement may grant the franchisee the opportunity to cure an ordinary, curable breach within a certain period of time after notice to enable the franchisee to postpone, or even avoid, the termination of the contract. Could a franchisee's conduct so seriously undermine the basis of the agreement that the franchisor could cancel the contract despite a notice-and-cure provision? That was the issue in the following case.

---

7. Although a franchisor can require franchisees to purchase supplies from it, requiring a franchisee to purchase exclusively from the franchisor may violate federal antitrust laws (see Chapter 47).

CASE 36.2
LJL Transportation, Inc. v. Pilot Air Freight Corp.
Supreme Court of Pennsylvania, 599 Pa. 546, 962 A.2d 639 (2009).
www.courts.state.pa.us/T/SupremeCourt[a]

BACKGROUND AND FACTS • Pilot Air Freight Corporation moves freight through a network of company-owned and company-franchised locations at airports and other sites. Franchisees included LJL Transportation, Inc., which is owned by Louis Pektor and Leo Decker. The franchise agreement required LJL to assign all shipments to the Pilot network. The agreement also provided that "Pilot shall allow Franchisee an opportunity to cure a default within ninety (90) days of receipt of written notice." After eight years as a Pilot franchisee, LJL began to divert shipments to Northeast Transportation, a competing service owned by Pektor and Decker. On learning of the diversions, Pilot terminated the franchise agreement. LJL filed a suit in a Pennsylvania state court against Pilot, alleging breach of contract and asserting a right to cure. The court issued a summary judgment in Pilot's favor, and a state intermediate appellate court affirmed. LJL appealed.

IN THE LANGUAGE OF THE COURT
Justice *TODD.*
* * * *

* * * There is no Pennsylvania case law directly governing the resolution of the particular question presented in this appeal * * *. Courts from other jurisdictions appear to be in accord that * * * a termination clause affording the right to notice and cure is * * * a cumulative remedy which does not bar the non-breaching party from exercising

---

a. In the "Conducting Business with the Court" section, click on "Supreme Court Opinions." On that page, in the "Caption" box, type "LJL"; in the "Month" pull-down menu, select "January"; in the "Year" pull-down menu, choose "2009"; and click on "Search." In the result, click on the link to access the opinion. The Unified Judicial System of Pennsylvania maintains this Web site.

CASE 36.2 CONTINUED ➧ other remedies available to it in the event of a breach by the other party going directly to the heart of the contract, and destroying the fundamental trust upon which the contractual relationship is built.

＊ ＊ ＊ ＊

＊ ＊ ＊ [This] view [is] consistent with the law ＊ ＊ ＊ regarding the effect of material breaches, and likewise consistent with the policy ＊ ＊ ＊ requiring good faith and honesty in the performance and enforcement of contractual relations.

＊ ＊ ＊ ＊

＊ ＊ ＊ *Self-dealing is the antithesis [exact opposite] of that [policy] and it violates the relationship of trust necessarily underlying such agreements.* [Emphasis added.]

The franchisee's breach of its implied duty of honesty and fidelity [goes] to the heart of the contract. Merely requiring the franchisee to retroactively undo its wrongdoing ＊ ＊ ＊ would not be an adequate remedy. [Emphasis added.]

＊ ＊ ＊ ＊

＊ ＊ ＊ Consequently, we have no difficulty in concluding that when there is a breach of contract going directly to the essence of the contract, which is so exceedingly grave as to irreparably damage the trust between the contracting parties, the non-breaching party may terminate the contract without notice ＊ ＊ ＊ . Requiring such notice before termination under such circumstances would be a useless gesture, as such a breach may not reasonably be cured. Such a breach is so fundamentally destructive, it understandably and inevitably causes the trust which is the bedrock foundation and veritable lifeblood of the parties' contractual relationship to essentially evaporate. We find our law does not require a non-breaching party to prolong a contractual relationship under such circumstances.

DECISION AND REMEDY • *The Pennsylvania Supreme Court affirmed the lower court's judgment. A franchise agreement may be terminated immediately when there is a material breach of the contract so serious it goes directly to the heart and essence of the contract, rendering the breach incurable.*

THE ETHICAL DIMENSION • *From an ethical perspective, if LJL had been allowed to invoke the right-to-cure provision, could it have undone its wrongdoing so that the franchise relationship could have continued? Why or why not?*

WHAT IF THE FACTS WERE DIFFERENT? • *Suppose that Pilot had terminated its franchise agreement simply because it no longer wished to be bound. Would refusing to allow LJL to invoke the right-to-cure provision in that circumstance have been valid?*

Wrongful Termination

Because a franchisor's termination of a franchise often has adverse consequences for the franchisee, much franchise litigation involves claims of wrongful termination. Generally, the termination provisions of contracts are more favorable to the franchisor than to the franchisee. This means that the franchisee, who normally invests a substantial amount of time and financial resources in making the franchise operation successful, may receive little or nothing for the business on termination. The franchisor owns the trademark and hence the business. It is in this area that statutory and case law become important. The federal and state laws discussed earlier attempt, among other things, to protect franchisees from the arbitrary or unfair termination of their franchises by the franchisors.

In the following case, a group of service-station franchisees claimed that their franchisor had violated the Petroleum Marketing Practices Act (PMPA) of 1979, which limits the circumstances in which petroleum franchisors may terminate a franchise. The franchisees contended that changes in the rental provisions of the franchise contract had effectively increased their fuel costs, thereby "constructively" (in effect) terminating the franchises. The franchisees, however, had continued to operate their service stations. Under the PMPA, must a franchisee abandon its franchise in order to recover for constructive termination? That was the issue facing the United States Supreme Court.

✴ EXTENDED CASE 36.3 ✴
Mac's Shell Service, Inc. v. Shell Oil Products Co.

Supreme Court of the United States, ___U.S.___, 130 S.Ct. 1251, 176 L.Ed.2d 36 (2010).
www.supremecourt.gov[a]

IN THE LANGUAGE OF THE COURT

Justice *ALITO* delivered the opinion of the Court.

* * * *

This litigation involves a dispute between Shell Oil Company (Shell), a petroleum franchisor, and several Shell franchisees in Massachusetts. Pursuant to their franchise agreements with Shell, each franchisee was required to pay Shell monthly rent for use of the service-station premises. For many years, Shell offered the franchisees a rent subsidy that reduced the monthly rent by a set amount for every gallon of motor fuel a franchisee sold above a specified threshold. Shell renewed the subsidy annually through notices that "explicitly provided for cancellation [of the rent subsidy] with thirty days' notice." Nonetheless, Shell representatives made various oral representations to the franchisees "that the subsidy or something like it would always exist."

In 1998, Shell joined with two other oil companies to create Motiva Enterprises LLC (Motiva), a joint venture that combined the companies' petroleum-marketing operations in the eastern United States. Shell assigned to Motiva its rights and obligations under the relevant franchise agreements. * * * Effective January 1, 2000, Motiva ended the volume-based rent subsidy, thus increasing the franchisees' rent.

In July 2001, sixty-three Shell franchisees (hereinafter dealers) filed suit against Shell and Motiva in Federal District Court. Their complaint alleged that Motiva's

discontinuation of the rent subsidy constituted a breach of contract under state law. Additionally, the dealers asserted [a claim] under the PMPA [Petroleum Marketing Practices Act]. * * * They maintained that Shell and Motiva, by eliminating the rent subsidy, had "constructively terminated" their franchises in violation of the Act.

After a two-week trial involving eight of the dealers, the jury found against Shell and Motiva on all claims. Both before and after the jury's verdict, Shell and Motiva moved for judgment as a matter of law on the dealers' [PMPA claim]. They argued that they could not be found liable for constructive termination under the Act because none of the dealers had abandoned their franchises in response to Motiva's elimination of the rent subsidy—something Shell and Motiva said was a necessary element of any constructive termination claim. * * * The District Court denied [the motion], and Shell and Motiva appealed. [The U.S. Court of Appeals for the First Circuit affirmed the district court's judgment, and Shell and Motiva appealed to the United States Supreme Court.]

* * * *

The * * * question we are asked to decide is whether a service-station franchisee may recover for constructive termination under the PMPA when the franchisor's allegedly wrongful conduct did not force the franchisee to abandon its franchise. *For the reasons that follow, we conclude that a necessary element of any constructive termination claim under the Act is that the franchisor's conduct forced an end to the franchisee's use of*

the franchisor's trademark, purchase of the franchisor's fuel, or occupation of the franchisor's service station. [Emphasis added.]

When given its ordinary meaning, the text of the PMPA prohibits only that franchisor conduct that has the effect of ending a franchise. As relevant here, the Act provides that "no franchisor * * * may * * * terminate any franchise," except for an enumerated reason and after providing written notice.

The word "terminate" ordinarily means "put an end to." * * * The object of the verb "terminate" is the noun "franchise," a term the Act defines as "any contract" for the provision of one (or more) of the three elements of a typical petroleum franchise. Thus, when given its ordinary meaning, the Act is violated only if an agreement for the use of a trademark, purchase of motor fuel, or lease of a premises is "put [to] an end" * * * . Conduct that does not force an end to the franchise, in contrast, is not prohibited by the Act's plain terms.

* * * *

Requiring franchisees to abandon their franchises before claiming constructive termination is also consistent with the general understanding of the doctrine of constructive termination. As applied in analogous legal contexts—both now and at the time Congress enacted the PMPA—*a plaintiff must actually sever a particular legal relationship in order to maintain a claim for constructive termination.* For example, courts have long recognized a theory of constructive discharge in the field of employment law. Similarly, landlord-tenant law has long recognized the

---

a. Select "Opinions" under "Supreme Court Documents" in the left column. On the page that opens, under "Current Term," select "Latest Slip Opinions." In the list of cases that appears, scroll down to "30" and click on the case title to access the opinion. The United States Supreme Court maintains this Web site.

EXTENDED CASE 36.3 CONTINUED ➡

concept of constructive eviction. The general rule under that doctrine is that a tenant must actually move out in order to claim constructive eviction. [Emphasis added.]

As generally understood in these and other contexts, a termination is deemed "constructive" because it is the plaintiff, rather than the defendant, who formally puts an end to the particular legal relationship—not because there is no end to the relationship at all. There is no reason why a different understanding should apply to constructive

termination claims under the PMPA. At the time when it enacted the statute, Congress presumably was aware of how courts applied the doctrine of constructive termination in these analogous legal contexts. And in the absence of any contrary evidence, we think it reasonable to interpret the Act in a way that is consistent with this well-established body of law.

* * * *

We therefore hold that a necessary element of any constructive termination claim under the PMPA is that the complained-of conduct forced an end to the franchisee's use of the franchisor's trademark,

purchase of the franchisor's fuel, or occupation of the franchisor's service station. Because none of the dealers in this litigation abandoned any element of their franchise operations in response to Motiva's elimination of the rent subsidy, they cannot maintain a constructive termination claim on the basis of that conduct.

* * * *

The judgment of the Court of Appeals is reversed * * *. The cases are remanded for further proceedings consistent with this opinion.

It is so ordered.

QUESTIONS

1. The PMPA regulates only the circumstances in which service-station franchisors may terminate a franchise or decline to renew a franchise relationship. Are there any reasons why Congress might have limited the scope of the PMPA to just these two aspects of franchising? Explain.
2. Suppose that some of the service-station franchisees, on the expiration of their contracts with Shell, signed a renewal agreement with Motiva, even though the franchisees believed that the rental terms of the new agreement were unacceptable. Given the Court's reasoning on the issue of constructive termination, would the franchisees have been likely to succeed in a suit against the franchisor for "constructive nonrenewal" of the franchise agreement? Why or why not?

The Importance of Good Faith and Fair Dealing

Generally, both statutory law and case law emphasize the importance of good faith and fair dealing in terminating a franchise relationship. In determining whether a franchisor has acted in good faith when terminating a franchise agreement, the courts usually try to balance the rights of both parties. If a court perceives that a franchisor has arbitrarily or unfairly terminated a franchise, the franchisee will be provided with a remedy for wrongful termination. If a franchisor's decision to terminate a franchise was made in the normal course of the franchisor's business operations, however, and reasonable notice of termination was given to the franchisee, in most instances a court will not consider the termination wrongful.

CASE IN POINT Chapin Miller acquired Chic Miller's Chevrolet, a General Motors Corporation (GM) dealership. Chic Miller's entered into lending

agreements, commonly known as floor plan financing, to enable it to buy new vehicles from GM. At first, the dealership had floor plan financing through GM, but then it switched to Chase Manhattan Bank. In 2002, Chase declined to provide further financing, and Chic Miller's was unable to obtain a loan from any other lender, including GM. Under the franchise's "Dealer Sales and Service Agreement," GM could terminate a dealership for "Failure of Dealer to maintain the line of credit." In March 2003, GM terminated Chic Miller's franchise. Chic Miller's claimed that GM had failed to act in good faith in terminating the franchise, but the court held in GM's favor. GM had good cause to terminate the dealership because Chic Miller's failed to maintain floor plan financing, which was a material requirement under the franchise agreement.[8]

---

8. *Chic Miller's Chevrolet, Inc. v. General Motors, Inc.*, 352 F.Supp.2d 251 (D.Conn. 2005).

REVIEWING

Sole Proprietorships and Franchises

Carlos Del Rey decided to open a Mexican fast-food restaurant and signed a franchise contract with a national chain called La Grande Enchilada. The contract required the franchisee to strictly follow the franchisor's operating manual and stated that failure to do so would be grounds for terminating the franchise contract. The manual set forth detailed operating procedures and safety standards, and provided that a La Grande Enchilada representative would inspect the restaurant monthly to ensure compliance. Nine months after Del Rey began operating his restaurant, a spark from the grill ignited an oily towel in the kitchen. No one was injured, but by the time firefighters were able to put out the fire, the kitchen had sustained extensive damage. The cook told the fire department that the towel was "about two feet from the grill" when it caught fire. This was in compliance with the franchisor's manual that required towels be placed at least one foot from the grills. Nevertheless, the next day La Grande Enchilada notified Del Rey that his franchise would terminate in thirty days for failure to follow the prescribed safety procedures. Using the information presented in the chapter, answer the following questions.

1. What type of franchise was Del Rey's La Grande Enchilada restaurant?
2. If Del Rey operates the restaurant as a sole proprietorship, then who bears the loss for the damaged kitchen? Explain.
3. Assume that Del Rey files a lawsuit against La Grande Enchilada, claiming that his franchise was wrongfully terminated. What is the main factor that a court would consider in determining whether the franchise was wrongfully terminated?
4. Would a court be likely to rule that La Grande Enchilada had good cause to terminate Del Rey's franchise in this situation? Why or why not?

DEBATE THIS: *All franchisors should be required by law to provide a comprehensive estimate of the profitability of a prospective franchise based on the experiences of their existing franchisees.*

TERMS AND CONCEPTS

franchise 708   sole proprietorship 706
franchisee 708
entrepreneur 706   franchisor 708

QUESTIONS AND CASE PROBLEMS

36–1. Franchising Maria, Pablo, and Vicky are recent college graduates who would like to go into business for themselves. They are considering purchasing a franchise. If they enter into a franchising arrangement, they would have the support of a large company that could answer any questions they might have. Also, a firm that has been in business for many years would be experienced in dealing with some of the problems that novice businesspersons might encounter. These and other attributes of franchises can lessen some of the risks of the marketplace. What other aspects of franchising—positive and negative—should Maria, Pablo, and Vicky consider before committing themselves to a particular franchise?

36–2. QUESTION WITH SAMPLE ANSWER: Control of a Franchise.

National Foods, Inc., sells franchises to its fast-food restaurants, known as Chicky-D's. Under the franchise agreement, franchisees agree to hire and train employees strictly according to Chicky-D's standards. Chicky-D's regional supervisors are required to approve all job candidates before they are hired and all general policies affecting those employees. Chicky-D's reserves the right to terminate a franchise for violating the franchisor's rules. In practice, however, Chicky-D's regional supervisors routinely approve new employees and individual franchisees' policies. After several incidents of racist comments and conduct by Tim, a recently hired assistant manager at a Chicky-D's, Sharon, a counterperson at the restaurant, resigns. Sharon files a suit in a federal district court against National. National files a motion for summary judgment, arguing that it is not liable for harassment by franchise employees. Will the court grant National's motion? Why or why not?

- **For a sample answer to Question 36–2, go to Appendix I at the end of this text.**

36–3. The Franchise Contract Otmar has secured a high-quality ice cream franchise. The franchise agreement calls for Otmar to sell the ice cream only at a specific location; to buy all the ice cream from the franchisor; to order and sell all the flavors produced by the franchisor; and to refrain from selling any ice cream stored for more than two weeks after delivery by the franchisor, as the quality of the ice cream declines after that period of time. After two months of operation, Otmar believes that he can increase his profits by moving the store to another part of the city. He refuses to order even a limited quantity of the "fruit delight" flavor because of its higher cost, and he has sold ice cream that has been stored longer than two weeks without customer complaint. Otmar maintains that the franchisor has no right to restrict him in these practices. Discuss his claims.

36–4. Franchise Termination In the automobile industry, luxury-car customers are considered the most demanding segment of the market with respect to customer service. Jaguar Cars, a division of Ford Motor Co. until 2008, was the exclusive U.S. distributor of Jaguar luxury cars. Jaguar Cars distributes its products through franchised dealers. In April 1999, Dave Ostrem Imports, Inc., an authorized Jaguar dealer in Des Moines, Iowa, contracted to sell its dealership to Midwest Automotive III, LLC. A Jaguar franchise generally cannot be sold without Jaguar Cars' permission. Jaguar Cars asked Midwest Auto to submit three years of customer satisfaction index (CSI) data for all franchises with which its owners had been associated. (CSI data are intended to measure how well dealers treat their customers and satisfy their customers' needs. Jaguar Cars requires above-average CSI ratings for its dealers.) Most of Midwest Auto's scores fell below the national average. Jaguar Cars rejected Midwest Auto's application and sought to terminate the franchise, claiming that a transfer of the dealership would be "substantially detrimental" to the distribution of Jaguar vehicles in the community. Was Jaguar Cars' attempt to terminate this franchise reasonable? Why or why not? [*Midwest Automotive III, LLC v. Iowa Department of Transportation*, 646 N.W.2d 417 (Iowa 2002)]

36–5. The Franchise Contract On August 23, 1995, Climaco Guzman entered into a commercial janitorial services franchise agreement with Jan-Pro Cleaning Systems, Inc., in Rhode Island for a franchise fee of $3,285. In the agreement, Jan-Pro promised to furnish Guzman with "one (1) or more customer account(s) . . . amounting to $8,000.00 gross volume per year. . . . No portion of the franchise fee is refundable except and to the extent that the Franchisor, within 120 business days following the date of execution of the Franchise Agreement, fails to provide accounts." By February 19, Guzman had not received any accounts and demanded a full refund. Jan-Pro then promised "two accounts grossing $12,000 per year in income." Despite its assurances, Jan-Pro did not have the ability to furnish accounts that met the requirements. In September, Guzman filed a suit in a Rhode Island state court against Jan-Pro, alleging, in part, fraudulent misrepresentation. Should the court rule in Guzman's favor? Why or why not? [*Guzman v. Jan-Pro Cleaning Systems, Inc.*, 839 A.2d 504 (R.I. 2003)]

36–6. Sole Proprietorship James Ferguson operates Jim's 11#E Auto Sales in Jonesborough, Tennessee, as a sole proprietorship. In 1999, Consumers Insurance Co. issued a policy to "Jim Ferguson, Jim's 11#E Auto Sales" covering "Owned 'Autos' Only." *Auto* was defined to include "a land motor vehicle," which was not further explained in the policy. Coverage extended to damage caused by the owner or driver of an underinsured motor vehicle. In 2000, Ferguson bought and titled in his own name a 1976 Harley-Davidson motorcycle, intending to repair and sell the cycle through his dealership. In October 2001, while riding the motorcycle, Ferguson was struck by an auto driven by John Jenkins. Ferguson filed a suit in a Tennessee state court against Jenkins, who was underinsured with respect to Ferguson's medical bills, and Consumers. The insurer argued, among other things, that because the motorcycle was bought and titled in Ferguson's own name, and he was riding it at the time of the accident, it was his personal vehicle and thus was not covered under the dealership's policy. What is the relationship between a sole proprietor and a sole proprietorship? How might this status affect the court's decision in this case? [*Ferguson v. Jenkins*, 204 S.W.3d 779 (Tenn.App. 2006)]

36–7. CASE PROBLEM WITH SAMPLE ANSWER: Franchise Termination.

Walid Elkhatib, a Palestinian Arab, emigrated to the United States in 1971 and became a U.S. citizen. Eight years later, Elkhatib bought a Dunkin' Donuts, Inc., franchise in Bellwood, Illinois. Dunkin' Donuts began offering breakfast sandwiches with bacon, ham, or sausage through its franchises in 1984, but Elkhatib refused to sell these items at his store on the ground that his religion forbade the handling of pork. In 1995, Elkhatib opened a second franchise in Berkeley, Illinois, at which he also refused to sell pork products. The next year, at both locations, Elkhatib began selling meatless sandwiches. In 1998, Elkhatib opened a third franchise in Westchester, Illinois. When he proposed to relocate this franchise, Dunkin' Donuts refused to approve the new location and added that it

would not renew any of his franchise agreements because he did not carry the full sandwich line. Elkhatib filed a suit in a federal district court against Dunkin' Donuts and others. The defendants filed a motion for summary judgment. Did Dunkin' Donuts act in good faith in its relationship with Elkhatib? Explain. [*Elkhatib v. Dunkin' Donuts, Inc., 493 F.3d 827 (7th Cir. 2007)*]

• To view a sample answer for Problem 36–7, go to this book's Web site at www.cengage.com/blaw/clarkson, select "Chapter 36," and click on "Case Problem with Sample Answer."

36–8. Sole Proprietorship Julie Anne Gaskill is an oral and maxillofacial surgeon in Bowling Green, Kentucky. Her medical practice is a sole proprietorship that consists of Gaskill as the sole surgeon and an office staff. She sees every patient, exercises all professional judgment and skill, and manages the business. When Gaskill and her spouse, John Robbins, initiated divorce proceedings in a Kentucky state court, her accountant estimated the value of the practice at $221,610, excluding goodwill. Robbins's accountant estimated the value at $669,075, including goodwill. (Goodwill is the ability or reputation of a business to draw customers, get them to return, and contribute to future profitability.) How can a sole proprietor's reputation, skill, and relationships with customers be valued? Could these qualities be divided into "personal" and "enterprise" goodwill, with some goodwill associated with the business and some solely due to the personal qualities of the proprietor? If so, what might comprise each type? Is this an effective method for valuing Gaskill's practice? Discuss. [*Gaskill v. Robbins, 282 S.W.3d 306 (Ky. 2009)*]

36–9. Franchise Disclosure Peaberry Coffee, Inc., owned and operated about twenty company stores in the Denver area. The company began a franchise program and prepared a disclosure document as required by the Federal Trade Commission (FTC). Peaberry sold ten franchises, and each franchisee received a disclosure document. Later, when the franchises did not do well, the franchisees sued Peaberry, claiming that its FTC disclosure document had been fraudulent. Specifically, the franchisees claimed that Peaberry had not disclosed that most of the company stores were unprofitable and that its parent company had suffered significant financial losses over the years. In addition, the trial court found that an article in the *Denver Business Journal*—in which an

executive had said that Peaberry was profitable—was fraudulent. This article had been included in the franchisees' information packets. The district court dismissed the franchisees' complaint, noting that the FTC disclosure document had contained an exculpatory clause (see Chapter 13). This clause said that the buyers should not rely on any material that was not in the franchise contract itself. The franchisees appealed. Can a franchisor disclaim the relevance of the information it provides to franchisees? Why or why not? [*Colorado Coffee Bean, LLC v. Peaberry Coffee, Inc., ___ P.3d ___ (Colo.App. 2010)*]

36–10. A QUESTION OF ETHICS: Sole Proprietorship.

In August 2004, Ralph Vilardo contacted Travel Center, Inc., in Cincinnati, Ohio, to buy a trip to Florida in December for his family to celebrate his fiftieth wedding anniversary. Vilardo paid $6,900 to David Sheets, the sole proprietor of Travel Center. Vilardo also paid $195 to Sheets for a separate trip to Florida in February 2005. Sheets assured Vilardo that everything was set, but in fact no arrangements were made. Later, two unauthorized charges for travel services totaling $1,182.35 appeared on Vilardo's credit-card statement. Vilardo filed a suit in an Ohio state court against Sheets and his business, alleging, among other things, fraud and violations of the state consumer protection law. Vilardo served Sheets and Travel Center with copies of the complaint, the summons, a request for admissions, and other documents filed with the court, including a motion for summary judgment. Each of these filings asked for a response within a certain time period. Sheets responded once on his own behalf with a denial of all of Vilardo's claims. Travel Center did not respond. [*Vilardo v. Sheets, ___ Ohio App.3d ___ (2006)*]

(a) Almost four months after Vilardo filed his complaint, Sheets decided that he was unable to adequately represent himself and retained an attorney, who asked the court for more time. Should the court grant this request? Why or why not? Ultimately, what should the court rule?

(b) Sheets admitted that Travel Center, Inc., was a sole proprietorship. He also argued that liability might be imposed on his business but not on himself. How would you rule with respect to this argument? Why? Would there be anything unethical about allowing Sheets to avoid liability on this basis? Explain.

LEGAL RESEARCH EXERCISES ON THE WEB

Go to this text's Web site at www.cengage.com/blaw/clarkson, select "Chapter 36," and click on "Practical Internet Exercises." There you will find the following Internet research exercises that you can perform to learn more about the topics covered in this chapter.

Practical Internet Exercise 36–1: Legal Perspective
Starting a Business

Practical Internet Exercise 36–2: Management Perspective
Franchises

CHAPTER 37

Partnerships and Limited Liability Partnerships

Traditionally, the two most common forms of business organization selected by two or more persons entering into business together have been the partnership and the corporation. A *partnership* arises from an agreement, express or implied, between two or more persons to carry on a business for a profit. Partners are co-owners of the business and have joint control over its operation and the right to share in its profits. In this chapter, we examine several forms of partnership. (Corporations will be discussed in Chapters 39 through 41.)

We begin the chapter with an examination of traditional partnerships, or *general partnerships,* and the rights and duties of partners in this business entity.

We then examine some special forms of partnerships known as *limited partnerships* and *limited liability partnerships,* which receive a different treatment under the law.

SECTION 1
BASIC PARTNERSHIP CONCEPTS

Partnerships are governed both by common law concepts (in particular, those relating to agency) and by statutory law. As in so many other areas of business law, the National Conference of Commissioners on Uniform State Laws has drafted uniform laws for partnerships, and these have been widely adopted by the states.

Agency Concepts and Partnership Law

When two or more persons agree to do business as partners, they enter into a special relationship with one another. To an extent, their relationship is similar to an agency relationship because each partner is deemed to be the agent of the other partners and of the partnership. The agency concepts that were discussed in Chapters 32 and 33 thus apply—specifically, the imputation of knowledge of, and responsibility for, acts carried out within the scope of the partnership relationship. In their relationships with one another, partners, like agents, are bound by fiduciary ties.

In one important way, however, partnership law is distinct from agency law. In a partnership, two or more persons agree to commit some or all of their funds or other assets, labor, and skills to a business with the understanding that profits and losses will be shared. Thus, each partner has an ownership interest in the firm. In a nonpartnership agency relationship, the agent usually does not have an ownership interest in the business, nor is he or she obligated to bear a portion of ordinary business losses.

The Uniform Partnership Act

The Uniform Partnership Act (UPA) governs the operation of partnerships *in the absence of express agreement* and has done much to reduce controversies in the law relating to partnerships. Except for Louisiana, all of the states, as well as the District of Columbia, have adopted the UPA. A majority of the states have enacted the most recent version of the UPA to provide limited liability for partners in a limited liability partnership.[1] Excerpts from the latest version of the UPA are presented in Appendix E.

---

1. At the time this book went to press, more than two-thirds of the states, as well as the District of Columbia, Puerto Rico, and the U.S. Virgin Islands, had adopted the UPA with the 1997 amendments.

Definition of a Partnership

Parties sometimes find themselves in conflict over whether their business enterprise is a legal partnership. The UPA defines a **partnership** as "an association of two or more persons to carry on as co-owners a business for profit" [UPA 101(6)]. Note that the UPA's definition of *person* includes corporations, so a corporation can be a partner in a partnership [UPA 101(10)]. The *intent* to associate is a key element of a partnership, and one cannot join a partnership unless all other partners consent [UPA 401(i)].

When Does a Partnership Exist?

In resolving disputes over whether a partnership exists, courts usually look for the following three essential elements, which are implicit in the UPA's definition of a general partnership:

1. A sharing of profits or losses.
2. A joint ownership of the business.
3. An equal right to be involved in the management of the business.

If the evidence in a particular case is insufficient to establish all three factors, the UPA provides a set of guidelines to be used. For example, the sharing of profits and losses from a business creates a presumption that a partnership exists. No presumption is made, however, if the profits were received as payment of any of the following [UPA 202(c)(3)]:

1. A debt by installments or interest on a loan.
2. Wages of an employee or for the services of an independent contractor.
3. Rent to a landlord.
4. An annuity to a surviving spouse or representative of a deceased partner.
5. A sale of the **goodwill** (the valuable reputation of a business viewed as an intangible asset) of a business or property.

To illustrate: A debtor owes a creditor $5,000 on an unsecured debt. To repay the debt, the debtor agrees to pay (and the creditor, to accept) 10 percent of the debtor's monthly business profits until the loan with interest has been paid. Although the creditor is sharing profits from the business, the debtor and creditor are not presumed to be partners.

Joint Property Ownership and Partnership Status

Joint ownership of property does not in and of itself create a partnership. In fact, the sharing of gross returns and even profits from such ownership "does not by itself establish a partnership" [UPA 202(c)(1) and (2)].[2] Suppose that MacPherson and Bunker jointly own a piece of farmland and lease it to a farmer for a share of the profits from the farming operation in lieu of set rental payments. This arrangement normally would not make MacPherson, Bunker, and the farmer partners.

Note, though, that while the sharing of profits from ownership of property does not prove the existence of a partnership, sharing *both profits and losses* usually does. For example, two sisters, Zoe and Cienna, buy a restaurant together, open a joint bank account from which they pay for supplies and expenses, and share the proceeds (and losses) that the restaurant generates. Zoe manages the restaurant and Cienna handles the bookkeeping. After eight years, Cienna stops keeping the books and does no other work for the restaurant. Zoe claims that she and Cienna did not establish a partnership. In this situation, a court would find that a partnership existed because the sisters shared management responsibilities, had a joint account, and shared the profits and losses of the restaurant equally.

Entity versus Aggregate

At common law, a partnership was treated only as an aggregate of individuals and never as a separate legal entity. Thus, at common law a lawsuit could never be brought by or against the firm in its own name; each individual partner had to sue or be sued.

Today, in contrast, a majority of the states follow the UPA and treat a partnership as an entity for most purposes. For example, a partnership usually can sue or be sued, collect judgments, and have all accounting procedures in the name of the partnership entity [UPA 201, 307(a)]. As an entity, a partnership may hold the title to real or personal property in its name rather than in the names of the individual partners. Additionally, federal procedural laws permit the partnership to be treated as an entity in suits in federal courts and bankruptcy proceedings.

Tax Treatment of Partnerships

Modern law does treat a partnership as an aggregate of the individual partners rather than a separate legal entity in one situation—for federal income tax purposes. The partnership is a pass-through entity and not a taxpaying entity. A **pass-through entity**

---

2. See, for example, *In re Estate of Ivanchak,* 169 Ohio App.3d 140, 862 N.E.2d 151 (2006).

is a business entity that has no tax liability; the entity's income is passed through to the owners of the entity, who pay taxes on it. Thus, the income or losses the partnership incurs are "passed through" the entity framework and attributed to the partners on their individual tax returns. The partnership itself pays no taxes and is responsible only for filing an **information return** with the Internal Revenue Service. A partner's profit from the partnership (whether distributed or not) is taxed as individual income to the individual partner.

SECTION 2
PARTNERSHIP FORMATION

As a general rule, agreements to form a partnership can be *oral, written,* or *implied by conduct.* Some partnership agreements, however, must be in writing (or an electronic record) to be legally enforceable under the Statute of Frauds (see Chapter 15 for details). For example, a partnership agreement that authorizes the partners to deal in transfers of real property must be evidenced by a sufficient writing (or record).

The Partnership Agreement

A partnership agreement, also known as **articles of partnership,** can include almost any terms that the parties wish, unless they are illegal or contrary to public policy or statute [UPA 103]. The terms commonly included in a partnership agreement are listed in Exhibit 37–1 below.

Duration of the Partnership

The partnership agreement can specify the duration of the partnership by stating that it will continue until a designated date or until the completion of a particular project. This is called a *partnership for a term.* Generally, withdrawal from a partnership for a term prematurely (before the expiration date) constitutes a breach of the agreement, and the responsible partner can be held liable for any resulting losses [UPA 602(b)(2)].

If no fixed duration is specified, the partnership is a *partnership at will.* Any partner can dissolve this type of partnership at any time without violating the agreement and without incurring liability for losses to other partners that result from the termination.

EXHIBIT 37–1 • Terms Commonly Included in a Partnership Agreement

TERM	DESCRIPTION
Basic Structure	• Name of the partnership. • Names of the partners. • Location of the business and the state law under which the partnership is organized. • Purpose of the partnership. • Duration of the partnership.
Capital Contributions	• Amount of capital that each partner is contributing. • The agreed-on value of any real or personal property that is contributed instead of cash. • How gains and losses on contributed capital will be allocated and whether contributions will earn interest.
Sharing of Profits and Losses	• Percentage of the profits and losses of the business that each partner will receive. • When distributions of profit will be made and how net profit will be calculated.
Management and Control	• How management responsibilities will be divided among the partners. • Name(s) of the managing partner or partners and whether other partners have voting rights.
Accounting and Partnership Records	• Name of the bank in which the partnership will maintain its business and checking accounts. • Statement that an accounting of partnership records will be maintained and that any partner, or her or his agent, can review these records at any time. • The dates of the partnership's fiscal year (if used) and when the annual audit of the books will take place.
Dissociation and Dissolution	• Events that will cause the dissociation of a partner or dissolve the partnership, such as the retirement, death, or incapacity of any partner. • How partnership property will be valued and apportioned on dissociation and dissolution. • Whether an arbitrator will determine the value of partnership property on dissociation and dissolution and whether that determination will be binding.
Arbitration	• Whether arbitration is required for any dispute relating to the partnership agreement.

Partnership by Estoppel

Occasionally, persons who are not partners nevertheless hold themselves out as partners and make representations that third parties rely on in dealing with them. In such a situation, a court may conclude that a **partnership by estoppel** exists and impose liability—but not partnership *rights*—on the alleged partner or partners. Similarly, a partnership by estoppel may be imposed when a partner represents, expressly or impliedly, that a nonpartner is a member of the firm. Whenever a third person has reasonably and detrimentally relied on the representation that a nonpartner was part of the partnership, a partnership by estoppel is deemed to exist. When this occurs, the nonpartner is regarded as an agent whose acts are binding on the partnership [UPA 308].

CASE IN POINT Gary Chavers operated Chavers Welding and Construction (CWC). Gary's two sons began to work in the business after graduating from high school. CWC contracted with Epsco, Inc., to provide payroll services for CWC. Epsco extended credit to CWC, which the Chaverses represented was a partnership. When CWC's account was more than $80,000 delinquent, Epsco sued to recover payment. The father filed for bankruptcy, and his obligation to Epsco was discharged. The sons claimed that their father owned CWC as a sole proprietor and that they were not partners in the business. The court, however, held that the sons were liable for CWC's debts based on partnership by estoppel. Because the Chaverses had represented to Epsco that CWC was a partnership and Epsco had relied on this representation when extending credit, the sons were prevented from claiming that no partnership existed.[3]

SECTION 3
PARTNERSHIP OPERATION

The rights and duties of partners are governed largely by the specific terms of their partnership agreement. In the absence of provisions to the contrary in the partnership agreement, the law imposes the rights and duties discussed in the following subsections. The character and nature of the partnership business generally influence the application of these rights and duties.

Rights of Partners

The rights of partners in a partnership relate to the following areas: management, interest in the partnership, compensation, inspection of books, accounting, and property.

MANAGEMENT In a general partnership, all partners have equal rights in managing the partnership [UPA 401(f)]. Unless the partners agree otherwise, each partner has one vote in management matters *regardless of the proportional size of his or her interest in the firm*. In a large partnership, partners often agree to delegate daily management responsibilities to a management committee made up of one or more of the partners.

The majority rule controls decisions on ordinary matters connected with partnership business, unless otherwise specified in the agreement. Decisions that significantly affect the nature of the partnership or that are outside the ordinary course of the partnership business, however, require the *unanimous* consent of the partners [UPA 301(2), 401(i), 401(j)].

Unanimous consent is likely to be required for a decision to undertake any of the following actions:

1. To alter the essential nature of the firm's business as expressed in the partnership agreement or to alter the capital structure of the partnership.
2. To admit new partners or engage in a completely new business.
3. To assign partnership property to a trust for the benefit of creditors.
4. To dispose of the partnership's *goodwill* (defined on page 720).
5. To confess judgment against the partnership or to submit partnership claims to arbitration. (A **confession of judgment** is an act by a debtor that permits a judgment to be entered against him or her by a creditor, for an agreed sum, without the institution of legal proceedings.)
6. To undertake any act that would make further conduct of partnership business impossible.
7. To amend the terms of the partnership agreement.

INTEREST IN THE PARTNERSHIP Each partner is entitled to the proportion of business profits and losses that is specified in the partnership agreement. If the agreement does not apportion profits (indicate how the profits will be shared), the UPA provides that profits will be shared equally. If the agreement does not apportion losses, losses will be shared in the same ratio as profits [UPA 401(b)].

For example, Rico and Brett form a partnership. The partnership agreement provides for capital

---

3. *Chavers v. Epsco, Inc.*, 352 Ark. 65, 98 S.W.3d 421 (2003).

contributions of $60,000 from Rico and $40,000 from Brett, but it is silent as to how they will share profits or losses. In this situation, they will share both profits and losses equally. If their partnership agreement had provided that they would share profits in the same ratio as capital contributions, however, 60 percent of the profits would go to Rico, and 40 percent would go to Brett. If this agreement was silent as to losses, losses would be shared in the same ratio as profits (60 percent and 40 percent, respectively).

COMPENSATION Devoting time, skill, and energy to partnership business is a partner's duty and generally is not a compensable service. Rather, as mentioned, a partner's income from the partnership takes the form of a distribution of profits according to the partner's share in the business. Partners can, of course, agree otherwise. For example, the managing partner of a law firm often receives a salary—in addition to her or his share of profits—for performing special administrative or managerial duties.

INSPECTION OF THE BOOKS Partnership books and records must be kept accessible to all partners. Each partner has the right to receive (and the corresponding duty to produce) full and complete information concerning the conduct of all aspects of partnership business [UPA 403]. Each firm retains books for recording and securing such information. Partners contribute the information, and a bookkeeper typically has the duty to preserve it. The books must be kept at the firm's principal business office (unless the partners agree otherwise). Every partner, whether active or inactive, is entitled to inspect all books and records on demand and can make copies of the materials. The personal representative of a deceased partner's estate has the same right of access to partnership books and records that the decedent would have had [UPA 403].

ACCOUNTING OF PARTNERSHIP ASSETS OR PROFITS An accounting of partnership assets or profits is required to determine the value of each partner's share in the partnership. An accounting can be performed voluntarily, or it can be compelled by court order. Under UPA 405(b), a partner has the right to bring an action for an accounting during the term of the partnership, as well as on the partnership's dissolution and winding up.

PROPERTY RIGHTS Property acquired *by* a partnership is the property of the partnership and not of the partners individually [UPA 203]. Partnership property includes all property that was originally contributed to the partnership and anything later purchased by the partnership or in the partnership's name (except in rare circumstances) [UPA 204]. A partner may use or possess partnership property only on behalf of the partnership [UPA 401(g)]. A partner is *not* a co-owner of partnership property and has no right to sell, mortgage, or transfer partnership property to another [UPA 501].[4]

In other words, partnership property is owned by the partnership as an entity and not by the individual partners. Thus, a creditor of an individual partner cannot seek to use partnership property to satisfy the partner's debt. Such a creditor can, however, petition a court for a **charging order** to attach the individual partner's *interest* in the partnership (her or his proportionate share of the profits and losses and right to receive distributions) to satisfy the partner's obligation [UPA 502]. A partner can also assign her or his right to a share of the partnership profits to another to satisfy a debt.

Duties and Liabilities of Partners

The duties and liabilities of partners that we examine here are basically derived from agency law. Each partner is an agent of every other partner and acts as both a principal and an agent in any business transaction within the scope of the partnership agreement. Each partner is also a general agent of the partnership in carrying out the usual business of the firm "or business of the kind carried on by the partnership" [UPA 301(1)]. Thus, every act of a partner concerning partnership business and "business of the kind" and every contract signed in the partnership's name bind the firm. The UPA affirms general principles of agency law that pertain to the authority of a partner to bind a partnership in contract or tort.

FIDUCIARY DUTIES The fiduciary duties that a partner owes to the partnership and the other partners are the duty of care and the duty of loyalty [UPA 404(a)]. Under the UPA, a partner's *duty of care* is limited to refraining from "grossly negligent or reckless conduct, intentional misconduct, or a knowing violation of law" [UPA 404(c)].[5] A partner is not

---

4. Under the previous version of the UPA, partners were *tenants in partnership*. This meant that every partner was a co-owner with all other partners of the partnership property. The current UPA does not recognize this concept.

5. The previous version of the UPA touched only briefly on the duty of loyalty and left the details of the partners' fiduciary duties to be developed under the law of agency.

liable to the partnership for simple negligence or honest errors in judgment in conducting partnership business.

The *duty of loyalty* requires a partner to account to the partnership for "any property, profit, or benefit" derived by the partner in the conduct of the partnership's business or from the use of its property. A partner must also refrain from competing with the partnership in business or dealing with the firm as an adverse party [UPA 404(b)]. The duty of loyalty can be breached by self-dealing, misusing partnership property, disclosing trade secrets, or usurping a partnership business opportunity. The following case is a classic example.

CASE 37.1
Meinhard v. Salmon

Court of Appeals of New York, 249 N.Y. 458, 164 N.E. 545 (1928).
www.nycourts.gov/reporter/Index.htm[a]

BACKGROUND AND FACTS • Walter Salmon negotiated a twenty-year lease for the Hotel Bristol in New York City. To pay for the conversion of the building into shops and offices, Salmon entered into an agreement with Morton Meinhard to assume half of the cost. They agreed to share the profits and losses from the *joint venture* (see page 746), but Salmon was to have the sole power to manage the building. Less than four months before the end of the lease term, the building's owner, Elbridge Gerry, approached Salmon about a project to raze the converted structure, clear five adjacent lots, and construct a single building across the whole property. Salmon agreed and signed a new lease in the name of his own business, Midpoint Realty Company, without telling Meinhard. When Meinhard learned of the deal, he filed a suit in a New York state court against Salmon. The court ruled in Meinhard's favor, and Salmon appealed.

IN THE LANGUAGE OF THE COURT
CARDOZO, C.J. [Chief Justice]
* * * *

    Joint adventurers, like copartners, owe to one another, while the enterprise continues, the duty of the finest loyalty. Many forms of conduct permissible in a work-a-day world for those acting at arm's length are forbidden to those bound by fiduciary ties. * * * Not honesty alone, but the punctilio [strictness in observance of details] of an honor the most sensitive, is then the standard of behavior. As to this there has developed a tradition that is unbending and inveterate [entrenched]. Uncompromising rigidity has been the attitude of courts * * * when petitioned to undermine the rule of undivided loyalty.

    * * * The trouble about [Salmon's] conduct is that he excluded his coadventurer from any chance to compete, from any chance to enjoy the opportunity for benefit.

    * * * The very fact that Salmon was in control with exclusive powers of direction charged him the more obviously with the duty of disclosure, [because] only through disclosure could opportunity be equalized.

    * * * Authority is, of course, abundant that one partner may not appropriate to his own use a renewal of a lease, though its term is to begin at the expiration of the partnership. The lease at hand with its many changes is not strictly a renewal. Even so, the standard of loyalty for those in trust relations is without the fixed divisions of a graduated scale. * * * *A man obtaining [an]* * * * *opportunity* * * * *by the position he occupies as a partner is bound by his obligation to his copartners in such dealings not to separate his interest from theirs, but, if he acquires any benefit, to communicate it to them. Certain it is also that there may be no abuse of special opportunities growing out of a special trust as manager or agent.* [Emphasis added.]

    * * * Very likely [Salmon] assumed in all good faith that with the approaching end of the venture he might ignore his coadventurer and take the extension for himself. He had given to the enterprise time and labor as well as money. He had made it a success. Meinhard, who had given money, but neither time nor labor, had already been richly paid. * * * [But] Salmon had put himself in a position in which thought of self was to be renounced, however hard the

---

a. In the links at the bottom of the page, click on "Archives." In the result, scroll to the name of the case and click on it to access the opinion. The New York State Law Reporting Bureau maintains this Web site.

CASE 37.1 CONTINUED ➧ abnegation [self-denial]. He was much more than a coadventurer. He was a managing coadventurer. For him and for those like him the rule of undivided loyalty is relentless and supreme.

DECISION AND REMEDY • *The Court of Appeals of New York held that Salmon breached his fiduciary duty by failing to inform Meinhard of the business opportunity and secretly taking advantage of it himself. The court granted Meinhard an interest "measured by the value of half of the entire lease."*

WHAT IF THE FACTS WERE DIFFERENT? • *Suppose that Salmon had disclosed Gerry's proposal to Meinhard, who had said that he was not interested. Would the result in this case have been different? Explain.*

IMPACT OF THIS CASE ON TODAY'S LAW • *This landmark case involved a joint venture, not a partnership. At the time, a member of a joint venture had only the duty to refrain from actively subverting the rights of the other members. The decision in this case imposed the highest standard of loyalty on joint-venture members. The duty is now the same in both joint ventures and partnerships. The eloquent language in this case that describes the standard of loyalty is frequently quoted approvingly by courts in cases involving partnerships.*

BREACH AND WAIVER OF FIDUCIARY DUTIES A partner's fiduciary duties may not be waived or eliminated in the partnership agreement, and in fulfilling them each partner must act consistently with the obligation of good faith and fair dealing [UPA 103(b), 404(d)]. The agreement can specify acts that the partners agree will violate a fiduciary duty.

Note that a partner may pursue his or her own interests without automatically violating these duties [UPA 404(e)]. The key is whether the partner has disclosed the interest to the other partners. For example, a partner who owns a shopping mall may vote against a partnership proposal to open a competing mall, provided that the partner has fully disclosed her interest in the existing shopping mall to the other partners at the firm. A partner cannot make secret profits or put self-interest before his or her duty to the interest of the partnership, however.

AUTHORITY OF PARTNERS The UPA affirms general principles of agency law that pertain to a partner's authority to bind a partnership in contract. A partner may also subject the partnership to tort liability under agency principles. When a partner is carrying on partnership business or business of the kind with third parties in the usual way, apparent authority exists, and both the partner and the firm share liability.

The partnership will not be liable, however, if the third parties *know* that the partner has no such authority. For example, Patricia, a partner in a law firm, applies for a bank loan on behalf of the partnership without authorization from the other partners. If the bank manager knows that Patricia has no

authority to do so and nonetheless grants the loan, Patricia will be personally bound, but the partnership will not be liable.

A partnership may file in a designated state office a "statement of partnership authority" to limit a partner's capacity to act as the firm's agent or transfer property on its behalf [UPA 105, 303]. Any such limit on a partner's authority, however, normally does not affect a third party who does not know about the statement (except in real estate transactions when the statement has been recorded with the appropriate state office—see Chapter 50).

The agency concepts relating to apparent authority, actual authority, and ratification that were discussed in Chapter 33 also apply to partnerships. The extent of *implied authority* generally is broader for partners than for ordinary agents, however.

The Scope of Implied Powers. The character and scope of the partnership business and the customary nature of the particular business operation determine the implied powers of partners. For example, a *trading partnership* is a business that has goods in inventory and makes profits buying and selling those goods. A partner in a trading partnership has a wide range of implied powers, such as to advertise products, hire employees, and extend the firm's credit by issuing or signing checks (see Chapter 26).

In an ordinary partnership, the partners can exercise all implied powers reasonably necessary and customary to carry on that particular business. Some customarily implied powers include the authority to make warranties on goods in the sales business and the power to enter into contracts consistent with the firm's regular course of business. Most partners also have the implied authority to make admissions and representations concerning partnership affairs. A partner might also have the implied power to convey (transfer) real property in the firm's name when such conveyances are part of the ordinary course of partnership business.

Authorized versus Unauthorized Actions. If a partner acts within the scope of authority, the partnership is legally bound to honor the partner's commitments to third parties. For example, a partner's authority to sell partnership products carries with it the implied authority to transfer title and to make usual warranties. Hence, in a partnership that operates a retail tire store, any partner negotiating a contract with a customer for the sale of a set of tires can specify that "each tire will be warranted for normal wear for 40,000 miles." This same partner, however, does not have the authority to sell office equipment, fixtures, or the partnership's retail facility without the consent of all of the other partners.

In addition, because partnerships are formed to generate profits, a partner generally does not have the authority to make charitable contributions without the consent of the other partners. Such actions are not binding on the partnership unless they are ratified by all of the other partners.

LIABILITY OF PARTNERS One significant disadvantage associated with a traditional partnership is that the partners are *personally* liable for the debts of the partnership. Moreover, in most states, the liability is essentially unlimited because the acts of one partner in the ordinary course of business subject the other partners to personal liability [UPA 305]. The following subsections explain the rules on a partner's liability.

Joint Liability. At one time, each partner in a partnership generally was jointly liable for the partnership's obligations. **Joint liability** means that a third party must sue all of the partners as a group, but each partner can be held liable for the full amount.[6] If a third party sued a partner on a contractual debt, the lawsuit had to name all of the partners as defendants to seek partnership assets to pay any judgment. With joint liability, the partnership's assets must be exhausted before creditors can reach the partners' individual assets.[7]

Joint and Several Liability. In the majority of the states, under UPA 306(a), partners are both jointly and severally (separately, or individually) liable for all partnership obligations, including contracts, torts, and breaches of trust. **Joint and several liability** means that a third party has the option of suing all of the partners together (jointly) or one or more of the partners separately (severally). This is true even if a partner did not participate in, ratify, or know about whatever it was that gave rise to the cause of action. Normally, though, the partnership's assets must be exhausted before a creditor can enforce a judgment against a partner's separate assets [UPA 307(d)].

A judgment against one partner severally (separately) does not extinguish the others' liability. Those not sued in the first action normally may be sued subsequently, unless the court in the first action held that the partnership was in no way liable. If a plaintiff is successful in a suit against a partner or partners, he or she may collect on the judgment only against the assets of those partners named as defendants. A partner who commits a tort may be required to indemnify (reimburse) the partnership for any damages it pays—unless the tort was committed in the ordinary course of the partnership's business.

CASE IN POINT Nicole Moren was a partner in Jax Restaurant. After work one day, Moren was called back to the restaurant to help in the kitchen. She brought her two-year-old-son, Remington, and sat him on the kitchen counter. While she was making pizzas, Remington reached into the dough press. His hand was crushed, causing permanent injuries. Through his father, Remington filed a suit against the partnership for negligence. The partnership filed a complaint against Moren, arguing that it was entitled to indemnity (compensation or reimbursement) from Moren for her negligence. The court held in favor of Moren and ordered the partnership to pay damages to Remington. Moren was not required to indemnify the partnership because her negligence occurred in the ordinary course of the partnership's business.[8]

---

6. Under the previous version of the UPA, which is still in effect in a few states, partners were subject to joint liability on partnership debts and contracts, excluding partnership debts arising from torts. States that still follow the previous version of the UPA include Connecticut, West Virginia, and Wyoming. In these states, the partners are subject to *joint liability* on contracts and to *joint and several liability* (discussed next) on debts arising from torts.

7. For a case applying joint liability to a partnership, see *Shar's Cars, LLC v. Elder,* 97 P.3d 724 (Utah App. 2004).

8. *Moren v. Jax Restaurant,* 679 N.W.2d 165 (Minn.App. 2004).

Liability of Incoming Partners. A partner newly admitted to an existing partnership is not personally liable for any partnership obligation incurred before the person became a partner [UPA 306(b)]. In other words, the new partner's liability to existing creditors of the partnership is limited to her or his capital contribution to the firm.

For example, Smartclub, an existing partnership with four members, admits a new partner, Alex Jaff. He contributes $100,000 to the partnership. Smartclub has debts amounting to $600,000 at the time Jaff joins the firm. Although Jaff's capital contribution of $100,000 can be used to satisfy Smartclub's obligations, Jaff is not personally liable for partnership debts that were incurred before he became a partner. Thus, his personal assets cannot be used to satisfy the partnership's preexisting debt. If, however, the managing partner at Smartclub borrows funds for the partnership after Jaff becomes a partner, Jaff will be personally liable for those amounts, along with all other partners.

SECTION 4
DISSOCIATION OF A PARTNER

Dissociation occurs when a partner ceases to be associated in the carrying on of the partnership business. Although a partner always has the *power* to dissociate from the firm, he or she may not have the *right* to dissociate. Dissociation normally entitles the partner to have his or her interest purchased by the partnership, and terminates his or her actual authority to act for the partnership and to participate with the partners in running the business. After that, the partnership continues to do business without the dissociated partner.[9]

Events That Cause Dissociation

Under UPA 601, a partner can be dissociated from a partnership in any of the following ways:

1. By the partner's voluntarily giving notice of an "express will to withdraw." (Note that when a partner gives notice of her or his intent to withdraw, the remaining partners must decide whether to continue or give up the partnership business. If they do not agree to continue the partnership, the voluntary dissociation of a partner will dissolve the firm [UPA 801(1)].)

2. By the occurrence of an event specified in the partnership agreement.

3. By a unanimous vote of the other partners under certain circumstances, such as when a partner transfers substantially all of her or his interest in the partnership, or when it becomes unlawful to carry on partnership business with that partner.

4. By order of a court or arbitrator if the partner has engaged in wrongful conduct that affects the partnership business, breached the partnership agreement or violated a duty owed to the partnership or the other partners, or engaged in conduct that makes it "not reasonably practicable to carry on the business in partnership with the partner" [UPA 601(5)].

5. By the partner's declaring bankruptcy, assigning his or her interest in the partnership for the benefit of creditors, or becoming physically or mentally incapacitated, or by the partner's death. Note that although the bankruptcy or death of a partner represents that partner's "dissociation" from the partnership, it is not an *automatic* ground for the partnership's dissolution (*dissolution* will be discussed shortly).

Wrongful Dissociation

As mentioned, a partner has the power to dissociate from a partnership at any time, but if she or he lacks the right to dissociate, then the dissociation is considered wrongful under the law [UPA 602]. When a partner's dissociation breaches a partnership agreement, for instance, it is wrongful. Suppose that a partnership agreement states that it is a breach of the agreement for any partner to assign partnership property to a creditor without the consent of the other partners. If Janis, a partner, makes such an assignment, she has not only breached the agreement but has also wrongfully dissociated from the partnership. Similarly, if a partner refuses to perform duties required by the partnership agreement—such as accounting for profits earned from the use of partnership property—this breach can be treated as a wrongful dissociation.

A partner who wrongfully dissociates is liable to the partnership and to the other partners for damages caused by the dissociation. This liability is in addition to any other obligation of the partner to the partnership or to the other partners. Thus, a wrongfully dissociating partner is liable to the partnership

---

9. Under the previous version of the UPA, when a partner withdrew from a partnership, the partnership was considered dissolved, its business had to be wound up, and the proceeds had to be distributed to creditors and among partners. The new UPA provisions dramatically changed the law governing partnership breakups and dissolution by no longer requiring that the partnership end if one partner dissociates.

not only for any damages caused by breach of the partnership agreement, but also for costs incurred to replace the partner's expertise or to obtain new financing.

Effects of Dissociation

Dissociation (rightful or wrongful) terminates some of the rights of the dissociated partner, requires that the partnership purchase his or her interest, and alters the liability of the parties to third parties.

RIGHTS AND DUTIES On a partner's dissociation, his or her right to participate in the management and conduct of the partnership business terminates [UPA 603]. The partner's duty of loyalty also ends. A partner's duty of care continues only with respect to events that occurred before dissociation, unless the partner participates in winding up the partnership's business (which will be discussed shortly). For example, Debbie Pearson is a partner who is leaving an accounting firm, Bubb & Pearson. Pearson can immediately compete with the firm for new clients. She must exercise care in completing ongoing client transactions, however, and must account to the firm for any fees received from the old clients based on those transactions.

After a partner's dissociation, his or her interest in the partnership must be purchased according to the rules in UPA 701. The **buyout price** is based on the amount that would have been distributed to the partner if the partnership had been wound up on the date of dissociation. Offset against the price are amounts owed by the partner to the partnership, including damages for wrongful dissociation.

CASE IN POINT In 1978, Wilbur and Dee Warnick and their son Randall bought a ranch for $335,000 and formed a partnership to operate it. The partners' initial capital contributions totaled $60,000, of which Randall paid 34 percent. Over the next twenty years, each partner contributed funds to the operation and received cash distributions from the partnership. In 1999, Randall dissociated from the partnership. When the parties could not agree on a buyout price, Randall filed a lawsuit. The court awarded Randall $115,783.13— the amount of his cash contributions, plus 34 percent of the increase in the value of the partnership's assets above all partners' cash contributions. Randall's parents appealed, arguing that $50,000 should be deducted from the appraised value of the assets for the estimated expenses of selling them. The court affirmed the buyout price, however,

because "purely hypothetical costs of sale are not a required deduction in valuing partnership assets" to determine a buyout price.[10]

LIABILITY TO THIRD PARTIES For two years after a partner dissociates from a continuing partnership, the partnership may be bound by the acts of the dissociated partner based on apparent authority [UPA 702]. In other words, the partnership may be liable to a third party with whom a dissociated partner enters into a transaction if the third party reasonably believed that the dissociated partner was still a partner. Similarly, a dissociated partner may be liable for partnership obligations entered into during a two-year period following dissociation [UPA 703].

To avoid this possible liability, a partnership should notify its creditors, customers, and clients of a partner's dissociation. In addition, either the partnership or the dissociated partner can file a statement of dissociation in the appropriate state office to limit the dissociated partner's authority to ninety days after the filing [UPA 704]. Filing this statement helps to minimize the firm's potential liability for the former partner and vice versa.

SECTION 5
PARTNERSHIP TERMINATION

The same events that cause dissociation can result in the end of the partnership if the remaining partners no longer wish to (or are unable to) continue the partnership business. Only certain departures of a partner will end the partnership, though, and generally the partnership can continue if the remaining partners consent [UPA 801].

The termination of a partnership is referred to as **dissolution,** which essentially means the commencement of the winding up process. **Winding up** is the actual process of collecting, liquidating, and distributing the partnership assets.[11] Here, we discuss the dissolution and winding up of partnership business.

Dissolution

Dissolution of a partnership generally can be brought about by acts of the partners, by operation of law,

---

10. *Warnick v. Warnick,* 2006 WY 58, 133 P.3d 997 (2006).
11. Although "winding down" would seem to describe more accurately the process of settling accounts and liquidating the assets of a partnership, English and U.S. statutory and case law have traditionally used "winding up" to denote this final stage of a partnership's existence.

or by judicial decree [UPA 801]. Any partnership (including one for a fixed term) can be dissolved by the partners' agreement. Similarly, if the partnership agreement states that it will dissolve on a certain event, such as a partner's death or bankruptcy, then the occurrence of that event will dissolve the partnership. A partnership for a fixed term or a particular undertaking is dissolved by operation of law at the expiration of the term or on the completion of the undertaking.

Any event that makes it unlawful for the partnership to continue its business will result in dissolution [UPA 801(4)]. Under the UPA, a court may order dissolution when it becomes obviously impractical for the firm to continue—for example, if the business can only be operated at a loss [UPA 801(5)]. Note, however, that even when one partner has brought a court action seeking to dissolve a partnership, the partnership continues to exist until it is legally dissolved by the court or by the parties' agreement.

CASE IN POINT Ellin Curley and Lawrence Kaiser were married when they formed a general partnership, K&K Associates. Later, Curley and Kaiser were divorced and entered into an amended partnership agreement that stated that Curley owned 80 percent of the firm and Kaiser owned 20 percent. K&K invested part of its capital, but the investment suffered losses. When Kaiser refused to pay his share of the losses, Curley filed a suit for breach of contract and requested judicial dissolution of K&K. While the lawsuit was pending, Kaiser died, and his new wife was substituted as the defendant. A provision in the amended agreement stated that if Kaiser died while still a partner, K&K would terminate, and the value of Kaiser's ownership interest in the closing capital account would be zero. The defense argued that this provision was not enforceable because the partnership no longer existed. The court ruled that although the dissolution process had begun, the partnership still existed when Kaiser died. Therefore, the provision in the amended agreement effectively terminated the partnership and reduced the value of Kaiser's interest to zero.[12]

Winding Up and Distribution of Assets

After dissolution, the partnership continues for the limited purpose of the winding up process.[13] The

partners cannot create new obligations on behalf of the partnership. They have authority only to complete transactions begun but not finished at the time of dissolution and to wind up the business of the partnership [UPA 803, 804(1)].

Winding up includes collecting and preserving partnership assets, discharging liabilities (paying debts), and accounting to each partner for the value of his or her interest in the partnership. Partners continue to have fiduciary duties to one another and to the firm during this process. UPA 401(h) provides that a partner is entitled to compensation for services in winding up partnership affairs (and reimbursement for expenses incurred in the process) above and apart from his or her share in the partnership profits.

Both creditors of the partnership and creditors of the individual partners can make claims on the partnership's assets. In general, partnership creditors share proportionately with the partners' individual creditors in the partners' assets, which include their interests in the partnership. A partnership's assets are distributed according to the following priorities [UPA 807]:

1. Payment of debts, including those owed to partner and nonpartner creditors.
2. Return of capital contributions and distribution of profits to partners.[14]

If the partnership's liabilities are greater than its assets, the partners bear the losses—in the absence of a contrary agreement—in the same proportion in which they shared the profits (rather than, for example, in proportion to their contributions to the partnership's capital).

Partnership Buy-Sell Agreements

Before entering into a partnership, partners should agree on how the assets will be valued and divided in the event that the partnership dissolves. A **buy-sell agreement,** sometimes called simply a *buyout agreement,* provides for one or more partners to buy out the other or others, should the situation warrant. Agreeing beforehand on who buys what, under what circumstances, and, if possible, at what price may eliminate costly negotiations or litigation later. Alternatively, the agreement may specify that one

---

12. *Curley v. Kaiser,* 112 Conn.App. 213, 962 A.2d 167 (2009).
13. Note that at any time after dissolution but before winding up is completed, all of the partners may decide to continue the partnership business and waive the right to have the business wound up [UPA 802].

14. Under the previous version of the UPA, creditors of the partnership had priority over creditors of the individual partners. Also, in distributing partnership assets, third party creditors were paid before partner creditors, and capital contributions were returned before profits.

or more partners will determine the value of the interest being sold and that the other or others will decide whether to buy or sell.

Under UPA 701(a), if a partner's dissociation does not result in a dissolution of the partnership, a buyout of the partner's interest is mandatory. The UPA contains an extensive set of buyout rules that apply when the partners do not have a buyout agreement. Basically, a withdrawing partner receives the same amount through a buyout that he or she would receive if the business were winding up [UPA 701(b)].

SECTION 6
LIMITED LIABILITY PARTNERSHIPS

The **limited liability partnership (LLP)** is a hybrid form of business designed mostly for professionals who normally do business as partners in a partnership. The first state to enact an LLP statute was Texas, in 1991. Other states quickly followed suit, and by 1997, almost all of the states had enacted LLP statutes.

The major advantage of the LLP is that it allows a partnership to continue as a pass-through entity for tax purposes but limits the personal liability of the partners. The LLP is especially attractive for two categories of businesses: professional service firms and family businesses. In fact, all of the "Big Four" accounting firms—the four largest international accountancy and professional services firms—are organized as LLPs, including Ernst & Young, LLP, and PricewaterhouseCoopers, LLP.

Formation of an LLP

LLPs must be formed and operated in compliance with state statutes, which may include provisions of the UPA. The appropriate form must be filed with a central state agency, usually the secretary of state's office, and the business's name must include either "Limited Liability Partnership" or "LLP" [UPA 1001, 1002]. In addition, an LLP must file an annual report with the state to remain qualified as an LLP in that state [UPA 1003].

In most states, it is relatively easy to convert a traditional partnership into an LLP because the firm's basic organizational structure remains the same. Additionally, all of the statutory and common law rules governing partnerships still apply (apart from those modified by the LLP statute). Normally, LLP statutes are simply amendments to a state's already existing partnership law.

Liability in an LLP

An LLP allows professionals, such as attorneys and accountants, to avoid personal liability for the malpractice of other partners. A partner in an LLP is still liable for her or his own wrongful acts, such as negligence, however. Also liable is the partner who supervised the individual who committed a wrongful act. (This generally is true for all types of partners and partnerships, not just LLPs.)

Although LLP statutes vary from state to state, generally each state statute limits the liability of partners in some way. For example, Delaware law protects each innocent partner from the "debts and obligations of the partnership arising from negligence, wrongful acts, or misconduct." The UPA more broadly exempts partners from personal liability for any partnership obligation, "whether arising in contract, tort, or otherwise" [UPA 306(c)]. Although the language of these statutes may seem to apply specifically to attorneys, almost any group of professionals can organize as an LLP.

LIABILITY FROM STATE TO STATE When an LLP formed in one state wants to do business in another state, it may be required to register in the second state—for example, by filing a statement of foreign qualification [UPA 1102]. Because state LLP statutes are not uniform, a question sometimes arises as to which law applies if the LLP statutes in the two states provide different liability protection. Most states apply the law of the state in which the LLP was formed, even when the firm does business in another state, which is also the rule under UPA 1101.

SHARING LIABILITY AMONG PARTNERS When more than one partner in an LLP is negligent, there is a question as to how liability should be shared. Some states provide for proportionate liability—that is, for separate determinations of the negligence of the partners. For example, accountants Don and Jane are partners in an LLP, with Don supervising Jane. Jane negligently fails to file a tax return for one of their clients, Centaur Tools. Centaur files a suit against Don and Jane. Under a proportionate liability statute, Don will be liable for no more than his portion of the responsibility for the missed tax deadline. In a state that does not allow for proportionate liability, Don can be held liable for the entire loss.

Family Limited Liability Partnerships

A **family limited liability partnership (FLLP)** is a limited liability partnership in which the partners are related to each other—for example, as spouses, parents and children, siblings, or cousins. A person acting in a fiduciary capacity for persons so related can also be a partner. All of the partners must be natural persons or persons acting in a fiduciary capacity for the benefit of natural persons.

Probably the most significant use of the FLLP form of business organization is in agriculture. Family-owned farms sometimes find this form to their benefit. The FLLP offers the same advantages as other LLPs with certain additional advantages, such as, in Iowa, an exemption from real estate transfer taxes when partnership real estate is transferred among partners.[15]

SECTION 7
LIMITED PARTNERSHIPS

We now look at a business organizational form that limits the liability of *some* of its owners—the **limited partnership (LP).** Limited partnerships originated in medieval Europe and have been in existence in the United States since the early 1800s. In many ways, limited partnerships are like the general partnerships discussed at the beginning of this chapter, but they differ from general partnerships in several ways. For this reason, they are sometimes referred to as *special partnerships*.

A limited partnership consists of at least one **general partner** and one or more **limited partners.** A general partner assumes management responsibility for the partnership and has full responsibility for the partnership and for all its debts. A limited partner contributes cash or other property and owns an interest in the firm but does not undertake any management responsibilities and is not personally liable for partnership debts beyond the amount of his or her investment. A limited partner can forfeit limited liability by taking part in the management of the business. A comparison of general partnerships and limited partnerships appears in Exhibit 37–2 on the following page.[16]

Until 1976, the law governing limited partnerships in all states except Louisiana was the Uniform Limited Partnership Act (ULPA). Since 1976, most states and the District of Columbia have adopted the revised version of the ULPA, known as the Revised Uniform Limited Partnership Act (RULPA). Because the RULPA is the dominant law governing limited partnerships in the United States, we refer to it in the following discussion. Note, however, that amendments to make the RULPA more flexible were proposed to the states in 2001, and fifteen states have adopted the 2001 version of this law.

Formation of a Limited Partnership

In contrast to the informal, private, and voluntary agreement that usually suffices for a general partnership, the formation of a limited partnership is a public and formal proceeding that must follow statutory requirements. A limited partnership must have at least one general partner and one limited partner, as mentioned previously. Additionally, the partners must sign a **certificate of limited partnership,** which requires information such as the name, mailing address, and capital contribution of each general and limited partner. (The information required is similar to that found in a corporation's *articles of incorporation*—see Chapter 39.) The certificate must be filed with the designated state official—under the RULPA, the secretary of state. The certificate is usually open to public inspection.

Liabilities of Partners in a Limited Partnership

General partners, unlike limited partners, are personally liable to the partnership's creditors. Thus, at least one general partner is necessary in a limited partnership so that someone has personal liability. This policy can be circumvented in states that allow a corporation to be the general partner in a partnership. Because the corporation has limited liability by virtue of corporation statutes, if a corporation is the general partner, no one in the limited partnership has personal liability.

The liability of a limited partner, as mentioned, is limited to the capital that she or he contributes or agrees to contribute to the partnership [RULPA 502]. Limited partners enjoy this limited liability only so long as they do not participate in management [RULPA 303]. A limited partner who participates in management will be just as liable as a general partner to any creditor who transacts business with the limited partnership and believes, based on the limited partner's conduct, that the limited partner is a general partner [RULPA 303]. It is not always clear how much review and advisement a limited partner can engage in before being exposed to liability, though.

---

15. Iowa Statutes Section 428A.2.
16. Under the UPA, a general partnership can be converted into a limited partnership and vice versa [UPA 902, 903]. The UPA also provides for the merger of a general partnership with one or more general or limited partnerships [UPA 905].

EXHIBIT 37-2 • A Comparison of General Partnerships and Limited Partnerships

CHARACTERISTIC	GENERAL PARTNERSHIP (UPA)	LIMITED PARTNERSHIP (RULPA)
Creation	By agreement of two or more persons to carry on a business as co-owners for profit.	By agreement of two or more persons to carry on a business as co-owners for profit. Must include one or more general partners and one or more limited partners. Filing of a certificate with the secretary of state is required.
Sharing of Profits and Losses	By agreement; or, in the absence of agreement, profits are shared equally by the partners, and losses are shared in the same ratio as profits.	Profits are shared as required in the certificate agreement, and losses are shared likewise, up to the amount of the limited partners' capital contributions. In the absence of a provision in the certificate agreement, profits and losses are shared on the basis of percentages of capital contributions.
Liability	Unlimited personal liability of all partners.	Unlimited personal liability of all general partners; limited partners liable only to the extent of their capital contributions.
Capital Contribution	No minimum or mandatory amount; set by agreement.	Set by agreement.
Management	By agreement; or, in the absence of agreement, all partners have an equal voice.	Only the general partner (or the general partners). Limited partners have no voice or else are subject to liability as general partners (but only if a third party has reason to believe that the limited partner is a general partner). A limited partner may act as an agent or employee of the partnership and vote on amending the certificate or on the sale or dissolution of the partnership.
Duration	Terminated by agreement of the partners, but can continue to do business even when a partner dissociates from the partnership.	Terminated by agreement in the certificate or by retirement, death, or mental incompetence of a general partner in the absence of the right of the other general partners to continue the partnership. Death of a limited partner does not terminate the partnership, unless he or she is the only remaining limited partner.
Distribution of Assets on Liquidation— Order of Priorities	1. Payment of debts, including those owed to partner and nonpartner creditors. 2. Return of capital contributions and distribution of profit to partners.	1. Outside creditors and partner creditors. 2. Partners and former partners entitled to distributions of partnership assets. 3. Unless otherwise agreed, return of capital contributions and distribution of profit to partners.

Rights and Duties in a Limited Partnership

With the exception of the right to participate in management, limited partners have essentially the same rights as general partners. Limited partners have a right of access to the partnership's books and to information regarding partnership business. On dissolution of the partnership, limited partners are entitled to a return of their contributions in accordance with the partnership certificate [RULPA 201(a)(10)]. They can also assign their interests subject to the certificate [RULPA 702, 704] and can sue an outside party on behalf of the firm if the general partners with authority to do so have refused to file suit [RULPA 1001].

General and limited partners also owe each other a fiduciary duty to exercise good faith in transactions related to the partnership. Can this duty be waived through a provision in the partnership agreement? That was the issue in the following case.

CASE 37.2
1515 North Wells, LP v. 1513 North Wells, LLC

Appellate Court of Illinois, First District, 392 Ill.App.3d 863, 913 N.E.2d 1 (2009).

BACKGROUND AND FACTS • Thomas Bracken (owner of 1513 North Wells, LLC), Mark Sutherland, and Alex Pearsall were limited partners in 1515 North Wells, LP. Sutherland and Pearsall's company, SP Development Corporation, was 1515's general partner. The partnership was formed to build a condominium with residential and commercial space. SP chose another Sutherland and Pearsall company, Sutherland and Pearsall Development, to be the general contractor for the 1515 project. Meanwhile, Bracken borrowed $250,000 from 1515. When he did not repay the loan, 1515 filed a suit in an Illinois state court to collect. In response, Bracken filed a claim that included SP Development Corporation, alleging breach of fiduciary duty. The court ordered Bracken to repay the loan and SP to pay Bracken $900,000. SP appealed, arguing that a provision in 1515's partnership agreement, which allowed all partners to engage in "whatever activities they choose," effectively "relaxed" SP's fiduciary duty.

IN THE LANGUAGE OF THE COURT
Justice *CAHILL* delivered the opinion of the court:
* * * *
* * * Paragraph 1.7 of the limited partnership agreement * * * provided:

> The General Partner and each Limited Partner may, notwithstanding this Agreement, engage in whatever activities they choose, whether the same are competitive with the Partnership or otherwise, without having or incurring any obligation to offer any interest in such activities to the Partnership or any Partner.

* * * *

The general partner argues that paragraph 1.7 did in fact relax the parties' fiduciary duties to each other.
* * * *

A fiduciary relationship exists between partners and each is bound to exercise the utmost good faith in all dealings and transactions related to the partnership. To state a claim for breach of fiduciary duty, a plaintiff must establish (1) a fiduciary duty on the part of the defendant, (2) the defendant's breach of that duty, and (3) damages that were proximately caused by the defendant's breach.

Under Section 103(b)(3) of the Uniform Partnership Act, a partnership agreement may not "eliminate or reduce a partner's fiduciary duties." Language in an agreement that allows the partners discretion in certain areas does not metamorphose [transform] the document into an unrestricted license to engage in self-dealing at the expense of those to whom the managing partner owes such a duty. *There is no authority for the proposition that there can be a priori waiver of fiduciary duties in a partnership.* Nor is the practice of imposing purported advance waivers of fiduciary duties in limited partnership enterprises to be given judicial recognition. [Emphasis added.]

Here, there was ample evidence to support the [trial] court's finding of a breach of fiduciary duty, including the "cost plus fee" contract that the general partner awarded to the general contractor and the profits from condominium upgrades that went to the general contractor, not to the limited partnership. Paragraph 1.7 of the limited partnership agreement did not immunize the partners against liability for breach of fiduciary duty.

DECISION AND REMEDY • *The state intermediate appellate court affirmed the lower court's judgment. A partnership agreement cannot "contract away" the fiduciary duty that a general partner owes to limited partners.*

WHAT IF THE FACTS WERE DIFFERENT? • *Suppose that instead of choosing Sutherland and Pearsall Development to be the general contractor, SP had selected a party with no connection to any of 1515's partners. Is it likely that the result in this case would have been different? Why or why not?*

THE ETHICAL DIMENSION • *Did any of the parties involved in this case commit an ethical violation? Discuss.*

Dissociation and Dissolution

A general partner has the power to voluntarily dissociate, or withdraw, from a limited partnership unless the partnership agreement specifies otherwise. A limited partner theoretically can withdraw from the partnership by giving six months' notice unless the partnership agreement specifies a term, as most do. Also, some states have passed laws prohibiting the withdrawal of limited partners.

In a limited partnership, a general partner's voluntary dissociation from the firm normally will lead to dissolution *unless* all partners agree to continue the business. Similarly, the bankruptcy, retirement, death, or mental incompetence of a general partner will cause the dissociation of that partner and the dissolution of the limited partnership unless the other members agree to continue the firm [RULPA 801]. Bankruptcy of a limited partner, however, does not dissolve the partnership unless it causes the bankruptcy of the firm. Death or an assignment of the interest of a limited partner does not dissolve a limited partnership [RULPA 702, 704, 705]. A limited partnership can be dissolved by court decree [RULPA 802].

On dissolution, creditors' claims, including those of partners who are creditors, take first priority. After that, partners and former partners receive unpaid distributions of partnership assets and, except as otherwise agreed, amounts representing returns of their contributions and amounts proportionate to their shares of the distributions [RULPA 804].

In the following case, two limited partners wanted the business of the partnership to be sold on its dissolution, while another limited partner (actor Kevin Costner) and the general partner wanted it to continue.

✳ EXTENDED CASE 37.3 ✳
In re Dissolution of Midnight Star Enterprises, LP

Supreme Court of South Dakota, 2006 SD 98, 724 N.W.2d 334 (2006).

IN THE LANGUAGE OF THE COURT
SABERS, Justice.
* * * *
Midnight Star Enterprises, L.P. (Midnight Star) is a limited partnership, which operates a gaming, on-sale liquor and restaurant business in Deadwood, South Dakota. The owners of Midnight Star consist of: Midnight Star Enterprises, Ltd. (MSEL) as the general partner, owning 22 partnership units; Kevin Costner (Costner), owning 71.50 partnership units; and Francis and Carla Caneva (Canevas), owning 3.25 partnership units each. Costner is the sole owner of MSEL and essentially owns 93.5 partnership units.

The Canevas managed the operations of Midnight Star, receiving salaries and bonuses for their employment. According to MSEL, it became concerned about the Canevas' management and voiced concerns. Communications between the * * * partners broke down * * *.

MSEL * * * brought a Petition for Dissolution [in a South Dakota state court]. In order to dissolve, the fair market value of Midnight Star had to be assessed. MSEL hired Paul Thorstenson, an accountant, to determine the fair market value. * * * The Canevas solicited an "offer" from Ken Kellar, a Deadwood casino, restaurant, and hotel owner * * *.

* * * Thorstenson determined the fair market value was $3.1 million based on the hypothetical transaction standard of valuation. * * * The * * * court * * * found Kellar's offer of $6.2 million to be the fair market value * * * [and] ordered the majority owners to buy the business for $6.2 million within 10 days or the court would order the business to be sold on the open market. [MSEL appealed to the South Dakota Supreme Court.]
* * * *

[The] Canevas claim the partnership agreement does not allow the general partner to buy out their interest in Midnight Star. Instead, the Canevas argue, the agreement mandates the partnership be sold on the open market upon dissolution. * * * Article 10.4 provides:

> After all of the debts of the Partnership have been paid, the General Partner * * * may distribute in kind any Partnership property provided that a good faith effort is first made to sell * * * such property * * * at its estimated fair value to one or more third parties * * *.

* * * *

* * * This provision clearly states the General Partner "may distribute in kind any partnership property" if the property is first offered to a third party for a fair value. While the General Partner may offer the property on the open market, Article 10.4 does not require it.

This interpretation is reinforced when read together with Article 10.3.1 * * * [which] instructs that "no assets * * * shall be sold or otherwise transferred to [any

EXTENDED CASE 37.3 CONTINUED ➜

partner] unless the assets are valued at their then fair market value * * * ." *If Article 10.4 requires a forced sale, then there would be no need to have the fair market value provision of Article 10.3.1.* [Emphasis added.]

* * * Read as a whole, the partnership agreement does not require a mandatory sale upon dissolution. Instead, the general partner can opt to liquidate using either a sale or transfer under Article 10.3.1. * * * Because MSEL decided to pursue dissolution under Article 10.3.1, we decide the correct standard for determining the fair market value of the partnership.

* * * *

MSEL claims the correct standard * * * is the hypothetical

transaction analysis * * * . [The] Canevas argue that * * * the offer from Kellar represented the fair market value * * * .

* * * *

* * * *[There are] sound policy reasons why an offer cannot be the fair market value.* * * * What if a businessman, for personal reasons, offers 10 times the real value of the business? What if the partnership, for personal reasons, such as sentimental value, refuses to sell for that absurdly high offer? *These arbitrary, emotional offers and rejections cannot provide a rational and reasonable basis for determining the fair market value.* [Emphasis added.]

Conversely, the hypothetical transaction standard does provide a rational and reasonable basis for determining the fair market value

* * * by removing the irrationalities, strategies, and emotions * * * .

* * * *

Since it was error for the [lower] court to value Midnight Star at $6.2 million, it was also error to force the general partners to buy the business for $6.2 million or sell the business.

* * * *

* * * Instead of ordering the majority partners to purchase the whole partnership for the appraised value, the majority partners should only be required to pay any interests the withdrawing partner is due. * * * The majority partners should only be required to pay the Canevas the value of their 6.5 partnership units * * * .

* * * We reverse and remand for further proceedings * * * .

 QUESTIONS

1. Why did the court hold that a forced sale of the property of the limited partnership was not appropriate?
2. Under what circumstances might a forced sale of the property of a limited partnership on its dissolution be appropriate?

Limited Liability Limited Partnerships

A **limited liability limited partnership (LLLP)** is a type of limited partnership. An LLLP differs from a limited partnership in that a general partner in an LLLP has the same liability as a limited partner in a limited partnership. In other words, the liability of all partners is limited to the amount of their investments in the firm.

A few states provide expressly for LLLPs.[17] In states that do not provide for LLLPs but do allow for limited partnerships and limited liability partnerships, a limited partnership should probably still be able to register with the state as an LLLP.

---

17. See, for example, Colorado Revised Statutes Annotated Section 7-62-109. Other states that provide expressly for limited liability limited partnerships include Delaware, Florida, Georgia, Kentucky, Maryland, Nevada, Texas, and Virginia.

REVIEWING

Partnerships and Limited Liability Partnerships

Grace Tarnavsky and her sons, Manny and Jason, bought a ranch known as the Cowboy Palace in March 2007, and the three verbally agreed to share the business for five years. Grace contributed 50 percent of the investment, and each son contributed 25 percent. Manny agreed to handle the livestock, and Jason agreed to handle the bookkeeping. The Tarnavskys took out joint loans and opened a joint

REVIEWING CONTINUES ➜

bank account into which they deposited the ranch's proceeds and from which they made payments toward property, cattle, equipment, and supplies. In September 2011, Manny severely injured his back while baling hay and became permanently unable to handle livestock. Manny therefore hired additional laborers to tend the livestock, causing the Cowboy Palace to incur significant debt. In September 2012, Al's Feed Barn filed a lawsuit against Jason to collect $32,400 in unpaid debts. Using the information presented in the chapter, answer the following questions.

1. Was this relationship a partnership for a term or a partnership at will?
2. Did Manny have the authority to hire additional laborers to work at the ranch after his injury? Why or why not?
3. Under the current UPA, can Al's Feed Barn bring an action against Jason individually for the Cowboy Palace's debt? Why or why not?
4. Suppose that after his back injury in 2011, Manny sent his mother and brother a notice indicating his intent to withdraw from the partnership. Can he still be held liable for the debt to Al's Feed Barn? Why or why not?

DEBATE THIS: *A partnership should automatically end when one partner dissociates from the firm.*

TERMS AND CONCEPTS

articles of partnership 721
buyout price 728
buy-sell agreement 729
certificate of limited partnership 731
charging order 723

confession of judgment 722
dissociation 727
dissolution 728
family limited liability partnership (FLLP) 730
general partner 731
goodwill 720
information return 721

joint and several liability 726
joint liability 726
limited liability limited partnership (LLLP) 735
limited liability partnership (LLP) 730
limited partner 731

limited partnership (LP) 731
partnership 720
partnership by estoppel 722
pass-through entity 720
winding up 728

QUESTIONS AND CASE PROBLEMS

37–1. Partnership Formation Daniel is the owner of a chain of shoe stores. He hires Rubya to be the manager of a new store, which is to open in Grand Rapids, Michigan. Daniel, by written contract, agrees to pay Rubya a monthly salary and 20 percent of the profits. Without Daniel's knowledge, Rubya represents himself to Classen as Daniel's partner and shows Classen the agreement to share profits. Classen extends credit to Rubya. Rubya defaults. Discuss whether Classen can hold Daniel liable as a partner.

37–2. QUESTION WITH SAMPLE ANSWER: Partnership Dissolution.

Dorinda, Luis, and Elizabeth form a limited partnership. Dorinda is a general partner, and Luis and Elizabeth are limited partners. Consider the separate events below, and discuss fully whether each event constitutes a dissolution of the limited partnership.

(a) Luis assigns his partnership interest to Ashley.

(b) Elizabeth is petitioned into involuntary bankruptcy.

(c) Dorinda dies.

• **For a sample answer to Question 37–2, go to Appendix I at the end of this text.**

37–3. Distribution of Partnership Assets Meyer, Knapp, and Cavanna establish a partnership to operate a window-washing service. Meyer contributes $10,000 to the partnership, and Knapp and Cavanna contribute $1,000 each. The partnership agreement is silent as to how profits and losses will be shared. One month after the partnership begins operation, Knapp and Cavanna vote, over Meyer's objection, to purchase another truck for the firm. Meyer believes that because he contributed $10,000, the partnership cannot make any major commitment to purchase over his objection. In addition, Meyer claims that in the absence of any provision in the agreement, profits must be divided in the same ratio as capital contributions. Discuss Meyer's contentions.

37–4. Indications of Partnership At least six months before the 1996 Summer Olympic Games in Atlanta, Georgia, Stafford Fontenot, Steve Turner, Mike Montelaro, Joe Sokol, and Doug Brinsmade agreed to sell Cajun food at the Games and began making preparations. Calling themselves "Prairie Cajun Seafood Catering of Louisiana," on May 19 the group applied for a license with the Fulton County, Georgia, Department of Public Health–Environmental Health Services. Later, Ted Norris received for the sale of a mobile kitchen an $8,000 check drawn on the "Prairie Cajun Seafood Catering of Louisiana" account and two promissory notes, one for $12,000 and the other for $20,000. The notes, which were dated June 12, listed only Fontenot "d/b/a [doing business as] Prairie Cajun Seafood" as the maker. On July 31, Fontenot and his friends signed a partnership agreement, which listed specific percentages of profits and losses. They drove the mobile kitchen to Atlanta, but business was "disastrous." When the notes were not paid, Norris filed a suit in a Louisiana state court against Fontenot, seeking payment. What are the elements of a partnership? Did a partnership exist among Fontenot and the others? Why or why not? Who is liable on the notes? Why? [*Norris v. Fontenot*, 867 So.2d 179 (La.App. 3 Cir. 2004)]

37–5. Partnership Status Charlie Waugh owned and operated an auto parts junkyard in Georgia. Charlie's son, Mack, started working in the business part-time as a child and full-time when he left school at the age of sixteen. Mack oversaw the business's finances, depositing the profits in a bank. Charlie gave Mack a one-half interest in the business, telling him that if "something happened" to Charlie, the entire business would be his. In 1994, Charlie and his wife, Alene, transferred to Mack the land on which the junkyard was located. Two years later, however, Alene and her daughters, Gail and Jewel, falsely convinced Charlie, whose mental competence had deteriorated, that Mack had cheated him. Mack was ordered off the land. Shortly thereafter, Charlie died.

Mack filed a suit in a Georgia state court against the rest of the family, asserting, in part, that he and Charlie had been partners and that he was entitled to Charlie's share of the business. Was the relationship between Charlie and Mack a partnership? Is Mack entitled to Charlie's "share"? Explain. [*Waugh v. Waugh*, 265 Ga.App. 799, 595 S.E.2d 647 (2004)]

37–6. CASE PROBLEM WITH SAMPLE ANSWER: Indications of Partnership.

In August 2003, Tammy Duncan began working as a waitress at Bynum's Diner, which was owned by her mother, Hazel Bynum, and her stepfather, Eddie Bynum, in Valdosta, Georgia. Less than a month later, the three signed an agreement under which Eddie was to relinquish his management responsibilities, allowing Tammy to be co-manager. At the end of this six-month period, Eddie would revisit this agreement and could then extend it for another six-month period. The diner's bank account was to remain in Eddie's name. There was no provision with regard to the diner's profit, if any, and the parties did not change the business's tax information. Tammy began doing the bookkeeping, as well as waiting tables and performing other duties. On October 30, she slipped off a ladder and injured her knees. At the end of the six-month term, Tammy quit working at the diner. The Georgia State Board of Workers' Compensation determined that she had been the diner's employee and awarded her benefits under the diner's workers' compensation policy with Cypress Insurance Co. Cypress filed a suit in a Georgia state court against Tammy, arguing that she was not an employee, but a co-owner. What are the essential elements of a partnership? Was Tammy a partner in the business of the diner? Explain. [Cypress Insurance Co. v. Duncan, 281 Ga.App. 469, 636 S.E.2d 159 (2006)]

• **To view a sample answer for Problem 37–6, go to this book's Web site at www.cengage.com/blaw/clarkson, select "Chapter 37," and click on "Case Problem with Sample Answer."**

37–7. Partnership Dissolution Nine minority partners each owned one-half of 1 percent of J&J Celcom, a partnership with AT&T, which owned the rest. AT&T, using its majority power, voted to buy out the minority partners. It offered each partner a price that was slightly higher than the price provided by a third party's appraisal. Some of the partners accepted the offer, but others did not. AT&T then voted to dissolve the partnership, forcing the remaining minority partners to accept the appraisal price. Those partners sued. The trial court held for AT&T, and the minority partners appealed. The appeals court held that the price offered was the fair market price, but certified the following question to Washington State's highest court: "Does a controlling partner violate the duty of loyalty to the partnership or to dissenting minority partners where the controlling partner causes the partnership to sell all its assets" to another party? How should the Washington Supreme Court answer this question? Why? [*J&J Celcom v. AT&T Wireless Services, Inc.*, 162 Wash.2d 102, 169 P.3d 823 (Sup.Ct. 2007)]

37–8. Limited Partnership James Carpenter contracted with Austin Estates, LP, to buy property in Texas. Carpenter asked Sandra McBeth to invest in the deal. He admitted that a dispute had arisen with the city of Austin over water for the property, but he assured her that it would not be a significant obstacle. McBeth agreed to invest $800,000 to hold open the option to buy the property. She became a limited partner in StoneLake Ranch, LP. Carpenter acted as the firm's general partner. Despite his assurances to McBeth, the purchase was delayed due to the water dispute. Unable to complete the purchase in a timely manner, Carpenter paid the $800,000 to Austin Estates without notifying McBeth. Later, Carpenter and others—*excluding* McBeth—bought the property and sold it at a profit. McBeth filed a suit in a Texas state court against Carpenter. What is the nature of the fiduciary duty that a general partner owes a limited partner? Did Carpenter breach that duty in this case? Explain. [*McBeth v. Carpenter*, 565 F.3d 171 (5th Cir. 2009)]

37–9. Partnership Dissolution George Chaney and William Dickerson were partners in Bowen's Mill Landing, which purchased a large piece of land in the 1980s. The partners had planned to develop the property, but nothing was ever done. Chaney died in 1990, and his wife inherited his interest. When she died in 2004, her two sons, John and Dewey Lynch, inherited the half-interest in the partnership. Dickerson died in 1995, and his daughter, Billie Thompson, inherited his half-interest. In 2006, the Lynches filed a petition for partition, asking that a commission be appointed to make a fair division of the land, giving the Lynches half and Thompson half. In 2007, the commission reported on how to divide the land into two parts. Thompson objected that the land belonged to Bowen's Mill Landing and could not be divided. The trial court ordered Thompson to "effectuate the dissolution of any partnership entity and . . . to wind up the business and affairs of any partnership" so that the land could be divided. Thompson appealed. Can the court order the partnership to dissolve? Why or why not? [*Thompson v. Lynch*, 990 A.2d 432 (Sup.Ct.Del. 2010)]

37–10. A QUESTION OF ETHICS: Wrongful Dissociation.

Elliot Willensky and Beverly Moran formed a partnership to renovate and "flip" (resell) some property. According to their agreement, Moran would finance the purchase and renovation of the property, and Willensky would provide labor and oversight of the renovation work. Moran would be reimbursed from the profits of the sale, and the remainder of the profits would be divided evenly. Any losses would also be divided evenly. Moran paid $240,000 for a house and planned to spend $60,000 for its renovation. The parties agreed that the renovation would be completed in six months. Willensky lived in the house during the renovation. More than a year later, the project still was not completed, and the cost was much more than the $60,000 originally planned. Willensky often failed to communicate with Moran, and when she learned that her funds were nearly exhausted and the house nowhere near completion, she became worried. She told Willensky that he would have to pay rent and utility bills if he wished to continue to live in the house. Shortly thereafter, Willensky left for Florida due to a family emergency, saying that he would return as soon as he could. He never returned, however, and Moran lost touch with him. Moran took over the project and discovered that Willensky had left numerous bills unpaid, spent money on excessive or unnecessary items, and misappropriated funds for his personal use. After completing the project, paying all expenses relating to the renovation (in all, the renovation costs came to $311,222), and selling the property, Moran brought an action in a Tennessee state court to dissolve the partnership and to recover damages from Willensky for breach of contract and wrongful dissociation from the partnership. [Moran v. Willensky, ___ S.W.3d ___ (Tenn.Ct.App. 2010)]

(a) Moran alleged that Willensky had wrongfully dissociated from the partnership. When did this dissociation occur? Why was his dissociation wrongful?

(b) Which of Willensky's actions simply represent unethical behavior or bad management, and which constitute a breach of the agreement?

LEGAL RESEARCH EXERCISES ON THE WEB

Go to this text's Web site at **www.cengage.com/blaw/clarkson**, select "Chapter 37," and click on "Practical Internet Exercises." There you will find the following Internet research exercises that you can perform to learn more about the topics covered in this chapter.

Practical Internet Exercise 37–1: Legal Perspective
Liability of Dissociated Partners

Practical Internet Exercise 37–2: Economic Perspective
Taxation of Partnerships

Practical Internet Exercise 37–3: Management Perspective
Limited Partnerships and Limited Liability Partnerships

CHAPTER 38

Limited Liability Companies and Special Business Forms

I n the preceding chapters, we examined sole proprietorships, partnerships, and several forms of limited partnerships. Here, we examine a relatively new form of business organization called the *limited liability company (LLC)*. LLCs are becoming an organizational form of choice among businesspersons—

a trend encouraged by state statutes permitting their use.

In this chapter, we begin by examining the origins and evolution of the LLC. We then look at important characteristics of the LLC, including formation, jurisdictional requirements, and the advantages and disadvantages

of choosing to do business as an LLC. Next, we examine the operation and management options in an LLC. The chapter concludes with a discussion of various other special business forms, including joint ventures, syndicates, joint stock companies, business trusts, and cooperatives.

SECTION 1
THE LIMITED LIABILITY COMPANY

A **limited liability company (LLC)** is a hybrid form that combines the limited liability aspects of the corporation and the tax advantages of a partnership. These business forms are governed by state LLC statutes. These laws vary, of course, from state to state. In an attempt to create more uniformity among the states in this respect, in 1995 the National Conference of Commissioners on Uniform State Laws issued the Uniform Limited Liability Company Act (ULLCA), but less than one-fifth of the states adopted it. Some provisions are common to most state statutes, however, and we base our discussion of LLCs in this section on these common elements.

In 1977, Wyoming became the first state to pass legislation authorizing the creation of an LLC. Although LLCs emerged in the United States in the latter half of the 1900s, they have been used for more than a century in other foreign jurisdictions, including several European and South American nations. For example, the South American *limitada* is a form of business organization that operates

more or less as a partnership but provides limited liability for the owners. Japan has the *godo kaisha*, a limited liability type of business organization that is similar to an LLC.

Taxation of the LLC

In the United States, after Wyoming's adoption of an LLC statute, it still was unclear how the Internal Revenue Service (IRS) would treat the LLC for tax purposes. In 1988, however, the IRS ruled that Wyoming LLCs would be taxed as partnerships instead of corporations, providing that certain requirements were met. Before this ruling, only one additional state—Florida, in 1982—had authorized LLCs. The 1988 ruling encouraged other states to enact LLC statutes, and in less than a decade, all states had done so.

In 1997, IRS rules also encouraged more widespread use of LLCs in the business world. Under these rules, any unincorporated business with more than one owner is automatically taxed as a partnership unless it indicates otherwise on its tax form or fits into one of the exceptions. The exceptions involve publicly traded companies, companies formed under a state incorporation statute, and certain foreign-owned companies. If a business chooses to be taxed as a corporation, it can indicate this preference by checking a box on its tax form.

Part of the impetus behind creating LLCs in this country is that foreign investors are allowed to become LLC members. Thus, in an era increasingly characterized by global business efforts and investments, the LLC offers U.S. firms and potential investors from other countries flexibility and the opportunity for limited liability and increased tax benefits.

The Nature of the LLC

LLCs share many characteristics with corporations. Like corporations, LLCs are creatures of state statute. In other words, they must be formed and operated in compliance with state law. Like the shareholders of a corporation, the owners of an LLC, who are called **members,** enjoy limited liability [ULLCA 303].[1] Thus, if the LLC is sued for wrongful discharge, for example, its individual members, managers, and agents cannot be held liable based solely on their status in the LLC.[2]

Similar to corporations, LLCs are legal entities apart from their owners. As a legal person, the LLC can sue or be sued, enter into contracts, and hold title to property [ULLCA 201]. The terminology used to describe LLCs formed in other states or nations is also similar to that used in corporate law. For example, an LLC formed in one state but doing business in another state is referred to in the second state as a *foreign LLC.*

---

1. Members of an LLC can also bring derivative actions, which you will read about in Chapter 40, on behalf of the LLC [ULLCA 101]. As with a corporate shareholder's derivative suit, any damages recovered go to the LLC, not to the members personally.
2. See, for example, *McFarland v. Virginia Retirement Services of Chesterfield, LLC,* 477 F.Supp.2d 727 (2007).

The Formation of the LLC

As mentioned, LLCs are creatures of statute and thus must follow state statutory requirements. To form an LLC, **articles of organization** must be filed with a central state agency—usually the secretary of state's office [ULLCA 202].[3] Typically, the articles are required to include such information as the name of the business, its principal address, the name and address of a registered agent, the names of the owners, and information on how the LLC will be managed [ULLCA 203]. The business's name must include the words *Limited Liability Company* or the initials *LLC* [ULLCA 105(a)]. Although a majority of the states permit one-member LLCs, some states require at least two members.

Businesspersons sometimes enter into contracts on behalf of a business organization that is not yet formed. As you will read in Chapter 39, persons who are forming a corporation may enter into contracts during the process of incorporation but before the corporation becomes a legal entity. These contracts are referred to as *preincorporation contracts.* Once the corporation is formed and adopts the preincorporation contracts (by means of a *novation,* discussed in Chapter 17), it can enforce the contract terms.

In the following case, the question was whether the same principle extends to LLCs. A person in the process of forming an LLC entered into a preorganization contract under which it would be obligated to purchase a hotel. Once the LLC legally existed, the owners of the hotel refused to sell the property to the LLC, claiming that the contract was unenforceable.

---

3. In addition to requiring articles of organization to be filed, a few states require that a notice of the intention to form an LLC be published in a local newspaper.

CASE 38.1

02 Development, LLC v. 607 South Park, LLC

Court of Appeal of California, Second District, 159 Cal.App.4th 609, 71 Cal.Rptr.3d 608 (2008).

BACKGROUND AND FACTS • In 2004, 607 South Park, LLC, entered into a written agreement to sell Park Plaza Hotel to 607 Park View Associates, Ltd., for $8.7 million. The general partner of 607 Park View Associates was Creative Environments of Hollywood, Inc. In 2005, Creative Environments assigned the rights to the hotel purchase to another company, 02 Development, LLC. At the time, 02 Development did not yet exist; it was legally created several months later. When 607 South Park subsequently refused to sell the hotel, 02 Development sued 607 South Park for breach of the hotel purchase agreement. 607 South Park moved for summary judgment, arguing that no enforceable contract

CASE 38.1 CONTINUED ➧ existed because at the time of the assignment, 02 Development did not yet legally exist. Furthermore, 607 South Park argued that 02 Development suffered no damages because it was "not ready, willing, and able to fund the purchase of the hotel." The trial court granted the motion and entered judgment in favor of 607 South Park. 02 Development appealed.

IN THE LANGUAGE OF THE COURT
ROTHSCHILD, J. [Judge]

* * * *

It is hornbook law [black letter, or well-established, law] that a corporation can enforce preincorporation contracts made in its behalf, as long as the corporation "has adopted the contract or otherwise succeeded to it." * * * California law does not deviate from that well-established norm. *607 South Park does not argue that limited liability companies should be treated differently from corporations in this respect, and we are aware of no authority that would support such a position.* 607 South Park's first ground for its summary judgment motion—that there is no enforceable contract between 607 South Park and 02 Development because 02 Development did not exist when the assignment agreement was executed—therefore fails as a matter of law. [Emphasis added.]

607 South Park's principal contention to the contrary is that a nonexistent business entity cannot be a party to a contract. The contention is true but irrelevant. *When the assignment agreement was executed, 02 Development did not exist, so it was not then a party to the agreement. But once 02 Development came into existence, it could enforce any pre-organization contract made in its behalf, such as the assignment agreement, if it adopted or ratified it.* [Emphasis added.]

* * * *

In the trial court, 607 South Park contended that in order to prove causation, 02 Development would have to prove either that it had the $8.7 million necessary to fund the transaction or that it had legally binding commitments from third parties to provide the necessary funding.* * * 607 South Park disavows [this contention] on appeal.

Instead, 607 South Park now argues that its motion was based on the proposition that 02 Development "must present admissible evidence that it would have been financially able to close the transaction." But 607 South Park's evidence in support of its motion showed only that 02 Development had neither the $8.7 million to fund the transaction nor legally binding commitments from third parties to provide the funding. *607 South Park presented no evidence that 02 Development would have been unable to arrange for the necessary funding to close the transaction on time if 607 South Park had given it the opportunity instead of repudiating the contract in advance.* Because 607 South Park introduced no evidence to support an argument based on the proposition of law that 607 South Park is now advocating, the burden of production never shifted to 02 Development to present contrary evidence. For all of these reasons, the trial court erred when it granted 607 South Park's motion for summary judgment. [Emphasis added.]

DECISION AND REMEDY • *The California intermediate appellate court reversed the judgment and directed the trial court to enter an order denying 607 South Park's motion for summary judgment. According to the appellate court, limited liability companies should be treated the same as corporations with respect to preorganization contracts.*

THE LEGAL ENVIRONMENT DIMENSION • *Why did the appellate court dismiss 607 South Park's argument that 02 Development should be required to prove that it had funding commitments for $8.7 million?*

THE ETHICAL DIMENSION • *What might have been some of the reasons that 607 South Park refused to sell the property to 02 Development?*

Jurisdictional Requirements

One of the significant differences between LLCs and corporations involves federal jurisdictional requirements. Under the federal jurisdiction statute, a corporation is deemed to be a citizen of the state where it is incorporated and maintains its principal place of business. The statute does not mention the state citizenship of partnerships, LLCs, and other unincorporated associations, but the courts have tended to regard these entities as citizens of every state in which their members are citizens.

The state citizenship of an LLC may come into play when a party sues the LLC based on diversity of citizenship. Remember from Chapter 2 that when parties to a lawsuit are from different states and the amount in controversy exceeds $75,000, a federal court can exercise diversity jurisdiction. *Total* diversity of citizenship must exist, however.

Suppose that Jen Fong, a citizen of New York, wishes to bring a suit against Skycel, an LLC formed under the laws of Connecticut. One of Skycel's members also lives in New York. Fong will not be able to bring a suit against Skycel in federal court on the basis of diversity jurisdiction because the defendant LLC is also a citizen of New York. The same would be true if Fong was bringing a suit against multiple defendants and one of the defendants lived in New York.

Advantages of the LLC

The LLC offers many advantages to businesspersons, which is why this form of business organization has become increasingly popular.

LIMITED LIABILITY A key advantage of the LLC is that the liability of members is limited to the amount of their investments. Although the LLC as an entity can be held liable for any loss or injury caused by the wrongful acts or omissions of its members, the members themselves generally are not personally liable.

As you will read in Chapter 39, the courts on occasion make an exception to the limited liability of shareholders. In certain circumstances, a court will *pierce the corporate veil* and hold a shareholder personally liable for a corporate obligation.

Sometimes, the corporate veil is pierced when a corporation is deemed to be merely an "alter ego" of the shareholder-owner (see page 768). A court may apply the alter-ego theory when a shareholder commingles personal and corporate funds or fails to observe required corporate formalities.

Whether the alter-ego theory should be applied to an LLC was at issue in the following case.

✳ EXTENDED CASE 38.2 ✳
ORX Resources, Inc. v. MBW Exploration, LLC

Court of Appeal of Louisiana, Fourth Circuit, 32 So.3d 931 (2010).
www.la4th.org[a]

IN THE LANGUAGE OF THE COURT
Charles R. *JONES*, Judge.
* * * *
On January 16, 2003, ORX [Resources, Inc.,] entered into the "Clovelly Purchase Agreement" with Coastline Oil & Gas, Inc. Pursuant to this Agreement, ORX purchased certain oil, gas and mineral leases/interests in a tract of land located in Lafourche Parish, known as the "Clovelly Prospect." ORX partnered with other entities, including MBW [Exploration, LLC], to share in the expense and potential profits of the

venture to explore and develop the Clovelly Prospect. The partnering parties entered into a Joint Operating Agreement ("JOA") and the Clovelly Prospect Participation Agreement ("Participation Agreement"). Mr. [Mark] Washauer signed these documents in October of 2003 and December of 2004, respectively, on behalf of MBW, in his capacity as a "Managing Member." However, MBW did not come into existence until July of 2005, when its articles of organization were filed with the Louisiana Secretary of State.

The JOA provided that ORX was to serve as the "Operator" drilling a

well within the Clovelly Prospect. It further provided that the nonoperating working interest partners, like MBW, would pay their proportionate share of the costs in exchange for a corresponding working interest ownership share in the Clovelly Prospect. The drilled well was governed by the Participation Agreement, which provided that MBW had a working interest in the Clovelly Prospect whereby MBW would share in 2.5% of the costs incurred, and would gain a proportionate share of the returns, if any, produced by the well.

Later, ORX submitted an Authorization for Expenditure

---

a. In the "Case Searching Options" area of the screen, select "Opinions." When the search page opens, select "Search Case Year and Number" and then enter "2009" in the "Case Year" box and "0662" in the "Case Number" box. When the search result appears at the bottom of the screen, click on "Download Opinion." The Louisiana Court of Appeal for the Fourth Circuit maintains this Web site.

EXTENDED CASE 38.2 CONTINUED ➡

("AFE") to MBW for approval, which Mr. Washauer signed in his own name. Additionally, he paid MBW's participation fee with a check drawn from the account of another entity, MBW Properties, LLC.

In 2006, ORX, as the well Operator, began planning the Allain LeBreton Well No. 2 in the Clovelly Prospect, ("the Well"), which was the "initial well" called for in the Participation Agreement. * * * Mr. Washauer paid the full amount of MBW's share of an ORX cash call invoice of $59,325 with a personal check.

The well proved to be unsuccessful, and was ultimately plugged. MBW's unpaid share of expenses for said project amounted to $84,220.01, for which ORX demanded payment via correspondence, but to no avail. As a result, ORX filed suit for breach of contract against both MBW and Mr. Washauer ("the Appellants").

* * * [The trial court—a state district court—determined that Washauer operated MBW as his alter ego and allowed ORX to pierce the veil of the LLC. The court granted summary judgment in favor of ORX, holding that Washauer and MBW were liable, jointly and severally, to ORX in the amount of $84,220.01.]

The Appellants timely filed [an] appeal from this judgment.
* * * *

We first address whether the district court erred in ruling that the alter ego theory of the corporate veil piercing applied to Louisiana limited liability companies.
* * * *

The provisions of La. R.S. [Louisiana Revised Statutes] 12:1320(D) provide for the piercing of an LLC's veil when the situation so warrants.
* * * *

* * * *Piercing the veil of an LLC is justified to prevent the use of the LLC form to defraud creditors.* Under our * * * review, we find that the district court did not err in determining that the alter ego theory of corporate veil piercing applies to a Louisiana limited liability company, under the facts of this case, where it appears that Mr. Washauer used MBW as a shell and tried to avoid paying a legitimate debt of the LLC. [Emphasis added.]
* * * *

The Louisiana Supreme Court has identified *five nonexclusive factors to be used in determining whether to apply the alter ego doctrine: [commingling of corporate and shareholder funds; failure to follow statutory formalities for incorporating and transacting corporate affairs;*

undercapitalization; failure to provide separate bank accounts and bookkeeping records; and failure to hold regular shareholder and director meetings]. [Emphasis added.]
* * * *

In applying [these] factors, * * * we find that Mr. Washauer's activities on behalf of MBW do merit the piercing of the veil of this LLC. Commingling of the LLC's funds occurred with the funds of Mr. Washauer and a separate company of his. This commingling occurred because MBW was undercapitalized and did not have a separate bank account to transact its own affairs. Furthermore, at the time MBW began contracting with ORX, it was not yet recognized as an LLC by the Louisiana Secretary of State. Lastly, while LLCs are not bound by corporate laws to hold regular meetings, the fact that MBW has not had a meeting in over a year further evidences that Mr. Washauer was operating MBW at his leisure and direction. Thus, we find that the district court did not err in determining that MBW was being operated as the alter ego of Mr. Washauer under the [above-mentioned] factors, and therefore, he can be held personally liable jointly and solidarily [severally] with MBW.

For the foregoing reasons, * * * the judgment of the district court is affirmed * * * .

 QUESTIONS

1. One of the advantages of the LLC is that its members enjoy limited personal liability for the company's obligations. In view of this fact, does the possibility that a court may hold an LLC member personally liable for the LLC's debts reduce the utility of the LLC form of business organization? Explain.
2. What does "jointly and solidarily" (jointly and severally) mean in terms of liability? Would ORX prefer that Washauer and MBW be held personally liable jointly and severally, rather than that Washauer alone be held personally liable? Explain.

FLEXIBILITY IN TAXATION Another advantage of the LLC is its flexibility in regard to taxation. An LLC that has *two or more members* can choose to be taxed as either a partnership or a corporation. As will be discussed in Chapter 39, a corporate entity must pay income taxes on its profits, and the shareholders pay personal income taxes on profits distributed as

dividends. An LLC that wants to distribute profits to its members may prefer to be taxed as a partnership to avoid the "double taxation" that is characteristic of the corporate entity.

Unless an LLC indicates that it wishes to be taxed as a corporation, the IRS automatically taxes it as a partnership. This means that the LLC, as an entity, pays no taxes. Rather, as in a partnership, profits are "passed through" the LLC to the members, who then personally pay taxes on the profits. If an LLC's members want to reinvest profits in the business rather than distribute the profits to members, however, they may prefer to be taxed as a corporation. Corporate income tax rates may be lower than personal tax rates. Part of the attractiveness of the LLC is this flexibility with respect to taxation.

An LLC that has only *one member* cannot be taxed as a partnership. For federal income tax purposes, one-member LLCs are automatically taxed as sole proprietorships unless they indicate that they wish to be taxed as corporations. With respect to state taxes, most states follow the IRS rules.

MANAGEMENT AND FOREIGN INVESTORS Another advantage of the LLC for businesspersons is the flexibility it offers in terms of business operations and management—as will be discussed shortly. Because foreign investors can participate in an LLC, the LLC form of business is attractive as a way to encourage investment.

Disadvantages of the LLC

The main disadvantage of the LLC is that state LLC statutes are not uniform. Therefore, businesses that operate in more than one state may not receive consistent treatment in these states. Generally, most states apply to a foreign LLC (an LLC formed in another state) the law of the state where the LLC was formed. Nonetheless, difficulties can arise when one state's court must interpret and apply another state's laws.

SECTION 2
OPERATION AND MANAGEMENT OF AN LLC

As mentioned, an advantage of the LLC form of business is the flexibility it offers in terms of operation and management. Here, we discuss the operating agreement, management options, and general operating procedures of LLCs.

The LLC Operating Agreement

The members of an LLC can decide how to operate the various aspects of the business by forming an **operating agreement** [ULLCA 103(a)]. Operating agreements typically contain provisions relating to management, how profits will be divided, the

transfer of membership interests, whether the LLC will be dissolved on the death or departure of a member, and other important issues.

A WRITING IS PREFERRED In many states, an operating agreement is not required for an LLC to exist, and if there is one, it need not be in writing. Generally, though, LLC members should protect their interests by creating a written operating agreement. As with any business, disputes may arise over any number of issues. If there is no agreement covering the topic under dispute, such as how profits will be divided, the state LLC statute will govern the outcome. For example, most LLC statutes provide that if the members have not specified how profits will be divided, they will be divided equally among the members.

PARTNERSHIP LAW MAY APPLY When an issue, such as the authority of individual members, is not covered by an operating agreement or by an LLC statute, the courts often apply principles of partnership law. These principles can give the members broad authority to bind the LLC unless the operating agreement provides otherwise.

CASE IN POINT Clifford Kuhn, Jr., and Joseph Tumminelli formed Touch of Class Limousine Service as an LLC. They did not create a written operating agreement but orally agreed that Kuhn would provide the financial backing and that Tumminelli would manage the day-to-day operations. Tumminelli embezzled $283,000 from the company after cashing customers' checks at Quick Cash, Inc., a local check-cashing service. Kuhn sued Tumminelli and Quick Cash to recover the embezzled funds. He argued that Quick Cash was liable because Tumminelli did not have the authority to cash the company's checks. The court, however, held that in the absence of a written operating agreement to the contrary, a member of an LLC, like a partner in a partnership, has the authority to cash a firm's checks.[4]

Management of an LLC

Basically, LLC members have two options for managing the firm. It can be either a "member-managed" LLC or a "manager-managed" LLC. Most state LLC statutes and the ULLCA provide that unless the articles of organization specify otherwise, an LLC is assumed to be member managed [ULLCA 203(a)(6)].

In a *member-managed* LLC, all of the members participate in management, and decisions are made by majority vote [ULLCA 404(a)]. In a *manager-managed*

4. *Kuhn v. Tumminelli,* 366 N.J.Super. 431, 841 A.2d 496 (2004).

LLC, the members designate a group of persons to manage the firm. The management group may consist of only members, both members and nonmembers, or only nonmembers.

Under the ULLCA, managers in a manager-managed LLC owe fiduciary duties (the duty of loyalty and the duty of care) to the LLC and its members—just as corporate directors and officers owe fiduciary duties to the corporation and its shareholders [ULLCA 409(a), 409(h)]. But because not all states have adopted the ULLCA, some state statutes provide that managers owe fiduciary duties only to the LLC and not to the LLC's members. Although to whom the duty is owed may seem insignificant at first glance, it can have a dramatic effect on the outcome of litigation. See this chapter's *Insight into Ethics* feature below for further discussion of this issue.

Operating Procedures

An LLC's operating agreement can also include provisions governing decision-making procedures. For instance, the agreement can set forth procedures for choosing or removing managers. Although most LLC statutes are silent on this issue, the ULLCA provides that members may choose and remove managers by majority vote [ULLCA 404(b)(3)].

The members are also free to include in the agreement provisions designating when and for what purposes they will hold formal members' meetings. Most state LLC statutes have no provisions regarding members' meetings, which is in contrast to most state laws governing corporations, as you will read in Chapter 39.

Members may also specify in their agreement how voting rights will be apportioned. If they do not, LLC statutes in most states provide that voting rights are apportioned according to each member's capital contributions.[5] Some states provide that, in the absence of an agreement to the contrary, each member has one vote.

```
        ▲▲▲▲  SECTION 3  ◢◣◢◣
```

DISSOCIATION AND DISSOLUTION OF AN LLC

Recall from Chapter 37 that in the context of partnerships, *dissociation* occurs when a partner ceases to be associated in the carrying on of the partnership business. The same concept applies to LLCs. A member

---

5. In contrast, partners in a partnership generally have equal rights in management and equal voting rights unless they specify otherwise in their partnership agreement (see Chapter 37).

INSIGHT INTO ETHICS
Fiduciary Duties of LLC Managers

Fiduciary duties, such as the duty of loyalty and the duty of care, have an ethical component because they require a person to act honestly and faithfully toward another. In states that have adopted the ULLCA, the managers of a manager-managed LLC owe fiduciary duties to the members and thus basically are required to behave ethically toward them. In other states, however, the LLC statutes may not include such a requirement. Consequently, even when a manager has acted unfairly and unethically toward members, the members may not be able to sue the manager for a breach of fiduciary duties.

In North Carolina and Virginia, for example, the LLC statutes do not explicitly create fiduciary duties for managers to members. Instead, the statutes require that a manager exercise good business judgment in the best interests of the company. Because the statutes are silent on the manager's duty to members, in 2009 courts in those two states held that a manager-member owed fiduciary duties only to the LLC and not to the other members.[a] In contrast, in two other cases decided in 2009, courts in Idaho and Kentucky held that a manager-member owed fiduciary duties to the LLC's other members and that the members could sue the manager for breaching fiduciary duties.[b]

CRITICAL THINKING

INSIGHT INTO THE ETHICAL ENVIRONMENT
Why wouldn't a manager always owe a fiduciary duty to the members of an LLC?

---

a. *Remora Investments, LLC v. Orr,* 277 Va. 316, 673 S.E.2d 845 (2009), applying Virginia Code Sections 13.1–1024.1; and *Kaplan v. O.K. Technologies, LLC,* 675 S.E.2d 133 (N.C.App. 2009), applying North Carolina General Statutes Section 57C-3-22(b).
b. *Bushi v. Sage Health Care, LLC,* 146 Idaho 764, 203 P.3d 694 (2009), applying Idaho Code Sections 30-6-101 *et seq.;* and *Patmon v. Hobbs,* 280 S.W.3d 589 (Ky.App. 2009), applying Kentucky Revised Statutes Section 275.170.

of an LLC has the *power* to dissociate from the LLC at any time, but he or she may not have the *right* to dissociate. Under the ULLCA, the events that trigger a member's dissociation from an LLC are similar to the events causing a partner to be dissociated under the Uniform Partnership Act (UPA). These include voluntary withdrawal, expulsion by other members or by court order, bankruptcy, incompetence, and death. Generally, even if a member dies or otherwise dissociates from an LLC, the other members may continue to carry on the LLC business, unless the operating agreement provides otherwise.

Effect of Dissociation

When a member dissociates from an LLC, he or she loses the right to participate in management and the right to act as an agent for the LLC. The member's duty of loyalty to the LLC also terminates, and the duty of care continues only with respect to events that occurred before dissociation. Generally, the dissociated member also has a right to have his or her interest in the LLC bought out by the other members. The LLC's operating agreement may contain provisions establishing a buyout price, but if it does not, the member's interest is usually purchased at a fair value. In states that have adopted the ULLCA, the LLC must purchase the interest at fair value within 120 days after the dissociation.

If the member's dissociation violates the LLC's operating agreement, it is considered legally wrongful, and the dissociated member can be held liable for damages caused by the dissociation. Suppose that Chadwick and Barrow are members in an LLC. Chadwick manages the accounts, and Barrow, who has many connections in the community and is a skilled investor, brings in the business. If Barrow wrongfully dissociates from the LLC, the LLC's business will suffer, and Chadwick can hold Barrow liable for the loss of business resulting from her withdrawal.

Dissolution

Regardless of whether a member's dissociation was wrongful or rightful, normally the dissociated member has no right to force the LLC to dissolve. The remaining members can opt either to continue or to dissolve the business. Members can also stipulate in their operating agreement that certain events will cause dissolution, or they can agree that they have the power to dissolve the LLC by vote. As with partnerships, a court can order an LLC to be dissolved in certain circumstances, such as when the members have engaged in illegal or oppressive conduct, or when it is no longer feasible to carry on the business.

When an LLC is dissolved, any members who did not wrongfully dissociate may participate in the winding up process. To wind up the business, members must collect, liquidate, and distribute the LLC's assets. Members may preserve the assets for a reasonable time to optimize their return, and they continue to have the authority to perform reasonable acts in conjunction with winding up. In other words, the LLC will be bound by the reasonable acts of its members during the winding up process. Once all of the LLC's assets have been sold, the proceeds are distributed to pay off debts to creditors first (including debts owed to members who are creditors of the LLC). The members' capital contributions are returned next, and any remaining amounts are then distributed to members in equal shares or according to their operating agreement.

SPECIAL BUSINESS FORMS

In addition to the LLC and the other traditional business forms discussed in this unit, several other forms can be used to organize a business. For the most part, these special business forms are hybrid organizations—that is, they have characteristics similar to those of partnerships or corporations, or combine features of both. These forms include joint ventures, syndicates, joint stock companies, business trusts, and cooperatives.

Joint Venture

A **joint venture** is a relationship in which two or more persons or business entities combine their efforts or their property for a single transaction or project or a related series of transactions or projects. Unless otherwise agreed, joint venturers share profits and losses equally and have an equal voice in controlling the project. For instance, when several contractors combine their resources to build and sell houses in a single development, their relationship is a joint venture.

Joint ventures range in size from very small activities to multimillion-dollar joint actions carried out by some of the world's largest corporations. Large organizations often undertake new products or services by forming joint ventures with other enterprises. For example, Intel Corporation and Micron Technology,

Inc., formed a joint venture to manufacture NAND flash memory, a data-storage chip widely used in digital cameras, cell phones, and portable music players, including some iPods made by Apple, Inc. Similarly, Mitsubishi Chemical Corporation formed a joint venture with Exxon Chemical Corporation to start Mytex Polymers, a company that produces certain plastic compounds used by automakers in the United States and Japan.

SIMILARITIES TO PARTNERSHIPS The joint venture resembles a partnership and is taxed like a partnership. For this reason, most courts apply the same principles to joint ventures as they apply to partnerships. Joint venturers owe each other the same fiduciary duties, including the duty of loyalty, that partners owe each other. Thus, if one of the venturers secretly buys land that was to be acquired by the joint venture, the other joint venturers may be awarded damages for the breach of loyalty. A joint venturer can also be held personally liable for the venture's debts (because joint venturers share profits *and losses*).

Like partners, joint venturers have equal rights to manage the activities of the enterprise, but they can agree to give control of the operation to one of the members.[6] Joint venturers also have authority as agents to enter into contracts for the business that will bind the joint venture.

The question in the following case was whether two vintage aircraft makers had formed a joint venture.

---

6. See, for example, *PGI, Inc. v. Rathe Productions, Inc.,* 265 Va. 438, 576 S.E.2d 438 (2003).

CASE 38.3
SPW Associates, LLP v. Anderson

Supreme Court of North Dakota, 2006 ND 159, 718 N.W.2d 580 (2006).
www.ndcourts.com/search/opinions.asp[a]

BACKGROUND AND FACTS • In 1996, Murdo Cameron and Douglas Anderson entered into a written agreement to build two vintage airplanes. Cameron was to provide an engine for the first airplane and various other component parts for both airplanes, and Anderson was to design and manufacture additional parts and build the airplanes. On the first flight of one of the planes, Anderson was to pay Cameron for the engine, with the price dependent upon the amount of time it took Anderson to build the airplane. Although not expressly stated in the written agreement, Cameron and Anderson had agreed that each would keep one of the two completed airplanes. The parties intended to build additional planes for sale to the public. In 1997, Anderson entered into a loan agreement with SPW Associates, LLP, to finance the operation. The first airplane was pledged as security for the loan. Anderson did not disclose to SPW his agreement with Cameron and did not disclose to Cameron the loan transaction with SPW. The second airplane was never built. In 2002, after Anderson defaulted on the loan, SPW brought an action against Anderson, Cameron, and others in a North Dakota state court, seeking a declaratory judgment that it was entitled to possession of the aircraft. The court found that Anderson and Cameron had entered into a joint venture and that Anderson was authorized to grant SPW a security interest in the airplane, which was joint-venture property. The court found that SPW had a perfected security interest in the airplane superior to any rights of Cameron and was entitled to possession of the plane. Cameron appealed, claiming that there was no joint venture.

IN THE LANGUAGE OF THE COURT
VANDEWALLE, **Chief Justice.**
  * * * *A joint venture is generally considered akin to a partnership, although more limited in scope and duration, and principles of partnership law apply to the joint venture relationship.* [Emphasis added.]
  [North Dakota Century Code] Section 45-15-01(1) * * * provides that a partner is an agent of, and may bind, the partnership * * *.

---

a. In the "Title:" box, type "SPW" and click on "Execute." In the result, click on the name of the case to access the opinion. The North Dakota Supreme Court maintains this Web site.

CASE CONTINUES ▸

CASE 38.3 CONTINUED ➡   * * * Applying these principles in this case, if Anderson was a joint venturer with Cameron, he had the authority to grant a security interest in joint venture property and the security agreement would be valid.

For a business enterprise to constitute a joint venture, the following four elements must be present:

(1) contribution by the parties of money, property, time, or skill in some common undertaking * * * ; (2) a proprietary interest and right of mutual control over the engaged property; (3) an express or implied agreement for the sharing of profits * * * ; and (4) an express or implied contract showing a joint venture was formed.

* * * *

In this case there is no dispute on three of the four elements. Both parties made contributions to the enterprise, both exerted a degree of control over the enterprise, and there was a written contract evidencing the agreement. Cameron contends, however, that there was no evidence showing an agreement, either express or implied, to share profits.

In this case the parties admittedly contemplated building additional airplanes for sale to the public * * * . The parties' written agreement also expressly recognized that additional planes would be built for sale. For example, the agreement provided that Cameron would provide computerized documentation and lab test results on composite parts he manufactured to Anderson "and future aircraft purchasers," and Anderson was to "develop an inspection and documentation process on the first two airplanes, and all future airplanes purchased." The agreement further provided that construction of "all appliances" to be used in the manufacturing process "will be such that they can be used for multiple year production runs."

* * * *

We conclude the * * * court did not err in determining that Cameron and Anderson had entered into a joint venture.

DECISION AND REMEDY • *The Supreme Court of North Dakota affirmed the lower court's decision. Cameron and Anderson had entered into a joint venture, and SPW was entitled to possession of the plane.*

THE LEGAL ENVIRONMENT DIMENSION • *On what basis might Cameron maintain a suit against Anderson?*

WHAT IF THE FACTS WERE DIFFERENT? • *How might the outcome of this case have been different if Cameron had been merely an aircraft parts supplier, with his only profit to be from the sale of components to Anderson?*

DIFFERENCES FROM PARTNERSHIPS Joint ventures differ from partnerships in several important ways. The members of a joint venture have less implied and apparent authority than the partners in a partnership. In part, this is because a joint venture is typically created for a single project or series of transactions, whereas a partnership usually (though not always) involves an ongoing business. As discussed in Chapter 37, each partner is treated as an agent of the other partners. Because the activities of a joint venture are more limited than the business of a partnership, the members of a joint venture are presumed to have less power to bind their co-venturers. In Case 38.3 above, for instance, if Anderson's loan agreement with SPW had not been directly related to the business of building vintage planes, the court might have concluded that Anderson lacked the authority to bind the joint venture. Also, unlike most partnerships, a joint venture normally terminates when the project or transaction for which it was formed is completed, unless the members have otherwise agreed.

Syndicate

In a **syndicate,** or *investment group,* several individuals or firms join together to finance a particular project, such as the construction of a shopping center or the purchase of a professional basketball franchise. The form of such entities varies considerably. A syndicate may be organized as a corporation or as a general or limited partnership. In some instances, the members do not have a legally recognized business arrangement but merely purchase and own property jointly.

Joint Stock Company

A **joint stock company** is a true hybrid of a partnership and a corporation. It has many characteristics of a corporation in that (1) its ownership is represented by transferable shares of stock, (2) it is normally managed by directors and officers of the company or association, and (3) it can have a perpetual existence. Most of its other features, however, are more characteristic of a partnership, and it generally is treated as a partnership. As with a partnership, a joint stock company is formed by agreement (not statute). Property usually is held in the names of the members, and the owners (shareholders) have personal liability. In a joint stock company, however, shareholders are not considered to be agents of each other, as they would be in a true partnership.

Business Trust

A **business trust** is created by a written trust agreement that sets forth the interests of the beneficiaries and the obligations and powers of the trustees. Legal ownership and management of the trust's property stay with one or more of the trustees, and the profits are distributed to the beneficiaries.

The business trust form of organization was started in Massachusetts in an attempt to obtain the limited liability advantage of corporate status while avoiding certain restrictions on a corporation's ownership and development of real property. A business trust resembles a corporation in many respects. Beneficiaries of the trust, for example, are not personally responsible for the trust's debts or obligations. In fact, in a number of states, business trusts must pay corporate taxes.

Cooperative

A **cooperative** is an association that is organized to provide an economic service to its members (or shareholders). It may or may not be incorporated. Most cooperatives are organized under state statutes for cooperatives, general business corporations, or LLCs. Generally, an incorporated cooperative will distribute dividends, or profits, to its owners on the basis of their transactions with the cooperative rather than on the basis of the amount of capital they contributed. Members of incorporated cooperatives have limited liability, as do shareholders of corporations and members of LLCs. Cooperatives that are unincorporated are often treated like partnerships. The members have joint liability for the cooperative's acts.

The cooperative form of business is generally adopted by groups of individuals who wish to pool their resources to gain some advantage in the marketplace. Consumer purchasing co-ops are formed to obtain lower prices through quantity discounts. Seller marketing co-ops are formed to control the market and thereby enable members to sell their goods at higher prices. Co-ops range in size from small, local consumer cooperatives to national businesses such as Ace Hardware and Land O'Lakes, a well-known producer of dairy products.

See *Concept Summary 38.1* below for a review of the types of special business forms discussed in this chapter.

CONCEPT SUMMARY 38.1
Special Business Forms

Concept	Description
Joint Venture	An organization created by two or more persons in contemplation of a limited activity or a single transaction; similar to a partnership in many respects.
Syndicate	An investment group that undertakes to finance a particular project; may be organized as a corporation or as a general or limited partnership.
Joint Stock Company	A business form similar to a corporation in some respects (transferable shares of stock, management by directors and officers, perpetual existence) but otherwise resembling a partnership.
Business Trust	A business form created by a written trust agreement that sets forth the interests of the beneficiaries and the obligations and powers of the trustee(s). A business trust is similar to a corporation in many respects. Beneficiaries are not personally liable for the debts or obligations of the business trust.
Cooperative	An association organized to provide an economic service, without profit, to its members. A cooperative can take the form of a corporation or a partnership.

REVIEWING

Limited Liability Companies and Special Business Forms

The city of Papagos, Arizona, had a deteriorating bridge in need of repair on a prominent public roadway. The city posted notices seeking proposals for an artistic bridge design and reconstruction. Davidson Masonry, LLC, which was owned and managed by Carl Davidson and his wife, Marilyn Rowe, decided to submit a bid to create a decorative concrete structure that incorporated artistic metalwork. They contacted Shana Lafayette, a local sculptor who specialized in large-scale metal creations, to help them design the bridge. The city selected their bridge design and awarded them the contract for a commission of $184,000. Davidson Masonry and Lafayette then entered into an agreement to work together on the bridge project. Davidson Masonry agreed to install and pay for concrete and structural work, and Lafayette agreed to install the metalwork at her expense. They agreed that overall profits would be split, with 25 percent going to Lafayette and 75 percent going to Davidson Masonry. Lafayette designed numerous metal sculptures of salmon that were incorporated into colorful decorative concrete forms designed by Rowe, while Davidson performed the structural engineering. The group worked together successfully until the completion of the project. Using the information presented in the chapter, answer the following questions.

1. Would Davidson Masonry automatically be taxed as a partnership or a corporation?
2. Is Davidson Masonry member managed or manager managed?
3. When Davidson Masonry and Lafayette entered an agreement to work together, what kind of special business form was created? Explain.
4. Suppose that during construction, Lafayette had entered into an agreement to rent space in a warehouse that was close to the bridge so that she could work on her sculptures near the site where they would eventually be installed. She entered into the contract without the knowledge or consent of Davidson Masonry. In this situation, would a court be likely to hold that Davidson Masonry was bound by the contract that Lafayette entered? Why or why not?

DEBATE THIS: *Because LLCs are essentially just partnerships with limited liability for members, all partnership laws should apply.*

TERMS AND CONCEPTS

articles of organization 740
business trust 749

cooperative 749
joint stock company 748
joint venture 746

limited liability
  company (LLC) 739
member 740

operating agreement 744
syndicate 748

QUESTIONS AND CASE PROBLEMS

38–1. Limited Liability Companies John, Lesa, and Tabir form a limited liability company. John contributes 60 percent of the capital, and Lesa and Tabir each contribute 20 percent. Nothing is decided about how profits will be divided. John assumes that he will be entitled to 60 percent of the profits, in accordance with his contribution. Lesa and Tabir, however, assume that the profits will be divided equally. A dispute over the profits arises, and ultimately a court has to decide the issue. What law will the court apply? In most states, what will result? How could this dispute have been avoided in the first place? Discuss fully.

38–2. QUESTION WITH SAMPLE ANSWER: Special Business Forms.

Bateson Corp. is considering entering into two contracts—one with a joint stock company that distributes home products east of the

Mississippi River and the other with a business trust formed by a number of sole proprietors who are sellers of home products on the West Coast. Both contracts will require Bateson to make large capital outlays in order to supply the businesses with restaurant equipment. In both business organizations, at least two shareholders or beneficiaries are personally wealthy, but both organizations have limited financial resources. The owner-managers of Bateson are not familiar with either form of business organization. Because each form resembles a corporation, they are concerned about potential limits on liability in the event that either business organization breaches the contract by failing to pay for the equipment. Discuss fully Bateson's concern.

- **For a sample answer to Question 38–2, go to Appendix I at the end of this text.**

38–3. Diversity Jurisdiction and Limited Liability Companies Joe, a resident of New Jersey, wants to open a restaurant. He asks Kay, his friend, an experienced attorney and a New Yorker, for her business and legal advice in exchange for a 20 percent ownership interest in the restaurant. Kay helps Joe negotiate a lease for the restaurant premises and advises Joe to organize the business as a limited liability company (LLC). Joe forms Café Olé, LLC, and with Kay's help, obtains financing. Then, the night before the restaurant opens, Joe tells Kay that he is "cutting her out of the deal." The restaurant proves to be a success. Kay wants to file a suit in a federal district court against Joe and the LLC. Can a federal court exercise jurisdiction over the parties based on diversity of citizenship? Explain.

38–4. Fiduciary Duties Westbury Properties, Inc., and others (collectively, the Westbury group) owned, managed, and developed real property. Jerry Stoker and the Stoker Group, Inc. (the Stokers), also developed real property. The Westbury group entered into agreements with the Stokers concerning a large tract of property in Houston County, Georgia. The parties formed limited liability companies (LLCs), including Bellemeade, LLC (the LLC group), to develop various parcels of the tract for residential purposes. The operating agreements provided that "no Member shall be accountable to the [LLC] or to any other Member with respect to [any other] business or activity even if the business or activity competes with the [LLC's] business." The Westbury group entered into agreements with other parties to develop additional parcels within the tract in competition with the LLC group. The Stokers filed a suit in a Georgia state court against the Westbury group, alleging, among other things, breach of fiduciary duty. What duties do the members of an LLC owe to each other? Under what principle might the terms of an operating agreement alter these duties? In whose favor should the court rule? Discuss. [*Stoker v. Bellemeade, LLC*, 272 Ga.App. 817, 615 S.E.2d 1 (2005)]

38–5. Limited Liability Companies A "Certificate of Formation" (CF) for Grupo Dos Chiles, LLC, was filed with the Delaware secretary of state in February 2000. The CF named Jamie Rivera as the "initial member." The next

month, Jamie's mother, Yolanda Martinez, and Alfred Shriver, who had a personal relationship with Martinez at the time, signed an "LLC Agreement" for Grupo, naming themselves "managing partners." Grupo's business was the operation of Dancing Peppers Cantina, a restaurant in Alexandria, Virginia. Identifying themselves as Grupo's owners, Shriver and Martinez borrowed funds from Advanceme, Inc., a restaurant lender. In June 2003, Grupo lost its LLC status in Delaware for failing to pay state taxes, and by the end of July, Martinez and Shriver had ended their relationship. Shriver filed a suit in a Virginia state court against Martinez to wind up Grupo's affairs. Meanwhile, without consulting Shriver, Martinez paid Grupo's back taxes. Shriver filed a suit in a Delaware state court against Martinez, asking the court to dissolve the firm. What effect did the LLC agreement have on the CF? Did Martinez's unilateral act reestablish Grupo's LLC status? Should the Delaware court grant Shriver's request? Why or why not? [*In re Grupo Dos Chiles, LLC*, __ A.2d __ (Del.Ch. 2006)]

38–6. Limited Liability Companies A limited liability company (LLC) sold a Manhattan apartment building that it owned. The owners of 25 percent of the membership interests in the LLC filed a lawsuit on behalf of the LLC—called a derivative suit—claiming that those in majority control of the LLC had sold the building for less than its market value and had personally profited from the deal. The trial court dismissed the suit, holding that the plaintiffs individually could not bring a derivative suit "to redress wrongs suffered by the corporation" because such actions were permitted only for corporations and could not be brought for an LLC. An intermediate appellate court reversed, holding that derivative suits on behalf of LLCs are permitted. That decision was appealed. A key problem for the court was that the state law governing LLCs did not address the issue. How should such matters logically be resolved? Are the minority owners in an LLC at the mercy of the decisions of the majority owners? [*Tzolis v. Wolff*, 10 N.Y.3d 100, 884 N.E.2d 1005 (2008)]

38–7. CASE PROBLEM WITH SAMPLE ANSWER: Joint Venture.

Holiday Isle Resort & Marina, Inc., operated four restaurants, five bars, and various food kiosks at its resort in Islamorada, Florida. Holiday entered into a "joint-venture agreement" with Rip Tosun to operate a fifth restaurant called "Rip's—A Place for Ribs." The agreement gave Tosun authority over the employees and "full authority as to the conduct of the business." It also prohibited Tosun from competing with Rip's without Holiday's approval but did not prevent Holiday from competing. Later, Tosun sold half of his interest in Rip's to Thomas Hallock. Soon, Tosun and Holiday opened the Olde Florida Steakhouse next to Rip's. Holiday stopped serving breakfast at Rip's and diverted employees and equipment from Rip's to the Steakhouse, which then started offering breakfast. Hallock filed a suit in a Florida state court against Holiday. Did Holiday breach the joint-venture agreement? Did it breach the duties that joint venturers owe each other? Explain. [Hallock

v. Holiday Isle Resort & Marina, Inc., *4 So.3d 17 (Fla.App. 3 Dist. 2009)]*

- To view a sample answer for Problem 38–7, go to this book's Web site at **www.cengage.com/blaw/clarkson**, select "Chapter 38," and click on "Case Problem with Sample Answer."

38–8. LLC Dissolution Walter Van Houten and John King formed 1545 Ocean Avenue, LLC, with each managing 50 percent of the business. Its purpose was to renovate an existing building and construct a new commercial building. Van Houten and King quarreled over many aspects of the work on the properties. King claimed that Van Houten paid the contractors too much for the work performed. As the projects neared completion, King demanded that the LLC be dissolved and that Van Houten agree to a buyout. Because the parties could not agree on a buyout, King sued for dissolution. The trial court enjoined (prevented) further work on the projects until the dispute was settled. As the ground for dissolution, King cited the fights over management decisions. There was no claim of fraud or frustration of purpose. The trial court ordered that the LLC be dissolved, and Van Houten appealed. Should either of the owners be forced to dissolve the LLC before the completion of its purpose—that is, before the building projects are finished? Explain. [*In re 1545 Ocean Avenue, LLC, 893 N.Y.S.2d 590 (N.Y.A.D. 2 Dept. 2010)]*

38–9. A QUESTION OF ETHICS: Limited Liability Companies.

 Blushing Brides, LLC, a publisher of wedding planning magazines in Columbus, Ohio, opened an account with Gray Printing Co. in July 2000. On behalf of Blushing Brides, Louis Zacks, the firm's member-manager, signed a credit agreement that identified the firm as the "purchaser" and required payment within thirty days. Despite the agreement, Blushing Brides typically took up to six months to pay the full amount for its orders. *Gray printed and shipped 10,000 copies of a fall/winter 2001 issue for Blushing Brides but had not been paid when the firm ordered 15,000 copies of a spring/summer 2002 issue. Gray refused to print the new order without an assurance of payment. On May 22, Zacks signed a promissory note payable to Gray within thirty days for $14,778, plus interest at 6 percent per year. Gray printed the new order but by October had been paid only $7,500. Gray filed a suit in an Ohio state court against Blushing Brides and Zacks to collect the balance. [Gray Printing Co. v. Blushing Brides, LLC, __ N.E.2d __ (Ohio App. 10 Dist. 2006)]*

(a) Under what circumstances is a member of an LLC liable for the firm's debts? In this case, is Zacks personally liable under the credit agreement for the unpaid amount on Blushing Brides' account? Did Zacks's promissory note affect the parties' liability on the account? Explain.

(b) Should a member of an LLC assume an ethical responsibility to meet the obligations of the firm? Discuss.

(c) Gray shipped only 10,000 copies of the spring/summer 2002 issue of *Blushing Brides'* magazine, waiting for the publisher to identify a destination for the other 5,000 copies. The magazine had a retail price of $4.50 per copy. Did Gray have a legal or ethical duty to "mitigate the damages" by attempting to sell or otherwise distribute these copies itself? Why or why not?

38–10. SPECIAL CASE ANALYSIS: Limited Liability Companies.
Go to Extended Case 38.2, *ORX Resources, Inc. v. MBW Exploration, LLC, 32 So.3d 931 (2010)* on pages 742 and 743. Read the excerpt and answer the following questions.

(a) Issue: What was the main issue in this case?

(b) Rule of Law: What rule of law did the court apply?

(c) Applying the Rule of Law: Describe how the court applied the rule of law to the facts of this case.

(d) Conclusion: What was the court's conclusion?

LEGAL RESEARCH EXERCISES ON THE WEB

Go to this text's Web site at **www.cengage.com/blaw/clarkson**, select "Chapter 38," and click on "Practical Internet Exercises." There you will find the following Internet research exercises that you can perform to learn more about the topics covered in this chapter.

Practical Internet Exercise 38–1: Legal Perspective
Limited Liability Companies

Practical Internet Exercise 38–2: Economic Perspective
Joint Ventures

CHAPTER 39

✺
Corporate Formation and Financing

The corporation is a creature of statute. A corporation is an artificial being, existing only in law and neither tangible nor visible. Its existence generally depends on state law, although some corporations, especially public organizations, are created under federal law. Each state has its own body of corporate law, and these laws are not entirely uniform.

The Model Business Corporation Act (MBCA) is a codification of modern corporation law that has been influential in shaping state corporation statutes. Today, the majority of state statutes are guided by the most recent version of the MBCA, often referred to as the Revised Model Business Corporation Act (RMBCA). (Excerpts from the RMBCA are included in Appendix G of this text.) Keep in mind, however, that corporation laws vary considerably even among states that have used the MBCA or the RMBCA as a basis for

their statutes, and several states do not follow either act. Consequently, individual state corporation laws should be relied on to determine corporate law rather than the MBCA or RMBCA.

In this chapter, we examine the nature of the corporate form of business enterprise and the various classifications of corporations. We then discuss the formation and financing of today's corporation.

◢◤ SECTION 1 ◢◤
THE NATURE AND CLASSIFICATION OF CORPORATIONS

A corporation is a legal entity created and recognized by state law. This business entity can have one or more owners (called shareholders), and it operates under a name distinct from the names of its owners. The owners may be individuals, or *natural persons* (as opposed to the artificial *legal person* of the corporation), or other businesses. Although the corporation substitutes itself for its shareholders when conducting corporate business and incurring liability, its authority to act and the liability for its actions are separate and apart from the individuals who own it.

A corporation is recognized as a "person," and it enjoys many of the same rights and privileges under state and federal law that U.S. citizens enjoy. For example, corporations possess the same right of access to the courts as citizens and can sue or be sued. The constitutional guarantees of due process, free speech, and freedom from unreasonable searches and seizures also apply to corporations.

Corporate Personnel

In a corporation, the responsibility for the overall management of the firm is entrusted to a *board of directors,* whose members are elected by the shareholders. The board of directors makes the policy decisions and hires *corporate officers* and other employees to run the daily business operations of the corporation.

When an individual purchases a share of stock in a corporation, that person becomes a shareholder and an owner of the corporation. Unlike the partners in a partnership, the body of shareholders can change constantly without affecting the continued existence of the corporation. A shareholder can sue the corporation, and the corporation can sue a shareholder. Additionally, under certain circumstances, a shareholder can sue on behalf of a corporation. The rights and duties of corporate directors, officers, and shareholders will be examined in Chapter 40.

The Limited Liability of Shareholders

One of the key advantages of the corporate form is the limited liability of its owners. Normally, corporate shareholders are not personally liable for the obligations of the corporation beyond the extent of their investments. In certain limited situations, however, a court can *pierce the corporate veil* (see page 766) and impose liability on shareholders for the corporation's obligations. Additionally, creditors often will not extend credit to small companies unless the shareholders assume personal liability, as guarantors, for corporate obligations.

Corporate Earnings and Taxation

When a corporation earns profits, it can either distribute them to its shareholders in the form of **dividends** or retain the profits. These **retained earnings,** if invested properly, will yield higher corporate profits in the future and thus cause the price of the company's stock to rise. Individual shareholders can then reap the benefits of these retained earnings in the capital gains that they receive when they sell their stock.

CORPORATE TAXATION Whether a corporation retains its profits or passes them on to the shareholders as dividends, those profits are subject to income tax by various levels of government. Failure to pay taxes can lead to severe consequences. The state can suspend the entity's corporate status until the taxes are paid or even dissolve the corporation for failing to pay taxes.

Another important aspect of corporate taxation is that corporate profits can be subject to double taxation. The company pays tax on its profits, and then if the profits are passed on to the shareholders as dividends, the shareholders must also pay income tax on them (unless the dividends represent distributions of capital). The corporation normally does not receive a tax deduction for dividends it distributes. This double-taxation feature is one of the major disadvantages of the corporate form.

A taxation issue of increasing importance to corporations is whether they are required to collect state sales taxes on goods or services sold to consumers via the Internet. See this chapter's *Shifting Legal Priorities for Business* feature on the facing page for a discussion of this issue.

HOLDING COMPANIES Some U.S. corporations use holding companies to reduce or defer their U.S. income taxes. At its simplest, a **holding company** (sometimes referred to as a *parent company*) is a company whose business activity consists of holding shares in another company. Typically, the holding company is established in a low-tax or no-tax offshore jurisdiction, such as the Cayman Islands, Dubai, Hong Kong, Luxembourg, Monaco, or Panama.

Sometimes, a U.S. corporation sets up a holding company in a low-tax offshore environment and then transfers its cash, bonds, stocks, and other investments to the holding company. Generally, any profits received by the holding company on these investments are taxed at the rate of the offshore jurisdiction where the company is registered (not at the rates applicable to the corporation or its shareholders in their country of residence). Thus, deposits of cash, for example, may earn interest that is taxed at only a minimal rate. Once the profits are brought "onshore," though, they are taxed at the federal corporate income tax rate, and any payments received by the shareholders are also taxable at the full U.S. rates. In the federal government's 2011 budget, the Obama administration proposed measures that would restrict multinational companies from deferring the payment of taxes on profits earned overseas.

Torts and Criminal Acts

A corporation is liable for the torts committed by its agents or officers within the course and scope of their employment. This principle applies to a corporation exactly as it applies to the ordinary agency relationships discussed in Chapter 33. It follows the doctrine of *respondeat superior.*

Under modern criminal law, a corporation may also be held liable for the criminal acts of its agents and employees, provided the punishment is one that can be applied to the corporation. Although corporations cannot be imprisoned, they can be fined. (Of course, corporate directors and officers can be imprisoned, and many have been in recent years.) In addition, under sentencing guidelines for crimes committed by corporate employees (white-collar crimes), corporate lawbreakers can face fines amounting to hundreds of millions of dollars.[1]

CASE IN POINT Brian Gauthier worked as a dump truck driver for Angelo Todesca Corporation. Although the truck was missing its back-up alarm that automatically sounded when the truck was put

---

1. Note that the Sarbanes-Oxley Act of 2002 (see Chapter 5) stiffened the penalties for certain types of corporate crime and ordered the U.S. Sentencing Commission to revise the sentencing guidelines accordingly.

SHIFTING LEGAL PRIORITIES FOR BUSINESS
The Latest Recession Re-Ignites the Internet Taxation Debate

Governments at the state and federal levels have long debated whether states should be able to collect sales taxes on online sales to their residents. State governments claim that their inability to tax online sales has caused them to lose billions of dollars in sales tax revenue. The issue has taken on new urgency as the states search desperately for revenue in the wake of the economic recession that began in late 2007.

Supreme Court Precedent Requires Physical Presence

In 1992, the United States Supreme Court ruled that no individual state can compel an out-of-state business that lacks a substantial physical presence (such as a warehouse, office, or retail store) within that state to collect and remit state taxes.[a] The Court recognized that Congress has the power to pass legislation requiring out-of-state corporations to collect and remit state sales taxes, but Congress so far has chosen not to tax Internet transactions.

In fact, Congress temporarily prohibited the states from taxing Internet sales, and that ban was extended until 2014.[b] Thus, only online retailers that also have a physical presence within a state must collect state taxes on any Web sales made to residents of that state. (Otherwise, state residents are required to self-report their purchases and pay so-called use taxes to the state, which rarely occurs.)

New York Changed Its Definition of Physical Presence

In an effort to collect taxes on Internet sales made by out-of-state corporations, New York changed its tax laws in 2008 to redefine *physical presence.* Under the new law, if an online retailer pays any party within the state to solicit business for its products, that retailer has a physical presence in the state and must collect state taxes.[c] For example, Amazon.com, the largest U.S. online retailer, pays thousands of associates in New York to post ads that link to Amazon's Web site. Consequently, the law requires Amazon to collect tax on any sales to New York residents.

Both Amazon and Overstock.com, a Utah corporation, filed lawsuits in 2009 claiming that the new law was unconstitutional. A New York court dismissed Amazon's case, finding that the law provided a sufficient basis for requiring collection of New York taxes. As long as the seller has a substantial connection with the state, the taxes need not derive from in-state activity. The court also observed that "out-of-state sellers can shield themselves from a tax-collection obligation by altogether prohibiting in-state solicitation activities . . . on their behalf."[d] As a result, Amazon now collects and pays state sales taxes on shipments to New York.

Overstock also lost its lawsuit but has filed an appeal.[e] In the meantime, to avoid having to collect the sales tax, Overstock canceled agreements with its New York affiliates that were being paid to direct traffic to its Web site. In 2009 and 2010, Amazon ended its arrangements with affiliates in Colorado, North Carolina, and Rhode Island for the same reason. Fifteen other states, including California, Illinois, Iowa, Maryland, New Mexico, Vermont, and Virginia, are now considering passing laws similar to New York's.

MANAGERIAL IMPLICATIONS

Most states and municipal governments continue to struggle with budgets, so they will continue to seek additional sources of revenues. These governments will pass more laws to try to capture taxes from commercial activities on the Internet. Therefore, managers whose companies sell goods or services on the Internet must keep track of what lawmakers are planning in this contentious area.

---

a. See *Quill Corp. v. North Dakota,* 504 U.S. 298, 112 S.Ct. 1904, 119 L.Ed.2d 91 (1992).

b. Internet Tax Freedom Act, Pub. L. No. 105-277; 47 U.S.C. Section 151 note (1998); extended to 2014 by Pub. L. No. 110-108.

c. New York Tax Law Section 1101(b)(8)(vi).

d. *Amazon.com, LLC v. New York State Department of Taxation and Finance,* 23 Misc.3d 418, 877 N.Y.S.2d 842 (2009).

e. *Overstock.com, Inc. v. New York State Department of Taxation and Finance,* 2009 WL 1259061 (2009).

---

into reverse, Angelo allowed Gauthier to continue driving the truck. At a worksite, when Gauthier backed up to dump the truck's load, he struck and killed a police officer who was facing away from the truck. The state charged Angelo and Gauthier with the crime of vehicular homicide. Angelo argued that a corporation could not be guilty of vehicular homicide because it cannot operate a vehicle. The court ruled that if an employee commits a crime "while engaged in corporate business that the employee has been authorized to conduct," the corporation can be held liable for the crime. Hence, the court held that Angelo was liable for Gauthier's negligent operation of its truck, which resulted in a person's death.[2]

---

2. *Commonwealth v. Angelo Todesca Corp.,* 446 Mass. 128, 842 N.E.2d 930 (2006).

Classification of Corporations

Corporations can be classified in several ways. The classification of a corporation normally depends on its location, purpose, and ownership characteristics, as described in the following subsections.

DOMESTIC, FOREIGN, AND ALIEN CORPORATIONS A corporation is referred to as a **domestic corporation** by its home state (the state in which it incorporates). A corporation formed in one state but doing business in another is referred to in the second state as a **foreign corporation.** A corporation formed in another country (say, Mexico) but doing business in the United States is referred to in the United States as an **alien corporation.**

A corporation does not have an automatic right to do business in a state other than its state of incorporation. In some instances, it must obtain a *certificate of authority* in any state in which it plans to do business. Once the certificate has been issued, the corporation generally can exercise in that state all of the powers conferred on it by its home state. If a foreign corporation does business in a state without obtaining a certificate of authority, the state can impose substantial fines and sanctions on the corporation, and sometimes even on its officers, directors, or agents.

Note that most state statutes specify certain activities that are not considered "doing business" within the state. These statutes often allow foreign corporations to participate in lawsuits, hold meetings of directors or shareholders, own real or personal property, and maintain an office or bank account.[3] Normally, a foreign corporation can conduct isolated business transactions (but not repeated transactions) within a state without obtaining a certificate of authority to do business there.

PUBLIC AND PRIVATE CORPORATIONS A **public corporation** is a corporation formed by the government to meet some political or governmental purpose. Cities and towns that incorporate are common examples. In addition, many federal government organizations, such as the U.S. Postal Service, the Tennessee Valley Authority, and AMTRAK, are public corporations. Note that a public corporation is not the same as a *publicly held* corporation. A **publicly held corporation** (often called a *public company*) is any corporation whose shares are publicly traded in a securities market, such as the New York Stock Exchange or the NASDAQ (an electronic stock exchange founded by the National Association of Securities Dealers).

In contrast to public corporations, private corporations (such as publicly held companies) are created either wholly or in part for private benefit (for profit). Most corporations are private. Although they may serve a public purpose, as a public electric or gas utility does, they are owned by private persons rather than by the government.[4]

NONPROFIT CORPORATIONS Corporations formed for purposes other than making a profit are called *nonprofit* or *not-for-profit* corporations. Private hospitals, educational institutions, charities, and religious organizations, for example, are frequently organized as nonprofit corporations. The nonprofit corporation is a convenient form of organization that allows various groups to own property and to form contracts without exposing the individual members to personal liability.

CLOSELY HELD CORPORATIONS Most corporate enterprises in the United States fall into the category of closely held corporations (sometimes called close corporations). A **closely held corporation** is one whose shares are not publicly traded. In fact, there is no trading market for the shares. The shares are often held by family members or by a relatively small group of persons. Usually, the members of the small group constituting a closely held corporation are personally known to each other. Closely held corporations are also sometimes referred to as *privately held* corporations.

In practice, a closely held corporation is often operated like a partnership. Some states have enacted special statutory provisions that apply to these corporations and allow them to depart significantly from certain formalities required by traditional corporation law.[5]

Additionally, a provision in the RMBCA gives a closely held corporation considerable flexibility in determining its rules of operation [RMBCA 7.32]. If all of a corporation's shareholders agree in writing, the corporation can operate without directors, bylaws, annual or special shareholders' or directors' meetings, stock certificates, or formal records of shareholders' or directors' decisions.[6]

---

3. See, for example, Iowa Code Section 490.1501 and Texas Code Section 9.251.

4. The United States Supreme Court first recognized the property rights of private corporations and clarified the distinction between public and private corporations in the landmark case *Trustees of Dartmouth College v. Woodward,* 17 U.S. (4 Wheaton) 518, 4 L.Ed. 629 (1819).

5. For example, in some states (such as Maryland), a closely held corporation need not have a board of directors.

6. Shareholders cannot agree, however, to eliminate certain rights of shareholders, such as the right to inspect corporate books and records or the right to bring *derivative actions* (lawsuits on behalf of the corporation—see Chapter 40).

Management of Closely Held Corporations. A closely held corporation has a single shareholder or a tightly knit group of shareholders, who usually hold the positions of directors and officers. Management of a closely held corporation resembles that of a sole proprietorship or a partnership. As a corporation, however, the firm must meet all specific legal requirements set forth in state statutes.

To prevent a majority shareholder from dominating a closely held corporation, the company may require that more than a simple majority of the directors approve any action taken by the board. Typically, this would apply only to extraordinary actions, such as changing the amount of dividends or dismissing an employee-shareholder, and not to ordinary business decisions.

Transfer of Shares in Closely Held Corporations. By definition, a closely held corporation has a small number of shareholders. Thus, the transfer of one shareholder's shares to someone else can cause serious management problems. The other shareholders may find themselves required to share control with someone they do not know or like.

Suppose that three brothers, Terry, Damon, and Henry Johnson, are the only shareholders of Johnson's Car Wash, Inc. Terry and Damon do not want Henry to sell his shares to an unknown third person. To avoid this situation, the corporation could restrict the transferability of shares to outside persons. Shareholders could be required to offer their shares to the closely held corporation or the other shareholders before selling them to an outside purchaser. In fact, a few states have statutes that prohibit the transfer of closely held corporation shares unless certain persons—including shareholders, family members, and the corporation—are first given the opportunity to purchase the shares for the same price.

Shareholder Agreement to Restrict Stock Transfers. Control of a closely held corporation can also be stabilized through the use of a *shareholder agreement*. A shareholder agreement can provide that when one of the original shareholders dies, her or his shares of stock in the corporation will be divided in such a way that the proportionate holdings of the survivors, and thus their proportionate control, will be maintained. Agreements between shareholders can also restrict the transfer of a closely held corporation's stock in other ways.

CASE IN POINT The Kearns-Tribune Corporation, a closely held corporation owned by the Kearns-McCarthey family, owned *The Salt Lake Tribune*. In 1997, the family sold the corporation to cable company Tele-Communications, Inc. (TCI). As part of the agreement, the family received an option to repurchase the assets of *The Tribune* at a later date. After TCI merged with AT&T Corporation, giving AT&T control over Kearns-Tribune, the family attempted to exercise the option to repurchase *The Tribune*. The court denied the request, however, because Kearns-Tribune had previously signed another agreement with Deseret News to form the Newspaper Agency Corporation (NAC), with Kearns-Tribune and Deseret News each owning 50 percent of NAC. Under that contract, the shareholders agreed to prohibit the transfer of ownership of NAC stock. Therefore, the stock transfer restriction was an obstacle to the family's claim for specific performance of the option.[7]

Misappropriation of Closely Held Corporation Funds. Sometimes, a majority shareholder in a closely held corporation takes advantage of his or her position and misappropriates company funds. In such situations, the normal remedy for the injured minority shareholders is to have their shares appraised and to be paid the fair market value for them.

In the following case, two wronged minority shareholders pursued an additional remedy.

---

7. *Salt Lake Tribune Publishing Co. v. AT&T Corp.*, 320 F.3d 1081 (10th Cir. 2003).

CASE 39.1
Williams v. Stanford

District Court of Appeal of Florida, First District, 977 So.2d 722 (2008).

BACKGROUND AND FACTS • Two brothers, Paul and James Williams, together held 30 percent of the stock in Brown and Standard (B&S), Inc., a construction company. John Stanford owned the other 70 percent of the closely held corporation shares. The Williams brothers worked for B&S for five years when they became suspicious of Stanford's financial management. Stanford reported net losses

CASE CONTINUES ▶

CASE 39.1 CONTINUED ◆ for the company. When the brothers asked to see the B&S books, they were fired. Later, it was shown that Stanford had misappropriated at least $250,000 in B&S funds for his personal use. The Williams brothers brought a *shareholder's derivative suit* (see Chapter 40) on behalf of B&S, naming Stanford as the defendant and accusing him of breach of fiduciary duty. Before trial, Stanford resigned from B&S and closed the company. He gave the assets and liabilities of B&S to a new company he formed and owned, J. C. Stanford & Sons. He offered the Williams brothers $25,000 each for their stock in B&S. They responded with a request for $125,000 each. The trial court held that by law the Williams brothers, by making a counteroffer, had given up their rights to bring a suit against the company. Hence, the court granted summary judgment to Stanford. The Williams brothers appealed.

IN THE LANGUAGE OF THE COURT
KAHN, Judge.
* * * *

In the present case, the Williams brothers alleged sufficient acts of unfair dealing to withstand appellees' [Stanford and his wife, who served on the board of directors] motion for summary judgment, which the trial court should have denied.

In cases such as the present controversy, involving dissenting shareholders who seek more than appraisal of their shares in the wake of objectionable transactions, *courts must balance the principle that an adequate remedy should exist for a dissenting shareholder in an unfair transaction against the consideration that courts should not become bogged down in a wide range of disputes over the fairness of cash-out prices offered to minority shareholders who object to corporate transactions.* We have no question that, in the present case, we are not dealing with "a fair price complaint artfully disguised in the camouflage of procedural unfairness." As appellants' counsel pointed out during oral argument, the Williams brothers' complaint over the fairness of the transfer of B&S assets stems from the fact that, at the time appellants' statutory appraisal right crystallized, the company's treasury—and thus the corresponding value of their shares—had been all but eviscerated [reduced to practically no value] through several years of the Stanfords' alleged misappropriations and mismanagement of corporate funds, activities the Williams brothers did not detect until the company recorded a net loss in 2001. Contingent upon proof of the allegations, appraisal at the time of the November 2003 transfer of B&S assets, effectuated [accomplished] after years of allegedly value destroying activities on the Stanfords' part, would not have afforded the Williams brothers adequate recourse in this particular case. [Emphasis added.]

* * * *

We interpret the "fraud or material misrepresentation" exception in [Florida's corporation statute] to mean that a minority shareholder who alleges specific acts of "fraud, misrepresentation, self-dealing, or deliberate waste of corporate assets," may be entitled to equitable remedies beyond an appraisal proceeding if those allegations are proven true and if the alleged acts have so besmirched [tarnished] the propriety of the challenged transaction that no appraisal could fairly compensate the aggrieved minority shareholder. We adopt the entire fairness analysis developed in [other cases] to assess whether a corporate transaction avails aggrieved minority shareholders of rights beyond appraisal. The trial court erred in granting summary judgment as to appellants' claim for rescission of the transfer of assets; we reverse summary judgment and remand for factual determinations as to the truth of appellants' allegations of fraud, misrepresentation, and breaches of fiduciary duty on the Stanfords' part.

DECISION AND REMEDY • *The state appellate court reversed the trial court, holding that the Williams brothers were entitled to a trial to determine if they could prove abuse of the company by Stanford. Although this did not follow the usual procedure for appraisal of minority shares, given the strong suspicion of fraud in this instance, the court was willing to allow for greater review.*

THE ETHICAL DIMENSION • *Was it acceptable for the William brothers to demand $125,000 each for their shares? Why or why not?*

MANAGERIAL IMPLICATIONS • *No matter how friendly the shareholders of a closely held corporation may be, or how informal its formation, all owners, particularly minority owners, must insist from the beginning that the corporation establish written procedures that will enable them to carefully audit its financial activities. All shareholders should have continuing access to accounting information as well as the right to review bank statements.*

S CORPORATIONS A closely held corporation that meets the qualifying requirements specified in Subchapter S of the Internal Revenue Code can choose to operate as an **S corporation.** (A corporation will automatically be taxed under Subchapter C unless it elects S corporation status.) If a corporation has S corporation status, it can avoid the imposition of income taxes at the corporate level while retaining many of the advantages of a corporation, particularly limited liability. Among the numerous requirements for S corporation status, the following are the most important:

1. The corporation must be a domestic corporation.
2. The corporation must not be a member of an affiliated group of corporations.
3. The shareholders of the corporation must be individuals, estates, or certain trusts and tax-exempt organizations.
4. The corporation must have no more than one hundred shareholders.
5. The corporation must have only one class of stock, although all shareholders do not need to have the same voting rights.
6. No shareholder of the corporation may be a non-resident alien.

An S corporation is treated differently than a regular corporation for tax purposes. An S corporation is taxed like a partnership, so the corporate income passes through to the shareholders, who pay personal income tax on it. This treatment enables the S corporation to avoid the double taxation imposed on regular corporations.

In addition, the shareholders' tax brackets may be lower than the tax bracket that the corporation would have been in if the tax had been imposed at the corporate level. The resulting tax saving is particularly attractive when the corporation wants to accumulate earnings for some future business purpose. If the corporation has losses, the S election allows the shareholders to use the losses to offset other income. Nevertheless, because the limited liability company (see Chapter 38) and the limited liability partnership (see Chapter 37) offer similar tax advantages and greater flexibility, the S corporation has lost some of its appeal.

PROFESSIONAL CORPORATIONS Professionals such as physicians, lawyers, dentists, and accountants can incorporate. Professional corporations are typically identified by the letters *P.C.* (professional corporation), *S.C.* (service corporation), or *P.A.* (professional association).

In general, the laws governing the formation and operation of professional corporations are similar to those governing ordinary business corporations. There are some differences in terms of liability, however. For liability purposes, some courts treat a professional corporation somewhat like a partnership and hold each professional liable for any malpractice committed within the scope of the business by the others in the firm. With the exception of malpractice or a breach of duty to clients or patients, a shareholder in a professional corporation generally cannot be held liable for the torts committed by other professionals at the firm.

See *Concept Summary 39.1* on the following page for a review of the ways in which corporations are classified.

SECTION 2
CORPORATE FORMATION

Up to this point, we have discussed some of the general characteristics of corporations. We now examine the process by which corporations come into existence. Incorporating a business is much simpler today than it was twenty years ago. In fact, many states allow businesses to incorporate online.

One of the most common reasons for creating a corporation is the need for additional capital to finance expansion. Many Fortune 500 companies started as sole proprietorships or partnerships and then converted to corporate entities. Incorporation may be the best choice for an expanding business organization because a corporation can obtain more capital by issuing shares of stock. (Corporate financing will be discussed later in this chapter.)

Promotional Activities

In the past, preliminary steps were taken to organize and promote the business prior to incorporating. Contracts were made with investors and others on behalf of the future corporation. Today, however, due to the relative ease of forming a corporation in most states, persons incorporating their business rarely, if ever, engage in preliminary promotional activities.

Nevertheless, it is important for businesspersons to understand that they are personally liable for all preincorporation contracts made with investors, accountants, or others on behalf of the future corporation. A promoter may limit her or his potential liability in an initial promotional contract with a third party by including a provision that makes the corporation, once formed, assume liability under the contract. If the contract does not include such

Classification	Description
Domestic, Foreign, and Alien Corporations	A corporation is referred to as a *domestic corporation* in its home state (the state in which it incorporates). A corporation is referred to as a *foreign corporation* by any state that is not its home state. A corporation is referred to as an *alien corporation* if it originates in another country but does business in the United States.
Public and Private Corporations	A *public corporation* is formed by a government (for example, a city, town, or public project). A *private corporation* is formed wholly or in part for private benefit. Most corporations are private corporations.
Nonprofit Corporation	A corporation formed without a profit-making purpose (for example, charitable, educational, and religious organizations and hospitals).
Closely Held Corporation	A corporation that is owned by a family or a relatively small number of individuals. Because the number of shareholders is small and the transfer of shares usually is restricted, the shares are not traded in a public securities market. (Sometimes called a close corporation.)
S Corporation	A small domestic corporation (must have no more than one hundred shareholders) that, under Subchapter S of the Internal Revenue Code, is given special tax treatment. S corporations allow shareholders to enjoy the limited legal liability of the corporate form but avoid its double-taxation feature. (Shareholders pay taxes on the income at personal income tax rates, and the S corporation is not taxed separately.)
Professional Corporation	A corporation formed by professionals (for example, physicians or lawyers) to obtain the advantages of incorporation (such as tax benefits and limited liability). In most situations, the professional corporation is treated like other corporations, but sometimes the courts disregard the corporate form and treat the shareholders as partners, especially with regard to malpractice liability.

a provision, the promoter's personal liability continues. A promoter will remain personally liable for the preincorporation contract until the corporation assumes liability through a *novation* (a contract to substitute a third party in the place of one of the original contracting parties—see Chapter 17). A newly formed corporation is not liable for any preincorporation contract unless it has expressly agreed to its terms (in the initial contract or the novation).

Incorporation Procedures

Exact procedures for incorporation differ among states, but the basic steps are as follows: (1) select a state of incorporation, (2) secure the corporate name, (3) prepare the articles of incorporation, and (4) file the articles of incorporation with the secretary of state. These steps are discussed in more detail in the following subsections.

SELECT THE STATE OF INCORPORATION The first step in the incorporation process is to select a state in which to incorporate. Because state laws differ, individuals may look for the states that offer the most advantageous tax or incorporation provisions. Another consideration is the fee that a particular state charges to incorporate as well as the annual fees and the fees for specific transactions (such as stock transfers).

Delaware has historically had the least restrictive laws, along with provisions that favor corporate management. Consequently, many corporations, including a number of the largest, have incorporated there. Delaware's statutes permit firms to incorporate in that state and conduct business and locate their operating headquarters elsewhere. Most other states now permit this as well. Generally, though, closely held corporations, particularly those of a professional nature, incorporate in the state where their principal shareholders live and work. For reasons of convenience and cost, businesses often choose to incorporate in the state in which most of the corporation's business will be conducted.

SECURE THE CORPORATE NAME The choice of a corporate name is subject to state approval to ensure against duplication or deception. State statutes usually require that the secretary of state run a check on the proposed name in the state of incorporation. Some states require that the persons incorporating a firm, at their own expense, run a check on the proposed name, which can often be accomplished via Internet-based services. Once cleared, a name can be reserved for a short time, for a fee, pending the completion of the articles of incorporation.

Must Include Words That Disclose Corporate Status. All states require the corporation name to include the word *Corporation (Corp.)*, *Incorporated (Inc.)*, *Company (Co.)*, or *Limited (Ltd.)*. A firm's failure to disclose its corporate status through the use of one of these terms or abbreviations can result in the individual who signed a contract for the corporation being held personally liable (as an undisclosed principal—see Chapter 33).

Cannot Infringe on Another's Trademark Rights. A new corporation's name cannot be the same as (or deceptively similar to) the name of an existing corporation doing business within the state (see Chapter 8). Suppose that an existing corporation is named Digital Synergy, Inc. The state will not likely allow a new corporation to use the name Digital Synergy Company. That name is deceptively similar to the first and could cause confusion. This similar name could also transfer part of the goodwill established by the first corporate user to the second, thus infringing on the first company's trademark rights.

If those incorporating a firm contemplate doing business in other states—or over the Internet—they will also need to check existing corporate names in the other states in which they will do business to avoid liability for trademark infringement in those states. A related issue concerns the new firm's Internet domain name. Because the firm will want to use its name as a domain name, those incorporating the firm will need to make sure that the domain name is available by checking the ICANN database of domain names (see page 156).

PREPARE THE ARTICLES OF INCORPORATION The primary document needed to incorporate a business is the **articles of incorporation** (for an example, see Exhibit 39–1 on the next page). The articles include basic information about the corporation and serve as a primary source of authority for its future organization and business functions. The person or persons who execute (sign) the articles are called *incorporators*. Generally, the articles of incorporation *must* include the following information [RMBCA 2.02].

1. The name of the corporation.
2. The number of shares the corporation is authorized to issue.
3. The name and street address of the corporation's initial registered agent and registered office.
4. The name and address of each incorporator.

In addition, the articles *may* set forth other information, such as the names and addresses of the initial members of the board of directors, the duration and purpose of the corporation, a par value for shares of the corporation, and any other information pertinent to the rights and duties of the corporation's shareholders and directors. Articles of incorporation vary widely depending on the jurisdiction and the size and type of the corporation. Frequently, the articles do not provide much detail about the firm's operations, which are spelled out in the company's **bylaws** (internal rules of management adopted by the corporation at its first organizational meeting).

Shares of the Corporation. The articles must specify the number of shares of stock the corporation is authorized to issue [RMBCA 2.02(a)]. For instance, a company might state that the aggregate number of shares that the corporation has the authority to issue is five thousand. Large corporations often state a par value for each share, such as $.20 per share, and specify the various types or classes of stock authorized for issuance (see the discussion of *common* and *preferred stock* later in this chapter). Sometimes, the articles set forth the capital structure of the corporation and other relevant information concerning equity, shares, and credit. To allow for the raising of additional capital in the future, the articles of incorporation often authorize many more shares of stock than will initially be issued. This avoids the cumbersome and sometimes complicated task of amending the articles of incorporation at a later date.

Registered Office and Agent. The corporation must indicate the location and street address of its registered office within the state. Usually, the registered office is also the principal office of the corporation. The corporation must also give the name and address of a specific person who has been designated as an *agent*

EXHIBIT 39-1 • Articles of Incorporation Sample

| ARTICLE ONE | The name of the corporation is _____ . |

| ARTICLE TWO | The period of its duration is _____ (may be a number of years or until a certain date). |

ARTICLE THREE The purpose (or purposes) for which the corporation is organized is (are) _____
_____
_____ .

ARTICLE FOUR The aggregate number of shares that the corporation shall have the authority to issue is _____ with the par value of _____ dollar(s) each (or without par value).

ARTICLE FIVE The corporation will not commence business until it has received for the issuance of its shares consideration of the value of $1,000 (can be any sum not less than $1,000).

ARTICLE SIX The address of the corporation's registered office is _____ , and the name of its registered agent at such address is _____
_____ .

ARTICLE SEVEN The number of initial directors is _____ , and the names and addresses of the directors are
_____
_____ .

ARTICLE EIGHT The names and addresses of the incorporators are

_____   _____   _____
(Name)   (Address)   (Signature)

_____   _____   _____
(Name)   (Address)   (Signature)

_____   _____   _____
(Name)   (Address)   (Signature)

Sworn to on _____ by the above-named incorporators.
        (Date)

_____
                                        Notary Public
(Notary Seal)

and who can receive legal documents (such as orders to appear in court) on behalf of the corporation.

Incorporators. Each incorporator must be listed by name and address. The incorporators need not have any interest at all in the corporation, and sometimes signing the articles is their only duty. Many states do not have residency or age requirements for incorporators. In some states, only one incorporator is needed, but other states require as many as three. Incorporators frequently participate in the first organizational meeting of the corporation.

Duration and Purpose. A corporation has perpetual existence unless the articles state otherwise. The RMBCA does not require a specific statement of purpose to be included in the articles. A corporation

can be formed for any lawful purpose. Some incorporators include a general statement of purpose "to engage in any lawful act or activity," while others specify the intended business activities (such as "to engage in the production and sale of agricultural products"). The trend is toward allowing corporate articles to state that the corporation is organized for "any legal business," with no mention of specifics, to avoid the need for future amendments to the corporate articles [RMBCA 2.02(b)(2)(i), 3.01]. (Stating that a corporation is organized for any legal business also might avoid potential *ultra vires* issues, as discussed later in this chapter.)

Internal Organization. The articles can describe the corporation's internal management structure, although this usually is included in the bylaws adopted after the corporation is formed. The articles of incorporation commence the corporation. The bylaws are formed after commencement by the board of directors. Bylaws cannot conflict with the incorporation statute or the articles of incorporation [RMBCA 2.06].

Under the RMBCA, shareholders may amend or repeal the bylaws. The board of directors may also amend or repeal the bylaws unless the articles of incorporation or provisions of the incorporation statute reserve this power to the shareholders exclusively [RMBCA 10.20]. The bylaws typically describe such matters as voting requirements for shareholders, the election of the board of directors, and the methods of replacing directors. Bylaws also frequently outline the manner and time of holding shareholders' and board meetings (these corporate activities will be discussed in Chapter 40).

FILE THE ARTICLES WITH THE STATE Once the articles of incorporation have been prepared and signed by the incorporators, they are sent to the appropriate state official, usually the secretary of state, along with the required filing fee. In most states, the secretary of state then stamps the articles "Filed" and returns a copy of the articles to the incorporators. Once this occurs, the corporation officially exists. (Note that some states issue a *certificate of incorporation,* or *corporate charter,* which is similar to articles of incorporation, representing the state's authorization for the corporation to conduct business.[8] This procedure was typical under the unrevised MBCA.)

First Organizational Meeting to Adopt Bylaws

After incorporation, the first organizational meeting must be held. Usually, the most important function of this meeting is the adoption of bylaws, which, as mentioned, are the internal rules of management for the corporation. If the articles of incorporation named the initial board of directors, then the directors, by majority vote, call the meeting to adopt the bylaws and complete the company's organization. If the articles did not name the directors (as is typical), then the incorporators hold the meeting to elect the directors, adopt bylaws, and complete the routine business of incorporation (authorizing the issuance of shares and hiring employees, for example). The

business transacted depends on the requirements of the state's corporation statute, the nature of the corporation, the provisions made in the articles, and the desires of the incorporators.

Improper Incorporation

The procedures for incorporation are very specific. If they are not followed precisely, others may be able to challenge the existence of the corporation. Errors in incorporation procedures can become important when, for example, a third party who is attempting to enforce a contract or bring a suit for a tort injury learns of them. If a corporation has substantially complied with all conditions precedent to incorporation, the corporation is said to have *de jure* (rightful and lawful) existence. In most states and under RMBCA 2.03(b), the secretary of state's filing of the articles of incorporation is conclusive proof that all mandatory statutory provisions have been met [RMBCA 2.03(b)].

Sometimes, the incorporators fail to comply with all statutory mandates. If the defect is minor, such as an incorrect address listed on the articles of incorporation, most courts will overlook the defect and find that a corporation (*de jure*) exists. If the defect is substantial, however, such as a corporation's failure to hold an organizational meeting to adopt bylaws, the outcome will vary depending on the court. Some states, including Mississippi, New York, Ohio, and Oklahoma, still recognize the common law doctrine of *de facto* corporation.[9] In those states, the courts will treat a corporation as a legal corporation despite the defect in its formation if the following three requirements are met:

1. A state statute exists under which the corporation can be validly incorporated.
2. The parties have made a good faith attempt to comply with the statute.
3. The parties have already undertaken to do business as a corporation.

Many state courts, however, have interpreted their states' version of the RMBCA as abolishing the common law doctrine of *de facto* corporations. These states include Alaska, Arizona, the District of Columbia, New Mexico, Minnesota, Oregon, South Dakota, Tennessee, Utah, and Washington. In those states, if there is a substantial defect in complying with the incorporation statute, the corporation does

---

8. Under some circumstances, such as when a corporation fails to pay taxes, a state can revoke the firm's corporate charter, or status as a corporation.

9. See, for example, *In re Hausman,* 13 N.Y.3d 408, 921 N.E.2d 191, 893 N.Y.S.2d 499 (2009).

not legally exist, and the incorporators are personally liable.

Corporation by Estoppel

If a business holds itself out to others as being a corporation but has made no attempt to incorporate, the firm may be estopped (prevented) from denying corporate status in a lawsuit by a third party. This doctrine of corporation by estoppel is most commonly applied when a third party contracts with an entity that claims to be a corporation but has not filed articles of incorporation—or contracts with a person claiming to be an agent of a corporation that does not in fact exist. When justice requires, courts in some states will treat an alleged corporation as

if it were an actual corporation for the purpose of determining the rights and liabilities in particular circumstances.[10] Recognition of corporate status does not extend beyond the resolution of the problem at hand.

In the following case, a party sought to avoid liability on a contract with a firm that had not yet filed its articles of incorporation. Could the party escape liability on the ground that the corporation did not exist at the time of the contract?

---

10. Some states have expressly rejected the common law theory of corporation by estoppel, finding that it is inconsistent with their statutory law, whereas other states have abolished only the doctrines of *de facto* and *de jure* corporations. See, for example, *Stone v. Jetmar Properties, LLC,* 733 N.W.2d 480 (Minn.App. 2007).

CASE 39.2

Brown v. W. P. Media, Inc.

Supreme Court of Alabama, 17 So.3d 1167 (2009).

BACKGROUND AND FACTS • In 2001, W. P. Media, Inc., and Alabama MBA, Inc., agreed to form a joint venture—to be called Alabaster Wireless MBA, LLC—to provide wireless Internet services to consumers. W. P. Media was to create a wireless network and provide ongoing technical support. Alabama MBA was to contribute capital of $79,300, and W. P. Media was to contribute "proprietary technology" in the same amount. Hugh Brown signed the parties' contract on Alabama MBA's behalf as the chair of its board. At the time, however, Alabama MBA's articles of incorporation had not yet been filed. Brown filed the articles of incorporation in 2002. Later, Brown and Alabama MBA filed a suit in an Alabama state court, alleging that W. P. Media had breached their contract by not building the wireless network. The court issued a summary judgment in the defendant's favor. The plaintiffs appealed.

IN THE LANGUAGE OF THE COURT
SMITH, Justice.
* * * *

Corporate action may * * * be established under principles of estoppel, whether or not an entity or organization qualifies as a de facto corporation. The doctrine is based on conduct by a party that recognizes an organization as a corporation or an express or implied representation by a corporation that it is a corporation. In the first instance, estoppel cannot apply to one who has not dealt with the organization or in any way recognized it as having corporate existence, or who has participated in holding it out as a corporation. In the second instance, where a party has contracted or otherwise dealt with an organization, believing it to be a corporation, there may have been no holding out of corporate status by the organization. *In either instance, estoppel arises from the contract or course of dealing by the parties and is applicable in a suit by the party dealing with the organization, as well as in a suit by the organization.* [Emphasis added.]

Alabama MBA * * * argues that because W. P. Media treated Alabama MBA as a corporation, W. P. Media is now estopped from denying Alabama MBA's corporate existence.
* * * * *

W. P. Media entered into a contractual relationship with Alabama MBA to operate Alabaster Wireless. The operating agreement identified Alabama MBA as a corporation, was executed in Alabama MBA's corporate name, and was signed by Brown as Alabama MBA's "chairman of the board." W. P. Media further concedes * * * that Alabama MBA and Brown had essentially "represented" that Alabama MBA was "a viable, legal corporation" and that W. P. Media had

CASE 39.2 CONTINUED ➡ "no reason to doubt" those representations. Although Alabama MBA had not yet filed articles of incorporation at the time the operating agreement was executed in 2001, the articles of incorporation were subsequently filed in 2002. * * * At no time during the venture did W. P. Media challenge the validity of the operating agreement until after it was sued for breaching the operating agreement. Under the facts of this case, we hold that W. P. Media's actions of entering into a contract with Alabama MBA and participating with Alabama MBA in the joint venture before and after Alabama MBA's articles of incorporation were filed estop W. P. Media from denying Alabama MBA's corporate existence for purposes of challenging the validity of the operating agreement.

DECISION AND REMEDY • *The Alabama Supreme Court reversed the lower court's judgment and remanded the case. Under the principle of corporation by estoppel, W. P. Media could not deny Alabama MBA's corporate existence.*

THE LEGAL ENVIRONMENT DIMENSION • *Did Alabama MBA exist as a* de facto *corporation when it entered into the contract with W. P. Media? Why or why not?*

WHAT IF THE FACTS WERE DIFFERENT? • *Would the result in this case have been different if the parties' contract to build and operate a wireless network had been negotiated and agreed to entirely online? Discuss.*

SECTION 3
CORPORATE POWERS

Under modern law, a corporation generally can engage in any act and enter into any contract available to a natural person in order to accomplish the purposes for which it was formed. When a corporation is created, the express and implied powers necessary to achieve its purpose also come into existence.

Express Powers

The express powers of a corporation are found in its articles of incorporation, in the law of the state of incorporation, and in the state and federal constitutions. State statutes often give corporations a wide variety of powers, allowing a corporation to issue stocks and bonds, execute contracts and negotiable instruments, buy and sell (or lease) property, pay employee benefits, and make charitable contributions.

Corporate bylaws and the resolutions of the corporation's board of directors also grant or restrict certain powers. Because state corporation statutes frequently provide default rules that apply if the company's bylaws are silent on an issue, it is important that the bylaws set forth the specific operating rules of the corporation. In addition, after the bylaws are adopted, the corporation's board of directors will pass resolutions that also grant or restrict corporate powers.

The following order of priority is used if a conflict arises among the various documents involving a corporation:

1. The U.S. Constitution.
2. State constitutions.
3. State statutes.
4. The articles of incorporation.
5. Bylaws.
6. Resolutions of the board of directors.

Implied Powers

Certain implied powers arise when a corporation is created. Unless expressly prohibited by a constitution, a statute, or the articles of incorporation, the corporation has the implied power to perform all acts reasonably appropriate and necessary to accomplish its corporate purposes. For this reason, a corporation has the implied power to borrow funds within certain limits, lend funds, and extend credit to those with whom it has a legal or contractual relationship.

To borrow funds, the corporation acts through its board of directors to authorize the loan. Most often, the president or chief executive officer (see Chapter 40) of the corporation will execute the necessary papers on behalf of the corporation. Corporate officers such as these have the implied power to bind the corporation in matters directly connected with the *ordinary* business affairs of the enterprise. There is a limit to what a corporate officer can do, though. A corporate officer does not have the authority to bind the corporation to an action that will greatly affect the corporate purpose or undertaking, such as the sale of substantial corporate assets.

Ultra Vires Doctrine

The term ***ultra vires*** means "beyond the power." In corporate law, acts of a corporation that are beyond its express or implied powers are *ultra vires* acts. Under Section 3.04 of the RMBCA, the shareholders can seek an injunction from a court to prevent the corporation from engaging in *ultra vires* acts. The attorney general in the state of incorporation can also bring an action to obtain an injunction against the *ultra vires* transactions or to institute dissolution proceedings against the corporation on the basis of *ultra vires* acts. The corporation or its shareholders (on behalf of the corporation) can seek damages from the officers and directors who were responsible for the *ultra vires* acts.

In the past, most cases dealing with *ultra vires* acts involved contracts made for unauthorized purposes. Now, however, most private corporations are organized for "any legal business" and do not state a specific purpose, so the *ultra vires* doctrine has declined in importance in recent years. Today, cases that allege *ultra vires* acts usually involve nonprofit corporations or municipal (public) corporations.

CASE IN POINT Four men formed a nonprofit corporation to create the Armenian Genocide Museum & Memorial (AGM&M). The bylaws appointed them as trustees (similar to corporate directors) for life. One of the trustees, Gerard L. Cafesjian, became the chair and president of AGM&M. Eventually, the relationship among the trustees deteriorated, and Cafesjian resigned. The corporation then brought a suit claiming that Cafesjian had engaged in numerous *ultra vires* acts, self-dealing, and mismanagement. Among other things, although the bylaws required an 80 percent affirmative vote of the trustees to take action, Cafesjian had taken many actions without the board's approval. He had also entered into contracts for real estate transactions in which he had a personal interest. Because Cafesjian had taken actions that exceeded his authority and had failed to follow the rules set forth in the bylaws for board meetings, the court ruled that the corporation could go forward with its suit.[11]

---

11. *Armenian Assembly of America, Inc. v. Cafesjian,* 692 F.Supp.2d 20 (D.C. 2010).

PIERCING THE CORPORATE VEIL

Occasionally, the owners use a corporate entity to perpetrate a fraud, circumvent the law, or in some other way accomplish an illegitimate objective. In these situations, the courts will ignore the corporate structure and **pierce the corporate veil,** exposing the shareholders to personal liability [RMBCA 2.04].

Generally, when the corporate privilege is abused for personal benefit, the courts will require the owners to assume personal liability to creditors for the corporation's debts. The courts will also impose personal liability when the corporate business is treated so carelessly that the corporation and the controlling shareholders are no longer separate entities. In short, when the facts show that great injustice would result from the use of a corporation to avoid individual responsibility, a court will look behind the corporate structure to the individual shareholders.

Factors That Lead Courts to Pierce the Corporate Veil

The following are some of the factors that frequently cause the courts to pierce the corporate veil:

1. A party is tricked or misled into dealing with the corporation rather than the individual.
2. The corporation is set up never to make a profit or always to be insolvent, or it is too "thinly" capitalized—that is, it has insufficient capital at the time it is formed to meet its prospective debts or potential liabilities.
3. The corporation is formed to evade an existing legal obligation.
4. Statutory corporate formalities, such as holding required corporation meetings, are not followed.
5. Personal and corporate interests are mixed together, or **commingled,** to the extent that the corporation has no separate identity.

Although state corporation codes usually do not prohibit a shareholder from lending funds to her or his corporation, courts will scrutinize the transaction closely if the loan comes from an officer, director, or majority shareholder. Loans from persons who control the corporation must be made in good faith and for fair value.

A Potential Problem for Closely Held Corporations

The potential for corporate assets to be used for personal benefit is especially great in a closely held corporation, in which the shares are held by a single person or by only a few individuals, usually family members. In such a situation, the separate status of the corporate entity and the sole shareholder (or family-member shareholders) must be carefully preserved. Certain practices invite trouble for the one-person or family-owned corporation: the commingling of corporate and personal funds, the failure to hold board of directors' meetings and record the minutes, or the shareholders' continuous personal use of corporate property (for example, vehicles).

In the following case, a creditor asked the court to pierce the corporate veil and hold the sole shareholder-owner of the debtor corporation personally liable for a corporate debt.

✳ EXTENDED CASE 39.3 ✳
Schultz v. General Electric Healthcare Financial Services

Court of Appeals of Kentucky, ___ S.W.3d ___ (2010).

IN THE LANGUAGE OF THE COURT
STUMBO, Judge.

* * * *

[Thomas] Schultz was the president and sole shareholder/owner of Intra-Med [Services, Inc.], a Kentucky corporation that performed medical diagnostic imaging services, such as MRIs and CT scans. GE [General Electric Healthcare Financial Services, Inc.; General Electric Company; and General Electric Capital Corporation] entered into a contract to lease certain medical equipment to Intra-Med. In 2004, Intra-Med defaulted on the contract by failing to make the required lease payments to GE.

On July 8, 2004, GE filed a complaint against Intra-Med in Jefferson Circuit Court. On November 15, 2004, the court entered a judgment on the pleadings in favor of GE for over $4.7 million. GE was able to collect approximately $700,000 of the judgment.

While collecting on its judgment, GE learned of certain documents that Intra-Med had produced in discovery in another lawsuit. Those documents revealed that Mr. Schultz had used Intra-Med assets for his own purposes. For example, Mr. Schultz bought multiple pieces of property for himself using Intra-Med funds and when some of this property was later sold, Mr. Schultz kept the proceeds. GE intervened in this other lawsuit and filed a third-party complaint against Mr. Schultz seeking to pierce the corporate veil and hold him personally liable for the judgment against Intra-Med.

On April 17, 2007, GE filed a motion for partial judgment on the pleadings in which it requested a partial judgment in the amount of $1,150,000. This was allegedly the amount of Intra-Med funds which Schultz used improperly.

On August 10, 2007, the trial court held that Mr. Schultz's admissions in his answer to GE's third-party complaint support the conclusion that Schultz improperly used Intra-Med's funds. It also held that none of Mr. Schultz's affirmative defenses would preclude an entry of judgment against him. However, the court found that Mr. Schultz might have been entitled to receive some payments from Intra-Med because he personally loaned the company $700,000. Because of this possibility, the court denied GE's motion.

GE next filed a motion in which it stated it would settle for $450,000, the difference between $1,150,000 and the claimed $700,000 loan. GE also stipulated that it would voluntarily dismiss its remaining claims against Mr. Schultz if the court entered the $450,000 judgment. The court ultimately granted the motion on September 10, 2007. Mr. Schultz filed a motion to alter or amend, but it was denied. This appeal followed.

* * * *

Mr. Schultz admitted several facts in his answer to GE's third-party complaint. The relevant admitted facts are: on November 15, 2004, GE was awarded a judgment in the amount of $4,746,921.80, plus interest, against Intra-Med; Mr. Schultz had knowledge of the GE judgment on or after November 15, 2005; on or about December of 1998, Mr. Schultz, individually, purchased real property located at 7405 New LaGrange Road, Louisville, KY 40242, using Intra-Med funds; Intra-Med did not receive any of the proceeds from the subsequent sale of the New LaGrange Road property in March of 2004; on or about October of 2000, Mr. Schultz, individually, purchased and improved real property located at 8700 Dixie Highway, Louisville, KY 40258, using Intra-Med funds; after entry of the GE judgment, Mr. Schultz sold the Dixie Highway property, which had been purchased and renovated by Mr. Schultz with Intra-Med funds, for $850,000; Intra-Med did not receive any of the proceeds from the sale of the Dixie Highway property; on or about May 24, 2001, Mr. Schultz, individually, purchased a marina slip for $23,000 with Intra-Med

EXTENDED CASE CONTINUES ➡

EXTENDED CASE 39.3 CONTINUED ⬇

funds; and Intra-Med did not receive any of the proceeds from the subsequent sale of the marina slip. It is from these admitted facts that GE moved for a judgment on the pleadings.

"Three basic theories have been utilized to hold the shareholders of a corporation responsible for corporate liabilities. These have been labeled (1) the instrumentality theory; (2) the alter ego theory; and (3) the equity formulation." GE focused on the instrumentality theory in its motion.

Under the instrumentality theory three elements must be established in order to warrant a piercing of the corporate veil: (1) that the corporation was a mere instrumentality of the

shareholder; (2) that the shareholder exercised control over the corporation in such a way as to defraud or to harm the plaintiff; and (3) that a refusal to disregard the corporate entity would subject the plaintiff to unjust loss. The courts adopting this test have been virtually unanimous in requiring that these three elements co-exist before the corporate veil will be pierced. [Emphasis added.]

* * * *

The admitted facts * * * support the finding that the corporate veil should be pierced under the instrumentality theory. Mr. Schultz treated the corporation as a mere instrumentality by using corporate funds for his own individual purposes to purchase real estate and a boat slip. The admitted facts also demonstrate that Mr. Schultz

harmed GE by using corporate funds as his own even after GE obtained a monetary judgment against Intra-Med. Money that could have been used to satisfy that judgment was used by Mr. Schultz for his own purposes. Finally, not piercing the corporate veil would subject GE to an unjust loss. As previously stated, money that could have been used to satisfy GE's judgment against Intra-Med was removed from the company and used elsewhere. GE has only been able to recover around $700,000 from a $4.7 million judgment. Piercing the corporate veil appears to be the only method for GE to recover its judgment.

* * * *

For the foregoing reasons we affirm the trial court's judgment on the pleadings.

QUESTIONS

1. Schultz argued that even if the corporate veil should be pierced, the $450,000 judgment against him was too much and should be reduced. How might the court have responded to this argument?
2. Suppose that Schultz had turned over the proceeds from the sale of his properties to his corporation, Intra-Med, and used them to pay part or all of GE's judgment. In this situation, if the funds were insufficient to cover the debt, would the court have pierced the corporate veil to obtain the balance from Schultz personally? Explain.

The Alter-Ego Theory

Sometimes, courts pierce the corporate veil under the theory that the corporation was not operated as a separate entity, but was just another side (or alter ego) of the individual or group who actually controlled the corporation. This is called the alter-ego theory. The theory is applied when a corporation is so dominated and controlled by an individual or group that the separate identities of the person (or group) and the corporation are no longer distinct. Courts use the alter-ego theory to avoid injustice or fraud that would result if wrongdoers were allowed to hide behind the protection of limited liability.

CASE IN POINT Harvey and Barbara Jacobson owned Aqua Clear Technologies, Inc., which installed and serviced home water-softening systems. The Jacobsons consistently took funds out of the business for their personal expenses, including payments for their home, cars, health-insurance

premiums, and credit cards. Three weeks after Aqua filed a bankruptcy petition, Harvey formed another corporation called Discount Water Services, Inc. Discount appropriated Aqua's equipment and inventory (without buying it) and continued to service water-softening systems for Aqua's customers, even using the same phone number. The trustee appointed to Aqua's bankruptcy case sought to recover Aqua's assets on the ground that Discount was Aqua's alter ego. The court ruled that Discount was simply a continuation of Aqua's business (its alter ego) under a new name, and therefore held Discount liable for the claims asserted against Aqua in bankruptcy (totaling $108,732.64).[12]

---

12. *In re Aqua Clear Technologies, Inc.*, 361 Bankr. 567 (S.D.Fla. 2007).

SECTION 5
CORPORATE FINANCING

Corporations are financed by the issuance and sale of corporate **securities,** which include stocks and bonds. **Stocks,** or *equity securities,* represent the purchase of ownership in the business firm. **Bonds** (debentures), or *debt securities,* represent the borrowing of funds by firms (and governments). Of course, not all debt is in the form of debt securities. For example, some debt is in the form of accounts payable and notes payable, which typically are short-term debts. Bonds are simply a way for corporations to split up their long-term debt so that it can be more easily marketed.

Bonds

Bonds are issued by business firms and by governments at all levels as evidence of the funds they are borrowing from investors. Bonds normally have a designated *maturity date*—the date when the principal, or face amount, of the bond (or loan) is returned to the investor. They are sometimes referred to as *fixed-income securities* because their owners (that is, the creditors) receive fixed-dollar interest payments, usually semiannually, during the period of time prior to maturity.

Because debt financing represents a legal obligation on the part of the corporation, various features and terms of a particular bond issue are specified in a lending agreement, called a **bond indenture.**

A corporate trustee, often a commercial bank trust department, represents the collective well-being of all bondholders in ensuring that the corporation meets the terms of the bond issue. The bond indenture specifies the maturity date of the bond and the pattern of interest payments until maturity.

Stocks

Issuing stocks is another way for corporations to obtain financing [RMBCA 6.01]. The ways in which stocks differ from bonds are summarized in Exhibit 39–2 below.

Exhibit 39–3 on the following page offers a summary of the types of stocks issued by corporations. The two major types are *common stock* and *preferred stock.*

COMMON STOCK The true ownership of a corporation is represented by **common stock.** Common stock provides a proportionate interest in the corporation with regard to (1) control, (2) earnings, and (3) net assets. A shareholder's interest is generally in proportion to the number of shares he or she owns out of the total number of shares issued.

Any person who purchases common stock acquires voting rights—one vote per share held. Voting rights in a corporation apply to the election of the firm's board of directors and to any proposed changes in the ownership structure of the firm. For example, a holder of common stock generally has the right to vote in a decision on a proposed merger, as mergers can change the proportion of ownership.

EXHIBIT 39–2 • How Do Stocks and Bonds Differ?

STOCKS	BONDS
1. Stocks represent ownership.	1. Bonds represent debt.
2. Stocks (common) do not have a fixed dividend rate.	2. Interest on bonds must always be paid, whether or not any profit is earned.
3. Stockholders can elect the board of directors, which controls the corporation.	3. Bondholders usually have no voice in or control over management of the corporation.
4. Stocks do not have a maturity date; the corporation usually does not repay the stockholder.	4. Bonds have a maturity date, when the corporation is to repay the bondholder the face value of the bond.
5. All corporations issue or offer to sell stocks. This is the usual definition of a corporation.	5. Corporations do not necessarily issue bonds.
6. Stockholders have a claim against the property and income of the corporation after all creditors' claims have been met.	6. Bondholders have a claim against the property and income of the corporation that must be met before the claims of stockholders.

EXHIBIT 39-3 • Types of Stocks

TYPE	DEFINITION
Common Stock	Voting shares that represent ownership interest in a corporation. Common stock has the lowest priority with respect to payment of dividends and distribution of assets on the corporation's dissolution.
Preferred Stock	Shares of stock that have priority over common-stock shares as to payment of dividends and distribution of assets on dissolution. Dividend payments are usually a fixed percentage of the face value of the share. Preferred shares may or may not be voting shares.
Cumulative Preferred Stock	Preferred shares on which required dividends not paid in a given year must be paid in a subsequent year before any common-stock dividends can be paid.
Participating Preferred Stock	Preferred shares entitling the owner to receive (1) the preferred-stock dividend and (2) additional dividends after the corporation has paid dividends on common stock.
Convertible Preferred Stock	Preferred shares that, under certain conditions, can be converted into a specified number of common shares either in the issuing corporation or, sometimes, in another corporation.
Redeemable, or Callable, Preferred Stock	Preferred shares issued with the express condition that the issuing corporation has the right to repurchase the shares as specified.

State corporation law specifies the types of actions for which shareholder approval must be obtained.

Firms are not obligated to return a principal amount per share to each holder of common stock because no firm can ensure that the market price per share of its common stock will not decline over time. The issuing firm also does not have to guarantee a dividend; indeed, some corporations never pay dividends.

Holders of common stock are investors who assume a *residual* position in the overall financial structure of the business. In terms of receiving returns on their investments, they are last in line. They are entitled to the earnings that are left after federal and state taxes are paid and after preferred stockholders, bondholders, suppliers, employees, and other groups have been paid. Once those groups are paid, however, the owners of common stock may be entitled to *all* the remaining earnings. (The board of directors normally is not under any duty to declare the remaining earnings as dividends, however.)

PREFERRED STOCK **Preferred stock** is an equity security with *preferences*. Usually, this means that holders of preferred stock have priority over holders of common stock as to dividends and payment on dissolution of the corporation. The preferences must be stated in the articles of incorporation. Holders of preferred stock may or may not have the right to vote.

Preferred stock is not included among the liabilities of a business because it is equity. Like other equity securities, preferred shares have no fixed maturity date on which the firm must pay them off. Although firms occasionally buy back preferred stock, they are not legally obligated to do so. Investors who hold preferred stock have assumed a rather cautious position in their relationship to the corporation. They have a stronger position than common shareholders with respect to dividends and claims on assets, but they do not share in the full prosperity of the firm if it grows successfully over time. Preferred stockholders receive fixed dividends periodically, however, and they may benefit to some extent from changes in the market price of the shares.

The return and the risk for preferred stock lie somewhere between those for bonds and those for common stock. Preferred stock is more similar to bonds than to common stock, even though preferred stock appears in the ownership section of the firm's balance sheet. As a result, preferred stock is often categorized with corporate bonds as a fixed-income security, even though the legal status is not the same.

Venture Capital and Private Equity Capital

As discussed, corporations traditionally obtain financing through issuing and selling securities (stocks and bonds) in the capital market. Many investors do not want to purchase stock in a business that lacks a track record, however, and banks generally are reluctant to extend loans to high-risk enterprises. Numerous corporations fail because they are undercapitalized. Therefore, to obtain sufficient financing, many entrepreneurs seek alternative financing.

VENTURE CAPITAL Start-up businesses and high-risk enterprises often obtain venture capital financing. **Venture capital** is capital provided to new business ventures by professional, outside investors (*venture capitalists,* usually groups of wealthy investors and securities firms). Venture capital investments are high risk—the investors must be willing to lose their invested funds—but offer the potential for well-above-average returns at some point in the future.

To obtain venture capital financing, the start-up business typically gives up a share of its ownership to the venture capitalists. In addition to funding, venture capitalists may provide managerial and technical expertise, and are nearly always given

some control over the new company's decisions. Many Internet-based companies, such as Google and Amazon, were initially financed by venture capital.

PRIVATE EQUITY CAPITAL Private equity firms obtain their capital from wealthy investors in private markets. The firms use their **private equity capital** to invest in existing corporations. Usually, a private equity firm buys an entire corporation and may later reorganize it as a publicly held corporation. Sometimes, divisions of the purchased company are sold off to pay down debt. Ultimately, the private equity firm may sell shares in the reorganized (and perhaps more profitable) company to the public in an *initial public offering* (usually called an IPO—see Chapter 42). In this way, the private equity firm can make profits by selling its shares in the company to the public.

REVIEWING
Corporate Formation and Financing

William Sharp was the sole shareholder and manager of Chickasaw Club, Inc., an S corporation that operated a popular nightclub of the same name in Columbus, Georgia. Sharp maintained a corporate checking account but paid the club's employees, suppliers, and entertainers in cash out of the club's proceeds. Sharp owned the property on which the club was located. He rented it to the club but made mortgage payments out of the club's proceeds and often paid other personal expenses with Chickasaw corporate funds. At 12:45 A.M. on July 31, eighteen-year-old Aubrey Lynn Pursley, who was already intoxicated, entered the Chickasaw Club. A city ordinance prohibited individuals under the age of twenty-one from entering nightclubs, but Chickasaw employees did not check Pursley's identification to verify her age. Pursley drank more alcohol at Chickasaw and was visibly intoxicated when she left the club at 3:00 A.M. with a beer in her hand. Shortly afterward, Pursley lost control of her car, struck a tree, and was killed. Joseph Dancause, Pursley's stepfather, filed a tort lawsuit in a Georgia state court against Chickasaw Club, Inc., and William Sharp, seeking damages. Using the information presented in the chapter, answer the following questions.

1. Under what theory might the court in this case make an exception to the limited liability of shareholders and hold Sharp personally liable for the damages? What factors would be relevant to the court's decision?
2. Suppose that Chickasaw's articles of incorporation failed to describe the corporation's purpose or management structure as required by state law. Would the court be likely to rule that Sharp is personally liable to Dancause on that basis?
3. Suppose that the club extended credit to its regular patrons in an effort to maintain a loyal clientele, although neither the articles of incorporation nor the corporate bylaws authorized this practice. Would the corporation likely have the power to engage in this activity? Explain.
4. How would the court classify the Chickasaw Club corporation—domestic or foreign, public or private?

DEBATE THIS: *The sole shareholder of an S corporation should not be able to avoid liability for the torts of her or his employees.*

TERMS AND CONCEPTS

	closely held corporation 756	pierce the corporate veil 766
	commingle 766	preferred stock 770
alien corporation 756	common stock 769	private equity capital 771
articles of incorporation 761	dividends 754	public corporation 756
bond 769	domestic corporation 756	publicly held
bond indenture 769	foreign corporation 756	corporation 756
bylaws 761	holding company 754	retained earnings 754

S corporation 759
securities 769
stock 769
ultra vires 766
venture capital 771

QUESTIONS AND CASE PROBLEMS

39–1. Incorporation Jonathan, Gary, and Ricardo are active members of a partnership called Swim City. The partnership manufactures, sells, and installs outdoor swimming pools in the states of Arkansas and Texas. The partners want to continue to be active in management and to expand the business into other states as well. They are also concerned about rather large recent judgments entered against swimming pool companies throughout the United States. Based on these facts only, discuss whether the partnership should incorporate.

39–2. QUESTION WITH SAMPLE ANSWER: Preincorporation.

Cummings, Okawa, and Taft are recent college graduates who want to form a corporation to manufacture and sell personal computers. Peterson tells them he will set in motion the formation of their corporation. First, Peterson makes a contract with Owens for the purchase of a piece of land for $20,000. Owens does not know of the prospective corporate formation at the time the contract is signed. Second, Peterson makes a contract with Babcock to build a small plant on the property being purchased. Babcock's contract is conditional on the corporation's formation. Peterson secures all necessary subscription agreements and capitalization, and he files the articles of incorporation.

(a) Discuss whether the newly formed corporation, Peterson, or both are liable on the contracts with Owens and Babcock.

(b) Discuss whether the corporation is automatically liable to Babcock on formation.

• **For a sample answer to Question 39–2, go to Appendix I at the end of this text.**

39–3. *Ultra Vires* Doctrine Oya Paka and two business associates formed a corporation called Paka Corp. for the purpose of selling computer services. Oya, who owned 50 percent of the corporate shares, served as the corporation's president. Oya wished to obtain a personal loan

from her bank for $250,000, but the bank required the note to be cosigned by a third party. Oya cosigned the note in the name of the corporation. Later, Oya defaulted on the note, and the bank sued the corporation for payment. The corporation asserted, as a defense, that Oya had exceeded her authority when she cosigned the note on behalf of the corporation. Had she? Explain.

39–4. Corporate Powers InterBel Telephone Cooperative, Inc., is a Montana corporation organized under the Montana Rural Electric and Telephone Cooperative Act. This statute limits the purposes of such corporations to providing "adequate telephone service" but adds that this "enumeration . . . shall not be deemed to exclude like or similar objects, purposes, powers, manners, methods, or things." Mooseweb Corp. is an Internet service provider that has been owned and operated by Fred Weber since 1996. Mooseweb provides Web site hosting, modems, computer installation, technical support, and dial-up access to customers in Lincoln County, Montana. InterBel began to offer Internet service in 1999, competing with Mooseweb in Lincoln County. Weber filed a suit in a Montana state court against InterBel, alleging that its Internet service was *ultra vires*. Both parties filed motions for summary judgment. In whose favor should the court rule, and why? [*Weber v. InterBel Telephone Cooperative, Inc.*, 2003 MT 320, 318 Mont. 295, 80 P.3d 88 (2003)]

39–5. Torts and Criminal Acts Greg Allen is an employee, shareholder, and director of Greg Allen Construction Co., and its president. In 1996, Daniel and Sondra Estelle hired Allen's firm to renovate a home they owned in Ladoga, Indiana. To finance the cost, they obtained a line of credit from Banc One, Indiana, which required periodic inspections before it would disburse funds. Allen was on the job every day and supervised all of the work. He designed all of the structural changes, including a floor system for the bedroom over the living room, the floor system of the living room, and the stairway to the second floor. He did all of the electrical, plumbing, and carpentry work and installed all of the windows. He did most of the drywall taping and finishing and most of the painting. The Estelles found much of this work to be unacceptable, and the bank's inspector agreed that it was of poor quality. When Allen failed to act on the Estelles' complaints, they filed a suit in an Indiana state court against Allen Construction and Allen personally, alleging, in part, that his individual work on the project was negligent. Can both Allen and his corporation be held liable for this tort? Explain. [*Greg Allen Construction Co. v. Estelle,* 798 N.E.2d 171 (Ind. 2004)]

39–6. CASE PROBLEM WITH SAMPLE ANSWER: Torts and Criminal Acts.

 Thomas Persson and Jon Nokes founded Smart Inventions, Inc., in 1991 to market household con-sumer products. The success of their first product, the Smart Mop, continued with later products, which were sold through infomercials and other means. Persson and Nokes were the firm's officers and equal shareholders, with Persson responsible for product development and Nokes in charge of day-to-day operations. By 1998, they had become dissatisfied with each other's efforts. Nokes represented the firm as financially "dying," "in a grim state, . . . worse than ever," and offered to buy all of Persson's shares for $1.6 mil-lion. Persson accepted. On the day that they signed the agree-ment to transfer the shares, Smart Inventions began marketing a new product—the Tap Light—that was an instant success, generating millions of dollars in revenues. In negotiating with Persson, Nokes had intentionally kept the Tap Light a secret. Persson filed a suit in a California state court against Smart Inventions and others, asserting fraud and other claims. Under what principle might Smart Inventions be liable for Nokes's fraud? Is Smart Inventions liable in this case? Explain. [Persson v. Smart Inventions, Inc., *125 Cal.App.4th 1141, 23 Cal.Rptr.3d 335 (2 Dist. 2005)]*

- **To view a sample answer for Problem 39–6, go to this book's Web site at www.cengage.com/blaw/clarkson, select "Chapter 39," and click on "Case Problem with Sample Answer."**

39–7. Improper Incorporation

Denise Rubenstein and Christopher Mayor agreed to form Bayshore Sunrise Corp. (BSC) in New York to rent certain premises and operate a laundromat. BSC entered into a twenty-year commercial lease with Bay Shore Property Trust on April 15, 1999. Mayor signed the lease as the president of BSC. The next day—April 16—BSC's certificate of incorporation was filed with New York's secretary of state. Three years later, BSC defaulted on the lease, which resulted in its termination. Rubenstein and BSC filed a suit in a New York state court against Mayor, his brother-in-law Thomas Castellano, and Planet Laundry, Inc., claiming wrongful interference with a contractual relationship. The plaintiffs alleged that Mayor and Castellano con-spired to squeeze Rubenstein out of BSC and arranged the default on the lease so that Mayor and Castellano could form and operate their own business, Planet Laundry, at the same address. The defendants argued that they could not be liable on the plaintiffs' claim because there had never been an enforceable lease—BSC

lacked the capacity to enter into contracts on April 15. What theory might Rubenstein and BSC assert to refute this argument? Discuss. [*Rubenstein v. Mayor,* 41 A.D.3d 826, 839 N.Y.S.2d 170 (2 Dept. 2007)]

39–8. Piercing the Corporate Veil

Smith Services, Inc., was a corporation solely owned by Tony Smith. Bear, Inc., owned and operated Laker Express, a fueling station in Kentucky. Smith charged fuel to an account at Laker Express and owed approximately $35,000. There was no written agreement indicating who was liable on the account in the event of default, but all invoices had been issued to Smith Services. Smith later dissolved Smith Services and continued to run his business as a sole pro-prietorship. When Laker Express sued Smith Services to collect on the debt, there were no assets in the corpo-ration. Laker Express sued Tony Smith personally and asked the court to pierce the corporate veil, claiming that Smith was engaged in fraud and was using the corporate form only to protect himself. The trial court dismissed the case, and Laker Express appealed. Should the court pierce the corporate veil and hold Smith personally lia-ble for the unpaid corporate debt? Why or why not? Or should Laker Express have been more careful when deal-ing with clients? Explain. [*Bear, Inc. v. Smith,* 303 S.W.3d 137 (Ky.App. 2010)]

39–9. A QUESTION OF ETHICS: Improper Incorporation.

 Mike Lyons incorporated Lyons Concrete, Inc., in Montana, but did not file its first annual report, so the state involuntarily dissolved the firm in 1996. Unaware of the dissolution, Lyons continued to do business as Lyons Concrete. In 2003, he signed a written con-tract with William Weimar to form and pour a certain amount of concrete on Weimar's property in Lake County for $19,810. Weimar was in a rush to complete the entire proj-ect, and he and Lyons orally agreed to additional work on a time-and-materials basis. When scheduling conflicts arose, Weimar had his own employees set some of the forms, which proved deficient. Weimar also directed Lyons to pour concrete in the rain, which undercut its quality. In mid-project, Lyons submitted an invoice for $14,389, which Weimar paid. After the work was complete, Lyons sent Weimar an invoice for $25,731, but he refused to pay, claiming that the $14,389 covered everything. To recover the unpaid amount, Lyons filed a mechanic's lien as "Mike Lyons d/b/a Lyons Concrete, Inc." against Weimar's property. Weimar filed a suit in a Montana state court to strike the lien, and Lyons filed a counterclaim to reassert it. [Weimar v. Lyons, *338 Mont. 242, 164 P.3d 922 (2007)]*

(a) Before the trial, Weimar asked for a change of venue on the ground that a sign on the courthouse lawn advertised "Lyons Concrete." How might the sign affect a trial on the parties' dispute? Should the court grant this request?

(b) Weimar asked the court to dismiss the counter-claim on the ground that the state had dissolved Lyons Concrete in 1996. Lyons immediately filed new articles of incorporation for "Lyons Concrete,

Inc." Under what doctrine might the court rule that Weimar could not deny the existence of Lyons Concrete? What ethical values underlie this doctrine? Should the court make this ruling?

(c) At the trial, Weimar argued, in part, that there was no "fixed price" contract between the parties and that even if there were, the poor quality of the work, which required repairs, amounted to a breach, excusing Weimar's further performance. Should the court rule in Weimar's favor on this basis?

39–10. VIDEO QUESTION: Corporation versus LLC.

 Go to this text's Web site at **www.cengage.com/ blaw/clarkson** and select "Chapter 39." Click on "Video Questions" and view the video titled

Corporation or LLC: Which Is Better? Then answer the following questions.

(a) Compare the liability that Anna and Caleb would be exposed to as shareholders/owners of a corporation versus as members of an LLC.

(b) How does the taxation of corporations and LLCs differ?

(c) Given that Anna and Caleb conduct their business (Wizard Internet) over the Internet, can you think of any drawbacks to forming an LLC?

(d) If you were in Anna and Caleb's position, would you choose to create a corporation or an LLC? Why?

LEGAL RESEARCH EXERCISES ON THE WEB

Go to this text's Web site at **www.cengage.com/blaw/clarkson**, select "Chapter 39," and click on "Practical Internet Exercises." There you will find the following Internet research exercises that you can perform to learn more about the topics covered in this chapter.

Practical Internet Exercise 39–1: **Legal Perspective**
Corporate Law

Practical Internet Exercise 39–2: **Management Perspective**
Online Incorporation

CHAPTER 40

Corporate Directors, Officers, and Shareholders

A corporation joins together the efforts and resources of a large number of individuals for the purpose of producing greater returns than those persons could have obtained individually. Corporate directors, officers, and shareholders all play different roles within the corporate entity. Sometimes, actions that may benefit the corporation as a whole do not coincide with the separate interests of the individuals making up the corporation. In such situations, it is important to know the rights and duties of all participants in the corporate enterprise. This chapter focuses on these rights and duties and the ways in which conflicts among corporate participants are resolved.

SECTION 1
ROLES OF DIRECTORS AND OFFICERS

The board of directors is the ultimate authority in every corporation. Directors have responsibility for all policymaking decisions necessary to the management of all corporate affairs. Additionally, the directors must act as a body in carrying out routine corporate business. The board selects and removes the corporate officers, determines the capital structure of the corporation, and declares dividends. Each director has one vote, and customarily the majority rules. The general areas of responsibility of the board of directors are shown in Exhibit 40–1 on the following page.

Directors are sometimes inappropriately characterized as *agents* because they act on behalf of the corporation. No individual director, however, can act as an agent to bind the corporation. As a group, directors collectively control the corporation in a way that no agent is able to control a principal. In addition, although directors occupy positions of trust and control over the corporation, they are not *trustees* because they do not hold title to property for the use and benefit of others.

Few qualifications are required for directors. Only a handful of states impose minimum age and residency requirements. A director may be a shareholder, but that is not necessary (unless the articles of incorporation or bylaws require ownership interest).

Election of Directors

Subject to statutory limitations, the number of directors is set forth in the corporation's articles or bylaws. Historically, the minimum number of directors has been three, but today many states permit fewer. Normally, the incorporators appoint the first board of directors at the time the corporation is created, or the directors are named in the articles of incorporation. The initial board serves until the first annual shareholders' meeting. Subsequent directors are elected by a majority vote of the shareholders.

A director usually serves for a term of one year—from annual meeting to annual meeting. Most state statutes permit longer and staggered terms. A common practice is to elect one-third of the board members each year for a three-year term. In this way, there is greater management continuity.

REMOVAL OF DIRECTORS A director can be removed *for cause*—that is, for failing to perform a required duty—either as specified in the articles or bylaws or by shareholder action. The board of directors may also have the power to remove a director for cause, subject to shareholder review. In most states, a director cannot be removed without cause unless the shareholders have reserved the right to do so at the time of election.

EXHIBIT 40-1 • **Directors' Management Responsibilities**

RESPONSIBILITIES	EXAMPLES
Authorize Major Corporate Policy Decisions	• Oversee major contract negotiations and management-labor negotiations. • Initiate negotiations on the sale or lease of corporate assets outside the regular course of business. • Decide whether to pursue new product lines or business opportunities.
Select and Remove Corporate Officers and Other Managerial Employees, and Determine Their Compensation	• Search for and hire corporate executives and determine the elements of their compensation packages, including stock options. • Supervise managerial employees and make decisions regarding their termination.
Make Financial Decisions	• Make decisions regarding the issuance of authorized shares and bonds. • Decide when to declare dividends to be paid to shareholders.

VACANCIES ON THE BOARD Vacancies occur on the board if a director dies or resigns or when a new position is created through amendment of the articles or bylaws. In these situations, either the shareholders or the board itself can fill the vacant position, depending on state law or on the provisions of the bylaws. Note, however, that even when an election appears to be authorized by the bylaws, a court can invalidate the results if the directors were attempting to manipulate the election in order to reduce the shareholders' influence.

CASE IN POINT The bylaws of Liquid Audio, Inc., authorized a board of five directors, with two directors to be elected each year. Another company offered to buy all of Liquid Audio's stock, but the board rejected this offer. Fearing that the shareholders would elect new directors who would allow the sale, the directors amended the bylaws to increase the number of directors to seven, thereby diminishing the shareholders' influence in the upcoming election. When the shareholders challenged the election, the court ruled that the directors' action was illegal because they had attempted to diminish the shareholders' right to vote effectively in an election of directors.[1]

Compensation of Directors

In the past, corporate directors rarely were compensated, but today they are often paid at least nominal sums and may receive more substantial compensation in large corporations because of the time, work, effort, and especially risk involved. Most states

permit the corporate articles or bylaws to authorize compensation for directors. In fact, the Revised Model Business Corporation Act (RMBCA) states that unless the articles or bylaws provide otherwise, the board itself may set the directors' compensation [RMBCA 8.11]. Directors also gain through indirect benefits, such as business contacts and prestige, and other rewards, such as stock options.

In many corporations, directors are also chief corporate officers (president or chief executive officer, for example) and receive compensation in their managerial positions. A director who is also an officer of the corporation is referred to as an **inside director,** whereas a director who does not hold a management position is an **outside director.** Typically, a corporation's board of directors includes both inside and outside directors.

Board of Directors' Meetings

The board of directors conducts business by holding formal meetings with recorded minutes. The dates of regular meetings are usually established in the articles or bylaws or by board resolution, and ordinarily no further notice is required. Special meetings can be called, with notice sent to all directors. Today, most states allow directors to participate in board of directors' meetings from remote locations via telephone or Web conferencing, provided that all the directors can simultaneously hear each other during the meeting [RMBCA 8.20].

Normally, a majority of the board of directors must be present to constitute a *quorum* [RMBCA 8.24]. (A **quorum** is the minimum number of members of a body of officials or other group that must be present for business to be validly transacted.) Modern incorporation statutes, however, generally

---

1. *MM Companies, Inc. v. Liquid Audio, Inc.,* 813 A.2d 1118 (Del.Sup. Ct. 2003).

permit the articles of incorporation or bylaws to set a quorum at more or less than a majority.[2]

Once a quorum is present, the directors transact business and vote on issues affecting the corporation. Each director present at the meeting has one vote.[3] Ordinary matters generally require a simple majority vote; certain extraordinary issues may require a greater-than-majority vote. In other words, the affirmative vote of a majority of the directors present at a meeting binds the board of directors with regard to most decisions.

Rights of Directors

A corporate director must have certain rights to function properly in that position. The *right to participation* means that directors are entitled to participate in all board of directors' meetings and have a right to be notified of these meetings. Because the dates of regular board meetings are usually specified in the bylaws, no notice of these meetings is required. If special meetings are called, however, notice is required unless waived by the director [RMBCA 8.23].

A director also has a *right of inspection,* which means that each director can access the corporation's books and records, facilities, and premises. Inspection rights are essential for directors to make informed decisions and to exercise the necessary supervision over corporate officers and employees. This right of inspection is almost absolute and cannot be restricted (by the articles, bylaws, or any act of the board of directors).

When a director becomes involved in litigation by virtue of her or his position or actions, the director may also have a *right to indemnification* (reimbursement) for the legal costs, fees, and damages incurred. Most states allow corporations to indemnify and purchase liability insurance for corporate directors [RMBCA 8.51].

Committees of the Board of Directors

When a board of directors has a large number of members and must deal with myriad complex business issues, meetings can become unwieldy. Therefore, the boards of large, publicly held corporations typically create committees, appoint directors to serve on individual committees, and delegate certain tasks to these committees. Committees focus on individual subjects and increase the efficiency of the board. The most common types of committees are discussed next.

EXECUTIVE COMMITTEE The board members often elect an executive committee to handle interim management decisions between board meetings. The committee is limited to making management decisions about ordinary business matters and conducting preliminary investigations into proposals. It cannot declare dividends, authorize the issuance of shares, amend the bylaws, or initiate any actions that require shareholder approval.

AUDIT COMMITTEE The audit committee is responsible for the selection, compensation, and oversight of the independent public accountants who audit the corporation's financial records. The Sarbanes-Oxley Act of 2002 requires all publicly held corporations to have an audit committee (as will be discussed in Chapters 42 and 48).

NOMINATING COMMITTEE This committee chooses the candidates for the board of directors that management wishes to submit to the shareholders in the next election. The committee can nominate but cannot select directors to fill vacancies on the board (because only the shareholders can elect directors) [RMBCA 8.25].

COMPENSATION COMMITTEE The compensation committee reviews and decides the salaries, bonuses, stock options, and other benefits that are given to the corporation's top executives. The committee may also determine the compensation of directors.

LITIGATION COMMITTEE This committee decides whether the corporation should pursue requests by shareholders to file a lawsuit against some party that has allegedly harmed the corporation. The committee members investigate the allegations and weigh the costs and benefits of litigation.

In addition to appointing committees, the board of directors can also delegate some of its functions to corporate officers. In doing so, the board is not relieved of its overall responsibility for directing the affairs of the corporation. Instead, corporate officers and managerial personnel are empowered to make decisions relating to ordinary, daily corporate activities within well-defined guidelines.

---

2. See, for example, Delaware Code Annotated Title 8, Section 141(b); and New York Business Corporation Law Section 707. Both these state statutes allow corporations to set a quorum at less than a majority, but not less than one-third of the directors.

3. Except in Louisiana, which allows a director to vote by proxy under certain circumstances.

Corporate Officers and Executives

The board of directors hires officers and other executive employees. At a minimum, most corporations have a president, one or more vice presidents, a secretary, and a treasurer. In most states, an individual can hold more than one office, such as president and secretary, and can be both an officer and a director of the corporation. In addition to carrying out the duties articulated in the bylaws, corporate and managerial officers act as agents of the corporation, and the ordinary rules of agency (discussed in Chapters 32 and 33) normally apply to their employment.

Corporate officers and other high-level managers are employees of the company, so their rights are defined by employment contracts. Nevertheless, the board of directors normally can remove a corporate officer at any time with or without cause. If the directors remove an officer in violation of the terms of an employment contract, however, the corporation may be liable for breach of contract.

The duties of corporate officers are similar to those of directors because both groups are involved in decision making and are in similar positions of control. Hence, officers and directors are viewed as having the same fiduciary duties of care and loyalty in their conduct of corporate affairs, a subject to which we now turn.

For a synopsis of the roles of directors and officers, see *Concept Summary 40.1* below.

SECTION 2
DUTIES AND LIABILITIES OF DIRECTORS AND OFFICERS

Directors and officers are deemed to be fiduciaries of the corporation because their relationship with the corporation and its shareholders is one of trust and confidence. As fiduciaries, directors and officers owe ethical—and legal—duties to the corporation and

CONCEPT SUMMARY 40.1
Roles of Directors and Officers

Aspect	Description
Election of Directors	The incorporators usually appoint the first board of directors; thereafter, shareholders elect the directors. Directors usually serve a one-year term, although the term can be longer. Few qualifications are required; a director can be a shareholder but is not required to be. Compensation usually is specified in the corporate articles or bylaws.
Board of Directors' Meetings	The board of directors conducts business by holding formal meetings with recorded minutes. The dates of regular meetings are usually established in the corporate articles or bylaws; special meetings can be called, with notice sent to all directors. Usually, a quorum is a majority of the corporate directors. Once a quorum is present, each director has one vote, and the majority normally rules in ordinary matters.
Rights of Directors	Directors' rights include the rights of participation, inspection, compensation, and indemnification.
Board of Directors' Committees	Directors may appoint committees and delegate some of their responsibilities to the committees and to corporate officers and executives. For example, directors commonly appoint an *executive committee,* which handles ordinary, interim management decisions between board of directors' meetings. Directors might also appoint an *audit committee* to hire and supervise the independent public accountants who audit the corporation's financial records.
Role of Corporate Officers and Executives	The board of directors normally hires the corporate officers and other executive employees. In most states, a person can hold more than one office and can be both an officer and a director of a corporation. The rights of corporate officers and executives are defined by employment contracts.

the shareholders as a whole. These fiduciary duties include the duty of care and the duty of loyalty.

Duty of Care

Directors and officers must exercise due care in performing their duties. The standard of *due care* has been variously described in judicial decisions and codified in many state corporation codes. Generally, a director or officer is required to act in good faith, to exercise the care that an ordinarily prudent (careful) person would exercise in similar circumstances, and to do what she or he believes is in the best interests of the corporation [RMBCA 8.30(a), 8.42(a)]. Directors and officers whose failure to exercise due care results in harm to the corporation or its shareholders can be held liable for negligence (unless the *business judgment rule* applies, as will be discussed shortly).

DUTY TO MAKE INFORMED DECISIONS Directors and officers are expected to be informed on corporate matters and to conduct a reasonable investigation of the situation before making a decision. This means that they must do what is necessary to keep adequately informed: attend meetings and presentations, ask for information from those who have it, read reports, and review other written materials. In other words, directors and officers must investigate, study, and discuss matters and evaluate alternatives before making a decision. They cannot decide on the spur of the moment without adequate research.

Although directors and officers are expected to act in accordance with their own knowledge and training, they are also normally entitled to rely on information given to them by certain other persons. Most states and Section 8.30(b) of the RMBCA allow a director to make decisions in reliance on information furnished by competent officers or employees, professionals such as attorneys and accountants, and committees of the board of directors (on which the director does not serve). The reliance must be in good faith, of course, to insulate a director from liability if the information later proves to be inaccurate or unreliable.

DUTY TO EXERCISE REASONABLE SUPERVISION Directors are also expected to exercise a reasonable amount of supervision when they delegate work to corporate officers and employees. Suppose that Dale, a corporate bank director, fails to attend any board of directors' meetings for five years. In addition, Dale never inspects any of the corporate books or records and generally fails to supervise the activities of the bank president and the loan committee. Meanwhile,

Brennan, the bank president, who is a corporate officer, makes various improper loans and permits large overdrafts. In this situation, Dale (the corporate director) can be held liable to the corporation for losses resulting from the unsupervised actions of the bank president and the loan committee.

DISSENTING DIRECTORS Directors are expected to attend board of directors' meetings, and their votes should be entered into the minutes. Sometimes, an individual director disagrees with the majority's vote (which becomes an act of the board of directors). Unless a dissent is entered in the minutes, the director is presumed to have assented. If a decision later leads to the directors' being held liable for mismanagement, dissenting directors are rarely held individually liable to the corporation. For this reason, a director who is absent from a given meeting sometimes registers a dissent with the secretary of the board regarding actions taken at the meeting.

The Business Judgment Rule

Directors and officers are expected to exercise due care and to use their best judgment in guiding corporate management, but they are not insurers of business success. Under the **business judgment rule,** a corporate director or officer will not be liable to the corporation or to its shareholders for honest mistakes of judgment and bad business decisions. Courts give significant deference to the decisions of corporate directors and officers, and consider the reasonableness of a decision at the time it was made, without the benefit of hindsight. Thus, corporate decision makers are not subjected to second-guessing by shareholders or others in the corporation.

The business judgment rule will apply as long as the following occurred:

1. The director or officer took reasonable steps to become informed about the matter.
2. He or she had a rational basis for the decision.
3. There was no conflict of interest between the director's or officer's personal interest and that of the corporation.

In fact, unless there is evidence of bad faith, fraud, or a clear breach of fiduciary duties, most courts will apply the rule and protect directors and officers who make bad business decisions from liability for those choices. Consequently, if there is a reasonable basis for a business decision, a court is unlikely to interfere with that decision, even if the corporation suffers as a result. Note also that as a practical matter, corporate officers face liability more often than directors under this rule because they work at the corporation every day, whereas directors meet once a month or less. But does the business judgment rule ever provide too much protection for corporate decision makers? See this chapter's *Insight into Ethics* feature below for a discussion of this issue.

Duty of Loyalty

Loyalty can be defined as faithfulness to one's obligations and duties. In the corporate context, the duty of loyalty requires directors and officers to subordinate their personal interests to the welfare of the corporation. For instance, a director should not oppose a transaction that is in the corporation's best interest simply because pursuing it may cost the director her or his position. Directors cannot use corporate funds or confidential corporate information for personal advantage and must refrain from self-dealing. Cases dealing with the duty of loyalty typically involve one or more of the following:

1. Competing with the corporation.
2. Usurping (taking personal advantage of) a corporate opportunity.
3. Having an interest that conflicts with that of the corporation.
4. Using information that is not available to the public to make a profit trading securities (see *insider trading* on page 820).
5. Authorizing a corporate transaction that is detrimental to minority shareholders.
6. Selling control over the corporation.

The following classic case illustrates the conflict that can arise between a corporate official's personal interest and his or her duty of loyalty.

INSIGHT INTO ETHICS
Is the Business Judgment Rule Overly Protective?

The business judgment rule generally insulates corporate decision makers from liability for bad decisions even though this may seem to contradict the goal of greater corporate accountability. Is the rule fair to shareholders?

Citigroup—An Example

In 2009, a Delaware court ruled against shareholders of Citigroup, Inc., who claimed that the bank's directors had breached their fiduciary duties. The shareholders alleged that the directors had caused Citigroup to continue to engage in subprime lending (see Chapter 31) despite the steady decline of the housing market, the dramatic increase in foreclosures, the collapse of other subprime lenders, and other red flags that should have warned Citigroup to change its practices.

The shareholders claimed that the directors' failure to adequately protect the corporation's exposure to risk given these warning signs was a breach of their duties and resulted in significant losses to Citigroup. The court, however, found that "the warning signs alleged by plaintiffs are not evidence that the directors consciously disregarded their duties or otherwise acted in bad faith; at most they evidence that the directors made bad business decisions."[a] Thus, under the business judgment rule, the court dismissed the shareholders' claims of breach of fiduciary duty. The court, however, did allow the shareholders to maintain a claim for waste based on the directors' approval of a compensation package for the company's chief executive officer.

Lyondell Chemical—Another Example

Another 2009 case also involved the business judgment rule. Early in 2007, a foreign firm had announced its intention to acquire Lyondell Chemical Company. Over the next several months, Lyondell's directors did nothing to prepare for a possible merger. They failed to research Lyondell's market value and made no attempt to seek out other potential buyers. The $13 billion cash merger was negotiated and finalized in less than one week in July 2007.

At that time, the directors met for a total of only seven hours to discuss the transaction. Shortly afterward, shareholders filed a lawsuit alleging that the directors had breached their fiduciary duties by failing to maximize the sale price of the corporation. Nevertheless, the Delaware Supreme Court ruled that the directors were protected by the business judgment rule.[b]

CRITICAL THINKING

INSIGHT INTO THE LEGAL ENVIRONMENT
If courts were to ignore the business judgment rule, what might the consequences be?

a. *In re Citigroup, Inc., Shareholder Derivative Litigation,* 964 A.2d 106 (Del.Ch. 2009).

b. *Lyondell Chemical Co. v. Ryan,* 970 A.2d 235 (Del.Sup.Ct. 2009).

CASE 40.1
Guth v. Loft, Inc.
Supreme Court of Delaware, 23 Del.Ch. 255, 5 A.2d 503 (1939).

BACKGROUND AND FACTS • Loft, Inc., made and sold candies, syrups, beverages, and food from its offices and plant in Long Island City, New York. Loft operated 115 retail outlets in several states and also sold its products wholesale. Charles Guth was Loft's president. Guth and his family owned Grace Company, which made syrups for soft drinks in a plant in Baltimore, Maryland. Coca-Cola Company supplied Loft with cola syrup. Unhappy with what he felt was Coca-Cola's high price, Guth entered into an agreement with Roy Megargel to acquire the trademark and formula for Pepsi-Cola and form Pepsi-Cola Corporation. Neither Guth nor Megargel could finance the new venture, however, and Grace was insolvent. Without the knowledge of Loft's board, Guth used Loft's capital, credit, facilities, and employees to further the Pepsi enterprise. At Guth's direction, Loft made the concentrate for the syrup, which was sent to Grace to add sugar and water. Loft charged Grace for the concentrate but allowed forty months' credit. Grace charged Pepsi for the syrup but also granted substantial credit. Grace sold the syrup to Pepsi's customers, including Loft, which paid on delivery or within thirty days. Loft also paid for Pepsi's advertising. Finally, losing profits at its stores as a result of switching from Coca-Cola, Loft filed a suit in a Delaware state court against Guth, Grace, and Pepsi, seeking their Pepsi stock and an accounting. The court entered a judgment in the plaintiff's favor. The defendants appealed to the Delaware Supreme Court.

IN THE LANGUAGE OF THE COURT
LAYTON, Chief Justice, delivering the opinion of the court:
    * * * *
    Corporate officers and directors are not permitted to use their position of trust and confidence to further their private interests. * * * They stand in a fiduciary relation to the corporation and its stockholders. A public policy, existing through the years, and derived from a profound knowledge of human characteristics and motives, has established *a rule that demands of a corporate officer or director, peremptorily [not open for debate] and inexorably [unavoidably], the most scrupulous observance of his duty, not only affirmatively to protect the interests of the corporation committed to his charge, but also to refrain from doing anything that would work injury to the corporation * * * .* The rule that requires an undivided and unselfish loyalty to the corporation demands that there shall be no conflict between duty and self-interest. [Emphasis added.]
    * * * *
    * * * *If there is presented to a corporate officer or director a business opportunity which the corporation is financially able to undertake [that] is * * * in the line of the corporation's business and is of practical advantage to it * * * and, by embracing the opportunity, the self-interest of the officer or director will be brought into conflict with that of his corporation, the law will not permit him to seize the opportunity for himself. * * * In such circumstances, * * * the corporation may elect to claim all of the benefits of the transaction for itself, and the law will impress a trust in favor of the corporation upon the property, interests and profits so acquired.* [Emphasis added.]
    * * * *
    * * * The appellants contend that no conflict of interest between Guth and Loft resulted from his acquirement and exploitation of the Pepsi-Cola opportunity [and] that the acquisition did not place Guth in competition with Loft * * *. [In this case, however,] Guth was Loft, and Guth was Pepsi. He absolutely controlled Loft. His authority over Pepsi was supreme. As Pepsi, he created and controlled the supply of Pepsi-Cola syrup, and he determined the price and the terms. What he offered, as Pepsi, he had the power, as Loft, to accept. Upon any consideration of human characteristics and motives, he created a conflict between self-interest and duty. He made himself the judge in his own cause. * * * Moreover, a reasonable probability of injury to Loft resulted from the situation forced upon it. Guth was in the same position to impose his terms upon Loft as had been the Coca-Cola Company.

CASE CONTINUES ➡

* * * The facts and circumstances demonstrate that Guth's appropriation of the Pepsi-Cola opportunity to himself placed him in a competitive position with Loft with respect to a commodity essential to it, thereby rendering his personal interests incompatible with the superior interests of his corporation; and this situation was accomplished, not openly and with his own resources, but secretly and with the money and facilities of the corporation which was committed to his protection.

DECISION AND REMEDY • *The Delaware Supreme Court upheld the judgment of the lower court. The state supreme court was "convinced that the opportunity to acquire the Pepsi-Cola trademark and formula, goodwill and business belonged to [Loft], and that Guth, as its President, had no right to appropriate the opportunity to himself."*

WHAT IF THE FACTS WERE DIFFERENT? • *Suppose that Loft's board of directors had approved Pepsi-Cola's use of its personnel and equipment. Would the court's decision have been different? Discuss.*

IMPACT OF THIS CASE ON TODAY'S LAW • *This early Delaware decision was one of the first to set forth a test for determining when a corporate officer or director has breached the duty of loyalty. The test has two basic parts—whether the opportunity was reasonably related to the corporation's line of business, and whether the corporation was financially able to undertake the opportunity. The court also considered whether the corporation had an interest or expectancy in the opportunity and recognized that when the corporation had "no interest or expectancy, the officer or director is entitled to treat the opportunity as his own."*

Disclosure of Potential Conflicts of Interest

Corporate directors often have many business affiliations, and a director may sit on the board of more than one corporation. Of course, directors are precluded from entering into or supporting businesses that operate in direct competition with corporations on whose boards they serve. Their fiduciary duty requires them to make a full disclosure of any potential conflicts of interest that might arise in any corporate transaction [RMBCA 8.60].

Sometimes, a corporation enters into a contract or engages in a transaction in which an officer or director has a personal interest. The director or officer must make a *full disclosure* of the nature of the conflicting interest and all facts pertinent to the transaction, and must abstain from voting on the proposed transaction.

For example, Ballo Corporation needs office space. Stephanie Colson, one of its five directors, owns the building adjoining the corporation's headquarters. Colson can negotiate a lease for the space to Ballo if she fully discloses her conflicting interest and any facts known to her about the proposed transaction to Ballo and the other four directors. If the lease arrangement is fair and reasonable, Colson abstains from voting on it, and the other members of the corporation's board of directors unanimously approve it, the contract is valid. The rule is one of reason. Otherwise, directors would be prevented from ever having financial dealings with the corporations they serve.

Liability of Directors and Officers

Directors and officers are exposed to liability on many fronts. They can be held liable for negligence in certain circumstances, as previously discussed. They may also be held liable for the crimes and torts committed by themselves or by corporate employees under their supervision, as discussed in Chapters 9, 33, and 39.

Additionally, if shareholders perceive that the corporate directors are not acting in the best interests of the corporation, they may sue the directors, in what is called a *shareholder's derivative suit*, on behalf of the corporation. (This type of action will be discussed later in this chapter, in the context of shareholders' rights.) Directors and officers can also be held personally liable under a number of statutes, such as statutes enacted to protect consumers or the environment (see Chapters 45 and 46).

See *Concept Summary 40.2* on the facing page for a review of the duties and liabilities of directors and officers.

CONCEPT SUMMARY 40.2
Duties and Liabilities of Directors and Officers

Aspect	Description
Duties of Directors and Officers	1. *Duty of care*—Directors and officers are obligated to act in good faith, to use prudent business judgment in the conduct of corporate affairs, and to act in the corporation's best interests. If a director or officer fails to exercise this duty of care, he or she may be answerable to the corporation and to the shareholders for breaching the duty. The *business judgment rule* immunizes a director from liability for a corporate decision as long as it was within the power of the corporation and the authority of the director to make and was an informed, reasonable, and loyal decision. 2. *Duty of loyalty*—Directors and officers have a fiduciary duty to subordinate their own interests to those of the corporation in matters relating to the corporation. 3. *Conflicts of interest*—To fulfill their duty of loyalty, directors and officers must make a full disclosure of any potential conflicts between their personal interests and those of the corporation.
Liability of Directors and Officers	Corporate directors and officers are personally liable for their own torts and crimes (when not protected under the business judgment rule). Additionally, they may be held personally liable for the torts and crimes committed by corporate personnel under their direct supervision (see Chapters 9, 33, and 39). They may also be held personally liable for violating certain statutes, such as environmental and consumer protection laws, and can sometimes be sued by shareholders for mismanaging the corporation.

SECTION 3
THE ROLE OF SHAREHOLDERS

The acquisition of a share of stock makes a person an owner and a shareholder in a corporation. Shareholders thus own the corporation. Although they have no legal title to corporate property, such as buildings and equipment, they do have an equitable (ownership) interest in the firm.

As a general rule, shareholders have no responsibility for the daily management of the corporation, although they are ultimately responsible for choosing the board of directors, which does have such control. Ordinarily, corporate officers and other employees owe no direct duty to individual shareholders (unless some contract or special relationship exists between them in addition to the corporate relationship). Their duty is to act in the best interests of the corporation and its shareholder-owners *as a whole*. In turn, as you will read later in this chapter, controlling shareholders owe a fiduciary duty to minority shareholders.

In this section, we look at the powers of shareholders, which may be established in the articles of incorporation and under the state's general corporation law.

Shareholders' Powers

Shareholders must approve fundamental changes affecting the corporation before the changes can be implemented. Hence, shareholder approval normally is required to amend the articles of incorporation or bylaws, to conduct a merger or dissolve the corporation, and to sell all or substantially all of the corporation's assets. Some of these powers are subject to prior board approval. Shareholder approval may also be requested (though it is not required) for certain other actions, such as to approve an independent auditor.

Shareholders also have the power to vote to elect or remove members of the board of directors. As described earlier, the first board of directors is either named in the articles of incorporation or chosen by the incorporators to serve until the first shareholders' meeting. From that time on, selection and retention of directors are exclusively shareholder functions.

Directors usually serve their full terms; if the shareholders judge them unsatisfactory, they are simply not reelected. Shareholders have the inherent power, however, to remove a director from office *for cause* (breach of duty or misconduct) by a majority vote.[4] As noted earlier in this chapter, some state

---

4. A director can often demand court review of removal for cause, however.

statutes (and some articles of incorporation) permit removal of directors without cause by the vote of a majority of the shareholders entitled to vote.[5]

Shareholders' Meetings

Shareholders' meetings must occur at least annually. In addition, special meetings can be called to deal with urgent matters.

NOTICE OF MEETINGS A corporation must notify its shareholders of the date, time, and place of an annual or special shareholders' meeting at least ten days, but not more than sixty days, before the meeting date [RMBCA 7.05].[6] (The date and time of the annual meeting can be specified in the bylaws.) Notice of a special meeting must include a statement of the purpose of the meeting, and business transacted at the meeting is limited to that purpose. The RMBCA does not specify how the notice must be given (such as by mail or e-mail), but most corporations specify in their bylaws the acceptable methods of notifying shareholders about meetings. Also, some states' incorporation statutes outline the means of notice that a corporation can use in that jurisdiction. For example, in Alaska, notice may be given in person, by mail, or by various electronic transmission methods—including fax, e-mail, blog, or Web post—as long as the shareholder has agreed to that electronic method.[7]

PROXIES It usually is not practical for owners of only a few shares of stock of publicly traded corporations to attend a shareholders' meeting. Therefore, the law allows stockholders to appoint another person as their agent to vote their shares at the meeting. The signed appointment form or electronic transmission authorizing an agent to vote the shares is called a **proxy** (from the Latin *procurare,* meaning "to manage or take care of").

Management often solicits proxies, but any person can do so to concentrate voting power. Groups of shareholders have used proxies as a device for taking over a corporation (corporate takeovers will be discussed in Chapter 41). Proxies normally are revocable (can be withdrawn), unless they are specifically designated as irrevocable and coupled with an interest (such as when the person receiving the proxies from shareholders has agreed to buy their shares). Under RMBCA 7.22(c), proxies are valid for eleven months, unless the proxy agreement mandates a longer period.

SHAREHOLDER PROPOSALS When shareholders want to change a company policy, they can put their ideas up for a shareholder vote. They do this by submitting a shareholder proposal to the board of directors and asking the board to include the proposal in the proxy materials that are sent to all shareholders before meetings.

The Securities and Exchange Commission (SEC), which regulates the purchase and sale of securities (see Chapter 42), has special provisions relating to proxies and shareholder proposals. SEC Rule 14a-8 provides that all shareholders who own stock worth at least $1,000 are eligible to submit proposals for inclusion in corporate proxy materials. The corporation is required to include information on whatever proposals will be considered at the shareholders' meeting along with proxy materials. Only those proposals that relate to significant policy considerations, not ordinary business operations, must be included.

Under the SEC's e-proxy rules,[8] all public companies must post their proxy materials on the Internet and notify shareholders how to find that information. Although the law requires proxy materials to be posted online, public companies may still choose among several options—including paper documents or a DVD sent by mail—for actually delivering the materials to shareholders.

Shareholder Voting

Shareholders exercise ownership control through the power of their votes. Corporate business matters are presented in the form of resolutions, which shareholders vote to approve or disapprove. Unless there is a provision to the contrary, each common shareholder is entitled to one vote per share, although the voting techniques discussed next enhance the power of the shareholder's vote. The articles of incorporation can exclude or limit voting rights, particularly

---

5. Most states allow *cumulative voting* (see facing page) for directors. If cumulative voting is authorized, a director may not be removed if the number of votes against removal would be sufficient to elect a director under cumulative voting. See, for example, California Corporations Code Section 303A. See also Section 8.08(c) of the RMBCA.

6. The shareholder can waive the requirement of notice by signing a waiver form [RMBCA 7.06]. A shareholder who does not receive notice but who learns of the meeting and attends without protesting the lack of notice is said to have waived notice by such conduct.

7. Alaska Statutes Section 10.06.410 Notice of Shareholders' Meetings.

8. 17 C.F.R. Parts 240, 249, and 274.

for certain classes of shares. For example, owners of preferred shares are usually denied the right to vote [RMBCA 7.21]. If a state statute requires specific voting procedures, the corporation's articles or bylaws must be consistent with the statute.

QUORUM REQUIREMENTS For shareholders to act during a meeting, a quorum must be present. Generally, a quorum exists when shareholders holding more than 50 percent of the outstanding shares are present, but state laws often permit the articles of incorporation to set higher or lower quorum requirements. In some states, obtaining the unanimous written consent of shareholders is a permissible alternative to holding a shareholders' meeting [RMBCA 7.25].

Once a quorum is present, voting can proceed. A straight majority vote of the shares represented at the meeting is usually required to pass resolutions. Assume that Novo Pictures, Inc., has 10,000 outstanding shares of voting stock. Its articles of incorporation set the quorum at 50 percent of outstanding shares and provide that a majority vote of the shares present is necessary to pass ordinary matters. Therefore, for this firm, at the shareholders' meeting, a quorum of stockholders representing 5,000 outstanding shares must be present to conduct business, and a vote of at least 2,501 of those shares is needed to pass ordinary resolutions. Thus, if 6,000 shares are represented, a vote of 3,001 will be necessary.

At times, more than a simple majority vote will be required either by statute or by the articles of incorporation. Extraordinary corporate matters, such as a merger, a consolidation, or dissolution of the corporation (see Chapter 41), require a higher percentage of all corporate shares entitled to vote, not just a majority of those present at that particular meeting [RMBCA 7.27].

VOTING LISTS The RMBCA requires a corporation to maintain an alphabetical voting list of shareholders. The corporation prepares the voting list before each shareholders' meeting. Ordinarily, only persons whose names appear on the corporation's stockholder records as owners are entitled to vote.[9] The voting list contains the name and address of each shareholder as shown on the corporate records on a given cutoff date, or *record date*. (Under RMBCA 7.07, the bylaws or board of directors may fix a record date that is as much as seventy days before the meeting.) The voting list also includes the number of voting shares held by each owner. The list is usually kept at the corporate headquarters and must be made available for shareholder inspection [RMBCA 7.20].

CUMULATIVE VOTING Most states permit, and many require, shareholders to elect directors by *cumulative voting,* a voting method designed to allow minority shareholders to be represented on the board of directors.[10] With cumulative voting, each shareholder is entitled to a total number of votes equal to the number of board members to be elected multiplied by the number of voting shares that the shareholder owns. The shareholder can cast all of these votes for one candidate or split them among several nominees for director. All nominees stand for election at the same time. When cumulative voting is not required by statute or under the articles, the entire board can be elected by a majority of shares at a shareholders' meeting.

Suppose that a corporation has 10,000 shares issued and outstanding. The minority shareholders hold 3,000 shares, and the majority shareholders hold the other 7,000 shares. Three members of the board are to be elected. The majority shareholders' nominees are Alvarez, Beasley, and Caravel. The minority shareholders' nominee is Dovrik. Can Dovrik be elected to the board by the minority shareholders?

If cumulative voting is allowed, the answer is yes. The minority shareholders have 9,000 votes among them (the number of directors to be elected times the number of shares, or $3 \times 3,000 = 9,000$ votes). All of these votes can be cast to elect Dovrik. The majority shareholders have 21,000 votes ($3 \times 7,000 = 21,000$ votes), but these votes must be distributed among their three nominees. The result of cumulative voting is that no matter how the majority shareholders cast their 21,000 votes, they will not be able to elect all three directors if the minority shareholders cast all of their 9,000 votes for Dovrik, as illustrated in Exhibit 40–2 on the next page.

---

9. When the legal owner is deceased, bankrupt, mentally incompetent, or in some other way under a legal disability, his or her vote can be cast by a person designated by law to control and manage the owner's property.

10. See, for example, California Corporations Code Section 708. Some states, such as Nebraska, require cumulative voting in their state constitutions. Under RMBCA 7.28, no cumulative voting rights exist unless the articles of incorporation so provide.

EXHIBIT 40-2 • Results of Cumulative Voting

BALLOT	MAJORITY SHAREHOLDER VOTES			MINORITY SHAREHOLDER VOTES	DIRECTORS ELECTED
	Alvarez	*Beasley*	*Caravel*	*Dovrik*	
1	10,000	10,000	1,000	9,000	Alvarez, Beasley, Dovrik
2	9,001	9,000	2,999	9,000	Alvarez, Beasley, Dovrik
3	6,000	7,000	8,000	9,000	Beasley, Caravel, Dovrik

OTHER VOTING TECHNIQUES A group of shareholders can agree in writing prior to a shareholders' meeting, in a *shareholder voting agreement,* to vote their shares together in a specified manner. Such agreements usually are held to be valid and enforceable. A shareholder can also appoint a voting agent and vote by proxy, as mentioned previously.

Another technique is for shareholders to enter into a *voting trust.* A **voting trust** is an agreement (a trust contract) under which a shareholder assigns the right to vote his or her shares to a trustee, usually for a specified period of time. The trustee is then responsible for voting the shares on behalf of all the shareholders in the trust. The shareholder retains all rights of ownership (for example, the right to receive dividend payments) except the power to vote the shares [RMBCA 7.30].

Although shareholders are free to make voting agreements among themselves and with management, corporate managers must be careful that such agreements do not constitute a breach of their fiduciary duties. Agreements regarding voting must be in the corporation's best interests, or the corporate officers and directors can be sued.

CASE IN POINT Several shareholders of Cryo-Cell International, Inc., mounted a proxy contest in an effort to replace the board of directors. Another stockholder, Andrew Filipowski, agreed to support management in exchange for being included in management's slate of directors. The company's chief executive officer, Mercedes Walton, secretly promised Filipowski that if management's slate won, the board of directors would add another board seat to be filled by a Filipowski designee. After management won the election, Walton prepared to add Filipowski's designee to the board. When the dissident shareholders challenged the election results, the court held that the board's actions and Walton's secret agreement constituted serious breaches of fiduciary duty that tainted the election. The court therefore ordered a new election to be held.[11]

SECTION 4

RIGHTS OF SHAREHOLDERS

Shareholders possess numerous rights. A significant right—the right to vote their shares—has already been discussed. We look at some additional rights of shareholders in the following subsections.

Stock Certificates

In the past, corporations commonly issued **stock certificates** that evidenced ownership of a specified number of shares in the corporation. Today, however, most shares of stock are uncertificated—that is, no actual, physical stock certificates are issued [RMBCA 6.26]. Instead, the corporation keeps an official record of its shareholders and may send each of them a letter or other notice that contains the pertinent information that formerly was included on the face of stock certificates.

Stock is intangible personal property, and the ownership right has always existed independently of any stock certificate. Thus, if a stock certificate was lost or destroyed, ownership was not destroyed with it. A new certificate could be issued to replace the one that was lost or destroyed. Notice of shareholders' meetings, dividends, and operational and financial reports are all distributed according to the recorded ownership listed in the corporation's books, not on the basis of possession of a certificate.

Preemptive Rights

Sometimes, the articles of incorporation grant preemptive rights to shareholders. With **preemptive rights**, a shareholder receives a preference over all other purchasers to subscribe to or purchase a pro-rated share of a new issue of stock. In other words, the shareholder can purchase a percentage of the new shares that is equal to his or her current percentage of ownership in the corporation. Under RMBCA 6.30, preemptive rights do not exist unless provided for in the articles of incorporation. Preemptive rights do not apply to **treasury shares**—shares that are authorized and issued but are no longer outstanding

---

11. *Portnoy v. Cryo-Cell International, Inc.,* 940 A.2d 43 (Del.Ch. 2008).

because they have been redeemed (purchased back) by the corporation.

THE PURPOSE OF PREEMPTIVE RIGHTS Preemptive rights allow each shareholder to maintain her or his proportionate control, voting power, or financial interest in the corporation. Generally, preemptive rights apply only to additional, newly issued stock sold for cash, and the preemptive rights must be exercised within a specified time period, which usually is thirty days.

For example, Tron Corporation authorizes and issues 1,000 shares of stock, and Omar Loren purchases 100 shares, making him the owner of 10 percent of the company's stock. Subsequently, Tron, by vote of its shareholders, authorizes the issuance of another 1,000 shares (by amending the articles of incorporation). This increases its capital stock to a total of 2,000 shares. If preemptive rights have been provided, Loren can purchase one additional share of the new stock being issued for each share he already owns—or 100 additional shares. Thus, he can own 200 of the 2,000 shares outstanding, and his relative position as a shareholder will be maintained. If preemptive rights are not reserved, his proportionate control and voting power will be diluted from that of a 10 percent shareholder to that of a 5 percent shareholder because the additional 1,000 shares were issued.

PREEMPTIVE RIGHTS IN CLOSELY HELD CORPORATIONS Preemptive rights are most important in closely held corporations because each shareholder owns a relatively small number of shares but controls a substantial interest in the corporation. Without preemptive rights, it would be possible for a shareholder to lose his or her proportionate control over the firm. Nevertheless, preemptive rights can hinder a corporation from raising capital from new, outside investors who can provide needed expertise as well as capital.

Stock Warrants

Stock warrants are rights to buy stock at a stated price by a specified date that are given by the company. Usually, when preemptive rights exist and a corporation is issuing additional shares, it gives its shareholders stock warrants. Warrants are often publicly traded on securities exchanges.

Dividends

A **dividend** is a distribution of corporate profits or income *ordered by the directors* and paid to the shareholders in proportion to their respective shares in the corporation. Dividends can be paid in cash, property, stock of the corporation that is paying the dividends, or stock of other corporations.[12]

State laws vary, but each state determines the general circumstances and legal requirements under which dividends are paid. State laws also control the sources of revenue to be used; only certain funds are legally available for paying dividends. Once declared, a cash dividend becomes a corporate debt enforceable at law like any other debt. Depending on state law, dividends may be paid from the following sources:

1. *Retained earnings.* All states allow dividends to be paid from the undistributed net profits earned by the corporation, including capital gains from the sale of fixed assets. As mentioned in Chapter 39, the undistributed net profits are called *retained earnings*.
2. *Net profits.* A few states allow dividends to be issued from current net profits without regard to deficits in prior years.
3. *Surplus.* A number of states allow dividends to be paid out of any kind of surplus.

ILLEGAL DIVIDENDS Sometimes, dividends are improperly paid from an unauthorized account, or their payment causes the corporation to become insolvent. Generally, shareholders must return illegal dividends only if they knew that the dividends were illegal when the payment was received (or if the dividends were paid when the corporation was insolvent). Whenever dividends are illegal or improper, the board of directors can be held personally liable for the amount of the payment.

THE DIRECTORS' FAILURE TO DECLARE A DIVIDEND When directors fail to declare a dividend, shareholders can ask a court to compel the directors to meet and declare a dividend. To succeed, the shareholders must show that the directors have acted so unreasonably in withholding the dividend that their conduct is an abuse of their discretion.

Often, a corporation accumulates large cash reserves for a legitimate corporate purpose, such as expansion or research. The mere fact that the firm has sufficient earnings or surplus available to pay a dividend normally is not enough to compel the directors to distribute funds that, in the board's opinion, should not be distributed.[13] The courts are

---

12. On one occasion, a distillery declared and paid a dividend in bonded whiskey.
13. A striking exception to this rule was made in *Dodge v. Ford Motor Co.,* 204 Mich. 459, 170 N.W. 668 (1919), when Henry Ford, the president and major stockholder of Ford Motor Company, refused to declare a dividend notwithstanding the firm's large capital surplus. The court, holding that Ford had abused his discretion, ordered the company to declare a dividend.

reluctant to interfere with corporate operations and will not compel directors to declare dividends unless abuse of discretion is clearly shown.

Inspection Rights

Shareholders in a corporation enjoy both common law and statutory inspection rights. The RMBCA provides that every shareholder is entitled to examine specified corporate records, including voting lists [RMBCA 7.20, 16.02]. The shareholder's right of inspection is limited, however, to the inspection and copying of corporate books and records for a *proper purpose,* and the request to inspect must be made in advance. The shareholder may inspect in person, or an attorney, accountant, or other authorized assistant can do so as the shareholder's agent.

The power of inspection is fraught with potential abuses, and the corporation is allowed to protect itself from them. For example, a shareholder can properly be denied access to corporate records to prevent harassment or to protect trade secrets or other confidential corporate information.[14] Some states require that a shareholder must have held her or his shares for a minimum period of time immediately preceding the demand to inspect or must hold a minimum number of outstanding shares. A shareholder who is denied the right of inspection can seek a court order to compel the inspection.

CASE IN POINT Craig Johnson was the sole officer and director and the majority shareholder of Distributed Solutions, Inc. (DSI), which provided consulting services, including payroll services. Jeffrey Hagen was a minority shareholder. Johnson sold DSI's payroll services to himself and set up another payroll services company. Although DSI revenues had been $739,034 and $934,532 the two previous years, the following year all of DSI's assets were sold. Johnson told Hagen that he was dissolving the firm because it conducted no business and had no future prospects. Hagen asked to inspect the corporate records so that he could determine DSI's financial condition, the value of its stock, and whether any misconduct had occurred. When there was no response, Hagen filed a lawsuit to compel the inspection. An Illinois appellate court found that Hagen had shown a proper purpose and allowed him access to DSI's records.[15]

---

14. See, for example, *Disney v. Walt Disney Co.,* 857 A.2d 444 (Del. Ch. 2004).
15. *Hagen v. Distributed Solutions, Inc.,* 328 Ill.App.3d 132, 764 N.E.2d 1141, 262 Ill.Dec. 24 (1 Dist. 2002).

Transfer of Shares

Corporate stock represents an ownership right in intangible personal property. The law generally recognizes the right of an owner to transfer property to another person unless there are valid restrictions on its transferability. When shares are transferred, a new entry is made in the corporate stock book to indicate the new owner. Until the corporation is notified and the entry is complete, all rights—including voting rights, notice of shareholders' meetings, and the right to dividend distributions—remain with the current record owner.

Rights on Dissolution

When a corporation is dissolved and its outstanding debts and the claims of its creditors have been satisfied, the remaining assets are distributed to the shareholders in proportion to the percentage of shares owned by each shareholder. The articles of incorporation may provide that certain classes of preferred stock will be given priority. If no class of stock has been given preference in the distribution of assets, all of the stockholders share the remaining assets. (See Chapter 41 for a full discussion of the process of dissolution, including the circumstances under which shareholders may petition a court to have the corporation dissolved.)

The Shareholder's Derivative Suit

When the corporation is harmed by the actions of a third party, the directors can bring a lawsuit in the name of the corporation against that party. If the corporate directors fail to bring a lawsuit, shareholders can do so "derivatively" in what is known as a **shareholder's derivative suit.** Before shareholders can bring a derivative suit, they must submit a written demand to the corporation, asking the board of directors to take appropriate action [RMBCA 7.40]. The directors then have ninety days in which to act. Only if they refuse to do so can the derivative suit go forward.

The right of shareholders to bring a derivative action is especially important when the wrong suffered by the corporation results from the actions of the corporate directors and officers—because they, for obvious reasons, would probably be unwilling to take any action against themselves. Nevertheless, a court will dismiss a derivative suit if a majority of the directors or an independent panel determines in good faith that the lawsuit is not in the best interests of the corporation [RMBCA 7.44].

When shareholders bring a derivative suit, they are not pursuing rights or benefits for themselves personally but are acting as guardians of the corporate entity. Therefore, if the suit is successful, any damages recovered normally go into the corporation's treasury, not to the shareholders personally.[16]

The following case illustrates some of the hurdles that a plaintiff must overcome when undertaking a shareholder's derivative suit.

---

16. The shareholders may be entitled to reimbursement for reasonable expenses of the derivative lawsuit, including attorneys' fees.

✳ EXTENDED CASE 40.2 ✳
Bezirdjian v. O'Reilly

Court of Appeal of California, First District, 183 Cal.App.4th 316, 107 Cal.Rptr.3d 384 (2010).
www.courtinfo.ca.gov/courts/courtsofappeal/1stDistrict[a]

IN THE LANGUAGE OF THE COURT
DONDERO, J. [Justice]
* * * *

On May 22, 2007, plaintiff [Lawrence Bezirdjian] filed a shareholder derivative complaint on behalf of Chevron Corporation (Chevron) against [David O'Reilly and others] current and certain former members of its Board of Directors (Board). The complaint contains counts for breach of fiduciary duties, gross mismanagement, constructive fraud, and waste of corporate assets, in connection with illicit payments Chevron allegedly made to Saddam Hussein in exchange for Iraqi oil from 2000 to 2003. In the complaint, plaintiff acknowledged that the majority of his factual allegations were derived from an article published by the *New York Times* on May 8, 2007, entitled "Chevron Seen Settling Case on Iraq Oil." He also alleged that he was excused from making a prefiling demand on the Board to institute this action because such demand would be futile. Specifically, he stated "the [Board] cannot exercise independent objective judgment in deciding whether to bring this action or whether to vigorously

prosecute this action because each of its members participated personally in the wrongdoing or are dependent upon other Defendants who did."

On August 9, 2007, the trial court filed its order staying the action. The order includes a stipulation from the parties deeming the complaint to be a stockholder's demand to pursue the claims alleged therein, and giving the Board until December 1, 2007, to act on the demand. Plaintiff was granted leave to amend the complaint within 15 days upon the lifting of the stay. The matter was subsequently continued several times.

On June 17, 2008, plaintiff filed an amended shareholder derivative complaint. The amended complaint repeats the original complaint's allegations concerning the illicit [illegal] payments, deletes the allegation excusing a prefiling demand, and adds the following: "Plaintiff made demand on Chevron to commence legal action * * *. Plaintiff's demand was refused. Accordingly, plaintiff has made sufficient effort to get Chevron to bring this action and need do no more." This portion of the complaint goes on to state that the Board had formed a special committee of directors (Committee)

to consider and respond to plaintiff's demand. On April 30, 2008, the Committee reported to the Board "that it had concluded its investigation and * * * had determined it not to be in the best interests of Chevron or its stockholders to pursue the claims asserted herein." Thereafter, Chevron management was directed to seek dismissal of the action.

* * * *

[The trial court granted Chevron's motion for judgment on the pleadings and dismissed the action. The plaintiff appealed.]

* * * *

Before proceeding to plaintiff's contentions, we review some basic principles regarding shareholder derivative actions. Chevron is incorporated in the state of Delaware, and both parties agree that Delaware law applies [to] this lawsuit. "A basic principle of the General Corporation Law of the State of Delaware is that directors, rather than shareholders, manage the business and affairs of the corporation. The exercise of this managerial power is tempered by fundamental fiduciary obligations owed by the directors to the corporation and its shareholders. *The decision to bring a lawsuit or to refrain from litigating a claim on behalf of a*

---

a. Select "Case Information" in the left-hand column. On the search page, in the box under the heading "Search by Court of Appeal or Trial Court Case Number," enter "A124859" and click on "Search by Case Number." On the page showing the search results, under "Case Summary," select the PDF for the "Court of Appeal Opinion" to access the case. The California Court of Appeal for the First District maintains this Web site.

EXTENDED CASE CONTINUES ▶

EXTENDED CASE 40.2 CONTINUED ⬇

corporation is a decision concerning the management of the corporation. Consequently, such decisions are part of the responsibility of the board of directors." [Emphasis added.]

* * * "[Delaware law] requires that shareholders seeking to assert a claim on behalf of the corporation must first exhaust intracorporate [within the corporation itself] remedies by making a demand on the directors to obtain the action desired, or to plead with particularity why demand is excused. The purpose of pre-suit demand is to assure that the stockholder affords the corporation the opportunity to address an alleged wrong without litigation, to decide whether to invest the resources of the corporation in litigation, and to control any litigation which does occur."

Courts generally accord some deference to a corporation's decision to refuse a shareholder's demand: "[Because] a conscious decision by a board of directors to refrain from

acting may be a valid exercise of business judgment, where demand on a board has been made and refused, [courts] apply the business judgment rule in reviewing the board's refusal to act pursuant to a stockholder's demand to file a lawsuit. The business judgment rule is a presumption that in making a business decision, not involving self-interest, the directors of a corporation acted on an informed basis, in good faith and in the honest belief that the action taken was in the best interests of the company. *'The burden is on the party challenging the decision to establish facts rebutting [this] presumption.'"* [Emphasis added.]

* * * To rebut the presumption, a plaintiff must plead with particularity facts that create a reasonable doubt as to the good faith or reasonableness of a board's investigation. Mere conclusory allegations are insufficient. "If there is reason to doubt that the board acted independently or with due care in responding to the demand, the stockholder

may have the basis * * * to claim wrongful refusal. The stockholder then has the right to bring the underlying action * * *."

* * * *

Plaintiff contends that his complaint states a valid cause of action under Delaware law. Certainly, the allegations in his complaint with respect to Chevron's alleged payments to Saddam Hussein suggest corporate wrongdoing. Nevertheless, as we have already discussed, it was within the Board's power to refuse to undertake this lawsuit if it deemed the litigation would be contrary to the corporation's best interests. Thus, even assuming, as we must at this stage of the proceedings, that all of the allegations in the complaint are true, plaintiff's failure to rebut the presumption created by the business judgment rule is fatal to his complaint.

* * * *

The judgment is affirmed.

 QUESTIONS

1. Given that the shareholder was suing the directors and not a third party (an outsider to the corporation), was it fair to him to require that he first demand that the directors undertake the suit? Why or why not?
2. Assuming that the shareholder's accusations were true, what could he have done to prevent the case from being dismissed?

SECTION 5
LIABILITY OF SHAREHOLDERS

One of the hallmarks of the corporate form of organization is that shareholders are not personally liable for the debts of the corporation. If the corporation fails, the shareholders can lose their investments, but that generally is the limit of their liability. As discussed in Chapter 39, in certain instances of fraud, undercapitalization, or careless observance of corporate formalities, a court will pierce the corporate veil (disregard the corporate entity) and hold the shareholders individually liable. But these situations are the exception, not the rule.

A shareholder also can be personally liable in certain other rare instances. One relates to illegal dividends,

which were discussed previously. Another relates to *watered stock*. Still another concerns the duties majority shareholders owe to minority shareholders.

Concept Summary 40.3 on the facing page reviews the role, rights, and liability of shareholders in a corporation.

Watered Stock

When a corporation issues shares for less than their fair market value, the shares are referred to as **watered stock.**[17] Usually, the shareholder who

---

17. The phrase *watered stock* was originally used to describe cattle that were kept thirsty during a long drive and then were allowed to drink large quantities of water just before their sale. The increased weight of the watered stock allowed the seller to reap a higher profit.

receives watered stock must pay the difference to the corporation (the shareholder is personally liable). In some states, the shareholder who receives watered stock may be liable to creditors of the corporation for unpaid corporate debts.

For example, during the formation of a corporation, Gomez, one of the incorporators, transfers his property, Sunset Beach, to the corporation for 10,000 shares of stock at a par value of $100 per share for a total price of $1 million. After the property is transferred and the shares are issued, Sunset Beach is carried on the corporate books at a value of $1 million. On appraisal, it is discovered that the market value of the property at the time of transfer was only $500,000. The shares issued to Gomez are therefore watered stock, and he is liable to the corporation for the difference between the value of the shares and the value of the property.

Duties of Majority Shareholders

In some instances, a majority shareholder is regarded as having a fiduciary duty to the corporation and to the minority shareholders. This duty occurs when a single shareholder (or a few shareholders acting in concert) owns a sufficient number of shares to exercise *de facto* (actual) control over the corporation. In these situations, the majority shareholder owes a fiduciary duty to the minority shareholders.

When a majority shareholder breaches her or his fiduciary duty to a minority shareholder, the minority shareholder can sue for damages. A breach of fiduciary duties by those who control a closely held corporation normally constitutes what is known as *oppressive conduct*. A common example of a breach of fiduciary duty occurs when the majority shareholders "freeze out" the minority shareholders and exclude them from certain benefits of participating in the firm.

CASE IN POINT Brodie, Jordan, and Barbuto formed a closely held corporation to operate a machine shop. Each owned one-third of the shares in the company, and all three were directors. Brodie served as the corporate president for twelve years but thereafter met with the other shareholders only a few times a year. After disagreements arose, Brodie asked the company to purchase his shares, but his requests were refused. A few years later, Brodie died, and his wife inherited his shares in the company. Jordan and Barbuto refused to perform a valuation of the company, denied her access to the corporate

---

CONCEPT SUMMARY 40.3
Role, Rights, and Liability of Shareholders

Aspect	Description
Shareholders' Powers	Shareholders' powers include approval of all fundamental changes affecting the corporation and election of the board of directors.
Shareholders' Meetings	Shareholders' meetings must occur at least annually; special meetings can be called when necessary. Notice of the time and place of a meeting (and its purpose, if the meeting is specially called) must be sent to shareholders. A minimum number of shareholders (quorum) must be present to vote.
Shareholders' Rights	Shareholders have numerous rights, which may include the following: 1. Voting rights. 2. Preemptive rights (depending on the corporate articles). 3. The right to receive dividends (at the discretion of the directors). 4. The right to inspect the corporate records. 5. The right to transfer shares (this right may be restricted in closely held corporations). 6. The right to receive a share of corporate assets when the corporation is dissolved. 7. The right to sue on behalf of the corporation (bring a shareholder's derivative suit) when the directors fail to do so.
Shareholders' Liability	Shareholders may be liable for watered stock. In certain situations, majority shareholders may be regarded as having a fiduciary duty to minority shareholders and will be liable if that duty is breached.

information she requested, did not declare any dividends, and refused to elect her as a director. In this situation, a court found that the majority shareholders had violated their fiduciary duty to Brodie's wife.[18]

18. *Brodie v. Jordan*, 447 Mass. 866, 857 N.E.2d 1076 (2006).

How egregious must majority shareholders' misbehavior be to warrant an award of punitive damages, in addition to compensatory damages? The court in the following case set out the factors to consider and weighed the majority shareholders' acts against these standards.

CASE 40.3
Mazloom v. Mazloom
Court of Appeals of South Carolina, 382 S.C. 307, 675 S.E.2d 746 (2009).

BACKGROUND AND FACTS • Four brothers—Iraj, Ahmad, Manooch, and Aboli Mazloom—incorporated a business known as AMBI, Inc. AMBI owned real estate in South Carolina on which the brothers operated a Mini Mart, a liquor store, and a one-bedroom apartment. Each brother had a 25 percent interest in AMBI. After seventeen years, Ahmad, Manooch, and Aboli dissolved AMBI, filed articles of organization for a new firm—AMA, LLC—and transferred AMBI's assets to AMA for five dollars. When Iraj learned of the changes, he had Manooch and Aboli file an amendment to AMA's articles stating that "Iraj Mazloom owns 25% (or 1/4) shares of stock in AMA." Less than five months later, Ahmad sold his interest in AMA to Manooch and Aboli, who then sold AMA's assets to Ganesh Mini Mart, LLC, for $345,000. They paid Iraj nothing. He filed a suit in a South Carolina state court against Manooch and Aboli, claiming breach of fiduciary duty. The brothers asserted that Iraj did not own shares in AMBI or AMA. The court awarded Iraj 25 percent of the proceeds from the sale of AMA's assets and other amounts, including punitive damages of $50,000. Manooch and Aboli appealed.

IN THE LANGUAGE OF THE COURT
WILLIAMS, J. [Judge]
* * * *
   If punitive damages are awarded, the [court] should review the amount awarded by considering the * * * following: (1) defendant's degree of culpability [guilt]; (2) duration of the conduct; (3) defendant's awareness or concealment; (4) the existence of similar past conduct; (5) likelihood the award will deter the defendant or others from like conduct; (6) whether the award is reasonably related to the harm likely to result from such conduct; (7) defendant's ability to pay; and finally, (8) * * * other factors deemed appropriate. [Emphasis added.]
   * * * The [trial court] found the misconduct of the brothers warranted an award of punitive damages to Iraj. This conduct included selling all of AMA's assets to a third party without Iraj's knowledge or consent, filing an official document stating Iraj held a 25 percent interest in AMA and then taking an opposite position after the business' assets were sold, failing to hold the sales proceeds in trust and to provide Iraj with his share, and filing Articles of Termination for AMA without Iraj's knowledge or consent.
   Additionally, * * * the [court] found the brothers were completely culpable for the misconduct leading to the award of punitive damages and that the brothers were fully aware of this misconduct which they engaged in repeatedly. The [court] also found the award was likely to deter the brothers from similar conduct in the future, the brothers had the ability to pay the award based on their [receipt of proceeds from the transaction] with Ganesh and ownership interests in houses * * * , and the award was reasonably related to the harm.
   There is ample evidence in the record to support the [court's] findings. For example, Iraj testified he was not told about the sale of AMA's assets and was not given any of the proceeds. Iraj stated that after the sale he repeatedly asked the brothers to provide him with his 25 percent share which they had acknowledged he owned in the [amendment to AMA's articles], but the brothers refused to acknowledge his interest. Iraj also testified he was not consulted or included in the filing of the Articles of Termination for AMA.

CASE 40.3 CONTINUED ▶   **DECISION AND REMEDY** • *The state intermediate appellate court affirmed the award of punitive damages for Manooch and Aboli's breach of fiduciary duty to Iraj. Majority shareholders' breach of fiduciary duty owed to a minority shareholder can support an award of punitive damages*

THE LEGAL ENVIRONMENT DIMENSION • *Why is an award of punitive damages almost completely at the discretion of a jury and trial judge?*

THE ETHICAL DIMENSION • *The court awarded $50,000 in punitive damages. Given the repeated culpable behavior of the three brothers, was the damages award appropriate? Why or why not?*

REVIEWING

Corporate Directors, Officers, and Shareholders

David Brock is on the board of directors of Firm Body Fitness, Inc., which owns a string of fitness clubs in New Mexico. Brock owns 15 percent of the Firm Body stock and is also employed as a tanning technician at one of the fitness clubs. After the January financial report showed that Firm Body's tanning division was operating at a substantial net loss, the board of directors, led by Marty Levinson, discussed the possibility of terminating the tanning operations. Brock successfully convinced a majority of the board that the tanning division was necessary to market the clubs' overall fitness package. By April, the tanning division's financial losses had risen. The board hired a business analyst, who conducted surveys and determined that the tanning operations did not significantly increase membership. A shareholder, Diego Peñada, discovered that Brock owned stock in Sunglow, Inc., the company from which Firm Body purchased its tanning equipment. Peñada notified Levinson, who privately reprimanded Brock. Shortly thereafter, Brock and Mandy Vail, who owned 37 percent of the Firm Body stock and also held shares of Sunglow, voted to replace Levinson on the board of directors. Using the information presented in the chapter, answer the following questions.

1. What duties did Brock, as a director, owe to Firm Body?
2. Does the fact that Brock owned shares in Sunglow establish a conflict of interest? Why or why not?
3. Suppose that Firm Body brought an action against Brock claiming that he had breached the duty of loyalty by not disclosing his interest in Sunglow to the other directors. What theory might Brock use in his defense?
4. Now suppose that Firm Body did not bring an action against Brock. What type of lawsuit might Peñada be able to bring based on these facts?

⊛ **DEBATE THIS:** *Because most shareholders never bother to vote for directors, shareholders have no real control over corporations.*

TERMS AND CONCEPTS

	inside director 776	quorum 776	stock warrant 787
	outside director 776	shareholder's derivative	treasury share 786
business judgment rule 779	preemptive rights 786	suit 788	voting trust 786
dividend 787	proxy 784	stock certificate 786	watered stock 790

QUESTIONS AND CASE PROBLEMS

40–1. Conflicts of Interest Oxy Corp. is negotiating with the Wick Construction Co. for the renovation of the Oxy corporate headquarters. Wick, the owner of the Wick Construction Co., is also one of the five members of Oxy's board of directors. The contract terms are standard for this type of contract. Wick has previously informed two of the other directors of his interest in the construction company. Oxy's board approves the contract by a three-to-two vote, with Wick voting with the majority. Discuss whether this contract is binding on the corporation.

40–2. QUESTION WITH SAMPLE ANSWER: Liability of Directors.

AstroStar, Inc., has approximately five hundred shareholders. Its board of directors consists of three members (Eckhart, Dolan, and Macero). At a regular board meeting, the board selects Galiard as president of the corporation by a two-to-one vote, with Eckhart dissenting. The minutes of the meeting do not register Eckhart's dissenting vote. Later, an audit reveals that Galiard is a former convict and has embezzled $500,000 from the corporation that is not covered by insurance. Can the corporation hold directors Eckhart, Dolan, and Macero personally liable? Discuss.

- **For a sample answer to Question 40–2, go to Appendix I at the end of this text.**

40–3. Preemptive Rights Superal Corp. authorized 100,000 shares and issued all of them during its first six months in operation. Avril purchased 10,000 of the shares (10 percent). Later, Superal reacquired 10,000 of the shares it originally issued. With shareholder approval, Superal has now amended its articles so as to authorize and issue another 100,000 shares. It has also, by a resolution of the board of directors, made plans to reissue the 10,000 shares of treasury stock (the shares reacquired by the corporation). The corporate articles do not include a provision dealing with shareholders' preemptive rights. Because of her ownership of 10 percent of Superal, Avril claims that she has the preemptive right to purchase 10,000 shares of the new issue and 1,000 shares of the stock being reissued. Discuss her claims.

40–4. Rights of Shareholders Lucia has acquired one share of common stock of a multimillion-dollar corporation with more than 500,000 shareholders. Lucia's ownership interest is so small that she is not sure what her rights are as a shareholder. For example, she wants to know whether this one share entitles her to (1) attend and vote at shareholders' meetings, (2) inspect the corporate books, and (3) receive yearly dividends. Discuss Lucia's rights in these three matters.

40–5. Duties of Majority Shareholders Steve and Marie Venturini were involved in the operation of Steve's Sizzling Steakhouse in Carlstadt, New Jersey, from the day their parents opened it in the 1930s. By the 1980s, Steve, Marie, and her husband Joe were running it. The business was a corporation with Steve and Marie each owning half of the stock. Steve died in 2001, leaving his stock in equal shares to his sons Steve and Gregg. Son Steve had never worked there. Gregg had done occasional maintenance work until his father's death. Despite their lack of participation, the sons were paid more than $750 per week each. In 2002, Marie's son Blaise, who had obtained a college degree in restaurant management while working part-time at the steakhouse, took over its management. When his cousins became threatening, he denied them access to the business and its books. Marie refused Gregg and Steve's offer of about $1.4 million for her stock in the restaurant, and they refused her offer of about $800,000 for theirs. They filed a suit in a New Jersey state court against her, claiming, among other things, a breach of fiduciary duty. Should the court order the aunt to buy out the nephews or the nephews to buy out the aunt, or neither? Why? [*Venturini v. Steve's Steakhouse, Inc.*, __ N.J.Super. __, __ A.2d __ (Ch.Div. 2006)]

40–6. Fiduciary Duties and Liabilities Harry Hoaas and Larry Griffiths were shareholders in Grand Casino, Inc., which owned and operated a casino in Watertown, South Dakota. Griffiths owned 51 percent of the stock and Hoaas 49 percent. Hoaas managed the casino, which Griffiths typically visited once a week. At the end of 1997, an accounting showed that the cash on hand was less than the amount posted in the casino's books. Later, more shortfalls were discovered. In October 1999, Griffiths did a complete audit. Hoaas was unable to account for $135,500 in missing cash. Griffiths then kept all of the casino's most recent profits, including Hoaas's $9,447.20 share, and, without telling Hoaas, sold the casino for $100,000 and kept all of the proceeds. Hoaas filed a suit in a South Dakota state court against Griffiths, asserting, among other things, a breach of fiduciary duty. Griffiths countered with evidence of Hoaas's misappropriation of corporate cash. What duties did these parties owe each other? Did either Griffiths or Hoaas, or both of them, breach those duties? How should their dispute be resolved? How should their finances be reconciled? Explain. [*Hoaas v. Griffiths*, 2006 SD 27, 714 N.W.2d 61 (2006)]

40–7. Role of Directors The board of directors of Necanicum Investment Co., a property management corporation in Oregon, meets on a regular basis. Necanicum paid the directors $6,000 each in the third quarter of 2003. It did not report the payments as part of its payroll and did not pay unemployment tax on the payments. The Oregon Employment Department contended that the company owed $700 in unemployment taxes on the payments to the directors. Necanicum protested. The administrative law judge (ALJ) for the Employment Department held that the company owed the taxes because directors' fees are the same as wages for unemployment tax purposes. Necanicum appealed, but the court of appeals affirmed the ALJ's ruling. The company appealed again. Are payments to directors the same as wages for tax purposes?

Why or why not? [*Necanicum Investment Co. v. Employment Department*, 345 Or. 138, 190 P.3d 368 (2008)]

40–8. CASE PROBLEM WITH SAMPLE ANSWER: Duties of Directors and Officers.

First Niles Financial, Inc., is a company whose sole business is to own and operate a bank, Home Federal Savings and Loan Association of Niles, Ohio. First Niles's directors included bank officers William Stephens, Daniel Csontos, and Lawrence Safarek; James Kramer, president of an air-conditioning company that serviced the bank; and Ralph Zuzolo, whose law firm served the bank and whose title company participated in most of its real estate deals. First Niles's board put the bank up for sale and received three bids. Farmers National Bank Corp. stated that it would not retain the board. Cortland Bancorp indicated that it would terminate the directors but consider them for future service. First Financial Corp. said nothing about the directors. The board did not pursue Farmers' offer, failed to timely respond to Cortland's request, and rejected First Financial's bid. Leonard Gantler and other First Niles shareholders filed a suit in a Delaware state court against Stephens and the others. What duties do directors and officers owe to a corporation and its shareholders? How might those duties have been breached here? Discuss. [Gantler v. Stephens, 965 A.2d 695 (Del.Sup.Ct. 2009)]

- **To view a sample answer for Problem 40–8, go to this book's Web site at www.cengage.com/blaw/clarkson, select "Chapter 40," and click on "Case Problem with Sample Answer."**

40–9. Fiduciary Duty of Officers

Designer Surfaces, Inc., supplied countertops to homeowners who shopped at stores such as Lowe's and Costco. The homeowners paid the store, which then contracted with Designer to fabricate and install the countertops. Designer bought materials from Arizona Tile, LLC, on an open account. Designer's only known corporate officers were Howard Berger and John McCarthy. Designer became insolvent and could not pay Arizona Tile for all the materials it had purchased, including materials for which Designer had already received payment from the retail stores. Arizona Tile sued Designer and won a default judgment, but the company had no funds. Arizona Tile then sued Berger and McCarthy personally for diverting company funds that Designer had received in trust for payment to Arizona Tile. Arizona Tile argued that the use of the funds for other purposes was a breach of fiduciary duty. Berger and McCarthy argued that corporate law imposed neither a fiduciary duty on corporate officers nor personal liability for breach of a duty to suppliers of materials. Which argument is more credible and why? [*Arizona Tile, LLC v. Berger*, 223 Ariz. 491, 224 P.3d 988 (Ariz.App. 2010)]

40–10. A QUESTION OF ETHICS: Duties of Directors and Officers.

New Orleans Paddlewheels, Inc. (NOP), is a Louisiana corporation formed in 1982 when James Smith, Sr., and Warren Reuther were its only shareholders, with each holding 50 percent of the stock. NOP is part of a sprawling enterprise of tourism and hospitality companies in New Orleans. The positions on the board of each company were split equally between the Smith and Reuther families. At Smith's request, his son James Smith, Jr. (JES), became involved in the businesses. In 1999, NOP's board elected JES as president, to be in charge of day-to-day operations, and Reuther is chief executive officer (CEO), to be in charge of marketing and development. Over the next few years, animosity developed between Reuther and JES. In October 2001, JES terminated Reuther as CEO and denied him access to the offices and books of NOP and the other companies, literally changing the locks on the doors. At the next meetings of the boards of NOP and the overall enterprise, deadlock ensued, with the directors voting along family lines on every issue. Complaining that the meetings were a "waste of time," JES began to run the entire enterprise by taking advantage of an unequal balance of power on the companies' executive committees. In NOP's subsequent bankruptcy proceeding, Reuther filed a motion for the appointment of a trustee to formulate a plan for the firm's reorganization, alleging, among other things, misconduct by NOP's management. [In re New Orleans Paddlewheels, Inc., 350 Bankr. 667 (E.D.La. 2006)]

(a) Was Reuther legally entitled to have access to the books and records of NOP and the other companies? JES maintained, among other things, that NOP's books were "a mess." Was JES's denial of that access unethical? Why or why not?

(b) How would you describe JES's attempt to gain control of NOP and the other companies? Were his actions devious and self-serving in the pursuit of personal gain or legitimate and reasonable in the pursuit of a business goal? Discuss.

LEGAL RESEARCH EXERCISES ON THE WEB

Go to this text's Web site at **www.cengage.com/blaw/clarkson**, select "Chapter 40," and click on "Practical Internet Exercises." There you will find the following Internet research exercises that you can perform to learn more about the topics covered in this chapter.

Practical Internet Exercise 40–1: **Legal Perspective**
Liability of Directors and Officers

Practical Internet Exercise 40–2: **Management Perspective**
D&O Insurance

CHAPTER 41

Corporate Merger, Consolidation, and Termination

Although a corporation may grow simply by reinvesting retained earnings in more equipment or by hiring more employees, corporations may also expand their operations by engaging in various transactions with other corporations. These transactions include a merger, a consolidation, a share exchange, a purchase of assets, or a purchase of a controlling interest in another corporation. This chapter examines each

of these types of corporate expansion. We look at how each type of transaction is carried out, whether the approval of the shareholders and the board of directors is required, and the rights of shareholders who object to the proposed transaction.

In the latter part of the chapter, we discuss dissolution and winding up—the combined processes by which a corporation terminates its existence. Dissolution

may come about either voluntarily or involuntarily, and we will look at some typical reasons for dissolution and at the methods used in the termination process.

This chapter concludes with a brief comparison of the major forms of business organization discussed in Chapters 36 through 41. We present a summary of the advantages and disadvantages of each business form.

SECTION 1
MERGER, CONSOLIDATION, AND SHARE EXCHANGE

The terms *merger* and *consolidation* traditionally referred to two legally distinct proceedings. Today, however, people commonly use the term *consolidation* to refer to all types of combinations, including mergers (discussed below) and acquisitions (discussed later in this chapter). Whether a combination is a merger, a consolidation, or a share exchange, the rights and liabilities of shareholders, the corporation, and the corporation's creditors are the same. Note also that the power to merge, consolidate, and exchange shares is conferred by statute, and thus state law establishes the specific procedures.

Merger

A **merger** involves the legal combination of two or more corporations. After a merger, only one of the corporations continues to exist. For example, Corporation A and Corporation B decide to merge. They agree that A will absorb B. Therefore, after the

merger, B ceases to exist as a separate entity, and A continues as the **surviving corporation.** Exhibit 41–1 below graphically illustrates this process.

After the merger, Corporation A is recognized as a single corporation possessing all of the rights, privileges, and powers of itself and B. Corporation A automatically acquires all of B's property and assets without the necessity of a formal transfer. Corporation A also inherits B's preexisting legal

EXHIBIT 41–1 • Merger
Corporation A and Corporation B decide to merge. They agree that A will absorb B, so after the merger, B no longer exists as a separate entity, and A continues as the surviving corporation.

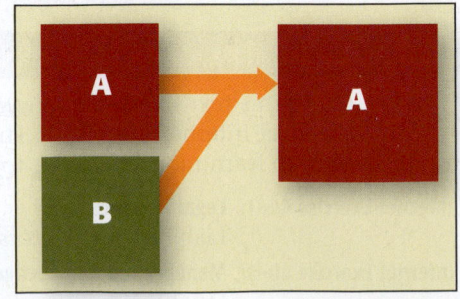

rights. Thus, if B had a right of action against a third party under tort or property law, for example, Corporation A can bring a suit after the merger to recover B's damages. Corporation A also becomes liable for all of B's debts and obligations. Finally, Corporation A's articles of incorporation are deemed amended to include any changes that are stated in the *articles of merger.*

Consolidation

In a **consolidation,** two or more corporations combine so that each corporation ceases to exist and a new one emerges. Corporation A and Corporation B consolidate to form an entirely new organization, Corporation C. In the process, A and B both terminate, and C comes into existence as a new entity. Exhibit 41–2 below graphically illustrates this process.

The results of a consolidation are similar to those of a merger—only one company remains—but it is a completely new entity (the *consolidated corporation*). Corporation C is recognized as a new corporation and a single entity; A and B cease to exist. C inherits all of the rights, privileges, and powers previously held by A and B. Title to any property and assets owned by A and B passes to C without a formal transfer. C assumes liability for all debts and obligations owed by A and B. The *articles of consolidation* take the place of A's and B's original corporate articles and are thereafter regarded as C's corporate articles.

When a merger or a consolidation takes place, the surviving corporation or newly formed corporation will issue shares or pay some fair consideration to the shareholders of the corporation or corporations that cease to exist. True consolidations have become less common among for-profit corporations because it is often advantageous for one of the firms to survive. In contrast, nonprofit corporations and associations may prefer consolidation because it suggests a new beginning in which neither of the two initial entities is dominant.

Share Exchange

In a **share exchange,** some or all of the shares of one corporation are exchanged for some or all of the shares of another corporation, but both corporations continue to exist. Share exchanges are often used to create *holding companies* (companies that own part or all of other companies' outstanding stock—see Chapter 39). For example, UAL Corporation is a large holding company that owns United Airlines. If one corporation owns *all* of the shares of another corporation, it is referred to as the *parent corporation,* and the wholly owned company is the *subsidiary corporation.*

Merger, Consolidation, and Share Exchange Procedures

All states have statutes authorizing mergers, consolidations, and share exchanges for domestic (in-state) and foreign (out-of-state) corporations. The procedures vary somewhat among jurisdictions. In some states, a consolidation resulting in an entirely new corporation simply follows the initial incorporation procedures discussed in Chapter 39, whereas other business combinations must follow the procedures outlined below.

The Revised Model Business Corporation Act (RMBCA) sets forth the following basic requirements [RMBCA 11.01–11.07]:

1. The board of directors of *each* corporation involved must approve the merger or share exchange plan.
2. The plan must specify any terms and conditions of the merger. It also must state how the value of the shares of each merging corporation will be determined and how they will be converted into shares or other securities, cash, property, or additional interests in another corporation.
3. The majority of the shareholders of *each* corporation must vote to approve the plan at a shareholders' meeting. If any class of stock is entitled to vote as a separate group, the majority of each separate voting group must approve the plan. As mentioned in Chapter 40, frequently a corporation's articles of incorporation or bylaws require approval by more than a majority once a quorum is present. In addition, some state statutes require the approval of two-thirds of the outstanding shares of voting stock (not just the shareholders present at the meeting), and others require a four-fifths approval.

EXHIBIT 41–2 • Consolidation
Corporation A and Corporation B consolidate to form an entirely new organization, Corporation C. In the process, A and B terminate, and C comes into existence.

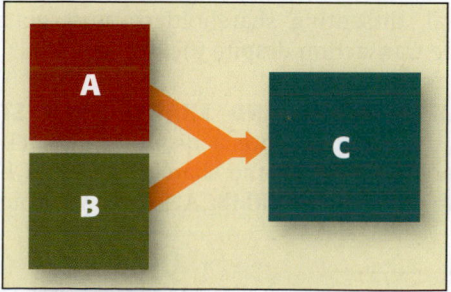

4. Once the plan is approved by the directors and the shareholders of both corporations, the surviving corporation files the plan (articles of merger, consolidation, or share exchange) with the appropriate official, usually the secretary of state.

5. When state formalities are satisfied, the state issues a certificate of merger to the surviving corporation or a certificate of consolidation to the newly consolidated corporation.

Short-Form Mergers

RMBCA 11.04 provides a simplified procedure for the merger of a substantially owned subsidiary corporation into its parent corporation. Under these provisions, a **short-form merger**—also referred to as a **parent-subsidiary merger**—can be accomplished *without* the approval of the shareholders of either corporation. The short-form merger can be used only when the parent corporation owns at least 90 percent of the outstanding shares of each class of stock of the subsidiary corporation. Once the board of directors of the parent corporation approves the plan, it is filed with the state, and copies are sent to each shareholder of record in the subsidiary corporation.

Shareholder Approval

As mentioned, except in a short-form merger, the shareholders of both corporations must approve a merger or other plan of consolidation. Shareholders invest in a corporation with the expectation that the board of directors will manage the enterprise and make decisions on *ordinary* business matters. For *extraordinary* matters, normally both the board of directors and the shareholders must approve the transaction.

Mergers and other combinations are extraordinary business matters, meaning that the board of directors must normally obtain the shareholders' approval and provide appraisal rights (discussed next). Amendments to the articles of incorporation and the dissolution of the corporation also generally require shareholder approval. Sometimes, a transaction can be structured in such a way that shareholder approval is not required, but if the shareholders challenge the transaction, a court might require shareholder approval. For this reason, the board of directors may request shareholder approval even when it might not be legally required.

Appraisal Rights

What if a shareholder disapproves of a merger or a consolidation but is outvoted by the other shareholders? The law recognizes that a dissenting shareholder should not be forced to become an unwilling shareholder in a corporation that is new or different from the one in which the shareholder originally invested. Dissenting shareholders therefore are given a statutory right to be paid the fair value of the number of shares they held on the date of the merger or consolidation. This right is referred to as the shareholder's **appraisal right.** So long as the transaction does not involve fraud or other illegal conduct, appraisal rights are the exclusive remedy for a shareholder who is dissatisfied with the price received for the stock.

Appraisal rights usually extend to regular mergers, consolidations, share exchanges, short-form mergers, and sales of substantially all of the corporate assets not in the ordinary course of business. Such rights can be particularly important in a short-form merger because the minority stockholders do not receive advance notice of the merger, the directors do not consider or approve it, and there is no vote.[1] Appraisal rights are often the only recourse available to shareholders who object to parent-subsidiary mergers.

APPRAISAL RIGHTS PROCEDURES Each state establishes the procedures for asserting appraisal rights in that jurisdiction. Generally, the corporation must notify shareholders that appraisal rights are or may be available [RMBCA 13.20]. Dissenting shareholders usually must then file a written notice of intent to demand payment with the corporation, before the shareholders' vote on the proposed transaction [RMBCA 13.21]. The "fair value of shares" normally is the value on the day prior to the date on which the vote was taken [RMBCA 13.21]. The corporation must make a written offer to purchase a dissenting shareholder's stock and must include a current corporate balance sheet and income statement with the offer. If the shareholder and the corporation do not agree on the fair value, a court will determine it.

Shareholders may lose their appraisal rights if they do not adhere precisely to the procedures prescribed by statute. When they lose the right to an appraisal, dissenting shareholders must go along with the transaction despite their objections.

APPRAISAL RIGHTS AND SHAREHOLDER STATUS Under the RMBCA, once a dissenting shareholder elects appraisal rights, the shareholder loses her or his shareholder status [RMBCA 13.23]. Without that

---

1. See, for example, *Glassman v. Unocal Exploration Corp.*, 777 A.2d 242 (Del.Sup.Ct. 2001).

status, the shareholder cannot vote, receive dividends, or sue to enjoin whatever action prompted the dissent. In some jurisdictions (and under the RMBCA), shareholder status may be reinstated if the shareholder decides to withdraw from the appraisal process. In other jurisdictions, shareholder status may not be reinstated until the appraisal is concluded.

SECTION 2
PURCHASE OF ASSETS

When a corporation acquires all or substantially all of the assets of another corporation by direct purchase, the purchasing, or *acquiring,* corporation simply extends its ownership and control over more assets. Because no change in the legal entity occurs, the acquiring corporation usually does not need to obtain shareholder approval for the purchase.[2]

Both the U.S. Department of Justice and the Federal Trade Commission, however, have issued guidelines that significantly constrain and often prohibit mergers that could result from a purchase of assets. (These guidelines are part of the federal antitrust laws that will be discussed in Chapter 47.)

Sales of Corporate Assets

Note that the corporation that is *selling* all of its assets is substantially changing its business position and perhaps its ability to carry out its corporate purposes. For that reason, the corporation whose assets are being sold must obtain approval from both its board of directors and its shareholders [RMBCA 12.02]. In most states and under RMBCA 13.02, dissenting shareholders of the selling corporation can demand appraisal rights.

Successor Liability in Purchases of Assets

Generally, a corporation that purchases the assets of another corporation is not automatically responsible for the liabilities of the selling corporation. Exceptions to this rule are made in certain circumstances, however.

In any of the following situations, the acquiring corporation will be held to have assumed *both* the assets and the liabilities of the selling corporation:

1. When the purchasing corporation impliedly or expressly assumes the seller's liabilities.
2. When the sale transaction is, in effect, a merger or consolidation of the two companies.[3]
3. When the purchaser continues the seller's business and retains the same personnel (same shareholders, directors, and officers).
4. When the sale is entered into fraudulently for the purpose of escaping liability.

The following case involved a sale of corporate assets. Although the parties agreed that the purchasing corporation was assuming the seller's liabilities as well, the parties disagreed as to whether the liabilities being assumed were limited to those that were existing and outstanding as of the closing date or also included liabilities that arose after the closing date. That was the question before the court.

---

2. Shareholder approval may be required in a few situations. If the acquiring corporation plans to pay for the assets with its stock but not enough authorized unissued shares are available, then shareholders must approve the issuance of additional shares. Also, if the acquiring corporation is one whose stock is traded on a national stock exchange and it will be issuing a significant number of shares (such as a number equal to 20 percent of outstanding shares), then shareholders must approve.

3. See, for example, *Cargo Partner AG v. Albatrans, Inc.,* 352 F.3d 41 (2d Cir. 2003) applying New York law on *de facto* mergers; and *Village Builders 96, LP v. U.S. Laboratories, Inc.,* 121 Nev. 261, 112 P.3d 1082 (2005).

CASE 41.1
American Standard, Inc. v. OakFabco, Inc.

Court of Appeals of New York, 14 N.Y.3d 399, 901 N.Y.S.2d 572 (2010).
www.courts.state.ny.us/decisions/index.shtml[a]

BACKGROUND AND FACTS • American Standard, Inc., sold its Kewanee Boiler division to OakFabco, Inc. The parties' agreement stated that OakFabco would purchase Kewanee assets subject to Kewanee liabilities. The phrase *Kewanee liabilities* was defined as "all the debts, liabilities, obligations,

---

a. Select "Court of Appeals" in the left-hand column. When the page opens, click on "April" in the 2010 calendar. In the search results, in the list under "April 6th, 2010," scroll down to the case title and open the link to access this opinion. The New York State court system maintains this Web site.

CASE CONTINUES ➡

CASE 41.1 CONTINUED ➤ and commitments (fixed or contingent) connected with or attributable to Kewanee existing and outstanding at the Closing Date." The boilers manufactured by Kewanee had been insulated with asbestos, and as a result, many tort claims were brought in the years and decades following the purchase of the business. Some of those claims were brought by plaintiffs who had suffered injuries after the closing of the transaction, allegedly attributable to boilers manufactured and sold before the closing. American Standard brought an action against OakFabco, asking the court for a declaratory judgment on the issue of whether liabilities for such injuries were among the Kewanee liabilities that OakFabco assumed. The trial court entered a declaratory judgment holding that OakFabco had assumed the liabilities. An intermediate appellate court affirmed the trial court's ruling, and OakFabco appealed to New York's highest court, the New York Court of Appeals.

IN THE LANGUAGE OF THE COURT
SMITH, J. [Judge]
* * * *

American Standard's position—that OakFabco assumed all tort liabilities arising out of boilers manufactured by the Kewanee Boiler division, whether the injury was suffered before or after American Standard sold the division—is strongly supported by the purpose of the transaction, as described in the agreement itself: *It was a purchase and sale of substantially all the assets of the Kewanee Boiler business "subject to all debts, liabilities, and obligations connected with or attributable to such business and operations."* Nothing in the nature of the transaction suggests that the parties intended OakFabco, which got all the assets, to escape any of the related obligations. [Emphasis added.]

OakFabco, however, argues that the definition of "Kewanee Liabilities"—the liabilities OakFabco assumed—is less broad than the purpose of the transaction would imply. It stresses the words "existing and outstanding" in the definition—"all the debts, liabilities, obligations and commitments * * * *existing and outstanding* at the Closing Date" (emphasis added [by the court]). According to OakFabco, a tort claim cannot be "existing and outstanding" before the tort plaintiff has been injured, because until then it is not possible for a tort lawsuit to be brought.
* * * *

That there was no such intention is made clear by a clause in the agreement relating to certain obligations owed to the boiler division's customers. The agreement said that the buyer would deliver at the closing:

An executed undertaking wherein the Buyer will assume and agree to pay, and defend and hold Seller harmless against, all Kewanee Liabilities, including, by way of specification but not limitation, the following:

* * * *

(iii) warranty, service, repair and return obligations of Kewanee, and other claims and complaints arising out of or in connection with any products manufactured, sold, leased or installed by Kewanee on or prior to the Closing Date[.]

This language clearly meant that the buyer would deal with any problems customers had after the closing date with boilers that had been installed previously. It would have been absurd for OakFabco to tell a customer whose boiler failed after the closing that, since the customer's claim was not "existing and outstanding" on the closing date, it was not OakFabco's problem. By including warranty, service, repair and return claims of this kind in the definition of "Kewanee Liabilities," the parties demonstrated that they were not reading the words "existing and outstanding" as OakFabco would have us read them.

We therefore agree with the [intermediate appellate court] that the liabilities assumed by OakFabco include claims brought by tort claimants injured after the closing date by boilers installed before that date.

DECISION AND REMEDY • *The New York Court of Appeals affirmed the appellate court's decision. The court concluded that the contract expressed the intention that OakFabco was to assume the liabilities of the selling corporation, including those claims that arose after the closing date.*

THE LEGAL ENVIRONMENT DIMENSION • *Generally, a corporation that purchases the assets of another is not automatically responsible for the liabilities of the selling corporation, with some exceptions. Which exception applied to this case? Explain.*

MANAGERIAL IMPLICATIONS • *This case illustrates the kinds of problems that can arise over contract interpretation. Business owners or managers who draft contracts should make sure that all contract clauses and terms are clearly defined and that the parties' intentions are clear. Before signing any contract drafted by another firm, business owners and managers should scrutinize it carefully for any wording that may be ambiguous or give rise to interpretational differences in the future.*

SECTION 3
PURCHASE OF STOCK

An alternative to the purchase of another corporation's assets is the purchase of a substantial number of the voting shares of its stock. This enables the acquiring corporation to control the **target corporation** (the corporation being acquired). The process of acquiring control over a corporation in this way is commonly referred to as a corporate **takeover.**

Tender Offers

In seeking to purchase the stock of the target corporation, the acquiring corporation deals directly with the target's shareholders by making a *tender offer.* A **tender offer** is a proposal to buy shares of stock from a target corporation's shareholders either for cash or for some type of corporate security of the acquiring company. The tender offer can be conditioned on the receipt of a specified number of outstanding shares by a certain date.

As a means of inducing shareholders to accept the offer, the tender price offered generally is higher than the market price of the target's stock before the tender offer was announced. For example, in the 2009 merger of two Fortune 500 pharmaceutical companies, Pfizer, Inc., paid $68 billion to acquire its rival, Wyeth. Wyeth shareholders reportedly received approximately $50.19 per share (part in cash and part in Pfizer stock), which amounted to a 15 percent premium over the market price of the stock.

Federal securities laws strictly control the terms, duration, and circumstances under which most tender offers are made. In addition, many states have passed antitakeover statutes. Generally, the offering corporation does not need to notify the Securities and Exchange Commission (SEC) or the target corporation's management until after the tender offer is made. The offeror must then disclose to the SEC the source of the funds used in the offer, the purpose of the offer, and the acquiring corporation's plans for the firm if the takeover is successful.

Responses to Tender Offers

A firm may respond to a tender offer in numerous ways. If the target firm's board of directors views the tender offer as favorable, the board will recommend that the shareholders accept it. Frequently, though, the target corporation's management opposes the proposed takeover. This is referred to as a *hostile takeover.*

To resist a takeover, a target company may make a *self-tender,* in which it offers to acquire stock from its own shareholders and thereby retain corporate control. The target corporation may also engage in a media campaign to persuade its shareholders that the tender offer is not in their best interests. Another possible defense is for the target firm to issue additional stock, thereby increasing the number of shares that the acquiring corporation must purchase to gain control. Several other tactics to resist a takeover are described in Exhibit 41–3 on the following page.

Concept Summary 41.1 on page 803 reviews all of the ways in which a corporation may expand its operations.

Takeover Defenses and Directors' Fiduciary Duties

As mentioned, the board of directors of the target corporation often opposes the takeover. Clearly, board members have an interest in keeping their jobs and control, but they also have a fiduciary duty to the corporation and its shareholders to act in the best interests of the company. In a hostile takeover attempt, sometimes directors' duties of care and loyalty collide with their self-interest. Then the shareholders, who would have received a premium for their shares as a result of the takeover, file lawsuits alleging that the directors breached their fiduciary duties in defending against the tender offer.

In this situation, courts apply the *business judgment rule* (see page 779 in Chapter 40) to analyze whether the directors acted reasonably in resisting the takeover attempt. The directors must show that they had reasonable grounds to believe that

EXHIBIT 41–3 • **The Terminology of Takeover Defenses**

TERM	DEFINITION
Crown Jewel	When threatened with a takeover, management makes the company less attractive to the raider by selling the company's most valuable asset (the "crown jewel") to a third party.
Golden Parachute	When a takeover is successful, top management usually is changed. With this in mind, a company may establish special termination or retirement benefits that must be paid to top managers if they are "retired." In other words, a departing high-level manager's parachute will be "golden" when he or she is forced to "bail out" of the company.
Greenmail	To regain control, a target company may pay a higher-than-market price to repurchase all of the stock that the acquiring corporation bought. When a takeover is attempted through a gradual accumulation of target stock rather than a tender offer, the intent may be to induce the target company to buy back the shares at a premium price—a concept similar to blackmail.
Pac-Man	Named after the Atari video game, this is an aggressive defense in which the target corporation attempts its own takeover of the acquiring corporation.
Poison Pill	The target corporation issues to its stockholders rights to purchase additional shares at low prices when there is a takeover attempt. This makes the takeover undesirably or even prohibitively expensive for the acquiring corporation.
White Knight	The target corporation solicits a merger with a third party, which then makes a better (often simply a higher) tender offer to the target's shareholders. The third party that "rescues" the target is the "white knight."

the tender offer posed a danger to the corporation's policies and effectiveness. In addition, the board's response must have been rational in relation to the threat posed.[4] Basically, the defensive tactics used must have been reasonable, and the board of directors must have been trying to protect the corporation and its shareholders from a perceived danger. If the directors' actions were reasonable under the circumstances, then they are not liable for breaching their fiduciary duties.

Takeovers and Antitrust Law

Sometimes, a target corporation will seek an injunction against an aggressor on the ground that the attempted takeover violates antitrust laws. This defense may succeed if a court finds that the takeover would result in a substantial increase in the acquiring corporation's market power. Because antitrust laws are designed to protect competition rather than competitors, incumbent managers who are able to avoid a takeover by resorting to the use of private antitrust actions are unintended beneficiaries of the laws.

As will be discussed in Chapter 47, antitrust challenges to mergers may also be brought by the government rather than by private parties. Hence, the antitrust considerations involved in a proposed takeover can exist apart from the consideration of defense tactics.

SECTION 4

TERMINATION

The termination of a corporation's existence has two phases—dissolution and winding up. **Dissolution** is the legal death of the artificial "person" of the corporation. *Winding up* is the process by which corporate assets are *liquidated,* or converted into cash and distributed among creditors and shareholders according to specific rules of preference.[5]

Voluntary Dissolution

Dissolution can be brought about voluntarily by the directors and the shareholders. State corporation statutes establish the procedures required for

---

4. For a landmark Delaware Supreme Court case applying the business judgment rule to hostile takeovers, see *Unocal Corp. v. Mesa Petroleum Co.,* 493 A.2d 946 (Del.Sup.Ct. 1985). See also *Shaper v. Bryan,* 371 Ill.App.3d 1079, 864 N.E.2d 876, 309 Ill. Dec. 635 (2007).

5. Some prefer to call this phase *liquidation,* but we use the term *winding up* to mean all acts needed to bring the legal and financial affairs of the business to an end, including liquidating the assets and distributing them among creditors and shareholders. See RMBCA 14.05.

CONCEPT SUMMARY 41.1
Methods of Expanding Corporate Operations and Interests

Method	Description

Merger and Consolidation	1. *Merger*—The legal combination of two or more corporations, with the result that the surviving corporation acquires all of the assets and obligations of the other corporation, which then ceases to exist.
	2. *Consolidation*—The legal combination of two or more corporations, with the result that each corporation ceases to exist and a new one emerges. The new corporation assumes all of the assets and obligations of the former corporations.
	3. *Share exchange*—A form of business combination in which some or all of the shares of one corporation are exchanged for some or all of the shares of another corporation, but both firms continue to exist.
	4. *Procedure*—Determined by state statutes. Basic requirements are the following:
	  a. The board of directors of each corporation involved must approve the plan of merger, consolidation, or share exchange.
	  b. The shareholders of each corporation must approve the merger or other consolidation plan at a shareholders' meeting.
	  c. Articles of merger or consolidation (the plan) must be filed, usually with the secretary of state.
	  d. The state issues a certificate of merger (or consolidation) to the surviving (or newly consolidated) corporation.
	5. *Short-form merger (parent-subsidiary merger)*—When the parent corporation owns at least 90 percent of the outstanding shares of each class of stock of the subsidiary corporation, shareholder approval is not required for the two firms to merge.
	6. *Appraisal rights*—Statutory rights of dissenting shareholders to receive the *fair value* for their shares when a merger or consolidation takes place. If the shareholder and the corporation do not agree on the fair value, a court will determine it.

Purchase of Assets	A purchase of assets occurs when one corporation acquires all or substantially all of the assets of another corporation. 1. *Acquiring corporation*—The acquiring (purchasing) corporation is not required to obtain shareholder approval. The corporation is merely increasing its assets, and no fundamental business change occurs. 2. *Acquired corporation*—The acquired (purchased) corporation is required to obtain the approval of both its directors and its shareholders for the sale of its assets because the sale will substantially change the corporation's business position.
Purchase of Stock	A purchase of stock occurs when one corporation acquires a substantial number of the voting shares of the stock of another (target) corporation. 1. *Tender offer*—A public offer to all shareholders of the target corporation to purchase their stock at a price generally higher than the market price of the target stock prior to the announcement of the tender offer. Federal and state securities laws strictly control the terms, duration, and circumstances under which most tender offers are made. 2. *Target responses*—The ways in which target corporations respond to takeover bids include self-tender (the target firm's offer to acquire its own shareholders' stock) and numerous other strategies (see Exhibit 41–3 on the previous page).

voluntarily dissolving a corporation. Basically, there are two possible methods: by the shareholders' unanimous vote to initiate dissolution proceedings[6] or by

---

6. Only some states allow shareholders to initiate corporation dissolution. See, for example, Delaware Code Annotated Title 8, Section 275(c).

a proposal of the board of directors that is submitted to the shareholders at a shareholders' meeting.

When a corporation is dissolved voluntarily, the corporation must file *articles of dissolution* with the state and notify its creditors of the dissolution. The corporation must also establish a date (at least 120 days after the date of dissolution) by which all claims against the corporation must be received [RMBCA 14.06].

A corporation's creditors want to be notified when the firm is dissolved so that they can file claims for payment. If a corporation is dissolved and its assets are liquidated without notice to a party who has a claim against the firm, who is liable for the debt? That was the question in the following case.

✳ EXTENDED CASE 41.2 ✳
Parent v. Amity Autoworld, Ltd.

New York District Court, Suffolk County, Third District, 15 Misc.3d 633, 832 N.Y.S.2d 775 (2007).

IN THE LANGUAGE OF THE COURT
C. Stephen *HACKELING,* J. [Judge]
* * * *

The plaintiff [Christine Parent] leased an automobile from Amity Autoworld, Ltd. (hereafter "Amity") [in Amityville, New York] in January 2002.

Amity sold all its Toyota automobile franchise assets * * * to respondent J S Autoworld, Ltd. (hereafter "Atlantic") pursuant to agreement in May 2002. * * * The alleged payments for the Amity dealership were made * * * directly to John Staluppi, Jr.

The plaintiff made a written claim for money damages to Amity on June 11, 2002.

The plaintiff commenced a small claims action [in a New York state court] against Amity via complaint dated March 9, 2005 and obtained a $2,643 * * * award.

The Suffolk County Sheriff returned the plaintiff's execution against Amity as unsatisfied on July 12, 2006, advising that the Toyota dealership is now owned by Atlantic.
* * * *

Amity's principal stockholder [was] John Staluppi, Jr., who is the son of Atlantic's principal stockholder John Staluppi, Sr. John

Staluppi, Jr. is listed with the N.Y. State Division of Corporation database as the "chairman, chief executive officer, executive officer and agent for process of Amity Autoworld, Ltd."
* * * *

* * * *Even in the absence of fraud, it [is] a violation of a duty on the part of the directors of a corporation to divest itself of all its property without affording a reasonable opportunity to its creditors to present and enforce their claims before the transfer becomes effective.* [Emphasis added.]

The assets of a corporation constitute a * * * fund for the payment of its debts. After the return of an unsatisfied execution against the defunct corporation, a creditor may maintain an action against a shareholder to reach assets received by him. *Directors incur derivative personal liability when they undertake to divest a corporation of all its property and in reality dissolve it without undertaking the proceedings for voluntary dissolution.* [Emphasis added.]

* * * [Section] 1007 of the [New York] Business Corporation Law * * * provides:

* * * *

[Section] 1007. Notice to creditors; filing or barring claims

(a) At any time after dissolution, the corporation may give a notice requiring all creditors and claimants * * * to present their claims

in writing and in detail at a specified place and by a specified day, which shall not be less than six months after the first publication of such notice. Such notice shall be published at least once a week for two successive weeks in a newspaper of general circulation in the county in which the office of the corporation was located * * *.

The Court notes that the use of the language "may give notice" to creditors in [Section] 1007 is permissive in nature. As such, * * * New York law allows for a corporation to informally dissolve by transferring all its assets without giving notice to creditors. However, * * * the cost of an informal dissolution is that directors cannot shield themselves against corporate creditor liability. Directors who undertake to divest a corporation of all its property without taking the proceedings for a voluntary dissolution do so at their peril.

In the matter presented, it is undisputed that Amity was informally liquidated and dissolved without notice to creditors and that John Staluppi, Jr. received in excess of $4,000,000 personally. * * * Accordingly, the Court authorizes the amendment of the plaintiff's complaint to include John Staluppi, Jr. as a * * * defendant and directs the Clerk of the Court to * * * schedule a trial of the matter.

QUESTIONS

1. A corporation may do business under a variety of names. How strictly should the law require a judgment to be issued against a corporation in its "true" name?
2. Could a corporation's former directors or shareholders, or its successors, avoid liability following its informal dissolution by claiming that they did all they felt was necessary to protect its creditors? Why or why not?

Involuntary Dissolution

Because corporations are creatures of statute, the state can also dissolve a corporation in certain circumstances. The secretary of state or the state attorney general can bring an action to dissolve a corporation that has failed to pay its annual taxes or to submit required annual reports, for example [RMBCA 14.20]. A state court can also dissolve a corporation that has committed fraud or misrepresentation to the state during incorporation or has engaged in mismanagement [RMBCA 14.30].

In some circumstances, a shareholder or a group of shareholders may petition a court to have the corporation dissolved. The RMBCA permits any shareholder to initiate an action for dissolution in any of the following circumstances [RMBCA 14.30]:

1. The directors are deadlocked in the management of corporate affairs, the shareholders are unable to break the deadlock, and the corporation is suffering irreparable injury as a result or is about to do so.
2. The acts of the directors or those in control of the corporation are illegal, oppressive, or fraudulent.
3. Corporate assets are being misapplied or wasted.

4. The shareholders are deadlocked in voting power and have failed, for a specified period (usually two annual meetings), to elect successors to directors whose terms have expired or would have expired with the election of successors.

CASE IN POINT Mt. Princeton Trout Club, Inc. (MPTC), was formed to own land in Colorado and provide recreational benefits to its shareholders. The articles of incorporation prohibited MPTC from selling or leasing any of its property without the approval of a majority of the directors. Nevertheless, MPTC officers entered into leases and contracts to sell corporate property without even notifying the directors. When a shareholder petitioned for dissolution, the court dissolved MPTC based on a finding that its officers had engaged in illegal, oppressive, and fraudulent conduct.[7]

The issue in the following case was whether the circumstances satisfied the statutory requirements for a court to dissolve a trucking corporation.

---

7. *Colt v. Mt. Princeton Trout Club, Inc.,* 78 P.3d 1115 (Colo.App. 2003).

CASE 41.3
Sartori v. S&S Trucking, Inc.
Supreme Court of Montana, 2006 MT 164, 332 Mont. 503, 139 P.3d 806 (2006).

BACKGROUND AND FACTS • Tony Stacy approached his friend Justin Sartori about buying a trucking business and operating it together. Sartori agreed, and because he had a good credit rating and Stacy did not, Sartori borrowed $78,493.68 from First Interstate Bank in Eureka, Montana, to buy the business. In September 2003, they formed S&S Trucking, Inc., and agreed to be its only directors, officers, and shareholders, with each owning an equal number of shares. Within weeks, however, they realized that they were incompatible. For example, Sartori often did not show up when and where Stacy expected, and they differed over the payment of earnings from S&S's income. In October, Sartori incorporated Brimstone Enterprise to undermine S&S. He had S&S's mail forwarded to Brimstone, transferred S&S's licenses to Brimstone, and attempted to attract S&S's customers to Brimstone. In mid-November, he quit working for S&S and filed a suit in a Montana state court against S&S and Stacy, demanding that the firm be dissolved. The court set a deadline for the dissolution. The defendants appealed to the Montana Supreme Court.

IN THE LANGUAGE OF THE COURT
Justice W. William *LEAPHART* delivered the opinion of the court.
* * * *

The [lower] Court dissolved S&S pursuant to [Montana Code Section] 35-1-938(2), which states that a * * * court may dissolve a corporation in a proceeding by a shareholder if it is established that:

(a) the directors are deadlocked in the management of the corporate affairs, the shareholders are unable to break the deadlock, and irreparable injury to the corporation is threatened or being suffered

CASE CONTINUES ➡

CASE 41.3 CONTINUED ➧ or the business and affairs of the corporation can no longer be conducted to the advantage of the shareholders generally because of the deadlock * * * .

Stacy maintains on appeal that, rather than dissolving the corporation, the * * * Court * * * should have simply removed Sartori as a shareholder and director of the corporation. While Stacy appears to concede that he and Sartori were unable to break their management deadlock as to corporate affairs, he argues that the court failed to find any harm to the corporation per the statutory language. Stacy stresses the fact that S&S is now a twelve-employee company that has thrived in the wake of Sartori's departure. Since there has been no corporate injury, Stacy argues, there can be no dissolution.

In making this argument, Stacy ignores relevant statutory language. Section 35-1-938(2)(a) * * * provides that *the court may order dissolution if "irreparable injury to the corporation is threatened or being suffered or the business and affairs of the corporation can no longer be conducted to the advantage of the shareholders generally because of the deadlock."* Stacy and Sartori were S&S's only shareholders. Although the corporation may not have suffered irreparable injury, the [lower] Court found that the management deadlock led Sartori to take numerous steps to sabotage the corporation. As a result, the business and affairs of S&S could no longer be conducted to the advantage of the shareholders, Stacy and Sartori. The court properly exercised its statutory authority when it dissolved S&S. [Emphasis added.]

DECISION AND REMEDY • *The Montana Supreme Court held that the dissolution of a corporation may be ordered without a finding that the firm has suffered or is threatened with an injury if its business can no longer be conducted to its shareholders' advantage. Thus, the order for the dissolution of S&S was correct, and the court affirmed the decision of the lower court.*

THE ETHICAL DIMENSION • *Did Sartori or Stacy behave unethically toward the other or toward the corporation? Discuss.*

THE LEGAL ENVIRONMENT DIMENSION • *At the time of the defendants' appeal, S&S had twelve employees, and, according to Stacy, its business was thriving. Should the court have taken these factors into consideration when deciding whether to order the dissolution of the firm? Explain.*

Winding Up

When dissolution takes place by voluntary action, the members of the board of directors act as trustees of the corporate assets. As trustees, they are responsible for winding up the affairs of the corporation for the benefit of corporate creditors and shareholders. This responsibility makes the board members personally liable for any breach of their fiduciary trustee duties.

When the dissolution is involuntary—or if board members do not wish to act as trustees of the assets—the court will appoint a **receiver** to wind up the corporate affairs and liquidate corporate assets. Courts may also appoint a receiver when shareholders or creditors can show that the board of directors should not be permitted to act as trustees of the corporate assets.

On dissolution, the liquidated assets are first used to pay creditors. Any remaining assets are distributed to shareholders according to their respective stock rights. Preferred stock has priority over common stock. Generally, the preferences are stated in the corporate articles.

SECTION 5
MAJOR BUSINESS FORMS COMPARED

As mentioned in Chapter 36, when deciding which form of business organization to choose, businesspersons normally consider several factors, including ease of creation, the liability of the owners, tax considerations, and the ability to raise capital. Each major form of business organization offers distinct advantages and disadvantages with respect to these and other factors.

Exhibit 41–4 on pages 807 and 808 summarizes the essential advantages and disadvantages of each of the forms of business organization discussed in Chapters 36 through 41.

EXHIBIT 41–4 • Major Forms of Business Compared

CHARACTERISTIC	SOLE PROPRIETORSHIP	PARTNERSHIP	CORPORATION
Method of Creation	Created at will by owner.	Created by agreement of the parties.	Authorized by the state under the state's corporation law.
Legal Position	Not a separate entity; owner is the business.	A traditional partnership is a separate legal entity in most states.	Always a legal entity separate and distinct from its owners—a legal fiction for the purposes of owning property and being a party to litigation.
Liability	Unlimited liability.	Unlimited liability.	Limited liability of shareholders— shareholders are not liable for the debts of the corporation.
Duration	Determined by owner; automatically dissolved on owner's death.	Terminated by agreement of the partners, but can continue to do business even when a partner dissociates from the partnership.	Can have perpetual existence.
Transferability of Interest	Interest can be transferred, but individual's proprietorship then ends.	Although partnership interest can be assigned, assignee does not have full rights of a partner.	Shares of stock can be transferred.
Management	Completely at owner's discretion.	Each partner has a direct and equal voice in management unless expressly agreed otherwise in the partnership agreement.	Shareholders elect directors, who set policy and appoint officers.
Taxation	Owner pays personal taxes on business income.	Each partner pays pro rata share of income taxes on net profits, whether or not they are distributed.	Double taxation—corporation pays income tax on net profits, with no deduction for dividends, and shareholders pay income tax on disbursed dividends they receive.
Organizational Fees, Annual License Fees, and Annual Reports	None or minimal.	None or minimal.	All required.
Transaction of Business in Other States	Generally no limitation.	Generally no limitation.[a]	Normally must qualify to do business and obtain certificate of authority.

a. A few states have enacted statutes requiring that foreign partnerships qualify to do business there.

EXHIBIT 41–4 CONTINUES ON THE FOLLOWING PAGE.

EXHIBIT 41–4 • Major Forms of Business Compared—Continued

CHARACTERISTIC	LIMITED PARTNERSHIP	LIMITED LIABILITY COMPANY	LIMITED LIABILITY PARTNERSHIP
Method of Creation	Created by agreement to carry on a business for profit. At least one party must be a general partner and the other(s) limited partner(s). Certificate of limited partnership is filed. Charter must be issued by the state.	Created by an agreement of the member-owners of the company. Articles of organization are filed. Charter must be issued by the state.	Created by agreement of the partners. A statement of qualification for the limited liability partnership is filed.
Legal Position	Treated as a legal entity.	Treated as a legal entity.	Generally, treated same as a traditional partnership.
Liability	Unlimited liability of all general partners; limited partners are liable only to the extent of capital contributions.	Member-owners' liability is limited to the amount of capital contributions or investments.	Varies, but under the Uniform Partnership Act, liability of a partner for acts committed by other partners is limited.
Duration	By agreement in certificate, or by termination of the last general partner (retirement, death, and the like) or last limited partner.	Unless a single-member LLC, can have perpetual existence (same as a corporation).	Remains in existence until cancellation or revocation.
Transferability of Interest	Interest can be assigned (same as a traditional partnership), but if assignee becomes a member with consent of other partners, certificate must be amended.	Member interests are freely transferable.	Interest can be assigned same as in a traditional partnership.
Management	General partners have equal voice or by agreement. Limited partners may not retain limited liability if they actively participate in management.	Member-owners can fully participate in management or can designate a group of persons to manage on behalf of the members.	Same as a traditional partnership.
Taxation	Generally taxed as a partnership.	LLC is not taxed, and members are taxed personally on profits "passed through" the LLC.	Same as a traditional partnership.
Organizational Fees, Annual License Fees, and Annual Reports	Organizational fee required; usually not others.	Organizational fee required; others vary with states.	Fees are set by each state for filing statements of qualification, statements of foreign qualification, and annual reports.
Transaction of Business in Other States	Generally no limitations.	Generally no limitation, but may vary depending on state.	Must file a statement of foreign qualification before doing business in another state.

REVIEWING

Corporate Merger, Consolidation, and Termination

In November 2005, Mario Bonsetti and Rico Sanchez incorporated Gnarly Vulcan Gear, Inc. (GVG), to manufacture windsurfing equipment. Bonsetti owned 60 percent and Sanchez owned 40 percent of the corporation's stock, and both men served on the board of directors. In January 2009, Hula Boards, Inc., owned solely by Mai Jin Li, made a public offer to Bonsetti and Sanchez to buy GVG stock. Hula offered 30 percent more than the market price per share for the GVG stock, and Bonsetti and Sanchez each sold 20 percent of their stock to Hula. Jin Li became the third member of the GVG board of directors. In April 2011, an irreconcilable dispute arose between Bonsetti and Sanchez over design modifications of their popular Baked Chameleon board. Sanchez and Jin Li voted to merge GVG with Hula Boards under the latter name, despite Bonsetti's dissent. Gnarly Vulcan Gear was dissolved, and production of the Baked Chameleon ceased. Using the information presented in the chapter, answer the following questions.

1. What rights does Bonsetti have (in most states) as a minority shareholder dissenting to the merger of GVG and Hula Boards?
2. Could the parties have used a short-form merger procedure in this situation? Why or why not?
3. What is the term used for Hula's offer to purchase GVG stock? By what method did Hula acquire control over GVG?
4. Suppose that after the merger, a person who was injured on a Baked Chameleon board sued Hula (the surviving corporation). Can Hula be held liable for an injury? Why or why not?

DEBATE THIS: *Corporate law should be altered to prohibit incumbent management from using most currently legal methods to fight takeovers.*

TERMS AND CONCEPTS

appraisal right 798

consolidation 797

dissolution 802

merger 796

parent-subsidiary merger 798

receiver 806

share exchange 797

short-form merger 798

surviving corporation 796

takeover 801

target corporation 801

tender offer 801

QUESTIONS AND CASE PROBLEMS

41–1. Corporate Acquisitions Gretz is the chair of the board of directors of Faraday, Inc., and Williams is the chair of the board of directors of Firebrand, Inc. Faraday is a manufacturing corporation, and Firebrand is a transportation corporation. Gretz and Williams meet to discuss the possibility of combining their corporations and activities into a single corporate entity. They consider two alternative courses of action: (1) Faraday acquires all of the stock and assets of Firebrand, or (2) the two corporations combine to form a new corporation, Farabrand, Inc. Both chairs are concerned about the necessity of a formal transfer of property, liability for existing debts, and the need to amend the articles of incorporation. Explain what the two

proposed combinations are called, and discuss the legal effect each has on the transfer of property, the liabilities of the combined corporations, and the need to amend the articles of incorporation.

41–2. QUESTION WITH SAMPLE ANSWER: Corporate Merger.

Alir owns 10,000 shares of Ajax Corp. Her shares represent a 10 percent ownership in Ajax. Zeta Corp. is interested in acquiring Ajax in a merger, and the board of directors of each corporation has approved the merger. The shareholders of Zeta have already approved the acquisition, and Ajax has called for a shareholders' meeting to approve the merger. Alir disapproves of the merger and does not want to accept Zeta shares for the Ajax shares she holds. The market price of Ajax shares is $20 per share the day before the shareholder vote and drops to $16 on the day the shareholders of Ajax approve the merger. Discuss Alir's rights in this matter, beginning with the notice of the proposed merger.

- **For a sample answer to Question 41–2, go to Appendix I at the end of this text.**

41–3. Corporate Takeover Alitech Corp. is a small midwestern business that owns a valuable patent. Alitech has approximately 1,000 shareholders with 100,000 authorized and outstanding shares. Block Corp. would like to have the use of the patent, but Alitech refuses to give Block a license. Block has tried to acquire Alitech by purchasing Alitech's assets, but Alitech's board of directors has refused to approve the acquisition. Alitech's shares are selling for $5 per share. Discuss how Block Corp. might proceed to gain the control and use of Alitech's patent.

41–4. Successor Liability In 1996, Robert McClellan, a licensed contractor doing business as McClellan Design and Construction, entered into a contract with Peppertree North Condominium Association, Inc., to do earthquake repair work on Peppertree's seventy-six-unit condominium complex in Northridge, California. McClellan completed the work, but Peppertree failed to pay. In an arbitration proceeding against Peppertree to collect the amount due, McClellan was awarded $141,000, plus 10 percent interest, attorneys' fees, and costs. McClellan filed a suit in a California state court against Peppertree to confirm the award. Meanwhile, the Peppertree board of directors filed articles of incorporation for Northridge Park Townhome Owners Association, Inc., and immediately transferred Peppertree's authority, responsibilities, and assets to the new association. Two weeks later, the court issued a judgment against Peppertree. When McClellan learned about the new association, he filed a motion asking the court to add Northridge as a debtor to the judgment. Should the court grant the motion? Why or why not? [*McClellan v. Northridge Park Townhome Owners Association, Inc.*, 89 Cal.App.4th 746, 107 Cal. Rptr.2d 702 (2 Dist. 2001)]

41–5. Corporate Dissolution Trans-System, Inc. (TSI), is an interstate trucking business. In 1994, to provide a source of well-trained drivers, TSI formed Northwestern Career Institute, Inc., a school for persons interested in obtaining a commercial driver's license. Tim Scott, who had worked for TSI since 1987, was named chief administrative officer and director. Scott, a Northwestern shareholder, disagreed with James Williams, the majority shareholder of both TSI and Northwestern, over four equipment leases between the two firms under which the sum of the payments exceeded the value of the equipment by not more than $3,000. Under four other leases, payments were $40,000 less than the value of the equipment. Scott also disputed TSI's one-time use, for purposes unrelated to the driving school, of $125,000

borrowed by Northwestern. Scott was terminated in 1998. He filed a suit in a Washington state court against TSI, seeking, among other things, the dissolution of Northwestern on the ground that the directors of the two firms had acted in an oppressive manner and misapplied corporate assets. Should the court grant this relief? If not, what remedy might be appropriate? Discuss. [*Scott v. Trans-System, Inc.*, 148 Wash.2d 701, 64 P.3d 1 (2003)]

41–6. Purchase of Assets Paradise Pools, Inc. (PPI), also known as "Paradise Pools and Spas," was incorporated in 1981. In 1994, PPI entered into a contract with Bromanco, Inc., to build a pool in Vicksburg, Mississippi, as part of a Days Inn Hotel project being developed by Amerihost Development, Inc. PPI built the pool, but Bromanco, the general contractor, defaulted on other parts of the project, and Amerihost completed the construction itself. Litigation ensued in Mississippi state courts, and Amerihost was awarded $12,656.46 against PPI. Meanwhile, Paradise Corp. (PC) was incorporated in 1995 with the same management as PPI, but different shareholders. PC acquired PPI's assets in 1996, without assuming its liabilities, and soon became known as "Paradise Pools and Spas." Amerihost obtained a writ of garnishment against PC to enforce the judgment against PPI. PC filed a motion to dismiss the writ on the basis that it was "not a party to the proceeding." Should the court dismiss the case? Why or why not? [*Paradise Corp. v. Amerihost Development, Inc.*, 848 So.2d 177 (Miss. 2003)]

41–7. Successor Liability In January 1999, General Star Indemnity Co. agreed to insure Indianapolis Racing League (IRL) race cars against damage during on-track accidents. In connection with the insurance, General Star deposited $400,000 with G Force, LLC (GFCO), a Colorado firm, to enable it to buy and provide parts for damaged cars without delay. GFCO agreed to return any unspent funds. Near the end of the season, Elan Motorsports Technologies (EMT) acquired GFCO. In 2000, EMT incorporated G Force, LLC, in Georgia (GFGA), and GFCO ceased to exist. GFGA renewed the arrangement with General Star and engaged in the same operations as GFCO, but EMT employees conducted GFGA's business at EMT's offices. In 2002, EMT assumed ownership of GFGA's assets and continued the business. EMT also assumed GFGA's liabilities, except for the obligation to return General Star's unspent funds. General Star filed a suit in a Georgia state court against EMT, seeking to recover its deposit. What is the rule concerning the liability of a corporation that buys the assets of another? Are there exceptions? Which principles apply in this case? Explain. [*General Star Indemnity Co. v. Elan Motorsports Technologies, Inc.*, 356 F.Supp.2d 1333 (N.D.Ga. 2004)]

41–8. CASE PROBLEM WITH SAMPLE ANSWER: Dissolution.

Clara Mahaffey operated Mahaffey's Auto Salvage, Inc., in Dayton, Ohio, as a sole proprietorship. In 1993, Kenneth Stumpff and Mahaffey's son, Richard Harris, joined the firm. Stumpff ran the

wrecker and bought the vehicles for salvage. Harris handled the day-to-day operations and the bookkeeping. They became the company's equal 50 percent shareholders on Mahaffey's death in 2002. Harris, who inherited the land on which the firm was located, increased the rent to $1,500 per month. Within two years of Mahaffey's death, and without consulting Stumpff, Harris raised the rent to $2,500. Stumpff's wife died, and he took a leave of absence, during which the company paid him $2,500 a month and provided health insurance. After two years, Harris stopped the payments, discontinued the health benefits, and fired Stumpff, threatening to call the police if he came on the premises. Stumpff withdrew $16,000 from the firm's account, leaving a balance of $113. Harris offered to buy Stumpff's interest in the business, but Stumpff refused and filed a suit in an Ohio state court against Harris. A state statute permits the dissolution of a corporation if the owners are deadlocked in its management. Should the court order the dissolution of Mahaffey's? Why or why not? [Stumpff v. Harris, __ N.E.2d __ (Ohio App. 2006)]

- **To view a sample answer for Problem 41–8, go to this book's Web site at www.cengage.com/blaw/clarkson, select "Chapter 41," and click on "Case Problem with Sample Answer."**

41–9. Successor Liability In 2004, the Watergate Hotel in Washington, D.C., obtained a loan from PB Capital. At this time, hotel employees were represented by a union (see Chapter 34), and under a collective bargaining agreement, the hotel agreed to make contributions to an employees' pension fund run by the union. In 2007, the hotel was closed due to poor business, although the owner stated that the hotel would reopen in 2010. Despite this expectation, PB Capital—which was still owed $40 million by the hotel owner—instituted foreclosure proceedings (see Chapter 31). At the foreclosure sale, PB Capital bought the hotel and reopened it under new management and with a new workforce. The union sued PB Capital, contending that it should pay $637,855 owed by the previous owner into the employees' pension fund. Should PB Capital, as the hotel's new owner,

have to incur the previous owner's obligation to pay into the pension fund under the theory of successor liability? Why or why not? [*Board of Trustees of Unite Here Local 25 v. MR Watergate, LLC*, 677 F.Supp.2d 229 (D.D.C. 2010)]

41–10. A QUESTION OF ETHICS: Purchase of Stock.

Topps Co. makes baseball and other cards, including the Pokemon collection, and distributes Bazooka bubble gum and other confections. Arthur Shorin, the son of Joseph Shorin, one of Topps's founders and the inspiration for "Bazooka Joe" (a character in the comic strip wrapped around each piece of gum), worked for Topps for fifty years and had served as its board chair and chief executive officer since 1980. Shorin's son-in-law, Scott Silverstein, served as Topps's president and chief operating officer. When Topps's financial performance began to lag, the board considered selling the company. Michael Eisner (formerly head of Disney Studios) offered to pay $9.75 per share and to retain Topps's management in a merger with his company. Upper Deck Co., Topps's chief competitor in the sports-card business, offered $10.75 per share but did not offer to retain the managers. Topps demanded that Upper Deck not reveal its bid publicly, but Topps publicized the offer, without accurately representing Upper Deck's interest and disparaging its seriousness. Upper Deck asked Topps to allow it to tell its side of events and to make a tender offer to Topps's shareholders. Topps refused and scheduled a shareholder vote on the Eisner offer. Topps's shareholders filed a suit in a Delaware state court against their firm, asking the court to prevent the vote. [In re Topps Co. Shareholders Litigation, 926 A.2d 58 (Del.Ch. 2007)]

(a) The shareholders contended that Topps's conduct had "tainted the vote." What factors support this contention? How might these factors affect the vote?

(b) Why might Topps's board and management be opposed to either of the offers for the company? Is this opposition ethical? Should the court enjoin (prevent) the scheduled vote? Explain.

LEGAL RESEARCH EXERCISES ON THE WEB

Go to this text's Web site at **www.cengage.com/blaw/clarkson**, select "Chapter 41," and click on "Practical Internet Exercises." There you will find the following Internet research exercises that you can perform to learn more about the topics covered in this chapter.

Practical Internet Exercise 41–1: **Legal Perspective**
Mergers

Practical Internet Exercise 41–2: **Management Perspective**
Golden Parachutes

CHAPTER 42

Securities Law and Corporate Governance

he stock market crash of October 29, 1929, and the ensuing economic depression caused the public to focus on the importance of securities markets for the economic well-being of the nation. Congress was pressured to regulate securities trading, and the result was the Securities Act of 1933[1] and the Securities Exchange Act of 1934.[2] Both acts were designed to

1. 15 U.S.C. Sections 77a–77aa.
2. 15 U.S.C. Sections 78a–78mm.

provide investors with more information to help them make buying and selling decisions about securities—generally defined as any instruments evidencing corporate ownership (stock) or debts (bonds)—and to prohibit deceptive, unfair, and manipulative practices in the purchase and sale of securities.

This chapter discusses the nature of federal securities regulation and its effect on the business world. We begin by looking at the federal administrative agency

that regulates securities transactions, the Securities and Exchange Commission. Next, we examine the major traditional laws governing securities offerings and trading.

We then discuss corporate governance and the Sarbanes-Oxley Act, which significantly affects certain types of securities transactions. In the concluding pages of this chapter, we look at how securities laws are being adapted to the online environment.

SECTION 1
THE SECURITIES AND EXCHANGE COMMISSION

The Securities Exchange Act of 1934 created the Securities and Exchange Commission (SEC) as an independent regulatory agency. The SEC administers the Securities Act of 1933 and the 1934 act. The SEC also plays a key role in interpreting the provisions of these acts (and their amendments) and in creating regulations governing the purchase and sale of securities. The basic functions of the SEC are as follows:

1. Interprets federal securities laws and investigates securities law violations.
2. Issues new rules and amends existing rules.
3. Oversees the inspection of securities firms, brokers, investment advisers, and ratings agencies.
4. Oversees private regulatory organizations in the securities, accounting, and auditing fields.
5. Coordinates U.S. securities regulation with federal, state, and foreign authorities.

Updating the Regulatory Process

The SEC is working to make the regulatory process more efficient and more relevant to today's securities trading practices. To this end, the SEC has embraced modern technology and communications methods, especially the Internet, more completely than many other federal agencies have. For example, the agency now requires companies to file certain information electronically so that it can be posted on the SEC's EDGAR (Electronic Data Gathering, Analysis, and Retrieval) database.

The SEC currently requires companies to make disclosures regarding climate change, as discussed in this chapter's *Shifting Legal Priorities for Business* feature on the facing page.

The SEC's Expanding Regulatory Powers

Since its creation, the SEC's regulatory functions have gradually been increased by legislation granting it authority in different areas. For example, to further curb securities fraud,

The Securities and Exchange Commission (SEC) requires companies to reveal the potential financial impacts of future events such as increased competition, changes in regulatory rules, and pending lawsuits. In short, publicly traded corporations must disclose material information about future developments that might affect their earnings so that investors can make sound investment decisions. Should that information include the potential impact of climate change related to global warming?

The Risks and Opportunities of Climate Change

Since 2007, environmental groups, large institutional investors such as state pension funds, and other groups have petitioned the SEC, asking the commission to require that publicly held companies disclose climate-related information that could materially affect their operations.[a] The groups cited a number of potential costs related to climate change, such as property losses in flooded coastal areas that would affect the property owners and their insurers, increased costs for food producers due to crop losses, and increased costs for pollution-control equipment to curb greenhouse gas emissions. At the same time, climate change could also present opportunities for companies that produce goods and services that can mitigate the effects of global warming or supply energy without generating emissions.

The SEC Responds

In 2010, the SEC decided that climate change had become a sufficiently important issue that publicly held companies should disclose their exposure to it. Accordingly, the SEC issued a guidance to aid companies in deciding when and whether to disclose the potential impacts of climate change on their future profitability.[b] In announcing the decision, Mary Schapiro, the SEC chair, pointed out that "we are not opining on whether the world's climate is changing, at what pace it might be changing, or due to what causes. Nothing that the commission does today should be construed as weighing in on these topics."

The SEC's guidance suggests that companies note in their quarterly and annual reports to shareholders any significant developments in federal and state legislation and regulations regarding climate change. For example, companies should disclose estimates for any material capital expenditures for pollution-control facilities. Risk factors related to existing or pending environmental legislation or regulations should be disclosed. In particular, companies should be "sensitive to greenhouse gas legislation or regulation."

The material impact of treaties or international conventions related to climate change should also be considered and disclosed. Companies whose businesses are "reasonably likely to be affected by such agreements should monitor the progress of any potential agreements and consider the possible impact."

Finally, the SEC suggested that companies consider changes in demand for their products or services, both existing and proposed, that might occur as a consequence of climate change or environmental legislation and regulations. For example, there might be a decrease in demand for services related to carbon-based energy, such as drilling or equipment maintenance services.

MANAGERIAL IMPLICATIONS

For the moment, only managers working in publicly held companies must worry about the SEC's guidelines with respect to climate change. Nonetheless, nonpublic companies sometimes "go public." Thus, managers in those companies should also monitor pending legislation, national and international, that might affect their businesses.

---

a. "File No. 4-547: Request for Interpretive Guidance on Climate Risk Disclosure." *www.sec.gov.* 18 Sep. 2007: n. p. Web.

b. 17 C.F.R. Parts 211, 231, and 241 (Release Nos. 33-9106 and 34-61469; FR-82).

Congress enacted the Securities Enforcement Remedies and Penny Stock Reform Act of 1990.[3] This act expands the SEC's enforcement options and allows SEC administrative law judges to hear cases involving more types of alleged securities law violations, such as fraudulent financial reporting and financial fraud. The Securities Acts Amendments of 1990 authorized the SEC to seek sanctions against those who violate foreign securities laws.[4]

The National Securities Markets Improvement Act of 1996 expanded the power of the SEC to exempt persons, securities, and transactions from the requirements of the securities laws.[5] The Sarbanes-Oxley Act of 2002, which you will read about later

---

3. 15 U.S.C. Section 77g.

4. 15 U.S.C. Section 78a.

5. 15 U.S.C. Sections 77z-3, 78mm.

in this chapter, further expanded the authority of the SEC. The Sarbanes-Oxley Act required the SEC to adopt new rules relating to corporate disclosure requirements and created an oversight board to regulate public accounting firms.

SECTION 2
THE SECURITIES ACT OF 1933

The Securities Act of 1933 governs initial sales of stock by businesses. The act was designed to prohibit various forms of fraud and to stabilize the securities industry by requiring that investors receive financial and other significant information concerning the securities being offered for public sale. Basically, the purpose of this act is to require disclosure. The 1933 act provides that all securities transactions must be registered with the SEC unless they are specifically exempt from the registration requirements.

What Is a Security?

Section 2(1) of the Securities Act of 1933 contains a broad definition of securities, which generally include the following:[6]

1. Instruments and interests commonly known as securities, such as preferred and common stocks, treasury stocks, bonds, debentures, and stock warrants.
2. Any interests commonly known as securities, such as stock options, puts, calls, or other types of privilege on a security or on the right to purchase a security or a group of securities in a national security exchange.
3. Notes, instruments, or other evidence of indebtedness, including certificates of interest in a profit-sharing agreement and certificates of deposit.
4. Any fractional undivided interest in oil, gas, or other mineral rights.
5. Investment contracts, which include interests in limited partnerships and other investment schemes.

In interpreting the act, the United States Supreme Court has held that an **investment contract** is any transaction in which a person (1) invests (2) in a common enterprise (3) reasonably expecting profits (4) derived *primarily* or *substantially* from others' managerial or entrepreneurial efforts. Known as the *Howey* test, this definition continues to guide the

determination of what types of contracts can be considered securities.[7]

For our purposes, it is convenient to think of securities in their most common form—stocks and bonds issued by corporations. Bear in mind, though, that securities can take many forms, including interests in whiskey, cosmetics, worms, beavers, boats, vacuum cleaners, muskrats, and cemetery lots. Almost any stake in the ownership or debt of a company can be considered a security. Investment contracts in condominiums, franchises, limited partnerships in real estate, and oil or gas or other mineral rights have qualified as securities.

CASE IN POINT   Alpha Telcom sold, installed, and maintained pay-phone systems. The company guaranteed buyers of the systems a 14 percent annual return. Alpha was operating at a net loss, however, and continually borrowed funds to pay investors the fixed rate of return it had promised. Eventually, the company filed for bankruptcy, and the SEC brought an action alleging that Alpha had violated the Securities Act of 1933. A federal court concluded that the pay-phone program was a security because it involved an investment contract.[8]

Registration Statement

Section 5 of the Securities Act of 1933 broadly provides that if a security does not qualify for an exemption, that security must be *registered* before it is offered to the public. Issuing corporations must file a *registration statement* with the SEC and must provide all investors with a *prospectus*. A **prospectus** is a disclosure document that describes the security being sold, the financial operations of the issuing corporation, and the investment or risk attaching to the security. The prospectus also serves as a selling tool for the issuing corporation. Recent SEC rules allow an issuer to deliver a prospectus to investors electronically via the Internet.[9] In principle, the registration statement and the prospectus supply sufficient

---

6. 15 U.S.C. Section 77b(1). Amendments in 1982 added stock options.

7. *SEC v. W. J. Howey Co.*, 328 U.S. 293, 66 S.Ct. 1100, 90 L.Ed. 1244 (1946).
8. *SEC v. Alpha Telcom, Inc.*, 187 F.Supp.2d 1250 (2002). See also *SEC v. Edwards*, 540 U.S. 389, 124 S.Ct. 892, 157 L.Ed.2d 813 (2004), in which the United States Supreme Court held that an investment scheme offering contractual entitlement to a fixed rate of return can be an investment contract and therefore can be considered a security under federal law.
9. Basically, an electronic prospectus must meet the same requirements as a printed prospectus. The SEC rules address situations in which the graphics, images, or audio files in or accompanying a printed prospectus cannot be reproduced in an electronic form. 17 C.F.R. Section 232.304.

information to enable unsophisticated investors to evaluate the financial risk involved.

CONTENTS OF THE REGISTRATION STATEMENT The registration statement must be written in plain English and fully describe the following:

1. The securities being offered for sale, including their relationship to the registrant's other capital securities.
2. The corporation's properties and business (including a financial statement certified by an independent public accounting firm).
3. The management of the corporation, including managerial compensation, stock options, pensions, and other benefits. Any interests of directors or officers in any material transactions with the corporation must be disclosed.
4. How the corporation intends to use the proceeds of the sale.
5. Any pending lawsuits or special risk factors.

All companies, both domestic and foreign, must file their registration statements electronically so that they can be posted on the SEC's EDGAR database (mentioned previously) and investors can access the information via the Internet. The EDGAR database includes material on *initial public offerings* (IPOs), proxy statements, corporations' annual reports, registration statements, and other documents that have been filed with the SEC.

REGISTRATION PROCESS The registration statement must be reviewed and approved by the SEC before it can become effective (unless it is filed by a *well-known seasoned issuer,* as will be discussed shortly). The 1933 act restricts the types of activities that an issuer can engage in at each stage of the registration process. If an issuer violates these restrictions, investors can rescind their contracts to purchase the securities. During the *prefiling period* (before filing the registration statement), the issuer normally cannot sell or offer to sell the securities. The issuer also cannot advertise its upcoming securities offering during the prefiling period.

Waiting Period. Once the registration statement has been filed, there is a waiting period of at least twenty days during which the SEC reviews the registration statement for completeness. Frequently, the staff members at the SEC who review the registration statement ask the registrant to make numerous changes and additions, which extends the length of the waiting period.

During the waiting period, the securities can be offered for sale but cannot be sold by the issuing

corporation. Only certain types of offers are allowed. All issuers can distribute a *preliminary prospectus,* called a **red herring prospectus.**[10] A red herring prospectus contains most of the information that will be included in the final prospectus but often does not include a price. General advertising is permitted, such as a **tombstone ad,** so named because historically the format resembled a tombstone. Such ads simply tell the investor where and how to obtain a prospectus.[11]

Most issuers can also use a *free-writing prospectus* during this period (although some inexperienced issuers will need to file a preliminary prospectus first).[12] A **free-writing prospectus** is any type of written, electronic, or graphic offer that describes the issuer or its securities and includes a legend indicating that the investor may obtain the prospectus at the SEC's Web site. The issuer normally must file the free-writing prospectus with the SEC no later than the first date it is used.

Posteffective Period. Once the SEC has reviewed and approved the registration statement and the waiting period is over, the registration is effective, and the *posteffective period* begins. The issuer can now offer and sell the securities without restrictions. If the company issued a preliminary or free-writing prospectus to investors, it must provide those investors with a final prospectus either before or at the time they purchase the securities. The issuer can require investors to download the final prospectus from a Web site if it notifies them of the appropriate Internet address.

Registration Process Review. To review the entire process, suppose that Delsey Corporation wants to make a public offering of its common stock. It files a registration statement and a prospectus with the SEC. On the same day, the company can make *offers* to sell the stock and start using a free-writing prospectus, but it cannot actually sell any of the stock. Delsey and its attorneys work with the SEC and provide additional information as requested for nearly six months. When the SEC finally indicates

---

10. The name *red herring* comes from the legend printed in red across the prospectus stating that the registration has been filed but has not become effective.
11. During the waiting period, the SEC also allows *road shows,* in which a corporate executive travels around speaking to institutional investors and securities analysts. In addition, electronic road shows are viewed via real-time communications methods, such as Web casting.
12. See SEC Rules 164 and 433. Note also companies that qualify as *well-known seasoned issuers* (see page 816) can even use a free-writing prospectus during the prefiling period.

that it has all the necessary information for the registration statement to be approved, Delsey can request that the twenty-day waiting period be accelerated. Only *after* the SEC declares the registration to be effective and the waiting period has elapsed or been accelerated can Delsey sell the first shares in the issue.

RESTRICTIONS RELAXED FOR WELL-KNOWN SEASONED ISSUERS In 2005, the SEC revised the registration process. The revisions created new categories of issuers based on size and presence in the market and provided a simplified registration process for large, experienced issuers.[13] The rules created new categories of issuers depending on their size and presence in the market and provided a simplified registration process for these issuers. The large, well-known securities firms that issue most securities have the greatest flexibility. A *well-known seasoned issuer* (WKSI) is a firm that has issued at least $1 billion in securities in the last three years or has at least $700 million of value of outstanding stock in the hands of the public. WKSIs can file registration statements the day they announce a new offering and are not required to wait for SEC review and approval. They can also use a free-writing prospectus at any time, even during the prefiling period.

Exempt Securities and Transactions

Certain types of securities are exempt from the registration requirements of the Securities Act of 1933. These securities—which generally can also be resold without being registered—are summarized in Exhibit 42–1 on the facing page under the heading "Exempt Securities."[14] The exhibit also lists and describes certain transactions that are exempt from registration requirements under various SEC regulations.

The transaction exemptions are the most important because they are very broad and can enable an issuer to avoid the high cost and complicated procedures associated with registration. Because the coverage of the exemptions overlaps somewhat, an offering may qualify for more than one. Therefore, many sales occur without registration. Even when a transaction is exempt from the registration requirements, the offering is still subject to the antifraud provisions of the 1933 act (as well as those of the 1934 act, to be discussed later in this chapter).

REGULATION A OFFERINGS An issuer's offering of up to $5 million in securities in any twelve-month period is exempt from registration.[15] Regulation A[16] provides a simplified registration process for issues of securities by small businesses (companies with annual revenues of less than $25 million). The issuer must file with the SEC a notice of the issue and an offering circular, which must also be provided to investors before the sale. This process is much less expensive than the procedures associated with full registration.

Companies are allowed to "test the waters" for potential interest before preparing the offering circular. To *test the waters* means to determine potential interest without actually selling any securities or requiring any commitment on the part of those who express interest. Small-business issuers can also use an integrated registration and reporting system that requires simpler forms than the full registration system.

Some companies have sold their securities via the Internet using Regulation A. In 1996, the Spring Street Brewing Company became the first company to sell securities via an online IPO. Spring Street raised about $1.6 million—without having to pay any commissions to brokers or underwriters. Such online IPOs are particularly attractive to small companies and start-up ventures that may find it difficult to raise capital from institutional investors or through underwriters. By making the offering online under Regulation A, the company can avoid both commissions and the costly and time-consuming filings required for a traditional IPO under federal and state law.

REGULATION D OFFERINGS The SEC's Regulation D contains several separate exemptions from registration requirements for limited offers (offers that either involve a small dollar amount or are made in a limited manner). Regulation D provides that any of these offerings made during any twelve-month period are exempt from the registration requirements.

Rule 504. Rule 504 is the exemption used by most small businesses. It provides that noninvestment company offerings up to $1 million in any twelve-month period are exempt.[17] Noninvestment

---

13. Securities Offering Reform, codified at 17 C.F.R. Sections 200, 228, 229, 230, 239, 240, 243, 249, and 274.

14. 15 U.S.C. Section 77c.

15. 15 U.S.C. Section 77c(b).

16. 17 C.F.R. Sections 230.251–230.263.

17. 17 C.F.R. Section 230.504. Small businesses in California may also be exempt under SEC Rule 1001. California's rule permits limited offerings of up to $5 million *per transaction,* if they satisfy the conditions of Section 25102(n) of the California Corporations Code. These offerings, however, can be made only to "qualified purchasers"—that is, knowledgeable, sophisticated investors.

EXHIBIT 42–1 • Exemptions for Securities Offerings under the 1933 Securities Act

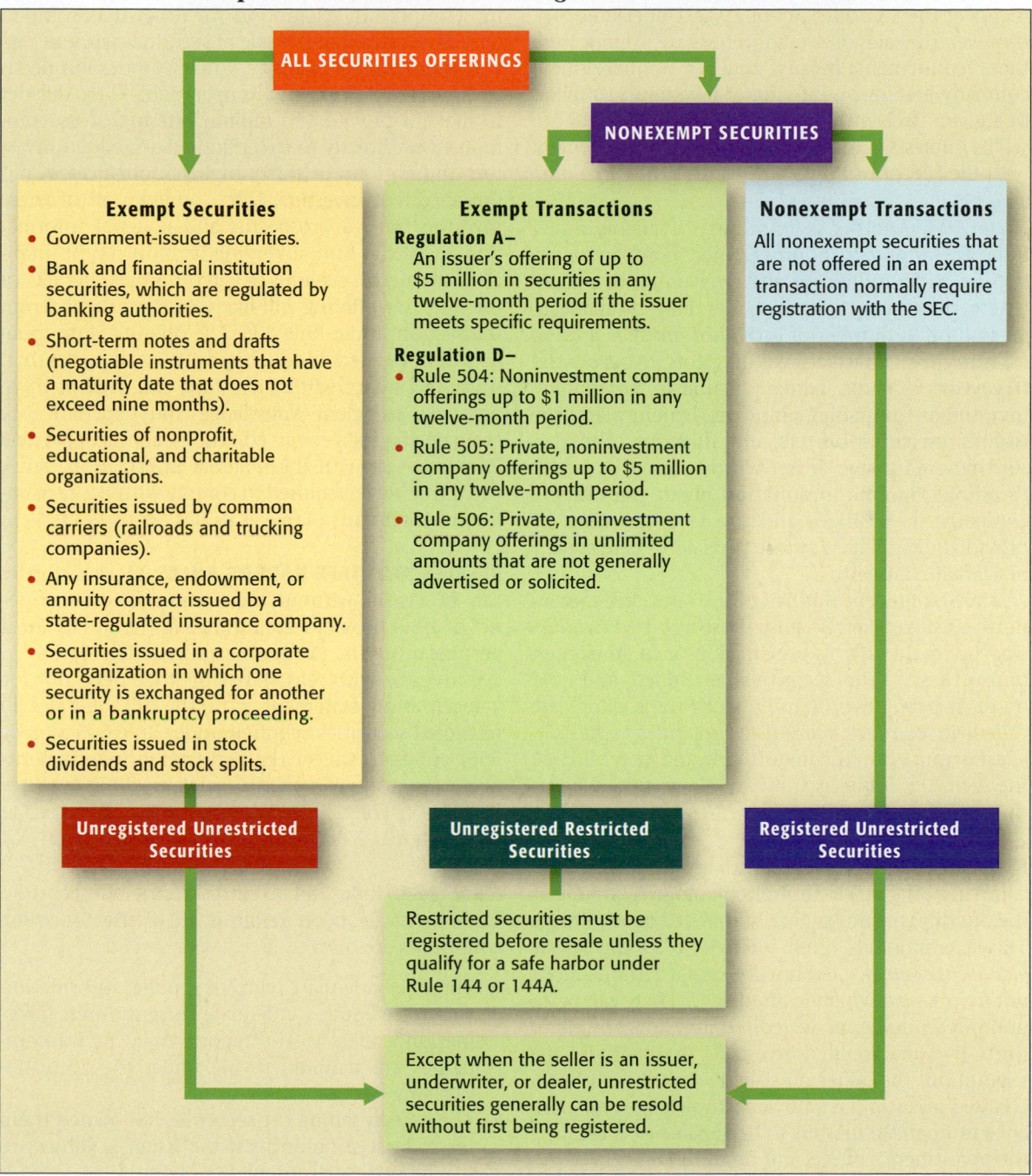

companies are firms that are not engaged primarily in the business of investing or trading in securities. (In contrast, an **investment company** is a firm that buys a large portfolio of securities and professionally manages it on behalf of many smaller shareholders/owners. A **mutual fund** is a well-known type of investment company.)

For example, Zeta Enterprises is a limited partnership that develops commercial property. Zeta intends to offer $600,000 of its limited partnership interests for sale between June 1 and next May 31. The buyers will become limited partners in Zeta. Because an interest in a limited partnership meets the definition of a security (discussed earlier in this chapter), its sale is subject to the registration and prospectus requirements of the Securities Act of 1933. Under Rule 504, however, the sales of Zeta's interests are exempt from these requirements because Zeta is a noninvestment company making an offering of less than $1 million in a given twelve-month period. Therefore, Zeta can sell its interests without filing a registration statement with the SEC or issuing a prospectus to any investor.

Rule 505. Another exemption is available under Rule 505 for private, noninvestment company offerings up to $5 million in any twelve-month period. Under this exemption, the offer may be made to an unlimited number of *accredited investors* and up to thirty-five unaccredited investors. **Accredited investors** include banks, insurance companies, investment companies, employee benefit plans, the issuer's executive officers and directors, and persons whose income or net worth exceeds a certain threshold. Specific information about the offering company, its business, and the securities must be provided to all buyers before the sale if there are *any* unaccredited investors.

The SEC must be notified of the sales, and precautions must be taken because these *restricted securities* may be resold only by registration or in an exempt transaction.[18] (The securities purchased and sold by most people who handle stock transactions are called, in contrast, *unrestricted securities*.) The purchasers must buy for investment and may not sell the securities for at least a year. No general solicitation or advertising is allowed.

Rule 506. Rule 506 exempts private, noninvestment company offerings in unlimited amounts, as long as the offerings are not generally solicited or advertised. This exemption is often referred to as the *private placement exemption* because it exempts "transactions not involving any public offering."[19] There can be an unlimited number of accredited investors and up to thirty-five unaccredited investors. To qualify for the exemption, the issuer must believe that each unaccredited investor has sufficient knowledge or experience in financial matters to be capable of evaluating the investment's merits and risks.[20]

The private placement exemption is perhaps the most important exemption for firms that want to raise funds through the sale of securities without registering them. For example, Citco Corporation needs to raise capital to expand its operations. Citco decides to make a private $10 million offering of its common stock directly to two hundred accredited investors and a group of thirty highly sophisticated, but unaccredited, investors. Citco provides all of these investors with a prospectus and material information about the firm, including its most recent financial statements. As long as Citco notifies the SEC of the sale, this offering will likely qualify as an exempt transaction under Rule 506. The offering is nonpublic and not generally advertised. There are fewer than thirty-five unaccredited investors, and each of them possesses sufficient knowledge and experience to evaluate the risks involved. The issuer has provided all purchasers with the material information. Thus, Citco will *not* be required to comply with the registration requirements of the Securities Act of 1933.

RESALES AND SAFE HARBOR RULES Most securities can be resold without registration. The Securities Act of 1933 provides exemptions for resales by most persons other than issuers or underwriters. The average investor who sells shares of stock need not file a registration statement with the SEC. Resales of restricted securities acquired under Rule 505 or Rule 506, however, trigger the registration requirements *unless the party selling them complies with Rule 144 or Rule 144A.* These rules are sometimes referred to as safe harbors.

Rule 144. Rule 144 exempts restricted securities from registration on resale if all of the following conditions are met:

1. There is adequate current public information about the issuer. ("Adequate current public information" refers to the reports that certain companies are required to file under the Securities Exchange Act of 1934.)
2. The person selling the securities has owned them for at least six months if the issuer is subject to the reporting requirements of the 1934 act.[21] If

---

18. Precautions to be taken against nonexempt, unregistered resales include asking the investor whether he or she is buying the securities for others; disclosing to each purchaser in writing, before the sale, that the securities are unregistered and thus cannot be resold, except in an exempt transaction, without first being registered; and indicating on the certificates that the securities are unregistered and restricted.
19. 15 U.S.C. Section 77d(2).
20. 17 C.F.R. Section 230.506.

---

21. Before 2008, when amendments to Rule 144 became effective, the holding period for restricted securities was one year if the issuer was subject to the reporting requirements of the 1934 act. See the revised SEC Rules and Regulations at 72 Federal Rules 71546-01, 2007 WL 4368599, Release No. 33-8869. This reduced holding period allows nonpublic issuers to raise capital electronically from private and overseas sources more quickly.

the issuer is not subject to the 1934 act's reporting requirements, the seller must have owned the securities for at least one year.

3. The securities are sold in certain limited amounts in unsolicited brokers' transactions.
4. The SEC is notified of the resale.[22]

Rule 144A. Securities that at the time of issue were not of the same class as securities listed on a national securities exchange or quoted in a U.S. automated interdealer quotation system may be resold under Rule 144A.[23] They may be sold only to a qualified institutional buyer (an institution, such as an insurance company or a bank, that owns and invests at least $100 million in securities). The seller must take reasonable steps to ensure that the buyer knows that the seller is relying on the exemption under Rule 144A. A sample restricted stock certificate is shown in Exhibit 42–2 below.

Violations of the 1933 Act

It is a violation of the Securities Act of 1933 to intentionally defraud investors by misrepresenting or omitting facts in a registration statement or prospectus. Liability is also imposed on those who

---

22. 17 C.F.R. Section 230.144.
23. 17 C.F.R. Section 230.144A.

are negligent in not discovering the fraud. Selling securities before the effective date of the registration statement or under an exemption for which the securities do not qualify results in liability.

CRIMINAL PENALTIES Criminal violations are prosecuted by the U.S. Department of Justice. Violators may be fined up to $10,000, imprisoned for up to five years, or both.

CIVIL SANCTIONS The SEC is authorized to impose civil sanctions against those who willfully violate the 1933 act. It can request an injunction to prevent further sales of the securities involved or ask a court to grant other relief, such as ordering a violator to refund profits.

Private parties who purchase securities and suffer harm as a result of false or omitted statements or other violations may bring a suit in a federal court to recover their losses and additional damages. If a registration statement or a prospectus contains material false statements or omissions, for example, damages may be recovered from those who signed the statement or those who provided information used in preparing the statement (such as accountants and other experts—see Chapter 48).

DEFENSES There are three basic defenses to charges of violations under the 1933 act. A defendant can

EXHIBIT 42–2 • **A Sample Restricted Stock Certificate**

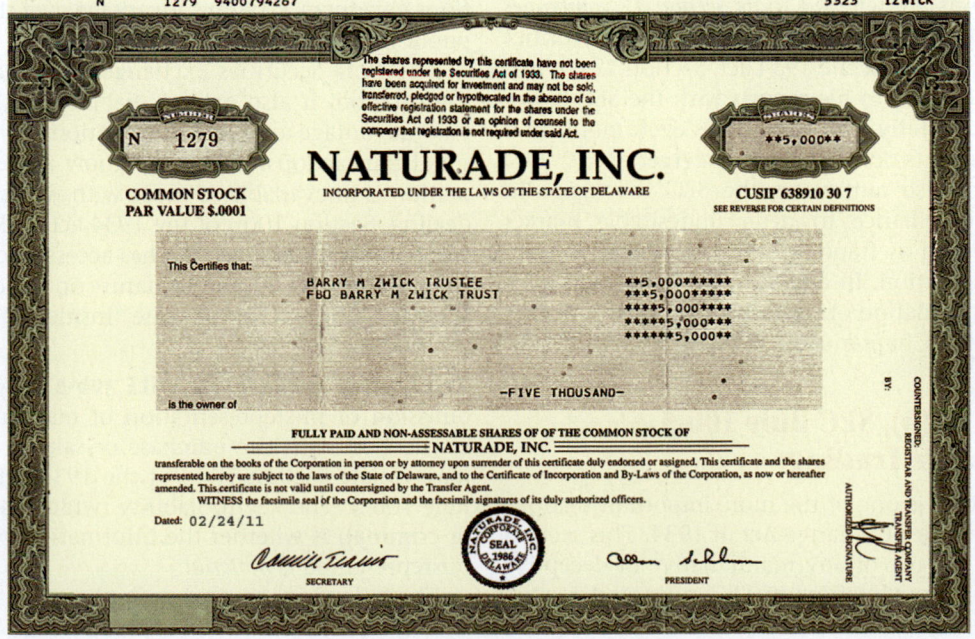

avoid liability by proving that (1) the statement or omission was not material, (2) the plaintiff knew about the misrepresentation at the time of purchasing the stock, or (3) the defendant exercised *due diligence* in preparing the registration and reasonably believed at the time that the statements were true.

The due diligence defense is the most important because it can be asserted by any defendant, except the issuer of the stock. The defendant must prove that she or he reasonably believed, at the time the registration statement became effective, that the statements in it were true and there were no omissions of material facts. (This defense will be discussed further in Chapter 48, in the context of the liability of accountants.)

SECTION 3
THE SECURITIES EXCHANGE ACT OF 1934

The Securities Exchange Act of 1934 provides for the regulation and registration of securities exchanges, brokers, dealers, and national securities associations, such as the National Association of Securities Dealers (NASD). Unlike the 1933 act, which is a one-time disclosure law, the 1934 act provides for continuous periodic disclosures by publicly held corporations to enable the SEC to regulate subsequent trading.

The Securities Exchange Act of 1934 applies to companies that have assets in excess of $10 million and five hundred or more shareholders. These corporations are referred to as *Section 12 companies* because they are required to register their securities under Section 12 of the 1934 act. Section 12 companies are required to file reports with the SEC annually and quarterly, and sometimes even monthly if specified events occur (such as a merger).

The act also authorizes the SEC to engage in market surveillance to deter undesirable market practices such as fraud, market manipulation, and misrepresentation. In addition, the act provides for the SEC's regulation of proxy solicitations for voting (discussed in Chapter 40).

Section 10(b), SEC Rule 10b-5, and Insider Trading

Section 10(b) is one of the more important sections of the Securities Exchange Act of 1934. This section prohibits the use of any manipulative or deceptive mechanism in violation of SEC rules and regulations. Among the rules that the SEC has promulgated

pursuant to the 1934 act is **SEC Rule 10b-5,** which prohibits the commission of fraud in connection with the purchase or sale of any security.

APPLICABILITY OF SEC RULE 10b-5 SEC Rule 10b-5 applies to almost all cases concerning the trading of securities, whether on organized exchanges, in over-the-counter markets, or in private transactions. Generally, the rule covers just about any form of security, including notes, bonds, agreements to form a corporation, and joint-venture agreements. The securities need not be registered under the 1933 act for the 1934 act to apply.

SEC Rule 10b-5 applies only when the requisites of federal jurisdiction—such as the use of stock exchange facilities or any means of interstate commerce—are present. Nevertheless, this requirement is easily met because almost every commercial transaction involves interstate contacts. In addition, the states have corporate securities laws, many of which include provisions similar to SEC Rule 10b-5.

INSIDER TRADING One of the major goals of Section 10(b) and SEC Rule 10b-5 is to prevent so-called **insider trading,** which occurs when persons buy or sell securities on the basis of information that is not available to the public. Corporate directors, officers, and others, such as majority shareholders, often have advance inside information that can affect the future market value of the corporate stock. Obviously, if they act on this information, their positions give them a trading advantage over the general public and other shareholders.

The 1934 Securities Exchange Act defines inside information. It also extends liability to those who take advantage of such information in their personal transactions when they know that the information is unavailable to those with whom they are dealing. Section 10(b) of the 1934 act and SEC Rule 10b-5 apply to anyone who has access to or receives information of a nonpublic nature on which trading is based—not just to corporate "insiders."

DISCLOSURE UNDER SEC RULE 10b-5 Any material omission or misrepresentation of material facts in connection with the purchase or sale of a security may violate Section 10(b) of the 1934 act and SEC Rule 10b-5. The key to liability (which can be civil or criminal) is whether the information omitted or misrepresented is *material*.

The following are some examples of material facts calling for disclosure under SEC Rule 10b-5:

1. Fraudulent trading in the company stock by a broker-dealer.
2. A dividend change (whether up or down).
3. A contract for the sale of corporate assets.
4. A new discovery, a new process, or a new product.
5. A significant change in the firm's financial condition.
6. Potential litigation against the company.

Note that any one of these facts, by itself, is not *automatically* considered material. Rather, it will be regarded as a material fact only if it is significant enough that it would likely affect an investor's decision as to whether to purchase or sell the company's securities.

For example, Sheen, Inc., is the defendant in a class-action product liability suit that its attorney, Paula Frasier, believes that the company will lose. Frasier has advised Sheen's directors, officers, and accountants that the company will likely have to pay a substantial damages award. Sheen plans to make a $5 million offering of newly issued stock before the date when the trial is expected to end. Sheen's potential liability and the financial consequences to the firm are material facts that must be disclosed because they are significant enough to affect an investor's decision as to whether to purchase the stock.

The case that follows is a landmark decision interpreting SEC Rule 10b-5. The SEC sued several of Texas Gulf Sulphur Company's directors, officers, and employees under SEC Rule 10b-5 after they purchased large amounts of the company's stock before the announcement of a rich ore discovery by the corporation. At issue was whether the ore discovery was a material fact that had to be disclosed under Rule 10b-5.

CASE 42.1
SEC v. Texas Gulf Sulphur Co.

United States Court of Appeals, Second Circuit, 401 F.2d 833 (1968).

BACKGROUND AND FACTS • Texas Gulf Sulphur Company (TGS) conducted aerial geophysical surveys over more than 15,000 square miles of eastern Canada. The operations indicated concentrations of commercially exploitable minerals. At one site near Timmins, Ontario, TGS drilled a hole that appeared to yield a core with an exceedingly high mineral content. TGS kept secret the results of the core sample. Officers and employees of the company made substantial purchases of TGS's stock or accepted stock options (rights to purchase stock) after learning of the ore discovery, even though further drilling was necessary to establish whether there was enough ore to be mined commercially. Several months later, TGS announced that the strike was expected to yield at least 25 million tons of ore. Subsequently, the price of TGS stock rose substantially. The Securities and Exchange Commission (SEC) brought a suit against the officers and employees of TGS for violating SEC Rule 10b-5. The officers and employees argued that the information on which they had traded had not been material at the time of their trades because the mine had not then been commercially proved. The trial court held that most of the defendants had not violated SEC Rule 10b-5, and the SEC appealed.

IN THE LANGUAGE OF THE COURT
WATERMAN, Circuit Judge.
* * * *
     * * * Whether facts are material within Rule 10b-5 when the facts relate to a particular event and are undisclosed by those persons who are knowledgeable thereof *will depend at any given time upon a balancing of both the indicated probability that the event will occur and the anticipated magnitude of the event in light of the totality of the company activity.* Here, * * * knowledge of the possibility, which surely was more than marginal, of the existence of a mine of the vast magnitude indicated by the remarkably rich drill core located rather close to the surface (suggesting mineability by the less expensive openpit method) within the confines of a large anomaly (suggesting an extensive region of mineralization) might well have affected the price of TGS stock and would certainly have been an important fact to a reasonable, if speculative, investor in deciding whether he should buy, sell, or hold. [Emphasis added.]
     * * * *

CASE CONTINUES ➡

CASE 42.1 CONTINUED ➡ * * * A major factor in determining whether the * * * discovery was a material fact is the importance attached to the drilling results by those who knew about it. * * * The timing by those who knew of it of their stock purchases * * *—purchases in some cases by individuals who had never before purchased * * * TGS stock—virtually compels the inference that the insiders were influenced by the drilling results.

DECISION AND REMEDY • *The appellate court ruled in favor of the SEC. All of the trading by insiders who knew of the mineral find before its true extent had been publicly announced violated SEC Rule 10b-5.*

IMPACT OF THIS CASE ON TODAY'S LAW • *This landmark case affirmed the principle that the test of whether information is "material," for SEC Rule 10b-5 purposes, is whether it would affect the judgment of reasonable investors. The corporate insiders' purchases of stock and stock options indicated that they were influenced by the drilling results and that the information about the drilling results was material. The courts continue to cite this case when applying SEC Rule 10b-5 to cases of alleged insider trading.*

WHAT IF THE FACTS WERE DIFFERENT? • *Suppose that further drilling had revealed that there was not enough ore at this site for it to be mined commercially. Would the defendants still have been liable for violating SEC Rule 10b-5? Why or why not?*

The Private Securities Litigation Reform Act.
One of the unintended effects of SEC Rule 10b-5 was to deter disclosure of forward-looking information. To understand why, consider an example. A company announces that its projected earnings in a certain time period will be $15 million. It turns out that the forecast is wrong. The earnings are in fact much lower, and the price of the company's stock is affected—negatively. The shareholders then bring a class-action suit against the company, alleging that the directors violated SEC Rule 10b-5 by disclosing misleading financial information.

In an attempt to rectify this problem and promote disclosure, Congress passed the Private Securities Litigation Reform Act (PSLRA) of 1995. Among other things, the PSLRA provides a "safe harbor" for publicly held companies that make forward-looking statements, such as financial forecasts. Those who make such statements are protected against liability for securities fraud as long as the statements are accompanied by "meaningful cautionary statements identifying important factors that could cause actual results to differ materially from those in the forward-looking statement."[24]

The Securities Litigation Uniform Standards Act.
After the PSLRA was passed, a number of class-action suits involving securities were filed in state courts to skirt its requirements. In response to this problem, Congress passed the Securities Litigation Uniform Standards Act (SLUSA) of 1998.[25] This act placed stringent limits on the ability of plaintiffs to bring class-action suits in state courts against firms whose securities are traded on national stock exchanges. The SLUSA not only prevents the purchasers and sellers of securities from bringing class-action fraud claims under state securities laws, but it also applies to investors who are fraudulently induced to hold on to their securities.[26]

OUTSIDERS AND SEC RULE 10b-5 The traditional insider-trading case involves true insiders—corporate officers, directors, and majority shareholders who have access to (and trade on) inside information. Increasingly, however, liability under Section 10(b) of the 1934 act and SEC Rule 10b-5 has been extended to include certain "outsiders"—those who trade on inside information acquired indirectly. Two theories have been developed under which outsiders may be held liable for insider trading: the *tipper/ tippee theory* and the *misappropriation theory*. In 2008, the United States Supreme Court heard a case in which the plaintiffs attempted to assert a third theory—*scheme liability*.

CASE IN POINT In 2000, management at the cable operator Charter Communications devised an accounting scheme that would artificially inflate its reported revenues. As part of the scheme, Charter's cable converter (set top) box suppliers, Scientific-Atlanta and Motorola, agreed to overcharge Charter for the cable boxes in exchange for additional advertising on Charter's cable network. A group

---

24. 15 U.S.C. Sections 77z-2, 78u-5.

25. Pub. L. No. 105-353. This act amended many sections of Title 15 of the *United States Code.*

26. *Merrill Lynch, Pierce, Fenner & Smith, Inc. v. Dabit,* 547 U.S. 71, 126 S.Ct. 1503, 164 L.Ed.2d 179 (2006).

of investors sued Scientific-Atlanta and Motorola, alleging violation of Section 10(b) of the Securities Exchange Act of 1934 and of SEC Rule 10b-5. The United States Supreme Court affirmed the dismissal of the suit, holding that Section 10(b)'s private right of action cannot be applied to suppliers or customers who seemingly "aid and abet" a scheme to show inflated sales revenues for a publicly traded company. The Court pointed out that the suppliers had no role in preparing or disseminating Charter's financial statements. The financial statements of both Scientific-Atlanta and Motorola were correct, and their deceptive acts were not communicated to the investing public. Consequently, the plaintiffs were unable to show reliance upon any of the actions of Scientific-Atlanta and Motorola "except in an indirect chain" that the Court found too remote to justify liability.[27]

Tipper/Tippee Theory. Anyone who acquires inside information as a result of a corporate insider's breach of his or her fiduciary duty can be liable under SEC Rule 10b-5. This liability extends to **tippees** (those who receive "tips" from insiders) and even remote tippees (tippees of tippees).

The key to liability under this theory is that the inside information must be obtained as a result of someone's breach of a fiduciary duty to the corporation whose shares are traded. The tippee is liable under this theory only if (1) there is a breach of a duty not to disclose inside information, (2) the disclosure is made in exchange for personal benefit, and (3) the tippee knows (or should know) of this breach and benefits from it.[28]

Misappropriation Theory. Liability for insider trading may also be established under the misappropriation theory. Under this theory, an individual who wrongfully obtains (misappropriates) inside information and trades on it for her or his personal gain is held liable because the individual stole information rightfully belonging to another.

The misappropriation theory has been controversial because it significantly extends the reach of SEC Rule 10b-5 to outsiders who ordinarily would not be deemed fiduciaries of the corporations in whose stock they trade. It is not always wrong to disclose material, nonpublic information about a company to a person who would not otherwise be privy to it. Nevertheless, a person who obtains the information and trades securities on it can be held liable.

CASE IN POINT Patricia Rocklage was the wife of Scott Rocklage, the chief executive officer of Cubist Pharmaceuticals, Inc. Scott had sometimes disclosed material, nonpublic information about Cubist to Patricia. She had always kept the information confidential. In 2001, however, when Scott told Patricia that one of Cubist's key drugs had failed its clinical trial, Patricia refused to keep the information secret. She warned her brother, William Beaver, who owned Cubist stock. Beaver sold his Cubist shares and tipped his friend David Jones, who sold his shares. When Cubist publicly announced the trial results, the price of its stock dropped. Beaver and Jones avoided significant losses by selling when they did. The SEC filed a lawsuit against Patricia, Beaver, and Jones. The defendants claimed that because Patricia had told her husband that she was going to tell her brother about the failed trial, they had not "misappropriated" the information. The court, however, determined that Patricia had "engaged in deceptive devices," because she had "tricked her husband into revealing confidential information to her so that she could, and did, assist her brother with the sale of his Cubist stock." The court therefore found all three defendants guilty of insider trading under the misappropriation theory.[29]

Insider Reporting and Trading—Section 16(b)

Section 16(b) of the 1934 act provides for the recapture by the corporation of all profits realized by certain insiders on any purchase and sale or sale and purchase of the corporation's stock within any six-month period. It is irrelevant whether the insider actually uses inside information; *all such short-swing profits must be returned to the corporation.* In this context, *insiders* means officers, directors, and large stockholders of Section 12 corporations (those owning 10 percent of the class of equity securities registered under Section 12 of the 1934 act).[30] To discourage such insiders from using nonpublic

---

27. *Stoneridge Investment Partners, LLC v. Scientific-Atlanta, Inc.,* 552 U.S. 148, 128 S.Ct. 761, 169 L.Ed.2d 627 (2008).

28. See, for example, *Chiarella v. United States,* 445 U.S. 222, 100 S.Ct. 1108, 63 L.Ed.2d 348 (1980); and *Dirks v. SEC,* 463 U.S. 646, 103 S.Ct. 3255, 77 L.Ed.2d 911 (1983).

29. *SEC v. Rocklage,* 470 F.3d 1 (1st Cir. 2006).

30. 15 U.S.C. Section 78*l*. Note that Section 403 of the Sarbanes-Oxley Act of 2002 shortened the reporting deadlines specified in Section 16(b).

information about their companies to their personal benefit in the stock market, they must file reports with the SEC concerning their ownership and trading of the corporation's securities.

Section 16(b) applies not only to stock but also to warrants, options, and securities convertible into stock. In addition, the courts have fashioned complex rules for determining profits. Note that the SEC exempts a number of transactions under Rule 16b-3.[31] For all of these reasons, corporate insiders should seek the advice of competent counsel before trading in the corporation's stock. Exhibit 42–3 below compares the effects of SEC Rule 10b-5 and Section 16(b).

Regulation of Proxy Statements

Section 14(a) of the Securities Exchange Act of 1934 regulates the solicitation of proxies (see Chapter 40) from shareholders of Section 12 companies. The SEC regulates the content of proxy statements. Whoever solicits a proxy must fully and accurately disclose in the proxy statement all of the facts that are pertinent to the matter on which the shareholders are to vote. SEC Rule 14a-9 is similar to the antifraud

---

31. 17 C.F.R. Section 240.16b-3.

provisions of SEC Rule 10b-5. Remedies for violations are extensive, ranging from injunctions to prevent a vote from being taken to monetary damages.

Violations of the 1934 Act

As mentioned earlier, violations of Section 10(b) of the Securities Exchange Act of 1934 and SEC Rule 10b-5, including insider trading, may lead to both criminal and civil liability. For either criminal or civil sanctions to be imposed, however, *scienter* must exist—that is, the violator must have had an intent to defraud or knowledge of his or her misconduct (see Chapter 14). *Scienter* can be proved if it is shown that the defendant made false statements or wrongfully failed to disclose material facts.

Violations of Section 16(b) include the sale by insiders of stock acquired less than six months before the time of sale (or less than six months after the sale, if selling short—that is, selling securities that one does not yet own). These violations are subject to civil sanctions. Liability under Section 16(b) is strict liability. Neither *scienter* nor negligence is required.

In the following case, the defendants were accused of securities fraud in violation of Section 10(b) and SEC Rule 10b-5. At issue was whether the defendants had acted with *scienter*.

EXHIBIT 42–3 • Comparison of Coverage, Application, and Liability under SEC Rule 10b-5 and Section 16(b)

AREA OF COMPARISON	SEC RULE 10b-5	SECTION 16(b)
What is the subject matter of the transaction?	Any security (does not have to be registered).	Any security (does not have to be registered).
What transactions are covered?	Purchase or sale.	Short-swing purchase and sale or short-swing sale and purchase.
Who is subject to liability?	Almost anyone with inside information under a duty to disclose—including officers, directors, controlling shareholders, and tippees.	Officers, directors, and certain shareholders who own 10 percent or more.
Is omission or misrepresentation necessary for liability?	Yes.	No.
Are there any exempt transactions?	No.	Yes, there are a number of exemptions.
Who may bring an action?	A person transacting with an insider, the SEC, or a purchaser or seller damaged by a wrongful act.	A corporation or a shareholder by derivative action.

⁂ EXTENDED CASE 42.2 ⁂
Gebhart v. SEC

United States Court of Appeals, Ninth Circuit, 595 F.3d 1034 (2010).
www.ca9.uscourts.gov/opinions[a]

IN THE LANGUAGE OF THE COURT

FISHER, Circuit Judge.

* * * *

In 1994, [Alvin Gebhart] began working at Mutual of New York (MONY) in San Diego, where he sold annuities and mutual funds. While at MONY, Gebhart met Jack Archer, a fellow MONY salesperson. In 1995, Archer told Gebhart about a business venture, Community Service Group (CSG), run by James Scovie. CSG was in the business of converting mobile home parks to resident ownership. CSG purchased parks from the owners and then assisted residents in purchasing them. In late 1996, Scovie and another person, David Mounier, created MHP Conversions, LLC (MHP), to facilitate the conversion process. MHP issued promissory notes that were sold to individual investors to raise funds for CSG's purchase of the parks. The MHP notes had one-year terms with fixed interest rates of 18 percent for new investments and 14 percent for reinvested funds. Each note stated that it would "ultimately be secured by a deed of trust" on the particular park to be purchased with the funds, but that "until such time as said deed of trust is recorded, the sole asset of [the issuer] will be a deed of trust for the property known as Eastern Trailer Park."

Archer told Gebhart about the MHP program, and * * * Gebhart arranged for Archer to make a presentation of the MHP program to three of his clients, all of whom made investments in the program.

In early 1996, Gebhart moved from MONY to another financial services firm, Mutual Service Corporation (MSC), a broker-dealer and member of the NASD [National Association of Securities Dealers]. His wife, Donna Gebhart, joined him at MSC, and the two opened and operated a MSC branch in Rancho Bernardo, California, where they sold insurance and annuities and provided financial planning services to clients. In October 1996, Archer approached the Gebharts about selling MHP notes to their MSC clients. * * * Archer told them that the MHP program had been approved by the compliance officer at Archer's firm, MONY. This was not true, however. Archer also told the Gebharts "that the parks were in good shape and he always assured us that they had a lot of equity in them * * * ."

The Gebharts conducted no independent investigation into the MHP program, either in 1996 or over the next four years, during which time they sold MHP [financial] notes to their clients. They failed to obtain any financial statements for CSG or MHP, ascertain who were the owners, officers, or shareholders of CSG or MHP, determine what compensation would be paid to CSG or MHP or their officers, verify that trust deeds securing the notes were being recorded, or obtain copies of recorded trust deeds. * * * Although the Gebharts believed that their clients' loans would be secured by second trust deeds, they did not inquire why they were not first trust deeds or who held the first trust deeds. In lieu of an independent investigation, the Gebharts relied on Archer's representations.

* * * *

Between the Gebharts' meeting with Archer in October 1996 and CSG's collapse in 2000, the Gebharts sold nearly $2.4 million in MHP promissory notes to 45 of their clients, earning about $105,000 in commission fees. The sales were based on several statements by the Gebharts that, it later became clear, were false. The Gebharts told their clients that the MHP notes were a proven investment that offered substantial returns and were secured by recorded deeds of trust. They said that in the worst case scenario their clients would be part owners of the mobile home parks and would be able to recover their investments. In fact, the trust deeds were not recorded and the parks were significantly over-encumbered [had excessive debt]. The Gebharts failed to disclose that their statements were based on information provided by Archer rather than their own, independent investigation.

* * * At the time of MHP's collapse [in 2000], the Gebharts' clients had over $1.5 million invested in outstanding MHP notes. MSC terminated the Gebharts' employment in August 2000.

As a result of these events, in 2002 the NASD's Department of Enforcement filed a complaint against the Gebharts for securities fraud. * * * A NASD hearing panel found that the Gebharts had acted in good faith and therefore rejected the fraud charges, but the NASD National Adjudicatory Council (NAC) reversed. The NAC found that the Gebharts had committed fraud, imposed a lifetime bar on Alvin Gebhart, and imposed a one-year suspension and a $15,000 fine on

---

a. Select the "Advanced Search" mode, enter "08-74943" in the "by Case No.:" box, and click on "Search." In the search results, click on the case title to access this opinion. The U.S. Court of Appeals for the Ninth Circuit maintains this Web site.

EXTENDED CASE CONTINUES ➡

EXTENDED CASE 42.2 CONTINUED →

Donna Gebhart. The SEC [Securities and Exchange Commission] upheld the NASD decision in 2006.

The Gebharts petitioned for review of the SEC decision.

* * * *

To establish a violation of Section 10(b) and Rule 10b-5, the SEC is required to "show that there has been a misstatement or omission of material fact, made with *scienter*." "The plaintiffs may establish *scienter* by proving either actual knowledge or recklessness."

* * * *

Scienter * * * *is a subjective inquiry. It turns on the defendant's actual state of mind. Thus, although we may consider the objective unreasonableness of the defendant's conduct to raise an inference of* scienter, *the ultimate question is whether the defendant knew his or her statements were false, or was consciously reckless as to their truth or falsity.* [Emphasis added.]

* * * *

The Gebharts contend that the SEC applied an erroneous *scienter* standard in this case by focusing exclusively on * * * objective

inquiry and disregarding evidence of subjective good faith. We disagree. The SEC considered all of the evidence bearing on the Gebharts' actual state of mind, including the Gebharts' extreme departure from ordinary standards of care, and found that the Gebharts were consciously aware of the risk that their statements were false. There was no error.

The SEC certainly considered the objective unreasonableness of the Gebharts' actions as *part* of its analysis. The SEC found that the Gebharts failed to perform any meaningful investigation into the MHP promissory notes—an extreme departure from ordinary standards of care that "created the substantial [and obvious] risk * * * that their representations were not true." The SEC found that the Gebharts "made no effort to investigate or understand why their clients were being sold second (and not first) deeds of trust; no effort to identify the first trust deed holders or the amounts of those outstanding trust deeds; and no effort to ensure their clients' investments were actually being secured by recorded trust deeds." The Gebharts made "no effort" to

corroborate [substantiate] Archer's representations that the parks were not overly encumbered.

The SEC properly considered the objective unreasonableness of the Gebharts' actions as some evidence supporting the inference that the Gebharts acted with *scienter*, but did not treat it as dispositive [a deciding factor]. The * * * [SEC] evaluated "the evidence the Gebharts put forward to demonstrate their good faith beliefs" as "part of the complete mix of facts bearing on an evaluation of their [actual] state of mind" and concluded that the "evidence from the Gebharts about their subjective belief [was] not sufficient to overcome" the inference of *scienter* created by the evidence as a whole. The Gebharts' assertions of good faith were "not plausible" and lacked "credibility." Based on the evidence as a whole, the SEC determined that the Gebharts "knew they had no direct knowledge of the truth or falsity" of their statements, and made their statements "despite not knowing whether they were true or false." The SEC correctly applied the appropriate *scienter* standard.

* * * *

PETITION DENIED.

QUESTIONS

1. At one point in the opinion (not included here), the court noted that "there is no evidence in the record that the Gebharts ever intended to defraud anyone." Why, then, did the court conclude that the Gebharts had acted with *scienter?*

2. According to the court, if the evidence before an agency is "susceptible to more than one rational interpretation," the court "may not substitute its judgment for that of the agency." Why do the courts show such deference to agency rulings?

CRIMINAL PENALTIES For violations of Section 10(b) and Rule 10b-5, an individual may be fined up to $5 million, imprisoned for up to twenty years, or both. A partnership or a corporation may be fined up to $25 million. Under Section 807 of the Sarbanes-Oxley Act of 2002, for a *willful* violation of the 1934 act the violator can be imprisoned for up to twenty-five years (in addition to being subject to a fine). For a defendant to be convicted in a criminal prosecution under the securities laws, there can be no reasonable doubt that the defendant knew he or she was acting wrongfully—a jury is not allowed

merely to speculate that the defendant may have acted willfully.

CASE IN POINT Martha Stewart, founder of a well-known media and homemaking empire, was once charged with intentionally deceiving investors based on statements she made at a conference. In December 2001, Stewart's stockbroker allegedly informed Stewart that the head of ImClone Systems, Inc., was selling his shares in that company. Stewart then sold her ImClone shares. The next day, ImClone announced that the Food and Drug Administration had failed to approve Erbitux, a greatly anticipated medication that the company had been developing. After the government began investigating Stewart's ImClone trades, she publicly stated at a Martha Stewart Living Omnimedia conference that she had previously instructed her stockbroker to sell her ImClone stock if the price fell to $60 per share. The government then filed a lawsuit, claiming that Stewart's statement showed she had the intent to deceive investors. The court, however, acquitted Stewart on this charge because "to find the essential element of criminal intent beyond a reasonable doubt, a rational juror would have to speculate."[32]

CIVIL SANCTIONS The SEC can also bring a civil action against anyone who violates or aids in a violation of the 1934 act or SEC rules by purchasing or selling a security while in the possession of material nonpublic information.[33] The violation must occur through the use of a national securities exchange or a broker or dealer.[34] The court may assess as a penalty as much as triple the profits gained or the loss

avoided by the guilty party.[35] The Insider Trading and Securities Fraud Enforcement Act of 1988 enlarged the class of persons who may be subject to civil liability for insider trading and gave the SEC authority to offer monetary rewards to informants.[36]

Private parties may also sue violators of Section 10(b) and Rule 10b-5. A private party may obtain rescission (cancellation) of a contract to buy securities or damages to the extent of the violator's illegal profits. Those found liable have a right to seek contribution from those who share responsibility for the violations, including accountants, attorneys, and corporations. (The liability of accountants and attorneys for violations of the securities laws is discussed in Chapter 48.) For violations of Section 16(b), a corporation can bring an action to recover the short-swing profits.

Recall from Chapter 14 that a required element of fraud is reliance. The innocent party must justifiably have relied on the misrepresentation. If an investor is aware of misrepresentations by corporate management and purchases shares in the firm anyway, can the investor still bring a lawsuit against the corporation for a violation of Rule 10b-5? That was the question in the following case.

---

32. *United States v. Stewart,* 305 F.Supp.2d 368 (S.D.N.Y. 2004). (Stewart was later convicted on other charges relating to her ImClone trading that did not require proof of intent.)
33. 15 U.S.C. Section 78u(d)(2)(A).
34. Transactions pursuant to a public offering by an issuer of securities are excepted.

35. 15 U.S.C. Section 78u(d)(2)(C).
36. 15 U.S.C. Section 78u-1.

CASE 42.3
Stark Trading v. Falconbridge, Ltd.

United States Court of Appeals, Seventh Circuit, 552 F.3d 568 (2009).
www.ca7.uscourts.gov[a]

COMPANY PROFILE • Brian Stark's interest in investing began in high school, when he worked for his father, an independent accountant. Together, they invested in the financial markets. Stark tested his own investment theories throughout college and law school, where he met Mike Roth. In 1992, Stark and Roth formed Stark Trading. Known today as Stark Investments, the firm invests in commodities, real estate, equity, and other markets. Its principals apply hedging and portfolio management techniques on behalf of their investors, including institutions, investment funds, and wealthy individuals. The firm has offices in cities around the world, including Hong Kong, London, Singapore, and Toronto.

BACKGROUND AND FACTS • Stark Trading was a minority shareholder in Falconbridge, Inc. Noranda, Inc., owned 59 percent of Falconbridge. Both were Canadian mining companies. Noranda offered its common stockholders preferred stock for their common stock. Noranda also offered to redeem the preferred stock for $25 per share, which exceeded the market value of the common stock. On the same day, Noranda offered minority shareholders in Falconbridge 1.77 shares of Noranda common stock for each share of Falconbridge common stock. Stark knew that Noranda's value was overstated in the offer to its common stockholders. Stark thought that the Falconbridge stock was

---

a. In the left-hand column, click on "Opinions." On that page, in the "Case Number:" boxes, type in "08" and "1327," and click on "List Case(s)." In the result, click on the appropriate link to access the opinion.

CASE CONTINUES ▶

CASE 42.3 CONTINUED ▶ undervalued in the market. This meant that Noranda was buying out Falconbridge's shareholders at a reduced price. Stark sent a letter explaining this to the Ontario Securities Commission. Nonetheless, Stark exchanged its Falconbridge shares for Noranda stock. Later, Noranda and Falconbridge merged to become Falconbridge, Ltd. Stark and others filed a suit in a federal district court against the new firm, alleging a violation of Rule 10b-5. The court dismissed the suit. The plaintiffs appealed.

IN THE LANGUAGE OF THE COURT
POSNER, Circuit Judge.
* * * *

   In a typical Rule 10b-5 case, the plaintiff buys stock at a price that he claims was inflated by misrepresentations by the corporation's management and sells his stock at a loss when the truth comes out and the price plummets. * * * [The plaintiffs] argue that * * * the offer to swap preferred stock in Noranda for common stock inflated the apparent value of Noranda stock, and therefore made the offer of Noranda stock for Falconbridge stock look generous. But they were not fooled. They knew that the tender offer undervalued Falconbridge— that Noranda was trying to buy out the minority shareholders (thus including the plaintiffs) cheap. [Emphasis added.]
   * * * *

   * * * We cannot find any basis for inferring that [the plaintiffs] relied on the defendants' [offer as a representation of the value] of Falconbridge. They knew better. They knew Falconbridge was worth a lot—that's why they invested. They thought the tender offer price was too low and that Noranda had resorted to fraud to make it succeed. They had known [when they bought their Falconbridge stock] they were buying into a company that had a majority shareholder, that it was a Canadian company, and therefore that a minority shareholder would not have the same legal protections (such as appraisal rights) that minority shareholders in U.S. corporations have. They also had to know that because they thought Falconbridge undervalued, so would Noranda, which would therefore try to buy out the minority shareholders before the market revalued Falconbridge upward. * * * And a week before the deadline for tendering their shares, the plaintiffs revealed in their letter to the [Canadian] securities commission the evidence that * * * Noranda [was] trying to pull a fast one on the minority shareholders.
   * * * *

   * * * Sophisticated investors, they must have considered the combination of the tender-offer price and a later suit (this suit) against the defendants a better deal than holding on to their shares and by doing so, and disseminating their doubts, trying to defeat the tender offer. That is not a strategy that the courts should reward in the name of rectifying securities fraud.

DECISION AND REMEDY • *The U.S. Court of Appeals for the Seventh Circuit upheld the lower court's decision. "So implausible is an inference of reliance from the complaint in this case * * * that the dismissal of the 10b-5 claim must be affirmed."*

THE GLOBAL DIMENSION • *Noranda and Falconbridge were Canadian companies. Falconbridge, Ltd., was later bought by Xstrata, a Swiss mining company. On what basis could a U.S. court exercise jurisdiction in this case?*

THE LEGAL ENVIRONMENT DIMENSION • *Stark's assessment of the value of Falconbridge proved correct. On the day the suit in this case was filed, the Noranda shares that Stark had received in exchange for its Falconbridge shares were worth about 50 percent more than what Stark had paid in accepting the offer. In other words, the plaintiffs could not allege that they had suffered a loss as a result of the trade. What effect does this fact have on their complaint?*

SECTION 4
STATE SECURITIES LAWS

Today, every state has its own corporate securities laws, or **blue sky laws,** that regulate the offer and sale of securities within its borders. (The phrase *blue sky laws* dates to a 1917 decision by the United States Supreme Court in which the Court declared that the purpose of such laws was to prevent "speculative schemes which have no more basis than so many feet of 'blue sky.'")[37] Article 8 of the Uniform

---

37. *Hall v. Geiger-Jones Co.,* 242 U.S. 539, 37 S.Ct. 217, 61 L.Ed. 480 (1917).

Commercial Code, which has been adopted by all of the states, also imposes various requirements relating to the purchase and sale of securities.

Requirements

Typically, state laws have disclosure requirements and antifraud provisions, many of which are patterned after Section 10(b) of the Securities Exchange Act of 1934 and SEC Rule 10b-5. State laws also provide for the registration of securities offered or issued for sale within the state and impose disclosure requirements. Methods of registration, required disclosures, and exemptions from registration vary among states. Unless an exemption from registration is applicable, issuers must register or qualify their stock with the appropriate state official, often called a *corporations commissioner.* Additionally, most state securities laws regulate securities brokers and dealers.

Concurrent Regulation

State securities laws apply mainly to intrastate transactions. Since the adoption of the 1933 and 1934 federal securities acts, the state and federal governments have regulated securities concurrently. Issuers must comply with both federal and state securities laws, and exemptions from federal law are not exemptions from state laws.

The dual federal and state system has not always worked well, particularly during the early 1990s, when the securities markets underwent considerable expansion. In response, Congress passed the National Securities Markets Improvement Act of 1996, which eliminated some of the duplicate regulations and gave the SEC exclusive power to regulate most national securities activities. The National Conference of Commissioners on Uniform State Laws then substantially revised the Uniform Securities Act to coordinate state and federal securities regulation and enforcement efforts. The new version was offered to the states for adoption in 2002. Seventeen states have adopted the Uniform Securities Act.[38]

---

38. At the time this book went to press, the Uniform Securities Act had been adopted in Georgia, Hawaii, Idaho, Indiana, Iowa, Kansas, Maine, Michigan, Minnesota, Mississippi, Missouri, New Mexico, Oklahoma, South Carolina, South Dakota, Vermont, and Wisconsin, as well as in the U.S. Virgin Islands. You can find current information on state adoptions at www. nccusl.org.

SECTION 5
CORPORATE GOVERNANCE

Corporate governance can be narrowly defined as the relationship between a corporation and its shareholders. According to a broader definition, corporate governance specifies the rights and responsibilities among different corporate participants (including stakeholders) and spells out the rules and procedures for making decisions on corporate affairs. Regardless of the way it is defined, effective corporate governance requires more than just compliance with laws and regulations.

Because corporate ownership (by shareholders) is separated from corporate control (by officers and managers), effective corporate governance is essential in large corporations. Otherwise, officers and managers may be able to advance their own interests at the expense of the shareholders. The well-publicized corporate scandals in the early 2000s clearly illustrate the reasons for concern about managerial opportunism. Indeed, corporate governance has become an issue of concern for corporate entities around the world. With the globalization of business, a corporation's bad acts (or lack of control systems) can have far-reaching consequences.

Attempts at Aligning the Interests of Officers with Those of Shareholders

Some corporations have sought to align the financial interests of their officers with those of the company's shareholders by providing the officers with **stock options,** which enable them to purchase shares of the corporation's stock at a set price. When the market price rises above that level, the officers can sell their shares for a profit. Because a stock's market price generally increases as the corporation prospers, the options give the officers a financial stake in the corporation's well-being and supposedly encourage them to work hard for the benefit of the shareholders.

Options have turned out to be an imperfect device for providing effective governance, however. Executives in some companies have "cooked" the company's books in order to keep share prices high so that they could sell their stock for a profit. Executives in other firms have had their options "repriced" so that they did not suffer any loss when the share price declined (and so that they could still profit from future increases above the lowered share price). Thus, although stock options theoretically can motivate officers to protect shareholder interests, stock option plans have sometimes become a way for officers to take advantage of shareholders.

The Goal Is to Promote Accountability

Effective corporate governance standards are designed to address problems such as those briefly discussed above and to motivate officers to make decisions that promote the financial interests of the company's shareholders. Generally, corporate governance entails corporate decision-making structures that monitor employees (particularly officers) to ensure that they are acting for the benefit of the shareholders. Thus, corporate governance involves, at a minimum:

1. The audited reporting of financial conditions at the corporation so that managers can be evaluated.
2. Legal protections for shareholders so that violators of the law who attempt to take advantage of shareholders can be punished for misbehavior and victims can recover damages for any associated losses.

Effective corporate governance can have considerable practical significance because corporate decision makers necessarily become more accountable for their actions to shareholders. Firms that are more accountable to shareholders typically report higher profits, higher sales growth, higher firm value, and other economic advantages. Thus, a corporation with better corporate governance and greater accountability to investors may also have a higher valuation than a corporation that is less concerned about governance.

Governance and Corporate Law

State corporation statutes set up the legal framework for corporate governance. Under the corporate law of Delaware, where most major companies incorporate, all corporations must have certain structures of corporate governance in place. The most important structure, of course, is the board of directors because the board makes the major decisions about the future of the corporation.

Some argue that shareholder democracy is the key to improving corporate governance. If shareholders could have more say on major corporate decisions, they presumably could have more control over the corporation. Essential to shareholder democracy is the election of the board of directors, usually at the corporation's annual meeting.

Although shareholders vote for directors, they often find it difficult to elect their nominees because organizing enough shareholders to sway an election can be very costly. In 2010, the SEC announced that it would work to modernize shareholder voting and proxy rules to reduce these costs and give shareholders direct access to other shareholders through the company's facilities for communicating with shareholders. The SEC's goal is to make the contest more even between the shareholders' candidates and the company's nominees.

THE BOARD OF DIRECTORS Under corporate law, a corporation must have a board of directors elected by the shareholders. Almost anyone can become a director, though some organizations, such as the New York Stock Exchange, require certain standards of service for directors of their listed corporations.

Directors are responsible for ensuring that the corporation's officers are operating wisely and in the exclusive interest of shareholders. Directors receive reports from the officers and give them managerial directions. In reality, though, corporate directors devote a relatively small amount of time to monitoring officers.

Ideally, shareholders would monitor the directors' supervision of the officers. In practice, however, it can be difficult for shareholders to monitor directors and hold them responsible for corporate failings. Although the directors can be sued if they fail to do their jobs effectively, directors are rarely held personally liable.

THE COMPENSATION COMMITTEE An important committee of the board of directors, mentioned in Chapter 40, is the *compensation committee,* which determines the compensation to be paid to the company's officers. As part of this process, the committee must assess the officers' performance and design a compensation system that will best align the officers' interests with those of the shareholders.

The Sarbanes-Oxley Act of 2002

As discussed in Chapter 5, in 2002, following a series of corporate scandals, Congress passed the Sarbanes-Oxley Act (see Appendix H for excerpts and explanatory comments). The act addresses certain issues relating to corporate governance. Generally, the act attempts to increase corporate accountability by imposing strict disclosure requirements and harsh penalties for violations of securities laws. Among other things, the act requires chief corporate executives to take personal responsibility for the accuracy of financial statements and reports that are filed with the SEC.

REPORTING ON EFFECTIVENESS OF INTERNAL CONTROLS The Sarbanes-Oxley Act requires all public companies to assess the effectiveness of their internal controls over financial reporting and to comply with certain procedures. Although the 2002 act initially required all public companies to have an independent auditor file a report with the SEC on management's assessment of internal controls, Congress enacted an exemption for smaller companies in 2010. In an effort to reduce compliance costs, public companies with a market capitalization, or public float, of less than $75 million no longer need to have an auditor report on management's assessment of internal controls.

OTHER PROVISIONS Additionally, the act requires that certain financial and stock-transaction reports be filed with the SEC earlier than was required under the previous rules. The act also created a new entity, called the Public Company Accounting Oversight Board, which regulates and oversees public accounting firms. Other provisions of the act established new private civil actions and expanded the SEC's remedies in administrative and civil actions.

Because of the importance of this act, we present some of its key provisions relating to corporate accountability in Exhibit 42–4 on the following page. (Provisions of the act that relate to public accounting firms and accounting practices will be discussed in Chapter 48, in the context of the liability of accountants.)

INTERNAL CONTROLS AND ACCOUNTABILITY The Sarbanes-Oxley Act includes some traditional securities law provisions but also introduces direct *federal* corporate governance requirements for public companies (companies whose shares are traded in the public securities markets). The law addresses many of the corporate governance procedures just discussed and creates new requirements in an attempt to make the system work more effectively. The requirements deal with independent monitoring of company officers by both the board of directors and the auditors.

Sections 302 and 404 of the act require high-level managers (the most senior officers) to establish and maintain an effective system of internal controls. Moreover, senior management must reassess the system's effectiveness on an annual basis. Some companies already had strong and effective internal

control systems in place before the passage of the act, but others had to take expensive steps to bring their internal controls up to the new federal standards. These include "disclosure controls and procedures" to ensure that the company's financial reports are accurate and timely. Assessment must involve documenting financial results and accounting policies before reporting the results. After the act was passed, hundreds of publicly held companies reported that they had identified and corrected shortcomings in their internal control systems.

CERTIFICATION AND MONITORING Section 906 requires that chief executive officers and chief financial officers certify the accuracy of the information in the corporate financial statements. These corporate officers are subject to both civil and criminal penalties for violations of this section. This requirement makes the officers directly accountable for the accuracy of their financial reporting and precludes any "ignorance defense" if shortcomings are later discovered.

The Sarbanes-Oxley Act also includes requirements to improve directors' monitoring of officers' activities. All members of the corporate audit committee for public companies must be outside directors. The New York Stock Exchange has a similar rule that also extends to the board's compensation committee. The audit committee must have a written charter that sets out its duties and provides for performance appraisal. At least one "financial expert" must serve on the audit committee, which must hold executive meetings without company officers being present. The audit committee must also establish procedures to encourage whistleblowers (see Chapter 34) to report violations. In addition to reviewing the internal controls, the committee also monitors the actions of the outside auditor.

SECTION 6

ONLINE SECURITIES FRAUD

A major problem facing the SEC today is how to enforce the antifraud provisions of the securities laws in the online environment. In 1999, in the first cases involving illegal online securities offerings, the SEC filed suit against three individuals for illegally offering securities on an Internet auction site.[39] In

---

39. *In re Davis,* SEC Administrative File No. 3-10080 (October 20, 1999); *In re Haas,* SEC Administrative File No. 3-10081 (October 20, 1999); and *In re Sitaras,* SEC Administrative File No. 3-10082 (October 20, 1999).

EXHIBIT 42–4 • **Some Key Provisions of the Sarbanes-Oxley Act of 2002 Relating to Corporate Accountability**

Certification Requirements: Under Section 906 of the Sarbanes-Oxley Act, the chief executive officers (CEOs) and chief financial officers (CFOs) of most major companies listed on public stock exchanges must certify financial statements that are filed with the SEC. CEOs and CFOs have to certify that filed financial reports "fully comply" with SEC requirements and that all of the information reported "fairly represents in all material respects, the financial conditions and results of operations of the issuer."

Under Section 302 of the act, CEOs and CFOs of reporting companies are required to certify that a signing officer reviewed each quarterly and annual filing with the SEC and that it contains no untrue statements of material fact. Also, the signing officer or officers must certify that they have established an internal control system to identify all material information and that any deficiencies in the system were disclosed to the auditors.

Effectiveness of Internal Controls on Financial Reporting: Under Section 404(a), all public companies are required to assess the effectiveness of their internal controls over financial reporting. Section 404(b) requires independent auditors to report on management's assessment of internal controls, but companies with a public float of less than $75 million are exempted from this requirement.

Loans to Directors and Officers: Section 402 prohibits any reporting company, as well as any private company that is filing an initial public offering, from making personal loans to directors and executive officers (with a few limited exceptions, such as for certain consumer and housing loans).

Protection for Whistleblowers: Section 806 protects "whistleblowers"—employees who report ("blow the whistle" on) securities violations by their employers—from being fired or in any way discriminated against by their employers.

Blackout Periods: Section 306 prohibits certain types of securities transactions during "blackout periods"—periods during which the issuer's ability to purchase, sell, or otherwise transfer funds in individual account plans (such as pension funds) is suspended.

Enhanced Penalties for:

- *Violations of Section 906 Certification Requirements*—A CEO or CFO who certifies a financial report or statement filed with the SEC knowing that the report or statement does not fulfill all of the requirements of Section 906 will be subject to criminal penalties of up to $1 million in fines, ten years in prison, or both. *Willful* violators of the certification requirements may be subject to $5 million in fines, twenty years in prison, or both.

- *Violations of the Securities Exchange Act of 1934*—Penalties for securities fraud under the 1934 act were also increased (as discussed earlier in this chapter). Individual violators may be fined up to $5 million, imprisoned for up to twenty years, or both.   violators may be imprisoned for up to twenty-five years in addition to being fined.

- *Destruction or Alteration of Documents*—Anyone who alters, destroys, or conceals documents or otherwise obstructs any official proceeding will be subject to fines, imprisonment for up to twenty years, or both.

- *Other Forms of White-Collar Crime*—The act stiffened the penalties for certain criminal violations, such as federal mail and wire fraud, and ordered the U.S. Sentencing Commission to revise the sentencing guidelines for white-collar crimes (see Chapter 9).

Statute of Limitations for Securities Fraud: Section 804 provides that a private right of action for securities fraud may be brought no later than two years after the discovery of the violation or five years after the violation, whichever is earlier.

essence, all three indicated that their companies would soon go public and attempted to sell unregistered securities via the Web auction site. All of these actions were in violation of Sections 5, 17(a)(1), and 17(a)(3) of the 1933 Securities Act. Since then, the SEC has brought a variety of Internet-related fraud cases and regularly issues interpretive releases to explain how securities laws apply in the online environment.

Investment Scams

As discussed in Chapter 9, the Internet has created a new vehicle for criminals to use to commit fraud and provided them with new ways of targeting innocent investors. The criminally inclined can use spam, online newsletters and bulletin boards, chat rooms, blogs, and tweets to spread false information and perpetrate fraud. For a relatively small cost, criminals can even build sophisticated Web pages to facilitate their investment scams.

Investment scams come in countless variations, but they almost always promise spectacular returns for small investments. A person might receive spam e-mail, for example, that falsely claims that a home business can "turn $5 into $60,000 in just three to six weeks." Another popular investment scam claims "a stimulus package has arrived" and promises individuals that they can make $100,000 a year using their home computer. Although most people today are dubious of the bogus claims made in spam messages, such offers can appear more attractive during times of economic recession. Often, investment scams are simply the electronic version of pyramid schemes in which the participants attempt to profit solely by recruiting new participants.

Online Investment Newsletters and Forums

Hundreds of online investment newsletters provide free information on stocks. Legitimate online newsletters can help investors gather valuable information, but some online newsletters are used for fraud. The law allows companies to pay people who write these newsletters to tout their securities, but the newsletters are required to disclose who paid for the advertising. Many fraudsters either fail to disclose or lie about who paid them. Thus, an investor reading an online newsletter may believe that the information is unbiased, when in fact the fraudsters will directly profit by convincing investors to buy or sell particular stocks.

The same deceptive tactics can be used on online bulletin boards (such as newsgroups and usenet groups), blogs, and social networking sites, including Twitter. While hiding their true identity, fraudsters may falsely pump up a company or reveal some "inside" information about a new product or lucrative contract to convince people to invest. By using multiple aliases on an online forum, a single person can easily create the illusion of widespread interest in a small stock.

Ponzi Schemes

In recent years, the SEC has filed an increasing number of enforcement actions against perpetrators of Ponzi schemes. In these scams, named after Charles Ponzi, the swindler promises high returns to investors and then uses their funds to pay previous investors. Ponzi schemes sometimes target U.S. residents and convince them to invest in offshore companies or banks. Other times, Ponzi schemes claim to offer risk-free or low-risk investments to lure investors.

CASE IN POINT Michael C. Regan told investors that he had an MBA and a proven track record of successful securities trading. As evidence, he offered fake financial statements and tax returns that showed high account balances. In reality, Regan did not have an MBA, was not a registered investment adviser, and had not traded any securities for several years. Regan promised investors returns averaging 20 percent with minimal risk and claimed to be using an investment strategy based on "short-term price trends." He used less than half of the funds entrusted to him for trading purposes and spent at least $2.4 million for his personal and family expenses. In 2009, the SEC filed a complaint alleging that Regan had engaged in a multimillion-dollar Ponzi scheme. Regan agreed to settle the case and return more than $8.7 million (plus interest) of the wrongfully acquired funds.[40]

---

40. "SEC Charges Investment Adviser in Multi-Million Dollar Ponzi Scheme." Litigation Release No. 21102. *www.sec.gov*. 24 June 2009: n. p. Web.

REVIEWING
Securities Law and Corporate Governance

Dale Emerson served as the chief financial officer for Reliant Electric Co., a distributor of electricity serving portions of Montana and North Dakota. Reliant was in the final stages of planning a takeover of Dakota Gasworks, Inc., a natural gas distributor that operated solely within North Dakota. Emerson went on a weekend fishing trip with his uncle, Ernest Wallace. Emerson mentioned to Wallace that he had been putting in a lot of extra hours at the office planning a takeover of Dakota Gasworks. When he returned from the fishing trip, Wallace purchased $20,000 worth of Reliant stock. Three weeks later, Reliant made a tender offer to Dakota Gasworks stockholders and purchased 57 percent of Dakota Gasworks stock. Over the next two weeks, the price of Reliant stock rose 72 percent before leveling out. Wallace then sold his Reliant stock for a gross profit of $14,400. Using the information presented in the chapter, answer the following questions.

REVIEWING CONTINUES ➡

REVIEWING

Securities Law and Corporate Governance, Continued

1. Would registration with the SEC be required for Dakota Gasworks securities? Why or why not?
2. Did Emerson violate Section 10(b) of the Securities Exchange Act of 1934 and SEC Rule 10b-5? Why or why not?
3. What theory or theories might a court use to hold Wallace liable for insider trading?
4. Under the Sarbanes-Oxley Act of 2002, who would be required to certify the accuracy of the financial statements Reliant filed with the SEC?

DEBATE THIS: *Insider trading should be legalized.*

TERMS AND CONCEPTS

	corporate governance 829	investment contract 814	SEC Rule 10b-5 820
	free-writing prospectus 815	mutual fund 817	stock option 829
accredited investor 818	insider trading 820	prospectus 814	tippee 823
blue sky laws 828	investment company 817	red herring prospectus 815	tombstone ad 815

QUESTIONS AND CASE PROBLEMS

42–1. Registration Requirements Estrada Hermanos, Inc., a corporation incorporated and doing business in Florida, decides to sell $1 million worth of its common stock to the public. The stock will be sold only within the state of Florida. José Estrada, the chair of the board, says the offering need not be registered with the Securities and Exchange Commission. His brother, Gustavo, disagrees. Who is right? Explain.

42–2. QUESTION WITH SAMPLE ANSWER: Registration Requirements.

Huron Corp. has 300,000 common shares outstanding. The owners of these outstanding shares live in several different states. Huron has decided to split the 300,000 shares two for one. Will Huron Corp. have to file a registration statement and prospectus on the 300,000 new shares to be issued as a result of the split? Explain.

- **For a sample answer to Question 42–2, go to Appendix I at the end of this text.**

42–3. Insider Trading David Gain was the chief executive officer (CEO) of Forest Media Corp., which became interested in acquiring RS Communications, Inc., in 2010.

To initiate negotiations, Gain met with RS's CEO, Gill Raz, on Friday, July 12. Two days later, Gain phoned his brother Mark, who bought 3,800 shares of RS stock on the following Monday. Mark discussed the deal with their father, Jordan, who bought 20,000 RS shares on Thursday. On July 25, the day before the RS bid was due, Gain phoned his parents' home, and Mark bought another 3,200 RS shares. The same routine was followed over the next few days, with Gain periodically phoning Mark or Jordan, both of whom continued to buy RS shares. Forest's bid was refused, but on August 5, RS announced its merger with another company. The price of RS stock rose 30 percent, increasing the value of Mark and Jordan's shares by $664,024 and $412,875, respectively. Did Gain engage in insider trading? What is required to impose sanctions for this offense? Could a court hold Gain liable? Why or why not?

42–4. Securities Laws In 1997, WTS Transnational, Inc., required financing to develop a prototype of an unpatented fingerprint-verification system. At the time, WTS had no revenue, $655,000 in liabilities, and only $10,000 in assets. Thomas Cavanagh and Frank Nicolois, who operated an investment banking company called U.S. Milestone (USM), arranged the financing using Curbstone Acquisition Corp. Curbstone had no assets but had registered approximately 3.5 million shares of stock with the Securities and Exchange Commission (SEC). Under the terms of the deal, Curbstone acquired WTS, and the resulting entity was named Electro-Optical Systems Corp. (EOSC). New EOSC shares were issued to all of the WTS shareholders. Only Cavanagh and others affiliated with USM could sell EOSC stock to the public, however. Over the next few months, these individuals issued false press releases, made small deceptive purchases of EOSC shares at high prices, distributed hundreds of thousands of shares to friends and relatives, and sold their own shares at inflated prices through third party companies they owned. When the SEC began to investigate, the share price fell to its actual value, and innocent investors lost more than $15 million. Were any securities laws violated in this case? If so, what might be an appropriate remedy? [*SEC v. Cavanagh*, 445 F.3d 105 (2d Cir. 2006)]

42–5. Securities Trading Between 1994 and 1998, Richard Svoboda, a credit officer for NationsBank N.A., in Dallas, Texas, evaluated and approved his employer's extensions of credit to clients. These responsibilities gave Svoboda access to nonpublic information about the clients' earnings, performance, acquisitions, and business plans in confidential memos, e-mail, credit applications, and other sources. Svoboda devised a scheme with Michael Robles, an independent accountant, to use this information to trade securities. Pursuant to their scheme, Robles traded in the securities of more than twenty different companies and profited by more than $1 million. Despite their agreement that Robles would do all of the trading, Svoboda also executed trades on his own and made profits of more than $200,000. Aware that their scheme violated NationsBank's policy, they attempted to conduct their trades so as to avoid suspicion. When NationsBank questioned Svoboda about his actions, he lied, refused to cooperate, and was fired. Did Svoboda or Robles commit any crimes? Is either of them subject to civil liability? If so, who could file a suit, and on what ground? What are the possible sanctions? What might be a defense? How should a court rule? Discuss. [*SEC v. Svoboda*, 409 F.Supp.2d 331 (S.D.N.Y. 2006)]

42–6. CASE PROBLEM WITH SAMPLE ANSWER: Duty to Disclose.

Orphan Medical, Inc., was a pharmaceutical company that focused on central nervous system disorders. Its major product was the drug Xyrem. In June 2004, Orphan merged with Jazz Pharmaceuticals, Inc., and Orphan shareholders received $10.75 per share for their stock. Before the merger was final, Orphan completed a phase of testing of Xyrem that indicated that the Food and Drug Administration (FDA) would allow the drug to proceed to the next stage of testing, which was necessary for the drug to be more widely marketed. If that happened, the value of the drug and Orphan would increase, and the stock would have been worth more than $10.75. Little Gem Life Sciences, LLC, was an Orphan shareholder that had received $10.75 per share for its stock. It sued,

claiming violations of federal securities laws because shareholders were not told, during the merger process, that the current stage of FDA tests had been successful. Little Gem claimed that if the information had been public, the stock price would have been higher. The federal district court dismissed the suit, holding that it did not meet the standards required by the Private Securities Litigation Reform Act. Little Gem appealed. Did Orphan's directors have a duty to reveal all relevant drug-testing information to shareholders? Why or why not? [*Little Gem Life Sciences LLC v. Orphan Medical, Inc., 537 F.3d 913 (8th Cir. 2008)*]

• **To view a sample answer for Problem 42–6, go to this book's Web site at www.cengage.com/blaw/clarkson, select "Chapter 42," and click on "Case Problem with Sample Answer."**

42–7. Violations of the 1934 Act To comply with accounting principles, a company that engages in software development must either "expense" the cost (record it immediately on the company's financial statement) or "capitalize" it (record it as a cost incurred in increments over time). If the project is in the pre- or post-development stage, the cost must be expensed. Otherwise it may be capitalized. Capitalizing a cost makes a company look more profitable in the short term. Digimarc Corp., which provides secure personal identification documents, announced that it had improperly capitalized software development costs over at least the previous eighteen months. The errors resulted in $2.7 million in overstated earnings, requiring a restatement of prior financial statements. Zucco Partners, LLC, which had bought Digimarc stock within the relevant period, filed a suit in a federal district court against the firm. Zucco claimed that it could show that there had been disagreements within Digimarc over its accounting. Is this sufficient to establish a violation of SEC Rule 10b-5? Why or why not? [*Zucco Partners, LLC v. Digimarc Corp.*, 552 F.3d 981 (9th Cir. 2009)]

42–8. Insider Trading Jabil Circuit, Inc., is a publicly traded electronics and technology company headquartered in St. Petersburg, Florida. In 2008, a group of shareholders who had owned Jabil stock from 2001 to 2007 sued the company and its auditors, directors, and officers for insider trading. Stock options were a part of Jabil's compensation for executives. In some situations, stock options were backdated to a point in time when the stock price was lower, making the options worth more to certain company executives. Backdating is legal as long as it is reported, but Jabil did not report the fact that backdating had occurred. Thus, expenses were understated and net income was overstated by millions of dollars. The shareholders claimed that by rigging the value of the stock options by backdating, the executives had engaged in insider trading and that there had been a general practice among the executives of selling stock before unfavorable news about the company was reported to the public. The shareholders, however, had no specific information about these stock trades or about when (or even if) a particular executive was aware of any accounting errors during the time of any backdating purchases. Were the shareholders' allegations sufficient to assert that insider trading had occurred under SEC Rule 10b-5? Why or why not? [*Edward J. Goodman Life Income Trust v. Jabil Circuit, Inc.,* 594 F.3d 783 (11th Cir. 2010)]

42–9. A QUESTION OF ETHICS: Violations of the 1934 Act.

 Melvin Lyttle told John Montana and Paul Knight about a "Trading Program" that purportedly would buy and sell securities in deals that were fully insured, as well as monitored and controlled by the Federal Reserve. Without checking the details or even verifying whether the Program existed, Montana and Knight, with Lyttle's help, began to sell interests in the Program to investors. For a minimum investment of $1 million, the investors were promised extraordinary rates of return—from 10 percent to as much as 100 percent per week—without risk. They were told, among other things, that the Program would "utilize banks that can ensure full bank integrity of The Transaction whose undertaking[s] are in complete harmony with international banking rules and protocol and who guarantee maximum security of a Funder's Capital Placement Amount." Nothing was required but the investors' funds and their silence—the Program was to be kept secret. Over a four-month period in 1999, Montana raised approximately $23 million from twenty-two investors. The promised gains did not accrue, however. Instead, Montana, Lyttle, and Knight depleted investors' funds in high-risk trades or spent the funds on themselves. [SEC v. Montana, 464 F.Supp.2d 772 (S.D.Ind. 2006)]

(a) The Securities and Exchange Commission (SEC) filed a suit in a federal district court against Montana and the others, seeking an injunction, civil penalties, and refund of profits with interest. The SEC alleged, among other things, violations of Section 10(b) of the Securities Exchange Act of 1934 and SEC Rule 10b-5. What is required to establish such violations? Describe how and why the facts in this case meet, or fail to meet, these requirements.

(b) It is often remarked, "There's a sucker born every minute!" Does that phrase describe the Program's investors? Ultimately, about half of the investors recouped the amount they invested. Should the others be considered at least partly responsible for their own losses? Why or why not?

42–10. VIDEO QUESTION: Disclosure under SEC Rule 10b-5.

 Go to this text's Web site at **www.cengage.com/ blaw/clarkson** and select "Chapter 42." Click on "Video Questions" and view the video titled *Real World Legal: Jack's Restaurant, Scene 1.* Then answer the following questions.

(a) Assuming that the companies involved in the merger are Section 12 companies, what statutory provisions prohibit Susan from trading company stock based on her inside knowledge of the merger with GTS?

(b) Did Susan breach a fiduciary duty to the corporation by telling the bartender about the proposed merger? Does the fact that she may be laid off by the company after the merger affect her duties? Explain.

(c) Under what legal theory might it be illegal for the bartender to buy shares in the company based on the information that he got from Susan? Analyze the owner's potential liability. Is there enough evidence of *scienter* in this scenario for the Securities and Exchange Commission to file criminal charges against Susan if the bartender buys the stock? Discuss.

LEGAL RESEARCH EXERCISES ON THE WEB

Go to this text's Web site at **www.cengage.com/blaw/clarkson**, select "Chapter 42," and click on "Practical Internet Exercises." There you will find the following Internet research exercises that you can perform to learn more about the topics covered in this chapter.

Practical Internet Exercise 42–1: **Legal Perspective**
Electronic Delivery

Practical Internet Exercise 42–2: **Management Perspective**
The SEC's Role

CHAPTER 43

Law for Small Business

Small businesses create much of the wealth and many of the new jobs in the United States. According to the U.S. Census Bureau, there are around 5 million firms with ten or fewer employees. The U.S. Small Business Administration (SBA) reports that small businesses employ half of all private-sector employees in the country, generate more than half of the nation's gross domestic product, and obtain a disproportionate number of patents. The SBA also reports, however, that more than half of small businesses fail within four years. A lack of understanding of legal issues and how to respond to them is one of the reasons that new businesses fail.

Some relatively new companies, such as Apple and Google, have become highly successful. Understanding business law and the legal environment has often been crucial to business success. Consider that Apple's and Google's growth is grounded to some extent in the smart decisions about contracts that those companies made in their early days.

For the most part, the laws of particular interest to small-business owners are the same general business laws covered throughout this text, and this chapter provides a review of some of those laws. In addition, we examine a number of the options and legal requirements faced by those who wish to start their own small businesses.

We also indicate how the general legal principles discussed throughout this book apply in the context of a small-business enterprise. Because legal compliance is crucial for any venture, we begin with a discussion of the importance of obtaining legal counsel.

SECTION 1
THE IMPORTANCE OF LEGAL COUNSEL

Nearly everyone who starts a business enterprise faces the following question: "Do I need an attorney?" The answer to this question will likely be "yes." Today, nonexperts find it almost impossible to keep up with the myriad rules and regulations that govern the conduct of business in the United States. Indeed, businesspersons sometimes incur penalties for violating laws or regulations of which they are totally unaware, as noted in Chapter 5. Obtaining competent legal counsel can help a small business avoid a number of pitfalls. An attorney may be very helpful when a business undertakes certain types of transactions, including the following:

1. Negotiating a franchise agreement;
2. Creating standard business forms, such as purchase orders and contract confirmations;
3. Buying or selling real property or a business;
4. Negotiating agreements to license intellectual property rights; and
5. Obtaining new outside investors.

Relevant questions thus include how to find the right attorney for one's needs and how to hold down legal costs as much as possible.

Although attorneys may seem expensive, the prudent business owner will make sure that he or she is not "penny wise and pound foolish." The consultation fee paid to an attorney may be a drop in the bucket compared with the potential liability facing a businessperson for violating a statutory law or regulation. Also, outside legal help may be essential for certain tasks associated with forming a new business, such as drafting and filing the documents necessary for incorporation. Failure to comply with specific state incorporation requirements may subject the owners of the new enterprise to personal liability for contracts or other obligations.

Find an Attorney

In selecting an attorney, most businesspersons rely on referrals from friends, business associates, and other local entities. Business networks, such as chambers of commerce and bar organizations, may also help identify knowledgeable attorneys. Attorneys and their areas of specialty are often listed in the Yellow Pages. Another good source of information is the *Martindale-Hubbell Law Directory,* which can be found at most law libraries. (It is also accessible online at www.martindale.com.) This directory lists the names, addresses, telephone numbers, areas of legal practice, and other information for more than 900,000 attorneys and law firms in the United States.

A number of lawyers specialize in small-business law. Many states now have certification programs that identify specialists in various legal areas.

Retain an Attorney

Retaining an experienced attorney will yield benefits beyond the resolution of legal problems. Many attorneys have advantageous contacts, including potential investors in your enterprise. An attorney may also have valuable business expertise. Furthermore, because the law protects the confidentiality of attorney-client communications, an attorney provides a useful sounding board for business plans.

Consider retaining an attorney at a large law firm. Such an attorney will be more expensive but may also have more ability and influence in the local business community than an attorney at a small firm. Furthermore, the attorney can draw on his or her firm's resources, and a letter on the letterhead of a large, well-known firm may carry more clout.

At the start-up stage, many entrepreneurs may feel that they do not have the financial resources to pay a lawyer, especially one who charges a high hourly rate. Attorneys have responded to this situation by offering innovative fee arrangements. Most attorneys will not charge for an initial consultation and typically will charge a flat fee for routine tasks, such as incorporating a business. Prospective clients should be careful to find out precisely what services the fee will cover, however. Some law firms offer prepaid legal service plans that cover many of the services that a small-business owner may require. An advantage of these plans is that the annual costs of legal representation for ordinary matters are predictable. Some attorneys will even provide a substantial amount of service in exchange for a promise of future legal business after the venture is established. Sometimes, an attorney may accept an equity (ownership) stake in the new business in lieu of a cash payment. Clients often have the opportunity to negotiate their attorney's compensation system to suit their needs.

Some small-business owners keep an attorney on **retainer.** This means that the client pays the attorney a fixed amount every month, and the attorney handles all necessary legal business that arises during the month. The amount of the retainer is negotiated with an eye toward expected legal needs. Thus, this approach probably will not save much overall, but it will make legal costs stable and predictable over time.

Hire an Accountant

In a new business, the proper management of accounts receivable and accounts payable is critical. There are software accounting programs to handle this job, but many small businesses hire professional accountants to do their bookkeeping. Although it is more expensive, having an accountant adds to your credibility with potential investors and lenders. Accurate bookkeeping is also legally important, as errors often provoke litigation.

SECTION 2
SELECTION OF THE BUSINESS ORGANIZATION

The various forms of business organization available to businesspersons were discussed in Chapters 36 through 42. We will now review them in the context of small businesses.

In the earliest stages, a small business may operate as a sole proprietorship, which requires few legal formalities. The law considers all new, single-owner businesses to be sole proprietorships, unless the owner affirmatively adopts some other form. Once business is under way, however, the sole proprietorship form may become problematic if additional investors are needed or the personal financial risks of the business become too great. The owner and any additional investors may then want to establish a more formal organization, such as a limited partnership (LP), a limited liability partnership (LLP), a limited liability company (LLC), or a corporation.

Each business form has its own advantages and disadvantages. Factors to consider when choosing a business form include liability, taxation, continuity of life, and the legal formalities and costs associated with starting the business.

Limitations on Liability

A key consideration in starting a business is whether the business form chosen will limit the owner's personal liability for business debts and obligations. If you form a limited liability entity, such as a corporation, you normally can avoid personal liability if, say, a customer slips and breaks his ankle in your store, sues your store, and is awarded damages by a court. Although the business entity may be liable for damages, you and the other owners normally will not be personally liable beyond the extent of your contributions to the firm. Legal limited liability generally is necessary for those who wish to raise outside capital.

Corporate business forms offer limited liability to the shareholder-owners. In a traditional, or general, partnership, however, there is no limited liability. Each partner is personally liable for the debts and obligations of the partnership. In an LP, the limited partners have limited liability; however, it must have at least one general partner who remains personally liable for the partnership's obligations. Note that limited personal liability does not obviate the need to obtain insurance for significant business liability risks (see Chapter 51). Limited liability organizations protect only personal assets, and a substantial uninsured liability can bankrupt the business and cause the owner to lose her or his entire investment. Moreover, limited personal liability may be lost by contract (such as when an individual personally guarantees payment of a business loan) or by failure to comply with the rules for a business form.

Today, all states permit businesspersons to conduct their business operations as LLCs, and most states provide for LLPs. These increasingly popular business forms also offer the advantage of limited personal liability for business debts and obligations (see Chapters 37 and 38).

Tax Considerations

Taxes are another critical factor to be considered in choosing a small-business form. A sole proprietorship is not a separate legal entity, and the owner pays taxes on business income as an individual. All revenues are taxable, but business expenses can be deducted, so the owner is taxed only once on the business's profits.

All corporations must pay certain state and local taxes—such as **franchise taxes** (annual taxes imposed for the privilege of doing business in a state)—but the key consideration involves corporate income taxes. The corporate form entails what is known as *double taxation.* The company must pay a corporate income tax on its profits, and the shareholder-owners must also pay individual income tax on any distributions of the remaining profits that they receive from the corporation. Double taxation is limited to distributions of profits, though, so corporations are taxed only once on retained earnings. (See Chapter 39 for a complete discussion of corporate taxation). Partnerships, LLCs, LLPs, and S corporations avoid double taxation and provide for "pass-through" taxation—that is, profits are passed through to the partners, members, or owners and are taxed only on their individual returns, not at the business level.

Continuity of Life

Continuity of life is another concern in selecting a business form. A business should prepare for the possibility that an owner may die, resign, be expelled, or become incapacitated. Corporations have continuity of life—that is, they survive their owners—except in the unusual event that the corporate documents provide otherwise. Normally, on the death of a corporate shareholder-owner, that shareholder's ownership interest simply passes to his or her heirs.

In many states, a partnership will not terminate on the death or withdrawal of a partner, unless the partners have expressly provided otherwise. (In those states that have not adopted the most recent version of the Uniform Partnership Act, however, the death of a partner will automatically dissolve the partnership—see Chapter 37.) By definition, a sole proprietorship terminates with the death of the sole proprietor.

Legal Formality and Expense

Additionally, businesspersons need to consider the legal formalities and expenses involved in starting a business. The requirements and costs associated with forming and operating as a corporation can be considerable. The expense of establishing an LP may also be significant. For these reasons, some individuals initially operate their businesses as sole proprietorships or traditional partnerships—and run considerable financial risk because of the personal liability associated with each of these business forms. Start-up formalities and costs generally are less extensive for LLCs than for corporations or limited partnerships.

REQUIREMENTS FOR ALL BUSINESS FORMS Although sole proprietorships and traditional partnerships avoid the legal formalities associated with incorporating or creating an LP, sole proprietors and partners must still comply with many laws. Any business, whatever its form, has to meet a variety of legal requirements, which typically relate to the following:

1. Business name registration.
2. Occupational licensing.
3. State tax registration (for example, to obtain permits for collecting and remitting sales taxes).
4. Health and environmental permits.
5. Zoning and building codes.
6. Import/export regulations.

If the business has employees, the owner must also comply with a host of laws governing the workplace. (We will look at several of these laws in the final section of this chapter.) Some small businesses, with few employees, are exempted from some of these laws. For example, the health-care legislation enacted in 2010 imposes a fine on employers that do not provide health insurance for their employees, but companies with fewer than fifty employees might remain exempt from this requirement.

FORMALIZING THE BUSINESS The owner should not overlook the potential benefits of establishing a business arrangement more formal than a sole proprietorship. Consider a family business that is owned and operated by a husband and wife. At the outset, the spouses should consider the possibility that they may have a falling-out in the future. If they run their enterprise as a sole proprietorship, it may be difficult to establish their respective ownership rights in the business should a dispute arise.

If they form a partnership, however, they can specify in a written partnership agreement how profits and losses will be shared, as well as the extent of each partner's ownership interest in the partnership. Alternatively, the spouses could incorporate and draw up a shareholder agreement (see page 848) that will provide for various eventualities and thus enable the company to continue. Formalizing the business is critical to its potential expansion as well.

SECTION 3
THE LIMITED LIABILITY COMPANY

The limited liability company (LLC) has been available for only a few decades, but it has become the preferred structure for many small businesses.

Indeed, since 2004, the LLC has been the first choice of most small-business owners who want a business form other than a sole proprietorship. The number of LLCs has increased so rapidly because they offer several advantages. For example, an LLC provides limited liability without the double taxation associated with a corporation. Forming an LLC is a much simpler process than setting up a corporation, although the owners of the LLC must still file a certificate with the state and pay a fee. We examined LLCs in Chapter 38, but the form has become so important for small businesses that we take a closer look at certain aspects of the LLC next.

The Basic Structure

The structure of an LLC roughly parallels that of a corporation. Instead of articles of incorporation, though, an LLC has *articles of organization*. In addition, it has an *operating agreement* that serves as the organization's charter. The owners of an LLC are called *members*, not shareholders. A member need not be a natural person but may be a separate corporation or other organized entity. Those who run the day-to-day operations of an LLC are known as *managers*. Two important aspects of an LLC's structure are its flexibility and the fiduciary duties of its members and managers.

FLEXIBILITY IN DETERMINING MEMBERS' RIGHTS
Under state law, LLCs have much more flexibility than corporations enjoy. Whereas corporations must comply with numerous requirements, the members of an LLC generally have the flexibility to decide what rules they will include in their operating agreement. Typically, the state statute includes default rules that will govern an LLC unless its operating agreement provides otherwise. For example, default rules often provide that profits, voting rights, and assets on liquidation will be apportioned according to the value of each member's financial contribution. An LLC's operating agreement, however, may apportion the members' voting rights equally or according to some criterion other than contributions. Similarly, the operating agreement may provide for profits and losses, and distributions to members, to be allocated on some other basis.

As another example, state statutes usually presume that an LLC's members will be its managers, but the agreement may provide otherwise. LLC membership interests normally cannot be transferred, and new memberships may not be issued, without the consent of all existing members. These default rules may also be modified by the agreement. Unlike a corporation, an LLC is not required by law to hold a formal annual meeting, but the agreement may require such a meeting. One leading case even found that the agreement could require all disputes among an

LLC's members to be resolved by arbitration, with no appeal of the decision to a court.[1]

The following case demonstrates how the rights of a terminated LLC member can be limited by the operating agreement.

_____

1. *Elf Atochem North America, Inc. v. Jaffari,* 727 A.2d 286 (Del.Sup. Ct. 1999).

✳ EXTENDED CASE 43.1 ✳
Mixon v. Iberia Surgical, LLC

Court of Appeal of Louisiana, Third Circuit, 956 So.2d 76 (2007).

IN THE LANGUAGE OF THE COURT
COOKS, Judge.
* * * *
Iberia Surgical [LLC] was formed, in August 1998, by a group of physicians practicing in Iberia Parish [Louisiana] for the purpose of establishing an ambulatory, outpatient surgery center. * * * Dr. [Tynes] Mixon was one of the original organizers and became the managing partner.

In June 1999, Iberia Surgical, in a joint ownership venture with Iberia Medical Center, formed New Iberia Surgery Center, L.L.C., an outpatient surgical facility.

Not long after the formation of Iberia Surgical, Dr. Mixon became dissatisfied with the operation of the new facility and management practices of his fellow physicians. * * * After months of discord, * * * on August 28, 2002, Dr. Mixon was terminated from Iberia Surgical by unanimous vote of the membership. Pursuant to the Buy-Out provisions of the Operating Agreement, Dr. Mixon was paid $71,356.85 * * *.

[Mixon filed a suit against Iberia Surgical in a Louisiana state court, presenting evidence that the fair market value of his interest in the business was $483,100. The trial court issued a summary judgment in the defendant's favor. Mixon

appealed to a state intermediate appellate court.]
* * * *
* * * Article 3.2(g) of the Operating Agreement provides:

> Termination Without Cause. A Member may be Terminated Without Cause, by unanimous vote in writing of the remaining Members of the Company.

* * * Dr. Mixon asserts the exercise of this contractual right by Iberia Surgical to terminate his membership was an abuse of right and violates moral rules, good faith, and elementary fairness. He also contends there was an absence of a serious or legitimate motive for the exercise of the right and, therefore, he concludes it was done to cause harm.
* * * *
* * * The members of Iberia Surgical, including Dr. Mixon, negotiated a business agreement the purpose of which was to establish a profitable outpatient surgery center. There is ample evidence in the record, including Dr. Mixon's own testimony, to establish he objected to the way the facility was being managed * * *. His views were not well received and represented the minority opinion within the organization. * * * A decision was made to buy-out Dr. Mixon's interest and sever financial ties with him.

The Operating Agreement, which Dr. Mixon negotiated and signed, gave Iberia Surgical the right to terminate one of its members without cause. Dr. Mixon has provided no evidence to suggest the termination was done to cause him harm or for any other reason than a legitimate business reason. The provisions of the Operating Agreement are straightforward * * *. There is no evidence to suggest the terms of the Operating Agreement violate moral rules, good faith, or elementary fairness.
* * * *
Dr. Mixon contends he was not adequately compensated for his interest in Iberia Surgical. The * * * Operating Agreement * * * provides:
* * * *

> (c) Purchase Price and Terms. The Purchase Price of a Former Member's Interest * * * shall be determined as follows:
>
> * * * *
>
> (ii) The "Book Value" means the "fair market value" of a Membership Interest computed in accordance with generally accepted accounting principles, of the net equity of the Company as of the end of the last full taxable year immediately preceding the year in which the Event giving rise to the purchase and sale of the Membership Rights or Interest occurred.

EXTENDED CASE CONTINUES ➡

EXTENDED CASE 43.1 CONTINUED ➡

Dr. Mixon contends "Book Value" is not synonymous with "Fair Market Value." He contends the Operating Agreement requires his membership share should be computed according to the "Fair Market Value," which he defines as the price a seller is willing to accept and a buyer is willing to pay on the open market.

We agree the terms "Book Value" and "Fair Market Value" are not

synonymous and have generally recognized meanings in accounting in valuation. * * * Under the terms of the Operating Agreement, the parties agreed to use the "book value" in determining the value of a member's interest, not fair market value. *The book value of a business has a well-defined meaning, is unambiguous, and is susceptible of only one construction. It is the value as shown by the books of the business, and no other value. Book value is calculated*

by measuring the assets of the business against its liabilities. Goodwill, actual value or value in the open market, is not considered in determining book value. [Emphasis added.]

* * * *

Based on the foregoing review of the record, we affirm the decision of the trial court granting summary judgment in favor of Iberia Surgical * * *.

QUESTIONS

1. What might Mixon and the other members of Iberia Surgical have done to avoid the litigation and its ultimate result in this case?
2. Does the outcome in this case illustrate the advantages or the disadvantages of the LLC form of business organization? Explain.

EXTENT OF FIDUCIARY DUTIES A key element of corporate law involves the fiduciary duties of directors and officers to shareholders. The nature and scope of these duties are not as fully defined for LLCs, but the states have imposed some requirements of fair and honest dealing by members and managers. Like many other aspects of the LLC, the duties of members and managers may be set out and limited in the LLC's operating agreement. If the agreement does not expressly limit or disavow the fiduciary duties of managers and members, then they have the same fiduciary duties as corporate managers (see Chapter 40).[2]

Converting an LLC into a Corporation

If a small business begins as an LLC and thrives, the owners may wish to convert it to a corporation. By incorporating, the larger business can attract more outside capital with public offerings of its equity. Because the company will likely be retaining its earnings to fund future growth, rather than distributing them to the owners, it will not experience the double-taxation disadvantage of the corporate form. In addition, the corporate structure facilitates the use of equity-based employee incentive plans, such

as grants of stock options, and a more expansive management structure.

If the LLC agreement does not provide otherwise, this conversion may require the unanimous consent of the members. The LLC must then file articles of dissolution with the state. The members will agree on a process to assign ownership interests in the new corporation by shareholdings. Then, they will go about forming the successor corporation, a procedure discussed in the next section.

SECTION 4

HOW TO FORM A BUSINESS ENTITY

As explained earlier in this chapter, the various forms of business organization differ considerably in the formalities and expenses required to create a business. There are no special legal requirements for creating a sole proprietorship, and a traditional partnership requires only an agreement between the partners. Forming an LLC involves only slightly more legal work but does require a filing with the state government. Forming an LP is somewhat more complicated. The limited partnership agreement, often called a *certificate of limited partnership*, must be prepared and recorded with the appropriate governmental authority. State laws also regulate the names of LPs, require certain record keeping, and

---

2. For example, in 2010, a decision by a Delaware court made clear that managers have fiduciary duties to LLC owners, unless the operating agreement explicitly disavows those duties. See *Kelly v. Blum,* 2010 WL 629850 (Del.Ch. 2010).

govern other aspects of the business. The procedures required for the creation of a corporation are perhaps the most complicated of all, so the remainder of this section is devoted to them.

Corporate Name

To incorporate, you first must choose a corporate name and file it with the appropriate state office, usually the office of the secretary of state. The name must be different from those used by existing businesses (even unincorporated businesses). Although private databases can be used to check names, the secretary of state's office should have all of the information necessary. The name of your new company should also include the word *Corporation, Company,* or *Incorporated* (abbreviated *Corp., Co.,* and *Inc.,* respectively).

Note that filing a name with the appropriate state official will protect the name as a trade name only within the state. Therefore, businesspersons who anticipate doing business nationally—via the Internet, for example—will want to make sure that their trade names will be protected under trademark law (to be discussed shortly).

Articles of Incorporation, Bylaws, and Initial Meeting

The second key step in incorporation is preparing and filing the articles of incorporation. Other steps involve drafting the corporate bylaws and holding the initial board of directors' meeting.

ARTICLES OF INCORPORATION As discussed in Chapter 39, states have different requirements as to the provisions that must be included in the articles. For example, some states require a minimum number of incorporators or directors, or a minimum capital contribution. As mentioned, entrepreneurs typically engage an attorney to help them draft and file the documents necessary to incorporate, including the articles of incorporation.

CORPORATE BYLAWS Another important step in the incorporation process is drafting the bylaws, which become the company's governing rules. The bylaws establish the dates on which annual meetings will be held, the number required for a voting quorum, and other rules. Incorporators generally include these rules in the bylaws rather than the articles of incorporation because the articles are relatively difficult to change. Bylaws are binding, but they are more

easily modified. Usually, bylaws can be changed by a majority vote of the shareholders. In some states, the bylaws can be modified by the board of directors.

THE INITIAL BOARD OF DIRECTORS' MEETING The new corporation then holds its first board of directors' meeting. The initial corporate directors are designated in the articles of incorporation. The directors adopt the agreed-on bylaws, appoint corporate officers and define their respective authority, issue stock, open a bank account, and take other necessary actions. The directors will continue to meet periodically and must stand for election at annual shareholders' meetings.

Corporate Records Book

The next step is to establish a corporate records book in which the corporation's important documents, such as the articles of incorporation and the minutes of directors' and shareholders' meetings, will be kept. If the state requires stock certificates, they will have to be printed and distributed to the owners. The corporation may also need a corporate seal because banks and other institutions sometimes require that seals be placed on certain documents. Again, an attorney typically handles these tasks as part of the incorporation process.

SECTION 5
INTELLECTUAL PROPERTY

Protecting rights in intellectual property is the central concern for some businesses. For example, software companies depend on their copyrights and patents to protect their investments in the research and development required to create new programs. Without copyright or patent protection, a competitor or a customer could simply copy the software. Laws governing rights in intellectual property were discussed in detail in Chapter 8. Here, we examine some aspects of intellectual property law that individuals should consider at the outset of any business venture.

Trademarks

Choosing a trademark or service mark and making sure that it can be protected under trademark law can be crucial to the success of a new business venture. A factor to consider in choosing a name for your business entity is whether you will use your business name as a trademark. Assume that you plan to incorporate your business. When the firm is incorporated, the secretary of state (or other state agency with which the business name is filed) approves your company's name only as a trade name—the name that you can use on checks, invoices, and letterhead stationery. You have legal ownership of your trade name only in that own state.

If you decide to use your business (trade) name as a trademark, then you need to follow the principles of trademark law. The general rule is that your trademark cannot be the same as another's mark or so similar that confusion might result.

Historically, the first business that actually used a trademark in the marketplace owned it. Today, for national trademark protection, the business must be the first to register the trademark with the U.S. Patent and Trademark Office (PTO) in Washington, D.C. First use still takes some precedence over federal registration, however. Suppose that you have used a particular trademark for two years but have not registered the mark with the PTO. If another company then registers the same mark with the PTO, you will probably have the traditional common law right to continue using that mark, but only in the geographic region in which you have been operating. Outside that region, the federal registrant will own the mark.

TRADEMARK SELECTION A trademark should be distinctive. Use of your name or a mere description of your product will probably receive, at most, only weak protection. If you have started a new online company, you cannot call it "Internet" and expect to receive protection. Although using a slight twist on the word may be tempting, this may lead to confusion. Thousands of companies already have the word *net* as part of their names. A distinctive made-up word (such as *Exxon* or *Kodak*) may be a good choice.

Once you have chosen a mark, you should do a trademark search to ensure that the mark is not too similar to existing marks. You can hire a trademark search firm or do the search yourself. Sources to consult include the Yellow Pages in any area in which you do business and *Brands and Their Companies* (available at www.gale.cengage.com or at your local library). You can also look at the federal trademark register, as well as the trademark register in your state. (Go to www.uspto.gov to check the PTO's online federal trademark register.) Other trademark databases, such as TrademarkScan, are also available on the Internet.

TRADEMARK REGISTRATION After selecting a trademark that appears to be available and that is not confusingly similar to an existing mark, you should register the mark with both the state government and the federal government. As explained earlier, if you do not register, your protection may be limited to the area in which you do business. Federal registration gives your trademark nationwide protection, provided that the trademark is already in use or will be used within six months. Even if your current business is only local, registration for national protection is important to protect your business's long-term growth.

To register your trademark with the PTO, you must submit an application that includes a specimen (picture) of your trademark, a list of marked goods and/or services, and the date on which you first used the trademark. You may want to register more than one mark. If your logo consists of a distinctive name as well as a graphic, you can register each item independently. For example, Apple, Inc., uses a rainbow-colored apple as a registered logo and the name *Apple* as a trademark. The apple logo and the Apple name could be registered separately to get independent protection. The PTO allows online filing through the Trademark Electronic Application System at www.uspto.gov/teas.

TRADEMARK PROTECTION After registering your trademark, you must take care of it. If your mark is federally registered, you may use the symbol ® with your mark; this puts others on notice of your registration. Even if you have not registered, you can use the symbol ™ with your mark. Five years after you initially register your mark, you should renew your registration with the PTO. Thereafter, you can renew at ten-year intervals. Filing for renewal informs the PTO that your mark is still in use and ensures that others cannot contest its validity.

To protect your mark, you must be alert to possible trademark infringement. If another company uses your trademark or a mark very similar to yours, you should take prompt action by sending a letter of complaint and consider filing a lawsuit for trademark infringement. If you ignore the problem, you may lose rights in your trademark. If, for example, a media outlet improperly refers to your trademark as if it were a generic word, send a letter of correction and keep a copy in your files. You may at some point need to demonstrate that you have consistently sought to enforce your rights in the mark, or it may be deemed abandoned.

Trade Secrets

Much of the value of a business may lie in its trade secrets. As discussed in Chapter 8, trade secrets are business secrets that have value and might be appropriated by another company, such as a competitor. Trade secrets may include information concerning product development, production processes and techniques, or customer lists. Preserving the secrecy of the information is necessary for legal protections.

As a practical matter, trade secrets must be divulged to key employees. Thus, any business runs the risk that those employees might disclose the secrets to competitors—or even set up competing businesses themselves. Generally, protecting against the possibility that valuable trade secrets will fall into the hands of others, especially competitors, presents an ongoing challenge for businesses, including new enterprises.

NONDISCLOSURE AND NONCOMPETE AGREEMENTS

To protect their trade secrets, companies may require employees who have access to trade secrets to agree in their employment contracts never to divulge those secrets. A company may also include a covenant not to compete in an employment contract. A noncompete covenant will help to protect against the possibility that a key employee will go to work for a competitor or set up a competing business— situations in which the company's trade secrets will likely be disclosed.

MISAPPROPRIATION As discussed in Chapter 8,

trade secrets are protected under the common law.[3] Thus, a company can sue an individual or a firm that has misappropriated its trade secrets. For example, two engineers developed new software for their company and then left to work at another firm. After the engineers developed a similar product for their new employer, the first company sued for infringement of trade secrets and prevailed in court.

SECTION 6
FINANCIAL CAPITAL

Raising financial capital is critical to the growth of most small businesses. In the early days of a business, the sole proprietor or partners may be able

to contribute sufficient capital, but if the business becomes successful, more funds may be needed. The owner or owners may want to raise capital from external sources to expand the business. One way to do this is to borrow funds. Another is to exchange equity (ownership rights) in the company in return for funds, either through private arrangements or through public stock offerings.

Loans

A small business may find it beneficial to obtain a bank loan because raising capital in this way allows the founder to retain full ownership and control of the business (though the bank may place some restrictions on future business decisions as a condition of granting the loan). Bank loans may not be available for some businesses, however. Banks are usually reluctant to lend significant sums to businesses that are not yet established. Even if a bank is willing to make such a loan, the bank may require personal guaranty contracts from the owners, putting their personal assets at risk (see Chapter 28).

Loans with desirable terms may be available from the U.S. Small Business Administration (SBA). One SBA program provides loans of up to $25,000 to businesspersons who are women, low-income individuals, or members of minority groups. Be aware that the SBA requires business owners to put some of their own funds at risk in the business. Some entrepreneurs have even used their credit cards to obtain initial capital.

The stimulus program that Congress enacted in 2009 also sought to assist small businesses, funneling $30 billion to smaller banks to support small-business lending. In addition, the government gave employers tax breaks for hiring new workers and eliminated the capital gains tax on investments in small business.

Venture Capital

As discussed in Chapter 39, many new businesses raise needed capital by exchanging equity in the firm for venture capital. In other words, an outsider contributes funds in exchange for an ownership interest in the company. **Venture capitalists,** often organized into major firms, seek out promising enterprises and fund them in exchange for equity stakes. Akin to venture capitalists are "angels," individuals who typically invest somewhat smaller sums in new businesses.

---

3. The theft of trade secrets is also a federal crime under the Economic Espionage Act of 1996 (see Chapter 9).

EXHIBIT 43–1 • Venture Capital Issues

ISSUE	DESCRIPTION
Type and Quantity of Stock	The venture capitalists will negotiate the *amount of stock* (which will determine their ownership share of the enterprise) and the *type of stock* (which usually will be preferred stock).
Stock Preferences	If the venture capitalists receive preferred shares, the shares generally will (1) provide for an annual per-share dividend to be paid before common stockholders receive any dividends and (2) give the venture capitalists priority among shareholders in the event of the firm's liquidation.
Conversion and Antidilution Rights	The preferred shares will be convertible into common stock at the option of the venture capitalists, and the company will be restrained from issuing new stock in an amount that would materially dilute the venture capitalists' ownership interests.
Board of Directors	The venture capitalists will define their proportionate representation on the board of directors.
Registration Rights	If the company conducts a public offering or registers its shares at a later date, the venture capitalists will have the right to have their shares registered also ("piggybacked"), making those shares more marketable.
Representations and Warranties	The owner will be required to make representations about the firm's capital structure, its possession of necessary government authorizations, its financial statements, and other material facts.

THE PROS AND CONS OF VENTURE CAPITAL FINANCING According to the U.S. National Venture Capital Association, U.S. venture capitalists invested $25.5 billion in nearly three thousand deals in 2007. The number of investments dropped precipitously during the Great Recession but should grow again as the economy recovers. On average, a venture capitalist invests about $5 million to $10 million in a company. In addition to providing needed financing, venture capitalists offer other advantages for businesses. Venture capitalists are often experienced managers who can provide invaluable assistance to entrepreneurs with respect to strategic business decisions, marketing, and important business contacts. Obtaining this assistance may be crucial to a new company's success.

The disadvantage is that a venture capitalist with a substantial equity stake will demand a corresponding degree of operational control over the company and a similar proportion of future profits.

CREATION OF A BUSINESS PLAN To attract outside venture capital, you will need a **business plan** that describes the company, its products, and its anticipated future performance. The plan should be relatively concise (typically fewer than fifty pages). After considering your plan, a venture capitalist may decide to investigate your venture further. This step may require you to disclose trade secrets, and you should insist that the potential investor sign a confidentiality agreement. If all goes well, you will then negotiate the terms of financing. A key point to be negotiated is how much ownership and control the venture capitalist will receive in exchange for the capital contribution. (Exhibit 43–1 above summarizes some key issues that may arise in negotiations with venture capitalists.)

Although venture capital may be crucial to a small business's growth, the prospect of venture capital may create new problems, as the following case illustrates.

CASE 43.2

Halo Technology Holdings, Inc. v. Cooper

United States District Court, District of Connecticut, ___ F.Supp.2d ___ (2010).

BACKGROUND AND FACTS • Halo Technology Holdings, Inc., is a Nevada corporation with its principal place of business in Connecticut. In 2005 and 2006, Halo acquired all of the shares of the entities that became HTH Emp., Inc., known as New Empagio, which was then a wholly owned subsidiary of Halo. Randall Cooper and other former employees of Halo (the Cooper Group) helped manage New Empagio. Halo sought to sell New Empagio to pay off a $20 million loan it had with Fortress Financial Corporation. Halo expected to receive at least $30 million from the sale. Cooper allegedly led potential buyers to believe that he had a right of first refusal, which led potential buyers not to submit bids. The Cooper Group then obtained venture capital financing from the Primus Group to buy New Empagio. The

CASE 43.2 CONTINUED ▶ Primus Group entered into a nondisclosure agreement with Halo and gained access to information on New Empagio. Unbeknownst to Halo, members of the Cooper Group provided inside information to the Primus Group and worked to obstruct other potential purchasers. They allegedly created a liquidity crisis at New Empagio, driving down its value. The Primus Group offered $14.5 million for New Empagio, which Halo rejected. Halo was unable to find any other purchasers by the time the Fortress loan came due, so it entered bankruptcy. New Empagio subsequently sold its assets for $16 million and also filed for bankruptcy. Halo filed a suit against Cooper and the Primus Group for breach of contract, interference, civil conspiracy, and violation of the Connecticut Unfair Trade Practices Act (CUTPA). New Empagio later intervened as an additional plaintiff. The defendants filed a motion to dismiss for failure to state a claim.

IN THE LANGUAGE OF THE COURT
UNDERHILL, District Judge.
* * * *

* * * Halo claims that the Primus Group intentionally breached the terms of the non-disclosure agreement by taking steps and actions constituting aggravating circumstances so substantial as to be immoral, oppressive, and unscrupulous in violation of CUTPA, and (b) the Primus Group conspired with the other defendants to breach that contract in violation of CUTPA.
* * * *

In Connecticut, a deceptive act that constitutes a breach of contract can form the basis for a CUTPA claim. A simple contract breach, however, does not constitute a violation of CUTPA. [There must also be a significant aggravating factor to establish a CUTPA claim.]
* * * *

At the motion to dismiss stage, the plaintiff must allege facts that form the basis of a plausible claim for relief. Halo alleges no fact that supports any inference that the Primus Group defendants actually breached the non-disclosure agreement. * * * The complaint makes no mention of what the Primus Group disclosed. Nor does it state which section of the agreement was violated.

* * * New Empagio alleges tortious interference with its business activities and conspiracy to commit tortious interference. *To survive a motion to dismiss * * *, New Empagio must show that it had a business relationship with another party, the Primus Group knew of that relationship, the Primus Group intentionally interfered with that relationship, and New Empagio suffered a resulting loss.*

* * * Halo cannot bring a claim for indirect harm and, at this stage of the litigation, Halo cannot bring a shareholder action for recovery because it no longer owns shares of New Empagio.
* * * *

Taking the facts in the complaint as true, New Empagio had a business relationship with its customers * * * and with its lender, Fortress. The Primus Group was aware of New Empagio's business relationship with its customers and lender. The Primus Group conspired with the Cooper Group to interfere in those relationships by delaying customer payments, instructing lower management to delay customer invoicing in order to induce a liquidity crisis, and taking steps to impede New Empagio's ability to repay Fortress.

DECISION AND REMEDY • *The court granted the motion to dismiss the claims brought by Halo but denied the motion to dismiss New Empagio's claims.*

THE ETHICAL DIMENSION • *There was an important legal distinction in the duties that the defendants owed to Halo and New Empagio. Was there a similar ethical distinction? Explain.*

THE LEGAL ENVIRONMENT DIMENSION • *Why did the court dismiss Halo's claims?*

Securities Regulation

Anyone raising capital needs to be aware of the regulations that govern securities. Many small-business owners raise funds from friends or business acquaintances instead of from venture capitalists. Whatever method is used, the investor exchanges capital for an interest in the enterprise. If this interest consists of shares of stock (or otherwise qualifies as a security under federal or state law), the business may become subject to extraordinarily detailed regulatory requirements. The securities may have to be registered with the Securities and Exchange Commission (SEC) or with the state in which the offering is made, unless the offering falls within an exemption to the securities laws.

PRIVATE OFFERINGS In certain circumstances, legal exemptions are available so that businesspersons need not worry about full registration or compliance with all of the securities regulations. (Securities regulations and exemptions were discussed in Chapter 42.) In short, the exemptions permit you to raise a limited amount of funds from a limited number of investors in what is sometimes called a *private offering.* If your offering qualifies, you need not register your shares as securities with the SEC. States have separate regulatory schemes and different terms for their exemptions from registration. In a private offering, capital typically is raised through a private placement memorandum distributed to selected potential investors.

PUBLIC OFFERINGS If your business proves especially successful, you may make a public offering in which a certain number of your shares are offered for purchase by members of the public at a price that you have set. Public offerings are highly regulated, but they may allow you to raise very large amounts of capital. Securities issued through public offerings must be registered with the SEC and applicable state regulatory agencies.

Full registration is complex, but the states and the SEC have jointly created a simplified securities registration process for small businesses. The Small Corporate Offering Registration (SCOR), which requires a form with only fifty questions, can be used for small offerings. Forty-three states have adopted the SCOR process, but their laws relating to use of the form vary.

SECTION 7
SHAREHOLDER AGREEMENTS AND KEY-PERSON INSURANCE

In the excitement of forming a new business, it is easy to overlook the possibility that partners or shareholders may die or become disabled or that disputes among partners or shareholders may make business decision making impossible. At the outset of any enterprise involving two or more owners, the owners should decide—and put in writing—how such problems will be resolved.

Shareholder Agreements

Even if a new company has only two owners, they should have a shareholder agreement that defines their relative ownership rights and interests. Such agreements are vital for small, closely held companies, in large part because shares in such entities cannot be readily sold to outsiders. This means that an owner may be locked into the investment against her or his will with little return.

A key aspect of the shareholder agreement is a *buy-sell agreement.* (This type of agreement was discussed in Chapter 37 in the context of a partnership agreement.)

BUY-SELL AGREEMENTS In a corporate shareholder agreement, a buy-sell agreement provides for the buyout of a shareholder and establishes criteria for the price to be paid for that shareholder's ownership interest. The death of a shareholder might trigger a buy-sell agreement, enabling the decedent's heirs to cash out the investment. Other common triggering events include a shareholder's bankruptcy, a shareholder's divorce, and the legal attachment of a shareholder's shares for other reasons.

BUY-SELL AGREEMENT PROVISIONS Buy-sell agreements can also resolve serious deadlocks that may develop between co-owners as the business grows. The agreement might provide that one owner has an option to buy out the others in the event that such a deadlock occurs. Alternatively, all co-owners might submit sealed bids to buy each other out, with the highest bidder being allowed to buy out the others.

The buy-sell agreement should include a provision for pricing the shares that will be sold. The price may be a set price or may be calculated according to a formula. The agreement might also include a provision for a *right of first refusal,* which restricts the transferability of the shares for a specified duration. Such a provision will prevent an owner from selling to a third party without first giving the other owners an opportunity to buy out his or her interest. An alternative to the right of first refusal is a "take-along right," which allows an investor to participate in any sale of shares to a third party. This right can protect relatively passive investors from the possibility that managing shareholders may "bail out" of the corporation by selling their shares to third parties.

Key-Person Insurance

Much of the value of a small enterprise may rest in the skills of one or a few employees (such as a software designer or a top management executive). To protect against the risk that these key persons may become disabled or die, business enterprises typically obtain *key-person insurance* (see Chapter 51). The proceeds of a key-person insurance policy can help cover the losses caused by the death or disability of essential employees. Venture capitalists or other investors may require that the company take out a key-person insurance policy as a condition of investing in the corporation.

SECTION 8
CONTRACT LAW AND SMALL BUSINESSES

Any business venture will require that contracts be formed and signed. For example, if you lease business premises, you will need to sign a lease contract. Any purchases or sales of equipment will also involve contracts. Understanding the basic contract law principles that were covered in Chapters 10 through 19 can help to ensure that any contracts you form will be valid and enforceable. As a general rule, you should make sure that any contractual agreement is in writing. Then, if a dispute arises, there will be written evidence of the contract's terms. Additionally, as discussed in Chapter 15, some contracts—such as contracts for the sale of goods priced at $500 or more[4]—fall under the Statute of Frauds, which means that they must be evidenced by a writing to be enforceable.

Contract Forms

Small-business owners often consult with their attorneys in creating contract forms for specific purposes. For example, a business may wish to provide a warranty for its products but also limit the scope of that warranty. This decision is best made through the mutual judgment of the businessperson and her or his attorney to ensure that both business and legal concerns are addressed. Standard-form contracts are available on the Internet, but they are only a starting point and should be adapted to the specific circumstances of the transaction.

---

4. There was an attempt in 2003 to raise this amount to $5,000 in a new version of Article 2 of the Uniform Commercial Code, but no state has adopted the newer version, so, for the moment, the relatively low $500 figure remains in force.

Potential Personal Liability

Contract law contains traps, and you should be aware of them. If you incorporate, you will want to enter into contracts as an agent of the corporation, not in your individual capacity. Otherwise, you may be held personally liable on the contracts. This principle applies to negotiable instruments as well. For example, if you sign a promissory note on behalf of the corporation, indicate that you are signing in a representative capacity (see Chapter 26 for further details on signature liability with respect to negotiable instruments). The same advice applies to partners and partnerships. Sometimes, personal liability may be unavoidable because other parties may not be willing to do business without a personal guaranty.

CASE IN POINT 1 Cache, LLC, applied for a line of credit with DBL Distributing, Inc. Gary and Aaron Bracken, officers and members of 1 Cache, signed the credit application on 1 Cache's behalf. The application contained the following clause: "The undersigned agrees to unconditionally guarantee payment of all sums owed pursuant to this Agreement." DBL gave 1 Cache the credit and then later requested that the Brackens sign an updated form, which stated, "The undersigned agrees to personally guarantee payment of all sums owed pursuant to this Agreement." When 1 Cache subsequently filed for bankruptcy, DBL filed a lawsuit against the Brackens claiming that they were personally liable for the company's debt. The court ruled that the Brackens' signatures on the updated credit application form provided an additional potential source of liability despite their claim that they signed on 1 Cache's behalf.[5]

SECTION 9
EMPLOYMENT ISSUES

Small businesses are exempt from some employment laws. For example, businesses with fewer than fifteen employees are exempt from federal laws prohibiting employment discrimination and certain other federal acts, such as the Family and Medical Leave Act of 1993.[6] Some state statutes have similar exemptions for small businesses. Nevertheless, even the smallest businesses are subject to many employment laws, so some knowledge of employment law is crucial for entrepreneurs starting up businesses.

---

5. *DBL Distributing, Inc. v. 1 Cache*, LLC, 147 P.3d 478 (Utah 2006).
6. 29 U.S.C. Sections 2601, 2611–2619, 2651–2654.

For example, the rather detailed regulations of the federal Occupational Safety and Health Administration have no small-business exemptions. Small businesses may be less likely to be inspected for violations, but if enforcement and penalties are applied, they can be far more disastrous for start-up companies than for larger, established firms that are in a better position to absorb these costs. Similarly, just one successful lawsuit against a small business can mean bankruptcy for the business.

Hiring Employees

Hiring good employees can be crucial to business success. Keep the following legal issues in mind during this process:

1. Be sure that the person you hire will not be disclosing any protected trade secrets of a former employer.
2. Do not make promises of job security unless you are sure you can keep them. If you promise that an employee's job will be permanent and the employee relies on your assurances, you may find it difficult to fire her or him.
3. Determine what screening tests are appropriate for the job. In some circumstances, you may be able to require the applicant to take a drug test.
4. Comply with all of the requirements imposed by federal immigration laws with respect to verifying whether workers are U.S. citizens and whether those who are not citizens are authorized to work in this country.

EMPLOYMENT CONTRACTS Usually, all employment agreements should be in writing. This generally is done in an offer letter that sets forth the basic terms of employment, including wages and benefits. An employment contract might specify that the contract is for at-will employment (see Chapter 34). At-will employment means that you can fire the employee at any time for any reason, provided that no employment laws are violated. In new businesses, an employee might want stock or options in lieu of part of his or her salary. Although granting equity to an employee saves scarce cash, it dilutes the other owners' interests. For high-level employees at least, it would be wise to consult an attorney regarding what contractual provisions should be included before awarding an equity interest in the firm.

VERIFICATION OF APPLICANTS' CREDENTIALS It goes without saying that you should contact former employers of job applicants and verify the applicants' credentials and job experience. You should also make sufficient inquiries to avoid a negligent-hiring lawsuit. Suppose that you hire a person who has been convicted twice for criminal assault. If that employee attacks a customer, the customer could sue your business for negligence in screening the worker's background during the hiring process. You therefore should check to see if a job applicant has any history of criminal conduct. You should also check a job applicant's driving record if the job involves driving a vehicle for business purposes. Additionally, actions of dishonest employees can cause a small business to suffer substantial economic losses. Thorough screening procedures will help you to avoid such problems.

Workers' Compensation

Most states require that employers carry workers' compensation insurance. If one of your employees is injured in the course of employment, the employee will be compensated for the injury by the state workers' compensation fund. That employee generally cannot sue you for further damages.

Workers' compensation insurance premiums are often high, and they may constitute one of a small business's greatest expenses. Premiums are initially based on the size of your payroll and the amount of risk involved in the business that you operate. After some time, your rates may be raised or lowered, depending on the safety record of your company. The fewer claims made against you, the lower your workers' compensation insurance costs will be.

Firing Employees

At one time or another, a small-business owner will probably find it necessary to fire a worker. Unless otherwise specified in employment contracts, your employees are presumptively at-will employees, and you can fire them without having to give any reason for doing so. Nevertheless, it is generally advisable to document good cause for terminating a worker—otherwise, he or she may succeed in a lawsuit against you for unlawful discrimination or some other legal violation.

EMPLOYEE FILES Generally, you should keep a file on each employee that includes the employee's application, performance reviews, and other relevant information. If you fire the employee, full documentation of why she or he was fired should be added to the file. Realize, though, that nearly half of the states have laws that allow employees to have access to their personnel records.

SEVERANCE PAY If you fire a worker, you might want to offer **severance pay,** which is a payment in addition to the employee's wages owed on termination. As a condition of receiving the severance pay, you might ask the employee to sign a release promising not to sue. Severance pay may be especially appropriate if the termination is not the employee's fault. Normally, you are not required to give severance pay (unless you have previously promised to do so or a union contract requires it). Most states have laws governing when you must provide the employee with his or her final paycheck, however.

WRONGFUL DISCHARGE Some states recognize a legal action for wrongful discharge (discussed in Chapter 35), but these actions generally are limited to terminations in bad faith. Be aware of any promises you made to an employee in a written contract, in an employee handbook, or even orally. These promises may prevent you from firing the employee without due process, good cause, or whatever else you may have promised.

Independent Contractors

Independent contractors are not considered to be employees, as was explained in Chapter 32. An independent contractor is a person who contracts with another to do something for him or her, but who is not controlled by the other with respect to his or her physical conduct in the performance of the undertaking.

BENEFITS OF INDEPENDENT CONTRACTORS The use of independent contractors offers many advantages to small businesses. For one thing, you need not withhold income taxes and Social Security and Medicare taxes from payments made to independent contractors, as you are required to do when you pay wages to employees. Furthermore, you need not match the amount withheld for Social Security and Medicare taxes, which can be costly for an employer.

Additionally, you need not pay premiums for workers' compensation insurance or unemployment insurance with respect to independent contractors.

Another important benefit of hiring independent contractors rather than employees is that you are not subject to laws governing employment relationships, including laws prohibiting discrimination. Normally, a court will not permit an independent contractor to bring a suit against you for age discrimination, for example, or for any other type of discrimination prohibited by federal or state laws governing employment relationships—because these laws protect only *employees,* not independent contractors.

LIABILITY FOR MISCLASSIFICATION OF WORKERS Of course, the trade-off in using independent contractors is that you cannot exercise a significant amount of control over how they perform their work. If you do, the Internal Revenue Service (IRS) or another government agency may decide that they are, in fact, employees and not independent contractors. Misclassification of an employee as an independent contractor can subject you to considerable tax liability, including penalties.

CASE IN POINT Microsoft Corporation was required to pay overdue employment taxes after the IRS reclassified as employees a number of workers that the company had designated as independent contractors. Then several hundred independent contractors sued the company to recover the benefits that Microsoft had made available to its employees but not to the independent contractors. The court held that the workers were entitled to participate in Microsoft's stock-purchase plan and other employee benefits—benefits worth millions of dollars.[7]

---

7. *Vizcaino v. U.S. District Court for the Western District of Washington,* 173 F.3d 713 (9th Cir. 1999). This case was also mentioned in Chapter 32 on page 627 in the discussion of the IRS's criteria for determining when an agent is an employee.

REVIEWING
Law for Small Business

APC, Inc., is a venture capital firm that invests in new businesses to help them grow. Wyatt Newmark owns and serves as a chef at "Earp's," a restaurant with a Western design that he operates as a sole proprietorship. Newmark has five employees at his restaurant—three servers, another chef, and a janitor. Newmark has had great success and hopes to expand or franchise the business. Newmark, who

REVIEWING CONTINUES ▶

REVIEWING
Law for Small Business, Continued

has not even retained an attorney for his small business, has approached APC for an investment. Using the information presented in the chapter, answer the following questions.

1. What approaches may APC take in order to invest in the restaurant, and what are the legal implications of each approach?
2. If APC takes an equity interest, the restaurant will need a new legal organizational form. What form would you recommend? Why?
3. In order to preserve the opportunity for growth and a possible franchise, what legal filings should Newmark's entity undertake?
4. What is the difference between employee status and independent-contractor status? Which form of employment relationship would be more advantageous to Newmark? Why should employers be cautious when designating workers as independent contractors?

DEBATE THIS: *The new penalty tax on employers that do not provide health insurance for their employees should apply to all employers, not just those with fifty or more employees.*

TERMS AND CONCEPTS

franchise tax 839	severance pay 851
retainer 838	venture capitalist 845

business plan 846

QUESTIONS AND CASE PROBLEMS

43–1. Business Forms George Overton has plans for establishing a new business with Elena Costanza. They will both be managers, and each will take an annual salary of $50,000. The company will have other expenses of $175,000. They expect to take in $375,000 in the first year of operation and share the profits equally. George and Elena have not yet decided whether to incorporate the new business or run it as a partnership. What are the tax differences between the two approaches?

43–2. QUESTION WITH SAMPLE ANSWER: Limited Liability Companies.

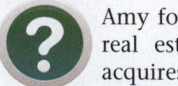

Amy forms Best Properties (BP), LLC, to own real estate as a long-term investment. BP acquires a 40,000-square-foot warehouse for $500,000, with the financing arranged for, and guaranteed by, Amy. Later, Carl and Dave become BP members. They sign a member's agreement, which states, "Amy shall own a 50 percent interest in the capital, profits, and losses of BP and shall have 50 percent of the voting rights. Carl and Dave, collectively, shall own

a 50 percent interest in the capital, profits, and losses of BP and shall have 50 percent of the voting rights." BP's sole asset is the warehouse. When relations among the members become strained, Amy executes a deed transferring the warehouse to Excel, LLC, for $500,000. Excel has two members—Amy, with a 60 percent interest, and Carl, with 40 percent. Neither Amy nor Carl discusses the warehouse transfer with Dave, but Amy mails him a check that purports to represent his 25 percent interest in the warehouse. Dave files a suit against Amy and Carl, alleging that the transfer was unfair. On what basis might the court rule in favor of the defendants? Why might the court decide in Dave's favor? Explain.

- **For a sample answer to Question 43–2, go to Appendix I at the end of this text.**

43–3. Officer Liability South Shore Imaging, Inc., agreed to lease a Konica laser imager machine from Key Equipment Finance. The lease contained a guaranty section to be signed by the officers. The officers returned the lease with their signatures but added their corporate titles in handwriting. Key then demanded that the document be reexecuted without the reference to corporate capacities. The officers did so. Key later sought to recover from the individual officers for breach of the lease. Should the court hold them liable? Explain. [*Key Equipment Finance v. South Shore Imaging, Inc.*, 69 A.D.3d 805, 893 N.Y.S.2d 574 (2010)]

43–4. Trade Secrets Hudson & Muma, Inc., was a small, family-owned insurance agency. Andrew Muma, the son of the founder, was an officer, shareholder, and director of the company. Andrew left the company and began working as a commissioned salesman for another insurance agency, Wolf-Hulbert Co. Hudson & Muma filed a suit against Wolf-Hulbert, alleging that Andrew had taken customer information that was a trade secret. Wolf-Hulbert argued that it had no knowledge of this, and the trial court granted a motion dismissing the action. Hudson & Muma appealed. How should the appellate court decide? Why? [*Hudson & Muma, Inc. v. Wolf-Hulbert Co.*, ___ N.W.2d ___ (Mich.App. 2010)]

43–5. Owner Liability Raynor Manufacturing Co. sold garage doors and related products. In 1983, it sold products to Kelly and Janet Stoner, doing business as Raynor Door Co. of Topeka. The Stoners, operating as a partnership, personally guaranteed payment of any balance to Raynor Manufacturing. The Stoners and Raynor Manufacturing continued doing business for more than a decade. In August 1992, the Stoners incorporated their partnership. In 2005, Raynor Manufacturing made a demand for a past due amount exceeding $223,000. It also sued the Stoners for failing to pay under their personal guaranty. The Stoners argued that their personal guaranty did not survive incorporation, but the district court found for Raynor Manufacturing. On appeal, what should be the result? Why? [*Raynor Manufacturing Co. v. Raynor Door Co.* 225 P.3d 780 (2010)]

43–6. Limited Partnerships Wall Street Technology Partners, LP, was a limited partnership, operating under a 2000 limited partnership agreement. Limited partners made capital contributions on joining the partnership. Under the agreement, they were obligated to make additional contributions as needed, when requested by the general partner. In December 2002, a capital call was sent to the limited partners, but they failed to respond. Wall Street brought an action to compel them to pay. They claimed that they had been promised that such contributions would not be required. Should they be compelled to pay? Why or why not? [*Wall Street Technology Partners, LP, v. Kanders*, ___ A.2d ___ (Conn.Super. 2010)]

43–7. CASE PROBLEM WITH SAMPLE ANSWER: Fraud.

Emil Cerullo owned a small diagnostic imaging center in Dallas, Texas. With one of the doctors who used the center, he formed a partnership to develop ambulatory centers for lap band surgeries for weight-loss patients. Cerullo and his partner approached Peter Gottlieb about building and managing a center, and he promised that he would do so. Gottlieb subsequently set up the center independently, without Cerullo and his partner, and Cerullo sued. A jury found that Gottlieb had committed fraud and awarded actual and punitive damages. Should this verdict stand on appeal? Explain why or why not. [*Cerullo v. Gottlieb*, 309 S.W.3d 160 (Tex. App. 2010)]

- To view a sample answer for Problem 43–7, go to this book's Web site at www.cengage.com/blaw/clarkson, select "Chapter 43," and click on "Case Problem with Sample Answer."

43–8. Limited Liability Companies Coco Investments, LLC, and other investors participated in a condominium conversion project to be managed by Zamir Manager River Terrace, LLC. The participants entered into a new LLC agreement for the project. The investors subsequently complained that Zamir had failed to disclose its plans for dramatic changes involving higher than expected construction costs and delays, had failed to provide financial information, and had restructured loans in a manner that allowed Zamir representatives to avoid personal liability. The investors sued Zamir on various grounds, including breach of contract and breach of fiduciary duty. Zamir moved for summary judgment. How should the court rule? Explain. [*Coco Investments, LLC v. Zamir Manager River Terrace, LLC*, 26 Misc.3d 1231 (N.Y.Sup. 2010)]

43–9. Limited Liability Companies PT China, LLC, joined with PT Korea, LLC, to form PT Holdings. Harrison Wang and Michael Kim, representing the two entities, were to be the managers. The agreements prohibited them from engaging in related outside business endeavors. PT China subsequently filed a suit against PT Korea and Kim, alleging that Kim had misappropriated funds. The defendants counterclaimed, alleging that Wang had breached his fiduciary duties of loyalty to the entity by usurping business opportunities. Wang moved to dismiss the counterclaim, contending that any allegation that he had violated his fiduciary duties was precluded by Kim's claim against him for breach of contract under the LLC's operating agreement. How should the court rule? Why? [*PT China, LLC v. PT Korea, LLC*, ___ A.2d ___ (Del.Ch. 2010)]

43–10. A QUESTION OF ETHICS: Taxation of LLCs.

Sean McNamee was the owner of an accounting firm, W. F. McNamee & Co., LLC (WFM), which he founded and formed in Connecticut as a limited liability company (LLC). For federal tax purposes, an LLC can elect to be treated as a corporation or as a sole proprietorship by checking the appropriate box on a certain tax form. A corporation's income is subject to double taxation—the corporation is taxed directly, and its shareholders are taxed on dividends paid to them from the income—but its owners normally are not liable if the firm does not pay its taxes. A sole proprietorship is taxed only once—the owner pays personal income tax on the business's income—but its owner is liable if the tax is not paid. In 2000, an LLC with a single owner that did not elect corporate treatment was taxed as a sole proprietorship. McNamee did not elect to have WFM treated as a corporation. During the last six months of 2000

and all of 2001, WFM employed an average of six persons but did not pay any payroll taxes. The unpaid total was $64,736.18. WFM went out of business in 2002. The U.S. Department of the Treasury, through the Internal Revenue Service (IRS), assessed the amount of the unpaid tax against McNamee personally. [McNamee v. Department of the Treasury, 488 F.3d 100 (2d Cir. 2007)]

(a) McNamee objected to the IRS's attempt to collect the tax from him, pointing to Connecticut statutes under which the members of an LLC are not personally liable for its debts. He argued that the IRS's action was "in direct conflict with the right of an LLC member." How would the IRS likely respond to this objection? Do you agree with McNamee or the IRS? Why? What might McNamee have done to avoid this dispute?

(b) In October 2005, the IRS proposed to amend the check-the-box regulation to relieve the owner of a single-member LLC from the possibility of personal liability for the LLC's payroll tax liability. Does this proposal show that the check-the-box regulation under which McNamee was personally assessed with the amount of the unpaid taxes was "unethical" or "wrong"? Why or why not?

LEGAL RESEARCH EXERCISES ON THE WEB

Go to this text's Web site at **www.cengage.com/blaw/clarkson**, select "Chapter 43," and click on "Practical Internet Exercises." There you will find the following Internet research exercises that you can perform to learn more about the topics covered in this chapter.

Practical Internet Exercise 43–1: **Legal Perspective**
The Entrepreneur's Options

Practical Internet Exercise 43–2: **Management Perspective**
Financing a Business

Every now and then, scandals in the business world rock the nation. Certainly, this was true in the first decade of the 2000s when the activities of Enron Corporation, AIG, and a number of other companies came to light. As noted in several chapters in this unit, Congress responded to public outcry in 2002 by passing the Sarbanes-Oxley Act, which imposed stricter requirements on corporations with respect to accounting practices and statements made in documents filed with the Securities and Exchange Commission (SEC). The lesson for the business world is, of course, that if business leaders do not behave ethically (and legally), the government will create new laws and regulations that force them to do so. We offered suggestions on how business decision makers can create an ethical workplace in Chapter 5. Here, we look at selected areas in which the relationships within specific business organizational forms may raise ethical issues.

The Emergence of Corporate Governance

The well-publicized corporate abuses of recent years provided the impetus for businesspersons to create their own internal rules for corporate governance (discussed in Chapter 42). Examples of these abuses make it clear why such rules are needed. In a few situations, officers have blatantly stolen from the corporation and its shareholders. More frequently, though, officers have received excessive benefits, or "perks," because of their position. To illustrate: Tyco International bought a $6,000 shower curtain and a $15,000 umbrella stand for its chief executive officer's apartment.

Corporate officers may be given numerous benefits, which they may or may not deserve. On several occasions, a leading corporate officer has received compensation of $50 million or more in a year when the company's share price actually declined. Even if corporate officers are scrupulously honest and have modest personal tastes, their behavior may still raise concerns: they may not be good managers, and they may make incompetent corporate decisions. They may be a little lazy and fail to do the hard work necessary to investigate the corporation's alternatives. Sometimes, officers may simply fail to appreciate the concerns of shareholders on certain matters, such as maximizing short-term versus long-term results.

Corporate governance controls are meant to ensure that officers receive only the benefits they earn. Governance monitors the actions taken by officers to make sure they are wise and in the best interests of the company. In this way, the corporation can be confident that it is acting ethically toward its shareholders.

Fiduciary Duties Revisited

The law of agency, as outlined in Chapters 32 and 33, permeates nearly all relationships within any partnership or corporation. An important duty that arises in the law of agency, and applies to all partners and corporate directors, officers, and management personnel, is the duty of loyalty. As caretakers of the shareholders' wealth, corporate directors and officers also have a fiduciary duty to exercise care when making decisions affecting the corporate enterprise.

The Duty of Loyalty   Every individual has his or her own personal interests, which may at times conflict with the interests of the partnership or corporation with which he or she is affiliated. In particular, a partner or a corporate director may face a conflict between personal interests and the interests of the business entity. Corporate officers and directors may find themselves in a position to acquire assets that would also benefit the corporation if acquired in the corporation's name. If an officer does purchase the asset without offering the opportunity to the corporation, however, she or he may be liable for usurping a corporate opportunity.[1]

Most courts also hold that a corporate officer or director has a fiduciary duty to disclose improper conduct to the corporation. The Supreme Court of Arkansas weighed in on this issue in 2007. Thomas Coughlin was a top executive in theft prevention at Wal-Mart who held several other high-level positions prior to becoming a member of the corporation's board of directors. He retired in 2005 and entered into a retirement agreement and release of claims with Wal-Mart under which he was to receive millions of dollars in benefits over the years.

Then Wal-Mart discovered that Coughlin, before his retirement, had abused his position of authority and conspired with subordinates to misappropriate hundreds of thousands of dollars in property and cash through various fraudulent schemes. Wal-Mart filed a lawsuit alleging that Coughlin had breached his fiduciary duty of loyalty by failing to disclose his misconduct before entering a self-dealing contract. Ultimately, the state's highest court agreed and held that the director's fiduciary duty obligated him to divulge material facts of *past* fraud to the corporation before entering the contract. The court stated, "We are persuaded, in addition, that the majority view is correct, which is that the failure of a fiduciary to disclose material facts of his fraudulent conduct to his corporation prior to entering into a self-dealing contract with that corporation will void that contract."[2]

---

1. For a landmark case on this issue, see *Guth v. Loft, Inc.,* 5 A.2d 503 (Del. 1939), presented as Case 40.1 in Chapter 40.
2. *Wal-Mart Stores, Inc. v. Coughlin,* 369 Ark. 365, 255 S.W.3d 424 (2007); also see *Blankenship v. USA Truck, Inc.,* 601 F.3d 852 (8th Cir. 2010) interpreting Arkansas law by applying the *Wal-Mart* case.

FOCUS ON ETHICS CONTINUES ➤

The Duty of Care   In addition to the duty of loyalty, every corporate director or officer owes a duty of care. *Due care* means that officers and directors must keep themselves informed and make businesslike judgments. Officers have a duty to disclose material information that shareholders need for competent decision making. Some courts have even suggested that corporate directors have a duty to detect and "ferret out" wrongdoing within the corporation.[3] In fact, a number of courts applying Delaware law have recognized that directors may be held liable for failing to exercise proper oversight.[4] For example, in 2009 a Delaware court held that shareholders of Citigroup, Inc., could sue the directors and officers for failure to exercise due care to adequately protect the corporation from exposure to the subprime lending market.[5] Corporate law also creates other structures to protect shareholder interests, such as the right to inspect books and records.

Although traditionally the duty of care did not require directors to monitor the behavior of corporate employees to detect and prevent wrongdoing, the tide may be changing. Since the corporate sentencing guidelines were issued in 1991, courts have had the power to impose substantial penalties on corporations and corporate directors for criminal wrongdoing. The guidelines allow these penalties to be mitigated, though, if a company can show that it has an effective compliance program in place to detect and prevent wrongdoing by corporate personnel. Since the Sarbanes-Oxley Act of 2002 required the sentencing commission to revise these guidelines, the penalties for white-collar crimes, such as federal mail and wire fraud, have increased dramatically.

Fiduciary Duties to Creditors   It is a long-standing principle that corporate directors ordinarily owe fiduciary duties only to a corporation's shareholders. Directors who favor the interests of other corporate "stakeholders," such as creditors, over those of the shareholders have been held liable for breaching these duties. The picture changes, however, when a corporation approaches insolvency. At this point, the shareholders' equity interests in the corporation may be worthless, while the interests of creditors become paramount. In this situation, do the fiduciary duties of loyalty and care extend to the corporation's creditors as well as to the shareholders? The answer to this question, according to some courts, is yes. In a leading case on this issue, a Delaware court noted that "the possibility of insolvency can do curious things to incentives, exposing creditors to risks of opportunistic behavior and creating complexities for directors." The court held that when a corporation is on the brink of insolvency, the directors assume a fiduciary duty to other stakeholders that sustain the corporate entity, including creditors.[6] When a corporation is insolvent, courts often require directors to consider the best interests of the whole corporate enterprise—including all its constituent groups—and not to give preference to the interests of any one group.[7]

Corporate Blogs and Tweets and Securities Fraud

In the fast-paced world of securities trading, there is a great demand for the latest information about companies, earnings, and market conditions. Corporations have adapted to technology by establishing Web sites and blogs, and using other interactive online media, such as Twitter and online shareholder forums. Nearly 20 percent of Fortune 500 companies sponsor blogs. Corporations that use the Internet to distribute information about the company to investors, however, need to make sure that they comply with the regulations issued by the SEC. The SEC treats statements by employees in online media, such as blogs and Twitter, the same as any other company statements for purposes of federal securities laws.

"Tweets" That Contain Financial Information   Some corporate blogs include links to corporate employees' Twitter accounts so that readers can communicate directly with, and get updates from, the individual who posted the information. For example, eBay, Inc., launched its corporate blog in 2008. A few months later, Richard Brewer-Hay, a seasoned blogger that eBay hired to report online, began "tweeting" (posting updates on Twitter) about eBay's quarterly earnings and what took place at Silicon Valley technology conferences. Brewer-Hay's tweets gained him a following, but then eBay's lawyers required him to include a regulatory disclaimer with certain posts to avoid problems with the SEC. Many of his followers were disappointed by the company's oversight, which put an end to his spontaneous, personal, and informal style.

3. *In re Caremark International, Inc. Derivative Litigation,* 698 A.2d 959 (Del.Ch. 1996); also *Forsyhe v. ESC Fund Management Co.* (U.S.), Inc., 2007 WL 2982247 (Del.Ch. 2007).

4. See, for example, *McCall v. Scott,* 239 F.3d 808 (6th Cir. 2001); *Guttman v. Huang,* 823 A.2d 492 (Del.Ch. 2003); *Landy v. D'Alessandro,* 316 F.Supp.2d 49 (D.Mass. 2004); and *Miller v. U.S. Foodservice, Inc.,* 361 F.Supp.2d 470 (D.Md. 2005).

5. *In re Citigroup, Inc., Shareholder Derivative Litigation,* 964 A.2d 106 (Del.Ch. 2009).

6. *Credit Lyonnais Bank Nederland N.V. v. Pathe Communications Corp.,* 1991 WL 277613 (Del.Ch. 1991). See also *Production Resources Group, LLC v. NCT Group, Inc.,* 863 A.2d 772 (Del.Ch. 2004); and *In re Amcast Industrial Corp.,* 365 Bankr. 91 (S.D. Ohio 2007).

7. See *Berg & Berg Enterprises, LLC v. Boyle,* 178 Cal.App.4th 1020, 100 Cal.Rptr.3d 875 (2009).

Brewer-Hay is now much more reserved in his tweets on financial matters and often simply repeats eBay executives' statements verbatim.[8]

A 2008 SEC Release Provides Guidance The reaction of eBay's lawyers to Brewer-Hay's tweets was prompted in part by an interpretive release issued by the SEC in August 2008. The SEC generally embraces new technology and encourages companies to use electronic communication methods. The SEC noted that "the use of the Internet has grown such that, for some companies in certain circumstances, posting of the information on the company's Web site, in and of itself, may be a sufficient method of public disclosure."

The release also addressed company-sponsored blogs, electronic shareholders' forums, and other "interactive Web site features." The SEC acknowledged that blogs and other interactive Web features are a useful means of ongoing communications among companies, their clients, investors, shareholders, and stakeholders. The SEC cautioned, though, that all communications made by or on behalf of a company are subject to the antifraud provisions of federal securities laws. "While blogs or forums can be informal and conversational in nature, statements made there . . . will not be treated differently from other company statements." In addition, the release stated that companies cannot require investors to waive protections under federal securities laws as a condition of participating in a blog or forum. (The release also cautioned companies that they can, in some situations, be liable for providing hyperlinks to third party information or inaccurate summaries of financial information on their Web sites.)[9]

The Sarbanes-Oxley Act and Insider Trading

The attorney-client privilege generally prevents lawyers from disclosing confidential client information—even when the client has committed an unlawful act. The idea is to encourage clients to be open and honest with their attorneys to ensure competent representation. The Sarbanes-Oxley Act of 2002, however, requires attorneys to report any material violations of securities laws to the corporation's highest authority.[10] The act does not require that the lawyer break client confidences, though, because the lawyer is still reporting to officials within the corporation.

In August 2003, the SEC went one step further than the Sarbanes-Oxley Act to permit attorneys to disclose confidential information to the SEC without the corporate client's consent in certain circumstances.[11] Although the American Bar Association modified its ethics rules to allow attorneys to break confidence with a client to report possible corporate fraud, not all state ethics codes allow attorneys to disclose client information to the SEC. Thus, by reporting possible violations of securities law to the SEC, corporate lawyers may violate the state ethics code of their profession.

DISCUSSION QUESTIONS

1. Three decades ago, corporations and corporate directors were rarely prosecuted for crimes, and penalties for corporate crimes were relatively light. Today, this is no longer true. Under the corporate sentencing guidelines and the Sarbanes-Oxley Act, corporate wrongdoers can receive substantial penalties. Do these developments mean that corporations are committing more crimes today than in the past? Will stricter laws be effective in curbing corporate criminal activity? How can a company avoid liability for crimes committed by its employees?

2. Do you agree that when a corporation is approaching insolvency, the directors' fiduciary obligations should extend to the corporation's creditors as well as to the shareholders?

3. When a company's executives offer opinions about the firm's financial status and future business prospects through blogs, Twitter, and other Internet forums, the SEC can hold the company liable for violating securities laws. Is this fair to investors who want to hear the straight scoop from the firm's executives? What arguments can you make in favor of this restriction? What arguments can you make against it?

4. Should corporate lawyers who become aware that someone at the client corporation may have violated securities laws report their suspicions only to persons within the corporation, or should they report their concerns to the SEC? Explain.

---

8. Cari Tuna. "Corporate Blogs and 'Tweets' Must Keep SEC in Mind. *online.wsj.com.* " April 27, 2009: n.p. Web.

9. SEC Release Nos. 34–58288, IC–28351, File No. S7–23–08. Commission Guidance on the Use of Company Web Sites.

10. See Section 307 of the Sarbanes-Oxley Act.

11. See 17 C.F.R. Part 205.3.

UNIT NINE

GOVERNMENT REGULATION

CONTENTS

BUSINESS LAW

CLARKSON · MILLER · CROSS

Government agencies established to administer the law have a great impact on the day-to-day operations of the government and the economy. In its early years, the United States had a simple, nonindustrial economy with few political demands for detailed regulations and therefore not very many administrative agencies. Today, in contrast, rules cover almost every aspect of a business's operation. Consequently, agencies have multiplied.

Administrative agencies issue rules, orders, interpretations, and decisions. The regulations make up the body of *administrative law.* You were introduced briefly to some of the main principles of administrative law in Chapter 1. In the following pages, we will look at these principles in much greater detail.

SECTION 1
THE PRACTICAL SIGNIFICANCE OF ADMINISTRATIVE LAW

Unlike statutory law, administrative law is created by administrative agencies, not by legislatures, but it is nevertheless of paramount significance for businesses. When Congress—or a state legislature—enacts legislation, it typically adopts a rather general statute and leaves its implementation to an administrative agency, which then creates the detailed rules and regulations necessary to carry out the statute. The administrative agency, with its specialized personnel, has the time, resources, and expertise to make the detailed decisions required for regulation.

Administrative Agencies Exist at All Levels of Government

Administrative agencies are spread throughout the government. At the federal level, the Securities and Exchange Commission regulates a firm's capital structure and financing, as well as its financial reporting. The National Labor Relations Board oversees relations between a firm and any unions with which it may deal. The Equal Employment Opportunity Commission also regulates employer-employee relationships. The Environmental Protection Agency and the Occupational Safety and Health Administration affect the way a firm manufactures its products, and the Federal Trade Commission influences the way it markets those products.

Added to this layer of federal regulation is a second layer of state regulation that, when not preempted, may cover many of the same activities as federal regulation or regulate independently the activities that federal regulation does not cover. If the actions of parallel state and federal agencies conflict, the actions of the federal agency will prevail under the supremacy clause of the U.S. Constitution. Agency regulations at the county or municipal level can also affect certain types of business activities.

Agencies Provide a Comprehensive Regulatory Scheme

Often, administrative agencies at various levels of government work together and share the responsibility of creating and enforcing particular regulations. For example, when Congress enacted the Clean Air Act (to be discussed in Chapter 46), it provided only general directions for the prevention of air pollution. The specific pollution-control requirements imposed on business are almost entirely the product of decisions made by the Environmental Protection Agency (EPA). Moreover, the EPA works with parallel environmental agencies at the state level to analyze existing data and determine the appropriate pollution-control standards.

Legislation and regulations have significant benefits—in the example of the Clean Air Act, a cleaner environment than existed in decades past. At the same time, these benefits entail considerable costs for business. The EPA has estimated the costs of compliance with the Clean Air Act at many tens of billions of dollars yearly. Although the agency has calculated that the overall benefits of its regulations often exceed their costs, the burden on business is substantial. Additionally, the costs are proportionately higher for small businesses because they cannot take advantage of the economies of scale (cost advantages that a firm obtains due to expansion) available to larger operations.

Given the costs that regulation entails, business has a strong incentive to try to influence the regulatory environment. Whenever new regulations are proposed, as happens constantly, companies may lobby the agency to try to persuade it not to adopt a particular regulation or to adopt one that is more cost-effective. At the same time, public-interest groups may be lobbying in favor of more stringent regulation.

SECTION 2

AGENCY CREATION AND POWERS

Congress creates federal administrative agencies. By delegating some of its authority to make and implement laws, Congress can monitor indirectly a particular area in which it has passed legislation without becoming bogged down in the details relating to enforcement—details that are often best left to specialists.

To create an administrative agency, Congress passes **enabling legislation,** which specifies the name, purposes, functions, and powers of the agency being created. Federal administrative agencies can exercise only those powers that Congress has delegated to them in enabling legislation. Through similar enabling acts, state legislatures create state administrative agencies, which commonly parallel federal agencies.

An agency's enabling statute defines its legal authority. An agency cannot regulate beyond the powers granted by the statute, and it may be required to take some regulatory action by the terms of that statute. When regulated groups oppose a rule adopted by an agency, they often bring a lawsuit arguing that the rule was not authorized by the enabling statute and is therefore void. Conversely, a group may file suit claiming that an agency has illegally *failed* to pursue regulation required by the enabling statute.

Enabling Legislation—An Example

Congress created the Federal Trade Commission (FTC) by enacting the Federal Trade Commission Act of 1914.[1] The act prohibits unfair methods of competition and deceptive trade practices. It also describes the procedures that the FTC must follow to charge persons or organizations with violations of the act, and it provides for judicial review of agency orders. The act grants the FTC the power to do the following:

1. To create "rules and regulations for the purpose of carrying out the Act."
2. To conduct investigations of business practices.
3. To obtain reports from interstate corporations concerning their business practices.
4. To investigate possible violations of federal antitrust statutes.[2]
5. To publish findings of its investigations.
6. To recommend new legislation.
7. To hold trial-like hearings to resolve certain kinds of trade disputes that involve FTC regulations or federal antitrust laws.

The authorizing statute for the FTC allows it to prevent the use of "unfair methods of competition," but does not define *unfairness.* Congress delegated that authority to the commission, thereby providing it with considerable discretion in regulating competition. The commission that heads the FTC is composed of five members, each of whom the president appoints, with the advice and consent of the Senate, for a term of seven years.

Types of Agencies

As discussed in Chapter 1, there are two basic types of administrative agencies: executive agencies and independent regulatory agencies. Federal *executive agencies* include the cabinet departments of the

---

1. 15 U.S.C. Sections 41–58.
2. The FTC shares enforcement of the Clayton Act with the Antitrust Division of the U.S. Department of Justice (see Chapter 47).

executive branch, which were formed to assist the president in carrying out executive functions, and the subagencies within the cabinet departments. The Occupational Safety and Health Administration, for example, is a subagency within the U.S. Department of Labor. Executive agencies usually have a single administrator, director, or secretary who is appointed by the president to oversee the agency and can be removed by the president at any time. Exhibit 44–1 below lists the cabinet departments and some of their most important subagencies.

Independent regulatory agencies are outside the federal executive departments (those headed by a cabinet secretary). Examples of independent agencies include the Federal Trade Commission and the Securities and Exchange Commission (SEC). Rather than having a single person as its head, an independent agency usually is run by a commission or board made up of several members, one of whom serves as the agency's chair. Commissioners or board members typically serve for fixed terms and cannot be removed without just cause. The SEC has five commissioners who serve

EXHIBIT 44–1 • Executive Departments and Important Subagencies

DEPARTMENT AND YEAR FORMED	SELECTED SUBAGENCIES
State (1789)	Passport Office; Bureau of Diplomatic Security; Foreign Service; Bureau of Human Rights and Humanitarian Affairs; Bureau of Consular Affairs; Bureau of Intelligence and Research
Treasury (1789)	Internal Revenue Service; U.S. Mint
Interior (1849)	U.S. Fish and Wildlife Service; National Park Service; Bureau of Indian Affairs; Bureau of Land Management
Justice (1870)[a]	Federal Bureau of Investigation; Drug Enforcement Administration; Bureau of Prisons; U.S. Marshals Service
Agriculture (1889)	Soil Conservation Service; Agricultural Research Service; Food Safety and Inspection Service; Forest Service
Commerce (1913)[b]	Bureau of the Census; Bureau of Economic Analysis; Minority Business Development Agency; U.S. Patent and Trademark Office; National Oceanic and Atmospheric Administration
Labor (1913)[b]	Occupational Safety and Health Administration; Bureau of Labor Statistics; Employment Standards Administration; Office of Labor-Management Standards; Employment and Training Administration
Defense (1949)[c]	National Security Agency; Joint Chiefs of Staff; Departments of the Air Force, Navy, Army; service academies
Housing and Urban Development (1965)	Office of Community Planning and Development; Government National Mortgage Association; Office of Fair Housing and Equal Opportunity
Transportation (1967)	Federal Aviation Administration; Federal Highway Administration; National Highway Traffic Safety Administration; Federal Transit Administration
Energy (1977)	Office of Civilian Radioactive Waste Management; Office of Nuclear Energy; Energy Information Administration
Health and Human Services (1980)[d]	Food and Drug Administration; Centers for Medicare and Medicaid Services; Centers for Disease Control and Prevention; National Institutes of Health
Education (1980)[d]	Office of Special Education and Rehabilitation Services; Office of Elementary and Secondary Education; Office of Postsecondary Education; Office of Vocational and Adult Education
Veterans Affairs (1989)	Veterans Health Administration; Veterans Benefits Administration; National Cemetery System
Homeland Security (2002)	U.S. Citizenship and Immigration Services; Directorate of Border and Transportation Services; U.S. Coast Guard; Federal Emergency Management Agency

a. Formed from the Office of the Attorney General (created in 1789).
b. Formed from the Department of Commerce and Labor (created in 1903).
c. Formed from the Department of War (created in 1789) and the Department of the Navy (created in 1798).
d. Formed from the Department of Health, Education, and Welfare (created in 1953).

for five-year terms that are staggered so that one term ends on June 5 of every year. The SEC's commissioners oversee its four divisions and nineteen offices. Selected independent regulatory agencies, as well as their principal functions, are listed in Exhibit 44–2 below.

Agency Powers and the Constitution

Administrative agencies occupy an unusual niche in the U.S. legal scheme because they exercise powers that normally are divided among the three branches of government. As mentioned earlier, agencies' powers include functions associated with the legislature (*rulemaking*), the executive branch (*enforcement*), and the courts (*adjudication*).

The constitutional principle of *checks and balances* allows each branch of government to act as a check on the actions of the other two branches. Furthermore, the U.S. Constitution authorizes only the legislative branch to create laws. Yet administrative agencies, to which the Constitution does not specifically refer, can make **legislative rules,** or *substantive rules,* that are as legally binding as laws that Congress passes. (Administrative agencies also issue **interpretive rules,** which simply declare policy and do not affect legal rights or obligations.)

THE DELEGATION DOCTRINE Article I of the U.S. Constitution authorizes Congress to delegate powers to administrative agencies. In fact, courts generally hold that Article I is the basis for all administrative law. Section 1 of that article grants all legislative powers to Congress and requires Congress to oversee the implementation of all laws. Article I, Section 8, gives Congress the power to make all laws necessary for executing its specified powers. The courts interpret these passages, under what is known as the **delegation doctrine,** as granting Congress the power to establish administrative agencies that can create rules for implementing those laws.

The three branches of government exercise certain controls over agency powers and functions, as discussed next, but in many ways administrative agencies function independently. For this reason, administrative agencies, which constitute the **bureaucracy,** are sometimes referred to as the fourth branch of the U.S. government.

EXECUTIVE CONTROLS The executive branch of government exercises control over agencies both through the president's power to appoint federal officers and through the president's veto power. The

EXHIBIT 44–2 • Selected Independent Regulatory Agencies

NAME AND YEAR FORMED	PRINCIPAL DUTIES
Federal Reserve System Board of Governors (the Fed)–1913	Determines policy with respect to interest rates, credit availability, and the money supply; starting in 2008, the Federal Reserve became involved in various "bailouts" of firms in the financial sector, including a "conservatorship" of two large mortgage institutions (Fannie Mae and Freddie Mac) and control of the world's largest insurance company, AIG.
Federal Trade Commission (FTC)–1914	Prevents businesses from engaging in unfair trade practices; stops the formation of monopolies in the business sector; protects consumer rights.
Securities and Exchange Commission (SEC)–1934	Regulates the nation's stock exchanges, in which shares of stock are bought and sold; enforces the securities laws, which require full disclosure of the financial profiles of companies that wish to sell stock and bonds to the public.
Federal Communications Commission (FCC)–1934	Regulates all communications by telegraph, cable, telephone, radio, satellite, and television.
National Labor Relations Board (NLRB)–1935	Protects employees' rights to join unions and bargain collectively with employers; attempts to prevent unfair labor practices by both employers and unions.
Equal Employment Opportunity Commission (EEOC)–1964	Works to eliminate discrimination in employment based on religion, gender, race, color, disability, national origin, or age; investigates claims of discrimination.
Environmental Protection Agency (EPA)–1970	Undertakes programs aimed at reducing air and water pollution; works with state and local agencies to help fight environmental hazards. (It has been suggested recently that its status be elevated to that of a department.)
Nuclear Regulatory Commission (NRC)–1975	Ensures that electricity-generating nuclear reactors in the United States are built and operated safely; regularly inspects operations of such reactors.

president may veto enabling legislation presented by Congress or congressional attempts to modify an existing agency's authority. In addition, the president has created a process whereby the Office of Information and Regulatory Affairs (OIRA) of the Office of Management and Budget reviews the cost-effectiveness of agency rules. The OIRA also reviews agencies' compliance with the Paperwork Reduction Act,[3] which requires agencies to minimize the paperwork burden on regulated entities.

LEGISLATIVE CONTROLS Congress also exercises authority over agency powers. Congress gives power to an agency through enabling legislation and can take power away—or even abolish an agency altogether—through subsequent legislation. Legislative authority is required to fund an agency, and enabling legislation usually sets certain time and monetary limits on the funding of particular programs. Congress can always revise these limits. In addition to its power to create and fund agencies, Congress has the authority to investigate the implementation of its laws and the agencies that it has created. Congress also has the power to "freeze" the enforcement of most federal regulations before the regulations take effect. Another legislative check on agency actions is the Administrative Procedure Act, which will be discussed shortly.

JUDICIAL CONTROLS The judicial branch exercises control over agency powers through the courts' review of agency actions. As you will read in the next section, the Administrative Procedure Act provides for judicial review of most agency decisions. Agency actions are not automatically subject to judicial review, however, and the courts can deny review under the two theories discussed next.

The Exhaustion Doctrine. The party seeking court review must first exhaust all of his or her administrative remedies under what is called the *exhaustion doctrine.* In other words, the complaining party normally must have gone through the administrative process (from complaint to hearing to final agency order, all of which will be discussed later in this chapter) before seeking court review.

Suppose that an employee who has a disability believes that she has suffered unlawful discrimination in the workplace (see Chapter 35). Under the exhaustion doctrine, before she can file a complaint in court, she must have filed a complaint with the Equal Employment Opportunity Commission (EEOC), and the EEOC must have issued its final ruling.

The Ripeness Doctrine. In addition, under what is known as the *ripeness doctrine,* a court will not review an administrative agency's decision until the case is "ripe for review." Generally, a case is ripe for review if the parties can demonstrate that they have met certain requirements. For example, the party bringing the action must have *standing to sue* the agency (the party must have a direct stake in the outcome of the judicial proceeding, as discussed in Chapter 2), and there must be an *actual controversy* at issue. A court can dismiss the action if the administrative agency has not yet issued a decision or if the party lacks standing.

━━◢ SECTION 3 ◣━━
THE ADMINISTRATIVE PROCEDURE ACT

All federal agencies must follow specific procedural requirements when fulfilling their three basic functions of rulemaking, enforcement, and adjudication. In this section, we focus on agency rulemaking (enforcement and adjudication will be discussed in a later section of this chapter). Sometimes, Congress specifies certain procedural requirements in an agency's enabling legislation. In the absence of any directives from Congress concerning a particular agency procedure, the Administrative Procedure Act (APA) of 1946[4] applies.

The Arbitrary and Capricious Test

One of Congress's goals in enacting the APA was to provide for more judicial control over administrative agencies. To that end, the APA provides that courts should "hold unlawful and set aside" agency actions found to be "arbitrary, capricious, an abuse of discretion, or otherwise not in accordance with law."[5] Under this standard, parties can challenge regulations as contrary to law or so irrational as to be arbitrary and capricious.

---

3. Pub. L. No. 104-13, May 22, 1995, 109 Stat. 163, amending 44 U.S.C. Sections 3501 *et seq.*

4. 5 U.S.C. Sections 551–706.
5. 5 U.S.C. Section 706(2)(A).

There is no precise definition of what makes a rule arbitrary and capricious, but the standard includes factors such as whether the agency has done any of the following:

1. Failed to provide a rational explanation for its decision.
2. Changed its prior policy without justification.

3. Considered legally inappropriate factors.
4. Entirely failed to consider a relevant factor.
5. Rendered a decision plainly contrary to the evidence.

In the following case, the United States Supreme Court considered the application of the arbitrary and capricious standard.

✳ EXTENDED CASE 44.1 ✳
Federal Communications Commission v. Fox Television Stations, Inc.
Supreme Court of the United States, ___ U.S. ___, 129 S.Ct. 1800, 173 L.Ed.2d 738 (2009).
www.supremecourt.gov/opinions/opinions.aspx[a]

IN THE LANGUAGE OF THE COURT

Justice *SCALIA* delivered the opinion of the Court.
* * * *
The Communications Act of 1934 established a system of limited-term broadcast licenses subject to various "conditions" * * *.

* * * [These conditions include] the indecency ban—the statutory proscription [prohibition] against "utter[ing] any obscene, indecent, or profane language by means of radio communication"—which Congress has instructed the [Federal Communications] Commission to enforce * * *.
* * * *

The Commission first invoked the statutory ban on indecent broadcasts in 1975, declaring a daytime broadcast of George Carlin's "Filthy Words" monologue actionably indecent. At that time, the Commission announced the definition of indecent speech that it uses to this day, prohibiting "language that describes, in terms patently offensive as measured by contemporary community standards for the broadcast medium, sexual or excretory activities or organs, at times of the day when there is a reasonable risk that children may be in the audience."
* * * *

Over a decade later, the Commission emphasized that the "full context" in which particular materials appear is "critically important," but that a few "principal" factors guide the inquiry, such as the "explicitness or graphic nature" of the material, the extent to which the material "dwells on or repeats" the offensive material, and the extent to which the material was presented to "pander," to "titillate," or to "shock." * * * "Where sexual or excretory references have been made once or have been passing or fleeting in nature, this characteristic has tended to weigh against a finding of indecency."

In 2004, the Commission took one step further by declaring for the first time that a nonliteral (expletive) use of the F- and S-Words could be actionably indecent, even when the word is used only once. The first order to this effect dealt with an NBC broadcast of the Golden Globe Awards, in which the performer Bono [lead singer of the rock group U-2] commented, "This is really, really, f***ing brilliant."
* * * *

The order acknowledged that "prior Commission and staff action have indicated that isolated or fleeting broadcasts of the 'F-Word' * * * are not indecent or would not be acted upon." It explicitly

ruled that "any such interpretation is no longer good law."

[The present case] concerns utterances in two live broadcasts aired by Fox Television Stations, Inc., * * * prior to the Commission's Golden Globes Order. The first occurred during the 2002 Billboard Music Awards, when the singer Cher exclaimed, "I've also had critics for the last 40 years saying that I was on my way out every year. Right. So f*** 'em." The second involved a segment of the 2003 Billboard Music Awards, [when Nicole Richie asked] the audience, "Why do they even call it 'The Simple Life?' Have you ever tried to get cow s*** out of a Prada purse? It's not so f***ing simple."

On March 15, 2006, the Commission released Notices of Apparent Liability for a number of broadcasts that the Commission deemed actionably indecent, including the two described above.
* * * *

* * * In the Commission's view, "granting an automatic exemption for 'isolated or fleeting' expletives unfairly forces viewers (including children)" to take "the first blow" and would allow broadcasters "to air expletives at all hours of a day so long as they did so one at a time."

Fox [appealed] to the Second Circuit [Court of Appeals] for review of the [order] * * *. The Court of

a. Under the heading "2008 Term," select "2008 Term Opinions of the Court." When the page opens, scroll down the list to "49" in the left-hand column and click on the case title to access the opinion. The Supreme Court of the United States maintains this Web site.

EXTENDED CASE CONTINUES ➡

EXTENDED CASE 44.1 CONTINUED ➡

Appeals reversed the agency's order, finding the Commission's reasoning inadequate under the Administrative Procedure Act. * * * We granted *certiorari.*

* * * *

The Administrative Procedure Act, which sets forth the full extent of judicial authority to review executive agency action for procedural correctness, permits (insofar as relevant here) the setting aside of agency action that is "arbitrary" or "capricious." *Under what we have called this "narrow" standard of review, we insist that an agency "examine the relevant data and articulate a satisfactory explanation for its action." We have made clear, however, that "a court is not to substitute its judgment for that of the agency," and should "uphold a decision of less than ideal clarity if the agency's path may reasonably be discerned."* [Emphasis added.]

In overturning the Commission's judgment, the Court of Appeals here relied in part on Circuit precedent requiring a more substantial explanation for agency action that changes prior policy. The Second Circuit has interpreted the Administrative Procedure Act and our opinion in [a previous case] as requiring agencies to make clear "why the original reasons for adopting the [displaced] rule or policy are no longer dispositive [a deciding factor]" as well as "why the new rule effectuates the statute as well as or better than the old rule." The Court of Appeals for the District of Columbia Circuit has similarly indicated that a court's standard of review is "heightened somewhat" when an agency reverses course.

We find no basis in the Administrative Procedure Act or in our opinions for a requirement that all agency change be subjected to more searching review. The Act mentions no such heightened standard. [Emphasis added.]

To be sure, the requirement that an agency provide reasoned explanation for its action would ordinarily demand that it display awareness that it *is* changing position. An agency may not, for example, depart from a prior policy *sub silentio* [under silence, without any notice of the change] or simply disregard rules that are still on the books. And of course the agency must show that there are good reasons for the new policy. But it need not demonstrate to a court's satisfaction that the reasons for the new policy are *better* than the reasons for the old one; it suffices that the new policy is permissible under the statute, that there are good reasons for it, and that the agency *believes* it to be better.

* * * *

Judged under the above-described standards, the Commission's new enforcement policy and its order finding the broadcasts actionably indecent were neither arbitrary nor capricious. First, the Commission forthrightly acknowledged that its recent actions have broken new ground, taking account of inconsistent "prior Commission and staff action" and explicitly disavowing them as "no longer good law." * * * There is no doubt that the Commission knew it was making a change. That is why it declined to assess penalties * * *.

Moreover, the agency's reasons for expanding the scope of its enforcement activity were entirely rational. It was certainly reasonable to determine that it made no sense to distinguish between literal and nonliteral uses of offensive words, requiring repetitive use to render only the latter indecent. * * * It is surely rational (if not inescapable) to believe that a safe harbor for single words would "likely lead to more widespread use of the offensive language."

* * * *

The judgment of the United States Court of Appeals for the Second Circuit is reversed, and the case is remanded for further proceedings consistent with this opinion.[b]

---

b. On remand, the U.S. Court of Appeals for the Second Circuit ruled that the FCC's indecency policies were unconstitutionally vague and violated the broadcast networks' First Amendment rights. See *Fox Television Stations, Inc. v. Federal Communications Commission,* 613 F.3d 317 (2010).

 QUESTIONS

1. Today, children are likely exposed to indecent language in various media far more often than they were in the 1970s, when the Federal Communications Commission first began to sanction indecent speech. Does this mean that we need more stringent—or less stringent—regulation of broadcasts? Explain.
2. Technological advances have made it easier for broadcasters to "bleep out" offending words in the programs that they air. Does this development support a more stringent—or less stringent—enforcement policy by the Federal Communications Commission? Explain.

Rulemaking

Today, the major function of an administrative agency is **rulemaking**—the formulation of new regulations, or rules. The APA defines a *rule* as "an agency statement of general or particular applicability and future effect designed to implement, interpret, or prescribe law and policy."[6] Regulations are sometimes said to be *legislative* because, like statutes, they

---

6. 5 U.S.C. Section 551(4).

have a binding effect. Like those who violate statutes, violators of agency rules may be punished. Because agency rules have such significant legal force, the APA established procedures for agencies to follow in creating rules. Many rules must be adopted using the APA's *notice-and-comment rulemaking* procedure.

Notice-and-comment rulemaking involves three basic steps: notice of the proposed rulemaking, a comment period, and the final rule. The APA recognizes some limited exceptions to these procedural requirements, but they are seldom invoked. If the required procedures are violated, the resulting rule may be invalid.

The impetus for rulemaking may come from various sources, including Congress, the agency itself, or private parties, who may petition an agency to begin a rulemaking (or repeal a rule). For example, environmental groups have petitioned for stricter air-pollution controls to combat emissions that may contribute to global warming.

NOTICE OF THE PROPOSED RULEMAKING When a federal agency decides to create a new rule, the agency publishes a notice of the proposed rulemaking proceedings in the *Federal Register,* a daily publication of the executive branch that prints government orders, rules, and regulations. The notice states where and when the proceedings will be held, the agency's legal authority for making the rule (usually its enabling legislation), and the terms or subject matter of the proposed rule. The APA requires an agency to make available to the public certain information, such as the key scientific data underlying the proposal. The proposed rule is also often reported by the news media and published in the trade journals of the industries that will be affected by the new rule.

COMMENT PERIOD After the publication of the notice of the proposed rulemaking proceedings, the agency must allow ample time for persons to comment in writing on the proposed rule. The comment period must be at least thirty days but is often sixty days or longer. An agency can extend the period to allow for more comments or shorten it in emergencies (such as when the Federal Aviation Administration changed airport security procedures after September 11, 2001).

The purpose of this comment period is to give interested parties the opportunity to express their views on the proposed rule in an effort to influence agency policy. Anyone can submit comments. The comments may be in writing or, if a hearing is held, may be given orally. All comments are logged in and become a public record that others can examine.

The agency need not respond to all comments, but it must respond to any significant comments that bear directly on the proposed rule. The agency responds by either modifying its final rule or explaining, in a statement accompanying the final rule, why it did not make any changes. In some circumstances, particularly when the procedure being used in a specific instance is less formal, an agency may accept comments after the comment period is closed. The agency should summarize these *ex parte* (private, "off-the-record") comments in the record for possible review.[7]

THE FINAL RULE After the agency reviews the comments, it drafts the final rule and publishes it in the *Federal Register.* The final rule must contain a "concise general statement of . . . basis and purpose" that describes the reasoning behind the rule.[8] The final rule may modify the terms of the proposed rule in light of the public comments, but if substantial changes are made, a new proposal and a new opportunity for comment are required. The final rule is later compiled along with the rules and regulations of other federal administrative agencies in the *Code of Federal Regulations.* Final rules have binding legal effect unless the courts later overturn them and for this reason are considered legislative rules. If an agency failed to follow proper rulemaking procedures when it issued the final rule, however, the rule may not be binding.

CASE IN POINT Members of the Hemp Industries Association (HIA) manufacture and sell food products made from hemp seed and oil. These products contain only trace amounts of tetrahydrocannabinols (THC, a component of marijuana) and are nonpsychoactive—that is, they do not affect a person's mind or behavior. In 2001, the U.S. Drug Enforcement Administration (DEA) published an interpretive rule declaring that "any product that contains any amount of THC is a Schedule I controlled substance [a drug whose availability is restricted by law]." Subsequently, without following formal rulemaking procedures, the DEA declared that two legislative rules relating to products containing natural THC were final. These rules effectively

---

7. *Ex parte* is a Latin term meaning "from one party." In the law, it usually refers to proceedings in which only one party to a dispute is present. *Ex parte* communications with judges (or administrative law judges) generally are prohibited. Thus, when agencies accept *ex parte* public comments, they must record them and make them available to others.

8. 5 U.S.C. Section 555(c).

banned the possession and sale of the food products of the HIA's members. The HIA petitioned for court review, arguing that the DEA rules should not have been enforced. A federal appellate court agreed and ruled in favor of the HIA. The DEA should have held hearings on the record concerning the rules, invited public comment, and then issued formal rulings on each finding, conclusion, and exception. Because the DEA did not follow its formal rulemaking procedures, the rules were not enforceable.[9]

Informal Agency Actions

Rather than take the time to conduct notice-and-comment rulemaking, agencies have increasingly been using more informal methods of policymaking, such as issuing interpretive rules and guidance documents. As mentioned previously, *legislative rules* are substantive in that they affect legal rights, whereas *interpretive rules* simply declare policy and do not affect legal rights or obligations. Agencies also issue various other materials, such as guidance documents, which advise the public on the agencies' legal and policy positions.

Informal agency actions are exempt from the APA's requirements because they do not establish legal rights—a party cannot be directly prosecuted for violating an interpretive rule or a guidance document. Nevertheless, an agency's informal action can be of practical importance because it warns regulated entities that the agency may engage in formal rulemaking if they fail to heed the positions taken informally by the agency.

SECTION 4

JUDICIAL DEFERENCE TO AGENCY DECISIONS

When asked to review agency decisions, courts historically granted some deference (significant weight) to the agency's judgment, often citing the agency's great expertise in the subject area of the regulation. This deference seems especially appropriate when applied to an agency's analysis of factual questions, but should it also extend to an agency's interpretation of its own legal authority? In *Chevron U.S.A., Inc. v. Natural Resources Defense Council, Inc.,*[10] the United States Supreme Court held that it should,

thereby creating a standard of broadened deference to agencies on questions of legal interpretation.

The Holding of the *Chevron* Case

At issue in the *Chevron* case was whether the courts should defer to an agency's interpretation of a statute giving it authority to act. The Environmental Protection Agency (EPA) had interpreted the phrase "stationary source" in the Clean Air Act as referring to an entire manufacturing plant, and not to each facility within a plant. The agency's interpretation enabled it to adopt the so-called bubble policy, which allowed companies to offset increases in emissions in part of a plant with decreases elsewhere in the plant—an interpretation that reduced the pollution-control compliance costs faced by manufacturers. An environmental group challenged the legality of the EPA's interpretation.

The Supreme Court held that the courts should defer to an agency's interpretation of *law* as well as fact. The Court found that the agency's interpretation of the statute was reasonable and upheld the bubble policy. The Court's decision in the *Chevron* case created a new standard for courts to use when reviewing agency interpretations of law, which involves the following two questions:

1. Did Congress directly address the issue in dispute in the statute? If so, the statutory language prevails.
2. If the statute is silent or ambiguous, is the agency's interpretation "reasonable"? If it is, a court should uphold the agency's interpretation even if the court would have interpreted the law differently.

When Courts Will Give *Chevron* Deference to Agency Interpretation

The notion that courts should defer to agencies on matters of law was controversial. Under the holding of the *Chevron* case, when the meaning of a particular statute's language is unclear and an agency interprets it, the court must follow the agency's interpretation as long as it is reasonable. This led to considerable discussion and litigation to test the boundaries of the *Chevron* holding. For instance, are courts required to give deference to all agency interpretations or only to those interpretations that result from adjudication or formal rulemaking procedures? Are informal agency interpretations issued through opinion letters and internal memoranda also entitled to deference?

CASE IN POINT   The United States has a tariff (tax) schedule that authorizes the U.S. Customs Service

---

9. *Hemp Industries Association v. Drug Enforcement Administration,* 357 F.3d 1012 (9th Cir. 2004).
10. 467 U.S. 837, 104 S.Ct. 2778, 81 L.Ed.2d 694 (1984).

to classify and fix the rate of duty on imports. "Ruling letters" set tariff classifications for particular imports. Mead Corporation imported "daily planners," which had been tariff-free for several years. The Customs Service issued a ruling letter reclassifying them as "bound diaries," which were subject to a tariff. Mead brought a lawsuit claiming that the ruling letter should not receive *Chevron* deference because it was not put into effect pursuant to notice-and-comment rulemaking. When the case reached the United States Supreme Court, the Court agreed that the ruling letter was *not* entitled to *Chevron* deference. For agencies to be assured of such judicial deference, they must meet the formal legal standards for notice-and-comment rulemaking.[11]

---

11. *United States v. Mead Corporation,* 533 U.S. 218, 121 S.Ct. 2164, 150 L.Ed.2d 292 (2001).

In the case that follows, an environmental organization brought an action challenging the U.S. Forest Service's decision to issue a special use permit to a business that conducts helicopter-skiing operations in two national forests. As you will read in Chapter 46, the National Environmental Policy Act requires federal agencies to prepare an environmental impact statement (EIS) that considers every significant aspect of the environmental impact of a proposed action. Although the Forest Service prepared an EIS before issuing the use permit, environmental groups claimed that the EIS did not sufficiently analyze increasing recreational pressures in the forests. The groups sought to have the court invalidate the permit. Although the *Chevron* precedent is not specifically mentioned, the court's analysis illustrates the way in which courts review agency decisions.

CASE 44.2
Citizens' Committee to Save Our Canyons v. Krueger
United States Court of Appeals, Tenth Circuit, 513 F.3d 1169 (2008).

BACKGROUND AND FACTS • Under the National Forest Management Act (NFMA), the U.S. Forest Service manages national forests in accordance with forest plans periodically developed for each forest. The plans for two national forests—the Wasatch-Cache and Uinta forests—were initially adopted in 1985 and revised in 2003. The Forest Service interpreted the 1985 forest plans as requiring the forests to allow helicopter skiing, and the plans expressly recognized helicopter skiing as a legitimate use of the national forests. Wasatch Powderbird Guides (WPG) has continuously operated a guided helicopter-skiing business in the Wasatch-Cache and Uinta national forests since 1973. It operates under the authority of special use permits periodically issued by the Forest Service. Citizens' Committee to Save Our Canyons and Utah Environmental Congress (referred to collectively as SOC) are nonprofit organizations whose members use the areas in which WPG operates for nonmotorized uses, such as backcountry skiing, snowshoeing, hiking, and camping. They claimed that their recreational opportunities and experiences were diminished by WPG's operations and argued that the Forest Service failed to comply with relevant laws when issuing WPG's most recent permit. The district court upheld the Forest Service permit, and SOC appealed.

IN THE LANGUAGE OF THE COURT
TYMKOVICH, Circuit Judge.
* * * *

Under the Administrative Procedure Act ("APA"), which governs judicial review of agency actions, * * * we set aside the agency's action * * * if it is "arbitrary, capricious, an abuse of discretion, or otherwise not in accordance with law." We will also set aside an agency action if the agency has failed to follow required procedures.

Our review is highly deferential [respectful of the agency's reasoning]. The duty of a court reviewing agency action under the "arbitrary or capricious" standard is to ascertain whether the agency examined the relevant data and articulated a rational connection between the facts found and the decision made. Furthermore, in reviewing the agency's explanation, the reviewing court must determine whether the agency considered all relevant factors and whether there has been a clear error of judgment. A presumption

CASE CONTINUES ➡

CASE 44.2 CONTINUED ▶ *of validity attaches to the agency action and the burden of proof rests with the appellants who challenge such action.* [Emphasis added.]

* * * *

NFMA requires the Forest Service to "develop, maintain, and, as appropriate, revise land and resource management plans for units of the National Forest System." All permits the Forest Service issues "for the use and occupancy of National Forest System lands shall be consistent with the land management plans."

* * * The EIS examined various options and concluded an acceptable balance between helicopter skiing and other uses could be reached by imposing certain restrictions on WPG's operations. These restrictions reflect no special consideration for WPG's economic viability beyond the goal of providing "a range of diverse, recreational opportunities" including helicopter skiing. The EIS thoroughly explains the Forest Service's approach, and the 2005 permit includes a number of reasonable restrictions on WPG with the goal of allowing both helicopter skiers and other backcountry users to enjoy the national forests. In the end, the Forest Service's permit reflected the "type and level" of heli-skiing it thought appropriately balanced the competing recreational uses in the forests.

Taking the interpretation of the forest plans represented by the EIS as a whole, the EIS and the ultimate permitting decision comply with the Forest Service's interpretation of its forest plans. The Forest Service properly considered how particular options would affect the range of recreational opportunities available in the forests and balanced interests in a way it believed promoted multiple forest uses.

* * * *

In sum, the Forest Service's EIS fully disclosed and considered the impact of its decision to issue a special use permit to WPG. *Our objective is not to "fly speck" the [EIS], but rather, to make a pragmatic judgment whether the [EIS]'s form, content and preparation foster both informed decision-making and informed public participation.* The [National Environmental Policy Act (NEPA)] process in this case, including extensive public comment, considered a variety of options and yielded a number of reasonable restrictions on WPG's operations designed to minimize conflict among forest users. This is all NEPA requires. [Emphasis added.]

DECISION AND REMEDY • *The U.S. Court of Appeals for the Tenth Circuit affirmed the district court's decision that upheld the Forest Service permit allowing WPG to conduct helicopter-skiing operations in two national forests. The Forest Service's EIS properly considered all relevant factors and allowed for public comment. Because the Forest Service's interpretation of the NFMA and NEPA was reasonable, the court found that the permit complied with federal laws.*

WHAT IF THE FACTS WERE DIFFERENT? • *Suppose that the Forest Service had granted WPG a permit for its helicopter-skiing operations on national forest land without preparing an EIS or soliciting public comment. How might that have changed the court's ruling?*

THE ETHICAL DIMENSION • *If it turned out that the helicopter-skiing operation had paid a substantial sum to the Forest Service official who prepared the EIS to influence the official's findings, would the court have been able to consider this fact and invalidate the permit? Why or why not?*

SECTION 5
ENFORCEMENT AND ADJUDICATION

Although rulemaking is the most prominent agency activity, enforcement of the rules is also critical. Often, an agency itself enforces its rules. It identifies alleged violators and pursues civil remedies against them in a proceeding held by the agency rather than in federal court, although the agency's determinations are reviewable in court.

Investigation

After final rules are issued, agencies conduct investigations to monitor compliance with those rules or the requirements of the enabling statute. A typical agency investigation of this kind might begin when a citizen reports a possible violation to the agency. (See this chapter's *Insight into Ethics* feature on the facing page for a discussion of how concern about violating regulations has made pharmaceutical companies reluctant to use Twitter and Facebook.)

Many agency rules also require considerable compliance reporting from regulated entities, and such

INSIGHT INTO ETHICS
Should Pharmaceutical Companies Be Allowed to Tweet?

Where do Americans go when they need medical information? More than 60 percent turn to the Internet, and half of those go to social networks, such as Twitter and Facebook, to consult with others about diagnosis and treatments. According to pharmaceutical companies, however, much of the information that potential customers are finding online is incorrect.

Consumers Lack Complete Information on Drugs

Drug companies are, of course, in the business of selling prescription drugs, and they have an incentive to ensure that consumers have correct information about those drugs. Yet drug manufacturers spend less than 5 percent of their consumer advertising budgets on Internet advertising. (More than 95 percent of the $4 billion that these companies spend on direct consumer advertising goes to traditional outlets, such as newspapers, magazines, and television.)

Similarly, drug companies have little or no presence on sites such as Facebook and Twitter. Why not? They fear that the U.S. Food and Drug Administration (FDA) will retaliate if they do not list all of the potential side effects when they mention their drugs on the Web.

Web Ads and Tweets Have Size Limits

The FDA requires advertisements for prescription drugs to disclose all of the potential negative side effects. A magazine ad for a prescription drug, for example, typically includes a large block of small print that details potential side effects. Display ads on the Web are not amenable to such lists. So, to avoid violating the FDA's regulations, pharmaceutical companies run only general, disease-related search ads on the Web. Because the ads only rarely mention a drug's brand name, consumers looking for information about a particular drug rarely click on or find such ads.

As a result, consumers have less information about available prescription drugs. For the same reason, drug companies are reluctant to tweet about their drugs. How could they possibly describe all of the potential side effects in only 140 characters?

CRITICAL THINKING

INSIGHT INTO THE E-COMMERCE ENVIRONMENT
Do pharmaceutical companies have an ethical responsibility to correct erroneous information about their products on sites such as Wikipedia?

---

a report may trigger an enforcement investigation. For example, environmental regulators often require reports of emissions, and the Occupational Safety and Health Administration requires companies to report any work-related deaths.

INSPECTIONS Many agencies gather information through on-site inspections. Sometimes, inspecting an office, a factory, or some other business facility is the only way to obtain the evidence needed to prove a regulatory violation. Administrative inspections and tests cover a wide range of activities, including safety inspections of underground coal mines, safety tests of commercial equipment and automobiles, and environmental monitoring of factory emissions. An agency may also ask a firm or individual to submit certain documents or records to the agency for examination. For example, the Federal Trade Commission often asks to inspect corporate records for compliance.

Normally, business firms comply with agency requests to inspect facilities or business records because it is in any firm's interest to maintain a good relationship with regulatory bodies. In some instances, however, such as when a firm thinks an

agency's request is unreasonable and may be detrimental to the firm's interest, the firm may refuse to comply with the request. In such situations, an agency may resort to the use of a subpoena or a search warrant.

SUBPOENAS There are two basic types of subpoenas. The subpoena *ad testificandum* ("to testify") is an ordinary subpoena. It is a writ, or order, compelling a witness to appear at an agency hearing. The subpoena *duces tecum*[12] ("bring it with you") compels an individual or organization to hand over books, papers, records, or documents to the agency. An administrative agency may use either type of subpoena to obtain testimony or documents.

There are limits on the information that an agency can demand. To determine whether an agency is abusing its discretion in its pursuit of information as part of an investigation, a court may consider such factors as the following:

1. *The purpose of the investigation.* An investigation must have a legitimate purpose. Harassment is an

---

12. Pronounced *doo*-suhs *tee*-kum.

example of an improper purpose. An agency may not issue an administrative subpoena to inspect business records if the agency's motive is to harass or pressure the business into settling an unrelated matter.

2. *The relevance of the information being sought.* Information is relevant if it reveals that the law is being violated or if it assures the agency that the law is not being violated.

3. *The specificity of the demand for testimony or documents.* A subpoena must, for example, adequately describe the material being sought.

4. *The burden of the demand on the party from whom the information is sought.* In responding to a request for information, a party must bear the costs of, for example, copying the documents that must be handed over. A business generally is not required to reveal its trade secrets, however.

SEARCHES DURING SITE INSPECTIONS As mentioned, agency investigations often involve on-site inspections. For example, the Environmental Protection Agency (EPA) frequently conducts inspections to enforce environmental laws. The EPA may inspect a site to determine if hazardous wastes are being stored properly or to sample a facility's wastewater to ensure that it complies with the Clean Water Act. Usually, companies do not resist such inspections, although in some circumstances they may do so.

Search Warrant Usually Required. The Fourth Amendment protects against unreasonable searches and seizures by requiring in most instances that a search warrant be obtained before a physical search for evidence is conducted. An agency typically must obtain a search warrant that directs law enforcement officials to search a specific place for a specific item and present it to the agency.

Some Warrantless Searches Legal. Agencies can conduct warrantless searches in several situations. Warrants are not required to conduct searches in certain highly regulated industries. Firms that sell firearms or liquor, for example, are automatically subject to inspections without warrants. Sometimes, a statute permits warrantless searches of certain types of hazardous operations, such as coal mines or liquid propane retailers. A warrantless inspection might also be considered reasonable in emergency situations or when a violation is potentially dangerous to human health or the environment. Finally, if procuring a warrant will defeat the purpose of the inspection (because evidence will be destroyed or concealed, for example), a search undertaken without a warrant may be reasonable. Note also that if a business gives a valid consent to an agency's request for an inspection and search, it has waived its right to object to the lack of a warrant.[13]

Adjudication

After an investigation reveals a suspected violation, an agency may begin to take administrative action against an individual or organization. Most administrative actions are resolved through negotiated settlements at their initial stages, without the need for formal **adjudication** (the process of resolving a dispute by presenting evidence and arguments before a neutral third party decision maker).

NEGOTIATED SETTLEMENTS Depending on the agency, negotiations may take the form of a simple conversation or a series of informal conferences. Whatever form the negotiations take, their purpose is to rectify the problem to the agency's satisfaction and eliminate the need for additional proceedings.

Settlement is an appealing option to firms for two reasons: to avoid appearing uncooperative and to avoid the expense involved in formal adjudication proceedings and in possible later appeals. Settlement is also an attractive option for agencies. To conserve their own resources and avoid formal actions, administrative agencies devote a great deal of effort to giving advice and negotiating solutions to problems.

FORMAL COMPLAINTS If a settlement cannot be reached, the agency may issue a formal complaint against the suspected violator. If the EPA, for example, finds that a factory is polluting groundwater in violation of federal pollution laws, the EPA will issue a complaint against the violator in an effort to bring the plant into compliance with federal regulations. This complaint is a public document, and a press release may accompany it. The factory charged in the complaint will respond by filing an answer to the EPA's allegations. If the factory and the EPA cannot agree on a settlement, the case will be adjudicated.

Agency adjudication may involve a trial-like arbitration procedure before an **administrative law judge (ALJ)**. The Administrative Procedure Act (APA) requires that before the hearing takes place, the agency must issue a notice that includes the facts and law on which the complaint is based, the legal authority for the hearing, and its time and place. The administrative adjudication process is described next and illustrated graphically in Exhibit 44–3 on the facing page.

---

13. See, for example, *Lakeland Enterprises of Rhinelander, Inc. v. Chao*, 402 F.3d 739 (7th Cir. 2005).

EXHIBIT 44-3 • The Process of Formal Administrative Adjudication

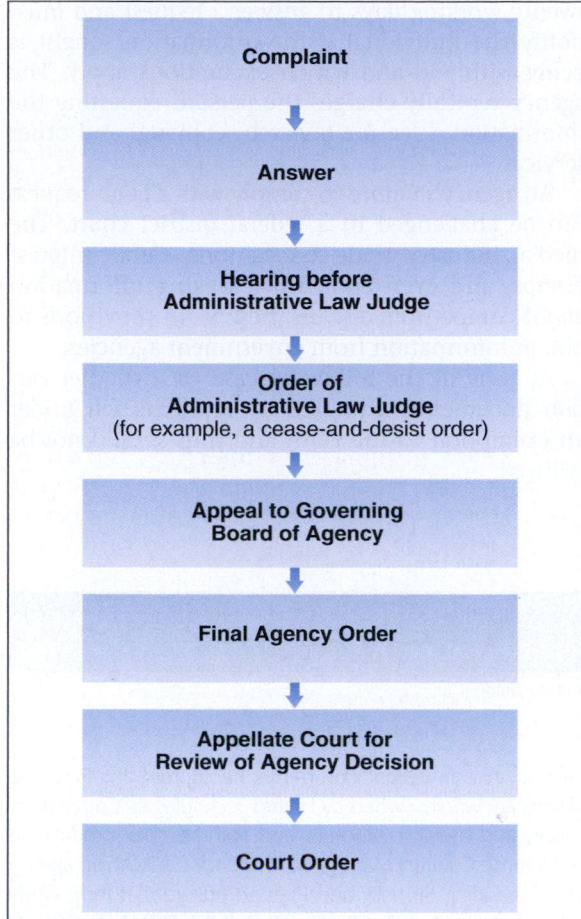

Complaint

↓

Answer

↓

Hearing before
Administrative Law Judge

↓

Order of
Administrative Law Judge
(for example, a cease-and-desist order)

↓

Appeal to Governing
Board of Agency

↓

Final Agency Order

↓

Appellate Court for
Review of Agency Decision

↓

Court Order

THE ROLE OF THE ADMINISTRATIVE LAW JUDGE An ALJ presides over the hearing and has the power to administer oaths, take testimony, rule on questions of evidence, and make determinations of fact. The law requires an ALJ to be an unbiased adjudicator (judge), even though the ALJ actually works for the agency prosecuting the case (in our example, the EPA). There are no juries in administrative hearings. The ALJ assumes the role of a judge and jury in a trial.

Certain safeguards prevent bias on the part of the ALJ and promote fairness in the proceedings. For example, the APA requires that the ALJ be separate from an agency's investigative and prosecutorial staff. The APA also prohibits *ex parte* (private) communications between the ALJ and any party to an agency proceeding, such as the EPA or the factory. Finally, provisions of the APA protect the ALJ from agency disciplinary actions unless the agency can show good cause for such an action.

HEARING PROCEDURES Hearing procedures vary widely from agency to agency. Administrative agencies generally exercise substantial discretion over the type of procedure that will be used. Frequently, disputes are resolved through informal adjudication proceedings. For example, the parties, their counsel, and the ALJ may simply meet at a table in a conference room to attempt to settle the dispute.

A formal adjudicatory hearing, in contrast, resembles a trial in many respects. Prior to the hearing, the parties are permitted to undertake discovery—involving depositions, interrogatories, and requests for documents or other information, as described in Chapter 3—although the discovery process is not quite as extensive as it would be in a court proceeding. The hearing itself must comply with the procedural requirements of the APA and must also meet the constitutional standards of due process. During the hearing, the parties may give testimony, present other evidence, and cross-examine adverse witnesses. A significant difference between a trial and an administrative agency hearing, though, is that normally much more information, including hearsay (secondhand information), can be introduced as evidence during an administrative hearing. The burden of proof in an enforcement proceeding is placed on the agency.

AGENCY ORDERS Following a hearing, the ALJ renders an **initial order,** or decision, on the case. Either party can appeal the ALJ's decision to the board or commission that governs the agency. If the factory in our example is dissatisfied with the ALJ's decision, it can appeal the decision to the EPA. If the factory is dissatisfied with the commission's decision, it can appeal the decision to a federal court of appeals. If no party appeals the case, the ALJ's decision becomes the **final order** of the agency. The ALJ's decision also becomes final if a party appeals and the commission and the court decline to review the case. If a party appeals and the case is reviewed, the final order comes from the commission's decision or (if that decision is appealed to a federal appellate court) that of the reviewing court.

SECTION 6
PUBLIC ACCOUNTABILITY

As a result of growing public concern over the powers exercised by administrative agencies, Congress passed several laws to make agencies more accountable through public scrutiny. Here, we discuss the most significant of these laws.

Freedom of Information Act

Enacted in 1966, the Freedom of Information Act (FOIA)[14] requires the federal government to disclose certain records to any person or entity on written request, even if no reason is given for the request. The FOIA exempts certain types of records, such as those pertaining to national security and those containing information that is confidential or personal. Under a 1996 amendment to the FOIA, all federal government agencies must make their records available electronically on the Internet and in other electronic formats. Any document an agency creates must be accessible by computer within a year after its creation. Agencies must also provide a clear index to all of their documents.

A request that complies with the FOIA procedures need only contain a reasonably specific description of the information sought. Many agencies now accept requests via e-mail, as well as by fax. The agency has twenty working days to answer a request and must notify the individual if the information sought is being withheld and which exemptions apply. The agency typically charges the person requesting the information a fee for research, copying, and other services.

An agency's failure to comply with a FOIA request can be challenged in a federal district court. The media, industry trade associations, public-interest groups, and even companies seeking information about competitors rely on these FOIA provisions to obtain information from government agencies.

At issue in the following case was whether certain documents requested by reporters fell under an exemption to the FOIA and thus should not be released.

---

14. 5 U.S.C. Section 552.

CASE 44.3
United Technologies Corp. v. U.S. Department of Defense

United States Court of Appeals, District of Columbia Circuit, 601 F.3d 557 (2010).
www.cadc.uscourts.gov/internet/home.nsf[a]

BACKGROUND AND FACTS • Sikorsky Aircraft Corporation makes helicopters, and Pratt and Whitney makes aircraft engines. Both companies are wholly owned by United Technologies Corporation. Both have various foreign and domestic military and civilian customers, and both sell their products to the U.S. Department of Defense (DoD). The Defense Contract Management Agency (DCMA), an agency within the DoD, monitors defense contractors, including Sikorsky and Pratt, to ensure that they satisfy their contractual obligations when providing services and supplies to the DoD. If the DCMA discovers a problem, it notifies the contractor and may issue a Corrective Action Request (CAR) or an audit report to the contractor to remedy the problem. In 2004, a reporter submitted a Freedom of Information Act (FOIA) request to the regional DCMA office for copies of all CARs that had been issued to Sikorsky during the previous year concerning Sikorsky's Black Hawk helicopter. Another reporter requested information, including a CAR and audit-related documents, concerning Pratt's airplane engine center at Middletown, Connecticut. Sikorsky and Pratt argued that the documents were exempt from FOIA disclosure. The DCMA disagreed and ruled that the documents could be disclosed. Sikorsky and Pratt filed separate suits against the DoD in a federal district court, arguing that the decision to release the documents was arbitrary, capricious, and contrary to law under the Administrative Procedure Act. They sought declaratory and injunctive relief preventing the documents' disclosure. The district court granted summary judgment to the DoD in both cases, and Sikorsky and Pratt appealed.

IN THE LANGUAGE OF THE COURT
Karen LeCraft *HENDERSON*, Circuit Judge.
* * * *

   Exemption 4 covers "trade secrets and commercial or financial information obtained from a person and privileged or confidential." * * * *For the documents to*

---

a. Select "Opinions" from the options. When the Search page opens, choose "March" and "2010" from the drop-down menus, and click on "Go!" Scroll down the list of search results to the case title and click on the link to the PDF to access the case. The U.S. Court of Appeals for the District of Columbia Circuit maintains this Web site.

CASE 44.3 CONTINUED ▶ *be exempt from disclosure, their release must be likely to cause the contractors "substantial competitive harm" or "impair the Government's ability to obtain necessary information in the future." [Emphasis added.]*

To qualify [as a "substantial competitive harm"], an identified harm must "flow from the affirmative use of proprietary information by competitors."

* * * *

* * * Sikorsky and Pratt maintain that the documents contain sensitive proprietary information about their quality control processes. Pratt's Director of Quality Military Engines attested that "a competitor with similar expertise could and would use the information to gain insights into the strengths and weaknesses of [Pratt's] quality control system as well as manufacturing techniques and use those insights to revise and improve its own quality control and manufacturing systems." Similarly, Sikorsky asserted that "proprietary information regarding Sikorsky's manufacturing process and procedures" is "inextricably intertwined with the quality control information" included in the CARs and it asserted that "release of this proprietary information would substantially harm Sikorsky's competitive position because its competitors would use this information to their advantage * * * ." In response, [the] DCMA simply stated that it had redacted [removed or obscured] all of the sensitive proprietary information and concluded that disclosure of the remaining information was not likely to cause the contractors substantial competitive harm.*

*We find [the] DCMA's response insufficient. The documents, even as redacted by [the] DCMA, appear to reveal details about Sikorsky's and Pratt's proprietary manufacturing and quality control processes. * * * The documents describe, in part, how the contractors build and inspect helicopters and/or engines. Once disclosed, competitors could, it appears, use the information to improve their own manufacturing and quality control systems, thus making "affirmative use of proprietary information" against which Exemption 4 is meant to guard.*

DECISION AND REMEDY • *The federal appellate court concluded that the DCMA had failed to provide a reasoned basis for its conclusion. The court remanded the case to the DCMA to examine the relevant data and give a satisfactory explanation for its decision, if it could, "including a rational connection between the facts found and the choice made."*

THE ETHICAL DIMENSION • *Sikorsky and Pratt also argued that if the documents were released, their competitors would use the documents to discredit them in the eyes of current and potential customers. Would such actions amount to a "substantial competitive harm"? Explain.*

MANAGERIAL IMPLICATIONS • *Businesses that contract with government agencies to provide goods or services can expect to have their processes and procedures monitored by these agencies. This means that proprietary information, including trade secrets, may find its way into various government reports or other documents. To protect this information from competitors, managers in such businesses would be wise to seek counsel as to what types of documents are exempt from disclosure under the FOIA.*

Government in the Sunshine Act

Congress passed the Government in the Sunshine Act,[15] or open meeting law, in 1976. It requires that "every portion of every meeting of an agency" be open to "public observation." The act also requires the establishment of procedures to ensure that the public is provided with adequate advance notice of scheduled meetings and agendas. Like the FOIA, the Sunshine Act contains certain exceptions. Closed meetings are permitted when (1) the subject of the meeting concerns accusing any person of a crime, (2) an open meeting would frustrate the implementation of agency actions, or (3) the subject of the meeting involves matters relating to future litigation or rulemaking. Courts interpret these exceptions to allow open access whenever possible.

Regulatory Flexibility Act

Concern over the effects of regulation on the efficiency of businesses, particularly smaller ones, led Congress to pass the Regulatory Flexibility Act[16] in

---

15. 5 U.S.C. Section 552b.

16. 5 U.S.C. Sections 601–612.

1980. Under this act, whenever a new regulation will have a "significant impact upon a substantial number of small entities," the agency must conduct a regulatory flexibility analysis. The analysis must measure the cost that the rule would impose on small businesses and must consider less burdensome alternatives. The act also contains provisions to alert small businesses—through advertising in trade journals, for example—about forthcoming regulations. The act reduces some record-keeping burdens for small businesses, especially with regard to hazardous waste management.

Small Business Regulatory Enforcement Fairness Act

The Small Business Regulatory Enforcement Fairness Act (SBREFA) of 1996[17] allows Congress to review

new federal regulations for at least sixty days before they take effect. This period gives opponents of the rules time to present their arguments to Congress.

The SBREFA also authorizes the courts to enforce the Regulatory Flexibility Act. This helps to ensure that federal agencies, such as the Internal Revenue Service, will consider ways to reduce the economic impact of new regulations on small businesses. Federal agencies are required to prepare guides that explain in plain English how small businesses can comply with federal regulations.

The SBREFA also set up the National Enforcement Ombudsman at the Small Business Administration to receive comments from small businesses about their dealings with federal agencies. Based on these comments, Regional Small Business Fairness Boards rate the agencies and publicize their findings.

---

17. 5 U.S.C. Sections 801 *et seq.*

REVIEWING
Administrative Law

Assume that the Securities and Exchange Commission (SEC) has a rule that it will enforce statutory provisions prohibiting insider trading only when the insiders make monetary profits for themselves. Then the SEC makes a new rule, declaring that it will now bring enforcement actions against individuals for insider trading even if the individuals did not personally profit from the transactions. In making the new rule, the SEC does not conduct a rulemaking procedure but simply announces its decision. A stockbrokerage firm objects and says that the new rule was unlawfully developed without opportunity for public comment. The brokerage firm challenges the rule in an action that ultimately is reviewed by a federal appellate court. Using the information presented in the chapter, answer the following questions.

1. Is the SEC an executive agency or an independent regulatory agency? Does it matter to the outcome of this dispute? Explain.
2. Suppose that the SEC asserts that it has always had the statutory authority to pursue persons for insider trading regardless of whether they personally profited from the transactions. This is the only argument the SEC makes to justify changing its enforcement rules. Would a court be likely to find that the SEC's action was arbitrary and capricious under the Administrative Procedure Act (APA)? Why or why not?
3. Would a court be likely to give *Chevron* deference to the SEC's interpretation of the law on insider trading? Why or why not?
4. Now assume that a court finds that the new rule is merely "interpretive." What effect would this determination have on whether the SEC had to follow the APA's rulemaking procedures?

✹ **DEBATE THIS:** *Because an administrative law judge (ALJ) acts as both judge and jury, there should always be at least three ALJs in each administrative hearing.*

TERMS AND CONCEPTS

adjudication 872

administrative law
   judge (ALJ) 872

bureaucracy 863

delegation doctrine 863

enabling legislation 861

final order 873

initial order 873

interpretive rule 863

legislative rule 863

notice-and-comment
   rulemaking 867

rulemaking 866

QUESTIONS AND CASE PROBLEMS

44–1. Rulemaking and Adjudication Powers
For decades, the Federal Trade Commission (FTC) resolved fair trade and advertising disputes through individual adjudications. In the 1960s, the FTC began promulgating rules that defined fair and unfair trade practices. In cases involving violations of these rules, the due process rights of participants were more limited and did not include cross-examination. Although anyone charged with violating a rule would receive a full adjudication, the legitimacy of the rule itself could not be challenged in the adjudication. Furthermore, a party charged with violating a rule was almost certain to lose the adjudication. Affected parties complained to a court, arguing that their rights before the FTC were unduly limited by the new rules. What would the court examine to determine whether to uphold the new rules?

44–2. QUESTION WITH SAMPLE ANSWER: Informal Rulemaking.

Assume that the Food and Drug Administration (FDA), using proper procedures, adopts a rule describing its future investigations. This new rule covers all future circumstances in which the FDA wants to regulate food additives. Under the new rule, the FDA is not to regulate food additives without giving food companies an opportunity to cross-examine witnesses. Later, the FDA wants to regulate methylisocyanate, a food additive. The FDA undertakes an informal rulemaking procedure, without cross-examination, and regulates methylisocyanate. Producers protest, saying that the FDA promised them the opportunity for cross-examination. The FDA responds that the Administrative Procedure Act does not require such cross-examination and that it is free to withdraw the promise made in its new rule. If the producers challenge the FDA in court, on what basis would the court rule in their favor?

• **For a sample answer to Question 44–2, go to Appendix I at the end of this text.**

44–3. Arbitrary and Capricious Test Lion Raisins, Inc., is a family-owned, family-operated business that grows raisins and markets them to private enterprises. In the 1990s,

Lion also successfully bid on more than fifteen contracts awarded by the U.S. Department of Agriculture (USDA). In May 1999, a USDA investigation reported that Lion appeared to have falsified inspectors' signatures, listed false moisture content, and changed the grade of raisins on three USDA raisin certificates issued between 1996 and 1998. Lion was subsequently awarded five more USDA contracts. Then, in November 2000, the company was the low bidder on two new USDA contracts for school lunch programs. In January 2001, however, the USDA awarded these contracts to other bidders and, on the basis of the May 1999 report, suspended Lion from participating in government contracts for one year. Lion filed a suit in the U.S. Court of Federal Claims against the USDA, seeking, in part, lost profits on the school lunch contracts on the ground that the USDA's suspension was arbitrary and capricious. What reasoning might the court employ to grant a summary judgment in Lion's favor? [*Lion Raisins, Inc. v. United States,* 51 Fed.Cl. 238 (2001)]

44–4. Investigation Maureen Droge began working for United Air Lines, Inc. (UAL), as a flight attendant in 1990. In 1995, she was assigned to Paris, France, where she became pregnant. Because UAL does not allow its flight attendants to fly during their third trimester of pregnancy, Droge was placed on involuntary leave. She applied for temporary disability benefits through the French social security system, but her request was denied because UAL does not contribute to the French system on behalf of its U.S.-based flight attendants. Droge filed a charge of discrimination with the U.S. Equal Employment Opportunity Commission (EEOC), alleging that UAL had discriminated against her and other Americans. The EEOC issued a subpoena, asking UAL to detail all benefits received by all UAL employees living outside the United States. UAL refused to provide the information, in part, on the grounds that it was irrelevant and compliance would be unduly burdensome. The EEOC filed a suit in a federal district court against UAL. Should the court enforce the subpoena? Why or why not? [*Equal Employment Opportunity Commission v. United Air Lines, Inc.,* 287 F.3d 643 (7th Cir. 2002)]

44–5. Judicial Controls Under federal law, when accepting bids on a contract, an agency must hold "discussions" with all offerors. An agency may ask a single offeror for "clarification" of its proposal, however, without holding "discussions" with the others. Regulations define *clarifications* as "limited exchanges." In March 2001, the U.S. Air Force asked for bids on a contract. The winning contractor would examine, assess, and develop means of integrating national intelligence assets with the U.S. Department of Defense space systems, to enhance the capabilities of the Air Force's Space Warfare Center. Among the bidders were Information Technology and Applications Corp. (ITAC) and RS Information Systems, Inc. (RSIS). The Air Force asked the parties for more information on their subcontractors but did not allow them to change their proposals. Determining that there were weaknesses in ITAC's bid, the Air Force awarded the contract to RSIS. ITAC filed a suit in the U.S. Court of Federal Claims against the government, contending that the postproposal requests to RSIS, and its responses, were improper "discussions." Should the court rule in ITAC's favor? Why or why not? [*Information Technology & Applications Corp. v. United States,* 316 F.3d 1312 (Fed. Cir. 2003)].

44–6. CASE PROBLEM WITH SAMPLE ANSWER: Investigation.

Riverdale Mills Corp. makes plastic-coated steel wire products in Northbridge, Massachusetts. Riverdale uses a water-based cleaning process that generates acidic and alkaline wastewater. To meet federal clean-water requirements, Riverdale has a system within its plant to treat the water. It then flows through a pipe that opens into a manhole-covered test pit outside the plant in full view of Riverdale's employees. Three hundred feet away, the pipe merges into the public sewer system. In October 1997, the Environmental Protection Agency (EPA) sent Justin Pimpare and Daniel Granz to inspect the plant. Without a search warrant and without Riverdale's express consent, the agents took samples from the test pit. Based on the samples, Riverdale and James Knott, the company's owner, were charged with criminal violations of the federal Clean Water Act. The defendants filed a suit in a federal district court against the EPA agents and others, alleging violations of the Fourth Amendment. What right does the Fourth Amendment provide in this context? This right is based on a "reasonable expectation of privacy." Should the agents be held liable? Why or why not? [Riverdale Mills Corp. v. Pimpare, 392 F.3d 55 (1st Cir. 2004)]

• **To view a sample answer for Problem 44–6, go to this book's Web site at www.cengage.com/blaw/clarkson, select "Chapter 44," and click on "Case Problem with Sample Answer."**

44–7. Rulemaking The Investment Company Act of 1940 prohibits a mutual fund from engaging in certain transactions in which there may be a conflict of interest between the manager of the fund and its shareholders. Under rules issued by the Securities and Exchange Commission (SEC), however, a fund that meets certain conditions may engage in an otherwise prohibited transaction. In June 2004, the SEC added two new conditions. A year later, the SEC reconsidered the new conditions in terms of the costs that they would impose on the funds. Within eight days, and without asking for public input, the SEC readopted the conditions. The Chamber of Commerce of the United States—which is both a mutual fund shareholder and an association with mutual fund managers among its members—asked the U.S. Court of Appeals for the Second Circuit to review the new rules. The Chamber charged, in part, that in readopting the rules, the SEC relied on materials not in the "rulemaking record" without providing an opportunity for public comment. The SEC countered that the information was otherwise "publicly available." In adopting a rule, should an agency consider information that is not part of the rulemaking record? Why or why not? [*Chamber of Commerce of the United States v. Securities and Exchange Commission,* 443 F.3d 890 (D.C.Cir. 2006)]

44–8. Agency Powers A well-documented rise in global temperatures has coincided with a significant increase in the concentration of carbon dioxide in the atmosphere. Some scientists believe that the two trends are related, because when carbon dioxide is released into the atmosphere, it produces a greenhouse effect, trapping solar heat. Under the Clean Air Act (CAA) of 1963, the Environmental Protection Agency (EPA) is authorized to regulate "any" air pollutants "emitted into . . . the ambient air" that in its "judgment cause, or contribute to, air pollution." Calling global warming "the most pressing environmental challenge of our time," a group of private organizations asked the EPA to regulate carbon dioxide and other "greenhouse gas" emissions from new motor vehicles. The EPA refused, stating, among other things, that Congress last amended the CAA in 1990 without authorizing new, binding auto emissions limits. The petitioners—nineteen states, including Massachusetts, and others—asked the U.S. Court of Appeals for the District of Columbia Circuit to review the EPA's denial. Did the EPA have the authority to regulate greenhouse gas emissions from new motor vehicles? If so, was its stated reason for refusing to do so consistent with that authority? Discuss. [*Massachusetts v. Environmental Protection Agency,* 549 U.S. 497, 127 S.Ct. 1438, 167 L.Ed.2d 248 (2007)]

44–9. Judicial Deference Dave Conley, a longtime heavy smoker, was diagnosed with lung cancer. He died two years later. His death certificate stated that the cause of death was cancer, but it also noted other significant conditions that had contributed to his death were a history of cigarette smoking and coal mining. Conley's wife filed for benefits under the Black Lung Benefits Act, which provides for victims of black lung disease caused by coal mining. To qualify for benefits under the act, the exposure to coal dust must be a substantially contributing factor leading to the person's death, which, under the statute, means "hastens death." The U.S. Department of Labor collected Conley's work and medical records. An administrative law judge (ALJ) reviewed the record and took testimony from several physicians about the cause of Conley's death. Only one physician testified that the coal dust was a substantial factor leading to Conley's lung cancer, but he offered no evidence other than his testimony to support his conclusion. The ALJ nevertheless ruled that coal mining had hastened Conley's death and awarded benefits to Mrs. Conley. Conley's employer appealed to the Benefits Review Board (BRB) for black lung claims. The BRB reversed the ALJ, finding that there was insufficient evidence to hold that coal dust was a substantial factor that triggered Conley's lung cancer. Mrs. Conley appealed to a federal appellate court. Should the federal court defer to the ALJ's decision on the cause of Conley's death? Why or why not? Which decision does the federal appellate court review, the ALJ's conclusions or the BRB's reversal? [*Conley v. National Mines Corp.*, 595 F.3d 297 (6th Cir. 2010)]

44–10. A QUESTION OF ETHICS: Rulemaking.

To ensure highway safety and protect driver health, Congress charged federal agencies with regulating the hours of service of commercial motor vehicle operators. Between 1940 and 2003, the regulations that applied to long-haul truck drivers were mostly unchanged. (Long-haul drivers are those who operate beyond a 150-mile radius of their base.) In 2003, the Federal Motor Carrier Safety Administration (FMSCA) revised the regulations significantly, increasing the number of daily and weekly hours that drivers could work. The agency had not considered the impact of the changes on the health of the drivers, however, and the revisions were overturned. The FMSCA then issued a notice that it would reconsider the revisions and opened them up for public comment. The agency analyzed the costs to the industry and the crash risks due to driver fatigue under different options and concluded that the safety benefits of not increasing the hours were less than the economic costs. In 2005, the agency issued a rule that was nearly identical to the 2003 version. Public Citizen, Inc., and others, including the Owner-Operator Independent Drivers Association, asked the U.S. Court of Appeals for the District of Columbia Circuit to review the 2005 rule as it applied to long-haul drivers. [*Owner-Operator Independent Drivers Association, Inc. v. Federal Motor Carrier Safety Administration*, 494 F.3d 188 (D.C.Cir. 2007)]

(a) The agency's cost-benefit analysis included new methods that were not disclosed to the public in time for comments. Was this unethical? Should the agency have disclosed the new methodology sooner? Why or why not?

(b) The agency created a graph to show the risk of a crash as a function of the time a driver spent on the job. The graph plotted the first twelve hours of a day individually, but the rest of the time was depicted with an aggregate figure at the seventeenth hour. This made the risk at those hours appear to be lower. Is it unethical for an agency to manipulate data? Explain.

LEGAL RESEARCH EXERCISES ON THE WEB

Go to this text's Web site at **www.cengage.com/blaw/clarkson**, select "Chapter 44," and click on "Practical Internet Exercises." There you will find the following Internet research exercises that you can perform to learn more about the topics covered in this chapter.

Practical Internet Exercise 44–1: Legal Perspective
The Freedom of Information Act

Practical Internet Exercise 44–2: Management Perspective
Agency Inspections

CHAPTER 45

Consumer Law

All statutes, agency rules, and common law judicial decisions that serve to protect the interests of consumers are classified as consumer law. Traditionally, in disputes involving consumers, it was assumed that the freedom to contract carried with it the obligation to live by the deal made. Over time, this attitude has changed considerably. Today, myriad federal and state laws protect consumers from unfair trade practices, unsafe products, discriminatory or unreasonable credit requirements, and other problems related to consumer transactions. Nearly every agency and department of the federal government has an office of consumer affairs, and most states have one or more such offices to help consumers. Also, typically the attorney general's office assists consumers at the state level.

In this chapter, we examine some of the major laws and regulations protecting consumers. Because of the wide variation among state consumer protection laws, our primary focus in this chapter is on federal legislation. Realize, though, that state laws often provide more sweeping and significant protections for the consumer than do federal laws. Exhibit 45–1 below indicates many of the areas of consumer law that are regulated by federal statutes.

EXHIBIT 45–1 • Selected Areas of Consumer Law Regulated by Statutes

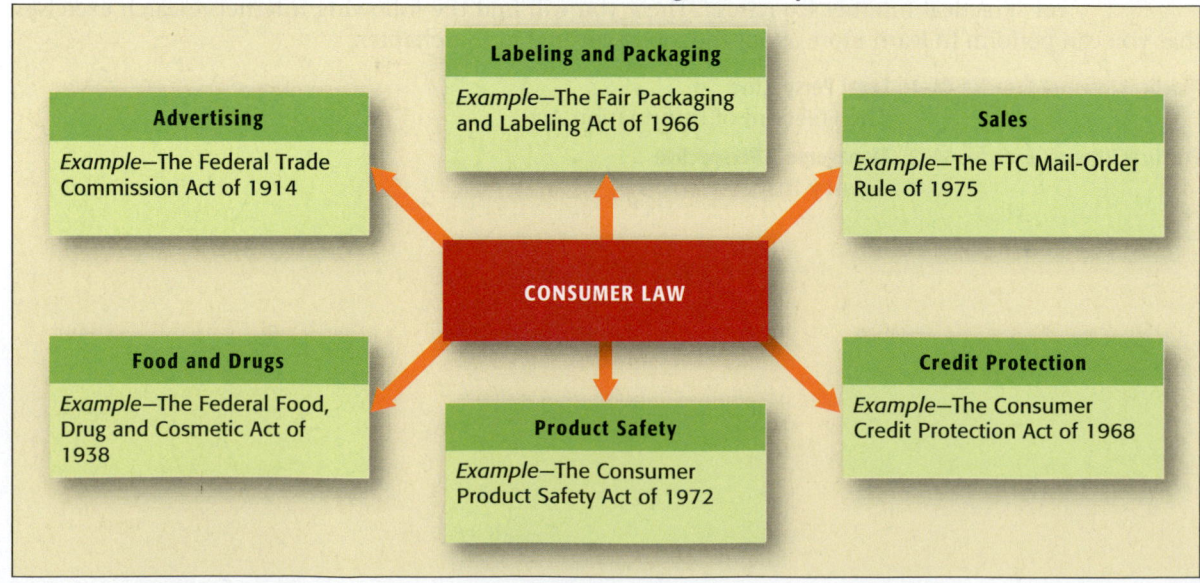

SECTION 1
DECEPTIVE ADVERTISING

One of the earliest federal consumer protection laws—and still one of the most important—was the Federal Trade Commission Act of 1914 (mentioned in Chapter 44).[1] The act created the Federal Trade Commission (FTC) to carry out the broadly stated goal of preventing unfair and deceptive trade practices, including deceptive advertising.[2]

Generally, **deceptive advertising** occurs if a reasonable consumer would be misled by the advertising claim. Vague generalities and obvious exaggerations are permissible. These claims are known as *puffery*. When a claim takes on the appearance of literal authenticity, however, it may create problems. Advertising that *appears* to be based on factual evidence but in fact is not reasonably supported by some evidence will be deemed deceptive.

Some advertisements contain "half-truths," meaning that the presented information is true but incomplete and therefore leads consumers to a false conclusion. For example, the maker of Campbell's soups advertised that "most" Campbell's soups are low in fat and cholesterol and thus helpful in fighting heart disease. What the ad did not say was that many Campbell's soups are high in sodium, and high-sodium diets may increase the risk of heart disease. Hence, the FTC ruled that Campbell's claims were deceptive. Advertising that contains an endorsement by a celebrity may be deemed deceptive if the celebrity does not actually use the product.

Even before the FTC brought the following case, *Wired* magazine had already put the product in question on its list of the top ten "snake oil gadgets."

---

1. 15 U.S.C. Sections 41–58.
2. 15 U.S.C. Section 45.

CASE 45.1
Federal Trade Commission v. QT, Inc.
United States Court of Appeals, Seventh Circuit, 512 F.3d 858 (2008).
www.ca7.uscourts.gov[a]

BACKGROUND AND FACTS • QT, Inc., heavily promoted the Q-Ray Ionized Bracelet on television infomercials and on its Web site. In its promotions, the company claimed that the bracelet offered immediate and significant or complete pain relief and could cure chronic pain. At trial, the U.S. district court labeled all such claims fraudulent; forbade further promotional claims; and ordered the company to pay $16 million, plus interest, into a fund to be distributed to customers. QT appealed to the U.S. Court of Appeals for the Seventh Circuit.

IN THE LANGUAGE OF THE COURT
EASTERBROOK, Chief Judge.

    * * * According to the district court's findings, almost everything that defendants have said about the bracelet is false. Here are some highlights:

• Defendants promoted the bracelet as a miraculous cure for chronic pain, but it has no therapeutic effect.

• Defendants told consumers that claims of "immediate, significant or complete pain relief" had been "test-proven"; they hadn't.

    * * * *

• Defendants represented that the therapeutic effect wears off in a year or two, despite knowing that the bracelet's properties do not change. This assertion is designed to lead customers to buy new bracelets. Likewise the false statement that the bracelet has a "memory cycle specific to each individual wearer" so that only the bracelet's original wearer can experience pain relief is designed to increase sales by eliminating the second-hand market and "explaining" the otherwise-embarrassing fact that the buyer's friends and neighbors can't perceive any effect.

---

a. Click on "Opinions" in the left-hand column. In the boxes for the case number, type "07" and "1662," and then click on "List Case(s)." Follow the links to access the opinion. The U.S. Court of Appeals for the Seventh Circuit maintains this Web site.

CASE CONTINUES ➡

CASE 45.1 CONTINUED ➡   The magistrate judge [the judge presiding over the trial] did not commit a clear error, or abuse his discretion, in concluding that the defendants set out to bilk unsophisticated persons who found themselves in pain from arthritis and other chronic conditions.

* * * *The Federal Trade Commission Act forbids false and misleading statements, and a statement that is plausible but has not been tested in the most reliable way cannot be condemned out of hand.* [Emphasis added.]

* * * For the Q-Ray Ionized Bracelet, * * * all statements about how the product works—Q-Rays, ionization, enhancing the flow of bio-energy, and the like—are blather [nonsense]. Defendants might as well have said: "Beneficent creatures from the 17th Dimension use this bracelet as a beacon to locate people who need pain relief, and whisk them off to their home-world every night to provide help in ways unknown to our science."

* * * *Proof is what separates an effect new to science from a swindle.* Defendants themselves told customers that the bracelet's efficacy had been "test-proven"; * * * but defendants have no proof of the Q-Ray Ionized Bracelet's efficacy. The "tests" on which they relied were bunk. * * * What remain are testimonials, which are not a form of proof * * *. That's why the "testimonial" of someone who keeps elephants off the streets of a large city by snapping his fingers is the basis of a joke rather than proof of cause and effect. [Emphasis added.]

* * * *

Physicians know how to treat pain. Why pay $200 for a Q-Ray Ionized Bracelet when you can get relief from an aspirin tablet that costs [one cent]?

DECISION AND REMEDY • *The federal appellate court affirmed the district court's decision. QT, Inc., was required to stop its deceptive advertising and to pay the $16 million, plus interest, so that its customers could be reimbursed.*

WHAT IF THE FACTS WERE DIFFERENT? • *Assume that the defendant had actually conducted scientific studies, but they were inconclusive. How might the judge have ruled in that situation?*

THE ETHICAL DIMENSION • *Most people have seen infomercials. Does the fact that QT used infomercials to make fraudulent promotional claims mean that all products "pitched" on television are suspect? Why or why not?*

Bait-and-Switch Advertising

The FTC has issued rules that govern specific advertising techniques. One of the most important rules is contained in the FTC's "Guides Against Bait Advertising,"[3] issued in 1968. The rule seeks to prevent **bait-and-switch advertising**—that is, advertising a very low price for a particular item that will likely be unavailable to the consumer, who will then be encouraged to purchase a more expensive item. The low price is the "bait" to lure the consumer into the store. The salesperson is instructed to "switch" the consumer to a different, more expensive item. Under the FTC guidelines, bait-and-switch advertising occurs if the seller refuses to show the advertised item, fails to have a reasonable quantity of the item in stock, fails to promise to deliver the advertised item within a reasonable time, or discourages employees from selling the item.

Online Deceptive Advertising

Deceptive advertising can occur in the online environment as well. The FTC actively monitors online advertising and has identified hundreds of Web sites that have made false or deceptive claims for products ranging from medical treatments for various diseases to exercise equipment and weight-loss aids.

The FTC has issued guidelines to help online businesses comply with existing laws prohibiting deceptive advertising.[4] These guidelines include three basic requirements:

1. All ads—both online and offline—must be truthful and not misleading.
2. The claims made in an ad must be substantiated; that is, advertisers must have evidence to back up their claims.
3. Ads cannot be unfair, which the FTC defines as "likely to cause substantial consumer injury that

---

3. 16 C.F.R. Part 238.

4. "Advertising and Marketing on the Internet: Rules of the Road." *www.ftc.com.* September 2000: n.p. Web.

consumers could not reasonably avoid and that is not outweighed by the benefit to consumers or competition."

The guidelines also call for "clear and conspicuous" disclosure of any qualifying or limiting information. The overall impression of the ad is important in meeting this requirement. The FTC suggests that advertisers should assume that consumers will not read an entire Web page. Therefore, to satisfy the "clear and conspicuous" requirement, the disclosure should be placed as close as possible to the claim being qualified or be included within the claim itself. If such placement is not feasible, the next-best location is on a section of the page to which a consumer can easily scroll. Generally, hyperlinks to a disclosure are recommended only for lengthy disclosures or for disclosures that must be repeated in several locations on the Web page.

FTC Actions against Deceptive Advertising

The FTC receives complaints from many sources, including competitors of alleged violators, consumers, consumer organizations, trade associations, Better Business Bureaus, government organizations, and state and local officials. When the agency receives numerous and widespread complaints about a particular problem, it will investigate.

THE COMPLAINT ORDER If the FTC concludes that a given advertisement is unfair or deceptive, it drafts a formal complaint, which is sent to the alleged offender. The company may agree to settle the complaint without further proceedings. If not, the FTC can conduct a hearing in which the company can present its defense (see Chapter 44).

THE CEASE-AND-DESIST ORDER If the FTC succeeds in proving that an advertisement is unfair or deceptive, it usually issues a **cease-and-desist order** requiring the company to stop the challenged advertising. In some circumstances, it may also impose a sanction known as **counteradvertising,** which requires the company to advertise anew—in print, on the Internet, on radio, and on television—to inform the public about the earlier misinformation. The FTC sometimes institutes a **multiple product order,** which requires a firm to cease and desist from false advertising in regard to all of its products, not just the product that was the subject of the original action. When a company's deceptive ad leads to wrongful payments by consumers, the FTC may seek other remedies, including restitution.

CASE IN POINT Verity International, Ltd., billed phone-line subscribers who accessed certain online pornography sites at the rate for international calls to Madagascar. When consumers complained about the charges, Verity told them that the charges were valid and had to be paid, or the consumers would face further collection activity. A federal appellate court held that this representation of "uncontestability" was deceptive and a violation of the FTC Act. The court ordered Verity to pay nearly $18 million in restitution to consumers.[5]

Telemarketing and Fax Advertising

The Telephone Consumer Protection Act (TCPA)[6] prohibits telephone solicitation using an automatic telephone dialing system or a prerecorded voice. In addition, most states have statutes regulating telephone solicitation. The TCPA also makes it illegal to transmit ads via fax without first obtaining the recipient's permission. (Similar issues have arisen with respect to junk e-mail, called *spam*—see Chapters 6 and 9.)

The Federal Communications Commission (FCC) enforces the act. The FCC imposes substantial fines ($11,000 each day) on companies that violate the junk fax provisions of the act and has even fined one company as much as $5.4 million.[7] The TCPA also gives consumers a right to sue for either $500 for each violation of the act or for the actual monetary losses resulting from a violation, whichever is greater. If a court finds that a defendant willfully or knowingly violated the act, the court has the discretion to treble (triple) the amount of damages awarded.

The Telemarketing and Consumer Fraud and Abuse Prevention Act of 1994[8] directed the FTC to establish rules governing telemarketing and to bring actions against fraudulent telemarketers. The FTC's Telemarketing Sales Rule (TSR)[9] requires a telemarketer to identify the seller's name, describe the product being sold, and disclose all material facts related to the sale (such as the total cost of the goods being sold). The TSR makes it illegal for telemarketers to misrepresent information or facts about their goods

---

5. *Federal Trade Commission v. Verity International, Ltd.,* 443 F.3d 48 (2d Cir. 2006).

6. 47 U.S.C. Sections 227 *et seq.*

7. See *Missouri ex rel. Nixon v. American Blast Fax, Inc.,* 323 F.3d 649 (8th Cir. 2003); *cert.* denied, 540 U.S. 1104, 124 S.Ct. 1043, 157 L.Ed.2d 888 (2004).

8. 15 U.S.C. 6101–6108.

9. 15 U.S.C. Sections 1331–1341.

or services. A telemarketer must also remove a consumer's name from its list of potential contacts if the customer so requests. An amendment to the TSR established the national Do Not Call Registry. Telemarketers must refrain from calling those consumers who have placed their names on the list. Significantly, the TSR applies to any offer made to consumers in the United States—even if the offer comes from a foreign firm. Thus, the TSR helps to protect consumers from illegal cross-border telemarketing operations.

SECTION 2
LABELING AND PACKAGING LAWS

A number of federal and state laws deal specifically with the information given on labels and packages. In general, labels must be accurate, and they must use words that are easily understood by the ordinary consumer. For example, a box of cereal cannot be labeled "giant" if that would exaggerate the amount of cereal contained in the box.

In some instances, labels must specify the raw materials used in the product, such as the percentage of cotton, nylon, or other fiber used in a garment. In other instances, the product must carry a warning. Cigarette packages and advertising, for example,

must include one of several warnings about the health hazards associated with smoking.[10]

Federal Statutes

Numerous federal laws regulate the labeling and packaging of products. These include the Wool Products Labeling Act of 1939,[11] the Fur Products Labeling Act of 1951,[12] the Flammable Fabrics Act of 1953,[13] and the Fair Packaging and Labeling Act of 1966.[14] The Comprehensive Smokeless Tobacco Health Education Act of 1986[15] requires producers, packagers, and importers of smokeless tobacco to include one of several warnings about the use of smokeless tobacco on the labels of their products.

The Energy Policy and Conservation Act of 1975[16] requires automakers to attach an information label to every new car. This label must include the Environmental Protection Agency's fuel economy estimate for the vehicle. In the following case, the buyer of a new car complained that the vehicle had failed to achieve the fuel economy estimate advertised in the automaker's brochure and listed on the label.

---

10. 15 U.S.C. Sections 1331–1341.
11. 15 U.S.C. Section 68.
12. 15 U.S.C. Section 69.
13. 15 U.S.C. Section 1191.
14. 15 U.S.C. Sections 1451 *et seq.*
15. 15 U.S.C. Sections 4501–4508.
16. 49 U.S.C. Section 32908(b)(1).

CASE 45.2
Paduano v. American Honda Motor Co.
California Court of Appeal, Fourth District, 169 Cal.App.4th 1453, 88 Cal.Rptr.3d 90 (2009).

BACKGROUND AND FACTS • In 2004, Gaetano Paduano bought a new Honda Civic Hybrid in California. The information label on the car stated that the fuel economy estimates from the Environmental Protection Agency (EPA) were forty-seven miles per gallon (mpg) and forty-eight mpg for city and highway driving, respectively. Honda's sales brochure added, "Just drive the Hybrid like you would a conventional car and save on fuel bills." Paduano soon became frustrated with the car's fuel economy, which was less than half of the EPA's estimate. When American Honda Motor Company refused to repurchase the vehicle, Paduano filed a suit in a California state court against the automaker, alleging deceptive advertising in violation of the state's Consumer Legal Remedies Act and Unfair Competition Law. Honda argued that the federal Energy Policy and Conservation Act (EPCA), which prescribed the EPA's fuel economy estimate, preempted Paduano's claims (preemption was discussed in Chapter 4). The court issued a summary judgment in Honda's favor. Paduano appealed to a state intermediate appellate court.

IN THE LANGUAGE OF THE COURT
AARON, J. [Judge]
* * * *

The basic rules of preemption are not in dispute: *Under the supremacy clause of the United States Constitution, Congress has the power to preempt state law concerning matters that lie within the authority of Congress. In determining whether federal law preempts state*

CASE 45.2 CONTINUED ⬦ *law, a court's task is to discern congressional intent.* Congress's express intent in this regard will be found when Congress explicitly states that it is preempting state authority. [Emphasis added.]

* * * *

Honda * * * argues that [the EPCA] prevents Paduano from pursuing his * * * claims. That provision states in pertinent part,

> When a requirement under [the EPCA] is in effect, a State or a political subdivision of a State may adopt or enforce a law or regulation on disclosure of fuel economy or fuel operating costs for an automobile covered by [the EPCA] only if the law or regulation is identical to that requirement.

* * * Honda goes on to assert that "Paduano's deceptive advertising and misrepresentation claims would impose *non* identical disclosure requirements."

Contrary to Honda's characterization * * *, Paduano's claims are based on statements Honda made in its advertising brochure to the effect that one may drive a Civic Hybrid in the same manner as one would a conventional car, and need not do anything "special," in order to achieve the beneficial fuel economy of the EPA estimates. * * * Paduano is challenging * * * Honda's * * * commentary in which it alludes to those estimates in a manner that may give consumers the misimpression that they will be able to achieve mileage close to the EPA estimates while driving a Honda hybrid in the same manner as they would a conventional vehicle. Paduano does not seek to require Honda to provide "additional alleged facts" regarding the Civic Hybrid's fuel economy, as Honda suggests, but rather, seeks to prevent Honda from making misleading claims about how easy it is to achieve better fuel economy. Contrary to Honda's assertions, if Paduano were to prevail on his claims, Honda would not have to do anything differently with regard to its disclosure of the EPA mileage estimates.

* * * *

* * * Allowing states to regulate false advertising and unfair business practices may further the goals of the EPCA, and we reject Honda's claim.

DECISION AND REMEDY • *The state intermediate appellate court concluded that federal law did not preempt Paduano's claims concerning Honda's advertising. The court reversed the judgment and remanded the case.*

THE ETHICAL DIMENSION • *Suppose that the defendant automaker had opposed this action solely to avoid paying for a car that had proved to be a "lemon." Would this have been unethical? Explain.*

THE LEGAL ENVIRONMENT DIMENSION • *What does the interpretation of the law in this case suggest to businesspersons who sell products labeled with statements mandated by federal or state law?*

Food Labeling

Because the quality and safety of food are so important to consumers, several statutes deal specifically with food labeling. The Fair Packaging and Labeling Act requires that food product labels identify (1) the product; (2) the net quantity of the contents and, if the number of servings is stated, the size of a serving; (3) the manufacturer; and (4) the packager or distributor. The act includes additional requirements concerning descriptions on packages, savings claims, components of nonfood products, and standards for the partial filling of packages.

Food products must bear labels detailing the nutritional content, including the number of calories and the amounts of various nutrients that the food contains. The Nutrition Labeling and Education Act of 1990[17] requires food labels to provide standard nutrition facts (including the amount and type of fat that the food contains) and regulates the use of such terms as *fresh* and *low fat*. The U.S. Food and Drug Administration (FDA) and the U.S. Department of Agriculture (USDA) are the primary agencies that issue regulations on food labeling. These rules are published in the *Federal Register* and updated annually.

New rules that became effective in 2009 require the labels on fresh meats, vegetables, and fruits to indicate where the food originated so that consumers can know whether their food was imported. See

---

17. 21 U.S.C. Section 343.1.

Tucked into the 2,700-page health-care reform bill that President Obama signed into law in March 2010 was a provision aimed at combating the problem of obesity in the United States. The provision requires all restaurant chains with twenty or more locations to post the caloric content of the foods on their menus so that customers will know how many calories they are eating.[a] The hope is that customers, armed with this information, will consider the number of calories when they make their food choices. The new federal law will supersede all state and local laws already in existence.

What the Law Does and Does Not Cover

The law now directs the U.S. Food and Drug Administration (FDA) to create a new national standard for menu labeling and to establish specific regulations supporting that standard—a task that will take at least a year. Nevertheless, the outlines of the new requirement are clear. Any restaurant to which the law applies will have to post the caloric content of the foods listed on its standard menu, menu boards, or menu lists for drive-thru windows. Signs will also have to be posted near salad bars and buffets, providing information on the foods offered there. Exempt from the rules are condiments, daily specials, and foods offered for only a limited period (less than sixty days). In addition, restaurants will be required to post standard guidelines on the number of calories that an average person requires daily so that customers can

determine what portion of a day's calories a particular food choice will provide.

The law applies to foods offered through vending machines. The foods most affected will be those that do not list the number of calories on the front of the package.

The Law Will Spur Innovations

Restaurant chains affected by the new law will likely be forced to innovate as customers discover how many calories some of their favorite foods contain. Some customers, for example, may be surprised to learn that a Big Mac hamburger from McDonald's provides 540 calories—more than a quarter of the 2,000 calories needed by an average adult each day. The restaurant chains will have to create lower-calorie foods that taste as good as their high-calorie popular items. Some chains are already doing just that. Dunkin' Donuts has launched a lower-calorie DDSmart option. KFC now offers grilled chicken, and Starbucks has switched to lower-fat milk for espresso-based drinks.

MANAGERIAL IMPLICATIONS

Although the new requirements currently apply only to restaurant chains with twenty or more locations, managers in other restaurant situations can anticipate that calorie-posting requirements will eventually affect them. The FDA may even decide to impose criminal penalties on those who violate the calorie-posting requirements. Therefore, managers throughout the food-services industry should start thinking now about how they are going to comply with any calorie-posting requirements in the future. It is always less costly to introduce change gradually than all at once.

a. See Section 4205 of the Patient Protection and Affordable Care Act, H.R. 3590, passed by Congress on March 21, 2010 (also see the Health Care and Education Reconciliation Act of 2010, H.R. 4872).

---

this chapter's *Shifting Legal Priorities for Business* feature above for a discussion of a new requirement imposed on restaurant chains by the health-care legislation enacted in 2010.

SECTION 3
SALES

A number of statutes protect consumers by requiring the disclosure of certain terms in sales transactions and providing rules governing unsolicited merchandise and various forms of sales, such as door-to-door

sales, mail-order sales, and referral sales. The FTC has regulatory authority in this area, as do other federal agencies. The Federal Reserve Board of Governors, for example, has issued **Regulation Z,**[18] which governs credit provisions associated with sales contracts, as will be discussed later in this chapter. Many states and the FTC have **"cooling-off" laws** that permit the buyers of goods sold door to door to cancel their contracts within three business days. The FTC rule further requires that consumers be notified in Spanish of this right if the oral negotiations for the sale were in that language.

---

18. 12 C.F.R. Sections 226.1–226.30.

Telephone and Mail-Order Sales

The FTC Mail or Telephone Order Merchandise Rule of 1993 amended the FTC Mail-Order Rule of 1975.[19] The rule provides specific protections for consumers who purchase goods over the phone, through the mail, online via computer, or by fax machine. Among other things, the rule requires merchants to ship orders within the time promised in their catalogues or advertisements and to notify consumers when orders cannot be shipped on time. The rule also requires merchants to issue a refund within a specified period of time when a consumer cancels an order.

In addition, under the Postal Reorganization Act of 1970,[20] a consumer who receives *unsolicited* merchandise sent by U.S. mail can keep it, throw it away, or dispose of it in any manner that she or he sees fit. The recipient will not be obligated to the sender.

Online Sales

The FTC and other federal agencies have brought numerous enforcement actions against those who perpetrate online fraud (see the discussion of wire fraud in Chapter 9). Nonetheless, protecting consumers from fraudulent and deceptive sales practices conducted via the Internet has proved to be a challenging task. The number of consumers who have fallen prey to Internet fraud has actually grown in recent years. Faced with economic recession, job losses, mounting debt, and dwindling savings, many consumers are looking for any source of income. Complaints to the FTC about sales of fraudulent business opportunities, such as work-at-home offers and real estate systems, nearly doubled from 2008 to 2009, and nearly tripled in the first six months of 2010.

SECTION 4
CREDIT PROTECTION

Credit protection is one of the more important aspects of consumer protection legislation. Nearly 80 percent of U.S. consumers have credit cards, and most carry a balance on these cards, which amounts to about $2.5 trillion of debt nationwide. In 2010, Congress established a new agency, the Consumer Financial Protection Bureau, which is dedicated to overseeing the practices of banks, mortgage lenders, and credit-card companies.[21] We discuss significant consumer credit protection legislation next.

The Truth-in-Lending Act

A key statute regulating the credit and credit-card industries is Title I of the Consumer Credit Protection Act,[22] which is commonly referred to as the Truth-in-Lending Act (TILA). The TILA has been amended several times, most recently in 2009, when Congress passed sweeping reforms to strengthen its consumer protections.[23]

The TILA is basically a *disclosure law*. It is administered by the Federal Reserve Board and requires sellers and lenders to disclose credit terms or loan terms so that individuals can shop around for the best financing arrangements. TILA requirements apply only to persons who, in the ordinary course of business, lend funds, sell on credit, or arrange for the extension of credit. Thus, sales or loans made between two consumers do not come under the protection of the act. Additionally, this law protects only debtors who are natural persons (as opposed to the artificial "person" of a corporation). It does not extend to other legal entities.

DISCLOSURE REQUIREMENTS The disclosure requirements are contained in Regulation Z. If the contracting parties are subject to the TILA, the requirements of Regulation Z apply to any transaction involving an installment sales contract that calls for payment to be made in more than four installments. Transactions subject to Regulation Z typically include installment loans, retail and installment sales, car loans, home-improvement loans, and certain real estate loans if the amount of financing is less than $25,000.

Under the provisions of the TILA, all of the terms of a credit instrument must be clearly and conspicuously disclosed. A lender must disclose the annual percentage rate (APR), finance charge, amount financed, and total payments (the sum of the amount loaned, plus any fees, finance charges, and interest at the end of the loan). The TILA provides for contract rescission (cancellation) if a creditor

---

19. 16 C.F.R. Sections 435.1–435.2.
20. 39 U.S.C. Section 3009.

21. Title 10 of the Restoring American Financial Stability Act of 2010, S.B. 3217, April 15, 2010.
22. 15 U.S.C. Sections 1601–1693r.
23. The TILA was amended in 1980 by the Truth-in-Lending Simplification and Reform Act. It was significantly amended again in 2009 by the Credit Card Accountability, Responsibility, and Disclosure Act of 2009, Pub. No. 111-24, 123 Stat. 1734, enacting 15 U.S.C. Sections 1616, 1651, 1665c–1665e, 1666b, 1666i-1, 1666i-2, and 1693l-1, and 16 U.S.C. Section 1a-7b, as well as amending many other provisions of the TILA.

fails to follow *exactly* the procedures required by the act.[24]

EQUAL CREDIT OPPORTUNITY In 1974, Congress enacted the Equal Credit Opportunity Act (ECOA)[25] as an amendment to the TILA. The ECOA prohibits the denial of credit solely on the basis of race, religion, national origin, color, gender, marital status, or age. The act also prohibits credit discrimination on the basis of whether an individual receives certain forms of income, such as public-assistance benefits.

Under the ECOA, a creditor may not require the signature of an applicant's spouse, except as a joint applicant, on a credit instrument if the applicant qualifies under the creditor's standards of credit-worthiness for the amount and terms of the credit request.

CASE IN POINT Tonja, an African American, applied for financing with a used-car dealer. The dealer looked at Tonja's credit report and, without submitting the application to the lender, decided that she would not qualify. Instead of informing Tonja that she did not qualify, the dealer told her that she needed a cosigner on the loan to purchase the car. She filed a complaint. According to a federal appellate court, the dealer qualified as a creditor in this situation because the dealer unilaterally denied the credit and thus could be held liable under the ECOA.[26]

CREDIT-CARD RULES The TILA also contains provisions regarding credit cards. One provision limits the liability of a cardholder to $50 per card for unauthorized charges made before the creditor is notified that the card has been lost. If a consumer receives an *unsolicited* credit card in the mail that is later stolen, the company that issued the card cannot charge the consumer for any unauthorized charges. Another provision requires credit-card companies to disclose the balance computation method that is used to determine the outstanding balance and to state when finance charges begin to accrue. Other provisions set forth procedures for resolving billing disputes with the credit-card company. These procedures are used if, for example, a cardholder thinks that an error has occurred in billing or wishes to withhold payment for a faulty product purchased by credit card.

ADDITIONAL CREDIT-CARD PROTECTION In 2009, President Barack Obama signed into law amendments to the credit-card protections of the TILA that became effective in 2010. The most significant provisions of the new rules impose the following requirements on credit-card companies:

1. A company may not retroactively increase the interest rates on existing card balances, unless the account is sixty days delinquent.
2. A company must provide forty-five days' advance notice to consumers before changing the credit-card terms.
3. Monthly bills must be sent to cardholders twenty-one days before the due date.
4. The interest rate charged on a customer's credit-card balance may not be increased except in specific situations, such as when a promotional rate ends.
5. A company may not charge over-limit fees except in specified situations.
6. When the customer has balances at different interest rates, payments in excess of the minimum amount due must be applied first to the balance with the highest rate (for example, a higher interest rate is commonly charged for cash advances).
7. A company may not compute finance charges based on the previous billing cycle (a practice known as double-cycle billing, which hurts consumers because they are charged interest for the previous cycle even though they have paid the bill in full).

CONSUMER LEASES The Consumer Leasing Act (CLA) of 1988[27] amended the TILA to provide protection for consumers who lease automobiles and other goods. The CLA applies to those who lease or arrange to lease consumer goods in the ordinary course of their business. The act applies only if the goods are priced at $25,000 or less and if the lease term exceeds four months. The CLA and its implementing regulation, Regulation M,[28] require lessors to disclose in writing (or by electronic record) all of the material terms of the lease.

The Fair Credit Reporting Act

The Fair Credit Reporting Act (FCRA)[29] protects consumers against inaccurate credit reporting and requires that lenders and other creditors report correct, relevant, and up-to-date information. The act

---

24. Note, however, that amendments to the TILA enacted in 1995 prevent borrowers from rescinding loans because of minor clerical errors in closing documents [15 U.S.C. Sections 1605, 1631, 1635, 1640, and 1641].
25. 15 U.S.C. Sections 1691–1691f.
26. *Treadway v. Gateway Chevrolet Oldsmobile, Inc.,* 362 F.3d 971 (7th Cir. 2004).

27. 15 U.S.C. Sections 1667–1667e.
28. 12 C.F.R. Part 213.
29. 15 U.S.C. Sections 1681–1681t.

provides that consumer credit reporting agencies may issue credit reports to users only for specified purposes, including the extension of credit, the issuance of insurance policies, and compliance with a court order, and in response to a consumer's request for a copy of his or her own credit report.

CONSUMER NOTIFICATION AND INACCURATE INFORMATION Any time a consumer is denied credit or insurance on the basis of her or his credit report, the consumer must be notified of that fact and of the name and address of the credit reporting agency that issued the report. The same notice must be sent to consumers who are charged more than others ordinarily would be for credit or insurance because of their credit reports.

Under the FCRA, consumers may request the source of any information used by the credit agency, as well as the identity of anyone who has received an agency's report. Consumers are also permitted to access the information about them contained in a credit reporting agency's files. If a consumer discovers that an agency's files contain inaccurate information, he or she should report the problem to the agency. On the consumer's written request, the agency must conduct a systematic examination of its records. Any unverifiable or erroneous information must be deleted within a reasonable period of time.

REMEDIES FOR VIOLATIONS A credit reporting agency that fails to comply with the act is liable for actual damages, plus additional damages not to exceed $1,000 and attorneys' fees.[30] Creditors and other companies that use information from credit reporting agencies may also be liable for violations of the FCRA. In 2007, the United States Supreme Court held that an insurance company's failure to notify new customers that they were paying higher insurance rates as a result of their credit scores was a *willful* violation of the FCRA.[31]

CASE IN POINT Rex Saunders obtained an auto loan from Branch Banking & Trust Company of Virginia (BB&T), which failed to give Saunders a payment coupon book and rebuffed his attempts to make payments on the loan. In fact, BB&T told him that it had not extended a loan to him. Eventually, BB&T discovered its mistake and demanded full payment, plus interest and penalties. When payment was not immediately forthcoming, BB&T declared that Saunders was in default. It then repossessed the car and forwarded adverse credit information about Saunders to credit reporting agencies, without noting that Saunders disputed the information. Saunders filed a lawsuit alleging violations of the FCRA and was awarded $80,000 in punitive damages. An appellate court found that the damages award was reasonable, given BB&T's willful violation.[32]

The Fair and Accurate Credit Transactions Act

In an effort to combat identity theft (discussed in Chapter 9), Congress passed the Fair and Accurate Credit Transactions (FACT) Act of 2003.[33] The act established a national fraud alert system so that consumers who suspect that they have been or may be victimized by identity theft can place an alert on their credit files. The act also requires the major credit reporting agencies to provide consumers with free copies of their own credit reports every twelve months.

Another provision requires account numbers on credit-card receipts to be truncated (shortened) so that merchants, employees, or others who may have access to the receipts do not have the consumers' names and full credit-card numbers. The act further mandates that financial institutions work with the FTC to identify "red flag" indicators of identity theft and to develop rules for the disposal of sensitive credit information.

The FACT Act gives consumers who have been victimized by identity theft some assistance in rebuilding their credit reputations. For example, credit reporting agencies must stop reporting allegedly fraudulent account information once the consumer establishes that identify theft has occurred. Business owners and creditors are required to provide consumers with copies of any records that can help the consumer prove that a particular account or transaction is fraudulent (records showing that a fraudulent signature was used in the creation of an account, for example). In addition, the act allows consumers to report the accounts affected by identity theft directly to creditors in order to help prevent the spread of erroneous credit information.

---

30. 15 U.S.C. Section 1681n.

31. *Safeco Insurance. Co. of America v. Burr,* 551 U.S. 47, 127 S.Ct. 2201, 167 L.Ed.2d 1045 (2007).

32. *Saunders v. Branch Banking & Trust Co. of Virginia,* 526 F.3d 142 (4th Cir. 2008).

33. Pub. L. No. 108-159, 117 Stat. 1952 (December 4, 2003).

The Fair Debt Collection Practices Act

In 1977, Congress enacted the Fair Debt Collection Practices Act (FDCPA)[34] in an attempt to curb perceived abuses by collection agencies. The act applies only to specialized debt-collection agencies and attorneys who regularly attempt to collect debts on behalf of someone else, usually for a percentage of the amount owed. Creditors attempting to collect debts are not covered by the act unless, by misrepresenting themselves, they cause debtors to believe they are collection agencies.

PROHIBITED DEBT COLLECTION TACTICS   Under the FDCPA, a collection agency may not do any of the following:

1. Contact the debtor at the debtor's place of employment if the debtor's employer objects.
2. Contact the debtor at inconvenient or unusual times (for example, at three o'clock in the morning) or at any time, if the debtor is being represented by an attorney.
3. Contact third parties other than the debtor's parents, spouse, or financial adviser about payment of a debt unless a court authorizes such action.
4. Harass or intimidate the debtor (by using abusive language or threatening violence, for example) or make false or misleading statements (such as posing as a police officer).

5. Communicate with the debtor at any time after receiving notice that the debtor is refusing to pay the debt, except to advise the debtor of further action to be taken by the collection agency.

NOTIFICATION AND BONA FIDE ERRORS   The FDCPA also requires a collection agency to include a **validation notice** whenever it initially contacts a debtor for payment of a debt or within five days of that initial contact. The notice must state that the debtor has thirty days in which to dispute the debt and to request a written verification of the debt from the collection agency. A debt collector who fails to comply with the act is liable for actual damages, plus additional damages not to exceed $1,000[35] and attorneys' fees.

Debt collectors who violate the act are exempt from liability if they can show that the violation was not intentional and "resulted from a bona fide error notwithstanding the maintenance of procedures reasonably adapted to avoid any such error." The "bona fide error" defense typically has been applied to mistakes of fact or clerical errors. Should the defense also apply to mistakes of law? In other words, if a debt collector violates the act because of a mistaken interpretation of the legal requirements of the FDCPA, can the debt collector avoid liability under the act? That was the issue in the following case.

---

34. 15 U.S.C. Section 1692.

35. According to the U.S. Court of Appeals for the Sixth Circuit, the $1,000 limit on damages applies to each lawsuit, not to each violation. See *Wright v. Finance Service of Norwalk, Inc.*, 22 F.3d 647 (6th Cir. 1994).

✷ EXTENDED CASE 45.3 ✷
Jerman v. Carlisle, McNellie, Rini, Kramer & Ulrich, LPA

Supreme Court of the United States, ___ U.S. ___, 130 S.Ct. 1605, 176 L.Ed.2d 519 (2010).
www.supremecourt.gov/opinions/opinions.aspx[a]

IN THE LANGUAGE OF THE COURT

Justice   *SOTOMAYOR* delivered the opinion of the Court.
* * * *

Respondents in this case are a law firm, Carlisle, McNellie, Rini, Kramer & Ulrich, L.P.A., [Legal Professional Association], and one of its attorneys, Adrienne S. Foster (collectively Carlisle). In April 2006, Carlisle filed a complaint in Ohio

state court on behalf of a client, Countrywide Home Loans, Inc. Carlisle sought foreclosure of a mortgage held by Countrywide in real property owned by petitioner Karen L. Jerman. The complaint included a "Notice," later served on Jerman, stating that the mortgage debt would be assumed to be valid unless Jerman disputed it in writing. Jerman's lawyer sent a letter disputing the debt, and Carlisle sought verification from Countrywide. When Countrywide

acknowledged that Jerman had, in fact, already paid the debt in full, Carlisle withdrew the foreclosure lawsuit.

Jerman then filed her own lawsuit seeking * * * damages under the FDCPA [Fair Debt Collection Practices Act], contending that Carlisle violated [the act] by stating that her debt would be assumed valid unless she disputed it in writing. While acknowledging a division of authority on the

---

a. Select "Latest Slip Opinions" under the heading "Current Term." On the page that opens, scroll down to "42" in the left-hand column and click on the case title to access the opinion. The United States Supreme Court maintains this Web site.

EXTENDED CASE 45.3 CONTINUED ➡

question, the District Court held that Carlisle had violated [the act] by requiring Jerman to dispute the debt in writing. The court ultimately granted summary judgment to Carlisle, however, concluding that Section 1692k(c) [of the FDCPA] shielded it from liability because the violation was not intentional, resulted from a bona fide error, and occurred despite the maintenance of procedures reasonably adapted to avoid any such error. The Court of Appeals for the Sixth Circuit affirmed. Acknowledging that the Courts of Appeals are divided regarding the scope of the bona fide error defense, and that the "majority view is that the defense is available for clerical and factual errors only," the Sixth Circuit nonetheless held that Section 1692k(c) extends to "mistakes of law."

* * * *

The parties disagree about whether a "violation" resulting from a debt collector's misinterpretation of the legal requirements of the FDCPA can ever be "not intentional" under 1692k(c). Jerman contends that when a debt collector intentionally commits the act giving rise to the violation (here, sending a notice that included the "in writing" language), a misunderstanding about what the Act requires cannot render the violation "not intentional," given the general rule that mistake or ignorance of law is no defense. Carlisle and the dissent, in contrast, argue that nothing in the statutory text excludes legal errors from the category of "bona fide error[s]" covered by 1692k(c) and note that the Act refers not to an unintentional "act" but rather an unintentional "violation." The latter

term, they contend, evinces [makes clear] Congress' intent to impose liability only when a party knows its conduct is unlawful. Carlisle urges us, therefore, to read 1692k(c) to encompass "all types of error," including mistakes of law.

We decline to adopt the expansive reading of Section 1692k(c) that Carlisle proposes. *We have long recognized the "common maxim, familiar to all minds, that ignorance of the law will not excuse any person, either civilly or criminally." Our law is therefore no stranger to the possibility that an act may be "intentional" for purposes of civil liability, even if the actor lacked actual knowledge that her conduct violated the law.* [Emphasis added.]

* * * When Congress has intended to provide a mistake-of-law defense to civil liability, it has often done so more explicitly than here. In particular, the FTC [Federal Trade Commission] Act's administrative-penalty provisions—which * * * Congress expressly incorporated into the FDCPA—apply only when a debt collector acts with "actual knowledge or knowledge fairly implied on the basis of objective circumstances" that its action was "prohibited by [the FDCPA]." Given the absence of similar language in Section 1692k(c), it is a fair inference that Congress chose to permit injured consumers to recover actual damages, costs, fees, and modest statutory damages for "intentional" conduct, including violations resulting from mistaken interpretation of the FDCPA, while reserving the more onerous penalties of the FTC Act for debt collectors whose intentional actions also reflected "knowledge fairly implied on the basis of objective circumstances" that the conduct was prohibited.

* * * *

We draw additional support for the conclusion that bona fide errors in Section 1692k(c) do not include mistaken interpretations of the FDCPA from the requirement that a debt collector maintain "procedures reasonably adapted to avoid any such error." The dictionary defines "procedure" as "a series of steps followed in a regular orderly definite way." In that light, the statutory phrase is more naturally read to apply to processes that have mechanical or other such "regular orderly" steps to avoid mistakes— for instance, the kind of internal controls a debt collector might adopt to ensure its employees do not communicate with consumers at the wrong time of day or make false representations as to the amount of a debt. * * * We do not dispute that some entities may maintain procedures to avoid legal errors. But legal reasoning is not a mechanical or strictly linear process. For this reason, we find * * * that the broad statutory requirement of procedures reasonably designed to avoid "any" bona fide error indicates that the relevant procedures are ones that help to avoid errors like clerical or factual mistakes. Such procedures are more likely to avoid error than those applicable to legal reasoning, particularly in the context of a comprehensive and complex federal statute such as the FDCPA that imposes open-ended prohibitions on, *inter alia* [among other things], "false, deceptive," or "unfair" practices.

* * * *

For the reasons discussed above, the judgment of the United States Court of Appeals for the Sixth Circuit is reversed, and the case is remanded for further proceedings consistent with this opinion.

QUESTIONS

1. One of the concerns raised by Carlisle was that if attorneys could be held liable for their reasonable misinterpretations of the FDCPA's requirements, there would be a "flood of lawsuits" against creditors' attorneys by plaintiffs seeking damages and attorneys' fees. Should this concern have any bearing on the outcome of this case? Why or why not?
2. Jerman's attorneys contended that if the Court agreed with Carlisle's argument (that the bona fide error defense included errors in legal interpretation), ethical debt collectors would be placed at a disadvantage. Why would this be?

Garnishment of Wages

Despite the increasing number of protections afforded debtors, creditors are not without means of securing payment on debts. One of these is the right to garnish a debtor's wages after the debt has gone unpaid for a prolonged period. Recall from Chapter 28 that in a garnishment process, a creditor directly attaches, or seizes, a portion of the debtor's assets (such as wages) that are in the possession of a third party (such as an employer).

State law governs the garnishment process, but the law varies among the states as to how easily garnishment can be obtained. Indeed, a few states, such as Texas, prohibit garnishment of wages except for child support and court-approved spousal maintenance. Constitutional due process and federal legislation under the TILA also provide certain protections against abuse.[36] In general, the debtor is entitled to notice and an opportunity to be heard. Moreover, wages cannot be garnished beyond 25 percent of the debtor's after-tax earnings, and the garnishment must leave the debtor with at least a specified minimum income.

SECTION 5
CONSUMER HEALTH AND SAFETY

The laws discussed earlier regarding the labeling and packaging of products are intended to promote consumer health and safety. Nevertheless, there is a significant distinction between regulating the information dispensed about a product and regulating the actual content of the product. The classic example is tobacco products. Producers of tobacco products are required to warn consumers about the hazards associated with the use of their products, but the sale of tobacco products has not been subjected to significant restrictions or banned outright, despite the obvious dangers to health.[37] Here, we examine various laws that regulate the actual products made available to consumers.

The Federal Food, Drug and Cosmetic Act

The first federal legislation regulating food and drugs was enacted in 1906 as the Pure Food and Drugs Act.

That law, as amended in 1938, exists today as the Federal Food, Drug and Cosmetic Act (FFDCA).[38] The act protects consumers against adulterated and misbranded foods and drugs. As to foods, in its present form, the act establishes food standards, specifies safe levels of potentially hazardous food additives, and sets classifications of foods and food advertising. Most of these statutory requirements are monitored and enforced by the Food and Drug Administration (FDA).

The FFDCA also charges the FDA with the responsibility of ensuring that drugs are safe and effective before they are marketed to the public. Because the FDA must ensure the safety of new medications, there is always a delay before drugs are available to the public, and this sometimes leads to controversy.

CASE IN POINT A group of terminally ill patients claimed that they were entitled, under the U.S. Constitution, to access to experimental drugs before the FDA completed its clinical tests. The court, however, found that the FDA's policy of limiting access to drugs undergoing tests was rationally related to protecting patients from potentially unsafe drugs. Therefore, the court held that terminally ill patients do not have a fundamental constitutional right of access to experimental drugs.[39]

The Consumer Product Safety Act

As early as 1953, Congress began enacting laws to protect consumers from specific classes of unsafe products, such as highly flammable clothing or materials. Then, in 1972, Congress enacted the Consumer Product Safety Act,[40] which created the first comprehensive scheme of regulation over matters of consumer safety. The act also established the Consumer Product Safety Commission (CPSC), which has far-reaching authority over consumer safety.

THE CPSC'S AUTHORITY   The CPSC conducts research on the safety of individual consumer products and maintains a clearinghouse on the risks associated with various products. The Consumer Product Safety Act authorizes the CPSC to:

1. Set safety standards for consumer products.
2. Ban the manufacture and sale of any product that the commission believes poses an "unreasonable risk" to consumers. (Products banned by the CPSC have included various types of fireworks,

36. 15 U.S.C. Sections 1671–1677.
37. We are ignoring recent civil litigation concerning the liability of tobacco product manufacturers for injuries that arise from the use of tobacco. See, for example, *Philip Morris USA v. Williams,* 549 U.S. 346, 127 S.Ct. 1057, 166 L.Ed.2d 940 (2007).

38. 21 U.S.C. Sections 301–393.
39. *Abigail Alliance for Better Access to Developmental Drugs v. von Eschenbach,* 495 F.3d 695 (D.C.Cir. 2007).
40. 15 U.S.C. Sections 2051–2083.

cribs, and toys, as well as many products containing asbestos or vinyl chloride.)

3. Remove from the market any products it believes to be imminently hazardous. The CPSC's authority is sufficiently broad to allow it to ban any product that it believes poses an "unreasonable risk" to consumers. The CPSC frequently works in conjunction with manufacturers to voluntarily recall defective products from stores.

4. Require manufacturers to report on any products already sold or intended for sale if the products have proved to be hazardous.

5. Administer other product-safety legislation, including the Child Protection and Toy Safety Act of 1969[41] and the Federal Hazardous Substances Act of 1960.[42]

NOTIFICATION REQUIREMENTS The Consumer Product Safety Act requires the distributors of consumer products to notify the CPSC immediately if they receive information that a product "contains a defect which . . . creates a substantial risk to the public" or "an unreasonable risk of serious injury or death."

CASE IN POINT A company that sold juicers received twenty-three letters from customers complaining that during operation the juicer had suddenly exploded, sending pieces of glass and razor-sharp metal across the room. Nevertheless, the company waited more than six months before notifying the CPSC. In a case filed by the federal government, the court held that a company is required to report a problem to the CPSC within twenty-four hours after receiving information about a threat. Even if it must investigate the allegations, the company should not take more than ten days to verify the information and report the problem. The court found that the company had violated the law and ordered it to pay damages.[43]

---

41. 15 U.S.C. Section 1262(e).
42. 15 U.S.C. Sections 1261–1273.

43. *United States v. Mirama Enterprises, Inc.*, 185 F.Supp.2d 1148 (S.D.Cal. 2002).

REVIEWING
Consumer Law

Leota Sage saw a local motorcycle dealer's newspaper advertisement offering a MetroRider EZ electric scooter for $1,699. When she went to the dealership, however, she learned that the EZ model had been sold out. The salesperson told Sage that he still had the higher-end MetroRider FX model in stock for $2,199 and would sell her one for $1,999. Sage was disappointed but decided to purchase the FX model. When Sage said that she wished to purchase the scooter on credit, she was directed to the dealer's credit department. As she filled out the credit forms, the clerk told Sage, who is an Asian American, that she would need a cosigner to obtain a loan. Sage could not understand why she would need a cosigner and asked to speak to the store manager. The manager apologized, told her that the clerk was mistaken, and said that he would "speak to" the clerk about that. The manager completed Sage's credit application, and Sage then rode the scooter home. Seven months later, Sage received a letter from the manufacturer informing her that a flaw had been discovered in the scooter's braking system and that the model had been recalled. Using the information presented in the chapter, answer the following questions.

1. Did the dealer engage in deceptive advertising? Why or why not?
2. Suppose that Sage had ordered the scooter through the dealer's Web site but that the dealer had been unable to deliver it by the date promised. What would the FTC have required the merchant to do in that situation?
3. Assuming that the clerk required a cosigner based on Sage's race or gender, what act prohibits such credit discrimination?
4. What organization has the authority to ban the sale of scooters based on safety concerns?

DEBATE THIS: *Laws against bait-and-switch advertising should be abolished because no consumer is ever forced to buy anything.*

TERMS AND CONCEPTS

bait-and-switch
advertising 882

cease-and-desist order 883
consumer law 880
"cooling-off" laws 886

counteradvertising 883
deceptive advertising 881
multiple product orders 883

Regulation Z 886
validation notice 890

QUESTIONS AND CASE PROBLEMS

45–1. Unsolicited Merchandise Andrew, a resident of California, received an advertising circular in the U.S. mail announcing a new line of regional cookbooks distributed by the Every-Kind Cookbook Co. Andrew didn't want any books and threw the circular away. Two days later, Andrew received in the mail an introductory cookbook entitled *Lower Mongolian Regional Cookbook,* as announced in the circular, on a "trial basis" from Every-Kind. Andrew was not interested but did not go to the trouble to return the cookbook. Every-Kind demanded payment of $20.95 for the *Lower Mongolian Regional Cookbook.* Discuss whether Andrew can be required to pay for the book.

45–2. Credit-Card Rules Maria Ochoa receives two new credit cards on May 1. She has solicited one of them from Midtown Department Store, and the other arrives unsolicited from High-Flying Airlines. During the month of May, Ochoa makes numerous credit-card purchases from Midtown Department Store, but she does not use the High-Flying Airlines card. On May 31, a burglar breaks into Ochoa's home and steals both credit cards, along with other items. Ochoa notifies the Midtown Department Store of the theft on June 2, but she fails to notify High-Flying Airlines. Using the Midtown credit card, the burglar makes a $500 purchase on June 1 and a $200 purchase on June 3. The burglar then charges a vacation flight on the High-Flying Airlines card for $1,000 on June 5. Ochoa receives the bills for these charges and refuses to pay them. Discuss Ochoa's liability for the charges.

45–3. QUESTION WITH SAMPLE ANSWER: Sales.

On June 28, a salesperson for Renowned Books called on the Gonchars at their home. After a very persuasive sales pitch by the agent, the Gonchars agreed in writing to purchase a twenty-volume set of historical encyclopedias from Renowned Books for a total of $299. A down payment of $35 was required, with the remainder of the cost to be paid in monthly payments over a one-year period. Two days later, the Gonchars, having second thoughts, contacted the book company and stated that they had decided to rescind the contract. Renowned Books said this would be impossible. Did Renowned Books violate

any consumer law by not allowing the Gonchars to rescind their contract? Explain.

• **For a sample answer to Question 45–3, go to Appendix I at the end of this text.**

45–4. Fair Credit Reporting Act Source One Associates, Inc., is based in Poughquag, New York. Peter Easton, Source One's president, is responsible for its daily operations. Between 1995 and 1997, Source One received requests from persons in Massachusetts seeking financial information about individuals and businesses. To obtain this information, Easton first obtained the targeted individuals' credit reports through Equifax Consumer Information Services by claiming that the reports would be used only in connection with credit transactions involving the consumers. From the reports, Easton identified financial institutions at which the targeted individuals held accounts. He then called the institutions to learn the account balances by impersonating either officers of the institutions or the account holders. The information was then provided to Source One's customers for a fee. Easton did not know why the customers wanted the information. The state ("commonwealth") of Massachusetts filed a suit in a Massachusetts state court against Source One and Easton, alleging, among other things, violations of the Fair Credit Reporting Act (FCRA). Did the defendants violate the FCRA? Explain. [*Commonwealth v. Source One Associates, Inc.,* 436 Mass. 118, 763 N.E.2d 42 (2002)]

45–5. Food Labeling One of the products that McDonald's Corp. sells is the Happy Meal®, which consists of a McDonald's food entree, a small order of french fries, a small drink, and a toy. In the early 1990s, McDonald's began to aim its Happy Meal marketing at children aged one to three. In 1995, McDonald's began making nutritional information for its food products available in documents known as "McDonald's Nutrition Facts." Each document lists each food item that the restaurant serves and provides a nutritional breakdown, but the Happy Meal is not included. Marc Cohen filed a suit in an Illinois state court against McDonald's, alleging, among other things, that the defendant had violated a state law prohibiting consumer fraud and deceptive business practices by failing to adhere to the Nutrition Labeling and Education Act (NLEA) of 1990. The NLEA sets out different requirements for products specifically intended for children under the age of four—generally, the products' labels cannot declare the percent of daily value of nutritional components. Would this requirement be readily understood by a consumer who is not familiar with nutritional standards? Why or why not? Should a state court impose such regulations? Explain. [*Cohen v. McDonald's Corp.*, 347 Ill.App.3d 627, 808 N.E.2d 1, 283 Ill.Dec. 451 (1 Dist. 2004)]

45–6. Debt Collection 55th Management Corp. in New York City owns residential property that it leases to various tenants. In June 2000, claiming that one of the tenants, Leslie Goldman, owed more than $13,000 in back rent, 55th retained Jeffrey Cohen, an attorney, to initiate nonpayment proceedings. Cohen filed a petition in a New York state court against Goldman, seeking recovery of the unpaid rent and at least $3,000 in attorneys' fees. After receiving notice of the petition, Goldman filed a suit in a federal district court against Cohen. Goldman contended that the notice of the petition constituted an initial contact that, under the Fair Debt Collection Practices Act (FDCPA), required a validation notice. Because Cohen did not give Goldman a validation notice at the time, or within five days, of the notice of the petition, Goldman argued that Cohen was in violation of the FDCPA. Should the filing of a suit in a state court be considered "communication," requiring a debt collector to provide a validation notice under the FDCPA? Why or why not? [*Goldman v. Cohen*, 445 F.3d 152 (2d Cir. 2006)]

45–7. CASE PROBLEM WITH SAMPLE ANSWER: Food Labeling.

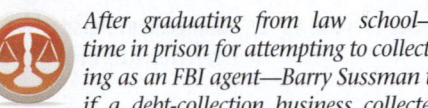

*The Nutrition Labeling and Education Act (NLEA) requires packaged food to have a "Nutrition Facts" panel that sets out "nutrition information," including "the total number of calories" per serving. Restaurants are exempt from this requirement. The NLEA also regulates nutritional content claims, such as "low sodium," that a purveyor might choose to add to a label. The NLEA permits a state or city to require restaurants to disclose nutrition information about the food they serve, but expressly preempts state or local attempts to regulate nutritional content claims. New York City Health Code Section 81.50 requires 10 percent of the restaurants in the city, including McDonald's, Burger King, and KFC, to post calorie content information on their menus. The New York State Restaurant Association (NYSRA) filed a suit in a federal district court, contending that the NLEA preempts Section 81.50. (Under the U.S. Constitution, state or local laws that conflict with federal laws are preempted.) Is the NYSRA correct? Explain. [*New York State Restaurant Association v. New York City Board of Health*, 556 F.3d 114 (2d Cir. 2009)]*

- **To view a sample answer for Problem 45–7, go to this book's Web site at www.cengage.com/blaw/clarkson, select "Chapter 45," and click on "Case Problem with Sample Answer."**

45–8. Deceptive Advertising Brian Cleary and Rita Burke filed a suit against the major cigarette maker Philip Morris USA, Inc., seeking class-action status for a claim of deceptive advertising. Cleary and Burke claimed that "light" cigarettes, such as Marlboro Lights, were advertised as safer than regular cigarettes, even though the health effects are the same. They contended that the tobacco companies concealed the true nature of light cigarettes. Philip Morris correctly claimed that it was authorized by the government to advertise cigarettes, including light cigarettes. Assuming that is true, should the plaintiffs still be able to bring a deceptive advertising claim against the tobacco company? Why or why not? [*Cleary v. Philip Morris USA, Inc.*, 683 F.Supp.2d 730 (N.D.Ill. 2010)]

45–9. A QUESTION OF ETHICS: Debt-Collection Practices.

*After graduating from law school—and serving time in prison for attempting to collect debts by posing as an FBI agent—Barry Sussman theorized that if a debt-collection business collected only debts that it owned as a result of buying checks written on accounts with insufficient funds (NSF checks), it would not be subject to the Federal Debt Collection Practices Act (FDCPA). Sussman formed Check Investors, Inc., to act on his theory. Check Investors bought more than 2.2 million NSF checks, with an estimated face value of about $348 million, for pennies on the dollar. Check Investors added a fee of $125 or $130 (more than the legal limit in most states) to the face amount of each check and aggressively pursued its drawer to collect. The firm's employees were told to accuse drawers of being criminals and to threaten them with arrest and prosecution. The threats were false. Check Investors never took steps to initiate a prosecution. The employees contacted the drawers' family members and used "saturation phoning"—phoning a drawer numerous times in a short period. They used abusive language, referring to drawers as "deadbeats," "retards," "thieves," and "idiots." Between January 2000 and January 2003, Check Investors netted more than $10.2 million from its efforts. [*Federal Trade Commission v. Check Investors, Inc.*, 502 F.3d 159 (3d Cir. 2007)]*

(a) The Federal Trade Commission filed a suit in a federal district court against Check Investors and others, alleging, in part, violations of the FDCPA. Was Check Investors a "debt collector," collecting "debts," within the meaning of the FDCPA? If so, did its methods violate the FDCPA? Were its practices unethical? What might Check Investors argue in its defense? Discuss.

(b) Are "deadbeats" the primary beneficiaries of laws such as the FDCPA? If not, how would you characterize debtors who default on their obligations?

45–10. VIDEO QUESTION: Deceptive Advertising.

Go to this text's Web site at **www.cengage.com/blaw/clarkson** and select "Chapter 45." Click on "Video Questions" and view the video titled *Advertising Communication Law: Bait and Switch.* Then answer the following questions.

(a) Is the auto dealership's advertisement for the truck in the video deceptive? Why or why not?

(b) Is the advertisement for the truck an offer to which the dealership is bound? Does it matter if Betty detrimentally relied on the advertisement?

(c) Is Tony committed to buying Betty's trade-in truck for $3,000 because that is what he told her over the phone?

LEGAL RESEARCH EXERCISES ON THE WEB

Go to this text's Web site at **www.cengage.com/blaw/clarkson**, select "Chapter 45," and click on "Practical Internet Exercises." There you will find the following Internet research exercises that you can perform to learn more about the topics covered in this chapter.

Practical Internet Exercise 45–1: Legal Perspective
The Food and Drug Administration

Practical Internet Exercise 45–2: Management Perspective
Internet Advertising and Marketing

CHAPTER 46

Environmental Law

oncern over the degradation of the environment has increased over time in response to the environmental effects of population growth, urbanization, and industrialization. Environmental protection is not without a price, however. For many businesses, the costs of complying with environmental regulations are high, and for some they may seem too high. A constant tension exists between the desire to increase profits and productivity and the need to protect the environment.

In this chapter, we discuss **environmental law,** which consists of all laws and regulations designed to protect and preserve our environmental resources. To a great extent, environmental law consists of statutes passed by federal, state, or local governments and regulations issued by administrative agencies. Before examining statutory and regulatory environmental laws, however, we look at the remedies against environmental pollution that are available under the common law.

SECTION 1
COMMON LAW ACTIONS

Common law remedies against environmental pollution originated centuries ago in England. Those responsible for operations that created dirt, smoke, noxious odors, noise, or toxic substances were sometimes held liable under common law theories of nuisance or negligence. Today, injured individuals continue to rely on the common law to obtain damages and injunctions against business polluters.

Nuisance

Under the common law doctrine of **nuisance,** persons may be held liable if they use their property in a manner that unreasonably interferes with others' rights to use or enjoy their own property. Courts typically balance the harm caused by the pollution against the costs of stopping it. Courts have often denied injunctive relief on the ground that the hardships that would be imposed on the polluter and on the community are greater than the hardships suffered by the plaintiff. For example, a factory that causes neighboring landowners to suffer from smoke, soot, and vibrations may be left in operation if it is the core of the local economy. The injured parties may be awarded only monetary damages, which may include compensation for the decline in the value of their property caused by the factory's operation.

A property owner may be given relief from pollution if he or she can identify a distinct harm separate from that affecting the general public. This harm is referred to as a "private" nuisance. Under the common law, individuals were denied standing (access to the courts—see Chapter 2) unless they suffered a harm distinct from the harm suffered by the public at large. Some states still require this. A public authority (such as a state's attorney general), however, can sue to stop a "public" nuisance.

Negligence and Strict Liability

An injured party may sue a business polluter in tort under the negligence and strict liability theories discussed in Chapters 6 and 7. The basis for a negligence action is a business's alleged failure to use reasonable care toward a party whose injury was foreseeable and was caused by the lack of reasonable care. For example, employees might sue an employer whose failure to use proper pollution controls contaminated the air, causing the employees to suffer respiratory illnesses. Lawsuits for personal injuries caused by exposure to a toxic substance, such as asbestos, radiation, or hazardous waste, have given rise to a growing body of tort law known as **toxic torts.**

Businesses that engage in ultrahazardous activities—such as the transportation of radioactive materials—are strictly liable for any injuries the activities cause. In a strict liability action, the injured party does not have to prove that the business failed to exercise reasonable care.

SECTION 2
FEDERAL, STATE, AND LOCAL REGULATIONS

All levels of government in the United States regulate some aspect of the environment. In this section, we look at some of the ways in which the federal, state, and local governments control business activities and land use in the interests of environmental preservation and protection.

State and Local Regulations

In addition to the federal regulation to be discussed shortly, many states have enacted laws to protect the environment. State laws may restrict a business's discharge of chemicals into the air or water or regulate its disposal of toxic wastes. States may also regulate the disposal or recycling of other wastes, including glass, metal, plastic containers, and paper. Additionally, states may restrict emissions from motor vehicles.

City, county, and other local governments also regulate some aspects of the environment. For instance, local zoning laws may be designed to inhibit or regulate the growth of cities and suburbs or to protect the natural environment. In the interest of safeguarding the environment, such laws may prohibit certain land uses. Even when zoning laws permit a business's proposed development, the proposal may have to be altered to lessen the development's impact on the environment. In addition, cities and counties may impose rules regulating methods of waste removal, the appearance of buildings, the maximum noise level, and other aspects of the local environment.

State and local regulatory agencies also play a significant role in implementing federal environmental legislation. Typically, the federal government relies on state and local governments to enforce federal environmental statutes and regulations such as those regulating air quality.

Federal Regulations

Congress has passed a number of statutes to control the impact of human activities on the environment. Exhibit 46–1 on the facing page lists and summarizes the major federal environmental statutes discussed in this chapter. Most of these statutes are designed to address pollution in the air, water, or land. Some of the laws specifically regulate toxic chemicals, including pesticides, herbicides, and hazardous wastes.

ENVIRONMENTAL REGULATORY AGENCIES The primary federal agency regulating environmental law is the Environmental Protection Agency (EPA), which was created in 1970 to coordinate federal environmental responsibilities. Other federal agencies with authority for regulating specific environmental matters include the Department of the Interior, the Department of Defense, the Department of Labor, the Food and Drug Administration, and the Nuclear Regulatory Commission. All federal agencies must take environmental factors into consideration when making significant decisions. In addition, as mentioned, state and local agencies play an important role in enforcing federal environmental legislation.

Most federal environmental laws provide that citizens can sue to enforce environmental regulations if government agencies fail to do so—or to limit enforcement actions if agencies go to far in their actions. Typically, a threshold hurdle in such suits is meeting the requirements for standing to sue (see page 35 in Chapter 2).

ENVIRONMENTAL IMPACT STATEMENTS The National Environmental Policy Act of 1969[1] requires that an **environmental impact statement (EIS)** be prepared for every major federal action that significantly affects the quality of the environment. An EIS must analyze (1) the impact on the environment that the action will have, (2) any adverse effects on the environment and alternative actions that might be taken, and (3) irreversible effects the action might generate.

An action qualifies as "major" if it involves a substantial commitment of resources (monetary or otherwise). An action is "federal" if a federal agency has the power to control it. Development of a ski resort by a private developer on federal land, for example, may require an EIS. Construction or operation of a nuclear plant, which requires a federal permit, or creation of a dam as part of a federal project requires an EIS. If an agency decides that an EIS is

---

1. 42 U.S.C. Sections 4321–4370d.

EXHIBIT 46–1 • **Major Federal Environmental Statutes**

POPULAR NAME	PURPOSE	STATUTE REFERENCE
Rivers and Harbors Appropriations Act (1899)	To prohibit ships and manufacturers from discharging and depositing refuse in navigable waterways.	33 U.S.C. Sections 401–418.
Federal Insecticide, Fungicide, and Rodenticide Act (1947)	To control the use of pesticides and herbicides.	7 U.S.C. Sections 136–136y.
Federal Water Pollution Control Act (1948)	To eliminate the discharge of pollutants from major sources into navigable waters.	33 U.S.C. Sections 1251–1387.
Clean Air Act (1963, 1970)	To control air pollution from mobile and stationary sources.	42 U.S.C. Sections 7401–7671q.
National Environmental Policy Act (1969)	To limit environmental harm from federal government activities.	42 U.S.C. Sections 4321–4370d.
Ocean Dumping Act (1972)	To prohibit the dumping of radiological, chemical, and biological warfare agents and high-level radioactive waste into the ocean.	16 U.S.C. Sections 1401–1445.
Endangered Species Act (1973)	To protect species that are threatened with extinction.	16 U.S.C. Sections 1531–1544.
Safe Drinking Water Act (1974)	To regulate pollutants in public drinking water systems.	42 U.S.C. Sections 300f–300j-25.
Resource Conservation and Recovery Act (1976)	To establish standards for hazardous waste disposal.	42 U.S.C. Sections 6901–6986.
Toxic Substances Control Act (1976)	To regulate toxic chemicals and chemical compounds.	15 U.S.C. Sections 2601–2692.
Comprehensive Environmental Response, Compensation, and Liability Act (1980)	To regulate the clean-up of hazardous waste–disposal sites.	42 U.S.C. Sections 9601–9675.
Oil Pollution Act (1990)	To establish liability for the clean-up of navigable waters after oil-spill disasters.	33 U.S.C. Sections 2701–2761.
Small Business Liability Relief and Brownfields Revitalization Act (2002)	To allow developers who comply with state voluntary clean-up programs to avoid federal liability for the properties that they decontaminate and develop.	42 U.S.C. Section 9628.

unnecessary, it must issue a statement supporting this conclusion. Private citizens, consumer interest groups, businesses, and others often use EISs as a means to challenge agency actions that they believe improperly threaten the environment.

SECTION 3
AIR POLLUTION

Federal involvement with air pollution goes back to the 1950s and 1960s, when Congress authorized funds for air-pollution research. In 1963, the federal government passed the Clean Air Act[2] to address multistate air pollution and provide assistance to the states. Later amendments to the act, especially those enacted in 1970, provide the basis for issuing regulations to control air pollution. The Clean Air Act covers both mobile sources (such as automobiles and other vehicles) and stationary sources (such as electric utilities and industrial plants) of pollution.

Mobile Sources

Regulations governing air pollution from automobiles and other mobile sources specify pollution standards and establish time schedules for meeting the standards. For example, 1990 amendments to the Clean Air Act required automobile manufacturers to cut new automobiles' exhaust emissions of nitrogen oxide by 60 percent and emissions of

---

2. 42 U.S.C. Sections 7401–7671q.

hydrocarbons and carbon monoxide by 35 percent by 1998. Beginning with 2004 models, the rules also applied to sport-utility vehicles (SUVs) and light trucks. The EPA periodically updates the pollution standards in light of new developments and data, reducing the amount of emissions allowed.

In 2009, the Obama administration announced a long-term goal of reducing emissions, including those from cars and SUVs, by 80 percent by 2050. In 2010, the administration ordered the EPA to develop national standards regulating fuel economy and emissions for medium- and heavy-duty trucks starting with 2014 models.

A growing concern among many scientists and others around the world is that greenhouse gases, such as carbon dioxide (CO_2), are contributing to global warming. The Clean Air Act, as amended, however, does not specifically mention CO_2 emissions. Therefore, up until 2009, the EPA did not regulate CO_2 emissions from motor vehicles.

CASE IN POINT In 2007, environmental groups and several states, including Massachusetts, sued the EPA in an effort to force the agency to regulate CO_2 emissions. When the case reached the United States Supreme Court, the EPA argued that the plaintiffs lacked standing because global warming has widespread effects and thus an individual plaintiff could not show the particularized harm required for standing. Furthermore, the agency maintained, it did not have authority under the Clean Air Act to address global climate change and regulate CO_2. The Court, however, ruled that Massachusetts had standing because its coastline, including state-owned lands, faced an imminent threat from rising sea levels caused by global warming. The Court also held that the Clean Air Act's broad definition of air pollutant gives the EPA authority to regulate CO_2 and requires the EPA to regulate any air pollutants that might "endanger public health or welfare." Accordingly, the Court ordered the EPA to determine whether CO_2 was a pollutant that endangered public health.[3] (In 2009, the EPA concluded that greenhouse gases, including CO_2 emissions, do constitute a public danger.)

Stationary Sources

The Clean Air Act also authorizes the EPA to establish air-quality standards for stationary sources (such as manufacturing plants) but recognizes that the primary responsibility for implementing these standards rests with state and local governments. The standards are aimed at controlling hazardous air pollutants—those likely to cause death or a serious, irreversible, or incapacitating condition such as cancer or neurological or reproductive damage.

LISTING OF HAZARDOUS AIR POLLUTANTS The Clean Air Act requires the EPA to list all hazardous air pollutants (HAPs) on a prioritized schedule. In all, nearly two hundred substances—including asbestos, benzene, beryllium, cadmium, and vinyl chloride—have been classified as hazardous. They are emitted from stationary sources by a variety of business activities, including smelting (melting ore to produce metal), dry cleaning, house painting, and commercial baking.

Mercury was added to the list of hazardous substances in 2000. The EPA attempted nonetheless to remove mercury from its list of designated HAPs emitted from steam-generating electricity plants. New Jersey and others challenged this delisting in the following case.

---

3. *Massachusetts v. Environmental Protection Agency,* 549 U.S. 497, 127 S.Ct. 1438, 167 L.Ed.2d 248 (2007).

CASE 46.1
State of New Jersey v. Environmental Protection Agency

United States Court of Appeals, District of Columbia Circuit, 517 F.3d 574 (2008).
www.cadc.uscourts.gov/bin/opinions/allopinions.asp[a]

BACKGROUND AND FACTS • The Environmental Protection Agency (EPA) published a rule—the Delisting Rule—that had the effect of removing from its regulation the emissions of mercury from steam-generating electricity plants that used coal or oil as their energy sources. This Delisting Rule ran counter to the EPA's own conclusions at the end of 2000 that it was "appropriate and necessary"

---

a. Select "February" and "2008" from the drop-down menus for "Month" and "Year" and click on "Go!" Scroll down to case number "05-1097" and click on the link to access the opinion. The U.S. Court of Appeals for the District of Columbia maintains this Web site.

CASE 46.1 CONTINUED ▶ to regulate mercury emissions. At that time, the agency placed mercury on its list of hazardous air pollutants (HAPs) to be monitored at electricity-generating sites. Later, however, the EPA tried to "delist" mercury from the HAPs list. New Jersey and fourteen other states, plus various state agencies, challenged the EPA's delisting action.

IN THE LANGUAGE OF THE COURT
ROGERS, Circuit Judge.
* * * *

First, Congress required EPA to regulate more than one hundred specific HAPs, including mercury and nickel compounds. Further, EPA was required to list and to regulate, on a prioritized schedule, "all categories and subcategories of major sources and areas sources" that emit one or more HAPs. *In seeking to ensure that regulation of HAPs reflects the "maximum reduction in emissions which can be achieved by application of [the] best available control technology," Congress imposed specific, strict pollution control requirements on both new and existing sources of HAPs.* [Emphasis added.]

Second, Congress restricted the opportunities for EPA and others to intervene in the regulation of HAP sources. For HAPs that result in health effects other than cancer, as is true of mercury, Congress directed that the Administrator "may delete any source category" from the section 112(c)(1) list only after determining that "emissions from no source in the category or subcategory concerned . . . exceed a level which is adequate to protect public health with an ample margin of safety and no adverse environmental effect will result from emissions from any source."
* * * *

EPA maintains that it possesses authority to remove EGUs [electrical generating units] from * * * [the] list under the "fundamental principle of administrative law that an agency has inherent authority to reverse an earlier administrative determination or ruling where an agency has a principled basis for doing so." EPA states in its brief that it has previously removed sources listed * * * without satisfying the requirements of [the statute]. But previous statutory violations cannot excuse the one now before the court. "We do not see how merely applying an unreasonable statutory interpretation for several years can transform it into a reasonable interpretation."

DECISION AND REMEDY • *The U.S. Court of Appeals for the District of Columbia Circuit ruled in favor of New Jersey and the other plaintiffs. The EPA was required to cancel its delisting of mercury.*

WHAT IF THE FACTS WERE DIFFERENT? • *Suppose that the EPA had carried out scientific tests that showed mercury was relatively harmless as a by-product of electricity generation. How might this have affected the court's ruling?*

THE GLOBAL DIMENSION • *Because air pollution knows no borders, how did this ruling affect our neighboring countries?*

AIR-POLLUTION CONTROL STANDARDS The EPA sets primary and secondary levels of ambient standards—that is, maximum permissible levels of certain pollutants—and the states formulate plans to achieve those standards. Different standards apply depending on whether the sources of pollution are located in clean areas or polluted areas and whether they are existing sources or major new sources.

Major new sources include existing sources modified by a change in a method of operation that increases emissions. Performance standards for major sources require the use of the *maximum achievable*

control technology, or MACT, to reduce emissions. The EPA issues guidelines as to what equipment meets this standard.[4]

Violations of the Clean Air Act

For violations of emission limits under the Clean Air Act, the EPA can assess civil penalties of up to $25,000 per day. Additional fines of up to $5,000

---

4. The EPA has also issued rules to regulate hazardous air pollutants emitted by landfills. See 40 C.F.R. Sections 60.750–60.759.

per day can be assessed for other violations, such as failure to maintain the required records. To penalize those who find it more cost-effective to violate the act than to comply with it, the EPA is authorized to impose a penalty equal to the violator's economic benefits from noncompliance. Persons who provide information about violators may be paid up to $10,000. Private citizens can also sue violators.

Those who knowingly violate the act may be subject to criminal penalties, including fines of up to $1 million and imprisonment for up to two years (for false statements or failure to report violations). Corporate officers are among those who may be subject to these penalties.

SECTION 4
WATER POLLUTION

Water pollution stems mostly from industrial, municipal, and agricultural sources. Pollutants entering streams, lakes, and oceans include organic wastes, heated water, sediments from soil runoff, nutrients (including fertilizers and human and animal wastes), and toxic chemicals and other hazardous substances.

Federal regulations governing water pollution can be traced back to the Rivers and Harbors Appropriations Act of 1899.[5] These regulations prohibited ships and manufacturers from discharging or depositing refuse in navigable waterways without a permit.[6] In 1948, Congress passed the Federal Water Pollution Control Act (FWPCA),[7] but its regulatory system and enforcement powers proved to be inadequate.

The Clean Water Act

In 1972, amendments to the FWPCA—known as the Clean Water Act (CWA)—established the following goals: (1) make waters safe for swimming, (2) protect fish and wildlife, and (3) eliminate the discharge of pollutants into the water. The CWA also set specific schedules, which were extended by amendment in 1977 and by the Water Quality Act of 1987.[8] Under these schedules, the EPA limits the discharge of various types of pollutants based on the technology available for controlling them.

---

5. 33 U.S.C. Sections 401–418.
6. The term *navigable waters* is interpreted today as including intrastate lakes and streams used by interstate travelers and industries, as well as coastal and freshwater wetlands.
7. 33 U.S.C. Sections 1251–1387.
8. This act amended 33 U.S.C. Section 1251.

FOCUS ON POINT-SOURCE EMISSIONS The CWA established a permit system, called the National Pollutant Discharge Elimination System (NPDES), for regulating discharges from "point sources" of pollution that include industrial, municipal (such as pipes and sewage treatment plants), and agricultural facilities.[9] Under this system, any point source emitting pollutants into water must have a permit. Pollution not from point sources, such as runoff from small farms, is not subject to much regulation. NPDES permits can be issued by the EPA and authorized state agencies and Indian tribes, but only if the discharge will not violate water-quality standards. NPDES permits must be reissued every five years. Although initially the NPDES system focused mainly on industrial wastewater, it was later expanded to cover storm water discharges.

In practice, the permit system under the CWA includes the following elements:

1. National effluent (pollution) standards set by the EPA for each industry.
2. Water-quality standards set by the states under EPA supervision.
3. A *discharge permit* program that sets water-quality standards to limit pollution.
4. Special provisions for toxic chemicals and for oil spills.
5. Construction grants and loans from the federal government for *publicly owned treatment works,* primarily sewage treatment plants.

STANDARDS FOR EQUIPMENT Regulations generally specify that the *best available control technology,* or BACT, be installed. The EPA issues guidelines as to what equipment meets this standard. Essentially, the guidelines require the most effective pollution-control equipment available. New sources must install BACT equipment before beginning operations. Existing sources are subject to timetables for the installation of BACT equipment and must immediately install equipment that utilizes the *best practical control technology,* or BPCT. The EPA also issues guidelines as to what equipment meets this standard.

The EPA must take into account many factors when issuing and updating its rules. Some provisions of the CWA instruct the EPA to weigh the cost of the technology required relative to the benefits achieved. The provision that covers power plants, however, neither requires nor prohibits a cost-benefit analysis. The question in the following case was whether the EPA could conduct such an analysis anyway.

---

9. 33 U.S.C. Section 1342.

CASE 46.2
Entergy Corp. v. Riverkeeper, Inc.

Supreme Court of the United States, __ U.S. __, 129 S.Ct. 1498, 173 L.Ed.2d 369 (2009).
www.findlaw.com/casecode/supreme.html[a]

BACKGROUND AND FACTS • As part of its implementation of the Clean Water Act, the Environmental Protection Agency (EPA) has developed two sets of rules that apply to the cooling systems of power plants. Phase I rules require new power plants to restrict their inflow of water "to a level commensurate with that which can be attained by a closed-cycle recirculating cooling water system." Phase II rules apply "national performance standards" to more than five hundred existing plants but do not require closed-cycle cooling systems. The EPA found that converting these facilities to closed-cycle operations would cost $3.5 billion per year. The facilities would then produce less power while burning the same amount of coal. Moreover, other technologies can attain nearly the same results as closed-cycle systems. Phase II rules also allow a variance from the national performance standards if a facility's cost of compliance "would be significantly greater than the benefits." Environmental organizations, including Riverkeeper, Inc., challenged the Phase II regulations, arguing that existing plants should be required to convert to closed-cycle systems. The U.S. Court of Appeals for the Second Circuit issued a ruling in the plaintiffs' favor. Power-generating companies, including Entergy Corporation, appealed to the United States Supreme Court.

IN THE LANGUAGE OF THE COURT
Justice *SCALIA* delivered the opinion of the Court.
* * * *

In setting the Phase II national performance standards and providing for site-specific cost-benefit variances, the EPA relied on its view that [the] "best technology available" standard permits consideration of the technology's costs and of the relationship between those costs and the environmental benefits produced.

* * * The "best" technology—that which is "most advantageous"—may well be the one that produces the most of some good, here a reduction in adverse environmental impact. But "best technology" may also describe the technology that most efficiently produces some good. *In common parlance one could certainly use the phrase "best technology" to refer to that which produces a good at the lowest per-unit cost, even if it produces a lesser quantity of that good than other available technologies.* [Emphasis added.]

* * * This latter reading is [not] precluded by the statute's use of the phrase "for minimizing adverse environmental impact." *Minimizing * * * is a term that admits of degree and is not necessarily used to refer exclusively to the "greatest possible reduction."* [Emphasis added.]

Other provisions in the Clean Water Act also suggest the agency's interpretation. When Congress wished to mandate the greatest feasible reduction in water pollution, it did so in plain language: The provision governing the discharge of toxic pollutants into the Nation's waters requires the EPA to set "effluent limitations which shall require the elimination of discharges of all pollutants * * * ." The less ambitious goal of "minimizing adverse environmental impact" suggests, we think, that the agency retains some discretion to determine the extent of reduction that is warranted under the circumstances. That determination could plausibly involve a consideration of the benefits derived from reductions and the costs of achieving them.

* * * [Under other Clean Water Act provisions that impose standards on sources of pollution,] the EPA is instructed to consider, among other factors, "the total cost of application of technology in relation to the * * * benefits to be achieved."
* * * *

This * * * comparison of * * * statutory factors * * * leads us to the conclusion that it was well within the bounds of reasonable interpretation for the EPA to conclude that cost-benefit analysis is not categorically forbidden.

---

a. In the "Browse Supreme Court Opinions" section, click on "2009." On that page, scroll to the name of the case and click on it to access the opinion. The United States Supreme Court maintains this Web site.

CASE CONTINUES ▶

CASE 46.2 CONTINUED ➡ * * * *

While not conclusive, it surely tends to show that the EPA's current practice is a reasonable and hence legitimate exercise of its discretion to weigh benefits against costs that the agency has been proceeding in essentially this fashion for over 30 years.

DECISION AND REMEDY • *The United States Supreme Court concluded that the EPA permissibly relied on a cost-benefit analysis to set national performance standards and to allow for variances from those standards as part of the Phase II regulations. The Court reversed the lower court's judgment and remanded the case.*

THE ETHICAL DIMENSION • *In this case, aquatic organisms were most directly at risk. Is it acceptable to apply cost-benefit analyses to situations in which the lives of people are directly affected? Explain.*

THE GLOBAL DIMENSION • *In analyzing the costs and benefits of an action that affects the environment, should a line be drawn at a nation's borders? Why or why not?*

WETLANDS The CWA prohibits the filling or dredging of **wetlands** unless a permit is obtained from the Army Corps of Engineers. The EPA defines *wetlands* as "those areas that are inundated or saturated by surface or ground water at a frequency and duration sufficient to support, and that under normal circumstances do support, a prevalence of vegetation typically adapted for life in saturated soil conditions." Wetlands are thought to be vital to the ecosystem because they filter streams and rivers and provide habitat for wildlife. In the past, the EPA's broad interpretation of what constituted a wetland generated substantial controversy, but the courts have considerably scaled back the CWA's protection of wetlands in recent years.[10]

In the following case, the court had to deal with the meaning of *wetlands* and whether the term included saturated land adjacent to so-called navigable-in-fact waters.

---

10. See, for example, *Rapanos v. United States,* 547 U.S. 715, 126 S.Ct. 2208, 165 L.Ed.2d 159 (2006).

✳ EXTENDED CASE 46.3 ✳
United States v. Lucas

United States Court of Appeals, Fifth District, 516 F.3d 316 (2008).

IN THE LANGUAGE OF THE COURT

Patrick E. *HIGGINBOTHAM,* Circuit Judge.
* * * *

Robert J. Lucas owned Big Hill Acres, Inc. (BHA, Inc.) and Consolidated Investments, Inc. Through these companies, he acquired Big Hill Acres (BHA), a large parcel of land in Jackson County, Mississippi, approximately eight miles from the Gulf of Mexico. He subdivided the property and sold mobile home lots under long-term installment plans. The property was not connected to a central municipal waste system,

and County law required Lucas to certify and install individual septic systems on each lot before they could establish electric hook-ups or sell the lots. In Jackson County, septic systems must be approved by an engineer with the Mississippi Department of Health (MDH) or by an independent licensed engineer. Lucas initially hired an MDH engineer to approve septic systems, but MDH withdrew many of its initial approvals when it found that the lots were on saturated soils. Lucas then hired a private licensed engineer, M. E. Thompson, Jr., to approve and certify the septic systems. Robbie Lucas Wrigley, Lucas's daughter, advertised the lots,

showed them to prospective buyers, and leased them.

The [U.S.] Army Corps of Engineers, the EPA [Environmental Protection Agency], the MDH, and the Mississippi Department of Environmental Quality (DEQ) became concerned that Defendants were selling house lots and installing septic systems on wetlands. These agencies issued several cease and desist orders against Lucas and Thompson, and the EPA sent letters to residents and organized a meeting of the residents to warn them of lot conditions and to tell them where wetlands were located on the property. It also met with BHA's counsel to attempt to designate the areas where they would allow development. These efforts were not fully successful.

The Government filed a forty-one-count indictment against Defendants * * * , charging filling of wetlands without a Section 404 permit from the [U.S. Army] Corps [of Engineers], failing to obtain Section 402 National Pollutant Discharge Elimination System (NPDES) Permits for the septic tanks, mail fraud, and conspiracy to commit mail fraud and to violate Sections 402 and 404 of the CWA [Clean Water Act]. * * * A jury convicted Defendants on all counts, and the court * * * sentenced Lucas, Wrigley, and [Thompson] to prison terms; placed BHA, Inc., and Consolidated Investments on probation; and ordered all Defendants to pay restitution, special assessments, and fines.

* * * *

The first and overarching [dominant] question is jurisdiction—whether the jury was properly required to find that the property at issue was subject to the CWA. * * * The instructions stated in relevant part,

* * * *

The term *wetlands* means those areas that are inundated or saturated by surface or groundwater at a frequency and duration sufficient to support, and that under normal circumstances do support,

a prevalence of vegetation typically adapted for life in saturated soil conditions * * * . * * * Wetlands that are waters of the United States are protected by the Clean Water Act. *Wetlands are considered waters of the United States if they are adjacent to a navigable body of open water. Wetlands are adjacent to a navigable body of water if there is a significant nexus [connection] between the wetlands in question and a navigable-in-fact waterway.* Some of the factors which you may wish to consider in determining whether there is a significant nexus include, but are not limited to: * * * flow rate of surface waters from the wetlands into a navigable body of water * * * when, or to what extent, contaminants from the wetlands have or will affect a navigable body of water * * * . [Emphasis added.]

Defendants argue that the court erred in not including their requested language that:

* * * adjacency implicates a "significant nexus" between the water in question and the navigable-in-fact waterway. If the government fails to prove beyond a reasonable doubt that the wetlands at issue in this case are in fact navigable or truly adjacent to [that is,] lying near, close, contiguous, or adjoining a navigable waterway, you must find the defendants not guilty * * * .

* * * *

* * * *A district court abuses its discretion in omitting a requested*

jury instruction only if the requested language "(1) is substantively correct; (2) is not substantially covered in the charge given to the jury; and (3) concerns an important point in the trial * * *."* [Emphasis added.]

The court's instructions were not in error, nor was the court's omission of Defendants' requested instructions. * * * The instructions substantially covered Defendants' requested instructions by requiring adjacency as defined by a significant nexus.

* * * *

The government has shown that there is a significant nexus between the wetlands on Big Hill Acres and navigable-in-fact waters. * * * The surface from the Big Hill Acres site drains in three directions. The western portions of the site drain into Bayou Costapia. Bayou Costapia empties into the Tchoutacabouffa River, which then empties into the Gulf of Mexico. The central portions of the Big Hill Acres development drained through tributaries into Old Fort Bayou Creek. And Old Fort Bayou Creek connects to Old Fort Bayou, which is a protected coastal preserve emptying into the Gulf of Mexico. And the eastern portions drain into the headwaters of Little Bluff Creek, which then connects to Bluff Creek, which flows into the Pascagoula River and on to the Gulf of Mexico. The court did not abuse its discretion in giving the CWA instructions.

 QUESTIONS

1. Assume that during most of the year, there was a solid strip of land around the property in question that was never under water or saturated. Would the outcome of this case have been the same? Why or why not?
2. According to the judge, what three characteristics of jury instructions does a federal appellate court examine to determine whether a district court has abused its discretion in omitting a requested jury instruction? Which of these three characteristics was at issue in this case?

VIOLATIONS OF THE CLEAN WATER ACT Because point-source water pollution control is based on a permit system, the permits are the key to enforcement. States have primary responsibility for enforcing the permit system, subject to EPA monitoring.

Discharging emissions into navigable waters without a permit, or in violation of pollution limits under a permit, violates the CWA. Firms that have discharge permits must monitor their own performance and file *discharge monitoring reports*. These reports are available for public inspection. Violators must report their violations and are subject to fines. Depending on the violation, civil penalties range from $10,000 to $25,000 per day, but not more than $25,000 per violation. Lying about a violation is more serious than admitting the truth about improper discharges.

Serious and intentional violations can result in criminal prosecutions, with substantial fines and imprisonment. Every year, violators—including some corporate officers—are sent to prison for dumping toxic pollutants. As with the Clean Air Act, citizens have the right to bring lawsuits for pollution that the EPA or a state environmental agency has not addressed properly. Injunctive relief and damages can also be imposed. The polluting party can be required to clean up the pollution or pay for the cost of doing so.

Drinking Water

The Safe Drinking Water Act[11] requires the EPA to set maximum levels for pollutants in public water systems. Operators of public water systems must come as close as possible to meeting the EPA's standards by using the best available technology that is economically and technologically feasible. The EPA is particularly concerned about contamination from underground sources, such as pesticides and wastes leaked from landfills or disposed of in underground injection wells. Many of these substances are associated with cancer and may cause damage to the central nervous system, liver, and kidneys.

The act was amended in 1996 to give the EPA greater flexibility in setting regulatory standards governing drinking water. These amendments also imposed certain requirements on suppliers of drinking water. Each supplier must send to every household it supplies with water an annual statement describing the source of its water, the level of any contaminants contained in the water, and any possible health concerns associated with the contaminants.

Ocean Dumping

The Marine Protection, Research, and Sanctuaries Act of 1972[12] (popularly known as the Ocean Dumping Act) regulates the transportation and dumping of material (pollutants) into ocean waters. It prohibits

entirely the ocean dumping of radiological, chemical, and biological warfare agents and high-level radioactive waste.

The act also established a permit program for transporting and dumping other materials, and designated certain areas as marine sanctuaries. Each violation of any provision or permit requirement in the Ocean Dumping Act may result in a civil penalty of up to $50,000. A knowing violation is a criminal offense that may result in a $50,000 fine, imprisonment for not more than a year, or both. A court may also grant an injunction to prevent an imminent or continuing violation.

Oil Pollution

When more than 10 million gallons of oil leaked into Alaska's Prince William Sound from the *Exxon Valdez* supertanker in 1989, Congress responded and passed the Oil Pollution Act of 1990.[13] (At that time, the *Exxon Valdez* disaster was the worst oil spill in U.S. history, but the British Petroleum oil spill in the Gulf of Mexico in 2010 surpassed it.) Under this act, any onshore or offshore oil facility, oil shipper, vessel owner, or vessel operator that discharges oil into navigable waters or onto an adjoining shore may be liable for clean-up costs, as well as damages. The act created an oil clean-up and economic compensation fund, and required oil tankers using U.S. ports to be double hulled by the year 2011 (to limit the severity of accidental spills).

Under the act, damage to natural resources, private property, and the local economy, including the increased cost of providing public services, is compensable. The penalties range from $2 million to $350 million, depending on the size of the vessel and on whether the oil spill came from a vessel or an offshore facility. The party held responsible for the clean-up costs can bring a civil suit for contribution from other potentially liable parties.

◣◤◢◥ **SECTION 5** ◣◤◢◥
TOXIC CHEMICALS

Originally, most environmental clean-up efforts were directed toward reducing smog and making water safe for fishing and swimming. Today, control of toxic chemicals used in agriculture and in industry has become increasingly important.

---

11. 42 U.S.C. Sections 300f to 300j-25.
12. 16 U.S.C. Sections 1401–1445.

13. 33 U.S.C. Sections 2701–2761.

Pesticides and Herbicides

The Federal Insecticide, Fungicide, and Rodenticide Act (FIFRA) of 1947[14] regulates pesticides and herbicides. Under FIFRA, pesticides and herbicides must be (1) registered before they can be sold, (2) certified and used only for approved applications, and (3) used in limited quantities when applied to food crops. The EPA can cancel or suspend registration of substances that are identified as harmful and may also inspect factories where the chemicals are made. Under 1996 amendments to FIFRA, a substance is deemed harmful if human exposure to the substance, including exposure through eating food, results in a risk of one in a million (or higher) of developing cancer.[15]

It is a violation of FIFRA to sell a pesticide or herbicide that is either unregistered or has had its registration canceled or suspended. It is also a violation to sell a pesticide or herbicide with a false or misleading label or to destroy or deface any labeling required under the act. For example, it is an offense to sell a substance that has a chemical strength different from the concentration declared on the label. Penalties for commercial dealers include imprisonment for up to one year and a fine of up to $25,000 (producers can be fined up to $50,000). Farmers and other private users of pesticides or herbicides who violate the act are subject to a $1,000 fine and incarceration for up to thirty days. Note that a state can also regulate the sale and use of federally registered pesticides.

CASE IN POINT The EPA conditionally registered Strongarm, a weed-killing pesticide. Dow Agrosciences, LLC, sold Strongarm to Texas peanut farmers. When the farmers applied it, however, Strongarm damaged their crops and failed to control the growth of weeds. The farmers sued Dow for violations of Texas law, but the lower courts ruled that FIFRA preempted their claims. The farmers appealed to the United States Supreme Court. The Court held that under a specific provision of FIFRA, a state can regulate the sale and use of federally registered pesticides so long as the regulation does not permit anything that FIFRA prohibits.[16]

Toxic Substances

The first comprehensive law covering toxic substances was the Toxic Substances Control Act of 1976.[17] The act was passed to regulate chemicals and chemical compounds that are known to be toxic—such as asbestos and polychlorinated biphenyls, popularly known as PCBs—and to institute investigation of any possible harmful effects from new chemical compounds.

The regulations authorize the EPA to require that manufacturers, processors, and other entities planning to use chemicals first determine their effects on human health and the environment. The EPA can regulate substances that may pose an imminent hazard or an unreasonable risk of injury to health or the environment. The EPA may require special labeling, limit the use of a substance, set production quotas, or prohibit the use of a substance altogether.

SECTION 6
HAZARDOUS WASTES

Some industrial, agricultural, and household wastes pose more serious threats than others. If not properly disposed of, these toxic chemicals may present a substantial danger to human health and the environment. If released into the environment, they may contaminate public drinking water resources.

Resource Conservation and Recovery Act

In 1976, Congress passed the Resource Conservation and Recovery Act (RCRA)[18] in response to growing concern about the effects of hazardous waste materials on the environment. The RCRA required the EPA to establish regulations to determine which forms of solid waste should be considered hazardous and to establish regulations to monitor and control hazardous waste disposal. The act also requires all producers of hazardous waste materials to label and package properly any hazardous waste to be transported. The RCRA was amended in 1984 and 1986 to decrease the use of land containment in the disposal of hazardous waste and to require smaller generators of hazardous waste to comply with the act.

Under the RCRA, a company may be assessed a civil penalty of up to $25,000 for each violation.[19] The penalty is based on the seriousness of the violation, the probability of harm, and the extent to which the violation deviates from RCRA requirements. Criminal penalties include fines of up to $50,000 for each day of violation, imprisonment for up to two years (in most instances), or both.

---

14. 7 U.S.C. Sections 136–136y.

15. 21 U.S.C. Section 346a.

16. *Bates v. Dow Agrosciences, LLC,* 544 U.S. 431, 125 S.Ct. 1788, 161 L.Ed.2d 687 (2005).

17. 15 U.S.C. Sections 2601–2692.

18. 42 U.S.C. Sections 6901–6986.

19. 42 U.S.C. Section 6928(a).

Criminal fines and the time of imprisonment can be doubled for certain repeat offenders.

Superfund

In 1980, Congress passed the Comprehensive Environmental Response, Compensation, and Liability Act (CERCLA),[20] commonly known as Superfund. The basic purpose of Superfund is to regulate the clean-up of disposal sites in which hazardous waste is leaking into the environment.

CERCLA, as amended, has four primary elements:

1. It established an information-gathering and analysis system that enables the government to identify chemical dump sites and determine the appropriate action.
2. It authorized the EPA to respond to hazardous substance emergencies and to arrange for the clean-up of a leaking site directly if the persons responsible for the problem fail to clean up the site.
3. It created a Hazardous Substance Response Trust Fund to pay for the clean-up of hazardous sites using funds obtained through taxes on certain businesses. (The name *Superfund* is sometimes used to refer just to the trust fund, but here we use it in the broader sense to refer to CERCLA as a whole.)
4. It allows the government to recover the cost of clean-up from the persons who were (even remotely) responsible for hazardous substance releases.

POTENTIALLY RESPONSIBLE PARTIES Superfund provides that when a release or a threatened release of hazardous chemicals from a site occurs, the following persons are responsible for cleaning up the site: (1) the person who generated the wastes disposed of at the site, (2) the person who transported the wastes to the site, (3) the person who owned or operated the site at the time of the disposal, or (4) the current owner or operator. A person falling within one of these categories is referred to as a **potentially responsible party (PRP).** If the PRPs do not clean up the site, EPA can clean up the site and recover the clean-up costs from the PRPs.

Superfund imposes strict liability on PRPs and that liability cannot be avoided through transfer of ownership. Thus, selling a site at which hazardous wastes were disposed does not relieve the seller of liability, and the buyer also becomes liable for the clean-up. Liability also extends to those that merge with or buy corporations that have violated CERCLA. Although a parent corporation is not automatically liable for the violations of its subsidiary, it can be held liable if the subsidiary was merely a shell company or if it participated in or controlled the facility.[21]

JOINT AND SEVERAL LIABILITY Liability under Superfund is usually joint and several—that is, a PRP who generated *only a fraction of the hazardous waste* disposed of at the site may nevertheless be liable for *all* of the clean-up costs. CERCLA authorizes a party who has incurred clean-up costs to bring a "contribution action" against any other person who is liable or potentially liable for a percentage of the costs.

MINIMIZING LIABILITY One way for a business to minimize its potential liability under Superfund is to conduct environmental compliance audits of its own operations regularly. A business can perform internal investigations of its own operations and lands to determine whether any environmental hazards exist.

The EPA encourages companies to conduct self-audits and promptly detect, disclose, and correct wrongdoing. Companies that do so are subject to lighter penalties (fines may be reduced as much as 75 percent) for violations of environmental laws. Under EPA guidelines, the EPA will waive all fines if a small company corrects environmental violations within 180 days after being notified of the violations (or 360 days if pollution-prevention techniques are involved). The policy does not apply to criminal violations of environmental laws, though, or to actions that pose a significant threat to public health, safety, or the environment.

DEFENSES There are a few defenses to liability under CERCLA. The most important is the innocent landowner defense.[22] Under this defense, an innocent property owner may be able to avoid liability by showing that he or she had no contractual or employment relationship with the person who released the hazardous substance on the land. Thus, if the property was transferred by contract from the third

---

20. 42 U.S.C. Sections 9601–9675.

21. The landmark case establishing the liability of a parent corporation under CERCLA is *United States v. Bestfoods,* 524 U.S. 51, 118 S.Ct. 1876, 141 L.Ed.2d 43 (1998).

22. 42 U.S.C. Section 9601(35)(B).

party who disposed of the substances to the current owner, the defense normally will not be available. To assert the defense, the landowner must be able to show that at the time the property was acquired, she or he had no reason to know that hazardous substances had been disposed of on it. The landowner must also show that at the time of the purchase, she or he undertook all appropriate investigation into the previous ownership and uses of the property to determine whether there was reason to be concerned about hazardous substances. In effect, this defense protects only property owners who took precautions and investigated the possibility of environmental hazards at the time they bought the property.

REVIEWING
Environmental Law

In the early part of the first decade of the 2000s, residents of Lake Caliopa, Minnesota, began noticing an unusually high number of lung ailments among their population. A group of concerned local citizens pooled their resources and commissioned a study of the frequency of these health conditions per capita in Lake Caliopa as compared with national averages. The study concluded that residents of Lake Caliopa experienced four to seven times the rate in the frequency of asthma, bronchitis, and emphysema as the population nationwide. During the study period, citizens began expressing concerns about the large volumes of smog emitted by the Cotton Design apparel manufacturing plant on the outskirts of town. The plant had opened its production facility two miles east of town beside the Tawakoni River in 1999 and employed seventy full-time workers by 2010.

Just downstream on the Tawakoni River, the city of Lake Caliopa operated a public water works facility, which supplied all city residents with water. In August 2010, the Minnesota Pollution Control Agency required Cotton Design to install new equipment to control air and water pollution. In May 2011, citizens brought a lawsuit in a Minnesota state court against Cotton Design for various respiratory ailments allegedly caused or compounded by smog from Cotton Design's factory. Using the information presented in the chapter, answer the following questions.

1. Under the common law, what would each plaintiff be required to identify in order to be given relief by the court?
2. Are air-quality regulations typically overseen by federal, state, or local governments?
3. What standard for limiting emissions into the air does Cotton Design's pollution-control equipment have to meet?
4. What information must the city send to every household that it supplies with water?

DEBATE THIS: *The courts should reject all cases in which the wetlands in question do not consist of actual bodies of water that exist during the entire year.*

TERMS AND CONCEPTS

environmental law 897
nuisance 897

potentially responsible
party (PRP) 908

toxic tort 898
wetlands 904

environmental impact
statement (EIS) 898

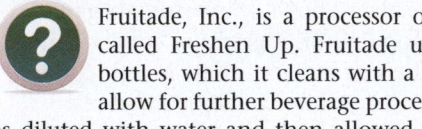

QUESTIONS AND CASE PROBLEMS

46–1. Clean Air Act Current scientific knowledge indicates that there is no safe level of exposure to a cancer-causing agent. In theory, even one molecule of such a substance has the potential for causing cancer. Section 112 of the Clean Air Act requires that all cancer-causing substances be regulated to ensure a margin of safety. Some environmental groups have argued that all emissions of such substances must be eliminated if a margin of safety is to be reached. Such a total elimination would likely shut down many major U.S. industries. Should the Environmental Protection Agency totally eliminate all emissions of cancer-causing chemicals? Discuss.

46–2. QUESTION WITH SAMPLE ANSWER: Environmental Laws.

Fruitade, Inc., is a processor of a soft drink called Freshen Up. Fruitade uses returnable bottles, which it cleans with a special acid to allow for further beverage processing. The acid is diluted with water and then allowed to pass into a navigable stream. Fruitade crushes its broken bottles and throws the crushed glass into the stream. Discuss fully any environmental laws that Fruitade has violated.

- **For a sample answer to Question 46–2, go to Appendix I at the end of this text.**

46–3. Environmental Laws Moonbay is a home-building corporation that primarily develops retirement communities. Farmtex owns a number of feedlots in Sunny Valley. Moonbay purchased 20,000 acres of farmland in the same area and began building and selling homes on this acreage. In the meantime, Farmtex continued to expand its feedlot business, and eventually only 500 feet separated the two operations. Because of the odor and flies from the feedlots, Moonbay found it difficult to sell the homes in its development. Moonbay wants to enjoin (prevent) Farmtex from operating its feedlot in the vicinity of the retirement home development. Under what common law theory would Moonbay file this action? Has Farmtex violated any federal environmental laws? Discuss.

46–4. Environmental Impact Statement Greers Ferry Lake is in Arkansas, and its shoreline is under the management of the U.S. Army Corps of Engineers, which is part of the U.S. Department of Defense (DOD). The Corps's 2000 Shoreline Management Plan (SMP) rezoned numerous areas along the lake, authorized the Corps to issue permits for the construction of new boat docks in the rezoned areas, increased by 300 percent the area around habitable structures that could be cleared of vegetation, and instituted a Wildlife Enhancement Permit to allow limited modifications of the shoreline. In relation to the SMP's adoption, the Corps issued a Finding of No Significant Impact, which declared that no environmental impact statement (EIS) was necessary. The Corps issued thirty-two boat dock construction permits under the SMP before Save Greers Ferry Lake, Inc., filed a suit in a federal district court against the DOD, asking the court to, among other things, stop the Corps from acting under the SMP and order it to prepare an EIS. What are the requirements for an EIS? Is an EIS needed in this case? Explain. [*Save Greers Ferry Lake, Inc. v. Department of Defense*, 255 F.3d 498 (8th Cir. 2001)]

46–5. CERCLA Beginning in 1926, Marietta Dyestuffs Co. operated an industrial facility in Marietta, Ohio, to make dyes and other chemicals. In 1944, Dyestuffs became part of American Home Products Corp. (AHP), which sold the Marietta facility to American Cyanamid Co. in 1946. In 1950, AHP sold the rest of the Dyestuffs assets and all of its stock to Goodrich Co., which immediately liquidated the acquired corporation. Goodrich continued to operate the dissolved corporation's business, however. Cyanamid continued to make chemicals at the Marietta facility, and in 1993, it created Cytec Industries, Inc., which expressly assumed all environmental liabilities associated with Cyanamid's ownership and operation of the facility. Cytec spent nearly $25 million on clean-up costs and filed a suit in a federal district court against Goodrich to recover, under CERCLA, a portion of the costs attributable to the clean-up of hazardous wastes that may have been discarded at the site between 1926 and 1946. Cytec filed a motion for summary judgment in its favor. Should the court grant Cytec's motion? Explain. [*Cytec Industries, Inc. v. B. F. Goodrich Co.*, 196 F.Supp.2d 644 (S.D. Ohio 2002)]

46–6. CASE PROBLEM WITH SAMPLE ANSWER: Superfund.

William Gurley was the president and majority stockholder in Gurley Refining Co. (GRC). GRC bought used oil, treated it, and sold it. The refining process created a by-product residue of oily waste. GRC disposed of this waste by dumping it at, among other locations, a landfill in West Memphis, Arkansas. In February 1992, after detecting hazardous chemicals at the site, the Environmental Protection Agency (EPA) asked Gurley about his assets, the generators of the material disposed of at the landfill, site operations, and the structure of GRC. Gurley refused to respond, except to suggest that the EPA ask GRC. In October, the EPA placed the site on its clean-up list and again asked Gurley for information. When he still refused to respond, the EPA filed a suit in a federal district court against him, asking the court to impose a civil penalty. In February 1999, Gurley finally answered the EPA's questions. Under CERCLA, a court may impose a civil penalty "not to exceed $25,000 for each day of noncompliance against any person who unreasonably fails to comply" with an information request. Should the court assess a penalty in this case? Why or why not? [United States v. Gurley, 384 F.3d 316 (6th Cir. 2004)]

- **To view a sample answer for Problem 46–6, go to this book's Web site at www.cengage.com/blaw/clarkson, select "Chapter 46," and click on "Case Problem with Sample Answer."**

46–7. Clean Water Act The Anacostia River, which flows through Washington, D.C., is one of the ten most polluted rivers in the country. For bodies of water such as the Anacostia, the Clean Water Act requires states (which, under the act, include the District of Columbia) to set a "total maximum daily load" (TMDL) for pollutants. A TMDL is to be set "at a level necessary to implement the applicable water-quality standards with seasonal variations." The Anacostia contains biochemical pollutants that consume oxygen, putting the river's aquatic life at risk for suffocation. In addition, the river is murky, stunting the growth of plants that rely on sunlight and impairing recreational use. The Environmental Protection Agency (EPA) approved one TMDL limiting the *annual* discharge of oxygen-depleting pollutants and a second limiting the *seasonal* discharge of pollutants contributing to turbidity. Neither TMDL limited daily discharges. Friends of the Earth, Inc. (FoE), asked a federal district court to review the TMDLs. What is FoE's best argument in this dispute? What is the EPA's likely response? What should the court rule, and why? [*Friends of the Earth, Inc. v. Environmental Protection Agency*, 446 F.3d 140 (D.C.Cir. 2006)]

46–8. Environmental Impact Statement The fourth largest crop in the United States is alfalfa, of which 5 percent is exported to Japan. RoundUp Ready alfalfa is genetically engineered to resist glyphosate, the active ingredient in the herbicide RoundUp. The U.S. Department of Agriculture (USDA) regulates genetically engineered agricultural products through the Animal and Plant Health Inspection Service (APHIS). APHIS concluded that RoundUp Ready alfalfa does not have any harmful health effects on humans or livestock and deregulated it. Geertson Seed Farms and others filed a suit in a federal district court against Mike Johanns (then the secretary of the USDA) and others, asserting that APHIS's decision required the preparation of an environmental impact statement (EIS). The plaintiffs argued, among other things, that the introduction of RoundUp Ready alfalfa might significantly decrease the availability of or even eliminate, all nongenetically engineered varieties. The plaintiffs were concerned that the RoundUp Ready alfalfa might contaminate standard alfalfa because alfalfa is pollinated by bees, which can travel as far as two miles from a pollen source. If contamination occurred, farmers would not be able to market "contaminated" varieties as "organic," which would affect the sales of "organic" livestock and exports to Japan, which does not allow the import of glyphosate-resistant alfalfa. Should an EIS be prepared in this case? Why or why not? [*Geertson Seed Farms v. Johanns,* __ F.Supp.2d __ (N.D.Cal. 2007)]

46–9. Environmental Impact Statement The U.S. National Park Service (NPS) manages the Grand Canyon National Park in Arizona under a management plan that is subject to periodic review. In 2006, after nine years of background work and the completion of a comprehensive environmental impact statement, the NPS issued a new management plan for the park. The plan allowed for the continued use of rafts on the Colorado River, which runs through the Grand Canyon. The number of rafts was limited, however. Several environmental groups criticized the plan because they felt that it still allowed too many rafts on the river. The groups asked a federal appellate court to overturn the plan, claiming that it violated the wilderness status of the national park. When can a federal court overturn a determination by an agency such as the NPS? Explain. [*River Runners for Wilderness v. Martin,* 593 F.3d 1064 (9th Cir. 2010)]

46–10. A QUESTION OF ETHICS: Clean Air Act.

 In the Clean Air Act, Congress allowed California, which has particular problems with clean air, to adopt its own standard for emissions from cars and trucks, subject to the approval of the Environmental Protection Agency (EPA) according to certain criteria. Congress also allowed other states to adopt California's standard after the EPA's approval. In 2004, in an effort to address global warming, the California Air Resources Board amended the state's standard to attain "the maximum feasible and cost-effective reduction of GHG [greenhouse gas] emissions from motor vehicles." The regulation, which applies to new passenger vehicles and light-duty trucks for 2009 and later, imposes decreasing limits on emissions of carbon dioxide through 2016. While EPA approval was pending, Vermont and other states adopted similar standards. Green Mountain Chrysler Plymouth Dodge Jeep and other auto dealers, automakers, and associations of automakers filed a suit in a federal district court against George Crombie (then the secretary of the Vermont Agency of Natural Resources) and others, seeking relief from the state regulations. [Green Mountain Chrysler Plymouth Dodge Jeep v. Crombie, 508 F.Supp.2d 295 (D.Vt. 2007)]

(a) Under the Environmental Policy and Conservation Act (EPCA) of 1975, the National Highway Traffic Safety Administration sets fuel economy standards for new cars. The plaintiffs argued, among other things, that the EPCA, which prohibits states from adopting separate fuel economy standards, preempts Vermont's GHG regulation. Do the GHG rules equate to the fuel economy standards? Discuss.

(b) Do Vermont's rules tread on the efforts of the federal government to address global warming internationally? Who should regulate GHG emissions? The federal government? The state governments? Both? Neither? Why?

(c) The plaintiffs claimed that they would go bankrupt if they were forced to adhere to the state's GHG standards. Should they be granted relief on this basis? Does history support their claim? Explain.

LEGAL RESEARCH EXERCISES ON THE WEB

Go to this text's Web site at **www.cengage.com/blaw/clarkson**, select "Chapter 46," and click on "Practical Internet Exercises." There you will find the following Internet research exercises that you can perform to learn more about the topics covered in this chapter.

Practical Internet Exercise 46–1: Legal Perspective
Nuisance Law

Practical Internet Exercise 46–2: Management Perspective
Complying with Environmental Regulation

Practical Internet Exercise 46–3: Ethical Perspective
Environmental Justice

CHAPTER 47

✳

Antitrust Law

Today's antitrust laws are the direct descendants of common law actions intended to limit restraints of trade (agreements between firms that have the effect of reducing competition in the marketplace). Concern over monopolistic practices arose following the Civil War with the growth of large corporate enterprises that attempted to reduce or eliminate competition. They did this by legally tying themselves together in *business trusts*, a type of business entity described on page 749 in Chapter 38. The participants in the most famous trust—the Standard Oil trust of the late 1800s—transferred their stock to a trustee and received trust certificates in exchange. The trustee then made decisions fixing prices, controlling production, and determining the control of exclusive geographic markets for all

of the oil companies that were members of the trust. Some argued that the trust wielded so much economic power that corporations outside the trust could not compete effectively.

Many states attempted to control such monopolistic behavior by enacting statutes outlawing the use of trusts. That is why all of the laws that regulate economic competition in the United States today are referred to as **antitrust laws**. At the national level, Congress recognized the problem in 1887 and passed the Interstate Commerce Act,[1] followed by the Sherman Antitrust Act[2] in 1890. In 1914, Congress passed the Clayton Act[3] and the Federal Trade Commission Act[4] to further curb

---

1. 49 U.S.C. Sections 501–526.
2. 15 U.S.C. Sections 1–7.
3. 15 U.S.C. Sections 12–27.
4. 15 U.S.C. Sections 41–58a.

anticompetitive or unfair business practices. Congress subsequently amended the 1914 acts to broaden and strengthen their coverage, and they continue to be an important element in the legal environment in which businesses operate.

This chapter examines these major antitrust statutes, focusing particularly on the Sherman Act and the Clayton Act, as amended, and the types of activities they prohibit. Remember in reading this chapter that the basis of antitrust legislation is the desire to foster competition. The law prohibits anticompetitive practices because of our belief that competition leads to lower prices, generates more product information, and results in a more equitable distribution of wealth between consumers and producers.

▶ SECTION 1 ◀

THE SHERMAN ANTITRUST ACT

The author of the Sherman Antitrust Act of 1890, Senator John Sherman, was the brother of the famed Civil War general and a recognized financial authority. He had been concerned for years about what he saw as diminishing competition within U.S. industry

and the emergence of monopolies. He told Congress that the Sherman Act "does not announce a new principle of law, but applies old and well-recognized principles of the common law."[5]

The common law regarding trade regulation was not always consistent. Certainly, it was not very familiar to the members of Congress. The public

---

5. 21 *Congressional Record* 2456 (1890).

concern over large business integrations and trusts was familiar, however, and in 1890 Congress passed "An Act to Protect Trade and Commerce against Unlawful Restraints and Monopolies"—more commonly referred to as the Sherman Antitrust Act, or simply the Sherman Act.

Major Provisions of the Sherman Act

Sections 1 and 2 contain the main provisions of the Sherman Act:

1. Every contract, combination in the form of trust or otherwise, or conspiracy, in restraint of trade or commerce among the several States, or with foreign nations, is hereby declared to be illegal [and is a felony punishable by fine and/or imprisonment].
2. Every person who shall monopolize, or attempt to monopolize, or combine or conspire with any other person or persons, to monopolize any part of the trade or commerce among the several States, or with foreign nations, shall be deemed guilty of a felony [and is similarly punishable].

Differences between Section 1 and Section 2

These two sections of the Sherman Act are quite different. Section 1 requires two or more persons, as a person cannot contract, combine, or conspire alone. Thus, the essence of the illegal activity is *the act of joining together.* Section 2, though, can apply either to one person or to two or more persons because it refers to "every person." Thus, unilateral conduct can result in a violation of Section 2.

The cases brought to the courts under Section 1 of the Sherman Act differ from those brought under Section 2. Section 1 cases are often concerned with finding an agreement (written or oral) that leads to a restraint of trade. Section 2 cases deal with the structure of a monopoly that exists in the marketplace. The term **monopoly** generally is used to describe a market in which there is a single seller or a very limited number of sellers. Whereas Section 1 focuses on agreements that are restrictive—that is, agreements that have a wrongful purpose—Section 2 looks at the so-called misuse of **monopoly power** in the marketplace.

Monopoly power exists when a firm has an extreme amount of **market power**—the ability to affect the market price of its product. Both Section 1 and Section 2 seek to curtail market practices that result in undesired monopoly pricing and output

behavior. For a case to be brought under Section 2, however, the "threshold" or "necessary" amount of monopoly power must already exist.

Jurisdictional Requirements

The Sherman Act applies only to restraints that have a significant impact on interstate commerce. Courts have generally held that any activity that substantially affects interstate commerce falls within the scope of the Sherman Act. As will be discussed later in this chapter, the Sherman Act also extends to U.S. nationals abroad that are engaged in activities that affect U.S. foreign commerce. State laws regulate local restraints on competition.

──────── SECTION 2 ────────

SECTION 1 OF THE SHERMAN ACT

The underlying assumption of Section 1 of the Sherman Act is that society's welfare is harmed if rival firms are permitted to join in an agreement that consolidates their market power or otherwise restrains competition. The types of trade restraints that Section 1 of the Sherman Act prohibits generally fall into two broad categories: *horizontal restraints* and *vertical restraints,* both of which will be discussed shortly. First, though, we look at the rules that the courts may apply when assessing the anticompetitive impact of alleged restraints of trade.

Per Se Violations versus the Rule of Reason

Some restraints are so substantially anticompetitive that they are deemed ***per se* violations**—illegal *per se* (inherently)—under Section 1. Other agreements, however, even though they result in enhanced market power, do not *unreasonably* restrain trade and are therefore lawful. Using what is called the **rule of reason,** the courts analyze anticompetitive agreements that allegedly violate Section 1 of the Sherman Act to determine whether they may, in fact, constitute reasonable restraints of trade. The need for a rule-of-reason analysis of some agreements in restraint of trade is obvious—if the rule of reason had not been developed, almost any business agreement could conceivably be held to violate the Sherman Act.

When analyzing an alleged Section 1 violation under the rule of reason, a court will consider several factors. These factors include the purpose of the agreement, the parties' power to implement the agreement to achieve that purpose, and the effect or potential effect of the agreement on competition. A court might also consider whether the parties could have relied on less restrictive means to achieve their purpose.

In the following case, the United States Supreme Court had to decide if a Section 1 violation had occurred. In addition, the Court had to determine whether the violation should have been considered a *per se* violation or whether it should have been analyzed under the rule of reason.

CASE 47.1
American Needle, Inc. v. National Football League

Supreme Court of the United States, ___ U.S. ___, 130 S.Ct. 2201, ___ L.Ed.2d ___ (2010).
www.supremecourt.gov[a]

BACKGROUND AND FACTS • The National Football League (NFL) includes thirty-two separately owned professional football teams. Each team has its own name, colors, and logo, and owns related intellectual property. In 1963, the teams formed National Football League Properties (NFLP) to develop, license, and market their trademarked items, such as caps and jerseys. Until 2000, the NFLP granted nonexclusive licenses to a number of vendors, permitting them to manufacture and sell apparel bearing team insignias. American Needle, Inc., was one of those licensees. In late 2000, the teams authorized the NFLP to grant exclusive licenses, and the NFLP granted Reebok International, Ltd., an exclusive ten-year license to manufacture and sell trademarked headwear for all thirty-two teams. It thereafter declined to renew American Needle's nonexclusive license. American Needle brought an action in a federal district court alleging that the agreements involving the NFL, its teams, the NFLP, and Reebok violated Sections 1 and 2 of the Sherman Act. In response, the defendants argued that they were incapable of conspiring within the meaning of Section 1 "because they are a single economic enterprise" as far as the marketing of trademarked goods was concerned. The district court granted summary judgment in favor of the defendants. American Needle appealed, and the U.S. Court of Appeals for the Seventh Circuit affirmed the trial court's decision. American Needle appealed to the United States Supreme Court.

IN THE LANGUAGE OF THE COURT
Justice *STEVENS* delivered the opinion of the Court.
* * * *

As the case comes to us, we have only a narrow issue to decide: whether the NFL respondents are capable of engaging in a "contract, combination * * * or conspiracy," as defined by Section 1 of the Sherman Act, or * * * whether the alleged activity by the NFL respondents "must be viewed as that of a single enterprise for purposes of Section 1."
* * * *

* * * The question is whether the agreement [among the teams with respect to the marketing of their intellectual property] joins together "independent centers of decision-making." If it does, the entities are capable of conspiring under Section 1, and the Court must decide whether the restraint of trade is an unreasonable and therefore illegal one.

* * * Each of the [NFL] teams is a substantial, independently owned, and independently managed business. "Their general corporate actions are guided or determined" by "separate corporate consciousnesses," and "their objectives are" not "common." The teams compete with one another, not only on the playing field, but to attract fans, for gate receipts and for contracts with managerial and playing personnel.

---

a. Select "Opinions" in the left-hand column, and when the sub-menu drops down, select "Latest Slip Opinions." In the results, scroll down the list of cases to "5/24/10" and click on the highlighted case title to access the opinion. The United States Supreme Court maintains this Web site.

CASE CONTINUES ➡

CASE 47.1 CONTINUED ▶

Directly relevant to this case, the teams compete in the market for intellectual property. To a firm making hats, the Saints and the Colts are two potentially competing suppliers of valuable trademarks. When each NFL team licenses its intellectual property, it is not pursuing the "common interests of the whole" league but is instead pursuing interests of each "corporation itself"; teams are acting as "separate economic actors pursuing separate economic interests," and each team therefore is a potential "independent center of decision-making." Decisions by NFL teams to license their separately owned trademarks collectively and to only one vendor are decisions that "depriv[e] the marketplace of independent centers of decision-making," and therefore of actual or potential competition.

* * * *

Respondents argue that * * * they constitute a single entity because without their cooperation, there would be no NFL football. * * * But the Court of Appeals' reasoning is unpersuasive.

The justification for cooperation is not relevant to whether that cooperation is concerted or independent action. *A "contract, combination * * * or conspiracy" that is necessary or useful to a joint venture is still a "contract, combination * * * or conspiracy" if it "deprives the marketplace of independent centers of decision-making."* Any joint venture involves multiple sources of economic power cooperating to produce a product. And for many such ventures, the participation of others is necessary. But that does not mean that necessity of cooperation transforms concerted action into independent action; a nut and a bolt can only operate together, but an agreement between nut and bolt manufacturers is still subject to Section 1 analysis. [Emphasis added.]

* * * *

Football teams that need to cooperate are not trapped by antitrust law. * * * The fact that NFL teams share an interest in making the entire league successful and profitable, and that they must cooperate in the production and scheduling of games, provides a perfectly sensible justification for making a host of collective decisions. But the conduct at issue in this case is still concerted activity under the Sherman Act that is subject to Section 1 analysis.

When "restraints on competition are essential if the product is to be available at all," *per se* rules of illegality are inapplicable, and instead the restraint must be judged according to the flexible Rule of Reason. In such instances, the agreement is likely to survive the Rule of Reason. And depending upon the concerted activity in question, the Rule of Reason may not require a detailed analysis; it "can sometimes be applied in the twinkling of an eye."

* * * *

Accordingly, the judgment of the Court of Appeals is reversed, and the case is remanded for further proceedings consistent with this opinion.

DECISION AND REMEDY • *The United States Supreme Court reversed the judgment of the court of appeals and remanded the case for further proceedings consistent with this opinion. The agreement among the NFL teams to license their intellectual property exclusively through the NFLP to Reebok constituted concerted activity subject to Section 1 analysis.*

THE LEGAL ENVIRONMENT DIMENSION • *What did the Court mean when it stated that "the agreement is likely to survive the Rule of Reason"?*

THE ECONOMIC DIMENSION • *Does the Court's ruling mean that the NFL teams' activities with respect to the marketing of their intellectual property through the NFLP were illegal? Explain.*

Horizontal Restraints

The term **horizontal restraint** is encountered frequently in antitrust law. A horizontal restraint is any agreement that in some way restrains competition between rival firms competing in the same market.

PRICE FIXING Any agreement among competitors to fix prices, or **price-fixing agreement,** constitutes a *per se* violation of Section 1 of the Sherman Act.

Perhaps the definitive case regarding price-fixing agreements is still the 1940 case of *United States v. Socony-Vacuum Oil Co.*[6] In that case, a group of independent oil producers in Texas and Louisiana were caught between falling demand due to the Great Depression of the 1930s and increasing supply from newly discovered oil fields in the region. In response

---

6. 310 U.S. 150, 60 S.Ct. 811, 84 L.Ed. 1129 (1940).

to these conditions, a group of the major refining companies agreed to buy "distress" gasoline (excess supplies) from the independents so as to dispose of it in an "orderly manner." Although there was no explicit agreement as to price, it was clear that the purpose of the agreement was to limit the supply of gasoline on the market and thereby raise prices.

There may have been good reasons for the agreement. Nonetheless, the United States Supreme Court recognized the potentially adverse effects that such an agreement could have on open and free competition. The Court held that the reasonableness of a price-fixing agreement is never a defense. Any agreement that restricts output or artificially fixes price is a *per se* violation of Section 1.

CASE IN POINT The manufacturer of the prescription drug Cardizem CD, which can help prevent heart attacks, was about to lose its patent on the drug. Another company had developed a generic version in anticipation of the patent's expiration. After the two firms became involved in litigation over the patent, the first company agreed to pay the second company $40 million per year not to market the generic version until their dispute was resolved. This agreement was held to be a *per se* violation of the Sherman Act because it restrained competition between rival firms and delayed the entry of generic versions of Cardizem into the market.[7]

GROUP BOYCOTTS A **group boycott** is an agreement by two or more sellers to refuse to deal with (boycott) a particular person or firm. Traditionally, the courts have considered group boycotts to constitute *per se* violations of Section 1 of the Sherman Act because they involve concerted action. To prove a violation of Section 1, the plaintiff must demonstrate that the boycott or joint refusal to deal was undertaken with the intention of eliminating competition or preventing entry into a given market. Although most boycotts are illegal, a few, such as group boycotts against a supplier for political reasons, may be protected under the First Amendment right to freedom of expression.

HORIZONTAL MARKET DIVISION It is a *per se* violation of Section 1 of the Sherman Act for competitors to divide up territories or customers. For example, manufacturers A, B, and C compete against one another in the states of Kansas, Nebraska, and Oklahoma. They agree that A will sell products only in Kansas, B only in Nebraska, and C only in Oklahoma. This concerted action reduces costs and allows each of the three (assuming there is no other competition) to raise the price of the goods sold in its own state. The same violation would take place if A, B, and C agreed that A would sell only to institutional purchasers (such as school districts, universities, state agencies and departments, and cities) in the three states, B only to wholesalers, and C only to retailers.

TRADE ASSOCIATIONS Businesses in the same general industry or profession frequently organize trade associations to pursue common interests. A trade association may engage in various joint activities, such as exchanging information, representing the members' business interests before governmental bodies, conducting advertising campaigns, and setting regulatory standards to govern the industry or profession. Generally, the rule of reason is applied to many of these horizontal actions. If a court finds that a trade association practice or agreement that restrains trade is nonetheless sufficiently beneficial both to the association and to the public, it may deem the restraint reasonable.

In *concentrated industries,* however, trade associations can be, and have been, used as a means to facilitate anticompetitive actions, such as fixing prices or allocating markets. A **concentrated industry** is one in which either a single firm or a small number of firms control a large percentage of market sales. When trade association agreements have substantially anticompetitive effects, a court will consider them to be in violation of Section 1 of the Sherman Act.

JOINT VENTURES Joint ventures undertaken by competitors are also subject to antitrust laws. As discussed in Chapter 38, a *joint venture* is an undertaking by two or more individuals or firms for a specific purpose. If a joint venture does not involve price fixing or market divisions, the agreement will be analyzed under the rule of reason. Whether the venture will then be upheld under Section 1 depends on an overall assessment of the purposes of the venture, a strict analysis of the potential benefits relative to the likely harms, and, in some cases, an assessment of whether there are less restrictive alternatives for achieving the same goals.[8]

---

7. *In re Cardizem CD Antitrust Litigation,* 332 F.3d 896 (6th Cir. 2003).

8. For a classic example of how courts judge joint ventures under the rule of reason, see *United States v. Morgan,* 118 F.Supp. 621 (S.D.N.Y. 1953).

Vertical Restraints

A **vertical restraint** of trade results from an agreement between firms at different levels in the manufacturing and distribution process. In contrast to horizontal relationships, which occur at the same level of operation, vertical relationships encompass the entire chain of production. The chain of production normally includes the purchase of inputs, basic manufacturing, distribution to wholesalers, and eventual sale of a product at the retail level. For some products, these distinct phases are carried on by different firms. In other instances, a single firm carries out two or more of the separate functional phases. Such enterprises are said to be **vertically integrated firms.**

Even though firms operating at different functional levels are not in direct competition with one another, they are in competition with other firms. Thus, agreements between firms standing in a vertical relationship may affect competition. Some vertical restraints are *per se* violations of Section 1. Others are judged under the rule of reason.

TERRITORIAL OR CUSTOMER RESTRICTIONS In arranging for the distribution of its products, a manufacturing firm often wishes to insulate dealers from direct competition with other dealers selling its products. To this end, the manufacturer may institute territorial restrictions or attempt to prohibit wholesalers or retailers from reselling the products to certain classes of buyers, such as competing retailers.

A firm may have legitimate reasons for imposing such territorial or customer restrictions. For example, a computer manufacturer may wish to prevent a dealer from reducing costs and undercutting rivals by offering computers without promotion or customer service, while relying on a nearby dealer to provide these services. In this situation, the cost-cutting dealer reaps the benefits (sales of the product) paid for by other dealers who undertake promotion and arrange for customer service. By not providing customer service, the cost-cutting dealer may also harm the manufacturer's reputation.

Territorial and customer restrictions were once considered *per se* violations of Section 1 of the Sherman Act.[9] In 1977, however, the United States Supreme Court reconsidered the treatment accorded to such vertical restrictions and held that they should be judged under the rule of reason.

CASE IN POINT GTE Sylvania, Inc., a manufacturer of television sets, limited the number of retail franchises that it granted in any given geographic area. It also required each franchisee to sell only Sylvania products from the location at which it was franchised. Sylvania retained sole discretion to increase the number of retailers in an area. When Sylvania decided to open a new franchise, it terminated the franchise of Continental T.V., Inc., an existing franchisee in that area that would have been in competition with the new franchise. Continental filed a lawsuit claiming that Sylvania's vertically restrictive franchise system violated Section 1 of the Sherman Act. The United States Supreme Court found that "vertical restrictions promote interbrand competition by allowing the manufacturer to achieve certain efficiencies in the distribution of his products." Therefore, Sylvania's vertical system, which was not price restrictive, did not constitute a *per se* violation of Section 1 of the Sherman Act.[10]

The *Continental* case above marked a definite shift from rigid characterization of territorial and customer restrictions to a more flexible, economic analysis of these vertical restraints under the rule of reason. This rule is still applied in most vertical restraint cases.

RESALE PRICE MAINTENANCE AGREEMENTS An agreement between a manufacturer and a distributor or retailer in which the manufacturer specifies what the retail prices of its products must be is known as a **resale price maintenance agreement.** Such agreements were once considered to be *per se* violations of Section 1 of the Sherman Act, but in 1997 the United States Supreme Court ruled that *maximum* resale price maintenance agreements should be judged under the rule of reason.[11] The setting of a maximum price that retailers and distributors can charge for a manufacturer's products may sometimes increase competition and benefit consumers.

The question before the United States Supreme Court in the following case was whether *minimum* resale price maintenance agreements should be treated as *per se* violations.

---

9. See *United States v. Arnold, Schwinn & Co.,* 388 U.S. 365, 87 S.Ct. 1856, 18 L.Ed.2d 1249 (1967).

10. *Continental T.V., Inc. v. GTE Sylvania, Inc.,* 433 U.S. 36, 97 S.Ct. 2549, 53 L.Ed.2d 568 (1977).

11. *State Oil Co. v. Khan,* 522 U.S. 3, 118 S.Ct. 275, 139 L.Ed.2d 199 (1997).

✳ EXTENDED CASE 47.2 ✳
Leegin Creative Leather Products, Inc. v. PSKS, Inc.

Supreme Court of the United States, 551 U.S. 877, 127 S.Ct. 2705, 168 L.Ed.2d 623 (2007).
www.law.cornell.edu/supct/index.htmla

IN THE LANGUAGE OF THE COURT

Justice *KENNEDY* delivered the opinion of the Court.

* * * *

Petitioner, Leegin Creative Leather Products, Inc. (Leegin), designs, manufactures, and distributes leather goods and accessories. In 1991, Leegin began to sell [products] under the brand name "Brighton."

Respondent, PSKS, Inc. (PSKS), operates Kay's Kloset, a women's apparel store in Lewisville, Texas. * * * It first started purchasing Brighton goods from Leegin in 1995.

* * * *

In December 2002, Leegin discovered Kay's Kloset had been marking down Brighton's entire line by 20 percent. * * * Leegin stopped selling [Brighton products] to the store.

PSKS sued Leegin in the United States District Court for the Eastern District of Texas. It alleged, among other claims, that Leegin had violated the antitrust laws by "enter[ing] into agreements with retailers to charge only those prices fixed by Leegin." * * * [The court] entered judgment against Leegin in the amount of $3,975,000.80.

The [U.S.] Court of Appeals for the Fifth Circuit affirmed. * * * We granted *certiorari* * * *.

* * * *

The rule of reason is the accepted standard for testing whether a practice restrains trade in violation of [Section] 1 [of the Sherman Act].

* * * *

Resort to per se *rules is confined to restraints* * * * *that would always or almost always tend to restrict competition and decrease output. To justify a per se prohibition a restraint must have manifestly anticompetitive effects, and lack* * * * *any redeeming virtue.* [Emphasis added.]

As a consequence, the *per se* rule is appropriate only after courts have had considerable experience with the type of restraint at issue, and only if courts can predict with confidence that it would be invalidated in all or almost all instances under the rule of reason.

* * * *

The reasoning of the Court's more recent jurisprudence has rejected the rationales on which [the application of the *per se* rule to minimum resale price maintenance agreements] was based. * * * [These rationales were] based on formalistic legal doctrine rather than demonstrable economic effect.

* * *

* * * Furthermore [the Court] treated vertical agreements a manufacturer makes with its distributors as analogous to a horizontal combination among competing distributors. * * * Our recent cases formulate antitrust principles in accordance with the appreciated differences in economic effect between vertical and horizontal agreements * * *.

* * * *

The justifications for vertical price restraints are similar to those for other vertical restraints. *Minimum resale price maintenance can stimulate interbrand competition* * * * *by reducing intrabrand competition* * * *. The promotion of interbrand competition is important because the primary purpose of the antitrust laws is to protect this type of competition. * * * *Resale price maintenance also has the potential to give consumers more options so that they can choose among low-price, low-service brands; high-price, high-service brands; and brands that fall in between.* [Emphasis added.]

* * * *

While vertical agreements setting minimum resale prices can have procompetitive justifications, they may have anticompetitive effects in other cases; and unlawful price fixing, designed solely to obtain monopoly profits, is an ever present temptation.

* * * *

Notwithstanding the risks of unlawful conduct, it cannot be stated with any degree of confidence that resale price maintenance always or almost always tends to restrict competition and decrease output. Vertical agreements establishing minimum resale prices can have either procompetitive or anticompetitive effects, depending upon the circumstances in which they are formed. * * * As the [*per se*] rule would proscribe a significant amount of procompetitive conduct, these agreements appear ill suited for *per se* condemnation.

* * * *

The judgment of the Court of Appeals is reversed, and the case is remanded for proceedings consistent with this opinion.

---

a. In the "Archive of Decisions" section, in the "By party" subsection, click on "1990–present." In the result, in the "2006–2007" row, click on "1st party." On the next page, scroll to the name of the case and click on it. On the next page, click on the appropriate link to access the opinion.

EXTENDED CASE CONTINUES ➡

EXTENDED CASE 47.2 CONTINUED ➡

 QUESTIONS

1. Should the Court have applied the doctrine of *stare decisis* to hold that minimum resale price maintenance agreements are still subject to the *per se* rule? Why or why not?

2. What factors might the courts consider in applying the rule of reason to minimum resale price maintenance agreements?

SECTION 3
SECTION 2 OF THE SHERMAN ACT

Section 1 of the Sherman Act proscribes certain concerted, or joint, activities that restrain trade. In contrast, Section 2 condemns "every person who shall monopolize, or attempt to monopolize." Thus, two distinct types of behavior are subject to sanction under Section 2: *monopolization* and *attempts to monopolize*. A tactic that may be involved in either offense is predatory pricing. **Predatory pricing** occurs when one firm (the predator) attempts to drive its competitors from the market by selling its product at prices substantially *below* the normal costs of production. Once the competitors are eliminated, the predator presumably will raise its prices far above their competitive levels to recapture its losses and earn higher profits.

Monopolization

The United States Supreme Court has defined **monopolization** as involving the following two elements: "(1) the possession of monopoly power in the relevant market and (2) the willful acquisition or maintenance of the power as distinguished from growth or development as a consequence of a superior product, business acumen, or historic accident."[12] To establish a violation of Section 2, a plaintiff must prove both of these elements—monopoly power and an *intent* to monopolize.

MONOPOLY POWER The Sherman Act does not define *monopoly*. In economic theory, monopoly refers to control of a specific market by a single entity. It is well established in antitrust law, however, that a firm may be a monopolist even though it is not the sole

seller in a market. Additionally, size alone does not determine whether a firm is a monopoly. For example, a "mom and pop" grocery located in an isolated desert town is a monopolist if it is the only grocery serving that particular market. Size in relation to the market is what matters because monopoly involves the power to affect prices and output.

Monopoly power may be proved by direct evidence that the firm used its power to control prices and restrict output.[13] Usually, however, there is not enough evidence to show that the firm intentionally controlled prices, so the plaintiff has to offer indirect, or circumstantial, evidence of monopoly power. To prove monopoly power indirectly, the plaintiff must show that the firm has a dominant share of the relevant market and that there are significant barriers for new competitors entering that market.

RELEVANT MARKET Before a court can determine whether a firm has a dominant market share, it must define the relevant market. The relevant market consists of two elements: (1) a relevant product market and (2) a relevant geographic market.

Relevant Product Market. The relevant product market includes all products that, although produced by different firms, have identical attributes, such as sugar. It also includes products that are reasonably interchangeable for the purpose for which they are produced. Products will be considered reasonably interchangeable if consumers treat them as acceptable substitutes.[14]

What should the relevant product market include? This is often the key issue in monopolization cases because the way the market is defined may determine whether a firm has monopoly power. By

---

12. *United States v. Grinnell Corp.*, 384 U.S. 563, 86 S.Ct. 1698, 16 L.Ed.2d 778 (1966).

13. See, for example, *Broadcom Corp. v. Qualcomm, Inc.*, 501 F.3d 297 (3d Cir. 2007).

14. See, for example, *Linzer Products Corp. v. Sekar*, 499 F.Supp.2d 540 (S.D.N.Y. 2007); and *HDC Medical, Inc. v. Minntech Corp.*, 474 F.3d 543 (8th Cir. 2007).

defining the product market narrowly, the degree of a firm's market power is enhanced.

CASE IN POINT Whole Foods Market, Inc., wished to acquire Wild Oats Markets, Inc., its main competitor in nationwide high-end organic food supermarkets. The Federal Trade Commission (FTC) filed a Section 2 claim against Whole Foods to prevent the merger. The FTC argued that the relevant product market consisted of only "premium natural and organic supermarkets" rather than all supermarkets, as Whole Foods maintained. An appellate court accepted the FTC's narrow definition of the relevant market and remanded the case to the lower court to decide what remedies were appropriate, as the merger had already taken place. Whole Foods later entered into a settlement with the FTC under which it was required to divest (sell or give up control over) thirteen stores, most of which were formerly Wild Oats outlets.[15]

Relevant Geographic Market. The second component of the relevant market is the geographic boundaries of the market in which the firm and its competitors sell the product or services. For products that are sold nationwide, the geographic boundaries of the market can encompass the entire United States. If transportation costs are significant or a producer and its competitors sell in only a limited area (one in which customers have no access to other sources of the product), then the geographic market is limited to that area. A national firm may thus compete in several distinct areas and have monopoly power in one geographic area but not in another.

Generally, the geographic market is that section of the country within which a firm can increase its price a bit without attracting new sellers or without losing many customers to alternative suppliers outside that area. Of course, the Internet is changing perceptions of the size and limits of a geographic market. It may become difficult to perceive any geographic market as local, except for products that are not easily transported, such as concrete.

THE INTENT REQUIREMENT Monopoly power, in and of itself, does not constitute the offense of monopolization under Section 2 of the Sherman Act. The offense also requires an *intent* to monopolize. A dominant market share may be the result of good business judgment or the development of a superior product. It may simply be the result of a historical

accident—for example, the first physician in town is by definition a monopolist, but only by historical accident. In these situations, the acquisition of monopoly power is not an antitrust violation. Indeed, it would be contrary to society's interest to condemn every firm that acquired a position of power because it was well managed and efficient and marketed a product desired by consumers.

If a firm possesses market power as a result of carrying out some purposeful act to acquire or maintain that power through anticompetitive means, then it is in violation of Section 2. In most monopolization cases, intent may be inferred from evidence that the firm had monopoly power and engaged in anticompetitive behavior.

CASE IN POINT Navigator, the first popular graphical Internet browser, used Java technology that was able to run on a variety of platforms. When Navigator was introduced, Microsoft Corporation perceived a threat to its dominance of the operating-system market. Microsoft developed a competing browser, Internet Explorer (IE), and then began to require computer makers that wanted to install the Windows operating system to install IE and exclude Navigator. Microsoft also included codes in Windows that would cripple the operating system if IE was deleted and paid Internet service providers to distribute IE and exclude Navigator. Because of this pattern of exclusionary conduct, a court found that Microsoft was guilty of monopolization. The court reasoned that Microsoft's pattern of conduct could be rational only if the firm knew that it possessed monopoly power.[16]

UNILATERAL REFUSALS TO DEAL As discussed previously, joint refusals to deal (group boycotts) are subject to close scrutiny under Section 1 of the Sherman Act. A single manufacturer acting unilaterally, though, normally is free to deal, or not to deal, with whomever it wishes.[17]

Nevertheless, in some instances, a unilateral refusal to deal will violate antitrust laws. These instances involve offenses proscribed under Section 2 of the Sherman Act and occur only if (1) the firm refusing to deal has—or is likely to acquire—monopoly power and (2) the refusal is likely to have an anticompetitive effect on a particular market.

---

15. *Federal Trade Commission v. Whole Foods Market, Inc.*, 548 F.3d 1028 (D.C.Cir. 2008); and 592 F.Supp.2d 107 (D.D.C. 2009).

16. *United States v. Microsoft Corp.*, 253 F.3d 34 (D.C.Cir. 2001). Microsoft has faced numerous antitrust claims and has settled a number of lawsuits in which it was accused of antitrust violations and anticompetitive tactics.

17. For a classic case in this area, see *United States v. Colgate & Co.*, 250 U.S. 300, 39 S.Ct. 465, 63 L.Ed. 992 (1919).

CASE IN POINT The owner of three of the four major ski areas in Aspen, Colorado, refused to continue its participation in a jointly offered "all Aspen" lift ticket. The United States Supreme Court ruled that the owner's refusal to cooperate with its smaller competitor was a violation of Section 2 of the Sherman Act. Because the company owned three-fourths of the local ski areas, it had monopoly power, and thus its unilateral refusal had an anticompetitive effect on the market.[18]

Attempts to Monopolize

Section 2 also prohibits **attempted monopolization** of a market. Any action challenged as an attempt to monopolize must have been specifically intended to exclude competitors and garner monopoly power. The attempt must also have had a "dangerous" probability of success—only *serious* threats of monopolization are condemned as violations. The probability cannot be dangerous unless the alleged offender possesses some degree of market power.[19]

As mentioned earlier, predatory pricing is a form of anticompetitive conduct that, in theory, could be used by firms that are attempting to monopolize. (Predatory pricing may also lead to claims of price discrimination, to be discussed shortly.) Predatory bidding involves the acquisition and use of *monopsony power,* which is market power on the *buy* side of a market. This may occur when a buyer bids up the price of an input too high for its competitors to pay, causing them to leave the market. The predatory bidder may then attempt to drive down input prices to reap above-competitive profits and recoup any losses it suffered in bidding up the prices.

The question in the following case was whether a claim of predatory bidding is sufficiently similar to a claim of predatory pricing that the same test should apply to both.

---

18. *Aspen Skiing Co. v. Aspen Highlands Skiing Corp.,* 472 U.S. 585, 105 S.Ct. 2847, 86 L.Ed.2d 467 (1985). See also *America Channel, LLC v. Time Warner Cable, Inc.,* 2007 WL 142173 (D.Minn. 2007).

19. See, for example, *Nobody in Particular Presents, Inc. v. Clear Channel Communications, Inc.,* 311 F.Supp.2d 1048 (D.Colo. 2004); and *City of Moundridge, Kansas v. Exxon Mobil Corp.,* 471 F.Supp.2d 20 (D.D.C. 2007).

CASE 47.3
Weyerhaeuser Co. v. Ross-Simmons Hardwood Lumber Co.

Supreme Court of the United States, 549 U.S. 312, 127 S.Ct. 1069, 166 L.Ed.2d 911 (2007).
www.findlaw.com/casecode/supreme.html[a]

BACKGROUND AND FACTS • Weyerhaeuser Company entered the Pacific Northwest's hardwood lumber market in 1980. By 2000, Weyerhaeuser owned six mills processing 65 percent of the red alder logs in the region. Meanwhile, Ross-Simmons Hardwood Lumber Company operated a single competing mill. When the prices of logs rose and those for lumber fell, Ross-Simmons suffered heavy losses. Several million dollars in debt, the mill closed in 2001. Ross-Simmons filed a suit in a federal district court against Weyerhaeuser, alleging attempted monopolization under Section 2 of the Sherman Act. Ross-Simmons claimed that Weyerhaeuser used its dominant position in the market to bid up the prices of logs and prevent its competitors from being profitable. Weyerhaeuser argued that the antitrust test for predatory pricing applies to a claim of predatory bidding and that Ross-Simmons had not met this standard. The district court ruled in favor of the plaintiff, the U.S. Court of Appeals for the Ninth Circuit affirmed, and Weyerhaeuser appealed to the United States Supreme Court.

IN THE LANGUAGE OF THE COURT
Justice *THOMAS* delivered the opinion of the Court.
* * * *

Predatory-pricing and predatory-bidding claims are analytically similar. This similarity results from the close theoretical connection between monopoly and monopsony. The kinship between monopoly and monopsony suggests that similar legal standards should apply to claims of monopolization and to claims of monopsonization.

---

a. In the "Browse Supreme Court Opinions" section, click on "2007." On that page, scroll to the name of the case and click on it to access the opinion.

CASE 47.3 CONTINUED ➡   * * * Both claims involve the deliberate use of unilateral pricing measures for anticompetitive purposes. And both claims logically require firms to incur short-term losses on the chance that they might reap supracompetitive profits [above-competitive rates] in the future.
* * * *
* * * *"Predatory pricing schemes are rarely tried, and even more rarely successful." Predatory pricing requires a firm to suffer certain losses in the short term on the chance of reaping supracompetitive profits in the future. A rational business will rarely make this sacrifice.* The same reasoning applies to predatory bidding. [Emphasis added.]
* * * *
* * * A failed predatory-pricing scheme may benefit consumers. * * * Failed predatory-bidding schemes can also * * * benefit consumers.

In addition, predatory bidding presents less of a direct threat of consumer harm than predatory pricing. A predatory-pricing scheme ultimately achieves success by charging higher prices to consumers. By contrast, a predatory-bidding scheme could succeed with little or no effect on consumer prices because a predatory bidder does not necessarily rely on raising prices in the output market to recoup its losses.
* * * *
* * * [Thus] our two-pronged [predatory pricing] test should apply to predatory-bidding claims.

* * * A plaintiff must prove that the alleged predatory bidding led to below-cost pricing of the predator's outputs. That is, the predator's bidding on the buy side must have caused the cost of the relevant output to rise above the revenues generated in the sale of those outputs. * * * Given the multitude of procompetitive ends served by higher bidding for inputs, the risk of chilling procompetitive behavior with too lax a liability standard is * * * serious * * * . Consequently, only higher bidding that leads to below-cost pricing in the relevant output market will suffice as a basis for liability for predatory bidding.

A predatory-bidding plaintiff also must prove that the defendant has a dangerous probability of recouping the losses incurred in bidding up input prices through the exercise of monopsony power. Absent proof of likely recoupment, a strategy of predatory bidding makes no economic sense because it would involve short-term losses with no likelihood of offsetting long-term gains.

Ross-Simmons has conceded that it has not satisfied [this] standard. Therefore, its predatory-bidding theory of liability cannot support the jury's verdict.

For these reasons, we vacate the judgment of the Court of Appeals and remand the case for further proceedings consistent with this opinion.

DECISION AND REMEDY • *The antitrust test that applies to claims of predatory pricing also applies to claims of predatory bidding. Because Ross-Simmons conceded that it had not met this standard, the United States Supreme Court vacated the lower court's judgment and remanded the case.*

WHAT IF THE FACTS WERE DIFFERENT? • *Logs represent up to 75 percent of a mill's total costs. Efficient equipment can increase both the speed at which lumber can be recovered from a log and the amount of lumber recovered. The Court noted that "Ross-Simmons appears to have engaged in little efficiency-enhancing investment." If Ross-Simmons had invested in state-of-the-art technology, how might the circumstances in this case have been different?*

THE ECONOMIC DIMENSION • *Why does a plaintiff alleging predatory bidding have to prove that the defendant's "bidding on the buy side caused the cost of the relevant output to rise above the revenues generated in the sale of those outputs"?*

SECTION 4
THE CLAYTON ACT

In 1914, Congress enacted the Clayton Act. The act was aimed at specific anticompetitive or monopolistic practices that the Sherman Act did not cover. The substantive provisions of the act deal with four distinct forms of business behavior, which are declared illegal but not criminal. For each provision, the act states that the behavior is illegal only if it tends to substantially lessen competition or to create monopoly power. The major offenses under the Clayton Act are set out in Sections 2, 3, 7, and 8 of the act.

Section 2—Price Discrimination

Section 2 of the Clayton Act prohibits **price discrimination,** which occurs when a seller charges different prices to competing buyers for identical goods or services. Congress strengthened this section by amending it with the passage of the Robinson-Patman Act in 1936. As amended, Section 2 prohibits direct and indirect price discrimination that cannot be justified by differences in production costs, transportation costs, or cost differences due to other reasons. In short, a seller is prohibited from charging a lower price to one buyer than is charged to that buyer's competitor.

REQUIRED ELEMENTS To violate Section 2, the seller must be engaged in interstate commerce, the goods must be of like grade and quality, and the goods must have been sold to two or more purchasers. In addition, the effect of the price discrimination must be to substantially lessen competition, tend to create a monopoly, or otherwise injure competition. Without proof of an actual injury resulting from the price discrimination, the plaintiff cannot recover damages.

Note that price discrimination claims can arise from discounts, offsets, rebates, or allowances given to one buyer over another. Moreover, giving favorable credit terms, delivery, or freight charges to only some buyers can also lead to allegations of price discrimination. For example, when a seller offers goods to different customers at the same price but includes free delivery for certain buyers, it may violate Section 2 in some circumstances.

DEFENSES There are several statutory defenses to liability for price discrimination.

1. *Cost justification.* If the seller can justify the price reduction by demonstrating that a particular buyer's purchases saved the seller costs in producing and selling the goods, the seller will not be liable for price discrimination.
2. *Meeting the price of competition.* If the seller charged the lower price in a good faith attempt to meet an equally low price of a competitor, the seller will not be liable for price discrimination.

   CASE IN POINT Water Craft was a retail dealership of Mercury Marine outboard motors. On discovering that Mercury was selling its outboard motors at a substantial discount to Water Craft's largest competitor, Water Craft filed a price discrimination lawsuit against Mercury. Mercury Marine was able show that the discounts were made in good faith to meet the low price charged

by another manufacturer of marine motors. Therefore, the court found that the "meeting competition defense" applied.[20]

3. *Changing market conditions.* A seller may lower its price on an item in response to changing conditions affecting the market for or the marketability of the goods concerned. Sellers are allowed to readjust their prices to meet the realities of the market without liability for price discrimination. Thus, if an advance in technology makes a particular product less marketable than it was previously, a seller can lower the product's price.

Section 3—Exclusionary Practices

Under Section 3 of the Clayton Act, sellers or lessors cannot sell or lease goods "on the condition, agreement or understanding that the . . . purchaser or lessee thereof shall not use or deal in the goods . . . of a competitor or competitors of the seller." In effect, this section prohibits two types of vertical agreements involving exclusionary practices—exclusive-dealing contracts and tying arrangements.

EXCLUSIVE-DEALING CONTRACTS A contract under which a seller forbids a buyer to purchase products from the seller's competitors is called an **exclusive-dealing contract.** A seller is prohibited from making an exclusive-dealing contract under Section 3 if the effect of the contract is "to substantially lessen competition or tend to create a monopoly."

CASE IN POINT Standard Oil Company, the largest gasoline seller in the nation in the late 1940s, made exclusive-dealing contracts with independent stations in seven western states. The contracts involved 16 percent of all retail outlets, whose sales were approximately 7 percent of all retail sales in that market. In a classic case decided in 1949, the United States Supreme Court said that the market was substantially concentrated because the seven largest gasoline suppliers all used exclusive-dealing contracts with their independent retailers and together controlled 65 percent of the market. Looking at market conditions after the arrangements were instituted, the Court found that market shares were extremely stable and that entry into the market was apparently restricted. Thus, the Court held that the Clayton Act had been violated because

---

20. *Water Craft Management, LLC v. Mercury Marine,* 457 F.3d 484 (5th Cir. 2006).

competition was "foreclosed in a substantial share" of the relevant market.[21]

Note that since the Supreme Court's 1949 decision, a number of decisions have called the holding in this case into doubt. Today, it is clear that to violate antitrust law, an exclusive-dealing agreement (or a tying arrangement, discussed next) must qualitatively and substantially harm competition. To prevail, a plaintiff must present affirmative evidence that the performance of the agreement will foreclose competition and harm consumers.

TYING ARRANGEMENTS In a **tying arrangement,** or *tie-in sales agreement,* a seller conditions the sale of a product (the tying product) on the buyer's agreement to purchase another product (the tied product) produced or distributed by the same seller. The legality of a tie-in agreement depends on many factors, particularly the purpose of the agreement and the agreement's likely effect on competition in the relevant markets (the market for the tying product and the market for the tied product).

Section 3 of the Clayton Act has been held to apply only to commodities, not to services. Tying arrangements, however, can also be considered agreements that restrain trade in violation of Section 1 of the Sherman Act. Thus, cases involving tying arrangements of services have been brought under Section 1 of the Sherman Act. Although earlier cases condemned tying arrangements as illegal *per se,* courts now evaluate tying agreements under the rule of reason.

CASE IN POINT Illinois Tool Works, Inc., made printing systems that included various patented components and used a specially designed, but unpatented, ink. It sold the systems to original equipment manufacturers (OEMs) that incorporated the systems into printers that were used in printing bar codes. As part of each deal, the OEMs agreed to buy ink exclusively from Illinois and not to refill the patented ink containers with ink of any other kind. Independent Ink, Inc., sold ink with the same chemical composition as Illinois's product at lower prices. Independent filed a suit against Illinois, alleging, among other things, that it was engaged in illegal tying in violation of the Sherman Act. Independent argued that because Illinois owned patents in the other components of the printing systems, market power could be presumed. The United States Supreme Court, however, ruled that a plaintiff that alleges an illegal tying arrangement involving a patented product must prove that the defendant has market power in the tying product. The Court therefore remanded the case to the trial court to give Independent an opportunity to offer such evidence.[22]

The decision in the *Illinois Tool Works* case above effectively reversed more than forty years of case law under which patent holders were presumed to have market power. In doing so, the Court recognized that tying arrangements can have legitimate business justifications.

Section 7—Mergers

Under Section 7 of the Clayton Act, a person or business organization cannot hold stock or assets in more than one business when "the effect . . . may be to substantially lessen competition." Section 7 is the statutory authority for preventing mergers that could result in monopoly power or a substantial lessening of competition in the marketplace. Section 7 applies to both horizontal and vertical mergers, as discussed in the following subsections.

A crucial consideration in most merger cases is **market concentration.** Determining market concentration involves allocating percentage market shares among the various companies in the relevant market. When a small number of companies share a large part of the market, the market is concentrated. For example, if the four largest grocery stores in Chicago accounted for 80 percent of all retail food sales, the market clearly would be concentrated in those four firms.

Competition is not necessarily diminished solely as a result of market concentration, however, and courts will consider other factors in determining if a merger violates Section 7. One factor of particular importance is whether the merger will make it more difficult for *potential* competitors to enter the relevant market.

HORIZONTAL MERGERS Mergers between firms that compete with each other in the same market are called **horizontal mergers.** If a horizontal merger creates an entity with a significant market share, the merger may be considered illegal because it increases market concentration.

21. *Standard Oil Co. of California v. United States,* 337 U.S. 293, 69 S.Ct. 1051, 93 L.Ed. 1371 (1949).

22. *Illinois Tool Works, Inc. v. Independent Ink, Inc.,* 547 U.S. 28, 126 S.Ct. 1281, 164 L.Ed.2d 26 (2006).

Factors to Determine Legality. When analyzing the legality of a horizontal merger, the courts also consider three other factors: the overall concentration of the relevant market, the relevant market's history of tending toward concentration, and whether the merger is apparently designed to establish market power or restrict competition.

The Federal Trade Commission (FTC) and the U.S. Department of Justice (DOJ) have established guidelines for determining which mergers will be challenged. Under the guidelines, the first factor to be considered is the degree of concentration in the relevant market. Other factors to be considered include the ease of entry into the relevant market, economic efficiency, the financial condition of the merging firms, and the nature and price of the product or products involved.

The Herfindahl-Hirschman Index. To determine market concentration, the FTC and the DOJ employ what is known as the **Herfindahl-Hirschman Index (HHI).** The HHI is computed by summing the squares of the percentage market shares of the firms in the relevant market. For example, if there are four firms with shares of 30 percent, 30 percent, 20 percent, and 20 percent, respectively, then the HHI equals 2,600 (900 + 900 + 400 + 400 = 2,600).

If the premerger HHI is less than 1,000, then the market is unconcentrated, and the merger is unlikely to be challenged. If the premerger HHI is between 1,000 and 1,800, the industry is moderately concentrated, and the merger will be challenged only if it increases the HHI by 100 points or more. If the HHI is greater than 1,800, the market is highly concentrated. In a highly concentrated market, a merger that produces an increase in the HHI of between 50 and 100 points raises "significant" competitive concerns. Mergers that produce an increase in the HHI of more than 100 points in a highly concentrated market are deemed likely to enhance market power.[23]

VERTICAL MERGERS A **vertical merger** occurs when a company at one stage of production acquires a company at a higher or lower stage of production. An example of a vertical merger is a company merging with one of its suppliers or retailers. Courts in the past have almost exclusively focused on "foreclosure" in assessing vertical mergers. *Foreclosure* may occur because competitors of the merging firms lose opportunities to sell to (or buy products from) the merging firms.

---

23. See, for example, *Chicago Bridge & Iron Co. v. Federal Trade Commission,* 534 F.3d 410 (5th Cir. 2008).

Today, whether a vertical merger will be deemed illegal generally depends on several factors, such as whether the merger creates a single firm that controls an undue percentage share of the relevant market. The courts also analyze whether the merger results in a significant increase in the concentration of firms in that market, barriers to entry into the market, and the apparent intent of the merging parties. Mergers that do not prevent competitors of either of the merging firms from competing in a segment of the market will not be condemned as foreclosing competition and are legal.

Section 8—Interlocking Directorates

Section 8 of the Clayton Act deals with *interlocking directorates*—that is, the practice of having individuals serve as directors on the boards of two or more competing companies simultaneously. Specifically, no person may be a director for two or more competing corporations at the same time if either of the corporations has capital, surplus, or undivided profits aggregating more than $25,844,001 or competitive sales of $2,584,100 or more. The Federal Trade Commission adjusts these threshold amounts each year. (The amounts given here are those announced by the commission in 2010.)

SECTION 5
ENFORCEMENT AND EXEMPTIONS

The federal agencies that enforce the federal antitrust laws are the U.S. Department of Justice (DOJ) and the Federal Trade Commission (FTC), which was established by the Federal Trade Commission Act of 1914. Section 5 of that act condemns all forms of anticompetitive behavior that are not covered under other federal antitrust laws.

Agency Actions

Only the DOJ can prosecute violations of the Sherman Act, which can be either criminal or civil offenses. Either the DOJ or the FTC can enforce the Clayton Act, but violations of that statute are not crimes and can be pursued only through civil proceedings. The DOJ or the FTC may ask the courts to impose various remedies, including **divestiture** (making a company give up one or more of its operations) and dissolution. A meatpacking firm, for example, might be forced to divest itself of control or ownership of butcher shops.

The FTC has sole authority to enforce violations of Section 5 of the Federal Trade Commission Act. FTC actions are effected through administrative orders, but if a firm violates an FTC order, the FTC can seek court sanctions for the violation.

The president, of course, plays a role in establishing enforcement policies at the agencies. The Obama administration has indicated that it will take a more active antitrust stance than the Bush administration did. The current administration is vigorously enforcing antitrust regulations—similar to the approach that the European Union has taken in recent years (to be discussed shortly).

Private Actions

A private party who has been injured as a result of a violation of the Sherman Act or the Clayton Act can sue for damages and attorneys' fees. In some instances, private parties may also seek injunctive relief to prevent antitrust violations. The courts have determined that the ability to sue depends on the directness of the injury suffered by the would-be plaintiff.

Thus, a person wishing to sue under the Sherman Act must prove (1) that the antitrust violation either caused or was a substantial factor in causing the injury that was suffered and (2) that the unlawful actions of the accused party affected business activities of the plaintiff that were protected by the antitrust laws. In 2007, the United States Supreme Court limited the ability of private parties to pursue antitrust lawsuits without presenting some evidence of facts that suggest that an illegal agreement was made.

CASE IN POINT A group of subscribers to local telephone and high-speed Internet services filed a class-action lawsuit against several regional telecommunication companies (including Bell Atlantic). The plaintiffs claimed that the companies had conspired with one another and engaged in *parallel conduct*—offering similar services and pricing—over a period of years to prevent other companies from entering the market and competing. The United States Supreme Court dismissed the case, finding that "without more, parallel conduct does not suggest conspiracy." A bare assertion of conspiracy is not enough to allow an antitrust lawsuit to go forward. The Court noted that more specificity is necessary to avoid potentially "massive" discovery costs, which are especially likely to occur when the suit is brought by a large class of plaintiffs.[24]

24. *Bell Atlantic Corp. v. Twombly,* 550 U.S. 544, 127 S.Ct. 1955, 167 L.Ed.2d 929 (2007).

Treble Damages

In recent years, more than 90 percent of all antitrust actions have been brought by private plaintiffs. One reason for this is that successful plaintiffs may recover treble damages—three times the damages that they have suffered as a result of the violation. In a situation involving a price-fixing agreement, normally each competitor is jointly and severally liable for the total amount of any damages, including treble damages if they are imposed.

Exemptions from Antitrust Laws

There are many legislative and constitutional limitations on antitrust enforcement. Most of the statutory and judicially created exemptions to the antitrust laws apply in such areas as labor, insurance, and foreign trade (see Exhibit 47–1 on the following page).

One of the most significant exemptions covers joint efforts by businesspersons to obtain legislative, judicial, or executive action. Under this exemption, for example, DVD producers can jointly lobby Congress to change the copyright laws without being held liable for attempting to restrain trade. Another exemption covers professional baseball teams.

SECTION 6
U.S. ANTITRUST LAWS IN THE GLOBAL CONTEXT

U.S. antitrust laws have a broad application. Not only may persons in foreign nations be subject to their provisions, but the laws may also be applied to protect foreign consumers and competitors from violations committed by U.S. business firms. Consequently, *foreign persons,* a term that by definition includes foreign governments, may sue under U.S. antitrust laws in U.S. courts.

The Extraterritorial Application of U.S. Antitrust Laws

Section 1 of the Sherman Act provides for the extraterritorial effect of the U.S. antitrust laws. The United States is a major proponent of free competition in the global economy, and thus any conspiracy that has a *substantial effect* on U.S. commerce is within the reach of the Sherman Act. The violation may even occur outside the United States, and foreign governments as well as individuals can be sued for violation of U.S. antitrust laws. Before U.S. courts will exercise jurisdiction and apply antitrust laws, it

EXHIBIT 47-1 • Exemptions to Antitrust Enforcement

EXEMPTION	SOURCE AND SCOPE
Labor	Clayton Act—Permits unions to organize and bargain without violating antitrust laws and specifies that strikes and other labor activities normally do not violate any federal law.
Agricultural Associations	Clayton Act and Capper-Volstead Act of 1922—Allow agricultural cooperatives to set prices.
Fisheries	Fisheries Cooperative Marketing Act of 1976—Allows the fishing industry to set prices.
Insurance Companies	McCarran-Ferguson Act of 1945—Exempts the insurance business in states in which the industry is regulated.
Exporters	Webb-Pomerene Act of 1918—Allows U.S. exporters to engage in cooperative activity to compete with similar foreign associations. Export Trading Company Act of 1982—Permits the U.S. Department of Justice to exempt certain exporters.
Professional Baseball	The United States Supreme Court has held that professional baseball is exempt because it is not "interstate commerce."[a]
Oil Marketing	Interstate Oil Compact of 1935—Allows states to set quotas on oil to be marketed in interstate commerce.
Defense Activities	Defense Production Act of 1950—Allows the president to approve, and thereby exempt, certain activities to further the military defense of the United States.
Small Businesses' Cooperative Research	Small Business Administration Act of 1958—Allows small firms to undertake cooperative research.
State Actions	The United States Supreme Court has held that actions by a state are exempt if the state clearly articulates and actively supervises the policy behind its action.[b]
Regulated Industries	Industries (such as airlines) are exempt when a federal administrative agency (such as the Federal Aviation Administration) has primary regulatory authority.
Businesspersons' Joint Efforts to Seek Government Action	Cooperative efforts by businesspersons to obtain legislative, judicial, or executive action are exempt unless it is clear that an effort is "objectively baseless" and is an attempt to make anticompetitive use of government processes.[c]

a. *Federal Baseball Club of Baltimore, Inc. v. National League of Professional Baseball Clubs,* 259 U.S. 200, 42 S.Ct. 465, 66 L.Ed. 898 (1922). A federal district court has held that this exemption applies only to the game's reserve system. (Under the reserve system, teams hold players' contracts for the players' entire careers. The reserve system generally is being replaced by the free agency system.) See *Piazza v. Major League Baseball,* 831 F.Supp. 420 (E.D.Pa. 1993).

b. *Parker v. Brown,* 317 U.S. 341, 63 S.Ct. 307, 87 L.Ed. 315 (1943).

c. *Eastern Railroad Presidents Conference v. Noerr Motor Freight, Inc.,* 365 U.S. 127, 81 S.Ct. 523, 5 L.Ed.2d 464 (1961); and *United Mine Workers of America v. Pennington,* 381 U.S. 657, 89 S.Ct. 1585, 14 L.Ed.2d 626 (1965). These two cases established the exception often referred to as the *Noerr-Pennington* doctrine.

must be shown that the alleged violation had a substantial effect on U.S. commerce. U.S. jurisdiction is automatically invoked, however, when a *per se* violation occurs.

If a domestic firm, for example, joins a foreign cartel to control the production, price, or distribution of goods, and this cartel has a *substantial effect* on U.S. commerce, a *per se* violation may exist. Hence, both the domestic firm and the foreign cartel could be sued for violation of the U.S. antitrust laws. Likewise, if a foreign firm doing business in the United States enters into a price-fixing or other anticompetitive agreement to control a portion of U.S. markets, a *per se* violation may exist.

The Application of Foreign Antitrust Laws

Large U.S. companies increasingly need to worry about the application of foreign antitrust laws as well. The European Union (EU), in particular, has stepped up its enforcement actions against antitrust violators in recent years.

EUROPEAN UNION ENFORCEMENT The EU's laws promoting competition are stricter in many respects than those of the United States and define more conduct as anticompetitive. The EU actively pursues antitrust violators, especially individual companies and cartels that engage in monopolistic conduct. For example, in 2009, the EU fined Intel, Inc., the world's largest semiconductor chip maker, $1.44 billion in an antitrust case. According to European regulators, Intel offered computer manufacturers and retailers price discounts and marketing subsidies if they agreed to buy Intel's chips rather than the chips produced by Intel's main competitor in Europe. The EU has also fined Microsoft Corporation more than $2 billion in the last ten years for anticompetitive conduct.

INCREASED ENFORCEMENT IN ASIA AND LATIN AMERICA Many other nations also have laws that promote competition and prohibit trade restraints. For example, Japanese antitrust laws forbid unfair trade practices, monopolization, and restrictions that unreasonably restrain trade. In 2008, China enacted its first antitrust rules, which restrict monopolization and price fixing (although the Chinese government may set prices on exported goods without violating these rules). Indonesia, Malaysia, South Korea, and Vietnam all have statutes protecting competition. Argentina, Brazil, Chile, Peru, and several other Latin American countries have adopted modern antitrust laws as well.

Most of the antitrust laws apply extraterritorially, as U.S. antitrust laws do. This means that a U.S. company may be subject to another nation's antitrust laws if the company's conduct has a substantial effect on that nation's commerce. For instance, in 2008, South Korea fined Intel $25 million for antitrust violations; Japan settled an antitrust case against Intel in 2005.

REVIEWING

Antitrust Law

The Internet Corporation for Assigned Names and Numbers (ICANN) is a nonprofit entity that organizes Internet domain names. It is governed by a board of directors elected by various groups with commercial interests in the Internet. One of ICANN's functions is to authorize an entity as a registry for certain "Top Level Domains" (TLDs). ICANN and VeriSign entered into an agreement that authorized VeriSign to serve as a registry for the ".com" TLD and provide registry services in accordance with ICANN's specifications. VeriSign complained that ICANN was restricting the services that it could make available as a registrar and blocking new services, imposing unnecessary conditions on those services, and setting the prices at which the services were offered. VeriSign claimed that ICANN's control of the registry services for domain names violated Section 1 of the Sherman Act. Using the information presented in the chapter, answer the following questions.

1. Should ICANN's actions be judged under the rule of reason or be deemed *per se* violations of Section 1 of the Sherman Act? Why?
2. Should ICANN's actions be viewed as a horizontal or a vertical restraint of trade? Why?
3. Does it matter that ICANN's directors are chosen by groups with a commercial interest in the Internet? Explain.
4. If the dispute is judged under the rule of reason, what might be ICANN's defense for having a standardized set of registry services that must be used?

DEBATE THIS: *The Internet and the rise of e-commerce have rendered our current antitrust concepts and laws obsolete.*

TERMS AND CONCEPTS

antitrust law 913	group boycott 917	monopoly 914	restraint of trade 913
attempted	Herfindahl-Hirschman	monopoly power 914	rule of reason 914
monopolization 922	Index (HHI) 926	*per se* violation 914	tying arrangement 925
concentrated industry 917	horizontal merger 925	predatory pricing 920	vertical merger 926
divestiture 926	horizontal restraint 916	price discrimination 924	vertical restraint 918
exclusive-dealing contract 924	market concentration 925	price-fixing agreement 916	vertically integrated firm 918
	market power 914	resale price maintenance	
	monopolization 920	agreement 918	

QUESTIONS AND CASE PROBLEMS

47–1. Group Boycott Jorge's Appliance Corp. was a new retail seller of appliances in Sunrise City. Because of its innovative sales techniques and financing, Jorge's caused the appliance department of No-Glow Department Store, a large chain store with a great deal of buying power, to lose a substantial amount of sales. No-Glow told a number of appliance manufacturers from whom it made large-volume purchases that if they continued to sell to Jorge's, No-Glow would stop buying from them. The manufacturers immediately stopped selling appliances to Jorge's. Jorge's filed a suit against No-Glow and the manufacturers, claiming that their actions constituted an antitrust violation. No-Glow and the manufacturers were able to prove that Jorge's was a small retailer with a small market share. They claimed that because the relevant market was not substantially affected, they were not guilty of restraint of trade. Discuss fully whether there was an antitrust violation.

47–2. QUESTION WITH SAMPLE ANSWER: Section 1 of the Sherman Act.

Allitron, Inc., and Donovan, Ltd., are interstate competitors selling similar appliances, principally in the states of Illinois, Indiana, Kentucky, and Ohio. Allitron and Donovan agree that Allitron will no longer sell in Indiana and Ohio and that Donovan will no longer sell in Illinois and Kentucky. Have Allitron and Donovan violated any antitrust laws? If so, which law? Explain.

- For a sample answer to Question 47–2, go to Appendix I at the end of this text.

47–3. Price Fixing Texaco, Inc., and Shell Oil Co. are competitors in the national and international oil and gasoline markets. They refine crude oil into gasoline and sell it to service station owners and others. Between 1998 and 2002, Texaco and Shell engaged in a joint venture, Equilon Enterprises, to consolidate their operations in the western United States and a separate venture, Motiva Enterprises, for the same purpose in the eastern United States. This ended their competition in the domestic refining and marketing of gasoline. As part of the ventures, Texaco and Shell agreed to pool their resources and share the risks and profits of their joint activities. The Federal Trade Commission and several states approved the formation of these entities without restricting the pricing of their gasoline, which the ventures began to sell at a single price under the original Texaco and Shell brand names. Fouad Dagher and other station owners filed a suit in a federal district court against Texaco and Shell, alleging that the defendants were engaged in illegal price fixing. Do the circumstances in this case fit the definition of a price-fixing agreement? Explain. [*Texaco Inc. v. Dagher*, 547 U.S. 1, 126 S.Ct. 1276, 164 L.Ed.2d 1 (2006)]

47–4. Restraint of Trade In 1999, residents of the city of Madison, Wisconsin, became concerned that overconsumption of liquor seemed to be increasing near the campus of the University of Wisconsin–Madison (UW), leading to more frequent use of detoxification facilities and calls for police services in the campus area. Under pressure from UW, which shared these concerns, the city initiated a new policy that imposed conditions on area taverns to discourage reduced-price "specials" believed to encourage high-volume and dangerous drinking. In 2002, the city began to draft an ordinance to ban all drink specials. Tavern owners responded by announcing that they had "voluntarily" agreed to discontinue drink specials on Friday and Saturday nights after 8 P.M. The city put its ordinance on hold. UW student Nic Eichenseer and others filed a suit in a Wisconsin state court against the Madison–Dane County Tavern League, Inc. (an association of local tavern owners), and others, alleging violations of antitrust law. On what might the plaintiffs base a claim for relief? Are the defendants in this case exempt from the antitrust laws? What should the court rule? Why? [*Eichenseer v. Madison–Dane County Tavern League, Inc.,* 2006 WI App 226, 725 N.W.2d 274 (2006)]

47–5. Price Discrimination The customers of Sodexho, Inc., and Feesers, Inc., are institutional food service facilities such as school, hospital, and nursing home cafeterias. Feesers is a distributor that buys unprepared food from suppliers for resale to customers who run their own cafeterias. Sodexho is a food service management company that buys unprepared food from suppliers; prepares the food; and sells the meals to the facilities, which it also operates, under contracts with its clients. Sodexho uses a distributor, such as Sysco Corp., to buy the food from a supplier, such as Michael Foods, Inc. Sysco pays Michael's list price and sells the food to Sodexho at a lower price—which Sodexho has negotiated with Michael—plus an agreed mark-up. Sysco invoices Michael for the difference. Sodexho resells the food to its facilities at its cost, plus a "procurement fee." In sum, Michael charges Sysco less for food resold to Sodexho than it charges Feesers for the same products, and thus Sodexho's customers pay less than Feesers's customers for these products. Feesers filed a suit in a federal district court against Michael and others, alleging price discrimination. To establish its claim, what does Feesers have to show? What might be the most difficult element to prove? How should the court rule? Why? [*Feesers, Inc. v. Michael Foods, Inc.,* 498 F.3d 206 (3d Cir. 2007)]

47–6. Tying Arrangement John Sheridan owned a Marathon gas station franchise. He sued Marathon Petroleum Co. under Section 1 of the Sherman Act and Section 3 of the Clayton Act, charging it with illegally tying the processing of credit-card sales to the gas station. As a condition of obtaining a Marathon dealership, dealers had to agree to let the franchisor process credit cards. They could not shop around to see if credit-card processing could be obtained at a lower price from another source. The district court dismissed the case for failure to state a claim. Sheridan appealed. Is there a tying arrangement? If so, does it violate the law? Explain. [*Sheridan v. Marathon Petroleum Co.,* 530 F.3d 590 (7th Cir. 2008)]

47–7. CASE PROBLEM WITH SAMPLE ANSWER: Monopolization.

When Deer Valley Resort Co. (DVRC) was developing its ski resort in the Wasatch Mountains near Park City, Utah, it sold parcels of land in the resort village to third parties. Each sales contract reserved the right of approval over the conduct of certain businesses on the property, including ski rentals. For fifteen years, DVRC permitted Christy Sports, LLC, to rent skis in competition with DVRC's ski rental outlet. When DVRC opened a new midmountain ski rental outlet, it revoked Christy's permission to rent skis. This meant that most skiers who flew into Salt Lake City and shuttled to Deer Valley had few choices: they could carry their ski equipment with them on their flights, take a shuttle into Park City and look for cheaper ski

*rentals there, or rent from DVRC. Christy filed a suit in a federal district court against DVRC. Was DVRC's action an attempt to monopolize in violation of Section 2 of the Sherman Act? Why or why not? [*Christy Sports, LLC v. Deer Valley Resort Co.,* 555 F.3d 1188 (10th Cir. 2009)]*

- To view a sample answer for Problem 47–7, go to this book's Web site at www.cengage.com/blaw/clarkson, select "Chapter 47," and click on "Case Problem with Sample Answer."

47–8. Price Fixing About 80 percent of the digital music purchased in the United States was controlled by several companies that produce, license, and distribute music sold as digital files over the Internet or on compact discs. The companies formed joint ventures called MusicNet and Duet to sell music to consumers. Through these ventures, the music sellers could communicate about pricing, terms, and use restrictions. Because the prices were so high, however, most consumers avoided them. Instead, song-by-song distribution over the Internet became more common. As a result, the music companies were forced to lower prices, but most sales were still done through MusicNet as the distributor. Eventually, the music companies agreed to a price of 70 cents wholesale for songs distributed on the Internet, but they refused to sell through another distributor, eMusic, which charged 25 cents per song. A group of consumers, including Kevin Starr, brought a lawsuit alleging that the music companies engaged in a conspiracy to restrain the distribution of Internet music and to fix and maintain artificially high prices. Do the consumers have a credible antitrust case to pursue in this situation? Discuss. [*Starr v. Sony BMG Music Entertainment,* 592 F.3d 314 (2d Cir. 2010)]

47–9. A QUESTION OF ETHICS: Section 1 of the Sherman Act.

*In the 1990s, DuCoa, L.P., made choline chloride, a B-complex vitamin essential for the growth and development of animals. The U.S. market for choline chloride was divided into thirds among DuCoa, Bioproducts, Inc., and Chinook Group, Ltd. To stabilize the market and keep the price of the vitamin higher than it would otherwise have been, the companies agreed to fix the price and allocate market share by deciding which of them would offer the lowest price to each customer. At times, however, the companies disregarded the agreement. During an increase in competitive activity in August 1997, Daniel Rose became president of DuCoa. The next month, a subordinate advised him of the conspiracy. By February 1998, Rose had begun to implement a strategy to persuade DuCoa's competitors to rejoin the conspiracy. By April, the three companies had reallocated their market shares and increased their prices. In June, the U.S. Department of Justice began to investigate allegations of price fixing in the vitamin market. Ultimately, a federal district court convicted Rose of conspiracy to violate Section 1 of the Sherman Act. [*United States v. Rose,* 449 F.3d 627 (5th Cir. 2006)]*

(a) The court "enhanced" Rose's sentence to thirty months' imprisonment, one year of supervised release, and a $20,000 fine based, among other things, on his role as "a manager or supervisor" in the conspiracy. Rose appealed this enhancement to the U.S. Court of Appeals for the Fifth Circuit. Was it fair to increase Rose's sentence on this ground? Why or why not?

(b) Was Rose's participation in the conspiracy unethical? If so, how might Rose have behaved ethically instead? If not, could any of the participants' conduct be considered unethical? Explain.

47–10. SPECIAL CASE ANALYSIS: Resale Price Maintenance Agreements.
Go to Extended Case 47.2, *Leegin Creative Leather Products, Inc. v. PSKS, Inc.*, 551 U.S. 877, 127 S.Ct. 2705,

168 L.Ed.2d 623 (2007), on pages 919 and 920. Read the excerpt and answer the following questions.

(a) **Issue:** The dispute in this case was between which parties and turned on what legal issue?

(b) **Rule of Law:** In resolving this dispute, what common law rule did the Court overturn, and what rule did the Court create to replace this rejected precedent?

(c) **Applying the Rule of Law:** What reasons did the Court give to justify its change in the law, and how did the new rule apply in this case?

(d) **Conclusion:** In whose favor did the Court rule and why?

LEGAL RESEARCH EXERCISES ON THE WEB

Go to this text's Web site at **www.cengage.com/blaw/clarkson**, select "Chapter 47," and click on "Practical Internet Exercises." There you will find the following Internet research exercises that you can perform to learn more about the topics covered in this chapter.

Practical Internet Exercise 47–1: **Legal Perspective**
The Standard Oil Trust

Practical Internet Exercise 47–2: **Management Perspective**
Avoiding Antitrust Problems

CHAPTER 48

Professional Liability and Accountability

Professionals such as accountants, attorneys, physicians, and architects are increasingly faced with the threat of liability. One of the reasons for this is that the public has become more aware that professionals are required to deliver competent services and are obligated to adhere to standards of performance commonly accepted within their professions.

Certainly, in the first decade of the 2000s, the dizzying collapse of Enron Corporation and the failure of other major companies called attention to the importance of abiding by professional accounting standards. As a result

of its failure to do so, Arthur Andersen, LLP, one of the world's leading public accounting firms, ceased to exist, and some 85,000 employees lost their jobs. Although the Sarbanes-Oxley Act of 2002 imposed stricter regulation and oversight on the public accounting industry, accounting fraud scandals have continued. Numerous corporations and former corporations—from American International Group (AIG), the world's largest insurance company, to HealthSouth, Goldman Sachs, Lehman Brothers, Tyco International, and India-based Satyam Computer Services—have been accused of engaging in accounting fraud. These

companies may have reported fictitious revenues, concealed liabilities and debts, or artificially inflated their assets.

Considering the many potential sources of legal liability that they face, accountants, attorneys, and other professionals should be very aware of their legal obligations. In this chapter, we look at the potential liability of professionals under both the common law and statutory law. The chapter concludes with a brief examination of the relationships of professionals, particularly accountants and attorneys, with their clients.

SECTION 1
POTENTIAL LIABILITY TO CLIENTS

Under the common law, professionals may be liable to clients for breach of contract, negligence, or fraud.

Liability for Breach of Contract

Accountants and other professionals face liability under the common law for any breach of contract. A professional owes a duty to her or his client to honor the terms of their contract and to perform the contract within the stated time period. If the professional fails to perform as agreed in the contract, then she or he has breached the contract, and the client has the right to recover damages from the professional. Damages include expenses incurred by

the client to hire another professional to provide the contracted-for services and any other reasonable and foreseeable losses that arise from the professional's breach. For example, if the client had to pay liquidated damages or penalties for failing to meet deadlines, the court may order the professional to pay an equivalent amount in damages to the client.

Liability for Negligence

Accountants and other professionals may also be held liable for negligence in the performance of their services. Recall from Chapter 7 that to establish negligence, the plaintiff must prove four elements: duty, breach, causation, and damages. These elements must be proved in negligence cases against professionals, which often focus on the standard of care exercised by the professional.

All professionals are subject to the standards of conduct and the ethical codes established by their profession, by state statutes, and by judicial decisions. They are also governed by the contracts they enter into with their clients. In performance of their contracts, professionals must exercise the established standards of care, knowledge, and judgment generally accepted by members of their professional group. Here, we look at the duty of care owed by two groups of professionals that frequently perform services for business firms: accountants and attorneys.

ACCOUNTANT'S DUTY OF CARE Accountants play a major role in a business's financial system. Accountants have the expertise and experience necessary to establish and maintain accurate financial records, as well as design, control, and audit record-keeping systems. They also have the appropriate education and training to prepare reliable statements that reflect an individual's or a business's financial status, give tax advice, and prepare tax returns. Generally, an accountant must possess the skills that an ordinarily prudent accountant would have and must exercise the degree of care that an ordinarily prudent accountant would exercise. The level of skill expected of accountants and the degree of care that they should exercise in performing their services are reflected in the standards discussed next.

GAAP and GAAS. In the performance of their services, accountants must comply with **generally accepted accounting principles (GAAP)** and **generally accepted auditing standards (GAAS).** The Financial Accounting Standards Board (FASB, usually pronounced "faz-bee") determines what accounting conventions, rules, and procedures constitute GAAP at a given point in time. GAAS are standards concerning an auditor's professional qualities and the judgment that he or she exercises in auditing financial records. The American Institute of Certified Public Accountants established GAAS. These standards are also reflected in the rules established by the Securities and Exchange Commission (see Chapter 42).

As long as an accountant conforms to GAAP and acts in good faith, the accountant normally will not be held liable to the client for a mistake in judgment. An accountant is not required to discover every impropriety, **defalcation,**[1] or fraud, in a client's books. If, however, the impropriety, defalcation, or fraud goes undiscovered because of the accountant's

negligence or failure to perform an express or implied duty, the accountant will be liable for any resulting losses suffered by the client. Therefore, an accountant who uncovers suspicious financial transactions and fails to investigate the matter fully or to inform the client of the discovery can be held liable to the client for the resulting loss.

A violation of GAAP and GAAS is considered *prima facie* evidence of negligence on the part of the accountant. Compliance with GAAP and GAAS, however, does not *necessarily* relieve an accountant from potential legal liability. An accountant may be held to a higher standard of conduct established by state statute and by judicial decisions.

Global Accounting Rules. In 2008, the Securities and Exchange Commission (SEC) unanimously approved a plan to require U.S. companies to use a set of global accounting rules established by the London-based International Accounting Standards Board. These rules, known as **International Financial Reporting Standards (IFRS),** will eventually be required for all of the financial reports that U.S. companies must file with the SEC. Under the plan, the use of GAAP will be phased out, with final approval of rules implementing the IFRS scheduled for 2011 or 2012.[2] To ease the transition, the SEC has set up a multiyear timetable for converting to the IFRS. The largest multinational companies are required to use the global rules by 2014, and the smallest publicly reporting companies must make the shift by 2016. The IFRS are simpler and more straightforward than GAAP and focus more on overriding principles than on specific rules.

Many countries already use the IFRS, so their adoption by the SEC will make it easier to compare the financial statements of U.S. and foreign companies. Nevertheless, the shift to the global rules has some drawbacks. It will be both costly and time consuming. Companies will have to upgrade their communications and software systems; study and implement the new rules; and train their employees, accountants, and tax attorneys. Another concern is that although the IFRS are simpler, they may not be better than GAAP. Because the global rules are broader and less detailed, they give companies more leeway in reporting, so less financial information may be disclosed. There are also indications that use of the IFRS can lead to wide variances in reported profits and tends to boost earnings above what they would have been under GAAP.

---

1. This term, pronounced deh-ful-*kay*-shun, is derived from the Latin *de* ("off") and *falx* ("sickle"—a tool for cutting grain or tall grass). In law, the term refers to the act of a defaulter or of an embezzler. As used here, it means embezzlement.

2. Although the original deadline to implement the international rules was June 2011, that deadline was pushed back, and the new rules may not be adopted until 2012.

Audits, Qualified Opinions, and Disclaimers.

One of the more important tasks that an accountant may perform for a business is an audit. An *audit* is a systematic inspection, by analyses and tests, of a business's financial records. The purpose of an audit is to provide the auditor with evidence to support an opinion on the reliability of the business's financial statements. A normal audit is not intended to uncover fraud or other misconduct. Nevertheless, an accountant may be liable for failing to detect misconduct if a normal audit would have revealed it. Also, if the auditor agreed to examine the records for evidence of fraud or other obvious misconduct and then failed to detect it, he or she may be liable. After performing an audit, the auditor issues an opinion letter stating whether, in his or her opinion, the financial statements fairly present the business's financial position.

In issuing an opinion letter, an auditor may *qualify* the opinion or include a disclaimer. An opinion that disclaims any liability for false or misleading financial statements is too general, however. A qualified opinion or a disclaimer must be specific and identify the reason for the qualification or disclaimer. For example, Richard Zehr performs an audit of Lacey Corporation. In the opinion letter, Zehr qualifies his opinion by stating that there is uncertainty about how a lawsuit against the firm will be resolved. In this situation, Zehr will not be liable if the outcome of the suit is unfavorable for the firm. Zehr could still be liable, however, for failing to discover other problems that an audit in compliance with GAAS and GAAP would have revealed. In a disclaimer, the auditor is basically stating that she or he does not have sufficient information to issue an opinion. Again, the auditor must identify the problem and indicate what information is lacking.

Unaudited Financial Statements.

Sometimes, accountants are hired to prepare unaudited financial statements. (A financial statement is considered unaudited if incomplete auditing procedures have been used in its preparation or if insufficient procedures have been used to justify an opinion.) Accountants may be subject to liability for failing, in accordance with standard accounting procedures, to designate a balance sheet as "unaudited." An accountant will also be held liable for failure to disclose to a client any facts or circumstances that give reason to believe that misstatements have been made or that a fraud has been committed.

Defenses to Negligence.

As discussed, an accountant may be held liable to a client for losses resulting from the accountant's negligence in performing various accounting services. An accountant facing a negligence claim, however, has several possible defenses, including the following:

1. That the accountant was not negligent.
2. If the accountant was negligent, this negligence was not the proximate cause of the client's losses (see the *Case in Point* example below).
3. The client was also negligent (depending on whether state law allows contributory negligence or comparative negligence as a defense—see Chapter 7).

CASE IN POINT Coopers & Lybrand, LLP, provided accounting services for Oregon Steel Mills (OSM), Inc. Coopers advised OSM to report a certain transaction as a $12.3 million gain on its financial statements. Later, when OSM planned to make a public offering of its stock, the SEC reviewed its financial statements, concluded that the accounting treatment of the transaction was incorrect, and required OSM to correct its statements. Because of the delay, the public offering did not occur on May 2, when OSM's stock was selling for $16 per share, but on June 13, when, due to unrelated factors, the price was $13.50. OSM filed a lawsuit against Coopers claiming that the negligent accounting resulted in the stock's being sold at a lower price. The court held, however, that although the accountant's negligence had delayed the stock offering, the negligence was not the proximate cause of the decline in the stock price. Thus, Coopers could not be held liable for damages based on the price decline.[3]

ATTORNEY'S DUTY OF CARE The conduct of attorneys is governed by rules established by each state and by the American Bar Association's Model Rules of Professional Conduct. All attorneys owe a duty to provide competent and diligent representation. Attorneys are required to be familiar with well-settled principles of law applicable to a case and to find relevant law that can be discovered through a reasonable amount of research. The lawyer must also investigate and discover facts that could materially affect the client's legal rights.

In judging an attorney's performance, the standard used will normally be that of a reasonably competent general practitioner of ordinary skill, experience, and capacity. If an attorney claims to have expertise in a particular area of law (for example, intellectual property), then the attorney's standard of care in that area is higher than those for attorneys without such expertise.

---

3. *Oregon Steel Mills, Inc. v. Coopers & Lybrand, LLP*, 336 Or. 329, 83 P.3d 322 (2004).

Misconduct. Generally, a state's rules of professional conduct for attorneys provide that committing a criminal act that reflects adversely on the person's "honesty or trustworthiness, or fitness as a lawyer in other respects" is professional misconduct. The rules often further provide that a lawyer should not engage in conduct involving "dishonesty, fraud, deceit, or misrepresentation." Under these rules, state authorities can discipline attorneys for many types of misconduct.

CASE IN POINT Michael Inglimo, who was licensed to practice law in Wisconsin, occasionally used marijuana with a person who later became his client in a criminal case. After the trial, the client claimed that Inglimo had been high on drugs during the trial and had not adequately represented him. Two years later, Inglimo was convicted for misdemeanor possession of marijuana. State authorities also discovered that Inglimo had written several checks for personal expenses out of his client trust account, commingled client funds, and engaged in other trust account violations. The state initiated disciplinary proceedings and asked the court to suspend Inglimo's license to practice for three years. Inglimo argued that he should not be suspended because his misconduct was related to his past use of controlled substances and he no longer used drugs. The court, however, concluded that the suspension was necessary to protect the public in light of Inglimo's "disturbing pattern of disregard" for his professional obligations.[4]

Liability for Malpractice. When an attorney fails to exercise reasonable care and professional judgment, she or he breaches the duty of care and can be held liable for *malpractice* (professional negligence). In malpractice cases—as in all cases involving allegations of negligence—the plaintiff must prove that the attorney's breach of the duty of care actually caused the plaintiff to suffer some injury. For example, if attorney Karen Boehmer allows the

---

4. *In re Disciplinary Proceedings against Inglimo*, 2007 WI 126, 305 Wis.2d 71, 740 N.W.2d 125 (2007).

statute of limitations to lapse on the claim of Beth Curl, a client, Boehmer can be held liable for malpractice because Curl can no longer pursue her claim and has lost a potential award of damages.

Liability for Fraud

Recall from Chapter 14 that fraud, or misrepresentation, involves the following elements:

1. A misrepresentation of a material fact.
2. An intent to deceive.
3. Justifiable reliance by the innocent party on the misrepresentation.
4. To obtain damages, an actual injury to the innocent party.

Both actual and constructive fraud are potential sources of legal liability for an accountant or other professional. A professional may be held liable for *actual* fraud when (1) he or she intentionally misstates a material fact to mislead a client and (2) the client is injured as a result of her or his justifiable reliance on the misstated fact. A material fact is one that a reasonable person would consider important in deciding whether to act.

In contrast, a professional may be held liable for *constructive* fraud whether or not he or she acted with fraudulent intent. Constructive fraud may be found when an accountant is grossly negligent in performing his or her duties. For example, Paula, an accountant, is conducting an audit of National Computing Company (NCC). Paula accepts the explanations of Ron, an NCC officer, regarding certain financial irregularities, despite evidence that contradicts those explanations and indicates that the irregularities may be illegal. Paula's conduct could be characterized as an intentional failure to perform a duty in reckless disregard of the consequences of such failure. This would constitute gross negligence and could be held to be constructive fraud.

In the following case, the court considered whether an accountant who had impersonated someone else could be sanctioned for fraudulent conduct by a state board of accountancy.

CASE 48.1

Walsh v. State

Nebraska Supreme Court, 276 Neb. 1034, 759 N.W.2d 100 (2009).

COMPANY PROFILE • The Nebraska Board of Public Accountancy was established in 1957 by the Nebraska Public Accountancy Act. The board's "vision" is "to protect the welfare of the citizens of the State of Nebraska by assuring the competency of persons licensed as Certified Public Accountants

CASE 48.1 CONTINUED ▶ (CPAs)." The board assures the competency of CPAs through examination, certification, licensure, registration, continuing professional education, and "quality review." Among other responsibilities, the board investigates and disciplines licensees who fail to comply with the board's requirements and standards, and the profession's ethical principles. The board's activities are self-supported through licensing fees.

BACKGROUND AND FACTS • Stephen Teiper wrote a letter to the Nebraska Board of Public Accountancy to accuse his brother-in-law, Michael Walsh, a CPA, of impersonating Teiper on the phone to obtain financial information from Teiper's insurance company. The board filed a complaint against Walsh for a violation of its rules. At a hearing, Walsh admitted that he had impersonated Teiper, but argued that Teiper had provided his personal information to Walsh for this purpose. The board found that Walsh had committed a "discreditable act" and concluded that his conduct was reprehensible and reflected adversely on his fitness to engage in the practice of public accountancy. As sanctions, the board reprimanded Walsh, placed him on probation for three months, and ordered him to attend four hours of continuing education in ethics. The board also ordered him to pay the costs of the hearing. Walsh petitioned a Nebraska state court, which affirmed the orders. Walsh appealed.

IN THE LANGUAGE OF THE COURT
WRIGHT, J. [Justice]
* * * *

[Under the Nebraska] Public Accountancy Act [the Nebraska Board of Public Accountancy] is * * * authorized to discipline the holders of certificates and permits who fail to comply with the technical or ethical standards of the public accountancy profession. The Board has the authority to adopt and promulgate [publicly issue] rules and regulations "of professional conduct appropriate to establish and maintain a high standard of integrity and dignity in the profession of public accountancy."
* * * *

* * * After notice and hearing, the Board may take disciplinary action against a permitholder for, among other reasons, violation of a rule of professional conduct * * * . The types of disciplinary action available to the Board include reprimand, suspension, probation, placement of limits on a permit or certificate, revocation of a permit or certificate, and imposition of a civil penalty and costs.
* * * *

Walsh claims there was not a sufficient nexus [connection] between the practice of public accountancy and Walsh's activity in lying to the insurance company for the Board to discipline him.

The Board's rules provide that "a licensee shall not commit an act that reflects adversely on his fitness to engage in the practice of public accountancy."

* * * Like attorneys or medical professionals, CPAs must demonstrate a high degree of moral and ethical integrity. * * * *A certificate as a CPA indicates to the public that the person holding such a certificate possesses the highest sort of qualifications and is one in whom may be placed the utmost trust and confidence.* * * * It is readily apparent that individuals rely upon honesty, integrity, sound professional judgment, and compliance with government regulations when they consult a CPA, even if the CPA may not be specifically acting as an accountant. [Emphasis added.]

The [lower] court found that a person could not knowingly impersonate another and make false statements without tainting the individual's reputation as a CPA and the reputation of the profession as a whole. We agree with the [lower] court.

DECISION AND REMEDY • *The Nebraska Supreme Court affirmed the lower court's decision. Walsh's actions reflected adversely on the accountancy profession, which demands a high level of honesty and integrity.*

WHAT IF THE FACTS WERE DIFFERENT? • *Suppose that Walsh had not been a CPA but had falsely advertised himself as a CPA. Could sanctions have been imposed under those circumstances? Explain why or why not.*

THE ETHICAL DIMENSION • *Was the specific reason for Walsh's impersonation significant to the result in this case? Why or why not?*

Limiting Professionals' Liability

Accountants and other professionals can limit their liability to some extent by disclaiming it. Depending on the circumstances, a disclaimer that does not meet certain requirements will not be effective, however; and in some situations, a disclaimer may not be effective at all.

Professionals may be able to limit their liability for the misconduct of other professionals with whom they work by organizing the business as a professional corporation (P.C.) or a limited liability partnership (LLP). In some states, a professional who is a member of a P.C. is not personally liable for a co-member's misconduct unless she or he participated in it or supervised the member who acted wrongly. The innocent professional is liable only to the extent of his or her interest in the assets of the firm. This is also true for professionals who are partners in an LLP. P.C.s were discussed in Chapter 39. LLPs were covered in Chapter 37.

SECTION 2
POTENTIAL LIABILITY TO THIRD PARTIES

Traditionally, an accountant or other professional owed a duty only to those with whom she or he had a direct contractual relationship—that is, those with whom she or he was in *privity of contract*. A professional's duty was only to her or his client. Violations of statutory laws, fraud, and other intentional or reckless acts of wrongdoing were the only exceptions to this general rule. Today, numerous third parties—including investors, shareholders, creditors, corporate managers and directors, and regulatory agencies—rely on the opinions of auditors (accountants) when making decisions. In view of this extensive reliance, many courts have all but abandoned the privity requirement in regard to accountants' liability to third parties.

In this section, we focus primarily on the potential liability of auditors to third parties. Understanding an auditor's common law liability to third parties is critical because often, when a business fails, its independent auditor (accountant) may be one of the few potentially *solvent* (able to pay expenses and debts) defendants. The majority of courts now hold that auditors can be held liable to third parties for negligence, but the standard for the imposition of this liability varies. Next, we discuss several different views of accountants' liability to third parties.

The *Ultramares* Rule

A general principle of contract law is that only the parties to a contract have rights under that contract. In other words, unless an exception applies, *privity of contract* must exist between a plaintiff and a defendant before the plaintiff can bring any action based on the contract.

THE REQUIREMENT OF PRIVITY   The traditional rule regarding an accountant's liability to third parties based on privity of contract was enunciated by Chief Judge Benjamin Cardozo of the New York Court of Appeals in 1931.

CASE IN POINT Fred Stern & Company had hired the public accounting firm of Touche, Niven & Company to review Stern's financial records and prepare a balance sheet for the year ending December 31, 1923.[5] Touche prepared the balance sheet and supplied Stern with thirty-two certified copies. According to the certified balance sheet, Stern had a net worth (assets less liabilities) of $1,070,715.26. In reality, however, Stern's liabilities exceeded its assets—the company's records had been falsified by insiders at Stern to reflect a positive net worth. In reliance on the certified balance sheets, Ultramares Corporation loaned substantial amounts to Stern. After Stern was declared bankrupt, Ultramares brought an action against Touche for negligence in an attempt to recover damages. The court refused to impose liability on Touche and concluded that Touche's accountants owed a duty of care only to those persons for whose "primary benefit" the statements were intended. In this case, the statements were intended only for the primary benefit of Stern. The court held that in the absence of privity or a relationship "so close as to approach that of privity," a party could not recover from an accountant.[6]

The court's requirement of privity has since been referred to as the *Ultramares* rule, or the New York rule. It continues to be used in some states.

CASE IN POINT Toro Company supplied equipment and credit to Summit Power Equipment Distributors and required Summit to submit audited reports indicating its financial condition. Accountants at Krouse, Kern & Company prepared the reports, which allegedly contained mistakes and omissions regarding Summit's financial condition. Toro extended large amounts of credit to Summit in reliance on the audited reports. When Summit was unable to repay

---

5. Banks, creditors, stockholders, purchasers, and sellers often rely on balance sheets when making decisions related to a company's business.

6. *Ultramares Corp. v. Touche,* 255 N.Y. 170, 174 N.E. 441 (1931).

these amounts, Toro brought a negligence action against Krouse and proved that the accountants knew the reports would be used by Summit to induce Toro to extend credit. Nevertheless, under the *Ultramares* rule, the court refused to hold the accounting firm liable because the firm was not in privity with Toro.[7]

MODIFICATION TO ALLOW "NEAR PRIVITY" The *Ultramares* rule was restated and somewhat modified in a 1985 New York case, *Credit Alliance Corp. v. Arthur Andersen & Co.*[8] In that case, the court held that if a third party has a sufficiently close relationship or *nexus* (link or connection) with an accountant, then the *Ultramares* privity requirement may be satisfied without the establishment of an accountant-client relationship. The rule enunciated in the *Credit Alliance* case is often referred to as the "near privity" rule. Only a minority of states have adopted this rule of accountants' liability to third parties.

The *Restatement* Rule

The *Ultramares* rule has been severely criticized because much of the work performed by auditors is intended for use by persons who are not parties to the contract. Thus, many assert that the auditors owe a duty to these third parties. Consequently, there has been an erosion of the *Ultramares* rule, and accountants have increasingly been exposed to potential liability to third parties. The majority of courts have adopted the position taken by the *Restatement (Second) of Torts*. Under the *Restatement*, accountants are subject to liability for negligence not only to their clients but also to foreseen, or known,

users—and users within a foreseen class of users—of their reports or financial statements.

Under Section 552(2) of the *Restatement (Second) of Torts*, an accountant's liability extends to:

1. Persons for whose benefit and guidance the accountant intends to supply the information or knows that the recipient intends to supply it, and
2. Persons whom the accountant intends the information to influence or knows that the recipient so intends.

For example, Steve, an accountant, prepares a financial statement for Tech Software, Inc., a client, knowing that the client will submit that statement to First National Bank to secure a loan. If Steve makes negligent misstatements or omissions in the statement, the bank may hold Steve liable because he knew that the bank would rely on his work product when deciding whether to make the loan.

Liability of Attorneys to Third Parties

Like accountants, attorneys may be held liable under the common law to third parties who rely on legal opinions to their detriment. Generally, an attorney is not liable to a nonclient unless the attorney has committed fraud (or malicious conduct). The liability principles stated in Section 552 of the *Restatement (Second) of Torts,* however, may apply to attorneys as well as to accountants.[9]

Should an attorney's duty of care extend to third party beneficiaries whose rights were harmed by the attorney's malpractice? That question was at issue in the following case.

---

7. *Toro Co. v. Krouse, Kern & Co.,* 827 F.2d 155 (7th Cir. 1987).
8. 65 N.Y.2d 536, 483 N.E.2d 110 (1985). A "relationship sufficiently intimate to be equated with privity" is enough for a third party to sue another's accountant for negligence.

9. See, for example, *North Fork Bank v. Cohen & Krassner,* 843 N.Y.S.2d 575, 44 A.D.3d 375 (N.Y.A.D. 1 Dept. 2007); and *Kastner v. Jenkins & Gilchrist, P.C.,* 231 S.W.3d 571 (Tex.App.—Dallas 2007).

✷ EXTENDED CASE 48.2 ✷
Perez[a] v. Stern

Nebraska Supreme Court, 279 Neb. 187, 777 N.W.2d 545 (2010).

IN THE LANGUAGE OF THE COURT
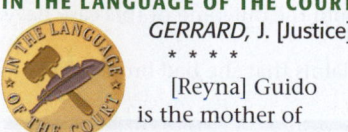
GERRARD, J. [Justice]
* * * *
[Reyna] Guido is the mother of

two minor children. [Domingo] Martinez, the children's father, died after he was run over by a car on July 8, 2001. Martinez was the victim of a hit-and-run accident.

Guido, as personal representative of Martinez's estate, retained [Sandra] Stern to file a wrongful death lawsuit. On July 8, 2003, Stern

EXTENDED CASE CONTINUES ➡

---

a. Esteban Perez was one of the minor children of Domingo Martinez, the man killed in the accident.

EXTENDED CASE 48.2 CONTINUED ◆

filed a wrongful death complaint in the district court. But Stern admits that she never perfected service of the complaint, and because the complaint was not served within six months of filing, the case was dismissed by operation of law.

* * * On February 6, 2007, Guido filed these legal malpractice claims against Stern on behalf of herself, the children, and the estate. Guido alleged that the wrongful death claim expired as a result of Stern's failure to timely perfect service of the complaint. Stern moved for summary judgment on the ground that the malpractice claims were barred by the two-year statute of limitations for professional negligence. Before the court ruled on the motion, Guido voluntarily dismissed her individual claim, but maintained claims as personal representative of the estate and next friend of the children.

The district court found that the malpractice claims accrued on May 7, 2004, when the wrongful death claim was dismissed. The court found that the estate's claim against Stern was time barred. In response to Guido's argument that the children's minority tolled [suspended] the statute of limitations with respect to them, the court found that because the children could not have brought the underlying wrongful death claim in their own names, the statute of limitations for the legal malpractice claims was not tolled by reason of the children's minority. The court granted summary judgment in favor of Stern and dismissed the complaint.

* * * *

Guido [appealed, claiming] that the district court erred in granting Stern's motion for summary judgment on her affirmative defense of the statute of limitations and, specifically, determining that the children had no independent standing to sue Stern and that Stern owed no independent duty to the minor children to protect their rights and interests.

We note that neither Guido's assignments of error nor the argument in her appellate brief challenges the district court's dismissal of Guido's claims as an individual and as personal representative of Martinez's estate. Therefore, those aspects of the court's judgment will be affirmed.

* * * *

The issue in this case is whether Stern owed an independent duty to the children, as Martinez's next of kin, to timely prosecute the underlying wrongful death claim.

* * * *

In Nebraska, *a lawyer owes a duty to his or her client to use reasonable care and skill in the discharge of his or her duties, but ordinarily this duty does not extend to third parties, absent facts establishing a duty to them.* [Emphasis added.]

But that does not end our analysis. * * * We have never said that privity [of contract] is an absolute requirement of a legal malpractice claim. Instead, we have said that a lawyer's duty to use reasonable care and skill in the discharge of his or her duties *ordinarily* does not extend to third parties, *absent facts establishing a duty to them.* On

the facts of this case, we conclude, as have other courts to have addressed this issue in the context of a wrongful death action, that the facts establish an independent legal duty from Stern to Martinez's statutory beneficiaries. [Emphasis in the original]

* * * Courts have repeatedly emphasized that *the starting point for analyzing an attorney's duty to a third party is determining whether the third party was a direct and intended beneficiary of the attorney's services.* [Emphasis added.]

* * * *

In this case, we conclude that Stern owed a duty to the children, as direct and intended beneficiaries of her services, to competently represent their interests. To hold otherwise would deny legal recourse to the children for whose benefit Stern was hired in the first place.

* * * Stern owed a legal duty to Martinez's minor children to exercise reasonable care in representing their interests. Therefore, they have standing to sue Stern for neglecting that duty, and their claims against Stern were tolled by their minority. The district court erred in concluding that their claims were time barred. We affirm the court's dismissal of Guido's individual claim and its determination that the estate's claim against Stern was time barred. But with respect to the children, this cause is reversed and remanded for further proceedings to fully adjudicate Guido's claims on behalf of the children * * *.

Affirmed in part, and in part reversed and remanded for further proceedings.

 QUESTIONS

1. If the children had suffered no harm as a result of the attorney's malpractice, would the outcome of this case have been different? Why or why not?
2. Why did the court affirm the dismissal of Guido's individual claim but not the claims that she had brought on behalf of the children?

CONCEPT SUMMARY 48.1

Common Law Liability of Accountants and Other Professionals

Concept	Nature of Liability
Liability to Clients	1. *Breach of contract*—An accountant or other professional who fails to perform according to his or her contractual obligations can be held liable for breach of contract and resulting damages. 2. *Negligence*—An accountant or other professional, in performance of her or his duties, must use the care, knowledge, and judgment generally used by professionals in the same or similar circumstances. Failure to do so is negligence. An accountant's violation of generally accepted accounting principles and generally accepted auditing standards is *prima facie* evidence of negligence. 3. *Fraud*—Intentionally misrepresenting a material fact to a client, when the client relies on the misrepresentation, is actual fraud. Gross negligence in performance of duties is constructive fraud.
Liability to Third Parties	An accountant may be liable for negligence to any third person the accountant knows or should have known will benefit from the accountant's work. The standard for imposing this liability varies, but generally courts follow one of the following rules: 1. The *Ultramares rule*—An accountant owes a duty of care to those persons for whose primary benefit the accountant's statements were intended. Liability will be imposed only if the accountant is in privity, or near privity, with the third party. 2. The *Restatement rule*—Extends liability to third parties whose reliance is foreseen or known and to third parties in a class of foreseen or known users. This includes persons for whose benefit and guidance the accountant intends to supply the information, and persons whom the accountant intends the information to influence. The majority of courts have adopted this rule. 3. *Liability of attorneys*—An attorney generally is not liable to a nonclient unless the attorney committed fraud or other malicious conduct. Although in some situations, an attorney may be liable to persons whose reliance is foreseen or known.

Concept Summary 48.1 above reviews the common law rules under which accountants, attorneys, and other professionals may be held liable.

SECTION 3

THE SARBANES-OXLEY ACT OF 2002

As previously mentioned, in 2002 Congress enacted the Sarbanes-Oxley Act. The act imposes a number of strict requirements on both domestic and foreign public accounting firms that provide auditing services to companies ("issuers") whose securities are sold to public investors. The act defines the term *issuer* as a company that has securities that are registered under Section 12 of the Securities Exchange Act of 1934, that is required to file reports under Section 15(d) of the 1934 act, or that has filed a registration

statement that has not yet become effective under the Securities Act of 1933.

The Public Company Accounting Oversight Board

Among other things, the Sarbanes-Oxley Act calls for an increased degree of government oversight of public accounting practices. To this end, the act created the Public Company Accounting Oversight Board, which reports to the Securities and Exchange Commission. The board consists of a chair and four other members. The purpose of the board is to oversee the audit of public companies that are subject to securities laws in order to protect public investors and to ensure that public accounting firms comply with the provisions of the Sarbanes-Oxley Act. The oversight board is uniquely situated in the federal government and has significant power to govern the accounting industry, which is why it was recently challenged as being unconstitutional. See this chapter's *Shifting Legal Priorities for Business* feature on the facing page for a complete discussion of this issue.

Applicability to Public Accounting Firms

Titles I and II of the act set forth the key provisions relating to the duties of the oversight board and the requirements relating to *public accounting firms*—defined by the act as firms and associated persons that are "engaged in the practice of public accounting or preparing or issuing audit reports."[10] These provisions are summarized in Exhibit 48–1 on page 944. (Provisions of the act that are more directly concerned with corporate fraud and the responsibilities of corporate officers and directors were listed and described in Exhibit 42–4 on page 832.)

Requirements for Maintaining Working Papers

While performing an audit for a client, an accountant accumulates **working papers**—the various documents used and developed during the audit. These include notes, computations, memoranda, copies, and other papers that make up the work product of an accountant's services to a client. Under the common law and the statutory law in a number of states, working papers remain the accountant's property. It is important for accountants to retain such records in the event that they need to defend against lawsuits for negligence or other actions in which their competence is challenged. The client also has a right to access an accountant's working papers because they reflect the client's financial situation. On a client's request, an accountant must return to the client any of the client's records or journals, and failure to do so may result in liability.

Section 802(a)(1) of the Sarbanes-Oxley Act provides that accountants must maintain working papers relating to an audit or review for seven years from the end of the fiscal period in which the audit or review was concluded. An accountant who knowingly violates this requirement may be fined, imprisoned for up to ten years, or both.

10. Recall from Chapter 42 that as of 2010, smaller companies with a public float of less than $75 million no longer need to file an auditor's report on management's assessment of internal controls under Section 404(b).

━━━━━ **SECTION 4** ━━━━━
POTENTIAL LIABILITY OF ACCOUNTANTS UNDER SECURITIES LAWS

Both civil and criminal liability may be imposed on accountants under the Securities Act of 1933, the Securities Exchange Act of 1934, and the Private Securities Litigation Reform Act of 1995.[11]

Liability under the Securities Act of 1933

The Securities Act of 1933 requires registration statements to be filed with the Securities and Exchange Commission (SEC) prior to an offering of securities (see Chapter 42).[12] Accountants frequently prepare and certify the issuer's financial statements that are included in the registration statement.

LIABILITY UNDER SECTION 11 Section 11 of the Securities Act of 1933 imposes civil liability on accountants for misstatements and omissions of material facts in registration statements. An accountant may be held liable if he or she prepared any financial statements included in the registration statement that "contained an untrue statement of a material fact or omitted to state a material fact required to be stated therein or necessary to make the statements therein not misleading."[13]

An accountant may be liable to anyone who acquires a security covered by the registration statement. A purchaser of a security need only demonstrate that she or he has suffered a loss on the security. Proof of reliance on the materially false statement or misleading omission ordinarily is not required, nor is there a requirement of privity between the accountant and the security purchaser.

The Due Diligence Standard. Section 11 imposes a duty on accountants to use **due diligence** in preparing financial statements included in the filed registration statements. After the purchaser has proved a loss on the security, the accountant has the burden of showing that he or she exercised due diligence

11. Civil and criminal liability may also be imposed on accountants and other professionals under other statutes, including the Racketeer Influenced and Corrupt Organizations Act (RICO). RICO was discussed in Chapter 9.
12. Many securities and transactions are expressly exempted from the 1933 act.
13. 15 U.S.C. Section 77k(a).

The Sarbanes-Oxley Act of 2002 created the Public Company Accounting Oversight Board (PCAOB) to set and police auditing standards for publicly held companies. The board, which conducts investigations of accounting firms and interprets the Sarbanes-Oxley Act, has a chair and four members. The chair is paid $654,000 per year, and the other members each make $532,000 per year—salaries that greatly exceed federal government pay scales. The salaries can be so high because the PCAOB was established as an independent nonprofit organization that is shielded from political influence.

Focusing on the Small Stuff Can Be Costly

One of the major functions of the PCAOB is to interpret and enforce Section 404 of the Sarbanes-Oxley Act, which requires companies to maintain internal controls aimed at preventing fraud. The PCAOB has interpreted its mandate to mean that it should review the minute details of a company's internal procedures. In one instance, the PCAOB investigated to determine which workers at a publicly held company were allowed to have office keys. On other occasions, it has told companies how often they should change computer access codes.

Of course, meeting the PCAOB's detailed demands for internal procedures can be costly. A study conducted by the Brookings Institute and the American Enterprise Institute found that the Sarbanes-Oxley Act has cost the U.S. economy more than $1 trillion in direct and indirect costs since 2002.

Some people also wonder whether all of the cost is justified. After all, even though Sarbanes-Oxley was enacted to prevent fraud, neither the act nor the PCAOB stopped the collapse of Refco, a major commodities firm, because of obvious accounting fraud. And the PCAOB completely missed the subprime mortgage disaster in 2007–2009, even though some of the firms that it investigates played major roles in the financial meltdown.

An Accountant Claims That the Act Is Unconstitutional

Recently, the PCAOB demanded a costly set of changes in the way the small auditing firm Beckstead and Watts, LLP, operated. Brad Beckstead, the accountant who had created the firm in Henderson, Nevada, decided to sue the PCAOB. His suit did not claim that the board had behaved improperly. Instead, he attacked the constitutionality of the way the PCAOB was formed, claiming that only the president has the power to oversee such an executive-level body.

The U.S. Constitution requires that the president appoint the heads of major federal agencies. The Sarbanes-Oxley Act, however, allows the Securities and Exchange Commission (SEC) to appoint the five members of the PCAOB. Hence, the board members are beyond presidential control and cannot be removed without good cause. The Constitution requires the president to "take care that the Laws be faithfully executed," but if the president cannot remove the members of the PCAOB, how can he or she ensure that the laws are "faithfully executed"?

The U.S. Court of Appeals for the District of Columbia Circuit upheld the PCAOB.[a] In 2009, the United States Supreme Court granted *certiorari*.

The Supreme Court Weighs In

In a five-to-four decision issued in 2010, the Supreme Court ruled that it was unconstitutional for the president to be unable to fire the members of the PCAOB. The Court nevertheless held that the board had been legally established and appointed, thereby leaving the Sarbanes-Oxley Act otherwise intact. The Court's focus seems to have been more on the proper limitations of executive power than on the deficiencies of the act.

The only portion of the act that the Court struck down was the "dual for-cause limitations" on the removal of board members. The Court stated that "the Act not only protects Board members from removal except for good cause, but withdraws from the President any decision on whether that good cause exists." The Court thought that this double layer of protection from presidential authority violated the Constitution. According to the Court, "the Constitution that makes the President accountable to the people for executing the laws also gives him the power to do so, and that power includes, as a general matter, the authority to remove those who assist him in carrying out his duties."[b] Essentially, the end result is that the Sarbanes-Oxley Act remains valid law, but the SEC can now remove board members at will (without having to show good cause).

MANAGERIAL IMPLICATIONS

The Supreme Court's decision in the *Free Enterprise* case did not have the monumental impact on the Sarbanes-Oxley Act that many businesspersons and accountants had hoped. Although PCAOB members will have a little less job security in the future, the board will function (and be compensated) as it has in the past. The costs of complying with the Sarbanes-Oxley Act remain unchanged. On the bright side, if the Court had invalidated the act completely so that Congress had to create new regulations governing accountants, firms would also have incurred significant costs to understand and comply with the new regulations.

---

a. *Free Enterprise Fund and Beckstead and Watts, LLP v. Public Company Accounting Oversight Board*, 537 F.3d 667 (2008).
b. *Free Enterprise Fund v. Public Company Accounting Oversight Board*, __ U.S. ___, 130 S.Ct. 3138, 177 L.Ed.2d 706 (2010).

EXHIBIT 48-1 • **Key Provisions of the Sarbanes-Oxley Act of 2002 Relating to Public Accounting Firms**

AUDITOR INDEPENDENCE

To help ensure that auditors remain independent of the firms that they audit, Title II of the Sarbanes-Oxley Act does the following:

- Makes it unlawful for Registered Public Accounting Firms (RPAFs) to perform both audit and nonaudit services for the same company at the same time. Nonaudit services include the following:
  1. Bookkeeping or other services related to the accounting records or financial statements of the audit client.
  2. Financial information systems design and implementation.
  3. Appraisal or valuation services.
  4. Fairness opinions.
  5. Management functions.
  6. Broker or dealer, investment adviser, or investment banking services.
- Requires preapproval for most auditing services from the issuer's (the corporation's) audit committee.
- Requires audit partner rotation by prohibiting RPAFs from providing audit services to an issuer if either the lead audit partner or the audit partner responsible for reviewing the audit has provided such services to that corporation in each of the prior five years.
- Requires RPAFs to make timely reports to the audit committees of the corporations. The report must indicate all critical accounting policies and practices to be used; all alternative treatments of financial information within generally accepted accounting principles that have been discussed with the corporation's management officials, the ramifications of the use of such alternative treatments, and the treatment preferred by the auditor; and other material written communications between the auditor and the corporation's management.
- Makes it unlawful for an RPAF to provide auditing services to an issuer if the corporation's chief executive officer, chief financial officer, chief accounting officer, or controller was previously employed by the auditor and participated in any capacity in the audit of the corporation during the one-year period preceding the date that the audit began.

DOCUMENT RETENTION AND DESTRUCTION

- The Sarbanes-Oxley Act provides that anyone who destroys, alters, or falsifies records with the intent to obstruct or influence a federal investigation or in relation to bankruptcy proceedings can be criminally prosecuted and sentenced to a fine, imprisonment for up to twenty years, or both.
- The act also requires accountants who audit or review publicly traded companies to retain all working papers related to the audit or review for a period of five years (now amended to seven years). Violators can be sentenced to a fine, imprisonment for up to ten years, or both.

---

in preparing the financial statements. To prove due diligence, an accountant must demonstrate that she or he did not commit negligence or fraud. To avoid liability, the accountant must show that he or she had, "after reasonable investigation, reasonable grounds to believe and did believe, at the time such part of the registration statement became effective, that the statements therein were true and that there was no omission of a material fact required to be stated therein or necessary to make the statements therein not misleading."[14] Failure to follow GAAP and GAAS (and presumably the IFRS, when they are required) is proof of a lack of due diligence.

In particular, the due diligence standard places a burden on accountants to verify information furnished by a corporation's officers and directors. Merely asking questions is not always sufficient to satisfy the requirement of due diligence. Accountants may be held liable, for example, for failing to detect danger signals in materials that, under GAAS, required further investigation under the circumstances, especially when the documents were furnished by corporate officers.[15]

Defenses to Liability. Besides proving that he or she has acted with due diligence, an accountant may raise the following defenses to Section 11 liability:

1. There were no misstatements or omissions.
2. The misstatements or omissions were not of material facts.
3. The misstatements or omissions had no causal connection to the plaintiff's loss.
4. The plaintiff-purchaser invested in the securities knowing of the misstatements or omissions.

---

14. 15 U.S.C. Section 77k(b)(3).

15. See, for example, *Escott v. BarChris Construction Corp.*, 283 F.Supp. 643 (S.D.N.Y. 1968); *In re Cardinal Health, Inc. Securities Litigation*, 426 F.Supp.2d 688 (S.D. Ohio 2006); and *In re WorldCom, Inc. Securities Litigation*, 352 F.Supp.2d 472 (S.D.N.Y. 2005).

LIABILITY UNDER SECTION 12(2) Section 12(2) of the Securities Act of 1933 imposes civil liability for fraud in relation to offerings or sales of securities.[16] Liability is based on communication to an investor, whether orally or in the written prospectus,[17] of an untrue statement or omission of a material fact.

Those who purchase securities and suffer harm as a result of a false or omitted statement, or some other violation, may bring a suit in a federal court to recover their losses and other damages. The U.S. Department of Justice brings criminal actions against those who commit willful violations. The penalties include fines up to $10,000, imprisonment up to five years, or both. The SEC is authorized to seek an injunction against a willful violator to prevent further violations. The SEC can also ask a court to grant other relief, such as an order to a violator to refund profits derived from an illegal transaction.

Liability under the Securities Exchange Act of 1934

Under Sections 18 and 10(b) of the Securities Exchange Act of 1934 and SEC Rule 10b-5, an accountant may be found liable for fraud. A plaintiff has a substantially heavier burden of proof under the 1934 act than under the 1933 act because under the 1934 act, an accountant does not have to prove due diligence to escape liability. The 1934 act relieves an accountant from liability if the accountant acted in "good faith."

LIABILITY UNDER SECTION 18 Section 18 of the 1934 act imposes civil liability on an accountant who makes or causes to be made in any application, report, or document a statement that at the time and in light of the circumstances was false or misleading with respect to any material fact.[18] Section 18 liability is narrow in that it applies only to applications, reports, documents, and registration statements filed with the SEC. In addition, it applies only to sellers and purchasers. Under Section 18, a seller or purchaser must prove one of the following:

1. The false or misleading statement affected the price of the security.
2. The purchaser or seller relied on the false or misleading statement in making the purchase or sale and was not aware of the inaccuracy of the statement.

An accountant will not be liable for violating Section 18 if he or she acted in good faith in preparing the financial statement. To demonstrate good faith, an accountant must show that he or she had no knowledge that the financial statement was false or misleading and that he or she lacked any intent to deceive, manipulate, defraud, or seek unfair advantage over another party. (Note that "mere" negligence in preparing a financial statement does not lead to liability under the 1934 act. This differs from the 1933 act, under which an accountant is liable for all negligent acts.)

In addition to the good faith defense, accountants can escape liability by proving that the buyer or seller of the security in question knew the financial statement was false and misleading. Sellers and purchasers must bring a cause of action "within one year after the discovery of the facts constituting the cause of action and within three years after such cause of action accrued."[19] A court also has the discretion to assess reasonable costs, including attorneys' fees, against accountants who violate this section.

LIABILITY UNDER SECTION 10(b) AND SEC RULE 10b-5 Accountants additionally face potential legal liability under the antifraud provisions contained in the Securities Exchange Act of 1934 and SEC Rule 10b-5. The scope of these antifraud provisions is very broad and allows private parties to bring civil actions against violators.

Section 10(b) makes it unlawful for any person, including an accountant, to use, in connection with the purchase or sale of any security, any manipulative or deceptive device or plan that is counter to SEC rules and regulations.[20] Rule 10b-5 further makes it unlawful for any person, by use of any means or instrumentality of interstate commerce, to do the following:

1. Employ any device, scheme, or strategy to defraud.
2. Make any untrue statement of a material fact or omit to state a material fact necessary to make the statements made, in light of the circumstances, not misleading.
3. Engage in any act, practice, or course of business that operates or would operate as a fraud or deceit on any person, in connection with the purchase or sale of any security.[21]

---

16. 15 U.S.C. Section 77*l*.
17. As discussed in Chapter 39, a *prospectus* contains financial disclosures about the corporation for the benefit of potential investors.
18. 15 U.S.C. Section 78r(a).

19. 15 U.S.C. Section 17r(c).
20. 15 U.S.C. Section 78j(b).
21. 17 C.F.R. Section 240.10b-5.

The Scope of Accountants' Liability. Accountants may be held liable only to sellers or purchasers of securities under Section 10(b) and Rule 10b-5. Privity is not necessary for a recovery. An accountant may be liable not only for fraudulent misstatements of material facts in written material filed with the SEC, but also for any fraudulent oral statements or omissions made in connection with the purchase or sale of any security.

Requirements for Recovering Damages. For a plaintiff to succeed in recovering damages under these antifraud provisions, he or she must prove intent (*scienter*) to commit the fraudulent or deceptive act. Ordinary negligence is not enough.

Under Section 10(b) and Rule 10b-5, do accountants have a duty to correct misstatements that they discover in *previous* financial statements if they know that potential investors are relying on those statements? That was the question in the following case.

CASE 48.3

Overton v. Todman & Co., CPAs, P.C.

United States Court of Appeals, Second Circuit, 478 F.3d 479 (2007).

BACKGROUND AND FACTS • From 1999 through 2002, Todman & Company, CPAs, P.C., audited the financial statements of Direct Brokerage, Inc. (DBI), a broker-dealer in New York registered with the Securities and Exchange Commission (SEC). Each year, Todman issued an unqualified opinion that DBI's financial statements were accurate. DBI filed its statements and Todman's opinions with the SEC. Despite the certifications of accuracy, Todman made significant errors that concealed DBI's largest liability—its payroll taxes—in the 1999 and 2000 audits. The errors came to light in 2003 when the New York State Division of Taxation subpoenaed DBI's payroll records, and it became clear that the company had not filed or paid its payroll taxes for 1999 and 2000. This put DBI in a precarious financial position, owing the state more than $3 million in unpaid taxes, interest, and penalties. To meet its needs, DBI sought outside investors, including David Overton, who relied on DBI's statements and Todman's opinion for 2002 to invest in DBI. When DBI collapsed under the weight of its liabilities in 2004, Overton and others filed a suit in a federal district court against Todman, asserting, among other things, fraud under Section 10(b) and Rule 10b-5. The court dismissed the complaint. The plaintiffs appealed to the U.S. Court of Appeals for the Second Circuit.

IN THE LANGUAGE OF THE COURT
STRAUB, Circuit Judge.
* * * *

A fundamental principle of securities law is that before an individual becomes liable for his silence, he must have an underlying duty to speak.

* * * *

* * * The Supreme Court [has] held that [Section] 10(b) does not authorize aiding and abetting liability. In order to be liable under [Section] 10(b), the Court held, an actor must himself "mak[e] . . . a material misstatement (or omission) or . . . commit . . . a manipulative act." The rationale underpinning this holding was that (1) by its terms, [Section] 10(b) requires the making of a statement or omission and (2) without such a statement or omission, the "critical" element of reliance would be absent.

Although the Court did not specifically discuss an auditor's duty to correct, it made clear that * * * secondary actors such as accountants may incur primary liability based on their omissions * * * .

* * * For many years we have recognized the existence of an accountant's duty to correct its certified opinions, but never squarely held that such a duty exists for the purposes of primary liability under [Section] 10(b) of the 1934 Act and Rule 10b-5. Presented with an opportunity to do so, we now so hold. Specifically, we hold that an accountant violates the "duty to correct" and becomes primarily liable under [Section] 10(b) and Rule 10b-5 when it (1) makes a statement in its certified opinion that is false or misleading when made; (2) subsequently learns or was reckless in not learning that the earlier statement was false or misleading; (3) knows or should know that potential investors are relying on the opinion and financial statements; yet (4) fails to take reasonable steps to correct or withdraw its opinion and/or the financial statements; and (5) all the other requirements for liability are satisfied.

CASE 48.3 CONTINUED ➧ ✶ ✶ ✶ ✶

In light of the above principles, we conclude that the District Court erred in dismissing the complaint. Plaintiffs pled that Todman's certified opinion and DBI's 2002 financial statements were misleading at the time they were issued, especially with respect to DBI's payroll tax liability; Todman ✶ ✶ ✶ subsequently learned that its certified opinion was false; Todman also knew that DBI was soliciting outside investors based in part on its 2002 certified financial statements and Todman's accompanying opinion; and that despite this knowledge, Todman took no action to correct or withdraw its opinion and/or DBI's financial statements. These allegations adequately state a claim of primary accountant liability under [Section] 10(b) and Rule 10b-5.

DECISION AND REMEDY • *The U.S. Court of Appeals for the Second Circuit held that an accountant is liable in these circumstances under Section 10(b) and Rule 10b-5. The court vacated the lower court's dismissal and remanded the case.*

WHAT IF THE FACTS WERE DIFFERENT? • *If Todman had conducted an audit for DBI but had not issued a certified opinion about DBI's financial statements, would the result in this case have been the same? Explain.*

THE LEGAL ENVIRONMENT DIMENSION • *Did Overton have a valid reason to sue DBI's auditors? Why or why not?*

The Private Securities Litigation Reform Act of 1995

The Private Securities Litigation Reform Act of 1995 made some changes to the potential liability of accountants and other professionals in securities fraud cases. Among other things, the act imposed a statutory obligation on accountants. An auditor must use adequate procedures in an audit to detect any illegal acts of the company being audited. If something illegal is detected, the auditor must disclose it to the company's board of directors, the audit committee, or the SEC, depending on the circumstances.[22]

PROPORTIONATE LIABILITY The 1995 act provides that, in most situations, a party is liable only for the proportion of damages for which he or she is responsible.[23] In other words, the parties are subject to proportionate liability rather than joint and several liability. Only if an accountant knowingly participated in defrauding investors will he or she be liable for the entire amount of the loss. Suppose that accountant Nina Chavez assisted the president and owner of Midstate Trucking Company in drafting financial statements that misrepresented Midstate's financial condition. If Nina did not knowingly participate in the fraud, she will be liable only for the proportion of damages for which she was responsible.

AIDING AND ABETTING The 1995 act also provides that aiding and abetting a violation of the Securities Exchange Act of 1934 is a violation in itself. Accountants aid and abet when they are generally aware that they are participating in an activity that is improper and knowingly assist the activity. Silence may constitute aiding.

If an accountant knowingly aids and abets a primary violator, the SEC can seek an injunction or monetary damages. For example, Smith & Jones, an accounting firm, performs an audit for Belco Sales Company that is so inadequate as to constitute gross negligence. Belco uses the financial statements provided by Smith & Jones as part of a scheme to defraud investors. When the scheme is uncovered, the SEC can bring an action against Smith & Jones for aiding and abetting on the ground that the firm knew or should have known that its audited statements contained material misrepresentations on which investors were likely to rely.

SECTION 5
POTENTIAL CRIMINAL LIABILITY OF ACCOUNTANTS

An accountant may be found criminally liable for violations of the Securities Act of 1933, the Securities Exchange Act of 1934, and the Internal Revenue Code. In addition, in most states, criminal penalties may be imposed for such actions as knowingly certifying false or fraudulent reports; falsifying, altering, or destroying books of account; and obtaining property or credit through the use of false financial statements.

---

22. 15 U.S.C. Section 78j-1.
23. 15 U.S.C. Section 78u-4(g).

Criminal Violations of Securities Laws

Under both the 1933 act and the 1934 act, accountants may be subject to criminal penalties for *willful* violations—imprisonment for up to five years and/or a fine of up to $10,000 under the 1933 act and up to ten years and $100,000 under the 1934 act. Under the Sarbanes-Oxley Act of 2002, for a securities filing that is accompanied by an accountant's false or misleading certified audit statement, the accountant may be fined up to $5 million, imprisoned for up to twenty years, or both.

Criminal Violations of Tax Laws

The Internal Revenue Code makes aiding or assisting in the preparation of a false tax return a felony punishable by a fine of $100,000 ($500,000 for a corporation's return) and imprisonment for up to three years.[24] This provision applies to anyone who prepares tax returns for others for compensation, not just

to accountants.[25] A penalty of $250 per tax return is levied on tax preparers for negligent understatement of the client's tax liability. For willful understatement of tax liability or reckless or intentional disregard of rules or regulations, a penalty of $1,000 is imposed.[26]

A tax preparer may also be subject to penalties for failing to furnish the taxpayer with a copy of the return, failing to sign the return, or failing to furnish the appropriate tax identification numbers.[27] In addition, those who prepare tax returns for others may be fined $1,000 per document for aiding and abetting another's understatement of tax liability (the penalty is increased to $10,000 for corporate returns).[28] The tax preparer's liability is limited to one penalty per taxpayer per tax year.

Concept Summary 48.2 below outlines the potential statutory liability of accountants and other professionals.

---

24. 26 U.S.C. Section 7206(2).

25. 26 U.S.C. Section 7701(a)(36).
26. 26 U.S.C. Section 6694.
27. 26 U.S.C. Section 6695.
28. 26 U.S.C. Section 6701.

CONCEPT SUMMARY 48.2
Statutory Liability of Accountants and Other Professionals

Statute	Nature of Liability
Sarbanes-Oxley Act of 2002	See Exhibit 48–1 on page 944 for the provisions of the act on auditor independence and document retention.
Securities Act of 1933, Sections 11 and 12(2)	Under Section 11 of the 1933 Securities Act, an accountant who makes a false statement or omits a material fact in audited financial statements required for registration of securities under the law may be liable to anyone who acquires securities covered by the registration statement. The accountant's defense is basically the use of due diligence and the reasonable belief that the work was complete and correct. The burden of proof is on the accountant. Willful violations of this act may be subject to criminal penalties. Section 12(2) of the 1933 act imposes civil liability for fraud on anyone who makes an untrue statement or omits a material fact when offering or selling a security to any purchaser of the security.
Securities Exchange Act of 1934, Sections 10(b) and 18	Under Sections 10(b) and 18 of the 1934 Securities Exchange Act, accountants are held liable for false and misleading applications, reports, and documents required under the act. The burden is on the plaintiff, and the accountant has numerous defenses, including good faith and lack of knowledge that what was submitted was false. Willful violations of this act may be subject to criminal penalties.
Internal Revenue Code	1. Aiding or assisting in the preparation of a false tax return is a felony. Aiding and abetting an individual's understatement of tax liability is a separate crime. 2. Tax preparers who negligently or willfully understate a client's tax liability or who recklessly or intentionally disregard Internal Revenue Code rules or regulations are subject to penalties. 3. Tax preparers who fail to provide a taxpayer with a copy of the return, fail to sign the return, or fail to furnish the appropriate tax identification numbers may also be subject to penalties.

CONFIDENTIALITY AND PRIVILEGE

Professionals are restrained by the ethical tenets of their professions to keep all communications with their clients confidential.

Attorney-Client Relationships

The confidentiality of attorney-client communications is protected by law, which confers a *privilege* on such communications. This privilege exists because of the need for full disclosure to the attorney of the facts of a client's case.

To encourage frankness, confidential attorney-client communications relating to representation are normally held in strictest confidence and protected by law. The attorney and her or his employees may not discuss the client's case with anyone—even under court order—without the client's permission. The client holds the privilege, and only the client may waive it—by disclosing privileged information to someone outside the privilege, for example.

Note, however, that since the Sarbanes-Oxley Act was enacted in 2002, the SEC has implemented new rules requiring attorneys who become aware that a client has violated securities laws to report the violation to the SEC. Reporting a client's misconduct could be a breach of the attorney-client privilege, however, so the new rules have created a potential conflict for some attorneys.

Accountant-Client Relationship

In a few states, accountant-client communications are privileged by state statute. In these states, accountant-client communications may not be revealed even in court or in court-sanctioned proceedings without the client's permission. The majority of states, however, abide by the common law, which provides that, if a court so orders, an accountant must disclose information about his or her client to the court. Physicians and other professionals may similarly be compelled to disclose in court information given to them in confidence by patients or clients.

Communications between professionals and their clients—other than those between an attorney and her or his client—are not privileged under federal law. In cases involving federal law, state-provided rights to confidentiality of accountant-client communications are not recognized. Thus, in those cases, in response to a court order, an accountant must provide the information sought.

REVIEWING
Professional Liability and Accountability

Superior Wholesale Corporation planned to purchase Regal Furniture, Inc., and wished to determine Regal's net worth. Superior hired Lynette Shuebke, of the accounting firm Shuebke Delgado, to review an audit that had been prepared by Norman Chase, the accountant for Regal. Shuebke advised Superior that Chase had performed a high-quality audit and that Regal's inventory on the audit dates was stated accurately on the general ledger. As a result of these representations, Superior went forward with its purchase of Regal. After the purchase, Superior discovered that the audit by Chase had been materially inaccurate and misleading, primarily because the inventory had been grossly overstated on the balance sheet. Later, a former Regal employee who had begun working for Superior exposed an e-mail exchange between Chase and former Regal chief executive officer Buddy Gantry. The exchange revealed that Chase had cooperated in overstating the inventory and understating Regal's tax liability. Using the information presented in the chapter, answer the following questions.

1. If Shuebke's review was conducted in good faith and conformed to generally accepted accounting principles, could Superior hold Shuebke Delgado liable for negligently failing to detect material omissions in Chase's audit? Why or why not?
2. According to the rule adopted by the majority of courts to determine accountants' liability to third parties, could Chase be liable to Superior? Explain.

REVIEWING CONTINUES ▶

REVIEWING

Professional Liability and Accountability, Continued

3. Generally, what requirements must be met before Superior can recover damages under Section 10(b) of the Securities Exchange Act of 1934 and SEC Rule 10b-5? Can Superior meet these requirements?
4. Suppose that a court determined that Chase had aided Regal in willfully understating its tax liability. What is the maximum penalty that could be imposed on Chase?

◉ DEBATE THIS: *Only the largest publicly held companies should be subject to the Sarbanes-Oxley Act.*

TERMS AND CONCEPTS

defalcation 934

due diligence 942

generally accepted
accounting principles
(GAAP) 934

generally accepted auditing
standards (GAAS) 934

International Financial
Reporting Standards
(IFRS) 934

working papers 942

QUESTIONS AND CASE PROBLEMS

48–1. The *Ultramares* Rule Larkin, Inc., retains Howard Patterson to manage its books and prepare its financial statements. Patterson, a certified public accountant, lives in Indiana and practices there. After twenty years, Patterson has become a bit bored with generally accepted accounting principles (GAAP) and has adopted more creative accounting methods. Now, though, Patterson has a problem, as he is being sued by Molly Tucker, one of Larkin's creditors. Tucker alleges that Patterson either knew or should have known that Larkin's financial statements would be distributed to various individuals. Furthermore, she asserts that these financial statements were negligently prepared and seriously inaccurate. What are the consequences of Patterson's failure to follow GAAP? Under the traditional *Ultramares* rule, can Tucker recover damages from Patterson? Explain.

48–2. QUESTION WITH SAMPLE ANSWER: The *Restatement* Rule.

The accounting firm of Goldman, Walters, Johnson & Co. prepared financial statements for Lucy's Fashions, Inc. After reviewing the various financial statements, Happydays State Bank agreed to loan Lucy's Fashions $35,000 for expansion. When Lucy's Fashions declared bankruptcy under Chapter 11 six months later, Happydays State Bank promptly filed an action against Goldman, Walters,

Johnson & Co., alleging negligent preparation of financial statements. Assuming that the court has abandoned the *Ultramares* approach, what is the result? What are the policy reasons for holding accountants liable to third parties with whom they are not in privity?

- For a sample answer to Question 48–2, go to Appendix I at the end of this text.

48–3. Accountant's Liability under Rule 10b-5 In early 2011, Bennett, Inc., offered a substantial number of new common shares to the public. Harvey Helms had a long-standing interest in Bennett because his grandfather had once been president of the company. On receiving a prospectus prepared and distributed by Bennett, Helms was dismayed by the pessimism it embodied. Helms decided to delay purchasing stock in the company. Later, Helms asserted that the prospectus prepared by the accountants was overly pessimistic and contained materially misleading statements. Discuss fully how successful Helms would be in bringing a cause of action under Rule 10b-5 against the accountants of Bennett, Inc.

48–4. Liability for Fraud In October 1993, Marilyn Greenen, a licensed certified public accountant (CPA), began working at the Port of Vancouver, Washington (the Port), as an account manager. She was not directly engaged in public accounting at the Port, but she oversaw the preparation of financial statements and supervised employees with accounting duties. At the start of her employment, she enrolled her husband for benefits under the Port's medical plan. Her marriage was dissolved in November, but she did not notify the Port of the change. In May 1998 and April 1999, the Port confronted her about the divorce, but she did not update her insurance information. After she was terminated, she reimbursed the Port for the additional premiums it had paid for unauthorized coverage for her former spouse. The Washington State Board of Accountancy imposed sanctions on Greenen for "dishonesty and misleading representations" while, in the words of an applicable state statute, "representing oneself as a CPA." Greenen asked a Washington state court to review the case. What might be an appropriate sanction in this case? What might be Greenen's best argument against the board's action? On what reasoning might the court uphold the decision? [*Greenen v. Washington State Board of Accountancy*, 824 Wash.App. 126, 110 P.3d 224 (2005)]

48–5. CASE PROBLEM WITH SAMPLE ANSWER: Accountant's Liability for Audit.

A West Virginia bank ran its asset value from $100 million to $1 billion over seven years by aggressively marketing subprime loans. The Office of the Comptroller of the Currency, a federal regulator, audited the bank and discovered that the books had been falsified for several years and that the bank was insolvent. The Comptroller closed the bank and brought criminal charges against its managers. The Comptroller fined Grant Thornton, the bank's accounting firm, $300,000 for recklessly failing to meet generally accepted auditing standards during the years it audited the bank. The Comptroller claimed Thornton violated federal law by "participating in . . . unsafe and unsound banking practice." Thornton appealed, contending that it was not involved in bank operations to that extent based on its audit function. What would be the key to determining if the accounting firm could be held liable for that violation of federal law? [Grant Thornton, LLP v. Office of the Comptroller of the Currency, 514 F.3d 1328 (D.C. Cir. 2008)]

- **To view a sample answer for Problem 48–5, go to this book's Web site at www.cengage.com/blaw/clarkson, select "Chapter 48," and click on "Case Problem with Sample Answer."**

48–6. Professional's Liability

Soon after Teresa DeYoung's husband died, her mother-in-law also died, leaving an inheritance of more than $400,000 for DeYoung's children. DeYoung hired John Ruggerio, an attorney, to ensure that her children would receive it. Ruggerio advised her to invest the funds in his real estate business. She declined. A few months later, $300,000 of the inheritance was sent to Ruggerio. Without telling DeYoung, he deposited the $300,000 in his account and began to use the funds in his real estate business. Nine months later, $109,000 of the inheritance was sent to Ruggerio. He paid this to DeYoung. She asked about the remaining amount. Ruggerio lied to hide his theft. Unable to access these funds, DeYoung's children changed their college

plans to attend less expensive institutions. Nearly three years later, DeYoung learned the truth. Can she bring a suit against Ruggerio? If so, on what ground? If not, why not? Did Ruggerio violate any standard of professional ethics? Discuss. [*DeYoung v. Ruggerio*, 185 Vt. 267, 971 A.2d 627 (2009)]

48–7. Professional Malpractice

Jeffery Guerrero hired James McDonald, a certified public accountant, to represent him and his business in an appeal to the Internal Revenue Service. The appeal was about audits that showed Guerrero owed more taxes. When the appeal failed, McDonald helped Guerrero prepare materials for an appeal to the Tax Court, which was also unsuccessful. Guerrero then sued McDonald for professional negligence in the preparation of his evidence for the court. Specifically, Guerrero claimed that McDonald had failed to adequately prepare witnesses and to present all the arguments that could have been made on his behalf so that he could have won the case. Guerrero contended that McDonald was liable for all of the additional taxes he was required to pay. Is Guerrero's claim likely to result in liability on McDonald's part? What factors would the court consider? [*Guerrero v. McDonald*, 302 Ga.App. 164, 690 S.E.2d 486 (2010)]

48–8. A QUESTION OF ETHICS: Liability for Negligence.

Portland Shellfish Co. processes live shellfish in Maine. As one of the firm's two owners, Frank Wetmore held 300 voting and 150 nonvoting shares of the stock. Donna Holden held the other 300 voting shares. Donna's husband Jeff managed the company's daily operations, including production, procurement, and sales. The board of directors consisted of Frank and Jeff. In 2001, disagreements arose over the company's management. The Holdens invoked the "Shareholders' Agreement," which provided that "[i]n the event of a deadlock, the directors shall hire an accountant at [Macdonald, Page, Schatz, Fletcher & Co., LLC] to determine the value of the outstanding shares. . . . [E]ach shareholder shall have the right to buy out the other shareholder(s)' interest." Macdonald Page estimated the stock's "fair market value" to be $1.09 million. Donna offered to buy Frank's shares at a price equal to his proportionate share. Frank countered by offering $1.25 million for Donna's shares. Donna rejected Frank's offer and insisted that he sell his shares to her or she would sue. In the face of this threat, Frank sold his shares to Donna for $750,705. Believing the stock to be worth more than twice Macdonald Page's estimate, Frank filed a suit in a federal district court against the accountant. [*Wetmore v. Macdonald, Page, Schatz, Fletcher & Co., LLC, 476 F.3d 1 (1st Cir. 2007)*]

(a) Frank claimed that in valuing the stock, the accountant disregarded "commonly accepted and reliable methods of valuation in favor of less reliable methods." He alleged negligence, among other things. Macdonald Page filed a motion to dismiss the complaint. What are the elements that establish negligence? Which is the most critical element in this case?

(b) Macdonald Page evaluated the company's stock by identifying its "fair market value," defined as "the price at which the property would change hands between a willing buyer and a willing seller, neither being under a compulsion to buy or sell and both having reasonable knowledge of relevant facts." The accountant knew that the shareholders would use its estimate to determine the price that one would pay to the other. Under these circumstances, was Frank's injury foreseeable?

(c) What factor might have influenced Frank to sell his shares to Donna even though he thought that Macdonald Page's "fair market value" figure was less than half of what it should have been? Does this factor represent an unfair, or unethical, advantage?

48–9. VIDEO QUESTION: Potential Liability to Third Parties.

 Go to this text's Web site at **www.cengage.com/ blaw/clarkson** and select "Chapter 48." Click on "Video Questions" and view the video titled *Accountant's Liability.* Then answer the following questions.

(a) Should Ray prepare a financial statement that values a list of assets provided by the advertising firm without verifying that the firm actually owns these assets?

(b) Discuss whether Ray is in privity with the company interested in buying Laura's advertising firm.

(c) Under the *Ultramares* rule, to whom does Ray owe a duty?

LEGAL RESEARCH EXERCISES ON THE WEB

Go to this text's Web site at **www.cengage.com/blaw/clarkson**, select "Chapter 48," and click on "Practical Internet Exercises." There you will find the following Internet research exercises that you can perform to learn more about the topics covered in this chapter.

Practical Internet Exercise 48–1: Legal Perspective
The Sarbanes-Oxley Act of 2002

Practical Internet Exercise 48–2: Management Perspective
Avoiding Legal Liability

If this text had been written a hundred years ago, it would have had little to say about federal government regulation. Today, in contrast, just about every area of economic activity is regulated by the government. Ethical issues in government regulation arise because regulation, by its very nature, means that some traditional rights and freedoms must be given up to ensure that other rights and freedoms are protected. Essentially, government regulation brings two ethical principles into conflict. On the one hand, deeply embedded in American culture is the idea that the government should play a limited role in directing our lives. On the other hand, one of the basic functions of government is to protect the welfare of individuals and the environment in which they live.

Ultimately, almost every law or rule regulating business represents a decision to give up certain rights in order to protect other perceived rights. In this *Focus on Ethics* feature, we look at some of the ethical aspects of government regulation.

Telemarketing and Consumers' Privacy Rights

A good example of how the rights of one group may conflict with those of another is the debate over the Do Not Call Registry discussed in Chapter 45. The do-not-call list allows consumers to register their telephone numbers with the Federal Trade Commission (FTC) to protect themselves from unwanted phone solicitations. Consumers, who had long complained about receiving unsolicited sales calls, have welcomed the Do Not Call Registry and the reduced number of calls that they receive as a result.

Telemarketers, in contrast, have strongly objected to the list. Business has sagged for numerous companies, causing jobs to be lost. Many firms have continued to contact individuals on the registry, making themselves vulnerable to fines of up to $11,000 whenever they dial a phone number on the list. Thus, protecting consumers' privacy rights has entailed significant restrictions on an industry's ability to conduct its business.

Some members of Congress have suggested creating a Do Not Spam bill, similar to the Do Not Call legislation. Though the idea holds promise in principle, in practice it would be hard to enforce. Even the FTC has concluded that such a list could actually increase the total amount of spam. Most spammers use offshore Internet servers to avoid being regulated by U.S. authorities. For the moment, there is no practical way to limit the large quantity of spam that fills e-mail inboxes each minute of every day.

Credit Reporting Agencies and "Blacklisting"

Today, some consumer credit reporting agencies will also conduct an online investigation of a person's history of credit disputes and litigation. Physicians and landlords frequently use such services to learn whether prospective patients or tenants have a history of suing their physicians or their landlords. One service, for example, allows physicians, for a fee, to perform more than two hundred online name searches to find out if a prospective patient was ever a plaintiff in a malpractice suit. Other services available to merchants (such as BadCustomer.com) keep a running tally of customers who have requested a credit-card reversal, called a *chargeback,* after paying a merchant. Even a single chargeback can cause merchants to reject a consumer's card in the future.

Users say that these services are an ideal way to screen out undesirable patients and applicants, and thereby reduce the risk of being sued. Consumer rights advocates, however, claim that the sale of such information is akin to "blacklisting"—discriminating against potential customers, patients, or tenants on the basis of previous disputes and litigation. In the last decade, these practices have led to complaints of unfairness, as well as lawsuits against reporting agencies. By and large, though, consumers have little recourse unless what is reported about them is inaccurate.

Consumer Safety

Consumers have become increasingly concerned about the safety of the products they buy, especially children's toys. Many of the toys—and other goods—sold in the United States are imported, often from China. Domestic manufacturers are unable or unwilling to compete with Chinese toy makers. After some well-publicized safety lapses with imported toys, many Americans have called for increased regulation of products from low-cost Chinese suppliers.

Certainly, there is an economic and even ethical trade-off here: accept lower-priced, less-than-perfect products from foreign low-cost producers or impose stricter regulations on imports and have the U.S. consumer pay a higher price. We might also note that not all problems are due to the foreign producers. Wal-Mart, which buys millions of Chinese toys each year, criticized its Chinese suppliers when defects were found in some toys. Later, though, Wal-Mart publicly apologized to the government of China because it turned out that the Chinese suppliers had followed Wal-Mart's specifications, which were the basis of the safety problems.

Environmental Law

Questions of fairness inevitably arise in regard to environmental law. Has the government gone too far—or not far enough—in regulating businesses in the interest of protecting the environment? At what point do the costs of environmental regulations become too burdensome for society to bear? Consider the problem of toxic waste. Although everybody is in favor

FOCUS ON ETHICS CONTINUES ▶

of cleaning up America's toxic waste dumps, nobody knows what this task will ultimately cost. Moreover, there is no agreed-on standard as to how clean a site must be before it no longer poses any threat. Must 100 percent of the contamination be removed, or would removal of some lesser amount achieve a reasonable degree of environmental quality?

Concerns over Pharmaceuticals in Drinking Water

The amount of pharmaceuticals used by the U.S. public and in agriculture (antibiotics and hormones given to livestock) has grown substantially in recent years. Now trace amounts of many drugs have been detected in our nation's water supply. In 2008, for example, the drinking water of at least 41 million Americans in twenty-four regions across the country was found to contain small amounts of prescription drugs. Some of these trace amounts came from unmetabolized drugs that had passed through the humans and animals that ingested them, but the rest had been flushed down the toilet. For years, pharmacists, physicians, and the federal government have recommended that people dispose of unused medications by flushing them away. This prevents children from accidentally ingesting the drugs and keeps controlled substances such as the painkillers oxycodone and morphine from falling into the hands of people who might abuse them. In making these recommendations, however, no one considered the long-term effect on the environment of adding pharmaceuticals to the water supply.

The quantities present in water now are far below medicinal doses, but no one knows how long-term exposure to random combinations of drugs will affect humans or wildlife. As yet, there is little scientific evidence about the long-term effects. The federal government does not require drinking water to be tested for drugs, so Americans do not know whether their drinking water is contaminated. Requiring that water be tested and that all traces of drugs be filtered from it would be enormously expensive.

Global Environmental Issues

Pollution does not respect geographic borders. Indeed, one of the reasons that the federal government became involved in environmental protection was that state regulation alone apparently could not solve the problem of air or water pollution. Pollutants generated in one state move in the air and water to other states. Nor does pollution respect national borders. Environmental issues, perhaps more than any others, bring home to everyone the fact that the world today is truly a global community. What one country does or does not do with respect to environmental preservation may be felt by citizens in countries thousands of miles away.

Global Warming. Another challenging—and controversial—issue is potential global warming. The fear is that emissions, largely from combustion of fossil fuels, will remain in the atmosphere and create a "greenhouse effect" by preventing heat from radiating outward. Concerns over this issue have led to many attempts to force all world polluters to "clean up their acts." For example, leaders of 187 nations have already agreed to reduce emissions of greenhouse gases in their respective countries. They did this when they ratified the Kyoto Protocol, which was drawn up at a world summit meeting held in Kyoto, Japan, in 1997. The Kyoto Protocol, which is often referred to as the global warming treaty, established different rates of reduction in greenhouse emissions for different countries or regions. Most nations, however, including the United States, will not meet the treaty's objectives. Many claim the treaty is not effective because it does not address the problem of curbing greenhouse gases from most of the developing world.

Is Economic Development the Answer? Economists have shown that economic development is the quickest way to reduce pollution worldwide. After a nation reaches a certain per capita income level, the more economic growth the nation experiences, the lower the pollution output. This occurs because richer nations have the resources to pay for pollution reduction. For example, industries in the United States pollute much less per unit of output than do industries in developing nations—because we are willing to pay for pollution abatement. Even among developed nations, the United States is a leader in curbing pollution. Indeed, in the last ten years, the United States saw a much smaller increase in greenhouse gases than did the European Union (EU).

DISCUSSION QUESTIONS

1. Does the national Do Not Call Registry adversely affect the way that business is conducted in this country? If so, how? Should Congress enact a Do Not Spam law? Why or why not?
2. If 90 percent of the toxic waste at a given site can be removed for $50,000, but removing the last 10 percent will cost $2 million, is it reasonable to require that the last 10 percent be removed? How would you address this question?
3. In a time of economic recession, should the government wait until there is scientific proof of the harmful effects on humans and wildlife before attempting to regulate pharmaceuticals in drinking water? Or should the government enact legislation to address the problem now—before it becomes worse? Discuss fully.
4. Can you think of a better way that the law can address the problem of global warming, which is clearly not just a national issue? Explain.

UNIT TEN

PROPERTY AND ITS PROTECTION

CONTENTS

CHAPTER 49

Personal Property and Bailments

Property consists of the legally protected rights and interests a person has in anything with an ascertainable value that is subject to ownership. Property would have little value (and the word would have little meaning) if the law did not define the rights of owners to use, sell, dispose of, control, and prevent others from trespassing on their property rights. In the United States, a substantial body of law protects the rights of property owners, but that protection is not absolute. As

you will read in this chapter and the next, property owners may have to prove that their ownership rights in a particular item of property are superior to the claims of others. In addition, through its police powers, the government can impose regulations and taxes on property, and can take or seize private property under certain circumstances.

In the first part of this chapter, we examine the differences between personal and real property. We then look at the methods of acquiring owner-

ship of personal property and issues relating to mislaid, lost, and abandoned personal property. In the second part of this chapter, we discuss bailment relationships. A *bailment* is created when personal property is temporarily delivered into the care of another without a transfer of title, such as when a person takes an item of clothing to the dry cleaners. The fact that there is no passage of title and no intent to transfer title is what distinguishes a bailment from a sale or a gift.

SECTION 1
PERSONAL PROPERTY VERSUS REAL PROPERTY

Real property (sometimes called *realty* or *real estate*) means the land and everything permanently attached to it, including structures and anything attached permanently to the structures. Everything else is **personal property** (sometimes referred to in case law as *personalty* or **chattel**). In essence, real property is immovable, whereas personal property is capable of being moved.

Personal property can be tangible or intangible. Tangible personal property, such as a flat-screen TV, heavy construction equipment, or a car, has physical substance. Intangible personal property represents some set of rights and interests, but it has no real physical existence. Stocks and bonds are intangible personal property. So, too, are patents, trademarks, and copyrights, as discussed in Chapter 8.

Both personal property and real property can be owned by an individual person or by an entity. When

two or more persons own real or personal property together, concurrent ownership exists. (The different types of joint or concurrent ownership will be discussed in Chapter 50.)

Why Is the Distinction Important?

The distinction between real and personal property is important for several reasons. First, the two types of property are usually subject to different types of taxes. Generally, each state assesses property taxes on real property. Typically, the tax rate is based on the market value of the real property and the various services provided by the city, state, and county in which the property is located (such as schools, roads, and libraries). Businesses usually pay taxes (both federal and state) on the personal property they own, use, or lease, including office or farm equipment and supplies. Individuals may pay sales tax when purchasing personal property, but generally they are not required to pay annual taxes on personal property that is not used for business.

Another reason for distinguishing between real and personal property has to do with the way the property is acquired or transferred. Personal property can be transferred with a minimum of formality, but real property transfers generally involve a written sales contract and a *deed* that is recorded with the state (deeds and real property transfers are discussed in Chapter 50). Similarly, establishing ownership rights is simpler for personal property than for real property. For example, if Mia gives Shawn an iPad as a gift, Shawn does not need to have any paperwork evidencing title (the ways to acquire ownership of personal property will be discussed shortly).

Conversion of Real Property to Personal Property

Sometimes, real property can be turned into personal property by detaching it from the land. For instance, the trees, bushes, and plants growing on land are considered part of the real property. If the property is sold, all the vegetation growing on the land normally is transferred to the new owner of the real property. Once the items are severed (removed) from the land, however, they become personal property. If the trees are cut from the land, the timber is personal property. If apples, grapes, or raspberries are picked from trees or vines growing on real property, they become personal property. (Note, however, that some crops that must be planted every year, such as corn and wheat, are considered to be personal property.) Similarly, if land contains minerals (including oil) or other natural resources such as silica or marble, the resources are part of the real property. But once removed, they become personal property. Conversely, personal property may be converted into real property by attaching it to the real property, as discussed next.

SECTION 2
FIXTURES

Certain personal property can become so closely associated with the real property to which it is attached that the law views it as real property. Such property is known as a **fixture**—a thing affixed to realty. A thing is affixed to realty when it is attached to the realty by roots; embedded in it; or permanently attached by means of cement, plaster, bolts, nails, or screws. The fixture can be physically attached to real property or attached to another fixture. It can even be an item, such as a statue, that is not physically attached to the land, as long as the owner *intends* the property to be a fixture.

Fixtures are included in the sale of land if the sales contract does not provide otherwise. The sale of a house includes the land and the house and garage on it, as well as the attached cabinets, plumbing, and windows. Because these are permanently affixed to the property, they are considered to be a part of it. Unless otherwise agreed, however, the curtains and throw rugs are not included. Items such as drapes and window-unit air conditioners are difficult to classify. Thus, a contract for the sale of a house or commercial property should indicate which items of this sort are included in the sale.

The issue of whether an item is a fixture (and thus real estate) or not a fixture (and thus personal property) often arises with respect to land sales, real property taxation, insurance coverage, and divorces. How the issue is resolved can have important consequences for the parties involved.

The Role of Intent

Generally, when the courts need to determine whether a certain item is a fixture, they examine the intention of the party who placed the object on the real property. If the facts indicate that the person intended the item to be a fixture, then it will normally be considered a fixture. When the intent of the party who placed the item on the realty is in dispute, the courts will usually deem that the item is a fixture if either or both of the following are true:

1. The property attached cannot be removed without causing substantial damage to the remaining realty.
2. The property attached is so adapted to the rest of the realty as to become a part of it.

Certain items can only be attached to property permanently. Such items are fixtures—it is assumed that the owner intended them to be fixtures because they had to be permanently attached to the property. A tile floor, cabinets, and carpeting are examples. Also, when an item of property is custom-made for installation on real property, as storm windows are, the item usually is classified as a fixture. In addition, an item that is firmly attached to the land and integral to its use, such as a mobile home or a complex irrigation system bolted to a cement slab on a farm, may be considered a fixture. The courts assume that owners, in making such installations, intend the objects to become part of their real property.

The following case illustrates the importance of intent in determining whether property is a fixture.

✷ EXTENDED CASE 49.1 ✷
APL Limited v. Washington State Department of Revenue

Court of Appeals of Washington, Division 1, 154 Wash.App. 1020 (2010).

IN THE LANGUAGE OF THE COURT

GROSSE, J. [Judge]

* * * *

On September 26, 1985, the Port of Seattle (Port) entered into a thirty-year lease with APL Limited, American President Lines, LTD, and Eagle Marine Services, LTD (collectively, APL) for premises at Terminal 5 for loading and unloading shipping container ships. Terminal 5 was substantially rebuilt and cranes were constructed and installed. The cranes at issue here are built to run on steel crane rails 100 feet apart, embedded in a concrete apron, and supported by specially designed steel-reinforced concrete and piers engineered specifically to support the cranes. The cranes themselves are steel structures that are 198 feet tall, 85 feet wide, more than 370 feet long and each weighs over 800 tons. They are hard wired to a dedicated high voltage electrical system that includes a power substation built specifically for Terminal 5 to power the cranes. The cranes are attached to the power substation by cables that are more than two inches thick. The cranes have been in use continuously on Terminal 5 since their construction over twenty years ago.

APL brought suit * * * for a refund of sales tax paid on the rent for the cranes. The State moved for summary judgment, arguing that the cranes were personalty [personal property] and, as such, subject to sales tax. The trial court granted the motion * * *.

APL appeals * * *.

* * * *

*Real property, for tax purposes, is defined as "the land itself * * * and all buildings, structures or improvements or other fixtures of whatsoever kind thereon."* [Emphasis added.]

* * * *

Case law dictates that to determine whether the cranes are personal property or real property, [that is,] fixtures, we apply the common law test. Under this test, we must consider the following three prongs:

(1) Actual annexation to the realty, or something appurtenant thereto; (2) application to the use or purpose to which that part of the realty with which it is connected is appropriated; and (3) the intention of the party making the annexation to make a permanent accession to the freehold.

All three prongs must be met for a chattel [movable property] to become a fixture. Both parties agree that the second prong is met in this instance but dispute the first and third prongs. [Emphasis added.]

Applying a confusing factual scenario, the trial court decided that the first prong, annexation, was not met and therefore it need not consider any of the other facts presented. This was error because *the determinative factor for whether a chattel annexed to real property becomes part of the real property or retains its character as personal property is the third prong: the intent with which the chattel was annexed to the land.* Intent can be determined from the nature of the chattel attached and its relation or necessity to the activity conducted on the land and the manner in which it is annexed. When the owner and the person that annexes the chattel are one and the same, a rebuttable presumption arises that the owner's intention was for the chattel to become part of the realty. [Emphasis added.]

* * * *

In its oral ruling, the trial court itself recognized that it had not examined the facts regarding the Port's intent to annex these cranes. Because annexation is so intertwined with the intent to annex, one cannot be examined without the other. * * * The factual inferences that can be drawn from the evidence presented should be permitted to be argued to the trial court. Because the trial court did not consider these inferences, summary judgment was inappropriate. We reverse.

QUESTIONS

1. Why did it matter to the parties in this lawsuit whether the cranes were fixtures or not?
2. Did the fact that the appellate court reversed the judgment of the trial court mean that the cranes were fixtures? Explain.

Trade Fixtures

Trade fixtures are an exception to the rule that fixtures are a part of the real property. A trade fixture is personal property that is installed for a commercial purpose by a tenant (one who rents real property from the owner, or landlord). Trade fixtures remain the property of the tenant, unless removal would irreparably damage the building or realty. A walk-in cooler, for example, purchased and installed by a tenant who uses the premises for a restaurant, is a trade fixture. The tenant can remove the cooler from the premises when the lease terminates but ordinarily must repair any damage that the removal causes or compensate the landlord for the damage.

SECTION 3
ACQUIRING OWNERSHIP OF PERSONAL PROPERTY

The most common way of acquiring personal property is by purchasing it. We have already discussed the purchase and sale of personal property (goods) in Chapters 19 through 22. Often, property is acquired by will or inheritance, a topic we cover in Chapter 52. Here, we look at additional ways in which ownership of personal property can be acquired, including acquisition by possession, production, gift, accession, and confusion.

Possession

Sometimes, a person can become the owner of personal property merely by possessing it. One example of acquiring ownership through possession is the capture of wild animals. Wild animals belong to no one in their natural state, and the first person to take possession of a wild animal normally owns it. A hunter who kills a deer, for example, has assumed ownership of it (unless he or she acted in violation of the law).

Those who find lost or abandoned property can also acquire ownership rights through mere possession of the property, as will be discussed later in this chapter. (Ownership rights in real property can also be acquired through *adverse possession*—to be discussed in Chapter 50.)

Production

Production is another means of acquiring ownership of personal property—that is, as the fruits of labor. For instance, writers, inventors, manufacturers, and others who produce personal property may thereby acquire title to it. (In some situations, though, as when a researcher is hired to invent a new product or technique, the researcher may not own what is produced—see Chapter 32.)

Gift

A **gift** is another fairly common means of acquiring or transferring ownership of property. A gift is essentially a *voluntary* transfer of property ownership for which no consideration is given. As discussed in Chapter 12, the presence of consideration is what distinguishes a contract from a gift. Gifts can be made during a person's lifetime or in a last will and testament. A gift made by will is called a *testamentary* gift.

For a gift to be effective, three requirements must be met: (1) donative intent on the part of the *donor* (the one giving the gift), (2) delivery, and (3) acceptance by the *donee* (the one receiving the gift). We examine each of these requirements next. Until these three requirements are met, no effective gift has been made. For example, Gary's aunt tells him that she is going to give him a new Mercedes-Benz for his next birthday. This is simply a promise to make a gift. It is not considered a gift until the Mercedes-Benz is delivered and accepted.

DONATIVE INTENT When a gift is challenged in court, the court will determine whether donative intent exists by looking at the language of the donor and the surrounding circumstances. A court may look at the relationship between the parties and the size of the gift in relation to the donor's other assets. When a person has given away a large portion of her or his assets, the court will scrutinize the transaction closely to determine the donor's mental capacity and look for indications of fraud or duress.

DELIVERY The gift must be delivered to the donee. Delivery may be accomplished by means of a third person who is the agent of either the donor or the donee. Naturally, no delivery is necessary if the gift is already in the hands of the donee (provided there is donative intent and acceptance). Delivery is obvious in most cases, but some objects cannot be relinquished physically. Then the question of delivery depends on the surrounding circumstances.

Constructive Delivery. When the physical object itself cannot be delivered, a symbolic, or constructive, delivery will be sufficient. **Constructive delivery** does not confer actual possession of the object in question, only the right to take actual possession. It is a general term for all of those acts that the law holds to be equivalent to acts of real delivery.

Suppose that Teresa wants to make a gift of various rare coins that she has stored in a safe-deposit box at her bank. Teresa certainly cannot deliver the box itself to the donee, and she does not want to take the coins out of the bank. In this situation, Teresa can simply deliver the key to the box to the donee and authorize the donee's access to the box and its contents. This constitutes symbolic, or constructive, delivery of the contents of the box.

Delivery of intangible personal property—such as stocks, bonds, insurance policies, and contracts, for example—must always be accomplished by constructive delivery. This is because the documents represent rights and are not, in themselves, the true property.

Relinquishing Dominion and Control. An effective delivery also requires that the donor give up control and **dominion** (ownership rights) over the subject matter of the gift. The outcome of disputes often turns on whether control has actually been relinquished. The Internal Revenue Service scrutinizes transactions between relatives, especially when one has given income-producing property to another who is in a lower marginal tax bracket. Unless complete control over the property has been relinquished, the "donor"—not the family member who received the "gift"—will have to pay taxes on the income from that property.

In the following classic case, the court focused on the requirement that a donor must relinquish complete control and dominion over property before a gift can be effectively delivered.

CASE 49.2
In re Estate of Piper
Missouri Court of Appeals, 676 S.W.2d 897 (1984).

BACKGROUND AND FACTS • Gladys Piper died intestate (without a will). At the time of her death, she owned personal property worth $5,150 in total, consisting of household goods, two old automobiles, farm machinery, and "miscellaneous" items. This did not include jewelry or cash. When Piper died, she had $206.75 in cash and her two diamond rings, known as the "Andy Piper" rings, in her purse. The contents of Piper's purse were taken by her niece, Wanda Brown, on Piper's death, allegedly to preserve them for the estate. Clara Kauffman, a friend of Gladys Piper, filed a claim against the estate for $4,800. For several years before Piper's death, Kauffman had taken Piper to the doctor, beauty salon, and grocery store; written her checks to pay her bills; and helped her care for her home. Kauffman maintained that Piper had promised to pay her for these services and that Piper had intended the diamond rings to be a gift to her. The trial court denied Kauffman's request for payment of $4,800 on the basis that the services had been voluntary. Kauffman then filed a petition for delivery of personal property (the rings), which was granted by the trial court. The defendants—Piper's heirs and the administrator of Piper's estate—appealed.

IN THE LANGUAGE OF THE COURT
GREENE, Judge.
* * * *

While no particular form is necessary to effect a delivery, and while the delivery may be actual, constructive, or symbolical, there must be some evidence to support a delivery theory. What we have here, at best, * * * was an intention on the part of Gladys, at some future time, to make a gift of the rings to Clara. Such an intention, no matter how clearly expressed, which has not been carried into effect, confers no ownership rights in the property in the intended donee. *Language written or spoken, expressing an intention to give, does not constitute a gift, unless the intention is executed by a complete and unconditional delivery of the subject matter, or delivery of a proper written instrument evidencing the gift.* There is no evidence in this case to prove delivery, and, for such reason, the trial court's judgment is erroneous. [Emphasis added.]

DECISION AND REMEDY • *The judgment of the trial court was reversed. No effective gift of the rings had been made because Piper had never delivered the rings to Kauffman.*

IMPACT OF THIS CASE ON TODAY'S LAW • *This classic case clearly illustrates the delivery requirement for making a gift. Assuming that Piper did, indeed, intend for Kauffmann to have the rings, it was unfortunate that Kauffmann had no right to receive them after Piper's death. Yet the alternative could lead to perhaps even more unfairness. The policy behind the delivery requirement is to protect alleged donors and their heirs from fraudulent claims based solely on parol evidence. If not for this policy, an alleged donee could easily claim that a gift was made when, in fact, it was not.*

CASE 49.2 CONTINUED ➡ **WHAT IF THE FACTS WERE DIFFERENT?** • *Suppose that Piper had told Kauffman that she was giving the rings to Kauffman but wished to keep them in her possession for a few more days. Would this have affected the court's decision in this case? Explain.*

ACCEPTANCE The final requirement of a valid gift is acceptance by the donee. This rarely presents any problems because most donees readily accept their gifts. The courts generally assume acceptance unless the circumstances indicate otherwise.

GIFTS *INTER VIVOS* AND GIFTS *CAUSA MORTIS* A gift made during the donor's lifetime is called a **gift inter vivos.** A **gift *causa mortis*** is a gift made in contemplation of imminent death. To be effective, a gift *causa mortis* must meet the three requirements of intent, delivery, and acceptance. A gift *causa mortis* does not become absolute until the donor dies from the contemplated illness. It is automatically revoked if the donor recovers from the illness. The gift is also revoked if the prospective donee dies before the donor.

Suppose that Steck is about to undergo surgery to remove a cancerous tumor. Before the operation, he delivers an envelope to Yang, a close business associate. The letter says, "I realize my days are numbered, and I want to give you this check for $1 million in the event that this operation causes my death." The business associate cashes the check. The surgeon performs the operation and removes the tumor. Steck recovers fully. Several months later, Steck dies from a heart attack that is totally unrelated to the operation. If Steck's personal representative (the party charged with administering Steck's estate) tries to recover the $1 million, normally she will succeed. The gift *causa mortis* to Yang is automatically revoked by Steck's recovery. The *specific event* that was contemplated in making the gift was death caused by a particular operation. Because Steck's death was not the result of this event, the gift is revoked, and the $1 million passes to Steck's estate.[1]

Accession

Accession means "something added." Accession occurs when someone adds value to an item of personal property by the use of either labor or materials. Generally, there is no dispute about who owns the property after accession occurs, especially when the accession is accomplished with the owner's consent. For example, Hoshi buys all the materials necessary to customize his Corvette. He hires Zach, a customizing specialist, to come his house to perform the work. Hoshi pays Zach for the value of the labor, obviously retaining title to the property.

If the improvement was made wrongfully—without the permission of the owner—the owner retains title to the property and normally does not have to pay for the improvement. This is true even if the accession increased the value of the property substantially. For example, Colton steals a car and puts expensive new tires on it. If the rightful owner later recovers the car, he obviously will not be required to compensate Colton, a car thief, for the value of the new tires.

If the accession is performed in good faith—and the improvement was made due to an honest mistake of judgment—the owner normally still retains title to the property but usually must pay for the improvement. In rare instances, when the improvement greatly increases the value of the property or changes its identity, the court may rule that ownership has passed to the improver. In those rare situations, the improver must compensate the original owner for the value of the property before the accession occurred.

Confusion

Confusion is the commingling (mixing together) of goods to such an extent that one person's personal property cannot be distinguished from another's. Confusion frequently occurs with *fungible goods,* such as grain or oil, which consist of identical units.[2]

If confusion occurs as a result of agreement, an honest mistake, or the act of some third party, the owners share ownership in the commingled goods in proportion to the amount each contributed. For example, five farmers in a small Iowa community enter into a cooperative arrangement. Each fall, the farmers harvest the same amount of number 2–grade yellow corn and store it in silos that are held by the cooperative. Each farmer thus owns one-fifth of the total corn in the silos. If a fire burns down one of the silos, each farmer will bear one-fifth of the loss. When goods are confused due to an intentional wrongful act, then the innocent party ordinarily acquires title to the whole.

---

1. For a classic case on the requirement that a donor die from the contemplated peril, see *Brind v. International Trust Co.,* 66 Colo. 60, 179 P. 148 (1919).

2. See Section 1–201(17) of the Uniform Commercial Code (UCC).

Concept Summary 49.1 below provides a review of the various ways in which personal property can be acquired.

SECTION 4
MISLAID, LOST, AND ABANDONED PROPERTY

As already noted, one of the methods of acquiring ownership of property is to possess it. Simply finding something and holding onto it, however, does not *necessarily* give the finder any legal rights in the property. Different rules apply, depending on whether the property was mislaid, lost, or abandoned.

Mislaid Property

Property that has been voluntarily placed somewhere by the owner and then inadvertently forgotten is **mislaid property.** A person who finds mislaid property does not obtain title to the goods.

Instead, the owner of the place where the property was mislaid becomes the caretaker of the property because it is highly likely that the true owner will return.[3] Suppose that Maya goes to a movie theater. While paying for popcorn at the concessions stand, she sets her iPhone on the counter and then leaves it there. The phone is mislaid property, and the theater owner is entrusted with the duty of reasonable care for it.

Lost Property

Property that is *involuntarily* left is **lost property.** A finder of lost property can claim title to the property against the whole world—*except the true owner.*[4] If the true owner is identified and demands that the lost property be returned, the finder must return it.

---

3. The finder of mislaid property is an *involuntary bailee* (as will be discussed later in this chapter).
4. For a landmark English case establishing finders' rights in property, see *Armory v. Delamirie,* 93 Eng.Rep. 664 (K.B. [King's Bench] 1722).

CONCEPT SUMMARY 49.1
Acquisition of Personal Property

Type of Acquisition	How Acquisition Occurs
By Purchase or by Will	The most common means of acquiring ownership in personal property is by purchasing it (see Chapters 19 through 22). Another way in which personal property is often acquired is by will or inheritance (see Chapter 52).
Possession	Ownership may be acquired by possession if no other person has ownership title (for example, capturing wild animals or finding abandoned property).
Production	Any product or item produced by an individual (with minor exceptions) becomes the property of that individual.
Gift	An effective gift is made when the following three requirements are met: 1. *Intent*—There is evidence of *intent* to make a gift of the property in question. 2. *Delivery*—The gift is delivered (physically or constructively) to the donee or the donee's agent. 3. *Acceptance*—The gift is accepted by the donee or the donee's agent.
Accession	When someone adds value to a piece of property by use of labor or materials, the added value generally becomes the property of the owner of the original property (when accessions are made in bad faith or wrongfully). Good faith accessions that substantially increase the property's value or change the identity of the property may cause title to pass to the improver, who compensates the original owner.
Confusion	In the case of fungible goods, if a person wrongfully and willfully commingles goods with those of another in order to render them indistinguishable, the innocent party acquires title to the whole. Otherwise, the owners share ownership of the commingled goods in proportion to the amount each contributed.

In contrast, if a third party attempts to take possession of the lost property, the finder will have a better title than the third party.

For example, Kayla works in a large library at night. As she crosses the courtyard on her way home, she finds a gold bracelet set with what seem to be precious stones. She takes the bracelet to a jeweler to have it appraised. While pretending to weigh the bracelet, the jeweler's employee removes several of the stones. If Kayla brings an action to recover the stones from the jeweler, she normally will win because she found lost property and holds title against everyone *except the true owner*.

CONVERSION OF LOST PROPERTY When a finder of lost property knows the true owner and fails to return the property to that person, the finder is guilty of the tort of *conversion* (see Chapter 6). In the example just mentioned, if Kayla knows that the gold bracelet she found belongs to Geneva and does not return the bracelet, Kayla is guilty of conversion. Many states require the finder to make a reasonably diligent search to locate the true owner of lost property.

ESTRAY STATUTES **Estray statutes** encourage and facilitate the return of property to its true owner and reward the finder for honesty if the property remains unclaimed. These laws provide an incentive for finders to report their discoveries by making it possible for them, after passage of a specified period of time, to acquire legal title to the property they have found.

Estray statutes usually require the finder or the county clerk to advertise the property in an attempt to help the owner recover what has been lost. Generally, the item must be lost property, not merely mislaid property, for the estray statute to apply. When the situation indicates that the property was probably lost and not mislaid or abandoned, loss is presumed as a matter of public policy, and the estray statute applies.

CASE IN POINT Drug smugglers often enter the United States illegally from Canada via a frozen river that flows through Van Buren, Maine. When two railroad employees in Van Buren found a duffel bag that contained $165,580 in cash, they reported their find to U.S. Customs agents, who took custody of it. A drug-sniffing dog gave a positive alert on the bag for the scent of drugs. The U.S. government claimed the property under forfeiture laws, which provide that cash and property involved in illegal drug transactions are forfeited to the government.

The two employees argued that they were entitled to the $165,580 under Maine's estray statute. The statute required finders to (1) provide written notice to the town clerk within seven days after finding the property, (2) post a public notice, and (3) advertise in the town's newspaper. Because the employees had not fulfilled these requirements, the court ruled they had not acquired title to the property. Thus, the federal government had a right to seize the cash.[5]

Abandoned Property

Property that has been *discarded* by the true owner, who has *no intention* of reclaiming title to it, is **abandoned property.** Someone who finds abandoned property acquires title to it, and that title is good against the whole world, *including the original owner*. The owner of lost property who eventually gives up any further attempt to find it is frequently held to have abandoned the property.

For example, Alexis is driving in her car on the freeway when a valuable scarf blows out the window. She retraces her route and looks for the scarf but cannot find it. She finally gives up her search and proceeds to her destination five hundred miles away. When Frye, a hitchhiker, finds the scarf six months later, he acquires title to it that is good even against Alexis. By completely giving up her search, Alexis abandoned the scarf just as effectively as if she had intentionally discarded it.

Note that if a person finds abandoned property while trespassing on another's property, the trespasser will not acquire title. In that situation, the owner of the real property on which the abandoned property was found will acquire title to it.

See *Concept Summary 49.2* on the following page for a comparison of mislaid, lost, and abandoned property.

SECTION 5

BAILMENTS

Many routine personal and business transactions involve bailments. A **bailment** is formed by the delivery of personal property, without transfer of title, by one person (called a **bailor**) to another (called a **bailee**). Bailment agreements usually are made for a particular purpose—for example, to loan, lease, store, repair, or transport the property. On

---

5. *United States v. One Hundred Sixty-Five Thousand Five Hundred Eighty Dollars ($165,580) in U.S. Currency,* 502 F.Supp.2d 114 (D.Me. 2007).

CONCEPT SUMMARY 49.2
Mislaid, Lost, and Abandoned Property

Concept	Description
Mislaid Property	Property that is placed somewhere voluntarily by the owner and then inadvertently forgotten. A finder of mislaid property will not acquire title to the goods, and the owner of the place where the property was mislaid becomes a caretaker of the mislaid property.
Lost Property	Property that is involuntarily left and forgotten. A finder of lost property can claim title to the property against the whole world *except the true owner.*
Abandoned Property	Property that has been discarded by the true owner, who has no intention of reclaiming title to the property in the future. A finder of abandoned property can claim title to it against the whole world, *including the original owner.*

completion of the purpose, the bailee is obligated to return the bailed property in the same or better condition to the bailor or a third person or to dispose of it as directed.

Although bailments typically arise by agreement, not all of the elements of a contract must necessarily be present (such as mutual assent and consideration). For example, if Dan lends his business law textbook to a friend, a bailment is created, but not by contract, because there is no consideration. Nevertheless, many commercial bailments, such as the delivery of clothing to the cleaners for dry cleaning, do involve contracts.

A bailment differs from a sale or a gift in that possession is transferred without passage of title or intent to transfer title. In a sale or a gift, title is intentionally transferred from the seller or donor to the buyer or donee.

Elements of a Bailment

Not all transactions involving the delivery of property from one person to another create a bailment. For such a transfer to become a bailment, the following three elements must be present:

1. Personal property.
2. Delivery of possession (without title).
3. Agreement that the property will be returned to the bailor or otherwise disposed of according to its owner's directions.

PERSONAL PROPERTY REQUIREMENT Only personal property, not real property or persons, can be the subject of a bailment. Although a bailment of your luggage is created when it is transported by an airline, as a passenger you are not the subject of a bailment. Although bailments commonly involve *tangible*

items—jewelry, cattle, automobiles, and the like—*intangible* personal property, such as promissory notes and shares of corporate stock, may also be bailed.

DELIVERY OF POSSESSION *Delivery of possession* means transfer of possession of the property to the bailee. For delivery to occur, the bailee must be given *exclusive possession and control* over the property, and the bailee must *knowingly* accept the personal property.[6] In other words, the bailee must *intend* to exercise control over it.

If either delivery of possession or knowing acceptance is lacking, there is no bailment relationship. For example, Ian is hurrying to catch his plane and wants to check a package at the airport. He arrives at the airport check-in station, but the person in charge has gone on a coffee break. Ian decides to leave the package on the counter. Even though there has clearly been a physical transfer of the package, the person in charge of the check-in station has not knowingly accepted the personal property. Therefore, there has not been an effective delivery.

The result is the same if, for example, Delacroix goes to a restaurant and checks her coat, leaving a $20,000 diamond necklace in the coat pocket. In accepting the coat, the bailee does not *knowingly* also accept the necklace. Thus, a bailment of the coat exists—because the restaurant has exclusive possession and control over the coat and knowingly accepted it—but not a bailment of the necklace.

---

6. We are dealing here with *voluntary bailments*. Under some circumstances, even if a person does not intentionally accept possession of someone else's personal property, the law imposes on him or her the obligation to return it. For example, if the owner of property accidentally and without negligence leaves it in another's possession, the person in whose possession the item has been left may be responsible for its return. This is referred to as an *involuntary bailment*.

Physical versus Constructive Delivery. Either *physical* or *constructive* delivery will result in the bailee's exclusive possession of and control over the property. As discussed earlier, in the context of gifts, constructive delivery is a substitute, or symbolic, delivery. What is delivered to the bailee is not the actual property bailed (such as a car) but something so related to the property (such as the car keys) that the requirement of delivery is satisfied.

Involuntary Bailments. In certain situations, a court will find that a bailment exists despite the apparent lack of the requisite elements of control and knowledge. One example of such a situation occurs when the bailee acquires the property accidentally or by mistake—as in finding someone else's lost or mislaid property. A bailment is created even though the bailor did not voluntarily deliver the property to the bailee. Such bailments are referred to as *constructive* or *involuntary* bailments.

Suppose that several corporate managers attend a meeting at the law firm of Jacobs & Matheson. One of the corporate officers, Kyle Gustafson, inadvertently leaves his briefcase behind at the conclusion of the meeting. In this situation, a court could find that an involuntary bailment was created even though Gustafson did not voluntarily deliver the briefcase and the law firm did not intentionally accept it. If an involuntary bailment exists, the firm is responsible for taking care of the briefcase and returning it to Gustafson.

The Bailment Agreement

Bailments for less than one year do not require a written agreement under the Statute of Frauds (see Chapter 15). Nevertheless, it is a good idea to have written contract, particularly when the bailed property is valuable. A bailment agreement can be *express* or *implied*.

The bailment agreement expressly or impliedly provides for the return of the bailed property to the bailor, or to a third person, or for disposal of the property by the bailee. The agreement presupposes that the bailee will return the identical goods originally given by the bailor. In certain types of bailments, though, such as bailments of fungible goods,[7] the property returned need only be equivalent property.

For example, if Hobson stores his grain (fungible goods) in Kwan's grain elevator, a bailment is created. At the end of the storage period, the grain elevator company is not obligated to return to Hobson exactly the same grain that was stored. As long as the company returns grain of the same type, grade, and quantity, the bailee company has performed its obligation.

SECTION 6
ORDINARY BAILMENTS

Bailments are either *ordinary* or *special (extraordinary)*. There are three types of ordinary bailments. They are distinguished according to *which party receives a benefit from the bailment*. This factor will dictate the rights and liabilities of the parties, and the courts may use it to determine the standard of care required of the bailee in possession of the personal property. The three types of ordinary bailments are listed below and described in the following subsections:

1. Bailment for the sole benefit of the bailor.
2. Bailment for the sole benefit of the bailee.
3. Bailment for the mutual benefit of the bailee and the bailor.

Bailment for the Sole Benefit of the Bailor

A bailment for the sole benefit of the bailor is a type of *gratuitous bailment*—meaning that it involves no consideration. The bailment is for the convenience and benefit of the bailor. Basically, the bailee is caring for the bailor's property as a favor. Therefore, the bailee owes only a slight duty of care and will be liable only if grossly negligent in caring for the property. (Negligence was discussed in Chapter 7.) For example, Allen asks his friend, Sumi, to store his car in her garage while he is away. If Sumi agrees to do so, then a gratuitous bailment is created because the bailment is for the sole benefit of the bailor (Allen). If the car is damaged while in Sumi's garage, Sumi will not be responsible for the damage unless it was caused by her gross negligence.

Bailment for the Sole Benefit of the Bailee

In a bailment for the sole benefit of the bailee, the bailor typically lends an article to a person (the

---

7. As mentioned earlier on page 961, *fungible goods* are goods that consist of identical particles, such as wheat. Fungible goods are defined in UCC 1–201(17).

bailee) solely for that person's convenience and benefit. Because the bailee is borrowing the item for her or his own benefit, the bailee owes a duty to exercise the utmost care and will be liable for even slight negligence. Suppose that Allen asks to borrow Sumi's boat so that he can take his girlfriend sailing over the weekend. The bailment of the boat is for Allen's (the bailee's) sole benefit. If Allen fails to pay attention and runs the boat aground, damaging its hull, he is liable for the costs of repairing the boat.

Mutual-Benefit Bailments

The most common kind of bailment is a bailment for the mutual benefit of the bailee and the bailor that involves some form of compensation for storing items or holding property. It is a contractual bailment and is often referred to as a *bailment for hire* or a *commercial bailment.*

In a commercial bailment, the bailee must exercise ordinary care, which is the care that a reasonably prudent (careful) person would use under the circumstances. If the bailee fails to exercise reasonable care, he or she will be liable for ordinary negligence. For example, Allen leaves his car at a service station for an oil change. Because the service station will be paid to change Allen's oil, this is a mutual-benefit bailment. If the service station fails to put the correct amount of oil back into Allen's car and the engine is damaged as a result, the service station will be liable for failure to exercise reasonable care. Many lease arrangements that involve goods (leases were discussed in Chapters 19 through 22) also fall into this category of bailment once the lessee takes possession.

Rights of the Bailee

Certain rights are implicit in the bailment agreement. Generally, the bailee has the right to take possession of the property and to utilize it for accomplishing the purpose of the bailment. The bailee also has a right to receive compensation (unless the bailment is intended to be gratuitous) and may be able to limit her or his liability for the bailed goods. These rights of the bailee are present (with some limitations) in varying degrees in all bailment transactions.

RIGHT OF POSSESSION A hallmark of the bailment agreement is that the bailee acquires the *right to control and possess the property temporarily.* The duration of a bailment depends on the terms of the agreement. If the bailment agreement specifies a particular period, then the bailment is continuous for that time period. Earlier termination by the bailor

is normally a breach of contract, and the bailee can recover damages from the bailor. If no duration is specified, the bailment ends when either the bailor or the bailee so demands and possession of the bailed property is returned to the bailor.

A bailee's right of possession, even though temporary, permits the bailee to recover damages from any third parties for damage or loss to the property. For example, No-Spot Dry Cleaners sends all suede leather garments to Cleanall Company for special processing. If Cleanall loses or damages any leather goods, No-Spot has the right to recover from Cleanall.

RIGHT TO USE BAILED PROPERTY Depending on the type of bailment and the terms of the bailment agreement, a bailee may also have a right to use the bailed property. When no provision is made, the extent of use depends on how necessary it is for the goods to be at the bailee's disposal for the ordinary purpose of the bailment to be carried out. When leasing drilling machinery, for example, the bailee is expected to use the equipment to drill. Similarly, if you borrow a car to drive a friend to the airport, you, as the bailee, would obviously be expected to use the car. In a bailment involving the long-term storage of a car, however, the bailee is not expected to use the car because the ordinary purpose of a storage bailment does not include use of the property. The bailee would be expected to use or move the car if necessary in an emergency to protect it from harm.

RIGHT OF COMPENSATION Except in a gratuitous bailment, a bailee has a right to be compensated as provided for in the bailment agreement, to be reimbursed for costs incurred and services rendered in keeping the bailed property, or both. In mutual-benefit bailments, the amount of compensation is often stated in the bailment contract. For example, in the rental (bailment) of a car, the contract provides for charges on the basis of time, mileage, or a combination of the two, plus other possible charges. In nonrental bailments, such as when a car is left at a gas station for an oil change, the bailee earns a service charge for the work performed.

Gratuitous Bailments. Even in a gratuitous bailment, a bailee has a right to be reimbursed or compensated for costs incurred in keeping the bailed property. For example, Hetta loses her pet dog, which is found by Jesse. Jesse takes Hetta's dog to his home and feeds it. Even though he takes good care of the dog, it becomes ill, and he takes it to a veterinarian. Jesse pays the bill for the veterinarian's services and the medicine. He is normally entitled to be reimbursed by Hetta for these reasonable costs incurred in keeping her dog.

The Bailee's Lien. To enforce the right of compensation, the bailee has a right to place a *possessory lien* (claim) on the specific bailed property until she or he has been fully compensated. This lien on specific bailed property is sometimes referred to as a **bailee's lien,** or artisan's lien (discussed in Chapter 28). If the bailor refuses to pay or cannot pay the charges (compensation), in most states the bailee is entitled to foreclose on the lien. This means that the bailee can sell the property and be paid the amount owed for the bailment out of the proceeds, returning any excess to the bailor.

For example, Sarito takes his car to a parking garage to be stored while he is out of the country. He pays storage fees for two months in advance. When he returns six months later, the garage tenders the car to Sarito, but because he is now unemployed, he cannot pay the fee. The garage has a right to retain possession of Sarito's car, exercising a bailee's lien. Unless Sarito can arrange for payment, the garage normally will be entitled to sell the car to obtain compensation for the storage.

RIGHT TO LIMIT LIABILITY In ordinary bailments, bailees have the right to limit their liability provided that the limitations are called to the attention of the bailor and are not against public policy. It is essential that the bailor be informed of the limitation in some way. Thus, a sign in Nikolai's garage stating that Nikolai will not be responsible "for loss due to theft, fire, or vandalism" may or may not be held to be notice to the bailor. Whether the notice will be effective will depend on the size of the sign, its location, and any other circumstances affecting the likelihood that customers will see it.

Even when the bailor knows of the limitation, courts consider certain types of disclaimers of liability to be against public policy and therefore illegal. As was discussed in Chapter 13, the courts carefully scrutinize *exculpatory clauses,* which limit a person's

liability for her or his own wrongful acts, and in bailments they are often held to be illegal. This is particularly true in bailments for the mutual benefit of the bailor and the bailee. For example, a receipt from a parking garage expressly disclaims liability for any damage to parked cars, regardless of the cause. Because the bailee (garage) has attempted to exclude liability for the bailee's own negligence, including a parking attendant's negligence, the clause will likely be deemed unenforceable because it is against public policy.

Duties of the Bailee

The bailee has two basic responsibilities: (1) to take appropriate care of the property and (2) to surrender the property to the bailor or dispose of it in accordance with the bailor's instructions at the end of the bailment. The bailee's duties are based on a mixture of tort law and contract law.

THE DUTY OF CARE The bailee must exercise reasonable care in preserving the bailed property (the duty of care was discussed in Chapter 7). As discussed earlier, what constitutes reasonable care in a bailment situation normally depends on the nature and specific circumstances of the bailment.

The courts determine the appropriate standard of care on the basis of the type of bailment involved. In a bailment for the sole benefit of the bailor, the bailee need exercise only a slight degree of care, whereas in a bailment for the sole benefit of the bailee, the bailee must exercise great care. Exhibit 49–1 below illustrates the degree of care required of bailees in bailment relationships. Determining whether a bailee exercised an appropriate degree of care is usually a question of fact for the jury or judge (in a nonjury trial). A bailee's failure to exercise appropriate care in handling the bailor's property results in tort liability.

DUTY TO RETURN BAILED PROPERTY At the end of the bailment, the bailee normally has a contractual duty to hand over the original property to either the

EXHIBIT 49–1 • Degree of Care Required of a Bailee

Bailment for the Sole Benefit of the Bailor	Mutual-Benefit Bailment	Bailment for the Sole Benefit of the Bailee
DEGREE OF CARE		
SLIGHT	REASONABLE	GREAT

bailor or someone the bailor designates or must otherwise dispose of it as directed.[8] Failure to give up possession at the time the bailment ends is a breach of contract and could result in a tort lawsuit for conversion or negligence.

If the bailed property has been lost or is returned damaged, a court will presume that the bailee was negligent. The bailee's obligation is excused, however, if the property was destroyed, lost, or stolen through no fault of the bailee (or claimed by a third party with a superior claim).

Because the bailee has a duty to return the bailed goods to the bailor, a bailee may be liable for conversion or misdelivery if the goods are given to the wrong person. Hence, a bailee must be satisfied that the person to whom the goods are being delivered is the actual owner or has authority from the owner to take possession of the goods.

A bailee's alleged negligence was at the heart of the following case.

---

8. As mentioned earlier, if the bailment involves fungible goods, such as grain, then the bailee is not required to return exactly the same goods to the bailor. Instead, the bailee must return goods of the same type, grade, and quantity.

CASE 49.3
LaPlace v. Briere

New Jersey Superior Court, Appellate Division, 404 N.J.Super. 585, 962 A.2d 1139 (2009).
www.lawlibrary.rutgers.edu/search.shtml[a]

BACKGROUND AND FACTS • Michael LaPlace boarded his horses, including a trained Quarter Horse named Park Me In First, at Pierre Briere's stable in New Jersey. Charlene Bridgwood also boarded a horse at the stable. About a dozen years earlier, LaPlace had boarded horses at the farm owned by Bridgwood's husband. Bridgwood had often lunged the horses, including those owned by LaPlace. (Lunging is a form of exercise in which the horse moves around the handler in a circle while attached to a long line.) In 2006, while LaPlace and Briere were at a horse show, Bridgwood offered to help Briere's shorthanded staff by lunging the horses, even though she was not an employee of the stable. During the exercise, Park Me In First suddenly reared up on his hind legs. He then collapsed with blood pumping from his nose and died. The veterinarian could not determine the cause of death without performing a necropsy (autopsy). Briere and Bridgwood offered to pay for the procedure, but none was performed because LaPlace did not authorize it until after the horse's remains had been removed. LaPlace filed a suit in a New Jersey state court against Briere, claiming negligence. The court issued a summary judgment in the defendant's favor. LaPlace appealed.

IN THE LANGUAGE OF THE COURT
CHAMBERS, J.A.D. [Judge, Appellate Division]
* * * *

 * * * In a bailment for mutual benefit, a bailee has a duty to exercise reasonable care for the safekeeping of the subject of the bailment and will be liable for any loss caused by its failure to do so. When proofs are presented showing that goods were damaged while in the care of a bailee, a presumption of negligence arises and in those circumstances, a *prima facie* case is established against the bailee. *The presumption of negligence, however, may be rebutted by the bailee with evidence showing that the loss was not caused by his negligence or that he exercised due care. The burden of proof always remains with the plaintiff.* [Emphasis added.]

 * * * Here plaintiff made out a *prima facie* [legally sufficient] case of negligence by showing that his horse died in Briere stable's care during the bailment. Briere stable then came forward with evidence showing that the horse was undergoing ordinary exercises by a person experienced in handling and exercising horses, when it died. These proofs presented by the Briere stable are devoid of any evidence of negligence causing the death of the horse, and thus rebut the presumption of negligence. Plaintiff has failed to come forward with any additional proofs to establish that the horse was negligently exercised or that the exercise was a proximate cause of its death.

---

a. In the "Search the N.J. Courts Decisions" section, in the "Please enter your search term(s) below:" box, type "LaPlace" and click on "Search!" In the result, click on the name of the case to access the opinion.

CASE 49.3 CONTINUED ▶   * * * Nor can we presume that proximate cause is present here. The rebuttable [refutable] presumption in favor of a bailor against a bailee for negligence * * * [is] in place because the chattel [personal property] is in the exclusive control of the bailee who is in a unique position to explain what happened to the chattel. Operation of that presumption on the issue of proximate cause in this case makes no sense since determining the cause of death was uniquely within the control of plaintiff. Since plaintiff owned the animal, his consent was required for further examination and a necropsy. Plaintiff still bears the ultimate burden of proof, and under a negligent cause of action, he must show both negligence and that the negligence was a proximate cause of the harm. This he cannot do.

DECISION AND REMEDY • *The state intermediate appellate court affirmed the lower court's judgment. Based on the lack of proof of negligence, Briere could not be held liable on that claim for the death of Park Me In First.*

THE LEGAL ENVIRONMENT DIMENSION • *At Briere's stable, LaPlace had access to, and control over, Park Me In First at any time. Could Briere thus deny that a bailment relationship existed? Explain.*

WHAT IF THE FACTS WERE DIFFERENT? • *Suppose that LaPlace could view his horses at any time via a Web camera installed in Briere's stable. Would the outcome of this case have been different? Why or why not?*

Duties of the Bailor

The duties of a bailor are essentially the same as the rights of a bailee. A bailor has a duty to compensate the bailee either as agreed or as reimbursement for costs incurred by the bailee in keeping the bailed property. A bailor also has an all-encompassing duty to provide the bailee with goods or chattels that are free from known defects that could cause injury to the bailee.

BAILOR'S DUTY TO REVEAL DEFECTS The bailor's duty to reveal defects to the bailee translates into two rules:

1. In a *mutual-benefit bailment,* the bailor must notify the bailee of all known defects and any hidden defects that the bailor knows of or could have discovered with reasonable diligence and proper inspection.
2. In a *bailment for the sole benefit of the bailee,* the bailor must notify the bailee of any known defects.

The bailor's duty to reveal defects is based on a negligence theory of tort law. A bailor who fails to give the appropriate notice is liable to the bailee and to any other person who might reasonably be expected to come into contact with the defective article.

Suppose that Rentco (the bailor) rents a tractor to Hal Iverson. Unknown to Rentco (but *discoverable* by reasonable inspection), the brake mechanism on the tractor is defective at the time the bailment is made.

Iverson uses the defective tractor without knowledge of the brake problem and is injured along with two other field workers when the tractor rolls out of control. In this situation, Rentco is liable for the injuries sustained by Iverson and the other workers because it negligently failed to discover the defect and notify Iverson.

WARRANTY LIABILITY FOR DEFECTIVE GOODS A bailor can also incur warranty liability based on contract law (see Chapter 22) for injuries resulting from the bailment of defective articles. Property that is leased from a bailor must be *fit for the intended purpose of the bailment.* The bailor's knowledge of or ability to discover any defects is immaterial. Warranties of fitness arise by law in sales contracts and have been applied by judicial interpretation in cases involving bailments "for hire." Article 2A of the Uniform Commercial Code (UCC) extends the implied warranties of merchantability and fitness for a particular purpose to bailments whenever those bailments include rights to use the bailed goods.[9]

SECTION 7
SPECIAL TYPES OF BAILMENTS

Although many bailments are the ordinary bailments that we have just discussed, a business is also

---

9. UCC 2A–212, 2A–213.

likely to engage in some special types of bailment transactions. These include bailments in which the bailee's duty of care is *extraordinary*—that is, the bailee's liability for loss or damage to the property is absolute—as is generally true for common carriers and innkeepers. Warehouse companies have the same duty of care as ordinary bailees; but like carriers, they are subject to extensive federal and state laws, including Article 7 of the UCC.

Common Carriers

Common carriers are publicly licensed to provide transportation services to the general public. In contrast, private carriers operate transportation facilities for a select clientele. A private carrier is not required to provide service to every person or company making a request. A common carrier, however, must arrange carriage for all who apply, within certain limitations.[10]

The delivery of goods to a common carrier creates a bailment relationship between the shipper (bailor) and the common carrier (bailee). Unlike ordinary bailees, the common carrier is held to a standard of care based on *strict liability,* rather than reasonable care, in protecting the bailed personal property. This means that the common carrier is absolutely liable, regardless of due care, for all loss or damage to goods—*except* damage caused by one of the following common law exceptions:

1. An act of God, such as a tornado or hurricane.
2. An act of a public enemy, such as pirates or terrorists who take or damage the goods.
3. An order of a public authority, such as when a nation's officials confiscate goods that are deemed potentially hazardous.
4. An act of the shipper, such as when the shipper fails to properly package or label goods in a way that the carrier cannot reasonably discover.
5. The inherent nature of the goods, such as when fruits or vegetables decay during transit.

Common carriers cannot contract away their liability for damaged goods. Subject to government regulations, however, they are permitted to limit their dollar liability to an amount stated on the shipment contract or rate filing.[11]

CASE IN POINT Treiber & Straub, Inc., a jewelry store in Wisconsin, shipped a diamond ring to a wholesaler in California via United Parcel Service, Inc. (UPS), and arranged shipment through UPS's Web site (www.ups.com). At the Web site, a customer has to click on two boxes to agree to "My UPS Terms and Conditions." Among these terms, UPS limits its liability and the amount of insurance coverage on packages to $50,000. UPS refuses to ship any items worth more than $50,000 and disclaims liability *entirely* for such items. The ring was worth $105,000. Undeterred, Treiber opted for the maximum coverage and indicated on the air bill that the value was "$50,000 or less." UPS lost the ring. Treiber filed a lawsuit against UPS to recover $50,000 under UPS's insurance policy. The court held that UPS's disclaimer was enforceable. Treiber had clear and reasonable notice of UPS's rules, which were repeated several times on the Web site. The court also found that Treiber had effectively breached the shipping contract when it misstated the insured value of the ring (as $50,000 rather than the actual value) on the air bill. Thus, Treiber & Straub was not entitled to any recovery from UPS.[12]

Warehouse Companies

Warehousing is the business of providing storage of property for compensation. Like ordinary bailees, warehouse companies are liable for loss or damage to property resulting from *negligence*. A warehouse company, though, is a professional bailee and is therefore expected to exercise a high degree of care to protect and preserve the goods. A warehouse company can limit the dollar amount of its liability, but the bailor must be given the option of paying an increased storage rate for an increase in the liability limit.[13]

Unlike ordinary bailees, a warehouse company can issue *documents of title*—in particular, *warehouse receipts*—and is subject to extensive government regulation, including Article 7 of the UCC.[14] A warehouse receipt describes the bailed property and the

---

10. A common carrier is not required to take any and all property anywhere in all instances. Public regulatory agencies govern common carriers, and carriers may be restricted to geographic areas. They may also be limited to carrying certain kinds of goods or to providing only special types of transportation equipment.

11. Federal laws require common carriers to offer shippers the opportunity to obtain higher dollar limits for loss by paying a higher fee for the transport.

12. *Treiber & Straub, Inc. v. United Parcel Service, Inc.,* 474 F.3d 379 (7th Cir. 2007).

13. UCC 7–204(1), (2).

14. A *document of title* is defined in UCC 1–201(15) as any "document which in the regular course of business or financing is treated as adequately evidencing that the person in possession of it is entitled to receive, hold, and dispose of the document and the goods it covers." A *warehouse receipt* is a document of title issued by a person engaged for hire in the business of storing goods.

terms of the bailment contract. It can be negotiable or nonnegotiable, depending on how it is written. It is negotiable if its terms provide that the warehouse company will deliver the goods "to the bearer" of the receipt or "to the order of" a person named on the receipt.[15] The warehouse receipt represents the goods (that is, it indicates title) and hence has value and utility in financing commercial transactions.

For example, Ossip delivers 6,500 cases of canned corn to Chaney, the owner of a warehouse. Chaney issues a negotiable warehouse receipt payable "to bearer" and gives it to Ossip. Ossip sells and delivers the warehouse receipt to Better Foods, Inc. Better Foods is now the owner of the corn and can obtain the cases by simply presenting the warehouse receipt to Chaney.

Innkeepers

At common law, innkeepers and hotel owners were strictly liable for the loss of any cash or property that guests brought into their rooms. Today, only those who provide lodging to the public for compensation as a *regular* business are covered under this rule of strict liability. Moreover, the rule applies only to those who are *guests*, as opposed to *lodgers*. A lodger

---

15. UCC 7–104.

is a permanent resident of the hotel or inn, whereas a guest is a traveler. A hotel owner also is not strictly liable for the safety of a guest's automobile, because the guest usually retains possession and control. If the innkeeper provides parking facilities, however, and the guest's car is entrusted to the innkeeper or to an employee, the rules governing ordinary bailments will apply.

In many states, innkeepers can avoid strict liability for loss of guests' cash and valuables by (1) providing a safe in which to keep them and (2) notifying guests that a safe is available. In addition, statutes often limit the liability of innkeepers with regard to articles that are not kept in the safe and may limit the availability of damages in the absence of innkeeper negligence. Most statutes require that the innkeeper post these limitations or otherwise notify guests. Such postings, or notices, are frequently found on the doors of the rooms in motels and hotels.

For example, Joyce stays for a night at the Harbor Hotel. When she returns to her room after breakfast, she discovers that her suitcase has been stolen and sees that the lock on the door between her room and the room next door was forced open. Joyce claims that the hotel is liable for her loss, but under state law, if the hotel was not negligent, it is not liable.

Concept Summary 49.3 below reviews the rights and duties of bailees and bailors.

CONCEPT SUMMARY 49.3
Rights and Duties of the Bailee and the Bailor

Concept	Description
Rights of a Bailee (Duties of a Bailor)	1. The right of possession allows actions against third parties who damage or convert the bailed property and allows actions against the bailor for wrongful breach of the bailment. 2. A bailee has the right to be compensated or reimbursed for keeping bailed property. This right is based in contract or quasi contract. 3. If the compensation or reimbursement is not paid, the bailee has a right to place a possessory lien on the bailed property and to foreclose on the lien. 4. A bailee has the right to limit his or her liability. An ordinary bailee can limit the types of risk, monetary amount, or both, provided proper notice is given and the limitation is not against public policy. In special bailments, limitations on the types of risk are usually not allowed, but limitations on the monetary amount of loss are permitted by regulation.
Duties of a Bailee (Rights of a Bailor)	1. A bailee must exercise reasonable care over property entrusted to her or him. A common carrier (special bailee) is held to a standard of care based on strict liability unless the bailed property is lost or destroyed due to (a) an act of God, (b) an act of a public enemy, (c) an act of a government authority, (d) an act of the shipper, or (e) the inherent nature of the goods.

CONCEPT SUMMARY CONTINUES ➡

CONCEPT SUMMARY 49.3
Rights and Duties of the Bailee and the Bailor, Continued

Concept	Description
Duties of a Bailee (Rights of a Bailor)—Continued	2. Bailed goods in a bailee's possession must be returned to the bailor or be disposed of according to the bailor's directions. Failure to return the property gives rise to a presumption of negligence.
	3. A bailee cannot use or profit from bailed goods except by agreement or in situations in which the use is implied to further the bailment purpose.

REVIEWING
Personal Property and Bailments

Vanessa Denai purchased forty acres of land in rural Louisiana with a 1,600-square-foot house on it and a metal barn near the house. Denai later met Lance Finney, who had been seeking a small plot of rural property to rent. After several meetings, Denai invited Finney to live on a corner of her property in exchange for Finney's assistance in cutting wood and tending her property. Denai agreed to store Finney's sailboat in her barn. With Denai's consent, Finney constructed a concrete and oak foundation on Denai's property. Finney then purchased a 190-square-foot dome from Dome Baja for $3,395. The dome was shipped by Doty Express, a transportation company licensed to serve the public. When it arrived, Finney installed the dome frame and fabric exterior so that the dome was detachable from the foundation. A year after Finney installed the dome, Denai wrote Finney a note stating, "I've decided to give you four acres of land surrounding your dome as drawn on this map." This gift violated no local land-use restrictions. Using the information presented in the chapter, answer the following questions.

1. Is the dome real property or personal property? Explain.
2. Is Denai's gift of land to Finney a testamentary gift, a gift *causa mortis,* or a gift *inter vivos?*
3. What type of bailment relationship was created when Denai agreed to store Finney's boat? What degree of care was Denai required to exercise in storing the boat?
4. What standard of care applied to the shipment of the dome by Doty Express?

DEBATE THIS: *Common carriers should not be able to limit their liability.*

TERMS AND CONCEPTS

abandoned property 963
accession 961
bailee 963
bailee's lien 967

bailment 963
bailor 963
chattel 956
confusion 961
constructive delivery 959
dominion 960

estray statute 963
fixture 957
gift 959
gift *causa mortis* 961
gift *inter vivos* 961
lost property 962

mislaid property 962
personal property 956
property 956
real property 956
trade fixture 958

QUESTIONS AND CASE PROBLEMS

49–1. Gifts Jaspal has a serious heart attack and is taken to the hospital. He is aware that he is not expected to live. Because he is a bachelor with no close relatives nearby, Jaspal gives his car keys to his close friend, Friedrich, telling Friedrich that he is expected to die and that the car is Friedrich's. Jaspal survives the heart attack, but two months later he dies from pneumonia. Jaspal's uncle, Sam, the executor of Jaspal's estate, wants Friedrich to return the car. Friedrich refuses, claiming that the car was given to him by Jaspal as a gift. Discuss whether Friedrich will be required to return the car to Jaspal's estate.

49–2. QUESTION WITH SAMPLE ANSWER: Bailments.

Curtis is an executive on a business trip to the West Coast. He has driven his car on this trip and checks into the Hotel Ritz. The hotel has a guarded underground parking lot. Curtis gives his car keys to the parking lot attendant but fails to notify the attendant that his wife's $10,000 fur coat is in a box in the trunk. The next day, on checking out, he discovers that his car has been stolen. Curtis wants to hold the hotel liable for both the car and the coat. Discuss the probable success of his claim.

• **For a sample answer to Question 49–2, go to Appendix I at the end of this text.**

49–3. Duties of the Bailee Discuss the standard of care required from the bailee for the bailed property in the following situations, and determine whether the bailee breached that duty.

(a) Benedetto borrows Tom's lawn mower because his own lawn mower needs repair. Benedetto mows his front yard. To mow the backyard, he needs to move some hoses and lawn furniture. He leaves the mower in front of his house while doing so. When he returns, he discovers that the mower has been stolen.

(b) Atka owns a valuable speedboat. She is going on vacation and asks her neighbor, Regina, to store the boat in one stall of Regina's double garage. Regina consents, and the boat is moved into the garage. Regina, in need of some grocery items for dinner, drives to the store. She leaves the garage door open, as is her custom. While she is at the store, the speedboat is stolen.

49–4. Duties of the Bailee Orlando borrows a gasoline-driven lawn edger from his neighbor, Max. Max has not used the lawn edger for two years. Orlando has never owned a lawn edger and is not familiar with its use. Max previously used this edger often, and if he had made a reasonable inspection, he would have discovered that the blade was loose. Orlando is injured when the blade becomes detached while he is edging his yard.

(a) Can Orlando hold Max liable for his injuries? Why or why not?

(b) Would your answer be different if Orlando had rented the edger from Max and paid a fee? Explain.

49–5. Gratuitous Bailment Raul, David, and Javier immigrated to the United States from Colima, Mexico, to find jobs and help their families. When they learned that a mutual friend, Francisco, planned to travel to Colima, they asked him to deliver various sums, totaling more than $25,000, to their families. During customs inspections at the border, Francisco told U.S. Customs officials that he was not carrying more than $10,000, when in fact, he carried more than $35,000. The government seized the cash and arrested Francisco. Raul, David, and Javier requested that the government return their cash, arguing that Francisco was a gratuitous bailee and that they still retained title. Are they right? Explain fully.

49–6. CASE PROBLEM WITH SAMPLE ANSWER: Found Property.

A. D. Lock owned Lock Hospitality, Inc., which in turn owned the Best Western Motel in Conway, Arkansas. Joe Terry and David Stocks were preparing the motel for renovation. As they were removing the ceiling tiles in room 118, with Lock present in the room, they noticed a dusty cardboard box near the heating and air-supply vent, where it had apparently been concealed. Terry climbed a ladder to reach the box, opened it, and handed it to Stocks. The box was filled with more than $38,000 in old currency. Lock took possession of the box and its contents. Terry and Stocks filed a suit in an Arkansas state court against Lock and his corporation to obtain the money. Should the money be characterized as lost, mislaid, or abandoned property? To whom should the court award it? Explain. [Terry v. Lock, *343 Ark. 452, 37 S.W.3d 202 (2001)*]

• **To view a sample answer for Problem 49–6, go to this book's Web site at www.cengage.com/blaw/clarkson, select "Chapter 49," and click on "Case Problem with Sample Answer."**

49–7. Gifts John Wasniewski opened a brokerage account with Quick and Reilly, Inc., in his son James's name. Twelve years later, when the balance was $52,085, the account was closed, and the funds were transferred to a joint account in the names of John and James's brother. Only after the transfer, when James received a tax form for the prior account's final year, did James learn of its existence. He filed a suit in a Connecticut state court against Quick and Reilly, alleging breach of contract and seeking to recover the account's principal and interest. What are the elements of a valid gift? Did John's opening of the account with Quick and Reilly constitute a gift to James? What is the likely result in this case, and why? [*Wasniewski v. Quick and Reilly, Inc.,* 292 Conn. 98, 971 A.2d 8 (2009)]

49–8. Bailment Obligation Don Gray, who ran an aircraft paint shop, was hired to repaint an airplane owned by Bob Moreland. When Moreland left the plane for the paint job, a bailment was created. The price agreed on was $9,470. When Moreland picked up the airplane, he was disappointed in the quality of the work and pointed out numerous defects. Gray had signed the airplane log-books, indicating that the work was complete. Moreland flew the plane to another paint shop, which redid the paint job and estimated the cost of repairing the damage caused by Gray to be about $7,000. Moreland refused to pay Gray, who then sued for payment for the work he had performed on the plane. Moreland made a counter-claim. The jury awarded Moreland damages of $9,385, plus attorneys' fees of $12,420. Gray appealed, contending that when Moreland took possession of the airplane after the job was completed, he was accepting the work that had been completed. Moreland had no right to take it to another shop without giving Gray a chance to repair any defects. Is that argument correct? Why or why not? [*Gray v. Moreland*, 2010 Ark.App. 207 (2010)]

49–9. A QUESTION OF ETHICS: Gifts.

Jason Crippen and Catharyn Campbell of Knoxville, Tennessee, were involved in a romantic relationship for many months. Their relationship culminated in an engagement on December 25, 2005, when Crippen placed an engagement ring on Campbell's finger and simultaneously proposed marriage. Campbell accepted the proposal, and the parties were engaged to be married. The engagement did not last, however. The parties broke up, their romantic relationship ended, and neither had any intent to marry the other. Crippen asked Campbell to return the ring. She refused. Crippen filed a suit in a Tennessee state court against Campbell to recover the ring. Both parties filed motions for summary judgment. The court ruled in Campbell's favor. Crippen appealed to a state intermediate appellate court. [Crippen v. Campbell, __ S.W.3d __ (Tenn. App. 2007)]

(a) Under what reasoning could the court affirm the award of the ring to Campbell? On what basis could the court reverse the judgment and order Campbell to return the ring? (Hint: Is an engagement ring a completed gift immediately on its delivery?) Which principles do you support and why?

(b) Should the court determine who was responsible for breaking off the engagement before awarding ownership of the ring? Why or why not?

(c) If, instead of Crippen, one of his creditors had sought the ring in satisfaction of one of his debts, how should the court have ruled? Why?

49–10. VIDEO QUESTION: Duties of the Bailee.

Go to this text's Web site at **www.cengage.com/blaw/clarkson** and select "Chapter 49." Click on "Video Questions" and view the video titled *Personal Property and Bailments*. Then answer the following questions.

(a) What type of bailment is discussed in the video?

(b) What were Vinny's duties with regard to the rug-cleaning machine? What standard of care should apply?

(c) Did Vinny exercise the appropriate degree of care? Why or why not? How would a court decide this issue?

LEGAL RESEARCH EXERCISES ON THE WEB

Go to this text's Web site at **www.cengage.com/blaw/clarkson**, select "Chapter 49," and click on "Practical Internet Exercises." There you will find the following Internet research exercises that you can perform to learn more about the topics covered in this chapter.

Practical Internet Exercise 49–1: **Legal Perspective**
Lost Property

Practical Internet Exercise 49–2: **Management Perspective**
Bailments

CHAPTER 50

Real Property and Landlord-Tenant Relationships

From the earliest times, property has provided a means for survival. Primitive peoples lived off the fruits of the land, eating the vegetation and wildlife. Later, as the wildlife was domesticated and the vegetation cultivated, property provided pastures and farmland. Throughout history, property has continued to be an indicator of family wealth and social position. In the Western world, the protection of an individual's right to his or her property has become one of our more important rights.

In this chapter, we first look at the nature of ownership rights in real property. We then examine the legal requirements involved in the transfer of real property, including the kinds of rights that are transferred by various types of deeds; the procedures used in the sale of real estate; and a way in which real property can, under certain conditions, be transferred merely by possession. (For information on the financial aspects of real estate transactions, see Chapter 31.) Realize that real property rights are never absolute. There is a higher right—that of the government to take, for compensation, private land for public use. This chapter discusses this right, as well as other restrictions on the ownership or use of property, including zoning laws. We conclude the chapter with a discussion of landlord-tenant relationships.

SECTION 1
THE NATURE OF REAL PROPERTY

As discussed in Chapter 49, real property (or realty) consists of land and everything permanently attached to it, including structures and other fixtures. Real property is immovable, but it also includes airspace and subsurface rights, as well as plant and vegetation rights.

Land and Structures

Land includes the soil on the surface of the earth and the natural products or artificial structures that are attached to it. Land further includes all the waters contained on or under its surface and much, but not necessarily all, of the airspace above it. The exterior boundaries of land extend down to the center of the earth and up to the farthest reaches of the atmosphere (subject to certain qualifications).

Airspace and Subsurface Rights

The owner of real property has relatively exclusive rights to both the airspace above the land and the soil and minerals underneath it. Any limitations on either airspace rights or subsurface rights, called *encumbrances,* normally must be indicated on the document that transfers title at the time of purchase. The ways in which ownership rights in real property can be limited will be examined later in this chapter.

AIRSPACE RIGHTS Disputes concerning airspace rights may involve the right of commercial and private planes to fly over property and the right of individuals and governments to seed clouds and produce artificial rain. Flights over private land normally do not violate property rights unless the flights are so low and so frequent that they directly interfere with the owner's enjoyment and use of the land. Leaning walls or projecting eave spouts or roofs may also violate the airspace rights of an adjoining property owner.

SUBSURFACE RIGHTS In many states, ownership of land can be separated from ownership of its subsurface. In other words, the owner of the surface may sell subsurface rights to another person. Subsurface rights can be extremely valuable, as these rights include the ownership of minerals, oil, or natural gas. But a subsurface owner's rights would be of little value if he or she could not use the surface to exercise those rights. Hence, a subsurface owner has a right, or a *profit* (see page 980), to go onto the surface of the land to, for example, find and remove minerals.

When ownership is separated into surface and subsurface rights, each owner can pass title to what she or he owns without the consent of the other owner. Of course, conflicts can arise between the surface owner's use of the property and the subsurface owner's need to extract minerals, oil, or natural gas. In that situation, one party's interest may become subservient (secondary) to the other party's interest either by statute or by case law. If the owners of the subsurface rights excavate, they are absolutely liable if their excavation causes the surface to collapse. Many states have statutes that also make the excavators liable for any damage to structures on the land. Typically, these statutes provide precise requirements for excavations of various depths.

Plant Life and Vegetation

Plant life, both natural and cultivated, is also considered to be real property. In many instances, the natural vegetation, such as trees, adds greatly to the value of realty. When a parcel of land is sold and the land has growing crops on it, the sale includes the crops, unless otherwise specified in the sales contract. When crops are sold by themselves, however, they are considered to be personal property or goods, as noted in Chapter 49. Consequently, the sale of crops is a sale of goods and governed by the Uniform Commercial Code (UCC, discussed in Chapters 19 through 22) rather than by real property law.

SECTION 2
OWNERSHIP AND OTHER INTERESTS IN REAL PROPERTY

Ownership of property is an abstract concept that cannot exist independently of the legal system. No one can actually possess, or *hold*, a piece of land, the air above, the earth below, and all the water contained on it. One can only possess *rights* in real property. Numerous rights are involved in real property ownership, which is why property ownership is often viewed as a bundle of rights. One who possesses the entire bundle of rights is said to hold the property in *fee simple,* which is the most complete form of ownership. When only some of the rights in the bundle are transferred to another person, the effect is to limit the ownership rights of both the transferor of the rights and the recipient.

Traditionally, ownership interests in real property were referred to as *estates in land,* which include fee simple estates, life estates, and leasehold estates. We examine these estates in land, forms of concurrent ownership, and certain other interests in real property that is owned by others in the following subsections.

Ownership in Fee Simple

In a **fee simple absolute,** the owner has the greatest aggregation of rights, privileges, and power possible. The owner can give the property away or dispose of the property by *deed* (see page 984) or by will (see Chapter 52). When there is no will, the fee simple passes to the owner's legal heirs on her or his death. A fee simple absolute is potentially infinite in duration and is assigned forever to a person and her or his heirs without limitation or condition.[1] The owner has the rights of *exclusive* possession and use of the property.

The rights that accompany a fee simple absolute include the right to use the land for whatever purpose the owner sees fit. Of course, other laws, including applicable zoning, noise, and environmental laws, may limit the owner's ability to use the property in certain ways. A person who uses his or her property in a manner that unreasonably interferes with others' right to use or enjoy their own property can be liable for the tort of *nuisance* (discussed in Chapter 46).

In the following case, the court had to decide whether the noise—including rock and roll music, conversation, and clacking pool balls—coming from a local bar unreasonably interfered with a neighboring property owner's rights.

---

1. Another type of estate, the *fee simple defeasible,* exists in which ownership in fee simple will automatically terminate if a stated event occurs, such as when property is conveyed (transferred) to a school board only as long as it is used for school purposes. In addition, the fee simple may be subject to a *condition subsequent,* meaning that if a stated event occurs, the prior owner of the property can bring an action to regain possession of the property.

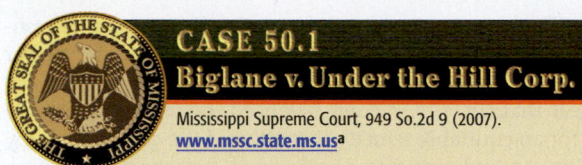

CASE 50.1
Biglane v. Under the Hill Corp.
Mississippi Supreme Court, 949 So.2d 9 (2007).
www.mssc.state.ms.us[a]

BACKGROUND AND FACTS • In 1967, Nancy and James Biglane bought and refurbished a building at 27 Silver Street in Natchez, Mississippi, and opened the lower portion as a gift shop. In 1973, Andre Farish and Paul O'Malley bought the building next door, at 25 Silver Street, and opened the Natchez Under the Hill Saloon.[b] Later, the Biglanes converted the upper floors of their building into an apartment and moved in. Although they installed insulated walls and windows, located the bedroom on the side of the building away from the Saloon, and placed the air-conditioning unit on the side nearest the Saloon, the Biglanes had a problem. The noise from the Saloon kept them wide awake at night. During the summer, the Saloon, which had no air-conditioning, opened its windows and doors, and live music echoed up and down the street. The Biglanes asked the Saloon to turn the music down, and it was. Additionally, thicker windows were installed, the loudest band was replaced, and the other bands were asked to keep their output below a certain level of decibels. Still dissatisfied, the Biglanes filed a suit in a Mississippi state court against the Saloon. The court enjoined the defendant from opening doors or windows when music was playing and ordered it to prevent its patrons from loitering in the street. Both parties appealed to the Mississippi Supreme Court.

IN THE LANGUAGE OF THE COURT
DIAZ, Justice, for the court.
* * * *

> An entity is subject to liability * * * when its conduct is a legal cause of an invasion of another's interest in the private use and enjoyment of land and that invasion is * * * intentional and unreasonable * * * . [Emphasis added.]

* * * [The trial court] found ample evidence that the Biglanes frequently could not use or enjoy their property—significantly, that Mrs. Biglane often slept away from the apartment on weekends to avoid the noise and that she could not have her grandchildren over on the weekends because of the noise. The audiologist [one who diagnoses hearing problems] who testified for the Biglanes concluded that the noise levels were excessive and unreasonable * * * .

* * * *

* * * The trial court weighed the fact that the Biglanes knew or should have known that there was going to be some sort of noise associated with living within five feet of a * * * saloon which provides live music on the weekends.

* * * *

* * * *A reasonable use of one's property cannot be construed to include those uses which produce obnoxious noises, which in turn result in a material injury to owners of property in the vicinity, causing them to suffer substantial annoyance, inconvenience, and discomfort.* [Emphasis added.]

Accordingly, even a lawful business—which the Under the Hill Saloon certainly is—may * * * [not interfere] with its neighbors' enjoyment of their property. We recognize that each * * * case must be decided upon its own peculiar facts, taking into consideration the location and the surrounding circumstances. Ultimately, it is not necessary that other property owners should be driven from their dwellings, because it is enough that the enjoyment of life and property is rendered materially uncomfortable and annoying.

* * * *

In the case at hand, the trial court exercised its power to permit continued operation of the Saloon while setting conditions to its future operation. Namely, it found that the Saloon could not operate its business with its doors and windows opened during any time that amplified

---

a. Under "Quick Links," click on "Decisions Search" in the "Supreme Court" section. When that page opens, select "Natural Language" and enter "Biglane" and click on "Search." Select the file from the Mississippi Supreme Court (decided 2/27/07) to view the decision. The Mississippi Judiciary maintains this Web site.

b. The term *saloon* was used during the mid- to late nineteenth century in the American West to indicate an establishment that served alcohol.

CASE CONTINUES ➡

CASE 50.1 CONTINUED ➧ music is being played inside the saloon. The * * * court found that such a limitation is reasonable in that it should help contain the noise within the saloon, and should discourage the bar patrons from congregating or loitering in the streets outside of the saloon.

From a review of the record it is clear that the * * * court balanced the interests between the Biglanes and the Saloon in a quest for an equitable remedy that allowed the couple to enjoy their private apartment while protecting a popular business and tourist attraction from over-regulation.

DECISION AND REMEDY • *The Mississippi Supreme Court affirmed the lower court's injunction. The Saloon unreasonably interfered with the Biglanes' rights. "One landowner may not use his land so as to unreasonably annoy, inconvenience, or harm others."*

THE ETHICAL DIMENSION • *At one point, the Biglanes blocked off two parking lots that served the Saloon. Was this an unreasonable interference with the Saloon's rights? Explain.*

THE LEGAL ENVIRONMENT DIMENSION • *Could repulsive odors emanating from a neighbor's property constitute unreasonable interference with a property owner's rights? Discuss.*

Life Estates

A **life estate** is an estate that lasts for the life of some specified individual. A **conveyance,** or transfer of real property, "to A for his life" creates a life estate.[2] In a life estate, the life tenant's ownership rights cease to exist on the life tenant's death. The life tenant has the right to use the land, provided that he or she commits no **waste** (injury to the land). In other words, the life tenant cannot use the land in a manner that would adversely affect its value. The life tenant can use the land to harvest crops or, if mines and oil wells are already on the land, can extract minerals and oil from it, but the life tenant cannot exploit the land by creating new wells or mines.

The life tenant can create liens, *easements* (see page 980), and leases. None can extend beyond the life of the tenant, however. In addition, with few exceptions, the owner of a life estate has an exclusive right to possession during his or her lifetime.

Along with these rights, the life tenant also has some duties—to keep the property in repair and to pay property taxes. In sum, the owner of the life estate has the same rights as a fee simple owner except that she or he must maintain the value of the property during her or his tenancy.

Concurrent Ownership

Persons who share ownership rights simultaneously in particular property (including real property and personal property) are said to have **concurrent ownership.** There are two principal types of concurrent ownership: *tenancy in common* and *joint tenancy.* Concurrent ownership rights can also be held in a tenancy by the entirety or as *community property,* although these types of concurrent ownership are less common.

TENANCY IN COMMON The term **tenancy in common** refers to a form of co-ownership in which each of two or more persons owns an undivided interest in the property. The interest is undivided because each tenant has rights in the whole property. On the death of a tenant in common, that tenant's interest in the property passes to her or his heirs.

For example, four friends purchase a condominium unit in Hawaii together as tenants in common. This means that each of them has an ownership interest (one-fourth) in the whole. If one of the four owners dies a year after the purchase, his ownership interest passes to his heirs (his wife and children, for example) rather than to the other tenants in common.

Unless the co-tenants have agreed otherwise, a tenant in common can transfer her or his interest in the property to another without the consent of the remaining co-owners. Generally, it is presumed that a co-tenancy is a tenancy in common unless there is a clear intention to establish a joint tenancy (discussed next).

JOINT TENANCY In a **joint tenancy,** each of two or more persons owns an undivided interest in the property, but a deceased joint tenant's interest passes to the surviving joint tenant or tenants. The right of a surviving joint tenant to inherit a deceased joint

---

2. A less common type of life estate is created by the conveyance "to A for the life of B." This is known as an estate *pur autre vie*— that is, an estate for the duration of the life of another.

tenant's ownership interest—referred to as a *right of survivorship*—distinguishes a joint tenancy from a tenancy in common. Suppose that Jerrold and Eva are married and purchase a house as joint tenants. The title to the house clearly expresses the intent to create a joint tenancy because it says "to Jerrold and Eva as joint tenants with right of survivorship." Jerrold has three children from a prior marriage. If Jerrold dies, his interest in the house automatically passes to Eva rather than to his children from the prior marriage.

Although a joint tenant can transfer her or his rights by sale or gift to another without the consent of the other joint tenants, doing so terminates the joint tenancy. In such a situation, the person who purchases the property or receives it as a gift becomes a tenant in common, not a joint tenant. For example, three brothers, Brody, Saul, and Jacob, own a parcel as joint tenants. Brody is experiencing financial difficulties and sells his interest in the property to Beth. The sale terminates the joint tenancy, and now Beth, Saul, and Jacob hold the property as tenants in common.

A joint tenant's interest can also be levied against (seized by court order, see Chapter 28) to satisfy the tenant's judgment creditors. If this occurs, the joint tenancy terminates, and the remaining owners hold the property as tenants in common. (Judgment creditors can also seize the interests of tenants in a tenancy in common.)

TENANCY BY THE ENTIRETY A **tenancy by the entirety** is a less common form of ownership that typically is created by a conveyance (transfer) of real property to a husband and wife. It differs from a joint tenancy in that neither spouse may separately transfer his or her interest during his or her lifetime unless the other spouse consents. In some states in which statutes give the wife the right to convey her property, this form of concurrent ownership has effectively been abolished. A divorce, either spouse's death, or mutual agreement will terminate a tenancy by the entirety.

COMMUNITY PROPERTY A limited number of states[3] allow property to be owned by a married couple as **community property.** If property is held as community property, each spouse technically owns an undivided one-half interest in the property. This type of ownership applies to most property acquired by the husband or the wife during the course of the marriage. It generally does not apply to property acquired prior to the marriage or to property acquired by gift or inheritance during the marriage. After a divorce, community property is divided equally in some states and according to the discretion of the court in other states.

Leasehold Estates

A **leasehold estate** is created when a real property owner or lessor (landlord) agrees to convey the right to possess and use the property to a lessee (tenant) for a certain period of time. In every leasehold estate, the tenant has a *qualified* right to exclusive, though *temporary,* possession (qualified by the landlord's right to enter onto the premises to ensure that the tenant is not causing damage to the property). The tenant can use the land—for example, by harvesting crops—but cannot injure it by such activities as cutting down timber to sell or extracting oil.

The respective rights and duties of the landlord and tenant that arise under a lease agreement will be discussed later in this chapter. Here, we look at the types of leasehold estates, or tenancies, that can be created when real property is leased.

FIXED-TERM TENANCY OR TENANCY FOR YEARS A **fixed-term tenancy,** also called a *tenancy for years,* is created by an express contract by which property is leased for a specified period of time, such as a month, a year, or a period of years. Signing a one-year lease to occupy an apartment, for instance, creates a tenancy for years. Note that the term need not be specified by date and can be conditioned on the occurrence of an event, such as leasing a cabin for the summer or an apartment during Mardi Gras. At the end of the period specified in the lease, the lease ends (without notice), and possession of the property returns to the lessor. If the tenant dies during the period of the lease, the lease interest passes to the tenant's heirs as personal property. Often, leases include renewal or extension provisions.

PERIODIC TENANCY A **periodic tenancy** is created by a lease that does not specify how long it is to last but does specify that rent is to be paid at certain intervals. This type of tenancy is automatically renewed for another rental period unless properly terminated. For example, Jewel, LLC, enters into a lease with Capital Properties. The lease states, "Rent is due on the tenth day of every month." This provision creates a periodic tenancy from month to

---

3. These states include Alaska, Arizona, California, Idaho, Louisiana, Nevada, New Mexico, Texas, Washington, and Wisconsin. Puerto Rico allows property to be owned as community property as well.

month. This type of tenancy can also extend from week to week or from year to year. A periodic tenancy sometimes arises when a landlord allows a tenant under a tenancy for years to *hold over* (retain possession after the lease term ends) and continue paying monthly or weekly rent.

Under the common law, to terminate a periodic tenancy, the landlord or tenant must give at least one period's notice to the other party. If the tenancy is month to month, for example, one month's notice must be given. State statutes often require a different period for notice of termination in a periodic tenancy, however.

TENANCY AT WILL In a **tenancy at will,** either the landlord or the tenant can terminate the tenancy without notice. This type of tenancy can arise if a landlord rents property to a tenant "for as long as both agree" or allows a person to live on the premises without paying rent. Tenancy at will is rare today because most state statutes require a landlord to provide some period of notice to terminate a tenancy (as previously noted). States may also require a landowner to have sufficient cause (reason) to end a residential tenancy. Certain events, such as the death of either party or the voluntary commission of *waste* (harm to the premises) by the tenant, automatically terminate a tenancy at will.

TENANCY AT SUFFERANCE The mere possession of land without right is called a **tenancy at sufferance.** A tenancy at sufferance is not a true tenancy because it is created when a tenant *wrongfully* retains possession of property. Whenever a tenancy for years or a periodic tenancy ends and the tenant continues to retain possession of the premises without the owner's permission, a tenancy at sufferance is created.

Nonpossessory Interests

In contrast to the types of property interests just described, some interests in land do not include any rights to possess the property. These interests, known as **nonpossessory interests,** include *easements*, *profits*, and *licenses*. Nonpossessory interests are basically interests in real property owned by others.

An **easement** is the right of a person to make limited use of another person's real property without taking anything from the property. The right to walk across another's property, for example, is an easement. In contrast, a **profit** is the right to go onto land owned by another and take away some part of the land itself or some product of the land.

For example, Akmed, the owner of Sandy View, gives Ann the right to go there and remove all of the sand and gravel that she needs for her cement business. Ann has a profit.

Easements and profits can be classified as either *appurtenant* or *in gross*. Because easements and profits are similar and the same rules apply to both, we discuss them together.

EASEMENT OR PROFIT APPURTENANT An easement or profit *appurtenant* arises when the owner of one piece of land has a right to go onto (or remove things from) an adjacent piece of land owned by another. The land that is benefited by the easement is called the *dominant estate,* and the land that is burdened is called the *servient estate*. Because easements appurtenant are intended to *benefit the land,* they run (are conveyed) with the land when it is transferred. Suppose that Owen has a right to drive his car across Green's land, which is adjacent to Owen's property. This right-of-way over Green's property is an easement appurtenant to Owen's land and can be used only by Owen. If Owen sells his land, the easement runs with the land to benefit the new owner.

EASEMENT OR PROFIT IN GROSS In an easement or profit *in gross,* the right to use or take things from another's land is given to one who does not own an adjacent tract of land. These easements are intended to *benefit a particular person or business,* not a particular piece of land, and cannot be transferred. For example, Avery owns a parcel of land with a marble quarry. Avery conveys to Classic Stone Corporation the right to come onto her land and remove up to five hundred pounds of marble per day. Classic Stone owns a profit in gross and cannot transfer this right to another. Similarly, when a utility company is granted an easement to run its power lines across another's property, it obtains an easement in gross.

CREATION OF AN EASEMENT OR PROFIT Most easements and profits are created by an express grant in a contract, deed, or will. This allows the parties to include terms defining the extent and length of time of use. In some situations, an easement or profit can also be created without an express agreement.

An easement or profit may arise by *implication* when the circumstances surrounding the division of a parcel of property imply its creation. For example, Barrow divides a parcel of land that has only one well for drinking water. If Barrow conveys the half without a well to Dean, a profit by implication arises because Dean needs drinking water.

An easement may also be created by *necessity*. An easement by necessity does not require division of property for its existence. A person who rents an apartment, for example, has an easement by necessity in the private road leading up to it.

An easement arises by *prescription* when one person exercises an easement, such as a right-of-way, on another person's land without the landowner's consent, and the use is apparent and continues for a period of time equal to the applicable statute of limitations. (In much the same way, title to property may be obtained by adverse possession, as will be discussed later in this chapter.)

TERMINATION OF AN EASEMENT OR PROFIT An easement or profit can be terminated or extinguished in several ways. The simplest way is to deed it back to the owner of the land that is burdened by it. Another way is to abandon it and create evidence of intent to relinquish the right to use it. Mere nonuse will not extinguish an easement or profit *unless the nonuse is accompanied by an overt act showing the intent to abandon.* Also, if the owner of an easement or profit becomes the owner of the property burdened by it, then it is merged into the property.

LICENSE In the context of real property, a **license** is the revocable right of a person to come onto another person's land. It is a personal privilege that arises from the consent of the owner of the land and can be revoked by the owner. A ticket to attend a movie at a theater is an example of a license. Assume that a Broadway theater owner issues a ticket to see a play to Alena. If Alena is refused entry because she is improperly dressed, she has no right to force her way into the theater. The ticket is only a revocable license, not a conveyance of an interest in property.

In essence, a license grants a person the authority to enter the land of another and perform a specified act or series of acts without obtaining any permanent interest in the land. When a person with a license exceeds the authority granted and undertakes some action on the property that is not permitted, the property owner can sue that person for trespass (discussed in Chapter 6).

CASE IN POINT A Catholic church granted Prince Realty Management, LLC, a three-month license to use a three-foot strip of its property adjacent to Prince's property. The license authorized Prince to "put up plywood panels," creating a temporary fence to protect Prince's property during the construction of a new building, and then restore the boundary line between the properties with a new brick fence.

During the license's term, Prince installed steel piles and beams on the licensed property. When Prince ignored the church's demands that these structures be removed, the church sued Prince for trespass. The court held that because the license allowed only temporary structures and Prince had exceeded its authority by installing steel piles and beams, the church was entitled to damages.[4]

See *Concept Summary 50.1* on the following page for a review of the interests that can exist in real property.

SECTION 3

TRANSFER OF OWNERSHIP

Ownership interests in real property are frequently transferred by sale, and the terms of the transfer are specified in a real estate sales contract. Often, real estate brokers or agents who are licensed by the state assist the buyers and sellers during the sales transaction. (For a discussion of special duties related to brokers and agents, see Chapter 32.) Real property ownership can also be transferred by gift, by will or inheritance, by possession, or by eminent domain. In the subsections that follow, we focus primarily on voluntary sales of real property. We then consider adverse possession, which is an involuntary method of transferring title to real property. Eminent domain will be discussed later in this chapter, and transfers by will or inheritance will be discussed in Chapter 52.

Listing Agreements

In a typical real estate transaction, the seller employs a real estate agent to find a buyer for the property by entering into a listing agreement with the agent. The listing agreement specifies the duration of the listing with that agent, the terms under which the seller will sell the property, and the amount of commission the seller will pay.

There are different types of listing agreements. If the contract gives the agent an exclusive right to sell the property, then only that real estate agent is authorized to sell the property for a specified period of time. For example, a seller might give the agent thirty days of exclusive agency. If a buyer is found within the thirty-day period, the agent will be paid the full amount of the commission even if the agent

---

4. *Roman Catholic Church of Our Lady of Sorrows v. Prince Realty Management, LLC,* 47 A.D.3d 909, 850 N.Y.S.2d 569 (2008).

Type of Interest	Description

Ownership Interests	1. *Fee simple absolute*—The most complete form of ownership.
	2. *Life estate*—An estate that lasts for the life of a specified individual.
	3. *Concurrent interests*—When two or more persons hold title to property together, concurrent ownership exists.
	   a. A tenancy in common exists when two or more persons own an undivided interest in property. On a tenant's death, that tenant's property interest passes to his or her heirs.
	   b. A joint tenancy exists when two or more persons own an undivided interest in property, with a right of survivorship. On the death of a joint tenant, that tenant's property interest transfers to the remaining tenant(s), not to the heirs of the deceased.
	   c. A tenancy by the entirety is a form of co-ownership between a husband and wife that is similar to a joint tenancy, except that a spouse cannot separately transfer her or his interest during her or his lifetime.
	   d. Community property is a form of co-ownership between a husband and wife in which each spouse technically owns an undivided one-half interest in property acquired during the marriage. This type of ownership occurs in only a few states.

Leasehold Estates	A leasehold estate is an interest in real property that is held for only a limited period of time, as specified in the lease agreement. Types of tenancies relating to leased property include the following: 1. *Fixed-term tenancy (tenancy for years)*—Tenancy for a period of time stated by express contract. 2. *Periodic tenancy*—Tenancy for a period determined by the frequency of rent payments; automatically renewed unless proper notice is given. 3. *Tenancy at will*—Tenancy for as long as both parties agree; no notice of termination is required. 4. *Tenancy at sufferance*—Possession of land without legal right.
Nonpossessory Interests	Interests that involve the right to use real property but not to possess it. Easements, profits, and licenses are nonpossessory interests.

was not responsible for finding that buyer. After the thirty-day period ends, if another real estate agent procures a buyer, the listing agent may have to split the commission. In an open listing, the seller agrees to pay a commission to the real estate agent who brings in a buyer. An open listing is nonexclusive, and thus agents with other real estate firms may attempt to find a buyer and share in the commission with the listing agent.

Although many sales of real estate involve listing agreements, it is not necessary for a property owner to list the property with a real estate agent. Many owners offer their properties for sale directly without an agent. The ability to advertise real properties for sale via the Internet has made it easier for an owner to find a buyer without using an agent. Because an agent is not essential, listing agreements

are not shown in Exhibit 50–1 on the facing page, which summarizes the steps involved in any sale of real property.

Real Estate Sales Contracts

The sale of real estate is in some ways similar to the sale of goods because it involves a transfer of ownership, often with specific warranties. In a sale of real estate, however, certain formalities are observed that are not required in a sale of goods. The sale of real estate is a complicated transaction. Usually, after substantial negotiation between the parties (offers, counteroffers, responses), the parties enter into a detailed contract setting forth their agreement. A contract for a sale of land includes such terms as the purchase price, the type of deed the buyer will

EXHIBIT 50-1 • Steps Involved in the Sale of Real Estate

BUYER'S PURCHASE OFFER
Buyer offers to purchase Seller's property. The offer may be conditioned on Buyer's ability to obtain financing, on satisfactory inspections of the premises, on title examination, and the like. Included with the offer is earnest money, which will be placed in an escrow account.

SELLER'S RESPONSE
If Seller accepts Buyer's offer, then a contract is formed. Seller could also reject the offer or make a counteroffer that modifies Buyer's terms. Buyer may accept or reject Seller's counteroffer or make a counteroffer that modifies Seller's terms.

PURCHASE AND SALE AGREEMENT
Once an offer or a counteroffer is accepted, a purchase and sale agreement is formed.

TITLE EXAMINATION AND INSURANCE
The examiner investigates and verifies Seller's rights in the property and discloses any claims or interests held by others. Buyer (and/or Seller) may purchase title insurance to protect against a defect in title.

FINANCING
Buyer may seek a mortgage loan to finance the purchase. Buyer agrees to grant lender an interest in the property as security for Buyer's indebtedness.

INSPECTION
Buyer has the property inspected for any physical problems, such as major structural or mechanical defects and insect infestation.

ESCROW
Buyer's purchase funds (including earnest money) are held in an escrow account by an escrow agent (such as a title company or a bank). This agent holds the deed transferring title received from Seller and any funds received from Buyer until all conditions of the sale have been met.

CLOSING
The escrow agent transfers the deed to Buyer and the proceeds of the sale to Seller. The proceeds are the purchase price less any amount already paid by Buyer and any closing costs to be paid by Seller. Included in the closing costs are fees charged for services performed by the lender, escrow agent, and title examiner. The purchase and sale of the property are complete.

---

receive, the condition of the premises, and any items that will be included.

CONTINGENCIES Unless the buyer pays cash for the property, the buyer must obtain financing through a mortgage loan. Real estate sales contracts are often made contingent on the buyer obtaining financing at or below a specified rate of interest. (Chapter 31 explains the disclosures necessary for residential financing and the special disclosures required for high-interest mortgage loans.) The contract may also be contingent on the buyer selling other real property, the seller obtaining a survey and title insurance, and the property passing one or more inspections. Normally, the buyer is responsible for having the premises inspected for physical or mechanical defects and for insect infestation.

CLOSING DATE AND ESCROW The contract usually fixes a date for performance, or **closing,** that

frequently is four to twelve weeks after the contract is signed. On this day, the seller conveys the property to the buyer by delivering the deed to the buyer in exchange for payment of the purchase price. Deposits toward the purchase price normally are held in a special account, called an **escrow account,** until all of the conditions of sale have been met. Once the closing takes place, the funds in the escrow account are transferred to the seller. The *escrow agent,* which may be a title company, bank, or special escrow company, acts as a neutral party in the sales transaction and facilitates the sale by allowing the buyer and seller to close the transaction without having to exchange documents and funds.

IMPLIED WARRANTIES IN THE SALE OF NEW HOMES
The common law rule of *caveat emptor* ("let the buyer beware") held that the seller of a home made no warranty as to its soundness or fitness (unless

the contract or deed stated otherwise). Today, however, most states imply a warranty—the **implied warranty of habitability**—in the sale of new homes. The seller of a new house warrants that it will be fit for human habitation even if the deed or contract of sale does not include such a warranty. Essentially, the seller is warranting that the house is in reasonable working order and is of reasonably sound construction. Under this theory, the seller of a new home can be liable if the home is defective. In some states, the warranty protects not only the first purchaser but any subsequent purchaser as well.

SELLER'S DUTY TO DISCLOSE HIDDEN DEFECTS In most jurisdictions, courts impose on sellers a duty to disclose any known defect that materially affects the value of the property and that the buyer could not reasonably discover. Failure to disclose such a material defect gives the buyer a right to rescind the contract and to sue for damages based on fraud or misrepresentation.

A dispute may arise over whether the seller knew of the defect before the sale, and there is normally a limit to the time within which the buyer can bring a suit against the seller based on the defect. For example, in Louisiana, the prescribed limit for a suit against a seller who knew, or can be presumed to have known, of the defect is one year from the day that the buyer discovered it. If the seller did not know of the defect, the limit is one year from the date of the sale.

CASE IN POINT Matthew Humphrey paid $44,000 for a house in Louisiana and partially renovated it. He then sold the house to Terry and Tabitha Whitehead for $67,000. A few months after the Whiteheads moved in, they discovered rotten wood behind the tile in the bathroom and experienced problems with the fireplace and the plumbing. Two years later, the Whiteheads filed a suit against Humphrey seeking to rescind the sale. They argued that the plumbing problems were a latent defect that the seller had failed to disclose. Evidence revealed that prior to the sale, the parties were made aware of issues regarding the sewer system and that corrective actions were taken. At the time of the sale, the toilets flushed, and neither side realized that the latent defects had not been resolved. The court ruled that rescission was not warranted for the sewer problems because the Whiteheads had waited too long after their discovery to file a claim against Humphrey. The court did order Humphrey to pay damages for the repairs to the fireplace and for replacing some of the rotten wood, however, because Humphrey knew about these defects at the time of the sale.[5]

Deeds

Possession and title to land are passed from person to person by means of a **deed**—the instrument used to transfer real property. A deed is a writing signed by an owner of real property by which title to it is transferred to another.[6] Deeds must meet certain requirements, but unlike a contract, a deed does not have to be supported by legally sufficient consideration. Gifts of real property are common, and they require deeds even though there is no consideration for the gift. To be valid, a deed must include the following:

1. The names of the *grantor* (the giver or seller) and the *grantee* (the donee or buyer).
2. Words evidencing the intent to convey (for example, "I hereby bargain, sell, grant, or give"). No specific words are necessary, and if the deed does *not* specify the type of estate being transferred, it presumptively transfers it in fee simple absolute.
3. A legally sufficient description of the land. The description must include enough detail to distinguish the property being conveyed from every other parcel of land. The property can be identified by reference to an official survey or recorded plat map, or each boundary can be described by *metes and bounds*. **Metes and bounds** is a system of measuring boundary lines by the distance between two points, often using physical features of the local geography—for example, "beginning at the southwesterly intersection of Court and Main Streets, then West 40 feet to the fence, then South 100 feet, then Northeast approximately 120 feet back to the beginning."
4. The grantor's (and usually his or her spouse's) signature.
5. Delivery of the deed.

WARRANTY DEEDS Different types of deeds provide different degrees of protection against defects of title. A **warranty deed** makes the greatest number

---

5. *Whitehead v. Humphrey,* 954 So.2d 859 (La.App. 2007).
6. Note that in some states when a person purchases real property, the bank or lender receives a *trust deed* on the property until the homeowner pays off the mortgage. Despite its name, a trust deed is not used to transfer property. Instead, it is similar to a mortgage in that the lender holds the property as security for a loan.

of warranties and thus provides the most extensive protection against defects of title. In most states, special language is required to create a warranty deed.

Warranty deeds include a number of *covenants,* or promises, that the grantor makes to the grantee. These covenants include a covenant that the grantor has the title to, and the power to convey, the property; a covenant of quiet enjoyment (a warranty that the buyer will not be disturbed in her or his possession of the land); and a covenant that transfer of the property is made without knowledge of adverse claims of third parties.

Generally, the warranty deed makes the grantor liable for all defects of title by the grantor and previous titleholders. For example, Julio sells a two-acre lot and office building by warranty deed. Subsequently, a third person appears, shows that she has better title than Julio had, and forces the buyer off the property. Here, the covenant of quiet enjoyment has been breached, and the buyer can sue Julio to recover the purchase price of the land, plus any other damages incurred as a result.

SPECIAL WARRANTY DEED In contrast to a warranty deed, a **special warranty deed,** which is frequently referred to as a *limited warranty deed,* warrants only that the grantor or seller held good title during his or her ownership of the property. In other words, the grantor does not warrant that there were no defects of title when the property was held by previous owners.

If the special warranty deed discloses all liens or other encumbrances, the seller will not be liable to the buyer if a third person subsequently interferes with the buyer's ownership. If the third person's claim arises out of, or is related to, some act of the seller, however, the seller will be liable to the buyer for damages.

QUITCLAIM DEED A **quitclaim deed** offers the least protection against defects in the title. Basically, a quitclaim deed conveys to the grantee whatever interest the grantor had. So, if the grantor had no interest, then the grantee receives no interest. Naturally, if the grantor had a defective title or no title at all, a conveyance by warranty deed or special warranty deed would not cure the defects. Such deeds, however, will give the buyer a cause of action to sue the seller.

A quitclaim deed can and often does serve as a release of the grantor's interest in a particular parcel of property. For instance, Sanchez owns a strip of waterfront property on which he wants to build condominiums. Lanz has an easement on a portion of the property that might interfere with Sanchez's plans for the development. Sanchez can negotiate with Lanz to deed the easement back to Sanchez. A quitclaim deed from Lanz would constitute such a transfer.

GRANT DEED With a **grant deed,** the grantor simply states, "I grant the property to you" or "I convey, or bargain and sell, the property to you." By state statute, grant deeds carry with them an implied warranty that the grantor owns the property and has not previously transferred it to someone else or encumbered it, except as set out in the deed.

SHERIFF'S DEED A **sheriff's deed** is a document giving ownership rights to a buyer of property at a sheriff's sale, which is a sale held by a sheriff when the owner of the property has failed to pay a court judgment against her or him. Typically, the property was subject to a mortgage or tax payments, and the owner defaulted on the payments. After a statutory period of time during which the defaulting owner can redeem the property (see Chapter 31), the deed is delivered to the purchaser.

Recording Statutes

Once the seller delivers the deed to the buyer (at closing), legal title to the property is conveyed. Nevertheless, the buyer should promptly record the deed with the state records office to establish superior ownership rights against any third parties who might make a claim to the property. Every state has a **recording statute,** which allows deeds to be recorded in the public record. Recording a deed involves a fee, which the buyer typically pays because he or she is the one who will be protected by recording the deed.

Recording a deed gives notice to the public that a certain person is now the owner of a particular parcel of real estate. By putting everyone on notice as to the true owner, recording a deed prevents the previous owners from fraudulently conveying the land to other purchasers. Deeds generally are recorded in the county in which the property is located. Many state statutes require that the grantor sign the deed in the presence of two witnesses before it can be recorded.

MARKETABLE TITLE The question of title to a particular parcel of property is especially important to the buyer. A grantor (seller) is obligated to transfer **marketable title,** or good title, to the grantee (buyer). Marketable title means that the grantor's ownership is free from encumbrances (except those disclosed by the grantor) and free of defects. If the buyer signs a real estate sales contract and then discovers that the seller does not have a marketable title, the buyer can withdraw from the contract. For example, Chan enters into an agreement to buy Fortuna Ranch from Hal. Chan then discovers that Hal has previously given Pearl an unexpired option to purchase the ranch. In this situation, the title is not marketable because Pearl could exercise the option and Hal would be compelled to sell the ranch to her. Therefore, Chan can withdraw from the contract to buy the property.

TITLE SEARCH Because each document affecting ownership of property is recorded, recording provides a chronological public record of all transactions concerning the property. A systematic examination of this record for transactions creating interests or rights in a specific parcel of real property is called a **title search.** A prospective buyer or lender generally performs a title search to determine whether the seller truly owns the interest that he or she is attempting to convey and whether anyone else has an interest in the property. A title search should—but does not always—reveal encumbrances on the property and the existence of an easement or lien.

METHODS OF ENSURING GOOD TITLE To ensure that the title is marketable, a grantee has several options depending on the state. The grantee may hire an attorney to examine an *abstract of title* (a history of what the public records show regarding the title to the property) and provide an opinion as to whether the title is marketable. If the title is defective, the attorney's opinion will specify the nature of the defects. The attorney is liable to the grantee for any loss caused by her or his negligence.

An alternative method available in a few states is the *Torrens system* of title registration. Under this system, the title is registered in a judicial proceeding. All parties claiming an interest in the property are notified of the proceeding and are given an opportunity to assert their claims. After the hearing, the court issues a certificate of title, which is similar to an automobile title, to the person found to be the owner. All encumbrances are noted on the certificate, and when the property is sold, the certificate is transferred to the grantee along with the deed.

The most common method of ensuring title is through **title insurance,** which insures the grantee against loss from defects in title to real property. When financing the purchase of real property, many lenders require title insurance to protect their interests in the collateral for the loan. Title insurance is becoming less significant because title information and records are now available electronically and thus are easy to access.

Adverse Possession

A person who wrongfully possesses (by occupying or using) the real property of another may eventually acquire title to it through adverse possession. **Adverse possession** is a means of obtaining title to land without delivery of a deed and without the consent of—or payment to—the true owner. Thus, adverse possession is a method of *involuntarily* transferring title to the property from the true owner to the adverse possessor.

Essentially, when one person possesses the real property of another for a certain statutory period of time (three to thirty years, depending on the state, with ten years being most common), that person acquires title to the land. For property to be held adversely, four elements must be satisfied:

1. *Possession must be actual and exclusive*—that is, the possessor must physically occupy the property. This requirement is clearly met if the possessor lives on the property, but it may also be met if the possessor builds fences, erects structures, plants crops, or even grazes animals on the land.
2. *The possession must be open, visible, and notorious, not secret or clandestine.* The possessor must occupy the land for all the world to see. This requirement of obviousness ensures that the true owner is on notice that someone is possessing the owner's property wrongfully.
3. *Possession must be continuous and peaceable for the required period of time.* This requirement means that the possessor must not be interrupted in the occupancy by the true owner or by the courts. *Continuous* does not mean constant—it simply means that the possessor has continuously occupied the property in some fashion for the statutory time. *Peaceable* means that no force was used to possess the land.
4. *Possession must be hostile and adverse.* In other words, the possessor cannot be living on the property with the owner's permission and must claim the property as against the whole world.

Additionally, some states have other requirements to show adverse possession. There are a number of public-policy reasons for the adverse possession doctrine. These include society's interest in resolving boundary disputes, in determining title when title to property is in question, and in assuring that real property remains in the stream of commerce. More fundamentally, the doctrine punishes owners who do not take action when they see adverse possession and rewards possessors for putting land to productive use.

In the following case, the question before the court was whether a landowner had obtained title to a portion of adjacent land by adverse possession.

CASE 50.2
Scarborough v. Rollins

Court of Appeals of Mississippi, ___ So.3d ___ (2010).
www.mssc.state.ms.us[a]

BACKGROUND AND FACTS • Charles T. Scarborough and Mildred T. Rollins were adjoining landowners, sharing one common boundary. Based on Rollins's survey of the property, Rollins believed that she owned a portion of a gravel road located to the south of the apartment buildings she owned. On the contrary, Scarborough believed that the gravel road was located totally on his property and that he owned some property north of the gravel road toward Rollins's apartment buildings. In July 2006, Scarborough filed a complaint seeking to quiet and confirm his title to the property. Rollins filed a counterclaim seeking to quiet and confirm her title. The court entered judgment for Rollins. Scarborough appealed.

IN THE LANGUAGE OF THE COURT
ISHEE, J. [Judge]
* * * *

Scarborough asserts that the trial court erred in finding that Rollins proved that she owned the property in dispute by adverse possession. Scarborough claims that Rollins failed to prove by clear and convincing evidence that her possession of the disputed grassy area down to the northern edge of the gravel road has been hostile, open, notorious, visible, continuing, exclusive, and peaceful. Scarborough also claims that Rollins's paying taxes and mowing the grass north of the gravel road by her and her predecessors in title, as well as [a prior owner's] installation of a gas line are not such adverse actions that gave him sufficient notice that he would know that Rollins was claiming the disputed area and that she was attempting to deny him ownership thereof and exclude him therefrom. Scarborough asserts that both he and Rollins used the disputed land, thus exercising joint use of the land; therefore, a claim of adverse possession is not supported. Scarborough also asserts that Rollins paid taxes only on the land situated north of her monumented south boundary line while he paid taxes on all of the land called for in his deed, including the gravel road and the land north of the gravel road up to Rollins's south boundary.

To succeed on a claim of adverse possession, the claimant has the burden to prove each element by clear and convincing evidence. * * * *Adverse possession requires the claimant to prove that her possession or occupancy was: (1) under claim of ownership; (2) actual or hostile; (3) open, notorious, and visible; (4) continuous and uninterrupted for a period of ten years; (5) exclusive; and (6) peaceful.*

1. Under Claim of Ownership

The deed to Rollins's property presented to the chancery court indicated that she owned the property at or near the disputed property. Evidence was provided to show that Rollins and her predecessors-in-title paid the taxes on all of the property north of the gravel road. However, Scarborough only paid taxes on the property that was south of the gravel road.

2. Actual or Hostile

Evidence was provided to the chancery court that for more than thirty-five years, no one other than Rollins and her predecessors-in-title, the Blacks, used this property.

---

a. Under "Quick Links" on the right-hand side of the page, click on "Decisions Search" in the "Court of Appeals" section. On the next page, click on "Natural Language." When that page opens, type "2008-CA-01579-COA" in the box and click on "Search." In the result, click on the second item in the list. The Mississippi Judiciary maintains this Web site.

CASE CONTINUES ➤

CASE 50.2 CONTINUED ▶

3. Open, Notorious, and Visible

[One witness] testified at trial that his family's ownership of that land was open and obvious. He stated that everyone in Starkville, who was around the apartments, knew that the apartment complex owned the yard up to the edge of the gravel road.

4. Continuous and Uninterrupted for a Period of Ten Years

Testimony at trial from [three witnesses] all provided that Rollins and her predecessors-in-title used the property for more than thirty-five years.

5. Exclusive

Testimony at trial * * * indicated that no one, until Scarborough, claimed to have used any part of the property in dispute.

6. Peaceful

Rollins testified that until September 2007, she and her predecessors-in-title enjoyed peaceful possession of the property.

We find that Rollins satisfied the elements required for adverse possession.

* * * *

The chancery court properly held that the gravel road which is to the north of Scarborough's property and to the south of Rollins's property was the boundary between the parties and that Rollins was entitled to an award of actual and punitive damages and attorney's fees due to the conversion of her property by Scarborough.

DECISION AND REMEDY • *The Court of Appeals of Mississippi affirmed the lower court's judgment and assessed all costs of the appeal to Scarborough. Rollins had proved title to the land by adverse possession.*

WHAT IF THE FACTS WERE DIFFERENT? • *Suppose that Rollins had not paid any taxes on the disputed land and that Scarborough had done so. Would the result have been different? Explain.*

THE E-COMMERCE DIMENSION • *How might the Internet have facilitated either party's claim to the disputed property?*

SECTION 4
LIMITATIONS ON THE RIGHTS OF PROPERTY OWNERS

No ownership rights in real property can ever really be absolute—that is, an owner of real property cannot always do whatever she or he wishes on or with the property. Nuisance and environmental laws, for example, restrict certain types of activities. Holding the property is also conditional on the payment of property taxes. Zoning laws and building permits frequently restrict one's use of the realty. In addition, if a property owner fails to pay debts, the property may be seized to satisfy judgment creditors. In short, the rights of every property owner are subject to certain conditions and limitations. We look here at some of the important ways in which owners' rights in real property can be limited.

Eminent Domain

Even ownership in fee simple absolute is limited by a superior ownership. Just as the king was the ultimate landowner in medieval England, today the government has an ultimate ownership right in all land in the United States. This right, known as **eminent domain,** is sometimes referred to as the *condemnation power* of government to take land for public use. It gives the government the right to acquire possession of real property in the manner directed by the U.S. Constitution and the laws of the state whenever the public interest requires it. Property may be taken only for public use, not for private benefit.

For example, when a new public highway is to be built, the government decides where to build it and how much land to condemn. After the government determines that a particular parcel of land is necessary for public use, it will first offer to buy the property. If the owner refuses the offer, the government brings a judicial (condemnation) proceeding to obtain title to the land. Then, in another proceeding, the court determines the *fair value* of the land, which usually is approximately equal to its market value.

When the government uses its power of eminent domain to acquire land owned by a private party, a

taking occurs. Under the *takings clause* of the Fifth Amendment to the U.S. Constitution, the government must pay "just compensation" to the owner. State constitutions contain similar provisions.

As just mentioned, the government can utilize its power of eminent domain to take property only for a public purpose. Clearly, a dam, a highway, or a national park would be considered a public purpose. But what about economic development? Is it also a public purpose that can be furthered through the use of the power of eminent domain? That was the question in the following case.

✳ EXTENDED CASE 50.3 ✳
Kelo v. City of New London, Connecticut

Supreme Court of the United States, 545 U.S. 469, 125 S.Ct. 2655, 162 L.Ed.2d 439 (2005).
www.findlaw.com/casecode/supreme.html[a]

IN THE LANGUAGE OF THE COURT

Justice *STEVENS* delivered the opinion of the Court.

* * * *

The city of New London (hereinafter City) sits at the junction of the Thames River and the Long Island Sound in southeastern Connecticut. Decades of economic decline led a state agency in 1990 to designate the City a "distressed municipality." In 1996, the Federal Government closed the Naval Undersea Warfare Center, which had been located in the Fort Trumbull area of the City and had employed over 1,500 people. In 1998, the City's unemployment rate was nearly double that of the State, and its population of just under 24,000 residents was at its lowest since 1920.

These conditions prompted state and local officials to target New London * * * for economic revitalization. * * * In February [1998] the pharmaceutical company Pfizer Inc. announced that it would build a $300 million research facility on a site immediately adjacent to Fort Trumbull; local planners hoped that Pfizer would draw new business to the area * * *.

* * * *

The city council approved [a] plan in January 2000 [to redevelop the area that once housed the federal facility]. The [City] successfully negotiated the purchase of most of the real estate in the 90-acre area, but its negotiations with [some of the property owners] failed. As a consequence, in November 2000, the [City] initiated * * * condemnation proceedings * * *.

* * * *

* * * Susette Kelo has lived in the Fort Trumbull area since 1997. * * * She prizes [her house] for its water view.

In December 2000 [Kelo and others] brought this action in [a Connecticut state court against the City and others]. They claimed, among other things, that the taking of their properties would violate the "public use" restriction in the [U.S. Constitution's] Fifth Amendment. * * * [The court issued a ruling partly in favor of both sides.]

* * * Both sides took appeals to the Supreme Court of Connecticut, [which] held * * * that all of the City's proposed takings were valid.

* * * *

We granted *certiorari* to determine whether a city's decision to take property for the purpose of economic development satisfies the "public use" requirement of the Fifth Amendment.

* * * *

* * * This Court long ago rejected any literal requirement that condemned property be put into use for the general public.

* * * Not only was the "use by the public" test difficult to administer (*e.g.*, what proportion of the public need have access to the property? at what price?), but it proved to be impractical given the diverse and always evolving needs of society. Accordingly, * * * this Court * * * *embraced the broader and more natural interpretation of public use as "public purpose."* [Emphasis added.]

The disposition of this case therefore turns on the question whether the City's development plan serves a "public purpose."

* * * *

Viewed as a whole, our jurisprudence has recognized that the needs of society have varied between different parts of the Nation, just as they have evolved over time in response to changed circumstances. * * * *For more than a century, our public use jurisprudence has wisely eschewed [avoided] rigid formulas and intrusive scrutiny in favor of affording legislatures broad latitude in determining what public needs justify the use of the takings power.* [Emphasis added.]

* * * *

Those who govern the City were not confronted with the need to remove blight in the Fort Trumbull area, but their determination that the area was sufficiently distressed to justify a program of economic

a. In the "Browse opinions by calendar year:" section, click on "2005." In the result, click on "Kelo v. New London" to access the opinion. The United States Supreme Court maintains this Web site.

EXTENDED CASE CONTINUES ➤

EXTENDED CASE 50.3 CONTINUED ◆

rejuvenation is entitled to our deference. The City has carefully formulated an economic development plan that it believes will provide appreciable benefits to the community, including—but by no means limited to—new jobs and increased tax revenue. As with other exercises in urban planning and development, the City is endeavoring to coordinate a variety of commercial, residential, and recreational uses of land, with the hope that they will form a whole greater than the sum of its parts. To effectuate this plan, the City has invoked a state statute that specifically authorizes the use of eminent domain to promote economic development. Given the comprehensive character of the plan, the thorough deliberation that preceded its adoption, and the limited scope of our review, it is appropriate for us * * * to resolve the challenges of the individual owners, not on a piecemeal basis, but rather in light of the entire plan. *Because that plan unquestionably serves a public purpose, the takings challenged here satisfy the public use requirement of the Fifth Amendment.* [Emphasis added.]

* * * *

The judgment of the Supreme Court of Connecticut is affirmed.

 QUESTIONS

1. Why did the United States Supreme Court grant *certiorari* in this case, and what did the Court hold with respect to the principal issue?
2. Considering the impact of the majority's ruling, what are some arguments against this decision?

Legislation Prohibiting Takings for Economic Development

The increasingly widespread use of eminent domain for economic development has generated substantial controversy. Although the United States Supreme Court approved this type of taking in the *Kelo* case (just discussed), the Court also recognized that individual states have the right to pass laws that prohibit takings for economic development. Forty-three states have done exactly that, limiting the government's ability to take private property and give it to private developers. At least eight states have amended their state constitutions, and a number of other states have passed ballot measures on this issue.

Restrictive Covenants

A private restriction on the use of land is known as a **restrictive covenant.** If the restriction is binding on the party who purchases the property originally and on subsequent purchasers as well, it is said to "run with the land." A covenant running with the land must be in writing (usually it is in the deed), and subsequent purchasers must have reason to know about it. Suppose that in the course of developing a fifty-lot suburban subdivision, Levitt records a declaration of restrictions that effectively limits construction on each lot to one single-family house. Each lot's deed includes a reference to the declaration with a provision that the purchaser and her or his successors are bound to those restrictions. Thus, each purchaser assumes ownership with notice of the restrictions. If an owner attempts to build a duplex (or any structure that does not comply with the restrictions) on a lot, the other owners may obtain a court order enjoining the construction.

Alternatively, Levitt might simply have included the restrictions on the subdivision's map, filed the map in the appropriate public office, and included a reference to the map in each deed. In this way, each owner would also have been held to have constructive notice of the restrictions.

Inverse Condemnation

Typically, a government agency exercises the power of eminent domain in order to seize private property through litigation or negotiation. If the agency obtains the private land through agreement or judgment, it then pays compensation to the landowner. **Inverse condemnation,** in contrast, occurs when a government simply takes private property from a landowner without paying any compensation at all. In this situation, the landowner is forced to sue the government for compensation for the lost value of the land. The taking can be accomplished physically, as when a government agency simply uses or occupies the land. Regulation issued by government agency may also result in a property losing much of its value.

CASE IN POINT In Walton County, Florida, water flows through a ditch from Oyster Lake to the Gulf of Mexico. When Hurricane Opal caused the water to rise in Oyster Lake, Walton County reconfigured the drainage to divert the overflow onto the nearby property of William and Patricia Hemby. The flow was eventually restored to pre-Opal conditions, but during a later emergency, water was diverted onto the Hembys' property again. This diversion was not restored. The Hembys filed a suit against the county. After their deaths, their daughter Cozette Drake pursued the claim. The court found that by allowing the water diversion, created during emergency conditions, to remain on Drake's property long after the emergency had passed, the county had engaged in a permanent or continuous physical invasion. This invasion rendered Drake's property useless and deprived her of its beneficial enjoyment. Drake was therefore entitled to receive compensation from the county.[7]

SECTION 5
ZONING AND GOVERNMENT REGULATIONS

The rules and regulations that collectively manage the development and use of land are known as **zoning laws.** Zoning laws were first used in the United States to segregate slaughterhouses, distilleries, kilns, and other businesses that might pose a nuisance to nearby residences. The growth of modern urban areas has led to an increased need to organize uses of land. Today, zoning laws enable the government of a municipality—a town, city, or county—to control the speed and type of development within its borders by creating different zones and regulating the use of property allowed in each zone.

The United States Supreme Court has held that zoning is a constitutional exercise of a government's police powers.[8] Therefore, as long as its zoning ordinances are rationally related to the health, safety, or welfare of the community, a municipal government has broad discretion to carry out zoning as it sees fit. Here, we look first at the scope of zoning laws and then at some common exceptions to these laws.

Purpose and Scope of Zoning Laws

The purpose of zoning laws is to manage the land within a community in a way that encourages sustainable and organized development while controlling growth in a manner that serves the interests of the community. One of the basic elements of zoning is the classification of land by permissible use as part of a comprehensive municipal plan, but zoning extends to other aspects of land use as well.

PERMISSIBLE USES OF LAND Municipalities generally divide their available land into districts according to the land's present and potential future uses. Typically, land is classified into three types of permissible uses: residential, commercial or business, and industrial. Conservation districts are also found in some municipalities. These districts are areas dedicated to carrying out local soil and water conservation efforts—for example, *wetlands* (see page 904) might be designated as a conservation district.

In areas dedicated for **residential use,** landowners can construct buildings for human habitation. Land assigned for business activities is designated as being for **commercial use,** sometimes called business use. For example, an area with a number of retail stores, offices, supermarkets, and hotels might be designated as a commercial or business district. Land used for entertainment purposes, such as movie theaters and sports stadiums, also falls into this category, as does land used for government activities.

The third major category is **industrial use,** which typically encompasses light and heavy manufacturing, shipping, and heavy transportation. For example, undeveloped land with easy access to highways and railroads might be classified as suitable for future use by industry. Although industrial uses can be profitable for a city seeking to raise tax revenue, such uses can also result in noise, smoke, or vibrations that interfere with others' enjoyment of their property. Consequently, areas zoned for industrial use generally are kept as far as possible from residential districts and some commercial districts.

A city's residential, commercial, and industrial districts may be divided, in turn, into subdistricts. For example, zoning ordinances regulate the type, density, size, and approved uses of structures within a given district. Thus, a residential district may be divided into low-density (single-family homes with large lots), high-density (single- and multiple-family homes with small lots), and planned-unit (condominiums or apartments) subdistricts.

OTHER ZONING RESTRICTIONS Zoning rules extend to much more than the permissible use of land. In residential districts, for example, an ordinance may require a house or garage to be set back a specific

---

7. *Drake v. Walton County,* 6 So.3d 717 (Fla.App. 2009).
8. *Village of Euclid v. Ambler Realty Co.,* 272 U.S. 365, 47 S.Ct. 114, 71 L.Ed. 303 (1926).

number of feet from a neighbor's property line. In commercial districts, zoning rules may attempt to maintain a certain visual aesthetic. Therefore, businesses may be required to construct buildings of a certain height and width so that they conform to the style of other commercial buildings in the area. Businesses may also be required to provide parking for patrons or take other measures to manage traffic. In some instances, municipalities limit construction of new businesses to prevent traffic congestion. Zoning laws may even attempt to regulate the public morals of the community. For example, cities commonly impose severe restrictions on the location and operation of adult businesses. The ethical ramifications of such rules will be discussed in this unit's *Focus on Ethics* feature on pages 1,039–1,041.

Exceptions to Zoning Laws

Zoning restrictions are not absolute. It is impossible for zoning laws to account for every contingency. The purpose of zoning is to enable the municipality to control development but not to prevent it altogether or limit the government's ability to adapt to changing circumstances or unforeseen needs. Hence, legal processes have been developed to allow for exceptions to zoning laws. Here, we look at these exceptions, known as *variances* and *special-use permits,* as well as at the *special incentives* that governments may offer to encourage certain kinds of development.

VARIANCES When a property owner wants to use his or her land in a manner not permitted by zoning rules, she or he can request a **variance,** which allows an exception to the rules. Property owners normally request variances in hardship situations. For example, a homeowner may want to replace her single-car garage with a two-car garage, but if she does so, the garage will be closer to her neighbor's property than is permitted by the zoning rules. Hence, she may ask for a variance. Similarly, a church might request a variance from height restrictions in order to erect a new steeple, or a furniture retail store might ask for a variance from footprint limitations so that it can expand its showroom (a building's *footprint* is the area of ground that it covers). Note that the hardship may not be self-created—that is, a person usually cannot buy property with zoning regulations in effect and then argue that a variance is needed for the property to be used for the owner's intended purpose.

In almost all instances, before a variance is granted, there must be a public hearing with adequate notice to neighbors who may object to the exception. The property owner requesting the variance must demonstrate that it is necessary for reasonable development, is the least intrusive solution to the problem, and will not alter the essential character of the neighborhood. After the public hearing, a hearing examiner appointed by the municipality (or the local zoning board or commission) determines whether to grant the exception. When a variance is granted, it applies only to the specific parcel of land for which it was requested and does not create a regulation-free zone.

SPECIAL-USE PERMITS Sometimes, zoning laws permit a use, but only if the property owner complies with specific requirements to ensure that the proposed use does not harm the immediate neighborhood. In such instances, the zoning board will issue **special-use permits,** also called *conditional-use permits.*

For example, an area is designated as a residential district, but small businesses are permitted to operate there so long as they do not affect the characteristics of the neighborhood. A bank asks the zoning board for a special-use permit to open a branch in the area. At the public hearing, the bank's managers demonstrate that the branch will be housed in a building that comforms to the style of other structures in the area, that adequate parking will be available, and that landscaping will shield the parking lot from public view. Unless there are strong objections from the branch's prospective neighbors, the board will likely grant the permit.

SPECIAL INCENTIVES In addition to granting exceptions to zoning regulations, municipalities may also wish to encourage certain kinds of development. To do so, they offer incentives, often in the form of lower tax rates or tax credits. For example, to attract new businesses that will provide jobs for local citizens and increase the tax base, a city may offer incentives in the form of lower property tax rates for a period of years. Similarly, homeowners may receive tax credits for historical preservation if they renovate and maintain older homes.

Municipalities also offer incentives to further environmental goals. For example, tax incentives are used to encourage property owners to replace aging buildings with new ones that minimize energy use, reduce resource consumption, and promote green transportation choices—such as by providing outlets for plugging in electric cars. Tax credits provided by cities and towns also encourage construction firms to participate actively in "green" construction. (For further discussion of the green movement in real estate development, see this chapter's *Shifting Legal Priorities for Business* feature on the following page.)

SECTION 6
LANDLORD-TENANT RELATIONSHIPS

The property interest involved in a landlord-tenant relationship is known as a leasehold estate, as discussed earlier in this chapter. A landlord-tenant relationship is established by a lease contract. A **lease** contract arises when a property owner (landlord) agrees to give another party (the tenant) the exclusive right to possess the property—usually for a price and for a specified term. In most states, statutes require leases for terms exceeding one year to be in writing. The lease should describe the property and indicate the length of the term, the amount of the rent, and how and when it is to be paid. State or local law often dictates permissible lease terms and establishes standards for structures offered for lease. For example, a statute or ordinance might prohibit the leasing of a structure that is in a certain physical condition or is not in compliance with local building codes.

Over the past forty years, landlord-tenant relationships, which were traditionally governed by contract law, have become more complex, as has the law governing them. In 1972, in an effort to create more uniformity in the law governing landlord-tenant relationships, the National Conference of Commissioners on Uniform State Laws issued the Uniform Residential Landlord and Tenant Act (URLTA). Twenty-one states have adopted variations of the URLTA. We look now at the respective rights and duties of landlords and tenants.

Parties' Rights and Duties

The rights and duties of landlords and tenants generally pertain to four broad areas of concern—the possession, use, maintenance, and, of course, rent of leased property.

POSSESSION A landlord is obligated to give a tenant possession of the property that the tenant has agreed to lease. Whether the landlord must provide actual physical possession (making sure that the previous tenant leaves) or the legal right to possession (leaving it to the new tenant to oust the previous tenant) depends on the particular state. After obtaining possession, the tenant retains the property exclusively until the lease expires, unless the lease states otherwise.

The covenant of quiet enjoyment mentioned previously also applies to leased premises. Under this covenant, the landlord promises that during the lease term, neither the landlord nor anyone having a superior title to the property will disturb the tenant's use and enjoyment of the property. This covenant forms the essence of the landlord-tenant relationship, and if it is breached, the tenant can terminate the lease and sue for damages.

If the landlord deprives the tenant of possession of the leased property or interferes with the tenant's use or enjoyment of it, an **eviction** occurs. An eviction occurs, for instance, when the landlord changes the lock and refuses to give the tenant a new key. A **constructive eviction** occurs when the landlord wrongfully performs or fails to perform any of the duties the lease requires, thereby making the tenant's further use and enjoyment of the property exceedingly difficult or impossible. Examples of constructive eviction include a landlord's failure to provide heat in the winter, light, or other essential utilities.

USE AND MAINTENANCE OF THE PREMISES If the parties do not limit by agreement the uses to which the property may be put, the tenant may make any use of it. This is true as long as the use is legal and reasonably relates to the purpose for which the property is adapted or ordinarily used and does not injure the landlord's interest.

The tenant is responsible for any damage to the premises that he or she causes, intentionally or negligently, and the tenant may be held liable for the cost of returning the property to the physical condition it was in at the lease's inception. Also, the tenant is not entitled to create a nuisance by substantially interfering with others' quiet enjoyment of their property rights. The tenant usually is not responsible for ordinary wear and tear, and the property's consequent depreciation in value.

In some jurisdictions, landlords of residential property are required by statute to maintain the premises in good repair. Landlords must also comply with applicable state statutes and city ordinances regarding maintenance and repair of commercial buildings.

IMPLIED WARRANTY OF HABITABILITY A landlord who leases residential property is required to

Like other U.S. businesses, firms in the construction industry are facing increasing pressure to "go green." Now, whenever they undertake a project, they must take into account a host of new developments including the following:

- Innovative designs for buildings that emphasize the interconnectivity of people and structures across an entire neighborhood.
- New types of financing, including renewable energy credits, public tax credits, and other financial incentives.
- Real estate valuations based on a life-cycle analysis of a building's costs and benefits.
- Regulations that set minimum levels of performance based on changing best industry practices.

All of these are aimed at ensuring that future real estate developments will be more sustainable than those of the past. In achieving that goal, integrated designs and life-cycle analysis are especially important.

Sustainability through Integrated Design and Life-Cycle Analysis

One of the hallmarks of green development is integrated design, which takes account of all of a building's stakeholders. These stakeholders include all of those who work on the design and construction of the project and those who will use the building it when it is completed. Thus, a building constructed with an integrated design will be cost-effective to build and maintain, accessible to persons with disabilities, aesthetically pleasing, safe—a matter of particular concern since 9/11—and functional.

To achieve all of these qualities requires an integrated team in which the members work together instead of focusing only on their specialties. Integrated teams include not only the architects, engineers, and contractors who do the initial design and construction but also the landscapers, maintenance personnel, and others who will maintain the building after its completion. The building's future occupants will have input as well.

Closely related to integrated design is life-cycle analysis of a building's costs and benefits. Instead of focusing only on the initial cost, life-cycle analysis takes into account all of the costs of acquiring, owning, and disposing of a building over its lifetime. Thus, an element that has a high initial cost might dramatically reduce the building's operating and maintenance costs over its lifetime. For example, a building's thermal load (the amount of heat that must be removed over a given time period) depends, in part, on its orientation to the sun. A change in the building's orientation may entail a higher cost initially but save substantially on air-conditioning expenses later.

Achieving Certified Green Building Status

Between 5 and 10 percent of the buildings started in 2010 incorporated green building techniques. A motive for building green is to obtain the LEED™ certification from the U.S. Green Building Council. (LEED stands for Leadership in Energy and Environmental Design.) To receive the certification, which was started almost two decades ago, a building or real estate development must use resources sustainably, achieve energy savings, conserve water, reduce carbon dioxide emissions, and obtain other environmentally friendly goals. A similar certification is available through the Green Globes program. To obtain either certification, the project must undergo a rigorous verification process.

The Legal Risks of Going Green

Although green building is the "right thing to do," it still may entail many risks for a construction firm or real estate developer. The builder may overpromise or fail to articulate what is meant by "green building." As a result, when the project is completed, the owner may be disappointed and threaten a lawsuit for breach of contract. If a subcontractor's work fails to conform to the requirements of the LEED rating system, certain federal, state, and local tax credits may not be available.

Some of these and other risks can be managed or limited by including express warranties and insurance provisions in contracts. Contracts should clearly identify the responsibilities of various team members to ensure that the project is truly green—or at least will meet certification requirements.

MANAGERIAL IMPLICATIONS

Wanting to help the planet is a laudable goal, but managers of real estate development projects must go further. Some will want to hire green specialists to oversee at least the preliminary stages of the project. Any manager of such a project must assess the risks. One way to do so is to hire a skilled attorney who has worked on other green projects.

ensure that the premises are habitable—that is, in a condition that is safe and suitable for people to live in. Additionally, the landlord must make repairs to maintain the premises in that condition for the lease's duration. Some state legislatures have enacted this warranty into law. In other jurisdictions, courts have based the warranty on the existence of a landlord's statutory duty to keep leased premises in good repair, or they have simply applied it as a matter of public policy. Generally, this warranty applies to major, or *substantial,* physical defects that the landlord knows or should know about and has had a reasonable time to repair—for example, a large hole in the roof.

RENT *Rent* is the tenant's payment to the landlord for the tenant's occupancy or use of the landlord's real property. Usually, the tenant must pay the rent even if she or he refuses to occupy the property or moves out, as long as the refusal or the move is unjustified and the lease is in force. Under the common law, if the leased premises were destroyed by fire or flood, the tenant still had to pay rent. Today, however, if an apartment building burns down, most states' laws do not require tenants to continue to pay rent.

In some situations, such as when a landlord breaches the implied warranty of habitability, a tenant may be allowed to withhold rent as a remedy. When rent withholding is authorized under a statute, the tenant must usually put the amount withheld into an *escrow account.* This account is held in the name of the depositor (the tenant) and an *escrow agent* (usually, the court or a government agency), and the funds are returned to the depositor if the third party (the landlord) fails to make the premises habitable.

Transferring Rights to Leased Property

Either the landlord or the tenant may wish to transfer her or his rights to the leased property during the term of the lease. If the landlord transfers complete title to the leased property to another, the tenant becomes the tenant of the new owner. The new owner may collect subsequent rent but must abide by the terms of the existing lease.

ASSIGNMENT The tenant's transfer of his or her entire interest in the leased property to a third person is an *assignment of the lease.* Many leases require that an assignment have the landlord's written consent. An assignment that lacks consent can be avoided (nullified) by the landlord. State statutes may specify that the landlord may not unreasonably

withhold consent, though. Furthermore, a landlord who knowingly accepts rent from the assignee may be held to have waived the consent requirement.

When an assignment is valid, the assignee acquires all of the tenant's rights under the lease. An assignment, however, does not release the assigning tenant from the obligation to pay rent should the assignee default. In addition, if the assignee exercises an option under the original lease to extend the term, the assigning tenant remains liable for the rent during the extension, unless the landlord agrees otherwise.

SUBLEASE The tenant's transfer of all or part of the premises for a period shorter than the lease term is a **sublease.** The same restrictions that apply to an assignment of the tenant's interest in leased property apply to a sublease. If the landlord's consent is required, a sublease without such permission is ineffective. In addition, a sublease does not release the tenant from her or his obligations under the lease any more than an assignment does.

For example, Derek, a student, leases an apartment for a two-year period. Although Derek had planned on attending summer school, he decides to accept a job offer in Europe for the summer months instead. Derek therefore obtains his landlord's consent to sublease the apartment to Ava. Ava is bound by the same terms of the lease as Derek, and the landlord can hold Derek liable if Ava violates the lease terms.

Termination of the Lease

Usually, a lease terminates when its term ends. The tenant surrenders the property to the landlord, who retakes possession. If the lease states the time it will end, the landlord is not required to give the tenant notice. The lease terminates automatically. In contrast, a *periodic tenancy* (a tenancy from month to month, for example) will renew automatically unless one of the parties gives timely notice (usually, one rental period) of termination. If the lease does not contain an option for renewal and the parties have not agreed that the tenant may stay on, the tenant has no right to remain. If the lease is renewable and the tenant decides to exercise the option, the tenant must comply with any conditions requiring notice to the landlord of the tenant's decision.

A lease may also be terminated in several other ways. For example, the landlord may agree that the tenant will purchase the leased property during the term or at its end, thus terminating the lease. The parties may agree to end a tenancy before it would otherwise terminate. The tenant may also *abandon* the premises—move out completely with no intention of returning before the lease term expires.

At common law and in many states, when a tenant abandons leased property, the tenant remains obligated to pay the rent for the remainder of the lease term—however long that might be. The landlord may refuse to lease the premises to an acceptable new tenant and let the property stand vacant. In a growing number of jurisdictions, however, the landlord is required to *mitigate* his or her damages—that is, the landlord is required to make a reasonable attempt to lease the property to another party. In these jurisdictions, the tenant's liability

for unpaid rent is restricted to the period of time that the landlord would reasonably need to lease the property to another tenant.[9] Damages may also be allowed for the landlord's costs in leasing the property again. What is considered a reasonable period of time with respect to leasing the property to another party varies with the type of lease and the location of the leased premises.

---

9. See, for example, *Danada Square, LLC v. KFC National Management Co.*, 392 Ill.App. 3d 598, 913 N.E.2d 33 (2009). For further discussion of mitigation of damages, see Chapter 18.

REVIEWING

Real Property and Landlord-Tenant Relationships

Vern Shoepke purchased a two-story home from Walter and Eliza Bruster in the town of Roche, Maine. The warranty deed did not specify what covenants would be included in the conveyance. The property was adjacent to a public park that included a popular Frisbee golf course. (Frisbee golf is a sport similar to golf but using Frisbees.) Wayakichi Creek ran along the north end of the park and along Shoepke's property. The deed allowed Roche citizens the right to walk across a five-foot-wide section of the lot beside Wayakichi Creek as part of a two-mile public trail system. Teenagers regularly threw Frisbee golf discs from the walking path behind Shoepke's property over his yard to the adjacent park. Shoepke habitually shouted and cursed at the teenagers, demanding that they not throw objects over his yard. Two months after moving into his Roche home, Shoepke leased the second floor to Lauren Slater for nine months. (The lease agreement did not specify that Shoepke's consent would be required to sublease the second floor.) After three months of tenancy, Slater sublet the second floor to a local artist, Javier Indalecio. Over the remaining six months, Indalecio's use of oil paints damaged the carpeting in Shoepke's home. Using the information presented in the chapter, answer the following questions.

1. What is the term for the right of Roche citizens to walk across Shoepke's land on the trail?
2. What covenants would most courts infer were included in the warranty deed that was used in the property transfer from the Brusters to Shoepke?
3. Suppose that Shoepke wants to file a trespass lawsuit against some teenagers who continually throw Frisbees over his land. Shoepke discovers, however, that when the city put in the Frisbee golf course, the neighborhood homeowners signed an agreement that limited their right to complain about errant Frisbees. What is this type of promise or agreement called in real property law?
4. Can Shoepke hold Slater financially responsible for the damage to the carpeting caused by Indalecio? Why or why not?

DEBATE THIS: *Under no circumstances should a local government be able to condemn property in order to sell it later to real estate developers for private use.*

TERMS AND CONCEPTS

adverse possession 986
closing 983
commercial use 991
community property 979
concurrent ownership 978
constructive eviction 993
conveyance 978
deed 984
easement 980
eminent domain 988
escrow account 983

eviction 993
fee simple absolute 976
fixed-term tenancy 979
grant deed 985
implied warranty of
   habitability 984
industrial use 991
inverse condemnation 990
joint tenancy 978
lease 993
leasehold estate 979
license 981
life estate 978

marketable title 985
metes and bounds 984
nonpossessory interests 980
periodic tenancy 979
profit 980
quitclaim deed 985
recording statute 985
residential use 991
restrictive covenant 990
sheriff's deed 985
special-use permit 992
special warranty deed 985
sublease 995

taking 989
tenancy at sufferance 980
tenancy at will 980
tenancy by the entirety 979
tenancy in common 978
title insurance 986
title search 986
variance 992
warranty deed 984
waste 978
zoning laws 991

QUESTIONS AND CASE PROBLEMS

50–1. Property Ownership Madison owned a tract of land, but he was not sure that he had full title to the property. When Rafael expressed an interest in buying the land, Madison sold it to Rafael and executed a quitclaim deed. Rafael properly recorded the deed immediately. Several months later, Madison learned that he had had full title to the tract of land. He then sold the land to Linda by warranty deed. Linda knew of the earlier purchase by Rafael but took the deed anyway and later sued to have Rafael evicted from the land. Linda claimed that because she had a warranty deed, her title to the land was better than that conferred by Rafael's quitclaim deed. Will Linda succeed in claiming title to the land? Explain.

50–2. Eviction James owns a three-story building. He leases the ground floor to Juan's Mexican restaurant. The lease is to run for a five-year period and contains an express covenant of quiet enjoyment. One year later, James leases the top two stories to the Upbeat Club, a discotheque. The club's hours run from 5:00 P.M. to 11:00 P.M. The noise from the Upbeat Club is so loud that it is driving customers away from Juan's restaurant. Juan has notified James of the interference and has called the police on a number of occasions. James refuses to talk to the owners of the Upbeat Club or to do anything to remedy the situation. Juan abandons the premises. James files suit for breach of the lease agreement and for the rental payments still due under the lease. Juan claims that he was constructively evicted and files a countersuit for damages. Discuss who will be held liable.

50–3. QUESTION WITH SAMPLE ANSWER: Deeds.

Wilfredo and Patricia are neighbors. Wilfredo's lot is extremely large, and his present and future use of it will not involve the entire area. Patricia wants to build a single-car garage and driveway along the present lot boundary. Because ordinances require buildings to be set back fifteen feet from an owner's property line, however, the placement of Patricia's existing structures prevents her from building the garage. Patricia contracts to purchase ten feet of Wilfredo's property along their boundary line for $3,000. Wilfredo is willing to sell but will give Patricia only a quitclaim deed, whereas Patricia wants a warranty deed. Discuss the differences between these deeds as they would affect the rights of the parties if the title to this ten feet of land later proves to be defective.

- **For a sample answer to Question 50–3, go to Appendix I at the end of this text.**

50–4. Implied Warranty of Habitability Sarah has rented a house from Frank. The house is only two years old, but the roof leaks every time it rains. The water that has accumulated in the attic has caused plaster to fall off ceilings in the upstairs bedrooms, and one ceiling has started to sag. Sarah has complained to Frank and asked him to have the roof repaired. Frank says that he has caulked the roof, but the roof still leaks. Frank claims that because Sarah has sole control of the leased premises, she has the duty to repair the roof. Sarah insists that repairing the roof is Frank's responsibility. Discuss fully who is responsible for repairing the roof and, if the responsibility belongs to Frank, what remedies are available to Sarah.

50–5. CASE PROBLEM WITH SAMPLE ANSWER: Eminent Domain.

The Hope Partnership for Education, a religious organization, proposed to build a private independent middle school in a blighted neighborhood in Philadelphia, Pennsylvania. In 2002, the Hope Partnership asked the Redevelopment Authority of the City of Philadelphia to acquire specific land for the project and sell it to the Hope Partnership for a nominal price. The land included a house at 1839 North Eighth Street owned by Mary Smith, whose daughter Veronica lived there with her family. The Authority offered Smith $12,000 for the house and initiated a taking of the property. Smith filed a suit in a Pennsylvania state court against the Authority, admitting that the house was a "substandard structure in a blighted area," but arguing that the taking was unconstitutional because its beneficiary was private. The Authority asserted that only the public purpose of the taking should be considered, not the status of the property's developer. On what basis can a government entity use the power of eminent domain to take property? What are the limits to this power? How should the court rule? Why? [Redevelopment Authority of City of Philadelphia v. New Eastwick Corp., 588 Pa. 789, 906 A.2d 1197 (2006)]

- **To view a sample answer for Problem 50–5, go to this book's Web site at** www.cengage.com/blaw/clarkson, **select "Chapter 50," and click on "Case Problem with Sample Answer."**

50–6. Ownership in Fee Simple Thomas and Teresa Cline built a house on a 76-acre parcel of real estate next to Roy Berg's home and property in Augusta County, Virginia. The homes were about 1,800 feet apart but in view of each other. After several disagreements between the parties, Berg equipped an 11-foot tripod with motion sensors and floodlights that intermittently illuminated the Clines' home. Berg also installed surveillance cameras that tracked some of the movement on the Clines' property. The cameras transmitted on an open frequency that could be received by any television within range. The Clines asked Berg to turn off, or at least redirect, the lights. When he refused, they erected a fence for 200 feet along the parties' common property line. The 32-foot-high fence consisted of 20 utility poles spaced 10 feet apart with plastic wrap stretched between the poles. This effectively blocked the lights and cameras. Berg filed a suit against the Clines in a Virginia state court, complaining that the fence interfered unreasonably with his use and enjoyment of his property. He asked the court to order the Clines to take the fence down. What are the limits on an owner's use of property? How should the court rule in this case? Why? [Cline v. Berg, 273 Va. 142, 639 S.E.2d 231 (2007)]

50–7. Commercial Lease Terms Gi Hwa Park entered into a lease with Landmark HHH, LLC, for retail space in the Plaza at Landmark, a shopping center in Virginia. The lease required the landlord to keep the roof "in good repair" and the tenant to obtain insurance on her inventory and absolve the landlord from any losses to the extent of the insurance proceeds. Park opened a store—The Four Seasons—in the space, specializing in imported men's suits and accessories. Within a month, and continuing for nearly eight years, water intermittently leaked through the roof, causing damage. Landmark eventually had a new roof installed, but water continued to leak into The Four Seasons. On a night of record rainfall, the store suffered substantial water damage, and Park was forced to close. On what basis might Park seek to recover from Landmark? What might Landmark assert in response? Which party's argument is more likely to succeed, and why? [Landmark HHH, LLC v. Gi Hwa Park, 277 Va. 50, 671 S.E.2d 143 (2009)]

50–8. Adverse Possession In 1974, the Mansells built a shed with a dirt floor, to be used as a three-car garage, at the back of their property. This shed went beyond the Mansells' property line and encroached approximately fourteen feet on the neighboring property. The neighbor knew of the encroachment and informally approved it, but did not transfer ownership of the property. In 2001, Betty Hunter bought the neighbor's property. The survey done at that time revealed the encroachment. In 2003, Hunter's attorney notified the Mansells about the encroachment, and the parties held some informal conversations but did not reach an agreement. In 2006, the Mansells installed a concrete foundation and ran electricity to the structure. Hunter then sought a declaratory judgment that she was the fee simple owner of the property partially covered by the garage that encroached on her property, and demanded the removal of the encroaching structure. The Mansells filed a counterclaim arguing that the possession of the property from 1974 to 2001 gave them ownership by adverse possession. The trial court held that the property still belonged to Hunter, but did not order removal of the garage. Hunter and Mrs. Mansell (whose husband had died in the meantime) both appealed. Did the open occupation of the property for twenty-eight years give Mansell title by adverse possession? Why or why not? [Hunter v. Mansell, ___ P.3d ___ (Colo.App. 2010)]

50–9. A QUESTION OF ETHICS: Seller's Duty to Disclose.

In 1999, Stephen and Linda Kailin bought the Monona Center, a mall in Madison, Wisconsin, from Perry Armstrong for $760,000. The contract provided, "Seller represents to Buyer that as of the date of acceptance Seller had no notice or knowledge of conditions affecting the Property or transaction" other than certain items disclosed at the time of the offer. Armstrong told the Kailins of the Center's eight tenants, their lease expiration dates, and the monthly and annual rent due under each lease. One of the lessees, Ring's All-American Karate, occupied about a third of the Center's space under a five-year lease. Because of Ring's financial difficulties, Armstrong had agreed to reduce its rent for nine months in 1997. By the time of the

sale to the Kailins, Ring owed $13,910 in unpaid rent, but Armstrong did not tell the Kailins, who did not ask. Ring continued to fail to pay rent and finally vacated the Center. The Kailins filed a suit in a Wisconsin state court against Armstrong and others, alleging, among other things, misrepresentation. [Kailin v. Armstrong, 2002 WI App 70, 252 Wis.2d 676, 643 N.W.2d 132 (2002)]

(a) Did Armstrong have a duty to disclose Ring's delinquency and default to the Kailins? Explain.

(b) What obligation, if any, did Ring have to the Kailins or Armstrong after failing to pay the rent and eventually defaulting on the lease? Discuss.

50–10. SPECIAL CASE ANALYSIS: Eminent Domain.
Go to Extended Case 50.3, *Kelo v. City of New London, Connecticut,* 545 U.S. 469, 125 S.Ct. 2655, 162 L.Ed.2d 439 (2005), on pages 989–990. Read the excerpt and answer the following questions.

(a) Issue: On what issue did the Court focus?

(b) Rule of Law: What does the Fifth Amendment to the U.S. Constitution, which the Court applied, require with respect to the legal issue in this case?

(c) Applying the Rule of Law: How did the Court apply the rule of law to the facts of this case?

(d) Conclusion: What was the Court's conclusion?

LEGAL RESEARCH EXERCISES ON THE WEB

Go to this text's Web site at **www.cengage.com/blaw/clarkson**, select "Chapter 50," and click on "Practical Internet Exercises." There you will find the following Internet research exercises that you can perform to learn more about the topics covered in this chapter.

Practical Internet Exercise 50–1: Legal Perspective
Eminent Domain

Practical Internet Exercise 50–2: Management Perspective
Fair Housing

Practical Internet Exercise 50–3: Social Perspective
The Rights of Tenants

※

CHAPTER 51

Insurance

Protecting against loss is a foremost concern of all property owners. No one can predict whether an accident or a fire will occur, so individuals and businesses typically protect their personal and financial interests by obtaining insurance.

Insurance is a contract in which the insurance company (the insurer) promises to pay a sum of money or give something of value to another (either the insured or the beneficiary) to compensate the other for a particular, stated loss. Insurance protection may provide for compensation for the injury or death of the insured or another, for damage to the insured's property, or for other types of losses, such as those resulting from lawsuits. Basically, insurance is an arrangement for *transferring and allocating risk.* In general, risk can be described as a prediction concerning potential loss based on known and unknown factors.

Risk management normally involves the transfer of certain risks from the individual to the insurance company by a contractual agreement. We examine the insurance contract and its provisions in this chapter. First, however, we look at some basic insurance terminology and concepts.

INSURANCE TERMINOLOGY AND CONCEPTS

Like other legal areas, insurance has its own special concepts and terminology, a knowledge of which is essential to an understanding of insurance law.

Insurance Terminology

An insurance contract is called a **policy.** The consideration paid to the insurer is called a **premium,** and the insurance company is sometimes called an **underwriter.** The parties to an insurance policy are the *insurer* (the insurance company) and the *insured* (the person covered by its provisions).

Insurance contracts usually are obtained through an *agent,* who normally works for the insurance company, or through a *broker,* who is ordinarily an *independent contractor.* When a broker deals with an applicant for insurance, the broker is, in effect, the applicant's agent (and not an agent of the insurance company). In contrast, an insurance agent is an agent of the insurance company, not an agent of the applicant. Thus, the agent owes fiduciary duties to the insurer (the insurance company), but not to the person who is applying for insurance. As a general rule, the insurance company is bound by the acts of its agents when they act within the scope of the agency relationship (see Chapters 32 and 33). In most situations, state law determines the status of all parties writing or obtaining insurance.

Classifications of Insurance

Insurance is classified according to the nature of the risk involved. For example, fire insurance, casualty insurance, life insurance, and title insurance apply to different types of risk. Furthermore, policies of these types protect different persons and interests. This is reasonable because the types of losses that are expected and the types that are foreseeable or unforeseeable vary with the nature of the activity.

Exhibit 51–1 on pages 1,002 and 1,003 provides a list of common insurance classifications.

Insurable Interest

A person must have an **insurable interest** in something in order to insure it. Without an insurable interest, there is no enforceable contract, and a transaction to purchase insurance coverage would have to be treated as a wager. The existence of an insurable interest is a primary concern in determining liability under an insurance policy.

LIFE INSURANCE In regard to life insurance, a person must have a reasonable expectation of benefit from the continued life of another to have an insurable interest in that person's life. The insurable interest must exist *at the time the policy is obtained*. The benefit may be pecuniary (monetary), or it may be founded on the relationship between the parties (by blood or affinity). Close family relationships give a person an insurable interest in the life of another. Generally, blood or marital relationships fit this category. For example, a husband can take out an insurance policy on his wife and vice versa, or parents can take out life insurance policies on their children. A policy that a person takes out on his or her spouse remains valid even if they divorce, unless a specific provision in the policy calls for its termination on divorce.

KEY-PERSON LIFE INSURANCE *Key-person insurance* is insurance obtained by an organization on the life of a person who is important to that organization. Because the organization expects to experience some financial gain from the continuation of the key person's life or some financial loss from the key person's death, the organization has an insurable interest. Typically, a partnership will insure the life of each partner because the firm will sustain some degree of loss if any partner dies. Similarly, a corporation has an insurable interest in the life of a key executive whose death would result in financial loss to the company. If a firm insures a key person's life and then that person leaves the firm and subsequently dies, the firm can collect on the insurance policy, provided it has continued to pay the premiums.

PROPERTY INSURANCE An insurable interest exists in real or personal property when the insured derives a pecuniary benefit from the preservation and continued existence of the property. Put another way, a person has an insurable interest in property when she or he would sustain a financial loss from its destruction. The owner of the property clearly has an insurable interest, but a party need not be the owner to have an insurable interest. Both a mortgagor and a mortgagee, for example, have an insurable interest in the mortgaged property, as do a landlord and a tenant in leased property, and a partner and the partnership in partnership property. A secured party has an insurable interest in the property in which he or she has a security interest. The existence of an insurable interest is a primary concern in determining liability under an insurance policy.

CASE IN POINT ABM Industries, Inc., operated the heating, ventilation, and air-conditioning systems at the World Trade Center (WTC) in New York City in 2001. Under its contracts to provide these services, ABM had office and storage space at the WTC. Zurich American Insurance Company insured ABM against losses resulting from "business interruption" caused by direct physical loss or damage "to property owned, controlled, used, leased or intended for use" by ABM. After the terrorist attacks on September 11, ABM filed a claim to recover for the loss of all income derived from its WTC operations. Zurich argued that the recovery should be limited to the income lost as a result of the destruction of ABM's office and storage space and supplies. A federal appellate court, however, ruled that ABM was entitled to compensation for the loss of all of its WTC operations. The court reasoned that the "policy's scope expressly includes real or personal property that the insured 'used,' 'controlled,' or 'intended for use.'" Because ABM's income depended on "the common areas and leased premises in the WTC complex," it had an insurable interest in that property at the time of the loss.[1]

SECTION 2
THE INSURANCE CONTRACT

An insurance contract is governed by the general principles of contract law, although the insurance industry is heavily regulated by each state.[2] Customarily, a party offers to purchase insurance by submitting an application to the insurance company. The company can either accept or reject the offer. Sometimes, the insurance company's acceptance is conditional—on the results of a life insurance applicant's medical examination, for example.

---

1. *Zurich American Insurance Co. v. ABM Industries, Inc.,* 397 F.3d 158 (2d Cir. 2005).
2. The states were given authority to regulate the insurance industry by the McCarran-Ferguson Act of 1945, 15 U.S.C. Sections 1011–1015.

EXHIBIT 51–1 • **Insurance Classifications**

TYPE OF INSURANCE	COVERAGE
Accident	Covers expenses, losses, and suffering incurred by the insured because of accidents causing physical injury and any consequent disability; sometimes includes a specified payment to heirs of the insured if death results from an accident.
All-Risk	Covers all losses that the insured may incur except those that are specifically excluded. Typical exclusions are losses due to war, pollution, earthquakes, and floods.
Automobile	May cover damage to automobiles resulting from specified hazards or occurrences (such as fire, vandalism, theft, or collision); normally provides protection against liability for personal injuries and property damage resulting from the operation of the vehicle.
Casualty	Protects against losses incurred by the insured as a result of being held liable for personal injuries or property damage sustained by others.
Credit	Pays to a creditor the balance of a debt on the disability, death, insolvency, or bankruptcy of the debtor; often offered by lending institutions.
Decreasing-Term Life	Provides life insurance; requires uniform payments over the life (term) of the policy, but with a decreasing face value (amount of coverage).
Disability	Replaces a portion of the insured's monthly income from employment in the event that illness or injury causes a short- or long-term disability. Some states require employers to provide short-term disability insurance. Benefits typically last a set period of time, such as six months for short-term coverage or five years for long-term coverage.
Employer's Liability	Insures an employer against liability for injuries or losses sustained by employees during the course of their employment. Covers claims not covered under workers' compensation insurance.
Fidelity or Guaranty	Provides indemnity against losses in trade or losses caused by the dishonesty of employees, the insolvency of debtors, or breaches of contract.
Fire	Covers losses to the insured caused by fire.
Floater	Covers movable property, as long as the property is within the territorial boundaries specified in the contract.
Group	Provides individual life, medical, or disability insurance coverage but is obtainable through a group of persons, usually employees. The policy premium is paid either entirely by the employer or partially by the employer and partially by the employee.

For the insurance contract to be binding, consideration (in the form of a premium) must be given, and the parties forming the contract must have the required contractual capacity to do so.

Application for Insurance

The filled-in application form for insurance is usually attached to the policy and made a part of the insurance contract. Thus, an insurance applicant is bound by any false statements that appear in the application (subject to certain exceptions). Because the insurance company evaluates the risk based on the information included in the insurance application, misstatements or misrepresentations can void a policy, especially if the insurance company can show that it would not have extended insurance if it had known the facts.

Effective Date

The effective date of an insurance contract—that is, the date on which the insurance coverage begins—is important. In some instances, the insurance applicant is not protected until a formal written policy is issued. For example, if the parties agree that the policy will be issued and delivered at a later time, the contract is not effective until the policy is issued and delivered. Thus, any loss sustained between the time of application and the delivery of the policy is not covered. In other situations, coverage begins when a *binder* is written (to be discussed shortly) or,

EXHIBIT 51–1 • Insurance Classifications, Continued

TYPE OF INSURANCE	COVERAGE
Health	Covers expenses incurred by the insured resulting from physical injury or illness and other expenses relating to health and life maintenance.
Homeowners'	Protects homeowners against some or all risks of loss to their residences and the residences' contents or liability arising from the use of the property.
Key-Person	Protects a business in the event of the death or disability of a key employee.
Liability	Protects against liability imposed on the insured as a result of injuries to the person or property of another.
Life	Covers the death of the policyholder. On the death of the insured, the insurer pays the amount specified in the policy to the insured's beneficiary.
Major Medical	Protects the insured against major hospital, medical, or surgical expenses.
Malpractice	A form of liability insurance that protects professionals (physicians, lawyers, and others) against malpractice claims brought against them by their patients or clients.
Marine	Covers movable property (including ships, freight, and cargo) against certain perils or navigation risks during a specific voyage or time period.
Mortgage	Covers a mortgage loan. The insurer pays the balance of the mortgage to the creditor on the death or disability of the debtor.
No-Fault Auto	Covers personal injuries (and sometimes property damage) resulting from automobile accidents, regardless of who was at fault. The insured submits his or her claims to his or her own insurance company, and is compensated for medical bills and lost wages (but usually not pain and suffering). Governed by state "no-fault" statutes. These laws generally prohibit a lawsuit against the at-fault driver except in specific circumstances, such as when a person's medical bills exceed a specific dollar amount or the damages exceed the policy limits.
Term Life	Provides life insurance for a specified period of time (term) with no cash surrender value. It usually is renewable.
Title	Protects against any defects in title to real property and any losses incurred as a result of existing claims against or liens on the property at the time of purchase.

depending on the terms of the contract, after a certain period of time has elapsed or a specified condition is met.

BROKERS VERSUS AGENTS   A broker is the agent of an applicant. Therefore, if the broker fails to procure a policy, the applicant normally is not insured. According to general principles of agency law, if the broker fails to obtain policy coverage and the applicant is harmed as a result, then the broker is liable to the harmed applicant-principal for the loss.

BINDERS AND CONDITIONS   A person who seeks insurance from an insurance company's agent is usually protected from the moment the application is made, provided—for life insurance—that some form of premium has been paid. Between the time the company receives the application and the time it is either rejected or accepted, the applicant is covered (possibly subject to certain conditions, such as passing a physical examination). Usually, the agent will write a memorandum, or **binder,** indicating that a policy is pending and stating its essential terms.

Parties may agree that a life insurance policy will be binding at the time the insured pays the first premium, or the policy may be expressly contingent on the applicant's passing a physical examination. If the applicant pays the premium and passes the examination, then the policy coverage is continuously in effect. If the applicant pays the premium but dies before having the physical examination, then in order to collect, the applicant's estate normally must show that the applicant would have passed the examination had he or she not died.

Provisions and Clauses

Some of the important provisions and clauses contained in insurance contracts are discussed in the following subsections and listed in Exhibit 51–2 below.

PROVISIONS MANDATED BY STATUTE If a statute mandates that a certain provision be included in insurance contracts, a court will deem that an insurance policy contains the provision regardless of whether the parties actually included it in the language of their contract. If a statute requires that any limitations regarding coverage be stated in the contract, a court will not allow an insurer to avoid liability for a claim through reliance on an unexpressed restriction.

INCONTESTABILITY CLAUSES Statutes commonly require that a policy for life or health insurance provide that after the policy has been in force for a specified length of time—often two or three years—the insurer cannot contest statements made in the application. This is known as an **incontestability clause.** Once a policy becomes incontestable, the insurer cannot later avoid a claim on the basis of, for example, fraud on the part of the insured, unless the clause provides an exception for that circumstance. The clause does not prevent an insurer from refusing or reducing payment for a claim due to nonpayment

of premiums, failure to file proof of death within a certain period, or lack of an insurable interest.

COINSURANCE CLAUSES Often, when taking out fire insurance policies, property owners insure their property for less than full value because most fires do not result in a total loss. To encourage owners to insure their property for an amount as close to full value as possible, fire insurance policies generally include a coinsurance clause. Typically, a *coinsurance clause* provides that if the owner insures the property up to a specified percentage—usually 80 percent—of its value, she or he will recover any loss up to the face amount of the policy. If the insurance is for less than the fixed percentage, the owner is responsible for a proportionate share of the loss. In effect, the owner becomes a coinsurer.

Coinsurance applies only in instances of partial loss. The amount of the recovery is calculated by using the following formula:

$$\text{Loss} \times \left(\frac{\text{Amount of Insurance Coverage}}{\text{Coinsurance Percentage} \times \text{Property Value}} \right) = \begin{array}{l}\text{Amount}\\\text{of Recovery}\end{array}$$

Thus, if the owner of property valued at $200,000 takes out a policy in the amount of $100,000 and suffers a loss of $80,000, the recovery will be $50,000. The owner will be responsible for (coinsure) the balance of the loss, or $30,000.

EXHIBIT 51–2 • Insurance Contract Provisions and Clauses

TYPE OF CLAUSE	DESCRIPTION
Antilapse Clause	An antilapse clause provides that a life insurance policy will not automatically lapse if no payment is made on the date due. Ordinarily, under such a provision, the insured has a *grace period* of thirty or thirty-one days within which to pay an overdue premium before the policy is canceled.
Appraisal Clause	Insurance policies frequently provide that if the parties cannot agree on the amount of a loss covered under the policy or the value of the property lost, an appraisal, or estimate, by an impartial and qualified third party can be demanded.
Arbitration Clause	Many insurance policies include clauses that call for arbitration of any disputes that arise between the insurer and the insured concerning the settlement of claims.
Coinsurance Clause	Many property insurance policies include a coinsurance clause that applies in the event of a partial loss and determines what percentage of the value of the property must be insured for an owner to be fully reimbursed for a loss. If the owner insures the property up to a specified percentage (typically 80 percent) of its value, she or he will recover any loss up to the face amount of the policy.
Incontestability Clause	An incontestability clause provides that after a policy has been in force for a specified length of time—usually two or three years—the insurer cannot contest statements made in the application.
Multiple Insurance Clause	Many insurance policies include a clause providing that if the insured has multiple insurance policies that cover the same property and the amount of coverage exceeds the loss, the loss will be shared proportionately by the insurance companies.

$$\$80{,}000 \times \left(\frac{\$100{,}000}{0.8 \times \$200{,}000} \right) = \$50{,}000$$

If the owner had taken out a policy in the amount of 80 percent of the value of the property, or $160,000, then according to the same formula, the owner would have recovered the full amount of the loss (the face amount of the policy).

APPRAISAL AND ARBITRATION CLAUSES Most fire insurance policies provide that if the parties cannot agree on the amount of a loss covered under the policy or on the value of the property lost, an *appraisal* can be demanded. An appraisal is an estimate of the property's value determined by a suitably qualified individual who has no interest in the property. Typically, two appraisers are used, with one appointed by each party. A third party, or umpire, may be called on to resolve differences. Other types of insurance policies also contain provisions for appraisal and arbitration when the insured and insurer disagree on the value of a loss.

MULTIPLE INSURANCE COVERAGE If an insured has *multiple insurance coverage*—that is, policies with several companies covering the same insurable interest—and the amount of coverage exceeds the loss, the insured can collect from each insurer only the company's proportionate share of the liability, relative to the total amount of insurance. Many fire insurance policies include a pro rata clause, which requires that any loss be shared proportionately by all carriers. For example, if Green insured $50,000 worth of property with two companies and each policy had a liability limit of $40,000, then on the property's total destruction, Green could collect only $25,000 from each insurer.

ANTILAPSE CLAUSES A life insurance policy may provide, or a statute may require a policy to provide, that it will not automatically lapse if no payment is made on the date due. Ordinarily, under an *antilapse provision,* the insured has a *grace period* of thirty

or thirty-one days within which to pay an overdue premium. If the insured fails to pay a premium altogether, there are alternatives to cancellation:

1. The insurer may be required to extend the insurance for a period of time.
2. The insurer may issue a policy with less coverage to reflect the amount of the payments made.
3. The insurer may pay to the insured the policy's **cash surrender value**—the amount the insurer has agreed to pay on the policy's cancellation before the insured's death. (This value depends on the period that the policy has already run, the amount of the premium, the insured's age and life expectancy, and amounts to be repaid on any outstanding loans taken out against the policy.)

When the insurance contract states that the insurer cannot cancel the policy, these alternatives are important.

Interpreting Provisions of an Insurance Contract

The courts recognize that most people do not have the special training necessary to understand the intricate terminology used in insurance policies. Therefore, when disputes arise, the courts will interpret the words used in an insurance contract according to their ordinary meanings in light of the nature of the coverage involved.

When there is an ambiguity in the policy, the provision generally is interpreted *against the insurance company*. Also, when it is unclear whether an insurance contract actually exists because the written policy has not been delivered, the uncertainty normally is resolved against the insurance company. The court presumes that the policy is in effect unless the company can show otherwise. Similarly, an insurer must make sure that the insured is adequately notified of any change in coverage under an existing policy.

Disputes over insurance often focus on the interpretation of an ambiguous provision in the policy, as the following case illustrates.

CASE 51.1
Cary v. United of Omaha Life Insurance Co.
Supreme Court of Colorado, 108 P.3d 288 (2005).

BACKGROUND AND FACTS • Fourteen-year-old Dena Cary shot herself under the chin in an unsuccessful suicide attempt because she suffered a major depressive episode of her diagnosed

CASE CONTINUES ➡

CASE 51.1 CONTINUED ➡ bipolar disorder. Her injuries required extensive medical treatment. Dena's father, Thomas Cary, sought payment for these costs under his medical insurance policy covering injury and illness, but the insurer denied the claim. The insurer argued that coverage was excluded under a provision reading: "Injury. Injury means accidental bodily injury which occurs independently of Illness. Injury does not include self-inflicted bodily injury, either while sane or insane." The Carys filed an action in a Colorado state court for bad faith denial of coverage. The trial court found that the injury was covered by the policy, but the state intermediate appellate court reversed. The Carys appealed to the state supreme court.

IN THE LANGUAGE OF THE COURT
RICE, Justice
* * * *
     * * * One reasonable interpretation of these definitions is * * * [that] the self-inflicted injury limitation in the second sentence of the "injury" definition modifies only the phrase "accidental bodily injury which occurs independently of Illness." As a result, injuries that occur as a result of illness, even if self-inflicted, are defined out of the "injury" definition and are covered by the Plan's promise to provide coverage for "treatment of an Illness."
* * * *
     However, an equally reasonable interpretation is that both sentences in the "injury" definition are of like definitional value, that is to say that one does not modify the other. Thus, to be covered, an injury must be [an] "accidental bodily injury which occurs independently of Illness" and must not be [a] "self-inflicted bodily injury, either while sane or insane." Accordingly, if an injury is accidental or is the result of an illness, it nonetheless would be excluded from coverage if it is self-inflicted.
     * * * Most importantly for our purposes, however, *the plan is ambiguous because it is susceptible to each equally reasonable interpretation. * * * Because we resolve ambiguities in favor of coverage, Dena's injuries are covered.* [Emphasis added.]

DECISION AND REMEDY • *The Colorado Supreme Court reversed the lower appellate court's decision, with instructions to return the case to the trial court for proceedings consistent with this opinion.*

WHAT IF THE FACTS WERE DIFFERENT? • *Suppose that there had not been an ambiguity in this policy and that it had been subject to only one reasonable interpretation. Would the result have been different? Explain.*

THE LEGAL ENVIRONMENT DIMENSION • *Should insurance policy provisions be interpreted to avoid ambiguities if possible? Why or why not?*

Cancellation

The insured can cancel a policy at any time, and the insurer can cancel under certain circumstances. When an insurance company can cancel its insurance contract, the policy or a state statute usually requires that the insurer give advance written notice of the cancellation. The same requirement applies when only part of a policy is canceled. Any premium paid in advance and not yet earned may be refundable on the policy's cancellation. The insured may also be entitled to a life insurance policy's cash surrender value.

     The insurer may cancel an insurance policy for various reasons, depending on the type of insurance. For example, automobile insurance can be canceled for nonpayment of premiums or suspension of the insured's driver's license. Property insurance can be canceled for nonpayment of premiums or for other reasons, including the insured's fraud or misrepresentation, gross negligence, or conviction for a crime that increases the risk assumed by the insurer. Life and health policies can be canceled because of false statements made by the insured in the application, but the cancellation must take place only before the effective date of an incontestability clause. An insurer cannot cancel—or refuse to renew—a policy for discriminatory reasons or other reasons that violate public policy, or because the insured has appeared as a witness in a case brought against the company.

Duties and Obligations of the Parties

Both parties to an insurance contract are responsible for the obligations they assume under the contract (contract law was discussed in Chapters 10 through 18). In addition, both the insured and the insurer have an implied duty to act in good faith.

DUTIES OF THE INSURED Good faith requires the party who is applying for insurance to reveal everything necessary for the insurer to evaluate the risk. In other words, the applicant must disclose all material facts, including all facts that an insurer would consider in determining whether to charge a higher premium or to refuse to issue a policy altogether. Many insurance companies today require that an applicant give the company permission to access other information, such as private medical records and credit ratings, for the purpose of evaluating the risk.

Once the insurance policy is issued, the insured has three basic duties under the contract: (1) to pay the premiums as stated in the contract, (2) to notify the insurer within a reasonable time if an event occurs that gives rise to a claim, and (3) to cooperate with the insurer during any investigation or litigation.

DUTIES OF THE INSURER Once the insurer has accepted the risk, and some event occurs that gives rise to a claim, the insurer has a *duty to investigate* to determine the facts. When a policy provides insurance against third party claims, the insurer is obligated to make reasonable efforts to settle such a claim. If a settlement cannot be reached, then regardless of the claim's merit, the insurer has a *duty to defend* any suit against the insured. Usually, a policy provides that in this situation the insured must *cooperate* in the defense and attend hearings and trials if necessary. The insurer also owes a *duty to pay* any legitimate claims up to the face amount of the policy.

An insurer has a duty to provide or pay an attorney to defend its insured when a complaint alleges facts that could, if proved, impose liability on the insured within the policy's coverage. In the following case, the question was whether a policy covered a dentist's potential liability arising from a practical joke that he played on an employee while performing a dental procedure.

CASE 51.2
Woo v. Fireman's Fund Insurance Co.

Supreme Court of Washington, 161 Wash.2d 43, 164 P.3d 454 (2007).

BACKGROUND AND FACTS • Tina Alberts worked for Robert Woo as a dental surgical assistant. Her family raised potbellied pigs, and she often talked about them at work. Sometimes, Woo mentioned the pigs, intending to encourage a "friendly working environment." Alberts interpreted the comments as offensive. Alberts asked Woo to replace two of her teeth with implants. The procedure required the installation of temporary partial bridges called "flippers." While Alberts was anesthetized, Woo installed a set of flippers shaped like boar tusks, as a joke, and took photos. Before Alberts regained consciousness, he inserted the normal flippers. A month later, Woo's staff gave Alberts the photos at a gathering to celebrate her birthday. Stunned, Alberts refused to return to work. Woo tried to apologize. Alberts filed a suit in a Washington state court against him, alleging battery and other torts. He asked Fireman's Fund Insurance Company to defend him, claiming coverage under his policy. The insurer refused. Woo settled the suit with Alberts for $250,000 and filed a suit against Fireman's, claiming that it had breached its duty to defend him. The court awarded him $750,000 in damages plus the amount of the settlement and attorneys' fees and costs. A state intermediate appellate court reversed the award. Woo appealed to the Washington Supreme Court.

IN THE LANGUAGE OF THE COURT
FAIRHURST, J. [Justice]
* * * *

The professional liability provision states that Fireman's will defend any claim brought against the insured "even if the allegations of the claim are groundless, false or fraudulent." It defines "dental services" as "all services which are performed in the

CASE CONTINUES ➤

CASE 51.2 CONTINUED ➡ practice of the dentistry profession as defined in the business and professional codes of the state where you are licensed." [Revised Code of Washington (RCW) Section] 18.32.020 * * * states:

> A person practices dentistry * * * who * * * undertakes by any means or methods to diagnose, treat, remove stains or concretions from teeth, operate or prescribe for any disease, pain, injury, deficiency, deformity, or physical condition of the same, or take impressions of the teeth or jaw, or * * * owns, maintains or operates an office for the practice of dentistry * * * .

* * * [Woo] claims the joke was "intertwined with employee and patient relationships, areas of Woo's ownership and operation of the dental office." Fireman's responds that the allegations in Alberts' complaint unambiguously establish that Woo's practical joke was not connected to treating Alberts' condition. It asserts the boar tusk flippers were not intended to replace Alberts' teeth—they were intended only as a practical joke. Fireman's also asserts that insertion of the boar tusk flippers was not covered under the professional liability provision because Woo "interrupted his rendering of dental services."

* * * *

* * * In addition to covering the rendering of dental services, *the professional liability provision covers ownership, maintenance, or operation of an office for the practice of dentistry* and Alberts' complaint alleged Woo's practical joke took place while Woo was conducting his dental practice. The insertion of the boar tusk flippers was also intertwined with Woo's dental practice because it involved an interaction with an employee. [Emphasis added.]

Moreover, Woo's practical joke did not interrupt the dental surgery procedure, as Fireman's argues. * * * The acts that comprised the practical joke were integrated into and inseparable from the overall procedure.

In sum, Alberts' complaint alleges that Woo inserted a flipper, albeit oddly shaped, during a dental surgery procedure while he was operating an office for the practice of dentistry. * * * Because [Revised Code of Washington Section] 18.32.020 defines the practice of dentistry so broadly, the fact that his acts occurred during the operation of a dental practice conceivably brought his actions within the professional liability provision of his insurance policy.

DECISION AND REMEDY • *The Washington Supreme Court held that Fireman's had a duty to defend Woo under the professional liability provision of his policy because "the insertion of boar tusk flippers in Alberts' mouth conceivably fell within the policy's broad definition of the practice of dentistry." The state supreme court reversed the decision of the lower court.*

THE ETHICAL DIMENSION • *Are the acts of the principal parties—Woo, Alberts, and Fireman's—ethically justifiable in the circumstances of this case? Discuss.*

THE LEGAL ENVIRONMENT DIMENSION • *In determining if an insurer has a duty to defend an insured, should a court ask whether the insured had a "reasonable expectation" of coverage? Explain.*

BAD FAITH ACTIONS Although insurance law generally follows contract law, most states now recognize a "bad faith" tort action against insurers. Thus, if an insurer in bad faith denies coverage of a claim, the insured may recover in tort an amount exceeding the policy's coverage limits and may also recover punitive damages. Some courts have held insurers liable for a bad faith refusal to settle claims for reasonable amounts within the policy limits, provided that there was affirmative misconduct by the insurer.[3]

Defenses against Payment

An insurance company can raise any of the defenses that would be valid in an ordinary action on a contract, as well as the following defenses:

1. If the insurance company can show that the policy was procured through fraud or misrepresentation, it may have a valid defense for not paying on a claim. (The insurance company may also have the right to disaffirm or rescind the insurance contract.)
2. An absolute defense exists if the insurer can show that the insured lacked an insurable interest—thus rendering the policy void from the beginning.

---

3. See, for example, *Columbia National Insurance Co. v. Freeman,* 347 Ark. 423, 64 S.W.3d 720 (2002); and *Selman v. Metropolitan Life Insurance Co.,* 372 Ark. 420, 277 S.W.3d 196 (2008).

3. Improper actions, such as those that are against public policy or that are otherwise illegal, can also give the insurance company a defense against the payment of a claim or allow it to rescind the contract.

In some situations, the insurance company may be prevented, or estopped, from asserting defenses that normally are available. For example, an insurance company ordinarily cannot escape payment on the death of an insured on the ground that the person's age was stated incorrectly on the application. Also, incontestability clauses prevent the insurer from asserting certain defenses.

SECTION 3
TYPES OF INSURANCE

There are four general types of insurance coverage: life insurance, fire and homeowners' insurance, automobile insurance, and business liability insurance. We now examine briefly the coverage available under each of these types of insurance.

Life Insurance

There are five basic types of life insurance:

1. **Whole life** provides protection with an accumulated cash surrender value that can be used as collateral for a loan. The insured pays premiums during his or her entire lifetime, and the beneficiary receives a fixed payment on the death of the insured. (It is also sometimes referred to as straight life, ordinary life, or cash-value insurance.)

2. **Limited-payment life** is a type of policy under which premiums are paid for a stated number of years. After that time, the policy is paid up and fully effective during the insured's life. For example, a policy might call for twenty payments. Naturally, premiums are higher than for whole life. This insurance also has a cash surrender value.

3. **Term insurance** is a type of policy for which premiums are paid for a specified term. Payment on the policy is due only if death occurs within the term period. Premiums are lower than for whole life or limited-payment life, and there usually is no cash surrender value. Frequently, this type of insurance can be converted to another type of life insurance.

4. **Endowment insurance** involves fixed premium payments that are made for a definite term. At the end of the term, a fixed amount is paid to the insured or, on the death of the insured during the specified period, to a beneficiary. Thus, this type of insurance represents both term insurance and a form of **annuity** (the right to receive fixed, periodic payments for life or—as in this instance—for a term of years). Endowment insurance has a rapidly increasing cash surrender value, but premiums are high because a payment must be made at the end of the term even if the insured is still living.

5. **Universal life** combines aspects of both term insurance and whole life insurance. From every payment, usually called a "contribution," the issuing life insurance company makes two deductions. The first is a charge for term insurance protection; the second is for company expenses and profit. The funds that remain after these deductions earn interest for the policyholder at a rate determined by the company. The interest-earning amount is called the policy's *cash value,* but that term does not mean the same thing as it does for a traditional whole life insurance policy. With a universal life policy, the cash value grows at a variable interest rate rather than at a predetermined rate.

The rights and liabilities of the parties to life insurance contracts are basically dependent on the specific contract. A few features deserve special attention.

LIABILITY The life insurance contract determines not only the extent of the insurer's liability but also, generally, whether the insurer is liable on the death of the insured. Most life insurance contracts exclude liability for death caused by suicide, military action during war, execution by a state or federal government, and even an event that occurs while the insured is a passenger in a commercial vehicle. In the absence of contractual exclusion, most courts today construe any cause of death to be one of the insurer's risks.

ADJUSTMENT DUE TO MISSTATEMENT OF AGE The insurance policy constitutes the agreement between the parties. The application for insurance is part of the policy and is usually attached to the policy. When the insured misstates his or her age on the application, an error is introduced, particularly as to the amount of premiums paid. As mentioned, misstatement of age is not a material error sufficient to allow the insurer to void the policy. Instead, on discovery of the error, the insurer will adjust the premium payments and/or benefits accordingly.

ASSIGNMENT Most life insurance policies allow the insured to change beneficiaries. When this is permitted, in the absence of any prohibition or notice requirement, the insured can assign the rights to the policy (for example, as security for a loan) without the consent of the insurer or the beneficiary. If the beneficiary's right is *vested*—that is, has become absolute, entitling the beneficiary to payment of the proceeds—the policy cannot be assigned without the beneficiary's consent. For the most part, life insurance contracts permit assignment and require notice only to the insurer to be effective.

CREDITORS' RIGHTS Unless insurance proceeds are exempt under state law, the insured's interest in life insurance is an asset that is subject to the rights of judgment creditors. These creditors generally can reach insurance proceeds payable to the insured's estate, proceeds payable to anyone if the payment of premiums constituted a fraud on creditors, and proceeds payable to a named beneficiary unless the beneficiary's rights have vested. Creditors, however, cannot compel the insured to make available the cash surrender value of the policy or to change the named beneficiary to that of the creditor. Almost all states exempt at least a part of the proceeds of life insurance from creditors' claims.

TERMINATION Although the insured can cancel and terminate the policy, the insurer generally cannot do so. Therefore, termination usually takes place only if one of the following occurs:

1. Default in premium payments that causes the policy to lapse.

2. Death and payment of benefits.
3. Expiration of the term of the policy.
4. Cancellation by the insured.

Fire and Homeowners' Insurance

There are basically two types of insurance policies for a home—standard fire insurance policies and homeowners' policies.

STANDARD FIRE INSURANCE POLICIES The standard fire insurance policy protects the homeowner against fire and lightning, as well as damage from smoke and water caused by the fire or the fire department. Most fire insurance policies are classified according to the type of property covered and the extent (amount) of the issuer's liability. Exhibit 51–3 below lists typical fire insurance policies, and the following subsections discuss specific features and provisions.

Liability. The insurer's liability is determined from the terms of the policy. Most policies, however, limit recovery to losses resulting from *hostile* fires—basically, those that break out or begin in places where no fire was intended to burn. A *friendly* fire—one burning in a place where it was intended to burn—is not covered. Therefore, smoke from a fireplace is not covered, but smoke from a fire caused by a defective electrical outlet is covered. Sometimes, owners add "extended coverage" to the fire policy to cover losses from "friendly" fires.

If the policy is a *valued* policy (see Exhibit 51–3 below) and the subject matter is completely destroyed, the insurer is liable for the amount

EXHIBIT 51–3 • Typical Fire Insurance Policies

TYPE OF POLICY	COVERAGE
Blanket	Covers a class of property rather than specific property, because the property is expected to shift or vary in nature. A policy covering the inventory of a business is an example.
Floater	Usually supplements a specific policy. It is intended to cover property that may change in either location or quantity. To illustrate, if the painting mentioned below under "specific policy" is to be exhibited during the year at numerous locations throughout the state, a floater policy would be desirable.
Open	A policy that does not state an agreed-on value for the property. The policy usually provides for a maximum liability of the insurer, but payment for loss is restricted to the fair market value of the property at the time of loss or to the insurer's limit, whichever is less.
Specific	Covers a specific item of property at a specific location. An example is a particular painting located in a residence or a piece of machinery located in a factory or business.
Valued	A policy that, by agreement, places a specific value on the subject to be insured to cover the eventuality of its total loss.

specified in the policy. If it is an *open* policy, then the extent of the actual loss must be determined, and the insurer is liable only for the amount of the loss or for the maximum amount specified in the policy, whichever is less. For partial losses, actual loss must always be determined, and the insurer's liability is limited to that amount. Most insurance policies permit the insurer to either restore or replace the property destroyed or to pay for the loss.

Proof of Loss. As a condition for recovery, fire insurance policies require the insured to file a proof of loss with the insurer within a specified period or immediately (within a reasonable time). Failure to comply *could* allow the insurance carrier to avoid liability. Courts vary somewhat on the enforcement of such clauses.

Occupancy Clause. Most standard policies require that the premises be occupied at the time of the loss. The relevant clause states that if the premises are vacant or unoccupied for a given period and the insurer's consent to the vacancy is not obtained, the coverage is suspended until the premises are reoccupied. Persons going on extended vacations should check their policies regarding this point.

In the following case, the court had to consider how long a house must be left vacant before it can be considered "unoccupied" and whether the risk of hazard is always greater when a home is unoccupied.

※ EXTENDED CASE 51.3 ※
Estate of Luster v. Allstate Insurance Co.

United States Court of Appeals, Seventh Circuit, 598 F.3d 903 (2010).
www.ca7.uscourts.gov[a]

IN THE LANGUAGE OF THE COURT
POSNER, Circuit Judge.
* * * *
This diversity suit for breach of an insurance contract was dismissed on summary judgment * * *, and the plaintiff's [Estate of Luster's] appeal presents issues of both contract interpretation and Indiana insurance law.

[Wavie] Luster was a widow living alone in her house in Merrillville, Indiana. She had a homeowner's insurance policy from Allstate [Insurance Company]. In October 2001, when she was eighty-three, she was injured in a fall, and after being released from the hospital moved into an extended-care facility. She executed a power of attorney to her lawyer, Rick Gikas, who is the representative of her estate in this litigation. She never returned home and died in April 2006, some four and a half years after her fall. Gikas had notified

Allstate of his power of attorney and had directed the company to bill the insurance premiums to his law office. No one lived in the house after she left it.

Three months after her death—her house still unoccupied—a fire caused extensive damage. Gikas submitted a claim on behalf of the estate. An investigation indicated that the fire may well have been started by burglars, but the plaintiff denies this and the district judge made no finding.

In the course of the investigation Allstate discovered that the house had been unoccupied for four and a half years before Mrs. Luster's death and denied the claim, precipitating [hastening] this suit. Allstate continued billing Gikas for premiums, however, and he continued paying them until October 2008, more than two years after the fire, when Allstate—which claims not to have known that the policy was still in force until its lawyers read the estate's summary-judgment brief

that month—purported to cancel the policy retroactively to November 2001, and returned the premiums for the subsequent period to the estate.

The appeal requires us to consider [certain] provisions of the insurance policy: [The policy required the insured to notify Allstate of any change in occupancy of the premises and excluded coverage for property loss caused by "any substantial change or increase in hazard" or by "vandalism or malicious mischief" if the insured's dwelling was unoccupied for more than thirty consecutive days immediately prior to the vandalism or malicious mischief.]
* * * *
Gikas argues that * * * the house was *not* unoccupied, because right up until her death Luster expressed the intention of returning to live there when her health permitted.
Regardless of the owner's intentions, * * * four and a half years of continuous absence of human occupation

a. Select "Opinions" under the "Case Information" heading. When that page opens, enter case number "09-2483" and click on "List Cases." In the result, click on the highlighted case number to access the opinion. The U.S. Court of Appeals for the Seventh Circuit maintains this Web site.

EXTENDED CASE CONTINUES ➤

EXTENDED CASE 51.3 CONTINUED →

constitutes a change in occupancy. [Emphasis added.]

The duty-to-notify provision entitled Allstate to cancel the policy in the event the house became unoccupied.

Although the policy expressly authorizes the insurer to cancel it for a violation of any of its terms, it also requires the insurer to give thirty days' notice of intention to cancel, and Allstate failed to do that after discovering in the wake of the fire that the house had been unoccupied for years. *The requirement of notice of intent to cancel is important; it gives the insured an opportunity to prevent a lapse of coverage, by taking steps to reinstate the policy or obtain a substitute policy from another insurer. Retroactive termination is inconsistent with the requirement of advance notice.* [Emphasis added.]

* * * *

The district judge ruled that leaving the house unoccupied constituted a "substantial change or increase in hazard" within the meaning [the policy]. The judge seems to have thought that to leave a house unoccupied for however

short a time causes an "increase in hazard" as a matter of law. Allstate takes the more moderate position that any gap in occupation of more than thirty days increases hazard as a matter of law.

Neither position is correct. Houses are rarely occupied continuously. A homeowner might take a thirty-one-day trip; Allstate implies that if a fire occurred during that period the insured would be uncovered. That is not the law.

Allstate's argument thus implies that if you have a second home the homeowner's policy on your primary residence is illusory; you're away a lot and so coverage lapses. That's nonsense. And even if the house is unoccupied in the relevant sense—the sense that triggers the duty to notify the insurance company of a change in occupancy—it doesn't follow that you have created a "substantial * * * increase in hazard." Maybe you fitted the house with an array of locks and alarms and hired a security company to check on the house daily and so made the house more secure than when you were living there—an especially plausible inference if you happen to be an elderly person who

might if in residence damage it inadvertently by leaving appliances on or failing to remove combustibles [flammable items] like cans containing paint or oil-soaked rags or to attend to defects in the electrical wiring of the house. *There is no rule that moving out of a house* per se *[in itself] increases the hazards against which the insurance company has insured you.* [Emphasis added.]

* * * *

There may well have been vandalism, by burglars, and if so it occurred more than thirty days after the house became unoccupied, whenever precisely occupancy ceased—sometime during the four and a half years between Luster's fall and her death. But we do not know whether the vandalism caused the loss—there is no judicial finding that the fire that was the immediate cause of the loss was the result of vandalism. To decide whether it was will require an evidentiary [relating to evidence] hearing, as will Allstate's alternative ground that nonoccupancy substantially increased the risk of loss.

* * * *

REVERSED AND REMANDED.

QUESTIONS

1. Why did the court conclude that an unoccupied house did not necessarily create a substantial increase in hazard?
2. Why did the court hold that Allstate's cancellation of the policy, retroactive to November 2001 (when Luster moved to an extended-care facility), was ineffective?

Assignment. Before a loss has occurred, a fire insurance policy is not assignable without the consent of the insurer. The theory is that the fire insurance policy is a personal contract between the insured and the insurer. The nonassignability of a policy is extremely important when a house is purchased. The purchaser must procure his or her own insurance. If the purchaser wishes to assume the seller's remaining period of insurance coverage, the insurer's consent is essential.

To illustrate: Ann is selling her home and lot to Jeff. Ann has a one-year fire policy with Ajax Insurance Company, with six months of coverage

remaining at the date on which the sale is to close. Ann agrees to assign the balance of her policy, but Ajax has not given its consent. One day after passage of the deed, a fire totally destroys the house. Can Jeff recover from Ajax?

The answer is no, as the policy is actually voided on the closing of the transaction and the deeding of the property. The reason the policy is voided is that Ann no longer has an insurable interest at the time of loss, and Jeff has no rights in a nonassignable policy.

HOMEOWNERS' POLICIES A homeowners' policy provides protection against a number of risks under a single policy, allowing the policyholder to avoid the cost of buying each protection separately. There are two basic types of homeowners' coverage: property coverage and liability coverage.

Property Coverage.

Property coverage includes the garage, house, and other private buildings on the policyholder's lot. It also includes the personal possessions and property of the policyholder at home, while traveling, or at work. It pays additional expenses for living away from home because of a fire or some other covered peril.

Perils insured under property coverage often include fire, lightning, wind, hail, vandalism, and theft (of personal property). Standard homeowners' insurance typically does not cover flood damage. In the absence of a specific provision, such items of personal property as motor vehicles, farm equipment, airplanes, and boats normally are not included under property coverage. Coverage for other property, such as jewelry and securities, usually is limited to a specified dollar amount.

Liability Coverage.

Liability coverage is for personal liability in the event that someone is injured on the insured's property, the insured damages someone else's property, or the insured injures someone else (unless the injury involves an automobile, which would be covered by automobile insurance). Liability coverage under a homeowners' policy applies when others are injured or property is damaged because of the unsafe condition of the policyholder's premises. It also applies when the policyholder is negligent.

Liability coverage normally does not apply, however, if the liability arises from business or professional activities or from the operation of a motor vehicle, which are subjects for separate policies. Also excluded is liability arising from intentional misconduct. Similar to liability coverage is coverage for the medical payments of others who are injured on the policyholder's property and for the property of others that is damaged by a member of the policyholder's family.

Renters' Policies.

Renters also take out insurance policies to protect against losses to personal property. Renters' insurance covers personal possessions against various perils and includes coverage for additional living expenses and liability.

Automobile Insurance

There are two basic kinds of automobile insurance: liability insurance and collision and comprehensive insurance.

LIABILITY INSURANCE Automobile liability insurance covers liability for bodily injury and property damage. Liability limits are usually described by a series of three numbers, such as 100/300/50. This means that, for one accident, the policy will pay a maximum of $100,000 for bodily injury to one person, a maximum of $300,000 for bodily injury to more than one person, and a maximum of $50,000 for property damage. Many insurance companies offer liability coverage in amounts up to $500,000 and sometimes higher.

Individuals who are dissatisfied with the maximum liability limits offered by regular automobile insurance coverage can purchase separate coverage under an *umbrella policy*. Umbrella limits sometimes go as high as $10 million. Umbrella policies also cover personal liability in excess of the liability limits of a homeowners' policy.

COLLISION AND COMPREHENSIVE INSURANCE Collision insurance covers damage to the insured's car in any type of collision. Usually, it is not advisable to purchase full collision coverage (otherwise known as *zero deductible*). The price per year is relatively high because it is likely that some small repair jobs will be required each year. Most people prefer to take out policies with a deductible of $100, $250, or $500, which costs substantially less than zero-deductible coverage.

Comprehensive insurance covers loss, damage, and destruction due to fire, hurricane, hail, vandalism, and theft. It can be obtained separately from collision insurance.

OTHER AUTOMOBILE INSURANCE Other types of automobile insurance coverage include the following:

1. *Uninsured motorist coverage.* Uninsured motorist coverage insures the driver and passengers against injury caused by any driver without insurance or by a hit-and-run driver. Some states require that it be included in all auto insurance policies sold.
2. *Accidental death benefits.* Sometimes referred to as *double indemnity,* accidental death benefits provide for a payment of twice the policy's face amount if the policyholder dies in an accident. This coverage generally costs very little, but it may not be necessary if the insured has a sufficient amount of life insurance.
3. *Medical payment coverage.* Medical payment coverage provided by an auto insurance policy pays hospital and other medical bills and sometimes funeral expenses. This type of insurance protects all the passengers in the insured's car when the insured is driving.

4. *Other-driver coverage.* An *omnibus clause,* or *other-driver clause,* protects the vehicle owner who has taken out the insurance and anyone who drives the vehicle with the owner's permission. This coverage may be held to extend to a third party who drives the vehicle with the permission of the person to whom the owner gave permission.

5. *No-fault insurance.* Under no-fault statutes, claims arising from an accident are made against the claimant's own insurer, regardless of whose fault the accident was. In some situations—for example, when injuries require expensive medical treatment—state laws may allow an injured party to seek recovery from another party or insurer.

Business Liability Insurance

A business may be vulnerable to all sorts of risks. A key employee may die or become disabled; a customer may be injured when using a manufacturer's product; the patron of an establishment selling liquor may leave the premises and injure a third party in an automobile accident; or a professional may overlook some important detail and be liable for malpractice. Should the first situation arise (for instance, if the company president dies), the firm may have some protection under a key-person insurance policy, discussed earlier. In the other circumstances, other types of insurance may apply.

GENERAL LIABILITY Comprehensive general liability insurance can encompass as many risks as the insurer agrees to cover. For example, among the types of coverage that a business might wish to acquire is protection from liability for injuries arising from on-premises events not otherwise covered, such as company social functions. Some specialized establishments, such as taverns, may be subject to liability in particular circumstances, and policies can be drafted to meet their needs. In many jurisdictions, for example, statutes impose liability on a seller of liquor when a buyer of the liquor becomes intoxicated as a result of the sale and injures a third party. Legal protection may extend not only to the immediate consequences of an injury, such as paralysis resulting from an automobile accident, but also to the loss of financial support suffered by a family because of the injuries. Insurance can provide coverage for these injuries and financial losses.

PRODUCT LIABILITY Manufacturers and retailers may be subject to liability for injuries resulting from the products they sell, and product liability insurance can be written to match specific products' risks. Coverage can be procured under a comprehensive general liability policy or under a separate policy. The coverage may include payment for expenses incurred to recall and replace a product that has proved to be defective. (For a comprehensive discussion of product liability, see Chapter 22.)

PROFESSIONAL MALPRACTICE Attorneys, physicians, architects, engineers, and other professionals have increasingly become the targets of negligence suits. Professionals purchase malpractice insurance to protect themselves against such claims. The large judgments in some malpractice suits have received considerable publicity and are sometimes cited in discussions of what has been called "the insurance crisis," because they have contributed to a significant increase in malpractice insurance premiums.

WORKERS' COMPENSATION Workers' compensation insurance covers payments to employees who are injured in accidents arising out of and in the course of employment (that is, on the job). State statutes govern workers' compensation, as discussed in detail in Chapter 34.

REVIEWING
Insurance

Provident Insurance, Inc., issued an insurance policy to a company providing an employee, Steve Matlin, with disability insurance. Soon thereafter, Matlin was diagnosed with "panic disorder and phobia of returning to work." He lost his job and sought disability coverage. Provident denied coverage, doubting the diagnosis of disability. Matlin and his employer sued Provident. During pretrial discovery, the insurer learned that Matlin had stated on the policy application that he had never been treated for any "emotional, mental, nervous, urinary, or digestive disorder" or any kind of heart disease. In fact, before Matlin filled out the application, he had visited a physician for chest pains and general anxiety,

REVIEWING

Insurance, Continued

and the physician had prescribed an antidepressant and recommended that Matlin stop smoking. Using the information presented in the chapter, answer the following questions.

1. Did Matlin commit a misrepresentation on his policy application? Explain.
2. If there was any ambiguity on the application, should it be resolved in favor of the insured or the insurer? Why?
3. Assuming that the policy is valid, does Matlin's situation fall within the terms of the disability policy? Why or why not?
4. If Matlin is covered by the policy but is also disqualified by his misrepresentation on the application for coverage, might the insurer still be liable for bad faith denial of coverage? Explain.

☀ **DEBATE THIS:** *Whenever an insurance company can prove that the applicant committed fraud during the application process, it should not have to pay on the policy.*

TERMS AND CONCEPTS

	endowment insurance 1009	policy 1000	underwriter 1000
annuity 1009	incontestability clause 1004	premium 1000	universal life 1009
binder 1003	insurable interest 1001	risk 1000	whole life 1009
cash surrender value 1005	insurance 1000	risk management 1000	
	limited-payment life 1009	term insurance 1009	

QUESTIONS AND CASE PROBLEMS

51–1. Insurable Interest Adia owns a house and has an elderly third cousin living with her. Adia decides she needs fire insurance on the house and a life insurance policy on her third cousin to cover funeral and other expenses that will result from her cousin's death. Adia takes out a fire insurance policy from Ajax Insurance Co. and a $10,000 life insurance policy from Beta Insurance Co. on her third cousin. Six months later, Adia sells the house to John and transfers title to him. Adia and her cousin move into an apartment. With two months remaining on the Ajax policy, a fire totally destroys the house; at the same time, Adia's third cousin dies. Both insurance companies claim they have no liability under the insurance contracts, as Adia did not have an insurable interest, and tender back (return) the premiums. Discuss their claims.

51–2. QUESTION WITH SAMPLE ANSWER: Insurer's Defenses.

Patrick contracts with an Ajax Insurance Co. agent for a $50,000 ordinary life insurance policy. The application form is filled in to show Patrick's age as thirty-two. In addition, the application form asks whether Patrick has ever had any heart ailments or problems. Patrick answers no, forgetting that as a young child he was diagnosed as having a slight heart murmur. A policy is issued. Three years later, Patrick becomes seriously ill and dies. A review of the policy discloses that Patrick was actually thirty-three at the time of the application and the issuance of the policy and that he erred in answering the question about a history of heart ailments. Discuss whether Ajax can void the policy and escape liability on Patrick's death.

• **For a sample answer to Question 51–2, go to Appendix I at the end of this text.**

51–3. Assignment Sapata has an ordinary life insurance policy on her life and a fire insurance policy on her house. Both policies have been in force for a number of years. Sapata's life insurance names her son, Rory, as beneficiary. Sapata has specifically removed her right to change beneficiaries, and the life insurance policy is silent on the right of assignment. Sapata is going on a one-year European vacation and borrows money from

Leonard to finance the trip. Leonard takes an assignment of the life insurance policy as security for the loan, as the policy has accumulated a substantial cash surrender value. Sapata also rents out her house to Leonard and assigns her fire insurance policy to him. Discuss fully whether Sapata's assignment of these policies is valid.

51–4. Fire Insurance Fritz has an open fire insurance policy on his home for a maximum liability of $60,000. The policy has a number of standard clauses, including the right of the insurer to restore or rebuild the property in lieu of a monetary payment, and it has a standard coinsurance clause. A fire in Fritz's house destroys a utility room and part of the kitchen. The fire was caused by the overheating of an electric water heater. The total damage to the property is $10,000. The property at the time of loss is valued at $100,000. Fritz files a proof-of-loss claim for $10,000. Discuss the insurer's liability in this situation.

51–5. Insurer's Defenses In 1990, the city of Worcester, Massachusetts, adopted an ordinance that required rooming houses to be equipped with automatic sprinkler systems no later than September 25, 1995. James and Mark Duffy owned a forty-eight-room lodging house in Worcester, with two retail stores on the first floor. In 1994, the Duffys applied to General Star Indemnity Co. for an insurance policy to cover the premises. The application indicated that the premises had sprinkler systems. General issued a policy that required, among other safety features, a sprinkler system. Within a month, the premises were inspected on behalf of General. On the inspection form forwarded to the insurer, in the list of safety systems, next to the word *sprinkler* the inspector had inserted only a hyphen. In July 1995, when the premises sustained more than $100,000 in fire damage, General learned that there was no sprinkler system. The insurer filed a suit in a federal district court against the Duffys to rescind the policy, alleging misrepresentation in their insurance application about the presence of sprinklers. How should the court rule, and why? [*General Star Indemnity Co. v. Duffy*, 191 F.3d 55 (1st Cir. 1999)]

51–6. Interpreting Provisions Valley Furniture & Interiors, Inc., bought an insurance policy from Transportation Insurance Co. (TIC). The policy provided coverage of $50,000 for each occurrence of property loss caused by employee dishonesty. An "occurrence" was defined as "a single act or series of related acts." Valley allowed its employees to take pay advances and to buy discounted merchandise, with the advances and the cost of the merchandise deducted from their paychecks. The payroll manager was to notify the payroll company to make the deductions. Over a period of six years, without notifying the payroll company, the payroll manager issued advances to other employees and herself and bought merchandise for herself, in amounts totaling more than $200,000. Valley filed claims with TIC for three "occurrences" of employee theft. TIC considered the acts a "series of related acts" and paid only $50,000. Valley

filed a suit in a Washington state court against TIC, alleging, in part, breach of contract. What is the standard for interpreting an insurance clause? How should this court define "series of related acts"? Why? [*Valley Furniture & Interiors, Inc. v. Transportation Insurance Co.*, 107 Wash. App. 104, 26 P.3d 952 (Div. 1 2001)]

51–7. Cancellation James Mitchell bought a building in Los Angeles, California, in February 2000 and applied to United National Insurance Co. for a fire insurance policy. The application stated, among other things, that the building measured 3,420 square feet, it was to be used as a video production studio, the business would generate $300,000 in revenue, and the building had no uncorrected fire code violations. In fact, the building measured less than 2,000 square feet; it was used to film only one music video over a two-day period; the business generated only $6,500 in revenue; and the city had cited the building for combustible debris, excessive weeds, broken windows, missing doors, damaged walls, and other problems. In November, Mitchell met Carl Robinson, who represented himself as a business consultant. Mitchell gave Robinson the keys to the property to show it to a prospective buyer. On November 22, Robinson set fire to the building and was killed in the blaze. Mitchell filed a claim for the loss. United denied the claim and rescinded the policy. Mitchell filed a suit in a California state court against United. Can an insurer cancel a policy? If so, on what ground might United have justifiably canceled Mitchell's policy? What might Mitchell argue to oppose a cancellation? What should the court rule? Explain. [*Mitchell v. United National Insurance Co.*, 127 Cal.App.4th 457, 25 Cal.Rptr.3d 627 (2 Dist. 2005)]

51–8. CASE PROBLEM WITH SAMPLE ANSWER: Interpreting Provisions.

Richard Vanderbrook's home in New Orleans, Louisiana, was insured through Unitrin Preferred Insurance Co. His policy excluded coverage for, among other things, "[f]lood, surface water, waves, tidal water, overflow of a body of water, or spray from any of these, whether or not driven by wind." The policy did not define the term flood. In August 2005, Hurricane Katrina struck along the coast of the Gulf of Mexico, devastating portions of Louisiana. In New Orleans, some of the most significant damage occurred when the levees along three canals—the 17th Street Canal, the Industrial Canal, and the London Avenue Canal—ruptured, and water submerged about 80 percent of the city, including Vanderbrook's home. He filed a claim for the loss, but Unitrin refused to pay. Vanderbrook and others whose policies contained similar exclusions asked a federal district court to order their insurers to pay. They contended that their losses were due to the negligent design, construction, and maintenance of the levees and that the policies did not clearly exclude coverage for an inundation of water induced by negligence. On what does a decision in this case hinge? What reasoning supports a ruling in the plaintiffs' favor? In the defendants' favor? [In re Katrina Canal Breaches Litigation, 495 F.3d 191 (5th Cir. 2007)]

- To view a sample answer for Problem 51–8, go to this book's Web site at www.cengage.com/blaw/clarkson, select "Chapter 51," and click on "Case Problem with Sample Answer."

51–9. Insurance Coverage PAJ, Inc., a jewelry company, had a commercial general liability (CGL) policy from Hanover Insurance Co. It covered, among other things, liability for advertising injury. The policy required PAJ to notify Hanover of any claim or suit against PAJ "as soon as practicable." Yurman Designs sued PAJ for copyright infringement because of the design of a particular jewelry line. Unaware that the CGL policy applied to this matter, PAJ did not notify Hanover of the suit until four to six months after litigation began. Hanover contended that the policy did not apply to this incident because the late notification had violated its terms. PAJ sued Hanover, seeking a declaration that it was obligated to defend and indemnify PAJ. The trial court held for Hanover, as did an intermediate appellate court. PAJ appealed. Does Hanover have an obligation to provide PAJ with assistance, or did PAJ violate the insurance contract? Explain. [*PAJ, Inc. v. The Hanover Insurance Co.*, 243 S.W.3d 630 (Sup.Ct.Tex. 2008)]

51–10. Duty to Cooperate Dr. James Bubenik, a dentist practicing in Missouri, had two patients die while under sedation within six months. Bubenik had medical malpractice insurance with Medical Protective Co. (MPC). The families of both patients sued Bubenik for malpractice. MPC pointed out to Bubenik that a clause in his policy stated that the "Insured shall at all times fully cooperate with the Company in any claim hereunder and shall attend and assist in the preparation and trial of any such claim." During the litigation, however, Bubenik refused to submit to depositions, answer interrogatories, or testify at trial, invoking the Fifth Amendment privilege against self-incrimination. He also refused to communicate with MPC and entered into an agreement with the plaintiffs, stating that he would assist them in pursuing judgment against MPC. MPC requested a declaratory judgment from the court. The insurance company contended that it had no duty to defend Bubenik or counter the claims brought against him because of his refusal to cooperate. Did Bubenik's constitutional right to invoke the Fifth Amendment take precedence over the insurance policy's duty-to-cooperate clause? Why or why not? [*Medical Protective Co. v. Bubenik*, 594 F.3d 1047 (8th Cir. 2010)]

51–11. A QUESTION OF ETHICS: Insurance Coverage.

Paul and Julie Leonard's two-story home in Pascagoula, Mississippi, is only twelve feet above sea level and fewer than two hundred yards from the Gulf of Mexico. In 1989, the Leonards bought a homeowners' insurance policy from Jay Fletcher, an agent for Nationwide Mutual Insurance Co. The policy covered any damage caused by wind. It excluded all damage caused by water, including flooding. With each annual renewal, Nationwide reminded the Leonards that their policy did not cover flood damage, but that such coverage was available. The policy also contained an anti-concurrent-causation (ACC) clause that excluded coverage for damage caused by the synergistic action of a covered peril such as wind and an excluded peril such as water. In August 2005, Hurricane Katrina battered Pascagoula with torrential rain and sustained winds in excess of one hundred miles per hour. Wind damage to the Leonards' home was modest, but the storm drove ashore a seventeen-foot storm surge that flooded the ground floor. When Nationwide refused to pay for the damage to the ground floor, the Leonards filed a suit in a federal district court against the insurer. [Leonard v. Nationwide Mutual Insurance Co., 499 F.3d 419 (5th Cir. 2007)]

(a) Nationwide argued that the storm surge was a concurrently caused peril—a wall of water pushed ashore by hurricane winds—and thus its damage was excluded under the ACC clause. How would you rule on this point? Should a court "enlarge" an insurer's policy obligations? Why or why not?

(b) When the Leonards bought their policy in 1989, Fletcher told them that all hurricane damage was covered. Ten years later, Fletcher told Paul Leonard that they did not need additional flood coverage. Did these statements materially misrepresent or alter the policy? Were they unethical? Discuss.

LEGAL RESEARCH EXERCISES ON THE WEB

Go to this text's Web site at www.cengage.com/blaw/clarkson, select "Chapter 51," and click on "Practical Internet Exercises." There you will find the following Internet research exercises that you can perform to learn more about the topics covered in this chapter.

Practical Internet Exercise 51–1: **Legal Perspective**
Disappearing Decisions

Practical Internet Exercise 51–2: **Management Perspective**
Risk Management in Cyberspace

CHAPTER 52
❋
Wills and Trusts

As the adage says, "You can't take it with you." After you die, all of the real and personal property that you own will be transferred to others. A person can direct the passage of his or her property after death by *will,* subject to certain limitations imposed by the state. If no valid will has been executed, the decedent is said to have died **intestate,** and state **intestacy laws** prescribe the distribution of the property among heirs or next of kin. If no heirs or kin can be found, the property will

escheat[1] (title will be transferred to the state). In addition, a person can transfer property through a *trust.* When a trust is created, the owner (who may be called the *grantor* or the *settlor*) of the property transfers legal title to a trustee, who has a duty imposed by law to hold the property for the use or benefit of another (the beneficiary).

Wills and trusts are two basic devices used in the process of **estate planning**—determining in advance

how one's property and obligations should be transferred on death. In this chapter, we examine wills and trusts in some detail. Estate planning may also involve powers of attorney and living wills, which we discuss at the conclusion of this chapter. Other estate-planning devices include life insurance (discussed in Chapter 51) and joint-tenancy arrangements (described in Chapter 50). Typically, estate planning involves consultations with professionals, including attorneys, accountants, and financial planners.

---

1. Pronounced is-*cheet.*

SECTION 1
WILLS

A **will** is the final declaration of how a person desires to have her or his property disposed of after death. It is a formal instrument that must follow exactly the requirements of state law to be effective. One who makes a will is known as a **testator** (from the Latin *testari,* "to make a will"). A will is referred to as a *testamentary disposition* of property, and one who dies after having made a valid will is said to have died **testate.**

A will can serve other purposes besides the distribution of property. It can appoint a guardian for minor children or incapacitated adults. It can also appoint a personal representative to settle the affairs of the deceased. An **executor** is a personal representative named in a will. An **administrator** is a personal representative appointed by the court for a decedent who dies without a will, fails to name an executor in the will, names an executor lacking

the capacity to serve, or writes a will that the court refuses to admit to probate. Exhibit 52–1 on the facing page presents excerpts from the will of Michael Jackson, the "King of Pop," who died from cardiac arrest in 2009 at the age of fifty. Jackson held a substantial amount of tangible and intangible property, including the publishing rights to most of the Beatles' music catalogue. The will is a "pour-over" will, meaning that it transfers all of his property (that is not already held in the name of the trust) into the Michael Jackson Family Trust (trusts will be discussed later in this chapter). Jackson's will also appoints his mother, Katherine Jackson, as the guardian of his three minor children.

Laws Governing Wills

Laws governing wills come into play when a will is probated. To **probate** (prove) a will means to establish its validity and carry out the administration of the estate through a process supervised by a probate

EXHIBIT 52-1 • Excerpts from Michael Jackson's Will

LAST WILL OF MICHAEL JOSEPH JACKSON

I, MICHAEL JOSEPH JACKSON, a resident of the State of California, declare this to be my last Will, and do hereby revoke all former wills and codicils made by me.

I.   I declare that I am not married. My marriage to DEBORAH JEAN ROWE JACKSON has been dissolved. I have three children now living, PRINCE MICHAEL JACKSON, JR., PARIS MICHAEL KATHERINE JACKSON and PRINCE MICHAEL JOSEPH JACKSON, II. I have no other children, living or deceased.

II.   It is my intention by this Will to dispose of all property which I am entitled to dispose of by will. I specifically refrain from exercising all powers of appointment that I may possess at the time of my death.

III.   I give my entire estate to the Trustee or Trustees then acting under that certain Amended and Restated Declaration of Trust executed on March 22, 2002 by me as Trustee and Trustor which is called the MICHAEL JACKSON FAMILY TRUST, giving effect to any amendments thereto made prior to my death. All such assets shall be held, managed and distributed as a part of said Trust according to its terms and not as a separate testamentary trust.

If for any reason this gift is not operative or is invalid, or if the aforesaid Trust fails or has been revoked, I give my residuary estate to the Trustee or Trustees named to act in the MICHAEL JACKSON FAMILY TRUST, as Amended and Restated on March 22, 2002, and I direct said Trustee or Trustees to divide, administer, hold and distribute the trust estate pursuant to the provisions of said Trust * * * .
* * * *

IV.   I direct that all federal estate taxes and state inheritance or succession taxes payable upon or resulting from or by reason of my death (herein "Death Taxes") attributable to property which is part of the trust estate of the MICHAEL JACKSON FAMILY TRUST, including property which passes to said trust from my probate estate shall be paid by the Trustee of said trust in accordance with its terms. Death Taxes attributable to property passing outside this Will, other than property constituting the trust estate of the trust mentioned in the preceding sentence, shall be charged against the taker of said property.

V.   I appoint JOHN BRANCA, JOHN McCLAIN and BARRY SIEGEL as co-Executors of this Will. In the event of any of their deaths, resignations, inability, failure or refusal to serve or continue to serve as a co-Executor, the other shall serve and no replacement need be named. The co-Executors serving at any time after my death may name one or more replacements to serve in the event that none of the three named individuals is willing or able to serve at any time.

The term "my executors" as used in this Will shall include any duly acting personal representative or representatives of my estate. No individual acting as such need post a bond.

I hereby give to my Executors, full power and authority at any time or times to sell, lease, mortgage, pledge, exchange or otherwise dispose of the property, whether real or personal comprising my estate, upon such terms as my Executors shall deem best, to continue any business enterprises, to purchase assets from my estate, to continue in force and pay any insurance policy * * * .

VI.   Except as otherwise provided in this Will or in the Trust referred to in Article III hereof, I have intentionally omitted to provide for my heirs. I have intentionally omitted to provide for my former wife, DEBORAH JEAN ROWE JACKSON.
* * * *

VIII.   If any of my children are minors at the time of my death, I nominate my mother, KATHERINE JACKSON as guardian of the persons and estates of such minor children. If KATHERINE JACKSON fails to survive me, or is unable or unwilling to act as guardian, I nominate DIANA ROSS as guardian of the persons and estates of such minor children.
* * * *

court. Probate laws vary from state to state. In 1969, to promote more uniformity among the states, the American Bar Association and the National Conference of Commissioners on Uniform State Laws issued the Uniform Probate Code (UPC).

The UPC codifies general principles and procedures for the resolution of conflicts in settling estates and relaxes some of the requirements for a valid will contained in earlier state laws. Almost half of the states have enacted some part of the UPC and incorporated it into their own probate codes. For this reason, references to its provisions will be included in this chapter. Several states have adopted amendments to the UPC that were issued in 2008.

Nonetheless, succession and inheritance laws still vary widely among the states, and one should always check the particular laws of the state involved.[2]

Gifts by Will

A gift of real estate by will is generally called a **devise,** and a gift of personal property under a will is called a **bequest,** or **legacy.** (For a discussion of whether a gift of cyberspace property can be made under a will, see this chapter's *Insight into Ethics* feature below.) The recipient of a gift by will is a *devisee* or a *legatee,* depending on whether the gift was a devise or a legacy.

TYPES OF GIFTS Gifts by will can be specific, general, or residuary. A *specific* devise or bequest (legacy) describes particular property (such as "Eastwood Estate" or "my Cartier watch") that can be distinguished from the rest of the testator's property. A *general* devise or bequest (legacy) uses less restrictive terminology. For example, "I devise all my lands" is a general devise. A general bequest often specifies a sum of cash instead of a particular item of property,

such as a watch or an automobile. For example, "I give to my nephew, Carleton, $30,000" is a general bequest. If a testamentary gift is conditioned on the commission of an illegal act or an act that is legally impossible to fulfill, the condition will be invalid.

CASE IN POINT A testator made a charitable bequest of $29 million to a nursing home on the condition that the funds be used only to help white patients. Because this condition was impossible to fulfill without violating laws prohibiting discrimination, the court ruled that the illegal portion of the gift was invalid. Essentially, the court invalidated the condition (that the funds be used for only white patients) and allowed the nursing home to receive the funds without any conditions on their use.[3]

Sometimes, a will provides that any assets remaining after specific gifts have been made and debts have been paid—called the *residuary* (or *residuum*) of the estate—are to be given to the testator's spouse, distributed to the testator's descendants, or disposed of

---

2. For example, California law differs substantially from the UPC.

3. *Home for Incurables of Baltimore City v. University of Maryland Medical System Corp.,* 369 Md. 67, 797 A.2d 746 (2002). Note that the same rule applies to *testamentary trusts* (see page 1,030) that include conditions that are illegal or against public policy. See, for example, *In re Estate of Robertson,* 859 N.E.2d 772 (Ind. App. 2007).

INSIGHT INTO ETHICS
Should Cyberspace Estates Be Passed On to Heirs?

Many people participate in virtual worlds in cyberspace through avatars (alter egos). Often, these avatars amass virtual property that has an actual value in the real world.

For example, in Second Life, a popular virtual world created by Linden Lab, Linden dollars are traded for real dollars at a ratio of 259 to 1. The virtual goods market in the United States is estimated to be worth at least $1 billion, and worldwide the value may be much as $5 billion. But who really owns the value of this virtual property? If you own a gold coin in the real world, it has a market value and can be passed on to your heirs. But if you own a "gold coin" in Second Life, will your heirs be able to inherit it after you die?

The fate of a decedent's virtual estate depends, in part, on the virtual world in which it was created. The administrators of some virtual worlds and some Internet service providers give a new account holder the option of requesting that her or his executor be given access to the account in the event of his or her death. Otherwise, the account is simply erased.

To create a virtual world in Second Life, however, the user has to agree to Linden Lab's terms of service, which give the company the right to erase all of the user's virtual property after his or her death. One way to avoid such a fate is to name a *digital executor* through Digital Beyond, a clearinghouse for the distribution of virtual assets after the owner's death. After the owner dies, Digital Beyond transfers his or her most recent passwords to the person named as digital executor, thereby proving access to all of the decedent's accounts.

CRITICAL THINKING
INSIGHT INTO THE E-COMMERCE ENVIRONMENT
A Facebook game, FarmVille, allows members to manage virtual crops together. Would there be any benefit in being able to pass on to one's heirs "the fruits of one's virtual labor"? Why or why not?

in some other way. If the testator has not indicated what party or parties should receive the residuary of the estate, the residuary passes according to state laws of intestacy.

ABATEMENT If the assets of an estate are insufficient to pay in full all general bequests provided for in the will, an *abatement* takes place. An abatement means that the legatees receive reduced benefits. For example, Julie's will leaves $15,000 each to her children, Tamara and Lynn. On Julie's death, only $10,000 is available to honor these bequests. By abatement, each child will receive $5,000. If bequests are more complicated, abatement may be more complex. The testator's intent, as expressed in the will, controls.

LAPSED LEGACIES If a legatee dies prior to the death of the testator or before the legacy is payable, a *lapsed legacy* results. At common law, the legacy failed. Today, the legacy may not lapse if the legatee is in a certain blood relationship to the testator (such as a child, grandchild, brother, or sister) and has left a child or other surviving descendant.

Note that if the testator has included a provision in the will addressing lapsed legacies, courts generally will enforce the provision in the way the testator intended.

CASE IN POINT Katherine Hagan executed a will in 1994 that left the residuary of her estate, including all lapsed legacies, to various organizations, such as the Humane Society. In 2001, Hagan inherited $830,000 from a relative. At this time, Hagan did not have the mental capacity to revise her will. When she died in 2005, Hagan's residuary estate was worth $1.48 million. Hagan's relatives, including Janice Benjamin, tried to invalidate the will's provisions regarding the residuary estate so that the funds would pass to them by intestacy laws. The court, however, found that Hagen's intent controlled. She had not intended to give any portion of her estate to her relatives. Because the will specifically stated that lapsed legacies should go into the residuary estate and be distributed to the charities, the court enforced these provisions (and Hagan's relatives received nothing).[4]

Requirements for a Valid Will

A will must comply with statutory formalities designed to ensure that the testator understood his or her actions at the time the will was made. These formalities are intended to help prevent fraud.

Unless they are followed, the will is declared void, and the decedent's property is distributed according to the laws of intestacy of that state.

Although the required formalities vary among jurisdictions, most states uphold certain basic requirements for executing a will. We now look at the basic requirements for a valid will, including references to the UPC when appropriate.

TESTAMENTARY CAPACITY AND INTENT For a will to be valid, the testator must have testamentary capacity—that is, the testator must be of legal age and sound mind *at the time the will is made*. The legal age for executing a will varies, but in most states and under the UPC, the minimum age is eighteen years [UPC 2–501]. Thus, the will of a twenty-one-year-old decedent written when the person was sixteen is invalid if, under state law, the legal age for executing a will is eighteen.

The "Sound-Mind" Requirement. The concept of "being of sound mind" refers to the testator's ability to formulate and to comprehend a personal plan for the disposition of property. Generally, a testator must (1) intend the document to be his or her last will and testament, (2) comprehend the kind and character of the property being distributed, and (3) comprehend and remember the "natural objects of his or her bounty" (usually, family members and persons for whom the testator has affection).

Intent. A valid will is one that represents the maker's intention to transfer and distribute her or his property. When it can be shown that the decedent's plan of distribution was the result of fraud or undue influence, the will is declared invalid. A court may sometimes infer undue influence when the named beneficiary was in a position to influence the making of the will. Suppose that the testator ignored blood relatives and named as a beneficiary a nonrelative who was in constant close contact with the testator. For example, Frieda is a nurse who was responsible for caring for Julie, the testator, during the last years of her life. After Julie's death, her family discovers that Julie has executed a new will in the last year that names Frieda as sole beneficiary and excludes all family members. If Julie's family challenges the validity of the will, the court might infer that Frieda unduly influenced Julie and declare the will invalid.

A testator's disposition of his or her property transfers all of the property that the testator was entitled to dispose of at the time of death. Thus, property that a testator does not own at the time of her or his death is not subject to transfer by will. These principles were applied in the following case.

---

4. *Benjamin v. JP Morgan Chase Bank, N.A.*, 305 S.W.3d 446 (Ky.App. 2010).

CASE 52.1

Shaw Family Archives, Ltd. v. CMG Worldwide, Inc.

United States District Court, Southern District of New York, 486 F.Supp.2d 309 (2007).

BACKGROUND AND FACTS • The actress Marilyn Monroe, a New York resident, died in California on August 5, 1962. Her will gave her estate's residuary assets to Lee Strasberg and two other beneficiaries. Lee died in 1982. On the death of Aaron Frosch (the executor of Monroe's estate), Lee's widow, Anna, was appointed administrator. In 2001, the residuary assets were transferred to Marilyn Monroe, LLC (MMLLC), which Anna formed to manage those assets. During Monroe's life, photographer Sam Shaw took photos of her. After his death, the photos descended to the Shaw Family Archives (SFA). With Bradford Licensing Associates, SFA maintained a Web site through which they licensed Monroe's picture, image, and likeness for commercial use. In 2006, T-shirts that bore her picture and SFA's inscription on the label were offered for sale in Indiana. MMLLC asserted that under Indiana's Right of Publicity Act (which creates a right of publicity that survives for one hundred years after a person's death), it owned a right of publicity bequeathed by the residuary clause of Monroe's will and that SFA had violated this right. SFA and others filed a suit in a federal district court against MMLLC and CMG Worldwide, Inc., contending that MMLLC did not own such a right. Both parties filed motions for summary judgment.

IN THE LANGUAGE OF THE COURT
McMAHON, District Judge.
* * * *

Descendible [inheritable] postmortem [after death] publicity rights were not recognized, in New York, California, or Indiana at the time of Ms. Monroe's death in 1962. *To this day, New York law does not recognize any common law right of publicity and limits its statutory publicity rights to living persons.* California recognized descendible publicity rights when it passed its postmortem right of publicity statute in 1984, 22 years after Ms. Monroe's death. Prior to that time, a common law right of publicity existed, but it was not freely transferable or descendible. Indiana first recognized a descendible, postmortem right of publicity in 1994, when it passed the Indiana Right of Publicity Act. Prior to that time, rights of publicity were inalienable [not transferable] in Indiana, since they could only be vindicated through a personal tort action for invasion of privacy. [Emphasis added.]

Thus, at the time of her death in 1962 Ms. Monroe did not have any postmortem right of publicity under the law of any relevant state. As a result, any publicity rights she enjoyed during her lifetime were extinguished at her death by operation of law. [Emphasis added.]

Nevertheless, MMLLC argues that her will should be construed as devising postmortem publicity rights that were later conferred on Ms. Monroe by statute. Such a construction is untenable [indefensible].

Indiana follows the majority rule that the law of the domicile of the testator at his or her death applies to all questions of a will's construction. * * * Neither New York nor California—the only two states in which Ms. Monroe could conceivably have been domiciled—permitted a testator to dispose by will of property she does not own at the time of her death.
* * * *

[MMLLC cited references to "after-acquired property" in New York cases to support its argument.] * * * A will is deemed to pass all of the property the testator owns at the time of his death, rather than only the property owned at the time when the will was executed. Thus, when * * * [New York] court[s] * * * refer to "after-acquired" property, the term signifies property acquired after the execution of the will and before the testator's death—not property acquired after the testator's death. *[No case or statute] stands for the proposition that any intent on the part of the testator can overcome his testamentary incapacity to devise property he does not own at the time of his death.* [Emphasis added.]

California law does not differ from New York's.
* * * *

* * * Even if a postmortem right of publicity in Marilyn Monroe's persona could have been created after her death, [none] of the statutes that arguably bestowed that right allows for it to

CASE 52.1 CONTINUED ➡ be transferred through the will of a "personality" who, like Ms. Monroe, was already deceased at the time of the statute's enactment.

DECISION AND REMEDY • *The court issued a summary judgment in SFA's favor, holding that MMLLC had not become the owner of a right of publicity in Marilyn Monroe's name, likeness, and persona through her will. Monroe did not have the testamentary capacity to bequeath such a right because she did not own it—such rights did not exist—at the time of her death.*

THE E-COMMERCE DIMENSION • *Did SFA and Bradford's online offer of licenses for the commercial use of Monroe's image have any effect on the court's decision in this case? Why or why not?*

THE LEGAL ENVIRONMENT DIMENSION • *How might the court have ruled if Monroe had phrased her residuary clause to clearly state an intent to devise property she did not then own? (Hint: Can people—during or after their lives—transfer property that they do not own?)*

WRITING REQUIREMENTS Generally, a will must be in writing. The writing itself can be informal as long as it substantially complies with the statutory requirements. In some states, a will can be handwritten in crayon or ink. It can be written on a sheet or scrap of paper, on a paper bag, or on a piece of cloth. A will that is completely in the handwriting of the testator is called a **holographic will** (sometimes referred to as an *olographic will*).

In some instances, a court may find an oral will valid. A **nuncupative will** is an oral will made before witnesses. It is not permitted in most states. Where authorized by statute, such wills are generally valid only if made during the last illness of the testator and are therefore sometimes referred to as *deathbed wills*. Normally, only personal property can be transferred by a nuncupative will. Statutes frequently permit members of the military to make nuncupative wills when on active duty.

SIGNATURE REQUIREMENTS A fundamental requirement is that the testator's signature must appear on the will, generally at the end. Each jurisdiction dictates by statute and court decision what constitutes a signature. Initials, an X or other mark, and words such as "Mom" have all been upheld as valid when it was shown that the testators *intended* them to be signatures.

WITNESS REQUIREMENTS A will normally must be *attested* (sworn to) by two, and sometimes three, witnesses. The number of witnesses, their qualifications, and the manner in which the witnessing must be done are generally set out in a statute. A witness may be required to be disinterested—that is, not a beneficiary under the will. The UPC, however, allows even interested witnesses to attest to a will [UPC 2–505]. There are no age requirements for witnesses, but they must be mentally competent.

The purpose of the witnesses is to verify that the testator actually executed (signed) the will and had the requisite intent and capacity at the time. A witness need not read the contents of the will. Usually, the testator and all witnesses must sign in the sight or the presence of one another, but there are exceptions.[5] The UPC does not require all parties to sign in the presence of one another and deems it sufficient if the testator acknowledges her or his signature to the witnesses [UPC 2–502].

PUBLICATION REQUIREMENTS A will is *published* by an oral declaration by the maker to the witnesses that the document they are about to sign is his or her "last will and testament." Publication is becoming an unnecessary formality in most states, and it is not required under the UPC.

Revocation of Wills

An executed will is revocable by the maker at any time during the maker's lifetime. The maker may revoke a will by a physical act, such as tearing up the will, or by a subsequent writing. Wills can also be revoked by operation of law. Revocation can be partial or complete, and it must follow certain strict formalities.

REVOCATION BY A PHYSICAL ACT OF THE MAKER The testator may revoke a will by *intentionally* burning, tearing, canceling, obliterating, or destroying it or by having someone else do so in the presence of the testator and at the testator's direction.[6] In some states, partial revocation by a physical act of

---

5. See, for example, *Slack v. Truitt,* 368 Md. 2, 791 A.2d 129 (2000).
6. The destruction cannot be inadvertent. The maker's intent to revoke must be shown. When a will has been burned or torn accidentally, it is normally recommended that the maker have a new document created so that it will not falsely appear that the maker intended to revoke the will.

the maker is recognized. Thus, those portions of a will that are lined out or torn away are dropped, and the remaining parts of the will are valid. At no time, however, can a provision be crossed out and an additional or substitute provision written in. Such altered portions require that the will be reexecuted (signed again) and reattested (rewitnessed).

To revoke a will by a physical act, it is necessary to follow the mandates of a state statute exactly.

When a state statute prescribes the specific methods for revoking a will by a physical act, those are the only methods that will revoke the will.

In the following case, the court had to decide whether the testator had intended to revoke part or all of her will by making certain changes to it after it was executed.

✷ EXTENDED CASE 52.2 ✷
Peterson v. Harrell

Supreme Court of Georgia, 690 S.E.2d 151 (2010).
www.gasupreme.us[a]

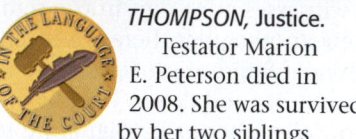

IN THE LANGUAGE OF THE COURT
THOMPSON, Justice.
Testator Marion E. Peterson died in 2008. She was survived by her two siblings [brother and sister], Arvin Peterson and Carolyn Peterson Basner (caveators[b]). After testator's death, Vasta Lucas, testator's longtime companion and executor of testator's estate, filed a petition to probate testator's will in solemn form. Lucas died during the pendency [pending period] of this appeal, and appellee Richard Harrell was appointed as successor executor and trustee for the estate. Caveators filed a caveat to the petition to probate, alleging the will was not properly executed or had been revoked due to obliterations. The trial court admitted the will to probate and caveators appealed.

OCGA [the Official Code of Georgia Annotated] Section 53-4-20(b) of the Revised Probate Code of 1998 provides that "a will shall be attested and subscribed in the presence of the testator by two or more competent witnesses." The record evidence in this case establishes that testator executed a will on

June 9, 1976. The will was witnessed by two subscribing witnesses, only one of whom was living at the time of trial. Having been provided a copy of testator's will, the surviving witness testified to its due execution by deposition testimony presented at trial and via written interrogatories filed with the court. Caveators presented no evidence challenging either the validity of the signatures on the will or testator's capacity at the time the will was executed. Accordingly, the evidence supports the trial court's finding that the will was duly executed.

The will contained a bequest to Lucas in the form of a trust and provided that upon Lucas's death the trustee shall distribute any remaining assets to four beneficiaries, including caveators. Some time after the will was executed, testator struck through with an ink pen the names of all successor beneficiaries of the trust estate, as well as language in the will nominating Richard Harrell as successor executor and trustee. None of the strike-throughs were witnessed or attested to. Near the end of the will, testator wrote, "My executrix is Julie Peterson." Caveators contend these alterations constitute material cancellations

that effect a revocation of the will.

To effect a revocation of a will by obliteration [elimination], caveators must show that testator made material obliterations to her will or directed another to do so and that testator intended for this act to revoke the will. *Joint operation of act and intention is necessary to revoke a will. The intent to revoke the will in its entirety shall be presumed from the obliteration or cancellation of a material portion of the will, but such presumption may be overcome by a preponderance of the evidence.* [Emphasis added.]

Even assuming, arguendo [for the sake of argument], that the alterations to testator's will constituted a material cancellation within the meaning of OCGA Section 53-4-44, we find no error in the trial court's conclusion that testator did not intend to revoke her entire will. The record supports the trial court's findings that caveators had no knowledge of the circumstances surrounding what they allege to be the revocation of the will, that testator never discussed revoking her will with caveators, and that caveators were not present when testator made the alterations to the will. Caveators presented no evidence of testator's intent other than the

---

a. Select "Opinions & Summaries" from the horizontal menu at the top of the page and then click on "2010 Opinions" in the drop-down menu. When that page appears, select the opinions for February 1. In the result, scroll down the page to the case title to access the opinion. The Georgia Supreme Court maintains this Web site.

b. In the context of wills, a *caveator* is one who files a *caveat* attacking the validity of an alleged will.

EXTENDED CASE 52.2 CONTINUED ➡

alterations themselves, and they satisfied their initial burden only by proving that testator made alterations to the will.

The record also shows, however, that the will was found in good condition on testator's desk among her personal papers. It bore the

signatures of both testator and her subscribing witnesses and set out a primary bequest to Lucas which remained intact. Handwritten alterations crossing out the names of the successor beneficiaries with a single line were initialed by testator and she added language to the will indicating her desire to substitute Julie Peterson as her executrix. As found

by the trial court, this evidence clearly indicates testator's intent to cancel only certain provisions of the will, not an intent to revoke the will in its entirety as required for revocation under OCGA Section 53-4-44.

* * * *

Judgment affirmed.

 QUESTIONS

1. Why would the caveators argue that the entire will should be revoked? How would the will's revocation benefit them?
2. What could the testator have done differently to clarify her intentions in her will?

REVOCATION BY A SUBSEQUENT WRITING A will may also be wholly or partially revoked by a **codicil,** a written instrument separate from the will that amends or revokes provisions in the will. A codicil eliminates the necessity of redrafting an entire will merely to add to it or amend it. A codicil can also be used to revoke an entire will. The codicil must be executed with the same formalities required for a will, and it must refer expressly to the will. In effect, it updates a will because the will is "incorporated by reference" into the codicil.

A new will (second will) can be executed that may or may not revoke the first or a prior will, depending on the language used. To revoke a prior will, the second will must use language specifically revoking other wills, such as, "This will hereby revokes all prior wills." If the second will is otherwise valid and properly executed, it will revoke all prior wills. If the express *declaration of revocation* is missing, then both wills are read together. If there are any discrepancies between the wills, the second will controls.

REVOCATION BY OPERATION OF LAW Revocation by operation of law occurs when a marriage, a divorce, an annulment, or the birth of a child takes place after a will has been executed. In most states, when a testator marries after executing a will that does not include the new spouse, on the testator's death the spouse can still receive the amount he or she would have taken had the testator died intestate (intestacy laws, which govern when there is no will, will be discussed shortly). In effect, this revokes the will to the point of providing the spouse with an intestate share. The rest of the estate is passed under the will

[UPC 2–301, 2–508]. If, however, the new spouse is otherwise provided for in the will (or by transfer of property outside the will), the new spouse will not be given an intestate amount.

At common law and under the law of most states, divorce does not necessarily revoke the entire will.[7] A divorce or an annulment occurring after a will has been executed revokes those dispositions of property made under the will to the former spouse [UPC 2–508].

If a child is born after a will has been executed and if it appears that the deceased parent would have made a provision for the child, that child may be entitled to a portion of the estate. Most state laws allow a child (born before or after execution of the will) to receive some portion of a parent's estate even if no provision is made in the parent's will. An exception is made when it is clear from the will's terms that the testator intended to disinherit the child. Under the UPC, the rule is the same.

Rights under a Will

The law imposes certain limitations on the way a person can dispose of property in a will. For example, a married person who makes a will generally cannot avoid leaving a certain portion of the estate to the surviving spouse (unless there is a valid prenuptial agreement—see Chapter 15). In most states, this is called an elective share or a forced share, and

---

7. Note that the 2008 amendments to the UPC, which have been adopted by only a few states, do provide for automatic revocation of testamentary devises on divorce [amended UPC 2–804].

it is often one-third of the estate or an amount equal to a spouse's share under intestacy laws.

Beneficiaries under a will have rights as well. A beneficiary can renounce (disclaim) his or her share of the property given under a will. Further, a surviving spouse can renounce the amount given under a will and elect to take the forced share when the forced share is larger than the amount of the gift—this is the widow's (or widower's) election, or right of election. State statutes provide the methods by which a surviving spouse accomplishes renunciation. The purpose of these statutes is to allow the spouse to obtain whichever distribution would be more advantageous. The UPC gives the surviving spouse an elective right to take a percentage of the total estate determined by the length of time that the spouse and the decedent were married to each other [UPC 2–201].

Probate Procedures

Typically, the procedures used to probate a will depend on the size of the decedent's estate.

INFORMAL PROBATE For smaller estates, most state statutes provide for the distribution of assets without formal probate proceedings. Faster and less expensive methods are then used. Property can be transferred by *affidavit* (a written statement taken in the presence of a person who has authority to affirm it), and problems or questions can be handled during an administrative hearing. Some states allow title to cars, savings and checking accounts, and certain other property to be transferred simply by filling out forms.

A majority of states also provide for *family settlement agreements,* which are private agreements among the beneficiaries. Once a will is admitted to probate, the family members can agree to settle among themselves the distribution of the decedent's assets. Although a family settlement agreement speeds the settlement process, a court order is still needed to protect the estate from future creditors and to clear title to the assets involved. The use of these and other types of summary procedures in estate administration can save time and expenses.

FORMAL PROBATE For larger estates, formal probate proceedings normally are undertaken, and the probate court supervises every aspect of the settlement of the decedent's estate. Additionally, in some situations—such as when a guardian for minor children must be appointed—more formal probate procedures cannot be avoided.

Formal probate proceedings may take several months or several years to complete, depending on the size and complexity of the estate and whether the will is contested. Factors that affect probate include the types of assets owned, the form of ownership, tax issues, the difficulty in locating the beneficiaries who inherit under the will, and marital property issues. When the will is contested, or someone objects to the actions of the personal representative (regardless of whether the person is the executor named in the will or an administrator appointed by the courts), the duration of probate is extended. As a result, a sizable portion of the decedent's assets (as much as 10 percent) may go to pay the fees charged by attorneys and personal representatives, as well as court costs.

Property Transfers outside the Probate Process

In the ordinary situation, a person can employ various **will substitutes** to avoid the cost of probate—for example, *living trusts* (see page 1,029), life insurance policies, or individual retirement accounts (IRAs) with named beneficiaries. One way to transfer property outside the probate process is to make gifts to children or others while one is still living.

Another method of accomplishing a property transfer without a will is through the joint ownership of property. For example, a person can hold title to certain real or personal property as a joint tenant with a spouse or other person. Recall from Chapter 50 that in a joint tenancy, when one joint tenant dies, the other joint tenant or tenants automatically inherit the deceased tenant's share of the property. This is true even if the deceased tenant has provided otherwise in her or his will.

In all of these situations, the person who sets up a living trust, arranges for a joint tenancy, or names a beneficiary for an IRA should be careful to ensure that the arrangement will benefit the intended person. A court will not apply the same principles when it reviews a transfer outside probate as it would apply to a testamentary transfer.

See *Concept Summary 52.1* on the facing page for a review of basic information about wills.

SECTION 2

INTESTACY LAWS

Each state regulates by statute how property will be distributed when a person dies intestate (without a valid will). These statutes are sometimes called

CONCEPT SUMMARY 52.1
Wills

Concept	Description
Terminology	1. *Intestate*—Describes one who dies without a valid will. 2. *Testator*—A person who makes a will. 3. *Personal representative*—A person appointed in a will or by a court to settle the affairs of a decedent. A personal representative named in the will is an *executor*. A personal representative appointed by the court for an intestate decedent is an *administrator*. 4. *Devise*—A gift of real estate by will; may be general or specific. The recipient of a devise is a *devisee*. 5. *Bequest, or legacy*—A gift of personal property by will; may be general or specific. The recipient of a bequest (legacy) is a *legatee*.
Requirements for a Valid Will	1. The testator must have testamentary capacity (be of legal age and sound mind at the time the will is made). 2. A will must be in writing (except for nuncupative wills). 3. A will must be signed by the testator, and usually several people must witness the signing, depending on the state statute. 4. A will may have to be *published*—that is, the testator may be required to announce to witnesses that this is his or her "last will and testament." Publication is not required in many states or under the UPC.

Revocation of Wills	1. *By a physical act of the maker*—Intentionally tearing up, canceling, obliterating, or deliberately destroying part or all of a will revokes it.
	 2. *By subsequent writing*—
	   a. Codicil—A formal, separate document that amends or revokes an existing will.
	   b. Second will, or new will—A new, properly executed will expressly revoking the existing will.
	 3. *By operation of law*—
	   a. Marriage—Generally revokes a will written before the marriage to the extent of providing for the spouse.
	   b. Divorce or annulment—Revokes dispositions of property made to the former spouse under a will made before the divorce or annulment.
	   c. Subsequently born child—It is inferred that the child is entitled to receive the portion of the estate granted under intestacy distribution laws.

Probate Procedures	To *probate* a will means to establish its validity and to carry out the administration of the estate through a court process. Probate laws vary from state to state. Probate procedures may be informal or formal, depending on the size of the estate and other factors, such as whether a guardian for minor children must be appointed.

statutes of descent and distribution or, more simply, intestacy laws, as mentioned in this chapter's introduction. Intestacy laws attempt to carry out the likely intent and wishes of the decedent. These laws assume that deceased persons would have intended that their natural heirs (spouses, children, grandchildren, or other family members) inherit their property. Therefore, intestacy statutes set out rules and priorities under which these heirs inherit the property. If no heirs exist, the state will assume ownership of the property.

The rules of descent vary widely from state to state. It is thus important to refer to the exact language of the applicable state statutes when addressing any problem of intestacy distribution.

Surviving Spouse and Children

Usually, state statutes provide that first the debts of the decedent must be satisfied out of the estate. Then the remaining assets pass to the surviving spouse and to the children. A surviving spouse usually receives only a share of the estate—typically, one-half if there is also a surviving child and one-third if there are two or more children.[8] Only if no children or grandchildren survive the decedent will a surviving spouse receive the entire estate.

Assume that Allen dies intestate and is survived by his wife, Betty, and his children, Duane and Tara. Allen's property passes according to intestacy laws. After his outstanding debts are paid, Betty will receive the homestead (either in fee simple or as a life estate) and ordinarily a one-third to one-half interest in all other property. The remaining real and personal property will pass to Duane and Tara in equal portions. Under most state intestacy laws and under the UPC, in-laws do not share in an estate. If a child dies before his or her parents, the child's spouse will not receive an inheritance on the parents' death. For example, if Duane died before his father (Allen), Duane's spouse would not inherit Duane's share of Allen's estate.

When there is no surviving spouse or child, the order of inheritance is grandchildren, then parents of the decedent. These relatives usually are called *lineal descendants*. If there are no lineal descendants, then *collateral heirs*—brothers and sisters, nieces and nephews, and aunts and uncles of the decedent—are the next groups that share. If there are no survivors in any of these groups, most statutes provide for the property to be distributed among the next of kin of the collateral heirs.

Stepchildren, Adopted Children, and Illegitimate Children

Under intestacy laws, stepchildren are not considered kin. Legally adopted children, however, are recognized as lawful heirs of their adoptive parents (as are children who are in the process of being adopted at the time of death). Statutes vary from state to state in regard to the inheritance rights of illegitimate children, or children born out of wedlock. Generally, an illegitimate child is treated as the child of the mother and can inherit from her and her relatives. Traditionally, the child usually was not regarded as the legal child of the father for inheritance purposes—unless paternity had been established through some legal proceeding prior to the father's death.

Given the dramatic increase in the number of children born out of wedlock in society today, many states have relaxed their laws of inheritance. A majority of states now consider a child born of any union that has the characteristics of a formal marriage relationship (such as unmarried parents who cohabit) to be legitimate. Under the revised UPC, a child is the child of the natural (biological) parents, regardless of their marital status, as long as the natural parent has openly treated the child as her or his offspring [UPC 2–114]. Although illegitimate children may have inheritance rights in most states, their rights are not necessarily identical to those of legitimate children.[9]

Distribution to Grandchildren

Usually, a will provides for how the decedent's estate will be distributed to descendants of deceased children (grandchildren). If a will does not include such a provision—or if a person dies intestate—the question arises as to what share the grandchildren of the decedent will receive. Each state designates one of two methods of distributing the assets of intestate decedents.

One method of dividing an intestate's estate is **per stirpes**.[10] Under this method, within a class or group of distributees (for example, grandchildren), the children of any one descendant take the share that their deceased parent *would have been* entitled to inherit. For example, Michael, a widower, has two children, Scott and Jillian. Scott has two children (Becky and Holly), and Jillian has one child (Paul). Scott and Jillian die before their father. When Michael dies, if his estate is distributed *per stirpes,* Becky and Holly each receive one-fourth of the estate (dividing Scott's one-half share). Paul receives one-half of the estate (taking Jillian's one-half share). Exhibit 52–2 on the top of the facing page illustrates the *per stirpes* method of distribution.

An estate may also be distributed on a **per capita**[11] basis—that is, each person in a class or group takes an equal share of the estate. If Michael's estate is distributed *per capita,* Becky, Holly, and Paul will each receive a one-third share. Exhibit 52–3 on the bottom of the facing page illustrates the *per capita* method of distribution.

---

8. UPC 2–102 has a formula for computing a surviving spouse's share that is contingent on the number of surviving children and parents. For example, if the decedent has no surviving children and one surviving parent, the surviving spouse takes the first $200,000, plus three-fourths of any balance of the intestate estate. UPC 2–102(2).

9. In the landmark case *Trimble v. Gordon,* 430 U.S. 762, 97 S.Ct. 1459, 52 L.Ed.2d 31 (1977), the United States Supreme Court ruled that state limitations on the inheritance rights of illegitimate children must be rationally related to a legitimate state interest.

10. *Per stirpes* is a Latin term meaning "by the roots" or "by stock." When used in estate law, it means proportionally divided between beneficiaries according to each beneficiary's deceased ancestor's share.

11. *Per capita* is a Latin term meaning "per person" or "for each head." When used in estate law, it means divided equally among beneficiaries within a class.

EXHIBIT 52-2 • *Per Stirpes* Distribution

Under this method of distribution, an heir takes the share that his or her deceased parent would have been entitled to inherit, had the parent lived. This may mean that a class of distributees—the grandchildren in this example—will not inherit in equal portions. Note that Becky and Holly receive only one-fourth of Michael's estate while Paul inherits one-half.

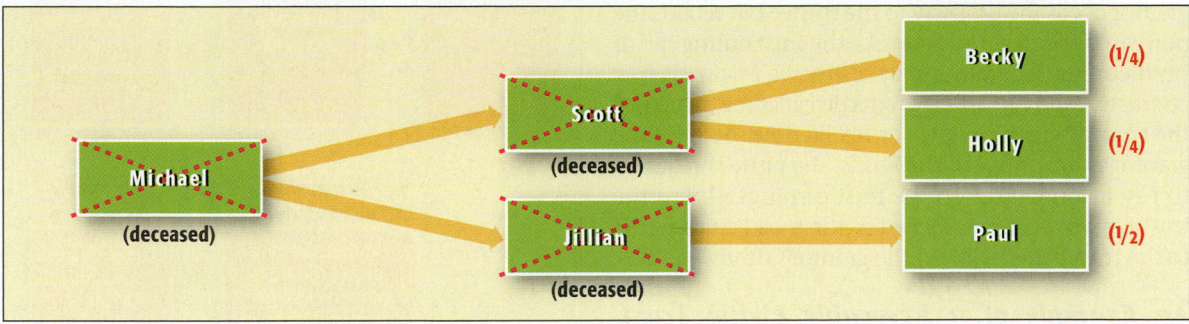

▰▰▰◢ **SECTION 3** ◣▰▰▰

TRUSTS

A **trust** is any arrangement by which property is transferred from one person to a trustee to be administered for the transferor's or another party's benefit. It can also be defined as a right of property (real or personal) held by one party for the benefit of another. A trust can be created to become effective during a person's lifetime or after a person's death. Trusts may be established for any purpose that is not illegal or against public policy.

Essential Elements of a Trust

The essential elements of a trust are as follows:

1. A designated beneficiary (except in charitable trusts, discussed shortly).
2. A designated trustee.
3. A fund sufficiently identified to enable title to pass to the trustee.

4. Actual delivery by the *settlor* or *grantor* (the person creating the trust) to the trustee with the intention of passing title.

Express Trusts

An express trust is created or declared in explicit terms, usually in writing. There are numerous types of express trusts, each with its own special characteristics.

LIVING TRUSTS A living trust—or *inter vivos* **trust** (*inter vivos* is Latin for "between or among the living")—is a trust created by a grantor during her or his lifetime. Living trusts have become a popular estate-planning option because at the grantor's death, assets held in a living trust can pass to the heirs without going through probate. Note, however, that living trusts do not necessarily shelter assets from estate taxes, and the grantor may still have to pay income taxes on trust earnings—depending on whether the trust is revocable or irrevocable.

EXHIBIT 52-3 • *Per Capita* Distribution

Under this method of distribution, all heirs in a certain class—in this example, the grandchildren—inherit equally. Note that Becky and Holly in this situation each inherit one-third, as does Paul.

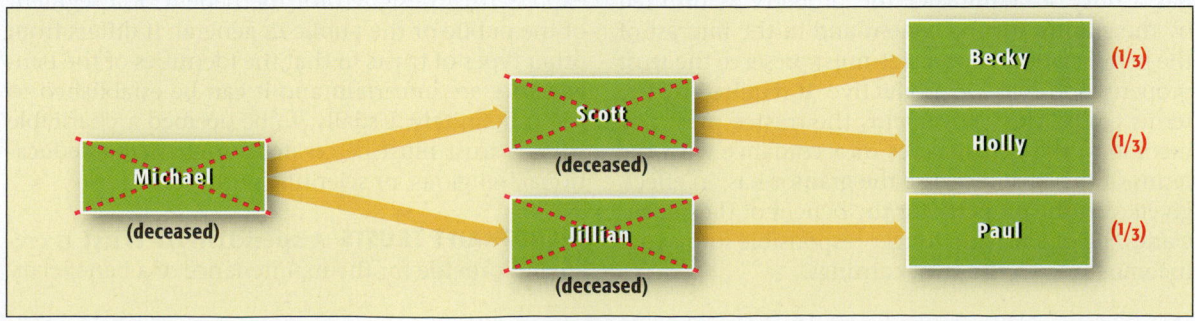

Revocable Living Trusts. Living trusts can be revocable or irrevocable. In a *revocable* living trust, which is the most common type, the grantor retains control over the trust property during her or his lifetime. The grantor deeds the property to the trustee but retains the power to amend, alter, or revoke the trust during her or his lifetime. The grantor may also serve as a trustee or co-trustee, and can arrange to receive income earned by the trust assets during her or his lifetime. Because the grantor is in control of the funds, she or he is required to pay income taxes on the trust earnings. Unless the trust is revoked, the principal of the trust is transferred to the trust beneficiary on the grantor's death.

An Example of a Revocable Living Trust. Suppose that James Cortez owns and operates a large farm. After his wife dies, James decides to create a living trust for the benefit of his three children, Alicia, Emma, and Jayden. He contacts his attorney, who prepares the documents creating the trust, executes a deed conveying the farm to the trust, and transfers the farm's bank accounts into the name of the trust. The trust designates James as the trustee and names his son Jayden as the *successor trustee,* who will take over the management of the trust when James dies or becomes incapacitated. James is the beneficiary during his lifetime and will receive an income from the trust (hence, he is called the *income beneficiary*).

On James's death, the farm will pass to his three children without having to go through probate (the children are referred to as *remainder beneficiaries).* By holding the property in a revocable living trust, James still has control over the farm during his life (and can make changes to, or end, the trust at any time). After his death, the trust becomes irrevocable, and Jayden, as trustee, must manage and distribute the trust property according to the trust's terms. This trust arrangement is illustrated in Exhibit 52–4.

Irrevocable Living Trusts. In an *irrevocable* living trust, in contrast, the grantor permanently gives up control over the property to the trustee. The grantor executes a trust deed, and legal title to the trust property passes to the named trustee. The trustee has a duty to administer the property as directed by the grantor for the benefit and in the interest of the beneficiaries. The trustee must preserve the trust property and make it productive. If required by the terms of the trust agreement, the trustee must pay income to the beneficiaries in accordance with the terms of the trust. Because the grantor has, in effect, given over the property for the benefit of the beneficiaries, he or she is no longer responsible for paying income taxes on the trust earnings.

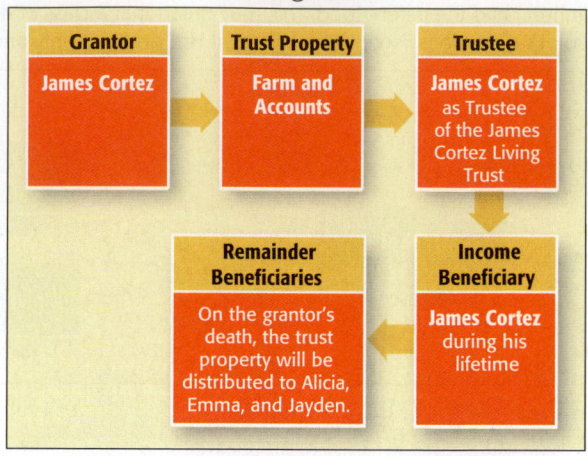

EXHIBIT 52–4 • A Revocable Living Trust Arrangement

TESTAMENTARY TRUSTS A **testamentary trust** is created by will and comes into existence on the grantor's death. Although a testamentary trust has a trustee who maintains legal title to the trust property, actions of the trustee are subject to judicial approval. This trustee can be named in the will or appointed by the court. Thus, a testamentary trust does not fail when the will does not name a trustee. The legal responsibilities of the trustee are the same as in an *inter vivos* trust.

If a court finds that the will setting up a testamentary trust is invalid, then the trust will also be invalid. The property that was supposed to be in the trust will then pass according to intestacy laws, not according to the terms of the trust.

If the court finds that a condition of the trust is invalid because it is illegal or against public policy, the court will invalidate the condition only and enforce the trust without it. For example, a condition of Herman's trust states "to my son if he never gets married." Because the condition is against public policy, the court will read the terms of the trust as not including the invalid restraint on marriage.

CHARITABLE TRUSTS A **charitable trust** is an express trust designed for the benefit of a segment of the public or the public in general. It differs from other types of trusts in that the identities of the beneficiaries are uncertain and it can be established to last indefinitely. Usually, to be deemed a charitable trust, a trust must be created for charitable, educational, religious, or scientific purposes.

SPENDTHRIFT TRUSTS A **spendthrift trust** is created to provide for the maintenance of a beneficiary by preventing him or her from being careless with the bestowed funds. Unlike the beneficiaries of other trusts, the beneficiary in a spendthrift trust is not permitted to transfer or assign his or her right to the trust's principal or future payments from the trust (*assignments* are discussed in Chapter 16). Essentially, the beneficiary can draw only a certain portion of the total amount to which he or she is entitled at any one time.

To qualify as a spendthrift trust, the trust must explicitly place restraints on the alienation—transfer to others—of the trust funds. A majority of the states allow spendthrift trust provisions that prohibit creditors from attaching such trusts, with a few exceptions, such as for payment of a beneficiary's domestic-support obligations. Additionally, creditors that have provided *necessaries* (see Chapter 13) to spendthrift trust recipients may request a court to compel payment from the trust income or principal.

TOTTEN TRUSTS A **Totten trust**[12] is created when a grantor deposits funds into an account in her or his own name with instructions that in the event of the grantor's death, whatever is in that account should go to a specific beneficiary. This type of trust is revocable at will until the depositor dies or completes

---

12. This type of trust derives its unusual name from *In the Matter of Totten*, 179 N.Y. 112, 71 N.E. 748 (1904).

the gift in her or his lifetime (by delivering the funds to the intended beneficiary, for example). The beneficiary has no access to the funds until the depositor's death, when the beneficiary obtains property rights to the balance on hand.

Implied Trusts

Sometimes, a trust is imposed (implied) by law, even in the absence of an express trust. Implied trusts include constructive trusts and resulting trusts.

CONSTRUCTIVE TRUSTS A **constructive trust** is imposed by a court in the interests of fairness and justice. In a constructive trust, the owner of the property is declared to be a trustee for the parties who are, in equity, actually entitled to the benefits that flow from the trust. If someone wrongfully holds legal title to property—because the property was obtained through fraud or in breach of a legal duty, for example—a court may impose a constructive trust. Courts often impose constructive trusts when someone who is in a confidential or fiduciary relationship with another person, such as a guardian to a ward, has breached a duty to that person.

In the following case, bank accounts and other financial assets with a value of about $500,000 were at the heart of a dispute over the imposition of a constructive trust.

CASE 52.3
Garrigus v. Viarengo

Appellate Court of Connecticut, 112 Conn.App. 655, 963 A.2d 1065 (2009).
www.jud.state.ct.us/index.html[a]

BACKGROUND AND FACTS • Stella Jankowski added her niece Genevieve Viarengo as a joint owner on several savings and checking accounts, certificates of deposit, and savings bonds. In executing a will, Jankowski told her attorney, John Wabiszczewicz, that she wanted her estate divided equally among her ten nieces, nephews, and cousins. She named Viarengo and Richard Golebiewski as co-executors. Wabiszczewicz was not aware of the jointly held accounts, and neither Jankowski nor Viarengo mentioned them. Jankowski died in 2001. Within days, Viarengo emptied Jankowski's safe and removed her financial records. Despite requests from Golebiewski and Wabiszczewicz, Viarengo did not reveal the contents of the safe or the records. Jankowski's estate—jewelry; a home in Waterbury, Connecticut; and the jointly held accounts—totaled about $600,000. The jointly owned assets were valued at about $500,000. Viarengo claimed that those accounts were hers. Diane Garrigus and other relatives filed a suit in a Connecticut state court against Viarengo. The court imposed a constructive trust. Viarengo appealed.

---

a. In the left-hand column, in the "Opinions" menu, select "Appellate Court." On that page, in the "Search the Archives:" section, click on "Appellate Court Archive." In the result, click on "2009." On that page, scroll to the "Published in Connecticut Law Journal – 2/17/09:" section and click on the number of the case to access the opinion. The State of Connecticut Judicial Branch maintains this Web site.

CASE CONTINUES ➡

CASE 52.3 CONTINUED ➡

IN THE LANGUAGE OF THE COURT
McLACHLAN, J. [Judge]
* * * *

A constructive trust arises * * * against one who, by fraud, actual or constructive, by duress or abuse of confidence, by commission of wrong, or by any form of unconscionable conduct, artifice, concealment, or questionable means, or who in any way against equity and good conscience, either has obtained or holds the legal right to property which he ought not, in equity and good conscience, hold and enjoy * * *. *A constructive trust arises whenever another's property has been wrongfully appropriated and converted into a different form * * * or when a person who holds title to property is subject to an equitable duty to convey it to another on the ground that he would be unjustly enriched if he were permitted to retain it.* [Emphasis added.]

In the present case, the court imposed a constructive trust on the assets held jointly by Stella [Jankowski] and the defendant after * * * finding that the plaintiff had proved by clear and convincing evidence that the defendant committed fraud in obtaining those assets and was unjustly enriched by holding the personal property that in equity and good conscience belonged to the ten beneficiaries of Stella's estate. * * * Stella told the defendant to divide the jointly held assets among her ten "children," * * * the defendant failed to do so and * * * the defendant was unjustly enriched because she obtained the bulk of Stella's estate.

* * * The defendant claims that "before the court can find that a constructive trust * * * should be imposed, the court must find, in addition to the element of fraud or misrepresentation, that a confidential relationship existed between Stella, as transferor, and the defendant, as transferee, at the time of the transfer of the property." Our case law does not support that position. In order for a constructive trust to be imposed, the plaintiff must allege and prove fraud, misrepresentation, imposition, circumvention, artifice or concealment, *or* abuse of confidential relations.

If fraud is established by clear and convincing evidence, which it was in this case, there is no additional requirement to prove the existence of a confidential relationship. The court imposed a constructive trust because it had found in favor of the plaintiff on his claim of fraud and because the defendant would be unjustly enriched if she retained the proceeds from the assets she had held jointly with Stella. The court did not address the issue of whether a confidential relationship existed; it was not necessary to do so.

DECISION AND REMEDY • *The state intermediate appellate court affirmed the lower court's judgment. A court can impose a constructive trust in the absence of a confidential relationship.*

THE LEGAL ENVIRONMENT DIMENSION • *What are the elements of fraud? Which facts in this case support the court's finding of fraud?*

WHAT IF THE FACTS WERE DIFFERENT? • *Suppose that by the time the court imposed a constructive trust on the joint accounts in this case, their value had decreased by $100,000. Should the defendant have been liable for the loss? Why or why not?*

RESULTING TRUSTS A **resulting trust** arises from the conduct of the parties. Here, the trust results, or is created, when circumstances raise an inference that the party holding legal title to the property does so for the benefit of another, unless the inference is refuted.

To illustrate: Glenda wants to put one acre of land she owns on the market for sale. Because she is going out of the country for two years and will not be available to deed the property to a buyer during that period, she conveys the property to her good friend Oscar. Oscar can then attempt to sell the property while Glenda is gone. The intent of the transaction in which Glenda conveyed the property to Oscar is neither a sale nor a gift. Consequently, Oscar will hold the property in a resulting trust for the benefit of Glenda. Therefore, on Glenda's return, Oscar will be required either to deed back the property to Glenda or, if the property has been sold, to turn over the proceeds (held in trust) to her.

Concept Summary 52.2 on the facing page provides a synopsis of basic information about trusts.

The Trustee

The trustee is the person holding the trust property. Anyone legally capable of holding title to, and dealing in, property can be a trustee. If the settlor of a

CONCEPT SUMMARY 52.2
Trusts

Concept	Description
Definition and Essential Elements	A trust is any arrangement by which property is transferred from one person to a trustee to be administered for another's benefit. The essential elements of a trust are (1) a designated beneficiary, (2) a designated trustee, (3) a fund sufficiently identified to enable title to pass to the trustee, and (4) actual delivery to the trustee with the intention of passing title.
Types of Trusts	1. *Living (inter vivos) trust*—A trust executed by a grantor during his or her lifetime. A living trust may be revocable or irrevocable. 2. *Testamentary trust*—A trust created by will and coming into existence on the death of the grantor. 3. *Charitable trust*—A trust designed for the benefit of a segment of the public or the public in general. 4. *Spendthrift trust*—A trust created to provide for the maintenance of a beneficiary by allowing her or him to receive only a certain portion of the total amount at any one time. 5. *Totten trust*—A trust created when one person deposits funds in his or her own name with instructions that the funds should go to a beneficiary on the depositor's death.
Implied Trusts	Implied trusts, which are imposed by law in the interests of fairness and justice, include the following: 1. *Constructive trust*—Arises by operation of law when a transaction occurs in which the person who takes title to property is, in equity, not entitled to enjoy the benefits from it. 2. *Resulting trust*—Arises from the conduct of the parties when an *apparent intention* to create a trust is present.

trust fails to name a trustee, or if a named trustee cannot or will not serve, the trust does not fail—an appropriate court can appoint a trustee.

TRUSTEE'S DUTIES A trustee must act with honesty, good faith, and prudence in administering the trust and must exercise a high degree of loyalty toward the trust beneficiary. The general standard of care is the degree of care a prudent person would exercise in his or her personal affairs.[13] The duty of loyalty requires that the trustee act in the exclusive interest of the beneficiary.

Among specific duties, a trustee must keep clear and accurate accounts of the trust's administration and furnish complete and correct information to the beneficiary. A trustee must keep trust assets separate from her or his own assets. A trustee has a duty to pay to an income beneficiary the net income

of the trust assets at reasonable intervals. A trustee also has a duty to limit the risk of loss from investments by reasonable diversification and to dispose of assets that do not represent prudent investments. Depending on the particular circumstances, prudent investment choices might include federal, state, or municipal bonds; corporate bonds; and shares of preferred or common stock.

TRUSTEE'S POWERS When a grantor creates a trust, he or she may set forth the trustee's powers and performance. State law governs in the absence of specific terms in the trust, and the states often restrict the trustee's investment of trust funds.[14] Typically, statutes confine trustees to investments in conservative debt securities such as government, utility,

---

13. Revised Uniform Principal and Income Act, Section 2(a)(3), which has been adopted by a majority of the states. See also *Restatement (Third) of Trusts (Prudent Investor Rule)*, Section 227.

14. As mentioned, a majority of the states have adopted the Revised Uniform Principal and Income Act, Section 2(a)(1). See also *Restatement (Third) of Trusts (Prudent Investor Rule)*, Section 227. Other uniform acts may also apply—for instance, more than twenty states have adopted the Uniform Trust Code, issued in 2000 and last amended in 2005.

and railroad bonds and certain real estate loans. Frequently, though, a grantor gives a trustee discretionary investment power. In that circumstance, any statute may be considered only advisory, with the trustee's decisions subject in most states to the prudent person rule.

A difficult question arises when the trust income proves to be insufficient to provide for the income beneficiary in an appropriate manner. In that situation, to what extent does the trustee have discretion to "invade" the principal and distribute it to the beneficiary? Conversely, if the trust income turns out to be more than adequate to provide for the beneficiary, can the trustee retain a portion of the income and add it to the principal? Generally, the answer to both questions is that the income beneficiary should be provided with a somewhat predictable annual income, but with a view to the safety of the principal. Thus, a trustee may make individualized adjustments in annual distributions.

Of course, a trustee is responsible for carrying out the purposes of the trust. If the trustee fails to comply with the terms of the trust or the controlling statute, he or she is personally liable for any loss.

ALLOCATIONS BETWEEN PRINCIPAL AND INCOME

Often, a grantor will provide one beneficiary with a life estate and another beneficiary with the remainder interest in the trust. A farmer, for example, may create a testamentary trust providing that the farm's income be paid to her surviving spouse and that, on the surviving spouse's death, the farm be given to their children. In this example, the surviving spouse has a *life estate* in the farm's income, and the children have a *remainder interest* in the farm (the principal). When a trust is set up in this manner, questions may arise between the income and principal beneficiaries as to how the receipts and expenses for the farm's management and the trust's administration should be allocated between income and principal.

When a trust instrument does not provide instructions, a trustee must refer to applicable state law. The general rule is that ordinary receipts and expenses are chargeable to the income beneficiary, whereas extraordinary receipts and expenses are allocated to the principal beneficiaries.[15] To illustrate: The receipt of rent from trust realty would be ordinary, as would the expense of paying the property's taxes. The cost of long-term improvements and proceeds from the property's sale, however, would be extraordinary.

---

15. Revised Uniform Principal and Income Act, Sections 3, 6, 8, and 13; and *Restatement (Third) of Trusts, (Prudent Investor Rule)* Section 227.

Trust Termination

The terms of a trust should expressly state the event on which the grantor wishes it to terminate—for example, the beneficiary's or the trustee's death. If the trust instrument does not provide for termination on the beneficiary's death, the beneficiary's death will not end the trust. Similarly, without an express provision, a trust will not terminate on the trustee's death.

Typically, a trust instrument specifies a termination date. For example, a trust created to educate the grantor's child may provide that the trust ends when the beneficiary reaches the age of twenty-five. If the trust's purpose is fulfilled before that date, a court may order the trust's termination. If no date is specified, a trust will terminate when its purpose has been fulfilled. Of course, if a trust's purpose becomes impossible or illegal, the trust will terminate.

SECTION 4
OTHER ESTATE-PLANNING ISSUES

Estate planning involves making difficult decisions about the future, such as who will inherit the family home and other assets and who will take care of minor children. It also involves preparing in advance for other contingencies. For example, what happens if you become incapacitated and cannot make your own decisions? Who will take care of your finances and other affairs? Do you want to be kept alive by artificial means, and who do you trust to make decisions about your health care in the event that you cannot? Preparing in advance for situations involving illness and incapacity can significantly ease the problems faced by family members. In this section, we discuss powers of attorney and living wills, both of which are frequently executed in conjunction with a will or trust.

Power of Attorney

As discussed in Chapter 33, a power of attorney is often used in business situations to give a person (an agent) authority to act on another's behalf. The powers usually are limited to a specific context, such as negotiating a deal with a buyer or entering into various contracts necessary to achieve a particular objective. Powers of attorney are commonly used in estate planning.

DURABLE POWER OF ATTORNEY One method of providing for future disability is to use a durable power of attorney. A **durable power of attorney** authorizes an individual to act on behalf of another when he or she becomes incapacitated. It can be drafted to take effect immediately or only after a physician certifies that the person is incapacitated. The person to whom the power is given can then write checks, collect insurance proceeds, and otherwise manage the incapacitated person's affairs, including health care.

For example, adult children may seek a durable power of attorney from their aging parents, particularly if the parents are becoming mentally incompetent or afflicted by Alzheimer's disease. A husband and wife may give each other a power of attorney to make decisions in the event that one of them is hospitalized and unable to express her or his wishes. A person who is undergoing an operation may sign a durable power of attorney to a loved one who can take over his or her affairs in the event of incapacity.

If you become incapacitated without having executed a durable power of attorney, a court may need to appoint a conservator to handle your financial affairs. Although a spouse may have some ability to write checks on joint accounts, for example, her or his power is often significantly limited. In most situations, it is better to have named a person you wish to handle your affairs in the event that you cannot.

HEALTH-CARE POWER OF ATTORNEY A **health-care power of attorney** designates a person who will have the power to choose what type of and how much medical treatment a person who is unable to make such decisions will receive. The health-care power of attorney is growing in importance as medical technology allows physicians and hospitals to keep people technically alive but in a so-called vegetative state for ever-increasing periods of time.

Consider the situation faced by the husband of Terri Schiavo, a Florida woman who was in a vegetative state from 1990 to 2005. It took more than twenty court hearings for the husband to convince the court that he had a right—against the wishes of Schiavo's mother and sister—to ask physicians to remove her feeding tube and let her die. If Schiavo had given her husband a health-care power of attorney, he would have had the right to make the decision to remove the feeding tube for her without going to court.

Living Will

A living will is not a will in the usual sense—that is, it does not appoint an estate representative, dispose of property, or establish a trust. Rather, a **living will** is an advance health directive that allows a person to control what medical treatment may be used after a serious accident or illness. Through a living will, a person can indicate whether he or she wants certain lifesaving procedures to be undertaken in situations in which the treatment will not result in a reasonable quality of life.

Most states have enacted statutes permitting living wills, and it is important that the requirements of state law be followed exactly in creating such wills. Typically, state statutes require physicians to abide by the terms of living wills, and living wills are often included with a patient's medical records.

REVIEWING
Wills and Trusts

In June 2009, Bernard Ramish set up a $48,000 trust fund through West Plains Credit Union to provide tuition for his nephew, Nathan Covacek, to attend Tri-State Polytechnic Institute. The trust was established under Ramish's control and went into effect that August. In December, Ramish suffered a brain aneurysm that caused frequent, severe headaches with no other symptoms. Shortly thereafter, Ramish met with an attorney to formalize in writing that he wanted no artificial life-support systems to be used should he suffer a serious illness. Ramish designated his cousin, Lizzie Johansen, to act on his behalf, including choosing his medical treatment, should he become incapacitated. In August 2011, Ramish developed heatstroke on the golf course at La Prima Country Club. After recuperating at the clubhouse, Ramish quickly wrote his will on the back of a wine list. It stated, "My last will and testament: Upon my death, I give all of my personal property to my friend Steve Eshom and my home to

REVIEWING CONTINUES ▶

REVIEWING

Wills and Trusts, Continued

Lizzie Johansen." He signed the will at the bottom in the presence of five men in the La Prima clubhouse, and all five men signed as witnesses. A week later, Ramish suffered a second aneurysm and died in his sleep. He was survived by his mother, Dorris Ramish; his son-in-law, Bruce Lupin; and his granddaughter, Tori Lupin. Using the information presented in the chapter, answer the following questions.

1. What type of trust did Ramish create for the benefit of Covacek? Was it revocable or irrevocable?
2. Would Ramish's testament on the back of the wine list meet the requirements for a valid will? Why or why not?
3. What would the order of inheritance have been if Ramish had died intestate?
4. Was Johansen granted a durable power of attorney or a health-care power of attorney for Ramish? Explain. Had Ramish created a living will?

⚙ **DEBATE THIS:** *Any changes to existing, fully witnessed wills should also have to be witnessed.*

TERMS AND CONCEPTS

administrator 1018
bequest 1020
charitable trust 1030
codicil 1025
constructive trust 1031
devise 1020
durable power of
  attorney 1035

escheat 1018
estate planning 1018
executor 1018
health-care power of
  attorney 1035
holographic will 1023
inter vivos trust 1029
intestacy laws 1018
intestate 1018

legacy 1020
living will 1035
nuncupative will 1023
per capita 1028
per stirpes 1028
probate 1018
resulting trust 1032
spendthrift trust 1030

testamentary trust 1030
testate 1018
testator 1018
Totten trust 1031
trust 1029
will 1018
will substitutes 1026

QUESTIONS AND CASE PROBLEMS

52–1. Wills and Intestacy Laws Benjamin is a widower who has two married children, Edward and Patricia. Patricia has two children, Perry and Paul. Edward has no children. Benjamin dies, and his typewritten will leaves all of his property equally to his children, Edward and Patricia, and provides that should a child predecease him, the grandchildren are to take per stirpes. The will was witnessed by Patricia and by Benjamin's lawyer and was signed by Benjamin in their presence. Patricia has predeceased Benjamin. Edward claims the will is invalid.
(a) Discuss whether the will is valid.
(b) Discuss the distribution of Benjamin's estate if the will is invalid.
(c) Discuss the distribution of Benjamin's estate if the will is valid.

52–2. Specific Bequests Gary Mendel drew up a will in which he left his favorite car, a 1966 red Ferrari, to his daughter, Roberta. A year prior to his death, Mendel sold the 1966 Ferrari and purchased a 1969 Ferrari. Discuss whether Roberta will inherit the 1969 Ferrari under the terms of her father's will.

52–3. QUESTION WITH SAMPLE ANSWER: Revocation of Wills.

While single, James made out a will naming his mother, Carol, as sole beneficiary. Later, James married Lisa.

(a) If James died while married to Lisa without changing his will, would the estate go to his mother, Carol? Explain.

(b) Assume that James made out a new will on his marriage to Lisa, leaving his entire estate to Lisa. Later, he divorced Lisa and married Mandis, but he did not change his will. Discuss the rights of Lisa and Mandis to James's estate after his death.

(c) Assume that James divorced Lisa, married Mandis, and changed his will, leaving his estate to Mandis. Later, a daughter, Claire, was born. James died without having included Claire in his will. Discuss fully whether Claire has any rights in the estate.

• **For a sample answer to Question 52–3, go to Appendix I at the end of this text.**

52–4. Intent Requirement Merlin Winters had three sons. Merlin and his youngest son, Abraham, had a falling out in 1994 and stopped speaking to each other. Merlin made a formal will in 1996, leaving all of his property to the two older sons and explicitly excluding Abraham. Merlin's health began to deteriorate, and by 1997, he was under the full-time care of a nurse, Julia. In 1998, he made a new will expressly revoking the 1996 will and leaving all of his property to Julia. On Merlin's death, the two older sons contest the 1998 will, claiming that Julia exercised undue influence over their father. Abraham claims that both wills are invalid because the first will was revoked by the second will, and the second will is invalid on the ground of undue influence. Is Abraham's contention correct? Explain.

52–5. Intestacy Laws In January 1993, three and a half years after Lauren and Warren Woodward were married, they were informed that Warren had leukemia. At the time, the couple had no children, and the doctors told the Woodwards that the leukemia treatment might leave Mr. Woodward sterile. The couple arranged for Mr. Woodward's sperm to be collected and placed in a sperm bank for later use. In October 1993, Warren Woodward died. Two years later, Lauren Woodward gave birth to twin girls who had been conceived through artificial insemination using Mr. Woodward's sperm. The following year, Mrs. Woodward applied for Social Security survivor benefits for the two children. The Social Security Administration (SSA) rejected her application, on the ground that she had not established that the twins were the husband's children within the meaning of the Social Security Act of 1935. Mrs. Woodward then filed a paternity action in Massachusetts, and the probate court determined that Warren Woodward was the twins' father. Mrs. Woodward resubmitted her application to the SSA but was again refused survivor benefits for the twins. She then filed an action in a federal district court to determine the inheritance rights, under Massachusetts's intestacy law, of children conceived from the sperm of a deceased individual and his surviving spouse. How should the court resolve this case? Should children conceived after a parent's death (by means of artificial insemination or *in vitro* fertilization) still inherit under intestate succession laws? Why or why not? [*Woodward v. Commissioner of Social Security*, 435 Mass. 536, 760 N.E.2d 257 (2002)]

52–6. Wills In 1944, Benjamin Feinberg bought a plot in Beth Israel Cemetery in Plattsburgh, New York. A mausoleum was built on the plot to contain six crypts. In 1954, Feinberg's spouse died and was interred in one of the crypts. Feinberg, his only son, one of his two daughters, and the daughter's son, Julian Bergman, began using the mausoleum regularly as a place of prayer and meditation. When Feinberg died, he was interred in the mausoleum. His two daughters were interred in two of the remaining crypts on their deaths. Feinberg's son died in 2001 and was interred in the fifth crypt. His widow, Laurie, then changed the locks on the mausoleum and refused access to Julian, who filed a suit in a New York state court against her to obtain a key. Feinberg and all of his children died testate, but none of them made a specific bequest of their interest in the plot to anyone. Each person's will included a residuary clause, however. Who owns the plot, who has access to it, and why? [*Bergman v. Feinberg*, 6 A.D.3d 1031, 776 N.Y.S.2d 611 (3 Dept. 2004)]

52–7. CASE PROBLEM WITH SAMPLE ANSWER: Wills.

 *James Lillard's first wife had a child whom James adopted when he married that child's mother. James fathered other children with her until they divorced in the early 1970s. In 1975, James married his second wife. During this marriage, each spouse's biological children remained the other's stepchildren because neither spouse adopted the other's children. James's second wife died in 2002, and he was diagnosed with terminal cancer in January 2004. In February, he executed a will that divided his property equally among all of his children and stepchildren. By October, James was living with his children, who managed his finances and administered his prescribed drugs, which impaired him mentally and physically. A hospice worker noted that on October 5 James had difficulty completing sentences and was forgetful. A visitor two days later described him as "morphined up." On this same day, he tore his first will in half and executed a new will that left most of his property to his children. James died on October 19. His children submitted the second will to a Georgia state court for probate. His stepchildren objected, alleging, among other things, that at the time of its execution, James lacked testamentary capacity. His children responded that the first will had been validly revoked. Which will should be declared valid? Why? [*Lillard v. Owens*, 281 Ga. 619 641 S.E.2d 511 (2007)]*

• **To view a sample answer for Problem 52–7, go to this book's Web site at www.cengage.com/blaw/clarkson, select "Chapter 52," and click on "Case Problem with Sample Answer."**

52–8. Intestacy Laws A Florida statute provides that the right of election of a surviving spouse can be waived by written agreement: "A waiver of 'all rights,' or equivalent language, in the property or estate of a present or prospective spouse . . . is a waiver of all rights to elective share." The day before Mary Ann Taylor married Louis Taylor in Florida, they entered into a prenuptial agreement. The agreement stated that all property belonging to each spouse would "forever remain his or her personal estate," "said property shall remain forever free of claim by the other," and the parties would retain "full rights and authority" over their property as they would have "if not married." After Louis died without a will, his only child, Joshua Taylor, filed a petition in a Florida state court for a determination of the beneficiaries of Louis's estate. How much of the estate can Mary Ann elect to receive? Explain. [*Taylor v. Taylor*, 1 So.3d 348 (Fla.App. 1 Dist. 2009)]

52–9. Wills Elnora Maxey became the guardian of Sean Hall after his parents died. In 1996, Maxey died, and her will left the two houses in her estate to Hall. Julia Jordan became Hall's new guardian, and when she died, her husband, John Jordan, became Hall's guardian. In 1998, when Hall was eighteen years old, he died intestate, and Jordan was appointed as the administrator of Hall's estate. The two houses had remained in Maxey's estate, but Jordan paid the mortgage and tax payments on the houses for Hall's estate because Hall had inherited the houses. Anthony Cooper, a relative of Maxey, petitioned the probate court to be appointed executor of Maxey's estate, stating that there was now no heir. The court granted the request. Jordan was not aware of the proceedings. Cooper then sold both houses in a sweetheart deal for $20,000 each to Quan Smith, without informing Jordan. The houses were then resold to JSD Properties, LLC, for $190,000. Learning of the sale, Jordan sued, contending that Cooper had breached his fiduciary duty and had lied to the court, as Maxey's will had clearly left the houses to Hall. Does Jordan have the right to demand that JSD return the property? What factors would be considered in making this decision? [*Witcher v. JSD Properties, LLC*, 286 Ga. 717, 690 S.E.2d 855 (2010)]

52–10. A QUESTION OF ETHICS: Wills.

Vickie Lynn Smith, an actress and model also known as Anna Nicole Smith, met J. Howard Marshall II in 1991. During their courtship, J. Howard lavished gifts and large sums of money on

Anna Nicole, and they married on June 27, 1994. J. Howard died on August 4, 1995. According to Anna Nicole, J. Howard intended to provide for her financial security through a trust, but under the terms of his will, all of his assets were transferred to a trust for the benefit of E. Pierce Marshall, one of J. Howard's sons. While J. Howard's estate was subject to probate proceedings in a Texas state court, Anna Nicole filed for bankruptcy in a federal bankruptcy court. Pierce filed a claim in the bankruptcy proceeding, alleging that Anna Nicole had defamed him when her lawyers told the media that Pierce had engaged in forgery and fraud to gain control of his father's assets. Anna Nicole filed a counterclaim, alleging that Pierce prevented the transfer of his father's assets to a trust for her by, among other things, imprisoning J. Howard against his wishes, surrounding him with security guards to prevent contact with her, and transferring property against his wishes. [Marshall v. Marshall, 547 U.S. 293, 126 S.Ct. 1735, 164 L.Ed.2d 480 (2006)]

(a) What is the purpose underlying the requirements for a valid will? Which of these requirements might be at issue in this case? How should it apply here? Why?

(b) State courts generally have jurisdiction over the probate of a will and the administration of an estate. Does the Texas state court thus have the sole authority to adjudicate all of the claims in this case? Why or why not?

(c) How should Pierce's claim against Anna Nicole and her counterclaim be resolved?

(d) Anna Nicole executed her will in 2001. The beneficiary—Daniel, her son, who was not J. Howard's child—died in 2006, shortly after Anna Nicole gave birth to a daughter, Dannielynn. In 2007, before executing a new will, Anna Nicole died. What happens if a will's beneficiary dies before the testator? What happens if a child is born after a will is executed?

LEGAL RESEARCH EXERCISES ON THE WEB

Go to this text's Web site at **www.cengage.com/blaw/clarkson**, select "Chapter 52," and click on "Practical Internet Exercises." There you will find the following Internet research exercises that you can perform to learn more about the topics covered in this chapter.

Practical Internet Exercise 52–1: Legal Perspective
Wills and Trusts

Practical Internet Exercise 52–2: Management Perspective
Social Security

Property rights have long been given extensive legal protection under both English and U.S. law. In the United States, the right to own property is closely associated with liberty, the pursuit of happiness, and other concepts that have played an integral role in American life. At the same time, conflicts often arise over who owns what and over how property should be used. In this *Focus on Ethics* feature, we explore some of the ethical dimensions of the laws pertaining to property, insurance, and inheritance.

Finders' Rights

The children's adage "finders keepers, losers weepers" is actually written into law—provided that the loser (the rightful owner) cannot be found, that is. A finder may acquire good title to found personal property against everyone *except the true owner.*

An early English case, *Armory v. Delamirie,*[1] is a landmark in Anglo-American jurisprudence concerning actions in *trover*—an early form of recovery of damages for the conversion of property. The plaintiff in this case was Armory, a chimney sweep who found a jewel in its setting during the course of his work. He took the jewel to a goldsmith to have it appraised. The goldsmith refused to return the jewel to Armory, claiming that Armory was not the rightful owner of the property. The court held that the finder, as prior possessor of the item, had rights to the jewel superior to those of all others except the rightful owner. The court said, "The finder of a jewel, though he does not by such finding acquire an absolute property or ownership, yet . . . has such a property as will enable him to keep it against all but the rightful owner, and consequently maintain trover."

The *Armory* case illustrates the doctrine of the *relativity of title.* Under this doctrine, if two contestants, neither of whom can claim absolute title to the property, come before the court, the one who can claim prior possession will likely have established sufficient rights to the property to win the case.

Bailee's Duty of Care

The standard of care expected of a bailee clearly illustrates how property law reflects ethical principles. For example, a friend asks to borrow your business law text for the weekend. You agree to loan your friend the book. In this situation, which is a bailment for the sole benefit of the bailee (your friend), most people would agree that your friend has an ethical obligation to take great care of your book. After all, if your friend lost your book, you would incur damages. You would have to purchase another one, and if you could not, you might

1. 93 Eng.Rep. 664 (K.B. [King's Bench] 1722).

find it difficult to do well on your homework assignments and examinations.

The situation would be different if you had loaned your book to your friend totally for your own benefit. Suppose that you are leaving town during the summer, and your friend offers to store several boxes of books for you until you return in the fall. In this situation, a bailment for the sole benefit of the bailor (you) exists. If your books are destroyed through the bailee's (your friend's) negligence and you sue the bailee for damages, a court will likely take into consideration the fact that the bailee was essentially doing you a favor by storing the books. Although bailees generally have a duty to exercise reasonable care over bailed property, what constitutes reasonable care in a specific situation normally depends on the surrounding circumstances, including the reason for the bailment and who stood to benefit from the arrangement.

Land-Use Regulations and the "Takings Clause"

When property owners claim that a "regulatory taking" has occurred, the courts usually decide the issue on a case-by-case basis. In other words, there is no general rule that indicates whether a specific situation will be deemed a taking.

In a case decided in 2010, a group of Florida beachfront property owners challenged the constitutionality of the state's decision to add seventy-five feet of sand to the shoreline. Under Florida law, the boundary between private beachfront property and state-owned land is ordinarily the average high-water line. The state owns any land submerged beneath the ocean or other navigable waters. It is common for storms to cause some fluctuation in the shoreline, however, as sand is deposited or washed away by waves. A change that occurs gradually and imperceptibly over time is called an *accretion,* whereas a sudden change is called an *avulsion.* If an accretion deposits more sand on the shore, the owners of private beachfront property automatically acquire ownership rights to more land—to the new high-water line. If an avulsion occurs, however, the property owners' boundaries remain the same, so the state owns the land abutting the water's edge.

As a result of several hurricanes, 6.9 miles of beach were eroded (an avulsion) in the city of Destin and Walton County. The state therefore requested and received a permit from the Florida Department of Environmental Protection to add seventy-five feet of dry sand on its side (the seaward side) of the high-water line. Owners of the private beachfront property in the area formed a nonprofit corporation to fight the proposed addition of sand, but they lost at an administrative hearing. They then filed a lawsuit claiming that the state's action constituted an unlawful taking of their beachfront property.

FOCUS ON ETHICS CONTINUES ➡

The Courts Disagree A Florida appellate court agreed with the property owners that the state had taken their rights to receive accretions and to have their property remain in contact with the water. The Florida Supreme Court reversed, and the United States Supreme Court granted *certiorari*.

The Supreme Court held that Florida had not engaged in an unconstitutional taking. According to the high court, there was no taking because the property owners did not show that their rights to future accretions and to contact with the water were superior to Florida's right to fill in its submerged land. The state did not relocate the property line to take private property, but simply added sand to property that it already owned (on the side toward the water). Therefore, the state had a right to restore the beach even though the addition of sand interfered with the property owners' rights to have their property touch the water.[2] Although a majority of the Supreme Court justices concurred in the result, there were substantial differences in their reasoning.

A Question of Fairness The question of whether private landowners should be compensated when their land is essentially "taken" for public use by environmental and land-use regulations clearly involves issues of fairness. On the one hand, states, cities, and other local governments want to preserve their natural resources and need some authority to regulate land use to achieve this goal. On the other hand, private property owners complain that they alone should not have to bear the costs of creating a benefit—such as more sandy beaches for recreation or environmental preservation[3]—that all members of the public enjoy.

Discrimination in Housing

The Fair Housing Act also presents issues of fairness. The act prohibits mortgage lenders from refusing to lend funds for the purchase of homes in certain areas. Prohibiting this practice, known as *redlining*, severely restricts lenders' ability to choose freely where (or where not) to invest their money. Should lenders be coerced by law into lending funds toward the purchase of homes that are located in neighborhoods where criminal activity is on the rise and property values are rapidly declining? The lender is in business to make a profit on its loan; it is not a charitable organization. The

public policy expressed in the Fair Housing Act protects disadvantaged borrowers, in this context, by making more housing available to them. Lenders, however, are forced to extend credit in areas that may increase their risk of loss.

Insurance

A number of ethical issues arise in the area of insurance, a few of which we examine here.

Insurance Agents and Fiduciary Duties When a person applies for insurance coverage through an insurance company's agent, is the agent obligated to advise that person as to what coverage she or he should obtain? If the agent does not advise a client about certain types of coverage, has the agent breached a fiduciary duty owed to the applicant? For example, suppose that someone applies for auto insurance, and the insurance agent does not advise her that she should obtain uninsured motorist coverage. Later, the client is involved in an accident with an uninsured motorist, and the insurance company refuses to compensate her for her injuries and losses. The client claims that the insurance agent was negligent in not advising her to sign up for uninsured motorist coverage. Was the agent negligent? Did the agent breach a duty owed to the client?

The answer to this question is no. As mentioned in Chapter 51, an insurance agent is an agent of the insurer (the insurance company), not of the party who applies for insurance. As such, the agent owes fiduciary duties to the insurer, but not to the insured. The agent's only duties to the insured are contractual in nature. Although this rule may seem unfair to insurance applicants, who may know less about the need for certain types of insurance coverage than the agent does, a contrary rule might create even more unfairness. An insurance agent could be held liable for failure to advise a client of every possible insurance option, and the insured would be relieved of any burden to take care of his or her own financial needs and expectations. Also, as one court noted, if the state legislature does not require such coverage, why should the courts require insurance companies to offer or explain available optional coverage?[4]

Life Insurance Policies on Rank-and-File Employees Nearly 20 percent of the life insurance policies issued each year are sold to corporations to cover the lives of their employees. These policies—known as *dead peasant policies, corporate-owned life insurance* (COLI), or

---

2. *Stop the Beach Renourishment, Inc. v. Florida Department of Environmental Protection,* ___ U.S. ___, 130 S.Ct. 2592, ___ L.Ed.2d ___ (2010).

3. See, for example, *Tahoe-Sierra Preservation Council v. Tahoe Regional Planning Agency,* 535 U.S. 302, 122 S.Ct. 1465, 152 L.Ed.2d 517 (2002).

---

4. *Jones v. Kennedy,* 108 S.W.3d 203 (Mo.App. 2003). See also *Richey v. Philipp Co.,* 259 S.W.3d 1 (W.D.Mo.App. 2008).

bank-owned life insurance (BOLI)—cover rank-and-file employees rather than key employees. Since the 1990s, insurance companies have marketed COLI plans as a way for businesses to reap profits and significant tax deductions from a small investment. The businesses could use the profits from the plans to fund employee benefits. For years, employers were allowed to take out dead peasant policies without notifying the employees whose lives were being insured. Then, some employees (or their families if the employees were deceased) who had been insured through these plans started bringing lawsuits, claiming that their employers lacked an insurable interest and had obtained the policies without the employees' consent. For example, Wal-Mart Stores, Inc., which purchased more than 350,000 COLI policies between 1993 and 1995, has faced numerous lawsuits (and no longer obtains COLI policies). Wal-Mart settled one class-action suit in 2004 for $10.3 million and another in 2006 for $5 million including $1.7 million in attorneys' fees.[5]

In 2006, Congress responded to the controversy by enacting a law that requires an employer to obtain an employee's consent before purchasing life insurance on her or him and to notify the employee of the maximum amount of the policy. Litigation over COLI policies continues, however. In 2009, Wal-Mart lost an appeal in a class-action case filed by a Louisiana widow whose late husband had been covered by a COLI plan.[6] Another case against Wal-Mart was dismissed in 2009, however, on procedural grounds. The federal district court found that Wal-Mart had lacked an insurable interest in the life of Rita Atkinson, a rank-and-file employee, and therefore the $66,000 insurance policy on her life was void. Consequently, the amount in controversy did not exceed $75,000, as is required for a federal court to exercise diversity jurisdiction.[7]

Inheritance Rights

New applications of technology often present thorny issues for the courts, from both a legal and an ethical perspective. A challenging issue has to do with the inheritance rights of posthumously conceived

children—children conceived through the use of a decedent's sperm that had been previously collected and stored in a sperm bank. Do such children have inheritance rights under state intestacy laws? Should they?[8]

The laws on this issue vary from state to state. A handful of states (including California, Colorado, Delaware, Florida, North Dakota, Texas, Virginia, Washington, and Wyoming) have enacted statutes that specifically address the inheritance rights of posthumously conceived children. Many of these state laws specify that a deceased person is not a parent of any posthumously conceived biological child—unless he or she consented in writing to being a parent after death. California further requires that the child be *in utero* within two years from the date of the decedent's death for a probate court to consider it a child of the deceased parent.[9] Courts in four states (Arizona, Massachusetts, New Jersey, and New York) have held that posthumously conceived children are heirs who are entitled to benefits under the Social Security Act.[10] Several states (including Colorado, Delaware, Texas, Virginia, and Washington) have amended their intestacy laws to allow posthumously conceived children to inherit.

DISCUSSION QUESTIONS

1. Do you think that the law strikes a fair balance between the rights of parties with respect to found property? Why or why not?
2. Do the different standards of care that apply to bailed goods reflect underlying ethical values? If so, how?
3. Do you believe that it is fair for courts to decide whether a regulatory taking has occurred on a case-by-case basis and not to articulate a general rule on which landowners can rely? Why or why not?
4. Should posthumously conceived children have the same inheritance rights as children born during the decedent's life? Why or why not? How can a balance be struck between the interests of children born during the lifetime of the decedent and those born after the parent's death?

---

5. See *Lewis v. Wal-Mart Stores, Inc.,* 2006 WL 3505851 (N.D.Okla. 2006), and 232 Federal Rules Decision 687 (N.D.Okla. 2005); *Mayo v. Hartford Life Insurance Co.,* 354 F.3d 400 (S.D.Tex. 2004).
6. *Richard v. Wal-Mart Stores, Inc.,* 559 F.3d 341 (5th Cir. 2009). The case was remanded for a new trial.
7. *Atkinson v. Wal-Mart Stores, Inc.,* 2009 WL 1458020 (M.D.Fla. 2009).

8. See, for example, *Woodward v. Commissioner of Social Security,* 435 Mass. 536, 760 N.E.2d 257 (2002), which was presented as Case Problem 52–5 on page 1,037.
9. Cal. Probate Code Section 249.5.
10. See *In re Martin B.,* 17 Misc.3d 198, 841 N.Y.S.2d 207 (N.Y.Sur. 2007); *Gillett-Netting v. Barnhart,* 371 F.3d 593 (9th Cir. 2004); *In re Estate of Kolacy,* 332 N.J.Super. 593, 753 A.2d 1257 (Ch. Div. 2000); and the *Woodward* case cited in Footnote 8.

How to Brief Cases and Analyze Case Problems

How to Brief Cases

To fully understand the law with respect to business, you need to be able to read and understand court decisions. To make this task easier, you can use a method of case analysis that is called *briefing*. There is a fairly standard procedure that you can follow when you "brief" any court case. You must first read the case opinion carefully. When you feel you understand the case, you can prepare a brief of it.

Although the format of the brief may vary, typically it will present the essentials of the case under headings such as those listed below.

1. **Citation.** Give the full citation for the case, including the name of the case, the date it was decided, and the court that decided it.
2. **Facts.** Briefly indicate (a) the reasons for the lawsuit; (b) the identity and arguments of the plaintiff(s) and defendant(s), respectively; and (c) the lower court's decision—if appropriate.
3. **Issue.** Concisely phrase, in the form of a question, the essential issue before the court. (If more than one issue is involved, you may have two—or even more—questions here.)
4. **Decision.** Indicate here—with a "yes" or "no," if possible—the court's answer to the question (or questions) in the *Issue* section above.
5. **Reason.** Summarize as briefly as possible the reasons given by the court for its decision (or decisions) and the case or statutory law relied on by the court in arriving at its decision.

An Example of a Briefed Sample Court Case

As an example of the format used in briefing cases, we present here a briefed version of the sample court case that was presented in Chapter 1 in Exhibit 1–6 on pages 23–25.

SINGER v. RAEMISCH
United States Court of Appeals, Seventh Circuit, 593 F.3d 529 (2010).

FACTS Kevin Singer, an inmate at Wisconsin's Waupun Correctional Institution, is a devoted player of Dungeons and Dragons (D&D), a fantasy role-playing game. In November 2004, the prison's gang expert received an anonymous letter stating that Singer and three other inmates were trying to recruit others to join a "gang" dedicated to playing D&D. Prison officials searched Singer's cell, confiscated all of his D&D materials, and prohibited him and other inmates from playing D&D. Singer filed a suit in a federal district court against the prison, alleging, in part, that the officials' actions violated his right to free speech under the First Amendment to the U.S. Constitution. The court concluded that the D&D ban was rationally related to a legitimate government interest and issued a judgment in the prison's favor. Singer appealed to the U.S. Court of Appeals for the Seventh Circuit.

ISSUE Can a prison, consistent with the First Amendment, restrict inmates' speech, when that restriction is reasonably viewed as promoting prison security?

DECISION Yes. The U.S. Court of Appeals for the Seventh Circuit affirmed the lower court's judgment.

REASON The court acknowledged that the prison's D&D ban was a restriction of Singer's and the other inmates' constitutional rights. But the court explained, "Prison regulations that restrict inmates' constitutional rights are nevertheless valid if they are reasonably related to legitimate penological interests,"[1] which concern prison management and the treatment of inmates. In this case, the

---

1. *Penological interests* relate to the branch of criminology dealing with prison management and the treatment of offenders.

D&D ban "bears a rational relationship" to those interests. The ban promotes prison security because games such as D&D can "mimic the organization of gangs and lead to their development." The court pointed out that this conclusion was based on the prison gang expert's testimony that D&D can "foster an inmate's obsession with escaping from the real life, correctional environment, fostering hostility, violence and escape behavior." This "can compromise not only the inmate's rehabilitation and effects of positive programming but also endanger the public and jeopardize the safety and security of the institution."

Review of Sample Court Case

Here, we provide a review of the briefed version to indicate the kind of information that is contained in each section.

CITATION The name of the case is *Singer v. Raemisch*. Singer is the plaintiff; Raemisch is the defendant. The U.S. Court of Appeals for the Seventh Circuit decided this case in 2010. The citation states that this case can be found in Volume 593 of the *Federal Reporter, Third Series*, on page 529.

FACTS The *Facts* section identifies the plaintiff and the defendant, describes the events leading up to this suit, the allegations made by the plaintiff in the initial suit, and the lower court's ruling and the party appealing (because this case is a decision of one of the federal appellate courts). The appellant's contention on appeal is also sometimes included here.

ISSUE The *Issue* section presents the central issue (or issues) decided by the court. In this case, the U.S. Court of Appeals for the Seventh Circuit considers whether a prison can restrict the speech of its inmates if that restriction is reasonably viewed as promoting prison security.

DECISION The *Decision* section includes the court's decision on the issues before it. The decision reflects the opinion of the judge or justice hearing the case. Decisions by appellate courts frequently are phrased in reference to the lower court's decision. That is, the appellate court may "affirm" the lower court's ruling or "reverse" it. Here, the court determined that the belief of the prison officials with respect to the effect of unrestricted speech was reasonable. The officials thought that unrestricted speech would compromise prison security. On that basis, the prison could legitimately ban the playing of D&D. The appellate court affirmed the ruling in the prison's favor.

REASON The *Reason* section includes references to the relevant laws and legal principles that were applied in coming to the conclusion arrived at in the case before the court. The relevant law here included the principle that prison regulations restricting inmates' constitutional rights are valid if they reasonably relate to legitimate penological interests. This section also explains the court's application of the law to the facts in this case.

Analyzing Case Problems

In addition to learning how to brief cases, students of business law and the legal environment also find it helpful to know how to analyze case problems. Part of the study of business law and the legal environment usually involves analyzing case problems, such as those included in this text at the end of each chapter.

For each case problem in this book, we provide the relevant background and facts of the lawsuit and the issue before the court. When you are assigned one of these problems, your job will be to determine how the court should decide the issue, and why. In other words, you will need to engage in legal analysis and reasoning. Here, we offer some suggestions on how to make this task less daunting. We begin by presenting a sample problem:

> While Janet Lawson, a famous pianist, was shopping in Quality Market, she slipped and fell on a wet floor in one of the aisles. The floor had recently been mopped by one of the store's employees, but there were no signs warning customers that the floor in that area was wet. As a result of the fall, Lawson injured her right arm and was unable to perform piano concerts for the next six months. Had she been able to perform the scheduled concerts, she would have earned approximately $60,000 over that period of time. Lawson sued Quality Market for this amount, plus another $10,000 in medical expenses. She claimed that the store's failure to warn customers of the wet floor constituted negligence and therefore the market was liable for her injuries. Will the court agree with Lawson? Discuss.

Understand the Facts

This may sound obvious, but before you can analyze or apply the relevant law to a specific set of facts, you must clearly understand those facts. In other words, you should read through the case problem carefully—more than once, if necessary—to make sure you understand the identity of the plaintiff(s) and defendant(s) in the case and the progression of events that led to the lawsuit.

In the sample case problem just given, the identity of the parties is fairly obvious. Janet Lawson is the one bringing the suit; therefore, she is the plaintiff. Quality Market, against whom she is bringing the suit, is the defendant. Some of the case problems you may work on have multiple plaintiffs or defendants. Often, it is helpful to use abbreviations for the parties. To indicate a reference to a plaintiff, for example, the *pi* symbol—π—is often used, and a defendant is denoted by a *delta*—Δ—a triangle.

The events leading to the lawsuit are also fairly straightforward. Lawson slipped and fell on a wet floor, and she contends that Quality Market should be liable for her injuries because it was negligent in not posting a sign warning customers of the wet floor.

When you are working on case problems, realize that the facts should be accepted as they are given. For example, in our sample problem, it should be accepted that the floor was wet and that there was no sign. In other words, avoid making conjectures, such as "Maybe the floor wasn't too wet," or "Maybe an employee was getting a sign to put up," or "Maybe someone stole the sign." Questioning the facts as they are presented only adds confusion to your analysis.

Legal Analysis and Reasoning

Once you understand the facts given in the case problem, you can begin to analyze the case. Recall from Chapter 1 that the IRAC method is a helpful tool to use in the legal analysis and reasoning process. IRAC is an acronym for Issue, Rule, Application, Conclusion. Applying this method to our sample problem would involve the following steps:

1. First, you need to decide what legal **issue** is involved in the case. In our sample case, the basic issue is whether Quality Market's failure to warn customers of the wet floor constituted negligence. As discussed in Chapter 7, negligence is a *tort*—a civil wrong. In a tort lawsuit, the plaintiff seeks to be compensated for another's wrongful act. A defendant will be deemed negligent if he or she breached a duty of care owed to the plaintiff and the breach of that duty caused the plaintiff to suffer harm.

2. Once you have identified the issue, the next step is to determine what **rule of law** applies to the issue. To make this determination, you will want to review carefully the text of the chapter in which the relevant rule of law for the problem appears. Our sample case problem involves the tort of negligence, which is covered in Chapter 7. The applicable rule of law is the tort law principle that business owners owe a duty to exercise reasonable care to protect their customers ("business invitees"). Reasonable care, in this context, includes either removing—or warning customers of—*foreseeable* risks about which the owner *knew* or *should have known*. Business owners need not warn customers of "open and obvious" risks, however. If a business owner breaches

this duty of care (fails to exercise the appropriate degree of care toward customers), and the breach of duty causes a customer to be injured, the business owner will be liable to the customer for the customer's injuries.

3. The next—and usually the most difficult—step in analyzing case problems is the **application** of the relevant rule of law to the specific facts of the case you are studying. In our sample problem, applying the tort law principle just discussed presents few difficulties. An employee of the store had mopped the floor in the aisle where Lawson slipped and fell, but no sign was present indicating that the floor was wet. That a customer might fall on a wet floor is clearly a foreseeable risk. Therefore, the failure to warn customers about the wet floor was a breach of the duty of care owed by the business owner to the store's customers.

4. Once you have completed Step 3 in the IRAC method, you should be ready to draw your **conclusion.** In our sample problem, Quality Market is liable to Lawson for her injuries, because the market's breach of its duty of care caused Lawson's injuries.

The fact patterns in the case problems presented in this text are not always as simple as those presented in our sample problem. Often, for example, a case has more than one plaintiff or defendant. A case may also involve more than one issue and have more than one applicable rule of law. Furthermore, in some case problems the facts may indicate that the general rule of law should not apply. For example, suppose that a store employee advised Lawson not to walk on the floor in the aisle because it was wet, but Lawson decided to walk on it anyway. This fact could alter the outcome of the case because the store could then raise the defense of assumption of risk (see Chapter 7). Nonetheless, a careful review of the chapter should always provide you with the knowledge you need to analyze the problem thoroughly and arrive at accurate conclusions.

APPENDIX B

The Constitution of the United States

Preamble

We the People of the United States, in Order to form a more perfect Union, establish Justice, insure domestic Tranquility, provide for the common defence, promote the general Welfare, and secure the Blessings of Liberty to ourselves and our Posterity, do ordain and establish this Constitution for the United States of America.

Article I

Section 1. All legislative Powers herein granted shall be vested in a Congress of the United States, which shall consist of a Senate and House of Representatives.

Section 2. The House of Representatives shall be composed of Members chosen every second Year by the People of the several States, and the Electors in each State shall have the Qualifications requisite for Electors of the most numerous Branch of the State Legislature.

No Person shall be a Representative who shall not have attained to the Age of twenty five Years, and been seven Years a Citizen of the United States, and who shall not, when elected, be an Inhabitant of that State in which he shall be chosen.

Representatives and direct Taxes shall be apportioned among the several States which may be included within this Union, according to their respective Numbers, which shall be determined by adding to the whole Number of free Persons, including those bound to Service for a Term of Years, and excluding Indians not taxed, three fifths of all other Persons. The actual Enumeration shall be made within three Years after the first Meeting of the Congress of the United States, and within every subsequent Term of ten Years, in such Manner as they shall by Law direct. The Number of Representatives shall not exceed one for every thirty Thousand, but each State shall have at Least one Representative; and until such enumeration shall be made, the State of New Hampshire shall be entitled to chuse three, Massachusetts eight, Rhode Island and Providence Plantations one, Connecticut five, New York six, New Jersey four, Pennsylvania eight, Delaware one, Maryland six, Virginia ten, North Carolina five, South Carolina five, and Georgia three.

When vacancies happen in the Representation from any State, the Executive Authority thereof shall issue Writs of Election to fill such Vacancies.

The House of Representatives shall chuse their Speaker and other Officers; and shall have the sole Power of Impeachment.

Section 3. The Senate of the United States shall be composed of two Senators from each State, chosen by the Legislature thereof, for six Years; and each Senator shall have one Vote.

Immediately after they shall be assembled in Consequence of the first Election, they shall be divided as equally as may be into three Classes. The Seats of the Senators of the first Class shall be vacated at the Expiration of the second Year, of the second Class at the Expiration of the fourth Year, and of the third Class at the Expiration of the sixth Year, so that one third may be chosen every second Year; and if Vacancies happen by Resignation, or otherwise, during the Recess of the Legislature of any State, the Executive thereof may make temporary Appointments until the next Meeting of the Legislature, which shall then fill such Vacancies.

No Person shall be a Senator who shall not have attained to the Age of thirty Years, and been nine Years a Citizen of the United States, and who shall not, when elected, be an Inhabitant of that State for which he shall be chosen.

The Vice President of the United States shall be President of the Senate, but shall have no Vote, unless they be equally divided.

The Senate shall chuse their other Officers, and also a President pro tempore, in the Absence of the Vice President, or when he shall exercise the Office of President of the United States.

The Senate shall have the sole Power to try all Impeachments. When sitting for that Purpose, they shall be on Oath or Affirmation. When the President of the United States is tried, the Chief Justice shall preside: And no Person shall be convicted without the Concurrence of two thirds of the Members present.

Judgment in Cases of Impeachment shall not extend further than to removal from Office, and disqualification to hold and enjoy any Office of honor, Trust, or Profit under the United States: but the Party convicted shall nevertheless be liable and subject to Indictment, Trial, Judgment, and Punishment, according to Law.

Section 4. The Times, Places and Manner of holding Elections for Senators and Representatives, shall be prescribed in each State by the Legislature thereof; but the Congress may at any time by Law make or alter such Regulations, except as to the Places of chusing Senators.

The Congress shall assemble at least once in every Year, and such Meeting shall be on the first Monday in December, unless they shall by Law appoint a different Day.

Section 5. Each House shall be the Judge of the Elections, Returns, and Qualifications of its own Members, and a Majority of each shall constitute a Quorum to do Business; but a smaller Number may adjourn from day to day, and may be authorized to compel the Attendance of absent Members, in such Manner, and under such Penalties as each House may provide.

Each House may determine the Rules of its Proceedings, punish its Members for disorderly Behavior, and, with the Concurrence of two thirds, expel a Member.

Each House shall keep a Journal of its Proceedings, and from time to time publish the same, excepting such Parts as may in their Judgment require Secrecy; and the Yeas and Nays of the Members of either House on any question shall, at the Desire of one fifth of those Present, be entered on the Journal.

Neither House, during the Session of Congress, shall, without the Consent of the other, adjourn for more than three days, nor to any other Place than that in which the two Houses shall be sitting.

Section 6. The Senators and Representatives shall receive a Compensation for their Services, to be ascertained by Law, and paid out of the Treasury of the United States. They shall in all Cases, except Treason, Felony and Breach of the Peace, be privileged from Arrest during their Attendance at the Session of their respective Houses, and in going to and returning from the same; and for any Speech or Debate in either House, they shall not be questioned in any other Place.

No Senator or Representative shall, during the Time for which he was elected, be appointed to any civil Office under the Authority of the United States, which shall have been created, or the Emoluments whereof shall have been increased during such time; and no Person holding any Office under the United States, shall be a Member of either House during his Continuance in Office.

Section 7. All Bills for raising Revenue shall originate in the House of Representatives; but the Senate may propose or concur with Amendments as on other Bills.

Every Bill which shall have passed the House of Representatives and the Senate, shall, before it become a Law, be presented to the President of the United States; If he approve he shall sign it, but if not he shall return it, with his Objections to the House in which it shall have originated, who shall enter the Objections at large on their Journal, and proceed to reconsider it. If after such Reconsideration two thirds of that House shall agree to pass the Bill, it shall be sent together with the Objections, to the other House, by which it shall likewise be reconsidered, and if approved by two thirds of that House, it shall become a Law. But in all such Cases the Votes of both Houses shall be determined by Yeas and Nays, and the Names of the Persons voting for and against the Bill shall be entered on the Journal of each House respectively. If any Bill shall not be returned by the President within ten Days (Sundays excepted) after it shall have been presented to him, the Same shall be a Law, in like Manner as if he had signed it, unless the Congress by their Adjournment prevent its Return in which Case it shall not be a Law.

Every Order, Resolution, or Vote, to which the Concurrence of the Senate and House of Representatives may be necessary (except on a question of Adjournment) shall be presented to the President of the United States; and before the Same shall take Effect, shall be approved by him, or being disapproved by him, shall be repassed by two thirds of the Senate and House of Representatives, according to the Rules and Limitations prescribed in the Case of a Bill.

Section 8. The Congress shall have Power To lay and collect Taxes, Duties, Imposts and Excises, to pay the Debts and provide for the common Defence and general Welfare of the United States; but all Duties, Imposts and Excises shall be uniform throughout the United States;

To borrow Money on the credit of the United States;

To regulate Commerce with foreign Nations, and among the several States, and with the Indian Tribes;

To establish an uniform Rule of Naturalization, and uniform Laws on the subject of Bankruptcies throughout the United States;

To coin Money, regulate the Value thereof, and of foreign Coin, and fix the Standard of Weights and Measures;

To provide for the Punishment of counterfeiting the Securities and current Coin of the United States;

To establish Post Offices and post Roads;

To promote the Progress of Science and useful Arts, by securing for limited Times to Authors and Inventors the exclusive Right to their respective Writings and Discoveries;

To constitute Tribunals inferior to the supreme Court;

To define and punish Piracies and Felonies committed on the high Seas, and Offenses against the Law of Nations;

To declare War, grant Letters of Marque and Reprisal, and make Rules concerning Captures on Land and Water;

To raise and support Armies, but no Appropriation of Money to that Use shall be for a longer Term than two Years;

To provide and maintain a Navy;

To make Rules for the Government and Regulation of the land and naval Forces;

To provide for calling forth the Militia to execute the Laws of the Union, suppress Insurrections and repel Invasions;

To provide for organizing, arming, and disciplining, the Militia, and for governing such Part of them as may be employed in the Service of the United States, reserving to the States respectively, the Appointment of the Officers, and the Authority of training the Militia according to the discipline prescribed by Congress;

To exercise exclusive Legislation in all Cases whatsoever, over such District (not exceeding ten Miles square) as may, by Cession of particular States, and the Acceptance of Congress, become the Seat of the Government of the United States, and to exercise like Authority over all Places purchased by the Consent of the Legislature of the State in which the Same shall be, for the Erection of Forts, Magazines, Arsenals, dock-Yards, and other needful Buildings;—And

To make all Laws which shall be necessary and proper for carrying into Execution the foregoing Powers, and all other Powers vested by this Constitution in the Government of the United States, or in any Department or Officer thereof.

Section 9. The Migration or Importation of such Persons as any of the States now existing shall think proper to admit, shall not be prohibited by the Congress prior to the Year one thousand eight hundred and eight, but a Tax or duty may be imposed on such Importation, not exceeding ten dollars for each Person.

The privilege of the Writ of Habeas Corpus shall not be suspended, unless when in Cases of Rebellion or Invasion the public Safety may require it.

No Bill of Attainder or ex post facto Law shall be passed.

No Capitation, or other direct, Tax shall be laid, unless in Proportion to the Census or Enumeration herein before directed to be taken.

No Tax or Duty shall be laid on Articles exported from any State.

No Preference shall be given by any Regulation of Commerce or Revenue to the Ports of one State over those of another: nor shall Vessels bound to, or from, one State be obliged to enter, clear, or pay Duties in another.

No Money shall be drawn from the Treasury, but in Consequence of Appropriations made by Law; and a regular Statement and Account of the Receipts and Expenditures of all public Money shall be published from time to time.

No Title of Nobility shall be granted by the United States: And no Person holding any Office of Profit or Trust under them, shall, without the Consent of the Congress, accept of any present, Emolument, Office, or Title, of any kind whatever, from any King, Prince, or foreign State.

Section 10. No State shall enter into any Treaty, Alliance, or Confederation; grant Letters of Marque and Reprisal; coin Money; emit Bills of Credit; make any Thing but gold and silver Coin a Tender in Payment of Debts; pass any Bill of Attainder, ex post facto Law, or Law impairing the Obligation of Contracts, or grant any Title of Nobility.

No State shall, without the Consent of the Congress, lay any Imposts or Duties on Imports or Exports, except what may be absolutely necessary for executing its inspection Laws: and the net Produce of all Duties and Imposts, laid by any State on Imports or Exports, shall be for the Use of the Treasury of the United States; and all such Laws shall be subject to the Revision and Controul of the Congress.

No State shall, without the Consent of Congress, lay any Duty of Tonnage, keep Troops, or Ships of War in time of Peace, enter into any Agreement or Compact with another State, or with a foreign Power, or engage in War, unless actually invaded, or in such imminent Danger as will not admit of delay.

Article II

Section 1. The executive Power shall be vested in a President of the United States of America. He shall hold his Office during the Term of four Years, and, together with the Vice President, chosen for the same Term, be elected, as follows:

Each State shall appoint, in such Manner as the Legislature thereof may direct, a Number of Electors, equal to the whole Number of Senators and Representatives to which the State may be entitled in the Congress; but no Senator or Representative, or Person holding an Office of Trust or Profit under the United States, shall be appointed an Elector.

The Electors shall meet in their respective States, and vote by Ballot for two Persons, of whom one at least shall not be an Inhabitant of the same State with themselves. And they shall make a List of all the Persons voted for, and of the Number of Votes for each; which List they shall sign and certify, and transmit sealed to the Seat of the Government of the United States, directed to the President of the Senate. The President of the Senate shall, in the Presence of the Senate and House of Representatives, open all the Certificates, and the Votes shall then be counted. The Person having the greatest Number of Votes shall be the President, if such Number be a Majority of the whole Number of Electors appointed; and if there be more than one who have such Majority, and have an equal Number of Votes, then the House of Representatives shall immediately chuse by Ballot one of them for President; and if no Person have a Majority, then from the five highest on the List the said House shall in like Manner chuse the President. But in chusing the President, the Votes shall be taken by States, the Representation from each State having one Vote; A quorum for this Purpose shall consist of a Member or Members from two thirds of the States, and a Majority of all the States shall be necessary to a Choice. In every Case, after the Choice of the President, the Person having the greater Number of Votes of the Electors shall be the Vice President. But if there should remain two or more who have equal Votes, the Senate shall chuse from them by Ballot the Vice President.

The Congress may determine the Time of chusing the Electors, and the Day on which they shall give their Votes; which Day shall be the same throughout the United States.

No person except a natural born Citizen, or a Citizen of the United States, at the time of the Adoption of this Constitution, shall be eligible to the Office of President; neither shall any Person be eligible to that Office who shall not have attained to the Age of thirty five Years, and been fourteen Years a Resident within the United States.

In Case of the Removal of the President from Office, or of his Death, Resignation or Inability to discharge the Powers and Duties of the said Office, the same shall devolve on the Vice President, and the Congress may by Law provide for the Case of Removal, Death, Resignation or Inability, both of the President and Vice President, declaring what Officer shall then act as President, and such Officer shall act accordingly, until the Disability be removed, or a President shall be elected.

The President shall, at stated Times, receive for his Services, a Compensation, which shall neither be increased nor diminished during the Period for which he shall have been elected, and he shall not receive within that Period any other Emolument from the United States, or any of them.

Before he enter on the Execution of his Office, he shall take the following Oath or Affirmation: "I do solemnly swear (or affirm) that I will faithfully execute the Office of President of the United States, and will to the best of my Ability, preserve, protect and defend the Constitution of the United States."

Section 2. The President shall be Commander in Chief of the Army and Navy of the United States, and of the Militia of the several States, when called into the actual Service of the United States; he may require the Opinion, in writing, of the principal Officer in each of the executive Departments, upon any Subject relating to the Duties of their respective Offices, and he shall have Power to grant Reprieves and Pardons for Offenses against the United States, except in Cases of Impeachment.

He shall have Power, by and with the Advice and Consent of the Senate to make Treaties, provided two thirds of the Senators present concur; and he shall nominate, and by and with the Advice and Consent of the Senate, shall appoint Ambassadors, other public Ministers and Consuls, Judges of the supreme Court, and all other Officers of the United States, whose Appointments are not herein otherwise provided for, and which shall be established by Law; but the Congress may by Law vest the Appointment of such inferior Officers, as they think proper, in the President alone, in the Courts of Law, or in the Heads of Departments.

The President shall have Power to fill up all Vacancies that may happen during the Recess of the Senate, by granting Commissions which shall expire at the End of their next Session.

Section 3. He shall from time to time give to the Congress Information of the State of the Union, and recommend to their Consideration such Measures as he shall judge necessary and expedient; he may, on extraordinary Occasions, convene both Houses, or either of them, and in Case of Disagreement between them, with Respect to the Time of Adjournment, he may adjourn them to such Time as he shall think proper; he shall receive Ambassadors and other public Ministers; he shall take Care that the Laws be faithfully executed, and shall Commission all the Officers of the United States.

Section 4. The President, Vice President and all civil Officers of the United States, shall be removed from Office on Impeachment for, and Conviction of, Treason, Bribery, or other high Crimes and Misdemeanors.

Article III

Section 1. The judicial Power of the United States, shall be vested in one supreme Court, and in such inferior Courts as the Congress may from time to time ordain and establish. The Judges, both of the supreme and inferior Courts, shall hold their Offices during good Behaviour, and shall, at stated Times, receive for their Services a Compensation, which shall not be diminished during their Continuance in Office.

Section 2. The judicial Power shall extend to all Cases, in Law and Equity, arising under this Constitution, the Laws of the United States, and Treaties made, or which shall be made, under their Authority;—to all Cases affecting Ambassadors, other public Ministers and Consuls;—to all Cases of admiralty and maritime Jurisdiction;—to Controversies to which the United States shall be a Party;—to Controversies between two or more States;—between a State and Citizens of another State;—between Citizens of different States;—between Citizens of the same State claiming Lands under Grants of different States, and between a State, or the Citizens thereof, and foreign States, Citizens or Subjects.

In all Cases affecting Ambassadors, other public Ministers and Consuls, and those in which a State shall be a Party, the supreme Court shall have original Jurisdiction. In all the other Cases before mentioned, the supreme Court shall have appellate Jurisdiction, both as to Law and Fact, with such Exceptions, and under such Regulations as the Congress shall make.

The Trial of all Crimes, except in Cases of Impeachment, shall be by Jury; and such Trial shall be held in the State where the said Crimes shall have been committed; but when not committed within any State, the Trial shall be at such Place or Places as the Congress may by Law have directed.

Section 3. Treason against the United States, shall consist only in levying War against them, or, in adhering to their Enemies, giving them Aid and Comfort. No Person shall be convicted of Treason unless on the Testimony of two Witnesses to the same overt Act, or on Confession in open Court.

The Congress shall have Power to declare the Punishment of Treason, but no Attainder of Treason shall work Corruption of Blood, or Forfeiture except during the Life of the Person attainted.

Article IV

Section 1. Full Faith and Credit shall be given in each State to the public Acts, Records, and judicial Proceedings of every other State. And the Congress may by general Laws prescribe the Manner in which such Acts, Records and Proceedings shall be proved, and the Effect thereof.

Section 2. The Citizens of each State shall be entitled to all Privileges and Immunities of Citizens in the several States.

A Person charged in any State with Treason, Felony, or other Crime, who shall flee from Justice, and be found in another State, shall on Demand of the executive Authority of the State from which he fled, be delivered up, to be removed to the State having Jurisdiction of the Crime.

No Person held to Service or Labour in one State, under the Laws thereof, escaping into another, shall, in Consequence of any Law or Regulation therein, be discharged from such Service or Labour, but shall be delivered up on Claim of the Party to whom such Service or Labour may be due.

Section 3. New States may be admitted by the Congress into this Union; but no new State shall be formed or erected within the Jurisdiction of any other State; nor any State be formed by the Junction of two or more States, or Parts of States, without the Consent of the Legislatures of the States concerned as well as of the Congress.

The Congress shall have Power to dispose of and make all needful Rules and Regulations respecting the Territory or other Property belonging to the United States; and nothing in this Constitution shall be so construed as to Prejudice any Claims of the United States, or of any particular State.

Section 4. The United States shall guarantee to every State in this Union a Republican Form of Government, and shall protect each of them against Invasion; and on Application of the Legislature, or of the Executive (when the Legislature cannot be convened) against domestic Violence.

Article V

The Congress, whenever two thirds of both Houses shall deem it necessary, shall propose Amendments to this Constitution, or, on the Application of the Legislatures of two thirds of the several States, shall call a Convention for proposing Amendments, which, in either Case, shall be valid to all Intents and Purposes, as part of this Constitution, when ratified by the Legislatures of three fourths of the several States, or by Conventions in three fourths thereof, as the one or the other Mode of Ratification may be proposed by the Congress; Provided that no Amendment which may be made prior to the Year One thousand eight hundred and eight shall in any Manner affect the first and fourth Clauses in the Ninth Section of the first Article; and that no State, without its Consent, shall be deprived of its equal Suffrage in the Senate.

Article VI

All Debts contracted and Engagements entered into, before the Adoption of this Constitution shall be as valid against the United States under this Constitution, as under the Confederation.

This Constitution, and the Laws of the United States which shall be made in Pursuance thereof; and all Treaties made, or which shall be made, under the Authority of the United States, shall be the supreme Law of the Land; and the Judges in every State shall be bound thereby, any Thing in the Constitution or Laws of any State to the Contrary notwithstanding.

The Senators and Representatives before mentioned, and the Members of the several State Legislatures, and all executive and judicial Officers, both of the United States and of the several States, shall be bound by Oath or Affirmation, to support this Constitution; but no religious Test shall ever be required as a Qualification to any Office or public Trust under the United States.

Article VII

The Ratification of the Conventions of nine States shall be sufficient for the Establishment of this Constitution between the States so ratifying the Same.

Amendment I [1791]

Congress shall make no law respecting an establishment of religion, or prohibiting the free exercise thereof; or abridging the freedom of speech, or of the press; or the right of the people peaceably to assembly, and to petition the Government for a redress of grievances.

Amendment II [1791]

A well regulated Militia, being necessary to the security of a free State, the right of the people to keep and bear Arms, shall not be infringed.

Amendment III [1791]

No Soldier shall, in time of peace be quartered in any house, without the consent of the Owner, nor in time of war, but in a manner to be prescribed by law.

Amendment IV [1791]

The right of the people to be secure in their persons, houses, papers, and effects, against unreasonable searches and seizures, shall not be violated, and no Warrants shall issue, but upon probable cause, supported by Oath or affirmation, and particularly describing the place to be searched, and the persons or things to be seized.

Amendment V [1791]

No person shall be held to answer for a capital, or otherwise infamous crime, unless on a presentment or indictment of a Grand Jury, except in cases arising in the land or naval forces, or in the Militia, when in actual service in time of War or public danger; nor shall any person be subject for the same offence to be twice put in jeopardy of life or limb; nor shall be compelled in any criminal case to be a witness against himself, nor be deprived of life, liberty, or property, without due process of law; nor shall private property be taken for public use, without just compensation.

Amendment VI [1791]

In all criminal prosecutions, the accused shall enjoy the right to a speedy and public trial, by an impartial jury of the State and district wherein the crime shall have been committed, which district shall have been previously ascertained by law, and to be informed of the nature and cause of the accusation; to be confronted with the witnesses against him; to have compulsory process for obtaining witnesses in his favor, and to have the Assistance of Counsel for his defence.

Amendment VII [1791]

In Suits at common law, where the value in controversy shall exceed twenty dollars, the right of trial by jury shall be preserved, and no fact tried by jury, shall be otherwise re-examined in any Court of the United States, than according to the rules of the common law.

Amendment VIII [1791]

Excessive bail shall not be required, nor excessive fines imposed, nor cruel and unusual punishments inflicted.

Amendment IX [1791]

The enumeration in the Constitution, of certain rights, shall not be construed to deny or disparage others retained by the people.

Amendment X [1791]

The powers not delegated to the United States by the Constitution, nor prohibited by it to the States, are reserved to the States respectively, or to the people.

Amendment XI [1798]

The Judicial power of the United States shall not be construed to extend to any suit in law or equity, commenced or prosecuted against one of the United States by Citizens of another State, or by Citizens or Subjects of any Foreign State.

Amendment XII [1804]

The Electors shall meet in their respective states, and vote by ballot for President and Vice-President, one of whom, at least, shall not be an inhabitant of the same state with themselves; they shall name in their ballots the person voted for as President, and in distinct ballots the person voted for as Vice-President, and they shall make distinct lists of all persons voted for as President, and of all persons voted for as Vice-President, and of the number of votes for each, which lists they shall sign and certify, and transmit sealed to the seat of the government of the United States, directed to the President of the Senate;—The President of the Senate shall, in the presence of the Senate and House of Representatives, open all the certificates and the votes shall then be counted;—The person having the greatest number of votes for President, shall be the President, if such number be a majority of the whole number of Electors appointed; and if no person have such majority, then from the persons having the highest numbers not exceeding three on the list of those voted for as President, the House of Representatives shall choose immediately, by ballot, the President. But in choosing the President, the votes shall be taken by states, the representation from each state having one vote; a quorum for this purpose shall consist of a member or members from two-thirds of the states, and a majority of all states shall be necessary to a choice. And if the House of Representatives shall not choose a President whenever the right of choice shall devolve upon them, before the fourth day of March next following, then the Vice-President shall act as President, as in the case of the death or other constitutional disability of the President.—The person having the greatest number of votes as Vice-President, shall be the Vice-President, if such number be a majority of the whole number of Electors appointed, and if no person have a majority, then from the two highest numbers on the list, the Senate shall choose the Vice-President; a quorum for the purpose shall consist of two-thirds of the whole number of Senators, and a majority of the whole number shall be necessary to a choice. But no person constitutionally ineligible to the office of President shall be eligible to that of Vice-President of the United States.

Amendment XIII [1865]

Section 1. Neither slavery nor involuntary servitude, except as a punishment for crime whereof the party shall have been duly convicted, shall exist within the United States, or any place subject to their jurisdiction.

Section 2. Congress shall have power to enforce this article by appropriate legislation.

Amendment XIV [1868]

Section 1. All persons born or naturalized in the United States, and subject to the jurisdiction thereof, are citizens of the United States and of the State wherein they reside. No State shall make or enforce any law which shall abridge the privileges or immunities of citizens of the United States; nor shall any State deprive any person of life, liberty, or property, without due process of law; nor deny to any person within its jurisdiction the equal protection of the laws.

Section 2. Representatives shall be apportioned among the several States according to their respective numbers, counting the whole number of persons in each State, excluding Indians not taxed. But when the right to vote at any election for the choice of electors for President and Vice President of the United States, Representatives in Congress, the Executive and Judicial officers of a State, or the members of the Legislature thereof, is denied to any of the male inhabitants of such State, being twenty-one years of age, and citizens of the United States, or in any way abridged, except for participation in rebellion, or other crime, the basis of representation therein shall be reduced in the proportion which the number of such male citizens shall bear to the whole number of male citizens twenty-one years of age in such State.

Section 3. No person shall be a Senator or Representative in Congress, or elector of President and Vice President, or hold any office, civil or military, under the United States, or under any State, who having previously taken an oath, as a member of Congress, or as an officer of the United States, or as a member of any State legislature, or as an executive or judicial officer of any State, to support the Constitution of the United States, shall have engaged in insurrection or rebellion against the same, or given aid or comfort to the enemies thereof. But Congress may by a vote of two-thirds of each House, remove such disability.

Section 4. The validity of the public debt of the United States, authorized by law, including debts incurred for payment of pensions and bounties for services in suppressing insurrection or rebellion, shall not be questioned. But neither the United States nor any State shall assume or pay any debt or obligation incurred in aid of insurrection or rebellion against the United States, or any claim for the loss or emancipation of any slave; but all such debts, obligations and claims shall be held illegal and void.

Section 5. The Congress shall have power to enforce, by appropriate legislation, the provisions of this article.

Amendment XV [1870]

Section 1. The right of citizens of the United States to vote shall not be denied or abridged by the United States or by any State on account of race, color, or previous condition of servitude.

Section 2. The Congress shall have power to enforce this article by appropriate legislation.

Amendment XVI [1913]

The Congress shall have power to lay and collect taxes on incomes, from whatever source derived, without apportionment among the several States, and without regard to any census or enumeration.

Amendment XVII [1913]

Section 1. The Senate of the United States shall be composed of two Senators from each State, elected by the people thereof, for six years; and each Senator shall have one vote. The electors in each State shall have the qualifications requisite for electors of the most numerous branch of the State legislatures.

Section 2. When vacancies happen in the representation of any State in the Senate, the executive authority of such State shall issue writs of election to fill such vacancies: *Provided,* That the legislature of any State may empower the executive thereof to make temporary appointments until the people fill the vacancies by election as the legislature may direct.

Section 3. This amendment shall not be so construed as to affect the election or term of any Senator chosen before it becomes valid as part of the Constitution.

Amendment XVIII [1919]

Section 1. After one year from the ratification of this article the manufacture, sale, or transportation of intoxicating liquors within, the importation thereof into, or the exportation thereof from the United States and all territory subject to the jurisdiction thereof for beverage purposes is hereby prohibited.

Section 2. The Congress and the several States shall have concurrent power to enforce this article by appropriate legislation.

Section 3. This article shall be inoperative unless it shall have been ratified as an amendment to the Constitution by the legislatures of the several States, as provided in the Constitution, within seven years from the date of the submission hereof to the States by the Congress.

Amendment XIX [1920]

Section 1. The right of citizens of the United States to vote shall not be denied or abridged by the United States or by any State on account of sex.

Section 2. Congress shall have power to enforce this article by appropriate legislation.

Amendment XX [1933]

Section 1. The terms of the President and Vice President shall end at noon on the 20th day of January, and the terms of Senators and Representatives at noon on the 3d day of January, of the years in which such terms would have ended if this article had not been ratified; and the terms of their successors shall then begin.

Section 2. The Congress shall assemble at least once in every year, and such meeting shall begin at noon on the 3d day of January, unless they shall by law appoint a different day.

Section 3. If, at the time fixed for the beginning of the term of the President, the President elect shall have died, the Vice President elect shall become President. If the President shall not have been chosen before the time fixed for the beginning of his term, or if the President elect shall have failed to qualify, then the Vice President elect shall act as President until a President shall have qualified; and the Congress may by law provide for the case wherein neither a President elect nor a Vice President elect shall have qualified, declaring who shall then act as President, or the manner in which one who is to act shall be selected, and such person shall act accordingly until a President or Vice President shall have qualified.

Section 4. The Congress may by law provide for the case of the death of any of the persons from whom the House of Representatives may choose a President whenever the right of choice shall have devolved upon them, and for the case of the death of any of the persons from whom the Senate may choose a Vice President whenever the right of choice shall have devolved upon them.

Section 5. Sections 1 and 2 shall take effect on the 15th day of October following the ratification of this article.

Section 6. This article shall be inoperative unless it shall have been ratified as an amendment to the Constitution by the legislatures of three-fourths of the several States within seven years from the date of its submission.

Amendment XXI [1933]

Section 1. The eighteenth article of amendment to the Constitution of the United States is hereby repealed.

Section 2. The transportation or importation into any State, Territory, or possession of the United States for delivery or use therein of intoxicating liquors, in violation of the laws thereof, is hereby prohibited.

Section 3. This article shall be inoperative unless it shall have been ratified as an amendment to the Constitution by conventions in the several States, as provided in the Constitution, within seven years from the date of the submission hereof to the States by the Congress.

Amendment XXII [1951]

Section 1. No person shall be elected to the office of the President more than twice, and no person who has held the office of President, or acted as President, for more than two years of a term to which some other person was elected President shall be elected to the office of President more than once. But this Article shall not apply to any person holding the office of President when this Article was proposed by the Congress, and shall not prevent any person who may be holding the office of President, or acting as President, during the term within which this Article becomes operative from holding the office of President or acting as President during the remainder of such term.

Section 2. This article shall be inoperative unless it shall have been ratified as an amendment to the Constitution by the legislatures of three-fourths of the several States within seven years from the date of its submission to the States by the Congress.

Amendment XXIII [1961]

Section 1. The District constituting the seat of Government of the United States shall appoint in such manner as the Congress may direct:

A number of electors of President and Vice President equal to the whole number of Senators and Representatives in Congress to which the District would be entitled if it were a State, but in no event more than the least populous state; they shall be in addition to those appointed by the states, but they shall be considered, for the purposes of the election of President and Vice President, to be electors appointed by a state; and they shall meet in the District and perform such duties as provided by the twelfth article of amendment.

Section 2. The Congress shall have power to enforce this article by appropriate legislation.

Amendment XXIV [1964]

Section 1. The right of citizens of the United States to vote in any primary or other election for President or Vice President, for electors for President or Vice President, or for Senator or Representative in Congress, shall not be denied or abridged by the United States, or any State by reason of failure to pay any poll tax or other tax.

Section 2. The Congress shall have power to enforce this article by appropriate legislation.

Amendment XXV [1967]

Section 1. In case of the removal of the President from office or of his death or resignation, the Vice President shall become President.

Section 2. Whenever there is a vacancy in the office of the Vice President, the President shall nominate a Vice President who shall take office upon confirmation by a majority vote of both Houses of Congress.

Section 3. Whenever the President transmits to the President pro tempore of the Senate and the Speaker of the House of Representatives his written declaration that he is unable to discharge the powers and duties of his office, and until he transmits to them a written declaration to the contrary, such powers and duties shall be discharged by the Vice President as Acting President.

Section 4. Whenever the Vice President and a majority of either the principal officers of the executive departments or of such other body as Congress may by law provide, transmit to the President pro tempore of the Senate and the Speaker of the House of Representatives their written declaration that the President is unable to discharge the powers and duties of his office, the Vice President shall immediately assume the powers and duties of the office as Acting President.

Thereafter, when the President transmits to the President pro tempore of the Senate and the Speaker of the House of Representatives his written declaration that no inability exists, he shall resume the powers and duties of his office unless the Vice President and a majority of either the principal officers of the executive department or of such other body as Congress may by law provide, transmit within four days to the President pro tempore of the Senate and the Speaker of the House of Representatives their written declaration that the President is unable to discharge the powers and duties of his office. Thereupon Congress shall decide the issue, assembling within forty-eight hours for that purpose if not in session. If the Congress, within twenty-one days after receipt of the latter written declaration, or, if Congress is not in session, within twenty-one days after Congress is required to assemble, determines by two-thirds vote of both Houses that the President is unable to discharge the powers and duties of his office, the Vice President shall continue to discharge the same as Acting President; otherwise, the President shall resume the powers and duties of his office.

Amendment XXVI [1971]

Section 1. The right of citizens of the United States, who are eighteen years of age or older, to vote shall not be denied or abridged by the United States or by any State on account of age.

Section 2. The Congress shall have power to enforce this article by appropriate legislation.

Amendment XXVII [1992]

No law, varying the compensation for the services of the Senators and Representatives, shall take effect, until an election of Representatives shall have intervened.

(Adopted in fifty-two jurisdictions—all fifty States, although Louisiana has adopted only Articles 1, 3, 4, 7, 8, and 9; the District of Columbia; and the Virgin Islands.)

The Code consists of the following articles:

Art.

1. General Provisions
2. Sales
2A. Leases
3. Negotiable Instruments
4. Bank Deposits and Collections
4A. Funds Transfers
5. Letters of Credit
6. Repealer of Article 6—Bulk Transfers and [Revised] Article 6—Bulk Sales
7. Warehouse Receipts, Bills of Lading and Other Documents of Title
8. Investment Securities
9. Secured Transactions
10. Effective Date and Repealer
11. Effective Date and Transition Provisions

Article 1

GENERAL PROVISIONS

Part 1 General Provisions

§ 1–101. Short Titles.

(a) This [Act] may be cited as Uniform Commercial Code.
(b) This article may be cited as Uniform Commercial Code-Uniform Provisions.

§ 1–102. Scope of Article.

This article applies to a transaction to the extent that it is governed by another article of [the Uniform Commercial Code].

§ 1–103. Construction of [Uniform Commercial Code] to Promote Its Purpose and Policies; Applicability of Supplemental Principles of Law.

(a) [The Uniform Commercial Code] must be liberally construed and applied to promote its underlying purposes and policies, which are:

(1) to simplify, clarify, and modernize the law governing commercial transactions;

(2) to permit the continued expansion of commercial practices through custom, usage, and agreement of the parties; and

(3) to make uniform the law among the various jurisdictions.

(b) Unless displaced by the particular provisions of [the Uniform Commercial Code], the principles of law and equity, including the law merchant and the law relative to capacity to contract, principal and agent, estoppel, fraud, misrepresentation, duress, coercion, mistake, bankruptcy, and other validating or invalidating cause, supplement its provisions.

§ 1–104. Construction Against Implicit Repeal.

This Act being a general act intended as a unified coverage of its subject matter, no part of it shall be deemed to be impliedly repealed by subsequent legislation if such construction can reasonably be avoided.

§ 1–105. Severability.

If any provision or clause of [the Uniform Commercial Code] or its application to any person or circumstance is held invalid, the invalidity does not affect other provisions or applications of [the Uniform Commercial Code] which can be given effect without the invalid provision or application, and to this end the provisions of [the Uniform Commercial Code] are severable.

§ 1–106. Use of Singular and Plural; Gender.

In [the Uniform Commercial Code], unless the statutory context otherwise requires:
(1) words in the singular number include the plural, and those in the plural include the singular; and
(2) words of any gender also refer to any other gender.

§ 1–107. Section Captions.

Section captions are part of [the Uniform Commercial Code].

§ 1–108. Relation to Electronic Signatures in Global and National Commerce Act.

This article modifies, limits, and supersedes the Federal Electronic Signatures in Global and National Commerce Act, 15 U.S.C. Sections 7001 *et seq.*, except that nothing in this article modifies, limits, or supersedes Section 7001(c) of that act or authorizes electronic delivery of any of the notices described in Section 7003(b) of that Act.

Part 2 General Definitions and Principles of Interpretation

§ 1–201. General Definitions.

Subject to additional definitions contained in the subsequent Articles of this Act which are applicable to specific Articles or Parts thereof, and unless the context otherwise requires, in this Act:

(1) "Action", in the sense of a judicial proceeding, includes recoupment, counterclaim, set-off, suit in equity, and any other proceedings in which rights are determined.

(2) "Aggrieved party" means a party entitled to resort to a remedy.

(3) "Agreement", as distinguished from "contract", means the bargain of the parties in fact, as found in their language or by implication from other circumstances, including course of performance, course of dealing, or usage of trade as provided in Section 1–303.

(4) "Bank" means a person engaged in the business of banking and includes a savings bank, savings and loan association, credit union, and trust company.

(5) "Bearer" means a person in control of a negotiable electronic document of title or a person in possession of a negotiable instrument, negotiable tangible document of title, or certificated security that is payable to bearer or indorsed in blank.

(6) "Bill of lading" means a document of title evidencing the receipt of goods for shipment issued by a person engaged in the business of directly or indirectly transporting or forwarding goods. The term does not include a warehouse receipt.

(7) "Branch" includes a separately incorporated foreign branch of a bank.

(8) "Burden of establishing" a fact means the burden of persuading the trier of fact that the existence of the fact is more probable than its nonexistence.

(9) "Buyer in ordinary course of business" means a person that buys goods in good faith, without knowledge that the sale violates the rights of another person in the goods, and in the ordinary course from a person, other than a pawnbroker, in the business of selling goods of that kind. A person buys goods in the ordinary course if the sale to the person comports with the usual or customary practices in the kind of business in which the seller is engaged or with the seller's own usual or customary practices. A person that sells oil, gas, or other minerals at the wellhead or minehead is a person in the business of selling goods of that kind. A buyer in ordinary course of business may buy for cash, by exchange of other property, or on secured or unsecured credit, and may acquire goods or documents of title under a pre-existing contract for sale. Only a buyer that takes possession of the goods or has a right to recover the goods from the seller under Article 2 may be a buyer in ordinary course of business. A person that acquires goods in a transfer in bulk or as security for or in total or partial satisfaction of a money debt is not a buyer in ordinary course of business.

(10) "Conspicuous", with reference to a term, means so written, displayed, or presented that a reasonable person against which it is to operate ought to have noticed it. Whether a term is "conspicuous" or not is a decision for the court. Conspicuous terms include the following:

(A) a heading in capitals equal to or greater in size than the surrounding text, or in contrasting type, font, or color to the surrounding text of the same or lesser size; and

(B) language in the body of a record or display in larger type than the surrounding text, or in contrasting type, font, or color to the surrounding text of the same size, or set off from surrounding text of the same size by symbols or other marks that call attention to the language.

(11) "Consumer" means an individual who enters into a transaction primarily for personal, family, or household purposes.

(12) "Contract", as distinguished from "agreement", means the total legal obligation that results from the parties' agreement as determined by [the Uniform Commercial Code] as supplemented by any other laws.

(13) "Creditor" includes a general creditor, a secured creditor, a lien creditor and any representative of creditors, including an assignee for the benefit of creditors, a trustee in bankruptcy, a receiver in equity and an executor or administrator of an insolvent debtor's or assignor's estate.

(14) "Defendant" includes a person in the position of defendant in a counterclaim, cross-action, or third-party claim.

(15) "Delivery" with respect to an electronic document of title means voluntary transfer of control and with respect to an instrument, a tangible document of title, or chattel paper means voluntary transfer of possession.

(16) "Document of title" means a record (i) that in regular course of business or financing is treated as adequately evidencing that the person in possession or control of the record is entitled to receive, control, hold, and dispose of the record and the goods the record covers and (ii) that purports to be issued by or addressed to a bailee and to cover goods in the bailee's possession which are either identified or are fungible portions of an identified mass. The term includes a bill of lading, transport document, dock warrant, dock receipt, warehouse receipt, and

order for delivery of goods. An electronic document of title means a document of title evidenced by a record consisting of information stored in an electronic medium. A tangible document of title means a document of title evidenced by a record consisting of information that is inscribed on a tangible medium.

(17) "Fault" means a default, breach, or wrongful act or omission.

(18) "Fungible goods" means:

(A) goods of which any unit, by nature or usage of trade, is the equivalent of any other like unit; or

(B) goods that by agreement are treated as equivalent.

(19) "Genuine" means free of forgery or counterfeiting.

(20) "Good faith," except as otherwise provided in Article 5, means honesty in fact and the observance of reasonable commercial standards of fair dealing.

(21) "Holder" means:

(A) the person in possession of a negotiable instrument that is payable either to bearer or to an identified person that is the person in possession;

(B) the person in possession of a negotiable tangible document of title if the goods are deliverable either to bearer or to the order of the person in possession; or

(C) the person in control of a negotiable electronic document of title.

(22) "Insolvency proceeding" includes an assignment for the benefit of creditors or other proceeding intended to liquidate or rehabilitate the estate of the person involved.

(23) "Insolvent" means:

(A) having generally ceased to pay debts in the ordinary course of business other than as a result of bona fide dispute;

(B) being unable to pay debts as they become due; or

(C) being insolvent within the meaning of federal bankruptcy law.

(24) "Money" means a medium of exchange currently authorized or adopted by a domestic or foreign government. The term includes a monetary unit of account established by an intergovernmental organization or by agreement between two or more countries.

(25) "Organization" means a person other than an individual.

(26) "Party", as distinguished from "third party", means a person that has engaged in a transaction or made an agreement subject to [the Uniform Commercial Code].

(27) "Person" means an individual, corporation, business trust, estate, trust, partnership, limited liability company, association, joint venture, government, governmental subdivision, agency, or instrumentality, public corporation, or any other legal or commercial entity.

(28) "Present value" means the amount as of a date certain of one or more sums payable in the future, discounted to the date certain by use of either an interest rate specified by the parties if that rate is not manifestly unreasonable at the time the transaction is entered into or, if an interest rate is not so specified, a commercially reasonable rate that takes into account the facts and circumstances at the time the transaction is entered into.

(29) "Purchase" means taking by sale, lease, discount, negotiation, mortgage, pledge, lien, security interest, issue or reissue, gift, or any other voluntary transaction creating an interest in property.

(30) "Purchaser" means a person that takes by purchase.

(31) "Record" means information that is inscribed on a tangible medium or that is stored in an electronic or other medium and is retrievable in perceivable form.

(32) "Remedy" means any remedial right to which an aggrieved party is entitled with or without resort to a tribunal.

(33) "Representative" means a person empowered to act for another, including an agent, an officer of a corporation or association, and a trustee, executor, or administrator of an estate.

(34) "Right" includes remedy.

(35) "Security interest" means an interest in personal property or fixtures which secures payment or performance of an obligation. "Security interest" includes any interest of a consignor and a buyer of accounts, chattel paper, a payment intangible, or a promissory note in a transaction that is subject to Article 9. "Security interest" does not include the special property interest of a buyer of goods on identification of those goods to a contract for sale under Section 2–401, but a buyer may also acquire a "security interest" by complying with Article 9. Except as otherwise provided in Section 2–505, the right of a seller or lessor of goods under Article 2 or 2A to retain or acquire possession of the goods is not a "security interest", but a seller or lessor may also acquire a "security interest" by complying with Article 9. The retention or reservation of title by a seller of goods notwithstanding shipment or delivery to the buyer under Section 2–401 is limited in effect to a reservation of a "security interest." Whether a transaction in the form of a lease creates a "security interest" is determined pursuant to Section 1–203.

(36) "Send" in connection with a writing, record, or notice means:

(A) to deposit in the mail or deliver for transmission by any other usual means of communication with postage or cost of transmission provided for and properly addressed and, in the case of an instrument, to an address specified thereon or otherwise agreed, or if there be none to any address reasonable under the circumstances; or

(B) in any other way to cause to be received any record or notice within the time it would have arrived if properly sent.

(37) "Signed" includes using any symbol executed or adopted with present intention to adopt or accept a writing.

(38) "State" means a State of the United States, the District of Columbia, Puerto Rico, the United States Virgin Islands,

or any territory or insular possession subject to the jurisdiction of the United States.

(39) "Surety" includes a guarantor or other secondary obligor.

(40) "Term" means a portion of an agreement that relates to a particular matter.

(41) "Unauthorized signature" means a signature made without actual, implied, or apparent authority. The term includes a forgery.

(42) "Warehouse receipt" means a document of title issued by a person engaged in the business of storing goods for hire.

(43) "Writing" includes printing, typewriting, or any other intentional reduction to tangible form. "Written" has a corresponding meaning.

As amended in 2003.

§ 1–202. Notice; Knowledge.

(a) Subject to subsection (f), a person has "notice" of a fact if the person:

    (1) has actual knowledge of it;

    (2) has received a notice or notification of it; or

    (3) from all the facts and circumstances known to the person at the time in question, has reason to know that it exists.

(b) "Knowledge" means actual knowledge. "Knows" has a corresponding meaning.

(c) "Discover", "learn", or words of similar import refer to knowledge rather than to reason to know.

(d) A person "notifies" or "gives" a notice or notification to another person by taking such steps as may be reasonably required to inform the other person in ordinary course, whether or not the other person actually comes to know of it.

(e) Subject to subsection (f), a person "receives" a notice or notification when:

    (1) it comes to that person's attention; or

    (2) it is duly delivered in a form reasonable under the circumstances at the place of business through which the contract was made or at another location held out by that person as the place for receipt of such communications.

(f) Notice, knowledge, or a notice or notification received by an organization is effective for a particular transaction from the time it is brought to the attention of the individual conducting that transaction and, in any event, from the time it would have been brought to the individual's attention if the organization had exercised due diligence. An organization exercises due diligence if it maintains reasonable routines for communicating significant information to the person conducting the transaction and there is reasonable compliance with the routines. Due diligence does not require an individual acting for the organization to communicate information unless the communication is part of the individual's regular duties or the individual has reason to know of the transaction and that the transaction would be materially affected by the information.

§ 1–203. Lease Distinguished from Security Interest.

(a) Whether a transaction in the form of a lease creates a lease or security interest is determined by the facts of each case.

(b) A transaction in the form of a lease creates a security interest if the consideration that the lessee is to pay the lessor for the right to possession and use of the goods is an obligation for the term of the lease and is not subject to termination by the lessee, and:

    (1) the original term of the lease is equal to or greater than the remaining economic life of the goods;

    (2) the lessee is bound to renew the lease for the remaining economic life of the goods or is bound to become the owner of the goods;

    (3) the lessee has an option to renew the lease for the remaining economic life of the goods for no additional consideration or for nominal additional consideration upon compliance with the lease agreement; or

    (4) the lessee has an option to become the owner of the goods for no additional consideration or for nominal additional consideration upon compliance with the lease agreement.

(c) A transaction in the form of a lease does not create a security interest merely because:

    (1) the present value of the consideration the lessee is obligated to pay the lessor for the right to possession and use of the goods is substantially equal to or is greater than the fair market value of the goods at the time the lease is entered into;

    (2) the lessee assumes risk of loss of the goods;

    (3) the lessee agrees to pay, with respect to the goods, taxes, insurance, filing, recording, or registration fees, or service or maintenance costs;

    (4) the lessee has an option to renew the lease or to become the owner of the goods;

    (5) the lessee has an option to renew the lease for a fixed rent that is equal to or greater than the reasonably predictable fair market rent for the use of the goods for the term of the renewal at the time the option is to be performed; or

    (6) the lessee has an option to become the owner of the goods for a fixed price that is equal to or greater than the reasonably predictable fair market value of the goods at the time the option is to be performed.

(d) Additional consideration is nominal if it is less than the lessee's reasonably predictable cost of performing under the lease agreement if the option is not exercised. Additional consideration is not nominal if:

    (1) when the option to renew the lease is granted to the lessee, the rent is stated to be the fair market rent for the use of the goods for the term of the renewal determined at the time the option is to be performed; or

(2) when the option to become the owner of the goods is granted to the lessee, the price is stated to be the fair market value of the goods determined at the time the option is to be performed.

(e) The "remaining economic life of the goods" and "reasonably predictable" fair market rent, fair market value, or cost of performing under the lease agreement must be determined with reference to the facts and circumstances at the time the transaction is entered into.

§ 1–204. Value.

Except as otherwise provided in Articles 3, 4, [and] 5, [and 6], a person gives value for rights if the person acquires them:

(1) in return for a binding commitment to extend credit or for the extension of immediately available credit, whether or not drawn upon and whether or not a charge-back is provided for in the event of difficulties in collection;

(2) as security for, or in total or partial satisfaction of, a preexisting claim;

(3) by accepting delivery under a preexisting contract for purchase; or

(4) in return for any consideration sufficient to support a simple contract.

§ 1–205. Reasonable Time; Seasonableness.

(a) Whether a time for taking an action required by [the Uniform Commercial Code] is reasonable depends on the nature, purpose, and circumstances of the action.

(b) An action is taken seasonably if it is taken at or within the time agreed or, if no time is agreed, at or within a reasonable time.

§ 1–206. Presumptions.

Whenever [the Uniform Commercial Code] creates a "presumption" with respect to a fact, or provides that a fact is "presumed," the trier of fact must find the existence of the fact unless and until evidence is introduced that supports a finding of its nonexistence.

Part 3 Territorial Applicability and General Rules

§ 1–301. Territorial Applicability; Parties' Power to Choose Applicable Law.

(a) In this section:

(1) "Domestic transaction" means a transaction other than an international transaction.

(2) "International transaction" means a transaction that bears a reasonable relation to a country other than the United States.

(b) This section applies to a transaction to the extent that it is governed by another article of the [Uniform Commercial Code].

(c) Except as otherwise provided in this section:

(1) an agreement by parties to a domestic transaction that any or all of their rights and obligations are to be determined by the law of this State or of another State is effective, whether or not the transaction bears a relation to the State designated; and

(2) an agreement by parties to an international transaction that any or all of their rights and obligations are to be determined by the law of this State or of another State or country is effective, whether or not the transaction bears a relation to the State or country designated.

(d) In the absence of an agreement effective under subsection (c), and except as provided in subsections (e) and (g), the rights and obligations of the parties are determined by the law that would be selected by application of this State's conflict of laws principles.

(e) If one of the parties to a transaction is a consumer, the following rules apply:

(1) An agreement referred to in subsection (c) is not effective unless the transaction bears a reasonable relation to the State or country designated.

(2) Application of the law of the State or country determined pursuant to subsection (c) or (d) may not deprive the consumer of the protection of any rule of law governing a matter within the scope of this section, which both is protective of consumers and may not be varied by agreement: (A) of the State or country in which the consumer principally resides, unless subparagraph (B) applies; or (B) if the transaction is a sale of goods, of the State or country in which the consumer both makes the contract and take delivery of those goods, if such State or country is not the State or country in which the consumer principally resides.

(f) An agreement otherwise effective under subsection (c) is not effective to the extent that application of the law of the State or country designated would be contrary to a fundamental policy of the State or country whose law would govern in the absence of agreement under subsection (d).

(g) To the extent that [the Uniform Commercial Code] governs a transaction, if one of the following provisions of [the Uniform Commercial Code] specifies the applicable law, that provision governs and a contrary agreement is effective only to the extent permitted by the law so specified: (1) Section 2–402; (2) Sections 2A–105 and 2A–106; (3) Section 4–102; (4) Section 4A–507; (5) Section 5–116; [(6) Section 6–103;] (7) Section 8–110; (8) Sections 9–301 through 9–307.

§ 1–302. Variation by Agreement.

(a) Except as otherwise provided in subsection (b) or elsewhere in [the Uniform Commercial Code], the effect of provisions of [the Uniform Commercial Code] may be varied by agreement.

(b) The obligations of good faith, diligence, reasonableness, and care prescribed by [the Uniform Commercial Code] may not be disclaimed by agreement. The parties, by agreement, may determine the standards by which the performance of those obligations is to be measured if those standards are not manifestly unreasonable. Whenever [the Uniform Commercial Code] requires an action to be taken within a reasonable time, a time that is not manifestly unreasonable may be fixed by agreement.

(c) The presence in certain provisions of [the Uniform Commercial Code] of the phrase "unless otherwise agreed", or words of similar import, does not imply that the effect of other provisions may not be varied by agreement under this section.

§ 1–303. Course of Performance, Course of Dealing, and Usage of Trade.

(a) A "course of performance" is a sequence of conduct between the parties to a particular transaction that exists if:

(1) the agreement of the parties with respect to the transaction involves repeated occasions for performance by a party; and

(2) the other party, with knowledge of the nature of the performance and opportunity for objection to it, accepts the performance or acquiesces in it without objection.

(b) A "course of dealing" is a sequence of conduct concerning previous transactions between the parties to a particular transaction that is fairly to be regarded as establishing a common basis of understanding for interpreting their expressions and other conduct.

(c) A "usage of trade" is any practice or method of dealing having such regularity of observance in a place, vocation, or trade as to justify an expectation that it will be observed with respect to the transaction in question. The existence and scope of such a usage must be proved as facts. If it is established that such a usage is embodied in a trade code or similar record, the interpretation of the record is a question of law.

(d) A course of performance or course of dealing between the parties or usage of trade in the vocation or trade in which they are engaged or of which they are or should be aware is relevant in ascertaining the meaning of the parties' agreement, may give particular meaning to specific terms of the agreement, and may supplement or qualify the terms of the agreement. A usage of trade applicable in the place in which part of the performance under the agreement is to occur may be so utilized as to that part of the performance.

(e) Except as otherwise provided in subsection (f), the express terms of an agreement and any applicable course of performance, course of dealing, or usage of trade must be construed whenever reasonable as consistent with each other. If such a construction is unreasonable:

(1) express terms prevail over course of performance, course of dealing, and usage of trade;

(2) course of performance prevails over course of dealing and usage of trade; and

(3) course of dealing prevails over usage of trade.

(f) Subject to Section 2–209 and Section 2A–208, a course of performance is relevant to show a waiver or modification of any term inconsistent with the course of performance.

(g) Evidence of a relevant usage of trade offered by one party is not admissible unless that party has given the other party notice that the court finds sufficient to prevent unfair surprise to the other party.

§ 1–304. Obligation of Good Faith.

Every contract or duty within [the Uniform Commercial Code] imposes an obligation of good faith in its performance and enforcement.

§ 1–305. Remedies to be Liberally Administered.

(a) The remedies provided by [the Uniform Commercial Code] must be liberally administered to the end that the aggrieved party may be put in as good a position as if the other party had fully performed but neither consequential or special damages nor penal damages may be had except as specifically provided in [the Uniform Commercial Code] or by other rule of law.

(b) Any right or obligation declared by [the Uniform Commercial Code] is enforceable by action unless the provision declaring it specifies a different and limited effect.

§ 1–306. Waiver or Renunciation of Claim or Right After Breach.

A claim or right arising out of an alleged breach may be discharged in whole or in part without consideration by agreement of the aggrieved party in an authenticated record.

§ 1–307. *Prima Facie* Evidence by Third-Party Documents.

A document in due form purporting to be a bill of lading, policy or certificate of insurance, official weigher's or inspector's certificate, consular invoice, or any other document authorized or required by the contract to be issued by a third party is *prima facie* evidence of its own authenticity and genuineness and of the facts stated in the document by the third party.

§ 1–308. Performance or Acceptance Under Reservation of Rights.

(a) A party that with explicit reservation of rights performs or promises performance or assents to performance in a manner demanded or offered by the other party does not thereby prejudice the rights reserved. Such words as "without prejudice," "under protest," or the like are sufficient.

(b) Subsection (a) does not apply to an accord and satisfaction.

§ 1–309. Option to Accelerate at Will.

A term providing that one party or that party's successor in interest may accelerate payment or performance or require collateral or additional collateral "at will" or when the party "deems itself insecure," or words of similar import, means that the party has power to do so only if that party in good faith believes that the prospect of payment or performance is impaired. The burden of establishing lack of good faith is on the party against which the power has been exercised.

§ 1–310. Subordinated Obligations.

An obligation may be issued as subordinated to performance of another obligation of the person obligated, or a creditor may subordinate its right to performance of an obligation by agreement with either the person obligated or another creditor of the person obligated. Subordination does not create a security interest as against either the common debtor or a subordinated creditor.

Article 2
SALES

Part 1 Short Title, General Construction and Subject Matter

§ 2–101. Short Title.

This Article shall be known and may be cited as Uniform Commercial Code—Sales.

§ 2–102. Scope; Certain Security and Other Transactions Excluded From This Article.

Unless the context otherwise requires, this Article applies to transactions in goods; it does not apply to any transaction which although in the form of an unconditional contract to sell or present sale is intended to operate only as a security transaction nor does this Article impair or repeal any statute regulating sales to consumers, farmers or other specified classes of buyers.

§ 2–103. Definitions and Index of Definitions.

(1) In this Article unless the context otherwise requires

(a) "Buyer" means a person who buys or contracts to buy goods.

(b) "Good faith" in the case of a merchant means honesty in fact and the observance of reasonable commercial standards of fair dealing in the trade.

(c) "Receipt" of goods means taking physical possession of them.

(d) "Seller" means a person who sells or contracts to sell goods.

(2) Other definitions applying to this Article or to specified Parts thereof, and the sections in which they appear are:

"Acceptance". Section 2–606.
"Banker's credit". Section 2–325.
"Between merchants". Section 2–104.
"Cancellation". Section 2–106(4).
"Commercial unit". Section 2–105.
"Confirmed credit". Section 2–325.
"Conforming to contract". Section 2–106.
"Contract for sale". Section 2–106.
"Cover". Section 2–712.
"Entrusting". Section 2–403.
"Financing agency". Section 2–104.
"Future goods". Section 2–105.
"Goods". Section 2–105.

"Identification". Section 2–501.
"Installment contract". Section 2–612.
"Letter of Credit". Section 2–325.
"Lot". Section 2–105.
"Merchant". Section 2–104.
"Overseas". Section 2–323.
"Person in position of seller". Section 2–707.
"Present sale". Section 2–106.
"Sale". Section 2–106.
"Sale on approval". Section 2–326.
"Sale or return". Section 2–326.
"Termination". Section 2–106.

(3) The following definitions in other Articles apply to this Article:

"Check". Section 3–104.
"Consignee". Section 7–102.
"Consignor". Section 7–102.
"Consumer goods". Section 9–109.
"Dishonor". Section 3–507.
"Draft". Section 3–104.

(4) In addition Article 1 contains general definitions and principles of construction and interpretation applicable throughout this Article.

As amended in 1994 and 1999.

§ 2–104. Definitions: "Merchant"; "Between Merchants"; "Financing Agency".

(1) "Merchant" means a person who deals in goods of the kind or otherwise by his occupation holds himself out as having knowledge or skill peculiar to the practices or goods involved in the transaction or to whom such knowledge or skill may be attributed by his employment of an agent or broker or other intermediary who by his occupation holds himself out as having such knowledge or skill.

(2) "Financing agency" means a bank, finance company or other person who in the ordinary course of business makes advances against goods or documents of title or who by arrangement with either the seller or the buyer intervenes in ordinary course to make or collect payment due or claimed under the contract for sale, as by purchasing or paying the seller's draft or making advances against it or by merely taking it for collection whether or not documents of title accompany the draft. "Financing agency" includes also a bank or other person who similarly intervenes between persons who are in the position of seller and buyer in respect to the goods (Section 2–707).

(3) "Between merchants" means in any transaction with respect to which both parties are chargeable with the knowledge or skill of merchants.

§ 2–105. Definitions: Transferability; "Goods"; "Future" Goods; "Lot"; "Commercial Unit".

(1) "Goods" means all things (including specially manufactured goods) which are movable at the time of identification to the contract for sale other than the money in which the price is to be paid, investment securities (Article 8) and things in action. "Goods" also includes the unborn young of animals and growing crops and other identified

things attached to realty as described in the section on goods to be severed from realty (Section 2–107).

(2) Goods must be both existing and identified before any interest in them can pass. Goods which are not both existing and identified are "future" goods. A purported present sale of future goods or of any interest therein operates as a contract to sell.

(3) There may be a sale of a part interest in existing identified goods.

(4) An undivided share in an identified bulk of fungible goods is sufficiently identified to be sold although the quantity of the bulk is not determined. Any agreed proportion of such a bulk or any quantity thereof agreed upon by number, weight or other measure may to the extent of the seller's interest in the bulk be sold to the buyer who then becomes an owner in common.

(5) "Lot" means a parcel or a single article which is the subject matter of a separate sale or delivery, whether or not it is sufficient to perform the contract.

(6) "Commercial unit" means such a unit of goods as by commercial usage is a single whole for purposes of sale and division of which materially impairs its character or value on the market or in use. A commercial unit may be a single article (as a machine) or a set of articles (as a suite of furniture or an assortment of sizes) or a quantity (as a bale, gross, or carload) or any other unit treated in use or in the relevant market as a single whole.

§ 2–106. Definitions: "Contract"; "Agreement"; "Contract for Sale"; "Sale"; "Present Sale"; "Conforming" to Contract; "Termination"; "Cancellation".

(1) In this Article unless the context otherwise requires "contract" and "agreement" are limited to those relating to the present or future sale of goods. "Contract for sale" includes both a present sale of goods and a contract to sell goods at a future time. A "sale" consists in the passing of title from the seller to the buyer for a price (Section 2–401). A "present sale" means a sale which is accomplished by the making of the contract.

(2) Goods or conduct including any part of a performance are "conforming" or conform to the contract when they are in accordance with the obligations under the contract.

(3) "Termination" occurs when either party pursuant to a power created by agreement or law puts an end to the contract otherwise than for its breach. On "termination" all obligations which are still executory on both sides are discharged but any right based on prior breach or performance survives.

(4) "Cancellation" occurs when either party puts an end to the contract for breach by the other and its effect is the same as that of "termination" except that the cancelling party also retains any remedy for breach of the whole contract or any unperformed balance.

§ 2–107. Goods to Be Severed From Realty: Recording.

(1) A contract for the sale of minerals or the like (including oil and gas) or a structure or its materials to be removed from realty is a contract for the sale of goods within this Article if they are to be severed by the seller but until severance a purported present sale thereof which is not effective as a transfer of an interest in land is effective only as a contract to sell.

(2) A contract for the sale apart from the land of growing crops or other things attached to realty and capable of severance without material harm thereto but not described in subsection (1) or of timber to be cut is a contract for the sale of goods within this Article whether the subject matter is to be severed by the buyer or by the seller even though it forms part of the realty at the time of contracting, and the parties can by identification effect a present sale before severance.

(3) The provisions of this section are subject to any third party rights provided by the law relating to realty records, and the contract for sale may be executed and recorded as a document transferring an interest in land and shall then constitute notice to third parties of the buyer's rights under the contract for sale.

As amended in 1972.

Part 2 Form, Formation and Readjustment of Contract

§ 2–201. Formal Requirements; Statute of Frauds.

(1) Except as otherwise provided in this section a contract for the sale of goods for the price of $500 or more is not enforceable by way of action or defense unless there is some writing sufficient to indicate that a contract for sale has been made between the parties and signed by the party against whom enforcement is sought or by his authorized agent or broker. A writing is not insufficient because it omits or incorrectly states a term agreed upon but the contract is not enforceable under this paragraph beyond the quantity of goods shown in such writing.

(2) Between merchants if within a reasonable time a writing in confirmation of the contract and sufficient against the sender is received and the party receiving it has reason to know its contents, its satisfies the requirements of subsection (1) against such party unless written notice of objection to its contents is given within ten days after it is received.

(3) A contract which does not satisfy the requirements of subsection (1) but which is valid in other respects is enforceable

(a) if the goods are to be specially manufactured for the buyer and are not suitable for sale to others in the ordinary course of the seller's business and the seller, before notice of repudiation is received and under circumstances which reasonably indicate that the goods are for the buyer, has made either a substantial beginning of their manufacture or commitments for their procurement; or

(b) if the party against whom enforcement is sought admits in his pleading, testimony or otherwise in court that a contract for sale was made, but the contract is not enforceable under this provision beyond the quantity of goods admitted; or

(c) with respect to goods for which payment has been made and accepted or which have been received and accepted (Sec. 2–606).

§ 2–202. Final Written Expression: Parol or Extrinsic Evidence.

Terms with respect to which the confirmatory memoranda of the parties agree or which are otherwise set forth in a writing intended by the parties as a final expression of their agreement with respect to such terms as are included therein may not be contradicted by evidence of any prior agreement or of a contemporaneous oral agreement but may be explained or supplemented

(a) by course of dealing or usage of trade (Section 1–205) or by course of performance (Section 2–208); and

(b) by evidence of consistent additional terms unless the court finds the writing to have been intended also as a complete and exclusive statement of the terms of the agreement.

§ 2–203. Seals Inoperative.

The affixing of a seal to a writing evidencing a contract for sale or an offer to buy or sell goods does not constitute the writing a sealed instrument and the law with respect to sealed instruments does not apply to such a contract or offer.

§ 2–204. Formation in General.

(1) A contract for sale of goods may be made in any manner sufficient to show agreement, including conduct by both parties which recognizes the existence of such a contract.

(2) An agreement sufficient to constitute a contract for sale may be found even though the moment of its making is undetermined.

(3) Even though one or more terms are left open a contract for sale does not fail for indefiniteness if the parties have intended to make a contract and there is a reasonably certain basis for giving an appropriate remedy.

§ 2–205. Firm Offers.

An offer by a merchant to buy or sell goods in a signed writing which by its terms gives assurance that it will be held open is not revocable, for lack of consideration, during the time stated or if no time is stated for a reasonable time, but in no event may such period of irrevocability exceed three months; but any such term of assurance on a form supplied by the offeree must be separately signed by the offeror.

§ 2–206. Offer and Acceptance in Formation of Contract.

(1) Unless other unambiguously indicated by the language or circumstances

(a) an offer to make a contract shall be construed as inviting acceptance in any manner and by any medium reasonable in the circumstances;

(b) an order or other offer to buy goods for prompt or current shipment shall be construed as inviting acceptance either by a prompt promise to ship or by the prompt or current shipment of conforming or nonconforming goods, but such a shipment of nonconforming goods does not constitute an acceptance if the seller seasonably notifies the buyer that the shipment is offered only as an accommodation to the buyer.

(2) Where the beginning of a requested performance is a reasonable mode of acceptance an offeror who is not notified of acceptance within a reasonable time may treat the offer as having lapsed before acceptance.

§ 2–207. Additional Terms in Acceptance or Confirmation.

(1) A definite and seasonable expression of acceptance or a written confirmation which is sent within a reasonable time operates as an acceptance even though it states terms additional to or different from those offered or agreed upon, unless acceptance is expressly made conditional on assent to the additional or different terms.

(2) The additional terms are to be construed as proposals for addition to the contract. Between merchants such terms become part of the contract unless:

(a) the offer expressly limits acceptance to the terms of the offer;

(b) they materially alter it; or

(c) notification of objection to them has already been given or is given within a reasonable time after notice of them is received.

(3) Conduct by both parties which recognizes the existence of a contract is sufficient to establish a contract for sale although the writings of the parties do not otherwise establish a contract. In such case the terms of the particular contract consist of those terms on which the writings of the parties agree, together with any supplementary terms incorporated under any other provisions of this Act.

§ 2–208. Course of Performance or Practical Construction.

(1) Where the contract for sale involves repeated occasions for performance by either party with knowledge of the nature of the performance and opportunity for objection to it by the other, any course of performance accepted or acquiesced in without objection shall be relevant to determine the meaning of the agreement.

(2) The express terms of the agreement and any such course of performance, as well as any course of dealing and usage of trade, shall be construed whenever reasonable as consistent with each other; but when such construction is unreasonable, express terms shall control course of performance and course of performance shall control both course of dealing and usage of trade (Section 1–205).

(3) Subject to the provisions of the next section on modification and waiver, such course of performance shall be relevant to show a waiver or modification of any term inconsistent with such course of performance.

§ 2–209. Modification, Rescission and Waiver.

(1) An agreement modifying a contract within this Article needs no consideration to be binding.

(2) A signed agreement which excludes modification or rescission except by a signed writing cannot be otherwise modified or rescinded, but except as between merchants such a requirement on a form supplied by the merchant must be separately signed by the other party.

(3) The requirements of the statute of frauds section of this Article (Section 2–201) must be satisfied if the contract as modified is within its provisions.

(4) Although an attempt at modification or rescission does not satisfy the requirements of subsection (2) or (3) it can operate as a waiver.

(5) A party who has made a waiver affecting an executory portion of the contract may retract the waiver by reasonable notification received by the other party that strict performance will be required of any term waived, unless the retraction would be unjust in view of a material change of position in reliance on the waiver.

§ 2–210. Delegation of Performance; Assignment of Rights.

(1) A party may perform his duty through a delegate unless otherwise agreed or unless the other party has a substantial interest in having his original promisor perform or control the acts required by the contract. No delegation of performance relieves the party delegating of any duty to perform or any liability for breach.

(2) Except as otherwise provided in Section 9–406, unless otherwise agreed, all rights of either seller or buyer can be assigned except where the assignment would materially change the duty of the other party, or increase materially the burden or risk imposed on him by his contract, or impair materially his chance of obtaining return performance. A right to damages for breach of the whole contract or a right arising out of the assignor's due performance of his entire obligation can be assigned despite agreement otherwise.

(3) The creation, attachment, perfection, or enforcement of a security interest in the seller's interest under a contract is not a transfer that materially changes the duty of or increases materially the burden or risk imposed on the buyer or impairs materially the buyer's chance of obtaining return performance within the purview of subsection (2) unless, and then only to the extent that, enforcement actually results in a delegation of material performance of the seller. Even in that event, the creation, attachment, perfection, and enforcement of the security interest remain effective, but (i) the seller is liable to the buyer for damages caused by the delegation to the extent that the damages could not reasonably by prevented by the buyer, and (ii) a court having jurisdiction may grant other appropriate relief, including cancellation of the contract for sale or an injunction against enforcement of the security interest or consummation of the enforcement.

(4) Unless the circumstances indicate the contrary a prohibition of assignment of "the contract" is to be construed as barring only the delegation to the assignee of the assignor's performance.

(5) An assignment of "the contract" or of "all my rights under the contract" or an assignment in similar general terms is an assignment of rights and unless the language or the circumstances (as in an assignment for security) indicate the contrary, it is a delegation of performance of the duties of the assignor and its acceptance by the assignee constitutes a promise by him to perform those duties. This promise is enforceable by either the assignor or the other party to the original contract.

(6) The other party may treat any assignment which delegates performance as creating reasonable grounds for insecurity and may without prejudice to his rights against the assignor demand assurances from the assignee (Section 2–609).

As amended in 1999.

Part 3 General Obligation and Construction of Contract

§ 2–301. General Obligations of Parties.

The obligation of the seller is to transfer and deliver and that of the buyer is to accept and pay in accordance with the contract.

§ 2–302. Unconscionable Contract or Clause.

(1) If the court as a matter of law finds the contract or any clause of the contract to have been unconscionable at the time it was made the court may refuse to enforce the contract, or it may enforce the remainder of the contract without the unconscionable clause, or it may so limit the application of any unconscionable clause as to avoid any unconscionable result.

(2) When it is claimed or appears to the court that the contract or any clause thereof may be unconscionable the parties shall be afforded a reasonable opportunity to present evidence as to its commercial setting, purpose and effect to aid the court in making the determination.

§ 2–303. Allocations or Division of Risks.

Where this Article allocates a risk or a burden as between the parties "unless otherwise agreed", the agreement may not only shift the allocation but may also divide the risk or burden.

§ 2–304. Price Payable in Money, Goods, Realty, or Otherwise.

(1) The price can be made payable in money or otherwise. If it is payable in whole or in part in goods each party is a seller of the goods which he is to transfer.

(2) Even though all or part of the price is payable in an interest in realty the transfer of the goods and the seller's obligations with reference to them are subject to this Article, but not the transfer of the interest in realty or the transferor's obligations in connection therewith.

§ 2–305. Open Price Term.

(1) The parties if they so intend can conclude a contract for sale even though the price is not settled. In such a case the price is a reasonable price at the time for delivery if

(a) nothing is said as to price; or

(b) the price is left to be agreed by the parties and they fail to agree; or

(c) the price is to be fixed in terms of some agreed market or other standard as set or recorded by a third person or agency and it is not so set or recorded.

(2) A price to be fixed by the seller or by the buyer means a price for him to fix in good faith.

(3) When a price left to be fixed otherwise than by agreement of the parties fails to be fixed through fault of one party the other may at his option treat the contract as cancelled or himself fix a reasonable price.

(4) Where, however, the parties intend not to be bound unless the price be fixed or agreed and it is not fixed or agreed there is no contract. In such a case the buyer must return any goods already received or if unable so to do must pay their reasonable value at the time of delivery and the seller must return any portion of the price paid on account.

§ 2–306. Output, Requirements and Exclusive Dealings.

(1) A term which measures the quantity by the output of the seller or the requirements of the buyer means such actual output or requirements as may occur in good faith, except that no quantity unreasonably disproportionate to any stated estimate or in the absence of a stated estimate to any normal or otherwise comparable prior output or requirements may be tendered or demanded.

(2) A lawful agreement by either the seller or the buyer for exclusive dealing in the kind of goods concerned imposes unless otherwise agreed an obligation by the seller to use best efforts to supply the goods and by the buyer to use best efforts to promote their sale.

§ 2–307. Delivery in Single Lot or Several Lots.

Unless otherwise agreed all goods called for by a contract for sale must be tendered in a single delivery and payment is due only on such tender but where the circumstances give either party the right to make or demand delivery in lots the price if it can be apportioned may be demanded for each lot.

§ 2–308. Absence of Specified Place for Delivery.

Unless otherwise agreed

(a) the place for delivery of goods is the seller's place of business or if he has none his residence; but

(b) in a contract for sale of identified goods which to the knowledge of the parties at the time of contracting are in some other place, that place is the place for their delivery; and

(c) documents of title may be delivered through customary banking channels.

§ 2–309. Absence of Specific Time Provisions; Notice of Termination.

(1) The time for shipment or delivery or any other action under a contract if not provided in this Article or agreed upon shall be a reasonable time.

(2) Where the contract provides for successive performances but is indefinite in duration it is valid for a reasonable time but unless otherwise agreed may be terminated at any time by either party.

(3) Termination of a contract by one party except on the happening of an agreed event requires that reasonable notification be received by the other party and an agreement dispensing with notification is invalid if its operation would be unconscionable.

§ 2–310. Open Time for Payment or Running of Credit; Authority to Ship Under Reservation.

Unless otherwise agreed

(a) payment is due at the time and place at which the buyer is to receive the goods even though the place of shipment is the place of delivery; and

(b) if the seller is authorized to send the goods he may ship them under reservation, and may tender the documents of title, but the buyer may inspect the goods after their arrival before payment is due unless such inspection is inconsistent with the terms of the contract (Section 2–513); and

(c) if delivery is authorized and made by way of documents of title otherwise than by subsection (b) then payment is due at the time and place at which the buyer is to receive the documents regardless of where the goods are to be received; and

(d) where the seller is required or authorized to ship the goods on credit the credit period runs from the time of shipment but post-dating the invoice or delaying its dispatch will correspondingly delay the starting of the credit period.

§ 2–311. Options and Cooperation Respecting Performance.

(1) An agreement for sale which is otherwise sufficiently definite (subsection (3) of Section 2–204) to be a contract is not made invalid by the fact that it leaves particulars of performance to be specified by one of the parties. Any such specification must be made in good faith and within limits set by commercial reasonableness.

(2) Unless otherwise agreed specifications relating to assortment of the goods are at the buyer's option and except as otherwise provided in subsections (1)(c) and (3) of Section 2–319 specifications or arrangements relating to shipment are at the seller's option.

(3) Where such specification would materially affect the other party's performance but is not seasonally made or where one party's cooperation is necessary to the agreed performance of the other but is not seasonally forthcoming, the other party in addition to all other remedies

(a) is excused for any resulting delay in his own performance; and

(b) may also either proceed to perform in any reasonable manner or after the time for a material part of his own performance treat the failure to specify or to cooperate as a breach by failure to deliver or accept the goods.

§ 2–312. Warranty of Title and Against Infringement; Buyer's Obligation Against Infringement.

(1) Subject to subsection (2) there is in a contract for sale a warranty by the seller that

(a) the title conveyed shall be good, and its transfer rightful; and

(b) the goods shall be delivered free from any security interest or other lien or encumbrance of which the buyer at the time of contracting has no knowledge.

(2) A warranty under subsection (1) will be excluded or modified only by specific language or by circumstances which give the buyer reason to know that the person selling does not claim title in himself or that he is purporting to sell only such right or title as he or a third person may have.

(3) Unless otherwise agreed a seller who is a merchant regularly dealing in goods of the kind warrants that the goods shall be delivered free of the rightful claim of any third person by way of infringement or the like but a buyer who furnishes specifications to the seller must hold the seller harmless against any such claim which arises out of compliance with the specifications.

§ 2–313. Express Warranties by Affirmation, Promise, Description, Sample.

(1) Express warranties by the seller are created as follows:

(a) Any affirmation of fact or promise made by the seller to the buyer which relates to the goods and becomes part of the basis of the bargain creates an express warranty that the goods shall conform to the affirmation or promise.

(b) Any description of the goods which is made part of the basis of the bargain creates an express warranty that the goods shall conform to the description.

(c) Any sample or model which is made part of the basis of the bargain creates an express warranty that the whole of the goods shall conform to the sample or model.

(2) It is not necessary to the creation of an express warranty that the seller use formal words such as "warrant" or "guarantee" or that he have a specific intention to make a warranty, but an affirmation merely of the value of the goods or a statement purporting to be merely the seller's opinion or commendation of the goods does not create a warranty.

§ 2–314. Implied Warranty: Merchantability; Usage of Trade.

(1) Unless excluded or modified (Section 2–316), a warranty that the goods shall be merchantable is implied in a contract for their sale if the seller is a merchant with respect to goods of that kind. Under this section the serving for value of food or drink to be consumed either on the premises or elsewhere is a sale.

(2) Goods to be merchantable must be at least such as

(a) pass without objection in the trade under the contract description; and

(b) in the case of fungible goods, are of fair average quality within the description; and

(c) are fit for the ordinary purposes for which such goods are used; and

(d) run, within the variations permitted by the agreement, of even kind, quality and quantity within each unit and among all units involved; and

(e) are adequately contained, packaged, and labeled as the agreement may require; and

(f) conform to the promises or affirmations of fact made on the container or label if any.

(3) Unless excluded or modified (Section 2–316) other implied warranties may arise from course of dealing or usage of trade.

§ 2–315. Implied Warranty: Fitness for Particular Purpose.

Where the seller at the time of contracting has reason to know any particular purpose for which the goods are required and that the buyer is relying on the seller's skill or judgment to select or furnish suitable goods, there is unless excluded or modified under the next section an implied warranty that the goods shall be fit for such purpose.

§ 2–316. Exclusion or Modification of Warranties.

(1) Words or conduct relevant to the creation of an express warranty and words or conduct tending to negate or limit warranty shall be construed wherever reasonable as consistent with each other; but subject to the provisions of this Article on parol or extrinsic evidence (Section 2–202) negation or limitation is inoperative to the extent that such construction is unreasonable.

(2) Subject to subsection (3), to exclude or modify the implied warranty of merchantability or any part of it the language must mention merchantability and in case of a writing must be conspicuous, and to exclude or modify any implied warranty of fitness the exclusion must be by a writing and conspicuous. Language to exclude all implied warranties of fitness is sufficient if it states, for example, that "There are no warranties which extend beyond the description on the face hereof."

(3) Notwithstanding subsection (2)

(a) unless the circumstances indicate otherwise, all implied warranties are excluded by expressions like "as is", "with all faults" or other language which in common understanding calls the buyer's attention to the exclusion of warranties and makes plain that there is no implied warranty; and

(b) when the buyer before entering into the contract has examined the goods or the sample or model as fully as he desired or has refused to examine the goods there is no implied warranty with regard to defects which an examination ought in the circumstances to have revealed to him; and

(c) an implied warranty can also be excluded or modified by course of dealing or course of performance or usage of trade.

(4) Remedies for breach of warranty can be limited in accordance with the provisions of this Article on liquidation or limitation of damages and on contractual modification of remedy (Sections 2–718 and 2–719).

§ 2–317. Cumulation and Conflict of Warranties Express or Implied.

Warranties whether express or implied shall be construed as consistent with each other and as cumulative, but if such construction is unreasonable the intention of the parties shall determine which warranty is dominant. In ascertaining that intention the following rules apply:

(a) Exact or technical specifications displace an inconsistent sample or model or general language of description.

(b) A sample from an existing bulk displaces inconsistent general language of description.

(c) Express warranties displace inconsistent implied warranties other than an implied warranty of fitness for a particular purpose.

§ 2–318. Third Party Beneficiaries of Warranties Express or Implied.

Note: If this Act is introduced in the Congress of the United States this section should be omitted. (States to select one alternative.)

Alternative A

A seller's warranty whether express or implied extends to any natural person who is in the family or household of his buyer or who is a guest in his home if it is reasonable to expect that such person may use, consume or be affected by the goods and who is injured in person by breach of the warranty. A seller may not exclude or limit the operation of this section.

Alternative B

A seller's warranty whether express or implied extends to any natural person who may reasonably be expected to use, consume or be affected by the goods and who is injured in person by breach of the warranty. A seller may not exclude or limit the operation of this section.

Alternative C

A seller's warranty whether express or implied extends to any person who may reasonably be expected to use, consume or be affected by the goods and who is injured by breach of the warranty. A seller may not exclude or limit the operation of this section with respect to injury to the person of an individual to whom the warranty extends.

As amended 1966.

§ 2–319. F.O.B. and F.A.S. Terms.

(1) Unless otherwise agreed the term F.O.B. (which means "free on board") at a named place, even though used only in connection with the stated price, is a delivery term under which

(a) when the term is F.O.B. the place of shipment, the seller must at that place ship the goods in the manner provided in this Article (Section 2–504) and bear the expense and risk of putting them into the possession of the carrier; or

(b) when the term is F.O.B. the place of destination, the seller must at his own expense and risk transport the goods to that place and there tender delivery of them in the manner provided in this Article (Section 2–503);

(c) when under either (a) or (b) the term is also F.O.B. vessel, car or other vehicle, the seller must in addition at his own expense and risk load the goods on board. If the term is F.O.B. vessel the buyer must name the vessel and in an appropriate case the seller must comply with the provisions of this Article on the form of bill of lading (Section 2–323).

(2) Unless otherwise agreed the term F.A.S. vessel (which means "free alongside") at a named port, even though used only in connection with the stated price, is a delivery term under which the seller must

(a) at his own expense and risk deliver the goods alongside the vessel in the manner usual in that port or on a dock designated and provided by the buyer; and

(b) obtain and tender a receipt for the goods in exchange for which the carrier is under a duty to issue a bill of lading.

(3) Unless otherwise agreed in any case falling within subsection (1)(a) or (c) or subsection (2) the buyer must seasonably give any needed instructions for making delivery, including when the term is F.A.S. or F.O.B. the loading berth of the vessel and in an appropriate case its name and sailing date. The seller may treat the failure of needed instructions as a failure of cooperation under this Article (Section 2–311). He may also at his option move the goods in any reasonable manner preparatory to delivery or shipment.

(4) Under the term F.O.B. vessel or F.A.S. unless otherwise agreed the buyer must make payment against tender of the required documents and the seller may not tender nor the buyer demand delivery of the goods in substitution for the documents.

§ 2–320. C.I.F. and C. & F. Terms.

(1) The term C.I.F. means that the price includes in a lump sum the cost of the goods and the insurance and freight to the named destination. The term C. & F. or C.F. means that the price so includes cost and freight to the named destination.

(2) Unless otherwise agreed and even though used only in connection with the stated price and destination, the term C.I.F. destination or its equivalent requires the seller at his own expense and risk to

(a) put the goods into the possession of a carrier at the port for shipment and obtain a negotiable bill or bills of lading covering the entire transportation to the named destination; and

(b) load the goods and obtain a receipt from the carrier (which may be contained in the bill of lading) showing that the freight has been paid or provided for; and

(c) obtain a policy or certificate of insurance, including any war risk insurance, of a kind and on terms then current at the port of shipment in the usual amount, in the currency of the contract, shown to cover the same goods covered by the bill of lading and providing for payment of loss to the order of the buyer or for the account of whom it may concern; but the seller may add to the price the amount of the premium for any such war risk insurance; and

(d) prepare an invoice of the goods and procure any other documents required to effect shipment or to comply with the contract; and

(e) forward and tender with commercial promptness all the documents in due form and with any indorsement necessary to perfect the buyer's rights.

(3) Unless otherwise agreed the term C. & F. or its equivalent has the same effect and imposes upon the seller the same obligations and risks as a C.I.F. term except the obligation as to insurance.

(4) Under the term C.I.F. or C. & F. unless otherwise agreed the buyer must make payment against tender of the required documents and the seller may not tender nor the buyer demand delivery of the goods in substitution for the documents.

§ 2–321. C.I.F. or C. & F.: "Net Landed Weights"; "Payment on Arrival"; Warranty of Condition on Arrival.

Under a contract containing a term C.I.F. or C. & F.

(1) Where the price is based on or is to be adjusted according to "net landed weights", "delivered weights", "out turn" quantity or quality or the like, unless otherwise agreed the seller must reasonably estimate the price. The payment due on tender of the documents called for by the contract is the amount so estimated, but after final adjustment of the price a settlement must be made with commercial promptness.

(2) An agreement described in subsection (1) or any warranty of quality or condition of the goods on arrival places upon the seller the risk of ordinary deterioration, shrinkage and the like in transportation but has no effect on the place or time of identification to the contract for sale or delivery or on the passing of the risk of loss.

(3) Unless otherwise agreed where the contract provides for payment on or after arrival of the goods the seller must before payment allow such preliminary inspection as is feasible; but if the goods are lost delivery of the documents and payment are due when the goods should have arrived.

§ 2–322. Delivery "Ex-Ship".

(1) Unless otherwise agreed a term for delivery of goods "ex-ship" (which means from the carrying vessel) or in equivalent language is not restricted to a particular ship and requires delivery from a ship which has reached a place at the named port of destination where goods of the kind are usually discharged.

(2) Under such a term unless otherwise agreed

(a) the seller must discharge all liens arising out of the carriage and furnish the buyer with a direction which puts the carrier under a duty to deliver the goods; and

(b) the risk of loss does not pass to the buyer until the goods leave the ship's tackle or are otherwise properly unloaded.

§ 2–323. Form of Bill of Lading Required in Overseas Shipment; "Overseas".

(1) Where the contract contemplates overseas shipment and contains a term C.I.F. or C. & F. or F.O.B. vessel, the seller unless otherwise agreed must obtain a negotiable bill of lading stating that the goods have been loaded on board or, in the case of a term C.I.F. or C. & F., received for shipment.

(2) Where in a case within subsection (1) a bill of lading has been issued in a set of parts, unless otherwise agreed if the documents are not to be sent from abroad the buyer may demand tender of the full set; otherwise only one part of the bill of lading need be tendered. Even if the agreement expressly requires a full set

(a) due tender of a single part is acceptable within the provisions of this Article on cure of improper delivery (subsection (1) of Section 2–508); and

(b) even though the full set is demanded, if the documents are sent from abroad the person tendering an incomplete set may nevertheless require payment upon furnishing an indemnity which the buyer in good faith deems adequate.

(3) A shipment by water or by air or a contract contemplating such shipment is "overseas" insofar as by usage of trade or agreement it is subject to the commercial, financing or shipping practices characteristic of international deep water commerce.

§ 2–324. "No Arrival, No Sale" Term.

Under a term "no arrival, no sale" or terms of like meaning, unless otherwise agreed,

(a) the seller must properly ship conforming goods and if they arrive by any means he must tender them on arrival but he assumes no obligation that the goods will arrive unless he has caused the non-arrival; and

(b) where without fault of the seller the goods are in part lost or have so deteriorated as no longer to conform to the contract or arrive after the contract time, the buyer may proceed as if there had been casualty to identified goods (Section 2–613).

§ 2–325. "Letter of Credit" Term; "Confirmed Credit".

(1) Failure of the buyer seasonably to furnish an agreed letter of credit is a breach of the contract for sale.

(2) The delivery to seller of a proper letter of credit suspends the buyer's obligation to pay. If the letter of credit is dishonored, the seller may on seasonable notification to the buyer require payment directly from him.

(3) Unless otherwise agreed the term "letter of credit" or "banker's credit" in a contract for sale means an irrevocable credit issued by a financing agency of good repute and, where the shipment is overseas, of good international repute. The term "confirmed credit" means that the credit must also carry the direct obligation of such an agency which does business in the seller's financial market.

§ 2–326. Sale on Approval and Sale or Return; Rights of Creditors.

(1) Unless otherwise agreed, if delivered goods may be returned by the buyer even though they conform to the contract, the transaction is

    (a) a "sale on approval" if the goods are delivered primarily for use, and

    (b) a "sale or return" if the goods are delivered primarily for resale.

(2) Goods held on approval are not subject to the claims of the buyer's creditors until acceptance; goods held on sale or return are subject to such claims while in the buyer's possession.

(3) Any "or return" term of a contract for sale is to be treated as a separate contract for sale within the statute of frauds section of this Article (Section 2–201) and as contradicting the sale aspect of the contract within the provisions of this Article or on parol or extrinsic evidence (Section 2–202).

As amended in 1999.

§ 2–327. Special Incidents of Sale on Approval and Sale or Return.

(1) Under a sale on approval unless otherwise agreed

    (a) although the goods are identified to the contract the risk of loss and the title do not pass to the buyer until acceptance; and

    (b) use of the goods consistent with the purpose of trial is not acceptance but failure seasonably to notify the seller of election to return the goods is acceptance, and if the goods conform to the contract acceptance of any part is acceptance of the whole; and

    (c) after due notification of election to return, the return is at the seller's risk and expense but a merchant buyer must follow any reasonable instructions.

(2) Under a sale or return unless otherwise agreed

    (a) the option to return extends to the whole or any commercial unit of the goods while in substantially their original condition, but must be exercised seasonably; and

    (b) the return is at the buyer's risk and expense.

§ 2–328. Sale by Auction.

(1) In a sale by auction if goods are put up in lots each lot is the subject of a separate sale.

(2) A sale by auction is complete when the auctioneer so announces by the fall of the hammer or in other customary manner. Where a bid is made while the hammer is falling in acceptance of a prior bid the auctioneer may in his discretion reopen the bidding or declare the goods sold under the bid on which the hammer was falling.

(3) Such a sale is with reserve unless the goods are in explicit terms put up without reserve. In an auction with reserve the auctioneer may withdraw the goods at any time until he announces completion of the sale. In an auction without reserve, after the auctioneer calls for bids on an article or lot, that article or lot cannot be withdrawn unless no bid is made within a reasonable time. In either case a bidder may retract his bid until the auctioneer's announcement of completion of the sale, but a bidder's retraction does not revive any previous bid.

(4) If the auctioneer knowingly receives a bid on the seller's behalf or the seller makes or procures such as bid, and notice has not been given that liberty for such bidding is reserved, the buyer may at his option avoid the sale or take the goods at the price of the last good faith bid prior to the completion of the sale. This subsection shall not apply to any bid at a forced sale.

Part 4 Title, Creditors and Good Faith Purchasers

§ 2–401. Passing of Title; Reservation for Security; Limited Application of This Section.

Each provision of this Article with regard to the rights, obligations and remedies of the seller, the buyer, purchasers or other third parties applies irrespective of title to the goods except where the provision refers to such title. Insofar as situations are not covered by the other provisions of this Article and matters concerning title became material the following rules apply:

(1) Title to goods cannot pass under a contract for sale prior to their identification to the contract (Section 2–501), and unless otherwise explicitly agreed the buyer acquires by their identification a special property as limited by this Act. Any retention or reservation by the seller of the title (property) in goods shipped or delivered to the buyer is limited in effect to a reservation of a security interest. Subject to these provisions and to the provisions of the Article on Secured Transactions (Article 9), title to goods passes from the seller to the buyer in any manner and on any conditions explicitly agreed on by the parties.

(2) Unless otherwise explicitly agreed title passes to the buyer at the time and place at which the seller completes his performance with reference to the physical delivery of the goods, despite any reservation of a security interest and even though a document of title is to be delivered at a different time or place; and in particular and despite any reservation of a security interest by the bill of lading

    (a) if the contract requires or authorizes the seller to send the goods to the buyer but does not require him to deliver them at destination, title passes to the buyer at the time and place of shipment; but

(b) if the contract requires delivery at destination, title passes on tender there.

(3) Unless otherwise explicitly agreed where delivery is to be made without moving the goods,

(a) if the seller is to deliver a document of title, title passes at the time when and the place where he delivers such documents; or

(b) if the goods are at the time of contracting already identified and no documents are to be delivered, title passes at the time and place of contracting.

(4) A rejection or other refusal by the buyer to receive or retain the goods, whether or not justified, or a justified revocation of acceptance revests title to the goods in the seller. Such revesting occurs by operation of law and is not a "sale".

§ 2–402. Rights of Seller's Creditors Against Sold Goods.

(1) Except as provided in subsections (2) and (3), rights of unsecured creditors of the seller with respect to goods which have been identified to a contract for sale are subject to the buyer's rights to recover the goods under this Article (Sections 2–502 and 2–716).

(2) A creditor of the seller may treat a sale or an identification of goods to a contract for sale as void if as against him a retention of possession by the seller is fraudulent under any rule of law of the state where the goods are situated, except that retention of possession in good faith and current course of trade by a merchant-seller for a commercially reasonable time after a sale or identification is not fraudulent.

(3) Nothing in this Article shall be deemed to impair the rights of creditors of the seller

(a) under the provisions of the Article on Secured Transactions (Article 9); or

(b) where identification to the contract or delivery is made not in current course of trade but in satisfaction of or as security for a pre-existing claim for money, security or the like and is made under circumstances which under any rule of law of the state where the goods are situated would apart from this Article constitute the transaction a fraudulent transfer or voidable preference.

§ 2–403. Power to Transfer; Good Faith Purchase of Goods; "Entrusting".

(1) A purchaser of goods acquires all title which his transferor had or had power to transfer except that a purchaser of a limited interest acquires rights only to the extent of the interest purchased. A person with voidable title has power to transfer a good title to a good faith purchaser for value. When goods have been delivered under a transaction of purchase the purchaser has such power even though

(a) the transferor was deceived as to the identity of the purchaser, or

(b) the delivery was in exchange for a check which is later dishonored, or

(c) it was agreed that the transaction was to be a "cash sale", or

(d) the delivery was procured through fraud punishable as larcenous under the criminal law.

(2) Any entrusting of possession of goods to a merchant who deals in goods of that kind gives him power to transfer all rights of the entruster to a buyer in ordinary course of business.

(3) "Entrusting" includes any delivery and any acquiescence in retention of possession regardless of any condition expressed between the parties to the delivery or acquiescence and regardless of whether the procurement of the entrusting or the possessor's disposition of the goods have been such as to be larcenous under the criminal law.

(4) The rights of other purchasers of goods and of lien creditors are governed by the Articles on Secured Transactions (Article 9), Bulk Transfers (Article 6) and Documents of Title (Article 7).

As amended in 1988.

Part 5 Performance

§ 2–501. Insurable Interest in Goods; Manner of Identification of Goods.

(1) The buyer obtains a special property and an insurable interest in goods by identification of existing goods as goods to which the contract refers even though the goods so identified are non-conforming and he has an option to return or reject them. Such identification can be made at any time and in any manner explicitly agreed to by the parties. In the absence of explicit agreement identification occurs

(a) when the contract is made if it is for the sale of goods already existing and identified;

(b) if the contract is for the sale of future goods other than those described in paragraph (c), when goods are shipped, marked or otherwise designated by the seller as goods to which the contract refers;

(c) when the crops are planted or otherwise become growing crops or the young are conceived if the contract is for the sale of unborn young to be born within twelve months after contracting or for the sale of crops to be harvested within twelve months or the next normal harvest season after contracting whichever is longer.

(2) The seller retains an insurable interest in goods so long as title to or any security interest in the goods remains in him and where the identification is by the seller alone he may until default or insolvency or notification to the buyer that the identification is final substitute other goods for those identified.

(3) Nothing in this section impairs any insurable interest recognized under any other statute or rule of law.

§ 2–502. Buyer's Right to Goods on Seller's Insolvency.

(1) Subject to subsections (2) and (3) and even though the goods have not been shipped a buyer who has paid a

part or all of the price of goods in which he has a special property under the provisions of the immediately preceding section may on making and keeping good a tender of any unpaid portion of their price recover them from the seller if:

(a) in the case of goods bought for personal, family, or household purposes, the seller repudiates or fails to deliver as required by the contract; or

(b) in all cases, the seller becomes insolvent within ten days after receipt of the first installment on their price.

(2) The buyer's right to recover the goods under subsection (1)(a) vests upon acquisition of a special property, even if the seller had not then repudiated or failed to deliver.

(3) If the identification creating his special property has been made by the buyer he acquires the right to recover the goods only if they conform to the contract for sale.

As amended in 1999.

§ 2–503. Manner of Seller's Tender of Delivery.

(1) Tender of delivery requires that the seller put and hold conforming goods at the buyer's disposition and give the buyer any notification reasonably necessary to enable him to take delivery. The manner, time and place for tender are determined by the agreement and this Article, and in particular

(a) tender must be at a reasonable hour, and if it is of goods they must be kept available for the period reasonably necessary to enable the buyer to take possession; but

(b) unless otherwise agreed the buyer must furnish facilities reasonably suited to the receipt of the goods.

(2) Where the case is within the next section respecting shipment tender requires that the seller comply with its provisions.

(3) Where the seller is required to deliver at a particular destination tender requires that he comply with subsection (1) and also in any appropriate case tender documents as described in subsections (4) and (5) of this section.

(4) Where goods are in the possession of a bailee and are to be delivered without being moved

(a) tender requires that the seller either tender a negotiable document of title covering such goods or procure acknowledgment by the bailee of the buyer's right to possession of the goods; but

(b) tender to the buyer of a non-negotiable document of title or of a written direction to the bailee to deliver is sufficient tender unless the buyer seasonably objects, and receipt by the bailee of notification of the buyer's rights fixes those rights as against the bailee and all third persons; but risk of loss of the goods and of any failure by the bailee to honor the non-negotiable document of title or to obey the direction remains on the seller until the buyer has had a reasonable time to present the document or direction, and a refusal by the bailee to honor the document or to obey the direction defeats the tender.

(5) Where the contract requires the seller to deliver documents

(a) he must tender all such documents in correct form, except as provided in this Article with respect to bills of lading in a set (subsection (2) of Section 2–323); and

(b) tender through customary banking channels is sufficient and dishonor of a draft accompanying the documents constitutes non-acceptance or rejection.

§ 2–504. Shipment by Seller.

Where the seller is required or authorized to send the goods to the buyer and the contract does not require him to deliver them at a particular destination, then unless otherwise agreed he must

(a) put the goods in the possession of such a carrier and make such a contract for their transportation as may be reasonable having regard to the nature of the goods and other circumstances of the case; and

(b) obtain and promptly deliver or tender in due form any document necessary to enable the buyer to obtain possession of the goods or otherwise required by the agreement or by usage of trade; and

(c) promptly notify the buyer of the shipment.

Failure to notify the buyer under paragraph (c) or to make a proper contract under paragraph (a) is a ground for rejection only if material delay or loss ensues.

§ 2–505. Seller's Shipment under Reservation.

(1) Where the seller has identified goods to the contract by or before shipment:

(a) his procurement of a negotiable bill of lading to his own order or otherwise reserves in him a security interest in the goods. His procurement of the bill to the order of a financing agency or of the buyer indicates in addition only the seller's expectation of transferring that interest to the person named.

(b) a non-negotiable bill of lading to himself or his nominee reserves possession of the goods as security but except in a case of conditional delivery (subsection (2) of Section 2–507) a non-negotiable bill of lading naming the buyer as consignee reserves no security interest even though the seller retains possession of the bill of lading.

(2) When shipment by the seller with reservation of a security interest is in violation of the contract for sale it constitutes an improper contract for transportation within the preceding section but impairs neither the rights given to the buyer by shipment and identification of the goods to the contract nor the seller's powers as a holder of a negotiable document.

§ 2–506. Rights of Financing Agency.

(1) A financing agency by paying or purchasing for value a draft which relates to a shipment of goods acquires to

the extent of the payment or purchase and in addition to its own rights under the draft and any document of title securing it any rights of the shipper in the goods including the right to stop delivery and the shipper's right to have the draft honored by the buyer.

(2) The right to reimbursement of a financing agency which has in good faith honored or purchased the draft under commitment to or authority from the buyer is not impaired by subsequent discovery of defects with reference to any relevant document which was apparently regular on its face.

§ 2–507. Effect of Seller's Tender; Delivery on Condition.

(1) Tender of delivery is a condition to the buyer's duty to accept the goods and, unless otherwise agreed, to his duty to pay for them. Tender entitles the seller to acceptance of the goods and to payment according to the contract.

(2) Where payment is due and demanded on the delivery to the buyer of goods or documents of title, his right as against the seller to retain or dispose of them is conditional upon his making the payment due.

§ 2–508. Cure by Seller of Improper Tender or Delivery; Replacement.

(1) Where any tender or delivery by the seller is rejected because non-conforming and the time for performance has not yet expired, the seller may seasonably notify the buyer of his intention to cure and may then within the contract time make a conforming delivery.

(2) Where the buyer rejects a non-conforming tender which the seller had reasonable grounds to believe would be acceptable with or without money allowance the seller may if he seasonably notifies the buyer have a further reasonable time to substitute a conforming tender.

§ 2–509. Risk of Loss in the Absence of Breach.

(1) Where the contract requires or authorizes the seller to ship the goods by carrier

   (a) if it does not require him to deliver them at a particular destination, the risk of loss passes to the buyer when the goods are duly delivered to the carrier even though the shipment is under reservation (Section 2–505); but

   (b) if it does require him to deliver them at a particular destination and the goods are there duly tendered while in the possession of the carrier, the risk of loss passes to the buyer when the goods are there duly so tendered as to enable the buyer to take delivery.

(2) Where the goods are held by a bailee to be delivered without being moved, the risk of loss passes to the buyer

   (a) on his receipt of a negotiable document of title covering the goods; or

   (b) on acknowledgment by the bailee of the buyer's right to possession of the goods; or

   (c) after his receipt of a non-negotiable document of title or other written direction to deliver, as provided in subsection (4)(b) of Section 2–503.

(3) In any case not within subsection (1) or (2), the risk of loss passes to the buyer on his receipt of the goods if the seller is a merchant; otherwise the risk passes to the buyer on tender of delivery.

(4) The provisions of this section are subject to contrary agreement of the parties and to the provisions of this Article on sale on approval (Section 2–327) and on effect of breach on risk of loss (Section 2–510).

§ 2–510. Effect of Breach on Risk of Loss.

(1) Where a tender or delivery of goods so fails to conform to the contract as to give a right of rejection the risk of their loss remains on the seller until cure or acceptance.

(2) Where the buyer rightfully revokes acceptance he may to the extent of any deficiency in his effective insurance coverage treat the risk of loss as having rested on the seller from the beginning.

(3) Where the buyer as to conforming goods already identified to the contract for sale repudiates or is otherwise in breach before risk of their loss has passed to him, the seller may to the extent of any deficiency in his effective insurance coverage treat the risk of loss as resting on the buyer for a commercially reasonable time.

§ 2–511. Tender of Payment by Buyer; Payment by Check.

(1) Unless otherwise agreed tender of payment is a condition to the seller's duty to tender and complete any delivery.

(2) Tender of payment is sufficient when made by any means or in any manner current in the ordinary course of business unless the seller demands payment in legal tender and gives any extension of time reasonably necessary to procure it.

(3) Subject to the provisions of this Act on the effect of an instrument on an obligation (Section 3–310), payment by check is conditional and is defeated as between the parties by dishonor of the check on due presentment.

As amended in 1994.

§ 2–512. Payment by Buyer Before Inspection.

(1) Where the contract requires payment before inspection non-conformity of the goods does not excuse the buyer from so making payment unless

   (a) the non-conformity appears without inspection; or

   (b) despite tender of the required documents the circumstances would justify injunction against honor under this Act (Section 5–109(b)).

(2) Payment pursuant to subsection (1) does not constitute an acceptance of goods or impair the buyer's right to inspect or any of his remedies.

As amended in 1995.

§ 2–513. Buyer's Right to Inspection of Goods.

(1) Unless otherwise agreed and subject to subsection (3), where goods are tendered or delivered or identified to the contract for sale, the buyer has a right before payment or

acceptance to inspect them at any reasonable place and time and in any reasonable manner. When the seller is required or authorized to send the goods to the buyer, the inspection may be after their arrival.

(2) Expenses of inspection must be borne by the buyer but may be recovered from the seller if the goods do not conform and are rejected.

(3) Unless otherwise agreed and subject to the provisions of this Article on C.I.F. contracts (subsection (3) of Section 2–321), the buyer is not entitled to inspect the goods before payment of the price when the contract provides

(a) for delivery "C.O.D." or on other like terms; or

(b) for payment against documents of title, except where such payment is due only after the goods are to become available for inspection.

(4) A place or method of inspection fixed by the parties is presumed to be exclusive but unless otherwise expressly agreed it does not postpone identification or shift the place for delivery or for passing the risk of loss. If compliance becomes impossible, inspection shall be as provided in this section unless the place or method fixed was clearly intended as an indispensable condition failure of which avoids the contract.

§ 2–514. When Documents Deliverable on Acceptance; When on Payment.

Unless otherwise agreed documents against which a draft is drawn are to be delivered to the drawee on acceptance of the draft if it is payable more than three days after presentment; otherwise, only on payment.

§ 2–515. Preserving Evidence of Goods in Dispute.

In furtherance of the adjustment of any claim or dispute

(a) either party on reasonable notification to the other and for the purpose of ascertaining the facts and preserving evidence has the right to inspect, test and sample the goods including such of them as may be in the possession or control of the other; and

(b) the parties may agree to a third party inspection or survey to determine the conformity or condition of the goods and may agree that the findings shall be binding upon them in any subsequent litigation or adjustment.

Part 6 Breach, Repudiation and Excuse

§ 2–601. Buyer's Rights on Improper Delivery.

Subject to the provisions of this Article on breach in installment contracts (Section 2–612) and unless otherwise agreed under the sections on contractual limitations of remedy (Sections 2–718 and 2–719), if the goods or the tender of delivery fail in any respect to conform to the contract, the buyer may

(a) reject the whole; or

(b) accept the whole; or

(c) accept any commercial unit or units and reject the rest.

§ 2–602. Manner and Effect of Rightful Rejection.

(1) Rejection of goods must be within a reasonable time after their delivery or tender. It is ineffective unless the buyer seasonably notifies the seller.

(2) Subject to the provisions of the two following sections on rejected goods (Sections 2–603 and 2–604),

(a) after rejection any exercise of ownership by the buyer with respect to any commercial unit is wrongful as against the seller; and

(b) if the buyer has before rejection taken physical possession of goods in which he does not have a security interest under the provisions of this Article (subsection (3) of Section 2–711), he is under a duty after rejection to hold them with reasonable care at the seller's disposition for a time sufficient to permit the seller to remove them; but

(c) the buyer has no further obligations with regard to goods rightfully rejected.

(3) The seller's rights with respect to goods wrongfully rejected are governed by the provisions of this Article on Seller's remedies in general (Section 2–703).

§ 2–603. Merchant Buyer's Duties as to Rightfully Rejected Goods.

(1) Subject to any security interest in the buyer (subsection (3) of Section 2–711), when the seller has no agent or place of business at the market of rejection a merchant buyer is under a duty after rejection of goods in his possession or control to follow any reasonable instructions received from the seller with respect to the goods and in the absence of such instructions to make reasonable efforts to sell them for the seller's account if they are perishable or threaten to decline in value speedily. Instructions are not reasonable if on demand indemnity for expenses is not forthcoming.

(2) When the buyer sells goods under subsection (1), he is entitled to reimbursement from the seller or out of the proceeds for reasonable expenses of caring for and selling them, and if the expenses include no selling commission then to such commission as is usual in the trade or if there is none to a reasonable sum not exceeding ten per cent on the gross proceeds.

(3) In complying with this section the buyer is held only to good faith and good faith conduct hereunder is neither acceptance nor conversion nor the basis of an action for damages.

§ 2–604. Buyer's Options as to Salvage of Rightfully Rejected Goods.

Subject to the provisions of the immediately preceding section on perishables if the seller gives no instructions within a reasonable time after notification of rejection the buyer may store the rejected goods for the seller's account or reship them to him or resell them for the seller's account with reimbursement as provided in the preceding section. Such action is not acceptance or conversion.

§ 2–605. Waiver of Buyer's Objections by Failure to Particularize.

(1) The buyer's failure to state in connection with rejection a particular defect which is ascertainable by reasonable inspection precludes him from relying on the unstated defect to justify rejection or to establish breach

(a) where the seller could have cured it if stated seasonably; or

(b) between merchants when the seller has after rejection made a request in writing for a full and final written statement of all defects on which the buyer proposes to rely.

(2) Payment against documents made without reservation of rights precludes recovery of the payment for defects apparent on the face of the documents.

§ 2–606. What Constitutes Acceptance of Goods.

(1) Acceptance of goods occurs when the buyer

(a) after a reasonable opportunity to inspect the goods signifies to the seller that the goods are conforming or that he will take or retain them in spite of their nonconformity; or

(b) fails to make an effective rejection (subsection (1) of Section 2–602), but such acceptance does not occur until the buyer has had a reasonable opportunity to inspect them; or

(c) does any act inconsistent with the seller's ownership; but if such act is wrongful as against the seller it is an acceptance only if ratified by him.

(2) Acceptance of a part of any commercial unit is acceptance of that entire unit.

§ 2–607. Effect of Acceptance; Notice of Breach; Burden of Establishing Breach After Acceptance; Notice of Claim or Litigation to Person Answerable Over.

(1) The buyer must pay at the contract rate for any goods accepted.

(2) Acceptance of goods by the buyer precludes rejection of the goods accepted and if made with knowledge of a non-conformity cannot be revoked because of it unless the acceptance was on the reasonable assumption that the non-conformity would be seasonably cured but acceptance does not of itself impair any other remedy provided by this Article for non-conformity.

(3) Where a tender has been accepted

(a) the buyer must within a reasonable time after he discovers or should have discovered any breach notify the seller of breach or be barred from any remedy; and

(b) if the claim is one for infringement or the like (subsection (3) of Section 2–312) and the buyer is sued as a result of such a breach he must so notify the seller within a reasonable time after he receives notice of the litigation or be barred from any remedy over for liability established by the litigation.

(4) The burden is on the buyer to establish any breach with respect to the goods accepted.

(5) Where the buyer is sued for breach of a warranty or other obligation for which his seller is answerable over

(a) he may give his seller written notice of the litigation. If the notice states that the seller may come in and defend and that if the seller does not do so he will be bound in any action against him by his buyer by any determination of fact common to the two litigations, then unless the seller after seasonable receipt of the notice does come in and defend he is so bound.

(b) if the claim is one for infringement or the like (subsection (3) of Section 2–312) the original seller may demand in writing that his buyer turn over to him control of the litigation including settlement or else be barred from any remedy over and if he also agrees to bear all expense and to satisfy any adverse judgment, then unless the buyer after seasonable receipt of the demand does turn over control the buyer is so barred.

(6) The provisions of subsections (3), (4) and (5) apply to any obligation of a buyer to hold the seller harmless against infringement or the like (subsection (3) of Section 2–312).

§ 2–608. Revocation of Acceptance in Whole or in Part.

(1) The buyer may revoke his acceptance of a lot or commercial unit whose non-conformity substantially impairs its value to him if he has accepted it

(a) on the reasonable assumption that its nonconformity would be cured and it has not been seasonably cured; or

(b) without discovery of such non-conformity if his acceptance was reasonably induced either by the difficulty of discovery before acceptance or by the seller's assurances.

(2) Revocation of acceptance must occur within a reasonable time after the buyer discovers or should have discovered the ground for it and before any substantial change in condition of the goods which is not caused by their own defects. It is not effective until the buyer notifies the seller of it.

(3) A buyer who so revokes has the same rights and duties with regard to the goods involved as if he had rejected them.

§ 2–609. Right to Adequate Assurance of Performance.

(1) A contract for sale imposes an obligation on each party that the other's expectation of receiving due performance will not be impaired. When reasonable grounds for insecurity arise with respect to the performance of either party

the other may in writing demand adequate assurance of due performance and until he receives such assurance may if commercially reasonable suspend any performance for which he has not already received the agreed return.

(2) Between merchants the reasonableness of grounds for insecurity and the adequacy of any assurance offered shall be determined according to commercial standards.

(3) Acceptance of any improper delivery or payment does not prejudice the party's right to demand adequate assurance of future performance.

(4) After receipt of a justified demand failure to provide within a reasonable time not exceeding thirty days such assurance of due performance as is adequate under the circumstances of the particular case is a repudiation of the contract.

§ 2–610. Anticipatory Repudiation.

When either party repudiates the contract with respect to a performance not yet due the loss of which will substantially impair the value of the contract to the other, the aggrieved party may

(a) for a commercially reasonable time await performance by the repudiating party; or

(b) resort to any remedy for breach (Section 2–703 or Section 2–711), even though he has notified the repudiating party that he would await the latter's performance and has urged retraction; and

(c) in either case suspend his own performance or proceed in accordance with the provisions of this Article on the seller's right to identify goods to the contract notwithstanding breach or to salvage unfinished goods (Section 2–704).

§ 2–611. Retraction of Anticipatory Repudiation.

(1) Until the repudiating party's next performance is due he can retract his repudiation unless the aggrieved party has since the repudiation cancelled or materially changed his position or otherwise indicated that he considers the repudiation final.

(2) Retraction may be by any method which clearly indicates to the aggrieved party that the repudiating party intends to perform, but must include any assurance justifiably demanded under the provisions of this Article (Section 2–609).

(3) Retraction reinstates the repudiating party's rights under the contract with due excuse and allowance to the aggrieved party for any delay occasioned by the repudiation.

§ 2–612. "Installment Contract"; Breach.

(1) An "installment contract" is one which requires or authorizes the delivery of goods in separate lots to be separately accepted, even though the contract contains a clause "each delivery is a separate contract" or its equivalent.

(2) The buyer may reject any installment which is nonconforming if the non-conformity substantially impairs the value of that installment and cannot be cured or if the non-

conformity is a defect in the required documents; but if the non-conformity does not fall within subsection (3) and the seller gives adequate assurance of its cure the buyer must accept that installment.

(3) Whenever non-conformity or default with respect to one or more installments substantially impairs the value of the whole contract there is a breach of the whole. But the aggrieved party reinstates the contract if he accepts a non-conforming installment without seasonably notifying of cancellation or if he brings an action with respect only to past installments or demands performance as to future installments.

§ 2–613. Casualty to Identified Goods.

Where the contract requires for its performance goods identified when the contract is made, and the goods suffer casualty without fault of either party before the risk of loss passes to the buyer, or in a proper case under a "no arrival, no sale" term (Section 2–324) then

(a) if the loss is total the contract is avoided; and

(b) if the loss is partial or the goods have so deteriorated as no longer to conform to the contract the buyer may nevertheless demand inspection and at his option either treat the contract as voided or accept the goods with due allowance from the contract price for the deterioration or the deficiency in quantity but without further right against the seller.

§ 2–614. Substituted Performance.

(1) Where without fault of either party the agreed berthing, loading, or unloading facilities fail or an agreed type of carrier becomes unavailable or the agreed manner of delivery otherwise becomes commercially impracticable but a commercially reasonable substitute is available, such substitute performance must be tendered and accepted.

(2) If the agreed means or manner of payment fails because of domestic or foreign governmental regulation, the seller may withhold or stop delivery unless the buyer provides a means or manner of payment which is commercially a substantial equivalent. If delivery has already been taken, payment by the means or in the manner provided by the regulation discharges the buyer's obligation unless the regulation is discriminatory, oppressive or predatory.

§ 2–615. Excuse by Failure of Presupposed Conditions.

Except so far as a seller may have assumed a greater obligation and subject to the preceding section on substituted performance:

(a) Delay in delivery or non-delivery in whole or in part by a seller who complies with paragraphs (b) and (c) is not a breach of his duty under a contract for sale if performance as agreed has been made impracticable by the occurrence of a contingency the nonoccurrence of which was a basic assumption on which the contract was made or by compliance in good faith with any applicable foreign or domestic governmental regulation or order whether or not it later proves to be invalid.

(b) Where the causes mentioned in paragraph (a) affect only a part of the seller's capacity to perform, he must allocate production and deliveries among his customers but may at his option include regular customers not then under contract as well as his own requirements for further manufacture. He may so allocate in any manner which is fair and reasonable.

(c) The seller must notify the buyer seasonably that there will be delay or non-delivery and, when allocation is required under paragraph (b), of the estimated quota thus made available for the buyer.

§ 2–616. Procedure on Notice Claiming Excuse.

(1) Where the buyer receives notification of a material or indefinite delay or an allocation justified under the preceding section he may by written notification to the seller as to any delivery concerned, and where the prospective deficiency substantially impairs the value of the whole contract under the provisions of this Article relating to breach of installment contracts (Section 2–612), then also as to the whole,

    (a) terminate and thereby discharge any unexecuted portion of the contract; or

    (b) modify the contract by agreeing to take his available quota in substitution.

(2) If after receipt of such notification from the seller the buyer fails so to modify the contract within a reasonable time not exceeding thirty days the contract lapses with respect to any deliveries affected.

(3) The provisions of this section may not be negated by agreement except in so far as the seller has assumed a greater obligation under the preceding section.

Part 7   Remedies

§ 2–701. Remedies for Breach of Collateral Contracts Not Impaired.

Remedies for breach of any obligation or promise collateral or ancillary to a contract for sale are not impaired by the provisions of this Article.

§ 2–702. Seller's Remedies on Discovery of Buyer's Insolvency.

(1) Where the seller discovers the buyer to be insolvent he may refuse delivery except for cash including payment for all goods theretofore delivered under the contract, and stop delivery under this Article (Section 2–705).

(2) Where the seller discovers that the buyer has received goods on credit while insolvent he may reclaim the goods upon demand made within ten days after the receipt, but if misrepresentation of solvency has been made to the particular seller in writing within three months before delivery the ten day limitation does not apply. Except as provided in this subsection the seller may not base a right to reclaim goods on the buyer's fraudulent or innocent misrepresentation of solvency or of intent to pay.

(3) The seller's right to reclaim under subsection (2) is subject to the rights of a buyer in ordinary course or other good faith purchaser under this Article (Section 2–403). Successful reclamation of goods excludes all other remedies with respect to them.

§ 2–703. Seller's Remedies in General.

Where the buyer wrongfully rejects or revokes acceptance of goods or fails to make a payment due on or before delivery or repudiates with respect to a part or the whole, then with respect to any goods directly affected and, if the breach is of the whole contract (Section 2–612), then also with respect to the whole undelivered balance, the aggrieved seller may

(a) withhold delivery of such goods;

(b) stop delivery by any bailee as hereafter provided (Section 2–705);

(c) proceed under the next section respecting goods still unidentified to the contract;

(d) resell and recover damages as hereafter provided (Section 2–706);

(e) recover damages for non-acceptance (Section 2–708) or in a proper case the price (Section 2–709);

(f) cancel.

§ 2–704. Seller's Right to Identify Goods to the Contract Notwithstanding Breach or to Salvage Unfinished Goods.

(1) An aggrieved seller under the preceding section may

    (a) identify to the contract conforming goods not already identified if at the time he learned of the breach they are in his possession or control;

    (b) treat as the subject of resale goods which have demonstrably been intended for the particular contract even though those goods are unfinished.

(2) Where the goods are unfinished an aggrieved seller may in the exercise of reasonable commercial judgment for the purposes of avoiding loss and of effective realization either complete the manufacture and wholly identify the goods to the contract or cease manufacture and resell for scrap or salvage value or proceed in any other reasonable manner.

§ 2–705. Seller's Stoppage of Delivery in Transit or Otherwise.

(1) The seller may stop delivery of goods in the possession of a carrier or other bailee when he discovers the buyer to be insolvent (Section 2–702) and may stop delivery of carload, truckload, planeload or larger shipments of express or freight when the buyer repudiates or fails to make a payment due before delivery or if for any other reason the seller has a right to withhold or reclaim the goods.

(2) As against such buyer the seller may stop delivery until

    (a) receipt of the goods by the buyer; or

    (b) acknowledgment to the buyer by any bailee of the goods except a carrier that the bailee holds the goods for the buyer; or

    (c) such acknowledgment to the buyer by a carrier by reshipment or as warehouseman; or

(d) negotiation to the buyer of any negotiable document of title covering the goods.

(3) (a) To stop delivery the seller must so notify as to enable the bailee by reasonable diligence to prevent delivery of the goods.

(b) After such notification the bailee must hold and deliver the goods according to the directions of the seller but the seller is liable to the bailee for any ensuing charges or damages.

(c) If a negotiable document of title has been issued for goods the bailee is not obliged to obey a notification to stop until surrender of the document.

(d) A carrier who has issued a non-negotiable bill of lading is not obliged to obey a notification to stop received from a person other than the consignor.

§ 2–706. Seller's Resale Including Contract for Resale.

(1) Under the conditions stated in Section 2–703 on seller's remedies, the seller may resell the goods concerned or the undelivered balance thereof. Where the resale is made in good faith and in a commercially reasonable manner the seller may recover the difference between the resale price and the contract price together with any incidental damages allowed under the provisions of this Article (Section 2–710), but less expenses saved in consequence of the buyer's breach.

(2) Except as otherwise provided in subsection (3) or unless otherwise agreed resale may be at public or private sale including sale by way of one or more contracts to sell or of identification to an existing contract of the seller. Sale may be as a unit or in parcels and at any time and place and on any terms but every aspect of the sale including the method, manner, time, place and terms must be commercially reasonable. The resale must be reasonably identified as referring to the broken contract, but it is not necessary that the goods be in existence or that any or all of them have been identified to the contract before the breach.

(3) Where the resale is at private sale the seller must give the buyer reasonable notification of his intention to resell.

(4) Where the resale is at public sale

(a) only identified goods can be sold except where there is a recognized market for a public sale of futures in goods of the kind; and

(b) it must be made at a usual place or market for public sale if one is reasonably available and except in the case of goods which are perishable or threaten to decline in value speedily the seller must give the buyer reasonable notice of the time and place of the resale; and

(c) if the goods are not to be within the view of those attending the sale the notification of sale must state the place where the goods are located and provide for their reasonable inspection by prospective bidders; and

(d) the seller may buy.

(5) A purchaser who buys in good faith at a resale takes the goods free of any rights of the original buyer even though the seller fails to comply with one or more of the requirements of this section.

(6) The seller is not accountable to the buyer for any profit made on any resale. A person in the position of a seller (Section 2–707) or a buyer who has rightfully rejected or justifiably revoked acceptance must account for any excess over the amount of his security interest, as hereinafter defined (subsection (3) of Section 2–711).

§ 2–707. "Person in the Position of a Seller".

(1) A "person in the position of a seller" includes as against a principal an agent who has paid or become responsible for the price of goods on behalf of his principal or anyone who otherwise holds a security interest or other right in goods similar to that of a seller.

(2) A person in the position of a seller may as provided in this Article withhold or stop delivery (Section 2–705) and resell (Section 2–706) and recover incidental damages (Section 2–710).

§ 2–708. Seller's Damages for Non-Acceptance or Repudiation.

(1) Subject to subsection (2) and to the provisions of this Article with respect to proof of market price (Section 2–723), the measure of damages for non-acceptance or repudiation by the buyer is the difference between the market price at the time and place for tender and the unpaid contract price together with any incidental damages provided in this Article (Section 2–710), but less expenses saved in consequence of the buyer's breach.

(2) If the measure of damages provided in subsection (1) is inadequate to put the seller in as good a position as performance would have done then the measure of damages is the profit (including reasonable overhead) which the seller would have made from full performance by the buyer, together with any incidental damages provided in this Article (Section 2–710), due allowance for costs reasonably incurred and due credit for payments or proceeds of resale.

§ 2–709. Action for the Price.

(1) When the buyer fails to pay the price as it becomes due the seller may recover, together with any incidental damages under the next section, the price

(a) of goods accepted or of conforming goods lost or damaged within a commercially reasonable time after risk of their loss has passed to the buyer; and

(b) of goods identified to the contract if the seller is unable after reasonable effort to resell them at a reasonable price or the circumstances reasonably indicate that such effort will be unavailing.

(2) Where the seller sues for the price he must hold for the buyer any goods which have been identified to the contract and are still in his control except that if resale becomes possible he may resell them at any time prior to the collection of the judgment. The net proceeds of any such resale must be credited to the buyer and payment of the judgment entitles him to any goods not resold.

(3) After the buyer has wrongfully rejected or revoked acceptance of the goods or has failed to make a payment due or has repudiated (Section 2–610), a seller who is held not entitled to the price under this section shall

nevertheless be awarded damages for non-acceptance under the preceding section.

§ 2–710. Seller's Incidental Damages.

Incidental damages to an aggrieved seller include any commercially reasonable charges, expenses or commissions incurred in stopping delivery, in the transportation, care and custody of goods after the buyer's breach, in connection with return or resale of the goods or otherwise resulting from the breach.

§ 2–711. Buyer's Remedies in General; Buyer's Security Interest in Rejected Goods.

(1) Where the seller fails to make delivery or repudiates or the buyer rightfully rejects or justifiably revokes acceptance then with respect to any goods involved, and with respect to the whole if the breach goes to the whole contract (Section 2–612), the buyer may cancel and whether or not he has done so may in addition to recovering so much of the price as has been paid

(a) "cover" and have damages under the next section as to all the goods affected whether or not they have been identified to the contract; or

(b) recover damages for non-delivery as pro-vided in this Article (Section 2–713).

(2) Where the seller fails to deliver or repudiates the buyer may also

(a) if the goods have been identified recover them as provided in this Article (Section 2–502); or

(b) in a proper case obtain specific performance or replevy the goods as provided in this Article (Section 2–716).

(3) On rightful rejection or justifiable revocation of acceptance a buyer has a security interest in goods in his possession or control for any payments made on their price and any expenses reasonably incurred in their inspection, receipt, transportation, care and custody and may hold such goods and resell them in like manner as an aggrieved seller (Section 2–706).

§ 2–712. "Cover"; Buyer's Procurement of Substitute Goods.

(1) After a breach within the preceding section the buyer may "cover" by making in good faith and without unreasonable delay any reasonable purchase of or contract to purchase goods in substitution for those due from the seller.

(2) The buyer may recover from the seller as damages the difference between the cost of cover and the contract price together with any incidental or consequential damages as hereinafter defined (Section 2–715), but less expenses saved in consequence of the seller's breach.

(3) Failure of the buyer to effect cover within this section does not bar him from any other remedy.

§ 2–713. Buyer's Damages for Non-Delivery or Repudiation.

(1) Subject to the provisions of this Article with respect to proof of market price (Section 2–723), the measure of damages for non-delivery or repudiation by the seller is the difference between the market price at the time when the buyer learned of the breach and the contract price together with any incidental and consequential damages provided in this Article (Section 2–715), but less expenses saved in consequence of the seller's breach.

(2) Market price is to be determined as of the place for tender or, in cases of rejection after arrival or revocation of acceptance, as of the place of arrival.

§ 2–714. Buyer's Damages for Breach in Regard to Accepted Goods.

(1) Where the buyer has accepted goods and given notification (subsection (3) of Section 2–607) he may recover as damages for any non-conformity of tender the loss resulting in the ordinary course of events from the seller's breach as determined in any manner which is reasonable.

(2) The measure of damages for breach of warranty is the difference at the time and place of acceptance between the value of the goods accepted and the value they would have had if they had been as warranted, unless special circumstances show proximate damages of a different amount.

(3) In a proper case any incidental and consequential damages under the next section may also be recovered.

§ 2–715. Buyer's Incidental and Consequential Damages.

(1) Incidental damages resulting from the seller's breach include expenses reasonably incurred in inspection, receipt, transportation and care and custody of goods rightfully rejected, any commercially reasonable charges, expenses or commissions in connection with effecting cover and any other reasonable expense incident to the delay or other breach.

(2) Consequential damages resulting from the seller's breach include

(a) any loss resulting from general or particular requirements and needs of which the seller at the time of contracting had reason to know and which could not reasonably be prevented by cover or otherwise; and

(b) injury to person or property proximately resulting from any breach of warranty.

§ 2–716. Buyer's Right to Specific Performance or Replevin.

(1) Specific performance may be decreed where the goods are unique or in other proper circumstances.

(2) The decree for specific performance may include such terms and conditions as to payment of the price, damages, or other relief as the court may deem just.

(3) The buyer has a right of replevin for goods identified to the contract if after reasonable effort he is unable to effect cover for such goods or the circumstances reasonably indicate that such effort will be unavailing or if the goods have been shipped under reservation and satisfaction of the security interest in them has been made or tendered. In the case of goods bought for personal, family,

or household purposes, the buyer's right of replevin vests upon acquisition of a special property, even if the seller had not then repudiated or failed to deliver.

As amended in 1999.

§ 2–717. Deduction of Damages From the Price.

The buyer on notifying the seller of his intention to do so may deduct all or any part of the damages resulting from any breach of the contract from any part of the price still due under the same contract.

§ 2–718. Liquidation or Limitation of Damages; Deposits.

(1) Damages for breach by either party may be liquidated in the agreement but only at an amount which is reasonable in the light of the anticipated or actual harm caused by the breach, the difficulties of proof of loss, and the inconvenience or nonfeasibility of otherwise obtaining an adequate remedy. A term fixing unreasonably large liquidated damages is void as a penalty.

(2) Where the seller justifiably withholds delivery of goods because of the buyer's breach, the buyer is entitled to restitution of any amount by which the sum of his payments exceeds

   (a) the amount to which the seller is entitled by virtue of terms liquidating the seller's damages in accordance with subsection (1), or

   (b) in the absence of such terms, twenty per cent of the value of the total performance for which the buyer is obligated under the contract or $500, whichever is smaller.

(3) The buyer's right to restitution under subsection (2) is subject to offset to the extent that the seller establishes

   (a) a right to recover damages under the provisions of this Article other than subsection (1), and

   (b) the amount or value of any benefits received by the buyer directly or indirectly by reason of the contract.

(4) Where a seller has received payment in goods their reasonable value or the proceeds of their resale shall be treated as payments for the purposes of subsection (2); but if the seller has notice of the buyer's breach before reselling goods received in part performance, his resale is subject to the conditions laid down in this Article on resale by an aggrieved seller (Section 2–706).

§ 2–719. Contractual Modification or Limitation of Remedy.

(1) Subject to the provisions of subsections (2) and (3) of this section and of the preceding section on liquidation and limitation of damages,

   (a) the agreement may provide for remedies in addition to or in substitution for those provided in this Article and may limit or alter the measure of damages recoverable under this Article, as by limiting the buyer's remedies to return of the goods and repayment of the price or to repair and replacement of nonconforming goods or parts; and

   (b) resort to a remedy as provided is optional unless the remedy is expressly agreed to be exclusive, in which case it is the sole remedy.

(2) Where circumstances cause an exclusive or limited remedy to fail of its essential purpose, remedy may be had as provided in this Act.

(3) Consequential damages may be limited or excluded unless the limitation or exclusion is unconscionable. Limitation of consequential damages for injury to the person in the case of consumer goods is *prima facie* unconscionable but limitation of damages where the loss is commercial is not.

§ 2–720. Effect of "Cancellation" or "Rescission" on Claims for Antecedent Breach.

Unless the contrary intention clearly appears, expressions of "cancellation" or "rescission" of the contract or the like shall not be construed as a renunciation or discharge of any claim in damages for an antecedent breach.

§ 2–721. Remedies for Fraud.

Remedies for material misrepresentation or fraud include all remedies available under this Article for non-fraudulent breach. Neither rescission or a claim for rescission of the contract for sale nor rejection or return of the goods shall bar or be deemed inconsistent with a claim for damages or other remedy.

§ 2–722. Who Can Sue Third Parties for Injury to Goods.

Where a third party so deals with goods which have been identified to a contract for sale as to cause actionable injury to a party to that contract

(a) a right of action against the third party is in either party to the contract for sale who has title to or a security interest or a special property or an insurable interest in the goods; and if the goods have been destroyed or converted a right of action is also in the party who either bore the risk of loss under the contract for sale or has since the injury assumed that risk as against the other;

(b) if at the time of the injury the party plaintiff did not bear the risk of loss as against the other party to the contract for sale and there is no arrangement between them for disposition of the recovery, his suit or settlement is, subject to his own interest, as a fiduciary for the other party to the contract;

(c) either party may with the consent of the other sue for the benefit of whom it may concern.

§ 2–723. Proof of Market Price: Time and Place.

(1) If an action based on anticipatory repudiation comes to trial before the time for performance with respect to some or all of the goods, any damages based on market price (Section 2–708 or Section 2–713) shall be determined according to the price of such goods prevailing at the time when the aggrieved party learned of the repudiation.

(2) If evidence of a price prevailing at the times or places described in this Article is not readily available the price prevailing within any reasonable time before or after the time described or at any other place which in commercial

judgment or under usage of trade would serve as a reasonable substitute for the one described may be used, making any proper allowance for the cost of transporting the goods to or from such other place.

(3) Evidence of a relevant price prevailing at a time or place other than the one described in this Article offered by one party is not admissible unless and until he has given the other party such notice as the court finds sufficient to prevent unfair surprise.

§ 2–724. Admissibility of Market Quotations.

Whenever the prevailing price or value of any goods regularly bought and sold in any established commodity market is in issue, reports in official publications or trade journals or in newspapers or periodicals of general circulation published as the reports of such market shall be admissible in evidence. The circumstances of the preparation of such a report may be shown to affect its weight but not its admissibility.

§ 2–725. Statute of Limitations in Contracts for Sale.

(1) An action for breach of any contract for sale must be commenced within four years after the cause of action has accrued. By the original agreement the parties may reduce the period of limitation to not less than one year but may not extend it.

(2) A cause of action accrues when the breach occurs, regardless of the aggrieved party's lack of knowledge of the breach. A breach of warranty occurs when tender of delivery is made, except that where a warranty explicitly extends to future performance of the goods and discovery of the breach must await the time of such performance the cause of action accrues when the breach is or should have been discovered.

(3) Where an action commenced within the time limited by subsection (1) is so terminated as to leave available a remedy by another action for the same breach such other action may be commenced after the expiration of the time limited and within six months after the termination of the first action unless the termination resulted from voluntary discontinuance or from dismissal for failure or neglect to prosecute.

(4) This section does not alter the law on tolling of the statute of limitations nor does it apply to causes of action which have accrued before this Act becomes effective.

Article 2A
LEASES

Part 1 General Provisions

§ 2A–101. Short Title.

This Article shall be known and may be cited as the Uniform Commercial Code—Leases.

§ 2A–102. Scope.

This Article applies to any transaction, regardless of form, that creates a lease.

§ 2A–103. Definitions and Index of Definitions.

(1) In this Article unless the context otherwise requires:

(a) "Buyer in ordinary course of business" means a person who in good faith and without knowledge that the sale to him [or her] is in violation of the ownership rights or security interest or leasehold interest of a third party in the goods buys in ordinary course from a person in the business of selling goods of that kind but does not include a pawnbroker. "Buying" may be for cash or by exchange of other property or on secured or unsecured credit and includes receiving goods or documents of title under a pre-existing contract for sale but does not include a transfer in bulk or as security for or in total or partial satisfaction of a money debt.

(b) "Cancellation" occurs when either party puts an end to the lease contract for default by the other party.

(c) "Commercial unit" means such a unit of goods as by commercial usage is a single whole for purposes of lease and division of which materially impairs its character or value on the market or in use. A commercial unit may be a single article, as a machine, or a set of articles, as a suite of furniture or a line of machinery, or a quantity, as a gross or carload, or any other unit treated in use or in the relevant market as a single whole.

(d) "Conforming" goods or performance under a lease contract means goods or performance that are in accordance with the obligations under the lease contract.

(e) "Consumer lease" means a lease that a lessor regularly engaged in the business of leasing or selling makes to a lessee who is an individual and who takes under the lease primarily for a personal, family, or household purpose [, if the total payments to be made under the lease contract, excluding payments for options to renew or buy, do not exceed $_____].

(f) "Fault" means wrongful act, omission, breach, or default.

(g) "Finance lease" means a lease with respect to which:

(i) the lessor does not select, manufacture or supply the goods;

(ii) the lessor acquires the goods or the right to possession and use of the goods in connection with the lease; and

(iii) one of the following occurs:

(A) the lessee receives a copy of the contract by which the lessor acquired the goods or the right to possession and use of the goods before signing the lease contract;

(B) the lessee's approval of the contract by which the lessor acquired the goods or the right to possession and use of the goods is a condition to effectiveness of the lease contract;

(C) the lessee, before signing the lease contract, receives an accurate and complete statement designating the promises and warranties, and any disclaimers of warranties, limitations or modifications of remedies, or liquidated damages, including those of a third party, such as the manufacturer of the goods, provided to the lessor by the person supplying the goods in connection with or as part of the contract by which the lessor acquired the goods or the right to possession and use of the goods; or

(D) if the lease is not a consumer lease, the lessor, before the lessee signs the lease contract, informs the lessee in writing (a) of the identity of the person supplying the goods to the lessor, unless the lessee has selected that person and directed the lessor to acquire the goods or the right to possession and use of the goods from that person, (b) that the lessee is entitled under this Article to any promises and warranties, including those of any third party, provided to the lessor by the person supplying the goods in connection with or as part of the contract by which the lessor acquired the goods or the right to possession and use of the goods, and (c) that the lessee may communicate with the person supplying the goods to the lessor and receive an accurate and complete statement of those promises and warranties, including any disclaimers and limitations of them or of remedies.

(h) "Goods" means all things that are movable at the time of identification to the lease contract, or are fixtures (Section 2A–309), but the term does not include money, documents, instruments, accounts, chattel paper, general intangibles, or minerals or the like, including oil and gas, before extraction. The term also includes the unborn young of animals.

(i) "Installment lease contract" means a lease contract that authorizes or requires the delivery of goods in separate lots to be separately accepted, even though the lease contract contains a clause "each delivery is a separate lease" or its equivalent.

(j) "Lease" means a transfer of the right to possession and use of goods for a term in return for consideration, but a sale, including a sale on approval or a sale or return, or retention or creation of a security interest is not a lease. Unless the context clearly indicates otherwise, the term includes a sublease.

(k) "Lease agreement" means the bargain, with respect to the lease, of the lessor and the lessee in fact as found in their language or by implication from other circumstances including course of dealing or usage of trade or course of performance as provided in this Article. Unless the context clearly indicates otherwise, the term includes a sublease agreement.

(l) "Lease contract" means the total legal obligation that results from the lease agreement as affected by this Article and any other applicable rules of law. Unless the context clearly indicates otherwise, the term includes a sublease contract.

(m) "Leasehold interest" means the interest of the lessor or the lessee under a lease contract.

(n) "Lessee" means a person who acquires the right to possession and use of goods under a lease. Unless the context clearly indicates otherwise, the term includes a sublessee.

(o) "Lessee in ordinary course of business" means a person who in good faith and without knowledge that the lease to him [or her] is in violation of the ownership rights or security interest or leasehold interest of a third party in the goods, leases in ordinary course from a person in the business of selling or leasing goods of that kind but does not include a pawnbroker. "Leasing" may be for cash or by exchange of other property or on secured or unsecured credit and includes receiving goods or documents of title under a pre-existing lease contract but does not include a transfer in bulk or as security for or in total or partial satisfaction of a money debt.

(p) "Lessor" means a person who transfers the right to possession and use of goods under a lease. Unless the context clearly indicates otherwise, the term includes a sublessor.

(q) "Lessor's residual interest" means the lessor's interest in the goods after expiration, termination, or cancellation of the lease contract.

(r) "Lien" means a charge against or interest in goods to secure payment of a debt or performance of an obligation, but the term does not include a security interest.

(s) "Lot" means a parcel or a single article that is the subject matter of a separate lease or delivery, whether or not it is sufficient to perform the lease contract.

(t) "Merchant lessee" means a lessee that is a merchant with respect to goods of the kind subject to the lease.

(u) "Present value" means the amount as of a date certain of one or more sums payable in the future, discounted to the date certain. The discount is determined by the interest rate specified by the parties if the rate was not manifestly unreasonable at the time the transaction was entered into; otherwise, the discount is determined by a commercially reasonable rate that takes into account the facts and circumstances of each case at the time the transaction was entered into.

(v) "Purchase" includes taking by sale, lease, mortgage, security interest, pledge, gift, or any other voluntary transaction creating an interest in goods.

(w) "Sublease" means a lease of goods the right to possession and use of which was acquired by the lessor as a lessee under an existing lease.

(x) "Supplier" means a person from whom a lessor buys or leases goods to be leased under a finance lease.

(y) "Supply contract" means a contract under which a lessor buys or leases goods to be leased.

(z) "Termination" occurs when either party pursuant to a power created by agreement or law puts an end to the lease contract otherwise than for default.

(2) Other definitions applying to this Article and the sections in which they appear are:

"Accessions". Section 2A–310(1).

"Construction mortgage". Section 2A–309(1)(d).

"Encumbrance". Section 2A–309(1)(e).

"Fixtures". Section 2A–309(1)(a).

"Fixture filing". Section 2A–309(1)(b).

"Purchase money lease". Section 2A–309(1)(c).

(3) The following definitions in other Articles apply to this Article:

"Accounts". Section 9–106.

"Between merchants". Section 2–104(3).

"Buyer". Section 2–103(1)(a).

"Chattel paper". Section 9–105(1)(b).

"Consumer goods". Section 9–109(1).

"Document". Section 9–105(1)(f).

"Entrusting". Section 2–403(3).

"General intangibles". Section 9–106.

"Good faith". Section 2–103(1)(b).

"Instrument". Section 9–105(1)(i).

"Merchant". Section 2–104(1).

"Mortgage". Section 9–105(1)(j).

"Pursuant to commitment". Section 9–105(1)(k).

"Receipt". Section 2–103(1)(c).

"Sale". Section 2–106(1).

"Sale on approval". Section 2–326.

"Sale or return". Section 2–326.

"Seller". Section 2–103(1)(d).

(4) In addition Article 1 contains general definitions and principles of construction and interpretation applicable throughout this Article.

As amended in 1990 and 1999.

§ 2A–104. Leases Subject to Other Law.

(1) A lease, although subject to this Article, is also subject to any applicable:

    (a) certificate of title statute of this State: (list any certificate of title statutes covering automobiles, trailers, mobile homes, boats, farm tractors, and the like);

    (b) certificate of title statute of another jurisdiction (Section 2A–105); or

    (c) consumer protection statute of this State, or final consumer protection decision of a court of this State existing on the effective date of this Article.

(2) In case of conflict between this Article, other than Sections 2A–105, 2A–304(3), and 2A–305(3), and a statute or decision referred to in subsection (1), the statute or decision controls.

(3) Failure to comply with an applicable law has only the effect specified therein.

As amended in 1990.

§ 2A–105. Territorial Application of Article to Goods Covered by Certificate of Title.

Subject to the provisions of Sections 2A–304(3) and 2A–305(3), with respect to goods covered by a certificate of title issued under a statute of this State or of another jurisdiction, compliance and the effect of compliance or noncompliance with a certificate of title statute are governed by the law (including the conflict of laws rules) of the jurisdiction issuing the certificate until the earlier of (a) surrender of the certificate, or (b) four months after the goods are removed from that jurisdiction and thereafter until a new certificate of title is issued by another jurisdiction.

§ 2A–106. Limitation on Power of Parties to Consumer Lease to Choose Applicable Law and Judicial Forum.

(1) If the law chosen by the parties to a consumer lease is that of a jurisdiction other than a jurisdiction in which the lessee resides at the time the lease agreement becomes enforceable or within 30 days thereafter or in which the goods are to be used, the choice is not enforceable.

(2) If the judicial forum chosen by the parties to a consumer lease is a forum that would not otherwise have jurisdiction over the lessee, the choice is not enforceable.

§ 2A–107. Waiver or Renunciation of Claim or Right After Default.

Any claim or right arising out of an alleged default or breach of warranty may be discharged in whole or in part without consideration by a written waiver or renunciation signed and delivered by the aggrieved party.

§ 2A–108. Unconscionability.

(1) If the court as a matter of law finds a lease contract or any clause of a lease contract to have been unconscionable at the time it was made the court may refuse to enforce the lease contract, or it may enforce the remainder of the lease contract without the unconscionable clause, or it may so limit the application of any unconscionable clause as to avoid any unconscionable result.

(2) With respect to a consumer lease, if the court as a matter of law finds that a lease contract or any clause of a lease contract has been induced by unconscionable conduct or that unconscionable conduct has occurred in the collection of a claim arising from a lease contract, the court may grant appropriate relief.

(3) Before making a finding of unconscionability under subsection (1) or (2), the court, on its own motion or that of a party, shall afford the parties a reasonable opportunity to present evidence as to the setting, purpose, and effect of the lease contract or clause thereof, or of the conduct.

(4) In an action in which the lessee claims unconscionability with respect to a consumer lease:

    (a) If the court finds unconscionability under subsection (1) or (2), the court shall award reasonable attorney's fees to the lessee.

    (b) If the court does not find unconscionability and the lessee claiming unconscionability has brought or maintained an action he [or she] knew to be groundless, the court shall award reasonable attorney's fees to the party against whom the claim is made.

(c) In determining attorney's fees, the amount of the recovery on behalf of the claimant under subsections (1) and (2) is not controlling.

§ 2A–109. Option to Accelerate at Will.

(1) A term providing that one party or his [or her] successor in interest may accelerate payment or performance or require collateral or additional collateral "at will" or "when he [or she] deems himself [or herself] insecure" or in words of similar import must be construed to mean that he [or she] has power to do so only if he [or she] in good faith believes that the prospect of payment or performance is impaired.

(2) With respect to a consumer lease, the burden of establishing good faith under subsection (1) is on the party who exercised the power; otherwise the burden of establishing lack of good faith is on the party against whom the power has been exercised.

Part 2 Formation and Construction of Lease Contract

§ 2A–201. Statute of Frauds.

(1) A lease contract is not enforceable by way of action or defense unless:

(a) the total payments to be made under the lease contract, excluding payments for options to renew or buy, are less than $1,000; or

(b) there is a writing, signed by the party against whom enforcement is sought or by that party's authorized agent, sufficient to indicate that a lease contract has been made between the parties and to describe the goods leased and the lease term.

(2) Any description of leased goods or of the lease term is sufficient and satisfies subsection (1)(b), whether or not it is specific, if it reasonably identifies what is described.

(3) A writing is not insufficient because it omits or incorrectly states a term agreed upon, but the lease contract is not enforceable under subsection (1)(b) beyond the lease term and the quantity of goods shown in the writing.

(4) A lease contract that does not satisfy the requirements of subsection (1), but which is valid in other respects, is enforceable:

(a) if the goods are to be specially manufactured or obtained for the lessee and are not suitable for lease or sale to others in the ordinary course of the lessor's business, and the lessor, before notice of repudiation is received and under circumstances that reasonably indicate that the goods are for the lessee, has made either a substantial beginning of their manufacture or commitments for their procurement;

(b) if the party against whom enforcement is sought admits in that party's pleading, testimony or otherwise

in court that a lease contract was made, but the lease contract is not enforceable under this provision beyond the quantity of goods admitted; or

(c) with respect to goods that have been received and accepted by the lessee.

(5) The lease term under a lease contract referred to in subsection (4) is:

(a) if there is a writing signed by the party against whom enforcement is sought or by that party's authorized agent specifying the lease term, the term so specified;

(b) if the party against whom enforcement is sought admits in that party's pleading, testimony, or otherwise in court a lease term, the term so admitted; or

(c) a reasonable lease term.

§ 2A–202. Final Written Expression: Parol or Extrinsic Evidence.

Terms with respect to which the confirmatory memoranda of the parties agree or which are otherwise set forth in a writing intended by the parties as a final expression of their agreement with respect to such terms as are included therein may not be contradicted by evidence of any prior agreement or of a contemporaneous oral agreement but may be explained or supplemented:

(a) by course of dealing or usage of trade or by course of performance; and

(b) by evidence of consistent additional terms unless the court finds the writing to have been intended also as a complete and exclusive statement of the terms of the agreement.

§ 2A–203. Seals Inoperative.

The affixing of a seal to a writing evidencing a lease contract or an offer to enter into a lease contract does not render the writing a sealed instrument and the law with respect to sealed instruments does not apply to the lease contract or offer.

§ 2A–204. Formation in General.

(1) A lease contract may be made in any manner sufficient to show agreement, including conduct by both parties which recognizes the existence of a lease contract.

(2) An agreement sufficient to constitute a lease contract may be found although the moment of its making is undetermined.

(3) Although one or more terms are left open, a lease contract does not fail for indefiniteness if the parties have intended to make a lease contract and there is a reasonably certain basis for giving an appropriate remedy.

§ 2A–205. Firm Offers.

An offer by a merchant to lease goods to or from another person in a signed writing that by its terms gives assurance it will be held open is not revocable, for lack of consideration, during the time stated or, if no time is stated, for a reasonable time, but in no event may the period of irrevocability exceed

3 months. Any such term of assurance on a form supplied by the offeree must be separately signed by the offeror.

§ 2A–206. **Offer and Acceptance in Formation of Lease Contract.**

(1) Unless otherwise unambiguously indicated by the language or circumstances, an offer to make a lease contract must be construed as inviting acceptance in any manner and by any medium reasonable in the circumstances.

(2) If the beginning of a requested performance is a reasonable mode of acceptance, an offeror who is not notified of acceptance within a reasonable time may treat the offer as having lapsed before acceptance.

§ 2A–207. **Course of Performance or Practical Construction.**

(1) If a lease contract involves repeated occasions for performance by either party with knowledge of the nature of the performance and opportunity for objection to it by the other, any course of performance accepted or acquiesced in without objection is relevant to determine the meaning of the lease agreement.

(2) The express terms of a lease agreement and any course of performance, as well as any course of dealing and usage of trade, must be construed whenever reasonable as consistent with each other; but if that construction is unreasonable, express terms control course of performance, course of performance controls both course of dealing and usage of trade, and course of dealing controls usage of trade.

(3) Subject to the provisions of Section 2A–208 on modification and waiver, course of performance is relevant to show a waiver or modification of any term inconsistent with the course of performance.

§ 2A–208. **Modification, Rescission and Waiver.**

(1) An agreement modifying a lease contract needs no consideration to be binding.

(2) A signed lease agreement that excludes modification or rescission except by a signed writing may not be otherwise modified or rescinded, but, except as between merchants, such a requirement on a form supplied by a merchant must be separately signed by the other party.

(3) Although an attempt at modification or rescission does not satisfy the requirements of subsection (2), it may operate as a waiver.

(4) A party who has made a waiver affecting an executory portion of a lease contract may retract the waiver by reasonable notification received by the other party that strict performance will be required of any term waived, unless the retraction would be unjust in view of a material change of position in reliance on the waiver.

§ 2A–209. **Lessee under Finance Lease as Beneficiary of Supply Contract.**

(1) The benefit of the supplier's promises to the lessor under the supply contract and of all warranties, whether express or implied, including those of any third party provided in connection with or as part of the supply contract, extends to the lessee to the extent of the lessee's leasehold interest under a finance lease related to the supply contract, but is subject to the terms warranty and of the supply contract and all defenses or claims arising therefrom.

(2) The extension of the benefit of supplier's promises and of warranties to the lessee (Section 2A–209(1)) does not: (i) modify the rights and obligations of the parties to the supply contract, whether arising therefrom or otherwise, or (ii) impose any duty or liability under the supply contract on the lessee.

(3) Any modification or rescission of the supply contract by the supplier and the lessor is effective between the supplier and the lessee unless, before the modification or rescission, the supplier has received notice that the lessee has entered into a finance lease related to the supply contract. If the modification or rescission is effective between the supplier and the lessee, the lessor is deemed to have assumed, in addition to the obligations of the lessor to the lessee under the lease contract, promises of the supplier to the lessor and warranties that were so modified or rescinded as they existed and were available to the lessee before modification or rescission.

(4) In addition to the extension of the benefit of the supplier's promises and of warranties to the lessee under subsection (1), the lessee retains all rights that the lessee may have against the supplier which arise from an agreement between the lessee and the supplier or under other law.

As amended in 1990.

§ 2A–210. **Express Warranties.**

(1) Express warranties by the lessor are created as follows:

   (a) Any affirmation of fact or promise made by the lessor to the lessee which relates to the goods and becomes part of the basis of the bargain creates an express warranty that the goods will conform to the affirmation or promise.

   (b) Any description of the goods which is made part of the basis of the bargain creates an express warranty that the goods will conform to the description.

   (c) Any sample or model that is made part of the basis of the bargain creates an express warranty that the whole of the goods will conform to the sample or model.

(2) It is not necessary to the creation of an express warranty that the lessor use formal words, such as "warrant" or "guarantee," or that the lessor have a specific intention to make a warranty, but an affirmation merely of the value of the goods or a statement purporting to be merely the lessor's opinion or commendation of the goods does not create a warranty.

§ 2A–211. **Warranties Against Interference and Against Infringement; Lessee's Obligation Against Infringement.**

(1) There is in a lease contract a warranty that for the lease term no person holds a claim to or interest in the goods that arose from an act or omission of the lessor, other than a claim by way of infringement or the like, which

will interfere with the lessee's enjoyment of its leasehold interest.

(2) Except in a finance lease there is in a lease contract by a lessor who is a merchant regularly dealing in goods of the kind a warranty that the goods are delivered free of the rightful claim of any person by way of infringement or the like.

(3) A lessee who furnishes specifications to a lessor or a supplier shall hold the lessor and the supplier harmless against any claim by way of infringement or the like that arises out of compliance with the specifications.

§ 2A–212. Implied Warranty of Merchantability.

(1) Except in a finance lease, a warranty that the goods will be merchantable is implied in a lease contract if the lessor is a merchant with respect to goods of that kind.

(2) Goods to be merchantable must be at least such as

(a) pass without objection in the trade under the description in the lease agreement;

(b) in the case of fungible goods, are of fair average quality within the description;

(c) are fit for the ordinary purposes for which goods of that type are used;

(d) run, within the variation permitted by the lease agreement, of even kind, quality, and quantity within each unit and among all units involved;

(e) are adequately contained, packaged, and labeled as the lease agreement may require; and

(f) conform to any promises or affirmations of fact made on the container or label.

(3) Other implied warranties may arise from course of dealing or usage of trade.

§ 2A–213. Implied Warranty of Fitness for Particular Purpose.

Except in a finance of lease, if the lessor at the time the lease contract is made has reason to know of any particular purpose for which the goods are required and that the lessee is relying on the lessor's skill or judgment to select or furnish suitable goods, there is in the lease contract an implied warranty that the goods will be fit for that purpose.

§ 2A–214. Exclusion or Modification of Warranties.

(1) Words or conduct relevant to the creation of an express warranty and words or conduct tending to negate or limit a warranty must be construed wherever reasonable as consistent with each other; but, subject to the provisions of Section 2A–202 on parol or extrinsic evidence, negation or limitation is inoperative to the extent that the construction is unreasonable.

(2) Subject to subsection (3), to exclude or modify the implied warranty of merchantability or any part of it the language must mention "merchantability", be by a writing, and be conspicuous. Subject to subsection (3), to exclude or modify any implied warranty of fitness the exclusion must be by a writing and be conspicuous. Language to exclude all implied warranties of fitness is sufficient if it is in writing, is conspicuous and states, for example, "There is no warranty that the goods will be fit for a particular purpose".

(3) Notwithstanding subsection (2), but subject to subsection (4),

(a) unless the circumstances indicate otherwise, all implied warranties are excluded by expressions like "as is" or "with all faults" or by other language that in common understanding calls the lessee's attention to the exclusion of warranties and makes plain that there is no implied warranty, if in writing and conspicuous;

(b) if the lessee before entering into the lease contract has examined the goods or the sample or model as fully as desired or has refused to examine the goods, there is no implied warranty with regard to defects that an examination ought in the circumstances to have revealed; and

(c) an implied warranty may also be excluded or modified by course of dealing, course of performance, or usage of trade.

(4) To exclude or modify a warranty against interference or against infringement (Section 2A–211) or any part of it, the language must be specific, be by a writing, and be conspicuous, unless the circumstances, including course of performance, course of dealing, or usage of trade, give the lessee reason to know that the goods are being leased subject to a claim or interest of any person.

§ 2A–215. Cumulation and Conflict of Warranties Express or Implied.

Warranties, whether express or implied, must be construed as consistent with each other and as cumulative, but if that construction is unreasonable, the intention of the parties determines which warranty is dominant. In ascertaining that intention the following rules apply:

(a) Exact or technical specifications displace an inconsistent sample or model or general language of description.

(b) A sample from an existing bulk displaces inconsistent general language of description.

(c) Express warranties displace inconsistent implied warranties other than an implied warranty of fitness for a particular purpose.

§ 2A–216. Third-Party Beneficiaries of Express and Implied Warranties.

Alternative A

A warranty to or for the benefit of a lessee under this Article, whether express or implied, extends to any natural person who is in the family or household of the lessee or who is a guest in the lessee's home if it is reasonable to expect that such person may use, consume, or be affected by the goods and who is injured in person by breach of the warranty. This section does not displace principles of law and equity that extend a warranty to or for the benefit of a lessee to other persons. The operation of this section may not be excluded, modified, or limited, but an exclusion, modification, or limitation of the warranty, including any with respect to rights and remedies, effective against the lessee is also effective against any beneficiary designated under this section.

Alternative B

A warranty to or for the benefit of a lessee under this Article, whether express or implied, extends to any natural person who may reasonably be expected to use, consume, or be affected by the goods and who is injured in person by breach of the warranty. This section does not displace principles of law and equity that extend a warranty to or for the benefit of a lessee to other persons. The operation of this section may not be excluded, modified, or limited, but an exclusion, modification, or limitation of the warranty, including any with respect to rights and remedies, effective against the lessee is also effective against the beneficiary designated under this section.

Alternative C

A warranty to or for the benefit of a lessee under this Article, whether express or implied, extends to any person who may reasonably be expected to use, consume, or be affected by the goods and who is injured by breach of the warranty. The operation of this section may not be excluded, modified, or limited with respect to injury to the person of an individual to whom the warranty extends, but an exclusion, modification, or limitation of the warranty, including any with respect to rights and remedies, effective against the lessee is also effective against the beneficiary designated under this section.

§ 2A–217. Identification.

Identification of goods as goods to which a lease contract refers may be made at any time and in any manner explicitly agreed to by the parties. In the absence of explicit agreement, identification occurs:

(a) when the lease contract is made if the lease contract is for a lease of goods that are existing and identified;

(b) when the goods are shipped, marked, or otherwise designated by the lessor as goods to which the lease contract refers, if the lease contract is for a lease of goods that are not existing and identified; or

(c) when the young are conceived, if the lease contract is for a lease of unborn young of animals.

§ 2A–218. Insurance and Proceeds.

(1) A lessee obtains an insurable interest when existing goods are identified to the lease contract even though the goods identified are nonconforming and the lessee has an option to reject them.

(2) If a lessee has an insurable interest only by reason of the lessor's identification of the goods, the lessor, until default or insolvency or notification to the lessee that identification is final, may substitute other goods for those identified.

(3) Notwithstanding a lessee's insurable interest under subsections (1) and (2), the lessor retains an insurable interest until an option to buy has been exercised by the lessee and risk of loss has passed to the lessee.

(4) Nothing in this section impairs any insurable interest recognized under any other statute or rule of law.

(5) The parties by agreement may determine that one or more parties have an obligation to obtain and pay for insurance covering the goods and by agreement may determine the beneficiary of the proceeds of the insurance.

§ 2A–219. Risk of Loss.

(1) Except in the case of a finance lease, risk of loss is retained by the lessor and does not pass to the lessee. In the case of a finance lease, risk of loss passes to the lessee.

(2) Subject to the provisions of this Article on the effect of default on risk of loss (Section 2A–220), if risk of loss is to pass to the lessee and the time of passage is not stated, the following rules apply:

(a) If the lease contract requires or authorizes the goods to be shipped by carrier

(i) and it does not require delivery at a particular destination, the risk of loss passes to the lessee when the goods are duly delivered to the carrier; but

(ii) if it does require delivery at a particular destination and the goods are there duly tendered while in the possession of the carrier, the risk of loss passes to the lessee when the goods are there duly so tendered as to enable the lessee to take delivery.

(b) If the goods are held by a bailee to be delivered without being moved, the risk of loss passes to the lessee on acknowledgment by the bailee of the lessee's right to possession of the goods.

(c) In any case not within subsection (a) or (b), the risk of loss passes to the lessee on the lessee's receipt of the goods if the lessor, or, in the case of a finance lease, the supplier, is a merchant; otherwise the risk passes to the lessee on tender of delivery.

§ 2A–220. Effect of Default on Risk of Loss.

(1) Where risk of loss is to pass to the lessee and the time of passage is not stated:

(a) If a tender or delivery of goods so fails to conform to the lease contract as to give a right of rejection, the risk of their loss remains with the lessor, or, in the case of a finance lease, the supplier, until cure or acceptance.

(b) If the lessee rightfully revokes acceptance, he [or she], to the extent of any deficiency in his [or her] effective insurance coverage, may treat the risk of loss as having remained with the lessor from the beginning.

(2) Whether or not risk of loss is to pass to the lessee, if the lessee as to conforming goods already identified to a lease contract repudiates or is otherwise in default under the

lease contract, the lessor, or, in the case of a finance lease, the supplier, to the extent of any deficiency in his [or her] effective insurance coverage may treat the risk of loss as resting on the lessee for a commercially reasonable time.

§ 2A–221. Casualty to Identified Goods.

If a lease contract requires goods identified when the lease contract is made, and the goods suffer casualty without fault of the lessee, the lessor or the supplier before delivery, or the goods suffer casualty before risk of loss passes to the lessee pursuant to the lease agreement or Section 2A–219, then:

(a) if the loss is total, the lease contract is avoided; and

(b) if the loss is partial or the goods have so deteriorated as to no longer conform to the lease contract, the lessee may nevertheless demand inspection and at his [or her] option either treat the lease contract as avoided or, except in a finance lease that is not a consumer lease, accept the goods with due allowance from the rent payable for the balance of the lease term for the deterioration or the deficiency in quantity but without further right against the lessor.

Part 3 Effect of Lease Contract

§ 2A–301. Enforceability of Lease Contract.

Except as otherwise provided in this Article, a lease contract is effective and enforceable according to its terms between the parties, against purchasers of the goods and against creditors of the parties.

§ 2A–302. Title to and Possession of Goods.

Except as otherwise provided in this Article, each provision of this Article applies whether the lessor or a third party has title to the goods, and whether the lessor, the lessee, or a third party has possession of the goods, notwithstanding any statute or rule of law that possession or the absence of possession is fraudulent.

§ 2A–303. Alienability of Party's Interest Under Lease Contract or of Lessor's Residual Interest in Goods; Delegation of Performance; Transfer of Rights.

(1) As used in this section, "creation of a security interest" includes the sale of a lease contract that is subject to Article 9, Secured Transactions, by reason of Section 9–109(a)(3).

(2) Except as provided in subsections (3) and Section 9–407, a provision in a lease agreement which (i) prohibits the voluntary or involuntary transfer, including a transfer by sale, sublease, creation or enforcement of a security interest, or attachment, levy, or other judicial process, of an interest of a party under the lease contract or of the lessor's residual interest in the goods, or (ii) makes such a transfer an event of default, gives rise to the rights and remedies provided in subsection (4), but a transfer that is prohibited or is an event of default under the lease agreement is otherwise effective.

(3) A provision in a lease agreement which (i) prohibits a transfer of a right to damages for default with respect to the whole lease contract or of a right to payment arising out of the transferor's due performance of the transferor's entire obligation, or (ii) makes such a transfer an event of default, is not enforceable, and such a transfer is not a transfer that materially impairs the propsect of obtaining return performance by, materially changes the duty of, or materially increases the burden or risk imposed on, the other party to the lease contract within the purview of subsection (4).

(4) Subject to subsection (3) and Section 9–407:

(a) if a transfer is made which is made an event of default under a lease agreement, the party to the lease contract not making the transfer, unless that party waives the default or otherwise agrees, has the rights and remedies described in Section 2A–501(2);

(b) if paragraph (a) is not applicable and if a transfer is made that (i) is prohibited under a lease agreement or (ii) materially impairs the prospect of obtaining return performance by, materially changes the duty of, or materially increases the burden or risk imposed on, the other party to the lease contract, unless the party not making the transfer agrees at any time to the transfer in the lease contract or otherwise, then, except as limited by contract, (i) the transferor is liable to the party not making the transfer for damages caused by the transfer to the extent that the damages could not reasonably be prevented by the party not making the transfer and (ii) a court having jurisdiction may grant other appropriate relief, including cancellation of the lease contract or an injunction against the transfer.

(5) A transfer of "the lease" or of "all my rights under the lease", or a transfer in similar general terms, is a transfer of rights and, unless the language or the circumstances, as in a transfer for security, indicate the contrary, the transfer is a delegation of duties by the transferor to the transferee. Acceptance by the transferee constitutes a promise by the transferee to perform those duties. The promise is enforceable by either the transferor or the other party to the lease contract.

(6) Unless otherwise agreed by the lessor and the lessee, a delegation of performance does not relieve the transferor as against the other party of any duty to perform or of any liability for default.

(7) In a consumer lease, to prohibit the transfer of an interest of a party under the lease contract or to make a transfer an event of default, the language must be specific, by a writing, and conspicuous.

As amended in 1990 and 1999.

§ 2A–304. Subsequent Lease of Goods by Lessor.

(1) Subject to Section 2A–303, a subsequent lessee from a lessor of goods under an existing lease contract obtains, to the extent of the leasehold interest transferred, the leasehold interest in the goods that the lessor had or had power to transfer, and except as provided in subsection (2) and Section 2A–527(4), takes subject to the existing lease contract. A lessor with voidable title has power to transfer a good leasehold interest to a good faith subsequent lessee

for value, but only to the extent set forth in the preceding sentence. If goods have been delivered under a transaction of purchase the lessor has that power even though:

(a) the lessor's transferor was deceived as to the identity of the lessor;

(b) the delivery was in exchange for a check which is later dishonored;

(c) it was agreed that the transaction was to be a "cash sale"; or

(d) the delivery was procured through fraud punishable as larcenous under the criminal law.

(2) A subsequent lessee in the ordinary course of business from a lessor who is a merchant dealing in goods of that kind to whom the goods were entrusted by the existing lessee of that lessor before the interest of the subsequent lessee became enforceable against that lessor obtains, to the extent of the leasehold interest transferred, all of that lessor's and the existing lessee's rights to the goods, and takes free of the existing lease contract.

(3) A subsequent lessee from the lessor of goods that are subject to an existing lease contract and are covered by a certificate of title issued under a statute of this State or of another jurisdiction takes no greater rights than those provided both by this section and by the certificate of title statute.

As amended in 1990.

§ 2A–305. Sale or Sublease of Goods by Lessee.

(1) Subject to the provisions of Section 2A–303, a buyer or sublessee from the lessee of goods under an existing lease contract obtains, to the extent of the interest transferred, the leasehold interest in the goods that the lessee had or had power to transfer, and except as provided in subsection (2) and Section 2A–511(4), takes subject to the existing lease contract. A lessee with a voidable leasehold interest has power to transfer a good leasehold interest to a good faith buyer for value or a good faith sublessee for value, but only to the extent set forth in the preceding sentence. When goods have been delivered under a transaction of lease the lessee has that power even though:

(a) the lessor was deceived as to the identity of the lessee;

(b) the delivery was in exchange for a check which is later dishonored; or

(c) the delivery was procured through fraud punishable as larcenous under the criminal law.

(2) A buyer in the ordinary course of business or a sublessee in the ordinary course of business from a lessee who is a merchant dealing in goods of that kind to whom the goods were entrusted by the lessor obtains, to the extent of the interest transferred, all of the lessor's and lessee's rights to the goods, and takes free of the existing lease contract.

(3) A buyer or sublessee from the lessee of goods that are subject to an existing lease contract and are covered by a certificate of title issued under a statute of this State or of another jurisdiction takes no greater rights than those provided both by this section and by the certificate of title statute.

§ 2A–306. Priority of Certain Liens Arising by Operation of Law.

If a person in the ordinary course of his [or her] business furnishes services or materials with respect to goods subject to a lease contract, a lien upon those goods in the possession of that person given by statute or rule of law for those materials or services takes priority over any interest of the lessor or lessee under the lease contract or this Article unless the lien is created by statute and the statute provides otherwise or unless the lien is created by rule of law and the rule of law provides otherwise.

§ 2A–307. Priority of Liens Arising by Attachment or Levy on, Security Interests in, and Other Claims to Goods.

(1) Except as otherwise provided in Section 2A–306, a creditor of a lessee takes subject to the lease contract.

(2) Except as otherwise provided in subsection (3) and in Sections 2A–306 and 2A–308, a creditor of a lessor takes subject to the lease contract unless the creditor holds a lien that attached to the goods before the lease contract became enforceable.

(3) Except as otherwise provided in Sections 9–317, 9–321, and 9–323, a lessee takes a leasehold interest subject to a security interest held by a creditor of the lessor.

As amended in 1990 and 1999.

§ 2A–308. Special Rights of Creditors.

(1) A creditor of a lessor in possession of goods subject to a lease contract may treat the lease contract as void if as against the creditor retention of possession by the lessor is fraudulent under any statute or rule of law, but retention of possession in good faith and current course of trade by the lessor for a commercially reasonable time after the lease contract becomes enforceable is not fraudulent.

(2) Nothing in this Article impairs the rights of creditors of a lessor if the lease contract (a) becomes enforceable, not in current course of trade but in satisfaction of or as security for a pre-existing claim for money, security, or the like, and (b) is made under circumstances which under any statute or rule of law apart from this Article would constitute the transaction a fraudulent transfer or voidable preference.

(3) A creditor of a seller may treat a sale or an identification of goods to a contract for sale as void if as against the creditor retention of possession by the seller is fraudulent under any statute or rule of law, but retention of possession of the goods pursuant to a lease contract entered into by the seller as lessee and the buyer as lessor in connection with the sale or identification of the goods is not fraudulent if the buyer bought for value and in good faith.

§ 2A–309. Lessor's and Lessee's Rights When Goods Become Fixtures.

(1) In this section:

(a) goods are "fixtures" when they become so related to particular real estate that an interest in them arises under real estate law;

(b) a "fixture filing" is the filing, in the office where a mortgage on the real estate would be filed or recorded, of a financing statement covering goods that are or are to become fixtures and conforming to the requirements of Section 9–502(a) and (b);

(c) a lease is a "purchase money lease" unless the lessee has possession or use of the goods or the right to possession or use of the goods before the lease agreement is enforceable;

(d) a mortgage is a "construction mortgage" to the extent it secures an obligation incurred for the construction of an improvement on land including the acquisition cost of the land, if the recorded writing so indicates; and

(e) "encumbrance" includes real estate mortgages and other liens on real estate and all other rights in real estate that are not ownership interests.

(2) Under this Article a lease may be of goods that are fixtures or may continue in goods that become fixtures, but no lease exists under this Article of ordinary building materials incorporated into an improvement on land.

(3) This Article does not prevent creation of a lease of fixtures pursuant to real estate law.

(4) The perfected interest of a lessor of fixtures has priority over a conflicting interest of an encumbrancer or owner of the real estate if:

(a) the lease is a purchase money lease, the conflicting interest of the encumbrancer or owner arises before the goods become fixtures, the interest of the lessor is perfected by a fixture filing before the goods become fixtures or within ten days thereafter, and the lessee has an interest of record in the real estate or is in possession of the real estate; or

(b) the interest of the lessor is perfected by a fixture filing before the interest of the encumbrancer or owner is of record, the lessor's interest has priority over any conflicting interest of a predecessor in title of the encumbrancer or owner, and the lessee has an interest of record in the real estate or is in possession of the real estate.

(5) The interest of a lessor of fixtures, whether or not perfected, has priority over the conflicting interest of an encumbrancer or owner of the real estate if:

(a) the fixtures are readily removable factory or office machines, readily removable equipment that is not primarily used or leased for use in the operation of the real estate, or readily removable replacements of domestic appliances that are goods subject to a consumer lease, and before the goods become fixtures the lease contract is enforceable; or

(b) the conflicting interest is a lien on the real estate obtained by legal or equitable proceedings after the lease contract is enforceable; or

(c) the encumbrancer or owner has consented in writing to the lease or has disclaimed an interest in the goods as fixtures; or

(d) the lessee has a right to remove the goods as against the encumbrancer or owner. If the lessee's right to remove terminates, the priority of the interest of the lessor continues for a reasonable time.

(6) Notwithstanding paragraph (4)(a) but otherwise subject to subsections (4) and (5), the interest of a lessor of fixtures, including the lessor's residual interest, is subordinate to the conflicting interest of an encumbrancer of the real estate under a construction mortgage recorded before the goods become fixtures if the goods become fixtures before the completion of the construction. To the extent given to refinance a construction mortgage, the conflicting interest of an encumbrancer of the real estate under a mortgage has this priority to the same extent as the encumbrancer of the real estate under the construction mortgage.

(7) In cases not within the preceding subsections, priority between the interest of a lessor of fixtures, including the lessor's residual interest, and the conflicting interest of an encumbrancer or owner of the real estate who is not the lessee is determined by the priority rules governing conflicting interests in real estate.

(8) If the interest of a lessor of fixtures, including the lessor's residual interest, has priority over all conflicting interests of all owners and encumbrancers of the real estate, the lessor or the lessee may (i) on default, expiration, termination, or cancellation of the lease agreement but subject to the agreement and this Article, or (ii) if necessary to enforce other rights and remedies of the lessor or lessee under this Article, remove the goods from the real estate, free and clear of all conflicting interests of all owners and encumbrancers of the real estate, but the lessor or lessee must reimburse any encumbrancer or owner of the real estate who is not the lessee and who has not otherwise agreed for the cost of repair of any physical injury, but not for any diminution in value of the real estate caused by the absence of the goods removed or by any necessity of replacing them. A person entitled to reimbursement may refuse permission to remove until the party seeking removal gives adequate security for the performance of this obligation.

(9) Even though the lease agreement does not create a security interest, the interest of a lessor of fixtures, including the lessor's residual interest, is perfected by filing a financing statement as a fixture filing for leased goods that are or are to become fixtures in accordance with the relevant provisions of the Article on Secured Transactions (Article 9).

As amended in 1990 and 1999.

§ 2A–310. Lessor's and Lessee's Rights When Goods Become Accessions.

(1) Goods are "accessions" when they are installed in or affixed to other goods.

(2) The interest of a lessor or a lessee under a lease contract entered into before the goods became accessions is superior to all interests in the whole except as stated in subsection (4).

(3) The interest of a lessor or a lessee under a lease contract entered into at the time or after the goods became accessions is superior to all subsequently acquired interests in the

whole except as stated in subsection (4) but is subordinate to interests in the whole existing at the time the lease contract was made unless the holders of such interests in the whole have in writing consented to the lease or disclaimed an interest in the goods as part of the whole.

(4) The interest of a lessor or a lessee under a lease contract described in subsection (2) or (3) is subordinate to the interest of

(a) a buyer in the ordinary course of business or a lessee in the ordinary course of business of any interest in the whole acquired after the goods became accessions; or

(b) a creditor with a security interest in the whole perfected before the lease contract was made to the extent that the creditor makes subsequent advances without knowledge of the lease contract.

(5) When under subsections (2) or (3) and (4) a lessor or a lessee of accessions holds an interest that is superior to all interests in the whole, the lessor or the lessee may (a) on default, expiration, termination, or cancellation of the lease contract by the other party but subject to the provisions of the lease contract and this Article, or (b) if necessary to enforce his [or her] other rights and remedies under this Article, remove the goods from the whole, free and clear of all interests in the whole, but he [or she] must reimburse any holder of an interest in the whole who is not the lessee and who has not otherwise agreed for the cost of repair of any physical injury but not for any diminution in value of the whole caused by the absence of the goods removed or by any necessity for replacing them. A person entitled to reimbursement may refuse permission to remove until the party seeking removal gives adequate security for the performance of this obligation.

§ 2A–311. Priority Subject to Subordination.

Nothing in this Article prevents subordination by agreement by any person entitled to priority.

As added in 1990.

Part 4 Performance of Lease Contract: Repudiated, Substituted and Excused

§ 2A–401. Insecurity: Adequate Assurance of Performance.

(1) A lease contract imposes an obligation on each party that the other's expectation of receiving due performance will not be impaired.

(2) If reasonable grounds for insecurity arise with respect to the performance of either party, the insecure party may demand in writing adequate assurance of due performance. Until the insecure party receives that assurance, if commercially reasonable the insecure party may suspend any performance for which he [or she] has not already received the agreed return.

(3) A repudiation of the lease contract occurs if assurance of due performance adequate under the circumstances of the particular case is not provided to the insecure party within a reasonable time, not to exceed 30 days after receipt of a demand by the other party.

(4) Between merchants, the reasonableness of grounds for insecurity and the adequacy of any assurance offered must be determined according to commercial standards.

(5) Acceptance of any nonconforming delivery or payment does not prejudice the aggrieved party's right to demand adequate assurance of future performance.

§ 2A–402. Anticipatory Repudiation.

If either party repudiates a lease contract with respect to a performance not yet due under the lease contract, the loss of which performance will substantially impair the value of the lease contract to the other, the aggrieved party may:

(a) for a commercially reasonable time, await retraction of repudiation and performance by the repudiating party;

(b) make demand pursuant to Section 2A–401 and await assurance of future performance adequate under the circumstances of the particular case; or

(c) resort to any right or remedy upon default under the lease contract or this Article, even though the aggrieved party has notified the repudiating party that the aggrieved party would await the repudiating party's performance and assurance and has urged retraction. In addition, whether or not the aggrieved party is pursuing one of the foregoing remedies, the aggrieved party may suspend performance or, if the aggrieved party is the lessor, proceed in accordance with the provisions of this Article on the lessor's right to identify goods to the lease contract notwithstanding default or to salvage unfinished goods (Section 2A–524).

§ 2A–403. Retraction of Anticipatory Repudiation.

(1) Until the repudiating party's next performance is due, the repudiating party can retract the repudiation unless, since the repudiation, the aggrieved party has cancelled the lease contract or materially changed the aggrieved party's position or otherwise indicated that the aggrieved party considers the repudiation final.

(2) Retraction may be by any method that clearly indicates to the aggrieved party that the repudiating party intends to perform under the lease contract and includes any assurance demanded under Section 2A–401.

(3) Retraction reinstates a repudiating party's rights under a lease contract with due excuse and allowance to the aggrieved party for any delay occasioned by the repudiation.

§ 2A–404. Substituted Performance.

(1) If without fault of the lessee, the lessor and the supplier, the agreed berthing, loading, or unloading facilities fail or the agreed type of carrier becomes unavailable or the agreed manner of delivery otherwise becomes commercially impracticable, but a commercially reasonable substitute is available, the substitute performance must be tendered and accepted.

(2) If the agreed means or manner of payment fails because of domestic or foreign governmental regulation:

(a) the lessor may withhold or stop delivery or cause the supplier to withhold or stop delivery unless the lessee provides a means or manner of payment that is commercially a substantial equivalent; and

(b) if delivery has already been taken, payment by the means or in the manner provided by the regulation discharges the lessee's obligation unless the regulation is discriminatory, oppressive, or predatory.

§ 2A–405. Excused Performance.

Subject to Section 2A–404 on substituted performance, the following rules apply:

(a) Delay in delivery or nondelivery in whole or in part by a lessor or a supplier who complies with paragraphs (b) and (c) is not a default under the lease contract if performance as agreed has been made impracticable by the occurrence of a contingency the nonoccurrence of which was a basic assumption on which the lease contract was made or by compliance in good faith with any applicable foreign or domestic governmental regulation or order, whether or not the regulation or order later proves to be invalid.

(b) If the causes mentioned in paragraph (a) affect only part of the lessor's or the supplier's capacity to perform, he [or she] shall allocate production and deliveries among his [or her] customers but at his [or her] option may include regular customers not then under contract for sale or lease as well as his [or her] own requirements for further manufacture. He [or she] may so allocate in any manner that is fair and reasonable.

(c) The lessor seasonally shall notify the lessee and in the case of a finance lease the supplier seasonally shall notify the lessor and the lessee, if known, that there will be delay or nondelivery and, if allocation is required under paragraph (b), of the estimated quota thus made available for the lessee.

§ 2A–406. Procedure on Excused Performance.

(1) If the lessee receives notification of a material or indefinite delay or an allocation justified under Section 2A–405, the lessee may by written notification to the lessor as to any goods involved, and with respect to all of the goods if under an installment lease contract the value of the whole lease contract is substantially impaired (Section 2A–510):

    (a) terminate the lease contract (Section 2A–505(2)); or

    (b) except in a finance lease that is not a consumer lease, modify the lease contract by accepting the available quota in substitution, with due allowance from the rent payable for the balance of the lease term for the deficiency but without further right against the lessor.

(2) If, after receipt of a notification from the lessor under Section 2A–405, the lessee fails so to modify the lease agreement within a reasonable time not exceeding 30 days, the lease contract lapses with respect to any deliveries affected.

§ 2A–407. Irrevocable Promises: Finance Leases.

(1) In the case of a finance lease that is not a consumer lease the lessee's promises under the lease contract become irrevocable and independent upon the lessee's acceptance of the goods.

(2) A promise that has become irrevocable and independent under subsection (1):

(a) is effective and enforceable between the parties, and by or against third parties including assignees of the parties, and

(b) is not subject to cancellation, termination, modification, repudiation, excuse, or substitution without the consent of the party to whom the promise runs.

(3) This section does not affect the validity under any other law of a covenant in any lease contract making the lessee's promises irrevocable and independent upon the lessee's acceptance of the goods.

As amended in 1990.

Part 5 Default

A. In General

§ 2A–501. Default: Procedure.

(1) Whether the lessor or the lessee is in default under a lease contract is determined by the lease agreement and this Article.

(2) If the lessor or the lessee is in default under the lease contract, the party seeking enforcement has rights and remedies as provided in this Article and, except as limited by this Article, as provided in the lease agreement.

(3) If the lessor or the lessee is in default under the lease contract, the party seeking enforcement may reduce the party's claim to judgment, or otherwise enforce the lease contract by self-help or any available judicial procedure or nonjudicial procedure, including administrative proceeding, arbitration, or the like, in accordance with this Article.

(4) Except as otherwise provided in Section 1–106(1) or this Article or the lease agreement, the rights and remedies referred to in subsections (2) and (3) are cumulative.

(5) If the lease agreement covers both real property and goods, the party seeking enforcement may proceed under this Part as to the goods, or under other applicable law as to both the real property and the goods in accordance with that party's rights and remedies in respect of the real property, in which case this Part does not apply.

As amended in 1990.

§ 2A–502. Notice After Default.

Except as otherwise provided in this Article or the lease agreement, the lessor or lessee in default under the lease contract is not entitled to notice of default or notice of enforcement from the other party to the lease agreement.

§ 2A–503. Modification or Impairment of Rights and Remedies.

(1) Except as otherwise provided in this Article, the lease agreement may include rights and remedies for default in addition to or in substitution for those provided in this Article and may limit or alter the measure of damages recoverable under this Article.

(2) Resort to a remedy provided under this Article or in the lease agreement is optional unless the remedy is expressly

agreed to be exclusive. If circumstances cause an exclusive or limited remedy to fail of its essential purpose, or provision for an exclusive remedy is unconscionable, remedy may be had as provided in this Article.

(3) Consequential damages may be liquidated under Section 2A–504, or may otherwise be limited, altered, or excluded unless the limitation, alteration, or exclusion is unconscionable. Limitation, alteration, or exclusion of consequential damages for injury to the person in the case of consumer goods is *prima facie* unconscionable but limitation, alteration, or exclusion of damages where the loss is commercial is not *prima facie* unconscionable.

(4) Rights and remedies on default by the lessor or the lessee with respect to any obligation or promise collateral or ancillary to the lease contract are not impaired by this Article.

As amended in 1990.

§ 2A–504. Liquidation of Damages.

(1) Damages payable by either party for default, or any other act or omission, including indemnity for loss or diminution of anticipated tax benefits or loss or damage to lessor's residual interest, may be liquidated in the lease agreement but only at an amount or by a formula that is reasonable in light of the then anticipated harm caused by the default or other act or omission.

(2) If the lease agreement provides for liquidation of damages, and such provision does not comply with subsection (1), or such provision is an exclusive or limited remedy that circumstances cause to fail of its essential purpose, remedy may be had as provided in this Article.

(3) If the lessor justifiably withholds or stops delivery of goods because of the lessee's default or insolvency (Section 2A–525 or 2A–526), the lessee is entitled to restitution of any amount by which the sum of his [or her] payments exceeds:

   (a) the amount to which the lessor is entitled by virtue of terms liquidating the lessor's damages in accordance with subsection (1); or

   (b) in the absence of those terms, 20 percent of the then present value of the total rent the lessee was obligated to pay for the balance of the lease term, or, in the case of a consumer lease, the lesser of such amount or $500.

(4) A lessee's right to restitution under subsection (3) is subject to offset to the extent the lessor establishes:

   (a) a right to recover damages under the provisions of this Article other than subsection (1); and

   (b) the amount or value of any benefits received by the lessee directly or indirectly by reason of the lease contract.

§ 2A–505. Cancellation and Termination and Effect of Cancellation, Termination, Rescission, or Fraud on Rights and Remedies.

(1) On cancellation of the lease contract, all obligations that are still executory on both sides are discharged, but any right based on prior default or performance survives, and the cancelling party also retains any remedy for default of the whole lease contract or any unperformed balance.

(2) On termination of the lease contract, all obligations that are still executory on both sides are discharged but any right based on prior default or performance survives.

(3) Unless the contrary intention clearly appears, expressions of "cancellation," "rescission," or the like of the lease contract may not be construed as a renunciation or discharge of any claim in damages for an antecedent default.

(4) Rights and remedies for material misrepresentation or fraud include all rights and remedies available under this Article for default.

(5) Neither rescission nor a claim for rescission of the lease contract nor rejection or return of the goods may bar or be deemed inconsistent with a claim for damages or other right or remedy.

§ 2A–506. Statute of Limitations.

(1) An action for default under a lease contract, including breach of warranty or indemnity, must be commenced within 4 years after the cause of action accrued. By the original lease contract the parties may reduce the period of limitation to not less than one year.

(2) A cause of action for default accrues when the act or omission on which the default or breach of warranty is based is or should have been discovered by the aggrieved party, or when the default occurs, whichever is later. A cause of action for indemnity accrues when the act or omission on which the claim for indemnity is based is or should have been discovered by the indemnified party, whichever is later.

(3) If an action commenced within the time limited by subsection (1) is so terminated as to leave available a remedy by another action for the same default or breach of warranty or indemnity, the other action may be commenced after the expiration of the time limited and within 6 months after the termination of the first action unless the termination resulted from voluntary discontinuance or from dismissal for failure or neglect to prosecute.

(4) This section does not alter the law on tolling of the statute of limitations nor does it apply to causes of action that have accrued before this Article becomes effective.

§ 2A–507. Proof of Market Rent: Time and Place.

(1) Damages based on market rent (Section 2A–519 or 2A–528) are determined according to the rent for the use of the goods concerned for a lease term identical to the remaining lease term of the original lease agreement and prevailing at the times specified in Sections 2A–519 and 2A–528.

(2) If evidence of rent for the use of the goods concerned for a lease term identical to the remaining lease term of the original lease agreement and prevailing at the times or places described in this Article is not readily available, the rent prevailing within any reasonable time before or after the time described or at any other place or for a different

lease term which in commercial judgment or under usage of trade would serve as a reasonable substitute for the one described may be used, making any proper allowance for the difference, including the cost of transporting the goods to or from the other place.

(3) Evidence of a relevant rent prevailing at a time or place or for a lease term other than the one described in this Article offered by one party is not admissible unless and until he [or she] has given the other party notice the court finds sufficient to prevent unfair surprise.

(4) If the prevailing rent or value of any goods regularly leased in any established market is in issue, reports in official publications or trade journals or in newspapers or periodicals of general circulation published as the reports of that market are admissible in evidence. The circumstances of the preparation of the report may be shown to affect its weight but not its admissibility.

As amended in 1990.

B. Default by Lessor

§ 2A–508. Lessee's Remedies.

(1) If a lessor fails to deliver the goods in conformity to the lease contract (Section 2A–509) or repudiates the lease contract (Section 2A–402), or a lessee rightfully rejects the goods (Section 2A–509) or justifiably revokes acceptance of the goods (Section 2A–517), then with respect to any goods involved, and with respect to all of the goods if under an installment lease contract the value of the whole lease contract is substantially impaired (Section 2A–510), the lessor is in default under the lease contract and the lessee may:

    (a) cancel the lease contract (Section 2A–505(1));

    (b) recover so much of the rent and security as has been paid and is just under the circumstances;

    (c) cover and recover damages as to all goods affected whether or not they have been identified to the lease contract (Sections 2A–518 and 2A–520), or recover damages for nondelivery (Sections 2A–519 and 2A–520);

    (d) exercise any other rights or pursue any other remedies provided in the lease contract.

(2) If a lessor fails to deliver the goods in conformity to the lease contract or repudiates the lease contract, the lessee may also:

    (a) if the goods have been identified, recover them (Section 2A–522); or

    (b) in a proper case, obtain specific performance or replevy the goods (Section 2A–521).

(3) If a lessor is otherwise in default under a lease contract, the lessee may exercise the rights and pursue the remedies provided in the lease contract, which may include a right to cancel the lease, and in Section 2A–519(3).

(4) If a lessor has breached a warranty, whether express or implied, the lessee may recover damages (Section 2A–519(4)).

(5) On rightful rejection or justifiable revocation of acceptance, a lessee has a security interest in goods in the lessee's possession or control for any rent and security that has been paid and any expenses reasonably incurred in their inspection, receipt, transportation, and care and custody and may hold those goods and dispose of them in good faith and in a commercially reasonable manner, subject to Section 2A–527(5).

(6) Subject to the provisions of Section 2A–407, a lessee, on notifying the lessor of the lessee's intention to do so, may deduct all or any part of the damages resulting from any default under the lease contract from any part of the rent still due under the same lease contract.

As amended in 1990.

§ 2A–509. Lessee's Rights on Improper Delivery; Rightful Rejection.

(1) Subject to the provisions of Section 2A–510 on default in installment lease contracts, if the goods or the tender or delivery fail in any respect to conform to the lease contract, the lessee may reject or accept the goods or accept any commercial unit or units and reject the rest of the goods.

(2) Rejection of goods is ineffective unless it is within a reasonable time after tender or delivery of the goods and the lessee seasonably notifies the lessor.

§ 2A–510. Installment Lease Contracts: Rejection and Default.

(1) Under an installment lease contract a lessee may reject any delivery that is nonconforming if the nonconformity substantially impairs the value of that delivery and cannot be cured or the nonconformity is a defect in the required documents; but if the nonconformity does not fall within subsection (2) and the lessor or the supplier gives adequate assurance of its cure, the lessee must accept that delivery.

(2) Whenever nonconformity or default with respect to one or more deliveries substantially impairs the value of the installment lease contract as a whole there is a default with respect to the whole. But, the aggrieved party reinstates the installment lease contract as a whole if the aggrieved party accepts a nonconforming delivery without seasonably notifying of cancellation or brings an action with respect only to past deliveries or demands performance as to future deliveries.

§ 2A–511. Merchant Lessee's Duties as to Rightfully Rejected Goods.

(1) Subject to any security interest of a lessee (Section 2A–508(5)), if a lessor or a supplier has no agent or place of business at the market of rejection, a merchant lessee, after rejection of goods in his [or her] possession or control, shall follow any reasonable instructions received from the lessor or the supplier with respect to the goods. In the absence of those instructions, a merchant lessee shall make reasonable efforts to sell, lease, or otherwise dispose of the goods for the lessor's account if they threaten to decline in value speedily. Instructions are not reasonable if on demand indemnity for expenses is not forthcoming.

(2) If a merchant lessee (subsection (1)) or any other lessee (Section 2A–512) disposes of goods, he [or she] is entitled to reimbursement either from the lessor or the supplier or out of the proceeds for reasonable expenses of caring for and disposing of the goods and, if the expenses include no disposition commission, to such commission as is usual in the trade, or if there is none, to a reasonable sum not exceeding 10 percent of the gross proceeds.

(3) In complying with this section or Section 2A–512, the lessee is held only to good faith. Good faith conduct hereunder is neither acceptance or conversion nor the basis of an action for damages.

(4) A purchaser who purchases in good faith from a lessee pursuant to this section or Section 2A–512 takes the goods free of any rights of the lessor and the supplier even though the lessee fails to comply with one or more of the requirements of this Article.

§ 2A–512. Lessee's Duties as to Rightfully Rejected Goods.

(1) Except as otherwise provided with respect to goods that threaten to decline in value speedily (Section 2A–511) and subject to any security interest of a lessee (Section 2A–508(5)):

   (a) the lessee, after rejection of goods in the lessee's possession, shall hold them with reasonable care at the lessor's or the supplier's disposition for a reasonable time after the lessee's seasonable notification of rejection;

   (b) if the lessor or the supplier gives no instructions within a reasonable time after notification of rejection, the lessee may store the rejected goods for the lessor's or the supplier's account or ship them to the lessor or the supplier or dispose of them for the lessor's or the supplier's account with reimbursement in the manner provided in Section 2A–511; but

   (c) the lessee has no further obligations with regard to goods rightfully rejected.

(2) Action by the lessee pursuant to subsection (1) is not acceptance or conversion.

§ 2A–513. Cure by Lessor of Improper Tender or Delivery; Replacement.

(1) If any tender or delivery by the lessor or the supplier is rejected because nonconforming and the time for performance has not yet expired, the lessor or the supplier may seasonably notify the lessee of the lessor's or the supplier's intention to cure and may then make a conforming delivery within the time provided in the lease contract.

(2) If the lessee rejects a nonconforming tender that the lessor or the supplier had reasonable grounds to believe would be acceptable with or without money allowance, the lessor or the supplier may have a further reasonable time to substitute a conforming tender if he [or she] seasonably notifies the lessee.

§ 2A–514. Waiver of Lessee's Objections.

(1) In rejecting goods, a lessee's failure to state a particular defect that is ascertainable by reasonable inspection precludes the lessee from relying on the defect to justify rejection or to establish default:

   (a) if, stated seasonably, the lessor or the supplier could have cured it (Section 2A–513); or

   (b) between merchants if the lessor or the supplier after rejection has made a request in writing for a full and final written statement of all defects on which the lessee proposes to rely.

(2) A lessee's failure to reserve rights when paying rent or other consideration against documents precludes recovery of the payment for defects apparent on the face of the documents.

§ 2A–515. Acceptance of Goods.

(1) Acceptance of goods occurs after the lessee has had a reasonable opportunity to inspect the goods and

   (a) the lessee signifies or acts with respect to the goods in a manner that signifies to the lessor or the supplier that the goods are conforming or that the lessee will take or retain them in spite of their nonconformity; or

   (b) the lessee fails to make an effective rejection of the goods (Section 2A–509(2)).

(2) Acceptance of a part of any commercial unit is acceptance of that entire unit.

§ 2A–516. Effect of Acceptance of Goods; Notice of Default; Burden of Establishing Default after Acceptance; Notice of Claim or Litigation to Person Answerable Over.

(1) A lessee must pay rent for any goods accepted in accordance with the lease contract, with due allowance for goods rightfully rejected or not delivered.

(2) A lessee's acceptance of goods precludes rejection of the goods accepted. In the case of a finance lease, if made with knowledge of a nonconformity, acceptance cannot be revoked because of it. In any other case, if made with knowledge of a nonconformity, acceptance cannot be revoked because of it unless the acceptance was on the reasonable assumption that the nonconformity would be seasonably cured. Acceptance does not of itself impair any other remedy provided by this Article or the lease agreement for nonconformity.

(3) If a tender has been accepted:

   (a) within a reasonable time after the lessee discovers or should have discovered any default, the lessee shall notify the lessor and the supplier, if any, or be barred from any remedy against the party notified;

   (b) except in the case of a consumer lease, within a reasonable time after the lessee receives notice of litigation for infringement or the like (Section 2A–211) the lessee shall notify the lessor or be barred from any remedy over for liability established by the litigation; and

   (c) the burden is on the lessee to establish any default.

(4) If a lessee is sued for breach of a warranty or other obligation for which a lessor or a supplier is answerable over the following apply:

(a) The lessee may give the lessor or the supplier, or both, written notice of the litigation. If the notice states that the person notified may come in and defend and that if the person notified does not do so that person will be bound in any action against that person by the lessee by any determination of fact common to the two litigations, then unless the person notified after seasonable receipt of the notice does come in and defend that person is so bound.

(b) The lessor or the supplier may demand in writing that the lessee turn over control of the litigation including settlement if the claim is one for infringement or the like (Section 2A–211) or else be barred from any remedy over. If the demand states that the lessor or the supplier agrees to bear all expense and to satisfy any adverse judgment, then unless the lessee after seasonable receipt of the demand does turn over control the lessee is so barred.

(5) Subsections (3) and (4) apply to any obligation of a lessee to hold the lessor or the supplier harmless against infringement or the like (Section 2A–211).

As amended in 1990.

§ 2A–517. Revocation of Acceptance of Goods.

(1) A lessee may revoke acceptance of a lot or commercial unit whose nonconformity substantially impairs its value to the lessee if the lessee has accepted it:

(a) except in the case of a finance lease, on the reasonable assumption that its nonconformity would be cured and it has not been seasonably cured; or

(b) without discovery of the nonconformity if the lessee's acceptance was reasonably induced either by the lessor's assurances or, except in the case of a finance lease, by the difficulty of discovery before acceptance.

(2) Except in the case of a finance lease that is not a consumer lease, a lessee may revoke acceptance of a lot or commercial unit if the lessor defaults under the lease contract and the default substantially impairs the value of that lot or commercial unit to the lessee.

(3) If the lease agreement so provides, the lessee may revoke acceptance of a lot or commercial unit because of other defaults by the lessor.

(4) Revocation of acceptance must occur within a reasonable time after the lessee discovers or should have discovered the ground for it and before any substantial change in condition of the goods which is not caused by the nonconformity. Revocation is not effective until the lessee notifies the lessor.

(5) A lessee who so revokes has the same rights and duties with regard to the goods involved as if the lessee had rejected them.

As amended in 1990.

§ 2A–518. Cover; Substitute Goods.

(1) After a default by a lessor under the lease contract of the type described in Section 2A–508(1), or, if agreed, after other default by the lessor, the lessee may cover by making any purchase or lease of or contract to purchase or lease goods in substitution for those due from the lessor.

(2) Except as otherwise provided with respect to damages liquidated in the lease agreement (Section 2A–504) or otherwise determined pursuant to agreement of the parties (Sections 1–102(3) and 2A–503), if a lessee's cover is by lease agreement substantially similar to the original lease agreement and the new lease agreement is made in good faith and in a commercially reasonable manner, the lessee may recover from the lessor as damages (i) the present value, as of the date of the commencement of the term of the new lease agreement, of the rent under the new lease agreement applicable to that period of the new lease term which is comparable to the then remaining term of the original lease agreement minus the present value as of the same date of the total rent for the then remaining lease term of the original lease agreement, and (ii) any incidental or consequential damages, less expenses saved in consequence of the lessor's default.

(3) If a lessee's cover is by lease agreement that for any reason does not qualify for treatment under subsection (2), or is by purchase or otherwise, the lessee may recover from the lessor as if the lessee had elected not to cover and Section 2A–519 governs.

As amended in 1990.

§ 2A–519. Lessee's Damages for Non-Delivery, Repudiation, Default, and Breach of Warranty in Regard to Accepted Goods.

(1) Except as otherwise provided with respect to damages liquidated in the lease agreement (Section 2A–504) or otherwise determined pursuant to agreement of the parties (Sections 1–102(3) and 2A–503), if a lessee elects not to cover or a lessee elects to cover and the cover is by lease agreement that for any reason does not qualify for treatment under Section 2A–518(2), or is by purchase or otherwise, the measure of damages for non-delivery or repudiation by the lessor or for rejection or revocation of acceptance by the lessee is the present value, as of the date of the default, of the then market rent minus the present value as of the same date of the original rent, computed for the remaining lease term of the original lease agreement, together with incidental and consequential damages, less expenses saved in consequence of the lessor's default.

(2) Market rent is to be determined as of the place for tender or, in cases of rejection after arrival or revocation of acceptance, as of the place of arrival.

(3) Except as otherwise agreed, if the lessee has accepted goods and given notification (Section 2A–516(3)), the measure of damages for non-conforming tender or delivery or other default by a lessor is the loss resulting in the ordinary course of events from the lessor's default as determined

in any manner that is reasonable together with incidental and consequential damages, less expenses saved in consequence of the lessor's default.

(4) Except as otherwise agreed, the measure of damages for breach of warranty is the present value at the time and place of acceptance of the difference between the value of the use of the goods accepted and the value if they had been as warranted for the lease term, unless special circumstances show proximate damages of a different amount, together with incidental and consequential damages, less expenses saved in consequence of the lessor's default or breach of warranty.

As amended in 1990.

§ 2A–520. Lessee's Incidental and Consequential Damages.

(1) Incidental damages resulting from a lessor's default include expenses reasonably incurred in inspection, receipt, transportation, and care and custody of goods rightfully rejected or goods the acceptance of which is justifiably revoked, any commercially reasonable charges, expenses or commissions in connection with effecting cover, and any other reasonable expense incident to the default.

(2) Consequential damages resulting from a lessor's default include:

(a) any loss resulting from general or particular requirements and needs of which the lessor at the time of contracting had reason to know and which could not reasonably be prevented by cover or otherwise; and

(b) injury to person or property proximately resulting from any breach of warranty.

§ 2A–521. Lessee's Right to Specific Performance or Replevin.

(1) Specific performance may be decreed if the goods are unique or in other proper circumstances.

(2) A decree for specific performance may include any terms and conditions as to payment of the rent, damages, or other relief that the court deems just.

(3) A lessee has a right of replevin, detinue, sequestration, claim and delivery, or the like for goods identified to the lease contract if after reasonable effort the lessee is unable to effect cover for those goods or the circumstances reasonably indicate that the effort will be unavailing.

§ 2A–522. Lessee's Right to Goods on Lessor's Insolvency.

(1) Subject to subsection (2) and even though the goods have not been shipped, a lessee who has paid a part or all of the rent and security for goods identified to a lease contract (Section 2A–217) on making and keeping good a tender of any unpaid portion of the rent and security due under the lease contract may recover the goods identified from the lessor if the lessor becomes insolvent within 10 days after receipt of the first installment of rent and security.

(2) A lessee acquires the right to recover goods identified to a lease contract only if they conform to the lease contract.

C. Default by Lessee

§ 2A–523. Lessor's Remedies.

(1) If a lessee wrongfully rejects or revokes acceptance of goods or fails to make a payment when due or repudiates with respect to a part or the whole, then, with respect to any goods involved, and with respect to all of the goods if under an installment lease contract the value of the whole lease contract is substantially impaired (Section 2A–510), the lessee is in default under the lease contract and the lessor may:

(a) cancel the lease contract (Section 2A–505(1));

(b) proceed respecting goods not identified to the lease contract (Section 2A–524);

(c) withhold delivery of the goods and take possession of goods previously delivered (Section 2A–525);

(d) stop delivery of the goods by any bailee (Section 2A–526);

(e) dispose of the goods and recover damages (Section 2A–527), or retain the goods and recover damages (Section 2A–528), or in a proper case recover rent (Section 2A–529)

(f) exercise any other rights or pursue any other remedies provided in the lease contract.

(2) If a lessor does not fully exercise a right or obtain a remedy to which the lessor is entitled under subsection (1), the lessor may recover the loss resulting in the ordinary course of events from the lessee's default as determined in any reasonable manner, together with incidental damages, less expenses saved in consequence of the lessee's default.

(3) If a lessee is otherwise in default under a lease contract, the lessor may exercise the rights and pursue the remedies provided in the lease contract, which may include a right to cancel the lease. In addition, unless otherwise provided in the lease contract:

(a) if the default substantially impairs the value of the lease contract to the lessor, the lessor may exercise the rights and pursue the remedies provided in subsections (1) or (2); or

(b) if the default does not substantially impair the value of the lease contract to the lessor, the lessor may recover as provided in subsection (2).

As amended in 1990.

§ 2A–524. Lessor's Right to Identify Goods to Lease Contract.

(1) After default by the lessee under the lease contract of the type described in Section 2A–523(1) or 2A–523(3)(a) or, if agreed, after other default by the lessee, the lessor may:

(a) identify to the lease contract conforming goods not already identified if at the time the lessor learned of the default they were in the lessor's or the supplier's possession or control; and

(b) dispose of goods (Section 2A–527(1)) that demonstrably have been intended for the particular lease contract even though those goods are unfinished.

(2) If the goods are unfinished, in the exercise of reasonable commercial judgment for the purposes of avoiding loss and of effective realization, an aggrieved lessor or the supplier may either complete manufacture and wholly identify the goods to the lease contract or cease manufacture and lease, sell, or otherwise dispose of the goods for scrap or salvage value or proceed in any other reasonable manner.

As amended in 1990.

§ 2A–525. Lessor's Right to Possession of Goods.

(1) If a lessor discovers the lessee to be insolvent, the lessor may refuse to deliver the goods.

(2) After a default by the lessee under the lease contract of the type described in Section 2A–523(1) or 2A–523(3)(a) or, if agreed, after other default by the lessee, the lessor has the right to take possession of the goods. If the lease contract so provides, the lessor may require the lessee to assemble the goods and make them available to the lessor at a place to be designated by the lessor which is reasonably convenient to both parties. Without removal, the lessor may render unusable any goods employed in trade or business, and may dispose of goods on the lessee's premises (Section 2A–527).

(3) The lessor may proceed under subsection (2) without judicial process if that can be done without breach of the peace or the lessor may proceed by action.

As amended in 1990.

§ 2A–526. Lessor's Stoppage of Delivery in Transit or Otherwise.

(1) A lessor may stop delivery of goods in the possession of a carrier or other bailee if the lessor discovers the lessee to be insolvent and may stop delivery of carload, truckload, planeload, or larger shipments of express or freight if the lessee repudiates or fails to make a payment due before delivery, whether for rent, security or otherwise under the lease contract, or for any other reason the lessor has a right to withhold or take possession of the goods.

(2) In pursuing its remedies under subsection (1), the lessor may stop delivery until

(a) receipt of the goods by the lessee;

(b) acknowledgment to the lessee by any bailee of the goods, except a carrier, that the bailee holds the goods for the lessee; or

(c) such an acknowledgment to the lessee by a carrier via reshipment or as warehouseman.

(3) (a) To stop delivery, a lessor shall so notify as to enable the bailee by reasonable diligence to prevent delivery of the goods.

(b) After notification, the bailee shall hold and deliver the goods according to the directions of the lessor, but

the lessor is liable to the bailee for any ensuing charges or damages.

(c) A carrier who has issued a nonnegotiable bill of lading is not obliged to obey a notification to stop received from a person other than the consignor.

§ 2A–527. Lessor's Rights to Dispose of Goods.

(1) After a default by a lessee under the lease contract of the type described in Section 2A–523(1) or 2A–523(3)(a) or after the lessor refuses to deliver or takes possession of goods (Section 2A–525 or 2A–526), or, if agreed, after other default by a lessee, the lessor may dispose of the goods concerned or the undelivered balance thereof by lease, sale, or otherwise.

(2) Except as otherwise provided with respect to damages liquidated in the lease agreement (Section 2A–504) or otherwise determined pursuant to agreement of the parties (Sections 1–102(3) and 2A–503), if the disposition is by lease agreement substantially similar to the original lease agreement and the new lease agreement is made in good faith and in a commercially reasonable manner, the lessor may recover from the lessee as damages (i) accrued and unpaid rent as of the date of the commencement of the term of the new lease agreement, (ii) the present value, as of the same date, of the total rent for the then remaining lease term of the original lease agreement minus the present value, as of the same date, of the rent under the new lease agreement applicable to that period of the new lease term which is comparable to the then remaining term of the original lease agreement, and (iii) any incidental damages allowed under Section 2A–530, less expenses saved in consequence of the lessee's default.

(3) If the lessor's disposition is by lease agreement that for any reason does not qualify for treatment under subsection (2), or is by sale or otherwise, the lessor may recover from the lessee as if the lessor had elected not to dispose of the goods and Section 2A–528 governs.

(4) A subsequent buyer or lessee who buys or leases from the lessor in good faith for value as a result of a disposition under this section takes the goods free of the original lease contract and any rights of the original lessee even though the lessor fails to comply with one or more of the requirements of this Article.

(5) The lessor is not accountable to the lessee for any profit made on any disposition. A lessee who has rightfully rejected or justifiably revoked acceptance shall account to the lessor for any excess over the amount of the lessee's security interest (Section 2A–508(5)).

As amended in 1990.

§ 2A–528. Lessor's Damages for Non-acceptance, Failure to Pay, Repudiation, or Other Default.

(1) Except as otherwise provided with respect to damages liquidated in the lease agreement (Section 2A–504) or otherwise determined pursuant to agreement of the parties (Section 1–102(3) and 2A–503), if a lessor elects to retain the goods or a lessor elects to dispose of the goods and the

disposition is by lease agreement that for any reason does not qualify for treatment under Section 2A–527(2), or is by sale or otherwise, the lessor may recover from the lessee as damages for a default of the type described in Section 2A–523(1) or 2A–523(3)(a), or if agreed, for other default of the lessee, (i) accrued and unpaid rent as of the date of the default if the lessee has never taken possession of the goods, or, if the lessee has taken possession of the goods, as of the date the lessor repossesses the goods or an earlier date on which the lessee makes a tender of the goods to the lessor, (ii) the present value as of the date determined under clause (i) of the total rent for the then remaining lease term of the original lease agreement minus the present value as of the same date of the market rent as the place where the goods are located computed for the same lease term, and (iii) any incidental damages allowed under Section 2A–530, less expenses saved in consequence of the lessee's default.

(2) If the measure of damages provided in subsection (1) is inadequate to put a lessor in as good a position as performance would have, the measure of damages is the present value of the profit, including reasonable overhead, the lessor would have made from full performance by the lessee, together with any incidental damages allowed under Section 2A–530, due allowance for costs reasonably incurred and due credit for payments or proceeds of disposition.

As amended in 1990.

§ 2A–529. Lessor's Action for the Rent.

(1) After default by the lessee under the lease contract of the type described in Section 2A–523(1) or 2A–523(3)(a) or, if agreed, after other default by the lessee, if the lessor complies with subsection (2), the lessor may recover from the lessee as damages:

　　(a) for goods accepted by the lessee and not repossessed by or tendered to the lessor, and for conforming goods lost or damaged within a commercially reasonable time after risk of loss passes to the lessee (Section 2A–219), (i) accrued and unpaid rent as of the date of entry of judgment in favor of the lessor (ii) the present value as of the same date of the rent for the then remaining lease term of the lease agreement, and (iii) any incidental damages allowed under Section 2A–530, less expenses saved in consequence of the lessee's default; and

　　(b) for goods identified to the lease contract if the lessor is unable after reasonable effort to dispose of them at a reasonable price or the circumstances reasonably indicate that effort will be unavailing, (i) accrued and unpaid rent as of the date of entry of judgment in favor of the lessor, (ii) the present value as of the same date of the rent for the then remaining lease term of the lease agreement, and (iii) any incidental damages allowed under Section 2A–530, less expenses saved in consequence of the lessee's default.

(2) Except as provided in subsection (3), the lessor shall hold for the lessee for the remaining lease term of the lease agreement any goods that have been identified to the lease contract and are in the lessor's control.

(3) The lessor may dispose of the goods at any time before collection of the judgment for damages obtained pursuant to subsection (1). If the disposition is before the end of the remaining lease term of the lease agreement, the lessor's recovery against the lessee for damages is governed by Section 2A–527 or Section 2A–528, and the lessor will cause an appropriate credit to be provided against a judgment for damages to the extent that the amount of the judgment exceeds the recovery available pursuant to Section 2A–527 or 2A–528.

(4) Payment of the judgment for damages obtained pursuant to subsection (1) entitles the lessee to the use and possession of the goods not then disposed of for the remaining lease term of and in accordance with the lease agreement.

(5) After default by the lessee under the lease contract of the type described in Section 2A–523(1) or Section 2A–523(3)(a) or, if agreed, after other default by the lessee, a lessor who is held not entitled to rent under this section must nevertheless be awarded damages for non-acceptance under Sections 2A–527 and 2A–528.

As amended in 1990.

§ 2A–530. Lessor's Incidental Damages.

Incidental damages to an aggrieved lessor include any commercially reasonable charges, expenses, or commissions incurred in stopping delivery, in the transportation, care and custody of goods after the lessee's default, in connection with return or disposition of the goods, or otherwise resulting from the default.

§ 2A–531. Standing to Sue Third Parties for Injury to Goods.

(1) If a third party so deals with goods that have been identified to a lease contract as to cause actionable injury to a party to the lease contract (a) the lessor has a right of action against the third party, and (b) the lessee also has a right of action against the third party if the lessee:

　　(i) has a security interest in the goods;

　　(ii) has an insurable interest in the goods; or

　　(iii) bears the risk of loss under the lease contract or has since the injury assumed that risk as against the lessor and the goods have been converted or destroyed.

(2) If at the time of the injury the party plaintiff did not bear the risk of loss as against the other party to the lease contract and there is no arrangement between them for disposition of the recovery, his [or her] suit or settlement, subject to his [or her] own interest, is as a fiduciary for the other party to the lease contract.

(3) Either party with the consent of the other may sue for the benefit of whom it may concern.

§ 2A–532. Lessor's Rights to Residual Interest.

In addition to any other recovery permitted by this Article or other law, the lessor may recover from the lessee an amount that will fully compensate the lessor for any loss of or damage to the lessor's residual interest in the goods caused by the default of the lessee.

As added in 1990.

Revised Article 3
NEGOTIABLE INSTRUMENTS

Part 1 General Provisions and Definitions

§ 3–101. Short Title.

This Article may be cited as Uniform Commercial Code–Negotiable Instruments.

§ 3–102. Subject Matter.

(a) This Article applies to negotiable instruments. It does not apply to money, to payment orders governed by Article 4A, or to securities governed by Article 8.

(b) If there is conflict between this Article and Article 4 or 9, Articles 4 and 9 govern.

(c) Regulations of the Board of Governors of the Federal Reserve System and operating circulars of the Federal Reserve Banks supersede any inconsistent provision of this Article to the extent of the inconsistency.

§ 3–103. Definitions.

(a) In this Article:

(1) "Acceptor" means a drawee who has accepted a draft.

(2) "Drawee" means a person ordered in a draft to make payment.

(3) "Drawer" means a person who signs or is identified in a draft as a person ordering payment.

(4) "Good faith" means honesty in fact and the observance of reasonable commercial standards of fair dealing.

(5) "Maker" means a person who signs or is identified in a note as a person undertaking to pay.

(6) "Order" means a written instruction to pay money signed by the person giving the instruction. The instruction may be addressed to any person, including the person giving the instruction, or to one or more persons jointly or in the alternative but not in succession. An authorization to pay is not an order unless the person authorized to pay is also instructed to pay.

(7) "Ordinary care" in the case of a person engaged in business means observance of reasonable commercial standards, prevailing in the area in which the person is located, with respect to the business in which the person is engaged. In the case of a bank that takes an instrument for processing for collection or payment by automated means, reasonable commercial standards do not require the bank to examine the instrument if the failure to examine does not violate the bank's prescribed procedures and the bank's procedures do not vary unreasonably from general banking usage not disapproved by this Article or Article 4.

(8) "Party" means a party to an instrument.

(9) "Promise" means a written undertaking to pay money signed by the person undertaking to pay. An acknowledgment of an obligation by the obligor is not a promise unless the obligor also undertakes to pay the obligation.

(10) "Prove" with respect to a fact means to meet the burden of establishing the fact (Section 1–201(8)).

(11) "Remitter" means a person who purchases an instrument from its issuer if the instrument is payable to an identified person other than the purchaser.

(b) [Other definitions' section references deleted.]

(c) [Other definitions' section references deleted.]

(d) In addition, Article 1 contains general definitions and principles of construction and interpretation applicable throughout this Article.

§ 3–104. Negotiable Instrument.

(a) Except as provided in subsections (c) and (d), "negotiable instrument" means an unconditional promise or order to pay a fixed amount of money, with or without interest or other charges described in the promise or order, if it:

(1) is payable to bearer or to order at the time it is issued or first comes into possession of a holder;

(2) is payable on demand or at a definite time; and

(3) does not state any other undertaking or instruction by the person promising or ordering payment to do any act in addition to the payment of money, but the promise or order may contain (i) an undertaking or power to give, maintain, or protect collateral to secure payment, (ii) an authorization or power to the holder to confess judgment or realize on or dispose of collateral, or (iii) a waiver of the benefit of any law intended for the advantage or protection of an obligor.

(b) "Instrument" means a negotiable instrument.

(c) An order that meets all of the requirements of subsection (a), except paragraph (1), and otherwise falls within the definition of "check" in subsection (f) is a negotiable instrument and a check.

(d) A promise or order other than a check is not an instrument if, at the time it is issued or first comes into possession of a holder, it contains a conspicuous statement, however expressed, to the effect that the promise or order is not negotiable or is not an instrument governed by this Article.

(e) An instrument is a "note" if it is a promise and is a "draft" if it is an order. If an instrument falls within the definition of both "note" and "draft," a person entitled to enforce the instrument may treat it as either.

(f) "Check" means (i) a draft, other than a documentary draft, payable on demand and drawn on a bank or (ii) a cashier's check or teller's check. An instrument may be a check even though it is described on its face by another term, such as "money order."

(g) "Cashier's check" means a draft with respect to which the drawer and drawee are the same bank or branches of the same bank.

(h) "Teller's check" means a draft drawn by a bank (i) on another bank, or (ii) payable at or through a bank.

(i) "Traveler's check" means an instrument that (i) is payable on demand, (ii) is drawn on or payable at or through a bank, (iii) is designated by the term "traveler's check" or by a substantially similar term, and (iv) requires, as a condition to payment, a countersignature by a person whose specimen signature appears on the instrument.

(j) "Certificate of deposit" means an instrument containing an acknowledgment by a bank that a sum of money has been received by the bank and a promise by the bank to repay the sum of money. A certificate of deposit is a note of the bank.

§ 3–105. Issue of Instrument.

(a) "Issue" means the first delivery of an instrument by the maker or drawer, whether to a holder or nonholder, for the purpose of giving rights on the instrument to any person.

(b) An unissued instrument, or an unissued incomplete instrument that is completed, is binding on the maker or drawer, but nonissuance is a defense. An instrument that is conditionally issued or is issued for a special purpose is binding on the maker or drawer, but failure of the condition or special purpose to be fulfilled is a defense.

(c) "Issuer" applies to issued and unissued instruments and means a maker or drawer of an instrument.

§ 3–106. Unconditional Promise or Order.

(a) Except as provided in this section, for the purposes of Section 3–104(a), a promise or order is unconditional unless it states (i) an express condition to payment, (ii) that the promise or order is subject to or governed by another writing, or (iii) that rights or obligations with respect to the promise or order are stated in another writing. A reference to another writing does not of itself make the promise or order conditional.

(b) A promise or order is not made conditional (i) by a reference to another writing for a statement of rights with respect to collateral, prepayment, or acceleration, or (ii) because payment is limited to resort to a particular fund or source.

(c) If a promise or order requires, as a condition to payment, a countersignature by a person whose specimen signature appears on the promise or order, the condition does not make the promise or order conditional for the purposes of Section 3–104(a). If the person whose specimen signature appears on an instrument fails to countersign the instrument, the failure to countersign is a defense to the obligation of the issuer, but the failure does not prevent a transferee of the instrument from becoming a holder of the instrument.

(d) If a promise or order at the time it is issued or first comes into possession of a holder contains a statement, required by applicable statutory or administrative law, to the effect that the rights of a holder or transferee are subject to claims or defenses that the issuer could assert against the original payee, the promise or order is not thereby made conditional for the purposes of Section 3–104(a); but if the promise or order is an instrument, there cannot be a holder in due course of the instrument.

§ 3–107. Instrument Payable in Foreign Money.

Unless the instrument otherwise provides, an instrument that states the amount payable in foreign money may be paid in the foreign money or in an equivalent amount in dollars calculated by using the current bank-offered spot rate at the place of payment for the purchase of dollars on the day on which the instrument is paid.

§ 3–108. Payable on Demand or at Definite Time.

(a) A promise or order is "payable on demand" if it (i) states that it is payable on demand or at sight, or otherwise indicates that it is payable at the will of the holder, or (ii) does not state any time of payment.

(b) A promise or order is "payable at a definite time" if it is payable on elapse of a definite period of time after sight or acceptance or at a fixed date or dates or at a time or times readily ascertainable at the time the promise or order is issued, subject to rights of (i) prepayment, (ii) acceleration, (iii) extension at the option of the holder, or (iv) extension to a further definite time at the option of the maker or acceptor or automatically upon or after a specified act or event.

(c) If an instrument, payable at a fixed date, is also payable upon demand made before the fixed date, the instrument is payable on demand until the fixed date and, if demand for payment is not made before that date, becomes payable at a definite time on the fixed date.

§ 3–109. Payable to Bearer or to Order.

(a) A promise or order is payable to bearer if it:

(1) states that it is payable to bearer or to the order of bearer or otherwise indicates that the person in possession of the promise or order is entitled to payment;

(2) does not state a payee; or

(3) states that it is payable to or to the order of cash or otherwise indicates that it is not payable to an identified person.

(b) A promise or order that is not payable to bearer is payable to order if it is payable (i) to the order of an identified person or (ii) to an identified person or order. A promise or order that is payable to order is payable to the identified person.

(c) An instrument payable to bearer may become payable to an identified person if it is specially indorsed pursuant to Section 3–205(a). An instrument payable to an identified person may become payable to bearer if it is indorsed in blank pursuant to Section 3–205(b).

§ 3–110. Identification of Person to Whom Instrument Is Payable.

(a) The person to whom an instrument is initially payable is determined by the intent of the person, whether or not authorized, signing as, or in the name or behalf of, the issuer of the instrument. The instrument is payable to the person intended by the signer even if that person is identified in the instrument by a name or other identification that is not that of the intended person. If more than one person signs in the name or behalf of the issuer of an instrument and all the signers do not intend the same person as payee, the instrument is payable to any person intended by one or more of the signers.

(b) If the signature of the issuer of an instrument is made by automated means, such as a check-writing machine, the payee of the instrument is determined by the intent of the person who supplied the name or identification of the payee, whether or not authorized to do so.

(c) A person to whom an instrument is payable may be identified in any way, including by name, identifying number, office, or account number. For the purpose of determining the holder of an instrument, the following rules apply:

(1) If an instrument is payable to an account and the account is identified only by number, the instrument is payable to the person to whom the account is payable. If an instrument is payable to an account identified by number and by the name of a person, the instrument is payable to the named person, whether or not that person is the owner of the account identified by number.

(2) If an instrument is payable to:

(i) a trust, an estate, or a person described as trustee or representative of a trust or estate, the instrument is payable to the trustee, the representative, or a successor of either, whether or not the beneficiary or estate is also named;

(ii) a person described as agent or similar representative of a named or identified person, the instrument is payable to the represented person, the representative, or a successor of the representative;

(iii) a fund or organization that is not a legal entity, the instrument is payable to a representative of the members of the fund or organization; or

(iv) an office or to a person described as holding an office, the instrument is payable to the named person, the incumbent of the office, or a successor to the incumbent.

(d) If an instrument is payable to two or more persons alternatively, it is payable to any of them and may be negotiated, discharged, or enforced by any or all of them in possession of the instrument. If an instrument is payable to two or more persons not alternatively, it is payable to all of them and may be negotiated, discharged, or enforced only by all of them. If an instrument payable to two or more persons is ambiguous as to whether it is payable to the persons alternatively, the instrument is payable to the persons alternatively.

§ 3–111. Place of Payment.

Except as otherwise provided for items in Article 4, an instrument is payable at the place of payment stated in the instrument. If no place of payment is stated, an instrument is payable at the address of the drawee or maker stated in the instrument. If no address is stated, the place of payment is the place of business of the drawee or maker. If a drawee or maker has more than one place of business, the place of payment is any place of business of the drawee or maker chosen by the person entitled to enforce the instrument. If the drawee or maker has no place of business, the place of payment is the residence of the drawee or maker.

§ 3–112. Interest.

(a) Unless otherwise provided in the instrument, (i) an instrument is not payable with interest, and (ii) interest on an interest-bearing instrument is payable from the date of the instrument.

(b) Interest may be stated in an instrument as a fixed or variable amount of money or it may be expressed as a fixed or variable rate or rates. The amount or rate of interest may be stated or described in the instrument in any manner and may require reference to information not contained in the instrument. If an instrument provides for interest, but the amount of interest payable cannot be ascertained from the description, interest is payable at the judgment rate in effect at the place of payment of the instrument and at the time interest first accrues.

§ 3–113. Date of Instrument.

(a) An instrument may be antedated or postdated. The date stated determines the time of payment if the instrument is payable at a fixed period after date. Except as provided in Section 4–401(c), an instrument payable on demand is not payable before the date of the instrument.

(b) If an instrument is undated, its date is the date of its issue or, in the case of an unissued instrument, the date it first comes into possession of a holder.

§ 3–114. Contradictory Terms of Instrument.

If an instrument contains contradictory terms, typewritten terms prevail over printed terms, handwritten terms prevail over both, and words prevail over numbers.

§ 3–115. Incomplete Instrument.

(a) "Incomplete instrument" means a signed writing, whether or not issued by the signer, the contents of which show at the time of signing that it is incomplete but that the signer intended it to be completed by the addition of words or numbers.

(b) Subject to subsection (c), if an incomplete instrument is an instrument under Section 3–104, it may be enforced according to its terms if it is not completed, or according to its terms as augmented by completion. If an incomplete instrument is not an instrument under Section 3–104, but, after completion, the requirements of Section 3–104 are met, the instrument may be enforced according to its terms as augmented by completion.

(c) If words or numbers are added to an incomplete instrument without authority of the signer, there is an alteration of the incomplete instrument under Section 3–407.

(d) The burden of establishing that words or numbers were added to an incomplete instrument without authority of the signer is on the person asserting the lack of authority.

§ 3–116. Joint and Several Liability; Contribution.

(a) Except as otherwise provided in the instrument, two or more persons who have the same liability on an instrument as makers, drawers, acceptors, indorsers who indorse as joint payees, or anomalous indorsers are jointly and severally liable in the capacity in which they sign.

(b) Except as provided in Section 3–419(e) or by agreement of the affected parties, a party having joint and several liability who pays the instrument is entitled to receive from any party having the same joint and several liability contribution in accordance with applicable law.

(c) Discharge of one party having joint and several liability by a person entitled to enforce the instrument does not affect the right under subsection (b) of a party having the same joint and several liability to receive contribution from the party discharged.

§ 3–117. Other Agreements Affecting Instrument.

Subject to applicable law regarding exclusion of proof of contemporaneous or previous agreements, the obligation of a party to an instrument to pay the instrument may be modified, supplemented, or nullified by a separate agreement of the obligor and a person entitled to enforce the instrument, if the instrument is issued or the obligation is incurred in reliance on the agreement or as part of the same transaction giving rise to the agreement. To the extent an obligation is modified, supplemented, or nullified by an agreement under this section, the agreement is a defense to the obligation.

§ 3–118. Statute of Limitations.

(a) Except as provided in subsection (e), an action to enforce the obligation of a party to pay a note payable at a definite time must be commenced within six years after the due date or dates stated in the note or, if a due date is accelerated, within six years after the accelerated due date.

(b) Except as provided in subsection (d) or (e), if demand for payment is made to the maker of a note payable on demand, an action to enforce the obligation of a party to pay the note must be commenced within six years after the demand. If no demand for payment is made to the maker, an action to enforce the note is barred if neither principal nor interest on the note has been paid for a continuous period of 10 years.

(c) Except as provided in subsection (d), an action to enforce the obligation of a party to an unaccepted draft to pay the draft must be commenced within three years after dishonor

of the draft or 10 years after the date of the draft, whichever period expires first.

(d) An action to enforce the obligation of the acceptor of a certified check or the issuer of a teller's check, cashier's check, or traveler's check must be commenced within three years after demand for payment is made to the acceptor or issuer, as the case may be.

(e) An action to enforce the obligation of a party to a certificate of deposit to pay the instrument must be commenced within six years after demand for payment is made to the maker, but if the instrument states a due date and the maker is not required to pay before that date, the six-year period begins when a demand for payment is in effect and the due date has passed.

(f) An action to enforce the obligation of a party to pay an accepted draft, other than a certified check, must be commenced (i) within six years after the due date or dates stated in the draft or acceptance if the obligation of the acceptor is payable at a definite time, or (ii) within six years after the date of the acceptance if the obligation of the acceptor is payable on demand.

(g) Unless governed by other law regarding claims for indemnity or contribution, an action (i) for conversion of an instrument, for money had and received, or like action based on conversion, (ii) for breach of warranty, or (iii) to enforce an obligation, duty, or right arising under this Article and not governed by this section must be commenced within three years after the [cause of action] accrues.

§ 3–119. Notice of Right to Defend Action.

In an action for breach of an obligation for which a third person is answerable over pursuant to this Article or Article 4, the defendant may give the third person written notice of the litigation, and the person notified may then give similar notice to any other person who is answerable over. If the notice states (i) that the person notified may come in and defend and (ii) that failure to do so will bind the person notified in an action later brought by the person giving the notice as to any determination of fact common to the two litigations, the person notified is so bound unless after seasonable receipt of the notice the person notified does come in and defend.

Part 2 Negotiation, Transfer, and Indorsement

§ 3–201. Negotiation.

(a) "Negotiation" means a transfer of possession, whether voluntary or involuntary, of an instrument by a person other than the issuer to a person who thereby becomes its holder.

(b) Except for negotiation by a remitter, if an instrument is payable to an identified person, negotiation requires transfer of possession of the instrument and its indorsement by the holder. If an instrument is payable to bearer, it may be negotiated by transfer of possession alone.

§ 3–202. Negotiation Subject to Rescission.

(a) Negotiation is effective even if obtained (i) from an infant, a corporation exceeding its powers, or a person without capacity, (ii) by fraud, duress, or mistake, or (iii) in breach of duty or as part of an illegal transaction.

(b) To the extent permitted by other law, negotiation may be rescinded or may be subject to other remedies, but those remedies may not be asserted against a subsequent holder in due course or a person paying the instrument in good faith and without knowledge of facts that are a basis for rescission or other remedy.

§ 3–203. Transfer of Instrument; Rights Acquired by Transfer.

(a) An instrument is transferred when it is delivered by a person other than its issuer for the purpose of giving to the person receiving delivery the right to enforce the instrument.

(b) Transfer of an instrument, whether or not the transfer is a negotiation, vests in the transferee any right of the transferor to enforce the instrument, including any right as a holder in due course, but the transferee cannot acquire rights of a holder in due course by a transfer, directly or indirectly, from a holder in due course if the transferee engaged in fraud or illegality affecting the instrument.

(c) Unless otherwise agreed, if an instrument is transferred for value and the transferee does not become a holder because of lack of indorsement by the transferor, the transferee has a specifically enforceable right to the unqualified indorsement of the transferor, but negotiation of the instrument does not occur until the indorsement is made.

(d) If a transferor purports to transfer less than the entire instrument, negotiation of the instrument does not occur. The transferee obtains no rights under this Article and has only the rights of a partial assignee.

§ 3–204. Indorsement.

(a) "Indorsement" means a signature, other than that of a signer as maker, drawer, or acceptor, that alone or accompanied by other words is made on an instrument for the purpose of (i) negotiating the instrument, (ii) restricting payment of the instrument, or (iii) incurring indorser's liability on the instrument, but regardless of the intent of the signer, a signature and its accompanying words is an indorsement unless the accompanying words, terms of the instrument, place of the signature, or other circumstances unambiguously indicate that the signature was made for a purpose other than indorsement. For the purpose of determining whether a signature is made on an instrument, a paper affixed to the instrument is a part of the instrument.

(b) "Indorser" means a person who makes an indorsement.

(c) For the purpose of determining whether the transferee of an instrument is a holder, an indorsement that transfers a security interest in the instrument is effective as an unqualified indorsement of the instrument.

(d) If an instrument is payable to a holder under a name that is not the name of the holder, indorsement may be made by the holder in the name stated in the instrument or in the holder's name or both, but signature in both names may be required by a person paying or taking the instrument for value or collection.

§ 3–205. Special Indorsement; Blank Indorsement; Anomalous Indorsement.

(a) If an indorsement is made by the holder of an instrument, whether payable to an identified person or payable to bearer, and the indorsement identifies a person to whom it makes the instrument payable, it is a "special indorsement." When specially indorsed, an instrument becomes payable to the identified person and may be negotiated only by the indorsement of that person. The principles stated in Section 3–110 apply to special indorsements.

(b) If an indorsement is made by the holder of an instrument and it is not a special indorsement, it is a "blank indorsement." When indorsed in blank, an instrument becomes payable to bearer and may be negotiated by transfer of possession alone until specially indorsed.

(c) The holder may convert a blank indorsement that consists only of a signature into a special indorsement by writing, above the signature of the indorser, words identifying the person to whom the instrument is made payable.

(d) "Anomalous indorsement" means an indorsement made by a person who is not the holder of the instrument. An anomalous indorsement does not affect the manner in which the instrument may be negotiated.

§ 3–206. Restrictive Indorsement.

(a) An indorsement limiting payment to a particular person or otherwise prohibiting further transfer or negotiation of the instrument is not effective to prevent further transfer or negotiation of the instrument.

(b) An indorsement stating a condition to the right of the indorsee to receive payment does not affect the right of the indorsee to enforce the instrument. A person paying the instrument or taking it for value or collection may disregard the condition, and the rights and liabilities of that person are not affected by whether the condition has been fulfilled.

(c) If an instrument bears an indorsement (i) described in Section 4–201(b), or (ii) in blank or to a particular bank using the words "for deposit," "for collection," or other words indicating a purpose of having the instrument collected by a bank for the indorser or for a particular account, the following rules apply:

(1) A person, other than a bank, who purchases the instrument when so indorsed converts the instrument unless the amount paid for the instrument is received by the indorser or applied consistently with the indorsement.

(2) A depositary bank that purchases the instrument or takes it for collection when so indorsed converts the instrument unless the amount paid by the bank with respect to the instrument is received by the indorser or applied consistently with the indorsement.

(3) A payor bank that is also the depositary bank or that takes the instrument for immediate payment over the counter from a person other than a collecting bank converts the instrument unless the proceeds of the instrument are received by the indorser or applied consistently with the indorsement.

(4) Except as otherwise provided in paragraph (3), a payor bank or intermediary bank may disregard the indorsement and is not liable if the proceeds of the instrument are not received by the indorser or applied consistently with the indorsement.

(d) Except for an indorsement covered by subsection (c), if an instrument bears an indorsement using words to the effect that payment is to be made to the indorsee as agent, trustee, or other fiduciary for the benefit of the indorser or another person, the following rules apply:

(1) Unless there is notice of breach of fiduciary duty as provided in Section 3–307, a person who purchases the instrument from the indorsee or takes the instrument from the indorsee for collection or payment may pay the proceeds of payment or the value given for the instrument to the indorsee without regard to whether the indorsee violates a fiduciary duty to the indorser.

(2) A subsequent transferee of the instrument or person who pays the instrument is neither given notice nor otherwise affected by the restriction in the indorsement unless the transferee or payor knows that the fiduciary dealt with the instrument or its proceeds in breach of fiduciary duty.

(e) The presence on an instrument of an indorsement to which this section applies does not prevent a purchaser of the instrument from becoming a holder in due course of the instrument unless the purchaser is a converter under subsection (c) or has notice or knowledge of breach of fiduciary duty as stated in subsection (d).

(f) In an action to enforce the obligation of a party to pay the instrument, the obligor has a defense if payment would violate an indorsement to which this section applies and the payment is not permitted by this section.

§ 3–207. **Reacquisition.**

Reacquisition of an instrument occurs if it is transferred to a former holder, by negotiation or otherwise. A former holder who reacquires the instrument may cancel indorsements made after the reacquirer first became a holder of the instrument. If the cancellation causes the instrument to be payable to the reacquirer or to bearer, the reacquirer may negotiate the instrument. An indorser whose indorsement is canceled is discharged, and the discharge is effective against any subsequent holder.

Part 3 **Enforcement of Instruments**

§ 3–301. **Person Entitled to Enforce Instrument.**

"Person entitled to enforce" an instrument means (i) the holder of the instrument, (ii) a nonholder in possession of the instrument who has the rights of a holder, or (iii) a person not in possession of the instrument who is entitled to enforce the instrument pursuant to Section 3–309 or 3–418(d). A person may be a person entitled to enforce the instrument even though the person is not the owner of the instrument or is in wrongful possession of the instrument.

§ 3–302. **Holder in Due Course.**

(a) Subject to subsection (c) and Section 3–106(d), "holder in due course" means the holder of an instrument if:

(1) the instrument when issued or negotiated to the holder does not bear such apparent evidence of forgery or alteration or is not otherwise so irregular or incomplete as to call into question its authenticity; and

(2) the holder took the instrument (i) for value, (ii) in good faith, (iii) without notice that the instrument is overdue or has been dishonored or that there is an uncured default with respect to payment of another instrument issued as part of the same series, (iv) without notice that the instrument contains an unauthorized signature or has been altered, (v) without notice of any claim to the instrument described in Section 3–306, and (vi) without notice that any party has a defense or claim in recoupment described in Section 3–305(a).

(b) Notice of discharge of a party, other than discharge in an insolvency proceeding, is not notice of a defense under subsection (a), but discharge is effective against a person who became a holder in due course with notice of the discharge. Public filing or recording of a document does not of itself constitute notice of a defense, claim in recoupment, or claim to the instrument.

(c) Except to the extent a transferor or predecessor in interest has rights as a holder in due course, a person does not acquire rights of a holder in due course of an instrument taken (i) by legal process or by purchase in an execution, bankruptcy, or creditor's sale or similar proceeding, (ii) by purchase as part of a bulk transaction not in ordinary course of business of the transferor, or (iii) as the successor in interest to an estate or other organization.

(d) If, under Section 3–303(a)(1), the promise of performance that is the consideration for an instrument has been partially performed, the holder may assert rights as a holder in due course of the instrument only to the fraction of the amount payable under the instrument equal to the value of the partial performance divided by the value of the promised performance.

(e) If (i) the person entitled to enforce an instrument has only a security interest in the instrument and (ii) the person obliged to pay the instrument has a defense, claim in recoupment, or claim to the instrument that may be asserted against the person who granted the security interest, the person entitled to enforce the instrument may assert rights as a holder in due course only to an amount payable under the instrument which, at the time of enforcement of the instrument, does not exceed the amount of the unpaid obligation secured.

(f) To be effective, notice must be received at a time and in a manner that gives a reasonable opportunity to act on it.

(g) This section is subject to any law limiting status as a holder in due course in particular classes of transactions.

§ 3–303. Value and Consideration.

(a) An instrument is issued or transferred for value if:

(1) the instrument is issued or transferred for a promise of performance, to the extent the promise has been performed;

(2) the transferee acquires a security interest or other lien in the instrument other than a lien obtained by judicial proceeding;

(3) the instrument is issued or transferred as payment of, or as security for, an antecedent claim against any person, whether or not the claim is due;

(4) the instrument is issued or transferred in exchange for a negotiable instrument; or

(5) the instrument is issued or transferred in exchange for the incurring of an irrevocable obligation to a third party by the person taking the instrument.

(b) "Consideration" means any consideration sufficient to support a simple contract. The drawer or maker of an instrument has a defense if the instrument is issued without consideration. If an instrument is issued for a promise of performance, the issuer has a defense to the extent performance of the promise is due and the promise has not been performed. If an instrument is issued for value as stated in subsection (a), the instrument is also issued for consideration.

§ 3–304. Overdue Instrument.

(a) An instrument payable on demand becomes overdue at the earliest of the following times:

(1) on the day after the day demand for payment is duly made;

(2) if the instrument is a check, 90 days after its date; or

(3) if the instrument is not a check, when the instrument has been outstanding for a period of time after its date which is unreasonably long under the circumstances of the particular case in light of the nature of the instrument and usage of the trade.

(b) With respect to an instrument payable at a definite time the following rules apply:

(1) If the principal is payable in installments and a due date has not been accelerated, the instru-ment becomes overdue upon default under the instrument for nonpayment of an installment, and the instrument remains overdue until the default is cured.

(2) If the principal is not payable in installments and the due date has not been accelerated, the instrument becomes overdue on the day after the due date.

(3) If a due date with respect to principal has been accelerated, the instrument becomes overdue on the day after the accelerated due date.

(c) Unless the due date of principal has been accelerated, an instrument does not become overdue if there is default in payment of interest but no default in payment of principal.

§ 3–305. Defenses and Claims in Recoupment.

(a) Except as stated in subsection (b), the right to enforce the obligation of a party to pay an instrument is subject to the following:

(1) a defense of the obligor based on (i) infancy of the obligor to the extent it is a defense to a simple contract, (ii) duress, lack of legal capacity, or illegality of the transaction which, under other law, nullifies the obligation of the obligor, (iii) fraud that induced the obligor to sign the instrument with neither knowledge nor reasonable opportunity to learn of its character or its essential terms, or (iv) discharge of the obligor in insolvency proceedings;

(2) a defense of the obligor stated in another section of this Article or a defense of the obligor that would be available if the person entitled to enforce the instrument were enforcing a right to payment under a simple contract; and

(3) a claim in recoupment of the obligor against the original payee of the instrument if the claim arose from the transaction that gave rise to the instrument; but the claim of the obligor may be asserted against a transferee of the instrument only to reduce the amount owing on the instrument at the time the action is brought.

(b) The right of a holder in due course to enforce the obligation of a party to pay the instrument is subject to defenses of the obligor stated in subsection (a)(1), but is not subject to defenses of the obligor stated in subsection (a)(2) or claims in recoupment stated in subsection (a)(3) against a person other than the holder.

(c) Except as stated in subsection (d), in an action to enforce the obligation of a party to pay the instrument, the obligor may not assert against the person entitled to enforce the instrument a defense, claim in recoupment, or claim to the instrument (Section 3–306) of another person, but the other person's claim to the instrument may be asserted by the obligor if the other person is joined in the action and personally asserts the claim against the person entitled to enforce the instrument. An obligor is not obliged to pay the instrument if the person seeking enforcement of the instrument does not have rights of a holder in due course and the obligor proves that the instrument is a lost or stolen instrument.

(d) In an action to enforce the obligation of an accommodation party to pay an instrument, the accommodation party may assert against the person entitled to enforce the instrument any defense or claim in recoupment under subsection (a) that the accommodated party could assert against the person entitled to enforce the instrument, except the defenses of discharge in insolvency proceedings, infancy, and lack of legal capacity.

§ 3–306. Claims to an Instrument.

A person taking an instrument, other than a person having rights of a holder in due course, is subject to a claim of a property or possessory right in the instrument or its proceeds, including a claim to rescind a negotiation and to recover the instrument or its proceeds. A person having rights of a holder in due course takes free of the claim to the instrument.

§ 3–307. Notice of Breach of Fiduciary Duty.

(a) In this section:

(1) "Fiduciary" means an agent, trustee, partner, corporate officer or director, or other representative owing a fiduciary duty with respect to an instrument.

(2) "Represented person" means the principal, beneficiary, partnership, corporation, or other person to whom the duty stated in paragraph (1) is owed.

(b) If (i) an instrument is taken from a fiduciary for payment or collection or for value, (ii) the taker has knowledge of the fiduciary status of the fiduciary, and (iii) the represented person makes a claim to the instrument or its proceeds on the basis that the transaction of the fiduciary is a breach of fiduciary duty, the following rules apply:

(1) Notice of breach of fiduciary duty by the fiduciary is notice of the claim of the represented person.

(2) In the case of an instrument payable to the represented person or the fiduciary as such, the taker has notice of the breach of fiduciary duty if the instrument is (i) taken in payment of or as security for a debt known by the taker to be the personal debt of the fiduciary, (ii) taken in a transaction known by the taker to be for the personal benefit of the fiduciary, or (iii) deposited to an account other than an account of the fiduciary, as such, or an account of the represented person.

(3) If an instrument is issued by the represented person or the fiduciary as such, and made payable to the fiduciary personally, the taker does not have notice of the breach of fiduciary duty unless the taker knows of the breach of fiduciary duty.

(4) If an instrument is issued by the represented person or the fiduciary as such, to the taker as payee, the taker has notice of the breach of fiduciary duty if the instrument is (i) taken in payment of or as security for a debt known by the taker to be the personal debt of the fiduciary, (ii) taken in a transaction known by the taker to be for the personal benefit of the fiduciary, or (iii) deposited to an account other than an account of the fiduciary, as such, or an account of the represented person.

§ 3–308. Proof of Signatures and Status as Holder in Due Course.

(a) In an action with respect to an instrument, the authenticity of, and authority to make, each signature on the instrument is admitted unless specifically denied in the pleadings. If the validity of a signature is denied in the pleadings, the burden of establishing validity is on the person claiming validity, but the signature is presumed to be authentic and authorized unless the action is to enforce the liability of the purported signer and the signer is dead or incompetent at the time of trial of the issue of validity of the signature. If an action to enforce the instrument is brought against a person as the undisclosed principal of a person who signed the instrument as a party to the instrument, the plaintiff has the burden of establishing that the defendant is liable on the instrument as a represented person under Section 3–402(a).

(b) If the validity of signatures is admitted or proved and there is compliance with subsection (a), a plaintiff producing the instrument is entitled to payment if the plaintiff proves entitlement to enforce the instrument under Section 3–301, unless the defendant proves a defense or claim in recoupment. If a defense or claim in recoupment is proved, the right to payment of the plaintiff is subject to the defense or claim, except to the extent the plaintiff proves that the plaintiff has rights of a holder in due course which are not subject to the defense or claim.

§ 3–309. Enforcement of Lost, Destroyed, or Stolen Instrument.

(a) A person not in possession of an instrument is entitled to enforce the instrument if (i) the person was in possession of the instrument and entitled to enforce it when loss of possession occurred, (ii) the loss of possession was not the result of a transfer by the person or a lawful seizure, and (iii) the person cannot reasonably obtain possession of the instrument because the instrument was destroyed, its whereabouts cannot be determined, or it is in the wrongful possession of an unknown person or a person that cannot be found or is not amenable to service of process.

(b) A person seeking enforcement of an instrument under subsection (a) must prove the terms of the instrument and the person's right to enforce the instrument. If that proof is made, Section 3–308 applies to the case as if the person seeking enforcement had produced the instrument. The court may not enter judgment in favor of the person seeking enforcement unless it finds that the person required to pay the instrument is adequately protected against loss that might occur by reason of a claim by another person to enforce the instrument. Adequate protection may be provided by any reasonable means.

§ 3–310. Effect of Instrument on Obligation for Which Taken.

(a) Unless otherwise agreed, if a certified check, cashier's check, or teller's check is taken for an obligation, the obligation is discharged to the same extent discharge would result if an amount of money equal to the amount of the instrument were taken in payment of the obligation. Discharge of the obligation does not affect any liability that the obligor may have as an indorser of the instrument.

(b) Unless otherwise agreed and except as provided in subsection (a), if a note or an uncertified check is taken for an obligation, the obligation is suspended to the same extent the obligation would be discharged if an amount of money equal to the amount of the instrument were taken, and the following rules apply:

(1) In the case of an uncertified check, suspension of the obligation continues until dishonor of the check or until it is paid or certified. Payment or certification of the check results in discharge of the obligation to the extent of the amount of the check.

(2) In the case of a note, suspension of the obligation continues until dishonor of the note or until it is paid. Payment of the note results in discharge of the obligation to the extent of the payment.

(3) Except as provided in paragraph (4), if the check or note is dishonored and the obligee of the obligation for which the instrument was taken is the person entitled to enforce the instrument, the obligee may enforce either the instrument or the obligation. In the case of an instrument of a third person which is negotiated to the obligee by the obligor, discharge of the obligor on the instrument also discharges the obligation.

(4) If the person entitled to enforce the instrument taken for an obligation is a person other than the obligee, the obligee may not enforce the obligation to the extent the obligation is suspended. If the obligee is the person entitled to enforce the instrument but no longer has possession of it because it was lost, stolen, or destroyed, the obligation may not be enforced to the extent of the amount payable on the instrument, and to that extent the obligee's rights against the obligor are limited to enforcement of the instrument.

(c) If an instrument other than one described in subsection (a) or (b) is taken for an obligation, the effect is (i) that stated in subsection (a) if the instrument is one on which a bank is liable as maker or acceptor, or (ii) that stated in subsection (b) in any other case.

§ 3–311. Accord and Satisfaction by Use of Instrument.

(a) If a person against whom a claim is asserted proves that (i) that person in good faith tendered an instrument to the claimant as full satisfaction of the claim, (ii) the amount of the claim was unliquidated or subject to a bona fide dispute, and (iii) the claimant obtained payment of the instrument, the following subsections apply.

(b) Unless subsection (c) applies, the claim is discharged if the person against whom the claim is asserted proves that the instrument or an accompanying written communication contained a conspicuous statement to the effect that the instrument was tendered as full satisfaction of the claim.

(c) Subject to subsection (d), a claim is not discharged under subsection (b) if either of the following applies:

(1) The claimant, if an organization, proves that (i) within a reasonable time before the tender, the claimant sent a conspicuous statement to the person against whom the claim is asserted that communications concerning disputed debts, including an instrument tendered as full

satisfaction of a debt, are to be sent to a designated person, office, or place, and (ii) the instrument or accompanying communication was not received by that designated person, office, or place.

(2) The claimant, whether or not an organization, proves that within 90 days after payment of the instrument, the claimant tendered repayment of the amount of the instrument to the person against whom the claim is asserted. This paragraph does not apply if the claimant is an organization that sent a statement complying with paragraph (1)(i).

(d) A claim is discharged if the person against whom the claim is asserted proves that within a reasonable time before collection of the instrument was initiated, the claimant, or an agent of the claimant having direct responsibility with respect to the disputed obligation, knew that the instrument was tendered in full satisfaction of the claim.

§ 3–312. Lost, Destroyed, or Stolen Cashier's Check, Teller's Check, or Certified Check.*

(a) In this section:

(1) "Check" means a cashier's check, teller's check, or certified check.

(2) "Claimant" means a person who claims the right to receive the amount of a cashier's check, teller's check, or certified check that was lost, destroyed, or stolen.

(3) "Declaration of loss" means a written statement, made under penalty of perjury, to the effect that (i) the declarer lost possession of a check, (ii) the declarer is the drawer or payee of the check, in the case of a certified check, or the remitter or payee of the check, in the case of a cashier's check or teller's check, (iii) the loss of possession was not the result of a transfer by the declarer or a lawful seizure, and (iv) the declarer cannot reasonably obtain possession of the check because the check was destroyed, its whereabouts cannot be determined, or it is in the wrongful possession of an unknown person or a person that cannot be found or is not amenable to service of process.

(4) "Obligated bank" means the issuer of a cashier's check or teller's check or the acceptor of a certified check.

(b) A claimant may assert a claim to the amount of a check by a communication to the obligated bank describing the check with reasonable certainty and requesting payment of the amount of the check, if (i) the claimant is the drawer or payee of a certified check or the remitter or payee of a cashier's check or teller's check, (ii) the communication contains or is accompanied by a declaration of loss of the claimant with respect to the check, (iii) the communication is received at a time and in a manner affording the bank a reasonable time to act on it before the check is paid, and (iv) the claimant provides reasonable identification if requested by the obligated

---

*[Section 3–312 was not adopted as part of the 1990 Official Text of Revised Article 3. It was officially approved and recommended for enactment in all states in August 1991 by the National Conference of Commissioners on Uniform State Laws.]

bank. Delivery of a declaration of loss is a warranty of the truth of the statements made in the declaration. If a claim is asserted in compliance with this subsection, the following rules apply:

(1) The claim becomes enforceable at the later of (i) the time the claim is asserted, or (ii) the 90th day following the date of the check, in the case of a cashier's check or teller's check, or the 90th day following the date of the acceptance, in the case of a certified check.

(2) Until the claim becomes enforceable, it has no legal effect and the obligated bank may pay the check or, in the case of a teller's check, may permit the drawee to pay the check. Payment to a person entitled to enforce the check discharges all liability of the obligated bank with respect to the check.

(3) If the claim becomes enforceable before the check is presented for payment, the obligated bank is not obliged to pay the check.

(4) When the claim becomes enforceable, the obligated bank becomes obliged to pay the amount of the check to the claimant if payment of the check has not been made to a person entitled to enforce the check. Subject to Section 4–302(a)(1), payment to the claimant discharges all liability of the obligated bank with respect to the check.

(c) If the obligated bank pays the amount of a check to a claimant under subsection (b)(4) and the check is presented for payment by a person having rights of a holder in due course, the claimant is obliged to (i) refund the payment to the obligated bank if the check is paid, or (ii) pay the amount of the check to the person having rights of a holder in due course if the check is dishonored.

(d) If a claimant has the right to assert a claim under subsection (b) and is also a person entitled to enforce a cashier's check, teller's check, or certified check which is lost, destroyed, or stolen, the claimant may assert rights with respect to the check either under this section or Section 3–309.

Added in 1991.

Part 4 Liability of Parties

§ 3–401. Signature.

(a) A person is not liable on an instrument unless (i) the person signed the instrument, or (ii) the person is represented by an agent or representative who signed the instrument and the signature is binding on the represented person under Section 3–402.

(b) A signature may be made (i) manually or by means of a device or machine, and (ii) by the use of any name, including a trade or assumed name, or by a word, mark, or symbol executed or adopted by a person with present intention to authenticate a writing.

§ 3–402. Signature by Representative.

(a) If a person acting, or purporting to act, as a representative signs an instrument by signing either the name of the represented person or the name of the signer, the represented person is bound by the signature to the same extent the represented person would be bound if the signature were on a simple contract. If the represented person is bound, the signature of the representative is the "authorized signature of the represented person" and the represented person is liable on the instrument, whether or not identified in the instrument.

(b) If a representative signs the name of the representative to an instrument and the signature is an authorized signature of the represented person, the following rules apply:

(1) If the form of the signature shows unambiguously that the signature is made on behalf of the represented person who is identified in the instrument, the representative is not liable on the instrument.

(2) Subject to subsection (c), if (i) the form of the signature does not show unambiguously that the signature is made in a representative capacity or (ii) the represented person is not identified in the instrument, the representative is liable on the instrument to a holder in due course that took the instrument without notice that the representative was not intended to be liable on the instrument. With respect to any other person, the representative is liable on the instrument unless the representative proves that the original parties did not intend the representative to be liable on the instrument.

(c) If a representative signs the name of the representative as drawer of a check without indication of the representative status and the check is payable from an account of the represented person who is identified on the check, the signer is not liable on the check if the signature is an authorized signature of the represented person.

§ 3–403. Unauthorized Signature.

(a) Unless otherwise provided in this Article or Article 4, an unauthorized signature is ineffective except as the signature of the unauthorized signer in favor of a person who in good faith pays the instrument or takes it for value. An unauthorized signature may be ratified for all purposes of this Article.

(b) If the signature of more than one person is required to constitute the authorized signature of an organization, the signature of the organization is unauthorized if one of the required signatures is lacking.

(c) The civil or criminal liability of a person who makes an unauthorized signature is not affected by any provision of this Article which makes the unauthorized signature effective for the purposes of this Article.

§ 3–404. Impostors; Fictitious Payees.

(a) If an impostor, by use of the mails or otherwise, induces the issuer of an instrument to issue the instrument to the impostor, or to a person acting in concert with the impostor, by impersonating the payee of the instrument or a person authorized to act for the payee, an indorsement of the instrument by any person in the name of the payee is effective as the indorsement of the payee in favor of a person who, in good faith, pays the instrument or takes it for value or for collection.

(b) If (i) a person whose intent determines to whom an instrument is payable (Section 3–110(a) or (b)) does not intend the person identified as payee to have any interest in the instrument, or (ii) the person identified as payee of an instrument is a fictitious person, the following rules apply until the instrument is negotiated by special indorsement:

(1) Any person in possession of the instrument is its holder.

(2) An indorsement by any person in the name of the payee stated in the instrument is effective as the indorsement of the payee in favor of a person who, in good faith, pays the instrument or takes it for value or for collection.

(c) Under subsection (a) or (b), an indorsement is made in the name of a payee if (i) it is made in a name substantially similar to that of the payee or (ii) the instrument, whether or not indorsed, is deposited in a depository bank to an account in a name substantially similar to that of the payee.

(d) With respect to an instrument to which subsection (a) or (b) applies, if a person paying the instrument or taking it for value or for collection fails to exercise ordinary care in paying or taking the instrument and that failure substantially contributes to loss resulting from payment of the instrument, the person bearing the loss may recover from the person failing to exercise ordinary care to the extent the failure to exercise ordinary care contributed to the loss.

§ 3–405. Employer's Responsibility for Fraudulent Indorsement by Employee.

(a) In this section:

(1) "Employee" includes an independent contractor and employee of an independent contractor retained by the employer.

(2) "Fraudulent indorsement" means (i) in the case of an instrument payable to the employer, a forged indorsement purporting to be that of the employer, or (ii) in the case of an instrument with respect to which the employer is the issuer, a forged indorsement purporting to be that of the person identified as payee.

(3) "Responsibility" with respect to instruments means authority (i) to sign or indorse instruments on behalf of the employer, (ii) to process instruments received by the employer for bookkeeping purposes, for deposit to an account, or for other disposition, (iii) to prepare or process instruments for issue in the name of the employer, (iv) to supply information determining the names or addresses of payees of instruments to be issued in the name of the employer, (v) to control the disposition of instruments to be issued in the name of the employer, or (vi) to act otherwise with respect to instruments in a responsible capacity. "Responsibility" does not include authority that merely allows an employee to have access to instruments or blank or incomplete instrument forms that are being stored or transported or are part of incoming or outgoing mail, or similar access.

(b) For the purpose of determining the rights and liabilities of a person who, in good faith, pays an instrument or takes it for value or for collection, if an employer entrusted an employee with responsibility with respect to the instrument and the employee or a person acting in concert with the employee makes a fraudulent indorsement of the instrument, the indorsement is effective as the indorsement of the person to whom the instrument is payable if it is made in the name of that person. If the person paying the instrument or taking it for value or for collection fails to exercise ordinary care in paying or taking the instrument and that failure substantially contributes to loss resulting from the fraud, the person bearing the loss may recover from the person failing to exercise ordinary care to the extent the failure to exercise ordinary care contributed to the loss.

(c) Under subsection (b), an indorsement is made in the name of the person to whom an instrument is payable if (i) it is made in a name substantially similar to the name of that person or (ii) the instrument, whether or not indorsed, is deposited in a depository bank to an account in a name substantially similar to the name of that person.

§ 3–406. Negligence Contributing to Forged Signature or Alteration of Instrument.

(a) A person whose failure to exercise ordinary care substantially contributes to an alteration of an instrument or to the making of a forged signature on an instrument is precluded from asserting the alteration or the forgery against a person who, in good faith, pays the instrument or takes it for value or for collection.

(b) Under subsection (a), if the person asserting the preclusion fails to exercise ordinary care in paying or taking the instrument and that failure substantially contributes to loss, the loss is allocated between the person precluded and the person asserting the preclusion according to the extent to which the failure of each to exercise ordinary care contributed to the loss.

(c) Under subsection (a), the burden of proving failure to exercise ordinary care is on the person asserting the preclusion. Under subsection (b), the burden of proving failure to exercise ordinary care is on the person precluded.

§ 3–407. Alteration.

(a) "Alteration" means (i) an unauthorized change in an instrument that purports to modify in any respect the obligation of a party, or (ii) an unauthorized addition of words or numbers or other change to an incomplete instrument relating to the obligation of a party.

(b) Except as provided in subsection (c), an alteration fraudulently made discharges a party whose obligation is affected by the alteration unless that party assents or is precluded from asserting the alteration. No other alteration discharges a party, and the instrument may be enforced according to its original terms.

(c) A payor bank or drawee paying a fraudulently altered instrument or a person taking it for value, in good faith and without notice of the alteration, may enforce rights with respect to the instrument (i) according to its original terms, or (ii) in the case of an incomplete instrument altered by unauthorized completion, according to its terms as completed.

§ 3–408. Drawee Not Liable on Unaccepted Draft.

A check or other draft does not of itself operate as an assignment of funds in the hands of the drawee available for its payment, and the drawee is not liable on the instrument until the drawee accepts it.

§ 3–409. Acceptance of Draft; Certified Check.

(a) "Acceptance" means the drawee's signed agreement to pay a draft as presented. It must be written on the draft and may consist of the drawee's signature alone. Acceptance may be made at any time and becomes effective when notification pursuant to instructions is given or the accepted draft is delivered for the purpose of giving rights on the acceptance to any person.

(b) A draft may be accepted although it has not been signed by the drawer, is otherwise incomplete, is overdue, or has been dishonored.

(c) If a draft is payable at a fixed period after sight and the acceptor fails to date the acceptance, the holder may complete the acceptance by supplying a date in good faith.

(d) "Certified check" means a check accepted by the bank on which it is drawn. Acceptance may be made as stated in subsection (a) or by a writing on the check which indicates that the check is certified. The drawee of a check has no obligation to certify the check, and refusal to certify is not dishonor of the check.

§ 3–410. Acceptance Varying Draft.

(a) If the terms of a drawee's acceptance vary from the terms of the draft as presented, the holder may refuse the acceptance and treat the draft as dishonored. In that case, the drawee may cancel the acceptance.

(b) The terms of a draft are not varied by an acceptance to pay at a particular bank or place in the United States, unless the acceptance states that the draft is to be paid only at that bank or place.

(c) If the holder assents to an acceptance varying the terms of a draft, the obligation of each drawer and indorser that does not expressly assent to the acceptance is discharged.

§ 3–411. Refusal to Pay Cashier's Checks, Teller's Checks, and Certified Checks.

(a) In this section, "obligated bank" means the acceptor of a certified check or the issuer of a cashier's check or teller's check bought from the issuer.

(b) If the obligated bank wrongfully (i) refuses to pay a cashier's check or certified check, (ii) stops payment of a teller's check, or (iii) refuses to pay a dishonored teller's check, the person asserting the right to enforce the check is entitled to compensation for expenses and loss of interest resulting from the nonpayment and may recover consequential damages if the obligated bank refuses to pay after receiving notice of particular circumstances giving rise to the damages.

(c) Expenses or consequential damages under subsection (b) are not recoverable if the refusal of the obligated bank to pay occurs because (i) the bank suspends payments, (ii) the obligated bank asserts a claim or defense of the bank that it has reasonable grounds to believe is available against the person entitled to enforce the instrument, (iii) the obligated bank has a reasonable doubt whether the person demanding payment is the person entitled to enforce the instrument, or (iv) payment is prohibited by law.

§ 3–412. Obligation of Issuer of Note or Cashier's Check.

The issuer of a note or cashier's check or other draft drawn on the drawer is obliged to pay the instrument (i) according to its terms at the time it was issued or, if not issued, at the time it first came into possession of a holder, or (ii) if the issuer signed an incomplete instrument, according to its terms when completed, to the extent stated in Sections 3–115 and 3–407. The obligation is owed to a person entitled to enforce the instrument or to an indorser who paid the instrument under Section 3–415.

§ 3–413. Obligation of Acceptor.

(a) The acceptor of a draft is obliged to pay the draft (i) according to its terms at the time it was accepted, even though the acceptance states that the draft is payable "as originally drawn" or equivalent terms, (ii) if the acceptance varies the terms of the draft, according to the terms of the draft as varied, or (iii) if the acceptance is of a draft that is an incomplete instrument, according to its terms when completed, to the extent stated in Sections 3–115 and 3–407. The obligation is owed to a person entitled to enforce the draft or to the drawer or an indorser who paid the draft under Section 3–414 or 3–415.

(b) If the certification of a check or other acceptance of a draft states the amount certified or accepted, the obligation of the acceptor is that amount. If (i) the certification or acceptance does not state an amount, (ii) the amount of the instrument is subsequently raised, and (iii) the instrument is then negotiated to a holder in due course, the obligation of the acceptor is the amount of the instrument at the time it was taken by the holder in due course.

§ 3–414. Obligation of Drawer.

(a) This section does not apply to cashier's checks or other drafts drawn on the drawer.

(b) If an unaccepted draft is dishonored, the drawer is obliged to pay the draft (i) according to its terms at the time it was issued or, if not issued, at the time it first came into possession of a holder, or (ii) if the drawer signed an incomplete instrument, according to its terms when completed, to the extent stated in Sections 3–115 and 3–407. The obligation is owed to a person entitled to enforce the draft or to an indorser who paid the draft under Section 3–415.

(c) If a draft is accepted by a bank, the drawer is discharged, regardless of when or by whom acceptance was obtained.

(d) If a draft is accepted and the acceptor is not a bank, the obligation of the drawer to pay the draft if the draft is dishonored by the acceptor is the same as the obligation of an indorser under Section 3–415(a) and (c).

(e) If a draft states that it is drawn "without recourse" or otherwise disclaims liability of the drawer to pay the draft, the drawer is not liable under subsection (b) to pay the draft if the draft is not a check. A disclaimer of the liability stated in subsection (b) is not effective if the draft is a check.

(f) If (i) a check is not presented for payment or given to a depositary bank for collection within 30 days after its date, (ii) the drawee suspends payments after expiration of the 30-day period without paying the check, and (iii) because of the suspension of payments, the drawer is deprived of funds maintained with the drawee to cover payment of the check, the drawer to the extent deprived of funds may discharge its obligation to pay the check by assigning to the person entitled to enforce the check the rights of the drawer against the drawee with respect to the funds.

§ 3–415. Obligation of Indorser.

(a) Subject to subsections (b), (c), and (d) and to Section 3–419(d), if an instrument is dishonored, an indorser is obliged to pay the amount due on the instrument (i) according to the terms of the instrument at the time it was indorsed, or (ii) if the indorser indorsed an incomplete instrument, according to its terms when completed, to the extent stated in Sections 3–115 and 3–407. The obligation of the indorser is owed to a person entitled to enforce the instrument or to a subsequent indorser who paid the instrument under this section.

(b) If an indorsement states that it is made "without recourse" or otherwise disclaims liability of the indorser, the indorser is not liable under subsection (a) to pay the instrument.

(c) If notice of dishonor of an instrument is required by Section 3–503 and notice of dishonor complying with that section is not given to an indorser, the liability of the indorser under subsection (a) is discharged.

(d) If a draft is accepted by a bank after an indorsement is made, the liability of the indorser under subsection (a) is discharged.

(e) If an indorser of a check is liable under subsection (a) and the check is not presented for payment, or given to a depositary bank for collection, within 30 days after the day the indorsement was made, the liability of the indorser under subsection (a) is discharged.

As amended in 1993.

§ 3–416. Transfer Warranties.

(a) A person who transfers an instrument for consideration warrants to the transferee and, if the transfer is by indorsement, to any subsequent transferee that:

(1) the warrantor is a person entitled to enforce the instrument;

(2) all signatures on the instrument are authentic and authorized;

(3) the instrument has not been altered;

(4) the instrument is not subject to a defense or claim in recoupment of any party which can be asserted against the warrantor; and

(5) the warrantor has no knowledge of any insolvency proceeding commenced with respect to the maker or acceptor or, in the case of an unaccepted draft, the drawer.

(b) A person to whom the warranties under subsection (a) are made and who took the instrument in good faith may recover from the warrantor as damages for breach of warranty an amount equal to the loss suffered as a result of the breach, but not more than the amount of the instrument plus expenses and loss of interest incurred as a result of the breach.

(c) The warranties stated in subsection (a) cannot be disclaimed with respect to checks. Unless notice of a claim for breach of warranty is given to the warrantor within 30 days after the claimant has reason to know of the breach and the identity of the warrantor, the liability of the warrantor under subsection (b) is discharged to the extent of any loss caused by the delay in giving notice of the claim.

(d) A [cause of action] for breach of warranty under this section accrues when the claimant has reason to know of the breach.

§ 3–417. Presentment Warranties.

(a) If an unaccepted draft is presented to the drawee for payment or acceptance and the drawee pays or accepts the draft, (i) the person obtaining payment or acceptance, at the time of presentment, and (ii) a previous transferor of the draft, at the time of transfer, warrant to the drawee making payment or accepting the draft in good faith that:

(1) the warrantor is, or was, at the time the warrantor transferred the draft, a person entitled to enforce the draft or authorized to obtain payment or acceptance of the draft on behalf of a person entitled to enforce the draft;

(2) the draft has not been altered; and

(3) the warrantor has no knowledge that the signature of the drawer of the draft is unauthorized.

(b) A drawee making payment may recover from any warrantor damages for breach of warranty equal to the amount paid by the drawee less the amount the drawee received or is entitled to receive from the drawer because of the payment. In addition, the drawee is entitled to compensation for expenses and loss of interest resulting from the breach. The right of the drawee to recover damages under this subsection is not affected by any failure of the drawee to exercise ordinary care in making payment. If the drawee accepts the draft, breach of warranty is a defense to the obligation of the acceptor. If the acceptor makes payment with respect to the draft, the acceptor is entitled to recover from any warrantor for breach of warranty the amounts stated in this subsection.

(c) If a drawee asserts a claim for breach of warranty under subsection (a) based on an unauthorized indorsement of the draft or an alteration of the draft, the warrantor may defend by proving that the indorsement is effective under Section 3–404 or 3–405 or the drawer is precluded under Section 3–406 or 4–406 from asserting against the drawee the unauthorized indorsement or alteration.

(d) If (i) a dishonored draft is presented for payment to the drawer or an indorser or (ii) any other instrument is presented for payment to a party obliged to pay the instrument, and (iii) payment is received, the following rules apply:

(1) The person obtaining payment and a prior transferor of the instrument warrant to the person making payment in good faith that the warrantor is, or was, at the time the warrantor transferred the instrument, a person entitled to enforce the instrument or authorized to obtain payment on behalf of a person entitled to enforce the instrument.

(2) The person making payment may recover from any warrantor for breach of warranty an amount equal to the amount paid plus expenses and loss of interest resulting from the breach.

(e) The warranties stated in subsections (a) and (d) cannot be disclaimed with respect to checks. Unless notice of a claim for breach of warranty is given to the warrantor within 30 days after the claimant has reason to know of the breach and the identity of the warrantor, the liability of the warrantor under subsection (b) or (d) is discharged to the extent of any loss caused by the delay in giving notice of the claim.

(f) A [cause of action] for breach of warranty under this section accrues when the claimant has reason to know of the breach.

§ 3–418. Payment or Acceptance by Mistake.

(a) Except as provided in subsection (c), if the drawee of a draft pays or accepts the draft and the drawee acted on the mistaken belief that (i) payment of the draft had not been stopped pursuant to Section 4–403 or (ii) the signature of the drawer of the draft was authorized, the drawee may recover the amount of the draft from the person to whom or for whose benefit payment was made or, in the case of acceptance, may revoke the acceptance. Rights of the drawee under this subsection are not affected by failure of the drawee to exercise ordinary care in paying or accepting the draft.

(b) Except as provided in subsection (c), if an instrument has been paid or accepted by mistake and the case is not covered by subsection (a), the person paying or accepting may, to the extent permitted by the law governing mistake and restitution, (i) recover the payment from the person to whom or for whose benefit payment was made or (ii) in the case of acceptance, may revoke the acceptance.

(c) The remedies provided by subsection (a) or (b) may not be asserted against a person who took the instrument in good faith and for value or who in good faith changed position in reliance on the payment or acceptance. This subsection does not limit remedies provided by Section 3–417 or 4–407.

(d) Notwithstanding Section 4–215, if an instrument is paid or accepted by mistake and the payor or acceptor recovers payment or revokes acceptance under subsection (a) or (b), the instrument is deemed not to have been paid or accepted and is treated as dishonored, and the person from whom payment is recovered has rights as a person entitled to enforce the dishonored instrument.

§ 3–419. Instruments Signed for Accommodation.

(a) If an instrument is issued for value given for the benefit of a party to the instrument ("accommodated party") and another party to the instrument ("accommodation party") signs the instrument for the purpose of incurring liability on the instrument without being a direct beneficiary of the value given for the instrument, the instrument is signed by the accommodation party "for accommodation."

(b) An accommodation party may sign the instrument as maker, drawer, acceptor, or indorser and, subject to subsection (d), is obliged to pay the instrument in the capacity in which the accommodation party signs. The obligation of an accommodation party may be enforced notwithstanding any statute of frauds and whether or not the accommodation party receives consideration for the accommodation.

(c) A person signing an instrument is presumed to be an accommodation party and there is notice that the instrument is signed for accommodation if the signature is an anomalous indorsement or is accompanied by words indicating that the signer is acting as surety or guarantor with respect to the obligation of another party to the instrument. Except as provided in Section 3–605, the obligation of an accommodation party to pay the instrument is not affected by the fact that the person enforcing the obligation had notice when the instrument was taken by that person that the accommodation party signed the instrument for accommodation.

(d) If the signature of a party to an instrument is accompanied by words indicating unambiguously that the party is guaranteeing collection rather than payment of the obligation of another party to the instrument, the signer is obliged to pay the amount due on the instrument to a person entitled to enforce the instrument only if (i) execution of judgment against the other party has been returned unsatisfied, (ii) the other party is insolvent or in an insolvency proceeding, (iii) the other party cannot be served with process, or (iv) it is otherwise apparent that payment cannot be obtained from the other party.

(e) An accommodation party who pays the instrument is entitled to reimbursement from the accommodated party and is entitled to enforce the instrument against the accommodated party. An accommodated party who pays the instrument has no right of recourse against, and is not entitled to contribution from, an accommodation party.

§ 3–420. Conversion of Instrument.

(a) The law applicable to conversion of personal property applies to instruments. An instrument is also converted if it is taken by transfer, other than a negotiation, from a person not entitled to enforce the instrument or a bank makes or obtains payment with respect to the instrument for a person not entitled to enforce the instrument or receive payment. An action for conversion of an instrument may not be brought by (i) the issuer or acceptor of the instrument or (ii) a payee or indorsee who did not receive delivery of the instrument either directly or through delivery to an agent or a co-payee.

(b) In an action under subsection (a), the measure of liability is presumed to be the amount payable on the instrument, but recovery may not exceed the amount of the plaintiff's interest in the instrument.

(c) A representative, other than a depositary bank, who has in good faith dealt with an instrument or its proceeds on behalf of one who was not the person entitled to enforce the instrument is not liable in conversion to that person beyond the amount of any proceeds that it has not paid out.

Part 5 Dishonor

§ 3–501. Presentment.

(a) "Presentment" means a demand made by or on behalf of a person entitled to enforce an instrument (i) to pay the instrument made to the drawee or a party obliged to pay the instrument or, in the case of a note or accepted draft payable at a bank, to the bank, or (ii) to accept a draft made to the drawee.

(b) The following rules are subject to Article 4, agreement of the parties, and clearing-house rules and the like:

(1) Presentment may be made at the place of payment of the instrument and must be made at the place of payment if the instrument is payable at a bank in the United States; may be made by any commercially reasonable means, including an oral, written, or electronic communication; is effective when the demand for payment or acceptance is received by the person to whom presentment is made; and is effective if made to any one of two or more makers, acceptors, drawees, or other payors.

(2) Upon demand of the person to whom presentment is made, the person making presentment must (i) exhibit the instrument, (ii) give reasonable identification and, if presentment is made on behalf of another person, reasonable evidence of authority to do so, and (. . .) sign a receipt on the instrument for any payment made or surrender the instrument if full payment is made.

(3) Without dishonoring the instrument, the party to whom presentment is made may (i) return the instrument for lack of a necessary indorsement, or (ii) refuse payment or acceptance for failure of the presentment to comply with the terms of the instrument, an agreement of the parties, or other applicable law or rule.

(4) The party to whom presentment is made may treat presentment as occurring on the next business day after the day of presentment if the party to whom

presentment is made has established a cut-off hour not earlier than 2 p.m. for the receipt and processing of instruments presented for payment or acceptance and presentment is made after the cut-off hour.

§ 3–502. Dishonor.

(a) Dishonor of a note is governed by the following rules:

(1) If the note is payable on demand, the note is dishonored if presentment is duly made to the maker and the note is not paid on the day of presentment.

(2) If the note is not payable on demand and is payable at or through a bank or the terms of the note require presentment, the note is dishonored if presentment is duly made and the note is not paid on the day it becomes payable or the day of presentment, whichever is later.

(3) If the note is not payable on demand and paragraph (2) does not apply, the note is dishonored if it is not paid on the day it becomes payable.

(b) Dishonor of an unaccepted draft other than a documentary draft is governed by the following rules:

(1) If a check is duly presented for payment to the payor bank otherwise than for immediate payment over the counter, the check is dishonored if the payor bank makes timely return of the check or sends timely notice of dishonor or nonpayment under Section 4–301 or 4–302, or becomes accountable for the amount of the check under Section 4–302.

(2) If a draft is payable on demand and paragraph (1) does not apply, the draft is dishonored if presentment for payment is duly made to the drawee and the draft is not paid on the day of presentment.

(3) If a draft is payable on a date stated in the draft, the draft is dishonored if (i) presentment for payment is duly made to the drawee and payment is not made on the day the draft becomes payable or the day of presentment, whichever is later, or (ii) presentment for acceptance is duly made before the day the draft becomes payable and the draft is not accepted on the day of presentment.

(4) If a draft is payable on elapse of a period of time after sight or acceptance, the draft is dishonored if presentment for acceptance is duly made and the draft is not accepted on the day of presentment.

(c) Dishonor of an unaccepted documentary draft occurs according to the rules stated in subsection (b)(2), (3), and (4), except that payment or acceptance may be delayed without dishonor until no later than the close of the third business day of the drawee following the day on which payment or acceptance is required by those paragraphs.

(d) Dishonor of an accepted draft is governed by the following rules:

(1) If the draft is payable on demand, the draft is dishonored if presentment for payment is duly made to the acceptor and the draft is not paid on the day of presentment.

(2) If the draft is not payable on demand, the draft is dishonored if presentment for payment is duly made to the acceptor and payment is not made on the day it becomes payable or the day of presentment, whichever is later.

(e) In any case in which presentment is otherwise required for dishonor under this section and presentment is excused under Section 3–504, dishonor occurs without presentment if the instrument is not duly accepted or paid.

(f) If a draft is dishonored because timely acceptance of the draft was not made and the person entitled to demand acceptance consents to a late acceptance, from the time of acceptance the draft is treated as never having been dishonored.

§ 3–503. Notice of Dishonor.

(a) The obligation of an indorser stated in Section 3–415(a) and the obligation of a drawer stated in Section 3–414(d) may not be enforced unless (i) the indorser or drawer is given notice of dishonor of the instrument complying with this section or (ii) notice of dishonor is excused under Section 3–504(b).

(b) Notice of dishonor may be given by any person; may be given by any commercially reasonable means, including an oral, written, or electronic communication; and is sufficient if it reasonably identifies the instrument and indicates that the instrument has been dishonored or has not been paid or accepted. Return of an instrument given to a bank for collection is sufficient notice of dishonor.

(c) Subject to Section 3–504(c), with respect to an instrument taken for collection by a collecting bank, notice of dishonor must be given (i) by the bank before midnight of the next banking day following the banking day on which the bank receives notice of dishonor of the instrument, or (ii) by any other person within 30 days following the day on which the person receives notice of dishonor. With respect to any other instrument, notice of dishonor must be given within 30 days following the day on which dishonor occurs.

§ 3–504. Excused Presentment and Notice of Dishonor.

(a) Presentment for payment or acceptance of an instrument is excused if (i) the person entitled to present the instrument cannot with reasonable diligence make presentment, (ii) the maker or acceptor has repudiated an obligation to pay the instrument or is dead or in insolvency proceedings, (iii) by the terms of the instrument presentment is not necessary to enforce the obligation of indorsers or the drawer, (iv) the drawer or indorser whose obligation is being enforced has waived presentment or otherwise has no reason to expect or right to require that the instrument be paid or accepted, or (v) the drawer instructed the drawee not to pay or accept the draft or the drawee was not obligated to the drawer to pay the draft.

(b) Notice of dishonor is excused if (i) by the terms of the instrument notice of dishonor is not necessary to enforce the obligation of a party to pay the instrument, or (ii) the party whose obligation is being enforced waived notice of dishonor. A waiver of presentment is also a waiver of notice of dishonor.

(c) Delay in giving notice of dishonor is excused if the delay was caused by circumstances beyond the control of the person giving the notice and the person giving the notice exercised reasonable diligence after the cause of the delay ceased to operate.

§ 3–505. Evidence of Dishonor.

(a) The following are admissible as evidence and create a presumption of dishonor and of any notice of dishonor stated:

(1) a document regular in form as provided in subsection (b) which purports to be a protest;

(2) a purported stamp or writing of the drawee, payor bank, or presenting bank on or accompanying the instrument stating that acceptance or payment has been refused unless reasons for the refusal are stated and the reasons are not consistent with dishonor;

(3) a book or record of the drawee, payor bank, or collecting bank, kept in the usual course of business which shows dishonor, even if there is no evidence of who made the entry.

(b) A protest is a certificate of dishonor made by a United States consul or vice consul, or a notary public or other person authorized to administer oaths by the law of the place where dishonor occurs. It may be made upon information satisfactory to that person. The protest must identify the instrument and certify either that presentment has been made or, if not made, the reason why it was not made, and that the instrument has been dishonored by nonacceptance or nonpayment. The protest may also certify that notice of dishonor has been given to some or all parties.

Part 6 Discharge and Payment

§ 3–601. Discharge and Effect of Discharge.

(a) The obligation of a party to pay the instrument is discharged as stated in this Article or by an act or agreement with the party which would discharge an obligation to pay money under a simple contract.

(b) Discharge of the obligation of a party is not effective against a person acquiring rights of a holder in due course of the instrument without notice of the discharge.

§ 3–602. Payment.

(a) Subject to subsection (b), an instrument is paid to the extent payment is made (i) by or on behalf of a party obliged to pay the instrument, and (ii) to a person entitled to enforce the instrument. To the extent of the payment, the obligation of the party obliged to pay the instrument is discharged even though payment is made with knowledge of a claim to the instrument under Section 3–306 by another person.

(b) The obligation of a party to pay the instrument is not discharged under subsection (a) if:

(1) a claim to the instrument under Section 3–306 is enforceable against the party receiving payment and

(i) payment is made with knowledge by the payor that payment is prohibited by injunction or similar process of a court of competent jurisdiction, or (ii) in the case of an instrument other than a cashier's check, teller's check, or certified check, the party making payment accepted, from the person having a claim to the instrument, indemnity against loss resulting from refusal to pay the person entitled to enforce the instrument; or

(2) the person making payment knows that the instrument is a stolen instrument and pays a person it knows is in wrongful possession of the instrument.

§ 3–603. Tender of Payment.

(a) If tender of payment of an obligation to pay an instrument is made to a person entitled to enforce the instrument, the effect of tender is governed by principles of law applicable to tender of payment under a simple contract.

(b) If tender of payment of an obligation to pay an instrument is made to a person entitled to enforce the instrument and the tender is refused, there is discharge, to the extent of the amount of the tender, of the obligation of an indorser or accommodation party having a right of recourse with respect to the obligation to which the tender relates.

(c) If tender of payment of an amount due on an instrument is made to a person entitled to enforce the instrument, the obligation of the obligor to pay interest after the due date on the amount tendered is discharged. If presentment is required with respect to an instrument and the obligor is able and ready to pay on the due date at every place of payment stated in the instrument, the obligor is deemed to have made tender of payment on the due date to the person entitled to enforce the instrument.

§ 3–604. Discharge by Cancellation or Renunciation.

(a) A person entitled to enforce an instrument, with or without consideration, may discharge the obligation of a party to pay the instrument (i) by an intentional voluntary act, such as surrender of the instrument to the party, destruction, mutilation, or cancellation of the instrument, cancellation or striking out of the party's signature, or the addition of words to the instrument indicating discharge, or (ii) by agreeing not to sue or otherwise renouncing rights against the party by a signed writing.

(b) Cancellation or striking out of an indorsement pursuant to subsection (a) does not affect the status and rights of a party derived from the indorsement.

§ 3–605. Discharge of Indorsers and Accommodation Parties.

(a) In this section, the term "indorser" includes a drawer having the obligation described in Section 3–414(d).

(b) Discharge, under Section 3–604, of the obligation of a party to pay an instrument does not discharge the obligation of an indorser or accommodation party having a right of recourse against the discharged party.

(c) If a person entitled to enforce an instrument agrees, with or without consideration, to an extension of the due date of the obligation of a party to pay the instrument, the extension discharges an indorser or accommodation party having a right of recourse against the party whose obligation is extended to the extent the indorser or accommodation party proves that the extension caused loss to the indorser or accommodation party with respect to the right of recourse.

(d) If a person entitled to enforce an instrument agrees, with or without consideration, to a material modification of the obligation of a party other than an extension of the due date, the modification discharges the obligation of an indorser or accommodation party having a right of recourse against the person whose obligation is modified to the extent the modification causes loss to the indorser or accommodation party with respect to the right of recourse. The loss suffered by the indorser or accommodation party as a result of the modification is equal to the amount of the right of recourse unless the person enforcing the instrument proves that no loss was caused by the modification or that the loss caused by the modification was an amount less than the amount of the right of recourse.

(e) If the obligation of a party to pay an instrument is secured by an interest in collateral and a person entitled to enforce the instrument impairs the value of the interest in collateral, the obligation of an indorser or accommodation party having a right of recourse against the obligor is discharged to the extent of the impairment. The value of an interest in collateral is impaired to the extent (i) the value of the interest is reduced to an amount less than the amount of the right of recourse of the party asserting discharge, or (ii) the reduction in value of the interest causes an increase in the amount by which the amount of the right of recourse exceeds the value of the interest. The burden of proving impairment is on the party asserting discharge.

(f) If the obligation of a party is secured by an interest in collateral not provided by an accommodation party and a person entitled to enforce the instrument impairs the value of the interest in collateral, the obligation of any party who is jointly and severally liable with respect to the secured obligation is discharged to the extent the impairment causes the party asserting discharge to pay more than that party would have been obliged to pay, taking into account rights of contribution, if impairment had not occurred. If the party asserting discharge is an accommodation party not entitled to discharge under subsection (e), the party is deemed to have a right to contribution based on joint and several liability rather than a right to reimbursement. The burden of proving impairment is on the party asserting discharge.

(g) Under subsection (e) or (f), impairing value of an interest in collateral includes (i) failure to obtain or maintain perfection or recordation of the interest in collateral, (ii) release of collateral without substitution of collateral of equal value, (iii) failure to perform a duty to preserve the value of collateral owed, under Article 9 or other law, to a debtor or surety or other person secondarily liable, or (iv) failure to comply with applicable law in disposing of collateral.

(h) An accommodation party is not discharged under subsection (c), (d), or (e) unless the person entitled to enforce the instrument knows of the accommodation or has notice under Section 3–419(c) that the instrument was signed for accommodation.

(i) A party is not discharged under this section if (i) the party asserting discharge consents to the event or conduct that is the basis of the discharge, or (ii) the instrument or a separate agreement of the party provides for waiver of discharge under this section either specifically or by general language indicating that parties waive defenses based on suretyship or impairment of collateral.

ADDENDUM TO REVISED ARTICLE 3
Notes to Legislative Counsel

1. If revised Article 3 is adopted in your state, the reference in Section 2–511 to Section 3–802 should be changed to Section 3–310.

2. If revised Article 3 is adopted in your state and the Uniform Fiduciaries Act is also in effect in your state, you may want to consider amending Uniform Fiduciaries Act § 9 to conform to Section 3–307(b)(2)(iii) and (4)(iii). See Official Comment 3 to Section 3–307.

Revised Article 4
BANK DEPOSITS AND COLLECTIONS

Part 1 General Provisions and Definitions

§ 4–101. Short Title.

This Article may be cited as Uniform Commercial Code—Bank Deposits and Collections.

As amended in 1990.

§ 4–102. Applicability.

(a) To the extent that items within this Article are also within Articles 3 and 8, they are subject to those Articles. If there is conflict, this Article governs Article 3, but Article 8 governs this Article.

(b) The liability of a bank for action or non-action with respect to an item handled by it for purposes of presentment, payment, or collection is governed by the law of the place where the bank is located. In the case of action or non-action by or at a branch or separate office of a bank, its liability is governed by the law of the place where the branch or separate office is located.

§ 4–103. Variation by Agreement; Measure of Damages; Action Constituting Ordinary Care.

(a) The effect of the provisions of this Article may be varied by agreement, but the parties to the agreement cannot disclaim a bank's responsibility for its lack of good faith or failure to exercise ordinary care or limit the measure of damages for the lack or failure. However, the parties may determine by agreement the standards by which the bank's responsibility is to be measured if those standards are not manifestly unreasonable.

(b) Federal Reserve regulations and operating circulars, clearing-house rules, and the like have the effect of agreements under subsection (a), whether or not specifically assented to by all parties interested in items handled.

(c) Action or non-action approved by this Article or pursuant to Federal Reserve regulations or operating circulars is the exercise of ordinary care and, in the absence of special instructions, action or non-action consistent with clearing-house rules and the like or with a general banking usage not disapproved by this Article, is *prima facie* the exercise of ordinary care.

(d) The specification or approval of certain procedures by this Article is not disapproval of other procedures that may be reasonable under the circumstances.

(e) The measure of damages for failure to exercise ordinary care in handling an item is the amount of the item reduced by an amount that could not have been realized by the exercise of ordinary care. If there is also bad faith it includes any other damages the party suffered as a proximate consequence.

As amended in 1990.

§ 4–104. Definitions and Index of Definitions.

(a) In this Article, unless the context otherwise requires:

(1) "Account" means any deposit or credit account with a bank, including a demand, time, savings, passbook, share draft, or like account, other than an account evidenced by a certificate of deposit;

(2) "Afternoon" means the period of a day between noon and midnight;

(3) "Banking day" means the part of a day on which a bank is open to the public for carrying on substantially all of its banking functions;

(4) "Clearing house" means an association of banks or other payors regularly clearing items;

(5) "Customer" means a person having an account with a bank or for whom a bank has agreed to collect items, including a bank that maintains an account at another bank;

(6) "Documentary draft" means a draft to be presented for acceptance or payment if specified documents, certificated securities (Section 8–102) or instructions for uncertificated securities (Section 8–102), or other certificates, statements, or the like are to be received by the drawee or other payor before acceptance or payment of the draft;

(7) "Draft" means a draft as defined in Section 3–104 or an item, other than an instrument, that is an order;

(8) "Drawee" means a person ordered in a draft to make payment;

(9) "Item" means an instrument or a promise or order to pay money handled by a bank for collection or payment. The term does not include a payment order governed by Article 4A or a credit or debit card slip;

(10) "Midnight deadline" with respect to a bank is midnight on its next banking day following the banking day

on which it receives the relevant item or notice or from which the time for taking action commences to run, whichever is later;

(11) "Settle" means to pay in cash, by clearing-house settlement, in a charge or credit or by remittance, or otherwise as agreed. A settlement may be either provisional or final;

(12) "Suspends payments" with respect to a bank means that it has been closed by order of the supervisory authorities, that a public officer has been appointed to take it over, or that it ceases or refuses to make payments in the ordinary course of business.

(b) [Other definitions' section references deleted.]

(c) [Other definitions' section references deleted.]

(d) In addition, Article 1 contains general definitions and principles of construction and interpretation applicable throughout this Article.

§ 4–105. "Bank"; "Depositary Bank"; "Payor Bank"; "Intermediary Bank"; "Collecting Bank"; "Presenting Bank".

In this Article:

(1) "Bank" means a person engaged in the business of banking, including a savings bank, savings and loan association, credit union, or trust company;

(2) "Depositary bank" means the first bank to take an item even though it is also the payor bank, unless the item is presented for immediate payment over the counter;

(3) "Payor bank" means a bank that is the drawee of a draft;

(4) "Intermediary bank" means a bank to which an item is transferred in course of collection except the depositary or payor bank;

(5) "Collecting bank" means a bank handling an item for collection except the payor bank;

(6) "Presenting bank" means a bank presenting an item except a payor bank.

§ 4–106. Payable Through or Payable at Bank: Collecting Bank.

(a) If an item states that it is "payable through" a bank identified in the item, (i) the item designates the bank as a collecting bank and does not by itself authorize the bank to pay the item, and (ii) the item may be presented for payment only by or through the bank.

Alternative A

(b) If an item states that it is "payable at" a bank identified in the item, the item is equivalent to a draft drawn on the bank.

Alternative B

(b) If an item states that it is "payable at" a bank identified in the item, (i) the item designates the bank as a collecting bank and does not by itself authorize the bank to pay the item, and (ii) the item may be presented for payment only by or through the bank.

(c) If a draft names a nonbank drawee and it is unclear whether a bank named in the draft is a co-drawee or a collecting bank, the bank is a collecting bank.

As added in 1990.

§ 4–107. Separate Office of Bank.

A branch or separate office of a bank is a separate bank for the purpose of computing the time within which and determining the place at or to which action may be taken or notices or orders shall be given under this Article and under Article 3.

As amended in 1962 and 1990.

§ 4–108. Time of Receipt of Items.

(a) For the purpose of allowing time to process items, prove balances, and make the necessary entries on its books to determine its position for the day, a bank may fix an afternoon hour of 2 P.M. or later as a cutoff hour for the handling of money and items and the making of entries on its books.

(b) An item or deposit of money received on any day after a cutoff hour so fixed or after the close of the banking day may be treated as being received at the opening of the next banking day.

As amended in 1990.

§ 4–109. Delays.

(a) Unless otherwise instructed, a collecting bank in a good faith effort to secure payment of a specific item drawn on a payor other than a bank, and with or without the approval of any person involved, may waive, modify, or extend time limits imposed or permitted by this [act] for a period not exceeding two additional banking days without discharge of drawers or indorsers or liability to its transferor or a prior party.

(b) Delay by a collecting bank or payor bank beyond time limits prescribed or permitted by this [act] or by instructions is excused if (i) the delay is caused by interruption of communication or computer facilities, suspension of payments by another bank, war, emergency conditions, failure of equipment, or other circumstances beyond the control of the bank, and (ii) the bank exercises such diligence as the circumstances require.

§ 4–110. Electronic Presentment.

(a) "Agreement for electronic presentment" means an agreement, clearing-house rule, or Federal Reserve regulation or operating circular, providing that presentment of an item may be made by transmission of an image of an item or information describing the item ("presentment notice") rather than delivery of the item itself. The agreement may provide for procedures governing retention, presentment, payment, dishonor, and other matters concerning items subject to the agreement.

(b) Presentment of an item pursuant to an agreement for presentment is made when the presentment notice is received.

(c) If presentment is made by presentment notice, a reference to "item" or "check" in this Article means the presentment notice unless the context otherwise indicates.

As added in 1990.

§ 4–111. Statute of Limitations.

An action to enforce an obligation, duty, or right arising under this Article must be commenced within three years after the [cause of action] accrues.

As added in 1990.

Part 2 Collection of Items: Depositary and Collecting Banks

§ 4–201. Status of Collecting Bank as Agent and Provisional Status of Credits; Applicability of Article; Item Indorsed "Pay Any Bank".

(a) Unless a contrary intent clearly appears and before the time that a settlement given by a collecting bank for an item is or becomes final, the bank, with respect to an item, is an agent or sub-agent of the owner of the item and any settlement given for the item is provisional. This provision applies regardless of the form of indorsement or lack of indorsement and even though credit given for the item is subject to immediate withdrawal as of right or is in fact withdrawn; but the continuance of ownership of an item by its owner and any rights of the owner to proceeds of the item are subject to rights of a collecting bank, such as those resulting from outstanding advances on the item and rights of recoupment or setoff. If an item is handled by banks for purposes of presentment, payment, collection, or return, the relevant provisions of this Article apply even though action of the parties clearly establishes that a particular bank has purchased the item and is the owner of it.

(b) After an item has been indorsed with the words "pay any bank" or the like, only a bank may acquire the rights of a holder until the item has been:

(1) returned to the customer initiating collection; or

(2) specially indorsed by a bank to a person who is not a bank.

As amended in 1990.

§ 4–202. Responsibility for Collection or Return; When Action Timely.

(a) A collecting bank must exercise ordinary care in:

(1) presenting an item or sending it for presentment;

(2) sending notice of dishonor or nonpayment or returning an item other than a documentary draft to the bank's transferor after learning that the item has not been paid or accepted, as the case may be;

(3) settling for an item when the bank receives final settlement; and

(4) notifying its transferor of any loss or delay in transit within a reasonable time after discovery thereof.

(b) A collecting bank exercises ordinary care under subsection (a) by taking proper action before its midnight deadline following receipt of an item, notice, or settlement. Taking proper action within a reasonably longer time may constitute the exercise of ordinary care, but the bank has the burden of establishing timeliness.

(c) Subject to subsection (a)(1), a bank is not liable for the insolvency, neglect, misconduct, mistake, or default of another bank or person or for loss or destruction of an item in the possession of others or in transit.

As amended in 1990.

§ 4–203. Effect of Instructions.

Subject to Article 3 concerning conversion of instruments (Section 3–420) and restrictive indorsements (Section 3–206), only a collecting bank's transferor can give instructions that affect the bank or constitute notice to it, and a collecting bank is not liable to prior parties for any action taken pursuant to the instructions or in accordance with any agreement with its transferor.

§ 4–204. Methods of Sending and Presenting; Sending Directly to Payor Bank.

(a) A collecting bank shall send items by a reasonably prompt method, taking into consideration relevant instructions, the nature of the item, the number of those items on hand, the cost of collection involved, and the method generally used by it or others to present those items.

(b) A collecting bank may send:

(1) an item directly to the payor bank;

(2) an item to a nonbank payor if authorized by its transferor; and

(3) an item other than documentary drafts to a nonbank payor, if authorized by Federal Reserve regulation or operating circular, clearing-house rule, or the like.

(c) Presentment may be made by a presenting bank at a place where the payor bank or other payor has requested that presentment be made.

As amended in 1990.

§ 4–205. Depositary Bank Holder of Unindorsed Item.

If a customer delivers an item to a depositary bank for collection:

(1) the depositary bank becomes a holder of the item at the time it receives the item for collection if the customer at the time of delivery was a holder of the item, whether or not the customer indorses the item, and, if the bank satisfies the other requirements of Section 3–302, it is a holder in due course; and

(2) the depositary bank warrants to collecting banks, the payor bank or other payor, and the drawer that the amount of the item was paid to the customer or deposited to the customer's account.

As amended in 1990.

§ 4–206. Transfer Between Banks.

Any agreed method that identifies the transferor bank is sufficient for the item's further transfer to another bank.

As amended in 1990.

§ 4–207. Transfer Warranties.

(a) A customer or collecting bank that transfers an item and receives a settlement or other consideration warrants to the transferee and to any subsequent collecting bank that:

(1) the warrantor is a person entitled to enforce the item;

(2) all signatures on the item are authentic andauthorized;

(3) the item has not been altered;

(4) the item is not subject to a defense or claim in recoupment (Section 3–305(a)) of any party that can be asserted against the warrantor; and

(5) the warrantor has no knowledge of any insolvency proceeding commenced with respect to the maker or acceptor or, in the case of an unaccepted draft, the drawer.

(b) If an item is dishonored, a customer or collecting bank transferring the item and receiving settlement or other consideration is obliged to pay the amount due on the item (i) according to the terms of the item at the time it was transferred, or (ii) if the transfer was of an incomplete item, according to its terms when completed as stated in Sections 3–115 and 3–407. The obligation of a transferor is owed to the transferee and to any subsequent collecting bank that takes the item in good faith. A transferor cannot disclaim its obligation under this subsection by an indorsement stating that it is made "without recourse" or otherwise disclaiming liability.

(c) A person to whom the warranties under subsection (a) are made and who took the item in good faith may recover from the warrantor as damages for breach of warranty an amount equal to the loss suffered as a result of the breach, but not more than the amount of the item plus expenses and loss of interest incurred as a result of the breach.

(d) The warranties stated in subsection (a) cannot be disclaimed with respect to checks. Unless notice of a claim for breach of warranty is given to the warrantor within 30 days after the claimant has reason to know of the breach and the identity of the warrantor, the warrantor is discharged to the extent of any loss caused by the delay in giving notice of the claim.

(e) A cause of action for breach of warranty under this section accrues when the claimant has reason to know of the breach.

As amended in 1990.

§ 4–208. Presentment Warranties.

(a) If an unaccepted draft is presented to the drawee for payment or acceptance and the drawee pays or accepts the draft, (i) the person obtaining payment or acceptance, at the time of presentment, and (ii) a previous transferor of the draft, at the time of transfer, warrant to the drawee that pays or accepts the draft in good faith that:

(1) the warrantor is, or was, at the time the warrantor transferred the draft, a person entitled to enforce the draft or authorized to obtain payment or acceptance of the draft on behalf of a person entitled to enforce the draft;

(2) the draft has not been altered; and

(3) the warrantor has no knowledge that the signature of the purported drawer of the draft is unauthorized.

(b) A drawee making payment may recover from a warrantor damages for breach of warranty equal to the amount paid by the drawee less the amount the drawee received or is entitled to receive from the drawer because of the payment. In addition, the drawee is entitled to compensation for expenses and loss of interest resulting from the breach. The right of the drawee to recover damages under this subsection is not affected by any failure of the drawee to exercise ordinary care in making payment. If the drawee accepts the draft (i) breach of warranty is a defense to the obligation of the acceptor, and (ii) if the acceptor makes payment with respect to the draft, the acceptor is entitled to recover from a warrantor for breach of warranty the amounts stated in this subsection.

(c) If a drawee asserts a claim for breach of warranty under subsection (a) based on an unauthorized indorsement of the draft or an alteration of the draft, the warrantor may defend by proving that the indorsement is effective under Section 3–404 or 3–405 or the drawer is precluded under Section 3–406 or 4–406 from asserting against the drawee the unauthorized indorsement or alteration.

(d) If (i) a dishonored draft is presented for payment to the drawer or an indorser or (ii) any other item is presented for payment to a party obliged to pay the item, and the item is paid, the person obtaining payment and a prior transferor of the item warrant to the person making payment in good faith that the warrantor is, or was, at the time the warrantor transferred the item, a person entitled to enforce the item or authorized to obtain payment on behalf of a person entitled to enforce the item. The person making payment may recover from any warrantor for breach of warranty an amount equal to the amount paid plus expenses and loss of interest resulting from the breach.

(e) The warranties stated in subsections (a) and (d) cannot be disclaimed with respect to checks. Unless notice of a claim for breach of warranty is given to the warrantor within 30 days after the claimant has reason to know of the breach and the identity of the warrantor, the warrantor is discharged to the extent of any loss caused by the delay in giving notice of the claim.

(f) A cause of action for breach of warranty under this section accrues when the claimant has reason to know of the breach.

As amended in 1990.

§ 4–209. Encoding and Retention Warranties.

(a) A person who encodes information on or with respect to an item after issue warrants to any subsequent collecting bank and to the payor bank or other payor that the information is correctly encoded. If the customer of a depositary bank encodes, that bank also makes the warranty.

(b) A person who undertakes to retain an item pursuant to an agreement for electronic presentment warrants to any subsequent collecting bank and to the payor bank or other payor that retention and presentment of the item comply with the agreement. If a customer of a depositary bank undertakes to retain an item, that bank also makes this warranty.

(c) A person to whom warranties are made under this section and who took the item in good faith may recover from the warrantor as damages for breach of warranty an amount equal to the loss suffered as a result of the breach, plus expenses and loss of interest incurred as a result of the breach.

As added in 1990.

§ 4–210. Security Interest of Collecting Bank in Items, Accompanying Documents and Proceeds.

(a) A collecting bank has a security interest in an item and any accompanying documents or the proceeds of either:

(1) in case of an item deposited in an account, to the extent to which credit given for the item has been withdrawn or applied;

(2) in case of an item for which it has given credit available for withdrawal as of right, to the extent of the credit given, whether or not the credit is drawn upon or there is a right of charge-back; or

(3) if it makes an advance on or against the item.

(b) If credit given for several items received at one time or pursuant to a single agreement is withdrawn or applied in part, the security interest remains upon all the items, any accompanying documents or the proceeds of either. For the purpose of this section, credits first given are first withdrawn.

(c) Receipt by a collecting bank of a final settlement for an item is a realization on its security interest in the item, accompanying documents, and proceeds. So long as the bank does not receive final settlement for the item or give up possession of the item or accompanying documents for purposes other than collection, the security interest continues to that extent and is subject to Article 9, but:

(1) no security agreement is necessary to make the security interest enforceable (Section 9–203(1)(a));

(2) no filing is required to perfect the security interest; and

(3) the security interest has priority over conflicting perfected security interests in the item, accompanying documents, or proceeds.

As amended in 1990 and 1999.

§ 4–211. When Bank Gives Value for Purposes of Holder in Due Course.

For purposes of determining its status as a holder in due course, a bank has given value to the extent it has a security interest in an item, if the bank otherwise complies with the requirements of Section 3–302 on what constitutes a holder in due course.

As amended in 1990.

§ 4–212. Presentment by Notice of Item Not Payable by, Through, or at Bank; Liability of Drawer or Indorser.

(a) Unless otherwise instructed, a collecting bank may present an item not payable by, through, or at a bank by sending to the party to accept or pay a written notice that the bank holds the item for acceptance or payment. The notice must be sent in time to be received on or before the day when presentment is due and the bank must meet any requirement of the party to accept or pay under Section 3–501 by the close of the bank's next banking day after it knows of the requirement.

(b) If presentment is made by notice and payment, acceptance, or request for compliance with a requirement under Section 3–501 is not received by the close of business on the day after maturity or, in the case of demand items, by the close of business on the third banking day after notice was sent, the presenting bank may treat the item as dishonored and charge any drawer or indorser by sending it notice of the facts.

As amended in 1990.

§ 4–213. Medium and Time of Settlement by Bank.

(a) With respect to settlement by a bank, the medium and time of settlement may be prescribed by Federal Reserve regulations or circulars, clearing-house rules, and the like, or agreement. In the absence of such prescription:

(1) the medium of settlement is cash or credit to an account in a Federal Reserve bank of or specified by the person to receive settlement; and

(2) the time of settlement is:

(i) with respect to tender of settlement by cash, a cashier's check, or teller's check, when the cash or check is sent or delivered;

(ii) with respect to tender of settlement by credit in an account in a Federal Reserve Bank, when the credit is made;

(iii) with respect to tender of settlement by a credit or debit to an account in a bank, when the credit or debit is made or, in the case of tender of settlement by authority to charge an account, when the authority is sent or delivered; or

(iv) with respect to tender of settlement by a funds transfer, when payment is made pursuant to Section 4A–406(a) to the person receiving settlement.

(b) If the tender of settlement is not by a medium authorized by subsection (a) or the time of settlement is not fixed by subsection (a), no settlement occurs until the tender of settlement is accepted by the person receiving settlement.

(c) If settlement for an item is made by cashier's check or teller's check and the person receiving settlement, before its midnight deadline:

(1) presents or forwards the check for collection, settlement is final when the check is finally paid; or

(2) fails to present or forward the check for collection, settlement is final at the midnight deadline of the person receiving settlement.

(d) If settlement for an item is made by giving authority to charge the account of the bank giving settlement in the bank receiving settlement, settlement is final when the charge is made by the bank receiving settlement if there are funds available in the account for the amount of the item.

As amended in 1990.

§ 4–214. Right of Charge-Back or Refund; Liability of Collecting Bank: Return of Item.

(a) If a collecting bank has made provisional settlement with its customer for an item and fails by reason of dishonor, suspension of payments by a bank, or otherwise to receive settlement for the item which is or becomes final, the bank may revoke the settlement given by it, charge back the amount of any credit given for the item to its customer's account, or obtain refund from its customer, whether or not it is able to return the item, if by its midnight deadline or within a longer reasonable time after it learns the facts it returns the item or sends notification of the facts. If the return or notice is delayed beyond the bank's midnight deadline or a longer reasonable time after it learns the facts, the bank may revoke the settlement, charge back the credit, or obtain refund from its customer, but it is liable for any loss resulting from the delay. These rights to revoke, charge back, and obtain refund terminate if and when a settlement for the item received by the bank is or becomes final.

(b) A collecting bank returns an item when it is sent or delivered to the bank's customer or transferor or pursuant to its instructions.

(c) A depositary bank that is also the payor may charge back the amount of an item to its customer's account or obtain refund in accordance with the section governing return of an item received by a payor bank for credit on its books (Section 4–301).

(d) The right to charge back is not affected by:

(1) previous use of a credit given for the item; or

(2) failure by any bank to exercise ordinary care with respect to the item, but a bank so failing remains liable.

(e) A failure to charge back or claim refund does not affect other rights of the bank against the customer or any other party.

(f) If credit is given in dollars as the equivalent of the value of an item payable in foreign money, the dollar amount of any charge-back or refund must be calculated on the basis of the bank-offered spot rate for the foreign money prevailing on the day when the person entitled to the charge-back or refund learns that it will not receive payment in ordinary course.

As amended in 1990.

§ 4–215. Final Payment of Item by Payor Bank; When Provisional Debits and Credits Become Final; When Certain Credits Become Available for Withdrawal.

(a) An item is finally paid by a payor bank when the bank has first done any of the following:

(1) paid the item in cash;

(2) settled for the item without having a right to revoke the settlement under statute, clearing-house rule, or agreement; or

(3) made a provisional settlement for the item and failed to revoke the settlement in the time and manner permitted by statute, clearing-house rule, or agreement.

(b) If provisional settlement for an item does not become final, the item is not finally paid.

(c) If provisional settlement for an item between the presenting and payor banks is made through a clearing house or by debits or credits in an account between them, then to the extent that provisional debits or credits for the item are entered in accounts between the presenting and payor banks or between the presenting and successive prior collecting banks seriatim, they become final upon final payment of the item by the payor bank.

(d) If a collecting bank receives a settlement for an item which is or becomes final, the bank is accountable to its customer for the amount of the item and any provisional credit given for the item in an account with its customer becomes final.

(e) Subject to (i) applicable law stating a time for availability of funds and (ii) any right of the bank to apply the credit to an obligation of the customer, credit given by a bank for an item in a customer's account becomes available for withdrawal as of right:

(1) if the bank has received a provisional settlement for the item, when the settlement becomes final and the bank has had a reasonable time to receive return of the item and the item has not been received within that time;

(2) if the bank is both the depositary bank and the payor bank, and the item is finally paid, at the opening of the bank's second banking day following receipt of the item.

(f) Subject to applicable law stating a time for availability of funds and any right of a bank to apply a deposit to an obligation of the depositor, a deposit of money becomes available for withdrawal as of right at the opening of the bank's next banking day after receipt of the deposit.

As amended in 1990.

§ 4–216. Insolvency and Preference.

(a) If an item is in or comes into the possession of a payor or collecting bank that suspends payment and the item has not been finally paid, the item must be returned by the receiver, trustee, or agent in charge of the closed bank to the presenting bank or the closed bank's customer.

(b) If a payor bank finally pays an item and suspends payments without making a settlement for the item with its customer or the presenting bank which settlement is or becomes final, the owner of the item has a preferred claim against the payor bank.

(c) If a payor bank gives or a collecting bank gives or receives a provisional settlement for an item and thereafter suspends payments, the suspension does not prevent or interfere with the settlement's becoming final if the finality occurs automatically upon the lapse of certain time or the happening of certain events.

(d) If a collecting bank receives from subsequent parties settlement for an item, which settlement is or becomes final and the bank suspends payments without making a settlement for the item with its customer which settlement is or becomes final, the owner of the item has a preferred claim against the collecting bank.

As amended in 1990.

Part 3 Collection of Items: Payor Banks

§ 4–301. Deferred Posting; Recovery of Payment by Return of Items; Time of Dishonor; Return of Items by Payor Bank.

(a) If a payor bank settles for a demand item other than a documentary draft presented otherwise than for immediate payment over the counter before midnight of the banking day of receipt, the payor bank may revoke the settlement and recover the settlement if, before it has made final payment and before its midnight deadline, it

(1) returns the item; or

(2) sends written notice of dishonor or non-payment if the item is unavailable for return.

(b) If a demand item is received by a payor bank for credit on its books, it may return the item or send notice of dishonor and may revoke any credit given or recover the amount thereof withdrawn by its customer, if it acts within the time limit and in the manner specified in subsection (a).

(c) Unless previous notice of dishonor has been sent, an item is dishonored at the time when for purposes of dishonor it is returned or notice sent in accordance with this section.

(d) An item is returned:

(1) as to an item presented through a clearing house, when it is delivered to the presenting or last collecting bank or to the clearing house or is sent or delivered in accordance with clearing-house rules; or

(2) in all other cases, when it is sent or delivered to the bank's customer or transferor or pursuant to instructions.

As amended in 1990.

§ 4–302. Payor Bank's Responsibility for Late Return of Item.

(a) If an item is presented to and received by a payor bank, the bank is accountable for the amount of:

(1) a demand item, other than a documentary draft, whether properly payable or not, if the bank, in any case in which it is not also the depositary bank, retains the item beyond midnight of the banking day of receipt without settling for it or, whether or not it is also the depositary bank, does not pay or return the

item or send notice of dishonor until after its midnight deadline; or

(2) any other properly payable item unless, within the time allowed for acceptance or payment of that item, the bank either accepts or pays the item or returns it and accompanying documents.

(b) The liability of a payor bank to pay an item pursuant to subsection (a) is subject to defenses based on breach of a presentment warranty (Section 4–208) or proof that the person seeking enforcement of the liability presented or transferred the item for the purpose of defrauding the payor bank.

As amended in 1990.

§ 4–303. When Items Subject to Notice, Stop-Payment Order, Legal Process, or Setoff; Order in Which Items May Be Charged or Certified.

(a) Any knowledge, notice, or stop-payment order received by, legal process served upon, or setoff exercised by a payor bank comes too late to terminate, suspend, or modify the bank's right or duty to pay an item or to charge its customer's account for the item if the knowledge, notice, stop-payment order, or legal process is received or served and a reasonable time for the bank to act thereon expires or the setoff is exercised after the earliest of the following:

(1) the bank accepts or certifies the item;

(2) the bank pays the item in cash;

(3) the bank settles for the item without having a right to revoke the settlement under statute, clearing-house rule, or agreement;

(4) the bank becomes accountable for the amount of the item under Section 4–302 dealing with the payor bank's responsibility for late return of items; or

(5) with respect to checks, a cutoff hour no earlier than one hour after the opening of the next banking day after the banking day on which the bank received the check and no later than the close of that next banking day or, if no cutoff hour is fixed, the close of the next banking day after the banking day on which the bank received the check.

(b) Subject to subsection (a), items may be accepted, paid, certified, or charged to the indicated account of its customer in any order.

As amended in 1990.

Part 4 Relationship Between Payor Bank and Its Customer

§ 4–401. When Bank May Charge Customer's Account.

(a) A bank may charge against the account of a customer an item that is properly payable from the account even though the charge creates an overdraft. An item is properly payable if it is authorized by the customer and is in accordance with any agreement between the customer and bank.

(b) A customer is not liable for the amount of an overdraft if the customer neither signed the item nor benefited from the proceeds of the item.

(c) A bank may charge against the account of a customer a check that is otherwise properly payable from the account, even though payment was made before the date of the check, unless the customer has given notice to the bank of the postdating describing the check with reasonable certainty. The notice is effective for the period stated in Section 4–403(b) for stop-payment orders, and must be received at such time and in such manner as to afford the bank a reasonable opportunity to act on it before the bank takes any action with respect to the check described in Section 4–303. If a bank charges against the account of a customer a check before the date stated in the notice of postdating, the bank is liable for damages for the loss resulting from its act. The loss may include damages for dishonor of subsequent items under Section 4–402.

(d) A bank that in good faith makes payment to a holder may charge the indicated account of its customer according to:

(1) the original terms of the altered item; or

(2) the terms of the completed item, even though the bank knows the item has been completed unless the bank has notice that the completion was improper.

As amended in 1990.

§ 4–402. Bank's Liability to Customer for Wrongful Dishonor; Time of Determining Insufficiency of Account.

(a) Except as otherwise provided in this Article, a payor bank wrongfully dishonors an item if it dishonors an item that is properly payable, but a bank may dishonor an item that would create an overdraft unless it has agreed to pay the overdraft.

(b) A payor bank is liable to its customer for damages proximately caused by the wrongful dishonor of an item. Liability is limited to actual damages proved and may include damages for an arrest or prosecution of the customer or other consequential damages. Whether any consequential damages are proximately caused by the wrongful dishonor is a question of fact to be determined in each case.

(c) A payor bank's determination of the customer's account balance on which a decision to dishonor for insufficiency of available funds is based may be made at any time between the time the item is received by the payor bank and the time that the payor bank returns the item or gives notice in lieu of return, and no more than one determination need be made. If, at the election of the payor bank, a subsequent balance determination is made for the purpose of reevaluating the bank's decision to dishonor the item, the account balance at that time is determinative of whether a dishonor for insufficiency of available funds is wrongful.

As amended in 1990.

§ 4–403. Customer's Right to Stop Payment; Burden of Proof of Loss.

(a) A customer or any person authorized to draw on the account if there is more than one person may stop payment of any item drawn on the customer's account or close the account by an order to the bank describing the item or account with reasonable certainty received at a time and in a manner that affords the bank a reasonable opportunity to act on it before any action by the bank with respect to the item described in Section 4–303. If the signature of more than one person is required to draw on an account, any of these persons may stop payment or close the account.

(b) A stop-payment order is effective for six months, but it lapses after 14 calendar days if the original order was oral and was not confirmed in writing within that period. A stop-payment order may be renewed for additional six-month periods by a writing given to the bank within a period during which the stop-payment order is effective.

(c) The burden of establishing the fact and amount of loss resulting from the payment of an item contrary to a stop-payment order or order to close an account is on the customer. The loss from payment of an item contrary to a stop-payment order may include damages for dishonor of subsequent items under Section 4–402.

As amended in 1990.

§ 4–404. Bank Not Obliged to Pay Check More Than Six Months Old.

A bank is under no obligation to a customer having a checking account to pay a check, other than a certified check, which is presented more than six months after its date, but it may charge its customer's account for a payment made thereafter in good faith.

§ 4–405. Death or Incompetence of Customer.

(a) A payor or collecting bank's authority to accept, pay, or collect an item or to account for proceeds of its collection, if otherwise effective, is not rendered ineffective by incompetence of a customer of either bank existing at the time the item is issued or its collection is undertaken if the bank does not know of an adjudication of incompetence. Neither death nor incompetence of a customer revokes the authority to accept, pay, collect, or account until the bank knows of the fact of death or of an adjudication of incompetence and has reasonable opportunity to act on it.

(b) Even with knowledge, a bank may for 10 days after the date of death pay or certify checks drawn on or before the date unless ordered to stop payment by a person claiming an interest in the account.

As amended in 1990.

§ 4–406. Customer's Duty to Discover and Report Unauthorized Signature or Alteration.

(a) A bank that sends or makes available to a customer a statement of account showing payment of items for the account shall either return or make available to the customer the items paid or provide information in the statement of account sufficient to allow the customer reasonably to identify the items paid. The statement of account provides sufficient information if the item is described by item number, amount, and date of payment.

(b) If the items are not returned to the customer, the person retaining the items shall either retain the items or, if the items are destroyed, maintain the capacity to furnish legible copies of the items until the expiration of seven years after receipt of the items. A customer may request an item from the bank that paid the item, and that bank must provide in a reasonable time either the item or, if the item has been destroyed or is not otherwise obtainable, a legible copy of the item.

(c) If a bank sends or makes available a statement of account or items pursuant to subsection (a), the customer must exercise reasonable promptness in examining the statement or the items to determine whether any payment was not authorized because of an alteration of an item or because a purported signature by or on behalf of the customer was not authorized. If, based on the statement or items provided, the customer should reasonably have discovered the unauthorized payment, the customer must promptly notify the bank of the relevant facts.

(d) If the bank proves that the customer failed, with respect to an item, to comply with the duties imposed on the customer by subsection (c), the customer is precluded from asserting against the bank:

(1) the customer's unauthorized signature or any alteration on the item, if the bank also proves that it suffered a loss by reason of the failure; and

(2) the customer's unauthorized signature or alteration by the same wrongdoer on any other item paid in good faith by the bank if the payment was made before the bank received notice from the customer of the unauthorized signature or alteration and after the customer had been afforded a reasonable period of time, not exceeding 30 days, in which to examine the item or statement of account and notify the bank.

(e) If subsection (d) applies and the customer proves that the bank failed to exercise ordinary care in paying the item and that the failure substantially contributed to loss, the loss is allocated between the customer precluded and the bank asserting the preclusion according to the extent to which the failure of the customer to comply with subsection (c) and the failure of the bank to exercise ordinary care contributed to the loss. If the customer proves that the bank did not pay the item in good faith, the preclusion under subsection (d) does not apply.

(f) Without regard to care or lack of care of either the customer or the bank, a customer who does not within one year after the statement or items are made available to the customer (subsection (a)) discover and report the customer's unauthorized signature on or any alteration on the item is precluded from asserting against the bank the unauthorized signature or alteration. If there is a preclusion under this subsection, the payor bank may not recover for breach or warranty under Section 4–208 with respect to the unauthorized signature or alteration to which the preclusion applies.

As amended in 1990.

§ 4–407. Payor Bank's Right to Subrogation on Improper Payment.

If a payor has paid an item over the order of the drawer or maker to stop payment, or after an account has been closed, or otherwise under circumstances giving a basis for objection by the drawer or maker, to prevent unjust enrichment and only to the extent necessary to prevent loss to the bank by reason of its payment of the item, the payor bank is subrogated to the rights

(1) of any holder in due course on the item against the drawer or maker;

(2) of the payee or any other holder of the item against the drawer or maker either on the item or under the transaction out of which the item arose; and

(3) of the drawer or maker against the payee or any other holder of the item with respect to the transaction out of which the item arose.

As amended in 1990.

Part 5 Collection of Documentary Drafts

§ 4–501. Handling of Documentary Drafts; Duty to Send for Presentment and to Notify Customer of Dishonor.

A bank that takes a documentary draft for collection shall present or send the draft and accompanying documents for presentment and, upon learning that the draft has not been paid or accepted in due course, shall seasonably notify its customer of the fact even though it may have discounted or bought the draft or extended credit available for withdrawal as of right.

As amended in 1990.

§ 4–502. Presentment of "On Arrival" Drafts.

If a draft or the relevant instructions require presentment "on arrival", "when goods arrive" or the like, the collecting bank need not present until in its judgment a reasonable time for arrival of the goods has expired. Refusal to pay or accept because the goods have not arrived is not dishonor; the bank must notify its transferor of the refusal but need not present the draft again until it is instructed to do so or learns of the arrival of the goods.

§ 4–503. Responsibility of Presenting Bank for Documents and Goods; Report of Reasons for Dishonor; Referee in Case of Need.

Unless otherwise instructed and except as provided in Article 5, a bank presenting a documentary draft:

(1) must deliver the documents to the drawee on acceptance of the draft if it is payable more than three days after presentment, otherwise, only on payment; and

(2) upon dishonor, either in the case of presentment for acceptance or presentment for payment, may seek and follow instructions from any referee in case of need designated in the draft or, if the presenting bank does not choose to utilize the referee's services, it must use diligence and good faith to ascertain the reason for dishonor, must notify its transferor of the dishonor and of the results of its effort to ascertain the reasons therefor, and must request instructions.

However, the presenting bank is under no obligation with respect to goods represented by the documents except to follow any reasonable instructions seasonably received; it has a right to reimbursement for any expense incurred in following instructions and to prepayment of or indemnity for those expenses.

As amended in 1990.

§ 4–504. Privilege of Presenting Bank to Deal With Goods; Security Interest for Expenses.

(a) A presenting bank that, following the dishonor of a documentary draft, has seasonably requested instructions but does not receive them within a reasonable time may store, sell, or otherwise deal with the goods in any reasonable manner.

(b) For its reasonable expenses incurred by action under subsection (a) the presenting bank has a lien upon the goods or their proceeds, which may be foreclosed in the same manner as an unpaid seller's lien.

As amended in 1990.

Article 4A
FUNDS TRANSFERS

Part 1 Subject Matter and Definitions

§ 4A–101. Short Title.

This Article may be cited as Uniform Commercial Code—Funds Transfers.

§ 4A–102. Subject Matter.

Except as otherwise provided in Section 4A–108, this Article applies to funds transfers defined in Section 4A–104.

§ 4A–103. Payment Order–Definitions.

(a) In this Article:

(1) "Payment order" means an instruction of a sender to a receiving bank, transmitted orally, electronically, or in writing, to pay, or to cause another bank to pay, a fixed or determinable amount of money to a beneficiary if:

(i) the instruction does not state a condition to payment to the beneficiary other than time of payment,

(ii) the receiving bank is to be reimbursed by debiting an account of, or otherwise receiving payment from, the sender, and

(iii) the instruction is transmitted by the sender directly to the receiving bank or to an agent,

funds-transfer system, or communication system for transmittal to the receiving bank.

(2) "Beneficiary" means the person to be paid by the beneficiary's bank.

(3) "Beneficiary's bank" means the bank identified in a payment order in which an account of the beneficiary is to be credited pursuant to the order or which otherwise is to make payment to the beneficiary if the order does not provide for payment to an account.

(4) "Receiving bank" means the bank to which the sender's instruction is addressed.

(5) "Sender" means the person giving the instruction to the receiving bank.

(b) If an instruction complying with subsection (a)(1) is to make more than one payment to a beneficiary, the instruction is a separate payment order with respect to each payment.

(c) A payment order is issued when it is sent to the receiving bank.

§ 4A–104. Funds Transfer–Definitions.

In this Article:

(a) "Funds transfer" means the series of transactions, beginning with the originator's payment order, made for the purpose of making payment to the beneficiary of the order. The term includes any payment order issued by the originator's bank or an intermediary bank intended to carry out the originator's payment order. A funds transfer is completed by acceptance by the beneficiary's bank of a payment order for the benefit of the beneficiary of the originator's payment order.

(b) "Intermediary bank" means a receiving bank other than the originator's bank or the beneficiary's bank.

(c) "Originator" means the sender of the first payment order in a funds transfer.

(d) "Originator's bank" means (i) the receiving bank to which the payment order of the originator is issued if the originator is not a bank, or (ii) the originator if the originator is a bank.

§ 4A–105. Other Definitions.

(a) In this Article:

(1) "Authorized account" means a deposit account of a customer in a bank designated by the customer as a source of payment of payment orders issued by the customer to the bank. If a customer does not so designate an account, any account of the customer is an authorized account if payment of a payment order from that account is not inconsistent with a restriction on the use of that account.

(2) "Bank" means a person engaged in the business of banking and includes a savings bank, savings and loan association, credit union, and trust company. A branch or separate office of a bank is a separate bank for purposes of this Article.

(3) "Customer" means a person, including a bank, having an account with a bank or from whom a bank has agreed to receive payment orders.

(4) "Funds-transfer business day" of a receiving bank means the part of a day during which the receiving bank is open for the receipt, processing, and transmittal of payment orders and cancellations and amendments of payment orders.

(5) "Funds-transfer system" means a wire transfer network, automated clearing house, or other communication system of a clearing house or other association of banks through which a payment order by a bank may be transmitted to the bank to which the order is addressed.

(6) "Good faith" means honesty in fact and the observance of reasonable commercial standards of fair dealing.

(7) "Prove" with respect to a fact means to meet the burden of establishing the fact (Section 1–201(8)).

(b) Other definitions applying to this Article and the sections in which they appear are:

"Acceptance"	Section 4A–209
"Beneficiary"	Section 4A–103
"Beneficiary's bank"	Section 4A–103
"Executed"	Section 4A–301
"Execution date"	Section 4A–301
"Funds transfer"	Section 4A–104
"Funds-transfer system rule"	Section 4A–501
"Intermediary bank"	Section 4A–104
"Originator"	Section 4A–104
"Originator's bank"	Section 4A–104
"Payment by beneficiary's bank to beneficiary"	Section 4A–405
"Payment by originator to beneficiary"	Section 4A–406
"Payment by sender to receiving bank"	Section 4A–403
"Payment date"	Section 4A–401
"Payment order"	Section 4A–103
"Receiving bank"	Section 4A–103
"Security procedure"	Section 4A–201
"Sender"	Section 4A–103

(c) The following definitions in Article 4 apply to this Article:

"Clearing house"	Section 4–104
"Item"	Section 4–104
"Suspends payments"	Section 4–104

(d) In addition, Article 1 contains general definitions and principles of construction and interpretation applicable throughout this Article.

§ 4A–106. Time Payment Order Is Received.

(a) The time of receipt of a payment order or communication cancelling or amending a payment order is determined by the rules applicable to receipt of a notice stated in Section 1–201(27). A receiving bank may fix a cut-off time or times on a funds-transfer business day for the receipt and processing of payment orders and communications cancelling or amending payment orders. Different cut-off times may apply to payment orders, cancellations, or amendments, or to different categories of payment orders, cancellations, or amendments. A cut-off time may apply to senders generally or different cut-off times may apply to different senders or categories of payment orders. If a payment order or communication cancelling or amending a payment order is received after the close of a funds-transfer business day or after the appropriate cut-off time on a funds-transfer business day, the receiving bank may treat the payment order or communication as received at the opening of the next funds-transfer business day.

(b) If this Article refers to an execution date or payment date or states a day on which a receiving bank is required to take action, and the date or day does not fall on a funds-transfer business day, the next day that is a funds-transfer business day is treated as the date or day stated, unless the contrary is stated in this Article.

§ 4A–107. Federal Reserve Regulations and Operating Circulars.

Regulations of the Board of Governors of the Federal Reserve System and operating circulars of the Federal Reserve Banks supersede any inconsistent provision of this Article to the extent of the inconsistency.

§ 4A–108. Exclusion of Consumer Transactions Governed by Federal Law.

This Article does not apply to a funds transfer any part of which is governed by the Electronic Fund Transfer Act of 1978 (Title XX, Public Law 95–630, 92 Stat. 3728, 15 U.S.C. § 1693 et seq.) as amended from time to time.

Part 2 Issue and Acceptance of Payment Order

§ 4A–201. Security Procedure.

"Security procedure" means a procedure established by agreement of a customer and a receiving bank for the purpose of (i) verifying that a payment order or communication amending or cancelling a payment order is that of the customer, or (ii) detecting error in the transmission or the content of the payment order or communication. A security procedure may require the use of algorithms or other codes, identifying words or numbers, encryption, callback procedures, or similar security devices. Comparison of a signature on a payment order or communication with an authorized specimen signature of the customer is not by itself a security procedure.

§ 4A–202. Authorized and Verified Payment Orders.

(a) A payment order received by the receiving bank is the authorized order of the person identified as sender if that person authorized the order or is otherwise bound by it under the law of agency.

(b) If a bank and its customer have agreed that the authenticity of payment orders issued to the bank in the name of the customer as sender will be verified pursuant to a security procedure, a payment order received by the receiving bank is effective as the order of the customer, whether or not authorized, if (i) the security procedure is a commercially reasonable method of providing security against unauthorized payment orders, and (ii) the bank proves that it accepted the payment order in good faith and in compliance with the security procedure and any written agreement or instruction of the customer restricting acceptance of payment orders issued in the name of the customer. The bank is not required to follow an instruction that violates a written agreement with the customer or notice of which is not received at a time and in a manner affording the bank a reasonable opportunity to act on it before the payment order is accepted.

(c) Commercial reasonableness of a security procedure is a question of law to be determined by considering the wishes of the customer expressed to the bank, the circumstances of the customer known to the bank, including the size, type, and frequency of payment orders normally issued by the customer to the bank, alternative security procedures offered to the customer, and security procedures in general use by customers and receiving banks similarly situated. A security procedure is deemed to be commercially reasonable if (i) the security procedure was chosen by the customer after the bank offered, and the customer refused, a security procedure that was commercially reasonable for that customer, and (ii) the customer expressly agreed in writing to be bound by any payment order, whether or not authorized, issued in its name and accepted by the bank in compliance with the security procedure chosen by the customer.

(d) The term "sender" in this Article includes the customer in whose name a payment order is issued if the order is the authorized order of the customer under subsection (a), or it is effective as the order of the customer under subsection (b).

(e) This section applies to amendments and cancellations of payment orders to the same extent it applies to payment orders.

(f) Except as provided in this section and in Section 4A–203(a)(1), rights and obligations arising under this section or Section 4A–203 may not be varied by agreement.

§ 4A–203. Unenforceability of Certain Verified Payment Orders.

(a) If an accepted payment order is not, under Section 4A–202(a), an authorized order of a customer identified as sender, but is effective as an order of the customer pursuant to Section 4A–202(b), the following rules apply:

(1) By express written agreement, the receiving bank may limit the extent to which it is entitled to enforce or retain payment of the payment order.

(2) The receiving bank is not entitled to enforce or retain payment of the payment order if the customer proves that the order was not caused, directly or

indirectly, by a person (i) entrusted at any time with duties to act for the customer with respect to payment orders or the security procedure, or (ii) who obtained access to transmitting facilities of the customer or who obtained, from a source controlled by the customer and without authority of the receiving bank, information facilitating breach of the security procedure, regardless of how the information was obtained or whether the customer was at fault. Information includes any access device, computer software, or the like.

(b) This section applies to amendments of payment orders to the same extent it applies to payment orders.

§ 4A–204. Refund of Payment and Duty of Customer to Report with Respect to Unauthorized Payment Order.

(a) If a receiving bank accepts a payment order issued in the name of its customer as sender which is (i) not authorized and not effective as the order of the customer under Section 4A–202, or (ii) not enforceable, in whole or in part, against the customer under Section 4A–203, the bank shall refund any payment of the payment order received from the customer to the extent the bank is not entitled to enforce payment and shall pay interest on the refundable amount calculated from the date the bank received payment to the date of the refund. However, the customer is not entitled to interest from the bank on the amount to be refunded if the customer fails to exercise ordinary care to determine that the order was not authorized by the customer and to notify the bank of the relevant facts within a reasonable time not exceeding 90 days after the date the customer received notification from the bank that the order was accepted or that the customer's account was debited with respect to the order. The bank is not entitled to any recovery from the customer on account of a failure by the customer to give notification as stated in this section.

(b) Reasonable time under subsection (a) may be fixed by agreement as stated in Section 1–204(1), but the obligation of a receiving bank to refund payment as stated in subsection (a) may not otherwise be varied by agreement.

§ 4A–205. Erroneous Payment Orders.

(a) If an accepted payment order was transmitted pursuant to a security procedure for the detection of error and the payment order (i) erroneously instructed payment to a beneficiary not intended by the sender, (ii) erroneously instructed payment in an amount greater than the amount intended by the sender, or (iii) was an erroneously transmitted duplicate of a payment order previously sent by the sender, the following rules apply:

(1) If the sender proves that the sender or a person acting on behalf of the sender pursuant to Section 4A–206 complied with the security procedure and that the error would have been detected if the receiving bank had also complied, the sender is not obliged to pay the order to the extent stated in paragraphs (2) and (3).

(2) If the funds transfer is completed on the basis of an erroneous payment order described in clause (i) or (iii) of subsection (a), the sender is not obliged to pay the order and the receiving bank is entitled to recover from the beneficiary any amount paid to the beneficiary to the extent allowed by the law governing mistake and restitution.

(3) If the funds transfer is completed on the basis of a payment order described in clause (ii) of subsection (a), the sender is not obliged to pay the order to the extent the amount received by the beneficiary is greater than the amount intended by the sender. In that case, the receiving bank is entitled to recover from the beneficiary the excess amount received to the extent allowed by the law governing mistake and restitution.

(b) If (i) the sender of an erroneous payment order described in subsection (a) is not obliged to pay all or part of the order, and (ii) the sender receives notification from the receiving bank that the order was accepted by the bank or that the sender's account was debited with respect to the order, the sender has a duty to exercise ordinary care, on the basis of information available to the sender, to discover the error with respect to the order and to advise the bank of the relevant facts within a reasonable time, not exceeding 90 days, after the bank's notification was received by the sender. If the bank proves that the sender failed to perform that duty, the sender is liable to the bank for the loss the bank proves it incurred as a result of the failure, but the liability of the sender may not exceed the amount of the sender's order.

(c) This section applies to amendments to payment orders to the same extent it applies to payment orders.

§ 4A–206. Transmission of Payment Order through Funds-Transfer or Other Communication System.

(a) If a payment order addressed to a receiving bank is transmitted to a funds-transfer system or other third party communication system for transmittal to the bank, the system is deemed to be an agent of the sender for the purpose of transmitting the payment order to the bank. If there is a discrepancy between the terms of the payment order transmitted to the system and the terms of the payment order transmitted by the system to the bank, the terms of the payment order of the sender are those transmitted by the system. This section does not apply to a funds-transfer system of the Federal Reserve Banks.

(b) This section applies to cancellations and amendments to payment orders to the same extent it applies to payment orders.

§ 4A–207. Misdescription of Beneficiary.

(a) Subject to subsection (b), if, in a payment order received by the beneficiary's bank, the name, bank account number, or other identification of the beneficiary refers to a nonexistent or unidentifiable person or account, no person has rights as a beneficiary of the order and acceptance of the order cannot occur.

(b) If a payment order received by the beneficiary's bank identifies the beneficiary both by name and by an identifying or bank account number and the name and number identify different persons, the following rules apply:

(1) Except as otherwise provided in subsection (c), if the beneficiary's bank does not know that the name and number refer to different persons, it may rely on the number as the proper identification of the beneficiary of the order. The beneficiary's bank need not determine whether the name and number refer to the same person.

(2) If the beneficiary's bank pays the person identified by name or knows that the name and number identify different persons, no person has rights as beneficiary except the person paid by the beneficiary's bank if that person was entitled to receive payment from the originator of the funds transfer. If no person has rights as beneficiary, acceptance of the order cannot occur.

(c) If (i) a payment order described in subsection (b) is accepted, (ii) the originator's payment order described the beneficiary inconsistently by name and number, and (iii) the beneficiary's bank pays the person identified by number as permitted by subsection (b)(1), the following rules apply:

(1) If the originator is a bank, the originator is obliged to pay its order.

(2) If the originator is not a bank and proves that the person identified by number was not entitled to receive payment from the originator, the originator is not obliged to pay its order unless the originator's bank proves that the originator, before acceptance of the originator's order, had notice that payment of a payment order issued by the originator might be made by the beneficiary's bank on the basis of an identifying or bank account number even if it identifies a person different from the named beneficiary. Proof of notice may be made by any admissible evidence. The originator's bank satisfies the burden of proof if it proves that the originator, before the payment order was accepted, signed a writing stating the information to which the notice relates.

(d) In a case governed by subsection (b)(1), if the beneficiary's bank rightfully pays the person identified by number and that person was not entitled to receive payment from the originator, the amount paid may be recovered from that person to the extent allowed by the law governing mistake and restitution as follows:

(1) If the originator is obliged to pay its payment order as stated in subsection (c), the originator has the right to recover.

(2) If the originator is not a bank and is not obliged to pay its payment order, the originator's bank has the right to recover.

§ 4A–208. Misdescription of Intermediary Bank or Beneficiary's Bank.

(a) This subsection applies to a payment order identifying an intermediary bank or the beneficiary's bank only by an identifying number.

(1) The receiving bank may rely on the number as the proper identification of the intermediary or beneficiary's bank and need not determine whether the number identifies a bank.

(2) The sender is obliged to compensate the receiving bank for any loss and expenses incurred by the receiving bank as a result of its reliance on the number in executing or attempting to execute the order.

(b) This subsection applies to a payment order identifying an intermediary bank or the beneficiary's bank both by name and an identifying number if the name and number identify different persons.

(1) If the sender is a bank, the receiving bank may rely on the number as the proper identification of the intermediary or beneficiary's bank if the receiving bank, when it executes the sender's order, does not know that the name and number identify different persons. The receiving bank need not determine whether the name and number refer to the same person or whether the number refers to a bank. The sender is obliged to compensate the receiving bank for any loss and expenses incurred by the receiving bank as a result of its reliance on the number in executing or attempting to execute the order.

(2) If the sender is not a bank and the receiving bank proves that the sender, before the payment order was accepted, had notice that the receiving bank might rely on the number as the proper identification of the intermediary or beneficiary's bank even if it identifies a person different from the bank identified by name, the rights and obligations of the sender and the receiving bank are governed by subsection (b)(1), as though the sender were a bank. Proof of notice may be made by any admissible evidence. The receiving bank satisfies the burden of proof if it proves that the sender, before the payment order was accepted, signed a writing stating the information to which the notice relates.

(3) Regardless of whether the sender is a bank, the receiving bank may rely on the name as the proper identification of the intermediary or beneficiary's bank if the receiving bank, at the time it executes the sender's order, does not know that the name and number identify different persons. The receiving bank need not determine whether the name and number refer to the same person.

(4) If the receiving bank knows that the name and number identify different persons, reliance on either the name or the number in executing the sender's payment order is a breach of the obligation stated in Section 4A–302(a)(1).

§ 4A–209. Acceptance of Payment Order.

(a) Subject to subsection (d), a receiving bank other than the beneficiary's bank accepts a payment order when it executes the order.

(b) Subject to subsections (c) and (d), a beneficiary's bank accepts a payment order at the earliest of the following times:

(1) When the bank (i) pays the beneficiary as stated in Section 4A–405(a) or 4A–405(b), or (ii) notifies the beneficiary of receipt of the order or that the account of the beneficiary has been credited with respect to the order unless the notice indicates that the bank is rejecting the order or that funds with respect to the order may not be withdrawn or used until receipt of payment from the sender of the order;

(2) When the bank receives payment of the entire amount of the sender's order pursuant to Section 4A–403(a)(1) or 4A–403(a)(2); or

(3) The opening of the next funds-transfer business day of the bank following the payment date of the order if, at that time, the amount of the sender's order is fully covered by a withdrawable credit balance in an authorized account of the sender or the bank has otherwise received full payment from the sender, unless the order was rejected before that time or is rejected within (i) one hour after that time, or (ii) one hour after the opening of the next business day of the sender following the payment date if that time is later. If notice of rejection is received by the sender after the payment date and the authorized account of the sender does not bear interest, the bank is obliged to pay interest to the sender on the amount of the order for the number of days elapsing after the payment date to the day the sender receives notice or learns that the order was not accepted, counting that day as an elapsed day. If the withdrawable credit balance during that period falls below the amount of the order, the amount of interest payable is reduced accordingly.

(c) Acceptance of a payment order cannot occur before the order is received by the receiving bank. Acceptance does not occur under subsection (b)(2) or (b)(3) if the beneficiary of the payment order does not have an account with the receiving bank, the account has been closed, or the receiving bank is not permitted by law to receive credits for the beneficiary's account.

(d) A payment order issued to the originator's bank cannot be accepted until the payment date if the bank is the beneficiary's bank, or the execution date if the bank is not the beneficiary's bank. If the originator's bank executes the originator's payment order before the execution date or pays the beneficiary of the originator's payment order before the payment date and the payment order is subsequently cancelled pursuant to Section 4A–211(b), the bank may recover from the beneficiary any payment received to the extent allowed by the law governing mistake and restitution.

§ 4A–210. Rejection of Payment Order.

(a) A payment order is rejected by the receiving bank by a notice of rejection transmitted to the sender orally, electronically, or in writing. A notice of rejection need not use any particular words and is sufficient if it indicates that the receiving bank is rejecting the order or will not execute or pay the order. Rejection is effective when the notice is given if transmission is by a means that is reasonable in the circumstances. If notice of rejection is given by a means that is not reasonable, rejection is effective when the notice is received. If an agreement of the sender and receiving bank establishes the means to be used to reject a payment order, (i) any means complying with the agreement is reasonable and (ii) any means not complying is not reasonable unless no significant delay in receipt of the notice resulted from the use of the noncomplying means.

(b) This subsection applies if a receiving bank other than the beneficiary's bank fails to execute a payment order despite the existence on the execution date of a withdrawable credit balance in an authorized account of the sender sufficient to cover the order. If the sender does not receive notice of rejection of the order on the execution date and the authorized account of the sender does not bear interest, the bank is obliged to pay interest to the sender on the amount of the order for the number of days elapsing after the execution date to the earlier of the day the order is cancelled pursuant to Section 4A–211(d) or the day the sender receives notice or learns that the order was not executed, counting the final day of the period as an elapsed day. If the withdrawable credit balance during that period falls below the amount of the order, the amount of interest is reduced accordingly.

(c) If a receiving bank suspends payments, all unaccepted payment orders issued to it are are deemed rejected at the time the bank suspends payments.

(d) Acceptance of a payment order precludes a later rejection of the order. Rejection of a payment order precludes a later acceptance of the order.

§ 4A–211. Cancellation and Amendment of Payment Order.

(a) A communication of the sender of a payment order cancelling or amending the order may be transmitted to the receiving bank orally, electronically, or in writing. If a security procedure is in effect between the sender and the receiving bank, the communication is not effective to cancel or amend the order unless the communication is verified pursuant to the security procedure or the bank agrees to the cancellation or amendment.

(b) Subject to subsection (a), a communication by the sender cancelling or amending a payment order is effective to cancel or amend the order if notice of the communication is received at a time and in a manner affording the receiving bank a reasonable opportunity to act on the communication before the bank accepts the payment order.

(c) After a payment order has been accepted, cancellation or amendment of the order is not effective unless the receiving bank agrees or a funds-transfer system rule allows cancellation or amendment without agreement of the bank.

(1) With respect to a payment order accepted by a receiving bank other than the beneficiary's bank, cancellation or amendment is not effective unless a conforming cancellation or amendment of the payment order issued by the receiving bank is also made.

(2) With respect to a payment order accepted by the beneficiary's bank, cancellation or amendment is not effective unless the order was issued in execution of an unauthorized payment order, or because of a mistake by a sender in the funds transfer which resulted in the issuance of a payment order (i) that is a duplicate of a payment order previously issued by the sender, (ii) that orders payment to a beneficiary not entitled to receive payment from the originator, or (iii) that orders payment in an amount greater than the amount the beneficiary was entitled to receive from the originator. If the payment order is cancelled or amended, the beneficiary's bank is entitled to recover from the beneficiary any amount paid to the beneficiary to the extent allowed by the law governing mistake and restitution.

(d) An unaccepted payment order is cancelled by operation of law at the close of the fifth funds-transfer business day of the receiving bank after the execution date or payment date of the order.

(e) A cancelled payment order cannot be accepted. If an accepted payment order is cancelled, the acceptance is nullified and no person has any right or obligation based on the acceptance. Amendment of a payment order is deemed to be cancellation of the original order at the time of amendment and issue of a new payment order in the amended form at the same time.

(f) Unless otherwise provided in an agreement of the parties or in a funds-transfer system rule, if the receiving bank, after accepting a payment order, agrees to cancellation or amendment of the order by the sender or is bound by a funds-transfer system rule allowing cancellation or amendment without the bank's agreement, the sender, whether or not cancellation or amendment is effective, is liable to the bank for any loss and expenses, including reasonable attorney's fees, incurred by the bank as a result of the cancellation or amendment or attempted cancellation or amendment.

(g) A payment order is not revoked by the death or legal incapacity of the sender unless the receiving bank knows of the death or of an adjudication of incapacity by a court of competent jurisdiction and has reasonable opportunity to act before acceptance of the order.

(h) A funds-transfer system rule is not effective to the extent it conflicts with subsection (c)(2).

§ 4A–212. Liability and Duty of Receiving Bank Regarding Unaccepted Payment Order.

If a receiving bank fails to accept a payment order that it is obliged by express agreement to accept, the bank is liable for breach of the agreement to the extent provided in the agreement or in this Article, but does not otherwise have any duty to accept a payment order or, before acceptance, to take any action, or refrain from taking action, with respect to the order except as provided in this Article or by express agreement. Liability based on acceptance arises only when acceptance occurs as stated in Section 4A–209, and liability is limited to that provided in this Article. A receiving bank is not the agent of the sender or beneficiary of the payment order it accepts, or of any other party to the funds transfer, and the bank owes no duty to any party to the funds transfer except as provided in this Article or by express agreement.

Part 3 Execution of Sender's Payment Order by Receiving Bank

§ 4A–301. Execution and Execution Date.

(a) A payment order is "executed" by the receiving bank when it issues a payment order intended to carry out the payment order received by the bank. A payment order received by the beneficiary's bank can be accepted but cannot be executed.

(b) "Execution date" of a payment order means the day on which the receiving bank may properly issue a payment order in execution of the sender's order. The execution date may be determined by instruction of the sender but cannot be earlier than the day the order is received and, unless otherwise determined, is the day the order is received. If the sender's instruction states a payment date, the execution date is the payment date or an earlier date on which execution is reasonably necessary to allow payment to the beneficiary on the payment date.

§ 4A–302. Obligations of Receiving Bank in Execution of Payment Order.

(a) Except as provided in subsections (b) through (d), if the receiving bank accepts a payment order pursuant to Section 4A–209(a), the bank has the following obligations in executing the order:

(1) The receiving bank is obliged to issue, on the execution date, a payment order complying with the sender's order and to follow the sender's instructions concerning (i) any intermediary bank or funds-transfer system to be used in carrying out the funds transfer, or (ii) the means by which payment orders are to be transmitted in the funds transfer. If the originator's bank issues a payment order to an intermediary bank, the originator's bank is obliged to instruct the intermediary bank according to the instruction of the originator. An intermediary bank in the funds transfer is similarly bound by an instruction given to it by the sender of the payment order it accepts.

(2) If the sender's instruction states that the funds transfer is to be carried out telephonically or by wire transfer or otherwise indicates that the funds transfer is to be carried out by the most expeditious means,

the receiving bank is obliged to transmit its payment order by the most expeditious available means, and to instruct any intermediary bank accordingly. If a sender's instruction states a payment date, the receiving bank is obliged to transmit its payment order at a time and by means reasonably necessary to allow payment to the beneficiary on the payment date or as soon thereafter as is feasible.

(b) Unless otherwise instructed, a receiving bank executing a payment order may (i) use any funds-transfer system if use of that system is reasonable in the circumstances, and (ii) issue a payment order to the beneficiary's bank or to an intermediary bank through which a payment order conforming to the sender's order can expeditiously be issued to the beneficiary's bank if the receiving bank exercises ordinary care in the selection of the intermediary bank. A receiving bank is not required to follow an instruction of the sender designating a funds-transfer system to be used in carrying out the funds transfer if the receiving bank, in good faith, determines that it is not feasible to follow the instruction or that following the instruction would unduly delay completion of the funds transfer.

(c) Unless subsection (a)(2) applies or the receiving bank is otherwise instructed, the bank may execute a payment order by transmitting its payment order by first class mail or by any means reasonable in the circumstances. If the receiving bank is instructed to execute the sender's order by transmitting its payment order by a particular means, the receiving bank may issue its payment order by the means stated or by any means as expeditious as the means stated.

(d) Unless instructed by the sender, (i) the receiving bank may not obtain payment of its charges for services and expenses in connection with the execution of the sender's order by issuing a payment order in an amount equal to the amount of the sender's order less the amount of the charges, and (ii) may not instruct a subsequent receiving bank to obtain payment of its charges in the same manner.

§ 4A–303. Erroneous Execution of Payment Order.

(a) A receiving bank that (i) executes the payment order of the sender by issuing a payment order in an amount greater than the amount of the sender's order, or (ii) issues a payment order in execution of the sender's order and then issues a duplicate order, is entitled to payment of the amount of the sender's order under Section 4A–402(c) if that subsection is otherwise satisfied. The bank is entitled to recover from the beneficiary of the erroneous order the excess payment received to the extent allowed by the law governing mistake and restitution.

(b) A receiving bank that executes the payment order of the sender by issuing a payment order in an amount less than the amount of the sender's order is entitled to payment of the amount of the sender's order under Section 4A–402(c) if (i) that subsection is otherwise satisfied and (ii) the bank corrects its mistake by issuing an additional payment order for the benefit of the beneficiary of the sender's order. If the error is not corrected, the issuer of the erroneous order is entitled to receive or retain payment from the sender of the order it accepted only to the extent of the amount of the erroneous order. This subsection does not apply if the receiving bank executes the sender's payment order by issuing a payment order in an amount less than the amount of the sender's order for the purpose of obtaining payment of its charges for services and expenses pursuant to instruction of the sender.

(c) If a receiving bank executes the payment order of the sender by issuing a payment order to a beneficiary different from the beneficiary of the sender's order and the funds transfer is completed on the basis of that error, the sender of the payment order that was erroneously executed and all previous senders in the funds transfer are not obliged to pay the payment orders they issued. The issuer of the erroneous order is entitled to recover from the beneficiary of the order the payment received to the extent allowed by the law governing mistake and restitution.

§ 4A–304. Duty of Sender to Report Erroneously Executed Payment Order.

If the sender of a payment order that is erroneously executed as stated in Section 4A–303 receives notification from the receiving bank that the order was executed or that the sender's account was debited with respect to the order, the sender has a duty to exercise ordinary care to determine, on the basis of information available to the sender, that the order was erroneously executed and to notify the bank of the relevant facts within a reasonable time not exceeding 90 days after the notification from the bank was received by the sender. If the sender fails to perform that duty, the bank is not obliged to pay interest on any amount refundable to the sender under Section 4A–402(d) for the period before the bank learns of the execution error. The bank is not entitled to any recovery from the sender on account of a failure by the sender to perform the duty stated in this section.

§ 4A–305. Liability for Late or Improper Execution or Failure to Execute Payment Order.

(a) If a funds transfer is completed but execution of a payment order by the receiving bank in breach of Section 4A–302 results in delay in payment to the beneficiary, the bank is obliged to pay interest to either the originator or the beneficiary of the funds transfer for the period of delay caused by the improper execution. Except as provided in subsection (c), additional damages are not recoverable.

(b) If execution of a payment order by a receiving bank in breach of Section 4A–302 results in (i) noncompletion of the funds transfer, (ii) failure to use an intermediary bank designated by the originator, or (iii) issuance of a payment order that does not comply with the terms of the payment order of the originator, the bank is liable to the originator for its expenses in the funds transfer and for incidental expenses and interest losses, to the extent not covered by subsection (a), resulting from the improper execution.

Except as provided in subsection (c), additional damages are not recoverable.

(c) In addition to the amounts payable under subsections (a) and (b), damages, including consequential damages, are recoverable to the extent provided in an express written agreement of the receiving bank.

(d) If a receiving bank fails to execute a payment order it was obliged by express agreement to execute, the receiving bank is liable to the sender for its expenses in the transaction and for incidental expenses and interest losses resulting from the failure to execute. Additional damages, including consequential damages, are recoverable to the extent provided in an express written agreement of the receiving bank, but are not otherwise recoverable.

(e) Reasonable attorney's fees are recoverable if demand for compensation under subsection (a) or (b) is made and refused before an action is brought on the claim. If a claim is made for breach of an agreement under subsection (d) and the agreement does not provide for damages, reasonable attorney's fees are recoverable if demand for compensation under subsection (d) is made and refused before an action is brought on the claim.

(f) Except as stated in this section, the liability of a receiving bank under subsections (a) and (b) may not be varied by agreement.

Part 4 Payment

§ 4A–401. Payment Date.

"Payment date" of a payment order means the day on which the amount of the order is payable to the beneficiary by the beneficiary's bank. The payment date may be determined by instruction of the sender but cannot be earlier than the day the order is received by the beneficiary's bank and, unless otherwise determined, is the day the order is received by the beneficiary's bank.

§ 4A–402. Obligation of Sender to Pay Receiving Bank.

(a) This section is subject to Sections 4A–205 and 4A–207.

(b) With respect to a payment order issued to the beneficiary's bank, acceptance of the order by the bank obliges the sender to pay the bank the amount of the order, but payment is not due until the payment date of the order.

(c) This subsection is subject to subsection (e) and to Section 4A–303. With respect to a payment order issued to a receiving bank other than the beneficiary's bank, acceptance of the order by the receiving bank obliges the sender to pay the bank the amount of the sender's order. Payment by the sender is not due until the execution date of the sender's order. The obligation of that sender to pay its payment order is excused if the funds transfer is not completed by acceptance by the beneficiary's bank of a payment order instructing payment to the beneficiary of that sender's payment order.

(d) If the sender of a payment order pays the order and was not obliged to pay all or part of the amount paid, the bank receiving payment is obliged to refund payment to the extent the sender was not obliged to pay. Except as provided in Sections 4A–204 and 4A–304, interest is payable on the refundable amount from the date of payment.

(e) If a funds transfer is not completed as stated in subsection (c) and an intermediary bank is obliged to refund payment as stated in subsection (d) but is unable to do so because not permitted by applicable law or because the bank suspends payments, a sender in the funds transfer that executed a payment order in compliance with an instruction, as stated in Section 4A–302(a)(1), to route the funds transfer through that intermediary bank is entitled to receive or retain payment from the sender of the payment order that it accepted. The first sender in the funds transfer that issued an instruction requiring routing through that intermediary bank is subrogated to the right of the bank that paid the intermediary bank to refund as stated in subsection (d).

(f) The right of the sender of a payment order to be excused from the obligation to pay the order as stated in subsection (c) or to receive refund under subsection (d) may not be varied by agreement.

§ 4A–403. **Payment by Sender to Receiving Bank.**

(a) Payment of the sender's obligation under Section 4A–402 to pay the receiving bank occurs as follows:

(1) If the sender is a bank, payment occurs when the receiving bank receives final settlement of the obligation through a Federal Reserve Bank or through a funds-transfer system.

(2) If the sender is a bank and the sender (i) credited an account of the receiving bank with the sender, or (ii) caused an account of the receiving bank in another bank to be credited, payment occurs when the credit is withdrawn or, if not withdrawn, at midnight of the day on which the credit is withdrawable and the receiving bank learns of that fact.

(3) If the receiving bank debits an account of the sender with the receiving bank, payment occurs when the debit is made to the extent the debit is covered by a withdrawable credit balance in the account.

(b) If the sender and receiving bank are members of a funds-transfer system that nets obligations multilaterally among participants, the receiving bank receives final settlement when settlement is complete in accordance with the rules of the system. The obligation of the sender to pay the amount of a payment order transmitted through the funds-transfer system may be satisfied, to the extent permitted by the rules of the system, by setting off and applying against the sender's obligation the right of the sender to receive payment from the receiving bank of the amount of any other payment order transmitted to the sender by the receiving bank through the funds-transfer system. The aggregate balance of obligations owed by each sender to each receiving bank in the funds-transfer system may be satisfied, to the extent permitted by the rules of the system, by setting off and applying against that balance the aggregate balance of obligations owed to the sender by other members of the system. The aggregate balance is determined after the right of setoff stated in the second sentence of this subsection has been exercised.

(c) If two banks transmit payment orders to each other under an agreement that settlement of the obligations of each bank to the other under Section 4A–402 will be made at the end of the day or other period, the total amount owed with respect to all orders transmitted by one bank shall be set off against the total amount owed with respect to all orders transmitted by the other bank. To the extent of the setoff, each bank has made payment to the other.

(d) In a case not covered by subsection (a), the time when payment of the sender's obligation under Section 4A–402(b) or 4A–402(c) occurs is governed by applicable principles of law that determine when an obligation is satisfied.

§ 4A–404. **Obligation of Beneficiary's Bank to Pay and Give Notice to Beneficiary.**

(a) Subject to Sections 4A–211(e), 4A–405(d), and 4A–405(e), if a beneficiary's bank accepts a payment order, the bank is obliged to pay the amount of the order to the beneficiary of the order. Payment is due on the payment date of the order, but if acceptance occurs on the payment date after the close of the funds-transfer business day of the bank, payment is due on the next funds-transfer business day. If the bank refuses to pay after demand by the beneficiary and receipt of notice of particular circumstances that will give rise to consequential damages as a result of nonpayment, the beneficiary may recover damages resulting from the refusal to pay to the extent the bank had notice of the damages, unless the bank proves that it did not pay because of a reasonable doubt concerning the right of the beneficiary to payment.

(b) If a payment order accepted by the beneficiary's bank instructs payment to an account of the beneficiary, the bank is obliged to notify the beneficiary of receipt of the order before midnight of the next funds-transfer business day following the payment date. If the payment order does not instruct payment to an account of the beneficiary, the bank is required to notify the beneficiary only if notice is required by the order. Notice may be given by first class mail or any other means reasonable in the circumstances. If the bank fails to give the required notice, the bank is obliged to pay interest to the beneficiary on the amount of the payment order from the day notice should have been given until the day the beneficiary learned of receipt of the payment order by the bank. No other damages are recoverable. Reasonable attorney's fees are also recoverable if demand for interest is made and refused before an action is brought on the claim.

(c) The right of a beneficiary to receive payment and damages as stated in subsection (a) may not be varied by agreement or a funds-transfer system rule. The right of a beneficiary to be notified as stated in subsection (b) may be varied by agreement of the beneficiary or by a funds-transfer system rule if the beneficiary is notified of the rule before initiation of the funds transfer.

§ 4A–405. Payment by Beneficiary's Bank to Beneficiary.

(a) If the beneficiary's bank credits an account of the beneficiary of a payment order, payment of the bank's obligation under Section 4A–404(a) occurs when and to the extent (i) the beneficiary is notified of the right to withdraw the credit, (ii) the bank lawfully applies the credit to a debt of the beneficiary, or (iii) funds with respect to the order are otherwise made available to the beneficiary by the bank.

(b) If the beneficiary's bank does not credit an account of the beneficiary of a payment order, the time when payment of the bank's obligation under Section 4A–404(a) occurs is governed by principles of law that determine when an obligation is satisfied.

(c) Except as stated in subsections (d) and (e), if the beneficiary's bank pays the beneficiary of a payment order under a condition to payment or agreement of the beneficiary giving the bank the right to recover payment from the beneficiary if the bank does not receive payment of the order, the condition to payment or agreement is not enforceable.

(d) A funds-transfer system rule may provide that payments made to beneficiaries of funds transfers made through the system are provisional until receipt of payment by the beneficiary's bank of the payment order it accepted. A beneficiary's bank that makes a payment that is provisional under the rule is entitled to refund from the beneficiary if (i) the rule requires that both the beneficiary and the originator be given notice of the provisional nature of the payment before the funds transfer is initiated, (ii) the beneficiary, the beneficiary's bank, and the originator's bank agreed to be bound by the rule, and (iii) the beneficiary's bank did not receive payment of the payment order that it accepted. If the beneficiary is obliged to refund payment to the beneficiary's bank, acceptance of the payment order by the beneficiary's bank is nullified and no payment by the originator of the funds transfer to the beneficiary occurs under Section 4A–406.

(e) This subsection applies to a funds transfer that includes a payment order transmitted over a funds-transfer system that (i) nets obligations multilaterally among participants, and (ii) has in effect a loss-sharing agreement among participants for the purpose of providing funds necessary to complete settlement of the obligations of one or more participants that do not meet their settlement obligations. If the beneficiary's bank in the funds transfer accepts a payment order and the system fails to complete settlement pursuant to its rules with respect to any payment order in the funds transfer, (i) the acceptance by the beneficiary's bank is nullified and no person has any right or obligation based on the acceptance, (ii) the beneficiary's bank is entitled to recover payment from the beneficiary, (iii) no payment by the originator to the beneficiary occurs under Section 4A–406, and (iv) subject to Section 4A–402(e), each sender in the funds transfer is excused from its obligation to pay its payment order under Section 4A–402(c) because the funds transfer has not been completed.

§ 4A–406. Payment by Originator to Beneficiary; Discharge of Underlying Obligation.

(a) Subject to Sections 4A–211(e), 4A–405(d), and 4A–405(e), the originator of a funds transfer pays the beneficiary of the originator's payment order (i) at the time a payment order for the benefit of the beneficiary is accepted by the beneficiary's bank in the funds transfer and (ii) in an amount equal to the amount of the order accepted by the beneficiary's bank, but not more than the amount of the originator's order.

(b) If payment under subsection (a) is made to satisfy an obligation, the obligation is discharged to the same extent discharge would result from payment to the beneficiary of the same amount in money, unless (i) the payment under subsection (a) was made by a means prohibited by the contract of the beneficiary with respect to the obligation, (ii) the beneficiary, within a reasonable time after receiving notice of receipt of the order by the beneficiary's bank, notified the originator of the beneficiary's refusal of the payment, (iii) funds with respect to the order were not withdrawn by the beneficiary or applied to a debt of the beneficiary, and (iv) the beneficiary would suffer a loss that could reasonably have been avoided if payment had been made by a means complying with the contract. If payment by the originator does not result in discharge under this section, the originator is subrogated to the rights of the beneficiary to receive payment from the beneficiary's bank under Section 4A–404(a).

(c) For the purpose of determining whether discharge of an obligation occurs under subsection (b), if the beneficiary's bank accepts a payment order in an amount equal to the amount of the originator's payment order less charges of one or more receiving banks in the funds transfer, payment to the beneficiary is deemed to be in the amount of the originator's order unless upon demand by the beneficiary the originator does not pay the beneficiary the amount of the deducted charges.

(d) Rights of the originator or of the beneficiary of a funds transfer under this section may be varied only by agreement of the originator and the beneficiary.

Part 5 Miscellaneous Provisions

§ 4A–501. Variation by Agreement and Effect of Funds-Transfer System Rule.

(a) Except as otherwise provided in this Article, the rights and obligations of a party to a funds transfer may be varied by agreement of the affected party.

(b) "Funds-transfer system rule" means a rule of an association of banks (i) governing transmission of payment orders by means of a funds-transfer system of the association or rights and obligations with respect to those orders, or (ii) to the extent the rule governs rights and obligations between banks that are parties to a funds transfer in which a Federal Reserve Bank, acting as an intermediary bank, sends a payment order to the beneficiary's bank. Except as otherwise provided in this Article, a funds-transfer system rule governing rights and obligations between participating banks using the system may be effective even if the rule conflicts with this Article and indirectly affects another party to the funds transfer who does not consent to the rule. A funds-transfer system rule may also govern rights and obligations of parties other than participating banks using the system to the extent stated in Sections 4A–404(c), 4A–405(d), and 4A–507(c).

§ 4A–502. Creditor Process Served on Receiving Bank; Setoff by Beneficiary's Bank.

(a) As used in this section, "creditor process" means levy, attachment, garnishment, notice of lien, sequestration, or similar process issued by or on behalf of a creditor or other claimant with respect to an account.

(b) This subsection applies to creditor process with respect to an authorized account of the sender of a payment order if the creditor process is served on the receiving bank. For the purpose of determining rights with respect to the creditor process, if the receiving bank accepts the payment order the balance in the authorized account is deemed to be reduced by the amount of the payment order to the extent the bank did not otherwise receive payment of the order, unless the creditor process is served at a time and in a manner affording the bank a reasonable opportunity to act on it before the bank accepts the payment order.

(c) If a beneficiary's bank has received a payment order for payment to the beneficiary's account in the bank, the following rules apply:

(1) The bank may credit the beneficiary's account. The amount credited may be set off against an obligation owed by the beneficiary to the bank or may be applied to satisfy creditor process served on the bank with respect to the account.

(2) The bank may credit the beneficiary's account and allow withdrawal of the amount credited unless creditor process with respect to the account is served at a time and in a manner affording the bank a reasonable opportunity to act to prevent withdrawal.

(3) If creditor process with respect to the beneficiary's account has been served and the bank has had a reasonable opportunity to act on it, the bank may not reject the payment order except for a reason unrelated to the service of process.

(d) Creditor process with respect to a payment by the originator to the beneficiary pursuant to a funds transfer may be served only on the beneficiary's bank with respect to the debt owed by that bank to the beneficiary. Any other bank served with the creditor process is not obliged to act with respect to the process.

§ 4A–503. Injunction or Restraining Order with Respect to Funds Transfer.

For proper cause and in compliance with applicable law, a court may restrain (i) a person from issuing a payment order to initiate a funds transfer, (ii) an originator's bank from executing the payment order of the originator, or (iii) the beneficiary's bank from releasing funds to the beneficiary or the beneficiary from withdrawing the funds. A court may not otherwise restrain a person from issuing a payment order, paying or receiving payment of a payment order, or otherwise acting with respect to a funds transfer.

§ 4A–504. Order in Which Items and Payment Orders May Be Charged to Account; Order of Withdrawals from Account.

(a) If a receiving bank has received more than one payment order of the sender or one or more payment orders and other items that are payable from the sender's account, the bank may charge the sender's account with respect to the various orders and items in any sequence.

(b) In determining whether a credit to an account has been withdrawn by the holder of the account or applied to a debt of the holder of the account, credits first made to the account are first withdrawn or applied.

§ 4A–505. Preclusion of Objection to Debit of Customer's Account.

If a receiving bank has received payment from its customer with respect to a payment order issued in the name of the customer as sender and accepted by the bank, and the customer received notification reasonably identifying the order, the customer is precluded from asserting that the bank is not entitled to retain the payment unless the customer notifies the bank of the customer's objection to the payment within one year after the notification was received by the customer.

§ 4A–506. Rate of Interest.

(a) If, under this Article, a receiving bank is obliged to pay interest with respect to a payment order issued to the bank, the amount payable may be determined (i) by agreement of the sender and receiving bank, or (ii) by a funds-transfer system rule if the payment order is transmitted through a funds-transfer system.

(b) If the amount of interest is not determined by an agreement or rule as stated in subsection (a), the amount is calculated by multiplying the applicable Federal Funds rate by the amount on which interest is payable, and then multiplying the product by the number of days for which interest is payable. The applicable Federal Funds rate is the average of the Federal Funds rates published by the Federal Reserve Bank of New York for each of the days for which interest is payable divided by 360. The Federal Funds rate for any day on which a published rate is not available is the same as the published rate for the next preceding day for which there is a published rate. If a receiving bank that accepted a payment order is required to refund payment to the sender of the order because the funds transfer was not completed, but the failure to complete was not due to any fault by the bank, the interest payable is reduced by a percentage equal to the reserve requirement on deposits of the receiving bank.

§ 4A–507. Choice of Law.

(a) The following rules apply unless the affected parties otherwise agree or subsection (c) applies:

(1) The rights and obligations between the sender of a payment order and the receiving bank are governed by the law of the jurisdiction in which the receiving bank is located.

(2) The rights and obligations between the beneficiary's bank and the beneficiary are governed by the law of the jurisdiction in which the beneficiary's bank is located.

(3) The issue of when payment is made pursuant to a funds transfer by the originator to the beneficiary is governed by the law of the jurisdiction in which the beneficiary's bank is located.

(b) If the parties described in each paragraph of subsection (a) have made an agreement selecting the law of a particular jurisdiction to govern rights and obligations between each other, the law of that jurisdiction governs those rights and obligations, whether or not the payment order or the funds transfer bears a reasonable relation to that jurisdiction.

(c) A funds-transfer system rule may select the law of a particular jurisdiction to govern (i) rights and obligations between participating banks with respect to payment orders transmitted or processed through the system, or (ii) the rights and obligations of some or all parties to a funds transfer any part of which is carried out by means of the system. A choice of law made pursuant to clause (i) is binding on participating banks. A choice of law made pursuant to clause (ii) is binding on the originator, other sender, or a receiving bank having notice that the funds-transfer system might be used in the funds transfer and of the choice of law by the system when the originator, other sender, or receiving bank issued or accepted a payment order. The beneficiary of a funds transfer is bound by the choice of law if, when the funds transfer is initiated, the beneficiary has notice that the funds-transfer system might be used in the funds transfer and of the choice of law by the system. The law of a jurisdiction selected pursuant to this subsection may govern, whether or not that law bears a reasonable relation to the matter in issue.

(d) In the event of inconsistency between an agreement under subsection (b) and a choice-of-law rule under subsection (c), the agreement under subsection (b) prevails.

(e) If a funds transfer is made by use of more than one funds-transfer system and there is inconsistency between choice-of-law rules of the systems, the matter in issue is governed by the law of the selected jurisdiction that has the most significant relationship to the matter in issue.

Revised Article 5
LETTERS OF CREDIT

§ 5–101 Short Title.

This article may be cited as Uniform Commercial Code—Letters of Credit.

§ 5–102. Definitions.

(a) In this article:

(1) "Adviser" means a person who, at the request of the issuer, a confirmer, or another adviser, notifies or requests another adviser to notify the beneficiary that a letter of credit has been issued, confirmed, or amended.

(2) "Applicant" means a person at whose request or for whose account a letter of credit is issued. The term includes a person who requests an issuer to issue a letter of credit on behalf of another if the person making the request undertakes an obligation to reimburse the issuer.

(3) "Beneficiary" means a person who under the terms of a letter of credit is entitled to have its complying presentation honored. The term includes a person to whom drawing rights have been transferred under a transferable letter of credit.

(4) "Confirmer" means a nominated person who undertakes, at the request or with the consent of the issuer, to honor a presentation under a letter of credit issued by another.

(5) "Dishonor" of a letter of credit means failure timely to honor or to take an interim action, such as acceptance of a draft, that may be required by the letter of credit.

(6) "Document" means a draft or other demand, document of title, investment security, certificate, invoice, or other record, statement, or representation of fact, law, right, or opinion (i) which is presented in a written or other medium permitted by the letter of credit or, unless prohibited by the letter of credit, by the standard practice referred to in Section 5–108(e) and (ii) which is capable of being examined for compliance with the terms and conditions of the letter of credit. A document may not be oral.

(7) "Good faith" means honesty in fact in the conduct or transaction concerned.

(8) "Honor" of a letter of credit means performance of the issuer's undertaking in the letter of credit to pay or deliver an item of value. Unless the letter of credit otherwise provides, "honor" occurs

(i) upon payment,

(ii) if the letter of credit provides for acceptance, upon acceptance of a draft and, at maturity, its payment, or

(iii) if the letter of credit provides for incurring a deferred obligation, upon incurring the obligation and, at maturity, its performance.

(9) "Issuer" means a bank or other person that issues a letter of credit, but does not include an individual who makes an engagement for personal, family, or household purposes.

(10) "Letter of credit" means a definite undertaking that satisfies the requirements of Section 5–104 by an issuer to a beneficiary at the request or for the

account of an applicant or, in the case of a financial institution, to itself or for its own account, to honor a documentary presentation by payment or delivery of an item of value.

(11) "Nominated person" means a person whom the issuer (i) designates or authorizes to pay, accept, negotiate, or otherwise give value under a letter of credit and (ii) undertakes by agreement or custom and practice to reimburse.

(12) "Presentation" means delivery of a document to an issuer or nominated person for honor or giving of value under a letter of credit.

(13) "Presenter" means a person making a presentation as or on behalf of a beneficiary or nominated person.

(14) "Record" means information that is inscribed on a tangible medium, or that is stored in an electronic or other medium and is retrievable in perceivable form.

(15) "Successor of a beneficiary" means a person who succeeds to substantially all of the rights of a beneficiary by operation of law, including a corporation with or into which the beneficiary has been merged or consolidated, an administrator, executor, personal representative, trustee in bankruptcy, debtor in possession, liquidator, and receiver.

(b) Definitions in other Articles applying to this article and the sections in which they appear are:

"Accept" or "Acceptance" Section 3–409

"Value" Sections 3–303, 4–211

(c) Article 1 contains certain additional general definitions and principles of construction and interpretation applicable throughout this article.

§ 5–103. Scope.

(a) This article applies to letters of credit and to certain rights and obligations arising out of transactions involving letters of credit.

(b) The statement of a rule in this article does not by itself require, imply, or negate application of the same or a different rule to a situation not provided for, or to a person not specified, in this article.

(c) With the exception of this subsection, subsections (a) and (d), Sections 5–102(a)(9) and (10), 5–106(d), and 5–114(d), and except to the extent prohibited in Sections 1–102(3) and 5–117(d), the effect of this article may be varied by agreement or by a provision stated or incorporated by reference in an undertaking. A term in an agreement or undertaking generally excusing liability or generally limiting remedies for failure to perform obligations is not sufficient to vary obligations prescribed by this article.

(d) Rights and obligations of an issuer to a beneficiary or a nominated person under a letter of credit are independent of the existence, performance, or nonperformance of a contract or arrangement out of which the letter of credit arises or which underlies it, including contracts or arrangements between the issuer and the applicant and between the applicant and the beneficiary.

§ 5–104. Formal Requirements.

A letter of credit, confirmation, advice, transfer, amendment, or cancellation may be issued in any form that is a record and is authenticated (i) by a signature or (ii) in accordance with the agreement of the parties or the standard practice referred to in Section 5–108(e).

§ 5–105. Consideration.

Consideration is not required to issue, amend, transfer, or cancel a letter of credit, advice, or confirmation.

§ 5–106. Issuance, Amendment, Cancellation, and Duration.

(a) A letter of credit is issued and becomes enforceable according to its terms against the issuer when the issuer sends or otherwise transmits it to the person requested to advise or to the beneficiary. A letter of credit is revocable only if it so provides.

(b) After a letter of credit is issued, rights and obligations of a beneficiary, applicant, confirmer, and issuer are not affected by an amendment or cancellation to which that person has not consented except to the extent the letter of credit provides that it is revocable or that the issuer may amend or cancel the letter of credit without that consent.

(c) If there is no stated expiration date or other provision that determines its duration, a letter of credit expires one year after its stated date of issuance or, if none is stated, after the date on which it is issued.

(d) A letter of credit that states that it is perpetual expires five years after its stated date of issuance, or if none is stated, after the date on which it is issued.

§ 5–107. Confirmer, Nominated Person, and Adviser.

(a) A confirmer is directly obligated on a letter of credit and has the rights and obligations of an issuer to the extent of its confirmation. The confirmer also has rights against and obligations to the issuer as if the issuer were an applicant and the confirmer had issued the letter of credit at the request and for the account of the issuer.

(b) A nominated person who is not a confirmer is not obligated to honor or otherwise give value for a presentation.

(c) A person requested to advise may decline to act as an adviser. An adviser that is not a confirmer is not obligated to honor or give value for a presentation. An adviser undertakes to the issuer and to the beneficiary accurately to advise the terms of the letter of credit, confirmation, amendment, or advice received by that person and undertakes to the beneficiary to check the apparent authenticity of the request to advise. Even if the advice is inaccurate, the letter of credit, confirmation, or amendment is enforceable as issued.

(d) A person who notifies a transferee beneficiary of the terms of a letter of credit, confirmation, amendment, or advice has the rights and obligations of an adviser under subsection (c). The terms in the notice to the transferee beneficiary may differ from the terms in any notice to the transferor beneficiary to the extent permitted by the letter of credit, confirmation, amendment, or advice received by the person who so notifies.

§ 5–108. Issuer's Rights and Obligations.

(a) Except as otherwise provided in Section 5–109, an issuer shall honor a presentation that, as determined by the standard practice referred to in subsection (e), appears on its face strictly to comply with the terms and conditions of the letter of credit. Except as otherwise provided in Section 5–113 and unless otherwise agreed with the applicant, an issuer shall dishonor a presentation that does not appear so to comply.

(b) An issuer has a reasonable time after presentation, but not beyond the end of the seventh business day of the issuer after the day of its receipt of documents:

(1) to honor,

(2) if the letter of credit provides for honor to be completed more than seven business days after presentation, to accept a draft or incur a deferred obligation, or

(3) to give notice to the presenter of discrepancies in the presentation.

(c) Except as otherwise provided in subsection (d), an issuer is precluded from asserting as a basis for dishonor any discrepancy if timely notice is not given, or any discrepancy not stated in the notice if timely notice is given.

(d) Failure to give the notice specified in subsection (b) or to mention fraud, forgery, or expiration in the notice does not preclude the issuer from asserting as a basis for dishonor fraud or forgery as described in Section 5–109(a) or expiration of the letter of credit before presentation.

(e) An issuer shall observe standard practice of financial institutions that regularly issue letters of credit. Determination of the issuer's observance of the standard practice is a matter of interpretation for the court. The court shall offer the parties a reasonable opportunity to present evidence of the standard practice.

(f) An issuer is not responsible for:

(1) the performance or nonperformance of the underlying contract, arrangement, or transaction,

(2) an act or omission of others, or

(3) observance or knowledge of the usage of a particular trade other than the standard practice referred to in subsection (e).

(g) If an undertaking constituting a letter of credit under Section 5–102(a)(10) contains nondocumentary conditions, an issuer shall disregard the nondocumentary conditions and treat them as if they were not stated.

(h) An issuer that has dishonored a presentation shall return the documents or hold them at the disposal of, and send advice to that effect to, the presenter.

(i) An issuer that has honored a presentation as permitted or required by this article:

(1) is entitled to be reimbursed by the applicant in immediately available funds not later than the date of its payment of funds;

(2) takes the documents free of claims of the beneficiary or presenter;

(3) is precluded from asserting a right of recourse on a draft under Sections 3–414 and 3–415;

(4) except as otherwise provided in Sections 5–110 and 5–117, is precluded from restitution of money paid or other value given by mistake to the extent the mistake concerns discrepancies in the documents or tender which are apparent on the face of the presentation; and

(5) is discharged to the extent of its performance under the letter of credit unless the issuer honored a presentation in which a required signature of a beneficiary was forged.

§ 5–109. Fraud and Forgery.

(a) If a presentation is made that appears on its face strictly to comply with the terms and conditions of the letter of credit, but a required document is forged or materially fraudulent, or honor of the presentation would facilitate a material fraud by the beneficiary on the issuer or applicant:

(1) the issuer shall honor the presentation, if honor is demanded by (i) a nominated person who has given value in good faith and without notice of forgery or material fraud, (ii) a confirmer who has honored its confirmation in good faith, (iii) a holder in due course of a draft drawn under the letter of credit which was taken after acceptance by the issuer or nominated person, or (iv) an assignee of the issuer's or nominated person's deferred obligation that was taken for value and without notice of forgery or material fraud after the obligation was incurred by the issuer or nominated person; and

(2) the issuer, acting in good faith, may honor or dishonor the presentation in any other case.

(b) If an applicant claims that a required document is forged or materially fraudulent or that honor of the presentation would facilitate a material fraud by the beneficiary on the issuer or applicant, a court of competent jurisdiction may temporarily or permanently enjoin the issuer from honoring a presentation or grant similar relief against the issuer or other persons only if the court finds that:

(1) the relief is not prohibited under the law applicable to an accepted draft or deferred obligation incurred by the issuer;

(2) a beneficiary, issuer, or nominated person who may be adversely affected is adequately protected against loss that it may suffer because the relief is granted;

(3) all of the conditions to entitle a person to the relief under the law of this State have been met; and

(4) on the basis of the information submitted to the court, the applicant is more likely than not to succeed under its claim of forgery or material fraud and the person demanding honor does not qualify for protection under subsection (a)(1).

§ 5–110. Warranties.

(a) If its presentation is honored, the beneficiary warrants:

(1) to the issuer, any other person to whom presentation is made, and the applicant that there is no fraud or forgery of the kind described in Section 5–109(a); and

(2) to the applicant that the drawing does not violate any agreement between the applicant and beneficiary or any other agreement intended by them to be augmented by the letter of credit.

(b) The warranties in subsection (a) are in addition to warranties arising under Article 3, 4, 7, and 8 because of the presentation or transfer of documents covered by any of those articles.

§ 5–111. Remedies.

(a) If an issuer wrongfully dishonors or repudiates its obligation to pay money under a letter of credit before presentation, the beneficiary, successor, or nominated person presenting on its own behalf may recover from the issuer the amount that is the subject of the dishonor or repudiation. If the issuer's obligation under the letter of credit is not for the payment of money, the claimant may obtain specific performance or, at the claimant's election, recover an amount equal to the value of performance from the issuer. In either case, the claimant may also recover incidental but not consequential damages. The claimant is not obligated to take action to avoid damages that might be due from the issuer under this subsection. If, although not obligated to do so, the claimant avoids damages, the claimant's recovery from the issuer must be reduced by the amount of damages avoided. The issuer has the burden of proving the amount of damages avoided. In the case of repudiation the claimant need not present any document.

(b) If an issuer wrongfully dishonors a draft or demand presented under a letter of credit or honors a draft or demand in breach of its obligation to the applicant, the applicant may recover damages resulting from the breach, including incidental but not consequential damages, less any amount saved as a result of the breach.

(c) If an adviser or nominated person other than a confirmer breaches an obligation under this article or an issuer breaches an obligation not covered in subsection (a) or (b), a person to whom the obligation is owed may recover damages resulting from the breach, including incidental but not consequential damages, less any amount saved as a result of the breach. To the extent of the confirmation, a confirmer has the liability of an issuer specified in this subsection and subsections (a) and (b).

(d) An issuer, nominated person, or adviser who is found liable under subsection (a), (b), or (c) shall pay interest on the amount owed thereunder from the date of wrongful dishonor or other appropriate date.

(e) Reasonable attorney's fees and other expenses of litigation must be awarded to the prevailing party in an action in which a remedy is sought under this article.

(f) Damages that would otherwise be payable by a party for breach of an obligation under this article may be liquidated by agreement or undertaking, but only in an amount or by a formula that is reasonable in light of the harm anticipated.

§ 5–112. Transfer of Letter of Credit.

(a) Except as otherwise provided in Section 5–113, unless a letter of credit provides that it is transferable, the right of a beneficiary to draw or otherwise demand performance under a letter of credit may not be transferred.

(b) Even if a letter of credit provides that it is transferable, the issuer may refuse to recognize or carry out a transfer if:

(1) the transfer would violate applicable law; or

(2) the transferor or transferee has failed to comply with any requirement stated in the letter of credit or any other requirement relating to transfer imposed by the issuer which is within the standard practice referred to in Section 5–108(e) or is otherwise reasonable under the circumstances.

§ 5–113. Transfer by Operation of Law.

(a) A successor of a beneficiary may consent to amendments, sign and present documents, and receive payment or other items of value in the name of the beneficiary without disclosing its status as a successor.

(b) A successor of a beneficiary may consent to amendments, sign and present documents, and receive payment or other items of value in its own name as the disclosed successor of the beneficiary. Except as otherwise provided in subsection (e), an issuer shall recognize a disclosed successor of a beneficiary as beneficiary in full substitution for its predecessor upon compliance with the requirements for recognition by the issuer of a transfer of drawing rights by operation of law under the standard practice referred to in Section 5–108(e) or, in the absence of such a practice, compliance with other reasonable procedures sufficient to protect the issuer.

(c) An issuer is not obliged to determine whether a purported successor is a successor of a beneficiary or whether the signature of a purported successor is genuine or authorized.

(d) Honor of a purported successor's apparently complying presentation under subsection (a) or (b) has the consequences specified in Section 5–108(i) even if the purported successor is not the successor of a beneficiary. Documents signed in the name of the beneficiary or of a disclosed successor by a person who is neither the beneficiary nor the successor of the beneficiary are forged documents for the purposes of Section 5–109.

(e) An issuer whose rights of reimbursement are not covered by subsection (d) or substantially similar law and any confirmer or nominated person may decline to recognize a presentation under subsection (b).

(f) A beneficiary whose name is changed after the issuance of a letter of credit has the same rights and obligations as a successor of a beneficiary under this section.

§ 5–114. Assignment of Proceeds.

(a) In this section, "proceeds of a letter of credit" means the cash, check, accepted draft, or other item of value paid or delivered upon honor or giving of value by the issuer or any nominated person under the letter of credit. The term does not include a beneficiary's drawing rights or documents presented by the beneficiary.

(b) A beneficiary may assign its right to part or all of the proceeds of a letter of credit. The beneficiary may do so before presentation as a present assignment of its right to receive proceeds contingent upon its compliance with the terms and conditions of the letter of credit.

(c) An issuer or nominated person need not recognize an assignment of proceeds of a letter of credit until it consents to the assignment.

(d) An issuer or nominated person has no obligation to give or withhold its consent to an assignment of proceeds of a letter of credit, but consent may not be unreasonably withheld if the assignee possesses and exhibits the letter of credit and presentation of the letter of credit is a condition to honor.

(e) Rights of a transferee beneficiary or nominated person are independent of the beneficiary's assignment of the proceeds of a letter of credit and are superior to the assignee's right to the proceeds.

(f) Neither the rights recognized by this section between an assignee and an issuer, transferee beneficiary, or nominated person nor the issuer's or nominated person's payment of proceeds to an assignee or a third person affect the rights between the assignee and any person other than the issuer, transferee beneficiary, or nominated person. The mode of creating and perfecting a security interest in or granting an assignment of a beneficiary's rights to proceeds is governed by Article 9 or other law. Against persons other than the issuer, transferee beneficiary, or nominated person, the rights and obligations arising upon the creation of a security interest or other assignment of a beneficiary's right to proceeds and its perfection are governed by Article 9 or other law.

§ 5–115. Statute of Limitations.

An action to enforce a right or obligation arising under this article must be commenced within one year after the expiration date of the relevant letter of credit or one year after the [claim for relief] [cause of action] accrues, whichever occurs later. A [claim for relief] [cause of action] accrues when the breach occurs, regardless of the aggrieved party's lack of knowledge of the breach.

§ 5–116. Choice of Law and Forum.

(a) The liability of an issuer, nominated person, or adviser for action or omission is governed by the law of the jurisdiction chosen by an agreement in the form of a record signed or otherwise authenticated by the affected parties in the manner provided in Section 5–104 or by a provision in the person's letter of credit, confirmation, or other undertaking. The jurisdiction whose law is chosen need not bear any relation to the transaction.

(b) Unless subsection (a) applies, the liability of an issuer, nominated person, or adviser for action or omission is governed by the law of the jurisdiction in which the person is located. The person is considered to be located at the address indicated in the person's undertaking. If more than one address is indicated, the person is considered to be located at the address from which the person's undertaking was issued. For the purpose of jurisdiction, choice of law, and recognition of interbranch letters of credit, but not enforcement of a judgment, all branches of a bank are considered separate juridical entities and a bank is considered to be located at the place where its relevant branch is considered to be located under this subsection.

(c) Except as otherwise provided in this subsection, the liability of an issuer, nominated person, or adviser is governed by any rules of custom or practice, such as the Uniform Customs and Practice for Documentary Credits, to which the letter of credit, confirmation, or other undertaking is expressly made subject. If (i) this article would govern the liability of an issuer, nominated person, or adviser under subsection (a) or (b), (ii) the relevant undertaking incorporates rules of custom or practice, and (iii) there is conflict between this article and those rules as applied to that undertaking, those rules govern except to the extent of any conflict with the nonvariable provisions specified in Section 5–103(c).

(d) If there is conflict between this article and Article 3, 4, 4A, or 9, this article governs.

(e) The forum for settling disputes arising out of an undertaking within this article may be chosen in the manner and with the binding effect that governing law may be chosen in accordance with subsection (a).

§ 5–117. Subrogation of Issuer, Applicant, and Nominated Person.

(a) An issuer that honors a beneficiary's presentation is subrogated to the rights of the beneficiary to the same extent as if the issuer were a secondary obligor of the underlying obligation owed to the beneficiary and of the applicant to the same extent as if the issuer were the secondary obligor of the underlying obligation owed to the applicant.

(b) An applicant that reimburses an issuer is subrogated to the rights of the issuer against any beneficiary, presenter, or nominated person to the same extent as if the applicant were the secondary obligor of the obligations owed to the issuer and has the rights of subrogation of the issuer to the rights of the beneficiary stated in subsection (a).

(c) A nominated person who pays or gives value against a draft or demand presented under a letter of credit is subrogated to the rights of:

    (1) the issuer against the applicant to the same extent as if the nominated person were a secondary obligor of

the obligation owed to the issuer by the applicant;

(2) the beneficiary to the same extent as if the nominated person were a secondary obligor of the underlying obligation owed to the beneficiary; and

(3) the applicant to same extent as if the nominated person were a secondary obligor of the underlying obligation owed to the applicant.

(d) Notwithstanding any agreement or term to the contrary, the rights of subrogation stated in subsections (a) and (b) do not arise until the issuer honors the letter of credit or otherwise pays and the rights in subsection (c) do not arise until the nominated person pays or otherwise gives value. Until then, the issuer, nominated person, and the applicant do not derive under this section present or prospective rights forming the basis of a claim, defense, or excuse.

§ 5–118. Security Interest of Issuer or Nominated Person.

(a) An issuer or nominated person has a security interest in a document presented under a letter of credit to the extent that the issuer or nominated person honors or gives value for the presentation.

(b) So long as and to the extent that an issuer or nominated person has not been reimbursed or has not otherwise recovered the value given with respect to a security interest in a document under subsection (a), the security interest continues and is subject to Article 9, but:

(1) a security agreement is not necessary to make the security interest enforceable under Section 9–203(b)(3);

(2) if the document is presented in a medium other than a written or other tangible medium, the security interest is perfected; and

(3) if the document is presented in a written or other tangible medium and is not a certificated security, chattel paper, a document of title, an instrument, or a letter of credit, the security interest is perfected and has priority over a conflicting security interest in the document so long as the debtor does not have possession of the document.

As added in 1999.

Transition Provisions

§ [ ]. Effective Date.

This [Act] shall become effective on _____, 20__.

§ [ ]. Repeal.

This [Act] [repeals] [amends] [insert citation to existing Article 5].

§ [ ]. Applicability.

This [Act] applies to a letter of credit that is issued on or after the effective date of this [Act]. This [Act] does not apply to a transaction, event, obligation, or duty arising out of or associated with a letter of credit that was issued before the effective date of this [Act].

§ [ ]. Savings Clause.

A transaction arising out of or associated with a letter of credit that was issued before the effective date of this [Act] and the rights, obligations, and interests flowing from that transaction are governed by any statute or other law amended or repealed by this [Act] as if repeal or amendment had not occurred and may be terminated, completed, consummated, or enforced under that statute or other law.

Repealer of Article 6

BULK TRANSFERS and [Revised] ARTICLE 6 BULK SALES (States to Select One Alternative)

Alternative A

§ 1. Repeal

Article 6 and Section 9–111 of the Uniform Commercial Code are hereby repealed, effective _____.

§ 2. Amendment

Section 1–105(2) of the Uniform Commercial Code is hereby amended to read as follows:

(2) Where one of the following provisions of this Act specifies the applicable law, that provision governs and a contrary agreement is effective only to the extent permitted by the law (including the conflict of laws rules) so specified:

Rights of creditors against sold goods. Section 2–402.

Applicability of the Article on Leases. Section 2A–105 and 2A-106.

Applicability of the Article on Bank Deposits and Collections. Section 4–102.

Applicability of the Article on Investment Securities. Section 8–106.

Perfection provisions of the Article on Secured Transactions. Section 9–103.

§ 3. Amendment.

Section 2–403(4) of the Uniform Commercial Code is hereby amended to read as follows:

(4) The rights of other purchasers of goods and of lien creditors are governed by the Articles on Secured Transactions (Article 9) and Documents of Title (Article 7).

§ 4. Savings Clause.

Rights and obligations that arose under Article 6 and Section 9–111 of the Uniform Commercial Code before their repeal remain valid and may be enforced as though those statutes had not been repealed.]

§ 6–101. Short Title.

This Article shall be known and may be cited as Uniform Commercial Code—Bulk Sales.

§ 6–102. Definitions and Index of Definitions.

(1) In this Article, unless the context otherwise requires:

(a) "Assets" means the inventory that is the subject of a bulk sale and any tangible and intangible personal property used or held for use primarily in, or arising from, the seller's business and sold in connection with that inventory, but the term does not include:

(i) fixtures (Section 9–102(a)(41)) other than readily removable factory and office machines;

(ii) the lessee's interest in a lease of real property; or

(iii) property to the extent it is generally exempt from creditor process under nonbankruptcy law.

(b) "Auctioneer" means a person whom the seller engages to direct, conduct, control, or be responsible for a sale by auction.

(c) "Bulk sale" means:

(i) in the case of a sale by auction or a sale or series of sales conducted by a liquidator on the seller's behalf, a sale or series of sales not in the ordinary course of the seller's business of more than half of the seller's inventory, as measured by value on the date of the bulk-sale agreement, if on that date the auctioneer or liquidator has notice, or after reasonable inquiry would have had notice, that the seller will not continue to operate the same or a similar kind of business after the sale or series of sales; and

(ii) in all other cases, a sale not in the ordinary course of the seller's business of more than half the seller's inventory, as measured by value on the date of the bulk-sale agreement, if on that date the buyer has notice, or after reasonable inquiry would have had notice, that the seller will not continue to operate the same or a similar kind of business after the sale.

(d) "Claim" means a right to payment from the seller, whether or not the right is reduced to judgment, liquidated, fixed, matured, disputed, secured, legal, or equitable. The term includes costs of collection and attorney's fees only to the extent that the laws of this state permit the holder of the claim to recover them in an action against the obligor.

(e) "Claimant" means a person holding a claim incurred in the seller's business other than:

(i) an unsecured and unmatured claim for employment compensation and benefits, including commissions and vacation, severance, and sick-leave pay;

(ii) a claim for injury to an individual or to property, or for breach of warranty, unless:

(A) a right of action for the claim has accrued;

(B) the claim has been asserted against the seller; and

(C) the seller knows the identity of the person asserting the claim and the basis upon which the person has asserted it; and

(States to Select One Alternative)

Alternative A

[(iii) a claim for taxes owing to a governmental unit.]

Alternative B

[(iii) a claim for taxes owing to a governmental unit, if:

(A) a statute governing the enforcement of the claim permits or requires notice of the bulk sale to be given to the governmental unit in a manner other than by compliance with the requirements of this Article; and

(B) notice is given in accordance with the statute.]

(f) "Creditor" means a claimant or other person holding a claim.

(g)(i) "Date of the bulk sale" means:

(A) if the sale is by auction or is conducted by a liquidator on the seller's behalf, the date on which more than ten percent of the net proceeds is paid to or for the benefit of the seller; and

(B) in all other cases, the later of the date on which:

(I) more than ten percent of the net contract price is paid to or for the benefit of the seller; or

(II) more than ten percent of the assets, as measured by value, are transferred to the buyer.

(ii) For purposes of this subsection:

(A) delivery of a negotiable instrument (Section 3–104(1)) to or for the benefit of the seller in exchange for assets constitutes payment of the contract price pro tanto;

(B) to the extent that the contract price is deposited in an escrow, the contract price is paid to or for the benefit of the seller when the seller acquires the unconditional right to receive the deposit or when the deposit is delivered to the seller or for the benefit of the seller, whichever is earlier; and

(C) an asset is transferred when a person holding an unsecured claim can no longer obtain through judicial proceedings rights to the asset that are superior to those of the buyer arising as a result of the bulk sale. A person holding an unsecured claim can obtain those superior rights to a tangible asset at least until the buyer has an unconditional right, under the bulk-sale agreement, to possess the asset, and a person holding an unsecured claim can obtain those superior rights to an intangible asset at least until the buyer has an unconditional right, under the bulk-sale agreement, to use the asset.

(h) "Date of the bulk-sale agreement" means:

(i) in the case of a sale by auction or conducted by a liquidator (subsection (c)(i)), the date on which the seller engages the auctioneer or liquidator; and

(ii) in all other cases, the date on which a bulk-sale agreement becomes enforceable between the buyer and the seller.

(i) "Debt" means liability on a claim.

(j) "Liquidator" means a person who is regularly engaged in the business of disposing of assets for businesses contemplating liquidation or dissolution.

(k) "Net contract price" means the new consideration the buyer is obligated to pay for the assets less:

(i) the amount of any proceeds of the sale of an asset, to the extent the proceeds are applied in partial or total satisfaction of a debt secured by the asset; and

(ii) the amount of any debt to the extent it is secured by a security interest or lien that is enforceable against the asset before and after it has been sold to a buyer. If a debt is secured by an asset and other property of the seller, the amount of the debt secured by a security interest or lien that is enforceable against the asset is determined by multiplying the debt by a fraction, the numerator of which is the value of the new consideration for the asset on the date of the bulk sale and the denominator of which is the value of all property securing the debt on the date of the bulk sale.

(l) "Net proceeds" means the new consideration received for assets sold at a sale by auction or a sale conducted by a liquidator on the seller's behalf less:

(i) commissions and reasonable expenses of the sale;

(ii) the amount of any proceeds of the sale of an asset, to the extent the proceeds are applied in partial or total satisfaction of a debt secured by the asset; and

(iii) the amount of any debt to the extent it is secured by a security interest or lien that is enforceable against the asset before and after it has been sold to a buyer. If a debt is secured by an asset and other property of the seller, the amount of the debt secured by a security interest or lien that is enforceable against the asset is determined by multiplying the debt by a fraction, the numerator of which is the value of the new consideration for the asset on the date of the bulk sale and the denominator of which is the value of all property securing the debt on the date of the bulk sale.

(m) A sale is "in the ordinary course of the seller's business" if the sale comports with usual or customary practices in the kind of business in which the seller is engaged or with the seller's own usual or customary practices.

(n) "United States" includes its territories and possessions and the Commonwealth of Puerto Rico.

(o) "Value" means fair market value.

(p) "Verified" means signed and sworn to or affirmed.

(2) The following definitions in other Articles apply to this Article:

(a) "Buyer."	Section 2–103(1)(a).
(b) "Equipment."	Section 9–102(a)(33).
(c) "Inventory."	Section 9–102(a)(48).
(d) "Sale."	Section 2–106(1).
(e) "Seller."	Section 2–103(1)(d).

(3) In addition, Article 1 contains general definitions and principles of construction and interpretation applicable throughout this Article.

As amended in 1999.

§ 6–103. Applicability of Article.

(1) Except as otherwise provided in subsection (3), this Article applies to a bulk sale if:

(a) the seller's principal business is the sale of inventory from stock; and

(b) on the date of the bulk-sale agreement the seller is located in this state or, if the seller is located in a jurisdiction that is not a part of the United States, the seller's major executive office in the United States is in this state.

(2) A seller is deemed to be located at his [or her] place of business. If a seller has more than one place of business, the seller is deemed located at his [or her] chief executive office.

(3) This Article does not apply to:

(a) a transfer made to secure payment or performance of an obligation;

(b) a transfer of collateral to a secured party pursuant to Section 9–503;

(c) a disposition of collateral pursuant to Section 9–610;

(d) retention of collateral pursuant to Section 9–620;

(e) a sale of an asset encumbered by a security interest or lien if (i) all the proceeds of the sale are applied in partial or total satisfaction of the debt secured by the security interest or lien or (ii) the security interest or lien is enforceable against the asset after it has been sold to the buyer and the net contract price is zero;

(f) a general assignment for the benefit of creditors or to a subsequent transfer by the assignee;

(g) a sale by an executor, administrator, receiver, trustee in bankruptcy, or any public officer under judicial process;

(h) a sale made in the course of judicial or administrative proceedings for the dissolution or reorganization of an organization;

(i) a sale to a buyer whose principal place of business is in the United States and who:

(i) not earlier than 21 days before the date of the bulk sale, (A) obtains from the seller a verified and dated list of claimants of whom the seller has notice three days before the seller sends or delivers the list to the buyer or (B) conducts a reasonable inquiry to discover the claimants;

(ii) assumes in full the debts owed to claimants of whom the buyer has knowledge on the date the buyer receives the list of claimants from the seller or on the date the buyer completes the reasonable inquiry, as the case may be;

(iii) is not insolvent after the assumption; and

(iv) gives written notice of the assumption not later than 30 days after the date of the bulk sale by sending or delivering a notice to the claimants identified in subparagraph (ii) or by filing a notice in the office of the [Secretary of State];

(j) a sale to a buyer whose principal place of business is in the United States and who:

(i) assumes in full the debts that were incurred in the seller's business before the date of the bulk sale;

(ii) is not insolvent after the assumption; and

(iii) gives written notice of the assumption not later than 30 days after the date of the bulk sale by sending or delivering a notice to each creditor whose debt is assumed or by filing a notice in the office of the [Secretary of State];

(k) a sale to a new organization that is organized to take over and continue the business of the seller and that has its principal place of business in the United States if:

(i) the buyer assumes in full the debts that were incurred in the seller's business before the date of the bulk sale;

(ii) the seller receives nothing from the sale except an interest in the new organization that is subordinate to the claims against the organization arising from the assumption; and

(iii) the buyer gives written notice of the assumption not later than 30 days after the date of the bulk sale by sending or delivering a notice to each creditor whose debt is assumed or by filing a notice in the office of the [Secretary of State];

(l) a sale of assets having:

(i) a value, net of liens and security interests, of less than $10,000. If a debt is secured by assets and other property of the seller, the net value of the assets is determined by subtracting from their value an amount equal to the product of the debt multiplied by a fraction, the numerator of which is the value of the assets on the date of the bulk sale and the denominator of which is the value of all property securing the debt on the date of the bulk sale; or

(ii) a value of more than $25,000,000 on the date of the bulk-sale agreement; or

(m) a sale required by, and made pursuant to, statute.

(4) The notice under subsection (3)(i)(iv) must state:(i) that a sale that may constitute a bulk sale has been or will be made; (ii) the date or prospective date of the bulk sale; (iii) the individual, partnership, or corporate names and the addresses of the seller and buyer; (iv) the address to which inquiries about the sale may be made, if different from the seller's address; and (v) that the buyer has assumed or will assume in full the debts owed to claimants of whom the buyer has knowledge on the date the buyer receives the list of claimants from the seller or completes a reasonable inquiry to discover the claimants.

(5) The notice under subsections (3)(j)(iii) and (3)(k)(iii) must state: (i) that a sale that may constitute a bulk sale has been or will be made; (ii) the date or prospective date of the bulk sale; (iii) the individual, partnership, or corporate names and the addresses of the seller and buyer; (iv) the address to which inquiries about the sale may be made, if different from the seller's address; and (v) that the buyer has assumed or will assume the debts that were incurred in the seller's business before the date of the bulk sale.

(6) For purposes of subsection (3)(l), the value of assets is presumed to be equal to the price the buyer agrees to pay for the assets. However, in a sale by auction or a sale conducted by a liquidator on the seller's behalf, the value of assets is presumed to be the amount the auctioneer or liquidator reasonably estimates the assets will bring at auction or upon liquidation.

As amended in 1999.

§ 6–104. Obligations of Buyer.

(1) In a bulk sale as defined in Section 6–102(1)(c)(ii) the buyer shall:

(a) obtain from the seller a list of all business names and addresses used by the seller within three years before the date the list is sent or delivered to the buyer;

(b) unless excused under subsection (2), obtain from the seller a verified and dated list of claimants of whom the seller has notice three days before the seller sends or delivers the list to the buyer and including, to the extent known by the seller, the address of and the amount claimed by each claimant;

(c) obtain from the seller or prepare a schedule of distribution (Section 6–106(1));

(d) give notice of the bulk sale in accordance with Section 6–105;

(e) unless excused under Section 6–106(4), distribute the net contract price in accordance with the undertakings of the buyer in the schedule of distribution; and

(f) unless excused under subsection (2), make available the list of claimants (subsection (1)(b)) by:

(i) promptly sending or delivering a copy of the list without charge to any claimant whose written request is received bly the buyer no later than six months after the date of the bulk sale;

(ii) permitting any claimant to inspect and copy the list at any reasonable hour upon request received by the buyer no later than six months after the date of the bulk sale; or

(iii) filing a copy of the list in the office of the [Secretary of State] no later than the time for giving a notice of the bulk sale (Section 6–105(5)). A list filed in accordance with this subparagraph must state the individual, partnership, or corporate name and a mailing address of the seller.

(2) A buyer who gives notice in accordance with Section 6–105(2) is excused from complying with the requirements of subsections (1)(b) and (1)(f).

§ 6–105. Notice to Claimants.

(1) Except as otherwise provided in subsection (2), to comply with Section 6–104(1)(d) the buyer shall send or deliver a written notice of the bulk sale to each claimant on the list of claimants (Section 6–104(1)(b)) and to any other claimant of which the buyer has knowledge at the time the notice of the bulk sale is sent or delivered.

(2) A buyer may comply with Section 6–104(1)(d) by filing a written notice of the bulk sale in the office of the [Secretary of State] if:

(a) on the date of the bulk-sale agreement the seller has 200 or more claimants, exclusive of claimants holding secured or matured claims for employment compensation and benefits, including commissions and vacation, severance, and sick-leave pay; or

(b) the buyer has received a verified statement from the seller stating that, as of the date of the bulk-sale agreement, the number of claimants, exclusive of claimants holding secured or matured claims for employment compensation and benefits, including commissions and vacation, severance, and sick-leave pay, is 200 or more.

(3) The written notice of the bulk sale must be accompanied by a copy of the schedule of distribution (Section 6–106(1)) and state at least:

(a) that the seller and buyer have entered into an agreement for a sale that may constitute a bulk sale under the laws of the State of _____ ;

(b) the date of the agreement;

(c) the date on or after which more than ten percent of the assets were or will be transferred;

(d) the date on or after which more than ten percent of the net contract price was or will be paid, if the date is not stated in the schedule of distribution;

(e) the name and a mailing address of the seller;

(f) any other business name and address listed by the seller pursuant to Section 6–104(1)(a);

(g) the name of the buyer and an address of the buyer from which information concerning the sale can be obtained;

(h) a statement indicating the type of assets or describing the assets item by item;

(i) the manner in which the buyer will make available the list of claimants (Section 6–104(1)(f)), if applicable; and

(j) if the sale is in total or partial satisfaction of an antecedent debt owed by the seller, the amount of the debt to be satisfied and the name of the person to whom it is owed.

(4) For purposes of subsections (3)(e) and (3)(g), the name of a person is the person's individual, partnership, or corporate name.

(5) The buyer shall give notice of the bulk sale not less than 45 days before the date of the bulk sale and, if the buyer gives notice in accordance with subsection (1), not more than 30 days after obtaining the list of claimants.

(6) A written notice substantially complying with the requirements of subsection (3) is effective even though it contains minor errors that are not seriously misleading.

(7) A form substantially as follows is sufficient to comply with subsection (3):

Notice of Sale

(1) _____, whose address is _____, is described in this notice as the "seller."

(2) _____, whose address is _____, is described in this notice as the "buyer."

(3) The seller has disclosed to the buyer that within the past three years the seller has used other business names, operated at other addresses, or both, as follows:

_____ .

(4) The seller and the buyer have entered into an agreement dated _____, for a sale that may constitute a bulk sale under the laws of the state of _____.

(5) The date on or after which more than ten percent of the assets that are the subject of the sale were or will be transferred is _____, and [if not stated in the schedule of distribution] the date on or after which more than ten percent of the net contract price was or will be paid is _____ .

(6) The following assets are the subject of the sale:

_____ .

(7) [If applicable] The buyer will make available to claimants of the seller a list of the seller's claimants in the following manner: _____ .

(8) [If applicable] The sale is to satisfy $ _____ of an antecedent debt owed by the seller to _____ .

(9) A copy of the schedule of distribution of the net contract price accompanies this notice.

[End of Notice]

§ 6–106. Schedule of Distribution.

(1) The seller and buyer shall agree on how the net contract price is to be distributed and set forth their agreement in a written schedule of distribution.

(2) The schedule of distribution may provide for distribution to any person at any time, including distribution of the entire net contract price to the seller.

(3) The buyer's undertakings in the schedule of distribution run only to the seller. However, a buyer who fails to distribute the net contract price in accordance with the buyer's undertakings in the schedule of distribution is liable to a creditor only as provided in Section 6–107(1).

(4) If the buyer undertakes in the schedule of distribution to distribute any part of the net contract price to a person other than the seller, and, after the buyer has given notice in accordance with Section 6–105, some or all of the anticipated net contract price is or becomes unavailable for distribution as a consequence of the buyer's or seller's having complied with an order of court, legal process, statute, or rule of law, the buyer is excused from any obligation arising under this Article or under any contract with the seller to distribute the net contract price in accordance with the buyer's undertakings in the schedule if the buyer:

> (a) distributes the net contract price remaining available in accordance with any priorities for payment stated in the schedule of distribution and, to the extent that the price is insufficient to pay all the debts having a given priority, distributes the price pro rata among those debts shown in the schedule as having the same priority;

> (b) distributes the net contract price remaining available in accordance with an order of court;

> (c) commences a proceeding for interpleader in a court of competent jurisdiction and is discharged from the proceeding; or

> (d) reaches a new agreement with the seller for the distribution of the net contract price remaining available, sets forth the new agreement in an amended schedule of distribution, gives notice of the amended schedule, and distributes the net contract price remaining available in accordance with the buyer's undertakings in the amended schedule.

(5) The notice under subsection (4)(d) must identify the buyer and the seller, state the filing number, if any, of the original notice, set forth the amended schedule, and be given in accordance with subsection (1) or (2) of Section 6–105, whichever is applicable, at least 14 days before the buyer distributes any part of the net contract price remaining available.

(6) If the seller undertakes in the schedule of distribution to distribute any part of the net contract price, and, after the buyer has given notice in accordance with Section 6–105, some or all of the anticipated net contract price is or becomes unavailable for distribution as a consequence of the buyer's or seller's having complied with an order of court, legal process, statute, or rule of law, the seller and any person in control of the seller are excused from any obligation arising under this Article or under any agreement with the buyer to distribute the net contract price in accordance with the seller's undertakings in the schedule if the seller:

> (a) distributes the net contract price remaining available in accordance with any priorities for payment stated in the schedule of distribution and, to the extent that the price is insufficient to pay all the debts having a given priority, distributes the price pro rata among those debts shown in the schedule as having the same priority;

> (b) distributes the net contract price remaining available in accordance with an order of court;

> (c) commences a proceeding for interpleader in a court of competent jurisdiction and is discharged from the proceeding; or

> (d) prepares a written amended schedule of distribution of the net contract price remaining available for distribution, gives notice of the amended schedule, and distributes the net contract price remaining available in accordance with the amended schedule.

(7) The notice under subsection (6)(d) must identify the buyer and the seller, state the filing number, if any, of the original notice, set forth the amended schedule, and be given in accordance with subsection (1) or (2) of Section 6–105, whichever is applicable, at least 14 days before the seller distributes any part of the net contract price remaining available.

§ 6–107. **Liability for Noncompliance.**

(1) Except as provided in subsection (3), and subject to the limitation in subsection (4):

> (a) a buyer who fails to comply with the requirements of Section 6–104(1)(e) with respect to a creditor is liable to the creditor for damages in the amount of the claim, reduced by any amount that the creditor would not have realized if the buyer had complied; and

> (b) a buyer who fails to comply with the requirements of any other subsection of Section 6–104 with respect to a claimant is liable to the claimant for damages in the amount of the claim, reduced by any amount that the claimant would not have realized if the buyer had complied.

(2) In an action under subsection (1), the creditor has the burden of establishing the validity and amount of the claim, and the buyer has the burden of establishing the amount that the creditor would not have realized if the buyer had complied.

(3) A buyer who:

> (a) made a good faith and commercially reasonable effort to comply with the requirements of Section 6–104(1) or to exclude the sale from the application of this Article under Section 6–103(3); or

> (b) on or after the date of the bulk-sale agreement, but before the date of the bulk sale, held a good faith and commercially reasonable belief that this Article does not apply to the particular sale is not liable to creditors for failure to comply with the requirements of Section 6–104. The buyer has the burden of establishing the

good faith and commercial reasonableness of the effort or belief.

(4) In a single bulk sale the cumulative liability of the buyer for failure to comply with the requirements of Section 6–104(1) may not exceed an amount equal to:

(a) if the assets consist only of inventory and equipment, twice the net contract price, less the amount of any part of the net contract price paid to or applied for the benefit of the seller or a creditor; or

(b) if the assets include property other than inventory and equipment, twice the net value of the inventory and equipment less the amount of the portion of any part of the net contract price paid to or applied for the benefit of the seller or a creditor which is allocable to the inventory and equipment.

(5) For the purposes of subsection (4)(b), the "net value" of an asset is the value of the asset less (i) the amount of any proceeds of the sale of an asset, to the extent the proceeds are applied in partial or total satisfaction of a debt secured by the asset and (ii) the amount of any debt to the extent it is secured by a security interest or lien that is enforceable against the asset before and after it has been sold to a buyer. If a debt is secured by an asset and other property of the seller, the amount of the debt secured by a security interest or lien that is enforceable against the asset is determined by multiplying the debt by a fraction, the numerator of which is the value of the asset on the date of the bulk sale and the denominator of which is the value of all property securing the debt on the date of the bulk sale. The portion of a part of the net contract price paid to or applied for the benefit of the seller or a creditor that is "allocable to the inventory and equipment" is the portion that bears the same ratio to that part of the net contract price as the net value of the inventory and equipment bears to the net value of all of the assets.

(6) A payment made by the buyer to a person to whom the buyer is, or believes he [or she] is, liable under subsection (1) reduces pro tanto the buyer's cumulative liability under subsection (4).

(7) No action may be brought under subsection (1)(b) by or on behalf of a claimant whose claim is unliquidated or contingent.

(8) A buyer's failure to comply with the requirements of Section 6–104(1) does not (i) impair the buyer's rights in or title to the assets, (ii) render the sale ineffective, void, or voidable, (iii) entitle a creditor to more than a single satisfaction of his [or her] claim, or (iv) create liability other than as provided in this Article.

(9) Payment of the buyer's liability under subsection (1) discharges pro tanto the seller's debt to the creditor.

(10) Unless otherwise agreed, a buyer has an immediate right of reimbursement from the seller for any amount paid to a creditor in partial or total satisfaction of the buyer's liability under subsection (1).

(11) If the seller is an organization, a person who is in direct or indirect control of the seller, and who knowingly, intentionally, and without legal justification fails, or causes the seller to fail, to distribute the net contract price in accordance with the schedule of distribution is liable to any creditor to whom the seller undertook to make payment under the schedule for damages caused by the failure.

§ 6–108. Bulk Sales by Auction; Bulk Sales Conducted by Liquidator.

(1) Sections 6–104, 6–105, 6–106, and 6–107 apply to a bulk sale by auction and a bulk sale conducted by a liquidator on the seller's behalf with the following modifications:

(a) "buyer" refers to auctioneer or liquidator, as the case may be;

(b) "net contract price" refers to net proceeds of the auction or net proceeds of the sale, as the case may be;

(c) the written notice required under Section 6–105(3) must be accompanied by a copy of the schedule of distribution (Section 6–106(1)) and state at least:

(i) that the seller and the auctioneer or liquidator have entered into an agreement for auction or liquidation services that may constitute an agreement to make a bulk sale under the laws of the State of _____ ;

(ii) the date of the agreement;

(iii) the date on or after which the auction began or will begin or the date on or after which the liquidator began or will begin to sell assets on the seller's behalf;

(iv) the date on or after which more than ten percent of the net proceeds of the sale were or will be paid, if the date is not stated in the schedule of distribution;

(v) the name and a mailing address of the seller;

(vi) any other business name and address listed by the seller pursuant to Section 6–104(1)(a);

(vii) the name of the auctioneer or liquidator and an address of the auctioneer or liquidator from which information concerning the sale can be obtained;

(viii) a statement indicating the type of assets or describing the assets item by item;

(ix) the manner in which the auctioneer or liquidator will make available the list of claimants (Section 6–104(1)(f)), if applicable; and

(x) if the sale is in total or partial satisfaction of an antecedent debt owed by the seller, the amount of the debt to be satisfied and the name of the person to whom it is owed; and

(d) in a single bulk sale the cumulative liability of the auctioneer or liquidator for failure to comply with the requirements of this section may not exceed the amount of the net proceeds of the sale allocable to inventory and equipment sold less the amount of the portion of any part of the net proceeds paid to or applied for the benefit of a creditor which is allocable to the inventory and equipment.

(2) A payment made by the auctioneer or liquidator to a person to whom the auctioneer or liquidator is, or believes he [or she] is, liable under this section reduces pro tanto the auctioneer's or liquidator's cumulative liability under subsection (1)(d).

(3) A form substantially as follows is sufficient to comply with subsection (1)(c):

Notice of Sale

(1) _____, whose address is _____, is described in this notice as the "seller."

(2) _____, whose address is _____ , is described in this notice as the "auctioneer" or "liquidator."

(3) The seller has disclosed to the auctioneer or liquidator that within the past three years the seller has used other business names, operated at other addresses, or both, as follows: _____ .

(4) The seller and the auctioneer or liquidator have entered into an agreement dated _____ for auction or liquidation services that may constitute an agreement to make a bulk sale under the laws of the State of _____ .

(5) The date on or after which the auction began or will begin or the date on or after which the liquidator began or will begin to sell assets on the seller's behalf is _____, and [if not stated in the schedule of distribution] the date on or after which more than ten percent of the net proceeds of the sale were or will be paid is _____ .

(6) The following assets are the subject of the sale: _____ .

(7) [If applicable] The auctioneer or liquidator will make available to claimants of the seller a list of the seller's claimants in the following manner: _____ .

(8) [If applicable] The sale is to satisfy $ _____ of an antecedent debt owed by the seller to _____ .

(9) A copy of the schedule of distribution of the net proceeds accompanies this notice.

[End of Notice]

(4) A person who buys at a bulk sale by auction or conducted by a liquidator need not comply with the requirements of Section 6–104(1) and is not liable for the failure of an auctioneer or liquidator to comply with the requirements of this section.

§ 6–109. What Constitutes Filing; Duties of Filing Officer; Information from Filing Officer.

(1) Presentation of a notice or list of claimants for filing and tender of the filing fee or acceptance of the notice or list by the filing officer constitutes filing under this Article.

(2) The filing officer shall:

(a) mark each notice or list with a file number and with the date and hour of filing;

(b) hold the notice or list or a copy for public inspection;

(c) index the notice or list according to each name given for the seller and for the buyer; and

(d) note in the index the file number and the addresses of the seller and buyer given in the notice or list.

(3) If the person filing a notice or list furnishes the filing officer with a copy, the filing officer upon request shall note upon the copy the file number and date and hour of the filing of the original and send or deliver the copy to the person.

(4) The fee for filing and indexing and for stamping a copy furnished by the person filing to show the date and place of filing is $ _____ for the first page and $ _____ for each additional page. The fee for indexing each name beyond the first two is $ _____ .

(5) Upon request of any person, the filing officer shall issue a certificate showing whether any notice or list with respect to a particular seller or buyer is on file on the date and hour stated in the certificate. If a notice or list is on file, the certificate must give the date and hour of filing of each notice or list and the name and address of each seller, buyer, auctioneer, or liquidator. The fee for the certificate is $ _____ if the request for the certificate is in the standard form prescribed by the [Secretary of State] and otherwise is $ _____ . Upon request of any person, the filing officer shall furnish a copy of any filed notice or list for a fee of $ _____ .

(6) The filing officer shall keep each notice or list for two years after it is filed.

§ 6–110. Limitation of Actions.

(1) Except as provided in subsection (2), an action under this Article against a buyer, auctioneer, or liquidator must be commenced within one year after the date of the bulk sale.

(2) If the buyer, auctioneer, or liquidator conceals the fact that the sale has occurred, the limitation is tolled and an action under this Article may be commenced within the earlier of (i) one year after the person bringing the action discovers that the sale has occurred or (ii) one year after the person bringing the action should have discovered that the sale has occurred, but no later than two years after the date of the bulk sale. Complete noncompliance with the requirements of this Article does not of itself constitute concealment.

(3) An action under Section 6–107(11) must be commenced within one year after the alleged violation occurs.

Conforming Amendment to Section 2–403

States adopting Alternative B should amend Section 2–403(4) of the Uniform Commercial Code to read as follows:

(4) The rights of other purchasers of goods and of lien creditors are governed by the Articles on Secured Transactions (Article 9), Bulk Sales (Article 6) and Documents of Title (Article 7).

Article 7
Warehouse Receipts, Bills of Lading and Other Documents of Title

Part 1 General

§ 7–101. Short Title.

This Article shall be known and may be cited as Uniform Commercial Code–Documents of Title.

§ 7–102. Definitions and Index of Definitions.

(1) In this Article, unless the context otherwise requires:

(a) "Bailee" means the person who by a warehouse receipt, bill of lading or other document of title acknowledges possession of goods and contracts to deliver them.

(b) "Consignee" means the person named in a bill to whom or to whose order the bill promises delivery.

(c) "Consignor" means the person named in a bill as the person from whom the goods have been received for shipment.

(d) "Delivery order" means a written order to deliver goods directed to a warehouseman, carrier or other person who in the ordinary course of business issues warehouse receipts or bills of lading.

(e) "Document" means document of title as defined in the general definitions in Article 1 (Section 1–201).

(f) "Goods" means all things which are treated as movable for the purposes of a contract of storage or transportation.

(g) "Issuer" means a bailee who issues a document except that in relation to an unaccepted delivery order it means the person who orders the possessor of goods to deliver. Issuer includes any person for whom an agent or employee purports to act in issuing a document if the agent or employee has real or apparent authority to issue documents, notwithstanding that the issuer received no goods or that the goods were misdescribed or that in any other respect the agent or employee violated his instructions.

(h) "Warehouseman" is a person engaged in the business of storing goods for hire.

(2) Other definitions applying to this Article or to specified Parts thereof, and the sections in which they appear are:

"Duly negotiate". Section 7–501.

"Person entitled under the document". Section 7–403(4).

(3) Definitions in other Articles applying to this Article and the sections in which they appear are:

"Contract for sale". Section 2–106.

"Overseas". Section 2–323.

"Receipt" of goods. Section 2–103.

(4) In addition Article 1 contains general definitions and principles of construction and interpretation applicable throughout this Article.

§ 7–103. Relation of Article to Treaty, Statute, Tariff, Classification or Regulation.

To the extent that any treaty or statute of the United States, regulatory statute of this State or tariff, classification or regulation filed or issued pursuant thereto is applicable, the provisions of this Article are subject thereto.

§ 7–104. Negotiable and Non-Negotiable Warehouse Receipt, Bill of Lading or Other Document of Title.

(1) A warehouse receipt, bill of lading or other document of title is negotiable

(a) if by its terms the goods are to be delivered to bearer or to the order of a named person; or

(b) where recognized in overseas trade, if it runs to a named person or assigns.

(2) Any other document is nonnegotiable. A bill of lading in which it is stated that the goods are consigned to a named person is not made negotiable by a provision that the goods are to be delivered only against a written order signed by the same or another named person.

§ 7–105. Construction Against Negative Implication.

The omission from either Part 2 or Part 3 of this Article of a provision corresponding to a provision made in the other Part does not imply that a corresponding rule of law is not applicable.

Part 2 Warehouse Receipts: Special Provisions

§ 7–201. Who May Issue a Warehouse Receipt; Storage Under Government Bond.

(1) A warehouse receipt may be issued by any warehouseman.

(2) Where goods including distilled spirits and agricultural commodities are stored under a statute requiring a bond against withdrawal or a license for the issuance of receipts in the nature of warehouse receipts, a receipt issued for the goods has like effect as a warehouse receipt even though issued by a person who is the owner of the goods and is not a warehouseman.

§ 7–202. Form of Warehouse Receipt; Essential Terms; Optional Terms.

(1) A warehouse receipt need not be in any particular form.

(2) Unless a warehouse receipt embodies within its written or printed terms each of the following, the warehouseman is liable for damages caused by the omission to a person injured thereby:

(a) the location of the warehouse where the goods are stored;

(b) the date of issue of the receipt;

(c) the consecutive number of the receipt;

(d) a statement whether the goods received will be delivered to the bearer, to a specified person, or to a specified person or his order;

(e) the rate of storage and handling charges, except that where goods are stored under a field warehousing arrangement a statement of that fact is sufficient on a non-negotiable receipt;

(f) a description of the goods or of the packages containing them;

(g) the signature of the warehouseman, which may be made by his authorized agent;

(h) if the receipt is issued for goods of which the warehouseman is owner, either solely or jointly or in common with others, the fact of such ownership; and

(i) a statement of the amount of advances made and of liabilities incurred for which the warehouseman claims a lien or security interest (Section 7–209). If the precise amount of such advances made or of such liabilities incurred is, at the time of the issue of the receipt, unknown to the warehouseman or to his agent who issues it, a statement of the fact that advances have been made or liabilities incurred and the purpose thereof is sufficient.

(3) A warehouseman may insert in his receipt any other terms which are not contrary to the provisions of this Act and do not impair his obligation of delivery (Section 7–403) or his duty of care (Section 7–204). Any contrary provisions shall be ineffective.

§ 7–203. Liability for Non-Receipt or Misdescription.

A party to or purchaser for value in good faith of a document of title other than a bill of lading relying in either case upon the description therein of the goods may recover from the issuer damages caused by the non-receipt or misdescription of the goods, except to the extent that the document conspicuously indicates that the issuer does not know whether any part or all of the goods in fact were received or conform to the description, as where the description is in terms of marks or labels or kind, quantity or condition, or the receipt or description is qualified by "contents, condition and quality unknown", "said to contain" or the like, if such indication be true, or the party or purchaser otherwise has notice.

§ 7–204. Duty of Care; Contractual Limitation of Warehouseman's Liability.

(1) A warehouseman is liable for damages for loss of or injury to the goods caused by his failure to exercise such care in regard to them as a reasonably careful man would exercise under like circumstances but unless otherwise agreed he is not liable for damages which could not have been avoided by the exercise of such care.

(2) Damages may be limited by a term in the warehouse receipt or storage agreement limiting the amount of liability in case of loss or damage, and setting forth a specific liability per article or item, or value per unit of weight, beyond which the warehouseman shall not be liable; provided, however, that such liability may on written request of the bailor at the time of signing such storage agreement or within a reasonable time after receipt of the warehouse receipt be increased on part or all of the goods thereunder, in which event increased rates may be charged based on such increased valuation, but that no such increase shall be permitted contrary to a lawful limitation of liability contained in the warehouseman's tariff, if any. No such limitation is effective with respect to the warehouseman's liability for conversion to his own use.

(3) Reasonable provisions as to the time and manner of presenting claims and instituting actions based on the bailment may be included in the warehouse receipt or tariff.

(4) This section does not impair or repeal . . .

Note: *Insert in subsection (4) a reference to any statute which imposes a higher responsibility upon the warehouseman or invalidates contractual limitations which would be permissible under this Article.*

§ 7–205. Title Under Warehouse Receipt Defeated in Certain Cases.

A buyer in the ordinary course of business of fungible goods sold and delivered by a warehouseman who is also in the business of buying and selling such goods takes free of any claim under a warehouse receipt even though it has been duly negotiated.

§ 7–206. Termination of Storage at Warehouseman's Option.

(1) A warehouseman may on notifying the person on whose account the goods are held and any other person known to claim an interest in the goods require payment of any charges and removal of the goods from the warehouse at the termination of the period of storage fixed by the document, or, if no period is fixed, within a stated period not less than thirty days after the notification. If the goods are not removed before the date specified in the notification, the warehouseman may sell them in accordance with the provisions of the section on enforcement of a warehouseman's lien (Section 7–210).

(2) If a warehouseman in good faith believes that the goods are about to deteriorate or decline in value to less than the amount of his lien within the time prescribed in subsection (1) for notification, advertisement and sale, the warehouseman may specify in the notification any reasonable shorter time for removal of the goods and in case the goods are not removed, may sell them at public sale held not less than one week after a single advertisement or posting.

(3) If as a result of a quality or condition of the goods of which the warehouseman had no notice at the time of deposit the goods are a hazard to other property or to the warehouse or to persons, the warehouseman may sell the goods at public or private sale without advertisement on reasonable notification to all persons known to claim an interest in the goods. If the warehouseman after a reasonable effort is unable to sell the goods he may dispose of them in any lawful manner and shall incur no liability by reason of such disposition.

(4) The warehouseman must deliver the goods to any person entitled to them under this Article upon due demand made at any time prior to sale or other disposition under this section.

(5) The warehouseman may satisfy his lien from the proceeds of any sale or disposition under this section but must hold the balance for delivery on the demand of any person to whom he would have been bound to deliver the goods.

§ 7–207. Goods Must Be Kept Separate; Fungible Goods.

(1) Unless the warehouse receipt otherwise provides, a warehouseman must keep separate the goods covered by each receipt so as to permit at all times identification and delivery of those goods except that different lots of fungible goods may be commingled.

(2) Fungible goods so commingled are owned in common by the persons entitled thereto and the warehouseman is severally liable to each owner for that owner's share. Where because of overissue a mass of fungible goods is insufficient to meet all the receipts which the warehouseman has issued against it, the persons entitled include all holders to whom overissued receipts have been duly negotiated.

§ 7–208. Altered Warehouse Receipts.

Where a blank in a negotiable warehouse receipt has been filled in without authority, a purchaser for value and without notice of the want of authority may treat the insertion as authorized. Any other unauthorized alteration leaves any receipt enforceable against the issuer according to its original tenor.

§ 7–209. Lien of Warehouseman.

(1) A warehouseman has a lien against the bailor on the goods covered by a warehouse receipt or on the proceeds thereof in his possession for charges for storage or transportation (including demurrage and terminal charges), insurance, labor, or charges present or future in relation to the goods, and for expenses necessary for preservation of the goods or reasonably incurred in their sale pursuant to law. If the person on whose account the goods are held is liable for like charges or expenses in relation to other goods whenever deposited and it is stated in the receipt that a lien is claimed for charges and expenses in relation to other goods, the warehouseman also has a lien against him for such charges and expenses whether or not the other goods have been delivered by the warehouseman. But against a person to whom a negotiable warehouse receipt is duly negotiated a warehouseman's lien is limited to charges in an amount or at a rate specified on the receipt or if no charges are so specified then to a reasonable charge for storage of the goods covered by the receipt subsequent to the date of the receipt.

(2) The warehouseman may also reserve a security interest against the bailor for a maximum amount specified on the receipt for charges other than those specified in subsection (1), such as for money advanced and interest. Such a security interest is governed by the Article on Secured Transactions (Article 9).

(3)(a) A warehouseman's lien for charges and expenses under subsection (1) or a security interest under subsection (2) is also effective against any person who so entrusted the bailor with possession of the goods that a pledge of them by him to a good faith purchaser for value would have been valid but is not effective against a person as to whom the document confers no right in the goods covered by it under Section 7–503.

(b) A warehouseman's lien on household goods for charges and expenses in relation to the goods under subsection (1) is also effective against all persons if the depositor was the legal possessor of the goods at the time of deposit. "Household goods" means furniture, furnishings and personal effects used by the depositor in a dwelling.

(4) A warehouseman loses his lien on any goods which he voluntarily delivers or which he unjustifiably refuses to deliver.

§ 7–210. Enforcement of Warehouseman's Lien.

(1) Except as provided in subsection (2), a warehouseman's lien may be enforced by public or private sale of the goods in bloc or in parcels, at any time or place and on any terms which are commercially reasonable, after notifying all persons known to claim an interest in the goods. Such notification must include a statement of the amount due, the nature of the proposed sale and the time and place of any public sale. The fact that a better price could have been obtained by a sale at a different time or in a different method from that selected by the warehouseman is not of itself sufficient to establish that the sale was not made in a commercially reasonable manner. If the warehouseman either sells the goods in the usual manner in any recognized market therefor, or if he sells at the price current in such market at the time of his sale, or if he has otherwise sold in conformity with commercially reasonable practices among dealers in the type of goods sold, he has sold in a commercially reasonable manner. A sale of more goods than apparently necessary to be offered to ensure satisfaction of the obligation is not commercially reasonable except in cases covered by the preceding sentence.

(2) A warehouseman's lien on goods other than goods stored by a merchant in the course of his business may be enforced only as follows:

(a) All persons known to claim an interest in the goods must be notified.

(b) The notification must be delivered in person or sent by registered or certified letter to the last known address of any person to be notified.

(c) The notification must include an itemized statement of the claim, a description of the goods subject to the lien, a demand for payment within a specified time not less than ten days after receipt of the notification, and a conspicuous statement that unless the claim is paid within the time the goods will be advertised for sale and sold by auction at a specified time and place.

(d) The sale must conform to the terms of the notification.

(e) The sale must be held at the nearest suitable place to that where the goods are held or stored.

(f) After the expiration of the time given in the notification, an advertisement of the sale must be published once a week for two weeks consecutively in a newspaper of general circulation where the sale is to be held. The advertisement must include a description of the goods, the name of the person on whose account they are being held, and the time and place of the sale. The sale must take place at least fifteen days after the first publication. If there is no newspaper of general circulation where the sale is to be held, the advertisement must be posted at least ten days before the sale in not less than six conspicuous places in the neighborhood of the proposed sale.

(3) Before any sale pursuant to this section any person claiming a right in the goods may pay the amount necessary to satisfy the lien and the reasonable expenses incurred under this section. In that event the goods must not be sold, but must be retained by the warehouseman subject to the terms of the receipt and this Article.

(4) The warehouseman may buy at any public sale pursuant to this section.

(5) A purchaser in good faith of goods sold to enforce a warehouseman's lien takes the goods free of any rights of persons against whom the lien was valid, despite noncompliance by the warehouseman with the requirements of this section.

(6) The warehouseman may satisfy his lien from the proceeds of any sale pursuant to this section but must hold the balance, if any, for delivery on demand to any person to whom he would have been bound to deliver the goods.

(7) The rights provided by this section shall be in addition to all other rights allowed by law to a creditor against his debtor.

(8) Where a lien is on goods stored by a merchant in the course of his business the lien may be enforced in accordance with either subsection (1) or (2).

(9) The warehouseman is liable for damages caused by failure to comply with the requirements for sale under this section and in case of willful violation is liable for conversion.

As amended in 1962.

Part 3 Bills of Lading: Special Provisions

§ 7–301. Liability for Non-Receipt or Misdescription; "Said to Contain"; "Shipper's Load and Count"; Improper Handling.

(1) A consignee of a non-negotiable bill who has given value in good faith or a holder to whom a negotiable bill has been duly negotiated relying in either case upon the description therein of the goods, or upon the date therein shown, may recover from the issuer damages caused by the misdating of the bill or the nonreceipt or misdescription of the goods, except to the extent that the document indicates that the issuer does not know whether any part of all of the goods in fact were received or conform to the description, as where the description is in terms of marks or labels or kind, quantity, or condition or the receipt or description is qualified by "contents or condition of contents of packages unknown", "said to contain", "shipper's weight, load and count" or the like, if such indication be true.

(2) When goods are loaded by an issuer who is a common carrier, the issuer must count the packages of goods if package freight and ascertain the kind and quantity if bulk freight. In such cases "shipper's weight, load and count" or other words indicating that the description was made by the shipper are ineffective except as to freight concealed by packages.

(3) When bulk freight is loaded by a shipper who makes available to the issuer adequate facilities for weighing such freight, an issuer who is a common carrier must ascertain the kind and quantity within a reasonable time after receiving the written request of the shipper to do so. In such cases "shipper's weight" or other words of like purport are ineffective.

(4) The issuer may by inserting in the bill the words "shipper's weight, load and count" or other words of like purport indicate that the goods were loaded by the shipper; and if such statement be true the issuer shall not be liable for damages caused by the improper loading. But their omission does not imply liability for such damages.

(5) The shipper shall be deemed to have guaranteed to the issuer the accuracy at the time of shipment of the description, marks, labels, number, kind, quantity, condition and weight, as furnished by him; and the shipper shall indemnify the issuer against damage caused by inaccuracies in such particulars. The right of the issuer to such indemnity shall in no way limit his responsibility and liability under the contract of carriage to any person other than the shipper.

§ 7–302. Through Bills of Lading and Similar Documents.

(1) The issuer of a through bill of lading or other document embodying an undertaking to be performed in part by persons acting as its agents or by connecting carriers is liable to anyone entitled to recover on the document for any breach by such other persons or by a connecting carrier of its obligation under the document but to the extent that the bill covers an undertaking to be performed overseas or in territory not contiguous to the continental United States or an undertaking including matters other than transportation this liability may be varied by agreement of the parties.

(2) Where goods covered by a through bill of lading or other document embodying an undertaking to be performed in part by persons other than the issuer are received by any such person, he is subject with respect to his own performance while the goods are in his possession to the

obligation of the issuer. His obligation is discharged by delivery of the goods to another such person pursuant to the document, and does not include liability for breach by any other such persons or by the issuer.

(3) The issuer of such through bill of lading or other document shall be entitled to recover from the connecting carrier or such other person in possession of the goods when the breach of the obligation under the document occurred, the amount it may be required to pay to anyone entitled to recover on the document therefor, as may be evidenced by any receipt, judgment, or transcript thereof, and the amount of any expense reasonably incurred by it in defending any action brought by anyone entitled to recover on the document therefor.

§ 7–303. Diversion; Reconsignment; Change of Instructions.

(1) Unless the bill of lading otherwise provides, the carrier may deliver the goods to a person or destination other than that stated in the bill or may otherwise dispose of the goods on instructions from

   (a) the holder of a negotiable bill; or

   (b) the consignor on a non-negotiable bill notwithstanding contrary instructions from the consignee; or

   (c) the consignee on a non-negotiable bill in the absence of contrary instructions from the consignor, if the goods have arrived at the billed destination or if the consignee is in possession of the bill; or

   (d) the consignee on a non-negotiable bill if he is entitled as against the consignor to dispose of them.

(2) Unless such instructions are noted on a negotiable bill of lading, a person to whom the bill is duly negotiated can hold the bailee according to the original terms.

§ 7–304. Bills of Lading in a Set.

(1) Except where customary in overseas transportation, a bill of lading must not be issued in a set of parts. The issuer is liable for damages caused by violation of this subsection.

(2) Where a bill of lading is lawfully drawn in a set of parts, each of which is numbered and expressed to be valid only if the goods have not been delivered against any other part, the whole of the parts constitute one bill.

(3) Where a bill of lading is lawfully issued in a set of parts and different parts are negotiated to different persons, the title of the holder to whom the first due negotiation is made prevails as to both the document and the goods even though any later holder may have received the goods from the carrier in good faith and discharged the carrier's obligation by surrender of his part.

(4) Any person who negotiates or transfers a single part of a bill of lading drawn in a set is liable to holders of that part as if it were the whole set.

(5) The bailee is obliged to deliver in accordance with Part 4 of this Article against the first presented part of a bill of lading lawfully drawn in a set. Such delivery discharges the bailee's obligation on the whole bill.

§ 7–305. Destination Bills.

(1) Instead of issuing a bill of lading to the consignor at the place of shipment a carrier may at the request of the consignor procure the bill to be issued at destination or at any other place designated in the request.

(2) Upon request of anyone entitled as against the carrier to control the goods while in transit and on surrender of any outstanding bill of lading or other receipt covering such goods, the issuer may procure a substitute bill to be issued at any place designated in the request.

§ 7–306. Altered Bills of Lading.

An unauthorized alteration or filling in of a blank in a bill of lading leaves the bill enforceable according to its original tenor.

§ 7–307. Lien of Carrier.

(1) A carrier has a lien on the goods covered by a bill of lading for charges subsequent to the date of its receipt of the goods for storage or transportation (including demurrage and terminal charges) and for expenses necessary for preservation of the goods incident to their transportation or reasonably incurred in their sale pursuant to law. But against a purchaser for value of a negotiable bill of lading a carrier's lien is limited to charges stated in the bill or the applicable tariffs, or if no charges are stated then to a reasonable charge.

(2) A lien for charges and expenses under subsection (1) on goods which the carrier was required by law to receive for transportation is effective against the consignor or any person entitled to the goods unless the carrier had notice that the consignor lacked authority to subject the goods to such charges and expenses. Any other lien under subsection (1) is effective against the consignor and any person who permitted the bailor to have control or possession of the goods unless the carrier had notice that the bailor lacked such authority.

(3) A carrier loses his lien on any goods which he voluntarily delivers or which he unjustifiably refuses to deliver.

§ 7–308. Enforcement of Carrier's Lien.

(1) A carrier's lien may be enforced by public or private sale of the goods, in bloc or in parcels, at any time or place and on any terms which are commercially reasonable, after notifying all persons known to claim an interest in the goods. Such notification must include a statement of the amount due, the nature of the proposed sale and the time and place of any public sale. The fact that a better price could have been obtained by a sale at a different time or in a different method from that selected by the carrier is not of itself sufficient to establish that the sale was not made in a commercially reasonable manner. If the carrier either sells the goods in the usual manner in any recognized market therefor or if he sells at the price current in such market at the time of his sale or if he has otherwise sold in conformity with commercially reasonable practices among dealers in the type of goods sold he has sold in a commercially reasonable manner. A sale of more goods than apparently necessary to be offered to ensure satisfaction of the

obligation is not commercially reasonable except in cases covered by the preceding sentence.

(2) Before any sale pursuant to this section any person claiming a right in the goods may pay the amount necessary to satisfy the lien and the reasonable expenses incurred under this section. In that event the goods must not be sold, but must be retained by the carrier subject to the terms of the bill and this Article.

(3) The carrier may buy at any public sale pursuant to this section.

(4) A purchaser in good faith of goods sold to enforce a carrier's lien takes the goods free of any rights of persons against whom the lien was valid, despite noncompliance by the carrier with the requirements of this section.

(5) The carrier may satisfy his lien from the proceeds of any sale pursuant to this section but must hold the balance, if any, for delivery on demand to any person to whom he would have been bound to deliver the goods.

(6) The rights provided by this section shall be in addition to all other rights allowed by law to a creditor against his debtor.

(7) A carrier's lien may be enforced in accordance with either subsection (1) or the procedure set forth in subsection (2) of Section 7–210.

(8) The carrier is liable for damages caused by failure to comply with the requirements for sale under this section and in case of willful violation is liable for conversion.

§ 7–309. Duty of Care; Contractual Limitation of Carrier's Liability.

(1) A carrier who issues a bill of lading whether negotiable or nonnegotiable must exercise the degree of care in relation to the goods which a reasonably careful man would exercise under like circumstances. This subsection does not repeal or change any law or rule of law which imposes liability upon a common carrier for damages not caused by its negligence.

(2) Damages may be limited by a provision that the carrier's liability shall not exceed a value stated in the document if the carrier's rates are dependent upon value and the consignor by the carrier's tariff is afforded an opportunity to declare a higher value or a value as lawfully provided in the tariff, or where no tariff is filed he is otherwise advised of such opportunity; but no such limitation is effective with respect to the carrier's liability for conversion to its own use.

(3) Reasonable provisions as to the time and manner of presenting claims and instituting actions based on the shipment may be included in a bill of lading or tariff.

Part 4 Warehouse Receipts and Bills of Lading: General Obligations

§ 7–401. Irregularities in Issue of Receipt or Bill or Conduct of Issuer.

The obligations imposed by this Article on an issuer apply to a document of title regardless of the fact that

(a) the document may not comply with the requirements of this Article or of any other law or regulation regarding its issue, form or content; or

(b) the issuer may have violated laws regulating the conduct of his business; or

(c) the goods covered by the document were owned by the bailee at the time the document was issued; or

(d) the person issuing the document does not come within the definition of warehouseman if it purports to be a warehouse receipt.

§ 7–402. Duplicate Receipt or Bill; Overissue.

Neither a duplicate nor any other document of title purporting to cover goods already represented by an outstanding document of the same issuer confers any right in the goods, except as provided in the case of bills in a set, overissue of documents for fungible goods and substitutes for lost, stolen or destroyed documents. But the issuer is liable for damages caused by his overissue or failure to identify a duplicate document as such by conspicuous notation on its face.

§ 7–403. Obligation of Warehouseman or Carrier to Deliver; Excuse.

(1) The bailee must deliver the goods to a person entitled under the document who complies with subsections (2) and (3), unless and to the extent that the bailee establishes any of the following:

(a) delivery of the goods to a person whose receipt was rightful as against the claimant;

(b) damage to or delay, loss or destruction of the goods for which the bailee is not liable [, but the burden of establishing negligence in such cases is on the person entitled under the document];

Note: *The brackets in (1)(b) indicate that State enactments may differ on this point without serious damage to the principle of uniformity.*

(c) previous sale or other disposition of the goods in lawful enforcement of a lien or on warehouseman's lawful termination of storage;

(d) the exercise by a seller of his right to stop delivery pursuant to the provisions of the Article on Sales (Section 2–705);

(e) a diversion, reconsignment or other disposition pursuant to the provisions of this Article (Section 7–303) or tariff regulating such right;

(f) release, satisfaction or any other fact affording a personal defense against the claimant;

(g) any other lawful excuse.

(2) A person claiming goods covered by a document of title must satisfy the bailee's lien where the bailee so requests or where the bailee is prohibited by law from delivering the goods until the charges are paid.

(3) Unless the person claiming is one against whom the document confers no right under Sec. 7–503(1), he must surrender for cancellation or notation of partial deliveries any outstanding negotiable document covering the goods,

and the bailee must cancel the document or conspicuously note the partial delivery thereon or be liable to any person to whom the document is duly negotiated.

(4) "Person entitled under the document" means holder in the case of a negotiable document, or the person to whom delivery is to be made by the terms of or pursuant to written instructions under a non-negotiable document.

§ 7–404. No Liability for Good Faith Delivery Pursuant to Receipt or Bill.

A bailee who in good faith including observance of reasonable commercial standards has received goods and delivered or otherwise disposed of them according to the terms of the document of title or pursuant to this Article is not liable therefor. This rule applies even though the person from whom he received the goods had no authority to procure the document or to dispose of the goods and even though the person to whom he delivered the goods had no authority to receive them.

Part 5 Warehouse Receipts and Bills of Lading: Negotiation and Transfer

§ 7–501. Form of Negotiation and Requirements of "Due Negotiation".

(1) A negotiable document of title running to the order of a named person is negotiated by his indorsement and delivery. After his indorsement in blank or to bearer any person can negotiate it by delivery alone.

(2)(a) A negotiable document of title is also negotiated by delivery alone when by its original terms it runs to bearer.

(b) When a document running to the order of a named person is delivered to him the effect is the same as if the document had been negotiated.

(3) Negotiation of a negotiable document of title after it has been indorsed to a specified person requires indorsement by the special indorsee as well as delivery.

(4) A negotiable document of title is "duly negotiated" when it is negotiated in the manner stated in this section to a holder who purchases it in good faith without notice of any defense against or claim to it on the part of any person and for value, unless it is established that the negotiation is not in the regular course of business or financing or involves receiving the document in settlement or payment of a money obligation.

(5) Indorsement of a nonnegotiable document neither makes it negotiable nor adds to the transferee's rights.

(6) The naming in a negotiable bill of a person to be notified of the arrival of the goods does not limit the negotiability of the bill nor constitute notice to a purchaser thereof of any interest of such person in the goods.

§ 7–502. Rights Acquired by Due Negotiation.

(1) Subject to the following section and to the provisions of Section 7–205 on fungible goods, a holder to whom a negotiable document of title has been duly negotiated acquires thereby:

(a) title to the document;

(b) title to the goods;

(c) all rights accruing under the law of agency or estoppel, including rights to goods delivered to the bailee after the document was issued; and

(d) the direct obligation of the issuer to hold or deliver the goods according to the terms of the document free of any defense or claim by him except those arising under the terms of the document or under this Article. In the case of a delivery order the bailee's obligation accrues only upon acceptance and the obligation acquired by the holder is that the issuer and any indorser will procure the acceptance of the bailee.

(2) Subject to the following section, title and rights so acquired are not defeated by any stoppage of the goods represented by the document or by surrender of such goods by the bailee, and are not impaired even though the negotiation or any prior negotiation constituted a breach of duty or even though any person has been deprived of possession of the document by misrepresentation, fraud, accident, mistake, duress, loss, theft or conversion, or even though a previous sale or other transfer of the goods or document has been made to a third person.

§ 7–503. Document of Title to Goods Defeated in Certain Cases.

(1) A document of title confers no right in goods against a person who before issuance of the document had a legal interest or a perfected security interest in them and who neither

(a) delivered or entrusted them or any document of title covering them to the bailor or his nominee with actual or apparent authority to ship, store or sell or with power to obtain delivery under this Article (Section 7–403) or with power of disposition under this Act (Sections 2–403 and 9–307) or other statute or rule of law; nor

(b) acquiesced in the procurement by the bailor or his nominee of any document of title.

(2) Title to goods based upon an unaccepted delivery order is subject to the rights of anyone to whom a negotiable warehouse receipt or bill of lading covering the goods has been duly negotiated. Such a title may be defeated under the next section to the same extent as the rights of the issuer or a transferee from the issuer.

(3) Title to goods based upon a bill of lading issued to a freight forwarder is subject to the rights of anyone to whom a bill issued by the freight forwarder is duly negotiated; but delivery by the carrier in accordance with Part 4 of this Article pursuant to its own bill of lading discharges the carrier's obligation to deliver.

As amended in 1999.

§ 7–504. Rights Acquired in the Absence of Due Negotiation; Effect of Diversion; Seller's Stoppage of Delivery.

(1) A transferee of a document, whether negotiable or non-negotiable, to whom the document has been delivered but

not duly negotiated, acquires the title and rights which his transferor had or had actual authority to convey.

(2) In the case of a nonnegotiable document, until but not after the bailee receives notification of the transfer, the rights of the transferee may be defeated

(a) by those creditors of the transferor who could treat the sale as void under Section 2–402; or

(b) by a buyer from the transferor in ordinary course of business if the bailee has delivered the goods to the buyer or received notification of his rights; or

(c) as against the bailee by good faith dealings of the bailee with the transferor.

(3) A diversion or other change of shipping instructions by the consignor in a nonnegotiable bill of lading which causes the bailee not to deliver to the consignee defeats the consignee's title to the goods if they have been delivered to a buyer in ordinary course of business and in any event defeats the consignee's rights against the bailee.

(4) Delivery pursuant to a nonnegotiable document may be stopped by a seller under Section 2–705, and subject to the requirement of due notification there provided. A bailee honoring the seller's instructions is entitled to be indemnified by the seller against any resulting loss or expense.

§ 7–505. Indorser Not a Guarantor for Other Parties.

The indorsement of a document of title issued by a bailee does not make the indorser liable for any default by the bailee or by previous indorsers.

§ 7–506. Delivery Without Indorsement: Right to Compel Indorsement.

The transferee of a negotiable document of title has a specifically enforceable right to have his transferor supply any necessary indorsement but the transfer becomes a negotiation only as of the time the indorsement is supplied.

§ 7–507. Warranties on Negotiation or Transfer of Receipt or Bill.

Where a person negotiates or transfers a document of title for value otherwise than as a mere intermediary under the next following section, then unless otherwise agreed he warrants to his immediate purchaser only in addition to any warranty made in selling the goods

(a) that the document is genuine; and

(b) that he has no knowledge of any fact which would impair its validity or worth; and

(c) that his negotiation or transfer is rightful and fully effective with respect to the title to the document and the goods it represents.

§ 7–508. Warranties of Collecting Bank as to Documents.

A collecting bank or other intermediary known to be entrusted with documents on behalf of another or with collection of a draft or other claim against delivery of documents warrants by such delivery of the documents only its own good faith and authority. This rule applies even though the intermediary has purchased or made advances against the claim or draft to be collected.

§ 7–509. Receipt or Bill: When Adequate Compliance With Commercial Contract.

The question whether a document is adequate to fulfill the obligations of a contract for sale or the conditions of a credit is governed by the Articles on Sales (Article 2) and on Letters of Credit (Article 5).

Part 6 Warehouse Receipts and Bills of Lading: Miscellaneous Provisions

§ 7–601. Lost and Missing Documents.

(1) If a document has been lost, stolen or destroyed, a court may order delivery of the goods or issuance of a substitute document and the bailee may without liability to any person comply with such order. If the document was negotiable the claimant must post security approved by the court to indemnify any person who may suffer loss as a result of non-surrender of the document. If the document was not negotiable, such security may be required at the discretion of the court. The court may also in its discretion order payment of the bailee's reasonable costs and counsel fees.

(2) A bailee who without court order delivers goods to a person claiming under a missing negotiable document is liable to any person injured thereby, and if the delivery is not in good faith becomes liable for conversion. Delivery in good faith is not conversion if made in accordance with a filed classification or tariff or, where no classification or tariff is filed, if the claimant posts security with the bailee in an amount at least double the value of the goods at the time of posting to indemnify any person injured by the delivery who files a notice of claim within one year after the delivery.

§ 7–602. Attachment of Goods Covered by a Negotiable Document.

Except where the document was originally issued upon delivery of the goods by a person who had no power to dispose of them, no lien attaches by virtue of any judicial process to goods in the possession of a bailee for which a negotiable document of title is outstanding unless the document be first surrendered to the bailee or its negotiation enjoined, and the bailee shall not be compelled to deliver the goods pursuant to process until the document is surrendered to him or impounded by the court. One who purchases the document for value without notice of the process or injunction takes free of the lien imposed by judicial process.

§ 7–603. Conflicting Claims; Interpleader.

If more than one person claims title or possession of the goods, the bailee is excused from delivery until he has had a reasonable time to ascertain the validity of the adverse claims or to bring an action to compel all claimants to interplead and may compel such interpleader, either in defending an action for nondelivery of the goods, or by original action, whichever is appropriate.

Revised (1994) Article 8

INVESTMENT SECURITIES

Part 1 Short Title and General Matters

§ 8–101. Short Title.

This Article may be cited as Uniform Commercial Code—Investment Securities.

§ 8–102. Definitions.

(a) In this Article:

(1) "Adverse claim" means a claim that a claimant has a property interest in a financial asset and that it is a violation of the rights of the claimant for another person to hold, transfer, or deal with the financial asset.

(2) "Bearer form," as applied to a certificated security, means a form in which the security is payable to the bearer of the security certificate according to its terms but not by reason of an indorsement.

(3) "Broker" means a person defined as a broker or dealer under the federal securities laws, but without excluding a bank acting in that capacity.

(4) "Certificated security" means a security that is represented by a certificate.

(5) "Clearing corporation" means:

(i) a person that is registered as a "clearing agency" under the federal securities laws;

(ii) a federal reserve bank; or

(iii) any other person that provides clearance or settlement services with respect to financial assets that would require it to register as a clearing agency under the federal securities laws but for an exclusion or exemption from the registration requirement, if its activities as a clearing corporation, including promulgation of rules, are subject to regulation by a federal or state governmental authority.

(6) "Communicate" means to:

(i) send a signed writing; or

(ii) transmit information by any mechanism agreed upon by the persons transmitting and receiving the information.

(7) "Entitlement holder" means a person identified in the records of a securities intermediary as the person having a security entitlement against the securities intermediary. If a person acquires a security entitlement by virtue of Section 8–501(b)(2) or (3), that person is the entitlement holder.

(8) "Entitlement order" means a notification communicated to a securities intermediary directing transfer or redemption of a financial asset to which the entitlement holder has a security entitlement.

(9) "Financial asset," except as otherwise provided in Section 8–103, means:

(i) a security;

(ii) an obligation of a person or a share, participation, or other interest in a person or in property or an enterprise of a person, which is, or is of a type, dealt in or traded on financial markets, or which is recognized in any area in which it is issued or dealt in as a medium for investment; or

(iii) any property that is held by a securities intermediary for another person in a securities account if the securities intermediary has expressly agreed with the other person that the property is to be treated as a financial asset under this Article.

As context requires, the term means either the interest itself or the means by which a person's claim to it is evidenced, including a certificated or uncertificated security, a security certificate, or a security entitlement.

(10) "Good faith," for purposes of the obligation of good faith in the performance or enforcement of contracts or duties within this Article, means honesty in fact and the observance of reasonable commercial standards of fair dealing.

(11) "Indorsement" means a signature that alone or accompanied by other words is made on a security certificate in registered form or on a separate document for the purpose of assigning, transferring, or redeeming the security or granting a power to assign, transfer, or redeem it.

(12) "Instruction" means a notification communi-cated to the issuer of an uncertificated security which directs that the transfer of the security be registered or that the security be redeemed.

(13) "Registered form," as applied to a certificated security, means a form in which:

(i) the security certificate specifies a person entitled to the security; and

(ii) a transfer of the security may be registered upon books maintained for that purpose by or on behalf of the issuer, or the security certificate so states.

(14) "Securities intermediary" means:

(i) a clearing corporation; or

(ii) a person, including a bank or broker, that in the ordinary course of its business maintains securities accounts for others and is acting in that capacity.

(15) "Security," except as otherwise provided in Section 8–103, means an obligation of an issuer or a share, participation, or other interest in an issuer or in property or an enterprise of an issuer:

(i) which is represented by a security certificate in bearer or registered form, or the transfer of which may be registered upon books maintained for that purpose by or on behalf of the issuer;

(ii) which is one of a class or series or by its terms is divisible into a class or series of shares, participations, interests, or obligations; and

(iii) which:

(A) is, or is of a type, dealt in or traded on securities exchanges or securities markets; or

(B) is a medium for investment and by its terms expressly provides that it is a security governed by this Article.

(16) "Security certificate" means a certificate representing a security.

(17) "Security entitlement" means the rights and property interest of an entitlement holder with respect to a financial asset specified in Part 5.

(18) "Uncertificated security" means a security that is not represented by a certificate.

(b) Other definitions applying to this Article and the sections in which they appear are:

Appropriate person	Section 8–107
Control	Section 8–106
Delivery	Section 8–301
Investment company security	Section 8–103
Issuer	Section 8–201
Overissue	Section 8–210
Protected purchaser	Section 8–303
Securities account	Section 8–501

(c) In addition, Article 1 contains general definitions and principles of construction and interpretation applicable throughout this Article.

(d) The characterization of a person, business, or transaction for purposes of this Article does not determine the characterization of the person, business, or transaction for purposes of any other law, regulation, or rule.

§ 8–103. Rules for Determining Whether Certain Obligations and Interests Are Securities or Financial Assets.

(a) A share or similar equity interest issued by a corporation, business trust, joint stock company, or similar entity is a security.

(b) An "investment company security" is a security. "Investment company security" means a share or similar equity interest issued by an entity that is registered as an investment company under the federal investment company laws, an interest in a unit investment trust that is so registered, or a face-amount certificate issued by a face-amount certificate company that is so registered. Investment company security does not include an insurance policy or endowment policy or annuity contract issued by an insurance company.

(c) An interest in a partnership or limited liability company is not a security unless it is dealt in or traded on securities exchanges or in securities markets, its terms expressly provide that it is a security governed by this Article, or it is

an investment company security. However, an interest in a partnership or limited liability company is a financial asset if it is held in a securities account.

(d) A writing that is a security certificate is governed by this Article and not by Article 3, even though it also meets the requirements of that Article. However, a negotiable instrument governed by Article 3 is a financial asset if it is held in a securities account.

(e) An option or similar obligation issued by a clearing corporation to its participants is not a security, but is a financial asset.

(f) A commodity contract, as defined in Section 9–102(a) (15), is not a security or a financial asset.

As amended in 1999.

§ 8–104. Acquisition of Security or Financial Asset or Interest Therein.

(a) A person acquires a security or an interest therein, under this Article, if:

(1) the person is a purchaser to whom a security is delivered pursuant to Section 8–301; or

(2) the person acquires a security entitlement to the security pursuant to Section 8–501.

(b) A person acquires a financial asset, other than a security, or an interest therein, under this Article, if the person acquires a security entitlement to the financial asset.

(c) A person who acquires a security entitlement to a security or other financial asset has the rights specified in Part 5, but is a purchaser of any security, security entitlement, or other financial asset held by the securities intermediary only to the extent provided in Section 8–503.

(d) Unless the context shows that a different meaning is intended, a person who is required by other law, regulation, rule, or agreement to transfer, deliver, present, surrender, exchange, or otherwise put in the possession of another person a security or financial asset satisfies that requirement by causing the other person to acquire an interest in the security or financial asset pursuant to subsection (a) or (b).

§ 8–105. Notice of Adverse Claim.

(a) A person has notice of an adverse claim if:

(1) the person knows of the adverse claim;

(2) the person is aware of facts sufficient to indicate that there is a significant probability that the adverse claim exists and deliberately avoids information that would establish the existence of the adverse claim; or

(3) the person has a duty, imposed by statute or regulation, to investigate whether an adverse claim exists, and the investigation so required would establish the existence of the adverse claim.

(b) Having knowledge that a financial asset or interest therein is or has been transferred by a representative imposes no duty of inquiry into the rightfulness of a transaction and is not notice of an adverse claim. However, a person who knows that a representative has transferred a financial asset or interest therein in a transaction that is, or whose proceeds are being used, for the individual benefit of the representative or otherwise in breach of duty has notice of an adverse claim.

(c) An act or event that creates a right to immediate performance of the principal obligation represented by a security certificate or sets a date on or after which the certificate is to be presented or surrendered for redemption or exchange does not itself constitute notice of an adverse claim except in the case of a transfer more than:

(1) one year after a date set for presentment or surrender for redemption or exchange; or

(2) six months after a date set for payment of money against presentation or surrender of the certificate, if money was available for payment on that date.

(d) A purchaser of a certificated security has notice of an adverse claim if the security certificate:

(1) whether in bearer or registered form, has been indorsed "for collection" or "for surrender" or for some other purpose not involving transfer; or

(2) is in bearer form and has on it an unambiguous statement that it is the property of a person other than the transferor, but the mere writing of a name on the certificate is not such a statement.

(e) Filing of a financing statement under Article 9 is not notice of an adverse claim to a financial asset.

§ 8–106. Control.

(a) A purchaser has "control" of a certificated security in bearer form if the certificated security is delivered to the purchaser.

(b) A purchaser has "control" of a certificated security in registered form if the certificated security is delivered to the purchaser, and:

(1) the certificate is indorsed to the purchaser or in blank by an effective indorsement; or

(2) the certificate is registered in the name of the purchaser, upon original issue or registration of transfer by the issuer.

(c) A purchaser has "control" of an uncertificated security if:

(1) the uncertificated security is delivered to the purchaser; or

(2) the issuer has agreed that it will comply with instructions originated by the purchaser without further consent by the registered owner.

(d) A purchaser has "control" of a security entitlement if:

(1) the purchaser becomes the entitlement holder;

(2) the securities intermediary has agreed that it will comply with entitlement orders originated by the purchaser without further consent by the entitlement holder; or

(3) another person has control of the security entitlement on behalf of the purchaser or, having previously acquired control of the security entitlement,

acknowledges that it has control on behalf of the purchaser.

(e) If an interest in a security entitlement is granted by the entitlement holder to the entitlement holder's own securities intermediary, the securities intermediary has control.

(f) A purchaser who has satisfied the requirements of subsection (c) or (d) has control, even if the registered owner in the case of subsection (c) or the entitlement holder in the case of subsection (d) retains the right to make substitutions for the uncertificated security or security entitlement, to originate instructions or entitlement orders to the issuer or securities intermediary, or otherwise to deal with the uncertificated security or security entitlement.

(g) An issuer or a securities intermediary may not enter into an agreement of the kind described in subsection (c)(2) or (d)(2) without the consent of the registered owner or entitlement holder, but an issuer or a securities intermediary is not required to enter into such an agreement even though the registered owner or entitlement holder so directs. An issuer or securities intermediary that has entered into such an agreement is not required to confirm the existence of the agreement to another party unless requested to do so by the registered owner or entitlement holder.

As amended in 1999.

§ 8–107. Whether Indorsement, Instruction, or Entitlement Order Is Effective.

(a) "Appropriate person" means:

(1) with respect to an indorsement, the person specified by a security certificate or by an effective special indorsement to be entitled to the security;

(2) with respect to an instruction, the registered owner of an uncertificated security;

(3) with respect to an entitlement order, the entitlement holder;

(4) if the person designated in paragraph (1), (2), or (3) is deceased, the designated person's successor taking under other law or the designated person's personal representative acting for the estate of the decedent; or

(5) if the person designated in paragraph (1), (2), or (3) lacks capacity, the designated person's guardian, conservator, or other similar representative who has power under other law to transfer the security or financial asset.

(b) An indorsement, instruction, or entitlement order is effective if:

(1) it is made by the appropriate person;

(2) it is made by a person who has power under the law of agency to transfer the security or financial asset on behalf of the appropriate person, including, in the case of an instruction or entitlement order, a person who has control under Section 8–106(c)(2) or (d)(2); or

(3) the appropriate person has ratified it or is otherwise precluded from asserting its ineffectiveness.

(c) An indorsement, instruction, or entitlement order made by a representative is effective even if:

(1) the representative has failed to comply with a controlling instrument or with the law of the State having jurisdiction of the representative relationship, including any law requiring the representative to obtain court approval of the transaction; or

(2) the representative's action in making the indorsement, instruction, or entitlement order or using the proceeds of the transaction is otherwise a breach of duty.

(d) If a security is registered in the name of or specially indorsed to a person described as a representative, or if a securities account is maintained in the name of a person described as a representative, an indorsement, instruction, or entitlement order made by the person is effective even though the person is no longer serving in the described capacity.

(e) Effectiveness of an indorsement, instruction, or entitlement order is determined as of the date the indorsement, instruction, or entitlement order is made, and an indorsement, instruction, or entitlement order does not become ineffective by reason of any later change of circumstances.

§ 8–108. Warranties in Direct Holding.

(a) A person who transfers a certificated security to a purchaser for value warrants to the purchaser, and an indorser, if the transfer is by indorsement, warrants to any subsequent purchaser, that:

(1) the certificate is genuine and has not been materially altered;

(2) the transferor or indorser does not know of any fact that might impair the validity of the security;

(3) there is no adverse claim to the security;

(4) the transfer does not violate any restriction on transfer;

(5) if the transfer is by indorsement, the indorsement is made by an appropriate person, or if the indorsement is by an agent, the agent has actual authority to act on behalf of the appropriate person; and

(6) the transfer is otherwise effective and rightful.

(b) A person who originates an instruction for registration of transfer of an uncertificated security to a purchaser for value warrants to the purchaser that:

(1) the instruction is made by an appropriate person, or if the instruction is by an agent, the agent has actual authority to act on behalf of the appropriate person;

(2) the security is valid;

(3) there is no adverse claim to the security; and

(4) at the time the instruction is presented to the issuer:

(i) the purchaser will be entitled to the registration of transfer;

(ii) the transfer will be registered by the issuer free from all liens, security interests, restrictions, and claims other than those specified in the instruction;

(iii) the transfer will not violate any restriction on transfer; and

(iv) the requested transfer will otherwise be effective and rightful.

(c) A person who transfers an uncertificated security to a purchaser for value and does not originate an instruction in connection with the transfer warrants that:

(1) the uncertificated security is valid;

(2) there is no adverse claim to the security;

(3) the transfer does not violate any restriction on transfer; and

(4) the transfer is otherwise effective and rightful.

(d) A person who indorses a security certificate warrants to the issuer that:

(1) there is no adverse claim to the security; and

(2) the indorsement is effective.

(e) A person who originates an instruction for registration of transfer of an uncertificated security warrants to the issuer that:

(1) the instruction is effective; and

(2) at the time the instruction is presented to the issuer the purchaser will be entitled to the registration of transfer.

(f) A person who presents a certificated security for registration of transfer or for payment or exchange warrants to the issuer that the person is entitled to the registration, payment, or exchange, but a purchaser for value and without notice of adverse claims to whom transfer is registered warrants only that the person has no knowledge of any unauthorized signature in a necessary indorsement.

(g) If a person acts as agent of another in delivering a certificated security to a purchaser, the identity of the principal was known to the person to whom the certificate was delivered, and the certificate delivered by the agent was received by the agent from the principal or received by the agent from another person at the direction of the principal, the person delivering the security certificate warrants only that the delivering person has authority to act for the principal and does not know of any adverse claim to the certificated security.

(h) A secured party who redelivers a security certificate received, or after payment and on order of the debtor delivers the security certificate to another person, makes only the warranties of an agent under subsection (g).

(i) Except as otherwise provided in subsection (g), a broker acting for a customer makes to the issuer and a purchaser the warranties provided in subsections (a) through (f). A broker that delivers a security certificate to its customer, or causes its customer to be registered as the owner of an uncertificated security, makes to the customer the warranties provided in subsection (a) or (b), and has the rights and privileges of a purchaser under this section.

The warranties of and in favor of the broker acting as an agent are in addition to applicable warranties given by and in favor of the customer.

§ 8–109. Warranties in Indirect Holding.

(a) A person who originates an entitlement order to a securities intermediary warrants to the securities intermediary that:

(1) the entitlement order is made by an appropriate person, or if the entitlement order is by an agent, the agent has actual authority to act on behalf of the appropriate person; and

(2) there is no adverse claim to the security entitlement.

(b) A person who delivers a security certificate to a securities intermediary for credit to a securities account or originates an instruction with respect to an uncertificated security directing that the uncertificated security be credited to a securities account makes to the securities intermediary the warranties specified in Section 8–108(a) or (b).

(c) If a securities intermediary delivers a security certificate to its entitlement holder or causes its entitlement holder to be registered as the owner of an uncertificated security, the securities intermediary makes to the entitlement holder the warranties specified in Section 8–108(a) or (b).

§ 8–110. Applicability; Choice of Law.

(a) The local law of the issuer's jurisdiction, as specified in subsection (d), governs:

(1) the validity of a security;

(2) the rights and duties of the issuer with respect to registration of transfer;

(3) the effectiveness of registration of transfer by the issuer;

(4) whether the issuer owes any duties to an adverse claimant to a security; and

(5) whether an adverse claim can be asserted against a person to whom transfer of a certificated or uncertificated security is registered or a person who obtains control of an uncertificated security.

(b) The local law of the securities intermediary's jurisdiction, as specified in subsection (e), governs:

(1) acquisition of a security entitlement from the securities intermediary;

(2) the rights and duties of the securities inter-mediary and entitlement holder arising out of a security entitlement;

(3) whether the securities intermediary owes any duties to an adverse claimant to a security entitlement; and

(4) whether an adverse claim can be asserted against a person who acquires a security entitlement from the securities intermediary or a person who purchases a security entitlement or interest therein from an entitlement holder.

(c) The local law of the jurisdiction in which a security certificate is located at the time of delivery governs whether an adverse claim can be asserted against a person to whom the security certificate is delivered.

(d) "Issuer's jurisdiction" means the jurisdiction under which the issuer of the security is organized or, if permitted by the law of that jurisdiction, the law of another jurisdiction specified by the issuer. An issuer organized under the law of this State may specify the law of another jurisdiction as the law governing the matters specified in subsection (a)(2) through (5).

(e) The following rules determine a "securities intermediary's jurisdiction" for purposes of this section:

(1) If an agreement between the securities inter-mediary and its entitlement holder specifies that it is governed by the law of a particular jurisdiction, that jurisdiction is the securities intermediary's jurisdiction.

(2) If an agreement between the securities inter-mediary and its entitlement holder does not specify the governing law as provided in paragraph (1), but expressly specifies that the securities account is maintained at an office in a particular jurisdiction, that jurisdiction is the securities intermediary's jurisdiction.

(3) If neither paragraph (1) nor paragraph (2) applies and an agreement between the securities intermediary and its entitlement holder governing the securities account expressly provides that the securities account is maintained at an office in a particular jurisdiction, that jurisdiction is the securities intermediary's jurisdiction.

(4) If none of the preceding paragraph applies, the securities intermediary's jurisdiction is the jurisdiction in which the office identified in an account statement as the office serving the entitlement holder's account is located.

(5) If none of the preceding paragraphs applies, the securities intermediary's jurisdiction is the jurisdiction in which the chief executive office of the securities intermediary is located.

(f) A securities intermediary's jurisdiction is not determined by the physical location of certificates representing financial assets, or by the jurisdiction in which is organized the issuer of the financial asset with respect to which an entitlement holder has a security entitlement, or by the location of facilities for data processing or other record keeping concerning the account.

As amended in 1999.

§ 8–111. Clearing Corporation Rules.

A rule adopted by a clearing corporation governing rights and obligations among the clearing corporation and its participants in the clearing corporation is effective even if the rule conflicts with this [Act] and affects another party who does not consent to the rule.

§ 8–112. Creditor's Legal Process.

(a) The interest of a debtor in a certificated security may be reached by a creditor only by actual seizure of the security certificate by the officer making the attachment or levy, except as otherwise provided in subsection (d). However, a certificated security for which the certificate has been surrendered to the issuer may be reached by a creditor by legal process upon the issuer.

(b) The interest of a debtor in an uncertificated security may be reached by a creditor only by legal process upon the issuer at its chief executive office in the United States, except as otherwise provided in subsection (d).

(c) The interest of a debtor in a security entitlement may be reached by a creditor only by legal process upon the securities intermediary with whom the debtor's securities account is maintained, except as otherwise provided in subsection (d).

(d) The interest of a debtor in a certificated security for which the certificate is in the possession of a secured party, or in an uncertificated security registered in the name of a secured party, or a security entitlement maintained in the name of a secured party, may be reached by a creditor by legal process upon the secured party.

(e) A creditor whose debtor is the owner of a certificated security, uncertificated security, or security entitlement is entitled to aid from a court of competent jurisdiction, by injunction or otherwise, in reaching the certificated security, uncertificated security, or security entitlement or in satisfying the claim by means allowed at law or in equity in regard to property that cannot readily be reached by other legal process.

§ 8–113. Statute of Frauds Inapplicable.

A contract or modification of a contract for the sale or purchase of a security is enforceable whether or not there is a writing signed or record authenticated by a party against whom enforcement is sought, even if the contract or modification is not capable of performance within one year of its making.

§ 8–114. Evidentiary Rules Concerning Certificated Securities.

The following rules apply in an action on a certificated security against the issuer:

(1) Unless specifically denied in the pleadings, each signature on a security certificate or in a necessary indorsement is admitted.

(2) If the effectiveness of a signature is put in issue, the burden of establishing effectiveness is on the party claiming under the signature, but the signature is presumed to be genuine or authorized.

(3) If signatures on a security certificate are admitted or established, production of the certificate entitles a holder to recover on it unless the defendant establishes a defense or a defect going to the validity of the security.

(4) If it is shown that a defense or defect exists, the plaintiff has the burden of establishing that the plaintiff or some person under whom the plaintiff claims is a person against whom the defense or defect cannot be asserted.

§ 8–115. Securities Intermediary and Others Not Liable to Adverse Claimant.

A securities intermediary that has transferred a financial asset pursuant to an effective entitlement order, or a broker or other agent or bailee that has dealt with a financial asset at the direction of its customer or principal, is not liable to a person having an adverse claim to the financial asset, unless the securities intermediary, or broker or other agent or bailee:

(1) took the action after it had been served with an injunction, restraining order, or other legal process enjoining it from doing so, issued by a court of competent jurisdiction, and had a reasonable opportunity to act on the injunction, restraining order, or other legal process; or

(2) acted in collusion with the wrongdoer in violating the rights of the adverse claimant; or

(3) in the case of a security certificate that has been stolen, acted with notice of the adverse claim.

§ 8–116. Securities Intermediary as Purchaser for Value.

A securities intermediary that receives a financial asset and establishes a security entitlement to the financial asset in favor of an entitlement holder is a purchaser for value of the financial asset. A securities intermediary that acquires a security entitlement to a financial asset from another securities intermediary acquires the security entitlement for value if the securities intermediary acquiring the security entitlement establishes a security entitlement to the financial asset in favor of an entitlement holder.

Part 2 Issue and Issuer

§ 8–201. Issuer.

(a) With respect to an obligation on or a defense to a security, an "issuer" includes a person that:

(1) places or authorizes the placing of its name on a security certificate, other than as authenticating trustee, registrar, transfer agent, or the like, to evidence a share, participation, or other interest in its property or in an enterprise, or to evidence its duty to perform an obligation represented by the certificate;

(2) creates a share, participation, or other interest in its property or in an enterprise, or undertakes an obligation, that is an uncertificated security;

(3) directly or indirectly creates a fractional interest in its rights or property, if the fractional interest is represented by a security certificate; or

(4) becomes responsible for, or in place of, another person described as an issuer in this section.

(b) With respect to an obligation on or defense to a security, a guarantor is an issuer to the extent of its guaranty, whether or not its obligation is noted on a security certificate.

(c) With respect to a registration of a transfer, issuer means a person on whose behalf transfer books are maintained.

§ 8–202. Issuer's Responsibility and Defenses; Notice of Defect or Defense.

(a) Even against a purchaser for value and without notice, the terms of a certificated security include terms stated on the certificate and terms made part of the security by reference on the certificate to another instrument, indenture, or document or to a constitution, statute, ordinance, rule, regulation, order, or the like, to the extent the terms referred to do not conflict with terms stated on the certificate. A reference under this subsection does not of itself charge a purchaser for value with notice of a defect going to the validity of the security, even if the certificate expressly states that a person accepting it admits notice. The terms of an uncertificated security include those stated in any instrument, indenture, or document or in a constitution, statute, ordinance, rule, regulation, order, or the like, pursuant to which the security is issued.

(b) The following rules apply if an issuer asserts that a security is not valid:

(1) A security other than one issued by a government or governmental subdivision, agency, or instrumentality, even though issued with a defect going to its validity, is valid in the hands of a purchaser for value and without notice of the particular defect unless the defect involves a violation of a constitutional provision. In that case, the security is valid in the hands of a purchaser for value and without notice of the defect, other than one who takes by original issue.

(2) Paragraph (1) applies to an issuer that is a government or governmental subdivision, agency, or instrumentality only if there has been substantial compliance with the legal requirements governing the issue or the issuer has received a substantial consideration for the issue as a whole or for the particular security and a stated purpose of the issue is one for which the issuer has power to borrow money or issue the security.

(c) Except as otherwise provided in Section 8–205, lack of genuineness of a certificated security is a complete defense, even against a purchaser for value and without notice.

(d) All other defenses of the issuer of a security, including nondelivery and conditional delivery of a certificated security, are ineffective against a purchaser for value who has taken the certificated security without notice of the particular defense.

(e) This section does not affect the right of a party to cancel a contract for a security "when, as and if issued" or "when distributed" in the event of a material change in the character of the security that is the subject of the contract or in the plan or arrangement pursuant to which the security is to be issued or distributed.

(f) If a security is held by a securities intermediary against whom an entitlement holder has a security entitlement with respect to the security, the issuer may not assert any defense that the issuer could not assert if the entitlement holder held the security directly.

§ 8–203. Staleness as Notice of Defect or Defense.

After an act or event, other than a call that has been revoked, creating a right to immediate performance of the principal obligation represented by a certificated security or setting a date on or after which the security is to be presented or surrendered for redemption or exchange, a purchaser is charged with notice of any defect in its issue or defense of the issuer, if the act or event:

(1) requires the payment of money, the delivery of a certificated security, the registration of transfer of an uncertificated security, or any of them on presentation or surrender of the security certificate, the money or security is available on the date set for payment or exchange, and the purchaser takes the security more than one year after that date; or

(2) is not covered by paragraph (1) and the purchaser takes the security more than two years after the date set for surrender or presentation or the date on which performance became due.

§ 8–204. Effect of Issuer's Restriction on Transfer.

A restriction on transfer of a security imposed by the issuer, even if otherwise lawful, is ineffective against a person without knowledge of the restriction unless:

(1) the security is certificated and the restriction is noted conspicuously on the security certificate; or

(2) the security is uncertificated and the registered owner has been notified of the restriction.

§ 8–205. Effect of Unauthorized Signature on Security Certificate.

An unauthorized signature placed on a security certificate before or in the course of issue is ineffective, but the signature is effective in favor of a purchaser for value of the certificated security if the purchaser is without notice of the lack of authority and the signing has been done by:

(1) an authenticating trustee, registrar, transfer agent, or other person entrusted by the issuer with the signing of the security certificate or of similar security certificates, or the immediate preparation for signing of any of them; or

(2) an employee of the issuer, or of any of the persons listed in paragraph (1), entrusted with responsible handling of the security certificate.

§ 8–206. Completion of Alteration of Security Certificate.

(a) If a security certificate contains the signatures necessary to its issue or transfer but is incomplete in any other respect:

(1) any person may complete it by filling in the blanks as authorized; and

(2) even if the blanks are incorrectly filled in, the security certificate as completed is enforceable by a purchaser who took it for value and without notice of the incorrectness.

(b) A complete security certificate that has been improperly altered, even if fraudulently, remains enforceable, but only according to its original terms.

§ 8–207. Rights and Duties of Issuer with Respect to Registered Owners.

(a) Before due presentment for registration of transfer of a certificated security in registered form or of an instruction requesting registration of transfer of an uncertificated security, the issuer or indenture trustee may treat the registered owner as the person exclusively entitled to vote, receive notifications, and otherwise exercise all the rights and powers of an owner.

(b) This Article does not affect the liability of the registered owner of a security for a call, assessment, or the like.

§ 8–208. Effect of Signature of Authenticating Trustee, Registrar, or Transfer Agent.

(a) A person signing a security certificate as authenticating trustee, registrar, transfer agent, or the like, warrants to a purchaser for value of the certificated security, if the purchaser is without notice of a particular defect, that:

(1) the certificate is genuine;

(2) the person's own participation in the issue of the security is within the person's capacity and within the scope of the authority received by the person from the issuer; and

(3) the person has reasonable grounds to believe that the certificated security is in the form and within the amount the issuer is authorized to issue.

(b) Unless otherwise agreed, a person signing under subsection (a) does not assume responsibility for the validity of the security in other respects.

§ 8–209. Issuer's Lien.

A lien in favor of an issuer upon a certificated security is valid against a purchaser only if the right of the issuer to the lien is noted conspicuously on the security certificate.

§ 8–210. Overissue.

(a) In this section, "overissue" means the issue of securities in excess of the amount the issuer has corporate power to issue, but an overissue does not occur if appropriate action has cured the overissue.

(b) Except as otherwise provided in subsections (c) and (d), the provisions of this Article which validate a security or compel its issue or reissue do not apply to the extent that validation, issue, or reissue would result in overissue.

(c) If an identical security not constituting an overissue is reasonably available for purchase, a person entitled to issue or validation may compel the issuer to purchase the security and deliver it if certificated or register its transfer if uncertificated, against surrender of any security certificate the person holds.

(d) If a security is not reasonably available for purchase, a person entitled to issue or validation may recover from the issuer the price the person or the last purchaser for value paid for it with interest from the date of the person's demand.

Part 3 Transfer of Certificated and Uncertificated Securities

§ 8–301. Delivery.

(a) Delivery of a certificated security to a purchaser occurs when:

(1) the purchaser acquires possession of the security certificate;

(2) another person, other than a securities intermediary, either acquires possession of the security certificate on behalf of the purchaser or, having previously acquired possession of the certificate, acknowledges that it holds for the purchaser; or

(3) a securities intermediary acting on behalf of the purchaser acquires possession of the security certificate, only if the certificate is in registered form and is (i) registered in the name of the purchaser, (ii) payable to the order of the purchaser, or (iii) specially indorsed to the purchaser by an effective indorsement and has not been indorsed to the securities intermediary or in blank.

(b) Delivery of an uncertificated security to a purchaser occurs when:

(1) the issuer registers the purchaser as the registered owner, upon original issue or registration of transfer; or

(2) another person, other than a securities intermediary, either becomes the registered owner of the uncertificated security on behalf of the purchaser or, having previously become the registered owner, acknowledges that it holds for the purchaser.

As amended in 1999.

§ 8–302. Rights of Purchaser.

(a) Except as otherwise provided in subsections (b) and (c), upon delivery of a certificated or uncertificated security to a purchaser, the purchaser acquires all rights in the security that the transferor had or had power to transfer.

(b) A purchaser of a limited interest acquires rights only to the extent of the interest purchased.

(c) A purchaser of a certificated security who as a previous holder had notice of an adverse claim does not improve its position by taking from a protected purchaser.

As amended in 1999.

§ 8–303. Protected Purchaser.

(a) "Protected purchaser" means a purchaser of a certificated or uncertificated security, or of an interest therein, who:

(1) gives value;

(2) does not have notice of any adverse claim to the security; and

(3) obtains control of the certificated or uncerti-ficated security.

(b) In addition to acquiring the rights of a purchaser, a protected purchaser also acquires its interest in the security free of any adverse claim.

§ 8–304. Indorsement.

(a) An indorsement may be in blank or special. An indorsement in blank includes an indorsement to bearer. A special indorsement specifies to whom a security is to be transferred or who has power to transfer it. A holder may convert a blank indorsement to a special indorsement.

(b) An indorsement purporting to be only of part of a security certificate representing units intended by the issuer to be separately transferable is effective to the extent of the indorsement.

(c) An indorsement, whether special or in blank, does not constitute a transfer until delivery of the certificate on which it appears or, if the indorsement is on a separate document, until delivery of both the document and the certificate.

(d) If a security certificate in registered form has been delivered to a purchaser without a necessary indorsement, the purchaser may become a protected purchaser only when the indorsement is supplied. However, against a transferor, a transfer is complete upon delivery and the purchaser has a specifically enforceable right to have any necessary indorsement supplied.

(e) An indorsement of a security certificate in bearer form may give notice of an adverse claim to the certificate, but it does not otherwise affect a right to registration that the holder possesses.

(f) Unless otherwise agreed, a person making an indorsement assumes only the obligations provided in Section 8–108 and not an obligation that the security will be honored by the issuer.

§ 8–305. Instruction.

(a) If an instruction has been originated by an appropriate person but is incomplete in any other respect, any person may complete it as authorized and the issuer may rely on it as completed, even though it has been completed incorrectly.

(b) Unless otherwise agreed, a person initiating an instruction assumes only the obligations imposed by Section 8–108 and not an obligation that the security will be honored by the issuer.

§ 8–306. Effect of Guaranteeing Signature, Indorsement, or Instruction.

(a) A person who guarantees a signature of an indorser of a security certificate warrants that at the time of signing:

(1) the signature was genuine;

(2) the signer was an appropriate person to indorse, or if the signature is by an agent, the agent had actual authority to act on behalf of the appropriate person; and

(3) the signer had legal capacity to sign.

(b) A person who guarantees a signature of the originator of an instruction warrants that at the time of signing:

(1) the signature was genuine;

(2) the signer was an appropriate person to originate the instruction, or if the signature is by an agent, the agent had actual authority to act on behalf of the appropriate

person, if the person specified in the instruction as the registered owner was, in fact, the registered owner, as to which fact the signature guarantor does not make a warranty; and

(3) the signer had legal capacity to sign.

(c) A person who specially guarantees the signature of an originator of an instruction makes the warranties of a signature guarantor under subsection (b) and also warrants that at the time the instruction is presented to the issuer:

(1) the person specified in the instruction as the registered owner of the uncertificated security will be the registered owner; and

(2) the transfer of the uncertificated security requested in the instruction will be registered by the issuer free from all liens, security interests, restrictions, and claims other than those specified in the instruction.

(d) A guarantor under subsections (a) and (b) or a special guarantor under subsection (c) does not otherwise warrant the rightfulness of the transfer.

(e) A person who guarantees an indorsement of a security certificate makes the warranties of a signature guarantor under subsection (a) and also warrants the rightfulness of the transfer in all respects.

(f) A person who guarantees an instruction requesting the transfer of an uncertificated security makes the warranties of a special signature guarantor under subsection (c) and also warrants the rightfulness of the transfer in all respects.

(g) An issuer may not require a special guaranty of signature, a guaranty of indorsement, or a guaranty of instruction as a condition to registration of transfer.

(h) The warranties under this section are made to a person taking or dealing with the security in reliance on the guaranty, and the guarantor is liable to the person for loss resulting from their breach. An indorser or originator of an instruction whose signature, indorsement, or instruction has been guaranteed is liable to a guarantor for any loss suffered by the guarantor as a result of breach of the warranties of the guarantor.

§ 8–307. Purchaser's Right to Requisites for Registration of Transfer.

Unless otherwise agreed, the transferor of a security on due demand shall supply the purchaser with proof of authority to transfer or with any other requisite necessary to obtain registration of the transfer of the security, but if the transfer is not for value, a transferor need not comply unless the purchaser pays the necessary expenses. If the transferor fails within a reasonable time to comply with the demand, the purchaser may reject or rescind the transfer.

Part 4 Registration

§ 8–401. Duty of Issuer to Register Transfer.

(a) If a certificated security in registered form is presented to an issuer with a request to register transfer or an instruction is presented to an issuer with a request to register transfer of an uncertificated security, the issuer shall register the transfer as requested if:

(1) under the terms of the security the person seeking registration of transfer is eligible to have the security registered in its name;

(2) the indorsement or instruction is made by the appropriate person or by an agent who has actual authority to act on behalf of the appropriate person;

(3) reasonable assurance is given that the indorsement or instruction is genuine and authorized (Section 8–402);

(4) any applicable law relating to the collection of taxes has been complied with;

(5) the transfer does not violate any restriction on transfer imposed by the issuer in accordance with Section 8–204;

(6) a demand that the issuer not register transfer has not become effective under Section 8–403, or the issuer has complied with Section 8–403(b) but no legal process or indemnity bond is obtained as provided in Section 8–403(d); and

(7) the transfer is in fact rightful or is to a protected purchaser.

(b) If an issuer is under a duty to register a transfer of a security, the issuer is liable to a person presenting a certificated security or an instruction for registration or to the person's principal for loss resulting from unreasonable delay in registration or failure or refusal to register the transfer.

§ 8–402. Assurance That Indorsement or Instruction Is Effective.

(a) An issuer may require the following assurance that each necessary indorsement or each instruction is genuine and authorized:

(1) in all cases, a guaranty of the signature of the person making an indorsement or originating an instruction including, in the case of an instruction, reasonable assurance of identity;

(2) if the indorsement is made or the instruction is originated by an agent, appropriate assurance of actual authority to sign;

(3) if the indorsement is made or the instruction is originated by a fiduciary pursuant to Section 8–107(a) (4) or (a)(5), appropriate evidence of appointment or incumbency;

(4) if there is more than one fiduciary, reasonable assurance that all who are required to sign have done so; and

(5) if the indorsement is made or the instruction is originated by a person not covered by another provision of this subsection, assurance appropriate to the case corresponding as nearly as may be to the provisions of this subsection.

(b) An issuer may elect to require reasonable assurance beyond that specified in this section.

(c) In this section:

(1) "Guaranty of the signature" means a guaranty signed by or on behalf of a person reasonably believed by the issuer to be responsible. An issuer may adopt standards with respect to responsibility if they are not manifestly unreasonable.

(2) "Appropriate evidence of appointment or incumbency" means:

(i) in the case of a fiduciary appointed or qualified by a court, a certificate issued by or under the direction or supervision of the court or an officer thereof and dated within 60 days before the date of presentation for transfer; or

(ii) in any other case, a copy of a document showing the appointment or a certificate issued by or on behalf of a person reasonably believed by an issuer to be responsible or, in the absence of that document or certificate, other evidence the issuer reasonably considers appropriate.

§ 8–403. Demand That Issuer Not Register Transfer.

(a) A person who is an appropriate person to make an indorsement or originate an instruction may demand that the issuer not register transfer of a security by communicating to the issuer a notification that identifies the registered owner and the issue of which the security is a part and provides an address for communications directed to the person making the demand. The demand is effective only if it is received by the issuer at a time and in a manner affording the issuer reasonable opportunity to act on it.

(b) If a certificated security in registered form is presented to an issuer with a request to register transfer or an instruction is presented to an issuer with a request to register transfer of an uncertificated security after a demand that the issuer not register transfer has become effective, the issuer shall promptly communicate to (i) the person who initiated the demand at the address provided in the demand and (ii) the person who presented the security for registration of transfer or initiated the instruction requesting registration of transfer a notification stating that:

(1) the certificated security has been presented for registration of transfer or the instruction for registration of transfer of the uncertificated security has been received;

(2) a demand that the issuer not register transfer had previously been received; and

(3) the issuer will withhold registration of transfer for a period of time stated in the notification in order to provide the person who initiated the demand an opportunity to obtain legal process or an indemnity bond.

(c) The period described in subsection (b)(3) may not exceed 30 days after the date of communication of the notification. A shorter period may be specified by the issuer if it is not manifestly unreasonable.

(d) An issuer is not liable to a person who initiated a demand that the issuer not register transfer for any loss the person suffers as a result of registration of a transfer pursuant to an effective indorsement or instruction if the person who initiated the demand does not, within the time stated in the issuer's communication, either:

(1) obtain an appropriate restraining order, injunction, or other process from a court of competent jurisdiction enjoining the issuer from registering the transfer; or

(2) file with the issuer an indemnity bond, sufficient in the issuer's judgment to protect the issuer and any transfer agent, registrar, or other agent of the issuer involved from any loss it or they may suffer by refusing to register the transfer.

(e) This section does not relieve an issuer from liability for registering transfer pursuant to an indorsement or instruction that was not effective.

§ 8–404. **Wrongful Registration.**

(a) Except as otherwise provided in Section 8–406, an issuer is liable for wrongful registration of transfer if the issuer has registered a transfer of a security to a person not entitled to it, and the transfer was registered:

(1) pursuant to an ineffective indorsement or instruction;

(2) after a demand that the issuer not register transfer became effective under Section 8–403(a) and the issuer did not comply with Section 8–403(b);

(3) after the issuer had been served with an injunction, restraining order, or other legal process enjoining it from registering the transfer, issued by a court of competent jurisdiction, and the issuer had a reasonable opportunity to act on the injunction, restraining order, or other legal process; or

(4) by an issuer acting in collusion with the wrongdoer.

(b) An issuer that is liable for wrongful registration of transfer under subsection (a) on demand shall provide the person entitled to the security with a like certificated or uncertificated security, and any payments or distributions that the person did not receive as a result of the wrongful registration. If an overissue would result, the issuer's liability to provide the person with a like security is governed by Section 8–210.

(c) Except as otherwise provided in subsection (a) or in a law relating to the collection of taxes, an issuer is not liable to an owner or other person suffering loss as a result of the registration of a transfer of a security if registration was made pursuant to an effective indorsement or instruction.

§ 8–405. **Replacement of Lost, Destroyed, or Wrongfully Taken Security Certificate.**

(a) If an owner of a certificated security, whether in registered or bearer form, claims that the certificate has been lost, destroyed, or wrongfully taken, the issuer shall issue a new certificate if the owner:

(1) so requests before the issuer has notice that the certificate has been acquired by a protected purchaser;

(2) files with the issuer a sufficient indemnity bond; and

(3) satisfies other reasonable requirements imposed by the issuer.

(b) If, after the issue of a new security certificate, a protected purchaser of the original certificate presents it for registration of transfer, the issuer shall register the transfer unless an overissue would result. In that case, the issuer's liability is governed by Section 8–210. In addition to any rights on the indemnity bond, an issuer may recover the new certificate from a person to whom it was issued or any person taking under that person, except a protected purchaser.

§ 8–406. **Obligation to Notify Issuer of Lost, Destroyed, or Wrongfully Taken Security Certificate.**

If a security certificate has been lost, apparently destroyed, or wrongfully taken, and the owner fails to notify the issuer of that fact within a reasonable time after the owner has notice of it and the issuer registers a transfer of the security before receiving notification, the owner may not assert against the issuer a claim for registering the transfer under Section 8–404 or a claim to a new security certificate under Section 8–405.

§ 8–407. **Authenticating Trustee, Transfer Agent, and Registrar.**

A person acting as authenticating trustee, transfer agent, registrar, or other agent for an issuer in the registration of a transfer of its securities, in the issue of new security certificates or uncertificated securities, or in the cancellation of surrendered security certificates has the same obligation to the holder or owner of a certificated or uncertificated security with regard to the particular functions performed as the issuer has in regard to those functions.

Part 5 Security Entitlements

§ 8–501. **Securities Account; Acquisition of Security Entitlement from Securities Intermediary.**

(a) "Securities account" means an account to which a financial asset is or may be credited in accordance with an agreement under which the person maintaining the account undertakes to treat the person for whom the account is maintained as entitled to exercise the rights that comprise the financial asset.

(b) Except as otherwise provided in subsections (d) and (e), a person acquires a security entitlement if a securities intermediary:

(1) indicates by book entry that a financial asset has been credited to the person's securities account;

(2) receives a financial asset from the person or acquires a financial asset for the person and, in either case, accepts it for credit to the person's securities account; or

(3) becomes obligated under other law, regulation, or rule to credit a financial asset to the person's securities account.

(c) If a condition of subsection (b) has been met, a person has a security entitlement even though the securities intermediary does not itself hold the financial asset.

(d) If a securities intermediary holds a financial asset for another person, and the financial asset is registered in the name of, payable to the order of, or specially indorsed to the other person, and has not been indorsed to the securities intermediary or in blank, the other person is treated as holding the financial asset directly rather than as having a security entitlement with respect to the financial asset.

(e) Issuance of a security is not establishment of a security entitlement.

§ 8–502. Assertion of Adverse Claim against Entitlement Holder.

An action based on an adverse claim to a financial asset, whether framed in conversion, replevin, constructive trust, equitable lien, or other theory, may not be asserted against a person who acquires a security entitlement under Section 8–501 for value and without notice of the adverse claim.

§ 8–503. Property Interest of Entitlement Holder in Financial Asset Held by Securities Intermediary.

(a) To the extent necessary for a securities intermediary to satisfy all security entitlements with respect to a particular financial asset, all interests in that financial asset held by the securities intermediary are held by the securities intermediary for the entitlement holders, are not property of the securities intermediary, and are not subject to claims of creditors of the securities intermediary, except as otherwise provided in Section 8–511.

(b) An entitlement holder's property interest with respect to a particular financial asset under subsection (a) is a pro rata property interest in all interests in that financial asset held by the securities intermediary, without regard to the time the entitlement holder acquired the security entitlement or the time the securities intermediary acquired the interest in that financial asset.

(c) An entitlement holder's property interest with respect to a particular financial asset under subsection (a) may be enforced against the securities intermediary only by exercise of the entitlement holder's rights under Sections 8–505 through 8–508.

(d) An entitlement holder's property interest with respect to a particular financial asset under subsection (a) may be enforced against a purchaser of the financial asset or interest therein only if:

(1) insolvency proceedings have been initiated by or against the securities intermediary;

(2) the securities intermediary does not have sufficient interests in the financial asset to satisfy the security entitlements of all of its entitlement holders to that financial asset;

(3) the securities intermediary violated its obligations under Section 8–504 by transferring the financial asset or interest therein to the purchaser; and

(4) the purchaser is not protected under subsection (e).

The trustee or other liquidator, acting on behalf of all entitlement holders having security entitlements with respect to a particular financial asset, may recover the financial asset, or interest therein, from the purchaser. If the trustee or other liquidator elects not to pursue that right, an entitlement holder whose security entitlement remains unsatisfied has the right to recover its interest in the financial asset from the purchaser.

(e) An action based on the entitlement holder's property interest with respect to a particular financial asset under subsection (a), whether framed in conversion, replevin, constructive trust, equitable lien, or other theory, may not be asserted against any purchaser of a financial asset or interest therein who gives value, obtains control, and does not act in collusion with the securities intermediary in violating the securities intermediary's obligations under Section 8–504.

§ 8–504. Duty of Securities Intermediary to Maintain Financial Asset.

(a) A securities intermediary shall promptly obtain and thereafter maintain a financial asset in a quantity corresponding to the aggregate of all security entitlements it has established in favor of its entitlement holders with respect to that financial asset. The securities intermediary may maintain those financial assets directly or through one or more other securities intermediaries.

(b) Except to the extent otherwise agreed by its entitlement holder, a securities intermediary may not grant any security interests in a financial asset it is obligated to maintain pursuant to subsection (a).

(c) A securities intermediary satisfies the duty in subsection (a) if:

(1) the securities intermediary acts with respect to the duty as agreed upon by the entitlement holder and the securities intermediary; or

(2) in the absence of agreement, the securities intermediary exercises due care in accordance with reasonable commercial standards to obtain and maintain the financial asset.

(d) This section does not apply to a clearing corporation that is itself the obligor of an option or similar obligation to which its entitlement holders have security entitlements.

§ 8–505. Duty of Securities Intermediary with Respect to Payments and Distributions.

(a) A securities intermediary shall take action to obtain a payment or distribution made by the issuer of a financial asset. A securities intermediary satisfies the duty if:

(1) the securities intermediary acts with respect to the duty as agreed upon by the entitlement holder and the securities intermediary; or

(2) in the absence of agreement, the securities intermediary exercises due care in accordance with reasonable commercial standards to attempt to obtain the payment or distribution.

(b) A securities intermediary is obligated to its entitlement holder for a payment or distribution made by the issuer of a financial asset if the payment or distribution is received by the securities intermediary.

§ 8–506. Duty of Securities Intermediary to Exercise Rights as Directed by Entitlement Holder.

A securities intermediary shall exercise rights with respect to a financial asset if directed to do so by an entitlement holder. A securities intermediary satisfies the duty if:

(1) the securities intermediary acts with respect to the duty as agreed upon by the entitlement holder and the securities intermediary; or

(2) in the absence of agreement, the securities intermediary either places the entitlement holder in a position to exercise the rights directly or exercises due care in accordance with reasonable commercial standards to follow the direction of the entitlement holder.

§ 8–507. Duty of Securities Intermediary to Comply with Entitlement Order.

(a) A securities intermediary shall comply with an entitlement order if the entitlement order is originated by the appropriate person, the securities intermediary has had reasonable opportunity to assure itself that the entitlement order is genuine and authorized, and the securities intermediary has had reasonable opportunity to comply with the entitlement order. A securities intermediary satisfies the duty if:

(1) the securities intermediary acts with respect to the duty as agreed upon by the entitlement holder and the securities intermediary; or

(2) in the absence of agreement, the securities intermediary exercises due care in accordance with reasonable commercial standards to comply with the entitlement order.

(b) If a securities intermediary transfers a financial asset pursuant to an ineffective entitlement order, the securities intermediary shall reestablish a security entitlement in favor of the person entitled to it, and pay or credit any payments or distributions that the person did not receive as a result of the wrongful transfer. If the securities intermediary does not reestablish a security entitlement, the securities intermediary is liable to the entitlement holder for damages.

§ 8–508. Duty of Securities Intermediary to Change Entitlement Holder's Position to Other Form of Security Holding.

A securities intermediary shall act at the direction of an entitlement holder to change a security entitlement into another available form of holding for which the entitlement holder is eligible, or to cause the financial asset to be transferred to a securities account of the entitlement holder with another securities intermediary. A securities intermediary satisfies the duty if:

(1) the securities intermediary acts as agreed upon by the entitlement holder and the securities intermediary; or

(2) in the absence of agreement, the securities intermediary exercises due care in accordance with reasonable commercial standards to follow the direction of the entitlement holder.

§ 8–509. Specification of Duties of Securities Intermediary by Other Statute or Regulation; Manner of Performance of Duties of Securities Intermediary and Exercise of Rights of Entitlement Holder.

(a) If the substance of a duty imposed upon a securities intermediary by Sections 8–504 through 8–508 is the subject of other statute, regulation, or rule, compliance with that statute, regulation, or rule satisfies the duty.

(b) To the extent that specific standards for the performance of the duties of a securities intermediary or the exercise of the rights of an entitlement holder are not specified by other statute, regulation, or rule or by agreement between the securities intermediary and entitlement holder, the securities intermediary shall perform its duties and the entitlement holder shall exercise its rights in a commercially reasonable manner.

(c) The obligation of a securities intermediary to perform the duties imposed by Sections 8–504 through 8–508 is subject to:

(1) rights of the securities intermediary arising out of a security interest under a security agreement with the entitlement holder or otherwise; and

(2) rights of the securities intermediary under other law, regulation, rule, or agreement to withhold performance of its duties as a result of unfulfilled obligations of the entitlement holder to the securities intermediary.

(d) Sections 8–504 through 8–508 do not require a securities intermediary to take any action that is prohibited by other statute, regulation, or rule.

§ 8–510. Rights of Purchaser of Security Entitlement from Entitlement Holder.

(a) An action based on an adverse claim to a financial asset or security entitlement, whether framed in conversion, replevin, constructive trust, equitable lien, or other theory, may not be asserted against a person who purchases a security entitlement, or an interest therein, from an entitlement holder if the purchaser gives value, does not have notice of the adverse claim, and obtains control.

(b) If an adverse claim could not have been asserted against an entitlement holder under Section 8–502, the adverse claim cannot be asserted against a person who purchases a security entitlement, or an interest therein, from the entitlement holder.

(c) In a case not covered by the priority rules in Article 9, a purchaser for value of a security entitlement, or an interest therein, who obtains control has priority over a purchaser of a security entitlement, or an interest therein, who does not obtain control. Except as otherwise provided in subsection (d), purchasers who have control rank according to priority in time of:

(1) the purchaser's becoming the person for whom the securities account, in which the security entitlement is carried, is maintained, if the purchaser obtained control under Section 8–106(d)(1);

(2) the securities intermediary's agreement to comply with the purchaser's entitlement orders with respect to security entitlements carried or to be carried in the securities account in which the security entitlement is carried, if the purchaser obtained control under Section 8–106(d)(2); or

(3) if the purchaser obtained control through another person under Section 8–106(d)(3), the time on which priority would be based under this subsection if the other person were the secured party.

(d) A securities intermediary as purchaser has priority over a conflicting purchaser who has control unless otherwise agreed by the securities intermediary.

As amended in 1999.

§ 8–511. Priority among Security Interests and Entitlement Holders.

(a) Except as otherwise provided in subsections (b) and (c), if a securities intermediary does not have sufficient interests in a particular financial asset to satisfy both its obligations to entitlement holders who have security entitlements to that financial asset and its obligation to a creditor of the securities intermediary who has a security interest in that financial asset, the claims of entitlement holders, other than the creditor, have priority over the claim of the creditor.

(b) A claim of a creditor of a securities intermediary who has a security interest in a financial asset held by a securities intermediary has priority over claims of the securities intermediary's entitlement holders who have security entitlements with respect to that financial asset if the creditor has control over the financial asset.

(c) If a clearing corporation does not have sufficient financial assets to satisfy both its obligations to entitlement holders who have security entitlements with respect to a financial asset and its obligation to a creditor of the clearing corporation who has a security interest in that financial asset, the claim of the creditor has priority over the claims of entitlement holders.

Part 6 Transition Provisions for Revised Article 8

§ 8–601. Effective Date.

This [Act] takes effect . . . .

§ 8–602. Repeals.

This [Act] repeals . . . .

§ 8–603. Savings Clause.

(a) This [Act] does not affect an action or proceeding commenced before this [Act] takes effect.

(b) If a security interest in a security is perfected at the date this [Act] takes effect, and the action by which the security interest was perfected would suffice to perfect a security interest under this [Act], no further action is required to continue perfection. If a security interest in a security is perfected at the date this [Act] takes effect but the action by which the security interest was perfected would not suffice to perfect a security interest under this [Act], the security interest remains perfected for a period of four months after the effective date and continues perfected thereafter if appropriate action to perfect under this [Act] is taken within that period. If a security interest is perfected at the date this [Act] takes effect and the security interest can be perfected by filing under this [Act], a financing statement signed by the secured party instead of the debtor may be filed within that period to continue perfection or thereafter to perfect.

Revised Article 9
SECURED TRANSACTIONS

Part 1 General Provisions

[Subpart 1. Short Title, Definitions, and General Concepts]

§ 9–101. Short Title.

This article may be cited as Uniform Commercial Code— Secured Transactions.

§ 9–102. Definitions and Index of Definitions.

(a) In this article:

(1) "Accession" means goods that are physically united with other goods in such a manner that the identity of the original goods is not lost.

(2) "Account", except as used in "account for", means a right to payment of a monetary obligation, whether or not earned by performance, (i) for property that has been or is to be sold, leased, licensed, assigned, or otherwise disposed of, (ii) for services rendered or to be rendered, (iii) for a policy of insurance issued or to be issued, (iv) for a secondary obligation incurred or to be incurred, (v) for energy provided or to be provided, (vi) for the use or hire of a vessel under a charter or other contract, (vii) arising out of the use of a credit or charge card or information contained on or for use with the card, or (viii) as winnings in a lottery or other game of chance operated or sponsored by a State, governmental unit of a State, or person licensed or authorized to operate the game by a State or governmental unit of a State. The term includes health-care insurance receivables. The term does not include

(i) rights to payment evidenced by chattel paper or an instrument, (ii) commercial tort claims, (iii) deposit accounts, (iv) investment property, (v) letter-of-credit rights or letters of credit, or (vi) rights to payment for money or funds advanced or sold, other than rights arising out of the use of a credit or charge card or information contained on or for use with the card.

(3) "Account debtor" means a person obligated on an account, chattel paper, or general intangible. The term does not include persons obligated to pay a negotiable instrument, even if the instrument constitutes part of chattel paper.

(4) "Accounting", except as used in "accounting for", means a record:

(A) authenticated by a secured party;

(B) indicating the aggregate unpaid secured obligations as of a date not more than 35 days earlier or 35 days later than the date of the record; and

(C) identifying the components of the obligations in reasonable detail.

(5) "Agricultural lien" means an interest, other than a security interest, in farm products:

(A) which secures payment or performance of an obligation for:

(i) goods or services furnished in connection with a debtor's farming operation; or

(ii) rent on real property leased by a debtor in connection with its farming operation;

(B) which is created by statute in favor of a person that:

(i) in the ordinary course of its business furnished goods or services to a debtor in connection with a debtor's farming operation; or

(ii) leased real property to a debtor in connection with the debtor's farming operation; and

(C) whose effectiveness does not depend on the person's possession of the personal property.

(6) "As-extracted collateral" means:

(A) oil, gas, or other minerals that are subject to a security interest that:

(i) is created by a debtor having an interest in the minerals before extraction; and

(ii) attaches to the minerals as extracted; or

(B) accounts arising out of the sale at the wellhead or minehead of oil, gas, or other minerals in which the debtor had an interest before extraction.

(7) "Authenticate" means:

(A) to sign; or

(B) to execute or otherwise adopt a symbol, or encrypt or similarly process a record in whole or in part, with the present intent of the authenticating person to identify the person and adopt or accept a record.

(8) "Bank" means an organization that is engaged in the business of banking. The term includes savings banks, savings and loan associations, credit unions, and trust companies.

(9) "Cash proceeds" means proceeds that are money, checks, deposit accounts, or the like.

(10) "Certificate of title" means a certificate of title with respect to which a statute provides for the security interest in question to be indicated on the certificate as a condition or result of the security interest's obtaining priority over the rights of a lien creditor with respect to the collateral.

(11) "Chattel paper" means a record or records that evidence both a monetary obligation and a security interest in specific goods, a security interest in specific goods and software used in the goods, a security interest in specific goods and license of software used in the goods, a lease of specific goods, or a lease of specific goods and license of software used in the goods. In this paragraph, "monetary obligation" means a monetary obligation secured by the goods or owed under a lease of the goods and includes a monetary obligation with respect to software used in the goods. The term does not include (i) charters or other contracts involving the use or hire of a vessel or (ii) records that evidence a right to payment arising out of the use of a credit or charge card or information contained on or for use with the card. If a transaction is evidenced by records that include an instrument or series of instruments, the group of records taken together constitutes chattel paper.

(12) "Collateral" means the property subject to a security interest or agricultural lien. The term includes:

(A) proceeds to which a security interest attaches;

(B) accounts, chattel paper, payment intangibles, and promissory notes that have been sold; and

(C) goods that are the subject of a consignment.

(13) "Commercial tort claim" means a claim arising in tort with respect to which:

(A) the claimant is an organization; or

(B) the claimant is an individual and the claim:

(i) arose in the course of the claimant's business or profession; and

(ii) does not include damages arising out of personal injury to or the death of an individual.

(14) "Commodity account" means an account maintained by a commodity intermediary in which a commodity contract is carried for a commodity customer.

(15) "Commodity contract" means a commodity futures contract, an option on a commodity futures

contract, a commodity option, or another contract if the contract or option is:

(A) traded on or subject to the rules of a board of trade that has been designated as a contract market for such a contract pursuant to federal commodities laws; or

(B) traded on a foreign commodity board of trade, exchange, or market, and is carried on the books of a commodity intermediary for a commodity customer.

(16) "Commodity customer" means a person for which a commodity intermediary carries a commodity contract on its books.

(17) "Commodity intermediary" means a person that:

(A) is registered as a futures commission merchant under federal commodities law; or

(B) in the ordinary course of its business provides clearance or settlement services for a board of trade that has been designated as a contract market pursuant to federal commodities law.

(18) "Communicate" means:

(A) to send a written or other tangible record;

(B) to transmit a record by any means agreed upon by the persons sending and receiving the record; or

(C) in the case of transmission of a record to or by a filing office, to transmit a record by any means prescribed by filing-office rule.

(19) "Consignee" means a merchant to which goods are delivered in a consignment.

(20) "Consignment" means a transaction, regardless of its form, in which a person delivers goods to a merchant for the purpose of sale and:

(A) the merchant:

(i) deals in goods of that kind under a name other than the name of the person making delivery;

(ii) is not an auctioneer; and

(iii) is not generally known by its creditors to be substantially engaged in selling the goods of others;

(B) with respect to each delivery, the aggregate value of the goods is $1,000 or more at the time of delivery;

(C) the goods are not consumer goods immediately before delivery; and

(D) the transaction does not create a security interest that secures an obligation.

(21) "Consignor" means a person that delivers goods to a consignee in a consignment.

(22) "Consumer debtor" means a debtor in a consumer transaction.

(23) "Consumer goods" means goods that are used or bought for use primarily for personal, family, or household purposes.

(24) "Consumer-goods transaction" means a consumer transaction in which:

(A) an individual incurs an obligation primarily for personal, family, or household purposes; and

(B) a security interest in consumer goods secures the obligation.

(25) "Consumer obligor" means an obligor who is an individual and who incurred the obligation as part of a transaction entered into primarily for personal, family, or household purposes.

(26) "Consumer transaction" means a transaction in which (i) an individual incurs an obligation primarily for personal, family, or household purposes, (ii) a security interest secures the obligation, and (iii) the collateral is held or acquired primarily for personal, family, or household purposes. The term includes consumer-goods transactions.

(27) "Continuation statement" means an amend-ment of a financing statement which:

(A) identifies, by its file number, the initial financing statement to which it relates; and

(B) indicates that it is a continuation statement for, or that it is filed to continue the effectiveness of, the identified financing statement.

(28) "Debtor" means:

(A) a person having an interest, other than a security interest or other lien, in the collateral, whether or not the person is an obligor;

(B) a seller of accounts, chattel paper, payment intangibles, or promissory notes; or

(C) a consignee.

(29) "Deposit account" means a demand, time, savings, passbook, or similar account maintained with a bank. The term does not include investment property or accounts evidenced by an instrument.

(30) "Document" means a document of title or a receipt of the type described in Section 7–201(2).

(31) "Electronic chattel paper" means chattel paper evidenced by a record or records consisting of information stored in an electronic medium.

(32) "Encumbrance" means a right, other than an ownership interest, in real property. The term includes mortgages and other liens on real property.

(33) "Equipment" means goods other than inventory, farm products, or consumer goods.

(34) "Farm products" means goods, other than standing timber, with respect to which the debtor is engaged in a farming operation and which are:

(A) crops grown, growing, or to be grown, including:

(i) crops produced on trees, vines, and bushes; and

(ii) aquatic goods produced in aquacultural operations;

(B) livestock, born or unborn, including aquatic goods produced in aquacultural operations;

(C) supplies used or produced in a farming operation; or

(D) products of crops or livestock in their unmanufactured states.

(35) "Farming operation" means raising, cultivating, propagating, fattening, grazing, or any other farming, livestock, or aquacultural operation.

(36) "File number" means the number assigned to an initial financing statement pursuant to Section 9–519(a).

(37) "Filing office" means an office designated in Section 9–501 as the place to file a financing statement.

(38) "Filing-office rule" means a rule adopted pursuant to Section 9–526.

(39) "Financing statement" means a record or records composed of an initial financing statement and any filed record relating to the initial financing statement.

(40) "Fixture filing" means the filing of a financing statement covering goods that are or are to become fixtures and satisfying Section 9–502(a) and (b). The term includes the filing of a financing statement covering goods of a transmitting utility which are or are to become fixtures.

(41) "Fixtures" means goods that have become so related to particular real property that an interest in them arises under real property law.

(42) "General intangible" means any personal property, including things in action, other than accounts, chattel paper, commercial tort claims, deposit accounts, documents, goods, instruments, investment property, letter-of-credit rights, letters of credit, money, and oil, gas, or other minerals before extraction. The term includes payment intangibles and software.

(43) "Good faith" means honesty in fact and the observance of reasonable commercial standards of fair dealing.

(44) "Goods" means all things that are movable when a security interest attaches. The term includes (i) fixtures, (ii) standing timber that is to be cut and removed under a conveyance or contract for sale, (iii) the unborn young of animals, (iv) crops grown, growing, or to be grown, even if the crops are produced on trees, vines, or bushes, and (v) manufactured homes. The term also includes a computer program embedded in goods and any supporting information provided in connection with a transaction relating to the program if (i) the program is associated with the goods in such a manner that it customarily is considered part of the goods, or (ii) by becoming the owner of the goods, a person acquires a right to use the program in connection with the goods. The term does not include a computer program embedded in goods that consist solely of the medium in which the program is embedded. The term also does not include accounts, chattel paper, commercial tort claims, deposit accounts, documents, general intangibles, instruments, investment property, letter-of-credit rights, letters of credit, money, or oil, gas, or other minerals before extraction.

(45) "Governmental unit" means a subdivision, agency, department, county, parish, municipality, or other unit of the government of the United States, a State, or a foreign country. The term includes an organization having a separate corporate existence if the organization is eligible to issue debt on which interest is exempt from income taxation under the laws of the United States.

(46) "Health-care-insurance receivable" means an interest in or claim under a policy of insurance which is a right to payment of a monetary obligation for health-care goods or services provided.

(47) "Instrument" means a negotiable instrument or any other writing that evidences a right to the payment of a monetary obligation, is not itself a security agreement or lease, and is of a type that in ordinary course of business is transferred by delivery with any necessary indorsement or assignment. The term does not include (i) investment property, (ii) letters of credit, or (iii) writings that evidence a right to payment arising out of the use of a credit or charge card or information contained on or for use with the card.

(48) "Inventory" means goods, other than farm products, which:

(A) are leased by a person as lessor;

(B) are held by a person for sale or lease or to be furnished under a contract of service;

(C) are furnished by a person under a contract of service; or

(D) consist of raw materials, work in process, or materials used or consumed in a business.

(49) "Investment property" means a security, whether certificated or uncertificated, security entitlement, securities account, commodity contract, or commodity account.

(50) "Jurisdiction of organization", with respect to a registered organization, means the jurisdiction under whose law the organization is organized.

(51) "Letter-of-credit right" means a right to payment or performance under a letter of credit, whether or not the beneficiary has demanded or is at the time entitled to demand payment or performance. The term does not include the right of a beneficiary to demand payment or performance under a letter of credit.

(52) "Lien creditor" means:

(A) a creditor that has acquired a lien on the property involved by attachment, levy, or the like;

(B) an assignee for benefit of creditors from the time of assignment;

(C) a trustee in bankruptcy from the date of the filing of the petition; or

(D) a receiver in equity from the time of appointment.

(53) "Manufactured home" means a structure, transportable in one or more sections, which, in the traveling mode, is eight body feet or more in width or 40 body feet or more in length, or, when erected on site, is 320 or more square feet, and which is built on a permanent chassis and designed to be used as a dwelling with or without a permanent foundation when connected to the required utilities, and includes the plumbing, heating, air-conditioning, and electrical systems contained therein. The term includes any structure that meets all of the requirements of this paragraph except the size requirements and with respect to which the manufacturer voluntarily files a certification required by the United States Secretary of Housing and Urban Development and complies with the standards established under Title 42 of the United States Code.

(54) "Manufactured-home transaction" means a secured transaction:

(A) that creates a purchase-money security interest in a manufactured home, other than a manufactured home held as inventory; or

(B) in which a manufactured home, other than a manufactured home held as inventory, is the primary collateral.

(55) "Mortgage" means a consensual interest in real property, including fixtures, which secures payment or performance of an obligation.

(56) "New debtor" means a person that becomes bound as debtor under Section 9–203(d) by a security agreement previously entered into by another person.

(57) "New value" means (i) money, (ii) money's worth in property, services, or new credit, or (iii) release by a transferee of an interest in property previously transferred to the transferee. The term does not include an obligation substituted for another obligation.

(58) "Noncash proceeds" means proceeds other than cash proceeds.

(59) "Obligor" means a person that, with respect to an obligation secured by a security interest in or an agricultural lien on the collateral, (i) owes payment or other performance of the obligation, (ii) has provided property other than the collateral to secure payment or other performance of the obligation, or (iii) is otherwise accountable in whole or in part for payment or other performance of the obligation. The term does not include issuers or nominated persons under a letter of credit.

(60) "Original debtor", except as used in Section 9–310(c), means a person that, as debtor, entered into a security agreement to which a new debtor has become bound under Section 9–203(d).

(61) "Payment intangible" means a general intangible under which the account debtor's principal obligation is a monetary obligation.

(62) "Person related to", with respect to an individual, means:

(A) the spouse of the individual;

(B) a brother, brother-in-law, sister, or sister-in-law of the individual;

(C) an ancestor or lineal descendant of the individual or the individual's spouse; or

(D) any other relative, by blood or marriage, of the individual or the individual's spouse who shares the same home with the individual.

(63) "Person related to", with respect to an organization, means:

(A) a person directly or indirectly controlling, controlled by, or under common control with the organization;

(B) an officer or director of, or a person performing similar functions with respect to, the organization;

(C) an officer or director of, or a person performing similar functions with respect to, a person described in subparagraph (A);

(D) the spouse of an individual described in subparagraph (A), (B), or (C); or

(E) an individual who is related by blood or marriage to an individual described in subparagraph (A), (B), (C), or (D) and shares the same home with the individual.

(64) "Proceeds", except as used in Section 9–609(b), means the following property:

(A) whatever is acquired upon the sale, lease, license, exchange, or other disposition of collateral;

(B) whatever is collected on, or distributed on account of, collateral;

(C) rights arising out of collateral;

(D) to the extent of the value of collateral, claims arising out of the loss, nonconformity, or interference with the use of, defects or infringement of rights in, or damage to, the collateral; or

(E) to the extent of the value of collateral and to the extent payable to the debtor or the secured party, insurance payable by reason of the loss or nonconformity of, defects or infringement of rights in, or damage to, the collateral.

(65) "Promissory note" means an instrument that evidences a promise to pay a monetary obligation, does not evidence an order to pay, and does not contain an

acknowledgment by a bank that the bank has received for deposit a sum of money or funds.

(66) "Proposal" means a record authenticated by a secured party which includes the terms on which the secured party is willing to accept collateral in full or partial satisfaction of the obligation it secures pursuant to Sections 9–620, 9–621, and 9–622.

(67) "Public-finance transaction" means a secured transaction in connection with which:

(A) debt securities are issued;

(B) all or a portion of the securities issued have an initial stated maturity of at least 20 years; and

(C) the debtor, obligor, secured party, account debtor or other person obligated on collateral, assignor or assignee of a secured obligation, or assignor or assignee of a security interest is a State or a governmental unit of a State.

(68) "Pursuant to commitment", with respect to an advance made or other value given by a secured party, means pursuant to the secured party's obligation, whether or not a subsequent event of default or other event not within the secured party's control has relieved or may relieve the secured party from its obligation.

(69) "Record", except as used in "for record", "of record", "record or legal title", and "record owner", means information that is inscribed on a tangible medium or which is stored in an electronic or other medium and is retrievable in perceivable form.

(70) "Registered organization" means an organization organized solely under the law of a single State or the United States and as to which the State or the United States must maintain a public record showing the organization to have been organized.

(71) "Secondary obligor" means an obligor to the extent that:

(A) the obligor's obligation is secondary; or

(B) the obligor has a right of recourse with respect to an obligation secured by collateral against the debtor, another obligor, or property of either.

(72) "Secured party" means:

(A) a person in whose favor a security interest is created or provided for under a security agreement, whether or not any obligation to be secured is outstanding;

(B) a person that holds an agricultural lien;

(C) a consignor;

(D) a person to which accounts, chattel paper, payment intangibles, or promissory notes have been sold;

(E) a trustee, indenture trustee, agent, collateral agent, or other representative in whose favor a security interest or agricultural lien is created or provided for; or

(F) a person that holds a security interest arising under Section 2–401, 2–505, 2–711(3), 2A–508(5), 4–210, or 5–118.

(73) "Security agreement" means an agreement that creates or provides for a security interest.

(74) "Send", in connection with a record or notification, means:

(A) to deposit in the mail, deliver for transmission, or transmit by any other usual means of communication, with postage or cost of transmission provided for, addressed to any address reasonable under the circumstances; or

(B) to cause the record or notification to be received within the time that it would have been received if properly sent under subparagraph (A).

(75) "Software" means a computer program and any supporting information provided in connection with a transaction relating to the program. The term does not include a computer program that is included in the definition of goods.

(76) "State" means a State of the United States, the District of Columbia, Puerto Rico, the United States Virgin Islands, or any territory or insular possession subject to the jurisdiction of the United States.

(77) "Supporting obligation" means a letter-of-credit right or secondary obligation that supports the payment or performance of an account, chattel paper, a document, a general intangible, an instrument, or investment property.

(78) "Tangible chattel paper" means chattel paper evidenced by a record or records consisting of information that is inscribed on a tangible medium.

(79) "Termination statement" means an amendment of a financing statement which:

(A) identifies, by its file number, the initial financing statement to which it relates; and

(B) indicates either that it is a termination statement or that the identified financing statement is no longer effective.

(80) "Transmitting utility" means a person primarily engaged in the business of:

(A) operating a railroad, subway, street railway, or trolley bus;

(B) transmitting communications electrically, electromagnetically, or by light;

(C) transmitting goods by pipeline or sewer; or

(D) transmitting or producing and transmitting electricity, steam, gas, or water.

(b) The following definitions in other articles apply to this article:

"Applicant."	Section 5–102
"Beneficiary."	Section 5–102
"Broker."	Section 8–102

"Certificated security."	Section 8–102
"Check."	Section 3–104
"Clearing corporation."	Section 8–102
"Contract for sale."	Section 2–106
"Customer."	Section 4–104
"Entitlement holder."	Section 8–102
"Financial asset."	Section 8–102
"Holder in due course."	Section 3–302
"Issuer" (with respect to a letter of credit or letter-of-credit right).	Section 5–102
"Issuer" (with respect to a security).	Section 8–201
"Lease."	Section 2A–103
"Lease agreement."	Section 2A–103
"Lease contract."	Section 2A–103
"Leasehold interest."	Section 2A–103
"Lessee."	Section 2A–103
"Lessee in ordinary course of business."	Section 2A–103
"Lessor."	Section 2A–103
"Lessor's residual interest."	Section 2A–103
"Letter of credit."	Section 5–102
"Merchant."	Section 2–104
"Negotiable instrument."	Section 3–104
"Nominated person."	Section 5–102
"Note."	Section 3–104
"Proceeds of a letter of credit."	Section 5–114
"Prove."	Section 3–103
"Sale."	Section 2–106
"Securities account."	Section 8–501
"Securities intermediary."	Section 8–102
"Security."	Section 8–102
"Security certificate."	Section 8–102
"Security entitlement."	Section 8–102
"Uncertificated security."	Section 8–102

(c) Article 1 contains general definitions and principles of construction and interpretation applicable throughout this article.

Amended in 1999 and 2000.

§ 9–103. Purchase-Money Security Interest; Application of Payments; Burden of Establishing.

(a) In this section:

(1) "purchase-money collateral" means goods or software that secures a purchase-money obligation incurred with respect to that collateral; and

(2) "purchase-money obligation" means an obligation of an obligor incurred as all or part of the price of the collateral or for value given to enable the debtor to acquire rights in or the use of the collateral if the value is in fact so used.

(b) A security interest in goods is a purchase-money security interest:

(1) to the extent that the goods are purchase-money collateral with respect to that security interest;

(2) if the security interest is in inventory that is or was purchase-money collateral, also to the extent that the security interest secures a purchase-money obligation incurred with respect to other inventory in which the secured party holds or held a purchase-money security interest; and

(3) also to the extent that the security interest secures a purchase-money obligation incurred with respect to software in which the secured party holds or held a purchase-money security interest.

(c) A security interest in software is a purchase-money security interest to the extent that the security interest also secures a purchase-money obligation incurred with respect to goods in which the secured party holds or held a purchase-money security interest if:

(1) the debtor acquired its interest in the software in an integrated transaction in which it acquired an interest in the goods; and

(2) the debtor acquired its interest in the software for the principal purpose of using the software in the goods.

(d) The security interest of a consignor in goods that are the subject of a consignment is a purchase-money security interest in inventory.

(e) In a transaction other than a consumer-goods transaction, if the extent to which a security interest is a purchase-money security interest depends on the application of a payment to a particular obligation, the payment must be applied:

(1) in accordance with any reasonable method of application to which the parties agree;

(2) in the absence of the parties' agreement to a reasonable method, in accordance with any intention of the obligor manifested at or before the time of payment; or

(3) in the absence of an agreement to a reasonable method and a timely manifestation of the obligor's intention, in the following order:

(A) to obligations that are not secured; and

(B) if more than one obligation is secured, to obligations secured by purchase-money security interests in the order in which those obligations were incurred.

(f) In a transaction other than a consumer-goods transaction, a purchase-money security interest does not lose its status as such, even if:

(1) the purchase-money collateral also secures an obligation that is not a purchase-money obligation;

(2) collateral that is not purchase-money collateral also secures the purchase-money obligation; or

(3) the purchase-money obligation has been renewed, refinanced, consolidated, or restructured.

(g) In a transaction other than a consumer-goods transaction, a secured party claiming a purchase-money security interest has the burden of establishing the extent to which the security interest is a purchase-money security interest.

(h) The limitation of the rules in subsections (e), (f), and (g) to transactions other than consumer-goods transactions is intended to leave to the court the determination of the proper rules in consumer-goods transactions. The court may not infer from that limitation the nature of the proper rule in consumer-goods transactions and may continue to apply established approaches.

§ 9–104. Control of Deposit Account.

(a) A secured party has control of a deposit account if:

(1) the secured party is the bank with which the deposit account is maintained;

(2) the debtor, secured party, and bank have agreed in an authenticated record that the bank will comply with instructions originated by the secured party directing disposition of the funds in the deposit account without further consent by the debtor; or

(3) the secured party becomes the bank's customer with respect to the deposit account.

(b) A secured party that has satisfied subsection (a) has control, even if the debtor retains the right to direct the disposition of funds from the deposit account.

§ 9–105. Control of Electronic Chattel Paper.

A secured party has control of electronic chattel paper if the record or records comprising the chattel paper are created, stored, and assigned in such a manner that:

(1) a single authoritative copy of the record or records exists which is unique, identifiable and, except as otherwise provided in paragraphs (4), (5), and (6), unalterable;

(2) the authoritative copy identifies the secured party as the assignee of the record or records;

(3) the authoritative copy is communicated to and maintained by the secured party or its designated custodian;

(4) copies or revisions that add or change an identified assignee of the authoritative copy can be made only with the participation of the secured party;

(5) each copy of the authoritative copy and any copy of a copy is readily identifiable as a copy that is not the authoritative copy; and

(6) any revision of the authoritative copy is readily identifiable as an authorized or unauthorized revision.

§ 9–106. Control of Investment Property.

(a) A person has control of a certificated security, uncertificated security, or security entitlement as provided in Section 8–106.

(b) A secured party has control of a commodity contract if:

(1) the secured party is the commodity intermediary with which the commodity contract is carried; or

(2) the commodity customer, secured party, and commodity intermediary have agreed that the commodity intermediary will apply any value distributed on account of the commodity contract as directed by the secured party without further consent by the commodity customer.

(c) A secured party having control of all security entitlements or commodity contracts carried in a securities account or commodity account has control over the securities account or commodity account.

§ 9–107. Control of Letter-of-Credit Right.

A secured party has control of a letter-of-credit right to the extent of any right to payment or performance by the issuer or any nominated person if the issuer or nominated person has consented to an assignment of proceeds of the letter of credit under Section 5–114(c) or otherwise applicable law or practice.

§ 9–108. Sufficiency of Description.

(a) Except as otherwise provided in subsections (c), (d), and (e), a description of personal or real property is sufficient, whether or not it is specific, if it reasonably identifies what is described.

(b) Except as otherwise provided in subsection (d), a description of collateral reasonably identifies the collateral if it identifies the collateral by:

(1) specific listing;

(2) category;

(3) except as otherwise provided in subsection (e), a type of collateral defined in [the Uniform Commercial Code];

(4) quantity;

(5) computational or allocational formula or procedure; or

(6) except as otherwise provided in subsection (c), any other method, if the identity of the collateral is objectively determinable.

(c) A description of collateral as "all the debtor's assets" or "all the debtor's personal property" or using words of similar import does not reasonably identify the collateral.

(d) Except as otherwise provided in subsection (e), a description of a security entitlement, securities account, or commodity account is sufficient if it describes:

(1) the collateral by those terms or as investment property; or

(2) the underlying financial asset or commodity contract.

(e) A description only by type of collateral defined in [the Uniform Commercial Code] is an insufficient description of:

(1) a commercial tort claim; or

(2) in a consumer transaction, consumer goods, a security entitlement, a securities account, or a commodity account.

[Subpart 2. Applicability of Article]

§ 9–109. Scope.

(a) Except as otherwise provided in subsections (c) and (d), this article applies to:

(1) a transaction, regardless of its form, that creates a security interest in personal property or fixtures by contract;

(2) an agricultural lien;

(3) a sale of accounts, chattel paper, payment intangibles, or promissory notes;

(4) a consignment;

(5) a security interest arising under Section 2–401, 2–505, 2–711(3), or 2A–508(5), as provided in Section 9–110; and

(6) a security interest arising under Section 4–210 or 5–118.

(b) The application of this article to a security interest in a secured obligation is not affected by the fact that the obligation is itself secured by a transaction or interest to which this article does not apply.

(c) This article does not apply to the extent that:

(1) a statute, regulation, or treaty of the United States preempts this article;

(2) another statute of this State expressly governs the creation, perfection, priority, or enforcement of a security interest created by this State or a governmental unit of this State;

(3) a statute of another State, a foreign country, or a governmental unit of another State or a foreign country, other than a statute generally applicable to security interests, expressly governs creation, perfection, priority, or enforcement of a security interest created by the State, country, or governmental unit; or

(4) the rights of a transferee beneficiary or nominated person under a letter of credit are independent and superior under Section 5–114.

(d) This article does not apply to:

(1) a landlord's lien, other than an agricultural lien;

(2) a lien, other than an agricultural lien, given by statute or other rule of law for services or materials, but Section 9–333 applies with respect to priority of the lien;

(3) an assignment of a claim for wages, salary, or other compensation of an employee;

(4) a sale of accounts, chattel paper, payment intangibles, or promissory notes as part of a sale of the business out of which they arose;

(5) an assignment of accounts, chattel paper, payment intangibles, or promissory notes which is for the purpose of collection only;

(6) an assignment of a right to payment under a contract to an assignee that is also obligated to perform under the contract;

(7) an assignment of a single account, payment intangible, or promissory note to an assignee in full or partial satisfaction of a preexisting indebtedness;

(8) a transfer of an interest in or an assignment of a claim under a policy of insurance, other than an assignment by or to a health-care provider of a health-care-insurance receivable and any subsequent assignment of the right to payment, but Sections 9–315 and 9–322 apply with respect to proceeds and priorities in proceeds;

(9) an assignment of a right represented by a judgment, other than a judgment taken on a right to payment that was collateral;

(10) a right of recoupment or set-off, but:

(A) Section 9–340 applies with respect to the effectiveness of rights of recoupment or set-off against deposit accounts; and

(B) Section 9–404 applies with respect to defenses or claims of an account debtor;

(11) the creation or transfer of an interest in or lien on real property, including a lease or rents thereunder, except to the extent that provision is made for:

(A) liens on real property in Sections 9–203 and 9–308;

(B) fixtures in Section 9–334;

(C) fixture filings in Sections 9–501, 9–502, 9–512, 9–516, and 9–519; and

(D) security agreements covering personal and real property in Section 9–604;

(12) an assignment of a claim arising in tort, other than a commercial tort claim, but Sections 9–315 and 9–322 apply with respect to proceeds and priorities in proceeds; or

(13) an assignment of a deposit account in a consumer transaction, but Sections 9–315 and 9–322 apply with respect to proceeds and priorities in proceeds.

§ 9–110. Security Interests Arising under Article 2 or 2A.

A security interest arising under Section 2–401, 2–505, 2–711(3), or 2A–508(5) is subject to this article. However, until the debtor obtains possession of the goods:

(1) the security interest is enforceable, even if Section 9–203(b)(3) has not been satisfied;

(2) filing is not required to perfect the security interest;

(3) the rights of the secured party after default by the debtor are governed by Article 2 or 2A; and

(4) the security interest has priority over a conflicting security interest created by the debtor.

Part 2 Effectiveness of Security Agreement; Attachment of Security Interest; Rights of Parties to Security Agreement

[Subpart 1. Effectiveness and Attachment]

§ 9–201. General Effectiveness of Security Agreement.

(a) Except as otherwise provided in [the Uniform Commercial Code], a security agreement is effective according to its terms between the parties, against purchasers of the collateral, and against creditors.

(b) A transaction subject to this article is subject to any applicable rule of law which establishes a different rule for consumers and [insert reference to (i) any other statute or regulation that regulates the rates, charges, agreements, and practices for loans, credit sales, or other extensions of credit and (ii) any consumer-protection statute or regulation].

(c) In case of conflict between this article and a rule of law, statute, or regulation described in subsection (b), the rule of law, statute, or regulation controls. Failure to comply with a statute or regulation described in subsection (b) has only the effect the statute or regulation specifies.

(d) This article does not:

(1) validate any rate, charge, agreement, or practice that violates a rule of law, statute, or regulation described in subsection (b); or

(2) extend the application of the rule of law, statute, or regulation to a transaction not otherwise subject to it.

§ 9–202. Title to Collateral Immaterial.

Except as otherwise provided with respect to consignments or sales of accounts, chattel paper, payment intangibles, or promissory notes, the provisions of this article with regard to rights and obligations apply whether title to collateral is in the secured party or the debtor.

§ 9–203. Attachment and Enforceability of Security Interest; Proceeds; Supporting Obligations; Formal Requisites.

(a) A security interest attaches to collateral when it becomes enforceable against the debtor with respect to the collateral, unless an agreement expressly postpones the time of attachment.

(b) Except as otherwise provided in subsections (c) through (i), a security interest is enforceable against the debtor and third parties with respect to the collateral only if:

(1) value has been given;

(2) the debtor has rights in the collateral or the power to transfer rights in the collateral to a secured party; and

(3) one of the following conditions is met:

(A) the debtor has authenticated a security agreement that provides a description of the collateral and, if the security interest covers timber to be cut, a description of the land concerned;

(B) the collateral is not a certificated security and is in the possession of the secured party under Section 9–313 pursuant to the debtor's security agreement;

(C) the collateral is a certificated security in registered form and the security certificate has been delivered to the secured party under Section 8–301 pursuant to the debtor's security agreement; or

(D) the collateral is deposit accounts, electronic chattel paper, investment property, or letter-of-credit rights, and the secured party has control under Section 9–104, 9–105, 9–106, or 9–107 pursuant to the debtor's security agreement.

(c) Subsection (b) is subject to Section 4–210 on the security interest of a collecting bank, Section 5–118 on the security interest of a letter-of-credit issuer or nominated person, Section 9–110 on a security interest arising under Article 2 or 2A, and Section 9–206 on security interests in investment property.

(d) A person becomes bound as debtor by a security agreement entered into by another person if, by operation of law other than this article or by contract:

(1) the security agreement becomes effective to create a security interest in the person's property; or

(2) the person becomes generally obligated for the obligations of the other person, including the obligation secured under the security agreement, and acquires or succeeds to all or substantially all of the assets of the other person.

(e) If a new debtor becomes bound as debtor by a security agreement entered into by another person:

(1) the agreement satisfies subsection (b)(3) with respect to existing or after-acquired property of the new debtor to the extent the property is described in the agreement; and

(2) another agreement is not necessary to make a security interest in the property enforceable.

(f) The attachment of a security interest in collateral gives the secured party the rights to proceeds provided by Section 9–315 and is also attachment of a security interest in a supporting obligation for the collateral.

(g) The attachment of a security interest in a right to payment or performance secured by a security interest or other lien on personal or real property is also attachment of a security interest in the security interest, mortgage, or other lien.

(h) The attachment of a security interest in a securities account is also attachment of a security interest in the security entitlements carried in the securities account.

(i) The attachment of a security interest in a commodity account is also attachment of a security interest in the commodity contracts carried in the commodity account.

§ 9–204. After-Acquired Property; Future Advances.

(a) Except as otherwise provided in subsection (b), a security agreement may create or provide for a security interest in after-acquired collateral.

(b) A security interest does not attach under a term constituting an after-acquired property clause to:

(1) consumer goods, other than an accession when given as additional security, unless the debtor acquires rights in them within 10 days after the secured party gives value; or

(2) a commercial tort claim.

(c) A security agreement may provide that collateral secures, or that accounts, chattel paper, payment intangibles, or promissory notes are sold in connection with, future advances or other value, whether or not the advances or value are given pursuant to commitment.

§ 9–205. Use or Disposition of Collateral Permissible.

(a) A security interest is not invalid or fraudulent against creditors solely because:

(1) the debtor has the right or ability to:

(A) use, commingle, or dispose of all or part of the collateral, including returned or repossessed goods;

(B) collect, compromise, enforce, or otherwise deal with collateral;

(C) accept the return of collateral or make repossessions; or

(D) use, commingle, or dispose of proceeds; or

(2) the secured party fails to require the debtor to account for proceeds or replace collateral.

(b) This section does not relax the requirements of possession if attachment, perfection, or enforcement of a security interest depends upon possession of the collateral by the secured party.

§ 9–206. Security Interest Arising in Purchase or Delivery of Financial Asset.

(a) A security interest in favor of a securities intermediary attaches to a person's security entitlement if:

(1) the person buys a financial asset through the securities intermediary in a transaction in which the person is obligated to pay the purchase price to the securities intermediary at the time of the purchase; and

(2) the securities intermediary credits the financial asset to the buyer's securities account before the buyer pays the securities intermediary.

(b) The security interest described in subsection (a) secures the person's obligation to pay for the financial asset.

(c) A security interest in favor of a person that delivers a certificated security or other financial asset represented by a writing attaches to the security or other financial asset if:

(1) the security or other financial asset:

(A) in the ordinary course of business is transferred by delivery with any necessary indorsement or assignment; and

(B) is delivered under an agreement between persons in the business of dealing with such securities or financial assets; and

(2) the agreement calls for delivery against payment.

(d) The security interest described in subsection (c) secures the obligation to make payment for the delivery.

[Subpart 2. Rights and Duties]

§ 9–207. Rights and Duties of Secured Party Having Possession or Control of Collateral.

(a) Except as otherwise provided in subsection (d), a secured party shall use reasonable care in the custody and preservation of collateral in the secured party's possession. In the case of chattel paper or an instrument, reasonable care includes taking necessary steps to preserve rights against prior parties unless otherwise agreed.

(b) Except as otherwise provided in subsection (d), if a secured party has possession of collateral:

(1) reasonable expenses, including the cost of insurance and payment of taxes or other charges, incurred in the custody, preservation, use, or operation of the collateral are chargeable to the debtor and are secured by the collateral;

(2) the risk of accidental loss or damage is on the debtor to the extent of a deficiency in any effective insurance coverage;

(3) the secured party shall keep the collateral identifiable, but fungible collateral may be commingled; and

(4) the secured party may use or operate the collateral:

(A) for the purpose of preserving the collateral or its value;

(B) as permitted by an order of a court having competent jurisdiction; or

(C) except in the case of consumer goods, in the manner and to the extent agreed by the debtor.

(c) Except as otherwise provided in subsection (d), a secured party having possession of collateral or control of collateral under Section 9–104, 9–105, 9–106, or 9–107:

(1) may hold as additional security any proceeds, except money or funds, received from the collateral;

(2) shall apply money or funds received from the collateral to reduce the secured obligation, unless remitted to the debtor; and

(3) may create a security interest in the collateral.

(d) If the secured party is a buyer of accounts, chattel paper, payment intangibles, or promissory notes or a consignor:

(1) subsection (a) does not apply unless the secured party is entitled under an agreement:

(A) to charge back uncollected collateral; or

(B) otherwise to full or limited recourse against the debtor or a secondary obligor based on the nonpayment or other default of an account debtor or other obligor on the collateral; and

(2) subsections (b) and (c) do not apply.

§ 9–208. Additional Duties of Secured Party Having Control of Collateral.

(a) This section applies to cases in which there is no outstanding secured obligation and the secured party is not committed to make advances, incur obligations, or otherwise give value.

(b) Within 10 days after receiving an authenticated demand by the debtor:

(1) a secured party having control of a deposit account under Section 9–104(a)(2) shall send to the bank with which the deposit account is maintained an authenticated statement that releases the bank from any further obligation to comply with instructions originated by the secured party;

(2) a secured party having control of a deposit account under Section 9–104(a)(3) shall:

(A) pay the debtor the balance on deposit in the deposit account; or

(B) transfer the balance on deposit into a deposit account in the debtor's name;

(3) a secured party, other than a buyer, having control of electronic chattel paper under Section 9–105 shall:

(A) communicate the authoritative copy of the electronic chattel paper to the debtor or its designated custodian;

(B) if the debtor designates a custodian that is the designated custodian with which the authoritative copy of the electronic chattel paper is maintained for the secured party, communicate to the custodian an authenticated record releasing the designated custodian from any further obligation to comply with instructions originated by the secured party and instructing the custodian to comply with instructions originated by the debtor; and

(C) take appropriate action to enable the debtor or its designated custodian to make copies of or revisions to the authoritative copy which add or change an identified assignee of the authoritative copy without the consent of the secured party;

(4) a secured party having control of investment property under Section 8–106(d)(2) or 9–106(b) shall send to the securities intermediary or commodity intermediary with which the security entitlement or commodity contract is maintained an authenticated record that releases the securities intermediary or commodity intermediary from any further obligation to comply with entitlement orders or directions originated by the secured party; and

(5) a secured party having control of a letter-of-credit right under Section 9–107 shall send to each person having an unfulfilled obligation to pay or deliver proceeds of the letter of credit to the secured party an authenticated release from any further obligation to pay or deliver proceeds of the letter of credit to the secured party.

§ 9–209. Duties of Secured Party If Account Debtor Has Been Notified of Assignment.

(a) Except as otherwise provided in subsection (c), this section applies if:

(1) there is no outstanding secured obligation; and

(2) the secured party is not committed to make advances, incur obligations, or otherwise give value.

(b) Within 10 days after receiving an authenticated demand by the debtor, a secured party shall send to an account debtor that has received notification of an assignment to the secured party as assignee under Section 9–406(a) an authenticated record that releases the account debtor from any further obligation to the secured party.

(c) This section does not apply to an assignment constituting the sale of an account, chattel paper, or payment intangible.

§ 9–210. Request for Accounting; Request Regarding List of Collateral or Statement of Account.

(a) In this section:

(1) "Request" means a record of a type described in paragraph (2), (3), or (4).

(2) "Request for an accounting" means a record authenticated by a debtor requesting that the recipient provide an accounting of the unpaid obligations secured by collateral and reasonably identifying the transaction or relationship that is the subject of the request.

(3) "Request regarding a list of collateral" means a record authenticated by a debtor requesting that the recipient approve or correct a list of what the debtor believes to be the collateral securing an obligation and reasonably identifying the transaction or relationship that is the subject of the request.

(4) "Request regarding a statement of account" means a record authenticated by a debtor requesting that the recipient approve or correct a statement indicating what the debtor believes to be the aggregate amount of unpaid obligations secured by collateral as of a specified date and reasonably identifying the transaction or relationship that is the subject of the request.

(b) Subject to subsections (c), (d), (e), and (f), a secured party, other than a buyer of accounts, chattel paper, payment intangibles, or promissory notes or a consignor, shall comply with a request within 14 days after receipt:

(1) in the case of a request for an accounting, by authenticating and sending to the debtor an accounting; and

(2) in the case of a request regarding a list of collateral or a request regarding a statement of account, by authenticating and sending to the debtor an approval or correction.

(c) A secured party that claims a security interest in all of a particular type of collateral owned by the debtor may comply with a request regarding a list of collateral by sending to the debtor an authenticated record including a statement to that effect within 14 days after receipt.

(d) A person that receives a request regarding a list of collateral, claims no interest in the collateral when it receives the request, and claimed an interest in the collateral at an earlier time shall comply with the request within 14 days after receipt by sending to the debtor an authenticated record:

(1) disclaiming any interest in the collateral; and

(2) if known to the recipient, providing the name and mailing address of any assignee of or successor to the recipient's interest in the collateral.

(e) A person that receives a request for an accounting or a request regarding a statement of account, claims no interest in the obligations when it receives the request, and claimed an interest in the obligations at an earlier time shall comply with the request within 14 days after receipt by sending to the debtor an authenticated record:

(1) disclaiming any interest in the obligations; and

(2) if known to the recipient, providing the name and mailing address of any assignee of or successor to the recipient's interest in the obligations.

(f) A debtor is entitled without charge to one response to a request under this section during any six-month period. The secured party may require payment of a charge not exceeding $25 for each additional response.

As amended in 1999.

Part 3 Perfection and Priority

[Subpart 1. Law Governing Perfection and Priority]

§ 9–301. Law Governing Perfection and Priority of Security Interests.

Except as otherwise provided in Sections 9–303 through 9–306, the following rules determine the law governing perfection, the effect of perfection or nonperfection, and the priority of a security interest in collateral:

(1) Except as otherwise provided in this section, while a debtor is located in a jurisdiction, the local law of that jurisdiction governs perfection, the effect of perfection or nonperfection, and the priority of a security interest in collateral.

(2) While collateral is located in a jurisdiction, the local law of that jurisdiction governs perfection, the effect of perfection or nonperfection, and the priority of a possessory security interest in that collateral.

(3) Except as otherwise provided in paragraph (4), while negotiable documents, goods, instruments, money, or tangible chattel paper is located in a jurisdiction, the local law of that jurisdiction governs:

(A) perfection of a security interest in the goods by filing a fixture filing;

(B) perfection of a security interest in timber to be cut; and

(C) the effect of perfection or nonperfection and the priority of a nonpossessory security interest in the collateral.

(4) The local law of the jurisdiction in which the wellhead or minehead is located governs perfection, the effect of perfection or nonperfection, and the priority of a security interest in as-extracted collateral.

§ 9–302. Law Governing Perfection and Priority of Agricultural Liens.

While farm products are located in a jurisdiction, the local law of that jurisdiction governs perfection, the effect of perfection or nonperfection, and the priority of an agricultural lien on the farm products.

§ 9–303. Law Governing Perfection and Priority of Security Interests in Goods Covered by a Certificate of Title.

(a) This section applies to goods covered by a certificate of title, even if there is no other relationship between the jurisdiction under whose certificate of title the goods are covered and the goods or the debtor.

(b) Goods become covered by a certificate of title when a valid application for the certificate of title and the applicable fee are delivered to the appropriate authority. Goods cease to be covered by a certificate of title at the earlier of the time the certificate of title ceases to be effective under the law of the issuing jurisdiction or the time the goods become covered subsequently by a certificate of title issued by another jurisdiction.

(c) The local law of the jurisdiction under whose certificate of title the goods are covered governs perfection, the effect of perfection or nonperfection, and the priority of a security interest in goods covered by a certificate of title from the time the goods become covered by the certificate of title until the goods cease to be covered by the certificate of title.

§ 9–304. Law Governing Perfection and Priority of Security Interests in Deposit Accounts.

(a) The local law of a bank's jurisdiction governs perfection, the effect of perfection or nonperfection, and the priority of a security interest in a deposit account maintained with that bank.

(b) The following rules determine a bank's jurisdiction for purposes of this part:

(1) If an agreement between the bank and the debtor governing the deposit account expressly provides that a particular jurisdiction is the bank's jurisdiction for purposes of this part, this article, or [the Uniform Commercial Code], that jurisdiction is the bank's jurisdiction.

(2) If paragraph (1) does not apply and an agreement between the bank and its customer governing the deposit account expressly provides that the agreement is governed by the law of a particular jurisdiction, that jurisdiction is the bank's jurisdiction.

(3) If neither paragraph (1) nor paragraph (2) applies and an agreement between the bank and its customer

governing the deposit account expressly provides that the deposit account is maintained at an office in a particular jurisdiction, that jurisdiction is the bank's jurisdiction.

(4) If none of the preceding paragraphs applies, the bank's jurisdiction is the jurisdiction in which the office identified in an account statement as the office serving the customer's account is located.

(5) If none of the preceding paragraphs applies, the bank's jurisdiction is the jurisdiction in which the chief executive office of the bank is located.

§ 9–305. Law Governing Perfection and Priority of Security Interests in Investment Property.

(a) Except as otherwise provided in subsection (c), the following rules apply:

(1) While a security certificate is located in a jurisdiction, the local law of that jurisdiction governs perfection, the effect of perfection or nonperfection, and the priority of a security interest in the certificated security represented thereby.

(2) The local law of the issuer's jurisdiction as specified in Section 8–110(d) governs perfection, the effect of perfection or nonperfection, and the priority of a security interest in an uncertificated security.

(3) The local law of the securities intermediary's jurisdiction as specified in Section 8–110(e) governs perfection, the effect of perfection or nonperfection, and the priority of a security interest in a security entitlement or securities account.

(4) The local law of the commodity intermediary's jurisdiction governs perfection, the effect of perfection or nonperfection, and the priority of a security interest in a commodity contract or commodity account.

(b) The following rules determine a commodity intermediary's jurisdiction for purposes of this part:

(1) If an agreement between the commodity intermediary and commodity customer governing the commodity account expressly provides that a particular jurisdiction is the commodity intermediary's jurisdiction for purposes of this part, this article, or [the Uniform Commercial Code], that jurisdiction is the commodity intermediary's jurisdiction.

(2) If paragraph (1) does not apply and an agreement between the commodity intermediary and commodity customer governing the commodity account expressly provides that the agreement is governed by the law of a particular jurisdiction, that jurisdiction is the commodity intermediary's jurisdiction.

(3) If neither paragraph (1) nor paragraph (2) applies and an agreement between the commodity intermediary and commodity customer governing the commodity account expressly provides that the commodity account is maintained at an office

in a particular jurisdiction, that jurisdiction is the commodity intermediary's jurisdiction.

(4) If none of the preceding paragraphs applies, the commodity intermediary's jurisdiction is the jurisdiction in which the office identified in an account statement as the office serving the commodity customer's account is located.

(5) If none of the preceding paragraphs applies, the commodity intermediary's jurisdiction is the jurisdiction in which the chief executive office of the commodity intermediary is located.

(c) The local law of the jurisdiction in which the debtor is located governs:

(1) perfection of a security interest in investment property by filing;

(2) automatic perfection of a security interest in investment property created by a broker or securities intermediary; and

(3) automatic perfection of a security interest in a commodity contract or commodity account created by a commodity intermediary.

§ 9–306. Law Governing Perfection and Priority of Security Interests in Letter-of-Credit Rights.

(a) Subject to subsection (c), the local law of the issuer's jurisdiction or a nominated person's jurisdiction governs perfection, the effect of perfection or nonperfection, and the priority of a security interest in a letter-of-credit right if the issuer's jurisdiction or nominated person's jurisdiction is a State.

(b) For purposes of this part, an issuer's jurisdiction or nominated person's jurisdiction is the jurisdiction whose law governs the liability of the issuer or nominated person with respect to the letter-of-credit right as provided in Section 5–116.

(c) This section does not apply to a security interest that is perfected only under Section 9–308(d).

§ 9–307. Location of Debtor.

(a) In this section, "place of business" means a place where a debtor conducts its affairs.

(b) Except as otherwise provided in this section, the following rules determine a debtor's location:

(1) A debtor who is an individual is located at the individual's principal residence.

(2) A debtor that is an organization and has only one place of business is located at its place of business.

(3) A debtor that is an organization and has more than one place of business is located at its chief executive office.

(c) Subsection (b) applies only if a debtor's residence, place of business, or chief executive office, as applicable, is located in a jurisdiction whose law generally requires information concerning the existence of a nonpossessory security interest to be made generally available in a filing, recording, or registration system as a condition or result of the security interest's obtaining priority over the rights of a lien creditor with respect to the collateral. If subsection (b) does not apply, the debtor is located in the District of Columbia.

(d) A person that ceases to exist, have a residence, or have a place of business continues to be located in the jurisdiction specified by subsections (b) and (c).

(e) A registered organization that is organized under the law of a State is located in that State.

(f) Except as otherwise provided in subsection (i), a registered organization that is organized under the law of the United States and a branch or agency of a bank that is not organized under the law of the United States or a State are located:

(1) in the State that the law of the United States designates, if the law designates a State of location;

(2) in the State that the registered organization, branch, or agency designates, if the law of the United States authorizes the registered organization, branch, or agency to designate its State of location; or

(3) in the District of Columbia, if neither paragraph (1) nor paragraph (2) applies.

(g) A registered organization continues to be located in the jurisdiction specified by subsection (e) or (f) notwithstanding:

(1) the suspension, revocation, forfeiture, or lapse of the registered organization's status as such in its jurisdiction of organization; or

(2) the dissolution, winding up, or cancellation of the existence of the registered organization.

(h) The United States is located in the District of Columbia.

(i) A branch or agency of a bank that is not organized under the law of the United States or a State is located in the State in which the branch or agency is licensed, if all branches and agencies of the bank are licensed in only one State.

(j) A foreign air carrier under the Federal Aviation Act of 1958, as amended, is located at the designated office of the agent upon which service of process may be made on behalf of the carrier.

(k) This section applies only for purposes of this part.

[Subpart 2. Perfection]

§ 9–308. When Security Interest or Agricultural Lien Is Perfected; Continuity of Perfection.

(a) Except as otherwise provided in this section and Section 9–309, a security interest is perfected if it has attached and all of the applicable requirements for perfection in Sections 9–310 through 9–316 have been satisfied. A security interest is perfected when it attaches if the applicable requirements are satisfied before the security interest attaches.

(b) An agricultural lien is perfected if it has become effective and all of the applicable requirements for perfection in Section 9–310 have been satisfied. An agricultural lien

is perfected when it becomes effective if the applicable requirements are satisfied before the agricultural lien becomes effective.

(c) A security interest or agricultural lien is perfected continuously if it is originally perfected by one method under this article and is later perfected by another method under this article, without an intermediate period when it was unperfected.

(d) Perfection of a security interest in collateral also perfects a security interest in a supporting obligation for the collateral.

(e) Perfection of a security interest in a right to payment or performance also perfects a security interest in a security interest, mortgage, or other lien on personal or real property securing the right.

(f) Perfection of a security interest in a securities account also perfects a security interest in the security entitlements carried in the securities account.

(g) Perfection of a security interest in a commodity account also perfects a security interest in the commodity contracts carried in the commodity account.

Legislative Note: Any statute conflicting with subsection (e) must be made expressly subject to that subsection.

§ 9–309. Security Interest Perfected upon Attachment.

The following security interests are perfected when they attach:

(1) a purchase-money security interest in consumer goods, except as otherwise provided in Section 9–311(b) with respect to consumer goods that are subject to a statute or treaty described in Section 9–311(a);

(2) an assignment of accounts or payment intangibles which does not by itself or in conjunction with other assignments to the same assignee transfer a significant part of the assignor's outstanding accounts or payment intangibles;

(3) a sale of a payment intangible;

(4) a sale of a promissory note;

(5) a security interest created by the assignment of a health-care-insurance receivable to the provider of the health-care goods or services;

(6) a security interest arising under Section 2–401, 2–505, 2–711(3), or 2A–508(5), until the debtor obtains possession of the collateral;

(7) a security interest of a collecting bank arising under Section 4–210;

(8) a security interest of an issuer or nominated person arising under Section 5–118;

(9) a security interest arising in the delivery of a financial asset under Section 9–206(c);

(10) a security interest in investment property created by a broker or securities intermediary;

(11) a security interest in a commodity contract or a commodity account created by a commodity intermediary;

(12) an assignment for the benefit of all creditors of the transferor and subsequent transfers by the assignee thereunder; and

(13) a security interest created by an assignment of a beneficial interest in a decedent's estate; and

(14) a sale by an individual of an account that is a right to payment of winnings in a lottery or other game of chance.

§ 9–310. When Filing Required to Perfect Security Interest or Agricultural Lien; Security Interests and Agricultural Liens to Which Filing Provisions Do Not Apply.

(a) Except as otherwise provided in subsection (b) and Section 9–312(b), a financing statement must be filed to perfect all security interests and agricultural liens.

(b) The filing of a financing statement is not necessary to perfect a security interest:

(1) that is perfected under Section 9–308(d), (e), (f), or (g);

(2) that is perfected under Section 9–309 when it attaches;

(3) in property subject to a statute, regulation, or treaty described in Section 9–311(a);

(4) in goods in possession of a bailee which is perfected under Section 9–312(d)(1) or (2);

(5) in certificated securities, documents, goods, or instruments which is perfected without filing or possession under Section 9–312(e), (f), or (g);

(6) in collateral in the secured party's possession under Section 9–313;

(7) in a certificated security which is perfected by delivery of the security certificate to the secured party under Section 9–313;

(8) in deposit accounts, electronic chattel paper, investment property, or letter-of-credit rights which is perfected by control under Section 9–314;

(9) in proceeds which is perfected under Section 9–315; or

(10) that is perfected under Section 9–316.

(c) If a secured party assigns a perfected security interest or agricultural lien, a filing under this article is not required to continue the perfected status of the security interest against creditors of and transferees from the original debtor.

§ 9–311. Perfection of Security Interests in Property Subject to Certain Statutes, Regulations, and Treaties.

(a) Except as otherwise provided in subsection (d), the filing of a financing statement is not necessary or effective to perfect a security interest in property subject to:

(1) a statute, regulation, or treaty of the United States whose requirements for a security interest's obtaining priority over the rights of a lien creditor with respect to the property preempt Section 9–310(a);

(2) [list any certificate-of-title statute covering automobiles, trailers, mobile homes, boats, farm tractors, or the like, which provides for a security interest to be indicated on the certificate as a condition or result of perfection, and any non-Uniform Commercial Code central filing statute]; or

(3) a certificate-of-title statute of another jurisdiction which provides for a security interest to be indicated on the certificate as a condition or result of the security interest's obtaining priority over the rights of a lien creditor with respect to the property.

(b) Compliance with the requirements of a statute, regulation, or treaty described in subsection (a) for obtaining priority over the rights of a lien creditor is equivalent to the filing of a financing statement under this article. Except as otherwise provided in subsection (d) and Sections 9–313 and 9–316(d) and (e) for goods covered by a certificate of title, a security interest in property subject to a statute, regulation, or treaty described in subsection (a) may be perfected only by compliance with those requirements, and a security interest so perfected remains perfected notwithstanding a change in the use or transfer of possession of the collateral.

(c) Except as otherwise provided in subsection (d) and Section 9–316(d) and (e), duration and renewal of perfection of a security interest perfected by compliance with the requirements prescribed by a statute, regulation, or treaty described in subsection (a) are governed by the statute, regulation, or treaty. In other respects, the security interest is subject to this article.

(d) During any period in which collateral subject to a statute specified in subsection (a)(2) is inventory held for sale or lease by a person or leased by that person as lessor and that person is in the business of selling goods of that kind, this section does not apply to a security interest in that collateral created by that person.

Legislative Note: This Article contemplates that perfection of a security interest in goods covered by a certificate of title occurs upon receipt by appropriate State officials of a properly tendered application for a certificate of title on which the security interest is to be indicated, without a relation back to an earlier time. States whose certificate-of-title statutes provide for perfection at a different time or contain a relation-back provision should amend the statutes accordingly.

§ 9–312. Perfection of Security Interests in Chattel Paper, Deposit Accounts, Documents, Goods Covered by Documents, Instruments, Investment Property, Letter-of-Credit Rights, and Money; Perfection by Permissive Filing; Temporary Perfection without Filing or Transfer of Possession.

(a) A security interest in chattel paper, negotiable documents, instruments, or investment property may be perfected by filing.

(b) Except as otherwise provided in Section 9–315(c) and (d) for proceeds:

(1) a security interest in a deposit account may be perfected only by control under Section 9–314;

(2) and except as otherwise provided in Section 9–308(d), a security interest in a letter-of-credit right may be perfected only by control under Section 9–314; and

(3) a security interest in money may be perfected only by the secured party's taking possession under Section 9–313.

(c) While goods are in the possession of a bailee that has issued a negotiable document covering the goods:

(1) a security interest in the goods may be perfected by perfecting a security interest in the document; and

(2) a security interest perfected in the document has priority over any security interest that becomes perfected in the goods by another method during that time.

(d) While goods are in the possession of a bailee that has issued a nonnegotiable document covering the goods, a security interest in the goods may be perfected by:

(1) issuance of a document in the name of the secured party;

(2) the bailee's receipt of notification of the secured party's interest; or

(3) filing as to the goods.

(e) A security interest in certificated securities, negotiable documents, or instruments is perfected without filing or the taking of possession for a period of 20 days from the time it attaches to the extent that it arises for new value given under an authenticated security agreement.

(f) A perfected security interest in a negotiable document or goods in possession of a bailee, other than one that has issued a negotiable document for the goods, remains perfected for 20 days without filing if the secured party makes available to the debtor the goods or documents representing the goods for the purpose of:

(1) ultimate sale or exchange; or

(2) loading, unloading, storing, shipping, transshipping, manufacturing, processing, or otherwise dealing with them in a manner preliminary to their sale or exchange.

(g) A perfected security interest in a certificated security or instrument remains perfected for 20 days without filing if the secured party delivers the security certificate or instrument to the debtor for the purpose of:

(1) ultimate sale or exchange; or

(2) presentation, collection, enforcement, renewal, or registration of transfer.

(h) After the 20-day period specified in subsection (e), (f), or (g) expires, perfection depends upon compliance with this article.

§ 9–313. When Possession by or Delivery to Secured Party Perfects Security Interest without Filing.

(a) Except as otherwise provided in subsection (b), a secured party may perfect a security interest in negotiable documents, goods, instruments, money, or tangible chattel paper by taking possession of the collateral. A secured party may perfect a security interest in certificated securities by taking delivery of the certificated securities under Section 8–301.

(b) With respect to goods covered by a certificate of title issued by this State, a secured party may perfect a security interest in the goods by taking possession of the goods only in the circumstances described in Section 9–316(d).

(c) With respect to collateral other than certificated securities and goods covered by a document, a secured party takes possession of collateral in the possession of a person other than the debtor, the secured party, or a lessee of the collateral from the debtor in the ordinary course of the debtor's business, when:

(1) the person in possession authenticates a record acknowledging that it holds possession of the collateral for the secured party's benefit; or

(2) the person takes possession of the collateral after having authenticated a record acknowledging that it will hold possession of collateral for the secured party's benefit.

(d) If perfection of a security interest depends upon possession of the collateral by a secured party, perfection occurs no earlier than the time the secured party takes possession and continues only while the secured party retains possession.

(e) A security interest in a certificated security in registered form is perfected by delivery when delivery of the certificated security occurs under Section 8–301 and remains perfected by delivery until the debtor obtains possession of the security certificate.

(f) A person in possession of collateral is not required to acknowledge that it holds possession for a secured party's benefit.

(g) If a person acknowledges that it holds possession for the secured party's benefit:

(1) the acknowledgment is effective under subsection (c) or Section 8–301(a), even if the acknowledgment violates the rights of a debtor; and

(2) unless the person otherwise agrees or law other than this article otherwise provides, the person does not owe any duty to the secured party and is not required to confirm the acknowledgment to another person.

(h) A secured party having possession of collateral does not relinquish possession by delivering the collateral to a person other than the debtor or a lessee of the collateral from the debtor in the ordinary course of the debtor's business if the person was instructed before the delivery or is instructed contemporaneously with the delivery:

(1) to hold possession of the collateral for the secured party's benefit; or

(2) to redeliver the collateral to the secured party.

(i) A secured party does not relinquish possession, even if a delivery under subsection (h) violates the rights of a debtor. A person to which collateral is delivered under subsection (h) does not owe any duty to the secured party and is not required to confirm the delivery to another person unless the person otherwise agrees or law other than this article otherwise provides.

§ 9–314. Perfection by Control.

(a) A security interest in investment property, deposit accounts, letter-of-credit rights, or electronic chattel paper may be perfected by control of the collateral under Section 9–104, 9–105, 9–106, or 9–107.

(b) A security interest in deposit accounts, electronic chattel paper, or letter-of-credit rights is perfected by control under Section 9–104, 9–105, or 9–107 when the secured party obtains control and remains perfected by control only while the secured party retains control.

(c) A security interest in investment property is perfected by control under Section 9–106 from the time the secured party obtains control and remains perfected by control until:

(1) the secured party does not have control; and

(2) one of the following occurs:

(A) if the collateral is a certificated security, the debtor has or acquires possession of the security certificate;

(B) if the collateral is an uncertificated security, the issuer has registered or registers the debtor as the registered owner; or

(C) if the collateral is a security entitlement, the debtor is or becomes the entitlement holder.

§ 9–315. Secured Party's Rights on Disposition of Collateral and in Proceeds.

(a) Except as otherwise provided in this article and in Section 2–403(2):

(1) a security interest or agricultural lien continues in collateral notwithstanding sale, lease, license, exchange, or other disposition thereof unless the secured party authorized the disposition free of the security interest or agricultural lien; and

(2) a security interest attaches to any identifiable proceeds of collateral.

(b) Proceeds that are commingled with other property are identifiable proceeds:

(1) if the proceeds are goods, to the extent provided by Section 9–336; and

(2) if the proceeds are not goods, to the extent that the secured party identifies the proceeds by a method of tracing, including application of equitable principles, that is permitted under law other than this article with respect to commingled property of the type involved.

(c) A security interest in proceeds is a perfected security interest if the security interest in the original collateral was perfected.

(d) A perfected security interest in proceeds becomes unperfected on the 21st day after the security interest attaches to the proceeds unless:

(1) the following conditions are satisfied:

(A) a filed financing statement covers the original collateral;

(B) the proceeds are collateral in which a security interest may be perfected by filing in the office in which the financing statement has been filed; and

(C) the proceeds are not acquired with cash proceeds;

(2) the proceeds are identifiable cash proceeds; or

(3) the security interest in the proceeds is perfected other than under subsection (c) when the security interest attaches to the proceeds or within 20 days thereafter.

(e) If a filed financing statement covers the original collateral, a security interest in proceeds which remains perfected under subsection (d)(1) becomes unperfected at the later of:

(1) when the effectiveness of the filed financing statement lapses under Section 9–515 or is terminated under Section 9–513; or

(2) the 21st day after the security interest attaches to the proceeds.

§ 9–316. Continued Perfection of Security Interest Following Change in Governing Law.

(a) A security interest perfected pursuant to the law of the jurisdiction designated in Section 9–301(1) or 9–305(c) remains perfected until the earliest of:

(1) the time perfection would have ceased under the law of that jurisdiction;

(2) the expiration of four months after a change of the debtor's location to another jurisdiction; or

(3) the expiration of one year after a transfer of collateral to a person that thereby becomes a debtor and is located in another jurisdiction.

(b) If a security interest described in subsection (a) becomes perfected under the law of the other jurisdiction before the earliest time or event described in that subsection, it remains perfected thereafter. If the security interest does not become perfected under the law of the other jurisdiction before the earliest time or event, it becomes unperfected and is deemed never to have been perfected as against a purchaser of the collateral for value.

(c) A possessory security interest in collateral, other than goods covered by a certificate of title and as-extracted collateral consisting of goods, remains continuously perfected if:

(1) the collateral is located in one jurisdiction and subject to a security interest perfected under the law of that jurisdiction;

(2) thereafter the collateral is brought into another jurisdiction; and

(3) upon entry into the other jurisdiction, the security interest is perfected under the law of the other jurisdiction.

(d) Except as otherwise provided in subsection (e), a security interest in goods covered by a certificate of title which is perfected by any method under the law of another jurisdiction when the goods become covered by a certificate of title from this State remains perfected until the security interest would have become unperfected under the law of the other jurisdiction had the goods not become so covered.

(e) A security interest described in subsection (d) becomes unperfected as against a purchaser of the goods for value and is deemed never to have been perfected as against a purchaser of the goods for value if the applicable requirements for perfection under Section 9–311(b) or 9–313 are not satisfied before the earlier of:

(1) the time the security interest would have become unperfected under the law of the other jurisdiction had the goods not become covered by a certificate of title from this State; or

(2) the expiration of four months after the goods had become so covered.

(f) A security interest in deposit accounts, letter-of-credit rights, or investment property which is perfected under the law of the bank's jurisdiction, the issuer's jurisdiction, a nominated person's jurisdiction, the securities intermediary's jurisdiction, or the commodity intermediary's jurisdiction, as applicable, remains perfected until the earlier of:

(1) the time the security interest would have become unperfected under the law of that jurisdiction; or

(2) the expiration of four months after a change of the applicable jurisdiction to another jurisdiction.

(g) If a security interest described in subsection (f) becomes perfected under the law of the other jurisdiction before the earlier of the time or the end of the period described in that subsection, it remains perfected thereafter. If the security interest does not become perfected under the law of the other jurisdiction before the earlier of that time or the end of that period, it becomes unperfected and is deemed never to have been perfected as against a purchaser of the collateral for value.

[Subpart 3. Priority]

§ 9–317. Interests That Take Priority over or Take Free of Security Interest or Agricultural Lien.

(a) A security interest or agricultural lien is subordinate to the rights of:

(1) a person entitled to priority under Section 9–322; and

(2) except as otherwise provided in subsection (e), a person that becomes a lien creditor before the earlier of the time:

(A) the security interest or agricultural lien is perfected; or

(B) one of the conditions specified in Section 9–203(b)(3) is met and a financing statement covering the collateral is filed.

(b) Except as otherwise provided in subsection (e), a buyer, other than a secured party, of tangible chattel paper, documents, goods, instruments, or a security certificate takes free of a security interest or agricultural lien if the buyer gives value and receives delivery of the collateral without knowledge of the security interest or agricultural lien and before it is perfected.

(c) Except as otherwise provided in subsection (e), a lessee of goods takes free of a security interest or agricultural lien if the lessee gives value and receives delivery of the collateral without knowledge of the security interest or agricultural lien and before it is perfected.

(d) A licensee of a general intangible or a buyer, other than a secured party, of accounts, electronic chattel paper, general intangibles, or investment property other than a certificated security takes free of a security interest if the licensee or buyer gives value without knowledge of the security interest and before it is perfected.

(e) Except as otherwise provided in Sections 9–320 and 9–321, if a person files a financing statement with respect to a purchase-money security interest before or within 20 days after the debtor receives delivery of the collateral, the security interest takes priority over the rights of a buyer, lessee, or lien creditor which arise between the time the security interest attaches and the time of filing.

As amended in 2000.

§ 9–318. No Interest Retained in Right to Payment That Is Sold; Rights and Title of Seller of Account or Chattel Paper with Respect to Creditors and Purchasers.

(a) A debtor that has sold an account, chattel paper, payment intangible, or promissory note does not retain a legal or equitable interest in the collateral sold.

(b) For purposes of determining the rights of creditors of, and purchasers for value of an account or chattel paper from, a debtor that has sold an account or chattel paper, while the buyer's security interest is unperfected, the debtor is deemed to have rights and title to the account or chattel paper identical to those the debtor sold.

§ 9–319. Rights and Title of Consignee with Respect to Creditors and Purchasers.

(a) Except as otherwise provided in subsection (b), for purposes of determining the rights of creditors of, and purchasers for value of goods from, a consignee, while the goods are in the possession of the consignee, the consignee is deemed to have rights and title to the goods identical to those the consignor had or had power to transfer.

(b) For purposes of determining the rights of a creditor of a consignee, law other than this article determines the rights and title of a consignee while goods are in the consignee's possession if, under this part, a perfected security interest held by the consignor would have priority over the rights of the creditor.

§ 9–320. Buyer of Goods.

(a) Except as otherwise provided in subsection (e), a buyer in ordinary course of business, other than a person buying farm products from a person engaged in farming operations, takes free of a security interest created by the buyer's seller, even if the security interest is perfected and the buyer knows of its existence.

(b) Except as otherwise provided in subsection (e), a buyer of goods from a person who used or bought the goods for use primarily for personal, family, or household purposes takes free of a security interest, even if perfected, if the buyer buys:

(1) without knowledge of the security interest;

(2) for value;

(3) primarily for the buyer's personal, family, or household purposes; and

(4) before the filing of a financing statement covering the goods.

(c) To the extent that it affects the priority of a security interest over a buyer of goods under subsection (b), the period of effectiveness of a filing made in the jurisdiction in which the seller is located is governed by Section 9–316(a) and (b).

(d) A buyer in ordinary course of business buying oil, gas, or other minerals at the wellhead or minehead or after extraction takes free of an interest arising out of an encumbrance.

(e) Subsections (a) and (b) do not affect a security interest in goods in the possession of the secured party under Section 9–313.

§ 9–321. Licensee of General Intangible and Lessee of Goods in Ordinary Course of Business.

(a) In this section, "licensee in ordinary course of business" means a person that becomes a licensee of a general intangible in good faith, without knowledge that the license violates the rights of another person in the general intangible, and in the ordinary course from a person in the business of licensing general intangibles of that kind. A person becomes a licensee in the ordinary course if the license to the person comports with the usual or customary practices in the kind of business in which the licensor is engaged or with the licensor's own usual or customary practices.

(b) A licensee in ordinary course of business takes its rights under a nonexclusive license free of a security interest in the general intangible created by the licensor, even if the security interest is perfected and the licensee knows of its existence.

(c) A lessee in ordinary course of business takes its leasehold interest free of a security interest in the goods created by the lessor, even if the security interest is perfected and the lessee knows of its existence.

§ 9–322. Priorities among Conflicting Security Interests in and Agricultural Liens on Same Collateral.

(a) Except as otherwise provided in this section, priority among conflicting security interests and agricultural liens in the same collateral is determined according to the following rules:

(1) Conflicting perfected security interests and agricultural liens rank according to priority in time of filing or perfection. Priority dates from the earlier of the time a filing covering the collateral is first made or the security interest or agricultural lien is first perfected, if there is no period thereafter when there is neither filing nor perfection.

(2) A perfected security interest or agricultural lien has priority over a conflicting unperfected security interest or agricultural lien.

(3) The first security interest or agricultural lien to attach or become effective has priority if conflicting security interests and agricultural liens are unperfected.

(b) For the purposes of subsection (a)(1):

(1) the time of filing or perfection as to a security interest in collateral is also the time of filing or perfection as to a security interest in proceeds; and

(2) the time of filing or perfection as to a security interest in collateral supported by a supporting obligation is also the time of filing or perfection as to a security interest in the supporting obligation.

(c) Except as otherwise provided in subsection (f), a security interest in collateral which qualifies for priority over a conflicting security interest under Section 9–327, 9–328, 9–329, 9–330, or 9–331 also has priority over a conflicting security interest in:

(1) any supporting obligation for the collateral; and

(2) proceeds of the collateral if:

(A) the security interest in proceeds is perfected;

(B) the proceeds are cash proceeds or of the same type as the collateral; and

(C) in the case of proceeds that are proceeds of proceeds, all intervening proceeds are cash proceeds, proceeds of the same type as the collateral, or an account relating to the collateral.

(d) Subject to subsection (e) and except as otherwise provided in subsection (f), if a security interest in chattel paper, deposit accounts, negotiable documents, instruments, investment property, or letter-of-credit rights is perfected by a method other than filing, conflicting perfected security interests in proceeds of the collateral rank according to priority in time of filing.

(e) Subsection (d) applies only if the proceeds of the collateral are not cash proceeds, chattel paper, negotiable documents, instruments, investment property, or letter-of-credit rights.

(f) Subsections (a) through (e) are subject to:

(1) subsection (g) and the other provisions of this part;

(2) Section 4–210 with respect to a security interest of a collecting bank;

(3) Section 5–118 with respect to a security interest of an issuer or nominated person; and

(4) Section 9–110 with respect to a security interest arising under Article 2 or 2A.

(g) A perfected agricultural lien on collateral has priority over a conflicting security interest in or agricultural lien on the same collateral if the statute creating the agricultural lien so provides.

§ 9–323. Future Advances.

(a) Except as otherwise provided in subsection (c), for purposes of determining the priority of a perfected security interest under Section 9–322(a)(1), perfection of the security interest dates from the time an advance is made to the extent that the security interest secures an advance that:

(1) is made while the security interest is perfected only:

(A) under Section 9–309 when it attaches; or

(B) temporarily under Section 9–312(e), (f), or (g); and

(2) is not made pursuant to a commitment entered into before or while the security interest is perfected by a method other than under Section 9–309 or 9–312(e), (f), or (g).

(b) Except as otherwise provided in subsection (c), a security interest is subordinate to the rights of a person that becomes a lien creditor to the extent that the security interest secures an advance made more than 45 days after the person becomes a lien creditor unless the advance is made:

(1) without knowledge of the lien; or

(2) pursuant to a commitment entered into without knowledge of the lien.

(c) Subsections (a) and (b) do not apply to a security interest held by a secured party that is a buyer of accounts, chattel paper, payment intangibles, or promissory notes or a consignor.

(d) Except as otherwise provided in subsection (e), a buyer of goods other than a buyer in ordinary course of business takes free of a security interest to the extent that it secures advances made after the earlier of:

(1) the time the secured party acquires knowledge of the buyer's purchase; or

(2) 45 days after the purchase.

(e) Subsection (d) does not apply if the advance is made pursuant to a commitment entered into without knowledge of the buyer's purchase and before the expiration of the 45-day period.

(f) Except as otherwise provided in subsection (g), a lessee of goods, other than a lessee in ordinary course of business, takes the leasehold interest free of a security interest to the extent that it secures advances made after the earlier of:

(1) the time the secured party acquires knowledge of the lease; or

(2) 45 days after the lease contract becomes enforceable.

(g) Subsection (f) does not apply if the advance is made pursuant to a commitment entered into without knowledge of the lease and before the expiration of the 45-day period.

As amended in 1999.

§ 9–324. Priority of Purchase-Money Security Interests.

(a) Except as otherwise provided in subsection (g), a perfected purchase-money security interest in goods other than inventory or livestock has priority over a conflicting security interest in the same goods, and, except as otherwise provided in Section 9–327, a perfected security interest in its identifiable proceeds also has priority, if the purchase-money security interest is perfected when the debtor receives possession of the collateral or within 20 days thereafter.

(b) Subject to subsection (c) and except as otherwise provided in subsection (g), a perfected purchase-money security interest in inventory has priority over a conflicting security interest in the same inventory, has priority over a conflicting security interest in chattel paper or an instrument constituting proceeds of the inventory and in proceeds of the chattel paper, if so provided in Section 9–330, and, except as otherwise provided in Section 9–327, also has priority in identifiable cash proceeds of the inventory to the extent the identifiable cash proceeds are received on or before the delivery of the inventory to a buyer, if:

(1) the purchase-money security interest is perfected when the debtor receives possession of the inventory;

(2) the purchase-money secured party sends an authenticated notification to the holder of the conflicting security interest;

(3) the holder of the conflicting security interest receives the notification within five years before the debtor receives possession of the inventory; and

(4) the notification states that the person sending the notification has or expects to acquire a purchase-money security interest in inventory of the debtor and describes the inventory.

(c) Subsections (b)(2) through (4) apply only if the holder of the conflicting security interest had filed a financing statement covering the same types of inventory:

(1) if the purchase-money security interest is perfected by filing, before the date of the filing; or

(2) if the purchase-money security interest is temporarily perfected without filing or possession under Section 9–312(f), before the beginning of the 20-day period thereunder.

(d) Subject to subsection (e) and except as otherwise provided in subsection (g), a perfected purchase-money security interest in livestock that are farm products has priority over a conflicting security interest in the same livestock, and, except as otherwise provided in Section 9–327, a perfected security interest in their identifiable proceeds and identifiable products in their unmanufactured states also has priority, if:

(1) the purchase-money security interest is perfected when the debtor receives possession of the livestock;

(2) the purchase-money secured party sends an authenticated notification to the holder of the conflicting security interest;

(3) the holder of the conflicting security interest receives the notification within six months before the debtor receives possession of the livestock; and

(4) the notification states that the person sending the notification has or expects to acquire a purchase-money security interest in livestock of the debtor and describes the livestock.

(e) Subsections (d)(2) through (4) apply only if the holder of the conflicting security interest had filed a financing statement covering the same types of livestock:

(1) if the purchase-money security interest is perfected by filing, before the date of the filing; or

(2) if the purchase-money security interest is temporarily perfected without filing or possession under Section 9–312(f), before the beginning of the 20-day period thereunder.

(f) Except as otherwise provided in subsection (g), a perfected purchase-money security interest in software has priority over a conflicting security interest in the same collateral, and, except as otherwise provided in Section 9–327, a perfected security interest in its identifiable proceeds also has priority, to the extent that the purchase-money security interest in the goods in which the software was acquired for use has priority in the goods and proceeds of the goods under this section.

(g) If more than one security interest qualifies for priority in the same collateral under subsection (a), (b), (d), or (f):

(1) a security interest securing an obligation incurred as all or part of the price of the collateral has priority over a security interest securing an obligation incurred for value given to enable the debtor to acquire rights in or the use of collateral; and

(2) in all other cases, Section 9–322(a) applies to the qualifying security interests.

§ 9–325. Priority of Security Interests in Transferred Collateral.

(a) Except as otherwise provided in subsection (b), a security interest created by a debtor is subordinate to a security interest in the same collateral created by another person if:

(1) the debtor acquired the collateral subject to the security interest created by the other person;

(2) the security interest created by the other person was perfected when the debtor acquired the collateral; and

(3) there is no period thereafter when the security interest is unperfected.

(b) Subsection (a) subordinates a security interest only if the security interest:

(1) otherwise would have priority solely under Section 9–322(a) or 9–324; or

(2) arose solely under Section 2–711(3) or 2A–508(5).

§ 9–326. Priority of Security Interests Created by New Debtor.

(a) Subject to subsection (b), a security interest created by a new debtor which is perfected by a filed financing statement that is effective solely under Section 9–508 in collateral in which a new debtor has or acquires rights is subordinate to a security interest in the same collateral which is perfected other than by a filed financing statement that is effective solely under Section 9–508.

(b) The other provisions of this part determine the priority among conflicting security interests in the same collateral perfected by filed financing statements that are effective solely under Section 9–508. However, if the security agreements to which a new debtor became bound as debtor were not entered into by the same original debtor, the conflicting security interests rank according to priority in time of the new debtor's having become bound.

§ 9–327. Priority of Security Interests in Deposit Account.

The following rules govern priority among conflicting security interests in the same deposit account:

(1) A security interest held by a secured party having control of the deposit account under Section 9–104 has priority over a conflicting security interest held by a secured party that does not have control.

(2) Except as otherwise provided in paragraphs (3) and (4), security interests perfected by control under Section 9–314 rank according to priority in time of obtaining control.

(3) Except as otherwise provided in paragraph (4), a security interest held by the bank with which the deposit account is maintained has priority over a conflicting security interest held by another secured party.

(4) A security interest perfected by control under Section 9–104(a)(3) has priority over a security interest held by the bank with which the deposit account is maintained.

§ 9–328. Priority of Security Interests in Investment Property.

The following rules govern priority among conflicting security interests in the same investment property:

(1) A security interest held by a secured party having control of investment property under Section 9–106 has priority over a security interest held by a secured party that does not have control of the investment property.

(2) Except as otherwise provided in paragraphs (3) and (4), conflicting security interests held by secured parties each of which has control under Section 9–106 rank according to priority in time of:

(A) if the collateral is a security, obtaining control;

(B) if the collateral is a security entitlement carried in a securities account and:

(i) if the secured party obtained control under Section 8–106(d)(1), the secured party's becoming the person for which the securities account is maintained;

(ii) if the secured party obtained control under Section 8–106(d)(2), the securities intermediary's agreement to comply with the secured party's entitlement orders with respect to security entitlements carried or to be carried in the securities account; or

(iii) if the secured party obtained control through another person under Section 8–106(d)(3), the time on which priority would be based under this paragraph if the other person were the secured party; or

(C) if the collateral is a commodity contract carried with a commodity intermediary, the satisfaction of the requirement for control specified in Section 9–106(b)(2) with respect to commodity contracts carried or to be carried with the commodity intermediary.

(3) A security interest held by a securities intermediary in a security entitlement or a securities account maintained with the securities intermediary has priority over a conflicting security interest held by another secured party.

(4) A security interest held by a commodity intermediary in a commodity contract or a commodity account maintained with the commodity intermediary has priority over a conflicting security interest held by another secured party.

(5) A security interest in a certificated security in registered form which is perfected by taking delivery under Section 9–313(a) and not by control under Section 9–314 has priority over a conflicting security interest perfected by a method other than control.

(6) Conflicting security interests created by a broker, securities intermediary, or commodity intermediary which are perfected without control under Section 9–106 rank equally.

(7) In all other cases, priority among conflicting security interests in investment property is governed by Sections 9–322 and 9–323.

§ 9–329. Priority of Security Interests in Letter-of-Credit Right.

The following rules govern priority among conflicting security interests in the same letter-of-credit right:

(1) A security interest held by a secured party having control of the letter-of-credit right under Section 9–107 has priority to the extent of its control over a conflicting security interest held by a secured party that does not have control.

(2) Security interests perfected by control under Section 9–314 rank according to priority in time of obtaining control.

§ 9–330. Priority of Purchaser of Chattel Paper or Instrument.

(a) A purchaser of chattel paper has priority over a security interest in the chattel paper which is claimed merely as proceeds of inventory subject to a security interest if:

(1) in good faith and in the ordinary course of the purchaser's business, the purchaser gives new value and takes possession of the chattel paper or obtains control of the chattel paper under Section 9–105; and

(2) the chattel paper does not indicate that it has been assigned to an identified assignee other than the purchaser.

(b) A purchaser of chattel paper has priority over a security interest in the chattel paper which is claimed other than merely as proceeds of inventory subject to a security interest if the purchaser gives new value and takes possession of the chattel paper or obtains control of the chattel paper under Section 9–105 in good faith, in the ordinary course of the purchaser's business, and without knowledge that the purchase violates the rights of the secured party.

(c) Except as otherwise provided in Section 9–327, a purchaser having priority in chattel paper under subsection (a) or (b) also has priority in proceeds of the chattel paper to the extent that:

(1) Section 9–322 provides for priority in the proceeds; or

(2) the proceeds consist of the specific goods covered by the chattel paper or cash proceeds of the specific goods, even if the purchaser's security interest in the proceeds is unperfected.

(d) Except as otherwise provided in Section 9–331(a), a purchaser of an instrument has priority over a security interest in the instrument perfected by a method other than possession if the purchaser gives value and takes possession of the instrument in good faith and without knowledge that the purchase violates the rights of the secured party.

(e) For purposes of subsections (a) and (b), the holder of a purchase-money security interest in inventory gives new value for chattel paper constituting proceeds of the inventory.

(f) For purposes of subsections (b) and (d), if chattel paper or an instrument indicates that it has been assigned to an identified secured party other than the purchaser, a purchaser of the chattel paper or instrument has knowledge that the purchase violates the rights of the secured party.

§ 9–331. Priority of Rights of Purchasers of Instruments, Documents, and Securities under Other Articles; Priority of Interests in Financial Assets and Security Entitlements under Article 8.

(a) This article does not limit the rights of a holder in due course of a negotiable instrument, a holder to which a negotiable document of title has been duly negotiated, or a protected purchaser of a security. These holders or purchasers take priority over an earlier security interest, even if perfected, to the extent provided in Articles 3, 7, and 8.

(b) This article does not limit the rights of or impose liability on a person to the extent that the person is protected against the assertion of a claim under Article 8.

(c) Filing under this article does not constitute notice of a claim or defense to the holders, or purchasers, or persons described in subsections (a) and (b).

§ 9–332. Transfer of Money; Transfer of Funds from Deposit Account.

(a) A transferee of money takes the money free of a security interest unless the transferee acts in collusion with the debtor in violating the rights of the secured party.

(b) A transferee of funds from a deposit account takes the funds free of a security interest in the deposit account unless the transferee acts in collusion with the debtor in violating the rights of the secured party.

§ 9–333. Priority of Certain Liens Arising by Operation of Law.

(a) In this section, "possessory lien" means an interest, other than a security interest or an agricultural lien:

(1) which secures payment or performance of an obligation for services or materials furnished with respect to goods by a person in the ordinary course of the person's business;

(2) which is created by statute or rule of law in favor of the person; and

(3) whose effectiveness depends on the person's possession of the goods.

(b) A possessory lien on goods has priority over a security interest in the goods unless the lien is created by a statute that expressly provides otherwise.

§ 9–334. Priority of Security Interests in Fixtures and Crops.

(a) A security interest under this article may be created in goods that are fixtures or may continue in goods that become fixtures. A security interest does not exist under this article in ordinary building materials incorporated into an improvement on land.

(b) This article does not prevent creation of an encumbrance upon fixtures under real property law.

(c) In cases not governed by subsections (d) through (h), a security interest in fixtures is subordinate to a conflicting interest of an encumbrancer or owner of the related real property other than the debtor.

(d) Except as otherwise provided in subsection (h), a perfected security interest in fixtures has priority over a conflicting interest of an encumbrancer or owner of the real property if the debtor has an interest of record in or is in possession of the real property and:

(1) the security interest is a purchase-money security interest;

(2) the interest of the encumbrancer or owner arises before the goods become fixtures; and

(3) the security interest is perfected by a fixture filing before the goods become fixtures or within 20 days thereafter.

(e) A perfected security interest in fixtures has priority over a conflicting interest of an encumbrancer or owner of the real property if:

(1) the debtor has an interest of record in the real property or is in possession of the real property and the security interest:

(A) is perfected by a fixture filing before the interest of the encumbrancer or owner is of record; and

(B) has priority over any conflicting interest of a predecessor in title of the encumbrancer or owner;

(2) before the goods become fixtures, the security interest is perfected by any method permitted by this article and the fixtures are readily removable:

(A) factory or office machines;

(B) equipment that is not primarily used or leased for use in the operation of the real property; or

(C) replacements of domestic appliances that are consumer goods;

(3) the conflicting interest is a lien on the real property obtained by legal or equitable proceedings after the security interest was perfected by any method permitted by this article; or

(4) the security interest is:

(A) created in a manufactured home in a manufactured-home transaction; and

(B) perfected pursuant to a statute described in Section 9–311(a)(2).

(f) A security interest in fixtures, whether or not perfected, has priority over a conflicting interest of an encumbrancer or owner of the real property if:

(1) the encumbrancer or owner has, in an authenticated record, consented to the security interest or disclaimed an interest in the goods as fixtures; or

(2) the debtor has a right to remove the goods as against the encumbrancer or owner.

(g) The priority of the security interest under paragraph (f)(2) continues for a reasonable time if the debtor's right to remove the goods as against the encumbrancer or owner terminates.

(h) A mortgage is a construction mortgage to the extent that it secures an obligation incurred for the construction of an improvement on land, including the acquisition cost of the land, if a recorded record of the mortgage so indicates. Except as otherwise provided in subsections (e) and (f), a security interest in fixtures is subordinate to a construction mortgage if a record of the mortgage is recorded before the goods become fixtures and the goods become fixtures before the completion of the construction. A mortgage has this priority to the same extent as a construction mortgage to the extent that it is given to refinance a construction mortgage.

(i) A perfected security interest in crops growing on real property has priority over a conflicting interest of an encumbrancer or owner of the real property if the debtor has an interest of record in or is in possession of the real property.

(j) Subsection (i) prevails over any inconsistent provisions of the following statutes:

[List here any statutes containing provisions inconsistent with subsection (i).]

Legislative Note: States that amend statutes to remove provisions inconsistent with subsection (i) need not enact subsection (j).

§ 9–335. Accessions.

(a) A security interest may be created in an accession and continues in collateral that becomes an accession.

(b) If a security interest is perfected when the collateral becomes an accession, the security interest remains perfected in the collateral.

(c) Except as otherwise provided in subsection (d), the other provisions of this part determine the priority of a security interest in an accession.

(d) A security interest in an accession is subordinate to a security interest in the whole which is perfected by compliance with the requirements of a certificate-of-title statute under Section 9–311(b).

(e) After default, subject to Part 6, a secured party may remove an accession from other goods if the security interest in the accession has priority over the claims of every person having an interest in the whole.

(f) A secured party that removes an accession from other goods under subsection (e) shall promptly reimburse any holder of a security interest or other lien on, or owner of, the whole or of the other goods, other than the debtor, for the cost of repair of any physical injury to the whole or the other goods. The secured party need not reimburse the holder or owner for any diminution in value of the whole or the other goods caused by the absence of the accession removed or by any necessity for replacing it. A person entitled to reimbursement may refuse permission to remove until the secured party gives adequate assurance for the performance of the obligation to reimburse.

§ 9–336. Commingled Goods.

(a) In this section, "commingled goods" means goods that are physically united with other goods in such a manner that their identity is lost in a product or mass.

(b) A security interest does not exist in commingled goods as such. However, a security interest may attach to a product or mass that results when goods become commingled goods.

(c) If collateral becomes commingled goods, a security interest attaches to the product or mass.

(d) If a security interest in collateral is perfected before the collateral becomes commingled goods, the security interest that attaches to the product or mass under subsection (c) is perfected.

(e) Except as otherwise provided in subsection (f), the other provisions of this part determine the priority of a security interest that attaches to the product or mass under subsection (c).

(f) If more than one security interest attaches to the product or mass under subsection (c), the following rules determine priority:

(1) A security interest that is perfected under subsection (d) has priority over a security interest that is unperfected at the time the collateral becomes commingled goods.

(2) If more than one security interest is perfected under subsection (d), the security interests rank equally in proportion to the value of the collateral at the time it became commingled goods.

§ 9–337. Priority of Security Interests in Goods Covered by Certificate of Title.

If, while a security interest in goods is perfected by any method under the law of another jurisdiction, this State issues a certificate of title that does not show that the goods are subject to the security interest or contain a statement that they may be subject to security interests not shown on the certificate:

(1) a buyer of the goods, other than a person in the business of selling goods of that kind, takes free of the security interest if the buyer gives value and receives delivery of the goods after issuance of the certificate and without knowledge of the security interest; and

(2) the security interest is subordinate to a conflicting security interest in the goods that attaches, and is perfected under Section 9–311(b), after issuance of the certificate and without the conflicting secured party's knowledge of the security interest.

§ 9–338. Priority of Security Interest or Agricultural Lien Perfected by Filed Financing Statement Providing Certain Incorrect Information.

If a security interest or agricultural lien is perfected by a filed financing statement providing information described in Section 9–516(b)(5) which is incorrect at the time the financing statement is filed:

(1) the security interest or agricultural lien is subordinate to a conflicting perfected security interest in the collateral to the extent that the holder of the conflicting security interest gives value in reasonable reliance upon the incorrect information; and

(2) a purchaser, other than a secured party, of the collateral takes free of the security interest or agricultural lien to the extent that, in reasonable reliance upon the incorrect information, the purchaser gives value and, in the case of chattel paper, documents, goods, instruments, or a security certificate, receives delivery of the collateral.

§ 9–339. Priority Subject to Subordination.

This article does not preclude subordination by agreement by a person entitled to priority.

[Subpart 4. Rights of Bank]

§ 9–340. Effectiveness of Right of Recoupment or Set-Off against Deposit Account.

(a) Except as otherwise provided in subsection (c), a bank with which a deposit account is maintained may exercise any right of recoupment or set-off against a secured party that holds a security interest in the deposit account.

(b) Except as otherwise provided in subsection (c), the application of this article to a security interest in a deposit account does not affect a right of recoupment or set-off of the secured party as to a deposit account maintained with the secured party.

(c) The exercise by a bank of a set-off against a deposit account is ineffective against a secured party that holds a security interest in the deposit account which is perfected by control under Section 9–104(a)(3), if the set-off is based on a claim against the debtor.

§ 9–341. Bank's Rights and Duties with Respect to Deposit Account.

Except as otherwise provided in Section 9–340(c), and unless the bank otherwise agrees in an authenticated record, a bank's rights and duties with respect to a deposit account maintained with the bank are not terminated, suspended, or modified by:

(1) the creation, attachment, or perfection of a security interest in the deposit account;

(2) the bank's knowledge of the security interest; or

(3) the bank's receipt of instructions from the secured party.

§ 9–342. Bank's Right to Refuse to Enter into or Disclose Existence of Control Agreement.

This article does not require a bank to enter into an agreement of the kind described in Section 9–104(a)(2), even if its customer so requests or directs. A bank that has entered into such an agreement is not required to confirm the existence of the agreement to another person unless requested to do so by its customer.

Part 4 Rights of Third Parties

§ 9–401. Alienability of Debtor's Rights.

(a) Except as otherwise provided in subsection (b) and Sections 9–406, 9–407, 9–408, and 9–409, whether a debtor's rights in collateral may be voluntarily or involuntarily transferred is governed by law other than this article.

(b) An agreement between the debtor and secured party which prohibits a transfer of the debtor's rights in collateral or makes the transfer a default does not prevent the transfer from taking effect.

§ 9–402. Secured Party Not Obligated on Contract of Debtor or in Tort.

The existence of a security interest, agricultural lien, or authority given to a debtor to dispose of or use collateral, without more, does not subject a secured party to liability in contract or tort for the debtor's acts or omissions.

§ 9–403. Agreement Not to Assert Defenses against Assignee.

(a) In this section, "value" has the meaning provided in Section 3–303(a).

(b) Except as otherwise provided in this section, an agreement between an account debtor and an assignor not to assert against an assignee any claim or defense that the account debtor may have against the assignor is enforceable by an assignee that takes an assignment:

(1) for value;

(2) in good faith;

(3) without notice of a claim of a property or possessory right to the property assigned; and

(4) without notice of a defense or claim in recoupment of the type that may be asserted against a person entitled to enforce a negotiable instrument under Section 3–305(a).

(c) Subsection (b) does not apply to defenses of a type that may be asserted against a holder in due course of a negotiable instrument under Section 3–305(b).

(d) In a consumer transaction, if a record evidences the account debtor's obligation, law other than this article requires that the record include a statement to the effect that the rights of an assignee are subject to claims or defenses that the account debtor could assert against the original obligee, and the record does not include such a statement:

(1) the record has the same effect as if the record included such a statement; and

(2) the account debtor may assert against an assignee those claims and defenses that would have been available if the record included such a statement.

(e) This section is subject to law other than this article which establishes a different rule for an account debtor who is an individual and who incurred the obligation primarily for personal, family, or household purposes.

(f) Except as otherwise provided in subsection (d), this section does not displace law other than this article which gives effect to an agreement by an account debtor not to assert a claim or defense against an assignee.

§ 9–404. Rights Acquired by Assignee; Claims and Defenses against Assignee.

(a) Unless an account debtor has made an enforceable agreement not to assert defenses or claims, and subject to subsections (b) through (e), the rights of an assignee are subject to:

(1) all terms of the agreement between the account debtor and assignor and any defense or claim in recoupment arising from the transaction that gave rise to the contract; and

(2) any other defense or claim of the account debtor against the assignor which accrues before the account debtor receives a notification of the assignment authenticated by the assignor or the assignee.

(b) Subject to subsection (c) and except as otherwise provided in subsection (d), the claim of an account debtor against an assignor may be asserted against an assignee under subsection (a) only to reduce the amount the account debtor owes.

(c) This section is subject to law other than this article which establishes a different rule for an account debtor who is an individual and who incurred the obligation primarily for personal, family, or household purposes.

(d) In a consumer transaction, if a record evidences the account debtor's obligation, law other than this article requires that the record include a statement to the effect that the account debtor's recovery against an assignee with respect to claims and defenses against the assignor may not exceed amounts paid by the account debtor under the record, and the record does not include such a statement, the extent to which a claim of an account debtor against the assignor may be asserted against an assignee is determined as if the record included such a statement.

(e) This section does not apply to an assignment of a health-care-insurance receivable.

§ 9–405. Modification of Assigned Contract.

(a) A modification of or substitution for an assigned contract is effective against an assignee if made in good faith. The assignee acquires corresponding rights under the modified or substituted contract. The assignment may provide that the modification or substitution is a breach of contract by the assignor. This subsection is subject to subsections (b) through (d).

(b) Subsection (a) applies to the extent that:

(1) the right to payment or a part thereof under an assigned contract has not been fully earned by performance; or

(2) the right to payment or a part thereof has been fully earned by performance and the account debtor has not received notification of the assignment under Section 9–406(a).

(c) This section is subject to law other than this article which establishes a different rule for an account debtor who is an individual and who incurred the obligation primarily for personal, family, or household purposes.

(d) This section does not apply to an assignment of a health-care-insurance receivable.

§ 9–406. Discharge of Account Debtor; Notification of Assignment; Identification and Proof of Assignment; Restrictions on Assignment of Accounts, Chattel Paper, Payment Intangibles, and Promissory Notes Ineffective.

(a) Subject to subsections (b) through (i), an account debtor on an account, chattel paper, or a payment intangible may discharge its obligation by paying the assignor until, but not after, the account debtor receives a notification, authenticated by the assignor or the assignee, that the amount due or to become due has been assigned and that payment is to be made to the assignee. After receipt of the notification, the account debtor may discharge its obligation by paying the assignee and may not discharge the obligation by paying the assignor.

(b) Subject to subsection (h), notification is ineffective under subsection (a):

(1) if it does not reasonably identify the rights assigned;

(2) to the extent that an agreement between an account debtor and a seller of a payment intangible limits the account debtor's duty to pay a person other than the seller and the limitation is effective under law other than this article; or

(3) at the option of an account debtor, if the notification notifies the account debtor to make less than the full amount of any installment or other periodic payment to the assignee, even if:

(A) only a portion of the account, chattel paper, or payment intangible has been assigned to that assignee;

(B) a portion has been assigned to another assignee; or

(C) the account debtor knows that the assignment to that assignee is limited.

(c) Subject to subsection (h), if requested by the account debtor, an assignee shall seasonably furnish reasonable proof that the assignment has been made. Unless the assignee complies, the account debtor may discharge its obligation by paying the assignor, even if the account debtor has received a notification under subsection (a).

(d) Except as otherwise provided in subsection (e) and Sections 2A–303 and 9–407, and subject to subsection (h), a term in an agreement between an account debtor and an assignor or in a promissory note is ineffective to the extent that it:

(1) prohibits, restricts, or requires the consent of the account debtor or person obligated on the promissory note to the assignment or transfer of, or the creation, attachment, perfection, or enforcement of a security interest in, the account, chattel paper, payment intangible, or promissory note; or

(2) provides that the assignment or transfer or the creation, attachment, perfection, or enforcement of the security interest may give rise to a default, breach, right of recoupment, claim, defense, termination, right of termination, or remedy under the account, chattel paper, payment intangible, or promissory note.

(e) Subsection (d) does not apply to the sale of a payment intangible or promissory note.

(f) Except as otherwise provided in Sections 2A–303 and 9–407 and subject to subsections (h) and (i), a rule of law, statute, or regulation that prohibits, restricts, or requires the consent of a government, governmental body or official, or account debtor to the assignment or transfer of, or creation of a security interest in, an account or chattel paper is ineffective to the extent that the rule of law, statute, or regulation:

(1) prohibits, restricts, or requires the consent of the government, governmental body or official, or account debtor to the assignment or transfer of, or the creation, attachment, perfection, or enforcement of a security interest in the account or chattel paper; or

(2) provides that the assignment or transfer or the creation, attachment, perfection, or enforcement of the security interest may give rise to a default, breach, right of recoupment, claim, defense, termination, right of termination, or remedy under the account or chattel paper.

(g) Subject to subsection (h), an account debtor may not waive or vary its option under subsection (b)(3).

(h) This section is subject to law other than this article which establishes a different rule for an account debtor who is an individual and who incurred the obligation primarily for personal, family, or household purposes.

(i) This section does not apply to an assignment of a health-care-insurance receivable.

(j) This section prevails over any inconsistent provisions of the following statutes, rules, and regulations:

[List here any statutes, rules, and regulations containing provisions inconsistent with this section.]

Legislative Note: States that amend statutes, rules, and regulations to remove provisions inconsistent with this section need not enact subsection (j).

As amended in 1999 and 2000.

§ 9–407. Restrictions on Creation or Enforcement of Security Interest in Leasehold Interest or in Lessor's Residual Interest.

(a) Except as otherwise provided in subsection (b), a term in a lease agreement is ineffective to the extent that it:

(1) prohibits, restricts, or requires the consent of a party to the lease to the assignment or transfer of, or the creation, attachment, perfection, or enforcement of a security interest in an interest of a party under the lease contract or in the lessor's residual interest in the goods; or

(2) provides that the assignment or transfer or the creation, attachment, perfection, or enforcement of the security interest may give rise to a default, breach, right of recoupment, claim, defense, termination, right of termination, or remedy under the lease.

(b) Except as otherwise provided in Section 2A–303(7), a term described in subsection (a)(2) is effective to the extent that there is:

(1) a transfer by the lessee of the lessee's right of possession or use of the goods in violation of the term; or

(2) a delegation of a material performance of either party to the lease contract in violation of the term.

(c) The creation, attachment, perfection, or enforcement of a security interest in the lessor's interest under the lease contract or the lessor's residual interest in the goods is not a transfer that materially impairs the lessee's prospect of obtaining return performance or materially changes the duty of or materially increases the burden or risk imposed on the lessee within the purview of Section 2A–303(4) unless, and then only to the extent that, enforcement actually results in a delegation of material performance of the lessor.

As amended in 1999.

§ 9–408. Restrictions on Assignment of Promissory Notes, Health-Care-Insurance Receivables, and Certain General Intangibles Ineffective.

(a) Except as otherwise provided in subsection (b), a term in a promissory note or in an agreement between an account debtor and a debtor which relates to a health-care-insurance receivable or a general intangible, including a contract, permit, license, or franchise, and which term prohibits, restricts, or requires the consent of the person obligated on the promissory note or the account debtor to, the assignment or transfer of, or creation, attachment, or perfection of a security interest in, the promissory note, health-care-insurance receivable, or general intangible, is ineffective to the extent that the term:

(1) would impair the creation, attachment, or perfection of a security interest; or

(2) provides that the assignment or transfer or the creation, attachment, or perfection of the security interest may give rise to a default, breach, right of recoupment, claim, defense, termination, right of termination, or remedy under the promissory note, health-care-insurance receivable, or general intangible.

(b) Subsection (a) applies to a security interest in a payment intangible or promissory note only if the security interest arises out of a sale of the payment intangible or promissory note.

(c) A rule of law, statute, or regulation that prohibits, restricts, or requires the consent of a government, governmental body or official, person obligated on a promissory note, or account debtor to the assignment or transfer of, or creation of a security interest in, a promissory note, health-care-insurance receivable, or general intangible, including a contract, permit, license, or franchise between an account debtor and a debtor, is ineffective to the extent that the rule of law, statute, or regulation:

(1) would impair the creation, attachment, or perfection of a security interest; or

(2) provides that the assignment or transfer or the creation, attachment, or perfection of the security interest may give rise to a default, breach, right of recoupment, claim, defense, termination, right of termination, or remedy under the promissory note, health-care-insurance receivable, or general intangible.

(d) To the extent that a term in a promissory note or in an agreement between an account debtor and a debtor which relates to a health-care-insurance receivable or general intangible or a rule of law, statute, or regulation described in subsection (c) would be effective under law other than this article but is ineffective under subsection (a) or (c), the creation, attachment, or perfection of a security interest in the promissory note, health-care-insurance receivable, or general intangible:

(1) is not enforceable against the person obligated on the promissory note or the account debtor;

(2) does not impose a duty or obligation on the person obligated on the promissory note or the account debtor;

(3) does not require the person obligated on the promissory note or the account debtor to recognize the security interest, pay or render performance to the secured party, or accept payment or performance from the secured party;

(4) does not entitle the secured party to use or assign the debtor's rights under the promissory note, health-care-insurance receivable, or general intangible, including any related information or materials furnished to the debtor in the transaction giving rise to the promissory note, health-care-insurance receivable, or general intangible;

(5) does not entitle the secured party to use, assign, possess, or have access to any trade secrets or confidential information of the person obligated on the promissory note or the account debtor; and

(6) does not entitle the secured party to enforce the security interest in the promissory note, health-care-insurance receivable, or general intangible.

(e) This section prevails over any inconsistent provisions of the following statutes, rules, and regulations:

[List here any statutes, rules, and regulations containing provisions inconsistent with this section.]

Legislative Note: States that amend statutes, rules, and regulations to remove provisions inconsistent with this section need not enact subsection (e).

As amended in 1999.

§ 9–409. Restrictions on Assignment of Letter-of-Credit Rights Ineffective.

(a) A term in a letter of credit or a rule of law, statute, regulation, custom, or practice applicable to the letter of credit which prohibits, restricts, or requires the consent of an applicant, issuer, or nominated person to a beneficiary's assignment of or creation of a security interest in a letter-of-credit right is ineffective to the extent that the term or rule of law, statute, regulation, custom, or practice:

(1) would impair the creation, attachment, or perfection of a security interest in the letter-of-credit right; or

(2) provides that the assignment or the creation, attachment, or perfection of the security interest may give rise to a default, breach, right of recoupment, claim, defense, termination, right of termination, or remedy under the letter-of-credit right.

(b) To the extent that a term in a letter of credit is ineffective under subsection (a) but would be effective under law other than this article or a custom or practice applicable to the letter of credit, to the transfer of a right to draw or otherwise demand performance under the letter of credit, or to the assignment of a right to proceeds of the letter of credit, the creation, attachment, or perfection of a security interest in the letter-of-credit right:

(1) is not enforceable against the applicant, issuer, nominated person, or transferee beneficiary;

(2) imposes no duties or obligations on the applicant, issuer, nominated person, or transferee beneficiary; and

(3) does not require the applicant, issuer, nominated person, or transferee beneficiary to recognize the security interest, pay or render performance to the secured party, or accept payment or other performance from the secured party.

As amended in 1999.

Part 5 Filing

[Subpart 1. Filing Office; Contents and Effectiveness of Financing Statement]

§ 9–501. Filing Office.

(a) Except as otherwise provided in subsection (b), if the local law of this State governs perfection of a security interest or agricultural lien, the office in which to file a financing statement to perfect the security interest or agricultural lien is:

(1) the office designated for the filing or recording of a record of a mortgage on the related real property, if:

(A) the collateral is as-extracted collateral or timber to be cut; or

(B) the financing statement is filed as a fixture filing and the collateral is goods that are or are to become fixtures; or

(2) the office of [ ] [or any office duly authorized by [ ]], in all other cases, including a case in which the collateral is goods that are or are to become fixtures and the financing statement is not filed as a fixture filing.

(b) The office in which to file a financing statement to perfect a security interest in collateral, including fixtures, of a transmitting utility is the office of [ ]. The financing statement also constitutes a fixture filing as to the collateral indicated in the financing statement which is or is to become fixtures.

Legislative Note: The State should designate the filing office where the brackets appear. The filing office may be that of a governmental official (e.g., the Secretary of State) or a private party that maintains the State's filing system.

§ 9–502. Contents of Financing Statement; Record of Mortgage as Financing Statement; Time of Filing Financing Statement.

(a) Subject to subsection (b), a financing statement is sufficient only if it:

(1) provides the name of the debtor;

(2) provides the name of the secured party or a representative of the secured party; and

(3) indicates the collateral covered by the financing statement.

(b) Except as otherwise provided in Section 9–501(b), to be sufficient, a financing statement that covers as-extracted collateral or timber to be cut, or which is filed as a fixture filing and covers goods that are or are to become fixtures, must satisfy subsection (a) and also:

(1) indicate that it covers this type of collateral;

(2) indicate that it is to be filed [for record] in the real property records;

(3) provide a description of the real property to which the collateral is related [sufficient to give constructive notice of a mortgage under the law of this State if the description were contained in a record of the mortgage of the real property]; and

(4) if the debtor does not have an interest of record in the real property, provide the name of a record owner.

(c) A record of a mortgage is effective, from the date of recording, as a financing statement filed as a fixture filing or as a financing statement covering as-extracted collateral or timber to be cut only if:

(1) the record indicates the goods or accounts that it covers;

(2) the goods are or are to become fixtures related to the real property described in the record or the collateral is related to the real property described in the record and is as-extracted collateral or timber to be cut;

(3) the record satisfies the requirements for a financing statement in this section other than an indication that it is to be filed in the real property records; and

(4) the record is [duly] recorded.

(d) A financing statement may be filed before a security agreement is made or a security interest otherwise attaches.

Legislative Note: Language in brackets is optional. Where the State has any special recording system for real property other than the usual grantor-grantee index (as, for instance, a tract system or a title registration or Torrens system) local adaptations of subsection (b) and Section 9–519(d) and (e) may be necessary. See, e.g., Mass. Gen. Laws Chapter 106, Section 9–410.

§ 9–503. Name of Debtor and Secured Party.

(a) A financing statement sufficiently provides the name of the debtor:

(1) if the debtor is a registered organization, only if the financing statement provides the name of the debtor indicated on the public record of the debtor's jurisdiction of organization which shows the debtor to have been organized;

(2) if the debtor is a decedent's estate, only if the financing statement provides the name of the decedent and indicates that the debtor is an estate;

(3) if the debtor is a trust or a trustee acting with respect to property held in trust, only if the financing statement:

(A) provides the name specified for the trust in its organic documents or, if no name is specified, provides the name of the settlor and additional information sufficient to distinguish the debtor

from other trusts having one or more of the same settlors; and

(B) indicates, in the debtor's name or otherwise, that the debtor is a trust or is a trustee acting with respect to property held in trust; and

(4) in other cases:

(A) if the debtor has a name, only if it provides the individual or organizational name of the debtor; and

(B) if the debtor does not have a name, only if it provides the names of the partners, members, associates, or other persons comprising the debtor.

(b) A financing statement that provides the name of the debtor in accordance with subsection (a) is not rendered ineffective by the absence of:

(1) a trade name or other name of the debtor; or

(2) unless required under subsection (a)(4)(B), names of partners, members, associates, or other persons comprising the debtor.

(c) A financing statement that provides only the debtor's trade name does not sufficiently provide the name of the debtor.

(d) Failure to indicate the representative capacity of a secured party or representative of a secured party does not affect the sufficiency of a financing statement.

(e) A financing statement may provide the name of more than one debtor and the name of more than one secured party.

§ 9–504. Indication of Collateral.

A financing statement sufficiently indicates the collateral that it covers if the financing statement provides:

(1) a description of the collateral pursuant to Section 9–108; or

(2) an indication that the financing statement covers all assets or all personal property.

As amended in 1999.

§ 9–505. Filing and Compliance with Other Statutes and Treaties for Consignments, Leases, Other Bailments, and Other Transactions.

(a) A consignor, lessor, or other bailor of goods, a licensor, or a buyer of a payment intangible or promissory note may file a financing statement, or may comply with a statute or treaty described in Section 9–311(a), using the terms "consignor", "consignee", "lessor", "lessee", "bailor", "bailee", "licensor", "licensee", "owner", "registered owner", "buyer", "seller", or words of similar import, instead of the terms "secured party" and "debtor".

(b) This part applies to the filing of a financing statement under subsection (a) and, as appropriate, to compliance that is equivalent to filing a financing statement under Section 9–311(b), but the filing or compliance is not of itself a factor in determining whether the collateral secures an obligation. If it is determined for another reason that the collateral secures an obligation, a security interest held by the consignor, lessor, bailor, licensor, owner, or buyer which attaches to the collateral is perfected by the filing or compliance.

§ 9–506. Effect of Errors or Omissions.

(a) A financing statement substantially satisfying the requirements of this part is effective, even if it has minor errors or omissions, unless the errors or omissions make the financing statement seriously misleading.

(b) Except as otherwise provided in subsection (c), a financing statement that fails sufficiently to provide the name of the debtor in accordance with Section 9–503(a) is seriously misleading.

(c) If a search of the records of the filing office under the debtor's correct name, using the filing office's standard search logic, if any, would disclose a financing statement that fails sufficiently to provide the name of the debtor in accordance with Section 9–503(a), the name provided does not make the financing statement seriously misleading.

(d) For purposes of Section 9–508(b), the "debtor's correct name" in subsection (c) means the correct name of the new debtor.

§ 9–507. Effect of Certain Events on Effectiveness of Financing Statement.

(a) A filed financing statement remains effective with respect to collateral that is sold, exchanged, leased, licensed, or otherwise disposed of and in which a security interest or agricultural lien continues, even if the secured party knows of or consents to the disposition.

(b) Except as otherwise provided in subsection (c) and Section 9–508, a financing statement is not rendered ineffective if, after the financing statement is filed, the information provided in the financing statement becomes seriously misleading under Section 9–506.

(c) If a debtor so changes its name that a filed financing statement becomes seriously misleading under Section 9–506:

(1) the financing statement is effective to perfect a security interest in collateral acquired by the debtor before, or within four months after, the change; and

(2) the financing statement is not effective to perfect a security interest in collateral acquired by the debtor more than four months after the change, unless an amendment to the financing statement which renders the financing statement not seriously misleading is filed within four months after the change.

§ 9–508. Effectiveness of Financing Statement If New Debtor Becomes Bound by Security Agreement.

(a) Except as otherwise provided in this section, a filed financing statement naming an original debtor is effective to perfect a security interest in collateral in which a new debtor has or acquires rights to the extent that the financing statement would have been effective had the original debtor acquired rights in the collateral.

(b) If the difference between the name of the original debtor and that of the new debtor causes a filed financing statement that is effective under subsection (a) to be seriously misleading under Section 9–506:

(1) the financing statement is effective to perfect a security interest in collateral acquired by the new debtor before, and within four months after, the new debtor becomes bound under Section 9B–203(d); and

(2) the financing statement is not effective to perfect a security interest in collateral acquired by the new debtor more than four months after the new debtor becomes bound under Section 9–203(d) unless an initial financing statement providing the name of the new debtor is filed before the expiration of that time.

(c) This section does not apply to collateral as to which a filed financing statement remains effective against the new debtor under Section 9–507(a).

§ 9–509. Persons Entitled to File a Record.

(a) A person may file an initial financing statement, amendment that adds collateral covered by a financing statement, or amendment that adds a debtor to a financing statement only if:

(1) the debtor authorizes the filing in an authenticated record or pursuant to subsection (b) or (c); or

(2) the person holds an agricultural lien that has become effective at the time of filing and the financing statement covers only collateral in which the person holds an agricultural lien.

(b) By authenticating or becoming bound as debtor by a security agreement, a debtor or new debtor authorizes the filing of an initial financing statement, and an amendment, covering:

(1) the collateral described in the security agreement; and

(2) property that becomes collateral under Section 9–315(a)(2), whether or not the security agreement expressly covers proceeds.

(c) By acquiring collateral in which a security interest or agricultural lien continues under Section 9–315(a)(1), a debtor authorizes the filing of an initial financing statement, and an amendment, covering the collateral and property that becomes collateral under Section 9–315(a)(2).

(d) A person may file an amendment other than an amendment that adds collateral covered by a financing statement or an amendment that adds a debtor to a financing statement only if:

(1) the secured party of record authorizes the filing; or

(2) the amendment is a termination statement for a financing statement as to which the secured party of record has failed to file or send a termination statement

as required by Section 9–513(a) or (c), the debtor authorizes the filing, and the termination statement indicates that the debtor authorized it to be filed.

(e) If there is more than one secured party of record for a financing statement, each secured party of record may authorize the filing of an amendment under subsection (d).

As amended in 2000.

§ 9–510. Effectiveness of Filed Record.

(a) A filed record is effective only to the extent that it was filed by a person that may file it under Section 9–509.

(b) A record authorized by one secured party of record does not affect the financing statement with respect to another secured party of record.

(c) A continuation statement that is not filed within the six-month period prescribed by Section 9–515(d) is ineffective.

§ 9–511. Secured Party of Record.

(a) A secured party of record with respect to a financing statement is a person whose name is provided as the name of the secured party or a representative of the secured party in an initial financing statement that has been filed. If an initial financing statement is filed under Section 9–514(a), the assignee named in the initial financing statement is the secured party of record with respect to the financing statement.

(b) If an amendment of a financing statement which provides the name of a person as a secured party or a representative of a secured party is filed, the person named in the amendment is a secured party of record. If an amendment is filed under Section 9–514(b), the assignee named in the amendment is a secured party of record.

(c) A person remains a secured party of record until the filing of an amendment of the financing statement which deletes the person.

§ 9–512. Amendment of Financing Statement.

[Alternative A]

(a) Subject to Section 9–509, a person may add or delete collateral covered by, continue or terminate the effectiveness of, or, subject to subsection (e), otherwise amend the information provided in, a financing statement by filing an amendment that:

(1) identifies, by its file number, the initial financing statement to which the amendment relates; and

(2) if the amendment relates to an initial financing statement filed [or recorded] in a filing office described in Section 9–501(a)(1), provides the information specified in Section 9–502(b).

[Alternative B]

(a) Subject to Section 9–509, a person may add or delete collateral covered by, continue or terminate the effectiveness of, or, subject to subsection (e), otherwise amend the information provided in, a financing statement by filing an amendment that:

(1) identifies, by its file number, the initial financing statement to which the amendment relates; and

(2) if the amendment relates to an initial financing statement filed [or recorded] in a filing office described in Section 9–501(a)(1), provides the date [and time] that the initial financing statement was filed [or recorded] and the information specified in Section 9–502(b).

[End of Alternatives]

(b) Except as otherwise provided in Section 9–515, the filing of an amendment does not extend the period of effectiveness of the financing statement.

(c) A financing statement that is amended by an amendment that adds collateral is effective as to the added collateral only from the date of the filing of the amendment.

(d) A financing statement that is amended by an amendment that adds a debtor is effective as to the added debtor only from the date of the filing of the amendment.

(e) An amendment is ineffective to the extent it:

(1) purports to delete all debtors and fails to provide the name of a debtor to be covered by the financing statement; or

(2) purports to delete all secured parties of record and fails to provide the name of a new secured party of record.

Legislative Note: States whose real-estate filing offices require additional information in amendments and cannot search their records by both the name of the debtor and the file number should enact Alternative B to Sections 9–512(a), 9–518(b), 9–519(f), and 9–522(a).

§ 9–513. Termination Statement.

(a) A secured party shall cause the secured party of record for a financing statement to file a termination statement for the financing statement if the financing statement covers consumer goods and:

(1) there is no obligation secured by the collateral covered by the financing statement and no commitment to make an advance, incur an obligation, or otherwise give value; or

(2) the debtor did not authorize the filing of the initial financing statement.

(b) To comply with subsection (a), a secured party shall cause the secured party of record to file the termination statement:

(1) within one month after there is no obligation secured by the collateral covered by the financing statement and no commitment to make an advance, incur an obligation, or otherwise give value; or

(2) if earlier, within 20 days after the secured party receives an authenticated demand from a debtor.

(c) In cases not governed by subsection (a), within 20 days after a secured party receives an authenticated demand from a debtor, the secured party shall cause the secured party of record for a financing statement to send to the debtor a termination statement for the financing statement or file the termination statement in the filing office if:

(1) except in the case of a financing statement covering accounts or chattel paper that has been sold or goods that are the subject of a consignment, there is no obligation secured by the collateral covered by the financing statement and no commitment to make an advance, incur an obligation, or otherwise give value;

(2) the financing statement covers accounts or chattel paper that has been sold but as to which the account debtor or other person obligated has discharged its obligation;

(3) the financing statement covers goods that were the subject of a consignment to the debtor but are not in the debtor's possession; or

(4) the debtor did not authorize the filing of the initial financing statement.

(d) Except as otherwise provided in Section 9–510, upon the filing of a termination statement with the filing office, the financing statement to which the termination statement relates ceases to be effective. Except as otherwise provided in Section 9–510, for purposes of Sections 9–519(g), 9–522(a), and 9–523(c), the filing with the filing office of a termination statement relating to a financing statement that indicates that the debtor is a transmitting utility also causes the effectiveness of the financing statement to lapse.

As amended in 2000.

§ 9–514. Assignment of Powers of Secured Party of Record.

(a) Except as otherwise provided in subsection (c), an initial financing statement may reflect an assignment of all of the secured party's power to authorize an amendment to the financing statement by providing the name and mailing address of the assignee as the name and address of the secured party.

(b) Except as otherwise provided in subsection (c), a secured party of record may assign of record all or part of its power to authorize an amendment to a financing statement by filing in the filing office an amendment of the financing statement which:

(1) identifies, by its file number, the initial financing statement to which it relates;

(2) provides the name of the assignor; and

(3) provides the name and mailing address of the assignee.

(c) An assignment of record of a security interest in a fixture covered by a record of a mortgage which is effective as a financing statement filed as a fixture filing under Section 9–502(c) may be made only by an assignment of record of the mortgage in the manner provided by law of this State other than [the Uniform Commercial Code].

§ 9–515. Duration and Effectiveness of Financing Statement; Effect of Lapsed Financing Statement.

(a) Except as otherwise provided in subsections (b), (e), (f), and (g), a filed financing statement is effective for a period of five years after the date of filing.

(b) Except as otherwise provided in subsections (e), (f), and (g), an initial financing statement filed in connection with a public-finance transaction or manufactured-home transaction is effective for a period of 30 years after the date of filing if it indicates that it is filed in connection with a public-finance transaction or manufactured-home transaction.

(c) The effectiveness of a filed financing statement lapses on the expiration of the period of its effectiveness unless before the lapse a continuation statement is filed pursuant to subsection (d). Upon lapse, a financing statement ceases to be effective and any security interest or agricultural lien that was perfected by the financing statement becomes unperfected, unless the security interest is perfected otherwise. If the security interest or agricultural lien becomes unperfected upon lapse, it is deemed never to have been perfected as against a purchaser of the collateral for value.

(d) A continuation statement may be filed only within six months before the expiration of the five-year period specified in subsection (a) or the 30-year period specified in subsection (b), whichever is applicable.

(e) Except as otherwise provided in Section 9–510, upon timely filing of a continuation statement, the effectiveness of the initial financing statement continues for a period of five years commencing on the day on which the financing statement would have become ineffective in the absence of the filing. Upon the expiration of the five-year period, the financing statement lapses in the same manner as provided in subsection (c), unless, before the lapse, another continuation statement is filed pursuant to subsection (d). Succeeding continuation statements may be filed in the same manner to continue the effectiveness of the initial financing statement.

(f) If a debtor is a transmitting utility and a filed financing statement so indicates, the financing statement is effective until a termination statement is filed.

(g) A record of a mortgage that is effective as a financing statement filed as a fixture filing under Section 9–502(c) remains effective as a financing statement filed as a fixture filing until the mortgage is released or satisfied of record or its effectiveness otherwise terminates as to the real property.

§ 9–516. What Constitutes Filing; Effectiveness of Filing.

(a) Except as otherwise provided in subsection (b), communication of a record to a filing office and tender of the filing fee or acceptance of the record by the filing office constitutes filing.

(b) Filing does not occur with respect to a record that a filing office refuses to accept because:

(1) the record is not communicated by a method or medium of communication authorized by the filing office;

(2) an amount equal to or greater than the applicable filing fee is not tendered;

(3) the filing office is unable to index the record because:

(A) in the case of an initial financing statement, the record does not provide a name for the debtor;

(B) in the case of an amendment or correction statement, the record:

(i) does not identify the initial financing statement as required by Section 9–512 or 9–518, as applicable; or

(ii) identifies an initial financing statement whose effectiveness has lapsed under Section 9–515;

(C) in the case of an initial financing statement that provides the name of a debtor identified as an individual or an amendment that provides a name of a debtor identified as an individual which was not previously provided in the financing statement to which the record relates, the record does not identify the debtor's last name; or

(D) in the case of a record filed [or recorded] in the filing office described in Section 9–501(a)(1), the record does not provide a sufficient description of the real property to which it relates;

(4) in the case of an initial financing statement or an amendment that adds a secured party of record, the record does not provide a name and mailing address for the secured party of record;

(5) in the case of an initial financing statement or an amendment that provides a name of a debtor which was not previously provided in the financing statement to which the amendment relates, the record does not:

(A) provide a mailing address for the debtor;

(B) indicate whether the debtor is an individual or an organization; or

(C) if the financing statement indicates that the debtor is an organization, provide:

(i) a type of organization for the debtor;

(ii) a jurisdiction of organization for the debtor; or

(iii) an organizational identification number for the debtor or indicate that the debtor has none;

(6) in the case of an assignment reflected in an initial financing statement under Section 9–514(a) or an amendment filed under Section 9–514(b), the record does not provide a name and mailing address for the assignee; or

(7) in the case of a continuation statement, the record is not filed within the six-month period prescribed by Section 9–515(d).

(c) For purposes of subsection (b):

(1) a record does not provide information if the filing office is unable to read or decipher the information; and

(2) a record that does not indicate that it is an amendment or identify an initial financing statement to which it relates, as required by Section 9–512, 9–514, or 9–518, is an initial financing statement.

(d) A record that is communicated to the filing office with tender of the filing fee, but which the filing office refuses to accept for a reason other than one set forth in subsection (b), is effective as a filed record except as against a purchaser of the collateral which gives value in reasonable reliance upon the absence of the record from the files.

§ 9–517. Effect of Indexing Errors.

The failure of the filing office to index a record correctly does not affect the effectiveness of the filed record.

§ 9–518. Claim Concerning Inaccurate or Wrongfully Filed Record.

(a) A person may file in the filing office a correction statement with respect to a record indexed there under the person's name if the person believes that the record is inaccurate or was wrongfully filed.

[Alternative A]

(b) A correction statement must:

(1) identify the record to which it relates by the file number assigned to the initial financing statement to which the record relates;

(2) indicate that it is a correction statement; and

(3) provide the basis for the person's belief that the record is inaccurate and indicate the manner in which the person believes the record should be amended to cure any inaccuracy or provide the basis for the person's belief that the record was wrongfully filed.

[Alternative B]

(b) A correction statement must:

(1) identify the record to which it relates by:

(A) the file number assigned to the initial financing statement to which the record relates; and

(B) if the correction statement relates to a record filed [or recorded] in a filing office described in Section 9–501(a)(1), the date [and time] that the initial financing statement was filed [or recorded] and the information specified in Section 9–502(b);

(2) indicate that it is a correction statement; and

(3) provide the basis for the person's belief that the record is inaccurate and indicate the manner in which the person believes the record should be amended to cure any inaccuracy or provide the basis for the person's belief that the record was wrongfully filed.

[End of Alternatives]

(c) The filing of a correction statement does not affect the effectiveness of an initial financing statement or other filed record.

Legislative Note: States whose real-estate filing offices require additional information in amendments and cannot search their records by both the name of the debtor and the file number should enact Alternative B to Sections 9–512(a), 9–518(b), 9–519(f), and 9–522(a).

[Subpart 2. Duties and Operation of Filing Office]

§ 9–519. Numbering, Maintaining, and Indexing Records; Communicating Information Provided in Records.

(a) For each record filed in a filing office, the filing office shall:

(1) assign a unique number to the filed record;

(2) create a record that bears the number assigned to the filed record and the date and time of filing;

(3) maintain the filed record for public inspection; and

(4) index the filed record in accordance with subsections (c), (d), and (e).

(b) A file number [assigned after January 1, 2002,] must include a digit that:

(1) is mathematically derived from or related to the other digits of the file number; and

(2) aids the filing office in determining whether a number communicated as the file number includes a single-digit or transpositional error.

(c) Except as otherwise provided in subsections (d) and (e), the filing office shall:

(1) index an initial financing statement according to the name of the debtor and index all filed records relating to the initial financing statement in a manner that associates with one another an initial financing statement and all filed records relating to the initial financing statement; and

(2) index a record that provides a name of a debtor which was not previously provided in the financing statement to which the record relates also according to the name that was not previously provided.

(d) If a financing statement is filed as a fixture filing or covers as-extracted collateral or timber to be cut, [it must be filed for record and] the filing office shall index it:

(1) under the names of the debtor and of each owner of record shown on the financing statement as if they were the mortgagors under a mortgage of the real property described; and

(2) to the extent that the law of this State provides for indexing of records of mortgages under the name of the mortgagee, under the name of the secured party as if the secured party were the mortgagee thereunder, or, if indexing is by description, as if the financing statement were a record of a mortgage of the real property described.

(e) If a financing statement is filed as a fixture filing or covers as-extracted collateral or timber to be cut, the filing office shall index an assignment filed under Section 9–514(a) or an amendment filed under Section 9–514(b):

(1) under the name of the assignor as grantor; and

(2) to the extent that the law of this State provides for indexing a record of the assignment of a mortgage under the name of the assignee, under the name of the assignee.

[Alternative A]

(f) The filing office shall maintain a capability:

(1) to retrieve a record by the name of the debtor and by the file number assigned to the initial financing statement to which the record relates; and

(2) to associate and retrieve with one another an initial financing statement and each filed record relating to the initial financing statement.

[Alternative B]

(f) The filing office shall maintain a capability:

(1) to retrieve a record by the name of the debtor and:

(A) if the filing office is described in Section 9–501(a)(1), by the file number assigned to the initial financing statement to which the record relates and the date [and time] that the record was filed [or recorded]; or

(B) if the filing office is described in Section 9–501(a)(2), by the file number assigned to the initial financing statement to which the record relates; and

(2) to associate and retrieve with one another an initial financing statement and each filed record relating to the initial financing statement.

[End of Alternatives]

(g) The filing office may not remove a debtor's name from the index until one year after the effectiveness of a financing statement naming the debtor lapses under Section 9–515 with respect to all secured parties of record.

(h) The filing office shall perform the acts required by subsections (a) through (e) at the time and in the manner prescribed by filing-office rule, but not later than two business days after the filing office receives the record in question.

[(i) Subsection[s] [(b)] [and] [(h)] do[es] not apply to a filing office described in Section 9–501(a)(1).]

Legislative Notes:

1. States whose filing offices currently assign file numbers that include a verification number, commonly known as a "check digit," or can implement this requirement before the effective date of this Article should omit the bracketed language in subsection (b).

2. In States in which writings will not appear in the real property records and indices unless actually recorded the bracketed language in subsection (d) should be used.

3. States whose real-estate filing offices require additional information in amendments and cannot search their records by both the name of the debtor and the file number should enact Alternative B to Sections 9–512(a), 9–518(b), 9–519(f), and 9–522(a).

4. A State that elects not to require real-estate filing offices to comply with either or both of subsections (b) and (h) may adopt an applicable variation of subsection (i) and add "Except as otherwise provided in subsection (i)," to the appropriate subsection or subsections.

§ 9–520. Acceptance and Refusal to Accept Record.

(a)A filing office shall refuse to accept a record for filing for a reason set forth in Section 9–516(b) and may refuse to accept a record for filing only for a reason set forth in Section 9–516(b).

(b) If a filing office refuses to accept a record for filing, it shall communicate to the person that presented the record the fact of and reason for the refusal and the date and time the record would have been filed had the filing office accepted it. The communication must be made at the time and in the manner prescribed by filing-office rule but [, in the case of a filing office described in Section 9–501(a)(2),] in no event more than two business days after the filing office receives the record.

(c) A filed financing statement satisfying Section 9–502(a) and (b) is effective, even if the filing office is required to refuse to accept it for filing under subsection (a). However, Section 9–338 applies to a filed financing statement providing information described in Section 9–516(b)(5) which is incorrect at the time the financing statement is filed.

(d) If a record communicated to a filing office provides information that relates to more than one debtor, this part applies as to each debtor separately.

Legislative Note: A State that elects not to require real-property filing offices to comply with subsection (b) should include the bracketed language.

§ 9–521. Uniform Form of Written Financing Statement and Amendment.

(a) A filing office that accepts written records may not refuse to accept a written initial financing statement in the following form and format except for a reason set forth in Section 9–516(b):

[NATIONAL UCC FINANCING STATEMENT (FORM UCC1) (REV. 7/29/98)]

[NATIONAL UCC FINANCING STATEMENT ADDENDUM (FORM UCC1Ad)(REV. 07/29/98)]

(b) A filing office that accepts written records may not refuse to accept a written record in the following form and format except for a reason set forth in Section 9–516(b):

[NATIONAL UCC FINANCING STATEMENT AMENDMENT (FORM UCC3)(REV. 07/29/98)]

[NATIONAL UCC FINANCING STATEMENT AMENDMENT ADDENDUM (FORM UCC3Ad)(REV. 07/29/98)]

§ 9–522. Maintenance and Destruction of Records.

[Alternative A]

(a) The filing office shall maintain a record of the information provided in a filed financing statement for at least one year after the effectiveness of the financing statement has lapsed under Section 9–515 with respect to all secured parties of record. The record must be retrievable by using the name of the debtor and by using the file number assigned to the initial financing statement to which the record relates.

[Alternative B]

(a) The filing office shall maintain a record of the information provided in a filed financing statement for at least one year after the effectiveness of the financing statement has lapsed under Section 9–515 with respect to all secured parties of record. The record must be retrievable by using the name of the debtor and:

(1) if the record was filed [or recorded] in the filing office described in Section 9–501(a)(1), by using the file number assigned to the initial financing statement to which the record relates and the date [and time] that the record was filed [or recorded]; or

(2) if the record was filed in the filing office described in Section 9–501(a)(2), by using the file number assigned to the initial financing statement to which the record relates.

[End of Alternatives]

(b) Except to the extent that a statute governing disposition of public records provides otherwise, the filing office immediately may destroy any written record evidencing a financing statement. However, if the filing office destroys a written record, it shall maintain another record of the financing statement which complies with subsection (a).

Legislative Note: States whose real-estate filing offices require additional information in amendments and cannot search their records by both the name of the debtor and the file number should enact Alternative B to Sections 9–512(a), 9–518(b), 9–519(f), and 9–522(a).

§ 9–523. Information from Filing Office; Sale or License of Records.

(a) If a person that files a written record requests an acknowledgment of the filing, the filing office shall send to the person an image of the record showing the number assigned to the record pursuant to Section 9–519(a)(1) and the date and time of the filing of the record. However, if the person furnishes a copy of the record to the filing office, the filing office may instead:

(1) note upon the copy the number assigned to the record pursuant to Section 9–519(a)(1) and the date and time of the filing of the record; and

(2) send the copy to the person.

(b) If a person files a record other than a written record, the filing office shall communicate to the person an acknowledgment that provides:

(1) the information in the record;

(2) the number assigned to the record pursuant to Section 9–519(a)(1); and

(3) the date and time of the filing of the record.

(c) The filing office shall communicate or otherwise make available in a record the following information to any person that requests it:

(1) whether there is on file on a date and time specified by the filing office, but not a date earlier than three business days before the filing office receives the request, any financing statement that:

(A) designates a particular debtor [or, if the request so states, designates a particular debtor at the address specified in the request];

(B) has not lapsed under Section 9–515 with respect to all secured parties of record; and

(C) if the request so states, has lapsed under Section 9–515 and a record of which is maintained by the filing office under Section 9–522(a);

(2) the date and time of filing of each financing statement; and

(3) the information provided in each financing statement.

(d) In complying with its duty under subsection (c), the filing office may communicate information in any medium. However, if requested, the filing office shall communicate information by issuing [its written certificate] [a record that can be admitted into evidence in the courts of this State without extrinsic evidence of its authenticity].

(e) The filing office shall perform the acts required by subsections (a) through (d) at the time and in the manner prescribed by filing-office rule, but not later than two business days after the filing office receives the request.

(f) At least weekly, the [insert appropriate official or governmental agency] [filing office] shall offer to sell or license to the public on a nonexclusive basis, in bulk, copies of all records filed in it under this part, in every medium from time to time available to the filing office.

Legislative Notes:

1. States whose filing office does not offer the additional service of responding to search requests limited to a particular address should omit the bracketed language in subsection (c)(1)(A).

2. A State that elects not to require real-estate filing offices to comply with either or both of subsections (e) and (f) should specify in the appropriate subsection(s) only the filing office described in Section 9–501(a)(2).

§ 9–524. Delay by Filing Office.

Delay by the filing office beyond a time limit prescribed by this part is excused if:

(1) the delay is caused by interruption of communication or computer facilities, war, emergency conditions, failure of equipment, or other circumstances beyond control of the filing office; and

(2) the filing office exercises reasonable diligence under the circumstances.

§ 9–525. Fees.

(a) Except as otherwise provided in subsection (e), the fee for filing and indexing a record under this part, other than an initial financing statement of the kind described

in subsection (b), is [the amount specified in subsection (c), if applicable, plus]:

(1) $[X] if the record is communicated in writing and consists of one or two pages;

(2) $[2X] if the record is communicated in writing and consists of more than two pages; and

(3) $[1/2X] if the record is communicated by another medium authorized by filing-office rule.

(b) Except as otherwise provided in subsection (e), the fee for filing and indexing an initial financing statement of the following kind is [the amount specified in subsection (c), if applicable, plus]:

(1) $_____ if the financing statement indicates that it is filed in connection with a public-finance transaction;

(2) $_____ if the financing statement indicates that it is filed in connection with a manufactured-home transaction.

[Alternative A]

(c) The number of names required to be indexed does not affect the amount of the fee in subsections (a) and (b).

[Alternative B]

(c) Except as otherwise provided in subsection (e), if a record is communicated in writing, the fee for each name more than two required to be indexed is $_____.

[End of Alternatives]

(d) The fee for responding to a request for information from the filing office, including for [issuing a certificate showing] [communicating] whether there is on file any financing statement naming a particular debtor, is:

(1) $_____ if the request is communicated in writing; and

(2) $_____ if the request is communicated by another medium authorized by filing-office rule.

(e) This section does not require a fee with respect to a record of a mortgage which is effective as a financing statement filed as a fixture filing or as a financing statement covering as-extracted collateral or timber to be cut under Section 9–502(c). However, the recording and satisfaction fees that otherwise would be applicable to the record of the mortgage apply.

Legislative Notes:

1. To preserve uniformity, a State that places the provisions of this section together with statutes setting fees for other services should do so without modification.

2. A State should enact subsection (c), Alternative A, and omit the bracketed language in subsections (a) and (b) unless its indexing system entails a substantial additional cost when indexing additional names.

As amended in 2000.

§ 9–526. Filing-Office Rules.

(a) The [insert appropriate governmental official or agency] shall adopt and publish rules to implement this article. The filing-office rules must be[:

(1)] consistent with this article[; and

(2) adopted and published in accordance with the [insert any applicable state administrative procedure act]].

(b) To keep the filing-office rules and practices of the filing office in harmony with the rules and practices of filing offices in other jurisdictions that enact substantially this part, and to keep the technology used by the filing office compatible with the technology used by filing offices in other jurisdictions that enact substantially this part, the [insert appropriate governmental official or agency], so far as is consistent with the purposes, policies, and provisions of this article, in adopting, amending, and repealing filing-office rules, shall:

(1) consult with filing offices in other jurisdictions that enact substantially this part; and

(2) consult the most recent version of the Model Rules promulgated by the International Association of Corporate Administrators or any successor organization; and

(3) take into consideration the rules and practices of, and the technology used by, filing offices in other jurisdictions that enact substantially this part.

§ 9–527. Duty to Report.

The [insert appropriate governmental official or agency] shall report [annually on or before _____] to the [Governor and Legislature] on the operation of the filing office. The report must contain a statement of the extent to which:

(1) the filing-office rules are not in harmony with the rules of filing offices in other jurisdictions that enact substantially this part and the reasons for these variations; and

(2) the filing-office rules are not in harmony with the most recent version of the Model Rules promulgated by the International Association of Corporate Administrators, or any successor organization, and the reasons for these variations.

Part 6 Default

[Subpart 1. Default and Enforcement of Security Interest]

§ 9–601. Rights after Default; Judicial Enforcement; Consignor or Buyer of Accounts, Chattel Paper, Payment Intangibles, or Promissory Notes.

(a) After default, a secured party has the rights provided in this part and, except as otherwise provided in Section 9–602, those provided by agreement of the parties. A secured party:

(1) may reduce a claim to judgment, foreclose, or otherwise enforce the claim, security interest, or agricultural lien by any available judicial procedure; and

(2) if the collateral is documents, may proceed either as to the documents or as to the goods they cover.

(b) A secured party in possession of collateral or control of collateral under Section 9–104, 9–105, 9–106, or 9–107 has the rights and duties provided in Section 9–207.

(c) The rights under subsections (a) and (b) are cumulative and may be exercised simultaneously.

(d) Except as otherwise provided in subsection (g) and Section 9–605, after default, a debtor and an obligor have the rights provided in this part and by agreement of the parties.

(e) If a secured party has reduced its claim to judgment, the lien of any levy that may be made upon the collateral by virtue of an execution based upon the judgment relates back to the earliest of:

(1) the date of perfection of the security interest or agricultural lien in the collateral;

(2) the date of filing a financing statement covering the collateral; or

(3) any date specified in a statute under which the agricultural lien was created.

(f) A sale pursuant to an execution is a foreclosure of the security interest or agricultural lien by judicial procedure within the meaning of this section. A secured party may purchase at the sale and thereafter hold the collateral free of any other requirements of this article.

(g) Except as otherwise provided in Section 9–607(c), this part imposes no duties upon a secured party that is a consignor or is a buyer of accounts, chattel paper, payment intangibles, or promissory notes.

§ 9–602. Waiver and Variance of Rights and Duties.

Except as otherwise provided in Section 9–624, to the extent that they give rights to a debtor or obligor and impose duties on a secured party, the debtor or obligor may not waive or vary the rules stated in the following listed sections:

(1) Section 9–207(b)(4)(C), which deals with use and operation of the collateral by the secured party;

(2) Section 9–210, which deals with requests for an accounting and requests concerning a list of collateral and statement of account;

(3) Section 9–607(c), which deals with collection and enforcement of collateral;

(4) Sections 9–608(a) and 9–615(c) to the extent that they deal with application or payment of noncash proceeds of collection, enforcement, or disposition;

(5) Sections 9–608(a) and 9–615(d) to the extent that they require accounting for or payment of surplus proceeds of collateral;

(6) Section 9–609 to the extent that it imposes upon a secured party that takes possession of collateral without judicial process the duty to do so without breach of the peace;

(7) Sections 9–610(b), 9–611, 9–613, and 9–614, which deal with disposition of collateral;

(8) Section 9–615(f), which deals with calculation of a deficiency or surplus when a disposition is made to the

secured party, a person related to the secured party, or a secondary obligor;

(9) Section 9–616, which deals with explanation of the calculation of a surplus or deficiency;

(10) Sections 9–620, 9–621, and 9–622, which deal with acceptance of collateral in satisfaction of obligation;

(11) Section 9–623, which deals with redemption of collateral;

(12) Section 9–624, which deals with permissible waivers; and

(13) Sections 9–625 and 9–626, which deal with the secured party's liability for failure to comply with this article.

§ 9–603. Agreement on Standards Concerning Rights and Duties.

(a) The parties may determine by agreement the standards measuring the fulfillment of the rights of a debtor or obligor and the duties of a secured party under a rule stated in Section 9–602 if the standards are not manifestly unreasonable.

(b) Subsection (a) does not apply to the duty under Section 9–609 to refrain from breaching the peace.

§ 9–604. Procedure If Security Agreement Covers Real Property or Fixtures.

(a) If a security agreement covers both personal and real property, a secured party may proceed:

(1) under this part as to the personal property without prejudicing any rights with respect to the real property; or

(2) as to both the personal property and the real property in accordance with the rights with respect to the real property, in which case the other provisions of this part do not apply.

(b) Subject to subsection (c), if a security agreement covers goods that are or become fixtures, a secured party may proceed:

(1) under this part; or

(2) in accordance with the rights with respect to real property, in which case the other provisions of this part do not apply.

(c) Subject to the other provisions of this part, if a secured party holding a security interest in fixtures has priority over all owners and encumbrancers of the real property, the secured party, after default, may remove the collateral from the real property.

(d) A secured party that removes collateral shall promptly reimburse any encumbrancer or owner of the real property, other than the debtor, for the cost of repair of any physical injury caused by the removal. The secured party need not reimburse the encumbrancer or owner for any diminution in value of the real property caused by the absence of the goods removed or by any necessity of replacing them. A person entitled to reimbursement may refuse permission to remove until the secured party gives adequate assurance for the performance of the obligation to reimburse.

§ 9–605. Unknown Debtor or Secondary Obligor.

A secured party does not owe a duty based on its status as secured party:

(1) to a person that is a debtor or obligor, unless the secured party knows:

(A) that the person is a debtor or obligor;

(B) the identity of the person; and

(C) how to communicate with the person; or

(2) to a secured party or lienholder that has filed a financing statement against a person, unless the secured party knows:

(A) that the person is a debtor; and

(B) the identity of the person.

§ 9–606. Time of Default for Agricultural Lien.

For purposes of this part, a default occurs in connection with an agricultural lien at the time the secured party becomes entitled to enforce the lien in accordance with the statute under which it was created.

§ 9–607. Collection and Enforcement by Secured Party.

(a) If so agreed, and in any event after default, a secured party:

(1) may notify an account debtor or other person obligated on collateral to make payment or otherwise render performance to or for the benefit of the secured party;

(2) may take any proceeds to which the secured party is entitled under Section 9–315;

(3) may enforce the obligations of an account debtor or other person obligated on collateral and exercise the rights of the debtor with respect to the obligation of the account debtor or other person obligated on collateral to make payment or otherwise render performance to the debtor, and with respect to any property that secures the obligations of the account debtor or other person obligated on the collateral;

(4) if it holds a security interest in a deposit account perfected by control under Section 9–104(a)(1), may apply the balance of the deposit account to the obligation secured by the deposit account; and

(5) if it holds a security interest in a deposit account perfected by control under Section 9–104(a)(2) or (3), may instruct the bank to pay the balance of the deposit account to or for the benefit of the secured party.

(b) If necessary to enable a secured party to exercise under subsection (a)(3) the right of a debtor to enforce a mortgage nonjudicially, the secured party may record in the office in which a record of the mortgage is recorded:

(1) a copy of the security agreement that creates or provides for a security interest in the obligation secured by the mortgage; and

(2) the secured party's sworn affidavit in recordable form stating that:

(A) a default has occurred; and

(B) the secured party is entitled to enforce the mortgage nonjudicially.

(c) A secured party shall proceed in a commercially reasonable manner if the secured party:

(1) undertakes to collect from or enforce an obligation of an account debtor or other person obligated on collateral; and

(2) is entitled to charge back uncollected collateral or otherwise to full or limited recourse against the debtor or a secondary obligor.

(d) A secured party may deduct from the collections made pursuant to subsection (c) reasonable expenses of collection and enforcement, including reasonable attorney's fees and legal expenses incurred by the secured party.

(e) This section does not determine whether an account debtor, bank, or other person obligated on collateral owes a duty to a secured party.

As amended in 2000.

§ 9–608. Application of Proceeds of Collection or Enforcement; Liability for Deficiency and Right to Surplus.

(a) If a security interest or agricultural lien secures payment or performance of an obligation, the following rules apply:

(1) A secured party shall apply or pay over for application the cash proceeds of collection or enforcement under Section 9–607 in the following order to:

(A) the reasonable expenses of collection and enforcement and, to the extent provided for by agreement and not prohibited by law, reasonable attorney's fees and legal expenses incurred by the secured party;

(B) the satisfaction of obligations secured by the security interest or agricultural lien under which the collection or enforcement is made; and

(C) the satisfaction of obligations secured by any subordinate security interest in or other lien on the collateral subject to the security interest or agricultural lien under which the collection or enforcement is made if the secured party receives an authenticated demand for proceeds before distribution of the proceeds is completed.

(2) If requested by a secured party, a holder of a subordinate security interest or other lien shall furnish reasonable proof of the interest or lien within a reasonable time. Unless the holder complies, the secured party need not comply with the holder's demand under paragraph (1)(C).

(3) A secured party need not apply or pay over for application noncash proceeds of collection and enforcement under Section 9–607 unless the failure to do so would be commercially unreasonable. A secured party that applies or pays over for application noncash proceeds shall do so in a commercially reasonable manner.

(4) A secured party shall account to and pay a debtor for any surplus, and the obligor is liable for any deficiency.

(b) If the underlying transaction is a sale of accounts, chattel paper, payment intangibles, or promissory notes, the debtor is not entitled to any surplus, and the obligor is not liable for any deficiency.

As amended in 2000.

§ 9–609. Secured Party's Right to Take Possession after Default.

(a) After default, a secured party:

(1) may take possession of the collateral; and

(2) without removal, may render equipment unusable and dispose of collateral on a debtor's premises under Section 9–610.

(b) A secured party may proceed under subsection (a):

(1) pursuant to judicial process; or

(2) without judicial process, if it proceeds without breach of the peace.

(c) If so agreed, and in any event after default, a secured party may require the debtor to assemble the collateral and make it available to the secured party at a place to be designated by the secured party which is reasonably convenient to both parties.

§ 9–610. Disposition of Collateral after Default.

(a) After default, a secured party may sell, lease, license, or otherwise dispose of any or all of the collateral in its present condition or following any commercially reasonable preparation or processing.

(b) Every aspect of a disposition of collateral, including the method, manner, time, place, and other terms, must be commercially reasonable. If commercially reasonable, a secured party may dispose of collateral by public or private proceedings, by one or more contracts, as a unit or in parcels, and at any time and place and on any terms.

(c) A secured party may purchase collateral:

(1) at a public disposition; or

(2) at a private disposition only if the collateral is of a kind that is customarily sold on a recognized market or the subject of widely distributed standard price quotations.

(d) A contract for sale, lease, license, or other disposition includes the warranties relating to title, possession, quiet enjoyment, and the like which by operation of law accompany a voluntary disposition of property of the kind subject to the contract.

(e) A secured party may disclaim or modify warranties under subsection (d):

(1) in a manner that would be effective to disclaim or modify the warranties in a voluntary disposition of property of the kind subject to the contract of disposition; or

(2) by communicating to the purchaser a record evidencing the contract for disposition and including an express disclaimer or modification of the warranties.

(f) A record is sufficient to disclaim warranties under subsection (e) if it indicates "There is no warranty relating to title, possession, quiet enjoyment, or the like in this disposition" or uses words of similar import.

§ 9–611. Notification before Disposition of Collateral.

(a) In this section, "notification date" means the earlier of the date on which:

(1) a secured party sends to the debtor and any secondary obligor an authenticated notification of disposition; or

(2) the debtor and any secondary obligor waive the right to notification.

(b) Except as otherwise provided in subsection (d), a secured party that disposes of collateral under Section 9–610 shall send to the persons specified in subsection (c) a reasonable authenticated notification of disposition.

(c) To comply with subsection (b), the secured party shall send an authenticated notification of disposition to:

(1) the debtor;

(2) any secondary obligor; and

(3) if the collateral is other than consumer goods:

(A) any other person from which the secured party has received, before the notification date, an authenticated notification of a claim of an interest in the collateral;

(B) any other secured party or lienholder that, 10 days before the notification date, held a security interest in or other lien on the collateral perfected by the filing of a financing statement that:

(i) identified the collateral;

(ii) was indexed under the debtor's name as of that date; and

(iii) was filed in the office in which to file a financing statement against the debtor covering the collateral as of that date; and

(C) any other secured party that, 10 days before the notification date, held a security interest in the collateral perfected by compliance with a statute, regulation, or treaty described in Section 9–311(a).

(d) Subsection (b) does not apply if the collateral is perishable or threatens to decline speedily in value or is of a type customarily sold on a recognized market.

(e) A secured party complies with the requirement for notification prescribed by subsection (c)(3)(B) if:

(1) not later than 20 days or earlier than 30 days before the notification date, the secured party requests, in a commercially reasonable manner, information concerning financing statements indexed under the debtor's name in the office indicated in subsection (c)(3)(B); and

(2) before the notification date, the secured party:

(A) did not receive a response to the request for information; or

(B) received a response to the request for information and sent an authenticated notification of disposition to each secured party or other lienholder named in that response whose financing statement covered the collateral.

§ 9–612. Timeliness of Notification before Disposition of Collateral.

(a) Except as otherwise provided in subsection (b), whether a notification is sent within a reasonable time is a question of fact.

(b) In a transaction other than a consumer transaction, a notification of disposition sent after default and 10 days or more before the earliest time of disposition set forth in the notification is sent within a reasonable time before the disposition.

§ 9–613. Contents and Form of Notification before Disposition of Collateral: General.

Except in a consumer-goods transaction, the following rules apply:

(1) The contents of a notification of disposition are sufficient if the notification:

(A) describes the debtor and the secured party;

(B) describes the collateral that is the subject of the intended disposition;

(C) states the method of intended disposition;

(D) states that the debtor is entitled to an accounting of the unpaid indebtedness and states the charge, if any, for an accounting; and

(E) states the time and place of a public disposition or the time after which any other disposition is to be made.

(2) Whether the contents of a notification that lacks any of the information specified in paragraph (1) are nevertheless sufficient is a question of fact.

(3) The contents of a notification providing substantially the information specified in paragraph (1) are sufficient, even if the notification includes:

(A) information not specified by that paragraph; or

(B) minor errors that are not seriously misleading.

(4) A particular phrasing of the notification is not required.

(5) The following form of notification and the form appearing in Section 9–614(3), when completed, each provides sufficient information:

NOTIFICATION OF DISPOSITION OF COLLATERAL

To: *[Name of debtor, obligor, or other person to which the notification is sent]*

From: [Name, address, and telephone number of secured party]

Name of Debtor(s): [Include only if debtor(s) are not an addressee]

[For a public disposition:]

We will sell [or lease or license, as applicable] the [describe collateral] [to the highest qualified bidder] in public as follows:

Day and Date: _____

Time: _____

Place: _____

[For a private disposition:]

We will sell [or lease or license, as *applicable*] the [*describe collateral*] privately sometime after [*day and date*].

You are entitled to an accounting of the unpaid indebtedness secured by the property that we intend to sell [or lease or license, as applicable] [for a charge of $_____]. You may request an accounting by calling us at [telephone number].

[End of Form]

As amended in 2000.

§ 9–614. Contents and Form of Notification before Disposition of Collateral: Consumer-Goods Transaction.

In a consumer-goods transaction, the following rules apply:

(1) A notification of disposition must provide the following information:

(A) the information specified in Section 9–613(1);

(B) a description of any liability for a deficiency of the person to which the notification is sent;

(C) a telephone number from which the amount that must be paid to the secured party to redeem the collateral under Section 9–623 is available; and

(D) a telephone number or mailing address from which additional information concerning the disposition and the obligation secured is available.

(2) A particular phrasing of the notification is not required.

(3) The following form of notification, when completed, provides sufficient information:

[Name and address of secured party]

[Date]

NOTICE OF OUR PLAN TO SELL PROPERTY

[Name and address of any obligor who is also a debtor]

Subject: [Identification of Transaction]

We have your [describe collateral], because you broke promises in our agreement.

[For a public disposition:]

We will sell [describe collateral] at public sale. A sale could include a lease or license. The sale will be held as follows:

Date: _____

Time: _____

Place: _____

You may attend the sale and bring bidders if you want.

[For a private disposition:]

We will sell [describe collateral] at private sale sometime after [date]. A sale could include a lease or license.

The money that we get from the sale (after paying our costs) will reduce the amount you owe. If we get less money than you owe, you [will or will not, as applicable] still owe us the difference. If we get more money than you owe, you will get the extra money, unless we must pay it to someone else.

You can get the property back at any time before we sell it by paying us the full amount you owe (not just the past due payments), including our expenses. To learn the exact amount you must pay, call us at [telephone number].

If you want us to explain to you in writing how we have figured the amount that you owe us, you may call us at [telephone number] [or write us at [secured party's address]] and request a written explanation. [We will charge you $_____ for the explanation if we sent you another written explanation of the amount you owe us within the last six months.]

If you need more information about the sale call us at [telephone number] [or write us at [secured party's address]].

We are sending this notice to the following other people who have an interest in [describe collateral] or who owe money under your agreement:

[Names of all other debtors and obligors, if any]

[End of Form]

(4) A notification in the form of paragraph (3) is sufficient, even if additional information appears at the end of the form.

(5) A notification in the form of paragraph (3) is sufficient, even if it includes errors in information not required by paragraph (1), unless the error is misleading with respect to rights arising under this article.

(6) If a notification under this section is not in the form of paragraph (3), law other than this article determines the effect of including information not required by paragraph (1).

§ 9–615. Application of Proceeds of Disposition; Liability for Deficiency and Right to Surplus.

(a) A secured party shall apply or pay over for application the cash proceeds of disposition under Section 9–610 in the following order to:

(1) the reasonable expenses of retaking, holding, preparing for disposition, processing, and disposing, and, to the extent provided for by agreement and not prohibited by law, reasonable attorney's fees and legal expenses incurred by the secured party;

(2) the satisfaction of obligations secured by the security interest or agricultural lien under which the disposition is made;

(3) the satisfaction of obligations secured by any subordinate security interest in or other subordinate lien on the collateral if:

(A) the secured party receives from the holder of the subordinate security interest or other lien an authenticated demand for proceeds before distribution of the proceeds is completed; and

(B) in a case in which a consignor has an interest in the collateral, the subordinate security interest or other lien is senior to the interest of the consignor; and

(4) a secured party that is a consignor of the collateral if the secured party receives from the consignor an authenticated demand for proceeds before distribution of the proceeds is completed.

(b) If requested by a secured party, a holder of a subordinate security interest or other lien shall furnish reasonable proof of the interest or lien within a reasonable time. Unless the holder does so, the secured party need not comply with the holder's demand under subsection (a)(3).

(c) A secured party need not apply or pay over for application noncash proceeds of disposition under Section 9–610 unless the failure to do so would be commercially unreasonable. A secured party that applies or pays over for application noncash proceeds shall do so in a commercially reasonable manner.

(d) If the security interest under which a disposition is made secures payment or performance of an obligation, after making the payments and applications required by subsection (a) and permitted by subsection (c):

(1) unless subsection (a)(4) requires the secured party to apply or pay over cash proceeds to a consignor, the secured party shall account to and pay a debtor for any surplus; and

(2) the obligor is liable for any deficiency.

(e) If the underlying transaction is a sale of accounts, chattel paper, payment intangibles, or promissory notes:

(1) the debtor is not entitled to any surplus; and

(2) the obligor is not liable for any deficiency.

(f) The surplus or deficiency following a disposition is calculated based on the amount of proceeds that would have been realized in a disposition complying with this part to a transferee other than the secured party, a person related to the secured party, or a secondary obligor if:

(1) the transferee in the disposition is the secured party, a person related to the secured party, or a secondary obligor; and

(2) the amount of proceeds of the disposition is significantly below the range of proceeds that a complying disposition to a person other than the secured party, a person related to the secured party, or a secondary obligor would have brought.

(g) A secured party that receives cash proceeds of a disposition in good faith and without knowledge that the receipt violates the rights of the holder of a security interest or other lien that is not subordinate to the security interest or agricultural lien under which the disposition is made:

(1) takes the cash proceeds free of the security interest or other lien;

(2) is not obligated to apply the proceeds of the disposition to the satisfaction of obligations secured by the security interest or other lien; and

(3) is not obligated to account to or pay the holder of the security interest or other lien for any surplus.

As amended in 2000.

§ 9–616. Explanation of Calculation of Surplus or Deficiency.

(a) In this section:

(1) "Explanation" means a writing that:

(A) states the amount of the surplus or deficiency;

(B) provides an explanation in accordance with subsection (c) of how the secured party calculated the surplus or deficiency;

(C) states, if applicable, that future debits, credits, charges, including additional credit service charges or interest, rebates, and expenses may affect the amount of the surplus or deficiency; and

(D) provides a telephone number or mailing address from which additional information concerning the transaction is available.

(2) "Request" means a record:

(A) authenticated by a debtor or consumer obligor;

(B) requesting that the recipient provide an explanation; and

(C) sent after disposition of the collateral under Section 9–610.

(b) In a consumer-goods transaction in which the debtor is entitled to a surplus or a consumer obligor is liable for a deficiency under Section 9–615, the secured party shall:

(1) send an explanation to the debtor or consumer obligor, as applicable, after the disposition and:

(A) before or when the secured party accounts to the debtor and pays any surplus or first makes written demand on the consumer obligor after the disposition for payment of the deficiency; and

(B) within 14 days after receipt of a request; or

(2) in the case of a consumer obligor who is liable for a deficiency, within 14 days after receipt of a request, send to the consumer obligor a record waiving the secured party's right to a deficiency.

(c) To comply with subsection (a)(1)(B), a writing must provide the following information in the following order:

(1) the aggregate amount of obligations secured by the security interest under which the disposition was made, and, if the amount reflects a rebate of unearned interest or credit service charge, an indication of that fact, calculated as of a specified date:

(A) if the secured party takes or receives possession of the collateral after default, not more than 35 days before the secured party takes or receives possession; or

(B) if the secured party takes or receives possession of the collateral before default or does not take possession of the collateral, not more than 35 days before the disposition;

(2) the amount of proceeds of the disposition;

(3) the aggregate amount of the obligations after deducting the amount of proceeds;

(4) the amount, in the aggregate or by type, and types of expenses, including expenses of retaking, holding, preparing for disposition, processing, and disposing of the collateral, and attorney's fees secured by the collateral which are known to the secured party and relate to the current disposition;

(5) the amount, in the aggregate or by type, and types of credits, including rebates of interest or credit service charges, to which the obligor is known to be entitled and which are not reflected in the amount in paragraph (1); and

(6) the amount of the surplus or deficiency.

(d) A particular phrasing of the explanation is not required. An explanation complying substantially with the requirements of subsection (a) is sufficient, even if it includes minor errors that are not seriously misleading.

(e) A debtor or consumer obligor is entitled without charge to one response to a request under this section during any six-month period in which the secured party did not send to the debtor or consumer obligor an explanation pursuant to subsection (b)(1). The secured party may require payment of a charge not exceeding $25 for each additional response.

§ 9–617. **Rights of Transferee of Collateral.**

(a) A secured party's disposition of collateral after default:

(1) transfers to a transferee for value all of the debtor's rights in the collateral;

(2) discharges the security interest under which the disposition is made; and

(3) discharges any subordinate security interest or other subordinate lien [other than liens created under [cite acts or statutes providing for liens, if any, that are not to be discharged]].

(b) A transferee that acts in good faith takes free of the rights and interests described in subsection (a), even if the secured party fails to comply with this article or the requirements of any judicial proceeding.

(c) If a transferee does not take free of the rights and interests described in subsection (a), the transferee takes the collateral subject to:

(1) the debtor's rights in the collateral;

(2) the security interest or agricultural lien under which the disposition is made; and

(3) any other security interest or other lien.

§ 9–618. **Rights and Duties of Certain Secondary Obligors.**

(a) A secondary obligor acquires the rights and becomes obligated to perform the duties of the secured party after the secondary obligor:

(1) receives an assignment of a secured obligation from the secured party;

(2) receives a transfer of collateral from the secured party and agrees to accept the rights and assume the duties of the secured party; or

(3) is subrogated to the rights of a secured party with respect to collateral.

(b) An assignment, transfer, or subrogation described in subsection (a):

(1) is not a disposition of collateral under Section 9–610; and

(2) relieves the secured party of further duties under this article.

§ 9–619. **Transfer of Record or Legal Title.**

(a) In this section, "transfer statement" means a record authenticated by a secured party stating:

(1) that the debtor has defaulted in connection with an obligation secured by specified collateral;

(2) that the secured party has exercised its post-default remedies with respect to the collateral;

(3) that, by reason of the exercise, a transferee has acquired the rights of the debtor in the collateral; and

(4) the name and mailing address of the secured party, debtor, and transferee.

(b) A transfer statement entitles the transferee to the transfer of record of all rights of the debtor in the collateral specified in the statement in any official filing, recording, registration, or certificate-of-title system covering the collateral. If a transfer statement is presented with the applicable fee and request form to the official or office responsible for maintaining the system, the official or office shall:

(1) accept the transfer statement;

(2) promptly amend its records to reflect the transfer; and

(3) if applicable, issue a new appropriate certificate of title in the name of the transferee.

(c) A transfer of the record or legal title to collateral to a secured party under subsection (b) or otherwise is not of itself a disposition of collateral under this article and does not of itself relieve the secured party of its duties under this article.

§ 9–620. **Acceptance of Collateral in Full or Partial Satisfaction of Obligation; Compulsory Disposition of Collateral.**

(a) Except as otherwise provided in subsection (g), a secured party may accept collateral in full or partial satisfaction of the obligation it secures only if:

(1) the debtor consents to the acceptance under subsection (c);

(2) the secured party does not receive, within the time set forth in subsection (d), a notification of objection to the proposal authenticated by:

(A) a person to which the secured party was required to send a proposal under Section 9–621; or

(B) any other person, other than the debtor, holding an interest in the collateral subordinate to the security interest that is the subject of the proposal;

(3) if the collateral is consumer goods, the collateral is not in the possession of the debtor when the debtor consents to the acceptance; and

(4) subsection (e) does not require the secured party to dispose of the collateral or the debtor waives the requirement pursuant to Section 9–624.

(b) A purported or apparent acceptance of collateral under this section is ineffective unless:

(1) the secured party consents to the acceptance in an authenticated record or sends a proposal to the debtor; and

(2) the conditions of subsection (a) are met.

(c) For purposes of this section:

(1) a debtor consents to an acceptance of collateral in partial satisfaction of the obligation it secures only if the debtor agrees to the terms of the acceptance in a record authenticated after default; and

(2) a debtor consents to an acceptance of collateral in full satisfaction of the obligation it secures only if the debtor agrees to the terms of the acceptance in a record authenticated after default or the secured party:

(A) sends to the debtor after default a proposal that is unconditional or subject only to a condition that collateral not in the possession of the secured party be preserved or maintained;

(B) in the proposal, proposes to accept collateral in full satisfaction of the obligation it secures; and

(C) does not receive a notification of objection authenticated by the debtor within 20 days after the proposal is sent.

(d) To be effective under subsection (a)(2), a notification of objection must be received by the secured party:

(1) in the case of a person to which the proposal was sent pursuant to Section 9–621, within 20 days after notification was sent to that person; and

(2) in other cases:

(A) within 20 days after the last notification was sent pursuant to Section 9–621; or

(B) if a notification was not sent, before the debtor consents to the acceptance under subsection (c).

(e) A secured party that has taken possession of collateral shall dispose of the collateral pursuant to Section 9–610 within the time specified in subsection (f) if:

(1) 60 percent of the cash price has been paid in the case of a purchase-money security interest in consumer goods; or

(2) 60 percent of the principal amount of the obligation secured has been paid in the case of a non-purchase-money security interest in consumer goods.

(f) To comply with subsection (e), the secured party shall dispose of the collateral:

(1) within 90 days after taking possession; or

(2) within any longer period to which the debtor and all secondary obligors have agreed in an agreement to that effect entered into and authenticated after default.

(g) In a consumer transaction, a secured party may not accept collateral in partial satisfaction of the obligation it secures.

§ 9–621. Notification of Proposal to Accept Collateral.

(a) A secured party that desires to accept collateral in full or partial satisfaction of the obligation it secures shall send its proposal to:

(1) any person from which the secured party has received, before the debtor consented to the acceptance, an authenticated notification of a claim of an interest in the collateral;

(2) any other secured party or lienholder that, 10 days before the debtor consented to the acceptance, held a security interest in or other lien on the collateral perfected by the filing of a financing statement that:

(A) identified the collateral;

(B) was indexed under the debtor's name as of that date; and

(C) was filed in the office or offices in which to file a financing statement against the debtor covering the collateral as of that date; and

(3) any other secured party that, 10 days before the debtor consented to the acceptance, held a security interest in the collateral perfected by compliance with a statute, regulation, or treaty described in Section 9–311(a).

(b) A secured party that desires to accept collateral in partial satisfaction of the obligation it secures shall send its proposal to any secondary obligor in addition to the persons described in subsection (a).

§ 9–622. Effect of Acceptance of Collateral.

(a) A secured party's acceptance of collateral in full or partial satisfaction of the obligation it secures:

(1) discharges the obligation to the extent consented to by the debtor;

(2) transfers to the secured party all of a debtor's rights in the collateral;

(3) discharges the security interest or agricultural lien that is the subject of the debtor's consent and any subordinate security interest or other subordinate lien; and

(4) terminates any other subordinate interest.

(b) A subordinate interest is discharged or terminated under subsection (a), even if the secured party fails to comply with this article.

§ 9–623. Right to Redeem Collateral.

(a) A debtor, any secondary obligor, or any other secured party or lienholder may redeem collateral.

(b) To redeem collateral, a person shall tender:

(1) fulfillment of all obligations secured by the collateral; and

(2) the reasonable expenses and attorney's fees described in Section 9–615(a)(1).

(c) A redemption may occur at any time before a secured party:

(1) has collected collateral under Section 9–607;

(2) has disposed of collateral or entered into a contract for its disposition under Section 9–610; or

(3) has accepted collateral in full or partial satisfaction of the obligation it secures under Section 9–622.

§ 9–624. Waiver.

(a) A debtor or secondary obligor may waive the right to notification of disposition of collateral under Section 9–611 only by an agreement to that effect entered into and authenticated after default.

(b) A debtor may waive the right to require disposition of collateral under Section 9–620(e) only by an agreement to that effect entered into and authenticated after default.

(c) Except in a consumer-goods transaction, a debtor or secondary obligor may waive the right to redeem collateral under Section 9–623 only by an agreement to that effect entered into and authenticated after default.

[Subpart 2. Noncompliance with Article]

§ 9–625. Remedies for Secured Party's Failure to Comply with Article.

(a) If it is established that a secured party is not proceeding in accordance with this article, a court may order or restrain collection, enforcement, or disposition of collateral on appropriate terms and conditions.

(b) Subject to subsections (c), (d), and (f), a person is liable for damages in the amount of any loss caused by a failure to comply with this article. Loss caused by a failure to comply may include loss resulting from the debtor's inability to obtain, or increased costs of, alternative financing.

(c) Except as otherwise provided in Section 9–628:

(1) a person that, at the time of the failure, was a debtor, was an obligor, or held a security interest in or other lien on the collateral may recover damages under subsection (b) for its loss; and

(2) if the collateral is consumer goods, a person that was a debtor or a secondary obligor at the time a secured party failed to comply with this part may recover for that failure in any event an amount not less than the credit service charge plus 10 percent of the principal amount of the obligation or the time-price differential plus 10 percent of the cash price.

(d) A debtor whose deficiency is eliminated under Section 9–626 may recover damages for the loss of any surplus. However, a debtor or secondary obligor whose deficiency is eliminated or reduced under Section 9–626 may not otherwise recover under subsection (b) for noncompliance with the provisions of this part relating to collection, enforcement, disposition, or acceptance.

(e) In addition to any damages recoverable under subsection (b), the debtor, consumer obligor, or person named as a debtor in a filed record, as applicable, may recover $500 in each case from a person that:

(1) fails to comply with Section 9–208;

(2) fails to comply with Section 9–209;

(3) files a record that the person is not entitled to file under Section 9–509(a);

(4) fails to cause the secured party of record to file or send a termination statement as required by Section 9–513(a) or (c);

(5) fails to comply with Section 9–616(b)(1) and whose failure is part of a pattern, or consistent with a practice, of noncompliance; or

(6) fails to comply with Section 9–616(b)(2).

(f) A debtor or consumer obligor may recover damages under subsection (b) and, in addition, $500 in each case from a person that, without reasonable cause, fails to comply with a request under Section 9–210. A recipient of a request under Section 9–210 which never claimed an interest in the collateral or obligations that are the subject of a request under that section has a reasonable excuse for failure to comply with the request within the meaning of this subsection.

(g) If a secured party fails to comply with a request regarding a list of collateral or a statement of account under Section 9–210, the secured party may claim a security interest only as shown in the list or statement included in the request as against a person that is reasonably misled by the failure.

As amended in 2000.

§ 9–626. Action in Which Deficiency or Surplus Is in Issue.

(a) In an action arising from a transaction, other than a consumer transaction, in which the amount of a deficiency or surplus is in issue, the following rules apply:

(1) A secured party need not prove compliance with the provisions of this part relating to collection, enforcement, disposition, or acceptance unless the debtor or a secondary obligor places the secured party's compliance in issue.

(2) If the secured party's compliance is placed in issue, the secured party has the burden of establishing that the collection, enforcement, disposition, or acceptance was conducted in accordance with this part.

(3) Except as otherwise provided in Section 9–628, if a secured party fails to prove that the collection, enforcement, disposition, or acceptance was conducted in accordance with the provisions of this part relating to collection, enforcement, disposition, or acceptance, the liability of a debtor or a secondary obligor for a deficiency is limited to an amount by which the sum of the secured obligation, expenses, and attorney's fees exceeds the greater of:

> (A) the proceeds of the collection, enforcement, disposition, or acceptance; or

> (B) the amount of proceeds that would have been realized had the noncomplying secured party proceeded in accordance with the provisions of this part relating to collection, enforcement, disposition, or acceptance.

(4) For purposes of paragraph (3)(B), the amount of proceeds that would have been realized is equal to the sum of the secured obligation, expenses, and attorney's fees unless the secured party proves that the amount is less than that sum.

(5) If a deficiency or surplus is calculated under Section 9–615(f), the debtor or obligor has the burden of establishing that the amount of proceeds of the disposition is significantly below the range of prices that a complying disposition to a person other than the secured party, a person related to the secured party, or a secondary obligor would have brought.

(b) The limitation of the rules in subsection (a) to transactions other than consumer transactions is intended to leave to the court the determination of the proper rules in consumer transactions. The court may not infer from that limitation the nature of the proper rule in consumer transactions and may continue to apply established approaches.

§ 9–627. Determination of Whether Conduct Was Commercially Reasonable.

(a) The fact that a greater amount could have been obtained by a collection, enforcement, disposition, or acceptance at a different time or in a different method from that selected by the secured party is not of itself sufficient to preclude the secured party from establishing that the collection, enforcement, disposition, or acceptance was made in a commercially reasonable manner.

(b) A disposition of collateral is made in a commercially reasonable manner if the disposition is made:

> (1) in the usual manner on any recognized market;

> (2) at the price current in any recognized market at the time of the disposition; or

> (3) otherwise in conformity with reasonable commercial practices among dealers in the type of property that was the subject of the disposition.

(c) A collection, enforcement, disposition, or acceptance is commercially reasonable if it has been approved:

> (1) in a judicial proceeding;

> (2) by a bona fide creditors' committee;

> (3) by a representative of creditors; or

> (4) by an assignee for the benefit of creditors.

(d) Approval under subsection (c) need not be obtained, and lack of approval does not mean that the collection, enforcement, disposition, or acceptance is not commercially reasonable.

§ 9–628. Nonliability and Limitation on Liability of Secured Party; Liability of Secondary Obligor.

(a) Unless a secured party knows that a person is a debtor or obligor, knows the identity of the person, and knows how to communicate with the person:

> (1) the secured party is not liable to the person, or to a secured party or lienholder that has filed a financing statement against the person, for failure to comply with this article; and

> (2) the secured party's failure to comply with this article does not affect the liability of the person for a deficiency.

(b) A secured party is not liable because of its status as secured party:

> (1) to a person that is a debtor or obligor, unless the secured party knows:

> > (A) that the person is a debtor or obligor;

> > (B) the identity of the person; and

> > (C) how to communicate with the person; or

> (2) to a secured party or lienholder that has filed a financing statement against a person, unless the secured party knows:

> > (A) that the person is a debtor; and

> > (B) the identity of the person.

(c) A secured party is not liable to any person, and a person's liability for a deficiency is not affected, because of any act or omission arising out of the secured party's reasonable belief that a transaction is not a consumer-goods transaction or a consumer transaction or that goods are not consumer goods, if the secured party's belief is based on its reasonable reliance on:

> (1) a debtor's representation concerning the purpose for which collateral was to be used, acquired, or held; or

> (2) an obligor's representation concerning the purpose for which a secured obligation was incurred.

(d) A secured party is not liable to any person under Section 9–625(c)(2) for its failure to comply with Section 9–616.

(e) A secured party is not liable under Section 9–625(c)(2) more than once with respect to any one secured obligation.

Part 7 Transition

§ 9–701. Effective Date.

This [Act] takes effect on July 1, 2001.

§ 9–702. Savings Clause.

(a) Except as otherwise provided in this part, this [Act] applies to a transaction or lien within its scope, even if the transaction or lien was entered into or created before this [Act] takes effect.

(b) Except as otherwise provided in subsection (c) and Sections 9–703 through 9–709:

(1) transactions and liens that were not governed by [former Article 9], were validly entered into or created before this [Act] takes effect, and would be subject to this [Act] if they had been entered into or created after this [Act] takes effect, and the rights, duties, and interests flowing from those transactions and liens remain valid after this [Act] takes effect; and

(2) the transactions and liens may be terminated, completed, consummated, and enforced as required or permitted by this [Act] or by the law that otherwise would apply if this [Act] had not taken effect.

(c) This [Act] does not affect an action, case, or proceeding commenced before this [Act] takes effect.

As amended in 2000.

§ 9–703. Security Interest Perfected before Effective Date.

(a) A security interest that is enforceable immediately before this [Act] takes effect and would have priority over the rights of a person that becomes a lien creditor at that time is a perfected security interest under this [Act] if, when this [Act] takes effect, the applicable requirements for enforceability and perfection under this [Act] are satisfied without further action.

(b) Except as otherwise provided in Section 9–705, if, immediately before this [Act] takes effect, a security interest is enforceable and would have priority over the rights of a person that becomes a lien creditor at that time, but the applicable requirements for enforceability or perfection under this [Act] are not satisfied when this [Act] takes effect, the security interest:

(1) is a perfected security interest for one year after this [Act] takes effect;

(2) remains enforceable thereafter only if the security interest becomes enforceable under Section 9–203 before the year expires; and

(3) remains perfected thereafter only if the applicable requirements for perfection under this [Act] are satisfied before the year expires.

§ 9–704. Security Interest Unperfected before Effective Date.

A security interest that is enforceable immediately before this [Act] takes effect but which would be subordinate to the rights of a person that becomes a lien creditor at that time:

(1) remains an enforceable security interest for one year after this [Act] takes effect;

(2) remains enforceable thereafter if the security interest becomes enforceable under Section 9–203 when this [Act] takes effect or within one year thereafter; and

(3) becomes perfected:

(A) without further action, when this [Act] takes effect if the applicable requirements for perfection under this [Act] are satisfied before or at that time; or

(B) when the applicable requirements for perfection are satisfied if the requirements are satisfied after that time.

§ 9–705. Effectiveness of Action Taken before Effective Date.

(a) If action, other than the filing of a financing statement, is taken before this [Act] takes effect and the action would have resulted in priority of a security interest over the rights of a person that becomes a lien creditor had the security interest become enforceable before this [Act] takes effect, the action is effective to perfect a security interest that attaches under this [Act] within one year after this [Act] takes effect. An attached security interest becomes unperfected one year after this [Act] takes effect unless the security interest becomes a perfected security interest under this [Act] before the expiration of that period.

(b) The filing of a financing statement before this [Act] takes effect is effective to perfect a security interest to the extent the filing would satisfy the applicable requirements for perfection under this [Act].

(c) This [Act] does not render ineffective an effective financing statement that, before this [Act] takes effect, is filed and satisfies the applicable requirements for perfection under the law of the jurisdiction governing perfection as provided in [former Section 9–103]. However, except as otherwise provided in subsections (d) and (e) and Section 9–706, the financing statement ceases to be effective at the earlier of:

(1) the time the financing statement would have ceased to be effective under the law of the jurisdiction in which it is filed; or

(2) June 30, 2006.

(d) The filing of a continuation statement after this [Act] takes effect does not continue the effectiveness of the financing statement filed before this [Act] takes effect. However, upon the timely filing of a continuation statement after this [Act] takes effect and in accordance with the law of the jurisdiction governing perfection as provided in Part 3, the effectiveness of a financing statement filed in the same office in that jurisdiction before this [Act] takes effect continues for the period provided by the law of that jurisdiction.

(e) Subsection (c)(2) applies to a financing statement that, before this [Act] takes effect, is filed against a transmitting utility and satisfies the applicable requirements for perfection under the law of the jurisdiction governing perfection as provided in [former Section 9–103] only to the extent that Part 3 provides that the law of a jurisdiction other than the jurisdiction in which the financing statement is filed governs perfection of a security interest in collateral covered by the financing statement.

(f) A financing statement that includes a financing statement filed before this [Act] takes effect and a continuation statement filed after this [Act] takes effect is effective only to the extent that it satisfies the requirements of Part 5 for an initial financing statement.

§ 9–706. When Initial Financing Statement Suffices to Continue Effectiveness of Financing Statement.

(a) The filing of an initial financing statement in the office specified in Section 9–501 continues the effectiveness of a financing statement filed before this [Act] takes effect if:

(1) the filing of an initial financing statement in that office would be effective to perfect a security interest under this [Act];

(2) the pre-effective-date financing statement was filed in an office in another State or another office in this State; and

(3) the initial financing statement satisfies subsection (c).

(b) The filing of an initial financing statement under subsection (a) continues the effectiveness of the pre-effective-date financing statement:

(1) if the initial financing statement is filed before this [Act] takes effect, for the period provided in [former Section 9–403] with respect to a financing statement; and

(2) if the initial financing statement is filed after this [Act] takes effect, for the period provided in Section 9–515 with respect to an initial financing statement.

(c) To be effective for purposes of subsection (a), an initial financing statement must:

(1) satisfy the requirements of Part 5 for an initial financing statement;

(2) identify the pre-effective-date financing statement by indicating the office in which the financing statement was filed and providing the dates of filing and file numbers, if any, of the financing statement and of the most recent continuation statement filed with respect to the financing statement; and

(3) indicate that the pre-effective-date financing statement remains effective.

§ 9–707. Amendment of Pre-Effective-Date Financing Statement.

(a) In this section, "Pre-effective-date financing statement" means a financing statement filed before this [Act] takes effect.

(b) After this [Act] takes effect, a person may add or delete collateral covered by, continue or terminate the effectiveness of, or otherwise amend the information provided in, a pre-effective-date financing statement only in accordance with the law of the jurisdiction governing perfection as provided in Part 3. However, the effectiveness of a pre-effective-date financing statement also may be terminated in accordance with the law of the jurisdiction in which the financing statement is filed.

(c) Except as otherwise provided in subsection (d), if the law of this State governs perfection of a security interest, the information in a pre-effective-date financing statement may be amended after this [Act] takes effect only if:

(1) the pre-effective-date financing statement and an amendment are filed in the office specified in Section 9–501;

(2) an amendment is filed in the office specified in Section 9–501 concurrently with, or after the filing in that office of, an initial financing statement that satisfies Section 9–706(c); or

(3) an initial financing statement that provides the information as amended and satisfies Section 9–706(c) is filed in the office specified in Section 9–501.

(d) If the law of this State governs perfection of a security interest, the effectiveness of a pre-effective-date financing statement may be continued only under Section 9–705(d) and (f) or 9–706.

(e) Whether or not the law of this State governs perfection of a security interest, the effectiveness of a pre-effective-date financing statement filed in this State may be terminated after this [Act] takes effect by filing a termination statement in the office in which the pre-effective-date financing statement is filed, unless an initial financing statement that satisfies Section 9–706(c) has been filed in the office specified by the law of the jurisdiction governing perfection as provided in Part 3 as the office in which to file a financing statement.

As amended in 2000.

§ 9–708. Persons Entitled to File Initial Financing Statement or Continuation Statement.

A person may file an initial financing statement or a continuation statement under this part if:

(1) the secured party of record authorizes the filing; and

(2) the filing is necessary under this part:

(A) to continue the effectiveness of a financing statement filed before this [Act] takes effect; or

(B) to perfect or continue the perfection of a security interest.

As amended in 2000.

§ 9–709. Priority.

(a) This [Act] determines the priority of conflicting claims to collateral. However, if the relative priorities of the claims were established before this [Act] takes effect, [former Article 9] determines priority.

(b) For purposes of Section 9–322(a), the priority of a security interest that becomes enforceable under Section 9–203 of this [Act] dates from the time this [Act] takes effect if the security interest is perfected under this [Act] by the filing of a financing statement before this [Act] takes effect which would not have been effective to perfect the security interest under [former Article 9]. This subsection does not apply to conflicting security interests each of which is perfected by the filing of such a financing statement.

As amended in 2000.

APPENDIX D

The United Nations Convention on Contracts for the International Sale of Goods (Excerpts)

Part I. SPHERE OF APPLICATION AND GENERAL PROVISIONS

* * * *

Chapter II—General Provisions

* * * *

Article 8

(1) For the purposes of this Convention statements made by and other conduct of a party are to be interpreted according to his intent where the other party knew or could not have been unaware what that intent was.

(2) If the preceding paragraph is not applicable, statements made by and other conduct of a party are to be interpreted according to the understanding that a reasonable person of the same kind as the other party would have had in the same circumstances.

(3) In determining the intent of a party or the understanding a reasonable person would have had, due consideration is to be given to all relevant circumstances of the case including the negotiations, any practices which the parties have established between themselves, usages and any subsequent conduct of the parties.

Article 9

(1) The parties are bound by any usage to which they have agreed and by any practices which they have established between themselves.

(2) The parties are considered, unless otherwise agreed, to have impliedly made applicable to their contract or its formation a usage of which the parties knew or ought to have known and which in international trade is widely known to, and regularly observed by, parties to contracts of the type involved in the particular trade concerned.

* * * *

Article 11

A contract of sale need not be concluded in or evidenced by writing and is not subject to any other requirement as to form. It may be proved by any means, including witnesses.

* * * *

Part II. FORMATION OF THE CONTRACT

Article 14

(1) A proposal for concluding a contract addressed to one or more specific persons constitutes an offer if it is sufficiently definite and indicates the intention of the offeror to be bound in case of acceptance. A proposal is sufficiently definite if it indicates the goods and expressly or implicitly fixes or makes provision for determining the quantity and the price.

(2) A proposal other than one addressed to one or more specific persons is to be considered merely as an invitation to make offers, unless the contrary is clearly indicated by the person making the proposal.

Article 15

(1) An offer becomes effective when it reaches the offeree.

(2) An offer, even if it is irrevocable, may be withdrawn if the withdrawal reaches the offeree before or at the same time as the offer.

Article 16

(1) Until a contract is concluded an offer may be revoked if the revocation reaches the offeree before he has dispatched an acceptance.

(2) However, an offer cannot be revoked:

(a) If it indicates, whether by stating a fixed time for acceptance or otherwise, that it is irrevocable; or

(b) If it was reasonable for the offeree to rely on the offer as being irrevocable and the offeree has acted in reliance on the offer.

Article 17

An offer, even if it is irrevocable, is terminated when a rejection reaches the offeror.

Article 18

(1) A statement made by or other conduct of the offeree indicating assent to an offer is an acceptance. Silence or inactivity does not in itself amount to acceptance.

(2) An acceptance of an offer becomes effective at the moment the indication of assent reaches the offeror. An acceptance is not effective if the indication of assent does not reach the offeror within the time he has fixed or, if no time is fixed, within a reasonable time, due account being taken of the circumstances of the transaction, including the rapidity of the means of communication employed by the offeror. An oral offer must be accepted immediately unless the circumstances indicate otherwise.

(3) However, if, by virtue of the offer or as a result of practices which the parties have established between themselves or of usage, the offeree may indicate assent by performing an act, such as one relating to the dispatch of the goods or payment of the price, without notice to the offeror, the acceptance is effective at the moment the act is performed, provided that the act is performed within the period of time laid down in the preceding paragraph.

Article 19

(1) A reply to an offer which purports to be an acceptance but contains additions, limitations or other modifications is a rejection of the offer and constitutes a counter-offer.

(2) However, a reply to an offer which purports to be an acceptance but contains additional or different terms which do not materially alter the terms of the offer constitutes an acceptance, unless the offeror, without undue delay, objects orally to the discrepancy or dispatches a notice to that effect. If he does not so object, the terms of the contract are the terms of the offer with the modifications contained in the acceptance.

(3) Additional or different terms relating, among other things, to the price, payment, quality and quantity of the goods, place and time of delivery, extent of one party's liability to the other or the settlement of disputes are considered to alter the terms of the offer materially.

* * * *

Article 22

An acceptance may be withdrawn if the withdrawal reaches the offeror before or at the same time as the acceptance would have become effective.

* * * *

Part III.   SALE OF GOODS
Chapter I—General Provisions
Article 25

A breach of contract committed by one of the parties is fundamental if it results in such detriment to the other party as substantially to deprive him of what he is entitled to expect under the contract, unless the party in breach did not foresee and a reasonable person of the same kind in the same circumstances would not have foreseen such a result.

* * * *

Article 28

If, in accordance with the provisions of this Convention, one party is entitled to require performance of any obligation by the other party, a court is not bound to enter a judgment for specific performance unless the court would do so under its own law in respect of similar contracts of sale not governed by this Convention.

Article 29

(1) A contract may be modified or terminated by the mere agreement of the parties.

(2) A contract in writing which contains a provision requiring any modification or termination by agreement to be in writing may not be otherwise modified or terminated by agreement. However, a party may be precluded by his conduct from asserting such a provision to the extent that the other party has relied on that conduct.

* * * *

Chapter II—Obligations of the Seller
* * * *

Section II. Conformity of the Goods and Third Party Claims
Article 35

(1) The seller must deliver goods which are of the quantity, quality and description required by the contract and which are contained or packaged in the manner required by the contract.

(2) Except where the parties have agreed otherwise, the goods do not conform with the contract unless they:

(a) Are fit for the purposes for which goods of the same description would ordinarily be used;

(b) Are fit for any particular purpose expressly or impliedly made known to the seller at the time of the conclusion of the contract, except where the circumstances show that the buyer did not rely, or that it was unreasonable for him to rely, on the seller's skill and judgment;

(c) Possess the qualities of goods which the seller has held out to the buyer as a sample or model;

(d) Are contained or packaged in the manner usual for such goods or, where there is no such manner, in a manner adequate to preserve and protect the goods.

(3) The seller is not liable under subparagraphs (a) to (d) of the preceding paragraph for any lack of conformity of the goods if at the time of the conclusion of the contract the buyer knew or could not have been unaware of such lack of conformity.

* * * *

Article 64

(1) The seller may declare the contract avoided:

(a) If the failure by the buyer to perform any of his obligations under the contract or this Convention amounts to a fundamental breach of contract; or

(b) If the buyer does not, within the additional period of time fixed by the seller in accordance with paragraph (1) of article 63, perform his obligation to pay the price or take delivery of the goods, or if he declares that he will not do so within the period so fixed.

(2) However, in cases where the buyer has paid the price, the seller loses the right to declare the contract avoided unless he does so:

(a) In respect of late performance by the buyer, before the seller has become aware that performance has been rendered; or

(b) In respect of any breach other than late performance by the buyer, within a reasonable time:

(i) After the seller knew or ought to have known of the breach; or

(ii) After the expiration of any additional period of time fixed by the seller in accordance with paragraph (1) of article 63, or after the buyer has declared that he will not perform his obligations within such an additional period.

* * * *

Chapter IV—Passing of Risk

* * * *

Article 67

(1) If the contract of sale involves carriage of the goods and the seller is not bound to hand them over at a particular place, the risk passes to the buyer when the goods are handed over to the first carrier for transmission to the buyer in accordance with the contract of sale. If the seller is bound to hand the goods over to a carrier at a particular place, the risk does not pass to the buyer until the goods are handed over to the carrier at that place. The fact that the seller is authorized to retain documents controlling the disposition of the goods does not affect the passage of the risk.

(2) Nevertheless, the risk does not pass to the buyer until the goods are clearly identified to the contract, whether by markings on the goods, by shipping documents, by notice given to the buyer or otherwise.

* * * *

Chapter V—Provisions Common to the Obligations of the Seller and of the Buyer

Section I. Anticipatory Breach and Installment Contracts

Article 71

(1) A party may suspend the performance of his obligations if, after the conclusion of the contract, it becomes apparent that the other party will not perform a substantial part of his obligations as a result of:

(a) A serious deficiency in his ability to perform or in his creditworthiness; or

(b) His conduct in preparing to perform or in performing the contract.

(2) If the seller has already dispatched the goods before the grounds described in the preceding paragraph become

evident, he may prevent the handing over of the goods to the buyer even though the buyer holds a document which entitles him to obtain them. The present paragraph relates only to the rights in the goods as between the buyer and the seller.

(3) A party suspending performance, whether before or after dispatch of the goods, must immediately give notice of the suspension to the other party and must continue with performance if the other party provides adequate assurance of his performance.

Article 72

(1) If prior to the date for performance of the contract it is clear that one of the parties will commit a fundamental breach of contract, the other party may declare the contract avoided.

(2) If time allows, the party intending to declare the contract avoided must give reasonable notice to the other party in order to permit him to provide adequate assurance of his performance.

(3) The requirements of the preceding paragraph do not apply if the other party has declared that he will not perform his obligations.

Article 73

(1) In the case of a contract for delivery of goods by instalments, if the failure of one party to perform any of his obligations in respect of any instalment constitutes a fundamental breach of contract with respect to that instalment, the other party may declare the contract avoided with respect to that instalment.

(2) If one party's failure to perform any of his obligations in respect of any instalment gives the other party good grounds to conclude that a fundamental breach of contract will occur with respect to future instalments, he may declare the contract avoided for the future, provided that he does so within a reasonable time.

(3) A buyer who declares the contract avoided in respect of any delivery may, at the same time, declare it avoided in respect of deliveries already made or of future deliveries if, by reason of their interdependence, those deliveries could not be used for the purpose contemplated by the parties at the time of the conclusion of the contract.

Section II. Damages

Article 74

Damages for breach of contract by one party consist of a sum equal to the loss, including loss of profit, suffered by the other party as a consequence of the breach. Such damages may not exceed the loss which the party in breach foresaw or ought to have foreseen at the time of the conclusion of the contract, in the light of the facts and matters of which he then knew or ought to have known, as a possible consequence of the breach of contract.

Article 75

If the contract is avoided and if, in a reasonable manner and within a reasonable time after avoidance, the buyer has bought goods in replacement or the seller has resold the goods, the party claiming damages may recover the difference between the contract price and the price in the substitute transaction as well as any further damages recoverable under article 74.

Article 76

(1) If the contract is avoided and there is a current price for the goods, the party claiming damages may, if he has not made a purchase or resale under article 75, recover the difference between the price fixed by the contract and the current price at the time of avoidance as well as any further damages recoverable under article 74. If, however, the party claiming damages has avoided the contract after taking over the goods, the current price at the time of such taking over shall be applied instead of the current price at the time of avoidance.

(2) For the purposes of the preceding paragraph, the current price is the price prevailing at the place where delivery of the goods should have been made or, if there is no current price at that place, the price at such other place as serves as a reasonable substitute, making due allowance for differences in the cost of transporting the goods.

Article 77

A party who relies on a breach of contract must take such measures as are reasonable in the circumstances to mitigate the loss, including loss of profit, resulting from the breach. If he fails to take such measures, the party in breach may claim a reduction in the damages in the amount by which the loss should have been mitigated.

APPENDIX E

Minnesota Uniform Partnership Act (Excerpts)

The Uniform Partnership Act (UPA) was amended in 1997 to provide limited liability for partners in a limited liability partnership. More than half the states, including the District of Columbia, Puerto Rico, and the U.S. Virgin Islands, have adopted this latest version of the UPA. This apendix contains excerpts from the Minnesota Uniform Partnership Act.

Chapter 323A.

UNIFORM PARTNERSHIP ACT

323A.0101 DEFINITIONS.

* * * *

(8) "Partnership" means an association of two or more persons to carry on as co-owners a business for profit, including a limited liability partnership, formed under section 323A.0202, predecessor law, or comparable law of another jurisdiction.

(9) "Partnership agreement" means the agreement, whether written, oral, or implied, among the partners concerning the partnership, including amendments to the partnership agreement.

(10) "Partnership at will" means a partnership in which the partners have not agreed to remain partners until the expiration of a definite term or the completion of a particular undertaking.

(11) "Partnership interest" or "partner's interest in the partnership" means all of a partner's interests in the partnership, including the partner's transferable interest and all management and other rights.

(12) "Person" means an individual, corporation, business trust, estate, trust, partnership, association, joint venture, government, governmental subdivision, agency, or instrumentality, or any other legal or commercial entity.

* * * *

323A.0103 EFFECT OF PARTNERSHIP AGREEMENT; NONWAIVABLE PROVISIONS.

(a) Except as otherwise provided in subsection (b), relations among the partners and between the partners and the partnership are governed by the partnership agreement. To the extent the partnership agreement does not otherwise provide, this chapter governs relations among the partners and between the partners and the partnership.

(b) The partnership agreement may not:

(1) vary the rights and duties under section 323A.0105 except to eliminate the duty to provide copies of statements to all of the partners;

(2) unreasonably restrict the right of access to books and records under section 323A.0403(b);

(3) eliminate the duty of loyalty under section 323A.0404(b) or 323A.0603(b)(3), but:

(i) the partnership agreement may identify specific types or categories of activities that do not violate the duty of loyalty, if not manifestly unreasonable; or

(ii) all of the partners or a number or percentage specified in the partnership agreement may authorize or ratify, after full disclosure of all material facts, a specific act or transaction that otherwise would violate the duty of loyalty;

(4) unreasonably reduce the duty of care under section 323A.0404(c) or 323A.0603(b)(3);

(5) eliminate the obligation of good faith and fair dealing under section 323A.0404(d), but the partnership agreement may prescribe the standards by which the performance of the obligation is to be measured, if the standards are not manifestly unreasonable;

(6) vary the power to dissociate as a partner under section 323A.0602(a), except to require the notice under section 323A.0601(1), to be in writing;

(7) vary the right of a court to expel a partner in the events specified in section 323A.0601(5);

* * * *

323A.0105 EXECUTION, FILING, AND RECORDING OF STATEMENTS.

(a) A statement may be filed in the office of the secretary of state. A certified copy of a statement that is filed in an office in another state may be filed in the office of the secretary of state. Either filing has the effect provided in this chapter with respect to partnership property located in or transactions that occur in this state.

(b) A certified copy of a statement that has been filed and has been recorded has the effect provided for recorded statements in this chapter. A recorded statement that is not a certified copy of a statement filed in the office of the secretary of state does not provide knowledge or notice and does not have the effect provided for recorded statements in this chapter.

* * * *

323A.0106 GOVERNING LAW.

(a) Except as otherwise provided in subsection (b), the law of the jurisdiction in which a partnership has its chief executive office governs relations among the partners and between the partners and the partnership.

(b) The law of this state governs relations among the partners and between the partners and the partnership and the liability of partners for an obligation of a limited liability partnership.

* * * *

323A.0201 PARTNERSHIP AS ENTITY.

(a) A partnership is an entity distinct from its partners.

(b) A limited liability partnership continues to be the same entity that existed before the filing of a statement of qualification under section 323A.1001.

323A.0202 FORMATION OF PARTNERSHIP.

* * * *

(c) In determining whether a partnership is formed, the following rules apply:

(1) Joint tenancy, tenancy in common, tenancy by the entireties, joint property, common property, or part ownership does not by itself establish a partnership, even if the co-owners share profits made by the use of the property.

(2) The sharing of gross returns does not by itself establish a partnership, even if the persons sharing them have a joint or common right or interest in property from which the returns are derived.

(3) A person who receives a share of the profits of a business is presumed to be a partner in the business, unless the profits were received in payment:

(i) of a debt by installments or otherwise;

(ii) for services as an independent contractor or of wages or other compensation to an employee;

(iii) of rent;

(iv) of an annuity or other retirement or health benefit to a beneficiary, representative, or designee of a deceased or retired partner;

(v) of interest or other charge on a loan, even if the amount of payment varies with the profits of the business, including a direct or indirect present or future ownership of the collateral, or rights to income, proceeds, or increase in value derived from the collateral; or

(vi) for the sale of the goodwill of a business or other property by installments or otherwise.

323A.0203 PARTNERSHIP PROPERTY.

Property acquired by a partnership is property of the partnership and not of the partners individually.

323A.0204 WHEN PROPERTY IS PARTNERSHIP PROPERTY.

* * * *

(d) Property acquired in the name of one or more of the partners, without an indication in the instrument transferring title to the property of the person's capacity as a partner or of the existence of a partnership and without use of partnership assets, is presumed to be separate property, even if used for partnership purposes.

323A.0301 PARTNER AGENT OF PARTNERSHIP.

Subject to the effect of a statement of partnership authority under section 323A.0303:

(1) Each partner is an agent of the partnership for the purpose of its business. An act of a partner, including the execution of an instrument in the partnership name, for apparently carrying on in the ordinary course the partnership business or business of the kind carried on by the partnership binds the partnership, unless the partner had no authority to act for the partnership in the particular matter and the person with whom the partner was dealing knew or had received a notification that the partner lacked authority.

(2) An act of a partner which is not apparently for carrying on in the ordinary course the partnership business or business of the kind carried on by the partnership binds the partnership only if the act was authorized by the other partners.

* * * *

323A.0303 STATEMENT OF PARTNERSHIP AUTHORITY.

(a) A partnership may file a statement of partnership authority, which:

(1) must include:

(i) the name of the partnership;

(ii) the street address, including the zip code, of its chief executive office and of one office in this state, if there is one;

(iii) the names and mailing addresses, including zip codes, of all of the partners or of an agent appointed and maintained by the partnership for the purpose of subsection (b); and

(iv) the names of the partners authorized to execute an instrument transferring real property held in the name of the partnership; and

(2) may state the authority, or limitations on the authority, of some or all of the partners to enter into other transactions on behalf of the partnership and any other matter.

(b) If a statement of partnership authority names an agent, the agent shall maintain a list of the names and mailing addresses, including zip codes, of all of the partners and make it available to any person on request for good cause shown.

(c) If a filed statement of partnership authority is executed pursuant to section 323A.0105(c), and states the name of the partnership but does not contain all of the other information required by subsection (a), the statement nevertheless operates with respect to a person not a partner as provided in subsections (d) and (e).

(d) A filed statement of partnership authority supplements the authority of a partner to enter into transactions on behalf of the partnership as follows:

(1) Except for transfers of real property, a grant of authority contained in a filed statement of partnership authority is conclusive in favor of a person who gives value without knowledge to the contrary, so long as and to the extent that a limitation on that authority is not then contained in another filed statement. A filed cancellation of a limitation on authority revives the previous grant of authority.

(2) A grant of authority to transfer real property held in the name of the partnership contained in a filed statement of partnership authority, whether or not a certified copy of the filed statement is recorded, is conclusive in favor of a person who gives value without knowledge to the contrary, so long as and to the extent that a certified copy of a filed statement containing a limitation on that authority is not then of record. The recording of a certified copy of a filed cancellation of a limitation on authority revives the previous grant of authority.

(e) A person not a partner is deemed to know of a limitation on the authority of a partner to transfer real property held in the name of the partnership only if a certified copy of the filed statement containing the limitation on authority is of record.

(f) Except as otherwise provided in subsections (d) and (e) and sections 323A.0704 and 323A.0805, a person not a partner is not deemed to know of a limitation on the authority of a partner merely because the limitation is contained in a filed statement.

* * * *

323A.0305 PARTNERSHIP LIABLE FOR PARTNER'S ACTIONABLE CONDUCT.

(a) A partnership is liable for loss or injury caused to a person, or for a penalty incurred, as a result of a wrongful act or omission, or other actionable conduct, of a partner acting in the ordinary course of business of the partnership or with authority of the partnership.

(b) If, in the course of the partnership's business or while acting with authority of the partnership, a partner receives or causes the partnership to receive money or property of a person not a partner, and the money or property is misapplied by a partner, the partnership is liable for the loss.

323A.0306 PARTNER'S LIABILITY.

(a) Except as otherwise provided in subsections (b) and (c), all partners are liable jointly and severally for all obligations of the partnership unless otherwise agreed by the claimant or provided by law.

(b) A person admitted as a partner into an existing partnership is not personally liable for any partnership obligation incurred before the person's admission as a partner.

(c) An obligation of a partnership incurred while the partnership is a limited liability partnership, whether arising in contract, tort, or otherwise, is solely the obligation of the partnership. A partner is not personally liable, directly or indirectly, by way of contribution or otherwise, for such an obligation solely by reason of being or so acting as a partner. This subsection applies notwithstanding anything inconsistent in the partnership agreement that existed immediately before the vote required to become a limited liability partnership under section 323A.1001(b).

* * * *

323A.0307 ACTIONS BY AND AGAINST PARTNERSHIP AND PARTNERS.

(a) A partnership may sue and be sued in the name of the partnership.

* * * *

(d) A judgment creditor of a partner may not levy execution against the assets of the partner to satisfy a judgment based on a claim against the partnership unless the partner is personally liable for the claim under section 323A.0306; and

(1) a judgment based on the same claim has been obtained against the partnership and a writ of execution on the judgment has been returned unsatisfied in whole or in part;

(2) the partnership is a debtor in bankruptcy;

(3) the partner has agreed that the creditor need not exhaust partnership assets;

(4) a court grants permission to the judgment creditor to levy execution against the assets of a partner based on a finding that partnership assets subject to execution are clearly insufficient to satisfy

the judgment, that exhaustion of partnership assets is excessively burdensome, or that the grant of permission is an appropriate exercise of the court's equitable powers; or

(5) liability is imposed on the partner by law or contract independent of the existence of the partnership.

(e) This section applies to any partnership liability or obligation resulting from a representation by a partner or purported partner under section 323A.0308.

323A.0308 LIABILITY OF PURPORTED PARTNER.

(a) If a person, by words or conduct, purports to be a partner, or consents to being represented by another as a partner, in a partnership or with one or more persons not partners, the purported partner is liable to a person to whom the representation is made, if that person, relying on the representation, enters into a transaction with the actual or purported partnership. If the representation, either by the purported partner or by a person with the purported partner's consent, is made in a public manner, the purported partner is liable to a person who relies upon the purported partnership even if the purported partner is not aware of being held out as a partner to the claimant. If partnership liability results, the purported partner is liable with respect to that liability as if the purported partner were a partner. If no partnership liability results, the purported partner is liable with respect to that liability jointly and severally with any other person consenting to the representation.

(b) If a person is thus represented to be a partner in an existing partnership, or with one or more persons not partners, the purported partner is an agent of persons consenting to the representation to bind them to the same extent and in the same manner as if the purported partner were a partner, with respect to persons who enter into transactions in reliance upon the representation. If all of the partners of the existing partnership consent to the representation, a partnership act or obligation results. If fewer than all of the partners of the existing partnership consent to the representation, the person acting and the partners consenting to the representation are jointly and severally liable.

* * * *

323A.0401 PARTNER'S RIGHTS AND DUTIES.

* * * *

(b) Each partner is entitled to an equal share of the partnership profits and is chargeable with a share of the partnership losses in proportion to the partner's share of the profits.

* * * *

(f) Each partner has equal rights in the management and conduct of the partnership business.

(g) A partner may use or possess partnership property only on behalf of the partnership.

(h) A partner is not entitled to remuneration for services performed for the partnership, except for reasonable compensation for services rendered in winding up the business of the partnership.

(i) A person may become a partner only with the consent of all of the partners.

(j) A difference arising as to a matter in the ordinary course of business of a partnership may be decided by a majority of the partners. An act outside the ordinary course of business of a partnership and an amendment to the partnership agreement may be undertaken only with the consent of all of the partners.

* * * *

323A.0403 PARTNER'S RIGHTS AND DUTIES WITH RESPECT TO INFORMATION.

(a) A partnership shall keep its books and records, if any, at its chief executive office.

(b) A partnership shall provide partners and their agents and attorneys access to its books and records. It shall provide former partners and their agents and attorneys access to books and records pertaining to the period during which they were partners. The right of access provides the opportunity to inspect and copy books and records during ordinary business hours. A partnership may impose a reasonable charge, covering the costs of labor and material, for copies of documents furnished.

* * * *

323A.0404 GENERAL STANDARDS OF PARTNER'S CONDUCT.

(a) The only fiduciary duties a partner owes to the partnership and the other partners are the duty of loyalty and the duty of care set forth in subsections (b) and (c).

(b) A partner's duty of loyalty to the partnership and the other partners is limited to the following:

(1) to account to the partnership and hold as trustee for it any property, profit, or benefit derived by the partner in the conduct and winding up of the partnership business or derived from a use by the partner of partnership property, including the appropriation of a partnership opportunity;

(2) to refrain from dealing with the partnership in the conduct or winding up of the partnership business as or on behalf of a party having an interest adverse to the partnership; and

(3) to refrain from competing with the partnership in the conduct of the partnership business before the dissolution of the partnership.

(c) A partner's duty of care to the partnership and the other partners in the conduct and winding up of the partnership business is limited to refraining from engaging in grossly negligent or reckless conduct, intentional misconduct, or a knowing violation of law.

(d) A partner shall discharge the duties to the partnership and the other partners under this chapter or under the partnership agreement and exercise any rights consistently with the obligation of good faith and fair dealing.

(e) A partner does not violate a duty or obligation under this chapter or under the partnership agreement merely because the partner's conduct furthers the partner's own interest.

* * * *

323A.0405 ACTIONS BY PARTNERSHIP AND PARTNERS.

(a) A partnership may maintain an action against a partner for a breach of the partnership agreement, or for the violation of a duty to the partnership, causing harm to the partnership.

(b) A partner may maintain an action against the partnership or another partner for legal or equitable relief, with or without an accounting as to partnership business, to:

(1) enforce the partner's rights under the partnership agreement;

(2) enforce the partner's rights under this chapter, including:

(i) the partner's rights under section 323A.0401, 323A.0403, or 323A.0404;

(ii) the partner's right on dissociation to have the partner's interest in the partnership purchased pursuant to section 323A.0701 or enforce any other right under article 6 or 7; or

(iii) the partner's right to compel a dissolution and winding up of the partnership business under section 323A.0801 or enforce any other right under article 8; or

(3) enforce the rights and otherwise protect the interests of the partner, including rights and interests arising independently of the partnership relationship.

* * * *

323A.0501 PARTNER NOT CO-OWNER OF PARTNERSHIP PROPERTY.

A partner is not a co-owner of partnership property and has no interest in partnership property which can be transferred, either voluntarily or involuntarily.

323A.0502 PARTNER'S TRANSFERABLE INTEREST IN PARTNERSHIP.

The only transferable interest of a partner in the partnership is the partner's share of the profits and losses of the partnership and the partner's right to receive distributions. The interest is personal property.

323A.0503 TRANSFER OF PARTNER'S TRANSFERABLE INTEREST.

(a) A transfer, in whole or in part, of a partner's transferable interest in the partnership:

(1) is permissible;

(2) does not by itself cause the partner's dissociation or a dissolution and winding up of the partnership business; and

(3) does not, as against the other partners or the partnership, entitle the transferee, during the continuance of the partnership, to participate in the management or conduct of the partnership business, to require access to information concerning partnership transactions, or to inspect or copy the partnership books or records.

* * * *

323A.0504 PARTNER'S TRANSFERABLE INTEREST SUBJECT TO CHARGING ORDER.

(a) On application by a judgment creditor of a partner or of a partner's transferee, a court having jurisdiction may charge the transferable interest of the judgment debtor to satisfy the judgment. The court may appoint a receiver of the share of the distributions due or to become due to the judgment debtor in respect of the partnership and make all other orders, directions, accounts, and inquiries the judgment debtor might have made or which the circumstances of the case may require.

* * * *

323A.0601 EVENTS CAUSING PARTNER'S DISSOCIATION.

A partner is dissociated from a partnership upon the occurrence of any of the following events:

(1) the partnership's having notice of the partner's express will to withdraw as a partner or on a later date specified by the partner;

(2) an event agreed to in the partnership agreement as causing the partner's dissociation;

(3) the partner's expulsion pursuant to the partnership agreement;

(4) the partner's expulsion by the unanimous vote of the other partners if:

(i) it is unlawful to carry on the partnership business with that partner;

(ii) there has been a transfer of all or substantially all of that partner's transferable interest in the partnership, other than a transfer for security purposes, or a court order charging the partner's interest, which has not been foreclosed;

(iii) within 90 days after the partnership notifies a corporate partner that it will be expelled because it has filed a certificate of dissolution or the equivalent, its charter has been revoked, or its right to conduct business has been suspended by the jurisdiction of its incorporation, there is no revocation of the certificate of dissolution or no reinstatement of its charter or its right to conduct business; or

(iv) a partnership that is a partner has been dissolved and its business is being wound up;

(5) on application by the partnership or another partner, the partner's expulsion by judicial determination because:

(i) the partner engaged in wrongful conduct that adversely and materially affected the partnership business;

(ii) the partner willfully or persistently committed a material breach of the partnership agreement or of a duty owed to the partnership or the other partners under section 323A.0404; or

(iii) the partner engaged in conduct relating to the partnership business which makes it not reasonably practicable to carry on the business in partnership with the partner;

(6) the partner's:

(i) becoming a debtor in bankruptcy;

(ii) executing an assignment for the benefit of creditors;

(iii) seeking, consenting to, or acquiescing in the appointment of a trustee, receiver, or liquidator of that partner or of all or substantially all of that partner's property; or

(iv) failing, within 90 days after the appointment, to have vacated or stayed the appointment of a trustee, receiver, or liquidator of the partner or of all or substantially all of the partner's property obtained without the partner's consent or acquiescence, or failing within 90 days after the expiration of a stay to have the appointment vacated;

(7) in the case of a partner who is an individual:

(i) the partner's death;

(ii) the appointment of a guardian or general conservator for the partner; or

(iii) a judicial determination that the partner has otherwise become incapable of performing the partner's duties under the partnership agreement;

* * * *

323A.0602 PARTNER'S POWER TO DISSOCIATE; WRONGFUL DISSOCIATION.

(a) A partner has the power to dissociate at any time, rightfully or wrongfully, by express will pursuant to section 323A.0601(1).

(b) A partner's dissociation is wrongful only if:

(1) it is in breach of an express provision of the partnership agreement; or

(2) in the case of a partnership for a definite term or particular undertaking, before the expiration of the term or the completion of the undertaking:

(i) the partner withdraws by express will, unless the withdrawal follows within 90 days after another partner's dissociation by death or

otherwise under section 323A.0601(6) to (10) or wrongful dissociation under this subsection;

(ii) the partner is expelled by judicial determination under section 323A.0601(5);

(iii) the partner is dissociated by becoming a debtor in bankruptcy; or

(iv) in the case of a partner who is not an individual, trust other than a business trust, or estate, the partner is expelled or otherwise dissociated because it willfully dissolved or terminated.

(c) A partner who wrongfully dissociates is liable to the partnership and to the other partners for damages caused by the dissociation. The liability is in addition to any other obligation of the partner to the partnership or to the other partners.

323A.0603 EFFECT OF PARTNER'S DISSOCIATION.

(a) If a partner's dissociation results in a dissolution and winding up of the partnership business, article 8 applies; otherwise, article 7 applies.

(b) Upon a partner's dissociation:

(1) the partner's right to participate in the management and conduct of the partnership business terminates, except as otherwise provided in section 323A.0803;

(2) the partner's duty of loyalty under section 323A.0404(b)(3) terminates; and

(3) the partner's duty of loyalty under section 323A.0404(b)(1) and (2) and duty of care under section 323A.0404(c) continue only with regard to matters arising and events occurring before the partner's dissociation, unless the partner participates in winding up the partnership's business pursuant to section 323A.0803.

323A.0701 PURCHASE OF DISSOCIATED PARTNER'S INTEREST.

(a) If a partner is dissociated from a partnership without resulting in a dissolution and winding up of the partnership business under section 323A.0801, the partnership shall cause the dissociated partner's interest in the partnership to be purchased for a buyout price determined pursuant to subsection (b).

(b) The buyout price of a dissociated partner's interest is the amount that would have been distributable to the dissociating partner under section 323A.0807(b), if, on the date of dissociation, the assets of the partnership were sold at a price equal to the greater of the liquidation value or the value based on a sale of the entire business as a going concern without the dissociated partner and the partnership were wound up as of that date. Interest must be paid from the date of dissociation to the date of payment.

(c) Damages for wrongful dissociation under section 323A.0602(b), and all other amounts owing, whether or not presently due, from the dissociated partner to the partnership, must be offset against the buyout price. Interest must be paid from the date the amount owed becomes due to the date of payment.

* * * *

323A.0702 DISSOCIATED PARTNER'S POWER TO BIND AND LIABILITY TO PARTNERSHIP.

(a) For two years after a partner dissociates without resulting in a dissolution and winding up of the partnership business, the partnership, including a surviving partnership under article 9, is bound by an act of the dissociated partner which would have bound the partnership under section 323A.0301 before dissociation only if at the time of entering into the transaction the other party:

(1) reasonably believed that the dissociated partner was then a partner;

(2) did not have notice of the partner's dissociation; and

(3) is not deemed to have had knowledge under section 323A.0303(e) or notice under section 323A.0704(c).

(b) A dissociated partner is liable to the partnership for any damage caused to the partnership arising from an obligation incurred by the dissociated partner after dissociation for which the partnership is liable under subsection (a).

323A.0703 DISSOCIATED PARTNER'S LIABILITY TO OTHER PERSONS.

(a) A partner's dissociation does not of itself discharge the partner's liability for a partnership obligation incurred before dissociation. A dissociated partner is not liable for a partnership obligation incurred after dissociation except as otherwise provided in subsection (b).

(b) A partner who dissociates without resulting in a dissolution and winding up of the partnership business is liable as a partner to the other party in a transaction entered into by the partnership, or a surviving partnership under article 9, within two years after the partner's dissociation, only if the partner is liable for the obligation under section 323A.0306 and at the time of entering into the transaction the other party:

(1) reasonably believed that the dissociated partner was then a partner;

(2) did not have notice of the partner's dissociation; and

(3) is not deemed to have had knowledge under section 323A.0303(e) or notice under section 323A.0704(c).

* * * *

323A.0704 STATEMENT OF DISSOCIATION.

(a) A dissociated partner or the partnership may file a statement of dissociation stating the name of the partnership and that the partner is dissociated from the partnership.

(b) A statement of dissociation is a limitation on the authority of a dissociated partner for the purposes of section 323A.0303(d) and (e).

(c) For the purposes of sections 323A.0702(a)(3) and 323A.0703(b)(3), a person not a partner is deemed to have

notice of the dissociation 90 days after the statement of dissociation is filed.

* * * *

323A.0801 EVENTS CAUSING DISSOLUTION AND WINDING UP OF PARTNERSHIP BUSINESS.

A partnership is dissolved, and its business must be wound up, only upon the occurrence of any of the following events:

(1) in a partnership at will, the partnership's having notice from a partner, other than a partner who is dissociated under section 323A.0601(2) to (10), of that partner's express will to withdraw as a partner, or on a later date specified by the partner;

(2) in a partnership for a definite term or particular undertaking:

(i) within 90 days after a partner's dissociation by death or otherwise under section 323A.0601(6) to (10) or wrongful dissociation under section 323A.0602(b), the express will of at least half of the remaining partners to dissolve the partnership business, for which purpose a partner's rightful dissociation pursuant to section 323A.0602(b)(2)(i) constitutes the expression of that partner's will to dissolve;

(ii) the express will of all of the partners to wind up the partnership business; or

(iii) the expiration of the term or the completion of the undertaking;

(3) an event agreed to in the partnership agreement resulting in the winding up of the partnership business;

(4) an event that makes it unlawful for all or substantially all of the business of the partnership to be continued, but a cure of illegality within 90 days after notice to the partnership of the event is effective retroactively to the date of the event for purposes of this section;

(5) on application by a partner, a judicial determination that:

(i) the economic purpose of the partnership is likely to be unreasonably frustrated;

(ii) another partner has engaged in conduct relating to the partnership business which makes it not reasonably practicable to carry on the business in partnership with that partner; or

(iii) it is not otherwise reasonably practicable to carry on the partnership business in conformity with the partnership agreement; or

* * * *

323A.0802 PARTNERSHIP CONTINUES AFTER DISSOLUTION.

(a) Subject to subsection (b), a partnership continues after dissolution only for the purpose of winding up its business. The partnership is terminated when the winding up of its business is completed.

(b) At any time after the dissolution of a partnership and before the winding up of its business is completed, all of the partners, including any dissociating partner other than a wrongfully dissociating partner, may waive the right to have the partnership's business wound up and the partnership terminated. In that event:

(1) the partnership resumes carrying on its business as if dissolution had never occurred, and any liability incurred by the partnership or a partner after the dissolution and before the waiver is determined as if dissolution had never occurred; and

(2) the rights of a third party accruing under section 323A.0804(1), or arising out of conduct in reliance on the dissolution before the third party knew or received a notification of the waiver may not be adversely affected.

323A.0803 RIGHT TO WIND UP PARTNERSHIP BUSINESS.

(a) After dissolution, a partner who has not wrongfully dissociated may participate in winding up the partnership's business, but on application of any partner, partner's legal representative, or transferee, the court, for good cause shown, may order judicial supervision of the winding up.

(b) The legal representative of the last surviving partner may wind up a partnership's business.

(c) A person winding up a partnership's business may preserve the partnership business or property as a going concern for a reasonable time, prosecute and defend actions and proceedings, whether civil, criminal, or administrative, settle and close the partnership's business, dispose of and transfer the partnership's property, discharge the partnership's liabilities, distribute the assets of the partnership pursuant to section 323A.0807, settle disputes by mediation or arbitration, and perform other necessary acts.

323A.0804 PARTNER'S POWER TO BIND PARTNERSHIP AFTER DISSOLUTION.

Subject to section 323A.0805, a partnership is bound by a partner's act after dissolution that:

(1) is appropriate for winding up the partnership business; or

(2) would have bound the partnership under section 323A.0301 before dissolution, if the other party to the transaction did not have notice of the dissolution.

323A.0805 STATEMENT OF DISSOLUTION.

(a) After dissolution, a partner who has not wrongfully dissociated may file a statement of dissolution stating the name of the partnership and that the partnership has dissolved and is winding up its business.

(b) A filed statement of dissolution cancels a filed statement of partnership authority for the purposes of section 323A.0303(d)(1) and, if recorded, is a limitation on authority for the purposes of sections 323A.0303(d)(2) and 323A.0303(e).

(c) For the purposes of sections 323A.0301 and 323A.0804, a person not a partner is deemed to have notice of the dissolution and the limitation on the partners' authority as a result of the statement of dissolution 90 days after it is filed.

* * * *

323A.0807 SETTLEMENT OF ACCOUNTS AND CONTRIBUTIONS AMONG PARTNERS.

(a) In winding up a partnership's business, the assets of the partnership, including the contributions of the partners required by this section, must be applied to discharge its obligations to creditors, including, to the extent permitted by law, partners who are creditors. Any surplus must be applied to pay in cash the net amount distributable to partners in accordance with their right to distributions under subsection (b).

(b) Each partner is entitled to a settlement of all partnership accounts upon winding up the partnership business. In settling accounts among the partners, profits and losses that result from the liquidation of the partnership assets must be credited and charged to the partners' accounts. The partnership shall make a distribution to a partner in an amount equal to any excess of the credits over the charges in the partner's account. A partner shall contribute to the partnership an amount equal to any excess of the charges over the credits in the partner's account but excluding from the calculation charges attributable to an obligation for which the partner is not personally liable under section 323A.0306.

(c) If a partner fails to contribute the full amount required under subsection (b), all of the other partners shall contribute, in the proportions in which those partners share partnership losses, the additional amount necessary to satisfy the partnership obligations for which they are personally liable under section 323A.0306. A partner or partner's legal representative may recover from the other partners any contributions the partner makes to the extent the amount contributed exceeds that partner's share of the partnership obligations for which the partner is personally liable under section 323A.0306.

(d) After the settlement of accounts, each partner shall contribute, in the proportion in which the partner shares partnership losses, the amount necessary to satisfy partnership obligations that were not known at the time of the settlement and for which the partner is personally liable under section 323A.0306.

* * * *

323A.1001 STATEMENT OF QUALIFICATION.

(a) A partnership may become a limited liability partnership pursuant to this section.

(b) The terms and conditions on which a partnership becomes a limited liability partnership must be approved by the vote necessary to amend the partnership agreement except, in the case of a partnership agreement that expressly considers obligations to contribute to the partnership, the vote necessary to amend those provisions.

(c) After the approval required by subsection (b), a partnership may become a limited liability partnership by filing a statement of qualification. The statement must contain:

(1) the name of the partnership;

(2) the street address, including the zip code, of the partnership's chief executive office and, if different, the street address, including the zip code, of an office in this state, if any;

(3) if the partnership does not have an office in this state, the name and street address, including the zip code, of the partnership's agent for service of process. If an agent for service of process is listed, the limited liability partnership shall comply with section 5.36;

(4) a statement that the partnership elects to be a limited liability partnership; and

(5) a deferred effective date, if any.

* * * *

323A.1002 NAME.

The name of a limited liability partnership must meet the standard found in section 302A.115, except that the name must include "Registered Limited Liability Partnership," "Limited Liability Partnership," "R.L.L.P.," "L.L.P.," "RLLP," or "LLP" rather than the corporate designators found in section 302A.115, subdivision 1, paragraph (b).

323A.1003 ANNUAL RENEWAL.

(a) Each calendar year beginning in the calendar year following the calendar year in which a partnership files a statement of qualification or in which a foreign partnership becomes authorized to transact business in this state, the secretary of state may send annually to the partnership or foreign partnership, using the information provided by the limited liability partnership pursuant to section 5.002 or 5.34 or the limited liability partnership statement of qualification, a notice. The notice will announce the need to file the annual renewal and will inform the partnership or foreign partnership that the annual renewal may be filed online and that paper filings may also be made and that failure to file the notice by December 31 will result in the revocation of the statement of qualification of this limited liability partnership.

(b) A limited liability partnership, and a foreign limited liability partnership authorized to transact business in this state, shall file an annual renewal in the office of the secretary of state which contains the information required by section 5.34.

(c) An annual renewal must be filed once each calendar year beginning in the year following the calendar year in which a partnership files a statement of qualification or a foreign partnership becomes authorized to transact business in this state.

* * * *

323A.1101 LAW GOVERNING FOREIGN LIMITED LIABILITY PARTNERSHIP.

(a) The law under which a foreign limited liability partnership is formed governs relations among the partners and between the partners and the partnership and the liability of partners for obligations of the partnership.

* * * *

323A.1102 STATEMENT OF FOREIGN QUALIFICATION.

(a) Before transacting business in this state, a foreign limited liability partnership must file a statement of foreign qualification. The statement must contain:

(1) the name of the foreign limited liability partnership which satisfies the requirements of the state or other jurisdiction under whose law it is formed and ends with "Registered Limited Liability Partnership," "Limited Liability Partnership," "R.L.L.P.," "L.L.P.," "RLLP," or "LLP." If this name is unavailable, the foreign limited liability partnership may use an alternate name to transact business in the state if it delivers to the secretary of state a certified copy of the resolution of the partners adopting the alternate name;

(2) the street address, including the zip code, of the partnership's chief executive office and, if different, the street address, including the zip code, of an office of the partnership in this state, if any;

(3) if there is no office of the partnership in this state, the name and street address, including the zip code, of the partnership's agent for service of process. If an agent for service of process is listed, the limited liability partnership shall comply with section 5.36;

(4) a deferred effective date, if any;

* * * *

323A.1104 ACTIVITIES NOT CONSTITUTING TRANSACTING BUSINESS.

(a) Activities of a foreign limited liability partnership which do not constitute transacting business for the purpose of this article include:

(1) maintaining, defending, or settling an action or proceeding;

(2) holding meetings of its partners or carrying on any other activity concerning its internal affairs;

(3) maintaining bank accounts;

(4) maintaining offices or agencies for the transfer, exchange, and registration of the partnership's own securities or maintaining trustees or depositories with respect to those securities;

(5) selling through independent contractors;

(6) soliciting or obtaining orders, whether by mail or through employees or agents or otherwise, if the

orders require acceptance outside this state before they become contracts;

(7) creating or acquiring indebtedness, with or without a mortgage, or other security interest in property;

(8) collecting debts, including foreclosing mortgages, canceling contracts for deed, enforcing other security interests on property securing debts, accepting deeds or other instruments of title from debtors in lieu of foreclosure, cancellation or other enforcement, and holding, protecting, and maintaining property so acquired;

(9) conducting an isolated transaction that is completed within 30 days and is not one in the course of similar transactions; and

(10) transacting business in interstate commerce.

(b) For purposes of this article, the ownership in this state of income-producing real property or tangible personal property, other than property excluded under subsection (a), constitutes transacting business in this state.

* * * *

Section 101.

48-2a-101. Definitions.

As used in this chapter, unless the context otherwise requires:

(1) "Certificate of limited partnership" means:

    (a) a certificate referred to in Section 48-2a-201; and

    (b) a certificate as amended or restated.

(2) "Contribution" means any of the following that a partner contributes to a limited partnership in the partner's capacity as a partner:

    (a) cash; (b) property; (c) a service rendered; or (d) a promissory note or other binding obligation to: (i) contribute cash; (ii) contribute property; or (iii) perform a service.

(3) "Division" means the Division of Corporations and Commercial Code of the Department of Commerce.

(4) "Event of withdrawal of a general partner" means an event that causes a person to cease to be a general partner as provided in Section 48-2a-402.

(5) "Foreign limited partnership" means a partnership:

    (a) formed under the laws of a state other than this state; and (b) having as partners: (i) one or more general partners; and (ii) one or more limited partners.

(6) "General partner" means a person who is:

    (a) admitted to a limited partnership as a general partner in accordance with the partnership agreement; and (b) named in the certificate of limited partnership as a general partner.

(7) "Limited partner" means a person who is admitted to a limited partnership as a limited partner in accordance with the partnership agreement.

(8) "Limited partnership" and "domestic limited partnership" mean a partnership:

    (a) formed by two or more persons under the laws of this state; and (b) having: (i) one or more general partners; and (ii) one or more limited partners.

(9) "Partner" means a limited or a general partner.

(10) "Partnership agreement" means a valid agreement, written or oral, of the partners as to the affairs of a limited partnership and the conduct of its business.

(11) "Partnership interest" means: (a) a partner's share of the profits and losses of a limited partnership; and (b) the right to receive distributions of partnership assets.

(12) "Person" means an individual, general partnership, limited partnership, limited association, domestic or foreign trust, estate, association, or corporation.

* * * *

48-2a-102. Name.

(1) The name of each limited partnership as set forth in its certificate of limited partnership:

    (a) shall contain the terms: (i) "limited partnership"; (ii) "limited";(iii) "L.P."; or (iv) "Ltd.";

    (b) may not contain the name of a limited partner unless: (i) it is the name of a general partner; (ii) it is the corporate name of a corporate general partner; or (iii) the business of the limited partnership had been carried on under that name before the admission of that limited partner;

    (c) may not contain: (i) the words: (A) "association"; (B) "corporation"; or (C) "incorporated"; (ii) any abbreviation of a word listed in this Subsection (1)(c); or (iii) any word or abbreviation that is of like import to the words listed in Subsection (1)(c)(i) in any other language;

    (d) without the written consent of the United States Olympic Committee, may not contain the words: (i) "Olympic"; (ii) "Olympiad"; or (iii) "Citius Altius Fortius"; and

    (e) without the written consent of the Division of Consumer Protection issued in accordance with Section 13-34-114, may not contain the words: (i) "university"; (ii) "college"; or (iii) "institute" or "institution."

(2) (a) A person or entity other than a limited partnership formed or registered under this title may not use in

its name in this state any of the terms: (i) "limited"; (ii) "limited partnership"; (iii) "Ltd."; or (iv) "L.P."

(b) Notwithstanding Subsection (2)(a): (i) a foreign corporation whose actual name includes the word "limited" or "Ltd." may use its actual name in this state if it also uses: (A) "corporation"; (B) "incorporated"; or (C) any abbreviation of a word listed in this Subsection (2)(b)(i); (ii) a limited liability company may use in its name in this state the terms: (A) "limited"; (B) "limited company"; (C) "L.C."; (D) "L.L.C."; (E) "LC"; or (F) "LLC"; and (iii) a limited liability partnership may use the terms "limited liability partnership," "L.L.P.," or "LLP" in the manner allowed in Section 48-1-45.

(3) Except as authorized by Subsection (4), the name of a limited partnership must be distinguishable as defined in Subsection (5) upon the records of the division from:

(a) the name of any limited partnership formed or authorized to transact business in this state;

(b) the corporate name of any corporation incorporated or authorized to transact business in this state;

(c) any limited partnership name reserved under this chapter;

(d) any corporate name reserved under Title 16, Chapter 10a, Utah Revised Business Corporation Act;

(e) any fictitious name adopted by a foreign corporation or limited partnership authorized to transact business in this state because its real name is unavailable;

(f) any corporate name of a not-for-profit corporation incorporated or authorized to transact business in this state; and

(g) any assumed business name, trademark, or service mark registered by the division.

(4) (a) A limited partnership may apply to the division for approval to file its certificate under, or to reserve, a name that is not distinguishable upon the division's records from one or more of the names described in Subsection (3).

(b) The division shall approve of the name for which application is made under Subsection (4)(a) if: (i) the other person whose name is not distinguishable from the name under which the applicant desires to file: (A) consents to the filing in writing; and (B) submits an undertaking in a form satisfactory to the division to change its name to a name that is distinguishable from the name of the applicant; or (ii) the applicant delivers to the division a certified copy of the final judgment of a court of competent jurisdiction establishing the applicant's right to use in this state the name for which the application is made.

(5) A name is distinguishable from other names, trademarks, and service marks registered with the division if it contains one or more different letters or numerals from other names upon the division's records.

* * * *

48-2a-103. Reservation of Name.

(1) The exclusive right to a name may be reserved by:

(a) any person intending to organize a limited partnership under this chapter and to adopt that name;

(b) any domestic limited partnership or any foreign limited partnership registered in this state which, in either case, intends to adopt that name;

(c) any foreign limited partnership intending to register in this state and intending to adopt that name; and

(d) any person intending to organize a foreign limited partnership and intending to have it register in this state and adopt that name.

(2) The reservation shall be made by filing with the division an application, executed under penalty of perjury by the applicant, to reserve a specified name. If the division finds that the name is available for use by a domestic or a foreign limited partnership, it shall reserve the name exclusively for the applicant for a period of 120 days. The name reservation may be renewed for any number of subsequent periods of 120 days. The exclusive right to a reserved name may be transferred to any other person by filing with the division a notice of the transfer executed under penalty of perjury by the applicant for whom the name was reserved and specifying the name and address of the transferee.

* * * *

48-2a-105. Records to Be Kept.

Each limited partnership shall keep at its principal place of business, as specified in the certificate of limited partnership required by Section 48-2a-201, the following:

(1) a current list in alphabetical order of the full name and last known business address of each partner, separately identifying the general partners and the limited partners;

(2) a copy of the certificate of limited partnership and all certificates of amendment thereto, together with the executed copies of any powers of attorney pursuant to which the certificate has been executed;

(3) copies of the limited partnership's federal, state, and local income tax returns and reports, if any, for the three most recent years;

(4) copies of any then effective written limited partnership agreements and of any financial statements of the limited partnership for the three most recent years; and

(5) unless contained in a written partnership agreement, a writing setting out:

(a) the amount of cash and a description and statement of the agreed value of the other property or services contributed by each partner and which each partner has agreed to contribute;

(b) the times at which or events on the happening of which any additional contributions agreed to be made by each partner are to be made;

(c) any right of a partner to receive, or of a general partner to make, distributions to a partner which include a return of all or any of the partner's contribution; and

(d) any events upon the happening of which the limited partnership is to be dissolved and its affairs wound up.

48-2a-106. Nature of Business.

A limited partnership may carry on any business, except as otherwise prohibited by applicable provision of the Utah Code.

48-2a-107. Business Transactions of Partner with Partnership.

Except as provided in the partnership agreement, a partner may lend money to and transact other business with the limited partnership and, subject to other applicable law, has the same rights and obligations with respect thereto as a person who is not a partner.

* * * *

Section 201
48-2a-201. Certificate of Limited Partnerships.

(1) In order to form a limited partnership a certificate of limited partnership must be executed and filed with the division, setting forth:

(a) the name of the limited partnership;

(b) the information required by Subsection 16-17-203(1);

(c) the name and business address of each general partner;

(d) (i) the latest date upon which the limited partnership is to dissolve, if the duration of the limited partnership is to be limited; or (ii) a statement to the effect that the limited partnership is to have perpetual duration; and

(e) any other matters the general partners determine to include.

(2) A limited partnership is formed:

(a) at the time of the filing of the certificate of limited partnership with the division as evidenced by the stamped copy returned by the division pursuant to Subsection 48-2a-206(1); or

(b) at any later time specified in the certificate of limited partnership.

48-2a-202. Amendment to Certificate.

(1) (a) A certificate of limited partnership is amended by filing a certificate of amendment with the division.

(b) A certificate of amendment filed under this Subsection (1) shall state: (i) the name of the limited partnership; (ii) the date of filing the certificate; and (iii) the amendment to the certificate.

(2) An amendment to a certificate of limited partnership shall be filed within 60 days after the day the limited partnership continues business under Section 48-2a-801 after an event of withdrawal of a general partner.

(3) A general partner who knows or reasonably should know that any statement in a certificate of limited partnership or a certificate of amendment to a certificate of limited partnership was false at the time the certificate was executed making the certificate inaccurate in any respect, shall promptly amend the certificate.

(4) A certificate of limited partnership may be amended at any time for any other proper purpose the general partners determine.

(5) A person may not be held liable because an amendment to a certificate of limited partnership has not been filed under Subsection (2) if the amendment is filed within the 60 days specified in Subsection (2).

(6) A restated certificate of limited partnership may be executed and filed in the same manner as a certificate of amendment.

* * * *

48-2a-203. Voluntary Cancellation of Certificate.

A certificate of limited partnership shall be canceled upon the dissolution and the completion of winding up of the partnership or at any other time there are no limited partners. A certificate of cancellation shall be filed with the division and shall set forth:

(1) the name of the limited partnership;

(2) the date of filing of its certificate of limited partnership;

(3) the reason for filing the certificate of cancellation;

(4) the effective date of cancellation, which shall be a date certain, if the cancellation is not to be effective upon the filing of the certificate; and

(5) any other information the general partners filing the certificate determine.

* * * *

48-2a-204. Execution of Certificates.

(1) Each certificate required by this chapter to be filed with the division shall be executed in the following manner:

(a) an original certificate of limited partnership must be signed under penalty of perjury by all general partners;

(b) a certificate of amendment must be signed under penalty of perjury by at least one general partner and by each other general partner designated in the certificate as a new general partner; and

(c) a certificate of cancellation must be signed under penalty of perjury by all general partners.

(2) Any person may sign a certificate by an attorney-in-fact, but a power of attorney to sign a certificate relating to the admission of a general partner must specifically describe the admission.

48-2a-205. Execution by Judicial Act.

If a person required by Section 48-2a-204 to execute any certificate fails or refuses to do so, any other person who is adversely affected by the failure or refusal may petition a district court having competent jurisdiction to direct the execution of the certificate. If the court finds that it is proper for the certificate to be executed and that any person so designated has failed or refused to execute the certificate, it shall order the division to record an appropriate certificate.

48-2a-206. Filing with the Division.

(1) An original and one copy of the certificate of limited partnership, and of any certificates of amendment or cancellation, or of any judicial decree of amendment or cancellation, shall be delivered to the division. A person who executes a certificate as an attorney-in-fact or fiduciary need not exhibit evidence of the person's authority as a prerequisite to filing. Unless the division finds that any certificate does not conform to law as to its form, upon receipt of all filing fees established under Section 63J-1-504, it shall:

(a) place on the original and the copy a stamp or seal indicating the time, day, month, and year of the filing, the director of the division's signature, and the division's seal, or facsimiles thereof, and the name of the division;

(b) file the signed original in its office; and

(c) return the stamped copy to the person who filed it or the person's representative.

(2) The stamped copy of the certificate of limited partnership and of any certificate of amendment or cancellation shall be conclusive evidence that all conditions precedent required for the formation, amendment, or cancellation of a limited partnership have been complied with and the limited partnership has been formed, amended, or canceled under this chapter, except with respect to an action for involuntary cancellation of the limited partnership's certificate for fraud under Subsection 48-2a-203.5(1)(a).

(3) Upon the filing of a certificate of amendment or judicial decree of amendment with the division, the certificate of limited partnership is amended as set forth in the certificate of amendment or judicial decree of amendment, and upon filing a certificate of cancellation, or of a judicial decree of cancellation, the division shall cancel the certificate of limited partnership effective as of the date the cancellation was filed or as of the date specified in the decree, unless a later effective date is specified in the cancellation.

48-2a-207. Liability for False Statement in Certificate.

If any certificate of limited partnership or certificate of amendment or cancellation contains a false statement, one who suffers loss by reasonable reliance on the statement may recover damages for the loss from:

(1) any person who executed the certificate, whether in his own name or on behalf of another as attorney-in-fact, who knew, or reasonably should have known, that the statement was false at the time the certificate was executed; and

(2) any general partner who at any time knew, or reasonably should have known, that the statement was false at the time the certificate was executed or knew or reasonably should have known that any arrangement or other fact described in the certificate had changed, making the statement inaccurate in any respect, if that general partner failed to cancel or amend the certificate, or to file a petition for its cancellation or amendment under Section 48-2a-202 or 48-2a-203, within 30 days of the date on which the general partner knew, or reasonably should have known, that the statement was false or that the change had occurred.

48-2a-208. Scope of Notice.

The fact that a certificate of limited partnership or amendment to a certificate of limited partnership is on file in the office of the division is notice that the partnership is a limited partnership and the persons designated as general partners are general partners, but it is not notice of any other fact.

48-2a-209. Delivery of Certificates to Limited Partners.

Upon the return by the division pursuant to Section 48-2a-206 of a stamped copy of any certificate, the general partners shall promptly deliver or mail a copy of the certificate of limited partnership and each certificate of amendment or cancellation to each limited partner unless the partnership agreement provides otherwise.

* * * *

Section 301

48-2a-301. Admission of Additional Limited Partners.

(1) A person becomes a limited partner on the later of:

(a) the date the original certificate of limited partnership is filed; or

(b) the date stated in the records of the limited partnership as the date that person becomes a limited partner.

(2) After the filing of a limited partnership's original certificate of limited partnership, a person may be admitted as an additional limited partner:

(a) in the case of a person acquiring a partnership interest directly from the limited partnership or in the case of an assignee of a partnership interest of a partner who does not have authority, as provided in Section 48-2a-704, to grant the assignee the right to become a limited partner, upon compliance with the partnership agreement or, if the partnership agreement does not so provide, upon the written consent of all partners; and

(b) in the case of an assignee of a partnership interest of a partner who has the authority, as provided in Section 48-2a-704, to grant the assignee the right to become a limited partner, upon the exercise of that authority and compliance with any conditions limiting the grant or exercise of the authority.

48-2a-302. Voting.

Subject to Section 48-2a-303, the partnership agreement may grant to all or a specified group of the limited partners the right to vote upon any matter on a per capita or other basis.

48-2a-303. Liability to Third Parties.

(1) Except as provided in Subsection (4), a limited partner is not liable for the obligations of a limited partnership unless he is also a general partner or, in addition to the exercise of his rights and powers as a limited partner, he participates in the control of the business. However, if the limited partner participates in the control of the business, he is liable only to persons who transact business with the limited partnership reasonably believing, based upon the limited partner's conduct, that the limited partner is a general partner.

(2) A limited partner does not participate in the control of the business within the meaning of Subsection (1) solely by doing one or more of the following:

(a) being a contractor for or an agent or employee of the limited partnership or of a general partner, or being an officer, director, or shareholder of a general partner that is a corporation;

(b) consulting with and advising a general partner with respect to the business of the limited partnership;

(c) acting as surety for the limited partnership or guaranteeing or assuming one or more specific obligations of the limited partnership;

(d) taking any action required or permitted by law to bring or pursue a derivative action in the right of the limited partnership;

(e) requesting or attending a meeting of partners;

(f) proposing, approving, or disapproving, by voting or otherwise, one or more of the following matters: (i) the dissolution and winding up of the limited partnership; (ii) the sale, exchange, lease, mortgage, pledge, or other transfer of all or substantially all of the assets of the limited partnership; (iii) the incurrence of indebtedness by the limited partnership other than in the ordinary course of its business; (iv) a change in the nature of the business; (v) the admission or removal of a general partner; (vi) the admission or removal of a limited partner; (vii) a transaction involving an actual or potential conflict of interest between a general partner and the limited partnership or the limited partners; (viii) an amendment to the partnership agreement or certificate of limited partnership; or (ix) matters related to the business of the limited partnership not otherwise enumerated in this subsection, which the partnership agreement states in writing may be subject to the approval or disapproval of limited partners;

(g) winding up the limited partnership pursuant to Section 48-2a-803; or

(h) exercising any right or power permitted limited partners under this chapter and not specifically enumerated in this subsection.

(3) The enumeration in Subsection (2) does not mean that the possession or exercise of any other powers by a limited partner constitutes participation by him in the business of the limited partnership.

(4) A limited partner who knowingly permits his name to be used in the name of the limited partnership, except under circumstances permitted by Subsection 48-2a-102(1)(b) is liable to creditors who extend credit to the limited partnership without actual knowledge that the limited partner is not a general partner.

48-2a-304. Person Erroneously Believing Himself to Be a Limited Partner.

(1) Except as provided in Subsection (2), a person who makes a contribution to a business enterprise and erroneously but in good faith believes that he has become a limited partner in the enterprise is not a general partner in the enterprise and is not bound by its obligations by reason of making the contribution, receiving distributions from the enterprise, or exercising any rights of a limited partner, if, on ascertaining the mistake, he:

(a) causes an appropriate certificate of limited partnership or a certificate of amendment to be executed and filed; or

(b) withdraws from future participation in the profits and losses of the enterprise by executing and filing with the division a certificate declaring withdrawal under this section; withdrawal under this subsection is without prejudice to the person's right to receive the return of his unreturned contribution.

(2) A person who makes a contribution under the circumstance described in Subsection (1) is liable as a general partner to any third party who transacts business with the enterprise before the person withdraws and an appropriate certificate is filed to show withdrawal or before an appropriate certificate is filed to show that he is not a general partner, but in either case only if the third party actually believed in good faith that the person was a general partner at the time of the transaction and acted in reasonable reliance on such belief and extended credit to the partnership in reasonable reliance on the credit of such person.

48-2a-305. Inspection of Records—Right to Information.

(1) Each limited partner has the right to:

(a) inspect and copy any of the partnership records required to be maintained by Section 48-2a-105;

(b) obtain from the general partners from time to time upon reasonable demand: (i) a copy of any of the partnership records required to be maintained by Section 48-2a-105; (ii) true and full information regarding the state of the business and financial condition of the limited partnership; (iii) promptly after becoming available, a copy of the limited partnership's federal, state, and local income tax returns for each year; and

(c) other information regarding the affairs of the limited partnership as is just and reasonable.

(2) Unless otherwise provided in the partnership agreement, the cost of providing the information described in this section shall be the responsibility of the partnership.

Section 401

48-2a-401. Admission of Additional General Partners.

After the filing of a limited partnership's original certificate of limited partnership, additional general partners may be admitted as provided in writing in the partnership agreement or, if the partnership agreement does not provide in writing for the admission of additional general partners, with the written consent of all partners.

48-2a-402. Events of Withdrawal.

Except as approved by the specific written consent of all partners at the time thereof with respect to Subsections (4) through (10), a person ceases to be a general partner of a limited partnership upon the happening of any of the following events of withdrawal:

(1) The general partner withdraws from the limited partnership as provided in Section 48-2a-602.

(2) The general partner ceases to be a member of the limited partnership as provided in Section 48-2a-702.

(3) The general partner is removed as a general partner in accordance with the partnership agreement.

(4) Unless otherwise provided in the partnership agreement, the general partner:

(a) makes an assignment for the benefit of creditors;

(b) files a voluntary petition in bankruptcy;

(c) is adjudicated as bankrupt or insolvent;

(d) files a petition or answer seeking for himself any reorganization, arrangement, composition, readjustment, liquidation, dissolution, or similar relief under any statute, law, or regulation;

(e) files an answer or other pleading admitting or failing to contest the material allegations of a petition filed against him in any proceeding described in Subsection (4)(d); or

(f) seeks, consents to, or acquiesces in the appointment of a trustee, receiver, or liquidator of the general partner or of all or any substantial part of his properties.

(5) Unless otherwise provided in the partnership agreement, if within 120 days after the commencement of any proceeding against the general partner seeking reorganization, arrangement, composition, readjustment, liquidation, dissolution, or similar relief under any statute, law, or regulation, the proceeding has not been dismissed, or if within 90 days after the appointment without his consent or acquiescence of a trustee, receiver, or liquidator of the general partner or of all or any substantial part of his properties, the appointment is not vacated or stayed or within 90 days after the expiration of any such stay, the appointment is not vacated.

(6) In the case of a general partner who is a natural person: (a) his death; or (b) the entry of an order by a court of competent jurisdiction adjudicating him incompetent to manage his person or his estate.

(7) In the case of a general partner who is acting as a general partner by virtue of being a trustee of a trust, the distribution by the trustee of the trust's entire interest in the partnership, but not merely the substitution of a new trustee.

(8) In the case of a general partner that is a separate partnership, the dissolution and completion of winding up of the separate partnership.

(9) In the case of a general partner that is a corporation, the issuance of a certificate of dissolution or its equivalent, or of a judicial decree of dissolution, for the corporation or the revocation of its charter.

(10) In the case of a person who is acting as a general partner by virtue of being a fiduciary of an estate, the distribution by the fiduciary of the estate's entire interest in the partnership.

48-2a-403. General Powers and Liabilities.

(1) Except as provided in this chapter or in the partnership agreement, a general partner of a limited partnership has the rights and powers and is subject to the restrictions of a partner in a partnership without limited partners.

(2) Except as provided in this chapter, a general partner of a limited partnership has the liabilities of a partner in a partnership without limited partners to persons other than the partnership and the other partners. Except as provided in this chapter or in the partnership agreement, a general partner of a limited partnership has the liabilities of a partner in a partnership without limited partners to the partnership and to the other partners.

48-2a-404. Contributions by General Partners.

A general partner of a limited partnership may make contributions to the partnership and share in the profits and losses of, and in distributions from, the limited partnership as a general partner. A general partner also may make contributions to and share in profits, losses, and distributions as a limited partner. A person who is both a general partner and a limited partner has the rights and powers, and is subject to the restrictions and liabilities, of a general partner and, except as provided in the partnership agreement, also has the rights and powers, and is subject to the restrictions and liabilities, of a limited partner to the extent of his participation in the partnership as a limited partner.

48-2a-405. Voting.

The partnership agreement may grant to all or certain identified general partners the right to vote, on a per capita or any other basis, separately or with all or any class of the limited partners, on any matter.

Section 501

48-2a-501. Form of Contribution.

The contribution of a partner may be in cash, property, or services rendered, or a promissory note or other obligation to contribute cash or property or to perform services.

48-2a-502. Liability for Contribution.

(1) A promise by a limited partner to contribute to the limited partnership is not enforceable unless set out in a writing signed by the limited partner.

(2) Except as provided in the partnership agreement, a partner is obligated to the limited partnership to perform any enforceable promise to contribute cash or property or to perform services, even if he is unable to perform because of death, disability, or any other reason. If a partner does not make the required contribution of property or services, he is obligated at the option of the limited partnership to contribute cash equal to that portion of the value, as stated in the partnership records required to be kept pursuant to Section 48-2a-105, of the stated contribution which has not been made.

(3) Unless otherwise provided in the partnership agreement, the obligation of a partner to make a contribution or return money or other property paid or distributed in violation of this chapter may be compromised only by consent of all partners. Notwithstanding the compromise, a creditor of a limited partnership who extends credit, or otherwise acts in reliance on that obligation after the partner signs a writing which reflects the obligation and before the amendment or cancellation thereof to reflect the compromise may enforce the original obligation.

48-2a-503. Sharing of Profits and Losses.

The profits and losses of a limited partnership shall be allocated among the partners, and among classes of partners, in the manner provided in writing in the partnership agreement. If the partnership agreement does not provide in writing, profits, and losses shall be allocated on the basis of the value, as stated in the partnership records required to be kept pursuant to Section 48-2a-105, of the contributions made by each partner to the extent they have been received by the partnership and have not been returned.

48-2a-504. Sharing of Distributions.

Distributions of cash or other assets of a limited partnership shall be made among the partners and among classes of partners in the manner provided in writing in the partnership agreement. If the partnership agreement does not provide in writing, distributions shall be made on the basis of the value, as stated in the partnership records required to be kept pursuant to Section 48-2a-105, of the contributions made by each partner to the extent they have been received by the partnership and have not been returned.

Section 601

48-2a-601. Interim Distributions.

Except as provided in this article, a partner is entitled to receive distributions from a limited partnership before his withdrawal from the limited partnership and before the dissolution and winding up thereof to the extent and at the times or upon the happening of the events specified in the partnership agreement.

48-2a-602. Withdrawal of General Partner.

A general partner may withdraw from a limited partnership at any time by giving written notice to the other partners, but if the withdrawal violates the partnership agreement, the limited partnership may recover from the withdrawing general partner damages for breach of the partnership agreement and offset the damages against the amount otherwise distributable to him.

48-2a-603. Withdrawal of Limited Partners.

A limited partner may withdraw from a limited partnership at the time or upon the happening of events specified in writing in the partnership agreement. If the agreement does not specify in writing the time or the events upon the happening of which a limited partner may withdraw or a definite time for the dissolution and winding up of the limited partnership, a limited partner may withdraw upon not less than six months prior written notice to each general partner at his address on the books of the limited partnership required to be kept under Section 48-2a-105.

48-2a-604. Distribution upon Withdrawal.

Except as provided in this article, upon withdrawal any withdrawing partner is entitled to receive any distribution to which he is entitled under the partnership agreement and, if not otherwise provided in the partnership agreement, he is entitled to receive, within a reasonable time after withdrawal, the fair value of his interest in the limited partnership as of the date of withdrawal based upon his right to share in distributions from the limited partnership.

48-2a-605. Distribution in Kind.

Except as provided in the partnership agreement, a partner, regardless of the nature of his contribution, has no right to demand and receive any distribution from the limited partnership in any form other than cash. Except as provided in writing in the partnership agreement, a partner may not be compelled to accept a distribution of any asset in kind from a limited partnership to the extent that the percentage of the asset distributed to him exceeds a percentage of that asset which is equal to the percentage in which he shares in distributions from the limited partnership.

48-2a-606. Right to Distribution.

At the time a partner becomes entitled to receive a distribution, he has the status of, and is entitled to all remedies available to, a creditor of the limited partnership with respect to the distribution.

48-2a-607. Limitations on Distributions.

A partner may not receive a distribution from a limited partnership to the extent that, after giving effect to the distribution, all liabilities of the limited partnership, other than liabilities to partners on account of their partnership interests, exceed the fair value of the partnership assets.

48-2a-608. Liability upon Return of Contribution.

(1) If a partner has received the return of any part of his contribution without violation of the partnership agreement or this chapter, he is liable to the limited partnership for a period of one year thereafter for the amount of the returned contribution, but only to the extent necessary to discharge the limited partnership's liabilities to creditors who extended credit to the limited partnership during the period the contribution was held by the partnership.

(2) If a partner has received the return of any part of his contribution in violation of the partnership agreement or this chapter, he is liable to the limited partnership for a period of six years thereafter for the amount of the contribution wrongfully returned.

(3) A partner receives a return of his contribution to the extent that a distribution to him reduces his share of the fair value of the net assets of the limited partnership below the value, as set forth in the partnership records required to be kept under Section 48-2a-105, of his contribution to the extent that it has been made, less any previous return of contributions.

Section 701

48-2a-701. Nature of Partnership Interest.

A partnership interest is personal property.

48-2a-702. Assignment of Partnership Interest.

Except as provided in the partnership agreement, a partnership interest is assignable in whole or in part. Except as set forth in Subsection 48-2a-801(4), an assignment of a partnership interest does not dissolve a limited partnership or entitle the assignee to become or to exercise any rights of a partner. An assignment entitles the assignee to receive, to the extent assigned, only the distribution to which the assignor would be entitled. Except as provided in the partnership agreement, a partner ceases to be a partner upon assignment of all of his partnership interest.

48-2a-703. Rights of Creditor.

On application to a court of competent jurisdiction by any judgment creditor of a partner, the court may charge the partnership interest of the partner with payment of the unsatisfied amount of the judgment with interest. To the extent it is the beneficiary of such a charging order, the judgment creditor has only the rights of an assignee of the partnership interest. This chapter does not deprive any partner of the benefit of any exemption laws applicable to his partnership interest.

48-2a-704. Right of Assignee to Become Limited Partner.

(1) An assignee of a partnership interest, including an assignee of a general partner, may become a limited partner if and to the extent that:

(a) the assignor gives the assignee that right in accordance with authority described in the partnership agreement and the conditions set forth in the partnership agreement are met; or

(b) all other partners consent.

(2) An assignee who has become a limited partner has, to the extent assigned, the rights and powers, and is subject to the restrictions and liabilities, of a limited partner under the partnership agreement and this chapter. An assignee who becomes a limited partner also is liable for the obligations of his assignor to make and return contributions as provided in Articles V and VI of this chapter. However, the assignee is not obligated for any other liabilities unknown to the assignee at the time he became a limited partner.

(3) If an assignee of a partnership interest becomes a limited partner, the assignor is not released from his liability to the limited partnership under Sections 48-2a-207, 48-2a-502, and 48-2a-608.

48-2a-705. Power of Estate of Deceased or Incompetent Partner.

If a partner who is an individual dies or a court of competent jurisdiction adjudges him to be incompetent to manage his person or his property, the partner's executor, administrator, guardian, conservator, or other legal representative may exercise all of the partner's rights for the purpose of settling his estate or administering his property, including any authority the partner had to give an assignee the right to become a limited partner. If a partner is a corporation, trust, or other entity and is dissolved or terminated, the powers of that partner may be exercised by its legal representative or successor.

Section 801

48-2a-801. Nonjudicial Dissolution.

A limited partnership is dissolved and its affairs shall be wound up upon the happening of the first to occur of the following:

(1) at the time specified in the certificate of limited partnership;

(2) upon the happening of events specified in writing in the partnership agreement;

(3) written consent of all partners;

(4) an event of withdrawal of a general partner unless:

(a) at the time there is at least one other general partner and the written provisions of the partnership agreement permit the business of the limited partnership to be carried on by the remaining general partner and that partner does so; or

(b) within 90 days after the event of withdrawal, all partners agree in writing to continue the business of the limited partnership and to the appointment of one or more additional general partners if necessary or desired; or

(5) entry of a decree of judicial dissolution under Section 48-2a-802.

48-2a-802. Judicial Dissolution.

On application by or for a partner or the director of the division, a district court having competent jurisdiction may decree dissolution of the limited partnership whenever it is not reasonably practicable to carry on the business in conformity with the partnership agreement or for failure to comply with the requirements of this chapter.

48-2a-803. Winding Up.

Except as provided in the partnership agreement, the general partners who have not wrongfully dissolved a limited partnership or, if none, the limited partners, may wind up the limited partnership's affairs; but a district court having competent jurisdiction may wind up the limited partnership's affairs upon application of any partner, his legal representative, or assignee.

48-2a-804. Distribution of Assets.

Upon the winding up of a limited partnership, the assets shall be distributed as follows:

(1) to creditors, including partners who are creditors, to the extent permitted by law, in satisfaction of liabilities of the limited partnership other than liabilities for distributions to partners under Section 48-2a-601 or 48-2a-604;

(2) except as provided in the partnership agreement, to partners and former partners in satisfaction of liabilities for distributions under Section 48-2a-601 or 48-2a-604; and

(3) except as provided in the partnership agreement, to partners with respect to their partnership interests: (a) for the return of their contributions; and (b) in the proportions in which the partners share in distributions.

Section 901

48-2a-901. Law Governing.

Subject to the Constitution of this state: (1) the laws of the state under which a foreign limited partnership is organized govern its organization and internal affairs and the liability of its limited partners; and (2) a foreign limited partnership may not be denied registration by reason of any difference between those laws and the laws of this state.

48-2a-902. Registration.

(1) (a) Before transacting business in this state, a foreign limited partnership shall register with the division.

(b) To register, a foreign limited partnership shall submit to the division in a form provided by the division:

(i) a certificate of good standing or similar evidence of its organization and existence under the laws of the state in which the foreign limited partnership is formed; and

(ii) an original and one copy of an application for registration as a foreign limited partnership, signed under penalty of perjury by a general partner and setting forth: (A) the name of the foreign limited partnership and, if that name is not available in this state, the name under which it proposes to register and transact business in this state; (B) the state and date of its formation; (C) the information required by Subsection 16-17-203(1); (D) the name and business address of each general partner; and (E) the street address of the office at which is kept a list of the names and addresses of the limited partners and their capital contributions, together with an undertaking by the foreign limited partnership to keep those records until the foreign limited partnership's registration in this state is canceled or withdrawn.

(2) Without excluding other activities that may not constitute transacting business in this state, a foreign limited partnership is not considered to be transacting business in this state, for the purposes of this chapter, by reason of carrying on in this state any one or more of the following activities:

(a) (i) maintaining or defending any action or suit or any administrative or arbitration proceeding; (ii) effecting the settlement of an action or proceeding; or (iii) effecting the settlement of a claim or dispute;

(b) holding a meeting of its general partners or limited partners or carrying on another activity concerning its internal affairs;

(c) maintaining a bank account;

(d) (i) maintaining an office or agency for the transfer, exchange, and registration of its securities; or (ii) appointing and maintaining a trustee or depository with relation to its securities;

(e) effecting sales through an independent contractor;

(f) soliciting or procuring an order, whether by mail or through an employee, agent, or otherwise, if the order requires acceptance without this state before becoming a binding contract;

(g) creating evidences of debt, mortgages, or liens on real or personal property;

(h) securing or collecting a debt or enforcing a right in property securing the property;

(i) transacting business in interstate commerce;

(j) conducting an isolated transaction completed within a period of 30 days and not in the course of a number of repeated transactions of like nature; or

(k) (i) acquiring, in a transaction outside this state or in interstate commerce, of conditional sale contracts or of debts secured by mortgages or liens on real or personal property in this state; (ii) collecting or adjusting of principal and interest payments on the conditional sale contract or debt described in Subsection (2)(k)(i); (iii) enforcing or adjusting a right in property provided for in the conditional sale contract or securing the debt; or (iv) taking an action necessary to preserve and protect the interest of the conditional vendor in the property covered by the conditional sales contract or the interest of the mortgagee or holder of the lien in the security, or any combination of the one or more transactions.

(3) (a) The division may permit a tribal limited partnership to register with the division in the same manner as a foreign limited partnership formed in another state.

(b) If a tribal limited partnership elects to register with the division, for purposes of this chapter, the tribal limited partnership shall be treated in the same manner as a foreign limited partnership formed under the laws of another state.

48-2a-903. Issuance of Registration.

(1) If the division finds that an application for registration conforms to law as to its form, and all requisite fees have been paid, it shall:

(a) place on the original and the copy of the application a stamp or seal indicating the time, month, day, and year of the filing, the director of the division's signature and the division's seal, or facsimiles thereof, and the name of the division;

(b) file in its office the signed original of the application; and

(c) issue a certificate of registration to transact business in this state to which is attached the stamped copy.

(2) The certificate of registration, together with the stamped copy of the application, shall be returned to the person who filed the application or his representative.

48-2a-904. Name.

A foreign limited partnership shall register with the division under the name under which it is registered in its state of organization; provided that the name includes the words "limited partnership", "limited", "L.P.", or "Ltd." and provided that the name could be registered by a domestic limited partnership.

48-2a-905. Changes and Amendments.

If any statement in the application for registration of a foreign limited partnership was false when made or any arrangements or other facts described in the statement have changed, making the application inaccurate in any respect, the foreign limited partnership shall promptly file with the division a certificate, signed under penalty of perjury by a general partner, correcting or amending the statement.

48-2a-906. Cancellation of Registration.

A foreign limited partnership may cancel its registration by filing with the division a certificate of cancellation signed under penalty of perjury by a general partner. A cancellation does not terminate the authority of the director of the division to accept service of process on the foreign limited partnership with respect to claims for relief and causes of action against the foreign limited partnership arising before the cancellation.

48-2a-907. Transaction of Business Without Registration.

(1) A foreign limited partnership transacting business in this state may not maintain any action, suit, or proceeding in any court of this state until it has registered in this state.

(2) The failure of a foreign limited partnership to register in this state does not impair the validity of any contract or

act of the foreign limited partnership or prevent the foreign limited partnership from defending any action, suit, or proceeding in any court of this state.

(3) A limited partner of a foreign limited partnership is not liable as a general partner of the foreign limited partnership solely by reason of the fact that the foreign limited partnership has transacted business in this state without registration or has otherwise become subject to the jurisdiction of the courts of this state.

(4) A foreign limited partnership, by transacting business in this state without registration, appoints the director of the division as its agent for service of process with respect to claims for relief and causes of action arising out of the transaction of business in this state.

48-2a-908. Action by Director of Division.

The director of the division may bring an action to restrain a foreign limited partnership from transacting business in this state in violation of this Article.

Section 1001

48-2a-1001. Right of Action.

A limited partner may bring an action in the right of a limited partnership to recover a judgment in its favor if general partners with authority to do so have refused to bring the action and the general partners' decision not to sue constitutes an abuse of discretion or involves a conflict of interest that prevents an unprejudiced exercise of judgment, or if an effort to cause those general partners to bring the action is not likely to succeed.

48-2a-1002. Proper Plaintiff.

In a derivative action, the plaintiff must be a partner at the time of bringing the action and:

(1) must have been a partner at the time of the transaction of which he complains; or

(2) his status as a partner must have devolved upon him by operation of law or pursuant to the terms of the partnership agreement from a person who was a partner at the time of the transaction.

48-2a-1003. Pleading.

In a derivative action, the complaint shall set forth with particularity the effort of the plaintiff to secure initiation of the action by a general partner or the reasons for not making the effort.

48-2a-1004. Expenses.

If a derivative action is successful, in whole or in part, or if anything is received by the plaintiff as a result of a judgment, compromise, or settlement of an action or claim, the court may award the plaintiff reasonable expenses, including reasonable attorneys' fees, and shall direct him to remit to the limited partnership the remainder of those proceeds received by him.

* * * *

Chapter 2.
INCORPORATION

§ 2.01 Incorporators

One or more persons may act as the incorporator or incorporators of a corporation by delivering articles of incorporation to the secretary of state for filing.

§ 2.02 Articles of Incorporation

(a) The articles of incorporation must set forth:

(1) a corporate name * * *;

(2) the number of shares the corporation is authorized to issue;

(3) the street address of the corporation's initial registered office and the name of its initial registered agent at that office; and

(4) the name and address of each incorporator.

(b) The articles of incorporation may set forth:

(1) the names and addresses of the individuals who are to serve as the initial directors;

(2) provisions not inconsistent with law regarding:

(i) the purpose or purposes for which the corporation is organized;

(ii) managing the business and regulating the affairs of the corporation;

(iii) defining, limiting, and regulating the powers of the corporation, its board of directors, and shareholders;

(iv) a par value for authorized shares or classes of shares;

(v) the imposition of personal liability on shareholders for the debts of the corporation to a specified extent and upon specified conditions;

(3) any provision that under this Act is required or permitted to be set forth in the bylaws; and

(4) a provision eliminating or limiting the liability of a director to the corporation or its shareholders for money damages for any action taken, or any failure to take any action, as a director, except liability for (A) the amount of a financial benefit received by a director to which he is not entitled; (B) an intentional infliction of harm on the corporation or the shareholders; (C) [unlawful distributions]; or (D) an intentional violation of criminal law.

(c) The articles of incorporation need not set forth any of the corporate powers enumerated in this Act.

§ 2.03 Incorporation

(a) Unless a delayed effective date is specified, the corporate existence begins when the articles of incorporation are filed.

(b) The secretary of state's filing of the articles of incorporation is conclusive proof that the incorporators satisfied all conditions precedent to incorporation except in a proceeding by the state to cancel or revoke the incorporation or involuntarily dissolve the corporation.

§ 2.04 Liability for Preincorporation Transactions

All persons purporting to act as or on behalf of a corporation, knowing there was no incorporation under this Act, are jointly and severally liable for all liabilities created while so acting.

§ 2.05 Organization of Corporation

(a) After incorporation:

(1) if initial directors are named in the articles of incorporation, the initial directors shall hold an organizational meeting, at the call of a majority of the directors, to complete the organization of the corporation by appointing officers, adopting bylaws, and carrying on any other business brought before the meeting;

(2) if initial directors are not named in the articles, the incorporator or incorporators shall hold an

organizational meeting at the call of a majority of the incorporators:

(i) to elect directors and complete the organization of the corporation; or

(ii) to elect a board of directors who shall complete the organization of the corporation.

(b) Action required or permitted by this Act to be taken by incorporators at an organizational meeting may be taken without a meeting if the action taken is evidenced by one or more written consents describing the action taken and signed by each incorporator.

(c) An organizational meeting may be held in or out of this state.

* * * *

Chapter 3.
PURPOSES AND POWERS

§ 3.01 Purposes

(a) Every corporation incorporated under this Act has the purpose of engaging in any lawful business unless a more limited purpose is set forth in the articles of incorporation.

(b) A corporation engaging in a business that is subject to regulation under another statute of this state may incorporate under this Act only if permitted by, and subject to all limitations of, the other statute.

§ 3.02 General Powers

Unless its articles of incorporation provide otherwise, every corporation has perpetual duration and succession in its corporate name and has the same powers as an individual to do all things necessary or convenient to carry out its business and affairs, including without limitation power:

(1) to sue and be sued, complain and defend in its corporate name;

(2) to have a corporate seal, which may be altered at will, and to use it, or a facsimile of it, by impressing or affixing it or in any other manner reproducing it;

(3) to make and amend bylaws, not inconsistent with its articles of incorporation or with the laws of this state, for managing the business and regulating the affairs of the corporation;

(4) to purchase, receive, lease, or otherwise acquire, and own, hold, improve, use, and otherwise deal with, real or personal property, or any legal or equitable interest in property, wherever located;

(5) to sell, convey, mortgage, pledge, lease, exchange, and otherwise dispose of all or any part of its property;

(6) to purchase, receive, subscribe for, or otherwise acquire; own, hold, vote, use, sell, mortgage, lend, pledge, or otherwise dispose of; and deal in and with shares or other interests in, or obligations of, any other entity;

(7) to make contracts and guarantees, incur liabilities, borrow money, issue its notes, bonds, and other obligations (which may be convertible into or include the option to purchase other securities of the corporation), and secure any of its obligations by mortgage or pledge of any of its property, franchises, or income;

(8) to lend money, invest and reinvest its funds, and receive and hold real and personal property as security for repayment;

(9) to be a promoter, partner, member, associate, or manager of any partnership, joint venture, trust, or other entity;

(10) to conduct its business, locate offices, and exercise the powers granted by this Act within or without this state;

(11) to elect directors and appoint officers, employees, and agents of the corporation, define their duties, fix their compensation, and lend them money and credit;

(12) to pay pensions and establish pension plans, pension trusts, profit sharing plans, share bonus plans, share option plans, and benefit or incentive plans for any or all of its current or former directors, officers, employees, and agents;

(13) to make donations for the public welfare or for charitable, scientific, or educational purposes;

(14) to transact any lawful business that will aid governmental policy;

(15) to make payments or donations, or do any other act, not inconsistent with law, that furthers the business and affairs of the corporation.

* * * *

Chapter 5.
OFFICE AND AGENT

§ 5.01 Registered Office and Registered Agent

Each corporation must continuously maintain in this state:

(1) a registered office that may be the same as any of its places of business; and

(2) a registered agent, who may be:

(i) an individual who resides in this state and whose business office is identical with the registered office;

(ii) a domestic corporation or not-for-profit domestic corporation whose business office is identical with the registered office; or

(iii) a foreign corporation or not-for-profit foreign corporation authorized to transact business in this state whose business office is identical with the registered office.

* * * *

§ 5.04 Service on Corporation

(a) A corporation's registered agent is the corporation's agent for service of process, notice, or demand required or permitted by law to be served on the corporation.

(b) If a corporation has no registered agent, or the agent cannot with reasonable diligence be served, the corporation may be served by registered or certified mail, return receipt requested, addressed to the secretary of the corporation at its principal office. Service is perfected under this subsection at the earliest of:

(1) the date the corporation receives the mail;

(2) the date shown on the return receipt, if signed on behalf of the corporation; or

(3) five days after its deposit in the United States Mail, if mailed postpaid and correctly addressed.

(c) This section does not prescribe the only means, or necessarily the required means, of serving a corporation.

Chapter 6.
SHARES AND DISTRIBUTIONS

* * * *

Subchapter B. Issuance of Shares

* * * *

§ 6.21 Issuance of Shares

(a) The powers granted in this section to the board of directors may be reserved to the shareholders by the articles of incorporation.

(b) The board of directors may authorize shares to be issued for consideration consisting of any tangible or intangible property or benefit to the corporation, including cash, promissory notes, services performed, contracts for services to be performed, or other securities of the corporation.

(c) Before the corporation issues shares, the board of directors must determine that the consideration received or to be received for shares to be issued is adequate. That determination by the board of directors is conclusive insofar as the adequacy of consideration for the issuance of shares relates to whether the shares are validly issued, fully paid, and nonassessable.

(d) When the corporation receives the consideration for which the board of directors authorized the issuance of shares, the shares issued therefor are fully paid and nonassessable.

(e) The corporation may place in escrow shares issued for a contract for future services or benefits or a promissory note, or make other arrangements to restrict the transfer of the shares, and may credit distributions in respect of the shares against their purchase price, until the services are performed, the note is paid, or the benefits received. If the services are not performed, the note is not paid, or the benefits are not received, the shares escrowed or restricted and the distributions credited may be cancelled in whole or part.

* * * *

§ 6.27 Restriction on Transfer or Registration of Shares and Other Securities

(a) The articles of incorporation, bylaws, an agreement among shareholders, or an agreement between shareholders and the corporation may impose restrictions on the transfer or registration of transfer of shares of the corporation. A restriction does not affect shares issued before the restriction was adopted unless the holders of the shares are parties to the restriction agreement or voted in favor of the restriction.

(b) A restriction on the transfer or registration of transfer of shares is valid and enforceable against the holder or a transferee of the holder if the restriction is authorized by this section and its existence is noted conspicuously on the front or back of the certificate or is contained in the information statement [sent to the shareholder]. Unless so noted, a restriction is not enforceable against a person without knowledge of the restriction.

(c) A restriction on the transfer or registration of transfer of shares is authorized:

(1) to maintain the corporation's status when it is dependent on the number or identity of its shareholders;

(2) to preserve exemptions under federal or state securities law;

(3) for any other reasonable purpose.

(d) A restriction on the transfer or registration of transfer of shares may:

(1) obligate the shareholder first to offer the corporation or other persons (separately, consecutively, or simultaneously) an opportunity to acquire the restricted shares;

(2) obligate the corporate or other persons (separately, consecutively, or simultaneously) to acquire the restricted shares;

(3) require the corporation, the holders of any class of its shares, or another person to approve the transfer of the restricted shares, if the requirement is not manifestly unreasonable;

(4) prohibit the transfer of the restricted shares to designated persons or classes of persons, if the prohibition is not manifestly unreasonable.

(e) For purposes of this section, "shares" includes a security convertible into or carrying a right to subscribe for or acquire shares.

* * * *

Chapter 7.
SHAREHOLDERS

Subchapter A. Meetings

§ 7.01 Annual Meeting

(a) A corporation shall hold annually at a time stated in or fixed in accordance with the bylaws a meeting of shareholders.

(b) Annual shareholders' meetings may be held in or out of this state at the place stated in or fixed in accordance with the bylaws. If no place is stated in or fixed in accordance with the bylaws, annual meetings shall be held at the corporation's principal office.

(c) The failure to hold an annual meeting at the time stated in or fixed in accordance with a corporation's bylaws does not affect the validity of any corporate action.

* * * *

§ 7.05 Notice of Meeting

(a) A corporation shall notify shareholders of the date, time, and place of each annual and special shareholders' meeting no fewer than 10 nor more than 60 days before the meeting date. Unless this Act or the articles of incorporation require otherwise, the corporation is required to give notice only to shareholders entitled to vote at the meeting.

(b) Unless this Act or the articles of incorporation require otherwise, notice of an annual meeting need not include a description of the purpose or purposes for which the meeting is called.

(c) Notice of a special meeting must include a description of the purpose or purposes for which the meeting is called.

(d) If not otherwise fixed * * *, the record date for determining shareholders entitled to notice of and to vote at an annual or special shareholders' meeting is the day before the first notice is delivered to shareholders.

(e) Unless the bylaws require otherwise, if an annual or special shareholders' meeting is adjourned to a different date, time, or place, notice need not be given of the new date, time, or place if the new date, time, or place is announced at the meeting before adjournment. * * *

* * * *

§ 7.07 Record Date

(a) The bylaws may fix or provide the manner of fixing the record date for one or more voting groups in order to determine the shareholders entitled to notice of a shareholders' meeting, to demand a special meeting, to vote, or to take any other action. If the bylaws do not fix or provide for fixing a record date, the board of directors of the corporation may fix a future date as the record date.

(b) A record date fixed under this section may not be more than 70 days before the meeting or action requiring a determination of shareholders.

(c) A determination of shareholders entitled to notice of or to vote at a shareholders' meeting is effective for any adjournment of the meeting unless the board of directors fixes a new record date, which it must do if the meeting is adjourned to a date more than 120 days after the date fixed for the original meeting.

(d) If a court orders a meeting adjourned to a date more than 120 days after the date fixed for the original meeting, it may provide that the original record date continues in effect or it may fix a new record date.

Subchapter B. Voting

§ 7.20 Shareholders' List for Meeting

(a) After fixing a record date for a meeting, a corporation shall prepare an alphabetical list of the names of all its shareholders who are entitled to notice of a shareholders' meeting. The list must be arranged by voting group (and within each voting group by class or series of shares) and show the address of and number of shares held by each shareholder.

(b) The shareholders' list must be available for inspection by any shareholder, beginning two business days after notice of the meeting is given for which the list was prepared and continuing through the meeting, at the corporation's principal office or at a place identified in the meeting notice in the city where the meeting will be held. A shareholder, his agent, or attorney is entitled on written demand to inspect and, subject to the requirements of section 16.02(c), to copy the list, during regular business hours and at his expense, during the period it is available for inspection.

(c) The corporation shall make the shareholders' list available at the meeting, and any shareholder, his agent, or attorney is entitled to inspect the list at any time during the meeting or any adjournment.

(d) If the corporation refuses to allow a shareholder, his agent, or attorney to inspect the shareholders' list before or at the meeting (or copy the list as permitted by subsection (b)), the [name or describe] court of the county where a corporation's principal office (or, if none in this state, its registered office) is located, on application of the shareholder, may summarily order the inspection or copying at the corporation's expense and may postpone the meeting for which the list was prepared until the inspection or copying is complete.

(e) Refusal or failure to prepare or make available the shareholders' list does not affect the validity of action taken at the meeting.

* * * *

§ 7.22 Proxies

(a) A shareholder may vote his shares in person or by proxy.

(b) A shareholder may appoint a proxy to vote or otherwise act for him by signing an appointment form, either personally or by his attorney-in-fact.

(c) An appointment of a proxy is effective when received by the secretary or other officer or agent authorized to tabulate votes. An appointment is valid for 11 months unless a longer period is expressly provided in the appointment form.

* * * *

§ 7.28 Voting for Directors; Cumulative Voting

(a) Unless otherwise provided in the articles of incorporation, directors are elected by a plurality of the votes cast by the shares entitled to vote in the election at a meeting at which a quorum is present.

(b) Shareholders do not have a right to cumulate their votes for directors unless the articles of incorporation so provide.

(c) A statement included in the articles of incorporation that "[all] [a designated voting group of] shareholders are entitled to cumulate their votes for directors" (or words of similar import) means that the shareholders designated are entitled to multiply the number of votes they are entitled to cast by the number of directors for whom they are entitled to vote and cast the product for a single candidate or distribute the product among two or more candidates.

(d) Shares otherwise entitled to vote cumulatively may not be voted cumulatively at a particular meeting unless:

(1) the meeting notice or proxy statement accompanying the notice states conspicuously that cumulative voting is authorized; or

(2) a shareholder who has the right to cumulate his votes gives notice to the corporation not less than 48 hours before the time set for the meeting of his intent to cumulate his votes during the meeting, and if one shareholder gives this notice all other shareholders in the same voting group participating in the election are entitled to cumulate their votes without giving further notice.

* * * *

Subchapter D. Derivative Proceedings

* * * *

§ 7.41 Standing

A shareholder may not commence or maintain a derivative proceeding unless the shareholder:

(1) was a shareholder of the corporation at the time of the act or omission complained of or became a shareholder through transfer by operation of law from one who was a shareholder at that time; and

(2) fairly and adequately represents the interests of the corporation in enforcing the right of the corporation.

§ 7.42 Demand

No shareholder may commence a derivative proceeding until:

(1) a written demand has been made upon the corporation to take suitable action; and

(2) 90 days have expired from the date the demand was made unless the shareholder has earlier been notified that the demand has been rejected by the corporation or unless irreparable injury to the corporation would result by waiting for the expiration of the 90 day period.

* * * *

Chapter 8.
DIRECTORS AND OFFICERS

Subchapter A. Board of Directors

* * * *

§ 8.02 Qualifications of Directors

The articles of incorporation or bylaws may prescribe qualifications for directors. A director need not be a resident of this state or a shareholder of the corporation unless the articles of incorporation or bylaws so prescribe.

§ 8.03 Number and Election of Directors

(a) A board of directors must consist of one or more individuals, with the number specified in or fixed in accordance with the articles of incorporation or bylaws.

(b) If a board of directors has power to fix or change the number of directors, the board may increase or decrease by 30 percent or less the number of directors last approved by the shareholders, but only the shareholders may increase or decrease by more than 30 percent the number of directors last approved by the shareholders.

(c) The articles of incorporation or bylaws may establish a variable range for the size of the board of directors by fixing a minimum and maximum number of directors. If a variable range is established, the number of directors may be fixed or changed from time to time, within the minimum and maximum, by the shareholders or the board of directors. After shares are issued, only the shareholders may change the range for the size of the board or change from a fixed to a variable-range size board or vice versa.

(d) Directors are elected at the first annual shareholders' meeting and at each annual meeting thereafter unless their terms are staggered under section 8.06.

* * * *

§ 8.08 Removal of Directors by Shareholders

(a) The shareholders may remove one or more directors with or without cause unless the articles of incorporation provide that directors may be removed only for cause.

(b) If a director is elected by a voting group of shareholders, only the shareholders of that voting group may participate in the vote to remove him.

(c) If cumulative voting is authorized, a director may not be removed if the number of votes sufficient to elect him under cumulative voting is voted against his removal. If cumulative voting is not authorized, a director may be removed only if the number of votes cast to remove him exceeds the number of votes cast not to remove him.

(d) A director may be removed by the shareholders only at a meeting called for the purpose of removing him and the meeting notice must state that the purpose, or one of the purposes, of the meeting is removal of the director.

* * * *

Subchapter B. Meetings and Action of the Board

§ 8.20 Meetings

(a) The board of directors may hold regular or special meetings in or out of this state.

(b) Unless the articles of incorporation or bylaws provide otherwise, the board of directors may permit any or all directors to participate in a regular or special meeting by, or conduct the meeting through the use of, any means of communication by which all directors participating may simultaneously hear each other during the meeting. A director participating in a meeting by this means is deemed to be present in person at the meeting.

* * * *

§ 8.22 Notice of Meeting

(a) Unless the articles of incorporation or bylaws provide otherwise, regular meetings of the board of directors may be held without notice of the date, time, place, or purpose of the meeting.

(b) Unless the articles of incorporation or bylaws provide for a longer or shorter period, special meetings of the board of directors must be preceded by at least two days' notice of the date, time, and place of the meeting. The notice need not describe the purpose of the special meeting unless required by the articles of incorporation or bylaws.

* * * *

§ 8.24 Quorum and Voting

(a) Unless the articles of incorporation or bylaws require a greater number, a quorum of a board of directors consists of:

(1) a majority of the fixed number of directors if the corporation has a fixed board size; or

(2) a majority of the number of directors prescribed, or if no number is prescribed the number in office immediately before the meeting begins, if the corporation has a variable-range size board.

(b) The articles of incorporation or bylaws may authorize a quorum of a board of directors to consist of no fewer than one-third of the fixed or prescribed number of directors determined under subsection (a).

(c) If a quorum is present when a vote is taken, the affirmative vote of a majority of directors present is the act of the board of directors unless the articles of incorporation or bylaws require the vote of a greater number of directors.

(d) A director who is present at a meeting of the board of directors or a committee of the board of directors when corporate action is taken is deemed to have assented to the action taken unless: (1) he objects at the beginning of the meeting (or promptly upon his arrival) to holding it or transacting business at the meeting; (2) his dissent or abstention from the action taken is entered in the minutes of the meeting; or (3) he delivers written notice of his dissent or abstention to the presiding officer of the meeting before its adjournment or to the corporation immediately after adjournment of the meeting. The right of dissent or abstention is not available to a director who votes in favor of the action taken.

* * * *

Subchapter C. Standards of Conduct

§ 8.30 General Standards for Directors

(a) A director shall discharge his duties as a director, including his duties as a member of a committee:

(1) in good faith;

(2) with the care an ordinarily prudent person in a like position would exercise under similar circumstances; and

(3) in a manner he reasonably believes to be in the best interests of the corporation.

(b) In discharging his duties a director is entitled to rely on information, opinions, reports, or statements, including financial statements and other financial data, if prepared or presented by:

(1) one or more officers or employees of the corporation whom the director reasonably believes to be reliable and competent in the matters presented;

(2) legal counsel, public accountants, or other persons as to matters the director reasonably believes are within the person's professional or expert competence; or

(3) a committee of the board of directors of which he is not a member if the director reasonably believes the committee merits confidence.

(c) A director is not acting in good faith if he has knowledge concerning the matter in question that makes reliance otherwise permitted by subsection (b) unwarranted.

(d) A director is not liable for any action taken as a director, or any failure to take any action, if he performed the duties of his office in compliance with this section.

* * * *

Subchapter D. Officers

* * * *

§ 8.41 Duties of Officers

Each officer has the authority and shall perform the duties set forth in the bylaws or, to the extent consistent with the bylaws, the duties prescribed by the board of directors or by direction of an officer authorized by the board of directors to prescribe the duties of other officers.

§ 8.42 Standards of Conduct for Officers

(a) An officer with discretionary authority shall discharge his duties under that authority:

(1) in good faith;

(2) with the care an ordinarily prudent person in a like position would exercise under similar circumstances; and

(3) in a manner he reasonably believes to be in the best interests of the corporation.

(b) In discharging his duties an officer is entitled to rely on information, opinions, reports, or statements, including financial statements and other financial data, if prepared or presented by:

(1) one or more officers or employees of the corporation whom the officer reasonably believes to be reliable and competent in the matters presented; or

(2) legal counsel, public accountants, or other persons as to matters the officer reasonably believes are within the person's professional or expert competence.

(c) An officer is not acting in good faith if he has knowledge concerning the matter in question that makes reliance otherwise permitted by subsection (b) unwarranted.

(d) An officer is not liable for any action taken as an officer, or any failure to take any action, if he performed the duties of his office in compliance with this section.

* * * *

Chapter 11.
MERGER AND SHARE EXCHANGE

§ 11.01 Merger

(a) One or more corporations may merge into another corporation if the board of directors of each corporation adopts and its shareholders (if required * * *) approve a plan of merger.

(b) The plan of merger must set forth:

(1) the name of each corporation planning to merge and the name of the surviving corporation into which each other corporation plans to merge;

(2) the terms and conditions of the merger; and

(3) the manner and basis of converting the shares of each corporation into shares, obligations, or other securities of the surviving or any other corporation or into cash or other property in whole or part.

(c) The plan of merger may set forth:

(1) amendments to the articles of incorporation of the surviving corporation; and

(2) other provisions relating to the merger.

* * * *

§ 11.04 Merger of Subsidiary

(a) A parent corporation owning at least 90 percent of the outstanding shares of each class of a subsidiary corporation may merge the subsidiary into itself without approval of the shareholders of the parent or subsidiary.

(b) The board of directors of the parent shall adopt a plan of merger that sets forth:

(1) the names of the parent and subsidiary; and

(2) the manner and basis of converting the shares of the subsidiary into shares, obligations, or other securities of the parent or any other corporation or into cash or other property in whole or part.

(c) The parent shall mail a copy or summary of the plan of merger to each shareholder of the subsidiary who does not waive the mailing requirement in writing.

(d) The parent may not deliver articles of merger to the secretary of state for filing until at least 30 days after the date it mailed a copy of the plan of merger to each shareholder of the subsidiary who did not waive the mailing requirement.

(e) Articles of merger under this section may not contain amendments to the articles of incorporation of the parent corporation (except for amendments enumerated in section 10.02).

* * * *

§ 11.06 Effect of Merger or Share Exchange

(a) When a merger takes effect:

(1) every other corporation party to the merger merges into the surviving corporation and the separate existence of every corporation except the surviving corporation ceases;

(2) the title to all real estate and other property owned by each corporation party to the merger is vested in the surviving corporation without reversion or impairment;

(3) the surviving corporation has all liabilities of each corporation party to the merger;

(4) a proceeding pending against any corporation party to the merger may be continued as if the merger did not occur or the surviving corporation may be substituted in the proceeding for the corporation whose existence ceased;

(5) the articles of incorporation of the surviving corporation are amended to the extent provided in the plan of merger; and

(6) the shares of each corporation party to the merger that are to be converted into shares, obligations, or other securities of the surviving or any other corporation or into cash or other property are converted and the former holders of the shares are entitled only to the rights provided in the articles of merger or to their rights under chapter 13.

(b) When a share exchange takes effect, the shares of each acquired corporation are exchanged as provided in the plan, and the former holders of the shares are entitled only to the exchange rights provided in the articles of share exchange or to their rights under chapter 13.

* * * *

Chapter 13.
DISSENTERS' RIGHTS

Subchapter A. Right to Dissent and Obtain Payment for Shares

* * * *

§ 13.02 Right to Dissent

(a) A shareholder is entitled to dissent from, and obtain payment of the fair value of his shares in the event of, any of the following corporate actions:

(1) consummation of a plan of merger to which the corporation is a party (i) if shareholder approval is required for the merger by [statute] or the articles of incorporation and the shareholder is entitled to vote on the merger or (ii) if the corporation is a subsidiary that is merged with its parent under section 11.04;

(2) consummation of a plan of share exchange to which the corporation is a party as the corporation whose shares will be acquired, if the shareholder is entitled to vote on the plan;

(3) consummation of a sale or exchange of all, or substantially all, of the property of the corporation other than in the usual and regular course of business, if the shareholder is entitled to vote on the sale or exchange, including a sale in dissolution, but not including a sale pursuant to court order or a sale for cash pursuant to a plan by which all or substantially all of the net proceeds of the sale will be distributed to the shareholders within one year after the date of sale;

(4) an amendment of the articles of incorporation that materially and adversely affects rights in respect of a dissenter's shares because it:

(i) alters or abolishes a preferential right of the shares;

(ii) creates, alters, or abolishes a right in respect of redemption, including a provision respecting a sinking fund for the redemption or repurchase, of the shares;

(iii) alters or abolishes a preemptive right of the holder of the shares to acquire shares or other securities;

(iv) excludes or limits the right of the shares to vote on any matter, or to cumulate votes, other than a limitation by dilution through issuance of shares or other securities with similar voting rights; or

(v) reduces the number of shares owned by the shareholder to a fraction of a share if the fractional share so created is to be acquired for cash * * * ; or

(5) any corporate action taken pursuant to a shareholder vote to the extent the articles of incorporation, bylaws, or a resolution of the board of directors provides that

voting or nonvoting shareholders are entitled to dissent and obtain payment for their shares.

(b) A shareholder entitled to dissent and obtain payment for his shares under this chapter may not challenge the corporate action creating his entitlement unless the action is unlawful or fraudulent with respect to the shareholder or the corporation.

* * * *

Subchapter B. Procedure for Exercise of Dissenters' Rights

* * * *

§ 13.21 Notice of Intent to Demand Payment

(a) If proposed corporate action creating dissenters' rights under section 13.02 is submitted to a vote at a shareholders' meeting, a shareholder who wishes to assert dissenters' rights (1) must deliver to the corporation before the vote is taken written notice of his intent to demand payment for his shares if the proposed action is effectuated and (2) must not vote his shares in favor of the proposed action.

(b) A shareholder who does not satisfy the requirements of subsection (a) is not entitled to payment for his shares under this chapter.

* * * *

§ 13.25 Payment

(a) * * * [A]s soon as the proposed corporate action is taken, or upon receipt of a payment demand, the corporation shall pay each dissenter * * * the amount the corporation estimates to be the fair value of his shares, plus accrued interest.

* * * *

§ 13.28 Procedure If Shareholder Dissatisfied with Payment or Offer

(a) A dissenter may notify the corporation in writing of his own estimate of the fair value of his shares and amount of interest due, and demand payment of his estimate (less any payment under section 13.25) * * * if:

(1) the dissenter believes that the amount paid under section 13.25 * * * is less than the fair value of his shares or that the interest due is incorrectly calculated;

(2) the corporation fails to make payment under section 13.25 within 60 days after the date set for demanding payment; or

(3) the corporation, having failed to take the proposed action, does not return the deposited certificates or release the transfer restrictions imposed on uncertificated shares within 60 days after the date set for demanding payment.

(b) A dissenter waives his right to demand payment under this section unless he notifies the corporation of his demand in writing under subsection (a) within 30 days after the corporation made or offered payment for his shares.

* * * *

Chapter 14.
DISSOLUTION

Subchapter A. Voluntary Dissolution

* * * *

§ 14.02 Dissolution by Board of Directors and Shareholders

(a) A corporation's board of directors may propose dissolution for submission to the shareholders.

(b) For a proposal to dissolve to be adopted:

(1) the board of directors must recommend dissolution to the shareholders unless the board of directors determines that because of conflict of interest or other special circumstances it should make no recommendation and communicates the basis for its determination to the shareholders; and

(2) the shareholders entitled to vote must approve the proposal to dissolve as provided in subsection (e).

(c) The board of directors may condition its submission of the proposal for dissolution on any basis.

(d) The corporation shall notify each shareholder, whether or not entitled to vote, of the proposed shareholders' meeting in accordance with section 7.05. The notice must also state that the purpose, or one of the purposes, of the meeting is to consider dissolving the corporation.

(e) Unless the articles of incorporation or the board of directors (acting pursuant to subsection (c)) require a greater vote or a vote by voting groups, the proposal to dissolve to be adopted must be approved by a majority of all the votes entitled to be cast on that proposal.

* * * *

§ 14.05 Effect of Dissolution

(a) A dissolved corporation continues its corporate existence but may not carry on any business except that appropriate to wind up and liquidate its business and affairs, including:

(1) collecting its assets;

(2) disposing of its properties that will not be distributed in kind to its shareholders;

(3) discharging or making provision for discharging its liabilities;

(4) distributing its remaining property among its shareholders according to their interests; and

(5) doing every other act necessary to wind up and liquidate its business and affairs.

(b) Dissolution of a corporation does not:

(1) transfer title to the corporation's property;

(2) prevent transfer of its shares or securities, although the authorization to dissolve may provide for closing the corporation's share transfer records;

(3) subject its directors or officers to standards of conduct different from those prescribed in chapter 8;

(4) change quorum or voting requirements for its board of directors or shareholders; change provisions for selection, resignation, or removal of its directors or officers or both; or change provisions for amending its bylaws;

(5) prevent commencement of a proceeding by or against the corporation in its corporate name;

(6) abate or suspend a proceeding pending by or against the corporation on the effective date of dissolution; or

(7) terminate the authority of the registered agent of the corporation.

* * * *

Subchapter C. Judicial Dissolution

§ 14.30 Grounds for Judicial Dissolution

The [name or describe court or courts] may dissolve a corporation:

(1) in a proceeding by the attorney general if it is established that:

(i) the corporation obtained its articles of incorporation through fraud; or

(ii) the corporation has continued to exceed or abuse the authority conferred upon it by law;

(2) in a proceeding by a shareholder if it is established that:

(i) the directors are deadlocked in the management of the corporate affairs, the shareholders are unable to break the deadlock, and irreparable injury to the corporation is threatened or being suffered, or the business and affairs of the corporation can no longer be conducted to the advantage of the shareholders generally, because of the deadlock;

(ii) the directors or those in control of the corporation have acted, are acting, or will act in a manner that is illegal, oppressive, or fraudulent;

(iii) the shareholders are deadlocked in voting power and have failed, for a period that includes at least two consecutive annual meeting dates, to elect successors to directors whose terms have expired; or

(iv) the corporate assets are being misapplied or wasted;

(3) in a proceeding by a creditor if it is established that:

(i) the creditor's claim has been reduced to judgment, the execution on the judgment returned unsatisfied, and the corporation is insolvent; or

(ii) the corporation has admitted in writing that the creditor's claim is due and owing and the corporation is insolvent; or

(4) in a proceeding by the corporation to have its voluntary dissolution continued under court supervision.

* * * *

Chapter 16.
RECORDS AND REPORTS

Subchapter A. Records

§ 16.01 Corporate Records

(a) A corporation shall keep as permanent records minutes of all meetings of its shareholders and board of directors, a record of all actions taken by the shareholders or board of directors without a meeting, and a record of all actions taken by a committee of the board of directors in place of the board of directors on behalf of the corporation.

(b) A corporation shall maintain appropriate accounting records.

(c) A corporation or its agent shall maintain a record of its shareholders, in a form that permits preparation of a list of the names and addresses of all shareholders, in alphabetical order by class of shares showing the number and class of shares held by each.

(d) A corporation shall maintain its records in written form or in another form capable of conversion into written form within a reasonable time.

(e) A corporation shall keep a copy of the following records at its principal office:

(1) its articles or restated articles of incorporation and all amendments to them currently in effect;

(2) its bylaws or restated bylaws and all amendments to them currently in effect;

(3) resolutions adopted by its board of directors creating one or more classes or series of shares, and fixing their relative rights, preferences, and limitations, if shares issued pursuant to those resolutions are outstanding;

(4) the minutes of all shareholders' meetings, and records of all action taken by shareholders without a meeting, for the past three years;

(5) all written communications to shareholders generally within the past three years, including the financial statements furnished for the past three years
* * * ;

(6) a list of the names and business addresses of its current directors and officers; and

(7) its most recent annual report delivered to the secretary of state * * *.

§ 16.02 Inspection of Records by Shareholders

(a) Subject to section 16.03(c), a shareholder of a corporation is entitled to inspect and copy, during regular business hours at the corporation's principal office, any of the records of the corporation described in section 16.01(e) if he gives the corporation written notice of his demand at least five business days before the date on which he wishes to inspect and copy.

(b) A shareholder of a corporation is entitled to inspect and copy, during regular business hours at a reasonable location specified by the corporation, any of the following records of the corporation if the shareholder meets the requirements of subsection (c) and gives the corporation written notice of his demand at least five business days before the date on which he wishes to inspect and copy:

(1) excerpts from minutes of any meeting of the board of directors, records of any action of a committee of the board of directors while acting in place of the board of directors on behalf of the corporation, minutes of any meeting of the shareholders, and records of action taken by the shareholders or board of directors without a meeting, to the extent not subject to inspection under section 16.02(a);

(2) accounting records of the corporation; and

(3) the record of shareholders.

(c) A shareholder may inspect and copy the records identified in subsection (b) only if:

(1) his demand is made in good faith and for a proper purpose;

(2) he describes with reasonable particularity his purpose and the records he desires to inspect; and

(3) the records are directly connected with his purpose.

(d) The right of inspection granted by this section may not be abolished or limited by a corporation's articles of incorporation or bylaws.

(e) This section does not affect:

(1) the right of a shareholder to inspect records under section 7.20 or, if the shareholder is in litigation with the corporation, to the same extent as any other litigant;

(2) the power of a court, independently of this Act, to compel the production of corporate records for examination.

(f) For purposes of this section, "shareholder" includes a beneficial owner whose shares are held in a voting trust or by a nominee on his behalf.

APPENDIX H

The Sarbanes-Oxley Act of 2002 (Excerpts and Explanatory Comments)

Note: The authors' explanatory comments appear in italics following the excerpt from each section.

SECTION 302

Corporate responsibility for financial reports[1]

(a) Regulations required

The Commission shall, by rule, require, for each company filing periodic reports under section 13(a) or 15(d) of the Securities Exchange Act of 1934 (15 U.S.C. 78m, 78o(d)), that the principal executive officer or officers and the principal financial officer or officers, or persons performing similar functions, certify in each annual or quarterly report filed or submitted under either such section of such Act that—

(1) the signing officer has reviewed the report;

(2) based on the officer's knowledge, the report does not contain any untrue statement of a material fact or omit to state a material fact necessary in order to make the statements made, in light of the circumstances under which such statements were made, not misleading;

(3) based on such officer's knowledge, the financial statements, and other financial information included in the report, fairly present in all material respects the financial condition and results of operations of the issuer as of, and for, the periods presented in the report;

(4) the signing officers—

(A) are responsible for establishing and maintaining internal controls;

(B) have designed such internal controls to ensure that material information relating to the issuer and its consolidated subsidiaries is made known to such officers by others within those entities, particularly during the period in which the periodic reports are being prepared;

(C) have evaluated the effectiveness of the issuer's internal controls as of a date within 90 days prior to the report; and

(D) have presented in the report their conclusions about the effectiveness of their internal controls based on their evaluation as of that date;

(5) the signing officers have disclosed to the issuer's auditors and the audit committee of the board of directors (or persons fulfilling the equivalent function)—

(A) all significant deficiencies in the design or operation of internal controls which could adversely affect the issuer's ability to record, process, summarize, and report financial data and have identified for the issuer's auditors any material weaknesses in internal controls; and

(B) any fraud, whether or not material, that involves management or other employees who have a significant role in the issuer's internal controls; and

(6) the signing officers have indicated in the report whether or not there were significant changes in internal controls or in other factors that could significantly affect internal controls subsequent to the date of their evaluation, including any corrective actions with regard to significant deficiencies and material weaknesses.

(b) Foreign reincorporations have no effect

Nothing in this section shall be interpreted or applied in any way to allow any issuer to lessen the legal force of the statement required under this section, by an issuer having reincorporated or having engaged in any other transaction that resulted in the transfer of the corporate domicile or offices of the issuer from inside the United States to outside of the United States.

(c) Deadline

The rules required by subsection (a) of this section shall be effective not later than 30 days after July 30, 2002.

EXPLANATORY COMMENTS: *Section 302 requires the chief executive officer (CEO) and chief financial officer (CFO) of each public company to certify that they have reviewed the company's quarterly and annual reports to be filed with the Securities and Exchange Commission (SEC). The CEO and CFO must certify that, based on their knowledge, the reports do not contain any untrue statement of a material fact or any half-truth that would make the report misleading, and that the*

---

1. This section of the Sarbanes-Oxley Act is codified at 15 U.S.C. Section 7241.

information contained in the reports fairly presents the company's financial condition.

In addition, this section also requires the CEO and CFO to certify that they have created and designed an internal control system for their company and have recently evaluated that system to ensure that it is effectively providing them with relevant and accurate financial information. If the signing officers have found any significant deficiencies or weaknesses in the company's system or have discovered any evidence of fraud, they must have reported the situation, and any corrective actions they have taken, to the auditors and the audit committee.

Section 306

Insider trades during pension fund blackout periods[2]

(a) Prohibition of insider trading during pension fund blackout periods

(1) In general

Except to the extent otherwise provided by rule of the Commission pursuant to paragraph (3), it shall be unlawful for any director or executive officer of an issuer of any equity security (other than an exempted security), directly or indirectly, to purchase, sell, or otherwise acquire or transfer any equity security of the issuer (other than an exempted security) during any blackout period with respect to such equity security if such director or officer acquires such equity security in connection with his or her service or employment as a director or executive officer.

(2) Remedy

(A) In general

Any profit realized by a director or executive officer referred to in paragraph (1) from any purchase, sale, or other acquisition or transfer in violation of this subsection shall inure to and be recoverable by the issuer, irrespective of any intention on the part of such director or executive officer in entering into the transaction.

(B) Actions to recover profits

An action to recover profits in accordance with this subsection may be instituted at law or in equity in any court of competent jurisdiction by the issuer, or by the owner of any security of the issuer in the name and in behalf of the issuer if the issuer fails or refuses to bring such action within 60 days after the date of request, or fails diligently to prosecute the action thereafter, except that no such suit shall be brought more than 2 years after the date on which such profit was realized.

(3) Rulemaking authorized

The Commission shall, in consultation with the Secretary of Labor, issue rules to clarify the application of this subsection and to prevent evasion thereof. Such rules shall provide for the application of the requirements of paragraph (1) with respect to entities treated as a single employer with respect to an issuer under section 414(b), (c), (m), or (o) of Title 26 to the extent necessary to clarify the application of such requirements and to prevent evasion thereof. Such rules may also provide for appropriate exceptions from the requirements of this subsection, including exceptions for purchases pursuant to an automatic dividend reinvestment program or purchases or sales made pursuant to an advance election.

(4) Blackout period

For purposes of this subsection, the term "blackout period", with respect to the equity securities of any issuer—

(A) means any period of more than 3 consecutive business days during which the ability of not fewer than 50 percent of the participants or beneficiaries under all individual account plans maintained by the issuer to purchase, sell, or otherwise acquire or transfer an interest in any equity of such issuer held in such an individual account plan is temporarily suspended by the issuer or by a fiduciary of the plan; and

(B) does not include, under regulations which shall be prescribed by the Commission—

(i) a regularly scheduled period in which the participants and beneficiaries may not purchase, sell, or otherwise acquire or transfer an interest in any equity of such issuer, if such period is—

(I) incorporated into the individual account plan; and

(II) timely disclosed to employees before becoming participants under the individual account plan or as a subsequent amendment to the plan; or

(ii) any suspension described in subparagraph (A) that is imposed solely in connection with persons becoming participants or beneficiaries, or ceasing to be participants or beneficiaries, in an individual account plan by reason of a corporate merger, acquisition, divestiture, or similar transaction involving the plan or plan sponsor.

(5) Individual account plan

For purposes of this subsection, the term "individual account plan" has the meaning provided in section 1002(34) of Title 29, except that such term shall not include a one-participant retirement plan (within the meaning of section 1021(i)(8)(B) of Title 29).

(6) Notice to directors, executive officers, and the Commission

---

2. Codified at 15 U.S.C. Section 7244.

In any case in which a director or executive officer is subject to the requirements of this subsection in connection with a blackout period (as defined in paragraph (4)) with respect to any equity securities, the issuer of such equity securities shall timely notify such director or officer and the Securities and Exchange Commission of such blackout period.

* * * *

EXPLANATORY COMMENTS: *Corporate pension funds typically prohibit employees from trading shares of the corporation during periods when the pension fund is undergoing significant change. Prior to 2002, however, these blackout periods did not affect the corporation's executives, who frequently received shares of the corporate stock as part of their compensation. During the collapse of Enron, for example, its pension plan was scheduled to change administrators at a time when Enron's stock price was falling. Enron's employees therefore could not sell their shares while the price was dropping, but its executives could and did sell their stock, consequently avoiding some of the losses. Section 306 was Congress's solution to the basic unfairness of this situation. This section of the act required the SEC to issue rules that prohibit any director or executive officer from trading during pension fund blackout periods. (The SEC later issued these rules, entitled Regulation Blackout Trading Restriction, or Reg BTR.) Section 306 also provided shareholders with a right to file a shareholder's derivative suit against officers and directors who have profited from trading during these blackout periods (provided that the corporation has failed to bring a suit). The officer or director can be forced to return to the corporation any profits received, regardless of whether the director or officer acted with bad intent.*

Section 402

Periodical and other reports[3]

* * * *

(i) Accuracy of financial reports

Each financial report that contains financial statements, and that is required to be prepared in accordance with (or reconciled to) generally accepted accounting principles under this chapter and filed with the Commission shall reflect all material correcting adjustments that have been identified by a registered public accounting firm in accordance with generally accepted accounting principles and the rules and regulations of the Commission.

(j) Off-balance sheet transactions

Not later than 180 days after July 30, 2002, the Commission shall issue final rules providing that each annual and quarterly financial report required to be filed with the Commission shall disclose all material off-balance sheet transactions, arrangements, obligations (including contingent obligations), and other relationships of the issuer

---

3. This section of the Sarbanes-Oxley Act amended some of the provisions of the 1934 Securities Exchange Act and added the paragraphs reproduced here at 15 U.S.C. Section 78m.

with unconsolidated entities or other persons, that may have a material current or future effect on financial condition, changes in financial condition, results of operations, liquidity, capital expenditures, capital resources, or significant components of revenues or expenses.

(k) Prohibition on personal loans to executives

(1) In general

It shall be unlawful for any issuer (as defined in section 7201 of this title), directly or indirectly, including through any subsidiary, to extend or maintain credit, to arrange for the extension of credit, or to renew an extension of credit, in the form of a personal loan to or for any director or executive officer (or equivalent thereof) of that issuer. An extension of credit maintained by the issuer on July 30, 2002, shall not be subject to the provisions of this subsection, provided that there is no material modification to any term of any such extension of credit or any renewal of any such extension of credit on or after July 30, 2002.

(2) Limitation

Paragraph (1) does not preclude any home improvement and manufactured home loans (as that term is defined in section 1464 of Title 12), consumer credit (as defined in section 1602 of this title), or any extension of credit under an open end credit plan (as defined in section 1602 of this title), or a charge card (as defined in section 1637(c)(4)(e) of this title), or any extension of credit by a broker or dealer registered under section 78o of this title to an employee of that broker or dealer to buy, trade, or carry securities, that is permitted under rules or regulations of the Board of Governors of the Federal Reserve System pursuant to section 78g of this title (other than an extension of credit that would be used to purchase the stock of that issuer), that is—

(A) made or provided in the ordinary course of the consumer credit business of such issuer;

(B) of a type that is generally made available by such issuer to the public; and

(C) made by such issuer on market terms, or terms that are no more favorable than those offered by the issuer to the general public for such extensions of credit.

(3) Rule of construction for certain loans

Paragraph (1) does not apply to any loan made or maintained by an insured depository institution (as defined in section 1813 of Title 12), if the loan is subject to the insider lending restrictions of section 375b of Title 12.

(l) Real time issuer disclosures

Each issuer reporting under subsection (a) of this section or section 78o(d) of this title shall disclose to the public on a rapid and current basis such additional information concerning material changes in the financial condition or operations of the issuer, in plain English, which may include trend and qualitative information and graphic presentations, as the Commission determines, by rule, is necessary or useful for the protection of investors and in the public interest.

EXPLANATORY COMMENTS: *Corporate executives during the Enron era typically received extremely large salaries, significant bonuses, and abundant stock options, even when the companies for which they worked were suffering. Executives were also routinely given personal loans from corporate funds, many of which were never paid back. The average large company during that period loaned almost $1 million a year to top executives, and some companies, including Tyco International and Adelphia Communications Corporation, loaned hundreds of millions of dollars to their executives every year. Section 402 amended the 1934 Securities Exchange Act to prohibit public companies from making personal loans to executive officers and directors. There are a few exceptions to this prohibition, such as home-improvement loans made in the ordinary course of business. Note also that while loans are forbidden, outright gifts are not. A corporation is free to give gifts to its executives, including cash, provided that these gifts are disclosed on its financial reports. The idea is that corporate directors will be deterred from making substantial gifts to their executives by the disclosure requirement—particularly if the corporation's financial condition is questionable—because making such gifts could be perceived as abusing their authority.*

Section 403

Directors, officers, and principal stockholders[4]

(a) Disclosures required

(1) Directors, officers, and principal stockholders required to file

Every person who is directly or indirectly the beneficial owner of more than 10 percent of any class of any equity security (other than an exempted security) which is registered pursuant to section 78l of this title, or who is a director or an officer of the issuer of such security, shall file the statements required by this subsection with the Commission (and, if such security is registered on a national securities exchange, also with the exchange).

(2) Time of filing

The statements required by this subsection shall be filed—

(A) at the time of the registration of such security on a national securities exchange or by the effective date of a registration statement filed pursuant to section 78l(g) of this title;

(B) within 10 days after he or she becomes such beneficial owner, director, or officer;

---

4. This section of the Sarbanes-Oxley Act amended the disclosure provisions of the 1934 Securities Exchange Act, at 15 U.S.C. Section 78p.

(C) if there has been a change in such ownership, or if such person shall have purchased or sold a security-based swap agreement (as defined in section 206(b) of the Gramm-Leach-Bliley Act (15 U.S.C. 78c note)) involving such equity security, before the end of the second business day following the day on which the subject transaction has been executed, or at such other time as the Commission shall establish, by rule, in any case in which the Commission determines that such 2-day period is not feasible.

(3) Contents of statements

A statement filed—

(A) under subparagraph (A) or (B) of paragraph (2) shall contain a statement of the amount of all equity securities of such issuer of which the filing person is the beneficial owner; and

(B) under subparagraph (C) of such paragraph shall indicate ownership by the filing person at the date of filing, any such changes in such ownership, and such purchases and sales of the security-based swap agreements as have occurred since the most recent such filing under such subparagraph.

(4) Electronic filing and availability

Beginning not later than 1 year after July 30, 2002—

(A) a statement filed under subparagraph (C) of paragraph (2) shall be filed electronically;

(B) the Commission shall provide each such statement on a publicly accessible Internet site not later than the end of the business day following that filing; and

(C) the issuer (if the issuer maintains a corporate website) shall provide that statement on that corporate website, not later than the end of the business day following that filing.

* * * *

EXPLANATORY COMMENTS: *This section dramatically shortens the time period provided in the Securities Exchange Act of 1934 for disclosing transactions by insiders. The prior law stated that most transactions had to be reported within ten days of the beginning of the following month, although certain transactions did not have to be reported until the following fiscal year (within the first forty-five days). Because some of the insider trading that occurred during the Enron fiasco did not have to be disclosed (and was therefore not discovered) until long after the transactions, Congress added this section to reduce the time period for making disclosures. Under Section 403, most transactions by insiders must be electronically filed with the SEC within two business days. Also, any company that maintains a Web site must post these SEC filings on its site by the end of the next business day. Congress enacted this section in the belief that if insiders are required to file reports of their transactions promptly with the SEC, companies will do more to police themselves and prevent insider trading.*

Section 404

Management assessment of internal controls[5]

(a) Rules required

The Commission shall prescribe rules requiring each annual report required by section 78m(a) or 78o(d) of this title to contain an internal control report, which shall—

(1) state the responsibility of management for establishing and maintaining an adequate internal control structure and procedures for financial reporting; and

(2) contain an assessment, as of the end of the most recent fiscal year of the issuer, of the effectiveness of the internal control structure and procedures of the issuer for financial reporting.

(b) Internal control evaluation and reporting

With respect to the internal control assessment required by subsection (a) of this section, each registered public accounting firm that prepares or issues the audit report for the issuer shall attest to, and report on, the assessment made by the management of the issuer. An attestation made under this subsection shall be made in accordance with standards for attestation engagements issued or adopted by the Board. Any such attestation shall not be the subject of a separate engagement.

EXPLANATORY COMMENTS: *This section was enacted to prevent corporate executives from claiming they were ignorant of significant errors in their companies' financial reports. For instance, several CEOs testified before Congress that they simply had no idea that the corporations' financial statements were off by billions of dollars. Congress therefore passed Section 404, which requires each annual report to contain a description and assessment of the company's internal control structure and financial reporting procedures. The section also requires that an audit be conducted of the internal control assessment, as well as the financial statements contained in the report. This section goes hand in hand with Section 302 (which, as discussed previously, requires various certifications attesting to the accuracy of the information in financial reports).*

Section 404 has been one of the more controversial and expensive provisions in the Sarbanes-Oxley Act because it requires companies to assess their own internal financial controls to make sure that their financial statements are reliable and accurate. A corporation might need to set up a disclosure committee and a coordinator, establish codes of conduct for accounting and financial personnel, create documentation procedures, provide training, and outline the individuals who are responsible for performing each of the procedures. Companies that were already well managed have not experienced substantial difficulty complying with this section. Other companies, however, have spent millions of dollars setting up, documenting, and evaluating their internal financial control systems. Although initially creating the internal financial control system is a one-time-only expense, the costs of maintaining and evaluating it are ongoing. Some corporations that spent considerable sums complying with Section 404 have been able to offset

these costs by discovering and correcting inefficiencies or frauds within their systems. Nevertheless, it is unlikely that any corporation will find compliance with this section to be inexpensive.

Section 802 (a)

Destruction, alteration, or falsification of records in Federal investigations and bankruptcy[6]

Whoever knowingly alters, destroys, mutilates, conceals, covers up, falsifies, or makes a false entry in any record, document, or tangible object with the intent to impede, obstruct, or influence the investigation or proper administration of any matter within the jurisdiction of any department or agency of the United States or any case filed under title 11, or in relation to or contemplation of any such matter or case, shall be fined under this title, imprisoned not more than 20 years, or both.

Destruction of corporate audit records[7]

(a) (1) Any accountant who conducts an audit of an issuer of securities to which section 10A(a) of the Securities Exchange Act of 1934 (15 U.S.C. 78j-1(a)) applies, shall maintain all audit or review workpapers for a period of 5 years from the end of the fiscal period in which the audit or review was concluded.

(2) The Securities and Exchange Commission shall promulgate, within 180 days, after adequate notice and an opportunity for comment, such rules and regulations, as are reasonably necessary, relating to the retention of relevant records such as workpapers, documents that form the basis of an audit or review, memoranda, correspondence, communications, other documents, and records (including electronic records) which are created, sent, or received in connection with an audit or review and contain conclusions, opinions, analyses, or financial data relating to such an audit or review, which is conducted by any accountant who conducts an audit of an issuer of securities to which section 10A(a) of the Securities Exchange Act of 1934 (15 U.S.C. 78j-1(a)) applies. The Commission may, from time to time, amend or supplement the rules and regulations that it is required to promulgate under this section, after adequate notice and an opportunity for comment, in order to ensure that such rules and regulations adequately comport with the purposes of this section.

(b) Whoever knowingly and willfully violates subsection (a)(1), or any rule or regulation promulgated by the Securities and Exchange Commission under subsection (a)(2), shall be fined under this title, imprisoned not more than 10 years, or both.

(c) Nothing in this section shall be deemed to diminish or relieve any person of any other duty or obligation imposed

---

5. Codified at 15 U.S.C. Section 7262.

6. Codified at 15 U.S.C. Section 1519.

7. Codified at 15 U.S.C. Section 1520.

by Federal or State law or regulation to maintain, or refrain from destroying, any document.

EXPLANATORY COMMENTS: *Section 802(a) enacted two new statutes that punish those who alter or destroy documents. The first statute is not specifically limited to securities fraud cases. It provides that anyone who alters, destroys, or falsifies records in federal investigations or bankruptcy may be criminally prosecuted and sentenced to a fine or to up to twenty years in prison, or both. The second statute requires auditors of public companies to keep all audit or review working papers for five years but expressly allows the SEC to amend or supplement these requirements as it sees fit. The SEC has, in fact, amended this section by issuing a rule that requires auditors who audit reporting companies to retain working papers for seven years from the conclusion of the review. Section 802(a) further provides that anyone who knowingly and willfully violates this statute is subject to criminal prosecution and can be sentenced to a fine, imprisoned for up to ten years, or both if convicted.*

This portion of the Sarbanes-Oxley Act implicitly recognizes that persons who are under investigation often are tempted to respond by destroying or falsifying documents that might prove their complicity in wrongdoing. The severity of the punishment should provide a strong incentive for these individuals to resist the temptation.

SECTION 804

Time limitations on the commencement of civil actions arising under Acts of Congress[8]

(a) Except as otherwise provided by law, a civil action arising under an Act of Congress enacted after the date of the enactment of this section may not be commenced later than 4 years after the cause of action accrues.

(b) Notwithstanding subsection (a), a private right of action that involves a claim of fraud, deceit, manipulation, or contrivance in contravention of a regulatory requirement concerning the securities laws, as defined in section 3(a)(47) of the Securities Exchange Act of 1934 (15 U.S.C. 78c(a)(47)), may be brought not later than the earlier of—

(1) 2 years after the discovery of the facts constituting the violation; or

(2) 5 years after such violation.

EXPLANATORY COMMENTS: *Prior to the enactment of this section, Section 10(b) of the Securities Exchange Act of 1934 had no express statute of limitations. The courts generally required plaintiffs to have filed suit within one year from the date that they should (using due diligence) have discovered that a fraud had been committed but no later than three years after the fraud occurred. Section 804 extends this period by specifying that plaintiffs must file a lawsuit within two years after they discover (or should have discovered) a fraud but no later than five years after the fraud's occurrence. This provision has prevented the courts from dismissing numerous securities fraud lawsuits.*

SECTION 806

Civil action to protect against retaliation in fraud cases[9]

(a) Whistleblower protection for employees of publicly traded companies.—

No company with a class of securities registered under section 12 of the Securities Exchange Act of 1934 (15 U.S.C. 78l), or that is required to file reports under section 15(d) of the Securities Exchange Act of 1934 (15 U.S.C. 78o(d)), or any officer, employee, contractor, subcontractor, or agent of such company, may discharge, demote, suspend, threaten, harass, or in any other manner discriminate against an employee in the terms and conditions of employment because of any lawful act done by the employee—

(1) to provide information, cause information to be provided, or otherwise assist in an investigation regarding any conduct which the employee reasonably believes constitutes a violation of section 1341, 1343, 1344, or 1348, any rule or regulation of the Securities and Exchange Commission, or any provision of Federal law relating to fraud against shareholders, when the information or assistance is provided to or the investigation is conducted by—

(A) a Federal regulatory or law enforcement agency;

(B) any Member of Congress or any committee of Congress; or

(C) a person with supervisory authority over the employee (or such other person working for the employer who has the authority to investigate, discover, or terminate misconduct); or

(2) to file, cause to be filed, testify, participate in, or otherwise assist in a proceeding filed or about to be filed (with any knowledge of the employer) relating to an alleged violation of section 1341, 1343, 1344, or 1348, any rule or regulation of the Securities and Exchange Commission, or any provision of Federal law relating to fraud against shareholders.

(b) Enforcement action.—

(1) In general.—A person who alleges discharge or other discrimination by any person in violation of subsection (a) may seek relief under subsection (c), by—

(A) filing a complaint with the Secretary of Labor; or

(B) if the Secretary has not issued a final decision within 180 days of the filing of the complaint and there is no showing that such delay is due to the bad faith of the claimant, bringing an action at law or equity for de novo review in the appropriate district court of the United States, which shall have

---

8. Codified at 28 U.S.C. Section 1658.

9. Codified at 18 U.S.C. Section 1514A.

jurisdiction over such an action without regard to the amount in controversy.

(2) Procedure.—

(A) In general.—An action under paragraph (1)(A) shall be governed under the rules and procedures set forth in section 42121(b) of title 49, United States Code.

(B) Exception.—Notification made under section 42121(b)(1) of title 49, United States Code, shall be made to the person named in the complaint and to the employer.

(C) Burdens of proof.—An action brought under paragraph (1)(B) shall be governed by the legal burdens of proof set forth in section 42121(b) of title 49, United States Code.

(D) Statute of limitations.—An action under paragraph (1) shall be commenced not later than 90 days after the date on which the violation occurs.

(c) Remedies.—

(1) In general.—An employee prevailing in any action under subsection (b)(1) shall be entitled to all relief necessary to make the employee whole.

(2) Compensatory damages.—Relief for any action under paragraph (1) shall include—

(A) reinstatement with the same seniority status that the employee would have had, but for the discrimination;

(B) the amount of back pay, with interest; and

(C) compensation for any special damages sustained as a result of the discrimination, including litigation costs, expert witness fees, and reasonable attorney fees.

(d) Rights retained by employee.—Nothing in this section shall be deemed to diminish the rights, privileges, or remedies of any employee under any Federal or State law, or under any collective bargaining agreement.

EXPLANATORY COMMENTS: *Section 806 is one of several provisions that were included in the Sarbanes-Oxley Act to encourage and protect whistleblowers—that is, employees who report their employer's alleged violations of securities law to the authorities. This section applies to employees, agents, and independent contractors who work for publicly traded companies or testify about such a company during an investigation. It sets up an administrative procedure at the Department of Labor for individuals who claim that their employer retaliated against them (fired or demoted them, for example) for blowing the whistle on the employer's wrongful conduct. It also allows the award of civil damages—including back pay, reinstatement, special damages, attorneys' fees, and court costs—to employees who prove that they suffered retaliation. Since this provision was enacted, whistleblowers have filed numerous complaints with the Department of Labor under this section.*

SECTION 807
Securities fraud[10]

Whoever knowingly executes, or attempts to execute, a scheme or artifice—

(1) to defraud any person in connection with any security of an issuer with a class of securities registered under section 12 of the Securities Exchange Act of 1934 (15 U.S.C. 78l) or that is required to file reports under section 15(d) of the Securities Exchange Act of 1934 (15 U.S.C. 78o(d)); or

(2) to obtain, by means of false or fraudulent pretenses, representations, or promises, any money or property in connection with the purchase or sale of any security of an issuer with a class of securities registered under section 12 of the Securities Exchange Act of 1934 (15 U.S.C. 78l) or that is required to file reports under section 15(d) of the Securities Exchange Act of 1934 (15 U.S.C. 78o(d)); shall be fined under this title, or imprisoned not more than 25 years, or both.

EXPLANATORY COMMENTS: *Section 807 adds a new provision to the federal criminal code that addresses securities fraud. Prior to 2002, federal securities law had already made it a crime—under Section 10(b) of the Securities Exchange Act of 1934 and SEC Rule 10b-5, both of which are discussed in Chapter 42—to intentionally defraud someone in connection with a purchase or sale of securities, but the offense was not listed in the federal criminal code. Also, paragraph 2 of Section 807 goes beyond what is prohibited under securities law by making it a crime to obtain by means of false or fraudulent pretenses any money or property from the purchase or sale of securities. This new provision allows violators to be punished by up to twenty-five years in prison, a fine, or both.*

SECTION 906
Failure of corporate officers to certify financial reports[11]

(a) Certification of periodic financial reports.—Each periodic report containing financial statements filed by an issuer with the Securities Exchange Commission pursuant to section 13(a) or 15(d) of the Securities Exchange Act of 1934 (15 U.S.C. 78m(a) or 78o(d)) shall be accompanied by a written statement by the chief executive officer and chief financial officer (or equivalent thereof) of the issuer.

(b) Content.—The statement required under subsection (a) shall certify that the periodic report containing the financial statements fully complies with the requirements of section 13(a) or 15(d) of the Securities Exchange Act of 1934 (15 U.S.C. 78m or 78o(d)) and that information contained in the periodic report fairly presents, in all material

---

10. Codified at 18 U.S.C. Section 1348.

11. Codified at 18 U.S.C. Section 1350.

respects, the financial condition and results of operations of the issuer.

(c) Criminal penalties.—Whoever—

(1) certifies any statement as set forth in subsections (a) and (b) of this section knowing that the periodic report accompanying the statement does not comport with all the requirements set forth in this section shall be fined not more than $1,000,000 or imprisoned not more than 10 years, or both; or

(2) willfully certifies any statement as set forth in subsections (a) and (b) of this section knowing that the periodic report accompanying the statement does not comport with all the requirements set forth in this section shall be fined not more than $5,000,000, or imprisoned not more than 20 years, or both.

EXPLANATORY COMMENTS: *As previously discussed, under Section 302 a corporation's CEO and CFO are required to certify that they believe the quarterly and annual reports their company files with the SEC are accurate and fairly present the company's financial condition. Section 906 adds "teeth" to these requirements by authorizing criminal penalties for those officers who intentionally certify inaccurate SEC filings. Knowing violations of the requirements are punishable by a fine of up to $1 million, ten years in prison, or both. Willful violators may be fined up to $5 million, sentenced to up to twenty years in prison, or both. Although the difference between a knowing and a willful violation is not entirely clear, the section is obviously intended to remind corporate officers of the serious consequences of certifying inaccurate reports to the SEC.*

APPENDIX I

Sample Answers for End-of-Chapter *Questions with Sample Answer*

1–2A. Question with Sample Answer

At the time of the Nuremberg trials, "crimes against humanity" were new international crimes. The laws criminalized such acts as murder, extermination, enslavement, deportation, and other inhumane acts committed against any civilian population. These international laws derived their legitimacy from "natural law." Natural law, which is the oldest and one of the most significant schools of jurisprudence, holds that governments and legal systems should reflect the moral and ethical ideals that are inherent in human nature. Because natural law is universal and discoverable by reason, its adherents believe that all other law is derived from natural law. Natural law therefore supersedes laws created by humans (national, or "positive," law), and in a conflict between the two, national or positive law loses its legitimacy. The Nuremberg defendants asserted that they had been acting in accordance with German law. The judges dismissed these claims, reasoning that the defendants' acts were commonly regarded as crimes and that the accused must have known that the acts would be considered criminal. The judges clearly believed the tenets of natural law and expected that the defendants, too, should have been able to realize that their acts ran afoul of it. The fact that the "positivist law" of Germany at the time required them to commit these acts is irrelevant. Under natural law theory, the international court was justified in finding the defendants guilty of crimes against humanity.

2–2A. Question with Sample Answer

Trial courts, as explained in the text, are responsible for settling "questions of fact." Often, when parties bring a case to court there is a dispute as to what actually happened. Different witnesses have different versions of what they saw or heard, and there may be only indirect evidence of certain issues in dispute. During the trial, the judge and the jury (if it is a jury trial) listen to the witnesses and view the evidence firsthand. Thus, the trial court is in the best position to assess the credibility (truthfulness) of the witnesses and determine the weight that should be given to various items of evidence. At the end of the trial, the judge and the jury (if it is a jury trial) decide what will be considered facts for the purposes of the case. Trial courts are best suited to this job, as they have the opportunity to observe the witnesses and evidence, and they regularly determine the reliability of certain evidence. Appellate courts, in contrast, see only the written record of the trial court proceedings and cannot evaluate the credibility of witnesses and the persuasiveness of evidence. For these reasons, appellate courts nearly always defer to trial courts' findings of fact. An appellate court can reverse a lower court's findings of fact, however, when so little evidence was presented at trial that no reasonable person could have reached the conclusion that the judge or jury reached.

3–2A. Question with Sample Answer

(a) After all of the pleadings (the complaint, answer, and any counterclaim and reply) have been filed, either party can file a motion for judgment on the pleadings. This may happen because it is clear from just the pleadings that the plaintiff has failed to state a cause of action. This motion is also appropriate when all the parties agree on the facts, and the only question remaining is how the law applies to those facts. The court may consider only those facts pleaded in the documents and stipulated (agreed to) by the parties. This is the difference between a motion for judgment on the pleadings and a motion for summary judgment (discussed below). In a motion for summary judgment, there may be some facts in dispute and the parties may supplement the pleadings with sworn statements and other materials.

(b) During the trial, at the conclusion of the plaintiff's case, the defendant may move for a directed verdict. If the defendant does this, he or she will argue to the court that the plaintiff presented inadequate evidence that he or she is entitled to the remedy being sought. In considering a motion for a directed verdict (federal courts use the term "motion for a judgment as a matter of law"), the judge looks at the evidence in the light most favorable to the plaintiff and grants the motion only if there is insufficient evidence to raise an issue of fact. These motions are rarely granted at this stage of a trial. At the end of the defendant's case, the parties have another opportunity to move for a directed verdict. This time, either party can seek the motion. The motion will be granted only if there is no reasonable way to find for the party against whom the motion is made. In other words, if, after the defense's case is concluded, the plaintiff asks the court to direct a verdict against the defendant, the court will do so if no reasonable interpretation of the evidence would allow the defendant to win the case.

(c) As noted in part (a) of this answer, a motion for summary judgment is similar to a motion for a judgment on the pleadings in that it asks the court to grant a judgment without a trial. Either party can file a summary judgment motion when the only question is how the law applies to the facts in a case. When a court considers a motion for summary judgment, it can take into account evidence outside the pleadings. The evidence may consist of sworn statements by parties or witnesses as well as documents. The use of this additional evidence distinguishes the motion for summary judgment from the motion for judgment on the pleadings. Summary judgment motions will be granted only when there are no questions of fact that need to be decided and the only question is a question of law, which requires a judge's ruling. These motions can be made before or during a trial.

(d) If a losing party has previously moved for a directed verdict, that party can make a motion for a judgment *n.o.v.* (notwithstanding the verdict) after the jury issues its verdict. The standards for granting a judgment n.o.v. are the same as those for granting a motion to dismiss a case or a motion for a directed verdict. Essentially, the losing party argues that even if the evidence is viewed in the light most favorable to the other party, a reasonable jury could not have found in that party's favor. If the judge finds this contention to be correct or decides that the law requires the opposite result, the motion will be granted.

4–2A. Question with Sample Answer

As the text points out, Thomas has a constitutionally protected right to his religion and the free exercise of it. In denying his unemployment benefits, the state violated these rights. Employers are obligated to make reasonable accommodations for their employees' beliefs, right or wrong, that are openly and sincerely held. Thomas's beliefs were openly and sincerely held. By placing him in a department that made military goods, his employer effectively put him in a position of having to choose between his job and his religious principles. This unilateral decision on the part of the employer was the reason Thomas left his job and why the company was required to compensate Thomas for his resulting unemployment.

5–2A. Question with Sample Answer

Factors for the firm to consider in making its decision include the appropriate ethical standard. Under the utilitarian standard, an action is correct, or "right," when, among the people it affects, it produces the greatest amount of good for the greatest number. When an action affects the majority adversely, it is morally wrong. Applying the utilitarian standard requires (1) a determination of which individuals will be affected by the action in question; (2) an assessment, or cost-benefit analysis, of the negative and positive effects of alternative actions on these individuals; and (3) a choice among alternatives that

will produce maximum societal utility. Ethical standards may also be based on a concept of duty—which postulates that the end can never justify the means and human beings should not be treated as mere means to an end. But ethical decision making in a business context is not always simple, particularly when it is determined that an action will affect, in different ways, different groups of people: shareholders, employees, society, and other stakeholders, such as the local community. Thus, another factor to consider is to whom the firm believes it owes a duty.

6–2A. Question with Sample Answer

To answer this question, you must first decide if there is a legal theory under which Harley may be able to recover. You may recall from your reading the intentional tort of "wrongful interference with a contractual relationship." To recover damages under this theory, Harley would need to show that he and Martha had a valid contract, that Lothar knew of this contractual relationship between Martha and Harley, and that Lothar intentionally convinced Martha to break her contract with Harley. Even though Lothar hoped that his advertisments would persuade Martha to break her contract with Harley, the question states that Martha's decision to change bakers was based solely on the advertising and not on anything else that Lothar did. Lothar's advertisements did not constitute a tort. Note, though, that while Harley cannot collect from Lothar for Martha's actions, he does have a cause of action against Martha for her breach of their contract.

7–2A. Question with Sample Answer

This is a causation question. You will recall from the chapter that four elements must be proved for a plaintiff to recover in a claim for negligence: that the defendant owed a duty of care, the defendant breached this duty, the plaintiff suffered a legally recognizable injury, and the defendant's breach of the duty of care caused the injury. Ruth did breach the duty of care that she owed Jim (and others in society) when she parked carelessly on the hill. Jim also clearly suffered an injury. The only remaining question, then, has to do with causation. Causation is broken down into two parts, causation in fact and proximate cause. In order for Jim to recover, he must prove that both kinds of causation existed in this case. Causation in fact is answered by the "but for" test and readily answered here. Ruth's car set into motion a chain of events without which the barn would not have fallen down. Meeting the proximate cause test will be more difficult for Jim. Recall that proximate cause exists only when the connection between an act and an injury is strong enough to justify imposing liability. Careless parking on a hill creates a risk that a reasonable person can foresee could result in harm. The question here is whether the electric spark, the grass fire, the barn full of dynamite, and the roof falling in are *foreseeable* risks stemming from a poor parking job. In this case, it would be a question of fact for a jury to determine whether there were enough intervening events between Ruth's parking and Jim's injury to defeat Jim's claim.

8–2A. Question with Sample Answer

(a) Ursula will not be held liable for copyright infringement in this case because her photocopying pages for use in scholarly research falls squarely under the "fair use" exception to the Copyright Act.

(b) While Ursula's actions are improper, they could constitute trademark infringement, not copyright infringement. Copyrights are granted for literary and artistic productions; trademarks are distinctive marks created and used by manufacturers to differentiate their goods from those of their competitors. Trademark infringement occurs when a mark is copied to a substantial degree, intentionally or unintentionally.

(c) As with the answer to (a) above, Ursula's actions fall within the "fair use" doctrine of copyright law. Her use of the taped television shows for teaching is the exact type of use the exception is designed to cover.

9–3A. Question with Sample Answer

This is fraud committed in e-mail sent via the Internet. The elements of the tort of fraud are (1) the misrepresentation of material facts or conditions made with knowledge that they are false or with reckless disregard for the truth, (2) the intent to induce another to rely on the misrepresentation, (3) justifiable reliance on the misrepresentation by the deceived party, (d) damages suffered as a result of the reliance, and (4) a causal connection between the misrepresentation and the injury. If any of this e-mailer's recipients reply to her false plea with money, it is likely that all of the requirements for fraud will have been met. The sort of fraud described in this problem is similar to the "Nigerian letter fraud scam" noted in the text. In this type of scam, an individual sends an e-mail promising its recipient a percentage of money held in a bank account or payable from a government agency or other source if he or she will send funds to help a fictitious official transfer the amount in the account to another bank. The details of the scam are often adjusted to current events, with perpetrators referring to news-making conflicts, tax refunds or payments, and other occurrences.

10–2A. Question with Sample Answer

According to the question, Janine was apparently unconscious or otherwise unable to agree to a contract for the nursing services she received while she was in the hospital. As you read in the chapter, however, sometimes the law will create a fictional contract in order to prevent one party from unjustly receiving a benefit at the expense of another. This is known as a *quasi contract* and provides a basis for Nursing Services to recover the value of the services it provided while Janine was in the hospital. As for the at-home services that were provided to Janine, because Janine was aware that those services were being provided for her, Nursing Services can recover for those services under an implied-in-fact contract. Under this type of contract, the conduct of the parties creates and defines the terms. Janine's acceptance of the services constitutes

her agreement to form a contract, and she will probably be required to pay Nursing Services in full.

11–2A. Question with Sample Answer

(a) Death of either the offeror or the offeree prior to acceptance automatically terminates a revocable offer. The basic legal reason is that the offer is personal to the parties and cannot be passed on to others, not even to the estate of the deceased. This rule applies even if the other party is unaware of the death. Thus, Schmidt's offer terminates on Schmidt's death, and Barry's later acceptance does not constitute a contract.

(b) An offer is automatically terminated by the destruction of the specific subject matter of the offer prior to acceptance. Thus, Barry's acceptance after the fire does not constitute a contract.

(c) When the offer is irrevocable, under an option contract, death of the offeror does not terminate the option contract, and the offeree can accept the offer to sell the equipment, binding the offeror's estate to performance. Performance is not personal to Schmidt, as the estate can transfer title to the equipment. Knowledge of the death is immaterial to the offeree's right of acceptance. Thus, Barry can hold Schmidt's estate to a contract for the purchase of the equipment.

(d) When the offer is irrevocable, under an option contract, death of the offeree also does not terminate the offer. Because the option is a separate contract, the contract survives and passes to the offeree's estate, which can exercise the option by acceptance within the option period. Thus, acceptance by Barry's estate binds Schmidt to a contract for the sale of the equipment.

12–2A. Question with Sample Answer

The legal issue deals with the preexisting duty rule, which basically states that a promise to do what one already has a legal or contractual duty to do does not constitute consideration, and thus the return promise is unenforceable. In this case, Shade was required contractually to build a house according to a specific set of plans for $53,000, and Bernstein's later agreement to pay an additional $3,000 for exactly what Shade was required to do for $53,000 is without consideration and unenforceable. One of the purposes of this general rule is to prevent commercial blackmail. There are four basic exceptions to this rule:

(a) If the duties of Shade are modified, for example, by changes made by Bernstein in the specifications, these changes can constitute consideration and bind Bernstein to pay the additional $3,000.

(b) Rescission and new contract theory could be applied, by which the old contract of $53,000 would mutually be canceled and a new contract for $56,000 would be made. Most courts would not apply this theory unless there was a clear intent to cancel the original contract. It appears here that the intent to cancel the $53,000 contract is lacking (there is merely an intent to modify), so this exception would not apply.

(c) A few states have statutes that allow any modification to be enforceable if it is in writing. The facts stated give no evidence that Bernstein's agreement to the additional $3,000 is in writing, but, if it is, Bernstein is bound in those states.

(d) The unforeseen difficulty or hardship rule could be argued. This rule, however, applies only to unknown risks not ordinarily assumed in business transactions. Because inflation and price rises are risks ordinarily assumed in business, this exception cannot be used by Shade.

13–2A. Question with Sample Answer

Contracts in restraint of trade are usually illegal and unenforceable. An exception to this rule applies to a covenant not to compete that is ancillary to certain types of business contracts in which some fair protection is deemed appropriate (such as in the sale of a business). The covenant, however, must be reasonable in terms of time and area to be legally enforceable. If either term is excessive, the court can declare that the restraint goes beyond what is necessary for reasonable protection. In this event, the court can either declare the covenant illegal or it can reform the covenant to make the terms of time and area reasonable and then enforce it. Suppose the court declares the covenant illegal and unenforceable. Because the covenant is ancillary and severable from the primary contract, the primary contract is not affected by such a ruling. In the case of Hotel Lux, the primary contract concerns employment; the covenant is ancillary and desirable for the protection of the hotel. The time period of one year may be considered reasonable for a chef with an international reputation. The reasonableness of the three-state area restriction may be questioned, however. If it is found to be reasonable, the covenant probably will be enforced. If it is not found to be reasonable, the court could declare the entire covenant illegal, allowing Perlee to be employed by any restaurant or hotel, including one in direct competition with Hotel Lux. Alternatively, the court could reform the covenant, making its terms reasonable for protecting Hotel Lux's normal customer market area.

14–2A. Question with Sample Answer

Four basic elements are necessary to prove fraud, thus rendering a contract voidable: (1) an intent to deceive, usually with knowledge of the falsity; (2) a misrepresentation of material facts; (3) a reliance by the innocent party on the misrepresentation; and (4) usually damage or injury caused by the misrepresentation. Statements of events to take place in the future or statements of opinions are generally not treated as representations of fact. Therefore, even though the prediction or opinion may turn out to be incorrect, a contract based on this type of statement would remain enforceable. Grano's statement that the motel would make at least $45,000 next year would probably be treated as a prediction or opinion; thus, one of the elements necessary to prove fraud—misrepresentation of facts—would be missing. The statement that the motel

netted $30,000 last year is a deliberate falsehood (with intent and knowledge). Grano's defense will be that the books in Tanner's possession clearly indicated that the figure stated was untrue, and therefore Tanner cannot be said to have purchased the motel in reliance on the falsehood. If the innocent party, Tanner, knew the true facts, or should have known the true facts because they were available to him, Grano's argument will prevail.

Finally, the issue centers on Grano's duty to tell Tanner of the bypass. Ordinarily, neither party in a nonfiduciary relationship has a duty to disclose facts, even when the information might bear materially on the other's decision to enter into the contract. Exceptions are made, however, when the buyer cannot reasonably be expected to discover the information known by the seller, in which case fairness imposes a duty to speak on the seller. Here, the court can go either way. If the court decides there was no duty to disclose, deems the prediction of future profits to be opinion rather than a statement of fact, and also decides there was no justifiable reliance by Tanner because the books available to Tanner clearly indicated Grano's profit statement for the last year to be false, then Tanner cannot get his money back on the basis of fraud.

15–2A. Question with Sample Answer

In this situation, Mallory becomes what is known as a *guarantor* on the loan; that is, she guarantees to the hardware store that she will pay for the mower if her brother fails to do so. This kind of collateral promise, in which the guarantor states that he or she will become responsible *only* if the primary party does not perform, must be in writing to be enforceable. There is an exception, however. If the main purpose in accepting secondary liability is to secure a personal benefit—for example, if Mallory's brother bought the mower for her—the contract need not be in writing. The assumption is that a court can infer from the circumstances of the case whether the main purpose was to secure a personal benefit and thus, in effect, to answer for the guarantor's own debt.

16–2A. Question with Sample Answer

Thrift is a creditor beneficiary. To be a creditor beneficiary one must be the creditor in a previously established debtor-creditor relationship, and then the debtor's subsequent contract terms with a third party must confer a benefit on the creditor. The contract made between the debtor and third party is not made expressly for the benefit of the creditor (as is required for a donee beneficiary). Rather, it is made for the benefit of the contracting parties. In this case, the original mortgage contract created a debtor-creditor relationship between Hensley and Thrift. Hensley's contract of sale in which Sylvia agreed to assume the mortgage payments conferred a benefit on Thrift as to payment of the debt. The primary purpose of the contract was strictly to benefit the contracting parties. Hensley was to receive money for the sale of the house, and Sylvia was to receive the low mortgage interest rate. Thrift still has the house and lot as security for the loan, can hold Hensley personally liable for the mortgage note, and as a creditor beneficiary can hold Sylvia personally liable on the basis of her contract with Hensley to assume the mortgage.

17–2A. Question with Sample Answer

A novation exists when a new, valid contract expressly or impliedly discharges a prior contract by the substitution of a party. Accord and satisfaction exists when the parties agree that the original obligation can be discharged by a substituted performance. In this case, Fred's agreement with Iba to pay off Junior's debt for $1,100 (as compared to the $1,000 owed) is definitely a valid contract. The terms of the contract substitute Fred as the debtor for Junior, and Junior is definitely discharged from further liability. This agreement is a *novation*.

18–2A. Question with Sample Answer

Generally, the equitable remedy of specific performance will be granted only if two criteria are met: monetary damages (under the situation) must be inadequate as a remedy, and the subject matter of the contract must be unique.

(a) In the sale of land, the buyer's contract is for a specific piece of real property. The land under contract is unique, because no two pieces of real property have the same legal description. In addition, money damages would not compensate a buyer adequately, as the same land cannot be purchased elsewhere. Specific performance is an appropriate remedy.

(b) The basic criteria for specific performance do not apply well to personal-service contracts. If the identical service contracted for is readily available from others, the service is not unique, and monetary damages for nonperformance are adequate. If, however, the services are so personal that only the contract party can perform them, the contract meets the test of uniqueness; but the courts will refuse to decree specific performance if (1) the enforcement of specific performance requires involuntary servitude (prohibited by the Thirteenth Amendment to the U.S. Constitution), or (2) it is impractical to attempt to force meaningful performance by someone against his or her will. In the case of Amy and Fred, specific performance is not an appropriate remedy.

(c) A rare coin is unique, and monetary damages for breach are inadequate, as Hoffman cannot obtain a substantially identical substitute in the market. This is a typical case in which specific performance is an appropriate remedy.

(d) The key issue here is that this is a closely held corporation. Therefore, the stock is not available in the market, and the shares become unique. The uniqueness of these shares is enhanced by the fact that if Ryan sells her 4 percent of the shares to Chang, Chang will control the corporation. Because of this, monetary damages for Chang are totally inadequate as a remedy. Specific performance is an appropriate remedy.

19–2A. Question with Sample Answer

The entire answer falls under UCC 2–206(1)(b), because the situation deals with a buyer's order to buy goods for prompt shipment. The law is that such an order or offer invites acceptance by a prompt promise to ship conforming goods. If the promise (acceptance) is sent by a medium reasonable under the circumstances, the acceptance is effective when sent. Therefore, a contract was formed on October 8, and it required Martin to ship 100 model Color-X television sets. Martin's shipment is nonconforming, and Flint is correct in claiming that Martin is in breach. Martin's claim would be valid if Martin had not sent its promise of shipment. The UCC provides that shipment of nonconforming goods constitutes an acceptance *unless* the seller seasonably notifies the buyer that such shipment is sent only as an accommodation. Thus, had a contract not been formed on October 8, the nonconforming shipment on the 28th would not be treated as an acceptance, and no contract would be in existence to breach.

20–2A. Question with Sample Answer

There is no question that the suit is in existence and identified to the contract. Nor do the facts indicate that there was an agreement as to when title or risk of loss would pass. Therefore, these situations deal with passage of title and risk of loss to goods that are "to be delivered" without physical movement of the goods by the seller and not represented by a document of title. The rules of law are that title passes to the buyer on the making of the contract, and risk of loss passes from a *merchant* seller to the buyer when the buyer *receives* the goods.

(a) In the case of the major creditor, title is with Sikora, and the major creditor cannot levy on the suit.

(b) The risk of loss on the suit destroyed by fire falls on Carson. Carson is a merchant, and because Sikora has not taken possession, Carson retains the risk of loss. This problem illustrates that title and risk of loss do not always pass from seller to buyer at the same time.

21–2A. Question with Sample Answer

Topken basically has the following remedies.

(a) Topken can identify the 500 washing machines to the contract and resell the goods [UCC 2–704].

(b) Topken can withhold delivery and proceed with other remedies [UCC 2–703].

(c) Topken can cancel the contract and proceed with other remedies [UCC 2–703 and 2–106(4)].

(d) Topken can resell the goods in a commercially reasonable manner (public or private sale with notice to Lorwin, holding Lorwin liable for any loss and retaining any profits) [UCC 2–706]. If Topken cannot resell after making a reasonable effort, Topken can sue for the purchase price [UCC 2–709 (1)(b)].

(e) Topken can sue Lorwin for breach of contract, recovering as damages the difference between the market price (at the time and place of tender) and the contract price, plus incidental damages [UCC 2–708].

The student should note the combination of remedies that would be most beneficial for Topken under the circumstances.

22–2A. Question with Sample Answer

The court should rule in favor of the manufacturer, finding that the gun did not malfunction but performed exactly as Clark and Wright expected. The court should also point out that Clark and Wright appreciated the danger of using the guns without protective eyewear. Clark offered no proof that the paintball gun used in the incident failed to function as expected. He was aware that there was protective eyewear available but he chose not to buy it. He was an active participant in shooting paintballs at other vehicles. The evening of the incident Clark carried his paintball gun with him for that purpose. Wright also knew it was dangerous to shoot someone in the eye with a paintball gun. But the most crucial testimony was Wright's statement that his paintball gun did not malfunction.

23–2A. Question with Sample Answer

Yes, it is a reasonable approach to rely on the producers' financial records, which are reasonably reflective of their costs because their normal allocation methodologies were used for a number of years. These records are historically relied upon to present important financial information to shareholders, lenders, tax authorities, auditors, and other third parties. Provided that the producers' records and books comply with generally accepted accounting principles and were verified by independent auditors, it is reasonable to use them to determine the production costs and fair market value of canned pineapple in the United States.

24–2A. Question with Sample Answer

For an instrument to be negotiable, it must meet the following requirements:

(a) Be in writing.

(b) Be signed by the maker or drawer.

(c) Be an unconditional promise or order.

(d) State a fixed amount of money.

(e) Be payable on demand or at a definite time.

(f) Be payable to bearer or order (unless it is a check).

The instrument in this case meets the writing requirement in that it is handwritten and on something with a degree of permanence that is transferable. The instrument meets the requirement of being signed by the maker, as Juan Sanchez's signature (his name in his handwriting) appears in the body of the instrument. The instrument's payment is not conditional and contains Juan Sanchez's definite promise to pay. In addition, the sum of $100 is both a fixed amount and payable in money (U.S. currency). Because the instrument is payable on demand and to bearer (Kathy Martin or any holder), it is negotiable.

25–2A. Question with Sample Answer

(a) The bank does qualify as a holder in due course (HDC) for the amount of $5,000. To qualify as an HDC

under UCC 3–302, one must take the instrument for value, in good faith, and without being put on notice that a defense exists against it, that it has been dishonored, or that it is overdue. In this situation the bank has given full value for the instrument—$4,850 ($5,000 – $150 discount). Therefore, the bank is entitled to be an HDC for the face value of the instrument ($5,000). In addition, the bank took the instrument in good faith and without notice of the original incompleteness of the instrument (completed when purchased by the bank) or the lack of authority of Hayden to complete the instrument in an amount over $2,000. The instrument was also taken before overdue (before the maturity date). Thus, First National Bank is an HDC.

(b) The sale to a stranger in a bar for $500 creates an entirely different situation. One of the requirements for the status of an HDC is that a holder take the instrument in good faith. *Good faith* is defined in the UCC as "honesty in fact in the conduct or transaction concerned" [UCC 1–201(19)]. Although the UCC does not provide clear guidelines to determine what is or is not good faith, both the amount paid (as compared to the face value of the instrument) and the circumstances under which the instrument is taken (as interpreted by a reasonable person) dictate whether the holder honestly believed the instrument was not defective when taken. In this case, taking a $5,000 note for $500 in a bar would raise a serious question of the stranger's good faith. Thus, the stranger would not qualify as a holder in due course.

26–3A. Question with Sample Answer

Frazier can recover the $1,500 from Kennedy if he is a holder in due course (HDC). He will be an HDC only if he, as a holder, took the check (a) for value, (b) in good faith, and (c) without notice that the check was overdue or dishonored or that a claim or defense against it exists. In this instance, Frazier qualifies for HDC status. First, he is a holder as the check was properly negotiated to him (by indorsement). Second, the facts indicate that he gave value. Third, there is nothing to indicate that he took the instrument in bad faith. Fourth, he was unaware of Niles's fraud (claim or defense), and he took the check before it was overdue (within thirty days of issue). Thus, Frazier is a holder in due course and can hold Kennedy liable.

27–2A. Question with Sample Answer

Citizens Bank will not have to recredit Gary's account for the $1,000 check and probably will not have to recredit his account for the first forged check for $100. Generally, a drawee bank is responsible for determining whether the signature of its customer is genuine, and when it pays on a forged customer's signature, the bank must recredit the customer's account [UCC 3–401, 4–406]. There are, however, exceptions to this general rule. First, when a customer's negligence substantially contributes to the making of an unauthorized signature (including a forgery), the drawee bank that pays the instrument in good faith will not be obligated to recredit the customer's account for the full amount of the check [UCC 3–406]. In addition, when a drawee bank sends to its customer a statement of account and canceled checks, the customer has a duty to exercise reasonable care and promptness in examining the statement to discover any forgeries and report them to the drawee bank. Failure of the customer to do so relieves the drawee from liability to the customer to the extent that the drawee bank suffers a loss [UCC 4–406(c)]. Therefore, Gary's negligence in allowing his checkbook to be stolen and his failure to report the theft or examine his May statement will preclude his recovery on the $100 check from the Citizens Bank. Under UCC 3–406(b) and 4–406(e), however, the bank could be liable to the extent that its negligence substantially contributes to the loss. Second, when a series of forgeries is committed by the same wrongdoer, the customer must discover and report the initial forgery within fourteen calendar days from the date that the statement of account and canceled checks (containing the initial forged check) are made available to the customer [UCC 4–406(d)(2)]. Failure to discover and report a forged check releases the drawee bank from liability for all additional forged checks in the series written after the thirty-day period. Therefore, Gary's failure to discover the May forged check by June 30 relieves the bank from liability for the June 20 check of $1,000.

28–2A. Question with Sample Answer

Three basic actions are available to Holiday:

(a) Attachment—a court-ordered seizure of nonexempt property prior to Holiday's reducing the debt to judgment. The grounds for granting the writ of attachment are limited, but in most states (when submitted), the writ is granted on introduction of evidence that a debtor intends to remove the property from the jurisdiction in which a judgment would be rendered. Holiday would have to post a bond and reduce its claim to judgment; then it could sell the attached property to satisfy the debt, returning any surplus to Kanahara.

(b) Writ of execution, on reducing the debt to judgment. The writ is an order issued by the clerk directing the sheriff or other officer of the court to seize (levy) nonexempt property of the debtor located within the court's jurisdiction. The property is then sold, and the proceeds are used to pay for the judgment and cost of sale, with any surplus going to the debtor (in this case, Kanahara).

(c) Garnishment of the wages owed to Kanahara by the Cross-Bar Packing Corp. Whenever a third person, the garnishee, owes a debt, such as wages, to the debtor, the creditor can proceed to have the court order the employer garnishee to turn over a percentage of the take-home pay (usually no more than 25 percent) to pay the debt. Garnishment actions are continuous in some states; in others, the action must be taken for each pay period.

Holiday can proceed with any one or a combination of these three actions. Because the property may be removed

from the jurisdiction, and perhaps Kanahara himself may leave the jurisdiction (he may quit his job), prompt action is important.

29–3A. Question with Sample Answer

No. The bank will prevail because it held a properly perfected security interest in Edward's entire inventory, not just in specific items or in the value of the inventory at the time the loan was made. The entire inventory (the present inventory and any inventory thereafter acquired) was given as collateral for the loan, and, regardless of the fact the inventory is now twice as large, the bank can rightfully take possession of the entire inventory on Edward's default in his payments on the loan.

30–3A. Question with Sample Answer

A trustee is given avoidance powers by the Bankruptcy Code. One situation in which the trustee can avoid transfers of property or payments by a debtor to a creditor is when such transfer constitutes a *preference*. A preference is a transfer of property or payment that favors one creditor over another. For a preference to exist, the debtor must be insolvent and must have made payment for a preexisting debt within ninety days of the filing of the petition in bankruptcy. The Code provides that the debtor is *presumed* to be insolvent during this ninety-day period. If the payment is made to an insider (and in this case payment was made to a close relative), the preference period is extended to one year, but the presumption of insolvency still applies only to the ninety-day period. In this case, the trustee has an excellent chance of having both payments declared preferences. The payment to Cool Springs was within ninety days of the filing of the petition, and it is doubtful that Cool Springs could overcome the presumption that Peaslee was insolvent at the time the payment was made. The $5,000 payment was made to an insider, Peaslee's father, and any payment made to an insider within one year of the petition of bankruptcy is a preference—as long as the debtor was insolvent at the time of payment. The facts indicate that Peaslee probably was insolvent at the time he paid his father. If he was not, the payment is not a preference, and the trustee's avoidance of the transfer would be improper.

31–2A. Question with Sample Answer

The answer is likely no. A court would most likely find that this issue was novel and permitted the plaintiff to survive a motion to dismiss. However, if the loan was split without the consumer's consent, prior court cases have found that such practices violate the TILA's mandate to group all disclosures for a single transaction into one writing. Even if the plaintiff acquiesced to splitting the loan, the practice appears to circumvent the purpose of HOEPA through an artificial restructuring of the loan transaction. If loan splitting were allowed to circumvent consumer protections, lenders would have a strong incentive to divide loans as necessary to keep individual loan costs as low as possible.

32–2A. Question with Sample Answer

Upon creation of an agency, the agent owes certain fiduciary duties to the principal. Two such duties are the duty of loyalty and the duty to inform or notify. The duty of loyalty is a fundamental concept of the fiduciary relationship. The agent must act solely for the benefit of the principal, not in the agent's own interest or in the interest of another person. One of the principles invoked by this duty is that an agent employed to sell cannot become a purchaser without the principal's consent. When the agent is a partner, contracting to sell to another partner is equivalent to selling to oneself and is therefore a breach of the agent's duty. In addition, the agent has a duty to disclose to the principal any facts pertinent to the subject matter of the agency. Failure to disclose to Peter the knowledge of the shopping mall and the increased market value of the property also was a breach of Alice's fiduciary duties. When an agent breaches fiduciary duties owed to the principal by becoming a recipient of a contract, the contract is voidable at the election of the principal. Neither Carl nor Alice can hold Peter to the contract, and Alice's breach of fiduciary duties also allows Peter to terminate the agency relationship.

33–2A. Question with Sample Answer

As a general rule, a principal and third party are bound only to a contract made by the principal's agent within the scope of the agent's authority. An agent's authority to act can come from actual authority given to the agent (express or implied), apparent authority, or authority derived from an emergency. Express authority is directly given by the principal to the agent. Implied authority is deemed customary or inferred from the agent's position. Apparent authority is created when a principal gives a third person reason to believe the agent possesses authority not truly possessed. In this case, no express authority was given, and certainly no implied authority exists for a purchasing agent of goods to acquire realty. Moreover, A&B did nothing to lead Wilson to believe that Adams had authority to purchase land on its behalf. In addition, there was no emergency creating a need for Adams to purchase the land. Therefore, although Adams indicated in the contract that she was an agent, she acted outside the scope of her authority. Because of this, the contract between Adams and Wilson is treated merely as an unaccepted offer. As such, neither Wilson nor A&B is bound unless A&B ratifies (accepts) the contract before Wilson withdraws (revokes) the offer. Ratification can take place only when the principal is aware of all material facts and makes some act of affirmation. If A&B affirms the contract before Wilson withdraws, A&B can enforce Adams's contract. If Wilson withdraws first, Adams's contract cannot be enforced by A&B.

34–2A. Question with Sample Answer

The Occupational Health and Safety Act (OSHA) requires employers to provide safe working conditions for employees. The act prohibits employers from discharging or discriminating against any employee who refuses to work when the employee believes in good faith that he or she will risk death or great bodily harm by undertaking the employment activity. Denton and Carlo had sufficient reason to believe that the maintenance job required of them by their employer involved great risk, and therefore, under OSHA, their discharge was wrongful. Denton and Carlo can turn to the Occupational Safety and Health Administration, which is part of the Department of Labor, for assistance.

35–2A. Question with Sample Answer

Under Title VII of the Civil Rights Act, an employer must offer a reasonable accommodation to resolve a conflict between an employee's sincere religious belief and a condition of employment. Reasonable accommodation is required unless such an accommodation would create an undue hardship for the employer's business. In this hypothetical scenario, the only accommodation that Caldwell considered reasonable was a complete exemption from the no-facial-jewelry policy. This could be construed to impose an undue hardship on Costco. The company's dress code could be based on the belief that employees reflect on their employers, especially employees who regularly interact with customers, as Caldwell did in her cashier position. Caldwell's facial jewelry could have affected Costco's public image. Under this reasoning and in such a situation, an employer has no obligation to offer an accommodation before taking other action. Thus, Caldwell is not likely to succeed in a lawsuit against Costco for religious discrimination.

36–2A. Question with Sample Answer

The court would likely conclude that National Foods was responsible for the acts of harassment by the manager at the franchised restaurant, on the ground that the employees were the agents of National Foods. An agency relationship can be implied from the circumstances and conduct of the parties. The important question is the degree of control that a franchisor has over its franchisees. Whether it exercises that control is beside the point. Here, National Foods retained considerable control over the new hires and the franchisee's policies, as well as the right to terminate the franchise for violations. That its supervisors routinely approved the policies would not undercut National Foods' liability.

37–2A. Question with Sample Answer

(a) A limited partner's interest is assignable. In fact, assignment allows the assignee to become a substituted limited partner with the consent of the remaining partners. The assignment, however, does not dissolve the limited partnership.

(b) Bankruptcy of the limited partnership itself causes dissolution, but bankruptcy of one of the limited partners does not dissolve the partnership unless it causes the bankruptcy of the firm.

(c) The retirement, death, or insanity of a general partner dissolves the partnership unless the business can be continued by the remaining general partners. Because Dorinda was the only general partner, her death dissolves the limited partnership.

38–2A. Question with Sample Answer

Although a joint stock company has characteristics of a corporation, it is usually treated as a partnership. Therefore, although the joint stock company issues transferable shares of stock and is managed by directors and officers, the shareholders have personal liability. Unless the shareholders transfer their stock and ownership to a third party, not only are the joint stock company's assets available for damages caused by a breach, but the individual shareholders' estates are also subject to such liability. The business trust resembles and is treated like a corporation in many respects. One similarity is the limited liability of the beneficiaries. Unless by state law beneficiaries are treated as partners, making them liable to business trust creditors, Bateson Corp. can look to only business trust assets in the event of breach.

39–2A. Question with Sample Answer

(a) As a general rule, a promoter is personally liable for all preincorporation contracts made by the promoter. The basic theory behind such liability is that the promoter cannot be an agent for a nonexistent principal (a corporation not yet formed). It is immaterial whether the contracting party knows of the prospective existence of the corporation, and the general rule of promoter liability continues even after the corporation is formed. Three basic exceptions to promoter liability are:

(1) The promoter's contract with a third party can stipulate that the third party will look only to the new corporation, not to the promoter, for performance and liability.

(2) The third party can release the promoter from liability.

(3) After formation, the corporation can assume the contractual obligations and liability by *novation*. (If it is by *adoption,* most courts hold that the promoter is still personally liable.)

Peterson is therefore personally liable on both contracts, because (1) neither Owens nor Babcock has released him from liability, (2) the corporation has not assumed contractual responsibility by novation, and (3) Peterson's contract with Babcock did not limit Babcock to holding only the corporation liable. (Peterson's liability was conditioned only on the corporation's formation, which did occur.)

(b) Incorporation in and of itself does not make the newly formed corporation liable for preincorporation contracts. Until the newly formed corporation assumes Peterson's contracts by novation (releasing Peterson from personal liability) or by adoption (undertaking to perform Peterson's contracts, which makes both the corporation and Peterson liable), Babcock cannot enforce Peterson's contract against the corporation.

40–2A. Question with Sample Answer

Directors are personally answerable to the corporation and the shareholders for breach of their duty to exercise reasonable care in conducting the affairs of the corporation. Reasonable care is defined as being the degree of care that a reasonably prudent person would use in the conduct of personal business affairs. When directors delegate the running of the corporate affairs to officers, the directors are expected to use reasonable care in the selection and supervision of such officers. Failure to do so will make the directors liable for negligence or mismanagement. A director who dissents to an action by the board is not personally liable for losses resulting from that action. Unless the dissent is entered into the board meeting minutes, however, the director is presumed to have assented. Therefore, the first issue in the case of AstroStar, Inc., is whether the board members failed to use reasonable care in the selection of the president. If so, and particularly if the board failed to provide a reasonable amount of supervision (and openly embezzled funds indicate that failure), the directors will be personally liable. This liability will include Eckhart unless she can prove that she dissented and that she tried to reasonably supervise the new president. Considering the facts in this case, it is questionable that Eckhart could prove this.

41–2A. Question with Sample Answer

Ajax apparently has given shareholder Alir notice of the meeting for approval of the merger. In addition, however, Ajax should have notified Alir of her right to dissent and of her right, should the merger be approved, to be paid a fair value for her shares. The law recognizes that a dissenting shareholder should not be forced to become an unwilling shareholder in a new corporation. If Alir adheres strictly to statutory procedures, she has appraisal rights for the Ajax shares she holds after approval of the merger. Alir's appraisal rights entitle her to be paid by Zeta the "fair value" of her shares. Fair value is the value of the shares on the day prior to the date on which the vote for merger is taken. This value must not reflect appreciation or depreciation of the stock in anticipation of the approval. If $20 is a true value (the market value on the day before the vote), Alir will receive $200,000 for her 10,000 Ajax shares.

42–2A. Question with Sample Answer

No. Under federal securities law, a stock split is exempt from registration requirements. This is because no sale of stock is involved. The existing shares are merely being split, and no consideration is received by the corporation for the additional shares created.

43–2A. Question with Sample Answer

A court might initially consider whether a member of a limited liability company (LLC) who has a material conflict of interest should be prohibited from dealing with matters of the LLC. Most likely, a court would conclude that a member—even a member with a conflict of interest—can vote to transfer LLC property, but must do so fairly. In this problem, the transfer of BP's sole asset by two of BP's members to themselves, disguised as Excel (a newly created LLC), represented a material conflict of interest. Not only did Amy and Carl engage in self-dealing, but in doing so, they increased their interests in Excel. This conflict did not prohibit Amy and Carl from voting to transfer BP's sole asset to Excel, however, so long as they dealt fairly with Dave. To judge the fairness, a court might consider the members' conduct, the end result, the purpose of the LLC, and the parties' expectations. Here, the transfer was arguably unfair in two respects. First, it was not an "arm's length transaction" because it did not occur on the open market. Second, the sale undercut BP's capacity to carry on its intended business (to own the property as a long-term investment). The court might still rule in favor of Amy and Carl if they could argue successfully that the transaction did not need to be, or could not be, at "arm's length" and that BP's investment capacity was not undercut.

44–2A. Question with Sample Answer

The court will consider first whether the agency followed the procedures prescribed in the Administrative Procedure Act (APA). Ordinarily, courts will not require agencies to use procedures beyond those of the APA. Courts will, however, compel agencies to follow their own rules. If an agency has adopted a rule granting extra procedures, the agency must provide those extra procedures, at least until the rule is formally rescinded. Ultimately, in this case, the court will most likely rule for the food producers.

45–3A. Question with Sample Answer

Yes. A regulation of the Federal Trade Commission (FTC) under Section 5 of the Federal Trade Commission Act makes it a violation for door-to-door sellers to fail to give consumers three days to cancel any sale. In addition, a number of state statutes require this three-day "cooling off" period to protect consumers from unscrupulous door-to-door sellers. Because the Gonchars sought to rescind the contract within the three-day period, Renowned Books was obligated to agree to cancel the contract. Its failure to allow rescission was in violation of the FTC regulation and of most state statutes.

46–2A. Question with Sample Answer

Fruitade has violated a number of federal environmental laws if such actions are being taken without a permit. First, because the dumping is in a navigable waterway, the River and Harbor Act of 1886, as amended, has been violated. Second, the Clean Water Act of 1972, as amended, has been violated. This act is designed to make the waters safe for swimming, to protect fish and wildlife, and to eliminate discharge of pollutants into the water. Both the crushed glass and the acid violate this act. Third, the Toxic Substances Control Act of 1976 was passed to regulate chemicals that are known to be toxic and could have an effect on human health and the environment. The acid in the cleaning fluid or compound could come under this act.

47–2A. Question with Sample Answer

Yes. The major antitrust law being violated is the Sherman Act, Section 1. Allitron and Donovan are engaged in interstate commerce, and the agreement to divide marketing territories between them is a contract in restraint of trade.

The U.S. Department of Justice could seek fines for up to $1 million for each corporation, and the officers or directors responsible could be imprisoned for up to three years. In addition, the U.S. Department of Justice could institute civil proceedings to restrain this conduct.

48–2A. Question with Sample Answer

Assuming that the court has abandoned the *Ultramares* rule, it is likely that the accounting firm of Goldman, Walters, Johnson & Co. will be held liable to Happydays State Bank for negligent preparation of financial statements. There are various policy reasons for holding accountants liable to third parties even in the absence of privity. The potential liability would make accountants more careful in the preparation of financial statements. Moreover, in some situations the accountants may be the only solvent defendants, and hence, unless liability is imposed on accountants, third parties who reasonably rely on financial statements may go unprotected. Accountants, rather than third parties, are in better positions to spread the risks. If third parties such as banks have to absorb the costs of bad loans made as a result of negligently prepared financial statements, then the cost of credit to the public in general will increase. In contrast, accountants are in a better position to spread the risk by purchasing liability insurance.

49–2A. Question with Sample Answer

For Curtis to recover against the hotel, he must first prove that a bailment relationship was created between himself and the hotel as to the car or the fur coat, or both. For a bailment to exist, there must be a delivery of the personal property that gives the bailee exclusive possession of the property, and the bailee must knowingly accept the bailed property. If either element is lacking, there is no bailment relationship and no liability on the part of the bailee hotel. The facts clearly indicate that the bailee hotel took exclusive possession and control of Curtis's car, and it knowingly accepted the car when the attendant took the car from Curtis and parked it in the underground guarded garage, retaining the keys. Thus, a bailment was created as to the car, and, because a mutual benefit bailment was created, the hotel owes Curtis the duty to exercise reasonable care over the property to and to return the bailed car at the end of the bailment. Failure to return the car creates a presumption of negligence (lack of reasonable care), and unless the hotel can rebut this presumption, the hotel is liable to Curtis for the loss of the car. As to the fur coat, the hotel neither knew nor expected that the trunk contained an expensive fur coat. Thus, although the hotel knowingly took exclusive possession of the car, the hotel did not do so with the fur coat. (But for a regular coat and other items likely to be in the car, the hotel would be liable.) Because no bailment of the expensive fur coat was created, the hotel has no liability for its loss.

50–3A. Question with Sample Answer

Wilfredo understandably wants a general warranty deed, as this type of deed will give him the most extensive protection against any defects of title claimed against the property transferred. The general warranty would have Patricia warranting the following covenants:

(a) Covenant of seisin and right to convey—a warranty that the seller has good title and power to convey.

(b) Covenant against encumbrances—a guaranty by the seller that, unless stated, there are no outstanding encumbrances or liens against the property conveyed.

(c) Covenant of quiet possession—a warranty that the grantee's possession will not be disturbed by others claiming a prior legal right. Patricia, however, is conveying only ten feet along a property line that may not even be accurately surveyed. Patricia therefore does not wish to make these warranties. Consequently, she is offering a quitclaim deed, which does not convey any warranties but conveys only whatever interest, if any, the grantor owns. Although title is passed by the quitclaim deed, the quality of the title is not warranted.

Because Wilfredo really needs the property, it appears that he has three choices: he can accept the quitclaim deed; he can increase his offer price to obtain the general warranty deed he wants; or he can offer to have a title search made, which should satisfy both parties.

51–2A. Question with Sample Answer

Ajax will probably not be able to void the policy. Most life insurance policies contain what is called an incontestability clause. Such a clause provides that a policy cannot be contested for misstatements by the insured after the policy has been in effect for a given period, usually two years. Even though the application is part of the policy (attached to the policy), Patrick's innocent error in answering the question dealing with heart problems or ailments can no longer be contested by the insurer, as the incontestability clause is now in effect (three years have passed since the issuance of the policy). In addition, a misstatement about age is not grounds in and of itself for Ajax to avoid the policy. Ajax does, however, have the right to adjust premium payments to reflect the correct age or to reduce the amount of the insurance coverage accordingly. Thus, Ajax cannot escape liability on Patrick's death, but it can reduce the $50,000 coverage to account for the premiums that should have been paid for a person who is thirty-three years old, not thirty-two years old.

52–3A. Question with Sample Answer

(a) State laws vary on whether a will written and executed before marriage is revoked by the marriage. Some states declare that the will is revoked by a subsequent marriage only if a child is born out of that marriage. Under the Uniform Probate Code, a subsequent marriage does not revoke a will; however, the new spouse is entitled to share the estate as if the deceased has died intestate, and the balance passes under the will. In this case, if the will is revoked by marriage, Lisa will receive the entire estate, and Carol, as James's mother, will receive nothing. If the marriage does not revoke the will, Lisa will probably receive one-half the estate under the laws of intestacy, and the balance will go to Carol.

(b) At common law and under the Uniform Probate Code, divorce does not in and of itself revoke a will made and executed during a previous marriage. If the divorce is accompanied by a property settlement, most states revoke that portion of the will that disposed property to the former spouse. Although this matter is frequently controlled by statute, in the absence of such a statute, if Lisa received a property settlement on divorce, the will of James would be revoked and Mandis would recover the entire estate by the laws of intestacy.

(c) If a child is born after a will has been executed and the child is not provided for in the will, the law will allow the child to inherit as if the testator had died intestate. The philosophy is that unless the child is specifically excluded by the will, the child was intended to inherit and was omitted in error. Therefore, Claire would receive one-half of the estate in most states.

Glossary

A

Abandoned property Property with which the owner has voluntarily parted, with no intention of recovering it.

Abandonment In landlord-tenant law, a tenant's complete departure from leased premises, with no intention of returning before the end of the lease term.

Abatement A process by which legatees receive reduced benefits if the assets of an estate are insufficient to pay in full all general bequests provided for in the will.

Acceleration clause (1) A clause in an installment contract that provides for all future payments to become due immediately on the failure to tender timely payments or on the occurrence of a specified event. (2) A clause in a mortgage loan contract that makes the entire loan balance become due if the borrower misses or is late making monthly mortgage payments.

Acceptance (1) In contract law, the offeree's notification to the offeror that the offeree agrees to be bound by the terms of the offeror's proposal. Although historically the terms of acceptance had to be the mirror image of the terms of the offer, the Uniform Commercial Code provides that even modified terms of the offer in a definite expression of acceptance constitute a contract. (2) In negotiable instruments law, the drawee's signed agreement to pay a draft when presented.

Acceptor The person (the drawee) who accepts a draft and who agrees to be primarily responsible for its payment.

Accession Occurs when an individual adds value to personal property by either labor or materials. In some situations, a person may acquire ownership rights in another's property through accession.

Accommodation party A person who signs an instrument for the purpose of lending his or her name as credit to another party on the instrument.

Accord and satisfaction An agreement for payment (or other performance) between two parties, one of whom has a right of action against the other. After the payment has been accepted or other performance has been made, the "accord and satisfaction" is complete and the obligation is discharged.

Accredited investors In the context of securities offerings, "sophisticated" investors, such as banks, insurance companies, investment companies, the issuer's executive officers and directors, and persons whose income or net worth exceeds certain limits.

Acquittal A certification or declaration following a trial that the individual accused of a crime is innocent, or free from guilt, and is thus absolved of the charges.

Act of state doctrine A doctrine that provides that the judicial branch of one country will not examine the validity of public acts committed by a recognized foreign government within its own territory.

Actionable Capable of serving as the basis of a lawsuit.

Actual authority Authority of an agent that is express or implied.

Actual malice A condition that exists when a person makes a statement with either knowledge of its falsity or a reckless disregard for the truth. In a defamation suit, a statement made about a public figure normally must be made with actual malice for liability to be incurred.

Actus reus (pronounced *ak*-tus *ray*-uhs) A guilty (prohibited) act. The commission of a prohibited act is one of the two essential elements required for criminal liability, the other element being the intent to commit a crime.

Adequate protection doctrine In bankruptcy law, a doctrine that protects secured creditors from losing their security as a result of an automatic stay on legal proceedings by creditors against the debtor once the debtor petitions for bankruptcy relief. In certain circumstances, the bankruptcy court may provide adequate protection by requiring the debtor or trustee to pay the creditor or provide additional guaranties to protect the creditor against the losses suffered by the creditor as a result of the stay.

Adhesion contract A "standard-form" contract, such as that between a large retailer and a consumer, in which the stronger party dictates the terms.

Adjudication The process of resolving a dispute by presenting evidence and arguments before a neutral third party decision maker in a court or an administrative law proceeding.

Adjustable-rate mortgage (ARM) A mortgage in which the rate of interest paid by the borrower changes periodically, often with reference to a predetermined government interest rate (the index). Usually, the interest rate for ARMs is initially low and increases over time, but there is a cap on the amount that the rate can increase during any adjustment period.

Administrative agency   A federal, state, or local government agency established to perform a specific function. Administrative agencies are authorized by legislative acts to make and enforce rules to administer and enforce the acts.

Administrative law   The body of law created by administrative agencies (in the form of rules, regulations, orders, and decisions) in order to carry out their duties and responsibilities.

Administrative law judge (ALJ)   One who presides over an administrative agency hearing and who has the power to administer oaths, take testimony, rule on questions of evidence, and make determinations of fact.

Administrative process   The procedure used by administrative agencies in the administration of law.

Administrator   One who is appointed by a court to handle the probate (disposition) of a person's estate if that person dies intestate (without a valid will) or if the executor named in the will cannot serve.

Adverse possession   The acquisition of title to real property by occupying it openly, without the consent of the owner, for a period of time specified by a state statute. The occupation must be actual, open, notorious, exclusive, and in opposition to all others, including the owner.

Affidavit   A written or printed voluntary statement of facts, confirmed by the oath or affirmation of the party making it and made before a person having the authority to administer the oath or affirmation.

Affirm   To validate; to give legal force to. *See also* Ratification

Affirmative action   Job-hiring policies that give special consideration to members of protected classes in an effort to overcome present effects of past discrimination.

Affirmative defense   A response to a plaintiff's claim that does not deny the plaintiff's facts but attacks the plaintiff's legal right to bring an action. An example is the running of the statute of limitations.

After-acquired evidence   A type of evidence submitted in support of an affirmative defense in employment discrimination cases. Evidence that, prior to the employer's discriminatory act, the employee engaged in misconduct sufficient to warrant dismissal had the employer known of it earlier.

After-acquired property   Property of the debtor that is acquired after the execution of a security agreement.

Age of majority   The age at which an individual is considered legally capable of conducting himself or herself responsibly. A person of this age is entitled to the full rights of citizenship, including the right to vote. In contract law, the age at which one is no longer an infant and can no longer disaffirm a contract.

Agency   A relationship between two parties in which one party (the agent) agrees to represent or act for the other (the principal).

Agency by estoppel   An agency that arises when a principal negligently allows an agent to exercise powers not granted to the agent, thus justifying others in believing that the agent possesses the requisite agency authority.

Agent   A person who agrees to represent or act for another, called the principal.

Agreement   A meeting of two or more minds in regard to the terms of a contract; usually broken down into two events—an offer by one party to form a contract, and an acceptance of the offer by the person to whom the offer is made.

Alien corporation   A designation in the United States for a corporation formed in another country but doing business in the United States.

Alienation   In real property law, the voluntary transfer of property from one person to another (as opposed to a transfer by operation of law).

Allegation   A statement, claim, or assertion.

Allege   To state, recite, assert, or charge.

Alternative dispute resolution (ADR)   The resolution of disputes in ways other than those involved in the traditional judicial process. Negotiation, mediation, and arbitration are forms of ADR.

Amend   To change through a formal procedure.

American Arbitration Association (AAA)   The major organization offering arbitration services in the United States.

Analogy   In logical reasoning, an assumption that if two things are similar in some respects, they will be similar in other respects also. Often used in legal reasoning to infer the appropriate application of legal principles in a case being decided by referring to previous cases involving different facts but considered to come within the policy underlying the rule.

Annual percentage rate (APR)   The cost of credit on a yearly basis, typically expressed as an annual percentage.

Annuity   An insurance policy that pays the insured fixed, periodic payments for life or for a term of years, as stipulated in the policy, after the insured reaches a specified age.

Annul   To cancel or to make void.

Answer   Procedurally, a defendant's response to the plaintiff's complaint.

Antecedent claim   A preexisting claim. In negotiable instruments law, taking an instrument in satisfaction of an antecedent claim is taking the instrument for value—that is, for valid consideration.

Anticipatory repudiation   An assertion or action by a party indicating that he or she will not perform an obligation that the party is contractually obligated to perform at a future time.

Antitrust law   The body of federal and state laws and statutes protecting trade and commerce from unlawful restraints, price discrimination, price fixing, and monopolies. The principal federal antitrust statues are the Sherman Act of 1890, the Clayton Act of 1914, and the Federal Trade Commission Act of 1914.

Apparent authority   Authority that is only apparent, not real. In agency law, a person may be deemed to have had the power to act as an agent for another party if the other party's manifestations to a third party led the third party to believe that an agency existed when, in fact, it did not.

Appeal   Resort to a superior court, such as an appellate court, to review the decision of an inferior court, such as a trial court or an administrative agency.

Appellant   The party who takes an appeal from one court to another.

Appellate court   A court having appellate jurisdiction.

Appellate jurisdiction   Courts having appellate jurisdiction act as reviewing courts, or appellate courts. Generally, cases can be brought before appellate courts only on appeal from an order or a judgment of a trial court or other lower court.

Appellee   The party against whom an appeal is taken—that is, the party who opposes setting aside or reversing the judgment.

Appraisal right   The right of a dissenting shareholder, if he or she objects to an extraordinary transaction of the corporation (such as a merger or consolidation), to have his or her shares appraised and to be paid the fair value of his or her shares by the corporation.

Appraiser   An individual who specializes in determining the value of certain real or personal property.

Appropriation   In tort law, the use by one person of another person's name, likeness, or other identifying characteristic without permission and for the benefit of the user.

Arbitrary and capricious test   A court reviewing an informal administrative agency action applies this test to determine whether or not that action was in clear error. The court gives wide discretion to the expertise of the agency and decides if the agency had sufficient factual information on which to base its action. If no clear error was made, then the agency's action stands.

Arbitration   The settling of a dispute by submitting it to a disinterested third party (other than a court), who renders a decision. The decision may or may not be legally binding.

Arbitration clause   A clause in a contract that provides that, in the event of a dispute, the parties will submit the dispute to arbitration rather than litigate the dispute in court.

Arraignment   A procedure in which an accused person is brought before the court to answer criminal charges. The charge is read to the person, and he or she is asked to enter a plea—such as "guilty" or "not guilty."

Arson   The malicious burning of another's dwelling. Some statutes have expanded this to include any real property regardless of ownership and the destruction of property by other means—for example, by explosion.

Articles of incorporation   The document filed with the appropriate governmental agency, usually the secretary of state, when a business is incorporated; state statutes usually prescribe what kind of information must be contained in the articles of incorporation.

Articles of organization   The document filed with a designated state official by which a limited liability company is formed.

Articles of partnership   A written agreement that sets forth each partner's rights and obligations with respect to the partnership.

Artisan's lien   A possessory lien given to a person who has made improvements and added value to another person's personal property as security for payment for services performed.

Assault   Any word or action intended to make another person fearful of immediate physical harm; a reasonably believable threat.

Assignee   The person to whom contract rights are assigned.

Assignment   The act of transferring to another all or part of one's rights arising under a contract.

Assignor   The person who assigns contract rights.

Assumption of risk   A defense against negligence that can be used when the plaintiff was aware of a danger and voluntarily assumed the risk of injury from that danger.

Attachment   (1) In the context of secured transactions, the process by which a security interest in the property of another becomes enforceable. (2) In the context of judicial liens, a court-ordered seizure and taking into custody of property prior to the securing of a judgment for a past-due debt.

Attempted monopolization   Any actions by a firm to eliminate competition and gain monopoly power.

Authenticate   To sign a record, or with the intent to sign a record, to execute or to adopt an electronic sound, symbol, or the like to link with the record. A *record* is retrievable information inscribed on a tangible medium or stored in an electronic or other medium.

Authority   In agency law, the agent's permission to act on behalf of the principal. An agent's authority may be actual (express or implied) or apparent. *See also* Actual authority; Apparent authority

Authorization card   A card signed by an employee that gives a union permission to act on his or her behalf in negotiations with management. Unions typically use authorization cards as evidence of employee support during union organization.

Authorized means   In contract law, the means of acceptance authorized by the offeror.

Automatic stay   In bankruptcy proceedings, the suspension of virtually all litigation and other action by creditors against the debtor or the debtor's property; the stay is effective the moment the debtor files a petition in bankruptcy.

Award   In the context of litigation, the amount of money awarded to a plaintiff in a civil lawsuit as damages. In the context of arbitration, the arbitrator's decision.

B

Bailee   One to whom goods are entrusted by a bailor. Under the Uniform Commercial Code, a party who, by a bill of lading, warehouse receipt, or other document of title, acknowledges possession of goods and contracts.

Bailee's lien   A possessory lien, or claim, that a bailee entitled to compensation can place on the bailed property to ensure that he or she will be paid for the services provided. The lien is effective as long as the bailee retains possession of the bailed goods and has not agreed to extend credit to the bailor. Sometimes referred to as an artisan's lien.

Bailment   A situation in which the personal property of one person (a bailor) is entrusted to another (a bailee), who is obligated to return the bailed property to the bailor or dispose of it as directed.

Bailor   One who entrusts goods to a bailee.

Bait-and-switch advertising   Advertising a product at a very attractive price (the bait) and then informing the consumer, once he or she is in the store, that the advertised product is either not available or is of poor quality; the customer is then urged to purchase (switched to) a more expensive item.

Balloon mortgage   A loan that allows the debtor to make small monthly payments for an initial period, such as eight years, but then requires a large balloon payment for the entire remaining balance of the mortgage loan at the end of that period.

Banker's acceptance   A negotiable instrument that is commonly used in international trade. A banker's acceptance is drawn by a creditor against the debtor, who pays the draft at maturity. The drawer creates a draft without designating a payee. The draft can pass through many parties' hands before a bank (drawee) accepts it, transforming the draft into a banker's acceptance. Acceptances can be purchased and sold in a way similar to securities.

Bankruptcy court   A federal court of limited jurisdiction that handles only bankruptcy proceedings. Bankruptcy proceedings are governed by federal bankruptcy law.

Bankruptcy trustee   A person who is either appointed by the U.S. Department of Justice or by creditors in bankruptcy cases.   In all bankruptcies under Chapters 7, 12, or 13, a trustee is appointed by the U.S. Trustee, who is an officer of the Department of Justice. Chapter 11 bankruptcies allow the debtor to continue to manage the property as a "debtor in possession," but this person can be replaced for cause with a bankruptcy trustee.

Bargain   A mutual undertaking, contract, or agreement between two parties; to negotiate over the terms of a purchase or contract.

Basis of the bargain   In contract law, the affirmation of fact or promise on which the sale of goods is predicated, creating an express warranty.

Battery   The unprivileged, intentional touching of another.

Bearer   A person in the possession of an instrument payable to bearer or indorsed in blank.

Bearer instrument   Any instrument that is not payable to a specific person, including instruments payable to the bearer or to "cash."

Beneficiary   One to whom life insurance proceeds are payable or for whose benefit a trust has been established or property under a will has been transferred.

Bequest   A gift by will of personal property (from the verb—to bequeath).

Beyond a reasonable doubt   The standard used to determine the guilt or innocence of a person criminally charged. To be guilty of a crime, one must be proved guilty "beyond and to the exclusion of every reasonable doubt." A reasonable doubt is one that would cause a prudent person to hesitate before acting in matters important to him or her.

Bilateral contract   A type of contract that arises when a promise is given in exchange for a return promise.

Bill of lading   A document that serves both as evidence of the receipt of goods for shipment and as documentary evidence of title to the goods.

Bill of Rights   The first ten amendments to the U.S. Constitution.

Binder   A written, temporary insurance policy.

Binding authority   Any source of law that a court must follow when deciding a case. Binding authorities include constitutions, statutes, and regulations that govern the issue being decided, as well as court decisions that are controlling precedents within the jurisdiction.

Blank indorsement   An indorsement that specifies no particular indorsee and can consist of a mere signature. An order instrument that is indorsed in blank becomes a bearer instrument.

Blue sky laws   State laws that regulate the offer and sale of securities.

Bona fide   Good faith. A bona fide obligation is one made in good faith—that is, sincerely and honestly.

Bona fide occupational qualification (BFOQ)   Identifiable characteristics reasonably necessary to the normal operation of a particular business. These characteristics can include gender, national origin, and religion, but not race.

Bond   A certificate that evidences a corporate (or government) debt. It is a security that involves no ownership interest in the issuing entity.

Bond indenture   A written agreement between a bond issuer and the bondholders, normally consisting of a specified interest rate, maturity date, and other terms; sometimes simply called an indenture.

Botnet   Short for *robot network*—a group of computers that run an application that is controlled and manipulated only by the software source. Although sometimes a legitimate network, usually this term is reserved for a group of computers that have been infected by malicious robot software. In a botnet, each connected computer becomes a zombie, or drone.

Boycott   A concerted refusal to do business with a particular person or entity in order to obtain concessions or to express displeasure with certain acts or practices of that person or business. *See also* Secondary boycott

Breach   To violate a law, by an act or an omission, or to break a legal obligation that one owes to another person or to society.

Breach of contract The failure, without legal excuse, of a promisor to perform the obligations of a contract.

Bribery The offering, giving, receiving, or soliciting of anything of value with the aim of influencing an official action or an official's discharge of a legal or public duty or (with respect to commercial bribery) a business decision.

Bridge loan A short-term loan that allows a buyer to make a down payment on a new home before selling her or his current home (the current home is used as collateral).

Brief A formal legal document submitted by the attorney for the appellant—or the appellee (in answer to the appellant's brief)—to an appellate court when a case is appealed. The appellant's brief outlines the facts and issues of the case, the judge's rulings or jury's findings that should be reversed or modified, the applicable law, and the arguments on the client's behalf.

Browse-wrap terms Terms and conditions of use that are presented to an Internet user at the time certain products, such as software, are being downloaded but that need not be agreed to (by clicking "I agree," for example) before being able to install or use the product.

Bureaucracy A large organization that is structured hierarchically to carry out specific functions.

Burglary The unlawful entry into a building with the intent to commit a felony. (Some state statutes expand this to include the intent to commit any crime.)

Business ethics Ethics in a business context; a consensus of what constitutes right or wrong behavior in the world of business and the application of moral principles to situations that arise in a business setting.

Business invitees Those people, such as customers or clients, who are invited onto business premises by the owner of those premises for business purposes.

Business judgment rule A rule that immunizes corporate management from liability for actions that result in corporate losses or damages if the actions are undertaken in good faith and are within both the power of the corporation and the authority of management to make.

Business necessity A defense to allegations of employment discrimination in which the employer demonstrates that an employment practice that discriminates against members of a protected class is related to job performance.

Business plan A document describing a company, its products, and its anticipated future performance. Creating a business plan is normally the first step in obtaining loans or venture-capital funds for a new business enterprise.

Business tort Wrongful interference with the business rights of another.

Business trust A voluntary form of business organization in which investors (trust beneficiaries) transfer cash or property to trustees in exchange for trust certificates that represent their investment shares.

Management of the business and trust property is handled by the trustees for the use and benefit of the investors. The certificate holders have limited liability (are not responsible for the debts and obligations incurred by the trust) and share in the trust's profits.

Buyer in the ordinary course of business A buyer who, in good faith and without knowledge that the sale violates the ownership rights or security interest of a third party in the goods, purchases goods in the ordinary course of business from a person in the business of selling goods of that kind.

Buyout price The amount payable to a partner on his or her dissociation from a partnership, based on the amount distributable to that partner if the firm were wound up on that date, and offset by any damages for wrongful dissociation.

Buy-sell agreement In the context of partnerships, an express agreement made at the time of partnership formation for one or more of the partners to buy out the other or others should the situation warrant—and thus provide for the smooth dissolution of the partnership.

Bylaws A set of governing rules adopted by a corporation or other association.

Bystander A spectator, witness, or person who was standing nearby when an event occurred and who did not engage in the business or act leading to the event.

C

C.I.F. or C.&F. Cost, insurance, and freight—or just cost and freight. A pricing term in a contract for the sale of goods requiring, among other things, that the seller place the goods in the possession of a carrier before risk passes to the buyer.

C.O.D. Cash on delivery. In sales transactions, a term meaning that the buyer will pay for the goods on delivery and before inspecting the goods.

Callable bond A bond that may be called in and the principal repaid at specified times or under conditions specified in the bond when it is issued.

Cancellation The act of nullifying, or making void. *See also* Rescission

Capital Accumulated goods, possessions, and assets used for the production of profits and wealth; the equity of owners in a business.

Carrier An individual or organization engaged in transporting passengers or goods for hire. *See also* Common carrier

Case law The rules of law announced in court decisions. Case law includes the aggregate of reported cases that interpret judicial precedents, statutes, regulations, and constitutional provisions.

Case on point A previous case involving factual circumstances and issues that are similar to those in the case before the court.

Cash surrender value The amount that the insurer has agreed to pay to the insured if a life insurance policy is canceled before the insured's death.

Cashier's check A check drawn by a bank on itself.

Categorical imperative   A concept developed by the philosopher Immanuel Kant as an ethical guideline for behavior. In deciding whether an action is right or wrong, or desirable or undesirable, a person should evaluate the action in terms of what would happen if everybody else in the same situation, or category, acted the same way.

Causation in fact   An act or omission without ("but for") which an event would not have occurred.

Cause of action   A situation or set of facts sufficient to justify a right to sue.

Cease-and-desist order   An administrative or judicial order prohibiting a person or business firm from conducting activities that an agency or court has deemed illegal.

Certificate of deposit (CD)   A note of a bank in which a bank acknowledges a receipt of money from a party and promises to repay the money, with interest, to the party on a certain date.

Certificate of limited partnership   The basic document filed with a designated state official by which a limited partnership is formed.

Certification mark   A mark used by one or more persons, other than the owner, to certify the region, materials, mode of manufacture, quality, or accuracy of the owner's goods or services. When used by members of a cooperative, association, or other organization, such a mark is referred to as a collective mark. Examples of certification marks include the "Good Housekeeping Seal of Approval" and "UL Tested."

Certified check   A check that has been accepted by the bank on which it is drawn. Essentially, the bank, by certifying (accepting) the check, promises to pay the check at the time the check is presented.

Certiorari   *See* Writ of *certiorari*

Chain-style business franchise   A franchise that operates under a franchisor's trade name and that is identified as a member of a select group of dealers that engage in the franchisor's business. The franchisee is generally required to follow standardized or prescribed methods of operation. Examples of this type of franchise are McDonald's and most other fast-food chains.

Chancellor   An adviser to the king at the time of the early king's courts of England. Individuals petitioned the king for relief when they could not obtain an adequate remedy in a court of law, and these petitions were decided by the chancellor.

Charging order   In partnership law, an order granted by a court to a judgment creditor that entitles the creditor to attach profits or assets of a partner on dissolution of the partnership.

Charitable trust   A trust in which the property held by a trustee must be used for a charitable purpose, such as the advancement of health, education, or religion.

Chattel   All forms of personal property.

Chattel paper   Any writing or writings that show both a debt and the fact that the debt is secured by personal property. In many instances, chattel paper consists of a negotiable instrument coupled with a security agreement.

Check   A draft drawn by a drawer ordering the drawee bank or financial institution to pay a certain amount of money to the holder on demand.

Checks and balances   The national government is composed of three separate branches: the executive, the legislative, and the judicial branches. Each branch of the government exercises a check on the actions of the others.

Choice-of-language clause   A clause in a contract designating the official language by which the contract will be interpreted in the event of a future disagreement over the contract's terms.

Choice-of-law clause   A clause in a contract designating the law (such as the law of a particular state or nation) that will govern the contract.

Citation   A reference to a publication in which a legal authority—such as a statute or a court decision—or other source can be found.

Civil law   The branch of law dealing with the definition and enforcement of all private or public rights, as opposed to criminal matters.

Civil law system   A system of law derived from that of the Roman Empire and based on a code rather than case law; the predominant system of law in the nations of continental Europe and the nations that were once their colonies. In the United States, Louisiana is the only state that has a civil law system.

Claim   As a verb, to assert or demand. As a noun, a right to payment.

Clearinghouse   A system or place where banks exchange checks and drafts drawn on each other and settle daily balances.

Click-on agreement   An agreement that arises when a buyer, engaging in a transaction on a computer, indicates his or her assent to be bound by the terms of an offer by clicking on a button that says, for example, "I agree"; sometimes referred to as a click-on license or a click-wrap agreement.

Closed shop   A firm that requires union membership by its workers as a condition of employment. The closed shop was made illegal by the Labor-Management Relations Act of 1947.

Closely held corporation   A corporation whose shareholders are limited to a small group of persons, often including only family members. The rights of shareholders of a closely held corporation usually are restricted regarding the transfer of shares to others.

Closing   The final step in the sale of real estate—also called settlement or closing escrow. The escrow agent coordinates the closing with the recording of deeds, the obtaining of title insurance, and other concurrent closing activities. A number of costs must be paid, in cash, at the time of closing, and they can range from several hundred to several thousand dollars, depending on the amount of the mortgage loan and other conditions of the sale.

Closing argument   An argument made after the plaintiff and defendant have rested their cases. Closing arguments are made prior to the jury charges.

Cloud computing   The delivery to users of on-demand services from third-party servers over a network. Cloud computing is a delivery model. The most widely used cloud computing services are Software as a Service (SaaS), which offers companies a cheaper way to buy and use packaged applications that are no longer run on servers in house.

Codicil A written supplement or modification to a will. A codicil must be executed with the same formalities as a will.

Collateral Under Article 9 of the Uniform Commercial Code, the property subject to a security interest.

Collateral promise A secondary promise that is ancillary (subsidiary) to a principal transaction or primary contractual relationship, such as a promise made by one person to pay the debts of another if the latter fails to perform. A collateral promise normally must be in writing to be enforceable.

Collecting bank Any bank handling an item for collection, except the payor bank.

Collective bargaining The process by which labor and management negotiate the terms and conditions of employment, including working hours and workplace conditions.

Collective mark A mark used by members of a cooperative, association, or other organization to certify the region, materials, mode of manufacture, quality, or accuracy of the specific goods or services. Examples of collective marks include the labor union marks found on tags of certain products and the credits of movies, which indicate the various associations and organizations that participated in the making of the movies.

Comity A deference by which one nation gives effect to the laws and judicial decrees of another nation. This recognition is based primarily on respect.

Comment period A period of time following an administrative agency's publication or a notice of a proposed rule during which private parties may comment in writing on the agency proposal in an effort to influence agency policy. The agency takes any comments received into consideration when drafting the final version of the regulation.

Commerce clause The provision in Article I, Section 8, of the U.S. Constitution that gives Congress the power to regulate interstate commerce.

Commercial impracticability A doctrine under which a seller may be excused from performing a contract when (1) a contingency occurs, (2) the contingency's occurrence makes performance impracticable, and (3) the nonoccurrence of the contingency was a basic assumption on which the contract was made. Despite the fact that UCC 2–615 expressly frees only sellers under this doctrine, courts have not distinguished between buyers and sellers in applying it.

Commercial paper *See* Negotiable instrument

Commercial use Use of land for business activities only; sometimes called business use.

Commingle To put funds or goods together into one mass so that the funds or goods are so mixed that they no longer have separate identities. In corporate law, if personal and corporate interests are commingled to the extent that the corporation has no separate identity, a court may "pierce the corporate veil" and expose the shareholders to personal liability.

Common area In landlord-tenant law, a portion of the premises over which the landlord retains control and maintenance responsibilities. Common areas may include stairs, lobbies, garages, hallways, and other areas in common use.

Common carrier A carrier that transfers people or goods for hire to the general public.

Common law That body of law developed from custom or judicial decisions in English and U.S. courts, not attributable to a legislature.

Common stock Shares of ownership in a corporation that give the owner of the stock a proportionate interest in the corporation with regard to control, earnings, and net assets; shares of common stock are lowest in priority with respect to payment of dividends and distribution of the corporation's assets on dissolution.

Community property A form of concurrent ownership of property in which each spouse technically owns an undivided one-half interest in property acquired during the marriage. This form of joint ownership occurs in only a minority of states and Puerto Rico.

Comparative negligence A theory in tort law under which the liability for injuries resulting from negligent acts is shared by all parties who were negligent (including the injured party), on the basis of each person's proportionate negligence.

Compensatory damages A money award equivalent to the actual value of injuries or damages sustained by the aggrieved party.

Complaint The pleading made by a plaintiff alleging wrongdoing on the part of the defendant; the document that, when filed with a court, initiates a lawsuit.

Complete performance Performance of a contract strictly in accordance with the contract's terms.

Composition agreement *See* Creditors' composition agreement

Computer crime Any wrongful act that is directed against computers and computer parties, or wrongful use or abuse of computers or software.

Concentrated industry An industry in which a large percentage of market sales is controlled by either a single firm or a small number of firms.

Concurrent conditions Conditions in a contract that must occur or be performed at the same time; they are mutually dependent. No obligations arise until these conditions are simultaneously performed.

Concurrent jurisdiction Jurisdiction that exists when two different courts have the power to hear a case. For example, some cases can be heard in either a federal or a state court.

Concurrent ownership Joint ownership.

Concurring opinion A written opinion outlining the views of a judge or justice to make or emphasize a point that was not made or emphasized in the majority opinion.

Condemnation The process of taking private property for public use through the government's power of eminent domain.

Condition A possible future event, the occurrence or nonoccurrence of which will trigger the performance of a legal obligation or terminate an existing obligation under a contract.

Condition precedent A condition in a contract that must be met before a party's promise becomes absolute.

Condition subsequent A condition in a contract that operates to terminate a party's absolute promise to perform.

Confession of judgment The act of a debtor in permitting a judgment to be entered against him or her by a creditor, for an agreed sum, without the institution of legal proceedings.

Confiscation A government's taking of privately owned business or personal property without a proper public purpose or an award of just compensation.

Conforming goods Goods that conform to contract specifications.

Confusion The mixing together of goods belonging to two or more owners so that the separately owned goods cannot be identified.

Conglomerate merger A merger between firms that do not compete with each other because they are in different markets (as opposed to horizontal and vertical mergers).

Consent Voluntary agreement to a proposition or an act of another. A concurrence of wills.

Consequential damages Special damages that compensate for a loss that is not direct or immediate (for example, lost profits). The special damages must have been reasonably foreseeable at the time the breach or injury occurred in order for the plaintiff to collect them.

Consideration Generally, the value given in return for a promise or a performance. The consideration, which must be present to make the contract legally binding, must be something of legally sufficient value and bargained for.

Consignment A transaction in which an owner of goods (the consignor) delivers the goods to another (the consignee) for the consignee to sell. The consignee pays the consignor for the goods when they are sold by the consignee.

Consolidation A contractual and statutory process in which two or more corporations join to become a completely new corporation. The original corporations cease to exist, and the new corporation acquires all their assets and liabilities.

Constitutional law Law that is based on the U.S. Constitution and the constitutions of the various states.

Construction loan A loan obtained by the borrower to finance the building of a new home. Construction loans are often set up to release funds at particular stages of the project.

Constructive condition A condition in a contract that is neither expressed nor implied by the contract but rather is imposed by law for reasons of justice.

Constructive delivery An act equivalent to the actual, physical delivery of property that cannot be physically delivered because of difficulty or impossibility; for example, the transfer of a key to a safe constructively delivers the contents of the safe.

Constructive discharge A termination of employment brought about by making an employee's working conditions so intolerable that the employee reasonably feels compelled to leave.

Constructive eviction A form of eviction that occurs when a landlord fails to perform adequately any of the undertakings (such as providing heat in the winter) required by the lease, thereby making the tenant's further use and enjoyment of the property exceedingly difficult or impossible.

Constructive trust An equitable trust that is imposed in the interests of fairness and justice when someone wrongfully holds legal title to property. A court may require the owner to hold the property in trust for the person or persons who rightfully should own the property.

Consumer credit Credit extended primarily for personal or household use.

Consumer-debtor An individual whose debts are primarily consumer debts (debts for purchases made primarily for personal or household use).

Consumer goods Goods that are primarily for personal or household use.

Consumer law The body of statutes, agency rules, and judicial decisions protecting consumers of goods and services from dangerous manufacturing techniques, mislabeling, unfair credit practices, deceptive advertising, and so on. Consumer laws provide remedies and protections that are not ordinarily available to merchants or to businesses.

Contingency fee An attorney's fee that is based on a percentage of the final award received by his or her client as a result of litigation.

Continuation statement A statement that, if filed within six months prior to the expiration date of the original financing statement, continues the perfection of the original security interest for another five years. The perfection of a security interest can be continued in the same manner indefinitely.

Contract An agreement that can be enforced in court; formed by two or more parties, each of whom agrees to perform or to refrain from performing some act now or in the future.

Contract implied in law *See* Quasi contract

Contract under seal A formal agreement in which the seal is a substitute for consideration. A court will not invalidate a contract under seal for lack of consideration.

Contractual capacity The threshold mental capacity required by the law for a party who enters into a contract to be bound by that contract.

Contribution *See* Right of contribution

Contributory negligence A theory in tort law under which a complaining party's own negligence contributed to or caused his or her injuries. Contributory negligence is an absolute bar to recovery in a minority of jurisdictions.

Conversion   The wrongful taking, using, or retaining possession of personal property that belongs to another.

Convertible bond   A bond that can be exchanged for a specified number of shares of common stock under certain conditions.

Conveyance   The transfer of a title to land from one person to another by deed; a document (such as a deed) by which an interest in land is transferred from one person to another.

Conviction   The outcome of a criminal trial in which the defendant has been found guilty of the crime.

"Cooling-off" laws   A set of federal and state laws designed to protect purchasers and leasees of goods or property. For example, the Federal Trade Commission's cooling-off period is three business days for purchases of goods or services from door-to-door salespersons. Cooling off periods vary for loans, mortgages, leases, etc.

Cooperative   An association that is organized to provide an economic service to its members (or shareholders). An incorporated cooperative is a nonprofit corporation. It will make distributions of dividends, or profits, to its owners on the basis of their transactions with the cooperative rather than on the basis of the amount of capital they contributed. Examples of cooperatives are consumer purchasing cooperatives, credit cooperatives, and farmers' cooperatives.

Co-ownership   Joint ownership.

Copyright   The exclusive right of authors to publish, print, or sell an intellectual production for a statutory period of time. A copyright has the same monopolistic nature as a patent or trademark, but it differs in that it applies exclusively to works of art, literature, and other works of authorship, including computer programs.

Corporate governance   The relationship between a corporation and its shareholders—specifically, a system that details the distribution of rights and responsibilities of those within the corporation and spells out the rules and procedures for making corporate decisions.

Corporate social responsibility   The concept that corporations can and should act ethically and be accountable to society for their actions.

Corporation   A legal entity formed in compliance with statutory requirements. The entity is distinct from its shareholders-owners.

Cosign   The act of signing a document (such as a note promising to pay another in return for a loan or other benefit) jointly with another person and thereby assuming liability for performing what was promised in the document.

Cost-benefit analysis   A decision-making technique that involves weighing the costs of a given action against the benefits of the action.

Co-surety   A joint surety. One who assumes liability jointly with another surety for the payment of an obligation.

Counteradvertising   New advertising that is undertaken pursuant to a Federal Trade Commission order for the purpose of correcting earlier false claims that were made about a product.

Counterclaim   A claim made by a defendant in a civil lawsuit that in effect sues the plaintiff.

Counteroffer   An offeree's response to an offer in which the offeree rejects the original offer and at the same time makes a new offer.

Course of dealing   Prior conduct between parties to a contract that establishes a common basis for their understanding.

Course of performance   The conduct that occurs under the terms of a particular agreement; such conduct indicates what the parties to an agreement intended it to mean.

Court of equity   A court that decides controversies and administers justice according to the rules, principles, and precedents of equity.

Court of law   A court in which the only remedies that could be granted were things of value, such as money damages. In the early English king's courts, courts of law were distinct from courts of equity.

Covenant against encumbrances   A grantor's assurance that there are no encumbrances on land conveyed—that is, that no third parties have rights to or interests in the land that would diminish its value to the grantee.

Covenant not to compete   A contractual promise to refrain from competing with another party for a certain period of time and within a certrain geographic area. Although covenants not to compete restrain trade, they are commonly found in partnership agreements, business sale agreements, and employment contracts. If they are ancillary to such agreements, covenants not to compete will normally be enforced by the courts unless the time period or geographic area is deemed unreasonable.

Covenant not to sue   An agreement to substitute a contractual obligation for some other type of legal action based on a valid claim.

Covenant of quiet enjoyment   A promise by a grantor (or landlord) that the grantee (or tenant) will not be evicted or disturbed by the grantor or a person having a lien or superior title.

Covenant of the right to convey   A grantor's assurance that he or she has sufficient capacity and title to convey the estate that he or she undertakes to convey by deed.

Covenant running with the land   An executory promise made between a grantor and a grantee to which they and subsequent owners of the land are bound.

Cover   A buyer or lessee's purchase on the open market of goods to substitute for those promised but never delivered by the seller. Under the Uniform Commercial Code, if the cost of cover exceeds the cost of the contract goods, the buyer or lessee can recover the difference, plus incidental and consequential damages.

Cram-down provision   A provision of the Bankruptcy Code that allows a court to confirm a debtor's Chapter 11 reorganization plan even though only one class of creditors has accepted it. To exercise the court's right under this provision, the court must demonstrate that the plan does not discriminate unfairly against any creditors and is fair and equitable.

Creditor A person to whom a debt is owed by another person (the debtor).

Creditor beneficiary A third party beneficiary who has rights in a contract made by the debtor and a third person. The terms of the contract obligate the third person to pay the debt owed to the creditor. The creditor beneficiary can enforce the debt against either party.

Creditors' composition agreement An agreement formed between a debtor and his or her creditors in which the creditors agree to accept a lesser sum than that owed by the debtor in full satisfaction of the debt.

Crime A wrong against society proclaimed in a statute and punishable by society through fines and/or imprisonment—or, in some cases, death.

Criminal act *See Actus reus*

Criminal intent *See Mens rea*

Criminal law Law that defines and governs actions that constitute crimes. Generally, criminal law has to do with wrongful actions committed against society for which society demands redress.

Cross-border pollution Pollution across national boundaries; air and water degradation in one nation resulting from pollution-causing activities in a neighboring country.

Cross-collateralization The use of an asset that is not the subject of a loan to collateralize that loan.

Cross-examination The questioning of an opposing witness during a trial.

Cumulative voting A method of shareholder voting designed to allow minority shareholders to be represented on the board of directors. With cumulative voting, the number of members of the board to be elected is multiplied by the total number of voting shares held. The result equals the number of votes a shareholder has, and this total can be cast for one or more nominees for director.

Cure Under the Uniform Commercial Code, the right of a party who tenders nonconforming performance to correct his or her performance within the contract period.

Cyber crime A crime that occurs online, in the virtual community of the Internet, as opposed to the physical world.

Cyber fraud Fraud that involves the online theft of credit card information, banking details, and other information for criminal use.

Cyber mark A trademark in cyberspace.

Cyber tort A tort committed via the Internet.

Cyberlaw An informal term used to refer to all laws governing electronic communications and transactions, particularly those conducted via the Internet.

Cybernotary A legally recognized authority that can certify the validity of digital signatures.

Cybersquatting The act of registering a domain name that is the same as, or confusingly similar to, the trademark of another and then offering to sell that domain name back to the trademark owner.

Cyberterrorist A hacker whose purpose is to exploit a target computer for a serious impact, such as the corruption of a program to sabotage a business.

D

Damages Money sought as a remedy for a breach of contract or for a tortious act.

Debenture bond A bond for which no specific assets of the corporation are pledged as backing; rather, the bond is backed by the general credit rating of the corporation, plus any assets that can be seized if the corporation allows the debentures to go into default.

Debit card A plastic card issued by a financial institution that allows the user to access his or her accounts online via automated teller machines.

Debtor Under Article 9 of the Uniform Commercial Code, any party who owes payment or performance of a secured obligation, whether or not the party actually owns or has rights in the collateral.

Debtor in possession (DIP) In Chapter 11 bankruptcy proceedings, a debtor who is allowed to continue in possession of the estate in property (the business) and to continue business operations.

Deceptive advertising Advertising that misleads consumers, either by making unjustified claims concerning a product's performance or by omitting a material fact concerning the product's composition or performance.

Declaratory judgment A court's judgment on a justiciable controversy when the plaintiff is in doubt as to his or her legal rights; a binding adjudication of the rights and status of litigants even though no consequential relief is awarded.

Decree The judgment of a court of equity.

Deed A document by which title to property (usually real property) is passed.

Deed in lieu of foreclosure An alternative to foreclosure in which the mortgagor, rather than fighting to retain possession, voluntarily conveys the property to the lender in satisfaction of the mortgage.

Defalcation The misuse of funds.

Defamation Any published or publicly spoken false statement that causes injury to another's good name, reputation, or character.

Default judgment A judgment entered by a court against a defendant who has failed to appear in court to answer or defend against the plaintiff's claim.

Defendant One against whom a lawsuit is brought; the accused person in a criminal proceeding.

Defense Reasons that a defendant offers in an action or suit as to why the plaintiff should not obtain what he or she is seeking.

Deficiency judgment A judgment against a debtor for the amount of a debt remaining unpaid after collateral has been repossessed and sold.

Delegatee One to whom contract duties are delegated by another, called the delegator.

Delegation The transfer of a contractual duty to a third party. The party delegating the duty (the delegator) to the third party (the delegatee) is still obliged to perform on the contract should the delegatee fail to perform.

Delegation doctrine A doctrine based on Article I, Section 8, of the U.S. Constitution, which has been construed to allow Congress to delegate some of its power to make and implement laws to administrative agencies. The delegation is considered to be proper as long as Congress sets standards outlining the scope of the agency's authority.

Delegator One who delegates his or her duties under a contract to another, called the delegatee.

Delivery In contract law, one party's act of placing the subject matter of the contract within the other party's possession or control.

Delivery order A written order to deliver goods directed to a warehouser, carrier, or other person who, in the ordinary course of business, issues warehouse receipts or bills of lading [UCC 7–102(1)(d)].

Demand deposit Funds (accepted by a bank) subject to immediate withdrawal, in contrast to a time deposit, which requires that a depositor wait a specific time before withdrawing or pay a penalty for early withdrawal.

De novo Anew; afresh; a second time. In a hearing *de novo,* an appellate court hears the case as a court of original jurisdiction—that is, as if the case had not previously been tried and a decision rendered.

Depositary bank The first bank to receive a check for payment.

Deposition The testimony of a party to a lawsuit or a witness taken under oath before a trial.

Destination contract A contract in which the seller is required to ship the goods by carrier and deliver them at a particular destination. The seller assumes liability for any losses or damage to the goods until they are tendered at the destination specified in the contract.

Devise To make a gift of real property by will.

Digital cash Funds contained on computer software, in the form of secure programs stored on microchips and other computer devices.

Dilution With respect to trademarks, a doctrine under which distinctive or famous trademarks are protected from certain unauthorized uses of the marks regardless of a showing of competition or a likelihood of confusion. Congress created a federal cause of action for dilution in 1995 with the passage of the Federal Trademark Dilution Act.

Direct examination The examination of a witness by the attorney who calls the witness to the stand to testify on behalf of the attorney's client.

Directed verdict *See* Motion for a directed verdict

Disaffirmance The legal avoidance, or setting aside, of a contractual obligation.

Discharge The termination of an obligation. (1) In contract law, discharge occurs when the parties have fully performed their contractual obligations or when events, conduct of the parties, or operation of the law releases the parties from performance. (2) In bankruptcy proceedings, the extinction of the debtor's dischargeable debts.

Discharge in bankruptcy The release of a debtor from all debts that are provable, except those specifically excepted from discharge by statute.

Disclosed principal A principal whose identity is known to a third party at the time the agent makes a contract with the third party.

Discovery A phase in the litigation process during which the opposing parties may obtain information from each other and from third parties prior to trial.

Dishonor To refuse to accept or pay a draft or a promissory note when it is properly presented. An instrument is dishonored when presentment is properly made and acceptance or payment is refused or cannot be obtained within the prescribed time.

Disparagement of property An economically injurious false statement made about another's product or property. A general term for torts that are more specifically referred to as slander of quality or slander of title.

Disparate-impact discrimination A form of employment discrimination that results from certain employer practices or procedures that, although not discriminatory on their face, have a discriminatory effect.

Disparate-treatment discrimination A form of employment discrimination that results when an employer intentionally discriminates against employees who are members of protected classes.

Dissenting opinion A written opinion by a judge or justice who disagrees with the majority opinion.

Dissociation The severance of the relationship between a partner and a partnership when the partner ceases to be associated with the carrying on of the partnership business.

Dissolution The formal disbanding of a partnership or a corporation. It can take place by (1) acts of the partners or, in a corporation, of the shareholders and board of directors; (2) the death of a partner; (3) the expiration of a time period stated in a partnership agreement or a certificate of incorporation; or (4) judicial decree.

Distributed network A network that can be used by persons located (distributed) around the country or the globe to share computer files.

Distribution agreement A contract between a seller and a distributor of the seller's products setting out the terms and conditions of the distributorship.

Distributorship A business arrangement that is established when a manufacturer licenses a dealer to sell its product. An example of a distributorship is an automobile dealership.

Diversity of citizenship Under Article III, Section 2, of the Constitution, a basis for federal court jurisdiction over a lawsuit between (1) citizens of different states, (2) a foreign country and citizens of a state or of different states, or (3) citizens of a state and citizens or subjects of a foreign country. The amount in controversy must be more than $75,000 before a federal court can take jurisdiction in such cases.

Divestiture The act of selling one or more of a company's parts, such as a subsidiary or plant; often mandated by the courts in merger or monopolization cases.

Dividend   A distribution to corporate shareholders of corporate profits or income, disbursed in proportion to the number of shares held.

Docket   The list of cases entered on a court's calendar and thus scheduled to be heard by the court.

Document of title   Paper exchanged in the regular course of business that evidences the right to possession of goods (for example, a bill of lading or a warehouse receipt).

Domain name   The series of letters and symbols used to identify site operators on the Internet; Internet "addresses."

Domestic corporation   In a given state, a corporation that does business in, and is organized under the laws of, that state.

Domestic relations court   A court that deals with domestic (household) relationships, such as adoption, divorce, support payments, child custody, and the like.

Dominion   Perfect control in the right of ownership of property; typically implies both title and possession. It requires the complete retention of control over the disposition of property.

Donee beneficiary   A third party beneficiary who has rights under a contract as a direct result of the intention of the contract parties to make a gift to the third party.

Double jeopardy   A situation occurring when a person is tried twice for the same criminal offense; prohibited by the Fifth Amendment to the Constitution.

Double taxation   A feature (and disadvantage) of the corporate form of business. Because a corporation is a separate legal entity, corporate profits are taxed by state and federal governments. Dividends are again taxable as ordinary income to the shareholders receiving them.

Down payment   The part of the purchase price of real property that is paid in cash up front, reducing the amount of the loan or mortgage.

Draft   Any instrument (such as a check) drawn on a drawee (such as a bank) that orders the drawee to pay a certain sum of money, usually to a third party (the payee), on demand or at a definite future time.

Dram shop act   A state statute that imposes liability on the owners of bars and taverns, as well as those who serve alcoholic drinks to the public, for injuries resulting from accidents caused by intoxicated persons when the sellers or servers of alcoholic drinks contributed to the intoxication.

Drawee   The party that is ordered to pay a draft or check. With a check, a financial institution is always the drawee.

Drawer   The party that initiates a draft (writes a check, for example), thereby ordering the drawee to pay.

Due diligence   A required standard of care that certain professionals, such as accountants, must meet to avoid liability for securities violations. Under securities law, an accountant will be deemed to have exercised due diligence if he or she followed generally accepted accounting principles and generally accepted auditing

standards and had, "after reasonable investigation, reasonable grounds to believe and did believe, at the time such part of the registration statement became effective, that the statements therein were true and that there was no omission of a material fact required to be stated therein or necessary to make the statements therein not misleading."

Due process clause   The provisions of the Fifth and Fourteenth Amendments to the Constitution that guarantee that no person shall be deprived of life, liberty, or property without due process of law. Similar clauses are found in most state constitutions.

Dumping   The selling of goods in a foreign country at a price below the price charged for the same goods in the domestic market.

Durable power of attorney   A document that authorizes a person to act on behalf of an incompetent person—write checks, collect insurance proceeds, and otherwise manage the disabled person's affairs, including health care—when he or she becomes incapacitated. Spouses often give each other durable power of attorney and, if they are advanced in age, may give a second such power of attorney to an older child.

Duress   Unlawful pressure brought to bear on a person, causing the person to perform an act that he or she would not otherwise perform.

Duty of care   The duty of all persons, as established by tort law, to exercise a reasonable amount of care in their dealings with others. Failure to exercise due care, which is normally determined by the "reasonable person standard," constitutes the tort of negligence.

E

E-agent   A computer program, electronic, or other automated means used to perform specific tasks without review by an individual.

E-commerce   Business transacted in cyberspace.

E-contract   A contract that is entered into in cyberspace and is evidenced only by electronic impulses (such as those that make up a computer's memory), rather than, for example, a typewritten form.

E-evidence   A type of evidence that consists of computer-generated or electronically recorded information, including e-mail, voice mail, spreadsheets, word-processing documents, and other data.

E-money   Prepaid funds recorded on a computer or a card (such as a *smart card*).

E-signature   As defined by the Uniform Electronic Transactions Act, "an electronic sound, symbol, or process attached to or logically associated with a record and executed or adopted by a person with the intent to sign the record."

Early neutral case evaluation   A form of alternative dispute resolution in which a neutral third party evaluates the strengths and weakness of the disputing parties' positions; the evaluator's opinion forms the basis for negotiating a settlement.

Easement   A nonpossessory right to use another's property in a manner established by either express or implied agreement.

Electronic fund transfer (EFT) A transfer of funds with the use of an electronic terminal, a telephone, a computer, or magnetic tape.

Emancipation In regard to minors, the act of being freed from parental control; occurs when a child's parent or legal guardian relinquishes the legal right to exercise control over the child. Normally, a minor who leaves home to support himself or herself is considered emancipated.

Embezzlement The fraudulent appropriation of money or other property by a person to whom the money or property has been entrusted.

Eminent domain The power of a government to take land for public use from private citizens for just compensation.

Employee A person who works for an employer for a salary or for wages.

Employer An individual or business entity that hires employees, pays them salaries or wages, and exercises control over their work.

Employment at will A common law doctrine under which either party may terminate an employment relationship at any time for any reason, unless a contract specifies otherwise.

Employment discrimination Treating employees or job applicants unequally on the basis of race, color, national origin, religion, gender, age, or disability; prohibited by federal statutes.

Enabling legislation A statute enacted by Congress that authorizes the creation of an administrative agency and specifies the name, composition, purpose, and powers of the agency being created.

Encryption The process by which a message (plaintext) is transformed into something (ciphertext) that the sender and receiver intend third parties not to understand.

Endowment insurance A type of insurance that combines life insurance with an investment so that if the insured outlives the policy, the face value is paid to him or her; if the insured does not outlive the policy, the face value is paid to his or her beneficiary.

Entrapment In criminal law, a defense in which the defendant claims that he or she was induced by a public official—usually an undercover agent or police officer—to commit a crime that he or she would otherwise not have committed.

Entrepreneur One who initiates and assumes the financial risks of a new enterprise and who undertakes to provide or control its management.

Entrustment The transfer of goods to a merchant who deals in goods of that kind and who may transfer those goods and all rights to them to a buyer in the ordinary course of business [UCC 2–403(2)].

Environmental impact statement (EIS) A statement required by the National Environmental Policy Act for any major federal action that will significantly affect the quality of the environment. The statement must analyze the action's impact on the environment and explore alternative actions that might be taken.

Environmental law The body of statutory, regulatory, and common law relating to the protection of the environment.

Equal dignity rule In most states, a rule stating that express authority given to an agent must be in writing if the contract to be made on behalf of the principal is required to be in writing.

Equal protection clause The provision in the Fourteenth Amendment to the Constitution that guarantees that no state will "deny to any person within its jurisdiction the equal protection of the laws." This clause mandates that state governments treat similarly situated individuals in a similar manner.

Equitable maxims General propositions or principles of law that have to do with fairness (equity).

Equitable right of redemption The right of a mortgagor who has breached the mortgage agreement to redeem or purchase the property prior to foreclosure proceedings.

Equity of redemption The right of a mortgagor who has breached the mortgage agreement to redeem or purchase the property prior to foreclosure proceedings.

Equity participation loan A loan that allows the lender to participate in some percentage of the increase in the equity value of a business or property; any loan that gives the lender the right to obtain an ownership interest in the project being financed.

Escheat The transfer of property to the state when the owner of the property dies without heirs.

Escrow account An account that is generally held in the name of the depositor and escrow agent; the funds in the account are paid to a third person only on fulfillment of the escrow condition.

Establishment clause The provision in the First Amendment to the U.S. Constitution that prohibits Congress from creating any law "respecting an establishment of religion."

Estate The interest that a person has in real and personal property.

Estate planning Planning in advance how one's property and obligations should be transferred on one's death. Wills and trusts are two basic devices used in the process of estate planning.

Estop To bar, impede, or preclude.

Estoppel The principle that a party's own acts prevent him or her from claiming a right to the detriment of another who was entitled to and did rely on those acts. *See also* Agency by estoppel; Promissory estoppel

Estray statute A statute defining finders' rights in property when the true owners are unknown.

Ethical reasoning A reasoning process in which an individual links his or her moral convictions or ethical standards to the particular situation at hand.

Ethics Moral principles and values applied to social behavior.

Eviction A landlord's act of depriving a tenant of possession of the leased premises.

Evidence Proof offered at trial—in the form of testimony, documents, records, exhibits, objects, and so on—for the purpose of convincing the court or jury of the truth of a contention.

Exclusionary rule In criminal procedure, a rule under which any evidence that is obtained in violation of the accused's constitutional rights guaranteed by the Fourth, Fifth, and Sixth Amendments, as well as any evidence derived from illegally obtained evidence, will not be admissible in court.

Exclusive distributorship A distributorship in which the seller and the distributor of the seller's products agree that the distributor has the exclusive right to distribute the seller's products in a certain geographic area.

Exclusive jurisdiction Jurisdiction that exists when a case can be heard only in a particular court or type of court, such as a federal court or a state court.

Exclusive-dealing contract An agreement under which a seller forbids a buyer to purchase products from the seller's competitors.

Exculpatory clause A clause that releases a contractual party from liability in the event of monetary or physical injury, no matter who is at fault.

Executed contract A contract that has been completely performed by both parties.

Execution An action to carry into effect the directions in a court decree or judgment.

Executive agency An administrative agency within the executive branch of government. At the federal level, executive agencies are those within the cabinet departments.

Executor A person appointed by a testator to see that his or her will is administered appropriately.

Executory contract A contract that has not as yet been fully performed.

Export To sell products to buyers located in other countries.

Express authority Authority expressly given by one party to another. In agency law, an agent has express authority to act for a principal if both parties agree, orally or in writing, that an agency relationship exists in which the agent had the power (authority) to act in the place of, and on behalf of, the principal.

Express contract A contract in which the terms of the agreement are fully and explicitly stated in words, oral or written.

Express warranty A seller's or lessor's oral or written promise, ancillary to an underlying sales or lease agreement, as to the quality, description, or performance of the goods being sold or leased.

Expropriation The seizure by a government of privately owned business or personal property for a proper public purpose and with just compensation.

Extension clause A clause in a time instrument that allows the instrument's date of maturity to be extended into the future.

F

F.A.S. Free alongside. A contract term that requires the seller, at his or her own expense and risk, to deliver the goods alongside the ship before risk passes to the buyer.

F.O.B. Free on board. A contract term that indicates that the selling price of the goods includes transportation costs (and that the seller carries the risk of loss)

to the specific F.O.B. place named in the contract. The place can be either the place of initial shipment (for example, the seller's city or place of business) or the place of destination (for example, the buyer's city or place of business).

Family limited liability partnership (FLLP) A limited liability partnership (LLP) in which the majority of the partners are persons related to each other, essentially as spouses, parents, grandparents, siblings, cousins, nephews, or nieces. A person acting in a fiduciary capacity for persons so related could also be a partner. All of the partners must be natural persons or persons acting in a fiduciary capacity for the benefit of natural persons.

Federal form of government A system of government in which the states form a union and the sovereign power is divided between a central government and the member states.

Federal question A question that pertains to the U.S. Constitution, acts of Congress, or treaties. A federal question provides a basis for federal jurisdiction.

Federal Reserve System A network of twelve central banks, located around the country and headed by the Federal Reserve Board of Governors. Most banks in the United States have Federal Reserve accounts.

Federal Rules of Civil Procedure (FRCP) The rules controlling procedural matters in civil trials brought before the federal district courts.

Fee simple An absolute form of property ownership entitling the property owner to use, possess, or dispose of the property as he or she chooses during his or her lifetime. On death, the interest in the property passes to the owner's heirs; a fee simple absolute.

Fee simple absolute An ownership interest in land in which the owner has the greatest possible aggregation of rights, privileges, and power. Ownership in fee simple absolute is limited absolutely to a person and his or her heirs.

Felony A crime—such as arson, murder, rape, or robbery—that carries the most severe sanctions, usually ranging from one year in a state or federal prison to the forfeiture of one's life.

Fictitious payee A payee on a negotiable instrument whom the maker or drawer does not intend to have an interest in the instrument. Indorsements by fictitious payees are not treated as unauthorized under Article 3 of the Uniform Commercial Code.

Fiduciary As a noun, a person having a duty created by his or her undertaking to act primarily for another's benefit in matters connected with the undertaking. As an adjective, a relationship founded on trust and confidence.

Fiduciary duty The duty, imposed on a fiduciary by virtue of his or her position, to act primarily for another's benefit.

Filtering software A computer program that includes a pattern through which data are passed. When designed to block access to certain Web sites, the pattern blocks the retrieval of a site whose URL or key words are on a list within the program.

Final order The final decision of an administrative agency on an issue. If no appeal is taken, or if the case is not reviewed or considered anew by the agency commission, the administrative law judge's initial order becomes the final order of the agency.

Financial institution An organization authorized to do business under state or federal laws relating to financial institutions. Financial institutions may include banks, savings and loan associations, credit unions, and other business entities that directly or indirectly hold accounts belonging to consumers.

Financing statement A document prepared by a secured creditor and filed with the appropriate government official to give notice to the public that the creditor claims an interest in collateral belonging to the debtor named in the statement. The financing statement must contain the names and addresses of both the debtor and the creditor, and describe the collateral by type or item.

Firm offer An offer (by a merchant) that is irrevocable without consideration for a period of time (not longer than three months). A firm offer by a merchant must be in writing and must be signed by the offeror.

Fitness for a particular purpose *See* Implied warranty of fitness for a particular purpose

Fixed-rate mortgage A standard mortgage with a fixed, or unchanging, rate of interest. The loan payments on these mortgages remain the same for the duration of the loan, which ranges between fifteen and forty years.

Fixed-term tenancy A type of tenancy under which property is leased for a specified period of time, such as a month, a year, or a period of years; also called a *tenancy for years*.

Fixture A thing that was once personal property but that has become attached to real property in such a way that it takes on the characteristics of real property and becomes part of that real property.

Floating lien A security interest in proceeds, after-acquired property, or property purchased under a line of credit (or all three); a security interest in collateral that is retained even when the collateral changes in character, classification, or location.

Forbearance An agreement between the lender and the borrower in which the lender agrees to temporarily cease requiring mortgage payments, to delay foreclosure, or to accept smaller payments than previously scheduled.

Force majeure (pronounced mah-*zhure*) **clause** A provision in a contract stipulating that certain unforeseen events—such as war, political upheavals, acts of God, or other events—will excuse a party from liability for nonperformance of contractual obligations.

Foreclosure A proceeding in which a mortgagee either takes title to or forces the sale of the mortgagor's property in satisfaction of a debt.

Foreign corporation In a given state, a corporation that does business in the state without being incorporated therein.

Foreseeable risk In negligence law, the risk of harm or injury to another that a person of ordinary intelligence and prudence should have reasonably anticipated or foreseen when undertaking an action or refraining from undertaking an action.

Forfeiture The termination of a lease, according to its terms or the terms of a statute, when one of the parties fails to fulfill a condition under the lease and thereby breaches it.

Forgery The fraudulent making or altering of any writing in a way that changes the legal rights and liabilities of another.

Formal contract A contract that by law requires a specific form, such as being executed under seal, to be valid.

Forum A jurisdiction, court, or place in which disputes are litigated and legal remedies are sought.

Forum-selection clause A provision in a contract designating the court, jurisdiction, or tribunal that will decide any disputes arising under the contract.

Franchise Any arrangement in which the owner of a trademark, trade name, or copyright licenses another to use that trademark, trade name, or copyright, under specified conditions or limitations, in the selling of goods and services.

Franchise tax A state or local government tax on the right and privilege of carrying on a business in the form of a corporation.

Franchisee One receiving a license to use another's (the franchisor's) trademark, trade name, or copyright in the sale of goods and services.

Franchisor One licensing another (the franchisee) to use his or her trademark, trade name, or copyright in the sale of goods or services.

Fraud Any misrepresentation, either by misstatement or omission of a material fact, knowingly made with the intention of deceiving another and on which a reasonable person would and does rely to his or her detriment.

Fraud in the execution In the law of negotiable instruments, a type of fraud that occurs when a person is deceived into signing a negotiable instrument, believing that he or she is signing something else (such as a receipt); also called fraud in the inception. Fraud in the execution is a universal defense to payment on a negotiable instrument.

Fraud in the inducement Ordinary fraud. In the law of negotiable instruments, fraud in the inducement occurs when a person issues a negotiable instrument based on false statements by the other party. The issuing party will be able to avoid payment on that instrument unless the holder is a holder in due course; in other words, fraud in the inducement is a personal defense to payment on a negotiable instrument.

Fraudulent misrepresentation (fraud) Any misrepresentation, either by misstatement or omission of a material fact, knowingly made with the intention of deceiving another and on which a reasonable person would and does rely to his or her detriment.

Free exercise clause The provision in the First Amendment to the U.S. Constitution that prohibits Congress from making any law "prohibiting the free exercise" of religion.

Free writing prospectus A free writing prospectus is any type of written, electronic, or graphic offer that describes the issuing corporation or its securities and includes a legend indicating that the investor may obtain the prospectus at the SEC's Web site.

Frustration of purpose   A court-created doctrine under which a party to a contract will be relieved of his or her duty to perform when the objective purpose for performance no longer exists (due to reasons beyond that party's control).

Full faith and credit clause   A clause in Article IV, Section 1, of the Constitution that provides that "Full Faith and Credit shall be given in each State to the public Acts, Records, and Judicial Proceedings of every other State." The clause ensures that rights established under deeds, wills, contracts, and the like in one state will be honored by the other states and that any judicial decision with respect to such property rights will be honored and enforced in all states.

Full warranty   A warranty as to full performance covering generally both labor and materials.

Fungible goods   Goods that are alike by physical nature, by agreement, or by trade usage. Examples of fungible goods are wheat, oil, and wine that are identical in type and quality.

G

Garnishment   A legal process used by a creditor to collect a debt by seizing property of the debtor (such as wages) that is being held by a third party (such as the debtor's employer).

General jurisdiction   Exists when a court's subject-matter jurisdiction is not restricted. A court of general jurisdiction normally can hear any type of case.

General partner   In a limited partnership, a partner who assumes responsibility for the management of the partnership and liability for all partnership debts.

General partnership   *See* Partnership

Generally accepted accounting principles (GAAP)   The conventions, rules, and procedures that define accepted accounting practices at a particular time. The source of the principles is the Financial Accounting Standards Board.

Generally accepted auditing standards (GAAS)   Standards concerning an auditor's professional qualities and the judgment exercised by him or her in the performance of an examination and report. The source of the standards is the American Institute of Certified Public Accountants.

Genuineness of assent   Knowing and voluntary assent to the terms of a contract. If a contract is formed as a result of a mistake, misrepresentation, undue influence, or duress, genuineness of assent is lacking, and the contract will be voidable.

Gift   Any voluntary transfer of property made without consideration, past or present.

Gift *causa mortis*   A gift made in contemplation of death. If the donor does not die of that ailment, the gift is revoked.

Gift *inter vivos*   A gift made during one's lifetime and not in contemplation of imminent death, in contrast to a gift *causa mortis*.

Good faith   Under the Uniform Commercial Code, good faith means honesty in fact; with regard to merchants, good faith means honesty in fact *and* the observance of reasonable commercial standards of fair dealing in the trade.

Good faith purchaser   A purchaser who buys without notice of any circumstance that would put a person of ordinary prudence on inquiry as to whether the seller has valid title to the goods being sold.

Good Samaritan statute   A state statute that provides that persons who rescue or provide emergency services to others in peril—unless they do so recklessly, thus causing further harm—cannot be sued for negligence.

Goodwill   In the business context, the valuable reputation of a business viewed as an intangible asset.

Grand jury   A group of citizens called to decide, after hearing the state's evidence, whether a reasonable basis (probable cause) exists for believing that a crime has been committed and whether a trial ought to be held.

Grant deed   A deed that simply recites words of consideration and conveyance. Under statute, a grant deed may impliedly warrant that at least the grantor has not conveyed the property's title to someone else.

Grantee   One to whom a grant (of land or property, for example) is made.

Grantor   A person who makes a grant, such as a transferor of property or the creator of a trust.

Group boycott   The refusal to deal with a particular person or firm by a group of competitors; prohibited by the Sherman Act.

Guarantor   A person who agrees to satisfy the debt of another (the debtor) only after the principal debtor defaults; a guarantor's liability is thus secondary.

H

Habitability   *See* Implied warranty of habitability

Hacker   A person who uses one computer to break into another. Professional computer programmers refer to such persons as "crackers."

Health-care power of attorney   A document that designates a person who will have the power to choose what type of and how much medical treatment a person who is unable to make such a choice will receive.

Hearsay   An oral or written statement made out of court that is later offered in court by a witness (not the person who made the statement) to prove the truth of the matter asserted in the statement. Hearsay is generally inadmissible as evidence.

Herfindahl-Hirschman Index (HHI)   An index measuring market concentration for purposes of antitrust enforcement; calculated by summing the squares of the percentage market shares held by the respective firms.

Historical school   A school of legal thought that emphasizes the evolutionary process of law and that looks to the past to discover what the principles of contemporary law should be.

Holder Any person in the possession of an instrument drawn, issued, or indorsed to him or her, to his or her order, to bearer, or in blank.

Holder in due course (HDC) A holder who acquires a negotiable instrument for value; in good faith; and without notice that the instrument is overdue, that it has been dishonored, that any person has a defense against it or a claim to it, or that the instrument contains unauthorized signatures, alterations, or is so irregular or incomplete as to call into question its authenticity.

Holding company A company whose business activity is holding shares in another company.

Holographic will A will written entirely in the signer's handwriting and usually not witnessed.

Home equity loan A loan in which the lender accepts a person's home equity (the portion of the home's value that is paid off) as collateral, which can be seized if the loan is not repaid on time. Borrowers often take out home equity loans to finance the renovation of the property or to pay off debt that carries a higher interest rate, such as credit-card debt.

Homeowners' insurance Insurance that protects a homeowner's property against damage from storms, fire, and other hazards. Lenders may require that a borrower carry homeowners' insurance on mortgaged property.

Homestead exemption A law permitting a debtor to retain the family home, either in its entirety or up to a specified dollar amount, free from the claims of unsecured creditors or trustees in bankruptcy.

Horizontal merger A merger between two firms that are competing in the same market.

Horizontal restraint Any agreement that in some way restrains competition between rival firms competing in the same market.

Hot-cargo agreement An agreement in which employers voluntarily agree with unions not to handle, use, or deal in nonunion-produced goods of other employers; a type of secondary boycott explicitly prohibited by the Labor-Management Reporting and Disclosure Act of 1959.

Hybrid (two-step) mortgage A mortgage that starts as a fixed-rate mortgage and then converts to an adjustable-rate mortgage.

I

I-551 Alien Registration Receipt Proof that a noncitizen has obtained permanent residency in the United States; the so-called green card.

I-9 verification A form from the Department of Homeland Security, U.S. Citizenship and Immigration Services, used for employment eligibility verification; a form that documents that each new employee is authorized to work in the United States

Identification In a sale of goods, the express designation of the specific goods provided for in the contract.

Identity theft The act of stealing another's identifying information—such as a name, date of birth, or Social Security number—and using that information to access the victim's financial resources.

Illusory promise A promise made without consideration, which renders the promise unenforceable.

Immunity A status of being exempt, or free, from certain duties or requirements. In criminal law, the state may grant an accused person immunity from prosecution—or agree to prosecute for a lesser offense—if the accused person agrees to give the state information that would assist the state in prosecuting other individuals for crimes. In tort law, freedom from liability for defamatory speech. *See also* Privilege

Implied authority Authority that is created not by an explicit oral or written agreement but by implication. In agency law, implied authority (of the agent) can be conferred by custom, inferred from the position the agent occupies, or implied by virtue of being reasonably necessary to carry out express authority.

Implied warranty A warranty that the law derives by implication or inference from the nature of the transaction or the relative situation or circumstances of the parties.

Implied warranty of fitness for a particular purpose A warranty that goods sold or leased are fit for a particular purpose. The warranty arises when any seller or lessor knows the particular purpose for which a buyer or lessee will use the goods and knows that the buyer or lessee is relying on the skill and judgment of the seller or lessor to select suitable goods.

Implied warranty of habitability An implied promise by a landlord that rented residential premises are fit for human habitation—that is, in a condition that is safe and suitable for people to live in.

Implied warranty of merchantability A warranty that goods being sold or leased are reasonably fit for the ordinary purpose for which they are sold or leased, are properly packaged and labeled, and are of fair quality. The warranty automatically arises in every sale or lease of goods made by a merchant who deals in goods of the kind sold or leased.

Implied-in-fact contract A contract formed in whole or in part from the conduct of the parties (as opposed to an express contract). Also known as implied contract.

Impossibility of performance A doctrine under which a party to a contract is relieved of his or her duty to perform when performance becomes impossible or totally impracticable (through no fault of either party). Also known as Implied contract.

Imposter One who, by use of the mail, telephone, or personal appearance, induces a maker or drawer to issue an instrument in the name of an impersonated payee. Indorsements by imposters are not treated as unauthorized under Article 3 of the Uniform Commercial Code.

***In personam* jurisdiction** Court jurisdiction over the "person" involved in a legal action; personal jurisdiction.

***In rem* jurisdiction** Court jurisdiction over a defendant's property.

Incidental beneficiary A third party who incidentally benefits from a contract but whose benefit was not the reason the contract was formed; an incidental beneficiary has no rights in a contract and cannot sue to have the contract enforced.

Incontestability clause A clause within a life or health insurance policy that states that after the policy has been in force for a specified length of time—most often two or three years—the insurer cannot contest statements made in the policyholder's application.

Indemnify To compensate or reimburse another for losses or expenses incurred.

Independent contractor One who works for, and receives payment from, an employer but whose working conditions and methods are not controlled by the employer. An independent contractor is not an employee but may be an agent.

Independent regulatory agency An administrative agency that is not considered part of the government's executive branch and is not subject to the authority of the president. Independent agency officials cannot be removed without cause.

Indictment (pronounced in-*dyte*-ment) A charge by a grand jury that a reasonable basis (probable cause) exists for believing that a crime has been committed and that a trial should be held.

Indorsee A person to whom a negotiable instrument is transferred by indorsement.

Indorsement A signature placed on an instrument for the purpose of transferring one's ownership rights in the instrument.

Indorser A person who transfers an instrument by signing (indorsing) it and delivering it to another person.

Industrial use Land use for light or heavy manufacturing, shipping, or heavy transportation.

Informal contract A contract that does not require a specified form or formality in order to be valid.

Information A formal accusation or complaint (without an indictment) issued in certain types of actions (usually criminal actions involving lesser crimes) by a law officer, such as a magistrate.

Information return A tax return submitted by a partnership that only reports the income earned by the business. The partnership as an entity does not pay taxes on the income received by the partnership. A partner's profit from the partnership (whether distributed or not) is taxed as individual income to the individual partner.

Infringement A violation of another's legally recognized right. The term is commonly used with reference to the invasion by one party of another party's rights in a patent, trademark, or copyright.

Initial order In the context of administrative law, an agency's disposition in a matter other than a rule-making. An administrative law judge's initial order becomes final unless it is appealed.

Injunction A court decree ordering a person to do or refrain from doing a certain act or activity.

Innkeeper An owner of an inn, hotel, motel, or other lodging.

Innkeeper's lien A possessory or statutory lien allowing an innkeeper to take the personal property of a guest, brought into the hotel, as security for nonpayment of the guest's bill (debt).

Innocent misrepresentation A false statement of fact or an act made in good faith that deceives and causes harm or injury to another.

Inside director A person on the board of directors who is also an officer of the corporation.

Insider A corporate director or officer, or other employee or agent, with access to confidential information and a duty not to disclose that information in violation of insider-trading laws.

Insider trading The purchase or sale of securities on the basis of "inside information" (information that has not been made available to the public) in violation of a duty owed to the company whose stock is being traded.

Insolvent Under the Uniform Commercial Code, a term describing a person who ceases to pay "his debts in the ordinary course of business or cannot pay his debts as they become due or is insolvent within the meaning of federal bankruptcy law" [UCC 1–201(23)].

Installment contract Under the Uniform Commercial Code, a contract that requires or authorizes delivery in two or more separate lots to be accepted and paid for separately.

Instrument *See* Negotiable instrument

Insurable interest An interest either in a person's life or well-being or in property that is sufficiently substantial that insuring against injury to (or the death of) the person or against damage to the property does not amount to a mere wagering (betting) contract.

Insurance A contract in which, for a stipulated consideration, one party agrees to compensate the other for loss on a specific subject by a specified peril.

Intangible property Property that is incapable of being apprehended by the senses (such as by sight or touch); intellectual property is an example of intangible property.

Integrated contract A written contract that constitutes the final expression of the parties' agreement. If a contract is integrated, evidence extraneous to the contract that contradicts or alters the meaning of the contract in any way is inadmissible.

Intellectual property Property resulting from intellectual, creative processes. Patents, trademarks, and copyrights are examples of intellectual property.

Intended beneficiary A third party for whose benefit a contract is formed; an intended beneficiary can sue the promisor if such a contract is breached.

Intentional tort A wrongful act knowingly committed.

***Inter vivos* gift** *See* Gift *inter vivos*

***Inter vivos* trust** A trust created by the grantor (settlor) and effective during the grantor's lifetime (that is, a trust not established by a will).

Interest-only (IO) mortgage A mortgage that gives the borrower the option of paying only the interest portion of the monthly payment and forgoing the payment of principal for a specified period of time, such as five years. After the interest-only payment option is exhausted, the borrower's payment will increase to include payments on the principal.

Intermediary bank Any bank to which an item is transferred in the course of collection, except the depositary or payor bank.

International Financial Reporting Standards (IFRS) A set of accounting standards created by the International Accounting Standards Board (IASB). Today, more than 120 nations and reporting jurisdictions either permit or require IFRS for domesticly listed companies. The Securities and Exchange Commission is working towards a convergence between the IASB and U.S. accounting standards.

International law The law that governs relations among nations. International customs and treaties are generally considered to be two of the most important sources of international law.

International organization In international law, a term that generally refers to an organization composed mainly of nations and usually established by treaty. The United States is a member of more than one hundred multilateral and bilateral organizations, including at least twenty through the United Nations.

Interpretive rule An administrative agency rule that simply declares a policy or explains the agency's position and does not establish any legal rights or obligations.

Interrogatories A series of written questions for which written answers are prepared and then signed under oath by a party to a lawsuit, usually with the assistance of the party's attorney.

Intestacy laws State statutes that specify how property will be distributed when a person dies intestate (without a valid will); statutes of descent and distribution.

Intestate As a noun, one who has died without having created a valid will; as an adjective, the state of having died without a will.

Inverse condemnation The taking of private property by the government without payment of just compensation as required by the U.S. Constitution. The owner must sue the government to recover just compensation.

Investment company A company that acts on behalf of many smaller shareholder-owners by buying a large portfolio of securities and professionally managing that portfolio.

Investment contract In securities law, a transaction in which a person invests in a common enterprise reasonably expecting profits that are derived primarily from the efforts of others.

Invitee A person who, either expressly or impliedly, is privileged to enter onto another's land. The inviter owes the invitee (for example, a customer in a store) the duty to exercise reasonable care to protect the invitee from harm.

Irrevocable offer An offer that cannot be revoked or recalled by the offeror without liability. A merchant's firm offer is an example of an irrevocable offer.

Issue The first transfer, or delivery, of an instrument to a holder.

J

Joint and several liability In partnership law, a doctrine under which a plaintiff may sue, and collect a judgment from, one or more of the partners separately (severally, or individually) or all of the partners together (jointly). This is true even if one of the partners sued did not participate in, ratify, or know about whatever gave rise to the cause of action.

Joint liability Shared liability. In partnership law, partners incur joint liability for partnership obligations and debts. For example, if a third party sues a partner on a partnership debt, the partner has the right to insist that the other partners be sued with him or her.

Joint stock company A hybrid form of business organization that combines characteristics of a corporation (shareholder-owners, management by directors and officers of the company, and perpetual existence) and a partnership (it is formed by agreement, not statute; property is usually held in the names of the members; and the shareholders have personal liability for business debts). Usually, the joint stock company is regarded as a partnership for tax and other legally related purposes.

Joint tenancy The joint ownership of property by two or more co-owners in which each co-owner owns an undivided portion of the property. On the death of one of the joint tenants, his or her interest automatically passes to the surviving joint tenants.

Joint venture A joint undertaking of a specific commercial enterprise by an association of persons. A joint venture is normally not a legal entity and is treated like a partnership for federal income tax purposes.

Judgment The final order or decision resulting from a legal action.

Judgment *n.o.v.* *See* Motion for judgment *n.o.v.*

Judgment rate of interest A rate of interest fixed by statute that is applied to a monetary judgment from the moment the judgment is awarded by a court until the judgment is paid or terminated.

Judicial foreclosure A court-supervised foreclosure proceeding in which the court determines the validity of the debt and, if the borrower is in default, issues a judgment for the lender.

Judicial lien A lien on property created by a court order.

Judicial process The procedures relating to, or connected with, the administration of justice through the judicial system.

Judicial review The process by which courts decide on the constitutionality of legislative enactments and actions of the executive branch.

Junior lienholder A person or business that holds a lien that is subordinate to one or more other liens on the same property.

Jurisdiction The authority of a court to hear and decide a specific action.

Jurisprudence The science or philosophy of law.

Justiciable controversy A controversy that is not hypothetical or academic but real and substantial. A requirement that must be satisfied before a court will hear a case.

K

King's court   A medieval English court. The king's courts, or *curiae regis,* were established by the Norman conquerors of England. The body of law that developed in these courts was common to the entire English realm and thus became known as the common law.

L

Laches   The equitable doctrine that bars a party's right to legal action if the party has neglected for an unreasonable length of time to act on his or her rights.

Landlord   An owner of land or rental property who leases it to another person, called the tenant.

Larceny   The wrongful taking and carrying away of another person's personal property with the intent to permanently deprive the owner of the property. Some states classify larceny as either grand or petit, depending on the property's value.

Last clear chance   A doctrine under which a plaintiff may recover from a defendant for injuries or damages suffered, notwithstanding the plaintiff's own negligence, when the defendant had an opportunity—a last clear chance—to avoid harming the plaintiff through the exercise of reasonable care but failed to do so.

Law   A body of enforceable rules governing relationships among individuals and between individuals and their society.

Lawsuit   The litigation process. *See* Litigation

Lease   In real property law, a contract by which the owner of real property (the landlord, or lessor) grants to a person (the tenant, or lessee) an exclusive right to use and possess the property, usually for a specified period of time, in return for rent or some other form of payment.

Lease agreement   In regard to the lease of goods, an agreement in which one person (the lessor) agrees to transfer the right to the possession and use of property to another person (the lessee) in exchange for rental payments.

Leasehold estate   An estate in realty held by a tenant under a lease. In every leasehold estate, the tenant has a qualified right to possess and/or use the land.

Legacy   A gift of personal property under a will.

Legal positivists   Adherents to the positivist school of legal thought. This school holds that there can be no higher law than a nation's positive law—law created by a particular society at a particular point in time. In contrast to the natural law school, the positivist school maintains that there are no "natural" rights; rights come into existence only when there is a sovereign power (government) to confer and enforce those rights.

Legal rate of interest   A rate of interest fixed by statute as either the maximum rate of interest allowed by law or a rate of interest applied when the parties to a contract intend, but do not fix, an interest rate in the contract. In the latter case, the rate is frequently the same as the statutory maximum rate permitted.

Legal realism   A school of legal thought that was popular in the 1920s and 1930s and that challenged many existing jurisprudential assumptions, particularly the assumption that subjective elements play no part in judicial reasoning. Legal realists generally advocated a less abstract and more pragmatic approach to the law, an approach that would take into account customary practices and the circumstances in which transactions take place. The school left a lasting imprint on American jurisprudence.

Legal reasoning   The process of reasoning by which a judge harmonizes his or her decision with the judicial decisions of previous cases.

Legatee   One designated in a will to receive a gift of personal property.

Legislative rule   An administrative agency rule that affects substantive legal rights and carries the same weight as a congressionally enacted statute.

Letter of credit   A written instrument, usually issued by a bank on behalf of a customer or other person, in which the issuer promises to honor drafts or other demands for payment by third persons in accordance with the terms of the instrument.

Leveraged buyout (LBO)   A corporate takeover financed by loans secured by the acquired corporation's assets or by the issuance of corporate bonds, resulting in a high debt load for the corporation.

Levy   The obtaining of money by legal process through the seizure and sale of property, usually done after a writ of execution has been issued.

Liability   Any actual or potential legal obligation, duty, debt, or responsibility.

Libel   Defamation in writing or other form (such as in a videotape) having the quality of permanence.

License   A revocable right or privilege of a person to come on another person's land.

Licensee   One who receives a license to use, or enter onto, another's property.

Lien (pronounced *leen*)   A claim against specific property to satisfy a debt.

Lien creditor   One whose claim is secured by a lien on particular property, as distinguished from a general creditor, who has no such security.

Life estate   An interest in land that exists only for the duration of the life of some person, usually the holder of the estate.

Limited jurisdiction   Exists when a court's subject-matter jurisdiction is limited. Bankruptcy courts and probate courts are examples of courts with limited jurisdiction.

Limited liability   Exists when the liability of the owners of a business is limited to the amount of their investments in the firm.

Limited liability company (LLC)   A hybrid form of business enterprise that offers the limited liability of the corporation but the tax advantages of a partnership.

Limited liability limited partnership (LLLP)   A type of limited partnership. The difference between a limited partnership and an LLLP is that the liability of the general partner in an LLLP is the same as the liability of the limited partner. That is, the liability of all partners is limited to the amount of their investments in the firm.

Limited liability partnership (LLP)   A form of partnership that allows professionals to enjoy the tax benefits of a partnership while limiting their personal liability for the malpractice of other partners.

Limited partner   In a limited partnership, a partner who contributes capital to the partnership but has no right to participate in the management and operation of the business. The limited partner assumes no liability for partnership debts beyond the capital contributed.

Limited partnership (LP)   A partnership consisting of one or more general partners (who manage the business and are liable to the full extent of their personal assets for debts of the partnership) and one or more limited partners (who contribute only assets and are liable only to the extent of their contributions).

Limited-payment life   A type of life insurance for which premiums are payable for a definite period, after which the policy is fully paid.

Limited warranty   A written warranty that fails to meet one or more of the minimum standards for a full warranty.

Liquidated damages   An amount, stipulated in the contract, that the parties to a contract believe to be a reasonable estimation of the damages that will occur in the event of a breach.

Liquidated debt   A debt that is due and certain in amount.

Liquidation   (1) In regard to bankruptcy, the sale of all of the nonexempt assets of a debtor and the distribution of the proceeds to the debtor's creditors. Chapter 7 of the Bankruptcy Code provides for liquidation bankruptcy proceedings. (2) In regard to corporations, the process by which corporate assets are converted into cash and distributed among creditors and shareholders according to specific rules of preference.

Litigant   A party to a lawsuit.

Litigation   The process of resolving a dispute through the court system.

Living will   A document that allows a person to control the methods of medical treatment that may be used after a serious accident or illness.

Long arm statute   A state statute that permits a state to obtain personal jurisdiction over nonresident defendants. A defendant must have "minimum contacts" with that state for the statute to apply.

Lost property   Property with which the owner has involuntarily parted and then cannot find or recover.

M

Magistrate's court   A court of limited jurisdiction that is presided over by a public official (magistrate) with certain judicial authority, such as the power to set bail.

Mailbox rule   A rule providing that an acceptance of an offer becomes effective on dispatch (on being placed in a mailbox), if mail is, expressly or impliedly, an authorized means of communication of acceptance to the offeror.

Main purpose rule   A rule of contract law under which an exception to the Statute of Frauds is made if the main purpose in accepting secondary liability under a contract is to secure a personal benefit. If this situation exists, the contract need not be in writing to be enforceable.

Majority   See Age of majority

Majority opinion   A court's written opinion, outlining the views of the majority of the judges or justices deciding the case.

Maker   One who promises to pay a certain sum to the holder of a promissory note or certificate of deposit (CD).

Malpractice   Professional misconduct or the failure to exercise the requisite degree of skill as a professional. Negligence—the failure to exercise due care—on the part of a professional, such as a physician or an attorney, is commonly referred to as malpractice.

Manufacturing or processing-plant franchise   A franchise that is created when the franchisor transmits to the franchisee the essential ingredients or formula to make a particular product. The franchisee then markets the product either at wholesale or at retail in accordance with the franchisor's standards. Examples of this type of franchise are Coca-Cola and other soft-drink bottling companies.

Marine insurance   Insurance protecting shippers and vessel owners from losses or damages sustained by a vessel or its cargo during the transport of goods by water.

Mark   See Trademark

Market concentration   A situation that exists when a small number of firms share the market for a particular good or service. For example, if the four largest grocery stores in Chicago accounted for 80 percent of all retail food sales, the market clearly would be concentrated in those four firms.

Market power   The power of a firm to control the market price of its product. A monopoly has the greatest degree of market power.

Marketable title   Title to real estate that is reasonably free from encumbrances, defects in the chain of title, and other matters that affect title, such as adverse possession.

Market-share liability   A method of sharing liability among several firms that manufactured or marketed a particular product that may have caused a plaintiff's injury. Each firm's liability is proportionate to its respective share of the relevant market for the product. Market-share liability applies only if the injuring product is fungible, the true manufacturer is unidentifiable, and the unknown character of the manufacturer is not the plaintiff's fault.

Market-share test   The primary measure of monopoly power. A firm's market share is the percentage of a market that the firm controls.

Marshalling assets   The arrangement or ranking of assets in a certain order toward the payment of debts. In equity, when two creditors have recourse to the same property of the debtor, but one has recourse to other property of the debtor, that creditor must resort first to those assets of the debtor that are not available to the other creditor.

Material alteration *See* Alteration

Material fact A fact to which a reasonable person would attach importance in determining his or her course of action. In regard to tender offers, for example, a fact is material if there is a substantial likelihood that a reasonable shareholder would consider it important in deciding how to vote.

Mechanic's lien A statutory lien on the real property of another, created to ensure payment for work performed and materials furnished in the repair or improvement of real property, such as a building.

Mediation A method of settling disputes outside of court by using the services of a neutral third party, called a mediator. The mediator acts as a communicating agent between the parties and suggests ways in which the parties can resolve their dispute.

Member The term used to designate a person who has an ownership interest in a limited liability company.

Mens rea (pronounced *mehns ray*-uh) Mental state, or intent. A wrongful mental state is as necessary as a wrongful act to establish criminal liability. What constitutes a mental state varies according to the wrongful action. Thus, for murder, the *mens rea* is the intent to take a life. For theft, the *mens rea* must involve both the knowledge that the property belongs to another and the intent to deprive the owner of it.

Merchant A person who is engaged in the purchase and sale of goods. Under the Uniform Commercial Code, a person who deals in goods of the kind involved in the sales contract; for further definitions, see UCC 2–104.

Merger A contractual and statutory process in which one corporation (the surviving corporation) acquires all of the assets and liabilities of another corporation (the merged corporation). The shareholders of the merged corporation receive either payment for their shares or shares in the surviving corporation.

Meta tags Words inserted into a Web site's keywords field to increase the site's appearance in search engine results.

Minimum-contacts requirement The requirement that before a state court can exercise jurisdiction over a foreign corporation, the foreign corporation must have sufficient contacts with the state. A foreign corporation that has its home office in the state or that has manufacturing plants in the state meets this requirement.

Minimum wage The lowest wage, either by government regulation or union contract, that an employer may pay an hourly worker.

Mini-trial A private proceeding in which each party to a dispute argues its position before the other side and vice versa. A neutral third party may be present and act as an adviser if the parties fail to reach an agreement.

Mirror image rule A common law rule that requires, for a valid contractual agreement, that the terms of the offeree's acceptance adhere exactly to the terms of the offeror's offer.

Misdemeanor A lesser crime than a felony, punishable by a fine or imprisonment for up to one year in other than a state or federal penitentiary.

Mislaid property Property with which the owner has voluntarily parted and then cannot find or recover.

Misrepresentation A false statement of fact or an action that deceives and causes harm or injury to another. *See also* Fraudulent misrepresentation (fraud); Innocent misrepresentation

Mitigation of damages A rule requiring a plaintiff to have done whatever was reasonable to minimize the damages caused by the defendant.

Money laundering Falsely reporting income that has been obtained through criminal activity as income obtained through a legitimate business enterprise—in effect, "laundering" the "dirty money."

Monopolization The possession of monopoly power in the relevant market and the willful acquisition or maintenance of that power, as distinguished from growth or development as a consequence of a superior product, business acumen, or historic accident.

Monopoly A term generally used to describe a market in which there is a single seller or a limited number of sellers.

Monopoly power The ability of a monopoly to dictate what takes place in a given market.

Moral minimum The minimum degree of ethical behavior expected of a business firm, which is usually defined as compliance with the law.

Mortgage A written instrument that gives a creditor (the mortgagee) an interest in, or lien on, the debtor's (mortgagor's) real property as security for a debt. If the debt is not paid, the property can be sold by the creditor and the proceeds used to pay the debt.

Mortgage assignee An entity that purchases a mortgage from the current mortgage holder and assumes all rights and liabilities of that mortgage, including the right to collect and foreclose.

Mortgage bond A bond that pledges specific property. If the corporation defaults on the bond, the bondholder can take the property.

Motion A procedural request or application presented by an attorney to the court on behalf of a client.

Motion for a directed verdict In a state court, a party's request that the judge enter a judgment in her or his favor before the case is submitted to a jury because the other party has not presented sufficient evidence to support the claim. The federal courts refer to this request as a *motion for judgment as a matter of law*.

Motion for a new trial A motion asserting that the trial was so fundamentally flawed (because of error, newly discovered evidence, prejudice, or other reason) that a new trial is necessary to prevent a miscarriage of justice.

Motion for judgment as a matter of law In a federal court, a party's request that the judge enter a judgment in her or his favor before the case is submitted to a jury because the other party has not presented sufficient evidence to support the claim. The state courts refer to this request as a *motion for a directed verdict*.

Motion for judgment *n.o.v.* A motion requesting the court to grant judgment in favor of the party making the motion on the ground that the jury verdict against him or her was unreasonable and erroneous.

Motion for judgment on the pleadings A motion by either party to a lawsuit at the close of the pleadings requesting the court to decide the issue solely on the pleadings without proceeding to trial. The motion will be granted only if no facts are in dispute.

Motion for summary judgment A motion requesting the court to enter a judgment without proceeding to trial. The motion can be based on evidence outside the pleadings and will be granted only if no facts are in dispute.

Motion to dismiss A pleading in which a defendant asserts that the plaintiff's claim fails to state a cause of action (that is, has no basis in law) or that there are other grounds on which a suit should be dismissed.

Multiple product order An order issued by the Federal Trade Commission to a firm that has engaged in deceptive advertising by which the firm is required to cease and desist from false advertising not only in regard to the product that was the subject of the action but also in regard to all the firm's other products.

Municipal court A city or community court with criminal jurisdiction over traffic violations and, less frequently, with civil jurisdiction over other minor matters.

Mutual assent The element of agreement in the formation of a contract. The manifestation of contract parties' mutual assent to the same bargain is required to establish a contract.

Mutual fund A specific type of investment company that continually buys or sells to investors shares of ownership in a portfolio.

Mutual rescission An agreement between the parties to cancel their contract, releasing the parties from further obligations under the contract. The object of the agreement is to restore the parties to the positions they would have occupied had no contract ever been formed. *See also* Rescission

N

National law Law that pertains to a particular nation (as opposed to international law).

Natural law The belief that government and the legal system should reflect universal moral and ethical principles that are inherent in human nature. The natural law school is the oldest and one of the most significant schools of legal thought.

Necessaries Necessities required for life, such as food, shelter, clothing, and medical attention; may include whatever is believed to be necessary to maintain a person's standard of living or financial and social status.

Necessity In criminal law, a defense against liability; under Section 3.02 of the Model Penal Code, this defense is justifiable if "the harm or evil sought to be avoided" by a given action "is greater than that sought to be prevented by the law defining the offense charged."

Negative amortization Occurs when the payment made by the borrower is less than the interest due on the loan and the difference is added to the principal. The result of negative amortization is that the balance owed on the loan increases rather than decreases over time.

Negligence The failure to exercise the standard of care that a reasonable person would exercise in similar circumstances.

Negligence *per se* An act (or failure to act) in violation of a statutory requirement.

Negligent misrepresentation Any manifestation through words or conduct that amounts to an untrue statement of fact made in circumstances in which a reasonable and prudent person would not have done (or failed to do) that which led to the misrepresentation. A representation made with an honest belief in its truth may still be negligent due to (1) a lack of reasonable care in ascertaining the facts, (2) the manner of expression, or (3) the absence of the skill or competence required by a particular business or profession.

Negotiable instrument A signed writing that contains an unconditional promise or order to pay an exact sum of money, on demand or at an exact future time, to a specific person or order, or to bearer.

Negotiation (1) In regard to dispute settlement, a process in which parties attempt to settle their dispute without going to court, with or without attorneys to represent them. (2) In regard to instruments, the transfer of an instrument in such a way that the transferee (the person to whom the instrument is transferred) becomes a holder.

Nominal damages A small monetary award (often one dollar) granted to a plaintiff when no actual damage was suffered or when the plaintiff is unable to show such loss with sufficient certainty.

Nonconforming goods Goods that do not conform to contract specifications.

No-par shares Corporate shares that have no face value—that is, no specific dollar amount is printed on their face.

Normal trade relations (NTR) status A status granted through an international treaty by which each member nation must treat other members at least as well as it treats the country that receives its most favorable treatment. This status was formerly known as most-favored-nation status.

Notary public A public official authorized to attest to the authenticity of signatures.

Note A written instrument signed by a maker unconditionally promising to pay a fixed amount of money to a payee or a holder on demand or on a specific date.

Notice-and-comment rulemaking An administrative rulemaking procedure that involves the publication of a notice of a proposed rulemaking in the *Federal Register,* a comment period for interested parties to express their views on the proposed rule, and the publication of the agency's final rule in the *Federal Register.*

Notice of default A formal notice to a borrower who is behind in making mortgage payments that the borrower is in default and may face foreclosure if the payments are not brought up to date. The notice is filed by the lender in the county where the property is located.

Notice of Proposed Rulemaking A notice published (in the *Federal Register*) by an administrative agency describing a proposed rule. The notice must include information on when and where agency proceedings on the proposed rule will be held, a description of the nature of the proceedings, the legal authority for the proceedings (which usually is the agency's enabling legislation), and the terms or the subject matter of the proposed rule.

Notice of sale A formal notice to a borrower who is in default on a mortgage that the mortgaged property will be sold in a foreclosure proceeding. The notice is sent to the borrower by the lender and is also typically recorded with the county, posted on the property, and published in a newspaper.

Novation The substitution, by agreement, of a new contract for an old one, with the rights under the old one being terminated. Typically, there is a substitution of a new person who is responsible for the contract and the removal of an original party's rights and duties under the contract.

Nuisance A common law doctrine under which persons may be held liable for using their property in a manner that unreasonably interferes with others' rights to use or enjoy their own property.

Nuncupative will An oral will (often called a deathbed will) made before witnesses; usually limited to transfers of personal property.

O

Objective theory of contracts A theory under which the intent to form a contract will be judged by outward, objective facts (what the party said when entering into the contract, how the party acted or appeared, and the circumstances surrounding the transaction) as interpreted by a reasonable person, rather than by the party's own secret, subjective intentions.

Obligee One to whom an obligation is owed.

Obligor One that owes an obligation to another.

Offer A promise or commitment to perform or refrain from performing some specified act in the future.

Offeree A person to whom an offer is made.

Offeror A person who makes an offer.

Omnibus clause A provision in an automobile insurance policy that protects the vehicle owner who has taken out the insurance policy and anyone who drives the vehicle with the owner's permission.

Online Dispute Resolution (ODR) The resolution of disputes with the assistance of organizations that offer dispute-resolution services via the Internet.

Opening statement A statement made to the jury at the beginning of a trial by a party's attorney, prior to the presentation of evidence. The attorney briefly outlines the evidence that will be offered and the legal theory that will be pursued.

Operating agreement In a limited liability company, an agreement in which the members set forth the details of how the business will be managed and operated.

Opinion A statement by the court expressing the reasons for its decision in a case.

Option contract A contract under which the offeror cannot revoke his or her offer for a stipulated time period and the offeree can accept or reject the offer during this period without fear that the offer will be made to another person. The offeree must give consideration for the option (the irrevocable offer) to be enforceable.

Order for relief A court's grant of assistance to a complainant. In bankruptcy proceedings, the order relieves the debtor of the immediate obligation to pay the debts listed in the bankruptcy petition.

Order instrument A negotiable instrument that is payable "to the order of an identified person" or "to an identified person or order."

Ordinance A law passed by a local governing unit, such as a municipality or a county.

Original jurisdiction Courts having original jurisdiction are courts of the first instance, or trial courts—that is, courts in which lawsuits begin, trials take place, and evidence is presented.

Output contract An agreement in which a seller agrees to sell and a buyer agrees to buy all or up to a stated amount of what the seller produces.

Outside director A person on the board of directors who does not hold a management position at the corporation.

Overdraft A check written on a checking account in which there are insufficient funds to cover the amount of the check.

P

Parent-subsidiary merger A merger of companies in which one company (the parent corporation) owns most of the stock of the other (the subsidiary corporation). A parent-subsidiary merger (short-form merger) can use a simplified procedure when the parent corporation owns at least 90 percent of the outstanding shares of each class of stock of the subsidiary corporation.

Parol evidence A term that originally meant "oral evidence," but that has come to refer to any negotiations or agreements made prior to a contract or any contemporaneous oral agreements made by the parties.

Parol evidence rule A substantive rule of contracts under which a court will not receive into evidence the parties' prior negotiations, prior agreements, or contemporaneous oral agreements if that evidence contradicts or varies the terms of the parties' written contract.

Partially disclosed principal A principal whose identity is unknown by a third person, but the third person knows that the agent is or may be acting for a principal at the time the agent and the third person form a contract.

Participation loan A loan that gives the lender some equity rights in the property, such as the right to receive a percentage of revenue, rental income, or resale income. Also called an equity participation loan.

Partner A co-owner of a partnership.

Partnering agreement An agreement between a seller and a buyer who frequently do business with each other on the terms and conditions that will apply to all subsequently formed electronic contracts.

Partnership An agreement by two or more persons to carry on, as co-owners, a business for profit.

Partnership by estoppel A judicially created partnership that may, at the court's discretion, be imposed for purposes of fairness. The court can prevent those who present themselves as partners (but who are not) from escaping liability if a third person relies on an alleged partnership in good faith and is harmed as a result.

Par-value shares Corporate shares that have a specific face value, or formal cash-in value, written on them, such as one dollar.

Pass-through entity Any entity that does not have its income taxed at the level of that entity; examples are partnerships, S corporations, and limited liability companies.

Past consideration Something given or some act done in the past, which cannot ordinarily be consideration for a later bargain.

Patent A government grant that gives an inventor the exclusive right or privilege to make, use, or sell his or her invention for a limited time period. The word *patent* usually refers to some invention and designates either the instrument by which patent rights are evidenced or the patent itself.

Payee A person to whom an instrument is made payable.

Payor bank The bank on which a check is drawn (the drawee bank).

Peer-to-peer (P2P) networking The sharing of resources (such as files, hard drives, and processing styles) among multiple computers without necessarily requiring a central network server.

Penalty A sum inserted into a contract, not as a measure of compensation for its breach but rather as punishment for a default. The agreement as to the amount will not be enforced, and recovery will be limited to actual damages.

Per capita A Latin term meaning "per person." In the law governing estate distribution, a method of distributing the property of an intestate's estate in which each heir in a certain class (such as grandchildren) receives an equal share.

Per curiam By the whole court; a court opinion written by the court as a whole instead of being authored by a judge or justice.

Per se A Latin term meaning "in itself" or "by itself."

Per se violation A type of anticompetitive agreement—such as a horizontal price-fixing agreement—that is considered to be so injurious to the public that there is no need to determine whether it actually injures market competition; rather, it is in itself (*per se*) a violation of the Sherman Act.

Per stirpes A Latin term meaning "by the roots." In the law governing estate distribution, a method of distributing an intestate's estate in which each heir in a certain class (such as grandchildren) takes the share to which his or her deceased ancestor (such as a mother or father) would have been entitled.

Perfect tender rule A common law rule under which a seller was required to deliver to the buyer goods that conformed perfectly to the requirements stipulated in the sales contract. A tender of nonconforming goods would automatically constitute a breach of contract. Under the Uniform Commercial Code, the rule has been greatly modified.

Perfection The legal process by which secured parties protect themselves against the claims of third parties who may wish to have their debts satisfied out of the same collateral; usually accomplished by the filing of a financing statement with the appropriate government official.

Performance In contract law, the fulfillment of one's duties arising under a contract with another; the normal way of discharging one's contractual obligations.

Periodic tenancy A lease interest in land for an indefinite period involving payment of rent at fixed intervals, such as week to week, month to month, or year to year.

Personal defense A defense that can be used to avoid payment to an ordinary holder of a negotiable instrument but not a holder in due course (HDC) or a holder with the rights of an HDC.

Personal identification number (PIN) A number given to the holder of an access card (debit card, credit card, ATM card, or the like) that is used to conduct financial transactions electronically. Typically, the card will not provide access to a system without the number, which is meant to be kept secret to inhibit unauthorized use of the card.

Personal jurisdiction *See In personam* jurisdiction

Personal property Property that is movable; any property that is not real property.

Personalty Personal property.

Petition in bankruptcy The document that is filed with a bankruptcy court to initiate bankruptcy proceedings. The official forms required for a petition in bankruptcy must be completed accurately, sworn to under oath, and signed by the debtor.

Petitioner In equity practice, a party that initiates a lawsuit.

Petty offense In criminal law, the least serious kind of criminal offense, such as a traffic or building-code violation.

Phishing An online fraud action that allows criminals to pretend to be legitimate companies either by using e-mails or malicious Web sites that trick individuals and companies into providing useful information, such as bank account numbers, Social Security numbers, or credit card numbers.

Pierce the corporate veil To disregard the corporate entity, which limits the liability of shareholders, and hold the shareholders personally liable for a corporate obligation.

Plaintiff One who initiates a lawsuit.

Plea In criminal law, a defendant's allegation, in response to the charges brought against him or her, of guilt or innocence.

Plea bargaining The process by which a criminal defendant and the prosecutor in a criminal case work out a mutually satisfactory disposition of the case, subject to court approval; usually involves the defendant's pleading guilty to a lesser offense in return for a lighter sentence.

Pleadings Statements made by the plaintiff and the defendant in a lawsuit that detail the facts, charges, and defenses involved in the litigation; the complaint and answer are part of the pleadings.

Pledge A common law security device (retained in Article 9 of the Uniform Commercial Code) in which personal property is turned over to the creditor as security for the payment of a debt and retained by the creditor until the debt is paid.

Police powers Powers possessed by states as part of their inherent sovereignty. These powers may be exercised to protect or promote the public order, health, safety, morals, and general welfare.

Policy In insurance law, a contract between the insurer and the insured in which, for a stipulated consideration, the insurer agrees to compensate the insured for loss on a specific subject by a specified peril.

Positive law The body of conventional, or written, law of a particular society at a particular point in time.

Positivist school A school of legal thought whose adherents believe that there can be no higher law than a nation's positive law—the body of conventional, or written, law of a particular society at a particular time.

Possessory lien A lien that allows one person to retain possession of another's property as security for a debt or obligation owed by the owner of the property to the lienholder. An example of a possessory lien is an artisan's lien.

Potentially responsible party (PRP) A potentially liable party under the Comprehensive Environmental Response, Compensation and Liability Act (CERCLA). Any person who generated the hazardous waste, transported the hazardous waste, owned or operated a waste site at the time of disposal, or currently owns or operates a site may be responsible for some or all of the cleanup costs involved in removing the hazardous chemicals.

Power of attorney A written document, which is usually notarized, authorizing another to act as one's agent; can be special (permitting the agent to do specified acts only) or general (permitting the agent to transact all business for the principal).

Power of sale foreclosure A foreclosure procedure that is not court supervised; available only in some states.

Preauthorized transfer A transaction authorized in advance to recur at substantially regular intervals. The terms and procedures for preauthorized electronic fund transfers through certain financial institutions are subject to the Electronic Fund Transfer Act.

Precedent A court decision that furnishes an example or authority for deciding subsequent cases involving identical or similar facts.

Predatory pricing The pricing of a product below cost with the intent to drive competitors out of the market.

Predominant-factor test A test courts use to determine whether a contract is primarily for the sale of goods or for the sale of services.

Preemption A doctrine under which certain federal laws preempt, or take precedence over, conflicting state or local laws.

Preemptive rights Rights held by shareholders that entitle them to purchase newly issued shares of a corporation's stock, equal in percentage to shares presently held, before the stock is offered to any outside buyers. Preemptive rights enable shareholders to maintain their proportionate ownership and voice in the corporation.

Preference In bankruptcy proceedings, property transfers or payments made by the debtor that favor (give preference to) one creditor over others. The bankruptcy trustee is allowed to recover payments made both voluntarily and involuntarily to one creditor in preference over another.

Preferred creditor One who has received a preferential transfer from a debtor.

Preferred stock Classes of stock that have priority over common stock both as to payment of dividends and distribution of assets on the corporation's dissolution.

Prejudgment interest Interest that accrues on the amount of a court judgment from the time of the filing of a lawsuit to the court's issuance of a judgment.

Preliminary hearing An initial hearing used in many felony cases to establish whether it is proper to detain the defendant. A magistrate reviews the evidence and decides if there is probable cause to believe that the defendant committed the crime with which he or she has been charged.

Premium In insurance law, the price paid by the insured for insurance protection for a specified period of time.

Prenuptial agreement An agreement made before marriage that defines each partner's ownership rights in the other partner's property. Prenuptial agreements must be in writing to be enforceable.

Preponderance of the evidence A standard in civil law cases under which the plaintiff must convince the court that, based on the evidence presented by both parties, it is more likely than not that the plaintiff's allegation is true.

Presentment The act of presenting an instrument to the party liable on the instrument to collect payment; presentment also occurs when a person presents an instrument to a drawee for acceptance.

Presentment warranties Any person who presents an instrument for payment or acceptance impliedly warrants that (1) he or she is entitled to enforce the instrument or authorized to obtain payment or acceptance on behalf of a person who is entitled, (2) the instrument has not been altered, and (3) he or she has no knowledge that the signature of the drawer is unauthorized.

Pretrial conference A conference, scheduled before the trial begins, between the judge and the attorneys litigating the suit. The parties may settle the dispute, clarify the issues, schedule discovery, and so on during the conference.

Pretrial motion   A written or oral application to a court for a ruling or order, made before trial.

Price discrimination   Setting prices in such a way that two competing buyers pay two different prices for an identical product or service.

Price-fixing agreement   An agreement between competitors in which the competitors agree to fix the prices of products or services at a certain level; prohibited by the Sherman Act.

***Prima facie* case**   A case in which the plaintiff has produced sufficient evidence of his or her conclusion that the case can go to a jury; a case in which the evidence compels the plaintiff's conclusion if the defendant produces no evidence to disprove it.

Primary liability   In negotiable instruments law, absolute responsibility for paying a negotiable instrument. Makers and acceptors are primarily liable.

Prime offer rate   An interest rate that banks historically charged their most reliable customers. Today, it serves as a basis for pricing other commercial and residential loans.

Principal   In agency law, a person who agrees to have another, called the agent, act on his or her behalf.

Principle of rights   The principle that human beings have certain fundamental rights (to life, freedom, and the pursuit of happiness, for example). Those who adhere to this "rights theory" believe that a key factor in determining whether a business decision is ethical is how that decision affects the rights of others. These others include the firm's owners, its employees, the consumers of its products or services, its suppliers, the community in which it does business, and society as a whole.

Private equity capital   Private equity capital is a financing method by which a company sells equity in an existing business to a private or institutional investor.

Privatization   The replacement of government-provided products and services by private firms.

Privilege   In tort law, the ability to act contrary to another person's right without that person's having legal redress for such acts. Privilege may be raised as a defense to defamation.

Privileges and immunities clause   Special rights and exceptions provided by law. Article IV, Section 2, of the Constitution requires states not to discriminate against one another's citizens. A resident of one state cannot be treated as an alien when in another state; he or she may not be denied such privileges and immunities as legal protection, access to courts, travel rights, and property rights.

Privity of contract   The relationship that exists between the promisor and the promisee of a contract.

Pro rata   Proportionately; in proportion.

Probable cause   Reasonable grounds to believe the existence of facts warranting certain actions, such as the search or arrest of a person.

Probate   The process of proving and validating a will and the settling of all matters pertaining to administration, guardianship, and the like.

Probate court   A state court of limited jurisdiction that conducts proceedings relating to the settlement of a deceased person's estate.

Procedural due process   The requirement that any government decision to take life, liberty, or property must be made fairly. For example, fair procedures must be used in determining whether a person will be subjected to punishment or have some burden imposed on him or her.

Procedural law   Rules that define the manner in which the rights and duties of individuals may be enforced.

Procedural unconscionability   Occurs when, due to one contractual party's vastly superior bargaining power, the other party lacks knowledge or understanding of the contract terms due to inconspicuous print or the lack of an opportunity to read the contract or to ask questions about its meaning. Procedural unconscionability often involves an *adhesion contract,* which is a contract drafted by the dominant party and then presented to the other—the adhering party—on a take-it-or-leave-it basis.

Proceeds   Under Article 9 of the Uniform Commercial Code, whatever is received when the collateral is sold or otherwise disposed of, such as by exchange.

Product liability   The legal liability of manufacturers, sellers, and lessors of goods to consumers, users, and bystanders for injuries or damages that are caused by the goods.

Product misuse   A defense against product liability that may be raised when the plaintiff used a product in a manner not intended by the manufacturer. If the misuse is reasonably foreseeable, the seller will not escape liability unless measures were taken to guard against the harm that could result from the misuse.

Professional corporation   A corporation formed by professional persons, such as physicians, lawyers, dentists, or accountants, to gain tax benefits. Subject to certain exceptions (when a court may treat a professional corporation as a partnership for liability purposes), the shareholders of a professional corporation have the limited liability characteristic of the corporate form of business.

Profit   In real property law, the right to enter onto and remove things from the property of another (for example, the right to enter onto a person's land and remove sand and gravel therefrom).

Promise   A person's assurance that he or she will or will not do something.

Promisee   A person to whom a promise is made.

Promisor   A person who makes a promise.

Promissory estoppel   A doctrine that applies when a promisor makes a clear and definite promise on which the promisee justifiably relies; such a promise is binding if justice will be better served by the enforcement of the promise. *See also* Estoppel

Promissory note   A written promise made by one person (the maker) to pay a fixed sum of money to another person (the payee or a subsequent holder) on demand or on a specified date.

Promoter   A person who takes the preliminary steps in organizing a corporation, including (usually) issuing a prospectus, procuring stock subscriptions, making contract purchases, securing a corporate charter, and the like.

Property Legally protected rights and interests in anything with an ascertainable value that is subject to ownership.

Prospectus A document required by federal or state securities laws that describes the financial operations of the corporation, thus allowing investors to make informed decisions.

Protected class A class of persons with identifiable characteristics who historically have been victimized by discriminatory treatment for certain purposes. Depending on the context, these characteristics include age, color, gender, national origin, race, and religion.

Proximate cause Legal cause; exists when the connection between an act and an injury is strong enough to justify imposing liability.

Proxy In corporation law, a written agreement between a stockholder and another under which the stockholder authorizes the other to vote the stockholder's shares in a certain manner.

Proxy fight A conflict between an individual, group, or firm attempting to take control of a corporation and the corporation's management for the votes of the shareholders.

Public corporation A corporation owned by a federal, state, or municipal government—not to be confused with a publicly held corporation.

Public figures Individuals who are thrust into the public limelight. Public figures include government officials and politicians, movie stars, well-known businesspersons, and generally anybody who becomes known to the public because of his or her position or activities.

Public policy A government policy based on widely held societal values and (usually) expressed or implied in laws or regulations.

Public prosecutor An individual, acting as a trial lawyer, who initiates and conducts criminal cases in the government's name and on behalf of the people.

Publicly held corporation A corporation for which shares of stock have been sold to the public.

Puffery A salesperson's exaggerated claims concerning the quality of goods offered for sale. Such claims involve opinions rather than facts and are not considered to be legally binding promises or warranties.

Punitive damages Money damages that may be awarded to a plaintiff to punish the defendant and deter future similar conduct.

Purchase-money security interest (PMSI) A security interest that arises when a seller or lender extends credit for part or all of the purchase price of goods purchased by a buyer.

Q

Qualified indorsement An indorsement on a negotiable instrument in which the indorser disclaims any contract liability on the instrument; the notation "without recourse" is commonly used to create a qualified indorsement.

Quantum meruit (pronounced *kwahn*-tuhm *mehr*-oo-wuht) Literally, "as much as he deserves"—an expression describing the extent of liability on a contract implied in law (quasi contract). An equitable doctrine based on the concept that one who benefits from another's labor and materials should not be unjustly enriched thereby but should be required to pay a reasonable amount for the benefits received, even absent a contract.

Quasi contract A fictional contract imposed on parties by a court in the interests of fairness and justice; usually, quasi contracts are imposed to avoid the unjust enrichment of one party at the expense of another.

Question of fact In a lawsuit, an issue involving a factual dispute that can only be decided by a judge (or, in a jury trial, a jury).

Question of law In a lawsuit, an issue involving the application or interpretation of a law; therefore, the judge, and not the jury, decides the issue.

Quiet enjoyment *See* Covenant of quiet enjoyment

Quitclaim deed A deed intended to pass any title, interest, or claim that the grantor may have in the property but not warranting that such title is valid. A quitclaim deed offers the least amount of protection against defects in the title.

Quorum The number of members of a decision-making body that must be present before business may be transacted.

Quota An assigned import limit on goods.

R

Ratification The act of accepting and giving legal force to an obligation that previously was not enforceable.

Reaffirmation agreement An agreement between a debtor and a creditor in which the debtor reaffirms, or promises to pay, a debt dischargeable in bankruptcy. To be enforceable, the agreement must be made prior to the discharge of the debt by the bankruptcy court.

Real property Land and everything attached to it, such as foliage and buildings.

Reamortize Restart the amortization schedule (a table of the periodic payments the borrower makes to pay off a debt), changing the way the payments are configured.

Reasonable care The degree of care that a person of ordinary prudence would exercise in the same or similar circumstances.

Reasonable doubt *See* Beyond a reasonable doubt

Reasonable person standard The standard of behavior expected of a hypothetical "reasonable person." The standard against which negligence is measured and that must be observed to avoid liability for negligence.

Rebuttal The refutation of evidence introduced by an adverse party's attorney.

Receiver In a corporate dissolution, a court-appointed person who winds up corporate affairs and liquidates corporate assets.

Record According to the Uniform Electronic Transactions Act, information that is either inscribed on a tangible medium or stored in an electronic or other medium and that is retrievable. The Uniform Computer Information Transactions Act uses the term *record* instead of *writing*.

Recording statutes Statutes that allow deeds, mortgages, and other real property transactions to be recorded so as to provide notice to future purchasers or creditors of an existing claim on the property.

Red herring prospectus A preliminary prospectus that can be distributed to potential investors after the registration statement (for a securities offering) has been filed with the Securities and Exchange Commission. The name derives from the red legend printed across the prospectus stating that the registration has been filed but has not become effective.

Redemption A repurchase, or buying back. In secured transactions law, a debtor's repurchase of collateral securing a debt after a creditor has taken title to the collateral due to the debtor's default but before the secured party disposes of the collateral.

Reformation A court-ordered correction of a written contract so that it reflects the true intentions of the parties.

Regulation E A set of rules issued by the Federal Reserve System's Board of Governors under the authority of the Electronic Fund Transfer Act to protect users of electronic fund transfer systems.

Regulation Z A set of rules promulgated by the Federal Reserve Board to implement the provisions of the Truth-in-Lending Act.

Rejection In contract law, an offeree's express or implied manifestation not to accept an offer. In the law governing contracts for the sale of goods, a buyer's manifest refusal to accept goods on the ground that they do not conform to contract specifications.

Rejoinder The defendant's answer to the plaintiff's rebuttal.

Release A contract in which one party forfeits the right to pursue a legal claim against the other party.

Relevant evidence Evidence tending to make a fact at issue in the case more or less probable than it would be without the evidence. Only relevant evidence is admissible in court.

Remainder A future interest in property held by a person other than the original owner.

Remanded Sent back. If an appellate court disagrees with a lower court's judgment, the case may be remanded to the lower court for further proceedings in which the lower court's decision should be consistent with the appellate court's opinion on the matter.

Remedy The relief given to an innocent party to enforce a right or compensate for the violation of a right.

Remedy at law A remedy available in a court of law. Money damages are awarded as a remedy at law.

Remedy in equity A remedy allowed by courts in situations where remedies at law are not appropriate. Remedies in equity are based on settled rules of fairness, justice, and honesty, and include injunction, specific performance, rescission and restitution, and reformation.

Remitter A person who sends money, or remits payment.

Rent The consideration paid for the use or enjoyment of another's property. In landlord-tenant relationships, the payment made by the tenant to the landlord for the right to possess the premises.

Rent escalation clause A clause providing for an increase in rent during a lease term.

Repair-and-deduct statutes Statutes providing that a tenant may pay for repairs and deduct the cost of the repairs from the rent, as a remedy for a landlord's failure to maintain leased premises.

Replevin (pronounced rih-*pleh*-vin) An action to recover specific goods in the hands of a party who is wrongfully withholding them from the other party.

Reply Procedurally, a plaintiff's response to a defendant's answer.

Reporter A publication in which court cases are published, or reported.

Repudiation The renunciation of a right or duty; the act of a buyer or seller in rejecting a contract either partially or totally. *See also* Anticipatory repudiation

Requirements contract An agreement in which a buyer agrees to purchase and the seller agrees to sell all or up to a stated amount of what the buyer needs or requires.

Res ipsa loquitur (pronounced *rehs ehp*-suh *low*-quuh-tuhr) A doctrine under which negligence may be inferred simply because an event occurred, if it is the type of event that would not occur in the absence of negligence. Literally, the term means "the facts speak for themselves."

Resale price maintenance agreement An agreement between a manufacturer and a retailer in which the manufacturer specifies the minimum retail price of its products. Resale price maintenance agreements are illegal *per se* under the Sherman Act.

Rescind (pronounced rih-*sihnd*) To cancel. *See also* Rescission

Rescission (pronounced rih-*sih*-zhen) A remedy whereby a contract is canceled and the parties are returned to the positions they occupied before the contract was made; may be effected through the mutual consent of the parties, by their conduct, or by court decree.

Residential use Use of land for construction of buildings for human habitation only.

Residuary The surplus of a testator's estate remaining after all of the debts and particular legacies have been discharged.

Respondeat superior (pronounced ree-*spahn*-dee-uht soo-*peer*-ee-your) In Latin, "Let the master respond." A doctrine under which a principal or an employer is held liable for the wrongful acts committed by agents or employees while acting within the course and scope of their agency or employment.

Respondent In equity practice, the party who answers a bill or other proceeding.

Restitution An equitable remedy under which a person is restored to his or her original position prior to loss or injury, or placed in the position he or she would have been in had the breach not occurred.

Restraint of trade Any contract or combination that tends to eliminate or reduce competition, effect a monopoly, artificially maintain prices, or otherwise hamper the course of trade and commerce as it would be carried on if left to the control of natural economic forces.

Restrictive covenant A private restriction on the use of land that is binding on the party that purchases the property originally as well as on subsequent purchasers. If its benefit or obligation passes with the land's ownership, it is said to "run with the land."

Restrictive indorsement Any indorsement on a negotiable instrument that requires the indorsee to comply with certain instructions regarding the funds involved. A restrictive indorsement does not prohibit the further negotiation of the instrument.

Resulting trust An implied trust arising from the conduct of the parties. A trust in which a party holds the actual legal title to another's property but only for that person's benefit.

Retained earnings The portion of a corporation's profits that has not been paid out as dividends to shareholders.

Retainer An advance payment made by a client to a law firm to cover part of the legal fees and/or costs that will be incurred on that client's behalf.

Retaliatory eviction The eviction of a tenant because of the tenant's complaints, participation in a tenant's union, or similar activity with which the landlord does not agree.

Reverse To reject or overrule a court's judgment. An appellate court, for example, might reverse a lower court's judgment on an issue if it feels that the lower court committed an error during the trial or that the jury was improperly instructed.

Reverse discrimination Discrimination against majority groups, such as white males, that results from affirmative action programs, in which preferences are given to minority members and women.

Reverse mortgage A loan product typically provided to older homeowners that allows them to extract cash (in either a lump sum or multiple payments) for the equity in their home. The mortgage does not need to be repaid until the home is sold or the owner leaves or dies.

Reversible error An error by a lower court that is sufficiently substantial to justify an appellate court's reversal of the lower court's decision.

Revocation In contract law, the withdrawal of an offer by an offeror. Unless an offer is irrevocable, it can be revoked at any time prior to acceptance without liability.

Right of contribution The right of a co-surety who pays more than his or her proportionate share on a debtor's default to recover the excess paid from other co-sureties.

Right of entry The right to peaceably take or resume possession of real property.

Right of first refusal The right to purchase personal or real property—such as corporate shares or real estate—before the property is offered for sale to others.

Right of reimbursement The legal right of a person to be restored, repaid, or indemnified for costs, expenses, or losses incurred or expended on behalf of another.

Right of subrogation The right of a person to stand in the place of (be substituted for) another, giving the substituted party the same legal rights that the original party had.

Right-to-work law A state law providing that employees are not to be required to join a union as a condition of obtaining or retaining employment.

Risk A prediction concerning potential loss based on known and unknown factors.

Risk management Planning that is undertaken to protect one's interest should some event threaten to undermine its security. In the context of insurance, risk management involves transferring certain risks from the insured to the insurance company.

Robbery The act of forcefully and unlawfully taking personal property of any value from another; force or intimidation is usually necessary for an act of theft to be considered a robbery.

Rule of four A rule of the United States Supreme Court under which the Court will not issue a writ of *certiorari* unless at least four justices approve of the decision to issue the writ.

Rule of reason A test by which a court balances the positive effects (such as economic efficiency) of an agreement against its potentially anticompetitive effects. In antitrust litigation, many practices are analyzed under the rule of reason.

Rule 10b-5 *See* SEC Rule 10b-5

Rulemaking The process undertaken by an administrative agency when formally adopting a new regulation or amending an old one. Rulemaking involves notifying the public of a proposed rule or change and receiving and considering the public's comments.

Rules of evidence Rules governing the admissibility of evidence in trial courts.

S

S corporation A close business corporation that has met certain requirements as set out by the Internal Revenue Code and thus qualifies for special income tax treatment. Essentially, an S corporation is taxed the same as a partnership, but its owners enjoy the privilege of limited liability.

Sale The passing of title (evidence of ownership rights) from the seller to the buyer for a price.

Sale on approval A type of conditional sale in which the buyer may take the goods on a trial basis. The sale becomes absolute only when the buyer approves of (or is satisfied with) the goods being sold.

Sale or return A type of conditional sale in which title and possession pass from the seller to the buyer; however, the buyer retains the option to return the goods during a specified period even though the goods conform to the contract.

Sales contract A contract for the sale of goods under which the ownership of goods is transferred from a seller to a buyer for a price.

Satisfaction *See* Accord and satisfaction

Scienter (pronounced *sy-en-*ter) Knowledge by the misrepresenting party that material facts have been falsely represented or omitted with an intent to deceive.

Search warrant An order granted by a public authority, such as a judge, that authorizes law enforcement personnel to search particular premises or property.

Seasonably Within a specified time period, or, if no period is specified, within a reasonable time.

SEC Rule 10b-5 A rule of the Securities and Exchange Commission that makes it unlawful, in connection with the purchase or sale of any security, to make any untrue statement of a material fact or to omit a material fact if such omission causes the statement to be misleading.

Secondary boycott A union's refusal to work for, purchase from, or handle the products of a secondary employer, with whom the union has no dispute, for the purpose of forcing that employer to stop doing business with the primary employer, with whom the union has a labor dispute.

Secondary liability In negotiable instruments law, the contingent liability of drawers and indorsers. A secondarily liable party becomes liable on an instrument only if the party that is primarily liable on the instrument dishonors it or, in regard to drafts and checks, the drawee fails to pay or to accept the instrument, whichever is required.

Secured party A lender, seller, or any other person in whose favor there is a security interest, including a person to whom accounts or chattel paper has been sold.

Secured transaction Any transaction in which the payment of a debt is guaranteed, or secured, by personal property owned by the debtor or in which the debtor has a legal interest.

Securities Generally, corporate stocks and bonds. A security may also be a note, debenture, stock warrant, or any document given as evidence of an ownership interest in a corporation or as a promise of repayment by a corporation.

Security agreement An agreement that creates or provides for a security interest between the debtor and a secured party.

Security interest Any interest "in personal property or fixtures which secures payment or performance of an obligation" [UCC 1–201(37)].

Self-defense The legally recognized privilege to protect one's self or property against injury by another. The privilege of self-defense protects only acts that are reasonably necessary to protect one's self or property.

Seniority system In regard to employment relationships, a system in which those who have worked longest for the company are first in line for promotions, salary increases, and other benefits; they are also the last to be laid off if the workforce must be reduced.

Service mark A mark used in the sale or the advertising of services, such as to distinguish the services of one person from the services of others. Titles, character names, and other distinctive features of radio and television programs may be registered as service marks.

Service of process The delivery of the complaint and summons to a defendant.

Settlor One creating a trust; also called a *grantor*.

Severance pay A payment by an employer to an employee that exceeds the employee's wages due on termination.

Sexual harassment In the employment context, the granting of job promotions or other benefits in return for sexual favors or language or conduct that is so sexually offensive that it creates a hostile working environment.

Share A unit of stock. *See also* Stock

Share exchange In a share exchange, some or all of the shares of one corporation are exchanged for some or all of the shares of another corporation, but both corporations continue to exist. Share exchanges are often used to create *holding companies* (companies that own part or all of other companies' stock).

Shareholder One who purchases shares of a corporation's stock, thus acquiring an equity interest in the corporation.

Shareholder's derivative suit A suit brought by a shareholder to enforce a corporate cause of action against a third person.

Sharia Civil law principles of some Middle Eastern countries that are based on the Islamic directives that follow the teachings of the prophet Muhammad.

Shelter principle The principle that the holder of a negotiable instrument who cannot qualify as a holder in due course (HDC), but who derives his or her title through an HDC, acquires the rights of an HDC.

Sheriff's deed The deed given to the purchaser of property at a sheriff's sale as part of the foreclosure process against the owner of the property.

Shipment contract A contract in which the seller is required to ship the goods by carrier. The buyer assumes liability for any losses or damage to the goods after they are delivered to the carrier. Generally, all contracts are assumed to be shipment contracts if nothing to the contrary is stated in the contract.

Short-form merger A merger between a subsidiary corporation and a parent corporation that owns at least 90 percent of the outstanding shares of each class of stock issued by the subsidiary corporation. Short-form mergers can be accomplished without the approval of the shareholders of either corporation.

Short sale A sale of real property for an amount that is less than the balance owed on the mortgage loan, usually due to financial hardship. Both the lender and the borrower must consent to a short sale. Following a short sale, the borrower still owes the balance of the mortgage debt (after the sale proceeds are applied) to the lender unless the lender agrees to forgive the remaining debt.

Short-swing profits Profits made by officers, directors, and certain large stockholders resulting from the use of nonpublic (inside) information about their companies; prohibited by Section 12 of the 1934 Securities Exchange Act.

Shrink-wrap agreement An agreement whose terms are expressed in a document located inside a box in which goods (usually software) are packaged; sometimes called a *shrink-wrap license.*

Sight draft   In negotiable instruments law, a draft payable on sight—that is, when it is presented for payment.

Signature   Under the Uniform Commercial Code, "any symbol executed or adopted by a party with a present intention to authenticate a writing."

Slander   Defamation in oral form.

Slander of quality   The publication of false information about another's product, alleging that it is not what its seller claims.

Slander of title   The publication of a statement that denies or casts doubt on another's legal ownership of any property, causing financial loss to that property's owner. Also called trade libel.

Small claims courts   Special courts in which parties may litigate small claims (usually, claims involving $2,500 or less). Attorneys are not required in small claims courts, and in many states attorneys are not allowed to represent the parties.

Smart card   Prepaid funds recorded on a microprocessor chip embedded on a card. One type of *e-money.*

Sociological school   A school of legal thought that views the law as a tool for promoting justice in society.

Sole proprietorship   The simplest form of business, in which the owner is the business; the owner reports business income on his or her personal income tax return and is legally responsible for all debts and obligations incurred by the business.

Sovereign immunity   A doctrine that immunizes foreign nations from the jurisdiction of U.S. courts when certain conditions are satisfied.

Spam   Bulk, unsolicited (junk) e-mail.

Special indorsement   An indorsement on an instrument that indicates the specific person to whom the indorser intends to make the instrument payable; that is, it names the indorsee.

Special-use permit   A permit that allows for a specific exemption to zoning regulations for a particular piece of land in a location that has a particular zoning characteristic. Local zoning authorities grant special-use permits.

Special warranty deed   A deed in which the grantor only covenants to warrant and defend the title against claims and demands of the grantor and all persons claiming by, through, and under the grantor.

Specific performance   An equitable remedy requiring the breaching party to perform as promised under the contract; usually granted only when money damages would be an inadequate remedy and the subject matter of the contract is unique (for example, real property).

Spendthrift trust   A trust created to prevent the beneficiary from spending all the money to which he or she is entitled. Only a certain portion of the total amount is given to the beneficiary at any one time, and most states prohibit creditors from attaching assets of the trust.

Spot zoning   A zoning classification granted to a parcel of land that is different than the classification given to other land in the immediate area.

Stale check   A check, other than a certified check, that is presented for payment more than six months after its date.

Standing to sue   The requirement that an individual must have a sufficient stake in a controversy before he or she can bring a lawsuit. The plaintiff must demonstrate that he or she either has been injured or threatened with injury.

Stare decisis (pronounced *ster*-ay dih-*si*-ses)   A common law doctrine under which judges are obligated to follow the precedents established in prior decisions.

Statute of Frauds   A state statute under which certain types of contracts must be in writing to be enforceable.

Statute of limitations   A federal or state statute setting the maximum time period during which a certain action can be brought or certain rights enforced.

Statute of repose   Basically, a statute of limitations that is not dependent on the happening of a cause of action. Statutes of repose generally begin to run at an earlier date and run for a longer period of time than statutes of limitations.

Statutory law   The body of law enacted by legislative bodies (as opposed to constitutional law, administrative law, or case law).

Statutory lien   A lien created by statute.

Statutory period of redemption   A time period (usually set by state statute) during which the property subject to a defaulted mortgage, land contract, or other contract can be redeemed by the debtor after foreclosure or judicial sale.

Statutory right of redemption   A right provided by statute in some states under which mortgagors can redeem or purchase their property back after a judicial foreclosure for a limited period of time, such as one year.

Stock   An equity (ownership) interest in a corporation, measured in units of shares.

Stock buyback   Sometimes, publicly held companies use funds from their own treasuries to repurchase their own stock, with the result being that the price of the stock usually goes up.

Stock certificate   A certificate issued by a corporation evidencing the ownership of a specified number of shares in the corporation.

Stock option   *See* Stock warrant

Stock warrant   A certificate that grants the owner the option to buy a given number of shares of stock, usually within a set time period.

Stockholder   *See* Shareholder

Stop-payment order   An order by a bank customer to his or her bank not to pay or certify a certain check.

Strict liability   Liability regardless of fault. In tort law, strict liability may be imposed on defendants in cases involving abnormally dangerous activities, dangerous animals, or defective products.

Strike   An extreme action undertaken by unionized workers when collective bargaining fails; the workers leave their jobs, refuse to work, and (typically) picket the employer's workplace.

Subject-matter jurisdiction   Jurisdiction over the subject matter of a lawsuit.

Sublease   A lease executed by the lessee of real estate to a third person, conveying the same interest that the lessee enjoys but for a shorter term than that held by the lessee.

Subpoena   A document commanding a person to appear at a certain time and place or give testimony concerning a certain matter.

Subprime mortgage   A high-risk loan made to a borrower who does not qualify for a standard mortgage because of his or her poor credit rating or high debt-to-income ratio. Lenders typically charge a higher interest rate on subprime mortgages.

Subrogation   *See* Right of subrogation

Subscriber   An investor who agrees, in a subscription agreement, to purchase capital stock in a corporation.

Substantial performance   Performance that does not vary greatly from the performance promised in a contract; the performance must create substantially the same benefits as those promised in the contract.

Substantive due process   A requirement that focuses on the content, or substance, of legislation. If a law or other governmental action limits a fundamental right, such as the right to travel or to vote, it will be held to violate substantive due process unless it promotes a compelling or overriding state interest.

Substantive law   Law that defines the rights and duties of individuals with respect to each other, as opposed to procedural law, which defines the manner in which these rights and duties may be enforced.

Substantive unconscionability   Results from contracts, or portions of contracts, that are oppressive or overly harsh. Courts generally focus on provisions that deprive one party of the benefits of the agreement or leave that party without remedy for nonperformance by the other. An example of substantive unconscionability is the agreement by a welfare recipient with a fourth-grade education to purchase a refrigerator for $2,000 under an installment contract.

Suit   *See* Lawsuit; Litigation

Summary judgment   *See* Motion for summary judgment

Summary jury trial (SJT)   A method of settling disputes in which a trial is held, but the jury's verdict is not binding. The verdict acts only as a guide to both sides in reaching an agreement during the mandatory negotiations that immediately follow the summary jury trial.

Summons   A document informing a defendant that a legal action has been commenced against him or her and that the defendant must appear in court on a certain date to answer the plaintiff's complaint. The document is delivered by a sheriff or any other person so authorized.

Superseding cause   An intervening force or event that breaks the connection between a wrongful act and an injury to another; in negligence law, a defense to liability.

Supremacy clause   The provision in Article VI of the Constitution that provides that the Constitution, laws, and treaties of the United States are "the supreme Law of the Land." Under this clause, state and local laws that directly conflict with federal law will be rendered invalid.

Surety   A person, such as a cosigner on a note, who agrees to be primarily responsible for the debt of another.

Suretyship   An express contract in which a third party to a debtor-creditor relationship (the surety) promises to be primarily responsible for the debtor's obligation.

Surviving corporation   The remaining, or continuing, corporation following a merger. The surviving corporation is vested with the merged corporation's legal rights and obligations.

Syllogism   A form of deductive reasoning consisting of a major premise, a minor premise, and a conclusion.

Symbolic speech   Nonverbal conduct that expresses opinions or thoughts about a subject. Symbolic speech is protected under the First Amendment's guarantee of freedom of speech.

Syndicate   An investment group of persons or firms brought together for the purpose of financing a project that they would not or could not undertake independently.

T

Tag   In the context of the World Wide Web, a code in an HTML document. *See* Meta tags.

Takeover   The acquisition of control over a corporation through the purchase of a substantial number of the voting shares of the corporation.

Taking   The taking of private property by the government for public use. Under the Fifth Amendment to the Constitution, the government may not take private property for public use without "just compensation."

Tangible employment action   A significant change in employment status, such as firing or failing to promote an employee, reassigning the employee to a position with significantly different responsibilities, or effecting a significant change in employment benefits.

Tangible property   Property that has physical existence and can be distinguished by the senses of touch, sight, and so on. A car is tangible property; a patent right is intangible property.

Target corporation   The corporation to be acquired in a corporate takeover; a corporation to whose shareholders a tender offer is submitted.

Tariff   A tax on imported goods.

Technology licensing   Allowing another to use and profit from intellectual property (patents, copyrights, trademarks, innovative products or processes, and so on) for consideration. In the context of international business transactions, technology licensing is sometimes an attractive alternative to the establishment of foreign production facilities.

Tenancy at sufferance   A type of tenancy under which one who, after rightfully being in possession of leased premises, continues (wrongfully) to occupy the property after the lease has been terminated. The tenant has no rights to possess the property and occupies it only because the person entitled to evict the tenant has not done so.

Tenancy at will A type of tenancy under which either party can terminate the tenancy without notice; usually arises when a tenant who has been under a tenancy for years retains possession, with the landlord's consent, after the tenancy for years has terminated.

Tenancy by the entirety The joint ownership of property by a husband and wife. Neither party can transfer his or her interest in the property without the consent of the other.

Tenancy in common Co-ownership of property in which each party owns an undivided interest that passes to his or her heirs at death.

Tenant One who has the temporary use and occupation of real property owned by another person, called the landlord; the duration and terms of the tenancy are usually established by a lease.

Tender An unconditional offer to perform an obligation by a person who is ready, willing, and able to do so.

Tender of delivery Under the Uniform Commercial Code, a seller's or lessor's act of placing conforming goods at the disposal of the buyer or lessee and giving the buyer or lessee whatever notification is reasonably necessary to enable the buyer or lessee to take delivery.

Tender offer An offer to purchase made by one company directly to the shareholders of another (target) company; often referred to as a "takeover bid."

Term insurance A type of life insurance policy for which premiums are paid for a specified term. Payment on the policy is due only if death occurs within the term period. Premiums are less expensive than for whole life or limited-payment life, and there is usually no cash surrender value.

Testamentary trust A trust that is created by will and therefore does not take effect until the death of the testator.

Testate The condition of having died with a valid will.

Testator One who makes and executes a will.

Third party beneficiary One for whose benefit a promise is made in a contract but who is not a party to the contract.

Time draft A draft that is payable at a definite future time.

Tippee A person who receives inside information.

Title insurance Insurance commonly purchased by a purchaser of real property to protect against loss in the event that the title to the property is not free from liens or superior ownership claims.

Tombstone ad An advertisement, historically in a format resembling a tombstone, of a securities offering. The ad informs potential investors of where and how they may obtain a prospectus.

Tort A civil wrong not arising from a breach of contract. A breach of a legal duty that proximately causes harm or injury to another.

Tortfeasor One who commits a tort.

Totten trust A trust created by the deposit of a person's own money in his or her own name as a trustee for another. It is a tentative trust, revocable at will until the depositor dies or completes the gift in his or her lifetime by some unequivocal act or declaration.

Toxic tort A personal injury caused by exposure to a toxic substance, such as asbestos or hazardous waste. Victims can sue for medical expenses, lost wages, and pain and suffering.

Trade acceptance A draft that is drawn by a seller of goods ordering the buyer to pay a specified sum of money to the seller, usually at a stated time in the future. The buyer accepts the draft by signing the face of the draft, thus creating an enforceable obligation to pay the draft when it comes due. On a trade acceptance, the seller is both the drawer and the payee.

Trade dress The image and overall appearance of a product—for example, the distinctive decor, menu, layout, and style of service of a particular restaurant. Basically, trade dress is subject to the same protection as trademarks.

Trade fixture The personal property of a commercial tenant that has been installed or affixed to real property for a business purpose. When the lease ends, the tenant can remove the fixture but must repair any damage to the real property caused by the fixture's removal.

Trade libel The publication of false information about another's product, alleging it is not what its seller claims; also referred to as slander of quality.

Trade name A term that is used to indicate part or all of a business's name and that is directly related to the business's reputation and goodwill. Trade names are protected under the common law (and under trademark law, if the name is the same as the firm's trademark).

Trade secret Information or a process that gives a business an advantage over competitors who do not know the information or process.

Trademark A distinctive mark, motto, device, or implement that a manufacturer stamps, prints, or otherwise affixes to the goods it produces so that they may be identified on the market and their origins made known. Once a trademark is established (under the common law or through registration), the owner is entitled to its exclusive use.

Transfer warranties Implied warranties, made by any person who transfers an instrument for consideration to subsequent transferees and holders who take the instrument in good faith, that (1) the transferor is entitled to enforce the instrument, (2) all signatures are authentic and authorized, (3) the instrument has not been altered, (4) the instrument is not subject to a defense or claim of any party that can be asserted against the transferor, and (5) the transferor has no knowledge of any insolvency proceedings against the maker, the acceptor, or the drawer of the instrument.

Transferee In negotiable instruments law, one to whom a negotiable instrument is transferred (delivered).

Transferor In negotiable instruments law, one who transfers (delivers) a negotiable instrument to another.

Traveler's check   A check that is payable on demand, drawn on or payable through a bank, and designated as a traveler's check.

Treasure trove   Cash or coin, gold, silver, or bullion found hidden in the earth or other private place, the owner of which is unknown; literally, treasure found.

Treasury securities   Government debt issued by the U.S. Department of the Treasury. The interest rate on Treasury securities is often used as a baseline for measuring the rate on loan products with higher interest rates.

Treasury shares   Corporate shares that are authorized by the corporation but that have not been issued.

Treaty   An agreement formed between two or more independent nations.

Treble damages   Damages consisting of three times the amount of damages determined by a jury in certain cases as required by statute.

Trespass to land   The entry onto, above, or below the surface of land owned by another without the owner's permission or legal authorization.

Trespass to personal property   The unlawful taking or harming of another's personal property; interference with another's right to the exclusive possession of his or her personal property.

Trespasser   One who commits the tort of trespass in one of its forms.

Trial court   A court in which trials are held and testimony taken.

Trust   An arrangement in which title to property is held by one person (a trustee) for the benefit of another (a beneficiary).

Trust indorsement   An indorsement for the benefit of the indorser or a third person; also known as an agency indorsement. The indorsement results in legal title vesting in the original indorsee.

Two-step mortgage   A mortgage that starts as a fixed-rate mortgage and then converts to an adjustable-rate mortgage (ARM).

Tying arrangement   An agreement between a buyer and a seller in which the buyer of a specific product or service becomes obligated to purchase additional products or services from the seller.

U

U.S. trustee   A government official who performs certain administrative tasks that a bankruptcy judge would otherwise have to perform.

Ultra vires (pronounced *uhl*-trah *vye*-reez)   A Latin term meaning "beyond the powers"; in corporate law, acts of a corporation that are beyond its express and implied powers to undertake.

Unanimous opinion   A court opinion in which all of the judges or justices of the court agree to the court's decision.

Unconscionable (pronounced un-*kon*-shun-uh-bul) **contract or clause**   A contract or clause that is void on the basis of public policy because one party, as a result of his or her disproportionate bargaining power, is forced to accept terms that are unfairly burden-some and that unfairly benefit the dominating party. *See also* Procedural unconscionability; Substantive unconscionability

Underwriter   In insurance law, the insurer, or the one assuming a risk in return for the payment of a premium.

Undisclosed principal   A principal whose identity is unknown by a third person, and the third person has no knowledge that the agent is acting for a principal at the time the agent and the third person form a contract.

Unenforceable contract   A valid contract rendered unenforceable by some statute or law.

Uniform law   A model law created by the National Conference of Commissioners on Uniform State Laws and/or the American Law Institute for the states to consider adopting. If the state adopts the law, it becomes statutory law in that state. Each state has the option of adopting or rejecting all or part of a uniform law.

Unilateral contract   A contract that results when an offer can only be accepted by the offeree's performance.

Union shop   A place of employment in which all workers, once employed, must become union members within a specified period of time as a condition of their continued employment.

Universal defense   A defense that is valid against all holders of a negotiable instrument, including holders in due course (HDCs) and holders with the rights of HDCs. Universal defenses are also called real defenses.

Universal life   A type of insurance that combines some aspects of term insurance with some aspects of whole life insurance.

Unlawful detainer   The unjustifiable retention of the possession of real property by one whose right to possession has terminated—as when a tenant holds over after the end of the lease term in spite of the landlord's demand for possession.

Unliquidated debt   A debt that is uncertain in amount.

Unreasonably dangerous product   In product liability, a product that is defective to the point of threatening a consumer's health and safety. A product will be considered unreasonably dangerous if it is dangerous beyond the expectation of the ordinary consumer or if a less dangerous alternative was economically feasible for the manufacturer, but the manufacturer failed to produce it.

Usage of trade   Any practice or method of dealing having such regularity of observance in a place, vocation, or trade as to justify an expectation that it will be observed with respect to the transaction in question.

Usurpation   In corporation law, the taking advantage of a corporate opportunity by a corporate officer or director for his or her personal gain and in violation of his or her fiduciary duties.

Usury   Charging an illegal rate of interest.

Utilitarianism   An approach to ethical reasoning in which ethically correct behavior is not related to any absolute ethical or moral values but to an evaluation of the consequences of a given action on those who will be affected by it. In utilitarian reasoning, a "good" decision is one that results in the greatest good for the greatest number of people affected by the decision.

V

Valid contract A contract that results when elements necessary for contract formation (agreement, consideration, legal purpose, and contractual capacity) are present.

Validation notice An initial notice to a debtor from a collection agency informing the debtor that he or she has thirty days to challenge the debt and request verification.

Variance A form of a relief from zoning and other laws that is granted to a property owner; used to make up for any deficiency in real property so that it could prevent the property from complying with zoning regulations.

Vendee One who purchases property from another, called the vendor.

Vendor One who sells property to another, called the vendee.

Venture capital Capital (funds and other assets) provided by professional, outside investors (*venture capitalists,* usually groups of wealthy investors and investment banks) to start new business ventures.

Venture capitalist A person or entity that seeks out promising entrepreneurial ventures and funds them in exchange for equity stakes.

Venue (pronounced *ven*-yoo) The geographical district in which an action is tried and from which the jury is selected.

Verdict A formal decision made by a jury.

Vertical merger The acquisition by a company at one stage of production of a company at a higher or lower stage of production (such as its supplier or retailer).

Vertical restraint Any restraint on trade created by agreements between firms at different levels in the manufacturing and distribution process.

Vertically integrated firm A firm that carries out two or more functional phases—such as manufacture, distribution, retailing—of a product.

Vesting Under the Employee Retirement Income Security Act of 1974, a pension plan becomes vested when an employee has a legal right to the benefits purchased with the employer's contributions, even if the employee is no longer working for this employer.

Vicarious liability Legal responsibility placed on one person for the acts of another.

Virtual courtroom A courtroom that is conceptual and not physical. In the context of cyberspace, a virtual courtroom could be a location on the Internet at which judicial proceedings take place.

Virtual property Property that, in the context of cyberspace, is conceptual, as opposed to physical. Intellectual property that exists on the Internet is virtual property.

Virus Any program transmitted between computers via the Internet generally without the knowledge or consent of the recipient. Viruses attempt to do deliberate damage to systems and data.

Vishing The voice counterpart of phishing; vishers use an e-mail or a notice on a Web site that encourage persons to make a phone call which then triggers a voice response system that asks for valuable personal information such as credit card numbers.

Void contract A contract having no legal force or binding effect.

Voidable contract A contract that may be legally avoided (canceled, or annulled) at the option of one of the parties.

Voidable preference In bankruptcy law, a preference that may be avoided, or set aside, by the trustee.

Voir dire (pronounced *vwahr deehr*) A French phrase meaning, literally, "to see, to speak." In jury trials, the phrase refers to the process in which the attorneys question prospective jurors to determine whether they are biased or have any connection with a party to the action or with a prospective witness.

Voting trust An agreement (trust contract) under which legal title to shares of corporate stock is transferred to a trustee who is authorized by the shareholders to vote the shares on their behalf.

W

Waiver An intentional, knowing relinquishment of a legal right.

Warehouse receipt A document of title issued by a bailee-warehouser to cover the goods stored in the warehouse.

Warehouser One in the business of operating a warehouse.

Warranty A promise that certain facts are truly as they are represented to be.

Warranty deed A deed in which the grantor guarantees to the grantee that the grantor has title to the property conveyed in the deed, that there are no encumbrances on the property other than what the grantor has represented, and that the grantee will enjoy quiet possession of the property; a deed that provides the greatest amount of protection for the grantee.

Warranty disclaimer A seller's or lessor's negation or qualification of a warranty.

Warranty of fitness *See* Implied warranty of fitness for a particular purpose.

Warranty of merchantability *See* Implied warranty of merchantability.

Warranty of title An implied warranty made by a seller that the seller has good and valid title to the goods sold and that the transfer of the title is rightful.

Waste The abuse or destructive use of real property by one who is in rightful possession of the property but who does not have title to it. Waste does not include ordinary depreciation due to age and normal use.

Watered stock Shares of stock issued by a corporation for which the corporation receives, as payment, less than the fair market value of the shares.

Wetlands Areas of land designated by government agencies (such as the Army Corps of Engineers or the Environmental Protection Agency) as protected areas that support wildlife and that therefore cannot be filled in or dredged by private contractors or parties.

Whistleblowing An employee's disclosure to government, the press, or upper-management authorities that the employer is engaged in unsafe or illegal activities.

White-collar crime Nonviolent crime committed by individuals or corporations to obtain a personal or business advantage.

Whole life A life insurance policy in which the insured pays a level premium for his or her entire life and in which there is a constantly accumulating cash value that can be withdrawn or borrowed against by the borrower. Sometimes referred to as straight life insurance.

Will An instrument directing what is to be done with the testator's property on his or her death, made by the testator and revocable during his or her lifetime. No interests in the testator's property pass until the testator dies.

Willful Intentional.

Winding up The second of two stages involved in the termination of a partnership or corporation. Once the firm is dissolved, it continues to exist legally until the process of winding up all business affairs (collecting and distributing the firm's assets) is complete.

Workers' compensation laws State statutes establishing an administrative procedure for compensating workers' injuries that arise out of—or in the course of—their employment, regardless of fault.

Working papers The various documents used and developed by an accountant during an audit. Working papers include notes, computations, memoranda, copies, and other papers that make up the work product of an accountant's services to a client.

Workout agreement A formal contract between a debtor and his or her creditors in which the parties agree to negotiate a payment plan for the amount due on the loan instead of proceeding to foreclosure.

Worm A type of virus that is designed to copy itself from one computer to another without human interaction. Unlike the typical virus, a computer worm can copy itself automatically and can replicate in great volume and with great speed. Worms, for example, can send out copies of themselves to every contact in your e-mail address book.

Writ of attachment A court's order, prior to a trial to collect a debt, directing the sheriff or other officer to seize nonexempt property of the debtor; if the creditor prevails at trial, the seized property can be sold to satisfy the judgment.

Writ of *certiorari* (pronounced sur-shee-uh-*rah*-ree) A writ from a higher court asking the lower court for the record of a case.

Writ of execution A court's order, after a judgment has been entered against the debtor, directing the sheriff to seize (levy) and sell any of the debtor's nonexempt real or personal property. The proceeds of the sale are used to pay off the judgment, accrued interest, and costs of the sale; any surplus is paid to the debtor.

Wrongful discharge An employer's termination of an employee's employment in violation of an employment contract or laws that protect employees.

Z

Zoning The division of a city by legislative regulation into districts and the application in each district of regulations having to do with structural and architectural designs of buildings and prescribing the use to which buildings within designated districts may be put.

Zoning laws The rules and regulations that collectively manage the development and use of land.

Table of Cases

For your convenience and reference, here is a list of all the cases mentioned in this text, including those within the footnotes, features, and case problems. Any case that was an excerpted case for a chapter is given special emphasis by having its title **boldfaced.**

Index